ENCYCLOPEDIA OF AMERICAN LIVES

CSS

The SCRIBNER ENCYCLOPEDIA *of*

AMERICAN LIVES

The SCRIBNER ENCYCLOPEDIA *of*

AMERICAN LIVES

VOLUME ONE

1981–1985

KENNETH T. JACKSON
EDITOR IN CHIEF

KAREN MARKOE
GENERAL EDITOR

ARNOLD MARKOE
EXECUTIVE EDITOR

CHARLES SCRIBNER'S SONS
AN IMPRINT OF MACMILLAN LIBRARY REFERENCE USA
NEW YORK

Charles Scribner's Sons
An imprint of Macmillan Library Reference USA
1633 Broadway
New York, NY 10019

Library of Congress Cataloging-in-Publication Data

The Scribner encyclopedia of American lives / Kenneth T. Jackson,
    editor in chief ; Karen Markoe, general editor ; Arnold Markoe,
    executive editor.
        p.   cm.
    Includes bibliographical references and index.
    Contents: v. 1. 1981–1985
    ISBN 0-684-80492-1 (v. 1 : alk. paper)
    1. United States—Biography—Dictionaries.   I. Jackson, Kenneth
  T.   II. Markoe, Karen.   III. Markoe, Arnie.
CT213.S37   1998
920.073—dc21   98-33793
                                                                    CIP

1 3 5 7 9 11 13 15 17 19 20 18 16 14 12 10 8 6 4 2
PRINTED IN THE UNITED STATES OF AMERICA

The paper in this publication meets the minimum requirements of the American
National Standard for Information Services—Permanence of Paper for Printed
Library Materials, ANSI Z39.48-1992.

EDITORIAL *and* PRODUCTION STAFF

Managing Editor
TIMOTHY J. DEWERFF

Editorial Assistant and Photo Editor
ALEXANDER GOLDMAN

Editorial Assistants
AMELIA DEREZINSKY   ANDREW MCCARTHY   LAURA SMID

Editors
HANNAH BORGESON   JEFF CHEN   JOHN FITZPATRICK   STEPHEN WAGLEY

Copy Editors, Researchers
MELISSA A. DOBSON   LOUISE B. KETZ   MICHAEL LEVINE
JOHN B. ROSEMAN   LINDA SANDERS   ELIZABETH I. WILSON
BRIGIT DERMOTT   GEOFFREY GNEUHS   CHRISTINE M. GROVE   JOSEPH GUSTAITIS
JEAN F. KAPLAN   MARTHA SCHÜTZ   INGRID STERNER   SARAH VALDEZ

Proofreaders
CAROL HOLMES   GRETCHEN GORDON

Picture Researcher
ERMINE S. JONES

Production Manager
ROSE CAPOZZELLI

Designer
BRADY MCNAMARA

Executive Editor
SYLVIA K. MILLER

Publisher
KAREN DAY

PREFACE

The *Scribner Encyclopedia of American Lives* (*SEAL*) is a traditional book with unusual features. It is traditional in the sense that it profiles the careers and achievements of persons who have made significant contributions to our national past. Each essay appraises the circumstances and influences that shaped the life of an individual subject. The authors have provided basic biographical data, including the places and full dates of birth and death, the full names and occupations of parents, the number of siblings, the educational institutions attended and degrees granted, the names of spouses and the dates of marriages and divorces, and the number of children. Wherever possible, the entries also include information on residences, cause of death, and place of burial. The lengths of articles were determined both by the relative significance of the subjects and by the availability of biographical information, and the essays typically conclude with a brief analysis of the enduring legacy of the man or woman being remembered.

Unlike the *Dictionary of American Biography,* an earlier biographical reference work published by Scribners that remains in print, *SEAL* is being produced independently instead of under the auspices of the American Council of Learned Societies. *SEAL* also introduces a number of new features. First, almost every life story included in this volume is accompanied by a photograph of the subject. Second, each biography alerts readers to the significance of the subject's life at a glance by encapsulating his or her most important achievements in the opening paragraph. Finally, an index listing the subjects by occupation has been printed in the back matter of the volume that includes their biographies.

This first volume of *SEAL* contains the biographies of 494 persons who died in the five-year period between 1 January 1981 and 31 December 1985; future volumes will include subjects who died in subsequent five-year periods. The editors have as a rule included individuals, such as Ingrid Bergman, who made major professional or artistic contributions while living in the United States, whether or not they were born here or even actually became citizens. Conversely, we have not included persons who lived several years in the United States but whose major achievements took place in other countries.

In selecting a few hundred persons from the almost 10 million Americans who died in those years, the editors followed a rigorous process. First, they compiled a list of several thousand candidates from a variety of sources. Second, they classified the names according to profession or occupation. Third, they submitted the lists to specialists or groups of specialists who helped to rank the potential biographees. Fourth, an advisory board consisting of Stuart W. Bruchey of Columbia University, Joshua Lederberg of Rockefeller University, Vivian Perlis of Yale University, and Arthur M. Schlesinger, Jr., of the City University of New York reviewed the final list and made recommendations for additions or deletions.

The individuals who are profiled in this book obviously lived extraordinary lives and in conspicuous ways set themselves apart from the rest of us. Some won fame on the battlefield or in the halls of government. Others distinguished themselves by their books, their scientific research efforts, or their creative genius. Still others became household names because of their achievements as performing artists or sports heroes. But taken together, these unusual individuals reflect the diversity of the nation they called home. Representing virtually every race, ethnic group, and socioeconomic class, they came from every region of the United States. Many were born to privilege; others were born to sharecroppers or to penniless immigrants. All took advantage of their natural gifts to leave a permanent mark on a continental nation.

Some of the decisions to include certain subjects were easy, and many of the names in this book will be familiar to everyone. From the world of letters come Truman Capote, John Cheever, Alfred Knopf, Archibald MacLeish, and Ayn Rand; from motion pictures, Ingrid Bergman, Henry Fonda, William Holden, Rock Hudson, Grace Kelly, and Orson Welles; from the legitimate theater, Lynn Fontanne, Lillian Hellman, Ethel Merman, and Tennessee Williams; from government, Senators Sam Ervin and Henry ("Scoop") Jackson and Ambassador Henry Cabot Lodge; from sports, Paul ("Bear") Bryant, Jack Dempsey, and Joe Louis; from music, Count Basie, Thelonious Monk, Arthur Rubinstein, and Eugene Ormandy; and from industry and business, Ray Kroc, the founder of McDonald's, Donald Douglas, the founder of Douglas Aircraft, and Robert Woodruff, who made Coca-Cola a worldwide brand name. Persons interested in military history will note that this volume includes some of the last top commanders from World War II, including General of the Army Omar N. Bradley, who led 2 million American soldiers against Hitler's Wehrmacht in France and Germany, and General Mark Clark, who served as Allied Commander in Italy in 1944 and 1945.

In addition, this first volume of the *Scribner Encyclopedia of American Lives* includes persons who were not much in the news during their lifetimes, but who for particular reasons also deserve to be remembered. This book includes, for example, Helen Steiner Rice, author of thousands of greeting card poems; Karen Ann Quinlan, who was the tragic focus of the "right to die" issue; Dian Fossey, who wrote *Gorillas in the Mist* in an effort to save that endangered species; Al Schacht, the "Clown Prince of Baseball"; and Sally Stanford, the onetime madam who became the mayor of Sausalito, California.

As is the case in any large-scale research effort, *SEAL* could not have been produced without the cooperation and enthusiasm of hundreds of persons, some who were new to this venture, and others who have played important roles in previous Scribner reference efforts. Our 332 individual authors were unusually diligent in helping us to locate appropriate portraits of their subjects. Remarkably, the editors of this book all had previously worked together on similar ventures and willingly chose to do so again. The result is a volume that we hope will be useful, reliable, and readable for generations.

In particular, we wish to thank Timothy J. DeWerff, who managed the entire effort from his office at Scribners with his unique combination of wide intelligence, superb judgment, meticulous organization, and reliable good humor. Richard H. Gentile provided valuable insight and advice throughout the project. We also wish to acknowledge the generous counsel of William Gargan on literary subjects. Finally, we wish to record our gratitude to Karen Day, the publisher of Charles Scribner's Sons, whose personal commitment to the project was the essential ingredient in the creation of this new series. Everyone who uses this volume will be in her debt.

Kenneth T. Jackson
Karen E. Markoe
Arnold Markoe

CONTENTS

PREFACE   *vii*

BIOGRAPHIES   *1*

OCCUPATIONS INDEX   *911*

DIRECTORY OF CONTRIBUTORS   *919*

The SCRIBNER ENCYCLOPEDIA *of*

AMERICAN LIVES

A

ACE, Goodman (*b.* 15 January 1899 in Kansas City, Missouri; *d.* 25 March 1982 in New York City), broadcasting personality and humorist known for the urbane comedy of the radio show *Easy Aces* (done with his wife, Jane) and later for television writing and columns in the *Saturday Review*.

Goodman Ace's parents, Harry Aiskowitz, a haberdasher, and Anna Katzen, a homemaker, were Jewish immigrants who met in 1896 on the ship bringing them to New York City from Riga, Latvia. Goodman was the eldest of their three children who survived infancy.

Goodman graduated from Central High School in Kansas City. He briefly studied journalism at Kansas City Junior College. His father died in 1917, and Ace became the primary support for his mother and sisters. After a brief stint as a sales clerk at Wormser's clothing store, he became a reporter with the *Kansas City Post*. There he began using the name Goodman Ace, the name he used for the rest of his life. After a merger, Ace became the entertainment columnist for the *Kansas City Journal-Post,* a position he held until 1930.

Six feet tall, dark haired, and bespectacled, Ace enjoyed the life of an entertainment reporter, meeting and interviewing show business personalities, going out to clubs and theaters. On 16 November 1924 he married Jane Epstein (later known professionally as Jane Sherwood Ace), the attractive, blond, twenty-four-year-old daughter of a success-

ful clothing retailer. They lived fashionably and expensively in the Bellerive Hotel in Kansas City.

In 1928 Ace approached Kansas City radio station KMBC with proposals for two shows: a Friday night movie review program and a Sunday morning show on which he would read the funny papers. KMBC accepted both ideas and paid $10 per live fifteen-minute show. One day the network could not provide the next scheduled program, and Ace was forced to ad lib with Jane for fifteen minutes. From that experience he developed the idea for a situation comedy, building much of the humor on Jane's odd perceptions and malapropisms. KMBC liked the idea, and in 1929 *Easy Aces* appeared on the air for fifteen minutes three times a week. "Goody," as he was known, wrote the scripts and played the straight man. Jane got the laughs.

In the fall of 1931 the Aces took the show to Chicago and joined CBS's national schedule. Despite solid ratings, after two seasons in Chicago *Easy Aces* lost its sponsor. Producers Ann and Frank Hummert liked the program, however, so in 1933 the Aces moved to New York and went on NBC. *Easy Aces* stayed on network radio for the next twelve years. Ten of the best scripts from this period were later published as *Ladies and Gentlemen, Easy Aces* (1970). In the mid-1930s the Aces ventured to Hollywood, where they appeared in several "shorts" for RKO, including *Easy Aces* (1935).

Late in 1944, after a squabble with American Home Products, the show lost its sponsor, Anacin, and left the air

Goodman and Jane Ace sit at the bridge table from which they broadcast *Easy Aces, c.* 1941. ARCHIVE PHOTOS

in January 1945. Ace promptly began writing for other shows (e.g., *The Danny Kaye Show*) and in the years 1946–1947 worked as a programming executive for CBS. In 1948 he and Jane had a weekly comedy on CBS, *Mr. Ace and Jane,* but it was never successful. Although in 1951 and 1952 Jane briefly had a local radio program on a New York station, the Aces left network radio permanently in 1949.

Almost immediately, Ace went back to work as a writer, first for radio's *The Big Show* and then, from 1952 to 1955, for Milton Berle's TV program. Ace went on to write for a number of successful variety shows, establishing himself from 1955 to 1967 as chief writer for Perry Como's popular *Kraft Music Hall* and one of the highest-paid writers ($10,000 per script) in television. He also tried a number of other projects, including screenplays (e.g., *I Married a Woman* in 1957), TV specials, humorous books of nonfiction such as *The Fine Art of Hypochondria* (1966), and syndicated television series including a short-lived TV version of *Easy Aces.*

In 1952 Ace began writing regularly for the *Saturday Review,* and in 1955 he became a contributing editor. His humorous "Top of My Head" column became an established fixture of the magazine.

After the *Kraft Music Hall,* the Aces lived in comfortable semiretirement, splitting time between their apartment in Manhattan and vacations in Florida, with trips to visit family in the Midwest. They had no children, and when Jane died in November of 1974, five days before their fiftieth wedding anniversary, Ace felt the loss deeply. After a few months, however, he picked up the same life he had been living for decades, continuing his frequent correspondence with old friends and family, his afternoons at the Friars Club, and his magazine column.

After a period of declining health, Ace died in his apartment at the Ritz Towers. He was buried in Kansas City.

A classic American humorist, Ace brought to the electronic media a style of comedy that had less interest in easy laughs than in consistent character development and light but penetrating topical commentary. *Easy Aces,* for instance, though superficially similar to other "scatterbrain" comedies of the 1930s and 1940s, had a more trenchant wit than Burns and Allen or Marie Wilson's Irma. Jane's classic lines from *Easy Aces*—for instance, "Time wounds all heels"—are more than malapropian inversions; they contain a truth of their own. This quality helped make Goodman Ace particularly successful at writing for TV variety formats, especially for sensitive "stars" doing guest appearances. It also explains the success of his column in the *Saturday Review.* Though conventionally liberal on civil rights, for instance, his columns had little ideological content. They analyzed irrationalities among all sorts of people from ignorant network executives to bigoted taxi drivers. His statements on the art and frustrations of writing for broadcasting, collected in *The Book of Little Knowledge: More Than You Want to Know About Television* (1955) and *The Better of Goodman Ace* (1971), offer crisp, sometimes caustic, but enduringly valuable insights about radio and television.

★

Goodman Ace's papers, including 2,200 scripts for radio and television programs written between 1931 and 1967, are housed in the Manuscript Reading Room of the Library of Congress. His loving tribute to Jane in the *Saturday Review* (8 Feb. 1975) includes several important autobiographical details. By far the best source of information on Ace is the profile by Mark Singer, Ace's nephew and literary executor, originally published in the *New Yorker* (4 Apr. 1977) and reprinted as "Goodman Ace: Words Fool Me" in Singer's *Mr. Personality* (1989). Also of interest are the chapter "Scatterbrains" in Arthur Frank Wertheim, *Radio Comedy* (1979); "The Easy Aces" in John Dunning, *Tune in Yesterday: The Ultimate Encyclopedia of Old-Time Radio, 1925–1976* (1976); and Norman Cousins's editorial tribute, "Goody Ace," in the *Saturday Review* (June 1982). A substantial obituary is in the *New York Times* (26 Mar. 1982).

NICHOLAS A. SHARP

ADAMS, Ansel Easton (*b.* 20 February 1902 in San Francisco, California; *d.* 22 April 1984 in Monterey, California), photographer and environmentalist revered for his powerful black-and-white photographs of the American landscape and beloved for his commitment to the conservation of those lands.

Although Ansel Adams was born into a life of privilege, his father, Charles Hitchcock Adams, proved to be an unsuccessful businessman. By 1911 the family's fortune, ironically based on logging and lumber mills, had reversed to debt. Ansel's mother, Olive Bray, an unhappy woman, bitterly reproached her husband for the rest of her long life. Though his mother was cold and critical, his father proved to be a loving, nurturing parent.

A hyperactive child, Ansel Adams was primarily homeschooled by his father and an aunt, Mary Bray, who modeled their approach on the humanistic child-rearing theories of Herbert Spence and Robert Green Ingersoll. Always an avid reader, Adams valued the poems of Walt Whitman and the writings of philosopher Ralph Waldo Emerson. At age fifteen he received a grammar school degree from the Kate M. Wilkins Private School, his only earned diploma until the flood of honorary ones years later.

Adams, an only child, taught himself to play the piano when he was twelve years old. When he discovered his natural talent and deep affinity for music, he also found that he could personally create beauty. Previously overwhelmed by the chaos of life, he found order and meaning in the world through the discipline of serious musical study. He determined to become a professional classical pianist.

In 1916 the family vacationed in Yosemite National Park. Soon after their arrival, his parents presented Adams

Ansel Adams in Carmel, California, 1984. PHOTOGRAPH BY JIM ALINDER

with his first camera, a Kodak Box Brownie. The rapport among boy, camera, and Yosemite was immediate. A sickly child, he grew well and strong in the park and became convinced of its healing powers. He returned each summer to restore himself physically and mentally.

Adams became a member of the Sierra Club in 1920 after accepting the job of summer custodian at its Yosemite headquarters, the Le Conte Memorial Lodge, a position he held for four years. Created in 1892 by a group led by John Muir, the Sierra Club was founded to "explore, enjoy, and render accessible the mountain regions of the Pacific Coast." As Adams's photographs began appearing in the pages of the *Sierra Club Bulletin,* and he became a regular participant in the annual Sierra Club outings (two to three hundred members hiking and camping together for four weeks each summer), he grew to be a well-known, popular figure. Physically, he was striking, if not handsome; tall and skinny, he had protruding ears and a bent nose, broken in the San Francisco earthquake of 1906. At parties he starred; he was the first with a bawdy joke and could be counted upon to perform piano sonatas until dawn.

Invited by the Western landscape painter Harry Cassie Best during the summer of 1921 to practice on the piano in his Yosemite art gallery and studio, Adams met and fell in love with the artist's daughter, Virginia Rose Best. A consummate Yosemite girl who climbed mountains as bravely as any boy, the seventeen-year-old, blonde, blue-eyed Virginia was well-read and also possessed of a fine contralto voice. The young couple had much in common and after an on-again, off-again courtship were married in Yosemite on 2 January 1928. When their first child, Michael, was born in 1933, Adams was not by his wife's side, but hiking with his Sierra Club comrades, and when their daughter, Anne, their second and last child, was born in 1935, he was absent again, this time photographing Yosemite in winter.

Perhaps the biggest influence in the formation of this young artist was his friendship with Cedric Wright, a fellow Sierra Club member with whom he shared a great many values. Wright played the violin, read voraciously, spouted poetry, and loved the High Sierra. He introduced Adams to the writings of Edward Carpenter, who reaffirmed his own beliefs that nature was the source of all goodness by providing the succor of beauty. Together, the two comrades swore their lifelong devotion to the creation of beauty. Adams stuck by his promise.

Though he had considered photography an avocation and the piano his career, Adams realized small professional success in music. At a Sierra Club party in 1926, he was introduced to Albert Bender, a patron of the arts in San Francisco. After viewing a group of Adams's photographs, Bender announced he would sponsor his first portfolio, *Parmelian Prints of the High Sierras,* which was published in 1927 and included eighteen original gelatin-silver prints by Adams.

Believing he must include a definitive picture of Yosemite's grand centerpiece, Half Dome, Adams created his first masterpiece, *Monolith: The Face of Half Dome,* on 10 April 1927. After an arduous hike to the spot he had chosen, he discovered he had but two glass-plate negatives remaining. He made one exposure before he recognized that what he had captured was the apparent reality of the scene before him. The completed print would not possess the enormous power that he felt in the presence of Half Dome. For the final exposure, he placed a deep red filter before the lens. The effect was dramatic. No longer was a bland Half Dome seated before a pale sky; instead, the majestic cliff soared against a dark background, its inimitable granite face defined in shades of deepest gray. Adams had skewed the tonal values and with it the apparent reality. It was at this time that Adams formulated his important concept of visualization: that the photographer must see the finished photograph in his mind before the negative is exposed.

With the money he earned from the Parmelian portfolio, Adams opened a studio in his family's San Francisco home and began a career as a commercial photographer. When his mother learned of his decision to pursue photography, not music, she wailed, "But Ansel, photography cannot express the human soul!" Adams replied, "But mother, perhaps the photographer can."

Bender introduced his protégé to important people in the art world and also brought him along on trips, including a significant one to New Mexico in 1927. The American Southwest was second in Adams's affections only to California. In Santa Fe he met the writer Mary Hunter Austin and they agreed to collaborate on a book, his first. *Taos Pueblo,* with his original prints bound together with her descriptive prose, was published in 1930.

Without formal education in photography, Adams learned by doing. His training as a pianist had convinced him of the importance of practice and he applied this belief, coupled with an endlessly curious mind, as he learned the medium. He believed that an artist must be fluent in his craft before he can be fully expressive, progressing from craft to art. He often used musical analogies to express himself in photography, defining a negative as the score in music, and each print a new, potentially unique performance of that score.

The San Francisco Bay area was a hotbed of photography in the early 1930s. In 1932 Adams joined with Edward Weston, Imogen Cunningham, Willard Van Dyke, and two others to champion the cause of straight photography. They named themselves Group f/64, after a very small aperture setting intended to produce an image sharply focused throughout all planes of the photograph. They defined their style in a manifesto, written primarily by Adams, as

"possessing no qualities of technique, composition or idea, derivative of any other art form."

The leader of American photography during the first half of the twentieth century was Alfred Stieglitz, through his own photographs as well as his New York City galleries that exhibited the best of modern art in the form of photographs side-by-side with paintings. Adams journeyed cross-country in 1933 to show his work to Stieglitz, who was then sixty-nine. Their subsequent friendship proved pivotal. In 1936 Stieglitz presented a major exhibition of Adams's photographs at his Manhattan gallery, An American Place, in effect anointing the younger man as a photographer worthy of the attention of the world. This recognition was career-making for Adams as an artist, but since few people were yet buying creative photographs, he had to continue to work as a commercial photographer.

Adams moved into an influential position in creative photography with the publication of his first book on photographic technique in 1935. With its page after page of well-illustrated, clear instructions, *Making a Photograph* demonstrated how to become a practitioner of straight photography. After reading it, Stieglitz, usually parsimonious with praise, wrote, "It's so straight and intelligent and heaven knows the world of photography isn't any too intelligent—nor straight either."

In 1934 Adams was elected to the Sierra Club's board of directors and continued to serve until his resignation in 1971. Dressed in blue jeans and black basketball high-top shoes and never without his Stetson cowboy hat, he proved to be a captivating and influential lobbyist in Washington, D.C., on behalf of the Sierra Club's concerns, beginning in 1936 when he testified at congressional hearings to establish Kings Canyon National Park. An impassioned speaker, he proved even more effective when he showed his photographs of the grand wilderness that could be saved. In 1938 he published his first book of landscape photographs, *Sierra Nevada: The John Muir Trail.* Its many images from Kings Canyon provided convincing evidence to President Franklin D. Roosevelt and Secretary of the Interior Harold Ickes, whose combined leadership finally ensured the park's formation in 1940.

In late 1936 Adams's physical connection to Yosemite was made permanent when his father-in-law died. Adams's wife, Virginia, inherited Best's studio and moved with their two children to Yosemite so that she could manage the family business. Renamed the Ansel Adams Gallery in 1972, it remains in the Adams family, now managed by grandchildren, the longest-owned concession by one family in the national park system.

Many of Adams's best friends were artists as well, including Edward Weston, Dorothea Lange, and Georgia O'Keeffe (the wife of Stieglitz). His closest colleagues were the husband-wife team of Beaumont and Nancy Newhall.

In 1940 Adams, with Beaumont Newhall and David McAlpin, founded the first department of photography in the world in a major museum, the Museum of Modern Art in New York City. Adams collaborated with Nancy Newhall on a number of books, articles, and exhibitions. The most famous was the Sierra Club's first large format book, *This Is the American Earth* (1960).

Charles Adams had engraved in his son the old American West tradition of the importance of passing on to others what you have learned. From his own experience, Adams strongly believed in nontraditional education and spent a lifetime helping others learn. During a stint teaching at the Art Center School in Los Angeles in 1942 and 1943, he developed a number of teaching tools, including the Zone System, an arcane method of producing a full tonal range negative irrespective of lighting conditions. In 1946 he established the world's first department of photography in a major museum, at the California School of Fine Arts, later the San Francisco Art Institute.

During the 1930s Adams made many great images, including *Golden Gate Before the Bridge* (1932), *Frozen Lake and Cliffs* (1932), *Rose and Driftwood* (1933), and *Clearing Winter Storm* (1935). Too old for military service during World War II, he patriotically responded as an artist, creating a series of heroic landscapes that reflected what he believed to be the grand spirit of his beloved, endangered country. Adams was at his most commanding during the decade of the 1940s with the masterpieces *Surf Sequence* (1940), *Winter Sunrise* (1943), and *Mt. Williamson from Manzanar* (1945). He made his most famous photograph, *Moonrise, Hernandez, New Mexico,* on 1 November 1941 at 4:49:20 P.M. Mountain Standard Time, the date later determined by a computer model. Through *Moonrise,* the viewer stands beyond mankind to witness humanity's reach for the stars, for redemption, for God.

Though known almost exclusively as a landscape photographer, Adams, shocked by what he believed was a deeply tragic mistake by the American government, in 1943 and 1944 documented Manzanar, the Japanese-American internment camp situated on the east side of the Sierra. These images were published in 1944, along with Adams's impassioned text against racial prejudice, as the book *Born Free and Equal.*

Supported by a Guggenheim Fellowship in 1946 (renewed in 1948, and again awarded in 1958), Adams completed a lifelong dream to photograph U.S. national parks and monuments, creating a flurry of superb photographs, such as *Mt. McKinley and Wonder Lake* (1947); *Tenaya Creek, Dogwood, Rain* (1948); *Oak Tree, Snowstorm* (1948); and *Sand Dunes, Sunrise* (1948). In 1948 he produced the first of seven photographic portfolios, plainly titled *Portfolio I.*

After 1949 Adams made some images of consequence, such as *Aspens, Northern New Mexico* (1958), *Moon and Half Dome* (1960), and *El Capitan, Winter, Sunrise* (1968), but nothing like the abundance of masterpieces he produced in the 1930s and 1940s. Instead, he was fully occupied producing museum exhibitions, writing a series of technical books (massively revised shortly before his death), and consulting for corporations such as Polaroid and Hasselblad. He lectured and taught across the country, including his annual Yosemite workshop. After moving from San Francisco to Carmel, California, in 1962, he founded the Friends of Photography in 1967, which he saw grow into the largest nonprofit photography membership organization in the world.

By 1970 photography had finally become a popular and collectible art form. Adams's photographs were the most sought after of all and he spent the majority of his time making prints for a clamoring public. The rising value of a print of his *Moonrise* was used as the blue-chip stock indicator by which to measure the entire photographic market. With the publication of *Portfolio VII* in 1976, Adams announced he would no longer make photographs for sale, intending to devote himself to making prints from hitherto unknown negatives as well as writing books and teaching. With the promise of his photographic archive as its cornerstone, in 1974 the Center for Creative Photography was formed at the University of Arizona.

Even after he no longer served on the Sierra Club's board, Adams continued to be highly active in environmental concerns. Though a staunch Democrat, he was consulted by every president from Lyndon B. Johnson through Ronald Reagan. In 1980 President Jimmy Carter awarded Adams the Presidential Medal of Freedom, the country's highest civilian award, for his achievements in photography and conservation. And although he had never attended college, the nation's greatest universities, including the University of California at Berkeley (1961) and Harvard University (1981), bestowed honorary doctoral degrees upon him.

Adams was that rare artist who enjoyed fame during his lifetime. He was idolized by generations of photographers and environmentalists, and his achievements were recognized in 1979 with a major retrospective exhibition at the Museum of Modern Art, as well as the publication of an important book, *Yosemite and the Range of Light.* In September of that year his white-whiskered face, topped by his characteristic Stetson, smiled from the cover of *Time* magazine.

Still in the midst of publishing and environmental projects, active and vital until the end, Adams died of a heart attack. Shortly thereafter, Congress designated 229,334 acres in the Sierra next to Yosemite National Park as the Ansel Adams Wilderness Area. A year following his death, Mount Ansel Adams was named. On its summit Michael Adams placed his father's ashes.

Ansel Adams was a great twentieth-century artist whose maturation paralleled the creative photography and environmental movements. He was a model of the democratic citizen, believing that each of us is responsible for this world and that an individual can make a difference. But he will be best remembered for his photographs, two-dimensional, black-and-white images that transcend reality and time, providing an eternal wellspring of beauty.

★

The Ansel Adams archive at the Center for Creative Photography at the University of Arizona in Tucson, Arizona, holds negatives, original photographs, correspondence, manuscripts, awards, and memorabilia. For additional primary source material, see Mary Street Alinder and Andrea Gray Stillman, eds., *Ansel Adams: Letters and Images 1916–1984* (1988). Ansel Adams with Mary Street Alinder, *Ansel Adams: An Autobiography* (1985), was selected by the American Library Association as one of the 100 most important books published in the 1980s. Additional autobiographical information is in David Sheff and Victoria Sheff, "Ansel Adams: The Playboy Interview," *Playboy* (May 1983). Representative published works by Adams not mentioned in the text include *This Is the American Earth* (1960), cowritten with Nancy Newhall; *Yosemite and the Range of Light* (1979); *The Portfolios of Ansel Adams* (1981); and *Examples: The Making of Forty Photographs* (1983).

Nancy Newhall, *Ansel Adams: The Eloquent Light* (1963; rev. ed. 1980), is an excellent biography that, however, ends in 1939, when Adams was thirty-seven years old, and contains no index, footnotes, or bibliography. Jonathan Spaulding, *Ansel Adams and the American Landscape* (1985), is a valuable biography concerned with setting the artist within the social context of his time. Mary Street Alinder, *Ansel Adams: A Biography* (1996), is the first complete biography. See also Robert Hughes, "Master of the Yosemite," *Time* (3 Sept. 1979). "Conversations with Ansel Adams" is an oral history conducted in 1972, 1974, and 1975 by Ruth Teiser and Catherine Harroun (Bancroft Library, University of California at Berkeley, 1978). *Ansel Adams Photographer* (1981) is available on VHS cassette. An obituary is in the *New York Times* (24 Apr. 1984).

MARY STREET ALINDER

ADAMS, Harriet Stratemeyer (*b.* 11 December 1892 in Newark, New Jersey; *d.* 27 March 1982 in Pottersville, New Jersey), writer of young adult literature who produced nearly two hundred titles, including many for the Nancy Drew series.

Adams was one of the two daughters born to Magdalene Baker Van Camp and Edward L. Stratemeyer. Her father, the son of German immigrants, left school after completing the eighth grade but was a prolific dime novelist by the time Harriet was born. The colorful stories her father spun for his daughters both entertained and inspired young Harriet. Edward Stratemeyer soon realized that there was a

Harriet Stratemeyer Adams. COURTESY OF SIMON & SCHUSTER

market for juvenile fiction, especially series of fiction works for young girls. He founded the Stratemeyer Syndicate in 1906, and under his leadership the syndicate produced such series as Jack Ranger, the Bobbsey Twins, Nan Sherwood, and the Hardy Boys, which were published by several houses, including Grosset and Dunlap.

Following her graduation from Wellesley College in 1914, Adams convinced her father to let her work for his syndicate. She wanted to make her living by writing, just as he had done. At college she had worked toward that goal by majoring in English composition and serving as president of the Press Club.

In 1915 she married Russell Vroom Adams, a partner in the investment banking firm of Adams and Hinckley; they had two sons and two daughters. After her last child was born, Adams sought to rejoin the Stratemeyer Syndicate as a ghostwriter. Her father refused to allow it, believing that women belonged at home.

After her father's death in 1930, Adams followed the wishes of the syndicate's publishers and took over as senior partner. Her sister, Edith, was an active partner until 1942, when she resigned. The Stratemeyer Syndicate was by then a million-dollar enterprise.

Aside from moving the company's offices from lower Manhattan to a location nearer her home in East Orange, New Jersey, Adams seamlessly followed her father's lead. She recorded detailed proposals for her staff of ghostwriters to flesh out into stories, and she imitated her father's writing style, particularly in the series for young boys.

Adams made her mark with her contributions to the Nancy Drew series, which had been introduced in 1930. She considered the series' heroine her "fiction daugher" and, writing under the pseudonym of Carolyn Keene, made Nancy less bossy and bold than the character who had flowed from her father's pen. The series chronicled the lives of teenage sleuth Nancy Drew and her two comrades, Bess and George, who solved cases involving thieves, smugglers, and kidnappers. Nancy lived with her attorney father, Carson Drew, and a housekeeper named Hannah Gruen in the affluent town of River Heights. Although most of her cases centered in her hometown, Nancy had a reputation that was far-reaching. Even new acquaintances knew of her remarkable skills; her talents included the ability to pilot a plane, decipher an ancient inscription, and tap dance in Morse code. Driving around in her blue roadster, Nancy typified the modern woman's dreams of freedom and independence.

Adams also wrote the Bobbsey Twins series as Laura Lee Hope, the Hardy Boys as Franklin W. Dixon, and Tom Swift as Victor W. Appleton II. The pseudonyms were used by other authors. Beginning with *By the Light of the Study Lamp* (1934), Adams wrote some thirty books for the Dana Girls series, under the name Carolyn Keene. The series was the longest running of the ones she planned for the syndicate, lasting until 1979.

Several series were made into films. Walt Disney's *Mickey Mouse Club* serialized two Hardy Boys mysteries in the 1950s, and the series became the basis for a Saturday morning cartoon in 1969 and a television mystery series in 1977. In the 1970s the syndicate busily worked to find new outlets for series spin-offs. It devised puzzle books and cookbooks, detective and survival handbooks, and even picture books for children of elementary school age.

Although Adams's writings spanned decades that saw changes in American culture and values, she resisted suggestions that she modernize her stories. She felt that American children, even those living in the inner city, still wanted to curl up with a good story that allowed them to escape from their problems. She also believed that her books did not need to include sex, violence, profanity, or religious and political discussions to appeal to her readership. While her stories were not preachy, Adams tried to deliver a moral message within her gushy prose. She wanted readers to see that persistence paid off and that good could, and did, win over evil. In a filmstrip made in 1982, Adams remarked that she wanted the "young reader to see that life can be wholesome and beautiful."

Adams wanted her books, written in simple language, to be educational. She traveled throughout the Americas, Europe, Africa, and Hawaii, and used these places as settings for her stories. She also drew upon her studies in archaeology to educate her readers on everything from Nazca settlements in Peru to Ming vases.

Wellesley College awarded Adams its Alumnae Achievement Award in 1978, and the National Mother's Day Committee named her Mother of the Year in 1979. To commemorate her fiftieth anniversary as an author, Simon and Schuster, which had recently become the syndicate's paperback publisher, honored her with a party in 1980.

Adams continued to write and create new series for the Stratemeyer Syndicate right up to her death at the age of eighty-nine. She was watching *The Wizard of Oz* with her family when she suffered a fatal heart attack.

The successful literary formula her father had concocted, combined with her business acumen, writing skills, and market knowledge, enabled Adams to direct the syndicate's expansion into a global media operation over a period of fifty years. The Stratemeyer Syndicate knew how to survive in a changing world by resisting that change and promoting simple, traditional values. Its books used a basic vocabulary that enabled young and foreign readers to understand the action and message. Its titles gave young readers the familiarity and security they craved.

★

Papers of the Stratemeyer Syndicate are at the Yale University Library and the New York Public Library's Rare Book and Manuscripts Department. Carol Billman, *The Secret of the Stratemeyer Syndicate: Nancy Drew, the Hardy Boys, and the Million Dollar Fiction Factory* (1986), provides much information about the Stratemeyer Syndicate. Protean Productions made a filmstrip of an interview with Adams on the appeal of series fiction in 1982. An obituary is in the *New York Times* (29 Mar. 1982).

ANN LESLIE TUTTLE

ADLER, Luther (*b.* 4 May 1903 in New York City; *d.* 8 December 1984 in Kutztown, Pennsylvania), stage and film actor and cofounder of the Group Theatre; his theatrical career spanned seven decades.

Luther (born Lutha) Adler was the son of Jacob P. Adler, an actor, producer, and director in the Yiddish theater. His mother, Sarah Levitskaya Lewis, was an actress. He had one brother, four sisters, and two half brothers. Adler first appeared on the stage at the age of five in a Yiddish production of *Schmendrick* at the Thalia Theatre on the Bowery in Manhattan. He continued to act in the Yiddish theater throughout his childhood, often appearing in productions with his brother, Jay, and sisters Julia, Stella, Celia, and Frances. (Stella Adler later became a prominent stage personality and acting teacher.) He was educated at the Lewis Institute in Chicago.

Adler's adult acting debut took place at the Provincetown Playhouse in New York City on 5 December 1921 in *The Hand of the Potter*. The following year he toured in

Luther Adler in *Men in White*, 1933. MUSEUM OF THE CITY OF NEW YORK/ARCHIVE PHOTOS

Sonia, then returned to New York City to make his Broadway debut playing Leon Kantor in *Humoresque* at the Vanderbilt Theatre in February 1923. In this production he was billed for the first time as Luther Adler, the name he used for the rest of his life. Several additional appearances in New York City led to a tour of South Africa and England in 1927 with Harry Green in *The Music Master, Is Zat So?,* and *Give and Take.* Back in New York City, he appeared with his mother and siblings in several productions in his father's repertory. This fruitful period of apprenticeship led directly to appearances in a number of prominent productions, beginning in January 1929 when he played Sam in *Street Scene.* In December of the same year he appeared at the Martin Beck Theatre as Piotr in a Theatre Guild presentation of *Red Dust.*

In 1932 Adler became a founding member of the Group Theatre, which propelled him to stardom on the New York stage, notably in the plays of Clifford Odets. He played Joe Bonaparte, the title role in *Golden Boy* (1937), the story of a prizefighter who is also a talented violinist and has to make a choice between those two careers. Brooks Atkinson, drama critic for the *New York Times,* wrote of Adler's performance in *Golden Boy* that he played "the part of the headlong fighter with the speed and energy of an open-field runner." Adler made his London debut in 1938 at the Saint James's Theatre in the role of Joe Bonaparte.

Adler also played the roles of Moe Axelrod in *Awake and Sing!* (1935) and Dr. Benjamin in *Waiting for Lefty* (1935), both works by Odets. During this period other members of the Group Theatre included Elia Kazan, Morris Carnovsky, and Adler's sister Stella. During his years with the Group Theatre, Adler appeared in *Night over Taos* (1932), *Success Story* (1932), Katharine Cornell's production of *Alien Corn* (1933), *Men in White* (1933), *Gold Eagle Guy* (1934), and Odets's *Paradise Lost* (1935), among others.

While remaining chiefly a stage actor throughout his life, Adler appeared in more than thirty films over the course of his career. Primarily a character actor, Adler twice played the role of Adolf Hitler, in *The Desert Fox* (1951) opposite James Mason, who played Field Marshal Erwin Rommel, and in *The Magic Face* (1951). Other film appearances include *D.O.A.* (1950), *Von Ryan's Express* (1965), *The Girl in the Red Velvet Swing* (1955), *The Last Angry Man* (1959), *The Man in the Glass Booth* (1975), *Voyage of the Damned* (1976), and *Absence of Malice* (1981). Adler also made a number of television appearances in such series as the *U.S. Steel Hour, The Twilight Zone, The Untouchables, Mission Impossible,* and *Hawaii Five-O.*

Although Adler's theatrical prominence was tied chiefly to his work as an actor, he produced or directed a number of productions. In 1943 and 1944 he directed a touring production of *Jane Eyre* in which he also starred as Mr. Rochester. He staged *A Flag Is Born* at the Alvin Theater in New York City in 1946 and later replaced Paul Muni in the role of Tevye. He directed a stock production of *Angel Street* in which he played Mr. Manningham. It played in Atlantic City in the summer of 1955 and in Detroit the following year. Adler starred as Eddie Carbone in a Chicago production of *A View from the Bridge* (1957) and on a tour of the show that he directed in 1958 and 1959.

Many of Adler's most prominent roles were those he played in his fifties and sixties, and they gained him recognition by a new generation of theatergoers. In 1953 he starred as Shylock in a New York City Center production of *The Merchant of Venice.* In 1956 he played the role of the physician in *A Month in the Country* at the Phoenix Theatre in New York. Adler played Lenin in *The Passion of Josef D.,* by Paddy Chayefsky, opposite Peter Falk's Stalin at the Ethel Barrymore Theatre in New York City in 1964.

The role which perhaps required more courage than any other for Adler to assume was that of Tevye in *Fiddler on the Roof* (1965). He not only had to replace the formidable Zero Mostel, but to take the lead in a musical although he had never previously appeared in one. He rose to the occasion, however, and went on to head the national touring cast the following year.

Adler was married twice, first to the well-known actress Sylvia Sydney from 13 August 1938 until they divorced in 1947. They had one son, Jacob Luther. On 24 April 1959 he married Julia Hadley Roche, to whom he remained married until his death. They had no children.

An assessment of Adler's work and character was made in a letter to the *New York Times* (10 March 1985) written shortly after his death and signed by Marlon Brando, Paul Newman, Alexander Scourby, Jack Lord, Joseph Wiseman, and Joseph Buloff. It said, in part:

> Luther brought unusual emotional power to his work together with an extraordinary magnetism and charm. . . . Throughout his long career he gave a glamour, a touch of something larger than life, to every part he played. He was fun to work with, fun to be with—a good comrade-in-arms, generous, thrilled by every actor who played with talent. . . . He was secure in his own powers . . . not an idol of the moment, but an actor of enduring value.

★

Lula Rosenfeld, *Bright Star of Exile: Jacob Adler and the Yiddish Theatre* (1977), an account of the career and family life of Luther Adler's father, Jacob Adler, with some information on Luther, was written by one of Jacob's grandchildren. See also Walter Rigdon, *Notable Names in the American Theatre,* rev. ed. (1976). Obituaries are in the *New York Times* (9 Dec. 1984) and *Variety* (12 Dec. 1984).

NATALIE B. JALENAK

AIKEN, George David (*b.* 30 August 1892 in Dummerston, Vermont; *d.* 19 November 1984 in Montpelier, Vermont), horticulturist and U.S. senator from Vermont (1941–1975), one of the moderate Eastern Republicans who forged a bipartisan consensus on foreign policy after World War II.

Aiken was the son of Edward Webster Aiken and Myra Cook Aiken, local farmers. He graduated from Brattleboro High School in 1909, then opened a 500-acre nursery. He married Beatrice M. Howard in 1914, and they had four children: Dorothy, Marjorie, Howard, and Barbara. Aiken pioneered in the commercial cultivation of flowers, authoring two books on horticulture—*Pioneering with Wildflowers* (1933) and *Pioneering with Fruits and Berries* (1936). He maintained his farm throughout his life and was president of the Vermont Horticultural Society and a member of the Putney Grange.

Aiken's political career began in 1922, when he ran unsuccessfully for the Vermont state legislature, where three generations of Aikens had served. He was elected to the Vermont house of representatives in 1930, became speaker in 1933, and was elected lieutenant governor in 1935 and governor in 1937. In 1938, at the Vermont Republican Lincoln Day Dinner, he gained national attention by criticizing his party's leaders. He advised them to drop their anti-Roosevelt and anti–New Deal animus and to come up with a positive program. "The greatest praise I can give to Lincoln," he told his dinner audience, "is to say that he would be ashamed of his party's leadership today." As governor, Aiken instituted a pay-as-you-go budget and reduced Vermont's debt. He was an early proponent of the St. Lawrence Seaway project and created an industrial-labor council to head off strikes.

Aiken was elected to the U.S. Senate in 1940. He served throughout his career on the Agriculture and Forestry Committee and became a leader of the farm bloc. He backed soil conservation programs, food stamps for the poor, crop insurance schemes, and loan programs for farmers. He supported the Tennessee Valley Authority and the Rural Electrification Administration. He favored flexible price supports rather than fixed subsidies. In trade policies he favored low tariffs and an extension of the Reciprocal Tariff Act, in contrast to most of his party's members in the 1940s. In domestic affairs Aiken was a moderate. He sponsored bills for federal aid to education and federal grants for libraries, the Employment Act of 1946, and a minimum wage act in 1947. He opposed many of Senator Robert Taft's antilabor measures but eventually voted for the Taft-Hartley Act and to override President Harry S. Truman's veto. In 1948, fed up with his party's conservative stance, he called for the resignation of the national party chairman, B. Carroll Reese.

During the Dwight D. Eisenhower administration (1953–1961), Aiken helped fashion bipartisan legislation. The Anderson-Aiken Amendment to the Civil Rights Act of 1957 removed a proposal giving power to the U.S. attorney general to bring school-desegregation suits, a softening of the bill that enabled the measure to pass. In the Kennedy-Johnson era (1961–1969), Aiken compiled a moderate record. He voted in 1962 against President John F. Kennedy's plan for medical care for the aged but in 1965 voted for Lyndon B. Johnson's Medicare proposals. He voted for the Civil Rights Act of 1964 and the Voting Rights Act of 1965, but he opposed using federal funding of schools as a lever to end racial segregation, believing that it would involve too much coercive use of power by the national government. He voted for food stamps in 1965 and helped expand the food stamp program into a major income-subsidy program in the 1970s. He voted for rural environmental assistance programs and for the preservation of wilderness areas. During the Richard Nixon administration (1969–1974), Aiken voted to confirm Clement F. Haynsworth and G. Harrold Carswell for the Supreme Court (both nominations failed). While he often supported

George David Aiken, 1938. UPI/CORBIS-BETTMANN

the administration, he opposed funding the supersonic transport (SST) and voted against the Lockheed loan guarantee of 1971.

Aiken achieved his greatest influence in foreign affairs, serving on the Senate Foreign Relations Committee and rising to become its ranking Republican by 1965. He was a bipartisan internationalist. He voted for the United Nations Charter, the Bretton Woods monetary agreement, and the emergency loan to Great Britain. In 1947 he voted for aid to Greece and Turkey and strongly supported Truman's cold war initiatives, helping to forge a bipartisan internationalist coalition in the Senate.

In the 1960s Aiken became an opponent of the Vietnam War. Although he voted for the Gulf of Tonkin Resolution of 1964, he opposed the subsequent escalation of the war. He came out against Johnson's bombing of North Vietnam in 1966, telling reporters that the president should "declare the United States the winner and begin deescalation." Aiken was in favor of Nixon's Vietnamization plans to remove U.S. forces, but he denounced Nixon's invasion of Cambodia in 1970 and was cosponsor of the Cooper-

Church Amendment to cut off funds for combat operations in Cambodia. In February 1971 he proposed an all-Asian conference to end the war. In May 1972, when Nixon mined Haiphong harbor, Aiken denounced it as brinksmanship, but he opposed attempts at funding cutoffs for the fighting in Vietnam. He opposed the McGovern-Hatfield end-the-war amendment in 1970 and a similar proposal in the Senate Foreign Relations Committee in 1972. In May 1973, after the United States withdrew its combat forces from Vietnam, he observed, "What we got was essentially what I recommended six years ago—we said we had won, and we got out."

Aiken was helpful to Nixon's overall superpower strategy of détente. In 1969 he sponsored an amendment to a foreign-aid authorization stating the sense of Congress that recognition of a foreign government "does not imply that the United States approves of the form, ideology, or policy"of that government. This was an effort to provide Nixon with political cover if he decided to recognize the Communist government of the People's Republic of China. He supported Nixon's arms control negotiations with the Soviet Union. At other times he took an independent tack, as in 1971, when Aiken and Senator Mike Mansfield proposed to cut the number of troops in Europe. Mansfield and Aiken also proposed a single six-year term for the president. As Aiken put it, the proposal "would allow a president to devote himself entirely to the problems of the nation and would free him from the millstone of partisan politics." This was one of Aiken's few ideas that went nowhere.

Aiken resigned from the Senate in ill health in 1974 at the age of eighty-two. He died of respiratory ailments and was survived by his second wife, Lola Pierotti, whom he had married on 30 June 1967 (his first wife died in 1966). He was buried in Dummerston.

George Aiken was one of the key figures in forging a bipartisan consensus on maintaining and expanding the post–New Deal domestic and foreign policies. A moderating force within his own party and the Senate, he was a man of character, homespun dignity, rural wit, and common sense. He represented an era in the Senate when effective governance was more important than partisan advantage, when political compromise with opponents was considered honorable, and when Senate politics was not considered a form of warfare.

★

George Aiken, *Aiken: Senate Diary, January 1972–January 1975* (1976), is an autobiographical work. An obituary is in the *New York Times* (20 Nov. 1984).

RICHARD M. PIOUS

ALBERTSON, Jack (*b.* 16 June 1907 in Malden, Massachusetts; *d.* 25 November 1981 in Hollywood Hills, California), stage, film, and television actor and one of only three actors to win an Oscar, a Tony, and an Emmy.

Albertson was the son of Leo and Flora Albertson, but he never knew his father, who abandoned the family before Jack was born. Flora supported Jack and his sister, the future actress Mabel Albertson, on the minimal wages she earned working for a shoe factory in Lynn, Massachusetts. Albertson's mother eventually married again, this time to Alex Erlich, a barber in Lynn.

Albertson learned to shoot pool in the local pool halls around Lynn, where he grew up. He developed enough skill at the game to hustle local players, and Lynn area pool parlors banned him from their establishments. Undaunted, Albertson traveled throughout New England earning extra money as a pool shark. For a time he worked at the General Electric plant in Lynn and the shoe factory that employed his mother. He also shipped out on a freighter for a brief period before trying his luck in show business.

Albertson performed as a dancer in vaudeville, but he realized early the limits of his skill in this area. He shifted his focus to comedy, working as a straight man for such esteemed comedians as Milton Berle, Bert Lahr, and Bert Wheeler. He eventually teamed up with Phil Silvers and performed in the Catskill Mountain resorts in upstate New York. In their early act Silvers would play the saxophone while Albertson danced a soft-shoe.

Albertson moved to Hollywood in 1937 to further his career as an actor. That same year he landed his first film role in the chorus of Shirley Temple's *Rebecca of Sunnybrook Farm.* He returned east in 1940 to perform in *Meet the People,* a political revue that teamed Albertson with Eddie Johnson in a song-and-dance routine called "The Same Old South," which was critical of the South. Albertson later referred to the routine as a "sort of early civil-rights song." *Meet the People,* which opened at the Mansfield Theater on 25 December 1940, marked Albertson's debut on the New York stage. He had small parts in a number of shows for the next seven years before landing his first major Broadway role in a revival of *The Red Mill* (1945–1946), replacing an ailing Eddie Foy and establishing himself as a comedian in his own right.

In 1950 Albertson was praised for his performance in the revue *Tickets Please!* In 1951 he hooked up again with Silvers for the stage production of *Top Banana,* which eventually took them on the road. Albertson starred in the film version of *Top Banana* in 1954. Around this time, he married his third wife, Wallace Thomson. They had one daughter, Maura Dhu, who later became an actress and singer.

Albertson claimed that the turning point in his career, the moment "people finally started becoming aware of [him] as a legitimate actor," came when he starred in a

Jack Albertson in *Grandpa Goes to Washington,* 1978. ARCHIVE PHOTOS

Los Angeles production of Samuel Beckett's *Waiting for Godot* alongside Joey Faye. Years later, Albertson played the most acclaimed role of his long career in the New York stage production of Frank D. Gilroy's *The Subject Was Roses* (1964). Gilroy was largely responsible for casting Albertson in the role. He had seen Albertson perform in *Burlesque* at the University of California at Los Angeles while in Hollywood trying to find backers and talent for *The Subject Was Roses.* He was impressed enough with Albertson's performance to consider him for the lead in *The Subject Was Roses,* but he repeatedly had to defend his decision to producers, directors, and financial backers who wanted to cast a better-known actor. The play opened to favorable reviews, and Albertson won a Tony Award and went on to play the role in the Metro-Goldwyn-Mayer film of the same title, for which he won an Oscar for best supporting actor of 1968. In 1972 Albertson opened in the Broadway production of Neil Simon's *The Sunshine Boys* to sterling reviews.

Albertson also acted in many feature films, including *Miracle on 34th Street* (1947), *Days of Wine and Roses* (1962), *How to Murder Your Wife* (1965), *The Flim-Flam Man* (1967), *Willy Wonka and the Chocolate Factory* (1971), and *The Poseidon Adventure* (1972). He made numerous appearances on television shows, including roles for *Playhouse 90, I Love Lucy, The Jack Benny Show, Twilight Zone,* and *The Dick Van Dyke Show.* Albertson also starred in several television series, including *The Thin Man* (1957–1959), *En-*

sign O'Toole (1962–1963), *Room for One More* (1962), and *Grandpa Goes to Washington* (1978–1979), but he is best remembered for his role on *Chico and the Man* (1974–1978), for which he won one of his two Emmy Awards. His second Emmy was for a guest appearance on a Cher special. Albertson's last performance was in the ABC production of *My Body, My Child,* which aired after his death from cancer.

Albertson's work as an actor spanned nearly six decades and earned him a place in the history of film, theater, and television as one of America's most endearing talents.

★

Frank Daniel Gilroy, *About Those Roses; or, How Not to Do a Play and Succeed* (1965), traces Gilroy's association with Albertson regarding the production of *The Subject Was Roses* and provides valuable insight into Albertson's life just before the apex of his critical success. Articles on Albertson appeared in the *New York Times* (7 Jan. 1973) and *Washington Post* (15 Sept. 1974). Obituaries are in the *New York Times* and *Washington Post* (both 26 Nov. 1981) and in *Screen World* 33 (1982).

KEVIN ALEXANDER BOON

ALBION, Robert Greenhalgh (*b.* 15 August 1896 in Malden, Massachusetts; *d.* 9 August 1983 in Groton, Connecticut), maritime historian, educator, and author best known for pioneering the study of American maritime history and training a generation of maritime historians.

Albion was the eldest son of James Francis Albion, a Universalist minister, and Alice Marion Lamb. When he was eight years old, he and his family moved to South Portland, Maine, where Albion and his two sisters spent their youth. In 1918 he completed his studies at Bowdoin College and received his A.B. in economics. Albion served in the United States Army infantry during World War I and rose to the rank of second lieutenant. Following the war he continued his education at Harvard University, where he received his A.M. in 1920 and, four years later, his Ph.D. in English history.

Albion's career as an educator began in 1920 when he was named a teaching fellow at Harvard. In 1922 he joined the history department at Princeton as an instructor. He became a full professor in 1939 and remained a member of the Princeton faculty until 1949. He also served as the director of the summer session from 1929 to 1942 and as assistant dean of the faculty from 1929 to 1943.

On 16 August 1923 Albion married Jennie Barnes Pope. A skilled writer, she coauthored four books with him and served as his personal editor. Their collaboration began with his doctoral dissertation and continued through the publication of his sixteenth book in 1972. They had no children.

Although the courses Albion taught prior to 1936 fo-

Robert G. Albion. COURTESY MYSTIC SEAPORT MUSEUM, INC.

cused on military and economic history, he emphasized maritime concerns and activities and their role in history. With the introduction of his first maritime history course, Albion stressed the vital economic role played by shipping and maritime industries. Affectionately nicknamed "Boats," his course became a favorite with students throughout his teaching career.

Albion began his writing career with the publication of his dissertation in 1926. During the next five decades he wrote eighteen volumes, fifteen of which were on maritime topics. He considered his book *The Rise of New York Port, 1815–1860* (1939) to be his best work. In 1951 he privately and informally published his *Naval and Maritime History: An Annotated Bibliography* for use by his students. Within its ninety-four pages Albion listed 1,800 entries of books and dissertations on maritime topics. A valuable reference work, this book's fourth edition (1972) contained more than 5,000 entries. In addition to books, Albion contributed six chapters to cooperative works, submitted over twenty articles to professional and popular journals, authored a regular column in the *American Neptune* between 1952 and 1958, and wrote over eighty reference articles for the *Dictionary of American Biography* and various encyclopedias. Most of his publications dealt with maritime history.

In 1941 Albion opened a symposium on American defense at the University of Pennsylvania by stating that the United States Army was following pre-Verdun ideas and practicing a policy the English called "promotion of senility," in which an aged leadership perpetuated an outdated military strategy. Shortly after his talk, Albion was appointed to a number of advisory positions with the military. He served as president of the American Military Institute (1941–1945), as a consultant to the War Department (1943), and as the historian of Naval Administration (1943–1950), in which capacity he supervised the preparation of 200 volumes of unpublished analyses of the Navy's administrative history. In recognition of this work, President Harry S. Truman presented Albion with a Presidential Certificate of Merit in 1948. From 1946 to 1950 Albion also served as a trustee of the Naval Foundation.

Albion left Princeton in 1949 to become the first Gardiner Professor of Oceanic History and Affairs at Harvard University. In 1959 and 1960 Albion, in conjunction with the Harvard Extension Department, filmed *The Expansion of Europe*, a course stressing maritime history, which broke new ground in televised teaching. Albion received emeritus status in 1963 and retired. Between 1964 and 1972, he worked with the Harvard Polaris Program to create a series of television courses for use on naval vessels.

In addition to his duties at Harvard, Albion served as a member of the executive committee of the Maine Historical Society (1958–1976) and as a trustee of the Penobscot Marine Museum (from 1960 on). In 1955 he became the cofounder of the Munson Institute of Maritime History at Mystic, Connecticut. He served as the institute's coordinator between 1955 and 1966 and then as its director until 1975.

Following his retirement from Harvard in 1963, he remained involved in academia and the maritime community, serving as president of the Maine Historical Society (1963–1970); visiting lecturer at the University of Connecticut (1964–1965), Emory University (1966), Carleton College (1966), the University of Maine (1966–1972), and Bowdoin College (from 1971 on); as a consultant to the U.S. Naval War College (1965); vice chairman of the Maine Archives Committee (1965–1973); member of the advisory board for the South Street Seaport museum (from 1969); vice chairman of the Archives Advisory Board (1968–1973); and overseer of the Bath (Maine) Marine Museum (from 1973). Albion also served on the boards of the Peabody Museum, the Essex Institute, and the Maine Maritime Museum.

In October 1976 Albion's wife, Jennie Barnes Pope, died. He then sold their family home in South Portland and moved to Groton, Connecticut. At the time of his death Albion was a resident of the Groton Regency Convalescent Home. He left no immediate survivors. On 15 August 1983, what would have been his eighty-seventh birthday, Albion was laid to rest in the Mount Pleasant Cemetery in South Portland, Maine.

Albion played an important role in the development and growth of maritime studies in the United States. He gave depth, form, and orientation to a field that had previously focused on battles, strategy, and life at sea by emphasizing the administrative side and the economics of maritime affairs. Albion understood that the administrative skills of individuals like Pepys or Forrestal made possible the naval victories of officers like Farragut or Nimitz. He also recognized that the most important aspect of any commercial voyage was making port with a cargo or ship that could turn a profit. This philosophy permeated his writings and his teaching as he trained generations of maritime historians and influenced the development of naval and maritime studies in the United States.

John H. Kemble, "Maritime History in the Age of Albion," in *The Atlantic World of Robert G. Albion* (1975), edited by Benjamin W. Labaree, discusses the role Albion played in the development of maritime studies in the United States, and his influence on students, scholars, and the museum world; also in the Labaree text, Joan Bentinck-Smith, "The Writings of Robert G. Albion," offers a complete listing of Albion's writings up to 1975. See "Calls Army Behind Times," *New York Times* (9 July 1941). Tributes are in Archibald R. Lewis, "Robert G. Albion, 1896–1983: An Appreciation," *American Neptune* 44, no. 1 (winter 1984): 61–62; and "Robert G. Albion: An Appreciation," *Log of Mystic Seaport* 35, no. 4 (winter 1984): 144. Obituaries are in the *New York Times* (13 Aug. 1983) and the *Mariner's Mirror* 70, no. 2 (May 1984): 116.

DIANE E. COOPER

ALGREN, Nelson (*b.* 28 March 1909 in Detroit, Michigan; *d.* 9 May 1981 in Sag Harbor, New York), novelist, short story writer, poet, and essayist best known for his portrayal of the dispossessed in American society, particularly in Chicago.

Nelson Algren was the youngest of the three children of Gerson Abraham, a machinist at the Packard Auto Company, and Goldie Kalisher, who ran a candy and cigarette store. Born Nelson Ahlgren Abraham, he legally changed his name in 1944. In 1913 the family moved to Chicago, where they lived near 71st Street and South Park; in 1921 they moved to 4834 North Troy Street on the Northwest Side. Algren attended Park Manor Grammar School and Hibbard High School (now Roosevelt High), from which he graduated in 1927. From 1927 to 1931 he worked his way through the University of Illinois at Urbana, where he maintained a B average and received a B.S. in journalism.

Unable to find work in Chicago because of the Great Depression, Algren moved to New Orleans, where he sold coffee and then toiletries door-to-door. In the spring of 1932 he traveled by boxcar to southern Texas, where he picked

Nelson Algren. ROBERT LEE MCCULLOUGH

oranges and grapefruit, ran a gas station, and worked as a carnival shill. He returned to Chicago and began sending out stories under the name Nelson Algren. His first published story, "So Help Me," appeared in the August 1933 issue of *Story* magazine. His first book, *Somebody in Boots* (1935), was concerned with the underclass; it sold only 762 copies. Deeply depressed at this apparent failure, Algren attempted suicide. His fortunes then seemed to reverse: on 26 April 1935 he was elected to the National Congress of the League of American Writers, and also that year his short story "The Brother's House" was included in *O. Henry Memorial Prize Stories*. In September 1936 he began writing guidebooks for the Works Progress Administration's Federal Writers' Project.

Algren married Amanda Kontowicz in March 1937; they divorced in 1946, remarried in 1952, and divorced again in 1955. In 1938 he and Jack Conroy founded the literary magazine *The New Anvil,* a left-leaning publication that lasted about two years. In May 1940 he moved to Chicago's Polish "Triangle." He became identified with the Polish-American community in spite of his Swedish descent (his paternal grandfather had converted to Judaism and left Sweden in the mid-nineteenth century). Algren's *Never Come Morning* (1942), about a Chicago Polish prizefighter, was banned from Chicago libraries because of its perceived

negative portrayal of Poles. Algren was inducted into the U.S. Army in 1942 and subsequently served in the field artillery and medical corps in Wales, France, and Germany. He returned to Chicago in November 1945, and the following year his collection of stories *The Neon Wilderness* was published. In February 1947 Algren began a love affair with the French feminist writer Simone de Beauvoir that lasted until 1965. Through her he became acquainted with the philosopher Jean-Paul Sartre and his intellectual circle.

The Man with the Golden Arm, Algren's masterpiece about Frankie Machine, a Chicago card dealer and drug addict, was published in 1949. It earned *Time* magazine's award for the best novel of the year, and the first National Book Award in 1950. Although Algren wrote in the naturalist tradition of Frank Norris and James T. Farrell, he tried to raise the suffering of his Chicago poor to a more lyric height. The lives of his characters are not tragic, but certainly poignant. In 1951 *Chicago: City on the Make,* an insightful prose-poem, was published. In 1955 he went to Hollywood to work with Otto Preminger on the movie version of *The Man with the Golden Arm*. He lasted just a week and would resent Preminger's dismissive treatment of him for the rest of his life. A successful stage version of the novel was presented the following year in New York City.

A Walk on the Wild Side, a graphic portrayal of the seamy side of New Orleans, was published in 1956. In this novel Algren was unable to raise brothel life in the "Big Easy" above the tawdry; the characters do not seem nearly as real as his Chicago dispossessed. Algren next began work on a never completed novel titled "Entrapment." On 31 December 1956 Algren fell through the ice not far from his home in Miller Beach (Gary, Indiana), an "accident" surrounded by questionable circumstances. Although he recovered physically, he never seemed quite the same person again. In 1957 Algren sold the movie rights to *A Walk on the Wild Side* for $25,000, but within sixty days lost it all gambling. He began cutting off old friends.

Algren finished a travel book, *Who Lost an American?,* in 1963 and the following year published with H. E. F. Donohue an extensive and revealing series of interviews titled *Conversations with Nelson Algren*. In 1965 he married Betty Ann Jones, an actress; they were divorced in 1967. *Notes from a Sea Diary: Hemingway All the Way* (1965) included Hemingway criticism and an account of Algren's adventures in the Far East. In 1965 and 1966 Algren gave a number of lectures, many of them on college campuses (he also taught writing at Montana State University in 1965 and at the University of Iowa in 1966 and 1967). The Illinois Arts Council and the *Atlantic Monthly* funded a trip to Saigon to write about the war in Vietnam. He arrived there on 15 December 1968; in early 1969 he was so severely beaten in a price dispute that he had to return home without completing his assignment.

In 1973 Algren published *The Last Carousel,* a collection of stories and sketches. The next year he received the American Academy and Institute of Arts and Letters Award for the novel (he was inducted into the Academy in February 1981). He moved to New Jersey and became interested in the triple-murder case of Rubin "Hurricane" Carter. Algren received a $6,000 grant from the National Endowment for the Arts to write about the case, which forms the basis of *The Devil's Stocking,* a novel published posthumously in 1983. In June 1980 he moved to Sag Harbor, New York, where within a year he would die of a heart attack. He is buried in Oakland Cemetery, Sag Harbor.

Nelson Algren lived among and associated with society's outcasts nearly all of his life. He numbered among his acquaintances and friends addicts, prostitutes, and criminals—the dispossessed and desperate. He was himself a hobo and a migrant worker, and he even spent time in jail during the 1930s. He wanted to be and became one of America's preeminent writers about the agony of poverty. He was attracted to the communist movement (he joined the John Reed Club in the 1930s) as an alternative to a capitalist system that he thought created too many have-nots. Friends who shared his vision and cause included the writers Jack Conroy, Richard Wright, and Studs Terkel.

Though he wrote five novels, numerous short stories, and several essays on those in need, Algren's productivity was impaired by obsessive gambling and by an incessant and tumultuous search for a love that would be his redemption, but that he never quite found. Nevertheless, Ernest Hemingway considered him one of the great writers of the time. Algren never forgot the poor nor forgave the society that he held responsible for so many persons living invisibly in misery. Although this message became unfashionable during the affluent 1950s and later, his works remain a testament to his skill and empathy in portraying the underclass.

★

Algren's manuscripts and papers are at the Ohio State University Library in Columbus. H. E. F. Donohue (with Nelson Algren), *Conversations with Nelson Algren* (1964), contains many important insights into Algren's life and mind. Martha Heasley Cox and Wayne Chatterton, *Nelson Algren* (1975), is the first full-length biographical-critical study. Bettina Drew, *Nelson Algren: A Life on the Wild Side* (1989), is a definitive critical biography. Matthew J. Bruccoli, *Nelson Algren: A Descriptive Bibliography* (1985), thorough and precise, is an indispensable aid. James R. Giles, *Confronting the Horror: The Novels of Nelson Algren* (1989), suggests that Algren's work extended beyond the boundaries of naturalism into an existentialist and absurdist vision of reality. See also Richard Studing, "Researching and Collecting Nelson Algren," *American Book Collector* 3 (Jan./Feb. 1982); Paul Garon, "Nelson Algren in Paperback: A Checklist," *Paperback Quarterly*

5 (winter 1982); and Joe Pintauro, "Algren in Exile," *Chicago* 37 (Feb. 1988). An obituary is in the *New York Times* (10 May 1981).

MARVIN J. LaHOOD

ALSTON, Walter Emmons (*b.* 1 December 1911 in Venice, Ohio; *d.* 1 October 1984 in Oxford, Ohio), major league baseball manager for the Brooklyn and Los Angeles Dodgers from 1954 to 1976.

The son of William Emmons Alston, a tenant farmer and autoworker at a Ford Motor Company plant, and Lenora Neanover, Walter was the first of two children. In his autobiography, *Alston and the Dodgers* (1966), Walter claimed, "Next to farming, dad loved baseball best, which accounts for my being a baseball man." His fast pitching earned Alston the nickname "Smokey."

Alston played basketball and was a right-handed pitcher on the baseball team at Milford Township High School in Darrtown, Ohio. During his high school years, Walter also played semiprofessional baseball on a few local teams, alongside his father and uncles Stan Alston and Paul Neanover. After graduating from high school in 1929, Alston enrolled at nearby Miami University in Oxford, Ohio, for the fall 1929 semester, but he dropped out after the 1930

Walter Alston. NATIONAL BASEBALL HALL OF FAME LIBRARY, COOPERSTOWN, N.Y.

spring term. He married Lela Vaughn Alexander on 10 May 1930. At the time, he was only eighteen years old. The young couple moved in with his parents, while Alston worked odd jobs and played baseball on Sundays. They had one child. In 1932, the Reverend Ralph Jones, the local Methodist minister, encouraged Alston to re-enroll in college and gave him fifty dollars to cover his tuition. Alston returned to Miami University in the fall of 1932. He worked his way through college by driving a laundry truck and occasionally shooting pool.

Alston continued his athletic career, serving as captain of the baseball and basketball teams at Miami University. Frank Wilton, Miami's baseball manager, switched Alston from pitcher to infielder to take advantage of the six-foot-two-inch 210-pounder's right-handed power hitting. In the spring of 1935, Alston graduated with a baccalaureate degree in physical education and a teaching certificate.

On 19 June 1935, Frank Rickey, younger brother of the pioneering baseball executive Branch Rickey, signed Alston to the St. Louis Cardinals. Alston began his professional baseball career as the third baseman for the Cardinals' Class C team in Greenwood, Mississippi. In 1936 Alston played for Huntington, West Virginia (Class C), leading the Mid-Atlantic league in home runs (35), batting .326, and driving in 114 runs. The St. Louis Cardinals called up Alston in September 1936 for a closer look. His major league playing career consisted of one inning in the last game of the season against the Chicago Cubs. Alston struck out in his only at bat and in two chances at first base was credited with one putout and one error.

From 1937 through 1939, Alston played for Rochester, Houston, and Portsmouth (Ohio), all St. Louis farm teams. In 1940 Alston played first base and managed the Portsmouth team to a sixth-place finish. During the 1941 and 1942 seasons, he played first base and managed the Springfield, Ohio, team. Alston returned to Rochester, a Triple A team, in 1943 to play first and third bases, but not to manage. Injuries plagued Alston during the 1944 season at Rochester. The Cardinal organization released him during the season. He was thirty-two years old, and his baseball career seemed to be over, when Branch Rickey, now the president of the Brooklyn Dodgers, hired Alston to manage and play for the Dodgers' minor league team at Trenton, New Jersey. In 1948 Alston was asked to manage at the highest level of the minor league system, St. Paul in the American Association. At this point Alston decided to make his entire livelihood in baseball. From 1935 to 1940, Alston had worked in the off-season as a science, physical education, and industrial arts teacher and basketball coach at the New Madison School District (Ohio). He taught high school at Lewistown, Ohio, from 1940 to 1948. Alston returned to manage St. Paul in 1949, and he managed at Montreal, the Dodgers' top farm team, from 1950 to 1953.

On 24 November 1953 Alston became the Brooklyn Dodgers manager, replacing the outspoken Chuck Dressen, who left the Dodgers after being refused a multiyear contract. Although Alston had just led the Montreal Royals to the "Little World Series" championship, sportswriters and fans were surprised at his appointment. It had been assumed that the popular Dodgers shortstop Pee Wee Reese would take the helm, but Reese wanted to continue as a player. Then speculation shifted as to what other major league manager might fill the vacancy.

The Dodgers finished second in the National League in 1954, but in 1955 Alston led the team to a National League pennant and a World Series championship, defeating the New York Yankees four games to three. This was the Dodgers' first World Series championship in nine appearances. Alston was the first manager to defeat the Yankees' manager Casey Stengel, who had led the Yankees to World Series victories in his previous five efforts. In 1956 the Dodgers again captured the National League pennant, but lost to the Yankees in the World Series.

The Dodgers moved to Los Angeles after the 1957 season. In their initial year in Los Angeles, the team sank to a seventh-place finish, but in 1959 Alston captured another World Series, defeating the Chicago White Sox. Alston's Dodgers won two more World Series—in 1963 over the Yankees and in 1965 over the Minnesota Twins. He returned to the World Series in 1966 and 1974, losing to Baltimore and Oakland, respectively. After completing twenty-three consecutive one-year contracts with the Dodgers, Alston retired from baseball after the 1976 season, returning to Darrtown, Ohio. He was elected to the Baseball Hall of Fame in 1983; in April of that year he suffered a severe heart attack. He died eighteen months later and was buried in Darrtown.

During his tenure with the Dodgers, Alston's teams won seven National League pennants and four World Series championships. His managerial style was quiet; he usually played percentage baseball and relied upon his coaches. He adapted to the changing attributes of his teams. The Brooklyn teams featured the batting of Duke Snider, Gil Hodges, Roy Campanella, Carl Furillo, and Jackie Robinson. The Los Angeles teams of the 1960s relied heavily on the pitching of Don Drysdale and Sandy Koufax, and on the speed of Maury Wills and Willie Davis. During the 1970s, Alston fielded teams with sluggers Ron Cey and Steve Garvey, base stealer Davey Lopes, and pitchers Mike Marshall and Don Sutton. In a sport known for firing its managers when teams do not live up to expectations, Alston's twenty-three years with the same ball club are topped only by Connie Mack's fifty years with the Philadelphia Athletics and John McGraw's thirty-one years with the New York Giants.

★

The National Baseball Library in Cooperstown, New York, has a clippings file on Alston. The two autobiographies are (with Si Burdick) *Alston and the Dodgers* (1966) and (with Jack Tobin) *A*

Year at a Time (1976). Alston also wrote (with Don Weiskopf) *The Complete Baseball Handbook: Strategies and Techniques for Winning* (1972). Alston's records can be found in *The Baseball Encyclopedia,* 10th ed. (1996). A good short history of the Dodgers for the Alston years is in Peter C. Bjarkman, *Encyclopedia of Major League Baseball Team Histories,* vol. 2: *National League* (1991). Book chapters on Alston are in Harvey Frommer, *Baseball's Greatest Managers* (1985), and Hank Nuwer, *Strategies of the Great Baseball Managers* (1988). *Current Biography* (1954) provides background on Alston's life prior to becoming manager of the Dodgers. Newspaper and magazine articles offer different perspectives on Alston's personality and managerial skills. Robert Creamer, "The Trouble with Walter," *Sports Illustrated* (13 May 1963), argues Alston was a competent manager who suffered public ridicule in Los Angeles because of his "utterly colorless" personality. Melvin Durslag, "Walt Alston . . . Manager with a Hair Shirt," *Look* (30 July 1993), claims Alston was a "quietly tough, able" leader who was the "most harassed manager in baseball." Pat Jordan, "Strong, Silent, Enduring," *Sports Illustrated* (11 Mar. 1974), suggests Alston was not a brilliant manager. Dave Anderson, "The Legacy and the Bus," *New York Times* (7 Oct. 1984), presents an insightful tribute to Alston based on conversations with former Dodger players. Obituaries are in the *New York Times* (2 Oct. 1984), *Cincinnati Enquirer* (6 Oct. 1984), and *Sporting News* (15 Oct. 1984).

PAUL FRISCH

Leslie Arends. REPRODUCED FROM THE COLLECTIONS OF THE LIBRARY OF CONGRESS

ARENDS, Leslie Cornelius (*b.* 27 September 1895 near Melvin, Illinois; *d.* 16 July 1985 in Naples, Florida), congressman from Illinois who served as House Republican whip for more than thirty years and greatly influenced Republican party politics during his forty-year tenure.

Arends was born on his family's farm outside Melvin, Illinois. His father, George T. Arends, who worked the farm, and his mother, Talea Weiss, a housewife, raised six children in addition to Les, as he was familiarly known throughout his life. The Arends typified the small-town, agrarian mind-set, fusing frugality, individualism, civic-mindedness, and Midwest conservatism with their deeply held Methodism—all traits that would deeply effect Les.

After primary school Arends attended Melvin High School from 1909 to 1912, graduating in three years. In addition to his academic activities, he played baseball and basketball and was a clarinetist in the school band. His genial personality won him high praise from classmates and teachers alike.

In 1912 Arends entered Oberlin College in Ohio, where he studied liberal arts and continued his involvement in sports. It was there that he acquired his love for golf, a game that he would later play with political colleagues. He left Oberlin after a year, however, returning to Melvin in 1913. His father had started a grain business, and Les assisted him in this vocation. In addition, the young Arends worked

part time at a local bank. His father soon purchased enough stock in the bank to control it and renamed it the Commercial State Bank.

In part because of his German ancestry, Arends proved his patriotism by enlisting in the U.S. Navy when World War I broke out. He spent the war in the navy band. Discharged in 1919, Arends returned to Melvin and helped found the local American Legion Post. Rising rapidly through the Legion ranks, he gained local renown as a spirited public speaker. In addition to working at his father's bank, Arends worked for the Northwestern Life insurance company, purchased his own farm, and participated in local sports associations. He joined the Ford County Farm Bureau, an affiliate of the politically powerful Illinois Farm Bureau, remained active in his local Methodist Church, and joined the Masons. In 1934 he became president of Commercial State Bank.

With his personal charm and impressive professional credentials, Arends attracted the attention of local Republican officials, one of whom was Everett McKinley Dirksen, who had recently been elected to the U.S. House of Representatives. After some prompting from Dirksen, Arends ran for Congress in the 1934 election. Defeating four Republican primary opponents, he faced incumbent Democratic congressman Frank J. Gillespie in the general election. Arends conducted an energetic door-to-door campaign, and his magnetic personality and Midwestern charm and ideology won over his rural constituency. Despite the overwhelming popularity of President Franklin D. Roosevelt and the New Deal, Arends managed to win his election—he was the only Republican to unseat an incumbent Democratic congressman that year. Arends later claimed that his first campaign amounted to "six months of the hardest work I've ever put in in my life, day and night." Arends's district, the Illinois Seventeenth Congressional District, contained Bloomington, the largest city he represented in an otherwise rural seat. It comprised Ford, Iroquois, Kankakee, Livingston, McLean, Vermillion, and Woodford counties.

Arends found himself in two contradictory worlds in Congress. He began his political career at the height of the New Deal, and decried what he saw as needless deficit spending, wasteful bureaucratic programs, make-work agencies such as the Works Progress Administration, and, to him, menacingly socialistic creations like the Tennessee Valley Authority. He denounced the expanding federal government and supported states' rights. Arends also found himself, however, in the congenial atmosphere of a Washington that shed its partisanship after the votes were counted. In this good-old-boy network, Arends thrived. His charm, intellect, and self-effacing humor won him many friends on both sides of the aisle. Politicians from Richard M. Nixon to Thomas P. ("Tip") O'Neill counted Arends as a close friend.

While Arends stood as a preeminent critic of New Deal legislation, he could put his conservative political philosophy aside to serve his constituents. He supported the creation of a price-support system and other programs designed to aid farmers. His personality and effectiveness in office won him easy reelection, and his mastery of the "insider" politics of Washington and his close friendships with members of the Republican caucus led to Arends's election as Republican whip in 1943.

While keeping Republican members informed of upcoming legislation and rounding up votes, Arends learned the needs of each member of his caucus and weighed in with his brand of folksy charm to secure a vote when necessary. He continued as majority whip through the Republican majorities of 1947–1949 and 1953–1955, and served as minority whip for the rest of his time in Congress. On 21 April 1946, at the age of fifty-one, Arends married Betty Tychon; they had one daughter.

In foreign policy, Arends began as a strict isolationist and argued against Roosevelt's growing involvement in Europe. After World War II, however, he became a supporter of the cold war and backed President Harry S. Truman's efforts in Korea and President Lyndon B. Johnson's engagement in Vietnam.

The politicians who benefited most from Arends's sup-

port, both professionally and personally, were Republican presidents. Arends shepherded much of Dwight D. Eisenhower's legislative program through Congress, and he was one of the president's favored golfing partners. Arends was also a strong backer of Richard M. Nixon; he was among the last major political figures to ask the president not to resign. Nixon said of the moment he resigned from office: "The emotional level in the room was almost unbearable. . . . When I heard Les Arends, one of my closest and dearest friends, sobbing with grief, I could no longer control my emotions, and I broke into tears." Arends was also a strong supporter of President Gerald R. Ford, with whom he forged a close relationship when Ford was Republican leader in the House.

While he had vowed never to retire, Arends found his cherished congressional seat redistricted after the 1970 census. Although he won his 1972 election in a new district, the thrill of campaigning had left him. He retired from politics in 1975. He moved with his wife to Naples, Florida, and except for a brief appointment to President Ford's Foreign Intelligence Advisory Board in 1976, he bowed out of the political realm. Arends died of a heart attack and was buried in Melvin Cemetery in Melvin, Illinois.

Les Arends was instrumental to the inner workings of the Republican party for much of the forty years that he served in Congress. As whip for thirty years, Arends consistently advocated fiscal and moral conservatism and states' rights. From the 1940s until the 1970s, an internal battle for the soul of the Republican party was fought between so-called Rockefeller Republicans and those embracing a more conservative philosophy embodied by Arends. With perseverance and ability, Arends exerted strong behind-the-scenes influence on the House Republican caucus, ensuring that the conservative wing would play the dominant role in Republican party politics.

★

The Leslie C. Arends Papers at Illinois Wesleyan University, Bloomington, Illinois, is a comprehensive collection of Arends's correspondence and personal papers, as well as newspaper accounts. The *Danville Commercial News* (26 May 1960) includes an insightful interview of Arends by Frederick D. Drake. Edward L. Schapsmeier and Frederick H. Schapsmeier, "Serving Under Seven Presidents: Les Arends and His Forty Years in Congress," *Illinois Historical Journal* 85, no. 2 (1992): 105–118, provides an in-depth summary of Arends's political life. Midwestern attitudes and historical background are provided in Robert W. Frizzell, "Reticent Germans: The East Frisians of Illinois," *Illinois Historical Journal* 85, no. 3 (1992): 161–174. Obituaries are in the *New York Times,* the *Washington Post,* the *Chicago Tribune,* and the *St. Louis Post-Dispatch* (17 July 1985).

MARK SCHUSKY

ARMOUR, Norman (*b.* 14 October 1887 in Brighton, England; *d.* 27 September 1982 in New York City), Foreign Service officer who served as minister to Haiti and Canada and as ambassador to Chile, Argentina, Spain, Venezuela, and Guatemala.

Armour was one of four children of Harriette Foote and George Allison Armour, Americans on a visit to Great Britain when their son was born. Norman grew up in Princeton, New Jersey. George Armour had resided in Princeton for many years and was a generous contributor to Princeton University, of which he was an alumnus. Norman Armour attended Saint Paul's School in Concord, New Hampshire, for his preparatory education and then went on to Princeton, graduating in 1909 with an A.B. He received an LL.B. from Harvard Law School in 1913, then returned to Princeton, earning the graduate degree of A.M. in 1915. He would later become the first Princeton alumnus to receive the college's Woodrow Wilson Award, established in 1957.

Before entering Harvard Law School, Armour had served in the American embassy in Vienna, Austria, for three months. Although he was admitted to the New Jersey bar in 1914, he decided to follow a diplomatic career. In 1915 Armour joined the U.S. Foreign Service and became an attaché in the American embassy in Paris, France. He was there for less than a year.

Norman Armour examines state papers at his home in Camden, New Jersey, 1947. UPI/Corbis-Bettmann

In 1916 Armour was sent to Saint Petersburg, Russia, as third secretary of the American embassy, and in 1917 he was promoted to second secretary. Armour witnessed the disintegration of czarist Russia and was present in Saint Petersburg during the Bolshevik Revolution in the fall of 1917. He also witnessed the signing of the 1918 Brest-Litovsk Treaty that took Russia out of World War I. During this tumultuous period in Russia, Armour helped Princess Myra Koudacheff of Saint Petersburg escape to Sweden. He was imprisoned briefly by the Bolshevik authorities as a result but managed to escape and made his way to Finland. On 2 February 1919 Armour married Princess Myra in Stockholm, Sweden. The couple would have one son, also named Norman.

From 1919 to 1920 Armour served as second secretary to the U.S. embassy in Brussels, Belgium. He then served as first secretary of the U.S. legation at The Hague, Netherlands, in 1920. Soon he was transferred again, this time to Montevideo, Uruguay, where he was first secretary in 1921 and 1922. Beginning in 1922, Armour worked for two years as assistant to the undersecretary of state in Washington, D.C. He then became first secretary of the embassy in Rome, Italy, staying there from 1924 to 1925. Next, he became counselor of the embassy in Tokyo, Japan (1925–1928), and in Paris, France (1928–1932).

Armour was appointed U.S. minister to Haiti in October 1932 and played an important role there in bringing about normal relations with the United States. In 1932 the United States and Haiti were negotiating an agreement under which U.S. Marines were to be withdrawn, after having occupied Haiti since 1915. The withdrawal took place in August 1934, and in 1935 U.S. control of Haiti's financial affairs also was discontinued.

In June 1935 Armour became U.S. minister to Canada. He then became ambassador to Chile in January 1938. He served as chairman of the American delegation to the Third Pan-American Highway Conference at Santiago, Chile, in 1939. His next assignment was ambassador to Argentina between 1939 and 1944. This was a difficult posting, which involved negotiating the complex wartime relationship that existed between the United States and a country sympathetic to the Axis powers.

When relations with Argentina deteriorated, Armour was recalled to Washington. There, he became director of the State Department's Office of Latin American Affairs and worked on the Dumbarton Oaks Conference on world security affairs. Late in 1944 Armour was sent to Madrid as ambassador to Spain, but he quit after only nine months. He later claimed that he had left out of "disgust" with the fascist government there. He retired from the Foreign Service in January 1946. In 1947 Princeton University awarded him an honorary LL.D. degree.

President Harry S. Truman called Armour out of retirement in 1947 to became assistant secretary of state for political affairs. Armour was responsible for coordinating the State Department's four geographical divisions, centralizing Foreign Service operations, and assessing the skills of Foreign Service officers. Although his responsibilities were primarily administrative, Armour played an active role as an adviser on Latin American policy. He urged greater U.S. economic aid to Latin America at a time when many in the State Department focused on Europe. Armour believed that Latin America's dissatisfaction with American assistance had led to a deterioration of relations with the United States. Serving as a member of the U.S. delegation to the Ninth International Conference of the American States at Bogotá, Colombia, in 1948, Armour pushed Secretary of State George C. Marshall into assuring the Latin American countries that the United States had not forgotten their problems.

Armour retired once again in July 1948, at the age of sixty, but he was recalled in 1950, this time to serve as ambassador to Venezuela, where the United States was carrying on delicate oil negotiations. He served until 1951, when he again left the Foreign Service.

During the first days of Dwight D. Eisenhower's presidency, Armour joined other Foreign Service officers in protesting Senator Joseph R. McCarthy's attacks on the State Department. In March 1953, for example, after some senators challenged the nomination of Charles Bohlen as ambassador to the Soviet Union, Armour and others sent a letter to the Senate Foreign Relations Committee in support of Bohlen. In January 1954 Armour publicly joined four other career diplomats in denouncing the "sinister" effects of McCarthy's attacks on the Foreign Service. In that letter the five men charged that the government's loyalty, security, and personnel policies could produce "a Foreign Service competent to serve a totalitarian government."

In 1954 Armour was once more called out of retirement, this time to become ambassador to Guatemala. He arrived in that country just after the Central Intelligence Agency had helped overthrow the government of Jacobo Guzmán Arbenz. Armour's job was to aid the new government in restoring the Guatemalan economy. Claiming that the economic recovery of Guatemala was well under way, Armour retired again in May 1955. He was called out again, briefly, in October 1956; at that time Senator J. William Fulbright, chairman of the special Senate subcommittee investigating U.S. foreign aid, appointed Armour to a panel studying three U.S. aid recipients. Assigned to observe activities in Greece, Turkey, and Iran, Armour reported back to the committee in March 1957 that new foreign aid efforts were needed. Armour retired completely from public life after this fact-finding mission.

Norman Armour died at home in Manhattan in New York City and was buried in Princeton Cemetery in Prince-

ton, New Jersey. His religious affiliation was Episcopal. He was a member of the Princeton, Brook, Century, Metropolitan, Alibi, and Chevy Chase clubs.

A man of strong beliefs and morals, Norman Armour rose rapidly in his career, despite his many retirements. He worked tirelessly to improve U.S. relations with Latin America and had a significant impact on U.S. policy toward that region, but it was his strong sense of values that particularly stood out. In an interview in 1976, Armour claimed that "of all the memorable events in my career, I think that on balance I could say that I'm proudest of something I did after I retired," referring to the open letter of protest sent to Senator McCarthy in 1954.

★

Armour's personal papers are located at Princeton University, in the Seeley G. Mudd Manuscript Library. Discussion of Armour can be found in Randall B. Woods, *The Roosevelt Foreign-Policy Establishment and the "Good Neighbor": The United States and Argentina, 1941–1945* (1979), and Mario F. Russo, *United States–Spanish Relations, 1945: The Norman Armour Mission* (1984). An obituary is in the *New York Times* (29 Sept. 1982).

MICHELLE C. MORGAN

ASTAIRE, Adele Marie (*b.* 10 September 1898 in Omaha, Nebraska; *d.* 25 January 1981 in Phoenix, Arizona), acclaimed vaudeville and musical theater dancer and comedian whose stage career was spent performing with her brother, Fred Astaire.

Adele Marie Austerlitz, later known as Adele Astaire, was the first child of Frederic Austerlitz, an immigrant from Vienna, Austria, who settled in Omaha, Nebraska, in 1895, and Ann Geilus Austerlitz, an Omaha native of Alsatian descent. Frederic Austerlitz worked for the Storz Brewing Company. A second child, Frederick Austerlitz, Jr., later known as Fred Astaire, was born eighteen months after Adele.

Like many little girls in Omaha, Adele, nicknamed "Delly," enrolled in Chambers' Dancing Academy, where she learned easily and demonstrated talent. In 1904, Ann Austerlitz took the children, aged six and four, to New York City to see if Adele's dance potential might be developed into a marketable skill.

In New York, Adele and Fred enrolled in Claude Alvienne's dancing school and learned their school subjects from their mother. In 1905, with two electrically wired wedding-cake props, the children, costumed as bride and groom, toured the country on the Orpheum vaudeville circuit. The name "Astaire," chosen for its appeal on theater programs, was the maiden name of their paternal grandmother and became the children's new last name and later that of the parents. When angry at an audience, Adele backstage would stick out her tongue. In her leisure time she played with paper dolls.

As she neared her teen years Adele grew to be three inches taller than Fred, and bookings became hard to get. One theater manager reported that "the girl seems to have talent, but the boy can do nothing." For two years Adele and her brother retired to Weehawken, New Jersey, where for the only time in their lives they attended public school. After this hiatus they enrolled in Ned Wayburn's dancing school in New York, and in 1911 Wayburn devised a new vaudeville act for them entitled *A Rainy Saturday*.

In 1914, to improve chances of making the big time, a complete reworking of the act was begun. For six months Adele and Fred were coached by the vaudeville team of Aurelia Coccia and his wife, Minnie Amato. With the resulting act titled *Fred and Adele Astaire in New Songs and Smart Dances,* the juvenile image was shed and the two enjoyed their first showstopping success.

Between 1917 and 1932, Adele appeared with her brother in ten Broadway musicals, three of which went on to London productions: *Over the Top* (1917), *The Passing Show of 1918, Apple Blossoms* (1919), *The Love Letter* (1921), *For Goodness Sake* (1922), *The Bunch and Judy* (1922), *Stop Flirting* (1923, the London version of *For Goodness Sake*), *Lady, Be Good!* in New York (1924) and London (1926), *Funny Face* in New York (1927) and London (1928), *Smiles* (1930), and *The Band Wagon* (1931).

In *The Love Letter,* Adele and Fred first performed what would become their signature dance: the comic "runaround," in which the pair ran in ever-widening circles until they were offstage. *The Bunch and Judy,* their first show as stars, was a flop. In an attempt to promote the show with some publicity, on 9 December 1922, Charles Dillingham, the producer, threw a "twenty-first" birthday party for Adele, who was actually twenty-four years old. Among the gifts was a ton of coal from a Pittsburgh admirer.

During the eighteen-month run of *Stop Flirting,* which toured England and played in London, Adele and Fred were the toasts of the British capital. Their acquaintance was sought by the Prince of Wales and other royals, their names bought to endorse toothbrushes and cigarettes, and their opinions solicited by reporters. *Lady, Be Good!,* the Astaires' first Gershwin show, was a smash hit in New York and in London.

Throughout their adult partnership, Adele, who was never obsessive about rehearsals like her perfectionist brother, enjoyed nightclubs and socializing whenever she could. Onstage her charm covered up missteps that only her brother noticed. Offstage Adele often used the crude language she picked up in the theater. Despite their personality differences, Adele's relationship with her brother was always one of mutual love and support. When they

Adele and Fred Astaire in *Funny Face,* 1927. MUSEUM OF THE CITY OF NEW YORK/ARCHIVE PHOTOS

were apart, they constantly exchanged letters, gifts, and telephone calls.

On 9 July 1928, while on a weekend in Long Island, Adele suffered burns from a speedboat fire and was hospitalized. Despite rumors that her career was over, by 5 August she had reported to work for the London engagement of *Funny Face*. After another successful run in London, she and Fred were in an unsuccessful Florenz Ziegfeld show, *Smiles*. Adele had decided that as soon as she could retire from a hit she would marry Charles Cavendish, the younger son of the Duke of Devonshire. Her opportunity came with the next successful revue, *The Band Wagon,* and Adele's final performance was in Chicago on 5 March 1932.

On 9 May 1932, Astaire was married in England, and her principal residence became Lismore Castle in County Waterford, Ireland. In late September 1933 a daughter died shortly after birth, and in September 1935 twin newborn sons also died. Her tragedies continued when, on 24 March 1944, her husband, aged thirty-nine with a history of alcoholism, died from liver disease.

On 28 April 1947, Astaire married Kingman Douglass, a financier who from 1950 to 1952 was assistant director of the Central Intelligence Agency. The couple lived in Middleburg, Virginia, in New York City, and in Jamaica. After twenty-four years of marriage Douglass died of a heart ailment on 10 October 1971 in New York. Astaire then lived in Phoenix, Arizona, where on 6 January 1981 she suffered a stroke. She died on 25 January, never having regained consciousness. She was buried in Oakwood Memorial Park in Chatsworth, California.

As a performer in the 1920s, Adele Astaire enchanted audiences with her humor and lighthearted verve. She, along with her brother, personified qualities that appealed to a war-weary public, and the new popular music by the Gershwins and others perfectly suited their style. Her more lasting achievement is that she led her younger brother into show business. On 10 April 1981, when receiving a Life Achievement Award from the American Film Institute, Fred Astaire said that it was his sister who "was mostly responsible for my being in show business. She was the whole show, she really was, of all the vaudeville acts and the musical comedies we did together. Delly was the one that was the shining light, and I was just there pushing away." As Fred Astaire's first partner, Adele Astaire secured her place in the history of entertainment.

★

Fred Astaire, *Steps in Time* (1959), is a gentlemanly autobiography and the basic text for Astaire information. Other sources include Michael Freedland, *Fred Astaire* (1976), a trustworthy biography of Fred with details about Adele and especially good on her experiences in England; Bob Thomas, *Astaire, the Man, the Dancer* (1984), an entertaining biography of Fred with information about Adele; and Sara Giles, *Fred Astaire, His Friends Talk* (1988), a verbatim record of friends' comments on Fred and his family members, including Adele, that conveys a sense of her personality. Hugh Leamy, "The Ascending Astaires," *Collier's* (31 Mar. 1928), portrays Adele as a young whirlwind. Adele Astaire, "I'm Getting What I Want Out of Life," *Hearst's International Cosmopolitan* (Nov. 1935), contains Adele's account of her marriage and of English life. Lincoln Barnett, "Adele Astaire Comes Home," *Life* (19 Nov. 1945), reprinted in Lincoln Barnett, *Writing on Life: Sixteen Close-Ups* (1951), is an account of the middle-aged Adele returning to New York after World War II. An obituary is in the *New York Times* (26 Jan. 1981).

SUSAN MOWER

ATKINSON, (Justin) Brooks (*b.* 28 November 1894 in Melrose, Massachusetts; *d.* 13 January 1984 in Huntsville, Alabama), called the "conscience of the theater" as drama critic of the *New York Times* from 1925 to 1960, a cofounder in 1936 and first president of the New York Drama Critics Circle, and Pulitzer Prize–winning foreign correspondent.

The third of four children of Jonathan H. Atkinson, a self-styled merchandise broker, and Garafelia Taylor, a housewife, Justin regarded his father, a self-educated, compulsive reader, as "fabulously knowledgeable" and followed his example. As a Harvard freshman, he found that most of the books assigned in his English course were in his father's library.

The young Justin Atkinson (later self-recalled as "an objectionable little militarist" who loved flags, uniforms, and marching on patriotic occasions) had a happy suburban/semirural "puritan" boyhood despite a "certain anxiety about money hanging over the household." Career hunting at age ten, he considered preaching and forestry but discovered printing was "the most admirable of the crafts." On a toy typewriter, he typed a daily newspaper, *The Melrose Record;* a neighbor, Frank Swan, paid one cent to read it. A toy printing press arrived and the daily was abandoned for a biweekly magazine, *The Watchout,* read by Swan and twenty or thirty others. Swan gave Justin a book that Atkinson still treasured sixty-nine years later. Swan's death was the boy's first such loss; the sight of his elderly friend in a coffin brought hysterics.

At Harvard, Atkinson wrote pieces on George Bernard Shaw for the *Boston Herald.* After graduation (A.B., 1917) he worked as a reporter for the *Springfield Daily News,* leaving in the fall to teach English at Dartmouth College (1917–1918). In 1918 he served as a U.S. Army corporal in France. From 1919 to 1922 he was a police reporter at the *Boston Evening Transcript* and assistant to that newspaper's legendary drama critic H. T. Parker. From 1920 to 1922 Atkinson was associate editor of the *Harvard Alumni Bulletin.* In 1922, when his job inquiry to the *New York Times* brought an invitation to visit next time he was in New York, Atkinson "took the train the same day," interviewed, and joined the *Times* as editor of its Sunday book review section, occasionally also reviewing plays. He became drama critic in 1925, replacing Stark Young. In Manhattan, he enjoyed walks along the waterfront, about which he wrote in *Skyline Promenades: A Potpourri* (1925).

On 18 August 1926 he married Oriana MacIlveen, a writer. At their country house in the Catskill Mountains he spent happy summers enjoying the views and bird watching. Though the couple had no other children, stepson Bruce T. MacIlveen would later add five step-grandchildren and nine step-great-grandchildren to Atkinson's family.

From 1925 to 1931 "J. Brooks Atkinson" modeled himself on his mentor Parker, frequently writing "solemn and moralistic" reviews and articles of "staggering length," but on 27 October 1931 he surprised coworkers by finishing a negative review of a musical with the flippant remark: "As for the girls, they are O.K." Shortly thereafter he dropped the "J." from his byline and in 1932 he destroyed scrapbooks of his previous reviews, symbolizing the maturation of his personal style.

His new style featured brief, "erudite, witty" critiques in clear, carefully chosen, yet often colloquial language. Of *You Can't Take It with You* (1936) he wrote, "Mr. Hart and Mr. Kaufman . . . have never scooped up an evening of such

Brooks Atkinson. NEW YORK TIMES CO./ARCHIVE PHOTOS

tickling fun," and of Maurice Evans's *Hamlet* (1938), "Only the dopes will stay away from this one." The playwright S. N. Behrman called Atkinson's signature style recognizable "if any random paragraph were read aloud to you in a guessing game." Yet a "myth of sedateness" still surrounded Atkinson, possibly due to his exceptional moral integrity.

Dissatisfied with the 1935 Pulitzer Prizes in drama, Atkinson and a group of critics, including John Mason Brown and John Gassner, formed the New York Drama Critics' Circle in 1936. Atkinson was elected as its first president.

Atkinson preferred to come to each new play as "the public's delegate" with as few preconceptions as possible. "You can't be objectively wrong or right about a work of art," he said. "You can only have a personal reaction to what other people have done. The only mistake you can make is not to say what you think."

"The newspaper business is my real enthusiasm," Atkinson once said, but his writing ranged far beyond journalism. He wrote the biography *Henry Thoreau: The Cosmic Yankee* (1927), and in *East of the Hudson* (1931), he recalled making Manhattan his Walden and modeling his style on that of Thoreau. In 1934 he wrote *The Cingalese Prince; or,*

Around the World on a Freighter, a well-received travel book. He edited and wrote the introductions to *Walden and Other Writings of Henry David Thoreau* (1937) and *The Complete Essays and Other Writings of Ralph Waldo Emerson* (1940) and wrote about his pet dog in *Cleo for Short* (1940).

Rejected as too old when he tried to enlist after Pearl Harbor and restless reviewing plays during World War II, Atkinson asked for a leave of absence and assignment as foreign correspondent. Thereafter, he served in China (1942–1944) and the Soviet Union (1945–1946) for the *New York Times.* Returning home after ten months in Moscow, Atkinson infuriated the Soviet government with a series of articles describing its spirit as "fundamentally reactionary" and concluding that it "instinctively thinks in terms of force in external affairs." The series won Atkinson the 1947 Pulitzer Prize for correspondence.

His return to theater criticism in 1946 was welcomed by theater artists and producers, who valued his opinions and especially his genuine excitement and enthusiasm. These attributes, Atkinson felt, were the most valuable things a reviewer could bring to plays and communicate to readers, many of whom regarded Atkinson as a mentor as well as a reviewer.

Atkinson was not comfortable affecting people's livelihoods by influencing Broadway's box-office receipts. Although he stubbornly rejected pressure from superiors at the *Times* who disagreed with his opinions, he occasionally returned to re-review shows if he felt he had been too harsh, and he wrote extra Sunday pieces about plays he liked that were doing poorly. *Broadway Scrapbook* (1947) was a collection of his theater articles. *Once Around the Sun* (1951) observed a year of daily life in the city.

Leaving Broadway to see shows performed in converted basements and storefronts, Atkinson was the first major critic to report on off-Broadway theater, hastening the public's discovery of such new talents as the director José Quintero, producer Joseph Papp, and actors Colleen Dewhurst, Geraldine Page, George C. Scott, and Jason Robards. In 1955 Atkinson wrote the foreword to a play anthology, *New Voices in the American Theater.* On Atkinson's retirement, Quintero observed that "without his encouragement and criticism, there would not have been an off-Broadway theater."

Atkinson did not ordinarily mingle socially with theater folk, thinking it improper for a critic, but on 2 March 1958 he was lured to a surprise party at Sardi's restaurant arranged by colleagues to celebrate his thirty-sixth year at the *Times;* guests included Arthur Miller and Marilyn Monroe, Laurence Olivier, Helen Hayes, Katharine Cornell, and Thornton Wilder. In later years, after election to the Players Club, Atkinson found actors were "much more stimulating and delightful than I had imagined they would be."

In 1960, the year Atkinson relinquished the critic's chair,

Actors' Equity awarded him a life membership. In September the Mansfield Theater on West Forty-seventh Street was renamed the Brooks Atkinson Theater; he was the first critic so honored. In November he appeared on the television series *Play of the Week* to introduce Eugene O'Neill's *The Iceman Cometh.*

From 1960 to 1965, under the heading "Critic at Large," Atkinson wrote essays in the *New York Times* on whatever interested him. A collection of these pieces, ranging from nature and environmentalism through politics and Shakespearean scholarship, was published in 1963 as *Tuesdays and Fridays,* the days his column appeared. His last regular *Times* byline appeared on 30 April 1965. Then, according to former colleague John K. Hutchens, the *Times* "retired him altogether, with a shocking absence of public ceremony or even personal civility."

Atkinson wrote on American theater for the London *Daily Telegraph. Brief Chronicles* (1966) was another collection of his articles. A longtime admirer and champion of Sean O'Casey, he edited and wrote the foreword to *The O'Casey Reader: Plays, Autobiographies, Opinions* (1968). A major historical work, *Broadway* (1970), covered a century of American theater in Atkinson's breezy style, including biographies of producers, playwrights, stars, and critics, with critical comments on their place in America's theatrical culture. His love of America's natural landscape found expression in *This Bright Land: A Personal View* (1972).

On 29 November 1980 the Theater Committee for Eugene O'Neill awarded the frail, ill Atkinson a medal for "enriching the universal understanding of the playwright's work." Moved by this tribute, delivered to his rural Durham, New York, home by a busload of friends and associates, Atkinson called this the greatest moment of his life.

In 1981 the Atkinsons moved to Huntsville, Alabama, to be near Bruce MacIlveen and his family. Robert G. Lowery edited Atkinson's *Sean O'Casey: From Times Past* (1982), in which London's *Times Literary Supplement* (14 January 1983) found "enlightening insights" and "an intimate sense of O'Casey's art in relation to the movement of the theatre."

Variously described as a thin, mustached, bespectacled, pipe-smoking, and cordial person, Brooks Atkinson died at Crestwood Hospital in Huntsville after a bout with pneumonia. According to his wishes, his remains were cremated. There was no funeral service.

The Broadway stage was at its zenith during Atkinson's career, which began before talking films and television lured away the mass audience and when a whole generation of talented new theater artists was emerging. In 1973 Atkinson provided a delightful summary of his more than 3,000 opening nights as Broadway's most influential and popular reviewer by collaborating with the caricaturist Al Hirschfeld on *The Lively Years: Reviews and Drawings of the Most Significant Plays Since 1920.*

★

The Billy Rose Theater Collection at the New York Public Library for the Performing Arts, Lincoln Center, contains many volumes of uncatalogued newspaper clippings and magazine articles by and about Brooks Atkinson as well as memorabilia of his various honors. Atkinson's "A Puritan Boyhood," *Massachusetts Review* 15 (summer 1974): 339–380, is a vivid memoir ending soon after he decided that printing was his chosen vocation. Several copies of Atkinson's periodical *The Watchout* are in the Walter Hampden Library of the Players Club in the Gramercy Park neighborhood of Manhattan. Oriana Atkinson, *Over at Uncle Joe's* (1947), covers the couple's Soviet experiences. John K. Hutchens, "The Pleasantest Job in the World," *Theater Arts* 32 (spring 1948): 36–38, summarizes Atkinson's position in New York's theatrical world and his view of his job and includes a jovial Hirschfeld cartoon, "An Actor's View" of Atkinson on opening night. An interview in the *New Yorker* (14 May 1960) and Hutchens's *Saturday Review* article "The Boss" (8 Oct. 1966) provide additional detail. Obituaries in the *New York Times* (14 Jan. 1984) and *Variety* (18 Jan. 1984) offer informative, varied tributes.

DANIEL S. KREMPEL

AUSTIN, John Paul (*b.* 14 February 1915 in LaGrange, Georgia; *d.* 26 December 1985 in Atlanta, Georgia), chief executive officer of the Coca-Cola Company who diversified the firm's product line and expanded its sales throughout the world.

One of three children born to Samuel Yates Austin, a textile company executive, and Maude Jernigan, a homemaker, Austin grew up in LaGrange and Scarsdale, New York, where the family moved when he was ten years old. He received his secondary schooling at Culver Military Academy, from which he graduated in 1933. He was awarded the A.B. degree by Harvard College in 1937 and the law degree by Harvard in 1940. A six-foot, three-inch, broad shouldered athlete, Austin rowed on the Harvard crew and was a member of the U.S. rowing team at the Olympic Games held at Berlin in 1936.

Austin was admitted to the New York bar in 1940 and practiced with the Wall Street law firm of Rathbone, Perry, Kelley, and Drye until he joined the U.S. Navy in January 1942. He rose through the ranks from ensign to lieutenant commander and commanded a patrol torpedo boat in the Southwest Pacific. Following his discharge on 16 January 1946, he resumed the practice of law with his prewar employer.

In 1949 Austin was hired by the Coca-Cola Company at the behest of the company's chairman, Robert W. Woodruff, a close friend of his father's employer. Considered Woodruff's protégé by his coworkers, Austin was assigned initially to the legal department in Chicago. He married

John Paul Austin, 1962. ARCHIVE PHOTOS

Jeane Weed, a secretary in the Chicago office, on 12 July 1950. They had two sons.

Austin made his mark in the development of overseas markets for Coca-Cola. In 1954 he was posted to Johannesburg, South Africa, where he built a major market for the soft drink. He returned to New York City, headquarters of the export subsidiary, in 1958. That year Austin was elected executive vice president of the Coca-Cola Export Corporation, and the following two years he served as its president. In 1961 he was made an executive vice president of the Coca-Cola Company as well.

Elected president of Coca-Cola in 1962, Austin brought to corporate headquarters in Atlanta an analytical decision-making style that contrasted sharply with the intuitive style of the company's previous leaders. "We really zero in on a problem, pull all the legs off the centipede and see what he's like," Austin said of his decision-making process. He was noted for driving his subordinates and keeping them under constant pressure. Regardless of Austin's position—he was made chief executive officer in 1966 and chairman of the board in 1970—all important corporate decisions required the concurrence of Woodruff, who continued to dominate the corporation despite having officially retired as chairman in 1955. Austin always addressed Woodruff as

"Boss," both out of respect and in recognition of his place in the company's informal power structure.

Continued development of foreign markets for Coca-Cola was Austin's most notable achievement. He traveled extensively and met with political leaders all over the world, including a secret meeting in Havana, Cuba, with Fidel Castro in 1977. In 1966 he awarded the first Coca-Cola bottling franchise in Israel, an act that set off an Arab boycott of the company. Later, in 1977, he won Coke's reentry into Egypt through personal negotiations with President Anwar Sadat. In the early 1960s he had bowed to cold war pressure and suspended his efforts to sell Coke in the Soviet Union, only to see arch rival Pepsi-Cola win a monopoly agreement with the Soviet government a decade later. In 1978 Austin achieved two major triumphs—Coca-Cola's entry into both the Soviet Union and the People's Republic of China.

Austin's political connections proved valuable to his commercial efforts. An early supporter of Jimmy Carter's presidential ambitions, Austin sponsored Carter's membership in the Trilateral Commission, where the future president came into contact with business leaders from all over the Western world; he also provided introductions and Coca-Cola executives as escorts on Carter's global travels before he became president. To quell speculation that he would be named secretary of state when Carter was elected president, Austin quietly informed the transition team that he would not accept the job.

Austin escalated the diversification of Coca-Cola's product line, begun under his predecessor. A successful diet soft drink, Tab, and such diverse products as coffee, wine, farm-raised shrimp, water-desalination equipment, and plastic bags were added to Coca-Cola's product mix under his leadership. Nevertheless, 70 percent of corporate revenues came from the soft drink business. Political and social changes in the 1960s and 1970s transformed the environment in which Coca-Cola did business. Recognizing the potential impact of these trends was one of Austin's most valuable gifts as a manager. Fearing a boycott of Coca-Cola during the civil rights movement, Austin opened job categories previously closed to black employees and incorporated African Americans into Coca-Cola advertising for the first time. When the company was stung by televised reports of inhumane conditions for workers in the orange groves of its Minute Maid subsidiary, Austin announced that the company would improve housing, nutrition, and job opportunities. His acquisitions of the water treatment company Aqua-Chem and a plastic bag manufacturer were intended to position Coca-Cola to deal with anticipated environmental problems.

By the mid-1970s Austin was showing initial signs of Parkinson's and Alzheimer's diseases, but his efforts to mask the symptoms, accompanied by his fondness for alcohol, led his colleagues to believe that alcohol abuse was his principal problem. Austin reached Coca-Cola's mandatory retirement age of sixty-five just after the turbulent 1970s ended; because no consensus candidate had emerged to succeed him, he was asked by the board to remain one more year while a successor was chosen. In February 1981 he retired as chairman of Coca-Cola.

In retirement Austin's diseases took their toll, and he died of multiple causes at the age of seventy. He was buried in Arlington Memorial Park, Atlanta.

Although Austin never totally overcame the conservatism of Coca-Cola's aging board members, he stimulated innovation in a corporation noted for its resistance to change. Most innovative for Coca-Cola was his quest for diversification, which led to both profitable and unprofitable acquisitions. Most successful was his personal diplomacy, which opened markets around the world previously closed to Coke and expanded others. Austin stands as one of the key figures in the globalization of business in the twentieth century.

★

A collection of papers relating to Austin is in the Robert W. Woodruff papers in the Robert W. Woodruff Library at Emory University. Two histories of the Coca-Cola Company—Mark Pendergrast, *For God, Country, and Coca-Cola: The Unauthorized History of the Great American Soft Drink and the Company That Makes It* (1993), and Frederick Allen, *Secret Formula: How Brilliant Marketing and Relentless Salesmanship Made Coca-Cola the Best-Known Product in the World* (1994)—provide extensive coverage of Austin's career with Coca-Cola. Obituaries are in the *Atlanta Constitution* and the *New York Times* (both 27 Dec. 1985).

VAGN K. HANSEN

AVERILL, Howard Earl ("Rock") (*b.* 21 May 1902 in Snohomish, Washington; *d.* 16 August 1983 in Everett, Washington), baseball player elected to the Baseball Hall of Fame in 1975.

Averill's father, Joseph, was a logger who died when Earl, who never remembered being called Howard, was just eighteen months old. His mother Anne (Maddox) Averill and a grandmother raised Earl and his older brother, Forrest, on a small ranch in Snohomish, thirty-five miles north of Seattle. While pitching for his high school baseball team, Averill hurt his arm and, unable to compete, quit school and worked first with a florist and then in lumber camps and in a local shingle mill. On 15 May 1922 Averill married Gladys Loette Hyatt. They had four sons and remained together for sixty-one years until Earl's death. Meanwhile, Averill resumed play as an outfielder with the local team, the Snohomish Pilchuckers.

While attending a baseball tryout camp in Seattle in the

Earl ("Rock") Averill. COURTESY OF THE NATIONAL BASEBALL HALL OF FAME LIBRARY, COOPERSTOWN, N.Y.

spring of 1924, Averill landed a contract with the Bellingham, Washington, club in the Northwestern League at $15 per game. He split the 1925 season between Bellingham and Anaconda, Montana, in the Butte Mines League. The following year Averill began a three-year stint with the San Francisco Seals in the Pacific Coast League. Earning $300 per month, the left-handed hitting center fielder averaged .342 with the Seals, completing the 1928 season with 36 home runs, 173 runs batted in (RBIs), 178 runs scored, and 270 hits in 189 games. In San Francisco, Averill acquired the nickname "Rock," denoting his "rocklike" shoulders, arms, and wrists, which generated surprising power from the five-foot-ten-inch 170 pounder. Following the 1928 season, Averill was signed by the Cleveland Indians, who paid the Seals $50,000 for his contract, with $1,000 going to the player as a personal bonus.

The twenty-six-year-old rookie began his major league career in April 1929 with a bang, homering in his first at bat, up to then only the third player to do so. Averill became an instant fan favorite in Cleveland, playing in every game his rookie season, hitting .331 with 18 homers, a club record to that point; 97 RBIs; and a league-leading 388 putouts in center field. For his ten seasons in Cleveland through 1938, "Rock" batted .323, averaging 189 hits per season, including 23 home runs, 12 triples, and 37 doubles; 108 RBIs; 115 runs; and a .534 slugging percentage. He led the American League in putouts in 1929 and 1934, at bats in 1931, and hits and triples in 1936. From April 1931 to June 1935, Averill played in 673 consecutive games. His highlight year was 1936, with a batting average of .378, 232 hits, 28 home runs, 15 triples, 39 doubles, 136 runs, 126 RBIs, a .627 slugging percentage, and only 35 strikeouts. Averill's best personal day came in a 17 September 1930 doubleheader against the Washington Senators. He hit four home runs in five official at bats over the two games, with eleven RBIs.

"Rock" was the only outfielder chosen for the first six Major League All-Star games beginning in 1933. In these midseason contests Earl made four hits in fifteen at bats and was the hitting star of the 1934 American League 9–7 win, stroking a double and triple. However, Averill's most famous All-Star blow was a 1937 line drive off National League hurler Dizzy Dean's foot, which shortened that great pitcher's career.

In 1937 injuries began to take their toll on Averill. On 30 June he suffered momentary leg paralysis. X rays revealed a lifelong separation of the tailbone and spine, a condition that would not be repaired until surgery in 1960. Compensating for his injury, Averill changed his batting stance and hitting philosophy, adopting a lighter bat and becoming a "spray" hitter with considerably less power. His 1937 batting average fell to .299, but 1938 was a comeback year in which he hit .330, although slugging only 14 homers. Sensing the twilight of his Cleveland career, the fans held an Earl Averill Appreciation Day, showering him with gifts. On 14 June 1939 Averill was traded to the Detroit Tigers for pitcher Harry Eisenstat. A part-time player through 1940 with the Tigers, Earl batted .264 in 1939 and .280 in 1940. Nevertheless, the Tigers won the American League pennant in 1940 and Averill played in his only World Series, appearing three times without success as a pinch hitter. Released by Detroit, Earl signed with the Boston Red Sox for the 1941 season but played in only eight games before being sent to Seattle in the Pacific Coast League, where he hit .247 and retired. Over his thirteen-year major league career Averill appeared in 1,669 games, batted .318, collected 2,020 hits, scored 1,224 runs, drove in 1,165 runs, and slugged 238 home runs, thirteenth on the all-time list at his retirement. Earl's highest major league salary was $15,000.

In retirement Averill lived in Snohomish, first operating a greenhouse with his brother until 1949 and then opening the Earl Averill Motel. He retired in 1969. Meanwhile, he followed the baseball career of his son Earl, Jr., who spent seven years in the major leagues (1956–1963). In 1969 Cleveland sportswriters named the senior Averill to Cleveland's all-time outfield with Tris Speaker and "Shoeless Joe" Jackson. In 1975 Earl Averill was elected to the Baseball Hall of Fame in Cooperstown, New York, by the Committee on Veterans. He died of pneumonia and was buried in Everett, Washington.

★

Martin Appel and Burt Goldblatt, *Baseball's Best: The Hall of Fame Gallery* (1977), contains a short biographical sketch of Averill. Similar articles are found in the *Biographical Dictionary of American Sports: Baseball* (1987); John J. Ward, "That Phenomenal Rookie, Averill," *Baseball Magazine* (Feb. 1930); and Doug Simpson, "The Earl of Snohomish," *Baseball Research Journal* (1982). An obituary is in the *Seattle Times* (17 Aug. 1983).

DAVID BERNSTEIN

B

BAILEY, Thomas Andrew (*b*. 14 December 1902 in San Jose, California; *d*. 26 July 1983 in Menlo Park, California), historian of U.S. diplomacy best known as the author of *A Diplomatic History of the American People* (1940) and *The American Pageant* (1956).

Born to James Andrew Bailey, an engineer, and Annie Nelson Bailey, Thomas grew up in comfortable circumstances in San Jose. Perhaps because he was too young to serve in World War I, Bailey developed a lifelong fascination with the causes and results of America's participation in that epochal conflict. The war greatly influenced his decision to pursue the study of what was then a fledgling field of academic inquiry, diplomatic history. Nearly all of Bailey's scholarly writings were grounded in preoccupation with the forces and ideas shaping U.S. foreign policy before, during, and immediately after World War I.

Bailey was educated and, with several notable sojourns elsewhere, spent his entire academic career in California. He earned an A.B. degree summa cum laude from Stanford University in 1924 and immediately began graduate study in history at Stanford, earning an A.M. in 1925 and the Ph.D. in 1927. Bailey worked chiefly with Frank Golder and Herbert E. Bolton, pioneering scholars of frontier and borderlands history. Bailey's doctoral dissertation was on political factionalism in the U.S. Senate between 1865 and 1900. While working on his Ph.D. in 1925 and 1926 he taught at the University of California at Berkeley and after

its completion joined the faculty of the University of Hawaii. On 28 August 1928 he married Sylvia Dean; they had one child. He returned to Stanford in 1930, when he was appointed as assistant professor of history. Rising steadily through the ranks, he was promoted to associate professor in 1935, to professor in 1940, and to the Margaret Byrne Professorship of American History in 1952.

In 1940 Bailey produced the first of the two popular textbooks for which he is primarily remembered, *A Diplomatic History of the American People,* a work that greatly influenced several generations of secondary school teachers, college lecturers, and undergraduate students of American history. Frustrated that no satisfactory textbook existed for courses in American diplomatic history, Bailey signed a contract in 1935 for a one-volume text. He was determined that the work be both authoritative (with scholarly footnotes and extended bibliographical essays) and written in a lively style. Thus he interleaved traditional documentation with numerous anecdotes from popular magazines and newspapers, gleaned by a legion of undergraduates and graduate students. Bailey's avowed aim was to portray the history of American diplomacy "from the point of view of the people who lived it and made it." Students found the text an interesting and convincing exposition of the progressive development of America's role in world affairs, although some critics objected to the work as self-congratulatory, jingoistic, and racist. For a time, Bailey made a good faith effort to revise its contents in light of recent scholar-

Thomas A. Bailey, 1948. AP/WIDE WORLD PHOTOS

ship, but by the 1950s the text, though still widely used, contained much outdated scholarship and was out of step with contemporary academic emphases.

Most of Bailey's scholarly research, however, focused on the influence of public opinion and pressure groups in the making of American foreign policy. His *Policy of the United States Toward the Neutrals, 1917–1918* (1942) and *America's Foreign Policies: Past and Present* (1943) were models of historical scholarship but manifested deeply rooted nationalistic biases and cultural chauvinism. Similarly flawed was his groundbreaking study of public opinion and foreign policy, *The Man in the Street* (1948). Though persuaded that the "great unwashed" and recent immigrants had exerted powerful influence on American politics and diplomacy, Bailey was never quite comfortable with the reality of a pluralist democracy. His reputation as a scholar chiefly rests upon a two-volume study of President Woodrow Wilson and the League of Nations: *Woodrow Wilson and the Lost Peace* (1944) and *Woodrow Wilson and the Great Betrayal*

(1945). Written as a manifesto for the embryonic United Nations and as a case study of how to avoid the mistakes that had doomed the League of Nations, Bailey championed Wilsonian internationalism while simultaneously castigating the political naïveté and pride of Wilson himself.

To facilitate research in official records and archives on the East Coast, Bailey held visiting posts at George Washington University, the Institute for Advanced Study at Princeton, Harvard, and Cornell. In 1947 he lectured at the newly organized National War College and undertook a summer study trip to Europe, an experience he would memorialize many years later in a memoir-cum-history, *The Marshall Plan Summer* (1977).

In 1956 Bailey published *The American Pageant,* a general U.S. history textbook similar in conception to his *Diplomatic History of the American People.* Like the earlier book, it went through numerous editions and, invigorated when a second author was added in the 1970s, remained in print through the 1990s.

Although deeply involved in academic administration at Stanford, Bailey was active in professional organizations, serving as president of the Organization of American Historians in 1968. That same year he helped to found and was elected the first president of the Society of Historians of American Foreign Relations. The 1960s and 1970s also produced a second flood of scholarly articles and books from Bailey's Palo Alto study. Notable were *Presidential Greatness* (1966), in which he mused on presidential character; *Democrats vs. Republicans* (1968), a popular study of presidential politics, and *Essays Diplomatic and Undiplomatic of Thomas A. Bailey* (1969), an intriguing festschrift. Collaborations with Paul B. Ryan yielded the impressively balanced *Lusitania Disaster* (1975) and an overblown narrative entitled *Hitler vs. Roosevelt: The Undeclared Naval War* (1979).

Proud of the two popular and innovative texts he had authored, of his numerous scholarly contributions to the field, and of the several generations of graduate students he had mentored, Bailey rightly saw himself as one of that small band of historians who defined and legitimized the academic study of American foreign relations. Bailey remained professionally active for many years after his retirement in 1968.

★

Biographical information may be found in Thomas A. Bailey, *Essays Diplomatic and Undiplomatic* (1969), and Lester D. Langley, "The Diplomatic Historians: Bailey and Bemis," *Society for Historians of American Foreign Relations Newsletter* 10, no. 1 (Mar. 1979). An obituary is in the *New York Times* (29 July 1983).

THEODORE A. WILSON

BAINTON, Roland Herbert (*b.* 30 March 1894 in Ilkeston, Derbyshire, England; *d.* 13 February 1984 in New Haven,

Connecticut), one of the leading church historians of the twentieth century, noted for his many biographies of Reformation figures.

Bainton was one of two children of the Reverend James Herbert Bainton, a Congregational minister, and Charlotte Eliza Blackham, a homemaker. A pastor for eight years at the Ilkeston Congregational Church, James Bainton moved his family to Vancouver, British Columbia, and soon thereafter to Colfax, Washington, when Roland was a boy. The elder Bainton encouraged both a strong piety and intellectual curiosity in his son; as an adult Roland would fondly recall this influence in a biography of his father titled *Pilgrim Parson* (1958).

Bainton attended Colfax High School, graduating in 1910. He then entered Whitman College in Walla Walla, Washington, where he received a B.A. degree in classics in 1914. He then entered Yale Divinity School, where he received his Bachelor of Divinity degree in 1917. Further study was interrupted by the American entry into World War I. Like his father, Bainton was a pacifist. By then an ordained Congregational minister as well as an affiliate member of the Society of Friends (Quakers), he spent the duration of the war serving with the American Friends Service Committee under the Red Cross in France. After the war he returned to Yale, where he was appointed instructor in church history and New Testament in 1920 and received a Ph.D. in Semitics and Hellenistic Greek in 1921. That same year he married Ruth Mae Woodruff, a teacher who was also active in the Society of Friends; they would have five children.

At Yale, Bainton became an assistant professor in 1923, associate professor in 1932, and Titus Street Professor of Ecclesiastical History in 1936. Even as he rose in academic circles, however, he displayed a commitment to writing books that were grounded in scholarship but accessible to a lay audience, such as *The Church of Our Fathers* (1941), directed toward young people aged nine to nineteen. He also retained a strong commitment to pacifism, manifested, for example, by his lifelong membership in the Fellowship of Reconciliation and a long career spent writing and speaking about constructive means to build peace. He and his wife served as representatives of the American Friends Service Committee, and during World War II he counseled many young men in the Civilian Public Service camps, which had been organized by the nation's peace churches as an alternative to military service. He later suffered the abuse of the House Committee on Un-American Activities for his conscientious objection to war.

The postwar years were nevertheless a period of prodigious scholarly output for Bainton. He produced major biographies of key figures of the Reformation period, including *Here I Stand* (1950), which became the standard biography of Martin Luther, written in a style so accessible that it eventually sold more than a million copies; and *Erasmus of Christendom* (1969). His pacifism and devotion to religious toleration and ecumenism inspired his writings about "rebels" or "radicals" of the Reformation such as Michael Servetus in *Hunted Heretic* (1953). Bainton also wrote general church histories. *The Reformation of the Sixteenth Century* (1952) became the standard work on the Reformation, and his two-volume *Christendom: A Short History of Christianity and Its Impact on Western Civilization* (1966) was widely used as a textbook.

Steven Simpler is surely correct to say Bainton "uses history as a tool of Christian witness." Bainton claimed that as a historian he was interested in the religious experience of individuals. He believed that a historian cannot understand the religion of the past if he himself has no experience with God. As Simpler puts it, "For Bainton any interpretation which discounts the dynamics of religious experience is essentially invalid." At the same time, Bainton believed in examining history for the light it might cast on the present. *Christian Attitudes Toward War and Peace* (1960), for

Roland Bainton, 1965. SPECIAL COLLECTIONS, YALE DIVINITY SCHOOL LIBRARY, ROLAND BAINTON PAPERS, RECORD GROUP NO. 75

example, is a historical survey of conflict in which he urges contemporary readers to learn from the failures of the past.

Bainton's accomplishments as an author were equaled by those as a teacher during his long career at Yale, where his personal and scholarly influence was felt by several generations of students, in lectures that were a marvel of down-to-earth clarity and enlivened with humor. In 1957 he published *Yale and the Ministry: A History of Education for the Christian Ministry at Yale from the Founding in 1701.* He retired from Yale in 1962 but continued to live in New Haven, writing and publishing until his death in 1984.

Bainton's contributions to Reformation scholarship remain his primary public legacy. For those who knew him, however, he is remembered not only for his intelligence and scope of knowledge but also for his personal commitment to religious toleration, freedom of conscience, and the dignity of every individual.

★

Information about Bainton's childhood is contained in his biography of his father, *Pilgrim Parson: The Life of James Herbert Bainton* (1958). A fuller biographical sketch is Georgia Harkness, "Roland Bainton: A Biographical Appreciation," in Franklin Littell, ed., *Reformation Studies: Essays in Honor of Roland H. Bainton* (1962). Other essays in that work contain valuable analyses of Bainton's scholarly output, as does Steven H. Simpler, *Roland H. Bainton: An Examination of His Reformation Historiography* (1985).

TOM FORRESTER LORD

BALANCHINE, George (*b.* 22 January 1904 in Saint Petersburg, Russia; *d.* 30 April 1983 in New York City), the most important ballet choreographer of the twentieth century, known chiefly for the development of the plotless ballet, and with Lincoln Kirstein a co-founding director of the New York City Ballet.

He was born Georgi Melitonovich Balanchivadze, one of three children of Meliton Balanchivadze, a well-known Georgian-born composer, and Maria Vasilyeva Balanchivadze, with whom he first studied piano from an early age. Ironically, his entrance into a dancing career was accidental. His parents initially wished him to be admitted to the Imperial Naval Academy but missed the application deadline. In 1913, when his sister went to an audition at the Imperial Ballet School, his mother brought him along. There an acquaintance persuaded his mother to let him take the admitting examination as well. He was accepted and his sister was not. The uniform for the boys was exactly the same dark blue as that of the naval academy, except that the collar insignia was a lyre instead of an anchor. Depressed at first by loneliness at the school, he ran away and hid with an aunt, who persuaded him to return. His early appearances

George Balanchine and Margot Fonteyn rehearsing the *Ballet Imperial* at Covent Garden, London, 1950. HULTON-DEUTSCH COLLECTION/ CORBIS

onstage and glimpses of reigning ballerinas Tamara Karsavina, Agrippina Vaganova, and Elizaveta Gerdt in rehearsals fired his enthusiasm for the art, and he acquired a solid grounding in the pedagogical method of the Imperial School, which blended the vivacity of the Italian school and French precision with the emotional expressiveness inherent in Russian execution of the vocabulary.

The 1917 revolution caused the ballet school and theater to close for a year for lack of funds. During this period Balanchine accompanied silent movies on the piano, one of a number of such ad hoc survival jobs he and other students pursued. When the school reopened they resumed their studies, and Balanchine began to be asked by fellow students to arrange recital pieces and to accompany them in their performances. Shortly before his graduation from the ballet school in 1921, he also entered what was then called the Petrograd State Conservatory of Music, where he studied piano for another three years. This passionate interest in music would strongly guide his development as a choreographer; ultimately three-quarters of his ballets would bear musical titles.

The social revolution unleashed a sense of new beginnings throughout the society, even in the strongly traditional Imperial Ballet. Balanchine was in the forefront of such activity and incurred the displeasure of older administration staff members who wished to dismiss him from the school. The threatened expulsion, however, never occurred. A major creative influence on him at this time was the work of the choreographer Kasyan Goleizovsky, who favored unconventional athletic movement performed in abbreviated costumes. Balanchine was so taken by the novel approach that he wanted to open a studio with Goleizovsky. It never came to pass, but Balanchine did establish a small performance group, drawn from fellow students, that performed a few times as the Young Ballet. School authorities were sufficiently disapproving to threaten those who participated with dismissal, and it became apparent that his experimental approach would need a less traditional setting in which to develop. In 1922, at the age of eighteen, he married the dancer Tamara Geva, the first of his four wives (they later divorced).

In 1924 Vladimir Dimitriev, a singer from the former Imperial Opera, presented local Communist officials with the idea of forming a small company to tour abroad to display the continuing artistic achievements of the new regime. The tour of the newly formed Soviet State Musicians and Dancers was approved, and Alexandra Danilova, Tamara Geva, Nicholas Efimov, Balanchine, and Dimitriev, along with a group of musicians, sailed for Germany in the spring.

Almost immediately after landing in Germany, a telegram arrived ordering the whole company to return to Russia. The musicians left, but the dancers decided to stay and try their luck in the West. (Balanchine did not set foot in the Soviet Union again until 1964, when he returned with his own New York City Ballet as part of a major cultural exchange program.) The small company made a tour of spas in Germany then headed for London, where they briefly found work in music halls. While appearing there in 1925, the group received a telegram from the famed director of the Ballets Russes, Serge Diaghilev, inviting them to come to Paris to audition for his company. Diaghilev always had an eye out for Russian-trained dancers, and at this time he was also between choreographers. His former collaborators, Michel Fokine, Vaslav Nijinsky, Leonid Massine, and Bronislava Nijinska, were all unavailable.

At the audition Balanchine showed one of the works he had created for the Young Ballet and, at the age of twenty-one, he was immediately hired as company choreographer. Diaghilev's first concern was whether Balanchine could work quickly, for his company was contracted to begin its annual residency with the Monte Carlo opera company, supplying dance sequences as well as developing its own repertory. Balanchine's colleagues were taken on as members of the company, and Danilova subsequently assumed the lead performing position that formerly had been oc-

cupied by the legendary ballerinas Anna Pavlova and Tamara Karsavina.

During his time with the Ballets Russes, Balanchine worked with scores commissioned by Diaghilev from major composers of the day. For Balanchine the most significant of these was Igor Stravinsky's *Apollo* (originally *Apollon Musagète*). By his own testimony it changed his whole creative approach to choreography. It alerted him to the "family relationships" between steps and gave him the courage to simplify his work by retaining only that which was necessary rather than including every movement idea that came to him. Watching Balanchine assemble this ballet, Diaghilev observed that he was working in a manner that had not been seen since the days of Marius Petipa, the great nineteenth-century French-Russian choreographer. The style Balanchine introduced with *Apollo* became known popularly as neoclassicism.

When Diaghilev died in the summer of 1929, his company scattered. Balanchine worked in Europe with a variety of groups during the following four years. Les Ballets 1933 was the last of these, and during its London season the budding American impresario and ballet scholar Lincoln Kirstein invited Balanchine to found a school and a company in the United States. The initial plan to house the company in Hartford, Connecticut, was quickly abandoned when Balanchine demanded the venue of a large, cosmopolitan city. The School of American Ballet opened in New York City in 1934 and eventually became one of the world's leading ballet schools. The following year saw the first incarnation of the ballet company Balanchine and Kirstein had envisioned, which they called the American Ballet.

From the start, Balanchine created a body of work that would both instruct his dancers in the new style he was developing and display them to best advantage onstage. *Serenade* was the first ballet he made in the United States. Although he was notoriously unsentimental about preserving his past work, Balanchine's fondness for *Serenade* was obvious, since it was expanded and modified over the years and kept in repertory almost continuously. It is a lyrical celebration of dancing as a way of life. In the opening movement this is indicated when the seventeen women of the corps de ballet signal their entry to a career by assuming the first position of classical ballet after a farewell gesture to what has preceded.

The early years of the company were marked by a series of disappointments and new beginnings. An early tour collapsed for lack of bookings. In 1938 the group served as the resident ballet company of the Metropolitan Opera, but its contract for the next year was not renewed. Short seasons and temporary fill-in jobs became a way of life. Many company members danced in a show called *A Thousand Times Neigh*, advertising Ford Motors products at the New York World's Fair of 1939–1940. Beginning in 1936, Balanchine worked sporadically on Broadway and in the movies. A six-month "goodwill" tour of South America in 1941 was arranged through the State Department. The United States entered World War II in December 1941, two months after the return of the company, and it was disbanded for the duration. Ballet Society, a private subscription organization, was formed by Kirstein and Balanchine in 1946 and danced at a variety of locations in New York City. When the company perfomed at the New York City Center for Music and Drama in 1948, it caught the eye of Morton Baum, chairman of the finance committee. He invited it to become a constituent member of the center. Its name was changed to New York City Ballet and remained at the theater on West Fifty-fifth Street for the next seventeen years, building an audience.

The establishment of a home base for the company ushered in the most prolific creative period of Balanchine's career. During the 1950s he choreographed ballets ranging from the musically leading-edge *Ivesiana, Movements for Piano and Orchestra*, and *Agon* to the familiar Sousa marches used in *Stars and Stripes* and folk melodies in *Western Symphony*. He created an entire repertory while beginning to shape a company totally trained in his style of dance. The company attack was fast, sharp-edged, athletically demanding, and fluently musical. One could see the music visualized in the movement analogues that Balanchine constructed to accompany the scores he chose.

In 1964 the company was invited to open the New York State Theater in the emergent Lincoln Center for the Performing Arts. Balanchine now had an opera house–size stage and proceeded to add several full-length ballets to a repertory that already included *A Midsummer Night's Dream* and *The Nutcracker. Jewels* (1967) was clearly the most successful of the expanded works. It consisted of three movements, each celebrating the spirit of one of the nations in which he had worked. The first, "Emeralds," had a score drawn from Gabriel Fauré's *Pelléas et Mélisande* and *Shylock,* and demonstrated the precise reserve of the French school. The second, "Rubies," with Stravinsky's *Capriccio for Piano and Orchestra,* reflected the playful hijinks Balanchine associated with American movie musicals. The third, "Diamonds," set to Tchaikovsky's *Symphony No. 3* (omitting the first movement), suggested an homage to the elevated Imperial Ballet style in which he had grown up.

At age sixty, Balanchine, fondly referred to as "Mr. B" by his company, retained his trim physique and morning-to-midnight work schedule. Despite his artistic prominence, he always found time to discuss everyday professional problems with even the youngest members of his company who approached him for guidance. To the world outside the company he was a man of few words and certain formulaic responses to press queries.

Whenever asked to describe his work as a choreographer

Balanchine compared it to a variety of craftsmanlike occupations, most often to that of a cook preparing an interesting variety of dishes for the audience. No matter what career description he gave, the one constant in his approach was his cavalier-like attitude toward women, whom he thought more flexible than men in their dancing, and offered him more creative opportunities. Throughout his career, starting in Russia, Balanchine was attracted to young female dancers, beginning with Geva, Danilova (with whom he lived while still married to Geva), and Lydia Ivanova. In the Diaghilev company his first ballet was for the teenaged Alicia Markova. Later in the 1930s he worked with the youthful "baby ballerinas" Tamara Toumanova, Irina Baronova, and Tatiana Riabouchinska.

When he was working on Broadway in the 1940s the twenty-three-year-old Vera Zorina received his devoted attention (they were married from 1938 to 1946). She was succeeded by Maria Tallchief (his wife from 1946 to 1952), whom he totally remade as a dancer and who became the first star of New York City Ballet, bringing it national attention. She was the first dancer to whom he could and did devote his entire energies in working out his theories of dancing. For her he made a series of ballets, with *The Firebird* and *Scotch Symphony* being the most well known.

When Tallchief left the company Balanchine had the opportunity to work with several young dancers, notably Tanaquil LeClercq (*La Valse*), Diana Adams (*Agon*), and Allegra Kent (*The Unanswered Question*) in the 1950s; Gelsey Kirkland (*Suite No. 3*), Suzanne Farrell (*Meditation*) in the 1960s and 1970s; and Karin von Aroldingen (*Davidsbündlertänze*), the last of this line of inspiring muses, in 1980. LeClercq was his wife from 1952 to 1969, and for Farrell he created an unprecedented twenty-six ballets. To each he gave beautifully inventive vehicles which celebrated their personalities and extended their technical capabilities. He said at one time, "Ballet is woman," and did his creative best for those with whom he worked closely.

Among the most advanced works were those referred to as the "black and white" ballets, so called because they were costumed in what amounted to simple practice clothes. These include *Concerto Barocco, The Four Temperaments, Agon, Ivesiana, Episodes,* and *Symphony in Three Movements* and were the ballets in which he expanded the ballet vocabulary to the limit. The social ballets *Vienna Waltzes, Liebeslieder Waltzes, Stars and Stripes, Brahms Schoenberg Quartet,* and *Union Jack* were those in which he examined national character.

Balanchine's enormous love for the music of Tchaikovsky prompted him to choreograph *Mozartiana, Tchaikovsky Piano Concerto No. 2, Theme and Variations, Meditation, Tchaikovsky Pas de Deux, Allegro Brilliante, Swan Lake* (act 2), *The Sleeping Beauty* ("Garland Waltz"), and *The Nutcracker.* Versions of the latter have become standard offerings at Christmas by scores of ballet companies throughout the United States. Balanchine's rendition alone seriously delineates and celebrates the family rituals of inculcating manners to youngsters on their way to adulthood. The occasion is a family celebration uniting three generations, first in a realistic party gathering and then in a young girl's dream transformation of her innocent understanding of the process into an imaginary playland family.

Balanchine's major contribution to dance lay in the development of ballet in the twentieth century, but he made significant contributions to the popular musical on stage and in film. His first experience on Broadway was the Richard Rodgers–Lorenz Hart *On Your Toes* (1936), in which he requested and was given program credit as the show's choreographer. It was the first time the title had appeared in the commercial theater. His choreography for the show also integrated the dancing with the story line for the first time. Both innovations became commonplace in the Broadway musical. In Hollywood he created a small dance company on the Metro-Goldwyn-Mayer lot that kept a full complement of dancers employed for the months he worked on *The Goldwyn Follies.* Choreographer Jack Cole and others followed the pattern he established for their own film careers.

Television was a less satisfactory medium for Balanchine, although he was interested in mastering the technical aspects of presenting dance on the ubiquitous small screen. For a variety of reasons including technical camera limitations ("garage lighting" was his assessment of early studio conditions), he was unable to realize satisfactory productions on commercial television, although he did adapt a number of his stage ballets satisfactorily for noncommercial television.

Balanchine extended the Russian classic tradition established by Petipa while abandoning narrative in order to present his dancers in more universal, timeless settings. His core belief in the inherent expressive capabilities of dance steps alone led him to evaluate them individually, identify their familial affinities as a teacher, and use them in fresh combinations as a choreographer. He streamlined the ballet vocabulary to enable dancers to respond more closely to the brisk rhythmic demands of accompanying music. Most notably he drastically reduced the preparation time customary for the execution of spectacular, virtuosic steps, and acclerated the timing and variety of male support offered in partnered dancing.

To add to the visible excitement and freshness of such partnering, Balanchine increased the numbers of support points between male and female beyond the traditional nineteenth-century hand, waist, and shoulder contact. He also introduced the technique of off-balance partnering in which the female is supported beyond her normal balance point to extend spectacularly the range and scope of her gestures. With these modifications he was able to move dancers more efficiently to music of concert-level complexity in designs that demonstrated and expanded the creative expressiveness of classical ballet.

The pleasing structural balance and musical fluidity of his ballets are readily apparent, while full appreciation of their thematic content relies on closer attention to the meaningful language of movement itself. There are no characters whose roles are immediately identifiable by costume or setting. Instead, the dancers identify their roles continuously by the unfurling sequence of steps, poses, and gestures that establishes their place in the emotional or dramatic climate of the ballet. It is a beautifully distilled form of expression that communicates with the viewer directly through the classic vocabulary.

Balanchine's energy began to diminish in the late 1970s. He complained of feeling tired, and his eyesight and balance were affected. On 4 November 1982 he was admitted to Roosevelt Hospital in Manhattan. The nature of his illness was not diagnosed as Creutzfeldt-Jakob disease until after his death the following April. He is buried at Sag Harbor (Long Island), New York, near his home in Southampton.

★

Among the most informative books on Balanchine are Don McDonagh, *Balanchine* (1983); Richard Buckle, *Balanchine: Ballet Master* (1984) and *Choreography by George Balanchine: A Catalogue of Works* (1984); Bernard Taper, *Balanchine* (1984); and Francis Mason, *I Remember Balanchine: Recollections of the Ballet Master by Those Who Knew Him* (1991). Performances of his ballets are described in Arlene Croce, *Afterimages* (1977), *Going to the Dance* (1982), and *Sightlines* (1987). An obituary is in the *New York Times* (1 May 1983).

DON MCDONAGH

BALDWIN, Roger Nash (*b.* 21 January 1884 in Wellesley, Massachusetts; *d.* 26 August 1981 in Ridgewood, New Jersey), renowned civil libertarian who was the founder of the American Civil Liberties Union and its executive director for thirty years.

Baldwin came from a New England family deeply committed to reform. His father, Frank Fenno Baldwin, was a prosperous leather merchant. His mother, Lucy Cushing Nash, was a feminist. Baldwin was the oldest of their six children. He was raised a Unitarian, and by the time he was a teenager was working through the church on social reform. He graduated from Wellesley High School and entered Harvard University in 1901. He graduated from Harvard with both a B.A. and an M.A. in anthropology in 1905.

In 1906 Baldwin began his career as a social and civic reformer at the Self Culture Hall, a settlement house in St.

Roger Nash Baldwin. PRINCETON UNIVERSITY LIBRARY. PUBLIC POLICY PAPERS. DEPARTMENT OF RARE BOOKS AND SPECIAL COLLECTIONS, PRINCETON UNIVERSITY LIBRARY. PHOTO BY BLACKSTONE STUDIOS.

Louis. He also agreed to create a sociology department at Washington University and teach courses there. His work at the settlement house sent him into the St. Louis court system; in 1908 he accepted a position as chief probation officer of the juvenile court. His interest in the operation of the juvenile court system resulted in *Juvenile Courts and Probation* (1914), written with Bernard Flexner, which outlined a theory of juvenile justice used for the next several decades. Baldwin found his three jobs impossible to manage, so moved out of the settlement house and into a boardinghouse for young boys, which he ran with the mother of a Harvard classmate. Although the boardinghouse failed, he became the legal guardian of one of the boys who lived there, ten-year-old Otto ("Toto") Stolz. During his eleven years in St. Louis, Baldwin was a popular bachelor who, for a while, was engaged to radical activist Anna Louise Strong. In 1908 he met anarchist Emma Goldman. Later he would credit Goldman with having a profound philosophical impact on his life. Thereafter Baldwin became a lifelong pacifist and, increasingly, a radical. In 1910 he became director of the Civic League, which reformed the St. Louis city government to make it more democratic.

By the outbreak of World War I, Baldwin, like so many radicals, had become an opponent of the war. In 1917 he left St. Louis to accept a position with the American Union Against Militarism (AUAM), replacing Crystal Eastman. Baldwin became the AUAM's most determined crusader for conscientious objectors, organizing the Bureau for Conscientious Objectors (soon called the Civil Liberties Bureau) within the AUAM. His group was too radical for the other leaders of the AUAM, who divorced themselves from what became the National Civil Liberties Bureau.

Baldwin's fledgling group was raided by government agents in August 1918. Less than a month later, Baldwin refused to register for the draft and was arrested for willful violation of the Selective Service Act. He was found guilty and sentenced to a year in prison, beginning, ironically, on the day the war ended, 11 November 1918. Baldwin began his term at the Essex County (New Jersey) Jail but was transferred to the prison farm in Caldwell, New Jersey, after he organized the Prisoner's Welfare League at the first facility.

When Baldwin finished his term on 8 August 1919, he married a social worker, Madeleine Zabriskie Doty, in a ceremony presided over by the prominent socialist Norman Thomas. From the start, the marriage was unorthodox, and the Baldwins almost never resided together; for much of their marriage Doty lived in Geneva and worked for the Women's International League for Peace. Indeed, almost immediately after their honeymoon ended, Baldwin took off on a tour of the Midwest as a working man so that he might observe labor conditions and organizations firsthand.

Upon returning to New York City, Baldwin resumed his work at the National Civil Liberties Bureau, officially changing its name to the American Civil Liberties Union on 20 January 1920. Its sole commitment was to the Bill of Rights. The early ACLU was beleaguered by government because most of its clients were radicals and labor organizers. In 1925, however, the ACLU's fortunes took an upturn when it hired the flamboyant attorney Clarence Darrow to defend John Scopes in the so-called Monkey Trial in Tennessee. Although Scopes was found guilty, the case galvanized liberal public opinion and resulted in considerable positive publicity for the new organization. Although the ACLU was never involved in the defense of anarchists Nicola Sacco and Bartolomeo Vanzetti, Baldwin was personally involved in the Sacco and Vanzetti defense movement and a friend of Vanzetti's.

In 1926 Baldwin took a leave of absence from the ACLU to work for the International Committee for Political Prisoners in Europe. In 1927 he spent three months in the Soviet Union, collecting material for his book *Liberty Under the Soviets* (1928). In the book, Baldwin expressed a cavalier and tolerant attitude toward the Soviet government's repressions, a reflection of his increasingly radical views.

In 1935 Baldwin and Doty divorced. On 6 March 1936

he married Evelyn Preston, whom he had met in 1928 on Martha's Vineyard. They had one daughter. For years the Preston-Baldwin family (which included her two sons by a previous marriage) lived in adjoining houses on West 11th Street in New York City. Baldwin's sole contribution to the household till was to cover his personal expenses; everything else was paid for by Preston, who was independently wealthy.

The Great Depression further radicalized Baldwin and drew him into the orbit of communist "front" groups. He was active in the League Against War and Fascism and a number of pro-Loyalist Spanish Civil War organizations. Although the ACLU pursued a much more aggressive pro-labor position during the 1930s, not everyone on the ACLU board of directors shared Baldwin's views. In 1938 the ACLU board fought over whether the automobile manufacturer Henry Ford was entitled to proselytize his workers against unions, a battle emblematic of the tensions between anticommunist directors and those more sympathetic to the Popular Front (a communist-dominated coalition of leftist political parties). The next year the balance of power in the ACLU shifted when Baldwin, disillusioned with the Popular Front because of the Nazi-Soviet Pact, joined the anticommunist board faction. In February 1940 the ACLU board passed a resolution, composed by Baldwin, denying board membership to communists and members of other "totalitarian" organizations. In May, with Baldwin's support, the board expelled Elizabeth Gurley Flynn (who was, according to one scholar, his former lover), an overt communist. The action nearly split the organization in two.

During World War II, Baldwin struggled to reconcile his pacifism with his antifascism. The ACLU was one of the few organizations to defend the rights of the 110,000 Japanese and Japanese-Americans incarcerated in relocation camps. It oversaw two of the four Supreme Court cases concerning relocation, the Hirabayashi case (1943) and the Korematsu case (1944). Baldwin personally worked with government officials to improve conditions in the camps.

In 1947 General Douglas MacArthur invited Baldwin to come to Japan and consult on civil liberties matters with those establishing the postwar government there. While in Japan, Baldwin organized the Japan Civil Liberties Union. In 1948 he was invited to West Germany to consult on civil liberties matters.

Baldwin was never a particularly skilled administrator, and his long absences interfered with the ACLU's smooth functioning. He was persuaded to retire as executive director in November 1949. Thereafter he served as a kind of roving ambassador for the ACLU, concentrating particularly on international civil liberties. In 1950 Baldwin assumed the chairmanship of the International League for the Rights of Man and worked through the United Nations for civil liberties around the globe. He retired from that post in 1965. Thereafter he took occasional smaller jobs, such as teaching civil liberties law in Puerto Rico, where he spent his winters. Baldwin died of heart failure in Ridgewood, New Jersey, at the age of ninety-seven.

Baldwin's politics changed little over the course of his life. Virtually all of his work was aimed at protecting individual rights and assuring that those with dissident views would be allowed to voice them without reprisal or punishment. The U.S. government awarded Baldwin the Medal of Freedom in January 1981.

★

Baldwin's personal papers are housed at the Seeley G. Mudd Library at Princeton University. The ACLU papers, also at Princeton, contain another large collection of Baldwin's letters. His writings include *Juvenile Courts and Probation* (1914), *The Individual and the State* (1918), *Liberty Under the Soviets* (1928), and *A New Slavery* (1953). A combination biography and oral history of Baldwin is Peggy Lamson, *Roger Baldwin, Founder of the American Civil Liberties Union* (1976). A shorter profile is Dwight Macdonald, "The Defense of Everybody," *New Yorker* (11 and 18 July 1953). An oral history is at Columbia University. There is also a documentary film on the ACLU and Baldwin, *The Defense of Everybody* (1997). An obituary is in the *New York Times* (27 Aug. 1981).

JUDY KUTULAS

BANE, Frank B. (*b.* 7 April 1893 in Smithfield, Virginia; *d.* 23 January 1983 in Alexandria, Virginia), executive director of the Social Security Board and Council of State Governments, known for his role in the twentieth-century movement for efficient government management.

Named Robert Franklin Bane at birth, he was one of three children of Charles Lee Bane, a Methodist minister, and Carrie Howard Buchner, a homemaker. After graduating from high school at the age of seventeen he majored in history and political science at Randolph-Macon College in Ashland, Virginia, graduating with an A.B. and an LL.D. in 1914. He attended Columbia University Law School for the 1914–1915 academic year, where he audited a course on charity organization, thus forging a lifetime interest in social welfare. Returning to Virginia, Bane became a high school principal in Nansemond County and then its superintendent of schools. On 14 August 1918 he married Lillian Greyson Hoofnagle; they would have two children.

In 1920 Bane became director of the Virginia State Board of Charities, where he caught the attention of Louis Brownlow, a leader in scientific government and the city manager of Knoxville, the third largest city in Tennessee. Brownlow hired Bane as director of public welfare in 1923. In his three years there Bane converted what was called the

Frank Bane, 1983. FROM A PAINTING BY JOHN HUSBANDS. COURTESY OF THE SOCIAL SECURITY ADMINISTRATION HISTORY ARCHIVES.

"pest house" into a municipal hospital, built playgrounds, and consolidated the relief and institutional care of the poor. He raised city personnel standards by hiring physicians from established medical schools, trained nurses, supervisors for recreation, and trained social workers. In 1926 Bane became the commissioner of public welfare for the state of Virginia. After the Great Depression began in 1929, he also served for two years on President Herbert Hoover's Emergency Commission for Employment.

In the mixed system of public relief and private charity that then prevailed, professional social workers were notably hostile to what they viewed as the "pauperizing" tendencies of the public-relief system, which was generally administered through almshouses. Convinced that the future lay with the public sector, Bane, with help from the Laura Spelman Rockefeller Fund, in 1932 founded the American Public Welfare Association (APWA), an organization that represents state governments in matters of public welfare. He would later judge this action to be the most important of his career. He then served as a consultant to Harry L.

Hopkins, director of the Federal Emergency Relief Administration, established by the Franklin D. Roosevelt administration in May 1933. In that capacity, Bane convinced Hopkins that public funds required public administration, so many social workers were shifted from private organizations to state and local public agencies and were paid with tax moneys.

In November 1935 Bane became executive director of the Social Security Board. The board's responsibilities were a mixed bag of social insurance and welfare programs: Old Age Assistance; Old Age Insurance; Unemployment Compensation; Aid to Dependent Children; and Aid to the Blind. Assistance programs were carried out under federally approved state plans, with Washington matching state expenditures about fifty-fifty.

The board's early decision to separate policy making from administration did not work well in practice. Lengthy meetings were held every day to resolve technical fine points and difficult personnel issues. Bane and the bureau directors spent much time traveling to various states and cajoling governors to follow up efforts by novice and relatively powerless regional employees. According to a report by the Social Science Research Council, the board's impressive accomplishments—registering twenty-five million wage earners for old-age insurance and readying the states to assist the needy—occurred in "a crisis atmosphere." Bane's personal acquaintance with many governors proved extremely helpful, particularly in the drive to qualify states for federal public assistance. He also recruited APWA staff members to prepare model laws for state use.

Early in 1937 Bane became the center of a patronage conflict with Senator Carter Glass of Virginia, chairman of the powerful Senate Appropriations Committee. The Social Security Board did not receive its annual appropriation until Glass's own choice was hired, the board's chief of personnel was downgraded, and Bane's salary was cut. Bane resigned in 1938 in order to head the Council of State Governments in Chicago. Denying that his resignation was prompted by Senator Glass, Bane said that he made the move because the Social Security program was off to a good start, because the council was growing in membership and responsibilities, and because the salary was higher.

In Chicago, Bane and his staff dealt directly with governors and their staffs, bypassing time-consuming negotiations with legislatures and their committees in support of needed laws. According to Bane, the council succeeded in stopping "the silly business" of states' "running around from one foundation to another . . . getting little dabs of money." Instead, their research needs were pooled and presented directly to the states. Although the council was headquartered in Chicago, regional offices were added in San Francisco and Washington, D.C.

During World War II the Council of State Governments

participated in the organization and administration of all wartime agencies that involved state governments, including the Office of Price Administration (OPA), the Agricultural Adjustment Administration, and the War Manpower Administration. On leave from council duties, Bane served as director of food rationing at OPA. In the postwar years the Council of State Governments inaugurated comprehensive research on such emerging problems as mental hygiene, higher education, and statewide purchasing. Bane retired from the council in 1958 and later that year assumed the chairmanship of the Advisory Commission on Intergovernmental Relations, a position he held until he retired from government service in 1966.

A witty gentleman of the old school, a steadfast backer of professional women, a master of administrative planning, and an eminently successful negotiator, Bane was sometimes faulted as too courtly, too talkative, and too pleasant. Yet on balance, as the syndicated columnist Harold Pyle remarked, Bane was "a giant in the complex field of reconciling partisan and regional differences in issues of critical importance."

Bane died of cancer at Washington House, a retirement home in Alexandria, Virginia. He is buried in Arlington National Cemetery.

★

Bane's papers are located in the Alderman Library, University of Virginia at Charlottesville. Bane participated in several oral histories including "The Reminiscences of Frank Bane," at the Columbia University Oral History Research Office; Peter Corning, *Frank Bane* (1965), published by the Social History Project of the Columbia University Oral History Research Office; and James R. W. Leiby, *Frank Bane: Public Administration and Public Welfare* (1965), published by the University of California at Berkeley Regional Oral History Office. Works that contain valuable information on Bane are Louis B. Brownlow, *The Autobiography of Louis Brownlow: A Passion for Politics* (1955–1958); Charles McKinley and Robert W. Frase, *Launching Social Security: A Capture and Record Account, 1935–1937* (1970); and Blanche D. Coll, *Safety Net: Welfare and Social Security, 1929–1979* (1995). See also Linda Gordon, *Pitied but Not Entitled: Single Mothers and the History of Welfare, 1890–1935* (1994), and Michael Kernan, "The Father of Social Security," *Washington Post* (18 Jan. 1983). Obituaries are in the *Washington Post* (26 Jan. 1983) and the *New York Times* (29 Jan. 1983).

BLANCHE D. COLL

BARBER, Samuel Osborne, II (*b.* 9 March 1910 in West Chester, Pennsylvania; *d.* 23 January 1981 in New York City), major American composer known primarily for his symphonic works and art songs. The lyric beauty of his music, based mostly on traditional classical forms, was influenced by Romanticism.

Samuel Barber was named after his paternal grandfather. He and his younger sister grew up in a three-story brick house in West Chester with their father, Samuel Leroy Barber, a physician, and their mother, Marguerite McLeod Beatty, who played the piano and wrote down Barber's earliest compositions. Barber began studying piano at age six, wrote his first composition, "Sadness," a year later, and at age ten wrote the first act of an unfinished opera, "The Rose Tree," to a libretto by the family's Irish cook. At age eleven, he studied the pipe organ and the next year served briefly as organist at Westminster Presbyterian Church in West Chester. A maternal uncle, the composer Sidney Homer—whose wife, Louise, was a celebrated opera singer with the Metropolitan Opera—was Barber's mentor from 1922 until Homer's death in 1953. In their years of correspondence Homer gave encouragement, guidance, and vision to Barber, who wrote in greater depth to him than to anyone.

In 1924, at the age of fourteen, Barber entered the Curtis Institute of Music in Philadelphia, where he studied piano with Isabelle Vengerova, voice with Emilio de Gogorza, and composition and music theory with Rosario Scalero. He distinguished himself in all three areas. His nine years of rigorous tutelage under Scalero, a student of the eminent

Samuel Barber. ARCHIVE PHOTOS

Romanian-born Eusebius Mandyczewski, were a major influence on his music. The handsome, lanky, and bespectacled Barber was viewed as an extraordinary genius, the star among many talented students at the institute. He was well read, accomplished in foreign languages, and was considered affable and witty by his close friends, although he could also be shy and moody. He remained at the institute until 1932 and received a bachelor of music degree in 1934.

While at the Curtis Institute, Barber began an intimate, lifelong friendship with a talented Italian student, Gian Carlo Menotti. The Barber residence became Menotti's second home, and Barber spent many summers with the large Menotti family in Milan. This friendship led to a unique and productive personal and professional collaboration. They lived together most of their lives. Barber never married and had no children.

Upon leaving the institute, Barber tried singing and some teaching to support his composing and received help from his family and others. In later years he earned enough from his compositions in royalties, performance fees, commissions for new works, and awards to enable him to devote all his time to composing. His Sonata for Violoncello and Piano (1932) established a pattern that he repeated throughout his career of enlisting the cooperation of the performer during the compositional process, in this case cellist Orlando Cole, in discovering the idioms and scope of virtuosic possibilities of a particular instrument. He also collaborated closely in 1945 with cellist Raya Garbousova in composing the Concerto for Violoncello and Orchestra, one of the finest concertos for cello written during the twentieth century and one of the most challenging works in contemporary cello literature.

Barber's first piece for orchestra, *Overture to the School for Scandal* (1931), was given its world premiere in 1933 by the Philadelphia Orchestra under Alexander Smallens. Arturo Toscanini gave world premieres in 1938 of two Barber works, the *First Essay for Orchestra* and the orchestral version of the *Adagio for Strings,* which Barber had adapted from a movement of a string quartet written two years earlier. Recognition by other renowned conductors soon followed. The *Adagio for Strings* has earned a permanent and undisputed place in the American and international repertoire and is Barber's most frequently performed work. The *Adagio* was played at the funerals of President Franklin D. Roosevelt, Albert Einstein, and Princess Grace of Monaco, and was broadcast in South Africa upon the death of Jan Christian Smuts and in the United States for John F. Kennedy. (It was not, however, played at Barber's own funeral.) The Concerto for Violin and Orchestra, completed in 1939, is perhaps Barber's second most frequently performed work.

The choreographer and dancer Martha Graham invited Barber in 1946 to write the score for a ballet based on Eu-

ripides' *Medea,* to be performed at the second annual Festival of Contemporary Music. Following the world premiere in New York City in 1946, Graham revised the ballet and named it *Cave of the Heart.* Barber rearranged the ballet score into a seven-movement suite for full orchestra in 1947 and rescored it in 1955 into one continuous movement, renamed *Medea's Meditation and Dance of Vengeance.* Barber's Sonata for Piano (1949) was written for Vladimir Horowitz and commissioned in honor of the twenty-fifth anniversary of the League of Composers. The four-voice fugue in the last movement is a brilliant example of the compositional technique.

As a baritone who early in life explored a singing career, Barber wrote 103 solo songs, often composed spontaneously during periods when he was having difficulty beginning or revising a piece. Eleanor Steber, Jennie Tourel, and Leontyne Price performed many of his songs. The 1953 concert of *Hermit Songs* inaugurated Barber's long professional collaboration and friendship with Price. Over the next twenty years Barber was to write some of his most important and beautiful work for her, such as the soprano solo in *Prayers of Kierkegaard,* the opera role Cleopatra in *Antony and Cleopatra,* and the song cycle *Despite and Still.*

Barber selected song texts, mostly by Irish, English, and occasionally American poets, for their inherent musical interest or personal significance, and he occasionally wrote his own verses. Virtually all his large-scale orchestral works, with the exception of the two symphonies, carry literary allusions. Among the most performed of his works, the ten *Hermit Songs,* drawn from ancient Irish texts, focus on reclusion and his lifelong quest for solitude. His frequent use of melancholy is compelling in *Dover Beach* (1931), a cycle for voice and string quartet that uses the elegiac Matthew Arnold poem as text. He was inspired by other nineteenth-century poets, such as Shelley ("Music from a Scene from Shelley," 1933) and Gerard Manley Hopkins ("A Nun Takes the Veil," 1937). For *Reincarnations* (1942), a collection of choral works, he chose verses of three Irish poets (David O'Bruadair, Egan O'Rahilly, and Antoine O'Reachtaire) known as Raftery. The majority of his song texts reflect more modern poets and writers, such as James Joyce ("Fadograph of a Yestern Scene," from a line in *Finnegans Wake*; 1971), Rainer Maria Rilke (*Mélodies passagères*), and Stephen Spender ("A Stopwatch and an Ordnance Map," 1940). James Agee's prose poem "Knoxville: Summer of 1915" was used in Barber's work for orchestra and soprano solo by the same name, considered his "most American" work.

The successful *Vanessa,* Barber's first operatic essay and the first new American work produced by the Metropolitan Opera House since its opening in 1883, won Barber a Pulitzer Prize in 1958. Menotti, by then the foremost American operatic composer, created the libretto after Barber had discussed the project over many years with Dylan Thomas, Thornton Wilder, Agee, Spender, Tennessee Williams, and James Baldwin.

The Concerto for Piano and Orchestra (1962), written for John Browning and dedicated to Manfred Ibel, a long-time friend, premiered in the opening week of the new Philharmonic (now Avery Fisher) Hall at Lincoln Center. This work marked the high point in Barber's career, earned him a second Pulitzer Prize and a Music Critics Circle Award, and brought him the first invitation to an American composer to the biennial Congress of Soviet Composers.

His opera *Antony and Cleopatra,* commissioned for the opening of the Metropolitan Opera House at Lincoln Center in 1966, was viewed as a failure, partly because of technical problems with the new house's stage equipment and miscalculations by Franco Zeffirelli, director, stage designer, and librettist. Critics also found only rare moments of Barber's lyrical style and the lack of an overall sense of dramatic purpose and musical momentum. The third act, however, was considered brilliant because it contained the strongest emotional music and finest arias. Barber and Menotti later revised the opera. Another major disappointment to Barber was his Second Symphony, commissioned by the Army Air Forces while he was in the service in 1944.

Barber and Menotti shared for thirty years a house they named Capricorn in Mount Kisco, New York. They bought the mountainside chalet overlooking Croton Lake in 1943 when Barber was inducted into military service. Mary Curtis Bok, founder of the Curtis Institute and a patron of Barber, made the purchase possible. She also introduced him to Carl Engel at G. Schirmer, Inc., the firm that became his exclusive publisher. When the house that had been their creative, intellectual, and social center was sold in 1973, Barber moved to an apartment on Fifth Avenue in New York City. After a six-year creative hiatus, he resumed composing shortly before his death. His *Third Essay for Orchestra* (1978) was first performed in 1980 by the New York Philharmonic. The orchestration of the *Canzonetta for Oboe and String Orchestra,* completed posthumously by Barber's student and close friend Charles Turner, offers an appropriate elegy to the conclusion of Barber's career and pays tribute to the vocal inspiration that guided virtually all of his music.

Among American composers, the early, persistent, and enduring acclaim Barber received was exceptional, and his works, comprising forty-eight opus numbers and more than one hundred unpublished pieces, are among the most frequently performed. His music, primarily lyrical, was praised for its remarkable sense of form and well-crafted design. There was a lyrical quality even to his strictly instrumental pieces that from the first established him as a neo-Romantic. Although he incorporated elements of modernist language after 1940, such as dissonance, chro-

maticism, tonal ambiguity, limited serialism, and complex rhythms, he was insulated from the stylistic trends of his generation.

In addition to his two Pulitzer Prizes and the Music Critics Circle Award, Barber won two Joseph H. Bearns Prizes from Columbia University (1929 and 1933), the American Academy of Rome's Prix de Rome (1935), a Pulitzer traveling scholarship (1935–1936) with an extension, three Guggenheim Fellowships (1945, 1947, and 1949), and many commissions. He was the youngest member admitted to the National Institute of Arts and Letters (1941), was elected to the American Academy of Arts and Letters (1958), received the Henry Hadley Medal of the National Association for American Composers and conductors (1958), and was awarded an honorary doctorate from Harvard University (1959).

Samuel Barber died of cancer in New York City. During the last months of Barber's life, Menotti, Valentin Herranz, who was Barber's companion for twelve years, and many friends kept vigil and performed live music at his bedside. He was buried next to his mother in the Barber family plot at Oaklands Cemetery in West Chester.

★

All editions of Samuel Barber's compositions are published by G. Schirmer, Inc. Most of the unpublished works are at the Library of Congress in Washington, D.C. Nathan Broder, who knew Barber for fifteen years, wrote *Samuel Barber* (1954) based on information provided by Barber, his family, and newsletters from the Curtis Institute of Music. An excellent and complete biography is Barbara B. Heyman, *Samuel Barber: The Composer and His Music* (1992), which lists archives and special collections, interviews, taped radio broadcasts, and selected books and articles. Richard Jackson's general article on Barber in the *New Grove Dictionary of American Music,* edited by H. Wiley Hitchcock and Stanley Sadie (1986), builds on Broder's work and adds material through 1981. An obituary is in the *New York Times* (24 Jan. 1981).

PHYLLIS BADER-BOREL

BARNES, Djuna Chappell (*b.* 12 June 1892 in Cornwall on Hudson, New York; *d.* 19 June 1982 in New York City), novelist, journalist, dramatist, poet, and artist best known for her experimental lesbian novel, *Nightwood* (1936), and for the wit and style she brought to the avant-garde of Greenwich Village, Paris, and London.

Barnes, the daughter of Wald Barnes and Elizabeth Chappell, was born into a spectacularly unconventional family headed by her twice-divorced paternal grandmother, Zadel Barnes. A poet and journalist for *Harper's Monthly* magazine, Zadel Barnes was active in the feminist and temperance movements. Djuna's father was originally named Henry Budington, but after experimenting with various names, he settled on Wald Barnes, taking his mother's maiden name. Djuna's English-born mother had met Wald Barnes in London, where Zadel Barnes reputedly entertained such notable figures as Speranza Wilde, Oscar Wilde, and Robert Browning in a literary salon during the 1880s. In 1897 Fanny Faulkner moved into the family's log cabin in New York as Wald's second wife. Djuna had four brothers, two half brothers, and a half sister, most of them as creatively named as Djuna. All of the children were schooled at home. The family subsisted on Zadel Barnes's income and a desultory farm operation that shifted to Huntington, Long Island, in 1902. Wald Barnes played five musical instruments, composed operas, and tried his hand at poetry and watercolors but eschewed regular employment. The tempestuous dynamics of this ménage were represented in Djuna Barnes's later writing.

Barnes's first sexual experience probably came in bedding as a child with her grandmother Zadel. In 1910 her family imposed upon her a common-law marriage with Fanny's brother Percy Faulkner—an arrangement that lasted only a few months. The bigamous household persisted until 1912, when Elizabeth demanded that Wald make a choice and subsequently moved out.

Barnes's scant education included art classes at the Pratt Institute (1912–1913) and at the Art Students League of New York (1915–1916). She began her professional career as a journalist for the *Brooklyn Eagle* in 1913. Her participatory journalism included an interview with a young gorilla, forced feeding of the sort used with hunger-striking suffragettes, and a staged rescue from a burning building. She covered the ethnic cultures of New York City in articles featuring her own illustrations, and she initiated an innovative series of interviews with literary figures. She moved to Greenwich Village in 1915. That year, in the offbeat publishing house of Guido Bruno that evaded the censors, she produced *The Book of Repulsive Women,* sketches and poetry that unabashedly discussed prostitution and suicide. Among her lovers of the period were a German-born, Harvard-educated art dealer, Ernst "Putzi" Hanfstaengl (1914–1916), who later became a devotee of Adolf Hitler; and a socialist and drama critic for the Theatre Guild, Courtenay Lemon (1917–1919). She also wrote one-act plays for the Provincetown Players and reviews for the Drama Guild.

Barnes moved to Paris in 1921 with a commission from *McCall's* magazine. Impressed by James Joyce's *Ulysses* (1922), she interviewed Joyce for an independent article published in *Vanity Fair* in 1922. Her first major book, named simply *A Book* (1923), was composed of short stories, plays, and drawings. The years she spent in Paris provided material for *Nightwood,* which focuses on the life she shared there with Thelma Wood, the American silverpoint artist, from 1921 to 1929. Wood figured in the novel as

Djuna Barnes. OSCAR WHITE/CORBIS

Robin Vote and Barnes as Nora Flood. In 1927 Barnes purchased a flat and decorated it with church and circus trappings representative of her relationship with Wood.

In 1928 Barnes published *Ryder* and *Ladies Almanack,* two highly original, amusingly illustrated parodies. *Ryder* presents the philosophy and procreative adventures of Barnes's father, portrayed as Wendell Ryder, and a portrait of Zadel Barnes as Sophia, and it proclaims the release of the daughter Julie from reproduction. *Ladies Almanack* describes the lesbian exploits of such notable figures as Radclyffe Hall, Janet Flanner, and Solita Solano at Natalie Barney's Amazonian Paris salon. Subversively normative yet alternately mocking and celebratory of lesbianism, the controversial *Almanack* was treasured by Barney. Barnes resisted a lesbian label for herself, though she acknowledged her love for Wood.

During much of the 1930s, Barnes moved among Paris, New York, and London. Her lovers included Peter Negoe and Silas Glossip. She seems also to have loved Barney; Romaine Brooks, an artist; and Jane Heap, the editor of *Little Review.* Charles Henri Ford was her devoted friend, and together they traveled to Tangier, Munich, Vienna, and Budapest during 1931 to 1933. Barnes cared for and supported Baroness Elsa von Freytag Loringhoven, the eccentric dadaist, and eulogized her in *Transition* (December 1927). In 1932 Barnes attended a British summer writers' gathering at Hayford Hall in Devon that was sponsored by Peggy Guggenheim, who became Barnes's rather stinting patron. Amid the parlor games of Hayford Hall, Barnes began seriously writing *Nightwood*. Another writer in residence, Emily Holmes Coleman, one of the novel's chief advocates, convinced T. S. Eliot to publish it at Faber and Faber in London. Never legally married, Barnes had an abortion in 1933 but no children. Eliot became a loyal friend and helped keep tabs on Barnes's belongings after she returned to the United States in 1939.

Barnes derived her writing style from American folklore, the Bible, Elizabethan lyrics, and Jacobean plays. Her carnivalesque, palimpsestic narratives are populated by marginal characters and a menagerie of animals and are punctuated with similes and metaphors that challenge interpretation. Tall and slim with striking auburn hair, Barnes dressed stylishly in cast-off capes and cloche hats. She was a favorite of the photography of Man Ray, who called her a "stunning subject."

After her return from England, Barnes settled into a small, rent-controlled apartment at 5 Patchin Place in Greenwich Village. Eliot visited her throughout the 1940s, and she kept up with old friends, but otherwise she lived as a formidable recluse from 1940 until her death. She suffered from alcoholism until she gave up drinking in 1950. Eliot oversaw the production and publication of *The Antiphon* (1958), a drama that suggests several scenarios of sexual abuse during Barnes's childhood. The *New Yorker* published two of her short poems, "Quarry" (27 December 1969) and "The Walking-mort" (15 May 1971). She died of old age in New York City. Barnes was cremated, and her ashes were scattered among dogwoods on Storm King Mountain near her birthplace.

★

Barnes's papers are at the University of Maryland and the University of Delaware. Douglas Messerli compiled *Djuna Barnes: A Bibliography* (1975) and edited *At the Roots of the Stars: The Short Plays of Djuna Barnes* (1995). Some of Barnes's interviews are collected in Alyce Barry, ed., *Interviews of Djuna Barnes* (1985). An interview is "The Barnes Among Women," *Time* (18 Jan. 1943). Cheryl J. Plumb's edition of *Nightwood* (1995) appends some of the cuts made by Eliot and others for the Faber first edition. Biographies are Andrew Field, *Djuna, the Life and Times of Djuna Barnes: The Formidable Miss Barnes* (1983), and Phillip Herring, *Djuna: The Life and Work of Djuna Barnes* (1995). Mary Lynn Broe, ed., *Silence and Power: A Reevaluation of Djuna Barnes* (1991), is an important feminist collection. Also notable are James B. Scott, *Djuna Barnes* (1976), and Louis Kannenstein, *The Art of Djuna Barnes: Duality and Damnation* (1977). Significant segments on Barnes are in Kenneth Burke, *Language as Symbolic Action* (1968); Shari Benstock, *Women of the Left Bank* (1986); Gillian Hanscombe and Virginia L. Smyers, *Writing for Their Lives* (1987); and Bonnie Kime Scott, *The Gender of Modernism* (1990), a critical anthology, and *Refiguring Modernism* (1995). An obituary is in the *New York Times* (20 June 1982).

BONNIE KIME SCOTT

BARR, Alfred Hamilton, Jr. (*b.* 28 January 1902 in Detroit, Michigan; *d.* 15 August 1981 in Salisbury, Connecticut), first director of the Museum of Modern Art, New York City, known for reshaping the traditional museum by adding departments of film, photography, architecture, and design.

Barr was born to Alfred Hamilton Barr, a Presbyterian minister, and Annie Elizabeth Wilson, daughter of a Presbyterian minister. In 1911 the Barrs, along with the young Alfred and Andrew (two years younger), moved to Baltimore, where Alfred, Sr., had accepted a position as minister of the First Presbyterian Church.

An academic youth, Barr enjoyed collecting and studying butterflies and also began a lifelong love of ornithology.

Alfred H. Barr, Jr., director emeritus of the Museum of Modern Art, New York, wearing a paper tie designed for him by Pablo Picasso, at the opening of the exhibition "Picasso 75th Anniversary," The Museum of Modern Art, New York. May 1957. PHOTOGRAPH BY BARRY KRAMER, COURTESY THE MUSEUM OF MODERN ART, NEW YORK

After attending Boy's Latin School in Baltimore, Barr entered Princeton in 1918, intending to study paleontology. He completed a degree in art and archaeology in 1922, graduating Phi Beta Kappa. Barr continued his investigations of art at Princeton, receiving an M.A. in 1923. Later that year he began teaching art history at Vassar College. Barr and a friend traveled to Europe in the summer of 1924, carefully examining the masterpieces of art and architecture. In 1924, supported by a Thayer Fellowship, Barr passed his preliminary Ph.D. exams at Harvard University but withdrew from the program one year later for financial reasons. While taking courses at Harvard, Barr organized the first course in contemporary art at Wellesley College, which he began teaching in 1926.

Modern art was little known or comprehended by Americans in 1926, even in university art departments. Barr was growing increasingly concerned by this apparent national lack of interest in contemporary visual art, an observation enhanced by a study fellowship to Europe in 1927. On that trip he visited the progressive Bauhaus art school in Germany and also traveled to Russia, where he met film pioneer Sergei Eisenstein.

Barr's reputation as an effective teacher and scholar of modern art soon became well known. Articles were written about Barr's college courses in Boston newspapers, and he received publicity curating small exhibitions at the Fogg Art Museum in Boston. On the basis of a recommendation by Paul Sachs, in 1929 Abby Aldrich Rockefeller, Lillie P. Bliss, and Mary Sullivan invited the twenty-seven-year-old scholar to serve as director of the first museum dedicated to contemporary art in New York. Known as the Museum of Modern Art, it opened to the public on 9 November 1929 with Barr in that post. The energetic intellectual soon began to shape the image of the museum and of modern art. On an aggressive educational mission, Barr issued exhibition catalogs, public statements, articles, and letters to newspapers declaring modern art promising and worthy of study. In 1930 Barr met Margaret ("Marga") Scolari-Fitzmaurice, an Italian-born art historian studying at New York University; they were married on 8 May of that year. Barr and his wife made periodic trips to Europe, which had long been the center of Western artistic activity. Alarmed by escalating political turmoil in Europe, Barr tried to raise money to help scholars and artists flee Germany in the 1930s.

Nearly three years after the Museum of Modern Art opened, Barr created its Department of Architecture, appointing the architect Philip Johnson as its overseer. In 1935 the first film library to be established as part of a museum was opened at the Museum of Modern Art with Iris Barry as curator. Film had not previously been considered an artistic medium, and consequently many films were beginning to deteriorate. Many early American films that have survived owe their preservation to Barr and the original film department's foresight and conservation efforts.

In March 1936 Barr assembled the blockbuster exhibition "Cubism and Abstract Art," accompanied by a catalog of the same name. During the 1930s the Museum of Modern Art became tremendously popular, in large part because of Barr's zealous enthusiasm. Traveling exhibitions toured the country. In his catalogs, Barr's use of simple language illustrated a structured explanation of the history of modern art. He encouraged average Americans to take an interest in contemporary art by introducing coherent and rational concepts.

In 1937 his daughter (and only child) Victoria was born. Barr, who devoted countless hours to the museum, scholarly writing, and travel, did not consider himself family oriented. Unable to journey to Europe during World War II, Barr visited Central America, shedding light on largely unreceived Mexican and Cuban artists, such as Wilfredo Lam, José Clemente Orozco, Oswaldo Guayasamín, and Antonio Berni.

As the Museum of Modern Art's collection and staff grew, Barr was increasingly plagued by administrative burdens. He dedicated less and less time to writing while trying to maintain a balance between curating and managing the museum. In 1943, after running a deficit for two years and after numerous disagreements with the museum president, Barr was relieved of his duties as director because of careless management and poor administrative skills.

Still a member of the museum's board of trustees, Barr was assigned the post of advisory director. Without the burden of trivial administrative duties, Barr found time to deliver numerous public speeches, serve as a director of the College Art Association, and lecture frequently. He also produced *What Is Modern Painting?* (1943), a guide for the layman aimed at addressing the basic tenets of modern art. In 1946 he published *Picasso: Fifty Years of His Art,* a definitive text on the artist, for which Barr was awarded a Ph.D. from Harvard University in 1947. That year he also accepted a job as director of the Museum of Modern Art's collections.

Princeton University awarded Barr an honorary degree of humane letters in 1949. A workaholic, the slender and bespectacled Barr was ever devoted to the Museum of Modern Art, courting donors, assisting in purchases of art, and advising on exhibitions. He spent his free time obsessively searching for the works of artists in Europe and the United States to add to the museum's collection. From childhood on, Barr found relaxation in Greensboro, Vermont, spending each summer studying birds and other wildlife. He continued to give advice to scholars concerning the history and presentation of modern art. In the early 1960s Barr's health began to fail. In 1967 he retired after thirty-eight years of service to the Museum of Modern Art and was appointed an honorary councillor to its board of trustees.

In 1971 Barr was diagnosed with Alzheimer's disease and four years later was moved into a nursing home. He died in 1981 and was buried in Greensboro.

Barr was the driving force behind the structure and success of the Museum of Modern Art. His mission of education created an atmosphere of communication between an often incomprehensible field and the general public. Barr's strategy of offering exhibition catalogs, pamphlets, and wall texts sculpted the standard of an art exhibition. He explained modern art in an unpretentious and rational manner to a skeptical American audience. In his scholarly writings, Barr dissected and categorized the history of modern art. By assembling these art movements in a definitive system, he set the standard for modern art dissertation. He championed the recognition of contemporary art in universities, encouraging its acceptance as a legitimate area of discourse.

★

Colleen Hennessey and Rona Roob, *An Inventory of the Alfred H. Barr, Jr., Papers* (1985), contains a complete archival collection of Barr's papers and manuscripts, which are held at the Museum of Modern Art, New York. Alice Goldfarb Marquis, *Alfred H. Barr, Jr.: Missionary for the Modern* (1989), is a detailed account of Barr's personal and professional life. James Leggio, "Alfred H. Barr, Jr., As a Writer of Allegory, Art Criticism in a Literary Context," appears in *The Museum of Modern Art at Mid-Century: Continuity and Change* (1995). Katherine Kuh, "Alfred Barr: Modern Art's Durable Crusader," *Saturday Review* (30 Sept. 1967), is a short interview by a colleague and former student. *Alfred H. Barr, January 28, 1902–August 15, 1981: A Memorial Tribute, October 21, 1981, 4:30 P.M.* (Museum of Modern Art, 1981), is a recognition of Barr's extraordinary character and achievements by those who knew him.

RENÉE COPPOLA

BARR, (Frank) Stringfellow (*b.* 15 January 1897 in Suffolk, Virginia; *d.* 3 February 1982 in Alexandria, Virginia), educator and writer best known for introducing the Great Books Program at St. John's College in Annapolis, Maryland, and for advocating the creation of a world government.

"Winkie" Barr was the youngest of the three children of William Alexander Barr, an Episcopal minister, and Ida Stringfellow, a homemaker. Between 1897 and 1907 his family moved to Richmond, Norfolk, and then Lynchburg, Virginia. In 1910 the family ventured to New Orleans, where his father became the dean of the Episcopal Cathedral and where, from 1912 to 1913, Barr attended Tulane University. He transferred to the University of Virginia the

Stringfellow Barr (*left*) with Scott Buchanan on the campus of St. John's College, *c.* 1938. ST. JOHN'S COLLEGE LIBRARY COLLECTION

following year. While there he became an associate editor of the *University of Virginia Magazine,* the student literary monthly, and an assistant editor of *Corks and Curls,* the yearbook. Barr also boxed. He completed his B.A. in 1916 and his M.A. in 1917. Of medium height and medium build, the red-haired Barr could not get into the regular army during World War I because of flat feet. Instead, he became a sergeant attached to the U.S. Army Ambulance Service in 1917 and 1918 and the surgeon general's office in 1918 and 1919. He was discharged in April 1919.

Having won a Rhodes Scholarship, Barr attended Balliol College at Oxford University from 1919 to 1921 and received a B.A. in modern history with honors. On 13 August 1921 he married Gladys Josephine Baldwin, a Kings College (London) theology student whose father taught at Oxford. They had no children. Barr continued his studies at the University of Paris (the Sorbonne) and received a *diplôme* in 1922. In 1922 and 1923, armed with a fellowship in history, he studied at the University of Ghent (Belgium) under Henri Pirenne. In 1923 he returned to the United States to help his father recover from a severe illness in Asheville, North Carolina.

Barr's teaching career began at the University of Virginia in Charlottesville, where he was assistant professor (1924–1927), associate professor (1927–1930), and professor (1930–1936) of modern European history. He also was advisory editor (1926–1930 and 1934–1937) and editor (1930–

45

1934) of the *Virginia Quarterly Review.* He wrote *Mazzini: Portrait of an Exile* (1935), a book about the great mid-nineteenth-century Italian patriot. Between 1934 and 1935 Barr sat on the committee (with Scott Buchanan, a fellow Rhodes scholar) that proposed the introduction of an honors course at the University of Virginia. The recommended reading list for that course mirrored the one adopted by St. John's College several years later.

In 1936 Barr became visiting professor of liberal arts at the University of Chicago by invitation of its president, Robert Maynard Hutchins. Barr also sat on the committee commissioned by Hutchins to study the reform of undergraduate education in the United States. Scott Buchanan was the chairman of that committee.

At the request of the chairman of the board of trustees of St. John's College in Annapolis, Maryland, Barr and Buchanan became, respectively, president and dean of the institution in 1937. They quickly eliminated electives and intercollegiate sports and established a fixed curriculum based on the writings of those they regarded as the great American and Western European thinkers. They also required students to be proficient in several languages, in mathematics, and in laboratory science. While at St. John's, Barr became the spokesman for the Great Books Program. In May 1940 he inaugurated a Sunday afternoon radio program on CBS, titled *Invitation to Learning,* which discussed the Great Books. From 1944 to 1946 he was advisory editor for the Encyclopaedia Britannica Great Books series. Thinking St. John's had grown too large and fearing that some of its land would be seized by the U.S. Navy for its own academy, Barr and Buchanan resigned in 1946 and attempted to create a duplicate institution in the Berkshire Mountains of Massachusetts; this effort failed despite beautiful surroundings and the availability of a $4.5 million endowment.

Beginning in 1948 Barr focused his attention on the reform of the world's political structure. He established and was president of the Foundation for World Government from 1948 to 1958. He advocated the political unification of the world in *The Pilgrimage of Western Man* (1949), a historical survey about attempts made to unify Europe since the sixteenth century. Between 1950 and 1954 he traveled throughout South and Central America, Europe, Africa, and Asia under the auspices of the foundation. As a result of his globe-trotting, he produced the pamphlet, *Let's Join the Human Race* (1950), and his *Citizens of the World* (1952), which chastised American cold war policies for ignoring the problems of developing nations. Concurrent with his responsibilities at the foundation, Barr became visiting professor of political science at the University of Virginia at Charlottesville from 1951 to 1953.

As professor of humanities at Rutgers University at Newark from 1955 to 1964, Barr lectured about liberal education and American foreign policy. He wrote a cutting satire about life in a medium-sized university in *Purely Academic* (1958), and tried to show the relevance of ancient philosophy to twentieth-century learning in *The Will of Zeus* (1961), *The Three Worlds of Man* (1963), and *The Mask of Jove* (1966),

At the invitation of Robert M. Hutchins, Barr became a senior fellow at the Center for the Study of Democratic Institutions in Santa Barbara, California, from 1966 to 1969. While there, he lobbied for higher educators nationwide to be more sensitive to the underlying reasons for student unrest before reacting vehemently against it. Barr retired in 1969 and moved to Kingston, New Jersey. In retirement he published *Voices That Endured* (1971), which synthesized his ideas on the Great Books and the active life. Barr, a lifelong Democrat and Episcopalian, was the son, grandson, and nephew of Episcopalian ministers. In his spare time he enjoyed traveling and was deeply interested in organic agriculture and small-scale gardening. He died of pneumonia and was buried in Cismont, Virginia.

Stringfellow Barr provided an alternative voice in higher education and in world politics. His goal was to promote unity in knowledge and in global relations. His Great Books Program at St. John's College drew praise from those who believed that higher learning had become diluted by specialization and by the myriad of choices open to students. His program drew criticism from those who believed it inflexible and out of touch with the realities of twentieth-century life. Barr's advocacy of world government and the need for people to be responsible for one another was considered laudatory even by his critics. However, his vision of world unity had little chance of succeeding in an era dominated by the cold war.

★

Charles A. Nelson, *Stringfellow Barr: A Centennial Appreciation of His Life* (1997), provides a former student's view of Barr. J. Winfree Smith, *A Search for a Liberal College: The Beginnings of the St. John's Program* (1983), provides a faculty member's view of the first two decades of the Great Books Program and the impact Barr had on it. A biographical sketch is in Maxine Block, ed., *Current Biography 1940* (1941), and biographical data can be found in Ann Evory, ed., *Contemporary Authors,* New Revision Series, vol. 1 (1981). William Buchanan, "Educational Rebels in the Nineteen Thirties," *Journal of General Education* 37 (1985): 3–33, compares St. John's College with Olivet and Black Mountain Colleges. For obituaries, see the *New York Times* (5 Feb. 1982), and Jane Podell, ed., *The Annual Obituary, 1982* (1983). Transcripts of interviews with Stringfellow Barr from 24 August 1975 to 22 November 1975 are in the library at St. John's College in Annapolis, Maryland.

GLEN EDWARD AVERY

BARRETT, Emma ("Sweet Emma") (*b.* 25 March 1897 in New Orleans, Louisiana; *d.* 28 January 1983 in Metairie,

Louisiana), jazz pianist, singer, and bandleader who gained national fame through her performances at Preservation Hall in New Orleans.

An intensely private woman who rarely discussed her personal life, Barrett was one of at least four children of William B. Barrett, an Ohio-born white customhouse employee who she said was a Union army captain in the Civil War, and Emma (Kennedy) Barrett, a black woman born in Louisiana. At the age of seven Emma began tinkering on a piano originally purchased for a sister who never touched it, and her father arranged for piano lessons. She was twelve years old when she started playing in bands. She grew up to be an attractive young woman with a reedy figure, light complexion, and large expressive eyes. Although she was unable to read music, Barrett played with the top "reading bands" of New Orleans. By 1923 she belonged to the Original Tuxedo Orchestra, founded by trumpeter Oscar "Papa" Celestin. When trombonist William "Bebe" Ridgley left Celestin to form his own band in the mid-1920s, Barrett went with him and stayed about a decade. She also played in the bands of John Robichaux, trumpeter Sidney Desvigne, and the violinist, composer, and music publisher Armand J. Piron.

In the 1940s and 1950s Barrett mainly played in small groups at society gigs and familiar watering holes. In the 1950s she helped form the ensemble that would eventually be based at Preservation Hall in the French Quarter of New Orleans. Among the traditional jazz veterans who played with her were trumpeter and drummer Percy Humphrey and his clarinetist brother, Willie James Humphrey; tubist Jerry Green; and drummer Josiah "Cie" Frazier. Another longtime colleague, Ricard Alexis, had played trumpet with Ridgley and recorded with Celestin in 1927. Forced to switch to string bass after thugs broke his jaw in the 1930s, Alexis played with Barrett and others until his death in 1960. Barrett's son was Ricard Alexis, Jr.

In 1961, Preservation Hall opened and soon became a popular forum for traditional jazz. The success of the hall was due in no small part to Barrett, whose punchy keyboard rhythms, easygoing vocals, and feisty personality helped revive and broaden interest in the city's signature sound. By the 1960s she was known as "Sweet Emma the Bell Gal," a nickname that was stitched into her trademark red beanie and referred to bells attached to her garters that jangled as she kept time. Barrett could hammer a piano, summoning a big sound once compared to that of a calliope, heavy on chords with rinky-tink in the upper registers. She played from the wrist and sat low at the piano, graduating from stools to straight-back chairs, then finally to a wheelchair. She tailored her deep singing voice to fit the song. It could be clipped and sassy on upbeat tunes like "Bill Bailey," or slow and ponderous for a spiritual number such as "Just a Closer Walk with Thee."

Barrett relished the new level of popularity brought on by tourists, recordings, and spots on television and in the movies. In the mid-1960s she performed on the *Ed Sullivan Show* and played a number in *The Cincinnati Kid,* a movie starring Steve McQueen as a traveling card shark. The band traveled to such venues as Disneyland, the Guthrie Theater in Minneapolis, and Ellis Auditorium in Memphis. Some of her best-known recordings date to this period, among them *Sweet Emma and Her Preservation Hall Jazz Band* and *Sweet Emma at Disneyland* (both 1964).

Through it all Barrett stuck to her convictions, which could be as strong as her piano playing. She knew how to throw a tantrum if something important did not go her way, and she refused to fly, boarding trains even if the journey took a few extra days. She preferred to be paid in new bills and distrusted banks, carrying her life savings with her even after being robbed twice in the early 1960s. In 1967 she suffered a stroke that partially paralyzed her left side, confined her to bed for nearly two years, and limited her playing to just the right hand. She nevertheless returned to work, insisting on playing at Preservation Hall three times a week, often over the objections of concerned family and friends.

In recognition of the fact that Barrett was one of the

"Sweet Emma" Barrett. Preservation Hall, New Orleans

city's best-loved personalities, the New Orleans City Council asked the Preservation Hall Jazz Band to play in council chambers one day in June 1979 and proclaimed it Sweet Emma Day. Ten days after playing her last gig in January 1983, Barrett died at Bonnabel Hospital of complications from another stroke. Friends attended services at St. Raymond Catholic Church, and she was buried in St. Louis Cemetery No. 3. At her request, there was no jazz funeral.

Although Barrett was not the only female pianist identified with traditional New Orleans jazz or the most virtuosic musician to emerge from that city, she was a tenacious trouper who developed a lasting following. She enjoyed the income and fame that bypassed a number of her colleagues in their old age, and by continuing to play and record she also helped preserve a uniquely American musical legacy.

★

William Carter, *Preservation Hall: Music from the Heart* (1991), which profiles New Orleans jazz personalities, includes quotes from a rare interview Barrett gave to the jazz archivist William Russell as part of a Tulane University oral history project in 1968. Other biographical sources include Al Rose and Edmond Souchon, *New Orleans Jazz: A Family Album* (1967), a compendium of thumbnail sketches and vintage photographs of musicians, orchestras, brass bands, and venues; Barry Kernfeld, ed., *The New Grove Dictionary of Jazz,* vol. 1 (1988); and "Sweet Emma Has Her Day in New Orleans," *Times-Picayune/States-Item* (22 June 1979). Information about the races of her parents is from U.S. Census of 1880, Orleans Parish, New Orleans, Louisiana, Enumeration District 23, sheet 46, 16 June 1880. Obituaries are in the *Times-Picayune/States-Item* (29 Jan. 1983) and the *New York Times* (30 Jan. 1983).

WHITNEY SMITH

BASIE, William James ("Count") (*b.* 21 August 1904 in Red Bank, New Jersey; *d.* 26 April 1984 in Hollywood, Florida), bandleader, pianist, composer, and for more than fifty years one of the leading figures in big-band jazz.

Basie was raised in Red Bank, the second son of Harvey Basie, a caretaker and groundskeeper, and Lilly Childs Basie, a homemaker. Young Bill Basie left school after the eighth grade to pursue his music career. From 1924 to 1927 he toured in burlesque and vaudeville shows. In Harlem in New York City he played stride piano in small clubs and took theater-organ lessons from Fats Waller. In 1927 a black vaudeville tour took Basie to Tulsa, Oklahoma, where he heard the Blue Devils territory band. He saw this as the true beginning of his musical life. The Blue Devils imprinted on him the model of big-band swing, which he soon adopted and made his own. He joined the Blue Devils

as their regular pianist in 1928 and stayed with the band about a year, performing in Texas, Oklahoma, and the Southwest.

In 1929 Basie joined Bennie Moten's Kansas City–based band. He soon married a Kansas City girl, Vivian Wynn, but the marriage broke up quickly, and he was again living in hotels and rooming houses and was on the road with Moten's band. A 1932 national tour produced little money. A classic recording session that year for Victor Recording Company in Camden, New Jersey, included "Moten Swing" and "Toby," which displayed the propulsive rhythm and riff figures that would establish swing as the popular dance music of this era. Basie went to Little Rock, Arkansas, in early 1934 to lead his own band under Moten's sponsorship. In 1935, just as Benny Goodman's band was inaugurating the swing era, Moten died and his band (which Basie had just rejoined) broke up. Fortunately, Basie's job at the Reno Club in Kansas City gave him a base for building his own band, which eventually included many of the stars of the Blue Devils and Moten bands. Somewhere in this period Bill Basie became Count Basie and the name stuck for the rest of his career.

The critic and promoter John Hammond, who had helped launch the careers of Benny Goodman and the singer Billie Holiday, heard broadcasts of Basie's Reno Club band. Hammond put Basie in contact with the agent Willard Alexander, who brought Basie to the MCA agency. One of the biggest agencies in the band business, MCA rarely handled black bands, but Alexander arranged a set of engagements that brought the band to New York City by way of Chicago and Buffalo.

The band was still learning its craft. At the Grand Terrace in Chicago it had trouble playing for the nightclub show. During its New York opening in December 1936 at the Roseland Ballroom, Basie's band was panned by the critic George Simon for bad intonation. Like many black bands of the period, Basie's musicians could not afford the quality of instruments owned by most white bands. Also, Basie's blues and riff-based style sounded foreign to some New York ears.

Throughout 1937, Basie's band recorded extensively for Decca and toured the country. It was the first black band to play Pittsburgh's Chatterbox. Basie brought in new musicians and added more popular dance tunes to the repertoire. Audiences began to appreciate the loose, riff-based ensembles and virtuoso improvisations of the band. "One O'Clock Jump," recorded in July 1937, and other danceable instrumentals, often featuring the saxophonist Lester Young, established Basie's reputation. Jimmy Rushing's vocals, such as "Good Morning Blues" and "Sent for You Yesterday" added to Basie's popularity. Billie Holiday sang briefly with the band, but its main female voice on record was Helen Humes, who gave the band a complete swing-

Count Basie. METRONOME/ARCHIVE PHOTOS

era package. Basie's piano playing was now sparse and concise.

Basie's 1938 stay at the Famous Door in New York City established him as one of the four top black bandleaders in the country with Duke Ellington, Jimmie Lunceford, and Cab Calloway. Basie continued to record more hits for Decca. In December 1938 he headlined a concert at Carnegie Hall titled "From Spirituals to Swing," which, organized by Hammond, put jazz in its context of the African-American musical tradition and presented it to an educated interracial audience. With the onset of World War II, Basie continued to tour, even as Young and others left the band to join the army. Basie also broadcast and recorded V-discs to be played over loudspeakers at military bases.

In August 1942 in Seattle, Basie married Catherine ("Katie") Morgan, a dancer he had known on and off since his vaudeville days; they had one child. The couple moved into a Manhattan apartment on Fifth Avenue just south of 110th Street. Although the band's personnel frequently changed because of the draft, Basie retained the same solid sound as well as his popularity with both black and white audiences and critics. He won the *Metronome* magazine poll as favorite jazz pianist in 1942 and 1943. The band appeared in five Hollywood studio feature films in 1943, including *Reveille for Beverly* and *Top Man,* and made several soundies, short films for video jukeboxes. Basie recorded for Columbia from 1944 to 1945 and then for Victor from 1947 to 1949.

After the war the band business changed. Parents of the new baby-boom generation were moving to the suburbs and staying home with their kids rather than going out to ballrooms and nightclubs. Television began to take away the theater audience. All of this contributed to the extinction of the big bands. With Basie on the road, his wife moved their family from Harlem to Queens in this period. By 1950 Basie, like many of his contemporaries, was leading a small group.

Unlike many big-band leaders, however, by 1952 he had re-formed his big band, and he kept it in business for the rest of his life. New arrangers updated the swing sound with a lighter sound featuring section work by flutes and clarinets as well as saxophones. Basie's new sound emerged from a December 1953 recording date for modern-jazz entrepreneur Norman Granz, released as the album *Basie Dance Sessions.* The Basie sound carried over into the early rock era. The theme song for Dick Clark's *American Bandstand* television show was a reworking of Basie's "Jumpin' at the Woodside." Basie's own contribution to television history was an appearance on 8 December 1957 with members of his 1930s and 1950s bands on *The Sound of Jazz.* This CBS program was a great jazz event and became a classic album. With Basie's band constantly on the road, Katie Basie took over some of his business affairs, including a nightclub in Harlem. She also cared for his aging parents and arranged their funerals.

As rock and roll gained popularity, Basie played his danceable music for older audiences in concerts and at festivals. He toured Europe for the first time in 1954 and continued to do so on a regular basis into the 1980s. His band was rediscovered in the late 1950s by critics and audiences. Basie played regularly at the New York City club Birdland, and was featured at the Newport and other jazz festivals. Basie won the *Down Beat* magazine poll for best band every year between 1955 and 1961. Some consider the pinnacle of the 1950s work to be the 1957 Roulette album *The Atomic Mr. Basie,* with its great instrumentals and a mushroom-cloud album cover. Another hit album saw the band backing vocalese versions of Basie standards by the trio of Lambert, Hendricks, and Ross.

Basie's band played at President John F. Kennedy's inaugural ball in 1961; Basie's big solo hit of this period was "April in Paris," with its triple "one more time" ending borrowed from the organist Wild Bill Davis at a Birdland engagement. In this period the Basie band worked with many popular artists, including Ella Fitzgerald and Tony Bennett. The arranger Quincy Jones contributed to the 1960s Basie sound. The most important association of this decade was with Frank Sinatra, who recorded with the band and signed it to his own Reprise label. As Basie recorded popular songs and television and movie themes, won Grammy awards, and played Las Vegas and Caribbean cruises, some purists felt he had left jazz behind. From 1962 to 1965, Basie won the *Down Beat* dance-band award while Duke Ellington won the jazz award. Eventually Basie and his family moved to the Bahamas. The 1970 album *Afrique* showed his awareness of new directions in jazz and black consciousness.

In the 1970s Basie expanded his touring range with visits to Japan, Australia, and Southeast Asia. He also signed a new recording contract with Norman Granz's Pablo label and unleashed a flood of creativity in both big-band and small-group formats. He recorded with a wide assortment of small-group partners, including veterans of his band and modernists. Marvelous results came from his pairing with the pianist Oscar Peterson, whose style was as effusive as Basie's was sparse. Some of these sessions found Basie on organ, an instrument he had experimented with since his vaudeville days.

A heart attack in 1976 slowed Basie but he recovered and continued to tour for his last eight years, often using a motorized scooter on stage. His wife died a year before he did. Near the end of his life he collaborated on an autobiography entitled *Good Morning Blues* with the novelist and critic Albert Murray. Basie approved the first draft but did not live to see it completed; he died in Doctor's Hospital in Hollywood, Florida. His funeral was a Harlem event, complete with major media coverage. He was buried in Long Island, New York. The Count Basie Orchestra continued after his death, led by Frank Foster and other alumni.

Basie's impact on jazz is difficult to judge. He was not a prolific composer like Duke Ellington or an arranger like Fletcher Henderson or Benny Carter. His piano style was unique, but his real instrument was his band, which he kept tuned and focused with his rhythm, musicianship, and showmanship. As he said, "The thing about being the chief is that you get to call the tunes." By calling the tunes from vaudeville and swing to Newport, Las Vegas, Montreux, and Tokyo, Count Basie revealed the elements of African-American musical culture to a worldwide audience.

★

Count Basie and Albert Murray, *Good Morning Blues* (1985), tells Basie's own story. Biographical works include Stanley Dance, *The World of Count Basie* (1980); Chris Sheridan, *Count Basie: A Biodiscography* (1986); and Nathan W. Pearson, Jr., *Goin' to Kansas City* (1987). The impact of Basie's band is analyzed in Ross Russell, *Jazz Style in Kansas City and the Southwest* (1971); Albert J. McCarthy, *Big Band Jazz* (1974); Gunther Schuller, *The Swing Era* (1989); Thomas J. Hennessey, *From Jazz to Swing* (1994); David Stowe, *Swing Changes* (1994); and Lewis Erenberg, *Swinging the Dream* (1998). Basie's discography takes up eleven pages

in Richard Cook and Brian Morton, *The Penguin Guide to Jazz on CD* (1994). *The Complete Decca Recordings,* a three-CD boxed set, rates among the classic jazz recordings.

THOMAS J. HENNESSEY

BATTLES, Clifford Franklin ("Gyp") (*b.* 1 May 1910 in Akron, Ohio; *d.* 28 April 1981 in Seminole City, Florida), college and professional football player and coach, elected to both the National Football Foundation College Football Hall of Fame and the Pro Football Hall of Fame.

Battles's father was a laborer in the saltworks run by the Goodrich and Firestone Rubber companies. His mother was a housewife. Battles displayed athletic talent as a student at Kenmore High School in Akron but did not achieve significant recognition until enrolled at West Virginia Wesleyan College in 1928. Although he played primarily against small colleges, Battles's mixture of speed and power made him a noted breakaway runner. In 1930 he scored touchdowns of 90, 98, and 80 yards in a game against Waynesburg College, and 90 and 70 yards in a game against Georgetown University. That same year, playing against Salem College, he ran for 400 yards and scored seven touchdowns. In addition to football, Battles was a member of the swimming and tennis teams and earned a Phi Beta Kappa

Cliff Battles. PRO FOOTBALL HALL OF FAME

key for his academics. In 1932 he graduated with a degree in English.

Following his graduation, Battles signed a contract with George Preston Marshall's Boston Braves (later the Boston Redskins) of the National Football League (NFL). Battles's salary was $175 per game, and he was an instant success. During his rookie year Battles led the league in rushing with 576 yards in 148 carries. In 1934 he became the first person in NFL history to run for more than 200 yards in a game, gaining 215 against the New York Giants. At six-foot-one and weighing between 195 and 215 pounds, Battles was one of the larger ball carriers of his day. His combination of fullback power and halfback speed made him an exciting and durable runner. Battles won All-League honors for Boston in 1933 and 1936.

Although Battles prospered, his Boston team did not. Despite winning seasons and star players, few fans came to the games. In 1937 Marshall relocated the franchise to the nation's capital as the Washington Redskins. Marshall also signed the star passer Sammy Baugh that year. The combination of Baugh's passing and Battles's running gave the Redskins a balanced, unpredictable attack, and Battles enjoyed his finest season ever in 1937. He led the NFL with 216 carries, 874 rushing yards, and 5 rushing touchdowns. Once again he was named to the All-League team. Playing against the New York Giants in the Polo Grounds in the final regular season game of that year, with the Eastern Division championship at stake, Battles scored three touchdowns, on runs of 4 and 73 yards and a 76-yard interception return. The Redskins won, 49–14. The next week Battles ran 43 yards for a touchdown on the second play of the game, as the Redskins beat the Chicago Bears, 28–21, for the NFL championship.

Ironically, Battles's first championship would be his last. Redskins owner Marshall had tied up most of the team's payroll in signing Baugh, and when Columbia University offered Battles a position as an assistant coach at $1,000 above his playing salary, Marshall was unable to match the offer. By 1937 Battles was married to Edith Wann and needed the extra salary Columbia offered. The 1937 championship game was his last as a player. In his brief, six-year NFL playing career, Battles had carried the ball more times, for more yardage, than anyone up to that time.

Battles remained an assistant coach at Columbia University through the 1941 season. Following the Japanese attack on Pearl Harbor, he enlisted in the armed forces, serving as football coach at the El Toro, California, marine base. He concluded his coaching career in 1946 and 1947 as head coach of the Brooklyn Dodgers of the new All-American Football Conference.

After coaching the Dodgers, where he racked up a dismal 4–16–1 record, Battles left the world of athletics. He became manager of civic relations for General Electric, rep-

resenting the company as a congressional lobbyist until the late 1970s. Battles won election to the National Football Foundation College Football Hall of Fame (1955) and the Pro Football Hall of Fame (1968). Locally, he was president of the Washington, D.C., Touchdown Club and University Club and served on the board of governors of the Congressional Country Club. Battles often played golf with the former Supreme Court justice and NFL player Byron "Whizzer" White. He and his wife raised two daughters, Patricia and Judith. He was a Methodist.

After retiring from General Electric, Battles moved to Seminole City, Florida, a suburb of Clearwater, in 1979. He died from heart failure in 1981 and was buried in Rockville, Maryland.

Compared to the players of the modern consolidated NFL, Battles's football statistics do not appear especially impressive. During the 1930s, however, he was one of the dominant players of the game. The fact that after only six years he was able to retire with more career rushing yards than any other player demonstrates his success. Battles's talents were also vital to the survival of the Washington Redskins. The Depression drove many NFL teams out of business, but players like Battles gave the Redskins franchise the stability to survive.

★

Memorabilia and newspaper clippings relating to Battles are in the Pro Football Hall of Fame in Canton, Ohio. Brief biographical treatments appear in Don R. Smith, *Pro Football Hall of Fame All-Time Greats* (1988), and *The Coffin Corner* 18 (late summer 1996): 22–23. Interviews are found in Murray Goodman and Leonard Lewin, *My Greatest Day in Football* (1948), and Myron Cope, *The Game That Was: The Early Days of Pro Football* (1970). An obituary is in the *Washington Post* (29 Apr. 1981).

HAROLD W. AURAND, JR.

BAXTER, Anne (*b.* 7 May 1923 in Michigan City, Indiana; *d.* 12 December 1985 in New York City), actress with nearly a half century of experience on stage, in film, and on television. She was twice nominated for Academy Awards and in 1947 received the best supporting actress Oscar for her role in *The Razor's Edge* (1946).

Baxter was the only child of Kenneth Stuart Baxter, an executive with Frankford Distilleries, and Catherine Wright, who later gained recognition as a painter of Christmas scenes and an interior decorator. Baxter's mother was the daughter of famed architect Frank Lloyd Wright, with whom Anne had a close and caring relationship. One of her fondest recollections was of the dollhouse Wright designed for her. When Baxter was four, her family moved to White Plains, New York, then to other suburbs of New York City, and eventually relocated to Manhattan, where she at-

Anne Baxter. CORBIS-BETTMANN

tended private schools. Strict Presbyterians, her parents brought Baxter up to achieve success on her own rather than depending on her family for life's comforts. Once she saw Helen Hayes perform on the stage, Baxter had no doubt that she wanted to become an actress, and from 1934 to 1936 her parents enrolled her in Theodora Irvine's School of the Theatre, in White Plains. She attended the prestigious Brearly School in New York City in 1938 and 1939 and completed secondary school in Los Angeles.

Baxter made her Broadway debut in 1936 in *Seen But Not Heard*. Although the play was not a success, the noted drama coach Maria Ouspenskaya thought Baxter had promise and invited her to join her drama school. Baxter continued to seek parts on Broadway and in the summers of 1938 and 1939 performed at the Cape Playhouse in Dennis, Massachusetts. She had a role in the pre-Broadway run of *The Philadelphia Story*, but star Katharine Hepburn vetoed Baxter on the grounds that she overacted. In August 1939 she went to Hollywood to test for the lead in Alfred Hitchcock's *Rebecca* (1940). Although she was only sixteen, Hitchcock thought her acceptable as the woman with whom Laurence Olivier falls in love. Producer David O. Selznick believed that she did not appear mature enough

for the role and overrode Hitchcock. Twentieth Century–Fox officials, however, saw Baxter's test and signed her to a contract. After using her in a handful of bit parts, the studio began giving Baxter ingenue roles in such films as Jean Renoir's *Swamp Water* (1941) and loaned her to RKO for Orson Welles's *The Magnificent Ambersons* (1942). Many of her scenes in this film were deleted when RKO executives demanded extensive cuts in Welles's work.

During World War II Baxter had many screen credits, generally playing a wholesome girl-next-door type in such films as *Crash Dive* (1943), in which Tyrone Power and Dana Andrews compete for her attention; *Sunday Dinner for a Soldier* (1944); and *The Fighting Sullivans* (1944). Baxter's ability to deliver a plausible French accent gained her parts in *The Pied Piper* (1942) and in the behind-the-lines thriller *Five Graves to Cairo* (1943), and she played a Russian in *The North Star* (1943). On 7 July 1946 she married actor John Hodiak, her costar in *Sunday Dinner for a Soldier*. The couple had one daughter prior to divorcing in 1953.

With the end of the war the attractive, five-foot-three actress was eager for more diverse roles and won the coveted part of the alcoholic Sophie in *The Razor's Edge* (1946). For her role she won an Oscar for best supporting actress ahead of Ethel Barrymore and Lillian Gish. Baxter also received the Golden Globe award in the same category. Her Oscar apparently did little to raise her status at Fox, which cast her in films that did not place much demand on her acting skills. These included *The Luck of the Irish* (1948); the Western *Yellow Sky* (1949); and two musicals, *You're My Everything* (1949) and *A Ticket to Tomahawk* (1950).

Baxter's best role came unexpectedly when pregnancy caused actress Jeanne Crain to relinquish the part of Eve Harrington in the classic backstage drama *All About Eve* (1950). In this film Bette Davis plays Margo Channing, an established Broadway star entering middle age. Baxter plays the seemingly innocent Eve Harrington, who is actually very ambitious and manipulative. She insinuates herself into Margo's circle with a series of fabricated hard-luck tales and becomes Margo's understudy. From this position Eve vaults to stardom at Margo's expense. Although Eve was, and still is, recognized as Baxter's finest performance, she did not win the Oscar, largely because Davis was nominated for her role as Margo. Davis and studio executives urged Baxter to accept a nomination for supporting actress instead, but Baxter maintained that the part of Eve was central to the film. The two actresses split the vote, as Davis had feared, and the Oscar for best actress went instead to Judy Holliday.

Ironically, Baxter's career had peaked, even though she was not yet thirty. Baxter remarked that she was being stereotyped as what studio boss Darryl F. Zanuck thought of as a "librarian," a woman with an "intellect" who "lacked sex appeal," and was consequently being offered restricted parts. Therefore, she dyed her chestnut hair blonde and tried to develop a sexier image, but her ploy was not successful, because she had to compete at Fox with such other actresses as Crain, Gene Tierney, and Susan Hayward. When the studio would not even let her test for a part in the important new production *How to Marry a Millionaire* (1953), a film that catapulted Marilyn Monroe's career, Baxter asked for and got her release. Baxter continued to act, but with rare exceptions had little luck in getting roles worthy of her skills. She did have an important part as the temptress Queen Nefertari in Cecil B. DeMille's lavish *The Ten Commandments* (1956). Nevertheless, she was widely ridiculed for her "sex kitten" performance in the film, even though she acted the role as DeMille had directed.

On 18 February 1960 Baxter married Randolph Galt; the couple and Baxter's daughter from her first marriage moved to Galt's large ranch some 150 miles north of Sydney, Australia. There Baxter found life lonely and hard, as the couple lived in spartan conditions and she did many of the household and ranch chores. The couple had two daughters and eventually the entire family moved to a ranch in New Mexico in a vain effort to keep their faltering marriage alive. They were divorced in 1970.

Baxter continued to act on a reduced schedule while living in Australia, and after her divorce she attempted to pick up her career. She appeared many times on television as a guest star in such popular series as *Get Smart, Ironside,* and *Marcus Welby, M.D.,* and also starred in such dramatic anthologies as *GE Theater* and *Playhouse 90.* In addition, Baxter sought parts on the stage. In 1971 she replaced Lauren Bacall in the hit *Applause,* ironically playing the role of Margo Channing in this musical adaptation of *All About Eve.* Three years later Baxter performed in Noël Coward's *Suite in Two Keys.*

Baxter married David Klee, a New York banker, on 30 January 1977. He died the following year, but she chose to reside in what was to have been their country home in Easton, Connecticut, commuting into New York City as necessary for appearances in film, television, and the stage, where she was cast as Queen Gertrude in the American Shakespeare Theatre's 1982 production of *Hamlet.* She died in New York City of a stroke. At the time of her death she had a recurring role as Victoria Cabot, manager of the St. Gregory Hotel in the popular television series *Hotel.*

An actress since her early teens, Baxter was at the peak of her screen popularity in the five years after the Second World War. Even when her career in Hollywood declined, Baxter was thoroughly professional in her approach to her craft and continued working steadily for the rest of her life. Sometimes panned for overacting, she turned increasingly to the stage and to television where she earned several favorable reviews. A free-spirited person who described herself as "part Presbyterian, part Druid," Baxter had many interests and talents. A lover of nature, she was also involved in support for the symphony orchestra in Los Angeles and was a collector of Oriental decorative arts. She wrote the well-received *Intermission: A True Story* (1976) and at the time of her death had begun work on a manuscript dealing with her adored grandfather and his six children.

★

Baxter's papers were given to the University of Wyoming Library. Karin J. Fowler, *Anne Baxter: A Bio-Bibliography* (1991), is a good place to start for those seeking further information on the actress. Baxter herself wrote *Intermission: A True Story* (1976), a memoir of her experiences in Australia. James Robert Parish, *Fox Girls* (1972), contains a chapter on Baxter as well as a filmography. More on Baxter is in J. E. A. Bawden, "Anne Baxter," *Films in Review* (Oct. 1977). Several pertinent articles are Elizabeth Wilson, "Get Acquainted with Anne," *Silver Screen* (Feb. 1944); Anne Baxter, "Your Slip Always Shows," *Silver Screen* (Jan. 1951); Michael Sheridan, "Is Anne on a Merry-Go-Round," *Silver Screen* (Mar. 1954); and Helen Dudar, "Anne Baxter's Road to Shakespeare," *New York Times Biographical Service* (Aug. 1982). An obituary is in the *New York Times* (13 Dec. 1985).

LLOYD J. GRAYBAR

BEARD, James Andrew (*b.* 5 May 1903 in Portland, Oregon; *d.* 23 January 1985 in New York City), gourmet whose cookbooks and classes enabled Americans to develop their own national cuisine.

Beard was the only child of Jonathan A. Beard, an assistant appraiser of the port of Portland, and Mary Elizabeth Jones, who had formerly owned Portland's Gladstone Hotel. Their marriage had deteriorated by the time of his birth.

Under his mother's tutelage Beard's education centered on food. Beard later told friends that his mother had "had an uncanny sense of food and the talent to show others how to prepare it." He accompanied his mother to public markets, learned recipes from the Italian truck farmers who delivered fresh produce to his house, and heard his mother's instructions to butchers about cutting aged meat. She even showed him how to hang game birds and tend the smokehouse in their backyard. Summers were spent at a cottage in Gearhart, Oregon, where Beard gathered and fried oysters, steamed crabs, made flapjacks on a grill, and picked berries.

Beard later coined the phrase "taste memory" to explain his ability to imagine and then physically re-create the tastes of various foods he had eaten throughout his life. Even in his later years he could still recall the chicken jelly the family's Chinese cook made when Beard was three and the elaborate fare served at his mother's holiday meals.

James Beard (*right*), 1974. Irving Newman/Archive Photos

Because of his unusual and precocious upbringing, as well as his frequent illnesses and ever-increasing size, Beard was an oddity to his classmates. He claimed to have recognized his homosexuality by the age of ten. Over time Beard learned to use his uniqueness to his advantage. The theater became an outlet both to express himself and to transform himself into the flamboyant showman he became.

Beard entered Reed College in 1920 but was expelled for a prank before he had completed his studies. To avoid scandal, his mother sent her wayward son to study voice in England, where he made his singing debut in 1923. But his vocal cords developed nodes, and his mother, whose patience and purse strings were wearing thin, brought him back to Oregon the following year. Beard held a variety of jobs at local theaters and radio stations before joining the New York City theater community in 1937.

By 1938, after he had grown discouraged by the limited acting jobs he found, Beard began to rely on his culinary skills to support himself. At a party he met William Rhode, who had written a book on the dining habits of European nobles, and almost overnight the men developed plans to open a catering business on the Upper East Side of Manhattan. The shop offered fully prepared French, Italian, and Russian specialties for takeout. Barrows Publishers commissioned Beard to share the company's recipes with readers, and *Hors d'Oeuvres and Canapés, with a Key to the Cocktail Party* came out in 1940. The edition contained recipes for soon-to-be-standard fare like deviled eggs and open-faced sandwiches. It also tried to persuade Americans that with the demise of Prohibition, the cocktail party was "an institution as democratic as the subway."

Soon after the book's publication Beard's mother died and World War II broke out. Beard was drafted into the U.S. Army in 1942 and ran clubs for American military officers in the Panama Canal Zone, Puerto Rico, Rio de Janeiro, and Marseilles. In 1978 the French government would recognize his wartime contribution by naming him a Chevalier du Mérite Agricole. Rhode dissolved the business partnership with Beard in 1944.

Back in the United States after World War II, Beard, with a toque in one hand and rolling pin in the other, had a mission. In a preface to *The Fireside Cookbook* (1949), he expressed his wish for Americans to create a "truly national cuisine that will incorporate all that is best from our new, still-young nation." In his letters to Helen Evans Brown, a food writer, Beard decried the convenience foods that were becoming staples in American pantries: "God, the American palate is so immune to flavor that it is sinful to think of putting a good product on the market." He especially detested the shortcuts that women's magazines prescribed for their readers.

Beard drew upon his childhood memories and travels throughout Europe to refine the American palate. He briefly hosted a cooking segment on the television show *Elsie Presents*, which ran in 1946 and 1947. Ever the showman, he once substituted lighter fluid for brandy in his crepes Suzette, producing a stunning visual effect.

In his lifetime Beard published about twenty cookbooks on such topics as fowl and game cookery, barbecuing, outdoor cookery, and entertaining. His autobiographical *Delights and Prejudices* came out in 1964; *Beard on Bread* (1973) sold over 200,000 copies and was based on his taste memory. Like a consummate actor Beard conveyed his own voice in these productions, believing that too many cookbooks were "put together like paper dolls; there's no feeling of humanness in them."

Beard started a cooking school in his home in Manhattan's Greenwich Village in 1955 and another in Seaside, Oregon, in 1973. He recognized that home cooks did not have the time or patience to make elaborate meals, but he encouraged them to use fresh, regional ingredients and to balance food temperatures, tastes, and textures. Florida pompano, Maine lobster, and oysters from Oregon were some of the regional foodstuffs Beard incorporated into his recipes. He wanted the food itself to be the star on the American dinner plate, not a supporting player overwhelmed by sauces and seasonings.

In spite of his passionate feelings about freshness, Beard began to serve as a consultant and spokesman for several large food companies by the 1950s. His charisma made him a natural for the role, and his bald pate, portly face, and signature bow tie became associated with some of the items he endorsed. Advertisements for Green Giant produce, Planter's peanuts, and Spice Islands seasonings made him a household name. He also served as a consultant for Restaurant Associates and helped the firm plan menus for its restaurants, including the Four Seasons in New York City. Beard contributed articles to gourmet, women's, and even in-flight magazines.

Although food had traditionally been a domain relegated to women, Beard's success and teachings interested both men and women in this profession. The jacket copy for his 1941 book *Cook It Outdoors* proclaimed that it was "a man's book," and grilling became synonymous with the American male in the 1950s. Restaurateur Larry Forgione, cooking school instructor Peter Kump, and entrepreneur Chuck Williams (of Williams Sonoma) were some of Beard's associates, as was Marion Cunningham, who revised the classic Fannie Farmer cookbooks. Beard's friendliness, knowledge, and generous spirit drew these talented chefs to his side. By 1968 a food fraternity of sorts had developed, but with the big money that was now a part of this profession came backbiting and bickering that caused dissension and separation within its ranks.

Among his friends Beard was known for his large and elaborate private celebrations. During the Christmas season of 1953 he hosted four dinner parties, including a gathering for twenty people. Preparations for these parties might begin as early as November, when he would flavor ingredients like mincemeat with various liqueurs. One Thanksgiving,

he prepared a turkey in which he placed truffles under the bird's skin and made the stuffing from a mixture of minced parsley, pureed chestnuts, onions, bread crumbs, rice pilaf, and Madeira wine. By the 1980s, Americans had come to appreciate and emulate the good life that Beard represented. Fancy dinner parties and dining out at elaborate establishments were in vogue.

In his later years Beard, who usually weighed about 300 pounds, developed heart disease and other ailments. One of his last cookbooks reflected his new and healthier approach to food. For diners accustomed to medleys of precisely cut carrots and canned peas, the cookbook proved that foods did not have to be bland to be healthful. *The New James Beard* (1981), which sold over 100,000 copies, included vegetarian recipes and directions for replacing fat-derived flavors with low-fat, flavorful ingredients like yogurt and fresh herbs.

Beard was at work on a book titled *Menus and Memories* when he was hospitalized on 8 January 1985. He died at New York Hospital of cardiac arrest and was cremated. His home at 167 West Twelfth Street was converted into the headquarters of the James Beard Foundation, which annually recognizes the country's leading chefs and best cookbooks.

His obituary in the *New York Times* observed that Beard was a "pioneer in the postwar culinary awareness movement that turned tens of thousands of people into enthusiastic students and practitioners of the gastronomic arts." Called the "Father of American Gastronomy," he taught Americans to prize and use fresh, regional ingredients in straightforward, tasty recipes. In doing so, American cooks grew to love the experience of cooking and eating, wherein lay, according to Beard, the secret of good cooking.

★

Beard's papers are at the American Heritage Center at the University of Wyoming and at the library of the Oregon Historical Society. Beard's autobiography is *Delights and Prejudices: A Memoir with Recipes* (1964; repr. 1990 with a foreword by Barbara Kafka). Evan Jones, *Epicurean Delight: The Life and Times of James Beard* (1990), is a biography; Jones's wife served as Beard's editor at Alfred A. Knopf and both Joneses were his close friends. Robert Clark, *The Solace of Food: A Life of James Beard* (1993), provides the context of America's food history that enables social historians to better understand Beard's contribution. John Ferrone, ed., *Love and Kisses and a Halo of Truffles: Letters to Helen Evans Brown* (1994), is a compilation of the correspondence between Beard and Brown that shows their personal prejudices and goals for the national table. See also Russ Parsons, "The James Beard Style: Celebrating the Holidays with America's Butter Boy," *Los Angeles Times* (25 Nov. 1994); Evan Jones, "James Beard, the Man Who Loved to Eat: His Epicurean Adventure Shaped America's Taste" *Food and Wine* (Nov. 1990); *San Francisco Professional Food Society* (Feb./Mar. 1985); and *The NRN Fifty, A Hall of Fame: History*

Makers in Food Service (Feb. 1996): 25–26. An obituary is in the *New York Times* (24 Jan. 1985).

ANN LESLIE TUTTLE

BECK, Julian (*b.* 31 May 1925 in New York City; *d.* 14 September 1985 in New York City), actor, writer, and imaginative scenic designer; with his wife, Judith Malina, he organized and led the Living Theatre, the most experimental and controversial postwar American theater group.

Beck was the second son of Irving Beck, who ran an auto and motorcycle parts firm, and Mabel Blum, a schoolteacher, who were cultured and assimilated Jews of German ancestry. As a child, he was taken to the opera and the theater and began acting at the Horace Mann School, an elite preparatory institution. He enrolled at Yale College in 1942 but impulsively dropped out after his freshman year in reaction to its stuffy proprieties.

When Beck was summoned for a physical examination in the summer of 1943, he confessed to homosexual inclinations and received a 4-F classification. A psychiatrist, stressing the need for adjustment and taking the position that homosexuality was a treatable disease, recommended that he date women. Beck met an aspiring young performer named Judith Malina at an actors' club called Genius, Inc., in the Times Square area of New York City on 14 September 1943, and together they dreamed of a "poets' theater," whose plays would be written by poets, as opposed to the commercialized nature of Broadway. Judith studied with Erwin Piscator at the New School for Social Research, and Beck resumed classes at the City College of New York (1946–1949), although his main interest was in painting, particularly abstract impressionism (two of his paintings were exhibited at the Whitney Museum Beat retrospective in 1995).

Beck married Malina on 30 October 1948; they had two children. They began their theater in the living room of their Upper West Side apartment in the spring of 1951. By that time they were already closely connected with many members of the New York avant-garde, among them Paul Goodman, who introduced them to anarchist pacifism, and the composer John Cage. In 1952, using a $6,000 inheritance, Beck rented the Cherry Lane Theatre in Greenwich Village and presented plays by Gertrude Stein and poets Kenneth Rexroth and Paul Goodman. During a run of John Ashbery's *The Heroes,* the theater was closed when a fire department inspector found Julian's sets—constructed mostly of paper—hazardously flammable.

By 1955 a new location had been found: a loft on 100th Street and Broadway, where Beck and Malina staged W. H. Auden's *The Age of Anxiety,* August Strindberg's *Ghost Sonata,* and Luigi Pirandello's *Tonight We Improvise.* Produc-

Julian Beck carries his wife, Judith Malina, into court, 1964. Her leg had been cut by broken glass during a raid by IRS agents. UPI/CORBIS-BETTMANN

tion of the last of these was a key step in a search for a more spontaneous, improvisatory aesthetic allowing for the autonomy of the actors as a creative principle.

The loft was closed by the Department of Buildings in November 1955. While looking for a new location to be shared with John Cage and the choreographer Merce Cunningham, Beck and Malina became more politically active, protesting publicly against mandatory civil defense drills and nuclear testing. In June 1957 they found an empty department store on Fourteenth Street and Sixth Avenue that they renovated into a suitable space with the assistance of fellow actors and friends. At this time M. C. Richards was translating Antonin Artaud's *The Theatre and Its Double;* she showed her manuscript to Beck, leaving a powerful and formative impression of Artaud's vision of a "theater of cruelty" that could galvanize people living in a numbed age into feeling.

The new theater opened on 13 January 1959 with William Carlos Williams's *Many Loves,* a play that demonstrated an enduring concern with a poets' theater. But Beck and Malina's priorities had been affected by their own political involvements, and in "Why Vanguard," a piece by

Beck that appeared in the *New York Times* on 22 March 1959, he advocated a revolutionary theater. A big step in that direction was Jack Gelber's *The Connection,* a play about a group of heroin addicts performed on stage with jazz musicians. Concerning a taboo subject that most of the critics deplored, the play became an underground sensation, helped by favorable notices by Kenneth Tynan and Robert Brustein.

The Living Theatre became the artistic energy center of the off-Broadway movement, with readings by poets like Allan Ginsberg, LeRoi Jones (later known as Imamu Amiri Baraka), and Frank O'Hara; concerts by Cage; and lectures by Eric Bentley, Joseph Campbell, and Maya Deren. Performing *The Connection* in repertory with works by Bertolt Brecht and Pirandello, the company developed into a strongly committed group that included actors like Martin Sheen, Joseph Chaikin, and Warren Finnerty. Despite mounting financial difficulties, in 1961 Beck and Malina took the company to Paris, where they became the first Americans to win the Grand Prix of the Theatres des Nations.

In 1963 Beck and Malina decided to stage Kenneth Brown's *The Brig.* About the brutal incarceration of American Marines who had committed some infraction of the Marine code, the play was a highly naturalistic expression of Artaud's theater of cruelty. Suddenly, the theater was seized and closed by agents of the Internal Revenue Service for nonpayment of taxes, even though the Living Theatre was chartered as a nonprofit organization. Beck and Malina were jailed for contempt of court, and the rest of the company fled to Europe, where they remained for five years. When Beck and Malina rejoined the company, they gave it a new principle which was truly revolutionary though an extension of Artaud—the actors would now write the plays. They returned to the United States in 1968 with their new body of work, *Mysteries and Smaller Pieces,* in which they enacted Artaud's vision of the plague, *Frankenstein,* and *Paradise Now,* which depended on extreme political provocation.

In 1970 the entire company was thrown into prison by military despots in Brazil on charges they were using theater to induce political awareness. During most of the 1970s the group toured Italy and other European countries. In 1982, just as Jack Lang was trying to get them a permanent residency in Paris, Beck was diagnosed as having colon cancer. Following surgery, he rallied and brought the company back to America, but the cancer metastasized. In his last year Beck acted in Francis Ford Coppola's film *The Cotton Club,* in an episode of the television series *Miami Vice,* and in Samuel Beckett's *That Time,* a half-hour monodrama. He died on the anniversary of the day that he met Malina.

★

Works by Beck include *The Life of the Theatre* (1972); *Living in Volkswagen Buses* (1992); and *Theandric* (1992), edited by Erica Bilder. Beck and Judith Malina published *Living Theatre, Paradise Now: Collective Creation of the Living Theatre* (1971). Malina, *The Enormous Despair* (1972) and *The Diaries of Judith Malina, 1947–1957* (1984), provide information on Beck and Malina's life and work. An account of the Living Theatre is John Tytell, *The Living Theatre: Art, Exile, and Outrage* (1995). See also Aldo Rostagno, *We, the Living Theatre* (1979); and *The Living Book of the Living Theatre* (1971), with an introductory essay by Richard Schechner.

JOHN TYTELL

BEE, Clair Francis (*b.* 2 March 1900 in Grafton, West Virginia; *d.* 20 May 1983 in Cleveland, Ohio), legendary basketball coach, scholar, and author.

Born fewer than ten years after Dr. James Naismith invented the game of basketball, Bee was the only child of Clair Edward, a store manager, and Grace Louise (Skinner) Bee. His mother died of tuberculosis in St. Louis, Missouri, when he was six years old, and he too was stricken with the disease during his childhood. His father remarried after returning to Grafton, and Clair would eventually have five half brothers. His athletic career began at Grafton High School, where he played baseball, basketball, and football from 1914 to 1916. He attended Massanutten Military Academy in Woodstock, Virginia, during the 1916–1917 school year, before entering the U.S. Army and serving in the American Expeditionary Forces in France during World War I. He returned to Grafton High School upon his discharge in 1919 and graduated in 1920.

In 1922 Bee entered Waynesburg College in Waynesburg, Pennsylvania, on an athletic scholarship. He had spent the previous two years working in Ohio and playing semiprofessional football. Bee was not a big man. He stood five feet, ten inches tall and weighed less than 150 pounds. He lettered in football, wrestling, and baseball during his first year at Waynesburg but suffered a knee injury in 1923 that ended his playing career. He served as acting graduate manager of athletics during his junior and senior years and was also secretary to the president of the college in his senior year. Bee earned his bachelor's degree (Ph.B.) in 1925 and accepted a teaching and coaching position at Mansfield (Ohio) High School for the 1925–1926 school year.

In 1926 Bee became director of athletics and coach of baseball, basketball, and football at Rider College in Trenton, New Jersey. His basketball teams at Rider lost only seven games in three seasons (1928–1931) and his football teams compiled a record of 17–7–1, including an undefeated season in 1930. During his tenure at Rider, Bee also served as chairman of the accounting department and

Clair Bee, coach of the Long Island University basketball team, on the bench at Madison Square Garden, 1939. UPI/CORBIS-BETTMANN

earned an additional bachelor's degree (B.A.) from Waynesburg College in 1930, a master's degree (M.C.S.) from Rider in 1929, and began to work toward a second master's degree at Rutgers University (M.A.), which he earned in 1931. He was also awarded a bachelor's degree (B.C.S.) from Ohio State University in 1932.

In 1931 Bee became the director of athletics and coach of football and basketball at Long Island University in Brooklyn, New York. He coached the football team to a record of 8–1 in 1931, but it was as basketball coach that Bee led the LIU Blackbirds to national prominence. Bee's coaching tenure at LIU lasted until 1951. During that time, his teams won 357 games while losing only 79. He coached two undefeated teams (25–0 in 1935–1936; 23–0 in 1938–1939). Two of his teams (1938–1939 and 1940–1941) won the National Invitational Tournament, which at the time was tantamount to winning a national championship. His undefeated 1934–1935 team was the consensus national champion in the era before postseason play. LIU won 43 consecutive games between 1934 and 1936 and, astoundingly, won 139 consecutive home games between 1937 and 1951. His overall winning percentage as a college coach was .827 (410–86), the second highest of all time. During the decade of the 1930s, LIU won more games (201) and had a greater won-loss percentage (.841) than any team in the nation. Nearly all of these victories had come with Bee

as coach. In the 1940s, the Blackbirds continued to prosper, winning 179 games while losing only 49 for a won-loss percentage of .785. Only the University of Kentucky could claim to have done as well or better during this twenty-year period.

A self-described taskmaster, Bee was considered by his contemporaries to be the greatest defensive strategist in the game. He is credited with inventing the one-three-one zone defense and introducing the three-second rule. At Rider College he had been one of the first coaches to "scout" his opponents. Along with Joe Lapchick at St. John's University, Howard Cann at New York University, and Nat Holman at City College of New York, Bee made New York City the mecca of college basketball during the 1930s and 1940s.

As the public embraced the college game it became commonplace for the best teams to play one another in downtown arenas rather than in their own on-campus facilities. Media exposure of the game increased, and the crowds generated large amounts of revenue to be distributed between the arena owners, who promoted the games, and the colleges. Bee's Blackbirds were consistently rated among the top teams in the country during this period, yet Coach Bee himself was involved in a myriad of outside activities. He had started the nation's first sports camp for children in 1934, organized and directed coaching clinics beginning in

1936, and began a writing career which was to include more than fifty works with the publication of the five-volume *Clair Bee Basketball Library* in 1940. In 1939, Bee married Mary Margaret Miller; they had two children.

With the advent of World War II, Bee served as an officer in the United States Maritime Service, as assistant administrative supervisor of the Todd Shipyards in Hoboken, New Jersey, and as commander (administrative officer) at the Sheepshead Bay, New York, training facility. At the conclusion of the war he returned to coaching and became assistant to the president of LIU, a position he held from 1945 to 1951. Bee was named comptroller of Long Island University in 1951 and held this post until 1952.

During this era, however, the soaring popularity of college basketball and vast amounts of revenue the game was producing led to a series of betting scandals that tarnished the college game. Gamblers approached college players and offered them money either to lose games or ensure that their teams won by less than the number of points (or "spread") bookmakers had established as the betting line. There had been several bribery cases in the mid to late 1940s, but it was not until 1951 that a major scandal was uncovered. Players at seven colleges, LIU among them, were found to have accepted money in return for fixing games.

The scandal deeply wounded Coach Bee. He accepted personal responsibility, telling the *New York Times* columnist Ira Berkow that "I was so absorbed in the victory grail I lost sight of the educational purpose of athletics." In the wake of the scandal Long Island University canceled its intercollegiate sports program. Men's basketball was not reinstated at LIU until 1957.

In 1952 Bee became part-owner and coach of the Baltimore Bullets of the National Basketball Association. His team was not successful, compiling a 16–51 record in 1952–1953 and a 16–56 record in 1953–1954; it disbanded after fourteen games of the 1954–1955 season. He remained involved with the sport as a clinician, writer, camp director, and goodwill ambassador, traveling extensively to Europe, South America, and the Caribbean to give clinics for coaches and players. He also served as director of athletics at the New York Military Academy in Cornwall-on-Hudson from 1954 to 1967.

Bee was elected to the Helms Foundation Hall of Fame, the West Virginia Sports Writers Hall of Fame, the Madison Square Garden Hall of Fame, and the halls of fame at both Waynesburg College and Long Island University, in addition to his admittance to the Naismith Memorial Basketball Hall of Fame in 1968.

Bee's writing career continued with books on technical aspects of basketball as well as fiction for young readers. Between 1948 and 1964 he wrote the Chip Hilton Sports Series, encompassing twenty-three books. The hero of the series was an outstanding athlete whose character was beyond reproach. No matter what the sport, the reader could count on Chip Hilton to perform mightily, demonstrate excellent sportsmanship, and overcome various off-the-field obstacles. The character was modeled after the star player of Seton Hall University, Bob Davies, whom Bee admired both for his ability as a player and his demeanor on the court.

Bee spent his final years at his ranch in Roscoe, New York. His eyesight had deteriorated over the years due to glaucoma, which hampered his writing career. He died of cardiac arrest in Cleveland, Ohio, at the age of eighty-three and was buried in Roscoe. He had contributed greatly to the development of the game of basketball and had been overwhelmingly successful as a coach. Yet he was also a scholar who had earned five degrees, an administrator in college and in the armed forces, a patriot who had served in two wars, and an accomplished author. The first book of his Chip Hilton series bears a dedication to a former student-manager that reads: "Patriot, student, athlete, he gave all he had for his country and his team." The same could be said of Clair Bee.

★

Newspaper clippings and other biographical materials are on file at Edward J. and Gena G. Hickox Library of the Naismith Memorial Basketball Hall of Fame in Springfield, Massachusetts. Clair Bee, *The Science of Coaching* (1935), reveals the author's philosophy of basketball as well as his approach to the more technical aspects of the sport. For a biography of Bee, see Sandy Padwe, *Basketball's Hall of Fame* (1970). Neil D. Isaacs, *All the Moves* (1975), contains an analysis of the betting scandals. Obituaries are in the *New York Times* (21 May 1983) and *Sporting News* (6 June 1983).

DAVID J. HAYES, JR.

BEEBE, William Thomas (*b.* 26 January 1915 in Los Angeles, California; *d.* 9 June 1984 in Atlanta, Georgia), Delta Air Lines executive who presided over the air carrier through a period of expansion and profits in the 1970s.

Beebe was the son of Elsie Thomas and Dewey Sheldon Beebe, an investment banker; he had two sisters. Tall and broad shouldered with bushy eyebrows, a wide grin, and a commanding presence, he played high school football while growing up in Minneapolis until a knee injury sidelined him. In 1937 he graduated with a bachelor's degree in business administration from the University of Minnesota, where he edited the college yearbook. General Electric Company recruited Beebe in 1938, assigning him to personnel work at its plant in Bridgeport, Connecticut. After two years Beebe moved to the United Aircraft Corporation in Hartford as a personnel manager. During World War II he was in charge of personnel and labor relations at the navy-owned Pratt and Whitney Aircraft Company engine plant in Kansas City, Missouri.

In February 1947 Chicago and Southern Air Lines hired three top United Aircraft executives, including Beebe as director of personnel and labor relations. Based in Memphis, Tennessee, Chicago and Southern maintained routes from Chicago to New Orleans and from Detroit to Houston. By 1950 only six airlines in the United States were larger. Beebe gained experience consolidating staff and negotiating with unions, and when top management was overhauled in 1951 he was named a vice president. In Memphis on 3 February 1951, a month after the promotion, Beebe married Nancy Lee Gragg Jones, a widow. They had one child and Beebe adopted the two children from her earlier marriage.

When Delta and Chicago and Southern accomplished one of the largest airline mergers in the country's history in the spring of 1953, Beebe moved to Atlanta as personnel director of the combined firm. Within a year he was named a vice president. In his early years at Delta, Beebe oversaw employee relocation and fought unionization of the Air Line Pilots Association and the stewardesses. In many cases Beebe warded off organizing by meeting employee demands.

Longtime Delta chairman Collett Everman Woolman had maintained a firm grip on the airline, like his counterparts at several competing lines, but when he had a heart attack in the 1960s the business made a transition to collective management. As head of personnel Beebe helped put in place an organizational chart detailing the decision-making process. The strategy resulted in the promotion of numerous top corporate executives, including Beebe, who was elected to Delta's board of directors in 1966 and became senior vice president for administration in November 1967.

Beebe rose to the presidency of Delta Air Lines in January 1970. He became chairman of the board in October 1971, also serving as chief executive officer. Within the industry he was known for helping Delta produce annual profits in a decade when some air carriers were struggling. In 1972 his annual earnings were reported to be $110,000 plus stock options worth perhaps quadruple that sum. In one of the first major developments of Beebe's tenure as chairman, Delta absorbed the ailing Northeast Airlines, helping solidify its stature as one of the nation's largest trunk carriers. Deregulation was a major challenge for the industry at the time. Beebe opposed it on the grounds that it would cause financial havoc and dry up sources of capital investment even for large carriers. In his years at the helm Beebe was known to boast that Delta's employees were responsible for much of the airline's success. He retired as a Delta corporate officer in 1980, at age sixty-five, in keep-

ing with a policy he had instituted. He remained board chairman and kept an office at Delta headquarters at the Hartsfield Atlanta International Airport. Even after retiring as chairman in October 1983, he stayed active on the board of directors.

Beebe won national recognition as an executive on several fronts. In 1970 President Richard Nixon appointed him chairman of the National Alliance of Businessmen's Region IV, representing eight southeastern states. In 1974 he was honored for his handling of Delta during the fuel shortage that resulted from the oil crisis. He was named chief executive of the year for 1977 by *Financial World* magazine, which noted his open-door policy that encouraged anyone to bring problems to him. However, Sidney F. Davis, author of *Delta Air Lines: Debunking the Myth* and a onetime executive with the company, insisted that Beebe was reclusive and that the open-door policy had been Woolman's and would have been impractical to continue with tens of thousands of employees.

Beebe was fond of fine clothes, sports cars, fishing, and showing horses. He was a member of the Multiple Sclerosis Society's national advisory council, the National Park

William Beebe. COURTESY OF THE DELTA AIR TRANSPORT HERITAGE MUSEUM, INC.

Foundation, the Air Transport Association, the University of Minnesota Foundation Board, and the Atlanta Board of Education. He was chairman of the Georgia Society for the Prevention of Blindness and a director of the Citizens and Southern National Bank. He was an Episcopalian. Beebe suffered from heart problems for years and died of a heart attack following abdominal surgery at Doctors Memorial Hospital in Atlanta. He was buried at Arlington Memorial Park in Sandy Springs, Georgia.

Although he was president and chief executive officer of Delta Air Lines for a brief period compared to most of his predecessors and successors, Beebe was part of its inner circle of management during some its most prosperous years, some of its most challenging transitions, and its ascent to a leadership position in the industry.

★

The authors of *Delta: The History of an Airline* (1979), W. David Lewis and Wesley Phillips Newton, were Auburn University history professors with access to company records. See also *International Directory of Company Histories,* vol. 1 (1988); and Sidney F. Davis, *Delta Air Lines: Debunking the Myth* (1988), an unauthorized chronicle by a former navy pilot and former Delta executive that is critical of Beebe, saying he made few original contributions to the firm and did not adapt well to deregulation. Articles covering his business career are in the *New York Times* (30 Oct. 1971, 12 Mar. 1972, and 29 Oct. 1983) and the Memphis *Commercial Appeal* (16 Sept. 1970 and 17 Apr. 1977). Obituaries are in the *New York Times* and *Atlanta Journal* (both 11 June 1984).

WHITNEY SMITH

BELUSHI, John (*b.* 24 January 1949 in Wheaton, Illinois; *d.* 5 March 1982 in Hollywood, California), comedian and actor best known for his antics on television's *Saturday Night Live* and in the films *Animal House* and *The Blues Brothers.*

Belushi was the second of four children born to Albanian immigrants. His father, Adam Belushi, owned and managed restaurants, and his mother, Agnes, worked as a cashier in a local pharmacy. A brother, Jim Belushi, would also gain renown as a comedic actor. At Wheaton Central High School, Belushi was popular and was elected homecoming king and voted most humorous by his classmates. Despite being only five-foot-nine and 170 pounds, he was an all-conference middle linebacker and co-captain of the football team. He also played drums in a rock band, but his goal was to be an actor, and he starred in many school productions. Disregarding his father's wish that he join the family business, Belushi began acting in summer stock after graduating high school in 1967. He then attended the University of Wisconsin at Whitewater before transferring to

the College of DuPage in Illinois, where he graduated with an A.A. degree in 1970.

While in college, Belushi and his friends formed a comedy group called the West Compass Players and performed skits regularly at the student union and at local coffeehouses. In 1971 Belushi was hired by the Chicago-based improvisational group Second City, where his imitations of actor Marlon Brando, writer Truman Capote, singer Joe Cocker, and others soon made him the star of the show. Word spread of Belushi's talents, and in 1973 he was chosen by the counterculture humor magazine *National Lampoon* to appear in its off-Broadway production of *Lemmings* in New York City. *Lemmings* was a series of sketches that, among other things, parodied the Woodstock music festival and the administration of President Richard Nixon. The production was a box-office success, and Belushi's performance was praised by the *New York Times* and the *New Yorker.*

In 1975 Belushi was chosen by producer Lorne Michaels to be a cast member on the National Broadcasting Company's new variety television show *Saturday Night Live.* Belushi and Chevy Chase, Gilda Radner, Dan Aykroyd, Jane Curtin, Garrett Morris, and Laraine Newman became famous as the Not-Ready-for-Prime-Time Players, and the show grew in popularity among teenagers and young adults. Belushi's portrayals of Secretary of State Henry Kissinger, a grunting Japanese samurai warrior, and a gruff manager of a diner (based on his father) became classics of American comedy.

On 31 December 1976 Belushi married his high school sweetheart and longtime girlfriend Judith Jacklin. They lived in New York City's Greenwich Village and in 1979 purchased a summer home on Martha's Vineyard, Massachusetts. They had no children.

In 1978 Belushi's film career began when he played the role of Bluto, the crude yet lovable slob of the Delta fraternity, in *National Lampoon's Animal House.* The movie became one of the most popular comedies of all time and soon toga parties and food fights became popular on college campuses across the United States. Belushi appeared wearing his toga on the 23 October 1978 cover of *Newsweek* with the headline "College Humor Comes Back." *Newsweek* said of Belushi: "What you see onstage is also what you see off. He is a bundle of conflicting emotions. Yes, he wants success, money and stardom, but the punky kid in him recoils at the prospect of it all. Belushi enjoys operating at full throttle, on the edge, and he knows very well that his manic style has helped get him where he is." According to *Animal House* director John Landis, Belushi "abuses his body in ways that would kill bulls. . . . If he doesn't burn himself out, his potential is unlimited."

In 1979 Belushi left *Saturday Night Live* for Hollywood and starred in director Steven Spielberg's *1941.* This movie

John Belushi. ARCHIVE PHOTOS

was a failure, but in 1980 Belushi and his close friend Aykroyd returned to the screen as a pair of white soul singers known as the Blues Brothers. While *The Blues Brothers,* directed by Landis, received mostly negative reviews from film critics, the performances by Aretha Franklin, Cab Calloway, Ray Charles, and others in the movie led to a revival of interest in the blues. The Blues Brothers band, anchored by veteran musicians Matt Murphy, Donald Dunn, and Steve Cropper, released a record album titled *Briefcase Full of Blues,* which quickly sold more than a million copies, despite Belushi's limitations as a singer.

While Belushi was becoming a major star, appearing in a total of eight movies, it was increasingly apparent that he had developed an appetite for drugs, particularly cocaine, and it began to affect his personality and work. Belushi had begun smoking marijuana as a teenager and felt that it helped him perform. Drug use was rampant among the cast and crew of *Saturday Night Live,* and Belushi, responding to the stress of performing live each week and the excitement of his newfound fame, began to use cocaine and other narcotics at an increasing rate. In his best-selling book

Wired: The Short Life and Fast Times of John Belushi, reporter Bob Woodward documented Belushi's drug use and the inability of his wife and friends, also drug users, to stop him.

Belushi behaved in real life much like the scene-stealing, hard-partying characters he portrayed, often spending entire nights traveling from one nightclub to another in search of fun, loud music, and drugs. On 5 March 1982, while in California working on the screenplay for his next movie, the thirty-three-year-old Belushi was found dead in his room at the Hotel Chateau Marmont in Hollywood. The cause of death was determined by the Los Angeles County Coroner's office to be an overdose due to intravenous injections of heroin and cocaine.

Belushi was buried at Abel's Hill Cemetery near his Martha's Vineyard home on 9 March 1982.

★

Biographies of Belushi published after his death include Bob Woodward, *Wired: The Short Life and Fast Times of John Belushi* (1984), and Judith Jacklin Belushi, *Samurai Widow* (1990). Also see Doug Hill and Jeff Weingrad, *Saturday Night: A Backstage History of Saturday Night Live* (1986). An obituary is in the *New York Times* (6 Mar. 1982).

RICHARD L. DAVIDMAN

BENN, Ben (*b.* 27 December 1884 in Kaminetz Podolsk, Ukraine; *d.* 10 January 1983 in Connecticut), artist whose lyrical, richly colored paintings, though independent of twentieth-century stylistic movements, adapted certain elements of Postimpressionism, Cubism, and abstraction to his own painterly sensibility.

Benn, who was born Benjamin Rosenberg, emigrated with his family to New York City around 1894. Little detailed biographical information is available on Benn, but the critic Sidney Geist notes that the artist remembered having drawn on the walls and floors of his home as a child. He took his first drawing lessons at an evening high school on the Lower East Side of Manhattan in 1902. From 1904 to 1908 he studied at the National Academy of Design school, and before he had finished his course he was included in "Oils by Eight American Artists," an exhibition at the Artists' Gallery in 1907. Formal classes at the academy were supplemented by visits to the Metropolitan Museum of Art. The influence of Rembrandt, for example, shows strongly in his heavily shadowed *Self-Portrait with Cap* (1908); El Greco's exuberant brushwork—evident in works such as *Jamaica Flats* (1905)—was even more of an inspiration. By 1912 Benn's use of flattened forms and shallow spaces, and his richer palette, reveal an awareness of Postimpressionism. He never studied abroad; indeed, he never traveled far from New York City.

Benn was married in 1915 and thereafter painted several portraits of his wife, Velida, one of which was *Young Woman with Evening Cloak* (1921); the face is realistically represented, and the body is indicated by color (the enveloping red robe) and line. From the time of their marriage until 1930, when the Benns moved to 110 West Ninety-sixth Street on the Upper West Side of Manhattan, they lived in a studio on East Twenty-third Street in Manhattan that became a meeting place for artists and writers. Among their circle were the playwright Eugene O'Neill; the poet E. E. Cummings; the painters Marsden Hartley (Benn's closest friend), Charles Demuth, and Joseph Stella; and the sculptor Elie Nadelman, who bought a watercolor, the first piece Benn ever sold. A 1915 portrait of Hartley (one of several painted over the years) was a startling departure from Benn's other canvases, the most radically abstract work he ever painted.

With this exception Benn's was essentially a figurative, semiabstract style. His subjects were portraits, landscapes, and the still lifes that above all display his power and range within a set genre. Benn continued to paint with a loaded brush, building up a rich texture of high-keyed colors. He once commented, "You start with form, but . . . after a while color dictates form." He also worked in watercolor, pastel, and pen and ink, but rarely exhibited compositions in these media.

Benn's stature was confirmed when, in 1916, he was chosen as one of the seventeen artists (Hartley, the sculptor William Zorach, and the painter John Marin were among the others) shown in the Forum Exhibition of Modern American Painters at the Anderson Galleries. A landmark showing of the best of modern American art, the exhibition was designed as a response to the largely European representation at the famed 1913 Armory Show in New York City. Traces of Cubism (to which the latter exhibition introduced Americans) can be seen in a 1917 still life—one of the three paintings by Benn shown more than seven decades later at the Jewish Museum's "Painting a Place in America: Jewish Artists in New York 1900–1945" (1991)—and in some of his portraits of the 1920s. By then Henri Matisse's influence began to be evident in Benn's increasingly decorative still-life arrangements of flowers and fruits.

Benn's first solo exhibition was in 1925, at J. B. Neumann's New Art Circle Gallery. Some ten years later he took part in two important group shows: the 1933 "American Sources of Modern Art" at the Museum of Modern Art, and the 1935 "Abstract Painting in America" at the Whitney Museum of American Art. In the 1930s he also produced a group of cityscapes; continuing in the vein of his 1912 *Washington Square,* for example, they are very different from contemporary Socialist Realist, message-laden

urban scenes in that they simply record visual aspects of the New York he loved. At the same time Benn took delight in rural scenery, painting numerous compositions of forest glades and trees he had seen during summers spent in Woodstock, New York, in the mid-1930s. Shore scenes (fishing was a favorite pastime) were frequent subjects beginning in the 1920s, when he summered on the New Jersey coast.

From the 1940s on—Benn continued painting for another thirty years—his work continued to evolve. His colors became even juicier; a characteristic motif was introduced—the sinuous black lines superimposed with a palette knife on forms or color areas (as in the 1949 *Sea Gulls*); and Benn once again incorporated Cubist elements. In the 1955 self-portrait the head is multifaceted, built up of many planes of color; and there is the precipitously tilted perspective associated with Paul Cézanne or Georges Braque in compositions such as *Tray of Fruit* (1957).

The proliferation of exhibitions held in the last twenty years of Benn's life underscores his vitality. Notable among these are the one celebrating his ninetieth birthday, at the Hirshhorn Museum and Sculpture Garden in Washington, D.C., in 1974; "Ben Benn: The Octogenarian Decade," mounted in 1982 and 1983 at the Branchville Soho Gallery (by the administrators of his estate) in suburban Ridgefield, Connecticut; and retrospectives held at the Jewish Museum in 1965 and at the Hammer Gallery in 1983.

Long before these, however, Benn's participation in gallery and museum shows contributed to an impressively lengthy exhibition list. He is represented in the permanent collections of museums not only in New York City but elsewhere in the United States and, abroad, in the Kroller-Mueller Collection in The Hague. Benn received a Marjorie Peabody Waite Award, given by the National Institute of Arts and Letters to an older artist for continuing achievement, in 1971 and he was elected an associate of the National Academy of Design in 1980. He died in his ninety-ninth year at the home of his surviving sister in Connecticut.

Hilton Kramer, always a great admirer, unhesitatingly called Benn "one of the best painters in the U.S." By contrast Sidney Tillim contended that Benn's was a "prosaic vision" that offered only an example of "remarkable perseverance." On balance, however, Benn should be seen as a "painter's painter" held in great esteem by his fellow artists (if, in later years, overlooked by casual viewers) for his craftsmanship and for remaining true to his own credo— a desire to give joy to the viewer, a commitment to painting solely as a response to his own visual experience. The stages in his career were marked by subtle, self-engendered changes in that response, and he proved it possible to create a modern art without rigid adherence to prevailing aesthetic "isms."

★

The Art and Architecture Division of the New York Public Library's Center for the Humanities maintains a file of clippings relating to Benn's career. Published sources of information are Louis Lozowick, ed., *100 Contemporary American Jewish Painters and Sculptors* (1947), which quotes Benn's statements on the purposes of his art; the exhibition brochure *Ben Benn: Painter,* with an introduction by Hans van Weeren-Griek, a brief biographical note, and reproductions of the works included, issued by the Jewish Museum (1965); and Norman L. Kleeblatt and Susan Chevlowe, eds., *Painting a Place in America: Jewish Artists in New York 1900–1945* (1991), a catalog that, in addition to a sketch of Benn's career and a listing of his exhibitions, has reproductions of his three paintings included in the Jewish Museum show. The following articles provide a range of later critical opinion of the artist's work: Sidney Geist, "Profile: Ben Benn," *Art Digest* 28 (1 Oct. 1953): 25–28; Hilton Kramer, "The Achievements of Ben Benn," *Arts* 30 (Apr. 1956): 24–27, 29; Leslie Katz, "Ben Benn," *Arts Yearbook* 3 (1959): 118–119; Sidney Tillim, "Month in Review," *Arts Magazine* 37 (Mar. 1963): 58–60. An obituary is in the *New York Times* (11 Jan. 1983).

ELEANOR F. WEDGE

Robert Russell Bennett preparing orchestration for an NBC television series, *c.* 1950s. ARCHIVE PHOTOS

BENNETT, Robert Russell (*b.* 15 June 1894 in Kansas City, Missouri; *d.* 18 August 1981 in New York City), musical arranger, composer, and conductor who orchestrated the scores of more than three hundred Broadway musicals over a period spanning four decades.

Bennett was born into a musical family. His father, George Robert Bennett, played the trumpet and the violin in the Kansas City Philharmonic orchestra and his mother, May Bradford, was a piano teacher. He had one sister. Bennett began to exhibit his musical gifts early when, at the age of three, he picked out on the piano the melody of a Beethoven sonata that he had heard his mother play. The following year the family moved to a farm south of Kansas City to aid Bennett's recovery from polio. His parents provided most of his schooling. During this period his mother taught him to play the piano and his father gave him lessons on a number of brass and woodwind instruments. When the senior Bennett organized a local band, his son was proficient enough to sit in for any absent member.

When Bennett was fifteen, his family returned to Kansas City, where he became a student of the Danish-American musician Carl Busch, studying harmony, counterpoint, and composition. Between lessons he played second violin in the Kansas City Symphony under Busch's direction. (He also played third base for a local semipro ball team.) To pay for his musical education, Bennett played piano in dance

halls, movie theaters, and theatrical pit orchestras, discovering in the process his affinity for popular music.

In 1916 Bennett moved to New York City with just $200 in savings in his pocket. Again, he supported himself playing the piano in restaurants and dance halls. His first serious musical employment was with the music publishing house George Schirmer, Inc., where he was hired as a copyist. When the United States entered World War I, Bennett was able to enlist in the army infantry despite some lingering disabilities from polio. Assigned to a headquarters unit back in Kansas City because of a crippled foot, Bennett organized and conducted army bands and scored dance arrangements. After the armistice, Bennett returned to New York where, on 26 December 1919, he married Louise Merrill, daughter of the headmistress at a finishing school where he had given music lessons. They had one daughter, Beatrice Jean.

Bennett applied for a position as orchestrator at T. B. Harms and Company, at that time the top music publisher in Tin Pan Alley, the center of Manhattan's music industry. The interview won him a chance to audition; he was instructed to orchestrate a Cole Porter tune, "An Old Fashioned Garden," which became the biggest hit of 1919, and Bennett was hired. Soon he was orchestrating entire productions.

It has been said that Bennett is the reason why musical

arrangers get their names on theater programs today. His orchestrations embraced the work of every major composer of Broadway musicals for an entire generation: Rudolph Friml (*Rose Marie,* 1924); Vincent Youmans (*No, No, Nanette,* 1925); Jerome Kern (*Show Boat,* 1927; *Roberta,* 1933; and *Very Warm for May,* 1939); George Gershwin (*Of Thee I Sing,* 1931, and *Porgy and Bess,* 1935); Irving Berlin (*Annie Get Your Gun,* 1946); Cole Porter (*Kiss Me, Kate,* 1948); Burton Lane (*Finian's Rainbow,* 1947); and Kurt Weill (*Lady in the Dark,* 1941). He even reorchestrated Georges Bizet's opera *Carmen* for the all-black production, *Carmen Jones* (1943). Perhaps his best-known work was with Richard Rodgers, for whom he orchestrated *Oklahoma!* (1943), *Carousel* (1945), *South Pacific* (1949), *The King and I* (1951), and *The Sound of Music* (1959), among others. The best-known works of the latter part of his career are his orchestrations for Fritz Loewe's *My Fair Lady* (1956) and *Camelot* (1960). For both of these shows, Bennett collaborated with Philip J. Lang.

Bennett's astonishingly rapid method of orchestration was legendary. Watching a number two or three times in rehearsal, he was able to score it from memory, often turning out eighty pages of orchestrations a day. Thus, he occasionally had more than twenty shows running at the same time and almost never fewer than four or five per season.

In 1926, after successfully orchestrating more than sixty musicals, Bennett threw over this lucrative career to go to Paris to study classical composition with Nadia Boulanger. In 1927 and 1928 he won Guggenheim Fellowships enabling him to continue these studies. During this period he composed two symphonies, a ballet, and a one-act opera. In 1931 he was among the winners (along with Aaron Copland, Ernest Bloch, and Louis Gruenberg) of a contest sponsored by RCA for the best musical work by an American. The following year he collaborated with Robert A. Simon on a full-length opera, *Maria Malibran,* which opened at the Juilliard School of Music in New York City in 1935 to mixed reviews. Ironically, the RCA award led to many commissions as an arranger; so many, in fact, that his work as a composer languished. However, in the late 1930s Bennett provided original music as well as orchestrations for a number of Hollywood productions, including *Show Boat* (1936), *The Hunchback of Notre Dame* (1939), and *Rebecca* (1940). During this period he composed the music for the Lagoon of Nations at the New York World's Fair in 1939 and 1940. In 1943 Bennett was commissioned by the *Saturday Evening Post* to write a symphony on *The Four Freedoms,* based on the famous Norman Rockwell painting done for that magazine. Eugene Ormandy, conductor of the Philadelphia Orchestra, played it many times, as did other orchestras throughout the country during World War II.

The new medium of television gave additional scope to Bennett's abilities. In 1952 he orchestrated the Richard Rodgers score for the naval history of World War II, called *Victory at Sea.* Recordings of this score continued to sell well for many years. During the 1950s Bennett again worked periodically in Hollywood. For one of his orchestrations, *Oklahoma!* (1955), he won an Oscar. Tall, slender, and distinguished, Bennett was sometimes likened to the film star Ronald Colman. His hobbies were tennis, baseball, and pool, and every morning he studied the racing form to place bets. He died in New York City at the age of eighty-seven.

Conservative in both style and outlook, Bennett avoided the atonal mode of much serious twentieth-century music. His compositions are generally structured and melodic. Unlike the many composers with whom he worked, Bennett did not place great value on his efforts as an orchestrator. "The orchestrator's value is his sensitiveness to melody," he said once. "If the melody has something to say, he can put colors into the outlines. If the melody has nothing to say, he is powerless." Bennett took a rather snobbish view of Broadway show tunes. "Don't confuse this with music," he once told an interviewer. "I make my living with the Gershwins, the Porters, and the Kerns, but for my own consumption, no. When I have time to myself, I study the scores of the great masters." The passage of time has proven him wrong on two counts: both on what constitutes "music" and on the value of his contribution to it.

★

A biographical sketch is in Charles Moritz, ed., *Current Biography 1962* (1963). See also Lucy Greenbaum, "About an Arranger," *New York Times* (24 Oct. 1943), and John E. Vacha, "The Sound of Musicals: How Orchestrator Robert Russell Bennett Helped Orchestrate Many a Broadway Show," *Opera News* (July 1993). An obituary is in the *New York Times* (19 Aug. 1981).

NATALIE B. JALENAK

BENSON, Elmer Austin (*b.* 22 September 1895 in Appleton, Minnesota; *d.* 13 March 1985 in Minneapolis, Minnesota), governor of Minnesota and U.S. senator from Minnesota, best known as a leader of the Farmer-Labor party.

Benson was one of the six children of Thomas Helga Benson and Dora Jacobson Benson. His father, an immigrant from Norway, was successively a farmer, owner and manager of a liquor store, and proprietor of a general store.

Benson, a Lutheran, attended public schools in Appleton and received an LL.B. from St. Paul College of Law in 1918. He was a private in the U.S. Army from 16 April 1918 to 28 January 1919, and served overseas. He was admitted to the bar in 1919 but never practiced law.

On 14 October 1922 Benson married Frances Miller; they had a daughter and a son. Benson was an assistant cashier in the First National Bank of Appleton from 1922 to 1923 and a partner in a clothing business from 1919 to 1933. He was a cashier of the Farmers and Merchants Bank in Appleton from 1923 to 1933.

Benson was friendly, mild-mannered, and respected, with a streak of radicalism in his political philosophy. He was a close friend of the old-line Democratic editor of the *Appleton Press,* Martin J. McGowan, who did his best to advance Benson's political career.

Governor Floyd B. Olson, of the Farmer-Labor party, appointed Benson commissioner of securities (1933) and then as commissioner of banks (1933 to 1935). When Republican Senator Thomas David Schall died on 23 December 1935, following an automobile accident in Washington, it was Olson's responsibility to name an interim senator. When Olson chose Benson to succeed Schall in the Senate, it was with the tacit understanding that Benson would "keep the seat warm" until Olson could be elected to a six-year term in 1936. Benson was to step aside for Olson and, as the Farmer-Labor candidate, would succeed Olson as governor.

Benson served in the Second Session of the Seventy-fourth Congress, from 3 January 1936 until 3 November 1936, though Congress was in session only until 30 June. He was active during his brief tenure: he delivered addresses entitled "An American Future for American Youth" and "Cooperation and Cooperative Growth," and read into the *Congressional Record* a number of papers and speeches by others. He presented a wide variety of petitions and resolutions from Minnesotans, and delivered several radio addresses.

Olson died on 22 August 1936, and Lieutenant Governor Hjalmar Petersen challenged Benson for the gubernatorial nomination. Benson won the party's nomination and the election, defeating Martin A. Nelson, the Republican candidate, 680,342 votes (60.7 percent of the vote cast) to 431,841. Since he was not seeking reelection to the Senate, Benson resigned on 3 November 1936, the day he won election as governor. Benson was governor from 4 January 1937 until 2 January 1939.

Republican resurgence began during Benson's administration. A "People's Lobby," including some communists, invaded the Capitol in St. Paul and attempted to intimidate the lawmakers. When the regular session of the legislature ended, it had not even enacted appropriations measures for running the state. A deadlocked legislature forced Benson to call a special session. Laws passed during his governorship included mandatory workmen's compensation insurance for employers, the establishment of the State Geographic Board (to standardize names of natural features throughout the state), the abolition of state levies on homesteads, in-

Minnesota governor Elmer Benson visits the White House, 1937. UPI/ Corbis-Bettmann

creased taxes on mining companies, the establishment of county welfare boards, and increased relief payments and aid to farmers.

Benson sought reelection as governor, but in 1938 thirty-one-year-old Republican Harold E. Stassen garnered 678,839 votes (59.9 percent) to Benson's 387,263—the biggest shift in the state since 1904.

During Benson's administration the Farmer-Labor party was torn by dissension and entered a period of decline from which it never recovered. Many Farmer-Laborites—quiet during the Benson administration—intensely disliked the entry of communists into their party. They regarded the role of communists in the Popular Front wing of their movement as a betrayal of the democratic principles of their party. Popular Front supporters, led by former governor Benson, held on to party leadership from 1941 until the merger of their party with the Democratic party in 1944. Benson initially resisted when Franklin Roosevelt's administration and Elmer F. Kelm (one of the first German-Americans to break the near monopoly of Minnesota Democratic party leadership by Irish-Americans) wanted a merger in 1943, but pressure from his closest allies—the Congress of Industrial Organizations and the communists—caused him to change his position. In April 1944 the merger was made, with Kelm as the first chairman of the new Democratic-Farmer-Labor (DFL) party.

Benson was an unsuccessful candidate for election to the U.S. Senate in 1940 and 1942 but was elected state chairman of the Farmer-Labor Association in 1942. He devoted only a portion of his time to the office, letting the day-to-day activities of the party be managed by Viena P. Johnson, the party's state secretary and the first woman to exercise considerable statewide political power in Minnesota.

Following the merger of the Farmer-Labor party with the Democratic party, Benson's work was rewarded by President Harry S. Truman with a patronage appointment as collector of customs for the port of Duluth.

At the end of World War II the Democratic-Farmer-Labor party split into factions. In 1946 the DFL's Popular Front wing, still led by Benson, took control of the party's leadership. Benson's faction, with its significant communist presence, sought American accommodation with the Soviet Union. When Henry A. Wallace announced his opposition to President Truman's anticommunist foreign policy, Benson led his forces into the Wallace camp. When Wallace decided to run for the presidency in 1948, Benson became national chairman of Wallace's new Progressive party. He announced in Minnesota that his faction would take the DFL out of the Democratic party and affiliate it with the Progressives. This factional brawl resulted in the victory of Hubert Humphrey, an anticommunist liberal, over the DFL party and Minnesota's labor movement.

Benson opposed many popular figures (he referred to Humphrey as a "war criminal" for his support of the war in Vietnam) and championed many unpopular causes—saying, for example, that if Stalin had not done some of the things he did, the Soviet Union might have fallen to the Nazis. These and other factors contributed to Benson's loss of political power. Meanwhile, Benson's feuds with Hjalmar Petersen and Humphrey denied him a position of respect in the political history of Minnesota.

Eventually, his political career at an end, Benson returned to Appleton and spent the rest of his life as a farmer. He died at the age of eighty-nine and was buried in the Appleton City Cemetery.

★

There are a few primary sources dealing with Benson in the Minneapolis Public Library's vertical file. Useful government publications include *Congressional Record* for the Seventy-fourth Congress and *Biographical Directory of the American Congress, 1774–1961* (1961). The only full-length biography of Benson is James M. Shields, *Mr. Progressive: A Biography of Elmer Austin Benson* (1971). This work is reviewed by Lila M. Johnson in *Minnesota History* 42, no. 6 (1971): 236. George H. Mayer, *The Political Career of Floyd B. Olson* (1951), contains a great deal on Benson. See also Robert Sobel and John Raimo, eds., *Biographical Directory of the Governors of the United States, 1789–1978,* 4 vols. (1978), and Roy R. Glashan, comp., *American Governors and Gubernatorial Elections, 1775–1978* (1979). State histories with considerable material on Benson's gubernatorial and senatorial careers are Theodore Blegen, *Minnesota: A History of the State* (1963); Val Björnson, *The History of Minnesota,* 4 vols. (1969); Clifford E. Clark, Jr., ed., *Minnesota in a Century of Change: The State and Its People Since 1900* (1989). Benson also is treated in Eleanora W. Schoenebaum, ed., *Political Profiles: The Truman Years* (1978). An obituary is in the *New York Times* (15 Mar. 1985).

NORMAN E. TUTOROW

BERGMAN, Ingrid (*b.* 29 August 1915 in Stockholm, Sweden; *d.* 29 August 1982 in London, England), actress whose luminous performances and incandescent beauty made her an international film star.

The only child of German-born Friedel Adler and Justus Bergman, who owned a camera store, Ingrid Bergman was orphaned by the age of eleven, when she went to live with an aunt and uncle. Shortly before he died, her father had taken her to the theater, and from then on Bergman knew instinctively that she wanted to be an actress. Her deeply religious uncle, however, was horrified by her theatrical aspirations. Bergman attended the Stockholm Lyceum for Girls, a private school.

Ingrid Bergman, *c.* 1948. JERRY VERMILYE

In late 1931, when she was sixteen, Bergman worked as a film extra, and two years later she auditioned for, and was accepted by, the Royal Dramatic Theatre, Sweden's prestigious national theater. In 1934 she won her first movie role in a comedy called *The Count of the Monk's Bridge*. She was then offered a film contract by Svensk Filmindustri, Sweden's leading film company, and played small roles in a number of movies.

A major break in her career occurred when she won the leading role in her sixth Swedish film, *Intermezzo* (1936). Playing opposite the popular actor Gösta Ekman, she revealed an ethereal quality as a young pianist who falls in love with a renowned violinist. At first her career continued on a steady course; she made several more Swedish films, then agreed to make three movies with UFA, the major German film company (only one was ever completed). At the same time her personal life changed. On 10 July 1937 she married Petter Lindstrom, a dentist who was studying to be a physician. In 1938 their daughter Pia was born; she would become a television news broadcaster in the United States.

When Kay Brown, the East Coast story editor for the producer David O. Selznick, saw *Intermezzo* she urged Selznick to sign Bergman to a contract. Selznick was impressed by her talent and beauty and decided to remake *Intermezzo* in English, with Leslie Howard as her leading man. Bergman came to America to make the film, then returned to Sweden. To clear up any confusion as to what an "intermezzo" might be, Selznick renamed the film *Intermezzo: A Love Story* (1939). As the lovelorn pianist, Bergman enchanted American critics and filmgoers—her star potential was visible in every frame—and Selznick touted her as his latest discovery.

Reluctantly, Bergman returned to America, only to learn that Selznick had no immediate plans for her. Disappointed and disheartened, she decided to play opposite Burgess Meredith in a 1940 New York City stage revival of Ferenc Molnar's *Liliom* (which later became the musical *Carousel*). Selznick agreed to lend her to other studios, but neither *Adam Had Four Sons* (1941) nor *Rage in Heaven* (1941) advanced her career. She did, however, create something of a stir as the ill-fated barmaid Ivy in MGM's version of *Dr. Jekyll and Mr. Hyde* (1941), opposite Spencer Tracy.

Bergman was now famous but bored and restless, and she felt unfulfilled as an actress. Finally, after heavy negotiations, Selznick released her to play a leading role in Warner Brothers' movie *Casablanca* (1942). There was no indication that the film would be more than a standard melodrama, but it succeeded in fusing all of its elements—story, cast, photography, direction, and music—into a movie that became a legend. As the alluring Ilsa, torn between two men in wartime Casablanca, Bergman brought a palpably romantic feeling to her scenes with Humphrey Bogart's Rick. From then on she was a major film star.

Bergman could now choose her roles carefully, although they seemed to be dictated by the public's perception of her as a noble, even saintly woman. She won an Oscar nomination as the war-damaged, passionate young Maria in an adaptation of Ernest Hemingway's *For Whom the Bell Tolls* (1943), received her first Oscar as the tormented wife in *Gaslight* (1944), and played a demure psychiatrist unraveling the secret of her lover's mental illness in Alfred Hitchcock's *Spellbound* (1945). She starred as a nun in *The Bells of St. Mary's* (1945), a role that seemed to crystallize her saintly persona, and was again Oscar-nominated. It may have been something of a shock, therefore, for audiences to see her as the promiscuous daughter of a convicted Nazi in Alfred Hitchcock's riveting melodrama, *Notorious* (1946).

Around this time Bergman's marriage to Petter Lindstrom was beginning to unravel. As always driven and ambitious, she appeared to be setting her career above their marriage. She had also had affairs with various men, including director Victor Fleming, photographer Robert Capa, and harmonica performer Larry Adler. Lindstrom himself was deeply involved in changing careers; in Los Angeles he was studying to become a surgeon. (Years later, he would become a prominent neurosurgeon in Los Angeles.) Their lives seemed to be drifting apart.

With her film career temporarily on the wane (a 1946 film version of Erich Maria Remarque's *Arch of Triumph*, not released until 1948, was a dire failure), Bergman agreed to depict Joan of Arc in Maxwell Anderson's play *Joan of Lorraine*, which opened on Broadway in November 1946. Bolstered by its success, she then decided to bring her conception of the Maid of Orleans to the screen. But the resulting film, *Joan of Arc* (1948), though spectacular, was surprisingly heavy-handed. Bergman did, nonetheless, receive an Oscar nomination for her performance.

The year 1948 proved to be momentous for Bergman. That spring she had seen the Italian director Robert Rossellini's film *Paisan* (1948) and had been overwhelmed by its raw power. Two years earlier she had been equally stunned by his film *Open City* (1946). She wrote to Rossellini, offering to appear in any film he would make. He was both flattered and pleased, and after she filmed Alfred Hitchcock's *Under Capricorn* (1949)—another failure—she went to Rome in March 1949 to meet him.

Thus began the most tumultuous period of Bergman's career. She had a passionate affair with Rossellini which triggered an international scandal, with the press hounding them as they made *Stromboli* (1950), their first film together. Her pregnancy caused an extraordinary storm of wrath and condemnation, culminating in a denunciation of Bergman by U.S. Senator Edwin C. Johnson as "a powerful influence for evil." He also demanded that she be barred from the country for "moral turpitude."

Following the birth of her son Robertino in February 1950, Bergman obtained a Mexican divorce from Petter Lindstrom and in May 1950 married Rossellini by proxy in Mexico. In June 1952 Bergman gave birth to twin daughters, Isabella and Isotta (better known as Ingrid); the former became a well-known actress and model. Meanwhile, her film career faltered as she made a series of movies with Rossellini that met with critical and public disfavor. *Europa '51* (*The Greatest Love,* 1951), *Viaggio in Italia* (*Strangers,* 1954), and *Angst* (*Fear,* 1955), among others, were largely regarded as turgid efforts.

Totally possessive and subject to volatile rages, Rossellini continued to dominate Bergman's life and career, allowing her to appear only in Jean Renoir's French film *Elena et Les Hommes* (*Paris Does Strange Things,* 1956) and in a Paris stage production of *Tea and Sympathy* in 1956 and 1957. But as their marriage disintegrated, Bergman considered restarting her film career. She accepted an offer to star in a film adaptation of the play *Anastasia*. In the 1956 film she gave a sterling performance as a mysterious woman who claims to be the daughter of Russia's assassinated czar, Nicholas II. In January 1957 Bergman made a triumphant return to the United States to accept the New York Film Critics prize for best actress. She also won her second Oscar for best actress.

Her life and career now took a happier turn. Although her films following *Anastasia* were not all successful, she made notable appearances, her beauty still intact, in *Indiscreet* (1958), *Inn of the Sixth Happiness* (1958), and other movies. She also starred in several television and stage productions. Her marriage to Rossellini was annulled, and on 21 December 1958 she married Swedish theatrical producer Lars Schmidt. (They were divorced in 1975.)

Throughout the 1960s and 1970s Bergman alternated between the theater and films, acting in such movies as *Cactus Flower* (1969), *A Walk in the Spring Rain* (1970), and *Murder on the Orient Express* (1974)—for which she won an Oscar for best supporting actress, her third Academy Award—and in such plays as Somerset Maugham's *The Constant Wife* and Eugene O'Neill's *More Stately Mansions*. After being diagnosed with breast cancer, she continued to perform, giving a brilliant, Oscar-nominated performance in Ingmar Bergman's *Autumn Sonata* (1978). She made her final theatrical appearance as Israel's prime minister Golda Meir in the four-hour television series *A Woman Called Golda* (1982). She died of cancer in a London hospital on her sixty-seventh birthday. She was buried in Sweden.

A gifted actress and a legendary beauty, Ingrid Bergman reached the heights of success, then tumbled into harsh scandal as the world watched and whispered. With dignity and courage she succeeded in making her way back to the top, where her radiant image as one of the screen's greatest actresses still glows.

★

Ingrid Bergman's autobiography, *Ingrid Bergman: My Story* (1981), was written with Alan Burgess. Other books on her life and career include Lawrence J. Quirk, *The Films of Ingrid Bergman* (1970); Curtis F. Brown, *Ingrid Bergman* (1973); John Russell Taylor, *Ingrid Bergman* (1983); Laurence Leamer, *As Time Goes By: The Life of Ingrid Bergman* (1986); and Donald Spoto, *Notorious: The Life of Ingrid Bergman* (1997). Obituaries appear in the *New York Times* (31 Aug. 1982) and *Variety* (1 Sept. 1982).

TED SENNETT

BERMAN, Emile Zola (*b.* 3 November 1902 in New York City; *d.* 3 July 1981 in New York City), lawyer specializing in negligence who defended Marine Staff Sergeant Matthew C. McKeon, court-martialed in 1956 for the drowning of six recruits during a disciplinary march, and Sirhan Sirhan, the assassin of Senator Robert F. Kennedy convicted in 1969.

Berman, the eldest of three children of political refugees Eli and Elizabeth Berman, was born on Cherry Street on

Emile Zola Berman in his office in New York, 1959. AP/WIDE WORLD PHOTOS

the Lower East Side of Manhattan shortly after his parents arrived from Brest-Litovsk, Russia. He was named in honor of the novelist Émile Zola for his impassioned defense of Captain Alfred Dreyfuss, who in the 1890s had been unjustly accused of treason against France. His brother, Alfred, was named after Dreyfuss himself. Eli Berman, an architectural woodworker who owned his own firm, designed the interior wall paneling for the William L. Harkness Hall at Yale University.

Soon after his birth, the Bermans moved to the Bronx, New York City, where Emile grew up. Nicknamed "Zuke," he thrived at Evander Childs High School, where he was a miler and cross-country runner as well as captain of the chess team. Berman discovered his aptitude for the law in his elocution class.

Berman received a B.S. degree in 1923 and an LL.B. in 1924 from New York University. Admitted to the New York bar in 1925, he joined a law firm the next year that specialized in insurance work. Between 1926 and 1956, Berman became a top trial lawyer specializing in negligence cases. He was invited to lecture on courtroom tactics for bar groups across the United States and began teaching the subject in 1935 at the Practicing Law Institute of New York City. During World War II he served as a combat intelligence officer with the Tenth Air Force in China, Burma, and India. As a result of his service, he was awarded the Distinguished Flying Cross and the Bronze Star. He was discharged in 1946 as a lieutenant colonel.

On 20 October 1944 Berman married Alice Rose Gaines, a model originally from Clinton, South Carolina, whom he had met in 1938. They soon settled at 22 Schoolhouse Lane in Roslyn Heights, in Nassau County, Long Island. They adopted two children, Eli and Eliza. After the war, Berman resumed his law and teaching practice. As well as teaching at the Practicing Law Institute (1946–1968), he lectured from 1950 to 1955 at the law schools of New York University, Columbia University, and the University of Texas.

The year 1956 was an important one for Berman. He cofounded the firm of Berman & Frost, and in his specialty of negligence law he won the largest award to that time against the City of New York ($350,000) for a woman struck by a speeding police car. But it was the case of Marine Staff Sergeant Matthew C. McKeon that year that brought Berman national attention. One of the country's most famous court-martial cases, McKeon was brought up on charges stemming from a disciplinary night march at Parris Island, South Carolina, that resulted in six deaths. Berman volunteered to defend McKeon at no charge. While public opinion was squarely against McKeon before the trial, Berman garnered sympathy for his client through a public media campaign and by conducting a defense strategy that painted McKeon as a scapegoat for sadistic but common

military practices. The trial, which began on 16 July 1956, enabled Berman to combine his litigation skills and military background. Berman scored a coup for his client by convincing retired Lieutenant General Lewis B. ("Chesty") Puller, the Marines' most decorated contemporary hero, and Marine Corps commandant General Randolph McC. Pate, who had recommended the court-martial in the first place, to testify for the defense. On 4 August McKeon, found guilty only of drinking on duty and simple negligence, was given a comparatively light sentence.

By 1962 Berman was reportedly earning $250,000 a year. Looking for a new challenge, he ran as an independent Democrat for district attorney in staunchly Republican Nassau County. He lost by 84,000 votes.

In May 1964 he defended Camille Cravelle, a poor fourteen-year-old African American charged with aggravated rape of a sixty-seven-year-old spinster from the leading family of Alexandria, Louisiana. Arguing before an all-white jury, with his client looking at the death penalty, the case seemed doomed. "I was the Jew from New York and he was a Negro kid," Berman later recalled. "It was tough, I can tell you." But at the end of the trial a few weeks later, Cravelle received a three-year sentence, later reduced to two years. By 1967 Berman was divorced from Alice and had married Virginia Anne Berman. They lived in Westhampton, Long Island, and New York City.

Berman made national headlines again when he became the third member of the legal team defending Sirhan Bishara Sirhan, a Palestinian Arab accused in the 1968 murder of Senator Robert F. Kennedy during his presidential primary campaign. All three lawyers worked for free. "The worst cases and the worst crimes make the best law and this one represents everything I've been working for all my life," Berman noted. "Sirhan is a symbol of every man's right to a fair trial and this right needs constant reinforcement by people qualified to do it." On 14 February 1969 Berman delivered the defense's opening statement. The defense team's argument of "diminished capacity" was unsuccessful. Found guilty on 17 April 1969, Sirhan was sentenced to death. The sentence was later changed to life imprisonment.

Berman was a sociable, dapper, balding hawk-nosed man with red hair and a mustache, described as "a living version of Ichabod Crane." A colleague called him "a terrier in the courtroom, who shines in rebuttal and cross-examination." Considered one of New York's sharpest legal minds, he usually left pretrial work to subordinates, concentrating on the trial itself. Berman served on many professional committees and organizations. He did not maintain a religious affiliation.

Berman retired in 1972. Ill for several years, he died from complications from a stroke in the DeWitt Nursing Home in New York City.

★

The most comprehensive overview of Emile Zola Berman's life is found in Charles Moritz, ed., *Current Biography 1972*. Profiles of Berman appeared during his famous trials. The best for the McKeon trial is Joe McCarthy, "The Man Who Helped the Sergeant," *Life* (13 Aug. 1956). Others include "The Sergeant's Lawyer," *New York Times* (20 July 1956), and Stan Opotowsky, "Berman—The DI's Darrow," *New York Post Magazine* (29 July 1956). The best features on Berman during the Sirhan trial are Lacey Fosburgh, "Advocate for Sirhan," *New York Times* (15 Feb. 1969), and *Time* (17 Jan. 1969). An obituary is in the *New York Times* (5 July 1981).

SHARONA A. LEVY

BERNARD, Anna Jones (*b.* 21 April 1897 in Newark, New Jersey; *d.* 14 September 1983 in White Plains, New York), the first African-American woman admitted to the New York State Bar Association.

Bernard was the eldest of seven siblings born to Lewis Woodward Jones, a bricklayer and plasterer, and Mattie Lightfoot, a schoolteacher, who instilled in their children a thirst for knowledge and the determination to excel. When Bernard was three years old her family moved from New Jersey to New Rochelle, New York. In 1900 Bernard and her parents were among the first African Americans to integrate the suburbs of Westchester County, and in 1915 Bernard became the first African American to graduate from New Rochelle High School.

The following fall Bernard matriculated at Hunter College in New York City. Shortly after receiving her bachelor's degree in 1919, Bernard was certified by the New York State Department of Education and embarked on a teaching career in the New York City public school system that would last more than forty years. During her early years as a schoolteacher, Bernard resided in Harlem and taught elementary, junior high, and high school classes. Most of her career, however, was spent teaching English at Frederick Douglass Junior High School, where one of her more notable students was the author James Baldwin.

Although Bernard found teaching to be a fulfilling profession, she harbored a strong desire to help people still further. Known for her indomitable will and intelligence, Bernard applied to New York University Law School and was accepted at a time when she and one other woman became the first African-American women to enroll at the law school. The year was 1919 and Bernard found that her professors at the law school had no interest in her as a student or as a future attorney. "No particular interest was paid to us as women or as blacks. We were just not taken very seriously," Bernard said later.

Nevertheless, this lack of institutional support did not deter the outgoing, strong-willed Bernard from pursuing her J.D. degree. She taught classes in Harlem in the mornings so that she would not miss her afternoon classes at law school. Bernard graduated in 1923 and later that year became the first African-American woman admitted to the New York State Bar Association. But Bernard's search for work as an attorney was fruitless because during the 1920s it was unheard of for most law firms to hire female or African-American attorneys.

Bernard did not allow her inability to work as an attorney prevent her from realizing her potential as a leader and role model. For more than forty years as a teacher she encouraged discipline among her students and inspired them to realize their potential, regardless of societal limitations. Bernard's commitment to education was steadfast because she firmly believed that all students could learn if given the opportunity, and that education was the key to personal and professional fulfillment.

In 1924 Bernard married Woodruff J. Robinson, a dentist. Five years later she and her husband relocated to the upper-middle-class suburb of Greenburgh, New York, and became the first African Americans in this Westchester

Anna Bernard. COURTESY OF KENNETH JONES. PHOTO BY OTTO SCHMIDT.

community. After sixteen years of marriage, Bernard was divorced from her first husband in 1940. Five years later she married Lloyd Bernard. She had no children.

In 1960, at the age of sixty-three, Bernard retired from teaching and opened a private law practice and real estate agency at her home in Greenburgh, working in conjunction with the White Plains firm of Blazi and Zimmerman. At this time, Bernard also became the first African-American trustee at Westchester Community College, in Valhalla, N.Y., serving from 1969 to 1978. It was here that Bernard was able fully to realize her goals as an educator and administrator: to afford all young people the opportunity for an education, regardless of race, creed, or socioeconomic status; to force the college to realize its commitment toward an open-door policy, and to expand students' education with the inclusion of enriching extracurricular programs. She supported remedial reading, writing, and math so that students with special needs would be able to obtain a college education. She advocated a needs-based financial aid system and was instrumental in the expansion of the college's counseling staff. During Bernard's tenure as trustee, seven new campus buildings were built, the minority student population increased from 2 percent to 14 percent, and the college's budget increased significantly.

From the 1960s to the early 1980s Bernard was also very active in her community and held a number of notable positions in Greenburgh and in the neighboring towns of Westchester County. She was a vice chairperson of the Greenburgh Housing Authority, where she played an active role in getting lower- and moderate-income housing built; a director of the American Lung Association of Hudson Valley, a member of Greenburgh's Victory Gardens and Town Beautification committees; and a member of the Carver Gardens Club of White Plains, which was one of the earliest African-American social clubs in Westchester. A petite, attractive woman, she collected Asian and African-American art and was affiliated with the African Methodist Episcopal church.

After a two-month illness Anna Jones Bernard died of cancer in her home. She is buried in Beechwood Cemetery in White Plains, New York.

★

Obituaries of Bernard appear in Gannett Westchester Newspapers (15 Sept. 1983), the *New York Times* (17 Sept. 1983), and the (Westchester Community College) *Viking* (22 Sept. 1983). Oral interviews were conducted with the following family members: Lewis Jones, Helen Tynes, and Kenneth Jones. Also interviewed was Dr. Julius Ford of Westchester Community College.

LaRose T. Parris

BERNBACH, William (*b.* 13 August 1911 in New York City; *d.* 2 October 1982 in New York City), advertising executive considered among the most influential persons in the advertising industry and an "acknowledged leader of the revolution in advertising," according to an American Advertising Federation award in 1977.

The son of Jacob Bernbach, a Bronx designer of women's clothing, and Rebecca Reiter, William attended New York City public schools and graduated from New York University in 1933 with a bachelor's degree in English. He had two brothers and a sister. On 5 June 1938 he married Evelyn Carbone. The couple had two sons, John Lincoln and Paul Anthony. The couple lived in the Bay Ridge section of Brooklyn until their children were grown. Later they moved to an apartment in the UN Plaza in Manhattan.

Bill Bernbach's career in advertising began during the Great Depression. While working in the Schenley Distillers Company mail room, he wrote an ad, sent it to the firm's advertising agency, and eventually saw it published in the *New York Times*. Schenley president Lewis Rosenstiel discovered that Bernbach was responsible and rewarded the young man's talent and initiative with a raise and an assignment to the advertising department.

In 1939 and 1940 he worked as a researcher and writer in the promotion department of the New York World's Fair. After that job ended, he joined the William H. Weintraub agency, where the renowned graphic artist Paul Rand was

William Bernbach. RICHARD TINO

then a young art director. The two became friends, and Rand encouraged Bernbach's interest in art and graphics. Together, Bernbach and Rand worked to change advertising from what Bernbach said seemed to be "illustrations in a magazine, without that powerful graphic look," to a more modern appearance with dramatic impact.

Bernbach spent two years in the U.S. Army during World War II, stationed at Fort Eustis, a training and supply center in Virginia. After his early release because of a "bad heartbeat," as he called it, Bernbach returned to civilian life and became director of postwar planning for Coty, Inc. In 1945 he took a copywriting position at Grey Advertising, Inc., and quickly became that agency's vice president of copy and art. At Grey he met and befriended another vice president, Ned Doyle, who shared Bernbach's philosophy that an agency's work in creating an advertising message should not be compromised to curry favor with clients.

On 1 June 1949 Bernbach, Doyle, and Maxwell Dane, who had run a small agency of his own, formed Doyle Dane Bernbach (also known as DDB) with less than $500,000 in billings. Bernbach was named president, a title he held until 1968, when he became chairman and chief executive officer. From 1976 until his death he was chairman of the firm's executive committee.

Among Doyle Dane Bernbach's first accounts was Ohrbach's, a New York and Los Angeles low-priced department store, formerly at Grey. Other accounts at that time included Levy's Jewish rye bread, Thom McAn shoes, Benson and Hedges cigarettes, and Utica Club beer. Later Volkswagen and Avis Rent A Car were added.

By the time the company's stock was offered to the public in 1964, it was billing more than $100 million annually, and its clients had included American Airlines, Canadian Lord Calvert whiskey, Colombian coffee, Crackerjacks, Heinz ketchup, International Silver, Mobil Oil, Rheingold beer, Ronson lighters, Sony electronic products, and U.S. Royal tires.

Doyle Dane Bernbach's advertising for these and other clients was highly regarded and often displayed at other agencies. At Bernbach's death the agency was the nation's tenth largest, with billings of $1.2 billion, nearly 3,000 employees, and subsidiary offices in sixteen countries in Europe, Asia, Australia, and North and Central America. In August 1986 the agency merged with Needham Harper and Steers to become DDB Needham, part of the DDB Needham Worldwide Communications Group.

DDB took on causes as well as commercial products. One was SANE, the Committee for a Sane Nuclear Policy. A Democrat, Bernbach ran the agency's 1964 campaign for Lyndon B. Johnson and the Democratic party. During the Vietnam War he was a major supporter of Advertising People Against the War.

Bernbach believed strongly in the importance of the role of professional communicators in bettering society. In his speech at his induction into the Advertising Hall of Fame on 9 February 1977, he said:

> Men of good will are not necessarily good communicators. And that can be a tragedy. You can be the answer to that. You have the skill, the talent, and the knowledge to reach people and to touch their minds and hearts. I urge you to jump into the fray. . . . You have a great contribution to make to the welfare of mankind.

Considered the conscience of the advertising world, Bernbach held that "the most powerful element in advertising is the truth." He also believed that fresh advertising sold product advantages better than advertising that lacked originality.

He was the Copywriters Hall of Fame man of the year in 1963, 1965, and 1966 and Pulse Inc. man of the year in 1966. Voted top advertising agency president in a nationwide poll conducted by *Ad Daily* in 1967, he won the Madden Memorial Award in 1968 and four years later the Parsons School of Design Diamond Jubilee Award for "his creative contribution to the graphics communications industry and for his influence on the development of so many outstanding talents in the industry."

Active in professional and civic affairs, Bernbach was vice president and member of the board of the Educational Foundation of the Association of American Advertising Agencies. He was vice chairman and member of the board of Citizens Committee for New York City Inc. He was on the board and the executive committee of the Salk Institute for Biological Studies and was chairman of the Municipal Art Society of New York. He was vice chairman of the Lincoln Center Film Committee and board member of the International Eye Foundation, the Legal Aid Society, and the Mary Manning Walsh Home. A Distinguished Adjunct Professor at New York University, he also lectured at the Harvard Business School and the Massachusetts Institute of Technology. He was also a member of the advisory committee of the Kennedy School of Government at Harvard and the Communications Committee of the Harvard Medical School.

Physically, Bernbach was five feet, seven inches tall and 155 pounds, with very light blue eyes and a widow's peak. He was described as mild mannered, quiet, reserved, well balanced, "uneccentric," but with a strong ego. He was well read—enjoying literary criticism, sociology, and philosophy—and listened to jazz and classical music. His religious affiliation was Jewish.

Bernbach died of leukemia at New York Hospital.

★

A book devoted to Bernbach is *William Bernbach, American Advertising Agency President,* by Leonard L. Bartlett (1977). Three books have extensive coverage of Bernbach: Bart Cummings, *The Benevolent Dictators, Interviews with Advertising Greats* (1984); Stephen Fox, *The Mirror Makers* (1984); and Denis Higgins, *The Art of Writing Advertising* (1989). Articles about him appear in *Time* (31 Mar. 1958), *Madison Avenue* (Aug. 1959), *Newsday* (2 Oct. 1965), and *Advertising Age* (8 Nov. 1982 and 11 Aug. 1986). Obituaries are in the *New York Times* (3 Oct. 1982) and *Advertising Age* (11 Oct. 1982).

RICHARD L. TINO

BILLINGTON, Ray Allen (*b.* 28 September 1903 in Bay City, Michigan; *d.* 7 March 1981 in San Marino, California), historian of the frontier and the American West whose writings, starting with *Westward Expansion* (1949), chronicled and stressed the impact of westward emigration on America's development.

The only child of Nina Allen and Cecil Billington, a Detroit newspaperman, Billington attended local schools in Detroit and while in high school showed a penchant for writing; many of his poems, essays, and editorials were published in the school paper. In 1921 the blue-eyed, effervescent youth enrolled at the University of Michigan with the goal of becoming a journalist. One of his printed pieces aroused the ire of the college administration, however, and he was expelled.

In 1924 Billington entered the University of Wisconsin to study literature, but he soon developed an interest in history through the courses of Carl Fish and the frontier historian Frederic Paxton; he received his B.A. degree in philosophy in 1926. Although continuing to write for several Detroit papers, he returned to the University of Michigan the same year and was awarded an M.A. in history in 1927.

Also in 1927 he made a total commitment to the study of history when he was accepted into Harvard University to study for a doctorate. During his studies there, Billington took a frontier history course taught together by Frederick Merk, the successor of Frederick Jackson Turner at Harvard, and John B. Hedges, but his chief interest became intellectual history. His doctoral dissertation, written under Arthur Schlesinger, Sr., and completed in 1933, was later published as *Protestant Crusade, 1800–1860: A Study in the Origins of American Nativism* (1938). On 6 September 1928 he married Mabel Ruth Crotty; their two children were named Anne and Allen.

Billington began his teaching career at Clark University in 1931 and moved on to Smith College in 1937. The next year he was approached by Hedges, his former Harvard professor, to coauthor a book on the American frontier. Hedges was to write about expansion west of the Mississippi River, while Billington was to cover expansion from the Atlantic Ocean to the Mississippi. This proved to be a turning point in Billington's professional career, and for most of the next decade he read extensively on early American migration westward. Ultimately, he wrote all but three chapters of the work because Hedges did not wish to complete his portion. The result was *Westward Expansion: A History of the American Frontier* (1949). Calling the work a "synthesis," Billington tried to produce a book modeled on the ideas expressed in the writings of Turner (especially *The Significance of the Frontier in American History,* published in 1893, which pictured the frontier as a series of concentric lines spreading across the United States from the colonial period onward to about 1890 and influencing the development of American political, economic, and social institutions), the work that Turner might have written but never did.

Between 1944 and 1963 Billington taught at Northwestern University. His courses were social and intellectual history, as well as introductory American history and history of the American West; he taught both undergraduate and graduate students. He was an outstanding professor, well liked by his students. In his seminars he stressed not only research and writing skills but also analysis and criticism. In sum he was mentor for approximately twenty-four Ph.D.s. In 1953 and 1954 he served as Harmsworth Professor of History at Oxford.

During his years at Northwestern, Billington wrote and edited other books on various areas of America's past, including *The United States: American Democracy in World Perspective,* as coauthor (1947); *The Journal of Charlotte L. Forten,* as editor (1953); *The Far Western Frontier, 1830–1860* (1956); and *The Westward Movement in the United States* (1959). In 1962 he was elected president of the Mississippi Valley Historical Association (later the Organization of American Historians), and in the same year served as the first president of the Western History Association, which he had helped to establish.

Between 1963 and his death, Billington was senior research associate at the Huntington Library in San Marino, California. These were very productive years in which he finally drew on manuscript sources in his writings. In 1966 Billington wrote *America's Frontier Heritage,* in which he applied the latest social science data to Turner's thesis. During the 1970s he produced two books on his model, Turner, whose papers were deposited in the Huntington Library: he edited *"Dear Lady,": The Letters of Frederick Jackson Turner and Alice Forbes Perkins Hooper, 1910–1932* (1970), and wrote the biography *Frederick Jackson Turner* (1973), which won the Bancroft Prize and National Book Award. Just a month before his death, *Land of Savagery, Land of Promise* (1981) appeared. In it he contrasted the fictional writings of Europeans, who portrayed the American frontier as a savage and lawless place, with nonfictional European works that pictured the American West as a place of freedom, opportunity, and promise. He died as a result of a heart ailment and is buried in Los Angeles County, California.

In his writings on the American frontier, Ray Billington did not produce an original work or construct new themes and patterns. His talent lay in his ability to synthesize the writings of others and to present them in a well-written and structured narrative. He was a follower of the ideas of Turner and, while acknowledging the faults and errors of this historian, argued nevertheless that the frontier as it moved across the expanse of the United States was a strong force in shaping American character and institutions.

Billington was a diligent researcher and writer; his works contained ample bibliographies, and his output was enormous. He possessed a fine sense of humor (he was an adept limerick composer), and his enthusiasm and zeal did much to promote an interest in the history of the American West.

★

Ray A. Billington, "The Frontier and I," *Western Historical Quarterly* 1 (Jan. 1970): 5–20, contains autobiographical data on the development of Billington's interest in the writing on the American West; Richard E. Oglesby, "Ray Allen Billington," in *Historians of the American Frontier: A Bio-Bibliographical Sourcebook*, edited by John R. Wunder (1988), presents an exhaustive bibliography of Billington's writings, as well as biographical data and an analysis of his works; Martin Ridge, "Frederick Jackson Turner, Ray Allen Billington, and American Frontier History," *Western Historical Quarterly* 19 (Jan. 1988): 5–20, analyzes the writings of the two men and provides biographical information; Patricia N. Limerick, "Persistent Traits and the Persistent Historian: The American Frontier and Ray Allen Billington," in *Writing Western History: Essays on Major Western Historians,* edited by Richard W. Etulain (1991), mentions some biographical details but is mainly devoted to a detailed criticism of Billington's chief works and his adherence to Turner's ideas; Wilbur R. Jacobs, *On Turner's Trail: 100 Years of Writing Western History* (1994), supplies some details on Billington's relations with his colleagues, as well as on his writings; Martin Ridge, "Ray Allen Billington (1903–1981)," *Western Historical Quarterly* 12 (July 1981): 245–250, is a tribute to Billington just after his death by a former student and colleague; Richard E. Oglesby, "A Dedication to the Memory of Ray Allen Billington," *Arizona and the West* 28 (summer 1986): 103–106, is written by a former student who presents biographical data as well as recollections of his mentor; Martin Ridge, "Ray Allen Billington: Western History and American Exceptionalism," *Pacific Historical Review* 56 (Nov. 1987): 495–511, discusses the writings of Billington in a favorable light.

Obituaries are in the *New York Times* (8 Mar. 1981), *Los Angeles Times* (9 Mar. 1981), and *Washington Post* (14 Mar. 1981).

ALLAN NELSON

BLACK, William (*b.* 6 June 1900 in Brooklyn, New York; *d.* 7 March 1983 in New York City), businessman and philanthropist whose Chock Full O'Nuts coffee company evolved from a Manhattan nut stand.

William Black was one of three children of a grocery store owner. Young William began working as a delivery boy for the family store at age six and as a teenager had a summer job delivering laundry in the Catskill Mountains resort area. Educated in the New York City public schools, Black graduated from Brooklyn's Bushwick High School and then enrolled in Columbia University, where he earned a B.S. degree in engineering in 1926.

To finance his education Black worked twelve-hour shifts unloading produce trucks at lower Manhattan's Washington Market. Unable to find a position in his chosen field, he became an entrepreneur. His first business venture, capitalized with $250, was a tiny nut stand on the lower level of a building at Broadway and Forty-third Street in Manhattan's theater district. The stand was so successful that Black quickly expanded, opening eighteen Chock Full O'Nuts outlets by 1932. Plummeting sales during the Great Depression caused the short, solidly built young entrepreneur to reconfigure his business. What emerged, in 1933, was a chain of luncheonettes featuring coffee and nut and cream cheese sandwiches on raisin bread. Each item cost five cents. In time the menu was expanded to include pie, soup, and doughnuts. Besides being known for the affordability and quality of their food, the restaurants were renowned for their cleanliness, attributable in part to Black's secret nocturnal visits to various outlets and to the practice of preparing food with utensils rather than allowing employees' hands to touch anything served to customers. "Where Hands Never Touch the Food You Eat" soon became a Chock Full O'Nuts advertising slogan. Meanwhile, in 1930 he had married Lillian Mandl; they had two children.

With his restaurant business firmly established, Black in 1953 introduced a line of coffee bearing the same name as the restaurants. The coffee, which was roasted in the company's own Brooklyn plant, was an all-purpose grind. Competitors continued to offer a choice of drip, percolator, or regular grinds but their products were less appealing to many buyers, who evidently agreed with Black's claim that his coffee was superior. According to the *New York Times* (14 April 1956): "Mr. Black is proud of the quality of his coffee. The advertising campaign, 'Don't spend the extra money for this coffee unless you're just plain crazy about good coffee,' emphasizes the appeal to the connoisseur." Within a decade Chock Full O'Nuts coffee sales revenue exceeded that of the still highly profitable restaurants. A good product and extensive advertising, which included a

William Black. COURTESY OF MRS. PAGE MORTON BLACK

popular jingle sung by Black's second wife, Jean Martin (whom he married in 1951 following his divorce from Lillian Mandl Black), accounted for the success of the "heavenly coffee" (Black's term). They had one child and were divorced in 1960; on 27 March 1962 Black married his third wife, Page Morton. A professional entertainer, she subsequently sang the Chock Full O'Nuts jingle and throughout their marriage assisted her husband by reading and summarizing business reports and periodical articles.

At the time Chock Full O'Nuts was expanding into the vacuum-packed and instant coffee businesses, it experienced problems regarding its hiring policies. Although justly renowned for its generous benefits package, which included health and life insurance, pensions and vacations, no-interest loans, stock options, financial incentives to discourage absenteeism, and birthday bonus holidays, the company was charged with discrimination against white workers. At the time more than 80 percent of its workers were nonwhite. (Notably, African-American former baseball star Jackie Robinson was vice president for personnel from 1957 through 1964.) In the interest of settling the reverse discrimination charges, the company acceded to the request made by the New York City Commission on Human Relations to strive for a more equitable racial balance in its staffing.

Aside from his business, to which he devoted his full attention from noon until late at night, philanthropy was the only other interest that claimed William Black's attention. When a friend and corporate officer of Chock Full O'Nuts was diagnosed with Parkinson's disease, Black established the Parkinson's Disease Foundation in 1957. The foundation, which initially received $100,000 from Black, sponsored an international symposium in March 1960. Earlier in the year Black had given Columbia University, his alma mater, $5 million, the largest gift made up to that time by an alumnus. The funds were used for the William Black Medical Research Building. In recognition of his contributions and his life achievements, Columbia University awarded Black an honorary doctorate of humane letters in 1967. Continuing his generosity to medical institutions, Black, whose estate, Bon Repos, was located on the shore of Long Island Sound in suburban New Rochelle, donated a floor to the New Rochelle Hospital and a building for the Lenox Hill Hospital nursing school in 1961. Mount Sinai Hospital's Page and William Black Postgraduate School of Medicine was also funded by William Black. In his philanthropy Black emulated steel magnate Andrew Carnegie in believing that it was incumbent upon a wealthy man to distribute his fortune during his lifetime rather than bequeath the bulk of his estate to his heirs.

At Black's death, from cancer, Chock Full O'Nuts was worth $116 million. Only months before his death, the company had fended off a takeover attempt by a group of dissident shareholders headed by Jerry Finkelstein, publisher of the *New York Law Journal* and chairman of a company that manufactured power plant equipment. Black was buried in Woodlawn Cemetery in the Bronx, New York.

To the end, William Black was a contrarian. The graduate engineer who never held a job in the field for which he was trained—but who, according to the *New York Times* (8 February 1959), derived "his biggest kicks ... supervising the construction of a restaurant, coffee plant, or bakery—" was well known for his unique approach to the challenges and opportunities that came his way. In 1955, for example, the principled Black had advocated a coffee boycott by Americans to protest what he alleged was a deliberate attempt by Latin American growers to drive up the wholesale price of coffee by withholding supplies. Even in his philanthropic activities Black's approach was unique: the sole stipulation of his $5 million gift to Columbia, for instance, had been that the interest earnings be diverted to the Parkinson's Disease Foundation until the university actually began construction of the medical building. Black remarked that he included this incentive because he wanted "to see with my own eyes the results of my good intentions."

Black was able to do just that during the last quarter century of an extremely productive life. Despite major challenges at different times, he retained his marvelous sense of humor. (His widow Page Morton Black said, "When he was really happy, he'd sing 'Too-ra-loo-ra-loo-ral.'") Vigorous, energetic, and always projecting a youthful image, Black lived to be an octogenarian.

★

A substantial biographical article about William Black appears in Charles Moritz, *Current Biography 1964* (1965). His business career is discussed in the *New York Times* (14 Apr. 1956, 8 Feb. 1959, and 4 Jan. 1960); *Time* (18 Jan. 1960); and *Nation's Restaurant News* (8 Nov. 1982 and 3 Jan. 1983). Obituaries are in the *New York Times* (8 Mar. 1983) and *Time* (21 Mar. 1983).

MARILYN E. WEIGOLD

BLACKWELL, Randolph Talmadge (*b.* 10 March 1927 in Greensboro, North Carolina; *d.* 21 May 1981 in Atlanta, Georgia), civil rights activist, architect and organizer of self-help economic development among poor African Americans, and recipient of the Martin Luther King, Jr., Nonviolent Peace Prize.

One of eight children of Joe Blackwell and Blanche Mary Donnell, Randolph Blackwell married Elizabeth Knox on 24 December 1954. They had one child, a daughter. Returning from army service in 1947, Blackwell received a bachelor's degree in sociology from the North Carolina Agricultural and Technical State University in 1949 and a law degree from Howard University in 1953. After teaching economics for a year at Alabama Agricultural and Mechanical College, he became an associate professor of social sciences at Winston-Salem State University in 1954.

Blackwell's academic interests mirrored his social and political concerns. In 1962 he left his faculty position to become field director of the Atlanta-based Voter Education Project, an organization newly formed by the major civil rights organizations to register black voters in the South. After logging many thousands of miles across the region in less than two years, helping blacks become registered voters, he joined Martin Luther King, Jr., and his Southern Christian Leadership Conference (SCLC) as program director in 1963. In 1966 he founded and became director of Southern Rural Action, Inc., a nonprofit corporation dedicated to the economic development of poor blacks in the rural South.

His work with Southern Rural Action was the fulfillment of a long-standing preoccupation with helping small, poor, and, particularly, black communities to become more self-reliant. Blackwell felt that only by developing their own cooperatives could southern black farmers free themselves from their dependence on an exploitative commercial system. He envisioned a system of small manufacturing enterprises, fueled by pooled black resources, which would serve as an anchor for black agriculture, furnishing the necessary consumer goods, supplies, and markets.

Southern Rural Action received the support of labor unions, churches, and civil rights groups. Its first chairman was Walter Reuther, then president of the United Automobile Workers. Southern Rural Action's projects over the next decade, under Blackwell's leadership, included the initiation of garment factories, silk-screen printing shops, a roof-truss factory, brick-manufacturing plants, bakeries, and other small businesses in a number of southern states. Among other projects, it constructed hundreds of homes, helped establish a public housing complex, and founded accredited schools of photography and graphic arts in Atlanta. A striking example of the accomplishments of Blackwell's Southern Rural Action occurred during the mid-1960s in Plains, Georgia, in one of the state's poorest counties. The Plains project generated two factories that produced building construction materials, as well as fifteen new houses and a community center.

Although viewed by some as a disciple of Booker T. Washington, the first great African-American exponent of black industry and enterprise, Blackwell himself was more apt to associate his brand of black self-reliance with the views of reformers and activists such as W. E. B. Du Bois, Paul Robeson, and Martin Luther King, Jr. His parents, staunch disciples of Marcus Garvey's Back-to-Africa movement, were also instrumental in molding his social philosophy. Blackwell was critical of a black capitalism that depended upon government subsidies. He believed that government money tended to create the kind of businesses that take money out of the community rather than bring it in and that government subsidies to blacks as a class would result in black people becoming a servant caste.

A lifelong Democrat, in 1977 Blackwell accepted an appointment in President Jimmy Carter's administration as director of the Office of Minority Business Enterprise in the Department of Commerce. He resigned two years later and returned to Atlanta where, until his death, he was the local director of the Commerce Department's Office of Minority Business Programs.

A close friend of Martin Luther King, Jr., Blackwell was part of the tight inner circle of the Southern Christian Leadership Conference. In addition to his involvement with the SCLC, Blackwell was a longtime member of the Urban League and the National Association for the Advancement of Colored People. He was also a member of the board of directors of the Martin Luther King Center for Social Change. In 1976 he was named winner of the Martin Luther King, Jr., Nonviolent Peace Prize.

A dark-skinned black man of powerful build and commanding personality and a talented orator with an ironic sense of humor, Blackwell was described by Congressman and United Nations ambassador Andrew Young as a "renaissance man" who, among his other talents, could recognize almost any piece of classical music upon hearing no more than a few bars.

Blackwell died of cancer and was buried in Atlanta. He was eulogized by Coretta Scott King as "one of the unsung giants of the civil rights movement." His legacy is the influence that his perspective and accomplishments continue to have on the enduring debate over the rural South as a promising American environment for black commerce and industry.

★

There is no full-scale biography of Blackwell, although he is discussed in at least two major works on the civil rights movement: David J. Garrow, *Bearing the Cross: Martin Luther King, Jr., and the Southern Christian Leadership Conference* (1986), and Taylor Branch, *Parting the Waters: America in the King Years, 1954–1963* (1988). The most comprehensive journalistic account of his work with Southern Rural Action is in *Ebony* (Jan. 1975). Obituaries are in the *Atlanta Journal Constitution* (22 May 1981) and the *New York Times* (23 May 1981). Transcripts and audiotapes of a Blackwell lecture and a discussion with Stokely Carmichael of the Student Nonviolent Coordinating Committee are housed, respectively, at Mercer University in Macon, Georgia, and Spelman College in Atlanta. This article is based to some extent on the author's personal knowledge.

JACK HANDLER

BLAKE, Eugene Carson (*b.* 7 November 1906 in St. Louis, Missouri; *d.* 31 July 1985 in Stamford, Connecticut), American Presbyterian ecumenical leader best known for social activism and efforts toward Christian unity in the 1960s.

Blake, the youngest of three children of Lulu Carson and Orville Prescott Blake, grew up in a devout Presbyterian home in St. Louis, where his father was a steel company salesman and his mother a housewife and active churchwoman. Six feet tall, broad-shouldered, and affable, Blake was educated at the Lawrenceville School in Lawrenceville, New Jersey; Princeton University (A.B., 1928), where he played on the varsity football team; New College in Edinburgh; and Princeton Theological Seminary (D.M., 1932).

Blake married Valina Gillespie on 12 September 1929, following a short period of missionary service in British India. They had no children. In 1932 they moved to New York City, where Blake began his career as assistant pastor

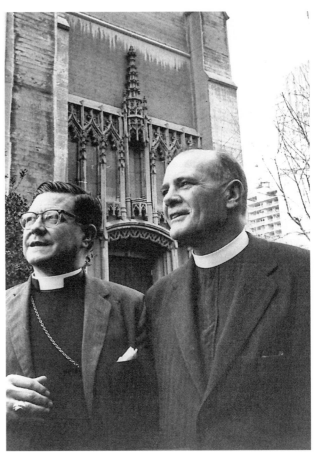

Eugene Carson Blake (*right*) with Bishop James Pike, 1960. DEPARTMENT OF HISTORY AND RECORDS MANAGEMENT SERVICES, PRESBYTERIAN CHURCH (U.S.A.) (PHILADELPHIA)

of the Collegiate Church of St. Nicholas (Reformed Church in America). In 1935 he was called to become senior minister of the First Presbyterian Church of Albany, New York, and in 1940 he moved to southern California to assume leadership of the Pasadena Presbyterian Church. During his ten years there, the Pasadena church grew to be the third largest Presbyterian congregation in the United States, with about 4,500 members.

In Pasadena, Blake emerged as an outstanding preacher and denominational leader whose theology was greatly influenced by the ideas of Reinhold Niebuhr and the neo-orthodox movement. Revealing the strong interests in social activism that would mark his later national and international career, Blake spoke out from his pulpit against racial segregation, substandard housing, and the violation of civil liberties by "loyalty" investigations.

On 29 May 1951, Blake was elected by the General Assembly of the Presbyterian Church in the U.S.A. to the office of stated clerk, the highest executive position in that denomination. During his nearly fifteen years in that post, Blake, based in Philadelphia, expanded the range of its

power and influence, and he became the dominant spokesman for American Presbyterians as well as a highly visible
leader of mainline Protestantism in general. Disturbed by
the excesses of anticommunism in the McCarthy era, in
1953 he and John McKay, president of the Princeton Seminary, issued a "Letter to Presbyterians" denouncing allegations of communist sympathies that had been made
against Protestant clergymen. They defended the right and
duty of ministers to speak out on controversial social issues.
In a 1954 *Look* magazine article, Blake warned of uncritical
patriotism in the post–World War II religious upsurge, and
in 1960 he joined other Protestant leaders in condemning
attacks on the Roman Catholic background of presidential
candidate John F. Kennedy.

Unquestionably the two most famous events of Blake's
entire career were his proposal for Protestant church union
in 1960 and his arrest during a civil rights demonstration
in 1963. Accepting an invitation from Episcopal bishop
James A. Pike to preach at Grace (Protestant Episcopal)
Cathedral in San Francisco on 4 December 1960, Blake
proposed the merger of the Presbyterian, Episcopal, Methodist, and United Church of Christ denominations as the
first step in a process of reuniting the fragmented elements
of Christianity in the United States. He spoke out of his
already extensive ecumenical experience in the National
Council of Churches of Christ in the U.S.A. (he had been
its president in the years 1954–1955), and he believed that
these four denominations possessed sufficiently common
historical and theological traditions to overcome their differences in liturgy and church governance.

The Blake-Pike proposal, as it was called (although almost entirely the work of Blake alone), generated much
public attention. It led directly to the formation in 1962 of
the Consultation on Church Union (COCU), which eventually grew to include ten Protestant denominations. For a
few years hopes were high that obstacles to organizational
unity could be overcome, but in 1966 COCU failed to adopt
a timetable for full church union. Thereafter, Blake's vision
of organic merger gradually faded.

Blake's commitment to racial justice also became more
focused and active in the 1960s. Throughout the previous
decade he had urged Presbyterians to denounce segregation
and discrimination verbally, but the sight of the brutal treatment of civil rights demonstrators in Birmingham, Alabama, in May 1963 compelled him to take direct, personal
action. On 4 July 1963 Blake joined a racially mixed group
seeking to enter the segregated (whites-only) Gwynn Oak
Amusement Park in Baltimore. He was arrested for violating Maryland's criminal trespass law, taken to a police
station to be fingerprinted, and then released on bond. He
pleaded not guilty and the charges were ultimately
dropped, but the incident reverberated widely, because

Blake was the first national Protestant executive to take
such action.

Although some Presbyterians denounced him for "dis-
gracing" their church, Blake became a hero to the many
clergy who were active in the social causes of the 1960s. In
a speech he gave at the historic March on Washington for
civil rights on 28 August 1963, Blake lamented that white
Christians had been too slow to participate in the struggle
for racial justice, stating: "We come, and late we come." He
worked to overcome that hesitancy by laboring intensively
for passage of the Civil Rights Act of 1964 and committing
Presbyterians to establish and fund an ongoing agency for
racial reconciliation.

On 11 February 1966 Blake was elected general secretary
of the World Council of Churches in Geneva, Switzerland,
a position he held until his retirement in August 1972. During those years religious leaders from Asia, Africa, and
Latin America challenged the traditional European and
North American dominance in ecumenism. The World
Council, made up of Protestant and Orthodox churches,
also began to engage more intensively with Roman Catholics on matters of common theological and social concern.
These new developments were widely manifest at the Upp-
sala (Sweden) Assembly of the World Council in July 1968.
Blake sought to bridge the racial, economic, and genera-
tional divides with more emphasis on programs to deal with
poverty, racism, and international conflict, and to open
more dialogue with other world religions.

The council's Program to Combat Racism became controversial in the early 1970s, when charges were made that
its funds were going to armed guerrilla movements in several African countries. Blake denied the accusations and
strongly defended the concept of "secular ecumenism." Another historic moment during Blake's tenure was the visit
of Pope Paul VI in June 1969, the first visit to Geneva by
a Catholic pontiff in more than 400 years.

Blake returned to the United States upon his retirement
in 1972 and, following the death of his wife Valina in 1973,
married Jean Ware Hoyt of Stamford, Connecticut, on 14
June 1974. He lived in retirement in Stamford and became
active in Bread for the World, an ecumenical organization
concerned with world hunger and poverty. He enjoyed
swimming, golf, and watching sports. He died of complications from diabetes.

Blake's ecclesiastical career was entirely in the service of
liberal, denominational, and ecumenical Protestant Christianity. The high points of his service coincided with two
significant periods: the growth in popular religious interest
and activity in the United States in the two decades after
World War II, and the social activism and ecumenical enthusiasm of the mainline churches in the 1960s. Blake remained convinced that the institutional church was the best
setting for religious life and work, but came to believe that

the various denominations needed to find ways to make their expressions of faith serve common goals and purposes. From a later perspective the settings in which Blake worked came to seem overly bureaucratic, hierarchical, and male-dominated. Blake was, however, in the context of his time, an advocate and an example of openness to change that was rooted in historic Christian belief.

★

The Eugene Carson Blake Papers are located at the Presbyterian Historical Society in Philadelphia and the Archives of the World Council of Churches in Geneva. The most complete biography is R. Douglas Brackenridge, *Eugene Carson Blake: Prophet with Portfolio* (1978), which is based partly on the author's personal interviews with Blake. Various aspects of Blake's career are covered in Norman Goodall, *Ecumenical Progress: A Decade of Change in the Ecumenical Movement, 1961–1971* (1972); Harvey G. Cox, "The 'New Breed' in American Churches: Sources of Social Activism in American Religion," *Daedalus* 96 (winter 1967): 135–150; and Paul A. Crow, Jr., "Ecumenism and the Consultation on Church Union," *Journal of Ecumenical Studies* 4 (fall 1967): 581–602. An obituary is in the *New York Times* (1 Aug. 1985).

JOHN B. WEAVER

BLAKE, James Hubert ("Eubie") (*b.* 7 February 1883 in Baltimore, Maryland; *d.* 12 February 1983 in Brooklyn, New York), ragtime pianist and composer known for his partnership with Noble Sissle; during the ragtime revival of the 1960s he enjoyed renewed attention and embarked on a second career.

James Hubert Blake's parents, John Sumner Blake and Emily Johnson, were former slaves. Blake's father, who celebrated his fiftieth birthday the day Eubie was born, was a dockworker, and his mother supplemented the family income by working as a domestic helper. Eubie was the eleventh child born to the couple and the only one to survive infancy.

Blake's talent for music was first noticed at age six when he played an organ in a music store. Although John Blake was earning just $9 a week as a stevedore, Emily found a way to buy an organ and pay for music lessons for the boy. Eubie's mother raised him in a strict religious home, but it was only a matter of time until the boy discovered ragtime. The infectious syncopated rhythms of this music ended his interest in classical music, the focus of his organ lessons.

Small for his age, Eubie was known in the neighborhood as "Mouse." To survive, he had to learn to fight. His formal education ended in the eighth grade, when he was expelled from school for fighting over a girl. By the time he was fifteen, he was secretly working nights playing ragtime music in a local bordello. Blake decided that the piano could be his way out of the life of poverty and physical labor experienced by his family. When the secret got out, John Blake found that his son was making more than the rest of the family combined (Eubie had hidden hundreds of dollars under a carpet), so he gave the boy his blessing. Blake composed his first piece of music during this period. Initially named "Sounds of Africa," it was transcribed years later and published as "The Charleston Rag."

Blake spent his late teens building a reputation in Baltimore. His quiet charm, seemingly endless repertoire, and talent for improvisation thrilled audiences. Now known by the nickname Professor, he joined a touring company in 1902 and performed in New York City for the first time, working as a buck dancer. By 1907 he was playing the Goldfield Hotel, a new and elegant Baltimore nightspot. Three years later he married Avis Lee, a school acquaintance.

On 16 May 1915 Blake met Noble Sissle, a talented and well-educated black singer and lyricist. The two started a partnership that would last for decades. Within days they had written a song that was picked up by the singer Sophie Tucker for her vaudeville act. In 1916 Blake and Sissle joined James Reese Europe's Society Orchestra in New York. The mild-mannered Europe had quietly opened doors for black entertainers to play at wealthy society parties in Long Island, New York, and Newport, Rhode Island. Blake later said of Europe: "To colored musicians he was as important—he did as much for them as Martin Luther King did for the rest of the Negro people. He set up a way for them to get jobs . . . and he made them get paid more."

When the United States entered World War I, Blake was too old to join Sissle and Europe in the army, where they served in a military band entertaining near the trenches of the western front in France. Meantime, Blake found a new partner, Broadway Jones, and played the vaudeville circuit. Blake later remembered Jones for his finely polished performance and wardrobe—he was never seen in the same suit twice.

Shortly after Sissle and Europe came home from the war, Europe was killed in a dispute with a band member. Reunited as the Dixie Duo, Sissle and Blake made a long, successful vaudeville run, starting at the famed Palace Theater in New York City. They were proud that they could succeed with white audiences without resorting to the caricature that many black performers had previously used to gain acceptance.

The duo started working with another pair of African-American entertainers, Aubrey Lyles and Flournoy Miller, to create one of the first black-oriented Broadway musicals, *Shuffle Along*. Lyles and Miller wrote the book, Sissle wrote the lyrics, and Blake composed the music for the low-

Eubie Blake (*piano*) and Noble Sissle (*vocals*), 1926. FRANK DRIGGS COLLECTION/ARCHIVE PHOTOS

budget play. It opened on 23 May 1921 at the 63rd Street Theater in Manhattan and was an immediate hit, running for more than 500 performances. One measure of the show's influence was that it gave early exposure to such performers as Paul Robeson and Josephine Baker. One of its hit songs, "I'm Just Wild About Harry," became Harry Truman's theme song for his 1948 presidential campaign. Another hit from the show, "You Were Meant for Me," was adapted for the play *London Calling,* starring Gertrude Lawrence and Noël Coward.

Blake and Sissle eventually took *Shuffle Along* on the road for a very profitable run. The pair wrote another musical, *In Bamville* (later renamed *Chocolate Dandies*), which opened in 1924, shortly after *Shuffle Along* closed. While Blake thought this was the better work, audiences disagreed, and the show lost money.

Blake and Sissle revived their vaudeville act and took it on a European tour in 1925, playing the British Isles and France. Blake turned down additional projects in England because he was anxious to return to America. By 1927 Sissle became attracted by the more favorable climate for black entertainers in Europe, so he returned there without Blake, who suspected that Sissle's wife was pushing him to go solo. That same year, Blake's mother died. She had lived to see her son become a huge success but was never comfortable with his career.

After Sissle left, Blake worked with touring companies of *Shuffle Along,* with Broadway musicals, and with several short musical films for Warner Brothers. During this period, Blake teamed with lyricist Andy Razaf for several of his best-known songs, including "Memories of You." In 1932 Sissle returned to America, and the partnership resumed. The next year Blake and Sissle wrote *Shuffle Along of 1933,* but the new show fell victim to the Depression economy within weeks. They shortened the play and took it on the road, playing it as a supplement to movies, but it was still unsuccessful.

In 1938 Blake's wife's health started to deteriorate. When she died the next year, Blake was inconsolable. He kept active in show business, writing music with lyricist Joshua Milton Reddie for Works Progress Administration–sponsored musicals in the late 1930s. "Reddie was the best lyricist I ever worked with," Blake later recalled. He also conducted United Service Organizations (USO) shows for the troops during World War II.

At the end of his USO days, Blake met Marion Gant Tyler, a wealthy executive whose husband had recently died. They married on 27 December 1945 and moved into her Brooklyn brownstone. As Blake described it: "I got the coop with the chicken." In 1946, at the age of sixty-three, he enrolled at New York University (NYU) to study the Schillinger method of composition. He completed the degree program in two and a half years, graduating in 1949. He would return to NYU in later years as a teacher. In 1952 he worked on an updated version of *Shuffle Along,* but it failed after only four performances.

Blake seemed destined to spend the rest of his life in a prosperous and quiet retirement. However, in the 1960s there was a revived interest in ragtime music. Blake was the surviving giant of the field, and he rode the wave to a new level of adulation. In 1965 he and Sissle were honored by the American Society of Composers, Authors, and Publishers at a major event at Town Hall in New York. Two years later, Eubie was invited to the Ragfest exposition in St. Louis. The eighty-four-year-old pianist electrified the audience with an energetic and technically perfect performance. His success was attributed to his long, slim fingers that had not slowed with age.

In 1969 the record producer John Hammond commissioned Blake to record a two-album set of music that encompassed his entire career. Even at age ninety Blake was making up to forty appearances a year, including his first visit to the *Tonight Show*. His longevity could not be attributed to healthy habits. His diet was notoriously driven by a sweet tooth, he smoked heavily all his life, and he shunned exercise. His consumption of alcohol, however, was always considered moderate.

In 1975 Noble Sissle died. Blake continued as a solo act and performed until he was ninety-nine years old, playing "Memories of You" at a birthday concert in Rochester, New York. His last concert was on 19 June 1982. On his hundredth birthday, friends threw a concert/party at the Shubert Theater in New York City, but Blake was recovering from pneumonia and was unable to attend. He did, however, speak to the gathering through a telephone hookup. Five days later, he died. He had lived most of the history of ragtime music and helped to keep it alive for new generations of music lovers.

★

Two important books about Blake are Al Rose, *Eubie Blake* (1979), and Robert Kimball and William Bolcom, *Reminiscing with Sissle and Blake* (1973). Blake also figures in Rudi Blesh and Harriet Janis, *They All Played Ragtime* (1971), and Edward A. Berlin, *Ragtime: A Musical and Cultural History* (1980). An obituary is in the *New York Times* (13 Feb. 1983).

TERRY BALLARD

BLISS, Ray Charles (*b.* 16 December 1907 in Akron, Ohio; *d.* 6 August 1981 in Akron, Ohio), Ohio Republican party leader who served as chairman of the Republican National Committee from 1965 to 1969 and modernized its tactics for the media age.

Bliss was the sole surviving child of German immigrants, Emil Bliss and Emilie Wieland. In 1932 his father, an electrical worker, was killed in an explosion at the Ohio State Office Building. The ensuing strong bond that Bliss developed with his mother, a housewife, resulted in his maintaining his principal residence with her until her death in 1956.

After graduating from South High School in 1925, Bliss

Ray Charles Bliss. COURTESY OF THE RAY C. BLISS INSTITUTE OF APPLIED POLITICS, UNIVERSITY OF AKRON. PHOTO BY OTTO GANGLE.

enrolled in the University of Akron, where he discovered his talent for political organizing. He joined the Phi Kappa Tau fraternity, determined to build it into a political force at the university.

In 1931, when Ellen Palmer, his future wife, was a May Queen candidate, Bliss organized his fraternity brothers to solicit the absentee ballots of students who lived off campus. When it was discovered that these ballots, submitted in envelopes labeled by Bliss, were forged, he stepped forward to accept the blame, though no evidence connected him with the wrongdoing. Bliss was expelled from the university. In 1935 the university repealed his expulsion and granted him a baccalaureate degree. From 1933 to 1937 he was secretary-treasurer of Wells and Bliss.

In 1931 Bliss was a volunteer in the Akron mayoral election. He worked under Republican leader James A. Corey, an old-style operator who tutored him in precinct politics. He gained useful insights into public opinion by going door-to-door and by talking with bartenders and their patrons in establishments throughout the city. Later Bliss would pioneer in the use of professionally prepared and executed public opinion surveys. In 1932 he became the youngest Republican precinct committee member (a position he held until 1978); a member of the Summit County (Akron) GOP Executive Committee (until 1981); and a delegate to the state Republican convention (until 1978). In 1944 Bliss served as chairman of the state Platform Committee, and from May 1941 to May 1964 was the chairman of the Summit County Republican Central Committee. From December 1935 to December 1978 he was a member of the Summit County Board of Elections, and its chair in the years 1945–1946 and 1949–1950.

Having turned in 1947 to full-time involvement with his newly formed Akron insurance and real-estate firm, Tower Agencies, Bliss sat out the 1948 elections. Ohio went for Democratic president Harry Truman that year; the Republicans lost all their statewide campaigns and control of the state legislature. Aware of Bliss's past electoral successes in Akron, Senator Robert A. Taft, looking toward his impending reelection campaign, persuaded Bliss to reenter full-time public life in 1949 as chairman of the Ohio Republican party; Bliss held that post until April 1965 and also was a member of its Central and Executive Committee from 1944 to 1974.

Appreciating that political power flows from the control of money, Bliss maximized Republican ties with business contributors and centralized fund-raising. He funneled funds to local party committees and campaigns, ran training sessions for party workers in campaign techniques like handling the media and polling, and sent "field workers" into targeted races. Through meticulous planning and hardheaded political choices, Bliss consistently won electoral victories and earned a nationwide reputation. The results showed early: Taft won a major victory in 1950 through Bliss's use of television as an electoral tool; the Republicans won every state office except the governorship and gained control of both houses of the state legislature.

Working out of offices in the Deshler Hotel in downtown Columbus, Bliss eschewed a public role as party leader, being instead a "nuts and bolts" organizer, an "office chairman." This style seemed to accord well with his shyness, which perhaps was related to a slight speech impediment, lack of a good speaking voice, and poor eyesight that made it difficult for him to recognize faces easily. In marked contrast to his public awkwardness, his sense of humor and personal honesty endeared him to his political counterparts, who knew he wasn't a "puff-up." Round-faced, stocky, 175 pounds and five foot seven, and a chain-smoker who liked popcorn and worked long hours, the earnest Bliss engaged in an endless round of nervous phone calls and meetings.

Believing that the party organization could provide only about 40 percent of the votes needed to win, Bliss strengthened the Ohio GOP's women's division; he also appreciated the importance of middle-class volunteers and urged candidates to build campaigns and use "supplemental organizations" to reach specific constituent groups, independents, and Democrats. His political advertising programs produced 3 million pieces of literature in a typical

campaign, along with billboards, television ads, and slogans. His *Republican News,* the Ohio GOP newspaper, was the largest-circulation political weekly in the United States.

Though Bliss called himself a fiscal conservative, his desire to win in a state with large urban centers and many African-American, union, and ethnic voters made him keenly aware that the GOP needed to project a moderate or even liberal image. Thus he argued vehemently, though unsuccessfully, against placing a business-backed right-to-work referendum on the Ohio ballot in 1958. On 26 November 1959, Bliss finally married Ellen Palmer. They had no children.

Bliss had backed Richard Nixon during the 1952 "slush-fund" controversy and was an adviser to Nixon at the 1960 party convention. He urged Nixon to negotiate with New York governor Nelson A. Rockefeller over the platform, a move that angered party conservatives. Bliss's prowess was recognized during Nixon's 1960 presidential race; Ohio was the only state in which the state GOP ran Nixon's campaign. Through tight coordination of Nixon volunteers with party regulars and effective use of polling, Bliss pulled off Nixon's only win in a northern industrial state, further embellishing his national reputation.

After analyzing the 1960 vote Bliss became convinced that Nixon lost because too few urban Republicans turned up at the polls. This analysis served as the core of the 1961–1962 *Report on Big City Politics* produced for the Republican National Committee (RNC). Bliss was its principal author and chair of the subcommittee that produced it.

In the early 1960s Bliss refused several offers to serve as national Republican chair that came from both the party's moderate/liberal wing and from Senator Barry Goldwater of Arizona, the leader of the party's ideological right wing. Although Goldwater and Bliss had a long-standing friendship, Bliss did not support Goldwater's 1964 Republican presidential nomination because he didn't think he would win the general election. Bliss explained, "I'm to the right of Goldwater but I know you can't win on those types of issues. I was pragmatic about winning."

After Goldwater's electoral debacle, which left the GOP holding only 17 governorships, 32 Senate seats, and 141 House seats (a 38-seat loss), the party's moderate/liberal wing and even some conservatives and major backers of Goldwater pushed for the ouster of Dean Burch, Goldwater's former Senate aide who had become RNC chair in July 1964. Midwestern conservatives, who held the balance of power between the party's southern and western right wing and its "Eastern establishment," aided by former president Dwight Eisenhower and Nixon, convinced a reluctant Goldwater to replace Burch with Bliss. At the January 1965 RNC meeting Bliss was elected unanimously.

Bliss took over a bankrupt and disorganized national office in the Cafritz Office Building in Washington. During his four years at the RNC, he and his wife lived in an apartment at 4101 Cathedral Avenue, N.W. Bliss turned the national headquarters into a full-service center for state and local Republican party committees, aimed at "basement-up" party rebuilding. Using the Goldwater campaign's small-donor lists, he expanded the direct-mail program begun in 1962. He persuaded General Lucius D. Clay, an "Eastern establishment" figure, to head big-donor appeals.

To unify the various wings of the party, Bliss took up Representative Melvin Laird's suggestion to create the Republican Coordinating Committee. Its numerous position papers served as the basis of the GOP 1968 national platform. He led a party renewal measured by Republican gains of the White House, fourteen governorships, eleven Senate seats, and fifty-two House seats.

Ironically, Bliss's masterful orchestration of the 1968 GOP convention that nominated Richard Nixon was repaid with his ouster by President Nixon in 1969. Bliss's neutrality during the jockeying for the nomination had angered Nixon. Bliss had misgivings about Nixon's victory and his own contribution to it. He told his wife the day after the 1968 election, "I don't know whether I've done the country a service or a disservice."

Rejecting Nixon's offer of the ambassadorship to Denmark, Bliss moved with his wife to 2535 Addyston Road, Akron, and took over full-time management of Tower Agencies as its president. From 1970 until his death Bliss served on committees of the University of Akron (UA) and was its board of trustees' vice chairman from 1971 to 1981 and chairman in 1981. The university conferred the UA Alumni Honor Award in 1965 and a Doctor of Humane Letters degree in 1968. Bliss was an Episcopalian.

Bliss suffered a fatal heart attack at his Tower Agencies offices; he was buried at Mount Peace Cemetery in Akron. In 1986 the University of Akron established the Ray C. Bliss Institute of Applied Politics, to which his estate contributed funds.

As the Republican party rebuilt itself after the Watergate scandal, RNC chairman Bill Brock identified Bliss's organization-building, party modernization, and fund-raising as his model; in particular, Bliss's early and astute use of polling, television advertising, campaign training programs, national party assistance to local and state parties and candidates, and direct-mail solicitation of small donors were crucial. Though identifying himself as against "big government" and as a conservative on taxation and government spending, Bliss exemplified a centrist brand of politics, believing that in general a flexible, pragmatic, and moderate stance on issues and an avoidance of ideological polarization would elect Republican candidates. He conceived of the Republican party as a big tent accommodating a broad spectrum of views.

★

Ray C. Bliss Papers, MSS 768, Ohio Historical Society, is a rich collection containing many important documents related to national Republican politics. Ray C. Bliss, "The Role of the State Chairman," in James M. Cannon, ed., *Politics U.S.A.: A Practical Guide to the Winning of Public Office* (1960), is a useful spelling out of Bliss's approach to political and campaign organizing. Stephen Hess and David S. Broder, *The Republican Establishment: The Present and Future of the G.O.P.* (1967), a useful party history, describes Bliss and explains his importance in intraparty battles and politics. John C. Green, ed., *Politics, Professionalism, and Power: Modern Party Organization and the Legacy of Ray C. Bliss* (1994), based on papers given at a conference, constitutes a rich source on Bliss's life and the context in which he operated; it includes articles by people who worked with Bliss and extensive bibliographies. *New York Times* (13 Jan. 1965) announces Bliss's ascension to RNC chairman on p. 1 and has a profile on p. 38. David S. Broder, "Bliss Rides the Elephant," *New York Times Magazine* (21 Mar. 1965): 49–60, is an essential source. Alan L. Otten and Charles B. Seib, "The Minor Masterpiece of Ray C. Bliss," *The Reporter* (10 Feb. 1966): 35–38, is a generally positive assessment of Bliss's performance. Gene Jordan, "GOP's Ray Bliss Easing Out of Politics," *Columbus Dispatch Magazine* (6 July 1980): 6 ff., is an overview of Bliss's career. William Hershey, "The Party's Not Over," (Akron) *Beacon Journal* magazine (7 June 1981): 4–6, 10, 14, 16, includes extensive quotes, many details, and a comprehensive listing of Bliss's political posts. Obituaries and tributes are in the *New York Times* (7 Aug. 1981) and the *Washington Post* (12 Aug. 1981).

MARJORIE FREEMAN HARRISON

BLOCH, Felix (*b.* 23 October 1905 in Zurich, Switzerland; *d.* 10 September 1983 in Zurich, Switzerland), physicist, educator, and scientific administrator who shared the Nobel Prize in physics in 1952 (with Edward Mills Purcell) for the development of techniques for measuring the magnetic characteristics of atomic nuclei; his extensive theoretical and experimental research led to the important medical diagnostic system now known as MRI (magnetic resonance imaging).

Bloch was the son of Gustav Bloch, a wholesale grain merchant, and Agnes Mayer, a housewife. They were Jews of moderate to upper-middle-class economic means.

Bloch's interest and ability in scientific subjects, particularly astronomy and mathematics, were manifested at an early age, especially while attending the cantonal gymnasium of Zurich. (The curriculum was approximately equivalent to that of an American high school, supplemented with some undergraduate college work.) After completing his gymnasium studies in 1924, Bloch matriculated at the Federal Institute of Technology in Zurich (sometimes re-

Felix Bloch. RICE UNIVERSITY ARCHIVES, WOODSON RESEARCH CENTER, RICE UNIVERSITY LIBRARY, HOUSTON, TEXAS

ferred to in history-of-science literature by its German abbreviation ETH, for Eidgenossiche Technische Hochschule). The ETH was known for its educational excellence, distinguished faculty, and famous graduates.

Initially persuaded by his father's practical orientation to enroll as an engineering student, Bloch soon found his true career path through the introductory course in modern physics taught by Peter Debye. Bloch completed his work in the Division of Mathematics and Physics in 1927. At the urging of Debye, he enrolled that year at the University of Leipzig. He became the first graduate student of twenty-six-year-old Werner Heisenberg, newly appointed professor of theoretical physics.

With Heisenberg's encouragement, Bloch expanded some earlier work of Heisenberg relating to the radiation damping of electromagnetic wave packets. Bloch's first published paper, "Radiation Damping in Quantum Mechanics" (1928), made clear his firm grasp of the revolutionary applications of the new physics.

With Heisenberg as his adviser, Bloch continued work on the applications of quantum mechanics to solid-state physics. This became the basis of his Ph.D. dissertation

(1928): "Quantum Mechanics of Electrons in Crystal Lattices." Its publication resulted in his recognition as a theoretician of exceptional promise.

After receiving his Ph.D., Bloch returned to the Federal Institute of Technology in Zurich as a postgraduate assistant to Wolfgang Pauli, who had just been appointed professor of theoretical physics. Pauli enlisted Bloch to work on superconductivity, the vanishing of electrical resistance at temperatures approaching absolute zero. Bloch made decisive theoretical contributions in this area. Also while with Pauli he worked on aspects of the ferromagnetic behavior of free electrons.

In 1929 Bloch received a Lorentz Fund Fellowship at the University of Utrecht, where he continued research involving the temperature dependence of electrical resistance, ferromagnetism, and further theoretical applications of quantum mechanics.

In 1930 Heisenberg invited Bloch to return to the University of Leipzig. There Bloch pursued his work in ferromagnetism. This research formed the basis for his *Habilitationsschrift,* a dissertation that would enable him eventually to qualify for a professorship in a German university.

Bloch spent part of 1931 with Niels Bohr at Bohr's research institute in Copenhagen. This initial acquaintance led to a close friendship and frequent contacts between Bloch and Bohr until the latter died in 1962.

When Adolf Hitler became chancellor of Germany in January 1933, Bloch, who had returned to Leipzig as Heisenberg's assistant in 1932, realized that despite his growing scientific distinction, his professional life in Germany, like that of many other outstanding Jewish scientists, was over.

Bloch left Germany in 1933 and spent some time in Switzerland and France. He applied for and received a Rockefeller Fellowship, which enabled him to work with the physicist Enrico Fermi at the University of Rome. A remark by Fermi in 1933 to the then pure theoretician Bloch was acted upon with fruitful consistency by Bloch in his subsequent career. Fermi's suggestion, as reported later by Bloch was: "You really should start to do some experiments. They are fun!"

In 1934 Bloch accepted an appointment as associate professor of physics at Stanford University, where he remained until his retirement in 1971, with the exception of research between 1942 and 1945 at Los Alamos, New Mexico, in connection with the Manhattan Project atomic bomb development, and at Harvard University, where he worked on radar-related projects.

At Stanford, Bloch was promoted to professor in 1936. His activities there were varied, including work on gaseous discharges and X rays. With Arnold Nordsieck he wrote an important paper addressing the infrared catastrophe, one of the early unsolved problems of late-nineteenth-century classical physics; its resolution was part of the development of modern atomic theory.

However, Bloch's most vital work was in the field of nuclear magnetism, which began with his interest in the neutron. Experiments in 1933 by Otto Stern suggested that although it has no electrical charge, the neutron, surprisingly, has magnetic properties. In 1939, the year Bloch became a U.S. citizen, he and Luis W. Alvarez of the University of California at Berkeley measured the magnetic moment of the neutron, using Berkeley's cyclotron as a neutron source. In 1946 Bloch, applying advanced techniques learned while doing radar work during World War II, worked out a highly precise method for measuring nuclear magnetic moments. For this work he was awarded the Nobel Prize in 1952.

Essentially this technique depends on the magnetic moment of an atomic nucleus experiencing precession in a magnetic field, similar to the wobbling of a rotating top in a gravitational field. The frequency of nuclear precession which can be measured is a function of the strength of the magnetic field, and from these parameters the magnetic moment of the atomic nucleus can be calculated. The basic overall technique for achieving the desired measurement is known as nuclear magnetic resonance (NMR). NMR methods have had extensive applications in radio astronomy, analytic chemistry, and diagnosis of physiological disorders in devices known as magnetic resonance imaging (MRI).

In 1954 Bloch became the first director general of CERN (Conseil Européen de la Recherche Nucléaire; the European Commission for Nuclear Research), a multinational organization for both pure and applied physics research in Geneva, Switzerland. By virtue of his broad experience in both theoretical and experimental physics and his friendship with numerous first-rank scientists, Bloch was an excellent choice for a position he did not seek and, in fact, strenuously opposed accepting. Only the determined insistence of Bohr and Heisenberg persuaded him to take up this important administrative challenge.

Bloch made it clear that he was going to pursue his own scientific research at CERN as a working physicist, and that he would continue as executive head only until a suitable successor was found. CERN's subsequent success can be attributed in part to Bloch's vigorous stewardship during his tenure from April 1954 to September 1955.

Upon his return to Stanford, Bloch continued his work on the applications of what he called "nuclear induction" and what his co-Nobelist Edward Purcell designated "nuclear magnetic resonance absorption." A three-sentence summary of Bloch's most important scientific work was given in the presentation speech by a member of the Nobel Committee:

Since each kind of atom and its isotopes have a sharply defined and characteristic nuclear frequency, we can in any object placed between the poles of an electromagnet seek out and examine with radio waves all the various kinds of atoms and isotopes in question, and, which is the essential point, this without in any perceptible way affecting the same, its form, crystalline structure, etc. This form of analysis in situ is therefore probably not parallelled in any other known methods of analysis. Its extraordinary sensitiveness also makes it particularly well-adapted as a micro-method in many scientific and technical fields.

Bloch's influence extended well beyond his eighty published scientific papers. In 1948 he was elected to the (U.S.) National Academy of Sciences, and he became president of the American Physical Society in 1965. In 1961 he was named to the Max H. Stein endowed chair of physics. Among his numerous honors were honorary degrees from the University of Grenoble, the Hebrew University of Jerusalem, Brandeis University, and the University of Pavia, Italy. He was elected an honorary fellow of the Weizmann Institute of Science in 1958, an honorary member of the Royal Dutch Academy of Sciences in 1965, and a fellow of the Royal Society of Edinburgh in 1966.

On 14 March 1940 Bloch married Lore C. Misch, daughter of a professor and herself a physicist; they had three sons and one daughter. Among Bloch's interests were skiing, mountaineering, and music.

After his retirement from Stanford in 1971, Bloch returned to Zurich, where he died of a heart attack.

★

Papers by Bloch include "Radiation Damping in Quantum Mechanics," *Physikalische Zeitschrift* 29 (1928): 58 (in German); "Quantum Mechanics of Electrons in Crystal Lattices," *Zeitschrift für Physik* 52, nos. 7–8 (1928): 555 (in German); "Theory of Ferromagnetism," *Zeitschrift für Physik* 61, nos. 3–4 (1930): 206 (in German); "Mechanism of Unimolecular Electron Capture," *Physical Review* 48 (1935): 689, written with Norris E. Bradbury; "Radiation Field of the Electron," *Physical Review* 52 (1937): 54, written with Arnold Nordsieck; "Radar Reflections from Long Conductors," *Journal of Applied Physics* 17 (1946): 1015; "Relative Nuclear Moments of H^1 and H^2," *Physical Review* 72 (1947): 1125, letter written with E. C. Levinthal and M. E. Packard; "The Principle of Nuclear Induction," in *Nobel Lectures: Physics, 1942–1962* (1964), his Nobel lecture of 11 Dec. 1952; "Dynamical Theory of Nuclear Induction, II," *Physical Review* 102 (1956): 104. M. Chodorow, R. Hofstadter, and H. E. Rorschach, eds., *Felix Bloch and Twentieth Century Physics* (1980), is a compilation of fifteen papers by colleagues, former students, and other physicists. An obituary is in the *New York Times* (12 Sept. 1983).

LEONARD R. SOLON

BLOOD, Johnny. See McNally, John Victor.

BLOUGH, Roger Miles (*b*. 19 January 1904 in Riverside, Pennsylvania; *d*. 8 October 1985 in Hawley, Pennsylvania), lawyer and businessman who was chairman and chief executive officer of the U.S. Steel Corporation from 1955 to 1969.

Roger Blough (pronounced to rhyme with "plow") was born in a small town in eastern Pennsylvania, the fifth of seven children of Christian Emanuel Blough and Viola Nancy Hoffman Blough. Blough's father was a truck farmer and greenhouse operator, and his mother was a nurse. Like many people raised in farming communities, Blough lived a life shaped by close family ties, religion (his family was Lutheran), and hard work. Blough's parents had little extra money, and so at first he planned to stay in school only through the eighth grade. His academic performance so impressed Blough's teachers, however, that they persuaded him to continue his education, which he did by working his way through Susquehanna Academy and then

Roger Blough, 1963. ARCHIVE PHOTOS

Susquehanna University, both located in nearby Selinsgrove, Pennsylvania.

After graduating from college with an A.B. degree in 1925, Blough found a job as a basketball coach and teacher of mathematics and science in the public schools of Hawley, Pennsylvania, a small town in the state's northeast corner. During his three years as a schoolteacher, Blough considered entering a seminary for training as a Lutheran minister. Helping to change his mind was his courtship of Helen Decker, a domestic-science teacher in the Hawley schools. Her father was Hawley's leading lawyer, and his example, along with a desire to provide appropriately for Helen, seems to have persuaded Blough to pursue a career in law instead. He and Helen were married on 13 June 1928, shortly before he enrolled at Yale Law School. They later had two daughters.

Blough compiled a distinguished record in law school, where he became an editor of the *Yale Law Journal* and graduated with honors in June 1931. Even more impressive, Blough managed to land a job during the depths of the Great Depression at one of the leading New York City law firms, White & Case. His strong law school record gained him a job interview there, but his clean-cut and imposing appearance (he was just under six feet tall) and modest, soft-spoken manner convinced the firm to hire him.

Soon after Blough began practicing law, Irving S. Olds, a partner in White & Case who represented its client U.S. Steel, noticed Blough's analytical mind and began to mentor him. Blough first became heavily involved with U.S. Steel's affairs in 1939 and 1940, when he worked with its lawyers to defend the company from a congressional committee that was investigating monopolistic practices in U.S. industry. When Olds left White & Case in 1940 to become U.S. Steel's chief executive officer, Blough soon followed, moving to Pittsburgh. In 1942 he was appointed U.S. Steel's solicitor general (chief trial lawyer), a job that gave him a bird's-eye view of the company's vast and complex workings and facilitated his rise through the ranks there. In 1949 he prepared U.S. Steel president Benjamin Fairless to testify before another congressional investigating committee. Impressed, Fairless helped secure Blough's promotion in 1951 to executive vice president and secretary. When Fairless became chairman and chief executive officer the following year, Blough was named vice chairman. When Fairless retired on 8 May 1955, Blough succeeded him.

Blough's fourteen years as chief executive at U.S. Steel were dominated by a single, albeit very complicated, problem: maintaining the firm's competitiveness in a time of increasing technological innovation and foreign competition. Accomplishing this goal involved reducing the number of jobs for steelworkers, as machines replaced some of them, and slowing the growth in wages of those workers who remained. Although the cuts were necessary because of the technological advantages and lower labor costs of foreign competitors, Blough failed to develop a consensus for these policies with the leaders of the powerful United Steelworkers of America union, which represented U.S. Steel's blue-collar employees. Blough, who evidently believed that the union would never agree to such changes, tried instead to impose them unilaterally, a policy that led directly to a 116-day industry-wide steel strike in 1959, the biggest single industrial disturbance in U.S. history.

When that approach failed to yield sufficient concessions, Blough continued to press for job cuts and wage restraint while authorizing steel-price increases, a policy that led to a major confrontation with the Kennedy administration in the spring of 1962. Determined to hold down prices as well as wages, and in that way maintain U.S. industry's competitiveness, President John F. Kennedy induced the leaders of the United Steelworkers of America to sign a new contract in March 1962 that provided small wage increases in return for what he and union leaders believed was Blough's agreement to keep steel prices stable. When Blough appeared at the White House on 10 April to announce a $6-a-ton increase in steel prices, Kennedy felt betrayed and over the next three days publicly condemned Blough and deployed the full weight of the presidency to reverse Blough's decision. Although successful in persuading Blough to back down, the highly publicized confrontation strained business-government relations and produced no lasting change in the pricing policy of U.S. Steel. Over the next eighteen months, the firm gradually restored the increase to which Kennedy had objected.

This strong union and government opposition to Blough's initiatives during his final seven years as U.S. Steel chairman led to major changes in the firm's policies. Unable to get what he believed was necessary in terms of job cuts and wage restraint, Blough pushed the firm to diversify into other kinds of businesses· and to enter into joint ventures with foreign firms to make steel abroad. These changes succeeded in keeping U.S. Steel prosperous but led to a severe decline in the domestic steel industry during the 1970s and 1980s. By that point Blough had returned to White & Case, following his retirement from U.S. Steel in 1969, where he practiced law part-time until his death from heart failure. He was buried in Hawley.

Blough led one of the most important American corporations during a period of great change in the nation's economy and in so doing became one of the most influential business leaders of his time. Thanks to his extraordinary understanding of the steel industry's workings, he was able to perceive earlier than many others the major challenges U.S. industry and Americans more generally faced from technological innovation and foreign competition. An effective consensus builder for change within the business community, he proved, however, much less of one outside it.

★

See Blough's three books: *Free Man and the Corporation* (1959), which gives his views on the problems faced by U.S. business in the late 1950s; *Government Wage-Price Guideposts in the American Economy,* with George Meany and Neil H. Jacoby (1967); and *The Washington Embrace of Business* (1975), which contains Blough's explanation of his clash with the Kennedy administration. See, too, "Big Steel's New Top Man Has Job Cut Out," *Business Week* (7 May 1955); "Filling Big Steel's Big Job," *Newsweek* (16 May 1955); "U.S. Steel's Young New Chairman: He Believes in Change," *Fortune* (Jan. 1956); "Calling the Next Turn on Inflation," *U.S. News & World Report* (25 May 1959); "Man of Steel," *Time* (20 July 1959); and "Executive of the Year," *Dun's Review and Modern Industry* (Jan. 1962). An obituary is in the *New York Times* (10 Oct. 1985).

DAVID L. STEBENNE

BONI, Albert (*b.* 21 October 1892 in New York City; *d.* 31 July 1981 in Ormond Beach, Florida), a creative and occasionally controversial publisher who was an early and persistent champion of low-cost books and a pioneer in the use of microforms as commercial publishing media.

One of two sons of Charles Boni, an insurance executive, and Bertha Seltzer, Boni was brought up in Newark, New Jersey. He graduated from Barringer High School in 1909 and attended Cornell University in the 1909–1910 academic year, then attended Harvard from 1910 to 1912. Instead of returning to Harvard for his senior year in 1913 he borrowed money from his father and, with his brother, Charles, opened the Washington Square Book Shop at 137 MacDougal Street in Manhattan, which became a favorite gathering place for Greenwich Village literati. In the same year he published his first book, *Not Guilty,* by Robert Blatchford, of which 60,000 copies were sold. The brothers also published a poetry journal, *The Glebe,* edited by Alfred Kreymborg, which lasted a year (1913–1914). Another early Boni publishing venture, in a 1915 partnership with Harry Scherman (later founder of the Book-of-the-Month Club), was the Little Leather Library series, consisting of thirty tiny volumes (three inches wide and four inches high) bound in artificial leather, of selections from the works of Emerson, Kipling, Shakespeare, Shaw, and Dostoevsky. The books were initially distributed as premiums with Whitman's Samplers chocolates, then sold in Woolworth five-and-ten-cent stores, where sales approached a million copies. Another significant event at the bookstore, reflecting Boni's strong interest in the theater, was the formation, with Lawrence Langner and Lee Simonson, of the Washington

Albert Boni. CURCHACK-KARAYJIAN

Square Players, from which the Theatre Guild was descended in 1919.

In the spring of 1917 he joined Horace Liveright in establishing the firm of Boni and Liveright, which, he later recalled, published over a hundred titles during the years in which he was an active partner. Many of these were in the compact duodecimo format of the Modern Library of the World's Best Books, which originally sold for sixty cents each. The Boni and Liveright trade list included works of Oscar Wilde, Thornton Wilder, Rudyard Kipling, H. G. Wells, and H. L. Mencken, as well as Boni's own *Modern Book of French Verse in English Translations* (1920). In July 1918, after several disagreements, the partners decided to toss a coin to see who would buy the other out. Boni lost, and Liveright became the majority stockholder. Boni sold his interest to Liveright several months later, although Boni's uncle, Thomas Seltzer, who had been a member of the firm since its beginning, maintained a strong editorial influence until 1919. The Boni and Liveright name continued until 1928, by which time Bennett Cerf and Donald Klopfer bought the company, keeping the Modern Library imprint.

On 14 September 1917 Boni married Nell Van Leeuwen. They had four children. In 1919 they traveled to Europe, where he acquired translation and publication rights to Karl Kautsky's *Die deutsche Dokumente zum Kriegsausbruch,* drawn from German foreign office records of the beginning of World War I, and Kaiser Wilhelm II's memoirs, which he bought for *McClure's,* for $200,000. Also in

1919 Boni, who since high school had been an avowed Fabian Socialist, went to Russia, where he marched in a parade with Lenin, and was subsequently jailed for thirteen months as an American spy. His eventual release was a result of strenuous efforts by his wife Nell, Emma Goldman, and Beatrice and Sidney Webb.

In 1923 the brothers formed Albert and Charles Boni Publishers. Among their authors were Will Rogers, Thornton Wilder (whose *Bridge of San Luis Rey* became a bestseller), Romain Rolland, Ford Madox Ford, Marcel Proust, Mark Van Doren, and Upton Sinclair. In the spring of 1930, amid the Great Depression, the Bonis caused a considerable outcry from other members of the New York publishing community by starting a one-dollar book club and announcing that they would issue twelve paper books to subscribers for $5 per year. Albert Boni was president of the firm until 1935.

In the late 1930s, after his friend Manuel Komroff showed him remarkably clear prints, at several different enlargements, from a 35mm negative, Boni became interested in the possibility of publishing texts in microform, photographically reducing the contents to a small fraction of its original dimensions, printing it by offset, and devising an optical enlarger to restore it to a readable scale. On the advice of Upton Sinclair the Bonis moved, in the late 1930s, to Chester, Vermont, and Alfred continued to experiment with photography and offset printing techniques. In 1939, with the encouragement of Harry Miller Lydenberg, director of the New York Public Library, and Keyes Metcalfe (then reference librarian at the New York Public Library, later university librarian of Harvard), he announced the formation of the Readex Microprint Corporation and undertook the publication of Joseph Sabin's twenty-nine-volume *Dictionary of Books Relating to America.* This was a time when research libraries were particularly concerned by the rate at which they were outgrowing their stack space, and microforms offered great promise.

The Readex Microprint format, which Boni adopted after several years' research and experimentation, was a six-inch-by-nine-inch card, offset-printed on a finely calendered paper surface, from plates so composed from 35mm microfilm negatives that each card contained up to 100 pages of text. It was an intricate process, involving not only fine photography but also offset plates and presswork of unprecedented precision. When he was ready to go into production in 1950, Boni discovered that both the New York Public Library and the Columbia University copies of Sabin's work were too tattered to make adequate copies. The copy from which he published was borrowed from Lathrop Harper, a rare-book dealer. The Microprint copies sold for $35.

Readex proceeded to publish the nineteenth-century Sessional Papers of the British House of Commons and *Early American Imprints,* the actual texts of the books listed in Sabin's *Dictionary.* This was followed by United States, Russian, and United Nations documents, *Landmarks of Science, Nineteenth-Century English and American Plays,* and *American Women's Diaries.* Although space-saving had been a preeminent consideration when Readex began, Boni believed that publication of these large research sets in their entirety was the reason for his success. Although the Microprint cards themselves were inexpensive, they required a reading machine to magnify their images. In 1971 Boni wrote: "There was no possibility of selling a five dollar book for 25 cents if a person had to buy an apparatus that was going to cost $350 to read it. This determined our whole publishing policy of projects where saving would be so great that the cost of the projector was incidental."

Boni retired to Florida in 1974. His son, William F. Boni, succeeded him as president of Readex Microprint, which subsequently became a subsidiary of Newsbank, Inc., of New Canaan, Connecticut.

★

The UCLA Library has Boni's collections of books and papers related to the history of photography, and the Readex Microprint Corporation has additional papers, including Boni's unpublished manuscript "The Beginning of Readex Microprint" (1971). In addition to *The Modern Book of French Verse* (1920), Boni wrote two bibliographies on photography: *A Guide to the Literature of Photography* (1943) and *Photographic Literature: An International Bibliographic Guide* (1962). There is useful information about Boni's early career in Tom Dardis, *Firebrand: The Life of Horace Liveright*

(1995). Substantive articles are in the *New York Times* (30 May 1930 and 1 Dec. 1965); the *Key West Citizen* (19 Jan. 1969); and in Edgar L. Erickson, "Microprint: A Revolution in Printing," *Journal of Documentation* (Sept. 1951): 184–187. An obituary is in the *New York Times* (1 Aug. 1981).

DAVID W. HERON

BOYLE, William Anthony ("Tony") (*b.* 1 December 1901 in Marysville, Montana; *d.* 31 May 1985 in Wilkes-Barre, Pennsylvania), powerful trade union leader who, as president of the United Mine Workers of America, was convicted of embezzlement and of ordering the killings of a union rival and his family, thereby becoming the highest-ranking union executive ever convicted of murder.

Born in a Montana mining camp, Boyle was one of two sons of Catherine Mallin and James P. Boyle. His father, an Irish immigrant who would later die of tuberculosis, came from a family whose ancestors in Ireland and Scotland had for generations been going "down in the pits." As a teenager, young Tony Boyle was already working in the Montana mines after finishing high school. This experience cost him the small finger on his right hand and won the empathy of his fellow workers, who provided the black rock, or "buried sunshine," that the nation needed to heat buildings and create electricity and steel, too often at the personal cost of black lung disease. This disease, from fine coal dust that coats the lungs of miners, was a major breath-depriving health hazard.

As one of thousands of coal miners who produced annually over 500 million tons of coal, Tony Boyle worked a forty-eight-hour week in the early era of the United Mine Workers of America, which would become one of the strongest labor organizations in the country. Boyle's union sprung from the days when coal-mining companies provided the company stores where miners were forced to buy needed goods. Besides working as an underground coal miner, Boyle also labored in copper mines.

This first-generation American miner soon became an enthusiastic union organizer for the United Mine Workers, which represented workers in most of the coal mines, negotiating agreements with mine operators on working hours, rates of pay, and safety conditions in mines. On 3 June 1928 Boyle married Ethel V. Williams; they had a daughter, Antoinette. Meanwhile, the fiery union representative worked his way up through the ranks. In 1940 he was elected president of District 27 of the United Mine Workers in the West. He caught the eye of John L. Lewis, the legendary mine union patriarch, who admired Boyle's negotiating skills and candor. Boyle, who went to Washington, D.C., in 1948 as an administrative assistant to Lewis, was

Tony Boyle (*center*), with his daughter Antoinette Engebregson and his lawyer Charles Puerto, entering the courthouse in Media, Pennsylvania, for Boyle's second murder trial, 1977. UPI/CORBIS-BETTMANN

the only member of Lewis's staff who had the courage to speak plainly to him. Their friendship greatly benefited Boyle, who became the third most powerful executive in the union.

In 1960 Lewis retired from the union, although he remained influential as president emeritus. His successor, Thomas Kennedy, was ailing, so the day-to-day duties of the office fell to Boyle, who had become vice president upon Lewis's retirement. In 1963 Boyle ascended to the presidency of the 130,000-member union with the death of Kennedy, and in 1964 Boyle was elected to the post. So popular a president was he that on the event of a 1968 convention in Denver, the rank-and-file delegates proposed to double his $50,000 annual salary and presented him with gifts including $2,500 and a television. Subsequently, Boyle turned down all these offerings.

Lewis died in 1969 and so, too, his stewardship of the union. Dissident voices cried out for changes, particularly more benefits, better safety, and improved pensions. The most popular of these insurgents was Joseph "Jock" Yablonski, a fifty-nine-year-old miner from Pennsylvania, and a one-time protégé of Boyle. Yablonski challenged Boyle for his second term of the United Mine Workers leadership in a bitter election campaign, which included charges by Yablonski, who called Boyle "a crook and an embezzler." Boyle responded in kind with the appellation "cheap opportunist." Boyle handily won reelection by a two-to-one margin in December 1969.

On the night of 31 December 1969, three men entered the Yablonski home in Clarksville, Pennsylvania. Yablonski, his wife Margaret, and his daughter Charlotte were shot to death in their beds. The triple homicide captured national attention.

Although he denied it until his own death, Boyle was implicated in the murders from the beginning. Furthermore, Yablonski had lodged charges of election fraud and embezzlement before his death. After the killings the U.S. government declared the 1969 reelection void and ordered new balloting. In 1972 Boyle lost in his reelection bid to Arnold R. Miller. Indicted in 1971, Boyle was convicted of improper use of union funds and sentenced to five years in prison the following year. Meanwhile, the state of Pennsylvania, under prosecutor Richard A. Sprague, was working on the assassination of Yablonski and his family. Sprague began proceedings to extradite Boyle from Washington, D.C., to Pennsylvania. This, combined with the prospect of spending the next five years behind bars, resulted in Boyle's attempting suicide in 1973 in his home by taking a massive overdose of Amytal, a powerful barbiturate.

In September 1973 Boyle was indicted in Pennsylvania on charges that he conspired to murder Joseph Yablonski. In April 1974, sick and wizened, "Tough Tony" Boyle was convicted and sentenced to three consecutive life terms in prison. The conviction was appealed, however, on grounds that the judge should have allowed some contested testimony that may have cast doubts on Boyle's guilt. In January 1977 the Pennsylvania Supreme Court ordered a new trial. The following year Boyle, convicted of the same charges, received a duplicate of the original sentence and returned to jail. In ill health, he languished in a prison nursing home during the final months of his life. He died in Wilkes-Barre General Hospital of heart-lung disease at the age of eighty-three. He was cremated in Billings, Montana.

Boyle transformed the union hierarchy, which had been geared to deal with a relatively narrow range of mining issues, into an administrative, governing force equipped to take on the issues that were to represent the future for all unions: economic investment, political infrastructure, and health benefits. Tony Boyle, ultimately corrupted by power and tainted by violence, never enjoyed these benefits from his prison cell.

★

Two books, Arthur H. Lewis, *Murder by Contract: The People v. "Tough Tony" Boyle* (1975), and Stuart Brown, *A Man Named Tony: The True Story of the Yablonski Murders* (1976), detail the Yablonski murder trials. Obituaries are in the *New York Times* (1 June 1985) and the *Billings Gazette* (1 June 1985).

LOUISE CONTINELLI

BOYLSTON, Helen Dore (*b.* 4 April 1895 in Portsmouth, New Hampshire; *d.* 30 September 1984 in Trumbull, Connecticut), author of two popular series of books for younger readers, drawing upon her own experience to create heroines whose nursing and acting careers captivated several generations of preadolescent girls.

The daughter of Joseph and Fannie Dore (Wright) Boylston, she was educated in the Portsmouth public schools and attended Simmons College in Boston (1914–1915) before switching to a nursing curriculum. After graduating in 1917 from the Massachusetts General Hospital School of Nursing (a place she later used for a convincing background in the earlier Sue Barton books), Boylston joined the Harvard Medical Unit attached to the British Expeditionary Force in France during World War I. For two years she served as an anesthesiologist, attaining the rank of captain. In later years she looked back on this time with a kind of nostalgia for its intensity and camaraderie.

At the end of the war in 1918, Boylston returned to the United States, becoming head nurse and instructor in anesthesia at Massachusetts General until 1921. Finding this life lacking in adventure, she signed on as a nurse with the Red Cross and became involved in reconstruction work in Albania, Italy, Poland, and Germany until 1924. While working as a private duty nurse in New York City, she started to write the first book of the nursing series. The phenomenal success of *Sue Barton, Student Nurse* (1936) soon made other work unnecessary; it sold millions of copies in the United States and England over the next four decades. In the late 1940s, before writing the last two volumes in the seven-book series, Boylston returned briefly to

her original career, spending some time as head nurse in a Norwalk, Connecticut, hospital.

The romantic and nursing-life adventures of Boylston's witty and intrepid red-haired heroine continued in *Sue Barton, Senior Nurse* (1937), *Sue Barton, Visiting Nurse* (1938), *Sue Barton, Rural Nurse* (1939), and *Sue Barton, Superintendent of Nurses* (1940). *Sue Barton, Neighborhood Nurse* (1949) and *Sue Barton, Staff Nurse* (1952) attempted to pick up on the popularity of the five earlier volumes, written before her four-book Carol Page series concerning an aspiring young actress started in 1941.

A biographical entry written by Karen Nelson Hoyle in *Twentieth Century Children's Writers* (1983) makes an unsupported claim that Jane Cobb Berry should have received credit as coauthor of three of the Sue Barton books and all four of the Carol Page volumes. According to Boylston, the latter books—*Carol Goes Backstage* (1941), *Carol Plays Summer Stock* (1942), *Carol on Broadway* (1944), and *Carol on Tour* (1946)—were inspired and critiqued by a friend and neighbor, the noted actress and director Eva La Gallienne. Boylston never acknowledged—publicly, at least—any collaboration with Berry.

Despite the spectacular sales record of the Sue Barton books, both these and the Carol Page series received mixed reviews. Some critics welcomed them as the first to provide some genuine information and background for both the nursing and theater professions; others called them falsely glamorous. In any case, for preteen and early-teenage girls in the late 1930s to early 1950s, the criticism was irrelevant. Boylston's books were as loved, read, and reread as the Nancy Drew mysteries. They were funny, sad, and exciting. In keeping with the views of the times, of course, doctors were portrayed as godlike; even the gruff ones had twinkles in their eyes.

In discussing her books, Boylston said, "Nursing and acting have a romantic appeal, but young imaginations conjure up the most wildly inaccurate pictures of life in either profession. . . . Nursing is quite, *quite* different from anything girls imagine. The same is true with regard to the theatre. So, I proposed to give girls as *true* a picture as I was able."

Boylston's other publications include *Sister: The War Diary of a Nurse* (1927), taken from her World War I journal and first published in the *Atlantic Monthly* in 1920, and *Clara Barton: Founder of the American Red Cross* (1955), a "substantial" biography for young readers. Her *Travels with Zenobia* (1927), written with Rose Wilder Lane after they drove from Paris to Albania in a Model T Ford in 1926, was republished in 1982 by the University of Missouri Press.

Today the Sue Barton series, originally published by Little, Brown and Company, is mainly available in the form of a few worn-out paperback reprints (Popular Library,

1984) on library bookshelves. Whether or not the Sue Barton or Carol Page books fade into total obscurity depends on their finding publishers who wish to revive them. This is problematical since both the gender roles and ethnic understandings in these volumes fall woefully short of today's ideals. Some publisher with a ten-year-old daughter, however, might want to market test an updated *Sue Barton, Student Nurse* and find out if it still captures the imagination of young readers.

★

Information on Boylston is in *Contemporary Authors,* vols. 73–76, 113, and new rev. series 21. See also the entry by Karen Nelson Hoyle in *Twentieth Century Children's Writers,* 2d ed. (1983). An obituary is in the *New York Times* (5 Oct. 1984).

CAROL BURDICK

BRADLEY, Omar Nelson (*b.* 12 February 1893 near Clark, Missouri; *d.* 8 April 1981 in New York City), five-star general of the U.S. Army who served as commander of the Twelfth Army Group in Europe in World War II and chairman of the Joint Chiefs of Staff during the Korean War, known as the "GI's general."

Bradley's origins were humble but respectable. His father, John Smith Bradley, broke the family mold by leaving the farm to become a rural schoolteacher. He married one of his students, Sarah Elizabeth Hubbard, in 1892. Exactly nine months later, on 12 February 1893, Omar was born at his mother's family homestead near Clark, Missouri. When he was three years old his parents took into their home two female cousins who remained with the family for many years. His only sibling, a brother, did not survive infancy. In his early years Omar became accustomed to frequent moves as his father went from school to school in the region around Clark. Although the family did not engage in prayer or Bible reading they regularly attended the local Church of Christ and, Omar later recalled, shared a strong faith. From his father he inherited a love for books and sports, especially hunting and baseball. After his father's death, when Omar was fifteen years old, he and his mother moved to Moberly, where she supported the family through work as a seamstress.

Although Bradley initially considered a legal career, the lure of a free education and his mother's remarriage to a Moberly farmer, which relieved him of worries about leaving her alone, led him to apply for an appointment by his congressman to the U.S. Military Academy at West Point. When the leading candidate for the slot failed the entrance examination, Bradley received the appointment as an alternate. At West Point he distinguished himself in athletics, especially as a left fielder on the academy's baseball team.

General Omar N. Bradley. ARCHIVE PHOTOS

He sufficiently maintained his studies to graduate forty-fourth in a class of 164 in 1915. Known as "the class the stars fell on," graduates included seven future three-star generals, two future four-star generals, and another future five-star general and president, Dwight D. Eisenhower. Bradley received his commission as a second lieutenant in the infantry on 12 June 1915. During his three-month leave before reporting for duty with the Fourteenth Infantry at Fort George Wright near Spokane, Washington, he became engaged to a high school friend, the attractive, bright, and ambitious Mary Elizabeth Quayle. The Fourteenth Infantry soon deployed to Arizona in response to the crisis with Mexico, and it was not until 28 December 1916 that they exchanged vows. The Bradleys had one daughter.

Bradley's early career did not seem especially promising. He became a first lieutenant on 1 July 1916; a captain on 15 May 1917, one month after the United States intervened in World War I; and a temporary major on 17 June 1918. The Fourteenth Infantry, however, spent the war policing labor unrest in Montana mines and training in Des Moines, Iowa, for an overseas assignment that never materialized. Disappointed over missing combat duty, Bradley was an instructor of Reserve Officer Training Corps candidates at South Dakota State College beginning in August 1919.

With the postwar reductions in the army, he reverted to his prewar rank of captain on 22 January 1920. In September he became a mathematics instructor at West Point, where he began a serious study of military history and biography. After oscillating between captain and major, Bradley finally received his permanent promotion to major on 25 June 1924. From 1924 to 1925 he attended the senior officers' advanced course at the Infantry School at Fort Benning, Georgia. He then spent an enjoyable three years in Hawaii as a battalion commander in the Twenty-seventh Infantry and as the officer in charge of National Guard and Reserve affairs for the Hawaii Department. In 1929 he graduated from the Command and General Staff School at Fort Leavenworth, Kansas.

At this point, Bradley's career received a major break. After his return to the Infantry School at Fort Benning, his performance as chief of the school's weapons section caught the eye of Lieutenant Colonel George C. Marshall, then an assistant commandant at the school. In 1934 Bradley graduated from the Army War College in Washington, D.C. He then returned to West Point, teaching tactics and discipline. After twelve years as a major he at last became a lieutenant colonel on 26 June 1936. In June 1938 he returned to Washington to serve in the personnel section of the War Department General Staff. When Marshall became chief of staff the next year he called Bradley to his secretariat, a ministaff that organized the papers flooding into his office. Bradley thus played a central supporting role in Marshall's efforts to prepare the army and nation for the coming storm. Marshall rewarded him with an assignment as commandant of the Infantry School and a promotion, on 20 February 1941, to the temporary grade of brigadier general. At Fort Benning, Bradley established an infantry officers candidate school that produced thousands of officers during World War II. After the Japanese attack on Pearl Harbor, Bradley was elevated to the temporary rank of major general on 15 February 1942 and assigned to command the Eighty-second Infantry Division. Four months later he took over the Twenty-eighth Infantry Division. In both cases he achieved such success in whipping new formations into shape that he stood in line to take command of a corps.

On 16 February 1943, just as Bradley was reading the message assigning him to command the X Corps in Texas, he received a phone call ordering him to report instead to Washington, D.C., for overseas duty. The U.S. II Corps, which had landed in North Africa the previous November, was being rudely handled by the German Afrika Korps at Kasserine Pass, and General Eisenhower, the Allied commander in chief in Tunisia, had requested the War Department to send a general who would act as his observer at the front. Arriving in Tunisia on 27 February, Bradley concluded that American troops had much to learn about tactics, especially the use of tanks and close air support, and

he suggested that the II Corps get a new commander. Partly at Bradley's recommendation, Eisenhower sent Major General George S. Patton, Jr., to Tunisia as the new commander of the II Corps, with Bradley as his deputy. The flamboyant Patton left a rejuvenated II Corps to Bradley, who succeeded him as corps commander on 15 April. In his new post Bradley performed a difficult movement to the northern sector of the Tunisian front, and his careful planning paid dividends during the final offensive through the Tunisian mountains toward Bizerte. On 7 May, Bizerte fell to the II Corps, and on 13 May the remaining Axis in Tunisia surrendered.

Lauded by Eisenhower as "about the best rounded, well-balanced senior officer we have in the service," Bradley's stock was rising after North Africa. On 10 July 1943 his II Corps, part of Patton's Seventh Army, landed on the south coast of Sicily near Gela. As the Americans expanded their perimeter over the next few days, a strategic dispute erupted. The ground commander of the invasion, British field marshal Sir Harold Alexander, wanted the Seventh Army merely to guard the western flank of the British Eighth Army, which was driving on Messina at the northeast tip of the island. Patton instead expanded on Alexander's plan, sending the II Corps north to cut the island in two, while the Provisional Corps drove west on Palermo. For Bradley, the slow, hard advance across the Sicilian highlands only aggravated his irritation with the British, who appeared eager to monopolize the glory from the campaign, and with Patton, who seemed in Bradley's view to be playing for publicity. On 23 July the II Corps reached the northern coast. Bradley now turned his advance east toward Messina, fighting a bitter action at Troina and conducting amphibious landings along the north coast to outflank resistance. On 17 August, Allied troops entered Messina.

Patton's fall into disgrace after slapping a battle-fatigued soldier left Bradley, who had just been promoted to temporary lieutenant general on 2 June, as the logical choice for the most prominent U.S. field command in the coming invasion of France. On 2 September he was summoned to Eisenhower's headquarters, where he received word of his assignment to command the First Army in the invasion. Flying to England with selected members of his II Corps staff, he activated his headquarters in the west England port of Bristol on 20 October 1943. Under the supervision of General Sir Bernard L. Montgomery, the Allied ground commander for the invasion, Bradley and his staff scanned available intelligence, allocated shipping, and supervised the training of the invasion forces—just the kind of painstaking, methodical task for which they were well suited. On D day, 6 June 1944, as Bradley watched from the cruiser *Augusta,* the First Army landed at Utah and Omaha beaches. Stiff German resistance at Omaha almost led him to call off the attack, but naval gunfire support and excellent small-unit leadership enabled the assault troops to maintain a foothold.

On 8 June 1944 Bradley's daughter, Elizabeth, married Henry S. Beukema, an officer in the Army Air Forces, but her proud father could not attend. On 10 June the Allies linked up their beaches in Normandy. As the buildup accelerated, the First Army threw back German counterattacks and expanded its perimeter, completing a drive west across the base of the Cotentin Peninsula on 18 June and capturing Cherbourg at its tip on 26 June. Shifting his troops south, Bradley opened an offensive on 3 July, hoping to break through to more open country to the south. Lack of ammunition, an inability to concentrate forces, poor weather, and the rugged terrain of hedgerows bogged down the American attack. Frustrated, Bradley, about 8 July, personally prepared a plan that would break the German line and enable him to capture Brittany and its ports, the initial Allied objective. Based on Montgomery's overall design for a main effort in the west by the First Army, he conceived a massive attack by heavy bombers near St. Lô to blast a hole in the German line, then an attack and exploitation by six divisions of the U.S. VII Corps. The bombing mission on 25 July initially seemed to be a disaster, accidentally killing 111 American troops, but it achieved its purpose. By 1 August, American armored spearheads had reached Avranches, gateway to Brittany.

On 1 August, as the rampaging U.S. columns turned west into Brittany and east around the enemy's open flank, Bradley moved up to command the Twelfth Army Group, directly under Eisenhower. Until Eisenhower established his headquarters on the Continent, however, Montgomery coordinated the Allied ground forces. On 7 August, Adolf Hitler tried to recoup his fortunes by a counterattack west toward Avranches, hoping to cut off the Americans in Brittany from the Allied forces in Normandy. Holding firm against the German attack, Bradley seized the opportunity to send Patton's Third Army in an encircling maneuver from the area south of Avranches to the east and north, around the enemy flank. In one of his most controversial decisions, Bradley, concerned about a possible collision with Anglo-Canadian forces near Falaise, halted Patton short of a linkup on 13 August, permitting German forces to escape the closing trap. Over the next several days the Allies mopped up the remaining Germans in the "Falaise Pocket" while sending armor across the Seine. Paris fell on 25 August, and the Allies raced northeast toward the German frontier.

As the Allies drove toward the German frontier, Bradley became embroiled in a dispute over future strategy. Montgomery wanted to combine his Twenty-first Army Group with Bradley's Twelfth in a massive advance northeast into the Low Countries and thence eastward to the Ruhr industrial region. Bradley, motivated at least partly by the

threat Montgomery's plan posed to U.S. autonomy, wanted a secondary offensive in the north with the main effort by his Twelfth Army Group to be an advance east on Metz and the Saar industrial region. Eisenhower, who had assumed direct command after 1 September, decided for a more broad-front approach, but supply shortages, particularly of gasoline, slowed the Allied advance in September and October, allowing the enemy to recover. Once Bradley had built up his supplies he launched an offensive in November, but his armies, overly dispersed and bogged down in rugged terrain, such as the Huertgen Forest, made slow headway.

On 16 December the Germans launched the Battle of the Bulge, a surprise counteroffensive in the rugged Ardennes region of southern Belgium and Luxembourg. Bradley later called his weak front in the Ardennes a "calculated risk" to enable greater concentration elsewhere, but his reaction at the time indicated greater surprise than he later wished to admit. Four days later came another shock when Eisenhower, reacting to the depth of the enemy penetration, shifted Bradley's two armies north of the Bulge to Montgomery. Overcoming his pique, Bradley argued for the earliest possible counterattack on both shoulders of the Bulge. After the Allies had erased the Bulge and the First Army had returned to his command, Bradley supervised his army group's drive to the Roer River. During late February and early March his forces raced to the Rhine, seizing a windfall bridgehead at Remagen on 7 March. On 25 March, thirteen days after his temporary promotion to full general, Bradley broke out from his Rhine bridgeheads. By 1 April his armored spearheads had encircled the Ruhr. Reinforced by two more armies, he now led 1.3 million men, the most American troops under one field commander in U.S. history. This force carried out the main Allied effort across central Germany to a linkup with the Soviets near the Elbe on 25 April. The Twelfth Army Group's southern flank was driving into Czechoslovakia when, at 5:00 A.M. on 7 May, Bradley received word of Germany's surrender.

Bradley wanted to participate in the final campaign against Japan, but Marshall had other plans for him. On 15 August 1945 he appointed Bradley to head the Veterans Administration (VA). Aided by Major General Paul R. Hawley, Eisenhower's theater surgeon in World War II, Bradley reformed the antiquated VA medical system. He also revised and extended the educational benefits of the GI Bill, instituted job-training programs and loans for veterans, and administered the astounding growth in veterans insurance and disability pensions.

From the VA, Bradley moved to the post of army chief of staff on 7 February 1948. With the demobilization of the army, President Harry S. Truman's budget cuts, and the controversy over defense unification, it was a difficult time to be chief of staff. Bradley could not implement universal military training and direct U.S. Army control of the National Guard or get enough funds for weapons modernization, but cold war tensions enabled him to secure resumption of the Selective Service System. Despite budget cuts, he even managed to bring military pay into line with civilian pay scales.

After only eighteen months as army chief of staff, Bradley, on 16 August 1949, became the first chairman of the Joint Chiefs of Staff, the highest ranking officer in the U.S. armed forces. During his four years as chairman he played a critical role in the ongoing disputes over defense unification and service roles and missions. When the Atlantic powers formed the North Atlantic Treaty Organization (NATO) to contain communist expansion, Bradley became the first chairman of NATO's Military Committee. As President Truman's leading military adviser during the Korean War he played a critical role in formulating U.S. grand strategy, including the decision to limit the war to the Korean peninsula. Concerned that the war might be an attempt by the Soviets to divert the West from their true objective in central Europe, Bradley worked hard during the war years to build up NATO as a counter. He backed Truman's decision to relieve General Douglas MacArthur in April 1951, and he later appeared before Congress to defend the dismissal and the Truman Administration's limited war policy, at one point asserting that a broader war against Communist China was "the wrong war, at the wrong place, at the wrong time, and with the wrong enemy." Having been promoted to the permanent rank of full general on 31 January 1949, and to general of the army on 22 September 1950, Bradley retired on 15 August 1953.

Because generals of the army technically never retire, Bradley remained on active duty to his death, serving as a frequent adviser to presidents. He often represented the president or Defense Department at D day, Veterans Day, or Memorial Day commemorations. After retirement, he accepted a position as head of the research and development laboratories of the Bulova Corporation. In 1958 he became chairman of the board at Bulova, a position he held until 1973. Although his retirement years were generally comfortable, they were also marred by tragedy. On 19 January 1954 his son-in-law was killed in the crash of his jet fighter. Bradley's daughter and four grandchildren moved into the Bradley home in the Los Angeles area for about three years until her remarriage, which produced a fifth grandchild. Then, on 1 December 1965, Mary Bradley died. After a lonely ten months, the general married Esther Dora "Kitty" Buhler, a Hollywood writer, on 12 September 1966. Bradley's new wife brought a new, more lively lifestyle. They moved to Beverly Hills in 1968 and then to army quarters at Fort Bliss, Texas, in 1977. Having already written *A Soldier's Story* (1951), about his World War II expe-

riences, Bradley began work with the author Clay Blair on an autobiography but he did not live to finish it. On 8 April 1981 he died of a blood clot in the brain just minutes after receiving the Gold Medal Award from the National Institute of Social Sciences in New York City. He was buried in Arlington National Cemetery.

Tall, quiet, modest, a bit homely in his olive-drab uniform and spectacles, Bradley looked a bit like a country schoolteacher. His values—an emphasis on hard work and integrity, aversion to profanity and hard drinking, and idealization of the common man—reflected the small Midwest town where he had spent his boyhood. His image as the "GI's general"—a nickname given him by the popular war correspondent Ernie Pyle—has been overstated, but Bradley did possess empathy for the common soldier and his hardships. As a battlefield tactician he was careful and thorough. His plans reflected the strong influence of the Infantry School and higher-level schools of the interwar army and have since been criticized for lacking force, boldness, and imagination. But he did possess a keen sense of terrain, aptitude for numbers and logistics, appreciation for intelligence, and above all a strong character. His common touch enabled him to communicate well with people. Beneath the genial exterior, however, was a tough, calculating professional who did not hesitate to relieve from command those who, in his view, did not measure up. Calm even in a crisis, he projected an aura of serene confidence and common sense that reassured superiors and subordinates alike.

His distinguished service in World War II made Bradley one of the major figures in the army of the "American Century." He became one of the most prominent of the generation of officers that rose from low rank and obscurity to lead the largest armies ever fielded by the United States. His most lasting influence may well have come in the postwar years, when he reformed the Veterans Administration and played a key role in the debates over defense unification and development of the policies of containment and limited war. Still, he is most remembered as one of the pantheon—with Marshall, Eisenhower, MacArthur, and Patton—that led U.S. armies to victory in the greatest conflict in human history. For millions of Americans the calm, unassuming Missourian was the epitome of a soldier of democracy.

★

The two best books on Bradley's life are his memoir, *A Soldier's Story* (1951), and his collaborative effort with Clay Blair, *A General's Life* (1983). Also of interest is Charles Whiting, *Bradley* (1971). Several World War II books contain information on Bradley. The interested reader will probably wish to examine the U.S. Army's official histories, *The U.S. Army in World War II,* published by the Army Center of Military History in Washington, D.C.; from this series, see especially Martin Blumenson, *Breakout and Pursuit* (1961); Hugh M. Cole, *The Ardennes* (1965) and *The Lorraine Campaign* (1950); Albert N. Garland and Howard M. Smyth,

Sicily and the Surrender of Italy (1965); Gordon A. Harrison, *Cross Channel Attack* (1951); George F. Howe, *Northwest Africa* (1957); and Charles B. MacDonald, *The Siegfried Line Campaign* (1963) and *The Last Offensive* (1973). Other key works are Stephen E. Ambrose, *The Supreme Commander* (1970); Carlo D'Este, *Decision in Normandy* (1983) and *Bitter Victory* (1988); David Eisenhower, *Eisenhower at War* (1986); Nigel Hamilton's three-volume biography, *Monty* (1981–1987); and Russell F. Weigley, *Eisenhower's Lieutenants* (1981). Kent Roberts Greenfield, ed., *Command Decisions* (1960), closely analyzes Bradley's decision to halt Patton short of Falaise, and Martin Blumenson provides a critical view in *The Battle of the Generals* (1993). For Bradley's work during the Korean War, see James F. Schnabel, *Policy and Direction: The First Year* (1972), from the army's series on the U.S. Army in the Korean War. An obituary is in the *New York Times* (9 Apr. 1981).

DAVID W. HOGAN, JR.

BRAUTIGAN, Richard Gary (*b.* 30 January 1935 in Tacoma, Washington; *d.* September or October 1984 in Bolinas, California), poet and novelist best known for his work *Trout Fishing in America* (1967).

Richard Brautigan spent much of his childhood, which was marked by poverty, in Tacoma, Washington, other parts of the Pacific Northwest, and Montana. His mother, Lula Mary Keho, was a homemaker, and his father, Bernard F. Brautigan, was a common laborer who left his wife when

Richard Brautigan, 1982. CHRISTOPHER FELVER/ARCHIVE PHOTOS

she was pregnant with Richard. He had one younger sister, as well as a series of stepfathers while he was growing up. Brautigan did not attend college.

A tall, slim man with thick wire-rim glasses and sandy-blond longish hair, Brautigan in 1954 moved to San Francisco, the destination of many of the disaffected youth of his generation, and became involved in the Beat literary movement. While he had many of the same affinities as the members of this movement, such as an aversion to middle-class values, commercialism, and conformity, and an interest in mysticism and Zen Buddhism, he was never really a part of the group and is usually not classified by literary taxonomists as such. On 8 June 1957 he married Virginia Dionne Adler; they had one daughter, Ianthe. The couple divorced in July 1970.

In 1966 and 1967 Brautigan was poet-in-residence at the California Institute of Technology. In 1968, the year after *Trout Fishing in America* was published, he received a grant from the National Endowment for the Arts. In 1972 Brautigan left San Francisco and later bought a small ranch near Livingston, Montana. This move initiated an eight-year period during which Brautigan, who was capable of being intensely private and inward, largely shunned opportunities to give lectures at universities and refused all invitations to be interviewed. In 1976 he made his first trip to Japan, where he lived off and on until 1984. He married a Japanese woman named Akiko in 1978; that marriage, which was childless, ended in divorce in 1980.

In 1978 Brautigan's works became the center of a book-banning controversy in a northern California high school. The American Civil Liberties Union and his publisher, Delacorte Press, rallied behind students and teachers in a suit against the Shasta County school board after several of Brautigan's books were removed from the classroom. The case was decided in Brautigan's favor.

At the annual Modern Language Association meeting in San Francisco in December 1979, Brautigan appeared on a panel titled "Zen and Contemporary Poetry" with the poets Gary Snyder, Philip Whalen, Robert Bly, and Lucien Stryk to discuss the importance of Zen Buddhism to American literature. Brautigan was an instructor at Montana State University in Bozeman in 1982. The exact date of his death is not known. On 25 October 1984 his badly decomposed body was discovered at his home in Bolinas, California, twenty miles north of San Francisco; he had shot himself in the head with a Smith and Wesson .44 Magnum four to five weeks earlier.

Brautigan began his literary career as a poet but met with little success in that genre. His first poem to be published was titled "The Second Kingdom" (*Epos,* winter 1956). This was followed by several slim volumes of poetry, all published by small presses. Perhaps the most notable aspect of Brautigan's early poetry career was his participation in a volume titled *Please Plant This Book* (around 1968), which contained eight poems, all printed on the backs of seed packets that included full instructions for planting on the fronts. Other volumes of poetry include *The Return of the Rivers* (1957), *The Galilee Hitch-Hiker* (1958), *Lay the Marble Tea* (1959), *The Octopus Frontier* (1960), *All Watched Over by Machines of Loving Grace* (1967), *The Pill Versus the Springhill Mine Disaster* (1968), *Rommel Drives On Deep into Egypt* (1970), *Loading Mercury with a Pitchfork* (1976), and *June 30th, June 30th* (1978).

The title page of Brautigan's most famous, and arguably best, novel, *Trout Fishing in America,* features a telling typographical image: the novel's title appears in the shape of a hook. Most obviously, the design resonates with the idea of fishing expressed in the title, but it also conveys some sense of the book's ability to catch the imagination of American readers. Between 1967 and 1972 some 2,000 copies of the book were sold while it was still only available through a small, independent San Francisco–based publishing house called the Four Seasons Foundation. Despite its initially low sales, by 1970 the book had so touched the imagination of a generation that its title had become the namesake of a commune, a free school, and an underground newspaper, perhaps as much an indication of its popularity as of the general temper of the times. (Not a few sporting goods stores unwittingly stocked the novel and sold it to equally unsuspecting customers.)

Brautigan has been alternately classified as a beat, a hippie, and, more generically, a spokesman for the counterculture. But all of these labels seem unnecessarily limiting. In *Trout Fishing in America,* Brautigan creates his vision of America through a series of vignettes that range over a wide geographical, historical, and literary landscape. This vision is hardly one of complacent acceptance or rosy optimism. Rather it is one of recurrent disappointment, in which expectations, in terms both of society and of the confrontation between the imagination and reality, are repeatedly unfulfilled. Yet this pessimism does not lead to moroseness; in fact, a large part of the power and appeal of the novel (or "Brautigan," as one contemporary critic dubbed his difficult-to-classify works) derives from its subtle humor, which Brautigan expresses through felicitous turns of phrase and unexpected metaphors. The very title of the novel takes on an amorphous quality, appearing at various times throughout the book as an activity, a character, a place, a spirit, an imaginative construct. The slipperiness of this protean phrase suggests Brautigan's sense of the difficulty of defining the effect of America on the imagination.

Brautigan's other fiction includes *A Confederate General from Big Sur* (1964), *Revenge of the Lawn: Stories, 1962–1970* (1971), *The Abortion: An Historical Romance 1966* (1971), *The Hawkline Monster: A Gothic Western* (1974), *Willard and His Bowling Trophies: A Perverse Mystery* (1974),

Sombrero Fallout: A Japanese Novel (1976), *Dreaming of Babylon: A Private Eye Novel, 1942* (1977), *The Tokyo-Montana Express* (1980), and *So the Wind Won't Blow It All Away* (1982).

★

Terence Mallery, *Richard Brautigan* (1972), contains some biographical information and a discussion of Brautigan's works through 1971; Edward Halsey Foster, *Richard Brautigan* (1983), published the year before Brautigan's death, effectively reconstructs the social and cultural circumstances surrounding Brautigan's rise to popularity and contains excellent discussions of his works; and Jay Boyer, *Richard Brautigan* (1987), discusses Brautigan as a Western writer. See also John Stickney, "Gentle Poet of the Young," *Life* (14 Aug. 1970). Most articles in scholarly journals focus on individual works by Brautigan, but a single place with a collection of articles about different works is *Critique: Studies in Modern Fiction* 16, no. 1 (1974), a special issue devoted to Brautigan. Lawrence Wright, "The Life and Death of Richard Brautigan," is in *Rolling Stone* (11 Apr. 1985).

INGRID STERNER

BRETT, George Platt, Jr. (*b.* 9 December 1893 in Darien, Connecticut; *d.* 11 February 1984 in Southport, Connecticut), president of the Macmillan Publishing Company from 1931 to 1958.

Brett was the son of George Platt Brett, Sr., and Marie Louise Tostevan. George, Jr., was raised in Darien with his younger brother and two sisters, and attended the Salisbury School in Connecticut before going to the Collegiate School in New York City.

The Macmillan Company had been established in 1869 by Brett's grandfather, George Edward Brett, as part of Macmillan and Company of London. He managed the American branch for the English and Scottish booksellers, Alexander and Daniel Macmillan, until his death in 1890, at which time his son, George Platt Brett, Sr., turned down a partnership and a managerial position in favor of establishing a separate American company. Six years later, in 1896, the Macmillan Company became an autonomous corporation. Brett, Sr., served as president until 1921 and acquired such authors as Winston Churchill, Jack London, Edgar Lee Masters, Vachel Lindsay, and Owen Wister.

Although his father was president when George, Jr., went to work for Macmillan at age twenty, he started as a stock clerk and worked his way through various service departments. Before becoming a salesman for Macmillan's trade books, however, the blue-eyed, brown-haired, five-foot, eleven-inch Brett worked as a salesman for another publishing house, Doubleday, Page and Company, for a six-month stint in 1916. That same year the twenty-three-year-

George Brett (*left*), with Robert Degraff, president of Pocket Books Inc. (*center*), and James Thompson, executive vice president of McGraw Hill Co. (*right*), on a cultural relations tour of South America in 1943. UPI/ CORBIS-BETTMANN

old Brett postponed his developing publishing career to serve in the U.S. Army on the Mexican border. In 1917 he was commissioned as a second lieutenant after receiving officer training in Plattsburg, New York. From there, Brett went to France in the Seventy-seventh Division to fight in World War I. He was promoted quickly to first lieutenant in January 1918 and to captain in May of that year. He was discharged and sent home in May 1919, but remained in the reserve corps until 1943, when he resigned his commission as a lieutenant colonel in the New York National Guard so that he could take on an assignment for the State Department. Brett's military career came shortly after his marriage to Isabel Stevenson Yeomans on 18 August 1917. He and his wife had two children, George Platt Brett, 3d, and Bruce Yeomans Brett.

Upon returning home from the war, Brett went to work at the Chicago office of Macmillan. In ten months he was promoted to sales manager in the New York office and in 1924 he became the company's general manager. Brett served as general manager through the 1920s, during which time he established trade department branch offices in Chicago, Dallas, San Francisco, Atlanta, and Boston, all of which had previously been only distribution points. In Sep-

tember 1931 he was elected president of Macmillan, but he also continued to serve as general manager until 1934. His father, George Platt Brett, Sr., became chairman of the board when his son became president, serving until his death in 1936.

When Brett took over as president, Macmillan had already become known as a "department store of publishing" for its titles in education, medicine, and public health, children's and young person's literature, works on the outdoors, and particularly fiction, poetry, and biography. During his presidency Brett continued to expand the company's trade department branch offices, diversified publications, established an international sales department, and added such authors as Franklin Delano Roosevelt, Hamilton Fish Armstrong, Mary Ellen Chase, Rachel Field, Walter Lippmann, and Sara Teasdale. Brett's greatest publishing achievement, however, came early in his presidency. In 1935, after reviewing the manuscript of *Gone with the Wind,* Brett persuaded the author, Margaret Mitchell, to sell the rights to Macmillan, and thus made the company millions. The Civil War novel won the 1937 Pulitzer Prize, sold millions of copies worldwide, was translated into more than a dozen languages, and became the basis for one of the most successful films in motion-picture history.

During the 1940s Macmillan continued to grow under Brett's guidance. Presiding over nine major departments, or what he called his "nine-ring circus," Brett oversaw the production of approximately 13,000 active titles in that decade alone. Early in the 1950s the company went public, and Brett persuaded the British parent company, which still owned the majority of shares, to relinquish them to American stockholders.

Brett also took on several international and national publishing-related responsibilities. During World War II he conducted a study of book distribution in South America for the U.S. State Department, and was a member of the advisory committee on printing and publishing of the War Production Board. After the war he went to Germany to consult on the "rehabilitation of German intellectual life" and on the distribution of American textbooks in the American zone. In 1956 he served as chairman of the book committee of the People-to-People Program established by President Dwight D. Eisenhower. Brett also cofounded the American Textbook Publishers Institute.

In 1958 Brett became chairman of the board and his son, Bruce Yeomans, became president. Brett retained the position of director, however, until 1961, when Crowell-Collier took over Macmillan and replaced Brett, his son, and the nine department heads who served on the board. Brett went into retirement after the takeover, and although he remained active with his other projects, he never returned to publishing as a career. Meanwhile, the Brett dynasty at Macmillan ended with his son. An avid sailor and fisherman, Brett spent the remainder of his life in his Southport, Connecticut, home and in his summer home in Rainbow Lake, in the Adirondack Mountains of New York. He is buried in Southport.

★

A short biography is in Anna Rothe, ed., *Current Biography* (1948). A brief listing is in W. J. Burke and Will D. Howe, *American Authors and Books: 1640 to the Present,* 3d ed. (1972). Obituaries are in the *New York Times* (16 Feb. 1984), *Washington Post* (20 Feb. 1984), *Publisher's Weekly* (2 Mar. 1984), and Hal May, ed., *Contemporary Authors,* vol. 112 (1985).

JAMES P. MILLER

BREUER, Marcel Lajos (*b.* 21 May 1902 in Pécs, Austria-Hungary; *d.* 1 July 1981 in New York City), designer, architect, and educator whose "cesca" chair of 1928 became the best-known chair of the century and whose nine-year teaching career at Harvard University helped to revolutionize architectural education.

Marcel Breuer was the son of Jacob Breuer, a dental technician, and Franciska Kann. His family and close friends

Marcel Breuer. ARCHIVE PHOTOS

called him "Lajkó" even during his American years. He moved to Vienna in 1920 and briefly attended the Akademie der bildenden Künste but found it not to his liking. He then went to Weimar to attend the Bauhaus, an innovative design school that had been founded recently by Walter Gropius. Breuer flourished in the Bauhaus environment, and his entire career could be taken as a measure of the success of the Bauhaus.

At the Bauhaus, Breuer took the obligatory foundation course, meant to stimulate and nurture the creative powers of each individual student; he also enrolled in the carpentry workshop. In 1924 he completed the requirements for his journeyman's certificate, a goal the Bauhaus set for its students during its early years. Breuer's student work included experimental furniture of wood and fabric, most notably for two rooms of the Haus am Horn, built as part of a summer exhibition in 1923. Many of his student designs showed an influence from the Dutch de Stijl movement, resulting in, for example, chairs with seats, backs, and legs articulated as separate units. Breuer left Weimar for Paris in 1924, where he worked for an architect.

Gropius had decided to move the Bauhaus from Weimar to Dessau, where he designed a new building for it as well as housing for faculty nearby. Gropius brought Breuer to Dessau to head the furniture workshop and to design furniture for the new building and some of the faculty quarters. Having become fascinated by the bent-metal tubing used in bicycles, Breuer used metal tubing for folding chairs for the auditorium as well as for stools with bent-metal tubing frames and plywood seats. For the faculty duplex occupied by Wassily Kandinsky and his wife, Breuer designed a club chair consisting of a metal frame with suspended fabric panels. This soon became known as the "Wassily" chair and was manufactured, with choice of fabric or leather panels, by Standard-Möbel of Berlin beginning in 1927 and by the international Thonet firm from 1928. The following year Thonet bought Standard-Möbel, including its rights to all Breuer designs.

In 1926, Breuer designed his first cantilever chair, utilizing bent-metal tubing and stretched fabric, and showed it at an exhibition in Stuttgart the following year. The cantilever allowed the natural springiness of the metal tubes to make the chair more comfortable. Breuer refined the design in 1928, utilizing a seat and backrest with woven caning in wooden frames; shortly thereafter Thonet began mass production. The chair has been in production almost continuously since then and has been widely imitated. Thonet simply named it "B32," but a later manufacturer suggested that it be renamed, and in 1960 it became the "cesca" chair. The sitter's body does not touch the metal when seated; this was accomplished by using several materials, a practice suggested by tactile charts made as Bauhaus foundation-course exercises. (The tactile chart was assembled from contrasting materials, arranged in a sequence to be perceived by the sense of touch.)

Marcel Breuer and Martha Erps had met as students in Weimar, where they worked together on the design of the living room in the Haus am Horn, for which she designed the carpet. They were married in 1926. From his base in Dessau, Breuer began to design interiors, most notably for the Piscator apartment in Berlin in 1927. Breuer left the Bauhaus in 1928 and moved to Berlin, where he opened an architectural office. He was occupied with a few interior and exhibition designs but spent most of his time designing furniture for Thonet. His first architectural commission was in Wiesbaden in 1932 for the first Harnischmacher house. Breuer, who was born to a Jewish family, had begun to feel uncomfortable in Germany even though he was not a practicing Jew. Leaving Germany, he divided his time between Zurich and Budapest and also spent a good deal of time on the road in his new Ford automobile, studying traditional vernacular architecture. For a 1933 aluminum-furniture competition in Paris he designed an aluminum reclining chair with wooden arms and slats for the seat and back; it won a prize and went into mass production the following year. In Zurich, Breuer designed two apartment buildings in 1934, in collaboration with Alfred and Emil Roth. All three of these early buildings had boxy masses and smooth, light-hued walls, characteristic of the International Style then coalescing in the work of avant-garde architects. It was also in 1934 that Breuer and Erps were divorced.

Breuer moved in 1935 to England, where he worked with architect Francis Reginald Stevens Yorke; Gropius was already living in England. Yorke and Breuer's Gane's Exhibition Pavilion in Bristol (1936) utilized contrasting smooth walls and rough fieldstone walls; Breuer was here influenced by his studies of vernacular architecture as well as by Le Corbusier's De Mandrot house in Le Pradet, France (1930–1931), which Breuer visited during construction. In 1936, British Cement Industries commissioned exhibition models of concrete buildings for "a civic center of the future" from Breuer and Yorke; these models contained portents of Breuer's own future, including his signature Y-shaped buildings with exposed concrete walls. Also, Breuer produced numerous furniture designs for the British-Estonian firm Isokon, including some using bent plywood to produce early examples of biomorphic design. Advertisements for Breuer's furniture were designed by fellow Hungarian and former Bauhaus colleague László Moholy-Nagy, then also in London.

In 1937, Walter Gropius was invited to Harvard University as professor of architecture; soon thereafter he was asked to head the architecture department. He promptly invited Breuer to join him; together they replaced the outdated Beaux Arts curriculum with a successful and influential modern pedagogy. By the time Breuer left Harvard in 1946, the teaching of architecture in virtually every U.S. architectural school had been profoundly altered. Modernism in architecture had emerged from its avant-garde status to become mainstream. Breuer's students went on to become some of the best-known architects of the century: Philip Johnson, Paul Rudolph, and Edward Larrabee Barnes. It should be emphasized that while Gropius had a formal education in architecture, he had never taught it before, and that Breuer had no formal study of architecture, which was not even offered at the Bauhaus until after his student days there.

Although Breuer had worked for Gropius occasionally, they did not become partners until 1937. They remained partners until 1941, when Breuer set up his own office. Among the achievements of Gropius and Breuer were a number of small houses, including one for Gropius in 1938 and one for Breuer in 1939, both in Lincoln, Massachusetts, and both informed by Breuer's incorporation of New England examples into his continuing study of vernacular architecture. In 1940, Breuer and Constance Crocker Leighton were married; they had two children, Francesca and Tomas. Marcel Breuer was naturalized as a United States citizen in 1944.

Gropius and Breuer also achieved one of the key social goals of early modern architects, designing a low-income housing development of 250 units. This was Aluminum City Terrace of 1941 in New Kensington, Pennsylvania, originally built for families of workers employed by Alcoa in war production but still functioning as good housing for low-income families.

The first independent commission for Breuer came in 1945 with the Geller house, Lawrence, Long Island, New York. He soon received many commissions for small single-family houses, most in suburban or rural locations and usually on sites permitting picturesque views from generous windows. The most widely seen of these houses was constructed in 1949 in the sculpture garden of the Museum of Modern Art. It featured open planning, with its story-and-a-half massing sheltered under a single slanting slab roof. Surfaces included painted brick, fieldstone, wood, plaster, and glass bricks. Key pieces of furniture were designed by Breuer. Because of its timing during a construction boom, the house had a great deal of influence. (It was later reassembled on the Rockefeller estate in Tarrytown, New York.)

Breuer continued to be active as furniture designer, but most designs were site-specific and few were put into production. Nevertheless, the care that went into these designs can be illustrated by the chair Breuer entered in the Museum of Modern Art's International Competition for Low-Cost Furniture Design in 1948. Developed with technical assistance from the U.S. Forest Products Laboratory to assure the requisite strength, it was made of cut-out plywood with a curving woven-cane seat-and-back unit. Although not awarded a competition prize and never put into production, it was displayed in the house in the museum sculpture garden the following year.

Breuer opened an office in New York in 1946, situated at various locations in Manhattan; a Paris office was opened in 1964. Meanwhile, the Breuers moved to suburban New Canaan, Connecticut, and lived successively in two houses of his own design, the first dating from 1947 and the second from 1951.

The main block of the headquarters complex of the United Nations Educational, Scientific, and Cultural Organization (UNESCO) in Paris (1953–1958), designed in collaboration with Pier Luigi Nervi and Bernard Zehrfuss, was the first opportunity Breuer had to build a Y-shaped concrete building. This was followed by the headquarters of the Department of Housing and Urban Development in Washington, D.C. (1963–1968), designed with Herbert Beckhard and Nolen-Swinburne and Associates. Here, two Y shapes were used, joined at the stems. Both structures used precast units, with thick walls acting as sunshades.

For the Whitney Museum of American Art in New York (1963–1966), designed with Hamilton Smith, Breuer enlivened a corner site with a dramatic five-story concrete structure, most of it sheathed in gray granite, with bold cantilevers for the main (west) facades of the second, third, and fourth stories; the entrance is behind a bridge over the sunken sculpture court. Boldly scaled window frames in the form of truncated pyramids add to the drama; most are on the north facade. On the fourth floor the main gallery space is contrasted with small domestic-scaled galleries, and the offices on the fifth story are given a domestic touch with a patio-like terrace, open to the sky, for each office.

The best known of Breuer's religious buildings is the Abbey Church of St. John's University, Collegeville, Minnesota (1953–1961), designed with Smith. Towered over by a concrete "bell banner," the church has a folded-concrete shell, exposed inside and out, with gilding on the ceiling and upper inner walls. Breuer maintained that "church architecture at its best is always identical with the structural logic of the enclosure."

In addition to completing, with the aid of his office, Marcel Breuer and Associates, numerous buildings for a variety of clients in many countries, Breuer also left many unbuilt projects. One of these was the Franklin Delano Roosevelt Memorial in Washington, D.C., commissioned in 1966 but rejected the following year. The Roosevelt Memorial as completed in 1997 utilized designs of Lawrence Halprin.

Recognition for Breuer came from traveling retrospective exhibitions, including one that opened at the Museum of Modern Art in 1949 and another that opened at the Metropolitan Museum of Art in 1972. He received the Gold Medal of the American Institute of Architects in 1968. Breuer retired due to ill health in 1976 and moved to East Sixty-third Street in New York City. He died from a heart condition on 1 July 1981; later that month a large retrospective exhibition of his furniture and interiors opened at the Museum of Modern Art.

Breuer's furniture is regarded as among the very finest of the century. There is general enthusiasm about his buildings erected before 1953; no consensus has emerged about his later structures, and most of them, except for houses, have usually been ignored by critics and historians.

★

Marcel Breuer was not known as a writer; aside from a book of essays, *Sun and Shadow* (1954), his published writings consist of short essays and texts of lectures. Archival collections documenting his work include those at the George Arents Research Library at Syracuse University; the Archives of American Art in Washington, D.C.; and the Bauhaus-Archiv in Berlin. No single publication covers all of Breuer's life and career, but the best sources of information are Peter Blake, *Marcel Breuer: Architect and Designer* (1949); Whitney S. Stoddard, *Adventure in Architecture: Building the New Saint John's* (1958); Cranston Jones, ed., *Marcel Breuer: Buildings and Projects, 1921–1961* (1962); Tician Papachristou, *Marcel Breuer: Buildings and Projects, 1960–1970* (1970); Christopher Wilk, *Marcel Breuer: Furniture and Interiors* (1981); Katsuhiko Ichinowatari, *Process Architecture 32: The Legacy of Marcel Breuer* (1981); Magdelena Droste, *Marcel Breuer Design* (1992); and David Masello, *Architecture Without Rules: The Houses of Marcel Breuer and Herbert Beckhard* (1993). See also William H. Jordy, *American Buildings and Their Architects: The Impact of European Modernism in the Mid-Twentieth Century* (1972), especially chapter 3. Journal articles include Otakar Mácel, "Avant-garde Design and the Law: Litigation over the Cantilever Chair," *Journal of Design History* 3, nos. 2–3 (1990): 125–143; Kristin M. Szylvian, "Bauhaus on Trial: Aluminum City Terrace and Federal Defence Housing Policy During World War II," *Planning Perspectives* 9, no. 3 (July 1994): 229–254; and Isabelle Hyman, "Marcel Breuer and the Franklin Delano Roosevelt Memorial," *Journal of the Society of Architectural Historians* 54, no. 4 (December 1995): 446–458. An obituary is in the *New York Times* (2 July 1981).

LLOYD C. ENGELBRECHT

BRICKTOP (Ada Smith) (*b.* 14 August 1894 in Alderson, West Virginia; *d.* 31 January 1984 in New York City), vaudevillian, saloon entertainer, and nightclub owner whose clientele and friends included royalty, the wealthy, and the artistic elite.

Bricktop, born Ada Beatrice Queen Victoria Louisa Virginia Smith, was the third daughter and youngest of the five children of Thomas Smith, a black barber, and Harriet

"Bricktop" (Ada Smith) at the airport in Rome, 1961. UPI/CORBIS-BETTMANN

("Hattie") Elizabeth (Thompson) Smith. Her mother, seven-eighths white and of Irish descent, had been born a slave. Ada's lengthy name was an attempt to please many acquaintances. After her father died in 1898, the family moved to Chicago, where Hattie was a housekeeper and ran rooming houses. At the age of four or five, Ada made her stage debut in *Uncle Tom's Cabin* at the Haymarket Theatre in Chicago. She attended Keith public school and appeared in shows there. She also was fascinated with the saloons on State Street. When she was fourteen or fifteen, Ada joined the chorus at the Pekin Theatre but was forced to return to school.

At age sixteen Ada left school and began singing in vaudeville with Miller and Lyles. Later she toured the Theatre Owners' Booking Association and Pantage vaudeville circuits with McCabe's Georgia Troubadours, Ten Georgia Campers, the Kinky-Doo Trio, and the Oma Crosby Trio. The following year, in New York City, Ada met Barron Wilkins, the owner of Barron's Exclusive Club in Harlem; he nicknamed her "Bricktop" because of her flame-red hair. Later that year she performed at Roy Jones's saloon in Chicago and met the boxer Jack Johnson, for whom she worked at the Cabaret de Champion until it closed in 1912. Over the following years she appeared in many saloons, including the Panama Club, where she, Florence Mills, and Cora Green were known as the Panama Trio.

In 1917 Bricktop left the trio and went to Los Angeles. While working at the Watts Country Club she met Walter Delaney. They lived together until Delaney's history of arrests for selling drugs, gambling, and promoting prostitution forced them to move to San Francisco during a crackdown on vice in Los Angeles. Rather than drag her down with him, Delaney left Bricktop in San Francisco. She later moved to Seattle.

In 1922 Bricktop convinced Barron Wilkins to hire Elmer Snowden's Washingtonians, with pianist Duke Ellington, for his New York City Club. In 1924 she performed at the Café Le Grand Duc in Paris. One of her first acquaintances there was a busboy and struggling author named Langston Hughes. Visitors to Le Grand Duc included Zelda and F. Scott Fitzgerald, Fred Astaire, Ernest Hemingway, Man Ray, Pablo Picasso, John Steinbeck, Josephine Baker, Elsa Maxwell, and Cole and Linda Porter. In 1925 Bricktop taught the Charleston at the Porters' lavish Charleston parties, and they introduced her to the Paris elite. In the fall of 1926, after returning from the Porters' palazzo in Venice, Bricktop opened the Music Box saloon in Paris. It closed the same year, and she then took over Le Grand Duc. Wanting a more chic place, before the end of 1926 she opened Bricktop's, where guests such as Jascha Heifetz, Duke Ellington, Noël Coward, the Prince of Wales, and Paul Robeson, gave impromptu performances.

In 1927 Bricktop met saxophonist Peter Ducongé. They were married on 19 December 1929 and separated in 1933 but never divorced; they had no children. In 1931 Bricktop opened a bigger café, also named Bricktop's, with Mabel Mercer as her assistant. Following the custom of Montmartre cafés, Bricktop's closed for the summer; she opened another café during the summer in the resort of Biarritz. In 1934 the effects of the Great Depression forced her to move her café to a smaller location. By the fall of 1936 she could not afford to open for the season, so she and Mercer entertained at nightspots in Paris and Cannes.

From 1938 to 1939 Bricktop did radio broadcasts for the French government. In October 1939, at the insistence of the Duchess of Windsor and Lady Elsie de Wolfe Mendl, she fled the advancing war and returned to the United States, where she was reintroduced to American racial prejudice and segregation absent from her life in Paris. In New York City she worked at many cafés and attracted refugees from Paris. In 1940, when her following moved on, Bricktop helped open the Brittwood Café on 140th Street in Harlem. At first it was a success, drawing such celebrities and entertainers as Earl "Fatha" Hines, Anna Jones, Willie Grant, Minnie Hilton, and Robert Taylor. In 1943 Bricktop moved to Mexico City, where she lived for six years and was part owner of the Minuit and Chavez's clubs.

In 1949 Bricktop returned to Paris, and in May 1950 she opened a new Bricktop's on the Rue Fontaine. By Christmas it was closed. She then went to Rome, where in 1951 she opened Bricktop's on the Via Veneto, drawing Italian high society and royalty. While in Italy, Bricktop, who had converted to Catholicism in 1943, was involved with Catholic charity and fund-raising projects and became a friend of Bishop Fulton J. Sheen.

On 6 March 1964 Bricktop announced her retirement from the nightclub business because of poor health—she had arthritis and a heart condition. She returned to Chicago in 1965 to live with her sister Blonzetta. After Blonzetta's death in 1967, Bricktop settled in New York City. In 1972 she made her only recording, "So Long, Baby," with Cy Coleman. She also worked with Josephine Baker, a longtime friend, who was attempting a comeback, in 1973. In the same year Bricktop made the film documentary *Honeybaby, Honeybaby!* In 1975 she was awarded an honorary doctor of arts degree by Columbia College in Chicago. She continued to perform, but made few appearances after 1979 because of declining health. In 1983, on her last birthday, she was presented with the seal of New York City and a certificate of appreciation by Mayor Ed Koch. Just a few months later Bricktop died in her sleep at her Manhattan apartment. More than 300 people attended her funeral at St. Malachy's Church in Manhattan. She was buried at Woodlawn Cemetery in the Bronx.

T. S. Eliot is quoted as saying about the birth of Brick-

top: "And on that day Bricktop was born, and to her thorn, she gave a rose." Perhaps her most enduring contribution is herself. Although she was a stage entertainer and an early vaudevillian, Bricktop's special talent was to entertain and befriend some of the most famous and most talented people of the twentieth century, giving them a haven from their empty castles.

★

A collection of Bricktop's personal papers is at the Schomburg Center for Research in Black Culture of the New York Public Library. Her autobiography, *Bricktop by Bricktop* (1983), was written with James Haskins. Langston Hughes, *The Big Sea* (1963; repr. 1986), contains information on Bricktop's early days in Paris. An obituary is in the *New York Times* (1 Feb. 1984); an account of her funeral is in the *New York Times* (5 Feb. 1984).

RAYMOND L. ADAMS

BRODIE, Fawn McKay (*b.* 15 September 1915 in Ogden, Utah; *d.* 10 January 1981 in Santa Monica, California), historian known for her controversial biographies of prominent men.

The second of five children born to Thomas E. McKay, a farmer, and Fawn Brimhall, an artist, Brodie was raised in a picturesque farming community in northern Utah with her three sisters and brother. The family was devoutly Mormon and related to David O. McKay, a future president of the Church of Jesus Christ of Latter-day Saints. As a child, Brodie displayed precocious intelligence. While in grade school, she wrote poetry and at Weber High School excelled in public speaking. After graduating in 1930, she continued her education at Weber College before enrolling at the University of Utah. There she studied English and comparative literature and obtained her B.A. in 1934 at the age of eighteen. Brodie taught at Weber High School for a year, then left to attend the University of Chicago, where she pursued graduate study in English literature. In August 1936 she received an M.A. degree. That same month she wed outside the Mormon Church, marrying Bernard Brodie, a brilliant young graduate student majoring in political science and a nonpracticing Jew. The couple had three children.

In succeeding years, Brodie raised her family and accompanied Bernard as he completed his doctorate, conducted research at Princeton University, taught at Dartmouth College and Yale University, and worked at the Office of Naval Intelligence in Washington, D.C., during World War II. All the while Brodie was turning her hand to historical scholarship. With the assistance of an Alfred A. Knopf Fellowship awarded her in 1943, she undertook a biography of Joseph Smith. "I was . . . intrigued by the question of whether [he] was a prophet, and what he was like," she told an interviewer later in life. Published in 1945,

No Man Knows My History: The Life of Joseph Smith, the Mormon Prophet contended that Smith began as an outgoing and indolent man who spent his early years searching for buried treasure. He soon claimed to have received divine visions and unearthed gold plates that he "translated" as *The Book of Mormon*. Eventually, Smith called himself a true prophet, converted thousands to his faith, and attained martyrdom at the age of thirty-eight. If Brodie considered him something of an impostor, she nonetheless praised the physical grace and personal charm that enabled Smith to found a new, enduring religion. While non-Mormon scholars generally lauded her research, style, and sincerity, Mormon readers were deeply offended by the work, and Brodie was excommunicated by Mormon Church authorities in 1946 for her "apostasy."

Bernard Brodie's move to Southern California in 1951 to work at the RAND Corporation and the illnesses of Fawn's parents delayed publication of her second biography, *Thaddeus Stevens, Scourge of the South* (1959). In writing about an abolitionist who waged a relentless struggle against slavery, she was influenced by the nascent civil-rights movement. As with her life of Joseph Smith, Brodie carefully examined the formation of Stevens's youthful character. She explained his political behavior through psychoanalysis, speculating that his congenital clubfoot helped form his stern, unforgiving personality. Yet she also lauded Stevens as a champion of racial equality. Well researched and carefully written, the volume earned praise from many historians.

Brodie returned to Mormon history when her publisher asked that she edit a book about Salt Lake City written by the nineteenth-century English explorer Sir Richard Francis Burton. After *The City of the Saints, and Across the Rocky Mountains to California* appeared in 1963, she prepared a full-length life of this restless traveler who ventured to Mecca and sought the source of the Nile. For *The Devil Drives* (1967), Brodie tirelessly gathered materials to document Burton's life, particularly his unhappy childhood. She also consulted professional psychiatrists and physicians to explain his reckless behavior. A highly readable account, the book demonstrated that she had mastered the art of biography and could appeal to a general audience.

Although never entirely comfortable in the classroom, Brodie taught a course on American political biography at the University of California at Los Angeles from the late 1960s until she retired in 1977. Research done for class lectures led her to publish *Thomas Jefferson: An Intimate History* in 1974. In many ways a conventional biography, it was based on considerable research in primary and secondary sources. The work gained wide readership as well as notoriety because Brodie contended that Jefferson maintained a lengthy liaison with his slave Sally Hemings, who bore him several illegitimate children whom he never for-

Fawn Brodie. MANUSCRIPTS DIVISION, J. WILLARD MARRIOTT LIBRARY, UNIVERSITY OF UTAH

mally recognized. Traditional historians denounced both her assertions and her psychoanalytic explanation of Jefferson's character. Brodie felt she had presented a fair assessment, one that warmly praised Jefferson's intellect, rationality, democratic principles, natural simplicity, and antiwar policies.

In November 1978 cancer claimed the life of Brodie's husband, who had become a recognized authority on international power politics. Diagnosed with the same disease two years later, she hastened to complete her last biography, *Richard Nixon: The Shaping of His Character* (1981), for which she conducted numerous interviews with Nixon's associates and closely scrutinized his writings and speeches. Applying psychoanalytic methods to Nixon's childhood and adolescence, when his personality was formed by his harsh, unsuccessful father, his "saintly" mother, and the premature deaths of two brothers, Brodie concluded that the future president developed into a lonely, mistrustful, and vengeful adult, both duplicitous and moralistic in his public life. Always seeking the approval of others to gain power, Nixon alternated between self-destruction and rehabilitation. The biography was condemned by many reviewers, who strongly criticized her methods and conclusions. Brodie did not live to read the reviews. She died in Santa Monica and was cremated.

Brodie was five feet, ten inches tall with dark brown hair and brown eyes. Lacking a doctorate in history and self-trained in psychoanalytic method, she never fully gained confidence in her abilities, and admitted to an interviewer that she found it "incredibly hard to do research and write one really good paragraph." Yet her talent for producing substantial biographies of important historical figures, studies based on meticulous investigation of the sources and written in a lucid style, attests to her qualities as a serious, if controversial, scholar.

★

Brodie's papers and books are at the University of Utah library. She and her husband discussed their work in an interview with Marshall Berges, "Fawn and Bernard Brodie: They Write, Teach, Study, and Research," *Los Angeles Times Home Magazine* (20 Feb. 1977). In "Inflation Idyll: A Family Farm in Huntsville," *Utah Historical Quarterly* 40 (spring 1972): 112–121, Brodie fondly recalled her childhood years. She elaborated on her biography of Jefferson in an interview with Arnold Hano, "A Conversation with Fawn M. Brodie," *Book-of-the-Month Club News* (spring 1974), and that of Nixon in an interview with Tom Bourne, "In Search of Nixon," *Horizon* 24 (Feb. 1981): 42–45. Brodie reflected on her craft in a lecture, "Can We Manipulate the Past?" (1970), published by the Center for Studies in the American West, and in an article, "The Political Hero in America: His Fate and His Future," *Virginia Quarterly Review* 46 (winter 1970): 46–60. Her work is carefully evaluated by Newell G. Bringhurst in "Applause, Attack, and Ambivalence—Varied Responses to Fawn M. Brodie's *No Man Knows My History*," *Utah Historical Quarterly* 57 (winter 1989): 46–63, and "Fawn M. Brodie—Her Biographies as Autobiography," *Pacific Historical Review* 59 (May 1990): 203–229. Obituaries are in the *Los Angeles Times* (12 Jan. 1981), and *New York Times* (13 Jan. 1981).

JAMES FRIGUGLIETTI

BROOKS, (Mary) Louise (*b.* 14 November 1906 in Cherryvale, Kansas; *d.* 8 August 1985 in Rochester, New York), actress and writer who won cinematic fame as the amoral Lulu in the German film *Pandora's Box* (1929).

Louise Brooks was the second of four children of Leonard P. Brooks, an attorney, and Myra Rude, a homemaker. Myra Brooks had no interest in child care and spent most of her time in amateur cultural pursuits. She encouraged her children to read, however, and fostered young Louise's aptitude for dancing.

At age ten, Louise Brooks was a professional dancer. In November 1921 her mother took her to see the Denishawn Dancers at the Crawford Theater in Wichita, Kansas. The

Louise Brooks. ARCHIVE PHOTOS

company, formed by Ruth St. Denis and Ted Shawn, was the nation's premier modern-dance group. Shawn encouraged the petite fifteen-year-old to attend the Denishawn school in New York the following summer. She did so—and was asked to join the troupe in the fall of 1922. Brooks toured with Denishawn for two seasons, earning several featured roles. In the spring of 1924, however, St. Denis asked the seventeen-year-old dancer to leave the company—probably because she was unwilling to conform to Denishawn's strict moral code.

Brooks found a job on Broadway in the chorus of George White's *Scandals* in the summer of 1924. The hard-drinking, hard-playing dancer left the *Scandals* abruptly in the fall to sail to Europe. She danced briefly in London, then returned to New York. Early in 1925 Florenz Ziegfeld hired her to dance, first in a musical play, *Louie the 14th,* and then in the chorus of his famed *Follies*.

The photogenic Brooks also worked as a model and made a screen test for the 1925 film *Street of Forgotten Men*. The test was incorporated into the film, and Brooks signed a contract with Paramount Pictures. She made several comedies at Paramount's studios in the Astoria section of Queens. Meanwhile, she kept up her social whirl and embarked on a number of affairs, most notably one with Charlie Chaplin. In July 1926 Brooks married the film director A. Edward ("Eddie") Sutherland. The couple did not live together until Paramount closed the Astoria studios and transferred Brooks to Hollywood in 1927. They had no children and were divorced in 1928.

Brooks wrote later that she never felt at home in the unliterary, sweatshop atmosphere of Hollywood and never felt appreciated by her employers there. Most of her films were light fare. In 1928, two films gave her more substantial roles. In *A Girl in Every Port* she played a femme fatale, and in *Beggars of Life* she portrayed a girl on the lam, dressed as a boy.

When Brooks's contract came up for renewal, Paramount refused to give her a raise. Having heard that the German director G. W. Pabst was interested in hiring her, Brooks walked away from Hollywood. In October 1928 she went to Berlin to play the role for which she is best known. The search for a screen actress to play Lulu, the heroine of two plays by Frank Wedekind, had preoccupied Pabst for months. After seeing Brooks in *A Girl in Every Port,* he chose her over many German actresses, including, allegedly, Marlene Dietrich. Lulu is a femme fatale—but a surprisingly innocent one. She lives for pleasure and inspires lust and violence in all around her: she accidentally kills her husband, stirs a lover to homicide, and is finally slain by Jack the Ripper. Pabst had Brooks act in a playful, open manner, emphasizing her dancer's movements. Film historians have found her mesmerizing, but the film was not well received in its day. Brooks starred again for Pabst in *Diary of a Lost Girl* (1929), then went to France to make her first sound film, *Prix de Beauté* (released in 1930). Both garnered poor reviews.

Back in the United States late in 1929, Brooks looked for work but was hampered by her reputation as an uncooperative actress. She made a few low-budget movies, then turned down an offer to play the part eventually given to Jean Harlow in *The Public Enemy*. Biographer Barry Paris sees this decision as the end of her acting career.

In 1931 Brooks was offered the lead in a Broadway-bound play but was fired before it opened. The following year she declared bankruptcy. On 10 October 1933 she married Chicago playboy Deering Davis. The two performed briefly as a ballroom-dance duo and were divorced in 1934. They had no children.

After touring briefly with another dance partner, Brooks spent the years from 1936 to 1940 in Hollywood, making B pictures and dancing. In 1940 she returned to Wichita, where she worked sporadically for three years, including a stint running a dance studio; then she went back to New York. There Brooks acted briefly in radio soap operas and gathered stories for gossip columns. Most of her income in the 1940s and early 1950s, she admitted later, came from

men with whom she was romantically linked, although she did work as a salesclerk at Saks Fifth Avenue for two years. In 1954 a former lover, William S. Paley, president of the Columbia Broadcasting System, initiated a stipend to fund her attempts to establish herself as a writer.

In 1955, Brooks's renaissance began. A Paris exhibit marking the cinema's sixtieth anniversary prominently featured her. And archivist James Card of the George Eastman House International Museum of Photography initiated a worshipful, quasi-romantic relationship with Brooks, which led to her move in 1956 to Rochester. She began to write historical and autobiographical essays for film journals, many of which were collected in her book *Lulu in Hollywood* (1982).

Brooks's fame reached new heights in 1979, when Kenneth Tynan's *New Yorker* profile, "The Girl in the Black Helmet," publicized her as she liked to see herself—as a hard-talking maverick who had proved too strong for the Hollywood dream machine. Rediscovered but alone, Louise Brooks died in Rochester of a heart attack in 1985 and was buried there in Holy Sepulchre Cemetery.

Since her death, historians have agreed that Louise Brooks's performance in *Pandora's Box* was a landmark of the silent screen. David Thomson has written, "There is no more influential performance in screen history; no silent film so up to date; no movie better appreciated in hindsight." Brooks's life is harder to interpret. She viewed herself as free and anti-Hollywood; historians often speculate longingly about the paths her career might have taken had she ever shown any interest in it. As Barry Paris has observed, "Time and time again, Louise Brooks snatched obscurity from the jaws of fame."

★

Brooks's papers were left to George Eastman House; they are sealed until 2006. Her *Lulu in Hollywood* (1982) contains several autobiographical essays. Barry Paris, *Louise Brooks* (1989), attempts to find the parts of her life Brooks tried to keep hidden, with some success. Roland Jaccard, ed., *Louise Brooks: Portrait of an Anti-Star* (1986), is a series of essays about Brooks's film career. Kenneth Tynan's *New Yorker* profile (11 June 1979) is reprinted in his *Show People* (1979). Kevin Brownlow interviews Brooks extensively in *The Parade's Gone By* (1968). David Thomson's thoughts on the star appear in "Saint Lulu," *New Republic* (25 Dec. 1989).

TINKY "DAKOTA" WEISBLAT

BROWN, George Rufus (*b.* 12 May 1898 in Belton, Texas; *d.* 22 January 1983 in Houston, Texas), businessman and philanthropist who built an energy and construction empire.

George Rufus Brown was the son of Riney Louis Brown, owner of a general merchandise store, and Lucy Wilson

George Brown. RICE UNIVERSITY ARCHIVES, WOODSON RESEARCH CENTER, RICE UNIVERSITY LIBRARY, HOUSTON, TEXAS

(King) Brown, a housewife. In the years after his high school graduation he led a somewhat peripatetic life. He entered Rice University in 1916, where he was a member of the Student Army Training Corps. In 1917 he entered the Marine Officer Training School at the Georgia School of Technology, where he remained only about a year. After a semester at the University of Texas at Austin, he transferred to the Colorado School of Mines, from which he graduated in 1922. Brown next went to work as a mining engineer for the Anaconda Copper Company in Butte, Montana, but suffered a serious injury on the job. He returned to Texas and joined Brown and Root, a small construction company formed in 1919 by his brother Herman and Dan Root, Herman's brother-in-law. Brown married Alice Nelson Pratt on 25 November 1925; they had three daughters.

Following the death of Root in 1929, the Brown brothers purchased the firm. Brown and Root became one of the world's largest construction conglomerates. Initially it was principally a road-building company. In the late 1920s and early 1930s, when the Great Depression restricted funds for road construction, the Browns were forced to look for new business ventures. In 1936 they signed their largest contract to that date, to build the Marshall Ford Dam on the Col-

orado River. In 1942, as World War II pulled the nation out of its economic stagnation, the brothers formed the Brown Shipbuilding Company. The firm, located on the Houston Ship Channel, built more than 350 vessels for the U.S. Navy, employed 25,000 people, and was awarded the Army-Navy "E" award (for excellence) and a presidential citation. The Brown brothers also constructed an air and naval facility in Corpus Christi, Texas. Following World War II, when the federal government auctioned war surplus property, the brothers joined a group that successfully bid on the Big Inch and Little Inch pipelines that ran from Texas to New York. They converted these petroleum pipelines for the shipment of natural gas and formed the Texas Eastern Transmission Company.

When the oil and gas industry began to boost Houston's economy, Brown became an active participant in the economic, educational, and cultural development of the city. As a member of the board of trustees of Rice University, to which he was elected on 13 January 1943, he was involved in the location of the National Aeronautic and Space Administration facility, later named the Johnson Manned Space Flight Center, near Houston on land owned by Rice University (1961). With a group of businessmen Brown purchased land north of Houston that became the city's major airport.

Brown and Root became involved in several international projects, including air and naval bases in Guam, Spain, and France and military bases in Vietnam. Besides military projects the firm built offshore drilling facilities in the North Sea, as well as the required barges and pipelines. One of the firm's most interesting, although uncompleted, undertakings was Project Mohole, which sought to drill through Earth's crust in an effort to determine the composition of the core.

Brown was a member of the boards of directors of the Haliburton Company, First City Bancorporation of Texas, International Telephone and Telegraph, Armco Steel, Southland Paper, Texas Gulf, Trans World Airlines, Highland Resources, and Louisiana Land and Exploration. In 1982 he was awarded the American Petroleum Institute Gold Medal.

Brown was a generous benefactor of Rice University and of the Colorado School of Mines. At the latter he created the George R. Brown Computing Center. At Rice University, where he served on the board of trustees for twenty-five years, fifteen of them as chairman, the fruits of his generosity include George R. Brown Hall, a state-of-the-art biotechnology research facility, and the Alice Pratt Brown Music Building. On 11 November 1966 Brown and his wife were awarded Rice University's Gold Medal for distinguished service. The city of Houston named its convention center after him.

Brown died in Houston, shortly after suffering a heart attack.

★

Documents are available at the Brown Foundation and the Woodson Research Center, Fondren Library, Rice University, both in Houston. "Roadbuilders with a Flair for Other Jobs," *Business Week* (25 May 1957), includes a cover photo of the Brown brothers. See also Joseph A. Pratt and Christopher J. Castañeda, *Builders Herman and George R. Brown* (1998). An obituary is in the *New York Times* (24 Jan. 1983).

JAMES A. CASTAÑEDA

BRYANT, Paul William ("Bear") (*b*. 11 September 1911 in Moro Bottom, Arkansas; *d*. 26 January 1983 in Tuscaloosa, Alabama), football coach who compiled more victories than any other major college coach and who led the University of Alabama to six national championships during the 1960s and 1970s.

Paul Bryant, the eighth of nine surviving children of Wilson Monroe Bryant and Ida Mae Kilgore Bryant, was born in Moro Bottom, Arkansas, a rural community near the town of Fordyce. The Bryant's farm generated little cash income, and the family's extreme poverty was exacerbated by the chronic illness of Wilson Bryant, who died at age forty-six in 1931. Bryant often spoke reverentially about his mother's strength, religious piety, and hard work, which enabled his family to persevere amid continuing hardship. A physically imposing young man with a penchant for fighting, he acquired the nickname that epitomized his toughness as a fourteen-year-old, when he wrestled a carnival bear on the stage of the Lyric Theater in Fordyce. An indifferent student, he excelled as a football player at Fordyce High School.

In 1931, the assistant coach of the University of Alabama, Hank Crisp, recruited Bryant to play football there. After a semester at Tuscaloosa (Alabama) High School to pick up the last few credits needed for graduation, he entered the university in January 1932. He was an end on the Alabama varsity team from 1933 until 1935 under head coach Frank Thomas. Those three teams compiled a record of 23–3–2 and won two Southeastern Conference (SEC) championships. Led by Dixie Howell and Don Hutson, the 1934 team won the national title and defeated Stanford in the Rose Bowl. Bryant earned second-team all-SEC honors in 1935; his success was less a function of raw athletic talent than of his powerful work ethic and indomitable will to win. He displayed those traits in 1935, when he played in a game against the University of Tennessee despite having broken the fibula in his left leg the previous week.

Bryant married Mary Harmon Black of Birmingham on 2 June 1935. They had two children, Mae Martin and Paul

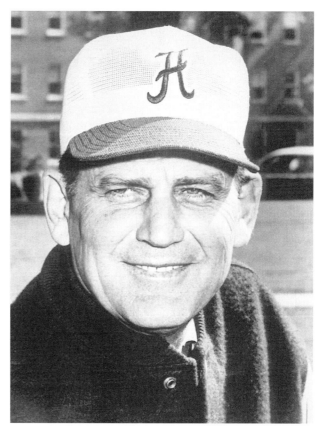

Paul ("Bear") Bryant. ARCHIVE PHOTOS

William, Jr. He worked as an assistant coach under Thomas at Alabama from 1936 until 1939, and as an assistant to Red Sanders at Vanderbilt University in Nashville, Tennessee, in 1940 and 1941. Bryant enlisted in the navy after Japan attacked Pearl Harbor. He served in North Africa in 1943 and worked as an instructor (as well as football coach) at the preflight training school for naval aviators at the University of North Carolina in 1944 and 1945.

The University of Maryland hired Bryant as its head football coach after his 1945 discharge from the navy. His 1945 team finished 6–2–1, but Bryant impetuously resigned in January 1946 amid a dispute with the University of Maryland president, Curly Byrd. Byrd, himself a former head football coach at Maryland, sought to exercise a degree of control over the program that Bryant found unacceptable.

Bryant accepted the head coaching job at the University of Kentucky in Lexington in 1946, and he energized a moribund program that had consistently been overshadowed by Adolph Rupp's basketball program. In eight seasons at Kentucky (1946–1953), Bryant's teams compiled a record of 60–23–5, played in four bowl games, and finished in the top twenty in each of his last five seasons there. His 1950 team went 11–1 and won the SEC title, the only time that a Kentucky team has accomplished this feat.

As the culmination of his long-standing rivalry with Rupp, Bryant resigned abruptly from Kentucky in February 1954 and accepted the head coaching job at Texas A&M. His grueling spring and summer practices drove all but 29 of the 115 scholarship players he inherited to quit the team, enhancing his reputation as a demanding taskmaster who required supreme effort and total dedication from his players. The woefully outmanned 1954 team finished 1–9, the only losing season of Bryant's career. As he had done at Kentucky, however, Bryant quickly turned the downtrodden A&M team into a winner. His 1956 team went undefeated and won the Southwest Conference championship. The A&M halfback, John David Crow, won the 1957 Heisman Trophy, the only Bryant-coached player to do so. Bryant's tenure at Texas A&M was partially tainted by his being implicated in a recruiting scandal, and the National Collegiate Athletic Association (NCAA) placed Texas A&M on two years' probation in 1955.

Bryant's success at Texas A&M contrasted sharply with the declining football fortunes of the University of Alabama, which had won only four games between 1955 and 1957. In the fall of 1957, the newly appointed Alabama president, Frank Rose, and numerous alumni pleaded with Bryant to become head coach at his alma mater. Bryant likened these entreaties to "Mama's call," and avowed that his loyalty to the institution that had elevated him from the crushing poverty of his youth was the only enticement that could induce him to break his contract with Texas A&M. He became head coach and athletic director at Alabama in January 1958, and held both positions until January 1983. In twenty-five seasons, he posted a record of 232–46–9 at Alabama, including six national championships, thirteen SEC championships, twenty-two top-twenty seasons, and twenty-four bowl appearances. Bryant's Alabama teams dominated their archrival Auburn University, also in Alabama, winning nineteen of their twenty-five games, including nine consecutive victories between 1973 and 1981.

The coach hailed as the Great Rehabilitator posted a 5–4–1 record in 1958 with a team that had been 2–7–1 in 1957. His efforts culminated in a national championship in 1961, when the Crimson Tide finished with an 11–0 record and a Sugar Bowl victory over the University of Arkansas. The defense, anchored by the linebacker Lee Roy Jordan, gave up only twenty-five points all year. Alabama continued this superlative performance for the next five years. It posted records of 10–1 in 1962 and 9–2 in 1963, finishing in the top ten nationally each season. Alabama won consecutive national championships in 1964 and 1965, and was denied an unprecedented third consecutive national title in the 1966 wire service polls despite being the only major college with an undefeated, untied record.

By the mid-1960s, Bryant had become a hero of mythic proportions to his millions of admirers. His critics, however, saw him as a contract-jumper and an unscrupulous recruiter who taught his teams to play with excessive brutality. The barrage of criticism culminated in a March 1963 article in the *Saturday Evening Post* alleging that he and the University of Georgia athletic director Wally Butts had conspired to fix the 1962 Alabama-Georgia game. Butts won a $406,000 libel judgment in federal court against the *Post*, and Bryant settled out of court for $300,000.

Racial controversies bedeviled Bryant during the 1960s as well. Bryant was a moderate who aligned himself with the southern business leaders who opposed the racial demagoguery of Alabama governor George Wallace. He broke the so-called unwritten law by allowing his team to play in the 1959 Liberty Bowl against a racially integrated Penn State team at the same time that the University of Alabama was fighting its doomed battle to remain segregated. Despite Bryant's stance, millions of southerners regarded his all-white championship teams as a vindication of white supremacy, and he was unwillingly associated with the resistance to desegregation. The national revulsion over the flagrant racial injustices in the state of Alabama cost Bryant's team the opportunity to play in the 1962 Rose Bowl, and many observers believed that it cost Alabama the 1966 national championship as well. Bryant moved cautiously when it came to desegregating his own team, however, preferring to allow other SEC programs to take the lead. In December 1969 the halfback Wilbur Jackson became the first black player to sign an athletic grant-in-aid at Alabama, and in September 1971 the defensive end John Mitchell became the first black player to play for the Alabama varsity team. Desegregation proceeded smoothly at Alabama, and by the mid-1970s Bryant was widely regarded as a symbol of the new southern paradigm of harmonious racial coexistence.

Alabama finished the 1960s with a record of 90–26–4, the best among major college football teams. It won three national championships and four SEC titles. Yet Alabama declined somewhat in the late 1960s, losing thirteen games between 1968 and 1970. Bryant dedicated himself to reviving the Alabama program, and his teams of the 1970s surpassed the extraordinary record compiled by their 1960s counterparts. He installed the wishbone offense in 1971, and a coach heretofore known for his defensive-mindedness fielded teams with offensive explosiveness. Alabama posted a 103–16–1 record during the 1970s, winning an unprecedented eight SEC titles and three national championships. Alabama and Notre Dame played one another for the first time in the 1973 Sugar Bowl, a thriller that Alabama lost by the score of 24–23. Another memorable game was the 1979 Sugar Bowl, in which a dramatic goal-line stand late in the fourth quarter sealed a 14–7 victory over Penn State and secured the national championship.

Bryant eclipsed Amos Alonzo Stagg's record for career victories by a collegiate coach by winning his 315th game against Auburn on 28 November 1981. He retired after the 1982 season. Bryant died of a heart attack at Tuscaloosa's Druid City Hospital on 26 January 1983. Hundreds of thousands of mourners lined the route of his funeral cortege from Tuscaloosa to Birmingham's Elmwood Cemetery in a massive and spontaneous outpouring of grief over the passing of Alabama's larger-than-life hero.

His career record of 323–85–17 included six national championships, fifteen conference championships, and twenty-nine bowl appearances. He was posthumously inducted into the College Football Hall of Fame in 1986. Scores of Bryant's players became stars in professional football, including George Blanda and Babe Parilli from Kentucky, John David Crow and Charlie Krueger from Texas A&M, and Lee Roy Jordan, Joe Namath, Kenny Stabler, Johnny Musso, John Hannah, Ozzie Newsome, Richard Todd, Sylvester Croom, and Bob Baumhower from Alabama. Forty-five men who played or coached for Bryant became head coaches of collegiate or professional teams, including Bum Phillips, Ray Perkins, Pat Dye, and Gene Stallings, who won a national championship as head coach at Alabama in 1993.

Bryant embodied the larger social and economic transformation of the twentieth-century South. He grew up amid the grinding poverty of the cotton-producing South and worked tirelessly to transcend his humble origins. He triumphed in the highly competitive, pressure-packed world of big-time college football and became a millionaire businessman. His financial interests included insurance, banking, meat packing, an automobile dealership, real estate, and product endorsements. Yet he never lost his affinity for the values and traditions of the agrarian world of his youth, and southerners loved him for it. He prospered for over two decades with all-white teams, but he successfully negotiated the difficult process of desegregation. He mellowed with age without losing the fire and drive that propelled him to the top. He was combative and controversial from the 1940s through the mid-1960s, but he diminished his authoritarian style during the late 1960s to adapt to the values of a new generation of college athletes. By the early 1980s, he possessed an avuncular, folksy image and was respected and admired by millions nationwide, reflecting the incorporation of the South into the mainstream of American society and culture.

★

Bryant's personal papers and related research materials are located at the Paul W. Bryant Museum in Tuscaloosa, Alabama. Two biographies of Bryant have been written: Keith Dunnavant, *Coach: The Life of Paul "Bear" Bryant* (1996), is comprehensive and solidly researched; and Mickey Herskowitz, *The Legend of Bear Bryant* (1987), is an engaging work by a Houston newspaperman who knew Bryant well. Paul W. Bryant and John Underwood, *Bear: The Hard Life and Good Times of Alabama's Coach Bryant* (1974), captures the essence of Bryant's character and personality and is one of the most entertaining and memorable sports autobiographies ever written. Bryant's *Building a Championship Football Team* (1960) is a coaching primer that reveals his coaching philosophy and systematic approach to the game. James Kirby, *Fumble: Bear Bryant, Wally Butts, and the Great College Football Scandal* (1986), is a comprehensive account of the *Saturday Evening Post* story and the ensuing lawsuit. John Forney, *Above the Noise of the Crowd* (1986), is a memoir by Alabama's longtime radio announcer that covers most of Bryant's career; Bryant figures prominently in John Forney and Steve Townsend, *Talk of the Tide: An Oral History of Alabama Football Since 1920* (1993). Thomas Stoddard, *Turnaround: The Untold Story of Bear Bryant's First Year at Alabama* (1996), recounts the 1958 season, and Geoffrey Norman, *Alabama Showdown: The Football Rivalry Between Auburn and Alabama* (1986), deals primarily with the years after Bryant's death but focuses on the Bryant years as well. An obituary is in the *New York Times* (27 Jan. 1983).

ANDREW DOYLE

BRYNNER, Yul (*b.* 11 July 1920 in Vladivostok, Russia; *d.* 10 October 1985 in New York City), virile screen and musical theater actor best known for the stage and film versions of *The King and I,* as well as film roles in *The Ten Commandments* and *Anastasia.*

He was born Youl Bryner (Yul Brynner became his name in 1946) to Boris Bryner, a mining engineer of Swiss-Mongolian ancestry, and his wife, Marousia Blagovidova Bryner. He had an older sister, Vera, who became an operatic and folk singer. When his parents separated around 1925, his mother and sister eventually moved to Harbin, Manchuria. In order to provide vocal training for her daughter, Brynner's mother took the children to Paris in 1934, where they associated with artistic White Russian circles as well as with the gypsy community of restaurateurs and musicians. Brynner enrolled at the Lycée Moncelle for two years, excelling in gymnastics, yoga, swimming, and waterskiing; he did not complete his formal education and, impressed by the cinema, resolved to become an actor.

For about two years he performed as a trapeze artist with the Cirque d'Hiver, until a somersault accident resulted in several cracked ribs and broken bones. He later created his own clown routine, but soon concentrated exclusively on singing and playing the guitar at Parisian cabarets, where he met Jean Cocteau and started to circulate with his group of artistic friends. Beginning in 1937 Brynner stayed for

Yul Brynner, 1978. POPPERFOTO/ARCHIVE PHOTOS

about a year with his maternal aunt and her daughter in Lausanne, Switzerland.

Upon his return to Paris, Brynner worked at sweeping floors, working on sets, sewing wigs and costumes, learning managerial duties, and studying pantomime and acting in French and Russian at Georges and Ludmilla Pitoëff's Théâtre des Mathurins. After Vera's marriage and relocation to New York, Brynner and his mother traveled in 1939 to Dalian, China, where his father resided with his former actress-companion and their adopted daughter.

As war approached, Brynner came to New York in 1940 with his mother in order to study with Michael Chekhov, who had moved his Chekhov Theatre Studio from England to Ridgefield, Connecticut. Speaking minimal English, Brynner learned lines phonetically and also drove the Chekhov Theatre Players' tour bus around the United States. He appeared in minor Shakespearean parts, such as Cornwall in *King Lear* and Fabian in *Twelfth Night;* the latter opened at New York's Little Theater (8 December 1941) for fifteen performances with Beatrice Straight and Hurd Hatfield. In order to keep up with medical expenses

for his mother, diagnosed with leukemia in 1941, Brynner bused tables, worked as a bouncer and usher, modeled for photographers, and performed his collection of gypsy songs. His mother died in 1943. During the war, he worked with the U.S. Office of War Information on broadcasts to the French Resistance.

Stage appearances included *L'Annonce faite à Marie* (a benefit performance, 20 May 1942, Barbizon Plaza Theater) and *The House in Paris* (Toronto, January 1944), both directed by Ludmilla Pitoëff, and *The Moon Vine* at the Morosco Theater (11 February 1943). On 6 September 1943 he married Broadway and film actress Virginia Gilmore. They had a son, Yul (Rock) Brynner, Jr., born in 1946.

Brynner made his Broadway debut as Tsai-Yong opposite Mary Martin in 142 performances of the esoteric musical play *Lute Song* (Plymouth Theater, 6 February 1946), in which he used the name "Yul Brynner" for the first time, and for which he won the Donaldson Award for the most promising new Broadway actor of 1946. After a yearlong American tour, he appeared in London in *Dark Eyes* (24 March 1947, Strand Theatre). Returning to New York, he reopened *Lute Song* at the Winter Garden (11 October 1948) for only twenty-four performances. In Hollywood he made his first screen test; in Paris he gave nightclub performances.

Around 1948 Brynner began a long association with television by working first with NBC and then CBS. He was associated with the earliest talk shows, sometimes working together with his wife; he also acted alone or with her in dramas for NBC's *Fireside Theater* and CBS's *Studio One.* His directorial responsibilities at CBS from 1948 to 1950 included fill-in work (including United Nations coverage); episodes of *Studio One, Somerset Maugham Theater,* and *Danger;* and the fifteen-minute children's series, *Snarky Parker* (January–September 1950).

His first film appearance was as a villain in *Port of New York* (1949), but then arose the careermaking role of his life, that of King Mongkut of Siam in *The King and I,* a musical play by Richard Rodgers and Oscar Hammerstein II based on Margaret Landon's *Anna and the King of Siam* (1944). Having been recommended by Mary Martin to the composer and lyricist, Brynner auditioned for the two at the Majestic Theatre; Brynner's "controlled ferocity" impressed Rodgers. After the pre-Broadway run in New Haven, Connecticut, Brynner went on to open on Broadway at the St. James Theatre on 29 March 1951. Success was immediate for the musical, its star (Gertrude Lawrence as Anna), and Brynner, who shaved his head for the part. For the rest of his life he would be associated with this award-winning role, for which he received the Donaldson Award for best actor and the Tony Award for best supporting actor. He received top billing after Miss Lawrence's death in September 1952; absent for three months in 1952, he continued until its final, 1,246th performance on 20 March 1954 and went on tour for a year.

Relocating his family from New York to the Los Angeles area, Brynner concentrated on his film career. First came a powerful performance as Rameses II in Cecil B. DeMille's remake of *The Ten Commandments;* then he reprised his stage role in the film version of *The King and I* and appeared as General Bounine in *Anastasia*. All three were released in 1956. For his screen re-creation of the King, he earned the 1956 best actor Academy Award and the best performer (musical) award of the National Board of Review of Motion Pictures.

Next, there was the less successful epic, *The Brothers Karamazov* (1958); despite daily discomfort from injuring his back on the set, he continued with the film. Subsequent films offered important roles, yet failed to match the grand quality of the three 1956 films: Jean Lafitte in *The Buccaneer* (1958); *The Journey* (1959); *The Sound and the Fury* (1959); and *Solomon and Sheba* (1959). The last, which was King Vidor's final feature film, was three-quarters finished when Tyrone Power, the original Solomon, died and Brynner agreed to assume the role; much of the ill-fated film had to be reshot. In several of these films, Brynner wore a wig or toupee, a fact humorously noted by the photographic press.

Unfortunately, out of the nearly forty films of his career, the quality of the 1956 ones remained unmatched; only *The Magnificent Seven* (1960) seemed to reestablish his former level of international acclaim. He played the Chairman in *The Madwoman of Chaillot* (1969) with Katharine Hepburn, and the robotic Gunslinger in Michael Crichton's *Westworld* and its sequel *Futureworld* (1973 and 1976, respectively).

Brynner served as special consultant to the United Nations High Commissioner for Refugees (1959–1960). He published *Bring Forth the Children* (1960), a narrative and photographic description of his visits to refugee camps. His experiences were the subject of "Rescue—with Yul Brynner," a CBS television special produced by Edward R. Murrow.

On 26 March 1960, his wife divorced him for incompatibility; five days later he married Doris Kleiner in Mexico City. Their daughter, Victoria, was born in 1962 in Lausanne, where they made their home. In May 1965 he renounced his U.S. citizenship, which he had acquired in 1947, having always maintained his Swiss citizenship. Brynner explained that it was easier for him to have the same citizenship as his wife and daughter, who were both Swiss. After his divorce from Kleiner, in 1971, he married Jacqueline de Thion de la Chaume de Croisset in Deauville, France, on 23 September 1971; their primary residence was a manor, Criqueboeuf, in Normandy. By the

spring of 1975, they had adopted two Vietnamese girls from Saigon, Mia and Melody.

Working again in the United States, Brynner starred in the CBS television series *Anna and the King* (17 September–31 December 1972). He played Odysseus in a new musical, *Home Sweet Homer,* which enjoyed a ten-month pre-Broadway tour until its Broadway opening—and closing—the same night (Palace Theater, 4 January 1976).

The final phase of his professional career was crowned by two major revivals and tours of *The King and I,* with Broadway openings on 2 May 1977 at the Uris Theater and 7 January 1985 at the Broadway Theater, along with performances at London's Palladium (June 1979). Upon his 4,500th performance as the King in 1985, he received a special Tony award.

After a third divorce, in 1983, Brynner married in April of that year Kathy Yam Choo (also known as Kathy Lee), a young dancer in the London production of *The King and I*. In September, the lifetime smoker (five cigarette packs a day) was informed about his inoperable lung cancer. He continued the tour of *The King and I* through Thanksgiving Day, whereupon he and his wife traveled to Europe. Radiation and other treatments seemed to place the cancer in remission, and the four-month Broadway run was extended to 30 June 1985, Brynner's 4,625th performance as the King of Siam; on that day the audience sang "Auld Lang Syne" in his honor.

Hospitalized after suffering a stroke in September 1985, Brynner died at New York Hospital–Cornell Medical Center in New York City. He was cremated. A secular memorial service was held at New York's Shubert Theater on 30 January 1986. Even after his death, Brynner's face and voice came through on television as the American Cancer Society aired a television commercial in which Brynner pronounced an ominous message against smoking.

Brynner's distinctive bearing and accented speech added an exotic luster to his acting on both stage and screen. His sturdy physique, disciplined demeanor, penetrating brown eyes, and steady intensity all combined to create unique, potent portrayals of different types of out-of-the-ordinary characters, even in his lesser films. Perhaps the very trademark of his ageless, shaved head and the commanding tones of his rich voice projected a sense of an almost steel-like dramatic starkness, an internalized sense of nobility, and an overwhelmingly masculine presence, which made him perfect as Pharaoh of Egypt and King of Siam.

★

Many of the facts of Brynner's life, especially his early life, are unknown or in doubt; he often provided conflicting information in various interviews. Two helpful biographies are Jhan Robbins, *Yul Brynner: The Inscrutable King* (1987) and Rock Brynner, *Yul, The Man Who Would Be King: A Memoir of Father and Son* (1989). His daughter Victoria Brynner published *Yul Brynner, Photogra-*

pher (1996), a wonderful collection of prints, many of which are rare candid shots of his famous friends. See also Richard G. Hubler, "Yul Brynner, Jack of All Mimes," *Coronet* (1957); "Yul Brynner, Golden Egghead," *Newsweek* (19 May 1958); Alvin H. Marill, "Yul Brynner: An Oriental Face and Bald Head Are Not His Only Assets," *Films in Review* 21, no. 8 (Oct. 1970): 457–472. Interesting interviews with Brynner include "Brynner Rex," *New Yorker* (21 Apr. 1951), Jon Whitcomb, "Bald Box-Office King," *Cosmopolitan* (May 1957), and Pete Martin, "I Call on Yul Brynner," *Saturday Evening Post* (22 Nov. 1958). Obituaries are in the *New York Times* (10 Oct. 1985), *Los Angeles Times* (10 Oct. 1985), *The Times* (London) (11 Oct. 1985), and *Variety* (16 Oct. 1985).

MADELINE SAPIENZA

BUNKER, Ellsworth (*b.* 11 May 1894 in Yonkers, New York; *d.* 27 September 1984 in Brattleboro, Vermont), ambassador to South Vietnam and diplomat who negotiated the treaties relinquishing U.S. control of the Panama Canal.

The elder son of Jeanie Polhemus Cobb, a housewife, and George Raymond Bunker, cofounder of the National Sugar Refining Company, Bunker spent his early years at the family home in Yonkers with his younger brother and sister

Ellsworth Bunker, 1972. AGENCE FRANCE PRESSE/ARCHIVE PHOTOS

and older half brother. After graduating from the Mackenzie School in Dobbs Ferry, New York, in 1912, he entered Yale College, where he majored in history and economics. At Yale he was a member of the rowing team and, despite poor vision resulting from a childhood attack of typhoid, participated in the Reserve Officers Training Corps. (He never served on active duty.)

After graduating from Yale with an A.B. degree in 1916, Bunker went to work for National Sugar Refining, initially as a laborer on its docks in Yonkers. Bunker rose rapidly through supervisory and management positions and was elected to the company's board of directors upon his father's death in 1927. Meanwhile, he had married Harriet Allen Butler on 24 April 1920; they had three children.

Bunker was named company secretary in 1931 and was promoted to vice president and treasurer in 1934. He became president of the company in 1940 and in 1948 rose to chairman of the board of directors. During World War II he headed the Cane Sugar Refiners War Committee and served on the boards of directors of sugar companies in Puerto Rico, Cuba, and Mexico.

A lifelong Democrat, Bunker was asked by Secretary of State Dean Acheson, a friend at Yale, to accept an appointment by President Harry Truman as U.S. ambassador to Argentina. In 1951 he resigned his position with National Sugar to take the ambassadorship. Argentina, at the time Latin America's richest and most powerful nation, was ruled by the anti-American Juan Domingo Perón, with whom the new ambassador took pains to cultivate friendly relations. Bunker perfected his Spanish in Argentina, immersed himself in the national culture, and soon won the respect and friendship of the populist dictator.

Tensions between the United States and Argentina had eased considerably when Truman named Bunker ambassador to Italy in 1952. In Rome, Bunker helped settle a dispute between the Italian government and foreign Protestant missionary groups before submitting his resignation in 1953, following the election of Republican Dwight D. Eisenhower as president.

Bunker was president of the American Red Cross from 1954 until 1956, when President Eisenhower appointed him ambassador to Nepal (until 1958) and India (until 1961). The austere and aristocratic Bunker, an avid reader of the novels of Joseph Conrad, got along well with Indian prime minister Jawaharlal Nehru; U.S.-Indian relations improved markedly during his ambassadorship. President John F. Kennedy employed Bunker as a diplomatic troubleshooter, first in the dispute between the Netherlands and Indonesia over West Irian (now Irian Barat) in 1962, then in the conflict between Saudi Arabia and Egypt in Yemen in 1963. Bunker's mediation produced settlements in both cases; the first lasted, but the second soon came apart. President Lyndon B. Johnson sent Bunker to Panama in 1964, to ease tensions exacerbated by anti-American student riots. Recognizing the need to deal forthrightly with issues of Panamanian sovereignty, Bunker initiated the process that would produce the Panama Canal treaties thirteen years later.

Also in 1964 Bunker was named U.S. representative to the Organization of American States (OAS). The next year the OAS was thrown into turmoil by the U.S. invasion of the Dominican Republic, in violation of the OAS Charter, to thwart a "pro-Communist" insurrection. Bunker managed to rally a majority of OAS members behind the U.S. position and then went to Santo Domingo as head of a three-man delegation to negotiate a settlement. Under the guns of the U.S.-led OAS peacekeeping force, the Dominican factions in 1965 agreed to elections that produced a pro-American government. For this feat Bunker was awarded his second Medal of Freedom by President Johnson in 1967 and was designated ambassador-at-large. In 1967 Johnson chose Bunker to be ambassador to South Vietnam. On 3 January 1967 he married Carol Clendening Laise, U.S. ambassador to Nepal. (His first wife had died in 1964.)

In Saigon, Bunker was virtually American proconsul: He ran the political-military war effort for Presidents Johnson and Richard M. Nixon from 1967 until 1973. He dealt effectively with South Vietnamese politicians and generals, employing an "iron fist in a velvet glove" to secure their compliance with policy handed down from Washington. Among his most impressive achievements was persuading President Nguyen Van Thieu to accept the Paris Peace Accords that called for the withdrawal of all U.S. forces from South Vietnam in 1973.

Bunker's prestige among the U.S. foreign policy establishment had reached new heights by the time he returned from Vietnam in 1973. Despite his efforts to avoid the limelight, he was well-known among the general public as well. Television and the print media supplied Americans with images of the tall, spare, white-haired diplomat, ramrod straight in a well-cut tropical business suit, rimless spectacles, and a Panama hat, standing cool as a refrigerator among sweating men in military fatigues. Bunker's self-control and aloofness were legendary, but among friends he was a jovial companion, wit, and raconteur.

Bunker's last and most important assignment was negotiating the Panama Canal Treaties from 1974 to 1977. In Vietnam he had implemented policy formulated in Washington, but in Panama he played an important role in recasting U.S. policy and in determining the eventual disposition of the canal. His experience in the aftermath of the Panamanian student riots of 1964 convinced him that the security of the canal required unequivocal U.S. recognition of Panama's sovereignty over the waterway. The treaties he negotiated with the government of General Omar

Torrijos provided for the turning over of management of the canal, and all U.S. military and civilian facilities in the Canal Zone, to Panama before the year 2000, while authorizing the United States to intervene militarily should the "neutrality" of the waterway be threatened. Bunker campaigned for the controversial treaties in the United States and was instrumental in persuading the Senate to ratify them in 1978.

After he retired from the foreign service in 1978, Bunker and his wife maintained a residence in Washington, D.C., where he was founding chairman of Georgetown University's Institute for the Study of Diplomacy and she was director general of the U.S. Foreign Service. They had a second home on a 600-acre dairy farm in Putney, Vermont. Bunker died of a viral infection and complications of old age and was buried in Dummerston, Vermont.

A self-described "old fashioned patriot," Bunker had a highly developed sense of duty. His diplomatic style was understated, circumspect, and secretive. He was goal-oriented: "The object of diplomacy," he maintained, is "not to win arguments but to achieve goals." He achieved most of the goals assigned to him.

★

"Ellsworth Bunker," in *Current Biography 1978,* written at the time of Bunker's definitive retirement from the foreign service, is the most complete account of his career. See also Douglas Pike, ed., *The Bunker Papers: Reports to the President from Vietnam, 1967–1973* (1990). Other useful sources include entries in John E. Findling, *Dictionary of American Diplomatic History,* 2d ed., rev. and enl. (1989); and Bruce Watterau, *The Presidential Medal of Freedom: Winners and Their Achievements* (1996). Obituaries are in the *New York Times* (28 Sept. 1984) and *National Review* (2 Nov. 1984).

NEILL MACAULAY

BURDEN, William Armistead Moale (*b.* 8 April 1906 in New York City; *d.* 10 October 1984 in New York City), Wall Street executive, U.S. ambassador to Belgium (1959–1961), president of New York City's Museum of Modern Art (1953–1959 and 1962–1965), and, as a trustee of the Smithsonian Institution (1962–1984), instrumental in founding the National Air and Space Museum.

Burden was the elder of two sons of William A. M. Burden and Florence Vanderbilt Twombly. His father, the grandson of the Scottish-born American inventor William Burden, died when William was very young, leaving him and his brother, Shirley, to be raised by their mother, a great-granddaughter of Cornelius Vanderbilt. Florence Burden never remarried, devoting herself instead to her two sons. In 1923, after a privileged if somewhat cloistered youth,

Mr. and Mrs. William Burden in Paris, 1955. AP/WIDE WORLD PHOTOS

sector. By the mid-1930s he had become one of the foremost experts on industry finances as well as on the military implications of air power. This reputation prompted his friend Nelson A. Rockefeller to ask him, in early 1941, to investigate and draft a report on the activities of Axis, particularly German-controlled, commercial airlines in Latin America. His conclusion—that these ostensibly civilian aircraft posed a serious military threat by virtue of their ability to collect and relay intelligence on Allied shipping to German naval forces—led to his appointment in June 1941 to the Defense Supplies Corporation (later subsumed by the Reconstruction Finance Corporation) with the mission of expelling Axis airlines from their South American bases. Initially obliged to proceed by indirection and, given the United States' noncombatant status, often in opposition to State Department policy, Burden quietly made the deals that, immediately after Pearl Harbor, enabled Washington to replace enemy-owned civilian airlines with U.S. government–controlled airlines, an achievement recounted in detail in his book *The Struggle for Airways in Latin America* (1943).

Burden served subsequently as aviation assistant to the Secretary of Commerce (1943–1947). Then, after a hiatus during which he founded his own venture-capital firm, he accepted an appointment as Undersecretary of Research and Development for the Air Force (1950–1952), with a portfolio that included nuclear weaponry and the then-fledgling space program. In 1959 he was once again summoned to serve the country, this time by President Dwight D. Eisenhower, and, at the urging of his friend Undersecretary of State C. Douglas Dillon, accepted appointment as U.S. ambassador to Belgium. A French-speaking Gallophile, Burden initially compared Brussels to the Paris mission he truly coveted to "going out with the sister of the woman you love." But as a man with a head for business, an eye for fine art, and a taste for good food and wine, he ultimately came to repudiate his assessment of the Belgian capital. Moreover, this diplomatic assignment proved unexpectedly challenging, because of the crisis brought on by Belgium's 1960 withdrawal from its Congo colony, the civil war that broke out there in the wake of Belgian evacuation, and the cold war jockeying for influence in postcolonial Africa that ensued. A calm, levelheaded analyst of the roots of the Congolese tragedy, Burden provided Washington with more than adequate representation, and if, in the end, he mistakenly identified Colonel Joseph Mobutu as a force for democratic stability in sub-Saharan Africa, he was hardly alone in doing so.

Apart from his business and public-service careers, Burden was an active patron of the arts. His association with New York City's Museum of Modern Art (MOMA) began when his wife-to-be took him to its opening show in January 1929. For the next half century his time, energy, and

young William went off, as had his father and grandfather before him, to Harvard, entering the college, as he recalled in his memoirs, "eager and innocent, without a father or a grandfather to advise me; a tee-totaler, sexually inexperienced, a non-athlete, and uninformed by the bull-sessions which prepare those in boarding schools [for campus life]." Despite these disadvantages, he adjusted well, both socially and academically, graduating cum laude in 1927, with an A.B. in humanities and a determination "to make a place" for himself in the world.

In 1928 he met Margaret ("Peggy") Livingston Partridge, the daughter of William Ordway Partridge, a wealthy American businessman turned sculptor, and a young woman of energy and ambition. They were married on 16 February and had four sons. During their marriage they maintained homes on Fifth Avenue in New York City as well as in Hobe Sound, Florida; Northeast Harbor, Maine; and Mount Kisco, New York. His wife's most immediate influence on him was to instill an appreciation of fine art, but he credited her as well with bringing focus to his heretofore vague career aspirations. Drawing on an enthusiasm for aviation that dated back to his youth, he went to work for Brown Brothers, a Wall Street brokerage firm, where he specialized in analyzing the emerging commercial-airline

administrative talents contributed to the museum's transformation from a small rented space for the exhibition of loaned paintings to the unrivaled permanent collection of art, photography, industrial design, and film it eventually became. Invited by Nelson A. Rockefeller to join the museum's Junior Advisory Committee in 1937, Burden became its chairman in 1940. In 1943 he was named a trustee and in 1953 was elected by his fellow trustees to succeed Rockefeller as president, the first of five successive annual terms. His presidency was marked by a major Salute to France exhibition of museum holdings mounted in L'Orangerie in Paris in 1955; a 1956 visit to the Soviet Union with MOMA's legendary director and head curator team of Alfred Hall and René d'Harnoncourt in one of the first (but ultimately abortive) attempts to arrange a cultural exchange with the Kremlin; a serious fire during renovation work in 1958, which killed one construction worker, destroyed two Monets, and forced the museum to shut down for four months; and a 1959 staff revolt pitting the Young Turks of the design, photography, film, and public-information departments against the policy-making Coordinating Committee, which was dominated by the painting and sculpture department. Burden told a *New York Times* interviewer in 1959 that his experience at MOMA was "as experimental and challenging as aviation to me." After his ambassadorial service, he returned to the presidency of MOMA, serving three more terms, which, if less eventful than his first five, were characterized by increased attendance and a growing endowment fund, to which Burden himself pledged $1 million. This gift, along with donations of two sculptures by Constantin Brancusi and paintings by Piet Mondrian, Georges Seurat, and Paul Cézanne, made him one of the institution's most generous benefactors as well.

Although publicly less well known, Burden's services on the board of regents of the Smithsonian Institution from 1962 to 1984 were capped by another great legacy, the founding of the National Air and Space Museum in Washington, D.C. Having originally proposed the idea during President John F. Kennedy's administration, he lobbied tirelessly in its behalf, personally commissioning an architect to design a building suitable for such a collection, persuading President Richard M. Nixon to request funds so that the museum might open as part of the nation's bicentennial celebration in 1976, and donating to it his vast collection of ballooning- and aviation-related books and memorabilia. Thanks to his efforts, this branch of the Smithsonian ultimately became the world's most-visited public collection of artifacts, edging out London's British Museum for that distinction.

In 1953 a *New Yorker* magazine profile of MOMA's new president marveled at Burden's ability "to juggle three not always compatible lives—that of businessman, lover of the arts, and conscientious citizen"—and suggested the following formula for his success: "He does the jobs he is fitted to do, he does them extremely well, and he takes pleasure and satisfaction in doing them." Born in an era when great wealth conferred a sense of social obligation that was generally expressed in philanthropic activity, Burden expanded the concept to encompass not only public service but work in the private sector as well. A young man of Burden's means with a passion for airplanes might easily have expressed that passion in a more self-indulgent way than by becoming a well-informed advocate for the commercial-aviation industry and its future (most presciently in the article "The Air Traffic of the Future," which he contributed to the *New York Times Magazine* of 20 February 1944). Similarly, he might have restricted his love of modern art, which was clearly deep and genuine, to building a private collection; instead, he chose to accept the very public and at times thankless task of heading a major cultural institution like MOMA. His philosophy, he once told an interviewer, was that a man "must not lie back, drifting and taking from life . . . [but must] contribute to knowledge and make life better for all"—a philosophy to which the chronicle of a long and active life would seem to stand in unimpeachable testimony.

Burden died of heart disease at age seventy-eight.

★

William A. M. Burden, *Peggy and I: A Life Too Busy for a Dull Moment* (1982), a self-published memoir with a foreword by General Maxwell Taylor, is a well-written and refreshingly modest account of the author's life. Additional information on the Burden family may be found in Shirley Burden, *The Vanderbilts in My Life: A Personal Memoir* (1981). Russell Lynes, *Good Old Modern: An Intimate Portrait of the Museum of Modern Art* (1973), and Alice Goldfarb Marquis, *Alfred H. Barr, Jr.: Missionary for the Modern* (1989), are not uncritical in their assessments of Burden's stewardship as president of MOMA, but both ultimately view him as one of the institution's more capable leaders. Useful short profiles of Burden include "Juggler," *New Yorker* (11 July 1959); "Envoy for the Air Age," *New York Times* (4 Sept. 1959); and "Man for Brussels," *Time* (14 Sept. 1959). On his MOMA service, see "Tribute to the Past—Plans for the Future," *Museum of Modern Art Bulletin* 22, nos. 1–2 (1954): 25–26, and, on the museum's twenty-fifth-anniversary celebration, *New York Times* (11 Aug. 1956). An exhaustive compendium of Burden's accomplishments, honors, and associations may be found in *William A. M. Burden, 1906–1984 in Memoriam* (1985), a volume available in the Rare Books Division of the New York Public Library. An obituary is in the *New York Times* (11 Oct. 1984).

RICHARD B. CALHOUN

BURROWS, Abe (*b.* 18 December 1910 in New York City; *d.* 17 May 1985 in New York City), writer, composer, and director who was a pioneer of musical theater; he is perhaps best known for coauthoring, with the composer and lyricist Frank Loesser, the script for *Guys and Dolls* (1950).

Born Abraham Solmon Borowitz to Louis Borowitz, a wallpaper and paint retailer, and Julia Salzburg Borowitz, Abe grew up on the immigrant Lower East Side of Manhattan. The family name was changed to Burrows in the 1930s. The eldest of three children, he was introduced to the stage by his father, who enjoyed vaudeville and often took his son to the theater. Abe attended Morris High School in the Bronx and graduated from New Utrecht High School in Brooklyn in 1928. He was a premed student at the City College of New York for two years, then transferred to New York University to study accounting, leaving before he obtained a degree to work as a clerk and later a bond salesman on Wall Street before being fired in 1934. He then worked briefly as a clerk in his father's store and as a salesman. In 1936 Burrows married Ruth Levinson; they had two children.

In his spare time, Burrows collaborated with a friend, Frank Galen, in developing comedy routines for nightclubs. He got into show business by performing summers in the Catskill Mountains in New York, on the so-called Borscht Circuit of Jewish hotels. In 1939 he went to Hollywood as a gag writer for *Texaco Star Theater* on the Columbia Broadcasting System (CBS). In the early 1940s Burrows scripted comic material for Rudy Vallee and Fred Allen, among others. In 1941 he collaborated on the creation of a radio show, *Duffy's Tavern*, which became a great popular success; Burrows spent the next four years as head writer for this show.

In 1946 and 1947 Burrows had his own radio show, the *Abe Burrows Show,* on which he performed comedy skits, played the piano, and sang songs, many of which were his original compositions. This show, which was taken off the air "by popular demand," in Burrows's words (despite having won the Radio Critics Award for best comedy show of 1947), was followed in 1949 by *Breakfast with Burrows* on CBS, which lasted only one year. In 1948 Burrows divorced his first wife, and in 1950 he married Carin Smith Kinzel; they had no children. In 1951 he got out of his contract with CBS to concentrate on his work in the theater.

During his radio years, Burrows also performed his music and comedy routines on the nightclub circuit. Throughout his career, he entertained at parties and informal gatherings, and he was a great favorite among his friends and acquaintances. Among his hits were such parodies of popular songwriting as "The Girl with the Three Blue Eyes" and "Put Your Lips Around Me, Honey," which he recorded on the Decca label in 1945 and 1950. *Current Biography* called these songs "travesties on the second-rate and the stereotyped in popular songmaking." Fellow hu-

Abe Burrows. ARCHIVE PHOTOS

morist Robert Benchley considered him "the country's greatest satirist."

In 1949 Broadway summoned Burrows. Frank Loesser had written the songs for a new musical based on the short stories of Damon Runyon, and Burrows was called in to collaborate on the dialogue with the guidance of playwright and director George S. Kaufman. He also collaborated with librettist Jo Swerling. *Guys and Dolls,* about small-time gamblers, Broadway lowlifes, and the civilizing influence of the Salvation Army, opened in Philadelphia in 1950 to rave reviews. With its pantheon of beloved characters and songs that became instant classics, *Guys and Dolls* was one of the greatest hits in the history of Broadway, with an initial run of 1,200 performances.

In 1953 Burrows wrote and directed another musical comedy, *Can-Can,* in collaboration with Cole Porter. The production, set in a Paris dance hall, was another success for Burrows, followed by *Silk Stockings* (1955), *Say, Darling* (1958), and *What Makes Sammy Run* (1964), also written and directed by Burrows. Another major hit came in 1961 with *How to Succeed in Business Without Really Trying,* again cowritten with Frank Loesser. Burrows and Loesser shared the Pulitzer Prize in 1962 for this production, and Burrows was also awarded two Tony Awards for the show, for best writer and best director. *How to Succeed in Business Without Really Trying* enjoyed a Broadway revival in the 1990s.

In 1951 and again in 1952 Burrows was called to testify before the House Committee on Un-American Activities, which was investigating alleged communist affiliation among people in the entertainment industry. Owen Vinson, a former radio director who had been treasurer of the Hollywood branch of the Communist party, had identified Burrows as a probable ex-communist. Burrows conceded that he had attended communist cultural events in the 1940s, but denied being a communist and characterized his former association with the Party as "naïve" and "downright stupid."

Burrows, who was described by the *New York Times* critic Robert D. McFadden as a "bald, bespectacled man with the wry wit, restless energy and New York accent of a Damon Runyon character," was highly respected as a so-called script doctor; he was called in on a number of Broadway productions to rewrite or direct after serious pre-opening problems had been identified. He directed numerous Broadway productions, including *Two on the Aisle* (1951), *Reclining Figure* (1954), *Forty Carats* (1968), and *Four on a Garden* (1971). In 1965 he brought *Cactus Flower*, his adaptation of a French comedy by Pierre Barillet and Jean-Pierre Gredy, to the stage. Burrows also directed this successful production, which starred Lauren Bacall and Barry Nelson.

Abe Burrows died of pneumonia at his Manhattan home; he was seventy-four and had been ill with Alzheimer's disease for several years. At his memorial service, the singer and lyricist Adolph ("Al") Green said: "His life was filled with energy, humanity, confidence, insecurity, humor, fretfulness, and intelligence. I never met such a combination. He had a strange surrealist quality, talking something like a mug and having a great intellect and frame of reference." The historian Arthur Schlesinger, Jr., said of him, "Few men in our time have given more delight to more people."

★

Burrows wrote a memoir, *Honest Abe; or, Is There Really No Business Like Show Business?* (1980). A profile by E. J. Kahn, Jr., is in the *New Yorker* (18 May 1957). Obituaries are in the *New York Times* and *New York Daily News* (both 19 May 1985).

WARREN E. DEDERICK

BURTON, Phillip (*b.* 1 June 1926 in Cincinnati, Ohio; *d.* 10 April 1983 in San Francisco, California), powerful congressman from San Francisco who played a pivotal role in welfare, labor, civil rights, reapportionment, congressional reform, and expansion of the national park system.

Raised in Milwaukee during the height of the Great Depression, Burton was one of three sons of Thomas P. and Mildred Marie Burton. An itinerant salesman who decided in his mid-thirties to become a physician, Thomas Burton studied medicine in Chicago, leaving the family for ex-

tended periods of time while Mildred sold advertising for the local Catholic diocese newspaper to support her boys. It was in progressive Milwaukee that Burton's liberal politics were first shaped. In this he was guided in large part by his father, an ardent New Dealer who always sided with the underdog and an exacting and withholding man whose approval young Phillip constantly sought. His youngest brother, John, later joined him in Congress.

After the family moved to San Francisco, Burton attended Washington High School, graduating in January 1944 and enrolling at the University of Southern California while enlisting in the U.S. Navy's V-12 program. He graduated with an A.B. degree in 1947 and returned home, where he sold oil leases by day and attended Golden Gate University Law School at night. He received an LL.B. degree in 1952 and was admitted to the bar that year.

He became active in local politics and a leader in the Young Democrats, where he met his future wife, Sala Galante, an émigré of Bialystock, Poland, several years his senior. They married in 1953. A tall man with a booming voice and the vocabulary of his dockworker constituents, Burton was already known for his intimidating and brusque manner, and Sala often had to smooth out his rough edges. They made a perfect political couple with no children of their own (she had a daughter from an earlier marriage) and no interests outside politics.

Burton lost his first race for the state assembly in 1954 but won two years later and served eight years in Sacramento, representing San Francisco and becoming a powerful rival to assembly speaker Jesse Unruh. Burton's most important legislation greatly liberalized California's welfare system. He was elected to Congress in February 1964. On leaving for Washington he quipped, "I already bankrupted one budget. I need a bigger one to play with." Burton moved quickly in the House, joining both the Education and Labor and the Interior committees. An early opponent of the Vietnam War and staunch supporter of civil rights, he helped pass legislation extending the minimum wage to millions of workers. He soon created what became known as the Burton Machine in San Francisco, which included his brother John and protégés George Moscone and Willie Brown.

By the early 1970s, Burton had become an important figure on Capitol Hill. He was key to passage of the Coal Mine Health and Safety Act of 1969, which greatly liberalized benefits to coal miners with black lung disease, and his legislation created the Supplemental Security Income program, or SSI, which provides benefits for the indigent aged or disabled. He was also the major figure in drawing new political boundaries for California congressmen in the 1960s, 1970s, and 1980s.

In 1971 Burton was elected chairman of the House Democratic Study Group, an important reform group that

Phillip Burton. REPRODUCED COURTESY OF THE LIBRARY OF CONGRESS

provided the impetus and strategy to democratize the House and reduce the power of committee chairmen. In 1973 he was elected chairman of the House Democratic Caucus and made it matter for the first time in sixty years. He was regarded as a likely candidate for Speaker of the House. On 6 December 1974, however, in probably the defining moment of his political career, Burton lost by one vote the election for House majority leader to Jim Wright of Texas. Many colleagues feared Burton would become too powerful and ride roughshod over them.

Assuming chairmanship of a minor House subcommittee on national parks in January 1977 and looking for a way to reestablish his power base, Burton over the next few years pushed through legislation that tripled the size of the national parks system and preserved critical pieces of wilderness—Mineral King in California, the Boundary Waters Canoe Area in Minnesota, the Pine Barrens in New Jersey, and many others—that environmentalists had for decades been trying to preserve. His technique became known as "park barrel," and his $1.4 billion National Parks and Recreation Act of 1978 contained projects in more than 200 congressional districts and 44 states.

Republicans were outraged by Burton's 1981 reapportionment of California's congressional districts. With two new seats to play with and a clever pen, he transformed what had been a state congressional delegation of twenty-two Democrats and twenty-one Republicans into a delegation of twenty-eight Democrats and seventeen Republicans. Thus, he added six new Democrats to the party's House majority, one-fourth of their national gains that year.

Burton was an unforgettable, uncontrollable, and incorruptible figure whose relentless day-and-night politicking distilled the raw essence of his profession. A heavy smoker and drinker who was often angry, Burton never forgot why he was in politics, which was to force government to provide services to those who need them, and never forgot his constituency, the poor and the disenfranchised. His redistributionist, Great Society politics and his bullying and often offensive personality went out of political fashion several years before his death in 1983. Nevertheless, millions of Americans who never heard his name enjoyed the fruits of his legislation. In many ways, his ascent in the House from the left presaged that of a later activist from the right—House Speaker Newt Gingrich, who continued some of the internal House reforms Burton began twenty years earlier.

Burton survived a difficult reelection challenge in 1982 and was again preparing to contest Jim Wright for House leadership when, on 10 April 1983, he collapsed and died in San Francisco of a ruptured abdominal aortic aneurysm. More than 110 members of Congress flew to his funeral service in City Hall in San Francisco, where a former aide eulogized, "Half of you are here to pay your respects, the other half to make sure he's really dead." Burton's cremated remains were interred in the National Cemetery of the Presidio in San Francisco.

The papers of Philip Burton are held at the Bancroft Library, University of California at Berkeley. See also *Phillip Burton: Memorial Addresses Delivered in Congress* (1983). John Jacobs, *A Rage for Justice: The Passion and Politics of Phillip Burton* (1995), is a full biography; and Laurence Leamer, *Playing for Keeps in Washington* (1977), contains a chapter on Burton. He is also profiled in Rian Malan, "BOSS: You Don't Want to Cross Phil Burton," *California Magazine* (Nov. 1981). An obituary is in the *New York Times* (11 Apr. 1983).

JOHN JACOBS

BUTTERFIELD, Lyman Henry (*b*. 8 August 1909 in Lyndonville, New York; *d*. 25 April 1982 in Boston, Massachusetts), historian and documentary specialist who was the initial editor in chief of the magisterial Adams Family Papers at the Massachusetts Historical Society.

One of three sons of Roy Lyman Butterfield and Ethel Place, Butterfield grew up in Lyndonville, where his father was the high school principal. Small of stature, Butterfield was more interested in libraries than playing fields, and he majored with relish in history at Harvard University, from which he graduated in 1930. He stayed in Cambridge to finish work on an M.A. degree, which he received in 1934.

Butterfield had teaching appointments at Harvard

(1930–1937, 1955–1964), Franklin and Marshall College (1937–1946), and the College of William and Mary (1951–1954). On 15 June 1935 he married Elizabeth Anne Eaton, daughter of the Cleveland industrialist Cyrus S. Eaton, Sr. They had two children. In 1946 he was appointed associate editor of the Thomas Jefferson Papers at Princeton University. For the next five years, working with the editor in chief, Julian P. Boyd, Butterfield was a key figure in planning and executing what became the landmark project in historical editing in the United States.

Boyd, a crusty librarian-turned-historian, found a perfect partner in Butterfield. Neither had gone on for a Ph.D. degree, and both seemed determined to show that their standards of editing were far beyond any previous documentary editions in American history. The Boyd-Butterfield team produced its first volume of *The Papers of Thomas Jefferson* in 1950 to critical acclaim. Thereafter, a score of editorial projects (including the Washington, Madison, and Hamilton Papers) were created in imitation of the Jefferson-Princeton program.

Although Butterfield kept in the background while at Princeton, he worked on his own time on the *Letters of Benjamin Rush* (2 vols., 1951), Rush being a Philadelphia physician who signed the Declaration of Independence and figured prominently in early American politics. Butterfield's edition of Rush's letters bore his strong editorial imprint.

With some regret but renewed energy, Butterfield left Princeton in 1951 to become director of the Institute of Early American History and Culture at Williamsburg, Virginia. In the afterglow of the country's victory in World War II, much attention was paid in educational circles to the role of the nation's founders in creating a triumphant democracy. Butterfield, conservative in dress, was liberal in his politics and was keenly interested in promoting historical research that would focus on the underpinnings of civil liberties in early America.

The Adams Family Papers at the Massachusetts Historical Society contained some of the key documents in early American history, spanned the period from 1753 to 1915, and needed organization. With his background and dedication, Butterfield accepted the helm of the unwieldy collection in 1954 and began an enormous reorganization. Under Butterfield's charge, the entire collection was microfilmed in more than 608 reels, giving scholars access to the materials far in advance of snail-paced published projects. Separate publication for the diaries and letters of John Adams and John Quincy Adams were undertaken and began to appear in 1961. They consisted of the *Diary and Autobiography of John Adams* (4 vols., 1961), *Adams Family Correspondence* (4 vols., 1963–1973), *Earliest Diary of John Adams* (1966), and *The Book of Abigail and John: Selected Letters of the Adams Family, 1762–1784* (1975). The high

Lyman Butterfield, 1954. AP/WIDE WORLD PHOTOS

quality of these volumes, collectively named the *Adams Papers,* was remarkable, both in editorial skills and elegant format.

Not the least of the *Adams Papers* admirers was President John F. Kennedy, who appeared at a Washington luncheon honoring publication of the first volumes. President Kennedy noted the scope of the 300,000-document project and remarked: "Four volumes out, and only 80 to 100 more to go. Obviously, the worst is over."

As the emphasis in academic history shifted away from politics to social studies, Butterfield recognized the contributions made by Abigail Adams, Charles Francis Adams, and Henry Adams to feminism, abolitionism, and social conduct. The Adamses, Butterfield once said, were important to any study dealing with how our ancestors "dressed, ate, played, talked, philosophized, worshipped, traveled, cared for themselves when they were sick, quarreled, made up, loved, married, and died." Such was the grist of the history that began to dominate the field from around 1965 onward.

Known for his dry wit, Butterfield often remarked that he had come to realize that all the Adamses "were different, and yet they are all alike." His insights were shared with others when he served on the White House Arts Committee (1960–1963), helped select books for the presidential library, and served as chief consultant for the acclaimed television production, *The Adams Chronicles*.

An eminent editor told friends he regarded Butterfield as "the most learned man I ever met." Behind his quiet dignity, Butterfield enjoyed the company of friends and welcomed those who could read to him in the evenings when his eyesight failed. Never one to act impulsively, he gloried in the adulation earned from his years of partnership with Julian Boyd. Boyd, unlike Butterfield, was a difficult scholar with a quick temper; his colleagues thought Butterfield was an excellent counterpoise and many regard the Jefferson Papers volumes they jointly produced as among the brightest jewels in the documentary editors' crowns. Among his peers, Butterfield was known as "the editors' editor."

Butterfield retired in 1975. His wife died in 1978, and he died four years later from heart and kidney failure. He was cremated. The Butterfields' son Fox became a prominent journalist.

★

Obituaries are in the *Boston Globe* and *New York Times* (both 26 Apr. 1982).

ROBERT ALLEN RUTLAND

CALDWELL, (Janet Miriam) Taylor (*b.* 7 September 1900 in Prestwich, Manchester, England; *d.* 30 August 1985 in Greenwich, Connecticut), prolific and best-selling writer, particularly of novels concerning rich and powerful families and of religious fiction.

Intellectually precocious and strong-willed even as a child, Caldwell moved to Buffalo, New York, at age six with her parents, Arthur Francis Caldwell, an artist, and Anna Marks, a homemaker, both natives of Glasgow, Scotland. She had one brother, five years younger. Caldwell reports being christened five times, including as a Methodist; by age nine she was a Roman Catholic, and she remained one for the rest of her life.

From 1904 to 1906 Caldwell attended a private school in Reddish, a Manchester suburb. There, at age six, she won a gold medal for an essay on Charles Dickens. She continued to write, beginning novels at age nine and completing one at age twelve, a romance about the lost continent of Atlantis that was rewritten by Jess Stearn and published in 1975. Arthur Caldwell, a commercial artist for the *Manchester Guardian,* failed to find good work in the United States; driven by a fear of poverty, a desire for accomplishment, and family pressure, Caldwell began a life of hard work in 1910, helping out at a local grocery. In addition to taking a full-time job in a factory at age fifteen, she pursued secretarial training and earned a high school degree in night classes. In 1918 and 1919 Caldwell served as a yeomanette in the U.S. Naval Reserve.

On 27 May 1919 Caldwell married a handsome West Virginian, William Fairfax Combs, and homesteaded with him in Kentucky; they had one child, Mary Margaret Combs. In 1923 Caldwell and her daughter moved back to Buffalo, where she became a court reporter for the New York State Department of Labor. In 1923 or 1924 Combs joined them. Caldwell began attending night classes at the University of Buffalo and received her B.A. in 1931.

Caldwell worked for the Department of Immigration and Naturalization in Buffalo from 1924 to 1931. She divorced Combs in 1931 and married a higher-ranked coworker, Marcus Reback, on 12 May 1931. Reback—a highly intelligent, Russian-born Jew—became Caldwell's adviser and helpmate; he was her business manager and assisted with research and perhaps with writing (her reports of this are contradictory). They had one child, Judith Ann Reback.

Reback was transferred to New York City in 1936. Caldwell started showing publishers her *Dynasty of Death,* begun in 1934, a novel of intrigue and romantic conflict between prestigious munitions families. The book, published in 1938, became a best-seller; reviews were mixed, and some critics suggested the book was written pseudonymously by an established male author. After Caldwell and Reback moved to Eggertville, New York, they revealed her identity. Magazines marveled at the best-seller by a housewife from the Buffalo suburbs.

Great popularity and mixed reviews continued throughout Caldwell's career, during which she published over thirty-five novels. Some books sold less well, such as *Time*

Taylor Caldwell. ARCHIVE PHOTOS

No Longer, which appeared under the pseudonym Max Reiner (1941), and her religious novel in monologue form, *The Listener* (1960). *The Devil's Advocate* (1952), a story of near-future tyranny, and *The Late Clare Beame* (1963), a mystery, were both less successful financially and panned critically.

Generally, however, Caldwell combined romance, conflict, and the feel of historical authenticity (regardless of accuracy) into powerful and popular novels. The story of the munitions families continued in *The Eagles Gather* (1940) and *The Final Hour* (1944). *Never Victorious, Never Defeated* (1954), concerning a Pennsylvania railroad millionaire family, won the Grand Prix Chatrain for 1956; and *Captains and the Kings* (1972), based on Joseph P. Kennedy's life, became a television miniseries. Caldwell also went further back in time, exploring different kinds of power in novels such as *The Earth Is the Lord's* (1941), about young Genghis Khan; *The Arm and the Darkness* (1943), about Cardinal Richelieu and the Huguenots in seventeenth-century France; and *A Pillar of Iron* (1965), with Cicero as the protagonist.

Caldwell also became famous for religious fiction. Besides *The Listener* and its sequel, *No One Hears but Him*

(1965), she wrote the epistolary *Dialogues with the Devil* (1967), obviously influenced by C. S. Lewis's *The Screwtape Letters* (1942) and Space Trilogy (1938–1945). Her best religious books, however, are biblical historical novels: *Dear and Glorious Physician* (1959), concerning the life of Saint Luke; *Great Lion of God,* about Saint Paul; and, written with Jess Stearn, *I, Judas* (1977).

Reback's death on 13 August 1970 devastated Caldwell. She married William Everett Stancell on 17 June 1972 and divorced him in 1973 for infidelity. In 1978 she married William Robert Prestie—her first marriage in the Catholic Church—with whom she moved to Greenwich, Connecticut, in 1980. Relationships with both daughters went badly. In September 1979 Judith Reback Goodman committed suicide after a five-year court battle with Caldwell over Reback's estate; and after Caldwell suffered an incapacitating stroke in May 1980, Mary Margaret Combs Fried fought Prestie for legal custody, despite enmity between mother and daughter.

Caldwell's final book, *Answer as a Man* (1981), based on the story of Job but featuring a turn-of-the-century rising businessman, was reminiscent of her nonreligious books. She died in Greenwich, Connecticut, of pulmonary failure resulting from lung cancer.

Caldwell is famous, or infamous, for both her popularity and her politics. While it is easy to fault her overwrought yet unrhythmical prose, her melodramatic plots, and her exaggerated characterizations, her vast readership—over 30 million copies of her books had been sold by 1980—cannot be dismissed. Perceptive critics note her talents for constructing narrative, for emotional effectiveness, and for evoking a setting.

Politically, Caldwell grew more conservative as society grew less so, a progression endearing her to some and alienating many more. She was honored by the John Birch Society as well as the National League of American Pen Women, by the anti-Semitic Liberty Lobby as well as the University of Buffalo. Even her historical novels carried overt comments on current issues. Ultimately, Caldwell's politics may prevent her from receiving the renewed critical attention that other female authors, and popular authors, were beginning to receive in the last three decades of the twentieth century.

★

Taylor Caldwell wrote autobiographically in a novel, *There Was a Time* (1947), and in the ostensibly nonfiction *On Growing Up Tough* (1971). The only full-length biography is the unsatisfactory but interesting *In Search of Taylor Caldwell* (1981), by her friend and sometime coauthor Jess Stearn. For perceptive contemporary reactions, see "Dear and Glorious . . . ," *Newsweek* (9 Mar. 1959); and Robert Wernick, "Queens of Fiction," *Life* (6 Apr. 1959). The best research aids are entries about her in *Current Biography 1940, Contemporary Literary Criticism* (1974), *Contemporary Authors,*

New Revised Series, Vol. 5 (1982), and *Twentieth-Century Romance and Historical Writers* (1994). See also Annette T. Rottenberg, "Obviously Bad," *English Journal* (Oct. 1963). An obituary is in the *New York Times* (2 Sept. 1985).

BERNADETTE LYNN BOSKY

CANADAY, John Edwin (*b.* 1 February 1907 in Fort Scott, Kansas; *d.* 19 July 1985 in New York City), art critic and author of mysteries best known for his resistance to dominant styles of abstract art and support of the classical tradition while he served as art editor of the *New York Times*.

John Canaday was one of five children of Agnes Florence Musson and William Franklin Canaday, a lawyer. When he was seven his family moved to San Antonio, Texas, where he grew up. An early interest in art led Canaday to pursue studies in painting at the University of Texas, where he received a B.A. in 1929, and at Yale University, which awarded him an M.A. in 1933. Following his college years Canaday went to Paris to study at the École du Louvre, returning to the United States with a desire to teach about

John Canaday, 1959. AP/WIDE WORLD PHOTOS

art rather than to become an artist. On 19 September 1935 Canaday married Katherine S. Hoover. They had two sons and three daughters. From 1938 to 1941 he was associate professor of art history at the University of Virginia in Charlottesville.

With the outbreak of World War II he interrupted his academic career to accept a number of overseas assignments. Canaday spent 1942 in the Belgian Congo working for the U.S. Bureau of Economic Warfare. In 1943 he served as a French interpreter in the Congo, the setting for the mystery novels Canaday began to write during this period under the pseudonym Matthew Head. Between 1943 and 1955 he produced seven mysteries. In 1944 Canaday enlisted in the Marine Corps and served as a first lieutenant in an air-warning squadron in the South Pacific until the war ended.

At the close of the war Canaday returned to his position at the University of Virginia, where he taught until 1950. In that year he moved to New Orleans, assuming the position of head of the art department at Newcomb College of Tulane University. In 1953 Canaday took the job of director of education at the Philadelphia Museum of Art, a post he held until 1959. His ability to make art accessible to the public attracted the attention of the Metropolitan Museum of Art, which commissioned him to write the text for its *Metropolitan Seminars in Art,* a multivolume series to promote public appreciation of Western art, which appeared between 1958 and 1960.

Canaday appeared trim and handsome, his urban style underpinning personal and professional self-confidence. On the other hand, he could be extremely witty and colloquial, with an ability to communicate with an audience beyond the arts community.

In September 1959 Canaday became an art critic for the *New York Times*. In that highly visible post he quickly gained a reputation for his often biting critiques of contemporary abstract expressionism, which had become the dominant style in the art world after World War II. Although he admired the best of the movement, he wrote in 1959: "Let us at least admit that the nature of Abstract Expressionism allows for exceptional tolerance of incompetence and deception."

Such views did not go unremarked. During Canaday's first year at the *Times,* he began to come under strong attack by artists and critics. The editor of the influential journal *Art News* articulated the views of many supporters of abstract art when he questioned Canaday's competence in evaluating art for a major newspaper. In perhaps the most public expression of dissatisfaction with Canaday, fifty artists, dealers, collectors, professors, and art historians and critics wrote a letter to the *New York Times* in March 1961 calling attention to specific writings of his that they believed amounted to attacks on the personal motives of those he was critiquing. Nonetheless, Canaday garnered much support for his views. Following the 1961 public letter to the *Times,* more than 300 letters were received at the newspaper in support of Canaday's position, far more than the number received from letter writers who endorsed his critics. Canaday also drew support from artists, some of whom were working against the abstract-expressionist tide. Edward Hopper, for example, called him "the best and most outspoken art critic the *Times* has ever had."

Canaday used his columns to criticize both art auction houses and art collectors for their roles in creating artificially inflated prices for contemporary works of art, which often were of questionable quality. Early in his tenure at the *Times,* Canaday also expressed his dissatisfaction with Frank Lloyd Wright's design of the Guggenheim Museum in New York City, saying that it provided one of the least satisfactory settings in which to appreciate paintings. Most important from his point of view, he advocated art that demonstrated mastery of craft. He judged twentieth-century painters by standards set by artists from the Renaissance to Picasso and condemned those who encouraged "difference as a fetish."

Canaday continued as a critic for the *Times* until 1977, when he retired to lecture and write. During his career he not only authored books that reflected his background in art but also served as a restaurant critic, a diversion he greatly enjoyed. His works include *Mainstreams of Modern Art* (1959), a widely used text; *The Lives of the Painters,* 4 vols. (1969), a reference collection; *Keys to Art* (1964), coauthored with his wife; *The Embattled Critic* (1962), a collection of his controversial articles for the *Times; Culture Gulch: Notes on Art and Its Public in the 1960s* (1969); and *The Artful Avocado* (1975), a fanciful treatment of his effort to grow avocados in his New York apartment.

One of Canaday's most significant achievements was creating in the art section of the *New York Times* a forum for serious art criticism. By his willingness to take risky and sometimes unpopular stands on contemporary art, he established a climate of credibility based on his recognized authority. By the time he retired from the *Times,* Canaday's reputation for fair art commentary was secure. He had not shirked the responsibility of a critic despite what some believed to be his early unprincipled attack on abstract expressionism. Rather, he widened his focus, writing more broadly about art history and criticism. In doing this he placed both his own role and that of the debates over contemporary art in historical perspective.

Canaday died in New York City of pancreatic cancer.

★

Biographical sources on Canaday are relatively slim. See the entry in Charles Moritz, ed., *Current Biography Yearbook 1962* (1963). An obituary is in the *New York Times* (21 July 1985).

CHARLES K. PIEHL

CANHAM, Erwin Dain (*b.* 13 February 1904 in Auburn, Maine; *d.* 3 January 1982 in Agana, Guam), journalist who rose to become editor in chief of the *Christian Science Monitor* and was the resident commissioner of the Northern Mariana Islands from 1976 to 1978.

Canham was the only child of Vincent Walter Canham, who was agricultural editor of the *Lewiston* (Maine) *Sun and Journal,* and Elizabeth May Gowell, who had been a schoolteacher in rural Maine during her teens and later helped her husband with newspaper work. Both his mother and father were brought up as Methodists.

When Canham was about two years old the family moved to a farm, where his father tried to combine farming with newspaper work, selling insurance, and other jobs. For a number of years Canham's father and mother were itinerant county correspondents, traveling from town to town, and often Erwin would be taken along. His earliest recollection of newspaper work was of his father taking stories by telephone and then typing them into copy on his ancient typewriter. Young Erwin would stand beside the typewriter, which he could barely reach, and let his hand ride back and forth along with the carriage. By age eight Canham himself stood on a chair by the telephone and took down items for publication, and by fourteen he was a general

Erwin Dain Canham. FABIAN BACHRACH

reporter for the *Sun and Journal* during the World War I manpower shortage.

Canham later noted that although he was born into a strong religious and moral tradition, the tradition was formal and stern, and mainly negative. According to Canham his mother's frequent illnesses cast a shadow over the family, while his father was restless and insecure. Canham himself was subject to illnesses. Their lives reached a crisis point when his mother took seriously ill with tumors or other growths in her throat, and the medical diagnosis allowed no hope of healing. Over the telephone she asked for the services of a Christian Science practitioner who lived more than 100 miles away, and during the first treatment the growth in her throat passed harmlessly away overnight. Canham wrote later that it was the beginning of good health both for her and himself. At that point the entire family began the study of Christian Science. The life of Canham's father was given new direction and purpose, and Erwin went to a city high school rather than the poor country school where he had begun his education. He had to take four entrance exams before being admitted into Bates College in Lewiston, Maine, but was on the honors list the first semester and continued his success. While at Bates he was a correspondent for eight daily newspapers in Portland, Boston, Philadelphia, and New York, and by the end of his junior year he was also writing for a resort magazine in Poland Spring, Maine, called the *Hill-Top*. He was captain of the debating team at Bates and as a sophomore took part in the first debate with Oxford University held in America. In the spring of his senior year, he traveled with his debate team to Great Britain and competed against a number of British universities. He was also a member of Phi Beta Kappa.

A few months after his graduation in 1925 he started working as state-house reporter at the *Christian Science Monitor,* a Boston newspaper founded by Mary Baker Eddy in 1908 to "spread confidence instead of fear, record the great good men do instead of magnifying and exploiting the regrettable evil," and "to injure no man, but to bless all mankind." Canham said in 1950 that the latter phrase, translated into operative journalism, gave a mandate to hold an undistorted mirror up to current history and to record the event and explain its meaning. While at the *Monitor,* the scholarly Canham was given the nickname "Spike" (because of its unlikeliness) by columnist Roscoe Drummond. He took a three-year leave of absence (1926–1929) to attend Oxford University as a Rhodes scholar, where he earned bachelor's and master's degrees, the latter in 1936; during the summers he covered the League of Nations in Switzerland for the *Monitor.* He then spent two years (1930–1932) as the *Monitor*'s Geneva correspondent. After his time in Europe, Canham returned to the United

States and continued his work for the *Monitor,* covering national and international events and serving as the paper's Washington bureau chief from 1932 to 1939. He returned to Boston as general news editor in 1939. In 1941 he became the managing editor and in 1945 was appointed editor, a position Canham held until named editor in chief in 1964. In 1974 he was appointed editor emeritus, and he retired in 1979.

The *Monitor* had a reputation for running more international news and analysis than most newspapers, analysis that would be relevant days or weeks later (an important feature for many overseas subscribers). Circulation was not large during Canham's editorship; it was 150,000 in the 1940s and 1950s. Its subscribers in the 1950s, however, included 4,000 editors and newspapers throughout the world. Canham wrote in his *Commitment to Freedom: The Story of the Christian Science Monitor* (1958) that the paper sought to give greatest emphasis to what is important and reduce the merely sensational to its place in an accurate system of values. As to certain words being taboo in the paper, he noted that "there is no word except a profane or obscene one that cannot be used in its proper context." Canham also believed that the balancing fact should be attached to the misleading assertion.

Canham's life outside the paper was suffused with civic involvement. He said at one point that he actually liked meetings and enjoyed an evening of trying to solve problems more than, say, an evening playing cards. He was involved early with the United Nations and in 1948 was the vice chairman of the U.S. delegation to the United Nations Conference on Freedom of Information. From 1948 to 1951 he was a member of the U.S. National Commission for UNESCO and in 1949 was an alternate delegate to the UN General Assembly. During the Dwight D. Eisenhower administration, Canham was the chairman of the National Manpower Council, and he was a member of the U.S. Advisory Commission on Information, which helped shape policy on information and propaganda from 1948 to 1951. He was named one of the eleven members of President Eisenhower's Commission on National Goals to identify great issues and the nation's objectives. Locally, during the Charlestown State Prison crisis in Massachusetts in 1955, he was called in as a mediator by prisoners holding hostages. Canham was also involved in many other local affairs.

Canham, described as gentle and scholarly, enjoyed reading, playing folk songs on the piano, and vacationing on Cape Cod. He was active in the Church of Christ, Scientist and taught Sunday school for many years. He served in the position of president of the church in 1966, at which time he went on an around-the-world speaking tour. He was also active on the board of directors of the U.S. Chamber of Commerce in the 1950s and was elected head of the Chamber of Commerce in 1959, where one of his goals, as the first journalist elected its head, was to put into words some of what the chamber felt to be the beliefs and problems of U.S. business. Canham served on the boards of individual businesses and was board chairman of the Federal Reserve Bank of Boston from 1962 to 1967. He was also elected chairman of the board of directors of Resources for the Future, a nonprofit organization involved in conservation and the development of natural resources.

Canham was president of the American Society of Newspaper Editors in 1948–1949. He won the Columbia Journalism Award and numerous other journalism awards. In Boston he moderated a local television program called *Starring the Editors,* which aired from the 1950s to the early 1970s. The 1949 George Foster Peabody Radio Awards ceremony gave a citation to Canham and his program *The Monitor Views the News* on ABC. Later he was a member of the board of the Public Broadcasting Service. In the 1970s Canham was a commentator for the Westinghouse Broadcasting Company. He received numerous awards from various kinds of groups, held nearly thirty honorary degrees at his retirement, and wrote or collaborated on several books.

Canham married Thelma Whitman Hart on 10 May 1930. In Boston they lived in an antebellum house at 6 Acorn Street. They had two daughters, Carolyn and Elizabeth. After his first wife's death in 1967, he married Patience M. Daltry on 23 June 1968. In his later years they had homes at Saipan in the Marianas and on Cape Cod. Canham died two weeks after abdominal surgery.

★

Canham's papers are located at the archives, Church History Department, First Church of Christ, Scientist, in Boston, Massachusetts. Information on his early years can be found in Louis Finkelstein, ed., *Thirteen Americans: Their Spiritual Autobiographies* (1969). Further information is contained in Kenneth N. Stewart and John Tebbel, *Makers of Modern Journalism* (1952). Obituaries are in the *Boston Globe* (3 Jan. 1982) and the *New York Times* (4 Jan. 1982).

ROBERT T. BRUNS

CAPOTE, Truman (*b.* 30 September 1924 in New Orleans, Louisiana; *d.* 25 August 1984 in Los Angeles, California), flamboyant media celebrity, short story writer, and novelist best known for his "nonfiction novel" *In Cold Blood.*

Capote was born Truman Streckfus Persons to Julian Arch Persons, a riverboat employee who became a New Orleans businessman, and Lillie Mae (Nina) Faulk Persons, a homemaker and former beauty queen. The couple married

Truman Capote, *c.* 1956. HULTON-DEUTSCH COLLECTION/CORBIS

in Monroeville, Alabama, on 23 August 1923. Arch was less than two weeks away from his twenty-sixth birthday; Lillie Mae was seventeen. People in Monroeville thought that Arch was a slick operator and regretted that the beautiful young woman had married him. Lillie Mae quickly came to share their opinion on her honeymoon, when Arch sent her home and did not return to her for more than a month. Realizing the failure of her marriage, Lillie Mae was unhappy to learn soon after that she was pregnant. Her only child was named Truman for Truman Moore, Arch's friend, and Streckfus for Arch's employer.

In the summer of 1930, a few months before Capote's sixth birthday, his parents separated. They divorced on 9 November 1931. From birth, the child had been shuffled among Lillie Mae's relatives in rural Monroeville; now he was left with them permanently—or for as long as anyone could foresee.

Capote found himself in an odd sort of household peculiar to the South at that time: three quarrelsome sisters (Jennie, Callie, and Sook) and their reclusive older brother, Bud. The air hung heavy with petty resentments, ancient secrets, and half a century of accumulated slights. Truman had only one companion his own age, Harper Lee, the youngest daughter of the family next door. United by their shared anguish at their family situations, the children were inseparable. Thirty years later, Harper Lee used Truman as the model for a character in *To Kill a Mockingbird.* Her description captures his childhood personality and appearance:

> He wore blue linen shorts that buttoned to his shirt, his hair was snow white and stuck to his head like dandruff; he was a year my senior but I towered over him. As he told us [an] old tale his blue eyes would lighten and darken; his laugh was sudden and happy; he habitually pulled at a cowlick in the center of his forehead. . . . We came to know [him] as a pocket Merlin, whose head teemed with eccentric plans, strange longings, and quaint fancies.

On 24 March 1932 Lillie Mae married Joseph Garcia Capote, a successful businessman born in Cuba. In September 1932 she sent for Truman to join her and Joe in New York City. Joe proved to be a loving and indulgent stepfather; on 14 February 1935 he adopted Truman, who was renamed Truman Garcia Capote. At the same time, Lillie Mae chose a more sophisticated first name, Nina.

Nina had never been close to Truman, chiefly because she was embarrassed by his effeminate ways. She terminated two pregnancies she conceived by Joe, saying, "I will not have another child like Truman and if I do have another child, it will be like Truman." Nina even took Truman to two psychiatrists in hopes of finding a drug or therapy that would turn him into a "real boy."

In September 1933 Truman began the fourth grade at the Trinity School, one of New York City's oldest and best private boys' schools. It was his first encounter with formal education. In the fall of 1936 Nina sent Truman to St. John's Military Academy in Ossining, New York, to make him into the masculine boy she wanted him to be. The experiment was a disaster, and in the fall of 1937 Nina sent Truman back to Trinity. In June 1939 the Capotes moved to Greenwich, Connecticut. That September, Truman entered Greenwich High School as a tenth grader. Though he became even more vividly unconventional, he made many friends there. He did poorly in all subjects except English.

In 1942 the Capotes moved back to New York City. Truman, whose poor grades prevented him from receiving a diploma with the rest of his high school class, began his senior year again at the Franklin School in New York City; again he did not graduate. At the same time, he took a part-time job with the *New Yorker* as a copyboy. At eighteen, Capote could pass for a child of twelve. He had not yet reached his adult height of five feet, three inches and had a high, childlike voice. William Shawn, the nonfiction editor on the magazine, thought that Capote seemed "like a small boy, almost like a child." Despite his lowly position in the company, Truman quickly commanded attention for his eccentric mannerisms and flamboyant clothing. The following year he was fired from the *New Yorker* for misrepresenting himself as a staff writer.

To deal with the loneliness of his uncertain upbringing, Capote had always invented stories. As an adult he claimed that he decided to become a professional writer when he was only ten years old. "I knew damned well I was going to be a famous writer," he later said. In June 1945 Capote published his first short story, "Miriam," in *Mademoiselle* magazine. The plot is interwoven with leitmotifs of isolation, dread, and psychological breakdown, typical concerns in Capote's early work. The prose is rich and precise, with gothic shadings. The story attracted widespread attention; it earned the O. Henry Memorial Award of 1946 and a book contract for its author.

In 1948 Capote finished the novel for which he had received the contract two years earlier. Called *Other Voices, Other Rooms,* it was an immediate critical and popular success. The book climbed to the top of the *New York Times* best-seller list, where it remained for nine weeks. Its author was only twenty-three years old. He became the darling of the New York literary circuit and was featured in *Life* magazine.

Success continued to come his way. His short story "Shut a Final Door" won first prize in the O. Henry Awards that year. That same year Capote and Jack Dunphy, a thirty-four-year-old dancer, became companions. Capote published his second novel, *The Grass Harp,* in 1951. Despite a flawed ending, this novel was as well received as *Other Voices, Other Rooms* had been. Capote adapted *The Grass Harp* as a play; it opened on 27 March 1952 and ran for thirty-six performances.

Capote next tried his hand at writing a script for the film *Indiscretion of an American Wife,* starring Montgomery Clift; the movie was a flop. A few weeks later Capote was hired to rewrite *Beat the Devil,* starring Humphrey Bogart. Although financially unsuccessful, this 1953 film was well regarded by many critics and has achieved the status of an offbeat classic.

Next Capote completed a stage show, *House of Flowers,* starring Pearl Bailey. The show ran for five months, closing on 22 May 1955, after 165 performances. By now Capote counted John and Jacqueline Kennedy, Arthur Miller and his wife Marilyn Monroe, Marlon Brando, and Elizabeth Taylor among his friends. He was allowed into the world of the rich and was feted on yachts, in chalets, and in penthouses.

In the midst of his wild social whirl, Capote began to develop a new approach to the role that nonfiction could have on his career and on literature in general. Late in 1955 he began his experiments along this line. First he accompanied the touring company of *Porgy and Bess* on their historical visit to Russia and filed reports with the *New Yorker*. The following year he combined these articles into a book, *The Muses Are Heard*. The book shows Capote's ability to guide his readers' responses to events and characters by his careful selection and arrangement of details. The same skill is evident in his 1957 interview with Marlon Brando, "The Duke in His Domain," which elevated the celebrity profile to an art form.

Breakfast at Tiffany's appeared in the spring of 1958. Within months, Holly Golightly, the novel's main character, had taken her place in American fiction's hall of fame. Although even as harsh a critic as Norman Mailer wrote that *Breakfast at Tiffany's* was so perfect that he would not change two words of it, Capote's greatest work and success was yet to come.

Capote secured his literary claim to fame in 1965, when the *New Yorker* published *In Cold Blood*. A gripping account of the mass murder of a Kansas farm family, the Clutters, the book follows the two young killers from the murder scene to their eventual execution five and a half years later. Capote's meticulous research—he had even befriended the murderers, Dick Hickock and Perry Smith, for five years before their execution in 1965—resulted in a literary landmark. Capote's "nonfiction novel" was received to extraordinary acclaim. The *New York Times* proclaimed the novel a "masterpiece"; paperback and movie rights were sold for record sums. *In Cold Blood* was published as a book in January 1966.

To celebrate the completion of *In Cold Blood*, Capote gave perhaps the most celebrated party of modern times, his masked "Black and White Ball" at the Plaza Hotel in Manhattan. One guest joked that the guest book read like "an international list for the guillotine." Those attending included publisher Katharine Graham, socialite Barbara Cushing Paley, decorator Billy Baldwin, Frank Sinatra, Mia Farrow, Tallulah Bankhead, Norman Mailer, and various princes and princesses.

In 1967 a televised version of Capote's short story "A Christmas Memory" earned great praise, as did the film version of *In Cold Blood*. He published hardcover versions of *A Christmas Memory* and *The Thanksgiving Visitor* (another story based on childhood memories) and became a frequent guest on talk shows. *The Dogs Bark*, a volume of previously published material, appeared in 1973. He also took a new companion, John O'Shea.

The last years of Capote's life were painful and difficult, punctuated by disaster. In 1975 Capote published "La Côte Basque, 1965," a chapter of *Answered Prayers*, a novel he was never to finish. In this work he broke the rules of the club by patterning his fiction on real people and real incidents that were socially important. In so doing, he had dredged up sordid events from his friends' lives. "Capote Bites the Hand That Feeds Him," the cover of *New York* magazine screamed. Just as it had once been fashionable to be seen with Capote, now it became fashionable to shun him.

In 1975 Capote finished work on the film *Murder by Death*. In 1977, exhausted and suffering from what he termed a "semi-nervous breakdown," Capote became so incoherent at a reading at Towson State College in Maryland that he was led off the stage. In 1984 he suffered two bad falls, one resulting in a cerebral concussion. He battled a host of physical problems, including emphysema and epilepsy. Alcoholism and drug addiction added to his difficulties. Capote published his final book, *Music for Chameleons,* in 1980, three years before his death from liver disease complicated by phlebitis and multiple drug intoxication. He was cremated.

Capote's *In Cold Blood* was a pioneer that opened up new literary territory. Other writers had used fictional techniques in nonfiction before, but no one had ever written a nonfiction book that could be read as a novel. In addition, Capote was a gifted prose stylist—"a fanatic on rhythm and language," he told one interviewer.

★

Biographies include Marie Rudisill and James C. Simmons, *Truman Capote* (1983), in which Rudisill, Capote's aunt, provides revealing incidents and anecdotes of Capote's early life; John Malcolm Brinnin, *Truman Capote: Dear Heart, Old Buddy* (1986), a personal and affectionate biography; and Gerald Clarke, *Capote: A Biography* (1988), the definitive biography. See also George Plimpton, *Truman Capote: In Which Various Friends, Enemies, Acquaintances and Detractors Recall His Turbulent Career* (1997). David L. Vanderwerken, "Truman Capote, 1943–1968: A Critical Bibliography," *Bulletin of Bibliography* 27 (July–Sept. 1970), lists Capote's works. An obituary is in the *New York Times* (27 Aug. 1984).

LAURIE ROZAKIS

CARMICHAEL, Howard Hoagland ("Hoagy") (*b.* 22 November 1899 in Bloomington, Indiana; *d.* 27 December 1981 in Rancho Mirage, California), composer of "Star Dust" and more than fifty other hit songs, notable for his lighthearted, jazz-influenced melodies and his twangy singing in movies and on the radio.

Carmichael was the oldest of the four children of Howard Clyde Carmichael and Lida Mary Robison. His journeyman father held numerous low-paying jobs, including hansom driver, telephone lineman, and electrician. Because he changed jobs frequently, the family lived in Indianapolis from time to time, and in 1909 moved to Montana for a short while, but always returned to Bloomington. Carmichael seems to have inherited his musical ability from

Hoagy Carmichael, 1946. METRONOME COLLECTION/ARCHIVE PHOTOS

his mother. She played piano for silent movies in Bloomington and often took young Hoagy to work with her. He was the envy of his schoolmates in the Bloomington public schools because he saw movies for free. By the age of sixteen he had become a proficient, self-taught piano player.

Unhappy in high school in Indianapolis, Carmichael quit to take a series of dead-end jobs, including a three-week stint as an entrails cleaner in a slaughterhouse. He also tried to enlist in the army several times during World War I but was turned down as underweight. He was finally accepted on 10 November 1918, one day before the armistice; the recruiting office sent him home.

The next year Carmichael reentered high school in Bloomington. He soon began to earn money playing in local bands with such friends as Harry Hostetter, Wad Allen, and Art Baker. He put himself through Indiana University by leading his own band on campus and at summer resorts, and by booking out-of-town bands for college dances. Through these activities, he met many important figures of early jazz, including Louis Armstrong, trumpeter Red Nichols, trombonist Jack Teagarden, drummer Gene Krupa, the Dorsey Brothers, Benny Goodman, and his idol, Bix Beiderbecke.

Carmichael and Beiderbecke became close friends. Beiderbecke's band, The Wolverines, made the first recording of a Carmichael song, "Free Wheelin'," in 1924, although they changed its name to "Riverboat Shuffle." In 1925 Carmichael wrote his first important song, "Washboard Blues." His friend Harry Hostetter took it to a local poet named Fred Callahan, who needed only twenty minutes to complete a lyric about an elderly black woman scrubbing clothes.

Both during his college years and after, Carmichael lived a frenetically rootless life. He gave minimal time to his studies, preferring all-night jam sessions, bootleg whiskey, and impulsive travel anywhere from New York to Havana. When Carmichael finally received his bachelor of law degree in 1926, he determined to put his hedonistic life behind him. Stuart Gorell, an old Bloomington friend who was a Miami journalist, persuaded him to establish a law practice in Florida. On his way from Indiana to Florida, however, he stopped by the New York City office of the music publisher Irving Mills to discuss the publication of "Washboard Blues."

After a round of partying and jamming in Manhattan jazz clubs, Carmichael eventually established a practice in West Palm Beach with attorney Wilbur Cook. But one day, after hearing jazz trumpeter Red Nichols's recording of "Washboard Blues," he abruptly abandoned law to return permanently to songwriting and playing.

In 1927 Carmichael added singing to his musical activities. Paul Whiteman asked him to play piano and do the vocal for what Whiteman called a "concert recording" of "Washboard Blues." Carmichael's voice was slightly nasal, but also light and musical. His singing style was unaffected, nonchalant, and charming. He preferred to call it "flatsy through the nose." At the same time, Whiteman had secretly asked one of the band's singers, the young Bing Crosby, to prepare the vocal in case Hoagy's recording was inadequate. Carmichael's performance proved satisfactory, and he and Crosby soon became close friends.

Carmichael continued to live a footloose life, mainly in Manhattan, through the late 1920s and early 1930s. He also played and sang with bands led by Jean Goldkette and Don Redman, although his goal was to establish himself as a songwriter. After Beiderbecke died in 1931, at the age of twenty-eight, Carmichael lost much of his interest in jazz. His songwriting after that was mainline pop, although he retained his affection for the jazz of his youth.

Carmichael wrote "Star Dust," his most famous song, in 1928 or 1929. The story of its composition is unclear. Carmichael wrote that it came about soon after Dorothy Kelly, a longtime sweetheart, had broken off their relationship. He said the melody came to him gradually as he sat on Indiana University's "spooning wall." Soon he rushed off to a piano in the Book Nook, a nearby college hangout, to finish it. Other sources say the song began as an up-tempo tune called "Barnyard Shuffle" but became "Star Dust" after substantial changes in mood and tempo. After several recordings demonstrated its continuing appeal, lyricist Mitchell Parish added the words in 1931. The most popular of its 500 different recordings was bandleader Artie Shaw's, which sold 2 million copies in 1940.

After Carmichael made several unsuccessful attempts to find work in Hollywood, Paramount Pictures hired him in 1936 to write an interpolated song for Crosby in a film version of Cole Porter's *Anything Goes* (1936). The result, "Moonburn," was soon forgotten and Carmichael returned to New York City. Later that year, Carmichael contributed one number, "Little Old Lady," to a Broadway revue called *The Show Is On*. When the song became a hit, Paramount put him under contract for $1,000 a week. On 14 March 1936, shortly before leaving New York for California, he married Chicago-born Ruth Mary Meinardi, whom he had met through a mutual friend. They had two sons, Hoagy Bix and Randy Bob. His life became more regular and more conventional. He and Ruth divorced in 1955. He married Wanda McKay on 20 June 1977.

In Hollywood, Carmichael worked with such lyricists as Frank Loesser ("Small Fry" for *Sing You Sinners*, 1938), Leo Robin, Sam Coslow, and Ned Washington ("The Nearness of You" for *Romance in the Dark*, 1938). He and Loesser also wrote "Two Sleepy People" (for *Thanks for the Memory*, 1938) and "Heart and Soul" (for *Some Like It Hot*, 1938), both sung by Bob Hope and Shirley Ross.

Carmichael had no single long-term collaborator. Occasionally, he wrote his own lyrics for such songs as "Rockin' Chair" (1930), which became jazz singer Mildred Bailey's signature song; "Blue Orchids" (1939), which rose to number one on the radio program *Your Hit Parade;* "I Get Along Without You Very Well" (1939); and "Hong Kong Blues" (1939). As early as 1933, Carmichael had begun to work off and on with his most important collaborator, Johnny Mercer. Sparked by their mutual interest in jazz and their imaginative affinity for rural America, they finished their first hit in twenty minutes when Mercer gave Carmichael the title "Lazy Bones." They went on to write such songs as "Moon Country" (1934), "Down t' Uncle Bill's" (1935), "Skylark" (1942), and "The Old Music Master" (1943). Carmichael's other important songs include "Georgia on My Mind" (1930; lyric by Stuart Gorell), "Lazy River" (1931; lyric by Sidney Arodin), "Lamplighter's Serenade" (1942; lyric by Paul Francis Webster), "Doctor, Lawyer, Indian Chief" (1945; lyric by Webster), "Baltimore Oriole" (1945; lyric by Webster), and "My Resistance Is Low" (1952; lyric by Harold Adamson).

Carmichael made his screen debut in *Topper* in 1937, playing the sort of droll, worldly-wise, laconic piano player he would most often portray in movies. His characters were not unlike Carmichael himself, and his performances usually included singing at least one of his songs. Carmichael's Hoosier twang, his slight build, and his long, lean poker face seemed to suit the characters he played. Perhaps his best-known performance is as Cricket, the piano player in Howard Hawks's version of Ernest Hemingway's *To Have and Have Not* (1944), which starred Humphrey Bogart and marked the screen debut of Lauren Bacall. Carmichael sang two of his own songs in the movie, "How Little We Know" (lyric by Mercer) and "Hong Kong Blues."

Carmichael especially enjoyed appearing in the 1946 Western *Canyon Passage,* because he played the mandolin rather than the piano, and he rode a mule rather than just sit in a bar. His song for that movie, "Ole Buttermilk Sky" (lyric by Jack Brooks), received an Academy Award nomination. Carmichael and Mercer won Carmichael's only Oscar for "In the Cool, Cool, Cool of the Evening," sung by Jane Wyman and Bing Crosby in the movie *Here Comes the Groom* (1951). His other notable movie appearances were in *Johnny Angel* (1945), *The Best Years of Our Lives* (1946), and *Young Man with a Horn* (1950).

Carmichael made only one attempt to write a score for a Broadway musical. *Walk with Music* opened at the Ethel Barrymore Theater on 4 June 1940. Although it ran for only fifteen performances, he and collaborator Johnny Mercer wrote several appealing tunes, including "Ooh, What You Said" and "Way Back in 1939 A.D."

In 1948 Carmichael began his own radio show in which he sang and chatted, and in 1953 he started a successful television show, *Saturday Night Review*. Although he was a frequent guest on television variety shows and the Western series *Laramie* from 1959 to 1963, his career languished in the loud new world of rock and roll, and his attempts at writing longer symphonic pieces were not greeted kindly by critics. He hosted a PBS children's series, *Hoagy Carmichael's Music Shop,* before retiring. In 1971 he was elected to the Songwriters' Hall of Fame; the following year Indiana University awarded him an honorary doctorate. He spent his later years playing tennis and golf. He died of a heart attack.

Most of Carmichael's best-known songs were written for undistinguished, long-forgotten movies. He wrote individual songs rather than scores, but their breezy charm and jazz-influenced rhythms made them both distinctive and memorable. Although "Star Dust" was a dreamily introspective ballad, Carmichael wrote less romantically than most major songwriters of his era. His work has a characteristic sunny, upbeat quality. Because he wrote often with a sense of the small town and the out-of-doors, his melodies feel rooted in common experience and familiar natural images. Somehow his own Hoosier twang always rests lightly atop his best songs.

★

Music manuscripts and sheet music of Carmichael's songs are located in the Archives of Traditional Music, Lilly Library, and School of Music Library, all at Indiana University. Hoagy Carmichael, *The Stardust Road* (1946) is a volume of informative, chatty, and occasionally introspective remembrances. Hoagy Carmichael, with Stephen Longstreet, *Sometimes I Wonder* (1965), is a similar volume. Alec Wilder, *American Popular Song: The Great Innovators 1900–1950* (1972), analyzes several of Carmichael's melodies and calls him "talented, inventive, sophisticated." Roy Hemming, *The Melody Lingers On: The Great Songwriters and Their Movie Musicals* (1986), examines Carmichael's work for the movies during the 1930s and 1940s. J. E. Hasse, *The Works of Hoagy Carmichael* (1983); Ronny S. Schiff, ed., *The Star Dust Melodies of Hoagy Carmichael* (1983); and "LP Recordings Devoted to Hoagy Carmichael," *Jazz Notes* (Oct. 1983), provide the most complete bibliographic information. An obituary is in the *New York Times* (28 Dec. 1981).

MICHAEL LASSER

CARPENTER, Karen Anne (*b.* 2 March 1950 in New Haven, Connecticut; *d.* 4 February 1983 in Downey, California), vocalist and musician, best known for her work with her brother, Richard, in the 1970s soft-rock duo the Carpenters.

The daughter of Harold Bertram Carpenter, a printer, and Agnes Reuwer Tatum, a homemaker, Karen was four years

Karen Carpenter, 1980. FOTOS INTERNATIONAL/ARCHIVE PHOTOS

younger than her brother Richard Lynn. Initially, Richard appeared to be the performer in the family; taking up piano at eight years old, by high school he had formed his first band and was also sitting in with groups at area clubs. Karen, although taking accordion lessons as a child, preferred playing sports.

In 1963 the family moved to Downey, California, a suburb of Los Angeles. The following year, Karen began playing glockenspiel in the school marching band, quickly moving on to drums. Richard continued playing in local clubs and after graduating from high school attended California State University in Long Beach. Karen also briefly attended Cal State, but neither Carpenter would graduate; both dropped out when their music careers took off.

In 1965 the two formed their first group, the jazz-influenced Richard Carpenter Trio, with Richard on piano, Karen on drums, and Wes Jacobs on tuba. The group played at dances, weddings, and local clubs; Karen occasionally sang, as did another vocalist, Margaret Shanor. In 1966 the group was signed to RCA after winning a "battle of the bands" contest held at the Hollywood Bowl. Although they recorded material for RCA, no album was released and the group was dropped. The trio broke up soon after. Karen released her first single in 1966, "Looking for Love"/"I'll Be Yours" (both written by Richard), on the small independent label Magic Lamp.

In 1967 Karen and Richard formed another group, Spectrum, which included John Bettis (who would later cowrite a number of Carpenters songs with Richard), Gary Sims, Danny Woodhams, and Leslie Johnston. Although the group broke into the lucrative Los Angeles club circuit, they could not find a record deal and soon disbanded. Karen and Richard then began recording their own material, and a demo tape made its way to Herb Alpert, one of the co-founders of the A&M Records label. He signed the two on 22 April 1969.

The Carpenters' first album, *Offering* (later repackaged as *Ticket to Ride*) was released in 1969 accompanied by the single "Ticket to Ride," a soft-rock reworking of the Beatles' hit. The single reached number 54 on the *Billboard* charts. But the group's next single, "Close to You," released in 1970, went straight to number one and became their first gold record. When the album of the same name reached number two, the Carpenters' success was solidified, and a string of hits followed over the next six years. The duo had twenty Top 40 singles, including eleven in the top five ("Top of the World," released in 1973, and "Please Mr. Postman," released in 1974, made it to number one), and seven Top 40 albums, including five in the top five (*The Singles 1969–1973,* released in 1973, topped the charts).

Other achievements included hosting their own television variety show, *Make Your Own Kind of Music,* in 1971, and a performance at the White House for President Richard Nixon during a state visit by West German chancellor Willy Brandt in 1974. The group also won three Grammy awards: best new artist of 1970; best contemporary vocal performance by a group (for "Close to You") in 1971; and best pop vocal performance by a group (for *The Carpenters*) in 1972.

But as the decade progressed, both Carpenters developed serious health problems. Richard became addicted to quaaludes, while Karen developed anorexia nervosa, an eating disorder. In 1975, with her weight at eighty pounds, Karen became too ill to perform, and two major overseas tours were canceled. The Carpenters stopped touring in 1978, and the following year Richard entered a treatment program for his addiction.

In addition to her illness, Karen faced other personal and professional difficulties. She married Thomas T. Burris, a real estate developer, on 31 August 1980, but by the end of 1981 the two had separated (Karen had an appointment to sign her divorce papers on the day of her death). The group's record sales had also fallen. During 1979 Karen recorded a solo album, but its release was canceled in favor of work on a new Carpenters album, *Made in America*, released in 1981. A single from the album, "Touch Me When We're Dancing," was the duo's last Top 40 hit.

In November 1981 Karen moved to New York City and entered therapy with Dr. Steven Levenkron (author of the book *The Best Little Girl in the World*, a study of anorexia). A year later, proclaiming herself cured, she moved back to California, but three months later, having spent the night with her parents, Karen was found by her mother passed out on the floor of her bedroom shortly before 9:00 A.M. on 4 February 1983. She was taken to the hospital, but could not be resuscitated. Karen's death was attributed to heart failure due to anorexia nervosa. Services were held on 8 February, and Karen was buried in Forest Lawn Cemetery, in Cypress, California.

The Carpenters were frequently derided during their years of success for their wholesome, all-American image (President Nixon lauded them as "Young America at its very best"), and their lush, melodic pop songs, which some critics dismissed as saccharine. In fact, however, Karen's vocal style was both distinctive and remarkably expressive, imbuing melancholy numbers like "Rainy Days and Mondays" and "Superstar" (both number-two hits) with a touching poignancy. A greater appreciation for Karen's work has developed in the years since her death, along with a clearer understanding of the difficulties lying beneath her wholesome facade and a greater awareness of the problem of anorexia nervosa. Notable collections of her work released since her death include *From the Top* (1990), a boxed set of hits, popular album tracks, and rarities, and *Karen Carpenter* (1996), the solo album she recorded in 1979.

★

Ray Coleman, *The Carpenters: The Untold Story* (1994), is the most comprehensive biography of Karen and Richard Carpenter, by a noted British music journalist. Robyn Archer and Diana Simmonds, *A Star Is Torn* (1987), is an examination of select female performers, including Carpenter. Gillian G. Gaar, *She's a Rebel: The History of Women in Rock & Roll* (1992), undertakes a feminist critique of rock history. An obituary is in the *New York Times* (5 Feb. 1983). The Carpenters, *From the Top* (1991), is a four-CD boxed set, with extensive liner notes.

GILLIAN G. GAAR

CASE, Clifford Philip (*b.* 16 April 1904 in Franklin Park, New Jersey; *d.* 5 March 1982 in Washington, D.C.), U.S. senator who, as a liberal Republican for more than three decades in Congress, championed important social and civil rights legislation and was an effective opponent of the Vietnam War.

The oldest of the six children of Clifford Philip Case, a Dutch Reformed minister, and Jeannette Benedict, Case grew up in the Hudson River valley, graduating from Poughkeepsie High School in 1921. He attended Rutgers University, where he played on the lacrosse team and was elected to Phi Beta Kappa. After graduating from Rutgers in 1925, he studied at the Columbia University School of Law and received an LL.B. degree in 1928. Case then joined the prestigious Wall Street law firm of Simpson, Thacher, and Bartlett, where he was a partner from 1939 until 1953.

Case married Ruth Miriam Smith on 13 July 1928; they had three children. In 1938 he was elected to the Rahway, New Jersey, common council. Four years later, he was elected to the state assembly.

In 1944 Case was elected to the U.S. House of Representatives, winning the first of five terms from northern New Jersey's Sixth District. He made his mark as an internationalist with a strong commitment to civil rights, sponsoring legislation to make lynching a federal crime in 1947. He also sought to repeal poll taxes in the Deep South that were used to keep blacks from voting. Case opposed the creation of the House Un-American Activities Committee as a permanent committee because of his concern that it could be used to abuse civil liberties. Case, who favored bipartisanship in foreign policy, supported the Marshall Plan and the Truman Doctrine. An early supporter of Dwight D. Eisenhower for the presidency in 1952, Case worked on his transition team.

After his reelection to the House in 1952, Case declared his candidacy for governor of New Jersey, but he had difficulty raising enough money and withdrew from the race before the 1953 primary election. On 14 August 1953 he quit the House to become president of the Fund for the

Clifford Case at a congressional hearing on Vietnam, 1973. ARCHIVE PHOTOS

Republic, an organization that had been awarded $15 million by the Ford Foundation to protect freedom of thought and expression "in the face of persistent international tension." Case resigned from the think tank in March 1954 to become a candidate for the U.S. Senate.

As a Senate candidate during the Army-McCarthy hearings, Case spoke out against Senator Joseph R. McCarthy. "The incident which triggered me off was Mr. McCarthy's unfair, unwarranted and slanderous personal attack on a young lawyer [Frederick G. Fisher] in the case," he recalled in a 1978 interview. McCarthy had charged that Fisher had once been a member of a communist front group. Case issued a 1,500-word denunciation of McCarthy in which he promised that, if elected, he would seek to remove McCarthy from any committee with investigative functions.

During the Senate campaign, Case was attacked by right-wingers as "a pro-communist Republicrat" and "Stalin's choice for senator." Case had anticipated this criticism, but he was stunned when the *Newark Star-Ledger,* which was pro-McCarthy, published allegations that Case's sister Adelaide had been a member of a communist front group during World War II. "Smear me if you can," Case responded. "Leave my sister alone."

Case narrowly won that election, squeaking through over Democratic Congressman Charles R. Howell with 48.7 percent and a plurality of just 3,507 votes out of more than 1.7 million. He held his Senate seat for twenty-four years, establishing a reputation as a force for good government in a state that had often been tainted by political corruption. Case decisively won reelection in 1960, 1966,

and 1972, winning more than 60 percent of the vote in the latter two races.

The tall, slender, craggy-faced Case became known as one of the most thoughtful and influential senators of his time. He was urbane, cultivated, and well-mannered. A 1960 survey of fifty leading Washington correspondents ranked him as one of the ten most able senators. By his second term, Case had gained slots on the Foreign Relations and Appropriations committees. In 1964 Case was among the first senators to sponsor an amendment calling for greater disclosure of personal and campaign finances. It was defeated.

Throughout his Senate career, Case made civil rights legislation a special priority. "A majority of the American people had made a decision that the old way was unacceptable," Case said of his role in the passage of the 1964 Civil Rights Act, "and the leadership of the civil rights movement was very wise in how they put together a coalition that handled the legislation. Everybody used a great deal of common sense and skill and persistence." Because of his efforts to fight racial discrimination, Case became estranged from the conservative wing of the Republican party. He declined to support 1964 Republican presidential nominee, Barry Goldwater, who opposed the Civil Rights Act.

On the Foreign Relations Committee, Case was low-key but effective in his opposition to the Vietnam War. Although he had voted in 1964 for the Gulf of Tonkin Resolution, which President Lyndon B. Johnson used as his authority to send troops into Vietnam, Case began to question the war's purpose. He went to Vietnam in June 1967 and concluded that the United States should end the war. "To me, it was a shocking and unacceptable waste of lives and money," he said in a 1978 interview. Case said in 1967 that Johnson had distorted and misused the Tonkin Gulf resolution as "a perpetual letter of credit." He cosponsored numerous amendments to end the war, including the 1973 Case-Church Act, which cut off funding for U.S. military activities "in, over, and off the shores" of Indochina, which ended American bombing on 16 August 1973.

Case was a favorite-son presidential candidate at the 1968 Republican National Convention in an effort to help deadlock the convention and prevent Richard M. Nixon's first-ballot nomination. When Nixon was elected, he sought to retaliate by not consulting Case on federal appointments. Case blocked one of these appointees from Senate confirmation and Nixon relented.

In New Jersey, Case nominated U.S. attorneys with a mandate to go after political corruption in both parties. In the 1970s, these officials sent to jail a former Newark mayor, a congressman, two former New Jersey secretaries of state, the former Republican state chairman, and the former Jersey City mayor and Democratic boss.

Case, who sought reelection to a fifth term in 1978, was upset in a low-turnout primary by a little-known conservative rival, Jeffrey Bell. He was viewed as too liberal by many Republicans. "I think I can honestly say that it's miraculous that I was in politics for forty years and managed to stay that long," Case said after the loss. "I've never been beaten in a general election, and I didn't think that the end would ever come. I still think that a small minority voted in the primary. But I can't be sure that a larger turnout would have made the difference."

He lectured at Rutgers University's Eagleton Institute of Politics and also resumed his law practice after leaving the Senate. Case died of lung cancer in Washington, D.C.

★

Case talked at length about his Senate career in "Reflections of an Honest Politician," *Philadelphia Inquirer Sunday Magazine* (28 Jan. 1979). Other useful sources include Case's articles "Changing Role of Congress: The Growing Concern with the Legislative Process," *George Washington Law Review* 32 (June 1964): 929–931, and "Congress and the Double Standard," *Federal Bar Journal* 24 (summer 1964): 257–263. An obituary is in the *New York Times* (7 Mar. 1982).

STEVE NEAL

CASEY, James E. (*b.* 29 March 1888 in Candelaria, Nevada; *d.* 6 June 1983 in Seattle, Washington), businessman and philanthropist who was a founder of United Parcel Service (UPS).

Casey was the eldest of four children of Annie E. and Henry J. Casey; his father was an innkeeper whose establishment served silver miners in Candelaria, Nevada. When gold was discovered in Alaska, Casey's father moved the family to Seattle and set off for the Klondike, hoping to strike it rich. He had no success and returned penniless and ill. Casey left school at age eleven to help support the family. His first job was as a department store delivery boy, which brought in $2.50 weekly. For a time in his teens Casey returned to Nevada and tried gold prospecting himself.

In 1907 Casey and a partner started a courier service, the American Messenger Company, in Seattle, employing six carriers and two bicycles and operating out of a basement under a saloon in what is now known as the city's underground. A free lunch counter served as both work space by day and as a bed at night. The company was soon serving local department stores as well as small businesses; its initial success was based on keeping clients accurately informed of the pickup times. The messenger service also picked up odd jobs, occasionally including a little detective work. In 1913 the company, after merging with a local delivery service, bought its first motor vehicle—a Model T Ford.

James Casey. COURTESY OF THE UNITED PARCEL SERVICE ARCHIVES. © 1960 BY YOUSUF KARSH.

Casey's partner, Claude Ryan, sold out in 1917, but by then Casey and his new partners had delivery agreements with every department store in Seattle. In 1919 the company expanded to Oakland and was renamed the United Parcel Service. At the suggestion of his partner Charles Soderstrom, Casey painted his trucks brown in emulation of Pullman coaches, hoping that this would, in his words, "make us equally famous on the streets of America." Soon, UPS trucks were rolling in all the big cities along the West Coast. In 1929 Casey experimented with using his trucks to feed shipments to airplanes, but the disruption of the airline industry by the stock market crash put an end to this innovation. Casey's focus on using air service remained a stumbling point with company directors until the time of his death.

In 1930 Casey brought his service to New York City, immediately picking up the prestigious Lord & Taylor department store as a principal customer. Soon Casey obtained contracts with nearly all of New York's great retail emporiums. Shortly thereafter, *Business Week* reported that the stores had scrapped their individual fleets of delivery equipment in favor of Casey's service because they could achieve savings of as much as 50 percent of previous costs (UPS generally bought the stores' fleets and hired some of the workers). By 1940 the company was serving thirty-seven

New York stores with 320 vehicles, including large trucks for furniture transport and several models of cars for special bulk items and package delivery. This use of specialized equipment was perhaps unique in the early trucking industry and led transportation planners to think in terms of the highly specialized equipment that would be required for highway conveyance of all commodities. Casey soon moved UPS corporate headquarters to Greenwich, Connecticut, and bought a modest two-bedroom home in the area. Later, he moved to an apartment in the Waldorf Towers in Manhattan.

Casey is considered a founder of modern management. He once cut out the side of a truck in order to observe how shipping clerks sorted and handled parcels. Casey eliminated 30 percent of worker movements this way. He would then establish work quotas based on his observations. When the firm went to computerized studies of worker productivity after Casey's death, some workers complained that these studies were less accurate than Casey's observations. A stickler for detail, Casey authored 138 employee rules. An employee in need of a haircut paid a fifty-cent fine; one who used profanity paid a dollar (one must remember that the UPS deliveryman usually arrived at a private home, not a business establishment).

Casey also had advice for his managers. "Each employee should be treated as a special asset that needs to be appreciated and developed—when someone leaves our company that's a failure," he wrote. He also insisted on promoting from the ranks, opening up management positions to employees. Casey established one of the first profit-sharing systems in the nation. By the time of his death United Parcel Service was one of the largest employee-owned companies in the world. Lower-level executives frequently attended conferences with Casey. "Ideals of our company cannot be carried out from the top alone," he wrote. Casey would sometimes anonymously stop a UPS truck and ask the driver how he liked his job.

After World War II, UPS expanded into new markets. Frequently, it did so not in its own name, but rather through a local affiliate. For example, in Philadelphia Casey's company called itself Common Carrier. The company started gaining interstate operating rights in 1957, and the system of regional carriers continued until the early 1970s, when the carrier applied to the Interstate Commerce Commission for permission to operate as a single entity. Beginning in 1975, the firm finally had interstate rights for the contiguous forty-eight states and functioned as a single operating entity.

Casey never married, he had no children, and he was reportedly somewhat of a recluse. He did, however, maintain strong community ties through his philanthropic activities, notably with the Annie E. Casey Foundation, named in honor of his mother, and the Casey Family Pro-

gram; the latter organization specialized in finding permanent homes for foster children. Casey also contributed $100,000 to the restoration of a park, Pioneer Square Triangle, in Seattle.

In the early 1960s Casey's dispute with UPS executives over air freight transportation led to his dismissal as chief executive officer. A series of bitter labor disputes with the Teamsters union had also weakened Casey's position with the firm. In the early 1980s the aging Casey was frequently hospitalized, and in 1983 Casey retired from the board of directors of United Parcel Service, becoming honorary director. Shortly thereafter, he died of undisclosed causes at a Seattle hospital at age ninety-five. He is interred at Holy-rood Mausoleum in Seattle. At the time of his death, United Parcel Service was delivering 6 million packages daily nationwide and had more than 115,000 employees.

★

C. L. Kane, *The Tightest Ship: UPS Exposé* (1993), is a polemic against the labor practices of the company since Casey's death; the opening chapter contains the best description of Casey's life available. *Fortune* (11 Mar. 1991) celebrates Casey's induction into the Business Hall of Fame. The Motor Carrier Reports of the Interstate Commerce Commission give glimpses into United Parcel Service operations under Casey, who generally eschewed regulatory battles. Obituaries are in the *New York Times* (7 June 1983) and *Seattle Post-Intelligencer* (8 June 1983).

JOHN DAVID HEALY

CATLEDGE, Turner (*b.* 17 March 1901 near New Prospect, Mississippi; *d.* 27 April 1983 in New Orleans, Louisiana), reporter and newspaper official whose tenure as managing editor and executive editor of the *New York Times* from 1951 to 1968 saw the newspaper solidify its place as the preeminent force in American journalism.

Catledge grew up in rural Mississippi, the younger of the two children of Willie Ann Turner, a seamstress, and Lee Johnston Catledge, a local politician and railroad clerk. His resourceful mother held the family together by running a boardinghouse during his father's periods of unemployment. Turner was brought up as a Presbyterian. He graduated from Philadelphia (Mississippi) High School in 1918 and then entered Mississippi A&M University (now Mississippi State University), from which he graduated with a business degree in 1922. After running several weekly and biweekly newspapers in Mississippi, he moved to Memphis, Tennessee, and worked as a reporter first at the *Memphis Press* and next at the *Memphis Commercial Appeal*. In 1927 his coverage of a flood on the Mississippi River brought him to the attention of Secretary of Commerce Herbert Hoover, who recommended him to the publisher of the *New York Times,* Adolf S. Ochs.

Catledge then spent two years at the *Baltimore Sun* before joining the *Times* in 1929, when President Hoover again urged Ochs to hire the young reporter. On 19 March 1931 Catledge married Mildred Turpin. The couple, who had two daughters, separated in 1949 and divorced in 1958. On 10 February 1958 Catledge married Abby Ray Izard.

From 1929 to 1941 Catledge covered Washington politics for Arthur Krock, head of the *Times*'s Washington bureau. James Reston later recalled that Catledge "took a tolerant and even amiable view of all politicians, regardless of their shenanigans, on the ground that they were at least more interesting than people in other walks of life and their blatant hypocrisy made good copy." President Franklin D. Roosevelt offered to become a prime news source for Catledge in 1936, thus circumventing Arthur Krock, whom the president disliked. Catledge informed Krock of what had occurred and did not accept Roosevelt's offer.

In 1937, when Roosevelt's "court-packing" plan became a Washington sensation, Catledge collaborated on a book about the episode with Joseph Alsop, the Washington correspondent for the *New York Herald-Tribune*. Their volume, *The 168 Days* (1938), presented an engrossing inside account of the struggle and made the best-seller list. In 1941 Catledge left the *Times* for a higher-paying position with the *Chicago Sun*. Unhappy in the new job, he returned to Washington and the *Times* at his old salary in mid-1943.

During World War II, Catledge traveled with the publisher of the *Times*, Arthur Hays Sulzberger, who had succeeded Ochs in 1935. As they drank together and even faced a Japanese sniper's bullet on the island of Pelileu in 1944, they became close friends. In December 1944 Catledge became assistant managing editor of the *Times*. By late 1951 he took over as managing editor after Edwin L. James died.

For the next thirteen years Catledge used the political skills he had developed as a reporter and his innate sense of where the *Times* should go to improve the newspaper in significant ways. He emphasized good writing through shorter, crisper sentences. He encouraged news analysis in the daily paper, and broadened the coverage of New York City and its metropolitan area. Catledge had a good eye for journalistic talent, and he built a staff that enabled the *Times* to cover the breaking stories of the 1950s and 1960s, such as the civil rights movement in the South and the social protests of the Kennedy-Johnson era. His guidance was gentle, and he gave great freedom to his editors and reporters. As a result, the morale of the men who worked with him was very high. "Catledge was the most affable of men, a gentlemanly editor with the gift of golden gab and the ability to mediate the many messes that confront editors," wrote Richard Shepard, a reporter who saw the rumpled, soft-spoken Catledge operate in this period.

For all his successes, Catledge had his blind spots and failures. He did little to encourage the hiring of women for

Turner Catledge, 1951. UPI/CORBIS-BETTMANN

the *Times* and once announced that a woman would never be a *Times* editor. In 1961 he watered down the revelations of the impending invasion of Cuba that became the Bay of Pigs disaster. President John F. Kennedy later said, "If you had printed more about the operation you would have saved us from a colossal mistake." On the other hand, Catledge did promote investigations of the Central Intelligence Agency in the 1960s and, despite his southern background, supported the newspaper's energetic reporting on civil rights issues.

Arthur Ochs Sulzberger became publisher of the *Times* in 1963, and he elevated Catledge to executive editor in charge of both the daily and Sunday editions of the paper a year later. In 1968 an internal controversy involving the Washington bureau produced a coolness between Sulzberger and Catledge that led to the latter's retirement two years earlier than anticipated. Catledge became a vice president of the New York Times Company and a member of its board of directors. He formally retired on 1 January 1970. His discreet memoir, *My Life and the Times,* appeared in 1971. A round-faced man of medium height, Catledge had a courtly southern manner and dry wit. In retirement he and his wife lived in New Orleans, where he died of a stroke.

Largely unknown to the general public during his lifetime, Turner Catledge was an excellent reporter and an influential editor. During his tenure the *New York Times* reached a level of authority and insight that gave it unequaled power as a newspaper in American politics and culture. Catledge's quiet but effective leadership allowed a talented staff of reporters and editors to produce a newspaper that often set the agenda for issues and shaped attitudes of the nation's political establishment. Catledge placed a large emphasis on thoroughness and objectivity as a managing editor, and these qualities helped the *Times* to one of the great periods in its history.

★

Catledge donated his papers to the Mitchell Library at Mississippi State University. The collection contains a large amount of his office files. Also indispensable are the archives of the *New York Times*. There is no biography. For aspects of Catledge's career in journalism, see Meyer Berger, *The Story of the New York Times, 1851–1951* (1951); Gay Talese, *The Kingdom and the Power* (1969); Harrison Salisbury, *Without Fear or Favor* (1980); Joseph C. Goulden, *Fit to Print: A. M. Rosenthal and His Times* (1988); James Reston, *Deadline: A Memoir* (1991); Nan Robertson, *The Girls in the Balcony: Women, Men, and the New York Times* (1992); and Richard F. Shepard, *The Paper's Papers: A Reporter's Journey Through the Archives of the New York Times* (1996). There is a lengthy obituary in the *New York Times* (28 Apr. 1983).

Lewis L. Gould

CELLER, Emanuel (*b.* 6 May 1888 in Brooklyn, New York; *d.* 15 January 1981 in Brooklyn, New York), influential Democratic congressman who served fifty years and was a champion of civil rights and liberal causes.

Of German-Jewish ancestry, Celler was one of four children born to Henry H. Celler, the owner of a whiskey-rectifying business, and Josephine Müller, a homemaker. Known as Mannie, he attended Boys High School in Brooklyn, where he graduated in 1906.

Celler's mother and father died within five months of each other soon after he entered Columbia College in Manhattan. A granduncle, Sam Grabfelder, helped to finance his education. He graduated in 1910 with a B.A. degree, and in 1912 he received an LL.B degree from Columbia University Law School. That year he became a member of the state bar of New York and began to practice law in New York City. On 30 June 1914 he married Stella B. Baar; they had two daughters, Jane and Judith, and remained married until her death in 1966.

Celler's first federal appointment was as an appeal agent under the Draft Act of 1917. Asked to run for Congress as the Democratic party candidate in Brooklyn's Tenth Congressional District in 1922, Celler accepted the nomination

Emanuel Celler. Archive Photos

even though the district had never elected a Democrat. Celler's slogan was "It's time for change," and he ran a campaign opposing Prohibition. In the November election, Celler won by 3,111 votes. He joined the Sixty-eighth Congress on 4 March 1923. Celler would continuously serve his district, which changed boundaries and population over the years as a result of reapportionment, for fifty years.

Early in his congressional career, Celler opposed national origins–based immigration quotas, monopolies, and abuses by big business. He introduced bills that, among others, facilitated interstate trade and commerce in copyrighted motion pictures and strengthened the Federal Trade Commission. During this early period he also served as a vice president of one bank and trustee and joint counsel of another.

After Franklin D. Roosevelt became president in 1933, Celler gave his support to the New Deal's National Recovery Act, reciprocal trade agreements, Social Security Act, Tennessee Valley Authority, and stock exchange control measures. Celler consistently supported pro-labor legislation. He opposed methods used by the House Special Committee to Investigate Un-American Activities, established in 1938, and seven years later he fought unsuccessfully against the measure that made it a standing committee.

In 1940 Celler became the House Judiciary Committee's ranking majority member. After World War II he supported the Full Employment Act (1945), the anti–poll tax bill (1945), the displaced person's bill (1948), and the Fair Employment Practices Act (1950). He voted against the Taft-Hartley Labor Management Relations Act (1947), the Mundt-Nixon communist registration bill (1948), and the Internal Security Act (1950). He voted against the Truman Doctrine (1947), which gave aid to Greece and Turkey, but supported the Marshall Plan (1948). Celler was a strong supporter of the State of Israel from its creation in 1948. He was the ranking minority member of the House Judiciary Committee during the Eightieth Congress (1947–1948), and when the Democrats regained control of the House after the 1948 election, Celler resumed the panel's chairmanship. He remained chairman for the remainder of his congressional career, except for the Eighty-third Congress (1953–1954), when the Republicans again were the majority in the House. A major piece of legislation that passed under Celler's chairmanship was the Celler-Kefauver Anti-Merger Act of 1950, a significant antitrust law.

An early supporter of civil rights, Celler backed the Civil Rights Act of 1957, the first piece of civil rights legislation enacted by Congress since 1875. It provided for a six-member Civil Rights Commission with the authority to subpoena and to investigate the denial of voting rights. However, it had no enforcement power. On 31 January 1964, debate opened on the Civil Rights Act of 1964. Celler presented the case for the bill. He said, "The grievances are real, the proof is in, the gathering of evidence has gone on for over a century." Title II banned discrimination in public accommodations; Title VII barred employment discrimination on the basis of race and gender; and Title VI banned federal aid to any organization practicing racial discrimination. It also made obstruction of court orders for school segregation a crime and gave added safeguards for voting rights. The House passed the bill on 2 February by a vote of 290 to 130. Celler said, "I feel like I've climbed Mount Everest" after passage. Celler led the way to final passage after the House received the bill from the Senate in June 1964. President Lyndon B. Johnson signed the Act on 2 July 1964.

When Representative Carl Vinson of Georgia retired in January 1965, Celler became the senior member of the House of Representatives in length of service. He outranked the Democratic speaker, John McCormack, by five years.

Representative Celler was a grandfatherly figure, mostly bald with sloped shoulders and bandy legs. In Congress he was a colorful and combative debater. Celler possessed a self-deprecating sense of humor. He regularly attended the opera and enjoyed reading biographies.

Celler lost the 1972 Democratic primary by just 562 votes to Elizabeth Holtzman, at the time a relatively little known political-reform candidate. After leaving his congressional seat he served as a member of the Commission on Revision of the Federal Appellate Court System from 1973 to 1975. He also resumed the practice of law. Celler died of pneumonia and was buried in Mount Neboh Cemetery in Cypress Hills, New York.

Throughout his exceptionally long congressional career, Celler remained true to the liberal views of his upbringing and his district's voters. In favoring laws on behalf of immigrants, labor, and ethnic and racial minorities, and by playing a lead role in passing significant civil rights legislation, Celler was to the end a champion of the common man.

★

Emanuel Celler, *You Never Leave Brooklyn: The Autobiography of Emanuel Celler* (1953), covers his early years and much of his public career. A biographical sketch appears in *Biographical Directory of the American Congress, 1774–1996* (1997). Obituaries are in the *New York Times* (16 Jan. 1981) and the *New York Daily News* (16 Jan. 1981).

MARTIN JAY STAHL

CHAPIN, Harry Forster (*b.* 7 December 1942 in New York City; *d.* 16 July 1981 near Jericho, New York), popular/folk singer and songwriter known for his hit songs "Taxi" and "Cat's in the Cradle" and for his work on behalf of various humanitarian causes.

The son of James "Big Jim" Chapin and Elspeth Burke, Harry Chapin grew up above a longshoremen's local in a working-class neighborhood in Greenwich Village. His father, a jazz drummer, was frequently out of town playing gigs, and the day-to-day task of raising Chapin and his three brothers, Steve, Tom, and James, was primarily left to his mother and grandmothers. When Chapin was six his parents legally separated and later divorced. The Chapin boys remained with their mother, who worked as a secretary and editor and in 1952 married journalist and editor Henry Hart, a strict and sometimes abusive disciplinarian.

In 1954, three months after the birth of Elspeth and Henry Hart's first son, Henry Hart, Jr. ("Jeb"), the family moved from Manhattan to Brooklyn Heights and Chapin joined the Brooklyn Heights Boys Choir. Two years later he began attending Brooklyn Technical High School, where his intelligence and strong will enabled him to excel. Loud, pushy, and attention-grabbing, but paradoxically a loner, he was known at school and his Episcopal church by the nickname "Gapin' Chapin." Having abandoned his first instrument, the trumpet, Chapin learned to play banjo and folk guitar. In 1958 Harry Chapin and his brothers Tom and Steve, calling themselves the Chapin Brothers, began performing in Grace Church choir concerts and then at open-mike night at the Bitter End in Greenwich Village.

Harry Chapin. COURTESY OF SANDY CHAPIN

Chapin graduated high school in January 1960, worked for a brief time at the New York Stock Exchange, and in June enrolled in the U.S. Air Force Academy in Colorado.

It was soon apparent, however, that Chapin was not cut out for military life. Academy officials granted his request to resign, and he was then admitted to the Cornell School of Architecture, where he enrolled for fall classes. But having no particular talent for design and lacking the patience and discipline necessary for drafting, he lost interest. Chapin was socially self-conscious; he was frequently rejected by women and was blackballed from the Sigma Nu fraternity. He did join an a cappella singing group, the Sherwoods, which performed on other campuses.

In January 1962 Chapin had to leave Cornell because of poor grades. He returned to New York City and went to work for his uncle, Richard Leacock, at Drew Associates, a documentary film company where he packed film crates and worked himself up to assistant film editor. This same year he met and fell in love with Clare MacIntyre, for whom he wrote his first song, "Stars Tangled in Her Hair." The relationship ended when Clare went to Europe in 1963.

Chapin re-enrolled in Cornell, where he continued to work on his music, learning to play the autoharp and harmonica and teaming up to give small concerts with schoolmates or his brothers. By 1964, when he once again withdrew from college, he was playing solo concerts six nights a week at Johnny's Big Red, a local Ithaca nightspot, as well as taking the lead in the Chapin Brothers and writing most of the group's music. In September, the Chapin Brothers, with "Big Jim" Chapin on drums, recorded their debut album *Chapin Music!* (1966).

In 1966 Chapin took a job with Big Fights, Inc., a Manhattan film company that produced boxing films, and at the suggestion of owner Bill Caton he created the boxing documentary *Legendary Champions,* completed in 1967 and nominated for an Academy Award for best feature documentary. Unsuited to the nine-to-five lifestyle, Chapin left Big Fights, Inc. after the completion of the documentary and did freelance jobs for Drew Associates, IBM, and Time-Life. In addition, he wrote music for his brothers' group, the Chapins, and for the ABC children's program *Make a Wish,* which was hosted by his brother Tom. He also placed an advertisement in the *Brooklyn Heights Press* offering to teach guitar lessons. Sandra Cashmore (born Sandra Gaston), a housewife and mother of three, became his pupil and his love interest as well. When her rocky marriage ended, she and Chapin started dating. They married on 28 November 1968.

Chapin was "discovered" at the Village Gate in Manhattan by Ann Purtill, a talent scout for Electra Records whose interest in Chapin prompted the attention of several other record companies. After a fourteen-day bidding war between Electra and Columbia Records, Chapin signed with Electra, having gained money and attention rare for a new artist. The extensive promotional efforts of the company and of Chapin himself paid off; his first solo album, *Heads and Tail* (1972), sold 250,000 copies, and the single "Taxi" from this album became a hit worldwide, despite its six-minute and forty-second length and lack of a catchy refrain.

With newfound financial security, Chapin moved with his wife, her three children from her first marriage, and their daughter Jennifer to suburban Huntington Bay, Long

Island, in 1972, shortly before the birth of their son Joshua. His second solo album, *Sniper and Other Love Songs,* released in 1972, was a commercial failure. His third, *Short Stories* (1973), fared considerably better thanks to the single "W*O*L*D," about an aging disc jockey. Meanwhile Chapin's marriage, already threatened by his frequent absences and his obsession with his career, was brought to crisis when his wife found Harry's "black book" containing women's phone numbers. The incident was a turning point for Chapin; it forced him to listen more closely to the concerns of his wife and to examine his role in the family. The *Billboard* number-one hit and Grammy nominee "Cat's in the Cradle" (from the 1974 album *Verities and Balderdash*) is based on a poem by Sandy Chapin about a man who is too busy to spend time with his son. Shifting his priorities, Chapin cut back on overnight absences, persuaded Sandy to attend marriage counseling, and became involved in the charitable causes that interested his wife.

A close friendship developed between Chapin and priest–disc jockey Father Bill Ayers, the Chapins' marriage counselor. The two men shared a common interest in the problems of hunger and poverty, and in 1974 they founded World Hunger Year (WHY), a nonprofit organization dedicated to hunger education and the redistribution of food. The organization made extensive use of its media contacts to raise money and awareness. In 1977 Chapin founded the Food Policy Center, a lobbying organization based in Washington, D.C., which resulted in the creation, by President Jimmy Carter, of a commission on hunger.

Chapin played 200 concerts a year, half of them benefits for the alleviation of world hunger, environmental and consumer causes, the Multiple Sclerosis Foundation, and numerous other organizations. He also found the time to get involved in the Long Island community, joining the Huntington Arts Council, of which Sandy was already a member, and working with an arts education group called the Performing Arts Foundation of Long Island, for which he performed benefits and raised tens of thousands of dollars, eventually becoming chairman of the board. Chapin served on the boards of the Long Island Philharmonic and the Eglevsky Ballet. He was a member of the Long Island Action Committee and the Cambodia Crisis Committee and a trustee of Hofstra University.

After recording his fourth solo album, *Verities and Balderdash,* Chapin tried the theater as an outlet for his talent, creating the Broadway multimedia show *The Night That Made America Famous* (1975), which won two Tony nominations, and *Chapin* (1977), a musical revue that played at the Improv Theatre in Hollywood. Chapin continued to write and record throughout the 1970s, completing eight more albums and starting another by the time of his death. His sequel to "Taxi" (called "Sequel") was particularly well received.

On 16 July 1981 Chapin was driving in his Volkswagen on the Long Island Expressway near Jericho, Long Island, on his way to perform at a free concert when his car was hit from behind by a tractor-trailer. He was taken to Nassau County Medical Center, where he was pronounced dead, most likely of a heart attack that occurred shortly before the impact of the crash. He was buried in Huntington, New York.

Musically, Harry Chapin is best remembered for his trademark "story songs," musical narratives about ordinary people, and dynamic live performances. Chapin was exceptional in his determination to use his talents to benefit society and was known for his credo, "When in doubt, do something."

★

Peter M. Coan, *Taxi: The Harry Chapin Story* (1987), is the only existing full-length biography of Chapin, written by his longtime confidant. Obituaries are in the *New York Times* (17 June 1981) and *Newsweek* (27 July 1981). A complete Harry Chapin discography as well as biographical information can be found on the Harry Chapin Fan Pages website at http://littlejason.com/chapin.

LAURA KATHLEEN SMID

CHARNEY, Jule Gregory (*b.* 1 January 1917 in San Francisco, California; *d.* 16 June 1981 in Boston, Massachusetts), meteorologist who revolutionized weather prediction and climate research through his work in atmospheric dynamics.

Charney was the only child of Ely Charney and Stella Litman, Russian immigrants who worked in the garment industry. Although his parents were not highly educated, they instilled an appreciation of intellectual values in their son and had high expectations for him. An apparently erroneous diagnosis of a heart condition led to Charney's having a somewhat protected childhood, during which he pursued his interests in science and mathematics. His high school years were primarily spent at Hollywood High School in Los Angeles.

At the age of seventeen Charney entered the University of California at Los Angeles (UCLA), where he received a B.A. degree in mathematics and physics in 1938, an M.A. in mathematics in 1940, and a Ph.D. in meteorology in 1946. His doctoral dissertation, "The Dynamics of Long Waves in a Baroclinic Westerly Current," was published (in revised form) in the *Journal of Meteorology* in October 1947.

In 1940, when Charney was beginning his doctoral work, the program in meteorology at UCLA was being developed by Jacob Bjerknees, with the assistance of Jorgen Holmboe and Morris Neiburger. The advice of Theodor von Kármán, who was then on the faculty of the California

Jule G. Charney. COURTESY OF MRS. NORA CHARNEY ROSENBAUM

Institute of Technology, led Charney to recognize the opportunities for personal and scientific advancement in meteorology and he became a teaching assistant as well as a doctoral candidate in the meteorology program in 1941. During World War II, Charney was part of the team at UCLA that trained members of the armed forces in weather forecasting.

Charney was introduced by his housemates to Elinor Kesting Frye, also a graduate student at UCLA (in the philosophy department), and they were married in 1946. Charney adopted her son from a previous marriage; they had a son and a daughter of their own. They were divorced in 1969. Charney married Lois Swirnoff in 1970; they were divorced in 1975.

In 1946 and 1947 Charney was a research assistant to the Swedish meteorologist Carl-Gustaf Rossby at the University of Chicago, and he held a National Research Fellowship at the University of Oslo in 1947 and 1948. In 1948 he was invited to join the faculty at the Institute for Advanced Study (IAS) in Princeton, New Jersey, where he was one of the first synoptic meteorologists to utilize the potential of the Electronic Numerical Integrator and Calculator (ENIAC). In cooperation with the mathematician and computer theorist John von Neumann, Charney developed a computer model of atmospheric behavior based on hy-

drodynamics. The model used the factors known at that time to affect atmospheric motion and weather. When the air force–navy numerical weather unit was created in 1954, the predictive three-dimensional model of cyclone formation that Charney had developed was adopted. From 1948 to 1956 Charney was the head of the Theoretical Meteorology Project.

In 1956 Charney became a professor of meteorology at the Massachusetts Institute of Technology (MIT). In his talk when the American Geophysical Union honored Charney as the thirty-eighth William Bowie Medalist in 1976, Joseph Smagorinsky reported that Charney remarked as he left for MIT, "My mother always said that every family should have a professor." Although Charney was never regarded as a polished classroom lecturer, his former students and colleagues praised his research, his ability to work with graduate students as well as his peers, and his superb writing style. His colleague Norman Phillips wrote: "Formal teaching in class by Jule was not a polished performance. But, those students fortunate to have had him as their thesis advisor received a personal indoctrination in the three factors that give life to creative conceptions in science: enthusiasm, rigor, and an obligation to compare theory with the real world whenever possible."

In 1961 the Global Atmospheric Research Program (GARP) became the first international program to carry out systematic observations of the atmosphere. Initiated under Charney's leadership, GARP was a response to President John F. Kennedy's proposal to the United Nations to find peaceful uses for satellites. Charney apparently had a strong dislike of violence and was involved in antiwar activities; thus the GARP project had special appeal for him. George Platzman (1990) quotes Charney as saying, "I found the idea of exploding atomic bombs in the atmosphere generally repugnant and sought for counter-arguments." The GARP project consisted of two major international field experiments, the Atlantic Tropical Experiment and the Global Weather Experiment.

During his twenty-five years at MIT, Charney made many contributions to meteorology. In addition to publishing more than seventy articles in scientific journals and conference proceedings, he served as a guest lecturer at institutions around the world. He was head of the Department of Meteorology at MIT from 1974 to 1977. From his election to Phi Beta Kappa during his junior year at UCLA (1937) to being named an honorary member of the Royal Meteorological Society in 1980, Charney was honored by all the major scholarly organizations in his field. The NASA Center for Computational Sciences has three Cray J932 systems, which are shared-memory architecture machines. One of these is the charney, named after Jule Charney. The American Meteorological Society presents the Jule

G. Charney Award each year to a researcher in meteorology, with an emphasis on atmospheric dynamics.

Charney died at the Dana-Farber Cancer Institute in Boston. He was cremated, and his ashes buried at a cemetery in Woods Hole, Massachusetts.

★

The Massachusetts Institute of Technology has several cartons and manuscript boxes of records covering the years 1940–1979 that include correspondence, reports, funding and research reports, personnel information, and memoranda relating to Charney. There are restrictions on access to portions of this collection. Richard S. Lindzen, Edward N. Lorenz, and George N. Platzman, eds., *The Atmosphere—a Challenge: The Science of Jule Gregory Charney* (1990), is a comprehensive source for information about Charney: his curriculum vitae, a list of his primary publications, recollections by several of his colleagues, and reprints of some of his most important scientific articles, including his dissertation. Norman A. Phillips, "Jule Charney's Influence on Meteorology," *Bulletin of the American Meteorological Society* 63 (1982): 492–498, is a tribute to Charney's work and life. Stephen H. Schneider, ed., *Encyclopedia of Climate and Weather,* vol. 1 (1996), 109–111, contains basic information on Charney, his research, and his contributions to dynamic meteorology. An obituary is in the *New York Times* (16 June 1981).

NANCY J. HERRINGTON

CHASE, Mary Coyle (*b.* 25 February 1907 in Denver, Colorado; *d.* 20 October 1981 in Denver, Colorado), dramatist who wrote the Pulitzer Prize–winning play *Harvey,* one of Broadway's most popular and longest-running hits, which along with her more than a dozen other comedies satirized contemporary American life.

Chase learned storytelling from her Irish-born mother, Mary McDonough Coyle, her father, and her uncles. Their fairy tales of banshees, leprechauns, cluiricaunes, and pookas would later reappear in her stories and plays. Her father, Frank Bernard Coyle, was a salesman for the Hungarian Flour Milling and Elevator Company of Colorado's premier Irish tycoon, John Kernan Mullen.

The youngest of four children, Mary attended Denver schools, graduating from West High School in 1922 at the age of fifteen. Her childhood home, a small, one-story cottage at 532 West Fourth Avenue in a working-class neighborhood, has been designated a Denver landmark in her honor. During her teen years, Chase fell in love with the theater district on Curtis Street, Denver's version of New York's Broadway.

Chase attended the University of Denver (1922–1924) and the University of Colorado in Boulder (1924–1925) before being hired by the *Rocky Mountain News,* Denver's oldest newspaper, in 1924. Of her journalistic career, Chase

said later that she had believed it would help her as a playwright by teaching her "how people speak at moments of crisis" and enabling her to view life "in a dramatic contrast and counterpoint."

An attractive, shapely, black-haired woman who dressed stylishly, Chase wrote a column for the paper called "Society Notes." Although initially confined to the feminine role of a society columnist, she later asserted herself as an investigative reporter. For example, when the Moffat Tunnel opened in 1928 as the first major railroad passage under the Rockies west of Denver, she was there. When male miners and tunnel workers feared a woman underground as bad luck, she talked a fellow reporter into loaning her a pair of pants. Adding a miner's cap, she headed into the tunnel after the final dynamite blast. Stumbling through smoke and fumes, she crawled up a mound of rock to grasp the hand of a reporter who had come in from the other side of the 6.2-mile-long tunnel underneath the Continental Divide.

At the *Rocky Mountain News* she met reporter Robert Lamont Chase, whom she married on 7 June 1928. Her husband later became the managing editor of the *News.* They had three sons, Michael, Colin, and Barry.

In 1931 Mary left the newspaper to pursue playwriting while working as a freelance correspondent for the International News Service and the United Press. The Federal Theater Project in Denver staged her first play, *Me Third,* in 1936. Producer Brock Pemberton purchased the play. Rewritten and renamed *Now You've Done It,* it opened on Broadway in 1937, directed by another Denver native, Antoinette Perry.

Chase's *Sorority House* (1939), produced by Samuel French and turned into a Hollywood screenplay, reflected her disappointment at never being asked to join a college sorority. This was followed by *Too Much Business* (1940) and *A Slip of a Girl* (1941).

Hoping to bring laughter to wartime America, Chase wrote a comedy about a six-foot-tall imaginary white rabbit. She originally called her play *The Pooka* for the large fairy of Irish folklore. In 1944 the play opened in Denver as *The White Rabbit.* The title was changed to *Harvey* for its opening on 1 November 1944 at the 48th Street Theater in New York City. Rave reviews greeted the comedy, produced by Brock Pemberton, directed by Antoinette Perry, and starring Frank Fay as Elwood P. Dowd, an alcoholic who finds a drinking companion in Harvey. Josephine Hull played Elwood's sister, Veta, who has her brother committed to a mental hospital but rescues him just before he is to be given an injection that will make Harvey go away. *Harvey* became one of the longest-running plays on Broadway, with 1,775 performances. Chase coauthored the movie version (1950), which starred Jimmy Stewart.

Chase's 1945 tragedy, *The Next Half Hour,* disappointed

Mary Coyle Chase, 1946. HULTON-DEUTSCH COLLECTION/CORBIS

critics and audiences, but she came back with a 1952 comedy, *Mrs. McThing,* starring Helen Hayes and child actor Brandon de Wilde as mother and son. Another 1952 comedy, *Bernardine,* became a 1957 movie starring Pat Boone and Terry Moore, with a screenplay by Chase. Her *Midgie Purvis* opened on Broadway in 1961 for a short run.

Chase also wrote children's books, including *Loretta Mason Potts* (1958), illustrated by Harold Berson, which was the basis for her 1969 play *Mickey,* and *The Wicked Pigeon Ladies in the Garden* (1968), illustrated by Don Bolognese. Her other plays included *Lolita* (1954), *The Prize Play* (1961), *The Dog Sitters* (1963), *Doll Face* (1966), *Cocktails with Mimi* (1974), and *The Terrible Tattoo Parlor* (1981).

Chase helped found the Denver chapter of the American Newspaper Guild and in 1941 and 1942 was the publicity director for the National Youth Administration in Denver. An active supporter of unions and the working class, she wrote a weekly radio program for the Teamsters Union from 1942 to 1944. In Denver she became legendary for joining picket lines in fancy hats and black satin dresses. She also wrote radio scripts, including a series on the sixty-three counties of Colorado. Her short pieces appeared in popular periodicals, such as the *Ladies Home Journal.*

A Democrat and a member of the Dramatists Guild, Chase collected musical recordings, Chinese art and furniture, doll houses, and dogs. Chase died of a heart attack in her home at 505 Circle Drive in Denver. She was buried at Crown Hill Cemetery in Denver.

An active advocate for the working class and poor in Colorado, she was a bright journalist and playwright. Having tried her hand at tragedies, Chase learned that she could draw more attention to serious social and spiritual issues with her outrageous sense of humor and farce. Recipient of several awards, she was the only Colorado writer ever to earn a Pulitzer Prize. "The greatest unacclaimed wit in America," as Dorothy Parker called her, Chase took her sense of humor to the grave; for her cemetery plot, she picked a site next to a large granite family stone inscribed "Harvey."

★

The Mary Coyle Chase Collection in the Western History Department of the Denver Public Library contains many articles on Chase, including some by her. See also Fay Abbott, *Famous Coloradans* (1990). Reference works with biographical information include *The National Cyclopedia of American Biography* (1964), Frances Carol Locher, ed., *Contemporary Authors,* vols. 77–80 (1979), and Lina Mainiero, ed., *American Women Writers: A Critical Reference Guide from Colonial Times to the Present,* vol. 1 (1979). An obituary is in the *New York Times* (23 Oct. 1981).

THOMAS J. NOEL

CHASE, Stuart (*b.* 8 March 1888 in Somersworth, New Hampshire; *d.* 16 November 1985 in Redding, Connecticut), economist, social critic, and professional writer whose books and articles popularized economic planning.

Chase was one of the two children of Harvey Stuart Chase, a leading engineer and accountant in New England, and Aaronette Rowe. He grew up in Newton and Haverhill, Massachusetts, graduating from Newton High School in 1906. He attended the Massachusetts Institute of Technology but transferred in 1908 to Harvard, where he received his B.S. cum laude in 1910. From 1910 to 1917 Chase was a partner in his father's accounting firm, Harvey S. Chase Company of Boston. Influenced by Henry George's *Progress and Poverty* (1879), which he first read in 1911, Chase, originally a supporter of President William Howard Taft, moved politically to the left, joining in sequence a Boston single-tax club, the Boston Fabian Society, and the Socialist Party of America. Chase married Margaret Hatfield on 5 July 1914; the couple had two children. Launching their marriage by living briefly in the slums of Rochester, New York, they coauthored an account of their experiences, *A Honeymoon Experiment* (1916).

In 1917 Chase became a staff member of the Federal Trade Commission (FTC). Given the position of chief examiner, he investigated violations of wartime regulations in the meatpacking industry. Chase found the major Chicago packers guilty of profiteering, but in 1920, with the FTC under severe attack from business interests, Chase was let go, ostensibly for lack of funds.

The experience radicalized Chase, who thenceforth used the popular press to expose business corruption and advocate a planned economy. In 1921 he moved to New York City, where he joined the Technical Alliance, dedicated to promoting the ideas of economist Thorstein Veblen and headed by engineer Howard Scott. Within a year Chase left the alliance, disillusioned with Scott's authoritarian personality and an ideology, Chase suspected, based on organizing engineers into a revolutionary body that would seize control of industry. In 1922, with economist George Soule, Chase established the Labor Bureau, Inc., a research agency for trade unions and cooperatives. Until the late 1930s, when Chase was able to depend solely on his writing, the bureau was his main source of income. During this time Chase contributed articles to the *Nation, New Republic,* and *Survey,* in which he covered topics as diverse as the grievances of coal miners and the attractions of nudism.

In Chase's first major book, *The Tragedy of Waste* (1925), he endorsed the British social critic R. H. Tawney, who had called for a functional society devoted primarily to supplying human wants. Chase believed that the creation of such a society was hindered by lack of jobs, inefficient methods of production and distribution, the depletion of natural resources, and the creation of nonessentials, in which category he put all military spending. *Your Money's Worth: A Study in the Waste of the Consumer's Dollar* (1927), written with engineer Frederick J. Schlink, attacked dishonest advertising and called for impartial standards. The book has been described as "the first articulate expression of the interests of a consumer society." In 1928 Chase and Schlink founded Consumers Research (later the Consumers Union), an organization that provided impartial laboratory tests on many products. *Men and Machines* (1929) found technology inadvertently introducing the menace of automated unemployment. He and his first wife divorced in 1929; the following year Chase married Marian Tyler, a fellow staffer on the *Nation* and subsequently Chase's critic, research assistant, and often coauthor. They had no children. Chase's *Mexico: A Study of Two Americas* (1931) favorably contrasted a society based on handicraft culture to one centered on manufacturing. In 1931 he moved to Redding, Connecticut, a small rural town, where he lived in a rebuilt barn furnished with Mexican rugs and handicrafts and commuted to New York City.

During the Great Depression, Chase found audiences more receptive to his ideas. No longer a supporter of the

Stuart Chase at home, 1931. UPI/CORBIS-BETTMANN

Socialist party, he became ardently pro-Roosevelt. His book *A New Deal* (1932) not only coined the phrase later used by Franklin D. Roosevelt's recovery program, but also presented Chase's schema for a radical reallocation of wealth and resources, directed by a disinterested "board of managers." An enthusiastic visitor to the Soviet Union in 1927, he was temporarily enamored by the Gosplan (state planning commission), which he called "the most interesting economic experiment in history." He asked: "Why should Russians have all the fun of remaking the world?" Such works as *Economy of Abundance* (1934), *Government in Business* (1935), and *Idle Money, Idle Men* (1940) further advanced his calls for rule by what he called "philosopher engineers." During the 1930s Chase repeatedly endorsed public control of banking and credit, massive public works projects, and national income redistribution. In *Rich Land, Poor Land: A Study of Waste in the Natural Resources of America* (1936), a stinging exposé of the impoverished American countryside, Chase found the Tennessee Valley Authority the model for state-directed economic development.

In 1938 Chase's thought took a new turn, with his *The*

Tyranny of Words, showing how the science of semantics could dissolve ideologies of both left and right. That same year he assisted the Securities and Exchange Commission in preparing a report for the Temporary National Economic Committee on the nation's financial and banking structure. A strong isolationist until the Japanese attacked Pearl Harbor, he espoused his belief in national self-sufficiency in *The New Western Front* (1939), coauthored with Marian Tyler, and in articles in the *Progressive.*

During World War II and immediately after, Chase wrote a series of books for the Twentieth Century Fund on the postwar economic outlook. After the war he moved to the political center; Chase no longer advocated economic management by social engineers instead of business executives but accepted that the former would merely advise the latter. He wrote well into the 1960s, advancing his favorite causes of environmentalism, semantics, and centralized planning. In *Live and Let Live: A Program for Americans* (1960), for example, he covered such topics as nationalism, nuclear warfare, the population explosion, automation, and racial tension. He strongly endorsed the Great Society programs of President Lyndon B. Johnson. Chase retired after the publication of his last book, *Danger—Men Talking!: A Background Book on Semantics and Communication* (1969).

Described as intelligent, alert, eager, friendly, and unpretentious, Chase was often superficial and naive, particularly in his belief in rule by impartial "experts," and he could be vague about such crucial concepts as nationalization. Yet because of his breezy and entertaining writing style, he had the ability to simplify the complex. Because of Chase, millions of middle-class Americans, who would never think of reading abstruse works by such "worldly philosophers" as Veblen and John Maynard Keynes, could understand complicated economic theories and view them with far less suspicion.

★

The papers of Stuart Chase are located in the Library of Congress. A short autobiographical sketch of Chase's conversion to radicalism is found in "Portrait of a Radical," *Century* 108 (July 1924): 295–304. James Carpenter Lanier, "Stuart Chase: An Intellectual Biography (1888–1940)" (Ph.D. diss., Emory University, 1971), is the only major work on any part of Chase's career. For brief treatments of Chase, see Arthur M. Schlesinger, Jr., *The Crisis of the Old Order, 1919–1933* (1957); Richard Pells, *Radical Visions and American Dreams: Culture and Social Thought in the Depression Years* (1973); and Geoffrey Perrett, *America in the Twenties: A History* (1982). Major scholarly articles include Robert B. Westbrook, "Tribune of the Technostructure: The Popular Economics of Stuart Chase," *American Quarterly* 32 (fall 1980): 387–408; and Linda J. Bradley and Barbara D. Merino, "Stuart Chase: A Radical CPA and the Meat Packing Investigation, 1917–1918," *Business and*

Economic History 23 (fall 1994): 190–200. An obituary is in the *New York Times* (17 Nov. 1985).

JUSTUS D. DOENECKE

CHAYEFSKY, Sidney Aaron ("Paddy") (*b.* 29 January 1923 in New York City; *d.* 1 August 1981 in New York City), writer of radio dramas, teleplays, plays, and films who achieved international recognition.

Chayefsky was the youngest of the three sons of Russian-Jewish immigrant parents, Harry Chayefsky, founder of Dellwood Dairy in Yonkers, New York, and Gussie Stuchevsky, a seamstress. He was raised on Tibbet Street, in the borough of the Bronx, in a neighborhood that was home to Irish, Italian, German, and Jewish families. His early experiences with these ethnic groups found their way into his writing through accents, cultural values, and language rhythms.

Chayefsky showed early promise as a writer in 1939, while he was attending De Witt Clinton High School, when he published his first two short stories, "No Dice" and "It's the Drummer in Me," in the *Magpie,* the school magazine. In "No Dice" he gave his characters French accents.

Upon graduating from high school at age sixteen and a half, Chayefsky entered City College of New York, from which he graduated in 1943 with a B.S. degree in the social sciences. During this time he earned money by playing semipro football for the Kingsbridge Trojans and by writing burlesque comedy and songs. He was not terribly successful at either venture.

In 1943 Chayefsky was drafted into the U.S. Army, which first trained him in the German language at Fordham University and then sent him to Europe with a combat unit. He was wounded in action at Aachen, Germany, and received the Purple Heart. While recuperating in England, he collaborated with a soldier named Jimmy Livingston on a musical comedy entitled *No T. O. for Love* (1945). This was Chayefsky's first attempt at playwriting. His name appeared on the script as "Paddy" Chayefsky. He had been given the name Paddy by an officer at Camp Carson when Chayefsky told him he could not perform kitchen police duty because he had to attend Catholic mass. When the officer pointed out that he was Jewish, Chayefsky lied and said that his mother was Irish. He kept the name "Paddy" for the rest of his professional career.

The script of *No T. O.* came to the attention of the famous director and playwright Garson Kanin, who invited Chayefsky to collaborate with him on a documentary film that he was writing, *The True Glory* (completed in 1945). The relationship continued when Kanin offered Chayefsky a $500 writing scholarship to help him learn his craft. He

Paddy Chayefsky. ARCHIVE PHOTOS

urged Chayefsky to write from his own experiences and to learn the formal play structure that would allow him to express his ideas dramatically. Chayefsky claimed that he learned the play form through copying by hand Lillian Hellman's *The Little Foxes* over and over until he understood the formal relationships among character, plot, theme, dialogue, and pace.

In 1946 Chayefsky completed the play *Put Them All Together.* The following year he was awarded a junior writer's contract by Universal International. In 1949 he published a short story, "The Great American Hoax," in *Cosmopolitan* magazine. On 24 February 1949 he married Susan Sackler, who endeavored to manage and direct his career; they had one son, Dan. Her influence on Chayefsky's career seemed to weaken during the 1950s as he became more successful as a writer.

In 1950 Chayefsky wrote a play entitled *The Man Who Made the Mountain Shake* (later titled *Fifth from Garibaldi*). Although the play was never produced, it demonstrated so much skill and creativity that Chayefsky was given a contract to write radio dramas for *Theatre Guild of the Air* and *Cavalcade of America.* In 1952 he wrote "The Meanest Man in the World," an adaptation of an Austin MacHugh story,

for *Theatre Guild of the Air* and "The Spectacle Lady" for *Cavalcade of America.* This led to his writing television scripts for two series, *Manhunt* and *Danger.*

In 1952 Chayefsky reached a turning point in his career when he signed a contract to write for a live television series, the prestigious and highly rated *Philco-Goodyear Television Playhouse.* From 1952 until 1963 Chayefsky wrote seventeen plays and films. For the *Philco-Goodyear Television Playhouse* he wrote "Holiday Song" and "The Reluctant Citizen" in 1952; "Printer's Measure," "The Bachelor Party," "The Sixth Year," "The Big Deal," "Catch My Boy on Sunday" in 1953; "The Mother" and "Middle of the Night" in 1954; and "Marty" and "The Catered Affair" in 1955.

In 1954 Chayefsky adapted his teleplay "Marty" as a motion picture, for which he received an Academy Award for the best screenplay of 1954. (*Marty* was also voted best picture.) During this time he established himself as one of the leading playwrights in the nation.

In 1956 Chayefsky turned to Broadway with a stage adaptation of his teleplay "Middle of the Night." Critically acclaimed as one of that year's best plays, it established him as a true Renaissance talent. In 1957 his film adaptation of "The Bachelor Party" met with both critical and commercial success. This was followed in 1958 by a release of his film *The Goddess,* which won the Critics' Prize at the Brussels Film Festival. The 1959 film version of "Middle of the Night" was not a commercial success. However, in the same year Chayefsky's *The Tenth Man* enjoyed critical praise and commercial success on Broadway.

In 1961 Chayefsky returned to the New York stage with *Gideon,* which received a lackluster response from the critics and very little interest from audiences. Chayefsky therefore set out to overturn what he perceived as criticism of his writing by creating a play that would dazzle the theater world.

In 1962 Chayefsky began working on a stage play entitled *The Passion of Josef D.,* based on the struggles between Lenin and Stalin. Not only did he write the script but he would direct the production as well. On 11 February 1964 *The Passion of Josef D.* opened to a capacity house in the Ethel Barrymore Theatre in New York City. Reviews were less than enthusiastic at best, and the play closed quickly with a financial loss of $160,000.

Although his film adaptation of William Bradford Huie's book, *The Americanization of Emily,* released by Metro-Goldwyn-Mayer in 1964, was a commercial and critical success, Chayefsky was still upset by *The Passion of Josef D.*'s rejection. In his opinion, the work had been seminal if not monumental. A long-running feud between Chayefsky and his critics, conducted in the *New York Times* "Letters to the Editor," culminated in Chayefsky's announcement on 17 January 1972 that he would never write another play for the New York theater. He was true to his word.

On 21 March 1968, at the Dallas Theatre Center, Chayefsky's *The Latent Heterosexual* was premiered. Reviews were mixed, and Chayefsky stopped writing plays for the legitimate theater, turning his talent to screenwriting.

In 1971 Chayefsky's blistering indictment of the medical industry, *The Hospital,* opened in New York City. It earned Chayefsky his second Academy Award for screenwriting. In 1975 Chayefsky submitted a treatment to United Artists entitled *Network,* a gut-wrenching, slashing attack on television news. The film was an unmitigated commercial and artistic success, and earned Chayefsky an unprecedented third Academy Award for best screenplay. Following the film's release in 1976 the *New York Daily News* film critic Rex Reed called it "a blazing, blistering indictment of television by the brilliant probing mind of Paddy Chayefsky."

Chayefsky next wrote a novel that he later adapted as a film. *Altered States,* published by Harper & Row in 1978, received mixed reviews. Chayefsky stubbornly refused to take advantage of numerous opportunities to advertise the book. In 1977, before he had written the last chapter of the novel, he had suffered a heart attack. This caused him to lose interest in the book, and instead he directed his energy into the completion of the motion picture script. Eventually Warner Brothers bought the rights to produce the film and hired Ken Russell to direct it. The antagonism that developed between Russell and Chayefsky was brutal. Before shooting was completed, Chayefsky demanded that his name be removed from the screen credits. His pseudonym, Sidney Aaron, would be listed as screenwriter. *Altered States* was released in 1980. Although Chayefsky hated it, the film was a commercial success, and critics gave it fair marks.

In January 1981 Chayefsky learned that he had cancer and needed surgery to save his life. He would not let the doctors operate on him. He died at the age of fifty-eight. His last words, written on a pad of paper to his wife, were "I tried. I really tried."

The death of Paddy Chayefsky was noted both nationally and internationally. His longtime associate and partner, Howard Gottfried, characterized Chayefsky as arrogant, demanding, vain, power-hungry, overly sensitive, and, at times, passionate to the point of near madness. Yet his contributions to stage and film were monumental. From *Marty,* a teleplay and motion picture that celebrated the triumph of the common man over loneliness and depression, to *Network,* a film that made famous the phrase "I'm mad as hell and I'm not going to take it anymore," Paddy Chayefsky's work is a legacy worthy of any artist.

★

Chayefsky's papers, consisting of seventeen boxes covering the period 1944–1964, are at the Wisconsin Center for Film and Theatre Research, Vilas Hall, University of Wisconsin at Madison.

John M. Clum, *Paddy Chayefsky* (1976), offers a detailed analysis of several of his plays. Shaun Considine, *Mad as Hell* (1994), is an excellent biography. Richard Corliss, *The Hollywood Screenwriters* (1977), compares Chayefsky with his contemporaries during the 1960s and 1970s. Helen Dudar, "Paddy Chayefsky: A *Post* Portrait," *New York Post* (4–7 January 1960), is an engrossing four-part series based on interviews with Chayefsky. John Gassner, *Theatre at the Crossroads: Plays and Playwrights of the Mid-Century American Stage* (1960), is an anthology of plays and play descriptions covering a time when Chayefsky was establishing himself as a successful playwright. William Goldman, *The Season* (1969), is an excellent analysis of the New York theater world. An obituary is in the *New York Times* (2 Aug. 1981).

EDWARD F. EMANUEL

CHEEVER, John William (*b.* 27 May 1912 in Quincy, Massachusetts; *d.* 18 June 1982 in Ossining, New York), short-story writer and novelist best known for his depiction of the spiritual poverty at the heart of the modern American Dream.

Born and raised in a middle-class Boston suburb, John Cheever was the younger of two sons of Frederick Lincoln Cheever and the English-born Mary Devereaux Liley. No relationship in John Cheever's life was more important than the troubled one he had with his brother, Fred, who was seven years older. Fraternal love-hate relationships are the most frequent recurring theme in Cheever's short stories and novels. Another standard theme is the fall of an honored family from social prominence to lower-class status, usually because of the father's irresponsible behavior in financial matters. Such a situation befell the Cheever family during the Great Depression, when, in 1932, Cheever's father lost his job as a successful traveling shoe salesman and with it the comfortable family home. Cheever's enterprising mother was able to sustain the family by creating her own gift shop and tearoom businesses, a skill both her husband and John came to resent deeply. All three Cheever men became alcoholics.

John Cheever's grandmother, Sarah Liley, was responsible for fostering his literary gifts by reading to him as a child the works of Jack London, Robert Louis Stevenson, and especially Charles Dickens. Although he was not a particularly gifted student at Wollaston Grammar School, he became known as the school's best storyteller. Many of the characters in those storytelling exercises—eccentric old women, ship captains, orphan boys—later became standard figures in his stories and novels. Certainly Captain Leander Wapshot and his cousin, Honora, of Cheever's first novel, *The Wapshot Chronicle* (1957), evolved out of his grammar school narratives. Ironically, Cheever asserted throughout his career that fiction should never be "crypto-autobiography."

If Cheever's grammar school years were undistinguished, his high school years were disastrous. He failed French and algebra at the prestigious Thayer Academy in South Braintree, Massachusetts, then dropped out in his junior year to attend Quincy High School. He returned to Thayer Academy for his senior year but was expelled in 1929. He was never forthright about the reason for his expulsion. He variously claimed that he was caught smoking, that it was his poor grades, and that he had seduced the son of one of the teachers. However, it was not unusual for Cheever to come up with divergent explanations for events in his early life. Certainly his casual treatment of facts about his life demonstrates the greater importance he placed on creativity and highlight his ability to entertain the fictive possibilities of a situation or character.

Cheever's adolescent trauma became the genesis of his first published story, appropriately entitled "Expelled," which he sent to the literary editor of the *New Republic,* Malcolm Cowley, who published it in the 1 October 1929 issue. Cheever was seventeen years old. He remained a close personal friend and professional colleague of Cowley, from whom he frequently sought advice and which he usually followed. With the continuing fall of his family into financial and emotional chaos, he decided against going to college and instead moved in with his brother, Fred, in Boston, remaining there from 1930 to 1934 and working in department stores and as a freelance journalist for several Boston newspapers. During these years he met some important members of the local literary set, including E. E. Cummings; Harry Dana, a Harvard professor and son of the novelist Richard Henry Dana; and Hazel Hawthorne Werner. Through these well-connected people he also met the editors of *Pagany* and *Hound & Horn,* where he published two early stories based on family conflicts similar to his own.

Cheever moved to New York City in 1934 after his relations with his brother became fractious; he later described their relationship as "morbidly close." His stories began to appear in the *New Yorker,* where he became, after John O'Hara, the most extensively published short-story writer in the magazine's history. After spending 1937 and 1938 in Washington, D.C., as a writer-editor for the Federal Writers' Project, he returned to New York and published stories in *Collier's,* the *Yale Review,* and *Story,* among others.

In 1939 Cheever met Mary Winternitz, who worked for his literary agent, Maxim Lieber. They fell in love and, after living together for two years, married on 22 March 1941. Mary was the daughter of Dr. Milton Winternitz, a well-known pathologist who eventually became dean of the Yale University Medical School. Mary's mother, Dr. Helen Watson, was one of the first women in the United States to earn a medical degree. Mary had been educated at Sarah Lawrence and was herself a fine poet. The Cheevers would

John Cheever. BERNARD GOTFRYD/ARCHIVE PHOTOS

have three children, two of whom, Susan and Benjamin, would also become writers. Being in love appears to have made Cheever productive; in 1940 he published fifteen stories, eleven in the *New Yorker* alone.

Just as his reputation was blossoming, World War II broke out. He immediately enlisted in the army, where he spent four uneventful years. His years in the service did result, however, in five or six early stories about military life. In March 1943 Random House published his first collection of short stories, *The Way Some People Live,* an event that caused his superior officers to recognize his talents and reassign him to the Signal Corps in Astoria, Queens. There he worked with other writers and movie producers and directors such as Stanley Kramer, William Saroyan, and Irwin Shaw, writing antifascist scripts for propaganda films. Had he remained with his original infantry unit he would have been shipped out to the European theater, where four out of five enlisted men in his outfit were wounded and half were killed by the end of the war.

After Cheever returned to civilian life in November

1945, he and his wife moved to an apartment in Manhattan on East Fifty-ninth Street, where they lived until 1950. In 1947 Cheever published "The Enormous Radio" and "Torch Song," landmark stories that exemplified his "new" style of writing, which moved away from his earlier naturalistic mode and into a more elaborate and mythically resonant one. Joan Harris, the dark, vampiric character in "Torch Song," is revealed upon closer scrutiny as the ancient Greek goddess Hecate, whose function is to lead souls to the underworld after death. Cheever often told students in creative-writing workshops that their primary purpose as writers was "to mythologize the commonplace," and with each new story collection and novel his own work became more mythic.

After winning a Guggenheim Fellowship in 1951, Cheever and his family relocated to the comfortable Westchester County suburb of Scarborough, a model of the many suburban communities he would write about for the next thirty years. Once away from the frenetic life of Manhattan, Cheever published his second collection, *The Enormous Radio and Other Stories* (1953), which met with mixed reviews but was later considered by many critics to be one of his most accomplished. He taught creative writing at Barnard College from 1954 to 1965 and continued to work on a novel that had been brewing since the late 1940s. According to his *Journals* (published posthumously in 1991), it was during this period that he began to feel the effects of his drinking as well as increasing guilt over his homosexual tendencies. Fortunately, Harper and Row bought his contract from Random House, giving him a substantial advance on his novel-in-progress and five years to finish it. He had already named it *The Wapshot Chronicle.* He also began winning prestigious literary awards: the Benjamin Franklin Magazine Award for his story "The Five-Forty-Eight" (1955) and the O. Henry Award for "The Country Husband" (1956). Both stories brilliantly depict the malaise of suburban life.

Two devastating occurrences took place in the middle of his literary achievements. The first was the death of his mother at the age of eighty-two; the second was the death of his editor at the *New Yorker,* Gus Lobrano. Both events took place within one week in 1956. The good news was a check for $40,000 from the head of Metro-Goldwyn-Mayer Studios, Dore Schary, for the film rights to "The Housebreaker of Shady Hill," which had been recently published and would serve as the title story of his next collection in 1958. The money enabled him to take his family to Italy for a year. A number of Italian stories came out of his year in Rome, the best known of which are "Boy in Rome" and "The Duchess." Cheever's pattern was to write about wherever he happened to be living at the time, and in that sense his writing often had a geographical basis.

In 1957 *The Wapshot Chronicle* was published by Harper and Row. Cheever was also elected to the National Institute of Arts and Letters. Although critics were divided over the merits of the novel, it won the National Book Award in 1958. He also won praise for *The Housebreaker of Shady Hill,* which contained some of his greatest stories: "The Sorrows of Gin," "The Five-Forty-Eight," and what is perhaps his most accomplished single story, "The Country Husband." The financial success of the novel and a second Guggenheim Fellowship enabled him to purchase a large and very old house in an upscale section of Ossining, New York. The comfortable, pastoral neighborhood, surrounded by pine forests, gave him a genuine sense of belonging and room to take his beloved dogs on long daily walks. Although the house had no swimming pool, his neighbors were happy to let him use theirs for his favorite exercise. Five feet, six inches tall, thin, and wiry, Cheever kept himself in good shape by walking and swimming daily, even during his heaviest drinking days.

His fourth story collection, *Some People, Places, and Things That Will Not Appear in My Next Novel,* was published in 1961. The critics were not pleased. A new, bitter tone had entered his work. One observer characterized Cheever as "a Gothic writer whose mind is poised at the edge of terror." His next novel, *The Wapshot Scandal* (1964), showed an even darker vision. Much of its apocalyptic darkness came out of his alcoholism and his unresolved homosexuality. His wife, Mary, was so frustrated by her husband's erratic behavior that she took a job teaching creative writing at nearby Briarcliff College, a move that she would say "saved my life." Although he had begun drinking even in the morning, he somehow managed to produce three of his finest stories: "The Swimmer," "The Music Teacher," and "The Angel of the Bridge."

Critics for the most part responded enthusiastically to the massive desolation of *The Wapshot Scandal* because of the brilliance of his satire and his ability to create entertainingly sardonic characters. *Time* magazine put him on its cover in March 1964, calling him "Ovid in Ossining," but his drinking was worsening and his family life was on the verge of collapse. Again, in spite of his self-destructiveness he had managed to sell stories to *Playboy, Esquire,* and the *Saturday Evening Post* as well as to the *New Yorker.* That same year, *The Brigadier and the Golf Widow* appeared. One of the stories in that collection, "The Swimmer," was quickly bought by the film director Frank Perry, who made it into a moderately successful movie starring Burt Lancaster; it earned Cheever a small fortune. During his time in Hollywood, Cheever fell in love with the actress Hope Lange, carrying on an affair that lasted many years. He also became less guarded about his affairs with young men. In the midst of all the chaos, *The Wapshot Scandal* won the Howells Medal of the American Academy of Arts and Letters in 1965.

Cheever made slow but significant progress on his next novel, *Bullet Park,* but also had a falling out with his long-time editor at the *New Yorker,* William Maxwell, over the effects of his drinking on the quality of his short stories. He also severed his relationship with Harper and Row and signed a contract with Alfred A. Knopf, which published *Bullet Park* in 1969 to mixed reviews. No previous novel of Cheever's had rendered a world so deeply divided between the conflicting demands of body and spirit, light and dark, good and evil. The names of the main characters, Hammer and Nailles, embody the crucifying agonies of a senseless world. The hostile critical reception of *Bullet Park* so overwhelmed Cheever that his drinking began to tell on his productivity. He published only one story in 1970, none in 1971, two in 1972, and one in 1973—meager results from a writer who normally published at least five stories a year. A collection of his works, *The World of Apples* (1973), was highly praised by most critics, however.

Because he had no future literary plans, he began teaching writing again in 1971, first at Sing Sing Prison, which was located in Ossining, then at the University of Iowa during the fall of 1973. He was hospitalized at the Phelps Memorial Hospital in May 1973 for acute alcoholism. Dismissing the suggestions of his family and doctors that he go to Alcoholics Anonymous, he took another teaching job at Boston University, where his drinking increased to such an extent that he was unable to finish the term. He was again detoxified at Phelps Hospital and his health became so precarious that he finally admitted himself to the Smithers Alcohol Rehabilitation Center in Manhattan in April 1975. He never touched alcohol again and became a faithful and participating member of AA.

Less than a year after he sobered up, Cheever was producing seven pages a day on his new novel, *Falconer,* published in 1977. *Falconer* takes place in a prison resembling Sing Sing, but Cheever later described it as the prison of himself. The main character faces his painfully bifurcated life and finally comes to terms—as Cheever did in his own life—with his self-destructive alcoholism and drug addiction, his bisexuality, and most importantly, his pathological love-hate relationship with his brother. Critics praised *Falconer,* and the novel's success made him wealthy. He appeared on the cover of *Newsweek* in March 1977 and also on the *Dick Cavett Show.* Paramount Pictures paid him $40,000 for the film rights for *Falconer* but never made the film. Cheever was delighted they never did. He received an honorary doctorate from Harvard as well as the Pulitzer Prize and National Book Critics Circle Award in 1979 for the *Stories of John Cheever* (1978), which renewed interest in Cheever's work. Knopf gave him a $500,000 advance on his next novel, *Oh What a Paradise It Seems,* published in 1982. Unfortunately, he was suffering from kidney and bone cancer so advanced that he could only write a short

version of what he had intended to be a much longer work. Cheever died quietly at his home in Ossining and was buried in Norwell, Massachusetts, in the Cheever family plot.

Although John Cheever struggled with his alcohol addiction all of his life and endured a loveless childhood and the agony of his bisexual impulses, he died a grateful man. He never lost the ability to change creative directions when he found himself in new circumstances and faced with new conflicts. No modern American writer has ever analyzed so compellingly the spiritual emptiness at the heart of the so-called American Dream.

★

Robert Gottlieb, ed., *The Journals of John Cheever* (1991), contains the definitive revelations of Cheever's deepest and most agonizing conflicts with alcoholism, his homosexual terrors, his conflicted relationships with his family, and the genesis of many of the stories and novels. Benjamin Cheever, ed., *The Letters of John Cheever* (1988), is his son's selection of letters to family members and fellow writers and friends such as John Updike, Malcolm Cowley, Saul Bellow, and Josephine Herbst. John D. Weaver, ed., *Glad Tidings: A Friendship in Letters: The Correspondence of John Cheever and John D. Weaver, 1945–1982* (1993), is a collection that reveals Cheever's public personality as told to one of his closest personal friends. Susan Cheever, *Home Before Dark* (1984), is his daughter's searingly honest biography of his troubled relationship with her and other family members, especially her mother's father. Scott Donaldson, *John Cheever: A Biography* (1988), artfully interweaves literary themes with biographical facts. George Hunt, *John Cheever: The Hobgoblin Company of Love* (1983), is a brilliant and erudite critical analysis of religious and mythic patterns in Cheever's work, mainly his novels. James E. O'Hara, *John Cheever: A Study of the Short Fiction* (1989), thoroughly uncovers recurring patterns in about sixty stories and is especially perceptive on critically neglected early stories. Patrick Meanor, *John Cheever Revisited* (1995), updates much of the scholarship and is the first full-length critical work to include material from Cheever's letters, journals, and biographies, demonstrating in detail how Cheever "mythologizes the commonplace" in the novels and many of the stories. An obituary is in the *New York Times* (24 June 1982).

PATRICK MEANOR

CHURCH, Frank Forrester (*b.* 25 July 1924 in Boise, Idaho; *d.* 7 April 1984 in Bethesda, Maryland), U.S. senator from Idaho who was a major opponent of the Vietnam War and a leader in intelligence reform.

Church's father, Frank Forrester Church II, was a dealer in sporting goods, and his mother, Laura Bilderback, was a homemaker. Church and his older brother Richard were grandsons of pioneers who had settled in Idaho after the Civil War. His family was strongly Republican, but Frank became a Democrat by arguing with his father at the dinner table. He graduated from Boise High School in 1942, as president of the student body and a first-prize winner of the American Legion national oratory contest. He went to Stanford University, but in October 1942, during his first semester, he enlisted in the U.S. army as a private for service in World War II. He was sent to Officers' Candidate School in Fort Benning, Georgia, and commissioned a second lieutenant in 1944, serving as a military intelligence officer in Burma, India, and China. He received his B.A. from Stanford in 1947, having been elected to Phi Beta Kappa. On 21 June 1947 he married Jean Bethine Clark, whose family had long been active in Democratic politics. They had two sons, Frank and Chase.

In the fall of 1947 Church began studies at Harvard Law School. He transferred to Stanford the following spring, and in 1948 he was diagnosed with testicular cancer. He was given six months to live but was subsequently successfully treated. He received a law degree from Stanford in 1950, and after returning to Idaho he became an associate in the Boise law firm of Langroise, Clark, and Sullivan. Church entered politics in 1952, losing a race for the Idaho legislature; that same year he was elected president of the Young Democrats of Idaho. In 1956 he ran for the U.S. Senate. He won the Democratic primary by defeating Glen Taylor, a former U.S. senator and the 1948 Progressive party vice presidential candidate. He then ran on a program of public ownership of electric power plants and a bipartisan internationalist foreign policy. Although Dwight D. Eisenhower carried the state in the presidential election, Church defeated the incumbent senator, Herman Welker, a right-wing Republican who had been a supporter of Senator Joseph R. McCarthy. At age thirty-two Church became the youngest person in the U.S. Senate, and the fourth youngest senator in American history. He was dubbed the "boy orator" by his colleagues.

Church was a liberal Democrat. His first Senate vote was on an unsuccessful attempt to make it easier to end the filibuster. In 1957 he introduced the "jury trial" amendment to ensure that blacks would not be discriminated against and could serve on federal juries. This amendment guaranteed liberal support for the bill and gained Church the gratitude of Senate Majority Leader Lyndon B. Johnson. Church also took care of his home state, making water development policy his major interest on the Senate Interior Committee. In 1957 he cosponsored a bill for a dam on the Snake River and also the Hell's Canyon Dam. In 1962 he sponsored the Bruces Eddy Dam on the Clearwater River. During Eisenhower's presidency Church played a bipartisan role. He voted for three-fifths of Eisenhower's program. He was a proponent of Alaskan and Hawaiian statehood. In 1960 he gave the keynote speech at the Democratic National Convention. In the 1960s he supported all of John F. Kennedy's and Johnson's domestic

programs and was one of the most liberal members of the Senate. He voted for an increase in the minimum wage, federal school aid, public housing, area redevelopment, and Medicare and Medicaid, and he developed programs to help the elderly. Church was a conservationist opposed by mining and lumber interests. In 1961 he was Senate floor manager of the National Wilderness System bill. In 1965 the National Wildlife Federation named him conservationist of the year. Church was not liberal on all issues, however. After the Supreme Court's *Roe* v. *Wade* decision, he sponsored an amendment in 1974 to health legislation allowing institutions that received federal funds to refuse to perform abortions and outlawed discrimination against hospital staff members who refused to perform abortions because of religious or ethical beliefs.

Church was an influential member of the Senate Foreign Relations Committee, on which he served from 1959. He was a strong supporter of Kennedy's Limited Test Ban Treaty of 1963 and other efforts for détente with the Soviet Union. Church was one of the first Democrats to break with President Johnson on the Vietnam War in 1965. "No

Senator Frank Church, 1976. OWEN FRANKEN/CORBIS

nation, not even our own," he argued, "possesses an arsenal so large or a treasury so rich as to damp down the fires of smoldering revolution throughout the whole, awakening world." In 1966 he was one of fifteen Democratic senators who urged Johnson to continue with his suspension of bombing in North Vietnam. As a result of Church's opposition, President Johnson remarked to reporters, "The next time Frank Church wants a dam in Idaho, let him ask Ho Chi Minh." Church called for negotiations with the Vietnamese communists, but he continued to vote for appropriations for the war and opposed unilateral withdrawal. In 1968 he defeated George V. Hansen for reelection. Church campaigned not as a war critic but as an effective representative for Idaho projects and on his success in blocking a plan to divert Idaho river waters to the Southwest.

Church opposed President Richard Nixon's war policies. In 1970 he introduced, with Senator John S. Cooper, the Cooper-Church Amendment to a military sales bill that would have barred funds for future military operations in Cambodia. The Senate passed it on 30 June by a vote of 58 to 37, after a seven-week debate that became one of the major congressional debates on the war. To forestall passage, President Nixon had agreed to withdraw forces from Cambodia by 30 June, but the Senate still passed the measure. The Senate defeated amendments to the bill by Senator Robert Dole that would have suspended its effect so long as American prisoners were being held in Cambodia and by Senator Robert Byrd that would have allowed the president to take action necessary to protect U.S. forces in South Vietnam. The House rejected the bill 237–153, but later the Senate passed an amendment offered by Church as part of a military appropriation bill, 73–17, which prohibited ground troops in Laos and Cambodia, although it allowed air strikes. This was the first limitation Congress had ever passed affecting the power of the president as commander in chief, although the language of the bill disingenuously stated that it was not intended to affect the commander in chief's constitutional authority and was "in line with the policy of the president." Later in 1970 Congress passed a Cooper-Church amendment to a foreign aid authorization bill prohibiting the use of funds to finance the introduction of U.S. ground forces into Cambodia, to provide advisers, or to fund Cambodian forces.

Church continued to propose antiwar amendments. In 1972 the Church-Case Amendment to a State Department appropriations bill, authorizing cutoff of funds for all combat operations in Indochina after 31 December, was passed by the Senate, but only after it was watered down so that it would go into effect only if a cease-fire had been negotiated. After the Paris Peace Accords ended U.S. military involvement in Vietnam, Church opposed any attempt to help South Vietnam. He sponsored legislation in 1975 that prevented any U.S. military aid to South Vietnam in response to the military successes of North Vietnam.

During the Nixon years Church was a strong opponent of many of the administration's foreign and defense policies. He voted in 1971 for a reduction of U.S. forces in Western Europe by 50,000, against deployment of an antiballistic missile system, against funding for the C5A cargo plane, and for reducing arms aid to right-wing dictators. In 1972 he advocated abrogating the Southeast Asia Treaty Organization (SEATO) to avoid future entanglements in Southeast Asia. Church was a strong supporter of Israel; in 1974 he held hearings on the secondary boycotts by U.S. companies complying with the Arab trade embargo against Israel. Church was skeptical of détente with the Soviet Union. In 1974 he proposed a legislative veto requiring prior congressional approval for credits to finance exports of equipment and services to develop the Soviet oil industry. In the 1975–1976 session his subcommittee held hearings on alleged bribery by U.S. corporations doing business abroad, which led to passage of legislation making such bribes illegal.

The most important legislative work performed by Church involved investigation of intelligence abuses. In 1975 Church headed the Senate Select Committee to Study Government Operations with Respect to Intelligence Activities, known as the Church committee. It heard testimony for eighteen months. Church fought to get access to confidential files and to get full cooperation from a reluctant administration. He widened the inquiry as much as possible, at times threatening to resign if he was not backed by committee and Senate leadership. The committee revealed Central Intelligence Agency (CIA) involvement in assassination plots against leaders of foreign governments, including Rafael Trujillo of the Dominican Republic, Fidel Castro of Cuba, Ngo Dinh Diem of the Republic of Vietnam, and Patrice Lumumba of the Democratic Republic of the Congo (none of these plots was successful) and CIA involvement in the coup against Chile's leftist government of Salvador Allende Gossens. The committee also found evidence of operations conducted by the Federal Bureau of Investigation (FBI) against domestic radical groups and leaders, such as Martin Luther King, Jr., including illegal wiretaps, break-ins, surveillance, harassment, burglaries, mail intercepts, and smear campaigns. It also found that all U.S. presidents since Franklin D. Roosevelt had used the FBI to obtain political intelligence on politicians, such as Adlai Stevenson and Paul Douglas. Church made the report public despite a letter from President Gerald Ford asking him to keep these matters confidential.

The Church committee's 651-page report was signed by nine of its eleven members. It concluded that U.S. intelligence operations often were without merit and initiated without adequate authorization. Presidents had pressured the CIA to produce intelligence estimates that would support policies. The director of central intelligence produced estimates for cabinet secretaries with vested interests in certain policies, particularly on arms control and Soviet military capabilities. It also claimed that the CIA had withheld information that the 1970 incursion into Cambodia would not halt infiltration. The committee faulted the CIA for too much current events reporting and not enough in-depth analysis. It warned against covert operations designed to avoid open debate about government policies, including the CIA's secret war in Laos. The committee criticized the CIA for its covert use of scholars on more than 100 campuses and for its links to fifty or so journalists and twenty-one members of the clergy. It found that the FBI had conducted at least 238 break-ins against domestic groups, some of them involved in civil rights and antiwar activities, between 1942 and 1968. These were "black bag" jobs that were known to be illegal. The Church committee recommendations involved new executive controls, including direct presidential authorization of all activities, laws to define limits of intelligence activities, restrictions on certain activities, and congressional oversight. In May 1976 the Senate voted to establish the Permanent Select Committee on Intelligence Activities. Church's work led to the laws creating a framework of oversight for intelligence committees and covert operations.

In 1976 Church entered the Democratic presidential primaries, defeating Jimmy Carter in Nebraska on 11 May, which led to a period in which Carter seemed in trouble. Church also won in Idaho, Montana, and Oregon, but Carter's victory in Ohio destroyed Church's credibility as a candidate; he dropped out of the race in June and endorsed Carter. During Carter's presidency Church was floor manager during the fight for Senate consent to the Panama Canal Treaties. He broke with Carter on plans to sell advanced weapons to Arab nations but supported Carter on the Strategic Arms Limitation Talks (SALT II). In 1979, as the newly elected chair of the Foreign Relations Committee, he demanded the withdrawal of Soviet combat forces from Cuba before a vote on SALT II. Carter believed Church had disclosed secret information just to protect himself politically in Idaho, but Church denied it.

In the late 1970s Church incurred the wrath of conservative timber and mining interests in Idaho when he sponsored a bill to make 2.2 million acres in Idaho protected wilderness under the River of No Return Wilderness bill. Conservative Republican groups such as the National Conservative Political Action Committee contributed funds in a negative campaign to defeat him in the Senate. They formed ABC, "Anyone but Church," and ran Steve D. Symms, a conservative Republican, to oppose him in the 1980 election. They claimed that Church had given the Panama Canal to the communists, leading Church to compare their campaign techniques to Hitler's Big Lie. Church received a great deal of money from liberals in New York for his campaign but lost because of the Idaho recession, the Sagebrush Rebellion (against federal control of Western lands), and the landslide election of Republican Ronald Reagan to the presidency.

After his defeat Church practiced international law at the Washington firm of Whitman and Ransom, representing multinational corporations doing business abroad. He died of pancreatic cancer at the age of fifty-nine and was buried in Morris Hill Cemetery in Boise, Idaho.

Frank Church exemplified the resurgence of congressional influence in the making of U.S. foreign policy in the 1960s and 1970s. The passage of his antiwar amendments marked the first time that the powers of the commander in chief were challenged by Congress. His congressional investigations of the intelligence apparatus resulted in significant changes in the laws, and it was the subsequent failure of the Reagan administration to comply with the new system of legislative oversight originated by Church that led to the Iran-Contra hearings in the 1980s.

★

F. Forrester Church, *Father and Son: A Personal Biography of Senator Frank Church of Idaho* (1985), is a portrait of the senator by his son. Loch K. Johnson, *A Season of Inquiry: The Senate Intelligence Investigation* (1985), provides a history of the Church committee and the efforts of its chairman by one of Church's senate staffers and committee investigators. LeRoy Ashby, *Fighting the Odds: The Life of Senator Frank Church* (1994), is a biographical treatment of Church that emphasizes his Senate career. An obituary is in the *New York Times* (8 Apr. 1984).

RICHARD M. PIOUS

CLARK, Mamie Phipps (*b.* 18 October 1917 in Hot Springs, Arkansas; *d.* 11 August 1983 in Hastings-on-Hudson, New York), psychologist and children's advocate whose research on racial identity and self-esteem played a key role in the landmark desegregation case *Brown* v. *Board of Education of Topeka, Kansas* (1954).

Clark was born Mamie Katherine Phipps, one of two children of Harold H. Phipps, a physician in Hot Springs, Arkansas, and Katie Smith Phipps, and grew up amid an extended family she would recall as warm and protective. She completed her secondary education at Langston High School in 1934, at the height of the Great Depression, but her prospects for attending college were slight, particularly in view of discrimination in admissions against African Americans by southern universities. With the assistance of a scholarship, however, she was able to travel to Washington, D.C., to attend Howard University, where she intended to major in mathematics.

At Howard she met Kenneth Bancroft Clark, a graduate

Mamie Phipps Clark. REPRODUCED COURTESY OF THE SIMON & SCHUS-
TER CORPORATE DIGITAL ARCHIVE

student and her future husband. It was he who first raised the possibility that she might pursue a career in psychology at Howard, where, under the leadership of Francis Cecil Sumner, the Department of Psychology was the leading undergraduate program for black students in this field. Switching majors, Clark performed part-time work in the department and also engaged in research with Max Meenes. In 1938 she graduated with a B.A. degree in psychology, magna cum laude. On 14 April of that year she married Kenneth Clark, who by this time was at Columbia University, where he would earn the Ph.D. in psychology in 1940, the first African American ever to do so. The couple had two children.

Remaining at Howard to do her master's work, Clark became involved in discussions with Ruth and Eugene L. Hartley that led to her thesis, *The Development of Consciousness of Self in Negro Pre-School Children*. She was awarded the M.A. in psychology in 1939. Together with her husband she developed a coloring test and a doll test of racial self-identification and submitted a proposal for funding to extend her master's research to the Julius Rosenwald Foundation, which was striving to encourage all-white colleges and universities to hire African Americans as professors. The financial support she received from the Rosenwald Foundation enabled her to pursue her Ph.D. at Columbia, and in 1940 she became the only black student

and one of only two women in the doctoral program in psychology. Her major adviser was Henry E. Garrett, a future president of the American Psychological Association who was a vigorous opponent of efforts to end the segregation of public schools. Nevertheless, under his supervision Clark completed her dissertation on the development of primary mental abilities in children, and in 1943 she became the second black person to earn a Ph.D. in psychology from Columbia.

In the mid-1940s Clark began to conduct psychological testing at the Riverdale Home for Children, a private agency in New York City for black homeless girls, an experience that made her keenly aware of the lack of availability of psychological services for minority children in New York. Thus in 1946 she and her husband established the Northside Center for Child Development, the first full-time child-guidance center offering psychological, psychiatric, and casework services for children and families in Harlem. The Northside Center soon became involved in the psychological testing of minority and deprived children in the New York City public schools. Illegally, and often without parental permission, these children were being shifted into classes for the mentally retarded. Testing showed that many were above the intelligence level for such placement, and they were eventually able to be returned to their normal classes. Thus the Northside Center quickly developed an activist and advocacy role in support of disadvantaged children. Psychological and psychiatric services were soon supplemented with a remedial reading and arithmetic program, a remarkable innovation for a mental health clinic in the 1940s.

Additional research she conducted with her husband made clear that African-American children were aware of their racial identity at a very early age and were acquiring a negative self-image. Her research on racial identity and self-esteem was described in "Racial Identification and Preference in Negro Children," in Theodore M. Newcomb and Eugene L. Hartley, eds., *Readings in Social Psychology* (1947), and in "Emotional Factors in Racial Identification and Preference in Negro Children," *Journal of Negro Education* 19 (1950), both with Kenneth Clark. These research findings were cited in expert testimony in school desegregation cases in South Carolina, Delaware, and Virginia.

Clark's research on racial identity and self-esteem in African-American children played a major role in the Supreme Court's 1954 decision in *Brown* v. *Board of Education of Topeka, Kansas,* which overturned legal segregation in U.S. public schools. Her research findings were part of a summary prepared by a group of prominent social scientists including Gordon Allport, Kenneth Clark, and Otto Klineberg of the negative effects upon children of racial segregation. This summary was submitted to the Supreme Court by Robert Carter, Thurgood Marshall, and other lawyers working with the National Association for the Advancement of Colored People, whose strategy was in part to demonstrate that segregation had detrimental effects on personality. In the Court's decision there was a summary description of Clark's 1947 and 1950 research findings: "To separate [children] from others of similar age and qualifications solely because of their race generates a feeling of inferiority as to their status in the community that may affect their hearts and minds in a way unlikely ever to be undone." The decision was noteworthy for being one of the first Supreme Court cases in which the decision was grounded in large part upon psychological arguments and evidence from psychological research.

In the years following the *Brown* decision Clark became an influential voice in both academic and social policy circles. Between 1958 and 1960 she was a visiting professor of experimental methods and research design at Yeshiva University in New York City. As executive director of the Northside Center, she helped bring about construction in the 1960s of Schomburg Plaza in Harlem, which included housing for 600 families. Clark served as the first woman trustee of Union Dime Savings Bank; as a member of several advisory groups including Harlem Youth Opportunities Unlimited and the National Headstart Planning Committee; and on the boards of Teachers College at Columbia University, the American Broadcasting Company, the New York Public Library, the Museum of Modern Art, the New York Mission Society, and the Phelps Stokes Fund. In 1957 Howard University presented Clark with its Alumni Achievement Award. In 1972 Williams College awarded her an honorary Doctor of Humane Letters degree. Clark was a member of Phi Beta Kappa, the American Psychological Association, and a fellow of the American Association of Orthopsychiatry. She retired in 1980 and died of cancer three years later.

During the course of her life Clark was able to move from childhood in a small, segregated southern town to positions of visibility within the profession of psychology and of leadership within the New York metropolitan area. Living at a time of extraordinary changes in the status of women and minorities within American society, Clark both reflected those changes in her own life and, through her scholarship and social activism, did much to reinforce and accelerate those changes.

★

Clark's revealing and engaging autobiography is in Agnes N. O'Connell and Nancy Felipe Russo, eds., *Models of Achievement: Reflections of Eminent Women in Psychology* (1983). A brief biography is included in Robert V. Guthrie, *Even the Rat Was White: A Historical View of Psychology* (1998). An obituary is in the *New York Times* (12 Aug. 1983).

JACK MEACHAM

CLARK, Mark Wayne (*b.* 1 May 1896 at Madison Barracks [now Fort Drum] near Watertown, New York; *d.* 17 April 1984 in Charleston, South Carolina), professional soldier and college president who served as General Dwight D. Eisenhower's deputy during the invasion of North Africa in World War II and eventually commanded all Allied forces in Italy; as commander of all United Nations forces, Clark signed the armistice ending the Korean War.

The second child and only son of Charles C. Clark, a member of the West Point class of 1890 who retired at the rank of colonel (1920), and Rebecca Ezekiels, the daughter of a Jewish immigrant from Central Europe, Clark was raised in army camps. He graduated from the United States Military Academy with a B.S. in April 1917, finishing 110th in a class of 139. Only the top graduates had their choice of service—the rest being assigned to infantry duty—but this presented no problem for Clark as he had always intended to follow in his father's footsteps by being commissioned in the infantry.

Because of America's entry into World War I, Clark was

Lieutenant General Mark Clark, *c.* 1945. THE NATIONAL ARCHIVES/ CORBIS

rapidly promoted to captain and given command of a company of the Eleventh Infantry Regiment, which was sent to France. In June 1918, as the Eleventh was approaching the front, Clark's battalion commander became ill and turned over command to Clark, who was barely twenty-two years old. Shortly after getting his unit into its trenches, a German artillery shell exploded near Clark, putting an end to his brief stint as a battalion commander and to his dreams of gaining glory on the battlefield. The severity of his wounds made it impossible for him to return to combat, and he finished out the war as a staff officer with the First Army's supply section.

After returning to the United States in 1919, Clark served as an infantry officer at Fort Snelling, Minnesota, and Fort Crook, Nebraska. In January 1921, much to his chagrin, Clark found himself in show business for nine months as commander of a detachment of United States Army soldiers of foreign birth, who performed on the Chautauqua circuit in an effort to maintain public support for the army.

While serving in the office of the assistant secretary of war between 1921 and 1924, Clark met Maurine Doran, a civilian employee of the Quartermaster Corps. The couple, who married in Washington, D.C., on 17 May 1924, eventually had two children. The newlyweds took up residence at Fort Benning, Georgia, where Clark completed the Advanced Officers Course before being transferred to the Presidio in San Francisco, where he remained from 1925 to 1928.

Between 1929 and 1933, Clark served as instructor and advisor to the Thirty-eighth Division of the Indiana National Guard in Indianapolis. Promoted to major in 1933, he attended the prestigious Command and General Staff School at Fort Leavenworth, Kansas (1933–1935), the stepping-stone to higher command. After brief service as a staff officer at Fort Sam Houston, Texas, and Fort Crook, Nebraska, he attended the Army War College in 1936 and 1937.

Clark was next assigned to the Third Division at Fort Lewis, Washington, where as plans and operations officer he devised and implemented the army's first full-division amphibious training exercise. The success of this operation attracted the attention of General Lesley McNair, who was interested in the concept of ship-to-shore operations. While at Fort Lewis, Clark also came into contact with General George C. Marshall, and he strengthened his ties to (then) Colonel Dwight D. Eisenhower, who had been an upperclassman when Clark entered West Point.

In 1940 Clark was promoted to lieutenant colonel and ordered to report to the Army War College in Washington, D.C., as an instructor. However, before he could leave Fort Lewis, all classes at the War College were canceled. In a quandary, Clark wired Washington for instructions. He received a terse reply from General Marshall, now army chief of staff, that he comply with orders.

As the threat of war loomed, Marshall was putting together a team, to be housed at the closed War College, to direct the expansion of the army. Clark was assigned to the plans and operations section (G-3) of this general headquarters, and promotion came rapidly.

In August 1941, even before the Japanese attack on Pearl Harbor, Clark was promoted to brigadier general, skipping the rank of colonel. In April 1942 Clark, who had already been named chief of staff, Army Ground Forces, received his second star. His swift rise meant he outranked many older officers who had long been his senior, a fact that stirred jealousy and sometimes caused problems in his relationship with older subordinates.

In June 1942 Clark journeyed to England to assume command of an American corps being formed there. However, his days as troop commander were short-lived, for in August General Eisenhower named him deputy supreme Allied commander, and Clark became involved in the planning of Operation Torch (the invasion of Vichy French North Africa), which was scheduled for November 1942.

Robert Murphy, an American diplomatic representative to North Africa, believed a deal might be struck with local Vichy French commanders, whereby they would not oppose the landings. A high-level officer, familiar with Operation Torch and with plenipotentiary powers, was needed to meet with these officers in the hope of arranging an armistice that would permit the Allies to land without resistance and give them the opportunity to occupy Tunisia before the German commander in North Africa, Field Marshall Erwin Rommel, could do so. Clark volunteered for the job, and this top secret mission, in which Clark and his party were transported from Gibraltar by a British submarine and landed by commandos in small boats, soon made Clark a celebrity—critics would call him a publicity hound—in a nation hungry for heroes in the dark days after Pearl Harbor.

Despite Clark's efforts, the Torch landings on 8 November 1942 were contested, and he returned to Algeria as Eisenhower's surrogate to continue efforts to secure an armistice. His was the unhappy task of signing an agreement with Vichy Admiral Jean-François Darlan, viewed by many as a collaborationist with the Nazis, while Eisenhower remained at his headquarters in Gibraltar aloof from this controversial step. In any case, Clark's actions in North Africa, more diplomatic than soldierly, won him his third star (November 1942) and, in January 1943, the command of the Fifth Army.

After the surrender of Axis forces in North Africa in May 1943, Clark's Fifth Army was assigned the task of invading Italy at Salerno on 9 September 1943. The Italian campaign, which many American military leaders opposed because they viewed it as a hindrance to the cross-Channel invasion they favored, would be beset with controversy, and Clark came in for his share of criticism for some of his decisions.

Ultra (the top-secret breaking of the German military cipher) intercepts had indicated that Hitler, anticipating a possible Allied invasion, did not plan to fight for southern Italy. However, Hitler, as on so many other occasions, confounded the Allies by changing his mind and giving his commander in Italy, Field Marshal Albert Kesselring, authority to fight rather than withdraw northward as originally planned. Kesselring's masterly defense, coupled with difficult terrain, meant that fighting in Italy would be long, hard, and bloody. In addition, as more and more resources were committed to Eisenhower's invasion of Normandy, Italy became, in Clark's view, the "forgotten front."

Clark's Fifth Army—a truly multinational force which eventually included four French divisions under General Alphonse Juin and a Polish corps under General Wladyslaw Anders—bogged down before the Germans' Gustav Line, which lay behind the Garigliano and Rapido Rivers. In an effort to break the stalemate by forcing a German withdrawal, an amphibious landing at Anzio (January 1944) was undertaken by the Sixth Corps under General John Lucas. Unfortunately, Lucas, who was not given clear instructions or objectives, established only a beachhead and made no effort to advance. The Germans soon organized defenses to contain the invasion force.

Meanwhile, in an effort to tie down German forces during the Anzio landing, Clark, despite its commander's protests, ordered an attack across the Rapido River by the Thirty-sixth Division, a Texas National Guard force, which was decimated by the German defenders. After the war, disgruntled veterans of the Thirty-sixth blamed General Clark for the bloodbath and demanded an investigation, but the army held that he had "exercised sound judgment" in planning and ordering the attack, and that it had helped make possible the landing at Anzio.

Controversy also arose over the Allied bombing of Monte Cassino, a Benedictine monastery behind the German lines. Clark, who referred to the destruction of the abbey as a "mistake," contended he had opposed the act as militarily unnecessary and that the British, not he, insisted on bombing it.

Further controversy developed over Clark's capture of Rome, on 4 June 1944. Dan Kurzman in *The Race for Rome* (1975) suggests that Clark was so obsessed with beating his British allies to the Italian capital that he failed to trap the retreating Germans before they could escape northward.

Whether or not significant enemy forces might have been cut off had Clark sent the Sixth Corps, which finally broke out from Anzio on 25 May 1944, eastward to cut German communications, instead of northward to Rome, remains a matter of dispute. However, the reason the Allied forces in Italy were unable to gain a decisive victory over the withdrawing Germans lay largely in factors beyond Clark's control. A planned Allied landing near St.-Tropez in southern France would take part of "his" Fifth Army. In response, Clark argued that a rapid victory in northern Italy would enable him to invade the Balkans and meet the Soviets far to the east.

When Allied strategists finally decided to launch the operation (Anvil-Dragoon, 15 August 1944) in southern France, Clark had to give up seven full divisions and a number of special units to the operation. Although he slowly acquired new forces as they became available, Clark would contend he lacked sufficient strength to force a rapid decision in Italy.

In December 1944 Clark was named commander of the Fifteenth Army Group (composed of his Fifth Army and the British Eighth Army), which in effect placed all Allied forces in Italy under his control, and in March 1945 he was given the four stars of a full general.

After the defeat of Germany, Clark became commander of United States forces in Austria as well as American High Commissioner. In these posts, he developed an abiding distrust of the Soviets who shared the occupation of Austria. Clark also played an important role in efforts to negotiate a peace treaty for that country, serving as deputy to George Marshall, then United States Secretary of State, at the Moscow meeting of the Council of Foreign Ministers in 1947.

In June 1947 Clark assumed command of the Sixth Army at the Presidio, San Francisco, California. In October 1949 he became chief of Army Field Forces, at Fort Monroe, Virginia, which placed him in charge of all training for the army.

In May 1952 Clark succeeded General Matthew B. Ridgway, a classmate of his at West Point, as commander of United Nations forces in Korea and of all United States forces in the Far East. He also assumed a task he did not relish—the negotiation of an armistice to bring the Korean War to an end. Clark believed that the United States should attempt to win the war as a means of preventing future ones. Although he would have preferred to go for victory, Clark bowed to civilian authority and signed an armistice on 27 July 1953. In *Captain's Bride, General's Lady* (1956), Clark's first wife, Maurine Doran Clark, portrayed Clark as a man agonizingly torn between his private feelings and his responsibility as an American officer sworn to defend the Constitution. "His duty was to sign the armistice, but his conviction was that victory was possible and would have been preferable in the long run. But he was also convinced that if there was no determination to win the war, then it was better to sign the armistice and stop the killing" (p. 255). On the night he returned to Tokyo after signing the armistice in Korea, she continued, Clark wept and told her of his intention to leave the army.

After retiring from the army after forty years of continuous service late in 1953, Clark publicly advocated the use of every weapon, including the atomic bomb, if the communists violated the armistice in Korea.

General Clark became president of the Citadel, the prestigious Charleston, South Carolina, military school, in 1954. He remained in this post until 1965. According to the *New York Times* (28 April 1984), Clark "believed his eleven-year presidency of the Citadel was his crowning achievement." He left a large portion of his estate, estimated to be worth $1 million, to that institution.

Clark's first wife died on 5 October 1966, and a year later, on 17 October 1967, he married Mary Millard Applegate, a family friend who had been widowed at about the same time as Clark. The couple had no children.

In 1968, Clark campaigned for Richard M. Nixon, and in 1969 the president appointed him to the American Battle Monuments Commission. During the 1970s, Clark, a staunch supporter of U.S. participation in the Vietnam War, made trips to Austria, Italy, and the Far East, and occasionally spoke out to denounce communism or to comment on military matters.

In March 1984 Clark was hospitalized and underwent tests for cardiovascular problems, which had plagued him for many years. However, his death, at the Medical University of South Carolina in Charleston, was the result of pancreatic cancer which had spread to his liver. He was buried on the campus of the Citadel.

★

Clark's papers are in the Daniel Library at the Citadel, in Charleston, South Carolina. Clark's two volumes of memoirs, *Calculated Risk* (1950) and *From the Danube to the Yalu* (1954), are good sources on his military career and his views of World War II strategy and American cold war policy, but are sketchy on his personal life. On the other hand, *Captain's Bride, General's Lady: The Memoirs of Mrs. Mark W. Clark* (1956), by Clark's first wife, Maurine Doran Clark, is somewhat vague on Clark's career, but provides an intimate glimpse of his private life. Although Michael Angelo Musmanno, a Pennsylvania jurist who served for a time as Clark's naval aide in Italy, published a brief sketch of Clark in Italian (*Il Generale Mark W. Clark: L'uomo e il soldato*, 1946), Martin Blumenson, *Mark Clark* (1984), which suffers from a lack of documentation, is the only full biographical treatment of Clark.

Godfrey B. Courtney, "General Clark's Secret Mission," *Life* (28 Dec. 1942), is by the British Commando captain who landed Clark and his party in Algeria from a British submarine and provides an eyewitness account of the highly publicized adventure that made Clark a celebrity. Milton Bracker, "General Mark Clark Gets the Tough Jobs," *New York Times Magazine* (19 Sept. 1943), paints an extremely favorable portrait of Clark as a man and a commander adored by the men of the Fifth Army. "Murder at the Rapido," *Time* (28 Jan. 1946), briefly discusses the charges of incompetence brought against Clark by veterans of the Thirty-sixth (Texas) Division for ordering an operation that cost the unit over 2,000 casualties in twenty-four hours. Sidney Mathews, "General Clark's Decision to Drive on Rome," *Command Decisions* (1960): 351–363, analyses Clark's motivation in evading the orders of his superior, British field marshal Sir Harold Alexander, by sending the bulk of the Sixth Corps toward Rome instead of eastward to cut Highway 6 at Valmontone. Obituaries are in the *New York Times* and the (Charleston, South Carolina) *News and Courier* (both 17 Apr. 1984) and the *Washington Post* (18 Apr. 1984).

ROMAN ROME

CLARKE, Kenny ("Klook") (*b.* 9 January 1914 in Pittsburgh, Pennsylvania; *d.* 26 January 1985 near Paris, France), innovative jazz drummer of the bebop era.

Clarke, one of two sons of Charles Spearman, a trombonist, and Martha Grace Scott, was born Kenneth Clarke Spearman in Pittsburgh. The city was then in its sooty prime as a steel town, and Clarke, who in later years exiled himself to Paris, recalled thinking about other places to live from a young age. Although his family could afford an organ and piano, on which Clarke learned his first music from his mother, his early life was haunted by the absence of his father, who ran off when Clarke was quite young, and the death of his mother when he was four or five. Clarke and his brother, Frank, were placed in Pittsburgh's Coleman Industrial Home for Negro Boys, where Clarke stayed until adolescence. Coleman luckily had a decent music program, and while there Clarke discovered the drums as a fair substitute for piano.

After living in several foster homes and a second try at staying with his Baptist preacher stepfather, when he was seventeen Clarke began playing the drums around Pittsburgh with the Leroy Bradley band, then briefly with Roy Eldridge. After drumming in St. Louis with the Jeter-Pillars Orchestra, he left Pittsburgh with his brother for New York in 1936. In his early gigging around the city Clarke also played the vibraphone, a percussion instrument that resembles the xylophone and may have allowed him to maintain a connection to his first love, the piano.

Like anyone who has studied piano, Clarke found most drummers too loud. Strangely, he thought little of drum solos and preferred to back his fellow musicians. "That's my job," he told his biographer, Mike Hennessey, in *Klook*. One who thrived on Clarke's daring rhythms early on was the trumpeter Dizzy Gillespie, with whom Clarke wrote the bebop standard "Salt Peanuts." Gillespie said: "It was Kenny Clarke who set the stage for the rhythmic content of our music. He was the first to make accents on the bass drum at specific points in the music. . . . Like, we called them dropping bombs." By the early 1940s Clarke's signature bombs and offbeat rim shot–bass drum couplets were so distinctive he had gained the nickname (from bandleader Teddy Hill and others) of "Klook-mop" or "Klook."

In New York in the mid-1930s he found a heady scene. Not every bandleader, however, wanted a drummer with his own ideas; Clarke's were beginning to form as he went from band to band, sometimes in the same night as drummer at the legendary Apollo Theatre in Harlem, as good an education in different rhythms as could be had. The bandleader Teddy Hill, who hired him in 1939 as a sound-alike for Count Basie's great drummer Jo Jones, did not always care for Clarke's unconventional playing and fired him the next year. (Hill would come around when they both worked at Minton's Playhouse in Harlem, the salon of the bebop revolution.) It was in the Teddy Hill band that Clarke first played with Gillespie, and the two soon worked more closely as part of the house band leading jam sessions at Minton's, where Clarke became musical director in 1941 and where famous regulars included Thelonious Monk (with whom Clarke shares cowriting credit for "Epistrophy"), the pianist Bud Powell, the saxophonist Charlie Parker, and the guitarist Charlie Christian. In 1941 and 1942 Clarke also had stints with Ella Fitzgerald, Louis Armstrong (briefly replacing the great Big Sid Catlet), and Benny Carter. After drumming for Red Allen in Chicago, Clarke enlisted in the U.S. Army, but in 1944 he went AWOL for three months, during which he played all over

Kenny "Klook" Clarke at Birdland in New York City, 1956. FRANK DRIGGS/ARCHIVE PHOTOS

New York and met Carmen McCrae, who was eighteen. The two got married before he was sent to Europe; they were divorced within a few years. After the war Clarke had not drummed in two years and was ready to quit music for good. He had also undergone a private conversion to Islam and took the name Liaquat Ali Salaam. Then he made a lucky call to Gillespie in the spring of 1946. Clarke replaced his onetime student Max Roach in Gillespie's big band, which toured Europe in 1948, and John Lewis, a piano player Clarke had met in the army, replaced Monk. Clarke also played in the United States with the band of singer Billy Eckstine, a fellow altar boy from Pittsburgh. In 1949 and 1950 Clarke shared drumming honors with Max Roach on the recording sessions of the Miles Davis Nonet, which resulted in the influential record, later called *Birth of the Cool,* that inspired the West Coast jazz movement.

In 1951 Clarke married Daisy Dina Wallbach in France; they had one son. (In 1950 Clarke had had a son out of wedlock by a young singer named Annie Ross.) Also in 1951 Clarke and his friend John Lewis helped found the Milt Jackson Quartet, which shortly evolved into the influential and commercially popular (by jazz standards) Modern Jazz Quartet. But the restless Clarke left the band after four years, before its greatest success. In 1956 Clarke, who claimed he had first dreamed of living in Paris when he was twelve, finally moved there permanently. He found a strong Paris jazz club scene in the late 1950s, when he played with Bud Powell's trio, among others. The life of the expatriate jazz musician suited his temperament, too, after the intolerance and rough experiences of American life. For thirteen years, he led the Kenny Clarke–Francy Boland Big Band, which included some Europeans and self-exiled Americans, such as Zoot Sims, Benny Bailey, Johnny Griffin, and others. In the later 1960s, however, the clubs in Paris began to change into discotheques, succumbing to rock and free jazz. Saddened though he was by the decline, in 1967 he founded the Kenny Clarke Drum School in Paris and led a series of jazz workshops. These and the occasional tour brought Clarke back to the United States several times over his final decades.

Clarke died of a heart attack, shortly after he turned seventy-one. His cremated remains were interred in the distinguished Père Lachaise cemetery in Paris, among French statesmen. According to Mike Hennessey, at the end Clarke could count thirty-eight notable bands he had played with during forty years in music. As he told a French interviewer in later years, "I never tried to become a celebrity. I wanted to be a musician and to please musicians. To be an accompanist—that's my greatest ambition. It is not the role of the drummer to be a star."

Although the drum set is traditionally considered the only instrument devised specifically for jazz music, it was not until Clarke's emergence in the 1930s and 1940s that the drums began to achieve equality with other pieces in the jazz ensemble. Instead of steadily thumping all four beats like a metronome, Clarke used his bass drum to accent and echo the other players, making the jazz drummer an independent improviser, while keeping time memorably, even sensually, on his ride cymbal. Clarke pioneered not only the freer drumming of bop but also the musical style itself through his work with fellow revolutionaries Dizzy Gillespie, Thelonious Monk, Charlie Parker, and others. As he simply characterized himself for his *Who's Who in America* entry years later: "creator modern conception of drumming; co-ordinated independence style for drummers."

★

Mike Hennessey, *Klook: The Story of Kenny Clarke* (1990), is a full-length biography. Also consult Barry Kornfeld, ed., *The New Grove Dictionary of Jazz* (1988), and Ian Carr, Digby Fairweather, and Brian Priestley, *Jazz: The Rough Guide* (1995). An obituary is in the *New York Times* (27 Jan. 1985).

NATHAN WARD

CLAUDE, Albert (*b.* 24 August 1898 in Longlier, Belgium; *d.* 22 May 1983 in Brussels, Belgium), a founder of modern cell biology, the first scientist to apply the electron microscope to the study of cells, pioneer in the use of centrifuges to separate the various components of the cell, and winner of the Nobel Prize in 1974.

Albert Claude was the son of Florentin Joseph Claude, a baker, and Marie-Glaudicine Wautriquant, who died of

Albert Claude, 1974. UPI/CORBIS-BETTMANN

cancer when he was only seven. As a child Claude's dream was to study medicine, but he never finished high school. During an economic depression in the years before World War I he moved with his father and three siblings to the manufacturing town of Athus, where he became an apprentice draftsman at a steelworks. During World War I Claude volunteered for the British Intelligence Service and was later cited for his bravery by War Minister Winston Churchill.

After the war the Belgian government decreed that war veterans could attend a university even if they had no high school diploma. In 1921 Claude passed an examination that allowed him to study at the School of Mining in Liège. In 1922 he entered the School of Medicine at the University of Liège and obtained his doctorate in medicine and surgery there in 1928. While at Liège he wrote a thesis on the effects of grafting mouse tumor cells onto rats, which won him a scholarship from the Belgian government for postgraduate study at the Cancer Institute in Berlin. Claude was forced to leave the institute prematurely, however, when he came into conflict with its director, who believed that cancer was caused by bacteria. He finished his scholarship in 1929 at the Kaiser Wilhelm Institute. While there Claude designed a research program and sent it to Simon Flexner, then director of the Rockefeller Institute for Medical Research (later Rockefeller University) in New York City. When Flexner accepted him, Claude received a scholarship from the U.S. government and in 1929 sailed to New York. He spent the next twenty years at the Rockefeller Institute, which became home to much of the great biomedical research and discoveries of the early twentieth century.

Claude, Belgian-born but a naturalized American from 1941, laid the foundation for modern cell biology with his work at the Rockefeller Institute between 1929 and 1949. Prior to that time cells were still largely scientific unknown territory. By using the recently developed electron microscope, Claude taught scientists to explore and map these miniature worlds. He also developed techniques for separating cell components in a centrifuge to help determine cell functions. Claude set the stage technically and conceptually for a whole area of biological investigation. By pursuing the new field of virology, he developed a technique using a high-speed centrifuge to spin fractionated (broken-up) cells infected with viruses in an attempt to isolate their agents.

One can scarcely appreciate the problems that faced these pioneering attempts at cell fractionation without having been there. The centrifuges were primitive. The patience of the operator, along with his determination, was strained by the inadequacies of the equipment. Claude, fortunately, had these ingredients in his character and the work went forward. He was able to fractionate various cell components that had never been separated before, preparing the way for new understanding of their varying functions. Though he never succeeded in fully isolating Peyton Rous's chicken sarcoma virus (RSV) within the cell structure, his discoveries became crucial to the study of cell biology. In fact, Claude and his colleagues proved in 1945 that mitochondria (an essential component of cells) are the powerhouses of all cells, from bacteria to liver cells, from plants to fungi to animals.

In 1942 Claude became convinced that the newly developed electron microscope would be useful in furthering his studies. He secured use of the only electron microscope in New York City, which was at the Interchemical Corporation, used there primarily for metallurgical purposes. The cells that Claude and his associate, Keith Porter, observed under the microscope showed the presence of a lacework structure that was eventually proven to be the major structural interior feature of all but bacterial cells. The lacework structure was also responsible in part for determining the shape of cells as well as the location for many granular cell components.

On the personal side, Claude was married to Joy Gilder on 20 June 1935. They had one child and were later divorced.

In 1948 Claude returned to Belgium and gave up active research for a time to become an administrator at the Université Libre de Bruxelles, and he spent the next twenty years developing a cancer research center. At the same time he headed the Institut Jules Bordet (1948–1971), where he resumed research on the fine structure of cells. Claude joined the faculty of Catholic University in Louvain in 1972 and also became the director of its Laboratory of Cellular Biology and Oncology.

In 1972 Rockefeller University awarded Claude emeritus standing. The 1974 Nobel Prize for physiology or medicine was shared by Claude, George E. Palade, and Christian de Duve "for their discoveries concerning the structural and functional organization of the cell."

Among the honors accrued over the span of his career were the Medal of the Belgian Academy of Medicine, the Louisa Gross Horwitz Prize of Columbia University, the Paul Ehrlich Award, and the Ludwig Darmstaedter Prize of Frankfurt. Claude was a full member of the Belgian and French academies of medicine and an honorary member of the American Academy of Arts and Science. He was a Roman Catholic. He died of natural causes and is buried in Brussels.

Albert Claude dedicated his life to the exploration of the basic unit of life, the cell. In his Nobel lecture he noted that the cell is an "autonomous and self-contained unit of living matter, which has acquired the knowledge and the power to reproduce; the capacity to store, transform, and utilize energy; and the capacity to accomplish physical works and to manufacture practically unlimited kinds of products." Claude was respected by his colleagues for his open-mindedness, tolerance, and fierce individuality. A determined and diligent student, he received his early education in a one-room schoolhouse and in later years was mostly self-taught. His dedication helped him overcome the hardships of having to use primitive equipment, or do without equipment, to further his research.

★

An excellent article on Claude is in Emily J. McMurray, ed., *Notable Twentieth-Century Scientists,* vol. 1 (1995). After Claude received the Nobel Prize in 1974, articles on his work appeared. Keith R. Porter wrote "The 1974 Nobel Prize for Physiology or Medicine," *Science* (8 Nov. 1974). Others include "Medicine: The World of the Cell," *Science News* (19 Oct. 1974), and "Explorers of the Cell," *Time* (21 Oct. 1974). Obituaries are in the *New York Times* and *Washington Post* (both 24 May 1983).

BEN DiRUSSO

CLEMENTS, Earle Chester (*b.* 22 October 1896 near Morganfield, Kentucky; *d.* 12 March 1985 in Morganfield, Kentucky), governor of Kentucky, congressman and U.S. senator, and Democratic party leader.

The sixth and last child of Aaron Waller Clements, a farmer and local official, and Sallie Anna Turley, a housewife, Clements came from a family with lengthy ties to the area and a strong interest in politics. After graduation from Morganfield High School in 1915, Clements went to State University (present-day University of Kentucky) and achieved prominence in football, winning honors as a center.

With the entry of the United States into World War I in 1917, Clements joined a National Guard unit that was activated but did not go overseas. He was discharged in 1919 as a captain. Rather than reenter the university, Clements worked from 1919 through 1920 in the Texas oilfields, then returned to his native Union County in January 1921. For eight years he served as a successful volunteer coach of the local football team.

In 1922 Clements entered public life, first serving as a deputy sheriff under his father. On the death of Aaron Clements in 1925, Earle Clements served as acting sheriff into 1926 and that year was elected county clerk. He served in that capacity for two terms until 1934. Meanwhile, on 18 January 1927 he married Sara Blue, herself the daughter of a Union County sheriff. They had one daughter, Elizabeth, who was later the social secretary to Lady Bird Johnson and executive assistant to Joan Mondale, wife of Vice President Walter Mondale. Clements and his wife attended the Christian church.

Clements continued to move steadily up the political ladder. In 1932 he was appointed to the Democratic State Central Executive Committee, where he made important

Senator Earle Clements, 1955. AP/WIDE WORLD PHOTOS

statewide contacts. The next year he won election as a county judge, the chief political post in the county, and served eight years. During that time he also made a decision that would shape his political future. In 1935 he agreed to serve as campaign chairman for what turned out to be the losing gubernatorial race of Thomas S. Rhea. Rhea's opponent, A. B. "Happy" Chandler, thereupon became Clements's bitter enemy for most of their lives, and the two would form opposing political factions within the usually dominant Democratic party.

In 1941 Clements won a seat in the state senate and in 1944 was named majority leader of that body. A Republican was serving as governor (a rarity in Kentucky at the time), and so Clements became one of the Democratic Party leaders and used that position to win a congressional seat in 1944. Indicative of Clements's growing power and ability to organize, incumbent Bev Vincent withdrew from the race before the election. Clements was reelected in 1946. During his brief career in the House, Clements served as a fairly liberal southern Democrat, voting against the Taft-Hartley Act of 1947, for antilynching and anti–poll tax bills, and with President Harry S. Truman on other civil rights issues.

Returning to Kentucky in 1947, the fifty-year-old Clements sought the governorship. His opponent in the pri-

mary was Harry Lee Waterfield, a young, strong candidate who focused on a parimutuel tax and on public development of electric power, both opposed by Clements. Backed by labor and a strong statewide organization, Clements won by nearly 25,000 votes. In the general election he swept to victory over Republican Eldon Dummit by a 100,000-vote margin and was inaugurated in December 1947.

As governor, Clements forged a progressive record. Additional funds that came into the state coffers through increased taxes on gasoline and distilled spirits went to roads, schools, and state parks. The professional Legislative Council (later the Legislative Research Commission) and a stronger state police force were created. Quietly the legislature amended the state's segregation law and made the first statutory moves to break down racial barriers.

Much of Clements's success came from the way he operated. A large man, nearly six feet tall and weighing around 220 pounds, he had a strong temper and could dominate those around him by his forceful presence. Neither an exceptional speaker nor a person with many personal friends, Clements was instead a masterful organizer who carefully prepared before acting. Called by one veteran correspondent "the most accomplished political operator that I know," he played the political game as well as anyone of his generation.

Clements used those abilities to gain higher office and in 1950 won election as U.S. senator over Charles I. Dawson. Resigning as governor on 27 November 1950, he immediately impressed those in Washington, D.C., with his skills. The freshman senator was made chairman of the Senate Democratic Campaign Committee in 1952, then party whip in 1953. When his close ally Lyndon B. Johnson experienced health problems, Clements temporarily replaced him as majority leader in 1955.

Attention to those additional duties, however, may have cost him politically. His extra work in Washington, opposition from now-governor Chandler, and a Republican upsurge led by President Dwight D. Eisenhower hurt Clements when he ran for reelection in 1956. In a shocking upset Clements lost his contest to Thruston B. Morton by some 7,000 votes. It was his only political loss and his last political race.

The next year Clements was named the executive director of the Democratic Senatorial Campaign Committee, a position he held until 1959, when he joined the gubernatorial administration of Bert Combs as Kentucky highway commissioner. Although widely viewed as the "kingmaker" behind Combs, Clements came under fire for what was said to be his pivotal role in a favorable truck contract that rewarded an ally of the administration. He resigned in September 1960, bitter over the governor's lack of support. He became a consultant for the American Merchant Marine Institute in 1961, then for the American Tobacco Institute three years after that. In 1966 he was named president of the Tobacco Institute and had a major influence in the nation's capital in the positions. After retirement Clements returned to his native county. His wife died in 1976. Long bothered by heart problems, he followed her in death nine years later and was buried in Morganfield Independent Order of Odd Fellows Cemetery.

From the 1930s into the 1960s, Clements led one of the two Democratic factions that controlled Kentucky. His progressive administration was one of the best of the century; his personal selections to succeed him continued that trend. Once in Washington he seemed destined to become a national figure, serving as acting majority leader in his first term; the *New York Times* named him one of the four top Democrats in Congress at that time. But a surprising defeat ended that opportunity, and Clements eventually became known for his effective defense of the tobacco industry.

★

Cautious about revealing himself in print, Clements did not disclose much of himself in writing. Nevertheless a sizable collection of his papers is at the University of Kentucky in Lexington. For a summary of these holdings see Charles C. Hay III and Victoria Walker, comps., *Guide to the Papers of Earle C. Clements* (1978). The most detailed study of his early career is Thomas H. Syvertsen, "Earle Chester Clements and the Democratic Party, 1920–1950" (Ph.D. diss., University of Kentucky, 1982). Extensive discussion of him is contained in John Ed Pearce, *Divide and Dissent: Kentucky Politics, 1930–1963* (1987). See also James C. Klotter, *Kentucky: Portrait in Paradox, 1900–1950* (1966); Lowell H. Harrison and James C. Klotter, *A New History of Kentucky* (1997); and Thomas H. Syvertsen, "Earle Chester Clements," in *Kentucky's Governors, 1792–1985,* edited by Lowell H. Harrison (1985). Numerous interviews focusing on Clements are also at the University of Kentucky. Analyses of his life appear in his obituaries in the *Lexington Herald-Leader* (13 Mar. 1985) and the *Louisville Courier-Journal* (13 Mar. 1985). See also the obituary in the *New York Times* (14 Mar. 1985).

JAMES C. KLOTTER

CODY, John Patrick (*b.* 24 December 1907 in St. Louis, Missouri; *d.* 25 April 1982 in Chicago, Illinois), Roman Catholic cardinal who served as archbishop of Chicago in the years immediately following the Second Vatican Council.

One of the two children of Thomas Cody, a fireman who became deputy chief of the St. Louis Fire Department, and Mary Begley, both Irish immigrants, young Cody attended the local parochial school in his St. Louis neighborhood. As a child his dream was to become a priest, and at age fourteen he entered the St. Louis Preparatory Seminary. Early on his teachers recognized that he was a very bright

John Cardinal Cody. CATHOLIC ARCHDIOCESE OF CHICAGO

and capable young man. In a very unusual move, they sent him to Rome in 1926 to attend the prestigious North American College to complete his studies for the priesthood. There he earned doctorates in philosophy, theology, and canon law, a remarkable achievement. He also learned to speak Italian and Latin fluently.

Cody was ordained a priest on 8 December 1931, the Feast of the Immaculate Conception. He was only twenty-three years old, an uncommonly young age to be ordained. During the next two years he continued his studies and in 1933 he was assigned to the staff of the Vatican secretariat of state, working for Monsignor Giovanni Battista Montini, the future Pope Paul VI; the two became the best of friends for the remainder of their lives. In 1938 Father Cody returned to the United States, becoming secretary to Archbishop John Glennon of St. Louis. Two years later he was appointed chancellor of the St. Louis archdiocese.

In 1943 Pope Pius XII named Cody a monsignor, and four years later Cody was consecrated a bishop in St. Louis. He served as auxiliary bishop to Archbishop Joseph E. Ritter. Thereafter, he steadily ascended in the American hierarchy. In 1954 he was named coadjutor bishop with the right of succession to Bishop Charles H. LeBlond of St. Joseph, Missouri, but instead was appointed bishop of the newly merged Kansas City–St. Joseph diocese in 1956. He quickly established a reputation as a builder. In just four months he raised $6 million to build ten elementary schools, a diocesan high school, ten churches and rectories, and eleven convents.

In 1961 Bishop Cody was transferred to New Orleans as coadjutor archbishop, with right of succession to Archbishop Joseph F. Rummel. When he became archbishop after Rummel's death in November 1964, Cody continued his bricks-and-mortar efforts by building more than $30 million worth of churches, schools, and convents in four years. But it was not only as an administrator that Cody attracted attention. He vigorously proclaimed church doctrine and directly immersed himself in controversy at the height of the civil rights movement of the 1960s. Archbishop Cody summarily desegregated Catholic schools in the archdiocese, earning a national reputation as a champion of civil rights. He also excommunicated Leander Perez, a leader of the segregationist opposition, and two other Catholics.

On 16 June 1965 Pope Paul VI appointed Cody archbishop of Chicago. He succeeded Cardinal Albert Meyer, who had died the previous April. On 24 August he was formally installed as head of the archdiocese of Chicago and spiritual leader of 2.5 million Catholics. As archbishop he lived in a redbrick Victorian mansion at North State Parkway and North Avenue, at Lincoln Park.

At the height of what was to be his longest assignment, Archbishop Cody entered the most trying period of his life. The Roman Catholic church in the summer of 1965 concluded the historic three-year ecumenical Second Vatican Council. Major reforms and changes were mandated in the life of the church, a two-thousand-year-old multinational, multicultural institution. Not since the Council of Trent in the sixteenth century had such changes taken place. This period in church history was a time of hope and renewal but also a period of disruption and confusion. Archbishop Cody was committed to instituting the council's directives, but he also, in temperament and in training, was a church bureaucrat used to exercising unquestioned authority. Cody personally was a man of great charm, kindness, and geniality but publicly he seemed stubborn and defensive. He was unprepared for the upheaval that was transforming American society, religious as well as civil, in a time in which all authority was challenged. The archbishop of Chicago was required to have the skills of a corporate executive and the charisma of a sensitive pastor and spiritual leader.

On 26 June 1967 Archbishop Cody was formally elevated to the College of Cardinals by Pope Paul VI. Cardinal Cody readily accepted the power and the glory and the challenge. He reformed the seminary system in Chicago, separating the college philosophy program from the theology school. He established a deacon program, instituted a pension plan for priests, and developed a so-called twin-ning program, whereby wealthier parishes directly assisted poor inner-city parishes. In 1975 he formed the Catholic Television Network. Moreover, he continued to be an outspoken critic of racism. In a pastoral letter to every parish in the archdiocese, he categorically stated that discrimination against minorities in any Catholic institution "must be rooted out." But Cardinal Cody encountered the anger of many blacks when in 1965 he asked Martin Luther King, Jr., not to march for open housing in all-white neighborhoods on the West and South sides of Chicago. Cardinal Cody feared, rightly as it turned out, that such marches would only exacerbate the inflammatory mood in that racially divided city. As a consequence, his reputation among liberals, both Catholic and non-Catholic alike, suffered. He was pained by the criticism, which he considered unfair in light of his courageous actions in New Orleans on behalf of racial justice.

Cardinal Cody's relations with the priests of the diocese were never good and only worsened with time. In 1971 the Association of Chicago Priests, an ad hoc group, voted by a slim margin to censure him because it felt he had not adequately represented their concerns at a meeting of the American bishops in Detroit that year. The cardinal became more obstinate and was criticized for not exercising his authority in the collegial spirit that had been encouraged by the Second Vatican Council.

In 1975 Cody's health began to deteriorate. The confrontations within the archdiocese were beginning to take a toll on him; a large and robust man, he lost a great amount of weight and became haggard and gaunt. Over the following years he was hospitalized several times. In a 1981 interview he reflected, "I did my duty and tried to make the most people happy. None of us is perfect. No one can solve all the problems."

On 10 September 1981 the *Chicago Sun-Times* ran a story about the cardinal's financial practices. It reported that the U.S. attorney's office in Chicago was investigating allegations that the cardinal had diverted $1 million in church funds to his stepcousin, Helen Dolan Wilson of St. Louis. The cardinal denied the charges and refused to answer subpoenas for his personal financial records. He felt there was a conspiracy against him engineered by some of his own priests to force him to resign or be dismissed by the Vatican. Thereafter, his health deteriorated rapidly and he entered the hospital. He insisted, however, on being released to celebrate mass on Christmas Eve on 24 December 1981 at Holy Name Cathedral. He said it was his "last hurrah." He was rehospitalized within days and died four months later of heart failure. He was buried in Queen of Heaven Mausoleum in Hillside, Illinois.

John Patrick Cardinal Cody was a consummate administrator and organizer. He was a noted fund-raiser who gave generously to the Vatican; he was a devoted churchman.

He enjoyed power and centralized it in himself. He was unprepared for the maelstrom that was American society in the 1960s and 1970s. Had he been born a generation earlier he no doubt would have been heralded as a great churchman in the tradition of an earlier predecessor, George Cardinal Mundelein, and beloved as well. But fortune's timing was neither propitious nor kind. Cardinal Cody died a broken, isolated, bewildered man.

★

The personal papers of Cardinal Cody are in the Archdiocesan Archives, St. Mary of the Lake Seminary, Mundelein, Illinois. For a rather unflattering portrait of Cody and his tenure in Chicago, see Charles W. Dahm, *Power and Authority in the Catholic Church: Cardinal Cody in Chicago* (1981). There are obituaries in the *New York Times* and the *Chicago Tribune* (both 26 Apr. 1982).

GEOFFREY GNEUHS

COHEN, Benjamin Victor (*b.* 23 September 1894 in Muncie, Indiana; *d.* 16 August 1983 in Washington, D.C.), lawyer and government official best known for drafting New Deal legislation enacted during the administration of President Franklin D. Roosevelt.

Cohen's parents, Moses Cohen and Sarah Ringold, were Jewish immigrants (from Poland and Lithuania, respectively), and Benjamin and his four siblings grew up in comfortable middle-class surroundings made possible by their father's successful scrap-iron business. He attended public schools in Muncie and later in Chicago, excelling in his studies and gaining entrance to the University of Chicago in 1910. He earned a Ph.B. degree in 1914 and, after achieving the highest marks ever recorded in the university's law school, was awarded a doctorate in jurisprudence in 1915. A year later, after graduate study at Harvard Law School with Felix Frankfurter, he became secretary to Federal Circuit Court judge Julian Mack, and through the handling of receivership cases learned much about the intricacies of corporate organization. In 1917 his weak eyes kept him out of military service, but he served the war government as an attorney for the U.S. Shipping Board (1917–1919). As counsel to the American Zionist Organization (1919–1921) he participated in the postwar peace negotiations concerning a British mandate in Palestine.

From 1922 to 1933 Cohen was in private practice in New York City, where he became "a lawyer's lawyer" whose work consisted chiefly of counseling other lawyers on litigation concerning corporate reorganization. In his own words, he also made a "great deal of money" in the stock market while losing only "some" of it. Politically he remained a "progressive," interested particularly in using the law to humanize the free enterprise system. He helped to organize a bank for New York clothing workers, and as unpaid counsel for the National Consumers League he wrote a model minimum-wage law for the state of New York.

Cohen entered the New Deal in April 1933, when Frankfurter brought him together with James Landis and

Benjamin Cohen, 1942. AP/WIDE WORLD PHOTOS

Thomas G. Corcoran to write a securities reform measure. Their handiwork became the Truth in Securities Act of 1933, and, more important, gave birth to the legendary team of Corcoran and Cohen, which from 1934 through 1938 functioned as the New Deal's unofficial legal firm, engaged not only in drafting major laws but also in lobbying them through, defending them in the courts, and influencing their administration. In their personalities the two men, both bachelors, were almost diametric opposites. But they lived and worked together harmoniously, with Corcoran's effervescence and gregariousness seemingly complementing Cohen's shyness and intellectuality, and as a team their performance earned them continuing assignments from the White House and a degree of notoriety as the "Brain Twins," the "Gold Dust Twins" (from the soap slogan "Let the Gold Dust Twins Do Your Work"), and the "Little Hot Dogs" (from their connection with Frankfurter).

Officially, Cohen was associate counsel to the Public Works Administration (1933–1934) and general counsel to the National Power Policy Committee (1934–1941). Unofficially, he acted as counsel to an array of New Deal lawyers and officials, who formed the habit of "talking it over with Ben," and he was known among them particularly for the artistry and brilliance that went into drafting such laws as the Securities Exchange Act of 1934, the Public Utility Holding Company Act of 1935, and the Fair Labor Standards Act of 1938; the ingenious litigation strategy that resulted in the Supreme Court's validation of the utilities law; and the imaginativeness demonstrated in fashioning such agencies as the Federal Housing Administration and the Electric Farm and Home Authority. In addition, he took some part, usually behind the scenes, as a draftsman of speeches, memoranda, and legislative proposals in the larger policy debates of the New Deal, siding in these with the "Brandeisians" and "Keynesians" against the "planners" and "budget-balancers."

As World War II approached, Cohen became an advocate of intervention. In 1940 he helped to find the legal basis for the destroyers-for-bases deal that sent fifty American destroyers to the British Royal Navy in exchange for bases. In 1941 he served briefly as counsel to the American Embassy in London, helping to implement the Lend-Lease Act. Subsequently, James F. Byrnes tapped him to serve as his assistant in the Office of Economic Stabilization (1942–1943) and as general counsel to the Office of War Mobilization (1943–1945). In 1944 Cohen was also a legal adviser to the Bretton Woods monetary conference and a delegate to the Dumbarton Oaks conference. He had hopes of becoming counsel to the State Department. Roosevelt disappointed him, however, and it was not until 1945, after Truman became president and Byrnes secretary of state, that Cohen got the position. Over the next two years he became

a regular participant in the postwar peace negotiations. He traveled with Byrnes to the international conferences in Potsdam, London, Moscow, and Paris, was dismayed by the worsening relations between the United States and the Soviet Union, and came to place most of his hopes for a lasting world peace with the newly formed United Nations. From 1948 to 1952 he was a member of the U.S. delegation to the UN General Assembly; in 1952 he served as the U.S. representative on the UN Disarmament Commission; and following his retirement from public service he continued to work for greater reliance on the UN. In 1961 he devoted his Oliver Wendell Holmes lectures at Harvard University to the organization's constitutional development and future possibilities and later was among those urging that the Vietnam issue be taken to it. In later years Cohen lived in a Dupont Circle apartment. He died of pneumonia and was buried in Muncie, Indiana.

In appearance Cohen was an unprepossessing figure, tall but habitually slouched, ill at ease, sad-faced, and careless of dress. He was also awkward and unlucky in his relationships with women and, despite several "loves," never married. Yet for those who came to know and admire his intellectual capacities, kindly gentleness, and enduring public spiritedness, he was a great and good man who was never properly rewarded for his accomplishments. In 1977 he recalled the New Deal years as being the "best years" of his life. Clearly he ranks among the major craftsmen of the New Deal's legislative legacy. Without his input the changes made in American governance would have differed, in some ways substantially.

★

The Cohen Papers are at the Library of Congress. Other manuscript collections containing relevant unpublished materials are the National Power Policy Committee Records at the National Archives, the Franklin D. Roosevelt Papers at the Roosevelt Presidential Library, and the Harold Ickes and Thomas Corcoran Papers at the Library of Congress. The fullest biographical account is in Joseph P. Lash, *Dealers and Dreamers: A New Look at the New Deal* (1988), but also helping to illuminate various aspects of Cohen's career are Joseph Alsop and Robert Kintner, *Men Around the President* (1939); Michael E. Parrish, *Securities Regulation and the New Deal* (1970); Philip J. Funigiello, *Toward a National Power Policy: The New Deal and the Electric Utility Industry, 1933–1941* (1973); and the memoirs in Katie Louchheim, ed., *The Making of the New Deal: The Insiders Speak* (1983). The most useful articles in periodicals and yearbooks are "'Twins': New Deal's Legislative Architects: Corcoran and Cohen," *Newsweek* (13 July 1935); Felix Belair, Jr., "Two of the 'Selfless Six,'" *Nation's Business* (July 1937); Blair Bolles, "Cohen and Corcoran: Brain Twins," *American Mercury* (Jan. 1938); Maxine Bloch, ed., *Current Biography 1941* (1942); "Men Around Byrnes," *Newsweek* (23 July 1945); John H. Crider, "Liaison Man for a 'Big-Three' Team," *New York Times Magazine* (12 Aug. 1945); and "Key Role of Benjamin Cohen in Shaping U.S. Foreign Policy," *U.S. News* (18 July 1947). An obituary is in the *New York Times* (17 Aug. 1983). Joseph P. Lash, "Ben Cohen, 'A Good Man,' " *New York Times* (5 Sept. 1983), is a moving tribute written shortly after Cohen's death.

ELLIS W. HAWLEY

COHEN, N(ehemiah) M(yer) (*b.* 10 September 1890 in Jerusalem, Palestine; *d.* 6 June 1984 in Washington, D.C.), pioneer in the American supermarket industry and founder of Giant Food, whose concept of self-service grocery shopping and lower food prices helped revolutionize the retail food business.

Named for the ancient Hebrew prophet, Cohen was the son of Joseph Cohen, a biblical scholar. His mother worked in the family butcher shop. He attended the Jerusalem Yeshiva and was ordained a rabbi at age seventeen. As a teacher in the elementary school of the small Mediterranean village of Rishon Le-Zion, he took great interest in the welfare of his community and the potential benefits of introducing new methods of scientific farming. In 1908 Cohen married Naomi Halperin; they had three children. While their two sons were still young, he traveled to England in 1914 to study new agricultural techniques.

The outbreak of World War I interrupted Cohen's education and his family life. Unable to return to Palestine (the Ottoman Empire, which controlled Palestine, was at war with the British), he traveled to the United States to continue his studies. Arriving in America in 1915, Cohen settled in Carnegie, Pennsylvania, where he earned his living as a rabbi, teacher, and *schochet,* a butcher skilled in preparing meat according to strict Jewish dietary laws. He soon opened his own kosher meat market in Carnegie and saved enough to bring his family to the United States after a seven-year separation. The family settled in Lancaster, Pennsylvania.

As in many immigrant families, children and parents worked in the shop, which was successful enough to spur the opening of two more stores in the area. Cohen's shops were thriving as the first supermarkets appeared in the eastern United States, offering customers a wider selection of products at dramatically lower prices by operating on a cash-only basis with high sales volume. The promise of the new industry appealed to Cohen, and in the midst of the Great Depression of the early 1930s, he sought the financial backing of Harrisburg, Pennsylvania, wholesale food distributor Jac Lehrman to open a supermarket. Given the economics of the time, the partners sought a city fueled by a substantial government payroll, and ultimately chose Washington, D.C., as the site of their new venture. On 6 February 1936, during one of the worst blizzards in the history of the city, Cohen and Lehrman opened Washington's first supermarket at 3509 Georgia Avenue, N.W. Within one year Giant Food had lowered area food prices by a staggering 35 percent. The second Giant Food store opened in December 1937; by the late 1950s Giant Food boasted a chain of over forty stores.

The heart of Giant's success was the personal philosophy of its founder. Cohen, most frequently called by his initials N.M., quickly became known for his meticulous attention to detail and to the needs of his customers. Every display needed to be perfect and every piece of fruit flawless. Giant Food customers came to count on a wide variety of quality food at the lowest possible prices, and friendly, pleasant service from employees who gave the company their loyalty in exchange for excellent salaries and benefits, profit-sharing plans, and genuine caring. Cohen was a shrewd businessman, a quiet and compassionate employer

N. M. Cohen with his sons, Manny and Izzy, and his daughter, Lillian, 1953. GIANT FOOD, INC.

with an uncanny, storekeeper's instinct that guided Giant Food through a steady growth period before and during World War II. Cohen became president of Giant Food in 1948, and under his leadership the company opened scores of stores in the growing Maryland and Virginia suburbs.

A staunch supporter of the state of Israel from its founding in 1948, Cohen was a regular visitor to his native Jerusalem. Because of his early rabbinical training he was fond of quoting biblical injunctions about the accuracy of a merchant's weights and measures and the need to deal ethically with all his customers. Cohen believed that Giant had an obligation to repay the region it served. In 1967 the Washington chapter of the Society for the Advancement of Management awarded Cohen its prestigious Management Achievement Award. The citation stated that "when businesses were failing across the nation, you had the courage and vision to come to the Washington area with a little-tried concept of the time. . . . Your faith in the principle of mass merchandising of foods at a low markup was more than vindicated by the success of your company."

However, Giant Food was not without its internal drama. In 1964, in a widely publicized struggle between Jac Lehrman and the Cohen family for control of the company, Cohen was elected to the newly created post of chairman of the board and general manager; Joseph B. Danzansky, outside general counsel for twenty years, succeeded Cohen as president. The Cohens gained operating control of Giant, and Lehrman retained a seat on the board of directors. In 1977 the reins of power were passed to Cohen's younger son, Israel ("Izzy"); Cohen was given the post of honorary chairman, which he retained until his death. By 1996 Giant Food employed 25,600 people, posted sales of $3.9 billion, and operated 169 stores serving over 3 million customers a week in Virginia, Maryland, Delaware, New Jersey, and the District of Columbia. Cohen died at Georgetown University Hospital four days after sustaining serious injuries in an automobile crash near his Washington home. He was buried in Adas Israel Cemetery in Washington, D.C.

An outstanding business executive in the classic American tradition, Cohen was the living embodiment of customer service, employee dedication, unshakable civic commitment, and, above all, devotion to product quality and customer service. By taking a high-risk business leap in the midst of the Great Depression, he opened a new chapter in American food merchandising.

★

Scott Sedar and Bari Sedar, *Fifty Years of Caring* (1986), was published by Giant Food's Office of Public Affairs on the company's fiftieth anniversary; and the Public Affairs Office of Giant Food issued *WE News Special Edition: Izzy* (1995). An obituary is in the *Washington Post* (6 June 1984).

RACHEL SNYDER

COLE, William Randolph ("Cozy") (*b.* 17 October 1909 in East Orange, New Jersey; *d.* 29 January 1981 in Columbus, Ohio), jazz drummer of the swing era.

Cole was the son of Reuben Cole and Carrie Johnson. Like two brothers who became professional piano players, he was attracted to music at an early age. He made his own drumsticks in a manual arts class and took private lessons. He received his nickname from chums on his school football team who called him "Colesy." While attending Wilberforce University in Columbus, Ohio (1927–1930), he began to perform professionally, playing briefly with the Wilbur Sweatman Orchestra and then leading his own band. Influenced by the drummer Sonny Greer of Duke Ellington's orchestra, Cole made his first recordings with Jelly Roll Morton's Red Hot Peppers in 1930, being featured on "Load of Cole." He joined vocalist Blanche Calloway and her Joy Boys in 1931, moving on to the Benny Carter Orchestra intermittently during 1933 and 1934.

By the time Cole became drummer for the swinging big band of Willie Bryant in 1935, he had established a reputation within the New York City jazz community for his light, driving rhythmic quality and showmanship. In demand for small pickup jazz recording groups on instrumental sessions and backing vocalists, Cole played drums for most of the groups led by pianist Teddy Wilson that accompanied jazz singer Billie Holiday between July 1935 and January 1939, the peak period of Holiday's creativity. He did the same on several records backing Mildred Bailey. His major instrumental group recordings were with vibraphonist Lionel Hampton (1937–1939) and assorted groups in 1944. He provided the rhythmic foundation for small recording bands led by trumpeters Henry "Red" Allen, Bunny Berigan, Frankie Newton, and Wingy Manone; saxophonist Chu Berry; guitarist Dick McDonough; and pianist Putney Dandridge.

Cole's excellence as a small band drummer made him a leading figure of New York's Fifty-second Street ("Swing Street") jazz scene after he joined the sextet led by violinist Stuff Smith at the Onyx Club early in 1936. The virtuosity of Smith, Cole, and trumpeter Jonah Jones was captured on their recordings as Stuff Smith and his Onyx Club Boys. He switched back to the big band format, playing drums for Cab Calloway's orchestra from November 1938 to August 1942. Cole's propulsive rhythm helped the Calloway band achieve the pinnacle of its musical success at the Cotton Club in Harlem, on the road, and on recordings, three of which featured Cole.

Cole moved in 1943 to the CBS radio band of Raymond Scott, who convinced him to take classes at the Juilliard School of Music studying timpani, drums, piano, and music theory. At nights he led his own trio at the new Onyx Club, where it also accompanied Billie Holiday. In 1943 Cole became perhaps the first black jazz musician to appear

"Cozy" Cole playing in a New York City nightclub, *c.* 1960. ROGER WOOD/© CORBIS

on stage, acting and playing in the Broadway musical *Carmen Jones* (he was on the 1954 soundtrack of the movie version as well). In the same period he appeared in the musical *The Seven Lively Arts* as a member of the Benny Goodman Quintet (1944–1945). With Goodman's quartet he also performed in the animated film *Make Mine Music* (1945). He freelanced in studio work and led small groups, including a *Drumboogie Revue* with dancers, until he joined Louis Armstrong's All Stars in 1949. In addition to two tours of Europe, the group appeared in the 1953 motion picture *The Glenn Miller Story,* in which Cozy performed a drum duet with Gene Krupa. On 18 July 1951 he married Evalena Kiggins; they had no children.

In 1953 Cole and Krupa began a twenty-year association operating a drum school in New York. Cole concurrently played gigs at the Metropole, appeared on Arthur Godfrey's radio show and several popular television variety programs, and, in 1957, toured Europe with Earl Hines and Jack Teagarden. In 1958 he made a two-sided single 45-rpm record of "Topsy," a riff and extended solo that—unusual for a jazz sideman and drummer—became a commercial hit. This resulted in leading his own quintet on tours that included Africa (1962–1963). From 1969 to 1976 he played and recorded with the Jonah Jones Quintet, after which he retired to Capital University in Columbus, Ohio, as artist in residence and to study arranging and harmony; he re-

mained there until his death, from cancer. An exciting, personable musician, Cole was admired by his peers also for his ability to play most styles of jazz, including bebop sessions with Charlie Parker.

★

Details of Cole's career may be found in standard reference works and discographies on jazz, some of which, however, incorrectly list him with the Fletcher Henderson Orchestra in 1937 and as performing on the 1951 motion picture soundtrack of *The Strip.* No published works have dealt primarily with Cole, although he is admired in several jazz histories, among them Arnold Shaw, *The Street That Never Slept* (1971); Barney Bigard, *With Louis and the Duke* (1985); and Gunther Schuller, *The Swing Era* (1989). His 1944 small-group recordings for Keynote and Savoy records have been issued as the CD "Cozy Cole 1944" (Classics 819). Cole's other work may be heard on many LPs and CDs of the artists for the appropriate years discussed above. "Topsy" was issued on the Love label. In addition to the films mentioned in the text, Cole appeared in a television production, "After Hours" (1961), with Coleman Hawkins and Roy Eldridge, and in "Cozy's Drums," part of a French film collection, *L'Aventure du jazz* (1970). An obituary is in the *New York Times* (31 Jan. 1981).

CLARK G. REYNOLDS

COLLINGWOOD, Charles Cummings (*b.* 4 June 1917 in Three Rivers, Michigan; *d.* 3 October 1985 in New York

171

City), pioneer radio and television journalist whose eye-witness reports emanated from locations all around the world and whose influential career spanned more than four decades.

Charles Collingwood was the oldest of six children of George Harris Collingwood, a forestry expert, and Jean Grinnell Cummings. His father's work apparently moved the family often. In 1934 Collingwood graduated from Central High School in Washington, D.C., and earned a three-year scholarship to attend Deep Springs School, a ranch school near Death Valley, California. He left Deep Springs in 1937 to complete his studies at Cornell University, where he majored in law and philosophy and graduated cum laude with an A.B. in 1939.

Collingwood's prowess as an athlete helped him win a Rhodes scholarship to study at New College at the University of Oxford. En route to Oxford in 1939, he journeyed to Geneva, Switzerland, on a summer fellowship. While Collingwood was there, the American consul advised him to contact Wally Carroll, a United Press employee, when he reached London. In September 1939 Collingwood began part-time work as a local correspondent for the United

Charles Collingwood. ARCHIVE PHOTOS

Press while he studied at New College. During school break, he worked in Amsterdam until the German occupation. When the Rhodes committee became aware of his press work, the members pressured him to choose between being a student or a journalist. He wrote to his family in May 1940 that the war had altered his priorities: "I am finding it harder and harder to care about medieval law with Armageddon coming closer and closer."

Collingwood chose to leave Oxford in June 1940 for full-time employment in London as a reporter for the United Press. In March 1941, Edward R. Murrow, who was assembling his legendary team of reporters to cover the European crisis for CBS news, convinced Collingwood to leave United Press for the CBS London bureau. Murrow reportedly at first hesitated to hire Collingwood because of his appearance as a fashionable dandy. Collingwood was a first-generation member of "the Murrow Boys," which included Eric Sevareid, William L. Shirer, Howard K. Smith, and other future luminaries of broadcast journalism. While working in London for CBS in 1941, Collingwood led the correspondents to a baseball victory over the Marine Corps baseball team. Known for his competitiveness, he raced to be the first to get a story to the wire.

Accompanying British troops on their triumphant drive across North Africa, Collingwood produced 2.5-minute broadcasts twice daily for the CBS radio network. He was the first to report from there the details of the assassination of Admiral Jean-Louis-Xavier-François Darlan on Christmas Eve 1942. Collingwood received the Headliners Award in 1942 and again in 1948. In February 1943, an article in *Newsweek* said of Collingwood: "Only 25 years old, the husky, blond-haired reporter now holds the top spot among radio reporters. He teams news sense with a natural radio voice . . . which many mistake for that of a man of 40. . . . Newspapers in both America and Britain have quoted him increasingly." In 1943 Collingwood won the George Foster Peabody Award for the best foreign news reporting. The citation said that he, "with the tools of inference, indignation, and fact, has conveyed to us through the screen of censorship an understanding of the troublesome situation in North Africa." In June 1944, he covered the D-day invasion in Normandy.

After the war, in May 1946, Collingwood married Louise Allbritton, an actress; she died in 1979. He returned to the United States in 1946 to serve as the first CBS news United Nations correspondent, and from 1948 to 1952, during the second administration of Harry S. Truman, he was White House correspondent. Taking a two-year leave in 1951 and 1952, he served as a special assistant to Averell Harriman, director of the Mutual Security Agency in Washington, D.C.

Collingwood easily made the transition to television. During the 1950s, as a radio and television reporter and commentator, he covered political conventions and read daily news segments on the *CBS Morning Show.* In 1954 he received the Alexander Hadden Medal for "promoting world understanding," and in 1957 the English Speaking Union presented him the Better Understanding Award. Collingwood became the first CBS London bureau chief in 1957 and, in 1959, followed Murrow as host of the *Person to Person* series.

On 14 February 1962 Collingwood produced a special, *A Tour of the White House with Mrs. John F. Kennedy.* Strolling through the public rooms of the presidential mansion and commenting on items of historical significance, Collingwood and the first lady drew an audience of 80 million viewers, and the program won a Peabody Award in 1963.

In 1962 Walter Cronkite became anchorman of CBS News, replacing Douglas Edwards, and Collingwood acted as Cronkite's second, along with Harry Reasoner, until the summer of 1963. During the CBS live, continuous coverage of the assassination of President John F. Kennedy on 22 November 1963, Collingwood anchored while Cronkite took a break.

From 1964 to 1975 Collingwood was the chief foreign correspondent for CBS. On 1 April 1964, he aired a show called "Vietnam: The Deadly Decision," looking at the escalating U.S. role in the war in Southeast Asia. As foreign correspondent, he covered Winston Churchill's funeral and Pope Paul VI's trip to the United States in 1965. That year he traveled to Vietnam on a special assignment, and between 1965 and 1969 he won journalism awards for the annual *Vietnam Perspective* television broadcasts. Assigned to report on the conflicts in the Middle East, he covered the 1967 Arab-Israeli war.

Collingwood applied for permission to travel to North Vietnam, but that country denied him for three consecutive years. Finally, in March 1968, the North Vietnamese government in Hanoi granted him a visa, and he became the first U.S. network correspondent to enter North Vietnam. Collingwood told his network audience, "It's my strong impression that my entry application was accepted because Hanoi wanted to make a move and decided to make it through CBS News and me." However, his trip was viewed with some disapproval by the administration of President Lyndon B. Johnson.

Reaching Hanoi in April, Collingwood immediately experienced six air-raid alerts. Nevertheless, he did not take cover in bomb shelters, explaining, "Look, you may not have any confidence in U.S. assurances that it will not hit population centers, but I do." The North Vietnamese assigned a French freelance cameraman, who had shot films favorable to the North Vietnamese, to work with Collingwood. He was taken to sites that had been bombed by the United States and shown survivors. Although he was not allowed to tour military sites, he moved freely about the country with its leaders, including Premier Pham Van Dong, and reported that they were "very courteous." On the last night of his eight-day visit to the country, Collingwood attended a banquet of, in his words, "a number of dishes, two of which were dog, which is a delicacy in North and South Vietnam." Drawing from his Vietnam experiences, he wrote *The Defector* (1970), a novel about CIA intrigue replete with descriptions and references to places he had experienced.

During the 1970s Collingwood was host-narrator of CBS series, including *Eyewitness, Chronicle,* and *Adventure.* In 1970 and 1971 he moderated the news in review productions at the end of the year. Broadcasting as anchorman and correspondent from Vietnam in late 1972 and early 1973, he filmed several documentaries, such as *Charles Collingwood's Report from Hanoi* and *Hanoi: A Report by Charles Collingwood.* He was the New York anchor for CBS coverage of President Richard Nixon's trip to China in 1972, and the following year he covered Princess Anne's marriage in England. Queen Elizabeth II made him an honorary commander of the British Empire in 1975 for his efforts toward British-American understanding.

Though Collingwood officially retired from CBS news on 30 June 1982, he held the title of special correspondent for the rest of his life. In June 1984, he married Tatiana Angelini Jolin, a Swedish singer; the marriage brought him two stepdaughters. Cornell University awarded him an honorary degree the same year. He received several awards from the Overseas Press Club and was decorated as a chevalier of the French Legion of Honor. A resident of Manhattan, he was a member of the Association of Radio News Analysts, the National Press Club, the Century Association, the Beefsteak and Garrick clubs in London, and the English Speaking Union. His hobbies included both modern and primitive art and archaeology. A fastidious dresser, he was frequently described as flamboyant, "Bonnie Prince Charlie," debonair, and a bon vivant. Upon her return from a United Service Organizations trip to Africa in 1943, the actress Kay Francis remarked that Collingwood was "the only man in Africa who knows where to get a suit pressed." He believed that "a well-rounded journalist should also be able to comport himself with savior faire in a drawing room or art gallery."

In late 1984 Collingwood underwent surgery for colon cancer. He died from cancer in Lenox Hill Hospital in Manhattan. He was cremated, and the ashes of the man who had spent his entire life traveling were scattered to the wind. A tombstone in the Jolin family grave in Stockholm, Sweden, bears his name.

Charles Collingwood's media world valued quality, content, and timeliness over ratings, visual impact, sound bites, or show business. His legacy is the yardstick of quality when contemporary broadcast journalists are assessed.

Cronkite commended his work with the broadcaster's union, the American Federation of Television and Radio Artists (AFTRA), during the blacklisting era, saying, "I think that almost as much as perhaps Ed Murrow's famed exposure of [Senator Joseph] McCarthy, Collingwood's leadership of AFTRA at that critical time was an important factor in breaking down and ending that terrible period." Charles Kuralt described Collingwood as "generous to others and he envied nobody. He was kind and helpful to all beneath him and to me when I was young and learning." Sidney Offit, curator of the George Polk Awards and broadcast commentator, called him "an authentic American, an elegant gentleman, one of the last of the television news commentators who had a profound sense of history and of the continuity of world events."

★

Collingwood's papers are in the Wisconsin State Historical Society Mass Communications Collection. He described his trip to North Vietnam in "Mission to Hanoi," *Time* (19 Apr. 1968). *Current Biography 1943* (1944) provides descriptions of Collingwood as a young man and is peppered with anecdotes. Stanley Cloud and Lynne Olson, *The Murrow Boys: Pioneers on the Front Lines of Broadcast Journalism* (1996), records their relationships and captures the essence of World War II broadcast reporting; see especially chapter 9, "Bonnie Prince Charlie." David Halberstam, *The Powers That Be* (1979), contains several references to Collingwood. Discussions of his early career are "Collingwood's Beats," *Newsweek* (1 Feb. 1943); "Charles Collingwood," *Time* (5 Apr. 1943); and Judy Dupuy, "Heard and Overheard: U.S. War Attitude Amazes Returning CBS Reporter," *PM* (18 Oct. 1943). See also Gene Ruffini, "Loving Farewell for Collingwood," *New York Post* (10 Oct. 1985). Obituaries are in the *New York Times* and *Washington Post* (both 4 Oct. 1985).

DONALD ALLPORT BIRD

COOGAN, John Leslie, Jr. ("Jackie") (*b.* 26 October 1914 in Los Angeles, California; *d.* 1 March 1984 in Santa Monica, California), actor best known as child star of silent films, who achieved fame as the title character in Charlie Chaplin's film *The Kid* (1921).

Coogan's parents were vaudeville performers. His father, John Coogan, Sr., originally of Syracuse, New York, was an actor and dancer, and his mother, Lillian Dolliver Coogan, from San Francisco, was a singer, who herself had been a child star billed as "Baby Lillian." Jackie had a younger brother, Robert.

As a young boy, Coogan appeared occasionally in his parents' stage acts and was discovered by Chaplin during a performance in Los Angeles in 1919. Chaplin cast Jackie in a short film, *A Day's Pleasure,* and then used the five-year-old in his first feature-length film, *The Kid,* made dur-

Jackie Coogan as a child actor. ARCHIVE PHOTOS

ing 1920. Coogan played an abandoned waif adopted by Chaplin's character, the tramp. The film was a huge success, and much of the credit was given to Coogan, memorable in an oversized cap and a Dutch bob haircut. "It is almost impossible to refrain from superlatives in referring to this child," wrote *Variety.* "In the title role his acting is so smooth as to give him equal honors with the star."

Over the next six years, Coogan capitalized on this success with a string of star vehicles—mainly reprising his lovable ragamuffin role—produced under the supervision of his father. The first six of these were produced by Sol Lesser for First National: *Peck's Bad Boy* in 1921; *Oliver Twist* (with Lon Chaney as Fagin), *My Boy,* and *Trouble* (with Wallace Beery as costar) in 1922; and *Daddy* and *Circus Days* in 1923. Coogan then signed a much-publicized contract with Metro Pictures (soon to become part of Metro-Goldwyn-Mayer, or MGM), which called for a $500,000 signing bonus—one of the largest salaries in Hollywood—and a percentage of the profits. At Metro/MGM, Coogan starred in *Long Live the King, Little Robinson Crusoe, A Boy of Flanders, The Rag Man,* and *Old Clothes* (which also starred the young Joan Crawford) from 1923 to 1925. As his adolescence approached, Coogan's popularity waned, and *Johnny Get Your Hair Cut* (1927), in which Coogan's emblematic bob was shorn, was the culmination of his career as a child star.

His popularity through the early 1920s made Coogan one of the highest-paid performers in Hollywood. Estimates of his earnings, from films and merchandising, vary from $2 million to $17 million. As Hollywood's reigning child star, Coogan toured the country and the world, meeting celebrities and heads of state and attracting widespread publicity. (His brother also appeared in several movies as a child star in the early 1930s.)

Coogan made the first of a lifelong series of comeback attempts with *Tom Sawyer* (1930) and *Huckleberry Finn* (1931), but these films marked the end of his career as a star. He attended Santa Clara College and the University of Southern California in the mid-1930s but did not receive a degree.

A sharp turning point in his life came in May 1935, when Coogan's father was killed in an automobile accident near San Diego, in which Coogan was also injured. His mother was subsequently married to the Coogan business manager, Arthur Bernstein. When Jackie turned twenty-one, his mother declared that none of the Coogan assets would be given to him, an action that was widely condemned. Coogan filed suit on 11 April 1938, but by the time the case was settled in 1939, the assets of Coogan Productions, Inc., had dwindled to less than $300,000, of which sum Jackie received less than half. The case inspired the California law known as the Coogan Act, which established court supervision over the earnings of child actors and required that 50 percent be put in trust.

Coogan was married to his first wife, the actress Betty Grable on 20 December 1937. He appeared in several films with her, including *College Swing* (1938) and *Million Dollar Legs* (1939). Coogan and Grable were separated in 1939 and divorced on 11 November 1940. Coogan's money troubles were widely cited as the reason. Inducted into the army in March 1941, he was trained as a glider pilot and graduated from the Army Air Forces Gliding School at Victorville, California, as a flight officer in January 1943. On 18 March 1944 he was among the first to fly British troops behind the Japanese lines in Burma.

Coogan married Flower Parry, an actress, on 10 August 1941, while he was in the service; they had a son and were divorced in 1943. His third wife was the singer Ann McCormack. They were married on 26 December 1946 and had a daughter. Coogan and McCormack were divorced 14 September 1950. His fourth and last wife was the dancer Dorothea (Dodie) Lanphere; they were married in Mexico in April 1952 and had two children.

After World War II, Coogan worked in various entertainment fields; he performed in a nightclub spoof of *The Kid* and appeared on Broadway in *Brother Rat*. His first television appearance was on *Pantomime Quiz* in the late 1940s. Through the 1970s, he appeared in dozens of television programs, winning an Emmy Award nomination in 1956 for a *Playhouse 90* appearance. He played the grotesque Uncle Fester in *The Addams Family*, a role he disliked, for two seasons in 1964 and 1965. He also appeared in nearly twenty films between 1947 and 1975, notably *The Joker Is Wild* (1957) and *Lonelyhearts* (1958).

In the early 1960s, Coogan was arrested several times on alcohol and drug charges; his brother was also arrested for narcotics possession in 1962. In his later years, Coogan lived in Palm Springs. He was an active sportsman, playing golf and going on hunting trips.

Coogan died after a heart attack at the Santa Monica Hospital. He had been hospitalized for two months prior to his death, after suffering for a number of years with heart and kidney ailments. He is buried in the Chapel of the Holy Cross Cemetery, Culver City, California.

Jackie Coogan led a peculiarly double life. He spent his childhood in the halcyon days of early Hollywood, making his family wealthy with the fruits of his phenomenal popularity. As he grew, he lost his boyish charm and the fortune built on his labors as a child. Had it been properly maintained, he could have retired at the age of thirteen. Instead, he spent the rest of his often difficult life as an entertainer in small, usually unflattering roles. Posterity will remember the two faces of Jackie Coogan: the adorable scamp with soulful eyes of *The Kid*, and the fat, bald, squeaky-voiced Uncle Fester of *The Addams Family*.

★

Norman J. Zierold devotes the first chapter of *The Child Stars* (1965) to Coogan, dwelling mostly on the 1938 lawsuit over Jackie's earnings. Chaplin recounts his discovery of Coogan in Charles Chaplin, *My Autobiography* (1964). "The Marvellous Boy of the Movies: Some Remarks on the Discovery of Jack Coogan, and the Picture Built Around Him," *Vanity Fair* (Jan. 1921), is Chaplin's contemporary account upon the release of *The Kid*. Of the two Betty Grable biographies, the superior is Spero Pastos, *Pin-Up: The Tragedy of Betty Grable* (1986), which devotes some attention to Coogan and Grable's marriage.

Coogan appeared regularly in fan magazines; notable is an entire issue of *Movie Weekly* devoted to him, the cover reading "Jackie Coogan Edits This Issue" (24 Mar. 1923).

An extensive interview with Coogan appeared in *Classic Film Collector* 52 (fall 1976): 6–9, although Coogan's memories are not always reliable. An article published during the run of *The Addams Family*, Arnold Hano, "The Kid Is Dead . . . Not Coogan: A Moving Account of the Career of that Bald Fellow Who Plays Uncle Fester," *TV Guide* (24 July 1965), remarks on some of the troubles Coogan suffered in the early 1960s. Aljean Harmetz, "Jackie Coogan—Remember?" *New York Times* (2 Apr. 1972), in addition to reviewing Coogan's film career, describes the active recreations of his later life. John Nangle, "Jackie Coogan 1914–1984," *Films in*

Review 35, no. 6 (June/July 1984): 347–352, is a sympathetic account of Coogan's life, emphasizing the ironies of his rise and fall. An obituary is in the *New York Times* (2 Mar. 1984).

Both the Museum of Modern Art, New York, and the New York Public Library at Lincoln Center have large clipping files on Coogan.

SAM STOLOFF

COOKE, Terence James (*b.* 1 March 1921 in New York City; *d.* 6 October 1983 in New York City), cardinal, bishop, and priest, whose fifteen-year tenure (1968–1983) as spiritual leader of metropolitan New York's then–1.8 million Roman Catholics was marked by traditionalism in theology, activism in social welfare programs, and dramatic changes in church governance.

Terence Cardinal Cooke was born into a poor, immigrant household, one of the three children of Michael Cooke, a

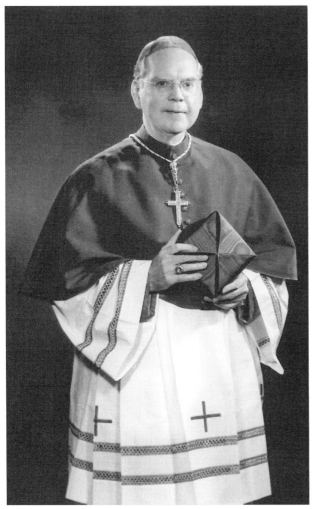

Terence Cardinal Cooke. COURTESY OF THE CARDINAL COOKE GUILD, CATHOLIC ARCHDIOCESE OF NEW YORK

sometime chauffeur and construction worker, and Margaret Gannon, a housewife, both from County Galway, Ireland. As the father's economic circumstances fluctuated, the family moved from La Salle Street in Upper Manhattan to the Throg's Neck section of the Bronx, and then up the Hudson River to suburban West Nyack, New York. After their mother's death in 1930, the three children were in the care of their maternal aunt, Mary Gannon, who moved into the Cooke household and, with their father, reinforced the deeply religious nature of their lives.

Despite his limited resources, the elder Cooke sent the three youngsters to parish schools run by the Benedictines and found additional money to provide Terence with violin lessons, thereby developing his lifelong love of music. (In later years, the cardinal, an unabashed opera buff, attended performances at the Metropolitan Opera as often as his schedule permitted.) He chose the priesthood while in elementary school and prepared for that role first at Cathedral High School and Cathedral College, both in Manhattan, and then at Saint Joseph's Seminary (known colloquially as Dunwoodie) in Yonkers, where he was a member of the string ensemble and (at slightly over six feet tall) a starting forward on the basketball team. He was ordained by Francis Cardinal Spellman on 1 December 1945 and, in the winter term, took course work in education, but no degree, at the University of Chicago. In the spring of 1946 he was sent as an assistant pastor to Saint Athanasius Church in the South Bronx, for the only time in his life serving full-time as a parish priest, and in 1947 was assigned to the chaplaincy at Saint Agatha's Home in Nanuet.

Cooke returned to formal studies later that year, earning an M.S. in social work in 1949 at Catholic University in Washington, D.C. For the next decade and a half, he accepted a broad range of administrative responsibilities within the New York archdiocese, which included Staten Island, Manhattan, the Bronx, and seven suburban counties north and west of the city. From 1949 to 1954 he was simultaneously assistant director of the Catholic Youth Organization, a director of youth activities and fund raising for Catholic Charities of New York, an assistant at Manhattan's Saint Jude Church, and a part-time instructor (through 1956) in the School of Social Service at Fordham University. In 1954 he returned to Dunwoodie as procurator (bursar), proving himself an able fiscal officer and deft manager.

In January 1957 he moved on to the Chancery Office of the archdiocese as personal secretary to Cardinal Spellman, the most powerful figure in the church's American hierarchy at that time. From May 1958 on, he lived in the cardinal's residence behind Saint Patrick's Cathedral and dined with the cardinal nearly every evening; they soon developed what Cooke himself called "a father-son relationship." Under Spellman's paternalistic eye, he began a rapid rise in status and authority. In 1958, now a monsignor, he was made a papal chamberlain and a vice-chancellor and given the special responsibility (which was his until 1968) of overseeing all building construction in the archdiocese. Named chancellor in 1961, he was made vicar general and consecrated as a bishop in 1965. When the archdiocese was reorganized in 1966 to promote administrative efficiency, Cooke, as auxiliary bishop of New York, was placed in charge of 175 city parishes in Manhattan and the Bronx, with the oversight of finances his principal concern. Obedient and discreet, he was, the historian of the archdiocese wrote, "the perfect number two man."

By then he had acquired a reputation among New York Catholics as one of "Spelly's boys," another of the many bishops throughout the country whose careers the conservative, autocratic cardinal had advanced, but who was unlikely to succeed him as head of the nation's oldest diocese because he lacked his mentor's political toughness and ecclesiastical flair. But Spellman, sometimes called "the American pope," had other ideas on the matter and, before his death in December 1967, made his preference known to Rome. On 8 March 1968 Pope Paul VI informed a thoroughly surprised Terence Cooke that he would be the seventh archbishop of New York.

His installation at Saint Patrick's Cathedral on 4 April 1968 took place just hours before Martin Luther King, Jr., was murdered in Memphis, Tennessee. The racial turmoil that followed King's death was but one of many social and political problems that Cooke would face during his pastorate. By the time he was elevated to the rank of cardinal on 28 April 1969, open challenges to institutional authority existed in every part of the United States. Opposition to the Vietnam War, some of it led by priests, had become increasingly violent. Also, both New York City and the archdiocese had entered a period of financial instability that bordered on insolvency, and nationally the church was faced with the resignation of a large number of priests and nuns over its clerical and social policies. In addition, there was the challenge of implementing the remarkable (some said radical) changes in liturgy and governance ordered by the Second Vatican Council in 1965 that sought to engage the laity more directly in worship and the work of the church. For the first time in the archdiocese's history, more Catholics lived in the suburbs than in the city and those who remained in the city were often poor. There were as well sharp doctrinal divisions concerning such matters as birth control and the ordination of women.

Unlike Spellman, Cooke did not meet these problems head-on. Never confrontational, he looked for local (rather than national) solutions within the established machinery of the archdiocese, working parish by parish to effect limited change. He restored the financial integrity of the archdiocese and granted his priests greater control in the management of their churches. Although he firmly upheld traditional Catholic teachings on sexual behavior, abortion, and a males-only priesthood, he welcomed the democratization of church ritual and encouraged an expanded role for the laity in church affairs. He supported the growth of ethnic parishes to reflect the changing face of New York's immigrant population by placing Spanish-speaking priests in inner-city neighborhoods and worked to extend the range of social services and welfare to the poor, especially by developing scholarship programs in parochial schools. But he never attempted to become, as Cardinal Spellman had been, a national and international voice for the church, and his influence rarely extended beyond the limits of the archdiocese. Not especially eloquent, he had no reputation as a theologian; his only book was a compilation of devotional readings, *Prayers for Today* (1971).

Within the archdiocese, Cardinal Cooke enjoyed great popularity once the initial skepticism about his ability to lead had passed. In contrast to his imperious predecessor, the blue-eyed, gray-haired prelate with the rimless glasses and a distinctive Bronx accent was everywhere perceived as mild-mannered and approachable. Following his death, Cooke was widely praised for his deep spirituality, priestly compassion, and personal courage.

Diagnosed with leukemia in 1973, the cardinal hid his illness for a decade, undergoing painful chemotherapy and blood transfusions in secret, his condition known only to his doctor and his personal confessor. Throughout those years, he kept to his established work schedule of eighteen-hour days, seven days a week, attending more than 200 board meetings a year. He died forty-one days after his illness was publicly announced. On 9 October 1984 his successor, John Cardinal O'Connor, at the urging of clergy and laity alike, formally initiated the complex and lengthy process of canonization that might one day lead to Cooke's designation as a saint. He is buried in St. Patrick's Cathedral.

★

The Terence Cardinal Cooke Archives are at Saint Joseph's Seminary in Yonkers, New York. Benedict J. Groeschel and Terrence L. Weber, *Thy Will Be Done: A Spiritual Portrait of Terence Cardinal Cooke* (1990), was prepared as one of the principal documents in the canonization process by a Capuchin friar (Groeschel), who was the cardinal's personal confessor, and by a Lutheran minister (Weber), the first archivist of the Cooke papers. Monsignor Florence D. Cohalan, *A Popular History of the Archdiocese of New York* (1983), gives the background to the Cooke years. Kenneth L. Woodward, *Making Saints: How the Catholic Church Determines Who Becomes a Saint, Who Doesn't, and Why* (1990), chapter 1, assesses the cardinal's effectiveness as leader of the archdiocese. Edward B. Fiske, "A Visit to Archbishop Cooke's

Domain," *New York Times Magazine* (13 Oct. 1968), examines Cooke's career at the beginning of his tenure; and Edward Tivnan, "A New Yorker Up for Sainthood," *New York Times Magazine* (30 Nov. 1986), looks at its aftermath. The most useful of the many articles about Cooke in the *New York Times* are the reports of his appointment as archbishop (9 Mar. 1968) and of his death (7 Oct. 1983).

ALLAN L. DAMON

COON, Carleton Stevens (*b.* 23 June 1904 in Wakefield, Massachusetts; *d.* 3 June 1981 in West Gloucester, Massachusetts), anthropologist and author who made major contributions in the fields of ethnology, physical anthropology, and prehistoric archaeology.

Coon was the eldest of three sons of John Lewis Coon, a businessman who specialized in textile machinery, and Bessie Carleton, a homemaker. The greatest influence in his early youth was his paternal grandfather, a blind veteran of the Civil War who was widely traveled and a great teller of tales that aroused Coon's love of adventure. Coon graduated in 1921 from the prestigious Phillips Academy in Andover, Massachusetts. There he read the *Iliad* in ancient Greek, began to teach himself Egyptian hieroglyphics, and became interested in archaeology.

Dr. Carleton S. Coon, 1952. UNIVERSITY OF PENNSYLVANIA MUSEUM (NEG. # S8-46924)

Coon next attended Harvard College, where he was encouraged to be a writer by his English professor Charles T. Copeland. The anthropologist Earnest A. Hooten caused him to change his concentration to anthropology, and he took every course in the department. Coon received his A.B. degree (magna cum laude) in 1925 and was elected to Phi Beta Kappa. He received the A.M. and Ph.D. degrees jointly from Harvard in 1928.

Coon married Mary Goodale in 1926. She joined him in many of his expeditions. They had two sons and were divorced in 1944. In 1945 Coon married Lisa Dougherty Geddes, who accompanied him on expeditions and drew the maps for his later books.

Coon was a member of the Harvard faculty from 1927 until 1948. During that period he undertook a wide range of fieldwork. Publications of this period include *Tribes of the Rif* (1931) based on his work in Morocco, and *Flesh of the Wild Ox* (1932), a work of fiction on the same subject. He also wrote *Ethiopia and Flight into Arabia* (1935), an account of the problems of fieldwork, as well as the classics *Races of Europe* (1939) and, with Eliot Dismore Chapple, *Principles of Anthropology* (1942).

During the war years from 1942 to 1945, Coon worked for the Department of State in the Office of Strategic Services with the rank of major. He had a series of incredible adventures that he recounted from memory and his diary in *A North African Story: The Anthropologist as an O.S.S. Agent 1941–1943* (1980). For these exploits he was elected an honorary member of the Association de la Liberation Française (1942) and received the Legion of Merit from the U.S. Army (1945).

From 1948 to 1963 Coon was professor of anthropology at the University of Pennsylvania and curator of ethnology at the University Museum. In the latter capacity he installed the Hall of Man at the museum, considered a major contribution to the presentation of anthropology to the public. He conducted many expeditions under museum auspices and continued to write on his experiences and his theories on race. During this period he produced *Races: A Study of the Problems of Race Formation in Man,* written with Stanley M. Garn and Joseph B. Birdsell (1950), which is considered a major landmark. *Caravan* (1951), which describes and analyzes the cultural bases of the Middle East, was used as a text by diplomats. *The Story of Man* (1954) was organized according to the order of exhibits in the Hall of Man. *The Seven Caves* (1957) is an archaeological exploration of the Middle East.

Coon's *Origin of Races* (1962) caused much controversy. His theory of five races of man before *Homo sapiens* evolving at different times and places was sometimes used by racists to back their theories. He steadily defended his ideas and explained his reasoning, firmly rejecting racist implications. (Today, this theory is generally discounted by scientists.) Nothing in his life supports the idea that he had any racist tendencies. *Anthropology A to Z* (1963), written with Edward E. Hunt, Jr., was based on their fieldwork.

With all this activity Coon yet found time to be president of the American Association of Physical Anthropology from 1961 to 1963. From 1949 to 1964 he appeared regularly on the television program *What in the World?* and was part of a panel that identified archaeological objects. The program won the Peabody Award in 1952. Other high points during this period were being awarded the Viking Medal in Physical Anthropology in 1951 and his election to the National Academy of Sciences in 1955.

Physically, Coon was a large and impressive man who loved to laugh and had a devilish sense of humor. He was a member of the Congregational Church and spoke ten languages, some of isolated tribes. In 1963 he retired from the University of Pennsylvania and moved to his summer home in West Gloucester, Massachusetts, where he kept an office. He maintained an affiliation with the Peabody Museum of Archaeology and Ethnology and he continued traveling and writing. With Edward E. Hunt, Jr., he wrote *The Living Races of Man* (1965), which describes physical attributes and tries to explain physiological differences. It received much less criticism than *Origin of Races. Hunting Peoples* (1971), based on his lecture notes, stresses the independence and self-reliance of early peoples. His delightful and witty autobiography is *Adventures and Discoveries: The Autobiography of Carleton S. Coon, Anthropologist and Explorer* (1981). He died at home of cancer and was buried in Beechbrook Cemetery in Gloucester, Massachusetts.

Coon was a master of both scholarly and popular writing. His aim was to make sense of human history in a way that could be understood by all readers. He used data from excavations to make his points, and his writing conveyed the excitement of fieldwork by including anecdotes about incidents that had occurred in the field.

★

The University Museum at the University of Pennsylvania has folders, obituaries, expedition reports, and videos of *What in the World?* The National Anthropological Archives at the Smithsonian Institution has forty-six linear feet of Coon's papers, reports, lecture notes, and letters. Obituaries are in the *New York Times* (6 June 1981); *American Journal of Physical Anthropology* 58 (July 1982) and 62 (Nov. 1983); *Journal of Anthropological Research* 40 (fall 1984); and *Biographical Memoirs. National Academy of Sciences* 58 (1989).

PATRICIA BRAUCH

COOPER, Charles Henry ("Chuck") (*b.* 29 September 1926 in Pittsburgh, Pennsylvania; *d.* 2 May 1984 in Pittsburgh, Pennsylvania), first black player to be drafted into the National Basketball Association (1950) and first black

director of the Department of City Parks and Recreation (1970) in Pittsburgh.

Cooper was the youngest of the five children of Daniel Webster Cooper, a mailman, and Emma Caroline Brown, who was a schoolteacher before Chuck was born. He graduated from Westinghouse High School in the East Liberty section of Pittsburgh on 3 February 1944, where he had played basketball for the first time. He attended West Virginia State College in Institute, West Virginia, and played for its basketball team (1944–1945) until drafted into the U.S. Navy, in which he served from July 1945 to October 1946.

After leaving the navy, Cooper entered Duquesne University in Pittsburgh, graduating in 1950 with a B.S. degree in education. He made the basketball team as a freshman, a very unusual accomplishment, and was the first black starter as well as an All-American. The Duquesne team compiled a 77–19 record during his four years. While on a three-week tour with the Harlem Globetrotters, after graduating, he was drafted in the second round and signed by the Boston Celtics for $7,500 on 25 April 1950. On 18 August 1951 he married Patsy Jayne Ware, a nurse from Pittsburgh. At six feet, five inches tall, Cooper played the

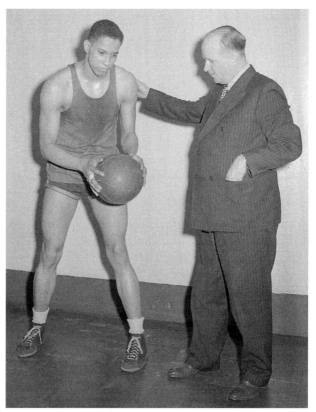

Charles Cooper with Duquesne University basketball coach Chick Davies, 1946. PITTSBURGH COURIER/CHARLES HARRIS/CORBIS

forward position with the Celtics from 1950 to 1954. Traded to the Milwaukee Hawks, he played for his new team in the 1954–1955 season. His first marriage ended in divorce at that time. There were no children. The Hawks moved to St. Louis for the 1955–1956 season, during which Cooper was traded to the Fort Wayne (Indiana) Pistons. That was his final National Basketball Association (NBA) season. His overall career average was 6.7 points per game. He then played for the Harlem Magicians, an offshoot of the Harlem Globetrotters, in 1956 and 1957.

On 28 March 1957 Cooper married Irva Lee. They had four children. Cooper and his family moved to Minnesota in 1959, and in 1961 he received a master of social work degree from the University of Minnesota. The family then moved back to Pittsburgh, where he held several social work jobs. He was acting executive director of Community Action of Pittsburgh (CAP) from 1966 to 1968 and again from 1971 to 1974, coordinator for Pittsburgh Community Action (1966–1969), and planning director for the Health and Welfare Association for Allegheny County (1969). He also worked with the Negro Education Emergency Drive (NEED) (1969–1970). In 1970 Pittsburgh mayor Pete Flaherty appointed Cooper director of the Department of City Parks and Recreation, where he worked until 1971. At the time of his death he was urban affairs officer for the Community Affairs Department at the Pittsburgh National Bank, responsible for ensuring the bank's compliance with the Community Reinvestment Act.

Despite his "black first" accomplishments in professional sports, Cooper downplayed his role as a pioneer or groundbreaker, giving credit for that to Jackie Robinson, who had broken the color barrier in baseball in 1947. Professional basketball was so lightly regarded in 1950 that no mention of Cooper's race appeared in the Boston newspapers when he was listed as a draftee or even in reports of the opening game. Cooper played his first game as a Celtic in Fort Wayne (Indiana) on 1 November 1950, coincidentally Arnold "Red" Auerbach's coaching debut with the team. He encountered racism in his college days as well as while playing in the NBA. In December 1946, the University of Tennessee team walked out of a game because Duquesne coach Chuck Davies refused to promise unconditionally not to play Cooper. Cooper remembers "a period when every time we played the game below the Mason-Dixon line, our team would be setting a precedent for a 'mixed' contest." Games in the deep southern states such as Alabama and Mississippi were "out of the question." He was refused service at "whites only" restaurants and hotels but was made to feel "at home" by Celtics coach Auerbach, team owner Walter Brown, and his teammates. Some Celtics, including roommate Bob Cousy, walked out of hotels and restaurants where Cooper was refused service. Cooper felt, after retiring from basketball, that racism was a reason

he was not offered the coaching jobs he wanted and for which he felt qualified.

A Baptist, Cooper was involved in community affairs in Pittsburgh and was honored by the city of Pittsburgh and Duquesne University. In 1964 he was named to the Duquesne All-Time team. In 1970 he was inducted into the Duquesne Hall of Fame and in 1978 was selected as one of the 100 Most Distinguished Living Alumni. In 1983 the Chuck Cooper Award was established to honor outstanding underclassmen on the basketball team. He was inducted into the Pennsylvania Sports Hall of Fame in 1974. The Pittsburgh City Council declared 26 February 1991 Chuck Cooper Day to honor him for his devotion to "recreation for young people" and as "a proven leader in his community."

Cooper's dedication to ending discrimination and to improving life in the black community is clear from the many positions he held. He was on the boards of trustees of the Citizens' Advisory Committee on Desegregation, the Urban League, the Hospital Council of Western Pennsylvania, and the Boy Scouts. He was the first and, at the time, the only black professional at Pittsburgh National Bank, where he was responsible for developing minority contacts and assisting the bank in meeting affirmative-action goals. His sports awards document his basketball achievements, but his life after professional sports shows that he should be remembered for being concerned with and giving back to the community, and for fighting racism and discrimination in both sports and in daily life. College and professional teammates, as well as acquaintances and coworkers, all described Cooper as kind and gentlemanly.

Cooper died of liver cancer and is buried in Homewood Cemetery in Pittsburgh.

★

The Duquesne University athletics department and the Boston Celtics maintain clipping files on Cooper. Edna Rust and Art Rust, Jr., *Art Rust's Illustrated History of the Black Athlete* (1985), contains a short first-person narrative by Cooper about his basketball career. Alex Sachare, ed., *The Official NBA Basketball Encyclopedia* (2d ed., 1989), has Cooper's NBA career statistics and other data. Roger Barry interviewed Bob Cousy about Cooper in the *Middlesex* (Massachusetts) *News* (13 Feb. 1986). Obituaries are in the *Boston Globe* and *New York Times* (both 7 Feb. 1984).

JANE BRODSKY FITZPATRICK

COOPER, Irving Spencer (b. 15 July 1922 in Atlantic City, New Jersey; d. 30 October 1985 in Naples, Florida), physician whose inventions of cryosurgery, the brain "pacemaker," and surgery to relieve the tremors of Parkinson's disease and dystonia made him the most innovative neurosurgeon of his time.

Cooper was one of two sons of Louis Cooper, who moved the family to Washington, D.C., in order to form a hotel kitchen equipment firm with several brothers, and Eleanor Lillian (Abramoff) Cooper, a homemaker. Irving was tall and handsome with wavy blond hair and blue eyes, an appearance that earned him the nickname "golden boy." It was also an apt description of his career, notable for serendipitous accident, good luck, brilliant insights, and compassion for the suffering. He was athletic and competitive in high school football and college lacrosse and an aggressive tennis player throughout his life. A scholar as well as athlete, he expressed lifelong passions for literature, poetry, science, the arts, and the sea.

He enrolled in Syracuse University in 1939, then transferred to the George Washington University for his third year of premedical studies, earning a B.A. degree in 1942. After entering the George Washington University School of Medicine, he married Mary Dan "Cherrie" Frost on 15 December 1944; they would have three children. He received his M.D. degree in 1945, then joined the United States Naval Reserve Medical Corps, serving a neurosurgical internship at St. Albans Naval Hospital in Queens, New York, and completing service as a lieutenant in 1948. Later that year he went to the Mayo clinic in Rochester, Minnesota, as a fellow. He completed his neurosurgery residency there in 1951, meanwhile obtaining both a master's and a Ph.D. degree in English literature from the University of Minnesota.

In 1951 Cooper joined the New York University postgraduate medical school as an assistant professor of neurosurgery. It was here that, on 9 October 1951, the young Dr. Cooper operated to relieve uncontrollable shaking in a forty-one-year-old truck driver. Following accepted technique, he was preparing to sever nerves in the midbrain, which would paralyze the trucker's shaking limbs, when a tiny artery was accidentally cut. The artery's function was little understood at the time, but Cooper had recently read a study of its importance to brain structures controlling movement. Closing the artery, he elected to end the operation and study the results of interrupting the artery's blood flow. As he recalled in *The Victim Is Always the Same* (1973), the next morning the anxious surgical team found the patient talking, his intellect intact, without paralysis and free from his shaking. It opened a new era in the physician's career and the field of neurosurgery.

In 1954 Cooper began a neurosurgery department in the small Bronx hospital called Home for Incurables, later renamed St. Barnabas Hospital for Chronic Disease. Among its meager facilities were two six-bed wards and a barber chair modified to serve as an operating table. As director of neurosurgery he performed thousands of operations there as the facility and his reputation grew. Concurrently, he was assistant professor of neurosurgery at the New York University postgraduate medical school from 1951 to 1957

Irving S. Cooper. COURTESY OF MRS. SISSEL H. COOPER

and director of neuromuscular diseases and professor of research surgery at the NYU-Bellevue Medical Center until 1966, when he became research professor of neuroanatomy at New York Medical College. Over the course of his career he would perform more than 10,000 surgeries on children and adults, relieving their painful, disfiguring, and disabling impairments. Many of those patients were conscious during their operation, since the brain feels no pain of incision. Despite the apparent risks Cooper's surgical mortality rate was 2 percent, about the same as gall-bladder surgery, while providing substantial relief or better to 75 percent. His surgical techniques were featured in *Life* magazine after he operated on the famous photographer Margaret Bourke-White, who suffered from Parkinson's disease. She was able to resume her work and lived for twelve more years.

To his dismay, Cooper's enthusiastic advocacy of his surgery met bitter rebuke and denial from some in his field. His autobiographical *The Vital Probe: My Life as a Brain Surgeon* (1981) included a defense of his achievements with detailed criticism of his detractors. He was just as quick to criticize colleagues who did not place patients' needs uppermost, writing that "modern medicine has lost sight of its purpose—the treatment of sick individuals who have come for help."

Cooper pioneered several other important medical techniques. He improved surgical precision by using a chemical treatment—injected through a thin tube—on diseased or aberrant brain cells. He invented the first cryosurgery device (to freeze tissue), modeling it after a wine-bottle cork opener he received for Christmas in 1960, which lifted the cork by injecting carbon dioxide gas into the bottle. He used liquid nitrogen flowing in a thin tube first to deaden, and then freeze, tremor-causing brain cells or tumors. The invention created a new field of surgery with applications for other areas of the body as well. In 1972 he invented a "pacemaker" that, once implanted, sent electrical impulses to specific sites in the brain to relieve epileptic seizures and reduce spasticity from cerebral palsy and in some cases rigidity following stroke. He was pleased to see medical therapy using the drug L-dopa begin to supersede his surgical procedures in 1968. However, neurosurgeons later returned to his pallidotomy and thalamotomy operations as the treatment of choice if L-dopa therapy failed.

In 1969 his wife, Cherrie, died in an automobile accident in Morocco. On 31 January 1970 he married Sissel Holm at his home at 76 Mount Tom Road in Pelham Manor, New York. They would have three sons. For all his success in the field of medicine, he remained, as one colleague put it, "a true Renaissance man." He was fluent in Spanish and Italian, read German, spoke some French, lectured in Russian, and studied Japanese. He loved opera and ballet, collected surrealist art, and wrote children's stories and papers on Shakespearean plays. He avidly read at least three books at a time, but still found time to fish and ski. Concerned about children's education, he and three friends founded the Community School of Naples, Florida. In 1974 he established the Cooper Institute for Advanced Studies in Medicine and the Humanities, a foundation dedicated to linking science and the humanities for medical treatment "that embraces the individual as a whole."

Cooper left St. Barnabas in 1978 to practice at Westchester County Medical Center in Valhalla, New York. He also continued to write, adding to a body of work that included, among others, *Involuntary Movement Disorders* (1969); *Living with Chronic Neurologic Disease: A Handbook for Patient and Family* (1976); and *It's Hard to Leave While the Music Is Playing* (1977), about a best friend's death from amyotrophic lateral sclerosis (Lou Gehrig's disease).

Cooper died in Naples, Florida, of lung cancer (though a nonsmoker) at the age of sixty-three. He is buried near his summer home in the Tannersville, New York, area of the Catskill Mountains.

Among scores of awards and honors, Cooper received the American Medical Association's Hektoen Bronze Medal (1957, 1958) and its certificate of merit (1961); the Lewis Harvey Taylor award of the American Therapeutic Society (1957); the Modern Medicine award (1960); the alumni achievement award (1960) and merit award of George Washington University (1967); the humanitarian award of the National Cystic Fibrosis Foundation (1962); and the merit award of the United Parkinson Foundation (1965).

Thousands of patients whose pain and tremors were relieved by Cooper's surgery amply validate his skill and dedication. Many of his peers considered him a leader in the development of neurosurgery. He was a pioneer in the crusade for medical ethics and greater sensitivity to the patient's perspective. Although he was sometimes the target of virulent criticism, such attacks may have stemmed from what his friend, the author C. P. Snow, described as "some envy, presumably because he appears to have all of the gifts that a man might conceivably wish for."

★

I. S. Cooper, *The Victim Is Always the Same* (1973), is an autobiographical chronicle of the ethical dilemmas and surgeries of several patients, and his *Vital Probe: My Life as a Brain Surgeon* (1981), is an autobiographical view of his career and controversies. See the *New York Times* (22 Sept. 1973), for a report on his brain pacemaker. An obituary is in the *New York Times* (4 Nov. 1985).

CHARLES A. ROND IV

CORCORAN, Thomas Gardiner (*b.* 29 December 1900 in Pawtucket, Rhode Island; *d.* 6 December 1981 in Washington, D.C.), lawyer, government official, and lobbyist best known for his work as a presidential adviser and strategist during the New Deal.

One of three children of Patrick Corcoran, a politician, and Mary O'Keefe, a housewife, Thomas grew up in Pawtucket, Rhode Island. After attending Brown University (B.A., 1921; M.A., 1922) and the Harvard Law School (LL.B., 1925; S.J.D., 1926), where he became a protégé of Felix Frankfurter's, Corcoran went to Washington as a clerk to Supreme Court justice Oliver Wendell Holmes, Jr., during the 1926 term. The following year he moved to New York City, where he specialized in holding companies and securities law with the firm of Cotton and Franklin until 1932. He then returned to Washington for a brief stint as counsel to the Reconstruction Finance Corporation, a position he nominally held again from 1934 to 1940. But in fact Corcoran, a lawyer of undisputed brilliance and a man of unlimited charm, was rarely at the RFC, as he was borrowed or assigned for special tasks in the Treasury and Justice Departments, or more usually, was put to work by President Franklin D. Roosevelt drafting key New Deal legislation.

This part of his career began in 1933, when Roosevelt

Thomas Corcoran. UPI/CORBIS-BETTMANN

asked Justice Frankfurter to oversee the drafting of a new truth-in-securities bill, and Frankfurter recruited three of his former students, James M. Landis, Benjamin V. Cohen, and Corcoran; they became the original core of Frankfurter's "Happy Little Hot Dogs." Corcoran then successfully lobbied for the bill's passage in Congress, and the following year helped draft and defend the Securities Exchange Act of 1934. Corcoran and Cohen became the most successful legislative duo in Washington, drafting all or part of such key New Deal measures as the Federal Housing Act of 1933, the Public Utility Holding Company Act of 1935, and the Fair Labor Standards Act of 1938.

After a White House dinner early in the Roosevelt administration, Corcoran won FDR's personal affection by serenading the president and his guests with a series of Irish ballads. For the next several years, "Tommy the Cork" was the "insiders' insider," advising the president, writing speeches, drafting legislation, and lobbying Congress, and helping to place dozens of bright young lawyers in the many New Deal agencies. It was Corcoran who penned the famous motto of Roosevelt's 1936 election campaign, "rendezvous with destiny."

Beginning in 1937, however, Corcoran's influence began to fade as he became a lightning rod for anti–New Deal sentiment. Although he had had nothing to do with Roosevelt's 1937 court-packing plan, he had supported it and

now took the blame for it. His power also went to his head; congressmen resented his threats that unless they supported the New Deal they would suffer politically. During the debate over the utilities bill, Republican congressman Owen Brewster of Maine accused Corcoran of threatening to stop construction of a dam in Brewster's district unless he supported the administration. In 1938 Corcoran played a major role in Roosevelt's unsuccessful efforts to purge the Democratic party of conservatives. He also led the drive during the late 1930s to draft Roosevelt for a third term, an idea that horrified conservatives of both parties. To help the president, Corcoran resigned from the RFC in 1940 and returned to New York City, where he worked almost anonymously in the Norris-LaGuardia Committee for the reelection of the president. He was thus able to help the 1940 campaign yet remain out of the spotlight.

Although still a personal favorite of Roosevelt's, by early 1941 Corcoran had become a political liability. The president, who needed support from conservatives for his preparedness program, could not afford to name Corcoran to any important government post. Corcoran reentered private practice in Washington, and for the next forty years he represented some of the most powerful corporate interests in the country before various government agencies. On 4 March 1940 he married one of his secretaries, Margaret Dowd. They had six children.

Within a short time Corcoran was accused of being an influence peddler. Called before a congressional committee, he testified that he had earned $100,000 during his first few months of private practice. He denied that he had done anything illegal, and in fact neither then nor at any other time could evidence be sustained that he had acted illegally. His influence came from his intricate knowledge of the government bureaucracy and of the people who staffed those agencies. When his clients needed administrative relief Corcoran knew where to go and how to secure it, a knowledge held by only a handful of Washington insiders.

Corcoran, like Justice Abe Fortas, became the living embodiment of those New Dealers who had come to Washington to do good and had stayed on to do well. In his four decades of practice he worked effectively for his clients and earned large fees from them. But he was repeatedly the subject of controversy. Admiral Hyman G. Rickover charged that Corcoran, as a representative of shipbuilding interests, had tried for years to force his retirement from the U.S. Navy; Corcoran denied the charge, and claimed that Rickover disliked him because he had opposed the admiral's efforts to "nationalize the shipyards."

In 1969 Corcoran supposedly tried to lobby Justices William J. Brennan and Hugo Black to reopen an antitrust case involving one of his clients. The episode came to light with the 1979 publication of Bob Woodward and Scott Armstrong's *The Brethren: Inside the Supreme Court,* and led to an investigation by the Board of Professional Responsibility of the District of Columbia Bar. The panel could find no evidence of improper behavior and did not recommend any disciplinary action.

Corcoran's problems, according to one friend, stemmed from the fact that he worked just as hard for his private clients as he had for the president of the United States. "He has never been able to make a distinction between them, or to realize that what might be justified within the Government cannot be from outside it."

Corcoran remained active in his law practice and in his advising of Democratic party officials until his death from a pulmonary blood clot suffered after surgery.

★

Corcoran's extensive papers are in the Library of Congress. There is no full-scale study of him other than an unpublished dissertation by Monica Lynne Niznik, "Thomas G. Corcoran: The Public Service of Franklin Roosevelt's 'Tommy the Cork'" (Notre Dame, 1981). An affectionate yet astute account of Corcoran and other key New Dealers is in Joseph P. Lash, *Dealers and Dreamers: A New Look at the New Deal* (1988). See also the profile by Monica L. Niznik in Otis L. Graham, Jr., and Meghan Robinson Wander, eds., *Franklin D. Roosevelt: His Life and Times, an Encyclopedic View* (1985). An obituary is in the *New York Times* (7 Dec. 1981).

MELVIN I. UROFSKY

CORI, Carl Ferdinand (*b.* 5 December 1896 in Prague, Austria-Hungary [in present-day Czech Republic]; *d.* 19 October 1984 in Cambridge, Massachusetts), biochemist and teacher who, with his wife, Gerty T. Cori, was awarded one half of the 1947 Nobel Prize in medicine or physiology for their analysis of the way the complex carbohydrate glycogen (sugar stored in the liver and in muscle tissue) is converted into glucose for immediate energy.

One of three children of Carl Isador Cori and Maria Lippich, Cori was raised in Prague and in Trieste, Italy, where his father was a professor of zoology and director of the Marine Biological Station. His mother was a homemaker. Carl attended the Trieste Gymnasium from 1906 until 1914, interrupting his studies during World War I to serve as a sanitation officer for the Austrian army on the Italian front. His future wife, Gerty Theresa Radnitz, daughter of a sugar manufacturer, was also born in Prague, on 15 August 1896 and was raised there and in Tetschen. They met shortly after both enrolled, in 1914, at the German University in Prague to study medicine. From the beginning of their relationship they were working partners, researching serum immunology.

In 1919, while still an undergraduate, Cori became an instructor at the second medical clinic in Prague. He and

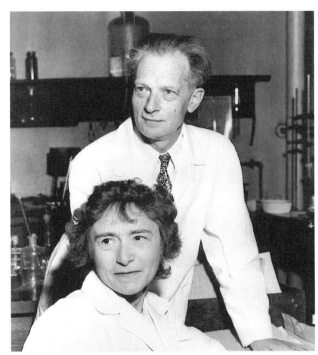

Drs. Carl and Gerty Cori, 1947. UPI/CORBIS-BETTMANN

Gerty were awarded M.D. degrees in 1920 and were married on 5 August that year. Not long after their marriage the couple moved to Vienna. They had already decided not to practice medicine in order to pursue laboratory research. From 1920 to 1922, Cori was an assistant in the first medical clinic of the University of Vienna and an assistant in pharmacology at the University of Graz. The Coris emigrated to the United States in 1922 after being invited to take staff positions as biochemists at the New York State Institute for the Study of Malignant Diseases in Buffalo. Cori was also an assistant professor of physiology at the University of Buffalo. There they discovered their main research interest, carbohydrate metabolism, an interest they would refine throughout the remaining thirty-four years of their working lives. Their first significant paper was published in Buffalo in 1923, entitled "Free Sugar Content of the Liver and its Relation to Glycogensynthesis and Glycogenolysis." In 1928 they became U.S. citizens.

They remained in Buffalo until 1931, when Cori was appointed professor of pharmacology and head of that department at the Washington University School of Medicine in St. Louis. Gerty was appointed a research associate in the same department. There they continued the study of glycogen and its conversion into glucose. In a series of jointly published papers in the 1930s they outlined their gradual discoveries of the mechanisms underlying the chemical conversion of glycogen by various enzymes and its hydrolysis into glucose usable by the body.

They achieved their first breakthrough in 1936 with the discovery of a previously unknown compound, glucose-1-phosphate, which became known as Cori-ester. This was the subject of their paper "The Formation of Hexose Phosphate Esters in Frog Muscle," which appeared in the *Journal of Biological Chemistry* (1936). Papers on other important discoveries subsequently appeared in that journal, including: "Crystalline Muscle Phosphorylase. III. Kinetics" (1943), written with A. A. Green and G. T. Cori; "The Enzymatic Conversion of Phosphorylase a to b"; and "Glucose 6-Phosphatase of the Liver in Glycogen Storage Disease" (1952).

The work and home lives of the Coris were almost inseparable, and their marriage was happy and successful. Their temperaments were complementary. He was described as shy, she as vivacious. They enjoyed such outdoor activities as fishing, swimming, tennis, skating, and mountain climbing, particularly in the American Rockies. At home they relaxed by working in their garden; Carl was responsible for the vegetables. In 1936, Gerty gave birth to their child, a son.

In 1941 Cori was appointed as a professor in biochemistry at Washington University and in 1946 became chairman of that department. In 1947 the Coris were awarded the Nobel Prize in medicine or physiology for "their discovery of the course of the catalytic conversion of glycogen." They shared the prize with an Argentine scientist, Dr. Bernardo Houssay, whose work was related to theirs. The Coris were one of only three couples ever to have won the Nobel Prize, the others being Pierre and Marie Curie (for physics, in 1903) and Irène (the Curies' daughter) and Frédéric Joliot-Curie (for chemistry, in 1935).

After receiving the prize, Cori won many more honors. He was awarded honorary doctorates by Western Reserve (later Case Western Reserve) University, Yale University, Boston University, Cambridge University, Gustavus Adolphus College, Brandeis, Washington University, and University of Trieste, among others. He received the Isaac Adler Prize (1943), the Lasker Award of the American Public Health Association (1946), the Sugar Foundation Prize (1947), the Squibb Award of the American Society of Endocrinologists (with Gerty Cori, 1947), and the Willard Gibbs Medal of the American Chemical Society (1948).

After suffering for several years from myelosclerosis, a painful bone marrow disease, Gerty Cori died in Glendale, Missouri, on 26 October 1957. Three years later, on 23 March 1960, Cori married Anne FitzGerald Jones, who had four children of her own. He remained at Washington as department head until his retirement in 1966, when he accepted a position at the Massachusetts General Hospital and the Harvard University School of Medicine.

Cori lived in Cambridge, Massachusetts, for the rest of his life. He held simultaneous posts from 1966 to 1984 as visiting lecturer of biological chemistry, director of the Enzyme Research Laboratory, and member of the faculty of Harvard Medical School. He died in Cambridge of natural causes and was buried there.

Cori's most significant contribution, inseparable from that of his wife Gerty, was to analyze the exact biochemical method by which the body converts glycogen into glucose and glucose into glycogen, a discovery of great significance in the treatment of diabetes. They brought to completion work that the French physiologist Claude Bernard had begun in the 1850s. Bernard had demonstrated that the body converts glucose into glycogen for storage and reconverts it back into glucose for immediate use. The Coris' experiments in the 1930s and 1940s gradually determined the entire conversion and reconversion process, which became known as the Cori cycle.

★

Carl F. Cori, "The Call of Science," *Annual Review of Biochemistry* 38 (1969): 1–20, and Bernardo A. Houssay, "Carl F. and Gerty T. Cori," *Biochemica et Biophysica Acta* 20 (1956): 11–16, contain personal information on Carl Cori and his wife. An obituary is in the *New York Times* (22 Oct. 1984).

STEVE TURTELL

CORNER, George Washington (*b.* 12 December 1889 in Baltimore, Maryland; *d.* 28 September 1981 in Huntsville, Alabama), anatomist and medical historian who was the codiscoverer in 1929 of progesterone, the hormone of gestation, and a key figure in the rise of reproductive endocrinology.

The eldest of three children of a prosperous Methodist family, Corner took pride in the numerous relatives who played prominent roles in the civic affairs of Baltimore. His parents, George Washington Corner II, a wholesale merchant, and Florence Evans, had a strong interest in Christian education and their son's intellectual development. When he began public schooling in the third grade, Corner was already a self-directed learner who loved reading and mechanical gadgets. He entered Boys' Latin School of Baltimore in 1903, graduated in three years, and enrolled at Johns Hopkins University in 1906.

Corner found his vocation as a biomedical scientist during the summer of 1907. While vacationing with his veterinarian uncle, he read the bacteriologist Theobald Smith's classic account of the discovery that Texas cattle fever is transmitted by ticks. When Corner returned to Johns Hopkins, he dropped Latin, declared himself a biologist, and although he served as editor of the undergraduate newspaper and was elected class poet, he took greatest pride in his identification with biomedical science. He received an A.B. in 1909.

Dr. George Corner, 1980. AP/WIDE WORLD PHOTOS

Corner's teachers urged him to pursue the Ph.D. and arranged for him to spend the postgraduate summer of 1909 on a research internship at a U.S. Bureau of Fisheries laboratory, where his observations of the death of protozoa led to the first of his 240 scientific journal articles. Persuaded by his parents, Corner elected to pursue an M.D. at the Johns Hopkins Medical School, so that he would have an alternative vocation if his research goals proved impractical. As he wrote later in his autobiography, *The Seven Ages of a Medical Scientist,* he believed that his parents, in advising him, were motivated by fear that "a career in biology might lead me away from the altars of home and church" (p. 33). And in fact Corner gradually shed both his Christian faith and his parents' evangelical suspicion of the pleasures of the flesh. But he retained their work ethic and high-mindedness, and avoided direct challenges to authority for the rest of his life, secure in his quiet confidence that the scientific method would reveal natural order.

As a medical student Corner throve on the enlightened pedagogy of Johns Hopkins, where students were provided with maximum opportunities for independent work and professors brought the excitement of recent discovery to even such traditionally numbing subjects as human anatomy. Under the influence of Franklin Paine Mall, who was transforming anatomy through physiological and cellular studies, Corner learned the traditional art of medicine and developed a strong research program of his own based on the description of embryonic tissues. He also internalized the university's enthusiasm for medical humanities, and he began a lifetime of research in the history of anatomy that allowed him to use his love of books and Latin as a source of perspective upon the secrets revealed by the microscope. Although his record as a medical student qualified Corner for a prestigious internship in gynecology, Mall convinced him that the surgical specialty needed new insight from those who were capable of delineating the basic mechanisms of mammalian reproductive physiology. After obtaining his medical degree in 1913, Corner postponed his internship to serve as assistant in anatomy under Mall (1913–1914) and began searching through thousands of mammalian organs harvested from slaughterhouses for the knowledge of ovulation, fertilization, and menstruation that would transform clinical practice. After completing his internship in gynecology at Johns Hopkins Hospital (1914–1915), he became assistant professor of anatomy at the University of California at Berkeley, which was building a new department modeled on the Johns Hopkins example.

Corner spent the summers of 1912 and 1913 as a medical volunteer at the Grenfell Labrador Mission in Newfoundland, Canada, where he fell in love with a fellow volunteer, Betsy Copping, a schoolteacher whose New England rearing as the daughter of a Congregational minister provided values quite compatible with those of the Baltimore Corners. They were married on 28 December 1915 and had two children. Betsy Corner died in 1976.

At Berkeley, Corner developed an aptitude for teaching anatomy that benefited generations of future medical leaders. Studies of the ovaries and uteri of sows led to publication of the first description of newly fertilized ova, but Corner's main focus was the corpus luteum. He would show this structure to be the gland of internal secretion that develops in the ruptured Graffian follicle after the mammalian egg leaves the ovary and that signals the uterus to prepare for nidification by the copious production of progesterone. In 1919 Corner returned to Johns Hopkins as an associate professor of anatomy, and in 1923 he helped found the medical school of the University of Rochester as its first professor of anatomy and chairman of the department. In Rochester, in collaboration with his protégé, biochemist Willard M. Allen, Corner proved the functional necessity of the corpus luteum for the maintenance and implantation of the embryo by isolating progesterone and demonstrating its effects on the uterus of female rabbits. An orally active, synthetic version of progesterone would be the main ingredient in the birth-control pill that was developed in the 1950s. Next, Corner pioneered the use of the rhesus monkey for studies of the menstrual cycle and led the intellectual community of endocrinologists who developed the hormonal theory of the menstrual cycle. In 1940 Corner returned to Baltimore as director of the Department of Embryology of the Carnegie Institution of Washington, where he continued to make fundamental observations of mammalian eggs and embryos.

Corner played important roles as a scientific executive and popular writer in the history of human sex research and education. In 1934 he became a member of the National Research Council's Committee for Research in Problems of Sex. As the chair of this committee from 1947 to 1957, he was a key supporter of Alfred Kinsey's work on human sexual behavior, but he was not interested in altering the gender system of modern America or in promoting sexual liberation. Wanting his adolescent children to have better information about their sexuality than had been available to him, Corner published *Attaining Manhood: A Doctor Talks to Boys About Sex* (1938) and *Attaining Womanhood* (1939). In *The Hormones in Human Reproduction* (1942), *Ourselves Unborn: An Embryologist's Essay on Man* (1944), and *Twenty-Five Years of Sex Research* (with Sophie D. Aberle, 1953), Corner interpreted contemporary developments in reproductive science for the educated public.

In 1956 Corner retired from the Carnegie Institution and began distinguished work in the history of science and medicine, including *A History of the Rockefeller Institute, 1901–1953: Origins and Growth* (1964). Beginning in 1960 he lived in Philadelphia, where he served as executive officer of the American Philosophical Society and, after his retirement from this post, as chairman of the society's research committee, whose small grants program aided thousands of scholars in many fields. Corner died of a stroke while visiting his son, a professor at the University of Alabama Medical School, and was buried in Sayre, Pennsylvania.

★

The Corner papers are in the American Philosophical Society Library in Philadelphia. Corner's two autobiographical works, *The Seven Ages of a Medical Scientist* (1981) and *Anatomist at Large: An Autobiography and Selected Essays* (1958), are reliable guides to his several careers and vast scholarly production. Obituaries are in the *New York Times* (1 Oct. 1981) and the *Philadelphia Inquirer* (29 Sept. 1981).

JAMES W. REED

CORNING, Erastus, 2d (*b.* 7 October 1909 in Albany, New York; *d.* 28 May 1983 in Boston, Massachusetts), mayor of Albany from 1942 until his death in 1983, serving the longest tenure of any big-city mayor in the United States.

A descendant of one of New York State's oldest families, Corning was the son of Edwin Corning, former lieutenant governor under Governor Alfred E. Smith, and Louise Maxwell. Corning's grandfather was an active Albany al-

Erastus Corning 2d in his office, 1980. UPI/CORBIS-BETTMANN

derman and civic leader and his great-grandfather, the first Erastus Corning, was mayor of Albany in the 1830s and the founder and president of the New York Central Railroad who gave his name to the city of Corning.

Corning was born in Albany, where he grew up with his two sisters. As heir to the family political dynasty, Corning was well educated. He attended the elite Albany Academy and Groton prep schools before enrolling at Yale, where he was a member of the Wolf's Head and Phi Beta Kappa societies and graduated with a B.A. in 1932. While a senior at Yale, Corning became engaged to Elizabeth Morris Platt, a prominent member of Philadelphia society who had been educated in Philadelphia and Florence, Italy, and whose ancestors included several mayors of Albany. Their wedding on 23 June 1932 was covered by the Philadelphia and New York society pages. Together they had two children, Elizabeth and Erastus, 3d.

The Cornings settled in Albany, where he began his career in politics. He initially served as an assemblyman and then briefly as a state senator in the 1930s. A few months before the bombing of Pearl Harbor, Corning ran for mayor as a candidate of the powerful Daniel P. O'Connell Democratic machine. Corning won and took office on 1 January 1942. The following year, while still serving his first term, he joined the army as a private. In Europe he earned the nickname "GI Mayor" and was elected for a second term in 1945 while still overseas. Corning would be reelected nine more times, usually with more than 70 percent of the vote. For many years, however, his success would be attributed to his association with the O'Connell machine.

Upon returning from Europe for his second term, Corning often found himself butting heads with the Republican governor, Thomas E. Dewey, who had run unsuccessfully against Franklin D. Roosevelt in the 1944 presidential race. Dewey and Corning each accused the other of being protected by "friends in government," Dewey by profiteers and Corning by the O'Connell machine. Dewey often lashed out at the machine, and Corning later recalled that "Governor Dewey did his damnedest to put every one of us in jail, but he spent a couple of million dollars just to prove we were honest."

Corning's closest election came in 1973 because of State Commission on Investigation inquiries in the years 1972 and 1973. At the time, Albany was considered the state's most corrupt city. The commission was investigating charges of municipal corruption, including a charge against Albany policemen for "systematic and organized burglaries, larcenies, and thefts of public funds." The commission, like Dewey twenty-five years earlier, lashed out at the Democratic machine and accused Corning of trying to delay and obstruct the investigation. Corning insisted that the charges against him were merely a publicity stunt, but he nearly lost the election to Republican opponent Carl Tuohey, defeating him with only 53 percent of the vote.

A tall, stately figure known for his courtliness of manner, Corning was nevertheless skillful in dealing with the largely blue-collar constituency of the O'Connell machine and remained heavily involved with it for three decades. Yet, when Daniel O'Connell passed away in 1977 and Corning faced his first Democratic challenger in thirty-six years with State Senator Howard Nolan, Jr., Corning easily won the nomination and went on to win overwhelmingly in the fall election. Winning both the Democratic nomination and election without O'Connell behind him proved to friends and foes alike that Albany was Mayor Corning's city.

When New York City mayor Ed Koch and Lieutenant Governor Mario Cuomo were battling it out for the Democratic gubernatorial nomination in 1982, Corning pledged his support for Cuomo early on. Corning's help was invaluable, and Cuomo recognized that by saying Corning was the only person to whom he felt a political debt. Governor Cuomo further recognized Corning's importance in March 1983, when he officially renamed the tallest building in Empire State Plaza, an ambitious urban-renewal project for which Corning was instrumental in arranging the financing, the Mayor Erastus Corning 2d Tower.

Corning fell ill in the spring of 1982 and was hospitalized in June for asthma, emphysema, and bronchitis. He was transferred to University Hospital in Boston in October 1982, where he died of an apparent heart attack seven months later. Eight thousand mourners gathered in Albany,

approximately 8 percent of the city's population, to pay respects to their mayor of forty-one years. Political figures from throughout the state attended the service at the Episcopal Cathedral of All Saints. Corning was buried in Albany.

The death of Erastus Corning 2d ended a political dynasty of four generations. (Corning's son, Erastus 3d, did not carry on the family tradition.) In 1981, during his last election campaign, Corning said if he felt as good as he did in four more years, he would run again. No doubt he would have won.

★

Paul Grondahl, *Mayor Corning: Albany Icon, Albany Enigma* (1997), is a full-length biography. Irene Neu, *Erastus Corning, Merchant and Financier, 1794–1872* (1960) is an interesting account of the patriarch of the Corning family. Biographical accounts of Erastus Corning, 2d, are available in M. A. Farber, "Erastus Corning 2d, Albany Mayor Since '42, Dies," *New York Times* (29 May 1983), and Michael Oreskes, "Erastus Corning and His Era Are Laid to Rest in Albany," *New York Times* (2 June 1983).

VALERIE L. DUNHAM

COVELESKI, Stanley Anthony ("Covey") (*b.* 13 July 1889 in Shamokin, Pennsylvania; *d.* 20 March 1984 in South Bend, Indiana), Hall of Fame baseball player.

Stanley was born Stanislaus Anthony Kowalewski, the son of immigrant Polish parents. At age twelve he worked as a slate picker in the mines and was paid five cents an hour for a seventy-two-hour week. After quitting time, he often threw rocks at a tin can tied to a tree by a string. Being the youngest of five brothers, four of whom played professional baseball, he worked hard on his baseball skills and soon developed a reputation for accurate throwing.

In 1907 his brother Harry became a major league pitcher and the following year Stan was called to the box office of a movie theater to sign a contract with Marty Hogan of the Atlantic League for $250 per month. The young right-hander, at five feet, eleven inches and 166 pounds, was not an impressive size but he pitched well in twelve games for Shamokin, winning six of eight decisions.

The next year, pitching 272 innings for Lancaster, Pennsylvania, of the Tri-State League, he led the league with 23 wins. The years 1910 and 1911 were also spent in Lancaster. For part of 1912 Coveleski pitched for Atlantic City until he was called up by Connie Mack to the Philadelphia Athletics. In his major league debut on 10 September, he beat Ty Cobb and the Detroit Tigers. But since there was no room for him on the excellent pitching staff of the Athletics, he was shipped to Spokane of the Northwest League in 1913. There he tied the league for most losses. Pitching again for Spokane in 1914, he was a 20-game winner and led the league in strikeouts. He was married that year as well and eventually had two sons.

By the next season Coveleski was well aware that he had to improve his pitching if he ever expected to join his brother Harry in the majors. Promoted to the Portland Beavers of the Pacific Coast League, he learned to throw a spitball. Later Coveleski remembered, "I could make [the spitball] do practically anything I wanted it to." That year he pitched in a league-leading 64 games. At season's end, his trip to the World's Fair in San Francisco became a chance for him to pitch in an All-Star game against big leaguers, where his spitball impressed players and coaches from both leagues. Because the Cleveland Indians had an agreement with Portland, Coveleski made it to the majors to stay in 1916 at the age of twenty-seven. From that year to the end of his career, Coveleski would be one of the American League leaders in many categories, including saves.

In 1917 Coveleski had the third lowest earned run average (ERA) in the league at 1.81. It was the first of six years in which his ERA would be under 3.00. He also gave up the fewest hits per nine innings (6.1); led in shutouts (9); and had the lowest opponents batting average, the league hitting but .194 against him.

Coveleski's first 20-win season came in 1918, when he had 22, and he was among the leaders in innings pitched with 311. From May 15 through May 24 of the 1919 season, he pitched 13 innings, then 20 innings, and then 19 innings in three starts. Winning 23 games, he was in the league's top five in five categories.

The next year was marked by the death of Coveleski's wife in May. In addition, his teammate Ray Chapman was killed by a pitched ball. But the Indians and their star pitcher found a way to win the American League pennant. Giving up very few walks (65) or hits (284 in 315 innings) and with a 2.49 ERA, Coveleski won 24 games and went on to pitch against the Brooklyn Superbas in the World Series. In 3 games Coveleski, a control expert, threw just 232 pitches, allowing 5 hits each game and 2 runs (for an 0.67 ERA) in his 3 complete-game victories. His performance remains as one of the most remarkable World Series accomplishments in a series marked by the only unassisted triple play in a World Series as well as the first World Series grand-slam home run.

In 1921 Coveleski was fourth in winning percentage (.639), fourth in innings pitched (315 ⅔), third in wins (23), and fourth in complete games (29). The next year Coveleski married his deceased wife's sister, Frances D. Shivetts, who had been taking care of his two boys. During the season he won 17 games with a 3.32 ERA. The 1923 season was an odd one. Although he led the league in both ERA (2.76) and shutouts (5), his pitching record was 13–14. The 1924 season was the second straight in which his won-lost per-

Stanley Coveleski. COURTESY OF THE NATIONAL BASEBALL HALL OF FAME LIBRARY, COOPERSTOWN, N.Y.

centage was under .500 (15–16) and his ERA was up to 4.04, so on 12 December he was traded to the Washington Senators. He had his best year ever with that team, winning 13 consecutive games and leading the league with a 2.85 ERA (the last time his ERA was under 3.0). He lost 2 games in the World Series, however, and his team lost the series to the Pittsburgh Pirates.

Pitching full time in 1926, Coveleski won 14 games and lost 11. The next year, however, in only 14 innings he managed but 2 wins. Traded to the New York Yankees powerhouse in 1928, he won 5 and lost 1, but had an ERA of 5.74 and was released before season's end. Offered a coaching job in South Bend, Indiana, and eager to keep his sons away from the mines where he had worked, Coveleski bought a house at 1038 North Napier Street, where he lived the rest of his life. For a while he operated a gas station, frequently playing games of catch out back. He was inducted into the National Baseball Hall of Fame on 28 July 1969 at the age of eighty.

Coveleski died in a nursing home. The next year the minor league ballyard in South Bend was named for him.

★

The library at the Baseball Hall of Fame in Cooperstown, New

York, holds primary source material on Coveleski. A chronological recounting of his career is in Martin Appel and Burt Goldblatt, *Baseball's Best: The Hall of Fame Gallery* (1980). Joseph L. Reichler, ed., *The Baseball Encyclopedia,* 8th ed. (1990), is the source for statistics. Bill James, *The Bill James Historical Baseball Abstract* (1985), is useful for rankings and comparative statistics. Oral histories can be found in Eugene Murdock, *Baseball Players and Their Times* (1991), and Lawrence S. Ritter, *The Glory of Their Times* (1992). An obituary is in the *New York Times* (21 Mar. 1984).

THOMAS BARTHEL

COWLES, Gardner, Jr. ("Mike") (*b.* 31 January 1903 in Algona, Iowa; *d.* 8 July 1985 in Southampton, New York), media executive, publisher, and journalist who founded *Look* magazine in 1937.

The last of six children born to Florence M. Call and Gardner Cowles, Sr., Gardner junior was nicknamed "Mike" while yet an infant because his father thought he looked like an Irishman. Before young Mike turned one year old, his family moved to Des Moines, Iowa, where his father assumed ownership of the *Register and Leader* newspaper. In 1908 Gardner senior purchased the *Des Moines Tribune*. By 1927 he had absorbed other competitors and his Register and Tribune Company dominated print journalism in Des Moines with its morning daily, the *Register*, and its after-

Gardner Cowles, 1962. UPI/CORBIS-BETTMANN

noon daily, the *Tribune*. When old enough, Mike followed his older brother John to Phillips Exeter Academy, where he edited the *Exonian*, the school newspaper. Mike graduated from Phillips Exeter in 1921 and entered Harvard University. There too he edited the school's newspaper, the *Crimson*, as his brother had done before him. Tall, handsome, athletic, intellectual, and gentlemanly, Mike Cowles graduated from Harvard in 1925.

While in college, Cowles had spent his summers as a reporter in Des Moines, and in 1925 he became city editor for the *Register*. A year later he advanced to news editor; in 1927 he became the associate managing editor. At that time Cowles had the company purchase an airplane so that pictures and news items from across Iowa and the Midwest could be rushed to Des Moines. Eventually, the company owned several airplanes, and the papers became well known for their photos and sports coverage, especially in the *Sunday Register*.

In 1925 Cowles had asked George Gallup, a young journalism instructor, to survey newspaper readers to find out what they liked most in the *Sunday Register*. The answer was stories with several accompanying pictures. Consequently, Cowles initiated the practice in the *Sunday Register* of presenting headlines followed by a series of photographs that told the story. Mike Cowles became the paper's executive editor in 1931, and in 1933 he established a picture service, with the Register and Tribune Syndicate supplying rotogravure pictures to other newspapers. As Cowles made his mark as a leader in photojournalism and the use of wire photos, the Register and Tribune Company established a Washington, D.C., bureau for the gathering of national political news. In all, not only did the *Register* and *Tribune* increase their statewide prominence, but an association of Iowa's other daily newspapers formed to counteract Cowles's endeavors. Such action, however, only highlighted the scope of Cowles's success.

Cowles also looked at expanding the family's media holdings by buying radio stations. And in 1935 the Cowles bought the *Minneapolis Evening Star*, which Mike's brother John took over in 1938. About the same time, Mike decided to create a mass circulation magazine based around photojournalism. The result of his efforts was *Look* magazine in 1937. While critics dubbed the publication's first offerings "cheesecake" and "sensationalism," the magazine soon offered serious articles and achieved a circulation of two million in its first year. Cowles held the titles of editor in chief and chairman of the board of Cowles Communications, which published the magazine. In 1940 Cowles moved the offices of *Look* to New York City, and in 1945 he relocated from Des Moines to New York while remaining associate publisher for the Register and Tribune Company, a title he had assumed in 1939.

Over the years, Cowles's personal life had also taken some turns. In 1926 he had married Helen Curtiss; they divorced in 1930. On 17 May 1933 he married Lois Thornburg, a young professional journalist on the *Register*'s staff. They had four children.

Mike and John Cowles were also active in Republican party politics, especially promoting internationalism. In 1940 they were impressed with Wendell Willkie and his dark horse candidacy for the Republican presidential nomination. They not only threw their support behind Willkie but also helped him develop a campaign strategy that resulted in his receiving the nomination.

After World War II began, President Franklin D. Roosevelt asked Willkie to undertake a world tour to bolster Allied war efforts. Mike Cowles went with him, met world leaders, and was even granted a rare interview with Joseph Stalin. After the trip, Cowles aided Joseph Barnes in helping Willkie write his best-selling *One World* (1943), which did much to convince Americans to support plans for postwar international cooperation.

Also in 1942, Cowles accepted President Roosevelt's offer of the deputy directorship of the Office of War Information in charge of domestic operations. He oversaw the supplying of information and articles to national publications. However, after a few significant writers left the bureau in 1943, protesting what they considered an advertising effort to "sell the war," Cowles resigned. That same year, he replaced his father as president of the Register and Tribune Company and initiated a statewide Iowa opinion poll—the first such undertaking by a single newspaper operation.

Cowles, who continued to live in New York City, divorced Lois in 1946 and married Fleur Fenton, an advertising agent. In the following years Cowles strove to turn Cowles Communications into a media leader. In 1950 he produced *Quick*, a pocket-sized news magazine. It was canceled eventually. A few years later, *Flair,* a women's magazine with innovative covers and photo features, was produced, but it also failed. *Venture*, a travel magazine, was also produced and then dropped. Cowles purchased *Family Circle*, a supermarket magazine, and expanded its production. In 1959 he established the *San Juan Star*, the first English-language newspaper in Puerto Rico. And as a resident of Long Island, he undertook founding the *Suffolk Sun*, a new daily for the region, which ultimately folded. Nonetheless, despite blatant failures, at its height Cowles Communications owned *Look*, *Family Circle*, several trade magazines, an educational book publishing firm, newspapers, television stations, and a publications subscription sales service.

Of course, the flagship of the enterprises was *Look*. In 1969, *Look* had a circulation of almost eight million, with its highest numbers coming in 1967 when it serialized William Manchester's *Death of a President*, which generated a demand for nine and a half million copies. However, as competition from television for advertising and readers' time grew and production and mailing costs increased, the magazine lost money. Cowles consequently began to sell off the corporation's holdings to save *Look*. It did not work. In 1971 *Look* ceased publication. Cowles sold the remainder of Cowles Communications' companies to the New York Times Company for 23 percent of Times stock. Cowles Communications was dissolved in 1978. Cowles served as a director for the *New York Times* from 1971 to 1974. In 1971 he gave up the presidency of the Register and Tribune Company but remained chairman of the board until 1973. Cowles continued to chair the board of Cowles Broadcasting, a Des Moines–based television and radio company, until 1983.

After 1978 Cowles spent much of his time directing the Cowles Charitable Trust. His personal life had also changed over the years. He and Fleur divorced in 1955, and the next year he married Jan Streate Cox. Their family included a daughter and a son by Jan's previous marriage. Mike Cowles died of a heart attack following a treatment for cancer.

Cowles had been a leader in American journalism. With his father and his brother he had helped make the *Des Moines Register* not only one of the few statewide newspapers in the nation but also nationally recognized for its quality. He pioneered photojournalism and promoted mass circulation magazines as well as special interest publications. He knew many of the great men of his time—Stalin, Churchill, Roosevelt, Chiang Kai-shek, and Khrushchev, to name a few—and functioned with prominent statesmen, politicians, businessmen, artists, journalists, and civic leaders. In part, his legacy to the communications industry was evinced by his view that not only must newspapers exhibit truth, fairness, and balance but they must also be "entertaining and friendly." Additionally, he contributed with his example of embracing innovation and his willingness to expand the type and scope of his operations as he helped foster change in the communications market.

★

Copies of Cowles's memoir—Gardner Cowles, *Mike Looks Back: The Memoirs of Gardner Cowles, Founder of Look Magazine* (1985)—are limited and hard to access. For further reading on Cowles, see George Mills, *Harvey Ingham and Gardner Cowles: Things Don't Just Happen* (1977); Don Gussow, *Divorce Corporate Style* (1972); Kenneth Stewart and John Tebbel, *Makers of Modern Journalism* (1952); William B. Friedricks, "The Newspaper That Captured a State: A History of the *Des Moines Register*, 1849–1985," *Annals of Iowa* 54 (fall 1995): 303–337; N. R. Kleinfield, "Publishing Patriarch: Gardner Cowles Looking Back at *Look*,"

New York Times (6 Feb. 1983); and William Barry Furlong, "The Midwest's Nice Monopolists John and Mike Cowles," *Harpers* (June 1963). Obituaries are in the *Des Moines Register* and the *New York Times* (9 July 1985).

THOMAS BURNELL COLBERT

CRABBE, Clarence Linden ("Buster") (*b.* 7 February 1908 in Oakland, California; *d.* 23 April 1983 in Scottsdale, Arizona), Olympic swimming gold medalist and movie and television portrayer of Tarzan, Buck Rogers, Billy the Kid, Flash Gordon, and Captain Gallant.

Crabbe was the elder of two sons of Edward Clinton Crabbe, a real estate agent, and Agnes Lucy McNamara, a homemaker. In 1910 the family moved to Hawaii, where the elder Crabbe had been hired to oversee a pineapple plantation. At the age of five, Crabbe learned to swim, and the proximity of the Pacific Ocean presented an opportunity to hone his skills in swimming and surfing. In 1927 he graduated from Puna Hou High School in Honolulu, his athletic versatility clearly distinguished by his collection of sixteen varsity letters in football, basketball, track, and swimming. While a freshman at the University of Hawaii, he won the light-heavyweight boxing championship of the islands in 1928. He transferred to the University of Southern California in 1929 and earned a B.A. there in

Buster Crabbe, 1932. UPI/CORBIS-BETTMANN

1932. He decided to forgo studying for a law degree in order to train for the Olympics and pursue a movie career.

A two-time Olympian, Crabbe was overshadowed in his Olympic debut by the great Johnny Weissmuller at the 1928 Olympics in Amsterdam. On 6 August 1928 he claimed his first Olympic medal by finishing third in the 1,500-meter freestyle event. Three days later, in the 400-meter freestyle, he missed winning a bronze medal by one-tenth of a second. In 1929 Crabbe teamed with his younger brother, Edward Clinton "Buddy" Crabbe, Jr., to represent the Outrigger Canoe Club of Honolulu at the National Amateur Athletic Union swimming championships. On 25 August 1929 the brothers had accumulated twenty-three points— Buster had won four championships and twenty-one points, and Buddy, two points—and the Outrigger Canoe Club claimed the rights to the national title.

During the summer of 1932 Crabbe earned $8 a week at Silverwood's clothing store in Los Angeles, where he was a stock clerk. He juggled his work schedule with an intense training program in preparation for the 1932 Olympic Games in Los Angeles. On 10 August 1932 Crabbe brought 10,000 screaming fans to their feet with a come-from-behind finish in the 400-meter freestyle. He became an instant celebrity by breaking the string of gold medal performances of the Japanese, who had dominated the swimming events in Los Angeles. Favored to win the event was Jean Taris of France, the world record holder in the 400-meter freestyle. Taris led until the final 25 meters, when the superbly conditioned Crabbe began to close in on the Frenchman. With a strong kick and precision arm motion, the determined Crabbe surged from second place and out-touched Taris by one-tenth of a second.

By the time Crabbe ended his amateur swimming career in his final Olympic race on 13 August 1932, a fifth-place finish in the 1,500-meter freestyle, he had claimed thirty-five national titles, annexed sixteen international championships, and set five world records. Years later, Crabbe reflected on his Olympic and world record achievement and credited the tenth-of-a-second margin of victory with changing his life. Shortly before the 1932 Games, Crabbe had been photographed by Paramount Pictures. His stunning Olympic performance and the resulting media blitz solidified an opportunity to become a movie actor. Three days after his gold medal Olympic performance, Paramount selected Crabbe to star in a series of adventure films. His Adonis-like physique and athletic ability made him a natural for lead roles in these films.

Crabbe married Adah Virginia Held on 13 April 1933. The couple had three children and remained married until Crabbe's death.

In addition to releases by Paramount Pictures, Crabbe appeared in motion pictures for Universal Studios and Producers Releasing Corporation. His superb talent in five sports was eclipsed by his appearance in no fewer than 175 movies. Among his most notable films were *Tarzan the Fearless* (1933), *King of the Jungle* (1933), *Nevada* (1936), *Flash Gordon's Trip to Mars* (1938), *Mars Attacks the World* (1938), *Buck Rogers* (1939), *Queen of Broadway* (1943), *Last of the Redmen* (1947), *Caged Fury* (1948), *Gunfighters of Abilene* (1959), and *Arizona Raiders* (1965). During the 1930s and 1940s he appeared in the serials *Buck Rogers, Flash Gordon,* and *Billy the Kid.*

Crabbe earned his greatest acclaim for his portrayals of the dashing personalities of Billy the Kid, Buck Rogers, and Captain Gallant. He joined other Olympic stars in the popular Billy Rose Aquacade swimming extravaganza at the 1939–1940 New York World's Fair. He remained physically fit and enthusiastically accepted the lead role in his final television series, *Captain Gallant of the French Foreign Legion.* The Legion's reputation for wild adventure had long fascinated Crabbe. In October 1953 he flew to Rabat, in what was then French Morocco, and spent nine months there while the entire series was being filmed. The thirty-nine episodes were syndicated by the National Broadcasting Company from 1955 to 1961. In 1956 Crabbe became vice president of Cascade Industries, maker of Buster Crabbe pools.

In his later years Crabbe promoted his lifelong interest in physical fitness through lectures and writings. He wrote two exercise books. The first, published in 1976, was *Energistics: The Simple Shape-Up Exercise Plan;* the second, *Buster Crabbe's Arthritis Exercise Book,* written with Raphael Cilento, was released in 1980. Crabbe experienced minor heart problems in his later years and died of a heart attack at his home in Scottsdale, Arizona.

Crabbe, who never had much regard for his dramatic talent, starred in roles that offered adventure to adults and attracted young people who admired him as a hero. Although best known as an actor, he was also a gifted athlete who excelled in every sport he attempted. When the gloom of the Great Depression threatened to dampen the spirit of the 1932 Olympic Games, Crabbe's victory, along with the success of other American Olympians, temporarily lifted the spirits of his compatriots. Although it was his gold medal performance at the 1932 Olympic Games that catapulted him into the spotlight, he remained immensely popular through the 1960s.

★

The Henning Library at the International Swimming Hall of Fame in Fort Lauderdale, Florida, has a collection of Crabbe's pictures, papers on his swimming career, and memorabilia. See also Don Shay, *Conversations,* vol. 1 (1969). Obituaries are in the *Los Angeles Times* (24 Apr. 1983); *New York Times* (24 Apr. 1983); *Washington Post* (24 Apr. 1983); and *Chicago Tribune* (25 Apr. 1983).

PAULA D. WELCH

CRISLER, Herbert Orin ("Fritz") (*b.* 12 January 1899 near Earlville, Illinois; *d.* 19 August 1982 in Ann Arbor, Michigan), football player, coach, and athletic administrator inducted into the College Football Hall of Fame.

Crisler was the only child of Catherine and Albert Crisler, a carpenter who farmed. The nephew of a country doctor, Crisler grew up wanting to be a physician. Sports were not a priority for the tall, thin youngster: as a high school freshman, he was six feet tall and weighed just ninety-two pounds. Of the fifteen boys enrolled in Earlville High School, Crisler and a handicapped youth were the only ones not on the football team. He later transferred to Mendota High, where studies remained his first concern. Crisler's goal was an academic scholarship. By maintaining a four-year average of 93.4, he earned a full-tuition scholarship to the University of Chicago, where he matriculated in 1917.

At Chicago, an encounter with Amos Alonzo Stagg, Chicago's coach and already a football legend, spawned Crisler's football career. As Crisler later recalled, "I was

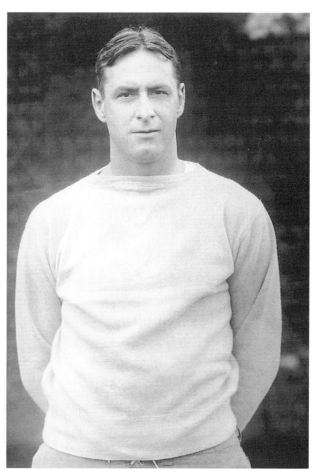

"Fritz" Crisler. PRO-FILE COLLECTION

wearing my green freshman beanie while watching practice. . . . A play came my way, [and] Mr. Stagg, avoiding the players, bumped into me and went down. He looked at me and asked why I wasn't out there with my classmates." Crisler responded that he had never played football. But Crisler was curious, so he drew equipment and reported to practice. He got "knocked from here to there" in a freshmen versus varsity scrimmage and promptly quit. Stagg saw him later and said, "I never figured you for a quitter." Crisler rejoined the team and would eventually earn nine varsity letters.

Crisler's rise to glory was neither smooth nor rapid. After competing on the frosh team, he, like many young men his age, spent 1918 in military service as the United States fought in World War I. Returning in 1919, he earned Stagg's wrath and a nickname. After Crisler repeatedly missed an assignment, he was rebuked by Stagg: "Crisler, there is a celebrated violinist whose name sounds like yours, but is spelled K-R-E-I-S-L-E-R. He's world renowned because he has genius, skill, coordination. From now on, Crisler, I'm going to call you Fritz, too, just to remind myself that you are his absolute opposite." The nickname stuck. In fact, a grandson of the coach was christened Fritz. Many knew coach Crisler was not the famous violinist, but few knew his given first name. Years later, when Fritz Kreisler was giving a concert in Ann Arbor, Michigan, the two met. They discussed family backgrounds and deduced that they were not related.

In 1922 Crisler graduated from Chicago with a B.A. in premedicine, after a solid, if not spectacular, football career. He almost made Phi Beta Kappa (several unexcused chapel "cuts" had cost him the honor points necessary for membership in the prestigious honor society). By this time, Stagg thought so highly of Crisler that he offered the young graduate a coaching position. Crisler married Dorothy Adams in 1923. Their only child, a son, Prescott ("Scotty"), recalls his father telling him a different version of the Fritz nickname: "My father said that Stagg told him after he [Crisler] missed several blocking assignments, 'I had a jackass [the closest Stagg ever got to using profanity] named Fritz; you remind me of him. So that's your name, Fritz.'"

Just two years after accepting the assistant's job at Chicago, Crisler was asked to coach at the University of Minnesota. Fritz turned down the offer when Stagg, after whom Crisler modeled his career, said, "Fritz, you're not ready to fly yet." Six years later, he accepted another Minnesota offer—with Stagg's blessing. His two-year record at Minnesota was 10–7–1.

When Princeton University courted Crisler in 1932, he left for New Jersey, but not before convincing Bernie Bierman to succeed him at Minnesota. Crisler said, "Little did I know at the time that that would come back to haunt me."

Princeton's Tigers were in the doldrums when Crisler arrived. In three previous seasons they had won a total of four games. Crisler immediately brought in a group of freshmen that included thirty high school and prep football captains. The star-studded group couldn't compete on the varsity in 1932, but Crisler, with his intricate "single-wing" offense, had a 2–2–3 record. Old Nassau's grads were mollified by a 7–7 tie with archrival Yale. The next three years, with the players in the class of 1936 maturing, were among the most notable in Princeton's long and storied history. The Tigers were undefeated in 1933, with a sizeable victory over Yale. Losing to Yale (7–0) was the only blemish in 1934. Undefeated again in 1935, Princeton thrashed Harvard, 35–0, and Yale, 38–7. The magic seemed to depart with the class of 1936. That fall the Tigers were 4–4–2, with a narrow (26–23) loss to Yale. After a 4–4 season in 1937, Crisler accepted an offer to be the University of Michigan's head coach.

At the time that Crisler became Michigan's coach, the Wolverines' gridiron fortunes had seen better days: the Maize & Blue had won only ten games between 1934 and 1937. With Tom Harmon and Forrest Evashevski, both All-American backs, Crisler produced immediate results in 1938 with a 6–1–1 record. The loss was to Bierman's Minnesota team. Minnesota also defeated Michigan in 1939 and in 1940, 7–6, to mar a perfect season.

Further developing his "spinner" series of plays and adding the "buck lateral" series, Crisler produced a single-wing attack that baffled opponents and dazzled fans. Crisler compiled a 71–16–3 record at Michigan, winning Big Ten championships in 1943 and 1947. In 1945 Crisler devised the "two-platoon system," which led to future specialization in football. Faced with the daunting task of playing the veteran team of Army, powered by "Touchdown Twins" Glenn Davis and Doc Blanchard, Crisler took his team of youngsters and divided them into two squads, one playing primarily on offense and another playing mainly on defense. Before the game, Crisler met the Cadets' coach, Colonel Earl ("Red") Blaik. As they parted, Crisler said, "May the best team win." Blaik said, "Don't you mean the better team?" Crisler said, "No, I mean best—I'm planning to use two myself." Michigan's youthful platoons proved no match for the Army juggernaut, and they were crushed. But that day a new approach to football was born.

With returning players in 1946, the Wolverines became a powerhouse again, peaking in 1947 when the Maize & Blue were undefeated, outscoring opponents 394 to 53. Voted national champions, the team capped the season with a 49–0 defeat of the University of Southern California in the Rose Bowl. Crisler, who was voted Coach of the Year, unexpectedly retired from coaching in 1948. He retained until 1968 his position as athletic director, a post he had held since 1941. In this position he oversaw the addition of many campus sports facilities. Perhaps his lasting legacy was the enlargement of Michigan Stadium to a capacity of 101,000, making it the largest on-campus football facility in the nation.

Crisler died at his Ann Arbor home of congestive heart failure. His remains were cremated, and his ashes were buried in Ann Arbor's Arborcreek Memorial Park.

Wherever Crisler coached, his records were among the best of his contemporaries. Not especially warm with those other than his family and close friends, Crisler was still highly respected by his players and opponents. Voted into the College Hall of Fame in 1954, he was also presented with the Touchdown Club of New York's highest honor— "for contributions of permanent value to the sport"—in 1955. His coaching record speaks for itself (116–32–9, lifetime), but as a life member of the National Collegiate Athletic Association football rules committee, he spearheaded the drive for many safety improvements, as well as the two-point conversion and the widening of the goalposts to encourage scoring. The University of Michigan honored Crisler in 1970 by naming its events building the Crisler Arena.

★

See Crisler's *Modern Football: Fundamentals and Strategy* (1949). His career is treated in Edwin Pope, *Football's Greatest Coaches* (1955); John D. McCallum and Charles H. Pearson, eds., *College Football USA* (1972); Tim Cohane, *Great College Football Coaches of the Twenties and Thirties* (1973); John D. McCallum, *Big Ten Football* (1976); and Melissa Larson, *College Football's Great Dynasties: Michigan* (1991). Obituaries are in the *New York Times* (21 Aug. 1982) and *Newsweek* (30 Aug. 1982).

JIM CAMPBELL

CRONIN, Joseph Edward (*b.* 12 October 1906 in San Francisco, California; *d.* 7 September 1984 in Osterville, Massachusetts), baseball player and manager who served as president of the American League and was elected to the National Baseball Hall of Fame.

Cronin was the youngest of three sons of Jeremiah Cronin, an Irish immigrant who drove a team of horses, and Mary Carolin, a native Californian of Irish descent. He grew up in the Excelsior district of San Francisco and developed into an outstanding all-around athlete on the playgrounds of the city. Although he won the San Francisco boys junior tennis championship in 1919, his first love was baseball.

Tall and rangy, with quick hands and a strong arm, Cronin became a standout shortstop on the sandlots and played for Mission High School for two years before the school burned down in 1923. He completed his secondary education at Catholic Sacred Heart High, where he starred in baseball, basketball, and soccer. After graduation in 1924, he spurned an athletic scholarship to nearby St. Mary's

Joseph Cronin. NATIONAL BASEBALL HALL OF FAME LIBRARY, COOPERSTOWN, N.Y.

College, because he believed that four more years of school would prevent him from earning money his family needed. Instead, Cronin took a job as an alternate instructor of the San Francisco Playground Commission and played in a semipro baseball league on Sundays for $12.50 per game. His superb fielding and timely hitting carried the Napa team to the league championship and brought him substantial offers from the hometown San Francisco Seals of the Pacific Coast League and the major league Pittsburgh Pirates. In September 1924 he signed a contract with the Pirates for a bonus of $200 and a salary of $400 per month.

Unable to dislodge Pirates regular Glenn Wright, one of the best shortstops in baseball, the slender, six-foot, 150-pound Cronin, who batted and threw right-handed, spent the better part of his first two professional seasons in the minor leagues. He hit for a .313 average at Johnstown (Pennsylvania) in the Middle Atlantic League in 1925 and .320 at New Haven (Connecticut) in the Eastern League in 1926. In 1927, his only full season with the Pirates, he appeared in just twelve games and batted an anemic .227.

Sold to the minor league Kansas City Blues of the American Association in 1928, Cronin played both shortstop and third base. He excelled in the field but his weak hitting continued, and he was about to be demoted further when scout Joe Engel negotiated his purchase by the Washington

Senators (then known as the Nationals or Nats) for $7,500. After backing up shortstop Bobby Reeves for most of the season, Cronin got the chance to play regularly when Reeves was moved to second base to replace manager Bucky Harris, who had been injured. Cronin fielded this position smoothly but struggled at the plate, batting only .242 in sixty-three games. In the off-season, he was nearly traded to the Boston Red Sox by Washington owner Clark Griffith along with four other players for Buddy Myer, a better-hitting shortstop. The Red Sox refused to take Cronin, however, and Griffith was forced to send Reeves to Boston to complete the deal. New manager Walter Johnson installed Myer at second base in 1929 and awarded Cronin the starting shortstop job. Cronin responded by leading the American League in assists and raising his batting average to a respectable .281.

From the outset of his career, Cronin worked tirelessly to become stronger physically and improve as a hitter. In addition to taking many hours of extra batting practice, he followed an off-season diet and exercise regimen that transformed him into a muscular 180-pounder. In 1930 Cronin's practice and conditioning paid dividends. He batted .346; led his team in hits, home runs, and runs batted in (RBIs); and was first among league shortstops in putouts, assists, and double plays. After almost single-handedly propelling the Senators up from fifth place to second, Cronin was chosen the American League's most valuable player by the *Sporting News*, beating out established stars Lou Gehrig of the New York Yankees and Al Simmons of the Philadelphia Athletics. Although he never again reached the dizzying heights of 1930, Cronin compiled batting averages of .306 in 1931, .318 in 1932, and .309 in 1933; led the American League in triples in 1932 and doubles in 1933; and drove in more than 100 runs for five consecutive seasons (1930–1934). He also outpaced other American League shortstops in putouts and double plays in 1931 and 1932, assists in 1932, and fielding percentage (.960) in 1933.

A fierce competitor, Cronin had firmly established himself as Washington's sparkplug and leader on the field by the time Griffith named him player-manager in 1932. The youngest field general in baseball history, the twenty-six-year-old Cronin led a talented Senators team that included Alvin Crowder, Goose Goslin, and Heinie Manush to the American League pennant in 1933, besting the powerful New York Yankees by seven games. Even though Cronin hit a sturdy .318 in the World Series, his team lost the championship to the New York Giants in five games.

In 1934 the Senators were plagued by injuries and plummeted to seventh place. Cronin was booed by Washington fans, and their abuse intensified after his engagement to the owner's niece (and adopted daughter) was announced. Griffith worried that his shortstop-manager would be under even greater pressure in Washington after the marriage

and dreaded the day when he might have to fire a member of his family. Consequently, when Thomas A. Yawkey, the wealthy new owner of the Boston Red Sox, offered the theretofore unheard-of sum of $250,000 (and shortstop Lyn Lary) for Cronin, Griffith accepted. On 27 September 1934, Cronin married Mildred June Robertson, Griffith's niece and secretary; they had four children.

With the Red Sox, the still-youthful Cronin had difficulty establishing his authority over the veteran players acquired from other clubs by Yawkey in his effort to rebuild the Boston team in the 1930s. Lefty Grove and Jimmie Foxx, who had played for Connie Mack on championship Philadelphia Athletics teams, often questioned their new manager's tactics and compared him unfavorably with Mack. At the same time, Yawkey, who became Cronin's friend as well as his patron, spoiled Grove, Foxx, and other recalcitrant stars and refused to discipline them. As a result, the Red Sox, in a state of constant turmoil, finished fourth in 1935, sixth in 1936, and fifth in 1937.

Cronin's situation improved after Yawkey and general manager Eddie Collins decided to reduce their reliance on older stars and develop young players in a farm system after 1937. The addition of stellar newcomers Ted Williams, Bobby Doerr, Dom DiMaggio, and Jim Tabor enabled Cronin to guide the Red Sox to four second-place finishes between 1938 and 1942. The playing manager, whose fielding skills had diminished noticeably after 1936, might have further strengthened the team if he had relinquished the shortstop position to Pee Wee Reese, another Boston farmhand. However, future Hall of Famer Reese was judged "too small" for the job and sold to the Brooklyn Dodgers in 1939. Cronin was the starting shortstop until 1942, when he finally named Johnny Pesky as his replacement.

Even as his fielding slipped, Cronin remained one of the best right-handed hitters in baseball. Taking advantage of the friendly left-field wall in Boston's Fenway Park, he batted .307 in 1937, .325 in 1938, .308 in 1939, and .311 in 1941; drove in over 100 runs in 1937, 1939, and 1940; and led the American League again in doubles in 1938. After leaving the starting lineup, Cronin set a league record with five pinch-hit home runs in 1943. A broken leg ended his playing career two years later. In twenty years in the major leagues, Cronin totaled 2,285 hits, 515 doubles, 118 triples, 170 home runs, and 1,424 RBIs. He had a lifetime batting average of .301 and a fielding mark of .953.

The return of Williams, Doerr, DiMaggio, Pesky, and pitching ace Tex Hughson from wartime service resulted in 104 victories (in 154 games) and a second American League pennant for Cronin in 1946. A World Series victory eluded him when the seemingly invincible Red Sox fell to the St. Louis Cardinals in seven games. After his club dropped to third in the standings in 1947, Yawkey moved Cronin up to the front office to replace Collins, whose health was failing. In fifteen seasons as a manager, Cronin's teams won 1,236 games and lost 1,055 (.540).

As Red Sox vice president and general manger from 1948 to 1959, Cronin directed a conservative organization that stressed hitting over pitching and defense. While Boston players were regularly among the leaders in batting average, home runs, and RBIs during these years, their one-dimensional ballclub won no pennants and finished no higher than third after 1949. Cronin and the Red Sox were also heavily criticized for being slow to sign and bring up black players. Boston was the last major league club to integrate, when infielder Pumpsie Green was promoted from the minors in 1959. Cronin's finest hour as a team executive came in 1952 when he sensitively handled the case of rookie outfielder Jim Piersall, who had suffered a nervous breakdown. After the Red Sox paid for his treatment, as well as a recuperative stay with his family in Florida, Piersall had six productive years for Boston and a seventeen-year big-league career.

Cronin was the first former player to become American League president, when, with Yawkey's backing, he was elected to succeed Will Harridge, who retired in 1959. During Cronin's two seven-year terms in office, the game on the field was almost overshadowed by news of franchise shifts, ownership changes, and labor disputes. At the same time, football gained substantially on baseball in the race for national popularity. Cronin oversaw the expansion of his league from eight to twelve teams by 1969; the controversial purchase of the Yankees by media giant CBS in 1966; and the transfer of franchises from Washington to Minnesota (1961), from Kansas City to Oakland (1968), and from expansion sites in Seattle and Washington to Milwaukee (1970) and Texas (1972), respectively. He also was on the negotiating team that hammered out basic agreements with the Major League Baseball Players Association (MLBPA) in 1966, 1969, and 1972. The initial refusal of Cronin and his colleagues to agree to the MLBPA's demand for a larger contribution by the owners to the players' pension fund precipitated the first strike in sports history in 1972. Innovations adopted to stem the rising tide of football during Cronin's league stewardship included divisional playoffs (1970) and the designated hitter rule (1973). After retiring from his post in 1973, Cronin chaired the American League board until 1984. He died of prostate cancer at his summer home on Cape Cod and was buried in St. Francis Xavier Cemetery in Centerville, Massachusetts.

Although Joe Cronin wore many hats during his nearly sixty-year career in baseball, he made his most significant contributions to the sport's history as a player. Named to the major league All-Star team by the Baseball Writers of America seven times between 1930 and 1940 and elected to the Hall of Fame in 1956, Cronin was the best shortstop of his baseball generation and had few peers as a clutch hitter.

On the latter point, the legendary Connie Mack once declared: "With a man on third and one out, I'd rather have Cronin hitting for me than anybody I've ever seen."

★

The National Baseball Hall of Fame Library in Cooperstown, N.Y., has a substantial clipping file on Cronin. Al Hirshberg, *From Sandlots to League President: The Story of Joe Cronin* (1962), is the only published biography. Cronin's life and career are discussed in some detail in Frederick G. Lieb, *The Boston Red Sox* (1947); Shirley Povich, *The Washington Senators* (1954); Ed Linn, *The Great Rivalry: The Yankees and the Red Sox, 1901–1990* (1991); and Peter Golenbock, *Fenway: An Unexpurgated History of the Boston Red Sox* (1992). See also Ed Linn, "Joe Cronin: The Irishman Who Made His Own Luck," *Sport* (Apr. 1956), and Bob Broeg, "None Better in the Clutch Than Cronin," *Sporting News* (22 Aug. 1970). Obituaries are in the *Boston Globe* and *New York Times* (both 8 Sept. 1984) and in *Sporting News* (17 Sept. 1984).

RICHARD H. GENTILE

CROWTHER, (Francis) Bosley, Jr. (*b.* 13 July 1905 in Lutherville, Maryland; *d.* 7 March 1981 in Mount Kisco, New York), film critic for the *New York Times* and author of five best-selling books on film history and criticism; he was one of the most influential and widely respected critics of the Golden Age of Hollywood.

Crowther was one of two children born to Francis Bosley Crowther, a sales manager in the oil business, and Eliza Leisenring Crowther; the family lived in a small community just outside Baltimore. Bosley grew up with the infant motion-picture industry, seeing his first film when he was five years old. He remembered a traveling exhibition of Lyman B. Howe, who supplemented his pictures with sound produced from a gramophone behind a screen.

Crowther took his schooling seriously, first in Lutherville, where his gifts in language and storytelling were often on display, and later in high schools in Winston-Salem, North Carolina, and Washington, D.C., where he began to cultivate a rich voice, a regal bearing, and a slightly patrician manner. The family's income allowed him to develop his skills as a writer at Woodberry Forest School in Woodberry Forest, Virginia, and at Princeton University, where he enrolled in 1924, served as editor of the *Daily Princetonian,* and, at five feet, seven inches and with a barrel chest, engaged in semiprofessional boxing activities. After graduating from Princeton with a B.A. degree in history in 1928, Crowther came to the *New York Times*, serving an apprenticeship as general reporter, feature writer, and rewrite man. On 20 January 1933 he married Florence Marks, who also worked at the *Times*; they would have three sons. He became the paper's film critic in 1940.

From the outset Crowther approached movie criticism with the same thoroughness of preparation and elegance in writing that had established his reputation as a journalist. His early appreciation of Walt Disney's *Fantasia* (1940) demonstrated an affinity for films in which their creators' "imaginative excursions" expanded the possibilities of cinema. As chairman of the New York Film Critics in 1940 he championed the cause of *The Grapes of Wrath* (1940), seeing John Ford's depiction of the victimization of the Great Depression era's agrarian class as a sociological study of mere man tenaciously fighting powerful adversaries. Critics divided over Charlie Chaplin's parody of Adolf Hitler in *The Great Dictator* (1940), but Crowther showed signs of things to come by naming Chaplin's "devastatingly matchless comic invention" the year's best.

During the war years Crowther came to recognize the power of his position as film critic of the nation's newspaper of record. It led to his scholarly search for "cinematic substance" and "artistry that moved the spirit through noble drama, humor, poetry, grace, and intelligence." He celebrated *Citizen Kane* (1941) for its "surprising inventions of cinema syntax" and defended its architect, the twenty-four-year-old "youthful genius" Orson Welles, against attacks in the newspapers of William Randolph Hearst, upon whom the film is loosely based. Crowther's favorable reception of *In Which We Serve* (1942), *Henry V* (1944), *Les Enfants du Paradis* (1945), and *Ivan the Terrible* (1945) showed his early advocacy of foreign films. At the height of the studio era the *New York Times* reviewed 500 films each year, nearly 200 of them made abroad, and most of these were seen by Crowther. He attended three to four films weekly and preferred writing reviews immediately afterward, often rushing back to his office and writing against a deadline.

The immediate postwar years brought the breakup of the system in which a handful of Hollywood studios controlled the production, distribution, and exhibition of motion pictures. The result was that studio profit margins diminished, fewer films were made, and longtime contract stars were left to fend for themselves. Crowther chronicled the collapse of the studio system and urged audiences to support the handful of quality films still being exhibited. In Billy Wilder's *The Lost Weekend* (1945), a bleak portrayal of alcoholism and delirium tremens, and *The Best Years of Our Lives* (1946), William Wyler's canvas of beleaguered servicemen home from the war, Crowther noted a new realism worthy of praise and emulation.

The power in moviemaking had shifted from the studio to the director, a trend Crowther was quick to recognize and encourage. His praise for John Huston's *The Treasure of the Sierra Madre* (1948), "a stark contemplation of the brutal consequences of sheer, raw greed," and Vittorio de Sica's *The Bicycle Thief* (1948), "a poignant survey of the desperate life of a poor bill-poster in Rome," focused on their "strong emotion and fresh vitality," which promised to rescue filmmakers and filmgoers from the encroach-

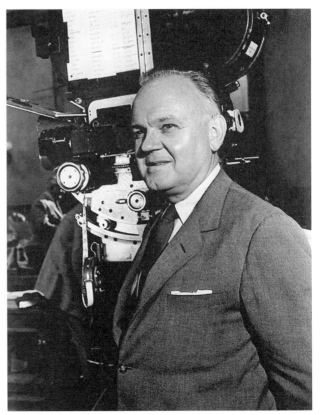

Bosley Crowther. ARCHIVE PHOTOS

ments of television. Crowther was contemptuous of television's tendency "to level the minds of everyone" by a ceaseless flow of programming designed to "damage and deaden" the taste of American audiences. He was certain that the rise of television as the nation's central cultural force in the 1950s and 1960s "contracted the audience's attention span" with a sameness that diminished viewers' recognition of and desire for quality.

Crowther deplored the rise of McCarthyism and the blacklisting of supposed communist sympathizers in Hollywood, and he excoriated the superpatriotic films of the early 1950s. He was an equally outspoken critic of film censorship and urged filmmakers to show social responsibility. Fred Zinnemann's *High Noon* (1952), "a stunning comprehension of a courageous man in a world of bullies and poltroons," and Elia Kazan's *On the Waterfront* (1954), celebrating a dockworker who "fearlessly breaks the rule of silence and inattention," were in Crowther's mind truly heroic films. Federico Fellini's *La Strada* (1956), Satyajit Ray's "Apu" trilogy (1956–1959), Alain Resnais's *Hiroshima, Mon Amour* (1959), and Luis Buñuel's *Viridiana* (1961) offered Crowther and filmgoers new heroes, who attempted to create meaning by simply surviving in a world that was alternately threatened by boredom and nuclear annihilation.

In two widely selling books, *The Lion's Share: The Story of an Entertainment Empire* (1957) and *Hollywood Rajah: The Life and Times of Louis B. Mayer* (1960), Crowther examined the growth and dissolution of Metro-Goldwyn-Mayer, the richest and most prestigious of the five Hollywood studios that had dominated moviemaking across four decades. Set against the landscape of industrial America, Crowther's story of the factory system that manufactured dreams and celebrity reveals "a long and lusty drama" of "giants and genius."

By the 1960s Crowther had solidified his place as the most powerful and widely quoted of U.S. film critics. He lectured widely and appeared on radio and television. He served three times as chairman of the New York Film Critics Circle and received the first award for film criticism given by the Screen Directors Guild. His movie reviews did not, however, go unchallenged. His praise for such Hollywood blockbusters as *Gigi* (1958), *Ben-Hur* (1959), *West Side Story* (1961), *Cleopatra* (1963), and *My Fair Lady* (1964) suggested to some younger reviewers that he had either sold out or was out of touch with where moviemaking was headed. When Crowther denounced Arthur Penn's acclaimed *Bonnie and Clyde* (1967) as a "pointless blending of farce with brutal killings," he was again alienated from the majority critical consensus.

The publication of his *Great Films: Fifty Golden Years of Motion Pictures* in 1967 coincided with his retirement as chief critic of the *Times*. The book celebrated film's unique ability to "stimulate and expand human experience." Crowther estimated that in twenty-seven years he had seen more than 7,000 films, the very best of them as important and lasting as anything produced in twentieth-century art. This was why he regarded movies as a resource worthy of the same care and preservation as the great literary and symphonic classics. It was the responsibility of film lovers of his generation, he argued in his last book, *Reruns: Fifty Memorable Films* (1978), to pass on the great films to the next generation as if handling a family heirloom.

Crowther served as critic emeritus of the *Times* beginning in January 1968. The Motion Picture Association of America and the Independent Film Importers and Distributors of America established an annual scholarship to honor his contribution to the understanding of film as an art form. Fifteen film critics from competing newspapers, magazines, and a broadcast network honored him with a special award. A weekly syndicated radio show hosted by Crowther was launched in March 1968. That summer the Museum of Modern Art ran a series of fifty films he had chosen as the movie industry's all-time best. In July the nation's theater operators honored Crowther for his critical contributions to excellence in film. In September, Crowther left the *Times* to serve as an executive consultant for Co-

lumbia Pictures, advising the company on the acquisition of novels, plays, and original scripts.

Crowther's death from a heart attack in 1981 came several days after he and his wife saw *Tess,* an elegant adaptation of the Thomas Hardy classic, the kind of film Crowther loved. His remains were cremated. During his career he had carefully chronicled the emergence of the Hollywood studio system as America's premier cultural institution and later had encouraged the development of independent filmmakers whose work would displace that of studios in the age of television. Throughout, Bosley Crowther's critical voice could be heard urging moviemakers to use the universal language of cinema to further "the eventual brotherhood of mankind."

★

A collection of Crowther's papers is at Brigham Young University. In addition to the books mentioned above, Crowther wrote *Vintage Films: Fifty Enduring Motion Pictures* (1977), a series of essays on selected movies. Many of his reviews are collected in *The New York Times Directory of the Film* (1971), with an introduction by Arthur Knight. Obituaries are in the *New York Times* and *Los Angeles Times* (both 8 Mar. 1981).

BRUCE J. EVENSEN

CUKOR, George Dewey (*b.* 7 July 1899 in New York City; *d.* 24 January 1983 in Los Angeles, California), director of many popular film comedies and melodramas, noted for eliciting memorable performances from Katharine Hepburn, Jean Harlow, Greta Garbo, and other actresses.

Cukor was the only son of Victor Cukor, an assistant district attorney in New York City, and Helen Gross, a homemaker. He had one sister. He was named after the Spanish-American War hero Admiral George Dewey, at the suggestion of his grandfather, a Hungarian-Jewish immigrant. After graduating from DeWitt Clinton High School in 1917, Cukor served briefly in the Student Army Training Corps at the City College of New York until November 1918.

A self-described "stage-struck kid," Cukor sought work in the theater. He began as an assistant stage manager for a touring Chicago company of *The Better 'Ole* in 1919, moved to Broadway as a stage manager in 1919, then went to Rochester, New York, as director and later manager of the Knickerbocker Players, a summer stock company, during most of the 1920s.

The introduction of sound into movies created a demand in Hollywood for dialogue experts, and Cukor went to work for Paramount Studios in 1929, initially as a dialogue director and later as a codirector. His early work included *All Quiet on the Western Front* (1930), *The Royal Family of Broadway* (1930), and *Tarnished Lady* (1931), his first film as principal director. He also directed *What Price Hollywood?* (1932) and *A Bill of Divorcement* (1932). The latter marked the screen debut of Katharine Hepburn, who recalled her impression of Cukor in her memoirs *Me: Stories of My Life* (1991): "He was really fat—about five feet eight inches and over 220 pounds. He was energetic, full of laughter and vitality. He summed me up very accurately for what I was: a lady, so-called—a sort of snob—and totally insecure. I summed him up too. Very bright—sharp as a tack and a good sense of humor." The film initiated a professional association that resulted in ten films, as well as a lifelong friendship.

Artistic differences with producer Ernst Lubitsch during the filming of *One Hour with You* (1932) caused Cukor to leave Paramount and join RKO. He worked closely at RKO with producer David O. Selznick, and later followed him to Metro-Goldwyn-Mayer (MGM). Cukor's films included the classic comedy *Dinner at Eight* (1933); *Little Women* (1933), a popular and critical success that marked his arrival as one of Hollywood's top directors; *David Copperfield* (1935); *Sylvia Scarlett* (1936); *Romeo and Juliet* (1936); *Camille* (1937); and *Holiday* (1938). Many of his films were adaptations of stage plays, which Cukor filmed with a minimal amount of camera movement. His guiding rule was: "Unless you have to move the camera, unless it does something for you, be quiet. When you cut, you have to do it delicately, not adventurously. You mustn't show off with the camera."

In 1938 Selznick selected Cukor to direct the widely anticipated *Gone with the Wind* (1939). Cukor spent a year on preproduction work, but directed only the first ten days of filming. The male lead, Clark Gable, felt that Cukor was overly attentive to Vivien Leigh and Olivia de Havilland, and feared that his own role would be overshadowed. One day Gable announced that he wouldn't be directed by "a fairy" and walked off the set; his box office clout forced Selznick (whom Gable privately referred to as "that Jewboy up there") to bring in Gable's friend Victor Fleming to finish directing the film.

Cukor immediately went to work on the film version of Clare Boothe Luce's hit play *The Women* (1939), although he spent his weekends still secretly coaching Leigh and de Havilland for their performances in *Gone with the Wind*. *The Women* was a popular and critical success and is now considered a comedy classic, as is *The Philadelphia Story* (1940). This highly successful film version of Philip Barry's comedy revived the career of Katharine Hepburn, who had been declared "box-office poison" after several earlier unsuccessful films, and earned her costar Jimmy Stewart an Academy Award.

Ruth Hussey's supporting role in *The Philadelphia Story* also earned an Academy Award nomination, which she attributed to Cukor's direction: "George didn't say, 'Well, let's try again.' . . . His corrections were more like 'A little more

George Cukor. ARCHIVE PHOTOS

color' or 'A little more depth,' or 'Lighten it up a bit.'" Hussey was also struck by Cukor's habit of mouthing the actors' parts during their filming: "His gestures were hilarious. If I was supposed to be smiling, he was smiling. If I was frowning, he was frowning. He just acted the whole thing."

After the United States entered into World War II, Cukor enlisted in the U.S. Army Signal Corps in October 1942 as a private and directed several propaganda and technical training films at the Astoria Studios in New York City. When his efforts to obtain an officer's commission were unsuccessful, he resigned in 1943 and returned to Hollywood. His next films were *Winged Victory* (1944), a revue celebrating the U.S. Army Air Corps, and *Gaslight* (1944), a sinister melodrama that earned Ingrid Bergman an Academy Award. Using this film as an illustration of his approach to directing, he told an interviewer: "If you're going to do a story about a murder in a Victorian house, you make it claustrophobic, clouded. You research the period, not just to reproduce things physically, but for the emotions to stir up. The text dictates the whole style."

Many of Cukor's films of the late 1940s were unmemorable, but he began a collaboration with screenwriters Garson Kanin and Ruth Gordon that resulted in several classic comedies. *Adam's Rib* (1949) starred Katharine Hepburn and Spencer Tracy and gave Judy Holliday her first important role. Cukor paired Hepburn and Tracy again in *Pat and Mike* (1952) and elicited further outstanding performances from Judy Holliday in *Born Yesterday* (1950), *The Marrying Kind* (1952), and *It Should Happen to You* (1954). He helped Judy Garland, rejected by the studios because of her addiction to drugs and alcohol, make a stunning comeback in *A Star Is Born* (1954), then he returned to Broadway briefly in 1955 to direct a stage production of *The Chalk Garden* at the Ethel Barrymore Theatre.

Cukor's films of the later 1950s and 1960s covered several genres, including adventure films like *Bhowani Junction* (1956) and *Wild Is the Wind* (1957); musicals like *Les Girls* (1957), *Let's Make Love* (1960), and *My Fair Lady* (1964), which won him an Academy Award for best director; and his only Western, *Heller in Pink Tights* (1960), which chronicled the misadventures of a theatrical troupe in the West. Although *Heller* was neither a critical nor a popular success, Cukor considered it one of his favorite films, along with *Little Women*.

Cukor formed his own film production company, GDC Enterprise, in 1962, but was unable to obtain sufficient financing for any of his projects. He returned to studio employment to direct *Justine* (1969) for Twentieth Century–Fox and *Travels with My Aunt* (1972) for MGM, neither of which was a popular success.

The University of California at Los Angeles awarded Cukor an honorary doctorate in 1967, Brandeis University bestowed a Creative Arts Award in 1979, and many museums and revival houses began retrospectives of his work in the 1970s. Ironically, just as the public honors began flowing, Cukor was having trouble finding further employment because of the decline of movie audiences and cutbacks in movie studios. He directed Katharine Hepburn again in *Love Among the Ruins* (1975), a made-for-television film that earned him an Emmy Award for best director. After directing *The Blue Bird* (1976), the first Russian-American coproduction and a box office failure, he made another television film with Hepburn, *The Corn Is Green* (1979), their last film together. His final motion picture was *Rich and Famous* (1981), which paired two newcomers from a younger generation of actresses, Candice Bergen and Jacqueline Bisset.

Cukor died of heart failure and was buried in the Goldwyn family crypt at Forest Lawn Memorial Park, Glendale, California, beside his close friend Frances Goldwyn, wife of the film producer Samuel Goldwyn. Cukor, who was homosexual, left no family; screenwriter and associate Garson Kanin declared that Cukor was "survived by his work."

Cukor's movie career spanned half a century. He was frequently characterized as a "woman's director," primarily because of his adroit handling of actresses, but he loathed the appellation and was always quick to point out that he also obtained consistently strong performances from actors like Cary Grant and Spencer Tracy. But fellow director

Joseph Mankiewicz noted: "What was special about George was his serene relationship with actresses . . . they knew he would never get them into bed. George was not threatening. . . . They knew he adored women." Mankiewicz also told an interviewer: "I don't know if you should quote me on this, but I mean it kindly. In a way, George Cukor was one of the first great female directors of Hollywood."

★

The George Cukor Special Collection is at the Academy of Motion Picture Arts and Sciences, Los Angeles; other primary sources are the papers of Stanley Musgrove (Cukor's publicist), the Warner Brothers collection, and the Norma Shearer collection, all in the Cinema-Television Archives at the University of Southern California. Two early biographies, Carlos Clarens, *George Cukor* (1976), and Gene D. Phillips, *Cukor* (1982), have been superseded by Patrick McGilligan, *George Cukor: A Double Life* (1991), and Emanuel Levy, *George Cukor: Master of Elegance* (1994), whose authors had access to Cukor's papers. Cukor's films, rather than his personal life, are the focus of Barbara Helen Battle, "George Cukor and the American Theatrical Film" (Ph.D. diss., Columbia University, 1969); Gary Carey, *Cukor and Company: The Films of George Cukor and His Collaborators* (1972); and James Bernardoni, *George Cukor: A Critical Study and Filmography* (1985). His work in genre films is mentioned in Stanley Clavell, *Pursuits of Happiness: The Hollywood Comedy of Remarriage* (1981), and Christine Gledhill, ed., *Home Is Where the Heart Is: Studies in Melodrama and the Woman's Film* (1987). For details about individual films, see Gavin Lambert, *GWTW: The Making of Gone with the Wind* (1973); Robert Darrel Jackson, "*Romeo and Juliet* on Film: A Comparative Analysis of Three Major Film Versions of Shakespeare's Play" (Ph.D. diss., Wayne State University, 1978); and Ronald Haver, *A Star Is Born: The Story of the Making of the 1954 Movie and Its 1983 Restoration* (1988). Also useful are Garson Kanin, *Tracy and Hepburn: An Intimate Memoir* (1971); Molly Haskell, *From Reverence to Rape: The Treatment of Women in the Movies* (1973); Neal Gabler, *An Empire of Their Own: How the Jews Invented Hollywood* (1988); A. Scott Berg, *Goldwyn* (1989); and David Thompson, *Showman: The Life of David O. Selznick* (1992).

Obituaries are in the *New York Times* (26 Jan. 1983) and *Variety* (26 Jan. 1983). Gavin Lambert, *On Cukor* (1972), and Gene D. Phillips, *The Movie Makers: Artists in an Industry* (1973), contain interviews with Cukor.

STEPHEN G. MARSHALL

CURRAN, Joseph Edwin (*b.* 1 March 1906 in New York City; *d.* 14 August 1981 in Boca Raton, Florida), labor union official who led the National Maritime Union from 1937 until 1973.

Curran was born on the Lower East Side of New York City. His father, Eugene Curran, died when Joseph was two; his mother, Ida Cohan Curran, became a cook in Westfield,

New Jersey, remarried, and sent Joseph to board with a family. Expelled from parochial school in the seventh grade for poor attendance, he worked as a caddy and a factory hand until, at the age of sixteen, he shipped out as an ordinary seaman. For fourteen years he made his living at sea, rising to the rank of able-bodied seaman and eventually earning the highest unlicensed rating, boatswain. In the latter rank he managed the crew, no easy task with many of the drifters and "performers" who then went to sea. But at six feet, two inches, and 220 pounds of visible muscle, Curran ran a tight ship, earning the epithet "No Coffee Time Joe" from seamen denied the customary twice-daily coffee breaks.

Curran catapulted to fame in March 1935 when he led a two-day sit-down strike in the port of San Pedro, California; the target was the SS *California,* which had sailed from New York City. The plight of the 400 passengers, who included celebrities, marooned on a luxury liner attracted national attention. The stoppage was planned by the Communist group within the International Seamen's Union (ISU), an affiliate of the American Federation of Labor (AFL).

Joseph Curran, 1957. ARCHIVE PHOTOS

Curran's subsequent emergence as a labor leader at the age of thirty-two was largely accidental. He was not, and never became, a communist, which worked heavily in his favor because the Communist party's policy was to push nonmembers to the heads of its dependent organizations (such as labor unions). In some ways Curran was an odd choice because he had no union background other than a few months in the ISU, which had a closed shop. But he had personal assets that included being a good seaman with tattoos on his hands and "a rough-looking appearance." Moreover, his friends and his enemies agreed upon his intelligence as well as his gifts as an extemporaneous speaker. Like many seamen he was an omnivorous reader. Throughout his union career Curran boasted that his favorite reading matter was *Robert's Rules of Order.* His mastery of parliamentary procedure contributed to his control of fractious union meetings. Although the Communist party had a number of gifted men in its organizing efforts to overthrow the ISU, Curran's leadership qualities, enhanced by his charisma, made him indispensable to the creation of the National Maritime Union (NMU).

The founding convention of the NMU took place in New York City in July 1937, and the new organization elected Curran its president. The NMU affiliated with the Congress of Industrial Organizations (CIO) and quickly became the largest organization of unlicensed seamen, claiming a probably exaggerated membership of 51,000 in 1939. By contrast, its national rival, the Seafarers International Union (SIU), chartered in 1938 by the AFL, had about 15,000 members in 1939.

Second only to Harry Bridges, head of the International Longshoremen's and Warehousemen's Union (ILWU), Curran was the favorite union leader of the Communist party, whose propaganda machine promoted him at every turn. Within the NMU, more than 100 of the 150 full-time officers, and nearly all appointed and staff personnel, were Communist party members, and those who were not Marxists were mostly fellow travelers whose views and activities were frequently indistinguishable from those of dues-paying communists. A number of other international unions and subordinate bodies were led or staffed by Communist party members, but in none was the party control so complete. Not unexpectedly the union followed the party line on all issues.

Curran married Retta Toble, a former shipmate, in 1939; they had one son. His wife died in 1963, and he married Florence B. Stetler in 1965.

In 1940 Curran was elected a national vice president of the CIO and the first president of the Greater New York Industrial Union Council, whose 118 affiliated local CIO unions represented more than 300,000 members. During World War II the NMU followed the Communist party line of no work stoppage under any circumstances. No matter what the provocation and heedless of its war-enhanced economic power, the NMU took pride in refraining even from threats of retaliation. The union paid a steep price for this rigidity, for despite winning bargaining rights with several major shipping companies in National Labor Relations Board elections, the companies' refusal to bargain effectively ended negotiations and the companies remained nonunion.

The wartime buildup of the U.S. merchant marine resulted in a vast increase in NMU membership, which reached more than 77,000 in 1945. The SIU announced at that time that its membership was around 60,000, undoubtedly an overstated figure. In 1945 the NMU was at the crest of its power, with a net worth in the millions of dollars and $2 million a year in dues income. Its communist leadership consisted of youthful, vigorous, and talented men with considerable achievements and reputations.

Within a year the Communist party domination of the NMU began to disintegrate. A major blow was the loss to the SIU of a bargaining election in the Isthmian Steamship Company, a subsidiary of U.S. Steel and by far the largest nonunion shipping company in the country with more than 100 vessels and 5,000 jobs. This was a crushing and unexpected defeat for the communist organizers, who had unlimited expense accounts and enjoyed the formidable resources of their national political party.

Curran was heartened at the damage to the Communist party's self-esteem and self-confidence, because he had become increasingly uneasy about his alliance with the party. In May 1946 the Communist party had selected Harry Bridges and Curran to head the Committee for Maritime Unity (CMU), a new organization ostensibly designed to be a national federation of all 215,000 maritime workers. In fact, however, it threatened to be an instrument to undermine his position within the NMU. The outbreak of the cold war and the disarray of the American Communist Party, which had expelled Earl Browder and other leading officials, shifted the political winds to an anticommunist direction. With the support of three top NMU officers who had just resigned from the Communist party and other disillusioned former communists, Curran, for the first time in his career, began to criticize the Communist party. By the end of 1946 he had resigned from the CMU, an act that not only destroyed that body but also was the irrevocable move in ending his collaboration with the communists.

Throughout 1947 Curran fought against the entrenched NMU officialdom, each side knowing that this was a life-and-death issue. No holds were barred, the outcome was touch-and-go, and not even the turbulent constitutional convention in the fall was conclusive, although its voting tilted in Curran's favor. In one major dispute Curran prevailed by only two votes (out of about 600), and he lost other ballots. The convention ended in disorder, with both

Curran and many of his enemies elected to major posts.

By the time of the next convention, in 1949, Curran was securely in control of the NMU. Communist officials were expelled from the union for one reason or another after he was able to secure passage of a constitutional amendment barring communists from membership. That loss of membership meant loss of employment for hundreds of professional seamen, and on civil liberties grounds the most prominent of Curran's allies in his struggle with the Communist party fought the ban. Curran saw to it that they were expelled from the union on trumped-up charges. Thus, over time both opponents and supporters suffered the same fate.

Curran was reelected president of the NMU at every convention until his retirement in 1973, but his reign was repeatedly challenged. He suffered a heart attack in 1953, and devoted less and less time to his union duties, delegating much of his authority to unelected staff assistants. In 1960, one year after the passage of the Landrum-Griffin legislation protecting union democracy, the Department of Labor charged that the last NMU election had been conducted without adequate safeguards. The case was settled on the basis that the union would reform its practices in the 1966 election. However, the federal government was forced to file suit in 1966 (and at every subsequent election), and the court ordered a new election. In it Curran ran far ahead of the rest of his slate and was elected to his fifteenth and last term. Although the election was severely criticized by some observers, the government accepted the result.

When Curran retired in 1973, he was making $85,000 annually, one of the highest salaries of any American union official. His retirement package, which occasioned an outcry at the 1973 convention and later a successful court suit, provided a lump-sum payment of $717,600, severance pay of $250,000, and an annual pension of $46,476. In 1979 a court ordered him to give back some of this, terming it excessive.

Shortly before Curran retired, the NMU membership was about 45,000; its rival, the SIU, reported over 80,000. The NMU's membership decline continued. Within twenty years of his retirement, the NMU disappeared as an independent union by becoming a subsidiary of the Marine Engineers Benevolent Association. Curran died of a heart attack at age seventy-five.

★

See Murray Kempton, *Part of Our Time* (1955); Joseph P. Goldberg, *The Maritime Story: A Study in Labor-Management Relations* (1958); Bert Cochran, *Labor and Communism: The Conflict That Shaped American Unions* (1977); Gary M. Fink, ed., *Labor Unions* (1977). An obituary is in the *New York Times* (15 Aug. 1981).

PHILIP ROSS

D

D'AMATO, Constantine ("Cus") (*b.* 17 January 1908 in New York City; *d.* 4 November 1985 in New York City), trainer, manager, and "boxing professor."

"Cus" D'Amato, the seventh of eight sons of Italian immigrants, was born in the South Bronx. His mother died when he was four, and he later described his father, an ice deliverer, as "the hardest, yet kindliest man I ever knew." While he did not last long in school, D'Amato's Bronx childhood, during which a neighborhood fight made him nearly blind in one eye, left him peculiarly qualified in later life to help street toughs transform themselves into disciplined boxers, sometimes into champions.

D'Amato started the Empire Boxing Club, with his friend Jack Barrow, at the Gramercy Gym on Manhattan's East Fourteenth Street in 1939. From the late 1930s to the early 1960s the Gramercy was the temple where he preached his philosophy of "elusive aggression" (the hands-under-chin, head-bobbing style made famous by boxers Floyd Patterson and, later, Mike Tyson) and where Cus often slept on a cot, guarded by a dog. After World War II (he claimed he cheated on the eye test to get into the army), one of D'Amato's best amateur prospects was a New York City fighter named Rocky Graziano, who left Cus when he turned professional and later became middleweight champion. Cus maintained a contractless policy with many of his fighters despite the bitter loss. He was less obliging with some of the rulers of boxing in the late 1940s and 1950s,

however, doing battle with mobsters and boxing officials and with the organizations where they fused, such as the International Boxing Club (IBC). As paranoid as he was brilliant, D'Amato feared attacks by gangsters much of his life.

In 1952 a Brooklyn delinquent named Floyd Patterson was brought to Cus by his coach at the Young Men's Christian Association. Later that year, Patterson won the Olympic gold medal at Helsinki as a middleweight. He then signed as a professional with D'Amato, who was criticized for developing Patterson against some underskilled competition. Nevertheless, Patterson took the heavyweight title four years later by knocking out Archie Moore in Chicago. At twenty-one, Patterson was the youngest heavyweight champ to date. These were full but frustrating years for D'Amato, and his unconventional style annoyed many sportswriters. During Patterson's first reign, the writer A. J. Liebling described D'Amato as "a middle-sized man of fifty or so, with a round head topped by white hair, which he wears close-cropped. He carries his head cocked argumentatively to one side, as if ready to slip a punch, and moves with brittle alacrity, like the straight man among the Fratellini clowns." Despite his brief education, D'Amato claimed a lifelong fondness for another American curmudgeon, Mark Twain.

In 1959, after having spent years fighting the notoriously corrupt International Boxing Commission (which had controlled the heavyweight championship before Rocky Mar-

Cus D'Amato, 1957. UPI/CORBIS-BETTMANN

ciano's retirement) and protecting his boxers, especially Patterson, from its influence, D'Amato went too far. He ran afoul of the New York State Athletic Commission for, among other things, breaking the rule in the first Floyd Patterson–Ingemar Johannson fight forbidding a promoter from also serving as a manager. D'Amato refused to appear at the hearing and was suspended. The suspension was moot, a court ruled, because D'Amato's license had already expired. Nevertheless, D'Amato refused to reapply to the commission and give anyone the chance to turn him down. From then on, others worked the corner for him as proxies; in later years these included Teddy Atlas and Kevin Rooney, wild youngsters whom D'Amato helped redirect into star trainers in their own right.

Despite his fighters' successes, D'Amato cared too little for money. In the late 1960s, during a time of financial trouble, he moved upstate with his longtime companion, the Ukrainian-born Camille Ewald, into a big Victorian house outside Catskill, New York, where he founded the Catskill Boxing Club above the town's police station. In 1980 an ex-fighter working at the nearby Tryon School for Boys told him about a promising but troubled twelve-year-old from Brooklyn who wanted to box. The similarities to the young Floyd Patterson were clear, and Cus made the career of Mike Tyson, whom he had adopted, the final project of his life. "I knew that a kid who loved pigeons couldn't be all bad," he told interviewers. "You had to peel away a few layers of mistrust and prejudice left by his tough experiences in Brooklyn." Cus did what he could.

D'Amato died of penumonia at New York's Mt. Sinai Hospital when he was seventy-seven. One of his champions, José Torres, who had recently become New York State athletic commissioner, gave the eulogy; D'Amato was buried in Catskill. Mike Tyson, undefeated in eleven bouts, claimed the title only months after D'Amato's death, beating Patterson's record as youngest heavyweight champion. Remembering D'Amato, Patterson told the writer Peter Heller: "I don't think that there'll be another . . . man as Cus, with his witty ways, his cleverness, his shrewdness." The city of New York agreed, naming the stretch of East Fourteenth Street where the Gramercy Gym had long stood Cus D'Amato Way in memoriam. Two lines from his headstone explain D'Amato as well as anything he did in his strange, accomplished life: "The boy comes to me with a spark of interest./I feed the spark and it becomes a flame."

★

Information on D'Amato can most easily be found in books about Mike Tyson; see especially Peter Heller, *Bad Intentions: The Mike Tyson Story* (1989); José Torres, *The Inside Story of Mike Tyson* (1989); and Reg Gutteridge and Norman Giller, *Mike Tyson: The Release of Power* (1995). An obituary is in the *Chicago Tribune* (6 Nov. 1985), and a remembrance by Ira Berkow is in the *New York Times* (7 Nov. 1985).

NATHAN WARD

DANIELS, Jonathan Worth (*b*. 26 April 1902 in Raleigh, North Carolina; *d*. 6 November 1981 in Hilton Head, South Carolina), liberal journalist, author, and presidential adviser who promoted progressive issues in a deeply conservative South.

Daniels was one of four sons—two daughters had died in infancy—of Addie Worth Bagley, a homemaker, and Josephus Daniels, owner and publisher of the *Raleigh News and Observer*. Having purchased the newspaper for $10,000 at a courthouse auction in 1894, Josephus Daniels turned it into a prosperous and influential state capital paper that the family would own for the next 101 years. A lifelong Democrat, he supported the Democratic party and its presidential candidates, beginning with William Jennings Bryan's first presidential campaign in 1896. The paper had an unusual tradition of putting a crowing red rooster on the front page when Democrats won major elections.

Jonathan Daniels was named after his maternal great-grandfather, Jonathan Worth, a Quaker opposed to slavery and governor of North Carolina during Reconstruction. The family lived in an older, racially mixed section of Raleigh in a big rambling house built by his paternal grandfather, who was a carpenter. Daniels attended Centennial

School, a one-story school and former governor's mansion, from 1908 until the family moved to Washington, D.C., in 1913. His father was appointed secretary of the navy for the newly elected president, Woodrow Wilson, and served two terms helping with naval preparations for World War I, aided by a young Franklin Roosevelt, whom he hired as assistant secretary of the navy. Daniels attended John Eaton School from 1913 to 1915 and St. Albans School from 1915 to 1918.

He entered the University of North Carolina and edited the university newspaper. He received a B.A. degree in 1921 and an M.A. degree in English in 1922, focusing on contemporary literature of the U.S. Midwest. The author Thomas Wolfe was a friend and classmate. Daniels attended Columbia University Law School in New York City (1922–1923) but did not graduate. Although he passed the North Carolina bar examination, he never practiced law, electing instead to pursue the family business, newspapers. On 5 September 1923 he married Elizabeth Bridgers; she died in 1929, leaving a daughter. He worked briefly on the *Louisville Courier-Journal* before returning to work at the *Raleigh News and Observer.* Daniels covered police and sports and then served as the paper's Washington correspondent from 1925 to 1928.

Daniels wrote his first book, *The Clash of Angels,* a satirical religious novel, in 1930; that year he also became one of the original journalists at *Fortune* magazine but left shortly after receiving a Guggenheim Fellowship in creative writing. He spent sixteen months in Europe but never published the novel. He then concentrated on nonfiction works and became the author of more than a dozen books noted for their meticulous research and readable prose. He briefly returned to *Fortune* before going back to the *News and Observer* in 1932 as associate editor. He replaced his father as editor the following year when the latter was appointed U.S. ambassador to Mexico by his former protégé President Franklin Roosevelt. In 1932 Jonathan married Lucy Billing Cathcart; they had three children.

The newspaper continued to be a family business. Daniels edited the paper while his brothers Josephus, Jr., and Frank handled business matters. This second generation helped the paper gain wider circulation and influence. Daniels supported Democratic candidates, organized labor, public education, better race relations, and a liberal agenda in a conservative southern state. Family ownership of the paper gave him unusual freedom and latitude to express unpopular opinions. Detractors called the influential paper "The Nuisance and Disturber."

Daniels began writing books and national magazine articles from a southern perspective, including *A Southerner Discovers the South* (1938), *A Southerner Discovers New England* (1940), and *Tar Heels: A Portrait of North Carolina* (1941). Between 1940 and 1942 he wrote the weekly col-

Jonathan Daniels. COURTESY OF THE HARRY S. TRUMAN LIBRARY

umn "A Native at Large" for the *Nation* as well as articles for national magazines.

With the onset of World War II, Daniels returned to Washington, D.C., and began a series of government-related jobs. He became assistant director of the Office of Civilian Defense (1942). His father had returned to the United States and resumed editorship of the paper. In 1943 Daniels became one of six presidential administrative assistants and worked three years in the Roosevelt administration. Daniels's versatility resulted in varied assignments, including an investigation of how race relations were affecting wartime production. Daniels became presidential press secretary in March 1945, a month prior to Roosevelt's death, and continued temporarily in that capacity for Harry Truman.

That summer Daniels returned to Raleigh and the newspaper and also spent time on book projects. In 1947 his father became ill and Daniels was named executive editor of the *Courier-Journal,* a post he would maintain, in addition to his numerous other activities, until his retirement in 1970. He joined the historic Truman whistle-stop campaign as consultant and speechwriter in 1948, a year in which southern Dixiecrats broke away from the Democratic party in a dispute over race relations. Daniels supported repeal of the poll tax, antilynching laws, protection against job discrimination, and elimination of segregation in public transportation. There were rumors of a major presidential appointment for Daniels but none occurred. He was recruited by Truman to write the president's authorized biography, *The Man of Independence* (1950), which shed new light on Truman's early career because the president urged family members and friends to cooperate with Daniels. Between 1948 and 1952 Daniels served on the Democratic National Committee, and he represented the United States on the United Nations Subcommission for the Prevention of Discrimination and the Protection of Minorities from 1947 to 1953.

The studious, bespectacled Daniels was five feet, eight inches tall and weighed 170 pounds. He worked mornings on his writing projects and afternoons at the newspaper. He wrote several children's books; an homage to his father and Roosevelt entitled *The End of Innocence* (1954); an exploration of the enmity among Thomas Jefferson, Alexander Hamilton, and Aaron Burr in *Ordeal of Ambition* (1970); and other volumes about twentieth-century U.S. political history.

In the 1960s he began spending more time at his Hilton Head, South Carolina, home. He moved there in 1971, although he remained editor emeritus of the *News and Observer* until his death. He helped establish a weekly, the *Hilton Head Island Packet,* to which he contributed a free weekly column. He died after a long illness and was buried in Six Oaks Cemetery on Hilton Head, preceded by his wife, Lucy, who had died in 1979.

Daniels was a rare combination of journalist, historian, and political insider who both observed and shaped dramatic changes in his region and the nation. He served as the progressive voice of the South, speaking forcefully against race discrimination, and his contemporary accounts of the policies and personal characters of presidents Roosevelt and Truman were major historical contributions to understanding the period.

★

The papers of Jonathan Worth Daniels are in the Southern Historical Collection at the University of North Carolina Library in Raleigh. His presidential papers and an oral history are at the Harry S. Truman Presidential Library in Independence, Missouri, along with extensive notes for *The Man of Independence* (1950). Daniels shared his experiences in wartime Washington, D.C., first in *Frontier on the Potomac* (1946) and later in *White House Witness, 1942–1945* (1975), his diary as a Roosevelt kitchen cabinet member. Charles W. Eagles, *Jonathan Daniels and Race Relations: The Evolution of a Southern Liberal* (1982), is a major biography and recounts his journalistic career focusing on the issue of race relations. An obituary is in the *New York Times* (7 Nov. 1981).

BRENT SCHONDELMEYER

DAVIS, (William) Allison (*b.* 14 October 1902 in Washington, D.C.; *d.* 21 November 1983 in Chicago, Illinois), psychologist and social anthropologist best known for challenging the cultural bias of standardized intelligence tests and educational programs in general, leading to changes in the use of intelligence testing and new thinking toward the education of socially and economically disadvantaged children.

The son of John Abraham Davis and Gabrielle Dorothy Beale, Allison Davis grew up in a time of economic prosperity and great social change in the United States, an age marked by increasing opportunities for young African Americans like himself. After excelling in high school he went on to Williams College in Massachusetts, where he was valedictorian of his graduating class, receiving a B.A. degree in English in 1924. He was elected to Phi Beta Kappa and was the highest prize winner in English. Davis continued his studies at Harvard University, where he earned an M.A. degree in English in 1925.

Davis immediately moved into a teaching career, instructing students in English literature at the historically African-American Hampton Institute (later University) of

Allison Davis. NYT PICTURES/NYT PERMISSIONS

Virginia from 1925 to 1932. One of his most renowned students was St. Clair Drake, who conducted research with Davis and went on to become a noted sociologist. Drake wrote that Davis gave magnificent lectures on English literature but more profoundly influenced the young people at Hampton when he published an article called "The Negro Deserts His People" in *Plain Talk* (1929), which said that the color line that had developed within the black community should be broken and that educated African Americans who had fled the South should return to work there. While teaching in Virginia, Davis married Alice Elizabeth Stubbs on 23 June 1929. Eventually they would have two sons, his only children. Davis and his wife returned to Harvard in 1932, where he completed a second M.A. degree, this time in anthropology. A fellowship awarded from the Julius Rosenwald Fund allowed Davis and his wife to move to London, where he pursued further graduate study with the distinguished British anthropologists Bronislaw Malinowski and Lancelot Hogben. Hogben was interested in the "nature versus nurture" question and published a population study called *Political Arithmetic* (1938), to which Davis contributed "The Distribution of Blood-Groups and Its Bearing on the Concept of Race."

The Davises returned to the United States in 1933, and they began research with fellow anthropologists Burleigh and Mary Gardner on the class and caste system in the South. They compared black and white communities in Natchez, Mississippi, and found that race relations and attitudes of whites toward blacks differed depending on their social class. For instance, while middle-class whites showed extreme prejudice toward blacks in an effort to impress wealthy whites, upper-class white landlords were willing to work with black landlords to take advantage of government programs and get more money from their tenants. The findings from this research were later published in *Deep South: A Social Anthropological Study of Caste and Class* (1941), which became a classic. The book also served to validate similar conclusions made by Davis and psychologist John Dollard from research during the same years, reported in *Children of Bondage: The Personality Development of Negro Youth in the Urban South* (1940). A preliminary publication based on Davis's research was an article he wrote with W. Lloyd Warner, "A Comparative Study of American Caste," published in *Race Relations and the Race Problem* (1939), edited by Edgar Thompson.

While conducting research in the South, Davis taught at Dillard University in New Orleans as professor of anthropology. In 1939, he received a fellowship to pursue a doctorate at the University of Chicago. He joined the university's Center on Child Development as a research associate and was named assistant professor of education at Chicago when he completed his Ph.D. in 1942. Davis stayed at the University of Chicago for the remainder of his teaching career.

Davis became interested in education while researching the class system within the African-American community. He came to see that an important role was played by familial, cultural, and societal values in the educational process. Children of the economic lower class learned from their families and teachers that they had little chance of improving their economic situation through education; consequently, they perceived education as having little value to them. Davis's research and writings then shifted to focus on the impact of culture and economics on education, and ways educators could devise to make instruction more valuable to children from disadvantaged groups. His *Father of the Man: How Your Child Gets His Personality,* written with Robert J. Havighurst, was published in 1947, the same year Davis was granted tenure as associate professor of education at the University of Chicago. He and Abram Lincoln Harris were the first two African Americans to be granted tenure at that institution.

In 1948 Davis was made full professor of education at the University of Chicago. Also that year he gave the annual Iglis Lecture at Harvard University, which gave him the opportunity to address the problem of the influence of social class on learning. The lecture, which pulled together his years of research in anthropology, sociology, and education, was published as *Social-Class Influences upon Learning* (1948).

During the 1950s Davis began to look at the nature of intelligence, supervising the publication of *Intelligence and Cultural Differences* (1951), together with Robert J. Havighurst and Ralph Tyler. He came to the conclusion that standardized intelligence tests created by middle-class whites were inherently biased against lower-class nonwhites, and he presented his solution to this problem in *The Davis-Eells Test of General Intelligence or Problem-Solving Ability* (1953), written with Kenneth Eells. The Davis-Eells Games Test, as it became known, was intended to be culturally fair in measuring intelligence.

Davis worked with Benjamin S. Bloom and Robert Hess in the 1960s, and together they published *Compensatory Education for Cultural Deprivation* (1964), the purpose being to "review what is known about the problems of education and cultural deprivation, to make recommendations about what might be done to solve some of these problems, and to suggest the critical problems for further research." In 1965, he was appointed to the President's Commission on Civil Rights. In 1967, the American Academy of Arts and Sciences elected Davis its first fellow from the field of education.

While he was achieving national recognition as an expert on social class and education, Davis suffered the loss of his wife, Alice, who passed away in 1966. He married

Lois L. Mason on 7 January 1969. The following year Davis was named the first John Dewey Distinguished Service Professor of Education at the University of Chicago. Other honors included the Teachers College Medal from Columbia University (1977) and the Solomon Carter Fuller award from the American Psychological Association (1977). He retired as professor emeritus from the University of Chicago in 1978 at the age of seventy-six.

Davis's last book, *Leadership, Love, and Aggression* (1983), was an analysis of the personalities of Frederick Douglass, W. E. B. Du Bois, Richard Wright, and Martin Luther King, Jr. He concluded that anger was a common motivating force for these men, which they transformed from negative emotion into positive action. A reviewer in the *West Coast Review of Books* described the work as "more than a psychobiography of the four but . . . also a descriptive analysis of the suffering of the American Black at the hands of the government and the larger society." Davis died following open heart surgery.

Allison Davis helped spur debates over standardized tests and the nature of intelligence that continue to this day. His pioneering research changed the thinking of educators with respect to cultural and societal influences on learning and led to such programs as Head Start, an early childhood education program in which three- and four-year-old children from poor families are prepared to be successful in school. The research of Allison Davis provides the theoretical foundation upon which many later goals and premises of multicultural education were built.

★

Michael R. Hillis, "Allison Davis and the Study of Race, Social Class, and Schooling," *Journal of Negro Education* 64, no.1 (1995), discusses the importance of Davis's research in relation to the multicultural education movement. Lewis C. Copeland, "Deep South: A Social Anthropological Study of Caste and Class" (book review), *American Journal of Sociology* 48, no. 3 (Nov. 1942): 432–433, provides a detailed analysis of one of Davis's most influential publications. See also St. Clair Drake, "In the Mirror of Black Scholarship: W. Allison Davis and *Deep South*," in *Education and Black Struggle: Notes from the Colonized World* (1974), pp. 42–54, by a student of Davis's at Hampton Institute who assisted him with sociological research in Natchez, Mississippi; and Andrea Marie Macaluso, "Allison Davis and the Historical Development of His Sociological Concepts: 'Cultural Deprivation' and 'Contemporary Education,' 1925–1983" (Ph.D. diss., Loyola University of Chicago, 1996). Hal May and Susan M. Trosky, eds., *Contemporary Authors,* vol. 125 (1989), provides a complete bibliography of Davis's works; biographical information including all honors, awards, and memberships; and brief analyses of Davis's most important publications. Obituaries are in the *New York Times* (22 Nov. 1983) and Hal May, ed., *Contemporary Authors*, vol. 111 (1984).

NAN POLLOT

DEAN, Paul ("Daffy") (*b*. 14 August 1913 in Lucas, Arkansas; *d*. 17 March 1981 in Springdale, Arkansas), baseball pitcher for the St. Louis Cardinals during the 1930s and the younger brother of Hall of Fame pitcher and broadcaster Jay "Dizzy" Dean.

Paul was one of three sons of Albert and Alma Nelson Dean. Albert Dean was an itinerant farmer who earned a living by picking cotton and laboring at other agricultural jobs. Despite what Paul called his brother Dizzy's exaggerations, the Deans were not poverty-stricken. The boys showed a talent for baseball, with Dizzy pitching and Paul playing shortstop. Both left school early to pursue paying employment. Paul earned a living as a migrant cotton picker across Arkansas and Texas, at which he was so successful that he was able to save $120 by 1929. He used this money to "pay" for Dizzy's release from the United States Army, a common practice during the 1930s.

In 1930 Dizzy signed with the St. Louis Cardinals and was sent to the St. Joseph, Missouri, team of the Western League. Paul followed his brother into the minor leagues a year later, joining Dizzy on the staff of the Texas League

"Daffy" Dean. NATIONAL BASEBALL HALL OF FAME LIBRARY, COOPERSTOWN, N.Y.

Houston Buffaloes. Paul then pitched for Springfield (Missouri) of the Western Association and Columbus (Ohio) of the American Association. In 1932, despite throwing a no-hitter on 30 August for Columbus against Kansas City, he ended the season with a 7–16 record. During the next season, however, he went 22–7 and led Columbus to the American Association pennant while topping the league in wins, strikeouts, and earned run average (ERA).

In 1934 Paul joined Dizzy on the pitching staff of the St. Louis Cardinals. Dizzy had already gained a reputation as one of the game's best pitchers, winning 18 and 20 games in 1932 and 1933, respectively. To complement Dizzy's nickname, Paul was called "Daffy" by the St. Louis sports-writers, although the name would not stick past his playing days. The Dean brothers, who resembled each other very closely, would have their best years as professionals during 1934. Dizzy went 30–7; Paul had an impressive record of 19–11 with an ERA of 3.43 during his rookie campaign. Despite his success Paul had a rough start to the season. After lasting only two innings in his first game and pitching poorly in relief during April, manager Frankie Frisch used Paul sparingly. On 3 May, Paul recorded his first major league win with a strong relief performance. Little over a week later, Paul solidified his spot in the starting rotation with a complete-game victory over the New York Giants in ten innings. Paul also pitched that season's only major league no-hitter in a game against the Brooklyn Dodgers on 21 September. Although overshadowed by his brother during the season, Paul took center stage during the team's 1934 World Series triumph over the Detroit Tigers. Paul tossed two complete-game wins and limited the Tigers with an ERA of 1.00. Dizzy pitched the other winning games, finishing the series 2–1 with an ERA of 1.73.

With the baseball season over, Dizzy and Paul Dean were heroes and in high demand. They formed the "Dizzy and Daffy Tour," which pitted the two pitchers and other players, mostly local, against barnstorming Negro League teams. In October they were signed to perform a vaudeville act, playing themselves, at the Roxy Theatre in New York City. The brothers also appeared in the Warner Brothers short film *Dizzy and Daffy*. In December 1934 Paul took time off the busy schedule to marry Dorothy Sandusky; they would have four children.

Paul Dean followed up his rookie year with another strong season with the Cardinals in 1935. He went 19–12 with an ERA of 3.37. After his second season, however, he gained a great deal of weight and developed shin splints. He never returned to the form that saw him post a 38–23 record during 1934 and 1935. He pitched in parts of the next four seasons with the Cardinals, then went to the New York Giants for the 1940 and 1941 seasons and to the St. Louis Browns in 1943, posting only a 12–11 record in 74 games over those seven seasons. His lifetime statistics were

50 wins, 34 losses, and a 3.75 ERA. He served in the United States Army between 1944 and 1946.

After the war Paul Dean remained in baseball as a minor-league general manager and part-time field manager for a number of different teams in the lower classifications of the minor leagues. In 1949 he became president and manager of the Clovis (New Mexico) Pioneers of the Class C West Texas–New Mexico League. As was the case with nearly every minor-league club he operated, Paul's wife, Dorothy, was the club secretary-treasurer. Paul also managed the team on the field, but the Pioneers finished in last place with a record of 53–87. In 1950 he remained as president but replaced himself as field manager. In 1951 and 1952 he was the general manager and business manager of the Lubbock Hubbers of the same league. He was let go after the 1952 season for reasons that included a large drop in attendance. In 1953 he served as general manager of the El Paso Texans of the Class C Arizona–Texas League and the following year became president and general manager of the Hot Springs (Arkansas) Bathers of the Class C Cotton States League.

In the mid-1960s Paul moved to Phoenix, Arizona, and operated his brother Dizzy's carpet store. The brothers would often spend time talking with fans and children about baseball. Paul left Dizzy's business in 1966 when he was hired as the baseball coach and athletic director of the expanding University of Plano (Texas). Late in life, he also operated filling stations in Springdale, Arkansas, where he lived until his death.

★

A file on Paul Dean is maintained at the National Baseball Hall of Fame Library, Cooperstown, New York. Vince Staten, *Ol' Diz: A Biography of Dizzy Dean* (1992), contains a good deal of information on Paul. For other accounts of his career, see Gene Karst and Martin J. Jones, Jr., *Who's Who in Professional Baseball* (1973); John E. DiMeglio, "Jay Hanna 'Dizzy' Dean" in David L. Porter, ed., *Biographical Dictionary of American Sports: Baseball* (1987); and Ed Rumill, "Paul Didn't Mind 'Playing Second Fiddle' to Diz," *Christian Science Monitor* (8 Mar. 1965).

COREY SEEMAN

DEBUS, Kurt Heinrich (*b.* 29 November 1908 in Frankfurt am Main, Germany; *d.* 10 October 1983 in Cocoa, Florida), rocket scientist who directed the early U.S. space program, including the launch of the first U.S. orbital satellite and of the first American into space, and headed the Kennedy Space Center, from which Americans were launched to the Moon.

The son of Heinrich P. J. Debus and Melly Graulich Debus, both of whom were merchants, Debus attended the Liebig Oberrealschule in Frankfurt and in 1929 entered the Technische Hochschule in Darmstadt, where he received a B.S. in mechanical engineering in 1933 and an M.S. in electrical engineering in 1935. Debus earned his doctorate (also in electrical engineering), summa cum laude, in 1939. In 1931 he became an instructor at the Technische Hochschule, and in 1936 he advanced to the rank of assistant professor (a post he held there until 1943). Meanwhile, Debus had married Irmgard Helene Brückmann on 30 June 1937; they had two children.

When Adolf Hitler began rearming Germany in the mid-1930s, Debus helped develop ballistic missiles under the direction of the brilliant rocket engineer Wernher von Braun. Some of the research for these missiles was conducted at the Darmstadt Technische Hochschule, where Debus directed wind-tunnel studies to perfect the V-2 rocket. In 1942, after repeated entreaties from von Braun, Debus joined the main V-2 development effort at the secret base of Peenumünde on the Baltic coast. He quickly became one of von Braun's most trusted assistants and served as V-2 flight-test director.

Debus was apparently a supporter of Hitler's regime. Although he later denied it, in 1939 he joined the SS, Hitler's elite force, and was assigned membership number 426559. In 1942 his colleague Richard Craemer was brought up on charges for making anti-Hitler statements. Craemer was sentenced to two years' imprisonment, but the sentence was suspended because of his value to the V-2 program. Debus claimed he had been responsible for that leniency, but Gestapo records suggest that Debus's derogatory testimony was the principal reason for Craemer's conviction in the first place and that his sentence was suspended only because of his supervisor's intervention.

At the end of World War II, Debus was one of 120 senior V-2 rocket developers who came with von Braun to the United States as part of a military operation, known as Project Paperclip, to secure German scientific and technical information. He and his German colleagues were taken to Fort Bliss, Texas, in November 1945 and spent the next five years experimenting with V-2 technology on the U.S. Army's White Sands Proving Grounds in New Mexico. In 1950 Debus and his German colleagues were transferred to the army's Redstone Arsenal in Huntsville, Alabama. He contributed significantly to the guidance system and launch success of the missiles developed by the von Braun team during these years. In both places Debus continued his close association with von Braun and became his de facto second in command. Debus became a naturalized citizen in 1951; although some questioned the propriety of this because of his Nazi background, his importance to the U.S. ballistic missile program prompted the government's Joint Intelligence Objectives Agency, charged with oversight of Germans brought to America at the end of the war, to approve his naturalization.

Dr. Kurt Debus stands beside a modified Jupiter missile that was the first stage of the Juno II rocket, Cape Canaveral, 1958. AP/WIDE WORLD PHOTOS

In 1952 Debus was appointed chief of the missile-firing laboratory of the Army Ballistic Missile Agency at Redstone Arsenal. During the next few years he scouted sites and constructed launch complexes for army missiles at a marshy backwater called Cape Canaveral, on Florida's eastern coast, and he headed the test program there. Debus recalled his first visit to Cape Canaveral: "At Cocoa, we drove east over a dreadful wooden bridge and came out the causeway to nothing. There were no houses, Cocoa Beach consisted principally of a traffic light. At Patrick [Air Force Base, located to the south], there were only a few temporary buildings."

Debus remade the area into the most advanced launch facility in the world. Beginning with the launch of the first Redstone missile on 20 August 1953, Debus's team fired eighty-three rockets from Cape Canaveral through 1960, seventy of them successfully. These included several historic flights, especially *Explorer I,* the first U.S. orbital satellite, launched on 31 January 1958, and *Pioneer I,* the first solar satellite, launched on 3 March 1959. He also launched two rhesus monkeys, Able and Baker, into space on 28 May 1959.

When President Dwight D. Eisenhower completed the transfer of the Army Ballistic Missile Agency in Huntsville to the National Aeronautics and Space Administration

(NASA) on 1 July 1960, Debus was named director of its Launch Operations Directorate at Cape Canaveral. From this facility NASA launched the first American into space on 5 May 1961; the fifteen-minute suborbital flight of Alan B. Shepard initiated the flight sequence of six piloted missions for Project Mercury, which included the first American orbital flight, by John H. Glenn on 22 February 1962.

Debus's launch complex was renamed the John F. Kennedy Space Center (KSC) in December 1963. President Kennedy's announcement on 25 May 1961 that the United States would send an American to the Moon before the end of the decade led to Project Apollo, the most sophisticated nonmilitary technological endeavor in U.S. history. It also required the construction of a massive vehicle preparation and launch complex at Debus's center. Under his direction, NASA constructed the Moonport facilities on Merritt Island, adjacent to the space center, from which to launch astronauts on missions to the Moon. This complex encompassed 88,000 acres of land, cost about $1 billion to build, and required an operational force of some 26,000 NASA and contractor personnel. Debus was the architect of the Moonport, making all major decisions about the infrastructure of launch complexes 39A and 39B; the Vehicle Assembly Building (VAB), where the rocket was assembled for flight; and the 6,000-ton crawler that transported the rocket from the VAB to the launch pad.

Debus presided over KSC throughout the Apollo program. All Mercury, Gemini, and Apollo missions were launched under his direction. On 26 January 1967 the center had its worst accident, when astronauts Gus Grissom, Ed White, and Roger Chaffee were burned to death in a flash fire while running ground simulations in an Apollo capsule. The Apollo program went into an eighteen-month hiatus for review and revision, then resumed in the fall of 1968. In December 1968 *Apollo 8* made the first circumlunar mission, and on 16 July 1969 *Apollo 11* lifted off from Debus's complex for the first lunar landing mission. Six more Apollo missions to the Moon were flown from KSC; all were successful except for *Apollo 13,* which suffered an explosion en route and had to abort its landing. The last *Apollo* flight (*Apollo 17*) took place in December 1972. Debus was also in charge of the launch complex in 1973 when *Skylab,* an orbital laboratory, was launched.

Debus retired from NASA on 9 October 1974 and settled into his home in Cocoa, Florida. He died there of a heart attack and was buried in Cocoa.

Kurt Debus was a significant figure in the development and use of rocket technology in the twentieth century. His role in developing the V-2 was pivotal, as was his management of launch operations for the United States at Cape Canaveral. At the time of his death, KSC's director Lee R. Scherer called Debus "a trailblazer—his contributions to the United States space program cannot be overempha-

sized. He brought a quiet, personal genius to this demanding work. His was the creative mind which conceived of the needs of a NASA launch center for decades to come—and it was under his direction that concepts and blueprints were transformed into the Spaceport, which we find so valuable a national asset today."

★

Collections of Debus's papers are at the Space and Rocket Center, Huntsville, Alabama; at the Kennedy Space Center Archives, Cape Canaveral, Florida; and at the NASA Historical Reference Collection, NASA Headquarters, Washington, D.C. Debus's Nazi past is detailed in the Debus Joint Intelligence Objectives Agency dossier, Record Group 330, and the IRR dossier XE034033, Record Group 319, both in the National Archives and Records Administration, Archives II, College Park, Md. Information about Debus in Germany is in Frederick I. Ordway III and Mitchell R. Sharpe, *The Rocket Team* (1979); Linda Hunt, *Secret Agenda: The United States Government, Nazi Scientists, and Project Paperclip, 1945 to 1990* (1991); and Michael J. Neufeld, *The Rocket and the Reich: Peenemünde and the Coming of the Ballistic Missile Era* (1995). His NASA career is related in Charles D. Benson and William Barnaby Faherty, *Moonport: A History of Apollo Launch Facilities and Operations,* NASA SP-4204 (1978); Roger E. Bilstein, *Stages to Saturn: A Technological History of the Apollo/ Saturn Launch Vehicles,* NASA SP-4206 (1980); and Arnold S. Levine, *Managing NASA in the Apollo Era,* NASA SP-4102 (1982). An obituary is in the *New York Times* (11 Oct. 1983).

ROGER D. LAUNIUS

DEDMON, Emmett (*b.* 16 April 1918 in Auburn, Nebraska; *d.* 18 September 1983 in Chicago), newspaper columnist, editor, and executive who ran the *Chicago Sun-Times* and the *Chicago Daily News* from 1968 to 1978.

The son of Roy Emmett Deadman, a clergyman, and Cora Christine Frank, he changed his surname to Dedmon in 1945. Bright and ambitious, while attending Fairbury High School, Dedmon received permission from the school's principal to revive the student newspaper, which had been discontinued because of the Depression. Starting with a mimeographed edition, the newspaper was such a success that it was soon published in the plant of the *Fairbury News.* Dedmon, who later described himself as "a brash young high school editor," said that he learned much about journalism from the editors of the *Fairbury News.* "They certainly get credit for keeping alive my first enthusiasm for newspapering," Dedmon wrote in 1961.

Dedmon became even more involved in journalism as a student at the University of Chicago. As a freshman he began writing for the *Daily Maroon,* which was then published four days a week. As a senior, Dedmon served as chairman of the newspaper's editorial board. On graduation from the university in 1939 with a degree in economics, Dedmon was awarded an exchange scholarship to the University of Geneva. Before he could begin his studies, World War II broke out in Europe and the scholarship was canceled. He sought for nearly a year to get a job on a Chicago newspaper and was hired in June 1940 as assistant foreign editor of the *Chicago Times.*

In November 1940 Dedmon enlisted as a private in the Army Air Forces and rose to the rank of captain. He was a squadron navigator in the first B-17 bomber group to fly nonstop across the Atlantic. Dedmon flew many combat missions and once returned safely to base in a burning plane. He was awarded the Air Medal for his combat service. While flying a mission to Hanover, Germany, in July 1943, his plane was shot down, and he parachuted into enemy territory, where he was captured. He spent two years as a prisoner of war in Stalag Luft II in Silesia. Dedmon kept a written record of his internment on the back of chocolate-bar wrappers, which he used in writing his 1946 novel, *Duty to Live.* He married Claire Lyons on 19 June 1945. They had a son, Jonathan.

Resuming his newspaper career, Dedmon joined the *Chicago Sun* as a book critic and columnist in 1946 and was promoted to literary editor in August 1947. When publisher Marshall Field III bought the *Chicago Times* in 1948 and created the *Chicago Sun-Times,* Dedmon was among Field's rising stars, and he became drama critic of the *Sun-Times* in 1950. *Fabulous Chicago,* Dedmon's highly readable history of Chicago, was published in 1953 to critical acclaim and was a national best-seller.

A talented innovator, Dedmon did much to establish the tabloid *Sun-Times* as one of the nation's more successful newspapers, with a daily circulation of more than a half million and more than 700,000 on Sunday. Marshall Field IV, who succeeded his father as editor and publisher in 1950, groomed Dedmon to run the newspaper. Dedmon's positions included assistant Sunday editor (1953–1955), assistant managing editor (1955–1958), managing editor (1958–1962), executive editor (1962–1965), editor (1965–1968), and executive vice president and editorial director of the *Sun-Times* and *Daily News* (1968–1978).

Skillful in resolving conflict, Dedmon was affable and thoughtful in dealing with other people, but he also had a temper. Under Dedmon's leadership, the *Sun-Times* covered the news with less sensationalism and more substance than had been the tradition among tabloid newspapers. He introduced a Sunday Viewpoint section that provided in-depth analysis of state, local, national, and world issues. With news coverage that was objective and brightly packaged, the *Sun-Times* surpassed the older *Tribune* in city circulation (in 1963) during Dedmon's editorship. Among the newspaper's more popular contributors were the columnists Rowland Evans and Robert Novak, Carl Rowan, Irv

Emmett Dedmon, 1973. STEVE NEAL

Kupcinet, Ann Landers, and political cartoonist Bill Mauldin.

A frequent public speaker, Dedmon enjoyed the limelight and took an active role as a civic leader. He was a trustee of the University of Chicago, national chairman of its alumni fund for twenty years, and chairman of its visiting committee of the Center for Far Eastern Studies. Dedmon was awarded the university's Alumni Service Medal in 1983. He was president of the YMCA of metropolitan Chicago, a trustee of the Chicago Historical Society, the Newberry Library, and the American Public Service Institute. Dedmon was vice president of the Economic Club of Chicago and served on the executive committees of the Chicago Club and the Commercial Club.

In September 1968 Dedmon moved to an executive position that put him in charge of the *Daily News* and the *Sun-Times.* He was succeeded as editor by Roy M. Fisher. With the death of Dedmon's close friend Marshall Field IV in September 1965, Dedmon lost his most valuable ally. He gradually lost influence, most notably in 1976 when James F. Hoge, Jr., was named by Marshall Field V as editor of both newspapers. In February 1978 Dedmon retired as vice president and editorial director, soon after the closing of the *Daily News* was announced. "With the impending demise of the *Daily News,* Emmett feels that much of the challenge of his job has been lost," Field said of Dedmon's departure.

Dedmon then joined Hill and Knowlton, the public relations firm, as a senior consultant. He wrote a new edition of his Chicago history that was published in 1981. Dedmon was inducted into the Chicago Press Club Hall of Fame in 1982.

Dedmon died of cancer at the University of Chicago Hospital. Field said, "Under Emmett Dedmon's leadership the *Sun-Times* earned a position among the great newspapers of this country."

★

Dedmon's papers are at the Chicago Historical Society. An obituary is in the *Chicago Sun-Times* (19 Sept. 1983).

STEVE NEAL

DELBRÜCK, Max Ludwig Henning (*b.* 4 September 1906 in Berlin, Germany; *d.* 10 March 1981 in Pasadena, California), biologist who was a leading pioneer of molecular biology and a winner of the Nobel Prize in Physiology or Medicine in 1969 for his studies concerning the multiplication in their host cells of bacterial viruses, called bacteriophages.

Delbrück was the youngest of seven children. His father, Hans Delbrück, was a distinguished historian and professor at the University of Berlin. Max grew up in a stimulating academic environment. His neighbors included the families of the noted theologians Dietrich Bonhoeffer and Adolf von Harnack and physicist Max Planck. Although the Delbrücks were intellectual, they had little interest in science

Max Delbrück. COURTESY OF THE ARCHIVES, CALIFORNIA INSTITUTE OF TECHNOLOGY

with the exception of Max, who from an early age developed an interest in astronomy. His mother made him a special robe for his nightly vigil on the porch with his telescope.

Delbrück's academic experiences were peripatetic. In 1924 he entered the University of Tübingen intending to study astonomy under Hans Rosenberg. He remained there for only one semester before traveling to Berlin, then to Bonn, then back to Berlin, and finally to the University of Göttingen, where he spent three years and wrote a thesis on the quantum mechanical theory of the lithium molecule. His interest shifted from astronomy to astrophysics to theoretical physics. He did not consider his thesis outstanding but it won him his Ph.D. in 1930.

Delbrück then spent eighteen months in Bristol, England, before receiving a Rockefeller fellowship to work first in Copenhagen with Niels Bohr and then in Zurich with Wolfgang Pauli. During this period his interest in biology was stimulated. He was attracted to and greatly influenced by Bohr's speculation concerning the implications of Werner Heisenberg's uncertainty principle for an understanding of the nature of life. When his fellowship terminated in 1932, Delbrück took a job in Berlin as an assistant to Lise Meitner, in part because Meitner's lab was near the Kaiser Wilhelm Institute for Chemistry, where he subsequently spent much of his time. Before returning to Berlin he had paid a short visit to Copenhagen to hear Bohr deliver his famous address "Light and Life," which confirmed Delbrück's decision to turn to biology.

His job with Meitner was as a consultant on theoretical physics during Meitner's experimental studies with Otto Hahn on neutron bombardment of uranium. Like other scientists at the time, Delbrück failed to see the first evidence of nuclear fission within the studies of Hahn and Meitner. Perhaps this was because his interest had shifted to biology and to his important activities with the Russian geneticist N. W. Timofeeff-Ressovsky and with K. G. Zimmer at the Kaiser Wilhelm Institute. Zimmer introduced Delbrück to drosophila (the fruit fly) as an experimental genetic tool. These studies were attempts to determine the properties of the gene by looking at its sensitivity to ionizing radiation. This work was highly technical and not well known among biologists but was later referred to in the 1940s in Erwin Schrödinger's widely read volume *What Is Life?* (1944). It maintained that Delbrück's model of the gene was the only possible one. Delbrück's reputation grew, especially among readers of the Schrödinger book, many of them physicists wanting to move into biology. It was not until the 1940s and early 1950s, however, that Delbrück helped many physicists make this transition.

In 1937 Delbrück was again awarded a Rockefeller fellowship, this time to support his study of biology at the California Institute of Technology. He accepted the fellowship, not only because of his hope to further his interest in biology, especially drosophila genetics, but also because a university career in Germany was not promising given the rise of the Nazis. At Caltech he spent a short time mastering the fundamentals of drosophila genetics from Alfred H. Sturtevant and Calvin Bridges before Emory L. Ellis introduced him to the study of bacteriophages, viruses that infect bacteria. Delbrück saw for the first time the multiplication of a single virus particle in a petri dish. He then turned his full attention to bacteriophage, or phage, the organism that was to occupy him for the next fifteen years, and he began his collaboration with Ellis to define the life cycle of a bacterial virus.

When Delbrück's fellowship expired in 1939, Vanderbilt University offered him a faculty position as an instructor and the Rockefeller Foundation agreed to pay part of his salary. He was a member of the faculty from 1940 until 1947, being promoted to associate professor. Vanderbilt permitted him to devote half his time to research. It was during this period that he began his collaboration with Salvador E. Luria, an Italian refugee working on bacteriophage in New York. The paper written by Luria and Delbrück in 1943 reporting their findings and conclusions is a landmark in molecular biology, because it provided the first true evidence that bacterial inheritance, like that of the cells of higher organisms, is mediated by genes and not by some mechanism of adaptation, as was widely held at the time. As William Hayes wrote in 1993, the finding signaled the birth of bacterial genetics, which became a basic tool for exploring the molecular basis of life.

At about this time, Luria initiated at Vanderbilt important studies of host-range mutations in phage, the results of which were published in 1945. Delbrück had become interested in the work done on phage by Alfred D. Hershey, a microbiologist in St. Louis, and in 1943 invited Hershey to join him at Vanderbilt. Delbrück, Luria, and Hershey thus formed the nucleus of the "Phage Group." In addition, a vital collaboration with Thomas F. Anderson, an electron microscopist, was established. The phage workers had begun spending summers at Cold Spring Harbor Laboratory in New York in 1941. The first Cold Spring Harbor phage course was offered in 1945 and was repeated twenty-six times. Delbrück also organized a series of phage meetings, the first three of which were held at Vanderbilt. The meetings rapidly grew in size.

When World War II ended, Delbrück's preeminent role in phage research led to his appointment as chair of biology at Caltech, a post he took up in 1947. In 1941 he had married Mary Adeline Bruce, who had grown up in a British environment on the Island of Cyprus. The couple had four children. Established and promising young investigators and scientists began research activities at Caltech during the early years of Delbrück's leadership. The rep-

utation of the program spread and those who attended soon realized they had become members of a friendly and hospitable international family related by social as well as by intellectual bonds, with Delbrück at the helm.

Delbrück's previous work on the one-step growth curve, which analyzed the multiplication of bacteria cells, had shown that, following phage infection of bacterial cells, a latent period of about twenty minutes elapses before the cells begin to burst and liberate a hundred or more progeny particles. Mutation had also been revealed by Luria as the cause of variation in phage, as well as in bacteria, as has already been shown. Then Delbrück and Hershey and W. T. Bailey, Jr., a student, independently demonstrated genetic recombination when bacteria were doubly infected with phages that differ in two characters. This was the important finding that led about ten years later to the ultimate genetic analysis of gene structure by Seymour Benzer.

Although Delbrück spent the remainder of his life at Caltech, he retained a strong interest in German science. He visited Germany frequently after the war and for two years (1961–1963) was director of the Institute for Genetics at the University of Cologne, an institute he helped to found.

In the early 1950s, as the field of phage genetics grew, Delbrück's attention to it diminished. He made a major change in his research efforts to the nature of the primary transducer processes of sense organs as manifested in the taxis of the fungus *Phycomyces*. He was particularly interested in phototropism. He pursued this research interest to the end of his life.

Delbrück's most significant research accomplishments were the collaborations with Ellis and later with Luria and others on the bacteriophage growth and the nature of the mutation process in bacteria. These studies laid the foundations for the fields of bacteriophage and bacterial genetics. Most important, new quantitative approaches to the study of microorganisms were developed—methodologies that allowed the analysis of individual as well as population phenomena and that did not confuse the two. This approach is exemplified by the Luria-Delbrück fluctuation analysis of mutational events in bacterial populations, the subject of their landmark 1943 paper. The fluctuation analysis is a method of demonstrating that genetic mutations are present in a population before they are selected, and it allows for the determination of mutation rates. Most bacteriophage and virus experiments that have been performed since are variations on the one-step growth experiment originally carried out by Ellis and Delbrück. For his bacteriophage work, Delbrück received many honors and awards, among them, with Luria and Hershey, the Nobel Prize in Physiology or Medicine in 1969.

Some believe that Delbrück's major contribution to science was his influence on the numerous scientists with whom he was associated. He was considered the father of the phage field. His sometimes brusque manner rose from a deep and persistent quest for understanding. His presence at a seminar or a meeting ensured its success; his questions were always penetrating and led to meaningful discussions. Science was serious business to him. If experiments did not help in answering important questions, they were not worth doing. The book *Phage and the Origins of Molecular Biology* (1966), a collection of articles by molecular biologists close to Delbrück and written for his sixtieth birthday, contains many anecdotes that substantiate Delbrück's powerful influence on his scientific friends.

Delbrück's dedication to science was but part of a larger appreciation of human values and the search for understanding. He gave his Nobel Prize honorarium to Amnesty International and in his later years spoke out increasingly about the limitations of science. Associates found Delbrück to be a witty, compassionate, and gregarious man who loved parties and practical jokes. He and his wife befriended countless postdoctoral students, opening their home to visitors and not infrequently including them on camping trips to the desert. A theoretician who lived to search for neat models and hypotheses to explain complex phenomena, Delbrück possessed a deep knowledge and appreciation of the arts. He was said to be the most active supporter of the art gallery on the campus at Caltech. Poetry was of particular interest to him, and he was invited in 1980 to lecture at the Poetry Center in New York, in the wake of such predecessors as T. S. Eliot and Dylan Thomas.

In 1977 Delbrück was appointed Board of Trustees Professor of Biology Emeritus at Caltech, where he continued the research of his *Phycomyces* group. Early in 1978 he found that he was suffering from multiple myeloma, a malignancy of the plasma cells of the bone marrow. This responded well to treatment, and he was able to travel to Paris in the spring of 1979 to be inducted as a foreign member of the French Académie des Sciences. Throughout his illness he retained the interest of a scientist toward his disease. A few months before his death he suffered a mild cerebrovascular accident that impaired his vision on one side. During the last few weeks of his life, Delbrück was engaged in the writing of his autobiography.

★

Discussion of Delbrück's scientific contributions can be found in John Cairns, Gunther S. Stout, and James D. Watson, eds., *Phage and the Origins of Molecular Biology* (1966), and Robert T. Lagermann, *History of the Physics-Astronomy Department at Vanderbilt University* (forthcoming). See also Robert S. Edgar, "Max Delbrück," *Annual Review of Genetics* 16 (1982): 501–505; and William Hayes, "Max Ludwig Henning Delbrück," *National Academy of Sciences. Biographical Memoirs* 62 (1993): 67–117. An obituary is in the *New York Times* (13 Mar. 1981).

HARRIS D. RILEY, JR.

DE MAN, Paul (*b.* 6 December 1919 in Antwerp, Belgium; *d.* 21 December 1983 in New Haven, Connecticut), scholar and literary critic best known as one of the foremost American advocates of deconstruction, a highly influential and controversial form of literary criticism.

Paul de Man was one of the two children of Robert Deman, a manufacturer of X-ray equipment, and Magdalena de Brey, both of whom were members of the Flemish upper class in Antwerp. In 1937 de Man enrolled in the Free University of Brussels, receiving his degree in science and philosophy in 1942, even though Germany had invaded Belgium on 10 May 1940. He and his future wife, Anaïde Baraghian, had attempted to flee the country but were turned back at the border.

Almost nothing was known about de Man's life in Europe until several years after his death. He married Baraghian, probably in 1940; they had three sons. By 1941 de Man was writing literary and other reviews for the largest daily Brussels newspaper, *Le Soir,* and for *Het Vlaamsche Land,* a Flemish weekly. He quit both by late 1942, then spent the remaining war years translating Flemish novels into French and *Moby-Dick* into Flemish (1945). In 1946 de Man invested heavily in Editions Hermès, an Antwerp publisher of art books, but by 1947 the business was bankrupt and he hastily left the city. His wife and children departed to join relatives in Argentina, while de Man went to New York City in 1948. For a little while he worked as a bookstore clerk, but by 1949 he had become a lecturer at Bard College in Annandale-on-Hudson, New York. In 1950, while at Bard, de Man married Patricia Kelley, a former student, even though he was not officially divorced from his first wife. The latter appeared at the college with one of his sons, a confrontation that prompted him to move to Boston in 1951. Kelley and de Man had two children.

In Boston, de Man taught French at Berlitz before becoming a graduate student at Harvard University, where he earned his doctorate in comparative literature in 1960. He taught at Cornell University from 1960 to 1967 and at Johns Hopkins University from 1967 to 1970. He was appointed Sterling Professor of French and Comparative Literature at Yale University in 1970. He was still teaching at Yale when he died of cancer; he was cremated.

In 1967 de Man met the French philosopher Jacques Derrida, who introduced the concept of deconstruction—a term de Man said Derrida "put on the map"—to the American intelligentsia. Deconstruction had part of its origins in the claim by the Swiss linguist Ferdinand de Saussure that there is no intrinsic relationship between a thing and its name. Objects and thoughts are fundamentally different from the words describing them; language in itself is arbitrary, although a kind of binary tension between thing and word is implied. Derrida accepted the basic

Paul de Man. COURTESY OF THE ESTATE OF PAUL DE MAN

premise of the arbitrariness of the "linguistic sign" but he stood the concept of binary relationships on its head. Because literature is language-based, no matter how vivid the events or ideas described in it, "reality" in writing is actually fiction. Metaphysical opposites like being and nothingness and truth and error are reversible constructs whose tensions are no longer between two opposing elements but, because of the ambiguity of language, are inherent within each.

In the mid-1950s both Derrida and de Man were examining the work of Martin Heidegger (who also was questioning traditional Western metaphysics) and the same text of Jean-Jacques Rousseau. In 1971, de Man published his first collection of essays, *Blindness and Insight: Essays in the Rhetoric of Contemporary Criticism,* which, expanded in 1983, contained essays on criticism by Heidegger and others and on Derrida's criticism of Rousseau; it was probably his most influential work. By now de Man had become a friend and in some ways a disciple of Derrida, and in this collection he demonstrated the principle of deconstructive reading. Because language is always ambiguous, a close exegesis of an original text can uncover contradictions within it, thereby exposing many assumptions unstated by the author. A second analysis, examining the criticism itself, could then discover the underlying assumptions hidden within that criticism. Thus, according to Carol Lynn DeKane, con-

struction affirmed the "radical notion that the meaning of the text resides as much in the interpretation as in the words of the text itself."

With *Blindness and Insight* de Man became a nationally known intellectual. By challenging the belief of a generation of literary critics that the text was the final reconciliation of language and being—that it was, in fact, redemptive—he and other deconstructionists at Yale changed both the path of American literary criticism and its scholarly importance. In this and subsequent books, *Allegories of Reading: Figural Language in Rousseau, Nietzsche, Rilke, and Proust* (1979), *The Rhetoric of Romanticism* (1984), *The Resistance to Theory* (1986), and *Aesthetic Ideology* (1988), de Man examined the delusions and randomness of language, a view that for him came to include the perception of the randomness of "deeds, words, thoughts," even death itself. Indeed, in one essay de Man wrote that one could not distinguish between "fictional discourse and empirical event," a view leading him to the fatal conclusion that this "indecision makes it possible to excuse the bleakest of crimes."

Despite the paucity of work published during his lifetime, the complexity of the subject, and the obscurity of much of the writing about it, de Man's influence on the practice and teaching of literary criticism in academic circles was profound. Although intensely private and scholarly, he inspired a passionate following, and devoted peers and colleagues concerned themselves with publishing much of his work posthumously. In the summer of 1987 Ortwin de Graef, a Belgian graduate student at the University of Louvain, was doing research for a thesis on de Man when he discovered the articles de Man had written for *Le Soir* between 1941 and November 1942. Although de Man had never spoken of these writings to anyone, it was now revealed that *Le Soir* and *Het Vlaamsche Land* had been controlled by the Nazis, and although most of de Man's roughly 170 articles were indeed reviews, there was at least one (4 March 1941) that was distinctly anti-Semitic. In "Jews and Contemporary Literature" in *Le Soir,* he discussed the question of whether Jews had "polluted" modern literature, concluding that "we can anticipate that a solution of the Jewish problem" resulting in the "creation of a Jewish colony isolated from Europe" would not have "regrettable consequences" for Western literary life.

Deconstructionists and de Man's friends were horrified by these discoveries and convened a conference in October 1987 at Tuscaloosa, Alabama, to assess their potential damage; in 1988 they published *Responses: On Paul de Man's Wartime Journalism* defending both man and theory. Meanwhile, the story appeared in the *New York Times* on 1 December 1987.

Even before these revelations the scholarly world had been deeply divided over the ethics of deconstruction. Detractors, citing passages from de Man and others, wrote that it was "apolitical and ultimately nihilistic," interpreting its emphasis on the "indeterminacy of meaning" as seeking to avert the reality and therefore the "culpability of error." The controversy about its underlying politics was reinforced by de Man's apparent sympathy with Nazi opinion coupled with the simultaneous discovery of Heidegger's close Nazi ties. Critics, in an attempt to "deconstruct de Man," maintained that by the end of 1942 few in Belgium could have been ignorant of the deportation of Jews to Germany. Nevertheless, although interrogated in May 1945 about his wartime activities by the Belgian military prosecutor's office, de Man was never charged, and those who had known him in both Europe and the United States uniformly insisted that he was "almost entirely without prejudice" in all his relationships.

An unsympathetic Jon Wiener, writing in the *Nation* (January 1988), said that "de Man's work had a tremendous appeal" because "it freed literature from context and history, opening it to complex new meanings in a way that was fertile [and] inventive" and engaging "the best of twentieth century [European] philosophy." Despite the revelations regarding de Man and Heidegger's past, deconstruction's repetitive reexamination of texts, and the abstruse prose enveloping it, deconstruction and postmodernism, one of its successors, continued to be taught at American universities in the mid-1990s. Nevertheless, deconstruction remained imbued with the enigma that was Paul de Man. Had it, as David Hirsch implied, been a veiled way for de Man to "obliterate" history and thus his own past? Or was Geoffrey Hartman correct when he suggested that de Man's critiques of "every tendency to totalize literature" was actually a "belated, but still powerful, act of conscience"?

★

Very little was known or written about Paul de Man's personal life until the revelations of 1987 in Belgium. The best account of de Man's life, and the one upon which others appear to be based, is James Atlas, "Paul de Man," *New York Times Magazine* (28 Aug. 1988). For the chronology and controversy surrounding the *Le Soir* discoveries, there are several sources: *New York Times* (1 Dec. 1987); John Wiener, "Deconstructing de Man," *Nation* (9 Jan. 1988); Geoffrey Hartman, "Blindness and Insight," *New Republic* (7 Mar. 1988); Scott Heller, "Scholars Grapple with Literary Critic's Early Writings for Pro-Nazi Periodical," *Chronicle of Higher Education* 34 (11 May 1988): A1, A6; Jonathan Culler, "It's Time to Set the Record Straight About Paul de Man and His Wartime Articles for a Pro-Fascist Newspaper," *Chronicle of Higher Education* 34 (13 July 1988): B1; and David H. Hirsch, *The Deconstruction of Literature: Criticism After Auschwitz* (1991). There is adequate literature on deconstruction itself, although much of it is almost incomprehensible. The best sources are Robert Alter, "Deconstruction in America," *New Republic* (25 Apr. 1983): 27–32; an interview with de Man by Robert Moynihan in *Yale Review*

73 (July 1984): 576–602; and Peter Shaw, "Devastating Developments Are Hastening the Demise of Deconstruction in Academe," *Chronicle of Higher Education* 37 (28 Nov. 1990): B1–2; and G. Douglas Atkins, *Reading Deconstruction: Deconstructive Reading* (1983). An obituary is in the *New York Times* (31 Dec. 1983).

SANDRA SHAFFER VANDOREN

DEMARA, Ferdinand Waldo, Jr. ("Fred") (*b*. 12 December 1921 in Lawrence, Massachusetts; *d*. 7 June 1982 in Anaheim, California), a high school dropout who successfully masqueraded as a college professor, a language teacher, a Roman Catholic monk, a prison reformer, and a Canadian naval surgeon—among other roles—in a twenty-year-long career of imposture during and after World War II.

Demara was born into a comfortable, middle-class family, the older child and only son of Ferdinand Waldo Demara, the owner of four movie theaters in Lawrence, Massachusetts, and Mary McNelly. An indifferent public school student, he was expelled from the fifth grade when he answered a threat from older boys with drawn (but unloaded) dueling pistols. He completed his elementary education at St. Augustine's parochial school.

In 1932, Demara's father lost his business and the family house, and thereafter the Demaras existed on charity and the income the elder Demara could eke out from odd jobs. These changes in the family's fortunes devastated young Demara, who years later could vividly recall the humiliations he suffered and the resentment he nursed in their aftermath. In 1936, he enrolled at Central Catholic High School in Lawrence. Demara was big for his age—full-grown he stood over six feet tall and weighed, at one point, 350 pounds—and thought himself brighter than his teachers; he withdrew from formal schooling before the end of his sophomore year. When his younger sister Elaine died suddenly in 1938, he left home for Valley Falls, Rhode Island, to enter a Trappist monastery.

Thereafter Demara lived much of his adult life under aliases, gaining employment for which he had no formal training by appropriating or forging birth certificates, college transcripts, and other credentials of men whose names he picked from newspaper stories or faculty listings in college catalogs. A self-confident autodidact, he acquired the skills he needed through reading and observation and, by many accounts, often performed his duties, whatever the field, with above average competence.

His first entry into religious life lasted a little over two years. As Frater Mary Jerome, he was unable to meet the Trappist order's strenuous rules governing diet, labor, and silence. He next joined the Brothers of Charity, a service order in Boston, and as Brother John Berchmans (a bor-

Ferdinand Waldo Demara, 1963. UPI/CORBIS-BETTMANN

rowed name) taught fourth grade at a children's shelter. Following a dispute with a superior in April 1941, he reassumed his own identity and enlisted in the U.S. Army.

While training in Biloxi, Mississippi, that fall, he impulsively stole personal papers from a friend and, using his friend's name, deserted the military for the Abbey of Our Lady of Gethsemani, the Trappists' main house, near Louisville, Kentucky. A week after his arrival, Demara believed he had been recognized by a visiting monk from Valley Falls and, rather than risk exposure, returned home to Lawrence. When the Japanese attacked Pearl Harbor, his father urged him to report to the army and own up to being absent without leave, but Demara instead enlisted under his real name in the navy, where he trained as a medical corpsman at Norfolk, Virginia. When a security check revealed his desertion from the army, he deserted the navy as well. Making his way back to Gethsemani and using the credentials of Dr. Robert Linton French—a research fellow at Yale—he reentered the Trappist order, only to fail its discipline again.

In November 1943, calling himself Dr. French—as he would for the next five years—he joined the Benedictines

in the Ozarks, where he taught science in a boys school. In early January 1944, he went to Chicago to yet another Catholic order and entered De Paul University for a year of graduate work in theology. In the autumn of 1945, he joined the Paulist fathers as Dean of the School of Philosophy at Gannon College in Erie, Pennsylvania. He became a popular and respected figure in the classroom and among civic groups in town but, after a clash with the college president, he moved to a Benedictine house in Peru, Illinois, then to hospital work in Los Angeles, and, in mid-1946, to teaching at St. Martin's Abbey and College near Olympia, Washington.

He was arrested by the Federal Bureau of Investigation in 1948 for his wartime desertion from the navy (the army dropped its charges) and served eighteen months of a six-year sentence in San Pedro, California. On his release, he resumed his impersonations. He enrolled for a time at Northeastern University's law school in Boston, Massachusetts (as Dr. Cecil Boyce Hamann), while working nights as an orderly under his own name at Boston's Massachusetts General Hospital. In the fall of 1950, using the name Brother John Payne, he trained parochial school teachers at Notre Dame Normal School in Alfred, Maine. Denied an administrative job, he bolted to Nova Scotia in March 1951 and as Joseph C. Cyr, M.D.—in reality, a New Brunswick physician whom he knew—accepted a commission as surgeon lieutenant in the Royal Canadian Navy and went to Korea on board the destroyer HMS *Cayuga*.

Knowing that he was in over his head as the ship's only medical officer, he asked the fleet's senior physicians to draw up a medical handbook listing common symptoms and treatments (ostensibly for a do-it-yourself guide he was publishing for woodcutters in doctorless logging camps across Canada). From it and other medical books he learned enough medicine to survive, suturing wounds and, on one occasion, removing a bullet from the chest of a Korean soldier. In 1980—long after his exposure as a fraud—the men of the *Cayuga* at one of their reunions called Demara "a life-saver" and praised his work.

While in Korea he voluntarily went ashore among the villagers, instructing them in sanitation and performing routine medical procedures, a story soon picked up by the Canadian press and published across Canada. The real Dr. Cyr came forward to expose Demara's impersonation, and on 21 November 1951 Canadian officials discharged him from naval service and ordered him out of the country. Two months later, *Life,* one of America's most widely circulated magazines, brought Demara's "colorful career" to millions of readers, giving him a notoriety he had long sought to avoid.

Under his own name, but using forged credentials, Demara worked at children's shelters and state hospitals in Massachusetts, Kansas, Pennsylvania, and New York, leaving each time his past caught up with him. In 1954 as Ben W. Jones, he joined the Texas Department of Corrections as an assistant warden at the state's maximum security prison in Huntsville and quickly gained a reputation for his humane and skilled treatment of prisoners. About to be promoted to warden, he was fired in December 1956, when an inmate found his picture in *Life*.

Heading north, he assumed the identity of Frank Kingston in a Brooklyn school for retarded children, and then as Martin Godgart taught Latin and French, first at North Haven, Maine, and then at a government school for Eskimos outside Point Barrow, Alaska. As Jefferson Baird Thorne, he taught English, French, and Latin in Winchendon, Massachusetts, in 1959. Later that year, acquiring the credentials of two civil engineers, Carl Shelby and R. C. Springarr, he went to Mexico in search of bridge-building contracts in the Yucatan, and then as B. J. Jones sought work in prison reform in Cuba. Unmasked, he was deported by the Batista government.

From that point on, he used his own name, settling in Anaheim, California, where, for the next fifteen years, he worked as a Baptist minister, a hospital counselor, and at various children's homes. He retired in 1980 for health reasons and died two years later from a heart attack. He never married.

Although he was charged at various times in a variety of jurisdictions with a broad range of felonies and misdemeanors, Demara was rarely prosecuted and, except for his wartime desertion, served little time in jail, largely because the authorities wished to avoid the embarrassment of a public trial or decided in the end that no great harm had been done by his deceptions and simply ordered him to move on to some other place and not return. In his later years, Demara defended himself by saying that he had never used his impostures for criminal ends and had always performed honestly whatever tasks he undertook.

★

As might be expected of a con-man whose first rules of survival were to "have an invisible past" and "never initiate remembrances," Demara constructed several versions of his life, each marked by vagaries, contradictions, and blurred chronology. The clearest account is Joe McCarthy, "The Master Impostor: An Incredible Tale," *Life* (28 Jan. 1952): 79–86. It was the source most often used to expose Demara over the next several years, when his activities were widely reported in newspapers and magazines. Robert Crichton, *The Great Impostor* (1960), a national best-seller, was repudiated as unreliable by Demara before his death; it is useful, if used with caution. The book served as the basis for the Universal Studio film, *The Great Impostor* (1960), which is more fiction than fact, beginning with the casting of Tony Curtis, who bore no resemblance to Demara. See also Robert Crichton, *The Rascal and the Road* (1961), the story of Crichton's and Demara's return to many of the places where Demara had carried out his impersonations. An excerpt appears in *Life* (6 July 1959): 96–98. An obituary is in the *New York Times* (9 June 1982).

ALLAN L. DAMON

DEMARET, James Newton ("Jimmy") (*b.* 24 May 1910 in Houston, Texas; *d.* 28 December 1983 in Houston, Texas), professional golfer and television commentator who was a three-time winner of the Masters tournament (1940, 1947, and 1950).

Demaret (pronounced de-MER-it) came from a generation of professional golfers who got their start in golf as caddies. The fourth of nine children of John O'Brien Demaret, a carpenter and house painter of Dutch-Irish stock, Jimmy caddied for the soldiers at the nearby Fort Logan golf course in Houston. He won his first caddie tournament there at age eleven. The next year at the Hermann Park public course he obtained employment in the pro shop, cleaning clubs and working as an apprentice club maker. While there he won the city caddie championship at age twelve and again at age fourteen, when he shot a 74. After working at the Golfcrest Country Club and the Colonial Country Club, he became assistant professional at the River Oaks Club in Houston at age sixteen, working under Jack Burke, Sr., as caddie master and starter. Demaret dropped out of Houston's North Side High School after two years.

In February 1934 Demaret asked a caddie named Charlie Schwartz to accompany him to the Texas PGA tournament in Dallas, offering him half his prospective winnings. They traveled by boxcar on a frigid night, arriving in Dallas very late. Demaret shot a record 286 for the four rounds and won the first-place prize of $25. He went on to win the Texas PGA tournament for the next four years.

After his Dallas success he obtained a position as club professional at the Galveston, Texas, municipal course and began to frequent the Hollywood Dinner Club, owned by Sam Maceo, who brought in many big-name bands of the day. Demaret would frequently jump up on the stand and sing with the orchestra, and the bandleader Ben Birnie eventually offered him a job singing. Maceo was impressed with his golf game, however, and proposed to back him on the professional tour (later in his career Demaret was offered $1,500 a week by the president of the William Morris Agency to sing at the Paramount Theater in New York; he chose to pursue golf then also). Demaret took off in a Model-T Ford for California with three other golfers and had some success in the tournaments there, although the car was lost in a pool game in El Paso. In December 1935 Jack Grout, later known as the teacher of Jack Nicklaus, pooled his resources with Demaret and agreed to split any prize money. In 1936 their winnings were meager. Demaret later said that "when I was broke, I was just what that word means."

Jimmy Demaret. ARCHIVE PHOTOS

In 1938 Demaret tried the tour again and gained his first major victory, defeating Sam Snead in the San Francisco Match Play Championship early in the year. In 1939 he was the Los Angeles Open champion. In 1940 Demaret finally blossomed as a top-flight tour player with a remarkable string of victories early in the year, winning the Oakland Open, the San Francisco Match Play tournament, the Western Open (which was played in his hometown), and the New Orleans Open in succession, and then the St. Petersburg Open and the Masters tournament. In the Masters he started out poorly, shooting a one-over-par 37 on the front nine, but he shot a six-under 30 on the back for an opening round of 67. During his stretch of six wins, Demaret spent money as he got it. In Miami he had to borrow funds to get back to his home in Houston and to his wife, Idella Adams Demaret, with whom he had a daughter.

Demaret developed an important friendship with fellow Texan Ben Hogan, whom he had known since 1932. Jimmy was an extrovert who would talk to the gallery in the days when the gallery was not roped off, while Hogan rarely said a word. Hogan and Demaret teamed together to win the 1941 Inverness Four-ball and won the event three more times, in addition to winning several other team events and

Ryder Cup matches together in 1947 and 1951. Demaret wrote a book with a title that reflected that experience: *My Partner, Ben Hogan* (1954).

Demaret was five feet, ten inches tall and weighed around 200 pounds in his prime, with a somewhat stocky build for his height and large forearms and hands. He kept his feet in a narrow stance when hitting the ball, even on long shots, and he hit with a "handsy" action. He struck the ball on a low flight, as did many players from Texas, but he could also hit it high and soft. He faded the ball from left to right.

Demaret was a leader in changing the dress code in golf from starched white shirts and ties to colorful lightweight tee shirts and slacks. He won the 1947 Masters dressed in canary yellow from head to foot, which complemented the kelly-green jacket that is given to the champion. In the late 1930s Demaret had discovered bolts of colorful, lightweight cloth at Harold Dryer's tailor shop in New York. He later produced his own clothing out of a tailor shop in Houston.

After the Japanese bombing of Pearl Harbor in 1941, Demaret joined the navy and spent, he wrote later, a "few frustrating years" before his discharge in 1946. After the war, he regained the golf form he had in 1940 and became one of the top touring pros. He led the tour in money earnings in 1947 with $27,937 and won the Vardon Trophy for the lowest scoring average with 69.80, while winning the Masters, Miami Four-ball, Inverness Four-ball, Miami Open, St. Petersburg Open, and Tucson Open. One of his greatest disappointments came in 1948 when he completed play on the last day of the U.S. Open with a potential new Open record of 278 but finished second to Ben Hogan's 276. In 1946 and 1953 he finished sixth in the Open, and in 1957 he had a chance to win it again, but finished one shot out of the lead. Gamely fighting fatigue in ninety-degree heat at a time when the Open had two rounds on the last day, the forty-seven-year-old Demaret finished birdie-par-birdie-par, but came up one shot short of Dick Mayer and Cary Middlecoff, who both birdied the last hole as Demaret watched. Demaret was also in the semifinals of the PGA tournament four times.

Demaret won the Bing Crosby National Pro-Am in 1952. It was one of his favorite tournaments because of his friendship with many of the Hollywood celebrities who played there, including Crosby. He shot a 74 that year in winds and rain when the rest of the field was having trouble breaking 80. Demaret also enjoyed playing golf in Latin America and won the Argentine Open in 1941 and the Havana Pro-Am in 1951. In his prime he went to Havana each year, and he also played in Brazil, Chile, Guatemala, Nicaragua, El Salvador, Panama, Venezuela, and Uruguay. One year he created international controversy by playing in the Mexican Open when it conflicted with a PGA tour event, and he was fined by the PGA. The president of the

Mexican PGA offered to take care of the fine, but Demaret shrugged off the controversy and paid it himself. In 1952 Demaret toured Australia with three other professionals.

In 1953, when playing the Tam-O-Shanter World Open, the tournament run by golf promoter George S. May in Chicago, Demaret finished early and returned to the last green, where Harry Wismer was announcing the first tournament televised live to several major cities. Demaret participated in the commentary, congratulating Chandler Harper on being about to win the $25,000 first prize, which was the largest in golf. Lew Worsham was about 125 yards away from the green and needed to birdie the hole to tie Harper, and Demaret told about a million viewers that he didn't think Worsham could do it. When Worsham hit his shot, the ball landed on the green, then skipped and hopped into the cup. Demaret yelled, "the sonofabitch went in!," which kicked off the era of live golf on national TV.

In the 1950s Demaret played a limited number of tournaments each year, usually about fourteen, and he retired from the tour in 1960. He still played in some tournaments and almost won the Bob Hope Desert Classic in 1964, at age fifty-four, finishing second to Tommy Jacobs. Demaret designed and built the Champions Golf Club in Houston, which opened in 1958, with Jack Burke, Jr. After he retired from the tour, Demaret designed the Onion Creek course in Austin, Texas, where the first Legends of Golf tournament was held in 1978. Demaret was instrumental, with Fred Raphael, in getting the Legends tournament started, and it turned into such a success with its two-person teams of over-fifty golfers that it led to the start of the Senior PGA Tour in the 1980s. Raphael was the executive producer of Shell's *Wonderful World of Golf* on television, which was filmed and announced by Gene Sarazen and Demaret at a series of championship courses around the world and ran from 1961 to 1970.

Demaret's place as a golf talent is defined by the tour rankings of the PGA Tour Statistical Project in 1989, which compiled the records of nearly 4,000 players from 1916 through 1988. The statistics concentrated on performance in significant events rather than money won. In percent of purse from 1916 to 1988 Demaret ranked twelfth; using the Ryder Cup point system he ranked ninth; and in lifetime points he ranked thirteenth. He was the winner of thirty-one official PGA tour tournaments and forty-three tournaments overall. He was a three-time member of the Ryder Cup team (1947, 1949, and 1951) and was voted a member of the PGA Hall of Fame (1960) and the World Golf Hall of Fame (1983). He died of a heart attack as he was getting into a golf cart to inspect his Champions course. His body was cremated.

★

Jimmy Demaret, *My Partner, Ben Hogan* (1954), contains valuable autobiographical material. Al Barkow, *Golf's Golden Grind:*

The History of the Tour (1974) and *History of the PGA Tour* (1989), covers Demaret, as does Curt Sampson, *Hogan* (1996). See also Charley Price, "Golf's Gorgeous Jester," *Saturday Evening Post* (10 June 1950); *Time* (11 Mar. 1940; 24 Nov. 1947); and Mike Purkey, "Jimmy Demaret," *Golf* (Nov. 1993). Obituaries are in the *New York Times, Chicago Tribune,* and *Houston Chronicle* (29 Dec. 1983).

ROBERT T. BRUNS

DEMPSEY, William Harrison ("Jack") (*b.* 24 June 1895 in Manassa, Colorado; *d.* 31 May 1983 in New York City), heavyweight boxing champion of the 1920s; he had a fan following that made "the Manassa Mauler" one of the most publicized figures of the Jazz Age.

Dempsey's parents called him Harry. He was an eleven-pound baby, one of eleven children born to Hyrum and Mary Celia Smoot Dempsey, pioneering parents who took their brood across the Colorado and Utah frontiers while in search of an elusive fortune. Hyrum had been a schoolteacher in West Virginia, and Mary, a no-nonsense Scotch Irishwoman, claimed Utah senator Reed Smoot as a distant relative. Both parents were part Indian and lived on and off the dole and through Mormon charity when farming, ranching, prospecting, and restaurant work could not be

Jack Dempsey. ARCHIVE PHOTOS

found. "You learned to work hard or starve," Dempsey remembered of the family's survival strategy. As a result, he did not go beyond grammar school.

As an adolescent in Lakeview, Utah, Jack shined shoes in a barbershop and was fired for accidentally breaking a comb. The experience fueled his "impatience to grow up." Other indignities followed. He shoveled dung, fed pigs, worked sugar-beet fields, and helped pitch circus tents. By sixteen he had joined his older brother Bernie as a copper-mine mucker, loading ore 3,000 feet down in Bingham County, Utah, and Cripple Creek, Colorado. Jack sparred with Bernie when his brother launched a brief boxing career as "Jack Dempsey," the name of an Irish middleweight who died the year of Jack's birth. The boy who would become the Jazz Age's Jack Dempsey sprinted against horses to test his speed and endurance. He followed Bernie's example by chewing gum to strengthen his jaw, and he bathed his face in beef brine to look older and meaner.

As "Kid Blackie" he took fights wherever he could get them for purses of $2, $5, and sometimes $10. For five years he rode the rails, living in hobo camps and always looking for a fight. The night in 1914 that he badly beat George Copelin in Cripple Creek was the first time he fought under the name "Jack Dempsey." A series of "crumby" fights followed, in which the untrained fighter fought hoping for "future rewards." Dempsey beat Slick Merrill in Tonopah, Nevada, but lost to Johnny Sudenberg in Goldfield, Nevada. He fought Sudenberg to a draw in Reno, beat the Boston Bearcat in a single round in Ogden, Utah, and upended Sudenberg in the second round of their fight in Ely, Nevada.

Dempsey built a four-foot-high cage and began sparring in it to perfect a stalking crouch that would become his signature in the ring. He intensified his training regimen by running six miles every morning. Three quick knockouts over highly regarded western fighters followed. Denver's Otto Floto and other sportswriters began to take notice. By June 1916 Dempsey felt on the verge of "becoming somebody." He arrived in New York City and toured the sports departments of the various newspapers with new fight manager Jack Price. Damon Runyon of the *American* and Nat Fleischer of the *Press* promoted Dempsey into an exhibition bout on his twenty-first birthday at the Fairmont Athletic Club in Chicago against ring veteran Andre Anderson. Each fighter decked the other several times in ten rounds, but Dempsey, always the aggressor, won the decision.

Dempsey's brawling bouts that summer with "Wild Bert" Kenny at the Fairmont and John Lester Johnson in Harlem, where he fought eight rounds with broken ribs, gave a glimpse of Dempsey's extraordinary tenacity. For these fights, he made only $150, which he evenly split with Price. It wasn't enough. A disappointed Price returned to

Salt Lake City; a few days later, after sleeping outside in Central Park, Dempsey followed.

On an impulse Dempsey married a piano player from a Commercial Street saloon on 9 October 1916. Maxine Cates from Walla Walla, Washington, was fifteen years Dempsey's senior. Hoping to restart his ring career, he was knocked down four times in the first round by "Fireman" Jim Flynn in Murray, Utah, on 13 February 1917 before his brother Bernie threw in the towel. His no-decision bouts against "Handsome" Al Norton and "Fat" Willie Meehan in Oakland seemed to confirm the impression that at age twenty-one, Dempsey was punched out.

After hiring out as a Seattle lumberjack and a Tacoma shipyard worker, Dempsey returned to Salt Lake City in the summer of 1917 after his younger brother Bruce was stabbed to death in a street fight. Maxine did not go with him, returning to saloon life. Broke, tired, beaten down by the fight game, Dempsey resigned himself to washing dishes, mining coal, picking fruit, and digging ditches. But a telegram from thirty-four-year-old John Leo McKernan, an Oakland fight manager known as "Doc" Kearns, offered Dempsey a second start. Kearns thought Dempsey "didn't know quit from spit" and might amount to something if handled right.

Dempsey moved in with Kearns, trained diligently, worked on quickness, developed his left hook, and learned how to finish a fighter. In the six months that followed Kearns craftily built up his protégé. A four-round decision over Meehan, twin wins over Kearns crony Norton, and a 2 October 1917 slugfest with "Gunboat" Smith in San Francisco's Mission Park began to attract press attention and crowds. When Dempsey, at six feet, one inch, and 187 pounds, dispatched the "Oklahoma Mastiff," six-foot, four-inch, 235-pound Carl Morris, at San Francisco's Dreamland Pavilion in four rounds on 1 November 1917, Kearns began to believe his hype that Dempsey might be championship material.

Through 1918, Kearns built Dempsey's knockout record to an impressive 60 percent by matching him with one-round wonders like Homer Rice, Tom Riley, and Kid McCarthy. Bouts against the better-known Bill Brennan and Billy Miske were fought when Kearns was certain the increasingly confident Dempsey was ready. His real target was heavyweight champion Jess Willard, the six-foot, six-inch "Pottawatomie Giant," who had taken the title from Jack Johnson in April 1915. Dempsey's knockout of number-one contender Fred Fulton in eighteen seconds of the first round on 27 July 1918 in suburban Harrison, New Jersey, brought press pressure for a Willard-Dempsey title fight. Kearns created the Jack Dempsey Revue for vaudeville houses to keep Dempsey's name in the papers, while cultivating through the nation's sports pages the image of Dempsey as an impregnable warrior.

Twenty-thousand people attended the Independence Day 1919 championship fight in Toledo, many watching in utter amazement as the sneering, stalking, saddle-colored Dempsey knocked Willard to the canvas seven times in the first round. When the badly battered Willard could not come out for the fourth round, Dempsey became, at twenty-four, the heavyweight champion of the world. Kearns immediately capitalized on Dempsey's celebrity status by signing his star to a $15,000 weekly contract to tour the Pantages vaudeville circuit. Hefty appearance fees followed. A West Coast studio, Pathé, planned to star Dempsey in a fifteen-episode serial, *Daredevil Jack,* but the project was shelved when Dempsey was indicted by a federal grand jury in February 1920 for evading the draft. Dempsey's former wife Maxine (they had divorced early in 1919), who charged Dempsey had not supported her during the war, later recanted her testimony and he was acquitted. The negative publicity haunted Dempsey. He had fought for himself, many papers wrote, while other able-bodied men had fought for their country.

Dempsey's 2 July 1921 match with French war hero Georges Carpentier, skillfully promoted by Kearns and boxing showman George "Tex" Rickard, produced great crowds at Boyle's Thirty Acres in Jersey City, New Jersey, and boxing's first $1 million gate. Dempsey's 1920 knockouts over Billy Miske and Bill Brennan, two fighters he had fought before, created nowhere near the excitement and drama of the Carpentier match. So taken was the press by pre-fight publicity pitting a great war hero against a reputed American war slacker that "the greatest battle since the Silurian Age," as a Chicago sportswriter described it, appeared to take on international significance. Dempsey's knockout victory over Carpentier and his July 1923 defeat of Tommy Gibbons seemed to solidify his growing reputation as a great fighting machine. It was, however, his ferocious battle with the "Wild Bull of the Pampas," Argentina's Luis Firpo, that left a lasting impression.

Eighty-eight thousand fight fans, including Babe Ruth, Ethel Barrymore, Kermit Roosevelt, William K. Vanderbilt, L. H. Rothschild, and the leading celebrities of the Jazz Age crowded into the Polo Grounds in New York City in September 1923 to witness one of the most memorable four-and-a-half minutes in ring history. The oversized Firpo was floored seven times in the first round, getting off the canvas to punch Dempsey through the ropes and onto the press table. A dozen reporters and leading stars on Broadway later claimed credit for hurling the enraged Dempsey back into the ring. The champion tore into his Argentine opponent and in the second round laid him out for good.

The $1 million gate for the Dempsey-Firpo fight reflected the degree to which boxing and Dempsey had become big commodities. In five years Dempsey had fought

thirty-nine rounds, totaling just short of two full hours. His total earnings of $1,257,000 during that time prorated to $32,231 a round, $10,744 a minute, $179 a second. For the pleasure of sending Firpo back to Buenos Aires, Dempsey earned $100,000 a minute. "Dempsey worship," sports columnist Ring Lardner wrote, had become "a national disease."

Adoring crowds closed in on Dempsey at every public appearance. He was a star. Men and women paid to shake his hand. Reporters and editors saw circulations soar in the weeks before and the days after a Dempsey title defense. Dempsey was in no hurry to return to the ring. He moved to Hollywood, acrimoniously broke his long professional relationship with Kearns, and married a beautiful, fast-fading, silent film actress, Estelle Taylor, in a highly publicized February 1926 wedding.

The bidding for Dempsey's return to the ring against the lightly regarded Gene Tunney involved Chicago, New York, and Philadelphia promoters. Twenty-five hundred millionaires joined some 120,000 other spectators in paying $2 million to see a visibly slowed Dempsey lose his championship to Tunney in a ten-round decision on 23 September 1926 in Philadelphia's Sesquicentennial Stadium. Listeners in homes, public parks, and storefronts heard the infant National Broadcasting Company's call of the contest. Nearly everyone had difficulty believing their generation's great "fighting machine" had been defeated.

Rumors immediately circulated that Dempsey's pre-fight meal had been drugged by gamblers. Dempsey knew, however, that the long layoff and soft lifestyle had made him a shadow of his former self. He returned gamely to the ring, knocking out future champion Jack Sharkey in the seventh round at Yankee Stadium on 21 July 1927 before a crowd of 72,000. The comeback fight against Tunney at Chicago's Soldier Field on 22 September 1927 produced a record $2.3 million gate and was heard by a worldwide audience that included three of every four adult Americans. It included what many would later regard as the most famous moment in the history of sports. Trailing by points in the seventh round, Dempsey momentarily flashed his former brilliance and caught Tunney with a looping left. An avalanche of lefts and rights left Tunney sitting and badly dazed. But instead of going to a neutral corner Dempsey towered over his fallen opponent, and the start of the referee's count was delayed more than six seconds. As a result, Tunney rose to his feet at the count of nine, nearly eighteen seconds after hitting the canvas, and held off Dempsey to retain his championship. The fairness of the "long count" would be argued for a generation.

Dempsey no longer needed to fight to make money. His classy acceptance of twin defeats further endeared him to millions. He starred with his wife, Estelle, in *The Big Fight,* a production of Broadway showman David Belasco, and it did good business during the summer of 1928. The death of Dempsey's crony Tex Rickard in January 1929 brought Dempsey back into promoting fights. But the collapse of the stock market, the onset of the Great Depression, a costly divorce, and $3 million in Florida real estate losses bankrupted the former champ. In 1931, at the age of thirty-six, he embarked on a series of boxing exhibitions designed to build him up for another title shot. A four-round beating by Kingfish Levinsky in Chicago Stadium finally persuaded Dempsey to end the pretense.

Dempsey then married singer Hannah Williams in 1933 and settled into domestic life. They had two daughters. As occasional actor and part-time wrestling referee, Dempsey rode out the Great Depression quietly. He made headlines by joining the Coast Guard while in his middle forties during World War II. By that time the cultural memory of Dempsey as slacker had been displaced by affection for a middle-aged boxing legend. In 1943 Dempsey and Williams were divorced.

Dempsey married Deanna Piatelli in 1958 and could be seen most evenings taking a familiar seat at his eponymous Broadway restaurant in midtown Manhattan.

There, he happily greeted the many who came to shake his hand or exchange mock blows beneath the fighting photos of his ring years. Before the restaurant closed in 1974, Dempsey had reconciled with Kearns, been honored by the Boxing Hall of Fame, and been named by the Associated Press as the greatest fighter of the half-century. His seventy-fifth birthday, staged at Madison Square Garden in June 1970, saw an outpouring of love for the man many still called champ.

The passing of Doc Kearns in 1963 and of Gene Tunney fifteen years later left only Dempsey of the boxing men whose personalities and performances elicited the tall tale-telling of sportswriters and promoters during America's prosperity decade. Heart problems in 1982 led to surgery and insertion of a pacemaker. His medical comeback was chronicled in the nation's newspapers, but the end came when his wife found Dempsey dead in their mid-Manhattan apartment following a heart attack. His wake elicited a final series of tributes, including President Ronald Reagan's observation that "our attachment to America's colorful past is weakened by the passing of Jack Dempsey." Burial was on Long Island.

When radio was in its infancy, the largest crowds in the history of North America gathered in municipal squares to listen to accounts of Jack Dempsey's title fights. People dressed as if for church. These civic spectacles testified to Dempsey's unique hold on the public imagination and his personal status as the quintessential American man of action. Modernity's demand for city living and bureaucratic management had created an appetite for individual feats of daring and drama that made Dempsey's rugged ring style the stuff of myth and legend.

★

Dempsey collaborated on three autobiographies: Jack Dempsey and Myron M. Stearns, *Round by Round* (1940); Jack Dempsey, Bob Considine, and Bill Slocum, *Dempsey: By the Man Himself* (1960); and Jack Dempsey with Barbara Piatelli Dempsey, *Dempsey* (1977). Biographical works include Nat Fleischer, *Jack Dempsey* (1972); Randy Roberts, *Jack Dempsey: The Manassa Mauler* (1979); and Bruce J. Evensen, *When Dempsey Fought Tunney: Heroes, Hokum, and Storytelling in the Jazz Age* (1996). Appreciations by Jazz Age sportswriters can be found in Allison Danzig and Peter Brandwein, eds., *Sport's Golden Age: A Close-up of the Fabulous Twenties* (1948); Grantland Rice, *The Tumult and the Shouting* (1954); and Paul Gallico, *The Golden People* (1965). The views of Dempsey's longtime manager and aide are in Jack Kearns and Oscar Fraley, *The Million Dollar Gate* (1966). The role of promotion in Dempsey's career is described in Maxine Rickard and Arch Oboler, *Everything Happened to Him: The Story of Tex Rickard* (1936). Dempsey's relation to cultural spectacle is described in Mel Heimer, *The Long Count* (1969). Dempsey's place in American culture is explored by Benjamin G. Rader, "Compensatory Sports Heroes: Ruth, Grange, and Dempsey," *Journal of Popular Culture* 16 (1983): 11–22, and Elliot J. Gorn, "The Manassa Mauler and the Fighting Marine: An Interpretation of the Dempsey-Tunney Fights," *Journal of American Studies* 19 (1985): 27–57. An obituary is in the *New York Times* (1 June 1983).

BRUCE J. EVENSEN

DENBY, Edwin Orr (*b.* 4 February 1903 in Tientsin, China; *d.* 12 July 1983 in Searsport, Maine), dancer, poet, and dance critic whose writings about dance transformed the nature of American dance criticism.

The son of Charles Denby and Martha Dalzell Orr, Denby was born in China, where his father served as the American consul in Shanghai. He had an older brother, James. Denby moved with his family to Vienna when he was seven. In 1916 he moved to the United States to attend the Hotchkiss School in Lakeville, Connecticut. In 1919 he entered Harvard University, where he stayed until December 1920 in his sophomore year. After leaving Harvard, Denby lived briefly in New York City and returned to Vienna in 1923 to study dance and psychoanalysis. Troubled and unstable, he sought help from Dr. Paul Federn, a disciple of Freud. Urged by Federn to pursue his love of dance, in 1925 Denby enrolled at the Hellerau-Laxenburg School. After graduating in 1928 he danced professionally, in Darmstadt, Germany, between 1928 and 1930; with Clare Eckstein in Berlin and Munich, Germany, between 1930 and 1933; and with Marietta von Meyenburg in Switzerland until 1935. As a dancer Denby was best known for his comic roles. In

Switzerland he met the photographer Rudolph Burckhardt in 1934, who would become a pioneer of avant-garde film in America. From then on Burckhardt was Denby's intimate life-long friend and cast him in nine movies, including *145 West 21* (1937), *Miracle on the BMT* (1963), *Lurk* (1964), *Money* (1967), *Tarzam* (1968), and *Inside Dope* (1971).

Repelled by Hitler's rise to power, Denby left Europe in 1936 and moved to New York City. He and Burckhardt moved into a walk-up apartment at 145 West Twenty-first Street, Denby's primary residence until his death. He commenced his career as a dance critic, contributing to *Modern Music,* edited by Minna Lederman. He wrote for that journal until 1942, when his friend the composer Virgil Thomson recommended that he temporarily replace critic Walter Terry at the *New York Herald Tribune* until Terry returned from service in the war. Many critics argue that Denby's journalistic dance writing for the *Herald Tribune* is his best. Under daily deadline pressure, Denby honed his critical style, characterized by a poet's sensibility for precision, vividness, and analogy. As a trained dancer writing criticism, he translated the kinesthetic and expressive effects of body movement into a terse, descriptive language understandable by dance audiences.

An excerpt from a 1945 review of George Balanchine's *Concerto Barocco* exemplifies his critical style:

> Against a background of chorus that suggests the look of trees in the wind before a storm breaks, the ballerina, with limbs powerfully outspread, is lifted by her male partner, lifted repeatedly in narrowing arcs higher and higher. Then, at the culminating phrase, from her greatest height he very slowly lowers her. You watch her body slowly descend, her foot and leg pointing stiffly downward, till her toe reaches the floor and she rests her full weight at last on this single sharp point and pauses. It is the effect at that moment of a deliberate and powerful plunge into a wound.

Dance scholar Marcia Siegel has asserted that "it wasn't *what* he saw but *how* he saw that gave his criticism authority. His insights went so deep, so far beyond ego projections or utilitarian accounts, that one was forced to stop and consider them."

Denby ceded his position to Terry in 1945 and thereafter wrote freelance. *Looking at the Dance* (1949), a collection of these early writings, established his genius. On its publication, *New York Times* dance critic John Martin wrote: "Here is the honest and courageous attitude of a highly cultivated, often keenly perceptive, mind toward a subject which he has studied closely and respects deeply." Denby's dance criticism is also published in two other collections: *Dancers, Buildings, and People in the Street* (1965) and the

Edwin Denby. PAUL HOSEFROS/NYT PICTURES

posthumous *Dance Writings* (1987), edited by Robert Cornfield and William MacKay.

During his early years as a critic, Denby pursued other artistic interests as well. He collaborated with Orson Welles on the libretto of *Horse Eats Hat* (1935); wrote the text for Aaron Copland's opera *The Second Hurricane* (1937); staged the "Negro" ballet in the 1938 production of Maxwell Anderson's *Knickerbocker Holiday;* and with Rita Matthias translated Ferdinand Bruckner's *The Criminals,* which opened in New York in 1941. Denby formed close bonds with other artists in the New York City avant-garde, in particular poets Frank O'Hara, Kenneth Koch, James Schuyler, John Ashbery, Ron Padgett, Anne Waldman, Alice Notley, and Ted Berrigan; painters Willem and Elaine de Kooning, Franz Kline, Alex Katz, Red Grooms, and Larry Rivers; composers Virgil Thomson, Aaron Copland, Roger Sessions, and John Cage; and choreographers Merce Cunningham, Paul Taylor, and Jerome Robbins.

Although he is best known for his writing on dance, Denby published several books of poetry: *In Public, in Private* (1948), *Mediterranean Cities* (1956), *Snoring in New York* (1974), and *Collected Poems* (1975). He also wrote a novel, *Mrs. W's Last Sandwich* (1972). Two works were published posthumously: *The Complete Poems* (1986) and "On the Soul's Reactions to Gymnastics," in *Ballet Review* (spring 1985). His honors include a Guggenheim Fellowship (1948), a *Dance* magazine award (1965), and the Brandeis University Notable Achievement Award (1979).

"To look at Edwin Denby, you would think him the mildest and frailest of men—an aristocrat, with his white hair and his Harvard accent, his disinterested way of wearing out-of-style clothes," recalled critic Marcia Siegel in her 1983 tribute to Denby in *Ballet News*. Denby suffered declining health in his later years. Although he remained involved in the New York art scene into the final months of his life, his faculties were failing. In 1983 Denby took his own life in his summer cabin in Searsport, Maine.

Denby's dance writing documents a pivotal moment in the history of modernism in dance. In the postwar period dance took a turn toward abstraction, in a move against the dominant expressionist mode that had characterized it since the turn of the century. Although Denby's taste was catholic, his bias toward an abstract classicism, embodied in the choreography of Balanchine, appears in his criticism. However, this preference does not render his written perceptions inaccessible or elitist. As dance critic Arlene Croce said, "Far from writing for a coterie, as he was sometimes accused of doing, he was working to broaden access to the subject on its deepest levels, both for the reader and for himself."

★

William MacKay, "Edwin Denby, 1903–1983," in *Edwin Denby: Dance Writings* (1986), edited by Robert Cornfield and William N. MacKay, offers a familiar perspective on Denby's life and work. Lois Draegin, "An Exemplary Life," *Harper's* (Feb. 1984), and David Kaufman, "Denby on Dance, Angst, and Beauty: The Life and Career of Dance Critic and Poet Edwin Denby," *Horizon* (July/Aug. 1987): 38–40, both explore Denby's activity in the mid-century New York art scene and synthesize other critical accounts of Denby's life and career. Marcia Siegel, "Edwin Denby: An Appreciation," *Ballet News* (Oct. 1983), provides profound insight into Denby's contribution to the field of dance criticism. For a collection of tributes to and reflections on Denby's life and work by those who knew him well see *Ballet Review* (spring 1984, summer 1984, fall 1984). In these issues entire sections are devoted to Denby. Arlene Croce, "Dancing Writings," *New Yorker* (13 Apr. 1987), reviews Denby's collected *Dance Writings* (1986) and evokes the art world in which he lived and worked. Mindy Aloff, "What One Writes About When One Writes About Dance," *Threepenny Review* (summer 1987): 17–21, comments on three books published after Denby's death. The obituary in the *New York Times* (14 July 1983) offers significant details about Denby's career and assesses his contribution to the fields of dance criticism and poetry.

REBEKAH J. KOWAL

DEUTSCH, Helene Rosenbach (*b.* 9 October 1884 in Przemysl, Austria-Hungary [present-day Poland]; *d.* 29 March 1982 in Cambridge, Massachusetts), psychoanalyst who underwent analysis with Sigmund Freud and was best known for her two-volume opus, *The Psychology of Women* (1944).

Raised in what was then the Polish part of the Austro-Hungarian Empire, Deutsch was one of four children born to Wilhelm Rosenbach and Regina Fass. She was the favorite of her father, a prominent Jewish lawyer who often took her with him to court. In later years she would attribute her thriving professional life to her identification with her father. In contrast, Deutsch openly despised her mother, a homemaker who, she claimed, beat her and thwarted her scholarly aspirations. Although she grew up in relative luxury, Deutsch was often isolated and unhappy, deriving much of her companionship and support from her father and an older sister.

As a teenager Deutsch was active in the socialist movement, even attempting at one point to join the Polish Worker's Party. At sixteen she met Herman Lieberman, a man who would become the center of her emotional life for many years. "Our love," she wrote in her autobiography, "was full of passion, happiness, and tragedy." Sixteen years her senior, Lieberman was a charismatic leader in the Social Democratic party; he had children and a wife who would not divorce him. Deutsch's affair enraged her mother, who plotted with Lieberman's wife to break up the relationship. In 1907 Deutsch left Poland to study medicine in Vienna. Lieberman, who was elected a delegate to Parliament that spring, would spend much of his political life in that same city.

One of a handful of women to enter medical school at the University of Vienna, Deutsch had originally planned to become a pediatrician but soon switched her focus to psychiatry. A lover of art and literature, she found that this latter study allowed her to indulge her creativity. She excelled at her work but suffered periodic emotional and physical disorders. Realizing that her relationship with Lieberman was stunting her psychic and professional development, she broke with him in 1911. On 14 April 1912 she married Felix Deutsch, a brilliant physician who specialized in internal medicine. Although the relationship lacked the tempestuous passion of her affair with Lieberman, it provided the peace and emotional stability she needed.

After she passed her first exam with "excellent success," her mother recognized her potential and allowed her father to support her financially. Deutsch always received good grades, although they were never very important to her. Graduating from medical school in 1913, she prepared for the field of psychiatry through exhaustive and systematic reading, often up to eight hours a day. During this time she became fascinated by the work of Sigmund Freud and began to think about a career in psychoanalysis. In 1914 Deutsch began working full-time at Wagner-Jauregg, the most prestigious psychiatric clinic in Vienna. The on-

Helene Deutsch, 1972. NYT PICTURES/NYT PERMISSIONS

slaught of World War I and the departure of other clinicians to the front brought new opportunities to Deutsch, and she rose to a prominence unprecedented for a woman in her post. She left the clinic in 1918 when she had the opportunity to undergo analysis with Freud. Her treatment ended abruptly after a year when Freud informed her that he needed her analytic hour to resume work with his former patient the "Wolf-Man." Deutsch always worried that her analysis bored Freud. Twice, she recalled, he fell asleep during her session. On 29 January 1917 Deutsch gave birth to her only child, Martin. Throughout her life she would be plagued by the difficulty of reconciling her professional life with her responsibilities as a mother.

The 1920s were Deutsch's most productive years. She emerged as a superb clinician, teacher, writer, and training analyst. In 1924 she garnered broad recognition after delivering her first essay on female psychology. That same year she was asked to head the newly established Vienna Training Institute. She remained director until the threat of Nazi occupation forced her to emigrate to America in 1935. Settling in Cambridge with her husband and son, Deutsch took a position at Massachusetts General Hospital. She served as president of the Boston Psychoanalytic Society and Institute from 1939 to 1941 and continued her clinical work as well as teaching and supervision until well into her eighties. Although psychoanalysis remained her true

passion, she continued her lifelong engagement in political activism, marching against the Vietnam War in the 1960s and 1970s. In 1973 she published her autobiography, *Confrontations with Myself*. She died in her home in Cambridge, Massachusetts, at the age of ninety-seven.

Helene Deutsch's most original clinical contribution was her notion of the "as if" personality. This concept referred to the patient who derived a sense of self only through identification with others. Although she used this concept to understand emotionally disaffected populations, she believed it could have more general applicability. In less theoretical circles Deutsch is best known for her two volumes on the psychology of women. At once her most substantial and most controversial contribution to the field, this project both derived and departed from Freudian notions of femininity and female sexuality. Deutsch believed that women are characterized by three essential traits—narcissism, passivity, and masochism—and that the conjunction of or conflict among these elements contributes to the formation of more "feminine" or "masculine" personalities. While her supporters praise her originality, her contribution to Freudian thought, and her exhaustive data, her detractors criticize her equation of passivity with femininity. Throughout her life Deutsch maintained that her psychoanalytic notions about female development contributed to the cause of women's emancipation.

★

Helene Deutsch, *Confrontations with Myself* (1973), is particularly revealing of her early years in Poland. Paul Roazen, *Helene Deutsch: A Psychoanalyst's Life* (1985), is an authorized biography that contains fascinating correspondence between Deutsch and her husband, Lieberman, and Freud. It is also useful in mapping the psychoanalytic community of Vienna at the beginning of the twentieth century. Janet Sayers, *Mothering Psychoanalysis: Helene Deutsch, Karen Horney, Anna Freud, and Melanie Klein* (1991), gives the best theoretical account of Deutsch's psychoanalytic concepts. Brenda S. Webster, "Helene Deutsch: A New Look," *Signs* 10, no. 3 (1985): 553–571, focuses on the contradictions and tensions between Deutsch's clinical findings and traditional psychoanalytic theory, while Nellie L. Thompson, "Helene Deutsch: A Life in Theory," *Psychoanalytic Quarterly* 56, no. 2 (1987): 317–353, examines Deutsch's understanding of identification. Suzanne Gordon, "Helene Deutsch and the Legacy of Freud," *New York Times* (30 July 1978), describes Deutsch's fraught relationship to feminism. Sanford Gifford, "Tribute to Helene Deutsch," *American Imago* 40, no. 1 (1983): 3–10, contains personal reminiscences. Obituaries are in the *New York Times* and *Washington Post* (both 1 Apr. 1982) and in *Time* (12 Apr. 1982).

GILLIAN SILVERMAN

DIAMOND, Selma (*b.* 5 August 1920 in London, Ontario, Canada; *d.* 13 May 1985 in Los Angeles, California), one of the few female comedy writers in the early days of television and an actress characterized by her uniquely gravel-voiced, dry delivery.

Selma Diamond grew up in Brooklyn, New York, and attended public schools there. Her father was a tailor, and she would become an excellent seamstress. Much of her later comic material related to the foibles of her New York Jewish relatives. As a teenager she sold jokes to comedians and cartoon ideas to the *New York Times*. After graduating from New York University she sold fiction and cartoons to magazines including the *New Yorker*.

From March 1943 through 1944, Diamond worked in Los Angeles for Groucho Marx's CBS radio show, *Blue Ribbon Town,* a comedy-variety show sponsored by Pabst Blue Ribbon. She was the only woman on the program's writing team, which included Artie Standar, Dick Mack, Bill Demling, and Robert Fisher. According to Fisher, in those days Diamond had a figure "like a goddess" but could handle the male locker-room type of humor that she encountered. According to Diamond, "My figure is the one thing I'm secure about." The men kidded her, and they liked her. The feeling was mutual. About men, she said, "I like them."

Diamond was also the lone female writer on radio's *Adventures of Ozzie and Harriet,* which started its ten-year run

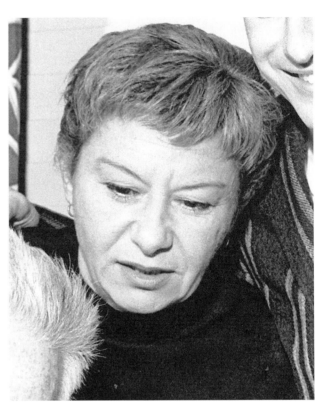

Selma Diamond, 1960. NYT PICTURES/NYT PERMISSIONS

on CBS in 1944. Groucho introduced her to Goodman Ace, a writer for the NBC radio program *The Big Show,* which aired in 1951 and 1952. Ace hired Diamond, who joined the writing team of Ace, Mort Green, and George Foster. The program, a weekly ninety-minute variety show starring Tallulah Bankhead and Fred Allen, featured an array of famous guests. Ace had expected that a female writer would contribute less raunchy and less censorable jokes than the men were prone to do. On Diamond's first show, however, she composed the following dialogue between Tallulah Bankhead and Judy Holliday:

> JUDY: "I've worn strapless evening gowns since I was twelve years old."
> TALLULAH: "Isn't twelve a little young for a strapless evening gown, darling?"
> JUDY: "If it stays up you're old enough."

On another show Diamond had Tallulah telling Groucho Marx that Tallulah likes a man of action who can fly a plane, race a boat, fight a duel. Groucho remarked that in the morning he got out of bed, went to the door, picked up the paper and the milk bottle and breakfast rolls and carried them inside without dropping anything.

> TALLULAH: "What's so remarkable about that?"
> GROUCHO: "No strings on my pajamas."

After *The Big Show* ended in 1952, Diamond went with Goodman Ace to NBC television, where she wrote for the *Milton Berle Show* with Ace, Aaron Rubin, Arnold Auerbach, and Jay Burton. From 1954 to 1957 she was part of the writing team of *Caesar's Hour,* starring Sid Caesar. Other writers for the show included Carl Reiner, Mel Brooks, Mel Tolkin, Larry Gelbart, and Sheldon Keller. Many of their skits were about postwar domestic life in the suburbs; dented fenders, in-laws, and charge accounts were typical topics. When Reiner created the *Dick Van Dyke Show,* which premiered in 1961, the character of Sally Rogers, the female member of a team of comedy writers, was a de-ethnicized version of Diamond.

Other television writing assignments included the *Adventures of Ozzie and Harriet* and the *Ed Sullivan Show.* Fond of children, Diamond recalled taking two little girls to an Ed Sullivan rehearsal,

> so they could meet Topo Gigio, the Italian mouse, whom I happen to know personally. As a matter of fact, I write his material when he appears on the Sullivan show. You think it's odd to be writing for a mouse? What about Ed Sullivan? He stands there and talks to him.

In the early 1960s she was working on the *Perry Como Show* with Goodman Ace and Jay Burton. About her career as a lone woman on a team of male writers she said, "It's like being Red China. I'm there. They just don't recognize me."

Between television seasons Diamond appeared as an actress in summer-stock productions of *Come Blow Your Horn, Funny Girl, Bye-Bye Birdie,* and *Barefoot in the Park.* In the early 1960s she began her guest appearances on Jack Paar's *Tonight Show* and continued after Johnny Carson became host. Her favorite subjects as a talk-show guest were her relatives and her dating problems. She was a single working woman, whose ideal of marriage was "an honest relationship between two people who like each other." She enjoyed the perks of her successful writing career, which included such luxuries as a mink coat and jacket, and an expensive New York apartment on exclusive Sutton Place on Manhattan's Upper East Side. A record album, *Selma Diamond Talks and Talks and Talks and Talks* (1960), was spliced together from anecdotes delivered on the Paar show. Regarding her sandpaperish, nasal voice, she said, "I think a mike distorts my voice, I really do. I never knew I sounded anything like that."

Diamond worked as a movie actress in *It's a Mad Mad Mad Mad World* (1963), as the telephone voice of Culpeper's wife; *Bang the Drum Slowly* (1973), as Tootsie; *My Favorite Year* (1982), as Lil; *Twilight Zone: The Movie* (1983), as Mrs. Weinstein; *Lovesick* (1983), as Harriet Singer; and *All of Me* (1984), as Margo. On television she appeared in *The Jetsons,* as the voice of Judy Jetson's talking diary, Di Di, in 1962 and 1963; *Magic Carpet* in 1971; *Too Close for Comfort,* as Mildred Rafkin in episodes 42 and 43, in 1980; *The Other Woman,* as Aunt Jeanette, in 1983; and *The Ratings Game,* as Francine's mother, in 1984.

Diamond's best-remembered role was also her last. She had a featured part as the gruff, chain-smoking bailiff, Selma Hacker, on the NBC sitcom *Night Court* during its first two seasons in 1984 and 1985. Reinhold Weege, creator of the series, said, "Selma was the only character I had cast in my mind before ever writing the first show. That's why the character's name is Selma." Carl Reiner characterized her style as "terse." "Even in her work on *Night Court*," he said, "she didn't go into any long routines. She would just walk in and drop a few plums." After completing the last program of the 1985 season, Diamond entered Cedars-Sinai Medical Center in Los Angeles on May 1. She died there of lung cancer and was buried at Hillside Memorial Park in Los Angeles.

Selma Diamond was a major comedy writer for some of America's most popular television shows, an unusual achievement for a woman during television's "golden age." Her popularity as a personality was based on humane humor, rooted in the mundane, delivered in a dry, world-weary style that audiences found captivating.

★

The Selma Diamond clipping file in the Billy Rose Theatre Collection, Lincoln Center Library for the Performing Arts in New York City, contains information about her life and career. Selma Diamond, *Nose Jobs for Peace* (1970), a collection of comic essays on a variety of topics, gives some details of Diamond's life as a writer and television personality. See also Mary Unterbrink, *Funny Women, American Comediennes, 1860–1985* (1987). Obituaries appear in the *Los Angeles Times, New York Times,* and *Washington Post* (all 14 May 1985).

SUSAN MOWER

DICK, Philip Kindred (*b.* 16 December 1928 in Chicago, Illinois; *d.* 2 March 1982 in Santa Ana, California), science fiction author whose explorations into the nature of consciousness and reality influenced a generation of writers and musicians.

Philip Kindred Dick and his twin sister, Jane Charlotte Dick, were born six weeks prematurely to Joseph Edgar and Dorothy Kindred Dick, who had difficulty feeding and caring for the infants. Baby Jane was burned by an electric blanket and Dorothy Dick could not get the feeding formula right. The fortuitous visit in 1929 of an insurance nurse checking on the welfare of the children, whose father had just taken out life insurance policies on them, saved Philip from death by malnutrition. The nurse rushed the babies to the hospital; Jane died on the way. The loss of his twin sister had a traumatic effect on Philip, chiefly because his mother often gloated about what a good thing it was that his "crippled" sister had died young. The phantom twin motif appears in many of Dick's books, especially those written after 1974.

In 1929 the Dicks moved to Berkeley, California. After his parents' divorce in 1933, Phil moved with his mother to Washington, D.C., where he attended boarding school for two years. He saw his mother only briefly each week, and his father not at all for more than five years until mother and son returned to Berkeley in 1939. Young Philip grew to idolize his distant, unapproachable father and to hate his cold and dominating mother. Still, it was Dorothy who encouraged him to write during his childhood.

In high school Dick read serious literature by Franz Kafka and John Dos Passos, along with pulp science fiction. He also discovered fine music. By 1944 he was working in the Art Music store in Berkeley, first as a janitor, then as a sales clerk. The job fostered his feelings of independence, and the staff served as a surrogate family, with his boss, Herbert G. Hollis, taking on a paternal role. Dick made many friends among the diverse student population of the University of California.

After graduating from Berkeley High School in 1945, Dick began a life of writing, women, and eventually mysticism. These three facets of his life were intimately interlinked, but are best discussed separately.

Phil Dick had five wives and numerous lovers. On 14 May 1948 he married Jeanette Marlin, an older woman of twenty-five. That marriage officially ended on 30 November 1948. In divorce court, Jeanette charged him with mental cruelty, which Dick did not contest. In 1950 he married Kleo Apostolides, a beautiful Greek girl who loved cats, cooking, and going to school. Dick stayed with her for eight years, but in 1958 Anne Williams Rubenstein lured him away from Berkeley to Point Reyes Station in Marin County. Dick and Kleo were divorced in 1959 and three weeks later he married Anne. Phil and Anne, already a mother of two, soon had a daughter, Laura. Dick stayed with Anne until 1963, when she divorced him for unfaithfulness. Anne kept custody of their daughter.

Dick then switched his affections to a nineteen-year-old girl named Nancy Hackett. He married her in 1966, and in 1967 they had a daughter, Isolde. Nancy divorced him in 1970, keeping custody of their child, leaving Dick to a series of brief affairs that ended in 1973 when he married Tessa Busby. He had a child by her, a son Christopher, later that year. Tessa stayed with Phil until 1976, when he drove her away with his adulteries. She was his last wife, but he continued to have brief, intense romantic encounters up until the time of his death.

Dick's writing career was similarly tumultuous. Although he had written continuously throughout his child-

Philip K. Dick, 1981. PHOTO BY FRANK RONAN

hood, his career as a science fiction author began in 1951 with the sale of his first short story, "Roog," to Anthony Boucher, the founder and first editor of the *Magazine of Fantasy and Science Fiction*. Although it was his first sale, seven stories were published in other magazines before "Roog" appeared in 1952. Dick wrote incessantly and had a wall full of rejection slips—he once got seventeen rejections back on the same day—but by 1952 he was selling regularly. From 1952 to 1954 he published sixty short stories, some under the pseudonym of Richard Phillips.

Solar Lottery was Dick's first novel. Written in 1954 and sold to Donald Wollheim, editor of Ace Books, it was published in 1955. From that point Dick turned out at least one novel per year. His 1962 offering, *The Man in the High Castle*, an "alternate world" story of an America conquered by the Axis Powers in World War II, was voted the Hugo Award for best science fiction novel in 1963. It remains, along with *Do Androids Dream of Electric Sheep?* (1968; also known as *Blade Runner*), one of the two novels on which his reputation rests. Dick continued to churn out novels until 1975. In that year, the trippy *Flow My Tears, the Policeman Said* won the John W. Campbell Award. That same year Paul Williams of *Rolling Stone* magazine conducted an extensive biographical interview with Dick that made him a folk hero with the counterculture.

Beginning with a vision of an eye in the sky in 1974 and continuing with the belief that a superintelligence reordered his life in 1975, Dick maintained for the remainder of his life the claim that he had entered a mystical state. He wrote as much as ever, but little got published in the six years between 1975 and 1981 while he tried to bring order to the vast revelations he was experiencing. Paradoxically, these were Dick's most prosperous years, since Gregg Press had republished his earlier paperback novels in hardcover and they were selling well. Best of all, the movie *Blade Runner* (1982), starring Harrison Ford, was in production. Two novels, *Valis* and *The Divine Invasion*, both based on occult revelations from the "superintelligence," saw print in 1981, and a mainstream novel, *The Transmigration of Timothy Archer*, was released in 1982.

But more than two decades of methamphetamine abuse along with a sedentary lifestyle finally had their effect on him. Philip K. Dick died suddenly of heart failure caused by a stroke on 2 March 1982 in Santa Ana, California. After his death several collections and novels appeared, some of which remained in print decades later. By the time of his death Dick had received considerable critical recognition and was regarded by many as the most brilliant writer in science fiction. With the success of the movie *Blade Runner* he became well known for the first time outside the science fiction subculture.

For twenty-seven years Philip K. Dick, voluptuary and mystic, explored the nature of consciousness and reality in more than thirty-five novels and six collections of short stories. His novels discussed the most serious issues of his time, including the nature of consciousness, reality, and God. He examined the moral consequences of future technologies such as cloning. His characters were common men in mind-bending situations, not superhumans out to save the galaxy. His works will undoubtedly continue to influence readers well into the twenty-first century.

★

Philip K. Dick, *The Shifting Realities of Philip K. Dick: Selected Literary and Philosophical Writings*, edited by Lawrence Sutin (1995), contains autobiographical fragments of Dick's writing, collected posthumously. An interview by Charles Platt is in *Dream Makers: The Uncommon People Who Write Science Fiction*, vol. 1 (1980). Gregg Rickman, *To the High Castle: Philip K. Dick, A Life, 1928–1962* (1989), is the most detailed examination of Dick's early life. Douglas A. Mackey, *Philip K. Dick* (1988), is primarily a critical reading of Dick's many novels and stories. Paul Williams, *Only Apparently Real: The World of Philip K. Dick* (1986), delves into Dick's mysticism and break from objective reality. See also James Gunn, ed., *New Encyclopedia of Science Fiction* (1988); Larry McCaffery, *Postmodern Fiction: A Bio-Bibliographic Guide* (1986); Baird Searles et al., *A Reader's Guide to Science Fiction* (1979); David Wingrove, ed., *The Science Fiction Source Book* (1984); and Noelle Watson and Paul E. Schellinger, *Twentieth Century Science-Fiction Writers*, 3d ed. (1991).

KENNETH E. ST. ANDRE

DIETZ, Howard (*b.* 8 September 1896 in New York City; *d.* 30 July 1983 in New York City), motion picture executive best known for his song lyrics for Broadway shows.

Howard Dietz was one of four children of Herman Dietz, a Jewish immigrant from Russia who worked in the jewelry business in New York City, and Julia Blumberg. He attended public elementary schools and Townsend Harris High School in New York City. As a teenager, he got a part-time job as a copyboy for the *New York American*. He attended the Columbia University School of Journalism from 1913 to 1917, paying his way in part as a university correspondent for the *New York American,* but did not graduate. During these years, he began contributing light verse to Franklin P. Adams's column in the *New York World,* as well as to other newspapers. He also won a prize of $500 offered by a tobacco company for the best advertisement by a college student for one of their cigarette brands.

After his stint at Columbia, Dietz worked briefly for the Philip Goodman Advertising Agency, where one of his first assignments was to create a trademark for Samuel Goldwyn's motion picture company, the Goldwyn Picture Cor-

Howard Dietz, 1976. UPI/CORBIS-BETTMANN

poration. The result was the famous roaring lion that appears at the beginning of every Goldwyn, and later Metro-Goldwyn-Mayer (MGM), motion picture. Dietz was married in 1917 to Elizabeth Bigelow Hall, and he served in the U.S. Navy in 1917 and 1918, spending most of his time working as a journalist for the magazine *Navy Life*. Following his discharge, he went to work in New York City as a publicist for the Goldwyn Picture Corporation.

In 1923 Dietz began another career, when he wrote the lyrics for the song "Alibi Baby," with music by Arthur Samuels, for the musical *Poppy*. Shortly thereafter, the well-known composer Jerome Kern asked him to write the lyrics for a musical, eventually entitled *Dear Sir*. Kern's show, which opened on Broadway on 3 September 1924, was not a success, running for only fifteen performances. Dietz's lyrics were favorably reviewed, however, and he was encouraged to continue his efforts in the musical theater. In 1924, when the Goldwyn Picture Corporation was merged into Metro-Goldwyn-Mayer, Dietz became director of advertising and publicity for the firm, working primarily in New York City. During his lengthy career with the company, he publicized such famous films as *Gone with the Wind* and a long line of famous movie stars, including Lon Chaney, Clark Gable, Greta Garbo, Judy Garland, Greer Garson, John Gilbert, Jean Harlow, Mickey Rooney, and Spencer Tracy.

In 1929 Dietz commenced a long and fruitful collaboration with lawyer-turned-composer Arthur Schwartz. Their first production was a musical revue, *The Little Show,* for which Schwartz wrote most of the music and Dietz most of the lyrics and sketches. The show ran for 321 performances on Broadway. Dietz's memorable songs included "I Guess I'll Have to Change My Plan," "Hammacher Schlemmer, I Love You," and "Moanin' Low." Thereafter, Schwartz and Dietz produced a new musical revue or book musical almost every year until the late 1930s. These included *The Second Little Show* (1930); *Three's a Crowd* (1930), which included the hit song "Something to Remember You By"; *The Band Wagon* (1931), which introduced the classic song "Dancing in the Dark"; *Flying Colors* (1932), which featured "A Shine on Your Shoes," "Alone Together," and "Louisiana Hayride"; *Revenge with Music* (1934), with the classic songs "If There Is Someone Lovelier Than You" and "You and the Night and the Music"; *At Home Abroad* (1935), with "Love Is a Dancing Thing"; and *Between the Devil* (1937), with another classic, "I See Your Face Before Me."

Dietz and his first wife were divorced in 1937, and that same year he married Tanis Guinness Montagu. They had one daughter (Dietz's only child). In 1940 he became vice president of publicity for MGM. His heavy commitments to MGM prevented any further collaborations with Schwartz in the late 1930s and early 1940s. In addition to

his work with MGM, Dietz undertook a number of patriotic activities to further the American war effort during World War II. He became a screen and radio consultant for the Treasury Department, promoting the sale of war bonds. He also wrote a show for the U.S. Coast Guard with the composer Vernon Duke in 1944, called *Tars and Spars*. Between 1943 and 1944, Dietz also worked with Duke on three commercial shows, none of which was successful. In 1948 he once more collaborated with Schwartz, on *Inside U.S.A.,* which ran for 399 performances on Broadway. Dietz wrote two more shows with Schwartz, *The Gay Life* (1961) and *Jennie* (1963); neither was a notable success.

In 1950 Dietz was commissioned by the Metropolitan Opera Company to provide English lyrics for a new production of Johann Strauss's operetta *Die Fledermaus*; his version had a modest success at the Metropolitan in the early 1950s. His English translation of Giacomo Puccini's opera *La Bohème* proved unpopular and had only seven performances during the Metropolitan Opera's 1952–1953 season.

Following his divorce from his second wife, Dietz married Lucinda Davis Goldsborough Balland on 31 July 1951. His activities during his last years were increasingly restricted by Parkinson's disease, which first afflicted him in 1954. He retired from MGM in 1957. He died at his home in New York City.

Howard Dietz had a successful and lucrative career as a mildly flamboyant motion picture executive and publicist. His enduring significance rests upon the songs he wrote for Broadway shows, primarily in collaboration with Arthur Schwartz and chiefly during the 1930s. The American composer Alec Wilder, in his classic examination of American popular songs, had special praise for both the sophisticated music of Schwartz and the equally sophisticated words of Dietz. Dietz's clever, often witty, and always beautifully crafted lyrics seem to have reflected the nature of the man: not always profound but always lively and interesting and frequently touching.

★

Howard Dietz, *Dancing in the Dark* (1974), an anecdotal autobiography, is by far the most extensive treatment of his life, although it contains disappointingly little detail about his longtime collaboration with Arthur Schwartz. Alec Wilder, *American Popular Song: The Great Innovators, 1900–1950* (1972), includes a brief but perceptive critical analysis of the songs written by Dietz and Schwartz. An obituary is in the *New York Times* (1 Aug. 1983).

JOHN E. LITTLE

DIRAC, Paul Adrien Maurice (*b.* 8 August 1902 in Bristol, England; *d.* 20 October 1984 in Tallahassee, Florida), theoretical physicist who received the Nobel Prize in 1933 for his work in atomic theory; his prediction in 1931 of the existence of the positive electron, or positron, the first known form of antimatter, is representative of his numerous fundamental contributions to quantum mechanics. Many aspects of his work stand at the theoretical bedrock of contemporary nuclear physics.

Dirac, one of three children, was the son of Charles Adrien Ladislas Dirac, who had emigrated from Switzerland to England in 1890. His mother was an Englishwoman, Florence Hannah Holten, the daughter of a ship's captain. English-born Dirac was registered as Swiss at birth and became a British citizen in 1919. His relationship with his dominating father was not at all favorable, and Dirac's childhood could be characterized as unhappy. His father taught French at the Merchant Venturer's Technical College in Bristol, England, where Dirac received his secondary schooling. From an early age he displayed strong ability in mathematics and science, but little interest in other subjects.

When he was sixteen Dirac undertook the study of electrical engineering at Bristol University, where he secured a B.Sc. degree in 1921. The economic depression in England following World War I made job finding difficult. Dirac thus elected to stay at Bristol University for another two

Paul Dirac. UPI/Corbis-Bettmann

years (1921–1923), having obtained a tuition-free scholarship in the mathematics department. During this period he was introduced to the theory of relativity, which Albert Einstein had published in 1905.

In 1923 Dirac entered St. John's College of Cambridge University to pursue graduate studies in mathematics and physics, and, in particular, to advance his understanding of relativity theory, which had been generated at Bristol and which was to influence his later research in many areas.

During his years as a graduate student (1923–1926), he had his first intensive exposure to the ideas of Einstein, Max Planck, Niels Bohr, Max Born, and Arnold Sommerfeld, which were the foundation of modern atomic physics. His dissertation adviser, Ralph Fowler, recognized Dirac's exceptional abilities and encouraged him to undertake research early in his studies. Less than a year after beginning his graduate work, Dirac began writing and publishing original research papers. He received his Ph.D. in 1926 with an unpublished thesis entitled simply "Quantum Mechanics." This thesis was seminal for Dirac's most famous publication, *The Principles of Quantum Mechanics*. Still widely employed as a textbook, in 1931 the work was praised by Einstein himself, who characterized it as the most logically perfect presentation of quantum mechanics in existence.

In 1928 he published what is now known as the Dirac equation, which represents, along with his prediction of antimatter, one of Dirac's two most important contributions to modern physics. Actually, the antimatter prediction was already implicit in the Dirac equation, which at its inception yielded apparent solutions reflecting negative energy states. Initially, these were regarded as mathematical anomalies that had no physical meaning. However, by 1931 after some false starts, Dirac interpreted the existence of these negative energy states as electrons with positive charge, later designated as positrons. The experimental verification of Dirac's hypothesis was first made by Carl Anderson at the California Institute of Technology; Anderson detected the positron in a single cloud-chamber photograph of cosmic ray events on 2 August 1932. With this discovery, Anderson also received the Nobel Prize. Several months later, the positron's existence was confirmed by Patrick Blackett in cloud-chamber measurements at the Cavendish Laboratory at Cambridge University. In fact, the existence of the positron—the first established antimatter particle—has led to compelling evidence that every particle of conventional matter may have an antimatter analogue. In his Nobel Prize lecture of 1933, Dirac postulated the existence of a negative proton or antiproton. High-energy particle accelerators now regularly generate antiprotons, antineutrons, and antimesons. The collision of a conventional particle and its antiparticle results in annihilation of both, with the release of electromagnetic energy in the form of photons.

Dirac's equation opened the entire field of antimatter physics.

Among other concepts bearing Dirac's name are the Dirac delta function and the Fermi-Dirac statistics. The Dirac delta function is a purely mathematical structure—zero at every place but the origin (in algebraic Cartesian coordinates $x = 0, y = 0$), but infinite at the origin. Its integrated value is finite, that is, having the value unity (or one). Dirac initially employed the function in 1927 in a paper demonstrating that the quantum mechanics of Werner Heisenberg and the wave mechanics of Erwin Schrödinger, who shared the Nobel Prize with Dirac in 1933, were two different ways of expressing the behavior of atomic particles and were equivalent to each other. Fermi-Dirac statistics were worked out independently but in a complementary way in 1926 by the two scientists who bear the concept's name. Enrico Fermi had earlier shown that electrons in an atom were subject to the Pauli exclusion principle. Dirac showed how the relevant statistical mechanics of atomic assemblies could be incorporated in Dirac's formalism of the new quantum mechanics.

In addition to quantum mechanics and its later related advanced formulation, characterized as quantum electrodynamics, Dirac, beginning in 1936, took a deep interest in cosmology and, in particular, the role of gravitation in the evolution of the universe. His interest in cosmology continued to the end of his life. He advanced the unusual hypothesis in 1978 that at least one of the fundamental forces of nature—gravitation—was not constant but had decreased in time with the age of the universe.

As important and enormously influential as Dirac was at a young age in the development of modern physics, his ability to communicate his ideas face-to-face as a teacher, as distinct from his attempts in numerous publications, was apparently subject to criticism. According to the physicist Victor F. Weisskopf, who knew Dirac at Cambridge, "Dirac . . . was absolutely useless for any student. You could not talk to him, or, if I talked to him, he would just listen and say, 'Yes.' From a student's point of view, Dirac was a lost experience."

When advised that he had won the Nobel Prize, Dirac's initial reaction was to decline the award because of his dislike of publicity. However, when Ernest Rutherford, winner of the Nobel Prize in chemistry in 1908, told Dirac that refusing the prize would guarantee more publicity than its acceptance, Dirac reluctantly agreed to the award. In addition to the Nobel Prize, Dirac received numerous honors, including the Royal Society's Royal Medal in 1939 and its Copley Medal in 1952. He was named to the National Academy of Sciences in 1949 and the Pontifical Academy of Sciences in 1961. He received Great Britain's Order of Merit in 1973.

Dirac, said to be reserved and even shy, was fond of solitude and long contemplative walks; these personal inclinations did not prevent him from becoming a well-traveled scientific scholar: his trips included numerous visits to universities in France, Japan, Poland, Canada, the Soviet Union, Israel, Australia, India, Ireland, and, most extensively and indeed finally, the United States. After receiving his Ph.D., he spent a year divided between Copenhagen with Niels Bohr and the Physics Institute at the University of Göttingen with Max Born. Returning to Cambridge, he was elected a fellow of St. John's College in 1928. In 1932 he was named Lucasian Professor of Mathematics at Cambridge, the chair once held by Isaac Newton and later by the astrophysicist Stephen Hawking. Dirac made his first of many invited visits to America in 1929, lecturing at several universities. In 1934 and 1935 he lectured at the Institute for Advanced Study in Princeton, New Jersey, where he met Margit Wigner Balasz, a divorcée and the sister of a Nobel Prize winner, Hungarian theoretical physicist Eugene Wigner. He married Balasz in London on 2 January 1937. Dirac adopted her two children from a previous marriage, and the couple had two additional children together.

In 1969 he retired from Cambridge to spend the remainder of his life in the United States. Although an American resident for more than fifteen years, Dirac never became a naturalized citizen. After appointments at the State University of New York at Stony Brook, in Long Island, and the University of Miami in Florida, he secured his last academic appointment as professor of physics at Florida State University in Tallahassee in 1971, a post he held for the remainder of his life. Dirac died in Tallahassee and is buried there.

In the firmament of outstanding scientists of the twentieth century, Dirac must be regarded as among the greatest. His mathematical formulations and exceptional innovations in the application of relativity theory to quantum mechanics have decisively influenced nuclear physics, cosmology, and related areas of contemporary science.

Probably the outstanding tribute to Dirac's integrity in his pursuit of scientific truth was made by Niels Bohr as reported by another eminent scientist, Sir Rudolph Peierls: "Of all physicists, Dirac has the purest soul."

★

Helge Kragh, *Dirac: A Scientific Biography* (1990), is an excellent readable biography containing information on both Dirac's personal history and his scientific work. J. G. Taylor, ed., *Tributes to Paul Dirac* (1987), comprises fifteen short essays, including an excellent biographical sketch by R. H. Dalitz and personal reminiscences by colleagues and students. See also R. H. Dalitz and R. Peierls, "Paul Adrien Maurice Dirac," *Biographical Memoirs of Fellows of the Royal Society* 32 (1986): 139–185; Behram N. Kursunoglu and Eugene P. Wigner, eds., *Reminiscences About a Great Physicist: Paul Adrien Maurice Dirac* (1987); and Peter Goddard, ed., *Paul Dirac: The Man and His Work* (1998). An obituary is in the *New York Times* (22 Oct. 1984).

LEONARD R. SOLON

DiSALLE, Michael Vincent (*b.* 6 January 1908 in New York City; *d.* 16 September 1981 in Pescara, Italy), Democratic politician best remembered as mayor of Toledo, Ohio (1948–1950), director of the Office of Price Stabilization under President Harry S. Truman (1950–1952), and governor of Ohio (1959–1963).

At the turn of the century Anthony DiSalle left Vasto, Italy, and immigrated to the United States, where he settled in New York City. Shortly after his arrival, he met Assunta D'Arcangelo, also an émigré from Vasto. The couple soon married and in 1908 Michael, the first of seven children, was born. The family moved to Toledo, Ohio, in 1911, where Anthony DiSalle founded the DiSalle Electroplating Company. Michael attended both public and private schools in Toledo, graduating in 1925 from Central Catholic High School. He enrolled at Georgetown University in Washington, D.C., where he completed the requirements for a law degree in 1931. While at Georgetown he met Myrtle Eugene England; they married on 19 December 1929. They had five children. To finance the purchase of a home and DiSalle's law school tuition, the couple began Lightning Messenger Service, a parcel-delivery business. Upon DiSalle's graduation the couple sold their business and returned to Toledo.

DiSalle taught commercial law at Central Catholic High School and read meters for the Toledo Water Department (1931–1932). He resigned his city position and ran an unsuccessful campaign for clerk of the municipal court. In 1932 he was admitted to the Ohio bar and established a private law practice in Toledo. A year later he became assistant district counsel for the Home Owners Loan Corporation (1933–1935).

DiSalle's entry into politics came in 1937, when he served a term as representative in the Ohio legislature (1937–1938). After an unsuccessful attempt at running for a seat in the upper house in 1938, he took the position of assistant city law director in Toledo (1939–1941). His quest for elective office never waned. He won a seat on the Toledo City Council and served from 1942 to 1944. He then held the office of vice mayor (1944–1947), in which capacity he earned nationwide acclaim for developing and chairing the Toledo Labor-Management Citizens Committee. The Toledo Plan, which this committee developed, arbitrated disputes between labor and management. The committee served as a model for other cities in arbitrating labor disputes and earned Toledo and DiSalle much acclaim. DiSalle also worked to make the city debt free by suggesting

a payroll tax, which voters approved. In 1946 he campaigned unsuccessfully for a seat in the U.S. House of Representatives.

The city council elected DiSalle mayor in 1947 and re-elected him in 1949. As mayor, he continued his efforts to make the city debt free and was instrumental in establishing one of the first clean-air acts for an industrialized city. DiSalle campaigned for the U.S. Senate in 1950 but lost in the Democratic primary to Joe Ferguson. He returned to his position as mayor of Toledo until he received a call from President Harry S. Truman to serve as director of the Office of Price Stabilization (1950–1952).

The Office of Price Stabilization was created during the Korean War and was responsible for establishing price ceilings on civilian and military goods so that the cost of living and cost of production could be managed throughout the war. DiSalle favored voluntary rather than enforced price controls but excessive inflation forced him to endorse a freeze on wages and prices.

He returned to Ohio politics in February 1952, when he ran for the U.S. Senate once again. This time he won the Democratic primary but was defeated by the Republican incumbent, John W. Bricker. DiSalle returned to Washington to serve the Truman administration as a special consultant to the Economic Stabilization Agency (1952–1953).

DiSalle returned to Toledo and resumed his law practice. In 1956 he ran an unsuccessful campaign for governor of Ohio against C. William O'Neill. He prevailed in his second race against O'Neill two years later, winning the

Michael V. DiSalle testifies before the Joint Congress Economic Committee on President Nixon's ninety-day wage freeze, 1971. UPI/CORBIS-BETTMANN

first four-year term as Ohio's governor (1959–1963). The DiSalle family then moved to Columbus.

When DiSalle became governor, Ohio faced financial crisis. He discovered that the state ranked low in expenditures for health and education programs. The new governor responded by increasing the excise tax on cigarettes, liquor, and gasoline, angering many conservatives who had voted for him. When he proposed further increases in the 1961–1963 budget, the conservative Ohio general assembly cut many of his projects. A compromise budget was approved, but without many of the increased expenditures favored by DiSalle.

DiSalle lost credibility with some of his supporters because he reversed his initial support of capital punishment. When the DiSalle family moved into the governor's mansion in 1959, the staff included convicted murderers serving life sentences. DiSalle took an interest in their cases and concluded that some of their convictions were tenuous at best. Working with the convicted murderers and seeing their contributions to society changed his mind about the death penalty. He approved five of the eleven appeals brought before him. After DiSalle left office he fully explained his argument against capital punishment in *The Power of Life or Death* (1965).

Despite losing political credibility in his own state, he gained political respect from the Democratic party in January 1960, when he endorsed John F. Kennedy for president. He was the first governor of a major state to do so. Unfortunately for DiSalle, Ohio voters favored Republican Richard M. Nixon, not Kennedy, in 1960. DiSalle was reluctant to run for another term and announced in the fall of 1961 he would not seek reelection. A citizen's committee cited his accomplishments in education, mental health services, and other areas as reasons why he should seek another term. Reluctantly, DiSalle agreed to run, but he was defeated by Republican James A. Rhodes, who campaigned against DiSalle's revenue increases.

The former governor returned to private life and opened a law practice in Columbus (1963–1966). He also published *Second Choice* (1966), which examined how and why vice presidents have been chosen throughout American history.

In 1966 DiSalle joined the Washington, D.C., firm of Chapman, Gadsby, Hannah and Duff (later Chapman, Duff and Paul), where he served as counsel (1966–1981). He split his time between Columbus and Washington, D.C., until his death. DiSalle continued to be active in the Democratic party and was appointed by President Lyndon B. Johnson to serve as a member of the Panel of Arbitrators and the Panel of Conciliators of the International Center for Settlement of Investment Disputes (1967–1974). He was a loyal supporter of the Kennedys and served as honorary chairman of Edward Kennedy's presidential campaign in 1980. DiSalle died of heart disease while visiting relatives in Pescara, Italy. He is interred at Calvary Cemetery in Toledo, Ohio.

Physically short in stature, DiSalle was never short on substance as a public servant. He was also quite outspoken about his views. Speaking his mind allowed him to experiment successfully with the Toledo Plan but at other times it had political costs. His backing of increased social expenditures and reversal on capital punishment had negative consequences for his gubernatorial reelection bid. DiSalle was a prominent leader of Ohio's Democrats and an important national voice among New Deal liberals.

★

The Michael V. DiSalle Papers are in the Manuscripts Department of the Ohio Historical Society, Columbus. Of the 467 linear feet of the collection, approximately half covers his term as governor of Ohio. The remainder documents the period when DiSalle was active in Toledo politics, his tenure in the Office of Price Stabilization, and DiSalle's role in various presidential elections. Diana Draur, "Michael V. DiSalle in Ohio Politics: 1950–1962" (M.A. thesis, University of Nebraska at Omaha, 1986), discusses the political career of DiSalle (Draur's father), with special emphasis on the 1958 gubernatorial election. In Michael V. DiSalle, "I Learned a Lesson from Murderers," *Parade* (7 June 1959), DiSalle discusses the evolution of his views on capital punishment. A biographical sketch appears in Ohio Historical Society, *The Governors of Ohio,* 2d ed. (1969). Victor Ullman, "Oh, How You'll Hate Him," *Saturday Evening Post* (17 Mar. 1951), contains early biographical information. An obituary is in the *New York Times* (17 Sept. 1981). In a 1964 interview with Ken Mack for the John F. Kennedy Library Oral History Program (Boston), DiSalle discussed his early endorsement of and association with John F. Kennedy. DiSalle discussed the relationship between Kennedy and Lyndon B. Johnson in a 1969 interview with T. H. Baker for the Lyndon B. Johnson Oral History Project.

JON E. TAYLOR

DOUGLAS, Donald Wills (*b.* 6 April 1892 in Brooklyn, New York; *d.* 1 February 1981 in Palm Springs, California), founder of Douglas Aircraft Corporation whose production of the DC-3 brought mass airline travel to the world.

From a very young age Donald Douglas showed his promise as a man who, as one associate described, "dipp[ed] into the future with the mind of a poet and the slide rule of an engineer." Donald was the second son and last child born to William Edward and Dorothy Locker Douglas. William was a banker of Scottish descent, whose own father had come to America from Glasgow and settled in Albany, New York, in 1813. Dorothy Locker's ancestors were from Germany and Scandinavia.

Don, as he was called all his life, attended a Brooklyn grammar school before beginning his college prep at Trinity

Chapel School in Manhattan, where he won awards for his writing and editorial skills on the school magazine. He developed an affection for reading, especially about anything pertaining to early flying experiments. Yet he also had a boyhood devotion to boats, influenced by his father, a member of the New York Yacht Club. Not surprisingly, it was his father who urged Douglas to apply for admission to the United States Naval Academy.

Upon graduating from Trinity Chapel in 1909, Douglas left for the United States Naval Academy in Annapolis, Maryland, where his elder brother, Harold, had preceded him two years earlier. There he began a career as a midshipman and made high grades, but his heart was not in seafaring problems and training cruises. In the summer before arriving at Annapolis, Douglas was part of a small group that witnessed the Wright brothers demonstrate their frail biplane to the army at Fort Myer, Virginia. Douglas saw the plane take off, circle the course, and land. He immediately began experimenting with his own models in hopes of interesting the navy in using the airplane as a naval weapon. Much to his irritation the navy was not interested in his airplanes, and Douglas, increasingly uninterested in its ships, resigned from the Academy in 1912. He then enrolled at the Massachusetts Institute of Technology.

In 1914 Douglas graduated from MIT with a B.S. degree in civil engineering. He remained at the school as an assistant to Professor Jerome C. Hunsaker of the aerodynamics department. There he worked with Hunsaker on the development of the first wind tunnel, which took the guesswork out of airplane performance. Douglas also coauthored with H. E. Rossell a chapter in the Hunsaker-Rossell report titled *Adjustment of Velocity Gradient Across a Section of the Wind Tunnel* (1916).

Douglas quickly moved on to join the Connecticut Aircraft Company in 1915, where he worked as a consultant on the D-1, the navy's pioneer dirigible. He stayed there only briefly before moving to Los Angeles to work for the Glenn L. Martin Company. As chief engineer there, Douglas contributed much to the design of the first Martin bomber, but he left Martin in 1916 to become chief civilian aeronautical engineer for the United States Signal Corps. He married Charlotte Marguerite Ogg of Indiana on 5 June 1916 and by 1917 was back as chief engineer at Martin, where he found some job stability. He remained at the new Cleveland factory of the Martin Company until 1920, rising to a vice presidency by age twenty-eight.

Douglas quit Martin in 1920 to try his luck in California as an aircraft manufacturer. With $600 in his pocket, a pleasing personality, and an impressive technological background, Douglas hoped someone with money would want an airplane. He found that man in David R. Davis, a wealthy Los Angeles sportsman who wanted to be the first

Donald Douglas holding a model of the DC-8. ARCHIVE PHOTOS

man to make a nonstop flight across the North American continent. The Davis-Douglas Company was born and Douglas set up an office in the rear of a barbershop in Santa Monica, California, to begin work on the Douglas Cloudster. The Cloudster was a single-bay biplane which had a streamlined body to increase airspeed, gas-dumping valves, and an effective instrument panel—all firsts in airplane design. Although Davis had to stop his cross-country flight in Texas because of engine trouble, he turned over his half interest in the company to Douglas along with a promissory note of $2,500.

It was with the Cloudster and the help of *Los Angeles Times* publisher Harry Chandler that Douglas got involved in military contracts. After the failed nonstop flight by Davis, Douglas went to Washington, where he was able to secure an order for three planes for the United States Navy. Although the contract would pay $120,000, Douglas was in need of capital to begin construction. He turned to Chandler, who was interested in supporting the project; they managed to convince other local businessmen to lend Douglas $1,000 each. With the capital secured, Douglas went to work and fulfilled the contract in 1921, changing the Davis-Douglas Company to the Douglas Company.

Success came quickly for the bright young man. In 1923 the army came to Douglas with a request for a plane that could fly around the world. Douglas had little problem fulfilling the request, and on 6 April 1924, four Douglas aircraft took off from Seattle, Washington, two of which completed the first successful round-the-world flight. The success brought international orders to the Douglas Company, including one from the Norwegian government. By 1928, with Douglas aircraft being used to fly the U.S. mail, Douglas was ready to reorganize, pay off his debts, and incorporate under the name Douglas Aircraft Company.

Douglas became president of the company and his father, a successful banker, came aboard as assistant treasurer. The company was able to make a profit even through the lean years of the 1930s. This was largely due to its new involvement in commercial air service. Signing a contract with Transcontinental and Western Airlines in 1932, Douglas Aircraft developed a series of twin-engine, all-metal airliners that placed Douglas Aircraft in a league all its own. The DC (Douglas Commercial) series began with the DC-1 in 1932, the modified DC-2 in 1934, and the groundbreaking DC-3 in 1936. The DC-3 was the first sleeper-transport plane, accommodating up to twenty passengers, and was the first airplane to profit from carrying passengers only. In essence, the DC-3 was to aviation what the Ford Model T was to the roadways, in that Douglas Aircraft controlled 95 percent of U.S. air traffic in the 1930s. The plane was so successful that Douglas won the Collier Award in 1936 for the "outstanding twin-engine transport plane." The DC-3 entered World War II in 1941 as the C-47 Skytrain. Built as a wartime transport, the plane was used primarily for carrying troops and equipment. Over 10,000 C-53 planes were built for the war effort.

The DC-3 was not the only Douglas plane to see action in World War II. At the outbreak of the war Douglas Aircraft canceled all foreign contracts with nations that were not Allies, and business was concentrated on the building of military aircraft for national defense. The DC-4, the largest land transport to date, had been built in 1938 at the request and expense of Pan American and the four largest domestic airlines. It entered the war in 1942 as the C-54 Skymaster, functioning as a transoceanic transport. Douglas Aircraft also developed a light bomber for the army (A-20 Havoc), a dive bomber for the navy (SBD Dauntless), and the army's fastest attack bomber (A-26 Invader), and collaborated with Boeing and Consolidated in the manufacture of the B-17 (Flying Fortress) and B-24 (Liberator). By the end of the war Douglas Aircraft had turned out over 29,000 airplanes, more military poundage than any other aircraft manufacturer. Although Douglas himself never attached a rivet or tightened a nut on any of those planes, he knew where every nut and bolt of each plane belonged.

In the decade after World War II, Douglas Aircraft Company was able to continue to produce more pounds of military aircraft than any other aircraft manufacturer. The four-engine DC-4, DC-6, and DC-7 ruled the skies through the

piston era, but the company's fortunes declined in the mid-1960s, when it was unable to compete with the Boeing 707 passenger jet, introduced in 1958. In 1967 Douglas Aircraft Company merged with the McDonnell Aircraft Corporation and Donald Douglas retired.

Douglas was a Republican and Episcopalian. He and Charlotte had four sons and one daughter. A tall, good-looking man with an athletic build and bronzed face, Douglas enjoyed life and rumor was that he chose to build his plant near Santa Monica because he wished to live near the smooth sailing waters in which he could enjoy fishing and yachting. A member of the Los Angeles Yacht Club and the Los Angeles Athletic Club, Douglas was able to pursue his boyhood devotion to boats. Douglas fell into poor health and passed away at the age of eighty-eight; he was buried in Palm Springs, California.

Douglas's domination of commercial aviation has never been matched. His contributions in aviation made the world smaller and helped the United States to win a war. Although the DC-3 was truly the "Model T of the skies," hundreds of the aircraft remained in service on the eve of the twenty-first century. Donald Douglas gave the world modern airline travel.

★

Frank Cunningham, *Sky Master: The Story of Donald Douglas* (1943), is an early account of his life. Anna Rothe, ed., *Current Biography* (1950), offers a more up-to-date account. An obituary in the *New York Times* (3 Feb. 1981) is a fitting tribute.

VALERIE L. DUNHAM

DOUGLAS, Melvyn (*b.* 5 April 1901 in Macon, Georgia; *d.* 4 August 1982 in New York City), actor whose stage and film career spanned six decades; his roles in over seventy films ranged from the suave, urbane leading men of the 1930s and 1940s to the crusty, eccentric oldsters of recent years.

Born Melvyn Edouard Hesselberg, Douglas was the son of Edouard Hesselberg, a Russian-born concert pianist, and Lena Shakelford, a homemaker. He attended schools in Nashville, Tennessee, Toronto, and Lincoln, Nebraska. During World War I, at age seventeen, he served in the U.S. Army as a medical orderly. After the armistice Douglas held a wide range of jobs until he decided to become an actor. After years of touring with stock and repertory companies, including a period as head of his own company, he joined the well-known troupe headed by Jessie Bonstelle. During the 1920s he was married briefly to Rosalind Hightower; they had one son.

Douglas made his Broadway debut in January 1928, playing a gambler in the melodrama *A Free Soul*. Two years later he was signed to appear opposite the popular actress

Melvyn Douglas, 1971. UPI/Corbis-Bettmann

Helen Gahagan in the comedy *Tonight or Never,* which was a success. Douglas and Gahagan were married on Easter in April 1931. The couple had two children. When *Tonight or Never* was bought as a film vehicle for Gloria Swanson, Douglas was signed to repeat his stage role.

From 1931 to 1942 Douglas was a romantic foil to many of the screen's leading ladies. His crisp speaking voice and air of ironic amusement served him well, whether he was playing a debonair suitor, a befuddled husband, or a fast-talking private detective. Among his more notable films were *Theodora Goes Wild* (1936), in which he freed Irene Dunne from her small-town constraints; *I Met Him in Paris* (1937), where he vied with Robert Young for the affection of Claudette Colbert; and especially *Ninotchka* (1939), in which he thawed Moscow's ice-cold, all-business communist emissary, Greta Garbo. He also starred opposite Joan Crawford in *A Woman's Face* (1941) and appeared with Garbo in her last film, *Two-Faced Woman* (1942). During this period Douglas returned occasionally to the theater, as producer or director.

Following America's entry into World War II, Douglas enlisted in the U.S. Army, only a few days before a law barring men older than thirty-eight from service went into effect. He was commissioned as a captain and named head of an army entertainment production unit that organized and staged camp shows throughout the China-Burma-India battle zone. Before the war ended, he was promoted to the rank of major.

In 1944 Helen Gahagan Douglas had been elected to the first of three terms in the U.S. House of Representatives. For years she and her husband, both New Deal Democrats, had championed liberal causes and advocated policies that had angered conservative politicians and organizations. Their close ties to Franklin and Eleanor Roosevelt made them suspect to these groups. Gahagan's involvement in politics reached its peak in 1950, when she ran for U.S. Senate from California and lost to Richard Nixon in a notably vicious campaign.

In 1946 Douglas coproduced the stage musical revue *Call Me Mister,* which celebrated the soldier's return to civilian life, and then resumed making films. Most of the movies, with the exception of *Mr. Blandings Builds His Dream House* (1948), were disappointing, and Douglas returned to the New York theater. Many of the plays in which he chose to appear (*Two Blind Mice,* 1949; *The Bird Cage,* 1950; *Time Out for Ginger,* 1952) were lightweight productions of little substance. He also began to act steadily on television.

It was not until 1955, when he replaced the ailing Paul Muni in the hit play *Inherit the Wind,* that Douglas was fully able to display his skill in character roles. As Henry Drummond, surrogate for famed lawyer Clarence Darrow at the notorious Scopes trial of 1925, he skewered the anti-evolution forces headed by Matthew Brady, a surrogate for William Jennings Bryan. Buoyed by the reception, Douglas continued working in the theater, replacing Ralph Richardson in the Jean Anouilh play *Waltz of the Toreadors* late in 1958 and winning a Tony Award for his performance as a presidential candidate in Gore Vidal's 1960 political drama *The Best Man.* In 1959 he sang in *Juno,* Marc Blitzstein's poorly received musical adaptation of Sean O'Casey's *Juno and the Paycock.*

When Douglas returned to films after a long absence, he was rewarded with roles that fully challenged his acting ability. In 1963 he won an Academy Award for his performance as a stubborn, principled old rancher in *Hud,* and the following year he played an eccentric admiral in *The Americanization of Emily.* He was also notable (and nominated for an Oscar) as a self-centered old man in *I Never Sang for My Father* (1970) and as Robert Redford's father in the political drama *The Candidate* (1972). During this period Douglas continued to act on television, repeating his stage role in an adaptation of *Inherit the Wind* (1965) and playing a feisty old man in *Do Not Go Gentle into That Good Night* (1968), for which he received an Emmy Award.

In his eighth decade, at an age when many actors would have retired, Douglas continued to win high praise for his performances. In 1979 he was splendid as a senator battling senility in *The Seduction of Joe Tynan,* and that same year he won a second Oscar for best supporting actor as a dying financier in *Being There.* His final film was *Ghost Story* (1981), a supernatural tale in which he costarred with Fred

Astaire and Douglas Fairbanks, Jr. He died in New York City of pneumonia complicated by a heart condition.

The actor's image flickers on the screen, and from this image we feel that we know him. But with Melvyn Douglas there were two distinct images over many years: one of the dapper young Frenchman coaxing Greta Garbo into amorous surrender in *Ninotchka,* the other of a proudly defiant old man, forced to destroy his diseased cattle in *Hud.* Both of these images reveal the elusive art of the consummate actor.

★

Douglas's autobiography, *See You at the Movies,* was published posthumously (1986), with Tom Arthur as coauthor and editor. Obituaries are in the *New York Times* and in *Variety* (both 5 Aug. 1981).

TED SENNETT

DOWNEY, Morton (*b.* 14 November 1902 in Wallingford, Connecticut; *d.* 25 October 1985 in Palm Beach, Florida), popular singer of the 1930s and 1940s whose soft Irish tenor voice earned him the nickname "the Irish thrush."

Downey was one of five children born to parents of Irish descent. His father, James Andrew Downey, was the Wal-

Morton Downey. ARCHIVE PHOTOS

lingford fire chief and owned a tavern. His mother, Elizabeth (Cox) Downey, was a homemaker and her son's first "employer": the story goes that she paid him a nickel for *not* disturbing her with his constant singing and whistling around the house. Her son nevertheless credited her with teaching him to sing Irish songs and even to play the harp. She coached him for his first public appearance, at the age of four, singing at the annual Fireman's Minstrel Show in Wallingford. A few years later he began to sing regularly at local social gatherings and for a while worked as a candy butcher on New Haven Railroad trains, earning extra money by singing as he sold his sweets.

After graduating from high school in Wallingford, Downey went to New York City to live with relatives and further his career. Befriended by James J. Hagan, a politician affiliated with the Tammany Hall political machine, he began to entertain at political rallies and in New York beer gardens and restaurants. In 1919, while he was singing at the Sheridan Square Theatre in Greenwich Village—billed as having come "direct from Ireland"—a friend of the well-known bandleader Paul Whiteman spotted him and persuaded Whiteman to hire the young performer.

Doing vocals with one or another of Whiteman's several bands, Downey scored his first major hit in 1922 during an engagement at the Palace, then New York's foremost vaudeville house. Over the next two years he toured the country with Whiteman's groups and made six transatlantic crossings as a vocalist with the SS *Leviathan* orchestra. Downey then went on tour in Europe, singing in supper clubs in Paris and London; on one occasion the Prince of Wales (later King Edward VIII and, following his abdication, the Duke of Windsor) heard him perform and repeatedly requested encores. Back in the United States by 1927, Downey went to Hollywood, where he was signed to sing and act in *Syncopation* (1929), generally identified as the first musical on film. He also starred in *Mother's Boy* in 1929 and two films in 1930, *Lucky in Love* (set in Ireland and New York) and *The Devil's Holiday.* While filming *Syncopation,* Downey met another member of the cast, Barbara Bennett, sister of the film stars Joan and Constance Bennett. The two married on 28 January 1928 and eventually had five children, of whom the second, Sean Morton (later Morton Downey, Jr.), became a well-known television personality. The Downeys were divorced in 1941, and in 1950 he married the heiress Margaret Schulze, who died in 1964. In 1970 he was married a third time, to Ann Van Gerbig.

Downey's start as one of the most popular singers in the golden age of radio came in 1930, when station WABC first broadcast his performances at Club Delmonico, a Manhattan nightspot he had helped finance. Soon thereafter he was featured on the *Camel Hour,* which was ranked as "the number one show of the airwaves." In the course of the decade Downey was the star of various other programs sponsored by leading manufacturers, including *Philip Morris Presents* and *Lucky Strike's Hit Parade*. As early as 1933 a *New York World Telegram* poll listed Downey as the male vocalist of the year. But by the decade's end, he left radio, thinking the public might grow tired of him. Appearances as the singing star of Billy Rose's *Aquacade* show at the New York World's Fair of 1939–1940 followed.

In 1942 Downey returned to radio, signing a five-year contract with the Coca-Cola Company, which eventually paid him more than $4,000 a week to sing on a show that was broadcast and transcribed nationwide. In 1949 he was made a director of the company, a post he held up to the time of his death. His earnings as a performer and businessman, augmented by years of careful investments, made Downey one of the wealthiest entertainers of his day. During the 1940s he also was a regular performer at such legendary New York nightspots as the Persian Room at the Plaza Hotel and the Wedgwood Room and Starlight Roof at the Waldorf-Astoria. Along with singing, Downey composed music and was a member of the American Society of Composers, Authors, and Publishers, with more than thirty songs to his credit. His most popular tunes were "That's How I Spell Ireland" and "Wabash Moon," which was his radio theme song. He was also a prolific recording artist; beginning as early as 1916 he cut some 1,500 records in all.

During World War II, in 1944 and 1945, Downey did a United Service Organizations tour entertaining U.S. servicemen at hospitals and camps in England and France. Three years later, in 1948, the NBC radio network premiered the *Morton Downey Show*. Broadcast three nights a week, the program appealed to a variety of tastes and eventually attracted one of the world's largest audiences. As television took over in the 1950s, however, he began to perform less frequently on radio.

Downey was somewhat stocky, with bright blue eyes, a ready smile, and a pleasant, light speaking voice. He died at the age of eighty-three, as the result of a stroke, in his home in Palm Beach. He was buried in his hometown of Wallingford. He had been a member of the Lambs Club and the American Guild of Variety Artists, serving as its president in 1941.

Contemporary reviews in the *New Yorker* and *Variety* noted that Downey's performances charmed even the most sophisticated audiences, who were won over not only by his mellifluous high tenor but also by his salty humor and the "zingy," "throw-away" manner in which he put his vocals across, never bogging down in sentiment.

★

The Music and Theater research divisions of the Lincoln Center Library for the Performing Arts in New York City maintain clipping files on Downey. Downey compiled a *Collection of Favorite Irish Songs* (1943), a group of thirty-two pieces with piano accompaniment. Obituaries are in the *New York Times* (27 Oct. 1985) and *Variety* (30 Oct. 1985).

ELEANOR F. WEDGE

DUBINSKY, David (*b.* 22 February 1892 in Brest-Litovsk, Russia [now Belarus]; *d.* 17 September 1982 in New York City), president (1932–1966) of the International Ladies' Garment Workers' Union (ILGWU) who introduced benefits for his members that became the standard for organized workers in many other industries.

Born Dovid Dobnievski, he was one of nine children of Zallel Dobnievski, a baker, and Shaine Wishingrad, a housewife. Although born on the eastern edge of what was then Russian-held Poland, Dubinsky grew up in the industrial center of Lodz. As a youngster he was fluent in Russian, Polish, and Yiddish; he never lost his Yiddish accent. When he was thirteen years old his father removed him from school, putting him to work in his bakery. By the age of fifteen the boy had become a master baker and was elected secretary of his bakers' union local. He was soon instrumental in organizing a strike, for which he was briefly

David Dubinsky. ARCHIVE PHOTOS

jailed. Upon his release he immediately returned to his former ways and was arrested again by Russian authorities a year later and exiled to a remote Siberian village where he was kept under close police surveillance. After a year and a half in Siberia he managed to elude the authorities, escape the gulag, and return to Lodz. He worked as a baker under an assumed name until 1911, when an older brother living in New York City provided the nineteen-year-old with boat passage to the United States. With his savings Dubinsky bought another ticket for a younger brother and paid smugglers to slip them both over the Russian border; the two then set out from Germany for New York.

Arriving in New York in the summer of 1911, Dubinsky went to work as a cutter in the garment industry, shaping cloth to be sewn into dresses. He joined Local 10 of the barely decade-old International Ladies' Garment Workers' Union (ILGWU) and quickly became a union activist. In 1915 he married Emma Goldberg; the couple would have one daughter.

A forceful, articulate, and determined man, Dubinsky rose steadily through the union hierarchy. He was elected to the executive board of Local 10 in 1918, manager of the local in 1921, a vice president of the ILGWU in 1922, and its secretary-treasurer in 1927. In an era when the American labor movement was marked by tumultuous socialist politics, his leadership was characterized by the comparatively moderate social-liberal beliefs he had held in Russia; he supported U.S. involvement in World War I as well as opposition to the Russian Revolution. When the American left split in 1920, its radical wing forming the Communist Party of the United States, he remained with the Socialist party and later successfully blocked an attempt by communists to take control of the ILGWU. By 1928 he had left the Socialist party and further distanced himself from the far left in 1932 by supporting the successful presidential campaign of the Democratic party candidate, Franklin D. Roosevelt. That same year he was elected president of the ILGWU, a position he would hold for the next thirty-four years.

When Dubinsky assumed the union's presidency it had fewer than 40,000 members and its treasury was almost totally empty. By 1935, aided by the New Deal and the National Industrial Recovery Act of 1933, a solvent Dubinsky-led ILGWU boasted well over 200,000 members.

In 1935, Dubinsky also became a vice president of the American Federation of Labor (AFL), the country's primary organization of affiliated labor unions, which had been created to respond to the specific needs of craft unions such as ILGWU. Dubinsky came to the conclusion that craft unions could not effectively organize or service workers in the country's mass-production industries, so he joined with other union presidents led by John L. Lewis of the United Mine Workers in creating the Committee for Industrial Organization (CIO), which later became the Congress of Industrial Organizations. Dubinsky took the ILGWU out of the AFL but declined to bring his union into the CIO because he had no wish to contend with the AFL for members and economic power. In 1940 the ILGWU reaffiliated with the AFL and Dubinsky again became a vice president of that organization.

In 1936 Dubinsky once again supported President Roosevelt for reelection, this time as a founding member of the American Labor Party (ALP), the mission of which was to give independent political clout to labor and to the liberal wings of the Democratic and Republican parties. Dubinsky and his union also endorsed Roosevelt through the ALP in the 1940 election. However, in 1944, because of increasing communist influence in the ALP, he rejected that party and became a major force in organizing the Liberal party and orchestrating its support for a fourth term for President Roosevelt.

Dubinsky's accomplishments on behalf of garment workers were momentous. Under his leadership the ILGWU membership grew to 450,000. Sweatshops were virtually eradicated, a thirty-five-hour workweek was instituted, and wages increased. Union garment workers received health, welfare, and retirement benefits as well as paid vacations and severance pay. The union provided its members with health centers, a recreation center in the Pennsylvania mountains, and cultural programs.

A short-statured man given to waving his arms excitedly as he exhorted listeners, Dubinsky also urged the American labor movement toward greater social responsibility. He was involved in a number of humanitarian projects. After World War II, at his prompting, the ILGWU spent several million dollars on relief in Israel and Italy. It also constructed an orphanage in China and endowed a trade union school in France. His crusade against the underworld penetration of a number of major unions resulted in the adoption of an antiracketeering code in 1957 by the then-merged AFL-CIO. And during the 1950s and 1960s he continued to play an activist role in the broader political landscape, serving on several government boards, acting as a consultant to the United Nations Economic and Social Council, and, through the Liberal party, supporting the successful New York City mayoral candidacy of John V. Lindsay in 1965.

In 1966, at the age of seventy-four, Dubinsky retired as president of the ILGWU. Following a long illness, he died in New York City in 1982. After Dubinsky's retirement the union's membership began a dramatic decline. Thirty years later, garment-industry sweatshops were flourishing anew both at home and abroad as the global economy enabled manufacturers to turn away from domestic unionized labor in favor of vast new pools of workers in low-wage countries.

★

With A. H. Raskin, Dubinsky wrote his autobiography, *David Dubinsky: A Life with Labor* (1977). Other useful works on Dubinsky and the ILGWU include John Dewey, *David Dubinsky: A Pictorial Biography* (1951); Max D. Danish, *The World of David Dubinsky* (1957); Gus Tyler, *Look for the Union Label: A History of the International Ladies' Garment Workers' Union* (1995); and Irving Howe, *World of Our Fathers* (1976). An extensive obituary is in the *New York Times* (18 Sept. 1982).

JACK HANDLER

DUBOS, René Jules (*b.* 20 February 1901 in Saint-Brice-sous-Forêt, France; *d.* 20 February 1982 in New York City), soil microbiologist, tuberculosis researcher, environmentalist, and a leader in the search for antibiotics who was concerned with the link between the environment and human welfare.

Dubos was the first of three children of Georges Alexandre Dubos and Adéline Madeleine de Bloëdt. He spent his early childhood in Henonville, a village in the Île-de-France region, where his father ran a butcher shop. During his early years, Dubos attended a one-room school, but an attack of rheumatic fever at the age of nine sharply restricted his activity for a year and caused damage to his heart valves. He read extensively, finding particular enjoyment in history, Western novels, and detective stories.

René Jules Dubos. CORBIS-BETTMANN

In 1914 the family moved to Paris, and with the outbreak of World War I, Dubos's father left to serve in the French army. He survived the war but died in 1919 in the great influenza epidemic. Dubos then helped his mother run their Paris meat shop as he continued his education.

After completing high school at Collège Chaptal in Paris in 1919, he had hopes of entering the École de Physique et Chimie but missed the entrance exam because of another bout of rheumatic fever. Once recovered, he learned that only the Institut National Agronomique was still accepting applicants for the 1919 academic year. He passed the entrance exam, placing fourth out of 400 students. He excelled in his classes with the exception of microbiology and chemistry, both of which he disliked, including the laboratory work.

After graduation in 1921, Dubos worked as an assistant editor at the International Institute of Agriculture in Rome, writing abstracts of articles from journals worldwide. He happened upon an article by the well-known Russian soil bacteriologist Sergei Winogradsky that set forth the shortcomings of studying microbes in the laboratory and recommended observing them in their own environment. This viewpoint made a deep impression on Dubos and influenced his decision to pursue a career in microbiology.

Before following that dream he embarked on another, a trip to the United States. Setting sail in 1924 on the SS *Rochambeau* bound for New York City, he encountered on the voyage the soil bacteriologist Selman Waksman, whom Dubos had met a few weeks earlier. Since Dubos had no specific plans, Waksman offered him a fellowship at Rutgers University, where he taught. Dubos accepted the offer and traveled with the Waksmans to New Brunswick, New Jersey, the very day the ship docked. Three years later, he earned his Ph.D., having written his dissertation on the ability of soil bacteria to break down cellulose.

Dubos then sought a National Research Council Fellowship but was turned down because he was not a U.S. citizen. A thoughtful secretary suggested that Dubos visit a fellow French scientist, Alexis Carrel, at the Rockefeller Institute for Medical Research in New York City. This small gesture made an enormous impact on the rest of his life, for it was at the Rockefeller Institute (later Rockefeller University) that Dubos worked for more than fifty years. For most of that time he lived a block away from the campus on the Upper East Side of Manhattan.

Dubos's meeting with Carrel led to an unexpected introduction to the noted bacteriologist Oswald Avery. In seeking a cure for lobar pneumonia, Avery was trying to decompose the complex polysaccharide capsule that enveloped the virulent type III pneumococcus, thus protecting the bacterium and enabling it to kill millions of people. Dubos believed that a microbe existed that could break down the barrier, reasoning "that if there were no enzyme that could decompose that capsular polysaccharide, it would accumulate in nature, and there would be mountains of it now."

Within weeks, Avery offered Dubos a position in his laboratory. After three years of experiments, Dubos was able to prove his hypothesis when he isolated an enzyme that decomposed the polysaccharide capsule from a soil sample from a cranberry bog that was rich in decomposing organic matter. Dubos transferred the enzyme to mice that had been injected with the type III pneumococcus; none of them became infected. Refining the enzyme for use in humans became unnecessary, however, because of the development of sulfa drugs (synthetic organic bacteria-inhibiting drugs).

Dubos later discovered that this enzyme could be induced into action under certain circumstances. Bacteria grew abundantly when he injected his medium with the standard food of peptones and sugars but no enzyme emerged. Only when the food source was limited to the polysaccharide capsule did the bacteria produce the specific enzyme. "It brought me face to face," Dubos wrote, "with one of the most interesting biological set of facts I have ever seen—namely, that cells have multiple potentialities [that] usually become manifest only when the cell is placed in an environment where it is compelled to use them."

Over the next several years Dubos attempted to isolate a microbe that would be toxic to other bacteria. Continuing to use soil samples, in 1939 he isolated the *Bacillus brevis,* from which he gleaned two antibacterial substances he called gramicidin and tyrocidine. Although tyrocidine was too toxic to be effectual, gramicidin could heal external wounds and bovine mastitis. These were the first antibiotics isolated from living bacteria in soil and the first sold on the market. Dubos's discovery and systematic technique were an impetus to scientists such as Howard Florey and Ernst Chain in their successful attempt to isolate penicillin, which Alexander Fleming had discovered but was unable to purify. Within a relatively short period, scientists produced a multitude of other antibiotics.

In 1942 Dubos accepted an offer to teach at the Harvard University Medical School and was named George Fabyan Professor of Comparative Pathology and professor of tropical medicine. His decision to take the job was due in part to his hope that a change would help his wife, Marie Louise Bonnet, whom he had married on 23 March 1934, to recover from tuberculosis. She died before they made the trip, however, and Dubos went on to Cambridge alone. He returned to the Rockefeller Institute in 1944 and opened a laboratory.

His wife's death drove Dubos to study the destructive tubercle bacilli, which he once referred to as "the captain of all the men of death." He pinpointed stress as a causative factor of tuberculosis when studies revealed a high inci-

dence of tuberculosis in turbulent times and fewer infections in more peaceful times. He determined that the environment in all its elements—physical, social, and emotional—contributed to the spread of the disease, an idea he elaborated on in *The White Plague: Tuberculosis, Man, and Society* (1952), which he wrote with his second wife, Letha Jean Porter, whom he had married on 16 October 1946.

Dubos believed that people overestimated the ability of medicine to cure disease. In *The Mirage of Health* (1959), he expressed his conviction that people who live by doing that which deeply matters to them and who can be resilient in the face of change will live healthfully. This did not mean, he added, a life free from struggle, danger, or disease.

In *So Human an Animal* (1968), Dubos wrote about the implications of our willingness to accept deteriorating surroundings and expounded on the dangers of advancing technology, and the underlying mythology, without regard for the consequences of such development. For this work, Dubos won the Pulitzer Prize in 1969.

Dubos devoted the last decade of his life to lecturing and writing on environmental issues. Activities beyond his work were limited for the most part to weekend retreats with his wife to his second home in Garrison, New York. There, in addition to writing, he enjoyed tending his trees and shrubs. Dubos felt completely at home in the United States and became a citizen in 1938. Nevertheless, he retained an affection for the French culture and countryside of his youth. He died of pancreatic cancer at New York Hospital. His cremated remains are buried in Garrison, New York.

Other scientists have made discoveries more far-reaching than those of Dubos but few have been so influential. Dubos wrote more than two dozen books and countless articles. His lectures were at times provocative, amusing, upsetting, and engrossing. He received forty-one honorary doctorates, three of which were M.D.s, and numerous awards. His staying power was his enthusiasm. Although distressed about the indifferent ravages of the earth, his unyielding faith in humanity never gave way to pessimism.

★

Dubos's manuscripts and personal papers are collected at the Rockefeller University Archives in New York City. Articles on his life and work are Saul Benison, "René Dubos and the Capsular Polysaccharide of Pneumococcus: An Oral History Memoir," *Bulletin of the History of Medicine* 50 (1976): 459–477; James G. Hirsch and Carol L. Moberg, "René Jules Dubos: February 20, 1901–February 20, 1982," *National Academy of Sciences of the United States of America: Biographical Memoirs* 58 (1989): 133–161; and Carol L. Moberg, "René Jules Dubos," *Research Profiles* 34 (1989): 1–6. An obituary is in the *New York Times* (21 Feb. 1982).

ELIZABETH MCKAY

DURANT, Will(iam) James (*b.* 5 November 1885 in North Adams, Massachusetts; *d.* 7 November 1981 in Los Angeles, California), and **DURANT, Ariel** (*b.* 10 May 1898 in Proskurov, Russia [present-day Ukraine]; *d.* 25 October 1981 in Los Angeles, California), historians best remembered for their collaborative work *The Story of Civilization* (1935–1975), an eleven-volume series that popularized and made accessible to the general public the history of humanity to the beginnings of the nineteenth century; the Durants were, to paraphrase *Time* magazine, the biographers of humanity, and their popular success can be inferred from the fact that all volumes of the series were still in print nearly two decades after their deaths.

Will Durant was born to Joseph and Marie Allors Durant, both of French Canadian stock, the sixth of eleven children, three of whom died in childhood. In 1892 the family moved from North Adams to industrial Kearny, New Jersey, and then to Arlington, New Jersey, about 1898. Durant's family belonged to the working class. Neither his father nor mother could read or write (not so unusual at the time), but his father became a factory technician and later superintendent of the "specialty" department in the celluloid factories of Kearny, which were later taken over by DuPont. In the autobiographical *Transition* (1927), Durant remembers the contrast between the farmers and the working class of North Adams. The former, descendants of the first European immigrants, had a hard existence with little hope of a better future and did not understand the new immigrants, the working class. The latter also had a difficult life, but remembering the hardships left behind in Europe, they looked to the future with greater confidence. This confidence both Will and Ariel shared throughout their lives.

The Durant children were educated by French Canadian Sisters of Charity in North Adams and Chicopee, Massachusetts, and Readsboro, Vermont. French was the language of instruction in the morning, English in the afternoon; until about 1900, the family spoke Canadian French at home. In Kearny and Arlington, the children attended public schools at first, then transferred to the parochial school attached to St. Cecilia's Church when it opened. At this school Durant met James Mooney, a priest who had a significant influence on his early life. Through the influence of his mother and Mooney, Durant decided to enter the priesthood. In 1900 he entered a contest for a scholarship at St. Peter's College in Jersey City, which he (along with two others) won.

Durant completed four years of secondary education and four years of college in seven years. He read voraciously in the college's library and made liberal use of the public libraries of Jersey City and Newark. Although he admired the Jesuits of St. Peter's as he had admired James Mooney,

Ariel and Will Durant embark on a world tour, 1932. UPI/CORBIS-BETTMANN

by his sophomore year at St. Peter's he had lost his faith and become a socialist. In his senior year, when he revealed his loss of faith, Mooney encouraged him to continue in his outward observances and pray for the return of his faith, which he did.

After graduating from St. Peter's College, Durant applied to Arthur Brisbane, one of the most influential columnists of the day, for a job as a reporter at the *New York Evening Journal*. Although there were many previous applicants, he was given the position. But a daily diet of the sordid side of life was distasteful to him, and he left the newspaper after four months. Mooney, now president of Seton Hall College and rector of its seminary, offered Durant a position as teacher of Latin, French, and geometry, which he accepted.

During his first year at Seton Hall, he conceived the idea of becoming a priest and reconciling the Catholic Church to socialism. So in 1908 he entered the seminary while continuing to teach in the college. He also was made librarian. In that capacity he read Baruch Spinoza's *Ethics Demonstrated in Geometrical Order* (1674), which he called the most influential book in his life after the Bible. He became convinced that he could not continue as a seminarian, so he left in January 1910, remaining as lay teacher at Seton Hall until June of that year. He then became a substitute teacher in Newark while living at home. During this time he helped found the Social Science Club, met Alden Freeman, the son of a Standard Oil millionaire, who would be his benefactor for a number of years, and began his career as lecturer. As a result of one of his lectures, "The Origins of Religion," delivered in January 1912, he was excommunicated by the bishop of Newark, and in consequence forced to leave home a few days later. Shortly after this he was offered the position of administrator and only teacher of the anarchist Francisco Ferrer Modern School (supported in part by Freeman), which he accepted. The summer of 1912 was spent touring Europe at Freeman's expense. When he returned to the Ferrer School in September 1912, one of his pupils was Ida Kaufman, the future Ariel Durant.

Ariel Durant (born Chaya Kaufman) was the fifth of seven children born to Joseph Michael Kaufman and Ethel Appel, the daughter of David Appel, a biblical and Talmudic scholar. Ethel Appel sat in the corner of her father's classes but also read liberally in Tolstoy and Russian radical literature, all of which she later used in stories for her children. Joseph Kaufman migrated to the United States in 1900, intending to send for the rest of the family later. When he did not do so, his pregnant wife and five of six children followed anyway in 1901 (the other child was sent over later). After a stopover in Liverpool and London for treatment of an eye disease that almost blinded Ariel, the family arrived in New York in November 1901. There, immigration officials changed Chaya's name to Ida and listed her and her three sisters as having been born two years apart, each on 10 May.

Joseph Kaufman worked at a newspaper stand, and his wife also began selling papers at Grand Central Station in Manhattan, their children also sharing in this occupation when not at school. Forced to work long hours seven days a week, Ariel's parents had little time to raise their family, which moved from one small apartment to another in the city, while the children were frequently left to roam the streets. After the birth of her seventh child, Ethel discouraged all attentions from her husband, leading to alienation. In 1907, heavily influenced by the anarchistic thinking of her brother Maurice and seeking escape from the drudgery of her life, Ethel left her family and moved into her own apartment. Ariel continued to see her mother, and it was from her that Ariel acquired the habit of reading and her passionate and high-spirited personality. Meanwhile, because of the family's frequent moves, Ariel attended one public school after the next. One day in 1912, while playing hooky in Central Park, she met a class from the Ferrer School. She joined the class and the school, and there met her future husband.

Ariel initiated the courtship, Will at first believing she was merely infatuated with him. However, he was soon persuaded of the depth of her commitment and returned her affection. Her family vigorously opposed the courtship because Will was not Jewish. Her mother finally gave her assent, and on 31 October 1913, the two were married. She was fifteen, he was nearly twenty-eight. She carried skates over her shoulder; he forgot the ring. They moved in with her mother at first; later in 1913 they moved (with her mother and brother Michael) into their own apartment. Will at first called his wife Puck, then Ariel; she adopted the latter as her legal name.

In September 1913 Will began graduate studies in philosophy, biology, and psychology at Columbia University, partially supported by Freeman. He was awarded the Ph.D. in philosophy in 1917. His thesis, *Philosophy and the Social Problem,* was published by Macmillan that year with a sale of 1,000 volumes guaranteed by Freeman; 100 were sold, and Will took home the remainder. He taught for a year at Columbia but World War I decreased the enrollment and he was not rehired.

Also in 1913, Will began to lecture regularly at the Labor Temple (a church loosely affiliated with the Presbyterian Church), which he did until 1927. He also had a full schedule of lectures across the United States; in 1923 he went to Kansas City to help Dan Coombs set up the Kansas City Academy. These were years in which nearly everyone believed in continuing education as a means of self-improvement. With no television, people eagerly attended lectures on almost every topic. Many of Will's lectures were concerned with politics; both he and Ariel were involved with politics much of their lives. On one occasion in 1915, Ariel entered the first New York City police station she could find and offered to have herself arrested so that she could "suffer with the many men and women the law has unjustly condemned." She found herself in Bellevue Hospital's mental ward for two days before being allowed to write a letter to her husband, who had been frantically looking for her. Over time, his socialism and her anarchism, more pragmatic than doctrinaire, gradually shifted to liberalism, a shift prompted in part, as they themselves knew, by their increasing prosperity and the responsibilities of parenthood. During this time the Durants lived in various apartments and houses in New York City and frequented bohemian Greenwich Village, where they mingled with the political, philosophical, literary, and artistic intelligentsia. Ariel continued to educate herself, and in 1918 she, too, began to lecture, at first with her husband, then independently. In 1926 she opened her own tearoom in Greenwich Village, the Gypsy Tavern. A daughter, Ethel, was born in 1919.

In 1922 Emanuel Haldeman-Julius, the publisher of a series of pamphlets known as "Little Blue Books," heard Will's lecture on Plato and asked him to rework it for publication in his series. With some hesitation, Will did so; this was followed by eleven more pamphlets on various philosophers. Then, in 1925, Max Schuster, cofounder of Simon and Schuster, asked Will to combine the pamphlets for publication as a single book. *The Story of Philosophy* (1926) was the result. It was immensely successful. In 1927 the Durants made their first of many trips abroad. In 1928 they moved to a colonial-style, eight-room shingle house at 44 North Drive in suburban Great Neck, Long Island, where they were to occupy several houses until 1943, and also adopted Ariel's nephew Louis. In 1929 they bought a summer house in Lake Hill, New York, near Woodstock.

Will had conceived, if only hazily, the idea of writing *The Story of Civilization* at the age of nineteen. Work on this project began shortly after the publication of *The Story of Philosophy* but was interrupted by a demanding schedule of lectures, the publication of other books, and time spent teaching two courses in philosophy at the University of California, Los Angeles, in the summer of 1935. Despite the interruptions, in 1935 the manuscript of the first volume, *Our Oriental Heritage,* was delivered to Simon and Schuster and published later that year; the introduction was also published separately the following year as *The Foundations of Civilization*. This and all subsequent volumes of *The Story of Civilization* were a tremendous success; some or all were translated into Spanish, Portuguese, French, Italian, German, Danish, Swedish, Chinese, Japanese, Arabic, and Persian. Occasionally the larger American volumes were divided into smaller, less expensive foreign volumes, especially in the years immediately following World War II.

The Story of Civilization was from the beginning a joint project. Will thought it would take twenty-five years and five volumes to complete. But it expanded to eleven volumes and took virtually the rest of the Durants' lives. In addition, both (especially Will) continued to lecture, and two books outside the series were published. For each volume Will would totally immerse himself in the subject, reading upward of 500 books, taking careful notes, then organizing the material, and finally writing. They also traveled extensively to visit the places about which they wrote. At first Ariel served as Will's research assistant, but by the seventh volume her contribution to research and organization had become such that she was given credit on the title page as coauthor (Will continued to write the final draft).

In 1943, after both children had grown, the Durants moved to California, buying a dilapidated thirteen-room Spanish-style mansion, named Casa della Vista by the architect, located at 5608 Briarcliff Road, Los Angeles, in the Hollywood Hills overlooking the city. This they renovated; it would be their last home. Will continued to lecture until 1957. Thereafter, their days were spent primarily working on *The Story of Civilization*. Their day began at 8 A.M. and ended at 10 P.M., with breaks only for meals, a nap at noon, and a midafternoon hike. The last volume, *The Age of Na-*

poleon, was completed in 1975, when Will was ninety and Ariel seventy-seven. They died six years later, thirteen days apart, she first, from what was described as a lingering illness, then he, following surgery and three weeks in intensive care; Will was never told of Ariel's death. On his deathbed, Will received confession from a Catholic priest.

The merits of *The Story of Civilization* have been debated ever since the publication of the first volume. There are serious omissions: the Americas before the conquest are not covered, nor is Africa, and the Far East shares only part of the first volume. It might more properly be titled "The Story of Western Civilization." Even so, the scope of the work is breathtaking. There are errors of fact, but when so much history is covered, this is perhaps unavoidable. Many scholars disliked it because so much of it was secondhand and synthetic, but this, too, seems unavoidable given the nature of the work. It is a reference book told in narrative style, something that had not been attempted before on this scale. The work put into the hands of ordinary men and women the whole history of western civilization. Not only were the major historical events covered, but the Durants tried to include the daily life of the common people, in all its sordid detail. This led to some incohesiveness and unevenness in treatment. Will's style was also the subject of criticism; some found it quite readable, others thought it convoluted and aphoristic. But the work as a whole seems to have withstood the test of time.

In addition to the works already mentioned, Will Durant wrote *The Mansions of Philosophy* (1929; republished in 1953, with some omissions, as *The Pleasures of Philosophy*), partly a collection of articles and lectures, with many new chapters; *The Case for India* (1930); *Adventures in Genius* (1931), largely a collection of previously published articles; *A Program for America* (1931); and *The Tragedy of Russia* (1933). Will and Ariel together wrote *The Lessons of History* (1968), *Interpretations of Life* (1970), and *A Dual Autobiography* (1977). Will also edited an abridgment of Arthur Schopenhauer's works titled *The Works of Schopenhauer* (1928), for which Thomas Mann wrote the introduction. All of Will's works were published by Simon and Schuster.

Both Will and Ariel Durant were honored with the Huntington Hartford Foundation Award for Literature in 1963 for *The Age of Louis XIV* (1963), volume 8 of *The Story of Civilization;* the Pulitzer Prize for general nonfiction literature in 1968 for *Rousseau and Revolution* (1967), volume 10 of *The Story of Civilization;* and the Medal of Freedom in 1977. Ariel Durant was named the *Los Angeles Times* Woman of the Year in Literature in 1965. Both Durants also received various honorary degrees.

★

Will and Ariel Durant, *A Dual Autobiography* (1977), is a highly detailed, personal account. Will Durant, *Transition* (1927), is a fictionalized autobiography of Will's early life. David Karsner, *Sixteen Authors to One* (1928; reprint 1968) includes an interview with Will Durant at the Durants' apartment shortly after the publication of *The Story of Philosophy*. *International Perspectives in Comparative Literature,* edited by Virginia M. Shaddy (1991), has a chapter by A. O. Aldridge on "Will Durant as Comparatist," dealing with the Durants' work. Jim Hicks, "Spry Old Team Does It Again," *Life* (18 Oct. 1963), and "Essence of the Centuries," *Time* (13 Aug. 1965), are among the magazine articles on the Durants. Jim Bishop, "The Philosopher and the Schoolgirl," *Reader's Digest* (Oct. 1969), gives a rather inaccurate account of the Durants' courtship and marriage. The *New York Times* (7 May 1977) includes coverage of the Durants' Pulitzer Prize. Lengthy obituaries appear in *Publishers Weekly* (6 and 20 Nov. 1981), *Time* (23 Nov. 1981), and *National Review* (22 Jan. 1982).

MICHAEL S. BORRIES

E

EISENHOWER, Milton Stover (*b.* 15 September 1899 in Abilene, Kansas; *d.* 2 May 1985 in Baltimore, Maryland), university president and government official who was an influential presidential adviser, especially to his brother, President Dwight D. Eisenhower.

Eisenhower was the son of David Eisenhower, a plant engineer, and Ida Stover. The youngest of six brothers, he attended public school in Abilene and entered Kansas State College in the summer of 1918. He left school that fall to earn expenses as a reporter and city editor at the *Abilene Daily Reflector.*

Milton returned to college in 1919 and later became campus correspondent for the *Kansas City Star* and editor of the *Kansas State Collegian.* After graduation in 1924 he took a job with the college as a journalism instructor; he quit later that year, however, to join the U.S. Foreign Service. He was assigned as a vice consul in Edinburgh, Scotland.

In 1926 Eisenhower left his diplomatic post for a sixteen-year career as a top official with the Department of Agriculture. William M. Jardine, who was president of Kansas State when Eisenhower was a student, had been appointed secretary of agriculture by President Calvin Coolidge. Milton was recruited by Jardine as his assistant. Eisenhower was reluctant to leave the Foreign Service because he was engaged to marry Helen Eakin and planned to start a family. They were wed on 12 October 1927 and had two chil-

dren, Milton and Ruth. "I couldn't accept a political appointment," Eisenhower said of that time. "I wasn't about to run any risks by taking a position with uncertain security." Accepting the job only after Jardine arranged for him to have a civil service classification, Eisenhower described himself as "the first career assistant to a cabinet member." His positions at the Department of Agriculture included assistant to the secretary (1924–1926), director of information (1937–1942), and coordinator of the land-use program (1937–1942). Eisenhower helped to shape legislation and was skillful in dealing with Congress and members of the news media.

The owlish and affable Eisenhower served under four secretaries of agriculture, two Republicans and two Democrats. After Jardine, Eisenhower enjoyed working most with Secretary Henry A. Wallace. "I never knew a man who possessed greater intellectual honesty than Henry Wallace," Milton said. "He was completely dedicated. He knew how to delegate authority, and he was an ideal administrator." Eisenhower had disdain for Wallace's successor, Claude R. Wickard, and made plans to quit the department.

President Franklin D. Roosevelt kept Eisenhower in government by making him one of the administration's troubleshooters. Through Wallace, Eisenhower had developed a friendship with Roosevelt that preceded his brother Dwight Eisenhower's rise to prominence. In June 1942 Roosevelt told General Eisenhower, "You know what I've been doing all morning? Well, I've been trying to decide

Milton Stover Eisenhower, 1963. ARCHIVE PHOTOS

among four competing bureaus where to put your baby brother. He's giving me an awful lot of trouble. I have to decide which will be lucky enough to get him."

Shortly after America's entry into World War II, Roosevelt asked Milton to draft plans for an Office of War Information. The president instructed Eisenhower to design a system that would provide an adequate flow of information to keep Americans and the Allies informed about the war. Eisenhower was also asked to recommend means of counteracting Axis propaganda. Milton proposed an agency with both foreign and domestic divisions.

In what Eisenhower would later describe as the most traumatic assignment of his public career, Roosevelt named him director of the War Relocation Authority on 10 March 1942 to oversee the wholesale evacuation of Japanese Americans from the Pacific Coast states and move them into internment camps. After failing in his effort to obtain more humane treatment of Japanese Americans, Eisenhower wanted out. He urged that Roosevelt "issue a strong public statement in behalf of the loyal American citizens who are now bewildered and wonder what is in store for them," and also recommended more liberal wages for the interned Japanese Americans. His advice was ignored.

Roosevelt then appointed him associate director of the Office of War Information (OWI). The *New York Herald Tribune* said Eisenhower had been chosen because he was "an expert in cutting snarled red tape" and had "a specialist's knowledge of which heads are useful and which should be lopped off." OWI director Elmer Davis, the former radio commentator, delegated administrative responsibilities to Eisenhower.

In the summer of 1943 Eisenhower began a second career in higher education, returning to Kansas State as its president. He persuaded the Kansas legislature to adopt an educational-building-fund tax that paid for a 50 percent expansion of the campus. A new library, a student union, and additional classrooms were constructed. Faculty salaries were boosted by 75 percent during his tenure. Graduate programs were expanded and the college's reputation was enhanced. Eisenhower moved quietly but forcefully to end racial discrimination. Blacks, who had been excluded from college housing, were admitted. Campus clubs and societies were warned by Eisenhower that their charters would be revoked if they racially discriminated.

Eisenhower moved on to the presidency of Pennsylvania State College in 1950. He embarked on a major building program there and raised academic standards by increasing the liberal arts requirement for technology students. Under his leadership, the college officially became a university in 1953.

That same year, his brother Dwight became president of the United States and Milton became his personal adviser. "I think I would rather take Milton's views than those of anyone else," the president said. During his brother's first year in the White House, he developed a system with the approval of university trustees that he would spend four days a week working for Penn State and three for his brother. He served on a three-member committee on government reorganization that was partly responsible for the creation of the Department of Health, Education, and Welfare, the United States Information Agency, the Small Business Administration, the Federal Aviation Administration, and the National Aeronautics and Space Agency. Milton also served as special ambassador to Latin America for his brother and made a ten-nation tour in 1953. He continued to serve as President Eisenhower's adviser through 1961.

Milton resigned the university presidency in June 1956 for "personal reasons," having lost interest in his work after his wife's death in 1954. He became president of Johns Hopkins University in 1956. With the university operating at a deficit, Eisenhower was recruited by trustees because of his reputation as a fund-raiser. Eisenhower met the challenge. In his eleven years at the helm, more than $75 million was spent to expand the physical plant and the university's endowment was doubled. Twelve endowed faculty chairs were created with private gifts, and faculty salaries became the fourth highest in the country. When he retired as president in 1967, the library was named in his honor. Four years later, he was called out of retirement after his successor ran up a $5 million debt and was cutting back faculty. As interim president in 1971 and 1972, Eisenhower slashed his own salary by two-thirds and in ten months cut the deficit to $2 million. "Many of the belt-tightening measures and reforms put into effect would probably not have been so effective or so willingly accepted if the man behind them had not possessed the humanity and ability the university needed in such crucial times," said an editorial in the *Johns Hopkins Magazine.*

In 1968 President Lyndon B. Johnson named Eisenhower chairman of a commission to study the causes of violence after the assassinations of Robert F. Kennedy and Martin Luther King, Jr. Among the commission's recommendations was a national firearms policy that would limit the availability of handguns.

Once described by Dwight Eisenhower as "the best qualified man to be president of the United States," Milton was courted by Kansas Republicans to run for the U.S. Senate in 1948 and for governor in 1950. After his move to Penn State that year, he was sought by Pennsylvania Republicans to run for the U.S. Senate in 1956 or the governorship in 1958, the first year that he would have been eligible under the Pennsylvania constitution. Following his move to Johns Hopkins, Milton seriously considered a 1962 bid for the U.S. Senate but decided against it. "When I was discussed as a candidate I felt it was simply because I was Ike's brother," he said in a 1976 interview. "If my name were Smith I doubt if they'd have been very interested." Eisenhower added: "I never really liked the idea of rough-and-tumble politics. I am somewhat sensitive, which might have worked against a political career but which helped give me a built-in radar system as a university president. I understood other people's feelings."

Eisenhower died of cancer at Johns Hopkins Hospital and was buried in State College, Pennsylvania.

★

Eisenhower's papers are at the Eisenhower Library in Abilene, Kansas. His book *The President Is Calling* (1974) covers his long career in education and government. *The Wine Is Bitter: The United States and Latin America* (1963) is a memoir of his service as Dwight D. Eisenhower's ambassador to Latin America. Stephen E. Ambrose and Richard H. Immerman, *Milton S. Eisenhower, Educational Statesman* (1983), is an insightful biography by authors who knew Eisenhower. Steve Neal, *The Eisenhowers* (1978), is a dual biography of Dwight and Milton. An obituary is in the *New York Times* (3 May 1985).

STEVE NEAL

ELLIOTT, James Francis ("Jumbo") (*b.* 8 July 1914 in Philadelphia, Pennsylvania; *d.* 22 March 1981 in Juno Beach, Florida), legendary coach who led the Villanova

University track team to more collegiate championships than any other school.

James Elliott was one of two children of James Michael Elliott, a local gas company meter reader who died when "Jumbo" was young, and Anna Anderson. He was born and raised around Fifty-sixth and Market Streets in West Philadelphia, an area some referred to as Shantytown. His lifelong association with track and field began as an elementary school child hawking Penn Relays programs at the nearby University of Pennsylvania. Although Elliott would ultimately live and work in the exclusive Main Line Philadelphia suburbs, the Relays became his annual spring homecoming and Franklin Field his Valhalla, where he could always be found high in the stands surrounded by family, friends, and admirers.

Fleet feet, useful in his rough-and-tumble neighborhood, carried Elliott on a successful running career at West Philadelphia Catholic High School. At the same time friends gave the lean, slightly stuttering athlete his enduring nickname after a contemporary, the rotund and unrelated "Jumbo" Jim Elliott, pitcher for the local Philadelphia Phillies baseball team. Naturally gifted as a runner, Elliott developed a strong work ethic supporting his poor family. Among other jobs, golf caddying at suburban country clubs offered Elliott the opportunity to learn a rich man's game. With a careful eye he honed his skills, watching the best

"Jumbo" Elliott. VILLANOVA UNIVERSITY

players attack the course and soon becoming a scratch golfer himself. Keen analytical ability and a disciplined work ethic, central to successful coaching, paid personal and professional dividends throughout Elliott's life.

The recipient of Villanova's first track scholarship, Elliott developed into a world-class middle-distance runner who went undefeated in collegiate 440-meter dual meets. In addition, he was a distinguished golfer and served as the football team trainer before assuming track-coaching duties during his junior year. Graduating from Villanova in 1935 with an economics degree, Elliott entered the U.S. Military Academy, having gained letters of recommendation from both Douglas MacArthur and Dwight Eisenhower. There he could continue to train for the 1936 Summer Olympic Games while preparing for an army career. Unfortunately, Elliott's sister, Catherine, died that fall, forcing him to forego West Point after only six months in order to help support his widowed mother. Continuing to train and compete when not working, Elliott roomed with sprinter Jesse Owens during the preparatory Olympic track tour. Although he was practically guaranteed a spot on the American squad, an untimely leg injury prevented him from making the team. Owens, however, remained a friend for life.

Returning to coach the Villanova track and golf teams, Elliott made most of his living from selling stocks and bonds, often on the golf course where his skill with a club and extroverted personality made him a sought-after tee partner. Commissioned into the U.S. Navy reserve as an athletic specialist in May 1942, Elliott toured with the likes of Byron Nelson in golf exhibitions to promote war bonds. On 9 March 1943 he married longtime sweetheart Catherine Rita O'Malley in the Villanova chapel; they had four children. After military service in North Africa and Europe, Lieutenant Commander Elliott returned to civilian life and began selling and leasing heavy construction equipment for the Frantz Company in 1947. Fifteen years later his hard work and business acumen led to partnership in a new enterprise, Elliott and Frantz, and made him a millionaire. Elliott also resumed duties as Villanova track coach following discharge and began to build a dynasty.

In 1948 quarter-miler George Guida and steeplechaser Browning Ross became the first of twenty-two Elliott protégés to participate in an unbroken streak of Summer Olympics lasting until the boycott of the 1980 Moscow Games. Guida and Browning were also instrumental in establishing Villanova's "Irish Connection" when they convinced Elliott to invite Jim Reardon, captain of Ireland's 1948 Olympic track team, to attend the school. Others followed, including Ron Delany, who set an Olympic record while winning the 1,500 meters in Melbourne (1956) and who became the first of more than a dozen Villanova runners to break the four-minute mile, and Eamonn Coghlan, who established an indoor mile world record.

Elliott's emphasis on middle-distance races at the expense of sprints and field events was a direct result of limited university funding for the sport. Nonetheless, three of his sprinters held world records. The coach trained his middle distancers for multiple events, thereby gaining maximum versatility from each athlete and enabling Villanova to defeat well-financed programs from other schools. Because Villanova teams lacked depth at any given distance, they typically were entered into major open competitions, such as invitationals and relay carnivals, rather than in dual meets. Elliott's uncanny knack for knowing which runner to enter in a particular race resulted from personal experience as a world-class athlete and intimate knowledge of each runner's abilities at any given moment during the track season.

Elliott had no patent regimen for his athletes. As an early advocate of interval training, where each runner varied the quantity (distance) and quality (pace) of training, Elliott focused on the individual simply because he knew that each runner had different requirements to reach peak performance. More rigid, however, was the coach's insistence upon maintaining academic standards and keeping a well-groomed appearance. Such self-discipline, Elliott believed, bred confidence that translated into success both on the track and after graduation.

Villanova's first national track titles were won in 1957 and earned Elliott honors as "Coach of the Year." Team titles amassed steadily from then on, including three Amateur Athletic Union national championships, eight National Collegiate Athletic Association national championships, thirty-nine Intercollegiate Association of Amateur Athletics of America (ICAAAA) championships, and seventy-five Championship of America Penn Relays titles. In 1961 Elliott led an American track delegation on a successful international tour that included victories in Moscow and Warsaw. The often outspoken Elliott, however, never coached an American Olympic track squad, believing that the Olympic team's coach and athletes should be selected by a panel of successful coaches and not by U.S. Olympic Committee administrators.

Elliott's many talented athletes collected six gold and three silver medals during Olympic competition, held dozens of American and world records, and won hundreds of national individual titles. The trio of Coghlan, Delany, and Marty Liquori won the Millrose Games' prestigious Wanamaker Mile eleven times in all. In addition, Liquori defeated the legendary miler Jim Ryun at the 1971 Martin Luther King Jr. Games in an electrifying race that became known as the "Mile of the Century." Not surprisingly, Elliott was later named "Coach of the Century" by the ICAAAA during its centennial in 1976.

Yet all was not well for the sage of the oval. Decades of combining a full workday in the construction equipment business with coaching an internationally recognized track team during its long competitive season, coupled with poor dietary habits, led to heart disease and high blood pressure. In 1968 he suffered a minor stroke, then a heart attack in 1976. More troubling for Elliott, however, was his wife's long, ultimately terminal, battle with cancer. In the end he survived Kay barely a month. He succumbed to coronary failure only days before the announcement of his induction into the Track and Field Hall of Fame. The Elliotts were buried in Calvary Cemetery in West Conshohocken, Pennsylvania.

Elliott brought international acclaim to the small private institution that first gave him the opportunity of a college education. Self-trained to world-class status in two sports, he overcame adversity through dedication, discipline, and desire. By ingraining that same ethic into the young men he coached, Jumbo Elliott prepared his athletes for success beyond the winner's platform. One Villanova track alumnus recalled his mentor's words: "When you are through running, people won't remember you for what you were but for what you are." That is the true Elliott legacy.

★

Theodore J. Berry, *Jumbo Elliott: Maker of Milers, Maker of Men* (1982), is a biography written by Elliott's close friend and personal physician. Three articles from late in Elliott's career are Tom Cushman, "Jumbo," *Philadelphia Daily News* (1 and 2 June 1978); Neil Amdur, "Jumbo Elliott: Ingenious Giant of U.S. Track," *New York Times* (23 Apr. 1979); and Rick Teleander, "Nobody's Bigger Than Jumbo," *Sports Illustrated* (10 Mar. 1980). Among many tributes are Craig Evans, "Jumbo Was Genuine Giant Even Beyond U.S. Borders," *Philadelphia Bulletin* (23 Mar. 1981); Lewis Freedman, "To His Athletes Elliott Was More Than Just Coach," *Philadelphia Inquirer* (23 Mar. 1981); Ira Berkow, "Elliott Is Given Final Tributes," *New York Times* (27 Mar. 1981); and "A Tribute to Jumbo Elliott: The End of an Era," *The Villanovan* (3 Apr. 1981). Obituaries are in the *New York Times, Philadelphia Bulletin*, and *Philadelphia Inquirer* (all 23 Mar. 1981).

WILLIAM E. FISCHER, JR.

ENDERS, John Franklin (*b.* 10 February 1897 in West Hartford, Connecticut; *d.* 8 September 1985 in Waterford, Connecticut), medical scientist best known for the discovery of the ability of poliomyelitis virus to grow in cultures of various tissues, for which he and Thomas H. Weller and Frederick C. Robbins were awarded the Nobel Prize in physiology or medicine.

The son of John Ostrum Enders, head of the Hartford National Bank, and Harriett Goulden Whitmore, a homemaker, Enders was the eldest of four children. The family maintained contacts with important figures in the field of literature; in particular, his father handled the financial affairs of Mark Twain.

In 1915 Enders graduated from St. Paul's Boarding School, where he preferred the humanities. That fall, at the age of eighteen years, with no defined academic objectives, he entered Yale College, where he was a member of Delta Kappa Epsilon social fraternity. After two years at Yale, he enlisted in the U.S. Naval Reserve Flying Corps and became a flight instructor.

After receiving his B.A. from Yale in 1920, Enders made a brief entry into the business world. He found business unexciting and enrolled in the Harvard Graduate School of Arts and Science, from which he received the M.A. degree in 1922. While exploring three different dissertation topics in the field of philology, he came under the influence of Hans Zinsser, chairman of the Department of Bacteriology and Immunology at Harvard Medical School. Enders, captivated by microbiology, decided to abandon his career in English literature and became a Ph.D. candidate under Zinsser. In 1930 he received his doctorate and was appointed an instructor in the department. His doctoral dissertation provided evidence that bacterial anaphylaxis and hypersensitivity of the tuberculin type are distinct phenomena.

In a tribute to Zinsser, published in the *Harvard Medical Alumni Bulletin,* Enders wrote warmly of life in his department. During staff lunches the conversation, led by Zinsser, would become quite lively and wide-ranging. In this favorable environment Enders slowly progressed up the academic ladder. He was an instructor from 1930 to 1935 and an assistant professor from 1935 to 1942.

At that early time Enders had developed well-established patterns in the laboratory. After arriving midmorning, carrying his lunch, he first reviewed any new observations. Although at the time he had no technician and only rarely participated actively in work at the bench, he took great interest in reviewing specimens and analyzing new data. Resources were limited, and Enders's entire research budget amounted to approximately $200 annually. Therefore, his junior associates spent much of their time washing and sterilizing glassware and devising other laboratory equipment.

Enders first directed his attention to bacterial diseases, especially of the pneumococcus, and made several important observations relating to its polysaccharide. In 1939 Dr. Alto E. Feller and Thomas H. Weller, then a senior medical student, undertook a research project under Enders, cultivating vaccinia virus in roller cultures of chicken tissues. Also in 1939 Enders published a paper with William McD. Hammon, a doctoral degree candidate, on panleukopenia, a virus disease. From that point on, Enders's attention was devoted almost exclusively to virus diseases; this led to a

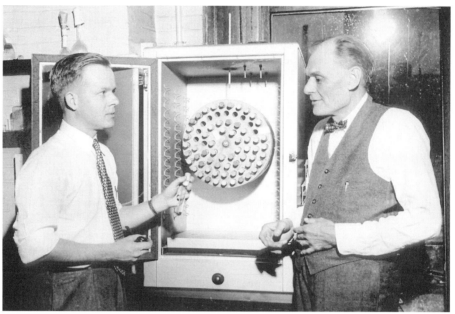

Dr. John Enders (*right*) with Dr. Thomas H. Weller. ARCHIVE PHOTOS

major emphasis in his laboratory—the application of tissue culture techniques to virology.

In 1940 Hans Zinsser died, ushering in a trying period for Enders. This was further accentuated by the unexpected death in 1943 of his wife, Sarah Frances Bennett, whom he had married on 17 September 1927 (they had two children), from acute myocarditis. From 1940 to 1942 Enders served as interim head of the department and in addition—with faculty departing during the war years—increased his own teaching duties. In 1942 he was made associate professor, and in 1943 his administrative duties, for which he had little liking, terminated with the appointment of Dr. J. Howard Mueller as permanent chairman of the department. Enders then expanded his own research on mumps, and with additional funding from military sources he was able for the first time to employ a personal technician and several junior associates. His laboratory showed that many cases of aseptic meningitis were due to mumps virus.

In 1947 Enders moved his laboratory from the Department of Bacteriology and Immunology to the Children's Hospital in Boston, where he established the Research Division of Infectious Diseases. He was soon joined by Dr. Thomas H. Weller and later by Dr. Frederick C. Robbins. Thus began Enders's long and productive association with the Children's Medical Center, where until 1972 he was chief of the Research Division of Infectious Diseases. In 1956 he was promoted to full professor at Harvard Medical School, and in 1962 he was named university professor, a title he held until 1967, when he became university professor emeritus.

Weller and Robbins have commented on Enders's demeanor in the laboratory:

> He developed a rather unique personal magnetism in the laboratory. This arose from the enjoyment he took in discussions with his associates. Deeply interested in medical problems, he would make astute observations regarding different diagnoses of a puzzling case. He had a unique capacity to identify and exploit significant findings and, in a low-key manner, could stimulate junior associates to further productive endeavors.
>
> Casual visitors observed Enders as a quiet, somewhat reticent individual of great personal charm. Stoop-shouldered he moved slowly about the laboratory, usually with a pipe in his mouth. He had a dry sense of humor and the occasional facetious remark was accompanied by a half-grin and a twinkle in his eyes.

In March 1948 Weller inoculated some unused cultures with Lansing strain (Type II) poliomyelitis virus. After twenty days in culture and three changes of medium, intracerebral inoculation of the fluids in the mice resulted in paralysis of all that were inoculated. Serial passage in vitro was readily accomplished. At Enders's suggestion, Robbins, who was interested in using tissue culture to identify a viral etiology of diarrhea in infants and children, used cultures of intestinal tissue obtained at the autopsy of a premature human infant and obtained similar results.

The potential significance of these observations was such that the laboratory directed its principal subsequent efforts to investigation of poliomyelitis. First, it was determined that Type I poliomyelitis virus could be similarly cultivated and supported in vitro by a completely differentiated, nonnervous tissue. It was also noted earlier that the polioviruses, when propagated in cultures, induced degenerative changes in the cells in which they grew. The virus could be detected, therefore, by both metabolic and morphologic changes—a phenomenon Enders termed the "cytopathic effect." The results were first published in *Science* in 1949.

Armed with these observations, the investigators were able to assay virus in vitro and assess the neutralizing capacity of antiserum. Tissue culture then could replace the experimental animal—usually a monkey. In June 1949 Robbins used the culture system successfully to isolate poliovirus from patients and a number of nonpolio enteroviruses from clinical cases of nonparalytic "polio." In the meantime Weller, concentrating on the long-term propagation of the polioviruses, obtained attenuated strains that had decreased variance. Other associates of Enders developed a complement fixation test for poliomyelitis using concentrated infected culture fluids as antigen. In 1954 the Nobel Prize in medicine or physiology was awarded to Enders, Weller, and Robbins for their epochal work.

From that time the race was on to develop a vaccine against poliomyelitis. The details have been provided by Robbins. These efforts have been enormously successful; as of the late 1990s the last case of paralytic poliomyelitis caused by wild virus that has been identified in the entire Western Hemisphere occurred in Peru in 1991.

Although poliomyelitis was the primary focus of the research effort in Enders's laboratory between 1948 and 1952, the researchers also explored other illnesses of possible viral etiology. These include studies that demonstrated that a Coxsackie virus was the etiologic agent of epidemic pleurodynia, that an unusual exanthematous illness was due to a viral agent later classified as ECHO 16 virus, and studies of measles (rubeola) vaccine. In 1954 the measles virus was isolated in cultures of human kidney cells and a complement fixing measles antigen was identified. In 1958 Enders, Samuel Katz, and Donald Medearis presented evidence that a strain of measles virus thus propagated became attenuated and that monkeys inoculated with this strain produced an antibody response with no viremia or recognizable disease. Enders immediately turned all the resources of his laboratory to the task of developing a measles vaccine based on the attenuated strain. Immunization with this agent produced a mild, modified infection resulting in protection. The publications relating to these studies provide the basis for studies that led to the licensing of the measles vaccine in 1963 in the United States.

Although the cultivation of poliomyelitis viruses was the reason that Enders, Weller, and Robbins were given the 1954 Nobel Prize, Enders later wrote that this work on measles was more personally satisfying to him and more socially significant.

As Enders's reputation spread, his laboratory became increasingly attractive and, although the number of trainees he accepted remained small, he was an influential force in the training of a generation of virologists. In 1967 a symposium was held in honor of his seventieth birthday, and more than a hundred associates and assistants from all parts of the world attended.

By 1959 Enders's group had once again shifted the focus of its investigations, first to problems with viral host-cell resistance, and to viral oncogenesis—the subject of the final segment of Enders's investigative career. These have been detailed by others.

In 1951, eight years after the death of Enders's first wife, he married Carolyn B. Keane. An autobiographical note written in 1953 lists carpentry, photography, and gardening among Enders's avocations, but his major nonscientific interests were fishing and playing the piano.

Enders received many honors in addition to the Nobel Prize. He was a member of the National Academy of Sciences, the Royal Society of England, and the French Academy of Sciences. He was awarded the Presidential Medal of Freedom in 1963. He received the Passano Award, the Lasker Award in 1954 and was selected as *Time* magazine's Man of the Year in 1961. He received honorary degrees from thirteen universities.

At the age of eighty Enders retired from laboratory work but continued to follow the patient literature closely and to enjoy discussions with scientific visitors to his home to the end. Enders died quietly at his summer home in Waterford, Connecticut, as he sat reading T. S. Eliot aloud to his wife and daughter. He is buried in Fairview Cemetery in West Hartford, Connecticut.

It is difficult to estimate the full impact of Enders's contributions because they will benefit future millions of children. The techniques developed in his laboratory, and since elaborated, provided the basis for the preparation of vaccines against poliomyelitis, measles, mumps, rubella, and varicella-zoster viruses. They have been important in providing simple and inexpensive methods of isolating viruses from biological and clinical specimens and for assaying antibodies. They are employed in studies of the molecular biology of viruses. Enders's laboratory served as an important training site for many infectious-disease trainees from all over the world. Those who worked with him found him to be a wise, imaginative loyal mentor who set a high standard of scientific and personal integrity. Enders's impact was felt both as a teacher and as a scientist. Millions of children are alive today and free of handicaps because of his work.

★

Obituaries or tributes include Frederick C. Robbins, "John F. Enders, 1897–1985: A Tribute," *Journal of Infectious Diseases* 153 (1986): 807–808; Thomas H. Weller and Frederick C. Robbins, "John Franklin Enders," *Biographical Memoirs. National Academy of Sciences* 60 (1991): 47–65, with an extensive bibliography; and Frederick C. Robbins, "John F. Enders," *Journal of Pediatrics* 124 (1994):155–157. His work and contributions are discussed in *Fields Virology,* edited by B. H. Fields, D. M. Knip, P. M. Holwey, et al. (1996), vol. 1, pp. 655–712.

HARRIS D. RILEY, JR.

ENGEL, A. Lehman (*b.* 14 September 1910 in Jackson, Mississippi; *d.* 29 August 1982 in New York City), conductor, composer, writer, and teacher who conducted the orchestras of a number of hit Broadway musicals and won acclaim as an interpreter of musical theater.

The only child of Ellis Engel, a clothing and shoe salesman, and Juliette Lehman, who helped to operate her brother's laundry, Engel was given the unusual first name of "A." in

Lehman Engel, 1962. UPI/CORBIS-BETTMANN

honor of his two grandfathers, whose names were Aaron and Abraham. He ceased to use his first name when he went away to school.

Small and shy as a child, Engel had little social contact with children other than his two cousins. He developed a love of music early in life, enthralled by the sounds of the small orchestra in Jackson's Majestic Theater during the era of silent films. He later said that this experience taught him to understand the "all-important interplay between drama and music." After studying piano with local teachers and graduating from Central High School in Jackson, Engel enrolled in the Cincinnati Conservatory of Music in 1926; he studied there for one year, then enrolled in the Cincinnati College of Music and the University of Cincinnati, where he studied for two more years. In 1929 he moved to New York City, intent on becoming a celebrated composer.

During his years in Cincinnati, Engel's childhood shyness had been replaced by a gregariousness and confidence that enabled him to make his way in New York's artistic community, where he gathered an ever-widening circle of friends. Almost from his arrival in New York, he composed and conducted while studying composition with Rubin Goldmark at the Juilliard Graduate School from 1930 to 1934 and in 1935 privately with Roger Sessions.

In 1931 Engel began to write music for Martha Graham, a rising young star of the dance; in 1934 he made his Broadway debut, conducting music he had composed for the Irish playwright Sean O'Casey's *Within the Gates*. From 1935 to 1939 he was employed by the Federal Music Project in a variety of positions, including director of a madrigal chorus. He became well known as a composer of incidental music for the theater, and composed, arranged, and conducted music for the popular radio show *Texaco Star Theater*.

In 1942 Engel enlisted in the U.S. Navy. He was assigned initially to the Great Lakes Naval Training Station, where he conducted a symphonic band, then to Washington, D.C., where, having been commissioned as an officer, he composed music for navy films.

Upon returning to New York in 1946, Engel was asked by Harold Rome to conduct the orchestra for his musical *Call Me Mister*. The play was Engel's first hit as a conductor, and it began a long-term professional relationship; Engel conducted several of Rome's subsequent musicals, including *Fanny* (1954) and *Destry Rides Again* (1959). *Fanny* was Engel's first collaboration with legendary producer David Merrick, with whom he worked frequently over the next eight years.

In 1950 Engel conducted the premiere of Gian Carlo Menotti's opera *The Consul* and won his first Tony Award. In 1953 he won Tonys for conducting *Wonderful Town,* with music by Leonard Bernstein, and for a series of Gilbert and Sullivan operettas. Other Broadway hits conducted by Engel included *Li'l Abner* (1956), *Take Me Along* (1959), *Do, Re, Mi* (1960), and *I Can Get It for You Wholesale* (1962).

Although Engel earned his reputation on Broadway, his conducting career was multifaceted. He conducted orchestras for more than eighty recordings, including the first recording on a major label of a Charles Ives composition, a number of television shows, symphony performances, and summer theater productions.

In addition to rehearsing and conducting the orchestra, a Broadway conductor has responsibility for auditioning and rehearsing singers and working with producers and directors on modifications to their show during pre-Broadway tryouts. Engel developed a reputation for understanding the relationship between drama and music that earned him multiple offers of employment every season. Unfortunately, he associated himself with as many flops as hits during the years, but he was always able to recover from the failures and move on with his career.

During the 1960s Engel became bored with Broadway conducting and increasingly intolerant of the production squabbles that characterized the tryout period. In 1966 he retired from the Broadway pit, but he continued to conduct in other venues. In 1969 the U.S. State Department sent him to Turkey to conduct a production of *Porgy and Bess* by the Turkish State Opera. Also in 1969 he reunited with Harold Rome and David Merrick to conduct their *Scarlett,* a musical version of *Gone with the Wind,* which opened in Tokyo in January 1970.

By the 1960s writing and teaching had become Engel's primary interests. His first book, *Planning and Producing the Musical Show,* had been published in 1957, during the height of his Broadway career. After 1966 he devoted more time to writing and published eight additional books, including *The American Musical Theatre* (1967), *Getting Started in the Theatre* (1973), and *The Making of a Musical* (1977). In 1961 Engel began workshops in New York for Broadcast Music, Inc. (BMI), to develop young composers, lyricists, and playwrights. Over the years the workshops were expanded to include regular sessions in Los Angeles and Toronto. His students wrote music for a number of Broadway hits, including *Raisin, The Best Little Whorehouse in Texas,* and *A Chorus Line.*

Engel was also a prolific composer, with more than seventy compositions to his credit. Most were incidental music for plays or scores for films, but he also wrote operas and music for chorus, piano, and orchestra. A number of his compositions were published, but their performances were limited.

Although he was ill for the last two years of his life, Engel continued to teach and write until just before his death from cancer. His ashes were buried next to his parents in Beth Israel Cemetery, Jackson, Mississippi. His last book, *Getting the Show On: The Complete Guidebook for Producing*

a Musical in Your Theater (1983), was published posthumously. He never married and had no children.

Despite a promising start in the 1930s, Engel never became the celebrated composer that he hoped to be. Instead, following the opportunities that presented themselves, he became a Broadway legend as a conductor, writer, and teacher. The *New York Times* drama critic Brooks Atkinson once declared, "Mr. Engel knows more about the American musical theatre than anyone else." Because of his innate understanding of the relationship between music and drama, Engel was known to many producers and directors as the person who could save a show that was in trouble. In the last part of his career he employed his skills as a writer and teacher to transmit his knowledge to the next Broadway generation and the public at large.

★

Most of Engel's papers are in the Music Library of Yale University. A smaller collection is in the Millsaps-Wilson Library of Millsaps College, Jackson, Mississippi. The Mississippi Department of Archives and History, in Jackson, has a substantial file consisting primarily of clippings. Engel's autobiography, *This Bright Day* (1974), provides insight into his personality as well as his career. Memorial tributes are in *BMI: The Many Worlds of Music,* no. 4 (1982). An obituary is in the *New York Times* (30 Aug. 1982).

VAGN K. HANSEN

ENGLE, Charles Albert ("Rip") (*b.* 26 March 1906 in Elk Lick, Pennsylvania; *d.* 7 March 1983 in Bellefonte, Pennsylvania), college athlete and football coach who brought Pennsylvania State University's football program into national prominence.

Engle, the son of Irvin Engle, a commercial building contractor, and Cora Newman, a housewife, became a mule driver in a coal mine at age fourteen and a mine supervisor by age nineteen. He attended Blue Ridge College in Maryland for one year and played in the first football game he ever saw. After Blue Ridge dissolved in 1925, he transferred to Western Maryland College and graduated in 1930. Dick Harlow coached Western Maryland to an 11–0 football mark in 1929, when Engle made the All-Maryland team as an end. Engle also captained the baseball and basketball teams and lettered in tennis. On 14 August 1931 he married Mary Webber "Sunny" Broughton, whom he had met at Western Maryland. They had one child.

Engle taught mathematics and coached football at Waynesboro High School in Pennsylvania from 1931 to 1941, posting an 86–17–5 record and compiling three undefeated seasons and eight conference titles. Engle pursued graduate work at Western Maryland College in 1941, serving as freshman football coach and varsity basketball coach.

Coach Rip Engle and team captain Ralph Baker, Penn State, 1963. AP/ WIDE WORLD PHOTOS

In 1942 he moved to Brown University as an assistant football coach to J. Neil "Skip" Stahley.

Engle became head football coach at Brown in 1944. He pioneered and perfected the winged-T offense, guiding the Bears through one of the most exciting periods in their football history. During his six-year tenure Brown's record was 28–20–4. In 1948 and 1949, the Bears conquered fifteen of eighteen opponents behind quarterback Joe Paterno. Brown finished 7–2 in 1948 for its best record in two decades and in 1949 lost only to Princeton University.

In April 1950 Engle replaced Joe Bedenk as head football coach at Penn State and named Paterno backfield coach. Paterno's leadership ability impressed Engle. Before Engle's arrival, Penn State did not rank among the nation's best football teams. Under Engle, however, the Nittany Lions did not have a losing season, compiling a 104–48–4 record from 1950 to 1965.

Engle installed the winged-T offense in 1950 and Penn State cracked the top twenty for the first time in 1954 with a 7–2 record. Upon switching to a multiple-T offense, Engle guided Penn State to twelfth place in 1959 with an 8–2 mark. Penn State that year made its first postseason appearance in over a decade, defeating Paul "Bear" Bryant's University of Alabama, 7–0, in the inaugural Liberty Bowl. Pollsters ranked the Nittany Lions sixteenth in 1960, when they finished 6–3 and routed the University of Oregon, 41–12, in the Liberty Bowl.

Penn State slipped one place in the 1961 polls after a 7–3 campaign and won its third consecutive postseason game, besting Georgia Tech, 30–15, in the Gator Bowl. The Nittany Lions vanquished nine of ten opponents in 1962 to crack the top ten for the only time under Engle, but lost, 17–7, to the University of Florida in the Gator Bowl. Pollsters rated Penn State sixteenth in 1963 with a 7–3 mark and fourteenth in 1964.

In 1964, after losing four of its first five games, Penn State conquered its last five foes to record the university's twenty-sixth consecutive winning season. Highlights included a 27–0 victory over Ohio State University and a 28–0 triumph over the University of Pittsburgh. Engle considered his 1964 6–4 team his most memorable and most indicative of his philosophy: "Success lies not in never failing, but in rising every time you fail." Engle retired following a disappointing 5–5 campaign in 1965. Penn State captured the Lambert Trophy as the best eastern college football team in 1961, 1962, and 1964. The Nittany Lions also won forty-one intersectional games and defeated five of their last seven Big Ten Conference opponents. Penn State upset Woody Hayes's Ohio State Buckeyes three times, winning 7–6 in 1956, 10–7 in 1963, and 27–0 in 1964. The Associated Press called the Nittany Lions's 1964 victory over the undefeated, second-ranked Buckeyes the biggest upset of that year in college football.

Engle coached six All-America players, including guard Sam Valentine in 1956, quarterback Richie Lucas in 1959, ends Bob Mitinger in 1961 and Dave Robinson in 1962, halfback Roger Kochman in 1962, and guard Glenn Ressler in 1964. Lucas was runner-up in the Heisman Trophy balloting and won the Maxwell Award in 1959, while Ressler received the Maxwell Award in 1964.

Engle served as president of the American Football Coaches Association, belonged to the NCAA Rules Committee, and chaired the Selection Committee for the East-West Shrine All-Star game. He conducted five overseas football clinics—two in Europe, two in Japan, and one in the Far East—for the U.S. Air Force and Army between 1950 and 1964. He shared head coaching responsibilities for the National All-Stars in the 1959 and 1960 Copper Bowl games and for the East aggregate in the first All-American Bowl in 1961.

The NCAA District 2 Coach-of-the-Year in 1962, Engle won the annual award of the Touchdown Club of New York and received the Amos Alonzo Stagg Award in 1970 for his contributions to football. He was elected to Brown University's Athletic Hall of Fame in 1972 and to the National Football Foundation's College Football Hall of Fame in 1974. Engle lived in State College near the Penn State campus during his retirement and summered at Cape Cod, where he enjoyed swimming and sailing. He died in a Bellefonte, Pennsylvania, nursing home after a long illness.

He is buried in Salisbury Cemetery in Somerset County, Pennsylvania.

Engle compiled 131 wins, 67 defeats, and 8 ties in twenty-four seasons at Brown and Penn State, ranking among the nation's twenty-five winningest coaches. His teams garnered the Lambert Trophy three times, performed in four bowls, produced six All-Americas, and never experienced a losing season. The magnetic mentor impressed others with his sincerity, humility, rugged exterior, smart football tactics, and undying interest in his players. The gentle, soft-spoken, reserved, likable coach with snow-white hair was not a strict disciplinarian but communicated effectively. To Engle, football meant both hard work and fun.

Engle delegated extensive responsibilities to his assistant coaches, retaining four for his entire sixteen years at Penn State. His ideas and philosophy profoundly influenced Paterno, who succeeded him as head coach in February 1966.

★

The Rip Engle files are at Penn State University, University Park, Pa. There is no full-length biography of Engle. Ken Rappoport, *The Nittany Lions: A Story of Penn State Football* (1973), and Ridge Riley, *Road to Number One* (1977), detail Engle's tenure at Penn State. Mervyn D. Hyman and Gordon S. White, *Joe Paterno: "Football My Way"* (1971), and Joe Paterno with Bernard Asbell, *Paterno by the Book* (1989), recount Paterno's experiences with Engle, while Frank Bilovsky, *Lion Country: Inside Penn State Football* (1982), provides reminiscences by several players. The (Penn State) *Daily Collegian* (19 Feb. 1966) summarizes Engle's career. Obituaries appear in the *Penn Stater* (May–June 1983), the (State College) *Centre Daily Times* (8 Mar. 1983), and the *New York Times* (8 Mar. 1983).

DAVID L. PORTER

ERNST, Hans-Ulrich ("Jimmy") (*b.* 24 June 1920 in Cologne, Germany; *d.* 6 February 1984 in New York City), abstract painter best known for his role as an exponent of the New York school.

Ernst spent his early childhood surrounded by key members of the European avant-garde art world who were friends of his father, the surrealist painter Max Ernst, and his mother, the art historian and journalist Louise Amalia Straus-Ernst. After his parents divorced in 1922, Ernst, an only child, remained with his mother in Germany and visited his father periodically in Paris, where Max had relocated. Ernst attended the Lindenthal Real-Gymnasium in Cologne from 1932 to 1936, and in 1935 he became apprenticed as a typographer in the firm of J. J. Augustin in Glückstadt. His project there entailed studies of Native American art. With the rise of the National Socialist party

Hans-Ulrich Ernst. OSCAR WHITE/CORBIS

in Germany, Ernst experienced the double persecution of being half Jewish on his mother's side and having a father whose art the Nazis had deemed "decadent." He obtained a visa and arrived in New York City on 9 June 1938. There he petitioned the Emergency Rescue Committee to help his parents escape from Europe. Whereas Max Ernst arrived in New York in 1941, Jimmy learned later in life that his mother had been on one of the last trains to the Nazi death camp at Auschwitz, where she died. His 1983 painting *Moments in Cell #12 (Requiem for L.S.E.)* is his epitaph for her.

In New York City the young Ernst rapidly assimilated into his new culture, becoming fluent in English. Even during his youth in Europe he had been enthralled by American culture, in particular jazz. In New York City he found himself squeezed into the upper mezzanine during the historic 1938 Carnegie Hall concert, "Spirituals to Swing." The equivalences between jazz and painting form one theme in his artistic oeuvre.

Soon after arriving in America Ernst became involved with the émigré art community. In 1939 he landed a job at the Museum of Modern Art, and by 1941 he was working as an assistant to art patron and collector Peggy Guggenheim, then the wife of Max Ernst. He became the director of Guggenheim's famed Art of This Century Gallery, which opened in 1942 and formed a major liaison between the American and European artists in New York at that time. The gallery showed both the surrealists and emerging American abstract expressionists such as Jackson Pollock. Ernst began as a self-taught painter in New York working in the surrealist style. He exhibited his early work, *The Flying Dutchman,* at the Marian Willard Gallery in 1942. He soon left Guggenheim's employment to organize, with Eleanor Lust, the Norlyst Gallery, which opened in 1943 on West Fifty-Seventh Street. Norlyst became an early New York school gallery showing some members of this New York–based movement that began in the 1940s. Ernst himself held his first one-person exhibition there called "Reflections on the Inner Eye" in 1943. Other shows of note which appeared in the gallery were "C*I*R*C*U*S*," which showcased the work of the then little known sculptor Louise Nevelsen, and "Documents France 1940–1944: Art-Literature-Press of the French Underground," a notable 1945 exhibition organized by the sculptor Louise Bourgeois. Ernst's work appeared again in 1946 in a one-person exhibition called "Black Music," containing works inspired by jazz and the blues. On 3 January 1947 he married an American, Edith Dallas Bauman Brody (called Dallas); they had two children.

Whereas in the 1940s Ernst had been surrounded by the European surrealists, by 1950 he joined his American colleagues in activities associated with the burgeoning New York school. He joined artists such as William Baziotes, Robert Motherwell, Barnett Newman, and others in a famed three-day symposium called "Artists Sessions at Studio 35." He joined the Irascible 18 (appearing in a reproduced photo of that group), protesting a perceived bias against abstraction on the part of the Metropolitan Museum of Art. In 1951 he began teaching at Brooklyn College along with Ad Reinhardt and other abstract expressionist painters. In 1952 he became an American citizen. He remained at Brooklyn College for decades until his retirement in 1978. At the end of his life he wrote a memoir, *A Not-So-Still Life,* which was published in 1984 before his death from a heart attack in New York City. He is buried in East Hampton, New York.

Ernst's early work was deeply inspired by surrealism. At the heart of his concerns was the role of the unconscious and the surrealists' notion of automatism, or purposefully uncontrolled methods, as a springboard to the unknown. Many other emerging abstract expressionist artists were inspired by this concept as well. Ernst began numerous paintings by using an automatic technique he called "sifflage," which involved blowing on thin oil paint until it spread in weblike patterns on the canvas. The improvisational component of jazz appealed to Ernst because of the primary role that automatism played in his art in the early 1940s. He clearly expressed the conjunction of jazz and automatism in paintings of 1944, such as *Blues from Chicago.* By combining the technique of sifflage with a notion of jazz improvisation, he found his own method of "blowing the blues." Ernst spoke as well of the intricate structures of boogie-woogie and the blues. His art became increasingly more architectonic after he abandoned sifflage and more obvious surrealist influences. His paintings, however, always manifest his quest for the unknown, the unconscious, and for the rendering of a haunting mood.

★

Jimmy Ernst, *A Not-So-Still Life: A Memoir* (1984), is a beautifully written and highly informative autobiography. Helen A. Harrison, *Jimmy Ernst, A Survey, 1942–1983* (1985), accompanied a major posthumous retrospective in East Hampton, N.Y., at the Guild Hall Museum. Robert D. Kinsman, *The Art of Jimmy Ernst, A Comprehensive Exhibition* (1963), covers an important exhibition at the Detroit Institute of Arts. Mona Hadler, "Jazz and the New York School," in *Representing Jazz,* edited by Krin Gabbard (1995), includes an examination of Ernst's interest in jazz. An obituary is in the *New York Times* (7 Feb. 1984).

MONA HADLER

ERVIN, Samuel James, Jr. (*b.* 27 September 1896 in Morganton, North Carolina; *d.* 23 April 1985 in Winston-Salem, North Carolina), senator who chaired the Watergate hearings that helped expose misdeeds committed by Richard M. Nixon and his aides, resulting in Nixon's historic resignation in 1974.

Sam Ervin was one of ten children of Laura Theresa Powe Ervin and Samuel James Ervin, Sr., stern Calvinists of Scotch-Irish descent. Growing up in Morganton, North Carolina, in the foothills of the Blue Ridge Mountains, Ervin inherited a suspicion of big government characteristic of the rural South. His father, an esteemed trial lawyer, passed on an ardent belief in the inviolability of constitutional liberties and a habit of quoting from memory passages from the law and great literature.

Ervin graduated from Morganton High School in 1913 and matriculated at the University of North Carolina at Chapel Hill, where he earned a B.A. (1917) and was elected president of his class. During World War I he saw combat as an infantryman in France, winning numerous medals, including the Purple Heart and the Distinguished Service Cross, for his valor. Although Ervin had already been admitted to the North Carolina bar, he enrolled at Harvard Law School after his discharge from the army, earning a law degree from Harvard in 1922.

While finishing his final exams in Cambridge, Ervin learned that the Burke County Democratic Party had nominated him, on the strength of his family name and precocious achievements, to run for state representative. Ervin accepted, returned to Morganton as he had planned, and won the seat. In 1924 he lost a primary bid for district attorney but managed to win reelection to the statehouse. Also that year, on 18 June, he wed Margaret Bruce Bell, his longtime sweetheart, to whom he stayed married his entire life. They had three children.

Over the next few decades, Ervin divided his time between politics and the law. He joined his father's practice, Ervin and Ervin, as the junior partner, and worked there for fifteen years. He was elected state representative for a third time in 1930, county judge in 1935, and North Carolina Superior Court judge in 1937. His first taste of national politics came in 1945, when his brother Joseph, a U.S. congressman from North Carolina, died. Sam ran unopposed in a special election to finish out his term. But when the term expired, he declined to seek the office on his own and returned to North Carolina. There he continued to ascend in state politics, serving from 1948 to 1954 on the state supreme court.

In 1954 another untimely passing brought Ervin back to Washington. When U.S. Senator Clyde R. Hoey died in May, North Carolina governor William B. Umstead chose Ervin to replace him. Just six weeks after assuming office on 11 June 1954, Ervin was named to serve on the select committee that was to consider censuring Senator Joseph R. McCarthy, whose unsubstantiated charges that various public officials were Communist party members were becoming increasingly intolerable to his colleagues. After holding hearings, the committee unanimously recommended censure on two counts, and on 2 December 1954 the full Senate adopted the censure resolution.

Two years later Ervin served on a committee of Southern senators who drafted a resolution that became known as the Southern Manifesto. The declaration condemned the U.S. Supreme Court's rulings that called for racial desegregation of Southern schools; the southerners contended that these edicts amounted to unwarranted judicial activism and a violation of states' rights. Though Ervin contributed little to the actual wording of the manifesto, he signed it, along with almost every other Southern congressman and senator. (Among Southern senators, only Lyndon B. Johnson of Texas and Albert Gore, Sr., and Estes Kefauver of Tennessee refused.) Ervin would adhere to this position throughout his career. He led the unsuccessful fight against the 1964 Civil Rights Act, which prohibited segregation in public places and created the Equal Employment Opportunity Commission. As late as 1984 Ervin wrote, "Civil rights are special privileges enacted by Congress, created by executive regulations, or manufactured by activist Supreme Court Justices for the supposed benefit of members of minority races on the basis of their race. . . .

Sam Ervin. WALLY MCNAMEE/CORBIS

They conferred on blacks superiority rather than equality under the law."

Ervin's fear of a tyrannical federal government allowed his defense of segregation on the grounds of states' rights to coexist, sometimes uneasily, with a belief in the protection of civil liberties. A religious man who frequently made reference to the Christian Bible, Ervin struggled over whether to support a constitutional amendment to allow prayer in public schools. He eventually concluded that such an amendment would harm religious freedom, and he threw his weight behind the campaign to defeat it. He also sought protections for groups such as the mentally ill and the criminally accused, although he railed against those Supreme Court decisions, under Chief Justice Earl Warren, that he believed amounted to legislation in the guise of adjudication.

In the 1960s and early 1970s, Ervin remained a conservative on most issues. On American involvement in the Vietnam War, he took a hawkish stance even after many of his Senate colleagues favored a military withdrawal. On labor issues, he supported "right-to-work" laws that allowed companies to hire nonunion workers, and he was generally on the side of business in employment disputes. He also vigorously opposed the Equal Rights Amendment for women as too sweeping in its scope, and he resisted extending the vote to citizens between the ages of eighteen and twenty-one.

Yet at the same time Ervin endeared himself to civil libertarians. Throughout the 1960s he championed an "Indian Bill of Rights" to guarantee Native Americans self-government while safeguarding their basic freedoms, a bill that became law in 1968. Despite his dislike of judicial rulings that allowed accused criminals to escape conviction on "technicalities," Ervin fought against "no-knock" laws that would weaken Fourth Amendment protections against warrantless searches. And as chairman of the Senate Subcommittee on Constitutional Rights, Ervin led the crusade against government surveillance of citizens. He publicized information about the army's spying on public officials and contributors to political campaigns, and he fought the creation of a computerized database to monitor political dissenters.

Ervin was thrust into the national spotlight in early 1973, when the new Congress, which convened in January, voted to appoint a select committee to investigate the burgeoning Watergate affair. On 17 June 1972 five individuals with ties to Nixon's campaign committee had been caught breaking in to Democratic party headquarters at Washington's Watergate building. Throughout the summer and fall, a small band of reporters, led by Bob Woodward and Carl Bernstein of the *Washington Post*, found increasing evidence of White House involvement in the Watergate break-in, its cover-up, and other illegal activities. Although the news did not stop Nixon from winning reelection by a landslide in November 1972, more disclosures trickled out over the winter, prompting the Senate to take action.

Senate majority leader Mike Mansfield tapped Ervin to head the seven-member investigative committee. The Senate Judiciary Committee, which might normally oversee such an inquiry, was headed by Mississippi senator James Eastland, a close friend of Nixon's. Mansfield himself had vocally criticized the administration's continuing prosecution of the Vietnam War, and other obvious choices for committee chair, such as Ted Kennedy of Massachusetts, might also be seen as excessively partisan. Ervin's reputation, on the other hand, was strong among both Democrats and Republicans, and he was known to harbor no presidential ambitions himself.

The Ervin hearings began on 17 May 1973 and immediately became a national event. Aired on television in the middle of the day, they held Americans spellbound, as one witness after another spilled more details about Watergate, for weeks on end. James McCord, one of the Watergate burglars, told the committee that John Dean, Nixon's counsel, and John Mitchell, his attorney general, had known about the break-in before it occurred. More major news came in late June when Dean testified; asked by Senator Howard Baker, the top Republican on the committee, "What did the president know and when did he know it?" Dean said he had personally discussed the cover-up with

Nixon himself as early as September 1972. Another bombshell came in July when Alexander Butterfield, a former White House aide who had been promoted to head of the Federal Aviation Administration, disclosed that Nixon secretly taped his White House conversations. The public also learned of plans to abuse the powers of the CIA and FBI, of the maintenance of an official White House "Enemies List," of secret wiretapping, of hush money paid to silence the burglars, and of much more. Amid these revelations, Nixon privately considered resigning.

The discovery of the tapes opened another chapter in the Watergate battles, in which Ervin's role again was critical. When Ervin's committee asked to hear the tapes, Nixon, in a letter to Ervin of 23 July 1973, refused, citing "executive privilege." Immediately, the committee voted to subpoena five of the recordings. Meanwhile, a federally appointed special prosecutor, Harvard law professor Archibald Cox, was pursuing indictments related to Watergate and obtained a subpoena of his own. In the course of the fight for the tapes, Nixon had Cox fired, a decision that backfired, turning public sentiment against the president even more strongly. Nixon finally surrendered some of the tapes to Cox's successor, Houston attorney Leon Jaworski, but Jaworski sought still more tapes, litigating all the way to the Supreme Court to win their release.

Through it all, Ervin became something of a national folk hero. His self-deprecating folksiness and down-home wit charmed viewers who watched him on television. Questioning witnesses, he would begin by saying, "Now I'm just an ol' country lawyer . . . ," as if to disavow any motive besides an innocent desire to unearth the truth. He quoted from Shakespeare and from the Bible and peppered his speech with aphorisms. Some admirers took to calling him "Uncle Sam" and sporting pins bearing that moniker. Sam Ervin T-shirts and wristwatches proliferated. During the height of the hearings, Ervin was receiving 5,000 pieces of mail a day—fan mail and hate mail, marriage proposals along with death threats. He reveled in his newfound celebrity, issuing a book, *Quotations from Chairman Sam*, and a record album, which included renditions of popular songs including "Bridge over Troubled Water," which he spoke in his familiar drawl.

At the height of his career, at age seventy-seven, Ervin chose to retire from public life. On 19 December 1973 he announced that he would not seek reelection in 1974. He was still chairing the Watergate committee, which was chartered to run through 30 June 1974. But, having brought to light an immense amount of information about the activities of Nixon and his aides, the committee had already made its main contribution to the untangling of the scandal. By this time a special prosecutor was seeking indictments and convictions of numerous White House and reelection campaign aides, and the House Judiciary Committee had undertaken hearings of its own to consider impeachment of the president.

Not wanting to prejudice the forthcoming trials or the House committee's work, Ervin decided that the Senate committee should issue a report that confined itself to a factual review of what the investigations had determined. Ervin filed the 1,094-page report on 27 June 1974. Several weeks later, on 8 August 1974, Nixon, having suffered a precipitous drop in congressional and popular support and facing almost certain impeachment, announced his resignation. Among Ervin's final achievements was the passage of the Privacy Act of 1974, signed into law by President Gerald Ford, which limited the extent to which federal agencies could collect data on private citizens.

Upon retirement, Ervin returned once more to Morganton. He continued to practice law. At first he had resolved not to write about Watergate, but after reading Nixon's memoirs, and believing them to be dishonest, he authored an account of Watergate, *The Whole Truth: The Watergate Conspiracy*, published in 1980. Later he also wrote a memoir, *Preserving the Constitution: The Autobiography of Senator Sam J. Ervin, Jr.*, published in 1985. Shortly after the latter book appeared, Ervin was beset by a series of medical problems, including emphysema and gall bladder and kidney failures. He succumbed to respiratory failure on 23 April 1985.

Dick Dabney, *A Good Man: The Life of Sam J. Ervin* (1976), is a less-than-thorough and somewhat dated biography of Ervin. For Watergate and the Ervin Committee, Theodore H. White, *Breach of Faith: The Fall of Richard Nixon* (1975), and Fred Emery, *Watergate: The Corruption of American Politics and the Fall of Richard Nixon* (1994), are useful guides. Feature articles about Ervin appear in the *New York Times* (13 May 1973), the *Washington Post* (17 May and 19 Aug. 1973), and *Time* (16 Apr. and 6 Aug. 1973). An obituary is in the *New York Times* (24 Apr. 1985).

DAVID GREENBERG

F

FARRAR, Margaret Petherbridge (*b.* 23 March 1897 in Brooklyn, New York; *d.* 11 June 1984 in New York City), an unassuming woman who served as crossword puzzle editor for the *New York Times* for nearly thirty years, thereby enormously influencing the way Americans spend their leisure time.

The daughter of Henry Wade Petherbridge, an executive with the National Licorice Company in Brooklyn, New York, and Margaret Elizabeth Furey, Margaret had one sibling, a sister. She graduated from the Berkeley Institute in Brooklyn in 1916 and from Smith College, where she majored in history, in 1919. She married the publisher and author John Chipman Farrar on 28 May 1926. The couple had three children, a son and two daughters.

Farrar's first job after receiving her B.A. degree was with the National City Bank of New York doing what she called "filing and figuring." A year later, after taking a brief secretarial course, she was hired by the Sunday editor of the *New York World*. In what Herbert Mitgang, who wrote Farrar's *New York Times* obituary, described as "almost an afterthought," the editor soon handed her the task of editing the daily crossword puzzles, a feature that had been inaugurated by the *World* in 1913. Farrar often involved some of her journalist friends (including the columnist Franklin Pierce Adams) in helping her find the best possible words for a particular puzzle. She also sought out celebrities and experts in many fields to construct puzzles built around such themes as current events, money, food, occupations, and sports.

After 1924, the now-syndicated crossword puzzles became a national addiction, a "fad" that has never failed. More and more Americans found a daily encounter with this particular form of wordplay necessary for their wellbeing. Working with two *World* writers, F. Gregory Hartswick and Prosper Buranelli, Farrar helped this increasing dependency on its way by editing the first crossword puzzle book; it was also the first book ever published by Simon and Schuster. This hit the open market in April 1924 and sold 350,000 copies in its first year. Today a biannual publication, it continues to be, despite many competitors, the longest-running series in American publishing history.

The *New York Times Sunday Magazine* added a puzzle page, under Farrar's editorship, as a regular feature in February 1942, and in September 1950 the book page in the daily *Times* started to include a crossword. "It looked," said Farrar triumphantly, "as if the crossword puzzle were here to stay!"

After her marriage to Farrar (a founding member of the publishing firm of Farrar, Straus & Giroux), she not only continued editing the *New York Times* puzzle page and the Simon and Schuster puzzle books, but also edited juveniles, cookbooks, and mysteries for her husband's publishing company. After his death in 1974, she became a member of

Margaret Farrar. NEW YORK TIMES PICTURES

the board of directors. Committee work occupied much of her time during her later years; she served such organizations as the Children's Book Committee of the Child Study Association, the Lincoln School, Scarborough School, and Smith College. A Republican and an Episcopalian, she wrote publicity for the Red Cross and the War Council during World War II.

In 1955 Farrar wrote that she was still, after thirty-five years of crossword puzzle work, "excited by the beauty and infinity of words. One of the pleasantest aspects [of my work] is the knowledge that a lot of people have a lot of fun with the puzzles."

Along with her groundbreaking efforts to popularize crossword puzzles, Farrar was largely responsible for making some enduring stylistic changes. She succeeded in moving the definitions used for clues from the commonplace and ordinary to more intriguing, intellectually challenging, and contemporary ones.

Farrar did not achieve literary fame and her name is no longer familiar to most of today's myriads of puzzle-solvers. Nonetheless, her contribution in establishing the crossword puzzle's definitive niche in American culture remains a remarkable achievement.

★

Brief sketches of Farrar appear in *Current Biography* (1955) and *Current Biography Yearbook* (1984). An obituary is in the *New York Times* (12 June 1984).

CAROL BURDICK

FELD, Irvin (*b.* 9 May 1918 in Hagerstown, Maryland; *d.* 6 September 1984 in Venice, Florida), entertainment promoter, showman, and owner of Ringling Bros. and Barnum & Bailey Circus, best remembered for turning the circus into a multimillion-dollar enterprise and founding Clown College to perpetuate traditional circus arts.

Irvin Feld was the fifth of six children of Isaac Feld and Jennie Mansch. His father ran a small clothing emporium in downtown Hagerstown that went bankrupt during the Great Depression. In the summer of 1931 Irvin and his only brother, Israel, sold snake oil from a Baltimore supply house at carnivals north and west of Hagerstown. The Feld boys earned enough money to help the family get through the winter. The following summer they increased the size of their stand and their profits.

After graduating from Park Forest High School in 1938, Irvin went to work full-time for the snake-oil company. A year later he borrowed $1,000 from his employer and, in partnership with his brother, opened his own drug-and-sundries store in a black neighborhood of Washington, D.C. When the National Association for the Advancement of Colored People offered to provide a pharmacist for his store, Feld expanded the operation to include a full pharmacy and the first integrated lunch counter in Washington, D.C.

On 5 March 1946 Feld married Adele Schwartz; they had a daughter, Karen, and a son, Kenneth. Following Adele's death in the late 1950s, Feld and his two small children moved in with Israel and his wife, Shirley. Together they raised Irvin's children and continued to build an entertainment empire.

By 1944 the Felds were producing record albums. Their fourth record, "Guitar Boogie," by the Arthur Smith Combo, sold 1 million copies. By 1949 Feld had opened four Super Music City stores in the Washington, D.C., area. That same year he began promoting musical groups with the booking of the Vaughn Monroe dance band at Constitution Hall in Washington.

In 1952 Feld booked his variety show in seven cities. Five years later he booked a similar show on a tour of eighty cities. As president and producer of Super Attractions, Inc., between 1954 and 1967, Feld pioneered the packaging of rock-and-roll and Motown tours. In 1957 he discovered, packaged, and became the personal manager of the singer Paul Anka. He remained Anka's manager until 1964.

Irvin Feld. CIRCUS WORLD MUSEUM, BARABOO, WISCONSIN

An ardent circus fan since childhood, Feld approached John Ringling North, the owner of Ringling Bros. and Barnum & Bailey Circus, in 1956 with a proposal to help the circus cut costs by booking it at auditoriums and indoor arenas. At first North refused the offer, but when he was forced to close down the circus in mid-season, North contacted Feld and together they began reshaping the circus. Feld's proposal required only that North deliver the circus on time to the places Feld booked and pay him a percentage of the gross ticket sales. In return, Feld would be responsible for booking, promoting, and advertising. By eliminating the canvas tent, the sideshow, and the menagerie, Feld reduced the number of circus employees, cut operating expenses by 30 percent, increased the performance schedule to forty-six consecutive weeks, and allowed North to pay off his debts.

Feld became concerned with the declining quality of the circus. Time had taken its toll. "Clown Alley," as the squad was known, had dwindled to thirteen aging clowns, and other performers were approaching retirement. Feld believed the only way he could make improvements was to purchase the show. On 11 November 1967 the Feld Corporation, consisting of Irvin and Israel Feld and Judge Roy Hofheinz, the operator of the Houston Astrodome, bought Ringling Bros. and Barnum & Bailey Circus from John Ringling North for $8 million.

To revitalize the circus, Feld in 1968 announced the formation of a second unit equal in quality and scale to the existing circus. To fulfill this promise of quality, Feld signed Gunther Gebel-Williams, the German animal trainer and owner of the Circus Williams, to a five-year contract by purchasing his entire circus for $2 million, moving it to the United States, and assigning all the acts and performers to the new Red Unit, a second circus equal in size and quality to the existing one, which became the Blue Unit. That same year Feld founded the Clown College in Venice, Florida, and began training a new generation of performers in the art of clowning. He also signed the first African-American circus act, the King Charles Troupe. In the years that followed, Feld hired performers from all over the world, creating a racially integrated organization.

After Israel Feld's death on 15 December 1972, Irvin's son, Kenneth, stepped in and eventually became Irvin's coproducer and business partner.

In addition to producing the circus, Feld conceived and built the Circus World theme park (1973–1984), was associate producer of the Broadway musicals *Barnum* (1980) and *The Three Musketeers* (1984), and produced the Las Vegas shows *Beyond Belief* (1981) and *One of a Kind* (1984). In 1979 he purchased *Ice Follies* and *Holiday on Ice,* which, starting in 1981, he developed into numerous Disney-themed ice shows in agreement with Disney Productions.

Throughout his life Feld contributed his time and talents to nonprofit organizations. He served on the endowment committee for the Circus World Museum, on the advisory council of the Wilmar Ophthalmology Institute, and on the board of the Johns Hopkins University School of Medicine, and he was a member of the Friars Club, the Variety Club, the Circus Saints and Sinners Club, and the National Press Club. In 1984 he received the Champion of Liberty Award from the B'nai B'rith Anti-Defamation League.

Feld died of a cerebral hemorrhage at the age of sixty-six.

Perhaps Feld's single most important contribution to the preservation of traditional circus acts was the founding of Clown College. In an interview he stated, "I would like to be remembered for having made a contribution to the continuance of the circus. It's practically all we have left of good, wholesome, clean entertainment that the whole family can enjoy." Feld's devotion to the circus ensured that the Greatest Show on Earth always would remain worthy of that name.

★

Mildred Sandison Fenner and Wolcott Fenner, comps., *The Circus: Lure and Legend* (1970), includes a short chapter on the Feld brothers. Dean Jensen, *The Biggest, the Smallest, the Longest, the Shortest: A Chronicle of the American Circus from Its Heartland* (1975), chronicles the history of the American circus, including a section on Feld's involvement with and eventual purchase of Ringling Bros. and Barnum & Bailey Circus. John Culhane, *The American Circus: An Illustrated History* (1990), traces the history of the circus in America, with numerous references to Feld. David Lewis Hammarstrom, *Big Top Boss: John Ringling North and the Circus* (1992), discusses Irvin Feld, his involvement with North, and his purchase of the circus. Ringling Bros. and Barnum & Bailey Circus Souvenir Programs, 1970–1984, contain articles about or interviews with Irvin Feld. See also "Three Purchase Ringling Circus," *New York Times* (12 Nov. 1967); "Behind the Spectacle, a Vigorous Producer," *New York Times* (25 Mar. 1970); and "The Man Who Saved the Circus," *New York Times* (11 Sept. 1984). An obituary is in the *New York Times* (7 Sept. 1984).

DIANE E. COOPER

FERGUSON, Homer Samuel (*b.* 25 February 1888 near Harrison City, Pennsylvania; *d.* 17 December 1982 in Grosse Pointe, Michigan), U.S. senator from Michigan, ambassador to the Philippines, and judge on the U.S. Court of Military Appeals, an indefatigable investigator who served on congressional committees instrumental in establishing the Central Intelligence Agency and the Department of Health, Education, and Welfare.

Senator Homer Ferguson. FROM BENTLEY HISTORICAL LIBRARY, UNIVERSITY OF MICHIGAN

"I was fortunate to love work," Ferguson wrote in 1973, "[and] to have parents who believed they had a duty and a privilege to teach their children moral and religious principles." Samuel and Margarete Bush Ferguson were farmers, but at fifteen Ferguson left the farm for a career in the coal mines; a mining accident, however, prompted him to try the professions instead. He began with schoolteaching, and even served briefly as a school principal. Homer grew up with one sister.

Ferguson attended the University of Pittsburgh in 1910 and 1911. Eventually, he "fell in love with the law" and entered the University of Michigan, where he received the bachelor of laws degree (LL.B.) in 1913. On 20 June 1913 he married Myrtle Jones and moved to Detroit. That same year he became a member of the Michigan state bar, practicing law in Detroit until 1929. From 1929 to 1939, Ferguson was a professor of law at the Detroit College of Law, while serving as a judge on the Wayne County (Michigan) Circuit Court from 1929 to 1942. During his tenure on the court Ferguson directed the one-man grand jury investigation that would launch his twelve-year career in the U.S. Senate.

In August 1939, when a clerk in a bookmaking joint committed suicide, leaving behind letters alleging corruption in Detroit municipal government, an aroused citizenry clamored for a grand jury investigation. Already a relentless investigator, Ferguson pursued the case for the next two years. When the case ended in 1941, Ferguson had secured more than 150 convictions, including the mayors of Detroit and Hamtramck, three city councillors, a district attorney, the Detroit chief of police, and various police officers. Impressed by the judge's handling of the case, Detroit voters launched a petition drive to draft Ferguson for the Senate. Running as a Republican, he defeated incumbent Democrat Prentiss Brown; Ferguson began his Senate career in January 1943.

Ferguson went to Washington determined to be a "why-man, not a yes-man." That resolve, with his reputation as a tough investigator, led to appointments on various investigative committees. His first notable assignment was the Senate Special Committee to Investigate the National Defense Program, known as the Truman Committee. Proposed by then-senator Harry S. Truman in February 1941, the task of the committee was to investigate defense contracts to achieve greater accountability and efficiency. As with the grand jury trials, Ferguson proved himself a tenacious interrogator, contributing significantly to the committee's effectiveness in saving the United States more than $1 billion in war production costs.

Ferguson also pushed for a formal investigation into the 1941 Japanese attack on Pearl Harbor to determine how U.S. forces could have been so unprepared. In June 1944 Congress issued a joint resolution directing the secretaries of war and navy to conduct such an investigation. Although both inquiries found "errors of judgment" sufficient to relieve navy admiral H. E. Kimmel and army lieutenant general Walter C. Short of their commands and demote them in rank, Ferguson was not satisfied. From the beginning, he had believed the Franklin D. Roosevelt administration guilty of forcing the attack in order to pull the United States into the war. However, because the army and navy investigations failed to implicate anyone in Washington, Ferguson was convinced that further investigation was needed. Consequently, in November 1944 he submitted a resolution calling for a congressional investigation. The subsequent hearings resulted in eight of the ten committee members filing a report that charged Short and Kimmel with failure to responsibly execute their commands; they also concluded that both army and navy intelligence practices were deficient.

However much he agreed with the majority report, Ferguson did not associate himself with it because he still was convinced that some blame lay in Washington. He and fellow senator Owen Brewster filed a minority report. Upon presenting it to Congress, Ferguson declared that even though he had no present desire to pursue the matter, "the time will come . . . when the people will learn, if it is possible . . . the whole story of the Pearl Harbor incident."

Responding to postwar fears of communism, Ferguson in March 1949 introduced a bill requiring communist organizations to register with the attorney general. The resulting Subversive Activities Control Act of 1950 was not a "thought-control bill," he asserted, but simply a measure to protect the American public from "innocent and unwitting collaboration" in un-American activities. Ferguson, however, was no McCarthyite. Always the fact seeker, he refused to support Senator Joseph McCarthy in his charges that communists were infiltrating the State Department. McCarthy, he said, had no facts to support his allegations.

Ferguson's remaining years in the Senate revolved chiefly around his work on the Hoover Commission and his 1954 reelection campaign. Actually two commissions, one formed in 1947 and one in 1953, the Hoover Commission on Organization of the Executive Branch of the Government saved some $10 billion in government expenditures and led to the establishment of the Department of Defense and the Department of Health, Education, and Welfare. Although Ferguson lost the 1954 election to Democrat Patrick V. McNamara, Congress voted to retain him on the commission until its work was completed in 1955.

Later that year, President Dwight D. Eisenhower appointed Ferguson ambassador to the Philippines but recalled him in 1956 to fill a vacant position on the U.S. Court of Military Appeals, which had been formed in 1951. Ferguson was an associate judge until 1971, then served as a senior judge until his retirement in 1976. Although the Fergusons had always kept in close contact with their daughter and her family, retirement—and residence in Grosse Pointe, Michigan—allowed more opportunity for family visits and enabled Ferguson to exercise a very different skill—oil painting. After his death of a heart ailment, Ferguson was buried at Woodlawn Cemetery in Detroit.

Uncomfortable with self-promotion, Ferguson was never a great politician. Nevertheless, Republican senator Robert A. Taft exaggerated little when he declared him "the hardest working man in Washington." Ferguson's tireless work on three major investigative committees—as well as numerous projects less prominent—caught the notice of President Eisenhower, who commended his "unusual record of achievement" and ensured Ferguson's long involvement in public service.

★

There are no full-length biographies of Homer Ferguson, and the most complete source material is the Homer Ferguson Papers, 1939–1976, housed at the Bentley Historical Library at the University of Michigan. Correspondence from Ferguson may be found in other Bentley Historical Library collections, most notably those of Owen J. Cleary, Shirley W. Smith, and Louis Carlisle Walker. A large body of material concerning the Hoover Commission, as well as correspondence from Ferguson, may be found in the library's James Kerr Pollack and Lawrence B. Lindemer collections. One autobiographical manuscript exists in the Ferguson papers, an incomplete recollection by Ferguson of the grand jury trials entitled "Fish in My Boots: The Story Behind the One-Man Grand Jury Investigation During the Years 1939, 1940 and 1941, Which Rocked the City of Detroit, Michigan," written around 1980. Thomas BeVier, "Homer Ferguson: The One-Man Grand Jury Who Nearly Indicted the Entire Municipal Government," *Detroit Free Press Magazine* (22 Jan. 1978), is an interview with Ferguson. Works discussing Ferguson's involvement with the Truman Committee and the Pearl Harbor Committee include Henry C. Clausen and Bruce Lee, *Pearl Harbor: Final Judgment* (1992), and David McCullough, *Truman* (1992). An obituary is in the *New York Times* (20 Dec. 1982).

MARILYN SAUDER MCLAUGHLIN

FETCHIT, Stepin (*b.* 30 May 1902 in Key West, Florida; *d.* 19 November 1985 in Los Angeles, California), actor who, in the 1930s, became the first African American to achieve star billing in United States film.

Lincoln Theodore Monroe Andrew Perry, known to movie audiences as Stepin Fetchit, was born just hours after his immigrant parents arrived in Key West from Nassau, the Bahamas. Employment opportunities drew his father, a cigar maker, to the United States. In 1908 the family, which also included a daughter, moved to Tampa, where Perry's father worked as a cook and a singer and his mother took in sewing. By the time Perry was eleven, both of his parents had died. He was placed in the care of a wealthy African-American woman who sent him to Saint Joseph's Academy, a private Catholic school in Montgomery, Alabama.

While his experiences at Saint Joseph's led him to embrace Catholicism, he was unhappy at the school. At thirteen, Perry ran away, joining first with the Ruben and Cherry Carnival and later with the Royal American Show, a traveling group of African-American performers providing entertainment for southern black sharecroppers and farmhands. During World War I, too young for military service, he took a job in a munitions factory in Toledo, Ohio.

After the war, Perry journeyed south, performing in a minstrel show under the name of Skeeter. While on tour in Texas, he lost all of his earnings at a racetrack. Friends then goaded him into betting his clothes against $30 on a horse that had never won a race. Miraculously, the horse, named Step and Fetch It, took first place. Perry claimed his $30 and composed a musical skit based on the incident. Shortly afterward he joined Dr. W. W. Taylor's traveling medicine show and performed the tunes of Bert Williams, America's most famous African-American vaudevillian.

In the early 1920s Perry teamed up with another black performer, Ed Lee. The duo first performed as "Lee and Skeeter" and later as "Step and Fetch It—Dixie Entertainers." They landed in Los Angeles in vaudeville in 1925; it was there that Perry decided to go solo under the name Stepin Fetchit. He struggled until he secured a part in a silent film in 1927. A series of small roles followed, and in 1929 he made his first major appearance, playing Gummy

in *Hearts in Dixie.* A romanticized view of the Old South, the film depicted blacks as happy, silly, and simpleminded, content with their subservient status. Fetchit's role epitomized this stereotype, and the actor went on to play the character repeatedly. Slow moving, slow talking, and dim-witted, with wide eyes and an exaggerated grin, Fetchit's character, who avoided work at all costs, shuffled, whined, and moaned his way through over thirty films. Fetchit received a studio contract, and by the mid-1930s he had emerged as a major motion picture star with a fortune of over $1 million. He purchased expensive suits, owned six homes attended by twelve Chinese servants, and maintained a fleet of high-priced cars, one a pink Rolls-Royce trimmed with neon lighting reading "Stepin Fetchit."

The actor was cast with the most popular stars of the era, including Shirley Temple, Jimmy Durante, and John Wayne. His appearances opposite Will Rogers won him many fans and the friendship of the cowboy star, who championed his career. Rogers's untimely death in 1935 jeopardized Fetchit's clout with the studio, and his career began to decline. He married, and a son was born in 1934; his first wife died in 1937. A series of scandals followed: he was arrested on several occasions for disorderly conduct and once for contributing to the delinquency of a minor. A palimony suit revealed he had fathered another son, Donald, in 1937. Rumors of extravagant parties and temperamental outbursts undermined his popularity. He had always challenged the white studio system, gaining a notoriety for being difficult on the set, habitually late and impossible to direct. But as his fame declined, so did his reputation. Ad-

Stepin Fetchit, 1935. TWENTIETH CENTURY–FOX/ARCHIVE PHOTOS

ditionally, by the late 1930s, African-American leaders were assailing Fetchit's reification of derogatory stereotypes. No longer a viable Hollywood commodity, he returned to vaudeville.

By 1943 Fetchit had depleted his fortune; a bankruptcy hearing revealed that he was over $3 million in debt. He opened his own production company, announcing he intended to produce films about African-American athletic heroes. But by 1947 this venture had landed him again in bankruptcy court. He hit the nightclub circuit and, during the 1950s, twice attempted to revive his film career but audiences' tastes had changed, and his character came to be commonly criticized as the symbol of racial oppression. In 1951 Fetchit married Bernice Sims of Tulsa, Oklahoma.

Fetchit became increasingly defensive, at one point even attacking civil rights leaders. In 1969 he filed a lawsuit against Bill Cosby and CBS for their documentary *Black History: Lost, Stolen, or Strayed*, alleging that their portrayal of him as a purveyor of racism was libelous. A federal judge dismissed the case in 1974, declaring that the documentary reflected on Fetchit's fictional character, not his person.

Fetchit's later years were marked by hardship. In 1964 he entered the charity ward of a Chicago hospital for prostate surgery. After recovering, he returned to the road. But in 1969 he suffered a crushing blow. While performing in a Kentucky night spot, he learned that his younger son, Donald, had committed suicide on the Pennsylvania Turnpike after shooting three people to death and wounding seventeen others.

The 1970s proved to be kinder. Fetchit appeared in two minor film roles and, in 1976, the Hollywood chapter of the National Association for the Advancement of Colored People honored him with a Special Image award. In 1978 he was elected to the Black Filmmaker's Hall of Fame. His health, however, had deteriorated. After suffering a stroke in 1976, he entered the Motion Picture Country House. In March of 1985 he was hospitalized at the Motion Picture and Television Hospital, where he died in November after fighting congestive heart failure and pneumonia. He was interred at Calvary Cemetery in Los Angeles.

Retrospective assessments of Fetchit's career are mixed. While acknowledging his character's degrading elements, some critics contend that his clownish style influenced many subsequent black comics. Others view his performance as an unimaginative attempt at marketing a demeaning image without regard to its detrimental impact on African Americans. Certainly Fetchit attempted to trade on the popularity of Bert Williams. But while Williams also employed black stereotypes, his performances contained subtle criticisms of white society, and his characters conveyed an element of humanity. Fetchit failed to achieve this depth of characterization and subversion. Yet his reputation for off-screen extravagance, his rebellion against his studio, and his fictional character, the black man who denied white society the labor it needed, does indicate defiance of white society's restrictions. But ultimately these more subversive elements were countered by the negative images perpetuated by Fetchit's on-screen persona.

★

Material on Stepin Fetchit is in a clippings file in the Margaret Herrick Library of the Academy of Motion Picture Arts and Sciences. Donald Bogle, *Toms, Coons, Mulattoes, Mammies, and Bucks: An Interpretative History of Blacks in American Films* (1973), views Fetchit's performance as negative but contends that he did forge a path for black comedians who followed him. For assessments focusing more on the demeaning aspects of his screen persona see Daniel J. Leab, *From Sambo to Superspade: The Black Experience in Motion Pictures* (1975), and Thomas Cripps, *Slow Fade to Black: The Negro in American Film, 1900–1942* (1977). Mel Watkins, *On the Real Side: Laughing, Lying, and Signifying* (1994), focuses on the relationship between the styles of Bert Williams and Fetchit. Obituaries are in the *New York Times* and the *Los Angeles Times* (both 20 Nov. 1985).

JILL WATTS

FIELDING, Temple Hornaday (*b.* 8 October 1913 in the Bronx, New York; *d.* 18 May 1983 in Palma, Majorca, Spain), travel writer who introduced Americans to the modern travel guide in 1948 with *Fielding's Travel Guide to Europe.*

Reared with an older sister and a younger brother in Stamford, Connecticut, Fielding was the son of George Thomas Fielding II, an electrical engineer, and Helen Ross Hornaday. His maternal grandfather, Dr. William Temple Hornaday, a pioneer conservationist, taxidermist, and animal collector, had helped found the Washington and Bronx zoos. A notable paternal ancestor was Henry Fielding, the English novelist. Fielding had a privileged upbringing, attending private schools in New York and Connecticut before his father suffered a financial loss in 1929 with the collapse of the stock market.

To support himself, Fielding at age sixteen began selling refrigerators around Stamford. But the company went bankrupt, and at the age of twenty-one he decided to finish high school in Stamford. One year later, in 1935, he entered Princeton University, working at odd jobs to supplement his student loans. Majoring in psychology and minoring in English, he was a leader and drum major of the Princeton University Band, a member of the senior editorial board of the *Tiger,* a contributing editor of *Nassau Lit,* captain and regimental adjutant of his ROTC unit, and a member of the Dial Lodge. In 1939 he graduated with honors and went to work as a salesman for the C.I.T. Corporation. On 17 October 1942 Fielding married Nancy Parker, a literary

Temple and Nancy Fielding with the Bay of Formentor in the background, Majorca, Spain, 1965. ARCHIVE PHOTOS

agent who was a devoted travel companion of her husband during their forty-one years of marriage. Their only child, Dodge Temple Fielding, born in 1939, became a professional writer and later joined his father's company.

In 1941 Fielding was called to active duty in the U.S. Army as a lieutenant, becoming one of the first officers to be stationed at the Field Artillery Replacement Training Center at Fort Bragg, North Carolina. During a period of five months, 550 new buildings had been constructed at the base. There was an urgent need for a guidebook for the thousands of arriving recruits, and four people tried unsuccessfully to write the guide. Brigadier General Edwin P. Parker gave the assignment to Fielding, and he successfully worked out his own format for the guide that became the model for a vast number of military-installation guides.

During World War II, Fielding was trained to be a propaganda specialist in enemy-occupied territories. He went to Algiers, Italy, and Yugoslavia to work with guerrilla forces. During 1944 he spent a considerable amount of time at Tito's headquarters. On 8 June 1945 he was discharged from the service with the rank of major. Two months before, his younger brother had been killed in action in Luzon.

Before entering the army, Fielding had begun his career as a writer with a publication in *Reader's Digest* in December 1940. He became a full-time writer in 1945 and traveled to the remote regions of Mexico for his first foreign assignment. In early 1946 he went to Europe and Africa on special

assignment for *Reader's Digest,* the *Saturday Evening Post,* and the International News Service. During the same year, he had a commission to produce a series of adventure advertisements for Canadian Club whiskey. For that purpose, he traveled in twenty-two countries and gained a wealth of information, which he later used for his first travel guide. Another assignment took Fielding across the United States, up to the Northwest Territories in Canada, to Cuba and the West Indies, and to every country in South America. In 1950 he toured Europe and Africa again. From 1946 to 1950 Fielding's work appeared in numerous magazines and newspapers, including *Cosmopolitan, Harper's Magazine, Coronet, Mademoiselle, Town and Country,* the *Baltimore Sun,* and the *Christian Science Monitor.*

Fielding's travels in foreign countries demonstrated to him the need for a book dealing with the practical aspects of touring. With the help of his wife, who provided much of the research, Fielding published *Fielding's Travel Guide to Europe* with William Sloane Associates in the spring of 1948. The guide adopted the tested format of his *Guide to Fort Bragg* and was revised annually. Fielding's manual radically departed from traditional handbooks by stressing the practical and hedonistic aspects of tourism, providing evaluations of hotels, restaurants, and airlines and steam ships, and including advice on tipping and shopping. This was achieved at the expense of coverage of cultural attractions such as museums and monuments, for Fielding believed that accommodations, meals, and shopping were the primary concerns of the pleasure traveler. "Sightseeing comes quite a bit down the list," he once remarked. Fielding told his readers where to shop and what to buy, where to stay and what to eat. His purpose was to "[ease] the path for good-hearted, well-meaning people who didn't know where they were going or what they were going to do when they got there."

Fielding spent five or six months a year, generally between November and June, in research travel, and five or six months, generally from June to November, writing at his home in Majorca, Spain, where he lived from 1951, first in a mountaintop estate in the beach resort of Formentor and, after 1982, in a penthouse in Palma. Meanwhile, the Fieldings crisscrossed Europe and traveled over a million miles, never accepting any special favors or compensation from the thousands of hotels, restaurants, and nightclubs profiled in the Fielding guides. In their travels, the Fieldings visited more than 130 countries and territories. Fielding's aim was to recommend noteworthy establishments to his readers. When he did so, he left new fortunes behind him. Because of this, he was feared by some, for his disapproval could hurt, even destroy, a business. In the preface of his guides, Fielding assured his readers that the writer of the book had slept before them in those hotels and eaten before them at those restaurants.

In addition to his travel guides, Fielding made a television series, *Fielding's in Europe,* on NBC in 1954. Beginning in 1950, *Fielding's Quick Currency Guide to Europe* was issued annually, followed in 1967 by *Currency Guide to the Far, Near, and Middle East.* Both Fieldings worked on the publication of *The Temple Fielding's Selective Shopping Guide,* which described about 1,000 regional shopping "best bets." This was begun in 1957 and was updated yearly. Nancy Fielding was also the coauthor of her husband's *Super-economy Guide to Europe,* first published in 1967.

Fielding also worked as a tour operator, organizing a luxury escorted tour in 1951 and a lower-priced guided world tour in 1954. In 1957 the Temple Fielding Epicure Club of Europe was established, offering its members a special introduction to thirty first-rank European restaurants.

In 1961, Joseph A. Raff, a former editor of the *Daily American,* published in Rome, and his wife, Judy, joined Fielding's working team. In 1966 Fielding set up his own publishing house in association with William Morrow Inc., of which William Sloane Associates was a subsidiary. In February 1983 Fielding sold his publishing corporation to Morrow with the agreement that he be retained as a consultant to the company.

Fielding's writing was unprecedented in the travel industry. A survey by the Danish National Tourist networks showed that between one-third and one-half of all American visitors to Denmark from 1948 to 1950 were directly influenced by *Fielding's Travel Guide.* The Danish government presented Fielding with the Danish Information Foundation Award, and Fielding and his family were invited to live in a house in Hornbaek on the Danish riviera and given a monthly allowance. Among his many honors, Fielding had been decorated by the governments of Spain, France, Sweden, and other countries.

A well-built man with wide shoulders and dark hair, Fielding was six feet tall and weighed 180 pounds. He had green eyes and poor eyesight, but he seldom wore glasses. He kept himself fit and enjoyed skin diving, deep-sea fishing, and duck hunting. Fielding died of a heart attack on 18 May 1983 in Palma, Majorca, Spain. He was buried in the town cemetery.

★

See Jane Howard, "The Tourist's Tourist: Close-up Guidebook Guru Temple Fielding," *Life* (3 May 1968), which features several impressive pictures illustrating Fielding's serious attitude toward his work; Edwin McDowell, "Fielding's Thirty-Five-Year Tour of Europe: His Books Won a Loyal 'Family'," *New York Times* (10 Apr. 1983); and John McPhee, "Profiles," *New Yorker* (6 Jan. 1968), and *A Roomful of Hovings and Other Profiles* (1968). An obituary is in the *New York Times* (19 May 1983).

Tian Xiao Zhang

FITZGERALD, Robert Stuart (*b.* 12 October 1910 in Geneva, New York; *d.* 16 January 1985 in Hamden, Connecticut), poet, translator, and teacher best known for his versions of Homer's *Iliad* and *Odyssey* in blank verse, which as works of art and scholarship rank among the most esteemed English translations of the ancient Greek epics.

The younger and only surviving son of Robert Emmet Fitzgerald, a lawyer, and Anne Montague Stuart, Fitzgerald grew up in Springfield, Illinois, where the family moved after his birth. He attended a Catholic elementary school and Springfield High School, where he began to write poetry, encouraged by a teacher who had known the poet Vachel Lindsay. It was Lindsay, a Springfield native, who later suggested that Fitzgerald submit his verse to the journal *Poetry,* which awarded him the Midland Author's Prize in 1931. In 1929 he finished high school at Choate, in Wallingford, Connecticut; one of his teachers was the poet and translator Dudley Fitts. As a freshman at Harvard University, Fitzgerald began to study Greek; his junior year (1931–1932; recalled in a June 1980 *Atlantic Monthly* article, "The Third Kind of Knowledge") was spent at Trinity College, Cambridge, where he read classics and philosophy. He received his A.B. from Harvard in 1933, the year T. S. Eliot was Norton lecturer. After reading some of Fitzgerald's verse, Eliot accepted two poems for publication in *Criterion.*

Certain that he wanted to write, Fitzgerald became a business reporter on the *New York Herald Tribune.* Finding this a dead end, however, he quit in 1935 to work on his first collection of lyric poetry. The somewhat mandarin tone and pessimism of *Poems* (1935) have been attributed to the influence of Ezra Pound and Eliot, but the work also reflects his own early experiences with loss: the death of his mother and younger brother before he was eight, and his father's long illness and death in 1929. The relationship of father and son is poignantly re-created in two short autobiographical stories published in the *New Yorker* in the 1970s: "Notes on a Distant Prospect" (23 February 1976) and "Light from the Bay Windows" (18 December 1978).

Shortly after the appearance of *Poems,* Fitzgerald, with his friend and mentor Fitts, did a translation of Euripides' *Alcestis* (1936), followed by one of Sophocles' *Antigone* (1939); both translations are still highly regarded for their lyricism and effectiveness as drama for modern audiences. The poets' third collaboration was on a version of Sophocles' *Oedipus Rex* (1949). During these years Fitzgerald worked intermittently as a writer and editor at *Time* magazine, taking a year's leave in 1940 and 1941 to finish his own translation of Sophocles' *Oedipus at Colonus* (1941). In 1943, the year his second volume of poetry was issued, he joined the U.S. Navy and served in the Pacific until 1946. *A Wreath for the Sea* (1943) displays the same craftsmanship

Robert Fitzgerald, 1957. AP/Wide World Photos

and precision of imagery as *Poems* but is somewhat less abstract and more mellow in tone.

On his return to civilian life Fitzgerald began his teaching career. He was an instructor in literature at Sarah Lawrence College in Bronxville, New York, from 1946 to 1953, concurrently serving (1948–1952) as poetry reviewer for the *New Republic* and as resident fellow at Princeton University (1950–1951), where he lectured on literary criticism. On 19 April 1947, a year after his divorce from the writer Eleanor Green (whom he had married in a civil ceremony in 1935), he returned to the Catholic faith and married Sarah Morgan. They had six children before separating in 1973 and were divorced in 1982.

In 1953, aware of the need for an English verse translation of the *Odyssey,* Fitzgerald decided to attempt one, and with the aid of a Guggenheim Fellowship spent the next seven years with his family in Italy, completing the project. Published in 1961, it won the Bollingen Award for Translation. Thirteen years later he did a translation of the *Iliad* (1974), which in 1976 was awarded the Harold Morton Landon Translation Prize of the Academy of American Poets. In 1976 Fitzgerald told a *New York Times* interviewer that he had used English iambic pentameter to "make something as . . . graceful [and] as sinewy" as the Greek lines, "and at the same time . . . avoid any stunting, metrical and otherwise, that might distract a reader from the main thing, which was always the dramatic action and narrative." Reviewers agreed that he had achieved his goal and that his work compared favorably with the classic translations of George Chapman and Alexander Pope, and with Richmond Lattimore's 1951 *Iliad,* while also providing "a Homer for our time." A 1976 recording of Fitzgerald reciting parts of his *Iliad* demonstrates its power as oral narrative.

Two years before his death Fitzgerald completed what some thought would be the definitive English version of Virgil's *Aeneid.* There were, as well, translations from the modern languages: the French of Paul Valéry and St.-John Perse, the Spanish of Cervantes and Jorge Luis Borges. His devotion to the art of translation has, in fact, led to the suggestion that it overshadowed his own poetry—notwithstanding receipt of the 1955 Shelley Memorial Award of the Poetry Society of America and numerous foundation grants over the years, as well as the publication of two more collections (both well received): *In the Rose of Time: Poems, 1931–1956* (1957) and *Spring Shade: Poems, 1931–1970* (1971).

As a critic, Fitzgerald's writings include *Enlarging the Change* (1985), which relates to his Princeton lectures; the "Postscripts" to his *Odyssey* and *Aeneid;* and the lengthy introductions to his editions of poetry and prose (both 1968) by James Agee, one of his colleagues at *Time,* and the short stories (1965) of Flannery O'Connor, for whom he acted as literary executor. With the *Odyssey* completed, and before essaying the *Iliad*, Fitzgerald returned to Harvard as a lecturer in 1964. The following year he was appointed Boylston Professor of Rhetoric and Oratory; he retired as emeritus professor in 1981. He was chancellor of the Academy of American Poets in 1968, a fellow of the National Institute of Arts and Letters and the American Academy of Arts and Sciences, and, in the last year of his life, consultant in poetry to the Library of Congress. A long illness prevented Fitzgerald from completing his two-year term in this post. He died at home, survived by his third wife, Penelope Laurans Fitzgerald, a former student whom he had married in 1982.

Fitzgerald is (so far) the only translator of all three classical epics into English verse. But the unique distinction of his re-creation of Homeric legend is that he narrates the experiences of the protagonists in supple, suitably colloquial language that conveys their differences in voice and character and makes them come alive. By thus preserving the dramatic impact of the original he carried on the oral tradition from which these narratives sprang and by means of which they were transmitted.

★

Penelope Laurans Fitzgerald, ed., *The Third Kind of Knowledge: Memoirs and Selected Writings* (1993), gathers Fitzgerald's short autobiographical sketches, his critical essays, and an interview published in the *Paris Review* issue devoted to "The Art of Translation" (winter 1984); the last is reprinted in George Plimpton, ed., *Writers at Work*, 8th ser. (1984). An interview with Fitzgerald in Edwin Honig, "Conversations with Translators, III," *Modern Language Notes* 91 (Dec. 1976): 1572–1602— like the *Paris Review* article—provides a firsthand account of what the poet set out to accomplish and his methods of translating. An obituary is in the *New York Times* (17 Jan. 1985).

ELEANOR F. WEDGE

FITZSIMMONS, Frank Edward (*b.* 7 April 1906 in Jeannette, Pennsylvania; *d.* 6 May 1981 in San Diego, California), union leader who succeeded Jimmy Hoffa as general president of the International Brotherhood of Teamsters, leading the nation's largest union through one of its most controversial periods.

Fitzsimmons was one of five children born to Frank and Ida May (Stabley) Fitzsimmons. His father worked in a brewery. The family moved to Detroit in the early 1920s hoping for better economic opportunities, but the health of the senior Fitzsimmons soon declined. After his father suffered a nearly fatal heart attack, the then sixteen-year-old Frank left high school and began working full-time in a factory. A year later his father died. Fitzsimmons never returned to school.

After working in an automobile hardware factory, Fitzsimmons became a bus driver for the Detroit Motor Company. In the early 1930s he took a job loading trucks and eventually became a long-haul truck driver for the CCC Trucking Company. He joined the Teamsters union in 1934 and was elected to the post of shop steward by his fellow drivers. It was in this position that he first met Jimmy Hoffa, then an ambitious business agent for Teamsters Local 299 in Detroit. Hoffa, whose own background did not include truck driving, found Fitzsimmons's ties to that sector of the union's membership useful and cultivated his support. In return Hoffa sponsored Fitzsimmons's climb up the union hierarchy. Fitzsimmons became business agent of Local 299 in 1937 and its vice president in 1940, as well as vice president of the Detroit Teamsters Joint Council. He gained regional and then national stature within the union after he became secretary-treasurer of the Michigan Conference of Teamsters in 1943. He was elected a vice president of the national Teamsters organization in 1961.

Fitzsimmons's loyalty to Hoffa, who had been elected general president of the Teamsters in 1957, was rewarded in 1966, when Hoffa, facing a thirteen-year jail sentence, positioned Fitzsimmons to lead the union in his stead. Convicted of jury tampering and mail fraud, Hoffa remained free while appealing his cases in 1966, but he faced the possibility of having to lead his union from a jail cell. To address that possibility Hoffa had the delegates to the 1966 Teamsters union convention amend the organization's constitution to create the new position of general vice president, an officer empowered to run the union in the name of the general president. Hoffa supported the election of Fitzsimmons, his loyal supporter and friend, to this new post. When Hoffa began serving his jail sentence in March 1967, Fitzsimmons became the union's acting president. He was described at the time as plodding, colorless, and weak, and many believed Hoffa had chosen him because he lacked the ability and ambition of other top Teamster leaders. It was thought that Fitzsimmons would simply do Hoffa's bidding and could be moved aside when Hoffa returned from prison.

The unassuming Fitzsimmons surprised many observers by adapting well to his new position. He was generally described as good natured and well liked, but he tended to become tongue-tied in public. Increasingly he ran the union in his own way and built up personal bonds of loyalty among the leadership that allowed him to stand in the office independently of Hoffa. Early in his tenure as acting president, Fitzsimmons told the union's executive board that he intended to let local and regional Teamster leaders operate with more autonomy. Hoffa had frequently intervened in local and regional matters, centralizing power in his office. Fitzsimmons, on the other hand, believed that his role was to serve as a spokesman for the organization

Frank Fitzsimmons, 1975. ARCHIVE PHOTOS

while exercising limited oversight of the union's operations. It was a view that the regional leadership found appealing. Fitzsimmons also won gains in the national trucking-industry contract negotiations in 1967 and 1970 and showed himself ready to set broad new policy agendas. In 1968 he negotiated with Walter Reuther of the United Automobile Workers to form a new national labor organization, the Alliance for Labor Action (founded in 1969), which they hoped would rival the conservative AFL-CIO.

Twice rejected for parole, Hoffa reasoned by summer 1971 that he would never be paroled as long as he retained his union positions. Reluctantly he resigned all of his union offices in June 1971, on the eve of the annual Teamsters convention. With Hoffa out of the picture (he would be released from prison soon thereafter), Fitzsimmons was unanimously elected as general president, a post he would hold until his death in 1981.

Controversy over the Teamsters grew steadily during Fitzsimmons's tenure. New currents of dissent emerged within the union itself in the early 1970s as younger members, apparently drawing on the same antiestablishment sentiments seen on college campuses, enlisted in insurgent organizations. Teamsters United Rank and File (TURF) and the Professional Road Drivers' Council (PROD) were founded in 1971, and Teamsters for a Decent Contract (later known as the Teamsters for a Democratic Union) began in 1975. Although their membership was relatively small, these groups proved adept at gaining press coverage for the charges of corruption and malfeasance they levied against the Fitzsimmons administration. A series of journalistic exposés on the union's largest pension plan, the Central States Pension Fund, highlighted questionable loan practices that had allegedly served to enrich various members of organized crime. Meanwhile, Jimmy Hoffa, who had been planning on running against Fitzsimmons for the presidency in 1976, disappeared in July 1975. It was assumed that he was abducted and killed by members of organized crime. His apparent murder reinforced popular suspicions that organized crime wielded great influence over the Teamsters.

Fitzsimmons vigorously defended the union against charges of corruption but undertook no substantive reform measures. Publicly he emphasized the union's achievements under his tenure. Membership had increased from 1.6 million in 1967 to 2.1 million by 1975. Wages were up and the investment return from the Central States Pension Fund compared favorably with that of other private investment funds. Stubbornly resisting calls for reform, Fitzsimmons viewed with frustration the union's continuing notoriety through the remainder of his presidency.

This notoriety extended into his family life. He and his first wife had two sons, Donald and Francis Richard. She later died, and in 1952 Fitzsimmons married Mary Patricia. Together they had two children, Gary and Carol Ann. Donald and Francis Richard became involved in union affairs, and eventually both were embroiled in charges of union corruption. Francis Richard was convicted of receiving a bribe from an employer. When Frank Fitzsimmons died of lung cancer in 1981 press reports focused on his achievements as a union leader, but they also repeated the charges of corruption and allegations that organized crime dominated the union.

★

Proceedings of the conventions of the International Brotherhood of Teamsters in 1961, 1966, 1971, 1976, and 1981 contain speeches by Fitzsimmons and personal reminiscences of those who knew him. His speeches to outside groups, collected in the union's archives in Washington, D.C., highlight his larger social vision and his response to charges of corruption. A chapter in Steven Brill, *The Teamsters* (1978), profiles Fitzsimmons, while Dan E. Moldea, *The Hoffa Wars: Teamsters, Rebels, Politicians, and the Mob* (1978), and Dan La Botz, *Rank and File Rebellion: Teamsters for a Democratic Union* (1990), contain much material about his administration and its contest with various dissident groups. A published account of his response to his critics can be found in a 1976 interview, "Cleaning Up the Teamsters: Interview with Union Chief Frank E. Fitzsimmons," *U.S. News & World Report* (26 Jan. 1976). An obituary is in the *New York Times* (7 May 1981).

DAVID S. WITWER

FIXX, James Fuller (*b.* 23 April 1932 in Flushing, New York; *d.* 20 July 1984 in Hardwick, Vermont), magazine editor and author of the best-selling *Complete Book of Running* (1977).

Jim Fixx was one of two children of Calvin Henry Fixx, a journalist for Time, Inc., and Marlys Virginia Fuller, a homemaker and graduate of Northwestern University. Fixx's father, who suffered his first heart attack at age thirty-five, died of a heart attack in 1953 at age forty-three. Jim Fixx attended the Garden Country Day School in Jackson Heights, New York, from 1947 to 1948 and Trinity School in New York City from 1948 until his graduation in June 1951. He attended Indiana University in Bloomington from 1951 to 1953 but withdrew after the death of his father, which had a profound effect on him. Fixx entered the U.S. Army on 5 February 1953; he was discharged on 23 December 1954.

Shortly after his discharge Fixx applied to and was accepted with advance standing at Oberlin College in Oberlin, Ohio, where he studied English and received his A.B. degree in 1957. At both Indiana and Oberlin, Fixx was an avid tennis player, an activity that led him, indirectly, to distance running. Fixx's Oberlin application indicates an early interest in writing fiction and essays, foretelling his future vocation in journalism. During the years 1955–1957, Fixx worked part-time during the school year and full-time during summers for the *Oberlin News-Tribune,* writing feature articles and reporting. Soon after graduation he married Mary Durling, an Oberlin classmate, with whom he had four children; the couple divorced in 1973. In 1974 he married Alice Kasman; they were later divorced.

Once out of college, Fixx was hired full-time by the *Sarasota* (Fla.) *Journal,* where he worked until 1959 as a $75-a-week reporter, feature writer, and drama critic; in the summer of 1958 he was hired as a stringer for Time, Inc. Fixx then worked briefly in 1959 as a textbook editor for Henry Holt and Co. in New York City. From 1959 to 1962 he served as a feature editor for *Saturday Review,* then as a book editor with Macmillan before returning to *Saturday Review,* where he remained until 1966. Hired as a senior editor for *McCall's* in 1966, within a month he advanced to executive editor and in 1967 was elevated to editor in chief, a position he held until 1969. That year, Fixx joined the editorial staff of *Life* and by September became senior editor. In the early 1970s, Fixx took various freelance writing, editing, and consulting assignments, contributing articles to *Newsweek, Reader's Digest,* and *Sports Illustrated.* In 1972 Doubleday published Fixx's *Games for the Superintelligent;* it was followed by *More Games for the Superintelligent* (1976) and *Solve It!* (1978). Fixx served as articles editor for *Audience* from 1971 to 1973 and after that magazine folded was hired as editor of *Horizon,* where he worked until 1976.

Fixx began running in 1967, both as a way to rehabilitate a muscle injured while playing tennis and out of concern for a hereditary predisposition to heart disease. The remarkable midlife physical transformation of Jim Fixx, a 220-pound, two-pack-a-day smoker, into a trim, 158-pound distance runner was nothing short of astonishing. In the foreword to his *Complete Book of Running,* Fixx promises to "first, introduce you to the extraordinary world of running, and second, to change your life." Fixx entered that world gradually in his late thirties, running just a half mile every three or four days. He finished last in his first-ever race, the 1967 Memorial Day road race in Greenwich, Connecticut. Within two years of first starting to run, Fixx won the Connecticut 10,000-meter title for his age category. Nevertheless, his best time at the marathon—three hours and ten minutes at Boston in 1975—placed him in the middle of the pack.

From the outset, Fixx studied the available literature on the physiological and psychological effects of long-distance running. During this period Americans generally began to focus greater attention on issues of health and diet. Dr. Ken Cooper's *Aerobics* (1968) helped launch a fitness boom in the United States during the mid-1970s, and American long-distance running had received a boost in 1972 when Frank Shorter won the Olympic gold medal in the marathon at Mexico City and a silver medal at Montreal in 1976. Although still considered more an eccentricity than a sport by some, a significant running and road-racing culture

Jim Fixx, 1978. UPI/Corbis-Bettmann

began developing in the 1970s, and Fixx himself became active in local running clubs and organizations. Hoping to liberate himself from his daily commute from Greenwich to New York City, with the aid of a $10,000 advance from Random House, Fixx devoted a year and a half to researching and writing *The Complete Book of Running*. The resulting compendium systematically covered all aspects of running, while offering the author's expertise and unique insights on the sport.

The enormous commercial success of *The Complete Book of Running* was serendipitous. Fixx's book appeared at the crest of the running boom that occurred in the late 1970s and early 1980s. It went through thirty printings and fourteen foreign editions within the first two years, selling more than one million copies and topping best-seller lists in the United States and abroad. In a highly readable, sometimes humorous, and painstakingly informed volume, Fixx explored all aspects of running for every level of runner, with an emphasis on the sport's myriad benefits. He offered readers the fresh insights of epidemiologists, psychologists, podiatrists, and fellow runners, but many of his observations were steeped in his own experience. Comprehensive yet accessible to a broad range of runners, and with particular attention devoted to women, children, and runners over forty, Fixx's book quickly became the standard text on the subject. *Jim Fixx's Second Book of Running* (1980) was inspired by the author's realization that "running possessed an importance that transcended its well-publicized physical and psychological benefits." This volume explores a wider range of subjects, such as the mind of the runner, running and the elderly, and strategies for overcoming inertia.

The financial success that *The Complete Book of Running* brought Fixx allowed him to work solely as a freelance writer from his home. A familiar face at road races in New York and Connecticut, Jim Fixx consistently ran sixty to eighty miles per week for nearly fifteen years and competed regularly in the New York and Boston marathons and at many other races in the United States and abroad. A tireless advocate for the sport and an approachable, supportive, and gracious member of the local running community, Fixx remained a reluctant celebrity and was especially uncomfortable with his new status as a "guru" of running. Nevertheless, a stream of product endorsements, nationally broadcast interviews, and lectures created a public persona synonymous with running. The irony of Jim Fixx's sudden death of a heart attack at age fifty-two, while on a solitary run in Hardwick, Vermont, prompted concern among many runners and was widely reported by the media. Fixx's family profile for coronary heart disease likely increased his vulnerability to heart attack. The question of whether running shortened Fixx's life was debated by physicians, trainers, editorial writers, and runners, though friends, family,

and supporters argued that running improved the quality of Fixx's life and may, in fact, have prolonged it.

Fixx also published *Jackpot!* (1982), an autobiographical account, and at the time of his death was at work on *The Complete Book of Sports Performance* (1985), which assembles training information for weekend athletes who do not have a coach. Fixx was a consultant to the President's Council on Physical Fitness and a member of the Governor's Council on Fitness in Connecticut. He served as president of Greenwich Fair Housing and was active in Oberlin College alumni affairs. In 1982 he donated money for building the Oberlin campus Fit-Trail, a jogging track with exercise stations. He also formed internships for creative-writing students and spoke on the Oberlin campus about running and fitness. Fixx considered himself an example of the ordinary runner—passionately dedicated to a daily activity that brought physical and spiritual sustenance, an avocation that matched perfectly with his vocation as editor and writer. The town of Greenwich hosts the annual Jim Fixx Memorial Run, the same race in which he had once finished last.

★

Archival information on Fixx is classified under Alumni Records, 1833–1995 (RG 28) in the Oberlin College Archives; Fixx's *Jackpot!* (1982) describes the unanticipated fame and fortune that his running books brought. See also Anna Quindlen, "Runner Can't Resist Telling the World About It," *New York Times* (14 Jan. 1978); Wayne Warga, "Taking Another Run at 'Complete,'" *Los Angeles Times* (3 June 1980); and Richard J. Pietschmann, "Probing Death on the Run," *Runner's World* (Nov. 1984), which explores generally the medical conditions concerning Fixx's sudden death. An obituary is in the *New York Times* (22 July 1984).

JONATHAN G. ARETAKIS

FLETCHER, Harvey (*b.* 11 September 1884 in Provo, Utah; *d.* 23 July 1981 in Provo, Utah), physicist, college professor, scientific administrator, and "father of modern acoustics."

Fletcher was one of nine children raised in a devout Mormon family by Elizabeth Miller Fletcher and Charles Eugene Fletcher, a carpenter until he lost his hearing during an illness contracted while traveling as a missionary, and later a farmer. Harvey attended Brigham Young Academy through eighth grade then saved up for tuition for Brigham Young Academy "upper school," which became Brigham Young University while he attended (1903). After receiving his B.S. degree in physics in 1907 he taught at Brigham Young in the 1907–1908 academic year. He married (Karen) Lorena Chipman of American Fork, Utah, on 9 September 1908. The couple moved to Chicago. Fletcher wanted to do graduate work at the University of Chicago

Harvey Fletcher. PHOTOGRAPHIC ARCHIVES, HAROLD B. LEE LIBRARY, BRIGHAM YOUNG UNIVERSITY, PROVO, UTAH

but the physics department would not accept his BYU degree as solid background. Dr. Robert A. Millikan permitted Fletcher to take graduate level courses on a trial basis, in which he excelled so that he became accepted as doctoral candidate.

While at Chicago, in 1909 Fletcher was introduced to a prevailing dilemma for progress in physics at that time, trying to measure the charge of the electron, denoted by *e*. Millikan, a professor in the physics department, was getting results using water droplets inserted between two parallel electronic field plates, but water evaporated too quickly for accuracy. Millikan suggested that Fletcher pursue other media as his doctoral thesis. Fletcher constructed an apparatus, purchased a perfume atomizer and watch oil from a drugstore, and began getting values for *e* that same day. He and Millikan spent years developing values for *e* and measuring and observing electrons in motion, about which Fletcher wrote five papers, one in his name for his thesis, one in Millikan's, and three coauthored.

The first paper that resulted from their collaboration described in detail the experiments (collectively known as the "Millikan Oil-Drop Experiment") leading to the exact evaluation of the charge of the electron. It was crucial in winning Millikan a Nobel Prize in physics in 1923, because it was an extremely vital step for electronics, technology,

and science. Fletcher was not bitter but grateful and utilized methods of coresearch for the rest of his life. In 1911 he received the Ph.D. summa cum laude in physics from the University of Chicago, the first to be so honored.

Devoted to the Church of Jesus Christ of Latter-day Saints and to his alma mater, Fletcher returned to Brigham Young to teach from 1911 to 1916, despite a job offer from a friend of Millikan's, Dr. Frank B. Jewett, head of research and development at AT&T. Fletcher served as department chair of physics at Brigham Young, influencing many students, including Vern O. Knudsen, who became an important architectural acoustician. In June 1916 Fletcher went to Western Electric Research Laboratories (Bell Laboratories after 1925) under Jewett, gradually taking over work on improving telephone system intelligibility.

Fletcher began unprecedented studies of speech and hearing, deaf people, degrees of deafness, linguistics, articulation, the physiology of the cochlea, and how we understand speech. Many physicists thought all there was to know about acoustics was known and that Fletcher should work on nuclear physics. However, Fletcher's studies during the 1920s resulted in many well-respected articles and the 2A audiometer. Used to measure the hearing of schoolchildren for forty years, it was a huge improvement over the tuning-fork method. He drew models of, and explained, the nonlinear filtration system for perception of sound in the cochlea and showed varying degrees of impaired hearing, which led to the field of otology, the science of the ear and its diseases. In 1924 Fletcher was awarded the Lewis Edward Levy Medal from the Franklin Institute of Philadelphia for his work in measuring audition.

Fletcher created the Linguistics Index (first in English, then other languages), which characterized, defined, organized, and grouped speech sounds by how they are produced. His index and research led to fields of psychoacoustics and speech perception (leading to artificial intelligence speech recognition) and became critical tools for poetic writing and voice lessons. He invented hearing aids, initially as large as a desk and employing vacuum tubes. Fletcher sought to make the telephone, which also used vacuum tubes, sound like the person speaking was only a meter away, a goal he ultimately realized by creating binaural speakers.

In 1925 he was appointed director of acoustical research at Bell Labs. His book *Speech and Hearing*, published in 1929, summed up his research and was the definitive work in the field. Around this point Fletcher's impact on technology becomes difficult to ascertain, because he instigated and delegated cutting-edge projects to talented colleagues and also codeveloped innumerable important ideas. A humble man, Fletcher did not demand credit for each project, but most sources readily acknowledge his contributions to the creation and development of microphones, amplifiers, phonographs, loudspeakers (woofers and tweeters), and recording devices during the 1920s and 1930s. Another example of his contributions includes those that led to the later crucial development of the transistor, originally signed under Fletcher's name at Bell Labs and later patented by the three scientists he grouped together to develop it. The transistor replaced the vacuum tube and made possible everything from the moon landing to the Internet.

Fletcher cofounded and was first president of the Acoustical Society of America (1929–1931). He also served as president of the American Federation of Organizations for the Hard of Hearing (1929–1930). In the late 1920s and early 1930s Fletcher was traveling to Hollywood frequently, working with Warner Brothers to perfect the first sound film, *The Jazz Singer* (1927), using what is now known as variable area optical sound, played on the same apparatus as the picture. For this Fletcher received the Progress Medal from the American Academy of Motion Pictures.

Fletcher's studies on loudness and his experiments with amplification branched out into work with W. A. Munson, which resulted in a definitive paper on loudness, published in 1933. Fletcher-Munson curves (commonly seen in microphone and stereo literature) accurately measure and interpret the ear's sensitivity to various frequencies at various levels, showing that the bottom end and extreme top of the range of audible frequencies disappear before the mid-range frequencies. Fletcher's loudness research determined noise thresholds and decibel standards for preventing damage to the ear. By 1933 Fletcher's work with the conductor Leopold Stokowski had resulted in the first demonstration of stereophonic sound transmission and reproduction. In 1933 Fletcher was appointed director of all physical research at Bell Labs, where he worked until he "retired" in 1949. For decades to come, however, he would still keep close tabs on and advise countless colleagues, who devotedly called him "Uncle Harvey." In 1937 Fletcher was elected vice president of the American Association for the Advancement of Science.

By April 1939 stereophonic recording had been perfected and was demonstrated at a concert in Carnegie Hall under Fletcher's careful supervision. In 1946 Fletcher presented "The Pitch, Loudness, and Quality of Musical Tones" before the American Physical Society (of which he served as president in 1945 and 1946) and other important organizations, a demonstration of a tone synthesizer. Fletcher then published an important summary of his research on musical acoustics. In 1949 he was elected an honorary member of the Audio Engineering Society. From 1949 to 1952 Fletcher served as professor of electrical engineering at Columbia University, creating the department of acoustical engineering. In 1953 *Speech and Hearing in Communication,* Fletcher's revised edition of his *Speech and Hearing* was published. It was an extremely definitive and uniquely comprehensive reference, forming the groundwork for advances in telecommunications. In 1952 he returned to Brigham Young University as dean of graduate research and then founder and first dean of the College of Engineering. Harvey Fletcher published 105 important articles and held 19 patents.

Fletcher held many positions in the Church of Latter-day Saints, and his book *The Good Life* is a compilation of his Sunday school lessons. He and his wife raised six children, of whom James was administrator of NASA from 1971 to 1977 and from 1986 to 1988. Fletcher's wife having died, he married her widowed sister, Fern Chipman Erying, in 1969. Fletcher was doing research until a month before his death, which resulted from causes incident to age at ninety-six. He is buried in American Fork, Utah.

Fletcher's pioneer research work in speech, hearing, and communication with various teams of Bell Labs scientists resulted in major breakthroughs in twentieth-century technology, including understanding of the ear, hearing aids, the artificial larynx, stereo recording, sound for movies, early television transmission, binaural headphones and headsets, amplifiers, speakers, microphones, microwave, radar, transistors, critical band theory, the Linguistic Index, the Articulation Index, Fletcher-Munson curves, huge improvements in the telephone and telecommunications, and his invention of the 2A audiometer.

★

The professional papers of Harvey Fletcher are housed at the Brigham Young University Library and University of Utah Science Archives, Salt Lake City. His personal papers are in the custody of the Fletcher family, who may be contacted through the University of Utah Science Archives. Harvey Fletcher, "My Work with Millikan on the Oil-Drop Experiment," *Physics Today* 35 (June 1982): 43–47, consists of excerpts from a manuscript autobiography. Short biographical sketches appear in the *National Cyclopedia of American Biography,* current vol. F, 1939–1942 (1942), and H. H. Sheldon and S. E. Farquhar, eds., *The Progress of Science: A Review of 1941* (1942). Obituaries are in the *New York Times* (25 July 1981), *Washington Post* (26 July 1981), and *Physics Today* 34 (Oct. 1981): 116. *The Caroling of Atoms* (1986–) is a video work-in-progress on Fletcher's life, available at the Brigham Young University Library.

J. S. CAPPELLETTI

FLORY, Paul John (*b.* 19 June 1910 in Sterling, Illinois; *d.* 9 September 1985 in Big Sur, California), physical chemist who received the 1974 Nobel Prize in chemistry for his theoretical and experimental achievements in the physical chemistry of macromolecules, which allowed the comparison of polymers, thus facilitating the development of new polymers.

Paul John Flory was the youngest of the four children of Ezra Flory and Martha (Brumbaugh) Flory. His father was a clergyman-educator; his mother had been a schoolteacher. Both of his parents were sixth-generation Americans descended from farmers and were the first in their respective families to attend college. Flory graduated from Elgin High School in 1927. He then attended Manchester College in North Manchester, Indiana, graduating in 1931 with a B.S. degree. He entered graduate school at Ohio State University, where he received his M.S. in 1931 and his Ph.D. in physical chemistry in 1934.

Flory began his professional career as a research chemist for E. I. du Pont de Nemours & Company at its experimental station in Wilmington, Delaware, joining a small group headed by Dr. Wallace H. Carothers, the inventor of nylon and neoprene. This work focused Flory's scientific pursuits on exploring the fundamentals of polymerization and polymeric materials, an area of research in its infancy in 1934. Flory married Emily Catherine Tabor on 7 March 1936. They had three children.

After the untimely death of Dr. Carothers, Flory left DuPont in 1938 and joined the Basic Science Research Laboratory of the University of Cincinnati as a research associate. After just two years, he returned to industry to assist in wartime research and development on synthetic rubber, which was in short supply at the outbreak of World War II. He worked from 1940 to 1943 as a research chemist at the Esso (now Exxon) Laboratories of the Standard Oil Development Company in Elizabeth, New Jersey. In 1943 he became director of fundamental research at the Research Laboratory of the Goodyear Tire and Rubber Company in Akron, Ohio, where he remained until 1948. Although these were industrial laboratories under severe pressure because of the war effort, Flory was able to conduct basic research and to publish much of what he was doing. Therefore, even while he was serving the vital wartime effort of the rubber industry, his reputation in the field of polymers continued to grow.

The chemistry department at Cornell University in Ithaca, New York, invited Flory to be the George Fisher Baker Non-Resident Lecturer in the spring of 1948. That fall he joined the department as professor of chemistry. Flory taught at Cornell until 1956, and while there he expanded on the Baker lectures and published his classic work *Principles of Polymer Chemistry* (1953). Concentrating on his own work, he presented a unified point of view that influenced polymer science for years. In 1956 Flory went to Pittsburgh, Pennsylvania, to become the executive director of research at the Mellon Institute. However, his attempts to undertake a "broad program of basic research" apparently were stymied by the withdrawal of promised support. This was the least productive period of his scientific life.

In 1961 Flory accepted the position of professor of

Paul Flory, 1971. STANFORD UNIVERSITY NEWS SERVICE

chemistry at Stanford University in Palo Alto, California, where he remained until his retirement. He served as chairman of the chemistry department from 1969 to 1971 and was named J. G. Jackson–C. J. Wood Professor in Chemistry in 1966. Flory was six feet tall and enjoyed swimming and playing golf.

Flory was awarded the Nobel Prize in chemistry in 1974, when he was sixty-four. The prize was awarded both for specific contributions and for a lifetime of achievement. Flory was cited for research that allowed quantification and comparison of polymers and other macromolecules. He showed that polymers dissolved in solvents achieved a kind of ideal state at a particular temperature, which became known as the Flory temperature, when the attraction forces between the links of the polymer chain balance the attractive forces between the chain and the molecules of the solvent. He demonstrated that the extension of a polymer chain in the solid state is the same as in solution at the Flory temperature. He also introduced a universal constant, known as Flory's universal constant, that quantitatively summarizes all the properties of polymer solutions. Flory used the prominence provided by the Nobel Prize to publicize human rights issues, focusing especially on the plight of Soviet scientists. He was awarded emeritus status at Stanford upon his retirement in 1976.

Flory and his wife remained in Portola Valley, California, after his retirement. Paul Flory died of a heart attack in Big Sur, California, where he was spending the weekend preparing a paper he planned to deliver to the American Chemical Society meeting in Chicago on 10 September 1985. He was cremated, and his ashes were scattered.

Flory's memory is honored by the American Chemical Society through the presentation of its Paul J. Flory Award in Polymer Education. His wife donated his personal science library to the University of Akron, Akron, Ohio, where the collection is housed in the Paul J. Flory Reading Room in the College for Polymer Science and Polymer Engineering.

All Americans have been influenced by what Flory learned about the physical chemistry of macromolecules, because the development of new polymers and the refinement of existing ones rely on his theories and techniques. Most plastics, synthetic fibers, and synthetic rubbers owe their existence, at least in part, to the pioneering work of Flory. Many of his ideas are also relevant to biological macromolecules, such as proteins and nucleic acids, which means that some important developments in health and medicine have been influenced by his work. His may not be a household name, but hardly a household has not been touched by this brilliant, committed, compassionate scientist.

★

A brief autobiography written by Flory when he received his Nobel Prize and the 15 October 1974 press release of the Royal Swedish Academy of Sciences are accessible at the following Internet site: http://nobel.sdsc.edu. His work is discussed in *Current Biography Yearbook 1975*. An obituary is in the *New York Times* (12 Sept. 1985).

JAMES R. VARNER

FONDA, Henry Jaynes (*b*. 16 May 1905 in Grand Island, Nebraska; *d*. 12 August 1982 in Los Angeles, California), stage and motion picture star noted for his sincerity and forthrightness in a time when national probity gave way to anxious questions about America's moral fiber; he was the recipient of two Academy Awards and the Life Achievement Award of the American Film Institute during a career that embraced the Depression, World War II, and ended not long after the war in Vietnam. Throughout that trajectory, he was the embodiment of honesty and decency.

Henry Fonda, known from an early age as "Hank," was the first of three children of Herberta Jaynes and William Brace Fonda. Before Henry was a year old, he moved with his parents to Omaha, Nebraska, where his father owned and operated a printing company.

Fonda had an ordinary childhood. He showed an early interest in writing, winning a short-story contest when he was ten. Upon graduating from high school in 1923, he worked his way through two years of journalism school at the University of Minnesota. In 1925, exhausted from the competing demands of academic assignments and employment, he quit and returned to Omaha. There he held a variety of jobs while attempting to find newspaper work.

Henry Fonda. POPPERFOTO/ARCHIVE PHOTOS

In 1925 Dorothy Brando, Marlon Brando's mother and a leader at the Omaha Community Playhouse, pursued Fonda to cast him as the juvenile lead in a production of Philip Barry's *You and I*. Fonda, shy and uninterested in acting, was reluctant to take the role, but Brando persisted. Although the play lasted only one week, Fonda, now hooked on acting, stayed with the theater for its nine-month season.

Merton of the Movies gave Fonda his first leading role with the Omaha Playhouse in 1927. His father, who had heretofore disapproved of his son's choice of careers, was impressed, whereupon Henry took off for New York City, where he saw nine plays in one week. He returned to Omaha and wrote a sketch for George Billings, a local impersonator, which included a part for himself. While on a three-month tour of the Midwest with Billings, Fonda made his professional debut in Des Moines, Iowa. He was promoted to assistant director upon his return to the Playhouse for the 1927–1928 season.

After three years of acting in Omaha, Fonda returned to New York. Unable to land work there, the neophyte went on to Cape Cod, where he became an assistant stage manager with the Cape Playhouse in Dennis, Massachusetts.

He played one lead, then joined the University Players, an undergraduate group from Princeton and Harvard, in Falmouth. The actors included such future notables as James Stewart, Margaret Sullavan, and Joshua Logan. As a Player, Fonda did everything from painting scenery to arranging lighting, while acting in more than forty shows and occasionally directing. When the other young actors went back to school, Fonda tried to crash New York. Even though he had no formal training, he insisted, "I was sure I was a damn good actor." His Broadway debut was a walk-on in *The Game of Love and Death* in 1929.

Critics noticed Fonda in *New Faces of 1934,* and Leland Hayward became his agent and manager. Hayward wanted him to meet Hollywood producer Walter Wanger, but the actor was not interested. The agent persisted and Fonda flew to Los Angeles; he insisted on being able to return to the theater, so Wanger included that guarantee in the contract. Fonda was about to ask for what he considered the exorbitant salary of $350 a week when Wanger offered him $1,000. Fonda was so surprised, he later said he did not remember signing the contract.

There were no films available at the moment, so Fonda returned to the stage and eventually secured the lead in *The Farmer Takes a Wife,* which opened on Broadway in October 1934. The play, which dealt with life along the Erie Canal in the 1850s, made Fonda a star. Brooks Atkinson, writing in the *New York Times,* said the performer gave "a manly, modest performance in a style of captivating simplicity."

James Stewart, Fonda's friend since the days of the University Players, appeared with him in *All Good Americans* on Broadway. The two actors roomed together and built model airplanes with fervor and glee, a practice they continued when Stewart arrived in Hollywood to begin his film career; in California, the two rented a house in Brentwood. When Fox bought the rights to *Farmer,* Fonda was the third choice to repeat his role, but he got the part, Wanger having agreed to loan him out. With his debut, Fonda's film career was secure.

From the beginning, Fonda displayed the hallmarks of an original, his dry voice and slow, thoughtful manner of speaking suggesting a man who had to investigate every possibility completely before he could even give voice to what he believed. When he reflected, it was either because the weight of the world rested on his shoulders or he was about to commit some hilarious gaffe. Fonda's thoughts were in his eyes. There's the blink as he digests the news that the Clantons have killed his brother in *My Darling Clementine* (1946), and there's the awestruck stare in *The Lady Eve* (1941) as he tries to figure out who the woman in his living room is.

In his film roles, Fonda's thoughtfulness masks a hidden sadness; the men he portrays are almost *too* sensitive, too caring. For them, intimacy can be dangerous; they seem to prefer solitude. If he can turn away from commitment in *Jezebel* (1938) and *Ash Wednesday* (1973), what will hold him? Not Clementine, whom he leaves to stride into the wilderness. Not the presidential office, which he rejects in *The Best Man* (1964). Not even his honesty, which he abandons in *There Was a Crooked Man* (1970).

His panther grace was as appropriate to the tattered overalls of a Tom Joad in *The Grapes of Wrath* (1940) as it was to the well-tailored suits of a twentieth-century businessman. There's the elegance of his Pres Dillard as he waltzes Bette Davis and her red dress to social doom in *Jezebel,* and there's the high-stepping stiffness of his Wyatt Earp maneuvering Cathy Downs, as Clementine, across raw planks in Dodge City.

In 1931 Fonda married the actress Margaret Sullavan, but by 1933 they were divorced. He married Frances Brokaw in 1936. In 1937 a daughter, Jane, was born; a son, Peter, followed in 1939. Both became famous as screen actors in the 1960s, with Jane winning two Academy Awards before her father had won his first. (Peter's daughter Bridget Fonda also became a movie star in the 1980s.) Frances, after a history of mental instability, committed suicide in 1950.

Susan Blanchard was Fonda's third wife. They were married in 1950, adopted a daughter, Amy, in 1953, and divorced in 1956. Of his fourth marriage, to Afdera Franchetti, Fonda said, "It was the craziest, most insane marriage anybody ever got into." Shirlee Mae Adams was in her late twenties when she married Fonda, who was then sixty-one. With the former airline attendant and model, he finally found happiness and stability. Of Shirlee, Fonda said, "She was worth the wait. I really feel she's the only wife I ever had."

If there is a quintessential Fonda character, it is the American outdoorsman, like the men he played in *The Grapes of Wrath* and *Drums Along the Mohawk* (1939). Western hero, sheriff, or saddle tramp, Fonda seemed connected to the soil. Although his flat, almost nasal voice limited his range, he possessed amazing versatility. Military hero, salt of the earth, Western gunman, aging sophisticate (*Sex and the Single Girl,* 1964)—he played them all with dignity and panache.

The Grapes of Wrath's Tom Joad is the role for which Fonda is best remembered. Although the Joads' indomitable mother exemplifies the family's strong bond, Tom is essentially a loner. He is taciturn, moody, and resentful. Bitter but hopeful, he leaves the family after killing the man who murdered the preacher Casy. After telling Ma, "Fella ain't got a soul of his own, just a little piece of a big soul," he explains what he envisions as his future. "I'll be all around in the dark. . . . Wherever there's a fight so hungry people can eat, I'll be there." Where the novelist John Steinbeck pleaded for justice for a powerless mass, John Ford's film made Tom the representative of that hungry multitude in its quest for a better life. After seeing Fonda in the movie, Steinbeck said, "A lean, hungry, dark-faced piece of electricity walked out on the screen and he had me. I believed my own story again."

Fonda enlisted as a seaman in the U.S. Navy in World War II. He earned a Bronze Star and presidential citation for his efforts in operations and air combat intelligence in the Pacific. In a line that presaged his role in *Mr. Roberts,* he told his chief petty officer, "I don't want to be an officer. I'll be stuck on some damn shore station doing public relations work for the rest of the war." He ended the war as a quartermaster third class.

During the middle of his career Fonda began to expand his repertoire, playing roles that explored the dark side of human nature. In *Fort Apache* (1948), he was the bristling martinet, Colonel Owen Thursday, whose refusal to see the Indians as human beings leads to the massacre of his troops. Fonda is stiff, obnoxious, and arrogant, qualities that are notable for their absence in *A Big Hand for the Little Lady* (1966), in which he portrays a lovable con man. *Firecreek* (1968) presents him for the first time as an out-and-out villain driven to live out his image as an archetype of Western individualism in the face of advancing civilization.

Fonda begins *There Was a Crooked Man* as a principled prison warden determined to rehabilitate his convicts, but then he tricks an escaped prisoner out of $500,000. The film that clinched his image as the devil on horseback was Sergio Leone's *Once Upon a Time in the West* (1969). His character starts by cold-bloodedly shooting a young boy, advances to raping the heroine, allows his crippled employer to die in the mud, and ends with a showdown with "the Man," whom he's been destined to confront from the beginning.

With the exception of his tenure at Twentieth Century–Fox from 1935 to 1947, which he mainly despised but for the work he did with director John Ford, Fonda was a free agent, a status that allowed him to return to Broadway when he wanted to. His most famous stage role was the lead in *Mr. Roberts,* which he played on Broadway for 1,077 performances beginning in 1948. He re-created the role of Doug Roberts, the World War II supply officer whose cargo ship sails "from Tedium to Apathy . . . with an occasional side trip to Monotony," for Hollywood in 1955. He is the quietly effective first officer whose job it is to plow through the backwaters of the Pacific during World War II, supplying the ships that go into battle, fights he would dearly love to be in the thick of. His second job is to oppose the petty cruelties of his captain, played with bombastic glee by James Cagney. Roberts is a quietly stirring role, a typical Fonda part, which shows him, as always, protecting his comrades from a superior's despotism.

Other notable Broadway performances included *Point of No Return* (1951), *The Caine Mutiny Court Martial* (1953), and *Two for the Seesaw* (1958). Fonda appeared with Olivia de Havilland in *A Gift of Time* (1962), which received glowing notices. Of this drama, he said, "It's the only play I've ever been in where they didn't applaud. ..... People found the play too painful to accept."

Miscast as Pierre in *War and Peace* (1956), the graceful, mature Fonda did his best to portray the man Tolstoy had depicted as a bumbling clod. The same year, in Alfred Hitchcock's *The Wrong Man,* Fonda was cast as a poor musician misidentified as a holdup man. Filmed as a semi-documentary, the movie is gritty and realistic. Again Fonda is an average man wrongly accused of a crime, buffeted by forces he is powerless to oppose. The film *12 Angry Men* (1957) is the only one Fonda ever produced (he starred in it as well). Adapted by Reginald Rose from his teleplay, the action takes place mostly in the confines of a jury room where twelve sharply contrasted men weigh the fate of a terrified boy accused of murder. Under Sidney Lumet's proficient direction the dynamic cast overcomes the contrivances of the story.

Otto Preminger's *Advise and Consent* (1962) is a panorama of Washington wheeling and dealing at its most Machiavellian. Fonda plays a nominee for secretary of state whose past as a putative communist propels the action. In the screen adaptation of Gore Vidal's play *The Best Man,* Fonda is a former secretary of state trying to secure a presidential nomination. It is a witty film à clef, in which Fonda depicts a man whose fervor to succeed taints his ideals. The performance is a mature version of his earlier roles, men whose best resolves lead to the worst results.

Henry Fonda made it to the presidency in *Fail Safe* (1964), but at a tremendous cost. When nuclear warheads are accidentally released over Moscow, Fonda annihilates New York City to avert a worldwide holocaust. It's as though Abe Lincoln had stalked into the twentieth century, only to be confronted by yet another situation he couldn't control.

Fonda appeared briefly in every episode of the television series *The Deputy* (1959–1961), but he starred in only a few. He then went on to *The Smith Family* (1971–1972). He starred in television specials and films, including *The Red Pony* (1972). In 1974 *Clarence Darrow* became his last theatrical appearance. It was a one-man show in which Fonda performed scenes from Darrow's famous trials. "All I knew about Darrow was that he defended Leopold [and] Loeb and was in the Scopes monkey trial," Fonda said. "So I went back and researched like I never remember doing for another part." The result of his studies was a portrayal not unlike his Abe Lincoln in *Young Mr. Lincoln* (1939). Both men were, like Fonda, from the Midwest, both were liberals, and both championed the oppressed. In April, near the end of this engagement, he collapsed backstage. He was fitted with a pacemaker and went through with the Los Angeles run that summer. The following year (1975), he took *Darrow* back to Broadway.

In the 1960s Fonda's children generated controversy, Jane for her position on the Vietnam War and espousal of radical causes, Peter for his association with the motorcycle and drug cult. In the 1970s their rebelliousness softened and the relationship improved. Fonda, described by both as a distant parent, said of himself, "I don't think I've been a particularly good father, but I've been lucky." Fonda saw himself as a liberal Democrat and supported Eugene McCarthy for president in 1968. Later, he backed George McGovern, but he always kept a low political profile.

"I'm not a religious man," Fonda said of *On Golden Pond* (1981), "but I thank God every morning that I lived long enough to play that role." The performance brought immense critical praise to Fonda, who played a cantankerous old codger who tries to reconcile with his estranged daughter, played by Jane Fonda. Echoes of the real-life difficulties of father and daughter resound throughout the film. Henry Fonda was an accomplished sketch artist, and when he was mulling over a suitable present to give his costar Katharine Hepburn, he hit on the idea of painting three of his hats, one of which had belonged to her late companion, Spencer Tracy. The actress was thrilled. "Working on [the film] was the best thing that could ever happen to us," Jane said. "It mirrors our own relationship."

Upon Fonda's receipt of the American Film Institute's Life Achievement Award in 1978, the actor Richard Widmark praised him as "the frontier American—part history, part folklore, part mythology." Three years later, the Academy of Motion Picture Arts and Sciences presented Fonda with an honorary Oscar for his lifetime contribution to film. The crowning glory of his career was the Oscar he won in 1982 for *On Golden Pond,* his last film. He was too ill to attend the ceremony; Jane Fonda accepted the honor for him, then rushed to present the award to her ghostlike father, who sat in a wheelchair and tried to control his tears.

Henry Fonda died of chronic heart disease at the age of seventy-seven. Americans mourned the passing of a man who for so long had reminded them of what was noblest about their country. James Cagney commented that "If [he] could do life all over again, he probably would do away with the knots that kept him from making stronger ties with more people." When tributes from his fellow actors poured in, Fonda's place in the movie community was most profoundly revealed. Jimmy Stewart said, "Hank will live in films for all time." In accordance with his wishes, Fonda's remains were cremated and no funeral service was held. He provided his own epitaph: "I ain't really Henry Fonda. Nobody could have that much integrity."

★

Fonda: My Life, as told to Howard Teichman (1981), is the result of two years of taped interviews in which the actor recounted his life, "warts and all," as he explained. See also David Shipman, *The Great Movie Stars: The Golden Years* (1970); John Shipman Springer, *The Fondas: The Films and Careers of Henry, Jane, and Peter Fonda* (1970); Michael Kerbel, *Henry Fonda* (1975); Danny Peary, *Close-Ups* (1978); Norm Goldstein, *Henry Fonda* (1982); Allen Roberts and Max Goldstein, *Henry Fonda: A Biography* (1984); Gerald Cole and Wes Farrell, *The Fondas* (1987); Tony Thomas, *The Films of Henry Fonda* (1990); Peter Collier, *The Fondas: A Hollywood Dynasty* (1991); and Kevin Sweeney, *Henry Fonda: A Bio-Bibliography* (1992). An obituary is in the *New York Times* (13 Aug. 1982).

JUDITH M. KASS

FONTANNE, Lynn (*b.* 6 December 1887 in Woodford, Essex County, England; *d.* 30 July 1983 in Genesee Depot, Wisconsin), the distaff side of the Lunts, the most famous husband-and-wife stage acting team in the world; in her sixty-one-year career, fifty-five years in partnership with her husband, Alfred Lunt, she won nearly every artistic honor and award in the field of entertainment, as well as the Presidential Medal of Freedom.

Lilly Louise Fontanne, renamed Lynn by her mother soon after her birth, was the youngest of four children (all girls) of Jules Pierre Antoine Fontanne, a type designer who owned a printing factory, and Frances Ellen Thornley Barnett. At a very early age Lynn demonstrated a talent for recitation. Her mother often allowed her to perform for guests at parties, which gave Lynn much pleasure. In school, however, she excelled in athletics rather than in the arts or sciences. She was an undistinguished student at both Buckstill School in Wessex and Windsor School. By the age of fifteen she had left school to pursue a career on the stage, for which she hitherto had received no training or education. Sophie Kean, a family friend, helped Lynn by writing a letter of introduction to Ellen Terry, one of the most famous actresses of the day. Lynn traveled to London and auditioned for Terry with Portia's mercy soliloquy from *The Merchant of Venice.* The audition so impressed Terry that she accepted Lynn as her private student.

On 26 December 1905, at the age of eighteen, Fontanne gave her first professional performance in *Cinderella,* a Christmas pantomime at the Theatre Royal, Drury Lane in London. She was only a member of the chorus but was allowed to understudy the lead role of the Fairy Queen and actually performed the role when the principal performer took ill. After her limited run in the holiday pantomime, Lynn was cast in a small role in a touring production of *Alice Sit-by-the-Fire.* In 1906 she had several small roles at the Savoy Theatre, beginning with *The Bond of Ninon,* featuring Lena Ashwell, another one of Terry's protégées. In

Lynn Fontanne. JOHN SPRINGER/CORBIS-BETTMANN

1907 she danced in *Monsieur Beaucaire* at the Lyric Theatre, where her name appeared as Viva Fontanne in the program.

Soon after, Fontanne appeared in another small role, in Beerbohm Tree's production of *The Mystery of Edwin Drood* at His Majesty's Theatre. Having difficulty in breaking out of the minor-character mode and into principal roles, she was forced to supplement her income by modeling for Wilfred and Jane de Glehn. The portrait titled *The Blue Coat,* which hangs in the Royal Academy in London, features Fontanne's likeness. On 4 January 1909 she premiered as the ingenue Rose Carlisle in Somerset Maugham's play *Lady Frederick,* which was followed by a small role in *The Peacemaker* by E. M. Bryant. Just when she thought she was on her way to larger and more significant roles, she found herself back in the chorus of *Where Children Rule* beginning 11 December 1909.

She had caught the attention, however, of Weedon Grossmith, a successful London producer, who hired her to play the role of the maid in his touring production of *Mr. Preedy and the Countess.* The tour began in March 1910 and eventually went to Montreal, Washington, D.C., and New York City. Lynn did so well in the role that Grossmith cast her in two more plays in 1911 and 1912. This led to an offer by the playwright Arnold Bennett to perform the

role of Gertrude Rhead in his *Milestones,* written with Edward Knoblock, in 1913. The show toured small villages and out-of-the-way hamlets in Great Britain and earned her little publicity. However, Knoblock featured her in another of his plays, *My Lady's Dress,* which teamed her with Edith Evans and Gladys Cooper, future stars of the British stage. On 31 October 1914 *Milestones* was revived for a London run with Fontanne reprising her touring role. This was followed by a string of minor roles in moderately successful productions, including the part of the nurse in *Searchlights,* by Horace Annesley Vachell, which opened at the Savoy Theatre in February 1915, followed by *The Terrorist, A War Committee, How to Get On,* and a musical called *The Starlight Express.*

Discouraged by the lack of success of these mediocre productions, Fontanne volunteered for military service in 1915 and was soon driving a British Army vehicle in Devonshire. Her military career was cut short when she received a cablegram from New York City inviting her to perform the role of Winifred in J. Hartley Manners's *The Wooing of Eve.* She immediately accepted the exceptionally high salary of $100 per week. This change of both country and lifestyle was the turning point in her career and personal life.

Starting on 27 November 1916 Fontanne performed the principal role of Olive Hood in another Manners play, *The Harp of Life.* The play was an outstanding success and Fontanne was highly praised in the press. This was followed by *Out There,* opening on 27 March 1917, and *Happiness,* premiering on 31 December 1917. Fontanne performed in *A Pair of Petticoats* in Chicago in 1918 and during the summer of 1918 established herself as one of the leading actresses of the New York theater with her performance of Mrs. Glendenning in the George Kaufmann play *Someone in the House.* Although a flu epidemic closed the run of the play, Fontanne's performance made her one of the most sought-after actresses on Broadway.

In the spring of 1919 Fontanne attended a rehearsal of her next play, *Made of Money,* at the New Amsterdam Theatre in New York City. It was here that she met Alfred Lunt, the play's costar, who became her husband and acting partner for life. On 26 May 1922 (one day before the announced wedding date) they were married. Fontanne had just finished her run in *Dulcy,* and Lunt's play *Intimate Strangers* was on a week's hiatus. In New York City they lived at 969 Lexington Avenue, and they established a second home, a Swedish-style farmhouse on a 120-acre farm, in Genessee Depot, Wisconsin, where Alfred Lunt's mother, Hattie, lived. The marriage brought Fontanne automatic U.S. citizenship. The Lunts were devoted to each other for the next fifty-five years; the union produced no children.

Upon their return to New York City in May 1923 the Lunts performed together in *Sweet Nell of Old Drury.* Although the obvious chemistry produced by their performances charmed critics and audiences, Lunt and Fontanne were not considered a permanent acting team until the opening on 13 October 1924 of the Theatre Guild's production of Ferenc Molnár's *The Guardsman,* in which Fontanne performed the leading role of the "actress" to her husband's title role. The play, which the Lunts also coproduced, was both an artistic and commercial success. Broadway now viewed the Lunts as an acting team, and the Theatre Guild was quick to offer the Lunts a lucrative contract that allowed Lunt and Fontanne to perform for other companies while providing them a home base with the Guild—a first in the history of actor-management contractual negotiations.

This artistic freedom resulted in Fontanne's performing for the Guild the roles of Raina in George Bernard Shaw's *Arms and the Man,* which opened on 14 September 1925; Stanja in *The Goat Song* (25 January 1926); Laura Pasquale in *At Mrs. Brown's* (26 April 1926); Eliza Doolittle in Shaw's *Pygmalion* (15 November 1926); Agrafena in *The Brothers Karamazov* (3 January 1927); Mrs. Frayne in *The Second Man* (11 April 1927), and Jennifer Dubedat in *The Doctor's Dilemma* (21 November 1927).

The Lunts' smashing success as an acting team dazzled the theater world and led to Fontanne's being offered in 1928 the character of Nina Leeds in Eugene O'Neill's *Strange Interlude.* Although Fontanne did not care much for the script and at first declined the role, Lunt urged her to accept the part because of the importance to her career of appearing in an O'Neill play—even though it would mean that they would not act as a team. Taking her husband's advice she performed the role and to her surprise received excellent reviews.

At the conclusion of *Strange Interlude* the Lunts became an acting team again and for the balance of their marriage, with *Caprice* in December 1928, *Meteor* in December 1929, *Elizabeth the Queen* in November 1930, and *Reunion in Vienna* in 1931. Perhaps the most significant decision in Fontanne's career occurred in 1931, when she and her husband reprised their roles in *The Guardsman* for a motion picture version. This could have been the beginning of a lucrative Hollywood career for the acting team, and the film world pursued them vigorously. But the Lunts rejected their suitors, claiming that they did not appreciate or embrace the artistic process of filmmaking. By rejecting films the acting artistry that the Lunts became known for was destined to be shared by relatively few people compared to what their fame could have been. The fact that both Fontanne and her husband shared each other's point of view about art and the theater so closely made them the perfect acting team.

On 24 January 1934 the Lunts returned to the stage by coproducing with Noël Coward and starring in the latter's *Design for Living* with Fontanne playing the role of Gilda. The Lunts and Coward were old friends, since before the Lunts were married. The three of them had often dreamed of the time when the Lunts would be a famous acting team and Coward would write plays for them. Their dreams came to fruition in *Design for Living,* which was the perfect comedy of manners and dialogue for the Lunts. Coward's clever, rapid-fire, witty dialogue perfectly suited Fontanne.

The following decade saw Fontanne in a repeat performance of Elena in *Reunion in Vienna,* a stunning performance in *Point Valaine* in the role of Linda Valaine, and an even more critically praised performance in the role of Katharina in *The Taming of the Shrew* on 30 September 1935, followed by the role of Irene in Robert Sherwood's Pulitzer Prize–winning play, *Idiot's Delight,* starting on 24 March 1936.

As the Lunts matured into the late 1930s and through World War II it was obvious that they were seeking more artistic challenges than their earlier romantic comedies had afforded them. The plays that followed show an evolutionary development that put Fontanne and Lunt alone at the top of their craft. These roles for Fontanne included Alkmena in *Amphitryon 38* in 1937, Irina in Anton Chekhov's *The Seagull* in 1938, a revival of *The Taming of the Shrew* in 1940, Miranda Valkonen in Sherwood's *There Shall Be No Night,* also in 1940, and Manuela in *The Pirate* in 1942.

Despite the danger of traveling between the United States and Great Britain during the war, Fontanne and Lunt performed *There Shall Be No Night* at the Aldwich Theatre in London, where she premiered in the role of Miranda on 15 December 1943. This was followed by the role of Olivia Brown in *Love in Idleness* at the Lyric Theatre beginning on 20 December 1944, followed by a tour of the play to Allied military bases in Europe in 1945. Although it would have been much less dangerous for the Lunts to continue their careers in the safe confines of Broadway, Fontanne had always thought that it was the duty of artists to commit themselves to uplifting the spirits of the population when times were hard and threatening.

After the war Lunt's health began to deteriorate. His lifelong eye problem was worsening and it was obvious to both Lynn and Alfred that they would have to choose their projects judiciously. Upon their return to the United States the Lunts agreed to perform on radio for the Theatre Guild on the Air. Between 1945 and 1952 they performed a number of broadcasts, including James Barrie's *The Old Lady Shows Her Medals.* Meanwhile, starting on 23 January 1946 Fontanne revived the character of Olivia Brown for the Empire Theatre in New York City, the play having been renamed *O Mistress Mine,* followed by a portrayal of Emily Chandler in *I Know My Love* in November 1949 and the Marchioness of Heronden in *Quadrille* in September 1952 and again in 1954. In January 1956 she performed Essie

Sebastian in *The Great Sebastians,* one of the most enjoyable characters in Fontanne's repertoire.

In 1957 the Lunts were offered a script entitled *Time and Again,* a new play by Friedrich Dürrenmatt. Fontanne knew that it might be Lunt's last performance. The roles of the female and male leads were powerful, artistic, and perfectly suited for them. Beginning on 4 January 1956 the Lunts toured the play in England with Fontanne playing the role of Claire Zachanassian. The Lunts and the play received excellent reviews and the play prepared for its American premier under the new title *The Visit.* On 1 April 1957 Fontanne revived her role of Essie in *The Great Sebastians* on television. It was carried live by the National Broadcasting System.

On 17 February 1958 the Lunts were given one of the highest honors actors can receive; the Globe Theatre in New York City was renamed the Lunt-Fontanne Theatre in their honor. Beginning on 5 May 1958 the Lunts recreated their roles in *The Visit* at the newly renamed theater, located at 205 West Forty-sixth Street. This was followed by a revival of *The Visit* at the New York City Center, premiering on 8 March 1960 and a tour to London at the Royalty Theatre beginning on 23 June 1960. In June 1963 the Lunts revived their radio broadcast of *The Old Lady Shows Her Medals* for the nationally televised *United States Steel Hour,* the television arm of the Theatre Guild. The show was greeted with critical success. Continuing with television, on 28 January 1965 the Lunts performed *The Magnificent Yankee* for the *Hallmark Hall of Fame.* Both Lunt and Fontanne received Emmy Awards for their portrayals. This performance was the last time that Fontanne and her husband acted as a team.

In September 1972 the Lunts announced their retirement from the stage. On 3 August 1977 Fontanne's husband of fifty-five years died. Six years later she died of pneumonia. She is buried in Forest Home Cemetery in Milwaukee, Wisconsin.

Lunt and Fontanne were the last of the actor-manager artists in America—performers who produced their own shows and booked their own tours, as well as playing the principal roles in the plays. Fontanne was noticed for her comedic technique and her execution of conversational dialogue that gave a sense of realism to her stage characters. During her extraordinary career she received honorary degrees from Dartmouth College, New York University, Beloit College, Carroll College, University of Wisconsin, and University of California at Los Angeles. She received a special medal for diction from the American Academy of Arts and Letters, and on 4 July 1964 President Lyndon B. Johnson awarded her the Presidential Medal of Freedom, the nation's highest civilian honor. In 1970 she received a special Tony Award for a lifetime of contribution to the theater, and in 1972 she received the American National Theatre

and Academy's first National Artist Award. On 6 December 1980 (her ninety-third birthday) she received the John F. Kennedy Center Honor for Lifetime Achievement.

★

George Freedly, *The Lunts* (1958), is a generalized but informative review of the Lunts' career and marriage. Aylesa Forsee, *My Love and I Together: The Story of Six Famous Marriages* (1961), offers an intimate look into the personal lives of the Lunts. Maurice Zolotow, *The Romance of Alfred Lunt and Lynn Fontanne* (1965), is an excellent biography of the Lunts that reviews their professional lives and includes personal details of their marriage. The definitive biography of Fontanne and Lunt is Jared Brown, *The Fabulous Lunts* (1986). Other books of interest include Walter Pritchard Eaton, *The Theatre Guild: The First Ten Years* (1929); Daniel Blum, *Great Stars of the Broadway Stage: A Pictorial Record* (1952), an interesting photographic review of major New York City Stage actors from the 1920s to the 1940s; and Brooks Atkinson, *Broadway* (1970), a thorough description of the New York stage. An obituary is in the *New York Times* (31 July 1983).

EDWARD EMANUEL

FOREMAN, Carl (*b.* 23 July 1914 in Chicago, Illinois; *d.* 26 June 1984 in Beverly Hills, California), screenwriter, producer, and director who worked on the classic films *High Noon* (1952), *The Bridge on the River Kwai* (1957), and *The Guns of Navarone* (1961).

One of two children of Isidore Foreman, a tailor, and Fanny Rozin, Russian Jewish immigrants, Foreman struggled for an education and a living during the Great Depression. After graduating from Chicago public schools, he attended the University of Illinois (1932–1933), Northwestern University (1935–1936), and John Marshall Law School (1936–1937), before seeking a career in show business. He began that career by working as a reporter, press agent, carnival barker, radio writer, little theater director, and writer of magazine fiction.

In 1938 Foreman moved to Hollywood, where his first jobs were story analyst and laboratory technician for Consolidated Film Industries. In addition he earned $85 a month by working for the Federal Writers Project. He studied screenwriting at the School for Writers, sponsored by the left-wing League of American Writers, where his mentors were writer-director Robert Rossen and writer-producer Dore Schary. In 1938 he married Estelle Barr; they had one child and were divorced in 1965.

In 1940 Foreman collaborated with Charles Marion, and they sold three scripts to Monogram Pictures for their Bowery Boys series. Although they were routine films, they qualified Foreman as a professional. He had stormed the magic castle of show business, and although he came in

Carl Foreman. AMERICAN STOCK/ARCHIVE PHOTOS

through the basement, now there was only one way to go—up.

When he entered the U.S. Army in 1942, Foreman was assigned to the prestigious Frank Capra unit as writer-producer of the Why We Fight orientation film series. He met two ambitious fellow soldiers who were to become his postwar partners, producer Stanley Kramer and publicist George Glass.

In 1945 Foreman sold *Dakota,* an original story written for John Wayne, to Republic Pictures. The following year Kramer, Glass, and Foreman established an independent film company, Screen Plays, Inc., with Foreman as writer, vice president, and treasurer. Their maiden effort was a script by Foreman and Herbert Baker. *So This Is New York* (1948), based on a Ring Lardner story, starred acerbic radio comedian Henry Morgan; it failed at the box office and with the critics. In 1949 Foreman's screenplay *Clay Pigeon* was produced by RKO. Later that year the group hit the jackpot with Foreman's hard-hitting screenplay of another Lardner story, *Champion,* which starred Kirk Douglas as a ruthless prizefighter. Foreman's career soared as he was nominated for both an Academy Award and a Writers Guild Award.

The fledgling production company followed *Champion* with another success, *Home of the Brave* (1949), Foreman's adaptation of the controversial Arthur Laurents play. The film dramatized discrimination against blacks in the U.S. Army and won Foreman his second Writers Guild nomination. The following year Foreman had three hits. He and Edmund North shared screenplay credit on another Douglas hit, *Young Man with a Horn,* which costarred Doris Day and Lauren Bacall and was based on a book portrayal of the legendary jazz musician Bix Beiderbecke. Then Foreman and his partners presented the plight of paraplegic World War II veterans in an original screenplay, *The Men,* which introduced Marlon Brando to the screen and won Foreman another pair of Academy Award and Writers Guild Award nominations. He was now rated among the most distinguished writers in Hollywood. The Kramer company next produced Foreman's screen version of the classic Edmond Rostand romantic drama *Cyrano de Bergerac,* starring Jose Ferrer (who won the Academy Award for best actor).

In 1951 Foreman wrote the script for one of the most important films of the decade, *High Noon* (1952), the story of a courageous marshal in the Old West who leaves retirement to defend his town against outlaws. Based loosely on the John Cunningham short story "The Tin Star," the film was intended to dramatize the conflict of an independent nation, like the United States, that has to fight to bring about peace in a world where it has no allies. The film starred Gary Cooper, who won the Academy Award as best actor, and was nominated as best picture. Foreman received another Academy Award nomination and won the Writers Guild Award.

In 1952, at the peak of his career, Foreman suddenly found himself a target of the House Committee on Un-American Activities (HUAC). Although he had been in the Communist party in the early 1940s, when summoned before the committee, he refused to acknowledge membership in the party or reveal names of other alleged members. For that refusal he was blacklisted in Hollywood. Foreman then ended his partnership with Kramer and Glass and sailed for England, where the State Department took away his passport. (It was returned to him in 1956, after an appearance before a member of HUAC.) In England he wrote *The Sleeping Tiger* (1954) with fellow blacklistee Harold Buchman, under the name Derek Frye. In 1957 he collaborated with Michael Wilson, also blacklisted, on the screenplay of one of the biggest hits of the year, *The Bridge on the River Kwai,* which starred William Holden and Alec Guinness. The screenplay won the Academy Award, which was given to Pierre Boulle, author of the novel on which the film was based, even though Boulle did not write in English.

Columbia Pictures ignored the blacklist and hired Foreman to write and produce a number of films. The first was

The Key (1958), starring Holden and Sophia Loren. For the second, an adaptation of an Alistair MacLean novel, *The Guns of Navarone* (1961), Foreman received an Academy Award nomination, this time under his own name. He worked steadily in England until 1975. His credits included *The Victors* (1963), which he also directed; *Mackenna's Gold* (1969); and *Young Winston* (1972), suggested by Winston Churchill after he saw *The Guns of Navarone*. This adventure story of Churchill's years in South Africa won Foreman his final Academy Award nomination. Foreman was also involved in the production of *The Mouse That Roared* (1959), *Born Free* (1966), *Otley* (1969), and *The Virgin Soldiers* (1969). In 1965 Foreman had married Evelyn Smith; they had two children. In the final decade of his life, back in Hollywood, Foreman made many deals but with few results. He received two writing credits: for the screenplay of *Force 10 from Navarone* (1978) and as cowriter with Stirling Silliphant of *When Time Ran Out* (1980).

Foreman's death was as dramatic as his life. As he lay dying of brain cancer, an old army friend, John D. Weaver, brought word that the Academy of Motion Picture Arts and Sciences was going to award him and Michael Wilson their Oscars for *The Bridge on the River Kwai*. As the writer Norman Corwin might have phrased it, he died on "a note of triumph." He was buried in Los Angeles.

★

Autobiographical articles include "The Road to the Victors," *Film and Filming* (Sept. 1963); "The Sense of Adventure," *Films and Filming* (Nov. 1969); and "Confessions of a Frustrated Screen Writer," *Film Comment* (winter 1970–1971). His blacklist experiences are described in Nancy Lynn Schwartz, *The Hollywood Writers' Wars* (1982). Obituaries are in the *New York Times* and the *Los Angeles Times* (both 27 June 1984).

MALVIN WALD

FORTAS, Abe (*b.* 19 June 1910 in Memphis, Tennessee; *d.* 5 April 1982 in Washington, D.C.), lawyer, public official, presidential adviser, and associate justice of the U.S. Supreme Court.

Fortas was the youngest of five children of Woolfe Fortas and Rachel Berzansky, Eastern Europe–born Jewish immigrants from England. His father, who changed his name to William, ran a furniture factory and later owned a men's clothing and jewelry store. The family continually struggled against economic adversity. Scholarships enabled Fortas to attend both Southwestern College at Memphis (B.A., 1930) and Yale Law School. Ranking second in his class and serving as editor in chief of the *Yale Law Journal,* he became a protégé of future Supreme Court justice William O. Douglas, then a Yale law professor. Fortas postponed an offer as assistant professor of law at Yale upon his gradua-

Abe Fortas, 1968. ARCHIVE PHOTOS

tion in 1933 to work in the administration of Franklin D. Roosevelt. He taught only one semester until 1935, when he returned to Yale for three years. Fortas moved to Washington in 1938, when he became general counsel of the Public Works Administration in the Department of the Interior, one of a series of posts mostly arranged by Douglas for him.

In 1942, having proved himself invaluable to Secretary of the Interior Harold L. Ickes, Fortas was named undersecretary of the interior. He oversaw the department's sprawling bureaucracy, engaging in numerous turf battles, supporting land reform, opposing the imposition of martial law in Hawaii, and fighting the internment of Japanese Americans. For a while, a Fortas biographer wrote, he "essentially ran Interior." He left government service in January 1946, having acquired a taste for power he never lost.

Fortas accepted an offer from Thurman Arnold, a former federal judge and assistant attorney general, to start a law firm. Two years later Paul Porter, former Federal Communications Commission chairman, joined them. Fortas was a new breed of Washington lawyer. He represented large corporate interests with as much ease and ardor as he did Owen Lattimore and other victims of the loyalty and blacklisting mania that marked the post–World War II Red

Scare. A superb legal strategist and meticulous craftsman, Fortas argued and won two landmark cases, *Durham* v. *United States* (1954), which modernized the legal definition of insanity, and before the U.S. Supreme Court, *Gideon* v. *Wainwright* (1963), which established a right to counsel regardless of ability to pay in all state felony cases. The latter decision brought him nationwide fame. To underlings he was a cold, demanding taskmaster, controlled and controlling. Fortas brought in three-quarters of the business and as managing partner ran the firm like a "benevolent dictator." Clients became his friends and he flattered influential individuals.

Prominent among these was then-senator Lyndon Johnson, whom Fortas had befriended in 1939. Johnson summoned Fortas to represent him when an opponent, Coke Stevenson, brought suit in federal court to block Johnson's eighty-seven-vote margin of victory in the 1948 Democratic senatorial primary in Texas. Fortas successfully developed the legal strategy to bring the matter in a summary way before Supreme Court Justice Hugo L. Black, who oversaw the judicial circuit of which Texas was a part. Black ruled in Johnson's favor, upholding the basic rule that federal courts have no jurisdiction in state elections. Thereafter Johnson considered Fortas "the best lawyer I know." As Senate majority leader in the 1950s Johnson regularly called on Fortas, who became Johnson's personal lawyer, for advice.

The relationship deepened during Johnson's presidency. Johnson wanted to name Fortas attorney general but Fortas refused, preferring to perform policy and legal tasks for Johnson that by 1965 were consuming nearly all his time. He also did not want to abandon an income that had reached $175,000 per year by 1964. President Johnson engineered Justice Arthur J. Goldberg's departure from the Supreme Court in July 1965 in order to appoint Fortas, which he had wanted to do for more than a year. Despite coveting the position, Fortas hesitated, which was in line with his lifelong habit of downplaying the things that mattered most to him. He claimed his firm needed him and that he could not afford the cut in salary. Johnson was persuasive, however, and Fortas was sworn in as an associate justice on 4 October 1965.

Once on the Supreme Court, Fortas immediately became part of its reformist, liberal majority. He expanded the right to symbolic speech in *Tinker* v. *Des Moines Independent Community School District* (1969), holding that students could wear black armbands to school to protest the Vietnam War. His dissent in *Time, Inc.* v. *Hill* (1967), a libel case, remains one of the strongest written defenses of the right of privacy; it reflects Fortas's aversion toward the press. His seminal opinion in *In re Gault* (1967) extended due process rights to minors in juvenile court proceedings. "Under our

Constitution the condition of being a boy does not justify a kangaroo court," he wrote.

Fortas's opinion for the Court in *Epperson* v. *Arkansas* (1968) struck down an Arkansas law that prohibited the teaching of evolution. His reason, that a prohibition brought into being due to a religious dogma or campaign could run afoul of the First Amendment's establishment-of-religion clause, raises the tantalizing possibility that had Fortas been on the Court when it later considered the abortion cases, he might have used this rationale to declare anti-abortion laws unconstitutional.

Fortas wrote these opinions while serving as principal adviser and best friend to Lyndon Johnson. He was a member of the administration in everything but name; President Johnson never made a major decision without consulting him. A private telephone line in Fortas's Supreme Court chambers connected him directly to the White House, where he spent much time, sleeping there on occasion. Every issue, foreign and domestic, even administration briefs to the Court itself, was in Fortas's bailiwick. He spoke with the president about at least three cases before the Court. In one case, *Fred Black* v. *United States* (1966), Fortas worked to protect Johnson, who was trying to place responsibility for wiretapping Black's lawyer on his political archenemy, Robert F. Kennedy.

In June 1968 Johnson nominated Fortas to replace retiring chief justice Earl Warren. Fortas became the first nominee for chief justice to appear before the Senate Judiciary Committee. Senators turned the hearings into a forum to criticize the Court's obscenity and criminal law decisions. Then came the disclosure that Fortas had received $15,000, raised by his law partner Porter from Fortas's friends and former clients, for teaching a seminar the previous summer at American University Law School. Opponents charged Fortas with lacking the necessary "sense of propriety." In October, after four days of discussion, the Senate voted to cut off debate. Fortas asked that his name be withdrawn. Johnson complied.

An article in *Life* magazine in 1969, written with the assistance of the Nixon administration, which wanted Fortas off the Court, revealed that Fortas had arranged with the foundation of a former client, Louis E. Wolfson, who had since been indicted for stock fraud, to receive $20,000 yearly during his life and that his wife, Carolyn Agger, a highly regarded tax lawyer and partner at his old firm, would receive the same if she outlived him. Justice Fortas publicly stated that he had returned the money, but the damage had been done. As the possibility of impeachment was raised, the administration claimed it had "far more serious" information than had been divulged and threatened instituting criminal charges against Fortas. The bluff worked. In May 1969 Fortas resigned to save the Supreme Court from further disgrace.

His downfall stemmed from greed and arrogance. Fortas wanted glory and money, partly to maintain a lifestyle to which he and his wife had become accustomed. "It's just as if an automobile hit me as I stepped off the curb," Fortas, who failed to acknowledge any ethical blindness, said after his resignation. "When a man goes into the White House," he later noted of Richard Nixon, "he forgets who he is and feels he can do no wrong." Few people who were not president knew the office better than Fortas.

Fortas had married Agger on 9 July 1935. They had met when Agger was an economist at the Agriculture Department in Washington. In 1938 she received her LL.B. degree from Yale Law School. They had no children. Law, politics, and music were Fortas's loves. As a child he was called "Fiddlin' Abe," and as an adult he played in regular Sunday evening chamber music sessions at his home. Even President Johnson took special care not to interrupt those sessions.

After his law firm refused to welcome him back, Fortas opened a small corporate law practice in Washington. It flourished, and in March 1982 he argued his first case before the Supreme Court since his resignation. Characteristically, he won; his generation knew no better lawyer. Fortas had the legal acumen, sympathy, courage, and rhetorical ability to become a great justice but, even aside from his short tenure on the Court, he lacked the temperament. He died in Washington of a heart attack.

★

Fortas's Supreme Court papers at Yale University will be opened in the year 2000. His law firm, now Arnold and Porter, has materials relating to his law practice. Laura Kalman, *Abe Fortas: A Biography* (1990) is a comprehensive account of Fortas's life and career. See also Robert Shogan, *A Question of Judgment: The Fortas Case and the Struggle for the Supreme Court* (1972), before publication of which Fortas threatened to sue the author for libel; and Bruce Allen Murphy, *Fortas: The Rise and Ruin of a Supreme Court Justice* (1988). On the Court for this period, see Bernard Schwartz, *Super Chief: Earl Warren and His Supreme Court—A Judicial Biography* (1983), and Roger K. Newman, *Hugo Black: A Biography* (1994). Anthony Lewis, *Gideon's Trumpet* (1964), is a classic study of *Gideon* v. *Wainwright*. Virtually every book on Lyndon Johnson mentions Fortas. See, for example, Joseph A. Califano, Jr., *The Triumph and Tragedy of Lyndon Johnson: The White House Years* (1991), and Clark Clifford with Richard Holbrooke, *Counsel to the President: A Memoir* (1991). Alexander Charns, *Cloak and Gavel: FBI Wiretaps, Bugs, Informers, and the Supreme Court* (1992) details Fortas's FBI activities. Articles on Fortas include Fred P. Graham, "The Many-Sided Justice Fortas" (4 June 1967), and Fred Rodell, "The Complexities of Mr. Justice Fortas" (28 July 1968), both from the *New York Times Magazine*.

Harold L. Ickes's diaries and papers at the Library of Congress mention Fortas frequently, as do numerous memoirs in the Columbia Oral History collection. There is much material about him in the papers of his Supreme Court colleagues and in various collections at the Lyndon B. Johnson Library, Austin, Texas, and a smaller amount in collections at the Franklin D. Roosevelt Library, Hyde Park, N.Y. An obituary is in the *New York Times* (7 Apr. 1982).

ROGER K. NEWMAN

FOSSEY, Dian (*b.* 16 January 1932 in San Francisco, California; *d.* c. 26 December 1985 in Karisoke Research Station, Ruhengeri, Rwanda, Africa), zoologist whose investigations of the mountain gorilla advanced knowledge of the great ape and spurred conservation efforts in Africa.

Dian Fossey was the only child of George Fossey III, a businessman, and Kitty Fossey, a model. Her parents divorced when Dian was just three years old, and she did not see her father again for some thirty years. As her mother needed to work, Dian was frequently left in the care of relatives.

When she was five years old, Richard Price, an entrepreneur, became her stepfather. Although Dian was now financially secure, her relationship with Price lacked intimacy. This childhood affected Dian personally for the remainder of her life. Needing affection and unsure of her relationships with others, she seemed insecure. Part of her social uncertainty came from her physical appearance; at fourteen, she was six feet, one inch tall. Uneasy around people, Dian often turned to animals for emotional support.

After completing high school, Dian began college at the University of California at Davis, majoring in animal husbandry. Two years later, concluding that her science grades were not high enough, Dian transferred to San Jose State University and changed her major to occupational therapy. After her graduation in 1954, she began work at the Kosair Crippled Children's Hospital in Louisville, Kentucky.

Shy and reserved, Dian worked well with the children. Through another worker at the hospital, she became part of the "family" surrounding Gaynee Henry, the matriarch of a large and active clan. The Henrys supplied the family life she had lacked. Still, Dian preferred to live alone with her pets.

Inspired by recent writings of George Schaller, Dian was determined to see gorillas in the wild. Thus, in 1963 she decided to go to Africa. Borrowing money, she planned a seven-week trip of travel with just a guide. In Africa she saw the gorillas and, in Olduvai Gorge in Tanzania, met Louis Leakey. A Louisville newspaper published several of her stories after she returned. When Leakey, who believed that women were ideal for studying apes, lectured at the University of Louisville in 1966, Dian met with him again and raised the issue of undertaking a study of the mountain gorilla.

Dian Fossey, Rwanda, Africa, 1985. YANN ARTHUS-BERTRAND/CORBIS

After some months of negotiations, and while Leakey sought funding for the study, Dian quit her job. She left for Africa in December 1966. Some questioned Leakey's choice; Fossey spoke none of the local languages, was ignorant of the difficult political situation in Zaire, where she was to be stationed, and had health problems that would make working in the mountains difficult. By mid-January 1967, she was alone at Kabara in the Virunga Mountains, beginning her investigation.

Although Fossey was pleased that her work had begun, she was isolated at the station and could communicate only through an English-speaking tribesman. Enamored of the gorillas, she was less than sympathetic to Africans and quickly developed a loathing for them and their culture. Fossey was uninterested in, and mostly ignorant of, the tense political situation in newly independent Zaire. As the civil war there became more vicious, most non-Africans were attacked or fled the country. Fossey was ordered off the mountain and spent about ten days in detention. She crossed into Uganda under guard but returned to Zaire.

On her return she was locked in an open cage for two days. During that period she was humiliated, terrorized, and probably sexually assaulted. She never made the extent of her ordeal totally clear but carried its scars through the rest of her life. Needing to get additional money and to register her vehicle, she managed to cross again into Uganda.

Despite her recent trauma, Fossey was determined to continue her gorilla studies at Karisoke on the Rwandan side of the border. She set up her new station under conditions that, in some ways, were more difficult than those

at the one in Zaire; Rwanda was one of the poorest and most densely populated countries in Africa. She had to overcome many problems, such as isolation, lack of funds, and lack of interest on the part of the government of Rwanda.

At Karisoke, Fossey was visited by Alan Root and John Hinde. Root filmed the dramatic sequences of Fossey making physical contact with gorillas; Hinde would become her graduate mentor at Cambridge University. As Fossey's fame spread, more and more students were sent to assist in the work. In the end, she seems to have broken with most of them, both personally and professionally.

In 1973, when she began graduate studies at Cambridge, other scholars and students felt that too much of her work was unscientific and made easy generalizations from a few experiences. It was unquantifiable and therefore could not be replicated. Nevertheless, her graduate studies continued sporadically over several years; she earned a Ph.D. in 1976. At Karisoke she exhibited increasingly hostile behavior toward Africans, both poachers and the herdsmen who encroached on the park boundaries.

A year and a half away from the field as visiting professor at Cornell University (March 1980–August 1982) did not ease the personal strain on Fossey, nor did it produce the book she had promised. Her major work, *Gorillas in the Mist,* was published in 1983. During these years, Fossey's health suffered and her asthma slowed the pace of her research; relations with others were increasingly strained. She was murdered in her cabin at Karisoke; questions remain concerning both killer and motive. Fossey was buried in the gorilla cemetery she had created at Karisoke.

Dian Fossey remains an enigma, personally and professionally. A seriously troubled woman, she spent almost twenty years studying the mountain gorilla. Hating Africans, she became devoted to the animals. No one who knew her remained neutral. Although she advanced our knowledge of this great ape, many of her colleagues questioned the scientific nature of her studies. From her own writing and letters, it is difficult to find the real Dian Fossey. She became petulant, querulous, and perhaps an alcoholic, but her life and horrible death continue to have meaning because of the world's awakened interest in the animals she loved.

★

Dian Fossey, *Gorillas in the Mist* (1983), is Fossey's personalized account of her encounters with the great ape and was the basis for a movie of the same title (1988). Harold T. P. Hayes, *The Dark Romance of Dian Fossey* (1990), is the most complete record of her life. Although sympathetic, it strives to be honest about a difficult subject. Bettyman Kevles, *Watching the Wild Apes: The Primate Studies of Goodall, Fossey, and Galdikas* (1976), consists of sections on the three students of Louis Leakey studying the great apes. This book reads as if written by Fossey's press agent. Alex Shoumatoff, *African Madness* (1988), covers some of the more serious problems facing Africa at the end of the twentieth century. In one long section it examines the work and death of Dian Fossey. Two of Fossey's articles are Dian Fossey, "More Years with Mountain Gorillas," *National Geographic* 140 (Oct. 1971), and "The Imperiled Mountain Gorilla," *National Geographic* 159 (Apr. 1981).

ART BARBEAU

FRICK, Helen Clay (*b.* 2 September 1888 in Pittsburgh, Pennsylvania; *d.* 9 November 1984 in Pittsburgh, Pennsylvania), founder of the Frick Art Reference Library and noted philanthropist.

The daughter of Henry Clay Frick and Adelaide Howard Childs, Frick, who had one brother, graduated from Miss Spence's School in New York City. Her father was a wealthy industrialist who contributed millions of dollars to a wide range of causes and founded the Frick Collection. He had a reputation for ruthlessness, however, because of his role as chairman of Carnegie Brothers and Company in the bloody Homestead strike of 1892.

Although Frick shared her father's interest in the arts from an early age, her first significant charitable endeavor was to start the Iron Rail Vacation Home for Working Girls in Wentham, Massachusetts, when she was twenty-one years old. The home offered working women from industrial communities in and around Boston a place for summer vacations. During World War I, she formed a Red Cross hospital unit and worked with it in France for six months during 1917.

Helen Clay Frick, 1919. UPI/CORBIS-BETTMANN

Frick's father died in 1919, and one year later Frick founded and financed the Frick Art Reference Library in Manhattan as a memorial to him. Inspired by her contact with art scholars, she started the library in the basement bowling alley of her posh Fifth Avenue home in New York City and eventually turned it into a major research center for the visual arts. In 1924 the library was opened to the public in a two-story building. In 1927 she founded the Frick Fine Arts Department at the University of Pittsburgh, and she financed the department for forty years. With Frick's assistance, the university built the Frick Fine Arts Library; in 1935 a thirteen-story structure was built to house the rapidly expanding Frick Art Reference Library.

During World War II, Frick and the library outlined important cultural monuments, sites, and treasures in Europe, and that information was useful in saving them from destruction by Allied bombing. The internationally renowned library, which is adjacent to the Frick Collection, holds 900,000 images of works of art, more than 72,000 auction catalogs, and more than 200,000 books and publications. Frick also served as a trustee of the Frick Collection for many years, taking an active role in directing and financing the expansion of the museum's collection.

Among her other projects, Frick purchased land around Frick Park in the east end of Pittsburgh to increase open space for public use; she restored the family mansion, Clayton, converting it into the Frick Art and Historical Center; and she backed various efforts to improve employer-employee relations in Pittsburgh. During the Great Depression, Frick led an effort called the Forty Plus Club of western Pennsylvania, which helped older unemployed men find jobs. A lifelong Republican, Frick took an active role in politics and a wide range of national causes.

In 1949 Frick marked the centennial of her father's birth by launching the well-regarded twelve-volume folio set *The Frick Collection: An Illustrated Catalogue of the Works of Art in the Collection of Henry Clay Frick* (1949–1956), which she wrote with the library and collection staff. By the time work was completed on the Frick Fine Arts Building at the University of Pittsburgh in 1965, however, relations between Frick and the university had deteriorated, and she withdrew her financial support and much of the artwork she had loaned to the school. She founded the Frick Art Museum in Pittsburgh in 1970. She remained a director of the Frick Art Reference Library until her retirement in 1983. Frick died of natural causes in Pittsburgh, where she is buried.

Much of Frick's work was dedicated to her father. In addition to advancing his name through contributions to various causes, she vigorously defended his reputation, particularly in Pittsburgh. She once sued a Pittsburgh newspaper for describing her father as a "robber baron," and in the 1960s she sought to suppress the distribution of a book that criticized her father's business ethics. Frick, who never married, played an instrumental role in advancing art scholarship. When she first started the Frick Art Reference Library and the Frick Fine Arts Department, art scholarship was not recognized as an academic pursuit and had an extremely limited audience. The work of these two institutions, however, played a major role in elevating the quality of art scholarship and in introducing it to a broader audience.

★

Further information on Frick is in Katherine McCook Knox, *The Story of the Frick Art Reference Library: The Early Years* (1979); Charles Ryskamp et al., *Art in the Frick Collection: Paintings, Sculpture, Decorative Arts* (1996); and Ray Anne Lockard, "Helen Clay Frick: Pittsburgh's Altruist and Gentlewoman Avenger," *Art Documentation* 16, no. 2 (1997).

ERIK BRUUN

FRIEDMAN, Benjamin ("Benny") (*b.* 18 March 1905 in Cleveland, Ohio; *d.* 23 November 1982 in New York City), college and professional football player, coach, and athletic administrator who was inducted into the College Football Hall of Fame in its charter class, 1951.

Friedman was one of six children of Louis and Mamie Atlevonik Friedman, immigrants from Russia. His father worked as a furrier and tailor and his mother was a homemaker. Benny's first athletic endeavors were street games with his brothers and other boys from his predominantly Jewish East Side neighborhood in Cleveland. Although compactly built, he was never tall. Impatiently waiting to grow, he exercised and went against the conventional wisdom of the day by lifting weights, which coaches feared would lead athletes to become "muscle bound." He threw heavy medicine balls and squeezed a handball to strengthen his grip. He raised a chair overhead by the bottom of one leg and tossed it from hand to hand. To widen his grip to accommodate the fat, melon-shaped football of his youth, he would press down his hand and force his thumb and little finger into a straight line, holding it in that position for as long as he could stand the considerable pain it caused.

As a sophomore at East Tech High School he was cut from the football squad after two weeks of preseason practice. When his family moved in 1921 to a new neighborhood, however, Friedman made the varsity at Cleveland's Glenville High. As a senior he stunned East Tech—and the coach who had deemed him too small—by trouncing

Benny Friedman as a Brooklyn Dodger, 1933. PRO-FILE COLLECTION

them 31–0, then led Glenville to a 13–0 win in the 1922 city football championship. Glenville went on to lay claim to what was touted as the national high-school championship by defeating Chicago's Oak Park High in a post-season game.

College representatives came to Cleveland to recruit the all-around athlete. Penn State turned lukewarm after deciding Friedman was too small at five feet, eight inches and 172 pounds. After a group of University of Michigan supporters suggested a visit to Ann Arbor, however, Friedman entered Michigan in the fall of 1923. To supplement his savings he played drums in a Chinese restaurant, was a theater ticket taker, and worked in the university bookstore for forty cents an hour. Later his godfather, Max Rosenblum, paid his tuition.

Friedman played well and honed his skills as a passer with the Wolverine freshman team, but at one time he was so discouraged that he seriously considered transferring to Dartmouth. His sophomore season under head coach George Little was even more discouraging; he did not play in the traditional rivalry game against the Michigan Aggies (now Michigan State). The next week, as Illinois and its star quarterback, Red Grange, victimized Michigan (Grange scored four touchdowns before the first quarter was over), Friedman played after the outcome was decided and threw several successful passes. Fielding Yost, who had retired from coaching the year before, instructed Little to start Friedman the next week against Wisconsin. Friedman led the Wolverines to a 21–0 victory as he ran for a touchdown and passed for two others.

In 1925 Little moved on to coach at Wisconsin and Yost came out of retirement to again coach at Michigan. Friedman now had a sophomore end, Bennie Oosterbaan, to catch his passes. At season's end, as Michigan breezed past all opponents but Northwestern (a 3–2 loss), Friedman and Oosterbaan became the first pass-catch combination to be named All-America. Years later Yost would say that his 1925 team was the best he ever had at Michigan. As a senior Friedman repeated as a consensus All-America, as did Oosterbaan, and the Wolverines had another fine season. Friedman's heroics were responsible for a pair of crucial victories. He threw for two touchdowns, kicked the extra points, and then won the Ohio State game 17–16 with a dramatic 43-yard field goal. Trailing Minnesota 6–0, Friedman's reliable toe kicked the winning conversion after Oosterbaan's 57-yard score to give Michigan a 7–6 victory. Only a 10–0 loss to Navy marred the season.

Friedman's career statistics (233 attempts and 86 completions for 1,688 yards) seem modest by modern standards, but his 27 touchdown passes remained an outstanding college record through most of the twentieth century. In any case, he earned a reputation as the greatest passer of his day in college football.

In 1927, now fully matured at five feet, ten inches and 183 pounds and with a B.A. degree in literature, Friedman joined the Cleveland Indians of the struggling National Football League (NFL). The next year he moved on to the Detroit Wolverines. He so impressed Tim Mara, owner of the New York Giants, that when Mara could not deal for Friedman he bought the entire team just to get the quarterback, paying him $10,000 a year, the highest salary in the league. From 1929 to 1931, Friedman was an outstanding team leader and drawing card.

NFL statistics did not become "official" until 1932, but subsequent research shows that from 1927 to 1930 Friedman threw 55 touchdown passes, leading the league each season—the second-place leaders in those years collectively accounted for 27. He gained 5,653 yards passing, again leading the league each year, with his closest rivals gaining 3,770. He made every All-Pro team of the era and revolutionized the game. Until then, passing was mainly a desperation measure on third down. As Giants owner Wellington Mara said of Friedman, "He changed the game. Benny would throw on first down, or any down. That was not done before." Friedman was hired by Yale University as backfield coach in 1930—the same year he married Shirley Immerman—but continued to play for the Giants and to keep the team in contention for the league championship.

In 1932, after Tim Mara would not allow him to buy into the team, Friedman became player-coach of the Brooklyn Dodgers. His passing statistics paled as his playing time lessened, but he still was the game's leading proponent and most successful practitioner of the forward pass. From 1934 to 1941 he coached football at City College of New York. After World War II he became the football coach and athletic director at Brandeis University in Waltham, Massachusetts. When Brandeis dropped the sport in 1963, Friedman left the football scene. In 1964, however, he started a football camp in Oxford, Maine, where he instructed aspiring young quarterbacks.

Despondent over the amputation of a leg, made necessary by poor circulation because of a heart condition, Friedman ended his life with a self-inflicted gunshot. He is buried in New York City.

Friedman's greatness is well documented. In 1930 he made the college All-Time All-America team. In 1947 he was chosen for the All-Time All-NFL team. He lobbied so enthusiastically for his own induction into the Pro Football Hall of Fame that he may have caused a backlash. However, in the late 1990s many football historians conceded—especially in light of previously unknown statistics of his early and best pro years—that he was worthy of serious consideration for induction.

★

Friedman's career is discussed in Harry A. March, *Pro Football, Its "Ups" and "Downs"* (1934); Don Smith, *New York Giants*

(1960); Barry Gottehrer, *The Giants of New York* (1963); Murray Olderman, *The Pro Quarterback* (1966); Myron Cope, *The Game That Was* (1970); Melissa Larson, *College Football's Great Dynasties: Michigan* (1991); and Stephen Fox, *Big Leagues* (1994).

JIM CAMPBELL

FRIEDRICH, Carl Joachim (*b.* 5 June 1901 in Leipzig, Germany; *d.* 19 September 1984 in Lexington, Massachusetts), educator and political philosopher best known for his works on constitutional government and federalism, especially *Constitutional Government and Politics* (1937; revised in 1941 as *Constitutional Government and Democracy*).

Friedrich was one of four sons born to Paul Leopold Friedrich, a distinguished professor of surgical medicine who died in 1916, and Charlotte, Baroness von Bülow, who raised the children alone after her husband's death. The economic difficulties the family underwent during the years of inflation in Germany had great influence on Friedrich, who interrupted his studies for a time to work in a coal mine. He finished his secondary education in Marburg.

The assassination in 1922 of Walther Rathenau, the Jewish foreign minister of Germany, was a profound shock to Friedrich, who later equated it with the assassination of John F. Kennedy. Friedrich attended the University of Heidelberg but, frustrated with the passivity of university life, took a leave of absence and attached himself to an international student movement that sponsored him on a lecture tour through North America in 1922. The following year he became active in the Institute for International Education in New York City, a group that sponsored academic exchange between German and American students. He fell in love with the country and with an American named Lenore Pelham. The two married on 6 October 1924; they had five children, four surviving into adulthood.

Friedrich earned his Ph.D. in history and economics from the University of Heidelberg in 1925, then emigrated to the United States and became a lecturer in the Government Department at Harvard University in 1926. He was promoted to a faculty position the following year, receiving tenure in 1931.

Any hopes he had about returning to Germany were canceled by Hitler's rise to power, and Friedrich became a naturalized U.S. citizen in 1938. A committed anti-Nazi, he vehemently opposed U.S. isolationism in the period before Pearl Harbor, calling the America First movement "fascist." Always publicly concerned about anti-Semitism, he published editorials about the plight of the European Jews in 1938 and, after World War II, spoke often in support of the foundation of the state of Israel.

Friedrich's intellectual interests focused primarily on is-

Carl J. Friedrich, 1962. AP/WIDE WORLD PHOTOS

sues of constitutional democracy and democratic state building. Influential among his early works was *The New Belief in the Common Man* (1942), which strongly emphasized his conviction that enlightened democratic rule was the strongest antidote to totalitarian violence.

Friedrich had the opportunity to test his theories during World War II. From 1943 to 1945 he served as the director of the School for Overseas Administration at Harvard, which trained military governors in anticipation of the occupation of former Axis countries. From 1946 to 1949 he served as a governmental adviser to the American military government in Germany with Henry Parkman and General Lucius Clay. Friedrich was particularly active in discussing the shape a future German constitutional government should take. Especially important was his awareness of both the weaknesses and potential strengths of Germany as a democratic nation within Europe and his willingness to voice these opinions to other influential Americans and Europeans. A strong advocate of the Marshall Plan, which provided U.S. assistance to help rebuild a ravaged postwar Europe, Friedrich authored many lectures on constitutional government and federalism and was an important American voice in discussions among the Allies about the future of the German state.

Friedrich's contribution to the drafting of the German Basic Law lay in his emphasis on the importance of the aggregate opinion of the common man, or the "working man" as he described him in his 1947 lecture "The Lasting Value of the Constitutional Idea." While Friedrich agreed that "unrestricted sovereignty of the people" can become the "worst of state orders," he nonetheless argued, in his advisory role as well as his academic one, that strong leadership regulated by a sensible populace was the road to democracy.

Friedrich remained a member of the Harvard faculty until 1971, serving jointly with the School of Public Administration and the John F. Kennedy School of Government. Throughout his later career he continued to write about constitutional issues, to boost democracy, and to criticize the Soviet Union and totalitarian rule. A wholehearted supporter of Radio Free Europe during the 1950s, Friedrich nonetheless urged the West to engage constructively with the Eastern Bloc.

In the 1950s Friedrich continued his work as a constitutional adviser and helped to formulate the constitutions of Puerto Rico and the U.S. Virgin Islands. He also prepared a draft constitution for the European Union as part of the ad hoc assembly of the Council of Europe. Through his affiliation with the Center for International Affairs at Harvard he worked to foster "informal processes" of community integration within Europe. During the 1960s he became increasingly involved in human rights issues, lecturing often at scholarly conferences and public events.

As a teacher Friedrich influenced many younger policymakers in the United States and Europe. Zbigniew Brzezinski, U.S. national security adviser from 1977 to 1981, was a student and coauthor of *Totalitarian Dictatorship and Autocracy* (1956). Friedrich also maintained close ties to universities in Germany and France. He served on the faculty of the University of Heidelberg from 1956 to 1966 and was visiting professor at the Sorbonne in Paris in 1955 and 1971.

Friedrich's most important contribution was his lifelong belief in the value of a critical allegiance to constitutional democracy. Highly respected in his native Germany, he published numerous editorials and commentaries on German politics. In recognition of his contributions to its constitution, the Federal Republic of Germany awarded Friedrich the Knight Commander's Cross of the German Order of Merit in 1967.

Friedrich lived in Cambridge, Massachusetts, after his retirement, enjoying his garden, his grandchildren, and his violoncello. He died in Pine Knoll Nursing Home in Lexington, Massachusetts, from sepsis due to Alzheimer's disease. His remains were cremated.

★

Three collections of Friedrich's papers are in the Harvard University Archives, including correspondence, lecture notes, newspaper clippings, and biographical material. Obituaries are in the *Harvard Gazette* and *Boston Globe* (both 21 Sept. 1984).

MARGARET E. MENNINGER

FULLER, R(ichard) Buckminster, Jr. (*b.* 12 July 1895 in Milton, Massachusetts; *d.* 1 July 1983 in Los Angeles, California), inventor, engineer, and philosopher best known for his design of the geodesic dome.

The second of four children of Richard Buckminster Fuller, a successful Boston tea and leather merchant, and Caroline Wolcott Andrews, a homemaker, Fuller was born into a prominent New England family (his forebears included the Transcendentalist social reformer Margaret Fuller and, on his mother's side, the colonial Connecticut governor Roger Wolcott). He was born with such poor vision that his view of the world was shaped by blurred images. Thus, when he received his first glasses at age four, it was an experience that dazzled and stimulated him for life. Two years later, while in kindergarten, he fashioned a tetrahedron-shaped device from dried peas and toothpicks that presaged his greatest architectural invention, the geodesic dome.

Fuller excelled in science and mathematics at Milton Academy but rebelled against traditional teaching methods. Following five generations of Fuller men to Harvard University in 1913, he deviated from the college's social norms by squandering his tuition money and allowance on an extravagant party for the Ziegfeld Follies chorus line in New York City and was promptly expelled. In 1914 his family sent him to work as an apprentice mechanic in a Canadian textile mill, where he so excelled in designing machine parts that he was readmitted to Harvard in 1915, only to be kicked out again for refusing to attend classes and other misdeeds.

Fuller's active mind worked best whenever it was challenged. After two years doing menial work for the Armour meatpacking company, in 1917 he obtained an ensign's commission in the wartime U.S. Navy through a ninety-day officer training course in scientific methodology at the U.S. Naval Academy. While assigned to command crash boats for naval aviation trainees at Newport News, Virginia, Fuller invented two devices to expedite air-sea rescues. He returned to Armour in 1919 as an export manager and in 1922 was briefly a national account manager with a trucking firm that soon went bankrupt.

Fuller married Anne Hewlett on 12 July 1917; they had a daughter in 1918. With his father-in-law, the prominent architect James Monroe Hewlett, he patented a method of constructing fibrous building blocks invented by Hewlett, and in 1922 they formed Stockade Building System in Chicago to produce them. His daughter suddenly died on her

R. Buckminster Fuller in front of his U.S. Pavilion at the Montreal World's Fair, 1967. UPI/Corbis-Bettmann

fourth birthday, a crushing blow that drove Fuller to become a workaholic by day and a heavy drinker by night. In 1927, soon after Fuller's second daughter was born, loss of profits forced Hewlett to sell his stocks; the new controlling stockholders blamed Fuller and discharged him. His life in ruins, he contemplated suicide.

Fuller rebounded through a personal transformation in which he vowed to reshape his thinking for the benefit of mankind. Living with his wife and child in a Chicago slum apartment for two years, he cut himself off from the world; for more than a year he spoke to no one, including his family, and he devoted his time and energy to rethinking the human condition and devising solutions to its problems. He stopped drinking, eschewed personal gain, and slept only two hours a night in order to apply his architectural skills to discovering ways for people to do more with less, as he put it. The result was what he later termed a "design-science revolution" of making machines that would liberate people from unnecessary work. Fuller coined the word "dymaxion" from "dynamic" and "maximum" and founded the Dymaxion Corporation in 1932. In 1927 and 1928 he designed a mass-produced, lightweight, hexagonal, "4-D" (fourth dimension) self-sufficient apartment house and the easily transported single-unit Dymaxion House, suspended from a central mast (to which he added a prefabricated modular bathroom in 1929). The

streamlined three-wheeled Dymaxion car, with a rear engine, was his major project from 1933 to 1935, when a fatal accident with a prototype caused such adverse publicity that Fuller had to cancel production after only three prototypes had been built. None of these inventions gained acceptance from the architectural or any other community.

From 1936 to 1938 Fuller was a research and design assistant for the Phelps Dodge Corporation, and from 1938 to 1940 he was a technical consultant for *Fortune* magazine. In 1940 he designed a steel and fiberglass Dymaxion military igloo that was produced during World War II, when he was chief of mechanical engineering for the Board of Economic Warfare. In 1943 Fuller applied his design principles to create the Dymaxion Air-ocean World Map, the first projection to depict the entire globe without visible distortion and the first of his designs to attract the interest of scientists. He founded the Dymaxion Dwelling Machines Company in 1944 to mass-produce the prefabricated Wichita House in anticipation of the postwar housing shortage but found no backers.

In 1947 and 1948 Fuller applied mathematics to his geometric use of triangles, tetrahedrons, and circles in his Dymaxion designs to develop the science of geodesics and synergetics, using tensional integrity ("tensegrity"): mutually supporting parts in the three shapes for a dome-shaped building whose lack of internal supports maximized space and whose appearance was new and aesthetically pleasing. He built the first fifty-foot-diameter geodesic dome at Black Mountain College, in North Carolina, in 1948 and incorporated Geodesics, Inc., in 1949. The Ford Motor Company commissioned Fuller in 1953 to design the ninety-three-foot plastic and aluminum dome for the rotunda of its Dearborn, Michigan, plant, an achievement that brought him international acclaim and more contracts: a helicopter-transported dome hangar for Marine Corps aircraft in 1954; radar enclosures (radomes) for the Air Force Dewline warning system across Alaska and northern Canada in 1955; and storage domes for the U.S. Navy in Antarctica in 1956, the same year that a 100-foot dome for an Afghanistan trade fair and subsequent exhibitions stimulated numerous orders.

Fuller founded Plydomes, Inc., in 1957 and the Tetrahelix Corporation in 1959 for further research and development. His largest domes, built in 1958, are the 384-foot structures covering oil-tank-car repair facilities in Louisiana and Illinois. Kaiser Aluminum had him build a 200-foot golden dome for the American Exchange Exhibition in Moscow in 1959; it dazzled Soviet leaders. His domes ranged from simple houses to immense structures at the 1962 Seattle World's Fair, the pavilion of the 1964 New York World's Fair, and the U.S. pavilion at Montreal's Expo 67 (designed with Shoji Sodao). From 1959 to 1970 Fuller was based at Southern Illinois University as research professor. From 1972 until his death he was World Fellow in residence at the University City Science Center in Philadelphia.

Fuller became a prolific commentator on "human engineering" and a guru of the counterculture with a plethora of works. Notable are *Ideas and Integrities* (1963); *Nine Chains to the Moon* (written with Robert Marks in 1938 but not acclaimed until it was reissued in 1963); *Operating Manual for Spaceship Earth, Utopia or Oblivion,* and his computerized World Game (all 1969); *I Seem to Be a Verb* (1970); *Synergetics* (with E. J. Applewhite, 1975); *On Education* (1979); and *Critical Path* (1981). Fuller also wrote three volumes of verse, and in the 1961–1962 academic year held a chair of poetry at Harvard University. He lectured widely, received numerous awards (notably the Presidential Medal of Freedom in 1983), and commanded a widespread cult following as the charismatic "Bucky." He ignored many critics who regarded him as a romantic and was not discouraged when certain of his ideas failed to gain acceptance. He held over 2,000 patents.

A small (five feet, two inches) and humble man with crewcut hair and thick glasses, Fuller held audiences spellbound for up to four hours at a stretch with a nonstop extemporaneous barrage of ideas and insights. A resident of Forest Hills, New York, in later life, he relaxed by sailing at his summer home on Bear Island, Maine. He died of a heart attack and was buried in Cambridge, Massachusetts.

★

Fuller's papers—his "chronofile"—are at Southern Illinois University. The standard biographies are Robert W. Marks, *The Dymaxion World of Buckminster Fuller* (1960); Hugh Kenner, *Bucky* (1973); and Alden Hatch, *Buckminster Fuller: At Home in the Universe* (1974). An obituary and an appreciation are in the *New York Times* (3 July 1983).

CLARK G. REYNOLDS

G

GALARZA, Ernesto, Jr. (*b.* 15 August 1905 in Jalcocotán, Nayarit, Mexico; *d.* 22 June 1984 in San Jose, California), educator and labor leader dedicated to improving the lives of agricultural workers.

Galarza was one of three children of Henriqueta and Ernesto Galarza, Sr.; his father was a hacienda manager in Miramar, Mexico, and his mother was a seamstress. After spending his earliest years traveling from place to place in Mexico, young Ernesto and his mother moved in 1911 to join relatives in Sacramento, California. There he quickly learned English, became a star pupil, and helped with family support by working a series of odd jobs. After the death of his mother Galarza continued on his own, finished high school, and began to spend his summers working in the fields near Sacramento. From this early experience he developed a lifelong commitment to ending the brutal and demeaning treatment experienced by native Hispanics and migrant Mexicans.

Throughout his life Galarza emphasized the importance of education in overcoming prejudice and empowering agricultural workers. He attended Occidental College on a scholarship, graduating with an A.B. degree in 1927, then completed an M.A. degree in history and political science at Stanford University in 1929. Shortly thereafter he married Mae Taylor, a teacher, with whom he eventually had two children.

From 1932 to 1936, Galarza and his wife codirected the Gardiner School, a progressive elementary school in the Jamaica neighborhood in the borough of Queens, New York City. In 1936 he became a research assistant with the Pan-American Union, an organization based in Washington, D.C., dedicated to promoting unity, peace, and trade. He later became chief of its Division of Labor and Social Information. Throughout this period he wrote and published extensively on Latin American affairs and especially on the problems of labor.

Following the completion of his Ph.D. in economics at Columbia University in 1947, Galarza turned his attention to migrant agricultural workers in California. He became active in the labor movement and began to write about the problems of farmworkers. In this arena he joined a dedicated coterie of such scholar-activists as George Sanchez, Arthur Campa, and Carlos Castañeda, all of whom dedicated their lives to using research and publication to counter stereotypes about Mexicans and Hispanic Americans. Through such books as *Strangers in Our Fields* (1956), *Merchants of Labor: The Mexican Bracero Story* (1964), and *Spiders in the House and Workers in the Field* (1970), Galarza effectively attacked stereotypes of Hispanic workers and demonstrated the brutal exploitation they experienced.

In addition to writing, Galarza in 1947 became one of the founding members of the National Farm Labor Union (NFLU). After some successful early organizing and support from the American Federation of Labor (AFL), the NFLU organized a strike against the Di Giorgio Vineyards in California, in an attempt to improve working conditions and gain better wages. Largely under Galarza's leadership, the NFLU aggressively conducted the strike along several creative fronts. It actively recruited and received support from other unions and coordinated boycotts of Di Giorgio products. The union also tried to build national support by picketing stores that sold the company's products. Union leaders worked with the Hollywood Film Council and the AFL to produce *Poverty in the Valley* (1949), a documentary about the problems faced by striking workers.

The strike failed, in part because use of the film back-fired. One result of gaining national attention was an investigation by the U.S. House of Representatives Committee on Education and Labor. The committee traveled to California on a fact-finding mission. Led by Congressman Richard M. Nixon, the committee produced a report condemning NFLU activities as illegal. Emboldened by the committee, Di Giorgio filed a successful libel suit against the union for its use of the film, effectively defeating the strike.

Throughout the 1950s, Galarza continued to call attention to the plight of farmworkers. He focused on ending the bracero program, which allowed for easy temporary migration of Mexican workers into the United States. Originally the program was intended to compensate for labor shortages during World War II, but after the war, growers lobbied successfully for its continuance. The end result was to depress wages and limit the possibility of successful labor organizing. Galarza used his writings and the NFLU to publicize the destructive nature of the program. He was able to attract national publicity and was a catalyst in the development of the influential documentary *Harvest of Shame* (1960), by the journalist Edward R. Murrow.

Galarza's efforts for the NFLU did not result in a major breakthrough. In 1960 the union surrendered its charter to the Agricultural Workers Organizing Committee (AWOC), which later combined with the United Farmworkers, led by César Chávez. Chávez was influenced by Galarza's methods and used many of them to win significant victories later in the decade, by which time Galarza had turned his attention to political rights for Hispanics. He served as a consultant to the U.S. Commission on Civil Rights and to the Ford Foundation. In 1963 and 1964 he worked as an adviser to the House Committee on Education and Labor, hoping that the Lyndon Johnson administration would work to ensure civil rights for Hispanics. Gradually, however, he despaired of the president's token support, and in 1967, when the Johnson administration held a major conference on Hispanics in El Paso, Texas, Galarza joined other militants in boycotting the meeting. During the same period, Galarza helped to form La Raza Unida and the Mexican-American Youth Organization, two major Chicano-rights organizations. Galarza served as the first chairman

Ernesto Galarza, Jr. STANFORD UNIVERSITY NEWS SERVICE

of La Raza Unida and used this forum to build community-based organizations to promote Hispanic causes.

In this vein, Galarza spent the early 1970s focusing his attention on community activities in the belief that the barrio and its citizens held the key to establishing Hispanic leadership. He also began to direct his activities to education. As a research associate at Notre Dame and San Jose State universities, he developed bilingual materials and wrote a series of children's books to build bridges between Hispanic and Anglo communities. Ever dedicated, Galarza continued to research, write, and advance the struggle for social justice until his death in 1984. He is buried in San Jose, California.

★

Ernesto Galarza's papers are in the Department of Special Collections of the Stanford University Libraries; see the department's *Guide to the Papers of Ernesto Galarza* (1994). Ernesto Galarza, *Barrio Boy* (1971), is an autobiographical and social history of his family's move from Mexico to the United States. Galarza's *Strangers in Our Fields* (1956) contains some autobiographical information; his *Spiders in the House and Workers in the Field* (1970) is a legal study of the Di Giorgio strike. Regional Oral History Office, Bancroft Library, University of California, *The Burning Light: Action and Organizing in the Mexican Community in California* (1982), is an oral history of Galarza and other organizers.

R. DAVID MYERS

GALLUP, George Horace (*b*. 18 November 1901 in Jefferson, Iowa; *d*. 26 July 1984 in Tschingel, Switzerland), pollster and public opinion statistician who pioneered reliable and accurate methods of public opinion sampling and was so identified with the field that his name became synonymous with polling.

The son of George Henry and Nettie (Davenport) Gallup, Gallup was raised in Jefferson, where his father speculated in farm and ranch lands and was an advocate of dry farming, a method of raising drought-resistant crops. Gallup worked his way through the University of Iowa at Iowa City and became editor of the campus newspaper, the *Daily Iowan*. A summer job in St. Louis for the D'Arcy Advertising Agency, canvassing local residents door to door to assess reader satisfaction with the *St. Louis Post-Dispatch*, started the young Gallup thinking about better ways to measure opinions. After earning his B.A. degree in 1923, he remained at Iowa as a journalism instructor while completing M.A. (1925) and Ph.D. (1928) degrees. His dissertation, "A New Technique for Objective Methods for Measuring Reader Interest in Newspapers," laid the groundwork for his future career in polling. Meanwhile, in 1925, Gallup married Ophelia Smith Miller, the daughter of a newspaper publisher. They had three children.

From 1929 to 1931 Gallup headed the journalism department at Drake University in Des Moines, Iowa. He then taught journalism and advertising at Northwestern University in Chicago for a year, while making a name for himself conducting reader-interest surveys for newspapers in the Midwest. He relocated to New York City as director of research for the Young and Rubicam advertising agency, where he worked from 1932 to 1947, becoming a vice president in 1937. He tested potential radio programs, books, and motion pictures on sample audiences. One study influenced Walt Disney's decision to produce *Alice in Wonderland*. Gallup accepted a visiting professorship at the Pulitzer School of Journalism at Columbia University, from 1935 to 1937, and founded Quill and Scroll, an international honor society for high school journalists in 1939.

His first foray into political opinion polling came in 1932 with a survey for his mother-in-law, Ola Babcock Miller, and her successful campaign for secretary of state of Iowa. It was the only time Gallup placed his polling techniques at the disposal of partisan politics. In 1935, while still working for Young and Rubicam, he and a partner, Harold R. Anderson, founded the American Institute of Public Opinion, headquartered in Princeton, New Jersey, with editorial offices in New York City, which began regular polling. The results were published in a weekly syndicated column, "America Speaks," which appeared in newspapers across the country. Today the Gallup organization operates in twenty-five countries. The Gallup Poll first gained prominence in 1936 by correctly predicting the failure of the *Literary Digest* straw poll, until then a generally accurate presidential poll. *Literary Digest* pollsters had mailed ballots to people selected from telephone directories and automobile registration lists—hardly a representative sample of the general population in the Great Depression year of 1936—and picked Republican Alf Landon to win. Gallup polled a more representative sample and correctly picked Franklin D. Roosevelt as the winner.

Since 1936 the Gallup Poll has correctly forecast the winner in all but two presidential races. In 1948, along with other pollsters, the Gallup organization predicted victory for the Republican candidate, Thomas E. Dewey, over President Harry S. Truman. Gallup attributed the error to a high number of undecided voters and the decision to discontinue polling in mid-October because Dewey had a substantial lead. Thereafter, presidential opinion polling has continued up to election day. The second error came in 1976, in a race that most pollsters said was too close to call. Gallup picked Gerald R. Ford to win 47 percent to 46 per-

George Gallup. ARCHIVE PHOTOS

cent, but Jimmy Carter was the winner with 50.1 percent of the vote. Gallup made numerous public appearances, published many articles, and wrote a number of books, including *The Pulse of Democracy: The Public-Opinion Poll and How It Works* (1940); *The Miracle Ahead* (1964); *The Sophisticated Poll Watcher's Guide* (1972); and *America Wants to Know: The Issues and the Answers of the Eighties* (1983).

Described as a friendly man, Gallup was an Episcopalian. He held honorary degrees from twelve colleges and universities, memberships in several professional societies, and was the recipient of numerous awards. He died of a heart attack near the Lake of Thun in central Switzerland and was buried in Princeton, New Jersey.

Gallup's major contribution was his demonstration that by interviewing a comparatively small but representative sample a public opinion poll could produce reliable results. The Gallup organization typically polls samples as small as 1,500 to 3,000 in the United States and 1,000 in European countries. Polling became so ubiquitous that a survey conducted in 1975 found that one in seven Americans over the age of eighteen had been interviewed in a public opinion poll. Gallup defended opinion polling as "one of the most useful instruments of democracy ever devised." Critics, however, often termed this a naive view and complained that polls exercised undue influence on political leaders, created a bandwagon effect, and were used by business and political leaders to manipulate public opinion. Gallup rejected such criticism, contending in *The Sophisticated Poll Watcher's Guide* that "polling is merely an instrument for gauging public opinion. When a President, or any other leader, pays attention to poll results, he is, in effect, paying attention to the views of the people. Any other interpretation is nonsense."

His populist views led him to favor term limits for federal officeholders, the abolition of the Electoral College, and the establishment of a national presidential primary. Toward the end of his life he spent summers in Switzerland, a country he loved not only for its scenic beauty but also for its reliance on political referenda—letting the people participate directly in decision making. In 1990 *Life* magazine listed Gallup as one of the 100 most important Americans of the twentieth century.

★

Rena Bartos's historic 1977 interview, "George Gallup: Mr. Polling," republished in the *Journal of Advertising Research* 26, no. 1 (Feb./Mar. 1986), offers Gallup's retrospective view of his life and career. "Dr. Gallup's Finger on America's Pulse," *Economist* (27 Sept. 1997), offers a view of Gallup's contributions to public opinion polling. Obituaries are in the *New York Times* and *Washington Post* (both 28 July 1984) and *Public Opinion Quarterly* 48 (winter 1984).

JERRY BORNSTEIN

GARDNER, John Champlin, Jr. (*b.* 21 July 1933 in Batavia, New York; *d.* 14 September 1982 in Susquehanna, Pennsylvania), teacher and writer best known for his novel *Grendel* (1971) and his provocative critical views notably articulated in *On Moral Fiction* (1978).

The eldest of four children, Gardner was the son of Priscilla Jones, a high school English teacher, and John Champlin Gardner, Sr., a dairy farmer and lay preacher. Life on a dairy farm in upstate New York did little to avert Gardner from intellectual and aesthetic pursuits. His parents instilled in him their own musical and literary interests; by the age of eleven he was writing stories and poetry. His brother Gilbert was killed in a tractor accident on 4 April 1945, and Gardner, the tractor's driver, claimed he used creative writing as a therapy in the years following the accident and wrote about the event in the short story "Redemption" (1977).

In 1951 Gardner entered DePauw University in Indiana. On 6 June 1953 he married Joan Louise Patterson, a music

John Gardner, Jr. FRANK CAPRI/SAGA/ARCHIVE PHOTOS

teacher and his second cousin; they had two children. Gardner left DePauw, completing his A.B. degree in 1955 at Washington University in St. Louis. Having won a prestigious Woodrow Wilson Fellowship, Gardner went on to earn an M.A. degree (1956) and a Ph.D. (1958) at the University of Iowa. During these years, Gardner focused primarily on literature, edging away from his interests in music and science. In 1958 Gardner submitted "The Old Men," an unpublished novel, as his doctoral dissertation.

Gardner's teaching career began in 1958 with a lectureship at Oberlin College in Ohio, where he taught English, world literature, and creative writing. From 1959 to 1962, he taught creative writing at Chico State College in California. Later, Gardner was a lecturer on medieval literature and creative writing at a variety of colleges, including the University of Detroit (1970), Northwestern University (1973), Bennington College (1974–1975), Skidmore College (1977), Williams College (1977), and George Mason University (1977). Beginning in 1974, Gardner also taught on an occasional basis at the Bread Loaf Writers' Conference in Vermont. Gardner's three most substantive positions were as assistant professor of medieval studies at San Francisco State (1962–1965), associate professor of Anglo-Saxon and medieval studies at Southern Illinois University (1965–1976), and director of the creative writing program at the State University of New York at Binghamton (1978–1982).

Despite his impressive teaching career, Gardner was known primarily for his writing, especially his criticism and fiction. That career developed slowly. Gardner's first two books of scholarship, *The Forms of Fiction* (1961) and *The Complete Works of the Gawain-Poet* (1965), secured Gardner academic positions without making an impact on academe. Likewise, Gardner's first two novels, *The Resurrection* (1966) and *The Wreckage of Agathon* (1970), went largely unnoticed.

Gardner broke through to a larger audience in September 1971, when he published two works, one of which was *Grendel*. That novel, a revision of *Beowulf* related from the monster's point of view, gave Gardner a reputation among critics, with Richard Locke of the *New York Times* proclaiming him "a major contemporary writer." *Grendel*'s success was followed by five major works of fiction in five years: *The Sunlight Dialogues* (1972), *Jason and Medea* (1973), *Nickel Mountain* (1973), *King's Indian* (1974), and *October Light* (1976). Of these works, *The Sunlight Dialogues, Nickel Mountain,* and *October Light* were best-sellers. In 1973 Gardner won a Guggenheim Fellowship and an award from the American Academy of Arts and Letters. Capping this period of public and critical acclaim, *October Light* won the National Book Critics Circle Award for outstanding fiction in 1976.

By 1976 Gardner was a major literary figure. After that,

however, his work gained him more notoriety than critical success. Although Gardner turned up everywhere, from the the *Dick Cavett Show* (May 1978) to the *New York Times Magazine* (July 1979), his reputation suffered. Gardner's next two books, *The Poetry of Chaucer* (1977) and *The Life and Times of Chaucer* (1977), lacked academic rigor. *On Moral Fiction* (1978), a polemic in which he attacked many of his peers and, more generally, postmodernism, had the largest readership of any of Gardner's critical works, but the book proved unpopular with critics, who found its harshness distasteful and its argument muddled, not to mention contrary to the postmodernist tendencies of Gardner's own novels.

Undeterred, Gardner continued to write with characteristic vigor. From 1977 to 1982 he published in an array of genres, including children's literature, poetry, short stories, film scripts, literary criticism, and even opera lyrics. In 1980 he founded *MSS,* a literary magazine for new writers, and he continually worked as an editor and translator. Critical attention, however, focused on his novels, including *Freddy's Book* (1980) and *Mickelsson's Ghosts* (1982), which were published during that period. Two more novels, *Stillness* (1986) and *Shadows* (1986), were published posthumously. None of these was a critical success.

In 1977 Gardner was diagnosed with colon cancer, which required immediate surgery. Gardner spent more than a month recovering at Johns Hopkins Hospital in Baltimore. At the same time, he was experiencing financial and marital difficulties. Gardner separated from his wife, Joan, in October 1976, divorcing her in 1979 after protracted litigation. On 17 February 1980 he married Elizabeth Rosenberg, an English professor. He divorced her on 8 September 1982. On 14 September 1982, Gardner died after losing control of his motorcycle near his home in Susquehanna, Pennsylvania. He was to have married Susan Thornton a few days later. He is buried in Grandview Cemetery, Batavia, New York.

Described in the *New York Times Magazine* as "a small, potbellied man" whose "white hair falls over his shoulders so he looks something like a pregnant woman trying to pass for a Hell's Angel," Gardner will especially be remembered for *Grendel,* which continues to gain popularity in college classrooms, and for the zeal with which he defended the intrinsic morality of fiction during the controversial period following the publication of *On Moral Fiction. Grendel* and *On Moral Fiction* are connected philosophically both by their spirited critiques of Sartrean existentialism, which Gardner believed led to nihilistic despair, and by their advocacy of art as the ultimate weapon against such despair. With luck, future readers will perceive that Gardner was driven to overly harsh critical statements (many of which he later recanted), not by malice or intolerance, but by his positive, energetic faith in art. This enthusiasm likewise informed his love of conversation, pipes, music, and motorcycles.

★

In the absence of a standard biography, Allan Chavkin, *Conversations with John Gardner* (1990), provides a source useful for its biographical chronology and its many personal interviews. John M. Howell, *John Gardner: A Bibliographical Profile* (1980), offers another useful chronology and gives a full listing through 1979 of primary works, including books, reviews, letters, and interviews. It also includes an afterword written by Gardner. Robert A. Morace, *John Gardner: An Annotated Secondary Bibliography* (1984), provides a full listing through 1983 of secondary works. Gregory L. Morris, *A World of Order and Light: The Fiction of John Gardner* (1984), is one of the earliest works of criticism dedicated to Gardner alone; Dean McWilliams, *John Gardner* (1990), and John M. Howell, *Understanding John Gardner* (1993), offer two more. Obituaries are in the *New York Times* (15 Sept. 1982) and *Annual Obituary* (1982).

DAVID ARTHUR ANDREWS

GARROWAY, David Cunningham, Jr. (*b.* 13 July 1913 in Schenectady, New York; *d.* 21 July 1982 in Swarthmore, Pennsylvania), the first host of the long-running morning program the *Today Show* and one of the most famous video personalities of the 1950s.

Dave Garroway. ARCHIVE PHOTOS

Garroway was the only child of Bertha Tanner, a homemaker, and David Cunningham Garroway, an engineer for General Electric. The family moved as the senior Garroway's assignments changed, finally settling in St. Louis, Missouri, in 1927. David, Jr., graduated from University High School in 1931 and from Washington University four years later. He held a number of jobs during the next few years and coedited a pamphlet of words that were frequently mispronounced, *You Don't Say ... Or Do You?* (1938). Garroway married Adele Dwyer on 15 February 1940. They had one daughter and were divorced in 1946.

In 1938 Garroway began work as a page at the National Broadcasting Company (NBC) and went through the network's announcing school, where he finished next to last in a class of twenty-four. His first job was with station KDKA in Pittsburgh. Two years later he went to work at station WMAQ in Chicago. Garroway spent three years in the U.S. Navy during World War II on a minesweeper and as a lieutenant in charge of a yeomen's school for radio technicians in Honolulu, Hawaii.

After the war Garroway returned to WMAQ as host of a record program that first aired in January 1946. His *11:60 Club* went on at midnight and featured the jazz records that he personally admired. Within a year Garroway had added an afternoon music program and a variety show on Sunday evenings to his duties. In the summer of 1947 Gar-

roway went on the NBC radio network with the *Dave Garroway Show,* and in April 1949 *Garroway at Large* began on Chicago television. Three months later the show was on the national network and won a large following. It featured singers, some guest comedians, but mostly Garroway's offbeat, quiet humor. Garroway was six feet, two inches tall, and weighed almost 200 pounds, but his agility and ease before the camera belied his size. His trademark striped bow tie and large glasses contributed to his avuncular appearance.

Garroway at Large lasted for more than two years before its sponsor dropped it in search of higher ratings. At the time Garroway learned that NBC's president, Sylvester "Pat" Weaver, was planning a two-hour morning program for which he needed a "communicator," or master of ceremonies. Garroway became the first host of *Today,* which went on the air on 14 January 1952. Although the show struggled to find an audience during its first several years, Garroway proved to be an ideal selection to handle the diverse demands of the new format. He was a superb interviewer, had an easy way with a commercial, and related well to the audience. His sign off with an upraised hand and an intoned "Peace" became a trademark moment.

By the mid-1950s, *Today* had become a steady money-maker for NBC and Garroway was a major television personality. The addition of a chimpanzee, J. Fred Muggs, added to the show's appeal. On 7 August 1956 Garroway married Pamela Wilde; they had one son, David, Jr., and Garroway became the stepfather of Michael, his wife's son by a previous marriage. Garroway also hosted *Wide, Wide World* on Sunday afternoons between 1955 and 1958 and was one of the highest-paid stars of network television in the 1950s. Although his shows were highly scripted, he had the ability to infuse apparent spontaneity into his daily appearances. "Where are my scripts?" he once asked. "How can I ad-lib without my scripts?"

The relentless routine of *Today,* which included rising every day at 4:00 A.M., and Garroway's ambivalence regarding his fame began to affect his health and performance. For years he had suffered from chronic depression and relied on amphetamines (which he called "The Doctor") to provide him with the energy to perform. By the late 1950s his addiction was beginning to affect his work and his personal life. His marriage encountered difficulties as the 1950s ended, and Pamela Garroway committed suicide by taking an overdose of sleeping pills in 1961.

Garroway had long been a temperamental performer. He fired writers and aides regularly, and several times behaved erratically on the air. In 1959 he delivered an impassioned public defense of Charles Van Doren, a major figure in the quiz-show scandals. After his wife's death he took a brief leave and then returned to *Today,* behaving even more strangely than before. He lay on the floor of his office and insisted that his demands for a greater salary and control of the show be met. Exasperated with Garroway's eccentric ways, NBC executives dismissed him in the summer of 1961.

For the next two decades Garroway made sporadic attempts at a comeback, but none of the programs attracted substantial audiences. From his home on East Sixty-third Street in Manhattan he spent time working on his passions—which included stamp and coin collecting, butterflies, astronomy, jazz, and classic automobiles (in 1960 he published *Fun on Wheels*)—but his loss of celebrity chafed at him. "Nobody cares for old Dave anymore," he told a friend on *Today.* He did endeavor to help others who suffered from depression, and the Lasker Foundation recognized his work in that field. He married Sarah Lee Lippincott on 29 February 1980. Despondent following open-heart surgery in July 1982, he killed himself with a shotgun.

Dave Garroway achieved a high degree of national prominence during the formative years of network television because of his understated style and skill as an interviewer. "He could look at the camera and make you feel he was talking only with you," recalled his colleague Barbara Walters. For a decade he had a unique platform from which to reach the American people, and he had much to do with shaping a television program that has become a morning institution. Yet Garroway found that television is a cruel medium in which the fame of a performer lasts only as long as the camera is on. When his personal foibles brought him down, he slipped into an obscurity that he could not escape.

★

Garroway's papers are at the American Heritage Center at the University of Wyoming. Some of his letters are in the Chet Huntley Papers at the State Historical Society of Wisconsin. The records of NBC at the State Historical Society of Wisconsin should also be consulted. The morgue of the *New York Herald-Tribune,* at the Center for American History, University of Texas at Austin, has a good file on Garroway, as does the morgue of the *Philadelphia Bulletin,* at the Urban Archives at Temple University. There is no biography. For coverage of Garroway's years on television, see Max Wilk, *The Golden Age of Television* (1976); Robert Metz, *The "Today" Show* (1977); Pat Weaver and Thomas Coffey, *The Best Seat in the House* (1994); and Jeff Kisseloff, *The Box: An Oral History of Television, 1920–1961* (1995). An obituary is in the *New York Times* (22 July 1982).

LEWIS L. GOULD

GATES, Thomas Sovereign, Jr. (*b.* 10 April 1908 in Germantown, Pennsylvania; *d.* 24 March 1983 in Philadelphia, Pennsylvania), secretary of the navy and secretary of defense in the administration of President Dwight D. Eisenhower and ambassador to the People's Republic of China in the administration of President Jimmy Carter.

Gates was the only child of Thomas Sovereign Gates, a lawyer and investment banker who served as the president of the University of Pennsylvania from 1930 to 1944, and Marie Rogers Gates, who died when her son was born. Young Gates attended Chestnut Hill Academy and then entered the University of Pennsylvania, where he was Phi Beta Kappa and was awarded an A.B. degree in 1928. That year he married Millicent Anne Brengle; they had three daughters.

After graduation Gates joined the investment firm of Drexel and Company, where he would become a partner in 1940. He entered the Naval Reserve in 1935 and was called to duty in April 1942, commissioned as a lieutenant. Trained in intelligence, he commanded a naval air intelligence school before serving as an air intelligence officer in both the Atlantic and Pacific theaters throughout World War II. For his naval service, Gates was awarded the Bronze Star and, in lieu of a second one, a Gold Star. Demobilized in May 1945 with the rank of commander, he was promoted to captain of the Naval Reserve soon after the war. He returned to Drexel and Company and also served as the

Thomas Sovereign Gates, Jr., 1959. COURTESY OF THE U.S. NAVAL IN-
STITUTE AT ANNAPOLIS

director of several Philadelphia corporations, as vice president and director of the Navy League, and as adviser to the
Bureau of Aeronautics. In 1953 Secretary of the Navy
Robert B. Anderson asked him to succeed Undersecretary
Charles Thomas. Gates's main challenge in this post was
deciding how much to spend to keep the fleet ready to fight
and how much to allocate to develop more modern hardware at a time when President Dwight D. Eisenhower
would not increase defense spending.

One of Gates's first duties was to head a board recommending changes in his department's organization, necessitated by the passage of Defense Reorganization Plan No.
6. The board concluded that four assistant secretaries—for
material, air, financial management, and manpower—
should aid the undersecretary.

On 1 April 1957 Gates assumed the post of secretary of
the navy. Buttressed by the chief of naval operations, Admiral Arleigh A. Burke, Gates faced the task of countering
a rejuvenated Soviet navy with a U.S. naval force consisting
mainly of ships dating back to World War II and reduced
in size since that time from 968 to 860 vessels (including

409 combatants). He nevertheless was able to support the
July 1958 landing by 7,000 U.S. marines at Beirut, Leba-
non, sent by President Eisenhower to shore up the faltering
Lebanese government; had ships stand by during the Tai-
wan Straits crisis of 1957–1958, involving the Chinese shell-
ing of Quemoy and Matsu; and sent annual cruises about
South America.

While Gates was secretary, the navy acquired two *Forrestal*-class carriers and modernized all the *Essex*-class carriers by fitting them with steam catapults and angled decks.
He had three "hunter-killer" groups ready to wage anti-
submarine warfare against Soviet submarines. Meanwhile,
older U.S. nuclear-powered submarines set new records for
speed, range, and dependability.

Gates bridled at legislation that sought to centralize
power in the Office of the Secretary of Defense and, by
deleting the service departments from the chain of command, merely required them to provide logistic support.
Testimony before Congress by Gates and others resulted in
preserving significant roles for the service secretaries and
for the Joint Chiefs of Staff.

President Eisenhower's prescription to achieve strength
with minimal spending caused Gates to compete for resources, particularly with the Air Force. Americans were
shocked when the Soviets launched the first intermediate-
range ballistic missile and then sent Sputnik into orbit on
4 October 1957. Although the navy's Vanguard program put
a satellite into orbit in May 1958, the Soviets had gained
the greater propaganda value. As recommended by a report
of the Science Advisory Committee, Gates speeded up the
Polaris program. By December 1961, three years ahead of
schedule, the nuclear submarine *George Washington* with its
1,200-mile Polaris intermediate-range ballistic missiles was
on station.

To bolster morale, Gates made visits to his personnel in
all oceans and created the ranks of senior petty officer (E8)
and master (E9); he also established the Navy Enlisted Special Education Program, which allowed selected men to
obtain a college education at government expense. To retain
young officers and alleviate the stagnation of promotions
of the most talented to the senior grades, he screened out
captains who had failed to be selected for promotion twice
and urged that younger officers be selected for flag rank
(promotion to rear admiral). He combined the Bureau of
Aeronautics and Bureau of Ordnance into a Bureau of
Weapons and replaced the assistant secretary of the navy
for air with an assistant secretary for research and development.

During his tenure, Gates arranged for the acquisition of
the nuclear-powered carrier *Enterprise* and guided-missile
cruiser *Long Beach,* replaced old destroyers with missile-
armed frigates, and decreed that all new submarines would
thenceforth be nuclear-powered. The Marine Corps mean-

while forged ahead with the development of vertical envelopment using helicopters and new assault ships

Gates, who was six feet, two inches tall and had an easygoing patrician manner, wanted to retire early in 1959 but delayed doing so because his designated successor, William B. Franke, was ill. In May, however, President Eisenhower asked him to succeed Deputy Secretary of Defense Don Quarles, who had died of a heart attack. After some hesitation Gates agreed, and he was quickly confirmed. Shortly thereafter, on 2 December 1959, he was elevated to secretary of defense, succeeding Neil McElroy.

A most important decision he made, one not relished by the navy, was to call for a coordinated plan for the use of nuclear weapons in which the navy would help the Strategic Air Command establish a Joint Strategic Target Planning Staff to select nuclear war targets and designate the delivery systems including Polaris—on condition that its deputy commander be a vice admiral. Gates also authorized the U-2 overflight of Russia by Francis Gary Powers, the 1960 incident in which Powers was shot down by a Russian missile, publicly revealing the use of such spy planes and leading to the cancellation by Soviet premier Nikita Khrushchev of a planned summit meeting with President Eisenhower.

Satisfied with his department's organization, Gates noted that he had the president's backing as well as plenary power because it was he who decided how to distribute funds. He established the Defense Communications Agency, a single-manager agency that was the forerunner of the Defense Supply and Defense Intelligence agencies. During his tenure he made full use of carrier air power to thwart possible Soviet intervention in the civil war in the Congo in 1960, sent additional attack carriers to the Mediterranean and Western Pacific, embargoed shipping to Cuba to prevent it from exporting communism, and sent a South Atlantic Amity Force to Africa as part of Eisenhower's "people to people" program.

Gates remained secretary of defense until 21 January 1961, when John F. Kennedy assumed the presidency. Gates joined the Morgan Guaranty Trust Company of New York, the nation's fifth-largest bank, where he subsequently served as director, chairman of the executive committee, and president. Many more directorships followed. He also twice again returned to government service, as head of a board offering recommendations for an all-volunteer force and head of the U.S. Liaison Office of the People's Republic of China—with the rank of ambassador—in 1976. He then finally retired to private life, having provided good leadership to both the U.S. Navy and the Department of Defense for eight years.

After a long illness, Gates died at the University of Pennsylvania Hospital in 1983. Although he lived in Devon, Pennsylvania, he was buried in Bryn Mawr, Pennsylvania.

★

Annual Reports of the Secretaries of Defense, 1953–1961 encompass the official work of the service secretaries as well as of the secretary of defense. Carl W. Borklund, "Thomas Gates (December 1959–January 1961)," in *Men of the Pentagon: From Forrestal to McNamara* (1966), offers a good character sketch of Gates, as does John R. Wadleigh, "Thomas Sovereign Gates, Jr., 1 April 1957–7 June 1959," in Paolo E. Coletta, Robert G. Albion, and K. Jack Bauer, eds., *American Secretaries of the Navy* (1981). A perceptive essay on the era is Allan Rosenberg, "Admiral Arleigh Albert Burke, 17 August 1955–1 August 1961," in Robert William Love, Jr., ed., *The Chiefs of Naval Operations* (1980). An obituary is in the *New York Times* (26 Mar. 1983).

PAOLO E. COLETTA

GAYE, Marvin Pentz (*b.* 2 April 1939 in Washington, D.C.; *d.* 1 April 1984 in Washington, D.C.), singer and songwriter and one of the most successful and popular soul artists during the early years of the Motown era.

Marvin Gaye (originally Gay) was the second of four children of Alberta and Marvin Gay, Sr., a minister. He grew up in a modest home in a poor, segregated section of the nation's capital. Raised by devout Seventh-Day Adventists, he was the product of a strict and often abusive upbringing. In contrast to Gay's mother, a strong, pious woman who left home each morning at 5 A.M. to work as a maid, his father was an uninspired, effeminate man who drank excessively and even beat his children. His fits of rage were tempered, ironically, by a millenarian religious devotion that prized restraint. Indeed, for much of their childhood, the Gay children were expected to immerse themselves in worship from Friday night until Sunday afternoon, making them the object of ridicule from schoolmates who considered their religion (and their father) peculiar. Nonetheless, at the age of three, Marvin began singing gospel hymns at the House of God, his father's church. As members of the congregation began to notice Marvin's considerable vocal and instrumental talents (he also played the organ), his father demanded that he pursue a religious vocation. Of his relationship with his father, Gaye would later say: "Living with my father was like living with a king, a very peculiar, changeable, cruel, and all-powerful king." That Marvin would, as a teenager, turn to more secular pleasures like sex, Viceroy cigarettes, and doo-wop music defied his father's uncompromising expectations.

Marvin attended Cardozo High School, where he studied drums, piano, and guitar. A shy, handsome adolescent, he immersed himself in musical pursuits, often skipping classes to watch singers like James Brown and Jackie Wilson perform at the Howard Theatre. An inconsistent student, he dropped out of school in 1957 and joined the air

Marvin Gaye. Fotos International/Archive Photos

force, where he hoped to learn how to fly. Once he realized that his unruly temperament was not fit for the military, Marvin wanted out. His honorable discharge (1957), read: "Marvin Gay cannot adjust to regimentation and authority." He did achieve one milestone while serving in the Air Force—he lost his virginity to a prostitute. This experience unleashed an internal struggle between physical desire and moral reserve that bedeviled him throughout his adult life.

When he returned to Washington in 1957, Gay joined with friends Reese Palmer, James Nolan, and Chester Simmons to form the Marquees, a doo-wop group that performed mostly in front of high school audiences. During their first year together, rhythm-and-blues pioneer Bo Diddley agreed to produce their first record, "Hey Little Schoolgirl," on the Columbia subsidiary label Okeh. Despite high expectations, their debut failed to reach the charts—a disappointment for Gay especially, who had long dreamed of becoming a "black Sinatra." After a number of humiliating months as a dishwasher at People's Drugstore, a local all-white establishment in Washington, D.C., Gay met Harvey Fuqua, a record promoter who had been impressed with his magnetic performance at a recent high school talent contest. Fuqua, who was then in the process of re-forming a group named the Moonglows, invited Gay and his friends to Chicago to sign with his label, Chess Records.

In 1959 the Marquees changed their name to Harvey and the Moonglows and recorded their first hit, "Ten Commandments of Love." It was as lead singer for Harvey and the Moonglows that Gay got his first exposure to the life of a road performer. Despite his initial excitement at this, experience soon taught him that opportunities for black performers came with profound limitations in Jim Crow America. "We ran into all kinds of racist shit," Marvin recalled. "I thought about Joseph and Mary being turned away, but that wasn't comfort enough. Jesus turned over tables in the temple, and I was ready to break down doors." This early period of Gay's professional life involved a search for identity, informed by the burdens of his own tortured past as well as the stark realities of a racially segregated society. Gay then decided to change his last name by adding an "e" to the end—at once a sign of independence from his father and a defiant response to those who had questioned his sexual identity.

In 1960 Gaye and Fuqua moved to Detroit, where they teamed up with Berry Gordy, Jr., the determined entrepreneur who had founded the Motown Record Corporation one year before. After about a year as a backup singer, studio musician, and drummer for Smokey Robinson's band and other Motown acts, Gaye signed a contract with the company as a solo artist. Shortly thereafter, he married Gordy's thirty-seven-year-old sister, Anna, a move that elicited severe criticism from those who saw the Gaye-Gordy marriage as blatant opportunism. Nonetheless, with Anna's encouragement, Gaye entered the studio and recorded his first album, *The Soulful Moods of Marvin Gaye* (1961), a modest collection of subdued, jazz-influenced ballads. After recording several more albums that failed to impress critics, Gaye was urged to modify his sound to conform to the increasingly popular genre of rhythm and blues (R&B) music. Somewhat begrudgingly, Gaye did so, recording his self-referential "Stubborn Kind of Fellow," which quickly reached the top-ten list. It was not until 1964, however, that Gaye got a taste of the kind of stardom he wanted, with hit singles like "Hitch Hike," "Can I Get a Witness," and especially "Pride and Joy," which climbed to the top ten on both the pop and rhythm-and-blues charts.

By this time Motown was growing into one of the most successful black-owned businesses in America. As the civil rights movement heated up during the summer of 1964, so did Marvin Gaye's career. Following his first batch of hits—including "How Sweet It Is (to Be Loved by You)" which soared to number six on the charts—Gaye began to do collaborative albums with some of Motown's hottest new female vocalists, including Mary Wells (*Together,* 1964) and Kim Weston (*It Takes Two,* 1967). His most successful collaboration, however, was with Tammi Terrell, a promising young R&B singer with whom Gaye recorded three albums in conjunction with the famous writing and production team of Ashford and Simpson. Their first hit single together, "Ain't No Mountain High Enough" (1967), was the first of nine songs to make the charts, including "Ain't Nothing Like the Real Thing" and "Your Precious Love" (both in 1968). By the time Terrell died of a brain tumor in March 1970 at age twenty-four, Gaye's marriage to Anna—despite the adoption of a son, Marvin Pentz Gaye III, in 1965—was disintegrating. He was bordering on depression (it was during this period that he first threatened suicide) and was involved with cocaine. "My heart was broken," he claimed. "My own marriage to Anna had proven a lie. In my heart I could no longer pretend to sing love songs for people. I couldn't perform. When Tammi became ill, I refused to sing in public."

Despite his personal torment, he continued to record hits. In 1968 Gaye finally hit number one with "I Heard It Through the Grapevine," which he followed with a deeply personal album, *M.P.G.* (1969), that exposed his marriage crisis and deepening depression. Continuing to abuse drugs, Gaye also grew more disillusioned with the state of the nation. Indeed, following the deaths of four protesters at Kent State University and his brother's return from Vietnam in 1971, Gaye was explosive. He recorded (and co-produced) his best-selling album *What's Going On,* a musically diverse and politically charged manifesto on the contemporary problems of racism, poverty, and war. Hailed as Motown's first "concept album," it contained soul-wrenching top-ten hits like "Inner City Blues (Make Me Wanna Holler)," "Mercy Mercy Me," and the famous title track, the lyrics of which spoke for a nation in chaos: "War is not the answer / Only love can conquer hate / We've got to find some way / to bring some lovin' here today." Because of the album's success, Gaye received *Billboard*'s Trendsetter of the Year award, *Cashbox*'s Male Vocalist of the Year award, and an NAACP Image Award in 1971. He followed this success two years later with *Let's Get It On,* an album whose sultry title song debuted at number one.

At the peak of his career, however, Gaye's personal life continued to crumble. Addicted to drugs and unwilling to perform in concert, he initiated a tumultuous affair in 1971 with sixteen-year-old Janis Hunter. Anna finally filed for divorce in 1975, at which point Janis was pregnant for a second time with Gaye's child. While Gaye was in Hawaii and Europe to avoid charges of tax evasion, Motown released an unfinished album, *In Our Lifetime,* without his permission. Furious, Gaye signed with CBS Records in 1981, ending an almost twenty-year partnership with Motown. In one last grasp for glory, he released *Midnight Lover* (1982), a compilation of love ballads that won him two Grammy Awards in 1983, for best male vocalist and best instrumental performance. The album's best-selling single, "Sexual Healing," remained at number one for four months, becoming the fastest-selling soul single in more

than five years. In 1983, during an erratic concert tour, Gaye was hospitalized for drug-related complications and developed an acute case of paranoia. He returned to Los Angeles, a broken man. On Sunday, 1 April 1984, the eve of his forty-fifth birthday, Gaye was shot to death by his father during a violent altercation about finances in his parents' home. Marvin Gay, Sr., was later acquitted of his son's murder, claiming that he acted in self-defense.

More than ten thousand people attended Gaye's open-casket funeral in Los Angeles, at which Stevie Wonder sang and Smokey Robinson read the Twenty-third Psalm. A longtime friend, Robinson later reflected on Gaye's legacy: "The tragic ending can only be softened by the memory of a beautiful human being. He could be full of joy sometimes, but at others, full of woe, but in the end how compassionate, how wonderful, how exciting was Marvin Gaye and his music."

★

Sources with information on Gaye include Nelson George, *Where Did Our Love Go? The Rise and Fall of the Motown Sound* (1985); David Ritz, *Divided Soul: The Life of Marvin Gaye* (1985); Gerald Early, *One Nation Under Groove: Motown and American Culture* (1995); and Pamela Des Barres, *Rock Bottom: Dark Moments in Music Babylon* (1996). An obituary is in the *New York Times* (2 Apr. 1984).

TIMOTHY P. MCCARTHY

GAYNOR, Janet (*b.* 6 October 1906 in Philadelphia, Pennsylvania; *d.* 14 September 1984 in Palm Springs, California), actress who won the first Academy Award for best actress in 1929.

Janet Gaynor was born Laura Augusta Gainer to Frank D. Gainer, a paperhanger, painter, and amateur actor, and Laura Buhl, a housewife. She had an older sister, Helen. The family lived in the Germantown section of Philadelphia. Following a divorce in 1914, Gaynor's mother moved to Chicago with her daughters. During World War I the sisters gave recitations at the Great Lakes Naval Training Station just north of Chicago along the Lake Michigan shore. After a severe bout of influenza, Gaynor spent several winters with her aunt in Melbourne, Florida, where she attended school and acted in amateur plays. Beginning in 1919 she attended Lakeview High School in Chicago.

In 1922 her mother married Harry C. Jones, who relocated the family to San Francisco, where Gaynor graduated with honors from Polytechnic High School the following year. Gaynor credited her stepfather for her movie career because he moved the family to Hollywood and encouraged Gaynor and her sister to enter the movie profession. The sisters studied at the Hollywood Secretarial School, becoming stenographers when not working as movie extras.

Gaynor made her first film appearance in the bathing-beauty two-reeler *All Wet* (1924). She changed her name to Janet Gaynor on the advice of her stepfather, who thought it more professional. Shortly thereafter she acted in many silent two-reelers for Hal Roach, Universal, and several other studios. Gaynor attained popularity with audiences charmed by her diminutive stature, large saucer eyes, dimples, wholesomeness, and vulnerability. These qualities attracted the Fox studio, which saw her as the next Mary Pickford. In 1926 Gaynor played the heroine Anna in *The Johnstown Flood,* her first billed role. After this well-received performance, she became a favorite of Fox's chief of production, Winkfield Sheehan, who signed her to a $100-a-week contract and cast her in important roles in such major films of 1926 as *The Shamrock Handicap, The Blue Eagle, The Midnight Kiss,* and *The Return of Peter Grimm.*

Gaynor always portrayed sweet, vulnerable child-women whose determination overcame in the end. She continued this role in the silent film classic *Sunrise* (1927), following which she commanded a $300-a-week salary. In 1927 Gaynor began her association with handsome costar Charles Farrell in the romance *Seventh Heaven.* The duo had chemistry on the screen and were dubbed the "world's favorite sweethearts." They went on to costar in a total of eleven romantic films, including *Street Angel* in 1928. For her work in *Seventh Heaven,* Gaynor received the first-ever Academy Award for best actress in May 1929.

During the transition from silent to talking films, Gaynor appeared in three part-talkies: *Four Devils* (1928, partial dialogue added in a 1929 rerelease); *Christina* (1929); and *Lucky Star* (1929). She passed the voice test for the 1929 musical *Sunny Side Up,* her first all-speaking and singing part. Not pleased with her performance, she took voice lessons, but the studio persuaded her to be herself. On 11 September 1929 Gaynor married Lydell Peck. She appeared in several mediocre musicals with Farrell in 1930. Gaynor, upset with the repetitive ingenue roles assigned her, left for Hawaii and promised to return only when given meatier parts. After holding out for seven months, she resumed the same roles that had made her famous. In 1931 and 1932 she acted in the remake of *Daddy Long Legs* (1931); in *The Man Who Came Back* (1931), with Farrell; and in four other films.

From 1933 to 1938, more naive-young-girl-makes-good roles followed, but three movies stood out: the original non-musical *State Fair* (1933), with Gaynor playing Will Rogers's daughter; *The Farmer Takes a Wife* (1935), as novice actor Henry Fonda's wife; and the original classic *A Star Is Born* (1937). In the last of these, Gaynor gave her most notable performance as rising star Esther Blodgett. For her performance, she received an Academy Award

Janet Gaynor. POPPERFOTO/ARCHIVE PHOTOS

nomination. Afterward, she acted in *Three Loves Has Nancy* (1938) and *The Young in Heart* (1938).

At the age of thirty-three, Gaynor retired from acting in 1939 as Hollywood's highest-paid actress, earning an annual salary of $252,583. After devoting seventeen years to the screen, she wanted to experience another life, fall in love, and have a child, her childless marriage to Peck having ended in divorce in 1935. Her popularity was also waning. Prewar viewers, wanting bolder and more sophisticated heroines, had begun to tire of the typical Gaynor film. On 14 August 1939, Gaynor married Gilbert Adrian. Gaynor and Adrian had one son, Robin, born in 1940. For the next twelve years, Gaynor traveled extensively with Adrian, assisting him with his fashion and furniture business. In 1952 they bought a ranch in Brazil, where for the next seven years they spent most of their time, with visits to their ranch in Palm Springs and a house in Hawaii.

Gaynor made a few professional appearances during World War II, participating in Victory Book Rallies in 1941 and 1942, a war bond tour, and a Navy Relief fund-raising tour. In 1951 she and Farrell reunited for a Lux Radio twenty-fifth anniversary production of "Seventh Heaven."

She made her final film appearance in 1957, playing Pat Boone's mother in *Bernardine*. During her later years, she attempted roles in three unsuccessful plays: *The Midnight Sun* (1959) and *Harold and Maude* (1980) on Broadway, and *On Golden Pond* (1981) in Chicago. She also appeared in several television productions, including *The Love Boat,* in 1981.

Adrian's death in 1959 left Gaynor devastated and ill. She credited her friend the producer Paul Gregory with her survival. They married on 24 December 1964 and made their home in Palm Springs, where Gaynor painted florals that she successfully exhibited. She also became a gourmet cook and merchandised a line of specialty foods. Gaynor died from pneumonia and complications from an auto accident in 1982 that had injured her husband Gregory and friend Mary Martin. She was buried in Palm Springs.

Despite her lack of professional training and beauty and her limited singing and dancing ability, Gaynor was one of Hollywood's most popular stars, performing in thirty-seven major films. She gave Depression-era audiences a sympathetic and loving heroine. In later years Gaynor said, "We were essences. ... I was the essence of young first love." She was honored with a special award at the 1978 Academy Awards for the "pleasure and entertainment" she had brought to film fans worldwide.

★

Gaynor's short autobiographical article "My Life So Far" can be found in *Photoplay* (Dec./Jan. 1928–1929). An interview with Gaynor appears in Roy K. Newquist, *Showcase* (1966). Connie Billup, *Janet Gaynor: A Bio-Bibliography* (1992), provides an uncritical biography with photographs and a comprehensive bibliography. Critical accounts of Gaynor's film work appear in Robert James Parish, *Fox Girls* (1972), and Ethan Mordden, *Movie Star: A Look at the Names Who Made Hollywood* (1983). John Gruen, "For Janet Gaynor, Broadway Is Seventh Heaven," *New York Times Biographical Service* (11 Feb. 1980), discusses Gaynor's stage work, and Lori Simmons Zelenko, "Janet Gaynor: A Talent for Making Pictures," *American Artist* 46 (Feb. 1982): 56–57, focuses on her painting. Obituaries are in *Variety* (19 Sept. 1984) and the *New York Times* (15 Sept. 1984). Gaynor discussed her career in an audiotape interview with Barbara Walters on the *Today Show* (18 May 1976).

Frances T. Giglio

GERNREICH, Rudi (*b.* 8 August 1922 in Vienna, Austria; *d.* 21 April 1985 in Los Angeles, California), fashion designer best known for his topless bathing suit and deconstructed and unisex styles that revolutionized women's clothing; he was a three-time winner of the Coty Fashion Award and a member of the Fashion Hall of Fame.

The only child of Siegmund Gernreich and Elisabeth Mueller, Rudi lived in Vienna until he was sixteen years old. His father, a hosiery manufacturer, committed suicide in 1930. In September 1938 he and his mother immigrated as Jewish refugees to the United States and settled in Los Angeles. Gernreich attended Los Angeles City College (1938–1941) and the Los Angeles Art Center School (1941–1942), where he studied design and dance. In 1943 he became a U.S. citizen.

In 1942 Gernreich started his career as a dancer and costume designer for the Lester Horton Company. He left the troupe in 1948 to find employment in New York City, and from 1949 to 1951 he worked for George Carmel, a coat and suit firm. Dissatisfied, Gernreich returned to Los Angeles in 1951. During his first significant employment as a designer for Walter Bass, Inc., a sportswear manufacturer, he persuaded Jack Hanson, owner of Jax, a posh Beverly Hills boutique, and Marjorie Griswold, the buyer for Lord & Taylor, to purchase his fashions. As a result, in 1952 he signed a seven-year contract with Bass.

In March 1952 Gernreich successfully introduced the first bra-free swimsuit, a wool jersey with tank top. In February 1953 a knitted tube dress earned him his first fashion credit in *Glamour*. Still working with Bass, he also contracted in March 1955 to do swimwear for Westwood Knitting Mills in Los Angeles. A tweed maillot with a low V neckline and five-button front became one of his most enduring designs. In 1956 *Sports Illustrated* gave him his first design citation.

In June 1956 Gernreich ventured into men's clothing with Chinese-styled beach and lounge jackets. In 1967 he added women's shoe designs. Believing that the face, leg, and foot would become the major fashion focal points, in 1958 he began designing hats, purses, shoes, and underwear. In February 1959 he introduced stripes and checks on nylon hosiery, becoming the first designer to do so.

In August 1960, after receiving a special Coty Award for swimwear design, Gernreich started his own business in Los Angeles, G. R. Designs, Inc., which, with Harmon Knitwear of Marinette, Wisconsin, produced his swimsuits. Like Italian designer Emilio Pucci, Gernreich juxtaposed bright colors: pink and orange, blue and green, red and purple. He also introduced unconventional graphics, such as checks and dots, stripes and diagonals, and unusual fabrics, such as vinyl and aluminum, while continuing to use knits. The Wool Knit Association honored him for his innovative "fabric manipulations in knitted dresses." In May 1963 he won the *Sports Illustrated* Sporting Look Award, and in June 1963 he won the Coty American Fashion Critics Award, called the Winnie, determined exclusively by the fashion media.

The fashion most responsible for Gernreich's notoriety was his topless swimsuit of 1964. Fearing that Pucci, who

Rudi Gernreich with the model Peggy Moffitt wearing a spring safari outfit he designed, New York City, 1970. UPI/Corbis-Bettmann

had predicted that in ten years women would wear topless swimsuits, would be first to design one, Gernreich agreed to a request at the end of 1963 from Susan Kirkland of *Look* that he create a topless suit for a layout on futuristic trends. He intended for his monokini, a suit with only straps attached to the bottom part, to be just a photograph, but Diana Vreeland, then fashion editor of *Harper's Bazaar,* advised him to manufacture it. The suits retailed for $25 apiece, and 3,000 were sold. The pope condemned it, which added to the designer's renown. In the September issue of *Town and Country,* Dr. Joyce Brothers wrote that women who wore it "were more to be pitied than censored." Gernreich's "no-bra" bra that year was also a success. In 1965 the *London Sunday Times* gave the designer its fashion award.

In 1966 Gernreich, objecting to couture prices, told Bernadine Morris of the *New York Times* that "it's bad taste to be expensively dressed." His dresses did not exceed $200, when couture cost $800. Also reacting against the notion of exclusivity, Gernreich sold his clothes to the Montgomery Ward discount chain. His knitted swimsuits with vinyl ap-

pliquéd stockings attached to vinyl garters, chiffon T-shirt dress, and turtle-necked swimsuits earned him a second Coty Award in 1966. That year he was the first designer to have his fashions featured in a video without commentary, called *Basic Black.*

On 30 June 1967 Gernreich received his third Coty Award, which automatically admitted him to the Fashion Hall of Fame. *Time* magazine (1 December 1967) characterized him as "the most way-out . . . designer in the U.S." and featured him with his two principal female models, Peggy Moffitt and Léon Bing, on the cover. He was also featured as "a modern artist of dress" in a 1967 exhibition at the Fashion Institute of Technology in New York. On 16 October 1968, needing relaxation, he announced a sabbatical year, which he spent in Morocco and Europe.

Invited by Helen Blagden, *Life* magazine editor, to present his futurist fashion concepts in the 1 January 1970 issue, Gernreich presented bodies shaved from head to toe, unisex clothing, women wearing pants, men wearing skirts, see-through clothes, and caftans for elderly men and women. Asked to make a fashion statement at Expo 70 in Osaka, Japan, he featured bald male and female models.

Gernreich's spring 1971 collection of knits accessorized by toy rifles, dog tags, and boots reflected the militancy of the feminist movement. Gernreich predicted that the new fashion direction would be "comfort over status, and the designer would be more technician than artist." In 1974 he designed the thong suit, the first women's bathing suit cut high on the thighs and exposing the buttocks. His washable jersey tube dresses, ornamented with nonscratching, acrylic-coated aluminum jewelry cuffs or necklaces, and his innovative jockey-styled briefs and boxer shorts for women were his most provocative fashions of 1975. His designs for Bella Lewitzky's dancers in the ballet *Inscape,* performed in 1976, included duotards that connected two dancers through a single costume.

Disappointed by the return to the constructed fashions of the 1970s, Gernreich diversified into furniture, quilts, cosmetics, leotards, kitchen accessories, rugs, bathroom accessories, and gourmet soups. He showed his last knitwear collection in 1981, and in March 1985 he showed his last fashion design, the "pubikini," a bathing suit emphasizing the dyed green pubic hair of the model. For his contribution to fashion, he was honored in 1985 by the Council of Fashion Designers of America.

Gernreich was five feet, six inches tall, compactly built, and always wore black. His home in Hollywood Hills was decorated with Mies van der Rohe and Charles Eames furniture. He enjoyed driving a white Bentley or Jaguar and smoking dark brown cheroots. He died of lung cancer at the Cedar Sinai Medical Center in Los Angeles, survived by his companion of thirty-one years, Oreste Pucciani. The estates of Gernreich and Pucciani endowed a trust to provide for litigation and education in the area of gay rights. Although Gernreich never publicized his homosexuality, he was one of the seven original members of the Mattachine Society, a forerunner of the gay movement, founded by Harry Hay, his lover from 1950 to 1952. Gernreich resigned from the society in 1953. His affiliation with the society was made public posthumously.

Gernreich's fashions were linked to those of Mary Quant and André Courrèges for structure and to Pucci for color. Initially vilified, his use of inner wear as outerwear and his unisex notions were fully realized by later designers. He claimed he was more influenced by watching young people than by any particular designer, although Claire McCardell, known for her fluid jersey dresses of the 1930s, was his first inspiration. Often called the "enfant terrible" of the fashion world and accused of the "desertion of the lady-like," he radicalized women's clothing, declaring that "fashion is an attitude" and "there are no rights and wrongs."

★

Peggy Moffit and William Claxton, *The Rudi Gernreich Book* (1991), with a lengthy essay by Marylou Luther, includes a detailed photographic record of Gernreich's fashions, information on his philosophy of design, biographical details, and the only comments on his homosexuality. Bernadine Morris, *The Fashion Makers: An Inside Look at America's Leading Designers* (1978), provides many of the fashion details Morris reported on for the *New York Times*. See also Colin McDowell, *Directory of Twentieth-Century Fashion* (1984); Caroline Rennolds Milbank, *New York Fashion: The Evolution of American Style* (1989); Joel Lobenthal, *Radical Rags: Fashions of the Sixties* (1990), which gives an excellent analysis of the designers of the decade and includes a lengthy essay on Gernreich; Richard Martin, ed., *Contemporary Fashion* (1995), which has a detailed list of the companies for which Gernreich designed and all of his awards; and Gloria Steinem, "Gernreich's Progress; or, Eve Unbound," *New York Times* (31 Jan. 1965). An obituary is in the *New York Times* (22 Apr. 1985).

BARBARA L. GERBER

GERSHWIN, Ira (*b.* 6 December 1896 in New York City; *d.* 17 August 1983 in Beverly Hills, California), lyricist, best known for his long collaboration with his younger brother, the composer George Gershwin.

Ira Gershwin (originally Israel Gershvin) was the eldest of four children born to Morris Gershvin (originally Moise Gershovitz) and Rose (Bruskin) Gershvin, both of whom had emigrated from Saint Petersburg, Russia, to the United States in the early 1890s. Morris Gershvin began work as a shoemaker and had numerous occupations as a worker and small businessman during his lifetime. Rose Gershvin was a housewife. The family moved frequently in Manhattan and Brooklyn during Ira's youth.

Ira Gershwin, 1932. THE NEW YORK TIMES CO./ARCHIVE PHOTOS

Gershwin attended the public schools of New York and from his early childhood was an omnivorous reader who also liked to write. He entered Townsend Harris Hall, a college preparatory high school, in 1910 and graduated in 1914. He then spent two years as an English major at the City College of New York. In both high school and college he was active in the institutional literary magazines and soon developed a great enthusiasm for writing light poetry. His brother George, two years younger, had become an enthusiastic and obviously talented piano player from about 1910 onward and in 1914 quit high school to become a song plugger for a Tin Pan Alley music publisher. George was soon writing songs of his own and getting them published and performed.

Ira took longer to find his career. After dropping out of college, he held a variety of jobs for varying periods of time, including cashier in a bathhouse owned by his father and business manager of a touring carnival show. He continued writing light verse, however, and began to turn his thoughts toward becoming a lyricist. In 1918 he crafted his first surviving lyric, "The Real American Folk Song (Is a Rag)." His brother George liked the piece and wrote music for it. Ira found that his words did not fit the music and rewrote the lyric. Thus began the close collaboration that lasted to the end of George's life. Ira soon decided that the music to a song must be written at least in part before he could set words to it, but when he had a melody to work with, the process became one of give-and-take between himself and the composer. "The Real American Folk Song" was inserted as an interpolation in a musical comedy, *Ladies First;* Ira first heard it in a pre-Broadway tryout in Trenton, New Jersey, but it was cut from the show before it reached Broadway.

In 1921 Ira (under the pseudonym Arthur Francis) wrote all the lyrics for the musical *A Dangerous Maid,* for which George wrote the music. The show closed in Pittsburgh during its pre-Broadway tour. For the next three years the brothers went their separate ways. Ira collaborated with the composer Vincent Youmans in 1921 on the show *Two Little Girls in Blue,* which had a respectable run of more than 100 performances on Broadway. In 1924 he worked with George S. Kaufman, Marc Connelly, and Lew Gensler on the musical *Be Yourself.* Later that year, however, George and Ira renewed their collaboration—permanently as it turned out. The first result was the romantic ballad "The Man I Love," which revealed a mature mastery in both George's music and Ira's lyrics. Although it was slow to catch on, being first inserted into and then cut from at least two shows by the Gershwins, it ultimately became a great hit in the late 1920s and is still considered one of the classic American popular ballads. The year 1924 also saw the opening (on 1 December) of George and Ira's first hit musical, *Lady, Be Good!* Starring the famous brother-and-sister dance team of Adele and Fred Astaire, the show ran for 330 performances on Broadway and included among its songs the title song "Oh, Lady, Be Good!" and another classic, "Fascinating Rhythm."

Ira and George Gershwin were involved in varying degrees in nine musical shows from 1925 to 1930. Their first major collaboration in this period was *Tip-Toes,* which premiered in New York on 28 December 1925 and won for Ira the first critical recognition of his increasingly sophisticated lyrics. The Gershwins' next major hit show was *Oh, Kay!,* which opened on Broadway on 8 November 1926. Designed to showcase the acting and musical talents of Gertrude Lawrence, this musical included another song destined to become a classic—"Someone to Watch Over Me." Despite his heavy involvement in writing and rehearsing *Oh, Kay!,* Ira found time to court Lenore Strunsky and to marry her on 14 September 1926. The marriage proved to be enduring and happy, but the couple had no children.

The Gershwins' next successful musical, *Funny Face,* premiered in New York on 22 November 1927. Fred and Adele Astaire again starred and the score included another classic song, "'S Wonderful." Their last important show in the traditional American musical revue style was *Girl Crazy,* which opened on Broadway on 14 October 1930. The production was fortunate to include two performers destined for greatness: Ethel Merman and Ginger Rogers, then aged eighteen and nineteen, respectively. There were two more classic songs, "Embraceable You" and "I Got Rhythm," and the score as a whole was the best yet done by the Gershwin brothers.

By the late 1920s and early 1930s, George and Ira Gershwin were growing discontented with the standard revue format of the Broadway musical show. They wanted to create a new kind of musical play, one that would integrate music and lyrics with a more rational plot that would treat serious subjects, such as contemporary social problems. They made their first venture in these new directions as early as 1927, when they collaborated with the playwright George S. Kaufman on *Strike Up the Band,* an often savage satire of war profiteering and the mindless patriotism and repression that Kaufman and, to a lesser extent, the Gershwins, felt had characterized the era of World War I in the United States. This effort proved too strong for the still upbeat audiences of the late 1920s, and the show closed before the end of its pre-Broadway tryouts.

The stock market crash of 1929 and the onset of the Great Depression, however, produced a new, more cynical and questioning view of American business and politics. A revised and toned-down version of *Strike Up the Band,* which opened 14 January 1930, achieved a respectable run of 191 performances on Broadway and the title song became a hit. The Gershwins, Kaufman, and Morrie Ryskind next created a good-natured satire of American politics and the presidency, *Of Thee I Sing.* Depicting the political campaign and presidency of one John P. Wintergreen, who had no campaign platform other than love, the show opened in New York on 8 December 1931 and ran for 441 performances, an amazing total for the Depression era. The songs "Wintergreen for President," "Of Thee I Sing, Baby," and "Who Cares?" achieved hit status. It was the first musical comedy to win the Pulitzer Prize. Kaufman, Ryskind, and the Gershwins collaborated on one more musical play, *Let 'Em Eat Cake,* a strong satire of political fanatics of both right and left. Opening on Broadway on 21 October 1933, the show was pervaded with a negative tone that proved too much even for Depression-era audiences and closed after ninety performances.

In 1926 George Gershwin read the novel *Porgy* by DuBose Heyward. He was so entranced by its depiction of black ghetto life set in Charleston, South Carolina, that he immediately wrote to Heyward, a white writer, proposing to make the story the basis of an opera. As it turned out, other commitments of both composer and author prevented them from undertaking the task until late 1933. At first Ira Gershwin was not involved in the project. Heyward himself created the libretto for the opera and wrote many of the song lyrics. However, he was not an experienced lyricist and hence often provided words that meshed awkwardly, if at all, with the music. Ira joined the collaboration in mid-1934, primarily to polish Heyward's lyrics. He soon found himself writing lyrics for some of the songs and coauthoring others with Heyward. He wrote all of the lyrics for "It Ain't Necessarily So" and, with Heyward, those for "I Got Plenty o' Nuthin'," In the end Ira was involved in one way or another with almost all of the songs in the opera.

Porgy and Bess was first performed in Boston on 30 September 1935 and opened on Broadway on October 10 of that year. The opera, substantially cut before opening in New York, ran for 124 performances and the production failed to break even financially. It was only much later that the opera came to be widely appreciated and performed. Many of the cut portions were restored in a Houston Grand Opera production of 1976. The opera achieved the ultimate tribute of a full-scale and substantially uncut production at the Metropolitan Opera in New York in 1985 and became a regular part of the Met's repertoire thereafter.

In 1934 Ira Gershwin collaborated with the composer Harold Arlen and the lyricist E. Y ("Yip") Harburg on a successful Broadway musical revue, *Life Begins at 8:40*. He worked with composer Vernon Duke on the *Ziegfeld Follies of 1936*. In mid-1936 George and Ira went to Hollywood for an extended stay. Their first project there was *Shall We Dance?* (1937), the latest in a highly successful series of RKO movies starring Fred Astaire and Ginger Rogers. The film proved to be the Gershwins' most successful movie production, featuring such hit songs as "Beginner's Luck," "They All Laughed," "Let's Call the Whole Thing Off," and "They Can't Take That Away from Me." The Gershwins also wrote music and lyrics for *A Damsel in Distress* (1937) and *The Goldwyn Follies* (1937). *Follies* included the classic songs "Love Is Here to Stay" and "Love Walked In." The latter proved to be the last song George and Ira wrote together. George Gershwin had begun to suffer severe headaches and other unusual symptoms during his last few months in Hollywood. A definitive diagnosis of a brain tumor was not made until after he had lapsed into a coma on 9 July 1937. He died two days later, a few hours after major surgery.

Ira Gershwin was devastated by his brother's death and felt guilty for not having realized the seriousness of George's illness. He had by this time decided to settle permanently in Beverly Hills, California. He wrote very little until 1940, when he agreed to produce lyrics for *Lady in the Dark,* a play about the psychoanalysis of a young woman written by Moss Hart, with extensive musical interludes by the German émigré composer Kurt Weill. Starring Gertrude Lawrence and featuring the young Danny Kaye, the work opened on Broadway on 23 January 1941, was hailed by the critics as a pathbreaking treatment of a serious subject, and ran for 467 performances. Gershwin collaborated, first with Weill on *Firebrand of Florence* (1945), and then with Arthur Schwartz on *Park Avenue* (1946), but neither was successful.

Most of his writing from 1944 to 1964 was done for Hollywood films. The successful movies included *Cover Girl* (1944), with music by Jerome Kern (which introduced the standard "Long Ago and Far Away"), and *The Barkleys of Broadway* (1949), the last of the films starring the team of Fred Astaire and Ginger Rogers, with music by Harry Warren. Ira served as consultant for the Academy Award–winning motion picture *An American in Paris* (1951), starring Gene Kelly, which brilliantly recycled earlier music and lyrics by the two Gershwins. Ira's last great collaboration was with Harold Arlen. Together they wrote songs for a new film version of *A Star Is Born* (1954), starring Judy Garland, and *The Country Girl* (1954), which featured Bing Crosby and Grace Kelly. The former included Ira's last classic song, "The Man That Got Away."

Ira Gershwin spent most of his last years collecting and organizing the music, lyrics, correspondence, and other manuscripts that he and his brother had created over their lifetimes into a comprehensive Gershwin archive that was eventually given to the Library of Congress. An important by-product of this effort was Ira's only book, *Lyrics on Several Occasions* (1959). His extensive annotations to this collection of what he considered his best lyrics provided not only his views on the craft of song writing but also valuable autobiographical notes on himself and on the many celebrated people with whom he and his brother had worked. Ira's last venture as a lyricist was the three songs with music by his brother for the Billy Wilder film *Kiss Me, Stupid* (1964). The University of Maryland awarded him an honorary degree in 1966. He died of old age at his home in Beverly Hills.

In contrast to his slender and highly energetic brother George, Ira Gershwin was a short, stout, placid man, who could often be seen smoking a pipe or cigars. He was, however, an enthusiastic swimmer, golfer, and tennis player.

Ira Gershwin was a modest and self-effacing man who always regarded his brother George as the truly great and important member of his family. However, the writer P. G. Wodehouse, himself a fine lyricist, wrote to Ira in 1959: "I've always considered you the best of the whole bunch." Moreover, there is ample evidence that George Gershwin fully recognized and acknowledged the importance of his brother's contributions to their artistic collaborations. Even on a mundane level, the uniting of words and music is an intricate and tricky business. Ira Gershwin's contribution was to demonstrate that, in the realm of American musical theater and popular song, this business could be raised into a genuine art form. The best of his songs, written with George and others, are likely to endure as classics of their kind.

★

Ira and George Gershwin's musical and prose manuscripts are at the Library of Congress, Washington, D.C. Ira Gershwin, *Lyrics on Several Occasions* (1959), contains not only a generous selection of his best lyrics but also extensive, often autobiographical, annotations thereon. Edward Jablonski, *Gershwin* (1987), is a very detailed biography of George that also contains much useful material on Ira. Deena Rosenberg, *Fascinating Rhythm: The Collaboration of George and Ira Gershwin* (1991) is a detailed study of both brothers. Phillip Furia, *Ira Gershwin: The Art of the Lyricist,* is a less-detailed biography and an analysis of Ira's lyrics. Obituaries appear in the *New York Times* and *Los Angeles Times* (both 18 Aug. 1983).

JOHN E. LITTLE

GESCHWIND, Norman (*b.* 8 January 1926 in New York City; *d.* 4 November 1984 in Brookline, Massachusetts), behavioral neurologist and educator who achieved international renown for his studies of the left and right hemispheres of the human brain and the relationship between the anatomy of the brain and behavior.

Norman's father, Morris Geschwind, and his mother, Hannah ("Anna") Blau, were immigrants from Galicia. When Norman was very young the family relocated from Manhattan to Borough Park in Brooklyn, where they were surrounded by Jewish friends and relatives. Morris Geschwind, a successful businessman in his family's feather business, died of pneumonia when Norman was four. Norman's mother took a job during the Great Depression as a saleswoman at May's department store and became a career woman, achieving the position of buyer. Norman and his older brother benefited from their close relationship with their extended family. Norman spoke English at home, Hebrew at school, and Yiddish with his grandfather, who lived with the family for a time. He attended Etz Chaim Yeshiva and then Boys High School, where he studied Greek, Latin, and French.

In 1942 Norman entered Harvard College on a Pulitzer scholarship, learning German and discovering the work of German neurologist Carl Wernicke. During World War II he served in Europe in 1944 and in Japan in 1945. He returned to Harvard and obtained his B.A. degree, graduating magna cum laude in 1947, and entered Harvard Medical School. Graduating cum laude in 1951, Geschwind served his medical internship at Boston's Beth Israel Hospital. From 1952 to 1955 he worked under Sir Charles Symonds at the National Hospital in London, first on a Moseley fellowship and then on a U.S. Public Health Service fellowship. In 1955 he returned to Boston as a chief neurology resident at Boston City Hospital under Derek Denny-Brown. On 8 September 1956 in Cambridge, Massachusetts, Geschwind married Patricia Dougan, a psychiatric nurse he had met in London. They had three children.

Geschwind joined the research team headed by Francis Schmitt at the Massachusetts Institute of Technology (MIT) as a research fellow in 1956, working on axonal physiology. By 1958 he had joined Fred Quadfasel as staff neurologist at Boston's Veterans Administration Hospital, shifting his focus to the psychological aspects of neurological studies. Geschwind was inspired by theories about particular regions of the brain responsible for speech, presented as early as 1861 by the French neuroanatomist Paul Broca and by Carl Wernicke, which had been largely dismissed by academics in the years since their introduction. During the 1960s Geschwind concluded in a paper, later included in *Cognitive Processes of Nonhuman Primates* (1971), edited by Leonard E. Jarrard, that dominance of one hemisphere of the brain over the other (and, more specifically, the left brain, with control of speech and language, dominating in right-handed persons) is unique to humans and not found in lesser-evolved primates.

Upon Quadfasel's retirement in 1963 Geschwind replaced him as chief of neurology. He served concurrently as associate professor of neurology at Boston University from 1962 to 1966. In 1965 Geschwind published a two-part article in the journal *Brain,* "Disconnexion Syndromes in Animals and Man," which established links between physical locations of the brain and behavioral results. Geschwind also distinguished human brains as having "cross-modal" associations, much more complex than in animals, linking brain areas responsible for stimulus (perception) and response (action) through secondary regions and making possible the unique power of speech. This pioneering work was largely responsible for the birth and development of the field of behavioral neurology, which explores the relationship between the mind and the brain.

By 1966 the Boston University Aphasia Center was established, and Geschwind was named director, professor, and chairman. During the late 1960s and early 1970s Geschwind produced at least sixty works dealing with language and aphasia, which established him as the single most influential figure in twentieth-century research on aphasia.

In 1969 Geschwind returned to Harvard as the James Jackson Putnam Professor of Neurology and director of the Harvard Neurological Unit of the Boston City Hospital. In 1975 the Harvard Medical School unit moved to the Beth Israel Hospital, where Geschwind remained as chief, serving as professor of neurology at Harvard and director of neurology at Beth Israel until his death. On sabbatical from Harvard, Geschwind returned to the National Hospital in London, where he taught and researched during 1976 and 1977. After 1978 Geschwind also served a dual professorship at MIT in psychology and in the School of Health Sciences and Technology. He also traveled to many countries, frequently lecturing in the local language, and corresponded with numerous researchers on countless projects. He was a witty and entertaining speaker, known for

and immune disorders. Well after Geschwind's death his extensive theories about dyslexia were carried into new research (he hypothesized that a hormonal trigger during pregnancy could reroute the speech and language center out of the "normal" left brain into other areas, thereby affecting the way the fetus perceives information for life). Besides his immediate impact on medical sciences, the importance of his research to increased popular understanding of the workings of different areas of the brain and left- and right-brain function is inestimable.

★

See *Behavioral Neurology and the Legacy of Norman Geschwind* (1997), edited by Steven C. Schacter and Orrin Devinsky, who also edited *Norman Geschwind: Selected Publications on Language, Epilepsy, and Behavior* (1997). Israel Rosenfield, "A Hero of the Brain," *New York Review of Books* (21 Nov. 1985) is a tribute. Obituaries are in the *Boston Globe* (5 Nov. 1984) and the *New York Times* (9 Nov. 1984).

J. S. CAPPELLETTI

GIAUQUE, William Francis (*b.* 12 May 1895 in Niagara Falls, Ontario, Canada; *d.* 28 March 1982 in Oakland, California), chemist who won the Nobel Prize in 1949 for pioneering work in the study of temperatures near absolute zero and proof of the third law of thermodynamics.

Giauque was the eldest of three children born to William Tecumseh Sherman Giauque and Isabella Jane (Duncan) Giauque. Although Giauque was born in Canada his parents were both U.S. citizens, and he spent the first thirteen years of his life in Michigan, attending public schools there. Following the death of his father in 1908 the family returned to Ontario, where Giauque continued his secondary education at the Niagara Falls Collegiate and Vocational Institute.

Planning to become an electrical engineer, he sought work in area power plants but was unsuccessful. Fortuitously, he answered a newspaper advertisement for a job at the Hooker Electro-Chemical laboratory in Niagara Falls. He worked there for two years, seeking solutions to process problems, and decided to pursue a career in chemical engineering.

Giauque entered the University of California at Berkeley and earned his B.S. degree in chemistry with highest honors in 1920. Continuing his studies at Berkeley under the tutelage of the eminent chemists Gilbert N. Lewis and G. E. Gibson, he completed a thesis on the behavior of materials at very low temperatures and received his Ph.D. in chemistry with a minor in physics in 1922.

Giauque joined the faculty at Berkeley as an instructor in chemistry in 1922 and was named assistant professor in 1927, associate professor in 1930, and full professor in 1934. Meanwhile, he married Muriel Frances Ashley, a physicist, on 19 July 1932. They had two sons and lived at 2643

Norman Geschwind. RUTH FREIMAN, ARCHIVAL SPECIALIST, BETH IS- RAEL DEACONESS MEDICAL CENTER, 330 BROOKLINE AVENUE, BOS- TON, MA 02215

associating diverse information from his vast store of experience and knowledge. Geschwind was fellow of the American Academy of Neurology and a member of the Academy of Aphasia and the American Neurological Association of Research.

His research on temporal lobe epilepsy demonstrated how disruption of the limbic system leads to psychiatric symptoms. Geschwind hypothesized that as many as 40 percent of mental patients in U.S. hospitals in 1976 were there because of physical disorders rather than emotional problems. In the decade before his death he was working on theories about correlations among left-handedness, sex hormones, and increased vulnerability to allergies, learning disabilities, speech disorders, migraines, and autoimmune diseases. A film on his work, *Left Brain, Right Brain,* produced by the Canadian Broadcasting Corporation, was released in 1981. Geschwind died from a sudden heart attack at his home in Brookline, Massachusetts, cutting short a brilliant research career. He is buried in Brookline.

In 1987 the Geschwind-Behan-Galaburda (GBG) theory of left-handedness was presented, which stimulated much debate and further research about the possible relationship of left-handedness with language, developmental,

Dr. William Giauque in his laboratory at the University of California at Berkeley, 1949. UPI/CORBIS-BETTMANN

Benvenue Avenue in Berkeley. Giauque was devoted to his work and spent the little free time he allowed himself swimming or attending sporting events with his sons. He spent his entire academic career at Berkeley, except for several years during World War II when he worked for the U.S. government designing a mobile unit for producing liquid oxygen.

Giauque determined accurately the entropy (a measure of disorder) of a large number of substances near absolute zero (minus 273.15 degrees Celsius), and he proved that the third law of thermodynamics—which states that at absolute zero a perfect crystal has a zero entropy—was a fundamental law of nature. He discovered how a strong magnet could be used to produce temperatures very close to absolute zero and devised new methods for accurately measuring very low temperatures.

While calculating the entropy of oxygen, Giauque and Herrick L. Johnson observed unexplained bands in the spectrum of oxygen, which led to their discovery of two new isotopes of the gas. For this discovery they shared the 1929 Pacific Division Prize of the American Association for the Advancement of Science.

Giauque tackled the difficulty of achieving extremely low temperatures by using magnetization and demagnetization to remove heat from susceptible molecules. This technique derived from his research into the control and measurement of entropy. He wrote that he specifically

"lowered the temperature of a dilute magnetic salt to approximately 1 degree Kelvin and then applied a magnetic field while allowing the resulting heat to flow to a surrounding liquid helium bath, thus reducing the entropy of the salt." Insulating the salt solution to prevent its regaining heat, he removed the magnetic field to cause a further drop in temperature (to as low as .003 Kelvin).

Giauque was awarded the Nobel Prize for chemistry on 10 December 1949 "for his contributions in the field of chemical thermodynamics, particularly concerning the behavior of substances at extremely low temperatures." Soon thereafter the University of California committed $500,000 to the establishment of a new low-temperature laboratory for his research.

He received many other awards, honors, and prizes during the course of his career, including an honorary doctor of science degree and the Chandler Medal from Columbia University in 1936, the Elliott Cresson Medal from the Franklin Institute in 1937, and the B. N. Lewis Medal in 1956. He received an LL.D. degree from the University of California at Berkeley in 1963 and was named an honorary Berkeley fellow. Giauque also produced some 200 papers in the course of his career, most dealing with research into the realm of extremely low temperatures. Giauque retired as professor emeritus in 1962 but continued to work at the low-temperature laboratory until the year before his death in 1982. He died in Oakland, California.

★

Giauque's papers are published as William F. Giauque, *The Scientific Papers of William F. Giauque,* vol. 1 (1969), and David Lyon, ed., *The Scientific Papers of William F. Giauque,* vols. 2 and 3 (1995), which appeared in conjunction with the centenary of Giauque's birth. See also William F. Giauque with G. E. Gibson, "The Third Law of Thermodynamics: Evidence from the Specific Heats of Glycerol," *Journal of the American Chemical Society* 45 (1923); William F. Giauque, "A Thermodynamic Treatment of Magnetic Effects: A Proposed Method of Producing Temperatures Considerably Below 1 Degree Absolute," *Journal of the American Chemical Society* (Dec. 1926), the proposal for the research methods that ultimately led to his Nobel Prize; William F. Giauque, R. W. Blue, and Roy Overstreet, "The Entropies of Methane and Ammonia," *Physical Review* 38 (1931); and William F. Giauque, "Temperatures Below 1 Degree Absolute," *Industrial and Engineering Chemistry* 28 (1936). See also William Jolly, *From Retorts to Lasers* (1987), with a chapter on Giauque; and *Dictionary of Scientific Biography: Supplement 2,* vol. 17 (1990), s.v. "Giauque, William Francis."

CHARLES A. ROND IV

GODFREY, Arthur Michael (*b.* 31 August 1903 in New York City; *d.* 16 March 1983 in New York City), radio and television personality of the 1940s and 1950s whose conversational style and easygoing charm on such programs as *Arthur Godfrey Time* and *Arthur Godfrey's Talent Scouts* had a humanizing influence on the evolution of radio and TV.

Arthur was the oldest of five children born to Arthur Hanbury Godfrey, an English-born sportswriter and racehorse touter, and Kathryn Morton Godfrey, a Scotch-Irish pianist and vocalist who performed in a local movie house. The family was desperately poor, moving to Hasbrouck Heights, New Jersey, in 1905, the first of many relocations necessitated by their attempts to evade bill collectors. Arthur remembered a particularly traumatic day when, coming home from school, he could not remember where his family lived. Arthur's mother attempted to be the breadwinner, selling homemade jams and jellies door to door. Arthur stole bottles of milk from neighborhood porches to feed the family and went to work at ten, driving a bakery wagon. He was dropped as captain of the high school debating team when the bakery job kept him out of school for three weeks.

Arthur's sisters remember being "the poorest family in town." Their brother's loaves of bread and their mother's optimism kept their spirits up, but poverty forced the family to move "twenty-six times" by 1918, the year Arthur abruptly quit school and drifted across the country. He became a typist in an army camp, a coal miner in Pennsylvania, a tire finisher in Akron, Ohio, and an architect's office boy. He feared he would become a bum.

The military changed his life. Godfrey graduated from

Arthur Godfrey. ARCHIVE PHOTOS

the Naval Radio School in Great Lakes, Illinois, shortly after the end of World War I, and then became a radio operator on the USS *Hatfield* in the Turkish Straits. Thriving in the navy's regimented structure, he was introduced to airplanes, which became a lifelong passion. A Hawaiian bunkmate taught him how to play the ukulele. He narrowly escaped an unexpected wedding date with a Turkish girl he had dated unchaperoned, and later claimed that a fortune-teller in Constantinople had confirmed his mother's claim that he would one day be a famous entertainer.

Godfrey was discharged from the navy in 1924, the year his father died, and he then became an insurance salesman. He liked selling, but his family found his "insistence on order" wearying. They had learned "not to cross Arthur when he was in a serious mood," particularly when "he ordered everybody about." Upset with the family's precarious financial footing, Arthur abruptly broke his engagement with a local woman and went west with his younger brother Charlie. He worked in a Detroit auto assembly plant, sold cemetery plots, became a short-order cook, wrote advertising copy, drove a cab, and eventually joined a

323

vaudeville troupe. He joined the Coast Guard in 1927 as a radioman. That year, while stationed in Connecticut, he married Catherine Collins. They had one child.

Godfrey's radio career began at a Baltimore speakeasy in 1929. He and several companions were listening to an amateur program on WFBR when they agreed that they were better than the on-air talent. The next week "Red Godfrey, the Warbling Banjoist" debuted on the station. He was good enough to be invited back. "The Warbling Banjoist and His Ukelele Club" became a twelve-minute, three-times-a-week show. Godfrey's birdseed sponsor paid him $5 a program. When his announcer did not show up one night, Godfrey did the selling himself, leading the station manager to observe that Arthur was a much better announcer than he was a musician. Godfrey was now a Coast Guardsman by day and a radio announcer at night.

Radio announcing became Godfrey's full-time work after his discharge in 1930. Later that year he and Catherine were divorced. Godfrey landed a job as staff announcer at NBC's Washington, D.C., affiliate WRC. His salary allowed Godfrey to pay for flying lessons. He was on his way to Congressional Airport on the morning of 26 September 1931 when his car collided with an oncoming truck. The accident crushed both of Godfrey's hips, shattered his knees, and broke six ribs, leaving him hospitalized for four months and forcing him to live with pain for the rest of his life.

From his hospital bed Godfrey listened to many radio programs and concluded that announcers "acted superior to their audience." They failed to realize that they were speaking not "to a mass audience" but to "individual people." And few interviewers, he observed, were very good listeners. When he returned to the air in early 1932, it was in the relaxed, conversational style that would become his trademark and revolutionize the industry. Godfrey became a favorite of listeners and even got an occasional boost in Walter Winchell's nationally syndicated column. By the late 1930s Godfrey was making several thousand dollars a week as host of a morning radio show. He bought a large farm in Leesburg, Virginia, and started his own flying school. On 24 February 1938 he married NBC receptionist Mary Bourke. They had two children and maintained an apartment in New York City in addition to their Virginia estate.

Godfrey was ambitious. He pushed CBS to give him a network show, but was turned down because executives thought of him as a local personality. That changed when Godfrey covered the funeral procession of President Franklin D. Roosevelt in April 1945. He sounded like an ordinary guy speaking from the heart when he somberly said, "Folks are havin' as tough a time as me watchin' this." Moments later when the new president came into view, Godfrey blurted out, "God bless you, Harry Truman." Two weeks after that broadcast *Arthur Godfrey Time* premiered on CBS

morning radio. He was to be a fixture for twenty-seven years.

The radio show proved a revelation. Godfrey's reassuring delivery played well to postwar audiences and was finely honed. "I knew I didn't have any talent," Godfrey later said. "I had to be someone upon whom you could depend." Whether selling Lipton tea or strumming the ukulele, Godfrey became, according to future broadcaster Larry King, "our uncle, our friend, our father." Godfrey had "a strange genius," his colleague Andy Rooney observed. "People were fascinated with him." Godfrey believed his hold on audiences was more than the affected charm of a welcome friend. "You had to believe what I told you," Godfrey noted, "because you knew it was true."

Much to his amazement Godfrey became a recording star. His singing of "The Too Fat Polka" in 1947 may have been an exercise in poor taste, but the song's success temporarily pushed Bing Crosby and Frank Sinatra from the top of the Hit Parade. The recording sold 3.5 million copies and became a Godfrey staple. On 9 December 1948 full-page ads in the nation's newspapers asked readers to "Take a Look at Godfrey Tonight." It was the television debut of *Arthur Godfrey's Talent Scouts*, the program that helped make Godfrey perhaps the most popular man in America and arguably the most powerful person in broadcasting.

Godfrey reached the peak of his popularity in the early 1950s. He was producing and starring in nine and a half hours of live TV each week, including a ninety-minute weekday morning show, the Monday night talent scout performance, and a Wednesday night variety program, which were seen by an audience of 82 million. Godfrey's shows generated $22 million for CBS annually, 12 percent of the network's total revenue. At a time when the average weekly income was $75, Godfrey made $2 million annually before taxes, yet retained the reputation of America's everyman. His red hair and freckled face and easygoing gait made him the guy next door. Even his mother was getting guest shots with Groucho Marx, Art Linkletter, and Lawrence Welk.

When hip surgery in the spring of 1953 took Godfrey temporarily off the air, he was flooded with 40,000 get-well cards and letters each week. Congregations lit candles and prayed for his recovery. At considerable expense, CBS and ATT built a transmission tower on Godfrey's estate so he could broadcast from his farm. His return was a moment of national rejoicing, leading *Broadcasting-Telecasting* to quip, "the deification of Arthur Godfrey has been underway for some time. It is only a matter of time before the second syllable of Godfrey will be forgotten."

A guest appearance on a Godfrey show meant national exposure that often led to stardom. Rosemary Clooney, Tony Bennett, Lenny Bruce, Patsy Cline, Don Knotts, and the McGuire Sisters were among the stars discovered on or greatly helped by Godfrey's shows. It was, however, Godfrey's relations with singer Julius LaRosa that marked a turning point in Godfrey's career. By the fall of 1953 LaRosa, one of the "Little Godfreys" and a regular on Arthur's morning show, was getting more fan mail than Godfrey. He hired an agent and a manager, against Godfrey's orders, and missed a rehearsal to attend to personal business. With the approval of management, Godfrey fired LaRosa on the air, referring to LaRosa's 19 October 1953 appearance on *Arthur Godfrey Time* as the singer's swan song with the show. At a later news conference, Godfrey, never known for his modesty, told reporters that the singer had been fired because "Julius has lost his humility."

Headlines battered Godfrey's high-handedness. Polls showed that viewers who had thought of Godfrey as a surrogate father now felt he had thrown his son out of the house. A segment of that audience never forgave him. In January 1954 the Federal Aviation Administration recommended revoking Godfrey's pilot license following his highly publicized buzzing of an air tower in New Jersey. The discovery that Florida's Kenilworth Hotel, which Godfrey partly owned, was restricted to Gentiles, led to charges he was anti-Semitic. Godfrey ordered that the policy be changed, but that action won little press attention.

On 1 May 1959 Godfrey made news when his left lung was removed during cancer surgery. He returned to the air in September, but fan interest was wearing thin. By the mid-1960s Godfrey was limited to guest appearances on talk shows and commercials. His daily radio shows became increasingly preachy, focusing on Godfrey passions such as ecology, but few listened. His final tearful program on 30 April 1972 had fewer than 1 million listeners.

Godfrey drifted out of America's consciousness in the 1970s. There were few television appearances, and ad agencies thought him too old to be their spokesman. Godfrey hoped for a show on cable, but he was limited to a five-minute nostalgia act during PBS pledge week in which he sang "The Too Fat Polka." After thirty years, his marriage to Mary ended in divorce. His health declined, and he was frequently hospitalized. He died in March 1983 in Mount Sinai Hospital in New York City, of emphysema and pneumonia; he was cremated. His passing produced few front-page headlines and led friend Andy Rooney to remark that "Arthur Godfrey is the single most forgotten man in the history of television." David Brinkley observed that no one had been more significant in recognizing the medium's communication potential. Noted Larry King, "Godfrey was the hugest broadcasting personality we have ever had in this country." Even LaRosa admitted, "America loved the man." Rooney agreed, "I don't think there was ever anyone more important to the medium than he was."

★

Appreciations of Godfrey's work include Jack O'Brian's *Godfrey the Great* (1951). Godfrey's own account of his success in broadcasting is chronicled in Arthur Godfrey, *Arthur Godfrey and His Gang* (1953). A family portrait of Arthur Godfrey appears in a book written by a sister and a sister-in-law. Jean Godfrey and Kathy Godfrey's *Genius in the Family* appeared in 1962. Godfrey's interest in environmental issues and organic farming is described in his *The Arthur Godfrey Environmental Reader* (1970). An obituary in the *New York Times* (17 Mar. 1983) cites his birth in 1903, but press accounts at the time of Godfrey's 1931 traffic accident report he was then thirty-one. Andy Rooney's appreciation of Godfrey is in the *Chicago Tribune* (24 Mar. 1983). Godfrey's reputation as "media champ" and "household icon" is the subject of Lewis Grossberger's article in *Rolling Stone* (28 Apr. 1983). Godfrey was the subject of a 1996 documentary on the Arts and Entertainment Network *Biography* series, titled "Arthur Godfrey: Broadcasting's Forgotten Giant."

BRUCE J. EVENSEN

GOFFMAN, Erving Manual (*b.* 11 June 1922 in Mannville, Alberta, Canada; *d.* 19 November 1982 in Philadelphia, Pennsylvania), professor of sociology and influential observer of everyday behavior, especially in modern urban settings, best known as the author of *The Presentation of Self in Everyday Life* (1959) and *Asylums* (1961).

Goffman was one of two children of Max Goffman, a shopkeeper, and his wife, Ann, a homemaker, who were two of 200,000 Ukrainians who moved to Canada between 1897 and 1914. Goffman was brought up in Dauphin, near Winnipeg, where he attended St. John's, a technical high school. For unknown reasons his friends called him "Pooky." Initially he showed an interest in chemistry, which he pursued after entering the University of Manitoba, in 1939. In 1943 and 1944 he worked at the National Film Board in Ottawa, where he met Dennis Wrong, an influential sociologist. Goffman soon moved to the University of Toronto, where he studied with C. W. M. Hart and Ray Birdwhistell, among others, receiving a B.A. degree in sociology in 1945.

Later that year he entered the University of Chicago for graduate work. His courses included Everett Hughes's seminar on work and occupations, where he first heard the expression "total institution," which would become the conceptual linchpin of *Asylums*. In Chicago, Goffman's acerbic wit earned him a new nickname, "the little dagger," which may also have been a reference to his small physical size. He completed his thesis, a survey project concerning audience reactions to a then-popular radio soap opera, and received his M.A. degree in 1949. Shortly thereafter he left for the Shetland Isles in Scotland. From December 1949 to May 1951 he lived on the island of Unst, where he collected ethnographic data for his doctoral dissertation. Masquerading as an American interested in agricultural techniques,

Erving Goffman. COURTESY OF THE AMERICAN SOCIOLOGICAL ASSO-
CIATION

he absorbed as much as he could about everyday life on this small island.

In May 1951 he moved to Paris, where he completed a draft of his doctoral dissertation. The following year he returned to Chicago, where he married Angelica Choate, whom he had met at the University of Chicago when she was a psychology student. The couple had two children. In 1953 Goffman successfully defended his dissertation, but his examiners had mixed reactions to his study. Several expected a detailed case study and were dismayed to receive what was primarily a general theory of face-to-face interaction. During this time Goffman completed the first draft of *The Presentation of Self in Everyday Life,* in which he describes everyday behavior as a performance, in which people are actors attempting to manipulate others and promote a favorable impression of themselves.

After working briefly as a research assistant, Goffman moved with his family to Washington, D.C., where in 1955 he began observations at St. Elizabeth's Hospital. He spent eighteen months there as assistant to the athletics director, a marginal position that gave him access to all parts of the hospital for an ethnographic research project sponsored by the National Institute of Mental Health. The chief administrator of St. Elizabeth's was the only one at the hospital who knew Goffman's true purpose—to understand the world of the mental hospital from the perspective of the patient. This fieldwork formed the basis of *Asylums* (1961).

On 1 January 1958 Goffman was hired as a visiting assistant professor at the University of California at Berkeley. He progressed rapidly, becoming a full professor in 1962. In addition to his academic interests he showed himself to be a shrewd stock-market analyst and a keen gambler. He was proud of his stock-picking abilities. Later in life he boasted that even though he was one of the highest-paid sociologists in the United States, he still earned a third of his income from investments and a third from royalties. By contrast, his gambling abilities remain unclear; there are reports that he was regularly beaten at poker by colleagues at the university, losses that he accepted with grace and good humor. He was a stronger blackjack player. Indeed, he later trained and worked as a blackjack dealer at the Station Plaza Casino in Las Vegas, where he was promoted to pit boss. His work in Las Vegas was actually fieldwork for a research study on gambling that was never published.

In 1964 his wife, Angelica, who had suffered from serious mental health problems for several years, committed suicide at the age of thirty-five. There is a parallel between Goffman's academic interest in mental illness and his personal observations of it at home. Perhaps nowhere is this clearer than in his 1970 essay, "The Insanity of Place," which describes the difficulties of family life when one member of the family is mentally ill.

In 1966 Goffman spent a sabbatical year at the Harvard Center for International Affairs, where he developed a friendship with Thomas Schelling, from whom he gained an understanding of game theory. He did not return to Berkeley, instead accepting a Benjamin Franklin chair in sociology at the University of Pennsylvania, moving to Philadelphia in 1968. The move did not slow down his research productivity. In 1971 he published *Relations in Public,* in which he brought together many of his ideas about the organization of everyday conduct. At this time he was also working to complete what he hoped would be his magnum opus, *Frame Analysis* (1974). Given the long gestation period, the lukewarm reception of the book by the sociological community must have been a disappointment. In later years, however, its ideas found a new audience among scholars interested in the study of social movements and collective behavior.

In 1981 he married the linguist Gillian Sankoff, with whom he had a daughter, Alice. In November 1982 he died of stomach cancer, a few weeks before he could deliver his presidential address to the American Sociological Association. The paper, "The Interaction Order," published in the *American Sociological Review* in 1983, was written from his hospital bed, and he knew that he was unlikely to live to deliver it in person. The title of the talk was carefully chosen: In 1953, Goffman had used it for the final chapter of his doctoral dissertation. This small gesture brought closure to his wide-ranging sociological ideas.

Goffman offered a persuasive account of everyday behavior based on a comparison to the theater. He extended our understanding of the experiences of the mentally ill in hospitals in the 1950s. His subtle criticisms of the institutional treatment of the mentally ill added impetus to the deinstitutionalization movement of the early 1960s. Goffman also transformed the study of face-to-face interaction into a field worthy of independent study.

★

A biographical work on Goffman is T. Burns, *Erving Goffman* (1992). For information on his work and research, see J. Ditton, ed., *The View from Goffman* (1980); P. Drew and A. Wootton, eds., *Erving Goffman: Exploring the Interaction Order;* and P. Manning, *Erving Goffman and Modern Sociology* (1992).

PHILIP MANNING

GOLDEN, Harry Lewis (*b.* 6 May 1903 in Milkulinsty, Galicia, Austria-Hungary [present-day Ukraine]; *d.* 2 October 1981 in Charlotte, North Carolina), civil libertarian who was the editor and publisher of the *Carolina Israelite,* which strongly influenced the civil rights movement, as well as a syndicated columnist and the author of several best-selling books of essays.

Harry Golden. UNC CHARLOTTE LIBRARY

Harry Golden was the third of seven children born to Leib and Anna Klein Goldhirsch. In 1905 the family emigrated to New York's Lower East Side, where Leib Goldhirsch became a Hebrew teacher and freelance writer and Anna a housewife and seamstress. His birth name of Herschele Lewis Goldhirsch was changed to Harry Lewis Goldhurst on the family's migration to America, and to Harry Golden upon his move to Charlotte, North Carolina. After graduating in 1917 from P.S. 20 in New York, Golden earned a diploma from East Side Evening High School around 1920 and attended night school at City College of New York, leaving about 1922 without a degree. From 1918 to 1923 he was profoundly influenced by the Round Table Literary Club, a discussion group started by an early employer, Oscar H. Geiger. On 17 March 1926 Golden married Genevieve Alice Marie Gallagher, an Irish Catholic schoolteacher. They had four children.

Golden held a number of jobs, including newspaper hawking and messaging, before working in his sister Clara's brokerage firm, which he left in 1926 to establish his own, Kable and Company. According to Golden's autobiography, *The Right Time* (1969), the firm was an illegal establishment purporting to buy and sell stock for customers. When, in the midst of the bull market of 1929, Golden's customers directed him to deliver proceeds from the sale of stocks he had not yet purchased on their behalf, his firm declared bankruptcy and Golden was indicted for mail fraud. He was surprised by the indictment and shocked by the unusually lengthy five-year prison sentence he received following his conviction. In his autobiography, Golden suggests that his sentence was influenced by political hostility between one of his customers, Bishop James Cannon, Jr., a staunch prohibitionist, and Virginia senator Carter Glass, who was strongly antiprohibitionist. Richard M. Nixon granted Golden a full presidential pardon in 1973.

Following his release after approximately three and a half years in prison (served at the Atlanta Penitentiary and then at Fort Meade, Indiana), Golden managed one of his brother's hotels and sold advertising for the *New York Daily Mirror* and the *New York Post.* By the early 1940s Golden had separated from his wife, though they were never divorced, and had relocated to Charlotte, North Carolina. Golden sold advertising for Charlotte newspapers but hoped to start his own paper, convinced that the South held the "big story," the sudden painful transformation of a society. Certain that southern newspapers would not report the true situation of black people, Golden undertook to provide it himself.

The *Carolina Israelite,* through which Golden hoped to bring Jews and Gentiles into the civil rights movement, first appeared in October 1942. The sixteen-page bimonthly newspaper, comprising 40 percent advertising and 60 percent editorial copy and written almost entirely by Golden, eventually had over 30,000 subscribers. Possibly the best-known piece published by the *Israelite* was "Golden's Vertical Negro Plan," written in response to the 1954 *Brown v. Board of Education* case. The essay prompted *Time* magazine on 1 April 1957 to comment on Golden's influence in civil rights issues. Reflecting Golden's ironic humor and his zealous fight against segregation, his plan suggested that, since whites found sitting with black people intolerable but did not seem to mind standing with them, all seats be removed from classrooms and restaurants. Golden continued this satiric needling in "White Baby Plan," advising black women to procure choice seats at movie theaters by "renting" white children to accompany them.

The *Carolina Israelite* brought Golden popularity and subscribers, but it was the publication of *Only in America* (1958), a compilation of essays from the *Israelite,* that put him on the best-seller list and precipitated an anonymous letter, published in the *Herald Tribune* on 18 September 1958, exposing his conviction for fraud, which he had up to then kept secret. The letter actually increased Golden's popularity. Adlai E. Stevenson, Carl Sandburg, Fannie Hurst, and Billy Graham came to his defense, and Dave Garroway and Jack Paar invited him to appear on their talk shows. Within six months of the appearance of *Only in America,* Golden's subscription list for the *Israelite* had more than doubled and included such notables as William Faulkner, Ernest Hemingway, Bertrand Russell, and Harry S. Truman. The book was turned into a Broadway play by Jerome Lawrence and Robert E. Lee in 1959, but opened to mixed reviews. Beginning in 1960, Golden began writing a syndicated column three times weekly, which appeared in sixty-four newspapers; his workload grew to be so great that he enlisted the assistance of his son Richard Goldhurst in preparing the columns. Golden also contributed articles to such journals as the *Nation, Commentary,* and *Life,* and covered the Adolf Eichmann trial for *Life* in 1961.

As a result of failing health and his conviction that "the romance had gone out of the civil rights movement," Golden ceased publication of the *Carolina Israelite* in 1968, a fact lamented by many, including Vice President Hubert H. Humphrey. Along the way, he received three honorary doctorates and, in 1979, the coveted North Carolina Award for Literature.

In addition to *Only in America,* Golden published a dozen other books, most of them in the humorous satirical style of the *Carolina Israelite.* Especially popular were *For 2 Cents Plain* (1959) and *Enjoy! Enjoy!* (1960). Golden also wrote several books focusing on topics of concern to Jews, including *The Israelis: Portrait of a People* (1971) and *Travels Through Jewish America* (1973, with son Richard Goldhurst). Golden enjoyed writing the biography *Carl Sandburg* (1961), describing it as not a definitive work but one that grew out of a rewarding friendship.

Golden once cautioned his readers against dying on Friday because acquaintances would consider their weekend "completely smashed up." Harry Golden died of a heart attack on Friday, 2 October 1981, in Charlotte, where he is buried in Hebrew Cemetery. Those who remember Golden describe him as a short, heavyset man, endlessly curious, quick, and entertaining, always ready to dismantle social and political complacency. Many Jews and Gentiles considered him the conscience of the South for over forty years and particularly enjoyed the spicy wit and humor of his satire. Among his admirers were a number of the major political players of the 1950s and 1960s, including John and Robert Kennedy, Richard Nixon, and Frank Porter Graham.

★

Golden's manuscripts, correspondence, and papers are in the J. Murray Atkins Library at the University of North Carolina at Charlotte. A few items are at the University of North Carolina at Chapel Hill. Materials related to Golden's trial for mail fraud can be found in the Carter Glass Papers, University of Virginia Manuscript Collection, and the James Cannon Jr. Papers, Manuscript Department, Duke University Library. A thorough analysis of the mail fraud episode appears in Robert A. Hohner, "The Other Harry Golden: Harry Goldhurst and the Cannon Scandals," *North Carolina Historical Review* 65, no. 2 (Apr. 1988): 155–172. The only full-length study of Golden's work is Clarence W. Thomas, *The Serious Humor of Harry Golden* (1997). Obituaries are in the *New York Times,* the *Chicago Tribune,* and the *Washington Post* (all 3 Oct. 1981).

MARY BOYLES

GOODRICH, Frances (*b.* 1891 in Belleville, New Jersey; *d.* 29 January 1984 in New York City), actress, playwright, and screenwriter best known for her thirty-year writing collaboration with her husband, Albert Hackett, on popular Hollywood films and the Pulitzer Prize–winning drama *The Diary of Anne Frank* (1955).

The daughter of Henry Wickes Goodrich, a Wall Street lawyer, and his wife, Madeleine Christy Lloyd, Goodrich was the oldest of two brothers and two sisters, but she never revealed her birthday. She attended private schools in New Jersey and graduated from Passaic Collegiate High School in 1908. Goodrich became interested in theater while attending Vassar College, where she received a B.A. degree in 1912. The following year she studied at the New York School of Social Service but left to become an actress with the Northampton Municipal Theater (1913–1916) in Massachusetts.

The dark-haired, hazel-eyed, five-foot, five-inch Goodrich made her Broadway acting debut in a 1917 production of *Come Out of the Kitchen.* On 3 May 1917, a month after her appearance on Broadway, she married film actor Robert Ames. The marriage ended in divorce in 1923. Goodrich worked steadily as an actress for the next twelve years. Her Broadway successes included *Queen Victoria* (1923), *The*

Showoff (1924), *A Good, Bad Woman* (1925), *Excess Baggage* (1927), and *Heavy Traffic* (1928). On 23 November 1927 Goodrich married the noted historian and author Henrik Willem Van Loon; they were divorced in 1930.

On 7 February 1931 Goodrich married fellow actor and aspiring writer Albert Hackett, and they forged the most successful husband-and-wife writing team in the history of Hollywood and the American theater. Goodrich and Hackett went on to collaborate on thirty-two films and four Broadway plays. They never wrote a film script or stage play outside of their collaboration.

Their play *Up Pops the Devil* (1930), a comedy about a bohemian couple living together in Greenwich Village and trying to write, was their first Broadway play and was a hit. Paramount Pictures purchased the play and in 1931 offered Hackett a Hollywood job as dialogue director on the filmed version, ignoring Goodrich's contribution to the play. Goodrich went with her husband to California and became a movie colony housewife. She was so depressed by her status that Hackett rejected a lucrative five-year Hollywood contract, and they returned to New York, where they wrote another Broadway play, *Bridal Wise* (1932). Although this script was never filmed, it led to a new contract that had Goodrich and Hackett returning to Hollywood as a screenwriting team.

The couple became hugely successful when their screenplays *The Thin Man* (1934) and its sequel, *After the Thin Man* (1936), became big hits and earned two Academy Award nominations, establishing Goodrich and Hackett as superb writers of witty and sophisticated dialogue. They received critical acclaim and another Academy Award nomination for their adaptation of the Eugene O'Neill play *Ah, Wilderness!* (1935). The Hollywood studio system ignored their writing strengths, however, and made them script the highly popular Jeanette McDonald–Nelson Eddy musicals *Naughty Marietta* (1935), *Rose Marie* (1936), and *The Firefly* (1937).

During the 1930s Goodrich was involved with the founding of the Screen Writers Guild (1933), serving on its board in 1936 and as its secretary in 1937 and 1938. As a result of this union activity and the numerous, uninspiring film adaptations they were being forced to write, Goodrich and Hackett lost their enthusiasm for Hollywood and returned in 1941 to New York, where they wrote *The Great Big Doorstep* (1942), their third Broadway play.

Finances forced Goodrich and Hackett to return to Hollywood in 1944. Despite Paramount Pictures' reputation for sophisticated comedies, Goodrich and Hackett's next two assignments were a semidocumentary and a Western for that studio. In 1946 the filmmaker Frank Capra put them to work on the Christmas classic *It's a Wonderful Life.* Goodrich hated working with Capra, describing this as the only unpleasant experience she ever had in Hollywood. Neither she nor Hackett ever watched the movie because,

Frances Goodrich. NEW YORK TIMES PICTURES

as she remarked, she did not want to be reminded of that "arrogant sonofabitch." Goodrich and Hackett wrote two widely successful musicals in 1948, *Easter Parade* (for which they gained their fourth Academy Award nomination) and *The Pirate.* They subsequently earned fifth and sixth Academy Award nominations, for their scripts of *Father of the Bride* (1950) and the musical *Seven Brides for Seven Brothers* (1955).

In 1955 the husband-wife writing team, still relatively unknown, achieved fame with the Broadway production of their drama *The Diary of Anne Frank.* Undertaking this theatrical adaptation of the diary had taken Goodrich through eight drafts of the script and two years of frequent crying for the young Holocaust victim who wrote it. The result of their years of meticulous research won Goodrich and Hackett the Pulitzer Prize, the New York Drama Critics Circle Award, and the Antoinette Perry (Tony) Award. Goodrich also received the Screen Writers Guild Laurel Award for Achievement in 1956. The couple's 1959 film adaptation of the play won the Screen Writers Guild Award and led to their seventh Academy Award nomination, but Goodrich and Hackett did not want their Holocaust drama turned into a film. They were satisfied with the stage version and did not see how a movie could get outside the walls of Anne's hiding place in the attic of an Amsterdam town house. Goodrich disliked the indifference with which director George Stevens treated the script in his attempt to make the lead actress, Millie Perkins, into a star.

Goodrich's disappointment with the filmed version of *The Diary of Anne Frank* and the poor critical and box-office reception of the motion picture that would be the final work of her career, *Five Finger Exercise* (1962), contributed to her decision to leave Hollywood. After a quarter century of writing some of the finest comedies and musicals ever filmed, Goodrich and Hackett were never offered another comedy or musical writing assignment because of the enormous success of their Holocaust drama. It was after they were asked to write a film about a gang rape that Goodrich and Hackett decided in disgust to return for the final time to New York City.

A well-liked and generous couple, Goodrich and Hackett were renowned for gracious entertaining inside their expansive duplex apartment on the Upper West Side of Manhattan overlooking Central Park. Goodrich died in her apartment of lung cancer at the age of ninety-three. She had no children and was survived by her husband and a younger brother, Lloyd, who was curator emeritus of the Whitney Museum of American Art.

Goodrich's life repeatedly testified to her fierce independence. Although she had been brought up with wealth and privilege, she left graduate school to become an actress in an era when the theater was not considered a respectable profession. Her marriage to Van Loon created something of a public scandal when newspapers published stories about their companionate marriage in which they lived in separate apartments. Her aggressive work on behalf of the fledgling Screen Writers Guild defied the threat of her being fired by studio executives and of losing an extremely lucrative income during the Great Depression. But most of all, her career as a playwright and screenwriter flourished during a time when women were not treated as the creative equals of men; even toward the end of her career, when she was awarded a Pulitzer Prize for drama, the $500 check that accompanied the citation was made out to her husband.

★

An insightful interview with Goodrich conducted just weeks before her death can be found in Pat McGilligan, *Backstory: Interviews with Screenwriters of Hollywood's Golden Age* (1986). Nancy Lynn Schwartz, *The Hollywood Writers' Wars* (1982), chronicles Goodrich's noncommunist, left-wing perspective on Hollywood politics and her activism on behalf of the Screen Writers Guild. John Chapman, "Good Hacks Find Out Two Pens Are Better Than One," *New York Daily News* (27 May 1956), is a wonderful article about the Goodrich and Hackett writing part-

nership, especially concerning their work on *The Diary of Anne Frank*. Ronald Bowers, "Frances Goodrich and Albert Hackett," *Films in Review* 28, no. 8 (8 Oct. 1977): 463–466, 490, offers an in-depth look at Goodrich's film writing career. An obituary is in the *New York Times* (31 Jan. 1984).

MARK A. BLICKLEY

GORDON, Ruth (*b.* 30 October 1896 in Quincy, Massachusetts; *d.* 28 August 1985 in Edgartown, Massachusetts), theater and film actress, playwright, and screenwriter, best remembered for her later film work in such movies as *Rosemary's Baby* (1969) and *Harold and Maude* (1971), and for her screenwriting collaboration with husband Garson Kanin.

Born Ruth Gordon Jones to a factory foreman, Clinton Jones, and Annie Tapley Ziegler, a former secretary, Gordon became stage-struck at age fifteen watching Hazel Dawn in a Boston production of *The Pink Lady*. As her autobio-

Ruth Gordon, 1968. SAM FALK/NEW YORK TIMES CO./ARCHIVE PHOTOS

graphical play *Years Ago* (1946) recounts, she persuaded her father to finance her drama training after high school. In 1914, he paid $400 to send her to New York's American Academy of Dramatic Arts; at year's end, Gordon was found unsuited to the stage by the school's directors and was dropped from the program.

But Gordon, by her own admission, "never faced facts," believing that "to be talented you have to want to be, aim high and when doubts come don't accept them." After working as a silent movie extra and haunting producers' offices, she debuted (on 21 December 1915) as one of the Lost Boys in Maude Adams's revival of *Peter Pan,* bringing her first Broadway review: *New York Times* critic Alexander Woollcott wrote, "Ruth Gordon was ever so gay as Nibs." Her naive thank-you letter to the critic began a friendship that lasted until Woollcott's death in 1943.

In 1916 and 1917, as part of a road company of *Fair and Warmer,* Gordon endured thirty-nine weeks of one-night stands. Her first Broadway lead, in Booth Tarkington's *Seventeen* (January 1918), provoked devastating comments. *Tribune* critic Heywood Broun wrote, "Anyone who looks like that and acts like that must get off the stage." But leading man Gregory Kelly, who had gotten her the part, married her on 24 December 1918. Gordon credited the "dazzlingly accomplished" Kelly with teaching her to act, although he felt she was "a heroine," unsuited to comedy. Gordon was small, dark haired, pert, vivacious, and witty. She was not conventionally pretty, but determined to do whatever was necessary to make herself into a star—in 1920, between acting engagements, she went so far as to have her bow legs broken and reset in a Chicago hospital.

Gordon and Kelly played the leads in *Clarence* (1920), then appeared in Indianapolis in 1921, establishing their own stock company there in 1922. The couple also starred on Broadway and on tour in *The First Year* (1922–1923) and then in *Tweedles* (1923), which had been written for them. After her success in *Mrs. Partridge Presents* (1925), Gordon said, "everyone knew I *could* play comedy." Escaping the "delicious moron" parts she had mastered, Gordon was appearing in *Saturday's Children* (1927), opposite Humphrey Bogart when her ailing husband died on 9 July 1927. Her next major role was the lead in *Serena Blandish* (January 1929).

In 1929 Gordon became pregnant during an affair with married Broadway producer Jed Harris and traveled to France to keep the birth of her son, Jones, a secret from the press and public. Returning to New York, she played in *Hotel Universe* (1930) for the Theatre Guild and had successful leading roles in *A Church Mouse* (1931), *Three-Cornered Moon* (1933), and *They Shall Not Die* (1934).

In Westport, Connecticut, in July 1935, Gordon appeared in her first period comedy, as Mrs. Pinchwife in *The Country Wife* (depicting, at Jed Harris's suggestion, "sex in terms of Minnie Mouse"). After a starring success in *Ethan Frome* (January 1936) opposite Raymond Massey, Gordon became the first American invited to act with the Old Vic company, making a sensational London debut in Tyrone Guthrie's production of *The Country Wife* (October 1936) with Michael Redgrave and Edith Evans. Bringing Mrs. Pinchwife to Broadway in December 1936 and playing Nora in Thornton Wilder's adaptation of Ibsen's *A Doll's House* (1937) established Gordon as one of the "first ladies" of the stage, along with her friends and contemporaries Helen Hayes, Lynn Fontanne, and Katharine Cornell.

Personally chosen for the role by playwright Robert Sherwood, Gordon made her first talking film appearance as Mary Todd Lincoln in *Abe Lincoln in Illinois* (1940), then played in *Dr. Ehrlich's Magic Bullet* (1940), *A Dispatch from Reuters* (1941), and in Greta Garbo's last film, *Two-Faced Woman* (1941).

On 4 December 1942, during final rehearsals as Natasha in Chekhov's *The Three Sisters* with Katharine Cornell and Judith Anderson, Gordon married Garson Kanin, a writer and director. She then acted in two 1943 films, *Edge of Darkness* and *Action in the North Atlantic.*

Gordon and Kanin's forty-three year marriage/partnership lasted until her death. Encouraged by Kanin, Gordon wrote and played the lead in *Over Twenty-One* (1944), wrote the play *Years Ago* (1946), wrote and starred in *The Leading Lady* (1948), and played the lead in Kanin's play *The Smile of the World* (1949), which he directed. She collaborated with Kanin on the screenplay for *A Double Life* (1948), a thriller about a Broadway star (Ronald Colman) who "became" his characters—in this case a murderous Othello. Their most famous collaborations were *Adam's Rib* (1949) and *Pat and Mike* (1952), two of the most popular films pairing Katharine Hepburn and Spencer Tracy, for which the writers won Oscar nominations. They also cowrote *The Marrying Kind* (1952). Gordon earned a reputation as a writer of witty dialogue, and she and Kanin were thought by friends on both coasts to represent the real-life models for the onscreen Tracy-Hepburn relationship. Gordon's screenplay of *Years Ago,* retitled *The Actress* (1953), starred Spencer Tracy as father to Jean Simmons's Ruth.

In 1938 Gordon had refused the leading role in *The Merchant of Yonkers,* a play that had been written for her by Thornton Wilder; in August 1954 she traveled to England to play Dolly Gallagher Levi in Wilder's revised version of the play, *The Matchmaker,* directed by Tyrone Guthrie. From Newcastle-on-Tyne to London, Edinburgh, Berlin, Broadway (December 1955), and a national tour ending in Hollywood in July 1957, Gordon triumphed in the role, directly inspiring the musical *Hello, Dolly!* Gordon's perfectionist discipline is revealed by Kanin's report of her "going over her part" before her final, 1,078th performance.

Gordon starred in *The Good Soup* (1960), *A Time to Laugh* (London, 1962) and *My Mother, My Father, and Me* (1963), then adapted Philippe Hériat's play *Les Joies de famille* as *A Very Rich Woman* (September 1965); Kanin produced and directed her in the title role.

After a twenty-three-year absence from the screen, Gordon returned to film acting, winning a Golden Globe Award for *Inside Daisy Clover* (1965) and appearing in *Lord Love a Duck* (1966). On Broadway, she played the title role in *The Loves of Cass McGuire* (October 1966). She won the 1968 best supporting actress Academy Award for *Rosemary's Baby* (1967), played in *What Ever Happened to Aunt Alice?* (1969), *Where's Poppa?* (1970), was Maude in the campus cult film *Harold and Maude* (1971), played Clint Eastwood's mother in *Every Which Way but Loose* (1978) and *Any Which Way You Can* (1980), and often appeared on television, winning an Emmy for a 1979 role on the situation comedy *Taxi*.

In 1976 Gordon wrote *Ho, Ho, Ho,* a two-act play. *Hardhat and Legs,* a Gordon-Kanin screenplay, was made into a TV movie in 1980. In addition to three autobiographies, Gordon also published a novel, *Shady Lady,* in 1981.

Gordon considered her life proof that talent was learned, not inborn. Joie de vivre and an antic wit characterized both her life and art. Accepting her Academy Award at age seventy-two, she wryly brought down the house with, "I can't tell ya how *encouragin'* a thing like this is!" She worked energetically for seventeen more years. Four new films were awaiting release when she told Kanin, "I'm in love with the past, but I'm having a love affair with the future." Three days later, she died of a stroke in her sleep. At her request, her body was cremated and the ashes scattered.

★

Scrapbooks of numerous clippings, articles, pictures, and interviews are in the Billy Rose Theater Collection at the New York Public Library for the Performing Arts, Lincoln Center. Ruth Gordon's earliest diaries provided material for her "Look in Your Glass" series of articles in *Atlantic Monthly* (Aug., Sept., and Oct. 1939). The same diaries were the basis of her play *Years Ago* (1946) and its film version *The Actress* (1953). These works and Gordon's autobiographies, *Myself Among Others* (1971), *My Side: The Autobiography of Ruth Gordon* (1976), and *Ruth Gordon: An Open Book* (1980), tell her story in vivid anecdotal detail, but other sources are often necessary for accurate dates, as Gordon was blithely unconcerned with specificity or chronology. Obituaries and tributes are in the *New York Times* (29 Aug. 1985 and 8 Sept. 1985), *Variety* (4 Sept. 1985), and *Washington Post* (29 Aug. 1985). Gordon's film performances are widely available on videocassettes, as are the films she wrote and on which she collaborated.

DANIEL S. KREMPEL

GOSDEN, Freeman Fisher (*b.* 5 May 1899 in Richmond, Virginia; *d.* 10 December 1982 in Los Angeles, California), the cocreator, with Charles J. Correll, of *Amos 'n' Andy,* the influential radio comedy of the 1930s.

The son of Walter W. Gosden, a bookkeeper, and Emma L. Smith, a homemaker, Freeman Gosden grew up in a stable, lower-middle-class family with deep roots in Virginia. The youngest of five children, Freeman attended the Ruffin School and John Marshall High School in Richmond. After Walter Gosden died in 1911, the Gosdens had to live frugally, and Freeman left school at age sixteen to work. When the United States entered World War I, he enlisted in the U.S. Navy.

After the war Gosden returned to Richmond and worked briefly as a tobacco salesman. In 1919 he joined the Joe Bren Company, which produced variety shows for community groups. Working on a show in North Carolina, he first met Charles J. Correll, another Bren employee. Thickset and curly haired, Correll presented a sharp contrast to the slim, sandy-haired Gosden. Correll's relaxed style complemented Gosden's nervous and energetic temperament. They became good friends.

In 1924 Gosden and Correll were promoted to Bren's Chicago office and decided to share an apartment. They worked up musical revues together, then developed a music act for local vaudeville houses. In March 1925 the Chicago radio station WEGH offered them a weekly radio show, and they began appearing in Midwestern theaters. During the summer of 1925 they resigned from the Bren Company to concentrate on their act.

In October radio station WGN in Chicago offered them $200 a week, and in November Correll and Gosden began a live radio program of songs and comedy. The show was successful, but the station wanted something different. Correll and Gosden proposed a show about two black American characters humorously struggling in the city. On 12 January 1926 *Sam 'n' Henry* began a two-year nightly series. The show's immediate success led Gosden and Correll to publish *Sam 'n' Henry* (1926), a book about the characters.

Early in 1928 the Chicago *Daily News* hired Gosden and Correll to do a nightly fifteen-minute show on its station. The new show, *Amos 'n' Andy,* went on WMAQ on 19 March 1928. Gosden and Correll retained much from their original *Sam 'n' Henry* concept. They changed the setting and the names of the characters but kept the same minstrel show voices. Gosden, with Correll's help, continued to do all of the writing.

Each episode focused on the misadventures of two African-American men who had come north, seeking better lives. Gosden played Amos Jones, an honest and hardworking character with a good deal of common sense. Cor-

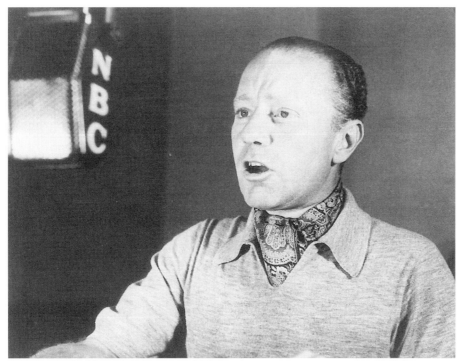

Freeman Gosden. UPI/CORBIS-BETTMANN

rell played Andrew H. Brown, a good-hearted but indolent character, easily led astray.

Amos 'n' Andy was astonishingly successful. Gosden and Correll wrote *All About Amos 'n' Andy* (1929) to answer listeners' questions. Advertisers took an interest, and on 19 August 1929 *Amos 'n' Andy* premiered nationally on NBC. The program became immensely popular and stayed on the air, basically unchanged, for fourteen years. Gosden and Correll became stars and, working in blackface, appeared in movies (*Check and Double Check* in 1930 and *The Big Broadcast of 1936* in 1935). In 1937 they moved their show from Chicago to Hollywood.

Eventually, *Amos 'n' Andy* lost popularity, leaving the air in February 1943. In October, Correll and Gosden were back with a weekly half-hour variety show that stayed on NBC until 1948. Then Gosden and Correll sold (for $2.5 million) CBS all rights to *Amos 'n' Andy* for twenty years, and they continued to receive "star" salaries for weekly CBS broadcasts. In 1954 their variety program ended, but they continued weekly CBS radio broadcasts of *Amos 'n' Andy's Music Hall* until 25 November 1960.

During the early 1950s CBS made a television version of *Amos 'n' Andy*. Featuring an all-African-American cast, the show premiered in June 1951 and immediately became embroiled in racial controversy. Although African Americans had generally approved the earliest broadcasts of *Amos 'n' Andy,* resentment over the portrayal of black characters

by white actors had grown rapidly. As early as 1931 African-American newspapers, especially the *Pittsburgh Courier,* had spoken out against the program. When the television series began, the National Association for the Advancement of Colored People protested vehemently. Correll and Gosden had always believed themselves to be friendly in their portrayal of African Americans, and the acrimony deeply distressed them. Though reasonably successful with audiences and critics, the television show left the air in 1953.

After their final radio broadcast on 25 November 1960, Correll and Gosden remained close friends until Correll's death in 1972. Gosden retired to Palm Springs, California. He had married Leta Marie Schreiber in June 1927; they had two children and were divorced. In September 1944 he married Jane Elizabeth Stoneham; they had two children. During the early 1970s he began suffering from heart trouble, and in 1982 he died of heart failure. He was buried in Los Angeles.

Amos 'n' Andy played a significant role in the development of radio and television. It demonstrated how immensely popular the medium could be, and it helped to establish the situation comedy as a staple in popular entertainment. Gosden, the primary creative talent for the show, was notoriously demanding in the standards he set for the quality of the program, and he deserves the lion's share of credit for the program's extraordinary success. The program's place in the history of American race relations, however, is profoundly problematic. It certainly traded on deeply racist stereotypes, conventions, and assumptions, yet it also often portrayed African Americans as struggling with many of the same Depression-era human and social issues as the rest of American society. Its real effect on race relations in a transitional era is probably important but complex and difficult to assess.

★

The bulk of Gosden's papers are at the Cinema-Television Library and Archives of Performing Arts at the Doheny Library of the University of Southern California. The authoritative study of Correll, Gosden, Amos, and Andy is Melvin Patrick Ely, *The Adventures of Amos 'n' Andy: A Social History of an American Phenomenon* (1991), which includes an exhaustive statement of primary sources. Gosden, Correll, and *Amos 'n' Andy* have been the subjects of much scholarly and popular interest. There is an excellent brief survey of that literature, especially concerning racial controversies, in Thomas Allen Greenfield, *Radio: A Reference Guide* (1989). Additional useful information is in John Dunning, *Tune In Yesterday: The Ultimate Encyclopedia of Old-Time Radio* (1976), and Arthur Frank Wertheim, *Radio Comedy* (1979). An obituary is in the *New York Times* (11 Dec. 1982).

NICHOLAS A. SHARP

GOULD, Chester (*b.* 20 November 1900 in Pawnee, Oklahoma; *d.* 11 May 1985 in Woodstock, Illinois), cartoon artist who created the "Dick Tracy" comic strip, which "shattered the American comic strip tradition" as the first deliberately unfunny strip.

Chester Gould was the eldest of three children of Gilbert R. Gould, manager of a Stillwater, Oklahoma, weekly newspaper, and Alice Miller, a housewife. As a child, Gould declared he wanted to be a cartoonist. He drew caricatures of local politicians at the age of seven and won $5 in a cartoon contest at the age of twelve. When he was fifteen, he took a mail-order cartooning course. Gould's cartoons were published in the *Tulsa Democrat* and the *Daily Oklahoman* (Oklahoma City), among others.

After graduating from high school in 1919, Gould attended Oklahoma A&M College (later, Oklahoma State University) in Stillwater for two years. In 1921 he left Oklahoma for Chicago to seek his fortune as a cartoonist. He said later, "I wanted to get rich, and the way to do that was to draw cartoons that the *Chicago Tribune* would syndicate."

One of his first acts upon arriving in Chicago was to enroll at Northwestern University, where he earned a diploma in commerce and marketing in 1923. While attending night classes, Gould also held a variety of newspaper jobs. He drew comic strips titled "Fillum Fables" and "Radio Cats" for the Hearst-owned *Chicago American* from

1924 to 1929 and worked as an advertisement illustrator for the *Chicago Daily News* from 1929 to 1931. On 6 November 1926 Gould married Edna Marie Gauger. They had one daughter, Jean.

In the late 1920s and early 1930s Gould was creating comic strip prototypes and submitting them to Captain Joseph Medill Patterson, copublisher of the *Chicago Tribune* and founder of the *New York Daily News*. Patterson was the era's recognized genius at developing popular comic strips, which were then distributed through the *Chicago Tribune–New York Daily News* syndicate.

Gould submitted some sixty unsuccessful ideas to Patterson until he presented the concept for an adventure strip featuring a police detective called "Plainclothes Tracy." Patterson liked the strip, but not the title. He changed the name to "Dick Tracy," "dick" being slang for a detective. The first "Dick Tracy" comic strip ran in the *Detroit Mirror* on 4 October 1931. The strip was launched in the *New York Daily News* on 12 October.

Gould's inspirations for the strip came from his fondness for the detective fiction of Edgar Allan Poe and Sir Arthur Conan Doyle, and from the day's newspapers, with their hard-boiled accounts of Chicago gangsters such as Al Capone. Gould, an ardent champion of law and order, decided to create a character who would "hunt these characters up and shoot 'em down."

Gould devoted the rest of his career to "Dick Tracy." As its popularity grew, the strip inspired Dick Tracy books, radio programs, movies, a television series, and toys. A poll of teenagers in the late 1940s found Dick Tracy to be the second best-known American, close behind Bing Crosby and ahead of President Harry S. Truman. At the height of its fame, "Dick Tracy" appeared in more than 1,000 newspapers around the world.

Gould had a serious interest in scientific law enforcement, taking college courses in forensics, fingerprinting, and ballistics to keep the strip realistic. In "Dick Tracy," Gould introduced such gadgetry as the two-way wrist radio and closed-circuit television years before such devices were used by police.

Gould, a stocky, five-foot-eight, bespectacled man with closely cropped naturally curly hair, lived in the Chicago suburb of Wilmette from 1926 to 1936. That year he bought a 130-acre farm in Woodstock, Illinois, sixty miles northwest of Chicago, where he worked and lived with his family the rest of his life. After he retired on Christmas Day 1977, associates continued the strip.

Although "Dick Tracy" was filled with brutality and violence, Gould personally was a loving and humorous man, according to his daughter. Others characterized him as cheerful and gregarious, but single-minded in his devotion to the strip. A Methodist, who did not attend church regularly, Gould read the Bible with his family every Sunday

Chester Gould with *Dick Tracy* comics, 1960. UPI/CORBIS-BETTMANN

evening. Gould died of congestive heart failure on 11 May 1985 in Woodstock, where he was buried.

Chester Gould revolutionized comic strips by bringing adventure, crime, and violence to the "funnies." The early "Dick Tracy" panels depicted the first murder in comic-strip history. Gould noted that "Dick Tracy" was the first strip to show a cop "fighting it out face to face with crooks via the hot lead route." But there were flashes of humor, too, that gave balance to the strip. "Dick Tracy's" strongest aspect was its compelling narrative. Indeed, Gould characterized himself as a "teller of tales." The strip had aspects of a morality play, pitting the forces of good, represented by Tracy and the police, against evil, represented by Tracy's underworld adversaries.

Those adversaries, a rogue's gallery of grotesque villains, were one of the strip's most popular aspects. The criminals' names and visages left no doubt of their evilness: Prune-face, whose features were obscured by wrinkles; the Blank, who had no face at all; the Mole who, rodentlike, stored his ill-gotten loot underground; Flyface, who was so rotten that flies swarmed around his head; and Flattop, whose head was as flat as the deck of an aircraft carrier. Tracy himself was as straight and spartan as his jutting, chiseled jaw implied. His devotion to crime fighting caused him to be shot twenty-seven times in the strip's first twenty-four years. He was also bludgeoned, buried, stabbed, burned, and gassed, among other abuses.

Gould's highly distinctive draftsmanship was considered bold, stark, and impressionistic. His liberal use of high-contrast black and white areas was said to symbolize the contrast between good and evil as spun out in Dick Tracy's adventures. The stark backgrounds and rare shadings made scenes appear as though illuminated by floodlights, critics said.

Gould, who created in Dick Tracy a national icon of law and order and fundamentally changed comic strips, received the Reuben Award of the National Cartoonists Society in 1959 and 1977, a special Edgar Award from the Mystery Writers of America in 1979, and many accolades from law-enforcement agencies.

★

Several books on comic-strip art and artists contain profiles of Gould and "Dick Tracy." Among the most extensive are Stephen Becker, *Comic Art in America* (1959); Jerry Robinson, *The Comics: An Illustrated History of Comic Strip Art* (1974); Richard Marschall, *America's Great Comic Strip Artists* (1989); and Rob Goulart, ed., *The Encyclopedia of American Comics* (1990). A sketch of Gould's career is in James Lesniak, ed., *Contemporary Authors,* New Revision Series, vol. 30 (1990). Obituaries appear in the *Chicago Tribune* (12 May 1985), *Los Angeles Times* (12 May 1985), *New York Times* (12 May 1985), *The Times* (London) (14 May 1985), *Newsweek* (20 May 1985), and *Time* (20 May 1985).

MARY ANN WESTON

GRACE, Princess, of Monaco. See Kelly, Grace.

GRASSO, Ella Rosa Giovianna Oliva Tambussi (*b.* 10 May 1919 in Windsor Locks, Connecticut; *d.* 5 February 1981 in Hartford, Connecticut), first woman elected a state governor who did not follow her husband's political career into office.

Ella Tambussi was the only child of Giacomo Tambussi, a baker, and Maria Oliva Tambussi, both immigrants from the Piedmont area of Italy. She was raised in modest circumstances and often referred to the economic hardships of being a "child of the Depression." Her birthplace in Connecticut was a tightly knit Italian community and remained her permanent residence for her entire life. She acknowledged the town as a source of her strong sense of identity and values, and, in one of her last letters, described Windsor Locks as "my strength, my life."

Grasso received her secondary education as a scholarship student at an exclusive local private girls' preparatory school, the Chaffee School, which later merged with the Loomis School for boys. The Chaffee yearbook significantly underestimated her talents, predicting she would be the first woman to be mayor of Windsor Locks. At Mount Holyoke College she was elected to Phi Beta Kappa in her junior year and graduated magna cum laude in 1940 with a B.A. degree in sociology and economics. She received her M.A. degree, also in economics and sociology, from Mount Holyoke in 1942. Grasso financed her college education through scholarships and by working as a baby-sitter, and, during her graduate studies, by working as a teaching assistant.

On 31 August 1942 she married Thomas A. Grasso, a schoolteacher who later became a school principal in East Hartford, Connecticut. They had two children. For three summers early in their marriage Ella and Thomas Grasso owned and operated the New Colony Movie Theater in Old Lyme, Connecticut; she sold tickets at the box office and he collected them at the door. From 1943 to 1946, Ella Grasso was the Assistant State Director of Research for the Federal War Manpower Commission.

In 1943 Grasso joined the League of Women Voters, an organization she credited with preparing her for public life by teaching her to understand political issues, formulate programs of political action, and learn legislative procedures. She believed one had to work within the political structure to translate legislative programs into actuality. She briefly joined the Republican party in the early 1940s before switching to the Democratic party, which "by inclination" she found more suitable to her ideology.

Grasso became a steadfast party worker, learning the political ropes under the tutelage of John M. Bailey, Connecticut's Democratic party chairman who later became party national chairman. With his endorsement, she successfully ran for the state General Assembly in 1952 and was reelected in 1954. As a member of the legislature she became a protégé of Bailey and a member of his informal "brain trust"; they worked closely on such projects as the elimination of county governments and the reorganization of the court system, measures Grasso had first embraced while active in the League of Women Voters. In 1955 Grasso was appointed assistant floor leader of the Connecticut House. The next year, at the state's Democratic convention, she was selected chairman of the party's platform committee and became chief architect of the platform; she held that chairmanship through 1968. She was also elected Connecticut's Democratic national committeewoman in 1956. She did not stand for reelection as a legislator that year even though she continued to play a strong role as a "volunteer" in working for Democratic legislative issues.

In 1958 Grasso resigned her post with the National Committee when she was elected Connecticut's secretary of state. She became the state's top female official and the chief legislative strategist for the General Assembly. Under her leadership, the secretary's office earned a popular reputation as a "people's lobby" for private citizens with problems, a style of representation that was Grasso's hallmark

Ella Grasso. ARCHIVE PHOTOS

in every government post she subsequently held. She served as secretary of state for three terms until 1970, receiving the highest number of votes cast in the state in both the elections of 1962 and 1966.

In the 1960s, Grasso's talents began to be recognized in national Democratic party circles. She was appointed by President John F. Kennedy to the Board of Foreign Scholarships, a post she held for six years. More important for her political future, however, was her appointment as cochairman of the Resolutions Committee at the Democratic National Conventions of 1964 and 1968. Afterward, Grasso's name was frequently discussed as a possible candidate for Congress, and in 1970 she was elected to the U.S. House of Representatives for the Sixth Congressional District of Connecticut. During her two terms in Washington she was considered more liberal in her political views than she had been in Connecticut. She was a supporter of progressive social policies as well as an advocate of spending programs designed to stimulate the economy.

In 1974 Grasso was elected governor of Connecticut. Her selection as the state's chief executive drew national attention, because she was the first woman to achieve such an office without having had a husband whose political career preceded her own and because her election was initially viewed as a political inroad for women's issues. Some women's groups were disappointed in her tenure, not only because of the small number of females she appointed to office, but also because of her antiabortion stance. She prohibited state financing of abortions under Medicaid, saying she did not "wish to be a party to killing the children of the poor."

In Connecticut matters, she was more of a traditionalist and a protector of the status quo than she had been on the national scene, but she successfully initiated programs to help the elderly and mentally retarded and made government more accessible to the public by championing a "sunshine law" that increased the public's ability to gain information about officials and records. To achieve her goal of keeping state spending low, she held increases in welfare benefits well below the rate of inflation and limited aid to cities. She received considerable criticism for actions she took in her economic austerity program in 1975, when she requested state employees increase their workweek by five hours without additional pay and when she laid off 500 state workers two weeks before Christmas. She insisted on budget cuts in her own office just as she did in other offices and, to illustrate her convictions, returned one-sixth of her salary to the state and discontinued the use of the governor's limousine in favor of a standard state police cruiser or a compact car.

Grasso was reelected to a second term as governor in 1978, having never lost an election in twenty-six years in political office. Part of the way through that four-year term

she learned she had incurable ovarian cancer and, despite the pain, resigned only when she reached the halfway mark of her term. She died a few weeks later in Hartford.

Grasso earned the public's respect as a "keenly intelligent woman" and a "natural politician." Although primarily concerned with issues, she understood the fundamentals of political organization, and her career achievements demonstrate the success of her approach to political office. She was not a fashionable woman, preferring a casual manner of dress and a simple hairstyle, but part of her appeal to the public was her lack of pretense coupled with her sense of personal interest in the lives of her constituents. Guided by a strong inner moral compass, she was a dedicated politician who was said to be "tenacious in her retention of values," a stance that repeatedly brought her the approval of the Connecticut citizenry. Although viewed by others as a pathbreaker for women seeking public office, her gender did not inform her political agenda, nor did she regard herself as a leader among women—she just happened to be a female.

★

There is no full-length biography of Ella Grasso, but she is one of ten women profiled in Peggy Lamson, *Few Are Chosen: American Women in Political Life Today* (1968). This source covers her career only through her years as Connecticut's secretary of state. She is mentioned briefly in *The Women's Book of World Records and Achievements* (1979). *The New York Times Index to Women* includes her political activities covered by the *New York Times* from 1965 to 1975. Of special interest are the profiles in the *New York Times* (22 July and 9 Nov. 1974) pertaining to her race for governor. The *Washington Post* reported on her last few weeks of illness (13 Jan. and 2 Feb. 1981) and published an obituary and profiles (5, 6, and 8 Feb. 1981). An obituary also is in the *New York Times* (6 Feb. 1981).

MARILYNN WOOD HILL

GREER, William Alexander ("Sonny") (*b.* 13 December 1902 in Long Branch, New Jersey; *d.* 23 March 1982 in New York City), jazz drummer who played with the Duke Ellington Orchestra from 1923 until 1951; his exotic percussive effects helped create the band's distinctive "jungle music" sound.

Greer grew up on the New Jersey shore, where his father, William Alexander Greer, Jr., was long employed as a master electrician for the Pennsylvania Railroad, and his mother was a modiste, or dressmaker, whose clients were primarily wealthy white women. Greer had one older and two younger siblings. At the local Chattle High School, Greer came under the influence of a stern taskmaster, Madame Briskie, who conducted the school's orchestra. Greer was one of the few African Americans in this racially integrated environment; he later noted that "Jersey was like Georgia then, it was so prejudiced."

From early on, Greer was an avid billiards player, possibly a pool shark. After hearing the vaudeville act of J. Rosamond Johnson at the Keith Theatre in Long Branch, Greer later met, played pool with, and beat its orchestra's drummer, Eugene Holland. Striking up a deal, the two exchanged lessons—drums for pool. Pool playing remained central throughout Greer's life. Making his professional debut with Harry Yerek during World War I, in 1918 he found employment at the Plaza Hotel on the boardwalk, in the then-fashionable Asbury Park resort, with the gifted young pianist Fats Waller.

After drifting to Washington, D.C., Greer was playing pool one afternoon when the manager of the nearby Howard Theatre frantically entered the poolroom seeking an emergency drum replacement for the pit band. Greer took the job, which lasted for three years, and it was during this time that he met the man his life revolved around for the next three decades—Duke Ellington.

Greer recalled approaching a group of musicians (including the young Duke Ellington) on a street corner: "I gave him [Ellington] a line of jive that set him back on his heels. From then on we were tight." Soon the group (including future Ellington saxophonist Otto Hardwicke) joined the combo of Wilbur Sweatman, a popular clarinet player and bandleader, which led them to New York City in 1923. They opened at Busoni's Balcanades opposite the Original Dixieland Jazz Band; the gig was an economic disaster and the group disbanded. Greer supported Ellington by playing pool for money. Their luck turned when the notorious Prohibition-era chanteuse "Bricktop" Ada Smith arranged work for them at Barron's, a Harlem nightspot on 134th Street. It was there that Ellington emerged as the group's leader, playing a piano style influenced by the then-popular Willie "the Lion" Smith and James P. Johnson. The band soon moved downtown to a better-paying speakeasy, the Kentucky Club, on Forty-ninth Street and Broadway; it was there that Greer recalled doing double duty, claiming "we had all kinds of people mixed there—show people, socialites, debutantes, musicians, and racketeers—it was still Prohibition, of course, and nobody could get a drink of booze in the place unless I gave the O.K. In all the time we were there, we never had a raid or a pinch."

In 1927 the Ellington orchestra moved back uptown to Harlem for a five-year residency at the legendary Cotton Club. There they became world famous and the partnership between Ellington and Greer began to flower as Greer became the unofficial cocaptain of the orchestra. As John S. Wilson wrote in the *New York Times,* "Greer was a very elegant and showmanly drummer. He sat slightly above and behind the rest of the Ellington band, enthroned on a stand on which he was surrounded by a glittering array of paraphernalia that included chimes, timpani, innumerable cymbals, tomtoms, snare drums and bass drums, and a huge gong set up in back of him as though to form a massive halo." Always elegantly dressed, the thin, dapper, frequently smiling Greer added greatly to the visual elegance of the orchestra. Ellington wrote in his autobiography, *Music Is My Mistress,* that Greer "was not the best reader of music" but rather he was "the world's best percussionist reactor. . . . When he heard a ping, he responded with the most apropos pong." Ellington further noted that "instead of following in his father's footsteps, Greer . . . banged on his mother's pots and pans, and developed his own style of drumming from those bim-banging beginnings. . . . A natural supporting artist with his pots and pans, he kept time with horses trotting, people sweeping, and people digging ditches." Sometime in the late 1920s Greer married his wife, Millicent, a Cotton Club dancer.

In 1951, having toured constantly for close to thirty years and recorded almost 2,000 records, Greer left the band, replaced by drummer Louis Bellson, who was followed by Sam Woodyard. Joining the new group of the alto sax great Johnny Hodges, made up largely of Ellington alumni, Greer recorded several critically acclaimed albums. Leaving after six months, Greer played with other small jazz combos in the 1950s and 1960s—with Henry "Red" Allen in 1952 and 1953, Tyree Glenn in 1959, and Eddie Barefield in the 1960s. In his later years Greer emerged as an elder statesman of jazz, becoming the epitome of the old Harlem pro, a raconteur, a jazz storyteller. A fixture of the New York City jazz club scene, he was employed regularly at the Embers, the Metropole, and the Stuyvesant Casino. In the late 1950s Greer was a regular on the Art Ford television show, played a small role in the film *The Night They Raided Minskys* (1968), and starred in the eleven-minute documentary *Sonny* for Signet Productions. From the early 1970s until his death, he played duet with the Ellington scholar and pianist Brooks Kerr at Gregory's in Manhattan (occasionally joined by Ellington alumnus Russell Procope on sax).

After suffering a series of strokes, Greer died of cancer at St. Luke's Hospital in Manhattan at the age of seventy-eight. He was buried at Woodlawn Cemetery in the Bronx, New York.

★

The engrossing autobiography *Music Is My Mistress,* by Duke Ellington (1973), contains a section full of Greer anecdotes, as does Stanley Dance, *The World of Duke Ellington* (1970). Factual data, recordings, and dates can be found in Brian Case, *The Illustrated Encyclopedia of Jazz* (1978) and Leonard G. Feather, *Encyclopedia of Jazz,* rev. ed. (1960). An extensive clippings file is available at Rutgers University's Institute of Jazz Studies in Newark, New Jersey, which also houses Stanley Crouch's oral history interviews with Greer. Several useful articles also at the institute include Burt Korall, "The Roots of the Duchy," *Down Beat* (1967); Jack Cooke, "Credit Is Due: A Short Study of Sonny," *Jazz Monthly* (1960); and Scott H. Fish, "Sonny Greer: The Elder Statesmen of Jazz," *Modern Drummer* (1981). *New Yorker* magazine critic Whitney Balliett wrote an interesting profile of Greer, republished in his *American Musicians: Fifty-six Portraits in Jazz* (1986). An obituary is in the *New York Times* (25 Mar. 1982).

JEFFREY S. ROSEN

GRILLO, Frank Raúl ("Machito"). See Machito.

GRIMES, Burleigh Arland (*b*. 18 August 1893 in Emerald, Wisconsin; *d*. 6 December 1985 in Clear Lake, Wisconsin), baseball player, manager, and scout, best known as an outstanding National League pitcher.

Grimes was one of the three children of Nick Grimes, a dairy farmer, and Ruth Tuttle, a homemaker. The younger Grimes attended Black Brook School in Clear Lake, Wisconsin. In his teens he played semiprofessional baseball and worked in a lumber camp from dawn to dusk for $1 a day. He was driving four horses hitched to a sled when a horse

Burleigh Grimes. COURTESY OF THE NATIONAL BASEBALL HALL OF FAME, COOPERSTOWN, N.Y.

tripped over a stump and buried him under seven tiers of sixteen-foot logs. Lumberjacks extricated Grimes, who was unhurt. His father, who had played some amateur baseball, gave him $15 to try professional ball.

Grimes began his professional baseball career in 1912 as a pitcher with the Eau Claire (Wisconsin) team in the Minnesota-Wisconsin League for $80 a month and toiled for Ottumwa (Iowa) of the Central Association in 1913. He was sold to the Detroit Tigers of the American League for $400 but spent only one week there and did not play. The five-foot, ten-inch, 195-pound right-hander hurled for Chattanooga of the Southern Association in 1913 and 1914, Richmond of the Virginia League in 1914, and Birmingham of the Southern Association in 1915 and 1916.

The Pittsburgh Pirates of the National League brought up Grimes in August 1916, but he lost sixteen games, including thirteen straight, for the last-place club in 1917. He scuffled with manager Hugo Bezdek aboard a Pullman train after being skipped for a starting assignment. In January 1918 the Pirates traded Grimes, Chuck Ward, and Al Mamaux to the Brooklyn Dodgers for Casey Stengel and George Cutshaw.

Grimes won 158 games for Brooklyn from 1918 to 1926, finishing 19–9 as a rookie and nearly pitching a no-hitter against the Philadelphia Phillies. He earned at least twenty victories four times with Brooklyn, compiling records of 23–11 in 1920, 22–13 in 1921, 21–18 in 1923, and 22–13 in 1924. Grimes helped the Dodgers win the 1920 National League pennant and blanked the Cleveland Indians, 3–0, in the second game of the 1920 World Series. In the fifth game, however, he surrendered the first grand-slam home run in World Series history to Elmer Smith in an 8–1 loss.

Grimes, a tough, aggressive, fearless competitor, looked on baseball as a battle for survival and clashed with opponents, teammates, managers, and reporters. He did not speak with Dodgers manager Wilbert Robinson. When it was his turn to pitch, Robinson relayed messages to Grimes through clubhouse boy Babe Hamberger or teammates. Grimes never permitted batters to dig in at the plate and often threw behind them or at their feet. He never shaved his beard on the days he pitched because the slippery elm he chewed to increase saliva irritated his skin. His growth of stubble added to his ominous mound presence and led to his nickname "Ol' Stubblebeard." He often brushed back Frankie Frisch of the St. Louis Cardinals and other batters who hit well against him.

Grimes and sixteen other major league pitchers who were already throwing the spitball were allowed to use the pitch after it was outlawed in 1920; often, however, he simply faked the pitch to keep batters guessing. Although primarily a fastball pitcher, he initially wore a cap a half size too small to disguise his spitball pitch. Before every pitch he held his glove to his mouth to shield his true intentions.

Manager Art Fletcher of the Philadelphia Phillies discovered one day that the tip of Grimes's hat moved whenever he threw the spitter and instructed his batters not to swing at that pitch. Grimes solved that problem by wearing a larger cap. Grimes pitched until age forty-two and was the last pitcher to throw legal spitters.

In January 1927 the New York Giants acquired Grimes for Butch Henline. Grimes compiled a 19–8 record in 1927 and won thirteen consecutive decisions, the longest winning streak of his major league career. Manager John McGraw taught Grimes an effective curve ball. McGraw liked his competitive spirit, but New York traded the aging veteran to the Pittsburgh Pirates in February 1928 for Vic Aldridge. Grimes starred for Pittsburgh, recording career bests with twenty-five victories in 1928 and a .708 winning percentage in 1929.

Grimes moved to the Boston Braves in April 1930 and the St. Louis Cardinals two months later, helping the latter win consecutive National League pennants with marks of 13–6 in 1930 and 17–9 in 1931. He lost two decisions, including a 2–0 heartbreaker on Jimmie Foxx's mammoth ninth-inning home run, to the Philadelphia Athletics in the 1930 World Series. Despite suffering an inflamed appendix, he defeated the Athletics twice in the 1931 World Series. He bested Lefty Grove, 5–2, on a two-hit masterpiece in game three, and George Earnshaw, 4–2, in the series finale.

Grimes struggled for the remainder of his major league career. In December 1931 St. Louis traded him to the Chicago Cubs for Hack Wilson and Bud Teachout. The Cardinals picked him up on waivers in August 1933. He divided his final major league campaign in 1934 between the St. Louis Cardinals, Pittsburgh Pirates, and New York Yankees.

After retirement as an active player, Grimes planned to umpire in the New York–Pennsylvania League, but Larry MacPhail and Branch Rickey of the St. Louis Cardinals persuaded him to become a manager in that team's farm system. He piloted Bloomington (Illinois) of the Three-I League in 1935 and Louisville of the American Association in 1936. Grimes replaced Casey Stengel as manager of the bedraggled Brooklyn Dodgers, guiding them to a 131–171 composite mark in 1937 and 1938. He protested the hiring of Babe Ruth as a first-base coach.

Subsequently, Grimes managed Montreal of the International League (1939), Grand Rapids of the Michigan State League (1940), Toronto of the International League (1942–1944, 1947, 1952–1953), and Rochester of the International League (1945–1946). He scouted for the New York Yankees (1947–1952), Kansas City Athletics (1956–1957), and Baltimore Orioles (1960–1971) and coached for the Kansas City Athletics (1955).

Grimes was married five times: to Florence Ruth in 1913 (divorced, 1931); to Laura Virginia in 1931 (divorced, 1939); to Inez Margaret Martin on 15 May 1940 (she died in 1964); to Zerita Brickell on 30 September 1965 (she died in 1974); and Lillian Gosselin in 1975. In retirement he lived in Holcombe, Wisconsin. Grimes, who had no children, died of cancer and is buried at Clear Lake Cemetery in Clear Lake.

The Veterans Committee elected Grimes to the Baseball Hall of Fame in 1964. The gruff, aggressive hurler won 270 games against only 212 losses over nineteen seasons for seven major league teams, attaining at least twenty victories on five occasions. His major league record included thirty-five shutouts, 314 games completed in 495 games started, 1,512 strikeouts in 4,179.2 innings pitched, and a 3.53 ERA.

Grimes led the National League four times in complete games (1921, 1923, 1924, 1928), three times in games started and innings pitched (1923, 1924, 1928), twice in victories (1921, 1928), appearances (1918, 1928), and hits allowed (1923, 1924), and once in winning percentage (1920), losses (1925), and strikeouts (1921). He helped the Brooklyn Dodgers, St. Louis Cardinals, and Chicago Cubs win four National League pennants, compiling a 3–4 record with a 4.29 ERA in World Series competition.

★

See the Burleigh Grimes files at the Burleigh Grimes Museum, Clear Lake, Wis.; the National Baseball Library in Cooperstown, N.Y., and the *Sporting News* in St. Louis, Mo. There is no full-length autobiography or biography of Grimes, but he reviewed his baseball career in Donald Honig, *The Man in the Dugout* (1977). For anecdotes about Grimes, see Frank Graham, *The Brooklyn Dodgers* (1945); Tom Meany, *Baseball's Greatest Pitchers* (1951); and Richard Goldstein, *Superstars and Screwballs* (1991). An obituary is in the *New York Times* (7 Dec. 1985).

DAVID L. PORTER

GROPPI, James Edward (*b.* 16 November 1930 in Milwaukee, Wisconsin; *d.* 4 November 1985 in Milwaukee, Wisconsin), Roman Catholic priest and civil rights leader whose open-housing marches focused attention on racial inequities and sparked debate on the interplay between religious faith and public policy.

Groppi was born in the working-class neighborhood of Bay View on Milwaukee's South Side near Lake Michigan. He was the eleventh of twelve children of Giocondo and Giorgina (Magri) Groppi. His father had immigrated to Milwaukee from Italy in 1913 and ran a grocery store in the family's largely Italian neighborhood. Young Jim worked in his father's store, attended a Catholic grade school, then spent four years at the public Bay View High School, where he was captain of the basketball team during his senior year.

Considering his environment, he had a relatively early awakening to racial injustice. Milwaukee's population in the late 1940s was only about 3 percent black, and almost all of those residents were crowded into an area known as the "inner core," north of downtown. The rest of the city was predominantly German and Polish. Like most of his neighbors, the teenage Groppi had little interaction with African Americans, but he was aware of the ribbing his father took for his thick Italian accent. For Jim Groppi that ridicule, however gentle, would come to symbolize the illogic of prejudice. At a Bay View basketball game, Groppi scuffled with, then apologized to, a visiting black player. The incident became the subject of a high school English paper, in which Groppi ruminated on the possibility of racial tolerance and understanding. After high school Groppi held a series of jobs and, searching for larger meaning in his life, decided to attend seminary. By the time he began attending Saint Francis (Wisconsin) Seminary in 1953, his racial sensitivities were sufficiently keen that he refused to attend a minstrel show put on by his classmates. Summer work at an inner-city Milwaukee youth center deepened his empathy for poor urban minorities.

Groppi received a bachelor's degree in theology in 1959 and was ordained the same year. He was assigned to Saint Veronica's, a white parish on Milwaukee's South Side. In 1963 he moved to Saint Boniface, on the North Side. Once heavily German, the Saint Boniface neighborhood had become mostly black with the influx of African Americans to Milwaukee after World War II.

As a young priest Groppi made civil rights the centerpiece of a militant ministry whose motto became, in Groppi's own words, "agitate, agitate, agitate." His conscience was inflamed, he later recalled, by a pilgrimage to Alabama in the company of other Milwaukee clergy in 1965. There he demonstrated against segregation and met the Reverend Martin Luther King, Jr. The key challenge of the era, many of Groppi's religious colleagues concurred, was not just to protest the apartheid system of the South, but to confront the de facto segregation and the hardened hearts that obstructed black progress everywhere in the United States.

Milwaukee, whose intensive segregation sprang from prejudice and social custom, more than from law, was an ideal venue for such a campaign. Groppi soon became active in the Milwaukee United School Integration Committee (MUSIC), which pushed for the integration of city schools. On 4 June 1965 Groppi was arrested for blocking a school bus that was transporting black children to segregated classes at an otherwise-white Milwaukee school. Three days later he enunciated his creed for what would become a radical Catholic ministry. A clergyman had to stand "with his people" in righting social wrongs, Groppi said, even if it meant going beyond "orderly procedures" of political involvement and into the realm of civil disobedience. During the next two years he would emerge as a

James Groppi in 1972 after the Supreme Court ruled that his imprisonment in 1969 had violated his constitutional right to due process. UPI/ CORBIS-BETTMANN

prominent civil rights leader, protesting, among other things, the membership of public officials in whites-only fraternal clubs and serving as adviser to the Milwaukee NAACP Youth Council.

But it was not until the open-housing marches of 1967 that Groppi rocketed to national prominence. Demanding a city ordinance banning racial discrimination in housing, Groppi and his growing army of activists, most of them young and black, organized a series of marches into the white South Side. In late August, Groppi and supporters marched on two consecutive nights, encountering white mobs that threw bottles, shouted obscenities, and hanged the priest in effigy. Reacting to the violence, Milwaukee mayor Henry Maier banned nighttime demonstrations; Groppi and 136 others were arrested the night of 31 August for marching in protest of the ban, which was lifted shortly afterward. Some called Milwaukee "the Selma of the North," a reference to the Alabama city whose local racial problems had drawn wide notoriety and an influx of out-of-town activists. With Saint Boniface Church as headquarters, and a Groppi-organized band of paramilitary "commandos" for security, the marches continued periodically through the autumn. Even after passage of a comparatively weak housing ordinance in December 1967, marches or rallies continued into the spring of 1968. That April, the Milwaukee Common Council passed a stronger open-housing ordinance.

Although Groppi was an activist for life, his influence waned thereafter. As a white man at the head of a black uprising, he was acutely aware of his tenuous leadership position, which would erode with the growth of the black power movement in the late 1960s. His subsequent causes included welfare rights, Vietnam War protests, and American Indian militancy. From 1970 to 1972 he served on the pastoral team at Saint Michael's, a racially mixed church on Milwaukee's North Side. Afterward, searching for direction, he entered Antioch Law School in Washington, D.C., and drove a taxi to earn a living. On 22 April 1976 Groppi married Margaret Rozga, thus giving up the active Catholic priesthood. (He was excommunicated from the church after his marriage, but the excommunication was lifted in 1983 after a change in church law.) In 1978 he studied for the Episcopal priesthood at the Virginia Theological Seminary, but found that he was emotionally unprepared to enter a new denomination. Raising a family, he found work driving a Milwaukee County Transit System bus and in 1983 became the leader of the drivers' union. He died of brain cancer, survived by his wife and three children. His burial site was not publicly disclosed, out of fear of vandalism.

A wiry man with a receding hairline, Groppi invariably was described as a passionate human being. Frank A. Aukofer, who covered Groppi's marches for the *Milwaukee Journal,* recalled that he could be "temperamental, annoying, and exasperating." But Groppi also had a "Pied Piper's" instincts for the needs of his flock, and his bond with children—especially poor black children—was "surreal," Aukofer wrote after Groppi's death.

Groppi's activism transcended city and state boundaries, and at the time of his death even his bitter adversaries gave him points for tenacity and moral courage. Much of what Groppi championed, including school desegregation and equal access to housing for all races, became law. (In another sort of vindication, two of his many arrests were appealed all the way to the U.S. Supreme Court, where they were ruled improper.) Human hearts, of course, were less subject to change than were mere words on paper. Faced with such intransigence, Groppi insisted repeatedly that his militancy was rooted in the imperatives of his faith. "Christ," he once said, "was not a peaceful, meek type of individual."

★

Groppi's papers (1964–1978) are housed in the Milwaukee manuscript collection of the State Historical Society of Wisconsin, on the campus of the University of Wisconsin-Milwaukee. Frank A. Aukofer, *City with a Chance* (1968), is a journalist's account of Groppi's upbringing and activism in Milwaukee through the open-housing marches of late 1967. A biographical sketch is in Nelson Lichtenstein, ed., *Political Profiles: The Johnson Years* (1976). A comprehensive obituary ran in the *Milwaukee Journal* (4 Nov. 1985). Obituaries also appear in the *Chicago Tribune* and *New York Times* (both 5 Nov. 1985).

JAMES KATES

GROSVENOR, Melville Bell (*b.* 26 November 1901 in Washington, D.C.; *d.* 22 April 1982 in Miami, Florida), author, editor, and president of the National Geographic Society.

The eldest of seven children born to Gilbert Hovey Grosvenor, editor and president of the National Geographic Society, and Elsie May Bell, daughter of Alexander Graham Bell, Melville Bell Grosvenor began a lifelong association with the society in 1902 when, as an infant held in the arms of his grandfather Bell, he "helped" lay the cornerstone of the original headquarters. The building, Hubbard Hall, was named in honor of his great-grandfather and the first society president, Gardiner Greene Hubbard. Most influential on young Grosvenor's development was his inseparable relationship with his grandfather Bell, who tutored

Melville Bell Grosvenor at Angkor Wat, Cambodia, 1959. BY ROBERT MOORE. © 1959 NATIONAL GEOGRAPHIC SOCIETY.

him and actively encouraged an interest in science. In addition to providing Grosvenor with a workbench in his laboratory, Bell appointed him "photographer of experiments," the first of many photographic assignments. Grosvenor's Scottish heritage was evidenced through Presbyterian faith.

Gilbert Grosvenor honed his son's writing and editing skills and spurred his interest in geography through world travel, encouraging an enthusiasm for sailing, charts, and maps on the family yacht during summers at Baddeck, Nova Scotia. Melville Grosvenor's love of the sea led to Annapolis, where he graduated from the U.S. Naval Academy in 1923. After serving aboard the battleships *Delaware* and *West Virginia,* he resigned his commission in 1924 to join the *National Geographic Magazine* staff as an assistant chief of the illustrations division. Earlier, on 4 January 1924, he married Helen North Rowland. They had three children, Helen, Alexander, and Gilbert, before the marriage ended. He married Anne Elizabeth Revis on 12 August 1950 and had two more children, Edwin and Sara.

Grosvenor's first of twenty-six *National Geographic* articles appeared in the September 1930 issue and featured the first successfully published natural-color aerial photographs, of Washington, D.C., and New York City, personally shot from two airships. Named an assistant editor in 1935, society trustee in 1945, and senior assistant editor in 1951, he became associate editor and vice president in 1954. Three years later the long apprenticeship culminated in election as editor and president. Between 1957 and 1967, he led the society through a period of sustained innovation and growth that one close associate fondly remembered as "that fabulous decade."

Although Grosvenor was fifty-six years old when he assumed the post of editor and had already spent more than three decades with the magazine, he retained an uncommon enthusiasm for his work. Orthodox in demanding quality text and images for publication, he otherwise endowed his staff with an inventiveness and curiosity that proved contagious. The evolving cover of *National Geographic,* where a shortened title and full-page color photography ultimately supplanted the staid acorns-and-oak-leaves border, was but the most visible evidence of a broader corporate renaissance. Magazine quality was further enhanced when printing was moved to Chicago to take advantage of new technology: high-speed film-set presses capable of producing millions of copies with every illustration in color. Through it all, however, the magazine maintained its genteel detachment from politics and controversy in general and continued to refuse alcohol and tobacco advertising.

Searching for new opportunities, Grosvenor inaugurated a monumental world atlas project, six years in the making, and the establishment of a special publications division to oversee development of topical books for the general reader. Both the atlas and the society's first-ever globe set high cartographic standards and were instant successes. Grosvenor increased funding tenfold for research and exploration during his ten-year tenure, supporting expeditions to all corners of the earth, including the first American conquest of Mount Everest. Anthropologist Louis S. B. Leakey, animal behaviorist Jane Goodall, and oceanographer Jacques-Yves Cousteau were but a few of the scientists who benefited from society sponsorship. In addition, he established the award-winning *National Geographic Television Special* series. The public demonstrated its favor for Grosvenor's visionary leadership by increasing membership from little over 2 million to 5.5 million. Such growth led to the construction in 1964 of a new Washington, D.C., headquarters building that included the popular Explorers Hall.

Satisfied with the direction he had provided *National Geographic* magazine and probably recalling his slow advancement under his father, who died in 1966, Grosvenor moved into the newly created post of editor in chief the following year. Magazine operations were turned over to a new editor, son Gilbert, then but thirty-nine years old. At the same time, the elder Grosvenor became chairman of the board of trustees; he was succeeded as president by Melvin M. Payne. No longer encumbered by publishing deadlines, Grosvenor had more time to skipper his beloved *White Mist.* With younger son Edwin often serving as first mate and photographer, the yawl became a means for continued exploration and, of course, additional *National Geographic* articles.

Publicly, Grosvenor's tireless effort to expand the society's frontiers earned international recognition. He received honorary degrees from universities including Miami (Sc.D., 1954), George Washington (LL.D., 1959), Boston (Litt.D., 1970), and New Brunswick (Sc.D., 1975). Among many awards were an International Oceanographic Foundation Gold Medal, a National Park Service Conservation award, and a Parks Canada National Heritage award for support in developing Nova Scotia's Alexander Graham Bell National Historic Park. Professional memberships included the Association of American Geographers, American Geographic Society, Royal Geographic Society (fellow), National Press Club, Overseas Press Club, and Explorers Club. Privately, Grosvenor belonged to the Cosmos, Chevy Chase, Metropolitan, Gibson Island, and Bath (Miami) Clubs, as well as the Cruising Club of America. He died of cardiac arrest at the age of eighty and was buried in Rock Creek Cemetery, Washington, D.C.

Grosvenor completed a transition begun by his grandfather, Alexander Graham Bell, that of converting the National Geographic Society from an obscure professional association into the world's largest nonprofit educational and scientific organization. Laboring for decades in subordinate magazine posts, Grosvenor nonetheless maintained an unquenchable thirst to fulfill the society's mandate "for the increase and diffusion of geographic knowledge." His leadership ensured that those less privileged would share in the adventure.

★

The National Geographic Society maintains a collection of Grosvenor's manuscripts and papers dealing with the organization. Charles McCarry, "Three Men Who Made the Magazine," *National Geographic* 174, no. 3 (Sept. 1988), examines Grosvenor's influence as editor. Bart McDowell, "A Decade of Innovation, a Lifetime of Service," *National Geographic* 162, no. 2 (Aug. 1982), is an illustrated tribute. Obituaries are in the *New York Times* and *Washington Post* (both 24 April 1982); *Chicago Tribune* (25 April 1982); and *Newsweek* and *Time* (both 3 May 1982).

WILLIAM E. FISCHER, JR.

GRUENTHER, Alfred Maximilian (*b.* 3 March 1899 in Platte Center, Nebraska; *d.* 30 May 1983 in Washington, D.C.), army officer who helped plan the Allied invasions of Europe and North Africa during World War II and who served as commander of the North Atlantic Treaty Organization (NATO) from 1953 to 1956.

Gruenther was the eldest of the six children of Mary Shea, a schoolteacher, and Christian M. Gruenther, editor of the *Platte Center Signal,* clerk of the district court, and president of the state Democratic club, in which capacity he managed William Jennings Bryan's third presidential campaign in Nebraska in 1908. Gruenther's parents instilled in their son

a sense of discipline and a thirst for knowledge. Alfred attended a parochial school and spent his high school years at Saint Thomas Academy in St. Paul, Minnesota. At age thirteen he took a summer correspondence course to improve his memory, followed by a course in public speaking. He completed eight months of study at the Army and Navy Preparatory School in Washington, D.C., and listed proficiency in German and Latin among his qualifications for admittance to the United States Military Academy at West Point, New York, where he matriculated in 1917. Because of U.S. involvement in World War I, Gruenther's class obtained their commissions after spending only eighteen months at West Point; in 1918 he graduated fourth in his class. Gruenther married Grace Elizabeth Crum on 22 August 1922. They had two sons, who became army officers.

Gruenther spent his early military career in teaching positions. He served three tours at West Point as an assistant professor of chemistry, mathematics, and electricity. He entered the army's postgraduate education establishment in 1926, serving through 1927 at the Command and General Staff School in Fort Leavenworth, Kansas. As a field artillery officer, he received a 1936 posting to further his graduate studies at the Army War College, where he remained through 1939. Gruenther's next career move came in 1941, with his posting to the Louisiana Maneuvers, large-scale war games that took place just months before the Japanese bombed Pearl Harbor. Gruenther's staff abilities earned him assignment as General Dwight D. Eisenhower's deputy in the maneuvers. Eisenhower brought Gruenther, nicknamed "the Brain" for his impressive memory and an-

General Alfred M. Gruenther on the CBS program *Face the Nation.* ARCHIVE PHOTOS

alytical skills, to London in 1942 to help General Mark W. Clark plan Operation Torch, the Allied invasion of North Africa. Gruenther went on to help plan the invasion of Sicily and Salerno and rode into Rome with General Clark in June 1944.

After World War II Gruenther became the first director of staff of the newly created Joint Chiefs of Staff and then the army's deputy chief of staff for plans and operations. When Eisenhower left the presidency of Columbia University in 1950 to become NATO's commander of Supreme Headquarters Allied Powers, Europe (SHAPE), he made Gruenther, who had never commanded anything larger than a battalion, his chief of staff, promoting him to four-star rank, making Gruenther at age fifty-three the youngest four-star general in the army's history. In 1953 President Eisenhower named him commander of SHAPE, to succeed General Matthew B. Ridgway.

Gruenther's impact on the NATO alliance was three-fold: organizational, tactical, and financial. In 1950 only one of NATO's fifteen military divisions was combat ready. There was no plan for the defense of Europe and no system of communication in place to implement such a plan. As one officer put it, all that stood between the Russians and the English Channel was "a group of committees." Gruenther established the New Approach Group (NAG) to devise a defense strategy and installed himself as chief planner. By 1956 NAG had a plan, a communications system, administrative resources, and a new advantage— American nuclear weapons.

The organizational network developed by Gruenther established the role of each nation in the alliance. He brought his formidable diplomatic skills to bear on convincing the Europeans that Copenhagen and Chicago were defended equally by a strongly supported NATO. He committed to memory an impressive store of information about the alliance, ranging from the productive capacities of an Italian tank factory to the results of a member nation's referendum on defense spending. When he visited one country to argue for increased military appropriations, Gruenther stunned his aides by addressing each parliamentarian by name and asking them specific personal questions, gleaned from his prior study of their biographical profiles, in order to establish a rapport with them.

General Gruenther, who was known for his keen sense of humor, eschewed the abrasive style of many high-ranking military figures but managed to be forceful in persuading member nations to strengthen their commitment to the NATO alliance. Gruenther, described by Eisenhower in his memoir *Mandate for Change: 1953–1956* as "one of the ablest all-around officers, civilian or military, I have encountered in my fifty years," retired from the army on 31 December 1956.

After his retirement he served as chairman of the English Speaking Union and sat on the boards of Dart Industries, Federated Department Stores, Pan American World Airways, and the New York Life Insurance Company. He also served on the presidential commissions for arms control and disarmament; heart disease, cancer, and stroke; and an all-volunteer armed force. Probably his most important civilian post was as president of the American Red Cross, in which capacity he served from 1957 to 1964.

Early in his military career, Gruenther had overheard a superior officer say that every young officer should learn how to play bridge. He promptly sent away for an instruction booklet on the game and soon became the best bridge player in the army; he was one of Eisenhower's favorite partners, and his skill with cards brought him recognition in *Time, Newsweek,* and the *New Yorker.* In 1933 he wrote *Duplicate Contract Complete,* considered a classic text on the game. His abilities with the pasteboards earned him an invitation to referee the celebrated Culbertson-Lenz bridge match of 1931. The bridge expert Julius Goldberg recognized Gruenther's talent as a tournament director and asked him to set up a match in New York City. Goldberg wanted "military discipline" imposed on the competition. Gruenther complied. On the day of the tournament Goldberg and his partner arrived late and under Gruenther's rules had to forfeit their seats. Later in life Gruenther served as honorary chairman of the World Bridge Federation.

Gruenther was a highly decorated military officer and received many civilian awards, including honorary doctorates from Harvard and Yale. The French Republic granted him its médaille militaire in 1956, making him only the fifth foreigner, after General John Pershing, President Franklin D. Roosevelt, Eisenhower, and Winston Churchill, to receive the award.

Gruenther, who lived in Washington, D.C., died of pneumonia at the Walter Reed Army Hospital there on 20 May 1983. He was buried with full military honors at Arlington National Cemetery.

★

Gruenther's papers are at the U.S. Military Academy and the Army War College. Obituaries are in the *New York Times* and *Washington Post* (both 31 May 1983).

LAWRENCE CARROLL ALLIN

GRUENTZIG, Andreas Roland (*b.* 25 June 1939 in Dresden, Germany; *d.* 27 October 1985 near Forsyth, Georgia), German-born physician whose development of percutaneous transluminal coronary angioplasty (PTCA) to clear blocked coronary arteries without resorting to open heart surgery transformed the practice of cardiology.

Andreas Gruentzig was born on the eve of World War II in a city that would be fire-bombed to near-extinction when he was kindergarten age. His father, Wilmar, was conscripted into the German army when Andreas was a baby and reportedly was killed in Berlin in 1945. Andreas learned to walk and talk in the rubble of war and, with his mother, Charlotte, and an older brother, relocated several times within Germany, moved to Argentina in 1950, and returned to Germany in 1952. He resumed his schooling first in Leipzig at the Thomas-Gymnasium (B.A. degree, 1957), then in Heidelberg, West Germany, at the Bunsen-Gymnasium (B.A. degree, 1958) and the University of Heidelberg Medical School (M.D, 1964).

Over the next six years Gruentzig continued his training and research in hospitals in Germany and England and in 1970 began an internal medicine fellowship in Zurich at the University Hospital in the department of angiology (the study of blood and lymph vessels). In August of that year he married Michaela Josefa Seebrunner; they had one daughter, Sonja.

Gruentzig progressed steadily up the academic ladder at University Hospital, advancing his expertise in radiology and cardiology. In 1971 he performed his first angioplasty— but in a femoral (thigh) artery. The procedure at the time was not often used and confined largely to the peripheral vessels to treat patients with intermittent claudication, a condition caused by arterial blockages that impede blood flow and make walking uncomfortable. His early studies, published in specialty medical journals in Europe and the United States, addressed the hemodynamics in the legs of such patients. Though peripheral angioplasty was an accepted procedure, it was considered inferior to surgery, and Gruentzig had to compete with surgeons for patients who might be treated either by scalpel or catheter.

The notion that the angioplasty technique could be adapted to the smaller and more vulnerable coronary anatomy to clear blockages was viewed skeptically by many cardiologists. Gruentzig worked ceaselessly—in the lab with dogs and human cadavers and in his apartment at his kitchen sink and table with catheters, wires, tubes, and balloon materials—to refine the technique and construct the device that would give form and substance to the concept of coronary angioplasty. He succeeded in fashioning a small, double-lumen catheter holding a tinier catheter with an inflatable balloon tip that could be threaded through an artery in the groin or upper arm and into the fatty plug within the target coronary. At this point the balloon would be inflated—to just the right size and exerting just the right amount of pressure—to flatten the plaque against the arterial wall, thereby restoring patency and blood flow to a blood-starved heart. The catheter would then be withdrawn.

Gruentzig came to the United States for the first time in November 1976, giving a presentation at the annual American Heart Association meeting on his canine coronary angioplasty experiments. His work and his projection of the procedure's human potential caused a stir, but many remained skeptical that it was actually possible. Several months later he performed intraoperative balloon dilatation in the involved coronary artery that had been bypassed in a coronary bypass surgery procedure, establishing that the physical maneuver was indeed possible in a living heart patient. Whether it would actually do the job in the absence of the definitive bypass procedure remained to be seen in the as yet unemergent first patient.

That patient soon presented himself, an insurance salesman whose optimism, confidence, and youth matched Gruentzig's own. With severe exercise-induced chest pain and angiographically demonstrated stenosis of the left anterior descending coronary artery, he opted for the risk of being the first coronary angioplasty patient over the known risks posed by standard coronary artery bypass surgery. Thus on 16 September 1977, Gruentzig successfully performed the procedure that would launch the new discipline of interventional cardiology. "Everyone was surprised about the ease of the procedure," he later recalled, "and I started to realize that my dreams had come true."

Two months after this feat, in November 1977, he returned to the American Heart Association meeting, this time with proof that coronary angioplasty was safe and effective for humans with coronary heart disease. He had not yet published his experience and many in the overflow crowd that attended his presentation were unaware of the details, or even that he had made the leap from dogs to humans. He began his discourse with what appeared to be a routine follow-up of his animal studies but ended with slides of the first human applications. Exclamations and thunderous applause filled the auditorium, and Andreas Gruentzig had secured his place in the medical archives. That he was movie-star handsome, with a quick and sparkling smile, did not diminish the considerable attention and adulation that followed him the rest of his life.

Over the next twelve months Gruentzig performed another thirty or so coronary angioplasties, oversaw the production and distribution of his angioplasty equipment, and started teaching the procedure to other cardiologists. The first commercial balloon catheter devices were manufactured on the proverbial shoestring in the garage outpost of a fledgling Swiss company, with the inventor serving as quality-control regulator. No physician could acquire an angioplasty balloon catheter without a signed training certificate from Andreas Gruentzig, attesting to successful completion of a hands-on course from the master.

Upon his return to Zurich from the American cardiology meeting, Gruentzig was besieged by a steady stream of visitors who wanted to view the procedure up close. He decided to establish biannual courses, and in March 1978 two American physicians taught by Gruentzig pioneered the procedure in the United States. From the beginning, he laid his procedure and his own skills on the line, conducting live demonstrations over closed-circuit television, a teaching technique that made its way into other areas of cardiology and medicine generally. Initially Gruentzig estimated that angioplasty would be a better alternative for 5 to 10 percent of patients who would otherwise undergo bypass surgery; by the time of his death, it had replaced 15 to 20 percent. A decade later, about a million procedures were performed annually worldwide, about half of them in the United States.

The U.S. medical community, especially, embraced both the man and his innovation, and several major U.S. research and teaching hospitals vied to attract Gruentzig to their faculty. Having been appointed physician in chief of cardiology at Zurich's University Hospital in 1979, he nevertheless was wooed away the following year to shape and direct the new discipline of interventional cardiology at Emory University in Atlanta and was accorded automatic U.S. citizenship upon his emigration to this country.

When Gruentzig arrived in the United States, he had his wife and daughter with him. But the Gruentzigs divorced and Michaela and Sonja returned to Switzerland before May 1983, when Gruentzig married Margaret Anne Thornton, age twenty-six, a physician and resident in radiology at Emory and the only child of a prominent Georgia family. In a thumbnail sketch he provided for Emory's files in 1981, Gruentzig listed among his "hobbies" being a pilot—"licensed in Switzerland, not yet in the U.S." He later secured his license and a twin-engine plane. On 27 October 1985, flying back from a weekend sojourn at their vacation home in Sea Island, Georgia, in the foggy, drizzly aftermath of Hurricane Juan, Andreas and Margaret Anne Gruentzig died in a plane crash. His death at age forty-six, at the height of a brilliant and charismatic career, devastated his colleagues and others who knew him or of him. Shortly after his death the board of trustees of Emory University approved the creation of the Andreas Gruentzig Cardiovascular Center at Emory University Hospital. He was buried in Macon, Georgia.

Andreas Gruentzig had the intelligence to perceive that the balloon catheter technique could be crafted to accommodate the coronary arteries, the diligence to build his own prototypes, and the will and charm to convince the rest of the world that this was an approach worth pursuing. Once he had succeeded, he undertook to train others in the technique and constantly sought to expose its weaknesses, analyze its relative usefulness, and improve upon its applications. From the onset of its use, coronary angioplasty was chosen instead of bypass surgery in increasingly complicated cases of coronary blockages, and successors in the

field continued to improve materials and techniques, often to great advantage of patients spared the trauma of open-heart surgery.

★

Gruentzig's scholarly works number in the hundreds and span the medical literature from 1971 to four years beyond the year of his death. Primary sources for information on his life and work are tributes by colleagues. Dr. J. Willis Hurst, "Tribute: Andreas Roland Gruentzig (1939–1985); A Private Perspective," *Circulation* (March 1986), is an account by Emory's chairman of medicine that traces Gruentzig's personal and professional odyssey from Dresden to Atlanta; another piece by the same author, "In Memory of Andreas Roland Gruentzig and Margaret Anne Thornton Gruentzig," *American Journal of Cardiology* (1 Feb. 1986), includes the recollections of Hurst and others of Gruentzig's coworkers. Spencer B. King III, "Angioplasty from Bench to Bedside to Bench," *Circulation* (1 May 1996) is an account of the development of angioplasty and the life of its inventor by the director of the Emory center dedicated to Gruentzig's memory.

FRAN POLLNER

GRUMMAN, Leroy Randle ("Roy") (*b.* 4 January 1895 in Huntington, New York; *d.* 4 October 1982 in Manhasset, New York), aeronautical engineer and aviation executive.

The descendant of seventeenth-century Scots-Irish immigrants, Roy Grumman was the son of George Tyson Grumman and Grace Ethel Conklin; his father was a carriage maker and postal clerk. He had one sister.

Grumman decided on an aviation career at an early age. When he graduated second in his class from the Huntington High School on Long Island in 1911, his salutatory address was entitled "The Aeroplane." Following his graduation from Cornell University in 1916 with a B.S. degree in mechanical engineering, he went to work in the engineering department of the New York Telephone Company. The following year he enlisted in the U.S. Navy as a machinist's mate second class and was sent first to Columbia University and then to the Massachusetts Institute of Technology (MIT) for additional study. He was subsequently accepted for flight training and graduated in September 1918 as Naval Aviator no. 1216 with a commission as ensign.

Grumman became a flight instructor to a bombing squadron at the Pensacola, Florida, Naval Air Training Station for a short time before returning to MIT at the navy's behest to study aeronautical engineering. In 1919 he was transferred to the Naval Aircraft Factory in Philadelphia, where he became a test pilot and a project engineer. While there, he met Grover and Albert Loening of the Loening Aeronautical Engineering Corporation of New York City. Impressed with the young man, they offered him a job as a test pilot and plant manager for their company. Grumman accepted and went to work for Loening in 1920.

Leroy Randle Grumman in a G-32A, 1938. Louis Eltscher. Courtesy of Grumman Corporation.

On 19 March 1921, he married Rose Marion Werther. They had three daughters and one son.

Loening sold his company in 1928 to the Keystone Aircraft Company of Bristol, Pennsylvania, which became part of the bigger Curtiss-Wright Corporation in 1929. Grumman had no desire to relocate and disliked the prospect of becoming part of a large bureaucratic organization. Hence, he decided to go into business for himself.

Accompanying him in this new venture were two men who had come to the Loening company in 1924 and who would figure prominently in Grumman's subsequent career. They were Leon A. "Jake" Swirbul and William T. Schwendler. Swirbul was the shop and production supervisor for Loening and Schwendler was an aeronautical engineer. The three men established the Grumman Aircraft Engineering Corporation on 6 December 1929, and opened for business on 2 January 1930 in a vacant building in Baldwin, Long Island. They agreed to pursue a cautious and conservative business strategy summarized as follows: "Let's do one thing at a time and do it well and let's keep everything under control." This was the hallmark of Grumman's managerial style for the next thirty-six years.

The company's first source of income was the repair and maintenance of the Loening Air Yacht, an amphibian airplane designed for wealthy sportsmen-pilots that was no longer being serviced by Loening. The company soon designed a new type of airplane float with a retractable land-

ing gear. This new airplane attracted the attention of the U.S. Navy, which purchased a small quantity to be used as scout planes. The navy also wanted to use the new landing gear in a fighter. Grumman had been working on such a design, and the navy on 28 March 1931 issued a contract for an experimental prototype, the XFF-1. A production contract for the FF-1 soon followed. It became the first in an unbroken line of Grumman-designed navy aircraft that extended to the end of the century. Roy Grumman's airplanes developed the reputation for being rugged and dependable. The Grumman plant was given the nickname "Iron Works" during World War II because of the durability of its products. Reputedly, Grumman aircraft shot down more than 60 percent of the Japanese aircraft destroyed in the Pacific theater of war.

Roy Grumman had envisioned a small familial company that would allow him to retain a high degree of personal control while preserving an informal managerial style. He believed that the maximum number of employees should not exceed 250. Survival in the airplane business demanded growth, however, and reluctantly accepting that reality, he consented to a public stock issue in order to finance expanded production. By 1945, the company that bore his name had over 22,000 workers on the payroll. It had long ago outgrown its tiny Baldwin plant and had moved first to Valley Stream, then to Farmingdale and finally to Bethpage, all on Long Island.

The Swirbul-Schwendler-Grumman team became well known for its ability to cut through bureaucratic red tape and maintain a high rate of production. These men complemented one another very well: "Grumman the creative engineer; Swirbul the employee-oriented production specialist; and Schwendler the problem solver" (Thruelsen, pp. 20–21). By the end of World War II, the Grumman Aircraft Engineering Corporation was one of the most highly regarded companies in the industry.

Its reputation failed to insulate it from the shocks of the retrenchment that accompanied postwar demobilization, however. In an attempt to remain viable, Grumman diversified into the civilian market with a line of aluminum products. Military aircraft remained the primary source of income, and Grumman soon produced a series of new designs that included jet fighters. The company also pursued guided-missile research and responded to the challenge of space exploration with a lunar landing module as one of its many space-related products.

Grumman relinquished the presidency of his company in 1946 and retired as board chairman in 1966. He remained a director until 1972 and held the title of honorary board chairman until his death, after a long illness. He is buried in Locust Valley Cemetery in Locust Valley, New York. Never interested in acquiring great wealth or executive power, he was the antithesis of the stereotypical business tycoon. He was shy and reserved by nature and was once described as "a quiet, reflective small-town man who dislikes big cities." He wanted to create a "small, intimately manageable, and innovative" aircraft company that would "contribute to aeronautical progress on its own terms." In fact, he created an aerospace empire that at the time of his retirement employed over 33,000 people and had $1 billion in sales.

Grumman received the Daniel Guggenheim Medal in 1948 "for outstanding achievement in successfully advancing aircraft design for naval and peacetime use." That same year he received the Presidential Medal of Merit for the company's wartime production record, the first aircraft manufacturer so honored. Additionally, he received an honorary D.Eng. degree from Polytechnic Institute of New York in Brooklyn in 1949 and an honorary LL.D. degree from Adelphi College in 1961. He was also given the Frank M. Hawks Memorial Award in 1958 and was named to the National Aviation Hall of Fame in 1972 and to the International Aerospace Hall of Fame in 1973. For his contributions to aeronautical engineering he became the first re-

cipient of the Hunsaker Medal of the National Academy of Sciences in 1968. He was also an Honorary Fellow in the Institute of Aeronautical Sciences and a member of the Society of Automotive Engineers.

★

Grumman's papers are available for scholarly research and are held at the History Center of the Northrop Grumman Corporation. The National Air and Space Museum in Washington, D.C., keeps a biographical file on Grumman. Other biographical information can be found in Richard Thruelsen, *The Grumman Story* (1976), a history of the Grumman Corporation. Articles on the Grumman company can be found in *Aero Digest* (Jan. 1940); *Time* (18 May 1942 and 11 Sept. 1944); and *Fortune* (June 1948).

Grumman aircraft are discussed in René Francillon, *Grumman Aircraft Since 1929* (1989); Terry C. Treadwell, *The Iron Works: A History of Grumman's Fighting Aeroplanes;* as well as numerous articles in *Wings* and *Airpower* magazines. An obituary is in the *New York Times* (5 Oct. 1982).

LOUIS R. ELTSCHER

H

HAGERTY, James Campbell (*b*. 9 May 1909 in Plattsburg, New York; *d*. 11 April 1981 in Bronxville, New York), newspaper reporter, press secretary to Governor Thomas E. Dewey of New York and President Dwight D. Eisenhower, and executive for the American Broadcasting Company.

Hagerty was born into a newspaper family; his father, James A. Hagerty, was chief political correspondent of the *New York Times*. His mother, the former Katherine S. Kearney, was a schoolteacher. He was one of three children. When the younger Hagerty was three years old the family moved to New York City, where the youth attended Evander Childs High School in the Bronx and, for his last two years of high school, Blair Academy in Blairstown, New Jersey. Upon graduation in 1928, he went to work at the New York Stock Exchange. Because of the market crash he went back to school, at Columbia University, where he graduated with an A.B. in 1934. On 15 June 1937 he married Marjorie Lucas; they had two sons.

While in college Hagerty was campus correspondent for the *New York Times,* and he joined the staff of the *Times* upon graduation, first with the city staff and then as legislative correspondent in Albany and deputy bureau chief. Possessed of a muscular and compact frame, conservatively dressed in dark double-breasted suits, Hagerty from the outset displayed a high charge of nervous energy and was constantly on the move. With his strong features, ruddy face, gray eyes with an owlish, inquisitive quality, framed in thick-lensed glasses, he was a man to watch.

In Albany politics beckoned, and in 1943 he became press secretary to Governor Thomas E. Dewey and thus learned the work of advancing a major state political leader into national notice. He helped manage Dewey's runs for the presidency in 1944 and 1948. In 1952 a group of reporters advanced his name to Dwight D. Eisenhower as a press secretary but the general was uncertain, fearing that to appoint him might link "Ike" with Dewey, who had lost the presidency twice. Eventually, Eisenhower decided to take him on because of Hagerty's experience in handling national publicity.

After Hagerty's appointment, announced in late November 1952, the bond between Eisenhower and his much younger assistant became close. The new president needed political advice, and Hagerty was full of it. There was almost a father-son relationship. "Jim, my boy . . . ," the president would begin a query or instruction. Hagerty, one should add, was a strong personality and did not hesitate to disagree with his senior. Eisenhower's well-known temper did not ruffle his press secretary, who, if he did not argue, nonetheless stood his ground. The president, an intelligent man, liked this relationship and profited from it.

As press secretary to a two-term president, Hagerty quickly gained the respect of the Washington press corps, because he himself had been a long-term newspaperman and knew the problems of reporters who had to work with deadlines and needed leads on stories that would save them time and avoid the need for complex inquiries. When Hagerty first met the press corps after Eisenhower became pres-

James Hagerty. ARCHIVE PHOTOS

ident, he set out the rules. "I would like to say to you fellows that I am not going to play any favorites," he said. He would not give out exclusive stories, nor would he lie to the reporters. "When I say to you, 'I don't know,' I mean I don't know. When I say, 'No comment,' it means I'm not talking, but not necessarily any more than that." Aside from that, he told them, he was there to help them get the news.

As press secretary, Hagerty abolished the long-standing practice that the president could not be directly quoted without specified permission. He knew that his boss was quite capable of dealing with reporters, for Eisenhower during the war years and afterward had met the press many times. Eisenhower was crisp and pointed when he wished to be, and also knew when to obfuscate. ("Don't worry, Jim," the president said after a briefing on an awkward subject, "I'll just go in there and confuse them.")

In addition to allowing the president to be quoted without limit, Hagerty in 1955 began allowing newsreel and television cameras into press conferences. Newspaper reporters objected vociferously, because for decades they had dominated presidential news. Although Hagerty was one of their own, he gave their objections no heed. Thenceforth, President Eisenhower was nationally televised, to the immense advantage of the administration, which could now more easily dominate the news.

When "Ike" took office in 1953 the Republican party was divided between adherents of the political center and the right. The latter possessed the principal chairmanships and other posts in Congress. Primarily because of Hagerty's skill with the media, however, Eisenhower was able virtually to create a moderate Republican party. The president also used Hagerty for special assignments, such as turning the Senate leadership against the machinations of Senator Joseph R. McCarthy of Wisconsin, whose Republican extremism was embarrassing to a middle-of-the-road GOP president. Through communication with senators and artful use of press conferences and private communication to reporters, Hagerty helped Eisenhower arrange a Senate censure of McCarthy in 1954 that virtually excluded him from further public influence.

Hagerty served as press secretary to the end of Eisenhower's presidency. Afterward, he was an executive at ABC's corporate headquarters in New York. He served as vice president of news, special events, and public affairs from 1961 to 1963 and as vice president for corporate relations from 1963 to 1975. During his ABC years he kept in occasional touch with Eisenhower, who died in 1969. His relaxations were poker and golf, which he continued into retirement beginning in 1975. Hagerty, an Episcopalian, died of heart failure in the New York suburb of Bronxville, where he had lived after retiring.

Hagerty's lasting influence was to place Eisenhower's public relations, primarily through newspapers and television, upon an unshakable foundation. Through Hagerty, the president reorganized the Republican party. Hagerty assisted on occasion as presidential hatchetman. What political advice he gave the president is difficult to know, but the success of the Eisenhower administration may well be testimony to advice that worked. Hagerty was the most successful presidential press secretary in the twentieth century, since institution of that office in 1939 during the Franklin D. Roosevelt administration. He was the only secretary to serve through two full presidential terms.

★

Hagerty's personal papers are in the Dwight D. Eisenhower Library in Abilene, Kansas. The first two boxes of the papers contain a diary for sixteen months during the Eisenhower presidency, for which see Robert H. Ferrell, ed., *The Diary of James C. Hagerty: Eisenhower in Mid-Course, 1954–1955* (1983). An obituary is in the *New York Times* (12 Apr. 1981). An oral history is in the Oral History Collection, Oral History Research Office, Butler Library, Columbia University.

ROBERT H. FERRELL

HALAS, George Stanley (*b.* 2 February 1895 in Chicago, Illinois; *d.* 31 October 1983 in Chicago, Illinois), sports executive who founded the Chicago Bears and is considered the father of professional football.

Halas was the youngest son of Bohemian immigrants who arrived in America in 1885 and settled on Chicago's West Side. His father, Frank J. Halas, ran a tailor shop; his mother, Barbara Poledna, sold groceries at the same location. In indoor arenas, his two older brothers involved young George in neighborhood softball games and other sports. He also had a sister. At Crane Technical High School and the University of Illinois, where he earned a degree in ceramic engineering in 1918, Halas excelled in baseball, basketball, and football.

In 1918 Halas enlisted in the U.S. Navy and was commissioned an ensign at the Great Lakes Naval Training Station, where he played football. He caught a touchdown pass in a victory over the Mare Island Marines in the 1919 Rose Bowl. Encouraged by the style of play exhibited by these former collegians, Halas believed football players could perform as professionals. A brief stint in 1919 with baseball's New York Yankees ended with a contract dispute and a hip injury.

In 1920 Halas found employment at the Staley Starch Works in Decatur, Illinois. Company owner A. E. Staley created an intramural athletic program to boost employee morale and advertise the company's products. To manage and organize the program, Staley appointed Halas as athletic director. When the enterprise was no longer economically feasible, Staley allowed Halas to keep the football team, giving him $5,000 to use the Staley name for one year. Halas then moved the squad to Chicago, renaming the team the Bears in honor of William Wrigley's baseball team, the Cubs. At that time professional football was a disorganized hodgepodge of teams with no set schedule and direction. More teams were held together by male bonding and barroom camaraderie than by loyalty or contractual obligation to a franchise. During the 1920 season, franchise owners—for the most part, businessmen—met in a Canton, Ohio, automobile dealership to establish the American Professional Football Association, the predecessor of the National Football League.

On 18 February 1922, Halas married Minnie Bushing, who served as team historian. They had two children. To earn a living and increase revenue to keep the team solvent, Halas worked as a car salesman while partner Edward "Dutch" Sternaman pumped gasoline. As player-coach, Halas set up schedules, served as publicist, sold programs, and collected tickets at the gate. In a game against the Oorang Indians, whose roster included names like Red Fang, Xavier Downwind, and Red Fox, Halas returned a Jim Thorpe fumble ninety-eight yards for a touchdown. Despite his efforts, the team lost $71.63 the first season. A marquee attraction was needed to increase ticket sales.

In 1925 Halas signed Harold "Red" Grange, who generated badly needed publicity. Grange had starred at the University of Illinois, where Grantland Rice dubbed him the "Galloping Ghost" for his elusive running style. As the greatest college football player of the age, Grange joined Charles Lindbergh, Babe Ruth, and Jack Dempsey in the pantheon of idolized heroes during the 1920s. At that time, professional football was a blue-collar sport associated with brawlers and barroom toughs. By signing Grange, Halas added credibility and respectability to professional football, which began to emerge as a major force in American culture.

After purchasing Sternaman's interest in the team in 1932, Halas and coach Ralph Jones began to experiment with the Bears' offense. Prior to 1940, football resembled trench warfare, a push-and-shove game in which muscle and brute force prevailed over finesse and speed. Formations like the single wing and the Notre Dame box placed the ends at the sides of the tackles and set the backfield three yards behind the line of scrimmage. Passing complemented goal-line offensive schemes and was used sparingly. Halas hired Stanford University coach Clark Shaughnessy as an offensive consultant to implement the new offense. Shaughnessy perfected the man-in-motion T formation, which placed the ends wide on either side of the line of scrimmage, the quarterback under center, and created the flanker, a back who moved laterally prior to the snap of the ball. With two remaining backs set behind the offensive line, the movement of the flanker placed the opposing defense in a quandary by giving the quarterback a variety of options. In the 1940 NFL championship game, the Bears

George Halas. PRO FOOTBALL HALL OF FAME

annihilated the Washington Redskins 73–0, heralding the modern age of professional football.

For their punishing, bruising play, the Bears became known as the "Monsters of the Midway." Halas endlessly prowled the sidelines in a heavy overcoat with a felt-brimmed hat on his bald head, scowling at players and officials through black, horn-rimmed glasses. A strict disciplinarian, he placed team loyalty high on his list of desirable human qualities. Halas once traded a player he overheard singing in the shower after a Bears loss. Contracts with players were negotiated on a one-to-one basis without agents. Halas even loaned players money to start businesses or to pay for educations as tribute for their loyalty.

In December 1942, Halas retired from football to serve as recreation director for the United States Pacific Fleet during World War II—one of three brief retirements before ending his career in 1968. Returning in November 1945, he coached the Bears to a league title, beating the New York Giants 24–14 in 1946. During the postwar era, intense competition for college talent and improved play in teams around the league hurt the Bears' chances for a league championship. During this period, Halas and the franchise were criticized for complacency and shortsightedness. Vindication came in 1963 when the Bears mauled the Giants 14–10 for the NFL championship. This game signified the rise of the middle linebacker as an integral component of defense strategy.

Although his coaching staff deserved part of the credit, Halas was responsible for many innovations. By selling broadcast rights to games, he was the first football executive to use the media to gain exposure. He was instrumental in initiating the college draft in 1936 to allow weaker teams to gain parity with stronger rivals. At his urging, the owners created the position of football commissioner to regulate and govern the league. Halas was the first to study game films, the first to cover the playing field to protect it from the elements, and one of the first to perfect the T formation, the predecessor of modern offenses. No fewer than twenty of his players were elected to the National Professional Football Hall of Fame, including Grange, Bronko Nagurski, Sid Luckman, Gale Sayers, Dick Butkus, and "Iron" Mike Ditka. All exhibited a tough, physical style of play, the mantra of Halas's teams. Halas was inducted into the Hall of Fame as a charter member in 1963; he compiled a lifetime coaching record of 325–151–31. After 1968 he remained active in the club's operations as owner, chairman of the board, and president until his death. When he died (from a variety of illnesses), the Bears franchise was worth an estimated $40 million. Halas is buried in Chicago.

His name will always be synonymous with Chicago, the football team he founded, and its mascot, an animal known for its great size, strength, and savage disposition. Halas's life also mirrored the evolution of professional football, where crude men first played in leather helmets on fields of dirt under rules dictated by primal instincts. He was relentless in pursuing his dream, gaining a reputation for being tough, conniving, and tightfisted. For his fiery demeanor as coach and fraternal influence in league affairs, he earned the nickname Papa Bear.

★

Halas (1979) is an autobiography written with Gwen Morgan and Arthur Veysey and provides insight into professional football history. The definitive study of the life of George Halas and the Bears franchise is George Vass, *George Halas and the Chicago Bears* (1971). Myron J. Smith, Jr.'s bibliography of related literature on Halas's life can be found in the Pro Football Hall of Fame Library, Canton, Ohio. An obituary is in the *New York Times* (1 Nov. 1983).

JEAN W. GRIFFITH, JR.

HALEY, William John, Jr. ("Bill") (*b.* 6 July 1925 in Highland Park, Michigan; *d.* 9 February 1981 in Harlingen, Texas), singer, guitarist, bandleader, known as the "father of rock and roll" because of his recordings, particularly "Rock Around the Clock."

The son of William Haley and Maude Green, Bill and his sister Margaret lived in Highland Park, a suburb of Detroit, until he was seven, when the family moved to Boothwyn, a suburb of Philadelphia. There Haley Sr. got a job at Sun shipyards. Bill was surrounded by music during his childhood. His father played the banjo, and his mother played the piano and organ. Haley was so fascinated by the music he heard around the house that he made a guitar out of cardboard. His parents, understanding Haley's enthusiasm, bought him a real guitar. He taught himself to play and to yodel as well.

As a schoolboy, Haley played country music on the guitar at local minstrel and variety shows. His first paid job was at the Booth Corners Auction Mart, a farmer's market, where he earned $1 a night playing the guitar. He was popular with the crowd and his salary was raised to $5 per night. With no future in sight other than working for the local Viscose factory, Haley focused on a career in music. By 1940 he had left school and started playing at small amusement parks in Pennsylvania, New Jersey, and Delaware. Then he signed with a "local" celebrity, Cousin Lee, who had a popular syndicated radio show and his own amusement park in the Wilmington area. While performing with Cousin Lee, Haley worked to improve his singing and playing and built up a small following of fans.

During World War II, Haley worked for Cousin Lee until 1944, when he answered an ad for a singing yodeler to replace Kenny Roberts in the Downhomers, a popular band in the Midwest. Roberts had been drafted but Haley,

Bill Haley, late 1950s. JOHN A. PLATT COLLECTION/ARCHIVE PHOTOS

who was blind in one eye, was not eligible for military service. Haley auditioned and got the job. He left the band in 1946 and traveled, performing country music with a variety of groups, including the Range Drifters. Haley returned home at age twenty-two, feeling he was not going to make it in show business.

Back in Pennsylvania, Haley lived in Chester and became a disc jockey at local radio station WPWA. By day Haley would sing on the air and pitch commercials for local merchants. At night he was singing and playing hillbilly music. Haley's first band, the Four Aces of Western Swing, consisted of Haley, an accordionist, a bassist, and another guitarist. In 1948 they recorded their first songs on the Cowboy label. "Too Many Parties, Too Many Pals" was followed by "Candy Kisses." In "My Sweet Little Girl From Nevada," Haley was a featured vocalist with Reno Browne and her Buckaroos. To save money Haley recorded in the studio at WPWA.

In 1949 Haley disbanded that group and assembled another with better musicians. To avoid confusion with another popular group from the same area, the Four Aces, Haley changed the name of the band to the Saddlemen; its members were the nucleus of Haley's future bands. At this time Haley was still yodeling and singing cowboy-hillbilly

music, and the group was playing at a variety of venues in the Philadelphia area.

But Haley had developed an interest in another type of music, rhythm and blues, associated with black musicians. He began to start his act with a rhythm and blues song called "Rock the Joint." Hillbilly fans loved it. Promoter Dave Miller offered the rhythm and blues song "Rocket 88" to Haley to do in a "white" version. Although it sold only 10,000 copies, the song, with its aggressive, rockabilly style, was a real departure for Haley. He followed up this modest success with more traditional country songs. Haley later said: "This was an era where there was very strong prejudice in music. If you sang what they called race music, why, you did only that. Or if it was country music, you did only that." It was Haley, however, who first fused white country-western music with black rhythm-and-blues music to form what was to become rock and roll.

In 1952 Haley recorded "Rock the Joint." With its heavy, driving beat, emphasizing the bass, and its "jive talk," it had the basic elements of the new rock and roll style. The record was a hit, and the band, which previously had an adult hillbilly following, started getting mail from high school kids. In fact, the song was described as an anthem for schoolkids, about having such a good time that nothing mattered: "We're gonna tear down the mailbox, rip up the floor / Smash out the windows and knock down the door."

With a new sound, the band needed a new look. The cowboy outfits were replaced by tuxedos, and the name was changed to Bill Haley and the Comets. During this time Haley was also writing songs. One, written with Danny Cedrone, was "Rock-a-Beatin-Boogie"; it had the line "Rock, rock, rock, everybody / Roll, roll, roll, everybody." This was the phrase that inspired Alan Freed, then disc jockey with WJW in Cleveland, Ohio, to coin the term "rock and roll." Haley wrote both words and music to his next major recording, "Crazy Man, Crazy." It was one of the big hits of the summer of 1953 and became the first rock-and-roll record to enter *Billboard*'s pop chart, reaching number five. That year was the beginning of stardom for Haley and the Comets.

In April 1954 Haley recorded "(We're Gonna) Rock Around the Clock" at Decca Record's Pythian Temple studio in New York City. The studio was a former ballroom with very high ceilings and a wood floor; the resulting sound was exceptional. However, "Rock Around the Clock," which was on the B side of "Thirteen Women (and Only One Man in town)" had just moderate success. Haley's next record, "Shake, Rattle, and Roll," reached number two on the rhythm-and-blues charts and sold a million copies. The song had previously been recorded by Joe Turner, but Haley used the blues element of the song, added some country flavor, and "cleaned up" the lyrics to make the song attractive to his growing audience of white fans. He once remarked, "We steer completely clear of anything suggestive." Many say that Haley's major contribution to the development of rock and roll was taking lyrics that were sexually obvious and toning them down for white listeners.

Because of the success of "Shake, Rattle, and Roll," Decca rereleased "Rock Around the Clock," which then became the national anthem of rock and roll and the largest selling rock-and-roll record in history. More than thirty million records by one hundred different groups were sold, but no version topped the original. What gave the song and Haley's career an even greater push was the song's inclusion on the soundtrack of the film *Blackboard Jungle* (1955). Within a year the record sold more than six million copies. It was inducted into the Grammy Hall of Fame in 1982. Haley's next hit song, "See You Later Alligator" (1956), cemented his reputation with the public. It sold a million copies in a single month, and the lyrics became part of American culture. When someone said "see you later alligator," the inevitable reply was "after a while crocodile," the following line in the song.

Bill Haley and the Comets were featured in the first rock-and-roll film, *Rock Around the Clock* (1956), a rags-to-riches story with a hastily written script. The film featured nine of Haley's best tunes, including the title track and "Razzle Dazzle." Teens loved the film, but it provoked riots, both in the United States and abroad. As a result, the film was banned in several communities. Banning the film was part of a growing backlash against rock and roll. *Variety* (11 April 1956) stated that rock and roll "may be getting too hot to handle" and that it "produced a staggering wave of juvenile violence and mayhem." A second film, *Don't Knock the Rock* (1956), attempted to show that rock and roll was a positive force in teenage life. Although the plot was weak, the music was a triumph.

In 1957 Bill Haley and the Comets began a series of successful world tours. In Australia they played to more than 330,000 fans during their three-week stay. Haley was the first U.S. rock star to tour the United Kingdom. His arrival in London was initially described as "the second battle of Waterloo" because of the huge crowds that greeted him at Waterloo Station. Queen Elizabeth II ordered a private screening of *Rock Around the Clock* to see what was causing such commotion in England. The tour was an overwhelming success. Crowds were drawn to Bill Haley and the Comets not only for the music, but also for their elaborate stage shows. Although Haley himself never moved around the stage much, Rudy Pompilli, the saxophonist, often played lying on his back, and Al Rex was renowned for his acrobatic displays on the standup bass.

Unruly crowds and riots were part of the tours, and Haley, a shy man, had difficulty with this type of notoriety. Haley also lacked business sense and spent money as

quickly as he earned it. Poor financial advice and troubles with the Internal Revenue Service began to plague him. His personal life also was not going well. He had married Dorothy Crowe in 1946; they had two children and divorced in 1951. The same year he married Barbara Joan Cupchack; they had three children and divorced in 1962.

Having lost all his property to creditors and taxes, Haley relocated to Mexico, where he was treated like a superstar. His record "Florida Twist," recorded for Orfeon in 1961, became the biggest-selling single in Mexico's history. Haley began to drink heavily and married Martha Velascao, a dancer performing with the band. They had one child.

Because of the advent of new performers, particularly Elvis Presley, Haley, with his "spit" curl in the middle of his forehead and chubby cheeks, did not have the dynamic charisma to retain his popularity in the United States. However, he continued to play to huge crowds in 1964, when he toured Germany, and on his 1966 European tour. When he returned to England in 1968 he was given a hero's welcome. In 1969 Bill Haley and the Comets began touring in Richard Nader's rock-and-roll revival shows in the United States. He was given an eight-minute standing ovation at Madison Square Garden. These shows are documented in the film *Let the Good Times Roll* (1973). Money problems still haunted Haley, and when Pompilli died in 1976, that was essentially the end for Haley as a performer. He retired that year but in 1979 returned to the concert stage with a moderately successful tour of England. Haley's final public appearances were in South Africa in 1980.

Toward the end of his life Haley became a recluse, drinking heavily and sometimes wandering the streets. He died of a heart attack and was cremated.

In 1987 Haley, who sold more than 60 million rock-and-roll recordings, was inducted into the Rock and Roll Hall of Fame. Whenever many people think of rock and roll, they think of Bill Haley. His hit song "Rock Around the Clock" was the song of the young establishing their own type of music. Haley was their first spokesperson.

★

The sole biography of Haley is John Swenson, *Bill Haley: The Daddy of Rock and Roll* (1982), which includes photographs and a discography. Sections on Haley are in Nik Cohn, *Rock from the Beginning* (1969); Dave Laing, *The Sound of Our Time* (1969); Dave Given, *The Dave Given Rock 'n' Roll Stars Handbook: Rhythm and Blues Artists and Groups* (1980); Stuart Colman, *They Kept on Rockin': The Giants of Rock 'n' Roll* (1982); Charles T. Brown, *Music U.S.A.: America's Country and Western Tradition* (1986); and Richard E. Jandrow, *What It Was Was Rockabilly: A History and Discography, 1927–1994* (1995). Obituaries are in the *New York Times* (10 Feb. 1981) and *Rolling Stone* (19 Mar. 1981).

MARCIA B. DINNEEN

HALL, Joyce Clyde (*b.* 29 December 1891 in David City, Nebraska; *d.* 29 October 1982 in Leawood, Kansas), businessman who founded Hallmark Cards, Inc., and created Crown Center as a city within a city in Kansas City, Missouri.

Hall was one of five children born to George Nelson Hall, an itinerant preacher, and Nancy Dudley. The first child died in infancy. With an invalid mother and an absentee father who provided little financial support, the three boys earned money to support the family at very young ages. Hall wrote, "We weren't poor because my father couldn't make a living—we were poor because he let us be. . . . He told my mother that she needn't worry, [that] 'the Lord would provide.' I found out then that it was a good idea to give the Lord a little help." From the age of eight, Hall worked at odd jobs, mostly in sales. In 1902 his brothers Rollie and William became partners in a bookstore in Norfolk, Nebraska, a larger town sixty miles north of David City. Joyce joined them after that school year; his mother and sister moved there shortly afterward. Times were hard for the family, but Hall's childhood memories were shaped by his belief that his experiences strengthened him. His autobiography, *When You Care Enough* (1979), includes a chapter on his early years called "The Gift of Poverty."

Working in the bookstore before and after school and during lunchtime, Hall learned the basics of retailing. He read and studied the advertisements in the books and magazines. Rollie was a candy salesman and took Joyce, when the latter was twelve, on his route through western Nebraska, Wyoming, and South Dakota. The following summer Hall worked part of Rollie's territory for him.

In 1905 he was introduced to picture postcards by a young salesman. Joyce quickly convinced William that they should sell the cards; they invested more than $150 each and committed the absent Rollie to the same amount. They immediately began selling wholesale, getting salesmen who came into the bookstore to sell the postcards to their other customers. The family's finances improved considerably, but Hall left high school in 1910 without graduating. He filled two shoeboxes with postcards and traveled to Kansas City. Within a year Rollie joined him to open a store and form Hall Brothers, Inc. In a few years picture postcard sales began to decline. Beginning in 1913 they added greeting cards, under the name Hallmark, to their wholesale business and soon began designing their own. Hall learned the greeting card business well. "I confess," he once said, "to an overwhelming prejudice in favor of the cards that sell best." What sold were cards with puppies and kittens, not people. Roses were good but a single rose was better, and pansies sold while geraniums did not.

In 1915 a fire destroyed their building and entire stock. The next year the brothers borrowed money, bought an

Joyce C. Hall, 1982. UPI/Corbis-Bettmann

engraving business, and began printing their own cards. Hall took an interest in all aspects of the business, from accounting to design to sales. The business grew steadily until the Great Depression, when revenues fell sharply. Hall refused to lay off workers and devised ways of continuing business in the face of new pressures. By 1936 the company had expanded enough so that the brothers purchased a six-story building in Kansas City.

On 25 March 1922 Hall married Elizabeth Ann Dilday, a former schoolmate of his sister. They had three children, the first born in July 1922. Hall wrote that his family wanted to name their one boy Joyce but he refused, saying he was grown before he was no longer ashamed of the name himself. (His mother had named him after a Methodist bishop.) The son, named Donald instead, became president of Hallmark when Hall retired. Hall became friends with public figures and world leaders. In addition to Harry Truman, who often spent time in Kansas City during his presidency, Hall also counted Walt Disney, Dwight Eisenhower, and Winston Churchill among his friends. In 1950 Churchill sold Hall twelve of his paintings to use on greeting cards.

In 1951 Hall took a bold step in deciding to sponsor a new television series, the *Hallmark Hall of Fame,* which brought opera and classic drama to the home screen. He had been advised to choose something more appealing to a mass audience, but the show was a success. Hall held subject approval and vetoed a production of Arthur Miller's

Death of a Salesman because he did not think it was suitable. Refusing to give in to southern boycott threats in 1957, he sponsored Marc Connelly's all-black *Green Pastures,* repeating it in 1959. The series received a total of forty-four Emmy Awards, including one to Hallmark Cards "for dedication to standards of quality and excellence."

Hall believed strongly that he could help revitalize central Kansas City. In the early 1960s he began planning Crown Center, modeled on Rockefeller Center in New York City. Ground was broken in 1968 for the 85-acre, $400 million development, which would grow to include the Hallmark headquarters, two hotels, a Halls department store and other retail space, and even an outdoor ice-skating rink. Situated between Kansas City's downtown business district and the Country Club Plaza shopping area, Crown Center dramatically changed the city's landscape.

Although Hall promoted employee ownership of corporate stock, some described him as reluctant to delegate authority. *Fortune* praised him as a man "who singlehandedly built a great corporation and then was forced to fight doggedly to prevent . . . [it] from swallowing him up." He resigned as company president in 1966 to devote more time to the Crown Center project, his legacy to Kansas City. He had built the company into a giant in the industry, helping to change the way Americans used greeting cards. When Hall died, Hallmark had 20,000 card shops and annual sales exceeding $1 billion and turned out 8 million greeting cards a day.

While Hall was first and foremost a businessman, he wrote that cards were "a way of giving less articulate people, and those who tend to disguise their feelings, a voice to express their love and affection." He died quietly in his sleep of causes related to old age and was buried in Forest Hill Cemetery, Kansas City, Missouri. He left over $100 million to charity. His estate sold nearly $94 million worth of Hallmark stock to employees, almost doubling the amount owned by employees and bringing the number of shares they held to about one-third of company stock. He was a hardworking, hardheaded businessman who believed that his business could contribute to the good of the community as well as to his own financial interests.

★

Hall's business papers and many personal papers, photographs, and mementos are held by the Hallmark Cards, Inc., archives. Joyce Clyde Hall (with Curtiss Anderson), *When You Care Enough* (1979), captures Hall's voice and persona and provides interesting anecdotes and a factually accurate account of his life. "Sponsor Who Cares," *Newsweek* (1 Nov. 1965), briefly discusses his connection with the *Hallmark Hall of Fame* program. Jane Howard, "Close-up: Joyce Hall, Greeting-card King," *Life* (Dec. 1968), examines the history of Hallmark through an interview with Hall. James McKinley, "If You've Got an Ounce of Feeling, Hallmark Has a Ton of Sentiment," *American Heritage* (Dec.

1982), has a less personal approach to the same subject. A series of articles on various aspects of Hall's life and career appear in the *Kansas City Star,* including an obituary (29 Oct. 1982), and articles on Hallmark and Kansas City, the *Hallmark Hall of Fame,* and Hall's moral qualities (all 30 Oct. 1982). An obituary is in the *New York Times* (30 Oct. 1982).

KEN LUEBBERING

HALPER, Albert (*b.* 3 August 1904 in Chicago, Illinois; *d.* 18 January 1984 in Poughkeepsie, New York), novelist and short-story writer known for his portrayal of urban and industrial life.

Halper's parents, Rebecca Alpert and Isaac Halper, immigrated from Lithuania to Chicago in the early 1890s; they settled on the West Side and opened a small grocery store on Lake Street. Halper was the next-to-youngest among six siblings. The Halpers moved their business often, finally settling at 426 North Kedzie Avenue. As the children grew, they attended grade and high school as well as services at a nearby synagogue. Young Halper attended Tilden Grammar School. He entered John Marshall High School in 1917 and graduated in 1921.

Working in the store, going to school, and living the local street life left indelible impressions on young Halper.

Albert Halper, New York, 1933. ALBERT HALPER PAPERS, MANUSCRIPTS AND ARCHIVES DIVISION, THE NEW YORK PUBLIC LIBRARY, ASTOR, LENOX AND TILDEN FOUNDATIONS

With accuracy and intensity he absorbed the sights and sounds and smells of a drab world that also included for him the glorious and magical changes of the seasons. Later in life he recalled he had come from "a raw slangy city" and "a raw slangy neighborhood." He learned from street life; he also read a lot and began a little scribbling. He enjoyed music, learned to play the piano, and loved to dance. He liked to draw and often visited the Art Institute of Chicago. When he was fourteen he worked after school as an errand boy at John T. Shayne and Company, a fur and haberdashery establishment in the famed Palmer House hotel on State Street.

After graduation Halper found work as an order picker at the Philipsborn Company, an early mail-order and catalog house, where he earned $13 a week. In the autumn of 1922 he found a new job at the Chicago Electrotype Company. As a shipping clerk he directed the errand boys and checked the electrotypes, but also listened to the stories and complaints of the bosses and the workers. He remained there for four years.

From September 1924 to June 1926, while still working, Halper attended evening classes at Northwestern University, studying writing, speech, psychology, and journalism. He began writing a little and reading extensively, especially Mark Twain, James Joyce, Sherwood Anderson, F. Scott Fitzgerald, and Ernest Hemingway. In 1927 he published at his own expense *Purple Pudding,* a small volume of poetry, which he later felt was not worth saving. He tried songwriting, without success.

Restless and dissatisfied, Halper worked at a number of odd jobs in 1926. After his mother died in 1927, however, he wanted something steady. For fourteen months he worked as a postal sorter on the night shift at Chicago's Central Post Office. But when Marianne Moore, editor of *Dial* magazine, accepted a sketch and a short story of his for publication, he quit immediately. He was determined to write. In October 1928 he boarded a bus for New York City; soon out of money, he returned to Chicago and found a job in a law office. By September 1929 he had saved enough to take a train to New York, never to live in Chicago again.

Halper moved frequently in Manhattan, soon meeting writers and editors. Fortunately, he began publishing a few stories and sketches that helped pay for food and rent, but his first novel, "Good-bye Again," was rejected. Then, in the summer of 1930, Clifton Fadiman recommended him for a residency at the Yaddo Artists' Colony in Saratoga Springs, New York, where he finished a second novel, "Windy City Blues." It would also remain unpublished, but he immediately started a third novel. Maxim Lieber, his literary agent, tried to interest him in joining the Communist party. Halper, however, was neither a joiner nor a political activist; he never championed causes or wrote for

them. During the summer of 1931 he worked as a waiter and skit writer at a camp for adults at Warrensburg, New York.

Ironically, the Chicago-born writer's first published novel was about New York. Halper's *Union Square* (1933) is the story of ten or more individuals who live near the square, on 14th Street in Manhattan, which is perhaps the real hero of the novel. It is the square that survives the social and historical conflicts that never end and the personal problems that are never solved. When the Literary Guild chose it for its March 1933 selection, Halper's success as a writer was assured. *On the Shore* (1934), comprising short stories about Chicago, widened his audience. With *The Foundry* (1934), based on his own experience and written in brisk and sometimes brash language, he became recognized as one of America's leading writers.

Having received a Guggenheim Fellowship in creative writing in 1934, Halper sailed for Great Britain in late August and began work on a new novel. After living in London, he visited the Soviet Union in April 1935, met a few writers, saw the May Day parade, and then returned to New York in early summer.

In his next three novels Halper drew on memories of life in Chicago. In *The Chute* (1937), bosses and workers at a mail-order house use cunning, speed, and skill to keep the huge cylinder, called the chute, filled with orders; as one worker says, "America is nothing but a big chute." In *Sons of the Fathers* (1940), an immigrant family in Chicago during World War I senses the economic waste and moral corruption that leads to personal disillusionment. *The Little People* (1942) explores the lives of workers and their jobs at a haberdashery store on Chicago's State Street.

World War II brought, Halper said, the "end of an era," and his own life took new directions. On 6 January 1942 he married Pauline Friedman, a textile designer, painter, and pianist. They had one child and were divorced in 1956. On 28 December 1956 he married Lorna Blaine Howard, an artist; they did not have children. The writing of novels had slowed. *Only an Inch from Glory* (1943) tells of four Greenwich Village bohemians, all with an itch for glamour and glory. *Atlantic Avenue* (1956), a short paperback novel, comments on the sleaze and violence of an area in Brooklyn. *The Fourth Horseman of Miami Beach* (1966) shows how retired "little" people try to renew their youth under the tropic sun.

Halper compiled two anthologies of essays and short stories, *This Is Chicago* (1952) and *The Chicago Crime Book* (1967). *The Golden Watch* (1953) included fifteen short stories of early life in Chicago. Two plays had short runs: *My Aunt Daisy* (with Joseph Schrank) ran in August 1954 in Westport, Connecticut; *Top Man* closed in Philadelphia in November 1955. In 1956 he taught a course in creative writing at the City College of New York. *Good-bye, Union*

Square: A Writer's Memoir of the Thirties (1970) was his last major work. *Post War* (1975), over seventy pen and ink drawings made in 1942, was privately printed in a limited edition. In his later years he lived in Pawling, New York. Halper died of leukemia and was cremated.

Halper's novels and stories are a sharp commentary on the urban and industrial life of mid-twentieth-century America. Writing at a time when social problems and radical causes stirred literary tradition, he spoke neither as proletarian nor propagandist, but as historian and commentator. He wrote of individuals, of those who earn their daily bread in "factories, stores, and offices," of ordinary people whose quirks and desires are sometimes tempered by wind and rain and sun. His memories shed light on the American past and on people everywhere.

★

Personal letters and other items are in the Manuscripts and Archives Section of the New York Public Library and the Special Collection of the University of Delaware Library, Newark. Albert Halper, *Good-bye, Union Square: A Writer's Memoir of the Thirties* (1970), begins with his coming to New York and is very selective. Albert Halper, "Thoughts on Being Twayned," *The American Scholar* 51 (winter 1981–1982): 105–114, includes biographical information. John E. Hart, *Albert Halper* (1980), is a critical and interpretative study with a bibliography and chronology. Freeman Champney, "Albert Halper and His Little People," *Antioch Review* 2 (Dec. 1942): 628–634, analyzes early writings. Obituaries are in the *New York Times* (20 Jan. 1984) and *Chicago Tribune* (24 Jan. 1984).

JOHN E. HART

HAMILTON, Margaret (*b.* 9 December 1902 in Cleveland, Ohio; *d.* 16 May 1985 in Salisbury, Connecticut), actress who appeared in more than seventy films, usually as waspish or crotchety women; she is best remembered for her performance as the Wicked Witch of the West in *The Wizard of Oz* (1939).

The youngest of the four children of Walter J. Hamilton, a prominent attorney, and Jennie Adams, an organist, Margaret Hamilton attended the Hathaway-Brown School for girls in Cleveland, where she made her stage debut as an elderly Englishman in a play called *Pomander Walk*. She was interested in acting from an early age but her father insisted that she learn a profession by which she could support herself. She decided to become a teacher, and after studying at the Wheelock Kindergarten Training School in Boston, she returned to Cleveland in 1923 to teach. For three years she ran her own kindergarten and nursery school in a church.

While pursuing her career as a teacher, her interest in

Margaret Hamilton holds a figurine of the *Wizard of Oz* character with which she is most identified, 1972. UPI/CORBIS-BETTMANN

the theater never waned. She continued to take occasional acting roles at the Cleveland Playhouse, and for a year, while teaching at the Country Day School in suburban Rye, New York, she took frequent excursions to nearby Manhattan to attend the Broadway theater. After her mother's death, she returned to Cleveland, where she appeared again with the Cleveland Playhouse, this time for three years.

On 13 June 1931 she married Paul Boynton Meserve, a landscape architect. They had one child and were divorced in 1938. Since Meserve worked for the Westchester County Park Commission, Hamilton spent part of the summer of 1931 in Rye. There she met producer Arthur J. Beckhard, who offered her a role in a stock production of *Hallam's Wives*, a play by Rose Franken. Although she had finally obtained a permanent teaching position, she decided to accept the role at her husband's encouragement. The play, retitled *Another Language,* was a surprise hit when it came to Broadway in 1932. When it was scheduled to be filmed, Hamilton was asked to repeat her role as Helen Hallam, a sharp-tongued member of the Hallam family.

Her performance in the movie version of *Another Language* (1933) launched her long career as a popular character actress. Her hawklike nose, pursed lips, and jutting chin, as well as her no-nonsense way of speaking, made her an appropriate choice to play a succession of prim, officious, and cantankerous women, although she also numbered many sympathetic characters among her performances. One of her most fondly recalled roles was Mrs. Gideon, the waspish nemesis of Mae West in the ramshackle but hilarious Western *My Little Chickadee* (1940). She also brought her forthright style to such films as *These Three* (1936), *Guest in the House* (1944), *State of the Union* (1948), *People Will Talk* (1951), and *Brewster McCloud* (1970). A favorite but largely forgotten movie was Preston Sturges's *The Sin of Harold Diddlebock* (1947), later reissued as *Mad Wednesday,* with the comedian Harold Lloyd.

In 1939 Hamilton was chosen to play the Wicked Witch of the West in MGM's lavish adaptation of L. Frank Baum's story *The Wizard of Oz.* After first selecting actress Gale Sondergaard to play a glamorous witch, the studio decided that an ugly witch—wicked and hateful—was more in keeping with the classic story, and Hamilton won the coveted role. During the filming, Hamilton suffered a near-fatal accident when, during the scene in which she disappears in a burst of red smoke and a clap of thunder, her hat and broom caught on fire, and she suffered severe burns on her face and one hand. Despite the mishap, she often remarked over the years that making the film was an experience she was delighted to share with the cast and crew. As the Wicked Witch, she appears on screen for only twelve minutes, but her character pervades the movie with her grotesque appearance and malicious cackle.

During her long career, Hamilton performed frequently in repertory and regional theater, and occasionally on Broadway (for many years she lived in an apartment building adjacent to Gramercy Park). She was also active in television, appearing in several series, including *The Egg and I* and *Ethel and Albert*, as well as in a number of television commercials as Cora, the New England storekeeper who sold only Maxwell House coffee. In her later years, she remained active with children, founding a kindergarten in a Beverly Hills, California, church and serving as president of that community's board of education. Hamilton died of a heart attack in 1985.

Throughout her career, Hamilton brought a bracing and welcome splash of vinegar to her many movie portrayals. To generations of moviegoers, however, she will forever be the Wicked Witch of the West, who never thought that "a good little girl" could destroy her "beautiful wickedness." And in fact, Hamilton's beautiful wickedness lives on, in a film destined to remain a Hollywood classic.

★

Further information on Margaret Hamilton can be found in two articles: Jerry Vermilye, "That Hamilton Woman," in *The Movie Buff's Book* (1975), and William S. Collins, "Margaret Hamilton," in *Films in Review* 28 (Aug./Sept. 1977). The pleasures and tribulations of making *The Wizard of Oz* are covered in Aljean Harmetz, *The Making of The Wizard of Oz* (1977), and Doug McClelland, *Down the Yellow Brick Road: The Making of The Wizard of Oz* (1976). An obituary is in the *New York Times* (17 May 1985).

TED SENNETT

HANKS, Nancy (*b.* 31 December 1927 in Miami Beach, Florida; *d.* 7 January 1983 in New York City), head of the National Endowment for the Arts from 1969 to 1977.

Bryan Cayce and Virginia Wooding Hanks named their first child after a distant relative, Nancy Hanks, the mother of Abraham Lincoln. As a lawyer and businessman, Bryan Hanks earned a comfortable living for his wife, a homemaker, and their two children. Hanks's early years were spent in Miami Beach. Although the family moved several times after that, from the time she was six years old Nancy had a consistent attachment to Cashiers, North Carolina, a small town in the Blue Ridge Mountains. She spent her childhood summers there and returned often as an adult.

At Duke University, which she entered in 1945, Hanks became a leader of campus life. As a senior, she was president of the student government. Her friendly personality was enhanced by her good looks. Of medium build with dark hair, she was among those elected May queen, a designation honoring Duke's most beautiful undergraduates. She received an A.B. degree magna cum laude, with a major in political science, in 1949.

In 1951 she secured a job in Washington, D.C., at the Office of Defense Mobilization. Early in 1953 she transferred to the President's Advisory Committee on Government Organization, headed by Nelson A. Rockefeller. Only months later, she became Rockefeller's assistant at the new Department of Health, Education, and Welfare, where he served as undersecretary until 1955. She continued as Rockefeller's assistant when he became President Dwight D. Eisenhower's special assistant for cold war strategy. As she picked up a workaholic lifestyle from Rockefeller, their relationship took on a romantic dimension.

Early in 1956, Rockefeller returned to New York City to enter electoral politics, and he took Hanks along. Although their intimate relationship soon deteriorated, Hanks worked for the Rockefeller family for the next thirteen years. Shortly after his return to New York, Rockefeller initiated a project that brought together experts and leaders from all areas of American life to write a series of reports on national problems and opportunities. Henry Kissinger came from Harvard University to direct the effort, and Hanks served as executive secretary of the staff and as a member of the planning committee.

When Rockefeller was elected governor of New York in 1958, Hanks went for a brief period to Albany, where she

Nancy Hanks, 1979. UPI/CORBIS-BETTMANN

played a part in drawing up a proposal for one of Rockefeller's pet projects—a state arts council. In 1961, at the request of Nelson's brother Laurance, she returned to Washington as an adviser to a congressional commission he headed, the Outdoor Recreation Resources Commission. Early in 1962, Hanks had a mastectomy, signaling the onset of her eventually terminal cancer. In mid-1963 she went to work for yet another of the Rockefeller brothers, John D., 3d, who had commissioned an investigation of American arts policy and funding. Published in 1965, the resulting document was a first step in developing programs to meet the nation's arts needs. Working on it brought Hanks into contact with the country's leaders in arts administration.

In the fall of 1969, Hanks was named chairman of the National Endowment for the Arts (NEA), which had been created in 1965. She came to the job through her administrative, political, and personal skills rather than through profound knowledge of the arts. Hanks set her style early by almost immediately proposing to double the budget for the following fiscal year. By the time she left eight years later, the budget was more than twelve times what it had been in 1969.

Hanks relentlessly advocated and realized expanded access to the arts across the country. Part of her success may be attributed to luck: She was in the right place when the country was ready to sponsor an arts agenda. But part of it was also because of her understanding of political realities. She knew it was important for arts support to be advan-

tageous to Congress and the president, and she made sure that every legislator could point with pride to some NEA program in his or her home district. She also fostered the concept of public-private partnership in support of the arts, a position that was palatable to those who opposed new government programs on principle.

At the NEA, Hanks oversaw innovation as well as growth in existing programs. For example, she initiated support for symphony orchestras, opera companies, museums, folk art, design, and programs for minorities and schoolchildren. She also devised a system of challenge grants to aid major arts institutions in raising the funds they needed to achieve long-term stability.

At the end of her second four-year term, Hanks was not reappointed by the recently elected president Jimmy Carter, who wanted to put his own stamp on the NEA. In addition, and surprisingly for one who understood Washington politics so well, Hanks had lost the support of many leaders among state and local arts groups. They were irritated that she had neglected the working relationships between federal and state agencies and had, they thought, arrogated too much power to herself.

After she left the NEA on 30 November 1977, Hanks returned to her position at the Rockefeller Brothers Fund in New York City and remained active in other charitable and corporate organizations. A bone scan revealed that the cancer that had recurred in 1974 was again spreading. Her health slowly failed, and on 12 November 1982 she entered the hospital where she died two months later.

Perhaps no single individual in U.S. history has done more than Hanks for the arts. Critics have pointed to weaknesses in her administrative procedures, and it is true that she relied on enthusiasm, instinct, and the spontaneous combustion of ideas. The NEA she left behind was unwieldy, and she never provided a systematic rationale for its multifarious activities, but under her leadership the NEA fueled an explosion of activity and artistic growth around the United States and institutionalized mechanisms for channeling public money to the arts. No other NEA chairman has been so effective.

★

Nancy Hanks's personal and professional papers are in the special collections of the Duke University Library. Michael Whitney Straight, *Nancy Hanks, An Intimate Portrait: The Creation of a National Commitment to the Arts* (1988) is the only book-length study of Hanks. Gaylen Moore, ed., with photographs by Lynn Gilbert, *Particular Passions: Talks with Women Who Have Shaped Our Times* (1981), includes Hanks's reflections on her career. Mary Devine, ed., *Annual Obituary* (1983) provides a useful profile. Obituaries are in the *New York Times* (8 Jan. 1983) and *Washington Post* (9 Jan. 1983).

ANN LEE MORGAN

HANSON, Howard Harold (*b*. 28 October 1896 in Wahoo, Nebraska; *d*. 26 February 1981 in Rochester, New York), Pulitzer Prize–winning composer, conductor, and music educator.

The son of Hans Hanson and Hilma Christina Eckstrom, both of Skåne, Sweden, Hanson studied piano and cello as a child, and his mother was one of his first teachers. The couple's firstborn child (a son) died before Howard's birth; he had no other siblings. Hanson attended Luther College in Wahoo; the University of Nebraska (1912–1913); the Institute of Musical Art in New York City (forerunner of the Juilliard School), where he studied piano under James Friskin and composition under Percy Goetschius and was encouraged to become a pianist; and Northwestern University, where he received a B.A. in music in 1916, after studying composition with Peter Lutkin and Arne Oldberg.

Upon graduation at the age of nineteen, Hanson became professor of music theory and composition at the College of the Pacific in San Jose, California, and, remarkably for such a young man, was appointed dean of its Conservatory of Fine Arts after only three years. In 1921 he won the first Prix de Rome in Music awarded by the American Academy for his incidental music to the ballet *California Forest Play of 1920* and his symphonic poem *Before the*

Howard Hanson, 1944. UPI/CORBIS-BETTMANN

Dawn. Taking up fellowship residence in Rome for three years, Hanson studied orchestration under Ottorino Respighi; devoted himself to composition, writing his Symphony no. 1 (*Nordic,* 1922) and two symphonic poems; and began work on his major choral piece, *The Lament for Beowulf,* which was completed in the United States in 1925.

While conducting the American premiere of his *Nordic* symphony with the Rochester Symphony Orchestra in 1923, Hanson met multimillionaire George Eastman, the founder of Eastman Kodak Company, who had recently endowed a school of music at the University of Rochester, and university president Rush Rhees. From Rome, Hanson accepted their offer of a directorship and held this position for forty years (1924–1964), making the Eastman School one of America's finest music institutions. Upon his retirement he became director of its Institute of American Music, which was renamed in Hanson's honor in 1996.

An extremely energetic man and dynamic teacher, Hanson simultaneously balanced his administrative, educational, and musical responsibilities and was deeply involved in the Eastman curriculum. Among his many students were the composers Jack Beeson, William Bergsma, and Peter Mennin. Many of his students, who marveled at his ability to sight-read instantaneously an orchestral score at the piano, went on to establish and run music departments in other colleges and universities.

Hanson made his conducting debut in 1919 with the Los Angeles Philharmonic, performing his *Symphonic Rhapsody,* and guest conducted all the major U.S. orchestras, usually in contemporary American works. His only opera, *Merry Mount,* which was strongly influenced by his Lutheran background, had its premiere at New York's Metropolitan Opera in 1934. Despite a very favorable public response (fifty curtain calls), it was dropped from the repertoire. Among Hanson's major compositions are seven symphonies, six pieces for chamber ensemble, a piano concerto, several songs set to the poetry of Walt Whitman, and sixteen choral works. Although his Symphony no. 4 (*Requiem*), which was dedicated to his father, won the Pulitzer Prize in 1944, his Symphony no. 2 (*Romantic*) is his most popular work.

Hanson was active in many professional organizations, serving as president of the National Association of Schools of Music and the Music Teachers National Association. While president of the National Music Council, he helped establish a composer-in-residence program in the public school system. He received honorary degrees from thirty institutions; won the first Alice M. Ditson Conductor's Award (1945), the George Foster Peabody Award (1946), the Laurel Leaf of the American Composers Alliance (1957), and the Huntington Hartford Foundation Award (1959); and was elected to the National Institute of Arts and Letters (1935) and to Sweden's Royal Academy of Music (1938). He was also editor in chief of the eleven-volume *New Scribner Music Library* (1972–1973).

On 24 July 1946 Hanson married Margaret "Peggy" Elizabeth Nelson, whom he had first met while conducting in Chautauqua, New York, and who was twenty years his junior. Peggy was an accomplished singer and played the piano and cello, although she did not pursue music professionally. The Hansons had no children and enjoyed spending vacations on Bold Island (off the Maine coast), which they owned. A tall, large man, Hanson grew his trademark goatee to look older while he was conducting the Rome Symphony Orchestra at the age of twenty-four. Hanson suffered from diabetes in later life and died after a short illness. He was buried on Bold Island.

Often referred to as the American Sibelius because of the somber (even bleak) harmonies and soaring romantic melodies of his compositions, Hanson also cited J. S. Bach and Edvard Grieg as major influences on his music, was an admirer of Ludwig van Beethoven and Antonín Dvořák, and absorbed Gregorian chant during his stay in Rome. Hanson was a vocal critic of dissonant and atonal music, which he called "anti-musica," and of music that was too cerebral, advocating instead a conservative, tonally centered approach to composition. He once observed: "Though I have a profound interest in theoretical problems, my own music comes from the heart and is a direct expression of my own emotional reactions." Hanson's theories are outlined in his 1960 book, *Harmonic Materials of Modern Music: Resources of the Tempered Scale.* Even though they did not appeal to him personally, Hanson included dissonant and atonal music in the programs at the American Music Festivals, which he instituted at the Eastman School in 1925.

A tireless proponent of American music, Hanson's greatest impact was undoubtedly through the Eastman School and the American Music Festivals, which enabled young composers, including Aaron Copland and Samuel Barber, to exhibit their work. In Rochester, Hanson presented more than 1,500 works by 700 composers, including the *Afro-American Symphony* by William Grant Still, the first symphony by an African American to be performed by a major orchestra. Hanson repeatedly used his prestige to proselytize for American music and, with the Eastman-Rochester Orchestra, recorded one of the most extensive series of American music ever undertaken (primarily for the Mercury Living Presence label), including the works of contemporaries, such as Charles Ives, Ferde Grofé, and William Schuman; predecessors, such as George W. Chadwick and Edward MacDowell; and his former students. Although the popularity of his music has waxed and waned, Hanson was a true giant in the field. As conductor Gerard Schwarz has observed, Hanson was "Mr. American Music."

★

The standard reference source for information on Hanson is James E. Perone, *Howard Hanson: A Bio-Bibliography* (1993), which provides citations for materials by and about Hanson, significant performances of his music, and a discography. Hanson's influence on music education is covered in Robert C. Monroe, "Howard Hanson: American Music Educator" (Ph.D. diss., Florida State University, 1970). Many other dissertations have been written on aspects of Hanson's music, including Barry Wayne Johnson, "An Analytical Study of the Band Compositions of Howard Hanson" (University of Houston, 1986), and William M. Skoog, "The Late Choral Music of Howard Hanson and Samuel Barber" (University of Northern Colorado, 1992). An earlier profile and interpretation of the composer is offered by Burnet C. Tuthill in "Howard Hanson," *Musical Quarterly* 22 (Apr. 1936): 140–153.

Fascinating insights into Hanson's style and blunt-talking personality are offered in David Russell Williams, *Conversations with Howard Hanson* (1988), based on a series of 1978 interviews. There are articles on Hanson in *The New Grove Dictionary of American Music,* 4 vols., ed. by H. Wiley Hitchcock and Stanley Sadie (1986); and *The New Grove Dictionary of Opera,* vol. 2, ed. by Stanley Sadie (1992). The most complete obituary appears in the *Rochester Democrat and Chronicle* (27 Feb. 1981); others appear in the *Washington Post* and *New York Times* (both 28 Feb. 1981).

JOHN A. DROBNICKI

HARBURG, Edgar Yipsel ("Yip") (*b.* 8 April 1896 in New York City; *d.* 5 March 1981 in Los Angeles, California), lyricist best known for his witty, introspective, and often politically charged words for such songs as "Over the Rainbow" and "Brother, Can You Spare a Dime?" and for such scores as *The Wizard of Oz* and *Finian's Rainbow.*

A product of Manhattan's Lower East Side, Harburg, born Isadore Hochberg, was the youngest of four children born to Lewis Hochberg and Mary Ricing, immigrants from Russia. His father worked in the garment industry while the family lived in a sixth-floor walk-up cold-water flat. During his childhood Harburg's active ways earned him the nickname Yip, a diminutive of *yipsel,* Yiddish for "squirrel."

He learned to love the theater from his father, who would set out for the synagogue with Yip on Friday nights and end up in the theater instead. One of his teachers at Public School 64 took young Harburg to see the actress Maude Adams as Peter Pan. His Orthodox parents later squelched his acting ambitions because they feared he would have to perform on Jewish holidays.

Harburg's excellent grades won him admission to Townsend Harris High School, where he met his lifelong friend and greatest influence, the lyricist Ira Gershwin. From the age of twelve, Harburg sold newspapers, packed

Edgar ("Yip") Harburg. UPI/Corbis-Bettmann

clothes in the sweatshop where his sister Anna worked, and lit gas lamps for the Edison Company. He also coedited, with Gershwin, the literary column in the *Academy Herald,* the high school's newspaper. Harburg lost his religious faith at fifteen, when his older brother Max, a physicist and mathematician, died of cancer at the age of twenty-eight.

At City College of New York, Harburg and Gershwin wrote light verse for the college newspaper, with Harburg signing his contributions Yip, and for the "The Conning Tower," Franklin P. Adams's column of light verse in the *New York World.*

After receiving his B.S. degree in 1918, Harburg lived in Montevideo, Uruguay, to avoid service in World War I, a conflict he opposed. There, he managed a department for the meatpacking firm Swift & Company and worked as a reporter until he returned to New York City in 1921 to establish an electrical-appliance company. In 1929, when the stock market crash undermined the economy, he turned to lyric writing, because, as he said, "I [had] had my fill of this dreamy abstract thing called business, and I decided to face reality and write lyrics."

On 23 February 1923 he married Boston-born Alice Richmond. They had two children in the mid-1920s and divorced in 1929. Harburg thereafter signed his work E. Y. Harburg and had his name legally changed in 1934.

Gershwin guided Harburg's early lyric writing, loaned him money, and introduced him to the composers Jay Gor-

ney, Vernon Duke, and Burton Lane. Harburg and composer Johnny Green had one hit song, "I'm Yours," in 1930. Harburg and Gorney began writing for early talkies and for Broadway revues, such as *Earl Carroll's Sketch Book* (1929). Their score for *Americana* (1932) included "Brother, Can You Spare a Dime?," one of the most powerful protest songs in American popular music.

Also in 1932 Harburg began to write comic lyrics for Willie Howard, Beatrice Lillie, and Bobby Clark, and he and Duke collaborated on Duke's first hit, "April in Paris," for the revue *Walk a Little Faster.* Their often fractious relationship soon ended, and in 1933 Harburg and his new collaborator, Harold Arlen, had their first hit, "It's Only a Paper Moon." They would work together for another twenty-five years.

After establishing himself by writing for a series of small, smart revues in the early 1930s, Harburg moved on to more sophisticated revues that featured such stars as Bert Lahr and Ray Bolger. For *Life Begins at 8:40* (1934), he and Arlen wrote "Let's Take a Walk Around the Block" and "You're a Builder-Upper."

Harburg moved to Hollywood, California, in 1934 to write songs and produce movies, but he was back in New York City in 1936 writing comic numbers for the revue *The Show Is On,* including Lahr's classic "Song of the Woodsman." Harburg spent the rest of his career moving between New York City and Hollywood.

In the 1937 Broadway revue *Hooray for What?* Harburg expressed his horror at the rise of fascism and his growing sense that another war was coming. The Arlen-Harburg score for this show included "In the Shade of the New Apple Tree," "Down with Love," and "God's Country." For the first time Harburg shaped the show's concept, political outlook, script, and lyrics. It marked the beginning of his transition from revues to full-length musicals in the 1940s.

In 1939 Arlen and Harburg collaborated on the score for the movie *The Wizard of Oz.* They won their first Oscar for best song for "Over the Rainbow," which became Judy Garland's signature number and one of America's best-loved songs. The score also included "We're Off to See the Wizard" and "Ding, Dong, the Witch Is Dead."

From the late 1930s through World War II, Harburg collaborated with Arlen on "Lydia, the Tattooed Lady" for Groucho Marx (*At the Circus,* 1939) and on his only important post-*Oz* movie, *Cabin in the Sky* (1943). The first mass-appeal film with an all-black cast, *Cabin in the Sky* was an adaptation of a 1940 Broadway show with a score by Vernon Duke and John La Touche. Among the songs Arlen and Harburg added was the Oscar-nominated "Happiness Is (Just) a Thing Called Joe." In 1944 Harburg and Jerome Kern's "More and More" from *Can't Help Singing* also received an Oscar nomination.

On 16 January 1943 Harburg married Edelaine Roden; they had no children.

After the war Harburg did almost all his important work on Broadway, largely because he was blacklisted in 1950 and was thus excluded from movies, radio, and television for twelve years. Although he was never a member of the Communist party and called himself a democratic socialist, he was active in organizations with communist members. In 1944 Harburg collaborated with left-wing folk composer Earl Robinson, with whom he wrote overtly political songs, including "Free and Equal Blues."

Among Harburg's successful later shows were *Bloomer Girl* with Arlen (1944); his masterpiece, *Finian's Rainbow,* with Lane (1947); and *Jamaica,* a vehicle for Lena Horne, also with Arlen (1957). Even though he continued to affirm his political convictions in a restrictive political climate, *Bloomer Girl* and *Finian's Rainbow* established Harburg as one of the Broadway musical's few major lyricists. He also wrote the book for several musicals, including *Finian's Rainbow* and *Flahooley* (1951, written with Fred Saidy). For *Bloomer Girl* his songs included "Evelina," "Right as the Rain," and "The Eagle and Me," and for *Finian's Rainbow,* "How Are Things in Glocca Morra?," "Old Devil Moon," "If This Isn't Love," and "Look to the Rainbow."

His work in the 1960s and 1970s in Hollywood and New York City was largely undistinguished, although he and Arlen composed songs for the animated feature *Gay Purree* in 1962. His last musical to reach Broadway, *Darling of the Day,* flopped in 1968. He also wrote an adaptation of *The Wizard of Oz* for the Bil Baird Puppet Theater in 1969.

Although he resisted the emergence of rock and roll, in 1978, at the age of eighty-two, Harburg wrote fifteen songs with the rock-oriented composer Phil Springer. He also tried unsuccessfully to produce *I Got a Song,* a revue based on his own work, and wrote his last song in 1980.

Harburg helped to found the musical theater program at New York University's Tisch School of the Arts. He received an honorary Litt.D. from the University of Vermont in 1972 and an honorary doctor of arts degree from Chicago's Columbia College in 1978. In 1973 he was elected to the Songwriter's Hall of Fame.

Harburg's other important songs include "I Like the Likes of You" (1934), "Last Night When We Were Young" (1936), "There's a Great Day Comin' Manana" (1940), "Poor You" and "I'll Take Tallulah" (1942), "Life's Full of Consequences" (1943), and "Here's to Your Illusions" (1951). He also published books of light verse in 1965 (*Rhymes for the Irreverent*) and 1976 (*At This Point in Rhyme*).

A small, energetic man of outspoken opinions, Harburg published 376 songs. His other collaborators included Arthur Schwartz, Sammy Fain, Jimmy Van Heusen, Milton Ager, and Peter DeRose. Only once in all his songs did he ever write the words "I love you." Like his great contemporaries Ira Gershwin, Lorenz Hart, and Cole Porter, Harburg struggled to be inventive and, more than anything, to avoid clichés. He softened his strong political views with engaging humor, dazzling wordplay, and a penchant for fantasy. His particular combination of the political and the fantastical gave him a unique voice among the major writers of the Broadway musical.

Nearing his eighty-fifth birthday, Harburg was driving alone on Sunset Boulevard in the Brentwood area of Los Angeles when he suffered a massive heart attack and died instantly. His remains were cremated and scattered over the Pacific Ocean.

★

The papers of E. Y. Harburg are in the Beinecke Library, Yale University, and the New York Public Library. Harold Meyerson and Ernest Harburg, *Who Put the Rainbow in the* Wizard of Oz?: *Yip Harburg, Lyricist* (1993), is the only full-length critical biography. Written by Harburg's son and his collaborator, the volume analyzes Harburg's contribution to musical theater as well as the themes and images that characterize his work.

Philip Furia, *The Poets of Tin Pan Alley: A History of America's Great Lyricists* (1990), and Thomas S. Hischak, *Word Crazy: Broadway Lyricists from Cohan to Sondheim* (1991), examine lyrics from a literary perspective. Both devote chapters to Harburg, although Furia's analysis is more extensive and penetrating. John Fricke, *The Wizard of Oz: The Official Fiftieth Anniversary Pictorial History* (1989), is a detailed history of the making of the movie, including information about Harburg's contribution. John Lahr, "The Lemon-Drop Kid," *New Yorker* (30 Sept. 1996), is a wittily insightful essay about the social and sexual innovations in Harburg's lyrics. Max Wilk, *They're Playing Our Song: Conversations with America's Classic Songwriters* (1991), is a book of interviews that includes the outspoken, eloquent Harburg. An obituary is in the *New York Times* (7 Mar. 1981).

MICHAEL LASSER

HARKNESS, Rebekah West (*b.* 17 April 1915 in St. Louis, Missouri; *d.* 17 June 1982 in New York City), dance patron and philanthropist whose Harkness Ballet Foundation supported such acclaimed dance companies as the Joffrey Ballet and influenced many distinguished artists and dancers.

Born into one of the leading families in St. Louis, Rebekah was the youngest of three children of Allen Tarwater West, a stockbroker, and Rebekah Semple West. Her paternal grandfather, Thomas Henry West, was the founder of the Union Trust Company of St. Louis. He acquired social prominence as the director of the local electric and gas companies and of the St. Louis–San Francisco Railroad company. Although the social norms of St. Louis society were restrictive for Rebekah, an impulsive and ambitious child, as part of her privileged upbringing she enjoyed traveling with her family to places like New York City and Miami Beach. She received her early education from private schools in St. Louis, the Rossman and the John Burroughs. Like other daughters from highly affluent families, Rebekah, familiarly known as Betty in her youth, then attended the Fermata, a finishing school in Aiken, South Carolina. Tall, blonde, and playful, Betty was the center of attention in her circle. Her interest in dancing unfolded early in her life when she started taking ballet lessons in order to reduce her weight. Soon after her graduation in 1932, she appeared in the chorus of a production of *Aïda* by the Chicago Opera Company in St. Louis. In 1937 she traveled around the world aboard the *Empress of Britain* with her twenty-nine-year-old brother, Allen West, Jr.

In 1938 Rebekah married a Yale graduate and an advertising executive for the firm of Color Photography, Charles Dickson Pierce, who was the son of a renowned St. Louis attorney. With Pierce, Rebekah had two children, born in 1940 and 1944. When her husband enlisted in the army during World War II, Rebekah, who wanted more than the circumscribed life of a mother, did volunteer work at Barnes Hospital in St. Louis as a nurse's aide and took up figure skating.

In 1946, two years after her divorce from Pierce, Rebekah visited the summer cottage of her parents at Watch Hill, Rhode Island. This visit changed the course of her life; at Watch Hill, Rebekah met William Hale Harkness, another Yale graduate, who was an heir to the fortunes of Standard Oil. On 1 October 1947 she and Harkness were married.

Although William Harkness concentrated most of his energies on his investment interests, the marriage was a happy one, and in 1948 the couple had a child. Their life together came to an abrupt end in 1954, however, when Harkness died of a heart attack at Westerly Hospital in Rhode Island. After her husband's death, Rebekah inherited his vast wealth. Now independent, she was determined to launch her artistic career, her passion for music and dance now backed by the Harkness wealth.

Rebekah initially devoted her talents to orchestral composition. She began receiving music lessons from Nadia Boulanger, the renowned French teacher of composition and harmony. Rebekah's works included *Safari Suite* (1955), based on her tour of Africa in 1952; *Macumba* (1965); *Journey to Love* (1958); and *Mediterranean Moods* (1956). Her first taste of success came when *Safari Suite* premiered at Carnegie Hall in New York in 1955. Three years later her ballet suite *Journey to Love* was performed by the company of the Marquis de Cuevas at the Brussels World's Fair in 1958.

In 1959 Harkness established the Rebekah Harkness Foundation, inaugurating her career as a patron of dance.

Rebekah Harkness (*right*) with the actress Paulette Goddard, 1965. AGENCE FRANCE PRESSE/ARCHIVE PHOTOS

With her beneficence, the Jerome Robbins' Ballet: USA emerged from a financial crisis and gained a new life as it performed throughout Europe and at home. One of the most important projects to come out of Harkness's commitment to dance was her summer workshops at Watch Hill, starting in 1962. These workshops embraced and extended support to troupes like the Robert Joffrey Company and many individual artists, such as Donald Saddler and Alvin Ailey. The Joffrey Ballet went on to achieve international acclaim. Harkness's largesse encompassed more than the world of dance. She also donated $2 million toward the construction of the William Hale Harkness Medical Research Building at New York Hospital.

Her success was problematic, however. Internal rivalry and disagreement over artistic direction (such as the use of her compositions) undermined her endeavors, and in April

1964 she formed her own ballet company, the Harkness Ballet, which consisted of some of the members of the Joffrey group. She was consequently blamed for co-opting members of the Joffrey company. In order to strengthen her own dancers and give them a permanent base in New York, she bought the mansion of IBM chief Thomas J. Watson for $625,000 and transformed it into a magnificent home, called the Harkness House for Ballet Arts, for the troupe. Harkness's aim of endowing ballet with power and prestige was accomplished through extravagant expenditure. "I want to give splendor back to ballet. I think today our artists deserve such elegance, for they are our true aristocrats. As an artist myself, I know that I am affected by my environment," she once commented to a reporter.

Despite its ups and downs, the Harkness School of Ballet produced many successful dancers. In 1968 Harkness diversified her artistic endeavor by starting a second company, the Harkness Youth Dancers, directed by choreographer Ben Stevenson. As Harkness's projects expanded, she felt financial strain, which caused her to cancel the Harkness Ballet's European tour under artistic director Lawrence Rhodes and choreographer Benjamin Harkarvy. Yet Harkness continued to acquire property in pursuit of her glamorous dream; she purchased the Old Colonial Theater in New York and furnished it with decorations imported from all over the world. The grand opening of the Harkness Theater in 1974 was attended by distinguished guests, including Lynda Bird Johnson and Salvador Dali. By 1976, however, the Harkness company had folded.

Meanwhile, Harkness's personal life went through many changes. In 1961 she married her third husband, Benjamin Harrison Kean, a physician. After her subsequent divorce in 1965, she married Niels Lauersen, also a physician, in 1974, but was again divorced in 1977. While none of her marriages offered her a stable relationship, she had developed an enduring romantic love for her onetime dance partner Robert Scevers in 1964. Scevers, who had had an ordinary upbringing in Texas and was twenty-five years younger than she, remained very close to Harkness and played a decisive role in her life. Rarely known for excellence in dance, Scevers nonetheless was in good favor with Harkness until her death; she chose him to succeed her as artistic director of the Harkness Ballet Foundation.

Rebekah Harkness died of cancer in 1982 in her Carlyle Hotel apartment in New York City. Her funeral was held at St. James Episcopal Church in Manhattan. A week after her death, a memorial service was held at Harkness House. Her ashes were supposed to be deposited in a jewel-studded golden urn designed by Salvador Dali, called the "Chalice of Life." But her remains finally found repose in the Harkness family mausoleum in Woodlawn Cemetery in the Bronx because of the insufficient capacity of the urn. The

urn was sold to the Mitsui Gallery in Tokyo. Harkness's summer house in Nassau and her chalet in Gstaad, Switzerland, were also sold upon her death, with the proceeds being donated to her foundation.

Although the artistic achievement of Rebekah Harkness was not profound, her philanthropy during her lifetime and after her death through the Harkness Ballet Foundation and the William Hale Harkness Foundation ensures her legacy as a patron of ballet. One alumnus of Harkness Ballet observed, "I maintain that for everything that went wrong, Mrs. Harkness gave more to dance than anyone since Diaghilev."

★

Craig Unger in his critical and comprehensive biography *Blue Blood* (1988) documents Harkness's career along with her at times troubled personal life, including her multiple divorces and the suicide of her daughter, Edith Harkness. *Current Biography* (1974) provides a detailed look at Harkness's professional development and her philanthropic contributions up to 1974. An obituary is in the *New York Times* (19 June 1982).

SAIYEDA KHATUN

HARRIS, Patricia Roberts Fitzgerald (*b*. 31 May 1924 in Mattoon, Illinois; *d*. 23 March 1985 in Washington, D.C.), activist, attorney, and educator who was the first African-American woman to be named a U.S. ambassador and who held two cabinet appointments in the administration of President Jimmy Carter.

Harris was the elder of two children born to Bert Fitzgerald, a Pullman car waiter, and Hildren Brodie Roberts, an insurance actuary. After Harris's father abandoned the family, she and her brother, Malcolm, were raised by their mother, who refused to define herself or her children by racist stereotypes. When Harris was six years old, she became aware of racism. Despite her exemplary academic record in primary school, Harris could not be named the top student on her school's honor roll because she was African American. It was her mother's unflagging support that provided Harris with the strength she needed as one of a handful of African Americans in the overwhelmingly white community of Mattoon, Illinois.

In 1942 Harris, a small, attractive, fair-skinned woman, graduated from Englewood High School in Chicago and entered Howard University in Washington, D.C. At Howard, Harris became active in the burgeoning civil rights movement and was among the first students to demonstrate and stage sit-ins to integrate the District of Columbia's restaurants, hotels, and department stores. This early involvement as a social activist laid the ideological foundation for Harris's future career in public service.

In 1945 Harris graduated summa cum laude from How-

Patricia Roberts Harris, 1965. ARCHIVE PHOTOS

ard with an A.B. degree in political science and economics. She then enrolled at the University of Chicago, where she received an M.A. degree in industrial relations in 1947. While pursuing her graduate studies there, Harris acted as program director of the Chicago Young Women's Christian Association from 1946 to 1949 and was instrumental in the creation of social programs to meet the needs of the city's postwar constituents. During the 1940s Harris also served on Chicago's Commission on Human Rights as well as in the Chicago Urban League.

In 1949 Harris relocated to Washington, D.C., where she took courses in public policy at American University from 1949 to 1950. She was assistant director of the American Council on Human Rights, located in Washington, from 1949 to 1953. She also became the executive director of Delta Sigma Theta, a national African-American public service society, from 1953 to 1959.

In 1955 Harris met District of Columbia attorney and Howard University law professor William Beasley Harris, and on 1 September of that year they were married. They had no children. Harris enrolled at the George Washington University Law School in 1957 and three years later was awarded the J.D. degree and the John Bell Larner Prize for graduating first in her class; she was also a member of Phi Beta Kappa and the Order of Coif Legal Honor Society.

From 1960 to 1961 Harris worked as a trial attorney in the U.S. Department of Justice Criminal Division. Harris then taught at Howard University Law School. After her brief career as a U.S. attorney and a law professor, Harris was named cochair of the National Women's Committee for Civil Rights by President John F. Kennedy in 1963. From 1964 to 1966 she served on President Lyndon B. Johnson's Commission on the Status of Puerto Rico. President Johnson named Harris to the position of U.S. ambassador to Luxembourg in 1965 and as an alternate delegate to the United Nations in 1966. She was the first African-American woman to be an ambassador and the first African American to hold her UN post.

Within political circles, Harris became known for her demanding, no-nonsense administrative style. Because she was a woman and an African American in positions of power in the traditionally white male domain of national politics, she was often described as arrogant and abrasive when, in fact, she was no more assertive than most of her colleagues. According to a former presidential aide: "You know why she's abrasive? She's abrasive because she's a black woman. There're not many people who like to have black women tell them what to do. They'll take much more guff from a white male."

Harris returned to Howard Law School in 1967. Although she became dean of the school in 1969, she resigned later that year in connection with student-administration conflict. One year later Harris became a partner in the prestigious Washington, D.C., law firm of Fried, Frank, Harris, Shriver and Kampelman, where she remained until 1977. From 1967 to 1977 Harris also served on the board of directors of the NAACP Legal Defense Fund and held board appointments with the American Civil Liberties Union, the national YWCA, National Educational Television, the Twentieth Century Fund, and Chase Manhattan.

Harris's political career did not end with her entrance into the private sector. In 1972 she became temporary chair of the Democratic party's credentials committee. In 1977 President Jimmy Carter appointed her secretary of housing and urban development (HUD). Ironically, despite her long advocacy for civil rights, during her nomination hearings Harris was accused of being unable to properly serve HUD's poor and minority constituents because of her success within the ranks of national policy-making organizations. She responded with her own personal credo:

> I am one of them. You do not seem to understand who I am. I am a black woman, the daughter of a dining car worker. . . . I did not start out as a member of a prestigious law firm, but as a woman who needed a scholarship to go to school. I have been a defender of women, of minorities, of those who have been outcasts of this society throughout my life. If

my life has any meaning at all, it is that those who start out as outcasts may end up being part of the system.

During her tenure as secretary of HUD, Harris worked tirelessly to help all Americans afford decent housing. Congress failed to support housing budgets proposed by HUD and approved by President Carter, however. In response, Harris, in her trademark forthright manner, asked: "How long will the people of this country be willing to put their heads in the sand and decide that they need not spend money to meet the needs of the poor?"

In an effort to close its budget gap, HUD under Harris's stewardship instituted several new policies to ensure that the government lived up to the promises made to the nation's poor during President Johnson's Great Society. Among these were the establishment of a Community Development Block Grants Program to fund community projects; the Urban Development and Action Grant Program to promote private investment in decaying cities; new regulations that committed the Federal National Mortgage Association to invest part of its assets into urban areas for low-income housing; and the first nationwide study of housing discrimination. From 1979 to 1981 Harris served as head of the Department of Health, Education, and Welfare, which was renamed the Department of Health and Human Services (HHS) in 1980.

Following President Carter's loss to Ronald Reagan in the 1980 election, Harris returned to George Washington University Law School as a full-time professor. In 1982 Harris ran in a mayoral race against Marion Barry in the District of Columbia. Despite her early association with civil rights activism as a young college student, her steadfast advocacy on behalf of the nation's poor and minorities, and her reputation as an effective administrator whose political victories reflected her commitment to improving the lives of all Americans, Harris was seen by many as a candidate of the middle class, both white and African American, and was never really considered an African-American leader. She lost the bitterly fought campaign to Barry, who was accepted as more of a grassroots leader.

During her impressive career as an attorney and civil rights advocate, Harris was awarded more than thirty-two honorary doctorate degrees from colleges and universities around the country, including Johns Hopkins University, Williams College, Brown University, the University of Maryland, and Georgetown University. She died of cancer at George Washington University Hospital. She is buried in Washington, D.C.

★

See Sylvia Dannett, *Profiles of Negro Womanhood* (1966); Wade Baskin and Richard N. Runes, *Dictionary of Black Culture* (1973); Harry Ploski, *Negro Almanac* (1976); and Darlene Clark Hine,

Black Women in America: An Historical Encyclopedia (1993). Also useful is Alex Poinsett, "Patricia Roberts Harris: HUD's Velvet-Gloved Iron Hand," *Ebony* (July 1979). Obituaries are in the *New York Times* (24 Mar. 1985), *Washington Post* (24 Mar. 1985), *Chicago Defender* (25 Mar. 1985), *Cleveland Call and Post* (28 Mar. 1985), and *Los Angeles Sentinel* (28 Mar. 1985).

LaRose T. Parris

HARTLINE, Haldan Keffer (*b.* 22 December 1903 in Bloomsburg, Pennsylvania; *d.* 17 March 1983 in Fallston, Maryland), medical doctor and professor of biophysics who was a cowinner of the 1967 Nobel Prize in physiology or medicine for his research on the electrophysiology of the retina.

Hartline attended the Bloomsburg State Normal School in Pennsylvania, where his parents, Daniel Schollenberger Hartline and Harriet ("Hallie") Franklin Keffer, were teachers. His father was professor and chairman of the department of biology and nature study and inspired his only son to pursue a career in the natural sciences. The Hartline Science Center, completed in 1968 at the Bloomsburg Campus, was named in honor of all three Hartlines. Keffer, as he was called by his family and friends, was fascinated with the organism his father had designated "King Crab." This arthropod, commonly known as the horseshoe crab (*Limulus polyphemus*), would later play an important role in the research that led to Hartline's award-winning studies on the visual system.

In 1923 Hartline graduated from Lafayette College in Easton, Pennsylvania, with a B.S. degree. Beverly Kunkel, Hartline's mentor and biology professor at Lafayette, encouraged him to further his studies of the visual responses of land isopods. In addition, Hartline spent several summers at the Marine Biological Laboratory in Woods Hole, Massachusetts, where Jacques Loeb, Selig Hecht, and Merkel H. Jacobs served as role models.

Hartline entered the medical school at Johns Hopkins University in the autumn of 1923, and he continued his work on vision in the department of physiology. Under the auspices of E. K. Marshall and C. D. Snyder, Hartline conducted research on insects, animals, and humans. Hartline completed his medical degree at Johns Hopkins in 1927 and that same year was presented with both the William H. Howell Award for Physiology and a National Research Council fellowship in the medical sciences, the latter enabling him to study mathematics and physics for the next two years. Hartline then became a student worker in A. H. Pfund's laboratory in the physics department at Johns Hopkins and attended mathematics classes with F. D. Murnaghan as well.

In 1929 Hartline received an Eldridge Reeves Johnson

Professor Haldan K. Hartline in his laboratory at Rockefeller University, 1967. UPI/CORBIS-BETTMANN

Traveling Fellowship from the University of Pennsylvania, which allowed him to go to Germany. He spent one semester at the University of Leipzig as part of a physics seminar headed by Werner Heisenberg and two semesters attending lectures by Arnold Sommerfeld at the University of Munich. On his return to the United States in the spring of 1931, Hartline was appointed assistant professor of medical physics by the Eldridge Reeves Johnson Foundation at the University of Pennsylvania. It was there that Hartline developed a longtime friendship and collaboration with Detlev W. Bronk; he also met with Ragnar Granit and Clarence Graham. Around the same time, Hartline spent the summer at Woods Hole, where he was introduced to George Wald.

In 1936, while teaching at the University of Pennsylvania, Hartline married Elizabeth Kraus, the daughter of the distinguished chemist C. A. Kraus. At that time she was an instructor of comparative psychology at Bryn Mawr College; they had three sons, all of whom worked in the biological or neurophysiological fields.

From 1940 to 1941 Hartline was an associate professor of physiology at the Cornell Medical College in New York City, where he conducted research for the military on night vision in humans. After receiving another Johnson Foundation award, Hartline returned to the University of Pennsylvania. In addition, the Society of Experimental Psychologists honored him with the Howard Crosby Warren Medal in 1948, which came with an honorary membership in the society. In 1949 Hartline accepted the position of professor of biophysics and chairman of the Thomas C. Jenkins Department at Johns Hopkins University. He remained there until 1953, when he joined the faculty at Rockefeller University, where Hartline, Bronk, and Frank Brink, Jr., created

a new division of biophysics that year. In 1954 Floyd Ratliff began a longtime collaboration with Hartline on the visual physiology of the *Limulus* eye.

Hartline continued his research at Rockefeller University until his retirement in 1974. The years were filled with many accolades, including an honorary doctor of science degree from Lafayette College in 1959; the Albert A. Michelson Award from the Case Institute of Technology in 1964; an honorary doctor of law degree from Johns Hopkins and the Lighthouse Award, both in 1969; and two honorary degrees in 1971—a doctor of science degree from the University of Pennsylvania and a doctor of medicine degree from the Albert-Ludwigs University at Freiburg im Breisgau. In 1972 Hartline obtained the Detlev W. Bronk Professorship from Rockefeller University; in 1982, he was presented with the George Washington Kidd Award from Lafayette. Hartline reached the pinnacle of his achievements in 1967 when he won the Nobel Prize in physiology or medicine, along with Ragnar Granit and George Wald, for their discoveries concerning the primary chemical and physiological visual processes in the eye.

Hartline was also an esteemed member of many learned societies, including the American Academy of Arts and Sciences, the American Philosophical Society, the American Physiological Society, the Biophysical Society, the National Academy of Sciences, the Optical Society of America, and the Royal Society, London. Hartline died of a heart attack at the Fallston General Hospital in Maryland. An exceptional individual in many ways, Hartline was highly intelligent and ambitious and published widely in his field. He also developed his own computer programs and was involved in setting up biological research guidelines for the National Aeronautics and Space Administration. What made him most extraordinary, however, is that despite his many achievements, he was able to maintain the shy and unassuming demeanor that had earned him the respect of both colleagues and students alike. His laboratory was described as "a slightly disorganized but extremely fertile chaos."

★

Floyd Ratliff, ed., *Studies on Excitation and Inhibition in the Retina* (1974), is a collection of Hartline's laboratory papers, with a foreword by Hartline. *Les Prix Nobel en 1967* (1968) contains a short biography of Hartline and other Nobel Prize winners, along with their articles. George W. Corner, *A History of the Rockefeller Institute, 1901–1953: Origins and Growth* (1964), briefly mentions Hartline's founding of the institute's division of biophysics. Werner Wiskari, "Three Get Nobel Prize for Eye Research," *New York Times* (19 Oct. 1967), focuses on the careers of the three Nobel laureates and offers some personal information. John E. Dowling and Floyd Ratliff, "Nobel Prize: Three Named for Medicine, Physiology Award," *Science* 158 (27 Oct. 1967), discusses the lives and research of Hartline, Granit, and Wald. An obituary is in the *New York Times* (19 Mar. 1983).

ADRIANA C. TOMASINO

HATHAWAY, Starke Rosecrans (*b.* 22 August 1903 in Central Lake, Michigan; *d.* 4 July 1984 in Minneapolis, Minnesota), psychology professor at the University of Minnesota best known for his collaboration with J. Charnley McKinley, a neuropsychiatrist, in developing the Minnesota Multiphasic Personality Inventory (MMPI), the most widely used personality test in the world.

Hathaway was the only child of Martin Walter Hathaway, a maintenance man, and Bertha Belle Rosecrans, a homemaker. Except for a few years in Kansas, he grew up in Marysville, a small town in central Ohio. His parents encouraged him in his lifelong interest in engineering, letting him experiment extensively with electrical and electronic gadgets. As a teenager he built radios for himself and for friends and relatives. Summers were spent working for power and telephone companies to earn money for college.

Hathaway entered Ohio University in Athens in 1923 to study engineering but, under the influence of James P. Porter, the chairman of the Department of Psychology, he changed his major to psychology. He received an A.B. degree in 1927 and an A.M. degree in 1928 with a major in psychology and a minor in statistics. He stayed on at Ohio University as an assistant professor, teaching courses in both psychology and physiology. While at Athens, Hathaway manufactured and sold psychogalvanometers and chronometers of his own invention. He married Virginia Riddle, a fellow psychology student at Ohio University in 1928; they had no children. Two years later he went to the University of Minnesota to study for his doctorate.

Portrait of Starke Hathaway. W. GRANT DAHLSTROM

As part of his graduate studies, Hathaway carried out anatomical and physiological research on the central nervous system. He also took courses at the School of Engineering. To investigate sleep patterns, he devised an action-activated camera for nightlong recording and, while collaborating in research with neurologists and neurosurgeons, he developed electronic devices for direct stimulation of the human cortex. These investigations led to work with Professor J. Charnley McKinley, chairman of the Department of Neuropsychiatry. Hathaway completed his doctoral work in 1932 and eventually gained tenure as a professor of psychology in neuropsychiatry. His neurological studies were integrated into a highly successful text in physiological psychology, published in 1942.

The collaboration between Hathaway and McKinley extended to the study of the effectiveness of psychological and medical treatment interventions for patients suffering from various forms of psychopathology. After trying out all available psychological measures to assess therapeutic outcomes, they decided that these tests were unsuited to this task. They found that the primary difficulty with these instruments was that the content and the scoring direction of the item statements were established a priori solely on the basis of the judgment of the test developers.

Hathaway and McKinley decided to employ an empirical approach to the development of a multifaceted instrument for this purpose. Using carefully selected samples of patients exhibiting some clear-cut emotional disorder, they analyzed the stable differences between that group and a heterogeneous group of "people in general" on about a thousand self-descriptive statements. Those items found to separate "normals" from those with the emotional disorder in question were collected into a scale. Each scale was then cross-validated on new samples of patients. Eventually ten such scales were assembled into a profile for the MMPI, together with several scales measuring the extent to which the test subjects were able to follow the instructions and willing to present themselves on the inventory. This instrument was published in 1940. It has been translated into more than forty languages and used in medical, educational, and employment screening, as well as in psychiatric settings. Computerized scoring and interpretive services in both the United States and abroad have been based on the MMPI. (The test was restandardized in 1989 and published as the MMPI-2; three years later the MMPI-A for adolescent clients was made available.)

After World War II, Hathaway established at the University of Minnesota one of the first graduate training programs in clinical psychology. He pioneered in the recording and analysis of psychotherapeutic interviews to train therapists and to evaluate treatment effectiveness. He initiated longitudinal research on juvenile delinquency, collaborating with the sociologist Elio D. Monachesi in testing more than 15,000 children with the MMPI in the ninth grade in the Twin Cities and around the state of Minnesota. (This work was in part facilitated by Hathaway's wife, who then held the position of director of psychological services in the Minneapolis school system.) It was published in 1953 as *Analyzing and Predicting Juvenile Delinquency with the MMPI.* A number of MMPI profile patterns have been found to predict later delinquencies as well as criminal, psychiatric, and substance abuse problems among these research subjects.

For several years prior to his retirement in 1971, Hathaway served as the executive director of the Department of Neuropsychiatry. He was honored by the American Psychological Association with its Distinguished Scientific Contribution Award in 1959 and the Distinguished Contribution for Applications in Psychology Award in 1977. Hathaway lived at 222 Melbourne Avenue, S.E., in Minneapolis. His death resulted from a series of strokes; his remains were cremated.

Hathaway's impact on students and colleagues assured long-lasting influence in the field of test development and personality assessment. In addition, the field of clinical psychology was fundamentally altered by his insistence on scientific openness and data-based techniques.

★

See Hathaway's essay "Through Psychology My Way," in T. S. Krawicc, ed., *The Psychologists: Autobiographies of Distinguished Living Psychologists,* vol. 3 (1978). A collection of essays edited by D. S. Nichols and P. A. Marks titled *Reflections and Remembrances: A Tribute to Starke R. Hathaway* was published by the University of Minnesota Press in 1992. Obituaries are in the *New York Times* (5 July 1984) and *American Psychologist* 41 (1986).

W. GRANT DAHLSTROM

HAYS, (Lawrence) Brooks (*b.* 9 August 1898 in Russellville, Arkansas; *d.* 11 October 1981 in Washington, D.C.), U.S. congressman from Arkansas who was a prominent figure in the controversy surrounding the racial integration of Little Rock Central High School in 1957 and was president of the Southern Baptist Convention (1957–1959).

Brooks Hays was the only child of Adelbert Steele Hays, a lawyer, and Sallie T. Butler. He was raised in the western frontier region of Arkansas, near the border with Oklahoma, itself only a few years removed from its designation as Indian Territory. His relatives were Democrats and Baptists, the dominant political and religious groups in Arkansas, and Hays was throughout his life identified with both groups. Hays attended the University of Arkansas in Fayetteville from 1915 to 1919, interrupting his studies briefly to serve in the army during the last months of World War I. He then attended George Washington University

Brooks Hays. REPRODUCED FROM THE COLLECTIONS OF THE LIBRARY OF CONGRESS

School of Law from 1919 to 1922, earning the LL.B. degree, and passed the Arkansas bar. On 2 February 1922 he married Marion Prather of Arkansas; they had two children. Just before his twenty-fourth birthday, he began the practice of law with his father's firm in Russellville, Arkansas; the firm's name became Hays, Priddy and Hays when he joined.

Finding the daily work in a law office tedious, Hays began almost immediately to dabble in politics, first managing an unsuccessful race for Congress by his father in 1922, then looking for his own chance to run for office. He was for a long time hampered by his youth, the fact that his family was known to oppose the activities of the Ku Klux Klan, and the opinion in his rural district that he was the child of a wealthy man, sent by his father to a fancy eastern law school. He persisted, however, because he was sure that politics was his calling. He began to hone his oratorical skills, which were enhanced by a disarming sense of humor.

In 1924 he managed the successful campaign of a candidate for Arkansas attorney general and was appointed the winner's assistant. He moved his family to Little Rock, where he began making regular appearances before the Arkansas Supreme Court. In 1927, although at the time of the primary election he was too young to take office, he ran for governor of Arkansas. He assured voters that he would reach the required age of thirty before the general election. Placing second in the Democratic primary, due in part to widespread voting fraud, he ran again in 1930 but once again placed second. In 1933, in what has been called "the most fraudulent election in Arkansas history," he lost a special election to Congress and in financial desperation accepted a job in 1934 with the New Deal Arkansas National Recovery Administration. He remained a political appointee for the next decade. He longed for the power of elective office but found fulfillment in New Deal activity because his work had a kind of ministerial flavor. He believed that he had both a political and a religious vocation, and during this "social work" period of his life each influenced the other.

In 1942, when the man who had defeated him in 1933 decided to run for the U.S. Senate, Hays sought and won the House of Representatives seat from the Fifth District of Arkansas. He won reelection seven times, serving in the House from 1943 to 1959. He was known in Congress for his sense of social justice, his political humor, and his spellbinding oratory. He served from the start on the Banking and Currency Committee, his third choice, but soon found a place on the Foreign Affairs Committee, where he spent much of his energy in the post–World War II and cold war eras. Foreign affairs, like his New Deal legal work, satisfied a need in him for "ministry." It was a political form of missionary work.

Hays was a deeply and publicly religious man, one of the most prominent in Congress during his years there. He was a devoted Baptist, a popular Sunday school teacher both in Little Rock and in Washington, and a lay minister. During their early, seventeenth-century days in England, Baptists depended on lay leadership, but twentieth-century Southern Baptists tended to elect ordained clergymen to administrative posts. It was therefore unusual for a layman like Hays, particularly a politician, to rise in Baptist ranks to serve on cardinal committees and to be elected president of the Southern Baptist Convention twice, in 1957 and 1958. While president he encouraged policies and introduced programs that were severely attacked by conservatives as communist and unchristian. But he used his famous humor to defuse most of the explosive confrontations and left the office highly respected.

Hays reached the top of his political career, and paradoxically its nadir as well, in 1957 and 1958, at the very time he was president of the Southern Baptist Convention. When Little Rock Central High School was ordered by the federal courts to integrate and Arkansas governor Orval Faubus opposed the decree and refused to maintain order, Hays, as the congressman representing Little Rock in Washington, felt compelled to step in and mediate the controversy. With violence possible, President Dwight D. Eisenhower sent in federal troops. At the next election, in 1958, with the Arkansas electorate seething over what it considered a federal invasion and what it perceived to be Hays's capitulation to the courts, Faubus forces organized a write-in vote in support of a challenger, Dale Alford, an outspoken segregationist, and Hays was turned out of office.

His final years, from age sixty to his death, were among his best. Eisenhower appointed him to the three-member board of the Tennessee Valley Authority, in which capacity he served from 1959 to 1961. President John F. Kennedy made him assistant secretary of state for congressional affairs (1961), where he became a troubleshooter for New Frontier policies. He worked for Great Society legislation as a special assistant to President Lyndon Johnson. He even returned to Arkansas in 1966 to run for governor at age sixty-eight, but once more, now considered a raving liberal, he was unsuccessful.

He went on to guest lectureships, a stint as director of the Ecumenical Institute at Wake Forest University in Winston-Salem, North Carolina (1968–1970), and even a final political race in 1972, for a North Carolina congressional seat, enlivening a lost cause with an energy remarkable for someone seventy-four. A greatly respected elder statesman, he died of a stroke at his Washington, D.C., apartment. He is buried at Oakland Cemetery in Russellville, Arkansas.

★

Collections of Hays's papers are at the University of Arkansas in Fayetteville (personal and professional), the Southern Baptist Sunday School Board Archives in Nashville, Tennessee (Baptist matters), the John F. Kennedy Presidential Library at Harvard University (White House years), and the Wake Forest University Library (later career). A biography by James T. Baker, *Brooks Hays* (1989), covers the political, religious, and personal dimensions of Hays's life. Hays, himself a prolific writer, provides biographical and philosophical information in four books: *This Word: A Christian's Workshop* (1958); *A Southern Moderate Speaks* (1959); the humorous *A Hotbed of Tranquility: My Life in Five Worlds* (1968); and *Politics Is My Parish: An Autobiography* (1981). A series of typeset interviews with Ronald Tonks from 1975 to 1977 are at the Sunday School Board Archives. An obituary is in the *New York Times* (13 Oct. 1981).

JAMES T. BAKER

HAYS, Lee Elhardt (*b.* 14 March 1914 in Little Rock, Arkansas; *d.* 26 August 1981 in Tarrytown, New York), singer, songwriter, and social activist who, as a member of the folk group the Weavers, helped bridge the gap between popular and folk music beginning in the 1950s.

Hays was the son of William Benjamin Hays, a Methodist minister, and Ellen Reinhardt Hays, who, prior to her marriage, had been the first woman court reporter in the state of Arkansas. He was the youngest of four children. His

The Weavers, including Lee Hays (*center*), Pete Seeger (*left*), Fred Halterman (*right*), and Miss Ronnie Gilbert, 1952. UPI/CORBIS-BETTMANN

eldest brother, Reuben, was the son of his father's first wife, who died soon after giving birth. The family moved frequently during Lee's childhood, and his earliest exposure to music was in the rural churches where his father preached. William Hays was killed in an auto accident when Lee was thirteen. Lee completed high school at the Emory Junior College Academy in Georgia.

Family economic hardship, as well as the emotional breakdowns of his mother and sister after his father's death, made it impossible for Hays to follow his older siblings to college. Instead, he traveled to Cleveland, Ohio, in September of 1930 to live with his brother, Reuben. He went to work shelving books in the Cleveland Public Library, reading voraciously during most of his working hours. Hays noted that "somewhere along in there, I became some kind of socialist. Just what kind I've never to this day figured out."

In 1934 Hays joined a group of young people who were followers of Claude Williams, a Presbyterian minister whose outspoken style, questioning of traditional religious dogma, and efforts to organize Arkansas coal miners in the town of Paris led to the loss of his pulpit. After a brief stint at the College of the Ozarks in 1934 and 1935, Hays took up residence at the Highlander Folk School in Tennessee, where the melodies of Southern mountain folk ballads and labor organizing songs formed an important part of the curriculum. Williams and Hays were reunited in the effort to organize sharecroppers through the Southern Tenant Farmers Union. Hays made a brief trip to New York City in 1935 to raise funds for a documentary film about this effort.

Hays and Williams returned to Arkansas in 1937 and began working at the Commonwealth Labor College, a cooperative school where Hays took on the varied tasks of teacher, songwriter, playwright, group singing leader, and cook. Commonwealth was proud of its labor and radical heritage, and its supporters often touted it as "more radical than Highlander." Under Williams's tutelage, Hays learned how to recast well-known gospel hymns and spirituals as union organizing songs. Realizing that all he often had to do was change the word "Jesus" to "union," Hays adapted many melodies familiar to poor Southern workers as he and Williams straddled the line between preaching and organizing, with labor versions of such songs as "We Shall Not Be Moved" and "Roll the Union On." When Commonwealth closed its doors in 1940, Hays traveled to New York, bringing his union songs and his radical politics with him. Hays had the support of his friends and colleagues, who raised the $65 he needed to travel north.

In New York, Hays began singing in union halls and anywhere else that he could get a hearing. He soon met Pete Seeger and, with the help of writer Millard Lampell and singer-songwriter Woody Guthrie, he joined Seeger in the Almanac Singers soon after the group's founding in 1941. The Almanac Singers took up residence in Manhattan's Greenwich Village, living, singing, and writing songs together. Before the United States entered World War II, they recorded an album of peace songs that reflected the position of the communist left of the period. After the Pearl Harbor attack, the group recorded "Dear Mr. President," which supported the war effort. The Almanac's best-known recording was "Talkin' Union," recorded early in 1941. Hays was said to have given the group its name when he quipped that the only books a country person needed were a Bible and a farmer's almanac. The Almanac Singers disbanded in 1942 when some of its members, most notably Pete Seeger, entered military service. Hays's most popular song of this period was the collaboration with Seeger on "If I Had a Hammer," written during a meeting of People's Songs, a group of radical and labor singers in New York City and throughout the United States.

After the war, Hays joined Seeger, Ronnie Gilbert, and Fred Hellerman in forming a new group, the Weavers, which bridged the gap between folk and popular music in the early 1950s and established a precedent of highly arranged music and lyrics of social commentary that was extended by many folk and protest groups and singers in the 1960s. Hays is credited with giving the group its name, and he helped to write or arrange many of its most popular hits. The poet Carl Sandburg commented, "When I hear America singing, the Weavers are there."

After their performance debut in December of 1949 in Greenwich Village, the Weavers made their first Decca Records recording of Woody Guthrie's Dust Bowl ballad "So Long, It's Been Good to Know You" and Leadbelly's (Huddie Ledbetter) "Good Night, Irene," which held the top place on the pop music charts for three months in 1950. They also recorded "Tzena, Tzena," which was a hit.

Mass market success brought enhanced exposure and more opportunity, but it also led to greater scrutiny of the political views of the Weavers in the early days of the cold war. They were signed to a contract for a weekly television show in 1950, but the sponsor backed out at the last minute because of allegations that Seeger and Hays were Communists. Blacklisting led to the Weavers' retirement in 1952 because they were unable to get concert bookings. On 16 August 1955 Hays appeared before the House Committee on Un-American Activities, asserting his rights under the Fifth Amendment and refusing to answer questions about his work, his beliefs, his personal and professional associations, and "Wasn't That a Time," the song about the cold war he had written with Walter Lowenfels.

In 1955 the Weavers were reunited for a Christmas concert arranged by their manager, Harold Leventhal. This Carnegie Hall appearance was historic for its expression of determination and optimism, even in the midst of the cold

war. They continued to perform and record with Seeger until 1958 and then with a number of replacement artists until 1963, when the members of the Weavers separated to pursue their own careers. Hays moved to suburban Croton-on-Hudson, New York, where he became a fixture in local folk music circles. In 1968 he played a bit part in the movie based on Arlo Guthrie's "Alice's Restaurant." He supported himself with the royalties from "If I Had a Hammer," songs written for his four albums of children's songs performed with the Baby Sitters, and other writings. He suffered from deteriorating health, the result of longtime drinking, diabetes, and the effects of tuberculosis contracted early in his life, which had permanently weakened him.

In 1980 the Weavers came together again at Carnegie Hall for a concert celebrating the twenty-fifth anniversary of their 1955 performance. Hays performed from a wheelchair, a screen covering his legs, which had been amputated because of gangrene from diabetes. Portions of the concert, historical footage of the Weavers, and vignettes featuring all of the members were compiled in the feature film, *Wasn't That a Time*, released in August 1981. On 26 August 1981 Lee Hays died of a heart attack in Tarrytown, New York. At his request, his ashes were scattered by friends in the compost pile of his garden.

Lee Hays was a prominent influence in American music of social commentary, telling *Sing Out!* magazine in 1979 that "the folksong tradition is so strong that when they're [folk songs] needed, they arise. They come up out of the earth."

★

Doris Willens, *Lonesome Traveler: The Life of Lee Hays* (1988) is a loving portrait of Hays, the title of which is taken from one of his songs. Willens had access to voluminous "songe poems, anecdotes, thoughts, recipes, essays, articles, short stories, letters, and photos" that Hays collected for his "posthumous memoirs," later called "Lee Hays' Commonplace Book." See also *The Weavers Song Book* (1960), *Sing Out!* (September/October 1980), and the entry on Hays in Irwin Stambler and Grelun Landon, *The Encyclopedia of Folk, Country, and Western Music*, 2d ed. (1983). An obituary is in the *New York Times* (27 Aug. 1981).

BARBARA L. TISCHLER

HEAD, Edith (*b.* 28 October 1897 in San Bernardino, California; *d.* 24 October 1981 in Hollywood, California), costume designer for films, nominee for thirty-five Academy Awards in motion-picture costume design, and recipient of eight Oscars during a career of fifty-eight years.

The only child of Max Posener and the former Anna Levy, she was originally named Edith Claire Posener. After her parents were divorced, her mother married an engineer named Spare. Edith took his name and converted to his Roman Catholic faith. At age twelve she moved with her family from Nevada to California. She earned an A.B. degree from the University of California, Berkeley, in 1919, and an M.A. degree in French from Stanford University in 1920. She then taught French and Spanish at two schools for girls in California. Also required to teach art, she attended the Otis Art Institute and later the Chouinard Art School in Los Angeles. In 1923 she married Charles Head, whom she divorced in 1938. She married Wiard ("Bill") Ihnen, an art director at Paramount, in a civil ceremony in Las Vegas on 8 September 1940. He died in 1979. She had no children.

Head's Hollywood career began in 1923 as a sketch artist. Howard Greer, the chief costume designer at Famous Players–Lasky, renamed the Paramount Studio in 1925, hired Head after seeing a portfolio of widely varied sketches, actually done by her classmates at Chouinard but bearing her signature. Travis Banton, trained in a custom design salon and engaged as the second major designer at Paramount a few months after Head had been hired, became her mentor. Under his tutelage she became especially known for her beaded gowns. Her first important assignment, in 1924, was the candy ball sequence in Cecil B. DeMille's *The Golden Bed* (1925). In 1927 Greer was replaced by Banton, who appointed Head as his assistant to dress minor film characters. During the 1930s she was also the designer of almost every "B" picture Paramount made.

Head's first film credit for costume design was *She Done Him Wrong* (1933), starring Mae West. Named chief designer at Paramount in the fall of 1938, she was the first woman to be exclusive director of a major studio's costume department. Her success with the twenty-five costume changes for Barbara Stanwyck in *The Lady Eve* (1941) established Head's reputation. Stanwyck was also important to Head because the actress helped improve Head's appearance by persuading her to replace two missing front teeth that had kept her from smiling.

The 1940s were Head's most prolific years. Her creativity showed in her costumes for Ginger Rogers in *Lady in the Dark* (1944); one featured a mink overskirt, lined with red and gold sequins, with a matching mink bolero and muff, costing $35,000. With *Notorious* (1946), Head began what became a thirty-year professional relationship with her favorite director, Alfred Hitchcock. In the second year that an Academy Award was presented for costume design, she won her first Oscar for *The Heiress* (1949), acknowledging that the award was for the designs that best advanced the story, "not necessarily for the most beautiful clothes." For *Samson and Delilah* (1949), one of the new wide-screen color films, Head received her second Oscar, but it did not make her proud as she knew the costumes were derivatives of *Lady Eve* and the 1917 version of *Cleopatra*. In 1949 she and Ihnen purchased Casa Ladera, a hacienda-style house in Beverly Hills.

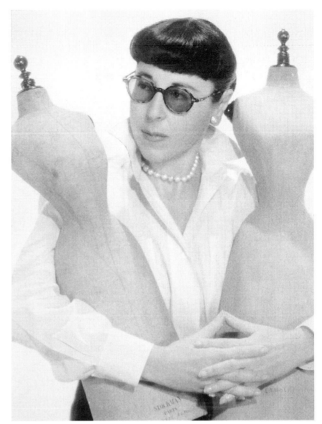

Edith Head. ARCHIVE PHOTOS

Sunset Boulevard (1950) did not win the Oscar for costumes, but Head thought her designs in it were more creative than the Oscar winner's. Her designs for Bette Davis in *All About Eve* (1950) also won her an Oscar, as did her designs for *A Place in the Sun* (1951), a black-and-white film with Elizabeth Taylor; Head said she was inspired by the Dior full-skirted look for Taylor's white tulle dress. In 1953 she was the first Hollywood designer to dress Audrey Hepburn, winning her fifth Oscar for *Roman Holiday*. The black dress with boat neckline and the white ball gown in that film, based on Givenchy sketches, were not credited to the Parisian designer by Head during the Academy Awards ceremony. Never again would Head dress Hepburn.

Head enjoyed dressing Grace Kelly in *The Bridges at Toko-ri, The Country Girl,* and *Rear Window,* all in 1954. In *To Catch a Thief* (1955), following Hitchcock's direction, she dressed Kelly as a princess in the fancy masquerade ball, with a dress of delicate gold mesh, a golden wig, and a golden mask, the most expensive and spectacular costuming Head had ever done. However, she won only the nomination, not the Oscar.

In the 1960s, although nominated for fourteen Oscars, she won only one, for *The Facts of Life* (1960). She played herself in the film *The Oscar* (1966) and won another nomination for the Academy Award in costume design. In 1967 she went to Universal Studios when Paramount did not renew her contract. In the 1970s Head won four nominations and one Oscar, for *The Sting* (1973). She was especially proud of winning this Academy Award, because *The Sting* starred Robert Redford and Paul Newman and had no female lead. Even in the 1940s, when male leads were expected to provide their own wardrobe, Head was unique in that she designed for Bob Hope and Bing Crosby in their "Road" films.

Throughout her career Head acknowledged that she was a better politician than designer, crediting her success to her effectiveness in dealing with directors. She saw her talent as adaptation, not creating couture designs. She said, "My concern is to change actors into characters, not to do fashion shows." For her ability to accomplish this, she became known as "the Doctor."

Head was all of five feet, one inch tall, her straight black hair typically pulled back in a chignon with bangs, and she wore thick-lensed horn-rimmed glasses and tailored suits. Head was once named by Hedda Hopper, an entertainment columnist, as one of Hollywood's worst-dressed women. She countered that her understated style was intentional. She was not the "eye-catcher"; her glamorous stars were. Louella Parsons, a rival of Hopper, spoke of Head's excellent taste and astute style sense.

Asked to offer advice on style to ordinary women, she did, first in 1945, on Art Linkletter's *House Party,* a radio show, and then in the 1950s on his television program of the same name. She later wrote books on the subject: *The Dress Doctor* (1959), coauthored with Jane Kesner Ardmore, and *How to Dress for Success* (1967), coauthored with Joe Hyams.

Head was the most prolific and longest-working costume designer in Hollywood. She won the most Oscars for costume design, was the only designer to be featured on a radio and television show, coauthored three books, and designed uniforms for Pan-American World Airways and United Nations tour guides. Head ended a distinguished career in 1981 with her 1,131st film (by her count) at Universal Studios, *Dead Men Don't Wear Plaid* (1982).

Head died at Good Samaritan Hospital in Hollywood from myeloid metaplasia, a progressive blood disease. She had no family and was survived only by her housekeeper of thirty-six years, Myrtle Tyson. Her funeral was preceded by a church service, in which she was eulogized by Bette Davis. She was buried in Forest Lawn Memorial Park, Glendale, California. Her will left an estate of $575,000, of which the Academy of Motion Picture Arts and Sciences, several cats, and a Dalmatian were the primary beneficiaries. She also left an ivory necklace to Elizabeth Taylor, who shared her love of pets.

★

Head's personal papers are in the Edith Head Archives of the Academy of Motion Pictures Library, Beverly Hills, California. For her life and career, see Edith Head and Paddy Calistro, *Edith Head's Hollywood* (1983), with a foreword by Bette Davis. See also David Chierichetti, *Hollywood Costume Design* (1976); Elizabeth Leese, *Costume Design in the Movies* (1976); Dale McConathy and Diana Vreeland, *The Hollywood Costume* (1976); and Robert W. LaVine, *The Fabulous Years of Costume Design* (1980). Donald Spoto, "Edith Head: The Award-Winning Costume Designer's Hacienda-Style Retreat in Beverly Hills," *Architectural Digest* (Oct. 1992), suggests her lifestyle at home. An obituary is in the *New York Times* (27 Oct. 1997).

BARBARA L. GERBER

HECHT, Harold (*b.* 1 June 1907 in New York City; *d.* 25 May 1985 in Beverly Hills, California), independent film producer who in 1955 successfully challenged the existing Hollywood star system with his low-budget, black-and-white, nonstar film *Marty.*

Hecht, the son of Joseph and Rose Lowey Hecht, was educated in the New York public school system. At age sixteen he enrolled in the American Laboratory Theater, where for three years he studied under actor-director Richard Boleslavsky, who made him his stage assistant. Until 1931 he was a dancer and a choreographer for a number of Broadway shows, including *The Lottery* and several productions of the *Grand Street Follies;* the Metropolitan Opera; the Martha Graham Dance Company; and other New York dance groups. With the development of sound technology, the movie industry turned its attention to musical films. Boleslavsky, who worked in both New York and California, brought Hecht to Hollywood. With the help of Busby Berkeley, Hecht started working as a freelance dancer and dance director for Metro-Goldwyn-Mayer, Paramount, RKO, and Universal. His work included two Marx Brothers classics—*Horse Feathers* (1932) and *Bottoms Up* (1934)—and an appearance with Mae West in *She Done Him Wrong* (1933).

In 1934 Hecht returned to New York City, where he would join the dance division of the Federal Theatre Project, a government organization headed by Hallie Flanagan and also employing John Houseman and Orson Welles in key artistic posts. He stayed with the dance project until its dissolution in 1938, then returned to Hollywood. He found a job at the offices of Nat Goldstone, where he was assigned the task of creating and heading a literary department for scriptwriters. For the next four years hundreds of film scripts passed through his hands. Hecht spent many days working with his authors, encouraging them, cajoling them, and trying to match their specific talents with the demands of the movie industry.

Harold Hecht signs Janette Scott to costar with Laurence Olivier, Burt Lancaster, and Kirk Douglas in *The Devil's Disciple,* 1958. LONDON TIMES/ARCHIVE PHOTOS

In 1942 Hecht was drafted into the U.S. Army, where he served until 1945. After his discharge in April, he returned to Hollywood and opened his own agency, representing only scriptwriters, directors, and producers. On a visit to New York in November of that year, Hecht went to see *A Sound of Hunting,* which had a three-week run at the Lyceum Theater. A young actor who was making his stage debut in a minor role caught Hecht's attention. The actor, a former circus acrobat, was untrained for the theater and unconvincing in his role. But, having been a dancer, Hecht appreciated his athletic build, his extraordinary agility, and his good looks, all of which were more important qualifications for Hollywood stardom than the ability to act. After the show Hecht was introduced to the young man, whose name was Burt Lancaster. He persuaded Lancaster to come to Hollywood, promising not only to make him a star but also that within five years they would be producing their own films. Hecht kept his promise. Indeed, their careers became so enmeshed that neither man can be understood without reference to the other.

Hecht's plan had three phases. In the first he negotiated contracts for Lancaster with major studios and independent producers. Within two years Lancaster acquired name rec-

ognition and was considered a budding star. With the profits from the contracts Hecht was able to fulfill his promise to Lancaster in 1948, when the partnership released its first independent production, *Kiss the Blood off My Hands.* Their second independent film, *The Flame and the Arrow* (1950), which Hecht produced, established Lancaster as a star. By that time the income from Lancaster's freelance acting and from Hecht's independent productions, which he made for distribution by the major studios, were such that Hecht could move on to his third step, creating the kind of films that for him constituted the very essence and purpose of his partnership with Lancaster. To that end he brought the scriptwriter to center stage of the creative process. Whenever Hecht made a film based on a book, a play, or a teleplay, he hired its writer to write the screenplay.

In 1955 Hecht premiered his groundbreaking film *Marty.* It was based on a teleplay by Paddy Chayefsky that had aired on NBC's *Philco Television Playhouse* on 24 May 1953. Hecht hired Chayefsky, one of the most gifted dramatists of the era, to adapt his story to the big screen, but Lancaster did not think much of it. To his amazement, *Marty* won four Academy Awards: best picture for Hecht, best director for Delbert Mann, best actor for Ernest Borgnine, and best script adapted from another medium for Chayefsky. Two years later Hecht made another film based on a Chayefsky teleplay, *The Bachelor Party.* Again he hired Chayefsky to write the screenplay; the film garnered high critical accolades and proved Hecht's thesis of the prime role of the author in creating a believable, character-centered motion picture.

Hecht was unable to produce a film in which Lancaster did not take a starring role, whether or not it suited him. More often than not Lancaster was miscast, as in *Separate Tables* (1958), based on a stage play by Terence Rattigan about people living in seedy gentility at a small English coastal inn. Lancaster insisted on playing the romantic lead, a complicated role that required many mood changes, emotional conflicts, a constant undercurrent of desperation, pathetic lying, and, generally, the ability to portray a man on his way down. The role was beyond Lancaster's scope. Similarly, when Hecht decided to produce George Bernard Shaw's *The Devil's Disciple* (1957), with Laurence Olivier and Kirk Douglas as the stars, Lancaster insisted on taking the role meant for Olivier. He had no preparation in the principles of the Shavian tradition, however, and Hecht saw one more of his films damaged by his partner.

None of these situations lessened the mounting tensions in the partnership. Lancaster felt that he was being outmaneuvered by Hecht and that he needed an ally who would side with him on every issue. Brushing aside Hecht's objections, he brought in screenwriter James Hill as an equal partner and producer, thus guaranteeing himself 2–1 voting majority in every decision. For Hecht this move signified the beginning of the end of their production company. In addition to Lancaster's growing insecurity, there were the seemingly endless quarrels with costars, writers, and directors over at least the previous five years. In *Vera Cruz* (1954) Lancaster tried to upstage Gary Cooper throughout the filming. Cooper turned down all subsequent offers to appear in the partnership's productions. Clark Gable walked off the set of *Run Silent, Run Deep* (1958) when Lancaster rewrote the script to cast his character in a more favorable light than Gable's, contrary to a clause in Gable's contract. An unsatisfactory compromise was reached and the film was completed, but Gable would never work with Lancaster again. Lancaster's uncontrolled temper, his ego, and his violent behavior—eyewitnesses asserted that Lancaster roughed up Hecht—tested Hecht's patience to the limit. The partnership finally came to an end in 1960.

In 1962 Hecht acquired the filming rights to *Birdman of Alcatraz,* the story of Robert Stroud, who was serving a life sentence for killing a man in Oregon and for the murder of a prison guard—and who, according to the story, through his interest in birds experienced a miraculous transformation. Hecht envisioned Marlon Brando as Stroud and Karl Malden as his nemesis, Warden Harvey Shoemaker. Unwisely, Hecht involved Lancaster in the project, and before he knew it, his former partner had grabbed the role of Stroud. Lancaster forced many changes in the script and interfered with the work of other actors, the director, and the producer until he had completely changed Hecht's original concept. He reduced Malden's role to a few episodic appearances, thus eliminating the powerful test of wills between them. The film was left with a single star. Nevertheless, Hecht managed to maintain the integrity and continuity of the film, and Lancaster received a nomination for the Academy Award for best actor. The critics reserved their accolades for Malden's brief performance. They pointed out Lancaster's frozen persona, which never revealed any emotion or development throughout the fifty-three years the film depicted. Hecht and Lancaster never worked together again.

Hecht's final break with Lancaster brought freedom to produce as he liked. He moved his offices to Columbia Pictures and sought out the best of the most promising young dramatists. One of his writers, Walter Newman, in collaboration with Frank R. Pierson, came up with the script for *Cat Ballou* (1965). Based on a novel by Roy Chanslor and directed by Elliot Silverstein, the film starred Jane Fonda, Lee Marvin, Michael Callan, Dwayne Hickman, and Nat King Cole. The film did for Marvin what *Marty* had done for Borgnine ten years earlier. He received the Academy Award for best actor and was established as a star of the first rank.

In 1967 Hecht produced *The Way West,* the script for which was written by Mitch Lindemann and Ben Meadow, based on an A. B. Guthrie, Jr., novel; it was directed by Andrew V. McLaglen. The cast included Kirk Douglas, Robert Mitchum, Richard Widmark, Lola Albright, and Sally Field. The film was a multimillion-dollar spectacular Wild West production, in very much the Hollywood tradition, aimed at the box office rather than at a select audience. Unfortunately the critics trashed it. After this experience Hecht's interest in the production side of the movie industry seemed to wane.

In later years Hecht started making plans to produce *Kid Sheleen,* a sequel to *Cat Ballou,* to which he wanted to add Bette Davis. He was also preparing a second project, *Jolly Roger,* which was to be a sequel to *The Crimson Pirate* (1952), a movie he had made with Lancaster. For television Hecht produced the movie *Flight from Ashiya,* with Yul Brynner, Richard Widmark, and George Chakiris. It was released for theater showing in 1964 and first aired on NBC in 1967 and again in 1974.

Hecht was married twice. On 1 November 1947 he married Gloria J. Buzell; they had three children and were divorced in 1960. On 1 November 1962 he married Martine Milner; they had three children and were divorced in September 1974.

Hecht spent fifteen of his most creative years tied to a partnership that crippled his career. Yet his influence on filmmaking has lasted. The idea of a film as an in-depth character study remains a powerful component in many motion picture schools and in the industry as a whole.

Hecht died of complications from cancer at his home in Beverly Hills, at age seventy-seven.

★

Hecht did not write his memoirs, and no one has written a book about his work. His papers are in the possession of his family. Obituaries are in the *Los Angeles Times* and *New York Times* (both 28 May 1985).

SHOSHANA KLEBANOFF

HELLMAN, Lillian Florence (*b.* 20 June 1905 in New Orleans, Louisiana; *d.* 30 June 1984 in Martha's Vineyard, Massachusetts), dramatist and essayist whose plays twice won the New York Drama Critics Circle Award and whose memoir, *An Unfinished Woman* (1969), won the National Book Award.

Hellman was the only child of Max Bernard Hellman, a shoe salesman who established his own company with the financial support of his wife, Julia Newhouse. After the Hellman Shoe Company failed, Max moved the family to New York City, where he became a clothing salesman. For several years, Lillian divided her time between her family on Manhattan's Upper West Side and her father's sisters in New Orleans. This division provided her with both a southern sensibility and a northern critique of that sensibility, which fueled much of her later writing.

Hellman attended New York University from 1922 to 1924 but was a desultory student and did not earn a degree. She did, however, read widely and determined to make a career as a writer. In 1924 and 1925 she worked as an assistant at Boni and Liveright, the prestigious publishing house that featured Ernest Hemingway, William Faulkner, and Eugene O'Neill. She reviewed manuscripts and made contacts in Manhattan literary circles but left after a year to marry writer and theatrical press agent Arthur Kober on 21 December 1925. Kober was raised in a poor Jewish neighborhood on the Lower East Side of Manhattan but aspired to write for the smart press and Broadway. He introduced Hellman to theatrical press agents and producers while she freelanced as a reviewer and critic.

Shortly after their marriage Kober was appointed editor of a new literary magazine, the *Paris Comet,* which intended to publish English and American fiction; Lillian followed her husband to Paris. There she sampled the famous Left Bank culture and dabbled in short stories and reviews for the *Comet,* but she was restless and desirous of finding some "shape" for her literary life. After a brief sojourn in Italy, she returned to New York without Kober, determined to make a mark on the literary and theatrical world that fascinated her.

She and Kober reconciled and rented a home in Douglaston, New York, and he had some modest success with *New Yorker* short stories while Lillian freelanced as a book reviewer for the *New York Herald Tribune* from 1925 to 1928. She also did publicity for an ill-fated musical revue, *The Bunk of 1926,* and from 1927 to 1930 read play manuscripts for producers whom Kober had befriended. In 1929 she became a publicist for the Cukor-Kondolph stock company in Rochester, New York, and that summer she made a brief visit to Germany, where in Bonn she encountered some of the anti-Semitic feeling that would become important in her later plays and that made her acutely conscious, for the first time, she claimed, of her identity as a Jew.

When the stock market collapsed in 1929, Kober was forced to take a job as press agent for Marc Connelly's play, *The Green Pastures,* but when Paramount Pictures offered him $450 per week to write screenplays, he jumped at the opportunity. At first Hellman refused to move to Hollywood, but eventually she relented, and at a more modest salary of $50 per week she finally found work as a script reader for Samuel Goldwyn. She wrote thoughtful synopses and learned a great deal about the craft of screenwriting. She also went to parties, entertained with Kober in a home they rented in Beverly Hills, and eventually met Dashiell Hammett, who was then at the height of his literary career as a writer of detective fiction.

Hammett had a huge influence on Hellman's career. They never married and their stormy relationship endured for thirty years despite alcohol abuse, philandering, and his political persecution. Hellman, who divorced Kober in 1932 and returned to New York, became the model for Nora Charles in Hammett's *The Thin Man* (1934). Hammett was a frequent editor of Hellman's plays and the subject of a moving essay in her best-selling memoir, *An Unfinished Woman: A Memoir* (1969).

It was Hammett who suggested the idea for her first Broadway success, *The Children's Hour,* which played for 691 New York performances beginning on 20 November 1934, and established her as an important new voice in American drama. Based on an actual episode, the play explored the terrifying consequence of a schoolgirl's lie on the lives of her teachers. Although *The Children's Hour* was controversial because of its lesbian overtones, what gave it power was the awful destructiveness brought about by human malevolence. It was a theme to which Hellman returned and that infused much of her theatrical writing. In 1939 her most successful production, *The Little Foxes,* also explored the landscape of human greed and ambition and featured a powerful scene in which a woman allows her stricken husband to die rather than fetching his heart medicine. Such moments caused some critics to speak of her work harshly as "melodrama," but Hellman, who had become increasingly political in the 1930s, believed that there was evil in the world and could not turn a blind eye to it.

Her political education was fostered by Hammett, who was a communist and who went to jail in 1951 rather than reveal the names of contributors to the communist-influenced Civil Rights Congress. But Hellman also was active in a variety of antifascist activities and saw the emerging totalitarian movements firsthand. In 1937 she journeyed to Soviet Russia and to Spain, where she witnessed the civil war. Like Hemingway and others, Hellman was an ardent Loyalist and outspoken critic of the Franco forces.

At home she explored the popular social protest theater in New York that dramatized workers' rights and the impact of labor unions. Her 1936 production *Days to Come* attempted to mirror the labor turmoil in a factory through the love triangle of its central characters. But the critics felt that it was too preachy, and it only played seven performances. Despite its failure, Hellman continued experimenting with a dramaturgy in which social problems were reflected in the moral struggles of her characters. In *The Searching Wind* (1944), she dramatized the liberal appeasement of Nazi Germany through the actions of a man who resists taking responsibility for either his personal or public life. Although the play ran for more than 300 performances, its heavy-handed ideology prevented it from repeating the triumph of its predecessor, *Watch on the Rhine* (1941).

Watch on the Rhine, Hellman's passionate plea for Amer-

Lillian Hellman, 1951. ARCHIVE PHOTOS

play for *Watch on the Rhine* (1943). Hellman wrote an original filmscript for *The North Star* (1943), a sympathetic look at the Russian people under German attack. Her pro-Russian stance, however, made Goldwyn nervous, and he altered the script during the filming. This version, renounced by Hellman, was released for television in 1957 under the title *Armored Attack,* with a prologue apologizing for any seemingly pro-Russian sentiments.

Following World War II, Hellman played an increasingly controversial role in the politics of the cold war. She campaigned for Henry Wallace in 1948 and was an active participant in the pro-Soviet Waldorf Conference, officially known as the Cultural and Scientific Conference for World Peace, in 1949. Although she denied ever being a member of the Communist party, she was sympathetic to the Soviet Union and an outspoken critic of the rising tide of McCarthyism. After the production of her eighth Broadway play, *The Autumn Garden* (1951), she made a celebrated appearance before the House Committee on Un-American Activities (HUAC) in 1952 where she refused to "name names." In a letter to HUAC she declared: "I cannot and will not cut my conscience to fit this year's fashions." Unlike some others, however, Hellman was not indicted for contempt, and her tough stance accorded her celebrity status in the next generation.

She was blacklisted in Hollywood, however, and was forced to sell her farm in Pleasantville, Westchester County, New York, where she and Hammett had entertained and written for a decade. In the theater her very first success, *The Children's Hour,* was revived successfully beginning in December 1952, running for 189 performances. It was followed by her adaptation of Jean Anouilh's *The Lark* (1955) and the book for a musical adaptation of *Candide* (1955), both of which had musical scores by Leonard Bernstein. Her final play, *Toys in the Attic* (1960), in which she turned back to the American South and the experiences of her spinster aunts, was a Broadway hit with 464 performances; it earned Hellman her second Drama Critics Circle Award.

Following Hammett's death in 1963 and the easement of cold war witch-hunting, Hellman entered a new phase of her literary career. She turned away from the theater and wrote a series of memoirs in which she revisited people and events in her remarkable life. The first, *An Unfinished Woman,* won the National Book Award and the second, *Pentimento* (1973), was selected for distribution by the Book-of-the-Month Club. *Pentimento* included a dramatic chapter, titled "Julia," about Hellman's ostensible wartime anti-Nazi smuggling; it was made into a successful 1977 film of the same name, starring Jane Fonda and Vanessa Redgrave.

It was with *Scoundrel Time* in 1976 that Hellman once again ignited the political passions on the American left and began a legal controversy that was unresolved at the

icans to wake up to the fascist threat, won the New York Drama Critics Circle Award and was widely praised as one of her strongest plays. Set in a comfortable suburb of Washington, D.C., the play dramatizes the Nazi threat to the Farrelly family when its son-in-law is revealed as a European freedom fighter. When his life is threatened by thugs in the German embassy, Hellman underscores how the war had already arrived on American shores. Like many of her plays, *Watch* is filled with carefully depicted good and evil people and is resolved with a dramatic murder. But the play's careful plotting and the courage of the Farrelly family attracted large audiences. In addition, its politics, during the last months of America's neutrality, were compelling. Hellman donated funds from a limited-edition publication of the play to the Joint Anti-Fascist Refugee Committee.

Meanwhile, her financial status had improved enormously. Following the box office success of *The Children's Hour,* Hellman signed a lucrative Hollywood contract with Samuel Goldwyn. Her screenplays for *The Dark Angel* (1935) and *Dead End* (1936), as well as an adaptation of *The Children's Hour* (*These Three,* 1936), were all successful and endeared her to Goldwyn. She and Hammett buttressed their income with screenplays as his literary career began to fade. In 1942 Hammett wrote a successful screen-time of her death. Buoyed by her celebrity status and a series of honors climaxing with election to the National Institute of Arts, Hellman retold her stories about HUAC and cold war blacklisting in a manner that rankled anticommunist patriots like Lionel and Diana Trilling, Mary McCarthy, and others. While admitting that she was "late" in denouncing Stalinism, she persisted in her belief that the anticommunist American "left" was largely responsible for the vilification of the Soviet Union and thus created the climate that led to the Vietnam War and the Watergate scandal. Many liberals resented Hellman's stance and argued that she had no business indicting them as the villains in her piece. When Mary McCarthy called her a liar on Dick Cavett's television show in January 1980, Hellman sued for libel, asking for $2.25 million.

McCarthy's attack led to a ransacking of Hellman's writings that exposed numerous contradictions and raised questions about people and events. In the most celebrated example, the whole portrait of "Julia" seemed to be largely fiction or else appropriated from the experiences of a Muriel Gardiner, whom Hellman had never met. Defenders pointed out that Hellman never claimed to be a historian and that the very title "pentimento" suggested perception rather than "fact." After her death, however, Hellman's credibility suffered with the publication of William Wright's 1986 biography, which analyzed "Julia," and Carl Rollyson's subsequent book in 1988, which clearly placed Hellman as a Communist party member in 1938, a claim she had repeatedly denied.

Despite controversy, however, Hellman enjoyed a legendary status among many Americans and spent her last years trying to "live well." Lionized for her courage before HUAC, wealthy from royalties, and glamorous because of the famous Blackgama mink coat advertisement ("What becomes a legend most?"), Hellman taught at Harvard and Yale universities, won the first round of her libel suit when a judge declined to dismiss it out of hand, and was awarded honorary doctoral degrees by New York University, Yale, Smith, and Columbia. She enjoyed cooking and fishing at her summer retreat on Martha's Vineyard, otherwise living in a town house on the Upper East Side of Manhattan. In the early 1980s her health worsened as she battled emphysema and poor eyesight. Hellman died of heart failure and was buried in Abel's Hill Cemetery in Chilmark, Massachusetts.

Hellman's literary reputation rests upon a handful of important plays, most notably *The Little Foxes, The Children's Hour,* and *Toys in the Attic,* and upon the memoirs that she wrote after Hammett's death. Although her work has been frequently criticized as being melodramatic, the fact remains that she did believe in evil, and good and bad characterized much of her view of people and events in the twentieth century. Her memoirs sparked debate about her

truthfulness, and her attack on the anticommunist left clouded her reputation. But Hellman's gifts as a writer of fiction were never questioned, and her later years were highlighted by a series of awards and honors that were testimony to her craft and her courage.

★

The Hellman Papers are part of the Humanities Research Center at the University of Texas at Austin. The most comprehensive biography is Carl Rollyson, *Lillian Hellman: Her Legend and Her Legacy* (1988), which expands upon some of the excellent work done by William Wright, *Lillian Hellman* (1986). Other useful biographies include Richard Moody, *Lillian Hellman, Playwright* (1972); Doris Faulk, *Lillian Hellman* (1978); Katherine Lederer, *Lillian Hellman* (1979); and Bernard Dick, *Hellman in Hollywood* (1982). In addition to her memoirs cited in the text, other important works include Jackson Bryer, ed., *Conversations with Lillian Hellman* (1986); Mark Estrin, ed., *Critical Essays on Lillian Hellman* (1989); and Robert P. Newman, *The Cold War Romance of Lillian Hellman and John Melby* (1989). An obituary is in the *New York Times* (1 July 1984).

BARRY B. WITHAM

HICKS, Granville (*b.* 9 September 1901 in Exeter, New Hampshire; *d.* 18 June 1982 in Franklin Park, near Princeton, New Jersey), literary critic who was one of the most famous intellectual converts to communism in the 1930s.

Hicks was the second of two children of Frank Stevens, the superintendent of a small factory, and Carrie Weston Horne, a homemaker. After Hicks's birth, his father's fortunes declined somewhat and the family moved several times, ending up in Framington, Massachusetts. From the beginning Hicks was an avid student, graduating as class valedictorian at Framingham High School in 1919. He graduated from Harvard University, summa cum laude, in 1923. An active Unitarian, he enrolled in Harvard Theological School in 1923, but two years later he decided against a ministerial career.

Hicks married Dorothy Dyer, his high school sweetheart, in June 1925; they had one daughter. Also in 1925 he began teaching religion and English at Smith College. While at Smith, Hicks formed a lifelong friendship with a fellow instructor, Newton Arvin. Arvin's politics influenced Hicks, who began to develop an interest in radicalism. In 1928 Hicks returned to Harvard to obtain a master's degree in English (1929). Thereafter, he became assistant professor of English at Rensselaer Polytechnic Institute in Troy, New York.

The Great Depression profoundly influenced Hicks's life. Jobs were scarce, so while he dreamed of a more satisfying teaching position, he had to be content at Rensselaer. Hoping to find a measure of personal security, he

Granville Hicks at work on his farm in Grafton, New York, *c.* 1938. UPI/
CORBIS-BETTMANN

bought an eight-room farmhouse in Grafton, New York. This would serve as his home for the rest of his life and a gathering place for such friends as Richard Rovere, Robert Gorham Davis, and Hope Hale Davis. His parents also moved to the Grafton farmhouse and remained there for the rest of their lives. In 1933 Hicks published *The Great Tradition,* an analysis of American literature since the Civil War. His career as a literary analyst, however, was somewhat slowed by his increasing interest in American communist politics. In 1932 he voted the Communist party ticket. He also joined virtually every significant Communist party front group of the 1930s, including the John Reed Club and the National Committee for the Defense of Political Prisoners.

Perhaps Hicks's greatest contribution to the literary community of the 1930s was his staunch championing of the communists' literary style, the so-called proletarian culture. Hicks officially joined the American Communist Party in 1935. Because he symbolized the kind of recruit the party sought during the Popular Front period (1935–1939), party functionaries used Hicks extensively to promote their causes. He became the literary editor of *The New Masses,* was a coeditor of the party's *Proletarian Literature in the United States* (1935), and with John Stuart wrote an authorized biography of the early communist John Reed in 1936. The communists asked him to speak at many public meetings, including the founding Congress of American Writers in 1935. His public politics cost him his job at Rensselaer in 1935. Thereafter, Hicks supported himself by working various jobs, including a brief stint teaching at Harvard University (1938–1939). In 1938 he published *I Like America,* a short book that described his communist politics in folksy terms.

The Nazi-Soviet Pact of 1939 triggered an ideological crisis in Hicks. He was stunned by the Communist party's quick reversal of its antifascist line on instructions from Moscow. In response, he publicly resigned from the party in the fall of 1939 and just as publicly tried—without much success—to organize an independent left-wing alternative.

During World War II, Hicks was an eager civil defense worker and avid local activist. Finally freed from the many tasks required of Communist party workers, he entered some of his most prolific years as a writer. He wrote a history of nineteenth-century British literature (*Figures of Transition*) in 1939, three novels—*The First to Awaken* (1940), *Only One Storm* (1942), and *Behold Trouble* (1944)—and a study of Grafton called *Small Town* in 1946.

Much of Hicks's postwar career was focused on explaining and interpreting his 1930s communism. He testified before an executive session of the House Un-American Activities Committee (HUAC) on 16 June 1952, and he talked about his Communist party cell at Harvard in an open session of HUAC on 25 February 1953. His memoir, *Where We Came Out* (1954), chronicles his political adventures. From the mid-1950s on, Hicks taught literature at various East Coast colleges. He also wrote for the *New Leader* and the *Saturday Review of Literature*. In 1965 he wrote his autobiography, *Part of the Truth,* which received mixed reviews.

After Hicks suffered a stroke in 1975, he and his wife moved near his daughter and her family in New Jersey. He suffered further strokes in 1978 and 1982 and entered a nursing home near his daughter's residence in Kendall Park, New Jersey. He died at the nursing home.

Hicks was one of the best-known and most influential intellectual communist converts in the 1930s, enjoying all the status and prestige the Communist party could confer. Because he was so widely known as a communist in the 1930s, he devoted much of the rest of his life to educating people about the drawbacks and weaknesses of communism.

★

Hicks's papers are at Syracuse University. Leah Levenson and Jerry Natterstad, *Granville Hicks: The Intellectual in Mass Society* (1993), is a biography. Terry Long, *Granville Hicks* (1981), offers a literary analysis of his major works. See also Robert Bricker, *Granville Hicks: An Annotated Biography* (1968), and the obituary in the *New York Times* (19 June 1982).

JUDY KUTULAS

HILL, (Joseph) Lister (*b.* 29 December 1894 in Montgomery, Alabama; *d.* 20 December 1984 in Montgomery, Alabama), congressman and U.S. senator from Alabama.

Hill was one of three children of Lilly Lyons Hill and Dr. Luther Leonidas Hill, Jr., the first American to suture the human heart successfully. Both his parents' families owned large expanses of land in central and southern Alabama, and Hill took the trappings of social position for granted. His mother, who was partly of Jewish ancestry, was a Catholic and raised her children in that faith. (As an adult Hill was affiliated with the Methodist church.) Despite his social standing, Lister never lost the feeling that he was a member of a minority. Politically, he identified with the powerless. As a child he embraced his stern, demanding father's desire that he become a senator. Lister received a B.A. from the University of Alabama in 1914 and, a quick study, LL.B. degrees from its law school in 1915 and from Columbia Law School in 1916.

Family connections immediately gained Hill a seat on the Montgomery board of education. In 1917 he became its president. Also in 1917, Hill enlisted in the U.S. Army, but when he reached France the fighting was nearly over. When the local congressman died in 1923, Hill won a special election for the House seat. He was the House sponsor of the 1933 bill to establish the Tennessee Valley Authority, having come around to Senator George Norris's belief in public power to operate the dams. A Democrat, he was known as a loyal New Deal supporter.

Hill's ultimate goal was to sit in the U.S. Senate. A cautious politician, he refused to run for either of Alabama's seats until he felt assured of winning. Then, in 1937, a spot opened up when President Franklin D. Roosevelt appointed Alabama senator Hugo L. Black to the Supreme Court. Hill was elected to fill the vacancy the next year.

His new colleagues made Hill assistant Democratic whip in 1939 and whip, second in command after majority leader, in 1941. He "literally fought like a tiger," always courteous yet firm, "until some reasonable semblance of what he was seeking was effectuated," noted his colleague Jacob Javits of New York. He applied blandishments. "A Bombay snake charmer could learn some lessons from the senator," a reporter wrote. To a friend, his oratory resembled "a holiness speaker weaving a trance." Hill often invoked as a farewell his father's horse-and-buggy rallying cry, "Chin up, tail over the dashboard!" A single purpose motivated him. "He wanted to pass laws," said an assistant. "That was his heaven on earth."

Hill ranks among the most productive legislators of his era. He sponsored the bill creating a federal program to bring telephone service to rural Americans and the Library Services Act for new libraries in rural and, later, urban areas. As chairman of the Senate Labor and Public Welfare Committee from 1955, he worked with Alabama congressman Carl Elliott in the aftermath of the launch of the Russian space satellite *Sputnik* to draft the National Defense Education Act (1958) and maneuver it through Congress.

It was in the medical field that Hill made his most lasting mark. His desire to advance the work of medicine was

Senator Lister Hill. Reproduced from the Collections of the Library of Congress

an outgrowth of his father's interests and it became his consuming passion. He originated the 1946 Hill-Burton Act to construct hospitals in impoverished regions, rural areas, and small towns. In the mid-1950s Hill guided the establishment of the National Institutes of Health, and federal funding for medical research increased twentyfold, to $1.5 billion annually, within a decade. Senator Hill was the moving force behind the vast array of medical care, facilities, education, and research legislation passed in the 1960s. During floor debate on a bill he introduced to increase medical research funds, sixteen senators of varying persuasions rose spontaneously to honor him. Hill had sponsored more "constructive legislation" than any senator ever, one of them noted.

Bills for medical research were much less controversial than the earlier bills he sponsored for federal aid to education and health insurance bills, with their unmistakable implications that their benefits would be available to Negroes as well as to whites. Hill also led the liberal forces in Alabama. He survived a heated 1944 primary battle against conservative James A. Simpson, who was well financed by industrial interests in and out of Alabama, but he was forced to stress his commitment to "the existing social order." (This was a mere euphemism for racial segregation.) By the late 1940s the politics of race were trapping him.

Democratic loyalists and party bolters were continually battling. A loyalist leader, Hill said equivocally, "I am an Alabama Democrat and will as always mark my cross under our rooster," the party emblem; above its head were the words "White Supremacy for the Right."

Poised to become the next Democratic majority leader, Hill resigned as whip in 1949. "I'm far too liberal for Alabama tastes," he said. This opened the way, two years later, for Lyndon B. Johnson to become whip and then Democratic leader, to Hill's immense bitterness and frustration. Like nearly all other senators, Hill thought he saw a potential president in the mirror, but in the Senate he frequently acknowledged his belief that a southerner could not be elected president. He was intensely disappointed when his junior Alabama colleague, John J. Sparkman, received the vice presidential nomination in 1952.

On 20 February 1928 Hill married Henrietta Fontaine McCormick, also from Alabama; they had two children. Hill easily won reelection in 1950 and 1956 but defeated a Republican by only 1 percent of the vote in 1962. By then, work had long been his life and, with his wife's health failing, Hill retired in 1968 after forty-five years in Congress. He died of pneumonia in Montgomery.

Personally conservative, tall, lean, and bald, usually dressed in a double-breasted suit, Hill always served what he called "the cause," helping people in need. He stands as a prime example of the southern tradition of liberalism held hostage to race. His views on all issues were those of a mainstream liberal. He never believed his considerable blather about segregation, a fact that did not bother him at all. "I'm doing more good for people staying here than if I went out front on the race issue," he noted. After his retirement he was apologetic, saying in a 1977 interview that "I had to do that to get elected." His life raises in dramatic form the age-old question of whether ends justify the means. But no assessment of Hill can overlook the improvements in medical care that he, more than anyone else, brought to millions of people.

★

Hill's papers are in the Gorgas Library of the University of Alabama in Tuscaloosa. Virginia Van der Veer Hamilton, *Lister Hill: Statesman of the New South* (1987), is the standard biography. Also see William D. Barnard, *Dixiecrats and Democrats: Alabama Politics, 1942–1950* (1974); Carl Elliott, Sr., and Michael D'Orso, *The Cost of Courage: The Journey of an American Congressman* (1992); and Roger K. Newman, *Hugo Black: A Biography* (1994). Useful articles include David L. Cohn, "The Gentleman from Alabama: Lister Hill," *Atlantic Monthly* (May 1944); and "Hill of Alabama," *New Republic* (1 May 1944). Of the few pieces that appeared under Hill's name, "My Father: Dr. Luther Leonidas Hill," *Alabama Review* 24 (Apr. 1971), which he wrote himself, is the most revealing.

ROGER K. NEWMAN

HIMES, Chester Bomar (*b*. 29 July 1909 in Jefferson City, Missouri; *d*. 12 November 1984 in Moraira, Spain), novelist and short-story writer best known for his contentious stories of racism in urban America.

Himes's father, Joseph Sandy Himes, a short, dark man, was a teacher of blacksmithing and wheelwrighting at southern land-grant schools for blacks. His mother, Estelle Charlotte Bomar, an octoroon, was criticized by some of her relatives for having married beneath her. The couple had three sons, of whom Chester was the youngest. Education in the Himes household was a priority. The father's profession and the mother's pretensions fostered a highly competitive environment of study.

Himes's early schooling was under the tutelage of his mother. In 1921, at the age of twelve, he entered classes at Branch Normal (later Arkansas A&M) College in Pine Bluff, Arkansas. When the family later moved to Cleveland, Ohio, Himes's father did odd jobs to support the family. In Cleveland, Himes attended East High School. His attitude toward school changed as he came under the influence of his peers. "I was unpopular with my teachers," Himes said, "and insufferably belligerent." Despite his shortcomings as

Chester B. Himes (*right*) with the French writer Jean Giono. ARCHIVE PHOTOS

a student, he entered Ohio State University after graduating from high school in 1926.

As a college student, Himes was a failure. The back-streets of the city were where he did most of his learning and where he picked up the dubious skills that led to his arrest and conviction for armed robbery. On 27 December 1928, at the age of nineteen, he was sentenced to twenty to twenty-five years of hard labor in the Ohio State Penitentiary. The ugliness he encountered and learned to survive when outside prison was just as prevalent inside. While in prison, Himes began to write and eventually submitted several short stories to African-American newspapers and magazines. These early stories centered on the criminal life he led prior to his incarceration and on what he had learned and seen while in prison. In 1934 he sold his first story, "Crazy in the Stir," to *Esquire* magazine.

After seven and a half years in prison, he was released to the care of his mother in May 1936. Needing to stabilize his life and desperate to avoid being sent back to prison because of possible parole violations, Himes married an old girlfriend, Jean Johnson, in 1936. The next year he found employment with the Works Project Administration (WPA) and eventually worked with the Ohio Writers' Project. Sensing Himes's feelings of vulnerability because of his past criminal experience, an editor of a Cleveland newspaper admonished him to get on with his life: "You have paid the penalty for your crime against society, now forget about it."

In 1945 Himes published his first novel, *If He Hollers Let Him Go,* which received mixed reviews. In 1946, while living on a ranch in California, he finished his second book, *Lonely Crusade,* which examines racial discrimination and violence in the wartime labor unions of California. When it was published in 1947, the novel sparked controversy because of its political theme. "It was then," Himes said, "that I decided to leave the United States forever."

By 1951, when his biographical family novel, *The Third Generation* (1954), was accepted for publication, his marriage had failed. His father's death in 1953 left him despondent. When he sold his prison novel, *Cast the First Stone* (1952), Himes took the advance money, bought a ticket, and sailed for Paris on 3 April 1953. On arrival, he began life as an expatriate and found himself among other black American artists, writers, and adventurers.

In 1954 Himes finished a manuscript titled "The End of a Primitive," which was published in 1955 as *The Primitive.* But Europe offered more distractions for Himes than opportunities. Two of his previous novels, *If He Hollers Let Him Go* and *Lonely Crusade,* were having some success in England and France. When approached by an editor of detective fiction to try his hand at detective stories, Himes was hesitant, but he wrote a story set in New York City's Harlem, where he had spent many months.

The publication of Himes's first detective novel, *The Five Cornered Square,* in 1957 launched his most successful period as a writer. He gained fame and recognition, things he craved. A series of fictions based in Harlem and featuring his two black detectives, Coffin Ed and Grave Digger Jones, followed and became staples of the genre. In 1958 he was awarded the French Grand Prize for Detective Fiction. The award boosted his popularity but did little for his financial status. Still struggling for money despite his growing fame, he turned out eight more detective stories.

In 1959, on the rebound from one of several stormy relationships, Himes met an English woman, Lesley Packard, whom he grew to depend on. She became his close companion, shielding him from unwanted attention and comforting him. During his time in Europe, Himes often felt isolated from other black expatriates, including his mentor, Richard Wright. He believed himself unappreciated in America and condescended to by Europeans. "I was becoming resentful of the way the Americans were treating me and resentful of the French who read my books and couldn't understand them," he said at one point.

In 1961, after a brief visit to New York City, Himes traveled to Mexico, where he became ill. Recovering in New York, he borrowed money and returned to France. He and Packard traveled around Europe before settling in Moraira, Spain. In February 1965 they were married. He never had children and died of an undisclosed illness. He is buried in Moraira.

Although Himes never achieved the worldwide recognition he sought, he gained fame among African-American writers, especially the younger ones of the 1960s. His works expressed a rage and torment with which his younger followers could identify. Assessments of Himes's work are mixed and still evolving. The author John A. Williams and the critic Bernard W. Bell suggest that Himes's most significant contribution to literature is his unstinting naturalism. Certainly there are ambiguities about the man himself that belie his perception of his life as absurd, a view he expressed in one of his autobiographies. But Himes is most noted as an obdurate, fiercely independent man who believed little in compromise. Still, his work has a definite literary legacy. The reissuing of his work attests to a renewed interest in his accomplishments.

★

Autobiographies include *The Quality of Hurt: The Early Years* (1972) and *My Life of Absurdity: The Later Years* (1976). Criticism of Himes's work is in Bernard W. Bell, *The Afro-American Novel and Its Tradition* (1987). See also John A. Williams, "My Man Himes: An Interview with Chester Himes," *Amistad I* (1970), documenting a wide-ranging conversation covering publishing, writers, and Himes's thoughts on America and Europe. An obituary is in the *New York Times* (14 Nov. 1984).

WILLIAM F. BROWNE

HINES, Earl Kenneth ("Fatha") (*b.* 28 December 1905 in Duquesne, Pennsylvania; *d.* 22 April 1983 in Oakland, California), innovative jazz pianist and orchestra leader.

Hines grew up with eleven relatives in a twelve-room house on Grant Avenue in Duquesne. His family was musically talented. Inspired by his father Joseph, a Pittsburgh dockworker, cornet player, and leader of the Eureka Brass Band, and a live-in uncle who played all brass instruments, Earl started playing cornet as a child. His stepmother Mary (his mother having died when he was three), an organist, enabled him to switch to piano and organ by giving him lessons. An aunt sang in light opera, and his half-brother Boots played piano, as did his half-sister Nancy, who also led a band in Pittsburgh in the 1930s. At age nine he began to study classical piano, intending to become a concert pianist and conductor. In high school he majored in music and played football, basketball, and baseball. He contemplated a baseball career until his parents insisted on music, a more respected occupation for middle-class black families of the day. One of very few African-American students in his grammar school, Hines seems rarely to have suffered from racial prejudice. While working odd jobs for spending money, he observed orchestras in order to augment his musical repertoire and skills.

In 1919 a visit to the Liederhouse, a Pittsburgh nightclub, exposed Hines to jazz rhythms and convinced him to change to jazz as his career calling. The next year he formed his own trio, including a violin and drums. The grueling schedule of learning and performing concert music and playing at school, social events, and nightclubs interfered with his schoolwork, so he welcomed the advice of several teachers to give up school for his career at age sixteen. The next year, 1922, he got his first steady job, at the Liederhouse with the band of male singer Lois B. Deppe. It was the first black orchestra to be broadcast over radio. Hines made his first recordings accompanying Deppe in 1923, during which year he toured with Deppe's Serenaders. In 1924 he briefly led his own band, which included saxophonist Benny Carter, at Pittsburgh's Grape Arbor club, then rejoined Deppe at the Elite No. 2 in Chicago. During this time he married Laura Badge, a singer, but they were soon divorced. For many years thereafter singer Kathryn Perry was his common-law wife. He had no children by either one.

Hines developed a distinctive jazz piano style while learning from musicians in these several bands and from others, notably trumpeter Joe Smith and Teddy Weatherford, dominant Chicago jazz pianist in the mid-1920s. Hines's classical training accounted for his remarkable technical skills, onto which he added a superior light touch, powerful rhythmic timing and dynamics, and inventive de-

Earl ("Fatha") Hines at the Savoy Ballroom in Harlem, 1939. CHARLES PETERSON/ARCHIVE PHOTOS

vices of single-note patterns, brief tremolos, and advanced harmonics. He did all these things while combining both hands in an integrated swing, ending the customary separation of the left hand playing ragtime, the right hand the melody line. His improvised solos, characterized by a complex, so-called trumpet style attack, redefined jazz piano as a solo instrument and influenced a generation of jazz pianists to build on his style.

After leading his own groups in Pittsburgh and Chicago, Hines joined Carroll Dickerson's orchestra at the Entertainer's Club in Chicago in 1925, then toured with him for more than nine months and returned to Chicago. There he played with Sammy Stewart's band at the Sunset Cafe and with Erskine Tate's Vendome Orchestra. When trumpet giant Louis Armstrong took over the Dickerson band in Chicago in 1927, Hines became musical director and featured pianist of Armstrong's reorganized quintet at the Savoy Ballroom and at a club they briefly owned together. The two men traded musical ideas and revolutionized jazz in the process. Hines next appeared with clarinetist Jimmie Noone at the Apex Club. In 1928 he recorded with that group; his own solos on piano rolls; and as part of the historic Louis Armstrong Hot 5 sessions, playing celeste as well as piano. The latter band's premier recording was "West End Blues." One of Hines's best solo recordings was "A Monday Date," his own composition.

On his twenty-third birthday Hines provided a ten-piece orchestra at the opening of the Grand Terrace Ballroom on Chicago's South Side, where it played for cabaret shows and dancing for the next decade. It dominated the Chicago jazz scene, expanding its appeal with the first tour of the South by a major black big band and with live coast-to-coast radio broadcasts of its performances starting in 1932. An announcer, piqued at Hines's fatherly advice, gave him his nickname "Fatha" on the air. Renowned for the hard-driving swing laid down by Hines on piano, the band drew on arrangements from Jimmy Mundy, Budd Johnson, and many others. Exceptional examples are "Pianology" and his most popular composition, "Rosetta." Outstanding among several major soloists were Omer Simeon on clarinet and Johnson on tenor sax. The band recorded and toured extensively.

During 1939 and 1940 the Hines orchestra achieved its peak in sheer excitement and popularity with its hit recording of "Boogie Woogie on the St. Louis Blues" and the addition of vocalist Billy Eckstine. His vocal on "Jelly Jelly" made the record an immense commercial success. In 1940 Hines bought his contract from the Grand Terrace manager, who had long exploited him, and relocated to New York City between road tours. In 1942 and 1943 the band became a proving ground for bebop, employing trumpeter Dizzy Gillespie, alto saxophonist Charlie Parker, tenor saxophonist Wardell Gray, and second pianist–vocalist Sarah Vaughan. Eckstine left in 1943. Unfortunately, a union ban on recordings prevented this period of Hines's musical creativity from being preserved. Ever the experimenter, in 1943 he added eleven women, including four violins, a harp, and a vocal quartet. He then turned from bebop to sweet sounds.

Serious injuries from an automobile accident forced Hines to curtail his activities in 1946, but he nevertheless continued to lead his twenty-four-piece orchestra for another year, after which he broke it up with the end of the big band era. He joined Louis Armstrong's All-Stars in 1948, and after appearing with them in the 1951 film *The Strip* he left, frustrated at being relegated to a sideman role. He married singer Janie Moses in 1947; they had two children. They were divorced in 1980.

Hines subsequently led a combo, with which he toured widely, and occasionally a big band, bringing both often to jazz festivals. In a Dixieland jazz format, he was based at the Club Hangover in San Francisco during the later 1950s and early 1960s and co-led a similar group with trombonist Jack Teagarden on a highly successful European tour in 1957. During the same decade he also conducted a weekly radio program for the U.S. Treasury Department, operated a short-lived club in Oakland, California, and made several television appearances, but recorded little. Then, in 1964, Hines received critical acclaim for three concerts in which he led a quartet at New York's Little Theater, followed by important gigs at Birdland that year and the Village Vanguard in 1965, both in Manhattan.

A hectic schedule of recordings, concerts, and tours ensued, with almost annual visits to Europe, Japan, and South America. That his pianistic prowess had not diminished was demonstrated at the Berlin jazz festival in 1966 when he soundly won a "battle" with jazz pianists Jaki Byard,

Bill Evans, John Lewis, Lennie Tristano, and Teddy Wilson. He then performed throughout the Soviet Union on a six-week tour for the U.S. State Department. The tours continued throughout the 1970s and early 1980s. He played his last gig in San Francisco the week before his death, from a heart attack.

An exciting showman who kept his band members impeccably attired, Earl Hines was tall, handsome, joyous, adorned with flashy smile and cigar; he occasionally sang while he played. He is universally recognized as one of the true pioneers and giants of jazz piano.

★

Stanley Dance, *The World of Earl Hines* (1977), is the standard biography, most of it transcribed interviews of Hines and several of his bandsmen. Dance's booklet for Time-Life's Giants of Jazz *Earl Hines* LP boxed album (1980) is an excellent abridgement. "Sunshine Always Opens Out" is an essay based on a 1964 interview of Hines by Whitney Balliett, reprinted in his *American Musicians: Fifty-six Portraits in Jazz* (1986). Hines's music is critically examined in Gunther Schuller, *Early Jazz: Its Roots and Musical Development* (1968), and *The Swing Era: The Development of Jazz, 1930–1945* (1989). His early period is included in William Howland Kenney, *Chicago Jazz: A Cultural History, 1904–1930* (1933). An obituary is in the *New York Times* (24 Apr. 1983).

Clark G. Reynolds

HIRSHHORN, Joseph Herman (*b.* 11 August 1899 in Mitau, Latvia; *d.* 31 August 1981 in Washington, D.C.), stock speculator, mining magnate, collector of modern art, and museum benefactor who created the Hirshhorn Museum in Washington, D.C.

Hirshhorn was one of thirteen children of Lazaar Hirshhorn, a merchant, and Amelia Friedlander. Lazaar died in Latvia when Joseph was still an infant, and in 1907 Amelia sailed with her children to New York City, where they settled in the Williamsburg neighborhood of Brooklyn. As soon as they were able, the children needed to contribute to the family income, because when a 1908 fire destroyed their tenement, the family was left destitute. Joseph worked selling newspapers and in a jewelry store. After a fifth-grade field trip to the New York Stock Exchange, he found himself fascinated with stocks and investing.

Hirshhorn soon took a job as an office boy on Wall Street and then charted stocks for an investment publication. In 1916 he established himself as a broker, invested $250 he had saved, and turned it into $168,000 within a year. He sold his seat on the New York Stock Exchange in 1924 and devoted himself to unlisted securities and bank stock. By the time he was twenty-nine years old he had accumulated a personal fortune of $1 million. In August 1929, just before the crash on Wall Street, he pulled out of the stock market with $4 million.

Joseph H. Hirshhorn, 1956. AP/WIDE WORLD PHOTOS

Although small in stature, Hirshhorn had what has been called an "outsize personality," with an insatiable curiosity and verbal command that allowed him to dominate any business, social, or personal situation. With capital to invest during the Great Depression, he decided to move into a new area, mining. He also changed the focus of his enterprise from New York to Canada, where he solidified his growing fortune and kept a second home in Toronto after 1933. Although Hirshhorn had no previous knowledge of mining, he applied the same principles he had used to get rich on the stock market, which meant finding undervalued assets and showing that they could perform with the proper infusion of investment. He attracted investors from around the world and also mastered the art of getting and controlling inside information.

Hirshhorn's initial success in this field came on the Toronto Stock Exchange, where he speculated on zinc, iron, tin, gas, and especially gold. When possible he gathered around him promoters, prospectors, and geologists to help assess opportunities and secure partners. He took over the virtually bankrupt Preston East Dome mine and recovered his investment many times over when a previously unknown source of gold ore turned up in 1936.

Not everything went well in Canada for Hirshhorn. His ability to buy and sell at opportune times led to an investigation by the Ontario Securities Commission in 1935. Ca-

nadian federal currency charges endangered his business endeavors in 1945, and he faced possible deportation to the United States. Although Hirshhorn was found guilty on relatively minor currency-trading charges, the record came back to haunt him ten years later when he faced possible deportation to the United States.

In the late 1940s Hirshhorn turned his attention to uranium mining. The coming of the nuclear age initiated a search for secure and abundant sources of uranium ore in order to meet what were expected to be dramatically increasing demands. Hirshhorn used his familiarity with Canada to address the need. As he drew together powerful international partners to help finance his plans, he began a secret search for a source of uranium ore that would allow him to dominate the market.

In the early 1950s, following a period of clandestine surveying, mapping, assaying, and filing of claims, Hirshhorn assumed title to what would become the monumental Algoma uranium mine in Ontario, near the northeast shore of Lake Huron. Within a short period of time Hirshhorn had a virtual monopoly on delivery of uranium to the United States, which was engaged in a massive expansion of the use of nuclear power for both military and nonmilitary uses. By the time the uranium market slumped in the late 1950s, Hirshhorn had secured yet another component of his fortune.

During this same period, he developed an obsession for collecting art. Although he had acquired rare books, manuscripts, and prints for many years without knowing much about the art world, he now approached it with the same enthusiasm he devoted to his financial interests. Although his knowledge was not that of a formally trained professional, he developed an appreciation for the art he collected and was not simply an art merchant who bought and sold. Soon Hirshhorn's various offices and several homes were full of paintings and sculptures.

Hirshhorn came to know some artists and dealers and to have preferences for the kind of art he wanted to collect. For example, he frequented Herman Baron's ACA Gallery in New York City to talk with artists. Sometimes he would buy their artworks by the dozens. Artists at the ACA generally reflected the social realist movement in art, which was falling out of favor when Hirshhorn began to buy their works. As a result, the artists were both grateful to and distrustful of this man who bought their creations with little apparent appreciation for the sentiment behind them.

By 1958 Hirshhorn's art collection—with its core of nineteenth-century French sculpture and American painting, a large selection of the first generation of the New York school of abstract expressionists, and representatives of social realism—totaled approximately 1,800 paintings and 450 sculptures and had a full-time curator. The owner continued to acquire and began to think of what he might do other than continue to amass artwork in warehouses where, increasingly, even he could not gain access to it. He decided to establish a museum that would contain his collection and bear his name. After weighing a wide variety of possible sites, Hirshhorn accepted an offer from the Smithsonian Institution to locate his museum on the Mall in Washington, D.C. In 1966 he presented almost 6,000 paintings and objects to the Hirshhorn Museum, which opened in October 1974 to mixed reviews from art critics, but which soon took its place among Washington, D.C., institutions as a miscellaneous museum of American and European art.

Hirshhorn was married four times in his life, with his first three marriages ending in divorce. His first wife was Jennie Berman, whom he married in 1922 and with whom he had four children; they were divorced in 1945. He married Lily Harmon in 1947; they adopted two children and were divorced in 1956. Brenda Hawley Heide became his third wife in 1956. After another divorce, in 1963, he married Olga Zatorsky in 1964. The couple lived in Greenwich, Connecticut, then moved to Washington, D.C., where he died of a heart attack.

★

Barry Hyams, *Hirshhorn: Medici from Brooklyn* (1979), is the only book-length work on Hirshhorn's life. A chapter is devoted to him in Aline B. Saarinen, *The Proud Possessors: The Lives, Times, and Tastes of Some Adventurous American Art Collectors* (1958). Articles that look at Hirshhorn from the perspective of his business enterprise and his activities as an art collector include Emmet J. Hughes, "Joe Hirshhorn, the Brooklyn Uranium King," *Fortune* (11 Feb. 1980), and Abram Lerner, "Joseph Hirshhorn," *Art News* (Dec. 1981). An obituary is in the *New York Times* (2 Sept. 1981).

CHARLES K. PIEHL

HOFFER, Eric (*b.* 25 July 1902 in New York City; *d.* 21 May 1983 in San Francisco, California), author and philosopher who worked for many years as a longshoreman, best known for his first book, *The True Believer* (1951).

Hoffer was the only son of Knut Hoffer, a cabinetmaker, and Elsa Goebel Hoffer, a homemaker, both Jewish immigrants from Germany. Knut Hoffer kept a small library of second-hand books, and Eric learned to read both German and English by the time he was five years old. That year, as he later told the story, his mother was carrying him down the stairs and fell. She died two years later, possibly as a result of that fall, and Eric, through some never-diagnosed physical or psychological injury, lost his sight. Blind for the next eight years, he did not attend school (he would have no formal education whatever) but instead remained at home in the care of a German-born nanny and housekeeper, Martha Bauer. She became his adoptive mother, encouraging the boy to think and speak philo-

sophically and praising him constantly for his brilliance. "If I am anything at all," he said later, "it is due to Martha." After the passage of many years, in 1967, he would refer to her in a television interview as "the woman who raised me," an awkward choice of words and a reminder that the woman who raised him was not his mother.

At the age of fifteen Hoffer regained his sight, and he began to read everything he could get his hands on. Martha Bauer returned to Germany, and in 1920 his father died. With no skills and no prospects, Hoffer took the $300 given him by his father's burial society and struck out for California. Taking a cheap room in a seedy section of Los Angeles, he began carving out a life that encompassed both skid row and the Los Angeles Central Library. Over the next twenty years his thinking would be formed equally by the people he met living "on the bum"—working as a migrant farmhand, railroad worker, lumberjack, dishwasher, gold prospector—and by his favorite authors and philosophers, including Bergson, de Tocqueville, and, especially, Montaigne, whose epigrammatic style deeply influenced his own writing. In 1942, rejected by the military because of a hernia, Hoffer began his twenty-five-year-long career as a longshoreman, loading and unloading ships on the docks of San Francisco, hard and sometimes dangerous work that nevertheless left him time for reading and writing.

Eric Hoffer, Washington, D.C., 1969. UPI/CORBIS-BETTMANN

In the late 1930s Hoffer had impressed an editor at Harper with a sample of his writing, and in 1951 the publisher released Hoffer's first book, *The True Believer*, which traces the origins of mass movements. In his sweeping, generalizing style, Hoffer wrote that mass movements, from religious wars to German fascism, historically arise at times of collective despair and are driven by people only superficially motivated by ideology. "The fanatic is not really a stickler to principle," he wrote. "He embraces a cause not primarily because of its justness or holiness but because of his desperate need for something to hold onto." Hoffer believed that the United States, in its single-minded pursuit of normalcy after World War II, was in danger of forgetting the causes of that war. "I can never forget," Hoffer wrote, speaking of Germany, "that one of the most gifted, best-educated nations in the world, of its own free will, surrendered its fate into the hands of a maniac."

Critical reception was overwhelmingly positive to *The True Believer* and to his next book, *The Passionate State of Mind* (1959), a collection of 280 philosophical aphorisms. These books established Hoffer's thorny and often ironic place in American letters: a thinker who was at once embraced by and contemptuous of intellectuals. To leftists of the era, still inclined to romanticize the "proletariat," he was something of a romantic figure: the self-educated roustabout with true working-class credentials, who spoke in nuggets of blunt, no-nonsense wisdom. He, in turn, thought of them as deluded ideologues out of touch with the reality of America. "It is remarkable," he wrote in *The Ordeal of Change* (1963), a collection of essays, "how closely the attitude of the intellectual toward the masses resembles the attitude of a colonial functionary toward the natives." One example of this uneasy relationship came in 1964, when he was invited by the University of California at Berkeley to hold weekly political science seminars, a position he called "gossiper in residence." When the seminars concluded in 1972, he said of his students, "they didn't have an idea in their heads—nothing."

Six feet tall and 220 pounds, with a strong face and vivid presence, Hoffer proved even more charismatic in person than on the page, as demonstrated by the popularity of a series of twelve programs aired by the public television station KQED in San Francisco in 1964 entitled "Conversations with Eric Hoffer." He had no interest in material wealth, living alone in a modest apartment in San Francisco even after his media success. He never married, but he did have an "adopted" family in his long relationship with Lili Osborne, a teacher, and her son, Eric, Hoffer's godson.

Forced by his age to retire from the docks in 1967, Hoffer was becoming increasingly controversial as an author. In *The Temper of Our Time* (1967) and *Working and Thinking on the Waterfront* (1969) he incited criticism with his comments on the civil rights movement, which he thought doomed to failure because of what he deemed a lack of self-respect among African Americans and reliance on "the alibi of discrimination." In 1967 he gave a nationally televised, one-hour interview with the commentator Eric Sevareid. In it, he said that he thought the embattled President Lyndon B. Johnson, whom he admired as a true "common man," would go down in history as "the foremost president of the twentieth century." Soon thereafter Johnson, beset by Vietnam War protests as well as rioting in America's inner cities, invited Hoffer to the White House for a fifty-minute meeting. The following year Hoffer was appointed as a member of the president's National Commission on the Causes and Prevention of Violence. Hoffer's extreme irascibility alienated the other members of the committee. As related by Hoffer biographer James T. Baker, in one "irrational and unfortunate exchange, a black witness said, 'We are full of rage,' and Hoffer shouted back, 'Mister, it is easy to be full of rage. It is not easy to go to work and *build* something.' He told the committee that he had lived half his life in poverty and had never asked for a handout." This, Baker continues, led one committee member to characterize Hoffer's comments as blatant racism, "indicative of the great racist pathology of our country."

Hoffer wrote a nationally syndicated column entitled "Reflections" between 1969 and 1971 and continued to produce books that included *First Things, Last Things* (1971), *In Our Time* (1976), and *Before the Sabbath* (1979). After the 1960s, however, because of his frank contempt for the progressive movements of the era and for what he saw as the lazy, spoiled, affluent youth of the 1960s generation, most of his admirers were to be found among American conservatives. Shortly before his death in May 1983, President Ronald Reagan awarded him the Presidential Medal of Freedom, the nation's highest civilian honor.

Hoffer's writings encompassed the major ideological currents of American life for forty years, from communism and fascism in the 1930s to the antiwar and social liberation movements of the 1960s and the rise of conservatism in the 1970s. Through it all, he remained committed not to a particular political ideology but to a particular vision of intellectual freedom. He summoned up the archetypal, if to some degree mythical, American working man: self-reliant, hardworking, and rational, too confident and hard-headed to be swayed by the glib emotional appeals of either politicians or preachers. Hoffer's critics, especially after the 1960s, believed that he ultimately reflected not the working man's wisdom but the working man's prejudices. At his best, however, Hoffer was a rare voice in American politics, an advocate who sought to sell people only on the idea of thinking for themselves.

★

Books about Hoffer include Calvin Tompkins, *Eric Hoffer: An American Odyssey* (1968), James D. Koerner, *Hoffer's America*

(1973), and the most complete biography, James T. Baker, *Eric Hoffer* (1982). An obituary is in the *New York Times* (22 May 1983).

ALEXANDER GOLDMAN

HOFHEINZ, Roy Mark (*b.* 10 April 1912 in Beaumont, Texas; *d.* 21 November 1982 in Houston, Texas), state legislator, judge, businessman, and mayor of Houston, remembered as a visionary entrepreneur who built Houston's Astrodome, the first major domed stadium.

Roy Hofheinz was the only child of Fritz Joseph Hofheinz and Englena Eliza Planchard. His father, a Wells Fargo employee, was descended from a German Lutheran minister; his mother, from a French Catholic family, was a homemaker. In 1924, hoping to begin a cleaning and pressing business, Fritz moved the family to Houston. He died in 1928 when Roy was sixteen.

At San Jacinto High School, Roy made money by printing the school's first athletic programs and by persuading a newspaper to pay him for a high school sports column. After his father's death he sold advertising on a radio amateur hour (which he hosted) and promoted dances. In his ramshackle Model-T, he became a familiar figure on Houston streets.

In 1928 Hofheinz entered Rice Institute (later Rice University) but transferred in 1929 to Houston Junior College (later the University of Houston) and in 1930 to the Houston Law School, graduating with honors in 1933. He married fellow graduate Irene Cafcalas on 19 July 1933. Although Hofheinz had been a Roman Catholic and Cafcalas a Greek Orthodox, the couple became Methodists. They had three children.

At age nineteen, two years before taking his law degree, Hofheinz passed the Texas bar exam and began a modest criminal-law practice; but at twenty-two, disillusioned with his clients, he took up civil law and in 1934 ran for the legislature in Austin. With support from labor and the black community, and a tabloid he printed himself, he defeated the candidate favored by all three Houston newspapers. Dubbed the "boy orator of Buffalo Bayou," he helped to pass bills in the assembly repealing Prohibition, creating old-age pensions, and reforming conditions in hospitals for the insane.

In 1936, at only twenty-four, he boldly sought and won election as county judge, serving from 1937 to 1945. He instigated progressive reforms that discontinued secret meetings of commissioners, attacked price-fixing by suppliers, and reassessed property valuations favoring wealthy families. Often traveling to Austin and Washington, he succeeded in creating a flood-control district, improving roads, and promoting juvenile justice reforms that brought him national recognition. As Harris County judge, Hofheinz presided over three courts and several municipal commissions, working eighteen-hour days and earning only $9,500 a year. As his second term neared an end in 1944, he told his family, "I'm not going into politics again until I am a millionaire."

In January 1945 he cofounded the Houston Slag Materials Company, which used waste from steel plants to build highways. A few months earlier he had opened his own radio station. Owning and running KTHT gave Hofheinz a profitable and independent public voice. He expanded his broadcast holdings and amassed real estate, using one property as collateral for the next. A partner warned him of "skating on thin ice"; others thought him arrogant, even ruthless. By 1950 Hofheinz, at age thirty-seven, was a millionaire. As a sign of his new wealth, he built "Huckster House," an ornate summer showplace where he enjoyed cooking and boating on Galveston Bay.

In 1952 he ran for mayor and won handily. With a sense of Houston's impending boom, he began building freeways, a new airport, and other public works. He also pursued his old progressive reforms, attempting to end secret council meetings, abuses in juvenile justice, and price-fixing among city suppliers. As mayor he operated autocratically, creating strains with city council members, whom Hofheinz dubbed the "cookie jar boys." In July 1954, when four councilmen boycotted a meeting, Hofheinz sent police to apprehend them. He was reelected later in the year. The following year the council voted for impeachment charges. Hofheinz retaliated with a televised rally and pushed through a charter amendment requiring municipal elections a year early. But the electorate, tired of incessant squabbling, ousted the mayor in the November 1955 election. To Hofheinz, the voters had "thrown out the warden and turned the city over to the inmates," all for the sake of "harmony."

After his defeat, Hofheinz formed an alliance with the oil millionaire R. E. "Bob" Smith. The two built a real-estate empire that culminated in the construction of Houston's Astrodome. In 1955 Hofheinz had visited the Colosseum in Rome and learned that on hot days the Romans had covered the structure for shade. He commented later, "I figured that a round facility with a cover was what we needed in the United States and that Houston would be the perfect spot for it because of its rainy, humid weather." Early in 1960 he and Smith were approached by investors who wished to bring major league baseball to Houston, and needed a stadium. Hofheinz went to the county commissioners to propose a tax-supported bond issue financing a domed stadium, then scarcely imaginable, to be built by the county and leased to Hofheinz and Smith's Houston Sports Association. The voters approved the issue in March 1961. After five years of plans and skirmishes, including a

Roy Hofheinz holds a news conference in the Astrodome, Houston, 1975. UPI/CORBIS-BETTMANN

second bond issue backed by the electorate in December 1962, problems with land acquisition, design snags, and the addition of an exhibition and convention hall, the Astrodome opened to the press in December 1964. It could seat up to 66,000 and featured a spectacular animated scoreboard. The elite sat in the first "skyboxes" to be built in a stadium; Hofheinz ordered them as an afterthought and had them individually designed on fantasy themes like "Bangkok," "Villa d'Este," and "Laverne Aloha." When his Astros baseball team complained of glare, Hofheinz painted the Dome's Lucite tiles with a translucent acrylic. When this killed the grass on the field, he accelerated his plans with Monsanto Chemical to use what he called "undertaker's grass" and got Astroturf, now used in hundreds of sports arenas.

During the Astrodome's first season in 1965, Bob Smith, irritated by his partner's headstrong attitude, sold Hofheinz his share in the Houston Sports Association. Then in December 1966, Hofheinz suffered his greatest personal loss in the death of his wife, Irene. He moved into his Astrodome suite and immersed himself in business.

His business was expansion. In September 1967 Hofheinz announced that he would build a theme park and a hotel complex, an Astrodomain, near the Astrodome. In November he acquired the Ringling Bros. and Barnum & Bailey Circus. On 9 April 1969, in the midst of constructing new luxury suites and ballrooms, Hofheinz married Mary Frances McMurtry Gougenheim, his secretary of seventeen years whom he called Kiddo. They had no children.

At the start of the 1970s Hofheinz had trouble renewing his loans. Rich in assets, he had little cash. Lenders pressed him to seek long-term financing for the theme park, hotels, and other projects. In May 1970, after a meeting with advisers, Hofheinz suffered a stroke that paralyzed his left arm and leg. In December he sold the Ringling Circus to Mattel Toys, bringing him $27 million in Mattel stock.

Suffering from paralysis and the increasing pressure of creditors, Hofheinz lost control of his empire. He secured long-term financing but at ruinous interest rates, and the proceeds from the circus eroded as the price of Mattel shares plummeted. In a landmark case Hofheinz successfully sued Mattel for misrepresenting its financial position, but the settlement was not enough to save him. In September 1976 he sold his holdings in Astrodomain, including all proprietary interests in the Astrodome he had built.

Hofheinz had been heartened by the 1973 election of his son Fred to the first of two terms as Houston's mayor. Now, after selling his holdings, he found himself at sixty-five in the strongest cash position of his career. He pursued new investments, made charitable donations, and followed the fortunes of his former ball club. In September 1979 he returned to the Astrodome for "Roy Hofheinz Night," rising from his wheelchair to throw out the first ball. He suffered a fatal heart attack three years later and is buried in Houston's Glenwood Cemetery.

Hofheinz's headstrong manner and extravagant tastes led easily to caricature, often concealing the stature of his accomplishments. A dark-haired, heavyset, intense man behind owlish glasses, he liked to describe himself as a "huckster." Yet Hofheinz successfully combined perseverance and ingenuity with a democratic political spirit, a spirit embodied in public works. As an entrepreneur he built an empire on handshakes and the trust of local banks, values that ceased to be relevant in the financial world of the 1970s. His legacy is his progressive, often visionary political leadership; his monument is the Astrodome.

★

Dene Hofheinz Mann, *You Be the Judge* (1965), is a short personal memoir by Hofheinz's daughter. The standard work on Hofheinz is Edgar W. Ray's carefully researched *The Grand Huckster: Houston's Judge Roy Hofheinz, Genius of the Astrodome* (1980). Brad Herzog, *The Sports 100: The One Hundred Most Important People in American Sports History* (1995), includes a short article on Hofheinz with a note on Astroturf. Obituaries appear in the *Houston Chronicle* (22 Nov. 1982); *Houston Post* (22, 23, and 24 Nov. 1982); and *New York Times* (23 Nov. 1982).

ALAN BUSTER

HOLDEN, William (*b*. 17 April 1918 in O'Fallon, Illinois; *d*. 16 November 1981 in Santa Monica, California), actor and conservationist.

Holden was born William Franklin Beedle, Jr., the eldest of three sons of William Beedle, an industrial chemist, and Mary Ball, a teacher. In 1921 the family moved to Monrovia, California, a suburb of Los Angeles, where Bill Beedle, Jr., flourished in the warm outdoors environment.

William Holden. ARCHIVE PHOTOS

Devoted to his family, he became interested in athletics (he was above average height and strongly built) and many other sporting activities. His first brush with acting came at the age of ten, when he played Rip Van Winkle in a grade-school play. In his teens Bill developed a passion for motorcycles and music, learning to perform moderately well on both the piano and clarinet.

Entering Pasadena Junior College in 1936, he studied chemistry with the idea that he might enter the same line of work as his father. He also took a course in radio drama and appeared in several shows for local station KECA. Later he acted in a theatrical production of *Manya,* a play about Marie Curie in which Bill performed as her eighty-year-old father-in-law. Something about the bewhiskered young man pretending to be decrepit appealed to a talent scout from Paramount Studios who was watching carefully in the audience. A few days later Bill arrived at Paramount to participate in a screen test. Successful, he was placed under contract at a salary of $50 per week. Unhappy with the name Beedle, the Paramount executives renamed him William Holden, after a local newspaperman.

Launched with a new career and moving in an entirely unexpected direction, Holden dropped out of college and found himself, along with a group of other promising hopefuls at Paramount, among those collectively dubbed the "Golden Circle." (Others included were Susan Hayward and Robert Preston.) In 1939 he received his big break. Columbia Pictures was searching for a new face to play the young lead in the film version of Clifford Odets's stage play *Golden Boy,* to be directed by Rouben Mamoulian. Paramount agreed to loan out Holden for testing, and he was cast in the role against Columbia president Harry Cohn's wishes. Mamoulian labored hard to extract a serviceable performance from the greenhorn, and with much help and encouragement from Barbara Stanwyck, the film's star, Holden pulled through. Critical notices were ultimately divided on the film's release, but the young man appeared to be on his way. In the early 1940s Holden, often on loan to other studios, played a succession of bland roles, the most notable of which was in *Our Town* (1940), for United Artists.

Under pressure from his family to find some stability and settle down, he met and fell in love with the actress Brenda Marshall, who was under contract to Warner Brothers and had played opposite Errol Flynn in *The Sea Hawk* (1940). Her real name was Ardis Ankerson, and together they flew to Las Vegas, where they were married on 13 July 1941. Ardis had a child from a previous marriage, and she had two sons with Holden.

In 1942 Holden joined the growing war effort, enlisting in the army and serving until 1945. He graduated from the Army Air Forces Officer Candidate School at Miami Beach, Florida. He was stationed in Connecticut and Texas, and his duty principally revolved around public relations and training films. In January 1944 his brother Bob, a fighter pilot, was shot down and killed during a raid on Kavieng in the South Pacific. This tragedy would be the first in a series of events to contribute to Holden's deepening feelings of guilt, low self-esteem, and self-loathing.

Increasingly discontent after demobilization, Holden endured a period of unemployment that lasted nearly a year. The studios had changed, and it was hard to pick up from where he had left off; he merely marked time hoping for a good role. It finally came in 1949, when he was cast as the opportunistic screenwriter Joe Gillis in Billy Wilder's *Sunset Boulevard* (1950). Unsure at first how to get a handle on his character, Wilder advised Holden to just be himself, and the screen persona that historically defines William Holden was forever established. Surrounded by legendary figures Wilder, Gloria Swanson, and Erich von Stroheim, Holden shone as the cynical Hollywood wanna-be, defeated and destroyed by hubris. He earned his first Academy Award nomination for best actor. The success and notoriety of *Sunset Boulevard*'s cruelly mordant and jaded comedy propelled Holden toward a decade of superstardom and a string of box-office hits.

Roles in *Born Yesterday* (1950), *Executive Suite* (1954), *Sabrina* (1954), *The Country Girl* (1954), *Love Is a Many-Splendored Thing* (1955), and *Picnic* (1956) helped him to hone and refine his image as a handsome leading man. David Ansen, the film critic for *Newsweek,* would later describe Holden's appeal as stemming from his being "courtly, cynical, possessed of a particularly American gallantry that was utterly free of airs." Billy Wilder said, "Holden was that rare creature, a beautiful American." The Academy Award for best actor would be his for his portrayal of the sly Sefton in another Wilder masterpiece, *Stalag 17* (1953). Sefton is an existential prisoner-of-war camp loner, wrongly thought by his campmates to be an enemy informer. Holden's unique ability to project ordinariness, coupled with a hard-edged survivalist mentality, showcased Sefton as a peculiarly American creation. The recognition helped his career to a new plateau, even as personal problems continued to gnaw at him.

During this period he also became active in other fields. Enamored of money and unhappy with the concept of being an actor, he diversified into various business endeavors. Shrewd with investments, he bought into import-export companies, stores, restaurants, and numerous real-estate holdings around the world. He described himself as a "businessman" on his many trips to exotic locales. He also became romantically involved with several of his leading ladies and developed lasting, intimate relationships with, among others, Grace Kelly and Audrey Hepburn. His dissatisfaction with life and his restless nature compelled him to seek refuge in foreign countries, sometimes for months at a stretch. His drinking, a habit that had been with him since his earliest days as an actor, began to exert a more insidious hold.

By 1957 Holden was astride the movie industry and his thirst for adequate remuneration resulted in some groundbreaking deals. For *The Bridge on the River Kwai* (1957) he received $300,000 plus 10 percent of the gross, payable at a maximum of $50,000 a year. When the movie took in more than $30 million at the box office, Holden was guaranteed a healthy annuity for life. As the dissolute Shears in *Kwai,* he also garnered some of his best notices.

In 1959, furious at the high level of personal income taxation, Holden moved his family to Switzerland to take advantage of recent tax-law changes. Thereupon, he was immediately vilified as a millionaire tax dodger. Even the Screen Actors Guild reproached him for supporting "runaway" or foreign-based production that took the emphasis away from Hollywood. Under pressure from the impact of television, the movie studios railed at their independent stars. Holden was unmoved, claiming that he worked hard for his money and was entitled to keep most of it. Members of Congress attacked Holden and others for "perverting the tax laws"; eventually, they changed the laws again by capping allowable tax exemptions for wealthy Americans living outside their country. Meanwhile, from his European base Holden expanded his enterprises and bought into a hotel called Cloudland situated at the foot of Mount Kenya, which he rechristened the Mount Kenya Safari Club. Also, as his disillusionment with the movie business grew, so did his fascination with Africa and big-game conservation.

In the 1960s Holden's films became less frequent and deteriorated markedly in quality. *The Counterfeit Traitor* (1962), *The Lion* (1962), *Paris When It Sizzles* (1964), and *The Seventh Dawn* (1964) were barely blips on the radar screen. His drinking went out of control. At the end of the shooting for *The Seventh Dawn,* he collapsed from acute alcohol poisoning and was airlifted to Switzerland for hospitalization. With him was his current love, the actress Capucine. His marriage all but over (he and his wife had separated), he yearned for some sense of coherence, but clearly his life was in decline. Recovering, he sought solace in Africa, founding a big-game reserve adjacent to the failing Safari Club. He stayed off the screen for two years. During this hiatus, his second brother, Dick, was killed in an airplane crash. The coincidence of both his younger brothers' dying in similar circumstances, and ahead of him, further eroded his self-esteem. Returning to film, he sleepwalked through the making of *Alvarez Kelly* (1966), but met Beverly Hills socialite Pat Stauffer, with whom he began a relationship that would last off and on for the remainder of his life.

In 1966, drunk at the wheel, Holden crashed his Ferrari into the back of a Fiat on the autostrada near Florence, Italy, killing the Fiat's driver. Holden's troubles with alcohol had plumbed a new depth. He was allowed home to

Switzerland but was found guilty of manslaughter and received a suspended prison sentence. His lawyers provided an out-of-court settlement for the victim's family. Needing to work, Holden rushed into some weak movie projects. A cameo appearance in the camp catastrophe *Casino Royale* (1967) was barely noticed; likewise, his role as the leader of an off-kilter platoon in the subpar World War II caper movie, *The Devil's Brigade* (1968). Salvation of a kind was at hand in 1968, however, when producer Phil Feldman raised Holden's name in conjunction with a new Warner Brothers Western, *The Wild Bunch* (1969). The pivotal part of Pike Bishop had just been turned down by Lee Marvin, and Feldman felt that the near-forgotten Holden was a viable replacement. *The Wild Bunch* was in the fiery charge of troubled director Sam Peckinpah, himself no stranger to the kinds of problems that plagued Holden. Eschewing Holden's recent reputation for chronic unreliability, Warner Brothers took a gamble on the production, placing Holden at the center of a stellar group of character actors that included Ernest Borgnine, Robert Ryan, Edmond O'Brien, Warren Oates, Ben Johnson, L. Q. Jones, and Strother Martin.

The finished film was a cause célèbre with tidal-wave repercussions that were still being felt a generation later. Peckinpah's epic revisionist Western helped to redefine the notion of traditional Western codes and opened the doors for a vivid new level of realistic screen violence. Virtually an allegory of the Vietnam War then raging at its height, *The Wild Bunch* tore a great hole in the American moviegoing psyche. Denounced by some, praised by others, the movie proved unforgettable and polarized opinions among everyone who saw it. Holden did not see what the fuss was about and attracted personal calumny by reviewers for his seemingly lackadaisical, unperturbed attitude. The film did give his career a much-needed boost, and his portrayal of the world-weary, aging bank robber who is consumed by guilt and failure struck uncomfortably close to Holden's real life. In the rheumy eyes of this sad, violent man, almost unknowingly seeking redemption in a bigger tragedy, lay the key to Holden's essentially unknowable personality.

By 1973 Holden's marriage had effectively ended. Citing irreconcilable differences, Brenda Marshall filed for divorce. Despite their separation in 1963, the couple had maintained a close relationship, and that relationship would continue until Holden's death. When he bought a house in Palm Springs, California, so did she, and they were regularly in each other's company. Around this time Holden made his television debut (apart from his guest appearance as himself on *I Love Lucy* in 1955) in the new format known as the miniseries. *The Blue Knight* (1973) was adapted from a novel by former policeman Joseph Wambaugh, who had become a best-selling author. Holden's weary, drink-ravaged features suited well the story of a beat patrolman near retirement, reluctant to give up his badge. His char-

acterization would reward him with an Emmy Award for best actor. His obsession with Africa grew unabated and a new love, actress Stefanie Powers, shared his passion for Kenya. Powers, like Pat Stauffer, would stay with him more or less, but she too would be defeated in time by Holden's inability to quit, or even modify, his drinking.

Feeling enthusiasm for his craft again, Holden appeared in a number of films. *Breezy* (1973), *Fedora* (1978), and *Ashanti* (1979) were attempts to re-create the persona of younger days, albeit shot through with middle-aged ennui. Ensemble pictures like *The Towering Inferno* (1974), *Escape to Athena* (1979), and *When Time Ran Out* (1980) kept Holden in the public eye. A third Academy Award nomination came his way for *Network* (1976), Paddy Chayefsky's acerbic look at the television industry. Holden felt he had a chance of winning, but was ultimately denied by Peter Finch, also nominated for *Network*.

Despite his protestations to the contrary, Holden's alcohol addiction consumed him. As the 1970s drew to a close, his constant blackouts and repeated spells in hospitals and clinics testified to the last stages of his condition. His game reserve in Africa grew in stature and reputation, but Holden's visits grew more sporadic and erratic. Director Blake Edwards recruited Holden for his satire on Hollywood, *S.O.B.* (1981), which gave Holden the pleasant experience of working with several old friends, including Robert Preston, Richard Mulligan, and Robert Webber. The movie turned out to be more of a convivial party than a story and Holden was relaxed, friendly, and on the set every day, even when he was not called. He regarded it as the start of a new period, one that would lead to choice roles befitting his older years. It was not to be, however. In November 1981 he was discovered dead in his Santa Monica, California, apartment. Holden had fallen in a drunken stupor, hitting his head on a coffee table. He had feebly tried to dab at his cut forehead with tissues, but unable to comprehend the seriousness of the wound, drifted into sleep and quietly passed away. His cremated ashes were scattered over the Pacific Ocean. He willed his game reserve in Kenya to an organization committed to his ideals and made substantial bequests to Stefanie Powers, Pat Stauffer, and Capucine, the three women who helped him the most in his long, losing battle with alcoholism.

★

See Bob Thomas, *Golden Boy: The Untold Story of William Holden* (1983), and Lawrence J. Quirk, *The Complete Films of William Holden* (1973). Obituaries are in the *New York Times* (17 Nov. 1981) and *Newsweek* (30 Nov. 1981).

NICK REDMAN

HOLLAND, Jerome Heartwell ("Brud") (*b.* 9 January 1916 in Auburn, New York; *d.* 13 January 1985 in New York City), educator, diplomat, and civil rights proponent who advocated education as the best means for African-

American youths to achieve economic and social advancement.

Holland was the son of Robert Howard Holland, a gardener and handyman, and Viola (Bagby) Holland, an occasional factory worker. One of thirteen children in a poor family, he began working for his father at age eight. He attended the Auburn public schools for his primary and secondary education, taking the commercial track that was encouraged for African Americans. Determined to continue his education after high school, he took a year of academic subjects after graduation to qualify for college admission.

Holland entered Cornell University in the fall of 1935, matriculating in the agricultural college, where tuition was less expensive. He became the university's first black football player. He earned his expenses working at odd jobs, including cleaning a fraternity house. He lived off campus because Cornell offered no housing for blacks. Holland majored in sociology and was a member of the junior and senior honor societies. He played varsity football and was All-America left end in 1937 and 1938. Unlike his peers of comparable academic and athletic standing, however, he was not recruited for business during campus job interviews in his senior year. As he later noted: "I was [the] exception. Nobody interviewed me. Nobody offered me a job. I am a Negro."

Holland found a position teaching sociology and coaching football from 1939 to 1942 at Lincoln University in

Jerome Holland, 1970. ARCHIVE PHOTOS

Oxford, Pennsylvania. During the summers he studied for his M.S. degree in sociology at Cornell, receiving it in 1941. About this time he married Madeline Smalls; they had two children before divorcing in 1944. After the entry of the United States into World War II, Holland was employed as the director of personnel for yard number 4 of the Sun Shipbuilding and Drydock Company of Pennsylvania, the construction yard for black workers, where he was employed until 1946. That year he joined the faculty of Tennessee State College in Nashville (now Tennessee Agricultural and Industrial State University), serving as chairman of the Department of Political and Social Sciences and football coach. He married Laura Mitchell of Boston on 22 August 1948 in Nashville; they had two children.

In 1950 Holland completed a Ph.D. in sociology from the University of Pennsylvania. The following year he became a social research consultant for the Pew Charitable Trust in Philadelphia, a foundation known for its contributions to black colleges. In 1953 he was appointed president of Delaware State College in Dover, a black college threatened with closure because of its small enrollment. Holland expanded the school's physical plant and enrollment, gaining accreditation for the college and achieving near parity in an integrated student body. In 1960 he was made president of Hampton Institute, a private college in Virginia. During his ten years at Hampton he increased its endowments and enlarged the physical facilities. In 1965 he was elected to the National Football Hall of Fame.

In 1970 President Richard M. Nixon appointed Holland ambassador to Sweden, a country whose relations with the United States had become strained because it criticized U.S. involvement in the Vietnam War and offered asylum to Americans fleeing the draft. Holland was publicly heckled in Sweden and called racial epithets he said he had previously heard only in "the most racially biased areas of the United States." In 1972, with relations between Sweden and the United States much improved, Holland resigned his post and returned to the United States. He moved to the Lawrence Park West community in Yonkers, New York.

Holland's subsequent career entailed serving on numerous business and volunteer boards. He was the first black to serve on the board of directors of the New York Stock Exchange (1972–1980) and as chair of the American Red Cross (1979–1985) and chair of National Planned Parenthood and World Population (1970). He also served on the boards of eleven major corporations, including AT&T, Chrysler, Federated Department Stores, General Foods, Union Carbide, and Manufacturers Hanover. He was a trustee and officer of the Institute of International Education, United Negro College Fund, northeast region of the National Council of Christians and Jews, Salvation Army, Cornell University, Massachusetts Institute of Technology, and American Academy of Arts and Sciences.

Holland was an imposing figure at six feet, two inches and 220 pounds. His friends described him as a gregarious man with a keen sense of humor and as a compelling speaker. Others described him as charismatic. He died of lung cancer in New York Hospital and was buried in the Fort Hill Cemetery in Auburn, New York.

From an early age Holland was conscious of the limitations in American society imposed by race, but his experiences at Cornell made the injustice of racial bias more vivid and the means of escaping that bias more certain. He believed that the route to black equality, opportunity, and success was through education and economic advancement, with education the more important of the two. This belief was a persistent theme in his life's work and was the thesis of his book *Black Opportunity* (1969), in which he noted that through education "we acquire and believe in our own dignity, self-respect, and assurance. . . . [We] accept equality as a natural right." Holland pursued this goal for his race through advocacy and, more notably, through personal example.

★

Some of Holland's papers are in the Cornell University Library; others, including those from his diplomatic years, are held by his family. His only book, *Black Opportunity,* contains some autobiographical information and is the source for quotations. A brief biographical sketch is included in Helen G. Edmonds, *Black Faces in High Places: Negroes in Government* (1971). The public relations office of the Athletic Department at Cornell University has a large folio of biographical data and news clippings. Information on Holland's appointment as ambassador to Sweden is in the *New York Times* (13, 18 Jan.; 17 Mar.; and 15 Apr. 1970). An obituary is in the *New York Times* (14 Jan. 1985).

MARILYNN WOOD HILL

HOLT, John Caldwell (*b.* 14 April 1923 in New York City; *d.* 14 September 1985 in Boston, Massachusetts), educator, author, and social reformer best known for his efforts in the late 1960s and early 1970s to reform American public schools.

Holt was the only son of Henry Holt, a wealthy insurance executive, and Elizabeth Crocker Holt. His family moved to suburban New Canaan, Connecticut, when John was a child. He attended exclusive private schools, including Le Rosey in Switzerland and from 1936 to 1938 Phillips Exeter Academy in New Hampshire. Holt later reflected that his early educational experiences blunted his imagination through regimented classroom structures. In 1939 Holt enrolled in Yale College and received a B.S. degree in industrial engineering in 1943. Upon graduation he entered the U.S. Navy and qualified for submarine warfare during World War II. Holt served as a junior officer on the sub-

John Holt, 1972. UPI/CORBIS-BETTMANN

marine USS *Barbero* and earned a Pacific theater of war combat ribbon. In 1946 he was honorably discharged from active duty.

Returning to civilian life, Holt moved to New York City and in 1946 began work with the United World Federalists, an international peace group that sought to prevent nuclear warfare through the creation of a single world government. From 1946 through 1952 Holt served this organization by speaking to groups throughout New York State and recruiting new members. By 1952 he was executive director of the New York State branch of the World Federalists, but he abruptly resigned during the Red Scare and spent the greater part of 1952 traveling in Europe.

From 1953 through 1957, Holt worked at the private Colorado Rocky Mountain School in Carbondale, Colorado, where he taught high school English, French, and mathematics and coached soccer and baseball. Holt later described himself as a conventional teacher who gradually grew disenchanted with the school's neglect of poorly performing students. In 1957 he became a fifth-grade teacher at the Shady Hill School in Cambridge, Massachusetts, but he was dismissed from this selective private school in 1959 because of his unconventional classroom presentations on mathematics, which sought to have the students understand the subject rather than engage in rote memorization. He then taught fifth grade at the Lesley Ellis School in Cambridge. Holt expanded his emerging educational theories by designing the entire elementary mathematics curriculum according to his innovative approaches. He also began to teach reading to first- and second-graders.

In 1964 Holt published *How Children Fail* for Pitman Press. This book, about his experiences at Shady Hill and Lesley Ellis, catapulted Holt to national prominence as a searing critic of the U.S. educational system. Holt condemned teachers and schools for blunting natural intelligence and curiosity through an oppressive regimen of rote learning that resulted in bored, confused, and alienated children. The study was heralded by many educators for its realistic portrait of classrooms and put Holt in demand as a lecturer and consultant to school systems.

In 1965 Holt became a high school English teacher at Boston's Commonwealth School. Over the next two years, he continued teaching and working on his next book. In *How Children Learn* (1967) Holt offered an optimistic sequel to his earlier manifesto, contending that children were naturally active and inquisitive learners. Through his narrative snapshots, Holt suggested broad reforms for the nation's schools. He recommended individualized instruction where children control their own learning. He advised teachers to be trusting and patient and to transform their role from master of knowledge to resource person. The success of this study put Holt in demand internationally as a lecturer and placed him in the vanguard of such educational reformers as Jonathan Kozol and Herbert Kohl, who advocated alternative schools and teaching methods during the late 1960s. In 1968 he was a visiting lecturer at Harvard's Graduate School of Education, and in 1969 he held a similar post at the University of California at Berkeley.

In 1969 Holt became president and founder of Holt Associates, Inc., an educational consulting firm that promoted radical proposals for school reform. Disillusioned with the piecemeal nature and lethargic pace of open education and the alternative-schools movement, Holt began to advocate in 1970 the radical vision of Ivan Illich's revolutionary educational theory of deinstitutionalizing education. In his 1972 study, *Freedom and Beyond,* Holt championed the "de-schooling movement," which called for an end to compulsory education in favor of individuals pursuing their own educational interests at their own paces and individual manners. Holt, in short, called for dismantling public education.

In 1976 Holt further advanced his de-schooling views in *Instead of Education: Ways to Help People Do Things Better.* Here he presented an array of alternative learning systems: home instruction by parents and children;

community-based learning centers; and removal of children from public schools. Over the next seven years, Holt continued to lecture, edit a detailed newsletter (*Growing Without Schooling*), and write books and articles for popular magazines promoting his faith in home instruction. Holt wrote eleven books, the last two of which were published posthumously. A bachelor and a shy person, Holt took up the cello at age forty and learned how to water-ski and ride a horse in his late forties. He died of cancer and is buried in Boston.

★

Holt's correspondence is reprinted in Susannah Sheffer, ed., *A Life Worth Living: Selected Letters of John Holt* (1990). Some of his major works are *How Children Fail* (1964); *How Children Learn* (1967); *What Do I Do Monday?* (1970); *Freedom and Beyond* (1972); *Instead of Education* (1976); and *Never Too Late: My Musical Life Story* (1978). See also his collected essays in his *The Underachieving School* (1969) and his bimonthly home-schooling newsletter, *Growing Without Schools,* launched in 1977. Assessments of Holt's impact on American education are offered in Diane Ravitch, *The Troubled Crusade: American Education, 1945–1980* (1983); Susan Douglas Franzosa, "The Best and Wisest Parent," *Urban Education* 19 (Oct. 1984): 227–244; and Herbert Kohl, "Tales Told In and About School," *Mothering* 61 (22 Sept. 1991). An obituary is in the *New York Times* (16 Sept. 1985).

RONALD LETTIERI

HOPKINS, Sam ("Lightnin'") (*b.* 15 March 1912 in Centerville, Texas; *d.* 30 January 1982 in Houston, Texas), blues singer, songwriter, and guitarist whose career spanned nearly six decades.

Hopkins grew up in a small farming town and worked in cotton fields. He built his first guitar at age eight and learned a few basic blues chords from his brother. Also at the age of eight he heard Blind Lemon Jefferson, a well-known Texas bluesman, perform at a General Association of Baptist Churches picnic. He heard Lemon on a number of subsequent occasions, and this exposure was a strong influence on his own artistry.

When Hopkins was not doing farm chores, he listened to the music of farmhands and sneaked into local bars to hear "real" musicians. He developed a guitar style that was uniquely his own—high-range runs accompanied by a hard-driving bass of erratic rhythms. He learned to sing by listening to his cousin Alger "Texas" Alexander, who began recording for Okeh Records in 1927.

Hopkins became a street singer, performing wherever he could but earning little money. He was forced to continue to hire out to farmers. An especially harsh experience working for landowner Tom Moore purportedly inspired a blues epic that was recorded on an early record:

You know I got a telegram this morning
It say your wife is dead.
I showed it to Mr. Moore, he says
Go ahead, nigger, you know you gotta
    plow a ridge.
That white man said it's been rainin'
Yes sir, I'm way behind.
I may let you bury that woman
On your dinner time.

I told him, no, Mr. Moore, somebody's
    got to go.
He said if you ain't goin' to plow, Sam,
    get up there and grab your hoe.

Hopkins went to Houston in 1946; there he made his first recordings, accompanying his cousin Texas and a piano player named Wilson "Thunder" Smith. Later in 1946 Sam and Thunder, calling themselves Thunder Smith and Lightnin' Hopkins, went to Hollywood to record for Aladdin Studios. From then on, he performed and recorded as Lightnin' Hopkins. His unusual, erratic, and improvisational approach to the blues and his autobiographical lyrics were at their best when performed with no accompaniment other than his own guitar playing, so he continued recording as a solo artist. In all, he recorded forty-three sides for Aladdin. Back in Houston he was also recording for Gold Star, sometimes recording the same songs for both labels.

Hopkins recorded regularly through 1954. Although he enjoyed the success of his records and the recognition that provided him with opportunities to perform throughout the South, Hopkins preferred working the beer joints and small clubs close to Houston. A growing number of blues experts recognized the fine quality of his work on his many recordings. Among the dozens of albums released in the 1950s were the double-record set *Lightnin' Hopkins and the Blues* on Imperial, *Lightnin' Strikes* on Vee-Jay, and *Goin' Away, Gotta Move Your Baby* on Bluesville. Hopkins managed money poorly, going rapidly through his earnings.

By the late 1950s the public had lost interest in country blues and Hopkins was down and out, moving from one furnished room to another. His wife had left him. He survived by playing for parties and was once again singing for his supper in small clubs. A folklorist named Mack McCormick, determined to bring Hopkins's singular, incredible talent to the widening folk/blues audience, sought him out and scheduled him to perform at Houston's Alley Theatre. The audience loved him, and soon Hopkins was performing for integrated audiences on college campuses. Sam Charters, a blues historian and record producer, encouraged him to begin recording in 1958, this time for Folkways. He later recorded for Prestige/Bluesville and other labels. Hopkins had found a new audience who appreciated his raw

Sam ("Lightnin'") Hopkins. PHOTOFEST

blues style and the natural, often bitter, poetry and wit of his narratives.

Hopkins debuted at Carnegie Hall on 14 October 1960, sharing the stage with new talents Bob Dylan and Joan Baez, and veteran folksinger Pete Seeger. After a long run at the Village Gate in New York City, he became a popular performer at college coffeehouses, at folk festivals, and on the blues club circuit. In 1964 he toured Europe with the American Folk Blues Festival before returning to New York for another performance at Carnegie Hall. In 1965 Hopkins was a featured artist at the Newport Folk Festival.

Hopkins's relentless recording schedule produced two or three LPs every year during the 1960s, some of them reissues of earlier recordings. Bluesville releases included *Blues in My Bottle* (1962), *Walkin' This Road by Myself* (1962), and *Smokes Like Lightnin'* (1963). His records for Verve included *Roots* (1965), *Lightnin' Strikes* (1966), and *Something Blue* (1967). He recorded an album with the Chambers Brothers and Barbara Dane for Arhoolie in 1966. During these years he also released LPs on Prestige, Vee-Jay Records, Tradition, and Jewel.

Throughout his career Hopkins performed and recorded for over twenty record labels, and he is widely recognized as having made more recordings than any other blues artist. He would record for any label that paid him cash up front. By the end of the 1970s it was estimated that the total number of songs he recorded had reached nearly 1,000.

Hopkins contributed his talents to the soundtrack of the movie *Sounder* (1972) and appeared in a number of blues documentaries that aired primarily on public television. He was featured in a short film by Les Blank entitled *The Blues Accordin' to Lightnin' Hopkins* (1970). He died of cancer in Houston.

Hopkins is widely regarded as one of the most significant and creative bluesmen ever recorded. A prolific songwriter and master storyteller, he was able to translate everyday events into compelling lyrics punctuated with an authentic wit and his own ragged, carefree style of guitar playing. He was a major influence on a number of white blues artists who emerged in the 1960s. They were drawn to his simple, soulful interpretation and his unique musicianship. His artistry turned the mundane events of a hard life into timeless masterpieces.

★

Samuel B. Charters, *The Country Blues* (1959), is a classic account by a well-known blues historian and record producer who was instrumental in Hopkins's reemergence in the 1960s. Irwin Stambler and Grelun Landon, *The Encyclopedia of Folk, Country, and Western Music* (1983), provides a comprehensive review of the uniquely American music of the 1950s and 1960s. An obituary is in the *New York Times* (1 Feb. 1982).

GAIL STRANGE THOMPSON

HOYT, Homer (*b.* 14 June 1895? in St. Joseph, Missouri; *d.* 29 November 1984 in Silver Spring, Maryland), land and real estate economist whose sector theory of urban development helped to shape post–World War II urban planning and whose demographic studies led to the creation of more than 200 shopping centers across the United States between 1946 and 1974.

An only child, Hoyt never knew the exact year of his birth nor—other than his last name—anything about his father. He was raised in neighborhoods in and around Kansas City, Kansas, by his hard-driving mother, Elizabeth Vath Hoyt, who early recognized his considerable intellect and moved frequently in search of the best possible schooling for him. Experiencing only hard times for much of his youth—at one point he and his mother lived in a tent in the eastern part of the city—he walked five miles a day as a first-grader to reach his classes and, for a three-year period (1902–1905), was taught by his mother at home because their small farm (purchased with a $300 mortgage) lay outside the city limits and the closest school district refused to admit him. Through his mother's persistence, he was allowed to attend Argentine High School on the city's periphery, where he ranked first in his class at the end of sophomore year (1907), and then Wyandotte High School downtown, from which he graduated in 1909. With his mother's help, he cobbled together the $15-dollar-a-year

Homer Hoyt, *c.* 1965. PHOTO BY MICHAEL HOYT. COURTESY OF MICHAEL HOYT.

tuition for the University of Kansas and in 1913, at age seventeen, earned an A.B., an A.M., and a Phi Beta Kappa key. Winning a fellowship, he went on to the University of Chicago (J.D., 1918) and was an instructor in economics at Beloit College in Wisconsin (1917–1918).

Following America's entry into World War I, Hoyt served as an economist in Washington, D.C., for the War Trade Board, one of several agencies President Woodrow Wilson assembled to manage the nation's war effort. After the armistice, Hoyt returned briefly to academic life as a professor of economics at Delaware College (now the University of Delaware) from 1919 to 1920. The following year he turned down an appointment at the University of Michigan to work as a statistician for the American Telephone and Telegraph Company in New York City. Bored by the sterility of the job, he went back to teaching economics, first at the University of North Carolina at Chapel Hill (1921–1923) and then at the University of Missouri at Columbia (1924–1925), in each case with the rank of associate professor.

In 1925 Hoyt reentered the private sector and thereafter combined his business interests with long stretches of public service and independent scholarship. His scholarly work in the next decade placed him in the forefront of urban historians, sociologists, and economists who had begun to examine the place of the city in modern American life. Like such pioneering writers as Arthur M. Schlesinger, Sr., Richard Hartshorne, Charles Merriam, W. Lloyd Warner, Robert and Helen Lynd, and Lewis Mumford, he was fascinated by the forces behind urban development and undertook to find economic models that would simultaneously explain past growth and aid future planning.

Working as a real estate broker and consultant in Chicago from 1925 to 1934, Hoyt completed his studies in economics at the University of Chicago (Ph.D., 1933) and published *One Hundred Years of Land Values in Chicago: 1830–1933* (1933; reprinted 1970), in which he provided historical perspective for the city's growth in relation to the value of its real estate. In so doing, he developed socioeconomic models of neighborhood change to show that real estate values were a function of the income, social standing, and race (or ethnicity) of a given area's residents—a concept that acquired importance among urban and economic historians.

From 1934 to 1940 Hoyt was the principal housing economist for the Federal Housing Administration (FHA), a key New Deal agency established under the National Housing Act (28 June 1934) to revive residential construction and upgrade building standards throughout the United States. Near the end of the decade, Hoyt published two influential books based on his studies of land values and land use for the FHA. One was a college text, *Principles of Urban Real Estate* (1939), written with Arthur Martin Weimer and (later) George F. Bloom. (The seventh and last edition published while he was alive appeared in 1978 under the title *Real Estate*.) The other, *The Structure and Growth of Residential Neighborhoods in American Cities,* was a report prepared for the FHA (1939; reprinted 1972). In each, Hoyt advanced his sector theory of urban development—first touched on in his doctoral dissertation—that challenged the prevailing theory of urban growth, advanced by Ernest C. Burgess in 1927, which held that cities grew outward from a central core in concentric rings defined by specific land use.

According to Hoyt, the entire city is a circle, and urban spatial patterns are typically wedge-shaped sectors (not rings) radiating from the center along established transportation corridors. Each sector is distinctively defined by a broad range of socioeconomic and geographic features, including the income and social status of its residents, the economic uses to which the land is put, and its topography. High-income residential areas, for example, tend to be on high ground and grow in the direction of open spaces; low-income areas develop on floodplains or in dead-end sections closed to further expansion. A stimulus to several de-cades of debate on urban planning, Hoyt's sector theory—since modified and recast by other theorists—provided a more detailed explanation of urban expansion than any prior formulation and, especially in its examination of the dynamics of growth, foreshadowed the postwar development of the nation's suburbs, urban expressways, and regional shopping centers.

From 1941 to 1943, Hoyt was director of research for the Chicago Plan Commission, and in 1943 he published *Master Plan of Residential Land Use of Chicago.* As director of economic studies for the Regional Plan Association in New York City (1943–1946), he wrote *The Economic Status of the New York Metropolitan Region in 1944* (1944). He was a visiting professor of land economics at the Massachusetts Institute of Technology and Columbia University (1944–1946).

In 1946 Hoyt, based in Larchmont, New York, established Homer Hoyt Associates, a land-economics consulting firm that provided demographic studies and real estate appraisals to local and county governments and private investors throughout the United States. Returning briefly to Chicago in 1951, Hoyt moved permanently to Washington, D.C., in 1953, where he was among the first planners to forecast the rapid postwar population and economic growth in the regions surrounding the nation's capital. In 1953, for example, he proposed developing a regional shopping center in Fairfax County, Virginia, when the area was still largely agricultural and, after extensive economic surveys in 1954, warned authorities in Maryland's rural Montgomery and Prince George's Counties that they faced a quarter century of suburban growth that, without careful planning, could overwhelm them. Over the next twenty years, Hoyt's consulting firm concentrated on commercial development and produced surveys, marketing studies, and maps that, by the early 1970s, had led to the construction of more than 200 shopping centers nationwide. After 1974 he was principally involved in real estate investment.

Throughout his business career, Hoyt continued his scholarly research and writing. He contributed a chapter on the effect of the automobile on urban growth and land values to Jean Labatut and Wheaton Joshua Lane, eds., *Highways in Our National Life: A Symposium* (1950) and published four books on his own: *An Economic Survey of the State of New Jersey* (1950); *World Urbanization: Expanding Population in a Shrinking World* (1962); *Where the Rich and the Poor People Live* (1966); and *According to Hoyt* (1966; revised 1970), a collection of his journal articles. In 1969 he wrote two monographs for the National Retail Merchants Association, *The Location of Additional Retail Stores in the United States in the Last One-Third of the Twentieth Century* and *People, Profits, Places.* In 1973 he published four specialized studies of historic land values in the American West produced as expert testimony for the U.S.

Department of Justice in the Indian Claims Commission cases: *Kootenai Tribe Lands in Northern Idaho and Montana, 1859; Nez Perce Tribe Lands in Northern Idaho, 1894; Northern Paiute Nation: Appraisal of Lands in Nevada and California, 1853–1863* (two volumes); and *Washoe Tribe of Indians: Appraisal of Lands in Nevada, 1862, and California, 1853.* Three other land-appraisal volumes appeared in 1974: *Cheyenne and Arapaho Lands in Colorado, Kansas, Wyoming, and Nebraska, 1865; Emigrant New York Lands in Illinois, 1832;* and *Emigrant New York Lands in Northeastern Wisconsin and Northwestern Michigan, 1832.* In addition, Hoyt was a regular contributor to professional journals, such as *American Journal of Sociology* and *Appraisal Journal,* and served on the editorial board of the journal *Land Economics* until his death. In 1967 he established the Homer Hoyt Institute, a nonprofit foundation, to underwrite university research on urban growth and land economics.

Hoyt married Gertrude O'Neill on 13 August 1941. Over time she became his principal business associate in charge of the day-to-day operations of his firm. They had one son together, and she had a son and daughter from a previous marriage. A widower for nine years, Hoyt died of pneumonia at Holy Cross Hospital in Silver Spring, Maryland, and was buried in Chicago.

★

Hoyt's papers, including his shopping-center maps and reports, are at Florida State University at Tallahassee and Marymount University in Arlington, Virginia. His son, Michael Hoyt, of Silver Spring, Maryland, who was interviewed by telephone (22 March and 14 April 1997), has twenty hours of taped reminiscences and microfilm copies of Hoyt's shopping-center studies. Obituaries are in the *Washington Post* (30 Nov. 1984) and *New York Times* (1 Dec. 1984).

ALLAN L. DAMON

HOYT, Waite Charles ("Schoolboy") (*b.* 9 September 1899 in Brooklyn, New York; *d.* 25 August 1984 in Cincinnati, Ohio), Hall of Fame baseball pitcher and baseball announcer.

Hoyt's father, Addison Hoyt, earned his living as a minstrel and a businessman; information on his mother is unavailable. Young Hoyt graduated in 1915 from Erasmus Hall High School in Brooklyn, where he attracted attention by pitching three no-hitters. At the age of fifteen he began pitching batting practice at the Polo Grounds, home of the famed New York Giants. Tired of the long subway rides and wanting more compensation, he asked manager John McGraw for a raise. Instead, McGraw gave Hoyt a contract that made him one of the country's youngest professional baseball players. He received a $5 signing bonus.

After several years in the minor leagues, Hoyt made his

Waite Hoyt. COURTESY OF THE NATIONAL BASEBALL HALL OF FAME LIBRARY, COOPERSTOWN, N.Y.

major league debut with the Giants in 1918. He struck out two of the three batters he faced in his first game and was immediately dubbed the "Schoolboy Wonder." Unimpressed, the Giants sent him to the minors. Hoyt refused to go and instead pitched semiprofessional ball. His pitching career with the Baltimore Drydocks was successful enough that he was signed by the Boston Red Sox. After two mediocre years with Boston, he was traded to the New York Yankees. This reunited him with Babe Ruth, his old Boston teammate and carousing companion. Hoyt's seasons with the Yankees were his golden years as a player. In the 1921 World Series he pitched twenty-seven innings without giving up an earned run. His best year, however, came in 1927 when he pitched for the greatest team in baseball history and led the American League in victories with twenty-two, against seven losses. In that year's World Series, which the Yankees swept four games to none, Hoyt won one game. The next year he had a record of twenty-three and seven. While a proud man with a strong will, he also knew how much he owed to his great Yankee teammates when he observed that "the secret of success as a pitcher is getting a job with the Yankees."

A man of great wit and charm, as well as possessing a command of the English language, Hoyt worked the off-season as a dancer and baritone soloist. Also, for two years he worked as a mortician dubbed the "Merry Mortician" and remarked, "I'm knocking 'em dead on Seventh Avenue while my partner is laying 'em out in Westchester."

Hoyt left the Yankees in 1930 after a dispute with the manager, Bob Shawkey, over how to pitch to heavy-hitting Al Simmons of the Philadelphia Athletics. Hoyt then pitched for several more teams: the Detroit Tigers (1930–1931); Philadelphia Athletics (1931); Brooklyn Dodgers (1932); New York Giants (1932); and Pittsburgh Pirates (1933–1937). He ended his major league career back with the Brooklyn Dodgers (1937–1938). His record of 237 wins and 182 losses gained him election to the Baseball Hall of Fame in 1969.

Hoyt was also the first pro ballplayer to make a successful transition to radio announcer. While in New York in 1927 he had a program on NBC, and in 1938 he had a show entitled *Grandstand and Bandstand* on New York's WNEW. The Cincinnati-based Burger Beer Company in 1942 signed him to broadcast the Cincinnati Reds games. He stayed at this until retirement in 1965.

At Cincinnati, Hoyt became a legend not only because of his accuracy ("When Hoyt says it's so, the Cincinnati public goes by what he says") but because of his rain-delay stories, whereby he revealed his intimate knowledge of baseball and his great narrative skills. Baseball broadcaster Red Barber observed that "Hoyt could tell baseball stories better than anybody who ever lived."

Hoyt married for a second time, wedding Betty Derie in 1983. He died of heart failure and is buried at Spring Grove Cemetery in Cincinnati.

★

There is no complete biography of Hoyt. Interviews by Eugene D. Murdock appear in the *New York Times* (4 June 1967 and 7 Feb. 1969). Obituaries appear in the *Cincinnati Enquirer* and *New York Times* (both 26 Aug. 1984).

RONALD H. RIDGLEY

HUDSON, Rock (*b.* 17 November 1925 in Winnetka, Illinois; *d.* 2 October 1985 in Beverly Hills, California), Academy Award–nominated actor who was the first major public figure to openly acknowledge that he had AIDS, bringing worldwide attention to the epidemic.

Rock Hudson was born Roy Harold Scherer, Jr., the only child of Roy Harold Scherer, Sr., an auto mechanic, and Katherine ("Kay") Wood, a homemaker who later worked as a telephone operator. The Scherers divorced when Hudson was four years old. His mother was remarried in 1932, to a former Marine Corps officer named Wallace Fitzgerald.

Rock Hudson. POPPERFOTO/ARCHIVE PHOTOS

Fitzgerald adopted Hudson, whose legal name became Roy Fitzgerald. That marriage also ended in divorce. Hudson had no siblings.

After graduating from Winnetka's New Trier High School in 1943, Hudson worked as a mail carrier. He served in the U.S. Navy from 1944 to 1946. After his discharge, he moved to California to pursue an acting career. Talent agent Henry Willson discovered Roy Fitzgerald and gave him the name Rock Hudson (a name the actor never liked). Willson was impressed by what he saw in the inexperienced but tall, good-looking, and eager newcomer. He signed the young man to a contract and sent him on countless auditions and interviews.

Director Raoul Walsh signed Rock Hudson to a personal contract and gave him a bit role in the motion picture *Fighter Squadron* (1948). The following year, Walsh sold Hudson's contract to Universal Pictures for $9,000, the amount he had spent trying to mold Hudson into a star. At Universal, Hudson studied acting, voice, fencing, and horseback riding, and was groomed for stardom alongside fellow contract players Tony Curtis, Jeff Chandler, and Piper Laurie.

In his early years at Universal, Hudson was mainly assigned minor roles in B pictures, including *Undertow* (1949), *I Was a Shoplifter* (1950), *Air Cadet* (1951), and *Tomahawk* (1951). As Hudson gained confidence and experience, he landed larger roles. After strong performances in supporting parts in *Iron Man* (1951), *Here Come the Nelsons* (1952), and *Bend of the River* (1952), he landed his first romantic leading role, in the 1952 adventure film *Scarlet Angel,* opposite Yvonne de Carlo. With *The Lawless Breed* (1952), Hudson achieved top billing for the first time in his career. In the picture, Hudson played outlaw John Wesley Hardin, who claimed in his autobiography to have killed at least forty men.

Hudson's career took an upward swing when he was cast opposite Jane Wyman in the melodrama *Magnificent Obsession,* a remake of the 1935 Irene Dunne–Robert Taylor classic. The 1954 update was a box office hit and turned Hudson into Universal's most profitable star. He received thousands of fan letters per week and was named the most popular actor of 1954 by *Modern Screen* magazine. To capitalize on Hudson's appeal with female filmgoers, Universal cast him in a series of romantic tearjerkers, including *One Desire* (1955), *All That Heaven Allows* (1955), and *Never Say Goodbye* (1956).

Hudson was one of the most popular matinee idols of the 1950s, and posters of his six-foot-four-inch muscular frame adorned many a teenage girl's bedroom. While he was romantically linked in the media with dozens of actresses, it was known within the entertainment industry that he was homosexual. On 9 November 1955, one month after *Life* magazine proclaimed him "Hollywood's Most Handsome Bachelor," Hudson married his agent Henry Willson's secretary, Phyllis Gates, in Santa Barbara, California. It is widely believed that the marriage was arranged to avert a threat by *Confidential* magazine to expose Hudson's secret. Gates always contended that it was a true marriage and that she had no knowledge of any arrangement. The marriage ended in divorce in 1958.

Hudson won the coveted role of Bick Benedict in the film version of Edna Ferber's *Giant* (1956) over such established stars as William Holden, Clark Gable, and Gary Cooper. It would prove to be the most important role of his career, earning him his only Academy Award nomination. Hudson lost the best actor statuette to Yul Brynner of *The King and I.* Hudson's costar in *Giant,* James Dean, was killed in an automobile accident during the production.

After earning accolades for his dramatic roles in *Battle Hymn* (1956), *Something of Value* (1957), and *A Farewell to Arms* (1957), Hudson opted for a change of pace. Though he had no prior experience with comedic acting, he accepted the starring role in the 1959 romantic comedy *Pillow Talk.* His leading lady, Doris Day, coached him, and the two launched a successful screen partnership, appearing together in *Lover Come Back* (1961) and *Send Me No Flow-*

ers (1964). Hudson, who then ranked as the top-grossing actor in the United States, also played romantic comedy leads in *Come September* (1961) and *Man's Favorite Sport?* (1964). He continued to take dramatic parts (including the role of an atheist who finally accepts God in 1962's *The Spiral Road*), but audiences preferred to see him in the "sex comedy" genre for which he was known.

The expiration of Hudson's contract with Universal Pictures in 1965 signaled the end of an era. He was the last major star under exclusive contract with a studio, and his decision to freelance after sixteen years at Universal marked the end of the studio-contract-player system. As a free agent, Hudson had the opportunity to choose from a wider selection of scripts. For his first film as a freelancer, he chose *Seconds* (1966), a dark drama far different from the frothy comedies the public had come to expect of him. Although Hudson received excellent reviews for his performance, the film was a box office failure. He fared better in *Ice Station Zebra* (1968), a grand-scale adventure film set at the North Pole.

Hudson's film career then began to decline. *The Undefeated* (1969), *Hornet's Nest* (1970), *Darling Lili* (1970), and *Pretty Maids All in a Row* (1971) were commercial and critical disappointments. With fewer film scripts being offered to him, he turned to other media. His biggest successes of the 1970s were in television and on the stage. Fulfilling a career-long ambition to do live theater, Hudson toured in stage productions of *I Do! I Do!, John Brown's Body*, and *On the Twentieth Century*. From 1971 to 1977 he played police commissioner Stewart McMillan on the television drama series *McMillan and Wife* (which was renamed *McMillan* in 1977 after costar Susan Saint James left the show). At $50,000 per episode, Hudson was the highest-paid actor on television at the time.

Although Hudson had lived with men both before and after his marriage to Phyllis Gates, Tom Clark was the first of Hudson's male paramours whom he went out with openly. A longtime friend, Clark moved in with Hudson in 1971, at which time he left his career as a publicist to become Hudson's personal manager. Because of their business relationship, the couple never aroused suspicion when they were seen together in public. The relationship ended in 1983, by which time Hudson had begun seeing Marc Christian, a self-described musicologist, who was living with Hudson at the time of the actor's death.

In the 1980s, Hudson starred in several high-rated television movies and miniseries, including *Arthur Hailey's Wheels* and *The Martian Chronicles*. On 2 November 1981 he underwent open-heart surgery. His surgery, compounded with production problems, resulted in a one-year delay of the debut of his short-lived detective drama series on television, *The Devlin Connection. The Ambassador*

(1984), Hudson's final motion picture, was withdrawn from general release after New York audiences booed it.

In June 1984 Rock Hudson was diagnosed with AIDS, a disease that at that time was believed to be confined to the homosexual community. For that reason, he kept the diagnosis a secret.

Despite his illness, Hudson accepted a role on the television series *Dynasty*. Due to the popularity of his character, the producers intended to star Hudson in a spin-off series, but signs of his weakening physical condition became evident. His *Dynasty* character was killed off after nine episodes. Hudson made his last television appearance on the cable talk show *Doris Day's Best Friends,* hosted by his good friend and former costar. Hudson's frail appearance at a press conference promoting the appearance caused reporters to speculate on the state of his health. It was variously reported that he was suffering from liver cancer, anemia, and the flu. On 25 July 1985, ten days after the press conference, Hudson's publicist announced that he had AIDS. The announcement stunned the world and made Rock Hudson the lead news story on the evening news throughout the world.

The following October, Hudson succumbed to the AIDS virus at his home at 9402 Beverly Crest Drive in Beverly Hills, where he had resided since the early 1960s. His body was cremated. A $250,000 donation Hudson made before his death helped establish the American Foundation for AIDS Research.

After Hudson's death, his lover Marc Christian filed a $10 million claim against the actor's estate, charging that Hudson continued their relationship after learning he had AIDS, without informing Christian of his illness. A jury awarded Christian $14.5 million but the estate appealed the decision. An out-of-court settlement was reached in August 1991, the terms of which were not disclosed.

Rock Hudson was a movie giant, one of the biggest stars Hollywood ever produced. His name topped the box office polls throughout the late 1950s and early 1960s. Though his career spanned thirty-seven years, with seventy-one films and hundreds of hours of television work to his credit, the revelation of his homosexuality and his death from AIDS have overshadowed his remarkable career in the memories of many moviegoers.

It was not until 1985 that the public learned of Rock Hudson's "double life." However, a *Films in Review* article ten years earlier had spoken of a dual life: "No matter how good a performance Rock Hudson ever gives, it is doubtful he will ever give as good a performance as the one which has been given by Roy Fitzgerald as Rock Hudson."

★

Rock Hudson and Sara Davidson, *Rock Hudson: His Story* (1986) was written by Davidson with Hudson's cooperation, although the star was already dying and was reportedly incoherent much of the six weeks that Davidson worked with him. Davidson interviewed many of Hudson's friends and associates and was granted access to his files and correspondence. Tom Clark, *Rock Hudson: Friend of Mine* (1990), with Dick Kleiner, is a recollection of the actor by Hudson's longtime companion. In Phyllis Gates and Bob Thom, *My Husband, Rock Hudson: The Real Story of Rock Hudson's Marriage to Phyllis Gates* (1987), Gates relates the story of her three-year union with Hudson. Mark Bego, *Rock Hudson, Public and Private: An Unauthorized Biography* (1986), written by the former editor in chief of *Modern Screen* magazine, offers an examination of Hudson's career and personal life. Brenda Scott Royce, *Rock Hudson: A Bio-Bibliography* (1995), presents a thorough examination of Hudson's life and career, with details on each of his film, television, and stage appearances.

James Robert Parish, *Hollywood's Great Love Teams* (1974) includes a lengthy chapter on Rock Hudson and Doris Day, with filmographies and biographical sketches. James Robert Parish and Don E. Stanke, with Michael R. Pitts, *The All-Americans* (1977), features an in-depth biographical essay on the star. Boze Hadleigh, *Conversations with My Elders* (1986), includes excerpts from two interviews with Hudson, in which the actor openly discusses his homosexuality. Jimmie Hicks, "Rock Hudson: The Film Actor as Romantic Hero," *Films in Review* (May 1975), is one of the most thorough magazine articles charting Hudson's career. An obituary is in the *New York Times* (3 Oct. 1985).

BRENDA SCOTT ROYCE

HUGHES, Emmet John (*b*. 26 December 1920 in Newark, New Jersey; *d*. 19 September 1982 in Princeton, New Jersey), journalist, author, political adviser, and professor who had a subtle yet influential impact upon American politics.

Hughes was the son of John L. Hughes, a county court judge, and Grace Freeman. After graduating summa cum laude from Princeton University with an A.B. degree in 1941, Hughes began graduate study in history with Professor Carlton J. Hayes at Columbia University. When Hayes was appointed U.S. ambassador to Spain in 1942, he made Hughes his press attaché. Hughes served from 1942 to 1946 in North Africa with the U.S. Army's Office of Strategic Services. He later resumed his service with Hayes as director of the Office of War Information in Madrid. In 1944 Hughes published *The Church and the Liberal Society* and in 1947 *Report from Spain,* both of which dealt with Catholicism and democracy. He assessed Francisco Franco's military rule in Spain as "a government without the people, above the people and against the people."

After World War II, Hughes became successively the Rome and Berlin bureau chief for Time-Life and developed a working relationship with Clare Boothe Luce. From 1949 to 1952, he was articles editor of *Life* magazine and a New Deal Democrat. However, during those three years, he

Emmet John Hughes. ARCHIVE PHOTOS

came to the conclusion that only a new Republican administration would have "the *freedom*—the *chance*—to think anew and to act anew."

Hughes joined Dwight D. ("Ike") Eisenhower's campaign in 1952, becoming what Eisenhower would describe as a "part-time word carpenter." Hughes, a self-avowed liberal who was aggressively anticommunist, was assigned to work on a speech Ike was scheduled to deliver at the Masonic Temple in Detroit on 24 October. Sherman Adams, Eisenhower's chief campaign adviser, remembered that the staff agreed on the need for a strong message attacking the Democratic administration's policies on the Korean War. Adams recalled: "While he was drafting the speech, Hughes was struck by the dramatic possibilities in having Eisenhower promise that he would make a personal trip to Korea. He built up a discussion of foreign policy centered on the Korean situation that came to a stirring finish with Eisenhower declaring, 'That job requires a personal trip to Korea. I shall make that trip. I shall go to Korea!'"

Hughes anticipated that General Eisenhower would criticize the draft as too provocative and flamboyant. Instead, Eisenhower reviewed it with animated and approv-

ing expressions and then reached for a pencil to enhance the dramatic impact of the key sentence. The candidate and his staff expected the speech to have a breathtaking impact on the campaign. Reporters who were given advance copies agreed; according to Adams, they said excitedly, "That does it—Ike is in." The speech had the same immediate effect on the audience in Detroit and on the television and radio audiences across the country. As Jack Bell, the Associated Press political reporter, wrote, "For all practical purposes, the contest ended that night."

During the first year of Eisenhower's administration, Hughes was the president's main speechwriter. Blanche W. Cook, a scholar of the Eisenhower presidency, contends that the president's "Chance for Peace" address to the American Society of Newspaper Editors on 16 April 1953 was a luminous appeal for "international harmony." Eisenhower thoughtfully scrutinized the speech, which was prepared by W. W. Rostow, D. D. Jackson, and Hughes. Although the president approved every word of each draft, he reluctantly acquiesced to his staff's skepticism about promoting détente. In his memoirs, Hughes explained that Eisenhower declined to propose a "U.S.-Soviet exchange of radio-and-TV time" because it was "too much of a publicity stunt" and omitted a "renewed offer to travel to meet Soviet leaders" because it tipped the "balance between *firm* and *conciliatory*" and might "suggest an over-anxiety far from our intentions." Adams, crediting Hughes with eloquently expressing Eisenhower's ideas, called the presentation to the newspaper editors "the most effective speech of Eisenhower's public career, and certainly one of the highlights of his presidency." The address, which urged the Soviet Union to work toward peace and arms control, received international praise.

Hughes's early characterization and assessment of Eisenhower in the 1950s has endured. "The man—and the President—was never more decisive," according to Hughes, "than when he held to a steely resolve *not* to do something that he sincerely believed wrong in itself or alien to his office." Subsequent historical scholarship on Eisenhower as president has conformed with that judgment of Ike's governing style. Some of Hughes's other insider perspectives proved troublesome. Eisenhower preferred empirically grounded realities, and Hughes thought Secretary of State John Foster Dulles provided only a lawyer's "surfeit of abstractions and generalizations." Hughes later acknowledged that his exuberant prediction that the Eisenhower-Dulles relationship would be short-lived was egregiously wrongheaded. Hughes returned to *Life* magazine as a special European correspondent in 1954.

Hughes's later criticisms of Eisenhower's "political naïveté" eventually led to their estrangement. They became so alienated that, after leaving office, Eisenhower minimized Hughes's role in composing the decisive 1952 campaign speech. Hughes wrote two books of bitter recollection, *America the Vincible* (1959) and *The Ordeal of Power* (1963), which convey a sense of his infuriation with the betrayal of close Eisenhower associates. In his memoir of Eisenhower's presidency, William Ewald wrote that Hughes's books had a "trenchant impact on the future course of American politics." Hughes's comments were used by John F. Kennedy, a Democrat, in the 1960 presidential campaign. In 1964 Hughes worked for the presidential campaign of Nelson A. Rockefeller, and consequently Eisenhower maintained a profound distrust of Rockefeller.

From 1963 to 1968, Hughes was a columnist for *Newsweek* and an editorial consultant for the *Washington Post,* then a special assistant to Rockefeller. In 1970 he became a professor of political science at the Eagleton Institute of Rutgers University. He published a respected set of reflections, *The Living Presidency,* in 1973. Hughes married three times and had five children; he died of heart disease.

★

The Emmet John Hughes Collection is at the Princeton University library. Robert A. Divine employs Hughes's recollections in *Eisenhower and the Cold War* (1981), which points out Eisenhower's self-restraint. Robert J. Donovan, *Eisenhower: The Inside Story* (1956), is an indispensable memoir by a journalist. Hughes is mentioned frequently in Sherman Adams, *Firsthand Report* (1961), and Henry Kissinger, *The Necessity for Choice: Prospects of American Foreign Policy* (1961). Eisenhower's personal comments on Hughes are in his *Mandate for Change: 1953–1956* (1963). On Hughes's anticommunism, see Whittaker Chambers's judgments in William F. Buckley, ed., *Odyssey of a Friend: Whittaker Chambers' Letters to William F. Buckley, Jr., 1954–1961* (1969). Blanche W. Cook, *The Declassified Eisenhower* (1981), characterizes Hughes as one of Eisenhower's "psychological warriors." The best contemporary perspective with a discerning historical assessment is William Bragg Ewald, Jr., *Eisenhower the President: Crucial Days, 1951–1960* (1981). See also Townsend Hoopes, *The Devil and John Foster Dulles* (1973), and Richard A. Melanson and David Mayers, eds., *Reevaluating Eisenhower: American Foreign Policy in the 1950s* (1987). An obituary is in the *New York Times* (20 Sept. 1982).

FRANK ANNUNZIATA

HUNTER, Alberta (*b.* 1 April 1895 in Memphis, Tennessee; *d.* 17 October 1984 in New York City), vocalist, entertainer, and composer of popular songs who performed with many noted musicians in a career that spanned much of the twentieth century.

One of three surviving children of Charles E. Hunter, a sleeping-car porter, and Laura Peterson, a housewife and chambermaid in a brothel, Hunter had little formal education and at the age of eleven ran away to Chicago, where she found work as a cook. The girl obtained her first sing-

Alberta Hunter, 1940s. ARCHIVE PHOTOS/FRANK DRIGGS COLLECTION

ing job at a bar known as Dago Frank's and performed at other venues in the city. On 27 January 1919 she married Willard Saxby Townsend. They had no children and were divorced on 23 March 1923.

Even in her twenties Hunter was influencing vocalists such as Al Jolson and Sophie Tucker. Her voice was mellow and not as strident as that of some of the so-called classic blues singers. At times she delivered the words in a semi-spoken manner and used a slight vibrato. She was equally adept at slow or up-tempo numbers using both polite and ribald lyrics. In 1921, while singing at the Dreamland Cafe in Chicago, she started recording for the Black Swan label, accompanied by Fletcher Henderson. Later, she sang backup with Eubie Blake and Louis Armstrong, among others. She also began writing music. One of her songs, "Down-Hearted Blues," was jazz singer Bessie Smith's first recording in 1923.

In that same year, Hunter moved to New York City, where she appeared in the all-black comedy *How Come?* at the Apollo Theater. After the closing of this production, she sang on radio for the first time in March 1924, on station WJZ. Later she toured with other black entertainers on the vaudeville circuit called TOBA (Theater Owners' Booking Association); they were humiliated and required to work under deplorable conditions. A longtime supporter of the National Association for the Advancement of Colored People, Hunter opposed segregation and racial discrimination.

On 5 August 1927 Hunter left for France and for what became an extended European stay. She viewed travel as a substitute for the formal education she never had. On 27 January 1928 she reached London and joined the cast of the musical *Show Boat,* which opened on 3 May 1928. She played the role of Queenie with Paul Robeson as the male lead. After the show closed, she sailed for New York City in May 1929.

Due in part to the racial prejudice, which had not abated in the United States, Hunter had to take whatever work she could find: recording for the Columbia label and touring on the vaudeville circuit. Moreover, the Great Depression of the 1930s took its toll on opportunities for work in the entertainment field, although, as her itinerary shows, she was employed both in the United States and in Europe, where she learned to speak several languages. From 1933 to 1938 she toured regularly in Europe and from 1938 to 1940 frequently appeared with the Henry Levine Orchestra on the *Alberta Hunter Show* on radio station WJZ in New York City. She also performed in a nonsinging role with Ethel Waters in the show *Mamba's Daughters* in 1939 and 1940.

During World War II and the Korean conflict, Hunter toured with United Service Organizations (USO) shows. In Germany in 1945 she provided a command performance for General Dwight Eisenhower and Russian marshal Georgi Zhukov. When not performing with the USO groups, she appeared in clubs and shows in the United States and Canada. In 1954 and 1955 she was an understudy for a role in the show *Mrs. Patterson,* starring Eartha Kitt.

In 1955 Hunter's mother died. The event prompted her to give up her singing career to become a volunteer at a Harlem Hospital so that she could, in her own words, "help humanity." On 16 December 1955 she passed her elementary school equivalency examination. Initially her application for study to become a nurse's aide was denied, but with persistence she was accepted in a Licensed Practical Nurse training program in 1956. She completed the courses and was duly licensed in August 1957. Hunter worked at New York City's Goldwater Memorial Hospital. The hospital personnel thought that they had a fifty-year-old woman starting a new career; she was really sixty-two. Few of her colleagues knew that she was a famous entertainer.

In January 1977 Hunter was told that she had reached the hospital's mandatory retirement age of seventy. In re-

ality, she was eighty-two. In May, Hunter was received back into the entertainment field. That summer, at a bon voyage party for singer Mabel Mercer hosted by pianist Bobby Short, Hunter was prevailed upon to sing. The guests were so enthusiastic that she was introduced to Barney Josephson, owner of a New York City club, the Cookery. He arranged for her to appear there, beginning on 10 October 1977. Subsequently her stay was extended indefinitely while she toured with Josephson as her manager and his club as her base of operations.

Shortly after her opening at the Cookery, movie producer Robert Altman commissioned Hunter to record the soundtrack for his film *Remember My Name,* which opened in Memphis in October 1978. She returned to Beale Street and was honored on "Alberta Hunter Day." On 23 March 1978 the Tennessee House of Representatives passed a resolution recognizing Hunter's contribution to the musical genre of the blues, and the following June she appeared at Carnegie Hall in a show that was part of the program of the twenty-fifth Newport Jazz Festival. On 7 January 1979 she sang at the Smithsonian Institution and at the end of February was invited to appear in a performance at the White House. Following these and other appearances, Hunter went on tour despite the misgivings of her friends, who believed that the program would be too strenuous for someone her age.

In June 1980 Hunter broke a wrist and a hip; in February 1981 she broke her left leg and had a pacemaker implanted. Despite these problems she continued to perform and to record for the Columbia label; she also received royalties for songs which she had written years earlier. On 16 November 1980 she received the Handy Award as traditional female blues artist of the year from the Blues Foundation of Memphis. In November 1980 she recorded a Voice of America program that would broadcast the story of her life overseas. Although she declined an invitation to attend a farewell party for President Jimmy Carter on 7 January 1981, she paid her respects by autographing a copy of an album of hers that included the song "Georgia on My Mind" and sending it to Carter.

In 1983 Hunter was invited to perform in São Paulo, Brazil. Her three-week appearance was a huge success, and at the end of May 1984 she returned to Brazil for another month's appearance. Back in New York City, she tried to continue working at the Cookery, but failing health prevented her from doing so. On her final television appearance, the *Good Morning America* show of 10 September 1984, her memory failed as she was singing. She died five weeks later from heart failure in her New York City apartment. Her remains were cremated, and the ashes were buried at Ferncliff Cemetery in Hartsdale, New York.

Although Alberta Hunter is credited with being a blues singer, she was more a performer of vaudeville than of the classic blues. She wrote some seventy songs, and her style was such that she returned from virtual obscurity to what amounted to a second career.

★

Frank C. Taylor with Gerald Cook, *Alberta Hunter: A Celebration in Blues* (1987), the only full-length biography, contains an extensive discography. Excellent, though brief, coverage is in Whitney Balliett, "Let It Be Classy: Alberta Hunter," in *American Singers* (1979); and Daphne Duval Harrison, "She's Got a Mind to Ramble: Alberta Hunter," in *Black Pearls: Blues Queens of the 1920s* (1988). Sheldon Harris, "Alberta Hunter," in *Blues Who's Who: A Biographical Dictionary of Blues Singers* (1979; rev. ed. 1993), provides detailed coverage of her tours and performances, as well as a photograph. Lawrence Cohn, *Nothing but the Blues: The Music and the Musicians* (1993), supplies the broad context within which Hunter performed. Gerald Clarke, "Good Tunes from an Old Violin: At Eighty-Seven Alberta Hunter Is Better Than Ever," *Time* (13 Dec. 1982), summarizes her life, with emphasis on her return to performing after her nursing career.

An obituary is in the *New York Times* (19 Oct. 1984); an editorial tribute is in the *New York Times* (21 Oct. 1984). Compact discs of her recordings are available. One that covers Hunter's earlier career is *Young Alberta Hunter: The 20s and 30s* (Mojo Records, 1996). A video is *Alberta Hunter: Jazz at the Smithsonian.* (Sony, 1982).

BARRETT G. POTTER

I-J

INGERSOLL, Ralph McAllister (*b.* 8 December 1900 in New Haven, Connecticut; *d.* 8 March 1985 in Miami Beach, Florida), journalist instrumental in the early development of the *New Yorker* and *Fortune* magazines, and the founding publisher of the crusading New York City tabloid *PM.*

Ralph Ingersoll was the youngest of three surviving children of Colin Mcrae Ingersoll, Jr., an engineer, and Theresa McAllister, a socialite. The family moved to New York City in 1906; his mother died four years later. Ingersoll attended local private schools and showed an early interest in writing. At age fifteen he entered prep school at Hotchkiss. In 1918 he enrolled in Yale University and its Sheffield Scientific School, where he studied science and engineering. After his graduation from Yale with a B.S. in 1921, he worked for mining companies in California, Arizona, and Mexico.

In the spring of 1923, Ingersoll returned to New York City, where he served a short stint as a reporter on the *New York American* (September 1923 to February 1924) and wrote a book, *In and Under Mexico* (1924). In June 1925 he landed a job at the *New Yorker,* then four months old. By the end of the year, he was editing the magazine's "Talk of the Town" section and was officially listed as its managing editor. On 18 November 1926 he married Mary Elizabeth Carden. She contracted tuberculosis less than a year later, and for most of their marriage Ingersoll saw her on weekends only. They had no children.

After building up Ingersoll into his right-hand man, *New Yorker* editor Harold Ross began to resent and denigrate him. So in the summer of 1930, when *Time* magazine publisher Henry Luce offered Ingersoll the position of associate editor with the newly founded *Fortune* magazine, Ingersoll accepted. By early 1932, Ingersoll was *Fortune*'s managing editor, and it had developed into one of the most exciting magazines of the 1930s, both visually and editorially.

Ingersoll's career took an unexpected turn in late 1935, when Luce named him vice president and general manager of Time Inc. Ingersoll essentially ran the company for a year, and it was during that year that the prototype for a new picture magazine, *Life,* was finalized. *Life* was launched on 19 November 1936, and its success nearly bankrupted the company, because its first-year advertising rates had been set artificially low by a cautious Luce. The crisis pulled Luce back into the trenches. He took over the running of *Life* himself and made Ingersoll the publisher of *Time,* where Ingersoll was responsible for making enough money to support the new magazine. Ingersoll agreed to the change, but with a caveat: when *Life* turned a profit, he would leave Time Inc.

By late 1937, *Life* was in the black. Luce offered Ingersoll $1 million in Time stock if he would stay for another five years. Ingersoll refused to commit to a full five years but offered to stay as long as Luce needed him. In return, Luce offered Ingersoll a sabbatical year of his own choosing, so that he might pursue a publication of his own.

Meanwhile, complications had developed in Ingersoll's personal life. In 1935 he had met playwright Lillian Hellman, and their mutual attraction quickly accelerated into an intense love affair. When Ingersoll asked for a divorce, however, his wife's tuberculosis flared up, setting a pattern that eventually put an end to his romance with Hellman. Ingersoll's divorce was not final until later in 1935, by which time his romance with Hellman was essentially over. During his involvement with Hellman, Ingersoll's politics, already liberal, had moved further left, and he began to envision a newspaper that would transform society. In 1937 Ingersoll became romantically involved with Laura Z. Hobson, then a promotion writer at Time, Inc. Their tumultuous three-year relationship sent both of them into analysis. In Hobson's first novel, *The Trespassers* (1943), the character of the radio tycoon Jason Crown was based, none too flatteringly, on Ingersoll.

In 1939 Ingersoll began his sabbatical from Time Inc. and raised the $1.5 million he estimated he needed to launch a newspaper: one that would report the news honestly and without sensationalism, deliver magazine quality in its articles and photography, and be so independent it would not contain advertising.

PM's first issue, on 18 June 1940, sold out, but a month later its circulation slipped below the 200,000 level that was needed to break even. The paper was saved by Marshall Field III, later the founding publisher of the *Chicago Sun,* who bought out the other investors. *PM* did begin to make its mark, however, not through the lofty aspirations with which it was launched but as the only major metropolitan daily in the United States that openly advocated U.S. involvement in World War II.

In the fall of 1940 Ingersoll went to Britain to cover the war. From 18 November to 9 December of that year, every issue of *PM* carried a major story from Ingersoll, and Simon & Schuster rushed a compilation of them, *Report on England* (1940), into print. A series of pro-interventionist articles were collected in another book, *America Is Worth Fighting For* (1941). Ingersoll traveled to Russia in 1941, and his Russia series was collected in *Action on All Fronts: A Personal Account of This War* (1942). After the United States entered the war, Ingersoll turned the paper's energies to exposing anything standing in the way of total mobilization, from lax munitions manufacturers to fascist sympathizers. In June 1942, when Ingersoll, then forty-one, was classified A-1 for service in the U.S. Army, he carried his argument that he was being drafted in retaliation for *PM's* political stances to the paper's front page, then enlisted.

Ingersoll thrived on army life, coming out of basic training a sergeant and rising to lieutenant colonel before the end of the war. During a military research trip to North Africa, he finagled his way to the front and wrote a book about the experience, *The Battle Is the Payoff* (1943). In England, he ran a special plans section that helped disguise the planned D-day invasion. Another notable Ingersoll deception project involved flooding the airwaves with enough false radio activity to mask the open movement of Patton's Third Army during the Battle of the Bulge. General Omar Bradley awarded him with the Legion of Merit for that contribution.

After the Allied victory in Europe, Ingersoll returned to the United States, where he fell in love with Elaine Keiffer Cobb, a staff writer at *Life* magazine. They were married in August 1945, at Lake Tahoe, Nevada, and settled in Lakeville, Connecticut, where Ingersoll worked on another book, *Top Secret* (1946), which argued that Bradley, not Dwight D. Eisenhower, deserved the greater part of the credit for the Allied victory in Europe.

In January 1946 Ingersoll returned to *PM,* which had continued publication in his absence, minus much of his verve. When Ingersoll tried to institute changes, a destructive battle with the Newspaper Guild and intense in-house fighting between the procommunist and anticommunist left, both well-represented at *PM,* resulted. That fall, when Field reversed the paper's no-advertising policy, Ingersoll was almost relieved to have an excuse to resign. The paper folded a few years later, in 1949.

Ingersoll set to work on a novel, *The Great Ones* (1948), which was widely viewed as a roman à clef about Henry and Clare Boothe Luce and received scathing reviews. Ingersoll's first child, Ralph II, was born in 1946. A second son, Jonathan III, was born on 1 April 1948; a few hours after the delivery, Elaine died.

His wife's death left Ingersoll shattered, and in its af-

Ralph Ingersoll. CORBIS-BETTMANN

termath he made a 180-degree career turn, devoting the rest of his professional life to making money. His avowed reason was that he owed it to Elaine to earn enough money to raise their sons properly. To former *PM* staffer Max Lerner, however, he gave another reason: "I wanted to beat those S.O.B.'s at their own game." Thereafter, frequently in partnership with others, he acquired a profitable string of small newspapers located primarily in the Northeast. He did not involve himself with the editorial policies of his purchases.

In November 1948 Ingersoll married Mary Hill Doolittle, largely because he felt that she would be a good mother to his sons. The marriage was not a happy one, and they divorced in 1962. In 1964 he married Thelma Bradford, the widow of artist Francis Scott Bradford; their marriage lasted until his death.

In 1975 Ralph II became the chief operating officer of Ingersoll Publications. Friction developed between him and his father, which culminated in an open split in 1982, when Ralph II and the other partners forced Ingersoll's resignation. Ingersoll died of complications arising from a stroke.

An abrasive bigger-than-life personality, Ingersoll contributed significantly to the early development of two of the most distinctive magazines in the twentieth century, the *New Yorker* and *Fortune.* Ironically, in his own publication, *PM,* he was unable to perform the service for himself that he had for Ross and Luce—transforming vision into reality.

★

Ingersoll's papers, which include several unpublished volumes of his autobiography, are at Boston University; papers relating to his years at Time Inc. are retained by the company. Roy Hoopes, *Ralph Ingersoll: A Biography* (1985), is the most complete source on Ingersoll's life and career. See also Ralph Ingersoll, *Point of Departure: An Adventure in Autobiography* (1961), the first and only published volume of a projected five-volume autobiography; Laura Z. Hobson, *Laura Z.: A Life* (1983) and *Laura Z: A Life— Years of Fulfillment* (1986); William Wright, *Lillian Hellman* (1986); and Wolcott Gibbs, "A Very Active Type Man," *New Yorker* (2 May and 9 May 1942). An obituary is in the *New York Times* (9 Mar. 1985).

LYNN HOOGENBOOM

IRISH, Edward Simmons, Sr. ("Ned") (*b.* 6 May 1905 in Lake George, New York; *d.* 21 January 1982 in Venice, Florida), sportswriter, sports promoter, and basketball executive, best known for popularizing college and professional basketball.

Irish, the son of Clifford Irish, who rented boats, and Madeleine Lancaster, a practical nurse and dermatologist, was left fatherless at age three and grew up in Brooklyn, New York. He graduated from Erasmus Hall High School in

Ned Irish, 1936. UPI/CORBIS-BETTMANN

Brooklyn in 1924 after covering high school sports for several local newspapers.

Irish worked his way through the University of Pennsylvania, serving as campus correspondent for the *Philadelphia Record.* After earning his B.S. degree in economics in 1928, he joined the *New York World-Telegram* sports staff. To supplement his $60-a-week salary, Irish served as public relations director for the New York Giants football club from 1930 to 1940 and operated the National Football League's information bureau. He wrote for the *World-Telegram* until becoming sports promoter of the Madison Square Garden Corporation in 1934. He later became acting president of the Garden from 1941 to 1945, executive vice president from 1945 to 1960, and president from 1960 to 1974. In 1931 Irish began assisting New York City mayor James J. Walker in promoting benefit basketball games at Madison Square Garden to raise money for unemployment relief. From 1931 to 1933 capacity Garden crowds watched three tripleheaders involving six New York City colleges.

Irish favored making college basketball more accessible to New Yorkers. Few schools owned facilities big enough to make college basketball profitable. Columbia University and Fordham University were the only metropolitan schools with gymnasiums seating more than 1,200 people. A 1933 basketball game at the tiny Manhattan College gymnasium convinced Irish that college basketball should be

415

moved into bigger quarters after, or so the story goes, he tore his trousers fighting his way into the cramped arena through an athletic department window.

Irish worked out a rental arrangement with Madison Square Garden, with a seating capacity just over 16,000, for the nation's first regular season college basketball doubleheader. With the consent of Garden president John Reed Kilpatrick, he invited premier college basketball teams from other sections of the country to play local college basketball powers at the Garden. Irish guaranteed the Garden $4,000, the average cost of renting the arena for one night. He handled scheduling, controlled ticket sales, and directed publicity. The Garden shared profits above the guarantee on a percentage basis.

Irish arranged the first intersectional college doubleheader at the Garden on 29 December 1934. That night, 16,188 fans watched New York University defeat the University of Notre Dame, 25–18, and Westminster College of Pennsylvania edge out St. John's University, 37–33. Ticket sales exceeded building rental costs by more than $4,000. Irish booked seven more doubleheaders that season, drawing more than 12,000 fans per contest. The Garden quickly became the showplace of college basketball. Record crowds watched eastern powers City College of New York, Long Island University, New York University, and St. John's challenge the nation's best intercollegiate basketball teams from 1935 to 1949. Irish's doubleheaders put college basketball on a sound financial footing, broadened the sport's audience, and sparked a tremendous upsurge in intersectional play.

Stanford University defeated Long Island University, 45–31, in a classic December 1936 intersectional game at the Garden. Hank Luisetti dazzled the 17,623 spectators with his running one-handed shots, propelling Stanford's innovative fast-break offense to victory and ending the LIU Blackbirds' forty-three-game winning streak. The contest, often considered the first modern college basketball game, revolutionized shooting and popularized the sport in the New York metropolitan area.

Under Irish's direction college basketball doubleheaders drew more than 500,000 spectators per season to the Garden from 1942 to 1949. Attendance reached a peak average of 18,196 per game in 1946. His intersectional college basketball doubleheaders stopped suddenly with the disclosure in 1951 of a point-shaving scandal involving thirty-two players from seven colleges. Thereafter, Garden doubleheaders matched only local college teams and drew small crowds.

In March 1938 Irish started the National Invitation Tournament (NIT). The best teams squared off at the Garden in the nation's first major postseason collegiate basketball tournament. Temple University defeated the University of Colorado, 60–36, in the title game. Oklahoma

A&M University, coached by the legendary Hank Iba, and New York University also participated. The National Collegiate Athletic Association (NCAA) tournament, begun in 1939, played second fiddle until the scandals discredited the NIT in 1951.

Irish also helped establish the eleven-team Basketball Association of America and the New York Knickerbockers in 1946. The BAA merged with the National Basketball League in 1949 to form the National Basketball Association (NBA). Irish insisted that home teams keep all gate receipts, an ideal arrangement for his Garden, with its large seating capacity. Irish served as Knicks president from 1946 to 1974. His club defeated the Toronto Huskies, 68–66, at Toronto in the first game in BAA history.

Irish built the Knickerbockers into a formidable franchise, signing Dick McGuire, Max Zaslofsky, Ernie Vandeweghe, Harry Gallatin, and Carl Braun. In 1950 he helped integrate the NBA by acquiring Nat "Sweetwater" Clifton from the Harlem Globetrotters. The Knicks reached the NBA finals three consecutive times, losing narrowly to the Rochester Royals in 1951 and the Minneapolis Lakers in 1952 and decisively to the Lakers in 1953. The Knicks struggled for the next decade until Irish shrewdly rebuilt the team. He drafted Willis Reed, Bill Bradley, Cazzie Russell, and Walt Frazier; acquired Dick Barnett, Dave DeBusschere, Jerry Lucas, and Earl Monroe in trades; and selected Red Holzman as coach. The rejuvenated Knicks won their first two NBA titles, defeating the Los Angeles Lakers in 1970 and 1973.

Irish favored merging the NBA with the rival American Basketball Association. He sought to persuade other NBA owners in 1969 that the rival leagues could not survive financially, but all-out bidding wars continued until the two leagues merged in 1976.

Irish, a sharp-featured, thin-lipped Brooklynite, possessed a brusque, serious manner. Contemporaries often regarded him as arrogant, tough, and aloof. He married Katharine B. Bridgman on 1 February 1929 and had one son. Irish was survived by his second wife, Jacqueline, whom he married in 1971. He received the National Association of Basketball Coaches Metropolitan Award in 1942 and was elected to the Naismith Memorial Basketball Hall of Fame in 1964. Irish died of a heart attack and was cremated.

A sportswriter, promoter, and executive, Irish popularized basketball as a spectator sport and made New York the mecca of college basketball. By sponsoring intersectional play, he nationalized the game. He also helped establish professional basketball leagues and guided the New York Knickerbockers through their formative period.

★

There is no book-length biography of Irish, but his file at the Naismith Memorial Basketball Hall of Fame in Springfield, Massachusetts, provides biographical data. Sandy Padwe, *Basketball's Hall of Fame* (1970), reviews his career. Brad Herzog, *The Sports 100* (1995), explains his importance in sports history. Stanley Frank, "Basketball's Big Wheel," *Saturday Evening Post* (15 Jan. 1949), and Roger Kahn, "Success and Ned Irish," *Sports Illustrated* (27 Mar. 1961), are accounts of his work. An obituary is in the *New York Times* (22 Jan. 1982).

DAVID L. PORTER

JACKSON, Henry Martin ("Scoop") (*b.* 31 May 1912 in Everett, Washington; *d.* 1 September 1983 in Everett, Washington), an expert on military, national security, and environmental affairs who profoundly influenced U.S. policy during a congressional career that spanned from January 1941 until September 1983.

Jackson was the youngest of five children born to Peter Jackson and Marine Anderson, both of whom immigrated to Washington State in the late nineteenth century from their native Norway. His father, a building contractor in Everett, was renowned for his reliability, and his mother, devoutly religious and doting, instilled in Henry Jackson the virtue of hard work and the ambition for achievement.

Senator Henry ("Scoop") Jackson, *c.* 1970. LIBRARY OF CONGRESS/CORBIS

As a teenager, Jackson achieved local fame for the record he set by delivering 74,880 copies of the *Everett Herald* without a single complaint. His oldest sister began calling him "Scoop" after a comic-strip character that he resembled. This name stuck with him for his entire life, even in Congress. At Everett High School, he excelled in history and debating. He worked his way through the University of Washington during the Great Depression, with the help of his sister Gertrude, and he earned a law degree there in 1935. He practiced law briefly in Everett before becoming the youngest prosecutor in the history of Snohomish County. Abstemious and serious, Jackson quickly earned the reputation as an incorruptible foe of prostitution, slot machines, and bootlegging that had plagued Everett since Prohibition.

Capitalizing on his prominence as a successful prosecutor, Jackson successfully ran for Congress in 1940 as a Democrat and an ardent supporter of President Franklin Roosevelt and the New Deal. The twenty-eight-year-old Jackson went to Washington, D.C., as the youngest member of the House, where he emerged as a specialist on public power, military affairs, and nuclear energy. An unswerving proponent of American vigilance in dealing with Soviet communism, a system he regarded as dangerous and evil, Jackson had an important role in the watershed 1949 recommendation of the Joint Committee on Atomic Energy that the United States build the hydrogen bomb lest the Soviet Union build one first.

Jackson won reelection to the House five times before he challenged Republican incumbent Harry P. Cain for the Senate in 1952. He defeated Cain by 135,000 votes amid a Republican landslide in the Pacific Northwest for President Eisenhower and Republican congressional candidates. Thus began Jackson's thirty-one-year tenure as a senator. Eventually, he became one of the Senate's most powerful members and probably its most influential member on military and foreign affairs. He also became one of the most successful politicians in the history of Washington State by dint of the lavish attention he paid to his constituents, his ability to deliver huge amounts of federal funds to his state through his positions on powerful committees, and his indefatigability for one-on-one campaigning. Jackson won the next five consecutive elections for the Senate by landslides, receiving a remarkable 84 percent of the vote in 1970 and never falling below 66 percent.

During the 1950s Jackson personified the outlook of the quintessential cold war liberal, an outlook he never abandoned. He believed fervently in the New Deal/Fair Deal economic policies. He supported organized labor and civil rights legislation unstintingly. He believed in global containment and anti-Soviet foreign policy, largely equating the Soviet Union with Nazi Germany. He was a leading advocate of the nuclear submarine program, as well as a main congressional defender of Admiral Hyman Rickover, the father of the nuclear navy. He worked to popularize the idea of a defense missile gap, on which his friend John F. Kennedy successfully campaigned for president in 1960. A strong civil libertarian who regarded the communist threat as external, Jackson abhorred Senator Joseph McCarthy and his witch-hunting methods and helped bring about McCarthy's censure with his probing questions during the Army-McCarthy hearings of 1954. He was Kennedy's first choice for vice president in 1960 but was supplanted by Lyndon Johnson because of the perceived need for a more conservative, southern running mate. As a consolation, Kennedy designated Jackson chairman of the Democratic party for the 1960 campaign. The workaholic Jackson finally ended his long bachelorhood six months shy of his fiftieth birthday, when he married Helen Hardin on 16 December 1961; they had two children.

During the 1960s, Jackson, elevated to chairman of the Interior Committee in January 1963, distinguished himself as a pioneer in environmental and energy policy. He warned presciently of an impending energy crisis years before the oil crisis of the 1970s. He wrote the landmark National Environmental Policy Act of 1969 (NEPA), managed the bill through the Senate, and crafted its most important provision—the requirement that federal agencies submit an environmental-impact statement before undertaking projects potentially damaging to the environment. For his work with NEPA and his role in expanding America's wilderness areas and national parks, Jackson in 1969 became the first politician ever to win the Sierra Club's John Muir Award. He also was a leading advocate of U.S. involvement in Southeast Asia and of antiballistic missile defense. By the end of the decade, Jackson's expertise and hard-line positions on foreign policy and defense issues had evoked increasing admiration from conservative Republicans. Republican president Richard Nixon even offered Jackson his choice of position as secretary of state or defense in 1968, partly in hopes of neutralizing Jackson as a political rival. Nixon in 1972 and President Gerald Ford in 1976 both considered Jackson to be their strongest potential political opponent.

Jackson performed badly, however, as a presidential candidate during both campaigns. By 1972 events surrounding the Vietnam War had moved Senator Jackson, unwavering in his belief in the compatibility of liberalism at home and robust anticommunism abroad, to an increasingly lonely position on the American political spectrum. A peerless legislator with a thirst for knowledge and detail but absolutely no charisma, Jackson also lacked the inclination or the skill to develop a style of campaigning appropriate for the mass media.

Politically, Jackson not only became the last of the 1940s liberals in Congress but also a transitional figure between traditional cold-war and blue-collar Democrats on one side and Reagan Democrats on the other. For the small but tremendously influential group of neoconservatives who inexorably gravitated to President Ronald Reagan, Jackson symbolized the best of the Democratic party's traditional vital center that, by their reckoning, had been repudiated by a younger generation of politicians.

Jackson had much greater success shaping the trajectory of U.S. foreign policy than he had running for president or trying to restore cold-war liberalism as the Democratic party's dominant paradigm. After 1968 he emerged as an intellectual and political leader in the perennial struggle of U.S. foreign policy to reconcile ideals with political interests. Jackson's approach to this dilemma defied easy classification. His active support of human rights and democracy abroad put him at odds with traditional realists, such as national security advisers Henry Kissinger and George Kennan, who lamented America's moralistic tradition of legal intervention in foreign policy. His emphasis on the importance of power and the eternally lurking danger of international conflict often put him at odds with those who, in Jackson's eyes, tended to depreciate the malevolence of America's totalitarian adversaries.

Unlike many liberals and conservatives, Jackson considered American ideals and self-interests complementary. Jackson opposed the Nixon and Ford administrations' policy of détente for its ideological diminution of the Soviet threat. The duty of the U.S. government to safeguard and encourage human rights in the Soviet Union arose, as Jackson saw it, from both moral and practical considerations. Nations, especially geopolitically powerful ones, that systematically repressed their citizens at home, he insisted, were likely to commit aggression abroad.

Jackson achieved great national attention for his efforts to mesh his concerns with his repugnance to anti-Semitism and unswerving support for a strong Israel, convictions forged by his mother and also by his visit as a congressman to the Buchenwald concentration camp in May 1945. The Jackson-Vanik Amendment to the Trade Act of 1974 prevailed despite attempts by the Ford administration to thwart the legislation, which made the Soviet Union's most-favored-nation status conditional on its permitting greater Jewish and Christian emigration. The Soviet Union's persistent refusal to comply and the decline in the rate of Jewish emigration were cited by critics as evidence of the flawed logic of the amendment. Soviet dissidents, however, hailed the amendment as a powerful blow that contributed mightily to the unraveling of the Soviet empire.

With equal ardor, Jackson opposed President Jimmy Carter's administration for slighting what he saw as the necessity of military preparedness. He considered Carter's human rights policy well-intentioned but deeply flawed in design and practice. He also felt that President Carter selectively applied human rights sanctions against rightist governments, partly as a pretext for imprudently abandoning the policy of containment, ignoring what Jackson felt were more systematic human rights violations by America's more dangerous adversaries.

Even Jackson's detractors concede the enormity of his impact. Secretary of State Kissinger considered Jackson his most persuasive and effective critic. Senator J. William Fulbright, Arkansas Democrat and paladin of the antiwar critique of U.S. foreign policy during the cold war, held Jackson most responsible for sabotaging détente as practiced by the Nixon, Ford, and Carter administrations—a policy Fulbright contended might otherwise have succeeded but for Jackson.

Jackson's defenders have emphasized the huge impact his thinking had on the foreign and defense policies of President Reagan, who largely saw eye-to-eye with him. During the 1980s the Reagan administration became a veritable haven for avowed former Jackson Democrats, among them United Nations ambassador Jeane Kirkpatrick, Undersecretary of Defense Richard Perle, Undersecretary of State Elliot Abrams, and Strategic Arms Reduction Talks (START) negotiator Max Kampelman. This group assisted Reagan in devising and implementing the president's strategy for the endgame of the cold war. The Jackson tradition in foreign affairs and national security lived on robustly in this wing of the Republican party rather than his own Democratic party.

Ironically, Jackson's influence in the U.S. Senate began to wane after 1980 just as his ideas on foreign and defense policy had triumphed. As a result of the Republican takeover of the Senate, Jackson lost the important committee chairmanships that had constituted an essential source of his clout. President Reagan had also preempted the themes that Jackson had championed in the fight during the 1970s in opposition to Presidents Nixon, Ford, Carter, and liberals in the Congress. In his final years, Jackson thus moved from a central to a supporting role in the debate over U.S. foreign and defense policies. His major contributions to Reagan included his support for the administration's defense budgets and arms control strategy, his opposition to the nuclear freeze, and his May 1983 proposal for a Central American commission to generate bipartisan support for combating mounting Soviet aggression in the Western Hemisphere.

Although many former Jackson Democrats later embraced Reagan's domestic agenda as well as his foreign and defense policies, Henry Jackson did not. He remained a New Deal/Fair Deal liberal who identified government as the solution to rather than the cause of the nation's most pressing domestic problems. Jackson decried President Reagan's 1982 decision to lift price controls on oil and natural gas, controls that Jackson, as chairman of the Interior and Energy Committees, had fought tenaciously to maintain

for a decade. In his last run for the senate in 1982, Jackson campaigned strenuously against both Reaganomics and Reagan's environmental policy.

The evolution of Jackson's views toward the People's Republic of China represents one of the few areas where his thinking fundamentally changed over the years. Originally as hostile to Chinese as to Soviet communism, Jackson had emerged by the early 1970s as a leading proponent of rapprochement with China as a counterweight to Soviet power. Jackson made four visits to China, the last just weeks before his death. He got along particularly well with China's leader, Deng Xiaoping, who largely shared his assessment of the Soviet threat.

A robust man with boundless energy and visible good health, Jackson died suddenly at his home in Everett of a ruptured aorta, just hours after delivering a blistering attack on the Soviet Union during his final press conference on Russia's shooting down of the Korean airliner KAL 007. He was buried in Everett. Liberal New York senator Daniel Patrick Moynihan extolled Jackson as proof that "at any moment in history, goodness in the world is preserved by thirty-six men who do not know that this was the role that the Lord had given them." Similarly, George F. Will, one of the nation's preeminent conservative commentators, called Jackson "the finest public servant" he had ever known, "[who] mastered the delicate balance of democracy, the art of being a servant to the vast public without being servile to any part of it."

Jackson ranks as one of the greatest senators in American history. With a congressional career spanning the tenure of nine presidents—from Roosevelt to Reagan—he served during watershed times in foreign and domestic politics: World War II, the cold war, Vietnam, the expansion of the welfare state, the civil rights and antiwar movements, and the slow but inevitable demise of President Roosevelt's New Deal coalition in presidential elections. He played a pivotal role in Soviet-American relations, national defense policy, human rights, arms control, China policy, the Arab-Israeli conflict, and the oil crisis. Between 1968 and 1981 he led the fight and offered the most compelling arguments against détente while waging an increasingly lonely battle against the isolationist impulse then regnant in the national Democratic party. Jackson was endowed with a national vision and was the most influential senator of his time who nevertheless failed to become president of the United States. His legacy will endure robustly into the twenty-first century.

★

The Henry M. Jackson Manuscript Archives are at the University of Washington, Seattle. The only full-length biography of Jackson is Robert G. Kaufman, *The Quiet Giant: Henry M. Jackson and the Transformation of American Liberalism from the New Deal* to the Present (1999). For two incomplete, journalistic accounts, see William Prochnau and Richard Larsen, *A Certain Democrat: Henry M. Jackson* (1972), and John Ognibene, *The Life and Times of Senator Henry M. Jackson* (1975). The Prochnau and Larsen book is by far the better of the two books.

ROBERT GORDON KAUFMAN

JACOBY, Oswald ("Ozzie") (*b.* 8 December 1902 in Brooklyn, New York; *d.* 27 June 1984 in Dallas, Texas), perhaps the greatest game player who ever lived; he was the winner of the first world team championship of contract bridge, winner of the Backgammon World Championship, and author of best-selling books on canasta, gin rummy, poker, and bridge.

Jacoby was always driven by competitive desire. In 1918, when he was only fifteen, he lied about his age in order to join the army, hoping to fight in World War I. The war ended two months later, and although he did not see action, he received the Victory Medal. Jacoby then entered Colum-

Oswald Jacoby. ARCHIVE PHOTOS

bia University, but he left in his junior year, having determined that a degree was unnecessary in his chosen occupation as an actuary. In 1924, he became the youngest person ever to pass the Society of Actuaries examination, and he went to work, first for the Metropolitan Life Insurance Company and then in 1929 for himself. Despite the Great Depression, he remained successful as a consulting actuary for the next forty years, even serving on the board of visitors of Harvard University.

Jacoby's first exploits at the bridge table occurred in 1929, when he won both the championship of the American Whist League and the Goldman Pairs championship of what was then called the American Bridge League. His rise to prominence, however, did not occur until 1931, when Sidney Lenz invited him to be his partner in a challenge match against bridge authority Ely Culbertson's team, which employed a rival bidding theory. After a series of disputes with Lenz, Jacoby walked out of the match, causing an uproar. Nevertheless, in 1933, he was invited to join the famous Four Aces team that, over the next ten years, would set a record of victories in national competition that has never been equaled. During that time span the Four Aces won the Spingold and Vanderbilt team championships five times each, the Grand National Open Teams three times, and assorted other titles, while Jacoby won seven additional championships in individual and pair events. To cap this record run, in 1935 at Madison Square Garden the Four Aces faced and defeated a team from France to win the first world team championship of bridge.

On 7 December 1941, Jacoby was playing in an open pairs event in Richmond, Virginia, when the news of the attack on Pearl Harbor was announced. He left the tournament and went straight to the enlistment office of the U.S. Navy. He spent World War II as a naval officer, dedicating his mathematical and analytical skills to the war effort and rising to the rank of lieutenant commander. In 1950, when the Korean conflict erupted, Jacoby again quit the bridge table for the rigors of Naval Intelligence, and served at Panmunjom.

These interruptions to his tournament career cost Jacoby his top spot in the masterpoint rankings, and in the 1950s he decided to redress that imbalance. Between 1959 and 1963, Jacoby won the McKenney Trophy, awarded to the top bridge competitor, four times. Not until the 1980s would a man of his age win the McKenney Trophy even once. In 1963 he achieved the then-unprecedented total of 1,034 masterpoints in a single year. When he reached a total of 10,000 masterpoints in 1967, Jacoby finally turned the McKenney Trophy race over to the younger generation.

Along the way Jacoby won the Spingold and Vanderbilt titles again, along with the master mixed teams, the men's teams, and the open pairs. One of his most cherished victories was a win in the Chicago Teams (since renamed the Reisinger Trophy championship) in 1955, partnered by his son James O. Jacoby. For these achievements, Jacoby was elected to the American Contract Bridge League Hall of Fame in 1965 and was made an honorary member of the American Contract Bridge League in 1967.

Jacoby did not retire from bridge altogether. He served as nonplaying captain of the North American bridge team in three world championships, winning twice. He also became interested in backgammon, writing a best-selling book on the subject and capturing the Backgammon World Championship in 1973. His remarkable competitive career was capped in 1983, when, already suffering from cancer, he nevertheless formed a team that won the Reisinger Trophy. For this achievement, among many others, he was named Bridge Personality of the Year by the International Bridge Press Association.

Jacoby began writing on bridge, and soon on other games, shortly after World War II. Jacoby made numerous contributions to bridge bidding theory, the best known of which are the Jacoby transfer bid and the weak jump overcall. In addition to four books on bridge, Jacoby wrote on all aspects of card playing, gambling, and mathematics. His *How to Win at Canasta* was the best-selling nonfiction book of 1949. In 1950 Jacoby became the daily bridge columnist for the Newspaper Enterprise Association, and proceeded to write columns continuously for more than thirty years. On 22 April 1982, his ten-thousandth column appeared. As a columnist, his name became perhaps better known to the general public even than that of Charles Goren, the renowned bridge popularizer.

On 25 April 1932 Jacoby married Mary Zita McHale, also a master bridge player. The couple had two sons, Jim (who also became a bridge champion, and cowrote the Jacoby bridge column for many years) and Jon. Jacoby died of cancer and was buried in his adopted home of Dallas, Texas.

Oswald Jacoby was a man who thrived in the intensely competitive worlds of championship bridge, and later high-stakes backgammon. Yet at the same time he was a patient and compassionate teacher, who dedicated a record percentage of his time to writing for the general public and who demonstrated his commitment to higher priorities with voluntary service in both world wars and the Korean conflict.

★

Victor Mollo included a chapter on Jacoby in his book, *The Bridge Immortals* (1967). A short obituary is in the *New York Times* (28 June 1984), followed by a fuller notice on 29 June. The American Contract Bridge League published a series of reminiscences and memorials in its *Bulletin* (Aug. 1984).

HARTLEY S. SPATT

JAMES, Harry Haag (*b.* 15 March 1916 in Albany, Georgia; *d.* 5 July 1983 in Las Vegas, Nevada), jazz trumpeter and orchestra leader.

James was born in a hotel while his parents were on the road with the Mighty Haag Circus, from which he received his middle name. His father, Everette Robert James, was the circus bandmaster and trumpet player; his mother, Maybelle Stewart, was a trapeze artist. At age four he began playing drums, on which he performed often throughout his career. He took up the trumpet at the age of eight and was schooled in the circus brass band musical tradition, unique for a major jazz soloist. After playing in his father's band, at age ten he became leader of the Christy Brothers Circus secondary band while his father directed the primary one. In 1929 the family settled in Beaumont, Texas, where Everette was a school music administrator and where James attended high school; young Harry soon won a statewide trumpet solo competition. He gigged with several dance bands in the Dallas–Galveston–New Orleans region, and was inspired to develop a jazz style by trumpet and cornet players Louis Armstrong, Muggsy Spanier, and Bunny Berigan.

James was discovered and hired in 1935 by bandleader Ben Pollack, for whom he composed the song "Peckin',"

Harry James, 1940s. FRANK DRIGGS COLLECTION/ARCHIVE PHOTOS

from which a popular dance step developed. He cut his first records with Pollack in September 1936. James's great technique, range, power, and sense of swing led Benny Goodman to hire him in January 1937 as his major trumpet soloist. James fit in so well with the other two men in the trumpet section, Ziggy Elman and Chris Griffin, that all three switched around playing lead in the arrangements and as soloists with equal facility. Together, they helped propel the Goodman orchestra to preeminence in the peak years of the swing era. As heard on hot showpiece numbers like "Sing, Sing, Sing" and "Roll 'Em," James provided a special kick that earned him popular acclaim behind only Goodman and drummer Gene Krupa in the band. He also displayed versatile talents in small jazz recording groups led by Teddy Wilson, notably on the blues "Just a Mood" in 1937. During 1937 and 1938 he made big band recordings under his own name using Goodman and Count Basie musicians and in December 1938 formed his own orchestra, partially financed by Goodman. He married vocalist Louise Tobin on 4 May 1935; they had two sons.

Harry James and His Music Makers, as he soon named the orchestra, played its first dance date and cut its initial recordings in February 1939. Though basically jazz oriented, it increasingly played romantic ballads, highlighted in June by the addition of unknown boy vocalist Frank Sinatra. Both band and singer were still honing their skills when Sinatra left later in the year to join Tommy Dorsey, but James replaced him with the highly polished Dick Haymes. At the start of 1941 James added four violins and in May recorded his first major hit, "You Made Me Love You," inspired by Judy Garland's recording of it but with James's warm trumpet solo replacing the lyric.

The popularity of the James orchestra soared, due largely to his eminently recognizable flashy trumpet solos; his tall, handsome, and dignified stage presence; and his appeal to wartime audiences' romantic preferences. Despite jazz purists who criticized him for compromising his creativity to satisfy commercial tastes, James emphasized soft, sweet ballads, although teenagers jitterbugged wildly to hit numbers like "Two O'Clock Jump." After adding Helen Forrest when Haymes left late in 1941, the band sold over one million copies of "I've Heard That Song Before," with Forrest on the vocal. In polls, record sales, and ballroom attendance the James orchestra was rated the best in America during the period 1942–1943. This enabled it to give up grueling road trips and settle in Hollywood late in 1942 for steady public appearances at the Hollywood Palladium ballroom, a continuous output of recordings, a thrice-weekly radio show, and participation in nine motion pictures between 1942 and 1950. In 1943 James divorced Louise Tobin in order to marry actress and pinup queen Betty Grable (on 5 July 1943); they had two children.

Musically, James's distinctive trumpet and wartime or-

chestra produced a big sound, averaging twenty-seven pieces: five trumpets (including James), three trombones, five reeds, four rhythm, a French horn, and from nine to fifteen strings, plus a male and a female singer. Forrest was followed by Helen Ward (1943–1944) and Kitty Kallen (1944–1945). In spite of his emphasis on slow and medium tempos, James and Ray Conniff arranged many swinging instrumentals which featured, in addition to James, tenor saxophonist Corky Corcoran (a seventeen-year-old child prodigy hired in 1942), Willie Smith on alto sax, and Juan Tizol on valve trombone. At the end of 1946, James reformed the band along jazz lines, and the new group played from 1947 to 1951. He served as musical adviser for the 1950 film *Young Man with a Horn,* in which his trumpet solos were dubbed for actor Kirk Douglas, and he had his own television program in 1952. The brief jazz octet he led in 1953 and 1954 and his big bands of the 1950s and 1960s had a swinging Basie flavor with arrangements by Neal Hefti and Ernie Wilkins, no vocalist, and exciting drummers in Buddy Rich and Louis Bellson.

Possessing flawless trumpet technique, James was the consummate swing band soloist and leader, admired by fellow musicians and fans alike. His musical spirit was equaled by a passion for baseball. He hit, pitched, and captained the championship Goodman team and his own in the informal big band league; he even broke a leg in one game. Beginning in the mid-1950s, James led his orchestra for dances, shows, and concerts in southern California and Nevada and tours of Europe, Japan, and Latin America. After settling in Las Vegas, he owned a stable of race horses. James and Betty Grable divorced in 1965. He married showgirl Joan Boyd on 27 December 1967; they had one son before divorcing. James played his last gig ten days before his death, from lymphatic cancer.

★

George T. Simon, *The Big Bands* (1967), includes a chapter on James. His musical skills are analyzed in James Lincoln Collier, *Benny Goodman and the Swing Era* (1989), and Gunther Schuller, *The Swing Era: The Development of Jazz, 1930–1945* (1989). For informative album liner notes, see Dan Morgenstern, "Harry James: First Team Player on the Jazz Varsity" (Savoy LP 2262, 1987). The orchestra's history is treated in Charles Garrod and Peter Johnson, *Harry James and His Orchestra* (1975). A personal perspective of James and the band is by Helen Forrest (with Bill Libby), *I Had the Craziest Dream* (1982). The relationship of Buddy Rich to the James orchestra is in Mel Tormé, *Traps: The Drum Wonder, The Life of Buddy Rich* (1991). An obituary is in the *New York Times* (6 July 1983).

CLARK G. REYNOLDS

JAWORSKI, Leon (*b.* 19 September 1905 in Waco, Texas; *d.* 9 December 1982 near Wimberley, Texas), lawyer and special prosecutor in the Watergate case, whose historic Supreme Court victory in 1974 paved the way for President Richard M. Nixon's resignation.

Leon Jaworski was one of four children born to Joseph and Marie Jaworski, European immigrants who settled in Texas. Marie, an Austrian by birth, died when Leon was five years old; Joseph, an evangelical minister from Poland, remarried four years later. Talented and hardworking, Leon graduated Waco High School at age fifteen and enrolled at Baylor University, where in 1925 he earned an LL.B. degree. He received an LL.M. degree from George Washington University in Washington, D.C., the next year, then returned to Texas to practice law.

The young Jaworski quickly settled into the community of attorneys and businessmen who dominated Texas's politics. In 1931, he married Jeannette Adam, with whom he would have three children. That same year he joined the Houston law firm of Fulbright, Crooker, Freeman, and Bates, where in 1934 he was named partner. Already known as a skilled litigator and courtroom performer, Jaworski served as an army colonel in World War II and subsequently helped prosecute the Nuremberg war crimes trials. He rejoined the firm in 1946 and became senior partner in 1951. The firm later changed its name to Fulbright and Jaworski.

Leon Jaworski. ARCHIVE PHOTOS

In the 1950s and 1960s, Jaworski grew close to his state's political, financial, and industrial movers and shakers. Like most Texas leaders of the period he was a Democrat, and in 1960 he oversaw the lawsuit that allowed U.S. Senate Majority Leader Lyndon Johnson to run for the senate and the vice presidency simultaneously. Politically moderate, Jaworski numbered mostly businessmen among his clients and criticized Chief Justice Earl Warren's Supreme Court for upholding controversial rights of the accused. He also, however, worked under Attorney General Robert F. Kennedy from 1962 to 1965, pressing charges against Mississippi Governor Ross Barnett for flouting a court order and trying to keep the University of Mississippi closed to blacks. Having served as president of the Houston Bar Association and the Texas Bar Association, Jaworski further burnished his professional reputation in July 1971, when he was named president of the American Bar Association. During his yearlong term he used the prominent position to warn against the growing disrespect for the law he perceived during those turbulent times.

Despite this distinguished career, Jaworski became a household name only when he was appointed special prosecutor in the Watergate case. Ever since five burglars tied to Nixon's reelection campaign had been caught breaking into Democratic party headquarters at the Watergate apartment-office complex on 17 June 1972, questions had been mounting about the administration's role in carrying out and covering up a slew of illegal activities, some with grave constitutional ramifications. In May 1973, Nixon's new attorney general, Elliot Richardson, appointed Harvard law professor Archibald Cox to investigate the charges and present the evidence to grand juries for possible indictments. When it came to light over the summer that Nixon had secretly taped his Oval Office conversations, Cox subpoenaed nine of those tapes. Nixon rebuffed the request and on 20 October 1973 ordered Richardson to fire Cox. Richardson refused, choosing instead to resign himself. So did his deputy, William Ruckelshaus. Finally, Solicitor General Robert Bork fired Cox, but the episode, dubbed the "Saturday Night Massacre," plunged the Nixon administration deeper into trouble.

Jaworski took over as special prosecutor on 5 November. Initially, many suspected the more conservative Jaworski wouldn't pursue the investigations as vigorously as Cox had. But he soon proved himself as determined as his predecessor. In February he prevailed upon the Watergate grand jury to indict several of Nixon's top aides, including former attorney general John Mitchell, Chief of Staff H. R. Haldeman, and advisers John Ehrlichman and Charles Colson. The grand jury named Nixon himself as an "unindicted coconspirator."

To pursue these indictments Jaworski sought more White House tapes. In April 1974 he obtained from Federal

District Judge John Sirica a subpoena for sixty-four of them. The White House stonewalled, but Jaworski pressed his case with Judge Sirica, who ordered Nixon to hand over the tapes by 31 May. Nixon appealed, and the matter went to the Supreme Court.

The United States of America v. *Richard M. Nixon, President* is considered one of the most important high-court cases in U.S. history. At stake was not simply the fate of Richard Nixon but a fundamental constitutional principle: whether the president could act according to his own reading of the law. On 8 July, Jaworski and his assistant, Philip Lacovara, and Nixon's attorney James St. Clair delivered oral arguments before a packed courtroom. Jaworski spelled out the central issue: "This nation's constitutional form of government is in serious jeopardy if the president, any president, is to say that the Constitution means what he says it does, and that there is no one, not even the Supreme Court, to tell him otherwise." St. Clair, on the other hand, claimed "executive privilege": The president, because of his unique position, could on his own choose to overrule a court edict. On 24 July the Supreme Court ruled 8–0 that Nixon had to turn over the tapes. (One justice, William Rehnquist, recused himself from the case.)

Jaworski's efforts accelerated Nixon's downfall. The tapes included the conversation of 23 June 1973 that became known as the "smoking gun." The tape recorded Nixon and Haldeman explicitly discussing how to cover up the administration's involvement in the Watergate break-in. Even before the tape's contents became public, the House Judiciary Committee on 27 July voted to bring its first article of impeachment against Nixon. When released, the smoking-gun tape wiped out most of what little support for the president remained in Congress. On 8 August 1974, Nixon announced his resignation, effective the next day.

Jaworski still had to decide whether to seek criminal charges against Nixon. While most of his staff wanted to do so, believing it important to show that the president was not above the law, Jaworski doubted Nixon could receive a fair trial. He was spared having to make this controversial decision, when President Gerald Ford, on 8 September, pardoned Nixon for all crimes he may have committed. Jaworski continued on as special prosecutor until 25 October 1974, at which point Henry Ruth took over the supervision of the remaining Watergate cases.

In 1977, House Speaker Tip O'Neill asked Jaworski to come back to Washington to investigate charges that Korean government officials had bribed U.S. congressmen. Although former congressman Richard T. Hanna ended up going to prison, the "Koreagate" hearings otherwise proved inconclusive. Jaworski returned to Texas to practice law, give lectures, and write his memoirs. He died on 9 December 1982 after a bout with pancreatic cancer.

★

Leon Jaworski, *The Right and the Power: The Prosecution of Watergate* (1976), an account of his career's most celebrated chapter, and *Confession and Avoidance: A Memoir* (1979) are both straightforward histories from Jaworski's point of view. James Doyle, *Not Above the Law: The Battles of Watergate Prosecutors Cox and Jaworski* (1977) covers the whole Watergate investigation, while Bob Woodward and Scott Armstrong, *The Brethren: Inside the Supreme Court* (1977), is excellent on the case *The United States of America* v. *Richard M. Nixon*. Among the numerous Watergate books, Theodore White, *Breach of Faith: The Fall of Richard Nixon* (1975), and the more up-to-date Fred Emery, *Watergate: The Corruption of American Politics and the Fall of Richard Nixon* (1994) are particularly useful. Profiles include *New York Times* (2 Nov. 1973), *Washington Post* (1 Nov. 1973), *Christian Science Monitor* (17 July 1980), and *Current Biography* (1974). An obituary is in the *New York Times* (10 Dec. 1982).

DAVID GREENBERG

JENKINS, Gordon Hill (*b.* 12 May 1910 in Webster Groves, Missouri; *d.* 1 May 1984 in Malibu, California), pianist, conductor, composer, and arranger whose lush, string-based orchestrations enhanced the performances of many popular music stars, including Nat King Cole, Louis Armstrong, and Frank Sinatra.

The son of William M. Jenkins, a church organist who also played piano for local movie theaters, and Angelica Lockwood Robinson, Jenkins was the youngest member of a musically inclined family. As a child, he learned to play practically every instrument and at age ten started his professional career as a relief organist for his father at a Chicago movie house.

In 1925 Jenkins won the amateur ukulele-playing contest, sponsored by "Ukulele-Ike" Edwards, in St. Louis. Still in his teens, Jenkins played banjo in his brother Marshall's band at a nearby summer resort. He dropped out of school to perform at a St. Louis speakeasy, wheeling his piano between the tables and collecting tips from the patrons. His style, at the time described as "rudimentary," became part of the one-finger piano technique he used in later orchestrations. Jenkins moved on to St. Louis radio station KMOX, where his multi-instrumental abilities were an asset. He opened the station at nine in the morning with fifteen minutes of piano music. Then, using a different name, he played the organ for another fifteen minutes. At 9:30 he took the name "Abe Snake, the Piano-Accordion Virtuoso." Fifteen minutes later, he was playing the ukulele. By ten o'clock, if the regular staff had not yet shown up, he began his act again.

Jenkins left Missouri for the first time in 1930 with Henry Santry's orchestra, but the job did not last long because the two disliked each other. When Jenkins left the

Gordon Jenkins. FRANK DRIGGS COLLECTION/ARCHIVE PHOTOS

Santry orchestra, he was close to New York City and went there to look for a job. After coming down with influenza, Jenkins returned home to Webster Groves and took a job at the local Fox theater, where he had the opportunity to write original material for the acts that played along with the talking pictures. He married his high school sweetheart, Nancy Harkey, in 1931.

In 1932 Jenkins had a major career break when he got the chance to fill in for the ailing pianist of the Isham Jones Orchestra while the orchestra was playing the Coronado Hotel in St. Louis. Shortly after the band returned to New York City, Jones sent for Jenkins as a permanent replacement for the pianist and as an orchestral arranger. Jenkins's arrangements were not always popular. A CBS station manager in Cleveland accused him of "bastardizing the airwaves" by jazzing up the classics and told Jones to "get that thin kid out of here." By 1936 Jenkins was chief arranger for the orchestra. For Jenkins, Jones was a role model who also encouraged him by giving Jenkins's early songs their first hearings. Through his association with Jones, Jenkins met fellow band member Woody Herman and composer, violinist, conductor, and arranger Victor Young. Young was present at a recording session that included songs Jenkins had orchestrated. In three hours, Jenkins later

said, he learned more from Young "than you could learn at college about practical writing," including when to let the singer sing and when to fill in with the orchestra.

During his years with Jones, Jenkins had been writing songs, including "You Have Taken My Heart" (1933) and "When a Woman Loves a Man" (1934). He wrote "Goodbye" (1935) for Benny Goodman, which became Goodman's closing theme. Jenkins also was doing arrangements for Paul Whiteman, Vincent Lopez, and Andre Kostelanetz. When Jones retired in 1936, many of his orchestra members went to the newly formed Woody Herman Band. Jenkins joined Herman as pianist and arranger. He had previously composed what was to become Herman's theme, "Blue Prelude" (1933)

In 1937 Jenkins began conducting for Vincente Minnelli's Broadway revue *The Show Is On,* starring Bea Lillie, but he grew bored with conducting the same music the same way every night and jumped at the chance to join the music staff at Paramount Pictures in 1938. This necessitated a move to California. After anonymously scoring the movies *The Big Broadcast of 1937* (1936), *Artists and Models* (1937), *Blossoms on Broadway* (1937), *College Swing* (1938), and others, Jenkins decided that he liked working in movies even less than Broadway and left for a job in radio with the National Broadcasting Company (NBC) in Hollywood in 1939.

At NBC, Jenkins was in charge of all musical direction for the West Coast from 1940 to 1944. He gave Skitch Henderson his first spot as a conductor and conducted a number of radio shows himself. With his own Gordon Jenkins Orchestra, he provided the music for *Signal Carnival* (1939–1941), a comedy variety show with Jack Carson, and *Little Ol' Hollywood* (1940–1942). He did the music for some early airings of *The Judy Canova Show* (1943–1953) and for *Mayor of the Town* (1942–1949), starring Lionel Barrymore. Jenkins's orchestra was featured on *The Fred Brady Show* (1943). His most significant affiliation with radio was *The Dick Haymes Show* (1944–1947), in which Jenkins, conducting a thirty-one-piece orchestra, first established himself as a distinctive orchestral stylist. As musical director, Jenkins persuaded Dick Haymes and his sponsor, Autolite, to present a series of "Autolite Operas," ten-minute pastiches, using Haymes, his occasional costar Helen Forrest, and the NBC orchestra and chorus. The "operas" were extended medleys of familiar songs with new lyrics as well as original material composed by Jenkins. The result was a musical narrative with connecting dialogue.

While working on the Haymes show, Jenkins met Beverly Mahr, who was the "Miss" in that show's vocal group Six Hits and a Miss. Jenkins divorced his first wife in 1946 and married Mahr in October of that year. They had four children.

During the 1940s Jenkins was involved in both writing

and recording music. In the early 1940s he was a nuts-and-bolts arranger for Decca Records, and in 1945 he officially joined the label's staff, first as a full-time conductor and then as musical director. At Decca he worked with a number of singers, including Louis Armstrong, Martha Tilton, Peggy Lee, Nat King Cole, and the Weavers, a folk singing group. At one point in the late 1940s, between recordings by Gordon Jenkins and His Orchestra, including the mega-hits "Maybe You'll Be There," "Again," and "Don't Cry Joe (Let Her Go, Let Her Go, Let Her Go)," and backings for various Decca pop singers, no less than five of the nation's top-ten singles were Jenkins productions.

Jenkins's major work as a composer during this era was *Manhattan Tower,* written over two years and first recorded for Decca in 1945. It was a multipart pop-song fantasia based on Jenkins's early experiences in New York City and narrated by the radio actor Eliot Lewis. This series of orchestral and choral impressions was an immediate best-seller. When Jenkins went to Capitol Records in 1956, he rewrote and rerecorded the work. The popularity of *Manhattan Tower* resulted in repeat performances in both New York City and Las Vegas. He conducted selections from *Manhattan Tower* on *The Ed Sullivan Show,* and it was a television special in 1956, featuring Ethel Waters, Cesar Romero, Phil Harris, Hans Conried, and Helen O'Connell. Two songs from these later versions of *Manhattan Tower* became hit singles: "Married I Can Always Get" and "Repeat After Me."

Other Jenkins Americana pieces reflect various moods of the country during and after World War II. They range from nostalgic, as in "Homesick That's All" (1945) and "P. S., I Love You," originally written in 1934 but revived more successfully in 1946, to the more upbeat "San Fernando Valley" (1943). The busy Jenkins returned to Hollywood, scoring the film *Strange Music* (1946), and to Broadway, scoring the musical *Along Fifth Avenue* (1949).

In 1950 three Jenkins records were in the top ten: "I Wanna Be Loved," "Bewitched," and "My Foolish Heart." His version of "Tzena, Tzena, Tzena" with the Weavers was also a top seller. Jenkins, who had an interest in folk songs, spotted the Weavers at the Village Vanguard in Greenwich Village in 1949. But when he wanted to bring them to Decca, top executive Dave Kapp turned him down. Jenkins was so sure of the Weavers' future success that he signed them to a personal contract, guaranteeing to pay them from his own pocket if their records did not sell. "Goodnight Irene" (1950), released by Gordon Jenkins and the Weavers, sold more than a million copies.

In the 1950s Jenkins worked in Las Vegas, composing and conducting the music for a series of casino and nightclub reviews at the Thunderbird, the Riviera, and the Tropicana. In 1953 he scored *Bwana Devil,* the first three-dimensional film. Jenkins also worked in television, staging the musical production numbers for *Holiday Hotel* (1950–

1951), a variety show that traced the art of music and comedy from vaudeville to the present. He returned to NBC as a television producer from 1955 to 1957 and did the music for *The Ballad of Louis the Louse* (1959), a sixty-minute special starring Phil Silvers. Jenkins's 1956 album with Nat King Cole, *Love Is the Thing,* recorded in the new stereo process, was a best-seller. In 1957 Jenkins conducted the orchestra for Judy Garland's London appearance. During this time he continued to write songs, and his "This Is All I Ask" (1958) became a standard for many popular singers, including Tony Bennett, whose 1963 release of the song was a best-seller.

Jenkins's finest work during the 1960s was with Frank Sinatra. Albums with Sinatra include *The Sinatra Christmas Album; Where Are You?,* which Sinatra described as "magnificent"; *No One Cares; All Alone; September of My Years;* and *She Shot Me Down.* Sinatra and Jenkins also collaborated on a number of other albums, including *Ol' Blue Eyes,* for which Jenkins scored six of the nine tracks. In 1965 Jenkins won a Grammy for his arrangement of Sinatra's hit "It Was a Very Good Year." In 1973 Jenkins arranged and conducted a Sinatra television special, *Magnavox Presents Frank Sinatra,* and in 1980 scored the film *The First Deadly Sin,* which starred Sinatra. His last major work was as composer of the "Future" section of Sinatra's *Trilogy* album in 1979.

After suffering for several years, Jenkins died of amyotrophic lateral sclerosis (Lou Gehrig's disease). He was cremated. Commenting on his former conductor, arranger, and songwriter, Sinatra described Jenkins as "one of the modern geniuses of good pop music."

★

To date, there is no biography of Jenkins. The section on him in Will Friedwald, *Sinatra! The Song Is You: A Singer's Art* (1995) includes information on Jenkins's life and his work with Sinatra. See entry on Jenkins in Roger D. Kinkle, *The Complete Encyclopedia of Popular Music and Jazz, 1900–1950* (1974) and the article "Fancy and Flashy," *Time* (26 June 1950). Full obituaries are in *Los Angeles Times* (2 May 1984), *St. Louis Post-Dispatch* (2 May 1984), *New York Times* (3 May 1984), *Variety* (9 May 1984), and *International Musician* (June 1984):13.

MARCIA B. DINNEEN

JENNER, William Ezra (*b.* 21 July 1908 in Marengo, Indiana; *d.* 9 March 1985 in Bedford, Indiana), Republican senator from Indiana in 1944–1945 and 1947–1959, best known nationally for his noninterventionist views on foreign relations in the aftermath of World War II and for his stalwart support of the domestic anticommunist agenda of Senator Joseph R. McCarthy during the 1950s.

Born to L. Lenwood ("Woody") Jenner and Jane (MacDonald) Jenner in a predominantly rural area of southern

Indiana, William almost died in infancy and was somewhat small for his age during childhood. Nevertheless, he had a fairly normal youth, attending the local public schools and becoming involved in extracurricular activities such as acting and singing. One of his earliest jobs was as a performer at Marengo Cave, a regional attraction near his home. He graduated from Lake Placid Preparatory School in New York State in 1926. Politics was an early passion for Jenner. His father, the Republican chairman of Crawford County, owned a general store. William could often be found there absorbing all the talk about regional politics. Among his early heroes were two senators from Indiana, Albert Beveridge and James Watson.

In 1926 Jenner enrolled at Indiana University, graduating with a B.A. degree in 1930. During his college years his interest in politics and the performing arts persisted. In the summer of 1930 he took night classes at George Washington University and held a job as an elevator operator in the old House Office Building in Washington, D.C., which offered a close look at the national political scene. Shortly thereafter he returned to Indiana University to study law, earning his LL.B. degree in 1932. He was admitted to the Indiana bar in the same year.

After opening his law practice (first in Paoli and then Shoals, Indiana), Jenner married Janet Cuthill on 30 June 1933; they had one child. In 1934 he embarked on his political career, first winning election to the state senate. His

William Jenner. REPRODUCED COURTESY OF THE LIBRARY OF CONGRESS

ambition, leadership skills, and party loyalty were soon rewarded. In 1937 and 1939, he served as minority leader of the state senate. When the Republicans captured control of that chamber in 1941, he became the president pro tempore.

The onset of U.S. involvement in World War II temporarily interrupted Jenner's rising political career. Resigning from the state senate in June 1942, he served in the Army Air Corps in Europe. Within weeks of his return to the United States for medical treatment and subsequent discharge from the army in October 1944, Jenner was elected to the U.S. Senate to fill out the remaining weeks of the term of the deceased senator Frederick Van Nuys. During his short stint with the Seventy-eighth Congress, Jenner served on the Labor Committee, Indian Affairs Committee, Committee on the District of Columbia, and Committee on Expenditures in the Executive Departments. Soon after returning to his law practice in Shoals, Jenner was elected Republican state chairman in February 1945. This position kept him in the public eye and helped launch his return to national politics. In the November 1946 election for the U.S. Senate, Jenner handily defeated the former governor of Indiana, M. Clifford Townsend, a Democrat.

Upon his return to Congress, Jenner was assigned to the Labor and Public Welfare Committee and the Rules and Administrative Committee of the Senate. Early in his first full six-year term on Capitol Hill, he demonstrated conservatism on most domestic issues and isolationism in the area of foreign affairs. For example, in May 1947 he voted for the Taft-Hartley Bill, many provisions of which were generally opposed by organized labor. As an isolationist, he voted against the Marshall Plan for Europe in March 1948. In the Eighty-first and Eighty-second Congresses (1949–1950 and 1951–1952), Jenner was assigned to the Senate Judiciary and the Rules and Administrative Committees. During this time his domestic conservatism and international isolationism were further exemplified. He opposed President Harry Truman's proposal for a department of welfare and voted against an amendment to a housing bill that would have given assistance in the form of loans to cooperatives and nonprofit organizations. He also voted to cut Marshall Plan funds and against ratification of the North Atlantic Security Pact.

The political rhetoric with which Jenner assailed the Truman administration became more extreme during these later Congresses. He referred to the president's 1950 State of the Union Address as a "soak-the-rich sales talk." After Truman removed General Douglas MacArthur from his command in 1951, Jenner exclaimed on the Senate floor: "I charge that this country today is in the hands of a secret inner coterie which is directed by agents of the Soviet Union. . . . Our only choice is to impeach President Truman and find out who is the secret invisible government." In 1950 he characterized former secretary of state General

George Marshall as "a living lie" and a "front man for traitors." Remarks like these were not inconsistent with much of the vitriolic rhetoric that characterized the ensuing McCarthyism in American politics. Indeed, Jenner was staunchly supportive of Senator McCarthy's investigations.

After winning reelection in Dwight D. Eisenhower's presidential landslide of 1952, Senator Jenner gained further notoriety and prominence as chairman of the Internal Security Subcommittee of the Senate Judiciary Committee. Here he investigated charges of communist infiltration of the teaching profession in the mid-1950s. Seemingly disenchanted with the direction of his party by the beginning of Eisenhower's second term, however, Jenner announced in 1957 that he would not seek reelection in 1958. In his farewell speech to the Senate, after chastising both the Republicans and the Democrats for yielding to "the men in the shadows behind them," he warned that "the American people are being pushed in the direction of catastrophic inflation by wild-eyed socialists, ambitious intellectuals, power-seeking demagogues and hidden Communists."

After retiring from politics, Jenner returned for a time to his law practice in Bedford, Indiana, where he died of respiratory ailments. He is buried in Bedford's Cresthaven Memorial Gardens.

William Ezra Jenner was a complex and controversial figure in twentieth-century American politics. While espousing positions during his active political life that have been labeled conservative, Jenner sometimes advocated policies and programs that could arguably be characterized as liberal. Thus, for example, even though he voted against the expressed interests of organized labor when he supported the Taft-Hartley Bill, he later tried to amend the Railway Labor Act in 1950 to deny the benefits of the act to unions practicing racial and religious discrimination. Moreover, when Indiana high schools would not allow black schools to participate in the state basketball tournament, Jenner helped push through the state senate a bill opening the tournament to all public and parochial schools. Jenner also had an uncanny ability to sense the political winds of his times. Given the volatile political climate of the 1940s and 1950s, even his political foes admitted that Jenner often exhibited a remarkably steady sense of political and personal loyalty.

★

Irving Leibowitz, *My Indiana* (1964), provides an interpretation of Jenner's political career and relates interesting anecdotes gleaned from personal interviews. Indiana Historical Bureau (eds. Frederick D. Hill et al.), *Their Infinite Variety: Essays on Indiana Politicians* (1981), discusses Jenner's career in terms of his impact on Indiana politics and other state politicians. An obituary is in the *New York Times* (11 Mar. 1985).

THOMAS D. KOTULAK

JESSEL, George Albert ("Georgie") (*b.* 3 April 1898 in New York City; *d.* 24 May 1981 in Los Angeles, California), entertainer who performed in vaudeville, musical theater, silent and sound films, and on radio and television; he was also a producer and writer whose cultivation of the role of master of ceremonies won him the popular title "toastmaster general of the United States."

Georgie Jessel, the son of playwright Joseph Aaron Jessel and Charlotte Schwartz, was named for a relative, Sir George Jessel, a British magistrate. His immigrant family, however, was poor, and Jessel grew up in the Manhattan neighborhood then known as Jewish Harlem. He had virtually no schooling, instead finding an education in show business. As early as age nine he was performing professionally as a tenor in the Imperial Trio, a child act that included two other future show-business figures, columnist Walter Winchell and Hollywood agent Jack Weiner. Before reaching his teenage years, Jessel had toured with Eddie Cantor on the vaudeville circuit as a member of Gus Edward's Girls and Boys, and he had even performed in a film directed by Thomas A. Edison, *Widow at the Races* (1911).

In 1914 the teenaged song-and-dance man went to London, where he found frequent bookings because the ranks of the British show business community were depleted by

George Jessel, 1939. ARCHIVE PHOTOS

World War I conscription. As he matured to adulthood his voice lost much of its charm. This caused him to shift the focus of his act toward the writing and performance of monologues and sketches.

Returning to the United States in 1917, Jessel played the vaudeville circuits, writing his own musical-comedy material. His first New York show, a revue titled *The Troubles of 1920,* was panned by the critics for its turgid sentimentality, a charge he would face for the rest of his career. He also wrote and produced *George Jessel's Troubles* (1922) and *Helen of Troy, New York* (1923), while continuing to perform onstage. He wrote several popular songs, including "If Ever I Lost You" and "As Long as I Love."

His major breakthrough came in the lead role of the Broadway production of *The Jazz Singer* (1925), a dramatic adaptation of Samson Raphaelson's short story concerning the son of an immigrant cantor who is caught between his family's tradition of religious vocation and a desire to use his vocal talents to become a popular American entertainer. In what some consider one of the great career blunders in show-business history, Jessel turned down the role in the 1927 film version, which then went to Al Jolson. As the first commercially released "talking picture," *The Jazz Singer* (1927) was a cinema landmark as well as an all-time box office smash.

Jessel had a second hit on the Broadway stage with *The War Song* (1928), which he cowrote with Bella Cohen and Samuel Spewack. Like *The Jazz Singer,* it focused on the theme of Jewish assimilation into American culture through show business, an issue that would remain at the heart of Jessel's concerns throughout his career. Other Broadway roles for Jessel included *Sweet and Low* (which he coauthored with Fanny Brice, 1930), *Show Time* (1942), and *Red, White, and Blue* (1950).

Despite his refusal of the *Jazz Singer* role, he appeared in many films during the late 1920s, including *Private Izzy Murphy* (1926), *Lucky Boy* (which he also wrote, 1927), *Ginzburg the Great* (1927), *Love, Live, and Laugh* (1929), and *Happy Days* (1930). In 1930 he formed the Jessel Producing Company, shifting his emphasis away from acting toward behind-the-scenes work, such as producing, writing, and songwriting. Preferring to perform in a medium where he could appear as himself rather than as a dramatic character, he became a mainstay of the diminishing vaudeville circuit, frequently playing such theaters as the Capitol and the Loew's State in New York during the last years of that type of stage entertainment. He also emceed variety radio programs for Reid's Ice Cream Company and Vitalis Hair Tonic. Between 1943 and 1963 he was frequently engaged by Twentieth Century–Fox as a producer and author.

Beginning with his friendship with Mayor Jimmy Walker in the 1920s, Jessel had a history of associations with New York Democratic party figures. His ubiquitous ap-pearances as master of ceremonies at political and show business banquets led President Franklin D. Roosevelt to dub him "toastmaster general of the United States," a title that he embraced so roundly that it became the center of his public persona for the rest of his life. Events that Jessel emceed raised a total exceeding $100 million for charitable organizations, and in 1970 Jessel received the Jean Hersholt Humanitarian Award of the Academy of Motion Picture Arts and Sciences.

Despite his lack of formal education, beginning in middle age Jessel became a prolific author of books. These included a half dozen autobiographical memoirs: *So Help Me* (1943), *This Way, Miss* (1955), *Jessel, Anyone?* (1960), *Elegy in Manhattan* (1961), *Halo over Hollywood* (1963), and *The World I Live In* (with John Austin, 1975). In these rambling autobiographies, the author takes great relish in attacking his critics, lauding his friends, and proclaiming the depths of his patriotism and his pride in the Jewish-American community. Jack Gould of the *New York Times* noted in his memoirs that Jessel had a "fixation" about reminding readers of "his way with the ladies." Other Jessel books include *The Toastmaster General's Guide to Successful Public Speaking* (1969) and *The Toastmaster General's Favorite Jokes: Openings and Closings for Speechmakers* (1973).

George Jessel was married and divorced four times and engaged several times more. His 1919 marriage to Florence Courtney ended in divorce in 1932. The couple had a daughter, his only child. Jessel's second and most celebrated marriage was to silent screen siren Norma Talmadge in 1934. Following their divorce in 1939, Jessel was married and divorced two more times, first to a sixteen-year-old showgirl, Lois Andrews, and then to Paula Jacobson. After that he remained single for the rest of his life.

By the time he had reached advanced age, Jessel's long career paralleling the development of modern entertainment media was for the most part overshadowed by his overbearing persona. Proclaiming his dedication to country, religion, family, and fundamental values, he often appeared in public, whether on a television talk show or at a celebrity funeral, wearing his "honorary" U.S. Air Force uniform, with a string of medals, earned for charity work, pinned to his chest. His fans saw him as a living embodiment of the American dream; his detractors dismissed him as a vainglorious buffoon. Jessel died in Los Angeles.

★

Jessel's several memoirs provide a vivid picture of their subject; add a grain or two of salt, and a bit of history emerges as well. A career sketch is in *Joe Franklin's Encyclopedia of Comedians* (1979). For a sample of Jessel's speaking style, listen to the 1953 RCA Victor record album, *Show Biz,* produced by Abel Green and Joe Laurie, Jr. An obituary is in the *New York Times* (26 May 1981).

DAVID MARC

JOHNSON, Edward Crosby, 2d (*b.* 19 January 1898 in Milton, Massachusetts; *d.* 2 April 1984 in Bourne, Massachusetts), lawyer-turned-investor who founded Fidelity Investments, which grew to be the largest mutual fund company in America.

Johnson was the only son of Samuel W. Johnson, an executive with C. F. Hovey & Co., a department store in Boston, and Josephine Forbush Johnson, a housewife. He and his four younger sisters were raised in a comfortable home on Randolph Avenue in Milton, a suburb of Boston. Johnson graduated from Milton Academy in 1916 and entered Harvard College that fall. After brief service in the naval reserve during World War I, he was graduated in 1920, then took a one-year course at the new Harvard Business School. In the fall of 1921 he entered Harvard Law School, and after graduation in 1924 he joined the firm of Ropes & Gray in Boston. On 18 October 1924 Johnson married his second cousin, Elsie Livingston Johnson; they had two children.

At Ropes & Gray, Johnson specialized in utility holding companies, but his real love was the stock market. He made a science of his hobby, tacking stock charts to his office walls and looking for patterns in the changing prices and trading

Edward C. Johnson 2d, 1960. COURTESY OF DIANA B. HENRIQUES. PHOTO BY BACHRACH.

volumes—an early example of what came to be known as technical analysis. His forecasts did not warn him of the 1929 crash, but he took pride in avoiding the much greater losses caused by the 1930–1932 market decline.

In 1935 Johnson became a legal adviser to the Boston firm of Incorporated Investors, one of the largest mutual fund companies of that day. Incorporated, founded in 1925, was one of the first true mutual funds, designed to reduce the risks small investors faced in the stock market. The fund industry at the time was dominated by investment trusts, later known as closed-end funds, which had a limited number of shares that traded on the stock exchange at prices that fluctuated with investor demand. By contrast, the new funds—first called "open-end funds"—had an unrestricted number of shares, which the fund would redeem at any time, at a price based on the portfolio's actual value. This type of fund gave small investors easier access to their savings.

By 1939 Johnson had left the law and become the treasurer of Incorporated Investors. In early 1943, while still an officer of Incorporated, he took control of the Fidelity Fund, a struggling fund with about $4 million in assets. By 1944 he was quietly selling Fidelity Fund shares to the public, in direct competition with Incorporated Investors. His boss and mentor, William A. Parker, discovered his sales activities in the late summer of 1945 and bitterly ended their relationship.

Johnson soon transformed the Fidelity Fund into a money machine. A robust economy and recovering stock market helped, of course. But Johnson was a masterful investor, and his Zenlike approach to the market fascinated the young managers who flocked to work for him. He saw investing as a study of "the mind of the crowd," a quest for the "thin air of the music we all heard." His letters to his shareholders became conversation pieces on Wall Street, where he was known as "Mister Johnson."

Johnson's most important contribution to the industry was his practice of giving young managers enormous latitude to manage investors' money. Elsewhere mutual funds were run by committees of market veterans who jointly decided what to buy and sell. Johnson thought this conservative approach was nonsense: "Two people can't play the violin," he would say. Investing was an individual art, in his view, and youth had an edge over age and experience. "A man is really at his best, his most fulfilled, when he's on the way to becoming what he's going to become," he once said. "After he's become it, he loses an infinitesimal bit of sharpness."

Fidelity became an incubator for young investment talent. In 1957 Johnson put Gerry Tsai, a young Chinese-born stock analyst, in charge of his new Fidelity Capital Fund, designed to take a riskier path to profit. By the early 1960s the enormously successful fund was outpacing the fund industry and Tsai was a media celebrity. Other fund companies copied Johnson's approach, and the media began to search for young managers who might warrant celebrity status. The Johnson model of single-handed management, with an emphasis on youth, dominated the industry well into the 1990s.

One of the most successful managers to emerge from Johnson's tutelage was his son, Edward 3d, known as Ned, whose track record eclipsed Tsai's. By 1972 Ned Johnson had taken charge of the family-owned business, which included more than a dozen separate funds containing a total of $4 billion. Ed Johnson remained chairman of the Fidelity Management board until his retirement in 1977. He died of pneumonia in 1984, after a long siege of Alzheimer's disease. He was buried in Forest Hills Cemetery, Boston.

By the time of his death, Johnson's $4 million fund had grown into the largest mutual fund management company in America, with more than $65 billion in assets; by the late 1990s the figure was nearly $500 billion. Fidelity's best-known fund, the Magellan Fund, became the largest single mutual fund in history during the 1980s.

★

For a full history of Fidelity, see Diana B. Henriques, *Fidelity's World: The Secret Life and Public Power of the Mutual Fund Giant* (1995). Joseph Nocera, *A Piece of the Action: How the Middle Class Joined the Money Class* (1994), looks at Fidelity during the 1970s and 1980s. Character portraits of Johnson are found in Adam Smith [George J. W. Goodman], *The Money Game* (1967), and John Brooks, *The Go-Go Years* (1973). Obituaries are in the *Boston Globe* (4 Apr. 1984) and *New York Times* (5 Apr. 1984).

DIANA B. HENRIQUES

JOHNSON, Paul Burney, Jr. (*b.* 23 January 1916 in Hattiesburg, Mississippi; *d.* 14 October 1985 in Hattiesburg, Mississippi), lawyer and politician who served as governor of Mississippi during the most intense period of the civil rights movement, encompassing the "Freedom Summer" of 1964.

Oldest of the three children of Paul Burney Johnson, Sr., a lawyer, and Corrine Venable, a homemaker, Johnson grew up in a politically prominent family. His father was elected governor of Mississippi in 1939 and died in office in 1943.

Johnson studied at the University of Mississippi, from which he received the LL.B. in 1940. The same year he began the practice of law in his hometown of Hattiesburg. On 8 February 1941 he married Dorothy Elizabeth Power in a ceremony at the Governor's Mansion; they had three children. Shortly after the attack on Pearl Harbor in December 1941, Johnson enlisted in the Marine Corps, serving from 1942 to 1946. He rose from private to captain and served in combat in the South Pacific.

Paul Burney Johnson. COURTESY OF MISSISSIPPI DEPARTMENT OF ARCHIVES AND HISTORY

In 1946 Johnson returned to Hattiesburg and resumed his law practice. The call of politics proved irresistible, and in 1947 he ran unsuccessfully for governor, then for U.S. senator when the death of Senator Theodore G. Bilbo created an opening that drew a field of six candidates. Known to voters only as the politically inexperienced son of a popular governor, Johnson placed a distant second in the Democratic primary for governor and a poor fourth in the special election for the Senate seat. From 1948 to 1951 he served as an assistant United States attorney for the Southern District of Mississippi.

In the 1950s Johnson emerged as the leader of an important political faction. As a one-party state in which Democrats held all offices and black residents were systematically denied the right to vote, the most enduring cleavage in Mississippi politics was between a populism that emphasized state activism to benefit small farmers and blue-collar workers and an antigovernment conservatism favored by businesspeople and owners of large plantations. Capturing the populist mantle once worn by his father, Johnson won a plurality in the first Democratic primaries for governor in 1951 and 1955, only to lose in runoffs to candidates favored by the conservative faction.

Johnson's dignified manner and lackluster speaking style set him in sharp contrast to the fiery demagogues, such as Bilbo and James K. Vardaman, who had dominated Mississippi populism for most of the century. Eschewing the overt racism that had characterized populism in the state, Johnson generally won the quiet support of the small number of black voters during the 1950s.

Frustrated by three failures to win the office held by his father, Johnson ran successfully for lieutenant governor in 1959. Serving with fiery segregationist governor Ross Barnett, Johnson found himself in the whirlwind when the University of Mississippi was ordered by a federal court to enroll James Meredith as its first black student in 1962. When federal marshals escorted Meredith to the campus on 26 September 1962, Johnson, accompanied by state law-enforcement officers, physically blocked their way. He was standing in for Governor Barnett, whose airplane had been grounded by bad weather. Previously considered suspect by segregationists, Johnson became a hero to opponents of civil rights.

As a candidate for governor again in 1963, Johnson skillfully exploited the incident. Since he lacked a suitable photograph, he commissioned an artist's drawing depicting him resolutely confronting Meredith and the chief federal marshal. Building his campaign on defiance of the federal government, Johnson encouraged the voters to "Stand Tall with Paul." This time he won the governorship, defeating not only the field of Democratic candidates, but also the first serious Republican challenger since Reconstruction.

Upon taking office on 21 January 1964, Johnson surprised both supporters and opponents with a conciliatory inaugural address. Devoting most of his speech to economic development, he declared that the state's economy "is not divisible . . . by race, color, or creed." In contrast to his campaign commitment to resist the civil rights movement, he declared, "If I must fight, it will not be a rear guard defense of yesterday . . . it will be an all out assault for our share of tomorrow."

During his four-year term as governor, Johnson attempted to focus on economic development, but events kept civil rights at the center of public attention. In 1964 civil rights organizations made Mississippi the focus of "Freedom Summer," a massive effort to mobilize black Mississippians with the assistance of volunteer civil rights workers from outside the state. Acts of violence, including murder and arson, by white resisters, especially a reinvigorated Ku Klux Klan, focused world attention on Mississippi.

Concerned that some local officials would be reluctant to protect black people and civil rights workers, Johnson won enactment of an unprecedented law permitting the governor to use state officers to enforce the law where local law enforcement proved unequal to the task. But he proved too timid to be effective when his state faced its greatest crisis: the murder of three civil rights workers near the small town of Philadelphia in June 1964. Only after President

Lyndon B. Johnson established an FBI office in Jackson in response to the murders did Johnson use the powers of his office to investigate and suppress Klan violence.

An innovator in economic development policy, Johnson focused his attention as governor, as much as possible, on the industrialization of Mississippi, the poorest state per capita in the United States. He established the state-operated Research and Development Center to apply technology to job creation and built a $130 million "shipyard of the future," owned by the state and leased to Litton Industries, to create 12,000 jobs on the Gulf Coast.

Barred by the state constitution from a second term, Johnson ran again for lieutenant governor in 1967. Unsuccessful, he returned to his home, "Tall Pines," in Hattiesburg and resumed the practice of law, forsaking active politics after seven campaigns in twenty years. After being in poor health for several years, he died of cardiac arrest and was buried in Hattiesburg.

As a political leader Johnson recognized that poverty was the greatest problem experienced by residents of his state, both black and white. Nevertheless, he shamelessly exploited racial prejudices to win the governorship. Too timid for the task of reconciliation when the civil rights movement challenged traditional racial policies, he missed opportunities to exercise responsible leadership in a critical period. His innovations in industrial development, however, made a lasting contribution to the economic well-being of his state and moved Mississippi closer to the national mainstream. Johnson early recognized the importance of technology to modern industry and worked to develop public-private partnerships to join the resources of both sectors for economic development.

★

Johnson's papers are housed in the University of Southern Mississippi Library. The Mississippi Department of Archives and History, in Jackson, has an extensive subject file, consisting primarily of newspaper clippings. Reid Stoner Derr examines Johnson's gubernatorial performance in "The Triumph of Progressivism: Governor Paul B. Johnson, Jr., and Mississippi in the 1960s" (Ph.D. thesis, University of Southern Mississippi, 1974). University of Mississippi professor James Silver critically surveys the political atmosphere in which Johnson rose to prominence in *Mississippi: The Closed Society* (1963). Earl Black examines Johnson's political career in the context of racial politics in *Southern Governors and Civil Rights: Racial Segregation as a Campaign Issue in the Second Reconstruction* (1976). Don Whitehead, *Attack on Terror: The FBI Against the Ku Klux Klan in Mississippi* (1970), and Seth Cagin and Philip Dray, *We Are Not Afraid: The Story of Goodman, Schwerner, and Chaney, and the Civil Rights Campaign for Mississippi* (1988), shed light on Johnson's role in the investigation of the Philadelphia murders. Erle Johnston, a state official under Johnson, offers a sympathetic account of Mississippi's efforts to preserve segregation in *Mississippi's Defiant Years, 1953–1973: An*

Interpretative Documentary with Personal Experiences (1990). An obituary is in the *New York Times* (15 Oct. 1985).

VAGN K. HANSEN

JOHNSON, Rachel Harris (*b.* 11 December 1887 in Worcester, Massachusetts; *d.* 9 August 1983 in Worcester, Massachusetts), civic worker who was founding president of the Girls Clubs of America.

Johnson was the daughter of Emma F. Dearborn, a community leader, and Henry F. Harris. The family's home, at 67 Lincoln Street in Worcester, became the first home of the Worcester Girls Club, founded in 1916, when Emma Harris donated it "as a clubhouse for the working girls of Worcester" in memory of her late husband. The club was for girls sixteen and over, to provide "ethical, educational, and social advantages to girls of lower income families." Emma Harris was very active in setting up the organization, particularly by securing the support of the Worcester branch of the National Civic Federation. She went on to serve as treasurer for about ten years.

Rachel Harris Johnson became secretary of the Worcester Girls Club in 1919. By then she had graduated from Smith College in 1909 and on 10 October 1912 had married J. Herbert Johnson, with whom she had two daughters. In 1919 the club became a charter member of the Community Chest of Worcester, which allowed the club's board to use fundraising revenue for improvements to the club rather than just for everyday operating expenses. In the mid-1920s the club expanded its membership to younger girls. During her years with the Worcester club, Johnson drafted the Girl's Bill of Rights, later published in *Thirty Years of Girls Club Experience* (1945), which she coauthored with Dora Estelle Dodge. The Girl's Bill of Rights reflected Johnson's belief that while preparing to become wives and mothers, young women deserved and should strive to be healthy, educated individuals with fulfilling lives.

The Worcester Girls Club continued to thrive in various capacities for many years, while similar organizations were developing in other cities throughout the nation. On 18 May 1945, nineteen girls clubs meeting in Springfield, Massachusetts, founded the national organization called Girls Clubs of America. The organization's two goals were to exchange information on programs for girls and to help communities establish new girls club centers. Johnson, who had been president of the Worcester Girls Club from 1934 to 1941 and had received the Isaiah Thomas Award from the Ad Club of Greater Worcester for distinguished service, became the national organization's first president. She retired in 1952.

After retirement Johnson continued to participate in Worcester civic and charitable organizations. In her lifetime

Rachel Harris Johnson. PHOTOGRAPH BY KEVIN GRINDER. COURTESY GIRLS, INC.

she was active in the local First Unitarian Church, Worcester Women's Club, Tatnuck Country Club, Foreign Policy Association, Women's Republican Club, Worcester Historical Society, Worcester Natural History Society, Worcester Art Museum, and Worcester County Musical Association. Johnson died at the Wayside Nursing Home in Worcester at the age of ninety-five. Her cremated remains were interred in Hope Cemetery in Worcester.

The initial headquarters of the Girls Clubs of America was a guest room in the Johnson family's Worcester home, and the group's initial assets amounted to $72.64. By 1990, when the organization's name became Girls Inc., with headquarters in New York City, it included more than 200 clubs in the United States and Canada with a membership of about 250,000. Thus, while Johnson lived and worked her entire life in Worcester, her efforts influenced the lives of tens of thousands of girls in North America during and after her lifetime.

★

Rachel Harris Johnson and Dora E. Dodge, *Thirty Years of Girls Club Experience* (1945), and Dora E. Dodge, *This Proud House: A Short History of the Early Days of the Worcester Girls Club* (1960), describe the origins, development, and programs of the Worcester club. Policy and Publications Committee of Girls Clubs of America, *Handbook for Organization and Administration of Girls*

Clubs (1969), provides some history of the Girls Clubs of America. Obituaries are in the *New York Times* (10 Aug. 1983), and Hal May, ed., *Contemporary Authors,* vol. 110 (1984).

NAN POLLOT

JORDAN, Leonard Beck ("Len") (*b.* 15 May 1899 in Mount Pleasant, Utah; *d.* 30 June 1983 in Boise, Idaho), Idaho governor (1951–1955) and U.S. senator (1962–1973).

Leonard Beck Jordan was born in Sanpete County, Utah, the son of Leonard Eugene Jordan and Irene (Beck) Jordan. The family moved to Enterprise, Oregon, where Jordan graduated from high school. He joined the United States Army during World War I, achieving the rank of lieutenant. Following the war, Jordan attended the University of Oregon. He majored in economics and lettered as a halfback on the varsity football team, graduating with an A.B. degree and Phi Beta Kappa honors in 1924. On 30 December 1924 he married Grace Edgington of Bend, Oregon. They had three children.

The Jordans moved to the rugged Hell's Canyon of the Snake River on the far western Idaho border and estab-

Len Jordan. REPRODUCED FROM THE COLLECTIONS OF THE LIBRARY OF CONGRESS

lished a sheep ranch. His wife later wrote a book, *Home Below Hell's Canyon* (1954), about family life in this very primitive area.

In 1941 Jordan moved to Grangeville, Idaho, an agricultural area nestled between the Clearwater River and the Snake River, where he established a farm implement business, a real estate agency, and an automobile dealership. Jordan won a seat in the state legislature in 1946, but suffered defeat in the predominantly Democratic area in 1948. That brief sojourn in the state's capital convinced Jordan to enter the 1950 Republican gubernatorial primary, which he won against four other candidates. In the fall election he defeated Calvin Wright by 10,000 votes, and he took office in January 1951. Because Idaho law prohibited a governor from succeeding himself, Jordan had one term to act.

Jordan's gubernatorial career featured four years of austerity measures. A postwar recession forced him to evaluate Idaho's higher education system, which led to the closing of the normal school at Albion in the southern part of the state. The legislature met only twice during his term, and this retrenchment policy on public education highlighted the first session. Jordan's own children were home-schooled by their mother at their Hell's Canyon home, so the governor felt local counties and districts should pay for the housing of students as well as building costs. The education lobby defeated many of his measures, but his cost-cutting put Idaho's finances on a sound footing. His initiatives during the second legislative session included an income tax cut and an attack on slot machines and punch cards, a form of a lottery. He defeated the gambling lobby and cut taxes, creating a deficit for his successor, Robert Smylie.

One of Jordan's primary interests was water development. He fought against federal attempts to dam Hell's Canyon but approved the Palisades Dam on the Snake River in eastern Idaho. Opposing President Harry Truman's desire for a Columbia Valley Authority, Jordan believed private power should develop water resources.

Upon leaving office in 1955, Jordan was appointed by President Dwight Eisenhower to chair the International Joint Commission (1955–1957), which deals with U.S.-Canada questions, and the International Development Advisory Board (1958–1959), which dealt primarily with the Saint Lawrence Seaway. He had barely returned to private life when Governor Smylie of Idaho appointed him to the U.S. Senate to serve out the term of the deceased Henry Dworshak in August 1962. Elected in his own right in 1966, he served in the Senate for a total of ten years.

As a senator, Jordan departed from his earlier position on private power and worked to create new federal dams in the northwestern United States, one on the Clearwater River and a second on the Teton River. Although a reluctant partner, he eventually joined Idaho colleague Frank Church in supporting the creation of the Sawtooth National Recreation Area in central Idaho. Jordan's tenure as a senator saw him take a moderate course on the Vietnam War, civil rights, and the War on Poverty. He tried to balance his conservative views of government with the activism of Presidents Lyndon Johnson and Richard Nixon. Jordan retired from the Senate in 1973 and returned to Boise for the last decade of his life. In recognition of his service, the Idaho legislature named a new government office building in Boise in his honor. He died of a stroke at age eighty-four and is buried at Cloverdale Cemetery in Boise.

★

Grace Jordan, *The Unintentional Senator* (1972), is a biography of Jordan written by his wife. A profile by Robert C. Sims is in *Idaho's Governors,* edited by Robert C. Sims and Hope Benedict (1992). An obituary is in the *New York Times* (2 July 1983).

F. ROSS PETERSON

K

KAHN, Herman (*b.* 15 February 1922 in Bayonne, New Jersey; *d.* 7 July 1983 in Chappaqua, New York), physicist, mathematician, "futurologist," lecturer and author, and founder of the Hudson Institute.

If Herman Kahn was to become famous, or in some circles infamous, for his blunt-spoken rejection of the doomsday and neo-Malthusian thinking that informed so much of the debate about managing risk in a thermonuclear, post-industrial age, his faith in humankind's capacity to rise above adversity was to some extent rooted in personal experience. His father, Abraham Kahn, a clothing manufacturer, and his mother, Yetta Koslowsky, a homemaker, divorced when he was very young. Abandoning his wife and three children, Abraham left them in poverty and dependent at various times during the Depression years on public assistance. When Kahn was thirteen, the family moved from New York City to Los Angeles. There, he attended high school while working almost full time in a number of menial jobs to help support his mother and two brothers. After graduation he enrolled at the University of Southern California, but his education was interrupted by World War II and a tour in Burma with the U.S. Army Signal Corps from 1943 to 1945. Upon discharge in 1945, he resumed his studies, transferring to the University of California at Los Angeles, from which he graduated with a B.A. in physics later that year. He then enrolled at the California Institute of Technology to pursue graduate work in applied mathematics, and began working part time as a research physicist in the aviation industry.

Obtaining an M.S. degree in 1948 from CalTech, Kahn obtained a job as staff physicist at the RAND Institute, a quasi-public consultant group doing military contract work, chiefly for the air force. Originally, he saw this job as a means of relieving his chronic impecuniousness while pursuing his doctoral studies en route to a career in academia. The opportunity RAND gave him to work under the brilliant mathematician John von Neumann, however, plus his meeting with Rosalie Jane Heilner, a coworker he would marry (on 31 March 1953), and the discovery of a personal affinity for the eccentric collegiality of the think-tank environment opened up new possibilities for him. Thus, when CalTech refused to accept his doctoral dissertation (sponsored by future Nobel laureate Richard P. Feynman), citing a policy against recognizing commercially sponsored research, he simply abandoned his ivory tower aspirations and embarked upon a trailblazing career as a contrarian thinker and philosophical provocateur.

During the first few years of his tenure at RAND, Kahn continued to work as a physicist, but by the mid-1950s his growing interest in economic and political issues led his superiors to create the position of roving consultant, freeing him to participate in those in-house projects in which he took particular interest. One of these, *A Study of Non-Military Defense* (1958), resulted in his being invited to give a series of lectures at Princeton's Center for International

Herman Kahn. CAMERA PRESS LTD./ARCHIVE PHOTOS

Studies in 1959. The thoroughly unconventional views expressed in these lectures were published by Princeton University Press the following year as *On Thermonuclear War.* This volume, the first of a trilogy on the subject, which also included *Thinking About the Unthinkable* (1962) and *On Escalation: Metaphors and Scenarios* (1965), not only elevated Kahn to the status of a major public figure but touched off a fierce, often vitriolic debate. Stripped of Kahn's own rhetorical excesses and his detractors' mischaracterizations, the book argued that while the probability of thermonuclear war actually breaking out was higher than anyone was prepared to acknowledge, there was no evidence to suggest that it would in fact be the all-annihilating holocaust so widely predicted, and that with proper planning based on realistic assessments of destruction, millions of lives that might otherwise be lost could be saved and prewar standards of living restored within a relatively short period of time.

Even stated in a manner far more tactful than Kahn's, such ideas were bound to stir up controversy. The issue was whether thermonuclear war would be made more survivable by taking prudent precautions, or more likely, by eliminating the "balance of terror" disincentive inherent in the

"total destruction" model. Thus, depending on which side one took, *On Thermonuclear War* either was "valuable because the author has taken off the blinders of self-deception and has faced up to the stark realities" (Jerome Spingarn in the *New York Times Book Review*), or raised the "question as to why we should be concerned with preserving a species of animal which can weigh coolly the concepts set forth in this book" (George Kirstein in the *Nation*). But for all the sound and fury, such academic debate was largely beside the point; in the corridors of power Kahn's "scenarios" (as he called his hypothesizations) evoked a highly favorable response, gaining him the title "father of deterrence theory" in the United States.

In 1961 he resigned from RAND, citing what he felt was its overdependence on military contracts, and with an investment of $10,000 established the Hudson Institute, first in White Plains and later in Croton-on-Hudson, New York. With typical immodesty he envisioned it as a "high-class RAND," staffed by a cadre of thinkers so varied he would be the only one capable of communicating with them all and devoted to the study of critical economic and social issues confronting the postindustrial world. His first significant essay in this direction was *The Year 2000* (1967), a "shape of things to come" manifesto commissioned by the American Academy of Arts and Sciences, in which he imagined a world at peace (the Soviet Union having collapsed because of its own economic shortcomings) and in the midst of unprecedented prosperity. It contained, to be sure, its share of far-fetched predictions, such as human control of weather, the ubiquity of household robots, and artificial moons to illuminate large regions of the earth at night. But as Art Kleiner observes in his book *The Age of Heretics* (1996), because Kahn "was so willing to scatter hypotheticals, he was the first to hit some targets," among them the social implications of the personal-computer revolution, breakthroughs in superconductivity, and the emergence of Japan as an economic superpower.

Kahn's optimism, his ultimate faith that technology, harnessed by private enterprise (in the form of multinational corporations), would usher in a "belle epoque" of global prosperity, brought him into conflict with the dominant "fragile earth" philosophy that had, since the early 1960s, energized active and influential "green" movements in the United States and Western Europe. These movements were championed, as Kahn saw it, by the same liberal intellectuals and their allies in the media, universities, and government bureaucracies he had earlier confronted in arguing for a less passive nuclear strategy. For Kahn, what had been a competition of ideas in the intellectual marketplace would, as Kleiner points out, over the next decade and a half become an increasingly bitter personal crusade against those he considered to constitute an out-of-touch elite seeking to preserve its own privileged position. "Have you ever seen a baby?" he would say to groups. "They're not known for tolerance, moderation. Babies will destroy the universe if they're empowered." Such views resonated strongly with proponents of anti-interventionist free-market growth and helped to provide the intellectual underpinnings for a movement that would put another unapologetic optimist, Ronald Reagan, in the White House in 1981. Indeed, as Kahn observed in an interview shortly before his death, "The Reagan administration is a clear response to and cause of new priorities for the nation. Much of its program can be characterized as a reaction to the excesses of the 1960s and 1970s."

From the time he founded the Hudson Institute until his death, from a heart attack, Kahn lived in Chappaqua. In a step that could not have surprised those familiar with his ideas, he had a fallout shelter built into his home. Kahn and his wife had two children. He enjoyed reading, conversation, swimming, and hiking.

An imposing physical presence at over six feet tall and more than three hundred pounds, Kahn cut a memorable figure on the lecture circuit. Blessed with a prodigious memory, he was a mesmerizing presence on the dais, part university don spouting abstruse information, part entertainer spinning out dramatizations and anecdotes to illustrate his points. To his opponents he was the very embodiment of the amoral technocrat and served as a frequent target for political satirists. Kahn (with a pinch of Werner von Braun added) was the inspiration for the title character in Stanley Kubrick's scathingly hilarious antiwar film, *Dr. Strangelove (Or How I Learned to Stop Worrying and Love the Bomb)* (1964). Indeed, he claimed to relish his role as bête noire of the liberal intellectual establishment, seeing in its ad hominem attacks on him proof of the unanswerability of his arguments. Yet for all his willingness to "think about the unthinkable," he was not without his own peculiar blind spots, some of which the critic and cultural historian Richard Kostelanetz enumerated in an otherwise admiring 1969 profile. These included tendencies to emphasize technological and organizational factors over equally significant cultural factors, to oversimplify for the sake of neat analysis or to exaggerate out of a desire to shock, to establish generalizations on the basis of a striking anecdote or to make arbitrary use of evidence to buttress a favored point of view, and to get carried away occasionally by his own ingenuity and espouse the same sorts of gimmicky solutions he so often decried in those with whom he disagreed.

Perhaps the best brief summation of Kahn's influence on his times and contemporaries was offered by *New York Times* business reporter Peter Passell in a review of his 1982 book, *The Coming Boom*. Passell wrote:

> Liberals got migraines contemplating his Strangelovean scenarios for nuclear war in *Thinking About the Unthinkable* [1962]. Environmentalists gnashed their teeth over *The Next Two Hundred Years* [1976], a rosy assessment of the world's long-term prospects. The Japanese, accustomed to awe from Westerners, were shocked by his prediction of big trouble ahead in *The Japanese Challenge* [1978]. What keeps them all coming back for more is that while Mr. Kahn irritates, he never fails to inform and entertain.

★

Richard Kostelanetz, *Master Minds: Portraits of Contemporary American Artists and Intellectuals* (1969), contains a highly readable, generally appreciative appraisal of Kahn at perhaps the apex of his influence. Robert L. Holmes, *On War and Morality* (1989), deals with Kahn as the "father of deterrence theory," offering a measured but uncompromising critique of his position. Art Kleiner, *The Age of Heretics: Heroes, Outlaws, and the Forerunners of Corporate Change* (1966), focuses on Kahn as one of a number of influences on the development of the modern multinational corporation, and while respectful of his contributions, finds at least as much to criticize as to praise. A useful early sketch of Kahn can be found in Charles Moritz, ed., *Current Biography 1962* (1963). Interviews with Kahn include the *New York Times* (13 Aug. 1982); S. N. Chakravarty, "Thinking About the Unthinkable," *Forbes* (22 Nov. 1982); and "Hudson Institute's Herman Kahn Foresees Likely Possibility of Widespread Revitalization," *Trusts and Estates* 122 (May 1983): 8–10. For biographical information, an overview of Kahn's literary output, and excerpts from leading reviews of his works, see Susan M. Trosky, ed., *Contemporary Authors,* vol. 44, New Revision Series (1994). Obituaries are in the *New York Times* (8 July 1983); *Time* (18 July 1983); *National Review* (5 Aug. 1983); and the *Futurist* 17 (Oct. 1983): 61–65.

RICHARD B. CALHOUN

KARDINER, Abram (*b.* 17 August 1891 in New York City; *d.* 20 July 1981 in Easton, Connecticut), leading American psychoanalyst who united psychoanalytic theory with cultural anthropology in research published in *The Individual and His Society* (1939) and *The Psychological Frontiers of Society* (1945).

Born on the Lower East Side of Manhattan, Abram Kardiner benefited from the educational policies of New York City. His mother had died when he was a toddler, and his father, a peddler, could not pay for a private school education. Kardiner attended Townsend Harris High School (a public high school with a curriculum designed to challenge highly competent students) and the tuition-free City College of New York, from which he graduated in 1912. He received his medical degree from Cornell Medical School in 1917, then served a two-year internship at Mount Sinai Hospital (1917–1919) and a psychiatric residency at

Abram Kardiner. NYT PICTURES/NYT PERMISSIONS

Manhattan State Hospital on Wards Island in New York City. While a resident he was medical examiner of Children's Court.

In 1921, the year he completed his residency, Kardiner was accepted as a student-patient by Sigmund Freud. He went to Vienna with five other young American psychiatrists for six months of psychoanalytic training, a personal and intellectual experience that influenced the rest of his life. In his analysis with Freud, Kardiner was distinguished from other student-patients by the fact that Freud talked to him. He attributed this difference in treatment to the fact that he told "a very interesting story" and "did not argue" with Freud's interpretation of the events in the story. When Kardiner returned to New York and worked with his own patients, he was selective in applying Freud's teachings; in particular he rejected Freud's emphasis on latent homosexuality. Throughout his life Kardiner was critical of aspects of orthodox psychoanalytic theory.

Kardiner's interests went beyond the private practice of psychiatry. In 1930, with Monroe Meyer and Bert Lewin, he founded the New York Psychiatric Institute, the first training school of its kind in the United States. Three years later he and several social scientists organized a seminar at the New York Psychoanalytic Society to study the processes by which culture is transmitted from one generation to the next. He started with two students; within three years there were 100 students. This seminar later moved to the department of anthropology at Columbia University, where Professor Ralph Linton, an anthropologist, shared in conducting the seminar. This collaboration resulted in the publication of *The Individual and His Society* (1939) and *The Psychological Frontiers of Society* (1945).

In studying primitive cultures Kardiner analyzed their mores in terms of their "basic disciplines": methods of child rearing, control of sex, psychological dependency, and attitudes toward aggression. Since he agreed with the broader aspects of Freud's theories that traced personality to childhood development, Kardiner concluded that the determinants of character and personality were linked to the nature of parent-child and intrafamilial relationships and that culture was transmitted to the child through the psychological processes inherent in these relationships. More than other theorists of his time, Kardiner emphasized the helplessness of the child and the child's resulting feelings of dependency. He concluded that pathological dependency resulted from failure to develop adequate resources or the unavailability of personal resources resulting from the person's neurotic difficulties. His ideas were forerunners of later theories concerning separation and individuation and, consequently, were an important influence on psychoanalytic thought.

Kardiner continued to study individual personality development. He collaborated with Dr. Lionel Ovesey on a study of twenty-five black individuals, *The Mark of Oppression: Explorations in the Personality of the American Negro* (1951). In this book the authors evaluated the impact of white sociocultural attitudes on black personality. With Edward Preble he wrote *They Studied Man* (1961), an evaluation of the lives and works of a number of anthropologists and other scholars. The authors concluded that "man has the capacity to invent new methods and ideas when the old ones fail him."

In the mid-1950s Kardiner was director of the psychoanalytic clinic at Columbia University (1955–1957) and a clinical professor of psychiatry there. In 1954 he published *Sex and Morality,* a book that examined the sexual mores of the American culture of that time. In 1977 he wrote a popular memoir of his psychoanalytical training sessions in Vienna, *My Analysis with Freud.*

In one of his last articles, "The Social Stress Syndrome," Kardiner commented on negative aspects of contemporary society that he considered to be symptoms of decline: violence, fanaticism, aberrant sexual behavior. He contended that such antisocial behavior, when it affected more than 10 or 15 percent of the adult population, weakened the pillars that supported the society. He held that individuals had an obligation to learn what the "breaking point" of their society was and to take steps to relieve or eliminate the pressures on that society.

Throughout his life Kardiner was actively engaged with all the arts, particularly with music. He played the piano and enjoyed a reputation as a fine amateur maker of violins. Kardiner died at his summer home in Easton, Connecticut, two months after sustaining a severe head injury during a fall.

Kardiner's contributions to psychoanalysis were both theoretical and clinical. From the clinical point of view, many of the persons who came to him for treatment became prominent in their professional careers, including Irving Bieber, S. Harmon Ephron, Harold Kelman, Judd Marmor, Daniel Schneider, and Alexander Wolf. From a theoretical point of view, he drew on sociological thought and anthropological research to enlarge psychological understanding of how the human animal becomes a social being. His research furthered the interpenetration of anthropology and psychoanalysis.

When he died, Kardiner was one of the last persons to have been analyzed by Freud. He thus represented the link between the mystique of Freud's consulting room in Vienna and the movement toward interdisciplinary research and thought in the twentieth-century social sciences.

★

See "Profile, Abram Kardiner," *Journal of the American Academy of Psychoanalysis* 5 (1977): 153–154. An obituary is in the *New York Times* (22 July 1981). See also Irving Bieber, "In Memory of Abram Kardiner (1891–1981)," *Journal of the American Academy of Psychoanalysis* 10 (1982): 285–288.

ANNETTE BENEDICT

KAUFMAN, Andrew Geoffrey ("Andy") (*b.* 17 January 1949 in New York City; *d.* 16 May 1984 in Los Angeles, California), actor and comedian best known for his role as the mechanic Latka Gravas on the television sitcom *Taxi*.

Kaufman grew up in Great Neck, New York, an affluent town on Long Island, the eldest of two sons of Stanley and Janice Kaufman. His talent for acting surfaced at a young age, and he was telling jokes and performing magic tricks for family and friends before the age of ten. After graduating from Great Neck North High School in 1967, Kaufman drove cabs and trucks on Long Island. In 1969 he

Andy Kaufman puts on a show for the camera, *c.* 1980. FOTOS INTERNATIONAL/ARCHIVE PHOTOS

enrolled at Grahm Junior College in Boston to study television and radio. There he starred in a campus radio show, *Uncle Andy's Fun House,* performed at coffeehouses, and appeared in *The Soul Time Review,* a show sponsored by a black student group.

Kaufman returned to New York in 1971 after college. He worked in nightclubs without pay until he was discovered in the early 1970s at My Father's Place, a Long Island club, by Budd Friedman, owner of the Improvisation comedy club. This connection landed Kaufman on the premier comedy club circuit, with appearances at the Improv and Catch a Rising Star in New York and Los Angeles. Following these successes he began practicing transcendental meditation to overcome shyness, a technique he continued throughout his life.

Kaufman's big break came when NBC invited him to audition for its new late-night comedy show *Saturday Night Live*. On the show's debut, 11 October 1975, Kaufman lip-synched the theme from *Mighty Mouse,* a cartoon show. He eventually made a dozen appearances on *Saturday Night Live*. His routines showcased his collection of odd personas, from Foreign Man, an awkward, would-be comedian whose helplessness and stage fright instilled a deep sense of pity and embarrassment in his audience, who transforms into Elvis Presley, to the World Inter-Gender Wrestling Champion, a virulent male chauvinist who challenged women to wrestle against him.

Kaufman committed himself to the unflinching portrayal of his many characters, or alter egos, no matter what reaction they engendered in his audience. Indeed, Kaufman's performances often provoked annoyance and even anger before laughter. He stated that he was not a comedian: "I never told a joke in my life." Instead, he aimed to blur the line between theater and reality and to rouse strong, genuine emotion in his audience.

Among Kaufman's most enduring characters was Tony Clifton, a minor-league lounge singer complete with mustache, sport coat, and toupee, a real-life performer whom Kaufman ostensibly discovered during a trip to Las Vegas in the early 1970s. Clifton's crass and obnoxious style tested the limits of his audience's patience. To the end Kaufman insisted, in vain, that he and Clifton were not the same person. After he died, friends revealed that although he did originally pose as Clifton, Kaufman passed on the role to friend and collaborator Bob Zmuda, who was responsible for most of Clifton's appearances.

Kaufman remains best known for the role of auto mechanic Latka Gravas on the television sitcom *Taxi*. From the first broadcast of *Taxi* on 12 September 1978 to the final show on 27 July 1983, Kaufman's Latka delighted audiences with his high-pitched, accented chatter and strange traditions from his never-named native land. An innocent but complex man prone to a wide variety of moods and personalities, Latka broke free from the traditional limitations put on sitcom characters. Even so, by the show's second season Kaufman had grown tired of Latka and the confinements of working from a script.

During his brief career Kaufman logged numerous television credits, including appearances on *The Tonight Show* and *Late Night,* as well as two television specials, *The Andy Kaufman Special: Andy's Funhouse* (1979) and *The Andy Kaufman Show* (1983). He also appeared in two feature-length films: *In God We Tru$t* (1980), as televangelist Armageddon T. Thunderbird, and *Heartbeeps* (1981), with Bernadette Peters, as a lovestruck robot.

Despite his television success Kaufman never abandoned the stage. On 26 April 1979 he appeared at Carnegie Hall in New York City, performing some of his best-known routines before an audience of 2,800. After the show Kaufman invited his fans to board twenty chartered buses waiting outside to take them to the New York School of Printing in Manhattan for milk and cookies. Hours later he resumed the show on the Staten Island ferry.

But for every ringing success in Kaufman's career there seemed to be a controversy. Most notorious, perhaps, was his guest-host appearance on *Fridays,* ABC's short-lived late-night answer to *Saturday Night Live,* on 20 February 1981. Beginning with the opening monologue, Kaufman departed from the script, leaving the show's cast and crew lost for the remainder of the live broadcast. By the last sketch, he had pushed some of the cast members to their limits, resulting in an on-air brawl. The audience sat in stunned silence as Kaufman was quickly escorted from the stage. Several members of the *Fridays* cast later admitted their complicity in Kaufman's prank, but it remains unclear just how many knew about it beforehand.

Kaufman reveled in controversies like the *Fridays* debacle. A week before the 20 November 1982 broadcast of *Saturday Night Live,* he engaged in a heated argument with its producers about his future on the show. At the beginning of the 20 November show, NBC executive Dick Ebersol announced a call-in referendum to decide whether Kaufman should be banned from *Saturday Night Live* for life. At the end of the night, viewers had voted Kaufman off the show, 195,544 to 169,186. He reportedly swallowed this bitter pill with a deep sense of betrayal; in fact, he had precipitated the entire conflict. He nevertheless respected the vote and never appeared on the show again.

Kaufman is remembered for his preoccupation with wrestling. He at first limited his wrestling exploits to female opponents, deriding his would-be challengers with chauvinist rhetoric and drawing the ire of feminists. Kaufman's antics ultimately provoked a feud with professional wrestler Jerry Lawler that culminated in a match at the Mid-South Coliseum in Memphis on 5 April 1982. Within minutes of the opening bell, Lawler knocked down the lanky Kaufman, who was rushed to the hospital with a serious cervical vertebrae injury. The story of Kaufman's brief wrestling career was depicted in the documentary film *I'm from Hollywood* (1983).

A nonsmoker, nondrinker, and health-food fanatic, Kaufman was diagnosed with a rare form of lung cancer in January 1984. The effects of his radiation therapy were obvious by the time his last film debuted on 20 March 1984. *My Breakfast with Blassie,* a takeoff on the cult classic *My Dinner with Andre,* featured Kaufman and professional wrestler Fred Blassie in conversation over breakfast at a Hollywood restaurant.

Kaufman died at Cedars-Sinai Medical Center in Los Angeles at the age of thirty-five. He was buried at the Beth David Cemetery in Elmont, New York.

★

See David Hirshey, "Andy Kaufman: Beyond Laughter," *Rolling Stone* (30 Apr. 1981). An obituary is in the *New York Times* (18 May 1984). See also Roger Wolmuth, "Andy Kaufman, 1949–1984," *People* (4 June 1984).

FRANK MORROW

KAUFMAN, Murray ("Murray the K") (*b.* 14 February 1922 in New York City; *d.* 21 February 1982 in Los Angeles, California), flamboyant disc jockey and rock and roll impresario.

Kaufman was the son of Max Kaufman, a leather merchant, and Jean Greenblatt, a vaudeville pianist who sometimes worked under the name Jean Greene. He dropped out of De Witt Clinton High School in the Bronx in the late 1930s and was briefly a baseball catcher in the New York Yankees farm system before serving on the home front organizing entertainment for troops during World War II. Kaufman launched his career in show business in the late 1940s, working as a freelance master of ceremonies at nightclubs in the Catskill Mountains of New York State. In the early 1950s he was hired as an announcer by radio station WMCA in New York City and occasionally hosted talk shows.

In 1958 Kaufman moved to WINS, the leading rock and roll station in New York, where he worked as a disc jockey

Murray Kaufman ("Murray the K"). ARCHIVE PHOTOS

on the overnight shift. His *Swingin' Soiree* program quickly won an avid following among the station's mostly youthful audience. In 1959 he was moved into the coveted 7 to 11 P.M. time slot that had once belonged to the legendary disc jockey Alan Freed. Kaufman displaced Freed's successor, Bruce ("Cousin Brucie") Morrow, who later became an immensely popular disc jockey at rival station WABC. Kaufman, who had dubbed himself "Murray the K," developed a colorful on-air persona: he blended a fanciful vocabulary (a journalist described it as "a sort of Pig Latin for teenagers") with zany, nonstop patter about "submarine races" and other nonsensical topics that made his adolescent listeners into loyal disciples.

Kaufman was fervently committed to spreading the gospel of rock and roll. In addition to his broadcasts, in which he often gave the first radio exposure to singles that later topped the charts, he hosted live shows in the late 1950s and early 1960s, first at Palisades Amusement Park in New Jersey, then at the Paramount Theater in Brooklyn, where he presented such artists as Marvin Gaye, Smokey Robinson and the Miracles, the Four Tops, and Martha and the Vandellas.

When the Beatles arrived in New York City on 7 February 1964 for their first U.S. appearance, Kaufman, wearing his signature porkpie hat, was among the throng of reporters, disc jockeys, and fans who turned out to greet them. He commandeered the group's initial press conference, firing questions from the foot of a makeshift platform. According to journalist Tom Wolfe's account of the event: "Some photographer would be yelling, 'Hey, how about . . . getting . . . a little closer . . . !' but . . . Murray the K would be singling out one Beatle like George Harrison and saying . . . , 'Hey George, baby, hey, . . . down here, how did this reception compare with the reception you got in Stockholm, baby?'" The Beatles reportedly admired Kaufman's initiative; their manager, Brian Epstein, appreciated the publicity Kaufman generated for a group that was not yet a household name in the United States.

During the Beatles' whirlwind stop in New York, Kaufman escorted the group to nightclubs and introduced them to such starlets as Stella Stevens and Tuesday Weld. At some point he apparently began referring to himself as "the Fifth Beatle." By another account, however, George Harrison supplied the moniker when he was asked by a reporter, during a visit by the Beatles to Washington, D.C. (accompanied by the ubiquitous Kaufman), "What the [expletive] is Murray the K doing here?" Kaufman later remarked, "This was the biggest thing in the history of popular music. Presley was never this big, neither was Sinatra. The fact that I was . . . associated with the Beatles the way I was, living with them, having George as my roommate—it caused such jealousy as I have never seen in my life."

Kaufman, an ambitious man, soon realized that his intense connection with the Beatles could prove detrimental to his career at a time when the musical tastes of his young listeners were rapidly changing. "I'm not riding the Beatles coattails," he told Tom Wolfe, "and if they go, I'm going to be ready for the next person who comes along." In 1965 he left WINS; the following year he became the program director of WOR-FM, New York City's first "progressive" rock music station. At WOR, Kaufman pioneered the concept of "free-form" radio, which quickly spread to other FM stations in New York and in other markets. Rather than adhere to a repetitive playlist, Kaufman played lengthier tracks from albums by such artists as Bob Dylan and the Jefferson Airplane. He toned down his rapid-fire delivery and became more attentive to the political tumult of the mid-1960s. After eighteen months at WOR, Kaufman was fired, reportedly for focusing too much attention on such controversial performers as Joan Baez and Richie Havens.

After leaving WOR, Kaufman opened short-lived discotheques on the Upper East Side of Manhattan and on Long Island. In the late 1960s and early 1970s he worked briefly as a disc jockey at CHUM in Toronto, WNBC in New York, and several other stations. In 1973 he contracted lymphoma, and over the next nine years he endured frequent chemotherapy treatments while attempting to revive his career by entering the radio nostalgia market as the host of a weekly syndicated program, *Soundtrack of the Sixties.* In 1981 his illness worsened and he could not continue the show; he died of cancer early in the following year.

Kaufman was married six times. His first wife (1943), Anna Mae Sytnyk, died giving birth to the first of his three sons in 1944. He married Anna Villi in 1946; they were divorced in 1949, when he had a brief third marriage and then a fourth, which lasted to 1959. In 1960 he married Jacqueline Hayes, whom he divorced in 1972. His last marriage, in 1978 to soap star Jacklyn Zeeman, lasted only a year.

Many people found Kaufman rather irascible, but few have questioned his stature as one of the most important disc jockeys in rock and roll history. Wolfman Jack, one of the many disc jockeys greatly influenced by Kaufman in the 1960s, called him a "rock and roll impresario." Dick Clark, longtime television host of *American Bandstand,* described Kaufman as "unique": "He combined his own special on-the-air talent with his ability to inspire the best of other people's talent."

★

Peter Altschuler, Kaufman's second son, manages the Murray the K archives. Tom Wolfe, *The Kandy-Kolored Tangerine-Flake Streamline Baby* (1965), contains an essay on Kaufman, "The Fifth Beatle." Richard Price, "Going Down with Murray the K," *Rolling Stone* (15 Apr. 1982), treats Kaufman's career from the perspective of his later years. Kurt Loder's obituary in *Rolling Stone* (15 Apr. 1982) is the most thorough published source of biographical information. See also the obituaries in the *New York Times* and *Washington Post* (both 23 Feb. 1982).

JAMES T. FISHER

KELLY, Charles E. ("Commando") (*b.* 23 September 1920 in Pittsburgh, Pennsylvania; *d.* 11 January 1985 in Pittsburgh, Pennsylvania), World War II hero and recipient of the Medal of Honor, two Silver Stars, and eight other awards.

Charles Kelly grew up in difficult circumstances that later made him an exceedingly tough soldier. Kelly, one of the nine sons of James and Irene (Reese) Kelly, came of age on the rough streets of Pittsburgh's North Side. After the death of Kelly's father, a blacksmith, his mother did her best to make their home, which lacked electricity and indoor plumbing, as hospitable as possible. Charles Kelly began working as a house painter's assistant immediately after grade school. In his off hours he ran the harsh streets of his neighborhood and had many petty scrapes with the law as a youngster.

On 26 May 1942 Kelly entered the U.S. Army and found himself in the environment in which he would achieve his greatest success. He chafed at authority, as he had in civilian life, and incurred many infractions (including a court-martial for being absent without leave for three weeks). He had, however, excellent military skills and, as he would demonstrate, an exceptional combat temperament.

Kelly's unit, the Thirty-sixth Infantry Division, arrived in North Africa in April 1943 but did not see heavy combat

Sergeant Charles Kelly with German rifles, Italy, 1944. UPI/CORBIS-BETTMANN

until it landed at Salerno, Italy, the following September. Corporal Kelly immediately proved to be an extraordinary combat soldier. His shooting skill and fearlessness made him a natural leader. He fought with cold detachment, noting in his memoir, *One Man's War* (1944), "I can remember no feeling about the German dead except curiosity . . . to us, they were just bundles of rags."

On 13 September 1943 Kelly's company found itself in a ferocious firefight in the town of Altavilla, six miles up from the Salerno beach. The men of the company had stockpiled ammunition in the mayor's house and now faced a withering German counterattack. Kelly moved from window to window, using up weapon after weapon, inflicting great losses on the assaulting enemy. When the Germans seemed poised to burst into the building, Kelly pulled the firing pins from 60-mm mortar shells and dropped the live rounds on the enemy below. He fought in a controlled frenzy and, when holding the position no longer proved possible, Kelly stayed until the last, firing to cover the withdrawal. He then made his escape and joined the remnants of his company, which had given up hope of his survival.

In the ensuing months Kelly would take part in some of the most intense combat that American troops experienced in the European theater. His efforts in the aborted crossing of the Rapido River earned him a Silver Star, and he fought with distinction in the Monte Cassino campaign. But it was his bravery on 13 September 1943 in Altavilla that led to the award of the nation's highest decoration for valor, the Medal of Honor. The citation drew upon eyewitness accounts to document Kelly's heroism and "intrepidity in battle." On 11 March 1944 General Mark Clark placed the pale blue ribbon holding the medal around the neck of the now-Sergeant Charles Kelly.

Four days later he was back in combat, but the army in May decided to return Kelly, now dubbed "Commando" by a *Stars and Stripes* correspondent, to the United States for war bond rallies and patriotic broadcasts. Kelly received a tumultuous welcome home in Pittsburgh, the largest parade in that city's history. He received $40,000 for a lengthy story in the *Saturday Evening Post* (published serially in July 1944) that was later expanded into *One Man's War.* He also received $25,000 for the film rights; later his memoir would, in fact, be made into a film. The instant fame had its draining effects, as well, and Kelly would write in his memoir of "getting pretty sick of my own story by this time." His sudden wealth allowed him to buy a home for his mother and purchase a gas station.

But Kelly would not find in peacetime the success he had at war. His business failed. His first wife, May Boish, with whom he had two children, died of cancer in 1951, and his second marriage, by which he had four children, ended in divorce. He moved from Pittsburgh to Louisville, Kentucky, in 1955 and lived in a public housing project.

After he was injured in an auto accident in the early 1970s, Pittsburgh veterans organizations raised money to get him an apartment in that city and a job as a maintenance man in a senior citizens facility. Kelly died at the Veterans Administration Hospital in Pittsburgh, suffering a heart attack following surgery. He is buried in Highwood Cemetery in Pittsburgh.

Charles Kelly, the self-proclaimed boy from "the other side of the tracks," became one of America's first World War II heroes. Pete Martin, who collaborated on Kelly's memoir, wrote in the memoir that "this war is not being fought exclusively by those voted 'most likely to succeed' by their graduating class. . . . A large chunk of this war is being fought by boys to whom Anzio and Cassino and Cherbourg were just bigger and tougher alley fights." America, for a time, celebrated this twenty-three-year-old hero home from the war, but that moment passed, and "Commando" Kelly never again found the steadiness of purpose that had served him so well as a warrior.

★

Charles E. Kelly and Pete Martin, *One Man's War* (1944), is a memoir of Kelly's war experiences, with some information about his prewar years. Edward F. Murphy, *Heroes of World War II* (1990), describes his major war exploits. Obituaries are in the *New York Times* (13 Jan. 1985) and *Washington Post* (14 Jan. 1985).

JOHN O'SULLIVAN

KELLY, George Lange ("Highpockets") (*b.* 10 September 1895 in San Francisco, California; *d.* 13 October 1984 in Burlingame, California), Hall of Fame baseball player, coach, and manager.

Kelly was one of nine children of police captain James Kelly and Mary Lange. His five older brothers were semiprofessional baseball players. He attended Madison Grammar School, graduated from Pacific Heights Junior High School, and then was enrolled in Polytechnic High School. Soon he was a member of two local baseball teams, the Ideal Billiard Parlor team and the Union Iron Works team.

Kelly left high school in 1914, his senior year, when his uncle, Bill "Little Eva" Lange, a Chicago Cubs player of the 1890s, helped Kelly find a first baseman's job with Victoria of the Northwest League. Although Kelly was a weak .250 hitter his first year, he showed a strong arm. In 1915 the manager of the New York Giants, John McGraw, read a favorable report on Kelly from scout Dick Kinsella, unaware that Kinsella had napped in his hotel room and written his report from what he had heard secondhand. At any rate, Kelly's .296 average and his fifteen home runs was persuasive to McGraw, who bought the contract of the nineteen-year-old for $1,200. Kelly played in his first game

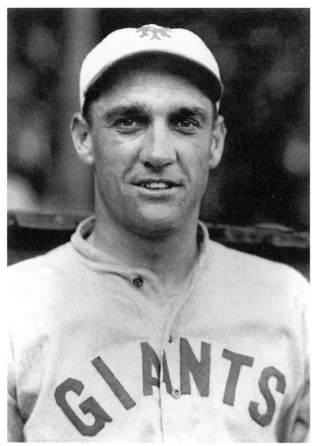

George Kelly. COURTESY OF THE NATIONAL BASEBALL HALL OF FAME LIBRARY, COOPERSTOWN, N.Y.

on 18 August 1915. From then through 1917 Kelly played a total of only eighty-five games.

McGraw saw the strength of Kelly's throwing arm and let him pitch in 1917, with Kelly getting five scoreless innings and a win; it was the only major league pitching he would do. "Those first two years I was with the Giants," Kelly later recalled, "McGraw kept me on the bench alongside him and talked to me about what was going on out there on the field, and I never learned so much about baseball." The Giants sent Kelly to Pittsburgh during 1917, but he lasted only twenty-three at bats before the Pirates sent him back to the Giants, who sent him down to the minor leagues. Kelly played for Rochester (New York) of the International League, where he made thirty-six hits in thirty-two games. He spent 1918 in the U.S. Army as a member of the ground unit at Kelly Field in San Antonio, Texas.

When Kelly returned to Rochester in 1919 he hit fifteen home runs and was batting .356 when the Giants called him back up to replace Hal Chase at first base in the last month of the season. Although Kelly hit .290 during that time, he was not as adroit a fielder as Chase and the fans

let him know it with their boos. But they were not aware that McGraw believed Chase was throwing games.

In 1920 Kelly became the Giants' first baseman, and because of his six-foot-four, 190-pound frame, he was nicknamed "Highpockets" by writer Damon Runyon. By now a powerful right-handed batter, his eleven home runs tied him for third in the National League. Kelly was in the top twenty in five offensive categories and led the National League with ninety-four runs batted in (RBIs) and was first in total chances per game as well as in putouts, double plays, and assists. Kelly set the league record for putouts and chances.

On 17 August 1921, when the Giants opened a five-game series with the league-leading Pittsburgh Pirates, Kelly's grand-slam homer in the seventh inning of the first game led New York to a sweep of the series and the first of four consecutive pennants. Kelly's twenty-three home runs that year made him first in the National League; "Long George," as he was called by the players, was also second in the league in both RBIs and doubles, as well as third in slugging percentage. He also played superbly in the field, being first in putouts, double plays, and assists. He began to take all the cutoff throws from the outfield, even those from left field.

In 1921 the Giants won the best-of-nine World Series against the New York Yankees by five games to three. With the Giants leading 1–0 in the bottom of the ninth of the eighth game, Kelly completed an unusual double play. Giants infielder Johnny Rawlings made a brilliant diving stop of a Frank Baker line drive and threw Baker out at first. Kelly flung the ball across the infield to third baseman Frankie Frisch, putting out the runner who was dashing from first and ending the series.

On 17 September 1922 Kelly hit three home runs in one game. That kind of power helped the Giants win another National League pennant. Kelly was fourth in the league in RBIs with 107, third in home runs with seventeen. A key asset on the field as well, he was first in assists and in total chances per game. After a second World Series victory over the Yankees, he visited Japan as part of an All-Star team.

The next year, the third straight pennant year for the Giants, Kelly again (on 14 June) hit three home runs, was fourth in RBIs with 103, first in putouts, and first in total chances per game. He played four positions. He also hit homers in six consecutive games. He made nineteen putouts in the World Series, but the Yankees took their first World Championship, four games to two. It was also a year that brought Kelly's younger brother Ren to pitch briefly for the Philadelphia Athletics.

McGraw insisted on putting Bill Terry into the lineup at first base in 1924 and so Kelly played 108 games as a second baseman. He helped make up a Hall of Fame infield, with Terry, Kelly, Travis Jackson at shortstop, and Freddie Lindstrom at third. Kelly was the cleanup hitter. He was first in the league in RBIs with 136, fourth in home runs with 21, and third in doubles with 37. He was sixth in the league in Most Valuable Player voting. In the 1924 World Series he played three different positions in a losing effort against the Washington Senators.

Although his offensive numbers fell in 1925, Kelly's general excellence was recognized when he came in third for the league's Most Valuable Player. In 1926 he fell to twenty-third in the balloting but hit .303 while finishing first in fielding average. The following year the Giants traded for second baseman Rogers Hornsby, the greatest right-handed hitter ever, who the Giants decided would replace Kelly, one future Hall of Fame player succeeding another. Kelly was then traded for yet another Hall of Famer, pitcher Edd Roush. Kelly's new team, the Cincinnati Reds, paid him $18,500 to share first base with Wally Pipp. After the season Kelly married Mary Helen O'Connor on 3 November 1927 at Mission Dolores in San Francisco; they had three children.

Kelly's production declined in 1928: his RBI total was only 58. That year he played ninety-nine games at his old position, first base. In 1929 Kelly was fourth in the league in doubles, setting a Reds record with forty-five. He became the first Reds' player to knock in 100 runs or more, driving in 103. Kelly, however, became too expensive for a losing Cincinnati team, and he was back in the minors in the years 1930 and 1931, playing for the Minneapolis Millers in AA ball. In 1931 he again visited Japan as part of an All-Star team. Kelly finished his major league playing career with a sixty-four-game stay with Brooklyn, completing the 1932 season at Jersey City of the International League.

In 1933 Kelly was hired by his old Cincinnati teammate Chuck Dressen, now the team's manager, to come back to the majors as a coach. He coached in Cincinnati until the end of the 1937 season and then with the Boston Braves from 1938 to 1943 under former Giant teammate Casey Stengel.

After working for a year as a machinist, Kelly scouted for the Reds in 1946, again coached the Reds for two years beginning in 1947, and scouted and coached for the Oakland Oaks of the Pacific Coast League from 1949 to 1953. He managed in 1954 in the Northwest League, where he had begun in back in 1914; he then retired from baseball, the owner of a fine collection of baseball memorabilia.

From 1955 to 1960 he worked as a dispatcher for ground transportation for San Francisco Airport, retiring in 1960. He died of a stroke and was buried in Millbrae, California.

In sixteen seasons Kelly hit 148 home runs and drove in 1,020 RBIs, while batting .297, twenty-ninth in lifetime batting average of all first basemen who ever played. He was third lifetime in total chances accepted per game,

fourth lifetime in putouts per game, eighth in all-time chances accepted per game for a season, and second in all-time putouts for one year. Kelly set single-season National League records for putouts, assists, double plays, and total chances. His putout record still stands.

When Kelly was inducted into the National Baseball Hall of Fame in 1973, the commissioner of baseball Bowie Kuhn said of Kelly: "He was by all odds one of the most versatile players our game has ever seen and surely he had one of the finest throwing arms in baseball history."

★

The National Baseball Hall of Fame Library in Cooperstown, N.Y., is the source of primary material concerning Kelly; *The Baseball Encyclopedia,* 8th ed. (1990), is the source for statistics. A chronological recounting is given in *Baseball's Best: The Hall of Fame Gallery* (1980), by Martin Appel and Burt Goldblatt. CD ROMs with information on Kelly include John Thorn and Peter Palmer, *Total Baseball* (1994); *Microsoft Complete Baseball* (1995); and Bill James, *Bill James Electronic Baseball Encyclopedia for Windows,* version 1.5 (1996). Obituaries are in the *Oakland Tribune* (15 Oct. 1984) and the *New York Times* (16 Oct. 1984).

THOMAS H. BARTHEL

KELLY, Grace Patricia (Princess Grace) (*b.* 12 November 1929 in Philadelphia, Pennsylvania; *d.* 14 September 1982 in the principality of Monaco), film actress and Princess of Monaco.

Kelly was born into a well-to-do family in the Germantown section of Philadelphia, the daughter of John Brendan Kelly, whose family had immigrated to the United States from county Mayo, Ireland, in 1867, and Margaret Majer of Philadelphia, the daughter of German immigrants. John Kelly was a sculling champion who won an Olympic gold medal; he became a building contractor and lost his bid for mayor of Philadelphia as a Democrat in 1935. Margaret Majer taught physical education at the University of Pennsylvania. She was also a magazine cover model.

Grace Kelly was raised along with her older brother and two older sisters in a family atmosphere charged with social ambition. Her siblings cultivated an aggressively patrician manner but failed to make any notable impression on Philadelphia society. Regardless of her father's economic climb from bricklayer to successful building contractor, it was through his children that John Kelly realized his social aspirations. His exclusion from the Diamond Sculls at Henley, England, was vindicated by his son's gaining second in this race in 1947; one is also tempted to say that his social snubs in Philadelphia were later compensated for by his daughter's royal title. Echoes of this early training were clearly present in the cool, richly monied nuances of the Grace Kelly persona in the Hollywood years, and she did little to dispel the press's assumption that her Philadelphia background was Main Line rather than Catholic, upper-middle class.

Kelly spent her childhood and adolescent years in a seventeen-room brick house at 3901 Henry Avenue in Germantown. She first attended the Ravenhill Academy, a convent school, then the Stevens School, a private institution, both located in Germantown. During the summers the Kelly family took up residence in a home that they owned in Ocean City, on the New Jersey shore. Throughout this period Grace's uncle, George Kelly, who was an actor and playwright, was a great influence on her. He was the author of *Craig's Wife* (1926), which won the Pulitzer Prize, and *The Torch Bearers,* in which Grace would later make her acting debut at the Bucks County Playhouse in 1949. With his encouragement she went to New York in 1947 and enrolled at the American Academy of Dramatic Arts, which was then housed at Carnegie Hall.

This period, during which Kelly lived at the Barbizon Hotel for women in New York, was an extremely productive one for her. She began to distill and market a personal brand of cool (some said icy) charm, flawless diction, and girl-next-door good looks, which were to become her trademark in the coming years. She was in great demand during the years 1947–1949 for print modeling and television commercials, and her more important credits include *Redbook, True Story,* and *Cosmopolitan.*

After making her stage debut in her uncle's *The Torch Bearers* in 1949, she enrolled later in the year in the Neighborhood Playhouse in New York, where she studied with drama coach Sanford Meisner. In the same year she also signed with agent Edith Van Cleve, played a music-hall singer on the radio program *Lights Out,* and made her Broadway debut in August Strindberg's *The Father.*

Although her performance in *The Father,* in the role of Raymond Massey's troubled daughter, did not create much of a critical stir, Brooks Atkinson of the *New York Times* found Kelly "charming and pliable." She was offered a screen test at Twentieth Century–Fox as a result of this play. A more immediate effect of Kelly's Broadway exposure, however, was that she began to work in television drama. Her first acting job in the new medium was for influential director Fred Coe in an adaptation of Sinclair Lewis's novel, *Bethel Merriday* (1940), in the *Philco Playhouse* series, broadcast in January 1950.

Throughout 1950 and 1951 Kelly worked in what were to become some of the classic venues of early television: the *Goodyear TV Playhouse, Studio One, Playhouse 90, Kraft Television Theater, Treasury Men in Action, The Web,* and *Suspense.* All told, she appeared in sixty television plays in a thirty-month period. She continued to do print ads, lending her unassailable "debutante" cachet to products including Ipana toothpaste, Old Gold cigarettes, various beers, and a great deal of fashion.

Grace Kelly. ARCHIVE PHOTOS

In 1951 she also made her first film, *Fourteen Hours,* for Twentieth Century–Fox. But she continued to affirm her primary interest in the stage, and in the summer of 1951, while appearing with Elich Gardens, a noted theater repertory company in Denver, Colorado, she was called to Hollywood to make *High Noon* (1952), produced by Stanley Kramer and directed by Fred Zinnemann. Kelly played Gary Cooper's Quaker bride, who shoots a man in the film's suspenseful conclusion. The film was an important step forward for Kelly because critics tended to view it as an "intellectual" Western, thus conferring on this lowbrow genre the kind of discussion generally reserved for classical tragedy.

In 1952 Kelly made *Mogambo* (1953), directed by John Ford. She had signed a contract with Twentieth Century–Fox for $750 a week but rejected many of the scripts that the studio suggested for her, and *Mogambo* was made on loan to Metro-Goldwyn-Mayer (MGM) at her insistence. The film was a remake of the hugely successful *Red Dust* (1932), starring Clark Gable and Jean Harlow. Gable also starred in the new version, this time opposite Ava Gardner. The filming took place in East Africa, where Kelly and Gable hunted together during breaks in the schedule and learned enough Swahili to order a meal.

While *Mogambo* was in production, *Dial M for Murder* was one of the great hits of the season on Broadway, and when Kelly returned to the United States, Alfred Hitchcock asked her to star in the film version. Kelly was to become the prototype for the cool Hitchcock blondes who were a feature of his films in the 1950s and 1960s. According to the Hitchcock biographer Donald Spoto, Hitchcock was probably in love with Kelly, and his customary attention to the most minute details of production created a showcase for her beauty.

The three films that Kelly made for Hitchcock, *Dial M for Murder* (1954), *Rear Window* (1954), and *To Catch a Thief* (1955), are by any standard a realization of the artistic ambitions that she had remained loyal to through the financially lucrative years of print advertising and the squabbles with Twentieth Century–Fox over inappropriate scripts. Hitchcock was attracted to and further enhanced the cool, patrician good looks that Kelly had by this time cultivated as a personal trademark. Since he storyboarded every shot in his films before the shooting began, he was able to create angles and lighting that showcased her unique beauty. No director had used the portrait shot in the kind of adoring way that Hitchcock did with Kelly since Josef von Sternberg had filmed Marlene Dietrich. Hitchcock lowered the pitch of her voice, which had previously been schoolteacherish at its worst, and the Quaker wife of *High Noon* became Lisa Fremont, the sexy woman of the world who unpacks her nightgown and serves a take-out dinner from "21" to James Stewart in *Rear Window.*

Kelly brought the same combination of playfulness, breeding, and intelligence to *Dial M for Murder* and *To Catch a Thief,* prompting Cary Grant, her costar in the latter, to comment that "she has a controlling interest in her own mind." *To Catch a Thief* was filmed on location on the French Riviera, where Kelly visited Monaco and gambled at Monte Carlo for the first time. All aspects of the film seemed to fall into place: Kelly had a great chemistry with her leading man; her wardrobe was by Edith Head and supervised by Hitchcock at every step of design; and the culmination of the film is a masked ball sequence at the center of which Kelly is radiant. None of this was lost on the critics, who had given her mixed or cool reviews in her earlier films but who gave her very good notices for this one. Critics also speculated that Kelly, who had been nominated for the Oscar for best supporting actress in 1953 for *Mogambo* and lost to Donna Reed in *From Here to Eternity,* would certainly be recognized for her Hitchcock films. Actually, she won the Academy Award for best actress for her portrayal of a hopeless drunkard's wife in Clifford Odets's *The Country Girl* (1954). The film also won the New York Film Critics Award. She next appeared with William Holden in *The Bridges of Toko-ri* (1955), about the Korean War.

Kelly reached the apogee of her critical success in this period. The media, as well as the American people, could not seem to get enough of her. She appeared on the cover of *Life* magazine in 1954, and the next year appeared on the covers of *Time, Look, Redbook, Collier's, Saturday Evening Post, Ladies Home Journal,* and *Cosmopolitan.*

In 1955 she made *The Swan* (1956), with Alec Guinness, for MGM, and the following year made *High Society* (1956), with Bing Crosby and Frank Sinatra, a remake of *The Philadelphia Story* (1940), starring Katharine Hepburn, Cary Grant, and James Stewart. In this version Kelly played Hepburn's role, that of a chilly Philadelphia debutante. The music was by Cole Porter. While the critics generally liked it, the film was to be Kelly's last. She was twenty-six.

During the hectic years during which Kelly moved from successful modeling to the New York stage and then to Hollywood, her family members found themselves in a position that grew increasingly difficult to negotiate. Their urge to climb socially was realized through the great success of their movie-star daughter, but the growing notoriety of her personal life became increasingly harder for them to ignore, particularly hard to reconcile with the rigid Catholicism that they had always maintained. For years, Kelly had carried on fairly public affairs with most of her leading men, including Clark Gable, William Holden, Ray Milland, and Bing Crosby. If this were not scandalous enough for the Kellys, some of these men were married and others, like the fashion designer Oleg Cassini, with whom she had an affair for several years, were recently divorced. Gossip columnist Hedda Hopper waged a personal campaign against Kelly during her affair with Bing Crosby. When Kelly attended the Cannes Film Festival in 1954, where *The Country Girl* was shown, newspapers and magazines on both sides of the Atlantic carried the story of her then-burgeoning affair with actor Jean-Pierre Aumont.

On a visit to Cannes in 1955, Kelly had a short meeting and photo session for the magazine *Paris Match* with thirty-two-year-old Prince Rainier. He was the absolute monarch of Monaco, a 370-acre principality about the size of Coney Island that borders on France and is best known for its gambling casinos. Just as Kelly was beginning to feel the pressure from her family in Philadelphia, the prince was under pressure for different reasons from the Monegasques, as his subjects were known. Rainier needed to produce an heir, of either sex, without whom the principality would revert to France, making them subject to taxes and military service. Neither of these situations was lost on the prince's spiritual adviser, Father Francis Tucker, a Catholic priest from the Philadelphia area who was a friend of John Kelly.

Tucker began a correspondence with the Kellys on the subject of a possible marriage between Grace Kelly and his "Lord Prince." Soon the prince and Kelly began an intense written and telephone correspondence of their own. In December 1955 the prince, Father Tucker, and the prince's physician arrived at the Kelly home for a Christmas celebration. It was during this visit that the prince had his intended bride's fertility certified and proposed marriage. What remained was for Father Tucker to negotiate a substantial cash dowry to be paid by the bride's father. This done, the couple's engagement was announced on 5 January 1956 to a world that had followed rumor and speculation about the romance for nearly a year.

On 4 April 1956 Kelly, along with an entourage of seventy-two family and friends, sailed on the USS *Constitution* for Monaco and the royal wedding. In Monaco a media circus of exceptional magnitude was unfolding. Every news service sent a battalion of reporters. NBC sent three more reporters than it had for D day, and it was quickly clear that coverage of the wedding would eclipse that of the coronation of Elizabeth II three years earlier. The culmination of this public spectacle was the wedding itself on 19 April 1956 (following a civil ceremony the preceding day), which was televised live to 30 million viewers. Grace Kelly's marriage to a prince was witnessed by more people than any other wedding in history up to that time. Many were served by the event: the columnist Earl Wilson referred to the bride's parents as "Queen Margaret and King John"; Monaco's sluggish tourist industry boomed; and Bob Hope had a year's worth of material for his comedy routines.

In the period that followed the marriage, reports from Monaco took on a more measured tone. On 23 January 1957 the couple's first child, a daughter, Caroline Louise Marguerite, was born. On 14 March 1958 Princess Grace gave birth to a son, Albert Alexandre Louis Pierre. With the birth of her first two children, Kelly settled into the role of mother and into the ceremonial and official duties as Her Serene Highness. Kelly took an active part in many charitable organizations. She established an annual Red Cross Ball, made successful in large part because of the large number of international celebrities that she brought to Monaco. She was particularly vocal about the agenda of La Leche League, a group that supported the breast feeding of babies. Later, she channeled the earnings from pressed flower collages, which she first made as a hobby and then exhibited and sold, into the Grace Kelly Foundation. Her *My Book of Flowers* (1980) was based on these collages. Perhaps most important to the well-being of her kingdom was the fact that in the first four years of her marriage the revenues from Monaco's tourist industry doubled.

In 1962 she accepted an offer from MGM to be directed by Alfred Hitchcock in *Marnie,* but when the news of it created an embarrassing stir of disapproval among her subjects, she withdrew from the project. Her third child was born on 1 February 1965, a daughter named Stephanie Marie Elizabeth.

In 1974 she took up part-time residence in Paris. Two years later she joined the board of directors of Twentieth Century–Fox, and traveled to their meetings, usually in New York City and Hollywood, four times a year.

From 1976 to 1981 Kelly was the subject of several documentaries, and she gave poetry readings of other people's works in Europe and America. On the morning of 13 September 1982, she and her daughter Stephanie left Roc Agel in France, where one of their homes was located, for a short drive to Monaco. Their automobile, which Kelly was driving, swerved, careened off a sharp turn in the highway, and crashed. Kelly was rushed to the hospital but died on the evening of 14 September 1982. After lying in state, she was buried in Monaco's cathedral.

★

Biographies of Kelly include Sarah Bradford, *Princess Grace* (1984); Steven Englund, *Grace of Monaco: An Interpretive Biography* (1984); James Spada, *Grace: The Secret Lives of a Princess* (1987); Howell Conant, *Grace* (1992); and Robert Lacey, *Grace* (1994), which also includes bibliographical references. Personal information is also in Judith B. Quine, *The Bridesmaids: Grace Kelly, Princess of Monaco, and Six Intimate Friends* (1989), and Jeannie Sakol and Caroline Latham, *About Grace: An Intimate Notebook* (1993). An obituary is in the *New York Times* (15 Sept. 1982).

DAVID COREY

KEMPER, James Scott (*b*. 18 November 1886 in Van Wert, Ohio; *d*. 17 September 1981 in Chicago, Illinois), insurance industry leader whose ideals and intuition helped him build one of the nation's largest property and casualty insurance empires.

Kemper was one of the three sons of Mary Jane Scott and of Hathaway Kemper, an attorney and a prominent Republican. Guests at the Kemper home included such GOP leaders as President William McKinley.

After graduating from Van Wert High School in 1905, "Jamie" Kemper dreamed of attending Harvard University but a friend's failure of the entrance exam discouraged him, and he signed on as a junior clerk with the Central Manufacturers Insurance Company in his hometown. Advancing quickly, he was managing the Chicago-based western division of the firm while still in his early twenties (1911). Concern that a youthful appearance might hold him back led him to grow a mustache that he wore for many years.

Kemper's expertise at servicing fire policy–holders led to his assignment to investigate a series of Chicago lumberyard fires. Eventually the nation's lumber interests sought

James S. Kemper, 1953. UPI/CORBIS-BETTMANN

his advice on how to lower insurance costs in connection with workers' compensation. In 1912 Chicago insurance executives approached him about managing Lumbermen's Mutal Casualty Company. He served as vice president and general manager until 1916, as president until 1945, as chairman until 1957, and thereafter as chairman of the board. He also developed and controlled a cluster of twenty or more insurance firms. He was president of the Kemper Insurance Group from 1920 to 1941, then chief executive officer until he retired in 1966. According to the firm, however, he never completely retired.

On 5 April 1913 Kemper married Mildred Estelle Hooper; they had three children. His first wife died in 1927, and on 17 January 1931 Kemper married Gertrude Ziesing Stout, who had a son by a prior marriage.

Short, stocky, and bald, and sporting an ever-present unlit cigar, Kemper had a reputation as a shirtsleeves executive. Proficient at cutting costs and emphasizing accident prevention, he favored several insurance practices that became popular. Among them were paying claims promptly to help avoid lengthy litigation and publishing details about company financial holdings to build confidence and sales. In 1980 the Kemper Group reported that it had assets of $5 billion and was the fourteenth largest property and casualty organization in the United States. As for his own

wealth, Kemper said little. In 1948 the Treasury Department listed his compensation from interests in Lumbermen's Mutual as $261,609. Apparently displeased at that disclosure, he reportedly took a nominal dollar-a-year salary from the firm thereafter and relied mainly on investment income.

Kemper belonged to the U.S. Chamber of Commerce for many years and rose to leadership positions in the organization. In speeches to business and government groups he was outspoken on labor relations and foreign affairs. In 1939–1940, as the organization's vice president, he opposed U.S. involvement in another world war, and as its president (1940–1941) he predicted dire financial consequences should the nation get involved. Kemper also opposed antistrike laws, on the grounds that they would be ineffective and would deny citizens their rights, and he urged employers to settle labor disputes amicably.

A great admirer of Benjamin Franklin, Kemper kept a portrait of the inventor, statesman, and insurance company founder in his office. Like Franklin, Kemper believed he had a role to play in public affairs. He worked for many local and national political campaigns and urged his thousands of employees to vote as they saw fit. Over the years he cultivated friendships with Presidents William Howard Taft, Herbert Hoover, and Dwight D. Eisenhower. In June 1953 Kemper was appointed U.S. ambassador to Brazil. The diplomat's business acumen impressed the South American business community, but apparently his outspoken remarks were not always diplomatic. Once he predicted a decline in coffee prices despite the Brazilian government's assurances to the contrary. On another occasion he withdrew an embassy dinner invitation to a congressman critical of U.S. economic policy toward Latin America. After a year and a half as ambassador, Kemper resigned in December 1954 and returned to his insurance interests, but he remained a devoted supporter of Republican causes. He served the Republican National Committee as treasurer for about two years starting in 1946 and was a convention delegate from 1936 to 1952, and again in 1964. While he believed that having a voice in politics could be good for business, Kemper also clearly relished the business of politics.

Well past his ninety-fourth birthday, Kemper died at his home on North Lake Shore Drive in Chicago. His funeral was at the Fourth Presbyterian Church, and he was buried in Chicago. Kemper was a past president of the Presbyterian Union of Chicago and a trustee of several theological organizations. He also was a director of the Community Fund of Chicago and a trustee of the James S. Kemper Foundation, which provides scholarships to insurance and nursing students.

Regardless of his many interests, Kemper was primarily an insurance man and an idea man who must have known he was in the right place at the right time. Rather than practice law as his father had, he struck out on his own and put his business instincts to work in a burgeoning insurance industry. Ultimately a large segment of that industry worked for him.

★

Coverage of Kemper's vice presidency of the U.S. Chamber of Commerce is in the *New York Times* (2 May 1939), and of his presidency, *New York Times* (3 May 1940). His resignation as ambassador is covered in the *New York Times* (29 Dec. 1954). An article on Kemper by Rosemary Cahill is in *Kemper Insurance Magazine* (Sept. 1981). Obituaries are in the *Chicago Tribune* and *New York Times* (both 19 Sept. 1981).

WHITNEY SMITH

KENNEDY, William Jesse, Jr. (*b.* 15 June 1889 in Andersonville, Georgia; *d.* 8 July 1985 in Durham, North Carolina), insurance executive.

The eldest son of William Jesse Kennedy, Sr., owner of a meat market, and Katie C. Kennedy, William, Jr., learned carpentry from his grandfather, a former slave who after emancipation continued working in his specialty of building bridges. William also learned something of business by working in his father's market in Andersonville. He was educated at the Americus Institute, Americus, Georgia, an American Baptist Home Academy, from which he graduated in 1912. Although he immediately went to work—first as a carpenter, then in sales for a custom-tailoring shop—Kennedy continued his education through a correspondence course from LaSalle University, did a year of legal studies, and took additional courses in business administration through Columbia University's extension division.

Kennedy's first insurance job was as an agent for Guaranty Mutual Health and Life Insurance Company in Athens, Georgia. He became district manager in his first year, then traveling inspector, then district manager of the firm's largest branch office, in Augusta, Georgia. While working there, he met the three leaders of North Carolina Mutual Life Insurance Company (the nation's leading African-American life insurance company)—John Merrick, Aaron Moore, and Charles Spaulding—who were touring Georgia, touting their company. Kennedy later claimed that they inspired him to move to life insurance, giving him a "zeal that never abated." He immediately set to work to learn all he could about life insurance, working through every major textbook on the field. In September 1916 Kennedy was named manager of North Carolina Mutual's Savannah office. He started with only $7,500 of life insurance in force; in two years Savannah led all districts, with more than $100,000 in force.

On 17 December 1917 Kennedy married Margaret Lillian Spaulding, daughter of Charles Spaulding; they had three children. In 1918 Kennedy served as corporal-clerk at battalion headquarters at Camp Holabird on Chesapeake Bay.

Given his accomplishments in Savannah, Kennedy was an obvious candidate for any opening at the home office in Durham, North Carolina. When John Merrick died in 1919, Aaron Moore moved to the presidency and Kennedy was appointed manager of the Ordinary Department, effective 18 October 1919. In January 1920 Kennedy was elected a director of the company; in 1923, after Moore died and Spaulding took over as president, Kennedy was appointed assistant secretary. Working under John Avery, he had the opportunity to learn every aspect of the company's operations. In 1924 he added the job of office manager for the home office and in 1931 became vice president and secretary.

From the time of his appointment as assistant secretary in 1923, Kennedy joined Avery and Spaulding in a loose hierarchy that managed the company. More significantly it fell to him to cope with a mountain of difficulties. The company had expanded rapidly and its success threatened a loss of control. Asa Spaulding later praised Kennedy's contribution: "What would have been the history of the company for the last decade without your stabilizing influence and foresight?" Kennedy formally remained in the same position of vice president and secretary until August 1952, when he assumed the presidency following the death of Charles Spaulding; he was the fourth man to lead the company.

North Carolina Mutual was socially active, expecting its agents to take a broad interest in the welfare of African Americans. For example, it once asked an agent to investigate the conditions under which African Americans were imprisoned in Charlotte, North Carolina. Kennedy shared this vision, working to establish Durham branches of the YWCA and the YMCA that would serve African Americans. He took a leading role in establishing the John Avery Boys Club and served as its president for more than twenty years. This led Kennedy into a prominent role with the Boys Club of America, which awarded him its Silver Keystone in 1974. Kennedy stepped down as president of North Carolina Mutual on 1 January 1959, although he continued to serve as chairman of the board until 1965. Asa Spaulding succeeded him as president.

Kennedy was active in Durham affairs, serving as president of Bankers Fire Insurance Company, as vice president of the Mutual Savings and Loan Association, and as a director of the Mechanics and Farmers Bank, Southern Fidelity Mutual Insurance Company, the James E. Sheppard Foundation, and the Durham Business and Professional Chain, the minority counterpart to the Durham Chamber of Commerce. He also served in several capacities with the

White Rock Baptist Church, where he taught the A. M. Moore Bible class for more than fifty years. In recognition of his service the church renamed the class the Moore-Kennedy Bible class in 1975. He also served on the North Carolina Recreation Commission from 1945 to 1956, and in 1955 Governor Luther Hodges appointed him to the newly created State Board of Higher Education. He was a trustee of Howard University and of the Boys Club of America and a member of the National Council of the United Negro College Fund. Kennedy founded the Durham chapter of the National Association for the Advancement of Colored People, which honored him at its Freedom Fund dinner in 1977. He died at his home in Durham in 1985.

During his long tenure at North Carolina Mutual, Kennedy played a central role in building a company that stood out as a leader among African-American owned and operated enterprises in America. He helped shape its unique mixture of business acumen and social activism and carried that activism into a wide array of community affairs. He thus also helped shape the cultural and social development of Durham and North Carolina and should be numbered among those who facilitated its emergence as perhaps the most dynamic southern state in the 1960s.

★

See Merah Steven Stuart, *An Economic Detour: A History of Insurance in the Lives of American Negroes* (1940); William J. Kennedy, Jr., *The North Carolina Mutual Story* (1970); and Walter B. Weare, *Black Business in the New South: A Social History of the North Carolina Mutual Life Insurance Company* (1973). An obituary is in the *New York Times* (13 July 1985).

FRED CARSTENSEN

KERTÉSZ, André (Andor) (*b.* 2 July 1894 in Budapest, Hungary; *d.* 28 September 1985 in New York City), pioneer photographer, father of photojournalism known for his Distortion Series, "photographic happenings," birds-eye views, and night scenes.

One of three sons of Leopold (Lipót) Kertész, a middle-class Jewish businessman, and his Christian wife, Ernestine (Ernesztin) Hoffman, Kertész, despite a lackluster student career, fulfilled family expectations by receiving his baccalaureate degree from the Hungarian Academy of Commerce in 1912 and taking a position as a clerk on the Budapest Stock Exchange. Unsuited to the business world, he was nevertheless able to realize a longtime dream and buy his first camera, an ICA box, and with no formal training he began shooting candid street scenes and folkloric subjects in the Hungarian countryside.

Drafted into the Austro-Hungarian army, Kertész served in World War I from 1914 to 1918. He captured many mov-

André Kertész. MUSEUM OF THE CITY OF NEW YORK/ARCHIVE PHOTOS

ing moments from the lulls between battles, lugging all his photography equipment in his backpack. Recovering in Esztergom after being wounded in 1915, he claims to have first noticed the effect of bent light rays on a body swimming underwater and produced his famous photograph *Underwater Swimmer,* precursor to his exploration of distortion photography in the 1930s. Unfortunately, most of these wartime negatives were lost or destroyed in the Hungarian Revolution of 1918.

The chaotic postwar years saw his return to the stock exchange in order to help support his widowed mother. Here he met his future wife, Elisabeth (Elizabet) Sali, and continued photographing in Budapest and the countryside, all the while yearning to join the artistic community in Paris. A self-portrait he submitted to the magazine *Borsszem Jankó* garnered his first prize in 1916, and in 1917 he published his first photographs in the magazine *Érdekes Újság* (Interesting news), where he would also have his first cover in 1925. In 1923, remaining true to his artistic vision, Kertész accepted a diploma from the Hungarian Amateur Photographers' Association instead of receiving a silver medal after he refused to reprint some photographs in the bromoil process, a soft-focus effect, then in vogue.

With his mother's blessing Kertész finally moved to Paris in 1925 at the age of thirty-one. The eleven years spent there proved most fruitful. He settled in the Montparnasse neighborhood, enjoyed the émigré bohemian life, and found bountiful work as a freelance photographer for magazines in France such as *Vogue, Le Sourire, Variétés, Le Matin,* and *L'Art vivant;* in Germany, *Uhu* and the illustrated magazines of Frankfurt, Berlin, Munich, and Leipzig; and in Great Britain, the *Times,* the *Sketch,* and the *Sphere.* He had his first one-man show in October 1927 in the gallery Sacre du Printemps in Paris and was included in the first Independent Salon of Photography in Paris in 1928, in the exhibition "Contemporary Photography" in Essen, and in the "Film und Foto" exhibition in Stuttgart in 1929. His work became so well known and popular in Germany that he was collected by museums in Berlin (Staatliche Museum/Bibliothek) and Zwickau (König-Albert Museum) and shown again in Munich (1930) and Essen (1931).

An innovator in the use of the small hand camera (he was one of the first to purchase the new Leica in 1928) and a pioneer in what is now called photojournalism, Kertész was a major influence on other photographers such as Henri Cartier-Bresson, Brassaï, and Robert Capa. In 1928 he also began a collaboration with Lucien Vogel on his journal, *Vu,* which lasted until 1935. Kertész's acquaintance with many of the artists and writers of that era, particularly the surrealists, led some to label him a surrealist—a designation he eschewed. He photographed and became acquainted with many of the great names of the day—Constantin Brancusi, Marc Chagall, Fernan Léger, Colette, Sergey Eisenstein, Maurice de Vlaminck, Piet Mondrian, Alexander Calder, Robert Delaunay, Man Ray, and Brassaï.

He was briefly (1928–1930) married to the photographer Rózsa Klein, known professionally as Rogie André. Little is known of her, and Kertész was at pains to keep it that way for the rest of his life. Elisabeth Sali joined him in Paris in 1931, and they married on 17 June 1933.

In 1932 thirty-five of his photographs were chosen for the "Modern European Photography" show at the Julien Levy Gallery in New York City. His first book, *Enfants,* followed in 1933, and he also completed more than 200 photographs in his Distortion Series for the magazine *Le Sourire.* Two more books followed: *Paris vu par André Kertész* (1934) and *Nos amies les bêtes* (1936).

At the height of his career, in October 1936, the Kertészes moved to New York City, where André fully expected to be warmly greeted and well respected. Instead he slipped into decades of obscurity and neglect in a country he had never wished to make his home. He entered into a one-year contract as a commercial studio photographer with Keystone Studios—an unhappy relationship he terminated in 1937. A lack of funds and the onset of World War II combined to end the Kertészes' plans to return to Europe and left them stranded in New York with enemy-alien status. Kertész found himself fingerprinted and forbidden to photograph anything outdoors for the duration of the war. The new magazine *Life* rejected his work, claiming that "you talk too much in your pictures"—that is, they did not act merely as background for the writer's material. He freelanced for *Look, Vogue, Harper's Bazaar, Colliers, House and Garden,* and *Coronet.* Elisabeth started a successful perfume business in 1941, and they assumed U.S. citizenship

in 1944. Kertész signed an exclusive contract with Condé Nast Publications that lasted from 1949 to 1962, years of rather routine assignments photographing models and architectural interiors, with little room for creative experimentation. In 1952 the Kertészes moved to an apartment at Two Fifth Avenue overlooking Washington Square, where he began a lifelong photographic study of the square. After recuperating from a severe illness in 1962 he decided to concentrate exclusively on art photography for the rest of his life, or as he put it, "to return to amateur status."

Recognition and honors followed a one-man show mounted by the Museum of Modern Art in 1964. He became a Guggenheim fellow in 1974 and was appointed Commander of the Order of Arts and Letters by the French government in 1976. He also received the New York City Mayor's Award of Honor for Arts and Culture (1977 and 1981); the Medal of the City of Paris (1980); an honorary doctorate of fine arts from Bard College (1980); and the Order of the Banner of the Hungarian People's Republic (1984). Elisabeth Sali Kertész died after a long illness on 21 October 1977, and André Kertész died at home on 28 September 1985 at the age of ninety-one. In recognition of the importance of France in his life, he bequeathed his negatives and correspondence to the French Ministry of Culture.

At the time of his death Kertész had lived longer than any other well-known photographer. His career flourished with the rise to prominence of the illustrated magazine in popular culture and spanned the evolution of photography from a technical procedure to a recognized art form. He spent a great many years in the United States filled with bitter disappointment when his modernist European style proved too advanced for the American postwar public. Happily, he lived long enough to see this trend reversed and to take his place in art history as one of the true innovators, who never stopped experimenting with new forms and new approaches to seeing the world.

★

Among the best books by Kertész are *André Kertész: A Lifetime of Perception* (1982) and *Kertész on Kertész: A Self-Portrait* (1985). Many others were produced in collaboration or cooperation with others: with John Szarkowski, *A. Kertész, Photographer* (1964); with Nicholas Ducrot, *J'aime Paris: Photographs Since the Twenties* (1974); with Hilton Kramer and Floyd Yearout, *Hungarian Memories* (1982); with Carole Kismaric, *André Kertész* (1993); with Pierre Borhan, ed., *André Kertész: His Life and Work* (1994); and with Weston Naef, ed., *In Focus: André Kertész; Photographs from the J. Paul Getty Museum* (1994). Other sources include Sandra S. Phillips, David Travis, and Weston J. Naef, *André Kertész: Of Paris and New York* (1985), as well as an obituary in the *New York Times* (30 Sept. 1985). André Kertész and John Musilli, *Everything Is Photograph: A Profile of André Kertész* (1989), is a color film of

Kertész at home and in his New York neighborhood, a delightful documentary notwithstanding the sometimes poor reproduction.

PAMELA ARMSTRONG LAKIN

KIERAN, John Francis (*b.* 2 August 1892 in New York City; *d.* 10 December 1981 in Rockport, Massachusetts), journalist, sportswriter, amateur naturalist, and polymath who became widely known during the 1930s and 1940s as a panel member of the radio program *Information Please.*

One of the seven children of James Michael Kieran, a school principal, college professor, and president of Hunter College, and of Kate Donohue Kieran, a teacher in the New York City public schools, Kieran grew up in a household where good books and learning were elements of daily life. Recalling his family's home in the Kingsbridge section of the Bronx, he wrote in *Not Under Oath:* "There was no electricity in the district. The streets were lighted with gas lamps. Telephones were still to come. Autos were unknown. Horses were necessary. Cows were common. There were chickens in many backyards, and it was a poor house that didn't have a little vegetable garden on the premises."

Although he lived and worked in New York City for most of his life, Kieran always was drawn to the country. He also remained faithful to what now may seem an old-

John Kieran. UPI/CORBIS-BETTMANN

fashioned ideal of learning. He was interested in a great many things—from the classics to science, biology, literature, farming, law, sports, and a great deal in between—and took every opportunity to study some more. Kieran was not shy in sharing with others the scope of his interests, the breadth of his knowledge, or his method of learning.

Kieran graduated from P.S. 103 in East Harlem and Townsend Harris High School. He attended the City College of New York and in 1912 graduated B.S. cum laude from Fordham University. He next raised chickens and grew apples at his family's farm in Dutchess County. He also taught at a nearby one-room school. After a year of modest success as a farmer, he returned to the city and took a job with a construction company.

In 1915, with the help of Frederick T. Birchall, a family friend and assistant managing editor at the *New York Times,* Kieran joined the sports department of that paper. In college he had played shortstop on the varsity baseball team and had been a member of the varsity swimming team. He also liked to play golf. When one day all sports events on the East Coast were rained out, a golf story Kieran had written came in handy. It was his first report to appear in print, and it landed him the job of golf writer for the *Times.*

As soon as the United States entered World War I in 1917, Kieran signed up with a volunteer engineer regiment (the Eleventh) specializing in railways. By the time he was discharged in 1919, he had risen from private to second lieutenant. He took advantage of his time in France to improve his command of French, a language he could read but not speak very well prior to 1917.

In 1919 Kieran married Alma Boldtmann; they had three children. He returned to his job at the *Times,* but in 1922 a colleague and friend, sportswriter Grantland Rice, lured him to the *New York Tribune* with the promise of a byline (something the *Times* did not give its sportswriters) as a baseball writer. Three years later, financial gain drew him to the *New York American,* a Hearst paper. In December 1926 the *Times* got Kieran back with the help of the same promise Rice had used to bring him to the *Tribune*— a byline as a sports columnist. On 1 January 1927 the first signed column in the history of the *New York Times* appeared under the title "Sports of the Times," a name chosen by Kieran. He produced a column every day until early 1943.

Kieran's only assignment was to turn out a column of about 1,100 words. Although the focus had to be sports, Kieran later admitted that, "As to subject matter, I rambled scandalously," incorporating discussions of all the great many things that interested him. He regularly used his column to try his hand at light verse. Nevertheless, he really did like sports and fully realized the advantages of his line of work. "I would go on a southern training trip. Weather permitting, I would watch a big league game every day during the regular season. I would cover the World Series. And I would be paid well . . . for having all that fun. Some are born lucky."

Kieran was more than a sportswriter. At heart he was an amateur student of everything, and in 1938 there came the perfect opportunity to put all his knowledge to work when he was recruited for the panel of the new radio quiz show *Information Please.* Panel members and prominent guests were challenged to answer questions, submitted by listeners, that were meant to "stump the experts." Judging from his memoirs, this, not his time as a sports columnist, was the highlight of Kieran's career—probably because it allowed him to deal with much more varied subject areas than sports and likely also because it allowed him to show off his range of knowledge.

In any case, starting in the late 1930s, Kieran began to move out of sports. Slowly but steadily he made the transition, not only to radio personality but also to independent author, particularly on nature. In his personal life, too, Kieran made a new start. His wife had died in 1944, and in April 1947 he married Margaret Ford, a newspaper reporter. After the outbreak of World War II, Kieran's involvement in a host of activities supporting the war effort caused him to leave the *Times.* For two years he wrote a general-interest column for the *New York Sun* (1943–1944). When *Information Please* ended in 1948, Kieran focused primarily on nature writing; in 1960 his output brought him the prestigious John Burroughs Society Medal for Natural History.

By that time Kieran had written books that included *The Story of the Olympic Games* (1936), *The American Sporting Scene* (1941), *John Kieran's Nature Notes* (1941), *Poems I Remember* (1942), *Footnotes on Nature* (1947), and the award-winning *A Natural History of New York City* (1959). He also had been an editor of *Information Please Almanac* and had contributed to many publications. He died of natural causes and was buried in Beech Grove Cemetery in Rockport, Massachusetts.

Kieran's significance in his own time may be the example he set for many through his erudition. His lasting influence is less clear, although his life and work, together with an awareness of his popularity, should help later generations understand how the prewar, pretelevision era differed from their own.

★

Kieran's memoir, *Not Under Oath* (1964), is very informative and revealing, as is an interview with Kieran in Jerome Holtzman, *No Cheering in the Press Box* (1973). Useful information is in the *New York Times* obituary (11 Dec. 1981).

RUUD VAN DIJK

KIMBALL, Spencer Woolley (*b.* 28 March 1895 in Salt Lake City, Utah; *d.* 5 November 1985 in Salt Lake City, Utah), president of the Church of Jesus Christ of Latter-day Saints (the LDS Church) from 1973 to 1985; he is best known for having authorized the ordination of males of African descent to the Mormon priesthood in 1978.

Spencer Kimball was the sixth of eleven children of Andrew Kimball and Olive Woolley. His paternal grandfather Heber C. Kimball was a member of the original Twelve Apostles and a counselor to Brigham Young. Andrew Kimball worked as a dry-goods salesman and served as president of the Indian Territory Mission of the LDS Church. In 1898 the family moved to Thatcher, Arizona, where Andrew served as president of an LDS stake, the Saint Joseph Stake. The family farmed, and Andrew sold various things including Bibles. Olive died in 1906, when Spencer was eleven years old. As a child and young adult Spencer had a number of diseases and accidents, including a near drowning, typhoid fever, and a facial paralysis.

Talented and likable, Spencer excelled in music, sports, and academics. At age fourteen he played piano in a dance band, and though he grew to be only five feet six inches tall, he led the Thatcher LDS Academy basketball team in

Spencer Kimball, 1976. AGENCE FRANCE PRESSE/ARCHIVE PHOTOS

scoring. The students elected him class president during all of his four years of high school.

Following his graduation from Latter-day Saints Academy in Thatcher in 1914, Kimball served as a missionary for the LDS Church in Independence, Missouri (1914–1917). In January 1917 he enrolled briefly in the University of Arizona at Tucson; the following fall he transferred to Brigham Young University. By this time the United States had entered World War I, and Kimball dropped out of school in midsemester to return to Arizona for preinduction processing.

Kimball married Camilla Eyring of Pima, Arizona, on 16 November 1917. In the summer of 1918 the couple traveled to Salt Lake City to have their marriage sealed in the LDS Temple. The first of their four children was born in August 1918.

The draft board did not call Kimball to active service, and so in 1917 he took a clerk's job at the Citizens Bank (in 1921 renamed the Arizona Trust and Savings Bank) in Thatcher. He became a teller and then an assistant cashier. He also played in an orchestra and was a bookkeeper at a local department store. In addition, he and Camilla wrote for a local newspaper.

Arizona Trust failed during a brief postwar depression in 1921, and the Kimballs lost the investment they had made in the bank. But in 1922 Spencer secured a position as chief teller at the Bank of Safford. He also continued to serve in the LDS Church, as Saint Joseph Stake clerk, as stake Sunday school chorister, as a counselor in the ward Sunday school superintendency, and as director of the ward choir. After the death of his father in 1924, Kimball became second counselor to the new Saint Joseph Stake president. In 1938 he became president of the newly organized Mount Graham Stake, which covered southeastern Arizona, southwestern New Mexico, and southwestern Texas.

In 1925, while employed by the Bank of Safford, Kimball and Joseph W. Greenhalgh began making small loans. In 1927 Kimball resigned from the bank to organize an insurance and real estate business in partnership with Greenhalgh. In 1935 he invested in the first radio station in Safford, KGLU. Active in public service, Kimball joined the Rotary Club in 1923, becoming club president in 1931 and, in 1936, district governor for Arizona. He served on the Safford city council, on the board of the Chamber of Commerce, as a Boy Scout executive, on the board of the Red Cross, and as a fund-raiser for Gila College.

In July 1943 Kimball was called by LDS president Heber J. Grant to the Quorum of Twelve Apostles of the LDS Church, the church's second-highest governing body after the First Presidency. He moved with his family to Salt Lake City.

Working as an administrator of churchwide programs, Kimball came to know the personal problems of church members quite intimately. He was particularly concerned about the influence of sin in the lives of people and about the failure to understand repentance, and he often gave talks on the subject. In 1969 he addressed the topic in a book, *The Miracle of Forgiveness.* Kimball's other major writings include: *Be Ye Clean! Five Steps to Repentance and Forgiveness* (1954); *Faith Precedes the Miracle: Based on the Discourses of Spencer W. Kimball* (1972); *My Beloved Sisters* (1979); and *The Teaching of Spencer W. Kimball, Twelfth President of the Church of Jesus Christ of Latter-day Saints* (1982).

Kimball concerned himself particularly with the problems of American Indians. In 1947 he inaugurated a program by which Latter-day Saint families would sponsor Indian children, inviting them into their homes so that they could attend public school.

He served as acting president (1970–1973) and as president (1972–1973) of the Quorum of Twelve Apostles in the LDS Church. After the death of church president David O. McKay in 1970 and of his successors Joseph Fielding Smith and Harold B. Lee in 1972 and 1973, Kimball was called as president on 30 December 1973.

During his service in the Quorum of Twelve Apostles, Kimball had become particularly sensitive to the policy of the church that prohibited blacks of African descent (as distinguished from Australian Aborigines or Tongans) from holding the priesthood, and he disapproved of attitudes and policies promoting racial discrimination. During the late 1960s and early 1970s, Brigham Young University came under extreme pressure because of the church's policy of denying the priesthood to blacks of African descent. Protests at athletic events preceded a decision by Stanford University to refuse to schedule games with BYU. Moreover, the church had begun to grow very rapidly in countries with large black populations like Brazil. Kimball counseled couples engaged in interracial romances that no church law prohibited them from marrying. During a visit to South America in 1959 Kimball was disturbed by the large number of black and mulatto church members who could not hold the priesthood. As LDS president he prayed about the matter, and on 8 June 1978 he announced a revelation that changed the Mormon Church's policy and allowed all worthy males regardless of race to receive the priesthood. He also called the first American Indian (1975) and Asian (1976) to the central leadership of the church as members of the First Quorum of the Seventy.

Concerned with the preservation of the family and of traditional sexual morality, as the leader of the LDS Church Kimball opposed the Equal Rights Amendment because he thought it too broad in its wording. Nevertheless, he favored equal treatment for women. To emphasize the administrative and spiritual role of women, he inaugurated semiannual all-church women's conferences in 1978 at which women gave the principal addresses. Also in 1978 he mandated that the church drop the long-standing practice of allowing only men to give prayers in Sacrament meetings, the church's principal worship service. He and others in the church leadership urged state legislatures to pass laws ensuring equal treatment of women.

In order to augment the number of proselytizing missionaries, Kimball urged increased attention to keeping the commandments for all men and women. During his presidency, the missionary force of the church increased from about 17,000 to about 32,000. He also emphasized the importance of spiritual service in the church, and he promoted the construction of new temples in various parts of the world. Concerned about international violence, in May 1981 the First Presidency (Kimball and his two counselors) issued a statement critical of the arms buildup in the United States and opposing the basing of MX missiles in the Utah-Nevada desert. In 1975, in order to reduce the secular responsibilities of the highest church leaders, Kimball resigned from the boards of corporations. He encouraged other church leaders to follow suit, but most did not.

Kimball made the church leadership more accessible to the general membership. Before he became LDS president, the church had conducted area conferences in places outside Salt Lake City on an average of once per year. Between 1975 and 1981 Kimball conducted fifty-nine area conferences, many of them in locations with large numbers of non-Caucasian members such as the Pacific islands, Asia, and Latin America.

Despite a long series of illnesses, Kimball served as an active leader of the LDS Church until 1982, when he suffered a third subdural hematoma. He believed that in 1950 a priesthood blessing had cured him of a throat disorder, but in 1957 he had surgery to remove a cancerous larynx. Thereafter his voice had a distinctive hoarseness, and in 1971 he received cobalt treatments for recurring throat cancer. In 1972 Kimball underwent heart bypass surgery, and in 1979 and 1981 he was again operated on for subdural hematomas. In 1981 he had a pacemaker installed, but his health deteriorated rapidly. He made his last public appearance in April 1982.

A man of deep and abiding spirituality, Spencer Kimball led the LDS Church toward equality by eliminating racial discrimination against black men and offering increased opportunities to women. He promoted educational opportunities for American Indians and opposed racial discrimination in marriage. He emphasized the importance of personal morality by opposing sexual promiscuity, while at the same time urging those who sinned to repent and return to full fellowship in the church.

★

A collection of Kimball's papers and diaries are in the archives of the Church of Jesus Christ of Latter-day Saints, Salt Lake City,

Utah. The most thorough and reliable biography is Edward L. Kimball and Andrew E. Kimball, Jr., *Spencer W. Kimball: Twelfth President of the Church of Jesus Christ of Latter-day Saints* (1977), by the subject's son and grandson. This should be supplemented by Edward L. Kimball, "The Administration of Spencer W. Kimball," *Sunstone* 11 (Mar. 1987): 8–14; and "Spencer W. Kimball," in *The Presidents of the Church,* edited by Leonard J. Arrington (1986). See also Francis M. Gibbons, *Spencer W. Kimball: Resolute Disciple, Prophet of God* (1995). An obituary is in the *New York Times* (7 Nov. 1985).

THOMAS G. ALEXANDER

KINARD, Frank Manning ("Bruiser") (*b.* 23 October 1914 in Pelahatchie, Mississippi; *d.* 7 September 1985 in Jackson, Mississippi), football player, coach, and athletic administrator who was inducted into the College Football Hall of Fame and Pro Football Hall of Fame.

F. M., as Kinard was known in his early childhood, was one of the seven children of Henry A. ("Major") Kinard, a farmer, and Pearl (Wooley) Kinard, a housewife. He first played organized sports in Mississippi as a tackle at Rolling Fork High School and later at Jackson Central. As a freshman, during one of his first practices, Kinard collided enthusiastically with an older teammate, Dave Ferguson. Picking himself up, Ferguson said, "You're a real bruiser." This would evolve into a lifelong nickname (so much so that when Kinard was asked how he wanted his Pro Football Hall of Fame ring to read, he said, "Better make it Bruiser. If it said Frank, no one would know it was mine"). Before graduation in 1934 from Central, where he was an all-around athlete (basketball and track and field in addition to football), Kinard married his high school sweetheart, Midge Frances Kirk of Jackson, on 10 December 1933. They had two children.

Kinard enrolled at the University of Mississippi (Ole Miss), where he was an outstanding player on the freshman team. As a sophomore he made an immediate impact on the varsity. His coach, Ed Walker, said at the time, "He is the best lineman ever to play the game." Not especially big, even in his era, at six feet, one inch and 205 pounds, Kinard was extremely durable (he once played 562 consecutive minutes and a total of 708 minutes out of a possible 720) and fast (he was clocked in full uniform in the 100-yard dash in 10.4 seconds). In his sophomore season (1935) Kinard and the Ole Miss Rebels posted a 9–2 record and lost the Orange Bowl to Catholic University, 20–19. Ole Miss had mediocre teams the next two seasons, but Kinard was still outstanding. Despite the team's 5–5–2 record in 1936, Kinard earned consensus All-America honors. The following year the Rebels slipped to 4–5–1, but his rugged, dominating style of play earned him repeat consensus All-

Frank ("Bruiser") Kinard. PRO FOOTBALL HALL OF FAME

America honors. While at Mississippi, Kinard was also a regular guard on the varsity basketball team and a quarter-miler in track. He earned his B.S. degree in 1938 and left the university with several "firsts." He was the first Rebel gridder to earn All-Southeast Conference recognition, the first Ole Miss All-America, and the first Rebel to play in the prestigious College All-Star game in Chicago. In 1938 Kinard and the collegians defeated the previous season's National Football League (NFL) champion Washington Redskins, 28–19.

Kinard was taken in the second round of the 1938 NFL player draft by the Brooklyn Dodgers. The team struggled during Kinard's first two seasons, but he was chosen as a tackle on the All-Pro team in his first season. His smothering style of defense and rugged offensive blocking would earn him All-Pro accolades in each subsequent year of his nine-year career. Kinard brought to the NFL the same durability he exhibited at Ole Miss.

Midway through the 1939 season the Dodgers waived several players and did not replace them. Kinard played the full sixty minutes in about a half-dozen games. While this was the single-platoon era, it was still unusual to play an entire game. It was during the 1939 season that Kinard and his fellow Dodgers were participants in the first NFL telecast. Their game at Ebbetts Field versus the Philadelphia Eagles on 22 October was televised by the National Broadcasting Company. With television in its infancy, the Dodgers' 23–14 victory was beamed, via one stationary camera, to approximately 500 television sets that existed at the time (all of them in New York City).

In 1940 the Dodgers' fortunes improved with the hiring of University of Pittsburgh coach John ("Jock") Bain Sutherland. The famous coach made his mark with a precision single-wing attack, a power formation ideally suited for Kinard's aggressive, speedy style. While he continued to excel as an all-encompassing defender, Kinard's exceptional speed elevated his offensive game under Sutherland, who designed special plays to skirt the opponents' flanks with Kinard as a lead blocker, pulling out from his tackle position. As Joe Stydahar of the Chicago Bears said, "Once Bruiser threw the lead block, there was daylight for the ballcarrier—and Bruiser never missed throwing that block." Ironically, it was Stydahar who caused Kinard to miss the only game in his career as a pro. During the 1940 season "Jumbo Joe" stepped on Bruiser's forearm, causing a nasty gash. Kinard bandaged it and practiced all week, but infection set in and he sat out the next Sunday's game.

While the Dodgers were never champions, they did finish second to the New York Giants in 1940 and 1941, thanks in great part to Kinard's All-Pro play. Wartime manpower shortages eroded the team, but because he was a welder at a shipyard, Kinard was still able to play with Brooklyn on Sundays for the 1942, 1943, and 1944 seasons. He entered the navy in 1945 and played on the storied Fleet City Bluejackets service team, earning All-Service honors.

Discharged in time for the 1946 season, Kinard joined the New York Yankees of the All-America Football Conference (AAFC). Again, Kinard helped make his team a viable contender, but the Yankees of 1946 and 1947 could not supplant the Cleveland Browns as league champions. Kinard, still not weighing above 218 pounds, was All-Pro in both of his final seasons, the last one spent as a player-coach. He was the only one of 100 players who jumped from the NFL to the AAFC to earn All-Pro recognition with both pro leagues. He retired as a player before the 1948 season and returned to his alma mater as a line coach. In 1971 he became director of athletics, retiring in 1978. Seven years later he died of Alzheimer's disease and was buried in Lakewood Cemetery in Jackson.

The honors Kinard attained speak to his greatness as one of football's true "immortals." He served as captain of his high school, freshman, and varsity teams, of the Dodgers and Yankees, and of his World War II service team. It is doubtful that any other athlete has been honored by captaincies at so many levels of the game. In addition to being inducted into the Pro Football Hall of Fame (1971), Kinard was a charter member of the College Football Hall of Fame (1951). He was also named to two college All-Time All-America teams. Once nearly universally regarded as "the South's finest lineman," he retained that honor in the eyes of many, long after his playing days were over.

★

Kinard's career is further discussed in John D. McCallum and Charles H. Pearson, eds., *College Football USA* (1972); Murray Olderman, *The Defenders* (1973); Bert Randolph Sugar, ed., *The SEC* (1979); Richard Whittingham, *The Game They Played* (1984); Mike Rathet and Don R. Smith, *Their Deeds and Dogged Faith* (1984); and Don R. Smith, *Pro Football Hall of Fame All-Time Greats* (1988). An obituary is in the *Canton* (Ohio) *Repository* (9 Sept. 1985).

JIM CAMPBELL

KING, Martin Luther, Sr. ("Daddy King") (*b.* 19 December 1899 in Stockbridge, Georgia; *d.* 11 November 1984 in Atlanta, Georgia), preacher, activist, and father of the civil rights leader Martin Luther King, Jr.

King was the second of nine surviving children born to James Albert King and Delia Linsey. His maternal grandfather, Jim Long, was a slave used for breeding, and after emancipation he maintained two families; his family with Jane Linsey resulted in the birth of King's mother. After his father's death in 1933, King, who was born Michael Luther King ("Mike" to his family and friends), changed his (and his son's) name to Martin Luther.

King's status and social position as the son of sharecroppers in the segregated South was marked by hard and violently enforced economic and social restrictions. As a child, King was beaten by the local mill owner for refusing to fetch water for his workers; in response, his mother beat the owner and his father threatened to kill the man. From this King learned the ability to fight discrimination but the way in which James King's stance forced the father to flee for his life reinforced the demonic nature of racism. Martin King also witnessed the lynching of a black man whose "crime" was the color of his skin.

In 1913 King left Stockbridge after a fight with his father and because of his general dissatisfaction with the life of a sharecropper. Jumping on a train passing through Stockbridge, King rode to Atlanta and found work in the Southern Railroad yard. Although he eventually went back to Stockbridge, the appeal of Atlanta remained with him, and he eventually returned there seeking opportunities in the ministry. King and his mother often attended local congregations and ultimately developed formal ties with the Floyd Chapel Baptist Church, where he sang and traveled locally with a gospel group. In 1917 he sought ordination, but because of his youth, the deacons of Floyd Chapel refused to license him. After he was offered the leadership of a small church outside Atlanta, the pressure to license and ordain him grew.

In 1918 King moved to Atlanta to explore the possibilities of ministry in the "big city." His sister Woodie was already in Atlanta, and King was able to stay with her while trying to establish his name on the preaching circuit and supporting himself by driving a delivery truck. In 1920 he founded the Second Baptist Church of College Park and pastored this church as well as the East Point Baptist Church until 1931. With the encouragement of those he respected, King recognized that additional academic training would enhance his ministry, and he decided to attend Bryant Preparatory School. Overcoming the awkwardness of being so much older than most students, King struggled through his lessons and resisted the urging of his father to return to the farm after the death of his mother in 1924.

Meanwhile, determined to marry Alberta Williams, the only daughter of the Reverend Adam Daniel and Jennie (Celeste) Williams, with whom Woodie King had boarded, King received his high school diploma in 1925 and married Alberta on Thanksgiving Day the following year; they had three children. Over the next several years, his reputation as a minister grew. In 1930 he received a B.A. degree in theology from Morehouse College.

Although recommended by his father-in-law, the Reverend Williams, on several occasions, King refused to accept an appointment as assistant pastor at Ebenezer Baptist Church; rather, he sought to develop ministerial skills and his reputation without "special treatment." However, with the death of Williams in 1931, King accepted the pastorate of Ebenezer Baptist Church. Over the years, he transformed this already prestigious church into Atlanta's leading black Baptist church, increasing the membership from 600 to 4,000. King's leadership role within Atlanta's religious community was marked by his selection as a delegate to the 1934 World Baptist Alliance Convention in Berlin, Germany. In addition, King was vice president and later president of the Atlanta Baptist Ministers' Union, president of the Atlanta District Baptist Young People's Union and Sunday School Convention, moderator of the Atlanta Missionary Baptist Association, and member of the National Baptist Convention's board of directors. In 1942 King was a key figure in the National Baptist Convention's efforts to get President Franklin Roosevelt to eliminate racial discrimination on railroad passenger trains. He eventually

Dr. Martin Luther King, Sr., gives the last sermon of his ministry at the Ebenezer Baptist Church in Atlanta, 1975. UPI/Corbis-Bettmann

broke with the National Baptist Convention and helped form the Progressive Baptist Convention in 1961, when the head of the National Baptist Convention refused to support a strong civil rights agenda. King lost his influence in the National Baptist Convention because he regarded social transformation—the fulfillment of democracy—as more important than personal position.

King was also active outside church circles as a member of the Atlanta executive committee of the National Association for the Advancement of Colored People (NAACP); a trustee of Morehouse College; an officer of the Atlanta Civic and Political League; and a trustee of Citizen's Trust Company, a black-owned bank in Atlanta. His confrontation with racial injustice marked him as one of the twentieth century's key religious leaders. Noteworthy activities included his leading Atlanta's first march to City Hall for voters rights in 1935 and his singlehanded and successful efforts to integrate the elevators in the Fulton County Court House that same year. He also led efforts to equalize black and white teachers' salaries in 1936. With time, the mayor of Atlanta and other officials came to depend upon his suggestions and insights, while his more confrontational activities resulted in a reference to King as "the leader of those dangerous radicals."

Despite tragic personal losses, including the deaths of his two sons (King, Jr., was assassinated in 1968 and Alfred Daniel drowned in 1969) and the murder of his wife during services at Ebenezer Baptist Church in June 1974, King maintained his commitment to social transformation and

a gospel of love. His labor on behalf of others was recognized with many awards, including the Clergyman of the Year Award in 1972 from the Georgia region of the National Conference of Christians and Jews. In 1975 he became the first black person to address a joint session of the Alabama state legislature, and in 1978 he was named the National Father of the Year in Religion.

Over the years, King maintained a hectic speaking schedule, gaining additional recognition and awards. After he retired from the active ministry at Ebenezer in 1975, he gave the benediction at the 1976 Democratic National Convention that nominated Jimmy Carter. As president, Carter regarded King as an invaluable adviser. King also gave the benediction at the 1980 Democratic National Convention, and his autobiography, *Daddy King,* was published during the same year. King died as the result of a heart attack and was interred in a white marble crypt in Atlanta.

King, considered "God's southern gentleman" by some, had a forceful presence that demanded respect and made things happen. Those who knew him remarked that his energy and commitment to progress were contagious and uncompromisingly maintained. His activities position him as a central figure in the struggle for justice and human rights during the twentieth century. King used churches, boycotts, and the ballot box as tools in the building of a democratic society that benefited all citizens. His son Martin Luther King, Jr., and others learned lessons from him that enabled them to maintain a creative vision and accomplish the changes that later generations would celebrate.

★

The Christine King Farris Collection, which is privately held, contains speeches and other material by King. The primary text about his life and philosophy is his autobiography, written with Clayton Riley, *Daddy King: An Autobiography* (1980). Also of interest is David Collins, *Not Only Dreamers: The Story of Martin Luther King, Sr., and Martin Luther King, Jr.* (1986). The introduction to *The Papers of Martin Luther King, Jr.,* vol. 1 (1992), written by Clayborne Carson, also provides important information on the elder King and the larger context of the King family. Although not solely devoted to King, Sr., Taylor Branch, *America in the King Years: Parting the Waters, 1954–1963* (1988), also provides interesting insights on King's public activities. King's attitude toward segregation and his efforts to stem this tide within his church dealings and family are presented by Lawrence D. Reddick, *Crusader Without Violence: A Biography of Martin Luther King, Jr.* (1959). King's involvement with the National Baptist Convention and the Progressive Baptist Convention is concisely presented in C. Eric Lincoln, *The Black Church in the African American Experience* (1990). An obituary is in the *New York Times* (12 Nov. 1984).

ANTHONY BERNARD PINN

KISTIAKOWSKY, George Bogdan (*b.* 18 November 1900 in Kiev, Ukraine [Russia]; *d.* 7 December 1982 in Cambridge, Massachusetts), physical chemist who, in connection with his work for the Manhattan Project, the American atomic bomb program, was the architect of key concepts that led to success in developing nuclear weapons.

Kistiakowsky, who was known as "Kisty" in his later career, was born into an upper-middle-class academic family. His father was Bogdan Kistiakowsky, a professor of legal philosophy at the University of Kiev; his mother was Mary Berenstam. Bogdan Kistiakowsky was described by his son as a sociologist deeply concerned with human rights.

Kistiakowsky attended public and private schools in Kiev and Moscow before his education was abruptly interrupted by the Russian Revolution. At the age of eighteen, he volunteered as a soldier in the anti-Bolshevik White Russian army, which sought to restore the overthrown czarist regime. Afflicted with typhus during the latter part of the revolutionary conflict, Kistiakowsky managed to escape the Red Army with a group of White Army soldiers and reached the Balkans and Turkey, where he spent much of 1919. Anticipating no professional future for himself in the USSR, he entered the University of Berlin as an undergraduate in 1920. He was a gifted student in the sciences and completed both his undergraduate and graduate work in less than four years. He received his Ph.D. in physical chemistry in 1925. Kistiakowsky's dissertation adviser was the prominent scientific leader of physical chemistry in

George Kistiakowsky, 1959. ARCHIVE PHOTOS

Germany, Max Bodenstein. The results of Kistiakowsky's important thesis work on the photochemical decomposition of chlorine monoxide and ozone were published in two separate papers in 1925 and 1926.

Upon Bodenstein's recommendation, Princeton University accepted Kistiakowsky as an International Education Board Fellow in 1925. In 1927 he was promoted to research associate and DuPont Fellow with the rank of instructor. During this period Kistiakowsky wrote *Photochemical Processes,* which was published by the American Chemical Society in 1928. It led to a recognition of Kistiakowsky's expertise in photochemistry and his promotion to the rank of assistant professor at Princeton.

In 1926, his first year at Princeton, he married Hildegard Moebius; they were divorced in 1942, having had one child, Vera, who became a professor of physics at the Massachusetts Institute of Technology. In 1945 Kistiakowsky married Irma E. Shuler. They were divorced in 1960. In 1962 he married Elaine Mahoney.

In 1930 James B. Conant, president of Harvard University, persuaded Kistiakowsky to leave Princeton for Harvard, where Kistiakowsky's academic career accelerated. In 1933 he was promoted to associate professor; in 1937 he became a full professor. Except for an eighteen-month interval between 1959 and 1961, during which he served as special adviser to President Dwight D. Eisenhower for science and technology, he remained at Harvard for the rest of his life.

At Harvard, Kistiakowsky became both a well-liked teacher and a first-rate researcher. In the latter sphere, he proved himself both a gifted practical experimentalist and a penetrating theoretician with strong mathematical aptitude. He extended his early Berlin work in using advanced spectroscopic and fluorescence techniques to probe fundamental photochemical interactions. His interests were expanded to include atomic reactions. His scientific work included important contributions in chemical kinetics, thermodynamics of organic molecules, unimolecular and bimolecular gas reactions, enzymatic chemistry, and chemiluminescence.

What was already a successful career in chemistry for Kistiakowsky took a dramatic new turn with the outbreak of World War II. In June 1940 President Franklin D. Roosevelt had established the National Defense Research Committee (NDRC) under the chairmanship of Vannevar Bush, former vice president of the Massachusetts Institute of Technology and then president of the Carnegie Institution. Its objective was to mobilize the scientific resources of the United States in areas of advanced military preparedness. Among the founding members of the NDRC was President Conant of Harvard; in 1941 Conant enlisted Kistiakowsky to be chief of the NDRC unit studying explosives and other munitions. Kistiakowsky held that post until February 1944, when he became leader of the Explosives Division of the Engineers' Manhattan District, developing components for the atomic bomb at Los Alamos, New Mexico.

Just prior to the official establishment of the NDRC by Roosevelt, a conference was held at the invitation of Vannevar Bush at the Carnegie Institution in Washington on 21 May 1940. The conference addressed a number of vital scientific questions of pressing military concern. Among the most important was the question of how to separate the fissionable isotope uranium-235—the only isotope of uranium capable of sustaining a chain reaction either as a fuel for a nuclear reactor or as an atomic bomb explosive.

During the conference Kistiakowsky suggested gaseous diffusion as the possible means for separating uranium-235 from the nonfissionable isotopes of uranium. Recognizing that neon and chlorine isotopes had been successfully separated by other scientists by recycling the gases through many stages, Kistiakowsky initiated research that, later pursued by scientists at Columbia University, became the basis for securing the substantial quantities of uranium-235 required for an atomic bomb explosive. Kistiakowsky is also credited with developing the explosive lenses of conventional (or "ordinary") chemical explosives that are required for the plutonium version of the atomic bomb.

The first nuclear explosion was the Trinity Test at Alamogordo, New Mexico, on 16 July 1945. The test employed plutonium-239 as the explosive fissionable material. The second, a true atomic bomb, which was used in the attack on Hiroshima on 6 August 1945, depended upon bringing together for nuclear detonation two subcritical masses of uranium. The second atomic bomb utilized the Trinity Test plutonium configuration and was exploded over Nagasaki on 9 August 1945. Both the Trinity Test and the Nagasaki weapon depended on implosion or compression to high density of the plutonium-239 to achieve chain-reacting fission and nuclear explosion. The extraordinarily difficult problem was addressed for successful theoretical resolution by mathematician John von Neumann but its empirical realization was turned over to Kistiakowsky, probably the leading chemical explosives expert in the United States.

When the Trinity Test of the plutonium atomic bomb detonated with an explosive yield of twenty kilotons of TNT—materially in excess of what had been generally anticipated—Kistiakowsky had two strongly conflicting reactions: joy at the project's success and deep concern with respect to the threatening aspects of nuclear war. He observed that day with prophetic awareness: "I am sure that at the end of the world, in the last millisecond of the earth's existence, Man will see what we have just seen."

In recognition of his wartime services, Kistiakowsky received the highest American civilian award, the Medal of Merit, from President Harry S. Truman in 1946. He also received the British Medal for Service in the Cause of Freedom in 1948. He returned to Harvard, where he became chairman of the department of chemistry, continuing and initiating important new areas of fundamental research. In addition to his academic work, Kistiakowsky's counsel as a scientific consultant was sought by federal government agencies in security areas, especially those dealing with nuclear weapons and ballistic missile delivery systems. He served on technical panels of the Atomic Energy Commission, the Department of Defense, and the Central Intelligence Agency.

On 14 July 1959 Kistiakowsky became the second presidential science adviser for science and technology. For the eighteen months that Kistiakowsky served in that position, President Dwight D. Eisenhower relied heavily upon his practical and frank advice for guidance in two conflicting areas: the generation of superior weapons and avoidance of surprise attack and the nonproliferation of nuclear weapons and an end to nuclear weapons testing.

On 20 January 1961, though a warm admirer of President Eisenhower, Kistiakowsky resigned in disillusion with what he regarded as obstructive positions of the military establishment in the public interest. His final break as a consultant to the Department of Defense came in 1968, when he resigned all his military advisory positions in protest against what he viewed as the government's immoral Vietnam policy and insufficiency in confronting the dangers of the arms race.

In later life Kistiakowsky served as chairman of the Council for a Livable World Education Fund, a position he held in 1982. In this capacity he urged a policy of curbing the arms race and especially the adoption of no-first-use of nuclear weapons by the United States.

Despite being afflicted with cancer in the last three years of his life, Kistiakowsky remained active in pursuit of weapons control and against nuclear proliferation. He died in Cambridge, Massachusetts, and he was cremated; his remains were scattered near his summer home on Cape Cod.

★

Kistiakowsky's *A Scientist at the White House: The Private Diary of President Eisenhower's Special Assistant for Science and Technology* (1976) furnishes insights into the dynamics of national policymaking as well as Kistiakowsky's exceptional character. Among his popular articles are "The Limitations of Strategic Arms," *Scientific American* (1972), and "The Arms Race: Is Paranoia Necessary for Security?" *New York Times Magazine* (27 Nov. 1977). Sir Frederick Dainton, "George Bogdan Kistiakowsky 1900–1982," *Biographical Memoirs of Fellows of the Royal Society* 31 (Nov. 1985): 377–407, provides a good summary of Kistiakowsky's life and a complete listing of his publications from 1925 to 1978. Kistiakowsky's activities in connection with the Manhattan Project are covered in the following books: Richard G. Hewlett and Oscar E. Anderson, *A History of the United States Atomic Energy Commission,* vol. 1, *The New World, 1939–1946* (1962); Leslie Groves, *Now It Can Be Told: The Story of the Manhattan Project* (1962); Lansing Lamont, *Day of Trinity* (1965); Stephane Groueff, *Manhattan Project: The Untold Story of the Making of the Atomic Bomb* (1967); and Richard Rhodes, *The Making of the Atomic Bomb* (1986), and *Dark Sun: The Making of the Hydrogen Bomb* (1995). An obituary is in the *New York Times* (8 Dec. 1982). A lead editorial, "George Kistiakowsky," is in the *Boston Globe* (9 Dec. 1982).

This writer acknowledges with appreciation some personal details of Kistiakowsky's life furnished in communication with his daughter, Dr. Vera Kistiakowsky.

LEONARD R. SOLON

KLINE, Nathan Schellenberg (*b.* 22 March 1916 in Philadelphia, Pennsylvania; *d.* 11 February 1983 in New York City), research psychiatrist and educator who pioneered the use of tranquilizers and antidepressant drugs in the treatment of mental illness.

Kline grew up in Atlantic City, New Jersey, with his sister and eight older half siblings, including Benjamin Kline, who developed the Kline test for syphilis. His father, Ignatz Kline, owned a chain of department stores, and his mother,

Florence Schellenberg, was a physician. Kline graduated from Atlantic City High School in 1934, then enrolled at Swarthmore College as an English major. He completed his English requirements in two years, then proceeded to take courses in philosophy and psychology. He received his B.A. degree with honors in 1938.

Fascinated with the relationship between mind and body, Kline studied psychology at Harvard Graduate School from 1938 to 1939. On the advice of Professor Mc-Fee Campbell, he enrolled in New York University's College of Medicine in 1939. He received his M.D. degree in 1943, and from 1943 to 1944 he served his internship and residency at St. Elizabeth's Hospital in Washington, D.C. In 1944 he entered the U.S. Public Health Service, which assigned him as an assistant surgeon to ships in the merchant marine. On these ships he observed emotionally disturbed men functioning usefully in their environment. The experience profoundly affected his approach to mental illness.

After his discharge from the Public Health Service in 1946, Kline studied for a year at Princeton University and worked part-time as a child psychiatrist at the Union County Mental Hygiene Society clinic in Plainfield, New Jersey. From 1946 to 1950 he was on staff at the Veterans' Administration hospital in Lyons, New Jersey, and from 1948 to 1950 he was a research assistant at the College of Physicians and Surgeons of Columbia University. In 1950 Kline became director of research at Worcester State Hospital in Massachusetts. He completed his studies at Clark University, obtaining an M.A. degree in psychology in 1951, and became a licensed psychiatrist in 1953. In 1952 Kline had left Worcester to become director of research at Rockland State Hospital in Orangeburg, New York. He resumed his association with Columbia the same year, serving as a research associate until 1957 and as clinical professor of psychiatry at the College of Physicians and Surgeons from 1957 until 1980.

Kline's discovery of tranquilizers was serendipitous. In 1953 he approached a friend at the pharmaceutical firm of E. R. Squibb and Sons for a grant to pay for a piece of equipment needed for his research. The company was testing derivatives of the Indian snakeroot plant *Rauwolfia serpentina* as a possible treatment for high blood pressure. Kline got the grant from Squibb after he agreed to study the plant's usefulness in sedating psychotic patients. At about the same time another drug company, Ciba, announced that its scientists had isolated and synthesized reserpine, apparently the active ingredient in *Rauwolfia*. Kline convinced the authorities at Ciba to allow him to include the new substance in his research. Initial findings were subtle, but when a concentrated, injectable form of reserpine was developed and tested, the results were dramatic. The drug enabled schizophrenic patients to cope

Nathan Kline, 1964. ARCHIVE PHOTOS

consciously with their environment. For his pioneer efforts in the use of psychoactive drugs, Kline was presented with the Albert Lasker Medical Research Award in 1957.

Beginning in May 1955 Kline made several widely publicized appearances before Congress to speak of his findings and to request a greater appropriation for additional research for mental health drugs. The psychiatric community was skeptical, but Kline reasoned that if there were drugs that could act as tranquilizers, there must also be drugs that could act as "psychic energizers" to relieve depression. He tested his ideas with a colleague and a drug called iproniazid, which had been noted to create a "mild euphoria" in the tuberculosis patients it was used to treat. By 1957 the drug, first in a class known as monoamine oxidase (MAO) inhibitors, gained widespread use; an estimated 400,000 people in the United States were treated with it in the first year. Kline won his second Lasker Award in 1964 for the introduction of iproniazid as an antidepressant. The award bore the inscription: "Literally hundreds of thousands of people are leading productive, normal lives who—

but for Dr. Kline's work—would be leading lives of fruitless despair and frustration."

Kline had a private practice in New York City for three decades. He was director of psychiatric services at Bergen Pines County Hospital in Paramus, New Jersey, from 1963 to 1975. He served as a consultant on psychiatry to many foreign governments and universities and was on the expert advisory panel to the World Health Organization from 1973 to 1983. Kline published more than 400 scientific books and articles. He was a member of the editorial boards of many publications, including *Excerpta Medica* (1955–1983). The research department at Rockland State Hospital officially became a separate unit, the Rockland Research Institute, in 1975, and Kline was its director until 1983.

Kline married Margot Hess on 29 June 1942; they had one child and were divorced in 1976. Kline was once described as almost theatrical in appearance, five feet, eight inches tall with blue eyes and thick gray hair. He was called bold, outspoken, and controversial, but also gregarious, articulate, and innovative. He collected modern paintings, abstract sculpture, and primitive artifacts and enjoyed literature, travel, and the theater. Kline died at University Hospital in New York City during heart surgery.

Kline's work in psychopharmacology revolutionized psychiatric practice in his time. His efforts helped many patients who were formerly considered untreatable to live normal lives outside of institutions. His idea that mental disorders could be treated in a manner similar to physical ailments began to change public perception of the nature of mental illness. Just eight months after his death, on 20 October 1983, the Rockland Research Institute acknowledged Kline's accomplishments by changing its name to the Nathan S. Kline Institute for Psychiatric Research.

★

See David Hendin, *Life Givers* (1976), and William Hoffman, *Doctors on the New Frontier* (1981). An article on Kline's work not treated here is Thomas Fleming, "The Computer and the Psychiatrist," *New York Times Magazine* (6 Apr. 1969). See also Donald Robinson, *One Hundred Most Important People in the World Today* (1970); "Out of the Mind's Darkness," in his *Miracle Finders* (1976); and *American Jewish Biographies* (1982). An obituary is in the *New York Times* (14 Feb. 1983).

VICTORIA TAMBORRINO

KNIGHT, John Shively (*b.* 26 October 1894 in Bluefield, West Virginia; *d.* 16 June 1981 in Akron, Ohio), newspaper editor and publisher who formed the Knight-Ridder newspaper chain, one of the country's largest and most influential media groups.

Knight's father, Charles Landon, worked his way up from advertising manager at the *Akron Beacon Journal* to become editor and publisher of the paper in 1909. "C.L." was known for his fiery editorials.

Knight graduated from Akron's Central High School in 1914, then prepped for a year at the Tome School in Port Deposit, Maryland, before entering Cornell University in Ithaca, New York. Knight interrupted his studies to enlist in the U.S. Army and saw military action in World War I in the Argonne Forest in France.

Upon his return to the United States, Knight won $5,000 shooting craps and headed to California, where he considered a career in the cattle business. But C. L. encouraged him to return to Ohio, where he gave him a job writing sports at the *Beacon Journal* in 1920. Lacking confidence, however, Knight used the pseudonym "Walker," once telling a friend, "I was ashamed of the stuff. I didn't write well enough."

In 1921 Knight married Katherine "Kitty" McLain. They had three sons, John Shively, Jr., Charles Landon, and Franklin. Kitty died unexpectedly in 1929, and three years later, Knight married Beryl Zoller Comstock.

Installed by his father as managing editor of the *Beacon Journal* in 1925, Knight inherited his father's position as editor and publisher when C. L. died in 1933. He then purchased the *Miami Herald* in 1937 for $2 million and, at the same time, he bought and closed the *Miami Tribune;* in 1938 he bought the Scripps-Howard *Akron Times Press.* In 1940 he garnered majority control of the *Detroit Free Press* and the *Chicago Daily News.*

Unlike other newspaper magnates of that time, such as William Randolph Hearst, Knight opposed centralizing the management of his growing empire. He demanded that each publication be the product and a reflection of its region. In Akron, for example, the *Beacon Journal* helped drive the economic development that transformed the small northeastern Ohio town into a center of industry along the Erie Canal. Knight expressed his views in a weekly column called "The Editor's Notebook," which he wrote for four decades.

Knight was elected president of the American Society of Newspaper Editors in 1944, an illustration of his competitors and colleagues' respect. During his term, he sent American reporters and editors on an international tour to interview foreign editors and public officials. A report from this trip concluded that the press is almost always used as a propaganda tool by governments, and that a fair and objective press could, among other things, reduce the likelihood of future wars.

Knight then took a one-year leave from his newspaper chain to become director of the United States Office of Censorship in London, where he was the country's liaison for Great Britain and North Africa. While Knight was in London only months before the war ended, his eldest son,

John S. Knight receiving the Americas Award, 1959. ARCHIVE PHOTOS

John Shively, Jr., a lieutenant in the army paratroopers, was killed in combat in Germany.

Knight returned to his property in Miami, the Fourth Estate Stables, and, in 1968 Columbia University awarded him a Pulitzer Prize—the profession's top honor. While he garnered the award for his column "The Editor's Notebook," he was also thrilled to learn that two of his newspapers, the *Detroit Free Press* and the *Charlotte Observer,* also won in other categories, making Knight the first publisher to ever win three Pulitzers in a single year.

His influence reached further in 1973, when Knight Newspapers merged with Ridder Publications, a California-based newspaper company. By that time, Knight Newspapers owned fifteen publications, including the *Philadelphia Inquirer, Philadelphia Daily News, Springfield Sun,* and *Tallahassee Democrat.* The merger with Ridder brought nineteen more publications to the chain.

While his business flourished, Knight was beset by tragedy again. In 1974 his second wife, Beryl, died, and the next year his grandson, John Shively III, the editor of the *Philadelphia Daily News,* was murdered in a robbery in his apartment.

In 1976 Knight married for a third time, wedding Frances Elizabeth Augustus, and he retired as editorial chairman of Knight-Ridder Newspapers, Inc. When he left the business, the company owned thirty newspapers with a total circulation of 9.5 million (13.6 million on Sundays), and had won twenty-six Pulitzer Prizes.

Knight enjoyed retirement by raising thoroughbred racehorses at the Fourth Estate Stables and by golfing in numerous club tournaments, several of which he won. He also oversaw the Knight Foundation, which he established in honor of his father in 1940.

Knight was the recipient of honorary doctorate degrees from the University of Akron, Northwestern University, Kent State University, Ohio State University, the University of Michigan, Oberlin College, and Colby College. He also was awarded the National Press Award and the Poor Richard Gold Medal of Achievement Award.

He was widowed a third time in December 1980, and on 16 June 1981, Knight suffered a massive heart attack at a friend's home in Akron and died at the age of eighty-six. The majority of his $245 million estate was left to the Knight Foundation.

Knight's legacy can be seen in the thirty-two newspapers and four television stations that Knight-Ridder owned fifteen years after his death. Following his lead, several other newspaper groups have formed, using major metropolitan dailies to generate revenue that allows their smaller publications to exist and compete.

★

See Charles Whited, *Knight: A Publisher in the Tumultuous Century* (1988). An obituary is in the *New York Times* (17 June 1981).

JONATHAN TAPPER

KNOPF, Alfred Abraham (*b*. 12 September 1892 in New York City; *d*. 11 August 1984 in Purchase, New York), editor, founder of the publishing company that bears his name, and publisher of the works of a number of major American writers; he also introduced many important European and Latin American authors to readers in the United States. The books he published won renown for the excellent craftsmanship that went into their making.

Alfred Knopf was the son of Samuel Knopf, a well-to-do advertising man and business consultant, and Ida Japhe, who died when Alfred was four. He had one sister and a half brother from his father's second marriage. Knopf attended DeWitt Clinton High School in New York City and graduated from the MacKenzie School in Dobbs Ferry, New York, in 1908. Later that year he entered Columbia University, from which he intended to go on to Harvard Law School. Although Knopf later remarked that he looked back on his time at Columbia "as an ex-convict might look back on Sing-Sing" (one of his complaints was that there

Alfred A. Knopf. KNOPF/RANDOM HOUSE

was not a single good restaurant in the area), it was his Columbia experience that developed his love of literature and history and eventually led to his career in publishing. Professor Joel E. Spingarn made an especially significant impression on the young man. Knopf's letter to the English author John Galsworthy, requesting information for a paper he was writing for one of Spingarn's courses, led to a continuing correspondence. During his senior year Knopf was advertising manager of the *Columbia Monthly*. By this time Knopf had clearly developed a distinguished sartorial sense; as teacher Carl Van Doren later remembered, Knopf was "color on the campus." His penchant for colored shirts and bright ties was to become a trademark throughout his life; Carl Van Vechten likened him to "a prince in a Persian miniature."

After his graduation in 1912 Knopf made his first trip to Europe, where he met Galsworthy. When Knopf returned to New York City, his plans to attend law school had been abandoned and he was determined to become involved in publishing. His career in the field began with an eight-dollar-a-week clerical position in the accounting department at Doubleday, Page and Company, a position he obtained with the help of a friend of his father. During his eighteen months at Doubleday, Knopf gained additional experience in several departments—manufacturing, advertising, and sales—that shortly would become invaluable.

Two significant experiences came out of his eighteen months at Doubleday: his promotion of a uniform edition of the works of Joseph Conrad and, more importantly, the beginning of his close friendship and collaboration with H. L. Mencken. After a brief association with Mitchell Kennerley, one of the more experimental publishers of the day, Knopf decided to found his own company. Thus, in the late spring of 1915, at the age of twenty-three, "full of chutzpah" and with $5,000, Knopf created an office in a single room in the Candler Building on West Forty-second Street in Manhattan. Blanche Wolf, whom he had met in his senior year at Columbia, became his all-around assistant, his fiancée, and on 4 April 1916 his wife.

Blanche shared Alfred's love of books, and the two supervised every detail in their publishing ventures, from soliciting authors to reading manuscripts, from designing the volumes to producing and advertising them. The Knopfs became the first husband-wife team in the history of book publishing. It was Blanche who early on suggested the borzoi, the Russian greyhound, as a symbol for the new firm. From the time the company adopted this label, the borzoi was acknowledged as a symbol of excellence in the publishing industry. A Knopf advertisement beginning with the words "Mr. Knopf has the honor to announce the following new Borzoi books" always marked an exciting new reading list.

The first publication to appear under the Knopf name was a translation from the French of four plays by Emile Augier. The volume immediately established two of Knopf's major objectives—to bring European literature to American readers and to produce beautiful books. It was, however, the publication in 1916 of W. H. Hudson's *Green Mansions,* with an introduction by John Galsworthy, that put the company "in business," Knopf would later say. Over the next few years Knopf brought the works of many more European writers to the United States, among them Thomas Mann, André Gide, Sigrid Undset, and Knut Hamsun. His American lists for those early years were equally impressive, with such names as T. S. Eliot, Ezra Pound, Wallace Stevens, and Willa Cather. Kahlil Gibran's *The Prophet,* which first appeared in 1923, would become Knopf's most successful publication. *The Borzoi 1925* (1925), commemorating the first ten years of the Knopf firm, is a remarkable testament to what the Knopfs had accomplished, both in terms of the works they had published and their dedication to the goal of printing physically attractive books. B. W. Huebsch, another of the distinguished publishers of the era, perhaps best described both

the personality and the significance of Knopf when he asserted, "Until Knopf blew in, like young Lochinvar, book publishing was a business; he made it a career." In 1928 the growth of the business necessitated a bigger office, and Knopf moved the firm to the Heckscher Building at 730 Fifth Avenue.

In 1923 Knopf helped found the *American Mercury,* the first issue of which appeared in January 1924, with Mencken and George Jean Nathan as its editors. Knopf's statement in the first issue was that the publication would offer "a comprehensive picture, critically presented, of the entire American scene," would avoid and attack "current platitudes," and would maintain the point of view of "the civilized minority." With its easily recognizable green cover, the *American Mercury* soon became extremely popular, particularly among college youth and their professors, and one of America's most respected publications. Within two years the magazine had a circulation of more than 74,000. Issues appeared until 1934, when the Great Depression brought about its end.

In the mid-1920s Knopf began printing a statement about the design and typographical characteristics of his books. From 1926 on every Knopf book included a page at the end with a description of the typeface that had been used in that volume and an explanation of the qualities of that typography. Knopf employed the very best craftsmen of the day, among them Rudolf Ruzicka, Elmer Adler, W. A. Dwiggins, Bruce Rogers, Warren Chappell, and George Salter, and regularly used the Plimpton Press as his printer. Publisher George Doran later commented that Knopf "not only made beautiful books but told the public they were beautiful books and thereby stimulated the public to require a more graceful format."

During the 1920s and the following decades the Knopf list continued to grow, with the addition of scholarly works, among them historical studies by Oswald Spengler, Thomas Beer, W. J. Cash, Oscar Handlin, Richard Hofstadter, David Donald, and Samuel Eliot Morison; works on music by Ernest Newman, J. W. N. Sullivan, and Alfred Einstein; and Mencken's *The American Language* (1921) and F. O. Matthiessen's *The James Family* (1947). At the same time the European list was headed by works of Camus, Sartre, Kafka, Mann, and de Beauvoir. Popular fiction included the works of Dashiell Hammett and Raymond Chandler. The Knopfs also were instrumental in publishing many major Latin American writers, thus opening a whole new area of interest to readers in the United States.

In 1959 the Knopfs' only child, Alfred A. ("Pat") Knopf, Jr., who had been involved in the family's business, left the firm to establish Atheneum Publishers. In early 1960 the senior Knopf, who had served as president then chairman of the board of Alfred A. Knopf, Inc. since 1918, agreed to a merger by which Knopf became a subsidiary of Random

House. Blanche Knopf died in 1966. On 20 April 1967 Knopf married Helen N. Hedrick in Rio de Janeiro. Knopf continued to serve as a member of the board of directors of Random House and to engage in various other interests and concerns, most notably in history, music, and conservation. He was awarded numerous honorary degrees by American colleges and universities and decorations and citations by various organizations. Knopf died of congestive heart failure at his home in suburban Purchase, Westchester County, New York, at the age of ninety-one. Knopf is buried in Ferncliff Cemetery in Westchester County, New York.

In his later years Knopf bemoaned the increasing commercialism in the publishing industry. He had long advocated printing fewer books as a way of maintaining quality in what was printed. Greed, he asserted, had taken over the business. Knopf was a shrewd businessman but as Knopf author John Updike declared upon his death, "He kept his eye on the matter of quality—quality in printing, quality in writing." During his tenure as the head of Alfred A. Knopf Publishers, the firm published more than 5,000 titles; sixteen Knopf authors were awarded Nobel Prizes and twenty-six were awarded Pulitzer Prizes. Mencken called Knopf "the perfect publisher." At a memorial service in 1984 another Knopf author, John Hersey, stated that he was simply "the greatest publisher this country has ever had."

★

The major collection of Knopf papers is in the Harry Ransom Humanities Research Center at the University of Texas at Austin. *Some Random Recollections: An Informal Talk Made at the Grolier Club, 21 October 1948* (1949) is one of Knopf's own accounts of how he came to be a publisher. This piece also includes several comments critical of the American book publishing industry at mid-century. "Publishing Then and Now: 1912–1964," one of the R. R. Bowker lectures, presented in November 1964, also covers much of the same material. Linda Kuehl, "Talking with Mr. Knopf," *New York Times Book Review* (24 Feb. 1974), provides some interesting information on Knopf's relationship with a number of authors and on the merger with Random House. Although there is no full-length biography of Knopf, two valuable sources of comment are *Alfred A. Knopf: Quarter Century* (1940), which contains comments by a number of Knopf authors and friends, and Geoffrey Hellman's *New Yorker* profile (20 and 27 Nov. 1948, 4 Dec. 1948). The Hellman portrait is the lengthiest and most informative biographical comment to date, providing a very good sense of the man and his career. Also particularly useful is Clifton Fadiman, ed., *Fifty Years: Being a Retrospective Collection* (1965). *Portrait of a Publisher, 1915–1965,* 2 vols. (1965), with an introduction by Paul A. Bennett, also contains essential biographical information. Remarks on Knopf in books on publishing history appear in Charles A. Madison, *Jewish Publishing in America: The Impact of Jewish Writing on American Culture* (1976), and John Tebbel, *The History of Book Publishing in the United States,* vol. 3, *The Golden Age Between Two Wars, 1920–1940* (1978). The obit-

uary in the *New York Times* (12 Aug. 1984) provides an overview of Knopf's career with appreciative statements by various authors and a list of all the Knopf authors who won Nobel and Pulitzer Prizes.

RICHARD C. HARRIS

KNOTT, Walter (*b.* 11 December 1889 in San Bernardino, California; *d.* 3 December 1981 in Buena Park, California), popularizer of the boysenberry and developer of the first theme park in the United States, Knott's Berry Farm.

Knott was the son of Elgin Columbus Knott and Margaret Virginia Dougherty. His father, a southern Methodist minister, died in 1896 after a train accident and suffering from tuberculosis. The older of two brothers, Walter Knott did his best to help his mother, who worked in a laundry after her husband died. At seven years old, Walter asked his neighbors if he could grow crops on their vacant lots and give the owners a share of his produce. He attended Po-

Walter Knott. © 1998 KNOTT'S BERRY FARM

mona High School from 1905 to 1906 but did not graduate. He married Cordelia L. Hornaday, his high school sweetheart, on 3 June 1911. They had four children and later adopted two more; they would remain married until her death in April 1974.

In 1909 Knott acquired his first full-time job, harvesting cantaloupes in the Imperial Valley while fighting mosquitoes and thirst. He homesteaded an initial 10 acres in 1911 and by 1917 had bought 160 acres on a spur of the Mojave Desert. As a farmer in Coachella, Knott eliminated the middleman. He picked up orders from Colton, the nearest town on the rail line, and delivered directly to wholesalers and grocers. Native American women worked for him for silver, and his commission man agreed to a fixed price for his produce, evening out the peaks and valleys of supply and demand. Since money was tight, Knott found additional employment as a carpenter, roadworker, and rancher in San Luis Obispo County. Cordelia sold homemade candies to raise money to purchase a car, and together they grew giant cabbages and dwarf Arizona Hopi corn.

In 1919 Knott formed a partnership with his cousin Jim Preston. They rented twenty acres in Buena Park, where they planted berries. The Knotts had a Model T Ford and $2,500 saved from months of austere living, which had included eating black-eyed peas flavored with salted pigs' jowls. The partners were successful with the youngberry, but frosts and skyrocketing land prices caused Preston to abandon the effort. Knott decided to make every effort, however, to retain his "berry patch." The Knotts could not survive farming in the Mojave so in 1922 they moved to Buena Park; the old homestead and the surrounding areas such as Calico mine later became part of Knott's theme park. Cordelia sold jams and jellies, and their children helped sell rhubarb and flowers to pay the mortgage. The family purchased ten more acres during the Great Depression. At the suggestion of a Department of Agriculture employee, Knott in 1927 contacted Rudolph Boysen concerning a hybrid plant, a blackberry, raspberry, and loganberry combination. Knott was successful with these vines, called boysenberries, which produced berries so large that twenty-five filled a standard half-pound basket.

By 1934 Cordelia Knott had started a successful fried chicken restaurant, while Walter Knott continued his berry production and began a mail-order nursery for plants. Knott foresaw that freezing would be a better way of packing fruit than canning. When the local banker denied him a loan to expand his business, Knott decided to proceed alone. By 1937 Knott had a new restaurant, and he turned down the local banker's offer to finance a national chain. Knott continued to buy produce from local farmers and emphasized local motifs with a mural in his restaurant depicting Indian chiefs, created by the artist Paul von Klieben.

Family settings ruled the day, and the grounds were kept free of litter.

In 1940, inspired by the pioneer stories his grandmother told him of covered wagon travel to the West, Knott built Ghost Town on his farm to capture those scenes. With whistling trains, braying burros, clanging cable cars, and people in costume telling stories, Ghost Town included a Wells Fargo Express, a livery barn, Ghost Town Boot Hill Cemetery, and a blacksmith shop. An irrigation pipe to the town was hidden inside a volcano and a cactus garden, and he moved an old hotel to his property from Prescott, Arizona.

In 1951 Knott turned the old mining town of Calico in the desert between Los Angeles and Las Vegas into a tourist attraction stocked by the real railroad, the Rio Grande Southern, and staffed by former employees of the railroad. There visitors sampled the flavor of the nineteenth century, rode the San Francisco Street Railway's cable cars, and mined for gold. When Disneyland opened nearby in 1955, Knott was sanguine, seeing competition as healthy. Indeed, as early as 1936 he instituted a profit-sharing program for his employees. In 1963 he built a replica of Philadelphia's Independence Hall, complete with a cracked "Liberty bell." In 1968 he built the Log Ride and, in 1971, the John Wayne Theater, which featured country-western shows and songs. The oldest theme park in the nation, Knott's Berry Farm was attracting more than 4 million tourists and employing more than 3,000 local workers by the 1980s. Knott's berry-preserves business was also still ongoing at the time of his death, from Parkinson's disease, in Buena Park, California. He is buried at Loma Vista Memorial Park in Fullerton, California.

Knott, a trim, feisty man with blue eyes, believed in himself, in God, and in following his dreams. His dream of farming in the desert, even though he lacked the financial resources for irrigation, was revived in a sense with his Calico Town (he never sold his old desert homestead). He was a pioneer in his love of the soil, in entrepreneurship, and in adapting to changing circumstances. His newsletter to his employees showed his marketing skills based on common sense and a love of people. Knott was known as a spokesman for constitutional rights and conservative causes, influenced by his distrust of big government. Even into his seventies, he worked from early to late, which spoke louder than his trumpeting of free enterprise against government regulations.

★

For more information on Knott, see F. J. Taylor, "One Man's Crusade for Everybody's Freedom," *Reader's Digest* (June 1964); Norman Eugene Nygaard, *Walter Knott: Twentieth-Century Pioneer* (1965); W. D. Woodson, "Saga of a Ghost Town Artist," *Design* (midsummer 1972); Helen Kooiman, *Walter Knott: Keeper of the Flame* (1973); and Willie Mae C. G. Caldwell, *The Genealogy of the Knott Family, 1617–1989* (1989). An obituary is in the *New York Times* (5 Dec. 1981).

AMY ANMEI B. WONG

KOOPMANS, Tjalling Charles (*b.* 28 August 1910 in Graveland, the Netherlands; *d.* 26 February 1985 in New Haven, Connecticut), economist, educator, and pioneer in the study of the optimum allocation of resources who shared the Nobel Prize in economic sciences in 1975.

Tjalling Koopmans (pronounced Challing KÜP-manz) was born in the Netherlands, the son of two teachers, Sjoerd Koopmans and Wijtske van der Zee. Young Tjalling, who had two older brothers, was a very good student. At the age of seventeen, in 1927, he went to study mathematics and physics at the University of Utrecht, which awarded him the M.A. degree in 1933. Although clearly a talented mathematician and theoretical physicist (he published an article in 1934 on quantum mechanics that he had written as a student), the young Koopmans searched for an application of his mathematical ability and intuition that would give him greater personal satisfaction.

He found the perfect outlet for his creativity in the emerging field of mathematical economics. Here his abstract reasoning and mathematical skills were brought to bear directly on the economic problems of the world—then suffering through the Great Depression. Luckily, perhaps the greatest mathematical economist of the day, Jan Tinbergen, was also a Netherlander. Koopmans went to study under Tinbergen in Amsterdam in 1934. He also had an opportunity to study briefly in 1935 with the other great European mathematical economist of the time, the Norwegian Ragnar Frisch, at the University of Oslo. Tinbergen and Frisch were two of the major architects of what became the field of econometrics—the application of mathematical and statistical techniques to modeling the economy through a system of equations and then estimating numerical values for the coefficients using historical data. Tinbergen and Frisch were later to share the Nobel Prize in economic sciences in 1969. The young Koopmans was there at the start of mathematical economics and was soon an important contributor to the field. For his dissertation "Linear Regression Analysis of Economic Time-Series" he was awarded the Ph.D. from the University of Leiden in 1936.

In October of the same year he married a fellow student, Truus Wanningen. During their life together they had two daughters and a son. Koopmans started an academic career with an appointment as a lecturer at the University of Rotterdam in 1936. But he soon moved on to Geneva and the League of Nations where he joined the financial section and worked with his mentor, Tinbergen, whom he succeeded as financial specialist at the League in 1938.

When Germany invaded its neighbors and World War II accelerated, Koopmans and his family took advantage of an opportunity to emigrate and moved in 1940 to the United States, which became his permanent home. He became a U.S. citizen in 1946.

During his first two years in America, Koopmans was a research associate at Princeton University but he also returned to teaching as a special lecturer at the school of business at New York University. For a year, he was an economist for the Penn Mutual Life Insurance Company and then, in 1942, he took a job in Washington, D.C., as a statistician for the British Merchant Shipping Mission (Combined Shipping Adjustment Board). It was while Koopmans worked for the mission, perhaps an unlikely place, that he made what turned out to be his most enduring contribution.

The shipping mission wanted Koopmans to reconfigure merchant shipping schedules in order to lessen Britain's losses to German submarine attack while also minimizing costs. While trying to determine the least costly way to ship

Tjalling Koopmans at home in Hamden, Connecticut, 1975. UPI/ CORBIS-BETTMANN

an assigned list of goods from a large number of starting points to a large number of destinations, Koopmans developed activity analysis, which was to revolutionize the study of resource allocation. Koopmans first stated his solution to the problem in a memorandum to his employer entitled "Exchange Ratios Between Cargoes on Various Routes" (1942).

Activity analysis is a particular way of formulating the linear-programming problem of maximizing or minimizing a function of several variables subject to various constraints (which can be stated as linear inequalities). Suppose some outcome can be achieved using several different processes or activities. Any particular result is the sum of the amounts contributed by each activity used at a particular level. The problem is to find the optimal "mix" subject to technological, resource, or other constraints. The class of problems which can be solved using these techniques is very large. Koopmans pioneered, in his later work, their application to very general issues of resource allocation and economic efficiency.

In 1944 Koopmans accepted a position with the Cowles Commission for Research in Economics. The commission was located in Chicago and was affiliated with the University of Chicago, where Koopmans joined the faculty and, in 1948, was made a professor. While at Chicago, Koopmans edited an important summary of his seminal work, *Activity Analysis of Production and Allocation* (1951). He also edited (with William C. Hood) a widely cited work on the foundations of econometrics, *Studies in Econometric Method* (1953).

When the Cowles Commission became the Cowles Foundation for Research in Economics and was moved to New Haven, Connecticut, Koopmans went along as the first holder of the Alfred Cowles Professorship in Economics at Yale University. The Cowles Commission/Foundation's motto was "Science Is Measurement" and was later changed to "Theory and Measurement." Koopmans spent the rest of his active scientific career associated with the Cowles Foundation producing both "theory" and empirical "measurement." One of the most widely read and influential economics books to appear during the 1950s was his *Three Essays on the State of Economic Science* (1957). It was on the bookshelf of virtually every economist.

Except for the academic year 1960–1961, which he spent as the Frank W. Taussig Professor of Economics at Harvard University, Koopmans remained at Yale. He was director of the Cowles Foundation from 1961 to 1967. The focus of his research shifted somewhat in the 1960s toward applying his theories of resource allocation to the study of efficiency in allocation over time—thus to the economic theory of growth and development to which he made many important contributions.

During World War II, as Koopmans was working on the problem of optimal shipping lanes, unknown to him in the Soviet Union, the Russian economist and mathematician Leonid Kantorovich was working on a similar problem regarding the Soviet railway system. Independently and yet almost at the same time, the two developed very similar solutions. For their work in creating activity analysis, the two shared the 1975 Nobel Prize in economic sciences.

Koopmans was named professor emeritus at Yale in 1981 when he retired from active teaching. He continued to live in nearby Hamden, Connecticut. At the age of seventy-four, after suffering a cerebral hemorrhage, he died at the Yale–New Haven Hospital. His body was cremated at Evergreen Crematory in New Haven.

The work that brought Koopmans his fame has a very wide application—ranging from the way individual corporations set up their production lines in manufacturing, distribution, or transportation to the way any kind of operation is optimally scheduled. The techniques apply in market economies, both capitalist and socialist, and also in centrally planned economies. Furthermore, they have broadened and deepened our knowledge of the very meaning of efficiency in resource allocation.

Koopmans was a tall, soft-spoken scholar who liked to play chess and the violin. He was interested in art and, especially, music and was an occasional composer. He was fellow and president of the Econometric Society, president of the American Economic Association, a fellow of the American Academy of Arts and Sciences, the American Statistical Association, the Royal Netherlands Academy of Arts and Sciences, and a member of the National Academy of Sciences. Many universities in Europe and the United States conferred honorary doctorates upon him. He remained throughout his life a quiet, modest person who cared deeply for his family, his students, and his colleagues.

★

A good place to read about the contribution that earned Koopmans the Nobel Prize and the circumstances in his life at the time it was developed, as well as its wide influence and many applications, is Herbert E. Scarf, "The 1975 Nobel Prize in Economics: Resource Allocation," *Science* 190 (14 Nov. 1975). Tyler Wasson, ed., *Nobel Prize Winners* (1987), includes a discussion of Koopmans's life and work. Obituary notices are in Hal May, ed., *Contemporary Authors* 115 (1985), and the *New York Times* (2 Mar. 1985).

EARL W. ADAMS

KRASNER, Lee (*b.* 27 October 1908 in Brooklyn, New York; *d.* 19 June 1984 in New York City), artist who was the only woman to achieve significant recognition in the first generation of abstract expressionist painters; she was also known for her personal and professional collaboration with the artist Jackson Pollock.

Lee Krasner was born Lena Krassner to Joseph Krassner and Anna Weiss, Russian-Jewish immigrants who operated a small food market in Brooklyn. Krasner, who had six siblings, received her early education in the New York City public schools. As a young woman, her lifelong independent spirit was evident in her decision to major in the nontraditional field of art. Krasner attended the Women's Art School of the Cooper Union from 1926 to 1928 and enrolled in the Art Students League in July 1928 and then, in September of that year, the National Academy of Design. In 1932 Krasner left the academy to attend the City College of New York to become certified to teach but continued to study at Greenwich House, a settlement house that offered art classes.

In January 1934, deciding against a teaching career, she applied to the Public Works of Art Projects (PWAP) and was employed off and on by the Works Progress Administration (WPA) until 1943. In 1937 she began studies with Hans Hofmann; in that same year she received her first opportunity to exhibit, at ACA Galleries, in a show organized by the Artists Union/Citizens Committee for Support of the WPA called "Pink Slips over Culture."

By the late 1930s Krasner was moving away from representational painting, and in 1940 she joined the American Abstract Artists group, which included her work in its annuals from 1940 to 1943. During this time, Krasner was meeting other artists who became important influences in her life and work—Piet Mondrian, John Graham (who included her work in his 1942 exhibition at the design firm McMillen Inc. entitled "French and American Painting"), and Jackson Pollock. She and Pollock were married on 25 October 1945 at the Marble Collegiate Church in New York City. They lived in a farmhouse in East Hampton, Long Island; they had no children. While Krasner was well-known to artists, critics, and dealers, she remained outside the center of the New York school during her early years, probably because she had a belligerent personality and was romantically linked to Pollock, from whom it was becoming increasingly difficult to separate her career. As was the case for many women artists, she received little critical attention.

In 1946 Krasner began her series of automatic, calligraphic paintings called "Little Images." In 1949 she and Pollock exhibited their work together at the Sidney Janis Gallery in a show called "Artists: Man and Wife." By this time, Pollock had had several one-person shows but Krasner, none. Pollock was drinking heavily, taxing Krasner's ego and energy, but she continued to push her aesthetic boundaries. Following a disappointing show at the Betty Parsons Gallery in 1951, in which none of her works were sold, she began to create large-scale collages incorporating fragments from her own work as well as from Pollock's drawings. In 1955 these were included in her first solo exhibition in New York City at Eleanor Ward's Stable Gallery.

Lee Krasner in front of her work. CHWATSKY/ART RESOURCE, N.Y.

Artistic successes were undercut by personal loss. In 1956 her first trip to Europe was cut short by Pollock's death in an automobile accident.

Krasner remained in the East Hampton farmhouse, moved into Pollock's studio, and began her first large abstract expressionist paintings. "The Seasons," her largest work, was included in her 1958 exhibition at the Martha Jackson Gallery in New York City. Also in 1958, Krasner received her first architectural commission, the design for two large mosaic panels for the Uris Building, a thirty-story corporate headquarters at 2 Broadway in Lower Manhattan. In 1959 a contract with Howard Wise Gallery brought Krasner solo shows in 1960 and 1962, featuring her Umber and White series, which Wise termed "mourning" pictures. A cerebral aneurysm in late 1962 and a broken arm in 1963 were challenges that Krasner readily overcame; by 1964 she was organizing work for a retrospective exhibition at Whitechapel Gallery in London that opened in October 1965 and traveled to five other venues.

The pace of Krasner's career then quickened. Beginning in 1966, she was represented by the Marlborough Gallery in New York, where she had the first of three exhibitions. In 1967 she was given a major exhibition at the University of Alabama. In 1969 the Museum of Modern Art curator William Rubin included her as the sole woman artist in his show "The New American Painting and Sculpture: The First Generation." In 1972, recognizing the demands made on her time in caring for Pollock's estate, she removed herself from that position. While not considering herself a political feminist, in that year Krasner chose to support colleagues by picketing the Museum of Modern Art in an attempt to influence its staff to show more women artists. In 1973 she was given her first solo show in a New York museum by the Whitney, curated by Marcia Tucker. Pace Gallery represented Krasner from 1976 to 1982, when she joined Robert Miller's Gallery.

In 1983, nearly twenty years after Pollock's death, the success of Krasner's independent career as a painter was at last confirmed by a major retrospective exhibition curated by Barbara Rose that opened at the Museum of Fine Arts, Houston, and traveled to four other venues, including the Museum of Modern Art. Krasner died at New York Hospital and is buried in Green River Cemetery on Long Island.

Krasner directed that her estate be used to establish the Pollock-Krasner Foundation to provide grants to artists around the world. The Pollock-Krasner House and Study Center in East Hampton, Long Island, now a National Historic Landmark, is managed by the Stony Brook Foundation and houses archival materials related to Krasner, Pollock, and the abstract expressionist movement. Krasner's work has been reassessed on its own merit; it reflects an artist's quest to redefine color and space in intensely personal yet heroic terms. Like its creator, Krasner's work is bold, intense, and radical. Her sustained aesthetic vision transcended personal anguish and continually transformed her work. Her recognition of the consuming nature of the creative process prompted her to come to the aid of artists in need.

★

Krasner's papers are in the collection of the Archives of American Art, Smithsonian Institution, Washington, D.C. Ellen G. Landau with Jeffrey D. Grove, *Lee Krasner: A Catalogue Raisonne* (1995), is the definitive work on the artist and includes an annotated chronology and extensive publication and exhibition history. Anne M. Wagner, "Fictions: Krasner's Presence, Pollock's Absence," in *Significant Others: Creativity and Intimate Partnership* (1993), is a feminist reevaluation of the personal and professional relationship of Krasner and Pollock. Sandor Kuthy and Ellen G. Landau, *Lee Krasner—Jackson Pollock: Kunstlerpaare-Kunstlerfreunde; Dialogues d'artistes—resonances* (1989), the catalog from an exhibition at the Kunstmuseum Bern (Switzerland), comprises an interesting parallel analysis of the two artists' careers. Barbara Rose, *Lee Krasner* (1983), accompanied the 1983 Krasner retro-

spective exhibition and contains in-depth essays and an extensive bibliography. There is also a film by Rose, *Lee Krasner: The Long View* (1978).

MARJORIE B. SEARL

KROC, Ray(mond) Albert (*b.* 5 October 1902 in Oak Park, Illinois; *d.* 14 January 1984 in San Diego, California), master salesman who developed the McDonald's global chain of restaurants, the largest such enterprise in the world.

Kroc was born in a suburb of Chicago, where his widowed, Bohemian grandmother had settled with her four children, including Ray's father, Louis Kroc, in the early 1890s. To help support the family, Louis Kroc quit school at age twelve. Despite his scanty formal education, he made a career as a minor executive in Western Union's subsidiary, the American District Telegraph. He also bought speculative real estate at bargain prices, but he was wiped out in the Great Depression. He died in 1932 of a cerebral hemorrhage at his desk at the Pyramid Vacant Real Estate Company. Ray's mother was Rose Mary Hrach, a piano teacher. Ray was the oldest child, with a brother and a sister, and

Ray Kroc, 1971. NEW YORK TIMES CO./ARCHIVE PHOTOS

one of his mother's best piano pupils. She taught him how to perform, which he enjoyed and which provided a source of extra income throughout his early career. Otherwise Kroc was not a highly motivated student. Bored by books, his most vivid memory of his high school days was his success as a debater. He dropped out of Oak Park High School at the end of his sophomore year.

Kroc worked one summer at his uncle's drugstore soda fountain in Oak Park. There he learned "that you could influence people with a smile and enthusiasm and sell them a sundae when they'd come for a cup of coffee." In the summer of 1917, soon after the United States entered World War I, Kroc lied about his age and enlisted in the Red Cross ambulance driver training program, then served overseas. After the armistice in 1918, he returned to Oak Park High School but dropped out again after only one semester. "Algebra," he wryly observed in later years, "had not improved in my absence." He yearned to be a salesman, and although he was still a teenager, he got a job traveling from city to city representing a ribbon novelty firm. On the side, he continued to look for piano "gigs."

In the summer of 1919, Kroc left the ribbon company to take a full-time job playing piano with a dance band at a Michigan resort called the Edgewater. There he met Ethel Fleming, whose parents owned a hotel on the other side of Paw-Paw Lake. Ray and Ethel's summer romance remained warm throughout the next year, and in 1922 they married. They had one child. Ray Kroc got a daytime job selling paper cups for Lily Tulip Company and a night job playing the piano on radio station WGES in Oak Park.

By 1925 Kroc had hit his stride as a salesman, but the paper cup business was traditionally slow in wintertime, and the Florida land boom beckoned him. He took a leave of absence from Lily, piled Ethel, her sister, and his baby into a new Model T Ford, and headed for the Sunshine State, where he quickly found employment with a real estate firm in Fort Lauderdale. His specialty consisted of rounding up wintertime tourists from the Chicago area. He showed them building lots still under water that were to be raised to the surface with earth dredged from the then uncompleted inland waterway. A "closer" lurked nearby to collect $500 deposits from the convinced.

When the Florida real estate boom turned to bust after a hurricane in 1926, Kroc found a job playing piano in a plush Miami nightclub. But Ethel and their daughter stayed home alone every night, and soon Kroc realized that his young family had to return to Chicago. He sent them ahead by train and set out alone in the Model T, traveling over primitive roads in miserable weather.

In 1926 Kroc returned to the Lily Tulip paper cup company and in time became the Midwest sales manager. His strong point was innovation. He persuaded Walgreen, the Midwest's foremost drugstore chain, to introduce take-out food service at its lunch counters, which enabled a drugstore to double the number of lunches sold during the rush hour. It also doubled the number of paper cups that Walgreen bought. Another of Kroc's large Chicago customers was the Prince's Castle chain of ice cream parlors. At Kroc's urging, the owner, Earl Prince, reluctantly introduced a new milk-shake formulation that, in Kroc's words, was "a colder and more viscous drink that people preferred to the thin, semi-cool conventional shake." Prince's chain was soon buying a million Lily cups a year from Kroc.

Meanwhile, Prince, who had been trained as a mechanical engineer, perfected a mixing machine that could make five milk shakes simultaneously. Kroc arranged for Lily Tulip to distribute the mixer, and Prince and Lily representatives signed a contract in 1939. When Lily Tulip's parent company in New York rejected the deal, Kroc decided to go ahead on his own. This was not easily accomplished. Securing the right to distribute the new mixer, called the Multimixer, cost him every nickel he could borrow, and he was forced to refinance the mortgage on his house in suburban Arlington Heights, Illinois. According to Kroc, the debt of almost $100,000 and the inherent risks of the new venture were too frightening for Ethel, and they began to drift apart.

Kroc was a superior salesman. His new company, started in 1941 as Prince Castle Multimixer Company and later called the Prince Castle Sales Division, prospered. But when the United States entered World War II, copper, an essential component of the mixer motors, disappeared from the civilian market. So did much of the sugar necessary to make ice cream, the basic ingredient of the drinks produced in the mixers. Kroc survived economically during the war years by finding and offering milk additives, based on corn syrup, that imitated the taste and texture of ice cream. After the war ended, the Multimixer business boomed once again, but not for long. Dairy Queen, Tastee-Freeze, and similar soft-ice-cream stands came into vogue, and this market had little use for milk-shake mixers. Indeed, the world of take-out food changed completely in the late 1940s and early 1950s. Americans were moving to the suburbs, miles away from the drugstore soda fountains and malted milk stands. At the same time, the idea of going out as a family to enjoy an inexpensive dinner became attractive to millions of parents with cars.

Most fast-food outlets required only one or two Multimixers, but Richard ("Dick") McDonald and Maurice ("Mac") McDonald, brothers who owned a hamburger stand in San Bernardino, California, purchased eight, enough to make forty shakes simultaneously. In 1954 Kroc went to San Bernardino to find out why they needed so much capacity. He found a spotlessly clean restaurant. The kitchen gleamed with immaculate stainless steel counters and custom-designed aluminum griddles. Service was swift. In only a minute or two, a customer could receive a tasty, freshly grilled hamburger (fifteen cents), crispy french fries (eight cents), and a sixteen-ounce milk shake (twenty cents) or a cup of coffee (a nickel). The stand had no pay phones, no vending machines, no carhops, and no place to "hang out." Nevertheless, customers, mostly young families, flocked to McDonald's. "I was amazed," Kroc said in later years, at "this little drive-in having people standing in line. The sales volume was incredible. . . . If they had a hundred stores like that one, I thought, I could sell them 800 Multimixers."

The McDonald brothers gave Kroc a thorough briefing, including a look at the architect's drawings of a new building surmounted by golden arches. The McDonalds' prior attempts at licensing had been disappointing, but Kroc urged them to franchise their name and unique assembly-line system. When Kroc returned to Chicago, he called Dick McDonald to ask if they were still looking for a franchise agent. "How about me?" Kroc asked.

Kroc's meeting with Dick and Mac McDonald was providential but by no means an accident. Kroc, who was fifty-two years old and suffered from diabetes and arthritis, needed to close a deal. He later said, "I was just carried away by the thought of McDonald's drive-ins proliferating like rabbits, with eight Multimixers in each one." Kroc was so carried away that he did not even bother to get his own lawyer. The McDonald brothers' attorney wrote the agreement that Kroc signed. It called for a franchise fee of $950 to be paid to Kroc's future company by each new franchisee. Operators were required to copy the San Bernardino store in every detail, including the sign, menu, and architecture. The smallest deviations were to be approved in writing by the McDonald brothers and sent by registered mail. Each franchise remitted 1.9 percent of its gross sales to the franchisor, of which 0.5 percent belonged to Dick and Mac McDonald, who had no other franchising function. Kroc's new franchising company kept the remaining 1.4 percent, which was not enough cash flow to finance growth, as Kroc learned.

On 2 March 1955, Kroc chartered McDonald's System Inc., which was later renamed McDonald's Corporation. On 15 April 1955 he and a golfing friend opened a "model" McDonald's in Des Plaines, Illinois, near Kroc's home. Kroc checked the store at 7:00 each morning before he caught the commuter train to his Multimixer office in downtown Chicago, and he visited it again on his way home. According to Fred Turner, the future McDonald's president who began his career as a grill man in Des Plaines: "Every night you'd see [Kroc] coming down the street, walking close to the gutter, picking up every McDonald's wrapper and cup along the way. He'd come into the store with both hands full." On weekends Kroc hosed down the parking lot, scrubbed the trash cans, and scraped chewing gum off the concrete.

In 1956 three franchised stores opened in Fresno, Los Angeles, and Reseda, California. It was easier, Kroc discovered, to close deals in California after franchisees visited the successful operation in San Bernardino. Nevertheless, during the last eight months of 1956, Kroc established eight more franchises, only one of which was in California. The most successful early McDonald's was in Waukegan, Illinois, on Lake Michigan north of Chicago. The day after the doors opened, the owner-manager ran out of cash register space for all the dollar bills that flooded in. Kroc publicized those results to attract the type of franchisee he wanted—working- or lower-middle-class family men who would devote their full time to the store.

During his years selling paper cups and milk-shake mixers, Kroc studied the emerging fast-food industry closely. He found that most franchisors sought quick income rather than long-lasting, mutually profitable relationships with their dealers. The franchise sellers profited from high license fees and marked-up supplies and foodstuffs that operators were required to buy exclusively from them. Kroc's approach was different. He strove to build up his franchisees rather than exploit them. McDonald's dealers ordered directly from approved suppliers, and McDonald's Systems earned nothing from these transactions.

Kroc was almost indifferent to money. He appeared to enjoy closing a sale more than its fruits. Until 1961 he drew neither salary nor expenses from McDonald's Systems, living on his modest Multimixer sales income alone. He was especially proud of his Hamburger University, which started in the early days of the McDonald's chain in the storeroom of a restaurant and eventually moved in 1983 to a $40 million campus in Elk Grove Village, Illinois. Much more than a public relations effort, it taught new franchise owners how to cook french fries and hamburgers according to McDonald's precise specifications as well as how to keep ledgers. Kroc compared his "university" to Harvard and Stanford, and its graduates became "bachelors of hamburgerology."

By 1957 Kroc had put together a small cadre of first-rate, young operating executives. Although McDonald's appeared poised for rapid growth, from a financial point of view it seemed headed for disaster. The cash flow was inadequate to handle the system's overhead or to generate a profit. Making McDonald's profitable was the achievement of Harry J. Sonneborn, who had scouted Kroc's model store in Des Plaines and foresaw the growth potential of the chain. He resigned a well-paid executive post at Tastee-Freeze in 1956 to work for Kroc at a starting salary of only $100 a week.

Sonneborn used a new leaseback system to turn McDonald's into a money machine. His staff selected sites, and restaurants were built and paid for by local real estate investors and their banks. McDonald's agreed in advance to lease the completed restaurants at a flat rent, then subleased them to new franchisees at a rent equivalent to 5 percent of sales or 140 percent of McDonald's rental cost, whichever was greater. The franchise fee, boosted by $550 in 1963, continued to be low. This system made it easier to fund new outlets and enabled Sonneborn to tell potential lenders and investors, who feared the vagaries of the restaurant business, that McDonald's was actually a real estate company.

Kroc's marriage to Ethel had become, in his own words, "a cold war." In 1957 he met Joan Smith, who played the electric organ in a nightclub in St. Paul, Minnesota. Her husband, Rawley Smith, a railroad engineer, was about to become a McDonald's restaurant manager. In love with Joan, Kroc moved out of his Arlington Heights house and proposed that they both get divorces so they could marry each other. At first Smith agreed, but under pressure from her mother and her fourteen-year-old daughter, she backed out. Kroc was devastated.

McDonald's continued to expand. By the end of 1957, 31 restaurants were in operation and by 1960 the number had increased to 228. However, the McDonald brothers' one-sided contract with Kroc remained a major stumbling block. Because the McDonalds never answered Kroc's letters, the "prior approval" clause of the contract was ignored out of necessity, but it hung over Kroc's head like a sword. In 1961 he asked the brothers to name a price for the exclusive right to the unfettered use of the McDonald's name and systems. They demanded $2.7 million in cash. "A million for me, a million for Mac, and $700,000 for Uncle Sam," was the way Dick McDonald put it. Raising so much money seemed impossible at the time, but Sonneborn convinced a group of institutional investors, including Princeton University, to lend Kroc the money.

In the spring of 1962 Kroc, by then divorced, moved to California because his leadership was needed on the booming West Coast, where imitators had slowed McDonald's growth to a trickle. That year he met Jane Dobbins Green, a script assistant to John Wayne. Two weeks later, they married and moved into a large house in Beverly Hills. They had no children. In 1965 Kroc purchased a ranch house in Santa Ynez, California, to use as a conference center for his senior executives.

By 1965 the total number of McDonald's restaurants was almost 700 and growing at the rate of 100 a year. To put some cash in Kroc and Sonneborn's pockets and to create a market for McDonald's stock, the corporation went public on 15 April 1965 at $22.50 per share. Kroc collected $3 million for the shares he sold at the offering price, but within a day the market price had risen to $30 a share. It quickly soared to nearly $50, and Kroc's remaining shares suddenly had a market value of $32 million. During the next twenty years, McDonald's experienced eight stock splits and one stock dividend. An investor who paid $2,250 for 100 shares in 1965 would have seen the value of that investment rise to more than $400,000 in 1986.

The McDonald's chain made restaurant and stock market history, but Sonneborn, who had become president in 1959, quit in 1967 after a series of bitter disagreements with Kroc. Turner, Kroc's levelheaded and loyal protégé, took over as president. Kroc retained the title of chairman until 1977, when his board named him senior chairman.

In the fall of 1968, Joan Smith and her husband attended a McDonald's convention in San Diego. Somehow, Rawley Smith was sequestered while Kroc and Joan Smith spent the night playing the piano and talking. Once again they agreed to divorce their mates and marry each other. This time they did. On 8 March 1969, they married in the ranch house in Santa Ynez. They had no children.

Kroc attended McDonald's dealer conventions, and his personal charm remained a key factor in the company's growth. A longtime colleague said that Kroc was the most inspiring extemporaneous speaker he had ever heard. Kroc was also obsessed with neatness and cleanliness. A former McDonald's executive declared, "When Ray read out an operator with a dirty store, you could hear him six blocks away."

In his later years Kroc turned his energies and some of his dollars to other activities. He lectured at Dartmouth College, which gave him an honorary doctorate. He celebrated his seventieth birthday by giving more than $7 million to such Chicago institutions as Children's Memorial Hospital, the Lincoln Park Zoo, and the Harvard Congregational Church in Oak Park, which he had attended as a child. He also gave substantial quantities of McDonald's stock to senior employees. In 1972 Kroc received the Horatio Alger Award from Norman Vincent Peale, the preacher and author. Kroc was hailed for "overcoming obstacles," as the inscription said, "through Diligence, Industry and Perseverance" on his way to a success achieved.

In 1974 Kroc fulfilled his lifelong dream of owning a major league baseball team when he bought the San Diego Padres. His frustrations as a team owner began at the first home game in 1974, during which the Padres made error after error, capped by a horrendous baserunning mistake. Kroc grabbed the stadium announcer's microphone, apologized to the fans, and berated the team.

In 1976 Kroc established the Kroc Foundation in Santa Ynez to support research in diabetes, arthritis, and multiple sclerosis and placed his younger brother, Robert L. Kroc, an endocrine expert, in charge. In 1977 Turner was elected chairman of the McDonald's board, and Kroc assumed the honorary title of senior chairman. In 1979, when the baseball league fined Kroc heavily for a violation of the free-agent rules, he became "disgusted" with baseball and, in midseason, placed operating control of the team in the hands of his son-in-law. By 1979 more than 6,000 McDonald's restaurants girdled the globe, and Kroc's personal fortune had grown to more than $500 million. Weakened by arthritis, Kroc died of a cardiac disorder in the Scripps Memorial Hospital in San Diego.

No doubt Kroc's qualities of perseverance and industry were important, but more than anything else his success can be attributed to strong self-dependence and his talents as a salesman. Like many other great salesmen, he was imaginative and willing to take risks. His career demonstrates that it is never too late to succeed.

★

In Ray Kroc with Robert Anderson, *Grinding It Out: The Making of McDonald's* (1977), Kroc depicts himself, "warts and all." Maxwell Boas and Steve Chain, *Big Mac: The Unauthorized Story of McDonald's* (1976), is not quite the muckrake implied by its title. John F. Love, *McDonald's: Behind the Arches* (1986), is a comprehensive and thoroughly researched narrative.

Magazine articles on Kroc include "McDonald's Makes Franchising Sizzle," *Business Week* (15 June 1968); "Appealing to a Mass Market," *Nation's Business* (4 July 1968); "Mirror, Mirror on the Wall," *Forbes* (1 Nov. 1970); J. A. Lucas, "As American As a McDonald's Hamburger on the Fourth of July," *New York Times Magazine* (4 July 1971); "America's Hamburger King," *Reader's Digest* (Oct. 1971); "Beef Against Big Mac," *Time* (27 Dec. 1971); "Rare Hamburger Headquarters," *Time* (28 Feb. 1972); M. A. Kellogg, "Making the Grade at Hamburger U," *Newsweek* (25 Sept. 1972); "For Ray Kroc, Life Began at 50. Or Was It 60?" *Forbes* (15 Jan. 1973); "Better Boys Burgers," *Ebony* (Mar. 1973); "Bull in the Hamburger Shop: D. Fujita of McDonald's Japan," *Forbes* (15 May 1973); "The Burger That Conquered the Country," *Time* (17 Sept. 1973); W. E. Sasser and S. H. Pettway, "The Case of Big Mac's Pay Plans," *Harvard Business Review* (July 1974); and "Big Mac Goes to School," *Newsweek* (4 Oct. 1976). The *McDonald's Corporation Annual Report* (1983) includes a lengthy tribute to Kroc. An obituary is in the *New York Times* (15 Jan. 1984).

FRANK VOS

KUZNETS, Simon Smith (*b.* 30 April 1901 in Pinsk, Russia; *d.* 8 July 1985 in Cambridge, Massachusetts), economist, educator, pioneering statistician, founder of national income measurement, and creator of quantitative economic history, for which he won the Nobel Prize in economic sciences in 1971.

Born in the Belarussian town of Pinsk, then controlled by czarist Russia, Simon Kuznets was the second of three sons of Abraham Kuznets, a furrier, and Pauline Friedman. The young Simon's early education was in a Jewish day school.

Simon Kuznets at home on the day he won the Nobel Prize for economics, 15 October 1971. UPI/CORBIS-BETTMANN

He completed gymnasium (high school) and entered University in Kharkov in the Ukraine, where the family had relocated. (Many sources incorrectly list Kharkov as Kuznets's place of birth.)

These were turbulent years in Kharkov. The onset of World War I, the Bolshevik Revolution of October 1917, and the occupation of the city by German troops in 1918 led to the closing of the university. Kuznets was in the second year of his economics studies. When the university closed, he took a position in the division of statistics of the Central Soviet of Trade Unions in Kharkov. During this time he wrote his first published article (in Russian), "Money Wages of Factory Employees in Kharkov in 1920" (1921).

With the signing of a Polish-Soviet treaty, those born in the territory of the newly configured country had the right to resettle in Poland. Thus, Simon and his brothers were able to make their way from Poland to the United States. They joined their father in New York City, where he had first immigrated in 1907.

Simon quickly learned English and in 1922 he matriculated at Columbia University with advanced standing. He was awarded the B.S. degree in 1923. Admitted to Columbia's graduate school, he earned the M.S. degree in 1924 and the Ph.D. in 1926. He prepared his dissertation under the direction of the eminent business-cycle scholar, Wesley C. Mitchell, with whom he was associated until Mitchell's death in 1948. For eighteen months Kuznets was a research fellow for the Social Science Research Council (1925–1927). In 1927, through Mitchell's good offices, he became associated with the newly formed National Bureau of Economic Research, an arrangement that lasted until 1961.

On 5 June 1929, Kuznets married Edith H. Handler, also an economist, whom he had met at the National Bureau. During their marriage they had a son and a daughter.

Kuznets's first academic appointment was in 1930 as an assistant professor of economic statistics at the University of Pennsylvania, where he progressed through the ranks to full professor and remained on the faculty until 1954. Much of Kuznets's work during the late 1920s was in business-cycle analysis and related areas. In his three works *Cyclical Fluctuations* (1926), *Secular Movements in Production and Prices* (1930), and *Seasonal Variations in Industry and Trade* (1933), Kuznets provides a complete analysis of economic data as they can be decomposed into their seasonal, cyclical, and secular-trend aspects. In the course of this monumental work, while analyzing long-term economic data for the United States, he discovered persistent cycles lasting from eighteen to twenty-five years that are now called "Kuznets cycles."

Many economic aggregates show a long-term (secular) trend. For example, production trends upward in a growing economy. There are alternating periods (cycles) when the rate of growth exceeds or falls short of its long-run average. If observations are taken within a year, such as monthly or quarterly, there is likely to be some recurring (seasonal) pattern. Thus, any particular economic datum is composed of secular, cyclical, and seasonal elements. This distinction is especially important in interpreting the meaning of a particular reported observation (such as the level of unemployment or output) and in extrapolating from current data in order to make a forecast.

"Kuznets cycles" are so-called because he first identified them. These cycles have since been observed in many economic, financial, and other measures during various periods in all developed countries. Kuznets did postulate a cause, but so have many others, whose explanations differ from his and each other's. It is not a well-understood phenomenon.

The next phase of Kuznets's research was his great work on national income accounting. It marked the beginning of the attempt to quantify the total output of a nation and culminated in the establishment of American national income accounts. Kuznets described the concepts behind the measurement of a nation's income and output in the classic article "National Income" for the *Encyclopedia of the Social Sciences* (1933). Various other works of this period—for example, *National Income, 1929–1932* (1934), *National Income and Capital Formation* (1937), and, most important, *National Income and Its Composition, 1919–1938* (1941)—

developed these ideas and the methodology of national income accounting.

During World War II (from 1942 to 1944) Kuznets was associate director of the Bureau of Planning and Statistics of the War Production Board. He had the awesome task of organizing the massive procurement required for the United States government's war mobilization.

The focus of Kuznets's work was about to shift, but one last seminal work on national income accounting appeared. In *National Income: A Summary of Findings* (1946), Kuznets reported his discovery that in the long run, when data are adjusted to account for variations due to the business cycle, the ratio of consumption to total income had remained constant (not declined, as was believed) as income increased. This was an important finding, which required a rethinking of the theory of how consumption is determined that had originated with the legendary John Maynard Keynes.

Most of Kuznets's research after World War II concerned economic growth. He examined, in great detail, the actual record of many countries over very long time spans, a task that occupied him for the rest of his life.

After nearly twenty-five years, Kuznets left the University of Pennsylvania in 1954 to become a professor of political economy at the Johns Hopkins University in Baltimore, Maryland. In 1960 he moved to Harvard University as a professor of economics. He retired from active teaching and was named professor emeritus in 1971.

His approach to the study of growth and many of his findings are best summarized in three major books of this period: *Six Lectures on Economic Growth* (1959), *Modern Economic Growth: Rate, Structure, and Spread* (1966), and *Economic Growth of Nations* (1971). Among many generalizations that Kuznets developed in this statistical extravaganza is the "Kuznets Curve or Law," which asserts that there is an increase in the inequality of income distribution during the early stages of economic development but that later there is a movement toward greater equality as a nation's economy matures.

He was awarded the Nobel Prize in economic sciences in 1971. Especially cited was his contribution to our understanding of the economic growth of nations. Kuznets continued his research after his retirement from Harvard and published *Population, Capital, and Growth* (1973), *Growth, Population, and Income Distribution* (1979), and *Growth and Structural Shifts* (1979) during these years.

After suffering a heart attack, Kuznets died at his home on Francis Avenue in Cambridge, Massachusetts, at the age of eighty-four. He is buried in Sharon Memorial Park in Sharon, Massachusetts.

Kuznets is credited with deriving the concept of gross national product, as well as the system of measurement used by the National Income Division of the United States

Department of Commerce in monitoring the nation's output and income. The same system is used by other countries, international agencies, and private economists to trace economic change. These measurements became the basis for macroeconomics, the study of the total economy and the relationships between its sectors. His work made an empirical science of economics possible.

During his lifetime Kuznets was widely recognized and honored. In addition to the Nobel Prize, he also received the Francis A. Walker Award in 1977—the highest honor the American Economics Association could bestow. He was President of the American Statistical Association and the American Economics Association, and a member of the American Philosophical Society, a Fellow of the Royal Statistical Society, the Econometric Society, the British Academy, and the American Academy of Arts and Sciences. Many universities awarded him honorary doctorates, among them Harvard, the University of Pennsylvania, Princeton, and the Hebrew University in Jerusalem.

Simon Kuznets was kindly and charming, a man with twinkling eyes and an engaging grin. He loved art, music, literature, and cigars. Although short in stature and soft of voice, he was truly a giant among economists.

★

Moses Abramovitz, "Nobel Prize for Economics: Kuznets and Economic Growth," *Science* 174 (29 Oct. 1971), is an appreciation of Kuznets's contribution by a distinguished colleague. A biographical essay with a particular interpretation of the Kuznets legacy is James H. Street, "The Contribution of Simon S. Kuznets to Institutionalist Development Theory," *Journal of Economic Issues* 22, no. 2 (June 1988): 499–509. Vibha Kapuria-Foreman and Mark Perlman, "An Economic Historian's Economist: Remembering Simon Kuznets," *Economic Journal* 105 (Nov. 1995): 1524–1547, provides an intellectual assessment of the life and work of Kuznets. Perlman was a close personal friend as well as a colleague of Kuznets. A very complete memorial with a comprehensive discussion of Kuznets's research is Moses Abramovitz, "Simon Kuznets 1901–1985," *Journal of Economic History* 46, no. 1 (Mar. 1986). An obituary is in the *New York Times* (11 July 1985).

EARL W. ADAMS

L

LADD, George Eldon (*b.* 31 July 1911 in Alberta, Canada; *d.* 5 October 1982 in Pasadena, California), theologian who had a major impact on American Evangelicalism and author of *Theology of the New Testament* (1974), one of only two full-scale theologies written by an American in the twentieth century.

Ladd was born in Canada and raised in New England by his parents, Elmer and Mary (Cowan) Ladd. His father was a country doctor who became a Christian just before his son was born. George became a Christian in 1929 and entered Gordon College in Massachusetts, where he earned a Bachelor of Theology degree in 1933. On 11 July of that year he married Winifred ("Winnie") Webber; they had two children.

Ladd then studied at Gordon Divinity School while pastoring at the First Baptist Church of Montpelier, Vermont. After receiving his Bachelor of Divinity degree in 1941, he and Winnie moved to Boston where he became pastor of the Blaney Memorial Church and studied classical Greek at Boston University. The next year he began teaching Greek at Gordon College, and in 1943 he entered Harvard University as a Ph.D. student. He continued teaching Greek and became head of the New Testament Department at Gordon Divinity School in 1946. His Ph.D. was completed in 1947 with a dissertation entitled "The Eschatology of the Didache."

Ladd's major goals were to raise the prestige of evangelical scholarship and make a lasting contribution to mainstream scholarship. To further those goals Ladd joined the faculty of Fuller Theological Seminary in 1950. Fuller, located in Pasadena, California, was in the process of challenging many aspects of Fundamentalism. Ladd's high standards for critical scholarship were both intimidating and inspirational to students. He would criticize a student mercilessly for using a Bible handbook, saying that "every preacher must be a theologian." Yet he was a man of deep faith and sentiment, sometimes weeping when telling of God's blessings in his own life.

His first book, *Crucial Questions About the Kingdom of God* (1952) was part of a lifelong endeavor to correct a popular Fundamentalist doctrine called dispensational eschatology. His second book, *The Blessed Hope* (1956), continued that discussion, executing what one scholar calls a "painstaking demolition" of pretribulationism. Yet Ladd always tried to be fair and suggested that differences of interpretation need not divide people. His third and fifth books, *The Gospel of the Kingdom: Scriptural Studies in the Kingdom of God* (1959) and *Jesus and the Kingdom: The Eschatology of Biblical Realism* (1964), are excellent examples of the two sides of Ladd: the critical scholar and the compassionate pastor.

The question of history in theological studies was another area of concentration for Ladd. Having studied German theology during sabbaticals in Heidelberg and Basel between 1958 and 1964, he addressed the influential writ-

George Eldon Ladd. FULLER THEOLOGICAL SEMINARY

ings of Rudolf Bultmann. He produced a number of articles and books, stressing that the revelation of God in the Bible relies on history. *Jesus Christ and History* (1963) defends the second coming of Christ and the establishment of a future kingdom. *Rudolf Bultmann* (1964) is a summary and critique of Bultmann's views. Ladd's third book dealing with history, *The New Testament and Criticism* (1967), influenced conservative Christians who had been taught that biblical criticism was adversative to faith. This book is often seen as a defense of Ladd's own academic work as an Evangelical. His view that "the Bible is the Word of God given in the words of men in history" placed him squarely between Fundamentalists and theological liberals.

It was Ladd's *Jesus and the Kingdom* that he hoped would be his major contribution to critical scholarship. His academic rigor and persuasive analysis are apparent in this work, which sought to understand eschatology from the biblical writers' point of view instead of imposing modern forms of thought. The book dealt with the mission and message of Jesus, God's Kingdom, and biblical eschatology. Although arguably one of the best books of its kind, it did not have the impact Ladd desired due to some unfortunate circumstances. Just before his book was finished, two major studies of the same topic were published. One of the authors of those new studies wrote a scathing review of Ladd's book in the journal *Interpretation*. He questioned Ladd's

exegesis and, more significantly, accused him of drawing conclusions based on presuppositions—exactly what Ladd attempted *not* to do. He was devastated. In the second edition of the book Ladd made a few changes and responded to the criticisms, but it never assuaged for the pain he experienced.

Despite this apparent setback, Ladd's standing as a scholar continued to grow. Gordon Divinity School awarded him an honorary Doctor of Divinity degree in 1970. That same year he was invited to contribute to the twenty-fifth anniversary issue of *Interpretation*. In 1974 he published his most ambitious work, *A Theology of the New Testament*, the first full-scale theology written by an American since George Barker Stevens's *Theology of the New Testament* (1910). Ladd's work received attention from non-Evangelicals and in a 1986 poll was ranked second in influence among Evangelicals after John Calvin's *Institutes of the Christian Religion*. After Winnie died unexpectedly in 1977, Ladd, slight of frame, began a physical and psychological decline. His final book, *The Last Things* (1978), was a popular work for the layperson and returned to the theme of eschatology. Ladd suffered a debilitating stroke in 1980 and could no longer read or write. He died on 5 October 1982 and was buried in Pasadena.

Although Ladd probably felt that he never achieved his goal of respectability for evangelical scholarship, most modern surveys of biblical theology include discussions of his work. There is widespread agreement that his impact on evangelical scholarship itself has resulted in previously unknown prestige. His *Theology of the New Testament* is almost unique in twentieth-century America. These three observations suggest that Ladd is one of America's premier theologians.

★

David A. Hubbard, "Biographical Sketch and Appreciation," in R. A. Guelich, ed., *Unity and Diversity in New Testament Theology: Essays in Honor of George Eldon Ladd* (1978), is a short summary of Ladd's life and work published before his death; see also the introduction by Guelich. Donald Hagner, "George Eldon Ladd," in W. Elwell, ed., *Handbook of Biblical Scholars* (forthcoming), is a penetrating and concise summary of Ladd's life and impact on biblical theology, written by the George Eldon Ladd Professor of New Testament at Fuller Theological Seminary. Two works that focus on the impact of Ladd's life and work are John A. D'Elia, "The Mediatorial Character of the New Evangelical Movement in the Life and Work of George Eldon Ladd" (Th.M. thesis, Fuller Theological Seminary, 1992), and Bradley J. Harper, "The Kingdom of God in the Theology of George Eldon Ladd: A Reflection of Twentieth-Century American Evangelicalism" (Ph.D. diss., St. Louis University, 1994). George M. Marsden, *Reforming Fundamentalism: Fuller Seminary and the New Evangelicalism* (1977), discusses Ladd's life and work within the context of Fuller Theological Seminary and the struggles of modern Evangelicalism.

MARKUS H. MCDOWELL

LANE, Frank Charles (*b.* 1 February 1896 in Cincinnati, Ohio; *d.* 19 March 1981 in Richardson, Texas), prominent baseball executive who served as general manager of the Chicago White Sox, St. Louis Cardinals, Cleveland Indians, and Kansas City Athletics.

Frank Lane was the only child of Frank J. Lane, a druggist who died when Frank was four years old; information on his mother is unavailable. By the time he was twelve he was working weekends and before and after school at a drugstore, where he earned $2.50 a week. A heavy child, Lane was inspired to become physically fit by Frank Merriwell, the fictional hero of a popular series of adventure

Frank Lane. COURTESY OF THE NATIONAL BASEBALL HALL OF FAME LIBRARY, COOPERSTOWN, N.Y.

stories. He worked diligently on exercise and turned himself into a fine local athlete, playing football in high school as well as for a Cincinnati semipro team when he was sixteen years old. After graduating from Woodward High School he did various kinds of work, including writing part-time for Cincinnati's *Commercial Tribune* and playing baseball with the Marion club of the Ohio State League in 1912. He was most successful as a sports official, becoming a sought-after referee for college football games. He worked local high school and college games as well as Big Ten and Southern Conference games, earning between $12,000 and $14,000 a year in the late 1920s. However, during the Great Depression, when his earnings for officiating games dropped to $5,000 per year, he sought a more secure line of work. Meanwhile, he met and married Selma Dent, with whom he would have a daughter, born in 1931.

At the age of thirty-eight in 1934, Lane became assistant general manager of the Cincinnati Reds. He was hired by the club's general manager, Larry MacPhail, who was also a fellow college football referee. Four years later Warren Giles became general manager of the Reds and assigned Lane to be general manager of the Durham Bulls, the organization's minor-league club in North Carolina. Lane's last position with the Reds, as director of their minor-league system, lasted four years.

He left the position with the American entry into World War II. He wanted to be a pilot but was turned down because of his age (forty-four). Instead, he was assigned to help direct the navy's physical-fitness program. After the war he left the service as a commander and rejoined MacPhail, now president of the New York Yankees. Lane became general manager of the Yankees farm club in Kansas City in 1946 and helped direct the western teams in the farm system with Yankees farm director George Weiss. In 1947 and 1948, Lane served as the president of the American Association, one of the leading minor leagues in the country.

Despite having a five-year contract, Lane left the league presidency in October 1948 to assume his first position as major-league general manager, hired by Charlie Comiskey of the Chicago White Sox. Taking over a team that was in eighth place and never drew more than a million fans, Lane spent seven seasons with the White Sox and built a solid American League contender. Called "Trader Lane" and "Frantic Frankie," Lane believed not in long-term team development, but rather that a general manager should do anything to improve the team immediately. He transformed the Sox by actively moving players, completing 241 trades involving 353 men and picking up such key players as Hall of Fame second baseman Nellie Fox and pitcher Billy Pierce, two key figures in the White Sox' 1959 American League championship team. More important, Lane improved the finances of the team with strong finishes and excellent attendance figures. In 1955 he left the Sox because of ongoing differences with the team's vice president, Chuck Comiskey.

In October 1955 Lane became the general manager of the St. Louis Cardinals, a position he held for two years. Through numerous trades, including one involving the popular Hall of Famer Red Schoendienst, Lane brought the Cardinals to fourth place from seventh the year before. In 1957 the Cardinals were in the pennant race until the end of the season, and Lane was designated Executive of the Year by the *Sporting News*. He left the Cardinals in November 1957, citing differences with team owner Gussie Busch.

His next job was as general manager of the Cleveland Indians, a position he held from 1958 through 1960. At Cleveland he completed two of his most controversial trades. Just prior to the opening of the 1960 season he traded the popular power-hitter Rocky Colavito to the Detroit Tigers for the 1959 American League batting champion, Harvey Kuenn. Despite Lane's contention that he traded "a hamburger for a steak," Cleveland fans took the news badly and immediately called for his job. In his other famous trade—one never repeated in baseball history—Lane orchestrated a trade of team managers, swapping Joe Gordon for Detroit's skipper, Jimmy Dykes.

In 1961 Lane became general manager of the Kansas City Athletics. With great fanfare, owner Charles O. Finley hired Lane to turn around the struggling franchise. Despite signing an eight-year contract, Lane lasted only eight months with Finley. Lane sued and won a significant severance package in court.

In May 1962 Lane joined the staff of the Chicago Packers of the National Basketball Association. He also worked for the Chicago Zephyrs through June 1963. He served in other positions in baseball, including director of baseball operations for the Milwaukee Brewers in the early 1970s, and was general scout for the Baltimore Orioles, San Diego Padres, and California Angels. In the last years of his life he primarily served as a consultant to teams and remained close to sportswriters, with whom he would always talk. He was living in a nursing home near Richardson, Texas, when he died at the age of eighty-five.

★

Newspaper clippings and other materials on Frank Lane are located in the Officials File of the National Baseball Hall of Fame Library, Cooperstown, New York. Summaries of Lane's career appear in Gene Karst and Martin J. Jones, Jr., *Who's Who in Professional Baseball* (1973), and Leverett T. Smith, Jr., "Frank C. Lane," in David L. Porter, ed., *Biographical Dictionary of American Sports: 1989–1992 Supplement* (1992). See also Bob Burnes, "Frank Lane—Marco Polo of Game," *Sporting News* (6 Sept. and 13 Sept. 1961); Mark Kram, "Would You Trade with This Man?," *Sports Illustrated* (26 Aug. 1968); and Harry T. Paxton, "Baseball's

Human Hurricane," *Saturday Evening Post* (30 May 1953). An obituary is in the *New York Times* (21 Mar. 1981).

COREY SEEMAN

LANGER, Susanne Katherina (*b.* 20 December 1895 in New York City; *d.* 17 July 1985 in Old Lyme, Connecticut), philosopher and educator whose theories on art and the nature of the imagination continue to influence work in the field of aesthetics; her first major book, *Philosophy in a New Key* (1942), became one of Harvard University Press's all-time best-sellers.

Born Susanne Katerina Knauth on Manhattan's Upper West Side to German immigrants Antonio Knauth and Else (Uhlich) Knauth, Langer grew up along with four siblings in a home rich in Teutonic culture. Her father, a well-to-do lawyer, maintained an active interest in the arts and played both the cello and the piano with proficiency. Though not as gifted a musician as her father, Langer soon learned to play the piano and later, while in college, took up the cello. Her passion and reverence for music became formative to her career as a philosopher. Continuing to play the cello throughout her life (and keeping her favorite instrument in a Victorian glass cabinet at her home in Old Lyme), she turned to an analysis of music as a way of working out her theory that man's life of feeling and experience is expressed symbolically in art.

A small, slight woman with bright blue eyes and close-cropped hair, Langer was frail as a child, weakened by a case of cocaine poisoning that she had suffered as an infant when a pharmacist misfilled a prescription. Her formal education began at the Veltin School, a private institution in Manhattan, though she often studied at home with private tutors, in part because of the continued weakness caused by the poisoning. While this attention to her education might suggest that her father was grooming her for a life of intellectual pursuit, nothing could be less true. Aristocratic in looks, formal and aloof in behavior, Langer's father abhorred bluestockings and was against any of his three daughters attending college. It was not until after his death, when Langer was twenty years old, that she enrolled in Radcliffe College and, with the blessing and encouragement of her mother, undertook serious formal study for the first time.

At Radcliffe, Langer studied philosophy and was drawn, in particular, to the discipline and rigor of logic. Also in Cambridge she met William Leonard Langer, a beginning graduate student in history at Harvard University. In 1921, a year after she had completed an A.B., the two married and together undertook a year of postgraduate study at the University of Vienna. (The couple would have two sons.) The following year, while her husband lectured at Clark

University in Worcester, Massachusetts, Langer brought her first book to completion. *The Cruise of the Little Dipper and Other Fairy Tales* (1923) was, as the title suggests, not a work of philosophy but a volume of children's stories. However, in light of Langer's notion that "myth is the primitive phase of metaphysical thought," her initial foray into the realm of princesses and heroes, of fantastic feats and mythical forces, presaged her works of serious philosophy that followed this first book with unceasing ambition till close to her death.

The couple returned in 1923 to Harvard, where Langer resumed her graduate work in philosophy, completing her M.A. in 1924 and her Ph.D. in 1926. Over the next fifteen years (1927–1942), while her husband taught history at Harvard, Langer worked as a tutor in philosophy at Radcliffe and systematically developed her thinking on man's drive to symbolize his experience of the world through art. Langer's first philosophical work, *The Practice of Philosophy* (1930), was intended not only as an introduction to philosophy and a diagnosis of the dead end to which the Cartesian *cogito* ("I think, therefore I am") had driven it, but also as a guide to the new direction philosophy was taking. Philosophy, as Langer saw it, is fundamentally a search for logical connections among meanings, and thus stands against the discipline of science, which seeks to detail empirical connections among facts. Though the contradistinction between meaning and fact suggests Langer's eventual

Susanne K. Langer, 1961. UPI/Corbis-Bettmann

devotion to aesthetics, it does not entail the conventional isolation of the imagination as a mystical, irrational mode of discovery and expression. On the contrary, she gave evidence at this early date of her conviction that, unlike the forms of knowledge limited by discursive syntactical languages, the "personal discovery of meanings through myth, ritual, and art is the very acme of logical procedure, and the refinement of intelligence."

In her second philosophical work, *An Introduction to Symbolic Logic* (1937), Langer offers a textbook summary of methods for analyzing the symbolic structure of abstract systems. But what these two initial works suggest about the importance of man's creative, symbolizing imagination, *Philosophy in a New Key* (1942) would take as its starting point: that symbolism in myth, religion, art, and science provides the key to understanding the diverse and seemingly chaotic phenomena of human experience and emotion. For Langer, a work of art "presents something like a direct vision of vitality, emotion, subjective reality," and it does so through a "symbolic transfer" of the data of human existence, a conversion to conceptual expression that can be achieved in the discourses of science and religion as well. In her next work, *Feeling and Form: A Theory of Art* (1953), Langer extended her axiomatic idea that art objectifies feeling by making categorical distinctions among the "primary illusions" created by each of the art forms she studied. If the work of the symbolizing imagination transforms the uncoded feelings of human experience into an artwork, constituted by symbols and evoking an illusion of the real, then it follows, Langer reasoned, that each genre is particularly suited to express a particular primary illusion. Music, for instance, expresses virtual duration, dance virtual power, and sculpture virtual space.

Langer taught at several universities, including the University of Delaware (1943) and Columbia University (1945–1950), following her divorce from William Langer and departure from Radcliffe in 1942. In 1953 she became professor of philosophy at Connecticut College, where she was appointed professor emeritus and research scholar in 1961. During the later part of her tenure at Connecticut College, Langer researched and wrote her magnum opus, *Mind: An Essay on Human Feeling,* published in three volumes in 1967, 1973, and 1982. In this culminating work Langer articulated her project as a search for a theory of mind in which the central problem "is the nature and origin of the veritable gulf that divides human from animal mentality, in a perfectly continuous course of development of life on earth that has no break." Her treatment of this crux involved evidence drawn from biology, biochemistry, psychology as well as other disciplines, all tending to prove "a special evolution of feeling in the hominid stock" which is thus set apart from the rest of the animal kingdom as a "being that is typified by language, culture, morality, and consciousness of life and death." Langer died at the age of eighty-nine in Old Lyme, Connecticut, where she was buried.

While considered a maverick by her contemporaries and never identified with a particular school of philosophical thought, Langer continues to exert an influence on thinkers in the diversified field of aesthetics because of the range and rigor of her analysis of art as a critical mode of expression, uniquely human and rigorously rational.

★

No full-length biography of Langer has yet been written. A lengthy portrait in the *New Yorker* (3 Dec. 1960) is the best source for biographical information. In addition to the works cited in the text, Langer wrote *Problems of Art* (1957) and *Philosophical Sketches* (1962). Scholarly studies of Langer's work are R. M. Liddy, *Art and Feeling: An Analysis and Critique of the Philosophy of Art of Susanne K. Langer* (1970), and Ranjan Ghosh, *Aesthetic Theory and Art: A Study in Susanne Langer* (1979). Obituaries are in the *New York Times* (19 July 1985), *Washington Post* (22 July 1985), and *Time* (29 July 1985).

G. ANDREW LYNCH

LANSKY, Meyer (*b.* 4 July? 1902 in Grodno, Byelorussia [now Belarus]; *d.* 15 January 1983 in Miami, Florida), crime figure best known for his financial skills in international money laundering and gambling enterprises.

Meyer Lansky, 1971. ARCHIVE PHOTOS

Lansky (born Maier Suchowljansky), a brother, and a sister were brought to the United States by their parents, Yetta and Max Suchowljansky, in 1911. As a youth he lived on the Lower East Side of New York City, where he attended Public School 34 and was considered a good student. On the streets of the Lower East Side, Lansky turned to crime. He was adept at numbers, and after he quit school at the age of sixteen, he became an enforcer for labor unions and on several occasions brutalized strikebreakers. At about this time he formed a friendship with another Jewish hoodlum, Benjamin "Bugsy" Siegel; they created the "Bug and Meyer Mob," which engaged in hijacking, robberies, burglaries, and extortion.

Lansky's first arrest for assault came in 1918. The victim of his attack was Salvatore Luciano, who years later, as Charles "Lucky" Luciano, became a leading figure in organized crime and close friend and associate of Lansky in criminal enterprises, including gambling casinos in Cuba and the Bahamas.

In 1921 Lansky met Arnold Rothstein—"the Brain"—who was mentor to many criminals and racketeers. Rothstein's success, from which Lansky absorbed important lessons, was largely dependent on the highly sophisticated legitimate business techniques he brought to the rackets and vices. Gambling, fencing of stolen goods, and political corruption formed the basis of Rothstein's operation. Through careful study of Rothstein's methods, Lansky acquired the sinister silkiness that became his trademark.

During his seven years with Rothstein, Lansky met important gangsters who would later emerge as "founding fathers" of the national crime syndicate. Rothstein played the role of broker between Tammany Hall and the gamblers and bootleggers and between two of New York's powerful political-criminal factions: one was headed by Jimmy Hines and had ties to Dutch Schultz; the other, also with a Tammany link, involved Italian gangsters such as Joe Masseria, Frank Costello, Lucky Luciano, and Salvatore Maranzano. Rothstein did favors for both—pistol permits, bail bonds, fencing, and "fixing" (influencing the local police).

Following Rothstein's assassination over a gambling debt in 1928, Lansky and his partners took over his businesses and his connections. Lansky's specialty was gambling. He became a naturalized citizen that year and launched a new type of criminal enterprise with Costello and Luciano. Known as "lakehouses," these forerunners of hotel-casinos in Florida, Havana, and Las Vegas were gambling establishments in Saratoga, New York, the fashionable resort that featured a famous race track. The best-known such establishment, the Piping Rock, was an immediate success, and Lansky earned a reputation for operating a fair establishment with neither tricks nor hustles.

On 9 May 1929 Lansky married Anna Citron, a religious woman who had no mob connections and very limited knowledge of her husband's reputation and occupation. They had three children. The Lanskys were divorced in 1947, and Lansky's ex-wife spent the rest of her life in a mental institution.

By 1930 the Italian-American underworld was in chaos. Lansky offered his services to his partners Luciano and Costello during the bloody Castellamarese War, which involved a struggle between two factions of the Sicilian mafia. Luciano had betrayed his boss to bring about peace and feared that his new master, Maranzano, distrusted him. Maranzano did plan to assassinate Luciano as a precaution against another betrayal. Lansky arranged for the murder of Maranzano instead. His plot succeeded, and Luciano emerged as the most powerful mafioso in New York.

Because he was Jewish rather than Italian, Lansky could never be part of the Cosa Nostra, but he did establish himself as a partner of Luciano and others in a host of rackets. In the 1930s Lansky was a central figure in the creation of a national crime syndicate that consolidated fragmented gangland empires into a flexible crime confederation one of whose more gruesome aspects was Murder, Inc.—a squad of professional assassins prepared to kill anywhere in the country at the behest of syndicate bosses. Lansky also arranged casino gambling in Cuba and in Hallandale, Florida. By the mid-1930s he had good reason to relocate his business outside of New York City: Luciano and other crime bosses had been prosecuted and convicted by the crusading district attorney Thomas E. Dewey. Lansky headed south with his brother, Jacob, and Cosa Nostra member Vincent "Jimmy Blue Eyes" Alo, who protected his operations.

When World War II began, Lansky dutifully registered for the draft but was not called. His contribution to the war effort involved secret maneuverings and negotiations with naval intelligence, as well as the help of Lucky Luciano and waterfront racketeers to ensure that Nazi sabotage and spies would not touch the docks of eastern ports. After the war Lansky concentrated on his investments in Cuba and Nevada, where his former associate Bugsy Siegel pioneered casino gambling. In 1948 he married Thelma Schwartz, a manicurist. They had no children.

The Kefauver Committee hearings in the U.S. Senate in 1950 and 1951 brought Lansky, Costello, and many other racketeers into the living rooms of millions of Americans. The unprecedented televised hearings conferred a kind of celebrity on Lansky, who always lived quietly, dressed conservatively, and never sought the limelight. He predictably took the Fifth Amendment against self-incrimination and said nothing. In 1953 he was convicted of illegal gambling in New York State and served less than three months.

In the 1950s Lansky concentrated on his interests in Cuba until Fidel Castro came to power in 1959. The Nacional, Lansky's plush casino in Havana, was seized along with its substantial assets when the charismatic Castro banned gambling.

In the 1960s, according to law enforcement sources, Lansky's skimming operations in Las Vegas yielded enormous profits for him and his partners. Lansky was able to attract legitimate investors because he built many businesses, even high-risk enterprises, solely on the strength of his word and fairness. Indeed, it was rumored that he was so successful that he had to maintain a full-time money manager in Switzerland to look after his accounts. The Department of Justice evidently took the rumors of Lansky's wealth seriously and created a "Lansky strike force" in 1962 to monitor his activities. At this time the Federal Bureau of Investigation overheard one of the most widely quoted remarks by a gangster when Lansky said to a confederate during a telephone conversation: "Organized crime is bigger than U.S. Steel."

Relentless government surveillance finally unnerved Lansky, and in June 1970, fearing indictment for tax evasion, he fled to Israel, where he claimed citizenship as a Jew under that nation's "law of return." The United States requested his extradition, and after a drawn-out legal battle, Israel declared him a "threat to the state" and denied his application for citizenship.

Because he could not stay in Israel, in 1972 Lansky left for Paraguay but was refused permission to deplane. Seven countries rejected his incredible offer of $1 million for sanctuary. Upon returning to the United States, Lansky was arrested in Miami for income tax evasion and contempt of court but was acquitted.

Lansky lived in relative seclusion in Miami. In 1973 a New England gambler and Costra Nostra associate, Vincent Teresa, alleged that he regularly delivered casino skim money to Lansky from establishments in London and Las Vegas. Lansky later was tried on the charge but was acquitted. After 1973 it became clear that he was, as he insisted, retired. Nevertheless, his name routinely surfaced in government hearings concerning mob influence in Atlantic City and other gambling venues or in connection with illegal loans from Teamster pension funds. On his deathbed he proudly said he never killed a man he did business with, but the fact remains that he made his living through men who murdered. Following his death, from cancer, none of the millions he was believed to have stashed away surfaced. He is buried in Mount Nebo Cemetery in West Miami, Florida.

★

Robert Lacey, *Little Man: Meyer Lansky and the Gangster Life* (1991), provides details on Lansky's youth and family life. Hank

Messick, *Lansky* (1971), describes his criminal career; and Robert J. Nash, *World Encyclopedia of Organized Crime* (1992), places Lansky and his activities in historical perspective. An obituary is in the *New York Times* (16 Jan. 1983).

ROBERT J. KELLY

LAWFORD, Peter Sydney Vaughn (*b.* 7 September 1923 in London, England; *d.* 24 December 1984 in Los Angeles, California), British-American film actor known for his association and playboy-style relationships with President John F. Kennedy, Robert Kennedy, Marilyn Monroe, Lana Turner, Judy Garland, Nancy Davis Reagan, and Frank Sinatra.

Lawford was the illegitimate son of Lieutenant-General Sir Sidney Lawford and May Somerville Aylen, the wife of a colonel who served under Lawford and committed suicide upon learning of May's affair (May and Sidney were married in 1924). An only child, Peter was said to have been privately educated by tutors in Great Britain, but it is suggested that these "tutors" were his nannies. After being raised as a girl in degrading circumstances, Lawford began his career on the British stage at the age of seven, in 1930.

Peter Lawford. ARCHIVE PHOTOS

A year later he made his film debut in an early British talkie, *Poor Old Bill.*

The family traveled extensively, and in 1938 Lawford moved to Hollywood, California, where he worked as an usher in a movie theater. The same year he played in *Lord Jeff.* His career took off in 1942 when he was in *Mrs. Miniver* and Metro-Goldwyn-Mayer (MGM) put him under contract. During the rest of the decade he appeared in the films *A Yank at Eton* (1942), *The White Cliffs of Dover* (1944), *The Picture of Dorian Gray* (1945), *Son of Lassie* (1945), *Good News* (1947), *Easter Parade* (1948), and *Little Women* (1949). His English accent, easy style, and dark good looks made him popular with young audiences. He married Patricia Kennedy, sister of John F. Kennedy, on 24 April 1954; they had four children and were divorced in 1966.

When Lawford's contract with MGM expired, he turned to television, appearing in the series *Dear Phoebe* (1956–1957) and *The Thin Man* (1957–1959). During this period he mainly played supporting roles, but he began to develop a playboy image reinforced by his debonair style on the screen and his jet-set lifestyle as a member of the Kennedy family and of Frank Sinatra's "clan."

In 1960 Lawford became a U.S. citizen. As an active supporter of his brother-in-law in that year's presidential campaign, he convinced other show-business personalities to join him and organized many fund-raising rallies. The same year he appeared in the film *Exodus.* The "clan"— often confused with the earlier "Rat Pack"—which consisted of Lawford, Frank Sinatra, Dean Martin, and Sammy Davis, Jr., created and appeared in *Ocean's Eleven* (1960) and *Sergeants 3* (1962). His membership in the "clan," his relationship with President John Kennedy and Attorney General Robert Kennedy, and his friendships with such high-profile celebrities as Marilyn Monroe put Lawford at the center of many controversies. Somehow he managed to avoid tainting his reputation while remaining highly visible and enhancing his playboy image. He also appeared in *The Longest Day* (1962), *Advise and Consent* (1962), *Dead Ringer* (1964), *Harlow* (1965), and *The Oscar* (1966). His production company, Chrislaw Productions, made films that included *Billie* (1965).

On 2 November 1971 Lawford married Mary Ann Rowan, daughter of comedian Dan Rowan; they were divorced in 1973. Among his later films are *That's Entertainment* (1974), *Rosebud* (1975), *Won Ton Ton* (1976), *Angels' Brigade* (1979), and *Body and Soul* (1981). His last role was a cameo as a talent agent in *Malice in Wonderland* (1985), a television movie. His television work also included *The Doris Day Show* (1971–1972) and a television production of *Ellery Queen* (1971).

In December 1983 his alcohol and drug addiction led Lawford to seek treatment at the Betty Ford Center in Rancho Mirage, California. The treatment program seemed to do little or no good. He was hospitalized in July 1984, the same month he married Patricia Seaton, and again hospitalized in November. On 16 December, Lawford entered Cedars-Sinai Medical Center in Los Angeles; he died there eight days later of cardiac arrest resulting from previous medical complications. On 26 December 1984 a memorial service was attended by the Kennedys and friends from his MGM days. His body was cremated and his ashes were placed in the Westwood Village Mortuary, Glendale, California. In May 1988 his wife had his body disinterred, claiming she could not pay the mortuary fees, and spread his ashes over the Pacific Ocean.

Lawford's movies exemplify neither extraordinary talent nor inventiveness; they are good examples of 1950s and 1960s entertainment and reveal why he never reached the stardom of many of his acquaintances. His fame and lasting significance lie in his tumultuous involvement with President Kennedy, Frank Sinatra, and Marilyn Monroe.

★

The Peter Lawford collection of work, papers, and memorabilia is in the Special Collections Division, Hayden Library, Arizona State University. Patricia Seaton Lawford with Ted Schwarz, *The Peter Lawford Story: Life with the Kennedys, Monroe, and the Rat Pack* (1988), offers a view of Lawford's life by the person who knew him best in his last years. Richard Gehmen, *Sinatra and His Rat Pack* (1961), is a contemporary view. Obituaries are in the *Los Angeles Times* and the *New York Times* (both 25 Dec. 1984).

RAYMOND L. ADAMS

LAY, Herman W. (*b.* 3 June 1909 in Charlotte, North Carolina; *d.* 6 December 1982 in Dallas, Texas), businessman who became a leader in the snack food industry through his own labeled items and creation of the Frito-Lay Company.

Herman Lay was the son of Jesse N. Lay and Bertha Erma Parr. Jesse Lay grew up on a farm and became a farm machinery salesman. His son later recalled how good a salesman his father was, selling "softly and with care. It was a pleasure to watch him because he did it so well." Herman's own first sales experience came when he was ten. The family had moved to Greenville, South Carolina, into a house across the street from the Greenville baseball park. Herman took advantage of the location by setting up a stand to sell soft drinks to fans. He did well and soon hired assistants to help run the stand, bought himself a bicycle, and opened his own bank account.

After graduating from public school, Lay won an athletic scholarship to Furman University in Greenville. He dropped out after two years, in 1928, and worked at a variety of jobs until 1932. By then he had managed to save enough to buy a 1928 Model A Ford, so he seized an op-

Herman Lay and Governor Ronald Reagan at the Waldorf-Astoria Hotel in New York City to receive Horatio Alger Awards, 1969. UPI/CORBIS-BETTMANN

portunity that required a car—the local distributorship covering the Nashville, Tennessee, region for Barrett Food Products Company of Atlanta. He soon had three salesmen working for him.

Despite the impact of the Great Depression, Lay was increasingly successful through the 1930s. In 1934 he created the H. W. Lay Distributing Company to handle his sales district. On 28 December 1935 he married Amelia Harper; they had three children. By 1937 he was employing fifteen salesman, and the company owned nine delivery trucks and had expanded to serve all of central Tennessee and southern Kentucky. Ironically, Barrett Food Products itself was struggling, so this same year Lay acquired Barrett, its plants in Atlanta and Memphis, and its Gardner's brand name. He followed this up in 1938 with the first product carrying the Lay's name, a french-fried popcorn labeled Lay's Tennessee Valley Popcorn.

In 1939 Lay consolidated his distributing company with Barrett to form the H. W. Lay Company, Inc. In 1941 the company became one of the first in the world to produce potato chips with continuous production technology when it installed in its Atlanta plant a Ferry continuous potato chip machine. Lay had also expanded his sales region throughout the Southeast. By 1944 he believed his own brand was established well enough that he could drop the

Gardner's name and market all his snack foods under the Lay's label. He strengthened his product line by introducing new products, including pretzels, and by acquiring an exclusive franchise to manufacture and distribute Fritos brand corn chips in the Southeast. (Fritos, founded in 1932, was well established in the West.) In 1956 Lay deepened his link with the Frito company by acquiring the Capital Frito Company of Maryland, which extended his franchise into the Middle Atlantic region.

During these years Lay had earned a reputation as a super salesman, one who persuaded both employees and customers to be enthusiastic about his products. He was also an innovative manager. His firm was among the first southern businesses to create professional personnel and benefit departments, institute formal training programs, and commit itself to providing steady year-round employment.

In 1959 Elmer Doolin, founder of the Frito Company, died. Given Lay's close ties to Frito—which had concentrated on just its corn chips and thus had no products competing with Lay's extensive list—it was natural for H. W. Lay to merge with Frito in 1961, creating the Frito-Lay Company, headquartered in Dallas, Texas, with Lay as president and chairman of the board. The merger also permitted Lay's Potato Chips to become the first nationally distributed chip.

By 1963, with thirty-two products now carrying the Frito-Lay name, the company had introduced a new advertising slogan for its Lay's potato chips, "Betcha can't eat just one," and hired actor-comedian Bert Lahr as official company spokesman. Frito-Lay also began developing foreign markets for its products. In 1964 Lay expanded further, acquiring Bell Products and Sevilla, both olive distributors. The company also announced introduction of a new strain of potato, the Monona, which it had developed through its research program. Frito-Lay was also now developing new strains of corn in an effort to enhance its corn chip products.

Frito-Lay was already established as the nation's leading snack food company, with 10,000 store routes nationally, when Lay met Donald Kendall, president of Pepsi Cola, at a grocer's convention in the early 1960s. In 1965 they agreed to merge their companies, creating a new firm, PepsiCo, Inc., with Frito-Lay as the snack food division. Kendall served as president and chief executive officer, Lay as chairman of the board. Over the next few years Frito-Lay introduced a host of new products, including Doritos tortilla chips, Cheetos, and Ruffles. In 1971 Lay moved to the position of chairman of the executive committee; he retired from PepsiCo in 1980. After leaving he started several businesses dealing in real estate, oil and gas exploration, and frozen foods. Two years after retiring, he died of cancer in Baylor Hospital in Dallas. He was buried in Dallas.

Lay received the Horatio Alger Award in 1969. He served as a director for a wide variety of companies, including Duke Power, Wilson Sporting Goods, Third National Bank of Nashville, First National Bank of Dallas, Southwestern Life Insurance Company, and Braniff Airlines. He was a strong advocate for entrepreneurship, a topic on which he gave many public talks. The U.S. Chamber of Commerce, in recognition of his leadership in that area, named its most substantial meeting room in its Washington, D.C., headquarters for him in 1984. Lay also endowed chairs in business administration at Baylor and Southern Methodist Universities.

★

See *Our First Fifty Years: The Frito-Lay Story, 1932–1982* (1982), a special fiftieth-anniversary issue of the Frito-Lay employee-relations magazine *Bandwagon*. Obituaries are in the *Dallas Morning News* and *New York Times* (both 7 Dec. 1982).

FRED CARSTENSEN

LENYA, Lotte (*b.* 18 October 1898 in Vienna, Austria; *d.* 27 November 1981 in New York City), actress and singer associated with the songs of Kurt Weill.

Born Karoline Wilhelmine Charlotte Blamauer, she was one of four children of Franz Paul Blamauer, a carriage driver, and Johanna Teuschel. She grew up in poverty, with an abusive father, and attended the local elementary school until transferring in 1908 to a school for gifted children. She made her performing debut dancing and playing the tambourine for a small traveling circus run by friends. At age thirteen she left school to work as an apprentice seamstress and then became a prostitute. She later claimed that this shaped her streetwise stage personality. Never a beauty, she radiated a much-remarked-upon sensuality—heightened by dyed red hair—that became a trademark.

In 1913 she moved to an aunt's in Zurich and studied ballet. Although not balletically gifted, her talent for pantomime and impersonation gained her walk-ons in Stadttheater productions. She returned briefly to Vienna, where her father had deserted her mother, but with the outbreak of World War I went back to Zurich's theater, living a carefree life with many lovers. Over the next seven years she played a succession of small roles. Richard Révy, the Schauspielhaus director, trained her in modern and classic roles and changed her stage name to Lotte Lenja (later revised to Lenya).

Lenya moved to Berlin in 1921 to seek stardom, but by 1926 her only significant job had been in a low-budget *Twelfth Night* (1923). Beginning in 1924 she was an au pair for the playwright Georg Kaiser. At the same time, the Roman Catholic Lenya fell in love with the Jewish composer Kurt Weill, whom she married in 1926. The marriage was unconventional, with both frequently engaged in extra-

Lotte Lenya, 1977. UPI/CORBIS-BETTMANN

End (1929), in which she made famous "Bilbao Song" and "Surabaya Johnny"; *The Song of Hoboken* (1930), a revue; Paul Kornfeld's *Jew Süss* (1930); and Valentin Katayev's *Squaring the Circle* (1931). She excelled in *Rise and Fall of the City of Mahagonny* (1931), as well as a special abbreviated version of that work shown in Vienna and a concert version in Paris (1932).

Endangered because Weill was Jewish, the couple fled Nazi Germany in 1933, settling in Paris. In exile Lenya starred in the Brecht-Weill combination of mime and song *The Seven Deadly Sins* (1933) in Paris and London. That year she divorced Weill, but they were reconciled by 1935, when they sailed to New York City. In December she debuted there in a concert of Weill's music. Lenya performed on radio and in nightclubs and had a small role in Max Reinhardt's spectacular production of Franz Werfel's *The Eternal Road* (1936), with music by Weill, whose career soared in America. The two remarried that year. In 1941, the Weills moved from Manhattan to suburban New City, New York, where they purchased a country estate called Brook House. Lenya became a U.S. citizen in 1944.

Lenya was praised for her small role in Maxwell Anderson's *Candle in the Wind* (1941) and toured with it to forty cities, sang in benefits on behalf of the war effort, made recordings of Weill's songs (her chain-smoker's voice growing ever huskier), and was widely thought to be miscast in Weill's flop musical *The Firebrand of Florence* (1945). Her career then froze as Weill's accelerated until his early death in 1950. There were no children. She subsequently devoted her time to the complex task of preserving and propagating his work. Lenya outlived her next three husbands, all homosexuals: George Davis, whom she married in 1951 and who died in 1957; Russell Detwiler, whom she married in 1962 and who died in 1969; and Richard Siemanowski, whom she wed in 1971, divorced in 1973, and who died in 1981.

Lenya's legend began to emerge as—despite chronic stage fright—she returned to performing in 1951. The five-foot-two, one-hundred-pound, craggy-faced actress-singer was seen in acclaimed American and European concerts, on Broadway in Maxwell Anderson's *Barefoot in Athens* (1951), and at off-Broadway's intimate Theatre de Lys, where she achieved her most brilliant success in Marc Blitzstein's long-running adaptation of *The Threepenny Opera* (1954). Her career blossomed with outstanding new Weill albums, including some made during return visits to Germany, where she was honored in 1957 with the Berlin Freedom Bell, and a New York revival of *The Seven Deadly Sins* (1958). She played unsavory characters in films including *The Roman Spring of Mrs. Stone* (1961), for which she earned an Oscar nomination, *From Russia with Love* (1964), *The Appointment* (1969), and *Semi-Tough* (1977). Other contributions included off-Broadway's *Brecht on Brecht*

marital dalliances, some of Lenya's being with other women. That year Lenya returned to the stage, understudying and sometimes playing Juliet in *Romeo and Juliet.*

Her career moved into high gear when Weill began to collaborate with the playwright Bertolt Brecht. Her idiosyncratic voice was perfect for "The Alabama Song" sung by the whore Jenny in *The Little Mahagonny* (later expanded to a full operatic version, *Rise and Fall of the City of Mahagonny*), performed at Baden-Baden (1927). Her big breakthrough arrived when she alternated as Jenny and Lucy in the Brecht-Weill *Threepenny Opera* (1928), which took Berlin by storm. As the prostitute Jenny she sang only "Tango-Ballad," but when she appeared in G. W. Pabst's 1931 movie version, the character also sang Polly's "Pirate Jenny," which became indelibly associated with Lenya's performance. This was reinforced by her recording of songs from the show. Lenya played important stage roles in Lion Feuchtwanger's *The Oil Islands* (1928); Leopold Jessner's staging of *Oedipus* (1929); Brecht's production of Marieluise Fleisser's *The Pioneers of Ingolstadt* (1929); George Büchner's *Danton's Death* (1929); the Brecht-Weill *Happy*

(1962), also seen in London and on tour; two productions of Brecht's *Mother Courage*, one in Germany (1966), and one with California university students (1971); a renowned performance as Fraülein Schneider in the Broadway musical *Cabaret* (1966); several television programs, dramatic and musical; and a final *Threepenny Opera*, at Florida State University (1972). She died of cancer two years after being inducted into the Theater Hall of Fame, and her grave is at Mount Repose Cemetery, Haverstraw, New York.

The quintessential performer of Weill's songs, Lenya—who considered herself more an actress than a singer—brought with her an unusual emotional ripeness and worldly edge. Her performances expressed a tough yet vulnerable Continental sophistication reminiscent of Berlin's decadent cabaret society, and it was largely through her efforts that Weill's music continued to be widely appreciated after his passing.

★

The chief sources for Lenya information are the Weill/Lenya Archive of the Yale University Music Library and the Weill-Lenya Research Center of the Kurt Weill Foundation for Music, New York City. Lenya's correspondence with Weill is collected in Lys Symonette and Kim H. Kowalke, eds., *Speak Low (When You Speak Love): The Letters of Kurt Weill and Lotte Lenya* (1996). The sole biography is Donald Spoto, *Lenya: A Life* (1989). A biographical summary is in *Current Biography, 1959* (1959–60). Among retrospective articles are Bob Matthew Walker, "The Legend of Lotte Lenya," *Plays and Players* 393 (June 1986), and Nancy Caldwell Sorel, "Lotte Lenya and Kurt Weill," *Atlantic* (Nov. 1992). An obituary is in the *New York Times* (28 Nov. 1981).

SAMUEL L. LEITER

LEVIN, Meyer (*b.* 8 October 1905 in Chicago, Illinois; *d.* 9 July 1981 in Jerusalem, Israel), writer of political novels, plays, and documentary films; also a film critic, translator, and editor who was regarded as "one of the best American writers working in the realistic tradition" by Norman Mailer.

The son of Joseph Levin, a tailor, and Goldie (Basiste) Levin, a housewife, Meyer Levin spent his childhood in the Jewish neighborhood of Chicago's West Side. Coming from an immigrant family, Levin remembered his childhood as being full of fear, shame, and constant derisive taunting and threats of beatings.

In 1921 Levin entered the University of Chicago, and with John Gunther formed a literary magazine, the *Circle*, which became the starting point of his writing career. From 1922 to 1929, while still a college student, Levin worked for the *Chicago Daily News* as a reporter, feature writer, and columnist. In 1924, he graduated from the University of Chicago and was sent to Paris as a reporter for the *Chicago*

Meyer Levin prepares for a radio show about the Leopold-Loeb murder case, 1957. UPI/CORBIS-BETTMANN

Daily News. There Levin briefly studied painting with the well-known artist Fernand Léger and the less-renowned Marek Szwarc, from whom Levin began to understand the rich and imaginative possibilities of an art form conceived within a religious framework.

In 1924 Levin visited Palestine for the first time, where he became fascinated by the pioneering lifestyle in the settlers' communes (the kibbutzim). In 1928, he returned to Palestine to live on a kibbutz. Based on his experience there, Levin published *Yehuda* (1931), a story dealing with life in an agricultural commune in Palestine. It was the first novel about modern Palestinian life to appear in English. Although Levin's first novel was *Reporter*, published in New York in 1929, *Yehuda* was the first to make Levin known as a Jewish American novelist.

In 1925 Levin attended art school at the Académie Moderne in Paris and wrote stories for the *Menorah Journal*, a journal of Jewish cultural life that later became the journal *Commentary*. In the early 1930s he opened his own experimental marionette theater in Chicago, and he later taught puppetry at the New School for Social Research in New York City. From 1933 to 1939 he worked as an associate editor for *Esquire* magazine in Chicago. His novel *The Old Bunch*, a story of the passage from adolescence to maturity of a group of Jewish boys and girls, was accepted by the Jewish community as a realistic portrayal of the lives of its youth. Joe Freedman, an artist, is an autobiographical character who makes a pilgrimage through Europe and Israel as Levin had done. *The Old Bunch* was published in 1937 and was followed by the publication of *Citizens* in 1940.

Levin had married Mabel Schamp Foy on 19 February 1935. This marriage ended in 1944, after which Mabel Levin worked as a chemistry professor at City College, New York, and later committed suicide. On 25 March 1948 Levin married Tereska Szwarc, a French novelist with the pen name Tereska Torres, who was the daughter of Marek Szwarc, the French artist of Polish descent with whom Levin had studied in Paris. The Levins lived part of each year in America, and part in Israel, with intervals in Paris. Tereska Levin had a daughter with her first husband, and Meyer and Tereska had two sons.

During World War II Levin served in the U.S. Office of War Information, worked on films in the United States and England, and served with the army's Psychological Warfare Division in France. He was a war correspondent—spending years literally under fire—for the Overseas News Agency and the Jewish Telegraphic Agency. Assigned to learn the fate of European Jews, Levin became an expert on the Nazi death camps and wrote reports, including *We Liberated Who's Who,* for various newspapers and magazines. Haunted by his war experience and the Holocaust, he made several film documentaries including *The Illegals, The Falashas,* and *Bus to Sinai.*

In 1947 Levin completed the manuscript of an autobiographical book *In Search,* but was unable to find a publisher until 1950. Albert Einstein wrote: "In this book the Jewish problem and fate have been grasped in all its depth." Shortly after the publication of *In Search,* Levin helped Otto Frank find an American publisher for his daughter's diary and then undertook a dramatization of *The Diary of Anne Frank.* Later, Levin filed a series of lawsuits against Otto Frank and the Broadway producers of the play *The Diary of Anne Frank* (1955), written by Frances and Albert Hackett. Levin believed that the play plagiarized his work. Levin eventually won a nominal judgment. Later, Levin gave Otto Frank all rights to his version of the play, but Frank's representatives did not permit Levin's version to be produced or even printed anywhere in the world. The story of Levin's twenty-year battle over the rejection and repression of his version of the play was the subject matter of another autobiographical book, *The Obsession,* which was published in 1973.

The publication of the novel *Compulsion* in 1956 brought Levin increased public attention. This best-seller about the 1920s Leopold-Loeb murder case was later made into a play and a film. The novel was also the cause of a $1.5 million lawsuit for damages filed against Levin by Nathan Leopold, who was paroled after serving a prison term for murdering Bobby Franks in 1924. Leopold accused Levin of unjustly using his name in the novel for profit. The court dismissed the case.

Haunted by the Holocaust, Levin wrote one novel after another: *Eva* (1959), *The Fanatic* (1964), *The Stronghold* (1966), *The Story of Israel* (1967), *The Settlers* (1972), and *The Harvest* (1978). All these novels concern the Holocaust, World War II, or Jewish history. Levin translated from French to English Tereska Torres's works: *Not Yet* (1957), *Dangerous Games* (1957), *The Golden Cage* (1959), *Women's Barracks* (1960), and *The Only Reason* (1962). His awards and honors include the Harry and Ethel Daroff Fiction award in 1966 for *The Stronghold* and the Isaac Siegel Memorial Juvenile Award of the Jewish Book Council of America in 1967 for *The Story of Israel.* He died of a stroke in Jerusalem.

The literary output of Meyer Levin includes more than twenty-five volumes. In the course of his career, which spanned almost six decades, Levin succeeded both in personalizing history and in viewing objective events within a subjective framework. In so doing, he was able to articulate not only his link with the Jewish past and its future, but also the cultural link between Jews and the world.

★

Steven J. Rubin, *Meyer Levin* (1982), is based on Levin's two autobiographical works and several interviews. Articles with treatment of Levin include Estelle Gilson, "An Authentic Jewish Writer," *Present Tense* 8, no. 4 (1981): 31–36, and Steven J. Rubin, "The Ghetto and Beyond: First-Generation American-Jewish Autobiography and Cultural History," in James Robert Payne, ed., *Multicultural Autobiography: American Lives* (1992): 178–206. An obituary is in the *New York Times* (11 July 1981).

TIAN XIAO ZHANG

LIEBMAN, Max (*b.* 2 August 1902 in Vienna, Austria; *d.* 21 July 1981 in New York City), television producer and director, best remembered as the producer and guiding light of *Your Show of Shows,* the most celebrated of the television variety programs of the 1950s.

Brought to the United States as a child, Liebman attended Boys High School in Brooklyn, where he was a member of the debating society and wrote class shows with Arthur Schwartz, the composer of future Broadway successes and popular songs.

In 1920 Liebman began to write sketches for vaudeville acts, and five years later he was hired as a social director at the Log Tavern in Pennsylvania. In 1932 he began his long association with Tamiment Lodge, a resort in the Poconos where he worked as theater director for fifteen seasons. He married Sonia Veskova, an opera singer, in 1935.

One of Liebman's Tamiment musicals, *The Straw Hat Revue,* for which he wrote and staged most of the sketch

Max Liebman. ARCHIVE PHOTOS

minute program that would be shown live, without tape or canned laughter, on Saturday nights. He reassembled many of the people who had worked with him on *The Admiral Revue,* headed by Caesar and Coca but also including comedians Carl Reiner and Howard Morris, writers Mel Tolkin and Lucille Kallen, and choreographer James Starbuck. Later, Tony Webster and the irrepressible Mel Brooks were added to the writing staff. (During one season, the staff also included Neil and Danny Simon.) *Your Show of Shows* premiered on 25 February 1950 and was an immediate success. A witty, sophisticated, Broadway-caliber blend of comedy, popular music, ballet, opera, and modern dance, the program became a focal point of Saturday night television viewing and enjoyed high praise from the critics.

Although *Your Show of Shows* featured many imaginative musical production numbers, often with such notable artists as Lily Pons and Lena Horne, the mainstay of the program was the comedy of Caesar and Coca. In solo or dual appearances, sly satire or broad slapstick, they never lost the core of humanity in their characters. By himself, Caesar could express joy, rage, insecurity, and pain in his monologues, or draw gales of laughter as "the Professor," the blustering Germanic "authority" on practically everything. By herself, Coca could turn into a frumpy stripper, a beaming model of ratty furs, or a poignant tramp. Together, Caesar and Coca often played Charlie and Doris Hickenlooper, a married couple with wildly disparate attitudes toward life. Or they could be strangers, meeting to spout a stream of hilarious cliches.

Your Show of Shows never underestimated the intelligence of its audience, and most programs featured wickedly funny satires of popular movies of the day, including *From Here to Eternity, A Place in the Sun,* and *A Streetcar Named Desire.* Frequently the show would offer on-target takeoffs of silent movies, with Caesar, Coca, and company in full bloom as they demonstrated unbridled passion, treachery, or familial devotion with such titles as *A Fool's Fate, Siren's Spell,* and *The Love Bandit.* Often, satire was put aside to make way for a full-scale musical production number.

After four triumphant years, *Your Show of Shows* ended on 5 June 1954, and Liebman moved on to other ventures in television. He produced and directed the situation comedy series *Stanley,* with Buddy Hackett and Carol Burnett, and also produced and directed several television "spectaculars," including "Satins and Spurs" and "The American Cowboy." An anthology of excerpts from *Your Show of Shows,* entitled *Ten from Your Show of Shows,* appeared in theaters in 1973. Liebman died of a heart attack in 1981.

A consummate showman, Liebman brought a new level of sophistication and imagination to television programming, especially with *Your Show of Shows.* At one point he said, "What really counts is taste, style, experience, and,

material, moved to Broadway in September 1939, where it introduced such future stars as Danny Kaye and Imogene Coca. Other talented people Liebman brought from the Poconos included performers Betty Garrett and Jules Munshin, as well as choreographer Jerome Robbins. During World War II, Liebman worked as a civilian director and sketch writer for United Service Organizations shows, producing and directing a revue called *Tars and Spars* for the U.S. Coast Guard in 1945. It was in this revue that Sid Caesar sparked his career by performing the air force movie parody he had fashioned with Liebman. After the war, Liebman directed Caesar in a Broadway revue, *Make Mine Manhattan* (1948).

Liebman came to television in 1949 with *The Admiral Broadway Revue,* a variety program that largely repeated the format of his Tamiment revues. Premiering on January 28 of that year, the show displayed the comedic gifts of Sid Caesar and Imogene Coca for the first time on television, along with showcasing such performers as Mary McCarty, Bobby Van, and Marge and Gower Champion. *The Admiral Broadway Revue* ran for one season, ending on 3 June 1949. The following year Liebman produced Bob Hope's television debut.

At this point Liebman was asked to create a new ninety-

above all, showmanship." In his life's work, Max Liebman displayed all of those qualities and more.

★

Information on Max Liebman and his role in the creation of *Your Show of Shows* can be found in Ted Sennett, *Your Show of Shows* (1977). Liebman also figures prominently in Sid Caesar's autobiography, *Where Have I Been?* (1982). An obituary is in the *New York Times* (24 July 1981).

TED SENNETT

LILIENTHAL, David Eli (*b.* 8 July 1899 in Morton, Illinois; *d.* 14 January 1981 in New York City), public administrator and international development executive known for leadership of the Tennessee Valley Authority (TVA), the Atomic Energy Commission (AEC), and economic development efforts throughout the world.

David Lilienthal was one of three sons of Minna Rosenak and Leopold Lilienthal, Jewish immigrants who came to the United States in the early 1890s from Bratislava, now in the Slovak Republic. Leo Lilienthal worked in or owned dry goods stores in Illinois and Indiana before settling in Michigan City, Indiana, in 1914. Minna helped in the stores but mainly kept the hearth. David always acknowledged his Jewish heritage, but like his father, never practiced the faith.

Lilienthal graduated from Isaac C. Elston High School in Michigan City in 1916 and enrolled in DePauw College in Greencastle, Indiana. Lilienthal was a good but not bril-

David Lilienthal. ARCHIVE PHOTOS

liant student. He was, however, an exceptional leader, winning several oratorical contests and serving as president of the forensic and drama clubs and his social fraternity. He was elected student body president his senior year. After graduating in 1920, Lilienthal enrolled in Harvard Law School, where he began a lifelong friendship with then law professor Felix Frankfurter. Lilienthal received his LL.B. in 1923 and on 4 September of that year married Helen Lamb, with whom he would have two children. The couple moved to Chicago, where Lilienthal worked three years for Donald Richberg, a progressive attorney and later adviser to Franklin Roosevelt. During this time, Lilienthal helped draft portions of the 1926 Railway Labor Act.

In 1926 Lilienthal founded his own firm, specializing in public-utility law. His numerous publications on public-utility reform, especially articles in the *Columbia Law Review* in 1929 and 1931, enhanced his reputation as a progressive, and in 1931 Wisconsin governor Philip La Follette appointed him as a state public-utility commissioner. In his two-year tenure in Madison, Lilienthal rewrote the state utility statutes and challenged scores of utility companies over rates, service levels, and relationships with out-of-state holding companies.

In spring 1933, President Franklin D. Roosevelt appointed Lilienthal to the TVA board, where he served first as a member and then as chairman between 1941 and 1946. While at TVA, Lilienthal became a champion of public power and regional development. His conflict with the private utilities over TVA's right to produce power became a national issue. In 1944, Lilienthal published his first book, *TVA: Democracy on the March,* a brilliant defense of the authority and a masterful example of political rhetoric.

On 23 January 1946 Lilienthal was named chairman of a U.S. State Department board of consultants regarding the internationalization of atomic energy. That same year, President Harry Truman appointed him as the first chairman of the AEC, a position he held from 1 January 1947 until 15 February 1950. Under Lilienthal the commission successfully transformed the locus of atomic-policy development from military to civilian control. In an increasingly conservative environment, however, he sparked considerable controversy by calling for open debate about atomic-energy policies. Near the end of his term he joined physicist J. Robert Oppenheimer in opposing the development of thermonuclear weapons.

After chairing the AEC, Lilienthal became an executive with the New York City investment firm Lazard Frères. While at Lazard, Lilienthal became president of a small industrial firm, traveled the world, and wrote extensively and approvingly about big business, especially in *Big Business: A New Era* (1953). Early in 1954, Lilienthal advised the Colombian government about a "TVA-like project" in the Cauca River Valley. Lilienthal's recommendation, titled

Plan Lilienthal, formed the basis for the Cauca Valley Corporation and marked the beginning of Lilienthal's career as an international development specialist. The Lilienthals lived in New York City from December 1952 to September 1957. They then moved to Princeton, New Jersey, where they lived until David Lilienthal's death.

In 1955, Lilienthal formed the Development and Resources (D&R) Corporation, a firm that developed contracts in more than thirty nations. D&R had contracts in Colombia, Brazil, and the Ivory Coast, and worked extensively in Iran. Until the fall of Mohammad Reza Pahlavi in late 1978, Lilienthal worked closely with the shah in developing the resources of the Khuzistan region in Western Iran. He also served the Lyndon B. Johnson and Richard M. Nixon administrations between February 1967 and April 1969 as director of the "postwar development initiative" in Vietnam, an unrealistic program to plan for economic development in Indochina after the war. The project was staggered first when the Tet offensive in January 1968 dashed all hopes for a foreseeable peace, and then by Nixon's failure to give anything more than lip service to his predecessor's initiative. During this time Lilienthal was also the target of vehement criticism from his children, other family members, and friends for associating with Johnson's ill-fated Vietnam policies. When revolutionaries took control of the Iranian government in early 1979, D&R lost most of its assets, ceased its programs, and Lilienthal resigned as president of the company.

Although Lilienthal kept an office in New York City, his failing health slowed him considerably. On 13 January 1981 he removed cataract-surgery dressings and retired to his Manhattan hotel, hoping to return to work the next day. Sometime that night he suffered a heart attack and died. A few days later, his family held a private interment on Martha's Vineyard, where the family had maintained a summer home for more than forty years.

Lilienthal was a significant figure in U.S. politics between 1930 and 1950. He was an unabashed liberal and advocate of enlarging the public realm on behalf of the public interest. In Wisconsin he fought the utilities and their parent holding companies for lower rates and better service for ordinary citizens. At the TVA he prevailed against powerful foes in extending electrical service throughout the region and in developing a national model for low-cost power. At the AEC, Lilienthal tried with less success to fight secrecy and oppressive security measures and to bring the atomic policy debate into the full light of day.

In his second career as an internationalist, Lilienthal's adventures reflected the best and worst instincts of American liberalism abroad. He was scrupulously honest in his dealings with other nations and expected everyone who worked with him to be the same. He had an unbounded optimism and believed that humankind could transform its world if it just tried. On the other hand he was a naive American who thought his brand of liberalism could easily adapt to other cultures. He believed that big development projects like his beloved TVA were the way to develop nations. He believed that the American experiment could easily take root in regions far different from his own—that economic development led inexorably to political development, then to democracy, and finally to a community of nations looking to the United States as the model for the world. That vision ultimately betrayed this very decent and caring citizen of the world in much the way it did many other Americans of good purpose and intent.

★

The Seeley G. Mudd Manuscript Library at Princeton University holds a large collection of Lilienthal's personal papers and a substantial number of D&R Corporation documents pertaining to the company's work in Iran. Other manuscript collections containing Lilienthal material include the presidential libraries of Herbert Hoover, Franklin D. Roosevelt, Harry S. Truman, and Lyndon B. Johnson. David E. Lilienthal, *The Journals of David E. Lilienthal* (1964–1983, seven volumes), is a comprehensive compilation of Lilienthal's observations from college years until a few days before his death. An early, generally positive biography is Willson Whitman, *David E. Lilienthal: Public Servant in a Power Age* (1948). Steven M. Neuse, *David E. Lilienthal: A Journey of an American Liberal* (1996), is the only complete biography of Lilienthal's life. Two other short works that consider specific periods of Lilienthal's career include Erwin C. Hargrove, "David Lilienthal and the Tennessee Valley Authority," in Jameson W. Doig and Erwin C. Hargrove, eds., *Leadership and Innovation: A Biographical Perspective on Entrepreneurs in Government* (1987), and Steven M. Neuse, "David Lilienthal: Exemplar of Public Purpose," *International Journal of Public Administration* 14, no. 6 (1991): 1099–1141. The best works on Lilienthal and the TVA include Thomas K. McCraw's *Morgan vs. Lilienthal: The Feud Within TVA* (1970) and *TVA and the Power Fight* (1971), and Roy Talbert, Jr., *FDR's Utopian: Arthur Morgan of the TVA* (1987). Lilienthal's struggle at the AEC is best told in Richard G. Hewlett and Francis Duncan, *A History of the United States Atomic Energy Commission: Atomic Shield, 1947–1952* (1962). A telling review of Lilienthal's relationship with the shah of Iran is in James A. Bill, *The Eagle and the Lion: The Tragedy of American-Iranian Relations* (1988).

STEVEN M. NEUSE

LINDSTROM, Frederick Charles, Jr. ("Lindy") (*b.* 21 November 1905 in Chicago, Illinois; *d.* 4 October 1981 in Chicago, Illinois), member of the Baseball Hall of Fame who was a flashy third baseman and outfielder who played thirteen seasons in the major leagues, nine of them with the New York Giants.

Lindstrom was the youngest of the five children of Frederick Lindstrom, Sr., a plumber, and Mary Sweeney. As a

Fred Lindstrom. FROM THE NATIONAL BASEBALL HALL OF FAME LIBRARY, COURTESY OF THE BETTMANN ARCHIVE

child Fred pitched in parochial schools and public parks, hoping one day to become a major league pitcher for his beloved Chicago White Sox. In high school, however, he switched to the infield and became a standout shortstop. His coach, Jake Weimer, was a close friend of the New York Giants manager, the legendary John McGraw. Weimer suggested that McGraw look at his "kid infielder." The scout sent by McGraw in 1922 astounded the young prospect and his father by offering to pay the sixteen-year-old $300 a month to play in the minor leagues, and even to pay for the necessary baseball shoes. The indignant father replied, "I've purchased this boy's shoes up to now and I'll continue to buy 'em even if you are going to pay him ... almost twice my salary." With a contract from the Giants and new shoes from his father, Freddie Lindstrom went to Toledo to become one of the youngest players ever in the American Association.

In 1924, after less than two years in the minors, Lindstrom was called up to the New York Giants as a backup infielder, eventually becoming the regular third baseman. The Giants won the pennant in 1924, and Lindstrom found himself under the pressure of a World Series; at age eigh-teen, he was the youngest player ever to appear in the fall classic. He batted .333 for the series, including four hits off the renowned Walter Johnson, an original Hall of Famer, and fielded twenty-three chances without an error. Lindstrom's joy was tempered by the Giants' loss of the series to the Washington Senators in the seventh game, when he watched two infield grounders find a pebble and take bizarre bounces over his head to bring in the tying and winning runs.

Despite his bad luck in the series, Lindstrom rapidly became a favorite of New York fans, who dubbed him the "Boy Wonder." They admired his good looks, flashing smile, and easy charm as well as his speed, range, and fielding and batting skills. He hit .358 in 1928 and .379 in 1930, collecting a remarkable 231 hits in each season, a feat equaled only by Rogers Hornsby and George Sisler, two of the greatest hitters in the history of the game. During his career Lindstrom hit .300 or better seven times, including six consecutive seasons, and compiled a .311 lifetime batting average.

On 14 February 1928 Lindstrom married his childhood sweetheart, Irene Kiedaisch. They had three sons. The youngest, Charles, was a professional ballplayer who caught for the Chicago White Sox for one game in 1958.

Fred Lindstrom was known for his intelligence, ready wit, and impetuous, independent spirit. He was one of the few players who dared to talk back to his manager, the fierce McGraw, also known as the "Little Napoleon." Lindy once slid into third base and broke his leg, and the irate manager berated his player for carelessness: "Breaking your leg? I always said you never learned to slide." An annoyed Lindstrom retorted, "Do you think this is fun? I hope you break your leg, too." This response so enraged McGraw that he stormed out of the hospital into the path of a taxi, breaking his leg. When Lindstrom hobbled in to visit his fallen leader, he couldn't resist quipping, "Breaking your leg? I always said you didn't know where you were going."

Although only the great Pie Traynor outranked Lindstrom as a third baseman at the time, McGraw decided to replace the latter at third in 1932. When Lindstrom protested, McGraw responded, "With your speed, throwing arm, and fielding ability, you can't miss becoming a great outfielder," a prediction that proved to be correct. Despite their many heated exchanges, the two men had great respect for each other. Lindstrom once declared that his greatest thrill was being named ninth on McGraw's list of his twenty all-time best players. His biggest disappointment occurred when McGraw resigned as manager in 1932. Lindstrom had been led to believe that he would be given the job; instead, McGraw offered it to Bill Terry. Although the two players had been close friends, the outspoken Lindstrom demanded to be traded. The reluctant Terry traded him to the Pittsburgh Pirates in December 1932.

Although he hit .310 in 1933, his first year with the Pirates, Lindstrom left his heart in the Polo Grounds in upper Manhattan, home of the Giants, and never again achieved the same heights of stardom. "I wasn't the same man, much less ballplayer," he explained. "I'd never experienced such a reversal." After two seasons with Pittsburgh, he was traded to the Chicago Cubs. There, he played a critical role with a twenty-one-game winning streak that propelled the Cubs to the National League pennant.

In 1936, hobbled with a bad back, Lindstrom found himself with the Brooklyn Dodgers, a team then known for its slapstick comedy, not its baseball talent. In one game, just as he set himself for a game-ending catch, his own shortstop ran into him, allowing the tying and winning runs to come in. Lindy lay on the ground laughing about "Dodger shenanigans," but the incident preyed on his mind and he soon retired from baseball at the age of thirty.

After two years conducting a radio sports program in Chicago, Lindstrom finally achieved his goal of managing, although on the minor league level, from 1940 to 1942. He then became baseball coach at Northwestern University, a position he held for twelve years. After that, he served as U.S. postmaster in Evanston, Illinois, for seventeen years.

Lindstrom was overlooked by the Baseball Writers Association of America when he became eligible for the Hall of Fame in 1942. In 1976 he was unanimously selected by the Committee on Veterans, which votes on players who have been retired for at least twenty-five years. "It's a real kick, a real honor," said Lindstrom when he was told of his selection as he returned from a golf course. "I didn't do much on the course. But that doesn't matter now."

Lindstrom died at Mercy Hospital in Chicago after a long illness.

★

Martin Appel and Burt Goldblatt, *Baseball's Best: the Hall of Fame Gallery* (1977); Frank Graham, *McGraw of the Giants* (1944); and Fred Stein and Nick Peters, *Day by Day in Giants' History* (1984), describe Lindstrom's accomplishments and contain anecdotes about his career. Additional stories can be found in the *New York Times* (26 Aug. 1954, 9 Jan. 1961, and 31 Jan. 1975), and in the *Sporting News* (1 Jan. 1966). An obituary is in the *New York Times* (6 Oct. 1981).

LOUISE A. MAYO

LINK, Edwin Albert (*b*. 26 July 1904 in Huntington, Indiana; *d*. 7 September 1981 in Binghamton, New York), inventor of pilot training and simulation devices and oceanographic exploration equipment.

One of three children of Edwin A. Link, Sr., an executive with a piano company, and Katherine Martin, Link moved to Binghamton, New York, in 1910 when his father purchased a bankrupt music firm that he renamed the Link Piano and Organ Company. Young Link showed little academic talent while attending local schools, but he early displayed an interest in mechanical devices. After his parents separated in 1918, Link lived with his mother and continued his education in Illinois, California, Pennsylvania, and West Virginia. In 1922 he moved back to Binghamton. After dropping out of high school in his senior year, Link went to work for Western Electric and then for his father's company, where he became skilled in organ building and repair.

Link had developed an interest in aviation following a flight in Los Angeles in 1920. He obtained his pilot's license in 1927. While learning to fly, Link had come to the conclusion that a mechanical device could be employed instead of actual time in the air as an inexpensive method for teaching rudimentary piloting skills. He began work on a trainer in the basement of his father's factory, using parts of organs and compressed air to construct a machine that simulated the motion of an airplane in flight. On 14 April 1929 he filed a patent application for his "pilot maker." Shortly thereafter he formed the Link Aeronautical Corporation to market his invention.

At first Link found little interest in his trainer among the aeronautical community, although he did sell several machines for use as coin-operated rides at amusement parks. In 1930 he organized the Link Flying School. With his trainer at the center of the curriculum, he guaranteed students that he would teach them to fly solo for the low cost of $85. But there were few takers during the early years of the Great Depression, even at a bargain price.

In 1931 Link married Marion Clayton, a reporter for a Binghamton newspaper. She promptly took over the business aspects of her husband's enterprises and thereafter acted as a partner in his later endeavors. They had two sons.

The turning point in Link's aeronautical career came in 1934 when the Army Air Corps suffered a number of highly publicized accidents while flying the mail. By this time Link had modified his trainer to serve as an instructional tool for instrument flying. The army ordered six of the instrument trainers, bringing Link's machine to public attention. Sales to Japan, the Soviet Union, and other foreign countries—with the required permission of the U.S. government—quickly followed. In 1935 he established Link Aviation Devices, Inc., to manufacture the instrument trainer.

The Link trainer came into widespread use during World War II. With factories in Binghamton and Gananoque, Ontario, Link employed 1,500 people and manufactured eighty trainers a week during peak wartime pro-

Edwin Link (*right*) stands by the flight simulator he invented, the Link Trainer, with Anne Morrow Lindbergh and Francis Kellogg, president of the Charles A. Lindbergh Fund, 1980. UPI/CORBIS-BETTMANN

duction. He once estimated that more than 500,000 pilots had used some 10,000 ANT-18 trainers, popularly known as "the blue box," between 1941 and 1945. Link also produced various specialized training devices, including a sophisticated celestial-navigation trainer.

After World War II the Link company developed electronic training devices suited to the performance of jet aircraft. The Link model C-11, introduced in 1949, represented a step between the wartime Link trainer and the later flight simulator.

In 1953, as Link's interest turned away from aeronautics, he gave up active management of his company and became chairman of the board of directors. He also established the Link Foundation to award grants to universities and nonprofit institutions for research in aeronautics and oceanography. Link sold Aviation Devices to the General Precision Equipment Corporation in 1954. Although he would serve as president of General Precision from 1958 to 1959, Link now applied his creative talents to the sea. Described as a "big man with a tanned face, a balding head, [and] a quiet, self-effacing manner," he maintained his primary residence in Binghamton but spent increasing amounts of time in the Bahamas and Florida.

Link's early interest in sailing and skin-diving had evolved by the 1950s into a second career in underwater archaeology and engineering. Link's fascination with Christopher Columbus led to a search for the *Santa Maria* and an attempt to establish the explorer's first landing site in the New World. The results of his archaeological work were published by the Smithsonian Institution Press in 1958 as *A New Theory on Columbus's Voyage Through the Bahamas* (with Marion C. Link). He later explored Caesarea, Israel, and Port Royal, Jamaica.

Applying his inventive skills to this new area of interest, Link developed a number of devices to facilitate the exploration of the sea, including a mobile, unmanned television camera to probe the sea bottom (the "Shark"); a small submarine (*Deep Diver*); and a submersible decompression chamber. Working with fellow diving enthusiast J. Steward Johnson, Link also developed the deep-diving submersible *Johnson-Sea-Link,* which was launched in January 1971. A slightly larger model, *Johnson-Sea-Link II,* appeared in 1975.

Link's passion for exploring the sea brought personal tragedy in 1973 when his son Clayton was killed during the operation of the *Johnson-Sea-Link* submersible. Although heartbroken, Link made a brave statement to the press. "We're not going to stop. This shows the magnitude of the problem and the challenge."

Link's quiet, self-effacing exterior masked an intensity for discovery and a creative talent that found outlets in both the air and sea. While his name will forever be connected with pilot training devices, his contributions to the exploration of the sea also brought well-deserved recognition in his later years. He died of cancer and was buried in Vestal, New York.

★

The major collection of Link papers may be found at the State University of New York at Binghamton. There is a smaller collection at the Roberson Museum and Science Center in Binghamton. The best account of Link's career is Martha Clark, *Edwin A. Link: A Register of His Papers with a Biography* (1981). Link's aeronautical activities are covered in Lloyd L. Kelly (as told to Robert B. Parke), *The Pilot Maker* (1970). For his oceanographic work, see Marion Clayton Link, *Sea Diver* (1964) and *Windows in the Sea* (1973); and Susan Van Hoek, *From Sky to Sea* (1993). An obituary is in the *New York Times* (9 Sept. 1981).

WILLIAM M. LEARY

LIVINGSTONE, Mary (*b.* 23 June 1906 in Seattle, Washington; *d.* 31 August 1983 in Holmby Hills, California), actress who performed on the radio and television programs of her husband, comedian Jack Benny.

Mary Livingstone was born Sadie Marks, the second of three children of David Marks, a storekeeper, and Esther Wagner, a housewife. She grew up in the Northwest, graduating from King George High School in Vancouver, British Columbia, Canada, around 1923. In that same year, her family moved to Los Angeles. Sadie took a job as a salesgirl at the May Company Department Store, where, legend has it, she met Jack Benny. According to accounts by Livingstone and several others, however, she had met him in 1921, when family friend Zeppo Marx brought Benny to dinner at the Marks home. The teenage Sadie grew angry with Benny for ignoring her, and she and her friends allegedly heckled him during his theater performance the next night. In 1926 the pair met again on a blind double date, and Benny was definitely smitten, showing up at the May Company to invite Marks out the next day. For the next few months, he saw her whenever he was in Los Angeles and telephoned her when he was not. The pair were married in Chicago on 14 January 1927.

According to Livingstone's later recollections, the early days of the marriage were not smooth. The thirty-two-year-old Benny had spent much of his vaudeville career as a ladies' man, and his wife had difficulties adjusting both to his travels and to his fellow performers. To alleviate the problem, in 1928 they hit upon the idea of incorporating Marks into Benny's act. Appearing first as a substitute for a sick performer and then on a permanent basis, she portrayed a "dumb Dora" character who provoked and reacted to Benny's comedy. She even clowned in a short film with her husband in 1928, billed as Marie Marsh.

Benny's career made great strides in the late 1920s, when he achieved stardom in films and on the Broadway stage. In March 1932, Ed Sullivan asked him to appear on the columnist's radio program, and Benny was a hit; by May 1932 he had his own program. He quickly brought his wife into the show. She played bit parts before hitting on the character Mary Livingstone in August 1932, playing a Jack Benny fan from Plainfield, New Jersey. The character, who had a distinctive laugh and talked about her crazy family

Mary Livingstone, 1935. ARCHIVE PHOTOS

members (most of whom could not stand Benny), proved popular with audiences.

Livingstone soon developed an acerbic identity. Benny recalled in his memoirs: "At first she played a dumb girl, but soon the character became sharper—in fact, sophisticated. She needled me constantly. She punctured my boasting. She saw through my little hypocrisies. Usually she would read a letter from her mother. And her delicious silver laughter was always there."

Livingstone became a pivotal member of Benny's radio ensemble company. Interactions with Livingstone and other stock characters enabled Benny and his writers to spotlight the comic faults of their everyman hero—a bragging penny pincher who was perpetually thirty-nine years old and tortured those around him with his dreadful violin playing. His wife's character, which evolved into what he termed a "heckler-secretary," was never a romantic interest for the fictional Jack Benny, who preferred working-class girls or showgirls to the middle-class, professional Mary Livingstone. Nevertheless, she was useful to his on-air persona, rescuing him from scrapes and commenting dryly on his foibles.

Off the air, of course, audience members knew that the Bennys were married. In 1934, they adopted a daughter, Joan, and built a stately home in Beverly Hills, California.

The woman who was increasingly known, even at home, only as Mary Livingstone (she changed her name legally in the late 1940s) became a prominent Hollywood hostess. She completed the transition from Sadie to Mary by lightening her hair and getting a nose job.

In the late 1940s, Livingstone began to develop "mike fright" during her radio broadcasts. When she had first performed in vaudeville and radio, she had not worried at all. "It was something that didn't matter to me in the least," she told a magazine interviewer in the 1950s, "and so I could do it without the slightest self-consciousness, like a child performer." As the years went by, however, performing in public became more difficult. The producers of Benny's radio program solved Livingstone's problem by recording her reading her lines at home, then splicing that recording into a tape of the rest of the cast performing before an audience.

When the Jack Benny program moved to television in 1950, however, Livingstone could no longer work at home. She therefore agreed to perform only in a limited number of programs per season. When her friend Gracie Allen retired from television in 1958, Livingstone decided to retire as well. She returned to the airwaves only for one special presentation in the late 1960s.

After her retirement, Mary Livingstone continued to engage in her favorite activities, entertaining and shopping. Little by little, however, she began to withdraw from the social scene, and after Benny's death in 1974, she became a recluse. She died of heart disease at her home in Holmby Hills (near Los Angeles) and was buried in Hillside Cemetery, Los Angeles.

After her death, the public learned of the less attractive side of the off-air Mary Livingstone. In his show-business histories, George Burns revealed that she had proved a demanding friend to him and Gracie Allen, and that they had put up with her mainly because of their friendship for Jack Benny. Benny's memoirs were completed in 1990 by his daughter, Joan, who also found her mother difficult. Nevertheless, she appreciated the professionalism of the untrained Mary Livingstone and expressed admiration for the glamour, spunk, and humor Livingstone exhibited off the air as well as on. Like the general public, she remembered her mother as a fit comedy partner for Jack Benny.

★

The University of California at Los Angeles Library and Film and Television Archives house a collection of clippings, scripts, recordings, and kinescopes related to Jack Benny and the Benny programs. Livingstone's own recollections of her life may be found in *Jack Benny* (1978), coauthored with Hilliard Marks and Marcia Borie, and "I Got Even With Jack Benny—I Married Him," as told to Jane Kesner Ardmore, in *Woman's Home Companion* (Feb. 1978). Other useful sources are *Sunday Nights at Seven,* a memoir by Jack Benny and Joan Benny (1990); Irving Fein, *Jack Benny:*

An Intimate Biography (1976); and George Burns, *Gracie: A Love Story* (1988).

TINKY "DAKOTA" WEISBLAT

LODGE, Henry Cabot, Jr. (*b.* 5 July 1902 in Nahant, Massachusetts; *d.* 27 February 1985 in Beverly, Massachusetts), journalist, U.S. senator, and diplomat best known as a Republican isolationist-turned-internationalist who repeatedly demonstrated his willingness to subordinate domestic partisan differences to U.S. foreign policy interests.

Lodge was the eldest of three children of George ("Bay") Lodge, a critically acclaimed poet who was the son of Senator Henry Cabot Lodge, and Mathilda Elizabeth ("Bessie") Frelinghuysen Davis, also descended from a distinguished American political family. Cabot, as he was called, had one brother, John Davis, and one sister, Helena. He had an idyllic and privileged childhood, spending summers in Nahant and winters in Washington, D.C. The Lodge household provided constant intellectual stimulation; French was often spoken in the home, and frequent visitors included such illustrious family friends as Henry Adams, Edith Wharton, and Henry James. Bay Lodge died suddenly when Cabot was seven, but his statesman-grandfather helped to fill the paternal void. Cabot's education,

Henry Cabot Lodge, *c.* 1950. HULTON-DEUTSCH COLLECTION/CORBIS

which reinforced the cosmopolitanism of his home, included two years of study in Paris, as well as stints at the prestigious St. Albans School in Washington and the Middlesex School in Concord, Massachusetts, from which he graduated in 1920.

In keeping with Lodge family tradition, Cabot entered Harvard University, where he majored in Romance languages and participated in glee club, crew, and the Signet Society. An excellent (though admittedly disinterested) student, he finished his course work in three years, graduating cum laude with his class after a one-year leave of absence.

Lodge's early career was as a journalist, first with the *Boston Transcript* (1923–1925), and then with the *New York Herald-Tribune* (1925–1932). Assignments at the *Tribune* involved him in issues of tremendous significance, such as the emergence of air power as a weapon and the convictions of anarchists Nicola Sacco and Bartolomeo Vanzetti, and included covering the White House, national political conventions, and the Navy and War Departments. On 1 July 1926 he married Emily Esther Sears; they had two sons.

After joining the U.S. Army Reserve following graduation from Harvard, Lodge developed an abiding interest in military preparedness. This commitment intensified after his first participation in summer maneuvers in 1930. Shortly afterward, he requested leave from the *Tribune* in order to write a book on preparedness. The resulting work, *The Cult of Weakness,* was published in 1932. Lodge never returned to journalism, instead launching a political career by running successfully for a seat in the lower house of the Massachusetts legislature (the General Court). Encouraged by Leverett Saltonstall, the Republican (GOP) speaker of the General Court, to take the chairmanship of the Labor and Industries Committee, Lodge distinguished himself by pushing through the state's first workers' compensation law. Easily reelected in 1934, he became a popular speaker at GOP functions and was soon well known across the state. In 1936 he defeated the colorful Democratic mayor of Boston, James Michael Curley, for the U.S. Senate seat previously held by the late Democrat Marcus Coolidge. His victory (by more than 135,000 votes) was the only Republican capture of a previously Democratic Senate seat in the year of President Franklin Roosevelt's landslide second-term reelection.

In the Senate, Lodge established himself as the brightest newcomer among the Republicans, rapidly emerging as the minority leader Charles McNary's most trusted legislative lieutenant. A moderate on domestic issues ("a practical progressive," as he described himself), Lodge energetically opposed Roosevelt's court-packing bill and interventionism abroad; he was one of only six senators to vote against cash-and-carry neutrality legislation in 1939, but—after extensive soul-searching—he broke ranks with other Senate isolationists and supported Roosevelt's lend-lease proposal to aid the Allies in 1941. After the Japanese attack on Pearl Harbor in December 1941, he vacillated no longer. His immediate preference was to go on active service with his army reserve unit, but by this time he had become so important an ally to the military in Congress that the armed forces leadership wanted him to remain there. When in 1942 President Roosevelt ordered that no member of Congress could go on active duty without resigning his seat, Lodge's options narrowed. Although reelected to the Senate in 1942, after two trips to the front in a civilian capacity, Lodge decided to resign and enter active service; on 2 February 1944 he so informed President Roosevelt.

Lodge served with distinction as a tank officer in World War II. Joining the Second Division of the IV Corps under his longtime friend General Willis Crittenberger, he performed reconnaissance work in the Italian campaign of 1944 and participated in the liberation of France and the occupation of Stuttgart, Germany, in 1945. He earned the Bronze Star, the Legion of Merit, the Croix de Guerre, and the Legion of Honor medal. During his military service Lodge renewed his acquaintance with General Dwight D. Eisenhower, with whom he had struck up a friendship while on field maneuvers in 1941.

After mustering out of the service with the rank of lieutenant colonel, Lodge sought reelection to the Senate in 1946. He easily defeated the longtime Democratic incumbent, David Walsh, who had been the best vote-getter in Massachusetts history. In his second term, as in his first, Lodge led moderate forces within his party. By this time he had converted to internationalism and, with his mentor, Senator Arthur Vandenberg of Michigan, he played an influential role among Republicans who backed President Harry Truman's early cold war policies, including aid to Greece and Turkey in 1947 (the Truman Doctrine), the Marshall Plan (1947), and American involvement in the first peacetime alliance in its history, the North Atlantic Treaty Organization (1949). Lodge also sponsored a bill to examine wastefulness in government (he set up the Hoover Commission) and, with less success, a bill to introduce a constitutional amendment to end the electoral college.

Lodge assumed an influential role within the Republican party, chairing its 1948 Platform Committee and ensuring the party a progressive platform on which presidential nominee Thomas Dewey could challenge President Truman. After Dewey's defeat, the disappointed Lodge wrote an article for a national news magazine entitled "What's the Matter with the Republicans." His commitment to keeping the GOP moderate and competitive led him to persuade General Eisenhower to accept the 1952 GOP presidential nomination. He succeeded in securing Eisenhower's blessing for a write-in campaign in the 1952 New Hampshire primary. The general's eventual convention victory owed much to Lodge, and thereafter the two enjoyed an even closer relationship. Ironically, as he was helping to mastermind Eisenhower's sweeping victory at the national level, Lodge lost his Senate seat to an attractive young Democrat, John F. Kennedy, in part because of disaffected conservative Republicans who resented Eisenhower's capture of the party. It was inevitable that Lodge would receive an important position in the new GOP administration, although not immediately clear what that position would be. At the urging of Secretary of State-designate John Foster Dulles, Eisenhower appointed Lodge United Nations ambassador, with cabinet rank.

The 1950s was the most interesting decade in the history of the United Nations; membership expanded from fifty nations to nearly double that number, most of the new members being nonaligned, newly independent Third World nations. This new reality posed a challenge to Lodge, who Eisenhower had appointed largely because of his eloquent and uncompromising opposition to communism (one historian has called Lodge "Eisenhower's answer to Joseph McCarthy"). Just as he had responded to the realities of World War II by converting from isolationism to internationalism, Lodge now proved adaptable to dealing with neutrals, demonstrating a capacity to view communist successes with the detachment of the nonaligned nations. In particular, he urged Eisenhower to strike a posture in the United Nations independent of the two major colonial powers, Great Britain and France, and to sponsor high-profile projects in the developing nations in order to counter Soviet appeal. Lodge retained direct access to the president throughout Eisenhower's administration, and in 1959 he was given the important assignment of hosting Soviet premier Nikita Khrushchev on his much-publicized visit to the United States.

Selected by GOP presidential candidate Richard M. Nixon for the second spot on the 1960 ticket, Lodge enjoyed great popularity among independent voters but campaigned in a largely lackluster fashion. After Nixon and Lodge were narrowly beaten by the Democratic ticket of John F. Kennedy and Lyndon B. Johnson, Lodge spent two years as director general of the Atlantic Institute, an organization dedicated to furthering economic cooperation and interparliamentary councils among European nations.

In 1963 Lodge was nominated by President Kennedy to a major post that would again enmesh him in issues of literally world-shaking importance—ambassador to Vietnam, just as Ngo Dinh Diem's regime was crumbling and just as the United States faced a fateful decision of whether to escalate military aid to the South Vietnamese regime. Lodge influenced Kennedy's support of Vietnamese leaders who were planning a coup against Diem (which succeeded almost three weeks before Kennedy's assassination in November 1963) and convinced Lyndon Johnson to approve a rapid escalation of U.S. military forces in Vietnam during 1964 and 1965. After being replaced in Saigon by General Maxwell Taylor from July 1964 to July 1965, Lodge served again as ambassador in the critical period from August 1965 to April 1967. He remained strongly supportive of the American military effort as others began to raise questions, but—as one of the "Wise Old Men" convened by Johnson to advise him in March 1968—finally agreed with the assessment that the war could not be won by conventional military means. During the last half-year of Johnson's presidency, Lodge served as ambassador to Germany—almost a respite after the tumultuous time in Saigon.

But Lodge was not finished giving important diplomatic service. After Nixon was elected president in 1968, he appointed his former running mate as chief U.S. negotiator at the Paris peace talks that were aimed at ending the Vietnam War. Still the ardent anticommunist, Lodge made little headway at the peace table; deeply frustrated, he resigned in December 1969. Thereafter he served Nixon as special envoy to the Vatican, a post that did not require him to live abroad but gave him the opportunity to conduct negotiations for the release of American prisoners of war. In 1970 he chaired a special presidential commission to study U.S. policy toward China; the resulting report urged Nixon to seek seating the People's Republic of China in the United Nations without expulsion of the Nationalist Chinese regime. Lodge's service as Vatican envoy ceased at the end of the administration of Nixon's successor, Gerald Ford, in 1977, and he retired to his home in Beverly, Massachusetts, where he lived until his death, due to congestive heart failure. He was buried in Cambridge, Massachusetts.

Refined and dignified (to the point of arrogance, said his detractors), Lodge was an imposing figure—strikingly handsome, patrician in bearing, erect in posture, and nearly six feet, three inches tall. He looked as much the president as any politician of his time, and everything about his lineage, training, and breadth of experience made him a logical presidential choice of his party. But his often brusque demeanor, his impatience with small talk, his diffidence as a campaigner—and, perhaps most of all, his "loner" instincts—militated against his success as a party politician. After 1960, except for a brief flurry of excitement around his write-in victory in the 1964 New Hampshire Republican primary, he was never a serious presidential contender, despite his continuing appeal to moderates and independents.

Still, few outside the White House played a more important part in shaping American diplomacy in the first decades of the cold war than this erudite statesman. A dominant force in constructing the bipartisan scaffolding for American policies toward the Soviets in the late 1940s, creating a realistic U.S. posture in the United Nations in the 1950s, and shaping the fateful decisions that led to the American military quagmire in Vietnam, Henry Cabot

Lodge was the quintessential cold warrior. As much as he embodied the instinctive and unrelenting anticommunism of his generation, however, and notwithstanding a formal and stiff demeanor that suggested rigidity, time and again during his career he demonstrated a remarkable capacity to adapt to changing world realities.

★

The main collection of Lodge's papers, 1920–1985, in the Massachusetts Historical Society, contains official and personal correspondence, World War II diaries, Senate files, speeches, UN papers, and papers related to Vietnam. Smaller microfilm collections are in the Dwight D. Eisenhower and Lyndon B. Johnson presidential libraries. Lodge's autobiography, *The Storm Has Many Eyes: A Personal Narrative* (1973), only occasionally reflects controversial episodes of his long career. A second volume, *As It Was: An Inside View of Politics and Power in the '50s and '60s* (1976), is episodic and provides little additional information. William J. Miller, *Henry Cabot Lodge: A Biography* (1967), is still the only full-scale biography of Lodge. An earlier, admiring work is Henry A. Zeiger, *The Remarkable Henry Cabot Lodge* (1964), obviously intended as a campaign biography. H. W. Brands, Jr., *Cold Warriors: Eisenhower's Generation and American Foreign Policy* (1988), contains a brief, favorable chapter on Lodge at the United Nations. A monograph more critical of Lodge's performance is Anne E. Blair, *Lodge in Vietnam: A Patriot Abroad* (1995). Informative obituaries of Lodge appear in the *New York Times, Washington Post,* and *Los Angeles Times* (all 28 Feb. 1985). Lodge contributed useful oral histories to the John Foster Dulles Oral History Project (Princeton University) and the John F. Kennedy Oral History Project (Kennedy Library, Boston).

GARY W. REICHARD

LODGE, John Davis (*b.* 20 October 1903 in Washington, D.C.; *d.* 29 October 1985 in New York City), film and stage actor, politician, and diplomat who won election to Congress and the governorship of Connecticut and was U.S. ambassador to three countries.

Lodge was the second of three children of George Cabot Lodge and Matilda Elizabeth Frelinghuysen Davis, both of whom came from politically prominent patrician families. His father, a poet, was the son of Senator Henry Cabot Lodge of Massachusetts. His mother was the granddaughter of Frederick Theodore Frelinghuysen, who had been a senator from New Jersey and secretary of state in the administration of President Chester A. Arthur. After George Cabot Lodge's death in 1909, John, his brother, Henry Cabot, Jr., and sister, Helena, were brought up in Washington and Nahant, Massachusetts, principally by their mother. In 1912 she moved her family to Paris, where the children attended private academies and received a rigorous European education. The Lodges returned to the United States (by way of England) following the outbreak of World

John Davis Lodge. ARCHIVE PHOTOS

War I in 1914. John and Cabot then spent an unsatisfactory year at St. Albans School in Washington before their grandfather enrolled them at the Middlesex School in Concord, Massachusetts. After having been in the same class throughout their early school years, the Lodge brothers were separated at Middlesex. John, who was fifteen months younger than his brother and had struggled in academic competition between the two, was held back and placed with boys his own age. He improved steadily in his studies until 1919, when a health breakdown caused him to be sent to the Evans School in Mesa, Arizona. There the climate and vigorous outdoor life promoted by the school helped him recover and graduate from Middlesex in the spring of 1921.

At Harvard College, Lodge was more interested in acting than scholarship. Tall (six feet, two inches), handsome, and more outgoing than his brother, he often played the lead in the theatricals put on by the Cercle Français (French Club). He also performed in the musical comedies of the Hasty Pudding Club and the serious dramas of the famed 47 Workshop of Professor George Pierce Baker. Although he toyed with the idea of making acting his life's work, Lodge opted for a legal career after receiving his A.B. in

1925. Accordingly, he attended classes at the École de Droit in Paris for a year and went on to Harvard Law School in the fall of 1926. Lodge graduated in 1929, and on 6 July of that year he married Francesca Braggiotti, an Italian-born professional dancer from Boston. They had three children.

Lodge was a clerk with the large New York City law firm of Cravath, De Gersdorff, Swaine and Wood for nearly two years before opening his own practice in 1931. A year later, he encouraged Francesca to accept an offer from Metro-Goldwyn-Mayer (MGM) in Hollywood to dub the film dialogue of Greta Garbo in French and Italian for the foreign market. While visiting his wife in California in August 1932, Lodge met Adeline Schulberg, the leading talent agent in Hollywood, and impressed her with his good looks and strong voice. She convinced him to make a screen test, and he received a motion picture contract offer from Paramount soon thereafter. Lodge, who had never been strongly committed to the practice of law, took the studio's offer, turned his clients over to colleagues, and moved to southern California that fall.

As John Lodge, he made his film debut with a small role in *The Woman Accused* (1933). He had secondary parts in two more films released in 1933—*Murders in the Zoo* and *Under the Tonto Rim*—before his contract option expired and Paramount released him. Some accounts of his career note that during this period Lodge declined the opportunity to play opposite Mae West in *She Done Him Wrong* (1933), because he thought himself too inexperienced for the role. The picture became a box office hit and a major breakthrough for West's eventual costar, Cary Grant.

Working as a freelance, Lodge won his first substantial supporting role in *Little Women* (1933), directed by George Cukor and starring Katharine Hepburn. At home in the nineteenth-century New England setting of the Louisa May Alcott novel, Lodge ably portrayed Brooke, the tutor who courts and marries the eldest of the March sisters. He then tested successfully for the male lead in *The Scarlet Empress* (1934), a garish film directed by Josef von Sternberg for his principal star, Marlene Dietrich. Under the exacting von Sternberg's coaching, a bewigged Lodge, as Count Alexei, the foremost lover of Catherine the Great of Russia, more than held his own opposite Dietrich's sultry Catherine. Despite these strong performances, Lodge became typecast as an aristocrat suited only for costume dramas and obtained no more leading parts in Hollywood. His last American motion picture appearance was as child star Shirley Temple's father in *The Little Colonel* (1935).

Determined to succeed as a screen actor, Lodge left California and sailed for Europe. After filming *Koenigsmark* (1936), a romance, in French and English versions for a studio in Paris, he went on to London, where he was given a wide range of roles and finally earned star billing. Lodge

made nine British films, including *Ourselves Alone* (1936), *The Tenth Man* (1936), adapted from a play by W. Somerset Maugham, *Bulldog Drummond at Bay* (1937), and *Bank Holiday* (1938), directed by Carol Reed. Although Graham Greene of the *Spectator* and other critics panned his acting as stiff and unconvincing, Lodge's performances were well-received by audiences and he achieved considerable popularity in England. He also traveled to Rome to do two pictures in Italian, one of which starred his wife. Lodge concluded his foreign odyssey playing the Austrian archduke Francis Ferdinand, whose violent death ignited World War I, in *From Mayerling to Sarajevo* (1940), a French production directed by Max Ophüls. In an eerie coincidence, the assassination sequence of the film was shot in August 1939 just before World War II began in Europe.

Back in the United States, Lodge left films to play in summer stock with his wife in 1940 and decided to try his luck on the New York stage the following year. His first Broadway show, the Shubert-produced operetta *Night of Love,* closed after only six performances. Director Herman Shumlin was impressed enough by Lodge, however, to cast him in the key role of aristocratic American lawyer David Farrelly in Lillian Hellman's anti-Nazi play *Watch on the Rhine.* He remained in the cast of the prize-winning drama from April 1941 until called to active duty in the navy in August 1942. Commissioned a lieutenant, Lodge first worked for the public relations division of the Third Naval District in New York. In 1943 he was transferred to the staff of Vice Admiral Henry Kent Hewitt, commander of the Eighth Fleet, and became Hewitt's liaison with Free French forces headquartered in Algiers. Subsequently, Lodge participated in Allied landings in Sicily and Salerno, Italy, and the invasion of southern France. He was discharged with the rank of lieutenant commander in January 1946.

Lodge's wartime experiences convinced him to give up acting and enter public service in his family's tradition. He took a research position with the American Economic Foundation in New York in order to familiarize himself with economic and other current issues early in 1946. That summer, Lodge became a candidate for Congress in Connecticut's Fourth District, which included the town of Westport, where he had owned a home since 1942. He easily captured the Republican nomination and defeated Democrat Henry A. Mucci, a war hero of Italian descent, in the election. Conducting a colorful campaign in which Francesca sang and danced at rallies, Lodge made speeches in fluent Italian and was able to neutralize Mucci's appeal to the sizable Italian-American community in the district; he won by 35,600 votes and was reelected in 1948.

In the House of Representatives, Lodge was a pragmatic moderate who voted with his party 82 percent of the time in his first term and 64 percent in his second term. He backed the Taft-Hartley Labor-Management Relations Act

(1947), the Mundt-Nixon Anti-Communist Bill (1948), the Anti–Poll Tax Bill (1949), and the National Housing Act (1950). As a member of the Foreign Affairs Committee, Lodge made fact-finding tours of eleven war-ravaged countries in 1947 and 1948 and strongly advocated the economic assistance of the Marshall Plan and the broadcasts of the Voice of America as antidotes for communism in Europe. To aid the faltering economy of Italy, which he viewed as especially vulnerable to "red infection" in 1947, Lodge co-sponsored legislation that returned $60 million worth of Italian ships and other property interned in the United States during World War II. He also worked behind the scenes with his brother Cabot (a senator from Massachusetts) for the inclusion of Italy in the North Atlantic Treaty Organization (NATO) in 1949.

Lodge ran for governor of Connecticut in 1950. Against the backdrop of war in Korea, he assailed liberal Democratic incumbent Chester Bowles for breaking a 1948 campaign promise to bring prices down and for being soft on communism. Lodge was elected by 17,014 votes. His governorship followed the moderate Republican formula of fiscal conservatism blended with liberal social policies. Aid to education, workmen's compensation, and unemployment benefits all were increased, and a state department of mental health was created during Lodge's four-year term. At the same time, his painstakingly crafted budgets transformed an inherited $11 million state deficit into a $17 million surplus, but his successes did not result in reelection. Lodge's aggressive promotion of General Dwight D. Eisenhower for the Republican presidential nomination in 1952 alienated conservative Connecticut supporters of Senator Robert A. Taft of Ohio. Their defection helped elect Democrat Abraham A. Ribicoff governor by 3,115 votes in 1954. President Eisenhower appointed Lodge ambassador to Spain soon after his defeat.

From 1955 to 1961, Lodge dutifully handled the job of maintaining friendly relations with the government of dictator Francisco Franco during construction in Spain of U.S. air and naval bases and other cold war defense installations authorized by the 1953 Treaty of Madrid. Even as he was scolded by American liberals for coddling an undemocratic former Axis collaborator, the multilingual Lodge won many friends among the Spanish populace by traveling the countryside making speeches and singing native songs. Francesca also gained admirers for her charity work.

After his return from Madrid, Lodge failed in two attempts to revive his political career in Connecticut, losing a bid for the Republican nomination for senator in 1962 and a race as the GOP candidate against Senator Thomas Dodd two years later. In 1968 Lodge's strong support of congressional friend Richard Nixon's candidacy for president led to another diplomatic appointment. Deemed too controversial a choice for the sensitive post of emissary to

the Organization of American States, he was named ambassador to Argentina by Nixon in 1969; he served until the fall of 1973. In Buenos Aires during a tumultuous period that saw two military coups and the election of former strongman Juan Perón as president, Lodge did his best to present a positive image of America to the Argentine people while avoiding close involvement with warring factions.

Lodge drifted to the political right in the late 1970s. It became his view that the accommodationist foreign policy of détente with the Soviet Union and a decline in traditional American values had sent the country "on a dangerous toboggan ride toward defeat, degradation and disaster." In 1980 he backed the successful presidential campaign of Ronald Reagan and was rewarded with the ambassadorship to Switzerland. Lodge served in this position from 1983 to 1985 and was a member of the U.S. delegation to the United Nations in 1983 and 1985. He suffered a fatal heart attack while making a speech in New York City and was buried in Arlington National Cemetery in Virginia.

Although Lodge was never celebrated for his acting, and his career in politics paled in comparison to that of his brother, he had a creditable record in both fields. He often remarked that his Hollywood and Broadway experience had been "of unique assistance" on the political and diplomatic stage. Thus, it seems appropriate that Lodge held his last important posts in the administration of the most successful actor-politician.

★

Lodge's papers are housed at the Hoover Institution for War, Revolution, and Peace at Stanford University. The Connecticut State Library in Hartford has a collection of his gubernatorial papers. The Margaret Herrick Library of the Academy of Motion Picture Arts and Sciences in Los Angeles has clippings and other material from Lodge's film career. Brief accounts of Lodge's life can be found in the periodic reports of the Harvard class of 1925, especially the *Twenty-fifth Anniversary Report* (1950) and the *Fiftieth Anniversary Report* (1975). A forthcoming work by Thomas A. DeLong is the only biography. Lodge's life and career are discussed at some length in Stephen Hess, *America's Political Dynasties from Adams to Kennedy* (1966) and Alden Hatch, *The Lodges of Massachusetts* (1973). The 1950 and 1954 campaigns and Lodge's governorship are reviewed in Albert E. Van Dusen, *Connecticut* (1961). Obituaries are in the *New York Times* and *Variety* (both 31 Oct. 1985). Interviews with Lodge are in the Columbia Oral History Collection and the Former Members of Congress Oral History Collection at the Library of Congress.

RICHARD H. GENTILE

LOEB, William (*b.* 26 December 1905 in Washington, D.C.; *d.* 13 September 1981 in Burlington, Massachusetts), newspaper publisher best known for his flamboyant right-wing views and vitriolic editorials, which were regularly on display during New Hampshire presidential primary campaigns from 1952 to 1980.

Born William Loeb, Jr., he was the only child of William Loeb, executive secretary to President Theodore Roosevelt, and Katharine Wilhelmina Dorr, a stenographer. The president and his wife, Edith Carow, were young Loeb's godparents. The elder Loeb, a Roosevelt intimate since the latter's New York governorship (1899–1901), often acted as chief of staff and coordinator of press relations at the White House between 1903 and 1909 and later served as collector of customs for the Port of New York and vice president of American Smelting and Refining Company. William, Jr., grew up in Washington and the elite communities of Oyster Bay and Mill Neck on Long Island in New York. He received his early education from private tutors before attending the Allen-Stevenson School in New York City and the Hotchkiss School in Lakeville, Connecticut. At both Hotchkiss, from which he graduated in 1923, and Williams College, where he studied philosophy and obtained his B.A. degree in 1927, Loeb had a reputation for abrasiveness and exhibitionism. He entered Harvard Law School in the fall of 1928 but left in 1930 without earning a degree. In that same year he also left his wife, Elizabeth V. Nagy, a philosophy instructor at Smith College whom he had married on 29 May 1926 while still an undergraduate at Williams.

William Loeb. UNION LEADER PHOTO

They were divorced in October 1932. Loeb's parents settled an alienation of affection suit his former wife had filed against them and also made their son's alimony payments after the divorce.

After leaving Harvard Law School, Loeb met with little success in journalism and business in the 1930s. Although he later claimed to have been a reporter for major national news bureaus, other accounts of his life indicate Loeb never rose above the rank of stringer for a few publications. After his father's death in 1937 he dropped the "Jr." from his name and made a brash attempt to gain control of the Reo Motor Car Company, in which the elder Loeb had been a substantial investor. His corporate reorganization plan was rejected by the directors of the company in 1938, however, and he was voted off the board. Loeb's only business success in this period came when his mother allowed him to handle her portfolio and keep half of the profits from the sale of securities.

Loeb also involved himself in politics during the Great Depression, usually traveling in liberal and left-wing circles. In 1932 he helped form a group to promote a boycott of goods imported to the United States from Japan to protest that country's occupation of Manchuria, and he was chosen chairman of a successor organization that extended the embargo to the purchase of German and Italian products in 1939. Many years later Loeb told interviewers he discovered that the executive committee of the American Boycott Against Aggressor Nations was a communist cell, and he set out to embarrass its members. He said he convinced the organization's national committee, which included such respected liberals as the philosopher John Dewey and the future U.S. senator Paul H. Douglas, to support a boycott of the Soviet Union for its invasion of Finland in 1939 and announced it to the press. When executive committee members vehemently protested the action, according to Loeb, he ended his career on the left. He noted that his principles were refined by this experience, and he became staunchly anticommunist.

In 1941 Loeb realized a long-held ambition to own a newspaper by purchasing the *St. Albans* (Vermont) *Daily Messenger* with the help of a loan from his mother. He added the financially weak *Burlington Daily News* (1942) and the *Vermont Sunday News* (1943) to his incipient empire. Loeb's early publishing effort, which an opponent characterized as a "strident pamphleteering sort of thing," had little appeal in Vermont. Intemperate attacks upon the respected senator Warren Austin for allegedly impeding the war effort and other offenses, as well as the front-page publication of Loeb's Episcopal baptismal certificate to rebut rumors of his Jewish heritage and to showcase the signatures of President and Mrs. Theodore Roosevelt, provoked only scorn. As a result, Loeb's Vermont newspapers struggled against well-established, better-financed competition, and all folded before their publisher's death. On 26 September 1942 Loeb married Eleanore McAllister, an equestrian instructor at the Foxcroft School in Virginia; they had one child.

Loeb's fortunes changed dramatically in 1946 when he bought the highly profitable Union-Leader Publishing Company of Manchester, New Hampshire, from Annie Reid Knox, the widow of his father's friend, Secretary of the Navy Frank Knox. Backed by the capital of Bernard, Joseph, and Victor Ridder, who owned the *New York Journal of Commerce* and other publications, Loeb outbid publishing magnates Frank Gannett and Marshall Field III and a prominent New Hampshire Republican, John McLane Clark, to take possession of the morning *Manchester Union* and afternoon *Manchester Leader* (the papers became the State Edition and City Edition of the *Manchester Union Leader* in 1951). He maneuvered the Ridders into selling their Union-Leader shares to him in 1947. Then, with a new partner, public relations executive Leonard Finder, Loeb purchased the *New Hampshire Sunday News* in 1948. Later that year he found another source of financing through the good offices of Senator Styles Bridges, a political ally, and ousted Finder. By luck and his own machinations, Loeb dominated the news business in New Hampshire by 1949. He was the owner of the only newspaper in Manchester, the state's largest city; he put out the only morning and Sunday editions; and his were the only papers distributed statewide.

Loeb divorced his second wife in June 1952 and wed Nackey Scripps Gallowhur, an artist and granddaughter of early newspaper baron Edward Wyllis Scripps, on 15 July 1952. Loeb and Gallowhur had begun seeing each other while both were married, and he was jailed briefly in 1949 as a result of an alienation of affection suit brought by her husband. After their marriage Loeb and Gallowhur purchased a ranch in Reno, Nevada, which became their legal residence, and a thirty-room mansion on 100 acres in Prides Crossing, Massachusetts, sixty miles south of Manchester. They had one child, and Loeb adopted Gallowhur's only child by her first marriage.

In the manner of the earlier generation of publishers that included Joseph Pulitzer and William Randolph Hearst, Loeb used his newspapers as personal instruments for the advancement of pet causes and the flaying of enemies. Although his Vermont papers were seen as "awkwardly New Dealish" during World War II, the *Union Leader,* Loeb's principal postwar vehicle, adopted a more extreme conservative political stance. In his own hardline editorials, dictated in a colloquial style, signed, and colorfully positioned on the front page, the publisher plumped for American individualism, traditional moral and religious values, and all-out resistance to communism at home and abroad. At the same time Loeb attacked big government

and its adherents as well as all those in public life he deemed insufficiently vigilant in the face of domestic and foreign threats to the nation. A self-styled "Teddy Roosevelt conservative," Loeb also expressed support for labor unions, trustbusting, and taxes on inherited wealth; opposed utility rate increases; and opened up an unusual amount of space in his New Hampshire paper for letters to the editor (more than 6,000 were published per year by the 1960s). The *Union Leader*'s circulation, which was 40,000 in the 1940s, had grown to 65,000 by the time of Loeb's death.

In 1950 and 1951 Loeb served as president of the American China Policy Association, the vanguard of the China Lobby, which led the attack on alleged communist sympathizers in the administration of President Harry S. Truman for the "loss" of China after the defeat of Chiang Kai-shek in 1949. At the same time he became a devotee of Senator Joseph R. McCarthy of Wisconsin, whose flippant, scattershot style of communist-baiting resembled his own. In May 1957 Loeb's lurid reaction to the discredited McCarthy's death (of cirrhosis of the liver) gained the publisher national notoriety. In a two-column, black-bordered box on page one of the *Union Leader,* he declared that his hero had been "murdered by the communists as surely as if he had been put up before a wall and shot." Loeb also held President Dwight D. Eisenhower responsible, denouncing him as a "stinking hypocrite" for having made McCarthy persona non grata at the White House after his censure by the Senate in 1954.

With the emergence of the New Hampshire primary as the first significant test of strength for presidential candidates of both major political parties, Loeb achieved even more celebrity. In addition to disproportionate coverage in the *Union Leader,* the campaigns of the publisher's conservative favorites, Republicans Robert A. Taft (1952), Richard M. Nixon (1960 and 1968), Barry Goldwater (1964), and Ronald Reagan (1976 and 1980), were aided by his editorial assaults against their opponents. Eisenhower, Nelson A. Rockefeller, George Romney, Gerald Ford, and George Bush all were on the receiving end of Loeb salvos over the years. The wealthy and liberal Rockefeller, whom the publisher especially disliked, was attacked most notably as a "wife swapper" in 1964 for having discarded his wife and married a younger divorcee.

Although most of Loeb's attention was focused upon the Republicans, he occasionally found time to make mischief in Democratic contests. His most famous foray into the Democratic race came in 1972, when he published a dubious letter accusing the front-runner, Senator Edmund Muskie of Maine, of referring to people of French-Canadian descent as "Canucks" during an appearance in Florida (the letter was later attributed to the "dirty tricks" division of the Nixon reelection committee) and then reproduced an unflattering gossip item from *Women's Wear Daily* about

Muskie's wife. By provoking a sobbing response from the candidate in front of the *Union Leader* building, Loeb damaged Muskie's campaign in New Hampshire and helped bring his presidential bid to a premature end.

By virtue of his newspaper's statewide circulation, Loeb also became a central figure in New Hampshire's politics. He directed his well-paid investigative reporters to expose corruption and waste in government and ferret out information embarrassing to his enemies. Even more important were Loeb's editorial tirades against broad-based taxes (income and sales) and their supporters, which had the lasting effect of inhibiting state officials and preventing expansion of government services. Consequently, low taxation caused development and new business to increase substantially in New Hampshire while aid to education and mental health programs lagged in the state. As a political kingmaker Loeb had a spotty record, but he did assist the elections of governors Wesley Powell (1959–1963), a conservative protégé of Senator Bridges, and Meldrim Thomson, Jr. (1973–1979), an obscure law book publisher who had never held public office. Perfectly in tune with Loeb, Thomson held the line on taxes and expedited the construction of the Seabrook nuclear power plant, which his benefactor had advocated over the objections of environmentalists.

Even as he exercised political power and gained national attention, Loeb's publishing enterprise was in constant financial turmoil. In addition to his Vermont newspapers, the *Connecticut Sunday Herald* (of Bridgeport) proved unsuccessful. However, most of Loeb's fiscal troubles stemmed from his reckless effort to set up a new paper in Haverhill, Massachusetts, to supplant the existing, strike-plagued *Haverhill Gazette* in 1957. Loeb entered into an agreement with city merchants to pay them a fee for advertising only in his *Haverhill Journal* and helping him defeat his more established rival. A consortium of New England publishers then purchased the *Gazette* in 1958, got it up and running, and blunted Loeb's Massachusetts offensive. Each side sued the other in federal court and the cases dragged on for seven years. Loeb was found in violation of antitrust law in 1965 and forced to pay a $1.25 million settlement. In the end, his failed Haverhill gambit cost almost $6 million. It resulted in the closing of the *Haverhill Journal* and the demise of a profit-sharing program Loeb had instituted for employees of the *Union Leader.* He was able to maintain ownership of the New Hampshire paper only because he received substantial loans in 1963 and 1965 from the Teamsters union's Central States, Southwest, Southeast Area Pension Fund. Subsequently, Loeb was among Teamsters president James Hoffa's stoutest defenders. After Hoffa's imprisonment for jury tampering in 1967, the *Union Leader* campaigned vigorously for his release.

In December 1977 the Jeep in which Loeb and his wife were riding overturned on an icy Nevada roadway. He was only slightly injured, but she became paralyzed from the waist down as a result of the accident. Four years later Loeb died of prostate cancer at the Lahey Clinic Medical Center and was cremated. His widow became administrator of the trust fund that held most of the *Union Leader* stock and took over as publisher.

Although his newspapers had a relatively small circulation, William Loeb was one of the most controversial figures in the history of American journalism. Described by a friend as a "throwback" to the "bare-knuckled journalism" of an earlier time, Loeb terrorized New Hampshire politicians and, at times, made and broke national candidates. He is probably remembered primarily for the vituperative epithets that he regularly launched in his editorials at Presidents Truman ("the little dictator"), Eisenhower ("dopey Dwight"), John F. Kennedy ("the No. 1 liar in the United States"), and Lyndon B. Johnson ("snake-oil Lyndon") and at other important public figures.

The only biography of Loeb is Kevin Cash, *Who the Hell Is William Loeb?* (1975), an exposé written by a former employee that is informative despite its bias. Assessments of Loeb's effect on the politics of his time can be found in Eric Veblen, *The Manchester Union Leader in New Hampshire Elections* (1975), and Neal R. Peirce, *The New England States: People, Politics, and Power in the Six New England States* (1976). Important articles on Loeb's life and career include Helen Kirkpatrick Milbank, "New Hampshire's Paper Tiger," *Columbia Journalism Review* (spring 1966); Bill Kovach, "Nixon's Too Left-Wing for William Loeb," *New York Times Magazine* (12 Dec. 1971); Jules Witcover, "William Loeb and the New Hampshire Primary: A Question of Ethics," *Columbia Journalism Review* (May/June 1972); and Gerry Nadel, "Citizen Loeb," *Boston Magazine* (May 1973). A tribute is "William Loeb, RIP," *National Review* (2 Oct. 1981). An obituary is in the *New York Times* (14 Sept. 1981).

RICHARD H. GENTILE

LOGAN, Rayford Whittingham (*b.* 7 January 1897 in Washington, D.C.; *d.* 4 November 1982 in Washington, D.C.), historian, educator, and pioneer in black studies.

The son of Arthur and Martha Whittingham Logan, Rayford attended public schools in Washington, D.C., before attending Williams College in Williamstown, Massachusetts, where he received his A.B. in 1917. Eager to serve in World War I, he enlisted immediately after graduation and rose from private to first lieutenant with the American Expeditionary Forces. He served in the all-black 93rd Infantry Division, which operated alongside French troops and was one of the few black commissioned officers in the war. An ear injury suffered in combat left him hearing-impaired.

After his discharge in 1919, Logan traveled in Europe

Rayford Logan. MOORLAND-SPINGARN RESEARCH CENTER, HOWARD UNIVERSITY

for five years and became associated with the Pan-African Congress movement, which aimed to unite the darker-skinned peoples in the United States, West Indies, and Africa to throw off European colonialism and advance the welfare of the black race. He served as secretary to congresses held in Paris (1921), London and Lisbon (1923), and New York City (1927), becoming acquainted with W. E. B. Du Bois and other movement leaders.

Upon returning to the United States in 1925, he accepted an appointment to teach history and modern languages at Virginia Union University, where he remained for five years. He earned two master's degrees in history, at Williams (1929) and Harvard University (1932), and his Ph.D. at Harvard in 1936 (he was also awarded a doctor of laws degree from Harvard in 1972). In 1927 he married Ruth Robinson; they had no children. Logan served a year as assistant to the editor of the *Journal of Negro History* (1932–1933) and then five years as head of the department of history at Atlanta University. In 1938 he moved to Howard University in Washington, D.C., where he remained for thirty-six years as professor of history, head of the history department (1942–1964), acting dean of the graduate school (1942–1944), and historian of the university (1965–1969).

From 1945 to 1948, Logan also was foreign affairs editor of the *Pittsburgh Courier*, a major black newspaper, and in 1945 he covered the founding of the United Nations in San Francisco. During and after World War II, he was a consultant for the U.S. government—as adviser to the coordinator of inter-American affairs (1941–1943) and as a member of the U.S. Commission for the United Nations Educational, Scientific, and Cultural Organization (1947–1950). From 1951 to 1952, he was an accredited observer for the National Association for the Advancement of Colored People (NAACP) at the UN General Assembly meeting in Paris.

Logan was a prolific scholar of African-American history, the African mandate system, and Haitian history. His many works include *The Operation of the Mandate System in Africa, 1919–1927, with an Introduction to the Problem of the Mandates in the Post-War World* (1942); *The Senate and the Versailles Mandate System* (1945); *The African Mandates in World Politics* (1948); *The Diplomatic Relations of the U.S. with Haiti, 1776–1891* (1941); and *Haiti and the Dominican Republic* (1968). He was one of the pioneering black scholars who in the early 1930s began to revise the traditional view of slavery as a benign experience and to emphasize the harsher aspects of American race relations. Other scholars were Carter G. Woodson, founder of the *Journal of Negro History* (which Logan edited from 1950 to 1951, along with the companion *Negro History Bulletin*), Alrutheus A. Taylor, E. Franklin Frazier, John Hope Franklin, and Benjamin Quarles.

Logan's many works on U.S. black studies include *The Negro and the Postwar World: A Primer* (1945); *The Negro in the United States: A Brief History* (1957); *The American Negro: Old World Background and New World Experience*, with Irving S. Cohen (1967); *Howard University: The First Hundred Years, 1867–1967* (1969); and the two-volume history *The Negro in the United States*, volume 1, *A History to 1945* (1970), and volume 2 (with Michael R. Winston), *Ordeal of Democracy, 1945–1970* (1971). His best-known work is *The Negro in American Life and Thought: The Nadir, 1877–1901* (1954), which was expanded and revised as *The Betrayal of the Negro: From Rutherford B. Hayes to Woodrow Wilson* (1965); this is an extensive study of white American racism and the depressed economic and social status of blacks in the late nineteenth and early twentieth centuries. Logan argued that northern desires for post–Civil War business expansion and reconciliation with the South resulted in the relegation of southern blacks to second-class citizenship, a view that became widely accepted.

Logan edited *The Attitude of the Southern White Press Toward Negro Suffrage, 1932–1940* (1940) and *What the Negro Wants* (1944), which includes fourteen essays by black American scholars and race leaders calling for first-class citizenship and full equality for American blacks. Other edited works are *Memoirs of a Monticello Slave* (1951), *Life and Times of Frederick Douglass* (1962), *W. E. B. Du Bois: A Profile* (1971), and (with Michael R. Winston) *Dictionary of American Negro Biography* (published posthumously, 1982).

Logan received numerous honors, including the Haitian National Order of Honor and Merit and the Spingarn Medal from the NAACP (1980), as well as honorary degrees from Williams (1965) and Howard (1972) and Fulbright and State Department grants for research in France and West Africa. He died of congestive heart failure and is buried in Fort Lincoln Cemetery, in Washington, D.C.

Logan is notable mainly for his lengthy list of scholarly publications, which contributed to a more accurate picture of American race relations. He also broke early barriers for his race in his service as a commissioned officer in World War I and as a consultant to the Roosevelt and Truman administrations and the United Nations. Lengthy service in academic administration at Howard, frequent attendance at international conferences, and periodic journalistic stints all bespeak a remarkable dedication and impressive work ethic.

★

Logan's papers are at Howard University in Washington, D.C. An obituary is in the *New York Times* (6 Nov. 1982).

WILLIAM F. MUGLESTON

LOOS, (Corinne) Anita (*b.* 26 April 1888 in Sisson [now Mount Shasta], California; *d.* 18 August 1981 in New York City), screenwriter, novelist, and playwright best known as the author of *Gentlemen Prefer Blondes*.

Although she would always maintain that she was born years later (up to 1894), Anita Loos was born in 1888, the middle of three children of R. Beers Loos, a journalist and theatrical entrepreneur, and Minerva Smith Loos, a housewife. Her charming, philandering father seldom made much money, and young Anita began to appear on stage at the age of six in order to supplement the family income, first in San Francisco and then in a San Diego theater her father first managed then owned.

The bookish Anita graduated from high school in San Diego in 1907 and was determined to become a writer. After a few years of freelance journalism, she sent a silent-film scenario to the Biograph Company in 1911. Biograph, the professional home of the director D. W. Griffith, accepted that script and went on to buy many more. By 1915 she had written more than 100 screenplays. Loos's first filmed screenplay was *The New York Hat,* a classic short comedy starring Mary Pickford and Lionel Barrymore.

She grew tired of the restrictions of life with her parents,

Anita Loos, 1970. ARCHIVE PHOTOS

and in 1915 she married Frank Pallma, a New Yorker spending the summer near San Diego, apparently merely to establish her independence. She left Pallma shortly after their marriage and divorced him some years later.

Loos moved to Los Angeles, then just becoming the capital of the American film industry, and worked more closely with Biograph, continuing to churn out stories for short comedies and melodramas and contributing title cards to other silent films, including Griffith's epic *Intolerance* (1916). She became known as the first writer whose titles were as witty and moving as the action in silent films.

In 1916 Loos began collaborating regularly with actor Douglas Fairbanks and director John Emerson on a series of comedic films that greatly enhanced Fairbanks's career. When the star moved on to more action-oriented pictures in 1918, Loos and Emerson continued working together on comedies. The couple married on 21 June 1920 and moved to New York City; they had no children. Emerson, who was fourteen years older than the petite Loos and looked like her father, was a man who, in his wife's words, "enjoyed ill health." He soon gave up directing, alternately resenting his wife's success and trying to horn in on it, either by living on her earnings or by inducing her to include his name in her screen credits.

To Emerson's chagrin, his wife's greatest success came not from a "shared" screenplay but from a series of stories first published in *Harper's Bazaar* in 1925 and then quickly put out as the book *Gentlemen Prefer Blondes* (1926). Loos later explained that the story of the novel's heroine, a blonde vamp named Lorelei Lee, was inspired by her own experience as an overlooked brunette observing a catered-to blonde birdbrain on a train trip. Instead of sulking, Loos took up a pencil and pad and began the sketch from which *Gentlemen Prefer Blondes* was born. A major best-seller, the book went into multiple printings in the United States and abroad. Loos adapted it into a play (1926), and it was rediscovered in 1949, when it was set to music. The Broadway musical solidified the career of Carol Channing, and the filmed musical (1953) gave Marilyn Monroe one of her most memorable roles. The book also inspired a sequel of sorts, *But Gentlemen Marry Brunettes* (1928), in which the author chronicles the adventures of Lorelei's best friend, Dorothy Shaw.

Despite the source of her inspiration, Lorelei Lee was neither a birdbrain nor a creature to be despised. She was a practical young woman who had internalized the materialism of the United States in the 1920s and therefore equated culture with cold cash and tangible assets. She tried to become as "cultured" as possible. The fools in the book were not Lorelei but men, who obligingly surrendered their hearts, their wits, and their precious jewelry to the siren who matter of factly delivered the novel's most co-opted line: "Kissing your hand may make you feel very very good but a diamond and safire [*sic*] bracelet lasts forever."

Thanks to the success of *Blondes,* Loos and Emerson took a vacation from work at the end of the 1920s and moved in leisurely fashion from New York to Europe to Palm Beach, Florida. The chic, clever Loos was a favorite with social, theatrical, and intellectual celebrities. In 1929, however, the Emersons lost their money in the stock-market crash, and Loos went back to work. In 1931 she signed a contract with Metro-Goldwyn-Mayer (MGM) and returned to Hollywood, where she would work on a number of notable sound screenplays, including *Red-Headed Woman* (1932), *San Francisco* (1936), and *The Women* (1939).

In 1943, Loos was let go by MGM and returned to New York, leaving the mentally and physically ailing Emerson in a California asylum, where he died in 1956. She wrote the Broadway play *Happy Birthday* (produced in 1946) for Helen Hayes, a close friend. Loos, who lived on West Fifty-seventh Street just opposite Carnegie Hall and the Russian Tea Room, went to on serve as an adviser for the Broadway musical version of *Gentlemen Prefer Blondes* (1949), to pro-

duce more fiction, and to write another successful play, her adaptation of Colette's novel *Gigi*, which debuted in New York in 1951 and made Audrey Hepburn a star.

When her theatrical career flagged, Loos produced three chatty books of memoirs, *A Girl Like I* (1966), *Kiss Hollywood Good-by* (1974), and *Cast of Thousands* (1977). Biographer Gary Carey notes: "She was a born storyteller and was always in peak form when reshaping a real-life encounter to make an amusing anecdote." Loos died of a heart attack in New York City and was cremated in Mount Shasta, California.

Flapper Anita Loos epitomized the witty, satirical 1920s in her writings, particularly in her memoirs and in her most famous (and most profitable) work, *Gentlemen Prefer Blondes*, which touched on many preoccupations of Americans of the jazz age, including the so-called threat of communism, the search for an "authentic" national literature, the growth of the film industry, the prominence of big business, Freudian psychology, and, of course, male-female relations. Upon first reading the stories of Lorelei Lee's adventures, H. L. Mencken told Loos, "Young lady, you're the first American writer ever to make fun of sex!"

★

Loos's autobiographies, listed above, provide entertaining if occasionally misleading sources on her life; the least useful is *A Cast of Thousands,* which generally only repeats previous material. Gary Carey's *Anita Loos: A Biography* (1988) tries to add to the anecdotes by showing the darker side of Loos—and by estimating her age more correctly. An interview with Loos is in *Publishers Weekly* (6 Dec. 1976). An obituary is in the *New York Times* (19 Aug. 1981).

TINKY "DAKOTA" WEISBLAT

LOUIS, Joe (*b*. 13 May 1914 near LaFayette, Alabama; *d*. 12 April 1981 in Las Vegas, Nevada), heavyweight boxing champion of the world from 1937 to 1949, first African-American athlete to win lasting fame and popularity, and a trailblazer for other black athletes.

Joseph Louis Barrow was the seventh of eight children born to Munroe Barrow and Lillie (Reese) Barrow, poor tenant farmers in Alabama's Buckalew Mountains. Two years after Joe's birth, his father was committed to the Searcy State Hospital for the Colored Insane. When Joe's father died a few years later, his mother married Pat Brooks, a widower with a large family of his own. Although poor, Joe was blessed with a strong family and a deeply religious, attentive, and strict mother and grew up to be generous and accepting of others. Although he would dominate an aggressive and angry sport, he had little anger in him.

In 1926 his family joined the African-American migration from the rural South to the urban North. Settling in Detroit, a large boy at age twelve and behind because of

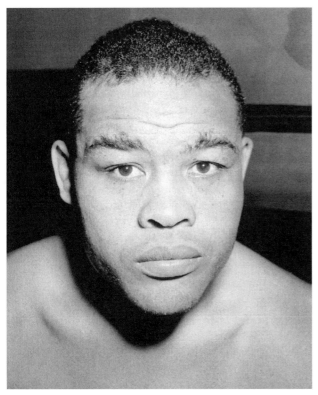

Joe Louis, 1950. ARCHIVE PHOTOS

his inadequate schooling in Alabama, Joe was embarrassed when he was assigned to classes with younger and smaller children. A speech impediment added to his discomfort in school. Within a few years his teachers shunted him off to Bronson Vocational School. As a teenager he worked at odd jobs and began boxing with neighborhood kids. He used the 50 cents a week his mother gave him for violin lessons to rent a locker at the Brewster Recreation Center, where he began a successful amateur boxing career under the name Joe Louis.

John Roxborough, the illegal numbers betting king in Detroit's black ghetto, decided to sponsor Louis's professional career. He enlisted the help of Julian Black, a Chicago speakeasy owner and numbers operator, and they moved Louis to Chicago to train with Jack Blackburn, a former lightweight boxer and skilled trainer who had already taken two white fighters to world championships in lower weight divisions. Blackburn patiently taught Louis a fundamental style of boxing that emphasized balanced but unspectacular footwork, a strong left jab, counterpunching, and throwing combination punches in rapid sequence. Until his death in 1942, Blackburn ensured that Louis ran six miles a day while in training, sparred with discipline, and maintained his physical superiority and confidence against all challengers.

By March 1935 Louis had won eighteen professional fights and was bumping up against the barrier of segrega-tion. Denied economic opportunity and political power, African Americans were invisible in America's emerging media age. With the exception of occasional tokens in track and field and college football, blacks had no opportunities to participate in major sports. Professional baseball and football were for whites only. In boxing, Louis had to live down the legacy of Jack Johnson, the first black heavyweight champion, who had caused race riots by humiliating former champion Jim Jeffries and national outrage by marrying white women. After Johnson lost his title in 1915, white promoters and fighters denied black contenders the opportunity to fight for the heavyweight title.

Mike Jacobs, a Jewish immigrant, helped Louis permanently trample the color line. Jacobs needed a heavyweight contender to break the Madison Square Garden Corporation's monopoly on big-time boxing and promised Louis that he would not have to throw fights to white opponents and would eventually get a chance at the title. Jacobs promoted five Louis tune-up fights, then brought Louis to New York City for a fight against former heavyweight champ Primo Carnera on 25 June 1935. Jacobs skillfully played on Louis's role as an ambassador for his race in the buildup to the Carnera fight, and when Louis, at six feet, one and one-half inches, and 197 pounds, destroyed his six-foot, six-inch, 260-pound opponent in six rounds, he became a media sensation.

On 24 September 1935, Louis married Marva Trotter in a brief private ceremony in a Harlem apartment and then drove to Yankee Stadium to fight Max Baer before a crowd of 80,000 people. Baer had lost the heavyweight title in an upset that summer but was still widely regarded as the best white fighter in the world. After taking a final ten-count on one knee in the fourth round, Baer told a reporter, "I could have struggled up once more, but when I get executed, people are going to have to pay more than twenty-five dollars a seat to watch it."

At a time when President Franklin Roosevelt refused to support antilynching legislation and African Americans were barely mentioned in the white media, Joe Louis suddenly was one of the most famous and written-about men in the world. The way white sportswriters wrote about Louis reveals how novel it was for a black to reach a position of prominence. The most sophisticated journalists of the day constantly mentioned Louis's race and gave him alliterative nicknames, such as the Brown Bomber, the Dark Destroyer, and the Tan Tornado. More racist reporters characterized Louis as a "jungle killer" and a cruel and savage fighter and quoted Louis in darkie dialect, saying that he had "pin-cushion lips" and writing about how much he ate and slept, implying that he was stupid and lazy.

Because Louis was the only black in the white world of fame and fortune, he became the symbol of his race to blacks and whites alike. For African Americans, Louis was the greatest of their small pantheon of heroes. Every time he stepped into the ring against a white opponent, Louis refuted theories of white superiority. From Martin Luther King, Jr., to Malcolm X, from Maya Angelou to Jesse Jackson—each of whom wrote eloquently about his impact on their lives—African Americans took hope and ambition from Joe Louis. After every Louis victory, blacks in urban ghettos across the United States filled the streets to cheer their hero.

Sportswriters believed that the white public would judge a whole people by Joe Louis's actions. With the help of a cooperative press, Louis and his managers carefully constructed a "well-behaved" public image for the fighter. Louis bought his mother a house, modestly downplayed his victories, complimented his white opponents, and presented an image of domestic tranquility with his classy black wife. White writers patronized Louis, calling him "a credit to his race."

Louis lost his reputation for invincibility on 11 June 1936, when he suffered his first professional loss to Max Schmeling of Germany. But Mike Jacobs outmaneuvered Schmeling and the Madison Square Garden Corporation by offering the heavyweight champion, James J. Braddock, a share of future promotional income from Louis's fights. Braddock agreed to defend his title against Louis instead of Schmeling. On 22 June 1937, in Chicago's Comiskey Park, Louis knocked out the courageous but overmatched Braddock in eight rounds.

Despite this victory, sports fans would have doubts about Louis's abilities until his rematch with Schmeling, the only man who had beaten him. Jacobs scheduled their rematch for 22 June 1938 in Yankee Stadium. The fight that would define Louis's career was also one of the most symbolic sporting events in history. Adolf Hitler had stepped up the pace of German rearmament and territorial expansion, annexing Austria in March 1938 and pressuring Czechoslovakia over the Sudetenland. Hitler's racist theories had received considerable press in the United States, partly because the American press had reported that Hitler had embraced Schmeling's 1936 victory over Louis as proof of Aryan racial superiority. Later in the summer of 1936, the Nazis hosted the Olympics in Berlin, and the American press reported that Hitler was counting Germany's overall medal victory as evidence of racial supremacy. The American press also noted that Hitler had snubbed Jesse Owens and other African-American track and field medal winners.

In an ironic twist, whites accepted Joe Louis as the representative of American values fighting against a symbol of Nazi racism. Upset with himself for losing to Schmeling in their first fight, angry that many people still believed that Schmeling was his boxing equal, determined to win a symbolic victory and personal vindication, Louis decided on a strategy that fit his mood. He planned to attack with-

out letup, not allowing Schmeling to set himself long enough to counterpunch with a right over Louis's jab, as Schmeling had done so successfully in their first fight. In the first round, Louis immediately drove Schmeling against the ropes with a sequence of combination punches and then landed an overhand right that had Schmeling out on his feet. Schmeling instinctively turned to avoid Louis, and as he turned Louis broke two of Schmeling's vertebrae with a roundhouse right to Schmeling's side. Louis knocked Schmeling down three times in rapid succession, and Schmeling's trainer, Max Machon, threw in the towel and rushed into the ring to protect his fighter. Referee Arthur Donovan called the fight at two minutes and four seconds into the first round, with Schmeling on his knees. More than 70,000 fans at Yankee Stadium and a huge international press contingent had witnessed a dominating athletic performance from a once-in-a-generation talent.

From January 1939 until the United States entered World War II, Louis defended his title fifteen times, fighting so often and so well that his overmatched opponents in early 1941 were called the "Bums of the Month." The only significant risk to Louis's title came on 18 June 1941, against light-heavyweight champion Billy Conn. Before the fight, Louis supposedly said of Conn, "He can run, but he can't hide." Weighing 170 pounds to Louis's 200, Conn used his lightning-quick hands to build a solid lead on points against Louis going into the thirteenth round. But Conn went for a knockout, continuing to trade punches until Louis interrupted a Conn combination with an overhand right that was solid enough to slow Conn. A two-minute volley of punches finished Conn with two seconds left in the round.

In early 1942, just after the United States entered World War II, Joe Louis enlisted in the U.S. Army. He went on morale-boosting tours for the army throughout the war, fighting exhibitions in the United States, Alaska, and Europe, and quietly broke racial barriers in the segregated armed services wherever he went.

After the war, the treatment of Louis by the white press changed. The alliterative nicknames disappeared, save the standard Brown Bomber and Dark Destroyer. White journalists now rarely identified him as a Negro and stereotyped references declined. Important newspapers praised Louis in editorials, and the praise had a more sincere and less condescending ring. Reporters began to call him a "credit to his race—the human race."

Louis left the army in 1945 as a beloved patriot but a bankrupt one. He had always been generous and free-spending to a fault, running through his huge prewar purses as quickly as they came in. During the war he borrowed heavily from Mike Jacobs and John Roxborough, and he had a large deferred tax bill. After the war, income tax rates on the top brackets rose as high as 90 percent as the

U.S. government tried to pay off its huge debt accumulated during the war.

On 19 June 1946, Louis knocked out Billy Conn in eight rounds in a much-anticipated rematch between two over-the-hill fighters. Louis's purse of $600,000 from the Conn rematch was a fantastic sum for those days but it was illusion. Mike Jacobs arranged to have Louis pay off his personal debts first, leaving Louis with an even larger unpaid tax liability. With upper tax brackets so high, Louis was running in quicksand, sinking under a tax bill that was above $1 million by the mid-1950s (it was never repaid).

Louis defended his title twice against Jersey Joe Walcott before retiring for the first time in 1949. Financial problems forced him back into the ring against new champion Ezzard Charles on 27 September 1950; Charles won a fifteen-round decision. After a series of wins over lesser lights, Louis fought for the last time against future champion Rocky Marciano on 26 October 1951. Louis outpointed Marciano until the eighth round, when he ran out of gas and was knocked out. Louis finished his career with sixty-eight wins, fifty-four by knockout, and three losses.

Of the forty-three men Louis fought before World War II, only one was black. The two heavyweight champions who followed him, Walcott and Charles, were black and were readily accepted by Americans as a result of Louis's well-crafted, inoffensive public image. Black athletes following Louis's example had integrated the National Football League in 1945, major league baseball in 1947, and the National Basketball Association in 1949. Louis opened sports to blacks and helped to make athletics a cutting edge of the civil rights movement.

Louis's first wife, Marva, with whom he had two children, divorced him in 1945, remarried him in 1946, and divorced him again in 1949. During the 1950s Louis lived a nomadic existence, making money from personal appearances and a brief stint as a professional wrestler. He was married to Rose Morgan, a successful beauty shop operator, from 1955 to 1958. In 1959 he married Martha Malone Jefferson, a successful black attorney, and moved into her home in Los Angeles. Martha cared for him through bouts of paranoia and drug abuse. After an involuntary commitment in a Colorado mental hospital in 1970, Caesars Palace in Las Vegas offered Louis a house and employment as a greeter in its casino. Louis lived there until his death from a massive heart attack. He was buried in Las Vegas. Jesse Jackson, who would later be the first African American to run for the presidency of the United States, told 3,000 assembled mourners that with "fist and character," Louis had "snatched down the cotton curtain."

Louis had followed a strategy of not speaking out against America's unrelenting racism in the 1930s in order to win white acceptance. In part because of the success of that strategy, white America became more aware of its own racism. In time, many African Americans became famous in sports, politics, and the arts, and the white media slowly came to accept black celebrities who spoke out against racism and refused to conform to stereotypes. A growing black militancy and rising white consciousness fed each other. In such a context, Joe Louis's image as inoffensive and popular with whites seemed dated and less worthy of respect.

Louis not only had to establish himself as a dominant athlete, but he also had to prove that blacks could compete on equal terms with dignity and without exacerbating racial tensions. Louis accepted that responsibility and performed so well that he became a challenge to segregation, the challenge that began to crack the system. When whites accepted Joe Louis, they accepted a black man at the height of his strength. They also accepted the possibility that other African Americans might do as well. Joe Louis was a revolutionary.

★

Louis's managers John Roxborough and Julian Black paid a professional clipping service to compile scrapbooks of press coverage of Louis from 1935 to 1941. Roxborough's set is housed in the Michigan Historical Collections on the campus of the University of Michigan at Ann Arbor. Black's set is available at the Smithsonian Institution in Washington, D.C. Louis wrote a tell-all autobiography, *Joe Louis: My Life,* with Edna and Art Rust, Jr. (1981). Biographies of Louis include Barney Nagler, *Brown Bomber* (1972), which chronicles Louis's bouts with mental illness and drugs in his later years; Gerald Astor, *". . . And a Credit to His Race": The Hard Life and Times of Joseph Louis Barrow, a.k.a. Joe Louis* (1974); Chris Mead, *Champion: Joe Louis, Black Hero in White America* (1985), which studies press coverage of Louis and its impact on American society; and *Joe Louis: Fifty Years an American Hero,* written by Louis's son, Joe Louis Barrow, Jr., and Barbara Munder (1988), which is an excellent source of affectionate personal detail about Louis's life from his family and friends.

CHRISTOPHER B. MEAD

LYND, Helen Merrell (*b.* 17 March 1896 in La Grange, Illinois; *d.* 30 January 1982 in Warren, Ohio), author and educator best known for the pioneering work *Middletown,* written with her husband, which became a basic text for sociology courses.

Lynd was one of three daughters of Edward Tracy Merrell, editor of the Congregationalist magazine *The Advance,* and Mabel Waite, a schoolteacher before her marriage. Lynd's upbringing was strict and family prayers were a part of each day. Although the family was not well off and lived "on the wrong side of the tracks," in a suburb of Chicago, Lynd received an excellent public school education at Lyons Township High School and was ready to enroll at North-

Helen Merrell Lynd. PHOTO SUPPLIED BY THE SARAH LAWRENCE COL-
LEGE ARCHIVES

western University when her father was offered a job in Framingham, Massachusetts. She then matriculated at Wellesley College. She was a commuter for her first two years, then lived on campus for the final two, waiting tables to pay her expenses.

For the strictly raised Lynd, Wellesley was "an emancipating experience." She joined the debating team and was president of the student government in her senior year. She studied under Mary S. Case, "the best teacher I ever had," who developed her interest in the philosophical system of Hegel. Case was instrumental in teaching Lynd how to question in order to see a variety of possibilities and to delve thoroughly into a subject. Lynd had a triple major in history, English, and philosophy and graduated Phi Beta Kappa in 1919, earning a B.A. degree.

Following graduation Lynd and her family vacationed in Randolph, New Hampshire, where she met her future husband, Robert Staughton Lynd, sociologist and educator. Both were hiking on Mount Washington, and an initial conversation about Thorstein Veblen's *Theory of the Leisure Class* sparked an interest that would result in their marriage. In the fall of 1919 Lynd taught at the Ossining School for

Girls, in Ossining, New York, which she later described as "a terrible place. . . . They didn't give you enough to eat." She taught eight courses. The next year she taught at Miss Master's School, in Dobbs Ferry, New York. Following her marriage to Lynd on 3 September 1921, they moved into her in-laws' apartment in New York City, and she completed an M.A. degree in history at Columbia University in 1922.

In 1924 the Institute for Social and Religious Research of the Rockefeller Foundation hired Robert Lynd to study the religious life of a small town. After a search for the appropriate community to investigate, the Lynds chose Muncie, Indiana, and moved there for a year and a half. Although Helen only had a half-time paid appointment, the resulting book, *Middletown: A Study in Contemporary American Culture* (1929), was a joint effort. Rather than focusing strictly on religion, the Lynds studied a variety of aspects of the community, comparing the changes in earning a living, homemaking, training the young, use of leisure time, and community activities from 1890 on. Their approach was original: they studied life in a contemporary American town by using the methods anthropologists use to study primitive tribes. Much of Helen Lynd's work in Muncie was researching the local newspapers and the records of various organizations. Interviewing the residents of Muncie, many of whom became friends, was, she said later, "one of the best things we did." When the Lynds returned to New York, they began the gigantic task of writing up their study. Each would write a chapter, and they would then exchange and rewrite each other's work. During this time Helen was also taking courses and writing exams toward her Ph.D. at Columbia, where her husband was a professor of sociology.

The institute, unhappy at how the Lynds had expanded the study's focus and seeing it as a "satire" on religion, refused to publish it, and the Lynds had to search for a new publisher. In the meantime Helen got a job doing research at the Lincoln School in New York City. When *Middletown* was finally published in 1929, it was an immediate success and went into six printings. Lynd's son Staughton, who would make a name for himself as an antiwar activist during the Vietnam War era, was born the same year.

Lynd also began teaching in 1929, initially part-time, at Sarah Lawrence, an "experimental" women's college founded in 1928 in Bronxville, New York. She soon became deeply involved in developing the new curriculum at the college, working five days a week and many evenings. Primarily, she taught social philosophy, which appealed to her because "I could follow any possible road to discovery." When Robert Lynd returned to Muncie in 1934, the year in which their second child was born, to study the effects on the community of ten years of industrial growth and the

Great Depression, Helen did not accompany him. She shared in the analysis of the material her husband returned with and in the writing of the resulting book, *Middletown in Transition: A Study in Cultural Conflicts* (1937).

Despite a heavy commitment at Sarah Lawrence, Lynd continued work on her Ph.D. dissertation, which she said "took forever" because she was "helping to start Sarah Lawrence and having two children." She received her Ph.D. in the history of ideas in 1944, and her dissertation, *England in the Eighteen-Eighties: Toward a Social Basis for Freedom,* an analysis of social change during a time of tremendous increases in economic power and social ferment, was published in 1945.

Lynd's book *Field Work in College Education* (1945) grew out of her experiences in building Sarah Lawrence and teaching there. At Sarah Lawrence faculty-student interaction was a basic part of the educational process, as teachers and students worked together to develop the student plans of study. Rather than giving standard grades, teachers wrote individual assessments of a student's strengths and weaknesses, incorporating suggestions for improvement and further avenues to explore. For Lynd, teaching enabled her to refine her ideas. At Sarah Lawrence she could always teach "at the front edge" of her thinking. Other innovations at Sarah Lawrence included faculty working together, jointly teaching courses to provide their particular insight into a subject. The new ideas at Sarah Lawrence and the stamp of "liberal" brought suspicion during the anticommunist crusade of the McCarthy era in the 1950s, when twelve faculty members at the college, from a total of only seventy, were suspected of being communists. When Lynd was asked to submit her "political history" to Harold A. Taylor, president of Sarah Lawrence, she refused.

Lynd's commitment to academic freedom and her opposition to those who would brand teachers as communists had been apparent in 1949, when she wrote "Truth at the University of Washington" for the *American Scholar* forum on "Communism and Academic Freedom." The forum was occasioned by the dismissal of three professors and the placing of three others on probation at the University of Washington. Lynd's article "Realism and the Intellectual in a Time of Crisis" (1952), also published in the *American Scholar,* continued to show her support for academic freedom. A member of the American Federation of Teachers and the American Civil Liberties Union, Lynd was also on the board of the New York Teachers Union for several years, "at a time when I think I may have been the only non-Party member on the board."

In 1953 Lynd was called before the Senate Internal Security subcommittee, chaired by William Jenner, who, like Senator Joseph McCarthy, was a leader in the anticommunist crusade. The hearing was described as a fishing expedi-

tion, looking for Lynd to implicate herself and other teachers at Sarah Lawrence. When Senator Jenner asked if she had ever been a member of the Communist party, she answered, "No." Later, Lynd regretted not taking the Fifth Amendment and publicly challenging the Jenner Committee.

On Shame and the Search of Identity (1958), Lynd's next book, grew out of her developing awareness of shame, which had not yet been explored by psychologists. The book, with its wealth of examples, demonstrates her knowledge of literature, psychology, philosophy, and history and explains the difference between guilt, caused by defying the constraints of society, and shame, caused by betraying one's own values. *Toward Discovery,* a collection of informal talks, articles, book reviews, and excerpts from her books was published in 1965. In an introductory essay, a colleague at Sarah Lawrence, Bert James Loewenberg, describes the book as "a record of [Lynd's] intellectual and spiritual growth."

Although Lynd formally retired from Sarah Lawrence in 1964, she continued to teach there part-time until a year before her death. During her retirement Lynd and her husband, who died in 1970, continued to write, working on their own projects in separate rooms. Lynd's proposed book, "Beyond Problem-Solving to Creativity," was never finished, although she had completed six chapters at the time of her death. The first two chapters are included in *Possibilities* (1983), written with the collaboration of Staughton Lynd and published posthumously. The title of the book accurately reflects Lynd's faith in mankind. *Possibilities* also includes personal reminiscences. Lynd remained in New York City until 1981, when she relocated to Ohio, where she died of a heart attack.

Lynd made significant contributions to the fields of sociology and education, but her work influenced other disciplines as well. Perhaps her greatest achievement was her encouraging generations of students toward discovery, to find out about their world.

★

A collection of Lynd's papers is at the Esther Rauschenbush Library, Sarah Lawrence College. Biographical material is in Irving Louis Horowitz, "Lynd, Robert S. and Helen Merrell," *International Encyclopedia of the Social Sciences, Biographical Supplement* (1979), and Mary Jo Deegan, "Helen Merrell Lynd," *Women in Sociology: A Bio-Bibliographical Sourcebook* (1991). Background material on *Middletown* is in John Madge, *The Origins of Scientific Sociology* (1962). "Reminiscences of Helen Merrell Lynd," interviews by Kitty Gellhorn (1973) and Elfie Karner Stock (1974), are in the Columbia University Oral History Collection. Obituaries are in the *New York Times* (1 Feb. 1982) and *Chicago Tribune* (2 Feb. 1982).

MARCIA B. DINNEEN

M

McBRIDE, Lloyd (*b*. 9 March 1916 in Farmington, Missouri; *d*. 6 November 1983 in Whitehall, Pennsylvania), labor leader who, as president of the United Steelworkers of America (USW) from 1977 to 1983, steered the union through a turbulent era.

McBride was born into a working-class family that moved to St. Louis, Missouri, when Lloyd was four. Until 1977, when he moved to the Pittsburgh area to take over the USW, St. Louis and its environs would be his home. He was educated in public schools there and graduated from Yeatman Junior High in 1930. The onset of the Great Depression had a significant influence on his life and that of his father. Instead of continuing his education, McBride left school at the age of fourteen and went to work full-time in the same steel-fabricating plant (Foster Brothers Manufacturing) that had recently laid off his father. The plant paid McBride a third of his father's seventy-five-cent-an-hour salary. It was a lesson to him in what powerful companies could do to their workers, in the "sort of indignity that workingmen had to endure in those days," as he once commented.

McBride began his labor activities by joining the union as soon as it came to Foster Brothers, in 1936, when he was twenty. In 1937 he married Dolores Neihaus, a Roman Catholic, and converted to his wife's faith. They had two children. In 1937, during contract negotiations, McBride helped to organize a sit-down to counteract a strikebreaking effort by management. At the end of the seven-week-old strike McBride was elected president of Local 1295, a post he kept until 1940. During this time he was also a member of the Steelworkers Organizing Committee.

For the rest of his career McBride held official positions in steelworkers' unions. He was president from 1940 to 1942 of the St. Louis Industrial Union Council of the Congress of Industrial Organizations (CIO) and from 1942 to 1944 of the Missouri CIO Industrial Union Council. The only interruption of his union activities occurred during World War II, when McBride enlisted in the U.S. Navy, serving from 1944 to 1946. From 1946 to 1958 he was a staff union representative of the United Steelworkers of America, a member of the American Federation of Labor–Congress of Industrial Organizations (AFL-CIO), in Granite City, Illinois. In 1958 he was made Granite City's subdistrict director; in 1965 he became district director for the entire area, District 34, headquartered in St. Louis. He remained in this post until his election in 1977 as president of the USW.

McBride's election as USW president was the most significant event in his career. During the rancorous campaign, he was depicted as an "establishment" candidate, handpicked by union officials determined to defend the status quo. His opponent, Edward Sadlowski of Chicago, was, like McBride, a member of USW's executive board and was the voice of those union members who opposed granting concessions to the industry. Sadlowski's followers

Lloyd McBride. UNITED STEELWORKERS OF AMERICA ARCHIVE, THE PENNSYLVANIA STATE UNIVERSITY

were particularly concerned with changing the "no-strike" agreement, which had been in effect since 1974. The no-strike agreement obligated labor and management to submit all conflicts to binding arbitration in an effort to prevent steel buyers from "hedge-buying," or laying in a large supply of steel in hopes of outlasting an anticipated or threatened strike or even eventual cost increases. Hedge-buying was a major factor in the boom-and-bust cycles that had plagued the industry throughout the 1960s. Resolving the issues of the no-strike agreement was especially important because negotiations for a new industrywide contract were scheduled to begin just weeks after the election. Sadlowski's campaign was, even according to some of his supporters, unfocused and unspecific, mainly dependent upon depicting the upper-echelon union officials as too close to management to adequately represent the workers. McBride had more money and had the support of every member of the executive board except for Sadlowski, a factor that contributed to McBride's slim victory.

McBride was installed as the USW leader on 1 June 1977, succeeding I. W. Abel, who had been president since 1965. Until his death in 1983, McBride continued at his post in spite of his heart ailment. The issues raised by the 1977 election were kept alive over the next several years by

the continued decline in the major steel producers' profits. By 1982 the industry wanted wage concessions that McBride was convinced were—in the face of increased foreign competition, new technologies, and lower sales—not only reasonable but necessary to keep plants open and jobs alive. But his proposal was resoundingly defeated at a historic 30 July 1982 meeting of some 400 local union presidents. In February of the next year, McBride was hospitalized for several weeks due to his heart condition, and a pacemaker was installed. He went back to work shortly thereafter. McBride was in the hospital by the fall of the same year; he had bypass surgery in October, stayed in the hospital for several weeks, and died a few days after release, at his home in Whitehall, Pennsylvania, in his sleep.

In addition to his efforts on behalf of steel industry unions, McBride was a member of many boards of directors and served on several important commissions. He was a delegate to meetings of the International Metalworkers Federation in Geneva, Switzerland; a member on the board of directors of the National Society for the Prevention of Blindness; a member of the board of governors of United Way; a trustee of the Human Resources Development Institute; and a member of the presidential commission to investigate the nuclear accident at Three Mile Island. He also held memberships in the Pay Advisory Board, the Committee for National Health Insurance, the Harry S. Truman Institute, and the steel tripartite commission of the Labor-Industry Coalition for International Trade.

In *And the Wolf Finally Came: The Decline of the American Steel Industry*, historian John P. Hoerr stated that "perhaps McBride's greatest contribution was in forcing the Steelworkers to face economic reality." He did not completely succeed—the rank-and-file membership overwhelmingly repudiated a contract McBride had negotiated on their behalf shortly after his election, a result he predicted would have dire consequences. Having risen through the ranks on the basis of his leadership abilities and raw intelligence, McBride's career was an illustration of the possibilities available in the early days of union organizing to someone who lacked formal education but had initiative and drive. He was known and respected by management as a shrewd, low-key, and trustworthy negotiator dedicated to the survival of an ailing industry, a survival workers depended upon. After his death the steelworkers' fortunes went into a steep decline, which McBride had foreseen and attempted to delay, even knowing that he could not completely forestall it.

★

There is no full-length biography of McBride, but substantial portraits can be pieced together from several works on the steel industry and the United Steel Workers Union, particularly John P. Hoerr, *And the Wolf Finally Came: The Decline of the American Steel Industry* (1988), and John Strohmeyer, *Crisis in Bethlehem:*

Big Steel's Struggle to Survive (1986), which include detailed accounts of his election and policies. In addition, there are many newspaper articles either about McBride or peripherally related to his tenure as president. See especially *Wall Street Journal* (30 Aug. 1976); *New York Times* (27 Sept. 1976), article by A. H. Raskin; *U.S. News and World Report* (17 Jan. 1977); *Business Week* (24 Jan. 1977); *New York Times* (11 Feb. 1977), article by Lee Dembert; *Business Week* (6 June 1977); *Steel Labor* (June 1977); *New York Times* (18 Oct. 1977), article by A. H. Raskin; *Current Biography* (1978). An obituary is in the *New York Times* (7 Nov. 1983).

STEPHEN TURTELL

McCAIN, John Sydney, Jr. (*b.* 17 January 1911 in Council Bluffs, Indiana; *d.* 22 March 1981 in an airplane en route from London to Loring Air Force Base, Maine), naval officer who was commander in chief of the Pacific Fleet (CINCPAC) during U.S. military operations in Vietnam and Cambodia in the early 1970s.

McCain was the youngest of three children of Admiral John Sydney McCain, Sr., and Katherine Vaulx. After graduating from Central High School in Washington, D.C., in 1927, he entered the U.S. Naval Academy at Annapolis. He graduated with a B.S. degree in 1931 and was assigned as an ensign on the battleship *Oklahoma* from 1931 to 1933. On 21 January 1933, he married Roberta Wright. They had

Vice Admiral John S. McCain, Jr. ARCHIVE PHOTOS

three children, one of whom, John McCain III, became a U.S. Senator from Arizona. McCain volunteered for submarine training in 1933 and attended the Submarine School in New London, Connecticut. He served on three submarines until 1938, when he returned to Annapolis to teach electrical engineering and physics for two years. In 1940 he returned to submarine service.

When Pearl Harbor was bombed by the Japanese in 1941, McCain was a submarine commanding officer. During World War II he commanded several submarines in the Atlantic and Pacific theaters of war, where he sunk a Japanese destroyer and more than 20,000 tons of enemy shipping. He was awarded the Bronze Star and Silver Star for distinguished service. After the war ended, McCain spent three years in the Pentagon as director of records in the Bureau of Naval Personnel, then served as commander of two submarine divisions. He spent part of 1950 as executive officer of a heavy cruiser, the *Saint Paul*. Later that year he returned to the Pentagon for two years to direct undersea warfare research development for the chief of naval operations during the Korean War (1950–1953). For the rest of the decade, McCain alternated between naval commands and service in the Pentagon. In 1959 he became a rear admiral and was appointed the navy's chief congressional liaison. From 1960 to 1962 he directed amphibious warfare training for the North Atlantic Treaty Organization (NATO), then returned to the Pentagon as chief of information.

In 1963 McCain was promoted to vice admiral and appointed commander of the amphibious forces of the Atlantic Fleet. As such, he was the operational commander of the U.S. forces that invaded the Dominican Republic during April and May 1965. Even though most commentators viewed the invasion as a hasty and unnecessary intervention, McCain accepted the rationale given by President Lyndon Johnson and told American audiences that the invasion was necessary "to see that Castro and the Cuban Communists do not get in." He was awarded the Legion of Merit.

For the next two years McCain served as military adviser to Arthur Goldberg, the U.S. delegate to the United Nations. Designated a full admiral in May 1967, McCain became commander in chief of U.S. naval forces in Europe. On 26 October 1967 his son, a naval pilot, was shot down and captured during a bombing raid over North Vietnam. On 11 April 1968 President Johnson appointed McCain as CINCPAC to replace Admiral U. S. Grant Sharp. At the same time Johnson named General Creighton W. Abrams to succeed General William Westmoreland as head of the U.S. ground forces in Vietnam. On 31 March 1968 Johnson had announced that he would not run for reelection, so McCain served most of his four years as CINCPAC under Johnson's successor, Richard Nixon.

In early 1969 McCain said in a *Reader's Digest* interview that the Vietnam War was a "testing ground" of a communist plan "to extend their domination over the world's peoples through wars of national liberation." Despite the 1968 Tet Offensive, he asserted: "We have the enemy licked now. He is beaten. We have the initiative in all areas. The enemy cannot achieve a military victory." His premature analysis was disavowed by the State Department.

With McCain's recommendation and support, Nixon enlarged the war through a joint U.S.–South Vietnamese invasion of Cambodia in 1970. The invasion failed to achieve its military objectives, caused extensive rioting in the United States, and led to a coup that toppled Cambodia's ruler, Prince Norodom Sihanouk. When the new Cambodian leader, Lon Nol, asked for U.S. military aid, McCain devised an extensive program to evade the Cooper-Church Amendment, with which Congress had prohibited the traditional type of military advisory group in Cambodia. McCain supported General Theodore Mataxis, the chief of the military aid team, who disregarded the advice of the U.S. ambassador to Cambodia, Mataxis's nominal superior. In late 1972, while Nixon and Henry Kissinger were negotiating the terms of the American withdrawal from Vietnam, McCain told a *U.S. News & World Report* writer: "There's no question that the South Vietnamese want us to stay. So do the Cambodians. As long as their independence is threatened by some external force, they're going to love the United States like a long-lost brother."

McCain retired on 1 November 1972 and was succeeded as CINCPAC by Admiral Noel Gaylor. McCain took up residence in Washington, D.C., where he served as president of the U.S. Strategic Institute, a think tank concerned with national security issues, and was publisher of *Strategic Review.* He also chaired the Veterans Administration's Monuments and Cemeteries Commission. While his son was a prisoner of war, McCain spent each Christmas at the demilitarized zone bordering North Vietnam.

In an exchange of prisoners in March 1973, the North Vietnamese released McCain's son, who had experienced more than five years of torture and close confinement. Several months later, a congressional investigation revealed that Admiral McCain and General Abrams, with the authorization of the Joint Chiefs of Staff, had ordered nighttime bombing raids targeting hospitals in North Vietnam and Cambodia in violation of the Geneva Convention. The results of the raids, which were excluded from the normal military after-action reports, were reported in "eyes only" messages to McCain and the chairman of the Joint Chiefs of Staff.

McCain took an active role in the 1978 debate over the two Panama Canal treaties signed by President Jimmy Carter. McCain and several other retired officers formed a Panama Canal Truth Squad and went on a speaking tour across the nation to criticize the treaties. McCain believed that transferring control of the canal to Panama would provide an opportunity for Soviet penetration of the Caribbean and Latin America and would jeopardize U.S. security.

McCain was returning from a vacation in Europe aboard a military transport when he experienced a heart attack. He was pronounced dead after the plane landed; he was buried in Arlington National Cemetery. In 1989 the U.S. Navy commissioned the USS *John S. McCain,* an Aegis-class destroyer named after McCain and his father.

★

McCain's naval records and some correspondence are at the Naval Historical Center, Washington Navy Yard, Washington, D.C. His correspondence with General Abrams is in the Abrams Collection, Center of Military History, Washington, D.C. McCain's role in the Dominican Republic invasion is mentioned in Abraham F. Lowenthal, *The Dominican Intervention* (1972). His work as CINCPAC is discussed in William Shawcross, *Sideshow: Kissinger, Nixon, and the Destruction of Cambodia* (1979), and Jeffrey J. Clarke, *United States Army in Vietnam: Advice and Support: The Final Years, 1965–1973* (1988). Interviews with McCain are John G. Hubbell, "In Vietnam, the Enemy Is Beaten," *Reader's Digest* (Feb. 1969); William F. Buckley, "Talk with an Admiral," *National Review* (Dec. 1969); John G. Hubbell, "Sentinel of the Pacific," *Reader's Digest* (Mar. 1970); and "If Vietnam War Ends," *U.S. News & World Report* (23 Oct. 1972). The congressional investigation of the hospital-bombing missions is described in the *New York Times* (9 Sept. 1973). Obituaries are in the *New York Times* and the *Washington Post* (both 24 Mar. 1981).

STEPHEN MARSHALL

McCALL, Thomas William Lawson (*b.* 22 March 1913 in Egypt, Massachusetts; *d.* 8 January 1983 in Portland, Oregon), governor of Oregon and environmentalist whose conservation policies had national influence.

The son of Dorothy Lawson and Henry McCall, who raised hay and alfalfa and operated a dairy, Thomas McCall, along with four siblings, grew up on his parents' 600-acre ranch near Prineville in central Oregon. He had two nationally prominent grandfathers, Samuel W. McCall, governor of Massachusetts, and the copper mogul Thomas W. Lawson. Although McCall was a lifelong Oregonian, he spoke with an upper-class New England accent.

From the age of four to eight, McCall had lived at Dreamwold, his grandfather Lawson's thousand-acre estate about thirty miles south of Boston. He attended the Derby Academy in Hingham, which was near the estate. When Lawson's fortunes declined and he lost the estate in 1922, the McCall children returned to Oregon.

McCall graduated from Redmond Union High School, where he was student body president, in 1932. Although

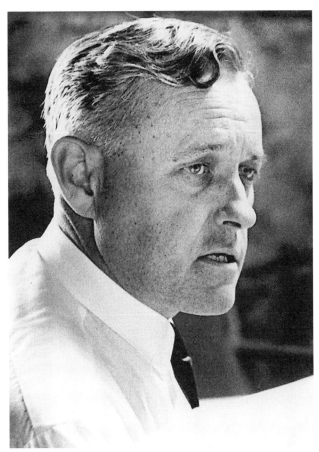

Thomas McCall. STEVE NEAL

his paternal grandfather's estate left funds for McCall's college education, his inheritance was insufficient to pay for an Ivy League education. While his grandfather Samuel had attended Dartmouth and his father had gone to Harvard, McCall attended the University of Oregon, graduating in 1936 with a bachelor's degree in journalism. Soon afterward, he was hired as a reporter by the *Bend Bulletin.* In February 1937 McCall moved to Idaho to work as a reporter for the Moscow *News-Review.* He married Audrey Owen on 20 May 1939. They had two sons, Thomas Lawson and Samuel Walker III, named for McCall's famous grandfathers.

In 1942 McCall joined the *Portland Oregonian* as a reporter. He covered police, sports, and the federal building. He also became a newscaster for KGW, an NBC radio station then owned by the *Oregonian.* During World War II, McCall enlisted in the navy and served as a correspondent in the Pacific in 1944 and 1945. Discharged as a seaman first class in January 1946, he resumed his career with radio station KEX in Portland.

From July 1949 until January 1952 McCall served as executive assistant to Oregon governor Douglas McKay. As McKay's chief aide, press spokesman, and troubleshooter, McCall ended a strike by inmates seeking better conditions at the state prison by offering to take their grievances to the state board of control. In late January 1952, he joined KGW radio as a political commentator and analyst.

In 1954 McCall ran as a Republican for the U.S. House of Representatives from Oregon's Third District. After upsetting sixteen-year incumbent Homer D. Angell in the primary, McCall narrowly lost the general election to Democrat Edith Green. He had gone into debt during the campaign, and now McCall had difficulty getting back into radio, as potential sponsors viewed him as too partisan. He worked briefly in public relations before being hired in June 1955 as a newscaster and commentator for Portland's KPTV. This job was also short-lived; he was fired in November 1956 for taking the side of a newsroom colleague in a dispute with management. From December 1956 until the spring of 1964, McCall was a commentator, a reporter, and the host of an interview program for KGW television. His most notable program was *Pollution in Paradise,* a 1961 documentary that showed how the Willamette River had become "an open sewer" for most of its 300 miles.

Still politically ambitious, McCall made his first bid for statewide office in 1964, winning election as Oregon's secretary of state. As a well-known television personality, he campaigned on the slogan "An old friend for a new task." In 1966, McCall moved up to the governorship, receiving 55.3 percent of the vote against Democratic state treasurer Robert W. Straub.

As governor, McCall launched a crusade to clean up and protect Oregon's environment. He broke precedent by testifying before a legislative committee on behalf of his environmental legislation and by naming himself as chairman of the State Sanitary Authority. "There is no more important task than to involve myself directly in the campaign against air and water pollution," he said. In the 1967 legislative session, McCall won approval for tougher standards of water quality and an enforcement plan for every industry and city on the state's waterways. He obtained $150 million in bonds for new sewage-treatment plants. The Willamette River became the focal point of McCall's effort. Within two years, salmon returned to the river and it was clean enough for swimming and boating.

When a 1967 court ruling questioned whether Oregon's 359 miles of Pacific beaches could be owned by the public, Governor McCall, with bipartisan support, signed a new law that protected public ownership and banned developers from construction on the shoreline.

In his first four years in office, McCall signed more than 100 environmental-protection measures into law. He led a successful protest in 1969 against the U.S. Army's plan to ship 13,000 tons of lethal nerve gas from Okinawa to a depot in eastern Oregon, filing a lawsuit against Defense

Secretary Melvin Laird before the Nixon administration backed down. Easily reelected in 1970, he pursued an ambitious agenda in his second term. In 1971 he signed the first state law in the nation that outlawed pull-tab cans and nonreturnable bottles. The law reduced the volume of highway litter by nearly half in its first two years and became a prototype for laws in other states.

McCall also dealt with the problems of uncontrolled land development and population growth. He declined to appear in commercials promoting Oregon tourism for this reason. Speaking before a national Jaycee convention in 1971, McCall invited the attendees to visit Oregon "again and again. But for heaven's sake, don't move here to live." He created the Land Conservation and Development Commission in 1973, giving the agency enforcement power. "The interests of Oregon for today and in the future must be protected from grasping wastrels of the land," McCall said. "Unlimited and unregulated growth leads inexorably to a lowered quality of life."

During the energy crisis of the 1970s, McCall was among the first political figures to show leadership in energy conservation. He lowered the state speed limit from seventy to fifty-five miles an hour, ordered a 20 percent cut in power consumption by state buildings, reduced highway lighting by half, and banned outdoor commercial lighting. In January 1974, McCall developed a program for voluntary gasoline rationing in which cars with odd- and even-numbered plates could get gasoline on alternate days. Most other states adopted McCall's plan.

A liberal Republican, McCall was among the first governors to call for Richard M. Nixon's resignation during the Watergate crisis. At six feet five inches, McCall was the tallest governor of his time and one of the more outspoken. He was ineligible under the Oregon constitution to run for a third consecutive term in 1974.

On leaving office, McCall taught for a year at Oregon State University, then moved to Portland in 1975 and joined KATU-TV as a news analyst and commentator. McCall attempted a political comeback in 1978 but lost the Republican primary for governor to Victor Aityeh. Conservatives and antienvironmental activists combined to help defeat McCall. He resumed his job as a television commentator and was involved in many environmental organizations. In the fall of 1982, although dying of cancer, McCall campaigned against a referendum that would have repealed his Oregon land-use planning law. McCall said he would rather die than "let the speculators build wall-to-wall condominiums." McCall won his last political battle. He died in Portland.

★

McCall's papers are at the Oregon Historical Society in Portland. The official records of his governorship are at the state archives in Salem. *Tom McCall: Maverick,* an autobiography with Steve Neal (1977), is an unusually candid political memoir. "Letter from Oregon" by E. J. Kahn, *New Yorker* (24 Feb. 1974), and "The Pacific Northwest" by Thomas Griffith, *Atlantic* (Apr. 1976), are useful portraits. An obituary is in the *New York Times* (9 Jan. 1983).

STEVE NEAL

McCORMICK, Frank Andrew ("Buck") (*b.* 9 June 1911 in the Bronx, New York; *d.* 21 November 1982 in Manhasset, New York), first baseman for the Cincinnati Reds, a seven-time all-star, and National League most valuable player in 1940.

McCormick was born in the Bronx, but his family moved to the Yorkville section of Manhattan before he began school. His father, Andrew McCormick, was a railroad worker and his mother, Ann McCormick, was a housewife; Frank had one sister. Athletic as a child, he attended St. Monica's parochial school in Yorkville, where he was a star

Frank McCormick. NATIONAL BASEBALL HALL OF FAME LIBRARY, COOPERSTOWN, N.Y.

basketball player. His first love was always baseball, however, and he practiced batting as a child by hitting stones outside his family's apartment.

After finishing high school McCormick worked packing antiques for the shipping department of the American Art Association on Fifty-seventh Street. In 1933 he took a week off to try out with the New York Giants at the Polo Grounds. Afterward McCormick received an unsigned letter saying that he would never master hitting the ball to right field. He was advised that, if he had a job, he should stop coming to the Polo Grounds, to avoid the risk of losing it. A tryout with the Yankees also failed to impress coaches.

Determined to be a professional ballplayer, he managed to land a spot on the roster of the semiprofessional Independents of Washington Heights in Manhattan, for whom he played the outfield. The manager of the Independents, George Halpin, encouraged him to switch to first base because of the overabundance of power-hitting outfielders in the major leagues. Halpin wrote letters to Bill Terry, manager of the Giants, and Joe McCarthy, manager of the Yankees, offering McCormick to either team for $100. Receiving no answer, Halpin wrote to Larry MacPhail, owner of the Cincinnati Reds, who passed McCormick's name to Frank Lane, head of the Reds' farm system. In the spring of 1934, McCormick was given a chance to try out with the Beckley, West Virginia, Class C minor league affiliate of the Reds. Borrowing $50 from his uncle for bus fare, McCormick landed a spot on the team and began his professional baseball career.

In 120 games for Beckley in 1934, McCormick batted .347, and after the minor league season ended he was called up to the Reds. In his first major league at bat against the Dodgers in Brooklyn, he smashed a single past second base. The Reds management was impressed, and the next season he reported to Toronto of the International League, a step below the majors. He fared poorly that season and was sent down to the Durham Bulls of the Piedmont League, where he hit .381 in 1936 and won the minor league batting title.

McCormick was again promoted to the Reds late in the 1937 season. In his first full year with the team in 1938 he batted .327 and played in every inning of every game. Remembering McCormick's letter of introduction, Reds owner Larry MacPhail sent George Halpin a check for $150 to cover the $100 Halpin had asked for McCormick and the $50 bus fare McCormick had borrowed from his uncle.

McCormick defied experts' predictions of a sophomore slump the next year by batting .332 and leading the league in runs batted in. In five of his eight seasons with the Reds he batted over .300. He led the league in hits in 1938, 1939, and 1940, in runs batted in during 1939, and in doubles in 1940, and he had the fewest strikeouts in 1938, 1939, and 1941. From 1938 through 1942, McCormick started in 652 consecutive games, at the time a record for a National

League first baseman. McCormick married Vera Preedy in Hamilton, Ohio, on 8 October 1938; the couple would have two daughters. They lived in Cincinnati during McCormick's playing, coaching, and broadcasting days and later settled on Long Island outside of New York City.

Tall, solidly built, and outgoing, McCormick resembled Lou Gehrig somewhat and was always willing to speak about his hitting. His best single year was 1940, when he hit .309 with 19 home runs and 127 runs batted in, led the league in doubles and hits, and was a driving force behind Cincinnati's World Series win. He won the National League Most Valuable Player award that year. Kept out of World War II because of a back problem, he continued with the Reds until the end of the 1945 season, after which he was sold to the Philadelphia Phillies. He played with the Phillies until he was released during the 1947 season. He joined the Boston Braves that year, playing part-time and helping them win the 1948 National League pennant. McCormick retired as a player at the end of the 1948 season, after being released by the Braves.

Following his career as a player, McCormick was a minor league manager with the Phillies from 1949 until 1951, when he became a scout for the Phillies. He rejoined the Reds as a scout the following year, remaining with them in that capacity through 1955. He coached for the Reds during the 1956 and 1957 seasons and was a television broadcaster for the team from 1958 until 1969. He returned to the New York City area in the early 1970s, living in Manhasset, Long Island. His last job was with the Yankees, where he worked in group- and season-ticket sales beginning in 1975. He was director of group sales from 1978 until shortly before his death, from cancer, at North Shore Hospital in Manhasset. He is buried in Manhasset.

McCormick had a long and impressive career as a baseball player. Over the course of thirteen seasons in the major leagues he batted .299, had 1,711 hits, 334 doubles, 128 home runs, and 954 runs batted in. He struck out only 189 times, an average of only once for every thirty at bats. Named to seven all-star teams, the six-feet-four-inch, 210-pound McCormick was surprisingly agile in the field. As a right-hander, McCormick was especially impressive at first base, a position usually reserved for left-handed fielders. Even late in his career he excelled at the position, playing 138 consecutive games without committing an error from 26 September 1945 to 23 September 1946.

★

The National Baseball Hall of Fame Library in Cooperstown, New York, maintains a file on McCormick with newspaper and magazine articles covering his career. Ira L. Smith, *Baseball's Famous First Basemen* (1956), Donald Honig, *Baseball When the Grass Was Real* (1975), and Richard Goldstein, *Spartan Seasons: How Baseball Survived the Second World War* (1980), all contain summaries of McCormick's major league accomplishments. Joseph L.

Reichler, ed., *The Baseball Encyclopedia* (1996), contains McCormick's statistical records. David L. Porter, ed., *The Biographical Dictionary of American Sports: Baseball* (1987), includes an entry on McCormick. An obituary is in the *New York Times* (24 Nov. 1982).

ANDREW S. TOMKO

MACDONALD, Dwight (*b*. 24 March 1906 in New York City; *d*. 19 December 1982 in New York City), editor, essayist, and critic known for his iconoclastic popular writings about politics, literature, and film.

Dwight Macdonald was born to what he called a "shabby-genteel" lineage—a once-prestigious Yankee family whose glory days and great wealth were behind it. His mother, Alice Hedges, was the daughter of an affluent Brooklyn, New York, merchant; his father, for whom he was named, was an attorney descended from a well-known New England family (the Dwights). He had one brother. Macdonald attended two top New York City private elementary schools, Collegiate School and Barnard School for Boys, and then Phillips Exeter Academy in New Hampshire. In 1924 he enrolled at Yale University, where he edited the humor magazine and wrote for the newspaper and literary magazine. He graduated in 1928 with a B.A. in history.

After an unfulfilling six months in an executive training program at Macy's department store in New York City, Macdonald began his journalistic career as an associate editor at the fledgling *Fortune* magazine, which was owned by the conservative publishing magnate Henry Luce. In the 1930s, Macdonald moved leftward in his politics, in part because of the influence of Nancy Gardiner Rodman, a Vassar graduate whom he married in 1934; they eventually had two sons. Reading Marx, Lenin, and Trotsky, Macdonald grew harshly critical of corporate capitalism and Luce's enthusiasm for it. While Macdonald succeeded in publishing an article that lauded the Communist party, he ended up resigning from *Fortune* in 1936, when his editors defanged a piece of his that assailed the "antiquated and inefficient practices" of the U.S. Steel Corporation.

Disenchanted with capitalism, Macdonald in 1937 joined with William Phillips, Philip Rahv, George L. K. Morris, and F. W. Dupee in reviving *Partisan Review*, a radical journal founded in 1934 that championed modernist culture and Marxist (specifically Trotskyist) politics. *Partisan Review* soon became the talk of the New York literary world for its original, trenchant, and wide-ranging thought, and over the next few decades, it became the premier forum for the essays of such writers as Sidney Hook, Mary McCarthy, Clement Greenberg, and Lionel Trilling, who later came to be known as the New York Intellectuals. Like the other editors at *Partisan Review*, Macdonald grew critical of

Dwight Macdonald. CORBIS-BETTMANN

Joseph Stalin's Soviet Union and the American Communist party, but Macdonald, ever the nonconformist, set out on his own idiosyncratic path, embracing anarchism and pacifism.

The political and intellectual battles among the New York Intellectuals were legend, and the question of U.S. involvement in World War II provoked heated debate. Many on the left, fearing Germany's fascism and anti-Semitism, signed on to the cause, but Macdonald dissented and in 1943 left *Partisan Review*. Macdonald's pacifism could both blind him and give him uncommon insight. When others rejoiced in America's victory over Japan, Macdonald boldly condemned the dropping of the atomic bomb, although that same moral righteousness was lacking earlier in the war, when he had downplayed Nazi atrocities against the Jews.

In February 1944, Dwight and Nancy Macdonald founded a new journal, *Politics*. By then his trademark style—witty, unsparing, often caustic, but always concerned with moral implications—had fully emerged. The Macdonalds ran *Politics* on a shoestring, and its out-of-the-garage feel was part of its appeal. Macdonald published influential essays by such thinkers as Hannah Arendt, Bruno Bettelheim, Albert Camus, and C. Wright Mills when they were still little known. Macdonald contributed one of his most enduring essays to the journal, entitled "The Root Is Man" (1946), which tried to reconcile Marxism and its deterministic laws with an individualistic humanism. That essay and a sequel were published as a book in 1953. He also wrote *Henry Wallace: The Man and the Myth* (1948), a profile of the left-wing vice president and presidential candidate that ridiculed Wallace's naiveté.

About this time, the Macdonalds were having marital problems, and, after folding *Politics* in 1949, they divorced in 1954. Soon after, he married Gloria Lanier, an art historian he had been seeing for some time. Meanwhile, in 1951 he had taken a job as a staff writer at the *New Yorker*, a magazine then regarded by intellectuals as lacking in heft. Macdonald, however, used his perch to preach rigorous cultural standards. Macdonald's critiques—a fusion of H. L. Mencken's contempt for the "booboisie" and the New York Intellectuals' post-Holocaust fear of mass movements—reached its apotheosis in his most famous essay, "Masscult and Midcult" (1960), which explicitly excoriated mass culture (crassly commercial work) and middlebrow culture (which masquerades as high art while dumbing it down for popular consumption). Another of his influential pieces extolled Michael Harrington's *The Other America: Poverty in the United States* (1962) and helped turn President John F. Kennedy's attention to the country's dire poverty. Macdonald collected these and earlier essays in *Memoirs of a Revolutionist* (1957) and *Against the American Grain* (1962); he also published a study of philanthropy, *The Ford Foundation: The Men and the Millions* (1956).

In the 1960s, Macdonald continued to harangue the purveyors of safe, unchallenging entertainment as a movie critic for *Esquire* magazine from 1960 to 1966 and for NBC's *Today Show*. Having earned a reputation as an incisive and exacting critic—memorably ridiculing such popular film stars as Charlton Heston and Paul Newman—he anthologized his film commentary in *Dwight Macdonald on Movies* (1969). In the 1960s, Macdonald also found a cause that renewed his interest in politics—the protest movement against the Vietnam War. In 1965 he accepted an invitation to a White House Festival of the Arts, at which he collected signatures for a petition against President Lyndon Johnson and the war. The next year, announcing it was time for a change, he traded in his film reviewing at *Esquire* for a political column. In 1967, the six-foot-tall Macdonald, sporting a white goatee, marched on the Pentagon, an event Norman Mailer immortalized in *The Armies of the Night* (1968). In 1969, when Columbia University students took over the president's office and other campus buildings, Macdonald, in contrast to his generally distraught peers, relished the upheaval. Told by his friend F. W. Dupee, a Columbia professor, to come see the spec-

tacle, Macdonald toured the campus like a celebrity and declared his "almost joyous excitement."

In 1970 he was elected to the National Institute of Arts and Letters, and the following year, he retired from the *New Yorker*. Macdonald's literary output began to decline, and he began drinking heavily. He sojourned in different parts of the country on visiting professorships. His final collection of writings, *Discriminations*, a survey of his life's work, appeared in 1974. He died of heart failure.

Macdonald's long and productive career, coupled with his fearlessness in writing about topics from politics to culture, made him the epitome of critics who engaged a wide, literate public. His cutting humor, exacting cultural standards, and continued devotion to the left (even as many of his peers moved rightward) ensured that his voice would remain distinctive and influential long after his death.

★

Macdonald's *Memoirs of a Revolutionist: Essays in Political Criticism* (1957) is less a memoir than a collection of essays, but that work and *Discriminations: Essays and Afterthoughts, 1938–1974* (1974) are valuable in tracing his life's work. Several of his other essays or collections of essays were also published as books. The definitive, if highly sympathetic, biography is Michael Wreszin, *A Rebel in Defense of Tradition: The Life and Politics of Dwight Macdonald* (1994). Stephen J. Whitfield, *A Critical American: The Politics of Dwight Macdonald* (1984), and Gregory Sumner, *Dwight Macdonald and the Politics Circle: The Challenge of Cosmopolitan Democracy* (1996) are narrower works.

For the life and times of the New York Intellectuals, see Alexander Bloom, *Prodigal Sons: The New York Intellectuals and Their World* (1986), and Alan Wald, *The New York Intellectuals: The Rise and Decline of the Anti-Stalinist Left from the 1930s to the 1980s* (1987). In newspapers and magazines, profiles and reviews of Wreszin's book provide useful biographical summaries, including *Commentary* (July 1994), *New Leader* (6 June 1994), and *New York Times* (1 May 1994). An obituary is in the *New York Times* (20 Dec. 1982).

DAVID GREENBERG

MACDONALD, Ross (*b.* 13 December 1915 in Los Gatos, California; *d.* 11 July 1983 in Santa Barbara, California), novelist noted for his hard-boiled detective series featuring private eye Lew Archer.

Ross Macdonald was born Kenneth Millar, the only child of John Macdonald Millar, a journalist, and Anne Moyer, a nurse. Not long afterward, the family moved to Vancouver, British Columbia, Canada, where John Millar worked as a harbor pilot. Millar deserted his family when Kenneth was three. Anne Millar, whose health was poor, could not support herself and her son. Kenneth lived with various relatives in western Canada and Ontario, sometimes with his mother, sometimes separated from her. He graduated from the Kitchener-Waterloo Collegiate and Vocational School in Kitchener, Ontario, in 1932 and was grateful to land a job working on a farm for meals and lodging.

His father died later that year and left Millar an insurance policy worth $2,500. The money enabled him to enroll in the University of Western Ontario in 1933. After his mother's death in 1935, he took a year off in 1936–1937 to travel in Europe. On his return he reencountered Margaret Ellen Sturm, whom he had known casually in high school. They married on 2 June 1938, the day after his graduation. He earned a teaching certificate at the University of Toronto in 1939 and their only child was born shortly thereafter. From 1939 to 1941 he taught English and history at the Kitchener-Waterloo school.

In 1941 Millar was awarded a graduate fellowship to study English at the University of Michigan. That same year Margaret Millar published her first mystery, *The Invisible Worm*. She eventually published twenty-six books, and Kenneth Millar always gave her a good deal of credit for his own subsequent success.

Millar earned his M.A. in English at the University of Michigan in 1942. In the fall of 1943 he wrote a spy thriller, *The Dark Tunnel* (1944). In 1944, Millar entered the U.S. Naval Reserve, serving as a communications officer on an escort carrier in the Pacific. While at sea he finished work on his second spy novel, *Trouble Follows Me* (1946). When Millar was discharged from the navy in March 1946, he joined his wife and daughter in Santa Barbara, California. During the next nine months, "in a kind of angry rapture," he wrote *Blue City* (1947), a hard-boiled mystery, and *The Three Roads* (1948), a psychological mystery. Both were published by Alfred A. Knopf.

Next, Millar tried to write a novel based on his Canadian youth but got hopelessly bogged down. In 1948 he decided to return to Michigan to complete work on his doctorate. To help finance the move he wrote *The Moving Target* (1949), a detective novel in the hard-boiled tradition of Dashiell Hammett and Raymond Chandler and featuring private eye Lew Archer. "I was in trouble, and Lew Archer got me out of it," he later wrote. Knopf considered *The Moving Target* a comedown from his previous two books and was reluctant to publish it. Millar suggested that his agents offer it to other publishers under a pseudonym. Knopf eventually published it, under the pseudonym John Macdonald (after Millar's father). In the second Lew Archer book the pseudonym became John Ross Macdonald to avoid confusion with John D. MacDonald, who also wrote private-eye fiction.

Millar wrote three Archer novels in the next three years—*The Drowning Pool* (1950), *The Way Some People Die* (1951), and *The Ivory Grin* (1952). He and his family returned to Santa Barbara after he completed work on his

Ph.D., which was awarded in 1952. His dissertation, which he never published, was titled "The Inward Eye: A Revaluation of Coleridge's Psychological Criticism." *Meet Me at the Morgue* (1953) was a non-Archer mystery. Lew Archer returned in *Find a Victim* (1954), and with *The Barbarous Coast* (1956) Millar settled on the pseudonym Ross Macdonald.

At this point many of Macdonald's hallmarks were already apparent. His novels were tough and unsentimental but contained little overt violence. His plotting was intricate. He specialized in the reverse (sometimes a double reverse or a triple reverse), in which an additional piece of information would turn previously known facts in a totally different direction.

Macdonald once again began toying with an autobiographical novel, but family problems intervened. In February 1956 his daughter, then seventeen, was involved in a vehicular homicide. She was given eight years probation and ordered to undergo psychiatric treatment. The family moved temporarily to Menlo Park near San Francisco, not far from where Macdonald had been born. "Seismic disturbances occurred in my life," he later wrote. "My half-suppressed Canadian years, my whole childhood and youth, rose like a corpse from the bottom of the sea to confront me." He underwent psychotherapy in 1956 and 1957. The personal turmoil changed his approach to his writing, and there would be echoes of his daughter, who died in 1970 of a cerebral hemorrhage, in the troubled teenagers who populated so many of his novels.

With *The Doomsters* (1958), Macdonald felt that he had begun to make a departure from the conventional hard-boiled detective novel. But he considered *The Galton Case* (1959) his real breakthrough: "I made up my mind that the convention of the detective novel, in which I had been working for fifteen years, would be able to contain the materials of my most ambitious and personal work so far." *The Ferguson Affair* (1960) was Macdonald's last non-Archer novel. Seven Lew Archer novels followed in the next nine years: *The Wycherly Woman* (1961); *The Zebra-Striped Hearse* (1962); *The Chill* (1964); *The Far Side of the Dollar* (1965); *Black Money* (1966); *The Instant Enemy* (1968); and *The Goodbye Look* (1969). It was with these novels that Macdonald truly hit his stride.

The sale of *The Moving Target* to the movies (where it became *Harper,* 1966) eased financial pressures. (Although both Ross Macdonald and Margaret Millar published regularly, their joint income had rarely exceeded that of a high-school teacher.) With *The Goodbye Look,* Macdonald finally received serious critical attention. In a front-page article in the *New York Times Book Review* (1 June 1969), William Goldman called the Archer novels "the finest series of detective novels ever written by an American." *The Goodbye Look* was Macdonald's first best-seller. *The Underground*

Man (1971) also received rave reviews and reached best-seller status. Macdonald was compared directly to Hammett and Chandler, and a few even argued that he was their superior.

With Macdonald's next novel, *Sleeping Beauty* (1971), the inevitable backlash set in, and several critics argued that his reputation was inflated. *The Blue Hammer* (1976), his last novel, was a bit mellower than the others, a deliberate decision according to Macdonald. Critical opinion of his last two books is mixed. Some consider them among his very best. Others feel they are a cut below his powerhouse books of the 1960s. In fact, Macdonald's output is remarkably consistent, and choosing the best of the Archer novels is very much a matter of personal taste.

Macdonald was unable to put the work he had intended into his collection of autobiographical essays, *Self-Portrait: Ceaselessly into the Past* (1981), because of the onset of Alzheimer's disease in 1980. He died of complications from the disease. His ashes were scattered in the Santa Barbara Channel.

★

Ross Macdonald, *Self-Portrait: Ceaselessly into the Past* (1981), contains valuable autobiographical information but is not a complete work. The most complete biography is Matthew J. Bruccoli, *Ross Macdonald* (1984). Valuable insights into Macdonald's life and personality can be found in the essays, many by close friends, in Ralph B. Sipper, ed., *Inward Journey: Ross Macdonald* (1984). Critical evaluations include Peter Wolfe, *Dreamers Who Live Their Dreams: The World of Ross Macdonald's Novels* (1976); Jerry Speir, *Ross Macdonald* (1978); Jeffrey Howard Mahan, *A Long Way from Solving That One: Psycho/Social and Ethical Implications of Ross Macdonald's Lew Archer Tales* (1990); and Bernard A. Schopen, *Ross Macdonald* (1990). A complete bibliography of published essays about Macdonald and reviews of his work is in Robert E. Skinner, *The Hard-Boiled Explicator: A Guide to the Study of Dashiell Hammett, Raymond Chandler, and Ross Macdonald* (1985). An obituary appears in the *New York Times* (13 July 1983).

LYNN HOOGENBOOM

MACHITO (Frank Raúl Grillo) (*b*. 16 February 1908? in Tampa, Florida; *d*. 15 April 1984 in London, England), the "King of Afro-Cuban jazz," vocalist and bandleader for the highly popular group Afro-Cubans.

Soon after his birth (which may have been in 1908, 1909, or 1912), Frank Raúl Grillo moved with his family to Havana, Cuba. He was nicknamed Machito, the diminutive form of Macho, because he was the first son after three daughters. His father, Rogelio Grillo, ran a restaurant, and the young Machito often played and sang with his father's employees as well as with the workers in the sugar mills to whom his father delivered meals of beans and rice—in ex-

Machito. METRONOME/ARCHIVE PHOTOS

change for invitations to night-long musical parties. He grew up in a black neighborhood of Havana where he heard complex rhythms of African origin and the drums on which they were played. Inspired by the leading Cuban musician Champito, Machito was determined to learn to play the maracas. He played them and sang backup with several groups in Havana before moving to New York City in 1937.

Machito found New York City, and Harlem in particular, "fantastic"; it was filled with musical energy, hope, and excitement. His close friend (and, later, brother-in-law) Mario Bauza, a trumpet player and arranger who would become a lifelong collaborator and musical partner, had already established himself on the jazz scene as musical director for Chick Webb and Cab Calloway. Machito moved in with Bauza and began going to the Savoy Ballroom every night (it was two blocks away) to hear Webb play "jazz you could dance to"; he also took in the music of other swing bands. He landed a brief job as a singer with Xavier Cugat, who was known for adapting Latin music to appeal to a non-Latin, more mainstream audience.

The poor economy in Puerto Rico, which had caused many Latinos to come to New York, led to creation of the El Barrio section of Harlem and a consequent strong demand for Latin music and radio programming. In July 1940 Bauza and Machito formed the Afro-Cubans, a band of black and Latin musicians who played authentic Cuban rhythms in the big-band style. While Machito served in the U.S. Army during 1943, Bauza continued to direct the Afro-Cubans, using his own orchestrations to take their music in a significantly new direction. He began combining Cuban sounds, rhythms, and percussion instruments (specifically, the conga drum) with American big-band harmonies, improvisational styles, and brass instruments. The result was "Cubop" or "Afro-Cuban" music; the tune "Tanga" (1943) was an immediate hit. When Machito returned (discharged from the army because of an injury), he welcomed Bauza's innovations and helped make the Afro-Cubans into a top dance band in New York. They established themselves as the house band for the club La Conga, and Machito's younger sister began to sing with the group.

In the mid-to-late 1940s, important years for jazz, bebop musicians were taking a serious interest in Machito's work. Machito and the Afro-Cubans collaborated and recorded with jazz greats such as Charlie Parker, Flip Phillips, Buddy Rich, and Dizzy Gillespie; their audience consequently expanded even further. Machito appeared in the Columbia picture *Tropical Nights* (1946). In 1947, to honor him, Stan Kenton wrote the song "Machito"; the same year Kenton and Machito combined forces in a historic concert at Town Hall in New York City. In "The Afro-Cuban Jazz Suite" (1948), which featured Parker and Phillips with Machito's band, the frenetic energies and precise execution of Cuban music provided rich rhythmic counterpoint to moody saxophone lines, thus proving wrong certain critics who claimed that Cubans could not play jazz. Machito's sounds and rhythms began to influence small jazz ensembles in addition to big bands. During this period the Afro-Cubans regularly played at the Royal Roost, Bop City, and the Apollo Theater.

At the same time, the Afro-Cubans continued to dominate the Latin dance scene, moving from playing rumbas and tangos in the 1940s to mambos in the 1950s and 1960s. In the 1950s a racially integrated group, often including celebrities, would go to the Palladium, "the birthplace of Latin music," for the Wednesday night mambo show. Machito and the Afro-Cubans also dominated the salsa scene of the 1970s and 1980s. Machito, whose artistic emphasis was on providing entertaining, danceable music, always considered his group a dance band. "In bad times, we have our music to sustain us," he said of the Latin community.

In their later years Machito and the Afro-Cubans inspired and guided a new generation of Latin musicians, including Tito Puente, who played with them briefly. In 1982 the recording *Machito and His Salsa Big Band* won a

Grammy Award; the same year Carlos Ortiz produced a documentary entitled *Machito*. Even after he became a successful and well-known musician, Machito continued to live in the Bronx, where neighbors considered him a down-to-earth, unpretentious man. Throughout his life Machito referred to his wife, Gilda Asther Porres, whom he married 19 April 1940, and their five children as his primary love in life. Until he suffered a fatal stroke while waiting to go on stage at a London club, the Afro-Cubans continued a rigorous international touring schedule.

Although he had fourteen recordings to his credit (over four decades) and a highly evident international influence, Machito was largely ignored by music scholars until the 1990s. It is now clear that his importance in the history of jazz and Latin music cannot be overestimated. With Bauza, Machito, always the more visible of the two, joined two worlds of music and forever changed jazz history. While some consider his musical contributions to be a continuation of "the Spanish Tinge," a trend started by Jelly Roll Morton in New Orleans, in truth the Machito phenomenon provided much more than a "tinge" to American jazz. In addition to his outstanding musical contributions, Machito's pride in Latin culture and his ability to cross cultural boundaries through music set valuable examples for musicians everywhere.

★

See *Machito: A Jazz Legacy,* a documentary by Carlos Ortiz (1982); Michael Erlewine, ed., *All Music Guide to Jazz,* 2d ed. (1996); Max Salazar, liner notes to *The Original Mambo Kings,* Polygram/Verve Records (1993). Obituaries are in the *New York Times* (17 Apr. 1984) and *Down Beat* (July 1984).

SARAH MARKGRAF

MacINNES, Helen Clark (*b.* 7 October 1907 in Glasgow, Scotland; *d.* 30 September 1985 in New York City), writer known for her best-selling espionage novels.

The only daughter of Donald McInnes, a businessman, and Jessica Cecilia Sutherland McDiarmid, Helen would later adopt a variant spelling of the family surname. When she was five years old, the family moved to Helensburgh, a residential town in Dumbartonshire, a popular resort at the entrance to the Gareloch on the Clyde estuary. For MacInnes and her only brother, Ian, it was an ideal setting in which to grow up. MacInnes graduated from the Hermitage School in Helensburgh in 1924, at age sixteen. She then attended the Girl's High School in Glasgow for a year before entering Glasgow University. In her first week as a freshman MacInnes met sophomore Gilbert Highet, who she married seven years later. While at the university, MacInnes continued her previous study of languages, and she graduated with an M.A. in French and German in 1928.

Helen MacInnes autographing copies of *Above Suspicion* for the British War Relief Society, 1941. UPI/
CORBIS-BETTMANN

After graduation, she became a member of the university library staff as a special cataloger of the Ferguson Collection of early printed books. She then worked a year for the Education Authority of Dumbartonshire, selecting books for libraries in the county. In 1930 MacInnes enrolled in the School of Librarianship of University College, London, earning her degree in librarianship in 1931. She later attributed her attention to detail and historical accuracy to her training as a librarian.

On 22 September 1932 MacInnes married Highet, a classics scholar. They had been engaged for seven years while Highet worked toward his degrees, first at Glasgow, then at Balliol College, Oxford. In those days an Oxford don, which Highet had become, was not allowed to marry, but the university made an exception in Highet's case. MacInnes noted in an interview: "I think we were the first ever to break that barrier." Their only child was born in 1933. The blue-eyed, dark-haired MacInnes often played lead roles in productions by the Oxford Dramatic Society and the Oxford Experimental Theatre. For the next few years Highet and MacInnes collaborated in translating books from German into English. *Sexual Life in Ancient Rome* by

Otto Kiefer was published in 1934 and *Friedrich Engels: A Biography* by Gustav Mayer in 1936. MacInnes published these translations under her married name, and the couple used the money to finance their European travels during the summers. Personal experiences during these travels would later become part of her novels.

In 1937 Highet was invited to teach at Columbia University in New York City for a year. Before the year was over, he had agreed to remain at Columbia as professor of Greek and Latin. In 1938 the family left Oxford and settled in New York City. Because Highet served in the British army during and after World War II, they did not become U.S. citizens until 1951.

During their honeymoon in Bavaria in 1932, just a few months before Adolf Hitler came to power, MacInnes and Highet were increasingly disturbed by the developing Nazi movement. Although MacInnes initially saw Hitler as "rather a comic figure," she changed her mind after witnessing the crowd's reaction to a speech he gave in Munich: "He got them." MacInnes began a journal documenting events and predicting what the Nazis would do. After reading it Highet suggested that "it's about time to write your novel." Some years before, MacInnes had started filling a notebook with information for a novel about Mad King Theodore of Abyssinia. She never wrote this novel, but in 1939 she began work on *Above Suspicion* (1941).

Above Suspicion is about an Oxford don and his wife (MacInnes insisted the novel was not autobiographical) who go to prewar Germany seeking a British anti-Nazi agent. MacInnes tells a good story, but what is significant about the novel is her depiction of the Germans' attitude on the eve of war and the refusal of many English to believe that another war would soon begin. The novel became a best-seller and was made into a film in 1943 starring Joan Crawford and Fred MacMurray. In an interview for *Publishers Weekly* some years later, MacInnes said about this film and others based on her books, "All the films of my books have been a mess. They always seem to change all the characters around. . . . [I]t makes the plots incomprehensible."

Her next book, *Assignment in Brittany* (1942), was also well received. Always conscious of making the settings of her novels "as factual as I can make them," she noted that after the war she met veterans who had tried to track down the places described in this book. Because the novel was about the French Resistance and might be read by Nazis, MacInnes was careful not to depict actual locations. What was "real" was her description of the difficulties of undercover work in an occupied country. The military used the novel to train Allied personnel who would be working covertly in German-occupied France. This novel was also made into a film in 1943 with Susan Peters and Jean-Pierre Aumont.

While MacInnes was writing these books, Highet was working for British intelligence. The novels were so accurate with reference to places, events, and espionage techniques that British authorities made a check on MacInnes to determine whether Highet had given away any official secrets. Her next book, *While Still We Live* (1944), which is set in Poland just before, during, and after the Nazi invasion, alarmed a Polish general who was worried about where she was getting her information. He was amazed that her names, places, and history were so accurate. During the war years she also wrote the novel *Horizon* (1945).

After World War II, following the advice of critics and publishers, MacInnes changed pace and wrote *Friends and Lovers* (1947), an autobiographical story of the Highets, and *Rest and Be Thankful* (1949), which is set in Wyoming. Neither was popular. Later she would write a play, her one venture into another genre. *Home Is the Hunter: A Comedy in Two Acts* (1964) is about the return of Ulysses to Ithaca. This, too, was not a popular success.

In 1951 MacInnes resumed writing spy thrillers. Allen Dulles, former head of the Central Intelligence Agency, described her as a master of the genre. Her novels were concerned with the threat of both physical and psychological aggression against the democratic system in the form of terrorist movements and war, lies and disinformation. Subjects ranged from the infiltration of the publishing industry by communists and fellow travelers in *Neither Five nor Three* (1951) to investigations into the activities of former Nazis and neo-Nazis in *The Salzburg Connection* (1968), which was made into a film in 1972 with Barry Newman and Anna Karina. The subject of *The Salzburg Connection*, like that of so many of her books, stemmed from her reading and analyzing newspaper articles. A newspaper account of an empty grave where a Nazi war criminal supposedly had been buried formed the germ of her novel *The Double Image* (1966). Reports of communist manipulation of the Algerian Organisation de L'Armée Secrète (OAS) for anti-West purposes led to *The Venetian Affair* (1963), which was made into a film in 1967 with Robert Vaughn and Elke Sommer.

Increasing concern with terrorism resulted in *The Hidden Target* (1980) and its sequel, *Cloak of Darkness* (1982). MacInnes's final novel, *Ride a Pale Horse* (1984), focuses on communist defectors and disinformation. The novel was near the top of the paperback best-seller list when MacInnes died from a stroke.

Despite some negative reviews from critics who believed her characters were too one-dimensional, her details too meticulous, and her political remarks, those of a self-admitted Jeffersonian Democrat, too frequent, MacInnes had a tremendous following of readers who awaited the publication of each novel. She became known as the "queen of international espionage fiction." Her twenty-one novels sold more than 23 million copies in the United States alone and were translated into twenty-two languages. The mixture of espionage, European settings, and romance did not fail to please, although the hero did not always get the girl. Yet, even the bittersweet ending of *Prelude to Terror* (1978), where the heroine is killed, has a feeling of hope in a job well done. That novel is dedicated to "Gilbert, my dear companion who has gone ahead on the final journey," and his death is reflected in the ending. The fictional lovers may be separated by death, but the remaining one will live as a reminder that liberty, according to MacInnes, is maintained only by personal sacrifice and "unceasing vigilance."

★

MacInnes's manuscripts are at Princeton University Library. Interviews with her include Robert Van Gelder, *Writers and Writing* (1946); Roy Newquist, *Counterpoint* (1964); and John F. Baker, "Helen MacInnes," *Publishers Weekly* (17 June 1974). A complete list of her writings is in *Contemporary Authors*, New Revision Series (1990). Biographical information is in Stanley J. Kunitz, ed., *Twentieth Century Authors, First Supplement: A Biographical Dictionary of Modern Literature* (1955); Harry Gilroy, "Doubling in Spies Suits Miss M'Innes," *New York Times* (8 Jan. 1966). Biographical information and critiques of her novels are in Frank N. Magill, ed., *Critical Survey of Mystery and Detective Fiction: Authors* (1988), and Gina Macdonald, "Helen MacInnes," in *British Mystery and Thriller Writers Since 1940, First Series,* edited by Bernard Benstock and Thomas F. Staley (1989). Excerpts of reviews of selected novels are in *Contemporary Literary Criticism* 27 (1984). For critiques of the novels as representative of the genre, see Mary H. Becker, "Politics in the Spy Novels of Helen MacInnes and Dorothy Gilman," *Proceedings of the Fifth National Convention of the Popular Culture Association* (1975): 748–754, and Mary K. Boyd, "The Enduring Appeal of the Spy Thrillers of Helen MacInnes," *Clues* 4 (fall/winter 1983): 66–75. Obituaries are in the *New York Times* (1 Oct. 1985) and *Chicago Tribune* and *Los Angeles Times* (both 2 Oct. 1985).

MARCIA B. DINNEEN

MACKEY, Joseph Creighton (*b.* 24 January 1910 near Lancaster, Ohio; *d.* 14 February 1982 in Davie, Florida), stunt pilot and aviation entrepreneur.

The son of William L. Mackey and Besse Creighton, Joseph grew up on a family farm doing chores and herding sheep. In 1921 the family moved to Columbus, Ohio, after which his father became president of the Maco Tile Company of Cleveland. He graduated from State High School in Cleveland. He began his flying career in Cleveland in 1926 under Cliff March, learning to pilot an OX-5 Eaglerock aircraft. He worked as an aviation mechanic for $2 a week and an hour's flight lesson. Determined to build a future in the air, by 1927 he had found employment with the Thompson Aeronautical Corporation and later with the Stewart Aircraft Corporation in Cleveland. In 1929 he joined the Curtiss Wright Flying Service at Port Columbus, where he served as an instructor, flew passengers, and did exhibition flying.

By 1931 Mackey and several associates had purchased the Golden Eagle factory at Port Columbus and moved it to Lancaster, where they built and sold twenty-seven airplanes at minimal profit. To earn more money Mackey began to stage air shows on Sunday afternoons. He also formed the Lancaster Flying Club, whose seventeen members he taught to fly during manufacturing lulls. He not only managed his small-town air shows but also carried about 120 passengers to them, two at a time in a Waco J-5, and then put on five exhibitions.

In 1935 Mackey started doing aerial advertising work for the Ohio Oil Company (later the Marathon Oil Company) by forming the Mackey Flying Service to do skywriting, neon-sign flying, and banner towing. Mackey named his aggregation of pilots the Linco Flying Aces after the brand of gasoline they hawked. The service later purchased a Laird Super-Solution, the winner of the 1931 Thompson Trophy Race. Mackey's Waco J-5, with an all-metal fuselage

Joseph Mackey in front of an airplane used for skywriting, 1936. UPI/ CORBIS-BETTMANN

rounded out for speed, was used for skywriting and low-level inverted flying, while a smaller Wasp-engine-powered Speed-wing Laird did skywriting and speed dashes at air meets. Several other ships did skywriting, towed signs, and carried neon signs after dark.

Mackey's ambitious, entrepreneurial spirit moved him to enroll in army correspondence courses, which led to a commission in the U.S. Army Air Corps Reserve in 1932. Lieutenant Mackey flew in several U.S. Army war games at Louisville and Indianapolis and was attached to the 308th Observation Squadron at Port Columbus. The year 1936 found him busier than ever, with six pilots working for him. That same year Mackey flew in the All-American Maneuvers at Miami, Florida, where he would spend much of the rest of his life. At the maneuvers he flew so well that he was awarded the Freddie Lund trophy for acrobatic flying and three other cups for outstanding airmanship. Later in 1936 Mackey represented the United States at the International Air Games in France. Mackey's airmanship delighted the French, and upon his departure he received two medals, a $10,000 check, and an air escort five miles out to sea. He married Frances Monarch on 28 August 1938 and had two children.

Because he had a competitive personality, and because he was asked by Roscoe Turner, a racer and a fellow pioneer aviator, Mackey entered the radial-engine-powered Golden Bullet Wendell-Williams No. 57 in the Thompson Trophy Race in 1939. He had lost the Bendix Trophy Race to Jackie Cochran in the same aircraft the year before. The Bullet's radial power plant overheated during the last part of the Thompson race, causing Mackey to throttle back to avoid damaging his engine, thus giving him a fourth-place finish in the grueling contest behind Turner's first place. This was the last of the truly great pre–World War II Cleveland National Air Races.

With the advent of World War II, Mackey entered the world of multiengine aircraft by ferrying bombers from Canada to England, during which time he endured several crashes. In 1941 he crashed in the Canadian wilderness, killing Sir Frederick Banting, the discoverer of insulin. Mackey survived for four days after the disaster by eating oranges. With his transoceanic experience and the rank of colonel, Mackey also took command of the Army Air Corps base at Miami, Florida, from which he dispatched aircraft and cargo across the South Atlantic to Africa and India.

In 1946 Mackey acquired three Lockheed Lodestars and put his wartime experience to use by starting Mackey Airline at Forman Field in Davie, Florida. For thirty-five years it served the Bahamas from south Florida airports. In 1967 he sold his airline for $19 million to Eastern Airlines. Unhappy with retirement, he founded Mackey International in 1968; it operated between Florida and smaller islands in the Bahamas. This new venture ran into trouble a decade later, filed for bankruptcy, and was taken over by Charter Air Corporation, a Gainesville, Florida-based carrier. Mackey stayed with the company briefly as president and chairman of the board but finally quit in 1978.

Having survived inverted flying, speed dashes, war, crashes, overheated engines, and mechanical failures, Mackey died of natural causes and was buried in Fort Lauderdale, Florida.

★

Mackey's papers are held by Eastern Airlines and Marathon Oil Company. His flying exploits are detailed in Bill Sweet, *They Call Me Mister Air Show* (1972), and *Antique Airplane News* of late 1956 and early 1957. There is an entry for Mackey in *Who's Who in Aviation 1942–1943* (1943). An obituary is in the *New York Times* (16 Feb. 1982).

LAWRENCE CARROLL ALLIN

MacLEISH, Archibald (*b.* 7 May 1892 in Glencoe, Illinois; *d.* 20 April 1982 in Boston, Massachusetts), poet, playwright, journalist, lawyer, statesman, and professor who was one of the most influential modern American men of letters.

MacLeish was the son of twice-widowed Andrew MacLeish and his third wife, Martha Hillard. His stern Glasgow-born father was an early settler of Chicago and had become a prosperous partner in a leading department store. His Vassar-educated mother, who traced her lineage to the *Mayflower* colonists, had been a college instructor. MacLeish, who had four full siblings and two stepsisters and a stepbrother, grew up in an affluent family that prized education. Initially a difficult child and mediocre student, MacLeish was sent at fifteen to start over at the Hotchkiss School in Lakeville, Connecticut. Although his four years at prep school were unhappy, he emerged as a leader in athletics, scholarship, and writing. In 1911 he entered Yale College.

MacLeish's achievements at Yale not only were outstanding in their own right, they also displayed the extraordinary diversity that distinguished his later career. Captain of the water-polo team, center of the football team, chair-

Archibald MacLeish, *c.* 1960. OSCAR WHITE/CORBIS

man of *Yale Literary Magazine,* and class poet, he was chosen for Skull and Bones, the university's elite secret society
(a membership that subsequently proved helpful on many
occasions). At graduation in 1915 fellow classmates overwhelmingly voted him "most brilliant" and "most versatile." By then MacLeish had already chosen his future wife,
Ada Taylor Hitchcock; recognized his poetic vocation; and
reluctantly planned a career in law.

By the time MacLeish graduated first in his class from
Harvard Law School in 1919, he had become a husband,
father, war veteran, and published poet. After successfully
completing his first year of law school, he gained his father's permission to marry Ada on 21 June 1916. They had
four children, one of whom died as an infant. When the
United States entered World War I a few months later, Mac-
Leish enlisted as a private in Yale's hospital unit, "so as to
do the right thing but not get hurt," but soon shifted to a
combat unit to pursue a commission. In the meantime Yale
University Press published his first collection of poems,
Tower of Ivory (1917). He returned from the war a captain.
After law school MacLeish briefly taught government at
Harvard before joining the Boston law firm of Choate,
Hall, and Stewart. He worked there for three busy years,
which left him with little time to write. In 1923 the thirty-
year-old poet resigned just as the firm offered him a part-
nership.

With his father's promise of support, he took his family
to Paris, where the favorable exchange rate allowed Americans to live cheaply. Planning to stay one year to write
poetry seriously and allow Ada, a gifted soprano, to pursue
her vocal studies, MacLeish remained for five years in "the
last of the great holy cities of the arts." He befriended fellow
American émigré writers of the Lost Generation—Ernest
Hemingway, John Dos Passos, F. Scott Fitzgerald, and E. E.
Cummings. MacLeish followed a strict and compulsive
schedule to transform himself into a modern poet. He
learned Italian to read Dante and systematically studied the
entire history of English-language poetry. Determined and
self-critical, MacLeish developed a lucid, compressed, and
sensuously evocative poetic style unlike the limp romanticism of his early work. Producing five books in five years,
he began to write the poems that would earn him a permanent place in American literature. The best poems of
his Parisian period—"Memorial Rain," "The End of the
World," "You, Andrew Marvell," and "Ars Poetica"—were
immediately recognized as modern classics and have never
left the anthologies. Indeed, the last two lines of "Ars Poetica" ("A poem should not mean/But be") probably rank
as the most frequently quoted couplet in twentieth-century
American poetry. The force, beauty, and originality of these
poems, however, eventually worked against MacLeish; later
critics carped that he never wrote this well again.

When MacLeish returned from Paris in 1928, he was
widely recognized as one of America's leading poets. His
fifth book of poems, *Streets in the Moon* (1926), had appeared to triumphant reviews. Still planning to spend half
of each year in Paris, he and his wife bought (with the help
of Ada's father) a house and farm in Conway, Massachusetts, where they would live for more than five decades.
MacLeish's critical reputation was ruffled by the publication of his book-length poem, *The Hamlet of A. MacLeish*
(1928), which not only occasioned bad reviews but eventually inspired Edmund Wilson's savage 1939 parody "The
Omelet of A. MacLeish." He quickly regained favor, however, with *New Found Land* (1930) and *Conquistador* (1932),
a book-length narrative of Hernán Cortés's plunder of
Mexico that won MacLeish the first of his three Pulitzer
Prizes.

The stock market crash of 1929 decimated MacLeish's
small private income. Not wanting to return to the law, he
accepted Henry Luce's offer to join the staff of *Fortune*
magazine, which had not yet published its first issue. *Fortune*'s original staff, which included the writer James Agee
and the political and cultural critic Dwight Macdonald,
remains legendary, but MacLeish, who usually worked only
part-time, soon emerged as the acknowledged star. Publishing nearly one hundred major articles, he became the
most influential writer at the nation's premier business
magazine. His liberal perspective helped make *Fortune*
sympathetic to many New Deal reforms, and the poet was
increasingly drawn into public affairs, especially the fight
against fascism.

In June 1938 MacLeish left *Fortune* to become the first
director of the Nieman journalism program at Harvard,
but the next spring President Franklin D. Roosevelt (advised by the poet's former law-school mentor, Supreme
Court justice Felix Frankfurter) asked MacLeish to become
the Librarian of Congress. The poet initially refused, but
Roosevelt viewed MacLeish as an articulate and well-
connected spokesman for the administration's policies who
could prove valuable in Washington, and the idealistic and
ambitious poet fell under the president's sway. For the next
six years he was Roosevelt's loyal public apologist. Not
without reason did one of MacLeish's key library associates
refer to him as "Roosevelt's minister of culture."

The American Library Association aggressively battled
MacLeish's nomination for professional reasons (he had no
training in library science), and Republican senators opposed him for his leftist associations, but Roosevelt's personal support secured his appointment. The previous librarian, Herbert Putnam, had occupied the post for forty
years, leaving behind the world's largest collection of books
(one-fourth of which had never been cataloged) and a vast
administrative mess. MacLeish quickly defined goals for
the library, reorganized the staff, updated services, and secured significantly greater funding. He also reconceived the

newly endowed position of poetry consultant. Gently ousting its mediocre occupant, he created a rotating appointment that soon became the most prestigious public position in American poetry. (Congress recognized its preeminence in 1986 by changing the consultantship's title to "Poet Laureate of the United States.") Previous librarians had kept a low profile, but MacLeish used his position to become a public advocate for progressive causes.

MacLeish's new determination "to integrate the role of the poet and the public man" proved disastrous to his poetry but beneficial to his political career. The poetry he published over the next decade addressed timely public issues, but it became overly rhetorical and verbally thin. He also returned to verse drama. His 1935 play, *Panic* (directed by John Houseman and starring Orson Welles), ran at the Phoenix Theatre in New York City ran for only three nights but occasioned huge controversy when communist organizations packed the final performance for a special critical symposium. Although MacLeish distrusted communists, he often made common cause with them during this period and even joined the League of American Writers, a communist-front organization—an action that complicated his later career in Washington politics. In collaboration with Dos Passos and Lillian Hellman, he wrote the screenplay for *The Spanish Earth,* a 1937 antifascist documentary. That same year, *The Fall of the City,* the first verse play ever written for radio, was broadcast nationally on CBS. Starring Welles and Burgess Meredith, the half-hour play scored a huge success and was rebroadcast a few months later from the Hollywood Bowl. Another radio play, *Air Raid,* followed less successfully in 1938.

Roosevelt soon expanded the poet's role in Washington. MacLeish joined Harry Hopkins, Sam Rosenman, and Robert Sherwood to write speeches for the president. (Most of the 1941 inaugural address, for example, was by MacLeish.) When the United States entered World War II, MacLeish was put in charge of the Office of Facts and Figures, a newly created bureau to disseminate accurate defense information. MacLeish assembled a celebrated staff that included the literary critic Malcolm Cowley, the historian Arthur Schlesinger, Jr., and the writer E. B. White to provide positive wartime propaganda. MacLeish was also appointed chairman of the Committee on War Information, made an overseer for the Office of Censorship, and was asked by Roosevelt to supervise preparations for the nation's official history of the war.

While fulfilling these duties, he continued as Librarian of Congress. In 1943 MacLeish joined a secret government committee to plan the postwar peace. The committee envisioned a central role for the still-nascent United Nations, which would be officially chartered in 1945. Leaving his library post in late 1944, MacLeish became (despite opposition from conservatives in both parties) assistant secretary of state for cultural and public affairs. A fervent one-world internationalist, he welcomed his official task of selling the American people on the United Nations. Among his many duties, MacLeish helped write the UN charter. (The preamble is almost entirely his work.) He also headed the U.S. delegation at the founding of the United Nations Educational, Scientific, and Cultural Organization (UNESCO) and became the first American member of UNESCO's executive council.

A year after Roosevelt's death, MacLeish returned to private life, nervously hoping he could resume writing poetry. *Actfive and Other Poems* (1948) received generally hostile reviews, but the author was gladdened by other news. Harvard offered him the Boylston Chair of Rhetoric and Oratory. His thirteen years at Harvard proved the happiest period of his life. He taught poetry and writing on a comfortable half-time basis. His students in English S (Harvard's code for creative writing) included Donald Hall, Robert Bly, George Plimpton, John Simon, and Edward Hoagland, although he twice rejected the young John Updike. In 1952 he published his *Collected Poems, 1917–1952* to exultant reviews. The book won every major prize, including the National Book Award, the Bollingen, and a second Pulitzer. A year later he was elected president of the American Academy of Arts and Letters.

MacLeish next returned to the theater. He wrote two short plays, *The Trojan Horse* (1952) and *This Music Crept by Me upon the Waters* (1953), for the BBC and then supervised their performance at the Poets Theater in Cambridge, Massachusetts. In 1958 his modern version of the Job story, *J. B.,* was first staged in New Haven, Connecticut. Much revised, the verse play opened on Broadway, directed by Elia Kazan. Despite a newspaper strike, *J. B.* became a huge hit and ran for a year before going on a national tour. Hailed as a modern classic, *J. B.* won both a Tony Award and a Pulitzer. The play also earned the poet more money than all of his books combined. MacLeish wrote other theatrical pieces, including *Herakles* (1967) and *Scratch* (1971), but had no commercial success. His screenplay for the documentary *The Eleanor Roosevelt Story* (1965), however, won him an Academy Award for best feature documentary, a unique honor for an American poet.

MacLeish's later years proved disappointing. After his mandatory retirement from Harvard at age seventy in 1962, he never found another satisfactory public position, and MacLeish thrived on activity. Although his critical reputation began to decline, MacLeish remained America's most visible public poet. President Gerald Ford awarded him the Medal of Freedom in 1977. MacLeish died of pneumonia a few weeks short of his ninetieth birthday. Celebrations planned in his honor became memorial services. He was buried alongside his sons at Pine Grove Cemetery in Conway, Massachusetts.

MacLeish's enduring reputation rests mainly on his short personal lyrics rather than on the long public poems of his middle years. His best work remains so strong and original that he ranks as a major figure in the second generation of American modernist poets. With the exception of *J. B.,* his verse plays are rarely performed, but his ambitious experiments in that genre make him the most influential figure in modern American poetic drama. His voluminous critical prose has dated badly, but it reflects the broad concerns of his political career. No American writer of similar distinction has ever played such an important role in public life.

★

MacLeish's papers are primarily at the Library of Congress. Significant material also resides in the Beinecke Library at Yale University. Scott Donaldson's exemplary biography, *Archibald MacLeish: An American Life* (1992), in collaboration with R. H. Winnick, provides a comprehensive and informed view of the poet's multifaceted career. Obituaries appear in the *New York Times* and *Washington Post* (both on 22 Apr. 1982).

DANA GIOIA

McNALLY, John Victor ("Johnny Blood") (*b.* 27 November 1903 in New Richmond, Wisconsin; *d.* 28 November 1985 in Palm Springs, California), professional football player and coach who was a charter inductee into the Pro Football Hall of Fame.

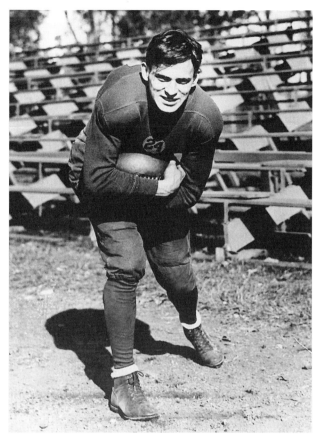

John McNally ("Johnny Blood"). PRO FOOTBALL HALL OF FAME

McNally's father was the manager of a flour mill in New Richmond, Wisconsin; his mother was a schoolteacher. He had three sisters. An excellent student, McNally graduated from high school at the age of fourteen. Considered too young for both college and organized sports, he enrolled in a local postsecondary commercial education program. A year later he entered River Falls Normal School in River Falls, Wisconsin, but was expelled for disciplinary reasons.

McNally next enrolled in St. John's University in Collegeville, Minnesota, where his athletic career began. He was captain of the school basketball team, participated in baseball and track, and was the star of the school's intramural football program. Outside of athletics, McNally joined the debate team and helped edit the school newspaper.

After three years at St. John's, McNally transferred to Notre Dame, but discipline problems again resulted in his expulsion. He used to say that his only contribution to the famous Notre Dame athletic tradition was that he wrote the English papers for his teammate Harry Stuhldreher, an All-American football player and one of the "Four Horsemen of Notre Dame." Believing his academic career was over, McNally then moved to Minneapolis, becoming a typesetter for the *Minneapolis Tribune,* owned by two ma-

ternal uncles. While in Minneapolis, he and a friend, Ralph Hanson, heard that a local semiprofessional football team called the 26th Street Liberties was in need of players. Because both thought they might have college eligibility remaining, they decided to adopt aliases. Using a marquee for the Rudolph Valentino movie *Blood and Sand* as his guide, John McNally became Johnny Blood.

In 1925, after playing for the 26th Street Liberties and another semiprofessional team in Ironwood, Michigan, McNally, still using the alias Johnny Blood, joined the Milwaukee Badgers of the National Football League (NFL). He spent parts of two seasons with Milwaukee, and then in 1926 and 1927 he played for the Duluth Eskimos. In 1928 he moved to the Pottsville (Pennsylvania) Maroons. McNally was considered to be a complete player. He ran, passed, punted, and played excellent defense.

Only when he joined the Green Bay Packers in 1929, however, did McNally truly come into his own. Packers coach Curly Lambeau was one of the early proponents of the forward pass. McNally's blazing speed made him an ideal receiver, and Lambeau made him an integral part of the Packer offense. With McNally leading the way, Green Bay won NFL championships in 1929, 1930, and 1931. It remains one of only two teams to win three straight titles. McNally was named to the All-League team in 1931 and led all players in touchdown receptions in 1930 and 1931.

While his play with the Packers was excellent, McNally was equally known for his colorful personality. Once described as "an uninhibited combination of scholar, esthete, bon vivant, and halfback," he loved to demonstrate the intelligence that had enabled him to graduate from high school at fourteen, and the quixotic behavior that got him expelled from two colleges by the time he was twenty. McNally would recite poetry, often from the tops of soapboxes outside the hotel where the team was staying. It was said that he had memorized most of Shakespeare, and he enjoyed all types of discussion and debate. Teammate Clarke Hinkle remembered McNally as someone who would hire every woman in a brothel just to enjoy their conversation. In the off-season McNally often went to the West Coast to work in a hotel or as a merchant seaman, only to return in time for preseason practice stowed away on a freight train.

McNally's wild lifestyle was a point of contention between him and Coach Lambeau. Lambeau offered him numerous incentives to quit drinking but rarely had success. Following the 1933 season, McNally was sent to the Pittsburgh Pirates but returned to Green Bay for 1935 and 1936. McNally concluded his NFL career as a player-coach with the Pirates from 1937 through 1939. Even at the end of his career McNally was a dangerous player. In his first game as Pirates coach, he returned the opening kickoff 100 yards for a touchdown. As a coach, however, he left much to be desired. He was notorious for missing practices, team trains, and even games, if he was suffering from a hangover.

When he retired in 1939, McNally had played more years than any other person in the NFL. He was officially credited with thirty-seven touchdowns, then also a record. The poor collection of statistics in the early days of the NFL almost guarantees he scored more. He was considered to be the first of the great pass receivers, a precursor of such later stars as Don Hutson and Jim Benton.

Once out of the NFL, McNally returned to semipro football. He was briefly a resident of a Winnebago, Wisconsin, mental hospital, where he wrote a book on economics. On his release he enlisted in the Army Air Corps for service in World War II. McNally saw action as a cryptographer in the Burmese theater of operations, and left with the rank of sergeant. In 1945 he failed in a comeback attempt with the Packers; in 1948 he married his first wife. In 1949 he returned to St. John's University to finish his undergraduate degree and eventually completed a master's degree in economics. Between 1950 and 1952 McNally coached the St. John's football team and taught classes in economics and history. Later he returned to New Richmond, Wisconsin, and opened an employment agency. In

1963 he was one of the charter inductees into the Pro Football Hall of Fame. McNally retired in Palm Springs, California, where he died of undetermined causes. He left behind his second wife (whom he married in 1966 after divorcing his first wife) and three sons.

McNally's career was one of the most successful and colorful of any professional football player. His unique skills helped turn the forward pass into a central component of the game instead of a desperation gamble. He was one of the keys to the Packer dynasty of the late 1920s and early 1930s. At the same time, McNally's personality epitomizes the "tramp athlete" of the early twentieth century. His willingness to shift from team to team, his casual off-season employments, and his less than reputable lifestyle reflect a time when sport was not a big business but a game played by big boys.

★

Memorabilia and newspaper clippings are in the Pro Football Hall of Fame in Canton, Ohio. There is a brief biographical sketch in Don R. Smith, *Pro Football Hall of Fame All-Time Greats* (1988). Interviews are printed in Myron Cope, *The Game That Was: The Early Days of Pro Football* (1970), and Richard Whittingham, *What a Game They Played* (1984). A major article on McNally is Gerald Holland's "Is That You Up There, Johnny Blood?" *Sports Illustrated* (2 Sept. 1963). McNally appears in the NFL Film's production *Old Leather* (1976). An obituary is in the *New York Times* (30 Nov. 1985).

HAROLD W. AURAND, JR.

McNAMARA, Margaret McKinstry Craig (*b.* 22 August 1915 in Seattle, Washington; *d.* 3 February 1981 in Washington, D.C.), civic worker and founder of the Reading Is Fundamental Program, a project designed to promote literacy by bringing books into the homes of disadvantaged children.

Margaret, nicknamed Margy, was one of two daughters born to Thomas J. Craig, an insurance executive, and Margaret McKinstry. When Margaret was a child the family moved to Alameda, California, in the San Francisco Bay Area. Occasionally she accompanied her grandfather on fishing trips, which likely helped foster her love for the outdoors.

A petite but athletic woman with wide cheekbones and smiling blue eyes, Margaret attended the University of California at Berkeley, majoring in physical education and graduating with a B.A. degree in 1937. From 1938 to 1940 she taught biology and health education at high schools in Alameda and San Rafael, California. She married Robert Strange McNamara on 13 August 1940; they moved to Boston, where he began his illustrious career as an assistant professor at Harvard University. The couple had three children.

Margaret McNamara. © READING IS FUNDAMENTAL, INC. USED WITH PERMISSION.

In August 1945, Margaret was stricken with polio, and the attack left her paralyzed from the waist down, with partial paralysis above the waist on her right side. Physicians gave her only a slim chance of recovery, but they sent her to a children's rehabilitation ward in Baltimore, and by February 1946 this determined and persistent woman was walking again. She soon rejoined her family in Ann Arbor, Michigan, where her husband had taken a job with the Ford Motor Company to keep up with Margaret's medical bills. Although a nurse and a therapist were hired and she continued rehabilitation, she retained a limp.

In Ann Arbor the family joined the Presbyterian church. Margaret tutored and was a member of the Juvenile Court from 1950 to 1960. Never one to stick to conventions when it came her turn to entertain other Ford Motor Company wives, she dispensed with the usual teas and did such things as taking the women on a tour of the University of Michigan cyclotron. In 1961, President John F. Kennedy persuaded her husband to join his cabinet as secretary of defense. In Washington the McNamaras settled into a large home on a wooded lot at 2412 Tracy Place, away from Georgetown's political homesteads.

When Margaret contracted polio, her recovery prompted the family's emphasis on exercise and outdoor activity. Unsuccessful at her attempts to maneuver on skis, she spent months building stamina to ski and climb mountains. In the 1960s, the McNamaras bought a cedar vacation home in Snowmass, Colorado, near Aspen. At Snowmass, Margaret had a view of the mountains, a place to visit with friends, and slopes for physical exercise. A relaxed and informal woman, Margaret sometimes drew criticism from politicians' wives for her nonconformity to Washington life. Unruffled, she plunged into organizational and volunteer work while helping her son overcome his problems with dyslexia. In 1959 she was named regional director of the White House Conference on Children and Youth. From 1964 to 1965 she served as director of Widening Horizons, a summer program for youth. She was a member of the National Advisory Council of the Office of Economic Opportunity from 1964 to 1968.

While tutoring two fifth-grade boys who had difficulty reading, McNamara was not surprised to find the boys had little interest in their simple, unexciting textbook. The following day she brought the boys a Jules Verne adventure book, which immediately drew their interest. When she discovered they had never owned a book, McNamara gave one of the boys the volume. Within months the child had become an enthusiastic reader, and McNamara had the impetus needed to start Reading Is Fundamental (RIF).

The RIF program allowed underprivileged children to select their own books and then keep them. McNamara felt that through "freedom of choice and pride of ownership" children would be more enthusiastic about the printed page. Within a year the program was functioning in sixty-one schools. RIF received funding from the Ford Foundation and other businesses and book donations from publishers. In 1976, Congress passed the Inexpensive Book Distribution Program, which enabled RIF to grow by adding federal matching funds to money raised in individual communities. The books were distributed to children in inner-city schools, hospitals, and on Indian reservations, inspiring the recipients and bringing the books into homes for families to share.

As antiwar demonstrations escalated during Robert McNamara's tenure as secretary of defense, tensions mounted at home. Margaret developed ulcers and had surgery in 1967. In 1968 Robert resigned to become president of the World Bank. Margaret continued her work as RIF's chairman of the board and traveled worldwide crusading for literacy.

From 1978 to 1979, she served on the advisory committee of the White House Conference on Library and Information Service. She was a trustee or member of the board of Smithsonian Associates, Chatham College, and the Agnes and Eugene Meyer Foundation. She served as a member of the National Committee on U.S.-China Relations and the Harvard University Visiting Committee for Far Eastern Studies. She received the Clarence Day Award (1975) and was designated *Ladies Home Journal* Woman of the Year in Education (1977) and Washingtonian of the Year (1977).

On 16 January 1981, President Carter awarded Margaret McNamara the nation's highest civilian honor, the Medal of Freedom, for founding RIF. She died only a few weeks later in Washington, D.C., from a rare form of cancer called mesothelioma. Her body was cremated and her ashes scattered in a meadow at Buckskin Pass near Snowmass.

After 1966, Margaret had traveled extensively. Whether she went to a local school in America or a remote area in Afghanistan, she spread RIF's message about the importance of books and of literacy. A valiant fighter, Margaret McNamara worked for world literacy as tenaciously as she had fought illness throughout her life. Never one to take credit for her own achievements, she gave praise to co-workers and volunteers of the Reading Is Fundamental program, which continued to grow after her death.

★

Details about Margaret McNamara are found in biographies and other writings on and by her husband, Robert McNamara. These include biographies by Henry L. Trewhitt, *McNamara* (1971), and Deborah Shapley, *Promise and Power: The Life and Times of Robert McNamara* (1993), which offers the more in-depth account of her. Two books primarily concerned with the period of the Vietnam War are Robert S. McNamara with Brian Van-DeMark, *In Retrospect: The Tragedy and Lessons of Vietnam* (1995), which includes brief memories of Margaret; and Paul Hendrickson, *The Living and the Dead: Robert McNamara and Five Lives of a Lost War* (1996), which gives more details about Margaret. Lady Bird Johnson, *A White House Diary* (1970), is a memoir of the first lady's White House years and mentions Margaret. Paul Hendrickson's interviews with Robert McNamara, "McNamara: The Jangling Riddles of a Man in Perpetual Motion," *Washington Post* (8 May 1984) and "Robert McNamara: Specters of Vietnam," *Washington Post* (10 May 1984) chronicle events in McNamara's life but also yield additional details about his wife. Information on Margaret McNamara's founding of and contribution to Reading Is Fundamental can be found in the *RIF Newsletter* (winter 1981) and a supplement of that issue, "A Tribute to Margaret McNamara." Other sources on McNamara's involvement with RIF are in Henry Brandon, "Mrs. McNamara's Crusade," *Saturday Review* (17 June 1967), and Phyllis Theroux, "The Great Book Giveaway," *New York Times* (27 April 1980). Obituaries are in the *New York Times* (4 February 1981) and *Publishers Weekly* (20 February 1981).

MARILYN ELIZABETH PERRY

MAGOWAN, Robert Anderson (*b.* 19 September 1903 in Chester, Pennsylvania; *d.* 17 December 1985 in Palm Beach, Florida), business executive who led Safeway Stores, Inc., a leading American supermarket chain, through a period of great expansion nationally and internationally.

Magowan was one of the two sons of Edward Thomas Magowan, a railroad stationmaster, and Estelle Smith, a homemaker. After attending the Kent School in Connecticut, he went to Harvard College, graduating in 1927 with a B.S. degree in economics. While at Harvard he managed the varsity baseball team and was an editor of the student newspaper. As a young man he also did some sports reporting for the *Boston Globe*.

Standing five feet, seven inches, with a trim build, handsome features, and intense blue eyes, Magowan was bright, funny, well-educated, and competitive. He embarked on his business career by accepting a $30 a week offer from R. H. Macy and Company shortly after graduating from Harvard. He worked there for several years at various assignments, including merchandise manager of the ready-to-wear departments. In 1934 he became a vice president of N. W. Ayer and Company, an advertising agency, staying there for a year.

On 15 June 1935 Magowan married Doris Merrill; they had five sons. The couple traveled extensively, participated in charitable activities, and played golf together. Magowan made no secret of the fact that the marriage also took his

Robert A. Magowan. UPI/CORBIS-BETTMANN

career to new levels. His father-in-law had consolidated a number of brokerage houses into the firm Merrill Lynch, Pierce, Fenner and Smith and had also cofounded Safeway. Early in his marriage Magowan took executive training with Safeway in San Francisco and worked there for three years. Then he joined the brokerage firm, working closely with his father-in-law until Merrill's death in the mid-1950s, except for a three-year stint as a navy air intelligence officer during World War II. During that conflict Magowan served in the South Pacific and rose to the rank of lieutenant. After the war he returned to Merrill Lynch. He became manager of the firm's sales division in 1948 and was securities and marketing services director when he left in 1955, although he remained a limited partner thereafter.

Magowan took over as chairman and chief executive of Safeway in 1955 with the goal of shoring up sagging sales. He assumed complete control of the business, which was based in Oakland, California, when he was named president in 1957. That year Safeway reached $2 billion in sales, which represented a doubling of total volume in a decade. One of Magowan's first major decisions was to sell the company's ailing New York division. Proceeds were used to expand into more profitable American markets and get the company started in Europe. By 1959 Safeway had moved into Alaska. At the beginning of the 1960s its ambitious construction program ensured that nearly half of its retail outlets were less than five years old. Magowan advised opening most of the new stores in shopping centers. Safeway's overseas expansion came with the acquisition of an eleven-store chain in England in 1962 and stores in Australia and West Germany two years later. In 1966, as Safeway celebrated its fortieth anniversary, it reported that it had reached $3 billion in annual sales. All of this attracted considerable national attention for Safeway and for Magowan, but he also made less visible internal changes to improve in-house communications. He developed a reputation as a hands-on manager who kept up on the supermarket empire by visiting stores himself and by talking with butchers and checkout clerks. In addition, he took popular steps to decentralize decision making. He encouraged division heads to consult each other more often and insisted that they start making major decisions affecting their divisions, rather than channeling everything through Oakland. Magowan stepped down as president of Safeway in 1966. He resigned as chief executive officer a few years later, staying on only as chairman of the executive committee before bowing out of active service in 1979. The following year Magowan's son Peter became chairman and CEO of the firm.

Long interested in sports, Magowan enjoyed skiing and golf but considered himself better at tennis. He and his wife were supporters of the San Francisco Opera and San Francisco Museum of Art. He was a director of R. H. Macy,

the Bank of California, Fibreboard Paper Products Corporation, Caterpillar Tractor, and Del Monte Properties and was on the executive committee of Southern Pacific Railroad Company. Magowan was an Episcopalian. As a trustee of the Charles E. Merrill Trust, he helped give away an estimated $100 million to colleges, churches, hospitals, and other recipients over a period of twenty-five years. In 1972 the trust and Magowan provided two grants totaling $1.5 million for the construction of a new athletic fieldhouse at the Kent School. Magowan also contributed to Stanford University.

Although Robert and Doris Magowan grew up on the East Coast, they eventually lived all over the country. In the 1960s they told an interviewer that they considered San Francisco, where they had moved in the mid-1950s, their principal residence, but they also kept homes on Manhattan's East Side, at Southampton on Long Island in New York, and in Palm Beach, Florida. It was in Palm Beach that Magowan died after suffering from heart trouble for three or four years. He was buried in Southampton.

Candid on the subject of his rise in the corporate world, Magowan was quoted as saying that he was "not one of those fellows who pulled himself by his bootstraps." His strong rapport with his father-in-law put him at the center of a considerable financial empire. Nonetheless he relied on his own drive, intelligence, and background in retail and advertising to help the Merrill Lynch brokerage firm advance and to make his own mark on the Safeway chain.

★

A profile by Vartanig G. Vartan appeared in the *New York Times* (27 Oct. 1963). Obituaries are in the *New York Times* (19 Dec. 1985) and the *Los Angeles Times* (20 Dec. 1985).

WHITNEY SMITH

MALTZ, Albert (*b.* 28 October 1908 in Brooklyn, New York; *d.* 26 April 1985 in Los Angeles, California), playwright, novelist, and short-story writer best known as one of the "Hollywood Ten" investigated by Congress for alleged communist ties and as screenwriter of *This Gun for Hire* (1942), *Pride of the Marines* (1945), *The Naked City* (1948), and the short, *The House I Live In* (1945).

Maltz was born of eastern European immigrant parents who settled in Brooklyn, New York, where his mother, Lena Sherry, worked in a sweatshop and his father, Bernard Maltz, eventually became a successful contractor. The Maltzes had two other sons, Ernest and Edward, but it was Albert who was destined for a career in the arts. He graduated from Brooklyn's Erasmus Hall High School in 1926 and from Columbia University in 1930, with a B.A. (Phi Beta Kappa) in philosophy. An undergraduate playwriting class inspired him to study drama at the Yale School of

Drama (1930–1932) under George Pierce Baker, founder of Harvard University's 47 Workshop, whose most famous student was Eugene O'Neill. At Yale, Maltz met George Sklar, with whom he collaborated on two plays, *Merry-Go-Round* (1931) and *Peace on Earth* (1933), whose themes of political corruption, exploitation, and pacifism reflected Maltz's radicalism that was nurtured by the Great Depression and led to his joining the Communist party in 1935. *Peace on Earth* was produced by the leftist Theatre Union, whose executive secretary, Margaret Larkin, became Maltz's first wife in 1937. The couple had two children, Peter and Katherine.

Maltz's later plays—*The Black Pit* (1934), *Rehearsal* (1938), and *Private Hicks* (1935)—while heartfelt, were little more than agitprop inveighing against social injustice. His better-crafted fiction includes his first short-story collection, *The Way Things Are* (1938), which, focusing on the interrelationship between environment and character, reveals his talents as a storyteller with a social conscience. Although Universal Pictures rejected Maltz and Sklar's adaptation of *Merry-Go-Round* (later filmed, in 1932, as *Afraid to Talk*, with a script by Tom Reed), Maltz did not give up on Hollywood. His early novels—*The Underground Stream* (1940) and *The Cross and the Arrow* (1944)—read like antifascist propaganda but used film techniques such as flashbacks, sequence-like chapters, crosscutting, and characterization through dialogue that revealed a genuine gift for screenwriting. When Maltz arrived in Hollywood in 1941, he discovered that film is a collaborative medium, in which screenplay credit is often shared, as happened with his first script, *This Gun for Hire* (1942). Maltz had a similar experience with *Destination, Tokyo* (1943). His first sole screenplay credit—and widely considered his best script— was the Academy Award–nominated *Pride of the Marines* (1945), based on the life of Al Schmid, a Marine blinded at Guadalcanal. That year also saw the release of his Oscar-winning short, *The House I Live In,* in which Frank Sinatra both sang the famous title song and gave some anti-Semitic boys a lesson in race relations.

In September 1947 Maltz's life changed dramatically when the House Committee on Un-American Activities began its investigation of alleged communist subversion of the movie industry on the grounds that Marxist sentiments and pro-Soviet allusions had been worked into American films. Maltz and others were subpoenaed to appear in Washington, D.C. Ten of the subpoenaed, including Maltz, invoked the First Amendment's freedom of expression clause. Believing that Congress had no authority to investigate an individual's politics, they refused to answer questions about their membership in the Communist party. The Hollywood Ten, as they came to be known, all received contempt citations and jail sentences. The notoriety resulted in Twentieth Century–Fox's decision not to film

Albert Maltz. COPYRIGHT WASHINGTON POST. REPRINTED BY PERMISSION OF THE D.C. PUBLIC LIBRARY.

Maltz's most highly regarded novel, *The Journey of Simon McKeever* (1949). In 1950 Maltz was sentenced to a year at West Virginia's Mill Point Prison Camp, of which he served ten months. Prior to his imprisonment and subsequent blacklisting, Maltz coauthored the script of *The Naked City* (1948), a classic semidocumentary, with Malvin Wald; he also adapted Lloyd C. Douglas's novel *The Robe,* eventually filmed in 1953 and credited to Philip Dunne, who mainly revised Maltz's script. The Motion Picture Association of America's refusal to credit Maltz for *The Robe* was in keeping with its policy of omitting names of blacklisted authors. In 1997 Maltz was given posthumous co-screenplay credit for *The Robe* and full credit for *Broken Arrow* (1950).

After his release from Mill Point, Maltz lived in Mexico from 1952 to 1962. He returned to fiction, producing two novels, *A Day in a Short Life* (1957) and *A Tale of One January* (1966), the latter dealing with the escape of inmates from the Auschwitz death camp. Once the blacklist ended in the early 1960s, he produced the scripts for *Two Mules for Sister Sara* (1970) and *Scalawag* (1973).

Maltz's marriage to Margaret Larkin ended in divorce

in 1963; a year later he married Rosemary Wylde, who died in 1968. In 1969 he married Esther Engelberg. Maltz died in Los Angeles in 1985 of complications from a stroke. At the time of his death, he was working on a World War II novel about the French Resistance, "Bel Canto," which remains unpublished.

Maltz could have been a successful fiction writer, as evidenced by his O. Henry Memorial Award–winning story, "The Happiest Man on Earth" (1938), and *The Journey of Simon McKeever,* the author's tribute to an arthritic sojourner who encounters a cross-section of America. But during the period that should have been his most productive (the 1930s and 1940s), he had become such a committed communist that, in 1946, when he argued in *New Masses* that writers should be judged by their art, not their politics, there was such an uproar from party members that he recanted. Maltz's screenwriting career was ultimately sabotaged by the cold war paranoia. His inability to subordinate politics to art, despite his belief that they are separate, resulted in a classic case of unfulfilled promise.

★

The Albert Maltz Collection, in the State Historical Society of Wisconsin, Madison, Wisconsin, consists of manuscripts of plays, various drafts of screenplays, and correspondence from 1932 to 1968. Walter B. Rideout, *The Radical Novel in the United States, 1900–1954: Some Interrelations of Literature and Society* (1956), contains an analysis of Maltz's early novels. Malcolm Goldstein, *The Political Stage: American Drama and Theater of the Great Depression* (1974), places Maltz's plays within the context of 1930s drama. See also Jack Salzman, *Albert Maltz* (1978); and Bernard F. Dick, *Radical Innocence: A Critical Study of the Hollywood Ten* (1989), which includes an evaluation of Maltz's fiction and screenplays, along with a bibliography and filmography. An obituary is in the *New York Times* (29 Apr. 1985).

BERNARD F. DICK

MANNE, Sheldon ("Shelly") (*b.* 11 June 1920 in New York City; *d.* 26 September 1984 in Los Angeles, California), jazz drummer who as bandleader and sideman, film studio musician, and nightclub owner played an important part in the West Coast world of "cool jazz" for three decades.

One of the two sons of Max Harold and Anna (Cozlin) Manne, Sheldon grew up, almost literally, in Tin Pan Alley (on Seventh Avenue and Forty-ninth Street in Manhattan), surrounded from childhood by professional musicians, friends of his family. His father, a contractor for Radio City Music Hall orchestras, and his two uncles were drummers. Educated in New York City public schools, Manne had no formal music training but started playing the alto saxophone as a boy.

Shelly Manne. FRANK DRIGGS/ARCHIVE PHOTOS

In 1937, after hearing Roy Eldridge's band at a Harlem club, Manne began to think about switching instruments; the following year a friend got him started playing drums. Three months later Manne was performing with bands on transatlantic liners; then he began sitting in with groups playing the jazz clubs along Fifty-second Street. In 1939 he was spotted at one of these clubs and hired to play with the Bobby Byrne band. In 1940 he substituted briefly for the drummer Dave Tough (whom Manne credited as one of his biggest influences) in Benny Goodman's Orchestra and then replaced Tough in Joe Marsala's band, with which he made a recording in 1941. Engagements with groups led by Raymond Scott (1941), Will Bradley (1941–1942), and Les Brown (1942) followed. During World War II, from 1942 to 1945, Manne served in the U.S. Coast Guard; in the interim, on 26 August 1943, he married Florence ("Flip") Butterfield, a Radio City Music Hall Rockette, and in the same year took part as a sideman in Coleman Hawkins's legendary recording of "The Man I Love."

For a year after the war Manne worked days at the NBC and CBS studios and at night played in various jazz spots. In 1946 he joined Stan Kenton's Orchestra and made his name, credited with establishing the "Kenton drum sound." From then on, between 1947 and 1962, Manne was regularly named top jazz drummer of the year in polls conducted by (among others) *Down Beat, Metronome,* and *Playboy* magazines; in 1949 he won out over famed jazz drummers Max Roach and Gene Krupa. Manne played and recorded with Kenton intermittently until 1952, also filling engagements with Charlie Ventura's band and a group led by George Shearing (1947), Bill Harris (1948–1949), and Woody Herman's Orchestra (1949). He also toured with Jazz at the Philharmonic in 1948 and 1949.

In 1952 Manne and his wife left New York for Los Angeles, partly (as he later tried to account for the move) because of the increased presence of drugs in the New York jazz world but also because of the demise of the Fifty-second Street clubs. Working as a freelance musician, he began to record for the Contemporary label in 1953; he was to do most of his important work for that company. Over the years Manne amassed an extensive discography, playing with his own groups or as sideman in other combos. As a member of a trio led by André Previn, for example, Manne is heard on recordings of jazz instrumentals based on Broadway musicals, including a very popular interpretation of *My Fair Lady* (1956) and *Pal Joey* (1957).

The start of Manne's long association with the movie industry came in 1954, when he played the background music for the Hitchcock thriller *Rear Window.* In 1955 he served as technical musical adviser for *The Man with the Golden Arm* and also had a role in it playing himself. Other movies in which he acted were *I Want to Live* (1958), *The Five Pennies* (1959), and *The Gene Krupa Story* (in which he played his idol Dave Tough). Films for which Manne composed music include *Trial of the Catonsville Nine* (1972) and *Trader Horn* (1973); he also composed music for the television series *Daktari* (1968).

By 1955 the musician had formed Shelly Manne and His Men, a quintet and the first of a series of his own small combos, which later included the Shelly Manne Quartet and the Poll Winners, a trio. He was established as a major exponent of "West Coast jazz," a form of bop actually developed (according to Manne) by transplanted New York musicians. His four-album set, *Shelly Manne and His Men at the Blackhawk,* recorded for Contemporary in San Francisco in 1959, is considered one of the finest examples of this laid-back, cool, but still swinging and smoky sound.

Manne's venture as a nightclub owner began in 1960 when he opened Shelly's Manne-Hole in Hollywood. For the next fourteen years it flourished as Los Angeles's premier jazz club, where he played on weekends with his own groups and which served as a venue for other bands during the week. When it folded in 1974 (because of problems with sound leaking into an adjacent recording studio), Manne started playing with other groups, such as the L.A. Four (until 1977), demonstrating his ability to switch from swing to progressive jazz and to jazz-rock fusion styles. Known internationally through his recordings, he also made tours abroad, took part in jazz festivals in Italy and London in 1970, and in 1980 traveled through Japan with Benny Carter's Gentlemen of Swing quartet.

Shelly Manne died suddenly of unspecified causes at his ranch home outside Los Angeles—only days after what the city mayor had proclaimed as Shelly Manne Day.

Considered one of the finest drummers of the postwar period, Shelly Manne was praised for his great sense of swing and elegant, restrained style. Never given to virtuoso performances, he was an ideal sideman as well as lead player. "Technique is only a means to get there," he felt; a colleague noted that "Shelly did not play drums, [he] played music." He was remembered after his death with great personal affection; younger players in particular honored him as a supportive, generous mentor and friend.

★

Shelly Manne published a short book, *Let's Play Drums,* in 1974. Biographical information is found in the article on Manne in *The New Grove Dictionary of Jazz,* vol. 2 (1988), and in the following periodical articles: "The Shelly Manne Story, as Told to Sinclair Traill," *Jazz Journal International* 32, no. 8 (1979): 21–23; D. Levine, "Shelly Manne," *Modern Drummer* 5, no. 7 (1981): 10–13; and C. M. Bernstein, "Shelly Manne: The Last Interview," *Modern Drummer* 9, no. 1 (1985): 14–19 (with a listing of his most important recorded performances and tributes from his colleagues). A selective discography is appended to the article on Manne in *The Guinness Encyclopedia of Popular Music,* 2d ed., vol. 4 (1995). Brief obituary notices are in the *New York Times* (27 Sept. 1984) and *Variety* (3 Oct. 1984).

ELEANOR F. WEDGE

MARGULIES, Lazar (*b.* 1895 in Galicia, Austria [now Poland]; *d.* 7 March 1982 in New York City), obstetrician-gynecologist who helped revolutionize contraceptive medicine with the development of the intrauterine device (IUD).

Margulies earned his degree in medicine at the University of Vienna after serving in the medical corps in the Austro-Hungarian army during World War I. He had an obstetrical and gynecologic practice in Vienna from 1929 until 1938, when, with World War II looming, he moved first to England and then to the United States, where he opened a practice in New York City in 1940.

Margulies served a fellowship in obstetrics at Mount Sinai Hospital in Manhattan in 1953. In 1958, having worked in Mount Sinai infertility clinic, he attended a lecture by Dr. John Rock. Margulies thought that the subject of the lecture was new techniques for infertility; instead, Rock discussed the dangers of overpopulation and the need for antifertility work. Intrigued, Margulies remembered reading about a contraceptive technique using an intrauterine device that was popular in other parts of the world. He attempted to obtain some of the devices from the manufacturer, but because of a lack of support for IUDs in the U.S. medical community, he had difficulty securing them. While intrauterine devices were in use throughout the world, they were condemned in the United States and in most of Europe because, as Rock stated, of their perceived "ineffectiveness, their potential source of infection and irritation, as well as their carcinogenic potentialities." Margulies researched articles in medical journals and was able to construct his own intrauterine devices. Having experimented with new designs and materials, Margulies developed a device that was less likely to cause complications while still preventing pregnancy. An IUD clinic was opened at Mount Sinai Hospital in 1961, after he had presented the results of a trial to test the effectiveness of his device on patients in his private practice. Among the patients in the trial was Margulies's wife, Kitty C. Herrman. (They had three children.)

Margulies spent a large part of his career as a researcher and teacher at Mount Sinai Hospital. He eventually became a lecturer in the Department of Obstetrics and Gynecology at the Mount Sinai School of Medicine as well as senior clinical assistant at Mount Sinai. He died at the Institute of Rehabilitation Medicine in Manhattan.

Margulies's creativity and persistence helped to revolutionize contraception. While his intrauterine device was found to be a preferred form of birth control, problems associated with other designs, including the Dalkon Shield, cast doubt in the public's mind about the safety of all intrauterine devices. The effectiveness worldwide of intrauterine devices led to a reexamination of the work of Margulies and his contemporaries as the basis for developing more effective methods of birth control.

★

Lazar Margulies, "History of Intrauterine Devices," *Bulletin of the New York Academy of Medicine* 51, no. 5 (May 1975): 662–667, discusses the difficulty early researchers encountered while developing and testing intrauterine devices. An obituary is in the *New York Times* (10 Mar. 1982).

NANCY M. FINN

MARIS, Roger Eugene (*b.* 10 September 1934 in Hibbing, Minnesota; *d.* 14 December 1985 in Houston, Texas), baseball player and holder of the single-season major league home-run record.

Maris (whose family name of Maras was legally changed in 1955) was the son of Rudolph Maris, Sr., a railroad mechanics supervisor, and Anne Corrine Sturbitz, a housewife. His family moved from Hibbing to Grand Forks, North Dakota, before settling in Fargo, North Dakota,

Roger Maris. NATIONAL BASEBALL HALL OF FAME LIBRARY, COOPERSTOWN, N.Y.

when Maris was in junior high school. Roger and Rudy, his older brother and only sibling, participated in all sports, encouraged by their father, a former semiprofessional hockey and baseball player.

Direct and uncomplicated, but sensitive, Maris revealed his superior athletic ability while playing for Bishop Shanley High School. He also displayed a stubborn streak that came out when he believed he had been ill-treated. In 1951 he established a national high school football record with four kickoff returns for touchdowns in one game. He also starred in basketball and track and was the most valuable player on the state champion American Legion baseball team in 1950.

Maris graduated from high school in 1952. A solidly built young man who would fill out to six feet and about 200 pounds at maturity, he was widely recruited to play college football; after visiting the University of Oklahoma, Maris realized he could not endure classroom confinement and returned home. But the multitalented Maris had also attracted the attention of professional baseball. Given the opportunity to try out by the Cleveland Indians organization, Maris impressed Cleveland's general manager Hank Greenberg. He was offered $5,000 to join the organization, with the promise of $10,000 more when he made the parent club.

An outfielder, Maris progressed steadily through the Cleveland organization, but he also developed a reputation for defiance, for example, by demanding to play with hometown Fargo (of the Class C Northern League) in 1953 and by walking off the field when he felt unjustly treated by his manager with Reading (Class A Eastern League) in 1955. Playing for Indianapolis (Class AAA American Association) in 1956, he starred in the minor league Little World Series.

Maris met Patricia Anne Carvell while attending Bishop Shanley High School. They were married on 13 October 1956 and had six children.

His minor league apprenticeship over, Maris played with the Cleveland Indians in 1957. He was having a good rookie year when he suffered broken ribs trying to break up a double play; he never regained his momentum that season. He would incur many injuries through aggressive play, adversely affecting his career. In June 1958, after a poor start in his sophomore season, Maris was traded to the Kansas City Athletics. Playing regularly before supportive fans in a relaxed atmosphere, he started well in 1959 but an emergency appendectomy and several prolonged slumps ruined a potentially great season.

By now Maris and his wife had started their family, bought a home, and settled in Raytown, Missouri. During the 1959 season, he voiced his desire to remain with the Athletics, but on 11 December 1959 he was traded to the New York Yankees. Although disappointed at the trade, Maris quickly provided the caliber of play desperately sought by the Yankees management. His all-out playing style and quiet, solid demeanor fit in well with his teammates and the image-conscious Yankees organization. He helped the team win the American League pennant in 1960 by batting .283, hitting 39 home runs (1 fewer than league-leading teammate Mickey Mantle), leading the league in runs batted in (112) and slugging percentage (.581), and winning the Most Valuable Player award.

Maris had a reasonable relationship with the press in 1960, but he was never at ease with aggressive reporters, and his terse responses to their questions were often misconstrued as rudeness. Meanwhile, Mantle, who held similar sentiments and who had been vilified during his disappointing 1959 season, was slowly regaining fan support and reaching an amicable accommodation he had never previously enjoyed with baseball writers.

By August 1960, Maris was hitting home runs at a rate that threatened Babe Ruth's mark of 60, established in 1927. Questioned at that time regarding the chances of breaking Ruth's record, Maris diplomatically answered that neither he nor anyone else would ever accomplish that feat. Rib

injuries shortly nullified whatever chance Maris had that year. But in 1961, both Maris and Mantle would capture the nation's attention as they each hit home runs at a record-breaking pace for much of the season. Ordered by Yankee management to concentrate on home runs, Maris hit 15 in June. By month's end, he had hit 27 and Mantle 25, and the nation's sportswriters started to treat their challenge to Ruth's record seriously. On 17 July, Baseball Commissioner Ford C. Frick, concerned that the newly expanded 162-game American League playing schedule might taint Ruth's record, ruled that a new home-run record would only be recognized if it was achieved within the first 154 games.

As the 1961 season unfolded, fans, active and former players, and writers debated the merits of Frick's decree. The home-run challenge brought out hordes of reporters wherever the Yankees played. Inundated with often simplistic, repetitive questions, badgered for interviews, and besieged by autograph-seekers, Maris withdrew deeper within himself to preserve his privacy. The self-perpetuating nature of the media furor led to inevitable inaccuracies, distortions, and misinterpretations of Maris's words. And Maris, taciturn by nature, harmed his own cause; his curt replies, once published, tended to suggest a surly, abrasive personality. Some writers attempted to play up the story of a feud between Maris and Mantle; in reality, the two men got along well and even shared an apartment that summer with teammate Bob Cerv.

Mantle kept pace with Maris for much of the season, but a hip abscess in September sidelined him and left Maris alone in the full glare of the media spotlight. Yankee officials did nothing to shield their player from media onslaughts as he neared the record. The pressure became almost intolerable for Maris; at one point, he suffered hair loss caused by nervous strain. He failed to equal Ruth's total in 154 games, but on 1 October 1961, the final game of the season, while facing Boston Red Sox pitcher Tracy Stallard at Yankee Stadium, Maris hit the record-breaking sixty-first home run. He went into the record book but his accomplishment was besmirched by an asterisk next to the number 61, keyed to a footnote announcing that Ruth's record for a 154-game season was still valid.

Maris was named Most Valuable Player for the second time in his career and received a plethora of other awards, but his phenomenal season had become a kind of curse. From the start of spring training in 1962, his problems with the press multiplied. Certain reporters portrayed him as a moody, surly complainer. Negative stories by Oscar Fraley and two particularly vicious pieces by sports columnist Jimmy Cannon, who had previously befriended him, deeply hurt and embittered Maris in his subsequent dealings with the media. Also in 1962, Maris became a target for fan abuse. Although he had an excellent season, finishing with 33 home runs and 100 runs batted in, and making a key fielding play that was instrumental in the team's World Series victory (over the San Francisco Giants), he was treated as if he was a failure because he did not match or surpass his 1961 totals. This problem of impossible expectations would blight the rest of his career.

Maris suffered from a variety of injuries that limited his playing time and productivity in 1963, but he finished strong in the final month of the 1964 season as the Yankees rallied to win their fifth consecutive American League championship. It would be his last statistically productive year. In 1965, Maris suffered a serious hand injury. X rays by several doctors failed to reveal any broken bones, but Maris claimed he was in considerable pain and unable to properly grip the bat. Under pressure from team management to play, and doubted by his teammates, baseball writers, and fans as a malingerer, Maris felt betrayed. The severity of his injury was finally discovered months later. He underwent surgery, but he never regained full strength in his right hand and lost partial feeling in several fingers. The incident further strained his already damaged relationship with team management.

After a dispiriting, injury-plagued season in 1966, during which he informed team management of his intention to retire, Maris was traded to the St. Louis Cardinals on 8 December 1966. He decided to postpone retirement and played for two more years. No longer able to hit for power, he contributed to the team's success with his professionalism, experience, and work ethic. In St. Louis, Maris found an appreciative management, respectful teammates, and supportive fans. Careful observers recognized that Maris was a complete player, doing the little things that help win games. In the 1967 World Series, his .385 batting average and 7 runs batted in played a major role in the Cardinals victory over the Red Sox. Maris retired after the 1968 World Series (the Cardinals lost to the Detroit Tigers) to operate with his brother an Anheuser-Busch beer distributorship in Gainesville, Florida.

In twelve seasons he batted .260 with 275 home runs. For several years, Maris kept his distance from baseball, occasionally participating in Old Timers Games, but resolutely declining all invitations tendered by the New York Yankees. Gradually, his attitude softened. On 12 April 1978 he appeared with Mantle at the Yankees home opener, where he received a warm fan reception. On 21 July 1984, his uniform, number 9, was officially retired in ceremonies at Yankee Stadium.

Maris was diagnosed with lymphoma in 1983. His illness went into brief remission after treatment but returned in the summer of 1985. He underwent experimental immune system treatments at the Franklin Clinic in Tennessee and died at the M. D. Anderson Tumor Institute in Houston. He was buried at Holy Cross Cemetery in Fargo.

Roger Maris was an unlikely hero, never comfortable with the demands of fame and the loss of privacy. An honest, straightforward family man of simple tastes, shy and uneasy among strangers, Maris was modest in regard to his own achievements. Unprepared for the media frenzy that enveloped him in 1961, he was badly scarred by the experience. He should be remembered as an excellent ballplayer of considerable courage who had the temerity to shatter the most revered single-season record in American sport and who faced the impossible tasks of living up to the mythical magnitude of his predecessor Ruth and his contemporary teammate, friend, and rival Mantle.

★

Roger Maris and Jim Ogle, *Roger Maris at Bat* (1962), is a colorless account of the 1961 season, offering no real insights into Maris's personality or character. Maury Allen, *Roger Maris: A Man for All Seasons* (1986), a sympathetic biography by a veteran sportswriter and friend, relies primarily on anecdotes and reminiscences of ex-teammates but fails to reveal the inner core of its subject. Harvey Rosenfeld, *Roger Maris*: *A Title to Fame* (1991), emphasizes insights from Maris's boyhood friends and best conveys his North Dakota origins. Tony Kubek and Terry Pluto, *Sixty-One: The Team, the Record, the Men* (1987), devotes more than fifty pages to Maris and underscores the respect and admiration he engendered among his teammates. Ralph Houk and Robert W. Creamer, *Season of Glory: The Amazing Saga of the 1961 New York Yankees* (1988), covers much the same ground as Kubek and Pluto but is clearly less sympathetic to Maris, influenced by his later problems with Houk in the 1965–1966 season. David Halberstam, *October 1964* (1994), adroitly probes the essence of Maris and the walls he constructed to keep the world at a distance.

Hal Lebovitz, "Maris Always Knew He Couldn't Miss," *Sporting News* (1 May 1957), describes the rookie Maris and the negative labels already being applied that would follow him throughout his baseball career. Roger Kahn, "Pursuit of #60: The Ordeal of Roger Maris," *Sports Illustrated* (2 Oct. 1961), best delineates the unrelenting pressure Maris faced in the final weeks of the 1961 season. Jim Ogle, "Fact and Legend of Roger Maris," *Sporting News* (14 Jan. 1967), by Maris's closest friend among sportswriters, is surprisingly frank about his personality quirks and his decline as a player. Rick Telander, "The Record Broke Him," *Sports Illustrated* (20 June 1977), depicts a still-embittered Maris as he began to reach out to his old baseball friends after years of unpleasant memories of his Yankee experience. Mike Bryan, "Reflections on the Game," *Sports Illustrated* (24 Apr. 1989), is a warmhearted appreciation of Maris from his most loyal fan, Andy Strasberg. An obituary is in the *New York Times* (15 Dec. 1985).

EDWARD J. TASSINARI

MARKHAM, Dewey ("Pigmeat") (*b.* 16 [18?] April 1904 [1906?] in Durham, North Carolina; *d.* 13 December 1981 in the Bronx, New York), African-American comedian and actor who originated the phrase "Here come de judge" and influenced American comedians as diverse as Milton Berle, Richard Pryor, and Eddie Murphy.

Markham's family and early life are obscure, and some facts are disputed. One source gives the year of his birth as 1904, another 1906. One has him running away at age thirteen to join a traveling circus. Another has him attending West Durham High School, writing and acting in school plays, and only leaving home after graduation to travel with carnivals for five years before joining the Florida Blossoms Minstrel Show sometime in the 1920s. In any case, after Markham's appearance with the Florida Blossoms, his career is, for the most part, traceable.

During the 1920s and 1930s Markham was a comic in the fading black-minstrel tradition. He left the Florida Blossoms to become the star comic for the Georgia-based Gonzelle White's Minstrel Show (Count Basie was the pianist). He acquired his nickname "Pigmeat" from a skit he performed: "Sweet Papa Pigmeat, with the River Jordan at

Publicity poster for a film starring Pigmeat Markham, 1946. PHOTOFEST/KISCH

my hips, and all the women is just run up to be baptized." Over the next two decades he moved into vaudeville and eventually the Broadway theater.

By his early twenties (1925–1927) Markham was touring with A. D. Price's *Sugar Cane Revue.* In the late 1920s he had a year-and-a-half-long run at the Alhambra Theater in New York City and later appeared at the Standard Theatre in Philadelphia, both with his straight man, George Wilshire. Their act was rooted in the minstrel tradition: "But yo' honor," Wilshire would plead in a typical exchange, "my wife got two buck teeth!" To which Pigmeat would reply: "I don't care how much they cost!" At the Alhambra, Markham introduced the "Here come de judge" routine for which he would eventually achieve national fame. The highlight is Markham's irascible judge who, approaching the bench wearing a magistrate's robe, his followers chanting, "Court's in session, here come de judge!," threatens everyone in the court, even himself: "This judge is high as a Georgia pine! Everybody's goin' to jail today! And to show you I don't mean nobody no good this morning, I'm givin myself six months! And if I'm gonna do six months, district attorney, you can imagine what you're gonna do!"

In 1930 Markham made his Broadway debut, starring in *Hot Rhythm.* Over the next ten years he performed in *Cocktails of 1932, Blackberries* (1932), *Sugar Cane* (1933), and *Ecstatic Ebony* (1939). It was during his years on Broadway that he began appearing in the venue he was to be associated with for the rest of his life, Harlem's famed Apollo, then a relatively new theater. He was on the bill every week from 1935 until 1938, when he moved to Hollywood.

In the 1940s Markham became a screen actor, performing exclusively in "race" (or all-black) movies produced by New York–based Toddy Pictures and aimed at the African-American film market. He first appeared in *Mr. Smith Goes Ghost* (1940), quickly followed by *Am I Guilty?* (1940) with Ralph Cooper, *That's My Baby* (1944), *Fight That Ghost* (1946), *House-Rent Party* (1946), *Look-Out Sister* (1946), *Killer Diller* (1948), and *Boarding House Blues* (1948). While in Hollywood he also had an association with the Andrews Sisters, appearing with them in *Moonlight and Cactus* (1944) and on their radio show, *Eight to the Bar,* playing Alamo, their chief cook.

During the 1950s, when production of all-black films was waning, Markham concentrated on live performances and television. He continued to appear (in fact, he did so well into his seventies) at the Apollo Theatre and began to do guest spots on television variety shows, including those hosted by Johnny Carson, Merv Griffin, and Mike Douglas. Preeminent among these programs was the *Ed Sullivan Show,* on which Markham was a guest more than thirty times during its twenty-three-year run.

In the 1960s, while continuing to appear in theater and on television, Markham began an association with Chess Records (a label specializing in rhythm and blues, jazz, and some comedy) and recorded the routines he had developed during thirty years of live performance. Chess issued nearly twenty records, and these remain his most permanent legacy. Beginning with *The Trial* (1961), Markham released at least an album a year: *Pigmeat Markham at the Party* (1961), *Anything Goes* (1962), *The World's Greatest Clown* (1963), *Moms Mabley and Pigmeat Markham* (1964), *Mr. Funny Man* (1965), *If You Can't Be Good, Be Careful* (1966), *Save Your Soul, Baby* and *Backstage* (1967), *Here Come de Judge* and *The Hustlers* (1968), and *Pigmeat 'Bag* (1969). He also issued two albums on the obscure Jewel label: *Would the Real Pigmeat Markham Please Sit Down* and *The Crap-Shootin' Rev.*

After Sammy Davis, Jr., recreated the "Here come de judge" routine on the 1960s television show *Rowan and Martin's Laugh-In,* it was an overnight sensation (a single derived from the album of the same name reached number 19 on Billboard's Top 100 in July 1968). The phrase entered the national lexicon.

Unfortunately, Markham's fame came near the end of his life. Although he continued to perform into the 1970s, his style quickly became unfashionable and his records were all out of print by the mid-1970s. The emergent Black Nationalists found his type of comedy degrading, a throwback to the Stepin Fetchit era, which catered to stereotypes of the shiftless and superstitious black clown, afraid of ghosts and apparitions. Markham died of a stroke at Montefiore Hospital in the Bronx. He was survived by his wife, the former Bernice Pinn, and their two children. He is buried in Woodlawn Cemetery in the Bronx, New York.

Markham's life spanned several eras of tumultuous show-business and social history. Changing fashions in the performing arts affected race relations, and those changes in turn influenced the arts, especially by broadening the possibilities for African-American artists. He began his career on the all-black minstrel circuit, in which the performers (including African Americans) had to wear blackface. (When this practice became unfashionable, a trend Markham at first resisted, his audiences were surprised to discover that he was lighter than the burnt cork had made him appear.) The minstrel circuit was almost completely removed from white society. Before long, Markham had moved over to vaudeville, where the audiences were more mixed even though the performers were still segregated. By the end of his life he achieved success outside these restricted milieus. However, his fame was never as large as his influence. He complained that other comedians used to steal his material: "The white comedians—Milton Berle, Joey Adams—all the guys came to Harlem . . . with a pencil and shorthand paper and steal comedy from all us boys.

They stole it and carried it into burlesque and kept it for years." It was not only whites who were accused. Claiming to have invented the comical dance walk "truckin'," Markham asserted: "I tried to keep it to myself. Then one day I saw an Al Jolson movie, and there in a big colored sequence was Cab Calloway and his band truckin all over heaven. There was my truck gone down the drain, just like 'Heah come de judge.' " His influence was invisible at first but strong and continuous. His rhythmical delivery, often over a musical accompaniment, was a precursor to rap music. His routines, built around stereotypes that are now dated, made fun of real-life situations, and his use of sexual material was a precursor to the freer, more outspoken styles that emerged in the 1970s and 1980s.

★

There is very little information available about Markham. Most of it is in the form of brief reminiscences of colleagues and is scattered throughout several books devoted to other topics. See especially Jack Schiffman, *Uptown: The Story of Harlem's Apollo Theatre* (1971); Ted Fox, *Showtime at the Apollo* (1983); and Jack Schiffman, *Harlem Heyday: A Pictorial History of Modern Black Show Business and the Apollo Theatre* (1984). Additional information can be found in Henry T. Sampson, *Blacks in Blackface: A Source Book on Early Black Musical Shows* (1980); and John Kisch and Edward Mapp, *A Separate Cinema: Fifty Years of Black-Cast Posters* (1992). Several of Markham's albums are still available, none, however, on compact disc. The following are all cassettes: *Would the Real Pigmeat Markham Please Sit Down,* Jewel 5012 (1973); *The Crap-Shootin' Rev,* Jewel 5007 (1972); *Live at the Apollo,* Jewel 5029 (1970); and *Here Come the Judge,* Chess 91557 (1984), which features his most famous routine and the top-twenty song based on it. An obituary is in the *New York Times* (16 Dec. 1981).

STEPHEN TURTELL

MARKS, John D. ("Johnny") (*b.* 10 November 1909 in Mount Vernon, New York; *d.* 3 September 1985 in New York City), composer of more than 175 songs, notably "Rudolph the Red-Nosed Reindeer."

Born to Louis B. Marks and Sadie Van Pragg, Johnny Marks was raised primarily in the Northeast. He was drawn to music at an early age and began composing songs at the age of thirteen. Music remained his central focus for the rest of his life. In 1931 he attended Colgate University in Hamilton, New York, where he earned a B.A. degree in 1935 and became a member of Phi Beta Kappa. He later studied music at Columbia University and in Paris but received no further academic degrees.

During the early part of his career, Marks supported himself by coaching singers and producing radio shows. By 1935 he was working full-time as a songwriter. In the early

Johnny Marks holding the sheet music and a Paul McCartney recording of his song *Rudolph the Red-Nosed Reindeer*, 1979. UPI/CORBIS-BETTMANN

1940s he worked alongside other composers in the Brill Building in the area of Manhattan known as Tin Pan Alley. For a time he shared an office with Dick Jacobs, who scored the arrangements for Gene Autry's version of "Rudolph the Red-Nosed Reindeer." Jacobs recounts in his 1988 book, *Who Wrote That Song?*, that he agreed to score arrangements for the song on speculation; Jacobs received nothing, with the understanding that if the song was successful, Marks would pay him double union scale. After the song became successful, Marks paid Jacobs the agreed amount plus, what Jacobs called, a "handsome bonus."

During his service in World War II, Marks produced shows for the army with the Twenty-sixth Special Service Company both in the United States and overseas. He was awarded a Bronze Star and four battle stars during his tour of duty. On 25 October 1947, Marks married Margaret Hope May. The couple had three children.

Marks formed St. Nicholas Music in 1949 in order to publish "Rudolph the Red-Nosed Reindeer." From the start, Marks was convinced of the song's potential, although some, most notably Autry, did not share his enthusiasm. Marks based the popular song on an advertising brochure given away by a Montgomery Ward store in Chicago in 1939, which included a story by Robert L. May, from which Marks derived his title. Marks reportedly carried the title with him for ten years before penning the song. His belief in the song's potential played a major role in its eventual success.

"Rudolph the Red-Nosed Reindeer" was first recorded by Autry, known as the "singing cowboy." Autry admitted later that he included it on the flip side of one of his records primarily because Autry's wife thought the song was good. Ironically, the A-side of the single disappeared into obscurity, while Autry's version of "Rudolph the Red-Nosed Reindeer" sold more than 12.5 million copies. It was later recorded by a number of other celebrities, and by 1998 more than 300 different versions of the song had been recorded, resulting in the sale of more than 150 million records. Meanwhile, more than 8 million copies of the sheet music and more than 25 million copies of choral and orchestral arrangements had been sold, making "Rudolph the Red-Nosed Reindeer" one of the best and most consistent-selling songs of all time.

Marks composed other hits, most with Christmas themes, including "Rockin' Around the Christmas Tree," composed in 1958 and recorded by Brenda Lee in 1960; "A Holly Jolly Christmas," written in 1963 and recorded by Burl Ives; and "I Heard the Bells on Christmas Day," recorded by Bing Crosby in 1956. Marks also wrote musical scores for television and commercials. The "Rudolph the Red-Nosed Reindeer" special, which Marks scored, was broadcast in 1963 and became one of the longest running specials in the history of television. He also wrote scores for "Ballad of Smokey the Bear," "The Tiny Tree," "Rudolph's Shiny New Year," and "Rudolph and Frosty."

In addition to his work as a composer and publisher, Marks served on the board of directors of the American Society of Composers, Authors and Publishers (ASCAP) and the Songwriters Hall of Fame. He even had a small part in the 1933 film *Harmony Row*. Marks died of complications from diabetes.

Marks was described by his friends as a gentle man. His work as a composer, publisher, and producer have earned him a permanent place in the musical heritage of America. Many of his compositions are deeply ingrained into American culture, and many of his melodies and lyrics have become inseparably associated with Christmas. Indeed, his works suffuse so much of the Christmas holidays that virtually the entire American population and much of the world population is intimately familiar with his work.

★

There is no full-length biography on Marks, but his life and work are frequently touched on in books on the music industry, such as the *ASCAP Biographical Dictionary* (1980), *The Complete Encyclopedia of Popular Music and Jazz, 1900–1950* (1974), and *Baker's Biographical Dictionary of Musicians* (1978), and are occasionally commented on in works by his friends and acquaintances, such as in Dick Jacobs, *Who Wrote That Song?* (1988). Obituaries are in the *New York Times* and the *Washington Post* (both 4 Sept. 1985).

KEVIN ALEXANDER BOON

MARRIOTT, J(ohn) Willard ("Bill") (*b.* 17 September 1900 in Marriott, Utah; *d.* 13 August 1985 in Wolfeboro, New Hampshire), restaurateur, founder of the Marriott Corporation, philanthropist, and religious leader.

The second of eight children born to Ellen Morris and Hyrum Willard "Will" Marriott, J. Willard "Bill" Marriott grew up west of Ogden in Marriott, Utah, which was named for his grandfather John Marriott. Both grandfathers, John Marriott and William Morris, had converted to the Church of Jesus Christ of Latter-day Saints (LDS) in England and had immigrated to Utah. A farmer, rancher, and local leader, Marriott's father served in the bishopric of the Marriott LDS ward and in the Utah state legislature. His mother was a homemaker.

While growing up, Bill farmed row crops, herded sheep and cattle, and attended school. Beginning at age fourteen, he marketed the family's sheep in San Francisco and Omaha. A good student and avid reader, he impressed his

J. Willard Marriott, *c.* 1983. UPI/CORBIS-BETTMANN

teachers at Slaterville School. Active in the LDS Church, at age nineteen he began two years of service as a proselytizing missionary in New England and New York.

On his return, Marriott found his father's family deeply in debt. Heavy borrowing and low agricultural prices after World War I had ravaged their farming and ranching operations. In part because of his early experiences and in part because of Ralph Waldo Emerson's writings on self-reliance and hard work, Marriott sought in education and entrepreneurship a way off the farm and out of poverty. Although he had not graduated from high school, he approached his former teacher Aaron Tracy, a professor and president-designate of Weber College, which had just added a junior-college curriculum. Tracy agreed to enroll him. Financing his education by selling advertisements for school publications and clerking at the college bookstore, Marriott graduated with the college's first class in June 1923.

After graduation, he worked as a clothing and woolens salesman in Nevada, northern California, and the Northwest. He continued to sell during the summers while finishing his education at the University of Utah, where he graduated in 1926. Tracy induced him to return briefly to Weber College as a teacher, treasurer, and manager.

During his senior year at the University of Utah, Marriott met Alice "Allie" Sheets, an honor student. Bill and Allie were married in the Salt Lake LDS Temple on 9 June 1927; they had two children.

On 10 May 1927 Marriott and Hugh Colton opened a small A & W Root Beer franchise stand in Washington, D.C. After their marriage Allie managed a second stand (also in Washington) and kept the company's books. To capture the winter trade, they renamed the restaurants the Hot Shoppes and offered Mexican-style fast foods. In 1928 Colton returned to Utah to practice law, and Marriott bought his share of the company. During the early 1930s Marriott opened additional Hot Shoppes in the greater Washington area and in Baltimore and Philadelphia.

Marriott contracted Hodgkin's disease in 1934. Given six months to live by his doctors, he called on two LDS leaders, who gave him a priesthood blessing. Before Christmas, tests showed him free of the disease.

Between 1937 and 1951 Marriott enlarged his food-service businesses. In 1937 his company began to furnish meals for airline passengers. During World War II he offered lunch-wagon services and opened cafeterias. In March 1947 the company started take-out service in Rosslyn, Virginia. During and after the war Marriott expanded his geographic base until by 1950 his companies operated in twelve states and the District of Columbia. In 1953 Hot Shoppes, Inc. (later renamed Marriott Corporation) offered stock to the public.

Marriott also engaged in professional, church, and civic activities. In 1948 he was president of the National Restaurant Association. After serving as second counselor in the presidency of the Washington, D.C., LDS stake from 1946 to 1948, he was called as stake president, a position he held for nine and a half years. Following his term, he was an Aaronic-priesthood adviser and Sunday-school teacher. He served on the committee to install the Brigham Young statue in the U.S. Capitol rotunda in 1950, and he worked actively in restoring buildings in Nauvoo, Illinois, the city from which the Mormons fled in 1846.

In 1957 the Marriott Corporation began to expand into the motor-hotel and specialty-restaurant business. Its first establishment was the Twin Bridges Motor Hotel in Arlington, Virginia. In November 1958 Marriott assigned his son Bill, Jr., to launch a multimillion-dollar motor-hotel program. The Marriotts opened hotels in various cities, including Dallas, Philadelphia, and Atlanta. They also opened Fairfield Inns and the Sirloin and Saddles and Kona Kai Hawaiian restaurants. Later they started fast-food restaurants and franchises, including the Roy Rogers and Big Boy chains.

In 1964, after continuing the company's expansion program, Marriott turned over the presidency of the corporation to his son, although he remained chairman of the board. Bill Jr. borrowed heavily for a rapid expansion of the hotel business; fearing debt, Marriott was not entirely pleased with such extensive borrowing.

Bill and Allie were lifelong Republicans. She served on the Republican National Committee and as convention treasurer in 1964, 1968, and 1972. They tended to support the moderate rather than the conservative wing of the party, favoring Dwight Eisenhower, associating with Nelson Rockefeller, and supporting George Romney, a personal friend. Despite bad health during the latter part of 1968, Marriott chaired Richard Nixon's 1969 inaugural committee, a post he held again in 1973.

During the 1960s and 1970s Marriott devoted considerable time to philanthropic and public affairs. He contributed $1 million each to the University of Utah for a library and to Brigham Young University for a basketball-activities center. In 1970, in the midst of the national turmoil over U.S. involvement in Vietnam, he chaired the Independence Day celebration in Washington, D.C., a service he repeated for the Bicentennial celebration of 1976. As he remained active in business and public affairs, his health continued to deteriorate. In late 1975 and early 1976 he suffered four heart attacks. Nevertheless, he participated in the opening of new hotels and in the first of three Marriott Great America theme parks.

Marriott suffered a heart attack at his family summer home on Lake Winnipesaukee in New Hampshire and was pronounced dead at Wolfeboro. He was buried in the Parklawn Memorial Park in Rockville, Maryland. At the time of his death, the Marriott Corporation had operations and franchises in fifty states and twenty-seven countries, including 125 hotels and 64 flight kitchens. It owned 667 restaurants and franchised 935 more. Beyond this, it operated 2 vacation resorts, 78 airport food-service facilities, 3 cruise ships, 2,097 catering accounts, and 19 shops.

Born to a family of moderate means but local prominence, Marriott worked to pay his way through college and saved and borrowed to enter business in Washington, D.C. A man of enormous energy and exceptional business sense, he succeeded largely through attending to economy, recognizing the changing role of the automobile in the lives of people, understanding the increasing importance of family dining and fast food, researching carefully locations for his businesses, and insisting on high quality for company products and services. A significant part of his success must also be attributed to his wife, Allie, who worked in the businesses and provided exceptional support and encouragement.

★

Marriott's papers are collected in the John Willard and Alice Sheets Marriott Papers, 1924–1984, Special Collections, Manuscripts, J. Willard Marriott Library, University of Utah, Salt Lake City. A collection of family photographs is in the John Willard Marriott Photograph Collection, ca. 1890–1980, in the same library. A full-length biography based on family records and interviews is Robert O'Brien, *Marriott: The J. Willard Marriott Story* (1977). A study of the family is found in Richard L. Jensen, *J. Willard Marriott's Ancestors,* Taskpapers in LDS History, no. 32 (1980). Ronna Romney's *Giving Time a Chance: The Secret of a Lasting Marriage* (1983) considers his marriage. See also the award citation in *Opportunity Still Knocks: Freedom's Living Proof of the Opportunities Under American Free Enterprise* (1975). An obituary is in *Deseret News* (14 Aug. 1985).

THOMAS G. ALEXANDER

MARTIN, Freddy (*b.* 9 October 1906 in Columbus, Ohio; *d.* 1 October 1983 in Newport Beach, California), musician, composer, and orchestra leader who helped shape the course of big-band music, particularly with his 1941 hit, "Tonight We Love," his adaptation of the Tchaikovsky Piano Concerto in B-flat.

Orphaned at age four, Freddy Martin was raised in the Knights of Pythias Orphanage in Springfield, Ohio. As a teenager, he became interested in music and at age sixteen moved to Cleveland to work in a music store. There he demonstrated the saxophone, which he taught himself to play from instruction books in the store. After an unsuccessful attempt to sell an alto saxophone to the bandleader Guy Lombardo and his brother Carmen, Martin became interested in performing music himself. Guy Lombardo became his mentor and encouraged him to form an orchestra.

Captain Freddy Martin and His Mariners opened in 1931 at the Hotel Bossert in Brooklyn, New York. Throughout the Great Depression the orchestra somehow managed to find regular work, usually through radio broadcasts that spread Martin's popularity across the country. Martin remained at the Hotel Bossert for four years before moving the Mariners to prominent hotels in New York City and Chicago, including the St. Regis, the Waldorf-Astoria, the Ritz-Carlton, the Roosevelt, and the Aragon Ballroom.

During his career as a big-band orchestra leader, Martin signed with several recording labels, including Columbia, Bluebird, and Capitol. During the 1930s the Mariners also recorded under pseudonyms to increase their sales; phony names included the Bellboys of Broadway, Vincent Rose, Freddie Stone, and Bob Causer's Cornellians. Freddy Martin and his orchestra signed with RCA Victor, one of the premier record labels, in July 1938 and continued that affiliation for more than two decades.

In 1938 Martin and his orchestra, now called the Freddy Martin Band, moved to the West Coast and played at the Cocoanut Grove in the Ambassador Hotel in Los Angeles. So beloved by local fans that he was nicknamed "Mr. Cocoanut Grove," Martin played in the room for many years. In 1948 the band established an extended stint playing at the Grove, which became an annual event. The "Back to the Grove" appearances continued until the mid-1960s.

Live radio broadcasts ensured the success of the Freddy Martin Band. Their popularity soared even further in 1941 when Martin heard pianist Vladimir Horowitz's live radio broadcast of a Tchaikovsky concerto and immediately adapted that piece, the Piano Concerto in B-flat, for the big-band sound. "Tonight We Love" became his biggest-selling record and a staple in the band's repertoire. Martin, along with his pianist Jack Fina, then began adapting other classics, including ones by Rimsky-Korsakov and Rachmaninoff.

"Tonight We Love" propelled the Freddy Martin Band into the ranks of other beloved big-band orchestras, such as those led by Jimmy Dorsey and Glenn Miller. Martin's orchestra continued its success in 1941 with "The Hut-Sut Song" and "Why Don't We Do This More Often?," both featuring singer Eddie Stone. The band's popularity took its toll on the musicians and led to a crisis. Martin, taking advantage of the popularity of "Tonight We Love," organized a grueling tour that involved some ninety one-night stands. Exhausted, more than half of his orchestra members quit. Martin took the opportunity to replace them with new faces, including singer Merv Griffin, who later gained fame as a television talk-show host and producer. By the mid-1940s Martin's new band had another slew of hits, in part because of the singing of Merv Griffin on "I've Got a Lovely Bunch of Cocoanuts" and "Deep in a Dream."

Martin was known in the musical business as a humble

Freddy Martin. ARCHIVE PHOTOS

and soft-spoken leader and was admired as both an orchestra leader and a performer. His playing was lauded by some of the great saxophone players of the era, including alto saxophonist Johnny Hodges of Duke Ellington's band and tenor saxophonist Leon ("Chu") Berry, who said that Martin was his favorite saxophone player. The smooth character of Martin's playing, along with the distinctive voices of Griffin and Stone, made his band instantly distinguishable to listeners.

By the 1960s the big-band era was over, but the Freddy Martin Band resisted splitting up and played charity balls and conventions throughout the decade. Martin played often in Las Vegas, stopping only briefly during 1965, when he had a heart attack.

In 1972 Martin organized the Big Band Cavalcade, a traveling musical production that highlighted three different bandleaders who rotated the conducting duties. The orchestra featured some of the most famous big-band musicians, with Martin, Bob Crosby, and Frankie Carle among the stars. The Cavalcade was so successful that the orchestra repeated the tour. In 1977 Martin was asked by the Guy Lombardo family to substitute for the ailing bandleader, who had remained Martin's friend. Martin agreed and led Lombardo's band, the Royal Canadians, until Lombardo died later that year.

In the 1980s Martin played few concerts and concentrated mainly on his publishing firm in Sherman Oaks, California. He also booked engagements for the Freddy Martin Band and kept a collection of its recordings in his possession. The Martin orchestra did play a few engagements a week and for one week a year played at Disneyland in Anaheim, California. Martin and his wife, Lillian, married for over half a century, lived in Newport Beach, California, enjoying retirement and sailing with their son and his family. Freddy Martin died from complications from strokes in Hoag Memorial Hospital in Newport Beach.

Freddy Martin is best known for his adaptation of classical themes for a pop music audience. He sparked new interest in the waning big-band sound with the Big Band Cavalcade. Martin was also regarded as a master on the saxophone and incorporated those sweet sounds into his distinctive musical arrangements.

★

Leo Walker, *The Big Band Almanac* (1978), includes a history of Martin's professional career and includes theme songs, recording affiliations, and media history. The jacket insert for the Franklin Mint Record Society's *Greatest Recordings of the Big Band Era* (album 18, nos. 69–72) contains a lengthy interview and expansive survey of Martin's life. Obituaries—containing some inaccuracies about Martin's personal life—are in the *New York Times* and *Washington Post* (both 1 Oct. 1983).

JUDITH A. PARKER

MASSEY, Raymond Hart (*b.* 30 August 1896 in Toronto, Canada; *d.* 29 July 1983 in Los Angeles, California), stage, film, and television actor.

Raymond Massey, 1940s. POPPERFOTO/ARCHIVE PHOTOS

Massey was one of two sons of Chester D. Massey, the head of an agriculture tool company, and Anna Vincent. Though his father was Canadian, Massey traced his American ancestry back to the Revolutionary War on both sides of his family. After graduating from Appleby School in Ontario in 1914, he served as a lieutenant in the Canadian army in World War I. Seriously wounded in France in 1916, he was sent home. After a lengthy recovery, he served from 1917 to 1918 as a gunnery instructor in the United States at Yale and Princeton Universities. From 1918 to 1919, he served in Siberia, where he organized a minstrel show to entertain the troops. His production was so successful that he was ordered to spend the rest of World War I putting on shows.

In 1919 Massey enrolled at the University of Oxford in England, where he studied for two years. He did some work in the school's theatrical productions but often lost the larger roles because he sounded too American. In 1921, he went back to Canada to work in the family firm. Realizing that he really wanted to act, Massey received his father's blessing and moved to London to look for work in the theater. Also in 1921, he married Margery Fremantle. They had one daughter.

In 1922, after only a few weeks of job hunting, Massey made his London theatrical debut in Eugene O'Neill's play *In the Zone*. Over the next few years, he worked steadily in the theater. Tall and lanky, he did not have the matinee-idol looks, but he still managed to get the leads in romantic and dramatic plays on the strength of his stage presence, stentorian voice, and talent. In 1924, he starred with Sybil Thorndyke in the premiere of George Bernard Shaw's play *St. Joan.*

In 1925, while also working as a stage manager, Massey got his first theatrical directing job with *Tunnel-Trench,* a war story in which he also acted. By the end of the 1920s, Massey was solidly established in the London West End theaters as a versatile actor and producer. In 1929 he divorced his first wife and married Adrienne Allen, an actress. In his second marriage, Massey had two children and gained a stepchild. In 1931, Massey debuted on Broadway in a new version of *Hamlet* adapted by Norman Bel Geddes. Both the play and Massey's performance took pound-ings from the critics. He returned to New York in 1934 and fared much better in Keith Winter's *The Shining Hour,* which also starred his wife.

In the mid-1930s Massey appeared in films, including H. G. Wells's production *Things to Come* (1935) and *The Prisoner of Zenda* (1937). Years later Massey's most vivid memory of *Things to Come* was of how uncomfortable the futuristic costumes were during the English summer. Robert Sherwood also approached Massey to star in a play about Abraham Lincoln, *Abe Lincoln in Illinois,* which was ready for its debut in 1938. Massey's performance was a triumph, winning him the New York Drama League Medal for Outstanding Performance. He then starred in the screen adaptation in 1940. In 1939, Massey divorced his second wife and married Dorothy Ludington Whitney. They had no children.

In 1941 Massey worked with the director Michael Powell in *The Invaders,* a thriller involving Nazi spies entering the United States at Niagara Falls. Its propaganda value was blunted by the fact that the United States had entered the war by the time the film was released. Even though he was in his mid-forties when the war started, Massey accepted a commission as a major in the Canadian army in 1942. Deciding that he was too old to be of any value to the war effort, he resigned the next year and concentrated on his work as an entertainer. In 1943 he starred with Humphrey Bogart in *Action in the North Atlantic,* a tribute to the merchant marine. On one occasion, the two lead actors convinced the director to let them do their own stunt scenes on a burning set.

Massey was working on Broadway when he became an American citizen on 21 March 1944. In 1945, during the final days of the war, he celebrated his citizenship by producing *Our Town* for the United Service Organizations (USO) and entertaining the troops in Europe with a play that effectively dramatized the ideals of the American experience. He worked again with Powell in the ensemble film *Stairway to Heaven* (1946), starring with David Niven and Kim Hunter. At the end of the war, he was working on a weekly radio variety show, *Harvest of Stars.* In the fall of 1945, Massey played Henry Higgins in a limited Broadway run of *Pygmalion,* with Gertrude Lawrence as Eliza Doolittle.

Massey joined Tyrone Power and Judith Anderson in a road show that dramatized Stephen Vincent Benét's poem *John Brown's Body* (1952). Backed up by a twenty-member chorus, the actors played engagements in eighty separate towns in the first year and went back on the road in 1953. After a relative dry spell in films, Massey in 1954 signed to play Adam Trask in an adaptation of John Steinbeck's book *East of Eden* (1955), directed by Elia Kazan. Massey had little patience for the method-acting style of his on-screen son James Dean, leading to tension between them on and off the set. Kazan deliberately used this tension to enhance the movie's drama, and the film won an Oscar nomination for best picture.

In 1960 Massey and his wife moved from Wilton, Connecticut, to Hollywood, where Massey played Dr. Gillespie in the television series *Dr. Kildare.* He had an easy rapport with his costar Richard Chamberlain, and the successful series ran until 1966. Thereafter, poor health confined Massey to sporadic work in the theater, such as a 1970 London production of Robert Anderson's play *I Never Sang for My Father.* The 1976 Los Angeles revival of *Night of the Iguana,* Massey's final stage work, reunited him with Chamberlain.

In the 1970s, Massey published two memoirs, *When I Was Young* (1976) and *A Hundred Different Lives* (1979). He died of pneumonia in Los Angeles. Massey's career had been successful in every facet of the entertainment industry.

★

In addition to Massey's memoirs, see his obituaries in the *New York Times* (31 July 1983) and *The Annual Obituary 1983* (1984).

TERRY BALLARD

MAYS, Benjamin Elijah (*b.* 1 August 1894 in Epworth, South Carolina; *d.* 28 March 1984 in Atlanta, Georgia), teacher, theologian, author, and college president who dedicated his life to defending the rights of black people and who examined the role of the church in black-white relationships in the South in several notable books.

The youngest of eight children born to S. Hezekiah and Louvenia Carter Mays, Benjamin grew up in a religious and loving sharecropper family. Raised in segregated rural South Carolina, he witnessed his father's fear of and humiliation by a mob of white men at age four, which made racial discrimination an inescapable issue throughout his life. Limited education was one of the many obstacles facing black children in the rural South (they attended classes only from November to February because of farm chores), but young Mays embraced the cultivation of mind over soil. He graduated high school in 1916 as class valedictorian from South Carolina State College (colleges in those days provided classes for students without high school facilities). Encouraged by his mother but opposed by his father, he attended Virginia Union University, then went north to Bates College in Lewiston, Maine. Diligent in his efforts, he graduated with honors and a B.A. degree in 1920. He began graduate studies at the University of Chicago School of Divinity but left to accept an offer to teach college math and high school algebra at Morehouse College in Atlanta, Georgia.

In 1922, after being ordained a Baptist minister, he became the pastor of nearby Shiloh Baptist Church. Three years later he returned to the University of Chicago, earning

The Reverend Dr. Benjamin E. Mays, 1963. UPI/CORBIS-BETTMANN

an M.A. in 1925. Further graduate studies were interrupted by an offer to teach English at the State College of South Carolina at Orangeburg (1925) and his position as executive secretary of the Tampa Urban League (1926). From 1928 to 1930, he served as national student secretary of the Young Men's Christian Association. His first wife, Ellen Harvin, had passed away after an operation in 1923, and on 9 August 1926 he married Sadie Gray, a teacher and social worker and his devoted companion until her death in 1969. Mays had no children.

Mays and Joseph W. Nicholson, a minister in the Colored Methodist Episcopal Church, studied the structure of the black church from 1930 to 1932, which resulted in Mays's first book, *The Negro's Church*, published in 1933. With Phi Beta Kappa honors officially awarded from Bates in 1935, Mays finished his doctoral studies that same year at the University of Chicago in Christian theology and ethics.

As dean of the School of Divinity at Howard University (1934–1940), his commitment to upgrade the school resulted in national and international attention among theologians, as well as the seminary's accreditation from the American Association of Theological Schools (1940). The school was later rededicated as the Benjamin E. Mays School of Divinity. Sought after as an emissary for the U.S. government, Mays traveled extensively throughout the

world during this period. His second book, *The Negro's God, as Reflected in His Literature,* a study of the black man's perception of God, was published in 1938. Carter G. Woodson wrote in his review in the *Journal of Negro History* (1939) that Mays's book was "the beginning of a much needed extensive study of the Negro's conception of God." In July 1940 Mays became the sixth president of Morehouse College in Atlanta. In 1942 he wrote: "The goals of education in the Negro liberal arts colleges must be defined in terms of social responsibility." He felt that African-American students should "believe and be taught that they can break through barriers however insurmountable they may seem." Faithful to the integrity that sustained him, Mays cultivated many unique alliances in his efforts to build a better Morehouse. One such relationship was with Margaret Mitchell, author of *Gone with the Wind*. In an exchange of letters with President Mays, Mitchell, a fellow Georgian, generously endowed Morehouse College with a $10,000 gift.

During World War II, when the college was fiscally threatened by the depleting pool of male students, Mays developed an early admission program for those too young for military service. In 1944, at the age of fifteen, Martin Luther King, Jr., came under Mays's wing as a candidate for early admittance to Morehouse. King deemed Mays his spiritual mentor and intellectual father, and on 9 April 1968, after King's assassination, Mays eulogized King, proclaiming "so close and so precious was he to me."

As a humanitarian who believed in educational and spiritual remedies to battle racial discrimination, Mays took his role as mentor very seriously. Often referred to as the "last of the great schoolmasters," Mays was a handsome, tall, quiet, and dignified man who believed that, in the wake of oppression, colleges should help black students understand religious values through curriculum, role modeling, and mandatory chapel services, and that Christianity transcended race. In 1944 he became the first black vice president of the Federal Council of the Churches of Christ in America. His tenure at Morehouse yielded many proud and committed black men. Honoring Mays in the U.S. House of Representatives on Mays's centennial birth date, Representative John Lewis of Georgia remarked: "He single-handedly cultivated an institution geared toward producing African-American leaders."

In 1969, at the age of seventy-five, Mays won election to the Atlanta Board of Education. A year later he became the first black president to oversee such a large public school system. After a long illness, he died in an Atlanta hospital. He was buried next to his wife in Southview Cemetery in Atlanta.

Mays received countless recognitions from public officials, academic institutions, associations, and religious affiliations around the world. Many distinguished men and women received scholarships, awards, fellowships, and a host of other pedagogical commendations bearing the name of Benjamin E. Mays from institutions of higher learning across the country.

★

The personal papers of Benjamin Elijah Mays are located at Moorland-Spingarn Research Center, Howard University, Washington, D.C. His autobiography is *Born to Rebel: An Autobiography* (1971). See also Marcus H. Boulware, *The Oratory of Negro Leaders, 1900–1968* (1969), and Ira J. Johnson and William J. Pickens, *Benjamin E. Mays and Margaret Mitchell: A Unique Legacy in Medicine* (1996). Journal articles that include biographical information on Mays are Joseph V. Baker, "Morehouse, Builder of Human Leadership," *Brown American* (Mar. 1942): a1–a8; Leon W. Lindsay, "The Views of Benjamin Mays," *Integrated Education* (May/June 1970): 50–53; "Dr. Benjamin E. Mays," *Ebony* (July 1971): 88–94; Jacob Worthham, "Benjamin E. Mays at Eighty-One," *Black Enterprise* (May 1977): 26–29; Pearl L. McNeil, "Baptist Black Americans and the Ecumenical Movement," *Journal of Ecumenical Studies* (1980): 103–117; Leonard Ray Teel, "Benjamin E. Mays: Teaching By Example, Leading Through Will," *Change* (Oct. 1982): 14–22; Charles V. Willie, "The Education of Benjamin Elijah Mays: An Experience," *Teacher College Record* 84 (summer 1983): 955–962; Freddie C. Colston, "Dr. Benjamin E. Mays: His Impact as Spiritual and Intellectual Mentor to Martin Luther King," *Black Scholar* 23 (summer 1993): 6–16; and Lerone Bennett, "Benjamin E. Mays: Last of the Great Schoolmasters," *Ebony* (Oct. 1994). Obituaries are in *Crisis* (Mar. 1984); the *New York Times* (29 Mar. 1984); *Christian Century* (11 Apr. 1984); and *Jet* (16 Apr. 1984).

GLORIA GRANT ROBERSON

MEDEIROS, Humberto Sousa (*b.* 6 October 1915 in Arrifes, São Miguel, Portuguese Azores; *d.* 17 December 1983 in Boston, Massachusetts), Roman Catholic cardinal and archbishop of Boston in the 1970s and 1980s, a period of racial turmoil.

Medeiros was the son of Antonio and Maria Medeiros; he had three siblings. The impoverished family emigrated from the Azores to Fall River, Massachusetts, in 1931. Medeiros swept factory floors to support his family during the Depression, teaching himself English, French, and algebra. He later went to high school and finished in less than three years, graduating first in a class of 651. He became a U.S. citizen in 1940.

After high school, Medeiros attended the Catholic University of America in Washington, D.C. He was ordained a priest on 15 June 1946 and returned to Fall River, serving in various Portuguese parishes for the next three years. He returned to Catholic University to complete his doctorate and went back to Fall River again in 1953. He held various positions over the next several years in the Fall River diocese. Then, in 1960, Medeiros was named pastor of St. Michael's Church, his childhood parish.

In April 1966 Pope Paul VI appointed him bishop of Brownsville, Texas. He arrived in the middle of a migrant farmworker strike led by César Chávez. Medeiros sided with the mostly Mexican and Catholic farmworkers. He said Mass in the fields and spent Christmas and Easter visiting local jails. He backed the workers' right to unionize; when criticized for associating with Chávez, Medeiros told the landowners, "If Christ were alive today, do you think he would cut himself off from MAYOS [Mexican American Youth Organization members] or the Black Panthers? He might not approve of everything they were doing, but he would not cut himself off from them."

During his tenure in Brownsville, Medeiros was a member of the American bishops' committees on Latin America and on farm labor. His efforts to conciliate farmworkers and landowners won plaudits from his superiors in Rome, and in September 1970 Pope Paul VI named him archbishop of Boston. With 2 million Catholics, the archdiocese was the second-largest in the United States. It had rapidly expanded into the suburbs after World War II and faced a crippling $42 million debt. Medeiros became the first non-Irish archbishop in Boston since 1848. In addition, his predecessor was Cardinal Richard Cushing, the legendary and enormously popular spiritual leader of Boston Catholics for twenty-six years. From the outset, Medeiros met resistance from some Irish Americans. Within hours of his arrival in October 1970, someone put a burning cross on the front lawn of archdiocese headquarters; arsonists set fire to the church television studios; and the next day police found a pipe bomb on the doorstep of Medeiros's residence.

In the early 1970s, civil rights activists filed suit against the city, saying it systematically put black students in low-quality schools with poor teachers. In 1974 U.S. District Judge W. Arthur Garrity, Jr., ordered the city to desegregate the schools by busing black and white students to different neighborhoods around Boston. White parents, especially in the Irish-Catholic neighborhoods of South Boston and Charlestown, were angered. They protested in the streets by the thousands, often violently and with nakedly racist epithets. They also rushed to transfer their children out of the public school system and into the church's extensive network of parochial schools. Medeiros, who had been elevated to cardinal in 1973, outraged many Catholics by ordering local parishes not to accept students fleeing the integrated schools. Some Catholics called for a boycott of the Annual Appeal, a yearly fund-raiser for the financially strapped church. Many pastors simply ignored the order. The archdiocese mailed out letters to pastors who flouted the no-transfer policy but never took any disciplinary action against them, leading to criticism from civil rights progressives that the cardinal was not serious about his policy.

Bishop Humberto Medeiros, Boston, 1970. UPI/CORBIS-BETTMANN

As the dispute reached its peak in 1975, Medeiros avoided firm statements on either side of the issue. At one point he publicly said he opposed busing. Later, he deferred to city politicians and Judge Garrity to let them solve the busing issue. Aftershocks of the busing crisis lingered well into the 1980s, but Medeiros had other problems to address. He wrestled with the archdiocese's debt. He loathed the back-slapping approach to raising money, but indirect fund-raising like the Annual Appeal fell short of his goals. Medeiros then turned to cutting the church budget. He slashed the budget by 40 percent from 1970 to 1977, which did little to win back Catholics already alienated by the busing crisis.

Medeiros also prodded Catholics in public policy. He believed Catholic voters were morally responsible for the policies of lawmakers they supported. Five days before the elections of 1980, he released a letter stating that "the law of God extends into the polling booth." The letter obviously referred to Barney Frank, a pro-choice, pro–gay rights politician running for the U.S. House of Representatives; Frank ultimately won.

On 5 September 1983, Medeiros was hospitalized for heart pains. Doctors performed surgery. When he showed little improvement, they operated again on 16 September. Medeiros died of heart failure the next day. His last words reportedly were, "Whatever God wants."

★

J. Anthony Lukas, *Common Ground: A Turbulent Decade in the Lives of Three American Families* (1985), describes the Boston racial crisis in great detail. Obituaries are in the *New York Times* and *Boston Globe* (both 18 Sept. 1983).

MATTHEW KELLY

MERCER, Mabel (*b.* 3 February 1900 in Burton-on-Trent, Staffordshire, England; *d.* 20 April 1984 in Pittsfield, Massachusetts), singer and cabaret entertainer best known for her interpretation of song lyrics and advocacy of many classic American theatrical and popular compositions.

Many of Mabel Mercer's maternal relations were painters, singers, and dancers; her English-Welsh mother performed in British music halls under the name of Mabel LaBlanche. Her father was an African-American traveling musician with the surname of Mercer who met LaBlanche on a trip to England; the union was very short-lived. Because her mother was constantly on tour, Mercer was raised by her grandmother in Liverpool; by age seven she was attending a convent boarding school in Manchester.

By 1914 Mercer was dancing in her aunt's vaudeville act. Minstrel-style entertainment and the newly emerging jazz music were already popular in the British Isles. Mercer's mixed racial heritage compelled her to work in shows featuring "colored" artists. Her study of piano and her inherent musicality soon put her in demand as a rehearsal accompanist and occasionally as an orchestra conductor. Mercer first visited Paris as a member of a singing group that specialized in Negro spirituals; by 1924 she was a featured singer at a Paris cabaret called Le Grand Duc. She sang and danced in the chorus of Lew Leslie's *Blackbirds of 1926* and, in 1927, acted in the London production of *Show Boat*.

In 1931 Mercer was hired by the cabaret performer and nightclub owner Ada "Bricktop" Smith as a hostess and entertainer at her new boîte located at 66 rue Pigalle, Paris. While working at Bricktop's, Mercer became a favorite among European royalty and the cream of American expatriates. This venue gave her an opportunity to develop an intimate manner of presenting song lyrics; it was at Bricktop's that she discovered the benefits of singing while seated.

Seeking a haven from the tumultuous political climate that produced World War II, she moved to New York City in 1938. Her first New York engagement was at Le Ruban Bleu. During an engagement in the Bahamas she met an African-American jazz pianist, Kelsey Pharr, whom she married on 21 January 1941. According to legend the marriage was arranged in order to obtain a visa for Mercer. (She became a naturalized citizen on 3 March 1952.) The marriage ended with Pharr's death in 1964. They had no children.

By 1942 Mercer was working at Tony's, a club located at 59 West Fifty-second Street in Manhattan. Due to wartime travel restrictions the ocean-hopping of New York's social elite was curtailed. The resulting boom in New York City's nightlife helped Mercer re-create the magic of her Paris days at Bricktop's. Not only did socialites flock to Tony's to hear Mercer, singers as diverse as Frank Sinatra, Billie Holiday, Nat "King" Cole, Bobby Short, Billy Daniels, and Sylvia Sims came to study her phrasing and diction. Singers also came to enrich their repertoires; many previously obscure American theatrical and popular songs have become standard numbers largely because Mabel Mercer chose to sing them. These songs include Richard Rodgers and Lorenz Hart's "Little Girl Blue," Cole Porter's "Ev'ry Time We Say Goodbye," Howard Dietz and Arthur Schwartz's "By Myself," Jerome Kern and Dorothy Fields's "Remind Me," Bart Howard's "Fly Me to the Moon," and the Irish folk song "The Kerry Dance." Perhaps Mercer's closest collaboration was with the composer Alec Wilder; his songs that were most associated with Mercer's performances include "Did You Ever Cross Over to Sneeden's," "It's So Peaceful in the Country," and "While We're Young."

After leaving Tony's in 1949, Mercer sang on a steady basis at the Byline Room until the East Side club burned down in 1952. During the remainder of the 1950s and throughout the 1960s she sang at the Bon Soir, the RSVP Room, the St. Regis Room, Upstairs at the Downstairs, the Café Carlyle, and the Roundtable's King Arthur Room. Despite the growing popularity of rock music and the demise of 1940s-style nightclubs, she maintained a dedicated following throughout her career. During the 1970s she added such numbers as Joni Mitchell's "Both Sides Now," Stephen Sondheim's "Send In the Clowns," and Joe Raposo's "Being Green," to a repertoire that easily exceeded a thousand songs. In 1977, after giving a concert in Carnegie Hall, Mercer returned to London for the first time in forty years. In addition to performing at clubs, she starred in the five-part BBC television film *Miss Mercer in Mayfair*. She performed at the Kool Jazz Festival in 1982 and participated in several National Public Radio series, including *Eileen Farrell's American Popular Singers*. Her honors include an honorary degree from the New England Conservatory of Music in 1980; a tribute by the Whitney Museum in 1981; and the Presidential Medal of Freedom (1983). She lived in a farmhouse in East Chatham, New York, for thirty years. After suffering from unstabilized angina, Mabel Mercer died of respiratory arrest at the Berkshire Medical Center in Pittsfield, Massachusetts. She is buried at Red Rock Cemetery in Red Rock, New York.

Although Mabel Mercer rarely performed outside of New York City after settling in the United States and never had a hit record, her influence on American popular singing and song repertoire was enormous. Mercer admitted that sensuous vocal beauty was not the strong point of her singing and that her voice could be an acquired taste. "People have to hear me two or three times before they like me," she said. "I grow on them like a barnacle." Frank Sinatra expressed a more commonly held critical viewpoint: "You are the best music teacher in the world; everyone who has ever raised his voice in song has learned from you." Her ability to make every listener feel as if being sung to directly is remembered by everyone who ever heard her.

★

Mabel Mercer's papers are located at the Schomburg Center for Research in Black Culture in New York City. This resource was used extensively by James Haskins in writing *Mabel Mercer: A Life* (1987), the only full-length biography of Mercer. There are numerous articles about Mercer, including "Mabel Mercer: Internationally Known Singer Woos Cult of Sophisticates in New York's Byline Room," *Ebony* (Sept. 1952); Gene Lees, "The Magic of Mabel Mercer," *Hi Fi/Stereo Review* (Sept. 1964); Rex Reed, liner notes for *Mabel Mercer and Bobby Short at Town Hall,* Atlantic Records (1968); Whitney Balliett, "Profiles: A Queenly Aura," *New Yorker* (18 Nov. 1972); William Livingstone, "Mabel Mercer: William Livingstone Visits with the Singer's Singer,"

Mabel Mercer. ARCHIVE PHOTOS

Stereo Review (Feb. 1975); and Boris Weintraub, "Mabel Mercer: Singer Who Needs No Voice," *Washington Star* (6 Oct. 1975). Obituaries are in the *New York Times* (21 Apr. 1984) and *New Yorker* (May 1984).

DAVID M. CARP

MERMAN, Ethel (*b.* 16 January 1909 in New York City; *d.* 15 February 1984 in New York City), Broadway musical and film star known for her clarion vocal powers.

Merman was born Ethel Agnes Zimmermann in the Astoria section of the borough of Queens, New York, the only child of Edward Zimmermann, an accountant for a dry goods company, and Agnes Gardner. (Accounts differ regarding the year of her birth.) Her parents encouraged her budding talents, and she sang at her father's Masonic lodge and at church socials. Her professional career began in 1917, when she performed for the troops at Camp Mills.

As a guarantee in case her singing career failed, she took commercial courses at William Cullen Bryant High School and became an expert stenographer. While working at the Bragg-Kliesrath Vacuum Booster Brake Company, she supplemented her income with late-night singing engagements. Her father grudgingly allowed her to change her name to Merman.

Ethel Merman. AMERICAN STOCK/ARCHIVE PHOTOS

In 1929 her engagement at the Little Russia speakeasy in Manhattan led to a contract to make movie shorts for Warner Brothers (Vitaphone), but she made only *The Cave Club* (1929). Merman gained attention at New York's Les Ambassadeurs nightclub, and her show at Brooklyn's Paramount Theater so impressed the producer Vinton Freedley that he introduced her to the composer George Gershwin, who cast her as Kate Fothergill in the musical play *Girl Crazy* (1930), in which Merman stole the show with her three songs: "I Got Rhythm," "Boy, What Love Has Done to Me!," and "Sam and Delilah." Listeners were amazed at her mighty projection and clarity of diction, although she had never taken a singing lesson. She eventually appeared in fourteen more Broadway shows, usually playing wisecracking and earthy, even brassy, women. Nightclubs, vaudeville, and radio increased her income and popularity, as did recordings.

Merman became a Broadway legend, not only for her talent, but for her professional discipline and unusual self-confidence. She rarely missed a show and always gave the same performance, sometimes, said her critics, to the point of inflexibility. She insisted on giving ticket buyers what they paid for and was infuriated when any performer gave anything less. While often supportive of newcomers, she was protective of her own position, and performers who upstaged her felt her wrath.

Some people, like Gershwin, believed her untrained voice would never last, but—apart from occasional throat problems—it retained its trumpetlike potency. She ultimately symbolized a time when Broadway stars did not require amplification. Cole Porter warned lyricists to write good lyrics for her "because everyone's going to hear them." Merman was continually praised for her breath control, articulation, atomic energy, magnetism, perfect timing, comic brio, emotional honesty, vivid smile and laughing eyes, and sense of enjoyment in her work.

She continued her Broadway career in the eleventh edition of *George White's Scandals* (1931), singing "Life Is Just a Bowl of Cherries." Her next show was *Humpty Dumpty*, which folded in Pittsburgh but was reworked and opened in New York as *Take a Chance* (1932). Merman, playing Wanda Brill, brought down the house with "Eadie Was a Lady," "Rise 'n Shine," and "You're an Old Smoothie." She began a professional relationship with Cole Porter when she starred as the flamboyant Reno Sweeney in his musical *Anything Goes* (1934). The title song, "Blow, Gabriel, Blow," "I Get a Kick out of You," and "You're the Top" provided her with rousing showstoppers. She repeated the role in the musically eviscerated film (1936).

Merman's first full-length movie was *Follow the Leader* (1930). She supported Bing Crosby and Carole Lombard in Hollywood's *We're Not Dressing* (1934); a spectacular number with elephants, "The Animal in Me," was cut but later appeared in *The Big Broadcast of 1936*. In 1934, she costarred with Eddie Cantor in *Kid Millions*. Her other films of the period, in which her roles were secondary, are *Strike Me Pink* (1936), with Eddie Cantor; *Happy Landing* (1938), with Sonja Henie and Don Ameche; *Alexander's Ragtime Band* (1938), with Tyrone Power; and *Straight, Place, and Show* (1938), with the Ritz Brothers. During this period she dyed her brunette hair a soft auburn, a color she retained, and later wore it piled high on her head to give her five-foot-five frame extra height. Still, her less-than-beauty-queen appearance and larger-than-life presence were not the stuff of movie stardom. Broadway theater was her métier.

Broadway in the 1930s got to see Merman as Nails O'Reilly Duquesne in Porter's *Red, Hot, and Blue!* (1936), in which she shared billing with Bob Hope and Jimmy Durante and sang "Down in the Depths on the 90th Floor," "Ridin' High," and "It's De-Lovely." She was Jeanette Adair in *Stars in Your Eyes* (1939), one of her rare flops, but she was tops again as May Daly and Du Barry in *Du Barry Was a Lady* (1939), singing Porter's "Do I Love You, Do I" and "Friendship," and sharing the laughs with Bert Lahr.

In 1940 she played Hattie Maloney in Porter's *Panama Hattie*, her first solo starring show, a hit in which she introduced "Let's Be Buddies" and "Make It Another Old-Fashioned, Please." In November of that year, she married the Hollywood agent William Jacob Smith, the first of her four marriages. The marriage ended quickly, and in the fall of 1941, she wed the New York newspaperman Robert D. Levitt; they had two children. Her only film role of the decade was a cameo in *Stage Door Canteen* (1943). She starred on Broadway as Blossom Hart in Porter's *Something for the Boys* (1943), another hit, but it did not compare with the success of Irving Berlin's *Annie Get Your Gun* (1946), in which she played sharpshooter Annie Oakley and sang such songs as "They Say It's Wonderful," "There's No Business Like Show Business," and "Anything You Can Do." In 1949 she hosted radio's *The Ethel Merman Show*.

Her Tony-winning role as Sally Adams in the Irving Berlin hit *Call Me Madam* (1950) was based on the life of Washington hostess and ambassador Perle Mesta. Among her nine songs was "You're Just in Love," a duet with Russell Nype. Her marriage to Levitt ended in 1952, and she wed airline executive Robert Foreman Six on 6 March 1953. (The marriage lasted until 1960.) She returned to film for Hollywood's version of *Call Me Madam* (1953). She appeared on the 1953 television "spectacular" *The Ford Fiftieth Anniversary Show*, costarring with Mary Martin, her friendly rival for the title of queen of Broadway musicals. The pair sang a memorable medley while sitting on stools, an idea that many others borrowed. Her other TV work of the period included an abbreviated remake of *Anything Goes* (1953), one of *Panama Hattie* (1954), several nonmusical dramatic roles, and numerous guest appearances. In 1954, Merman performed in the movie *There's No Business Like Show Business,* with a score by Berlin.

She returned to Broadway as Liz Livingston in *Happy Hunting* (1956), during which she feuded with costar Fernando Lamas and introduced the song "Mutual Admiration Society." This so-so show was succeeded by the Jule Styne–Stephen Sondheim hit *Gypsy* (1959). As Mama Rose, the overbearing—yet, as Merman played her, touchingly vulnerable—mother of stripper Gypsy Rose Lee, she had the crowning role of her career, one demanding dramatic power in addition to vocal dynamics. Her arialike "Rose's Turn" is an American musical highlight. She also introduced such songs as "Small World" and "You'll Never Get Away from Me." Merman was hurt when she failed to win the Tony Award (although she garnered the New York Drama Critics Award) and when Rosalind Russell was cast as Mama Rose in the movie version. During the run, she burst a blood vessel in her larynx, her first major physical problem.

Jerry Herman wrote *Hello, Dolly!* (1964) for her but she turned it down. In 1970, however, she became the eighth actress to play Dolly Levi, performing two new songs. During the 1960s she acted in the movie *It's a Mad, Mad, Mad, Mad World* (1963), debuted in Las Vegas, took *The Ethel Merman Show* to tents and outdoor venues across the country, made many television appearances (musical and dramatic), acted in the film *The Art of Love* (1965), toured Australia and England, traveled around the world, starred (at age fifty-eight) in a revival of *Annie Get Your Gun* (1966), gave concerts, and revived *Call Me Madam* (1969) several times outside of New York. She also endured a five-month marriage in 1964 to actor Ernest Borgnine and the death of her daughter in 1967 from a possibly suicidal drug overdose.

She won a special Tony Award for career achievement in 1972. During that decade, she continued to perform, especially in the *Ethel Merman in Concert* series with symphony orchestras. The television program *This Is Your Life* focused on Merman in 1977. She costarred with Mary Martin in *Together on Broadway* (1977), a highly successful benefit. In addition to various television shows, she had a cameo in the movie *Airplane!* (1980). Her final appearance was in a 1982 Carnegie Hall concert.

"La Merman," as journalists called her, was known for her thriftiness, love of bawdy jokes and profanity (but never onstage), dislike for giving autographs, feuds with leading show business figures such as Carol Channing and Richard Rodgers, and a lifelong devotion to her parents. In her later years, she was difficult and demanding. She suffered a stroke in April 1983 and underwent surgery for a brain tumor, which was deemed inoperable and was possibly the cause of her increasingly erratic behavior. She died ten months later and was cremated.

★

Merman wrote (with Pete Martin) the whitewashed autobiography *Who Could Ask for Anything More* (1955), based on a series of *Saturday Evening Post* articles, and (with George Eells) *Merman: An Autobiography* (1978). The standard biography is Bob Thomas, *I Got Rhythm: The Ethel Merman Story* (1985), but George B. Bryan, *Ethel Merman: A Bio-Bibliography* (1992) is very helpful for data and provides a fifty-five item discography. A Ph.D. dissertation is Sherri R. Dienstfrey, "Ethel Merman: Queen of Musical Comedy" (Kent State University, 1986). Worthwhile material can be found in Maurice Zolotow, *No People Like Show People* (1951); William C. Young, *Famous American Actors and Actresses on the American Stage,* vol. 1 (1978); Martin Gottfried, *Broadway Musicals* (1979); and Mary C. Robinson, Vera Mowry Roberts, and Millie S. Barranger, eds., *Notable Women in the American Theatre* (1989). Obituaries are in the *New York Times* (16 Feb. 1984) and *Variety* (22 Feb. 1984).

SAMUEL L. LEITER

MERRILL, John Putnam (*b.* 10 March 1917 in Hartford, Connecticut; *d.* 4 April 1984 at sea near the Bahamas), pioneer surgeon regarded as the father of nephrology, the scientific study of the kidney and its diseases, who helped develop the first clinically safe dialysis machine and led the team that performed the first successful kidney transplant.

John Putnam Merrill. NATIONAL LIBRARY OF MADISON, NIH

The son of Arthur Hodges Merrill, a physician, and Olive Grinnell Merrill, John Merrill studied at St. George's School in Newport, Rhode Island, and then went on to Dartmouth College in Hanover, New Hampshire. After graduating from Dartmouth in 1938, he entered Harvard Medical School in Boston because of "a family tradition of medicine" and "intellectual curiosity." In 1942 he graduated from Harvard and married Suzanne Strauss Nulsen; they had three children. Merrill served in the Army Air Forces as a major from 1943 to 1947. He was the flight surgeon to the crew of the *Enola Gay,* the World War II B-29 bomber that dropped the atomic bomb over Hiroshima, Japan, on 6 August 1945.

After his return to Boston, Merrill joined the staff of the Brigham and Women's (then Peter Bent Brigham) Hospital in 1947, and three years later became a member of the faculty at Harvard Medical School, where he became a full professor in 1970. In the mid-1950s a sabbatical took him to London and Paris to study immunology and the biochemistry of uremia, the complex of signs and symptoms involved in chronic kidney failure.

The search for an artificial kidney or a dialysis machine for people suffering from uremia had begun in the early 1900s. Dialysis involves the removal of certain unhealthy elements from the blood by virtue of the difference in the rates of their diffusion through a semipermeable membrane while the blood is circulated outside the body. At Brigham (under the direction of George Thorn), Carl Walter and Merrill modified a dialysis machine built by Willem J. Kolff, using more modern materials, such as plastic and stainless steel; the result was a safer machine. In May 1948 the age of successful kidney dialysis began when Merrill treated the first patient using the machine. Little was known, however, about the pathophysiology of uremia. Here, Merrill, now director of Harvard's Kidney Research Laboratory, exhibited his leadership, teamwork, guidance, mentoring skills, and calm persistence. Dialysis started to be quantified and methods found for a long-term treatment of acute uremic patients.

Merrill next set his sights on transplants as the appropriate solution to terminal kidney disease. In Europe and the United States, kidneys taken from cadavers had been transplanted into patients without real success because human bodies rejected foreign organs, even when newer drugs and improved techniques were used. In late 1954 opportunity knocked on Merrill's door. One of a set of identical twins was terminally ill with uremia.

Merrill did skin grafts on the twins as a test. Their success suggested that an organ transplant might also be successful. On 23 December 1954 Merrill, with the help of surgeons Joseph E. Murray and J. Hartwell Harrison, successfully transplanted Ronald Herrick's healthy kidney to his terminally ill twin, Richard. Richard lived a fairly normal life for seven years until succumbing to congestive heart failure at the age of twenty-nine. In 1959 Merrill's team performed a successful kidney transplant between fraternal twins. This time, in addition to drugs, irradiation was used to prevent rejection. In 1962 a successful kidney transplant was performed on unrelated people using immunosuppressive drug therapy. Since then hospitals around the world have performed this operation regularly.

Merrill guided more than sixty fellows and associates from some thirty countries and more than 100 trainees from throughout the United States. His students affectionately called him JPM and themselves Merrillophiles. The John P. Merrill Graduate Society, comprising these trainees, met annually and shared experiences. Merrill loved to hear about their successes in many branches of nephrology.

Merrill led a full life outside nephrology. He played tennis, sailed, skied, and even hunted African big game. He was a clarinet player, an accomplished musician who composed music and played Dixieland jazz in bands with his friends. He died by drowning in a boating accident in the Bahamas, where he was vacationing with his wife.

Merrill published more than 400 scientific papers and a landmark book, *The Treatment of Renal Failure;* with his wife he coauthored *Squirrel Island, Maine—The First Hundred Years, 1871–1971* (1973). He held many offices, most notably as director of the Kidney Research Laboratory. Among his many honors were the Alvarenga Prize of the Philadelphia Academy of Physicians (1960) and the Amory Prize of the American Academy of Arts and Sciences (1962). A member of many national and international academies, Merrill helped establish and presided over the American and the International Societies of Nephrology, the American and the International Societies of Artificial Internal Organs, and the International Transplantation Society. His historical reminiscences and addresses demonstrate his generosity in paying tributes to colleagues and sharing with them his triumphs and achievements. Eli A. Friedman, a Merrill trainee, summed up Merrill's contribution: "Were there a book of distinguished synonyms, the listing under nephrology would first be Merrill, J. P., and vice versa."

★

Merrill provided a bibliography of his writings in "Publications of John P. Merrill," *Nephron* 22, nos. 1–3 (1978): 267–280. See also Barbara K. Coleman and John P. Merrill, "The Artificial Kidney," *American Journal of Nursing* 52, no. 3 (Mar. 1952): 327–329; and Eli A. Friedman, "John P. Merrill: The Father of Nephrology as a Craft," *Nephron* 22, nos. 1–3 (1978): 6–8. *Artificial Organs* 11, no. 6 (Dec. 1987), contains three tributes to Merrill: Nancy Boucot Cummings, "John Putnam Merrill: An Appreciation," W. J. Kolff, "About John P. Merrill," and Gabriel Riches, "J. P. Merrill: A Founder of Scientific Clinical Nephrology."

SYED M. A. KHAN

MILGRAM, Stanley (*b.* 15 August 1933 in New York City; *d.* 20 December 1984 in New York City), social psychologist and essayist noted for his creative experiments on interpersonal behavior and for his works *Obedience to Authority* (1974) and *Individual in a Social World: Essays and Experiments* (1992).

Milgram was raised in a Bronx working-class home of first-generation Jewish-American parents from Eastern Europe, Adele Israel, a homemaker, and Samuel Milgram, a cake baker and shop owner. He had an elder sister, Marjorie, and a younger brother, Joel (later a professor of educational psychology at the University of Cincinnati). From childhood, he combined a playful attitude toward science with a talent for crafting new ideas and inventions. He attended James Monroe High School in the Bronx (1947–1950) and

Stanley Milgram. FROM THE COLLECTIONS OF THE LIBRARY OF CONGRESS AND THE SIMON & SCHUSTER CORPORATE DIGITAL ARCHIVE

earned an A.B. in political science at Queens College (1950–1954), where an admiring dean convinced him to switch to psychology. He studied scientific methods of interpersonal behavior with Solomon Asch and Gordon Allport at Harvard University, where he completed his doctorate in social psychology (1954–1960) with a dissertation on nationality and conformity. He married Alexandra Menkin, a psychiatric social worker, on 10 December 1961; they had two children.

Milgram began his remarkable academic career as assistant professor at Yale University (1960–1963), where he began his experiments on obedience to authority. In his laboratory at Linsly-Chittenden Hall he found that, in a study purportedly testing punishment's effect on learning ability, an experimenter in a gray lab coat could induce more than half of some 1,000 average people to administer what they believed were potentially fatal electric shocks to an unwilling stranger strapped into a chair in the next room. Because his findings were so alarming, articles on these experiments immediately became essential reading in social psychology following their release in 1963. The results became the hallmark example of "situationism," or how external situations override inner temperament in shaping our behavior, so that normal people behave abnormally in abnormal situations. These findings have been applied to understand German atrocities during the Nazi era. The studies received several awards for their revelations while also being criticized by some as unethical for their use of deception and stress in laboratory research.

From Yale, Milgram returned to Harvard (1963–1967), where he continued his stream of sociopsychological research using novel methods, such as the lost-letter technique and the small-world problem (both of which relate to the number of "degrees of separation" between any two randomly selected people). In 1967 Milgram moved from assistant professor at Harvard to professor and head of the social psychology doctoral program at the City University of New York (CUNY) Graduate School, where he was later appointed CUNY Distinguished Professor (1980); he remained there for the rest of his career, until 1984.

At CUNY, Milgram maintained a prolific research program, working closely with his doctoral students, to complete a total of five films, four books, and more than sixty articles or chapters involving imaginative methods or topics, such as urban overload, the lost child, subway norms, the image-freezing machine (that is, photography), queues, television violence, mental maps, familiar strangers, and Cyranoids. Besides his award-winning *Obedience to Authority: An Experimental View* (1974), he spawned the new subfield of urban psychology with his seminal article in *Science* (13 March 1970), titled "The Experience of Living in Cities."

Milgram's combination of a penetrating intellect, a high-intensity personality, and a deft pen shone across his many diverse activities in addition to research. As a teacher, his courses at three universities were noted for their passion and dynamism, generating many fascinating new ideas as well as alumni who became prolific psychologists. He was much sought internationally as a riveting public speaker. Milgram was an acclaimed man of letters, known for cogent essays as well as crisp technical reports, which have appeared in a dozen languages. He was also somewhat of a Renaissance man who wrote songs, short stories, and children's books; designed new board games and inventions; and produced several award-winning educational films, such as *The City and the Self* (1974).

Weakened by four heart attacks starting in 1980, Milgram died of heart failure after chairing a doctoral defense at CUNY. He was buried in Sharon Gardens, Kensico Cemetery, Valhalla, New York.

Milgram's obedience research is widely regarded as the single most powerful experiment ever completed in social psychology, if not in psychology in general. No introductory psychology textbook is complete without it. The controversy over the ethical aspects of his obedience experiments (in which subjects are deceived and discomforted) contributed to a reformulation of the ethical standards for informed consent in research, set by the American Psychological Association and by federal agencies. Since the 1970s the impact of Milgram's work has extended well beyond psychology, into popular culture in the United States and globally. Examples include the French film *I as in Icarus* (1977), the television movie *The Tenth Level* (1976), and a Broadway play, *Six Degrees of Separation* (1980). Unlike most behavioral researchers, his style of investigation was atheoretical, "to ask questions rather than to test hypotheses." Although he is best known for the obedience studies, his several other works are also widely cited, with broad influence on other social scientists. Milgram's most enduring legacy is likely his unmatched creativity in devising new experimental methods to reveal the causes underlying interpersonal behavior and his courage in passionately championing these methods when under fire.

★

Stanley Milgram's personal papers are cataloged in 150 boxes in Yale University's Sterling Memorial Library; they include his extensive teaching and research files from Yale, Harvard, and CUNY, spanning the years 1960 to 1984. Thomas Blass, "The Social Psychology of Stanley Milgram," in M. P. Zanna, ed., *Advances in Experimental Social Psychology,* vol. 25 (1992), limns the legacy of Milgram's obedience and other research. Biographical information is in Frances C. Locher, ed., *Contemporary Authors,* vol. 105 (1982). An obituary is in the *New York Times* (22 Dec. 1984).

HAROLD TAKOOSHIAN

MILLAR, Kenneth. See Ross Macdonald.

MILLER, Arnold Ray (*b.* 25 April 1923 in Cabin Creek, West Virginia; *d.* 12 July 1985 in Charleston, West Virginia), disabled veteran who served as the twelfth president of the United Mine Workers of America (UMWA) during the tumultuous years following the death of John L. Lewis and the subsequent murder conviction and imprisonment of Miller's predecessor, Tony Boyle.

Miller, one of two sons of George Matt Miller, a miner, and Lulu Hoy, a homemaker, grew up in the heart of coal country, twenty-two miles from Charleston, West Virginia. Arnold was a bright student, but the low miner's wages his father earned forced him to take a job in the mines and cut short his education. His first job was counting coal alongside his grandfather.

At nineteen, Miller enlisted in the U.S. Army as an infantryman. As part of the invasion force at Normandy on D day in 1944, he was severely wounded by machine-gun fire to the left side of his face that left him significantly scarred for the rest of his life. Honorably discharged in 1946, he returned to Cabin Creek and married Virginia

Arnold Miller, 1978. UPI/Corbis-Bettmann

Ruth Brown on 26 November 1948; they had two children. He took a job back in the mines as an electrician, at which he would work until 1970, when he was forced to retire after being diagnosed with arthritis and pneumoconiosis, or black lung disease.

During his years as a miner, Miller served as president of UMWA local 2903 near his home and ran unsuccessfully for the state legislature. After attempting to get help from the national headquarters in recognizing black lung as a compensable disability under state workers' compensation, he founded the Black Lung Association (BLA). In 1969 he led a three-week statewide sympathy strike and a march by the miners on the state capitol in Charleston. UMWA officials condemned the organization and branded the strike a wildcat action, urging state legislators to ignore it; the lawmakers, however, impressed by the number of miners who sympathized with the action, enacted state laws to compensate victims of the disease.

Miller's tenacity, organizing abilities, and courage found him favor with another dissident, Joseph ("Jock") Yablonski, who challenged Tony Boyle for the presidency of the UMWA in 1969. Miller immediately became an ardent Yablonski supporter. The battle for the union presidency was bitter. Yablonski leveled charges of corruption against Boyle, calling him "a crook and embezzler." Boyle responded in kind with the appellation of "cheap opportunist" and was reelected as president in December of that year.

On the night of 31 December 1969, Yablonski, his wife, and their daughter were shot to death in their beds. Although he denied it to his death, Boyle was implicated in the murder; furthermore, the U.S. government declared the Boyle victory void and ordered a new election. Miller was selected to become the new candidate for UMWA president. Because of his experience with bare-knuckle campaign tactics, Boyle ran a brutal campaign. The rank and file, stunned by the allegations, the corruption of the incumbent, and a promise by Miller to improve the miners' meager pensions, voted in Miller. He was sworn in on 22 December 1972.

Upon election Miller cut his salary from $50,000 to $35,000, sold the fleet of limousines that Boyle and his associates had acquired, and gave the rank and file a more democratic voice in union affairs, promising that all district representatives would have to return to their districts and stand for reelection. He also hosted a convention in 1973 to rewrite the outdated constitution. Miller made mine safety an issue and took steps to increase the UMWA safety division by allocating more manpower and money to it. He reinforced his sincerity in 1974 with a five-day national strike as a memorial to miners killed on the job.

In March 1975 Miller announced his intention to seek another five-year term in 1977, but shortly thereafter his organization started to collapse. His new democratic approach was resulting in wildcat strikes that he could not control. In private he was concerned about this behavior, but in public he suggested that the union's bylaws would resolve these strikes reasonably. West Virginia miners, his base of power, seemed to be the most militant, prowling the streets with weapons. There were shootings in Miller's hometown of Cabin Creek, and Governor John D. ("Jay") Rockefeller IV of West Virginia called for the FBI to investigate.

There were more charges of mismanagement leveled against the union officials by Miller's own vice president, Mike Trbovich. The U.S. Department of Labor investigated and cleared the administration of spending union funds for unlawful purposes in May 1976. In August 1977, Miller was hospitalized for exhaustion but was reelected president of the UMWA for a second term in October, defeating Lee Roy Patterson. Although Patterson filed charges of election irregularities, he did not pursue the charges and the Department of Labor confirmed the election.

Union coal production had fallen to about 55 percent from 74 percent of total production in 1974 because of wildcat strikes and Miller's inability to control the rank and file. In November 1977 the UMW international board adopted a recommendation by Trbovich that a convention be called to depose its president, but none was convened.

Miller's second term was characterized by a national strike that threatened to cripple the nation. Some of his fellow negotiators considered him unpredictable and slow to grasp technological issues. On 16 February 1978, 200 coal miners marched on Charleston, pleading for the ouster of Miller. On 20 February, President Jimmy Carter, though a Democrat and strong supporter of labor, sought support from Congress for an injunction under the Taft-Hartley Act to force the miners back to work. On 29 March 1978 Miller suffered a mild stroke and was again hospitalized. This was followed two weeks later by a heart attack. He did not return to work until July.

More allegations of irregularities surfaced in early 1979. These were no sooner put to rest when Bill Lamb, a member of the UMW international executive board who had been fired by Miller, was shot and wounded while driving to headquarters to protest his ouster. Finally, President Carter, cornered by dwindling coal reserves and the high price of oil imports, secured a Taft-Hartley injunction against the UMWA. Shortly afterward the strike was settled. Miller resigned as president of the UMWA on 16 November 1979, the day after he suffered yet another heart attack. His family was in shambles. He and his wife of thirty years had divorced. Miller continued to suffer from poor health. He died in the Charleston, West Virginia, Medical Center from complications brought on by his frail condition and was buried in Montgomery Memorial Park in London, West Virginia.

Most noted for his defeat of the old guard represented by Tony Boyle, Miller brought a sense of democracy to the United Mine Workers union. His polite, plainspoken, up-from-the-pits style won him the early admiration of union workers. But the speed of technological change, the desertions of those in his administration, and his illnesses contributed to his fall from favor and subsequent resignation in 1979.

★

Joseph Finley, *The Corrupt Kingdom* (1972), chronicles the history of the United Mine Workers union. See also the *Wall Street Journal* (12 Oct. 1977) and the *Washington Post* (25 Oct. 1983). An obituary is in the *New York Times* (13 July 1985).

ROBERT J. SMITH

MITCHELL, John James, Jr. (*b.* 28 April 1897 in Chicago, Illinois; *d.* 7 April 1985 in Santa Barbara, California), banker and a cofounder of National Air Transport, one of the predecessor companies of United Air Lines, Inc.

Mitchell was the son of John James Mitchell, Sr., a prominent Chicago businessman who was founder and president of the Illinois Merchants Bank, and Mary Louise Jewett, both of whom were killed in an automobile accident in 1927. He had two brothers and two sisters.

A graduate of the Hill School in Pottstown, Pennsylvania, "Jack" Mitchell attended Yale College but left when the United States became involved in World War I. He joined the Naval Air Corps and was designated a naval aviator, beginning a lifetime commitment to aviation. After the war, he returned to Yale and graduated in 1919 with a B.A. degree. He then went to work at his father's bank, the Illinois Merchants Trust and Savings Bank, which later became the Continental Illinois Bank and Trust Company. In 1925 he helped found National Air Transport.

Early in 1925 a group of airline promoters made an attempt to raise $2 million, a substantial amount of money at the time, to develop an airline operating between New York, Detroit, and Chicago. Mitchell's father was one of several railroad-minded Chicagoans contacted to help invest in this project but had no interest in risking money in the flying-machine business. One of the promoters noted that nearly every one of the attendees of a failed meeting of potential investors had a son in his twenties who had been a World War I aviator or had taken up flying since the war. A second meeting of young, up-and-coming businessmen was arranged. Among the group was John J. Mitchell, Jr., Phillip K. Wrigley, Lester Armour, and Earle Reynolds. Little effort was required to convince this group to become involved, a move that helped make Chicago a hub for the air transport business. When Mitchell told his father what he had done, his father replied, "I never thought I'd live to see my son in a fly-by-night business." The son's countering argument was that never in history had a faster means of transport failed to win out in competition with a slower form.

National Air Transport (NAT) was incorporated in Delaware on 21 May 1925, with John J. Mitchell, Jr., as secretary and treasurer. The airline began operations on 12 May 1926, with ten Curtiss Carrier Pigeon airplanes, thirty-five government surplus engines to power them, and only eight army-trained pilots. The Pigeons could carry a 1,000-pound payload. The management was initially more interested in carrying cargo and mail. It was more profitable and easier to carry cargo than passengers, but demand for passenger transport continued to grow despite the risks, discomforts, and dangers involved.

Mitchell served as NAT secretary-treasurer from 1925 to 1931, when NAT combined with three other carriers to become United Airlines. Mitchell resigned during the merger of NAT and United and left the Continental Illinois Bank to become vice president and treasurer of Universal Oil Products. He was elected a director of United in 1937 and continued in that position until 1970, when he became a director emeritus. He was named a director of UAL, Inc., when it was founded in 1969.

Mitchell married Lolita S. Armour, a meat-packing heiress and cousin of Lester in 1921. They had a daughter, Lolita, and a son, John James, Jr. In the 1920s they were considered among America's wealthiest couples, with an estimated fortune of greater than $120 million. They began spending vacations in Santa Barbara, California, and developed a fondness for horses and riding. A member of the Bohemian Grove (a social group in San Francisco devoted to the arts), he proposed a similar arrangement in the Santa Ynez Valley, based on horseback riding rather than the arts. Friends endorsed the idea, and the first ride, a three-day trek in the Santa Ynez Valley, was held in 1930. This ride developed into an annual adventure attracting hundreds of people, and Mitchell continued to actively participate until well into his seventies. In 1942 Mitchell and his wife divorced. Later that year, he married Olga V. Varchavsky, a Russian immigrant, and moved to Santa Barbara permanently. They had one son, James Jay. Mitchell became the founding president of the Rancheros Vistadores, a horse club in Santa Barbara, and served in that position until 1955. He became well known for his 8,600-acre ranch, Juan y Lolita, and devoted many hours to its operation.

In addition to his position with the Rancheros, Mitchell served on the advisory board of the Salvation Army in Chicago and in Santa Barbara for almost sixty years, a commitment later continued by his son John, Jr. Mitchell died of natural causes at his home in Santa Barbara on Easter Sunday, at the age of eighty-seven. He was buried in Santa Barbara.

John James Mitchell served his country in war, helped develop an industry which paved the way to the future, and had a love for nature and the outdoors. The inheritor of financial resources that put him in a position to make a difference, he confronted the challenges of industrial development during this century and devoted himself to valuable causes and personal pursuits that benefited those who were as fortunate as himself and many who were not.

★

Sources on Mitchell include United Air Lines, Inc., *Corporate and Legal History of United Air Lines and Its Predecessors and Subsidiaries, 1925–1945* (1953), and Frank J. Taylor, *High Horizons: Daredevil Flying Postmen to Modern Magic Carpet: The United Air Lines Story* (1964). An obituary is in the *New York Times* (10 Apr. 1985).

BRIAN CRADDOCK

MONK, Thelonious Sphere (*b.* 10 October 1917 in Rocky Mount, North Carolina; *d.* 17 February 1982 in Weehawken, New Jersey), pianist, composer, and bandleader who played a key role in the development of the "bebop" modern jazz style.

Thelonious Sphere Monk was the second of three children of Thelonious Monk and Barbara (Batts) Monk. The unusual middle name came from Barbara's father, Sphere Batts. Monk's father, who held a variety of manual-labor jobs, remains a mysterious figure. Barbara left him in 1922, moving with the children from North Carolina to New York City. After some years Thelonious senior migrated to New York as well, rejoining the family temporarily. Near the end of his life he spent time in a mental hospital and may have died there. Monk's parents were fairly musical: Thelonious senior played the ukulele, and Barbara sang in the church choir.

The Monks lived in an apartment in the Phipps housing project at 243 West Sixty-third Street, in an area of Manhattan then known as San Juan Hill. James P. Johnson, the composer and jazz pianist, lived in the neighborhood and was an early influence on Monk, as was the ragtime pianist Eubie Blake, who performed his musical *Shuffle Along* nightly in a local theater during Monk's teenage years. Monk lived in the apartment almost his entire life, remaining there after his mother's death in 1953. After Monk's death in 1982 the City of New York renamed the block where he had lived as Thelonious Sphere Monk Circle.

Monk taught himself to play the piano initially by imitating his older sister's lessons. Upon hearing him, the teacher recommended that the lessons be switched to Thelonious, then about five years old. Within a few years he was playing the organ in church. He attended Stuyvesant

Thelonious Monk, 1948. © WILLIAM GOTTLIEB. FROM THE COLLECTION OF THE LIBRARY OF CONGRESS, IRA & LEONORE S. GERSHWIN FUND.

High School, where he excelled in math, physics, and basketball. At the age of seventeen, possibly frustrated by the lack of a piano opening in the school orchestra, Monk dropped out. He took a job accompanying a gospel singing group and toured the United States extensively in 1934 and 1935. Returning to New York, he worked in various bars and restaurants, often as a solo pianist, honing his style.

Around 1938, possibly earlier, Monk began taking part in jam sessions at Minton's Playhouse, a Harlem bar where drummer Kenny Clarke led the house band. The harmonic and rhythmic underpinnings of bebop, the modern jazz form that evolved out of big-band swing in the years leading up to World War II, may be attributed in large part to the jam-session participants at Minton's, especially Monk, Clarke, and the pioneering electric guitarist Charlie Christian. By inverting and extending chords and substituting them for the stock chords found in popular songs, Monk changed the way jazz musicians thought about harmony. His techniques opened up new possibilities for improvising jazz soloists, leading directly to the spectacular melodic in-

novations in the 1940s by the alto saxophonist Charlie (Bird) Parker and the trumpeter Dizzy Gillespie.

The 1940s saw Monk putting his emerging style to the test in a variety of situations. He went on the road with Lucky Millinder's big band in 1942 but quit after a few months. He continued to play with the beboppers after bebop made its way downtown to the clubs on Fifty-second Street in Manhattan. His first major break came when tenor saxophonist Coleman Hawkins, an established star, hired Monk for his quartet. Monk made his debut on records in 1944 with Hawkins. The same year, the first recording of a Monk composition, "'Round Midnight," was made by the Cootie Williams orchestra, featuring Monk's influential young protégé, pianist Bud Powell. Monk played briefly with Andy Kirk's big band in 1945, then rejoined Hawkins for the first "Jazz at the Philharmonic" package tour. He played on Fifty-second Street and recorded with Dizzy Gillespie's big band in 1946. Monk was not drafted into military service during World War II, having been classified 4-F.

In 1947 Monk married Nellie Smith, a young woman from his neighborhood whom he had first met in the late 1930s; they would have two children. That same year he made his first recordings, for Blue Note Records, under his own name. Monk's six sessions for Blue Note, the last taking place in 1952, resulted in seminal works of art. Recordings such as "'Round Midnight," "Ruby, My Dear," "Well, You Needn't," "Straight No Chaser," "Introspection," "Off Minor," and "Epistrophy" established him as the most important jazz composer of his generation, although few critics realized it at the time.

Monk's playing style was virtuosic in its own way. Although considered a quintessentially modern stylist, he drew on an impressive knowledge of earlier piano styles from blues and gospel to ragtime and Harlem stride. He played with his fingers splayed out flat, not bent, which gave him a distinctive, percussive attack. His improvisations were often based on the melody of the tune he was playing, and he delighted in worrying a single phrase until it revealed all of its implications and permutations. He blurred the distinction between lead and accompanying voices, spelling out melodies with dissonant chords and clusters. His stride piano passages rang with authenticity in spite of their modern context, and decorative single-note runs revealed his debt to Art Tatum. The jazz pianist Geoff Keezer has called Monk "essentially a deconstructed stride pianist."

In 1950 Monk recorded for Verve Records with Charlie Parker and Dizzy Gillespie. He signed a contract with Prestige Records in 1952 and that year made important trio recordings. He led a quintet that included tenor saxophonist Sonny Rollins in 1953, then recorded as a sideman with trumpeter Miles Davis in 1954. Although the brief Prestige period yielded many valuable additions to the Monk oeuvre, among them "Little Rootie Tootie," "Monk's Dream," "Bemsha Swing," "Trinkle Tinkle," "Let's Call This," "Think of One," and "Blue Monk," it was not a satisfying period for Monk overall. The label wanted to capitalize on Monk's Fifty-second Street reputation as the "High Priest of Bop," a designation Monk detested, as it made his music seem all the more obscure and out of reach. Adding to Monk's difficulties at this time was the fact that his cabaret card, or work permit, had been revoked by the police, effectively barring him from performing in nightclubs. The ban stemmed from a conviction in 1951 when Monk had been arrested in a car in which heroin was found.

In 1954 Monk traveled to Paris, where he recorded solo piano. Returning home, Monk's cabaret-card problem did not prevent him from signing with Riverside Records, for which he recorded a string of classic jazz albums in the latter half of the 1950s. In 1956 a catastrophic fire in Monk's apartment destroyed all of his possessions, including his piano and musical scores. That year he made two of his greatest recordings: *The Unique Thelonious Monk,* a trio session that included the drummer Art Blakey, Monk's close friend and frequent collaborator; and *Brilliant Corners,* a quintet date featuring Sonny Rollins. Monk returned in 1957 with *Monk's Music,* a sextet recording featuring two tenor saxophonists, Coleman Hawkins and John Coltrane. That same year Monk hired a manager who succeeded in getting his cabaret card reinstated. In July, Monk opened at the Five Spot Café with a quartet featuring Coltrane. The group caused a sensation, playing six nights a week to a packed house and generating much well-timed publicity, as both men had been struggling to reach a wider audience. For Coltrane the gig was an apprenticeship in advanced jazz harmony; he later remarked that "working with Monk brought me close to a musical architect of the highest order." Monk capped off a successful year with an appearance in December on the acclaimed CBS television special *The Sound of Jazz.*

By the time of Monk's second contract with Riverside he had settled on the quartet of piano, bass, drums, and tenor saxophone as his preferred working unit. When Coltrane left Monk's group to rejoin Miles Davis, Monk replaced him with tenor saxophonist Johnny Griffin. Monk made several recordings with Griffin before replacing him, in late 1958, with a tenor saxophonist he knew from Minton's a decade earlier, Charlie Rouse. Rouse's partnership with Monk lasted twelve years, an indication both of Monk's increased ability to secure steady work and of Rouse's singular affinity for Monk's music. Monk was vindicated when, in 1958, he finally won the *Down Beat* magazine critics' poll. The following year he teamed with composer Hall Overton for a concert that featured Monk at the nucleus of a ten-piece band. The resultant album, *The Thelonious Monk Orchestra at Town Hall,* got mixed reviews. Monk and Overton waited until 1963 to try the large-band experiment again.

Monk's critical and popular success reached its zenith in the early 1960s. In 1962 he signed with Columbia Records, a move that guaranteed a larger and more mainstream audience for his music than Riverside had been able to reach. He recorded thirty times for Columbia between 1962 and 1965, in sessions supervised by producer Teo Macero. He also toured extensively in the United States and Europe and performed at summer jazz festivals. He went to Japan in 1963 and toured for a total of nine months in 1964. Monk's 1960s bands—the original quartet with Rouse, Butch Warren (bass), and Frankie Dunlop (drums) and the mid-1960s edition with Larry Gales (bass) and Ben Riley (drums)—performed as well-oiled machines, the result of heavy touring. Sonically, his interplay with Rouse had a consistency of texture not found in his previous recorded work. Like his Riverside recordings, Columbia albums such as *Monk's Dream* (1962) included a representative selection of early compositions, a few new originals, and one or two popular songs he favored, for example, Irving Caesar's "Just a Gigolo."

Monk stood six feet, four inches tall and carried himself regally. Solidly built as a young man, he became corporeal in middle age. He dressed well, with a penchant for unusual hats. He had always been eccentric: in concert he was known for standing up from the keyboard and performing an odd little dance by himself while the other musicians in his band soloed. Beginning in the late 1950s, however, musicians and family members began to observe that something was seriously wrong. He suffered from periodic attacks that caused him to withdraw totally from the people around him. At such times he would be unable to recognize his own children. He would become highly agitated, pacing the floor for days until he collapsed from exhaustion, unable to get out of bed. Between 1959 and his death he was hospitalized in psychiatric institutions approximately five times, usually for months at a time. It has been suggested that Monk's allegedly prodigious intake of drugs may have contributed to his condition. In spite of the encroaching darkness, on 28 February 1964, Monk achieved a level of fame rarely seen in jazz when his portrait appeared on the cover of *Time,* accompanied by an extensive feature article.

Compared to his arduous rise, Monk's decline was short and steep. His recording schedule was drastically curtailed after 1965 as Columbia shifted its focus from jazz to the more lucrative pop-music market. In 1968 he made a poorly received big-band recording with the commercially oriented arranger Oliver Nelson. When Monk's second Columbia contract expired in 1969 he left the label and was without a recording contract for the first time since 1947. Riley quit the group in 1970; Monk auditioned several drummers, then brought his son, Thelonious junior, into the band. Within a year Rouse had left as well; he was succeeded by Pat Patrick and Paul Jeffrey. Increasingly ill and hard to manage, Monk was moved by his wife and children into the New Jersey home of his close friend and patroness, Baroness Pannonica de Koenigswarter. Monk made European tours in 1971 and 1972 with an all-star group called the Giants of Jazz. In 1971, in England, he made his final recordings as a leader, alone and in a trio that included Art Blakey.

Monk was reclusive after 1973. He emerged in 1975 for two engagements, a concert at Carnegie Hall and a solo piano performance at the Newport Jazz Festival. He played the Newport festival again the following year to mixed reviews. He took the stage for the last time in 1976 at Carnegie Hall, where he made an unexpected cameo appearance at a concert by the pianist Barry Harris. Then he sank into an inconsolable depression from which he never emerged. He confined himself to his silent, darkened room on the top floor of the baroness's mansion, allowing few visitors and refusing to play the piano when asked. After six years of isolation and inaction he died of a brain hemorrhage and was buried in suburban Hartsdale, just north of New York City. Less than two years later his daughter, Barbara, a dancer and musician said to have inherited Monk's gifts, died of cancer.

Because of substantial publishing income from his compositions, many of which are jazz standards, Monk was one of the few jazz-era musicians able to leave his descendents a lasting financial legacy. Thelonious junior, known professionally as T. S. Monk, became the head of the Thelonious Monk Institute, a multimillion-dollar foundation with a philanthropic and educational mission. The crown jewel of the institute was its annual contest for jazz soloists, which played a major role in the resurgence of jazz in the 1990s by granting exposure and recording contracts to many talented young musicians. Other high-profile institute activities included a joint venture with the Walt Disney organization to establish a jazz museum at Disney World in Orlando, Florida. In 1995, Monk's portrait appeared on a U.S. postage stamp, a fitting tribute to a man who gave the world so much distinctly American music.

Monk's influence on subsequent generations of jazz musicians was enormous, challenging traditionally held concepts of melody, harmony, and rhythm and contributing to the paradigm of artistic integrity in jazz. Monk epitomizes the jazz musician who is willing to endure years of financial hardship and even ridicule in order to bring his idea of beauty into the world. Largely for this reason, Monk was celebrated as a patriarch by the abstract jazz avantgardists of the 1960s, Coltrane and the iconoclastic pianist Cecil Taylor among them. Like Duke Ellington, Monk influenced music beyond the borders of jazz. And, like Ellington, he must ultimately invite comparisons with the giants of European classical music. Monk reshaped the music of his time and, in doing so, brought new understanding to the concept of modernity.

★

In the late 1990s there were two biographies of Monk available, neither of them definitive. Laurent de Wilde, *Monk* (1997), by a French jazz pianist, is written in a casual, impressionistic style but covers the facets of Monk's life in a way that rings true most of the time. Leslie Gourse, *Straight, No Chaser: The Life and Genius of Thelonious Monk* (1997), is no more authoritative. The evolution of bebop, including Monk's role, is covered in detail in Ira Gitler, *Swing to Bop* (1985), an extensive oral history of the period. Original interviews with Monk are in *Down Beat* (25 July 1956, 10 Dec. 1963, and 28 Oct. 1971) and *Metronome* (Mar. 1957) magazines. Obituaries are in the *New York Times* (18 Feb. 1982), *New York Daily News* (18 Feb. 1982), *Rolling Stone* (1 Apr. 1982), and *Down Beat* (May 1982). Charlotte Zwerin's film *Thelonious Monk: Straight No Chaser* (1988) is an essential documentary.

GREG ROBINSON

MONROE, Marion (*b.* 4 February 1898 in Mount Vernon, Indiana; *d.* 25 June 1983 in Long Beach, California), child psychologist and reading specialist who is best known as the coauthor of the Dick and Jane reading series, used by millions of American schoolchildren from the 1940s through the early 1970s.

One of at least four children of Edwin S. and Laura Potter Monroe, Marion Monroe received her undergraduate degree from the University of Oklahoma in 1919, and her M.A. (1924) and Ph.D. in psychology (1929) from the University of Chicago, where she began her lifelong work of helping children learn to read. At Chicago, Monroe met the colleagues with whom she would continue working throughout her professional life, including William S. Gray, dean of the College of Education and a prominent reading authority.

Monroe was one of the early researchers studying reading disabilities. In 1928 she developed and standardized a battery of diagnostic tests. She noted that teachers assumed that children who could not learn to read were lazy or stupid. But with the advent of intelligence and achievement tests, many psychologists and educators began to investigate why children of average intelligence were not learning to read.

As a research psychologist at Chicago's Institute for Juvenile Research from 1929 to 1932, Monroe began a study of 415 persons who were having difficulties reading, and compared them with a control group of 101 schoolchildren in an average American school population. She devised and tested remedial methods to help the children who were not learning to read. This research study became her 1932 book, *Children Who Cannot Read: The Analysis of Reading Disabilities and the Use of Diagnostic Tests in the Instruction of Retarded Readers,* published by the University of Chicago Press. The text was organized and presented in a way that was helpful to teachers and parents alike. "Reading," Monroe wrote, "may be accomplished in many ways." Her remedial methods emphasized the value of individual attention and an understanding teacher. She also advocated having the child begin with easy tasks.

In 1932 Monroe went to Pittsburgh, where she worked as the chief psychologist at the Child Guidance Center until 1936. However, she would continue working with Dr. Gray as he developed educational materials for children. This association resulted in the basic-reading series Dick and Jane, which was developed in collaboration with authors, editors, and illustrators for the Scott, Foresman publishing company. Revised many times, the Dick and Jane series was used throughout the nation for the next forty years.

Unlike the dull, moralistic McGuffey readers previously used to teach children reading, the Dick and Jane stories featured bright, colorful pictures tied to simple plots relevant to children's lives, simple sentence structures, repetitive language, and a limited vocabulary. By the mid-1930s nearly half of America's students were learning to read with Dick and Jane, and by the 1950s over 80 percent of the nation's schools were using Dick and Jane materials. For children growing up in that era, learning was accomplished by reading sentences such as "See Spot run! Run, Spot, run!" which were accompanied by colorful pictures of a playful dog and happy children.

This program, which utilized the "look-see" method, emphasized the memorization of whole words, rather than the sounding out of parts of words, or syllables, which is the basis of phonics. Throughout the years the look-see method was criticized by researchers and educators; Dr. Rudolf Flesch, a leading authority on literacy, criticized the Dick and Jane series in his influential book *Why Johnny Can't Read* (1955), advocating instead the use of phonics to teach children to read. By the 1970s the Dick and Jane series seemed dated, racist, and sexist. Educators, who had once accepted without question Dick and Jane's white, middle-class life in the suburbs, began to understand that such exclusive images could no longer be used to teach America's children.

On 18 July 1942 Marion married William Wilbur Cox; she continued to use her maiden name in her subsequent writings. The couple adopted three children. In addition to her work with Scott, Foresman, Monroe was a consultant and a specialist in remedial reading who worked with public schools throughout the country. In 1945 she became director of the Reading Clinic at the University of Southern California at Los Angeles, and taught reading courses at UCLA and Berkeley. She developed the Monroe Reading Aptitude Tests and the Monroe Scales to Evaluate Oral Language, which were used to record, describe, analyze, and rate language skills. She also wrote *Growing Into Reading: How Readiness for Reading Develops at Home and at School* (1951) and coauthored *Foundations for Reading: Informal Pre-Reading Procedures* (with Bernice Rogers, 1964), both for Scott, Foresman.

Much of Monroe's published works came about through her association with the Scott, Foresman reading programs and followed the Dick and Jane formula. An example is *My Pictionary* (1970), written with W. Cabell Greet and Andrew Schiller, the first book of a series for beginning readers. It presented 535 words with labeled pictures, which were arranged in nine categories and color coded. Other books for young readers included *My First Picture Dictionary, The First Talking Alphabet*, the *Learn to Listen, Speak, and Write* series (written with others), and *The New Tall Tales* (with A. Sterl Artley).

The methods featured in Monroe's books are now an integral part of early-literacy programs. The Dick and Jane books may no longer be in use, but their look, organization, and structure have been widely adopted in the production of literature for the beginning reader.

Monroe died at age eighty-five in Long Beach, California.

★

Albert J. Harris, "Readings That Made a Difference: Those Who Taught Me About Reading," *Australian Journal of Reading* (Oct. 1979): 6–8, offers appreciation and background for Monroe's early work. Obituaries are in the *Chicago Tribune* (28 June 1983) and *New York Times* (29 June 1983).

JULIANNE CICARELLI

MONTGOMERY, Robert (*b.* 21 May 1904 in Beacon, New York; *d.* 27 September 1981 in New York City), actor and director of stage, screen, and television who portrayed playboys and played dramatic leads and became a critic of American television.

Robert Montgomery, born Henry Montgomery, Jr., was the elder of two children of Mary Weed Barney, a homemaker, and Henry Montgomery, Sr., a vice president of the New York Rubber Company who saw that his first son received the benefits of private tutors, the Pawling School, and a year in Europe. When the elder Henry died suddenly, having lost his fortune, his teenage heir became a mechanic's helper in the New York, New Haven, and Hartford railroad yards. An aspiring writer, he moved to Greenwich Village in New York City and soon went to sea in the engine room of an oil tanker. None of his stories and plays was successful. Returning to the Village, Robert Montgomery entered the theater world in September 1924, playing several parts in *The Mask and the Face*. Fired after only nine performances, he won parts in *Dawn* (1924) and *The Complex* (1925) before joining a Rochester repertory company. He mastered acting techniques by appearing in more than fifty roles in two years and worked another season in New England. On 14 April 1928 Montgomery married Elizabeth Bryan Allen, an actress. They had two children; daughter Elizabeth became a famous television star.

Montgomery's Broadway role in *Possession* (1928) brought him to the attention of Hollywood's Samuel Goldwyn of Metro-Goldwyn-Mayer, but his screen test with Vilma Banky was disastrous. Nevertheless, MGM liked Montgomery's potential and in 1929 offered him a contract at $350 a week; he remained at the studio with only a single loan-out for the next seventeen years. *So This Is College* (1930), his first film, was forgettable, but his performance in *The Big House* (1930) displayed leading-man qualities. As a contract actor Montgomery appeared in more than fifteen films by the end of 1931, often opposite Hollywood's leading ladies. At six feet tall with piercing blue eyes, Montgomery was typecast as a sophisticated playboy. His name was rarely above the title, but his popularity grew. Before the end of the 1930s, he had appeared five times each with Norma Shearer and Joan Crawford, as well as playing opposite Myrna Loy, Greta Garbo, Helen Hayes, and Marion Davies. By mid-decade he was a star lamenting that directors "put a cocktail shaker in my hands and kept me shaking for years."

Witty and acid tongued, Montgomery clashed with studio mogul Louis B. Mayer, who considered him an "ungrateful New York snob." The MGM management, which agreed to his large contract demands in 1934, was outraged when Montgomery assumed leadership of the small Screen Actors Guild. As president of SAG from 1935 to 1937, Montgomery fought for contract players, independent actors, and craft union members. His bravura performance as a labor leader forced the studios to recognize SAG in 1937. A vindictive Mayer punished Montgomery by casting him as a Cockney psychopath in *Night Must Fall* (1937), but the ploy backfired. Montgomery actually coveted the part, winning an Academy Award nomination and critical acclaim for broadening his range. MGM retaliated by not supporting Montgomery in the Oscar race and by virtually refusing to market his next film, *Yellow Jack* (1938). Most film historians consider these two performances the finest of Montgomery's career. When Mayer later attempted to break SAG by recognizing the International Alliance of Theatrical and Stage Employees, Montgomery proved the new organization's mob connections. Montgomery's evidence, published by Westbrook Pegler, won the journalist a Pulitzer Prize in 1941.

When World War II broke out in Europe, Montgomery

Robert Montgomery. CHAPMAN COLLECTION/ARCHIVE PHOTOS

was in London making *The Earl of Chicago* (1940). He drove an ambulance for the American Field Service until the Battle of Dunkirk in May 1940 and returned to lecture Americans on his experience. Originally a liberal Democrat, he supported Republican Wendell Willkie in 1940 and became increasingly conservative as years passed. Nominated for an Academy Award for the fantasy *Here Comes Mr. Jordan* (1941), Montgomery seemingly ended his career by accepting a commission in the naval reserve in August 1941. First dispatched to London as an attaché, he later commanded a PT boat and served in the Pacific both at Guadalcanal and in the Marshall Islands. In 1944 Montgomery narrated *This Is War* and was on the first destroyer to enter Cherbourg harbor on D day. Montgomery's military exploits earned him a Bronze Star and the Legion of Honor, and he rose to the rank of lieutenant commander. In 1945 Montgomery resumed acting in John Ford's military epic *They Were Expendable*. When Ford became ill, Montgomery demonstrated unexpected talent by directing its final three weeks. (During the filming, Montgomery was promoted to the rank of full commander.)

A decorated, bona fide movieland hero, Montgomery accepted another term as SAG president. In 1946 he directed the innovative *Lady in the Lake* (1946), using the camera as the eyes of his protagonist. Montgomery's director's credit for this "crucial bad film" forced him to resign from SAG, since he shared in *Lady*'s meager profits. Ronald Reagan replaced him as SAG leader, and in 1947 both men appeared as friendly witnesses before the House Un-American Activities Committee. Subsequently, Montgomery directed and starred for Universal in *Ride the Pink Horse* (1947), a film noir, and for Warner Brothers in *Your Witness* (1949). The latter was his last film role, but Montgomery, believing that "anyone who stands still in his . . . profession is lost," simply moved to new media.

In 1949 Montgomery, admitting an "innate desire not to keep my mouth shut," tried radio; his program, *Robert Montgomery Speaking,* was more charming than profound. Moving to New York City as executive producer of *Robert Montgomery Presents,* he introduced, starred in, and directed many of its 326 television episodes from 1950 to 1957. His twenty-two-year marriage ended in divorce in 1950, but his marriage to Elizabeth Grant Harkness on 9 December 1950 lasted until his death. Although his series endured, Montgomery became increasingly critical of television's ratings mania. He openly condemned the network "triopoly" for lack of quality and for pursuing personality over substance. He championed public television, suggesting it be financed by taxing commercial shows. He later wrote an *Open Letter from a Television Viewer* (1968), summarizing his scorn.

Long a Republican, Montgomery was President Dwight D. Eisenhower's television adviser from 1953 to 1961. Enjoying the prestige of a White House office but commuting from New York City, Montgomery began the practice of videotaping presidential press conferences for later broadcasting. Residence in New York rekindled Montgomery's love for live theater, and in 1955 he won a Tony for directing *The Desperate Hours.* Montgomery returned to Hollywood to direct his old friend James Cagney in *The Gallant Hours* (1960), the last of sixty-two Montgomery films. Two years later he directed the successful stage play *Calculated Risk.*

After Montgomery's show business career ended, he worked as communications consultant to John D. Rockefeller 3d from 1965 to 1969. He served a year as president of the Repertory Theater of Lincoln Center (1969–1970), and as trustee for the National Citizen's Committee on Broadcasting. Contemptuous of the networks, he fought against violent programming and found much to applaud in Vice President Spiro Agnew's denunciation of news coverage in the late 1960s and early 1970s. Happily relocated on a Canaan, Connecticut, farm, he occasionally delivered lectures about television or gave dramatic readings. He was an Episcopalian. After he died of cancer at Columbia-Presbyterian Hospital, the New York press posthumously awarded him a gold press card and heard Cagney eulogize a friend who always stood up to "the big guys." Montgomery's cremated remains were scattered over his farm in Connecticut.

★

There is no autobiography or adequate biography of Montgomery. Biographical information can be found in Anne Rothe, ed., *Current Biography 1948* (1949); *Who's Who in the Theater,* 15th ed. (1972); Liz-Anne Bowden, ed., *Oxford Companion to Film* (1976); and Hal May, ed., *Contemporary Authors,* vol. 108 (1983). Also see an article in *Collier's* (1 Apr. 1939). Obituaries are in the *New York Times* (28 Sept. 1981), *Newsweek* (12 Oct. 1981), and *Time* (12 Oct. 1981).

GEORGE J. LANKEVICH

MOORE, Stanford (*b.* 4 September 1913 in Chicago, Illinois; *d.* 23 August 1982 in New York City), biochemist who shared the 1972 Nobel Prize in chemistry with Christian B. Anfinsen and William H. Stein for their research on the molecular structure of proteins.

Stanford Moore grew up in Nashville, Tennessee, where his father, John Howard Moore, was a member of the faculty of the School of Law at Vanderbilt University. His mother was Ruth Fowler, a graduate of Stanford University. He grew up in an environment highly influenced by the intellectual achievements of his parents. He was raised in the Roman Catholic faith and attended a high school ad-

Stanford Moore, 1972. UPI/CORBIS-BETTMANN

ministered by the George Peabody College for Teachers in Nashville. Moore received his B. A. degree in chemistry from Vanderbilt in 1935, graduating summa cum laude. The faculty recommended him for a Wisconsin Alumni Research Foundation Fellowship, which took him to the University of Wisconsin. There he worked with Karl Paul Link and received his Ph.D. in organic chemistry in 1938. His thesis work was on the characterization of carbohydrates as benzimidazole derivatives.

In 1939 Moore went to New York City and joined the Rockefeller Institute for Medical Research (now Rockefeller University) to work with the German scientist Max Bergmann. After spending three years in this position, Moore was drawn out of the laboratory by World War II. He served as a junior administrative officer in Washington, D.C., for academic and industrial chemical projects administered by the Office of Scientific Research Development. In that capacity he studied the effects of mustard gas and other chemical warfare agents. By the end of the war, he was on duty with the Operational Research Section attached to the headquarters of the U.S. Armed Forces in the Pacific Ocean Area, Hawaii.

After the war Moore returned to the Rockefeller Institute, where he and his colleague William H. Stein were given laboratory space to pursue any area of research that interested them. This started a forty-year collaboration that led to the development of quantitative chromatographic methods for amino acid analysis, automation of these methods, and their utilization in research into protein chemistry. He continued his work at the Rockefeller Institute for the rest of his life, with some short breaks: tenure of the Francqui Chair at the University of Brussels in 1950; a six-month stay at the University of Cambridge in 1951; and a period in 1968 as visiting professor of health sciences at the Vanderbilt School of Medicine. Moore became a member of the Rockefeller Institute in 1952 and then full professor of chemistry.

Using column chromatography, in 1948 he and Stein separated amino acids by passing an amino acid solution through a column filled with potato starch. A year later they succeeded in separating amino acids from blood and urine by using a synthetic ion-exchange resin. They then applied the technique of chromatography to the analysis of amino acids and peptides obtained from proteins and biological fluids and used their analysis technique to determine the structure of enzymes. They were credited with making major contributions to the development of quantitative chromatographic procedures for the separation of amino acids, a technique that had not been used for the analysis of amino acids until Moore and Stein developed their approach.

In 1958, Moore and Stein contributed to the development of an automatic amino-acid analyzer and by the fol-

lowing year had determined the amino acid sequence of pancreatic ribonuclease, a digestive enzyme that breaks down ribonucleic acid (RNA), a compound that plays a major role in human heredity, so that its components can be reused. They were the first researchers to find that pancreatic nuclease consists of a chain of 124 amino acids and to demonstrate how those acids composed the molecule. This was the first complete description of the chemical structure of an enzyme ever done, and the discovery, which was vital to understanding how a biological malfunction might be repaired in the human body, led to Moore and Stein's sharing of the Nobel Prize in 1972. The research not only elucidated the detailed structural information of a specific enzyme but also led to the development of a methodology that revolutionized protein chemistry. The understanding of protein structure is essential to the understanding of biological function, and this knowledge opens the door to the study and treatment of different diseases. Moore and Stein's findings influenced research in neurochemistry and in the study of such diseases as sickle-cell anemia, cancer, and malaria.

Moore was editor of the *Journal of Biological Chemistry*, president of the American Society of Biological Chemistry, and a member of the National Academy of Sciences. He received the American Chemical Society Award in Chromatography and Electrophoresis in 1964 (shared with Stein), the Richards Medal of the American Chemical Society in 1972, and the Linderstrom-Lang Medal in 1972, as well as honorary degrees from the University of Paris and the University of Wisconsin.

In the early 1970s Moore was diagnosed with amytrophic lateral sclerosis (Lou Gehrig's disease), a progressive disease of the nerves and muscles. He committed suicide in his home in New York City. He never married nor had any children, and he left his estate to Rockefeller University, where he was John D. Rockefeller Professor at the time of his death.

★

Among Moore's published works are: "The Chemical Structure of Proteins" (with William Stein), *Scientific American* (Feb. 1961); "Chemical Structures of Pancreatic Ribonuclease and Deoxyribonuclease," *Science* (May 1973), which is the combined Nobel Prize lectures of Moore and Stein; and numerous other papers on protein and carbohydrate chemistry in various scientific journals. Additional information on Moore can be found in *The Nobel Prize Winners: Chemistry* (1990); and Emily J. McMurray, ed., *Notable Twentieth-Century Scientists* (1995). An obituary is in the *New York Times* (24 Aug. 1982).

MARIA PACHECO

MOOS, Malcolm Charles (*b.* 19 April 1916 in Saint Paul, Minnesota; *d.* 28 January 1982 at Ten Mile Lake in Hackensack, Minnesota), educator, author, and government official who was a speechwriter for President Dwight D. Eisenhower and president of the University of Minnesota from 1967 to 1974.

Moos was one of two children born to Charles John Moos and Katherine Isabelle Grant. His father was the postmaster of St. Paul between 1921 and 1933, then an insurance executive until 1959; he managed eleven successful Republican state campaigns in Minnesota.

Moos graduated from the University of Minnesota in 1937. As a teaching assistant, he engaged in a half-hour radio debate with Hubert H. Humphrey on the topic of Wendell L. Willkie versus Franklin D. Roosevelt. Moos commented, "Hubert took the first 27 minutes and I ended up with the last three." After receiving his master's degree from Minnesota in 1938, Moos was a research fellow at the university-affiliated League of Minnesota Municipalities. He produced the report *Nonpartisan Legislative and Judicial Elections in Minnesota* in 1938. In 1939 Moos obtained a teaching fellowship at the University of California, Berkeley, where he earned a doctorate in political science in 1942.

Malcolm Moos, 1967. UPI/CORBIS-BETTMANN

His first book, *State Penal Administration in Alabama* (1942), resulted from a study of road gangs for the University of Alabama's Bureau of Public Administration. Moos taught briefly at the University of Wyoming in Laramie before joining the Department of Political Science at Johns Hopkins University in Baltimore in 1942 as an assistant professor. He was made an associate professor in 1946 and a full professor in 1952, and he became a close friend of Milton S. Eisenhower, president of Johns Hopkins and brother of Dwight D. Eisenhower. On 29 June 1945 Moos married Margaret Tracy Gager, a student at Goucher College in Towson, Maryland. She worked as a librarian at the Baltimore Art Museum and was a Democratic, and later Republican, activist. They had five children.

Moos left academia in 1945 to become an associate editor of the *Baltimore Evening Sun,* where he knew H. L. Mencken, a man "born with his motor racing." Moos left the newspaper in 1948 and later edited a collection of Mencken's writing, *A Carnival of Buncombe* (1956). Moos belonged to the Prisoner's Aid Society from 1952 to 1958 and to the Baltimore City Jail Commission from 1953 to 1955. He also served as a consultant to the Maryland Commission on the Organization of State Government from 1952 to 1954.

Moos was appointed a visiting professor at the University of Michigan in 1955. In 1957 he became the director of the Research Commission on Government and Higher Education, which investigated the increasing role of government at American universities. He served as the chairman of the Republican State Central Committee in Baltimore between 1954 and 1958 and was an alternate delegate to the Republican National Convention in 1952 and a delegate in 1956. He wrote about American politics in a witty, uncomplicated style. His works include *A Grammar of American Politics: The National Government* (coauthored with Wilfred E. Binkley, 1949); *Politics, Presidents, and Coattails* (1952); *Power Through Purpose: The Bases of American Foreign Policy* (with Thomas L. Cook, 1954); *The Republicans: A History of Their Party* (1956); and *The Post–Land Grant University* (1981).

In 1957 presidential assistant Sherman Adams asked Moos to help Arthur Larson draft speeches for President Eisenhower. When Larson resigned in 1958, Moos became an administrative assistant to the president and his principal speechwriter. Moos is credited with inserting the term "military-industrial complex" in Eisenhower's famous farewell address on 17 January 1961.

Moos was a liberal Republican in a conservative era. He called himself "a left-wing Republican" and supported some New Deal legislation. In contrast to Eisenhower, he saw few major differences between Republicans and Democrats. His relations with Ike remained cordial, and Moos helped create a tough new image for the president. During this period Moos coauthored newspaper pieces with presidential assistant Stephen Hess, and the two wrote a history of presidential conventions, *Hats in the Ring* (1960).

President John F. Kennedy retained Moos as a member of the Presidential Commission on Campaign Costs, which completed its report on the fateful day of 22 November 1963. Moos became an adviser on public and political affairs to Rockefeller Brothers, Inc., in 1961, at the time Henry Kissinger was advising the Rockefellers on foreign affairs. Moos drafted speeches for New York governor Nelson A. Rockefeller's 1962 campaign and helped prepare his Godkin lectures on "The Future of Federalism," delivered at Harvard University in 1962. Moos assisted Governor William W. Scranton of Pennsylvania with speeches during his unsuccessful presidential campaign in 1964.

Moos returned to Johns Hopkins briefly in 1963. He accepted an appointment to teach public law and government at Columbia University later that year. Moos became the planning director of the Ford Foundation in 1964, establishing a division on government and law to develop more effectual forms of the democratic process. He persuaded the foundation to support the Legal Defense Fund of the National Association for the Advancement of Colored People.

In 1967 Moos succeeded O. Meredith Wilson as president of the University of Minnesota. He had served under J. L. Morrill, later president of the University of Minnesota, at Wyoming, and this connection presumably helped his candidacy. Moos was the first Minnesota graduate to assume the post. His seven-year term was a period of expansion during which the operating budget of the university increased from $98 million to $241 million, and day-college enrollment rose from about 60,000 to more than 63,000. The school's burgeoning size led to lecture classes of 5,000 students and televised lectures, most of which were abandoned after a few years.

Moos was a vigorous opponent of the Vietnam War, and only one major antiwar police-student riot occurred on campus during his tenure. He believed his most important achievement at the university was the advancement of women and minorities. In June 1968, when a midwestern summer storm blew up as thousands of students marched into Memorial Stadium for graduation ceremonies, Moos interrupted the benediction to announce, "All degrees are conferred," just as everybody scattered in the downpour.

Moos remained at Minnesota until 1974, when he resigned under pressure. The university budget had been cut four successive years, faculty had departed, and Moos refused to have his authority divided among administrators. He became president of the Fund for the Republic, Inc., in Santa Barbara, California, for a year, and then headed the Center for the Study of Democratic Institutions in Santa Barbara for another. He left after the center experienced financial difficulties.

In 1978 Moos failed to win the Republican nomination to run for the Senate seat being vacated by Muriel Humphrey. Only months before the election, 75 percent of the voters still had no idea whether Moos would make a good senator. He passed out moosehead buttons during the campaign.

Until 1974 Moos and his family lived in the University of Minnesota president's mansion, Eastcliff, near the bluffs of the Mississippi River. They spent their summers in Hackensack, Minnesota, in a cabin on Ten Mile Lake, where Moos enjoyed tennis and sailing. Moos was lanky and had bushy eyebrows and wavy white hair later in life. He once sued a neighbor who shot his golden retriever. Moos claimed that a pet was more valuable than mere property, but he lost the case. Coworkers described him alternately as gracious, pompous, ineffectual, gentle, proud, vain, amusing, nervous, unsure of himself, and a man committed to reason. Moos died after a heart attack at his summer home and was cremated.

★

Moos's papers are housed in the University of Minnesota archives. A good biographical account is the entry on Moos in *Current Biography* (1968). See also Burton Paulu, "A Speechwriter's Finest Phrase," *Minneapolis Star Tribune* (1 Feb. 1986).

JOHN L. SCHERER

MORGAN, Henry Sturgis ("Harry") (*b.* 24 October 1900 in London, England; *d.* 7 February 1982 in New York City), yachtsman and investment banker who was a founder of Morgan Stanley & Co., one of Wall Street's leading investment banks.

Morgan was the youngest of four children of John Pierpont Morgan, Jr., a famed Wall Street banker and financier, and Jane Norton Grew, daughter of a Boston banker and mill owner. After attending the Groton School, he graduated from Harvard in 1923. One week later, on 25 June 1923, he married Catherine Frances Adams, daughter of former secretary of the navy Charles Francis Adams and a descendant of Presidents John Adams and John Quincy Adams. They had five sons. Later that year he started working as a $15-a-week messenger boy at J. P. Morgan & Co., the bank founded by his grandfather. He rose steadily and became a partner in 1928, bringing him an annual income of $1 million.

The October 1929 stock market crash and ensuing depression created political pressure to break up Wall Street's concentration of financial power, and the Banking Act of 1933 (the Glass-Steagall Act) forced banks to choose be-

Henry Morgan at the Sleepy Hollow Country Club, Briarcliff Manor, New York, 1940. UPI/CORBIS-BETTMANN

tween investment banking and commercial banking. J. P. Morgan & Co. dissolved its bond department in June 1934, and the following year Harry Morgan and two other partners resigned from J. P. Morgan to create a new and independent investment bank, Morgan Stanley & Co. Harold Stanley became the president, William Ewing the vice president, and Morgan the treasurer and secretary. It opened for business on 16 September 1935, and during its first year captured one-quarter of the underwriting market. The new bank brought over about twenty employees from the commercial banking firm and was generally considered the unofficial successor to the investment branch of J. P. Morgan & Co.

Although the well-known Morgan name came first in the firm's title, the real power rested with Stanley, an expert in public utility and railroad financing who headed the firm until 1961. The company eventually became Wall Street's leader in the underwriting of heavy industry, mining, and foreign government bonds, the former specialties of J. P. Morgan & Co.

In the same year that Morgan Stanley was formed, Harry Morgan was elected to the board of overseers of Harvard University and became a member of the board of directors of the General Electric Corporation. He had been

a trustee of the Pierpont Morgan Library since 1924, and in 1960 he succeeded his brother as its president.

Morgan's income increased as business activities revived during the late 1930s, and in 1936 he bought 100 acres of land at Eaton's Neck on Long Island's North Shore to develop an estate containing a huge manor house, a swimming pool, cottages for the help, and an eight-car garage. He commuted to Wall Street by seaplane.

Morgan Stanley reorganized itself as a partnership in late 1941 in order to qualify for a seat on the New York Stock Exchange. Stanley's title changed from president to managing partner but he still headed the firm, with Morgan in a secondary role. Morgan considered himself "the brakeman on the Morgan Stanley express train," whose job was to make sure the firm maintained gentlemanly standards in an increasingly greedy business.

In September 1941, three months before the Japanese attack on Pearl Harbor, Morgan obtained a commission as commander with the United States Navy. During World War II he served in Washington as a naval representative to the War Production Board and the Office of Secret Services.

The economic recovery in the postwar period brought not only increased business to Morgan Stanley, but also government concern over the concentration of power on Wall Street. In 1947, Morgan was named as the lead defendant in *United States* v. *Henry Morgan et al.,* an antitrust prosecution against Morgan Stanley and sixteen other Wall Street investment banks. The trial lasted from November 1950 to May 1953, and although the defendant firms handled 70 percent of all Wall Street underwritings, the judge exonerated Morgan and the other defendants by dismissing all of the government's claims. In 1951, Morgan became a director of the Aetna Insurance Company, which his great-grandfather had founded in 1819.

Morgan's business interests, however, took a back seat to his passion for yachting. He was elected commodore of the New York Yacht Club in 1948, the same year in which his racing sloop, *Djinn,* won both the Astor Cup and the King's Cup.

In 1956 Morgan fought with other partners over making his son Charles a partner. Like his father, Charles did not appear to have an excessive interest in, or particular aptitude for, investment banking, leading one partner to later tell author Ron Chernow, "If ever two people, father and son, were miscast in life, it was Harry and Charlie Morgan." Several years later another of Morgan's sons was up for consideration as partner. The firm invoked a rarely used antinepotism rule to blackball him. According to Chernow, the other partners told Harry, "You've got Charlie, that's enough."

Following family tradition, Morgan marked his twenty-fifth anniversary with the firm in 1960 by giving everyone there a bonus. He had a fetish about privacy, which was believed to be the result of the federal government's investigation into Morgan finances during the 1930s and the antitrust prosecution of the 1950s. When Princeton University asked him in the 1960s about donating his papers, he responded that there were no Morgan papers because he had destroyed them to keep them out of the hands of future investigators.

Morgan's conservatism also led him to oppose proposals in the 1960s to move the firm's offices from 2 Wall Street to Midtown Manhattan, where the other partners believed they could have better access to their corporate clients. Morgan told his colleagues that he feared a Broadway address might lead his London friends to conclude he had become a theatrical producer.

In the late 1960s, Morgan Stanley decided to enter the lucrative business of mergers and acquisitions, and in order to obtain more capital, the firm transformed itself into a limited partnership in 1970. Although Morgan became a limited partner without a formal vote, he still exercised influence over the firm's affairs and successfully argued against a proposed buyout of the firm by American Express in the early 1970s.

In 1974 the firm abandoned a long-standing policy against financing hostile corporate takeovers, and Morgan retired from his partnership the following year. He retained the title of advisory director until the time of his death but devoted virtually all of his time to yachting. He was instrumental in 1958 in forming the United States International Sailing Association, which helped subsidize American participants in the Olympics and other competitions. The organization's name was changed in 1987 to United States Sailing Foundation. Shortly before his death he reversed his position about providing scholars access to family and business papers, and he donated an extensive collection to the Morgan Library.

Morgan, an Episcopalian, had an impressive appearance, notable for his pomaded hair, intense eyes, sharp chin, and expensive, tailor-made suits. He was a prototypical WASP banker, who benefited more from his inherited fortune, family connections, and amiable disposition than from his business abilities. He and his firm prospered enormously from the four decades of unbroken economic growth which followed the end of the Great Depression.

★

Morgan's family and business papers are located at the Pierpont Morgan Library in New York. Morgan and his bank are discussed in two books by Ron Chernow, *The House of Morgan: An American Banking Dynasty and the Rise of Modern Finance* (1990) and *The Death of the Banker: The Decline and Fall of the Great Financial Dynasties and the Triumph of the Small Investor* (1997). Morgan Stanley & Co., *Morgan Stanley Fiftieth Anniversary Review* (1985), is the bank's official history. Also useful are Harold

Medina, *Corrected Opinion . . .* (1954, repr. 1975); Vincent P. Carosso, *Investment Banking in America: A History* (1970); Matthew Josephson, *The Money Lords: The Great Finance Capitalists, 1925–1950* (1972); Michael C. Jenson, *The Financiers* (1976); William J. Kneisel, *Morgan Stanley & Co.: A Brief History* (1977); Paul Ferris, *The Master Bankers* (1984); Paul Hoffman, *The Dealmakers: Inside the World of Investment Banking* (1984); Institutional Investor, *The Way It Was: An Oral History of Finance, 1967–1987* (1988); and Nicholas von Hoffman, *Capitalist Fools: Tales of American Business, from Carnegie to Forbes to the Milken Gang* (1992). Useful articles include "The New Style at Morgan Stanley," *Business Week* (19 Jan. 1974): 47–54; "Morgan Stanley on the Move," *Financial World* (14 July 1971): 20; and Leslie Wayne, "The Heat's on Morgan Stanley," *New York Times* (21 Dec. 1982). Obituaries are in the *New York Times* and *Washington Post* (both 8 Feb. 1982).

STEPHEN MARSHALL

MORGANFIELD, McKinley. See Waters, Muddy.

MOROSS, Jerome (*b.* 1 August 1913 in Brooklyn, New York; *d.* 25 July 1983 in Miami, Florida), composer for the ballet (*Frankie and Johnny*), musical theater (*The Golden Apple*), and film (*The Big Country*).

Moross was the second of three sons born to Samuel and Molly Moross. Of Russian Jewish stock, his father was an electrician whose work in movie theaters eventually led him into the real estate business. Jerome attended DeWitt Clinton High School in Manhattan, where he began a lifelong friendship with Bernard Herrmann, a fellow musical iconoclast. The youths shared a love of music (especially the distinctive American sound of the little-known Charles Ives) and a rebellious streak that led them both to compose and perform adventurous works at New York University (NYU) and the Juilliard School. In 1931 Herrmann led a Juilliard student orchestra in the first performance of Moross's *Paeans,* a brashly avant-garde score that was later published in Henry Cowell's influential *New Music.*

Graduating from NYU at eighteen (1932), without any formal schooling in composition, Moross embraced life in the musical theater. Jobs as rehearsal pianist and pit musician supported his spare-time composition in a variety of forms. Early works included the cantata *Those Everlasting Blues* (1932), the *Biguine* for orchestra (1934), and *Paul Bunyan: An American Saga* (1934). The last two works originated as ballet scores for Charles Weidman. The 1935 revue *Parade* was developed by a Fourteenth Street "socialist" theater group and also enjoyed a brief uptown production by the Theatre Guild. Around this time, Moross, who was active in the informal Young Composers Group, was praised by its mentor, Aaron Copland, as "probably the

Jerome Moross. COURTESY OF SUSANNA TARJAN

most talented" composer of his generation, notable especially for the "sheer physicalness" of his music.

Ballet commissions continued, including *American Pattern* (1936) and the very successful *Notorious Life of Frankie and Johnny* (1938), both commissioned by Ruth Page and the Chicago Opera Ballet. Moross had met George Gershwin several years earlier and in 1937 was engaged as pianist for the road company of Gershwin's *Porgy and Bess*. It was his steadiest job during a lean decade. Moross's early travels also included a cross-country bus trip in 1936, during which he stopped at the little town of Albuquerque, New Mexico, and experienced an almost religious surge of wonder at the open spaces of the American West. Having early rejected modernism in favor of a blues- and folk-inflected nationalist style, Moross began to develop a distinctive Western sound. *A Tall Story* (1938) was his first orchestral piece in this vein.

Moross married Hazel Abrams on 28 August 1939 in New York City. The following year their only child was born in Hollywood. There, Copland invited Moross to help orchestrate his film music for *Our Town* (1940), opening a door to steady studio work for the young man. Moross worked for Warner Brothers for several years and then shuttled between New York and Hollywood for miscellaneous orchestrating jobs during the remainder of the 1940s. He always aligned himself with the New York theater, however,

and during this decade he joined with lyricist John Latouche in creating a series of musical theater pieces involving songs but no spoken dialogue: *Susanna and the Elders* (1940), *Willie the Weeper* (1945), *The Eccentricities of Davy Crockett,* and *Riding Hood Revisited* (both 1946). The first three of these works enjoyed an off-Broadway run as *Ballet Ballads* in 1948. The show later moved uptown, where its music was praised by Virgil Thomson for "a mastery that is both rare and welcome in the American theater."

In 1948 Moross finally got an opportunity to compose his own film scores, beginning with *Close-Up* and other B-pictures. By the mid-1950s he was offered more important subjects, such as *The Sharkfighters* (1956) and *The Proud Rebel* (1958). His greatest opportunity came with the epic Western *The Big Country* (1958). Feasting on his own love for the American West, Moross wrote a vigorous score whose muscular, balletic rhythms and sweeping lyricism have made it an enduring classic. Before *The Big Country*, Hollywood Westerns employed a thick-textured European sound; afterward Moross's lean, folk-based idiom became the norm. The music was nominated for an Academy Award and led Moross to further ambitious assignments on *The Cardinal* (1963), *The War Lord* (1965), and *Rachel, Rachel* (1968), as well as the popular theme for the television series *Wagon Train* (1962).

Despite these West Coast successes, including a symphony, premiered by Sir Thomas Beecham (Seattle, 1943), Moross remained a Hollywood outsider who never abandoned the New York musical world. Bolstered by successive Guggenheim fellowships (1947–1948), he again collaborated with Latouche to devise an operatic musical on the Helen of Troy legend recast in an American setting. *The Golden Apple,* including the song "Lazy Afternoon," was a Broadway success in 1954 and won the Drama Critics Circle Award for best musical. An even more ambitious production, *Gentlemen, Be Seated,* was staged by the New York City Opera in 1963. The poor critical reception of this minstrel-show and tap-dance retelling of the Civil War was a major disappointment for Moross. Another show, *Underworld* (about Chicago gangsters), and an innovative ballet, *The Last Judgment,* were never produced.

With serious film music in decline, Moross lost patience with the Hollywood of the late 1960s. He had always been pessimistic about the medium and even made a practice of overscoring all the scenes in the picture, believing that the filmmakers usually did not know what they wanted and could always delete the excess music anyway. Three last films helped finance the purchase of his West Side apartment in Manhattan, and then Moross withdrew from pictures altogether. His last film was *Hail, Hero* (1969). Moross's late years were dedicated to chamber music, including the four *Sonatinas for Divers Instruments* (1966–1970) for such unusual combinations as clarinet choir (no. 1) and double bass with piano (no. 2). Ill with heart disease and emphysema, Moross lived to complete a one-act opera, *Sorry, Wrong Number* (1977), based on Lucille Fletcher's radio drama, and to see a revival of interest in recordings of his early music. He died of heart failure while visiting his daughter in Miami and was buried in Long Island, New York.

An aggressive modernist in his youth—Oscar Levant once referred to himself, Bernard Herrmann, and Moross as "a little group . . . whose leitmotiv was bad manners"—Moross became a shy, diffident, pessimistic man who was never at ease with the vulgarity of Hollywood or the self-promotional aspects of show business. But his athletic, yearning, free-spirited music helped to transform the medium of film music and has found increasing admirers through a steady of stream of recordings released after his death.

★

The Moross papers are at Columbia University. The scanty published literature consists largely of incidental references in histories of film music and works about such colleagues as Aaron Copland, Charles Ives, and Bernard Herrmann. See Christopher Palmer's account of the life and works in *The New Grove Dictionary of American Music* (1986); the same author's "Popular Appeal Plus Musical Purpose: The Film Music of Jerome Moross," in *Crescendo International* 11 (1973); and Aaron Copland, "Our Younger Generation: Ten Years Later," in *Modern Music* 13 (1936). Liner notes for the numerous sound recordings are the chief source of biographical information, most notably those by John Caps for the Screen Classics release of *The Big Country* (1990). This article is based on broadcast interviews and correspondence with John Caps, Christopher Palmer, Mike Snell, Paul Snook, and Noah Andre Trudeau and on other materials provided by Susanna Moross Tarjan. An obituary is in the *New York Times* (27 July 1983).

JOHN FITZPATRICK

MORTON, Thruston Ballard (*b.* 19 August 1907 in Louisville, Kentucky; *d.* 14 August 1982 in Louisville, Kentucky), businessman and politician whose strident commitment to the worldwide policy of containment, as a U.S. senator in the 1960s, was shaken by America's failure in Vietnam.

A seventh-generation Kentuckian, Morton was one of three children of David Cummins Morton, a physician, and Mary Ballard, who hailed from a family established in the state's political and business segments. Morton's younger brother by seven years, Rogers C. B. Morton, served as a member of the House of Representatives from Maryland, chairman of the Republican National Committee, and a cabinet member in the presidential administrations of Richard Nixon and Gerald Ford. Thruston Morton traced his

Senator Thruston Ballard Morton, 1960. BYRON HULSEY

commitment to public service to his maternal grandfather, S. Thruston Ballard, whom President Woodrow Wilson appointed to a federal commission in 1914. Ballard was elected lieutenant governor of Kentucky in 1919, and Morton followed him to Frankfort to serve as a page in the general assembly. After attending the Louisville public schools, Morton finished his high school education at Woodberry Forest School near Orange, Virginia, in 1925.

Upon graduating from Yale with a B.A. in 1929, Morton entered the family business, Ballard and Ballard, the region's largest grain and flour mill. Climbing to the position of vice president and sales manager in 1932, Morton eventually became chairman of the board. An Episcopalian, Morton in April 1931 married Belle Clay Lyons; the couple had two children. Morton left Ballard and Ballard to join the U.S. Navy after the outbreak of World War II in 1941. He served primarily on a minesweeper in the Pacific. When he left the U.S. Naval Reserve in 1946, Morton had attained the rank of lieutenant commander.

Believing that a strong federal government threatened the nation's free economic institutions, Morton began his political career in 1946 by winning a seat in the U.S. House of Representatives in the same year the Republican party captured the Congress. Morton's six-year House career was unspectacular, but by voting for the Truman Doctrine and for antilynching legislation, he established himself as an internationalist and a moderate Republican. An ardent supporter of General Dwight D. Eisenhower's candidacy for the Republican nomination in 1952, Morton fell out of favor with Kentucky's GOP delegation, which except for Morton backed the more conservative Robert A. Taft, senator from Ohio. Morton chose not to run for reelection in 1952, opting instead to manage the successful Senate campaign of John Sherman Cooper and to promote Eisenhower's efforts to win the general election.

Morton intended to return to the family business, but Secretary of State John Foster Dulles persuaded the Kentuckian to serve the Eisenhower administration as assistant secretary of state for congressional relations. In this capacity Morton worked to gain conservative Republican support for Eisenhower's internationalist foreign policy. He marshaled opposition to the Bricker Amendment, an isolationist Republican proposal that would have limited the president's foreign policy power. He also resisted the excesses of Senator Joseph R. McCarthy and his anticommunist crusade. While Morton held that communism represented a threat to America's vital interests, he emphasized that "you cannot chip away part of the structure of liberty without beginning to destroy the entire structure."

With President Eisenhower's support, Morton launched a successful campaign for the U.S. Senate in 1956. On the hustings in rural Kentucky, the handsome Morton combined impressive storytelling abilities and an urbane appearance that won him the title "Alben Barkley in a Brooks Brothers suit." He benefited from Eisenhower's popularity and his association with the administration, and he profited as well from an intraparty dispute between his incumbent opponent Earle C. Clements and Kentucky's Democratic governor, A. B. Chandler. In the Senate, Morton continued to support the White House's agenda. Eisenhower wrote in a 1957 diary entry that Morton was one of several young Republicans who might succeed him in the White House and carry on the president's vision of modern Republicanism. Morton endorsed the administration's 1957 civil rights bill and upheld the president's efforts to win Senate approval of the Eisenhower Doctrine, which gave the president the power to use U.S. troops in the Middle East to thwart potential and actual communist aggression.

At Eisenhower's insistence, Morton in 1959 replaced the retiring Meade Alcorn as chairman of the Republican National Committee. He served in this capacity until 1961. In 1960 he worked for the election of GOP presidential nominee Richard Nixon, but Nixon distanced his campaign from the regular Republican organization by establishing the Nixon National Campaign Organization. In fact, Nixon held Morton responsible for the televised debates that most viewers believed were won by opponent John F.

Kennedy. Nixon later asserted that Morton's pledge that Nixon would debate Kennedy "under the right circumstances" hamstrung his campaign at a crucial time. For his part, Morton argued that the GOP's 1960 defeat derived from its poor showing in urban areas and with African-American voters.

While he supported the minimum wage bill and the nuclear test ban treaty in 1963, Morton opposed much of President Kennedy's domestic agenda. He voted against the White House's school aid and housing programs in 1961. He also battled Kennedy's medical care for the elderly plan in 1962. In that year Morton found himself in a bitter reelection contest against Kentucky's lieutenant governor Wilson Wyatt, one of the first cochairmen of the liberal Americans for Democratic Action (ADA). The Morton campaign circulated literature that condemned the ADA for its communist sympathies, and Morton himself argued that Wyatt's election "would give comfort and support to his old ADA friends who represent the policy of soft talk and concessions." Morton won a surprisingly comfortable 52.8 percent of the vote, remembering later: "In this game, you've got to hit. . . . [But] we did a lot of things that made my sensitive family unhappy."

Although many Republicans viewed Morton as a respected moderate balancing the extremes of the liberal Nelson Rockefeller and the conservative Barry Goldwater, Morton chose not to enter the 1964 presidential campaign. From the Senate he fought much of President Lyndon Johnson's Great Society program. Although he voted for the Appalachia Regional Development Act, which benefited rural Kentuckians, he opposed the Elementary and Secondary Education Act and the liberal attempt to repeal Section 14(b) of the Taft-Hartley Act. He continued to fight Democratic programs to provide federal medical insurance for the elderly. On the issue of race Morton worked to broaden the GOP's appeal. He supported the Civil Rights Acts of 1964, 1965, and 1968 and told an Alabama GOP meeting in April 1966 that the party would be mistaken to position itself "on the right of the [Southern] Democratic position on civil rights" because "there just isn't much room on their right!"

But it was in the area of foreign policy that Morton was to leave his most lasting mark. After his 1962 reelection and in the face of what he eventually deemed to be an unwinnable war in Southeast Asia, Morton softened his commitment to strident anticommunism. In 1967 he bucked the Republican leadership and led the Senate campaign to ratify the consular treaty with the Soviet Union. Later that year he became the nation's most respected and prominent Republican to break with the administration's Vietnam policy. In September he maintained that Johnson had been "brainwashed" by the military-industrial complex into believing that a military solution to the turmoil in Southeast Asia was the only way to promote U.S. interests.

At the height of his political career Morton shocked Washington's political establishment in 1968 by announcing his retirement. He told the media that he was "just plain track sore," but the *New York Times* reported that poor health had contributed to his decision. In 1968 he supported New York governor Nelson Rockefeller for the presidency, holding that he was the "only Republican candidate who can win . . . and who can thereafter unite a divided nation." In retirement Morton served as vice chairman of the Liberty National Bank and Trust Company and as chairman of Churchill Downs, Inc. He campaigned for President Gerald Ford in 1976 and backed Ronald Reagan in 1980. He died of cancer in his Louisville home and was buried in that city at Cave Hill Cemetery.

Although there were other Republican critics of the Vietnam War, none had the prestige of Morton. A committed cold warrior early in his career, Morton's reevaluation of America's policy of global containment gave credence to the similar misgivings of freshmen senators Mark Hatfield and Charles Percy. More important, Morton's reappraisal reflected the erosion of the cross-party consensus that had governed American foreign policy since the 1954 censure of Wisconsin senator Joseph McCarthy. For the Republican party, Morton's premature retirement signaled the decline of border-state moderation and the consolidation of Sun Belt conservatism.

★

The University of Kentucky libraries in Lexington house the Thruston Morton Papers. Sara Judith Smiley, *The Political Career of Thruston B. Morton: The Senate Years, 1956–1968* (Ph.D. diss., University of Kentucky, 1975), is the most complete account of Morton's importance to the Republican party. See also Robert L. Riggs, "Thruston Morton, the All-Purpose Republican," *New Republic* (27 June 1964). For two opposing views of Morton's reappraisal of President Lyndon Johnson's Vietnam policies, see "Morton the Realist," *Nation* (16 Oct. 1967), and "The Defection of Senator Morton," *National Review* (17 Oct. 1967). For a brief account that puts Morton's career in the context of Republican party history, see the *Washington Post* (17 Aug. 1982), p. A16. Obituaries are in the *New York Times* and the *Washington Post* (15 Aug. 1982). For the *Louisville Courier-Journal's* obituary, see *Congressional Record,* 97th Congress, 2d session, 16 Aug. 1982, pp. 21207–21209. The University of Kentucky libraries house an oral history collection chronicling Morton's life and career.

Byron C. Hulsey

MOSES, Robert (*b.* 18 December 1888 in New Haven, Connecticut; *d.* 29 July 1981 in West Islip, New York), park commissioner, highway builder, and public works czar, who remade New York for the automobile age.

Moses was one of three children of Emanuel Moses, a New Haven department store owner, and Bella Cohen Moses, both of German-Jewish descent. In 1897, Bella urged her husband to sell his store and the family moved to New York City, where she pursued Ethical Culture and did volunteer work at the Madison House settlement. Bella raised Robert with scant awareness of Judaism and an elite sense of public service. She sent him to private academies and to Yale College, from which he was graduated in 1909. He then went to Oxford University and studied English public administration for a thesis, *The Civil Service of Great Britain,* which he completed at Columbia University. After receiving the Ph.D. in 1914, Moses interned at the Bureau of Municipal Research in New York City, developing efficiency ratings for the Municipal Civil Service Commission, chaired by Madison House headworker Henry Moskowitz. Moses married a bureau secretary, Mary Louise Sims, on 15 August 1915, and soon had two daughters.

In 1919, Henry Moskowitz's wife, Belle Israels Moskowitz, a close adviser to the newly elected governor, Alfred E. Smith, summoned Moses for a job on the governor's Reconstruction Commission. Moses wrote the commission report, urging the creation of a strong gubernatorial office, an effort that brought the Republican reformer into the Democratic Smith's inner circle. After Smith lost his bid

Robert Moses. ARCHIVE PHOTOS

for reelection in 1920, Moses joined the good-government New York State Association and wrote its State Park Plan for New York (1922). When Smith regained the governorship in 1922, he supported Moses's draft of the legislation that created the State Council of Parks, and he named Moses chairman.

Although the state council was only supposed to coordinate eleven regional commissions (including the Long Island State Park Commission, which Moses also chaired), Moses soon made it the arbiter of parks and "parkways" (landscaped motor routes) across the state. He pushed construction of a giant radial system on Long Island, including the Southern State, Northern State, and Sagtikos parkways, and masterminded the condemnation of the Taylor Estate on the South Shore, a protracted struggle that made headlines for the people's right to recreation. By 1928 he was building 9,700 acres of parks on Long Island, a chain that eventually included Sunken Meadow and Montauk Point, the barrier beaches Gilgo State Park and Fire Island State Park, and Jones Beach State Park. Jones Beach, the Mediterranean lido completed in 1930, was Moses's masterpiece, complete with a Venetian campanile that hid a water tower, bathhouses for 15,000 people, and parking for 12,000 cars. When Governor Smith ran for president in 1928, Moses supervised Albany as the state's first appointed secretary of state.

For Moses's support in the 1933 municipal elections, Mayor Fiorello H. La Guardia named him city park commissioner. Moses drafted legislation ensuring that the post had jurisdiction over all five boroughs and would allow him to keep his state and Long Island positions. He avoided civil service rules against multiple public offices by accepting sumptuous benefits and perquisites instead of a salary, eventually holding twelve offices under state and city. During the Depression, Moses made the Park Department crucial to the New Deal in New York. Capturing federal grants, chiefly from the U.S. Works Progress Administration, Moses employed 80,000 on work-relief projects that refurbished Central Park and built 255 playgrounds and 11 outdoor pools, plus oceanfront beaches and outer-borough parkways. With $205 million drawn from city, state, and federal agencies he built the West Side Improvement, which buried railroad tracks under Riverside Park and ran the Henry Hudson Parkway from Manhattan to Westchester County.

In 1934 La Guardia appointed Moses chairman of the Triborough Bridge Authority, a toll project funded with $51 million from the U.S. Public Works Authority. Moses stretched the bridge grant to cover approach roads that connected with his parkways in the Bronx and Long Island, enriching the Triborough's toll collections. He applied the principle of open-ended mortgage refinance, common practice among public utilities, to Triborough refunding,

which gave the limited-purpose authority a perpetual covenant with its bondholders. Moses capitalized toll surpluses into other revenue producers, the Marine Parkway and Bronx-Whitestone bridges, which he connected with the Shore (Belt) Parkway around Brooklyn. He expected Triborough revenues to fund a suspension bridge between the Battery and Brooklyn in 1939 but settled for eventual control of a combined Triborough Bridge and Tunnel Authority, which built the Brooklyn-Battery Tunnel.

In the mid-1930s, when New York City could hardly afford $100 million per year for capital improvements, Moses was czar over $1.15 billion in federal public works. The key to his power was the Triborough chairmanship. It gave him command over a cadre of engineers and lawyers, loyal "Moses men" who slaved on blueprints, cost sheets, and legal briefs. When mayors and governors worried about landing New Deal grants, Moses presented them with budget estimates and slick brochures. He bypassed obstructionists by moving fast with his bulldozers. "Once you sink that first stake," he liked to say, "they'll never make you pull it up." The politicians were delighted with his ribbon-cutting ceremonies, and good-government groups could only applaud engineering marvels finished without scandal and on time. Critics wondered why he covered grass with asphalt and ran highways, such as the Henry Hudson, through parklands. He replied with ridicule that revealed his arrogant, mean spirit. When Republicans chose him to challenge Governor Herbert H. Lehman in 1934, his ill-mannered campaign lost by a record 808,000 votes.

In 1938, Moses urged Mayor La Guardia to put the New York City Housing Authority under a board to coordinate the construction of "housing and recreation." The mayor would not name Moses housing czar, but endorsed his talks with Metropolitan Life and other investors for medium-rent projects on the Lower East Side. When La Guardia appointed Moses to the City Planning Commission in late 1941, Moses used Triborough resources to prepare a list of postwar projects, including highways, parks, hospitals, and public housing sites. In 1943, Moses handed Metropolitan Life slum-clearance authority and tax relief on East Fourteenth Street to embark on the 8,755-unit Stuyvesant Town. It began reclamation of the Lower East Side for the middle class and was soon heralded as the prototype of postwar "urban redevelopment." Acknowledged housing coordinator and expediter of postwar plans, Moses was named city construction coordinator by Mayor William O'Dwyer in early 1946.

To this Promethean job Moses brought an urgency to rebuild New York for the automobile. As city negotiator with state and federal highway officials in 1947, he pushed urban arterials and the first mass evictions. He knocked down stands of tenements for the Cross-Bronx Expressway and moved scores of houses for the Van Wyck Expressway, which provided access to garden-apartment tracts in Queens. In 1955 he reached agreement with that other titan, the Port Authority of New York and New Jersey, to divide construction costs for a second deck on the George Washington Bridge, along with the Staten Island Expressway and the mammoth Verrazano-Narrows Bridge. As construction coordinator and Triborough chief, Moses crisscrossed the metropolitan area with thirteen vehicular spans and 416 miles of expressways.

Moses changed the environment in which New Yorkers lived and worked. With compliant allies on the New York City Housing Authority, he enforced his view that public housing should clear slums and not provide tools for racial integration. Moses concentrated the Housing Authority's spartan twelve- and fourteen-story structures in existing black and Puerto Rican ghettos, which hardened existing patterns of residential segregation. As construction coordinator he facilitated a land deal with the Rockefeller family to locate the United Nations on the East River; as park commissioner he allowed New York University to encroach on Washington Square; and as city planning commissioner he agreed that NYU and Bellevue Hospital should collaborate on a medical center on East Thirty-fourth Street. Moses cleared the land for what enthusiasts called the medical and political capitals of the postwar world.

Appointed by William O'Dwyer to chair the mayor's Committee on Slum Clearance, Moses huddled with private redevelopers to exploit Title I of the Housing Act of 1949. He unveiled projects for Corlear's Hook on the Lower East Side, Washington Square South, Manhattantown on West Ninety-seventh Street, and a half dozen other sites that required the relocation of thousands of blacks and Puerto Ricans to Housing Authority projects in Brooklyn and the Bronx. His bulldozers touched off protests in Greenwich Village and Manhattantown, where corrupt redevelopers removed 15,000 site tenants. Undaunted, he plowed ahead at Lincoln Center for the Performing Arts and at Seward Park and Penn South, where the garment unions sponsored medium-rent cooperative apartments. Moses enlarged campuses for New York University on Washington Square, Columbia University, Teacher's College and other academic institutions on Morningside Heights, and Fordham University at Lincoln Center. By 1959, sixteen Title I projects had replaced 314 blighted acres with towers containing 28,000 units.

In 1954 Governor Thomas E. Dewey appointed Moses chairman of the Power Authority of the State of New York. Moses then managed the $720 million Niagara River project, which condemned one fifth of the Tuscarora Indian Reservation for the Robert Moses Power Dam (completed in 1961), Lewiston State Park, and Robert Moses State Parkway overlooking the Niagara River. For the New York leg of the St. Lawrence Seaway he built another massive dam (also named for himself) at Massena, New York. He used state troopers against the Tuscarora resisters in 1958. As far as he was concerned, they were another band of pathetic critics.

Moses's high-handedness, however, ran against a city rediscovering small-scale neighborhood life. The Manhattantown Title I sparked a preference for brownstone rehabilitation that resulted in the West Side Urban Renewal. As park commissioner he enraged Greenwich Villagers with plans to run cars through Washington Square and affronted East Siders with parking lots in Central Park. He resigned as park commissioner and from the mayor's Committee on Slum Clearance in 1960 and was forced from the state park agencies and Power Authority by Governor Nelson A. Rockefeller in 1962. He busied himself at Flushing Meadows Park, as president of the corporation that developed the New York 1964–1965 World's Fair. After the death of his wife in 1966 he married Mary Grady, a Triborough staffer. He left his last redoubt, the Triborough, in 1968.

In retirement Moses fended off the growing disenchantment with his "projectitis" that culminated in Robert A. Caro's *The Power Broker: Robert Moses and the Fall of New York* (1974), a relentlessly critical biography. He dismissed naysayers as impotent carpers who could neither build nor use power. In 1981, at the age of 92, he collapsed from heart failure at his summer home at Gilgo Beach and died at Good Samaritan Hospital, West Islip, Long Island. He was buried at Woodlawn Cemetery in the Bronx.

For forty years Robert Moses was New York's and the nation's master builder, the selfless public servant who got things done. Admirers called him democracy's builder, who created ocean beaches and motorways and gave the masses weekends in the sun. His legion of enemies blamed him for sterile parks behind cyclone fences, superhighways that brought on the collapse of urban mass transit, and bulldozers that destroyed the heart of blue-collar New York. Both overlooked the debt which his ministry owed to liberal New York. Governor Smith gave him executive power; Mayor La Guardia the centralized, modern municipality; and progressive reformers government by special authority. Moses's excesses were those of his era, which believed in sculpted seashores, Saturday drives through the countryside, and parks for scientific recreation for adolescents. He believed that he was realizing the people's demands for a modern New York. He gave the city knowledge-sector redoubts such as NYU-Bellevue and Lincoln Center and lived to see white-collar professionals flock to the Title I apartments that rose on the Upper West Side. For the trade-union cooperatives and the United Nations that city politicians insisted were essential to Gotham's future, Moses swept away innumerable tenements. He was an era's public authority and public servant.

★

The Robert Moses Papers are in the Rare Books and Manuscripts Division, New York Public Library. Other major administrative archives are in the Park Department Records, New York Municipal Archives and Record Center; and the Triborough Bridge and Tunnel Authority headquarters on Randall's Island. Moses materials can also be found in the New York City Housing Authority Collection, Fiorello H. La Guardia Papers, and Robert F. Wagner, Jr., Papers, at the La Guardia and Wagner Archives, La Guardia Community College of the City University of New York. Moses was a prolific writer; his most characteristic statements are in his *Theory and Practice in Politics: The Godkin Lectures, 1939* (1939) and *Public Works: A Dangerous Trade* (1970). Biographical accounts include Cleveland Rodgers, *Robert Moses: Builder for Democracy* (1952), adulation by a loyal publicist; Robert A. Caro, *The Power Broker: Robert Moses and the Fall of New York* (1974), the study in villainy that won the Pulitzer Prize; and Joel Schwartz, *The New York Approach: Robert Moses, Urban Liberals, and the Redevelopment of the Inner City* (1993), which looks at Moses's supporters in the liberal city.

JOEL SCHWARTZ

MUELLER, Reuben Herbert (*b.* 2 June 1897 in St. Paul, Minnesota; *d.* 6 July 1982 in Franklin, Indiana), Methodist bishop and National Council of Churches official who played a key role in Protestant ecumenical and social justice activities in the 1960s.

Bishop Reuben H. Mueller. ARCHIVE PHOTOS

Mueller, the fourth of six children born to Reinhold M. Mueller and Emma Bunse, a homemaker, grew up in Faribault, Minnesota, where his father was a clergyman in the Evangelical Church. Reuben attended North Central College in Naperville, Illinois, a school affiliated with his denomination, and after interrupting his studies to serve in the military during World War I, he graduated in 1919; that same year, on 26 December, Mueller married C. Magdalene Stauffacher, a high school teacher. They had one daughter, Margaret, who served for a time as a missionary in Nigeria. From 1919 to 1924 Mueller taught in public high schools in Minnesota and Wisconsin, and from 1924 to 1926 he taught at North Central College.

Mueller's denomination, the Evangelical Church, was a small Protestant body with a Wesleyan (Methodist) theology and polity that had originated among German-speaking immigrants in eighteenth-century Pennsylvania. Following graduation in 1926 from the Evangelical Theological Seminary in Naperville, he served as pastor of two Evangelical churches, Grace Church in South Bend, Indiana, from 1924 to 1932, and First Church in Indianapolis from 1932 to 1937. In 1937 he began a series of administrative and executive assignments that eventually took him to the highest levels of Protestant leadership.

From 1937 to 1942 Mueller served as a superintendent of the Indiana conference of the Evangelical Church and in 1942 moved to Harrisburg, Pennsylvania, site of the denomination's headquarters, to assume the position of executive secretary of Christian education and evangelism. In 1946 the Evangelical Church merged with another small denomination with a similar theological and cultural background, the United Brethren, to form the Evangelical United Brethren Church (EUB). Mueller served as the executive secretary of Christian education in the new denomination until 1954, when he was elected a bishop of the EUB, assigned to the Indiana conference. He lived in Indianapolis during those years and published several books, including *Lay Leadership in the Evangelical Church* (1943) and *Christ Calls to Christian Growth* (1953).

Bishop Mueller had been active in the National Council of Churches of Christ in the U.S.A. (NCC) since its founding in 1950. This ecumenical umbrella organization was initially made up of more than thirty Protestant denominations, including the EUB, which were part of the mainline or moderate-to-liberal wing of American Protestantism. Eventually a number of Orthodox groups also joined the NCC. The NCC built on a tradition of Protestant ecumenism and worked in various social, educational, and theological ways to promote Christian unity and service to society. Although Mueller represented one of the smaller member-denominations in the NCC, he served as an officer in various positions in the organization in the 1950s and 1960s more frequently than anyone else. He was the recording secretary from 1950 to 1954, a vice president (for three terms) from 1954 to 1963, and president of the NCC from 1963 to 1966. His presidency coincided with some of the NCC's most intensive activities in the areas of civil rights and race relations.

Mueller's election as president took place at the NCC's triennial convention in Philadelphia on 7 December 1963, just a few weeks after the assassination of President John F. Kennedy. The civil rights bill proposed by the late president earlier that year had languished in Congress. Two days after Mueller's election as NCC president, he joined several colleagues in a meeting at the White House with President Lyndon B. Johnson to urge action on civil rights and offer their support for the bill's passage. Civil rights had become an important priority of the NCC in 1963, in the wake of protest marches and demonstrations led by the Reverend Martin Luther King, Jr., and others. During the next three years, under Mueller's leadership, the NCC created new departments and programs and hired new staff to work for racial justice and reconciliation, especially in Mississippi through the 1964 Freedom Summer campaign and the Delta Ministry. The NCC-led grassroots lobbying and letter-writing campaign, directed primarily toward Midwestern Republican congressmen and senators, had a major impact in bringing about final passage of the Civil Rights Act of 1964. Mueller supported all of these efforts, referring to racial segregation as the "major problem" in the United States.

He also vigorously defended other aspects of the NCC's social and political agenda, including efforts toward peace and nuclear disarmament with the Soviet Union. Various critics charged that the NCC was soft on communism and betrayed the beliefs of the lay members of its denominations. On the other hand, in his 1966 book *His Church,* considered his most important work, Mueller affirmed that the NCC was opposed to communism, and especially the atheist official policy of the Soviet Union. He also expressed concern that the political involvements of the NCC, while vital to its total mission, not overshadow its religious activities in evangelism, education, and theology.

Mueller continued to serve as an EUB bishop while involved with the NCC. At the time of the formation of the EUB in 1946, Methodist bishop G. Bromley Oxnam had invited the EUB to consider merging with the much larger Methodist Church. As president of the council of EUB bishops, Mueller attended the quadrennial Methodist General Conference in 1960 as an official observer. At that meeting the Methodists authorized their representatives to begin work on a Plan of Union with the EUB, and the

EUB took the same action in 1962. Thereupon Mueller and Methodist bishop Lloyd Wicke became cochairmen of the Joint Commission on Union, and by 1966 they had completed their work. Because the two denominations had essentially identical organizational structures and theological positions, the blueprint for merger did not require either side to undertake radical change in structure or program. The one exception was the EUB insistence, in which most Methodists concurred, that the last vestiges of racial segregation in the Methodist Church, in which predominantly black congregations were assigned to a separate "central jurisdiction," be abolished. In November 1966 the Methodists and EUB held simultaneous conferences in a Chicago hotel and voted to approve the plan of union. By June 1967 the necessary two-thirds of Methodist and three-fourths of EUB local conferences had given approval. When the United Methodist Church was officially proclaimed in Dallas, Texas, on 23 April 1968, Mueller became a bishop in the new denomination, continuing to serve in Indiana until his retirement in 1972. He urged United Methodists to continue to work for racial and social justice even as the political climate of the nation began to turn toward the right. Mueller lived in retirement in Franklin, Indiana, where he died of a heart attack.

An often repeated criticism of ecumenical agencies such as the NCC and the World Council of Churches is that they tend to become liberal political bureaucracies that lose touch with the day-to-day concerns of ordinary laypeople in local communities and parishes, and yet presume to speak in the name of Christians on many controversial social and political issues. Mueller, although for much of his career the kind of church executive presumed to "lose touch," remained keenly aware of the full mission of Christianity, both personal and social. As a pastor he encouraged evangelical expressions of personal religious commitment and always reminded his ecumenical colleagues of the need for balance in their various pursuits. He was proud of the pietistic, Wesleyan heritage of his own small denomination and believed that its strengths and contributions should be preserved.

★

Personal papers relating to Mueller's ecclesiastical career are in the manuscript collections of the United Methodist Church at Drew University in Madison, New Jersey, and of the National Council of Churches at the Presbyterian Historical Society in Philadelphia. There is no published biography. Mueller's role in denominational affairs is covered in J. Bruce Behney, *The History of the Evangelical United Brethren Church* (1979), and Nolan B. Harmon, ed., *The Encyclopedia of World Methodism* (1974). James Findlay, *Church People in the Struggle: The National Council of Churches and the Black Freedom Movement, 1950–1970* (1993) is a definitive account. See also Samuel M. Cavert, *The American Churches in the Ecumenical Movement, 1900–1968* (1968). An interview Mueller gave after his election to the NCC presidency is in "Mueller for Miller," *Time* (13 Dec. 1963). An obituary is in the *New York Times* (7 July 1982).

JOHN B. WEAVER

MUMFORD, Lawrence Quincy (*b.* 11 December 1903 in Hanrahan, North Carolina; *d.* 15 August 1982 in Washington, D.C.), first professionally trained librarian to serve as librarian of Congress.

Mumford was one of ten children born to Jacob Edward Mumford and Emma Luvenia Stocks and raised on a tobacco farm in Pitt County, North Carolina. He attended a one-room school in Hanrahan, then went to Grifton High School, where he displayed his talents as a debater and orator and was awarded a scholarship to Trinity College (later Duke University) in 1921. Mumford compiled an excellent academic record, was elected to Phi Beta Kappa, and graduated magna cum laude with an A.B. degree in 1925. He remained at Duke, earning an M.A. degree in English in 1928.

During his undergraduate years, Mumford had worked as an assistant in the college library. After receiving his undergraduate degree, he took a full-time position with the library in 1926. His mentor, librarian Louis T. Ibbotsen, encouraged Mumford to enroll in Columbia University's School of Library Science, which he did in 1928. Working part-time in Columbia's library to support himself, Mumford earned his B.S. degree in library science in 1929.

In early 1929 Mumford took a position as a reference assistant with the New York Public Library. Soon after joining the staff, he met Permelia Catherine Stevens, a children's librarian. They were married on 4 October 1930. The couple had one child. After a long illness, Permelia Mumford died in 1961. On 28 November 1969, Mumford married Betsy Perrin Fox; they had no children.

Among other responsibilities, Mumford served as chief of the Preparations Division, where he simplified the processing procedures for library materials. His new methods not only increased productivity but also saved time and money. His reforms attracted attention elsewhere, and he was asked to reorganize the processing division of the Library of Congress, a task he carried out in 1940 and 1941. Mumford's changes earned the praises of Librarian of Congress Archibald MacLeish, who said he had worked a "miracle in the processing department." Mumford then returned to the New York Public Library, where he headed the general services division and kept the library functioning efficiently despite wartime shortages.

In 1945 Mumford left New York to accept the assistant directorship of the Cleveland Public Library. In Cleveland he worked to increase the public's awareness of the library through branch libraries, bookmobiles, and television. By forging close relationships with city officials, Mumford raised the library's budget by 92 percent. Professionally, he gained prestige as well. Mumford was president of the Ohio Library Association (1947–1948) and the American Library Association (1954–1955).

On 22 April 1954 President Dwight D. Eisenhower nominated Mumford as his administration's candidate for librarian of Congress. Mumford was chosen in an attempt to rebuild congressional confidence in the library's administration. His predecessors had failed to cultivate strong relationships with members of Congress. During Mumford's confirmation hearings this problem was driven home. However, while promising to focus on the needs of the Congress, Mumford pointedly declared his own belief that the Library of Congress should also serve "the constituents of Members of Congress—the people."

Mumford was gradually able to overcome congressional distrust by cultivating personal contacts with members. In the first ten years of Mumford's administration, the library's appropriations increased from $9.4 million to $24.1 million and staff from 2,459 to 3,390. Mumford's strong relationship with Congress enabled him to reposition the library for a new national role. Under increasing pressure to make the library's sources promptly available to users, Mumford instituted a reform of the cataloging system. These changes, along with increased automation, allowed cataloging information to be more rapidly disseminated. Mumford also began such monumental bibliographic projects as the *National Union Catalog of Manuscript Collections* and the *Pre-1956 National Union Catalog*. Under his leadership the library also established the Preservation Office to provide for conversion to microfilm those printed materials prone to deterioration. Mumford also promoted new collective arrangements with other federal government libraries. Provisions were also made for the extension of the National Books for the Blind to include persons with other physical disabilities. Meanwhile, Mumford gathered support for the Library of Congress from such organizations as the Association of Research Libraries and the American Library Association.

Mumford also increased the library's international role. The Agricultural Trade Development and Assistance Act of 1954 was used by the library in 1958 to create overseas procurement centers to obtain publications for dispersal to libraries in the United States. The Higher Education Act of 1965 mandated the establishment of the National Program for Acquisitions and Cataloging, which increased the Library of Congress's foreign purchases and created a centralized system for cataloging foreign materials. By 1974 more than forty countries were cooperating with the program, which provided easier access to foreign scholarship while decreasing cataloging expenses.

The later years of Mumford's administration were marred by a variety of problems. While Congress authorized the James Madison Memorial Building in 1965, construction on the new building did not begin until 1971, leaving the library's two existing buildings overcrowded. Concerns about racial discrimination in staffing led the American Library Association to call for an investigation. These events left Mumford shaken and increasingly inaccessible. Nevertheless, Mumford was allowed to continue at his post past mandatory retirement age until 31 December 1974. He died of heart problems and was cremated; his ashes are located at the Oak Hill Cemetery in Georgetown, Washington, D.C.

Mumford forged a solid, mutually beneficial relationship between Congress and its library. Thanks to those ties, the library's budget increased to nearly $97 million by 1975. The holdings of the institution grew from 33,152,852 items in 1954 to 73,932,425 by 1974. All of this was achieved while increasing the library's outreach to the public. More than any of his predecessors, Mumford established the Library of Congress as one of the world's preeminent research libraries.

★

The Library of Congress holds Mumford's official papers in the Central Services Division and his personal papers are in the Manuscript Division. For short biographies, see John Y. Cole, "Lawrence Quincy Mumford," *Supplement to the Dictionary of American Library Biography* (1990), and Benjamin E. Powell, "Lawrence Quincy Mumford: Twenty Years of Progress," *Librarians of Congress, 1802–1974* (1977). Obituaries are in the *Washington Post* (17 Aug. 1982), *American Libraries* (Oct. 1982), *Library Journal* (1 Oct. 1982), and *Publishers Weekly* (3 Sept. 1982).

DAVID EKBLADH

MURRAY, Anna Pauline ("Pauli") (*b.* 20 November 1910 in Baltimore, Maryland; *d.* 1 July 1985 in Pittsburgh, Pennsylvania), clergywoman, lawyer, writer, and political activist best known for her civil rights and women's rights activities and her work as the first African-American women ordained in the Episcopal church.

Murray was the fourth of six children. In 1914 her mother, Agnes Fitzgerald Murray, a nurse, died of a cerebral hemorrhage, and Anna's father, William Henry Murray, a former principal in the Baltimore school system, sent her to live with her aunt Pauline Fitzgerald Dame and her grandparents, Cornelia and Robert Fitzgerald, in Durham, North Carolina.

Murray graduated from Hillside High School in Durham in 1926, and after completing additional courses at Richmond Hill High School in New York City, she began studies in 1928 at Hunter College. In 1930 she was briefly

Pauli Murray, 1946. UPI/CORBIS-BETTMANN

married to a man she referred to only as "Billy"; the marriage was later annulled and Murray never married again. She had no children. Despite setbacks, including financial difficulties and the illness of her Aunt Pauline, Murray received her B.A. degree in English in 1933, one of only four African Americans in her Hunter College class. In 1934 she published a poem, "Song of the Highway," in a collection entitled *Color*. With Pulitzer Prize–winning poet Stephen Vincent Benét's encouragement, Murray continued to write. In 1970 she published a volume of poetry entitled *Dark Testament and Other Poems*. Benét also helped with the refinement of what became her published family history, *Proud Shoes: The Story of an American Family* (1956). Much of the work for this volume was accomplished during her residency at the MacDowell Colony for Artists, where she was one of only two African Americans (the other being James Baldwin) admitted up to that time. Her literary interests found an outlet in her acquaintance with Countee Cullen, Langston Hughes, and other writers.

After Hunter College, Murray worked for *Opportunity* magazine (1933), the Works Progress Administration (1935–1939), and the Worker's Defense League. In the process, she met and established friendships with such prominent figures as Eleanor Roosevelt. These experiences inspired her to formally study the nature of race relations. She applied in 1938 to the University of North Carolina at Chapel Hill but was denied admission because of her race. Murray's work exposed the economic and political underbelly of American society including the plight of Odell Waller, a man sentenced to death in 1940 for murdering the white owner of the land he sharecropped; despite her efforts on his behalf, including raising money for defense, Waller was executed in 1942. In 1940 Murray was arrested in Petersburg, Virginia, for refusing to sit in the back of a Greyhound bus. After being jailed for three days, she was found guilty and fined. However, the nonviolent methods of protest she embraced during this time fostered attitudinal changes in prisoners and guards that captured Murray's imagination and renewed her academic interests.

In 1941 Murray enrolled in the Howard University Law School. While at Howard, Murray put her legal principles into action, for example participating in a student civil rights committee that fought for equal accommodations and an end to all forms of racial and gender discrimination. Much of what Murray and other students accomplished during these years predated similar efforts by attorneys for the National Association for the Advancement of Colored People (NAACP). Murray's experience of this period is expressed in her best-known poem, "Dark Testament," published in 1943.

Murray graduated first in her law school class in 1944, having served as class president and as a justice on the court of peers. She received a Rosenwald Fellowship but was rejected by Harvard Law School in what she saw as gender discrimination. Undaunted by Harvard's decision, Murray continued her education at the University of California at Berkeley, graduating with an L.L.M. degree in 1945. Remaining in California, Murray made history in 1946 as the first black deputy attorney general of California. She received numerous honors, including the National Council of Negro Women's Woman of the Year Award in 1946 and *Mademoiselle* magazine's selection as Woman of the Year in 1947.

Late in 1946 Murray moved to New York City, working as a law clerk because the big prestigious firms would not hire a black female attorney. In 1949 she opened her own law office, which was short-lived, and unsuccessfully ran for a seat as a city council member. In 1951 Murray published a legal text, *States' Laws on Race and Color,* which crystallized many of her legal ideas concerning jim crowism. Five years later Murray became the first female associate in the law firm Paul, Weiss, Rifkind, Wharton, and Garrison. This job provided security but it did not satisfy her interest in West African independence movements.

In 1960 Murray accepted a position as a senior lecturer in the newly formed law school at the University of Ghana; while there, she cowrote *The Constitution and Government of Ghana* (1961). She returned to the United States in 1961 to attend Yale Law School, and in 1965 she became the first African American to receive its doctor of juridical science degree. Her efforts on behalf of women and minorities, with friends such as Eleanor Holmes Norton and Marian Wright Edelman, were recognized through a 1962 appointment to the President's Commission on the Status of Women (the Committee on Civil and Political Rights). In 1965 she was appointed to the American Civil Liberties Union's board of directors; and in 1966 she became one of the founding members of the National Organization for Women (NOW). From 1966 to 1967 Murray was vice president and professor of political science at Benedict College in Columbia, South Carolina.

In 1968 Murray began teaching in Brandeis University's American studies program. During this period of civil rights activities, marked, for example, by the militancy of the Black Panthers, Murray's ideological stance and integrationist tactics were frequently questioned by African-American students who favored more aggressive approaches. From 1972 to 1973 Murray was the Louis Stulberg Professor of Law and Politics at Brandeis.

Disillusioned with her work and facing personal hardship—the death of her close friend Renee Barlow—Murray decided to alter the scope and direction of her life. She moved away from legal maneuvering—sociopolitical integration—and toward spiritual renewal and religious ministry. Leaving Brandeis in 1973, Murray began studies at the General Theological Seminary in New York City as the only black woman and the oldest student enrolled.

A lifelong Episcopalian, Murray openly condemned the church's discriminatory practices and sexist language, vowing to leave the church before bowing to its sexism. At one point, her discontent with the church resulted in a refusal to participate in worship. Yet Murray was fundamentally committed to transformation through confrontation and struggle. Hence, she returned to the church, and after the completion of her master of divinity degree in 1976, Murray was ordained a deacon; on 8 January 1977 she became the first black woman ordained an Episcopal priest. She spent the remainder of her life serving the Church of the Atonement in Washington, D.C., and the Church of the Holy Nativity in Baltimore. She retired from the ministry in January 1984 and moved to Pittsburgh. Murray died of cancer in Pittsburgh, Pennsylvania. Her autobiography, *Song in a Weary Throat: An American Pilgrimage,* was posthumously published in 1987.

In articles such as "Black, Feminist Theologies: Links, Parallels, and Tensions," published in *Christianity and Crisis* in 1980, Murray provides the early ideological and technical framework for one of the most important religious efforts of the twentieth century—liberation theology, a twentieth-century form of contextualized theological reflection that gives priority to the liberation of the oppressed. She strove to make sense of the social dynamics she encountered and extended this analysis to a larger community of the oppressed, highlighting the necessity of and potential for justice.

★

The Pauli Murray Papers are in Harvard University's Schlesinger Library. Murray's autobiography was reprinted as *Pauli Murray: The Autobiography of a Black Activist, Feminist, Lawyer, Priest, and Poet* (1989). Interesting secondary accounts include Jean M. Humez, "Pauli Murray's Histories of Loyalty and Revolt," *Black American Literature Forum* 24, no. 2 (summer 1990): 315–335, and Suzanne Hiatt, "Pauli Murray: May Her Song Be Heard At Last," *Journal of Feminist Studies in Religion* 4 (fall 1988): 69–73. For additional information on Murray's religious experience, see Regina Mooney's dissertation covering the religious and moral experience of Murray and Dorothy Day (Claremont Graduate School, 1992). An obituary is in the *New York Times* (4 July 1985).

ANTHONY BERNARD PINN

MYER, Dillon Seymour (*b.* 4 September 1891 in Hebron, Ohio; *d.* 21 October 1982 in Silver Spring, Maryland), federal administrator who supervised World War II Japanese-American internment camps as director of the War Relocation Authority and was later commissioner of the Bureau of Indian Affairs.

Myer's parents, John Hyson Myer and Harriet Estella Seymour, devout Methodists, farmed outside Hebron, and Dillon early decided to pursue an academic career in agronomy. He earned a B.S. degree in agricultural science from Ohio State University in 1914 and immediately accepted an appointment teaching crop management and other subjects at Kentucky Agricultural College. Myer joined the U.S. Department of Agriculture in 1916, becoming an agricultural extension agent in Vanderburgh County, Indiana. Returning to Ohio in 1920, Myer served as a county extension agent in Franklin, Ohio, for two years. Except for a leave of absence in 1925 and 1926 to earn an M.A. degree at Columbia University, he held the post of district supervisor for the Ohio State University Agricultural Extension Service from 1922 to 1934. With Ohio farmers mired in a decade-long agricultural depression, Myer, by now a dedicated member of the "helping professions," faced daunting tasks. In 1921 he married Jenness Wirt, a county home demonstrator agent; they had three children.

Recruited into the Agricultural Adjustment Administration in 1934, Myer moved to Washington as a civil servant with special expertise in soil conservation. That specialty led to his appointment as a division chief with the Soil Conservation Service (SCS) in 1935 and to promotion to the position of assistant chief. In the aftermath of the Jap-

Dillon Myer. THE NATIONAL ARCHIVES AND RECORDS ADMINISTRATION

anese attack on Pearl Harbor, Myer served the Department of Agriculture as acting administrator of all conservation and agricultural programs. To this point Myer had shown himself to be an efficient administrator and a quietly effective player in the game of Washington bureaucratic politics.

World War II brought a significant career change for Myer. The panicky roundup of Japanese Americans and the attending decision to incarcerate, without due process of law, a group mainly comprising U.S. citizens posed difficult problems for the administration of Franklin D. Roosevelt. When Milton S. Eisenhower, who had been Myer's mentor since he joined the Department of Agriculture headquarters staff, resigned as director of the euphemistically named War Relocation Authority in June 1942, he recommended Myer as his successor. Myer proved a noncontroversial choice, because he was viewed as apolitical and as a competent, fair administrator. At the time, Myer's performance in overseeing the compulsory removal from the West Coast of 110,000 people of Japanese descent received general praise, and his contributions were acknowledged by leaders of the Japanese-American community.

The establishment of "relocation centers," requiring construction of entire communities in remote areas, was done efficiently and, despite the primitive and humiliating conditions they were compelled to endure, the public perception was that Japanese Americans were treated humanely. In 1943 Myer inaugurated a work-release program that generated considerable anti-Japanese prejudice and also protests from inside the camps. This initiative, placing Japanese Americans in locales across the country, reflected the paternalistic attitude of Myer and other WRA officials toward their charges. In retrospect, it is clear that Myer was essentially a functionary (although he later admitted that the evacuation order had been a "regrettable" mistake), and that the WRA, nominally a civilian agency, was effectively controlled by the War Department.

A bureaucratic shuffle transferred the WRA to the Department of Interior in 1944 but left Myer in charge. At war's end he oversaw the dismantling of the camps and the relocation of those Japanese Americans who remained under WRA control. Two months after the WRA's dissolution, President Harry S. Truman in August 1946 named Myer head of the Federal Public Housing Authority (FPHA), responsible for administering low-rent housing and slum clearance programs. Once the most immediate housing needs of returning veterans and distressed families had been met, the FPHA proved vulnerable to the clamor for retrenchment, and Myer had to deal with an aggressive campaign against public housing by the private sector. Resigning as FPHA director in 1947, Myer was named president of the Institute of Inter-American Affairs, a Department of State–supervised organization that fostered hemispheric cooperation in education, agriculture, and health.

Returning to the Interior Department and to domestic public service, Myer in 1950 accepted a job he had twice previously declined—commissioner of the Bureau of Indian Affairs. Long a bureaucratic and political quagmire, the BIA was a fiefdom that exerted broad control over 200 Native American tribal groups and bands comprising some 450,000 people. Reporting to Secretary of the Interior Oscar L. Chapman, Myer launched a sweeping reorganization of the BIA, replacing experienced administrators with career bureaucrats from the SCS, WRA, and other agencies. The goal was the "emancipation" of Native Americans and their assimilation into American society. Achieving that end, Myer and other authoritarian liberals believed, required the termination of federal supervision. That the new policy flouted innumerable treaties and ignored the wishes of tribal communities was irrelevant, because the BIA believed it knew best. To prepare Native Americans for assimilation (and looking toward the BIA's eventual abolition), Myer won from Congress huge budget increases in 1951 and 1952. However, mounting opposition to the policy of termination led newly elected President Dwight D. Eisenhower (apparently influenced by a disillusioned Milton Eisenhower) to request Myer's resignation as BIA commissioner in March 1953.

Although disappointed about the way his career in public service had ended, Myer opted to stay in Washington as a lobbyist. He accepted the directorship of the Group Health Association, serving in that capacity until 1958. Various advisory appointments took Myer to Venezuela, South Korea, and Vietnam, and he returned briefly to federal service in 1961 to oversee the Cuban Refugee Program before retiring completely in 1964.

After his retirement Myer found himself increasingly beleaguered by groups he perceived as bent on besmirching his record of public service. His memoir, *Uprooted Americans: The Japanese Americans and the War Relocation Authority During World War II* (1971), was written in large part to rebut a growing chorus of criticism by Japanese Americans and historians about the WRA and its wartime policies. Myer vigorously disputed the characterization of the WRA centers as "concentration camps," but that portrayal largely prevailed. Comparable criticism of Myer's stewardship of the BIA emerged during the 1970s, as a more complete understanding emerged of the human costs and ethnocentric rationale for the policy of termination. While declining health silenced Myer, he apparently remained convinced of the correctness of the course pursued. But his career in public service testifies to the tragic limits of liberalism when joined with an unthinking ethnocentrism. He died of cardiac arrest in a Silver Spring, Maryland, nursing home and was buried in that city.

★

Dillon S. Myer, *Uprooted Americans: The Japanese Americans and the War Relocation Authority During World War II* (1971), is a defense of Myer's role at the WRA. Richard Drinnon, *Keeper of Concentration Camps: Dillon S. Myer and American Racism* (1987), is a highly critical examination of Myer's career. An obituary is in the *New York Times* (25 Oct. 1982).

THEODORE A. WILSON

N

NAGEL, Ernest (*b.* 16 November 1901 in Novomesto, Austria-Hungary; *d.* 20 September 1985 in New York City), philosopher and educator who was a founder of the logical empirical school of naturalism; Nagel is best remembered for his contributions to the philosophy of science, through such books as *The Structure of Science* (1961).

Nagel was one of two children of Isadore Nagel, a businessman, and Frieda (Weiss) Nagel. In 1911 the family immigrated to the United States and settled in New York City; Ernest became a naturalized citizen in 1919. Also in that year he entered City College of New York, from which he graduated Phi Beta Kappa with a B.S. in social studies in 1923. He then attended Columbia University, where he obtained his M.A. in mathematics in 1925 and his Ph.D. in 1931. On 23 January 1935 he married Edith Haggstrom, a physicist; they had two children.

Nagel began his teaching career in the New York City public school system, where he taught physics from 1923 to 1929. He next worked as an instructor of philosophy at City College of New York in 1930 and 1931. In 1931 he became an instructor of philosophy at Columbia University, beginning an association with Columbia that lasted for more than forty years. He was made assistant professor in 1937, associate professor in 1939, and full professor in 1946. In 1955 Nagel was named John Dewey Professor of Philosophy at Columbia, a position he held until 1966, when he became professor of philosophy at Rockefeller Univer-

sity. He returned to Columbia in 1967 as a university professor, and remained there until his retirement in 1970. He was professor emeritus at Columbia from 1970 to 1985.

Trained as a logician, Nagel made original contributions to discussions of logic and probability in his early books *On the Logic of Measurement* (1930), *Sovereign Reason* (1954), *Logic Without Metaphysics* (1957), and *Gödel's Proof* (with James R. Newman, 1958). His later publications dealt masterfully with methodology in philosophy, especially in *Teleology Revisited and Other Essays* (1978). His interests ranged from the natural sciences to the social sciences and the philosophy of law. His objective, to analyze philosophy's role in human inquiry, was attained not only by his published works but by his noted teaching career and his work as an editor of several leading philosophical journals: the *Journal of Philosophy* (1940–1956), the *Journal of Symbolic Logic* (1939–1945), and *Philosophy of Science* (1956–1959).

Nagel was a major figure in the school of philosophical naturalism in the United States, which flourished from 1945 to 1965 and had its headquarters at Columbia University. This school's major thinkers, including Nagel, John Dewey, Morris R. Cohen, and Sidney Hook, shared the common ground of materialism: the belief that in principal, nature alone, accessible to the inquiring mind solely by means of the sciences, contains the laws and powers operative throughout experience and society. Nagel was unique in this school in bringing logical positivism to bear

Ernest Nagel. SIDNEY NAGEL, © EVE ARNOLD/MAGNUM, MAGNUM PHOTOS INC.

on naturalism; indeed, he was among the first to bring the precepts of scientific empiricism to the United States, through his association with the Vienna Circle, a group of Austrian intellectuals engaged in analyzing the structure of scientific theory. He wrote at length about his findings in "Impressions and Appraisals of Analytic Philosophy in Europe," published in the *Journal of Philosophy* in 1936. His grafting of Viennese positivism on the indigenously American pragmatic movement enabled him to promote, almost without equal, the philosophy of science in developing American philosophical thought.

Highly respected for his precision of argument, Nagel engaged the attention of Bertrand Russell, who noted his vehement defense of common sense, the truth of his assertion that all science starts from common sense, and that science differs from common sense mainly by the fact that its percentage of mistakes is smaller.

Nagel confronted Thomism, the philosophy of Thomas Aquinas and its place in the Catholic tradition, in the person of Étienne Gilson, an exponent of Aquinas, in asserting the legitimacy of inquiring into the existence of the alleged Being, the pure Act of Existence. Those who reject such questioning as illegitimate are "dogmatically cutting short a discussion when the intellectual current runs against them," Nagel asserted in *Logic Without Metaphysics.* In that work he condemned the enormously popular metaphysician Lecomte du Noüy's position that certain facts of biology must be attributed to divine planning. He declared

that fideism, a view emphasizing the primacy of faith in achieving knowledge of the divine, was always impregnable to rational criticism.

Aligning himself with Albert Einstein as an unrepentant determinist, Nagel vigorously criticized Isaiah Berlin's strong attacks on determinism. His "A Defense of Atheism" was included in *Basic Beliefs* (1959), edited by J. E. Fairchild. Opposed to any kind of speculative metaphysics, Nagel described his own standpoint as "contextualistic naturalism" and considered himself in the broad sense of the word a materialist.

Nagel argued for a methodological naturalism and a logic without ontology in his most widely read book, often cited in studies of problems in the logic of scientific explanation, *The Structure of Science.* Also influential was his *Teleology Revisited and Other Essays,* in which he attempted to show the logic of scientific explanation as it developed in all sciences.

Nagel elaborated a logical empiricism that did not exclude feeling, ideas, imagination, and aspirations. His naturalism had two theses: that bodies (organized matter) were the necessary conditions for all events, qualities, and processes in nature, and that the manifest plurality and variety of things, including distinctive traits, were ultimate and real and cannot be reduced to any more ultimate reality.

A major contributor to the study of an evolving philosophy of science as a subject, Nagel emphasized in his theory of reduction that the laws of secondary science are approximately the same as those of primary science. Therefore, one can establish deductive relations between two sets of statements (those of primary and those of secondary science) that use a homogeneous vocabulary.

A formidable philosopher of science, Nagel was confident that exhibiting the logical flaws in theories that others found seductive comprised a sufficient intellectual contribution. His acuity, according to some critics, made him diffident in proposing theories of his own.

Nagel received numerous honors and awards. In 1954 he was elected president of the Eastern Division of the American Philosophical Association. He received the American Council of Learned Societies prize for distinguished scholarship in the humanities in 1959. A fellow of the American Academy of Arts and Sciences, he served as this organization's president from 1961 to 1963. He was also a member of the National Academy of Sciences. In 1980 he was awarded Columbia University's Nicholas Murray Butler Medal in Gold. Upon the award's presentation, Nagel summarized his view of philosophy's role in the realm of human inquiry: "Philosophy is in general not a primary inquiry into the nature of things. It is a reflection on the conclusion of those inquiries that may sometimes terminate, as it did in the case of Spinoza, in a clarified vision of man's place in the scheme of things."

Nagel died of heart failure at Columbia-Presbyterian Hospital in New York City at the age of eighty-three. He is buried in South Wardsboro, Vermont, the locale of his summer home, where he had done most of his writing.

★

See Andrew J. Reck, *The New American Philosophers: An Exploration of Thought Since World War II* (1968); *Handbook of World Philosophy*, edited by John R. Burr (1980); *A Modern Introduction to Philosophy: Readings from Classical and Contemporary Sources*, edited by Paul Edwards and Arthur Pap (1973); and *Logic, Methodology, and Philosophy of Science* (proceedings of the International Congress of Logic, Methodology, and Philosophy of Science, 1960 and 1964). An obituary is in the *New York Times* (22 Sept. 1985).

HENRY WASSER

NEARING, Scott (*b.* 6 August 1883 in Morris Run, Pennsylvania; *d.* 24 August 1983 in Harborside, Maine), pacifist writer and philosopher best known for his charismatic public speaking, political ideas and writings, and leadership of the back-to-the-land movement.

Scott Nearing was the oldest of six children born to Louis Nearing and Minnie Zabriskie. His grandfather, Winfield Scott Nearing, a mining engineer who ruled Morris Run as a "benevolent despot," influenced the young Scott in matters of Tolstoy, nature, travel, and economics. His father, not a prominent aspect of Scott's life, was a gentleman, businessman, and stockbroker. His mother, Minnie, introduced him to her cultured world and taught him about nature and the arts. He attended high school in Philadelphia and continued his education at the University of Pennsylvania's Wharton School of Finance and Economy. There, in 1903, he met the economist Simon Nelson Pat-

ton, who had a profound effect on Nearing's life. During this time Nearing joined the Grace Baptist Temple in Philadelphia and entertained the idea of becoming a minister. He taught sociology at Temple College from 1903 to 1905, while still an undergraduate at Wharton and while studying oratory at Temple. He graduated from both Temple and Wharton in 1905. Four years later Nearing received his Ph.D. in economics from Wharton, where he taught from 1906 to 1915. From 1908 to 1912 he also taught economics at Swarthmore, where he agitated for social change. In 1908 he married Nellie Marguerite Seeds, a feminist and pacifist. They raised two children, one adopted.

During the years 1906 to 1916, Nearing summered at the single-tax community of Arden, Delaware, espousing hard work and vegetarianism. He preached the virtues of the strenuous life to the leisure class during summers from 1912 to 1917 at Chautauqua, New York. In 1915 he was fired from Wharton for asserting that local businesses exploited children. Nearing then taught at Toledo University in Ohio until 1917, when he was discharged for his opposition to U.S. involvement in World War I. In 1917, after successfully publishing several books on Nearing's political philosophy, including child labor and the status of women, his publisher dropped him and remaindered his books. Shortly after that he became the chair of the People's Council of America for Democracy and Peace. In 1918 Nearing ran unsuccessfully against Fiorello La Guardia for Congress in New York's Fourteenth District under the Socialist party banner. That same year he was indicted by the federal government and charged under the Espionage Act for his antiwar stance but was acquitted in 1919. During this period he debated Clarence Darrow, Bertrand Russell, Hamilton Fish, and many others. Not long after visiting the

Scott and Helen Nearing at home, 1975. UPI/CORBIS-BETTMANN

Soviet Union in 1925, Nearing joined the Communist party. In 1929 he resigned from the party over his disagreement with Lenin's understanding of imperialism.

In 1927 Nearing met Helen Knothe and drifted away from his wife, Nellie, while remaining involved in his two boys' lives. In 1932 Scott and Helen, disillusioned with mainstream American life, moved to an old sixty-five-acre farm in Vermont with only $300 cash and an $800 mortgage, living in a stone house without electricity or a telephone. That same year his only piece of fiction was published: *Free Born: An Unpublishable Novel,* an attack on racial suppression. Scott and Nellie never divorced and only after her death did he and Helen marry, on 12 December 1947. Together with Helen, he wrote *The Maple Sugar Book* (1950), which remains an important source of information in that field.

Because of encroaching development, the Nearings moved to a rocky, coastal tree farm in Harborside, Maine, in 1952, where they continued their vegetable gardening and writing. With Helen's help he wrote *Living the Good Life* (1954; repr. 1970). They both lived a vegetarian lifestyle as a personal act of rebellion against violence, war, and mindless consumerism. His autobiographical treatise, *The Making of a Radical* (1972), reflecting his progressive ideas on the modern world, became the guidebook for a generation of activists. The short, craggy, often cranky old man turning compost and digging in his garden became a familiar sight in Harborside. The years until his death were spent in their organic gardens, receiving many admiring "back to the landers," lecturing around the country, and writing. In 1971 Nearing was given an award by the Maine State Commission on Arts and Humanities for his "life and work which have brought special distinction to our state." Two years later he was named honorary emeritus professor of economics at the University of Pennsylvania.

During his later years Nearing became estranged from his son, John, who had changed his name to John Scott because of differences in philosophy. In 1941 John was expelled from the Soviet Union, where he had been living, for slandering Soviet foreign policy. After working for *Time,* he became vice president of Radio Free Europe–Radio Liberty. Nearing was not pleased with John's change of allegiance and refused to communicate with him. John died in 1976.

Nearing and his wife built a stone house near the old farmhouse in Maine, including a stone wall enclosing a perfect fifty-by-fifty-foot organic garden, enough to feed the two of them. As he neared his hundredth birthday, Nearing decided he was ready to die and stopped eating. He went to bed, simply worn out, and Helen cared for him until his death. Nearing died on 24 August 1983 at the age of 100. He was cremated and his ashes scattered. Some of the ashes were held to mix with Helen's at her death and together, in 1995, they were spread on the garden at Forest Farm.

Nearing was a complex man, at once both a devout Christian and a socialist, both a sensitive naturalist and a hard-hearted parent, but he was true to his own strong ethics and lived the way he believed. On *Good Morning America* Nearing said, "Do the best that you can in the place that you are and be kind." During his lifetime he wrote some fifty books and 300 articles and pamphlets. He burned $60,000 in war bonds to protest the involvement of the United States in war. To his followers, he was the ultimate environmentalist, setting an example and leading the world in the pursuit of healthy living and hard work.

★

Personal papers of Scott Nearing can be found in the Peace Collection of Swarthmore College and the Boston University Archives. Scott Nearing, *The Making of a Radical: A Political Autobiography* (1972), goes back to his earliest experiences. Scott and Helen Nearing, *Living the Good Life: How to Live Sanely and Simply in a Troubled World* (1954; repr. 1970), recounts their experiences in Vermont, and their *Continuing the Good Life: Half a Century of Homesteading* (1979) updates their rural existence. Stephen J. Whitfield, *Scott Nearing: Apostle of American Radicalism* (1974), concentrates on his early days as a radical. John A. Saltmarsh, *Scott Nearing: An Intellectual Biography* (1991), is considered the definitive biography and includes a complete bibliography of his works. An obituary is in the *New York Times* (25 Aug. 1983).

CYNTHIA THAYER

NELSON, Eric Hilliard ("Rick") (*b.* 8 May 1940 in Teaneck, New Jersey; *d.* 31 December 1985 near DeKalb, Texas), rock and roll musician and actor; introduced on radio and television as the wisecracking younger son in *The Adventures of Ozzie and Harriet,* he was one of the nation's first teenage idols and one of the most popular rock stars of the late 1950s and early 1960s.

Rick Nelson's father, Oswald "Ozzie" Nelson, a bandleader, and his mother, Harriet Hilliard, an actress and singer, met in New York City on 31 December 1931 in the Edison Hotel Grand Ballroom, where she was an announcer. He hired her as a singer, and they married in 1935. By the time Rick was born at Holy Name Hospital in 1940, Harriet had given up singing and films to be home with him and her other son, David, although Ozzie continued to perform on the road. Show business required travel in those days and was in both Ozzie's and Harriet's blood: George Nelson, Ozzie's father, was an amateur singer and dancer; Ethel Nelson, Ozzie's mother, played ragtime piano. Roy and Hazel Hilliard, Harriet's parents, were itinerant actors.

Rick Nelson. ARCHIVE PHOTOS

Soon after Ricky was born the Nelsons bought a house in Tenafly, New Jersey. Within months, however, they moved to Hollywood, California. NBC radio offered Ozzie and Harriet a slot on *The Raleigh Cigarette Program,* starring the comedian Red Skelton. They were popular on Skelton's show and settled into a Cape Cod colonial resembling the house on their later television series. Ricky, who initially stayed in New Jersey with his grandmother Ethel Nelson, joined the family in 1942. Eric Nelson, known as Ricky to fans even after calling himself Rick, was a blond, blue-eyed, good-natured child, eager for attention but shy compared to his more outgoing brother. Ricky had asthma but recovered after several years.

When Skelton was drafted into World War II, a producer suggested that the Nelsons start their own radio show. From its beginnings in 1944, *The Adventures of Ozzie and Harriet* was known for its good, clean fun, reflecting the pleasures and pitfalls of the Nelsons. At first, child actors stood in for David and Ricky, but by February 1949 both boys were playing themselves. Ever the smarty-pants kid brother, Ricky got laughs with lines like "I don't mess around, boy." As television grew in popularity, Ozzie screen-tested his family for the feature film *Here Come the Nelsons.* It was successful, and the family made the leap to the small screen. The first telecast was on 3 October 1952. Over the years,

scripts rarely took real-life events into account but did reflect the off-camera activities of the boys. *The Adventures of Ozzie and Harriet* became one of the most popular domestic comedies of its day, along with *Father Knows Best, Make Room for Daddy,* and *Leave It to Beaver.* But more than the rest, *The Adventures of Ozzie and Harriet* idealized the American family, with unflappable characters whose problems were usually resolved in an episode.

The Nelson boys attended Gardner Street Public School. By the time Ricky got to Bancroft Junior High, he was winning tennis trophies. He took drum lessons, played the piano, and joined the school band's clarinet section. He attended Hollywood High for a time and graduated in June 1958, but a studio tutor, Randolph Van Scoyk, oversaw most of his secondary school education. Rick immersed himself in dating, sports, cars, and, of course, rock and roll. By the mid-1950s, his dark crew cut had evolved into a moderate pompadour, and his pouty sneers in publicity shots suggested shades of Elvis Presley. Certainly Nelson's music was influenced by Presley, as well as the rockabilly performers Carl Perkins, Jerry Lee Lewis, and Roy Orbison. At age fifteen Nelson was spending Saturday nights attending the television show *Town Hall Party* with Tex Ritter, Merle Travis, and Joe Maphis. At age seventeen he got a Martin D-35 guitar that he played for decades. He put together a band that rehearsed for hours in rooms filled with cigarette smoke he tried to hide from the abstemious Ozzie.

The athletic, hardworking, family-oriented older Nelson shaped, if not dominated, his sons' early entertainment careers. As a former law student, he negotiated lucrative contracts. Recognizing that the program's clean-cut, all-American lifestyle had broad appeal, he insisted that David and Ricky maintain the image off-camera, leaving the boys trying to distinguish between director and Dad. Occasionally Ricky rebelled, disagreeing with his parents' Republican politics and heading in his own musical direction, but he defended his father in the press. He told an interviewer that, contrary to popular belief, his father suggested that he begin singing on the show in 1957. The two-minute musical segments at the end of episodes developed an instant following and helped to sell as many as a million records in a week. On the initial music episode, "Ricky the Drummer" sang Fats Domino's hit "I'm Walkin'," which Nelson recorded with "A Teenager's Romance" on the flip side for Verve Records. On the Imperial label, he cut a gold record featuring "Be-Bop Baby" and "Have I Told You Lately That I Love You?" In the late 1950s and early 1960s, Nelson racked up more than two dozen pop hits. "Travelin' Man" (with "Hello, Mary Lou" on the flip) climbed to number one on the pop charts in 1961 and sold more than 5 million copies. Other favorites were "Stood Up," "Waitin' in School," "Believe What You Say," "Teenage Idol," "Everlovin'," "It's Up to You," "Lonesome Town," "I Got a Feeling," "It's Late," "Never Be Anyone Else but You," "Just a Little Too Much," and "Poor Little Fool." A major influence on Nelson's success was his band, perhaps especially James Burton, a guitarist on the *Louisiana Hayride* radio show who later played for Elvis Presley and on dozens of pop records. Nelson had substantial artistic control, steering clear of overproduction. He began touring in his teens and by 1963 had sold 35 million records. He made a few hits for Decca, but the mid-1960s marked the end of his greatest commercial success.

Toward the end of that era, Nelson married Kristin Harmon, an artist and daughter of the football player Tom Harmon and the actress Elyse Knox. The couple married on 20 April 1963 in a Catholic ceremony at St. Martin of Tours Church in Hollywood. They had met as children, and their parents were friends. Naturally, *The Adventures of Ozzie and Harriet* cast them as newlyweds. They had four children: Tracy, an actress; twins Matthew and Gunnar, who in the early 1990s formed the band Nelson; and a third son, Sam.

When the situation comedy ended after fourteen seasons, Nelson pursued other acting roles, although his film heyday was past. As a boy he had been kidnapped by robbers in the nonsensical comedy *Here Come the Nelsons*. At twelve he had starred with Ethel Barrymore and Leslie Caron in *The Story of Three Loves* (1953). In the John Wayne Western *Rio Bravo* (1959), Nelson played a cowhand who volunteered to find his boss's murderer. In *The Wackiest Ship in the Army* (1960) he was an ensign on the dubious hulk Jack Lemmon commanded on a secret mission against the Japanese. Five years later, Nelson starred with his wife in *Love and Kisses*. He did a little musical theater, including *How to Succeed in Business Without Really Trying* with Rudy Vallee, and television work, such as *Malibu U* and *Owen Marshall, Counselor at Law,* in which he played against his usual type by portraying an accused rapist.

But musically, Nelson was floundering. Overshadowed by the British invasion typified by the Beatles, he turned out several lackluster albums. He toured the Far East, where he remained popular, and experimented with country rock. Intrigued by that sound, he recruited players with backgrounds in folk, blues, pop, and country for his new Stone Canyon Band. It had a modest hit with Bob Dylan's "She Belongs to Me," and in 1970 he recorded *Rick Nelson in Concert,* a live album blending some of his old hits with songs by Dylan and others. Although critically acclaimed, the album had meager sales. Still, he was not content to rest on laurels and began writing more songs. Despite initial misgivings, he played a rock and roll revival concert at Madison Square Garden in New York City to promote Stone Canyon's *Rudy the Fifth* album. With his new band and his youthful face framed by shoulder-length hair, Rick

Nelson neither looked nor sounded exactly like Ricky. As he sang "Honky Tonk Women," some fans booed. Some thought they were objecting to rowdy concertgoers, but Nelson took it personally, assuming they wanted vintage hits. He considered the gig a disaster, but it inspired him to write a response in the song "Garden Party." Ironically, it was considered a comeback, but later efforts did not fare as well.

By the late 1970s, Nelson's marriage was on the rocks. The couple separated, reconciled, then separated again. Divorce proceedings were acrimonious, dragging on for two years before the couple signed a settlement agreement in December 1982. Continued money problems kept Nelson on the road at least two hundred days a year for the rest of his life, but he found ways to be content. He moved in with Helen Blair, a young model and animal trainer. They were engaged in 1984. He was also asked to join the finale of a Sun Records reunion album recorded in Memphis with Carl Perkins, Roy Orbison, Jerry Lee Lewis, Johnny Cash, and others.

Nelson played the Universal Amphitheatre in Los Angeles and attended the Sun session in the summer of 1985, then toured Australia and much of Great Britain that fall. Stone Canyon scheduled a short after-Christmas tour that was supposed to end with a New Year's Eve gig at a Dallas hotel. As it turned out, Nelson sang his last song, "Rave On," a day earlier at a small club in Guntersville, Alabama. En route to Dallas, the pilot of Nelson's private plane radioed for help as the cabin filled with smoke. The 1944 DC-3 jolted to a landing in a field near DeKalb, Texas, after plowing into some trees. The pilot and copilot escaped, but the cabin was engulfed in flames. Nelson perished with Blair and his five band members.

More than a thousand people attended the memorial service. He was buried in Hollywood's Forest Lawn Memorial Cemetery near his father. A few days later some newspapers reported that authorities were looking into several possible causes of the fire, including its passengers' free-basing cocaine. Toxicology reports indicated that the remains of Nelson and others contained traces of cocaine, but the inconclusive National Transportation Safety Board report released in May 1987 said a faulty cabin heater or an electrical short were the most likely causes. Nelson won a posthumous Grammy in 1986 for the Sun Records finale and was inducted into the Rock and Roll Hall of Fame in 1987.

With his slick good looks, unassuming charm, and plaintive singing voice, Rick Nelson developed a huge and lasting following among members of the baby-boom generation. His family's television series, which championed a utopian image of the home, helped sell millions of records for Nelson and eased parental acceptance of rock and roll. Like many of his generation, he did not fit the pasteurized, processed image projected by *The Adventures of Ozzie and Harriet* and rebelled against his father's expectation that he maintain a squeaky-clean lifestyle. Despite many attempts after age twenty-five, Nelson never again attained the extraordinary commercial success of his youth, but his early hits and his acting won him a permanent place in pop culture history.

★

Ozzie Nelson, *Ozzie* (1973), is a carefully worded autobiography that is useful for background on the Nelson family's entertainment heritage and on Ozzie's role in Rick's career. Biographies of Rick Nelson are Joel Selvin, *Ricky Nelson: Idol for a Generation* (1990), which contains analyses of Nelson's music and influence and contains a discography; and Philip Bashe, *Teenage Idol, Travelin' Man: The Complete Biography of Rick Nelson* (1992), for which the author interviewed an exhaustive list of Nelson's relatives and colleagues and in which he delves into such sensitive topics as Nelson's marriage. Sara Davidson, "The Happy, Happy, Happy Nelsons," *Esquire* (Sept. 1971), is a confrontational article that attempts to distinguish between the public image and private lives of the Nelsons and contains critical comments about the family from David Nelson. Jas Obrecht, "Q/A: Rick Nelson," *Guitar Player* (Sept. 1981), is an article based on a question-and-answer session in which Nelson reflected on early influences on his music, the extent of his artistic control, and his resistance to recording technology. See also Kent Demaret, "Rick Nelson, 1940–1985," *People Weekly* (20 Jan. 1986); and Patricia Romanowski and Holly George-Warren, eds., *The New Rolling Stone Encyclopedia of Rock and Roll* (1995). An obituary is in the *Los Angeles Times* (1 Jan. 1986), as is a remembrance (2 Jan. 1986).

WHITNEY SMITH

NEYMAN, Jerzy (*b.* 16 April 1894 in Bendery, Bessarabia [Russia]; *d.* 5 August 1981 in Oakland, California), mathematical statistician and educator who was among the pioneers of modern theoretical and applied statistics.

Both Neyman's father, Czeslaw Spława-Neyman, and mother, Kazimiera Lutosławaska, were of Polish descent and Roman Catholic. Born Jerzy Spława-Neyman, he dropped the Spława portion of his name when he was thirty years old. Neyman was the second son of four siblings. Jerzy's father was a judge in Bessarabia who had a lifelong interest in archaeology. As a child Neyman was often taken on field trips by his father. After Neyman's birth the family moved to different locations in Russia, as dictated by the requirements of his father's legal practice. Neyman did not enter a formal education program until the age of ten, when he attended the local gymnasium in the Crimean city of Simferopol. He was more advanced than most other students, except in Russian history and geography, and was especially competent in his command of Polish, Russian, French, German, and Ukrainian.

Jerzy Neyman. DEPARTMENT OF STATISTICS, UNIVERSITY OF CALIFORNIA AT BERKELEY

After his father's sudden death of a heart attack in 1906, economic necessity compelled Neyman's mother to quickly relocate to Kharkov in the Ukraine. There she took over the management of a large property belonging to one of her late husband's relatives and settled herself, her mother, and twelve-year-old Neyman in one of the houses on the property. Neyman was once again a superior student. In 1912 he graduated from the gymnasium and matriculated at the University of Kharkov (later Maxim Gorki University).

Intending to major in mathematics, he changed his focus to physics after hearing a report on Albert Einstein's special theory of relativity and of Marie Curie's Nobel Prize in physics in 1911 for the discovery of radium and that element's striking properties. However, an ineptitude in handling the apparatus of experimental physics coupled with an introduction by one of his Polish professors to a revolutionary advance in integral calculus by the French mathematician Henri-Léon Lebesgue led Neyman back to mathematics. In addition to studying the implications of Lebesgue's mathematical research, Neyman attended lectures on probability theory by the mathematician Serge N. Bernstein. The distinguished Bernstein had been relegated to being a docent, an academic position inferior to professor, because he was a Jew.

Neyman completed his undergraduate work in mathematics in September 1917 with the submission of a thesis entitled "Integral of Lebesgue." He continued graduate work at the University of Kharkov and concurrently secured a post as a mathematics lecturer at the Kharkov Institute of Technology. After a turbulent period, which included an unsuccessful effort to join the Russian army, an arrest for selling black-market matches for food, imprisonment as an enemy Polish alien, and marriage (4 May 1920) to a Russian Orthodox woman, Olga Solodovnikova, Neyman passed his examinations for a master's degree at the University of Kharkov in the fall of 1920. Although academic degrees had been officially abolished by the Soviet regime, examinations as a measure of scholarship attainment were still given. Following his success in the examinations, he was hired as a lecturer at the university and during the 1920–1921 academic year taught a variety of courses and seminars in higher algebra, integral calculus, set theory, and theory of functions of a real variable.

In 1921, with the conclusion of armed conflict between Poland and the Soviet Union, Neyman went with his wife, mother, and grandmother to Poland, which he always viewed as his own country. Between 1921 and 1923 he served as the single statistical expert at the National Institute for Agricultural Research in Bydgoszcz. Here he wrote the first of many papers on the application of mathematical statistics to agricultural problems, such as improving crop yield by judicious selection of plant mixtures, estimating the commercial value of sugar beets, and methods for testing the quality of various crops.

In 1923 Neyman became head of the Biometric Laboratory of the Nencki Institute for Experimental Biology in Warsaw. Concurrently, he became a special lecturer in mathematics and statistics at the Central College of Agriculture in Warsaw, as well as head of that institution's statistical laboratory.

In 1924 Neyman received his doctoral degree from the University of Warsaw, presenting as his dissertation two papers (in Polish with summaries in French) that he had written while associated with the National Institute for Agricultural Research: "On the applications of the theory of probability to agricultural experiments" and "Memoir on the application of mathematical statistics on resolving some agricultural problems." Asked in 1978 who had chaired his 1924 doctoral program, Neyman asserted "I am the student of Lebesgue," although he did not meet the mathematician until two years later, in 1926, when he attended Lebesgue's lectures at the Collège de France in Paris. Also in connection with his Ph.D. examination, when asked why he was not examined in statistics, he replied: "There was no one in Poland to examine me. I was *sui generis.*"

Subsequent to receiving his Ph.D., Neyman gave courses at the University of Warsaw, the Central College of Agriculture, and the University of Krakow. His colleagues at the University of Warsaw recognized Neyman's obvious talents, but not being in a position to evaluate his abundant statistical work or contribute to its development, they arranged for him to receive a postdoctoral fellowship from the Polish government for study abroad with Karl Pearson at University College London. Pearson is generally viewed as the primary founder of modern statistics.

Although disappointed during his initial stay at Pearson's laboratory at University College (1925–1926), Neyman met there William S. Gosset, whose assumed name of "Student" is coupled eponymously to the famous Student t-test, a method for securing a parameter to examine the statistical significance of errors introduced by taking the mean average of small samples from a sample population with a large number of members. The most important meeting for Neyman and his subsequent career was with Karl Pearson's son, Egon S. Pearson. Their collaboration was decisive in establishing a robust theory of hypothesis testing, utilizing the structure of modern mathematical statistics. Between 1926 and 1933 the Neyman-Pearson theory was developed by the two men, and beginning in 1928, it appeared in a series of jointly written papers in English scientific journals. The essential objective of the theory is how to secure a solution to the problem of accepting or rejecting an hypothesis about an aggregate universe of members when two types of errors are possible. The theory designates a Type I error, rejecting the hypothesis when it is true, and a Type II error, accepting the hypothesis when it is false.

In their papers the authors analyze how to minimize the risks of these errors for special situations employing what is now known as Neyman-Pearson statistics. The analysis leads to the probability of avoiding any errors reported quantitatively in what is characterized as "level of significance" and, later by Neyman, "confidence intervals."

After Neyman returned to his posts in Poland in 1927, the important collaboration of Neyman and Pearson, except for infrequent meetings in Paris and elsewhere, was principally by exchange of letters. Although Neyman's professional reputation had grown, and he had achieved the post of faculty docent at the University of Warsaw in June 1928, he was never offered a professorship in Poland at any time in his long career, presumably because, according to his biographer Constance Reid, "he was known as a nonbeliever who attributed to its Roman Catholic faith many of his country's troubles."

In 1934 Neyman returned to University College London as special lecturer. He was promoted to reader (equivalent to associate professor) in statistics in 1936 and to full professor in 1938 and was placed in charge of that institution's statistical laboratory. During his years in London, Neyman made further vital contributions to statistical science in addition to the Neyman-Pearson work. Among the problems addressed was the theory of propagation of contagion during epidemics. Work on sampling stratified populations yielded the statistical theory that led to development of the Gallup poll and related approaches to evaluating public opinion. Methods for randomized experiments in agriculture, biology, medicine, physics, and chemistry resulted from some of Neyman's investigations.

By 1938, Neyman had become recognized as one of the most important mathematical statisticians in the world. In that year he became professor of statistics at the University of California at Berkeley, where he eventually succeeded in having statistics and the statistical laboratory designated as independent entities, with Neyman as head of both. He remained active at Berkeley for the rest of his life and supervised thirty-nine Ph.D. students, many of whom became leading statisticians in their own right.

Beginning in March 1942 and lasting until the conclusion of World War II in August 1945, Neyman, who acquired U.S. citizenship in 1944, directly led Berkeley's Statistical Laboratory in computational work for the U.S. Army Air Forces to obtain optimum bombing patterns for aircraft attacking enemy trains and ships. This necessitated frequent separations from Berkeley and delegation of his teaching responsibilities to others.

Neyman formally retired in 1961, but the Berkeley administration waived its postretirement regulations to permit Neyman to continue as director of the Statistical Laboratory, accepting the recommendation of the tenured members of the Department of Statistics that "Neyman is preeminent among the world's mathematical statisticians, and the Laboratory and the University derive full benefit from his prestige only as long as he continues to serve as Director."

The spectrum of statistical application of Neyman's ideas was extraordinarily broad. He and Professor Elizabeth Scott, a longtime colleague at Berkeley and later in life a steady companion, had reviewed counts of galaxies showing their clustering. Employing statistical methods and reported astronomical observations, they were able to assist in the difficult problems of estimating the masses of distant galaxies. This class of research was reported in 1961 in the Fourth Berkeley Symposium on Mathematical Statistics and Probability, typical of one of the series of symposia that Neyman had initiated in 1949, and addressed in its various components statistical and probability theory, problems in the physical sciences, biology and health, and new methods of weather modification such as cloud seeding.

Outside of statistics, Neyman involved himself in what he viewed as compelling ethical and moral issues. So-called loyalty oaths, which constituted a disclaimer that the signer did not belong to organizations advocating the overthrow of the U.S. government, were required by the University of California. Although Neyman described himself as "color blind" on the subject and not believing in the oath, he signed it anyway. He nevertheless supported nonsigners at Berkeley whose tenure or continued employment had been threatened and was elated in 1951 when a federal court in California rendered a decision supporting the nonsigners.

In 1964 Neyman became actively opposed to the Vietnam War. Selected in 1965 as the recipient of the Samuel S. Wilks Medal by the American Statistical Association, he refused to attend the presentation ceremony because it was to be held at an army installation. Among Neyman's other awards were honorary doctorates from the University of Chicago (1959), University of California at Berkeley (1963), University of Stockholm (1964), and the University of Warsaw (1974). He received the Cleveland Prize of the American Association for the Advancement of Science in 1958 and the National Medal of Science in 1968.

Jerzy and Olga Neyman had one son. Although they separated in 1952, they lived less than a mile from each other in Berkeley and shared occasional visits and Easter dinners. Following a series of heart attacks, Neyman died at Kaiser Hospital in Oakland, California.

In addition to his contributions in mathematical statistics, Neyman is remembered for his kindness, hospitality, and humanitarian endeavors.

★

Neyman's papers are at the Department of Statistics, University of California at Berkeley. David G. Kendall, M. S. Bartlett, and T. L. Page, "Jerzy Neyman, 1894–1981," *Biographical Memoirs of Fellows of the Royal Society* 28 (1982): 379–412, is a good account of Neyman's early life and work. Of particular value is the complete bibliography of all of Neyman's work in English and other languages. Constance Reid, *Neyman from Life* (1982), is a splendid biography. See also Neyman's entry by Erich L. Lehmann in the *Dictionary of Scientific Biography,* vol. 18, suppl. 2 (1990). Edna E. Kramer, *The Nature and Growth of Modern Mathematics* (1970), provides a short account of Neyman-Pearson theory for nonexperts. An obituary is in the *New York Times* (13 Aug. 1981).

LEONARD R. SOLON

NIEL, Cornelis Bernardus van (*b.* 4 November 1897 in Haarlem, the Netherlands; *d.* 10 March 1985 in Carmel, California), microbiologist, educator, and author who was the first person to formulate a general chemical equation for the photosynthetic process in plants and bacteria.

Cornelis van Niel was born to Jan Hendrik van Niel and Geertien Gesiena Hagen. Growing up in the Netherlands, he served in the Dutch army from 1917 to 1919. After his discharge he attended the Delft University of Technology, also in the Netherlands. He graduated in 1922 with a degree in chemical engineering and in 1928 obtained his doctor of science degree from the same university. During his stay at Delft University, he worked as a research assistant in microbiology from 1922 to 1923. He worked as a conservator from 1925 to 1928. He married Christina van Hemert on 17 August 1925. They had three children: Jan, Ester, and Ruth.

After finishing his education at Delft University in 1928, van Niel and his family migrated to the United States. He then became an associate professor at Stanford University, where he remained until 1946, when he moved to Princeton University. In 1954 he accepted a position at Rutgers University in New Brunswick, New Jersey.

His studies were primarily devoted to the physiology and taxonomy of propionic acid bacteria and photosynthesizing bacteria. He was the first person to formulate a general chemical equation for the photosynthetic process in plants and bacteria.

Around 1930, while working at the Hopkins Marine Station of Stanford University at Pacific Grove, California, he demonstrated that purple and green sulfur bacteria can engage in photosynthesis without liberating oxygen. He also showed that in some bacteria, photosynthesis liberates sulfur rather than oxygen, as well as some more highly oxidized states of organic molecules, or, in some cases, no by-products at all.

He interpreted his research results by postulating that the process of photosynthesis can be represented by the following general reaction:

$$CO_2 + 2H_2A \longrightarrow (CH_2O) + 2A + H_2O$$

where the letter A represents oxygen in the oxygen-evolving photosynthetic reactions of green plants, and sulfur in the sulfur-producing photosynthetic reactions of purple bacteria. He went on to propose that the reaction takes place in two stages, known as the light and dark reactions, involving two different enzyme systems. The general equation he proposed was proved correct by various independent studies using isotopically labeled water and carbon dioxide.

Van Niel was elected to the prestigious National Academy of Sciences in 1945 and to the American Academy of Arts and Sciences in 1950. He was also a member of numerous professional organizations, such as the American Society of Microbiology and the American Society of Plant Physiology. Van Niel's awards include the National Medal of Science in 1964, the Emil Christian Hansen medal in 1964, the Rumford Medal of the American Academy of Arts and Sciences in 1967, and the Anthony Van Leeuwenhoek medal in 1970. His best-known scientific works are *The Propionic Acid Bacteria* (1928), with A. J. Kluyver, and *The*

Microbe's Contribution to Biology (1956), also with A. J. Kluyver. He also contributed to numerous professional journals.

The general understanding of the photosynthesis reaction rests largely on the elegant work of van Niel. His work gave rise to numerous other studies and greatly increased the general scientific knowledge of a very important field in both biology and chemistry. Cornelis van Niel died in Carmel, California.

★

The following represent some of the sources on van Niel's life and work: *The McGraw-Hill Modern Men of Science,* vol. 2 (1968); *Who's Who in America,* 39th ed. (1977); *Great Soviet Encyclopedia,* vol. 18 (1978); and Hal May, ed., *Contemporary Authors,* vol. 115 (1985). Some brief historical reference to his work can be found in biochemistry and microbiology textbooks.

MARIA PACHECO

NORTH, John Ringling (*b.* 14 August 1903 in Baraboo, Wisconsin; *d.* 4 June 1985 in Brussels, Belgium), showman, businessman, and president of Ringling Bros. and Barnum & Bailey Circus who brought the circus out of the big top and into indoor arenas.

John Ringling North was the eldest of three children born to Henry Whitestone North, an engineer with the Chicago and Northwestern Railroad, and Ida Lorena Wilhelmina Ringling, the youngest sibling and only sister of the famous Ringling brothers, whose circus had been founded in 1884. North grew up surrounded by the circus and held his first job at age thirteen selling at one of its candy stands.

North entered the University of Wisconsin in 1921 and transferred to Yale College in 1922. Following his marriage to Jane Connelly in September 1924, he had to leave Yale because undergraduates were not permitted to be married. He then joined a New York stock brokerage house. In 1926 North went to work for his uncle, circus president John Ringling, selling real estate in Sarasota, Florida, during the winter and spending his summers traveling with the circus, handling the organization's finances. Jane North never adjusted to the demands of circus life, and by 1927 their marriage was essentially over. They divorced three years later.

North returned to the brokerage house in 1929 and remained there until 1936. When debt and ill health forced John Ringling to turn the management of the circus over to creditors in 1932, North obtained his uncle's power of attorney and assumed responsibility for the circus's financial obligations. Suspicious of North's motives, John Ringling wrote a codicil to his will cutting Ida Ringling North and her two sons, John and Henry, off without a cent. Ringling's original will, however, named Ida and John executors and all three of them trustees of his estate. Because

John Ringling North, 1953. Circus World Museum, Baraboo, Wisconsin

Ringling neglected to cancel those provisions of his will, upon his death in 1936 the Norths managed to gain control of Ringling's estate and his 30 percent of the circus stock. North convinced the members of the extended Ringling family that the current management would bankrupt the circus, and, despite their distrust of North, they named him circus president in 1936.

Under North's direction the circus flourished. Within three seasons he paid off the organization's debts, regained complete ownership for the family, paid stockholders a dividend, and managed to save $1 million. North updated the circus, producing thematic shows with large-scale production numbers featuring theatrical lighting and showgirls. During a Paris blackout on Christmas Eve in 1939, North met the French movie star Germaine Aussey (born Germaine Agassis). They fell in love and were married in Philadelphia on 11 May 1940. Although Germaine joined North on the circus train for three seasons, she found circus life unsettling. In 1943 the couple separated and later divorced.

With the United States' entry into World War II, North feared rationing would create numerous management problems for the circus. His greatest concern was the availability of the chemicals required to flameproof the canvas tents. North recommended that the stockholders offer the circus to the government as a morale builder or else return it to winter quarters for the duration of the war. When they rejected both options, North reluctantly tendered his resignation as president. Under the leadership of North's cousin, Robert Ringling, the circus survived the early war years until the disastrous big-top fire at Hartford, Connecticut, in 1944, when 168 persons lost their lives. Five circus executives were indicted, tried, and convicted for neglect and public endangerment. At the April 1946 stockholders meeting North was reelected as vice president in charge of operations. In 1947 North gained control of 51 percent of the circus stock and the ability to appoint himself president for life.

By 1955 the circus was $1 million in debt. But the infusion of $1.3 million from the film *The Greatest Show on Earth* (1952) and the annual $100,000 fee paid by NBC for televising the dress rehearsal at Madison Square Garden kept the show from folding. The following year North faced increased opposition from the minority family stockholders who accused him of mismanaging the circus. At the same time, pressure from the Teamsters union threatened to shut down the production.

On 16 July 1956 in Pittsburgh, Pennsylvania, John Ringling North announced, "The tented circus as it now exists is, in my opinion, a thing of the past." He then closed the show in midseason and returned to winter quarters. By the time the circus train reached Sarasota, North was ready to talk with Irvin Feld, a promoter who had previously offered to help cut the circus operating costs by booking it into indoor auditoriums. Together they revamped the circus, moving it out of tents and into auditoriums.

Early in 1960 John Ringling North and his brother purchased their father's family home in Galway County, Ireland, and became Irish citizens. Two years later North left the United States permanently and took up residence in Zurich, Switzerland, with the Countess Ida von Zedlitz-Trützschler, who remained his companion until his death. Between 1962 and 1967 North served as president and owner of Ringling Bros. and Barnum & Bailey Circus in absentia, touring Europe for new acts while leaving the daily business affairs in the hands of his brother and the Feld Corporation.

Shortly after New Year's Day in 1967, North met with Irvin Feld in Rome, Italy, where he agreed to sell Feld the circus and to remain on as a producer. Feld, in partnership with his brother, Israel, and Judge Roy Hofheinz, purchased the circus from North for $8 million on 11 November 1967. The signing ceremony took place within the ruins of the Colosseum.

John Ringling North died of a stroke on 6 June 1985 in his hotel suite in Brussels, Belgium, while traveling. At the time he was residing in Geneva, Switzerland. He is buried in Sarasota, Florida.

During the three decades North headed the Ringling Bros. and Barnum & Bailey Circus organization, he proved himself an able showman and worthy successor of his uncles. North brought the circus into the modern age when he moved it into indoor arenas. He reinstated exotic animal acts and brought a touch of Broadway to the performance. With his eye for talent and his show business instincts, North traveled the world discovering and promoting new attractions for the Greatest Show on Earth.

★

David Lewis Hammarstrom, *Big Top Boss: John Ringling North and the Circus* (1992), relies heavily on one interview with North and numerous interviews with individuals who knew and worked with him. Fred Bradna as told to Hartzell Spense, *The Big Top: My Forty Years with the Greatest Show on Earth* (1952), is a ringmaster's personal reminiscences of life with Ringling Bros. and Barnum & Bailey Circus and working with John Ringling North. Henry Ringling North and Alden Hatch, *The Circus Kings: Our Ringling Family Story* (1960), traces the history of the Ringling family and their circus, with an emphasis on the John Ringling North era. Gene Plowden, *Those Amazing Ringlings and Their Circus* (1967), follows the career of the original Ringling brothers and their family circus up until North sold it. Another full-length history is Ernest J. Albrecht, *A Ringling by Any Other Name: The Story of John Ringling North and His Circus* (1989). Mildred Sandison Fenner and Wolcott Fenner, *The Circus: Lure and Legend* (1970), includes a short chapter on North; John Culhane, *The American Circus: An Illustrated History* (1990), contains numerous references to North. See also "North to Wed Actress," *New York Times* (5 Apr. 1940); "John R. North Weds Actress," *New York Times* (12 May 1940); and "Three Purchase Ringling Circus," *New York Times* (12 Nov. 1967). An obituary is in the *New York Times* (6 June 1985).

DIANE E. COOPER

NORTHROP, John Knudsen ("Jack") (*b.* 10 November 1895 in Newark, New Jersey; *d.* 19 February 1981 in Glendale, California), aircraft designer best known for developing the first all-metal monoplane and for the "Flying Wing," ancestor of the B-2 bomber.

John K. Northrop grew up intimately acquainted with long-distance transportation: his parents, Charles W. and Helen Knudsen Northrop, moved four times in his first nine years, eventually settling in California in 1905. There Northrop, an only child, would remain for the rest of his life. Northrop was a Roman Catholic. Three years after his graduation in 1913 from Santa Barbara High School, Northrop entered the fledgling aircraft industry, working with Allan and Malcolm Loughead as a mechanic and wood and metal worker. When the United States entered World War I, Northrop enlisted; he transferred quickly from the infan-

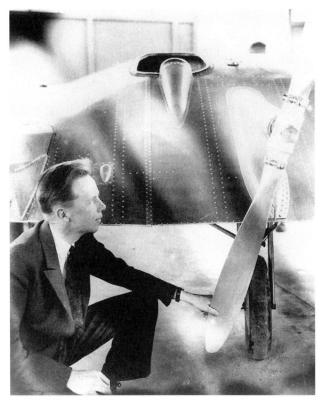

Aircraft designer John Northrop. UPI/CORBIS-BETTMANN

try to the Signal Corps, where he could continue to focus on aviation. Immediately after the war, Northrop married his high school sweetheart, Inez Harmer; they would have three children. He also went back into business with the Loughead brothers and a recent Czech immigrant, Anthony Stadlman. The inexperienced young men went out of business within a couple of years, but not before Northrop and Stadlman had begun work on the concept of tailless aircraft. Northrop's early training in materials and his military experience would also provide the foundation for later innovations in stressed-skin construction.

In 1923 Northrop began working for Douglas Aircraft, first as a draftsman, then as an engineer, and finally as a designer. Northrop's first task for Douglas was designing the fuel tanks for Douglas's round-the-world planes; it was perhaps at this time that he recognized the inherent structural rigidity of shaped metal, formed in what the French were calling *monocoque* construction (in which the outer skin bears most of the stress). He also continued his work on tailless airplanes, designing an all-wing glider as a pastime. In 1927 Northrop left Douglas to become chief designer for Allan Loughead, who had by then changed his name to Lockheed. His first design for Lockheed, an all-metal, high-wing monocoque airplane called the Vega, revolutionized the industry. The Vega, flown most famously by Wiley Post and Amelia Earhart, would set speed, altitude, and endurance records that were not broken until World War II.

Northrop wanted to proceed in the direction of all-metal construction set by the Vega, but policy differences between him and Lockheed led to his quitting the new company after only a year and forming a new company, the Avion Corporation, which was financed by the newspaper heir George Hearst. By 1929 Northrop had worked out designs for his first Flying Wing. This airplane was designed at first with the propellers pulling from the front, the conventional arrangement, but then was changed to have the propellers push from the rear, a feature that would remain constant in Northrop's later, much larger, all-wing planes. Like the Vega, the Flying Wing had all-metal stressed surfaces that provided both smooth airflow and structural strength. Thanks to the substantially reduced drag that his revolutionary design offered, its maximum speed was 25 percent greater than that of a conventional plane with equal power.

The coming of the Great Depression forced Northrop to sell his company to United Aircraft, for which he designed the Alpha, a long-wing commercial version of the Vega. But again Northrop chafed at having to work under someone else's direction, and in 1932 he founded a new corporation named after himself in El Segundo, California, designing and building conventional stressed-skin aircraft. There he developed commercial derivatives of the Alpha known as the Gamma and Delta, as well as military planes such as the A-17 attack plane and the BT-1 dive bomber. In 1938, Douglas Aircraft, a partner in Northrop's venture, bought out Northrop's share and renamed his dive bomber the Dauntless; under this name it became famous as the airplane that sank five Japanese aircraft carriers at the battles of the Coral Sea and Midway in 1942. Nearly 6,000 Dauntless dive bombers were produced during World War II.

Meanwhile, Northrop founded another company in Hawthorne, California, and developed two new military designs, the N-3PB patrol bomber and the P-61 Black Widow night fighter. The latter plane, of which more than a thousand were produced, was the fastest and, with its nose-mounted radar, deadliest propeller-driven combat aircraft of World War II. Funded by these successful designs, Northrop was able to resume work on the Flying Wing, now called the N-1M. The first flight of this one-third-scale effort occurred in July 1940, and Northrop filed a patent application in November. During this period Northrop also invented a new process for building airplanes out of ultralight welded magnesium, which he patented as the "Heliarc." With this new production process he built the XP-56 Black Bullet, the XP-79 Flying Ram, and the JB-1 Power Bomb, the first American cruise missile.

Northrop was known in the aircraft industry as a man who cared about his employees' working conditions. During World War II he hired wounded veterans to work in their hospitals or homes, paying them as if they were full-time resident workers. In 1943 he established a special research division to develop lightweight prosthetic arms and hands. And in 1942 he founded the Northrop Institute of Technology, now Northrop University, in Los Angeles, where students interested in more technical education could advance into the industry.

Northrop continued to work on his tailless designs throughout World War II, experimenting with rocket and turboprop propulsion as well as conventional propeller and jet engines. Eventually, in June 1946, a full-scale version of the Flying Wing, the XB-35, made its maiden flight; the YB-49, its jet-propelled sister ship, first flew a year and a half later. This immense yet nimble airplane weighed nearly fifty tons and had a wingspan of more than 170 feet, yet it could carry more than fifteen tons of bombs, could remain at high altitude for hours, and in 1949 flew cross-country at an average speed of 511 miles per hour. The time of the flight was only twelve minutes slower than the official jet fighter record at the time. Nevertheless, the Flying Wing project was canceled by the U.S. Air Force in November 1949. Because it was unconventional, it did not suit the traditionalists; because it could not carry nuclear weapons, it did not suit the modernists. Embittered by the fiasco, Northrop retired from leadership of his company in 1952, and although the company would go on to produce one more successful design, the F5A (best known in its T-38 trainer version), Northrop Aviation's greatest days were past. With the exception of a bitter interview he granted shortly before his death, Northrop put public life altogether behind him. He died of pneumonia and was buried in Santa Barbara Cemetery.

Ironically, Northrop's Flying Wing was restored to life some four decades after its cancellation, thanks to an unintended side effect of his design. In flight tests the XB-35 had proved to be nearly invisible to radar; therefore in the 1980s the project was renewed as the B-2 "Stealth" bomber. Built by the Northrop Corporation, it first flew in July 1989, and entered the U.S. Air Force fleet four years later. Northrop's career was finally complete.

★

Northrop's career has been well documented in two books: an internal company hagiography by Fred Anderson, *Northrop: An Aeronautical History* (1976), and E. T. Woolridge, *Winged Wonders: The Story of the Flying Wings* (1983). He was interviewed for *Current Biography 1949* before the cancellation of his Flying Wing contract. An obituary is in the *New York Times* (20 Feb. 1981).

HARTLEY S. SPATT

O

O'BRIEN, William Joseph, Jr. ("Pat") (*b.* 11 November 1899 in Milwaukee, Wisconsin; *d.* 15 October 1983 in Santa Monica, California), actor whose screen portrayals in more than 100 movies helped define the twentieth-century image of the all-American male with a heart of gold, albeit with a strong Irish tinge.

One of three children born to William Joseph O'Brien, a dry-goods clerk, and Margaret McGovern O'Brien, a housewife, "Pat" O'Brien grew up an only child after the early deaths of his two younger brothers. He assumed the name "Pat" in honor of his paternal grandfather who, according to appropriately dramatic family lore, was shot between the eyes while interceding in a barroom brawl. Devout and devoted, the O'Briens believed the family that prayed and played together stayed together. Mother, father, and son regularly patronized vaudeville performances, and the youngster soon showed a flair for school drama and recitations.

O'Brien attended parochial school, moving on to the Marquette Academy in Milwaukee, a Jesuit-operated secondary institution. There he met classmate Spencer Tracy, with whom he began a lifelong friendship based on a mutual love of theater. Enlisting in the U.S. Navy with Tracy in 1918, O'Brien spent World War I at the Great Lakes Naval Station. After the war he returned to complete his diploma at the Marquette Academy and then enrolled in Marquette University to pursue a law degree. But torts proved a weak rival to greasepaint. A university production of *Charley's Aunt* provided O'Brien his first significant lead. He snapped up an uncle's invitation to visit New York City in the summer of 1920 and stayed on, determined to make it on Broadway.

O'Brien persuaded Tracy to join him in the Big Apple, where both entered Sargent's School of Drama. His first professional role was as a chorus boy in the 1923 musical comedy *Adrienne*. He then landed a $50-a-week spot with a stock company in Plainfield, New Jersey. As he recalled in his autobiography, *The Wind at My Back* (1964), a new play was performed every week and actors juggled four assignments simultaneously, so that on any given day he was "playing a play, forgetting a play, studying a play, and rehearsing a play." His substantive Broadway debut came in the 1925 production *A Man's Man*.

After a string of stage successes, in December 1930 O'Brien was tapped for the role of the staccato-gruff reporter Hildy Johnson in Howard Hughes's movie of the Ben Hecht and Charles MacArthur drama *The Front Page*. During a two-hour break from shooting on 23 January 1931 he married the actress Eloise Taylor, whom he had met three years earlier when they worked together at the Delwyn Theater in Chicago. His portrait of the "get-the-news-at-all-costs" Johnson launched O'Brien toward cinematic stardom. He was selected by mogul Irving Thalberg for the lead in the movie *Flying High* (1931) at a salary of $1,750 per week and would appear in some fifty more films over the next decade.

With his square jaw and generous eyebrows, O'Brien

played soldiers, sailors, priests, football coaches, and newspapermen onscreen. Warner Brothers created box-office success by teaming him with his friend James Cagney in tough-guy action films, beginning with *Here Comes the Navy* in 1934. In *Angels with Dirty Faces* (1938), O'Brien's Father Connolly famously convinced Cagney's gangster figure, Rocky Sullivan, to whimper on his way to the electric chair so that the teenagers who had admired his hoodlum bravado would reject him as a role model. O'Brien's portrayal of the famed Notre Dame football coach Knute Rockne in *Knute Rockne—All American* (1940) culminated in the emotional halftime speech in which he urged his downtrodden team to "win one for the Gipper." With Ronald Reagan as the Gipper, the line passed into movie and political legend. (O'Brien and Reagan both received honorary degrees from the University of Notre Dame in 1981.)

O'Brien enjoyed playing a number of vivid real-life characters in biographical films during the 1940s. In addition to Rockne, he was Father Francis P. Duffy in *The Fighting 69th* (1940); Colonel Paddy Ryan, founder of the army bombardier school, in *Bombardier* (1943); Fordham University football coach Frank Cavanaugh in *The Iron Major* (1943); and Father Dunne in *Fighting Father Dunne* (1948). He worked for Columbia and RKO as well as Warner Brothers during this period. Too old for active service in World War II, he traveled tirelessly for the United Service Organizations, entertaining enlisted men in the Caribbean, North Africa, and the China-Burma-India war theater.

At the beginning of the 1950s, however, O'Brien found himself shut out of the Hollywood studios. Between 1950 and 1964 he would make only three pictures for major companies. He attributed this cold shoulder to the influence of the political left in the industry, feeling that he had been placed on a kind of reverse blacklist of people on the center and right. By this time he had four children and three households to maintain, having moved both his wife's and his own parents to California. So he went on the circuit with a nightclub act cobbled together from songs, poems, Irish stories, and set pieces from his biggest movies.

In 1957 he returned to the Broadway stage in *Miss Lonelyhearts,* an adaptation of the Nathanael West novel, in which he played another newspaperman. His 1960 television show about father-and-son lawyers, *Harrigan and Son,* lasted only one season. By then, however, he had prevailed upon his wife, Eloise, to come out of retirement to join him on the road, and they did summer stock together for more than twenty years. He came full circle in closing out his film career in 1981 with *Ragtime,* working again with old crony Cagney. He appeared in a dinner-theater production of *On Golden Pond* with his wife in 1983 at age 84. Later that year he suffered a heart attack and died in Santa Monica, California.

Pat O'Brien. AMERICAN STOCK/ARCHIVE PHOTOS

In a life spanning most of the twentieth century, O'Brien lived through the Great Depression and two world wars. Yet he never lost his basic optimism about the future of America, or for that matter about life in general. So many of the characters he played over his long acting career—strong religious and patriotic men of immigrant stock, willing to stand on principle, self-reliant and snappy—helped set the stage for America's confident and righteous attitude at mid-century. O'Brien was a grand character actor. What made him grand, beyond his Celtic sparkle and sweetness, was his popular reflection onscreen of American traits that his fellow citizens wanted to believe defined them as a people.

★

The Wisconsin Center for Film and Theatre Research at the Wisconsin State Historical Society at Madison holds many of O'Brien's contracts, and some correspondence, with Warner Brothers. His articulate autobiography, which he says he wrote himself with editorial help and advice from Stephen Longstreet, is *The Wind at My Back: The Life and Times of Pat O'Brien by Himself* (1964). Books that discuss O'Brien's films briefly while providing context for them include John Baxter, *The Gangster Film* (1970); Barry Norman, *The Hollywood Greats* (1979); and Robert Sklar, *City Boys: Cagney, Bogart, Garfield* (1992). An obituary is in the *New York Times* (16 Oct. 1983).

KEVIN P. REILLY

OCHSNER, (Edward William) Alton (*b*. 4 May 1896 in Kimball, South Dakota; *d*. 24 September 1981 in New Orleans, Louisiana), surgeon and teacher who cofounded the Ochsner Medical Institutions as a clinic and one of the first medical researchers to link smoking and lung cancer.

The only son and youngest of seven children of Edward Philip Ochsner, a merchant, and Clara Leda Shount, Alton Ochsner attended the public schools of Kimball, South Dakota, graduating in 1914. He received a B.A. degree (1918) from the University of South Dakota in Vermilion and an M.D. (1920) from Washington University in St. Louis, Missouri. He interned at Barnes Hospital, St. Louis (1920–1921) and externed at Augustana Hospital in Chicago (1921–1922) under his cousin Albert John Ochsner, who had a great impact on Alton's professional career. With his cousin's help, he studied for two years at the Kantonospital, University of Zurich (1922–1924). While in Switzerland, Ochsner demonstrated to the Swiss the technique of successful blood transfusions; from this came his first scientific paper. In Europe, he married Isabel Kathryn Lockwood on 13 September 1923; they had four children.

Alton Ochsner, 1980. UPI/CORBIS-BETTMANN

On his return to the United States, Ochsner became convinced that his talents were in teaching and research. After a short stint at Columbus and St. Mary's Hospitals (1925), he taught at Northwestern University as an instructor in surgical pathology (1925) and at the University of Wisconsin (1926–1927) as assistant professor of surgery. His greatest period of accomplishment was as chairman of surgery and head of the department of surgery at Tulane University (1927–1956). During this time, he authored or coauthored more than 500 articles on surgery and six books and trained more than 3,000 physicians. In 1936 he demonstrated a connection between smoking and carcinoma of the lung, one of the first researchers to make this link. He remained an influential opponent of cigarette smoking throughout his life. Ochsner also wrote on the treatment of liver abscess and the extraperitoneal approach to subphrenic access. He conducted important experimental heart surgery, successfully separated Siamese twins, and founded the journal *Surgery* in 1937.

The Ochsner Clinic, founded in New Orleans in 1942, began a new form of medical delivery in the South by grouping several specialists in one organization. Despite the opposition of many local physicians, the clinic was a success from the beginning.

Ochsner was described as an extremely dedicated surgeon who set high standards of skill, honesty, and loyalty. He held presidencies of the Southeastern Surgical Association (1944–1946), Southern Surgical Association (1944), American Association for Thoracic Surgery (1947–1948), American Cancer Society (1949–1950), American College of Surgeons (1951–1952), International Society of Angiography (1954–1956), Interstate Postgraduate Medical Assembly of North America (1955–1956), Pan Pacific Surgical Association (1961–1963), International Society of Surgery (1962–1963), and American Retired Physicians Association (1962–1977). He received the Distinguished Service Award of the American Medical Association in 1967.

His first wife died of lung cancer in 1968. In 1970 Ochsner married Jane Kellogg Sturdy, seventeen years his junior. He died of congestive heart failure and was buried in the Garden of Memories, in New Orleans.

★

The Alton Ochsner Papers are housed in Historic New Orleans, Louisiana. John Wilds and Ira Harkey, *Alton Ochsner: Surgeon of the South* (1990), is a thoroughly researched biography. Michael E. DeBakey, "Edwin William Alton Ochsner, Sr.," *Surgery* (Jan. 1982), is a moving salute by Ochsner's most famous pupil. Another collection of tributes from former students and President Reagan is *Journal of Thoracic and Cardiovascular Surgery* (July 1982). An obituary is in the *New York Times* (25 Sept. 1981).

RONALD H. RIDGLEY

OKADA, Kenzo (*b.* 28 September 1902 in Yokohama City, Kanagawa Prefecture, Japan; *d.* 25 July 1982 in Tokyo, Japan), a Japanese-American artist who participated in the heady, post–World War II atmosphere of the New York School and whose large-scale, yet delicate abstractions received international acclaim.

Okada's interest in art first manifested itself when as a child he discovered drawing. His first introduction to Western art came at Meijigakuin Middle School, which he attended from 1914 to 1920, when a teacher told him the story of nineteenth-century painter Jean-François Millet. At that moment he decided to become a painter, but Okada's father, a wealthy industrialist, felt that his son should join the family business. After the sudden death of his father, Okada immediately applied to the Tokyo Fine Arts University (now the Tokyo University of Arts). He was accepted in 1922. In addition to fine arts Okada studied art history, anatomy, language, and history, although he was only interested in his painting and drawing classes. In 1924 Okada moved to Paris, where he struggled with poverty and loneliness. At first Okada attended the Académie Paul Ranson and studied drawing. Although he did not paint much, Okada did submit an oil to the 1927 Salon d'Automne.

During his three years in Paris, Okada met artists as diverse as Alberto Giacometti, Moïse Kisling, Ossip Zadkine, Marie Laurencin, and, most significantly, the famous and colorful Japanese-French expatriate Tsuguharu Foujita, with whom he briefly studied. Okada's recollections of Paris were enigmatic; he probably operated on the fringes of the Parisian milieu, uncomfortable with the cultural demands Paris made on its artists.

In the fall of 1927 Okada returned to Japan as a figurative, impressionist painter. In less than two years he had his first solo exhibition at the Mitsukoshi Department Store. After his 1935 marriage to Kimi Kasomo, a dress designer (and his move into a new Tokyo studio), Okada became associated with the Nichido Gallery in Tokyo, where he received a solo exhibition in 1936. In 1937 Okada joined the Nika-kai Group, the largest organization of contemporary Japanese artists. From 1947 to 1950, Hokusyo Gallery in Tokyo held three one-person shows of his work. Okada taught at the Nippon University (1940–1942), Musashino Art Institute (1947 and 1950), and Tama Fine Arts College (1949–1950).

In the immediate aftermath of World War II, in which he did not serve, Okada lost interest in painting. Although "things" Western were now in vogue in Japan, Okada still found the art circles of Tokyo confining, and he turned his sights on the new artistic capital of the world, New York City. In August 1950 he and his wife emigrated. By 1951 Okada was ensconced in an apartment on East Ninth Street in Greenwich Village, a neighborhood where many contemporary artists lived and worked.

Okada found a freedom in New York art circles that he had not experienced in Paris or Japan. At first he painted little, preferring to draw while he absorbed the rough energy and massive scale of the city. One night, probably in 1952, he destroyed his "realist" drawings and began to paint his large-scale abstractions. At age fifty Okada finally began his mature work. He later told interviewers that at that time he felt the same purity of expression and excitement he had as a child.

Undoubtedly, much of Okada's success came from his close association with Betty Parsons, the famed dealer of the abstract expressionists. She gave Okada his first solo exhibition of his recent abstractions in October 1953 (followed by eleven more solo shows in her gallery between 1955 and 1978). Even more important, she introduced him to other New York School artists, including Mark Rothko, Barnett Newman, and Franz Kline. Their work provided the key to Okada's search for expression. He adopted their techniques—heavily worked surfaces, fields of color, and gestural accidents—and he understood their autobiograph-

Kenzo Okada. FROM THE BROCHURE FOR THE EXHIBITION "KENZO OKADA AND NATURE" AT THE MARISA DEL RE GALLERY, 1986

ical motives, namely, painting one's unconscious self in large-scale abstractions. For the first time Okada was able to address his Japanese heritage and experiences. He sought in his art a synthesis of Eastern and Western traditions which he described as "like black and white . . . which though opposites [were] still able to complement each other."

Okada's method of tapping into his unconscious was a process best described as stream of consciousness or what he repeatedly called "doing without knowing." He would work on four or more canvases at one time, with a variety of tools, including brushes, knives, and rollers, and with no preparatory drawings or preconceived ideas. This approach allowed him to move beyond his technical ability and long experience to tap into the essence of his subject, what Okada had termed by 1958 as Yugenism, a Japanese adjective meaning cryptic, profound, or mysterious.

Okada did not return to Japan until 1958. He became an American citizen in 1960, and by the late 1960s was dividing his time between New York and Japan, painting, however, only in his adopted country. In 1963 Okada purchased a home in Rensselaerville, outside of Albany, New York. "It is just like Japan," he said.

The 1960s and 1970s saw even greater recognition and fame for Okada, who received many awards and honors. His paintings were eagerly sought after by museums and collectors, especially in the early halcyon days of the New York School, and can be found in more than forty public and private institutions, from New York's Metropolitan Museum of Art to Rome's Galleria Nazionale d'Arte Moderna and Tokyo's National Museum of Modern Art. As Parsons wryly recalled, "Okada often paid my rent." In 1965 the Buffalo (New York) Academy of Fine Arts held Okada's first retrospective, which was then sent on a two-year international tour. In the spring of 1982 Okada received his second retrospective, hosted this time by a Japanese organization, the Seibu Museum of Art. Okada and his wife traveled to Tokyo for the exhibition. He died suddenly of a heart ailment and was buried in Japan.

Kenzo Okada was a quiet, subtle man whose works are like hidden treasures to be discovered and savored. Throughout his twenty-two-year New York career his powers of invention never faded. Okada remained true to his internal vision, turning the energy of abstract expressionist rhetoric and style into elusive, serenely magical works. As Okada stated, "I find myself in nature and nature in myself."

★

Of the many excellent exhibition catalogs on Okada, one of the best is Seibu Museum of Fine Art, *Kenzo Okada* (1982). Two excellent unpublished interviews with Kenzo Okada exist. For information on Okada's early experiences and career before coming to the United States, see the transcript of an interview con-

ducted by Forrest Selvig (22 Nov. 1968), Archives of American Art, Washington, D.C. For an understanding of Okada's working process and artistic aims, see the transcript of an interview conducted in 1966 by Arlene Jacobowitz, Brooklyn Museum of Art Archives, Records of the Department of Painting and Sculpture Exhibitions, "Listening to Pictures" (1968). Several interviews with Okada have been published: "Kenzo Okada," *Art Now: New York* 1, no. 4 (April 1969); "Kenzo Okada, Painter," in Chisaburoh F. Yamada, ed., *Dialogue in Art: Japan and the West* (1976); and Sumio Kuwabara, "Saka to kataru: Kenzo Okada to sono sakuhin" (Talking to the Author: Kenzo Okada and His Works), *Mizue* (Japan), no. 923 (summer 1982): 66–81, published shortly before his death on the occasion of his first retrospective in Japan. An obituary is in the *New York Times* (28 July 1982).

LEIGH BULLARD WEISBLAT

OLIN, John Merrill (*b*. 10 November 1892 in Alton, Illinois; *d*. 8 September 1982 in East Hampton, New York), chemical corporation executive, inventor, and philanthropist whose Olin Foundation helped change the political climate in the United States in the 1970s and 1980s.

Olin was the second of three sons of Franklin Walter Olin, a manufacturer of ammunition, and Mary Mott Moulton,

John Olin (*right*) with the newspaper publisher John Knight at the Belmont Park racetrack, New York, 1968. MORGAN COLLECTION/ARCHIVE PHOTOS

a housewife. Olin spent summer vacations at the New Hampshire farm of an uncle, Amos Merrill, who, Olin recalled in 1958, "gave me my first gun . . . I learned to work there." After graduating from the Cascadilla School in Ithaca, New York, in 1909, Merrill entered Cornell University and received a B.S. in chemistry in 1913.

Olin became a chemical engineer in 1913 at the Western Cartridge Company (which his father had founded) in East Alton, Illinois, a small city on the Mississippi River just north of St. Louis, Missouri. In 1914 he became assistant to his father, who was president of the company. On 29 September 1917, Olin married Adele Louise Levis; they had three children and divorced in 1935. On 11 May 1940, Olin married Evelyn Brown Niedringhaus.

In 1918 Olin became first vice president and a director of Western Cartridge. The company became a major manufacturer of sporting ammunition and firearms. For an executive, Olin had an unusually strong scientific background and was named as inventor (sometimes with others) on twenty-four patents. Olin said in 1958, "In the old days, I had two ways to prove a new bullet. I tested it in the laboratory. Then I went out and hunted with it. If it worked in both places, I knew I had a good bullet." Olin perfected a shotgun shell with increased velocity and range by using a progressive-burning smokeless powder. The popular Super-X shell was a financial as well as a technological breakthrough for Western Cartridge.

During World War II, Western Cartridge was an important manufacturer of military small arms and ammunition and helped develop raw materials for aluminum production. In 1944 Olin became president of Olin Industries, which was created by the merger of several firms, including Western Cartridge Company and Winchester Repeating Arms Company (which Olin had bought at the height of the Great Depression by borrowing $5 million). Frederick Olsen, whose patents improved Olin's ammunition, was vice president for research. In 1953 Olin Industries—working with Mathieson Chemical Corporation—made a major contribution to the U.S. space effort by conducting research on hydrazine, a rocket propellant.

In 1954 Olin became chairman of the board of Olin Mathieson Chemical Corporation, which was created by the merger of Mathieson Chemical Corporation and Olin Industries. Although the new company had headquarters in New York (and after 1967, Stamford, Connecticut), Olin continued to make his main residence in Alton, Illinois. He valued advice from executives John W. Hanes and Walter F. O'Connell and, later, from his attorney, George J. Gillespie III of Cravath, Swaine, and Moore. Olin acquired Squibb Pharmaceutical and Ecusta Paper Corporation of North Carolina, which made paper for cigarettes, and expanded into cellophane (through a licensing agreement with DuPont), aluminum, and lumber.

Near Alton, Olin built Nilo Kennels—the finest Labrador retriever training and breeding center in the United States—on 550 acres that became a wildlife preserve. He became a major conservationist and liked to hunt on his estate near Albany, Georgia. Olin's favorite Labrador, King Buck, won the National Retriever Field Trial Championship in 1952 and 1953 and appeared on a U.S. postage stamp. He was also a breeder of Thoroughbred racehorses; one of these, Cannonade, won the Kentucky Derby in 1974. Olin enjoyed fishing and belonged to the Moisie Salmon Club in Quebec and led a campaign to save the Atlantic salmon.

In 1963 Olin became honorary chairman of Olin Mathieson. His generosity was recalled by one of its senior scientists, Walter C. Saeman, who was surprised by the size of his first Christmas bonus. Olin made many donations to universities (including a research library at Cornell), museums, and hospitals and encouraged philanthropy among his employees by matching their gifts. Olin died of a heart attack.

Although he founded the John M. Olin Foundation in 1953, it was not until 1973 that he decided to use it (as he told his first executive director, Frank O'Connell) to promote the free-enterprise system that had made his success possible. According to William F. Buckley, Jr., "John Olin was blessed by inherited wealth which he creatively expanded, devoting himself to industry and to attempting to understand the freedoms within which industry, and employment, and economic progress flourish." Olin was opposed to the centralization of political power and "the tremendous growth of staffs in Washington." In 1977 William E. Simon, former secretary of the Treasury, became president of the Olin Foundation. Loyal executive directors—O'Connell, Michael Joyce, and James Piereson—ensured that grants went to conservative intellectuals who shared Olin's views on freedom and free enterprise, including Milton Friedman, Herbert Stein, Jeane Kirkpatrick, and Irving Kristol. According to Waldemar A. Nielsen in *Inside American Philanthropy,* "Olin was until his death in 1982 one of the most effective and influential philanthropists in recent times" and his foundation "became a model of focus and clarity."

The Olin Foundation focused on economics, politics, and the religious and cultural climate, while helping to change the political climate in the country. When Olin died at his home on Long Island, Ronald Reagan was president of the United States and was spreading his (and Olin's) vision of freedom and free markets throughout the world. Although successful in many fields, Olin was most influential as a philanthropist promoting his conservative philosophy. Olin was, in Buckley's words, "a singular man, of penetrating intelligence and understanding, who never forgot his debt to his country."

★

Olin gave interviews to Virginia Kraft, "A Man, a Dog, and a Crusade," *Sports Illustrated* (17 Nov. 1958); and Thomas E. Mullaney, "Olin: Staunch Fighter for Free Enterprise," *New York Times* (29 Apr. 1977). See also H. T. Sharp, "Men of the Month," *Chemical Engineering* (Aug. 1954). Waldemar A. Nielsen, *Inside American Philanthropy: The Dramas of Donorship* (1996), has a section on Olin, which includes a detailed analysis of his influential foundation. Obituaries are in the *New York Times* (10 Sept. 1982), *National Review* (1 Oct. 1982), *Cornell Alumni News* (Nov. 1982), and the *Olin Corporation Annual Report 1982*.

RALPH KIRSHNER

OPPEN, George (*b.* 24 April 1908 in New Rochelle, New York; *d.* 7 July 1984 in Sunnyvale, California), Pulitzer Prize–winning poet and craftsman best known as one of the founders and chief exponents of Objectivism, a major poetic movement of the 1930s.

Oppen was one of two children of middle-class Jewish parents, Elsie Rothfeld and George August Oppenheimer, a businessman. When he was four years old, Oppen's mother had a nervous breakdown and committed suicide. In 1918 the family moved to San Francisco, where Oppen lived through turbulent and anxious adolescent years. He attended the Warren Military Academy but was expelled after a serious car accident and a drinking charge. He went on to graduate from a small preparatory school.

In 1926 Oppen entered Oregon State University, where he met Mary Colby in a course on modern poetry. They stayed out all night on their first date and, after being disciplined by the school, left the university. They hitchhiked across the West, stopping in Dallas, Texas, on 7 October 1927 to be married. They were fleeing not only the academy, but also the restrictive social expectations of Oppen's wealthy family. Although they were only eighteen when they met, they remained together for the rest of their lives; they had one child. "I found George Oppen and poetry at one moment," writes Mary in her autobiography. "What happened to us, our joined lives, seems to us both choice and inevitability." From 1926 to 1929 they lived in New York, San Francisco, and Detroit. Rejecting his family background, Oppen held blue-collar positions throughout his life. He worked as a switchboard operator, factory worker, house builder, custom carpenter, and cabinet maker. His lifelong devotion to "craft" marked both his daily work and his poetry.

The Oppens moved to France in late 1929, settling in Le Beausset, near Marseilles. There they founded To Publishers, a short-lived venture, but one whose credits included works by Ezra Pound, William Carlos Williams, and Louis Zukofsky. Oppen's work began appearing in little magazines such as *Poetry,* and he started arranging his first volume.

It was at this time that Oppen helped develop Objectivism, which became one of the most important poetic trends following World War I. A general aesthetic, rather than a strict set of rules or practices, Objectivism can be understood in different ways. One has to do with the objectification of the poem—that is, making the poem into an object. Thus, Objectivists place emphasis on the way a poem looks on the page. Abandoning traditional prosody, they remain intensely interested in punctuation, lineation, and spacing. Oppen explained the importance of form: "The meaning of a poem is in the cadences and the shape of the lines and the pulse of the thought which is given by those lines." Objectivist verse also is particularly concerned with the exterior world and the commonplace objects of daily life. The poetry attempts to render these objects "objectively," without the interference of the poet's ego or personality.

Returning to New York City in 1933, Oppen began the Objectivist Press, which published, among other important works, his first collection, *Discrete Series* (1934). In his preface to this volume of short, precise, interconnected poems, Ezra Pound praised Oppen as a "serious craftsman" of original sensibility. Oppen's verse is marked by its slow, meditative pace; his use of unconventional punctuation and spacing, fragments, ellipses, and grammatical ambiguities adds to this effect. Although Oppen was already involved in left-wing causes, he chose to leave these political concerns out of his first volume, repudiating what he called "communist verse." For Oppen, poetry was an act of discovery, not a forum for didacticism. Thus, when he did choose to immerse himself in the world of politics, Oppen also chose to give up writing.

Concerned with widespread poverty and unemployment, the Oppens joined the Communist party in 1935. This marked the beginning of a twenty-five-year period of poetic silence. Oppen later said he gave up writing because of the "pressures of conscience" and because of a need for more life experience. Holding strong antifascist beliefs, Oppen provoked his induction into the U.S. Army in November 1942 by moving to Detroit from his aircraft industry job in New York. He served in the Rhineland and Central Europe campaigns as part of an antitank company. In April 1945 he was seriously wounded in Alsace, France, an experience he recounted in several poems. He was discharged with disability benefits and several decorations, including the Purple Heart.

After the war Oppen moved to Redondo Beach, California. In 1950, however, after several visits from the FBI and in the wake of hearings by the House Committee on Un-American Activities, the Oppens fled to Mexico City rather than betray friends or serve a prison term. (The FBI

George Oppen. AP/WIDE WORLD PHOTOS

maintained a file on Oppen for more than twenty-five years; even in Mexico he was occasionally harassed by U.S. officials.) Near the end of his exile, Oppen began to write again, a vocation he would take up with urgency on his permanent return to the United States by 1960.

The Materials (1962), Oppen's first volume after his long silence, reflects the intense life experience of the preceding years. Here, and in his seven subsequent volumes, Oppen discusses war, consumerism, the growth of a "city of corporations," as well as Jewish identity. For Oppen, the poem is never a revelation of something already known but rather an act of coming to awareness. *Of Being Numerous* (1968), winner of the Pulitzer Prize in 1969, is usually considered his greatest achievement. Here, he writes about the relationship between the individual and the community, singularity and "numerousness," a recurring concern in his poetry.

Oppen never received the same attention as the major Modernist poets of his generation. His suspicion of self-promotion and public appearances may account in part for his exclusion from important anthologies and from the canonical status enjoyed by many of his contemporaries. Nonetheless, after winning the Pulitzer Prize, his reputation grew. He received the PEN/West Rediscovery Award in 1982 and was honored by the American Academy and Institute of Arts and Letters in 1980 and by the National Endowment for the Arts. In a period of less than twenty years, Oppen created an important, if slender, body of work. His influence is most notable on the "Black Mountain" and "Language" poets who carried on and extended the Objectivist tradition.

By 1977 Oppen's health had begun to deteriorate. His wife helped him complete *Primitive* (1978), his last volume. At seventy-four years old, he was diagnosed with Alzheimer's disease. He died at Idlewood Convalescent Home in Sunnyvale, and his ashes were scattered on Tomales Bay, California.

Although some have found Oppen's poetry abstract and difficult, the poet believed he was writing for the widest possible audience. His interest in small-press publishing, in grassroots activism, and in people support this view of a populist writer. Oppen's life and work are about contacting the world outside through, as critic Jeffrey Peterson called it, a "world-opening act of witness." As an epigraph to *The Materials,* Oppen chose a quotation from the French philosopher Jacques Maritain that summarizes his commitments remarkably well: "We awake in the same moment to ourselves and to things."

★

Oppen's papers are in the Archive for New Poetry, Library of the University of California, San Diego. Mary Oppen's autobiography, *Meaning a Life* (1978), provides valuable information on both their lives. *The Selected Letters of George Oppen* (1990), edited by Rachel Blau DuPlessis, is an excellent source on Oppen's personality, poetics, history, and associations. Collections of essays, interviews, and bibliographies include Burton Hatlen, ed., *George Oppen: Man and Poet* (1981), and John Freeman, ed., *Not Comforts, but Vision: Essays on the Poetry of George Oppen* (1985). Several special issues of magazines have been devoted to Oppen's work: *Ironwood* 5 (1975) and 26 (1985) and *Paideuma* 10 (1981). His *Collected Poems* were published in London in 1972, and in New York as *The Collected Poems of George Oppen, 1929–1975* (1975). Charles Tomlinson edited a selection of his poetry, *Poems of George Oppen* (1990). An obituary is in the *New York Times* (9 July 1984).

MARK SILVERBERG

ORMANDY, Eugene (*b.* 18 November 1899 in Budapest, Hungary; *d.* 12 March 1985 in Philadelphia, Pennsylvania), conductor of Hungarian birth who is best known for his forty-two-year tenure as music director of the Philadelphia Orchestra.

The eldest of three sons, Eugene Ormandy, who was born Jenő Blau, received his early musical training from his father, Benjamin Blau, a dentist by profession. Eugene's two brothers were also trained musicians: one was a cellist with the New York Philharmonic and one was an accomplished harpist who became an orthopedic surgeon. A child prodigy, Eugene began playing the violin at age three. At age five, he was the youngest person ever admitted to the Royal Academy of Music in Budapest. Ormandy began violin studies with the virtuoso Jenő Hubay (for whom he had been named) when he was nine. His other teachers at the academy included Zoltán Kodály for composition and Leó Weiner for harmony and counterpoint.

Ormandy graduated at age fourteen and went on to further studies at the academy that earned him the title "artist violinist" three years later. In 1917 he toured Germany and Hungary as soloist with the Blüthner Orchestra. In 1919, when Hubay was named director of the Budapest Academy, Ormandy was appointed head of the violin department there. Ormandy also studied philosophy at Budapest University, receiving his degree in 1920. The following year he played a series of solo recitals, in which he was billed as Jenő B. Ormándy, in Austria and France. For one such concert, in Vienna on 12 March 1921, he performed a varied program of works by Beethoven, Zdeněk Fibich, Fritz Kreisler, Schubert, Henryk Wieniawski, and Hubay.

Ormandy arrived in New York on 2 December 1921, enticed by an offer of $30,000 for a 300-concert United States tour. The promoters of the tour proved to be insolvent, however, and the expected contract did not materialize. Within two weeks Ormandy was virtually penniless. A fellow Hungarian he met while making the rounds of New York City concert managers suggested he audition for Ernő Rapée, conductor of the orchestra at New York's Capitol Theater movie palace, owned by S. L. "Roxy" Rothafel. Eugene Ormandy Blau, as he was then known, was accepted and assigned a seat at the back of the second violin section. His virtuosity was immediately apparent, and he was moved to the concertmaster chair within the week. In 1922 he married Stephanie Goldner, a harpist in the orchestra, who joined the New York Philharmonic that same year. (She resigned in 1932 after Ormandy accepted the conductorship of the Minneapolis Symphony.) Ormandy made his conducting debut at the Capitol Theater in September 1924 with portions of Tchaikovsky's Fourth Symphony, when the orchestra's conductor, David Mendoza, fell ill. When, in 1926, Rapée left the Capitol to work at Rothafel's new theater, the Roxy, Ormandy was appointed associate director.

In 1927, the year in which he became a United States citizen, Ormandy met the celebrated and influential manager Arthur Judson while conducting the orchestra for an Anna Duncan (daughter of Isadora) dance recital. Judson was impressed with Ormandy (he later said, "I came to see a dancer and instead I heard a conductor"), and offered his managerial services. Ormandy remained at the Capitol until 1929 but from the time he met Judson he began to work in the expanding radio field on such programs as the Dutch Masters Hour, Jack Frost Melody Moments, and the McKesson-Robbins and Endicott Johnson programs. Judson also engaged Ormandy to conduct summer orchestral concerts and arranged appearances with the Philharmonic Symphony at New York's Lewisohn Stadium (1929) and the Philadelphia Orchestra at Fairmount Park's Robin Hood Dell (1930 and 1931).

The turning point in Ormandy's career came in October 1931 when, owing to illness, Arturo Toscanini withdrew from his guest conducting commitment in Philadelphia. Ormandy was approached after several established conductors, who did not want to risk their careers by substituting for the revered maestro, refused the engagement. Ormandy believed he had nothing to lose and everything to gain and accepted, despite Judson's warning that it might mean "suicide." Ormandy's daring paid off and the concerts were a success. Word quickly traveled across the country, catching the attention of the Minneapolis Symphony Orchestra, whose conductor Henri Verbrugghen had suffered a stroke. At the end of his weeklong Philadelphia engagement on 7 November, Ormandy headed directly for Minneapolis and what would be a five-year commitment.

While in Minneapolis, Ormandy revitalized the orchestra, improving the quality of its sound and expanding its repertory. He was largely responsible for arranging its 1934 recording contract with RCA Victor. Among the RCA releases were the first United States recordings of works by Mahler (Fourth Symphony), Rachmaninoff (Second Symphony), and Sibelius (First Symphony). In addition to assuring the future financial health of the orchestra, its recordings with RCA propelled Minneapolis from a provincial ensemble to international standing and elevated Ormandy to national prominence.

During his tenure in Minneapolis, Ormandy appeared as guest conductor in both Europe (in prewar Budapest, Linz, and Vienna) and the United States, most notably in Philadelphia (1932–1935). In December 1934 Leopold Stokowski made public his intention to resign as conductor of the Philadelphia Orchestra with an announcement that he would appear during only half of future concert seasons. Ormandy was part of a steady stream of guest conductors until the spring of 1936, when his appointment as co-conductor of the orchestra was announced. He was released from his Minneapolis contract, which had one more year to run, and for the next five concert seasons Ormandy and Stokowski shared the Philadelphia podium while maintaining a cordial, if distant, relationship. In 1938 Ormandy advanced one step closer to sole proprietorship of the or-

Eugene Ormandy. ARCHIVE PHOTOS

chestra when the board named him music director "in recognition of his splendid musical achievements that have made the last three years a succession of triumphs for conductor and orchestra alike." It was not until 1941, however, when Stokowski severed his ties to Philadelphia, that the "Ormandy era" officially began.

Ormandy inherited a virtuosic ensemble from Stokowski and continued to maintain a high artistic level throughout his tenure in Philadelphia. Small in stature, both energetic and graceful on the podium, Ormandy was known for his infallible ear and prodigious memory—he rarely conducted with a score. His primary influence was Toscanini, whose rehearsals he regularly attended in New York. Unsurpassed as an accompanist to the many soloists with whom he and the Philadelphia Orchestra performed, Ormandy was not a precise conductor; he was particularly known for his indefinite downbeat. He favored a baton through most of his career (with the exception of 1939–1953), but it was his violinist background that governed much of his technique; a distinctive conducting gesture of his was to bend his left arm and move his fingers tremulously, emulating a violinist's vibrato. The richness of tone he elicited from the orchestra's string sections soon became legend and was known variably as the "Ormandy" or "Philadelphia" sound.

Ormandy's repertory focused on late romantic and early-twentieth-century compositions. Under his direction, the Philadelphia Orchestra was responsible for many important world premieres, including Sergei Rachmaninoff's

Symphonic Dances (1941), Béla Bartók's Piano Concerto no. 3 (1946), and a number of works by American composers, among them Samuel Barber, Vincent Persichetti, Roger Sessions, and Virgil Thomson. Ormandy also conducted the United States premieres of works by, among others, Benjamin Britten, Sergei Prokofiev, and Dmitri Shostakovich. He was criticized for his habit of altering many of the compositions he conducted (particularly standard concert repertory) with additions to the orchestration, the doubling of instrumental parts, cuts, and reconceptions of rhythmic or melodic passages, but he was not alone in this practice, as recordings made by others of his generation testify. Ormandy also arranged many works for orchestra, among them a number of compositions for organ by J. S. Bach, which he programmed on orchestra concerts.

With the Philadelphia Orchestra, Ormandy made nine transcontinental tours between 1937 and 1977. He toured Europe five times, most notably in the summer of 1958, with performances in Romania, Poland, and the Soviet Union. He visited Latin America (1966), Japan (1967, 1972, and 1978), and Korea (1978). In 1973 the orchestra traveled to mainland China (1973), the first United States orchestra to do so, giving performances in Beijing and Shanghai. The tour was both a musical and political success.

As in Minneapolis, recordings were an important part of Ormandy's work in Philadelphia and a major source of revenue for the orchestra. Its long-standing relationship with RCA Victor continued until 1943, when Columbia's offer of a more profitable arrangement was accepted. Between 1944 and 1968, when the orchestra reverted to a new partnership with RCA, Ormandy and the Philadelphia Orchestra served as the foundation of the Columbia Records orchestral catalog, producing more than three hundred recordings. His Minneapolis and Philadelphia output soon made Ormandy one of the most prolific and widely known conductors on record. Radio and television appearances provided additional exposure and, in 1948, Ormandy conducted the first symphony concert telecast in America, beating Toscanini by one and a half hours on a rival network.

Ormandy was known to be extremely generous with orchestra members, offering all manner of assistance, including financial, when needed. His personal life reflected the same generosity. He and his wife, Stephanie, aided numerous European refugees during World War II, earning their home in the Philadelphia suburbs the designation "journey's end." The two were divorced in 1947 (the couple had two daughters, both of whom died in infancy due to a blood disorder), and in 1950 Ormandy married Margaret ("Gretel") Frances Hitsch. Born in Vienna, Gretel Ormandy was a naturalized American who had served in the U.S. Navy in World War II and was thoroughly devoted to her husband and his work until his death.

Although Ormandy remained in Philadelphia throughout the better part of each concert season, he continued to guest conduct, leading the major American and European orchestras and giving concerts in Australia (1944) and South America (1946). He made his Metropolitan Opera debut in New York in 1950, conducting Johann Strauss's *Die Fledermaus*.

Ormandy was the recipient of numerous awards in his lifetime, among them the Bruckner Society Medal (1936), the Presidential Medal of Freedom (1970), the Philadelphia Medal of Freedom (1980), and the Kennedy Center Honors (1982). He was made an *officier* of the French Legion of Honor (1952), promoted to commander (1958), and received several knighthoods: the Knight of the Order of Dannebrog, first class, by the King of Denmark (1952), Knight of the Order of the White Rose of Finland (1955), and Knight Commander of the Order of the British Empire by Queen Elizabeth II (1976).

Named conductor laureate upon his official retirement after an unprecedented forty-two years as music director of the Philadelphia Orchestra at the end of the 1979–1980 season, Ormandy continued to conduct, both in Philadelphia and elsewhere, until 1984. His last performance—which was with the Philadelphia Orchestra—took place at Carnegie Hall in Manhattan on 10 January 1984 when, already in failing health, he conducted Bartók's Concerto for Orchestra without a score. Two weeks later he had a heart attack, and for the subsequent fourteen months he suffered from complications of heart disease, finally succumbing to pneumonia at his home in Philadelphia.

Technically proficient, Ormandy was often criticized for a lack of depth in his interpretations, which were considered solid but not particularly insightful. But his polish and dedication to craft earned him an enduring popularity that has outlasted even his four decades in Philadelphia, and many of his recordings remain available. The continuity he brought through a career-long focus on a single ensemble was cherished by his audiences, and Ormandy will long be remembered as one of the last conductors of an era in which such continuity was a valued aspect of music making.

★

The Eugene Ormandy Papers and Oral History, Department of Special Collections, University of Pennsylvania Library, includes correspondence, administrative papers, programs and itineraries, clippings, awards, photographs, and recordings, dating from 1921 to 1991. The oral history collection includes tapes and transcripts of four interviews with Ormandy, as well as eighty-six interviews with conductors, soloists, composers, Philadelphia Orchestra members and administrative staff, and other professional colleagues, family, and friends. David Ewen, *Dictators of the Baton* (1943), written during Ormandy's early years in Philadelphia, provides an account of the conductor's initial success. Charles O'Connell, *The Other Side of the Record* (1947), is a candid portrait of the conductor written by a musical director of RCA Victor who worked closely with Ormandy for many years. John K. Sherman, *Music and Maestros: The Story of the Minneapolis Symphony Orchestra* (1952), provides the most comprehensive discussion available of Ormandy's tenure in Minneapolis. Hope Stoddard, *Symphony Conductors of the U.S.A.* (1957), is notable for the information it contains concerning Ormandy's early years. Herbert Kupferberg, *Those Fabulous Philadelphians: The Life and Times of a Great Orchestra* (1969), gives an in-depth account of Ormandy's accession to the Philadelphia podium as part of the orchestra's broader history. Deena Rosenberg and Bernard Rosenberg, *The Music Makers* (1979), includes an edited transcript of a 1977 interview. John L. Holmes, *Conductors on Record* (1982), details Ormandy's discographic history. Roger Dettmer, "Eugene Ormandy: In Memoriam," *Fanfare* 9, no. 1 (1985): 54–70, is the only available survey of Ormandy's entire career. Robert Chesterman, ed., *Conductors in Conversation* (1990), includes a 1971 interview. An obituary is in the *New York Times* (13 Mar. 1985).

MARJORIE HASSEN

OWINGS, Nathaniel Alexander (*b.* 5 February 1903 in Indianapolis, Indiana; *d.* 13 June 1984 in Santa Fe, New Mexico), architect, cofounder of the architectural firm Skidmore, Owings, and Merrill (SOM), and exponent of functionalism in U.S. architecture.

Owings was the son of Nathaniel Fleming Owings, who made a comfortable living importing, milling, and selling fine woods for furniture making, and Cora Alexander Owings, a housewife. Nathaniel had a younger sister, Eloise, who married his future partner, Louis Skidmore. When Nathaniel was thirteen, his father died, and the family was plunged into debt, but the strong-willed and competent Cora Owings enrolled in a correspondence course to learn bookkeeping, went to work, paid off her husband's debts, and thereafter supported herself and her children, although at a much more modest level than during her husband's lifetime.

Nathaniel attended Arsenal Technical High School in Indianapolis, graduating in 1920. An enthusiastic Boy Scout, he achieved Eagle rank. Indeed, it was through scouting that he discovered his vocation. Owings took part in the first International Boy Scout Jamboree, held in London in 1920, and then toured France with some fellow Boy Scouts. During this trip he was inspired by some of the great European cathedrals and other architectural masterpieces to pursue a career in architecture. He enrolled in the University of Illinois in 1921, but illness forced him to withdraw after one year. After recovering his health and working for a year with a pipe-laying company to earn money for college, he enrolled at Columbia University. He received his B.S. in architecture and engineering in 1927.

Nathaniel Owings stands before his architectural plans for the Mall in Washington, D.C., *c.* 1938. LIBRARY OF CONGRESS/CORBIS

Owings then took a job with the prominent New York City architectural firm York and Sawyer. His first assignment was designing the public restrooms for the new Department of Commerce building in Washington, D.C. Owings married Emily Hunting Otis on 5 September 1931. The couple had four children; the marriage ended in divorce in 1953. Owings then married Margaret Wentworth Millard on 31 December 1953.

After a year working on an aborted commission for a courthouse in Paterson, New Jersey, Owings moved to Chicago, where his brother-in-law Skidmore had been placed in charge of design for the 1933 Chicago Century of Progress exposition. The Great Depression had led to massive budget cuts for the exposition, and its viability was in doubt. Owings and Skidmore mastered the art of attracting wealthy patrons, and found unostentatious ways to solve building problems. They learned to build within severe financial constraints, even constructing display stands out of beaverboard in order to remain within their budget. They also learned to design not just exterior massings but the full range of interior details, lessons that would serve them well on future hotel, hospital, and university projects. Despite the Great Depression, the exposition was a financial success, establishing Skidmore and Owings as reliable overseers of massive projects.

Owings and Skidmore formed a partnership in 1936 and were joined three years later by John O. Merrill, an engineering specialist. The new firm decided to take a decentralized approach to operations, with Owings located in Chicago and Skidmore in New York, and to treat all their commissions as collaborative; it would be fifteen years before an individual architect received any credit for an SOM building. The only design Owings ever acknowledged as being his own work was a one-hundred-bed hospital in Petoskey, Michigan, and even on that building he shared credit with SOM's most famous architect, Gordon Bunshaft. Over the course of his career, Owings would become best known as a facilitator, famed for his ability to find resolutions to seemingly intractable conflicts of personality and philosophy and thereby keeping commissions on schedule.

SOM's first few commissions made little mark on the architectural world, even though the firm did design several smaller buildings for the 1939 World's Fair in New York City. Then World War II erupted, and in late 1942 SOM obtained the commission to build an entire town for the U.S. Army, at the top-secret uranium plant at Oak Ridge, Tennessee; eventually SOM built housing and related facilities for some 75,000 people. The town's site plan, with a series of neighborhood clusters feeding into central arteries that in turn led to the uranium works "downtown," served as a model for many planned suburban subdivisions in the postwar decades. Once the war ended and the veil of secrecy had been lifted, this commission made SOM famous.

The first major postwar commission received by SOM was a veterans hospital in Fort Hamilton, Brooklyn, New York. This was the first hospital built not only with reference to internal operating needs but also with respect to its external environment; every ward faced the sun and the ocean. There followed two major hotel commissions, in Cincinnati, Ohio, and Istanbul. Next came two commissions in New York City that made the International Style part of the American design vernacular. Both of them far transcended their relatively small scale to seize the attention of the world.

The first commission was a four-story bank building on Fifth Avenue, made memorable by its glass walls and monumental ground-floor vault. It was followed in 1952 by Lever House. This building was significant not only because of its beautiful glass curtain-wall design, used just previously by SOM in the Manufacturers Trust building, but also because it ushered in a long line of buildings with each erected on a relatively small portion of a site, reserving the remainder of the plot for public space. It was a design solution first introduced by Owings at a 1949 convention; it combined underground parking covered by plantings and walks with a slender, shaftlike, glass-walled, and fully air-conditioned building rising along one side of the plot. In less capable hands, the resulting "glass box" became the standard, featureless fixture of America's anonymous downtowns, not to be challenged until the new historicism of the 1980s restored stone and masonry to the commercial builder's inventory of building materials. But under the sensitive, creative guidance of Skidmore, Owings, and Merrill, this format would be used on such successful projects as the Chase Manhattan Bank building in lower Manhattan, the John Hancock Center in Chicago, and the Crown-Zellerbach building in San Francisco.

In the late 1950s Owings turned his interest to large-scale projects and increasingly focused on the relationship between human creations and the environment. He over-saw construction of the U.S. Air Force Academy in Colorado Springs, Colorado, where all service activities are kept separate from the focal points—the cadet facilities and their magnificent setting. He built homes for himself in the Big Sur region of California and the Hopi region of New Mexico, where he led fights against commercialization and introduced some of the first enlightened land-use codes in the country. In 1962 he was named chairman of the Commission on Pennsylvania Avenue in Washington, D.C. His most lasting achievement there was the design of a six-acre reflecting pool joining the Capitol and the Mall, where earlier a six-lane superhighway had been projected. He codified his decades of experience in two books, most notably *The American Aesthetic* (1969), a work that focuses on the fusion of architecture and ecology. He died of natural causes and was buried at his home, Festina Lente, in Santa Fe.

Owings is an anomaly among architects in that he left no specific monuments behind him. What he left was his organization, its belief that persistence in the details leads to beauty in performance, and his credo that the site and the situation must direct the architect.

★

Much of Owings's life story is analyzed in his professional autobiography *The Spaces in Between: An Architect's Journey* (1973). An obituary is in the *New York Times* (14 June 1984).

HARTLEY S. SPATT

P-Q

PADOVER, Saul Kussiel (*b.* 13 April 1905 in Vienna, Austria; *d.* 22 February 1981 in New York City), political scientist and educator who was a wartime intelligence officer and who wrote prolifically on America's founding fathers.

Saul Padover was the second child of Keva Padover, a U.S. citizen, and his Austrian wife, Fanny (Goldman) Padover. Shortly before Saul was born, his father returned to the United States, but his mother declined to accompany him. According to Padover, she was well educated and a "gentlewoman, a member of the local gentry" who believed that "only paupers and bankrupts went to America." Consequently, she took Saul and his older brother, Albert, to her father's farm in Bojanow, Austria, where they spent most of their childhood. The family was not reunited until 1920 when Fanny Padover and her sons left Europe to rejoin Keva in Detroit, Michigan, to escape the violence and anti-Semitism inflicted on them as residents of a Polish shtetl—Bojanow was shifted from Austrian to Polish control when the map of Europe was redrawn after World War I.

In Detroit, Padover attended Northeastern High School, from which he graduated in 1925. He then enrolled at Wayne State University, where he majored in history and English and developed an interest in journalism. A member of Phi Beta Kappa, he graduated cum laude from Wayne State in 1928. He attended Yale for one year of graduate work, after which he transferred to the University of Chicago; he remembered his time there as "some of the hap-

piest years of my life." Padover received his M.A. degree in 1930, having written his thesis on the Homestead strike. A university fellowship allowed him to remain at Chicago to pursue the Ph.D.; his dissertation was titled *Prince Kaunitz and the First Partition of Poland,* and he was awarded the doctorate in 1932. Also that year he published his first book, *Let the Day Perish,* a fictional but semiautobiographical account of how a Jewish mother living in Poland with her two sons eventually reached the United States.

While studying at Chicago, Padover was a research assistant at the university and taught history during summer sessions at West Virginia State University. He then accepted an appointment at the University of California, first as a research associate (1933–1936) and later as a lecturer in history (summer 1935). During the years 1936–1937 he held a Guggenheim Fellowship, which allowed him to continue his researches in Paris, London, and Vienna.

In 1938 Padover joined the staff of Secretary of the Interior Harold L. Ickes. He began as Ickes's confidential secretary, but by 1942 he was director of the Interior Department's Research Unit on Territorial Policy. Also while at Interior, he was appointed consultant to the Office of Facts and Figures.

Padover went to Great Britain in 1943 as the principal political analyst for the Federal Communications Commission. The Office of Strategic Services recruited him in 1944 as an intelligence officer attached to the Psychological Warfare Department of the First, Third, and Ninth Armies with the assimilated rank of lieutenant colonel. He landed in Normandy soon after D day and was thereafter in the midst of the fighting during the French and German campaigns. His principal duty in the Office of Strategic Services was interrogating German civilians to obtain military information, a task at which he excelled. For his wartime exploits, Padover earned a U.S. Army European Theater Ribbon with five battle stars. He also was awarded a Bronze Star citation for his interviewing work. President Harry Truman praised him for obtaining "at considerable risk" information that provided "interrogation reports of great value." The French government made him a chevalier of the Legion of Honor in 1947.

After World War II Padover began a new career as a journalist, serving as a foreign correspondent for the *Nation* and the *Toronto Star Weekly*. From 1946 to 1948 he wrote a signed column and served as an editorial writer and foreign correspondent for Marshall Field's New York newspaper, *PM*.

In 1948 Padover returned to academe, spending two years as a researcher and consultant at the Hoover Institution on War, Revolution, and Peace at Stanford University in Palo Alto, California. Simultaneously, he held an appointment as a lecturer at the New School for Social Research in New York City. In 1949 the Sorbonne appointed him visiting professor of American politics. After a year in France, Padover rejoined the New School's faculty as professor of history and politics. In 1950 he was named dean of that institution's School of Politics, a post he held until 1956. When he relinquished the deanship he remained on the New School's faculty but thereafter devoted himself to teaching and writing. John Everett, president of the New School, praised Padover as "one of the great intellectual leaders of the Graduate Faculty." During his tenure at the New School he also lectured at the Ethical Culture Society from 1949 to 1965 and at Quaker Seminars in Europe from 1949 to 1952. He served as research director for the Carnegie Endowment for International Peace from 1955 to 1956, and in 1973 Padover was a consultant to the Ervin Committee on the Presidency and to the Center for Democratic Institutions.

Padover was a prolific author and editor, publishing some forty books and innumerable articles in both popular and learned journals. His main subject was the nation's founders, especially Thomas Jefferson. He edited *Thomas Jefferson on Democracy* (1939), translated into a dozen languages, and wrote *Jefferson: A Biography* (1942), *Thomas Jefferson and the National Capitol* (1943), *A Jefferson Profile* (1956), and *Thomas Jefferson and the Foundations of American Freedom* (1965). His Jefferson studies were supplemented by volumes on George Washington (*The Washington Papers*, 1955), James Madison (*The Complete Madison*, 1953, and *James Madison: The Forging of American Federalism*,

Saul Padover. NEW SCHOOL FOR SOCIAL RESEARCH, OFFICE OF EXTERNAL AFFAIRS

1965), Alexander Hamilton (*The Mind of Alexander Hamilton*, 1958), and the founders as a group (*The World of the Founding Fathers*, 1960). He explained U.S. democracy to the French in *La Vie politique des États Unis* (1949) and French political life to Americans in *French Institutions, Values, and Politics* (1954). He also celebrated U.S. democracy in such books as *The Genius of America* (1960) and *The Meaning of Democracy* (1963). Surprisingly, perhaps, Karl Marx also captured his imagination, and he wrote or edited more than ten volumes on the father of scientific socialism. Unlike most academicians, Padover's writings were accessible to the general public; some 3 million copies of his books have been published in paperback.

Padover stood five feet, six inches tall and weighed about 155 pounds; his brown eyes sparkled below his dark head of hair. Padover's hobbies included chess and tennis. His first marriage to Irina Raben on 7 March 1942 ended with her death in May 1952. Margaret Thompson Fenwick, a screenwriter, became his second wife on 13 April 1957. Padover had no children. Padover died of a stroke in Lenox Hill Hospital in New York City. The nation lost a warm human being, an insightful scholar, and a dedicated teacher who enriched others' lives and the literature of his chosen fields.

★

There is no full-length biography of Padover but partial information sources about his life are *PM* (21 May 1946); *Current Biography* (1952); *New School for Social Research, News* (23 Feb. 1981); and Daniel Lerner, *Psychological Warfare Against Nazi Germany* (1949), a rich mine of information regarding Padover's war contributions. Padover's own *Experiment in Germany* covers the same material. An obituary is in the *New York Times* (24 Feb. 1981).

HAROLD L. WATTEL

PAIGE, Leroy Robert ("Satchel") (*b.* 7 July 1906 in Mobile, Alabama; *d.* 8 June 1982 in Kansas City, Missouri), one of the greatest pitchers in baseball history, who spent more than twenty years in the black baseball leagues and as a barnstormer; after the color barrier in baseball was broken in 1948, he played in the major leagues until 1953.

Paige grew up in an impoverished family in Mobile, Alabama, with ten brothers and sisters. His father was a gardener, and his mother did washing and ironing. At the age of seven, working as a baggage handler at the local railroad

Satchel Paige as a Kansas City Monarch. COURTESY OF THE NATIONAL BASEBALL HALL OF FAME LIBRARY, COOPERSTOWN, N.Y.

station, Paige earned small change and the nickname "Satchel," because he could handle so many bags at once using a sling harness he devised that his friends said he looked like a "satchel tree." He found little of interest attending the local school for black children and quickly found himself in bad company. When he was twelve years old, Paige was arrested for stealing toys, and the court sent him to the Industrial School for Negro Children at Mount Meigs, Alabama. He remained there for five years and learned to play baseball. He became a member of the school's team, starting out as a first baseman and then becoming a pitcher. A string bean at six feet, three inches and weighing only 140 pounds, Paige embarked on what was to be a stunning career.

Organized baseball being closed to blacks, in 1924 Paige joined the Mobile Tigers, a local black club on which one of his brothers also played. Almost immediately, he drew attention and became a crowd favorite as a "hot dog," affecting nonchalance with a studied slow gait as he stepped onto the pitcher's mound, then blasting the batters he faced with blinding fastballs. In time, batters would come to say that he could have the words "fast ball" painted on the sole of his left shoe, so that as he raised his foot high in his characteristic windup (he was a right-hander), the batter could know what was coming before he swung at the ball in vain. Periodically, Paige would call in his outfielders as if he did not need them and aim to strike out the side. He gradually developed a wondrous assortment of pitches, saying, "I got bloopers, loopers, and droopers. I got a jump ball, a be-ball, a screw ball, a wobbly ball, a whipsy-dipsy-do, a hurry-up ball, a nothin' ball and a bat dodger." His "be-ball," he explained, "is a be-ball 'cause it 'be' right where I want it, high and inside. It wiggles like a worm." On other occasions he called it a "bee-ball," because, he asserted, it hummed like a bee when it shot past the batters.

Determined to earn a living as a player, he joined the Chattanooga Black Lookouts in 1926 for $50 a month. Even though his pay was soon doubled, he was looking for greener pastures. With the Lookouts he learned the hesitation pitch, a delayed pitch in which the hurler strides forward and then holds back a second before throwing the ball. It became one of Paige's trademarks. Like many other black ballplayers scrambling to earn as much as possible for their talent, Paige jumped from team to team. Within a few years he had played with the Birmingham Black Barons, the Chicago American Giants, the Cleveland Cubs, and the Kansas City Monarchs. Seeking still more money, he fled to the Baltimore Black Sox. Regarding himself as a "traveling man," Paige also pitched countless games as a barnstormer wherever quality baseball was played in Latin America and the Caribbean. With the Pittsburgh Crawfords from 1931 to 1934, his battery mate was Josh Gibson, whose skill as a catcher was the stuff of legend. The heroics of both players were regularly reported in the African-American newspapers. Paige later said that the Crawfords owner put out advertising posters reading: "Josh Gibson and Satchel Paige, greatest battery in baseball—Josh Gibson guaranteed to hit two home runs and Satchel Paige guaranteed to strike out the first nine men." The team may have been the best in the history of black baseball, because, in addition to Paige and Gibson, it included three other future Baseball Hall of Famers—Cool Papa Bell, Judy Johnson, and Oscar Charleston. Paige was the publicity magnet, to the considerable resentment of his fellow stars. He was considered a lone wolf, ever on the lookout for betterment of his situation, and although widely admired among his peers, he was not beloved and had few close friends.

Paige, who could drink heavily, had many liaisons on his baseball odyssey, but on 26 October 1934 he married Janet Howard, a nineteen-year-old waitress working in a restaurant whose proprietor was the owner of the Crawfords. Paige, however, could not settle down and shortly the marriage foundered. In 1939 he became a member of the Kansas City Monarchs once again, and from then until 1942, the Monarchs—largely owing to Paige's superb pitching—won the championship of the Negro American League each year. In the 1942 Negro World Series, Paige was the winning pitcher in the final game against the Negro National League champions, the Homestead Grays. By now, however, Paige had passed his peak as a player, possibly suffering from burnout. No one could say how many games he had pitched. By some accounts, he had played in as many as 2,500 games, at least 10 percent of them shutouts, and had hurled forty-five no-hitters.

Paige had a disarming way of looking and sounding diffident while allowing his collielike eyes to droop, offering a thoughtful aphorism, like one for which he was renowned: "Don't look back. Something might be gainin' on you." For all his outward gaiety and nonchalance, Paige was deeply offended by the color line that kept him from playing in the major leagues. He resented the fact that only because of the color of his skin were his best years spent playing in ill-lit ballparks and on poorly tended grass, riding on beat-up buses all night before checking into fleabag hotels. Sometimes, when no lodging was available for blacks, the players had to make do by turning their autos into bedrooms. In the 1930s Paige could occasionally be seen fast asleep in his red roadster parked near the ballpark where he would pitch a few hours later.

Paige felt he belonged in the majors because he had pitched winning ball against many white professional players and had universally earned their esteem. When Joe DiMaggio, for example, was still a minor leaguer, he got a hit off Paige, and declared with satisfaction, "I know I can make the Yankees now." Thousands of white fans looked forward to the exhibition games between black all-stars and white all-stars, and Paige was a leading drawing card. Dizzy Dean, himself a showboat pitcher not noted for modesty, said after the first time he saw Paige pitch that he was the best he had ever watched. He could have added that few pitchers could bunt as well as Paige.

Paige was as profligate with money as with his talent. On 12 October 1947 he married Lahoma Brown, a long-time friend, in Hays, Kansas. She brought a measure of stability to Paige's life, and they settled into a handsome house in Kansas City, Missouri. They had one child. In 1947 Branch Rickey, the president and general manager of the Brooklyn Dodgers, signed Jackie Robinson to a contract, making him the first black ballplayer admitted into the major leagues. Paige, delighted at Robinson's good fortune, was nevertheless disappointed. He had hoped to be the first black man on a big league team: "It was my right," he wrote in his autobiography. It gave him much satisfaction the following year, however, when Bill Veeck, the owner of the American League's Cleveland Indians and an imaginative baseball promoter, signed Paige to a contract, making him the first black pitcher in the league. Many fans believed at first that this was just another of Veeck's stunts to help build attendance at Cleveland games, because Paige was then forty-two years old and would be the oldest rookie in the history of the game. "Myself, I never thought I'd make the majors," Paige later reflected. "I dreamed about it, of course, but I didn't figure it to happen." He won six games in his first season, losing only one—and that on an unearned run. The Indians won the World Series, and Paige pitched one inning. It was a high point of his life, to be cheered by the 87,000 fans who filled Municipal Stadium when he took his turn on the mound.

Paige played one more season for the Indians, and then he was dropped from the roster. He had become a burden to the team, absenting himself from games and missing trains. Plainly, he could not break his old nomadic habits, but Veeck continued to have faith in his "bad boy." When Veeck acquired the Saint Louis Browns in 1951, he signed Paige once again. Paige stayed for three seasons, finally retiring in 1953. He had accumulated twenty-eight major league wins. In the next few years, he played some minor league ball and did some barnstorming. He made many public appearances before worshipful audiences, for his humorous sallies and aphorisms were in the tradition of Yogi Berra and Will Rogers. In 1965, when Paige was almost sixty years old, he made a final big league appearance for the Kansas City Athletics, pitching three scoreless innings against the Boston Red Sox. It was clearly a publicity performance engineered by Charlie Finley, the eccentric owner of the A's, but it made Paige the oldest player ever to play in the major leagues.

In 1968 Paige was persuaded to run for a seat in the

Missouri state legislature, but he had no enthusiasm for the race. He was out of his element and lost. By then an ailing man, suffering from heart disease and emphysema, he was also broke. The president of the Atlanta Braves, William C. Bartholomay, in an act of appreciation and philanthropy, signed Paige as consultant and possible part-time pitcher. He pitched only a couple of innings near the end of the playing schedule. The Braves carried Paige on their roster into the 1969 season so that he could accrue a sufficient number of days to qualify for a major league pension.

When baseball finally celebrated Paige formally by electing him to the Baseball Hall of Fame in Cooperstown, New York, he was the first black so honored. He was soon joined by other black "greats" who had once been barred from playing in the big leagues, all their plaques placed in a separate section of the building—seemingly the victims of segregation still. Nevertheless, Paige said generously, "I don't feel segregated." Other accolades followed. In 1979 he was installed in the Missouri Sports Hall of Fame. He attended the ceremony in a wheelchair, his infirmities growing worse. On 5 June 1982, Kansas City dedicated its youth baseball field to him, naming it in his honor. Three days later, he died of a heart attack at his Kansas City home. He is buried in Forest Hills Cemetery in Kansas City.

Paige belongs in the select company of outstanding black American athletes of the twentieth century who were champions in the time of Jim Crow. Paige's exclusion from major league baseball because of his color was a personal tragedy as well as a loss to the nation and remains an indelible reminder of an unfortunate era in the country's history.

★

Norman L. Macht, *Satchel Paige* (1991), is the fullest, in-depth biography. John Holway, *Josh and Satch: The Life and Times of Josh Gibson and Satchel Paige* (1992), is a sentimental recounting of these intertwined careers. Kathryn L. Humphrey, *Satchel Paige* (1988), is a measured retelling of his story. David Shirley, *Satchel Paige* (1993), is another affectionate evocation of this interesting life. Hal Lebovitz, *Pitchin' Man: Satchel Paige's Own Story* (1948 and 1992), has the virtues and shortcomings of an as-told-to autobiography. David Lipman, *Maybe I'll Pitch Forever: A Great Baseball Player Tells the Hilarious Story Behind the Legend* (1962 and 1993), another ghost-written book, contains in an afterword to the revised edition a judicious evaluation of Paige. Mark Ribowsky, *Don't Look Back: Satchel Paige in the Shadows of Baseball* (1994), admirably places its man in the context of his times. Robert Rubin, *Satchel Paige: All-Time Baseball Great* (1974), is contemporaneous hagiography. Mike Shannon, *The Day Satchel Paige and the Pittsburgh Crawfords Came to Hertford, N.C.* (1992), recaptures some of the excitement and glory of all-black baseball. Patricia and Frederick McKissick, *Satchel Paige: The Best Arm in Baseball* (1992), and Lesa Ransome, *Satchel Paige* (1998), are children's books.

Obituaries are in the *New York Times* (9 June 1982), *Ebony* 37 (spring 1982), and *Sports Illustrated* 56 (21 June 1982).

HENRY F. GRAFF

PARSONS, Elizabeth Pierson ("Betty") (*b*. 31 January 1900 in New York City; *d*. 23 July 1982 in Southold, New York), art dealer and artist whose pioneering gallery played a major role in the development of the New York School of painting in the late 1940s and early 1950s.

Betty was the second of three daughters born to J. Fred Pierson, Jr., a businessman, and Suzanne Miles. Both her parents came from socially prominent families. In 1910 Betty was enrolled in Miss Chapin's School in Manhattan. A wayward, rebellious adolescent, Parsons traced the beginning of her passionate interest in art to the famous New York Armory Show of 1913, where she viewed works by Matisse, Picasso, Duchamp, and other artists of the European avant garde. Academically an undistinguished student, she completed her formal schooling in 1915. Fearing a college education would make her unmarriageable, Betty's parents refused to let her attend Bryn Mawr College in suburban Philadelphia. As a compromise she agreed to

Betty Parsons with items in her collection, 1979. UPI/CORBIS-BETTMANN

attend Mrs. Randall MacKeever's Finishing School, in New York City, if she could study with the sculptor Gutzon Borglum. On 8 May 1920 she married the New York socialite Schuyler Livingston Parsons. The marriage ended in divorce in 1923; there were no children.

Parsons spent the next eleven years in Paris, where she met many American expatriate artists and writers, including Gertrude Stein, Alexander Calder, Hart Crane, and Man Ray. She studied art at Bourdelle's Académie de la Grande Chaumière, where she met Constantin Brancusi and Alberto Giacometti. Parsons had been aware since adolescence of her sexual preference for women. Her most important relationship of this period was with Adge Baker, a woman whose deep interest in mysticism and spiritualism strengthened Parsons's own belief in the intuitive over the purely technical aspects of art.

The Great Depression, which caused Parsons considerable financial hardship, forced her to return to the United States in 1933. For most of her life she would rely on the generosity of a group of close women friends (whom she nicknamed "the Katinkas") for financial and emotional support. Encouraged by friends to pursue a career as a portraitist and art teacher, Parsons moved to Los Angeles in 1933, where she became a part of a sophisticated social circle that included Greta Garbo, Robert Benchley, and Dorothy Parker. In December 1933 Parsons showed watercolors and sculptures at her first professional exhibition, held at the Galerie des Quatre Chemins in Paris. Parsons failed to make a career as a portrait painter and returned to New York in 1935. She had her first New York exhibition in 1936 at the Midtown Gallery.

Parsons's career as a dealer began when she was hired by the Midtown Gallery to install and sell paintings. In 1937 she worked at a gallery owned by Mrs. Cornelius J. Sullivan, one of the founders of the Museum of Modern Art. In 1940 Parsons left Mrs. Sullivan to manage the gallery in the Wakefield Bookshop. She became friendly with some of the more notable artists who showed there: Saul Steinberg, Theodoros Stamos, Adolph Gottlieb, and Joseph Cornell. She represented these artists when she opened her own gallery several years later. In 1944 she fell in love with Strelsa von Scriver, with whom she had a relationship that lasted almost a decade. After the Wakefield Gallery closed in 1944, Parsons became the director of the modern division of the Mortimer Brandt Gallery, which specialized in Old Masters. With $4,500 of borrowed money and $1,000 of her own, Parsons opened her own gallery at 15 East Fifty-seventh Street in September 1946. The austere space of the new Betty Parsons Gallery reflected her innovative credo: "A gallery isn't a place to rest. It's a place to look at art. You don't come to my gallery to be comfortable." Her first exhibition was a show of Northwest Coast Indian art, for which Barnett Newman wrote the catalog. When Peggy

Guggenheim's famous gallery, Art of This Century, closed, her stable of artists—Barnett Newman, Jackson Pollock, Mark Rothko, and Clyfford Still—moved to the Parsons Gallery, which became the leading venue for abstract expressionist work. Over the next several years she showed work by Ad Reinhardt, Rothko, Hans Hoffmann, and Walter Murch. Hungry for more fame and money, Pollock, Rothko and the other "giants" left Parsons in 1951 to join the Sidney Janis Gallery. The artists who remained with Parsons (Stamos, Richard Pousette-Dart, Murch, Reinhardt, and Steinberg) while accomplished, lacked the stellar quality of the first generation of abstract expressionists. By 1954 Parsons began adding a wide variety of artists to her gallery, to the detriment, some felt, of its focus. In response to this criticism she stated that her gallery "dealt in the new, in abstraction, and in the spiritual aspects of art."

A woman of great energy, Parsons continued her own painting, finding the time to work during the summer when the gallery was closed. Throughout her life she thought of herself as an artist first and a dealer second.

During the 1950s she exhibited the work of Ellsworth Kelly, Richard Lindner, and Jack Youngerman. At a time when few women were represented by galleries, she showed work by Agnes Martin, Anne Ryan, and Hedda Sterne. In 1958 she opened a subsidiary space, Section 11 Gallery, on East Fifty-seventh Street; it closed after four years. In 1962 Parsons argued with Sidney Janis over gallery space. After losing a lawsuit against him in 1963, she was forced to give up her East Fifty-seventh Street gallery. She considered leaving the business, but with the encouragement of friends, she opened another space on West Fifty-seventh Street and took on new artists. In 1968 Finch College showed Parsons's personal collection of the paintings of other artists. Her own work was exhibited at Bennington College, Vermont, also in 1968, and that same year an exhibition of her work at the Whitechapel Gallery in London brought her acclaim as an artist and a dealer. In an interview in 1971 Parsons stated, "As a dealer, I have never been interested in trends, fashions or styles. I realize that I have always used my intuition rather than my judgment."

During the 1970s she showed the work of Paul Feeley, Cleve Gray, and Richard Tuttle. She received honorary degrees from Mount Holyoke College and Southampton College and awards from the Rhode Island School of Design, the National Arts Club, and the Parsons School of Design. In 1974 the Montclair (New Jersey) Art Museum held a retrospective exhibition of her work. During her last years Parsons continued to run her gallery and work as an artist (an exhibit of her painted driftwood sculpture was held at Kornblee/Truman Galleries in 1977). She died of a stroke in her home at Southold, on Long Island.

Parsons had a slim, boyish figure. In photos of her, even casual snapshots, she always appeared elegant and stylish.

At a time when there was little interest or prestige in exhibiting contemporary American painting, Betty Parsons tirelessly promoted the work of some of the greatest names in twentieth-century American art. Her taste and vision became synonymous with some of the best painting New York had to offer during the postwar years.

★

Lee Hall, *Betty Parsons: Artist, Dealer, Collector* (1981), is a detailed study of Parsons's life and work; Montclair Art Museum, *Betty Parsons Retrospective: An Exhibition of Paintings and Sculpture* (1974), is an exhibition catalog of her work, while the catalog Finch College, Museum of Art, *Betty Parsons' Private Collection* (1968), is devoted to Parsons as art collector; Lawrence Alloway, "Diary of an Art Dealer," *Vogue* (Oct. 1963), is an excerpt from a book on Parsons that was never published; Grace Lichtenstein, "Betty Parsons: Still Trying to Find the Creative World in Everything," *Art News* (Mar. 1979), profiles Parsons as dealer and artist; Ann Gibson, "Lesbian Identity and the Politics of Representation in Betty Parsons' Gallery. Part of a Symposium on Gay and Lesbian Studies in Art History," *Journal of Homosexuality* 27, nos. 1–2 (1994): 245–270, is an academic study; a tribute by John Russell, "Betty Parsons: An Artist Both in Life and Art," appears in the *New York Times* (15 Aug. 1982), as does an obituary (24 July 1982).

CHRISTINE STENSTROM

PARSONS, Johnnie (*b.* 1918; *d.* 8 September 1984 in Van Nuys, California), race-car driver, best known for his victory in the 1950 Indianapolis 500.

At the age of four Johnnie Parsons joined his parents' song-and-dance act. As Parsons and Parsons, his mother and father were a familiar fixture on the vaudeville circuits of Kentucky and Missouri. Young Johnnie performed sporting a top hat, tails, and a cane and developed a comic timing and an ease with the spotlight that later helped make him one of auto racing's most popular figures.

Parsons began his racing career on the sprint and midget car circuits of southern California in the late 1930s. Midget cars were actually full-sized racing vehicles, usually powered by four-cylinder engines and featured at a wide variety of racing venues, from one-tenth-mile tracks at indoor hockey rinks to mile-long ovals. Sprint cars were slightly larger than midgets and more powerful; featuring an exceptionally high power-to-weight ratio, they were generally considered the most dangerous racing cars ever devised.

Working from his home base in Van Nuys, Parsons successfully raced midget and sprint cars at such venues as Ascot Park in south central Los Angeles and Balboa Stadium in San Diego. In the years after World War II he also raced at Playland Park in Houston, where he competed against legendary drivers A. J. Foyt, Lloyd Ruby, and Rodger Ward. In the 1940s leading sprint car drivers were

Race-car driver Johnnie Parsons, 1951. UPI/CORBIS-BETTMANN

regularly hired by owners of cars designed to compete in the Indianapolis 500, the most prestigious and lucrative automobile race in the United States. Parsons was an especially strong candidate for graduation to the Indy car circuit; he not only had won numerous races against the best midget and sprint car drivers but had also greatly enhanced the image of race-car drivers. Parsons was one of the first drivers to routinely wear a uniform while competing rather than the usual T-shirt, and his attractive, gregarious personality made him a favorite among fans, journalists, and race promoters. "Guys like Sam Hanks, Duane Carter, Bob Sweikert, and myself wanted to upgrade auto racing," Parsons told a reporter in 1984. "I tried to buy the best clothes, stay in the best places and present a good image. It has come around to that today and I knew it would eventually."

Parsons made his Indianapolis 500 debut in 1949, in a rear-drive machine with a streamlined chassis built by Frank Kurtis, the leading designer of midget cars. Parsons closed strongly in the later stages of the race to finish second to Bill Holland. He went on to win the Automobile Club of America National Driving Championship for that year. Moments before the start of the 1950 Indy 500, Parsons discovered a tiny crack in the cylinder block of his Kurtis-

Kraft machine. He decided to race all-out from the opening lap, reasoning that because his car might break down at any time, he could at least earn lap prize money while hoping that the engine might endure for the entire race. Under threatening skies, Parsons immediately went into the lead, where he remained when a thunderstorm erupted at the 345-mile mark of the race. Parsons, who led challenger Holland by thirty-eight seconds, was declared the winner. Following the race, a wire service reporter asked Parsons if he now planned to retire from Indy car competition. "Are you kidding?" Parsons replied. "I just got here."

Parsons competed in eight more runnings of the Indianapolis 500, finishing fourth in 1956 and twelfth in his final appearance in 1958. In all he won eleven national championship races, placing him sixteenth on the all-time list. It was his Indy 500 triumph, however, that solidified his great popularity, which extended well beyond automobile racing circles. Always comfortable around celebrities and entertainers, Parsons earned a speaking part in the MGM film *To Please a Lady* (1950), parts of which were shot on location at the Indianapolis Motor Speedway in the weeks prior to the running of the 1950 race. Parsons became a goodwill ambassador for his sport, whether promoting midget races, driving the Indianapolis 500 pace car, or encouraging younger drivers.

Parsons's son, Johnny Parsons, Jr., became a professional driver, as did his grandson, Johnny Parsons III. In 1983 Parsons underwent quintuple heart bypass surgery. "They replaced five oil lines, rechecked the timing, and sewed me up," Parsons joked at the time. "I ought to be good for at least another 100,000 miles." He suffered a fatal heart attack the following year.

Johnnie Parsons was an important transitional figure in the history of American automobile racing. He took advantage of a winning personality in order to promote greater public recognition of his sport and respect for its drivers. The enormous increase in racing purse money since the 1950s and the great acclaim enjoyed by leading drivers may be attributed in large part to the pioneering efforts of Parsons and his compatriots.

★

Al Bloemker, *500 Miles to Go: The Story of the Indianapolis Speedway* (1961), and Bill Libby, *Champions of the Indianapolis 500* (1976), are useful. Stories in the *Los Angeles Times* (16 Mar. 1993) and *Indianapolis Star* (10 May 1996) provide information on different facets of Parsons's career. An obituary is in the *New York Times* (9 Sept. 1984).

JAMES T. FISHER

PATRIARCA, Raymond (*b.* 17 March 1908 in Worcester, Massachusetts; *d.* 11 July 1984 in Providence, Rhode Island), organized crime figure and head of the New England Cosa Nostra family for more than forty years.

The only child of Italian immigrants, Patriarca lived in Providence, Rhode Island, all his adult life, except when serving prison terms outside Rhode Island, but exercised influence over criminal activities throughout New England and played a role in Mafia activities across the United States. He left school at the age of eight to work as a shoeshine boy and bellhop but eventually found armed robbery and alcohol smuggling during Prohibition far more lucrative than menial labor. By the 1930s the Providence Board of Public Safety referred to Patriarca as public enemy number one and ordered the police to arrest him on sight. By 1938 he had apparently cultivated important political connections. Convicted of armed robbery in Massachusetts, Patriarca served less than six months of a long prison sentence before being pardoned by Governor Charles F. Hurley.

Just before America's entry into World War II, Patriarca consolidated his power and brought together numerous gangs engaged in gambling operations. In 1957 Robert F. Kennedy, then counsel for the U.S. Senate committee investigating mob infiltration and corruption within the Teamsters Union, questioned Patriarca aggressively about his jukebox business, which was suspected of being connected to the Teamsters and their underworld cronies. Patriarca falsely but coolly claimed that the capital required to launch that business came from his mother's inheritance.

Patriarca was influential in settling disputes between Cosa Nostra members and families and between criminal organizations outside the Mafia. In 1961 a war erupted in Boston between two Irish-American gangs—the McCleans and the McLaughlins. Patriarca intervened and brokered a peace treaty, and when the truce broke down, he "declared war" on the McLaughlins, a move that brought the conflict to a swift end. In 1963 he was also instrumental in bringing the Gallo-Profaci Mafia war in New York to a satisfactory conclusion. He intervened again in 1964 as an agent for the Cosa Nostra in the settlement of the Bonanno crime family dissolution after the family boss, Joseph Bonanno, had threatened the lives of two other Mafia leaders. A year earlier, Joseph Valachi, a Mafia turncoat, testified before the Senate subcommittee on labor racketeering and explained the national structure of the Cosa Nostra and how Patriarca rose to power in the American underworld.

Patriarca himself again testified before congressional committee members, who questioned him about the veracity of *The Godfather,* Mario Puzo's 1969 best-selling novel. Patriarca said that he thought it was a good book but "nothing but a lot of fiction." Turning the tables on the committee, he brazenly averred that the public's interest in the underworld should be laid at the doorstep of the government, which publicized and glamorized organized crime.

More notoriety surrounded New England's "godfather" in 1972. While serving a prison term for conspiracy to murder another mob member, Patriarca was subpoenaed by the

Raymond Patriarca, 1973. UPI/Corbis-Bettmann

House Select Committee on Crime to testify about alleged investments made by Frank Sinatra in a criminally suspect racetrack in Hanover, Massachusetts. He denied any knowledge of the track and its owners and claimed that he had never met Sinatra.

In the last part of his life, when his power and notoriety were at their height, Patriarca insisted that he was a legitimate businessman. He operated his vending machine business, the National Cigarette Service, from a location in the Little Italy section of Providence. The area around his headquarters was an armed camp that was impossible to move through without being spotted. Patriarca's reputation was such that no upstart gangster would venture to challenge him on his own turf. Although he never admitted to being a member of the Mafia, FBI wiretaps revealed his important role in the high councils of the Cosa Nostra. In 1981 he was indicted by a federal grand jury in Miami, Florida, on charges of labor racketeering. Federal and local law enforcement officials suspected Patriarca of loansharking, operating illegal numbers operations, trafficking in marijuana and cocaine, and smuggling illegal immigrants into the United States. At the time, Patriarca bitterly and accurately observed that government harassment would follow him to the grave. Three years later he died of natural causes; his son, Raymond Patriarca, Jr., became boss of the Cosa Nostra family (information about Patriarca's marriage is unavailable).

In the course of a criminal career that stretched across a half-century, Patriarca was arrested more than thirty times and served several prison sentences on charges ranging from bootlegging in the 1920s to conspiracy to commit murder in the late 1960s. Even while in prison, the New England crime boss maintained a firm grip on his organization. He continued to direct his criminal enterprises so effectively that his time away from "the office" was scarcely noticed. His businesses were a web of legal and illegal activities that he shrewdly mixed in order to confuse and deter law enforcement investigations.

★

Vincent Charles Teresa with Thomas C. Renner, *My Life in the Mafia* (1973), is a personal account of a Patriarca associate; Gerard O'Neil and Dick Lehr, *The Underboss: The Rise and Fall of a Mafia Family* (1989), describes a money-laundering operation conducted on behalf of Patriarca by his underboss using the city of Boston's oldest and largest bank. Additional material on organized crime in New England can be found in Stephen R. Fox, *Blood and Power: Organized Crime in Twentieth-Century America* (1989).

Robert J. Kelly

PAULEY, Edwin Wendell (*b.* 7 January 1903 in Indianapolis, Indiana; *d.* 28 July 1981 in Beverly Hills, California), oil producer and civic leader best known for his service in the Roosevelt and Truman administrations.

One of two sons born to Elbert L. Pauley, an executive of Standard Oil of Kentucky, and Ellen Eliza Van Petten, Edwin Pauley grew up in Birmingham, Alabama. He graduated from secondary school at Georgia Military Academy in 1918 and moved with his family to Pasadena, California, in 1919. Pauley attended Occidental College for one year,

Edwin Pauley. UPI/CORBIS-BETTMANN

then transferred to the University of California at Berkeley, where he won athletic letters in football and rowing. He received his B.S. degree in 1922 and his M.S. in 1923. After teaching economics briefly at the University of California, Pauley went to work for his father's business, Pauley Oil Company. On 10 June 1924 he married Norma Rae Barrett. They had one son.

After his father sold Pauley Oil, Edwin formed his own company, the Petrol Corporation, in 1928, and quickly rose to prominence as a spokesperson for the independent oil companies. In 1931, when the California legislature passed an oil conservation law, favored by the major firms but opposed by the independents, Pauley assumed a leading role in promoting a referendum through which the state's voters repealed the controversial statute.

On 3 October 1937 Pauley married Barbara Jean Mc-Henry. They had three children. Petrol Corporation prospered under Pauley's management despite the Great Depression, and Pauley diversified his business interests into land development and banking while escalating his political involvement. He served as president of California's Independent Petroleum Association from 1934 to 1938 and took an active role in Franklin D. Roosevelt's presidential reelection campaigns of 1936 and 1940, primarily as a fundraiser. He was named secretary (1941) and treasurer (1942) of the Democratic National Committee and quickly acquired renown within the party by wiping out a $750,000 deficit. A gregarious man with an athletic six-foot, three-

inch frame, Pauley was described as energetic, a ready talker, and a man who got along easily with people.

President Roosevelt brought Pauley into government as a dollar-a-year executive and assigned him responsibility for coordinating World War II oil supplies for beleaguered Great Britain and the Soviet Union. With Harold Ickes, Pauley also organized the Petroleum Administration for War, which managed U.S. oil supplies. The astute Pauley was accorded a place in Roosevelt's informal circle of advisers, where he was viewed as a spokesperson for the business interests whose contributions funded the Democratic party and Roosevelt's campaigns.

Pauley's role was especially prominent in the selection of a Democratic vice-presidential candidate in 1944. People close to Roosevelt doubted that he would live to complete a fourth term, and liberal vice president Henry Wallace was anathema to businesspeople and Southern Democrats. Pauley led the successful effort to supplant Wallace with Senator Harry S. Truman of Missouri.

After Truman assumed the presidency upon the death of Roosevelt on 12 April 1945, he engendered controversy by appointing Pauley to be the U.S. representative on the Allied Commission on Reparations, with the rank of ambassador and replacing Isador Lubin, a government statistician and favorite of the New Deal holdovers, who had been appointed to the post only six weeks earlier. Truman explained that he wanted a "tough negotiator" who would resist Soviet demands to strip Germany of its economic assets. The president subsequently sent Pauley on two missions to Asia—to Japan in November 1945 and to Korea and Manchuria in May and June 1946—as his chief adviser on war reparations.

Pauley was frequently mentioned in the press as a potential member of the president's cabinet, and when Truman nominated him to be undersecretary of the navy in January 1946, initial speculation focused on the likelihood that he would succeed Secretary of the Navy James Forrestal, who was expected to retire soon. Instead the Pauley nomination initiated a confirmation battle that split the administration and crippled Pauley as a Washington insider. Truman knew that the nomination would be controversial. Because of the significance of oil reserves to the fuel-intensive navy, having a leader of the petroleum industry in a policy-making position was thought by many to present an inherent conflict of interest. Secretary of Commerce Harold Ickes ignited a firestorm during Senate confirmation hearings when he declared under oath that Pauley had offered to raise about $300,000 from California oil interests for the 1944 presidential campaign if the federal government would discontinue its efforts to assert control over the state's offshore oil fields. The rift resulted in Ickes's resignation from the Truman cabinet, but Pauley had been irreparably damaged. Although Ickes's charges were never proven, after several weeks of delay Pauley agreed to have the nomination withdrawn.

Another charge of unethical conduct was leveled against Pauley in 1947, while he was serving as a special assistant to the secretary of the army. Harold Stassen, a Republican presidential hopeful, accused him of profiteering in food commodities. Pauley admitted to speculation but denied that he had used inside information available to him as a member of the government. Although he remained in Washington until 1948 as an adviser to the secretary of state on reparations, he could no longer exercise as powerful an influence in national government.

Pauley remained a major force in California, however. As a successful entrepreneur, most notably as president of Pauley Petroleum, Inc., which he formed in 1958 after selling the Petrol Corporation to his old adversary Standard Oil, Pauley generated impressive wealth. As a member of the board of regents of the University of California from 1939 to 1972, he influenced the university's policies during the years of its most intense growth and its most explosive controversies, including the student rebellions of the 1960s. In the early 1960s the *Los Angeles Times* observed that Pauley seemed to have more influence than the university president. While he vehemently opposed student demands for power, he made notable financial contributions to the university system, including million-dollar gifts toward the student union at Berkeley and the sports arena at Los Angeles, named the Edwin W. Pauley Pavilion. He led many civic drives and contributed to the Great Pauley Hall in the Art Museum at Los Angeles. He was a major influence in Democratic party politics in California, and in 1960 he was responsible for bringing the Democratic National Convention to Los Angeles.

A sportsman for most of his life, Pauley engaged in sailing, tennis, and other sports. In 1939 he won the Trans-Pacific Yacht Race from San Francisco to Honolulu. For several years he was co-owner of the Los Angeles Rams professional football team.

Pauley's health was poor, however, during the last decade of his life. He resigned from the University of California Board of Regents after three decades of service in 1972, in the second year of a sixteen-year term. He died at his Beverly Hills home after a lengthy illness and was buried in Forest Lawn Memorial Park, Glendale, California.

A self-made multimillionaire, Pauley devoted much of his talent, energy, and wealth to his city, state, and nation. As a member of Roosevelt's circle of advisers, he brought the perspectives of businesspeople into the councils of an administration sometimes hostile to business. Questions of ethics aborted his rise in national politics, but his return to California placed him in the midst of important developments such as the student movement of the 1960s. As a conservative Democrat in an era of liberal ascendancy, Pau-

ley viewed himself as a bulwark against unwelcome change, especially in his role as a policymaker for one of the nation's most significant public universities.

★

Pauley's diplomatic service to the Truman administration is analyzed in two master's theses: Philip A. Wright, "Edwin W. Pauley: A Profile in Politics and the Cold War, 1944–1946" (San Jose State University, 1974), and Martha Walker Samoza, "The Pauley Mission: A Study of German Reparations After World War II" (Northeast Louisiana University, 1978). Felix A. Nigro, "The Pauley Case," *Southwestern Social Science Quarterly* 41 (Mar. 1960): 341–349, chronicles the imbroglio over Pauley's appointment as undersecretary of the navy. Although Pauley never spoke publicly about his government service, interviews with prominent figures in the Roosevelt and Truman administrations in the Oral History Collection of Columbia University shed light on his role in national government. Interviews in the State Government Oral History Program of the University of California, Los Angeles, highlight his service as a regent of the University of California. Obituaries are in the *New York Times* and the *Los Angeles Times* (both 29 July 1981).

VAGN K. HANSEN

PECKINPAH, David Samuel ("Sam") (*b.* 21 February 1925 in Fresno, California; *d.* 28 December 1984 in Inglewood, California), film director best known for his revisionist, elegiac Westerns, by turns realistic and romantic, violent and lyrical, that depict the Old West in transition.

Peckinpah was born into a family of pioneers and entrepreneurs who settled in northern California after crossing the Great Plains in 1853–1854. His father, David Edward Peckinpah, a ranch foreman, married Fern Louise Church and became an attorney and eventually a superior court judge. The couple had another son and adopted two daughters. Peckinpah's childhood was unremarkable in most respects. The two salient influences upon his development as both a man and an artist were his Western ancestry and the combination of his mother's overweening protectiveness, his father's strict authoritarianism, and their troubled marriage. "I grew up sitting around a dining room table talking about law and order, truth and justice, on a Bible which was very big in our family," Peckinpah once said, "and I started to question them."

After graduating from military school in 1943, Peckinpah enlisted in the Marine Corps and did a tour of duty in China. Upon his return home in 1946, he enrolled as a history major at Fresno State University, where he met the actress Marie Selland. Within the year he changed his major to theater arts and married Marie.

In 1948 the couple moved to Los Angeles to attend graduate school at the University of Southern California.

The next year the first of their four children was born. Remembered by his academic adviser as "one of these fellows who has a burning desire to go into the theatre," with "a feeling for directing that few students have," Peckinpah spent the next five years alternating between course work and directing professional and semiprofessional theater.

After obtaining a masters degree in 1954 he became an assistant to the director Don Siegel, working on *Riot in Cell Block Eleven* (1954) and *Invasion of the Body Snatchers* (1956). Siegel recommended him as a writer for the television series *Gunsmoke,* and Peckinpah was soon in demand on other Western series. His first directing break came in 1958 on the series *Broken Arrow.* That same year he sold a script that became the pilot for *The Rifleman.* The next year he created another series, *The Westerner.* Its realistic, often dark portrait of a cowboy-drifter made Peckinpah a cult figure.

In 1961 he directed his first feature film, *The Deadly Companions.* Peckinpah believed the script needed rewriting but the producer forbade changes, and thus began a pattern of arguments with producers and executives that plagued the director his entire career. With his next film, *Ride the High Country* (1962), Peckinpah staked his claim to what would be a recurring theme in his films, of aging men of action living beyond their time in search of justification and redemption; the picture brought him international recognition when it won several prestigious awards, including best picture at the Belgium Film Festival.

Peckinpah's first attempt at epic filmmaking, the ambitious *Major Dundee* (1965) for Metro-Goldwyn-Mayer (MGM), resulted in a stark, gritty portrayal of horse soldiers on a punitive expedition into Mexico during the American Civil War; but the infighting between the director and the producer led to a studio recut that rendered the last third of the picture all but incoherent. Peckinpah again clashed with the producer of his next project, *The Cincinnati Kid* (1965), for Columbia. The director was fired after just four days of shooting. This together with his troubles at MGM led to his being blacklisted at every studio in Hollywood.

Peckinpah's personal life proved as turbulent as his professional life. He and Marie were divorced in 1962. In June 1964 he married the Mexican actress Begonia Palacios, with whom he had the most tempestuous relationship of his four wives (the couple were married and divorced twice). His drinking, a problem since his teenage years, was exacerbated by depression over being prevented from directing. The clouds lifted in 1966, when the producer Daniel Melnick took a chance and hired Peckinpah to write and direct what became a highly acclaimed adaptation of Katherine Anne Porter's *Noon Wine* for ABC television's *Stage 67* anthology series. "Suddenly," Peckinpah recalled, "I was back in business again."

In 1969 he returned to the big screen with *The Wild*

Sam Peckinpah in Mexico on the set of *The Wild Bunch,* 1968. COURTESY OF PAUL SEYDOR

Bunch, a visionary epic that became a landmark film, although it opened to enormous controversy owing to its unprecedented violence and the director's refusal to resolve his conflicted attitudes, at once exultant and horrified, toward that violence. But it was also a piercing character study—of American outlaws embroiled in the Mexican revolution of 1913—that allowed Peckinpah to give his ambiguous romantic realism its richest, most complex expression. *Sight and Sound* called it "a masterpiece of world cinema," a judgment that has stood the test of time.

The Wild Bunch initiated Peckinpah's most productive period. Between 1969 and 1978 he made a string of films—*The Ballad of Cable Hogue* (1970), *Straw Dogs* (1971), *The Getaway* (1972), *Junior Bonner* (1972), *Pat Garrett and Billy the Kid* (1973), *Bring Me the Head of Alfredo Garcia* (1974), *The Killer Elite* (1975), *Cross of Iron* (1977), and *Convoy* (1978)—that are marked by a prodigious thematic density, a bracing lyricism, a volatile preoccupation with violence, and an anguished, impassioned commitment to characters who are outcasts, loners, and misfits.

These years also bore witness to his worsening health, owing to his alcoholism and drug use (mostly cocaine); in 1979 a heart attack necessitated a pacemaker. His personal life was in greater turmoil than ever. In 1972 he married Joie Gould and was divorced six months later; in 1973 he and Begonia conceived a child but they were unmarried at the time; in 1980 he married his fourth wife, Marcy Blueher, and was divorced in a month. His only feature since 1978 was the disappointing *Osterman Weekend* in 1983. A year later, following a night of multiple heart attacks, he was dead. His remains were cremated, the ashes scattered at sea. Two months earlier he had finished a pair of music videos for the singer Julian Lennon. "My last movie," he told Begonia the day before he died, "was only two minutes long."

Peckinpah's depiction of the waning years of the Old West, the violent collision of mainstream society with men on the fringes, and the complex, labile relationship between history and myth, heroism and villainy, have rarely been equaled in cinema and never surpassed. Although his films are by no means uniform in their accomplishment, they speak with as original a voice as any filmmaker's: in the best of them, style, artistry, and vision establish Peckinpah as a seminal force in postwar cinema.

★

Peckinpah's papers and other materials are in the Peckinpah Collection at the library of the Academy of Motion Picture Arts and Sciences (Beverly Hills, Calif.), which contains scripts, correspondence, notes, memos, clippings, memorabilia, tapes, photographs, production reports, schedules, and trivia.

Garner Simmons's *Peckinpah: A Portrait in Montage* (1982), the first book about the director's career, has informative accounts of the making of each of his films through *Convoy*. The standard biography is David Weddle, *"If They Move, Kill 'Em": The Life and Times of Sam Peckinpah* (1994), which effectively balances sympathy and candor. None of the several critical studies is absolutely comprehensive. Paul Seydor, *Peckinpah: The Western Films: A Reconsideration* (1980, rev. ed. 1997) contains intensive analyses of the six western films, the only in-depth critical treatment of all the director's major television work, and full descriptions of the various versions of *Major Dundee, The Wild Bunch,* and *Pat Garrett and Billy the Kid*. Michael Bliss, *Justified Lives: Morality and Narrative in the Films of Sam Peckinpah* (1993), stands alone in covering all fourteen feature films. Bliss has also put together a useful anthology, *Doing It Right: The Best Criticism on Sam Peckinpah's "The Wild Bunch"* (1994), which collects important essays and interviews, concluding with an excellent overview of Peckinpah's career in Michael Sragow's obituary. A stimulating essay by a critic who knew him is Pauline Kael's "Notes on the Nihilistic Poetry of Sam Peckinpah" (1976; reprinted in her *For Keeps*).

A documentary, *The Wild Bunch: An Album in Montage,* written and directed by Paul Seydor and produced by Nick Redman (1996), features behind-the-scenes archival footage taken on the set in Mexico in 1968 showing Peckinpah directing the film; it is available as part of the deluxe laserdisc package of *The Wild Bunch* (Warner Home Video).

PAUL SEYDOR

PEERCE, Jan (*b.* 3 June 1904 in New York City; *d.* 15 December 1984 in New York City), one of America's most popular lyric tenors and a star of the Metropolitan Opera.

Jan Peerce was born Jacob Pincus Perelmuth on Orchard Street on New York City's Lower East Side to poor Russian-Jewish immigrants, Anna Posner and Louis Perelmuth, a garment presser. His mother's aspirations for Peerce intensified after the accidental death of his six-year-old brother in 1907. His sister Sara, one of three other siblings, married Richard Tucker, later Peerce's colleague at the Metropolitan Opera. "Pinye" was renowned for his beautiful alto voice as a child, singing in synagogue choirs on the Lower East Side and in Harlem. At nine he started taking violin lessons, which his mother paid for by opening a restaurant in their cold-water flat, charging five cents a meal. His parents eventually owned a successful kosher catering hall.

Despite the boy's obvious musical talent, his mother hoped he would become a physician, and he dutifully enrolled in Columbia University, after failing to take his final exams at DeWitt Clinton High School. He soon left academia without a backward glance.

From the age of fourteen, when he formed a four-piece jazz combo and made fifty cents a night playing dances at the Madison Street Settlement House, he began to create a career for himself as a freelance violinist. At fifteen, "Pinky Pearl," as he was now called, joined local 802 of the Musicians' Union, got a summer job in the Catskill Mountains playing with Pinky Pearl and His Society Dance Orchestra, and embarked on the grueling life of a musician working the Borscht Belt and Broadway. Increasingly, he put down his violin and sang solos with his band. In 1932, while performing with the New York Astor Hotel house band at a benefit for a vaudeville team, he so impressed Samuel "Roxy" Rothafel that the legendary showman asked him to join the company he was forming to appear in the soon-to-open Radio City Music Hall.

It was a risky career move for a man with a growing family. He had eloped with Alice Kalmanowitz, who was then barely sixteen, in 1928; they had three children. Alice supported his career choice and continued to be his fiercest partisan and critic throughout their fifty-six-year marriage. The couple first lived in the Bronx then moved to Manhattan's Upper West Side, ultimately settling in New Rochelle, New York, where they remained for forty years.

Roxy decided that the name "Pinky Pearl" would not do for a man with a fabulous voice and renamed the singer John Pierce. Pierce's career at Radio City began inauspiciously, because he was deemed too homely—short, stocky

Jan Peerce, 1967. UPI/CORBIS-BETTMANN

and bespectacled—to be a headliner. He was put behind the curtain, relegated to singing anonymously during intermissions. When he was allowed to sing onstage he was a hit and continued as the leading tenor at Radio City for eight years. It was an arduous apprenticeship of four shows a day, seven days a week and weekly broadcasts of *Radio City Music Hall of the Air*. Roxy changed the singer's name once more and this time the name, Jan Peerce, stuck. During the 1930s, he did a lot of radio work and was featured in movie shorts released by Universal Studios. In 1936, Peerce's recording of a song written for him by Sandor Harmati and Edward Heyman, "Bluebird of Happiness," became a million-selling crossover sensation, rivaled only by Enrico Caruso's World War I recording of "Over There." Peerce's voice was known to millions of Americans as a result of all this activity, and his repertoire, both classical and popular, was immense.

One of Peerce's radio fans was Arturo Toscanini, who was delighted with what he heard and invited the singer for an audition. Toscanini gave Peerce the coveted tenor role in a Carnegie Hall broadcast with the NBC Symphony Orchestra of Beethoven's Ninth Symphony on 6 February 1938. Thus began a fifteen-year association that produced operas, concerts, and sound recordings, including the an-

tifascist propaganda film *Hymn of the Nations* (1943), recordings of *La Traviata* and *La Bohème* that are still in print, and a two-part concert performance of *Ballo in maschera* on 17 and 24 January 1954, which was the last time Toscanini conducted an opera. Dubbed "Toscanini's tenor," Peerce was spiritually and emotionally close to the mercurial twentieth-century cultural icon. Peerce often said that he learned more about singing from Toscanini than from anyone else.

Peerce studied singing irregularly for fifteen years before he joined the Metropolitan Opera. His teachers included Eleanor McClellan, Emilio Roxas, and Giuseppe Boghetti. Although he gave his first concert recital in 1936 in Cleveland, it was not until 7 November 1939 that Peerce gave his New York debut recital, at Town Hall. By the late 1930s, Peerce's classical career was gaining momentum; he was concertizing extensively and singing with the traveling Columbia Opera Company, with which he sang—as the Duke in *Rigoletto*—his first full-length staged opera in Baltimore in 1938. Solomon Hurok was Peerce's manager, guiding him in his burgeoning operatic career from 1939 until the impresario's death in 1974. Milestones in Peerce's career that led to his being signed by the Metropolitan Opera were such performances as Rachmaninoff's "The Bells," with the composer conducting, in Philadelphia; an engagement in August 1941 as Alfredo in *Traviata* at the outdoor Hollywood Bowl; and a booking in October 1941 with the San Francisco Opera to do *Rigoletto* with Lawrence Tibbett and Lily Pons. After this performance both his costars sent wildly endorsing telegrams to the general manager of the Metropolitan Opera, Edward Johnson, urging him to hire Peerce.

At the advanced age of thirty-seven, Peerce was summoned to audition for the Metropolitan Opera in New York. His audition lasted only twenty minutes—including the unusual request that he sing encores—and he was given a contract that assigned him five leading roles for his first season. His debut performance, as Alfredo in *Traviata,* on Saturday afternoon, 29 November 1941, was broadcast nationally and was greeted enthusiastically by the New York critics. Not only were the beauty and power of his voice praised but also the dignity and restraint of his acting. So began Peerce's career with the world's premier opera company; it was a career that lasted twenty-seven years and encompassed 335 performances.

That an unabashed American Jew should become the Metropolitan Opera's leading tenor on the eve of World War II had tremendous symbolic significance. After the war, Peerce sang in thirty-seven countries and made thirty-six trips to Israel alone. Wherever he went, he made it a point to connect with the Jewish communities, never so poignantly as in 1956 when he traveled to the Soviet Union under Hurok's and the State Department's auspices. He was the first American musician to perform there since the start of the cold war. Peerce made an unscheduled appearance at the Great Synagogue of Moscow, where he sang the Sabbath prayers. It was a courageous act that gave unexpected hope to the oppressed Jews of Moscow. Peerce's second trip to the Soviet Union, in 1963, prompted an editorial on 14 May 1963 in the *New York Herald Tribune* that was later read into the *Congressional Record*.

Peerce was featured in several star-studded movie musicals: *Carnegie Hall* (1947), *Something in the Wind* (1947), and *Of Men and Music* (1951). They all had inane plots but the music was sublime. Jan and his brother Mac were given small but memorable parts in *Goodbye, Columbus* (1969) which was directed by his son, Larry Peerce.

Throughout the 1950s and 1960s, Peerce expanded his repertoire to include French and Baroque music. He was a member of the Bach Aria Group (with Eileen Farrell and Julius Baker, among others) from 1951 to 1964 and he sang regularly with the San Francisco Opera. Peerce recorded exclusively with RCA Victor from 1946 until 1962, when his contract ended, then began to record for the Westminster and Vanguard labels.

Peerce aged but his voice did not. Because he used his voice intelligently over the years, refusing to sing parts that were too "heavy," he had an instrument as glorious in his seventies as it had been thirty-five years earlier. It was his failing eyesight that forced Peerce to retire from the Metropolitan Opera in 1968. He continued to concertize, however, at a pace that would have killed a younger singer. He taught master classes at the Peabody Conservatory, the Manhattan School of Music, and in Israel. At the age of sixty-seven he played the role of Tevye in the Broadway production of *Fiddler on the Roof.* In 1975 he gave a recital at Alice Tully Hall that won him unanimous praise from the critics. In May 1982, less than four months after a Carnegie Hall recital, he had a stroke that partially paralyzed him, but he still vocalized every day and planned to sing publicly again. In early 1983, however, he succumbed to pneumonia, then lapsed into a coma. He died at the Jewish Home and Hospital for the Aged in Manhattan. He was buried in Mount Eden Cemetery in Valhalla, New York. Alice Peerce established the Jan Peerce Fellowships in the musical theater program at New York University's Tisch School of the Arts and the Jan Peerce Fellowships in Operatic Studies at New York University's School of Education.

Jan Peerce had a singing career unique in its diversity and longevity. His voice had a distinctive timbre, brilliant and clear, supported by a superb technique, impeccable diction, and sensitive musicianship. It was a resplendent voice belonging to a proud, practical, and courageous man.

★

There are three major collections of Peerce memorabilia in New York City, available to scholars by appointment. The Jan Peerce collection, housed in the American Music Collection of the New York Public Library at Lincoln Center, is an as-yet-unprocessed assortment of 150 boxes of letters, marked scores, scrapbooks, costumes, correspondence, honors, and citations. The Metropolitan Opera Archives at Lincoln Center in New York City has a collection of clippings, correspondence, and photographs. The Radio City Music Hall Archives, stored at 131 Varick Street in Manhattan, is a modest but fascinating collection of early reviews, interviews, and programs; access to this collection, however, requires considerable curatorial intervention.

Alan Levy, *The Bluebird of Happiness: The Memoirs of Jan Peerce* (1976), an as-told-to autobiography of immense interest and charm, is full of information and candid remarks, including interviews with Peerce's wife and son. Three magazine articles written after Peerce's death merit attention: Samuel Lipman, "Out of the Ghetto," *Commentary* 79, no. 3 (Mar. 1985): 56–62, a perceptive analysis of three first-generation Jewish-American musicians; Robert Jacobson, "Jan Peerce: June 3, 1904–December 15, 1984," *Opera News* (13 Apr. 1985), an eloquent tribute; and Leslie Rubinstein, "Believing," *Opera News* (29 Feb. 1992), includes unbuttoned commentary by Peerce's children. A front-page obituary by the music critic Harold Schoenberg is in the *New York Times* (17 Dec. 1984).

A valuable source of information and visual documentation is the film, *Jan Peerce: If I Were a Rich Man: The Life of Jan Peerce* (1990); hosted and narrated by Isaac Stern, it contains rare film clips, excerpts from concert and television performances, and extensive interviews with Peerce and his wife. Another film is *Toscanini: The Maestro,* appended to which is *Hymn of the Nations* (1943), featuring Peerce with the Westminster College Choir and the NBC Orchestra, with Toscanini conducting. The Oral History Library of the American Jewish Committee, now part of the Collection of the Dorot Jewish Division of the New York Public Library, includes two interviews with Jan Peerce, available to scholars and qualified researchers by appointment.

HONORA RAPHAEL WEINSTEIN

PERKINS, Dexter (*b.* 20 June 1889 in Boston, Massachusetts; *d.* 12 May 1984 in Rochester, New York), historian and teacher best known for his analysis of U.S. foreign policy and diplomatic history; his book *The Monroe Doctrine, 1823–1826* (1927) became a classic.

Perkins was the only child of Herbert W. Perkins, a merchant, and Cora Farmer, the sister of cookbook author Fannie Farmer. Perkins graduated from Boston Latin School (1905) and the Sanford School in Redding Ridge, Connecticut (1906). He received his A.B. in 1909 and his Ph.D. in 1914 from Harvard University. He also received a diploma from École des Sciences Politiques in Paris (1913).

Dexter Perkins. AMERICAN HISTORICAL ASSOCIATION ANNUAL MEETING PROGRAM, 1956. ALL RIGHTS RESERVED.

After a year at the University of Cincinnati in 1915, Perkins joined the history department at the University of Rochester in New York State, where he worked for much of the rest of his professional life. There, he met his wife, Wilma Lois Lord, with whom he had two children, including Bradford Perkins, a prominent historian at the University of Michigan. Shortly after their marriage on 2 May 1918, Perkins volunteered for infantry service in the U.S. Army during World War I as a private and was soon promoted to captain. Quite appropriately, he saw service in France at Chaumont with the historical section of General Headquarters, formed to record the history of battlefield strategy and tactics, and also attended some of the sessions of the Paris Peace Conference. Perkins's World War I experience forced him to relate to a cross-section of America's population while reinforcing his belief in the country's moral correctness in foreign relations.

Perkins returned to Rochester in 1919 to resume teaching. In 1925, he was promoted to chairman of the history department. By this time, he had acquired a reputation as a brilliant educator who possessed breadth and depth of knowledge, energy, idealism, and an ability to communicate the importance of history to the general public. Blessed with an ability to make and keep friends outside academe,

his advice carried considerable weight with university trustees and political leaders.

Balancing a commitment to teaching with a scholar's interest in research, he revised his Ph.D. dissertation for publication as *The Monroe Doctrine, 1823–1826* (1927). This groundbreaking study settled the doctrine's authorship question by crediting James Monroe and John Quincy Adams equally with its creation. Further, his research in European archives revealed that neither France nor the Holy Alliance had been a threat to intervene in Latin America in 1823, and he denied the received thesis that the United States had saved the Latin American revolutionaries from European intervention. Subsequent books by Perkins on the Monroe Doctrine would delineate the policy's evolution up to 1955. Some of Perkins's other books include *America and Two Wars* (1944); *The Evolution of American Foreign Policy* (1948; 2d ed., 1966); *Charles Evans Hughes and American Democratic Statesmanship* (1956); *The New Age of Franklin Roosevelt, 1932–1945* (1957); *The American Approach to Foreign Policy* (1962); *America's Quest for Peace* (1962); and *The Diplomacy of a New Age: Major Issues in U.S. Policy Since 1945* (1968). His most important speech, his address as president of the American Historical Association (AHA) in 1956 entitled "We Shall Gladly Teach," was an eloquent call for balance, measure, and commitment to a moral point of view in the teaching of history.

The accessibility of Perkins's prose and his commitment to the profession gained him many honors. In 1928 he was appointed secretary of the AHA and served in this influential position until 1939. His commitment to public history was recognized in 1936 by his appointment as city historian of Rochester. In 1937 he was named a lecturer on foreign policy at University College, London. In 1945 he served as a historian for the overseas branch of the Office of War Information at the United Nations Conference in San Francisco. During the fall term of 1945, he served as the first visiting Pitt Professor of American History and Institutions at Cambridge University.

After World War II, Perkins spent considerable time developing Rochester's first Ph.D. program, which taught scholars to teach effectively as well as to research and write. The graduate program became one of the most respected in the country. Concurrently, he was a key founder of the Rochester Association for the United Nations (RAUN) in 1946. Serving as its president and eventually its chairman, RAUN became a highly respected organization, advocating the ideals of collective security and problem solving.

In the 1950s, Perkins was elected to the Harvard Board of Overseers and became chairman of the Harvard Foundation for Advanced Study and Research. He also was elected moderator of the Unitarian Churches of the U.S. and Canada in 1952. In 1954, Perkins became emeritus professor of history at the University of Rochester and accepted the post of John L. Senior Professor in American Civilization at Cornell University, in Ithaca, New York.

In the 1950s and 1960s, Perkins spent considerable time on two large themes—the uniqueness of America's approach to foreign affairs and the unreliability of "revisionist" interpretations of the two world wars. Perkins argued in a paper delivered at a meeting of the AHA in December 1952 that in the United States there was a unique approach to foreign affairs that, on the whole, was admirable. The characteristics included: (1) The large role for public opinion, aspirations, and fears in the making of U.S. foreign policy; (2) the relative openness of debate and policy formation; (3) the unusual degree to which moral discourse and analysis informs U.S. diplomatic transactions; (4) the importance of general principles in explaining policy decisions to the American people—such accepted principles include the superiority of democracy, the immorality of aggression, the advantage of free access to foreign markets, and the importance of ethical behavior in international negotiations; (5) the pragmatic streak in foreign policy; (6) the peace-loving bent in American diplomacy; (7) the critical attitude toward foreign imperialism; and (8) the very broad definition of the concept of national security given by policymakers.

The other theme of Perkins's work was his notable critique of revisionist historiography. World War I revisionists, like Charles A. Beard, Harry Elmer Barnes, and Charles C. Tansill, argued that American intervention in the war was caused by powerful business and banking interests in the United States, not by a need to defend American security. World War II revisionists denied that either Germany or Japan had posed a serious threat to U.S. interests or security. President Franklin D. Roosevelt, they claimed, wanted war to build a powerful national security state, to ensure his reelection, to preserve the British Empire, and to expand American markets abroad. While finding the revisionist arguments stimulating and innovative, Perkins deplored "history by hypothesis" and the unempirical excesses of the revisionist school. On the whole, he found Roosevelt's diplomacy realistic, balanced, and honest. Indeed, in the 1950s, Perkins was a consistent spokesperson for the "consensus" school of historians. This school, led by Perkins, Louis Hartz, Richard Hofstadter, and Daniel Boorstin, was struck by the unifying framework of ideas and values that had always sustained Americans against the threat of alien ideologies and institutions. Most Americans, the school argued, had agreed on such basic values as the Lockean right of private property, the right of self-government, and the desirability of free market capitalism combined with recognized individual liberties. With Perkins, the consensus school called for balance, moderation, the retention of individuals as the fundamental category of analysis in historiography, and empirical rigor.

Perkins's approach to and conclusions about diplomatic history encountered fierce criticism by the new revisionists of the 1960s. Nonetheless, his historical conclusions, although superseded by new archival research and methodological approaches, continue to reward students of U.S. history.

Perkins died of heart failure and was buried in Rochester, New York.

★

Perkins's *Yield of the Years: An Autobiography* (1969) is the author's examination of his education, philosophy, and research interests. An obituary is in the *New York Times* (16 May 1984).

ALFRED L. CASTLE

PERRY, Lincoln. See Fetchit, Stepin.

PETRILLO, James Caesar (*b.* 16 March 1892 in Chicago, Illinois; *d.* 23 October 1984 in Chicago, Illinois), musician and longtime president of the American Federation of Musicians (AFM) who became famous and controversial during the 1940s and 1950s for his two bans on recorded music and his campaigns to bar nonunion musicians from performing in competition with AFM members.

One of five children of Italian immigrant parents, Petrillo was raised on the tough West Side of Chicago. At the age

James Petrillo. PHOTOGRAPH COURTESY OF THE AMERICAN FEDERATION OF MUSICIANS OF THE UNITED STATES AND CANADA

of eight, he received a cornet from his father and soon played in the bands of Jane Addams's Hull House and the newsboys' band of the *Chicago Daily News* with indifferent results. He was, as he said, "loud but lousy," and switched to drums. Petrillo also operated a cigar stand and a saloon before concentrating on labor politics. In 1916 he married Marie Frullate; they had four children. One of their sons died of an infection from a football injury at the age of thirteen, and the episode made the elder Petrillo obsessive about cleanliness and a germ-free existence.

The chubby, gregarious Petrillo joined the American Musicians Union (AMU) in 1906 and was soon a rising figure in the politics of the independent labor organization. In 1914 he won election as the AMU's president. Defeated for reelection in 1917, he switched his allegiance to Local 10 of the American Federation of Musicians (AFM) a year later. Elected vice president in 1919, he moved up to president in 1922, a post he held for forty years.

From the outset, Petrillo confronted the threat of technological changes to musicians that dominated his entire career. Talking motion pictures had reduced the number of jobs for musicians in movie theaters, and Petrillo sought job contracts for Local 10 members to be paid as standby musicians when members of other locals performed. He also forced radio stations, whose wide-ranging broadcasts effectively displaced local bands and orchestras, to hire only union members as disc jockeys. During the next eighteen years, Petrillo built up the power of Local 10 through a mixture of strikes and tough negotiations with theater owners and radio stations. He also ended the system of dual unions among musicians, which placed black and white players in different locals. Rumors circulated that Petrillo had links to organized crime and had once been kidnapped by the mob. Petrillo denied that the kidnapping had occurred, and his conduct of the union's affairs was honest, as even his critics recognized. When John L. Lewis of the United Mine Workers tried to organize remnants of the AMU for the Congress of Industrial Organizations, Petrillo easily vanquished his rival.

In 1940 Petrillo was elected national president of the AFM with an offensive against "canned music" as his main priority. In addition to his pay as national president, he retained his salary from the Chicago local, and his annual income of $46,000 made him the highest-paid union president in the country. His first move as AFM president was to bring the outstanding soloists who belonged to the American Guild of Musical Artists into his union. As he put it, "Since when is there a difference between [Jascha] Heifetz and a fiddler in a tavern?" Petrillo then moved toward a ban on all music recordings that started on 1 August 1942. The action made Petrillo a national figure and an object of vehement criticism for his allegedly dictatorial style. He became known as "Little Caesar" and the

"Mussolini of Music." After more than two years, the ban ended when all of the record companies agreed to contribute royalties on every recording to the Recording and Transcription Fund of the AFM, which in turn paid for free concerts across the country. Rank-and-file musicians thus received more employment.

Petrillo's efforts to curb competition from school orchestras and bands led him to bar radio broadcasts of the National Music Camp at Interlochen, Michigan, in 1942. Out of this heated quarrel with the camp director Joseph Maddy came congressional calls to curb Petrillo's power. During World War II, Petrillo's autocratic style and willingness to deny citizens a favorite diversion aroused strong antipathy. Committees of both houses of Congress probed his leadership practices with the AFM on several occasions. The result of these inquiries was the Lea Act of 1946, which banned unions from coercing radio stations and recording companies to use standby or unneeded performers. Petrillo tested the Lea Act by continuing his policies. When he was indicted for violating the law in 1947, the judge at his trial declared the law unconstitutional. The Supreme Court later upheld the law, and the Lea Act remained in force until 1980, when it was repealed.

The Taft-Hartley Act (1947) made the Recording and Transcription Fund illegal, and Petrillo imposed another recording ban in 1948 that led to the creation of the Music Performance Trust Fund. Because the fund favored the broad membership of the AFM, many of whom only occasionally worked in music, the more highly skilled musicians who could secure steady work, especially those in Los Angeles, became adamant opponents of the Trust Fund. In the 1950s, opposition to Petrillo also grew within the AFM. The split within the union led to Petrillo's decision in 1958 to step down as president of the AFM. He remained head of the Chicago local until he was ousted in 1962. Petrillo spent his retirement in his native Chicago, where he died of cancer and was buried.

Petrillo became a lightning rod for the antiunion attitudes of the 1940s because of his visibility and his impact on the music available to the American public. His blunt style of speech and his aggressive tactics in negotiations further contributed to his negative image. Even his opponents, however, conceded his honesty and sincerity as a labor leader. Some historians of popular music believe that Petrillo's first recording ban played a large role in ending the swing era of the big bands. His involvement with issues of a modernizing culture and technological change give his career historical significance.

★

Petrillo's personal papers are not available, but the records of the AFM are at the Robert F. Wagner Labor Archives at New York University. The Harry S. Truman Presidential Library in Independence, Missouri, also has a substantial amount of data on Petrillo. For Petrillo's philosophy as a union leader, see his testimony in "Investigation of James C. Petrillo, the American Federation of Musicians, et al.," U.S. Congress, House of Representatives, *Hearings Before the Special Subcommittee of the Committee on Education and Labor,* 80th Cong., 1st Sess. (1947): 178–216.

The only book-length study is Robert D. Leiter, *The Musicians and Petrillo* (1953). Other treatments of his career include Wellington Roe, *Juggernaut: American Labor in Action* (1948); Paul S. Carpenter, *Music, an Art and a Business* (1950); Donald Spivey, ed., *Union and the Black Musician: The Narrative of William Everett Samuels and Chicago Local 208* (1984); George Seltzer, *Music Matters: The Performer and the American Federation of Musicians* (1989); and James P. Kraft, "The 'Pit' Musicians: Mechanization in the Movie Theaters, 1926–1934," *Labor History* 35 (1994): 66–89. An obituary is in the *New York Times* (25 Oct. 1984).

Lewis L. Gould

PHILLIPS, Marjorie Acker (*b.* 25 October 1894 in Bourbon, Indiana; *d.* 19 June 1985 in Washington, D.C.), artist and cofounder of the Phillips Collection, the oldest existing museum of modern art in America.

Born at a relative's home while traveling, Marjorie Acker was one of five children of Charles Ernest Acker, an electro-chemical engineer, manufacturer, and inventor, and Alice Beal Acker, a homemaker and society matron. The family eventually settled in Ossining, New York. From the age of eleven, Marjorie later recalled, she painted from "the sheer need to paint." Her father did not approve of her inclinations, but her mother was warmly encouraging. Two of her uncles were well-established artists; one of them, Gifford Beal, was president of the Art Students League in New York. Marjorie spent hours in her uncles' studio at her grandparents' estate overlooking the Hudson River.

Because of family obligations she did not begin art school until about 1918, entering the Art Students League at age twenty-three. There she studied composition with Boardman Robinson and oil painting with Kenneth Hayes Miller. She also looked at contemporary art while she had the chance, visiting commercial galleries and museums.

In January 1921 her life took an unexpected turn when she was invited to New York City by her uncle Gifford to an exhibition at the Century Association of Duncan Phillips's nascent art collection, the nucleus of his recently incorporated museum. He asked to see her work, and they met again at her uncle's midtown studio, where Duncan purchased her painting *The Hudson at Ossining,* the first step in a period of intense courtship. On 8 October 1921 they were married at her family home in Ossining. Marjorie Phillips moved into her husband's townhouse at 1600 Twenty-first Street in Washington, D.C. In November the museum quietly opened to the public in two newly renovated galleries on the second floor.

Marjorie Phillips, 1920s. The Phillips Collection

From the moment they met, Duncan relied on Marjorie's perspective as an artist. In May 1921 he added her to his recently organized Committee of Scope and Plan, which was to set the goals of his new museum. She served as the museum's associate director from 1925 to 1966, accompanying him on all buying trips. She shared in every major decision of the museum, from renovation of the galleries to both major and minor acquisitions.

In the summer of 1923 the couple visited Paris. There they acquired the painting that became the centerpiece of the museum, Pierre-Auguste Renoir's *Luncheon of the Boating Party* (1880–1881). Over the next few years they branched out into other arenas of collecting, admiring the shimmering color of Pierre Bonnard, the classic cubism of Georges Braque, and the linear wit of Paul Klee. When they visited Alfred Stieglitz's gallery in New York City they discovered American modernists Arthur Dove, John Marin, and Georgia O'Keeffe. By the fall of 1930 the collection had grown so large that the Phillipses, by now with two children, moved to a home on Foxhall Road overlooking the Potomac River.

Although Marjorie devoted time to her family and the museum, she spent most mornings painting in her studio. She considered herself a realist sensitive to the nuances of color and design. Her work—landscapes, still lifes, and intimate family scenes—reflected her careful study of Bonnard's translucent color, deft technique, and preference for domestic scenes of leisure. Marjorie received her first solo exhibition in 1924 at the Kraushaar Galleries, New York, followed by one in 1925 at the Phillips.

The Phillipses continued to travel together in search of new art. Her special province was to develop exhibitions for two galleries, which, though called the "print rooms," often housed new work by contemporary artists. In these and other exhibitions Marjorie showed a discerning eye for modern sculpture and current trends in art. She helped her husband shift the purpose of his collection from a memorial in honor of his father and brother to a vital museum focusing on living artists. Duncan acknowledged Marjorie's role, writing in *The Artist Sees Differently* (1931) that he relied on frequent "consultations of her mind and eye." Marjorie, who later recalled that Duncan "took a great interest in everything I did," noted his pointed interest in the abstract expressionist Mark Rothko when she included six of his color-field paintings in a 1957 show she had organized of three New York School artists. The couple purchased Rothko's *Green and Maroon* (1953) from this show.

During the 1960s Marjorie began to take on a more active role in the museum, and upon her husband's death in May 1966 she became director of the Phillips Collection. Her exhibitions and acquisitions reflected her predisposition toward recent work of contemporary sculptors and painters, from Alexander Calder and Henry Moore to Clyfford Still and Jack Youngerman. She also began the book *Duncan Phillips and His Collection* (1970), which chronicles the creation of a museum that reflected their shared passion for art.

In February 1971 Marjorie Phillips oversaw the opening of a large Paul Cézanne retrospective she had organized in honor of the museum's fiftieth anniversary. The following year she retired, and her son, Laughlin Phillips, became the new director. Her second and final retrospective was held in 1973 at the Marlborough Fine Art gallery in London. Also that year Smith College awarded her an honorary doctorate of fine arts. She painted full-time until 1982, when her eyesight failed. In 1984 she and her niece began preparation of a book about the one arena that was completely her own, her painting. It was published in 1985, shortly before her quiet death of pulmonary heart failure at her home on Foxhall Road. She was buried in Old Rock Creek Cemetery in Washington, D.C. Her last act was a large bequest of the best works from the couple's personal art collection to the museum.

More than anyone else, Marjorie Phillips was responsible for helping Duncan Phillips maintain his focus on contemporary artists and respond to art from an artist's perspective. Although their personal and professional lives were endlessly entwined, at times her discriminating eye was apparent, as for example in April 1967, when several large stabiles by Calder stood under the cherry blossoms gracing the museum's exterior. Marjorie Phillips was a beloved figure in Washington, for whom "*surprise,* mystery, indefiniteness," as she put it, represented a guiding principle in art.

★

Material on Marjorie Acker Phillips is located in the archives, registrar's office, and curatorial records of the Phillips Collection, Washington, D.C. For the best account of how the Phillipses built the museum's collection, see Marjorie Phillips, *Duncan Phillips and His Collection* (1970, rev. 1982), and for an autobiographical account focused on her family and artistic life, see Sylvia Partridge, ed., *Marjorie Phillips and Her Paintings* (1985). There are a number of catalogs for Marjorie Phillips's exhibitions; see, for example, Guy Pène du Bois, *Exhibition of Paintings by Marjorie Phillips,* Kraushaar Galleries (1924); Thomas C. Howe, *Marjorie Phillips,* exhibition catalogue, California Palace of the Legion of Honor (1959); and Susan Drysdale, *Marjorie Phillips,* Marlborough Fine Art Limited (1973). In addition to obituaries in the *New York Times* (21 June 1985), *Washington Post* (20 June 1985), and *Washington Times* (20 June 1985), the Washington papers published several pieces in appreciation of her legacy, the most perceptive being Sarah Booth Conroy, "Appreciation: Memories of Marjorie Phillips as Washington Grande Dame, Painter, and Patron," *Washington Post* (20 June 1985).

LEIGH BULLARD WEISBLAT

PIDGEON, Walter (*b.* 23 September 1897 in East St. John, New Brunswick, Canada; *d.* 25 September 1984 in Santa Monica, California), actor who is best remembered for film roles of the 1940s, especially with costar Greer Garson in movies such as *Mrs. Miniver* (1942) and *Madame Curie* (1943), which brought him two Academy Award nominations.

Pidgeon was one of three sons of Caleb Pidgeon, a haberdasher, and Hannah Sanborn, a homemaker. He entered the University of New Brunswick in 1914 but dropped out after a year to enlist in the Canadian army for service in World War I.

Injured in an accident in training camp, Pidgeon was laid up for well over a year; he was invalided out of the military without seeing combat. He then moved to Boston, where he got a job as a book messenger. In 1922 he married his childhood sweetheart, Edna Pickles, who had preceded him to Boston to study art. She died in childbirth the following year, and Pidgeon's mother raised their daughter.

Pidgeon remained in Boston as a bond trader and joined a repertory group and took voice lessons at the New England Conservatory of Music. At a party Pidgeon attended, Fred Astaire, already a star on Broadway, was so impressed with his singing that he recommended Pidgeon to a the-

Walter Pidgeon. ARCHIVE PHOTOS

atrical agent in New York City. Eventually, Pidgeon landed a job with Elsie Janis's troupe and performed with her in various shows until 1925 (they were reported to be lovers). He then moved to Hollywood. Six-foot-three and handsome, Pidgeon landed his first billed role in the Paramount production *Mannequin* in 1926. He had no trouble finding employment thereafter, usually as a "good-looking clothes-horse" in undemanding roles. The transition to talking movies helped Pidgeon, who sang in several operettas and became known as First National Pictures' house baritone. In 1931 he married Ruth Hollister Walker, a nonprofessional who avoided the Hollywood social scene. The couple had no children.

In the early 1930s, with audiences tiring of the operettas that had been his forte, Pidgeon's career declined as First National Pictures sought vehicles suitable to exploit the dramatic talents of James Cagney, Paul Muni, and Edward G. Robinson. Pidgeon turned to the stage to develop a new image, appearing at the Hollywood Playhouse and finally on Broadway. His best New York reviews were for two 1935 productions, *The Night of January 16,* in which he played a gangster, and *There's Wisdom in Women,* in which his role was the unfaithful husband.

Returning to Hollywood in 1936, Pidgeon signed with Universal, which used him as a leading man in several low-budget films. His work came to the attention of Metro-Goldwyn-Mayer (MGM) head Louis B. Mayer, also from New Brunswick, who purchased his contract in 1937. MGM kept Pidgeon busy, often calling upon him to woo Myrna Loy or one of the studio's other leading ladies, whom Pidgeon inevitably lost, in films such as *Saratoga* (1937) and *Too Hot to Handle* (1938), to a star like Clark Gable.

Distinguished by his height and by his deep, reassuring voice, Pidgeon nevertheless remained in the second echelon of MGM's roster of performers until breaking through to stardom with a series of strong performances in films that were successful at the box office. On loan to Republic Pictures for *Dark Command* (1940), he played John Wayne's adversary, a schoolteacher turned border-raider in Kansas during the Civil War era. In *Man Hunt* (1941) he played a big-game hunter who for sport stalks Hitler, carrying an empty gun. In this film Pidgeon soon becomes the hunted, evading the Gestapo in a long and suspenseful chase sequence through the countryside of pre–World War II England. The film concludes with the suggestion that he will again pursue Hitler, and that this time his gun will be loaded. Pidgeon played a minister in John Ford's highly regarded production *How Green Was My Valley* (1941).

It was in the early 1940s that Pidgeon was first paired with MGM's dignified new leading lady, Greer Garson. Their first vehicle was *Blossoms in the Dust* (1941), and in 1942 they starred in *Mrs. Miniver.* Although cliché-ridden, the film was just what Americans wanted to see: decent Englishmen finding the resolve to stand up against the Nazi onslaught of 1940 and 1941. Pidgeon and Garson soon appeared together again in *Madame Curie* (1943) and in *Mrs. Parkington* (1944). Audience reaction to the comedy *Julia Misbehaves* (1948) and the dramas *That Forsyte Woman* (1949), *The Miniver Story* (1950), and *Scandal at Scourie* (1953), other Pidgeon-Garson films, showed that the pair was losing its popularity by the early 1950s. Seven of their eight films, however, opened at New York's prestigious Radio City Music Hall.

Physically ineligible for the draft, Pidgeon, who became a U.S. citizen in December 1943, devoted considerable time to entertaining American troops during both World War II and the Korean War. At the height of his fame in the 1940s, Pidgeon appeared without Garson in films such as *Week-End at the Waldorf* (1945), *If Winter Comes* (1947), *Red Danube* (1949), and *Command Decision* (1949), a powerful drama about the burdens placed on officers who send their men to combat in the air knowing that they face a high probability of death. Although investments had made him financially independent, Pidgeon wanted to continue acting and as good roles on the screen became scarcer (MGM dropped his contract in 1956), he turned again to Broadway where he earned favorable reviews for his performance in *The Happiest Millionaire* (1956) and in the musical *Take Me Along* (1959), based on Eugene O'Neill's *Ah! Wilderness*. Although Jackie Gleason, then at the height of his television popularity, was nominally the star, reviewers praised Pidgeon's singing and acting. Pidgeon also began appearing on television in dramatic roles and in guest spots on talk shows, where his warm personality and droll wit made him popular. He still made an occasional screen appearance, including *Advise and Consent* (1962) and *Funny Girl* (1968), in which he portrayed Florenz Ziegfeld, providing him with his best roles since his heyday at MGM. Late in 1977 Pidgeon experienced a serious fall that led to a blood clot on his brain. He underwent surgery but did not make a full recovery, and he spent the last decade of his life in semi-seclusion at his Bel Air home in Los Angeles. He died of a stroke at a Santa Monica Hospital. His body was donated to the UCLA Medical Center.

Nominated for Oscars for best actor for his roles in *Mrs. Miniver* and *Madame Curie* (on neither occasion did he win), Pidgeon achieved fame after fifteen years of work in silents, early musicals, and a variety of other film genres including the popular Nick Carter detective series. Stephen Hanson wrote: "By making astute use of his suave good looks, rich speaking voice, and intelligent demeanor [the studios were] able to cast him in a series of thoughtful wartime roles that were immensely popular and made him a star." Had Gable and many other prewar matinee idols not been absent due to wartime service, stardom might not have come to Pidgeon. He enjoyed the acclaim, but prominence in the credits was never as important to him as the chance to perform, and he was willing to accept lesser roles as his career began to decline in the 1950s. He continued to work steadily as an actor until his injury and forced retirement.

★

The best source for information about his career is the essay on Pidgeon in James Robert Parish, with Gregory W. Mank, *The Hollywood Reliables* (1980), which also includes a filmography. A. H. Marill, "Walter Pidgeon," *Films in Review* (Nov. 1969), is a cut above other material on Pidgeon. The star is profiled in James Robert Parish and Ronald L. Bowers, *The MGM Stock Company: The Golden Era* (1973), and David Shipman, *The Great Movie Stars: The Golden Years* (1970). M. Mann, "Bank on Pidgeon," *Screen Book* (Apr. 1939), and Hedda Hopper, "His Married Life," *Photoplay* (May 1943), provide examples of the approach taken in fan magazines. Dorothy Manners, "His Sob-Story," *Motion Picture Classic* (29 Aug. 1930), is an amalgam of fact and fiction. An obituary is in the *New York Times* (26 Sept. 1984).

LLOYD J. GRAYBAR

PILLSBURY, Philip Winston (*b.* 16 April 1903 in Minneapolis, Minnesota; *d.* 14 June 1984 in Minneapolis, Min-

nesota), corporate leader who transformed the Pillsbury Grain Milling Company into one of the largest diversified food concerns in the world.

Pillsbury was the only son of Charles Stinson Pillsbury and Helen Nelle Pendleton Winston. His first paternal American ancestor, William Pillsbury, had come to America from England seven generations earlier, in 1640. In 1869 Pillsbury's grandfather, Charles Alfred Pillsbury, arrived in Minneapolis, Minnesota, and purchased a share in the flour-milling business of his uncle, John Sargent Pillsbury, who was a prominent state politician and successful businessman. A few years later, when the uncle became governor of Minnesota, the management of the milling business was given to Charles Alfred. At this time various forces were about to transform the milling industry. Charles Alfred played a major role in taking advantage of these changes. In 1872 he, his uncle (John Sargent), and his father organized C. A. Pillsbury & Company, producing one of the leaders in the milling industry. By 1889, an English syndicate purchased the Pillsbury Mills, together with those of Senator W. D. Washburn, combining them to form the Pillsbury-Washburn Flour Mills Company. Under the management of Charles Alfred, the company soon became the largest milling firm in the world.

Charles Alfred's children, John Sargent II and Charles

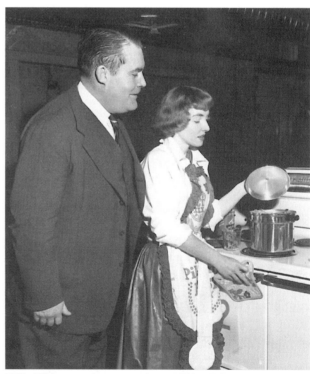

Philip Pillsbury watches a competitor in Pillsbury's Eightieth Anniversary Grand National Recipe Contest at the Waldorf-Astoria Hotel in New York City, 1949. AP/WIDE WORLD PHOTOS

Stinson, got involved in the management and operation of the company from early ages. As the twins' relationship with the company matured, they decided to reorganize in order to wrest control away from the English syndicate and to return it to American and family control. The process proved to be lengthy. In the meantime, John Sargent Pillsbury had eight children, and Charles Stinson Pillsbury had four—three daughters and a son, Philip Winston. These children were to become a new generation of Pillsbury Company leaders.

After receiving his preliminary education at Blake School (Hopkins, Minnesota), and Hotchkiss School (Lakeville, Connecticut), Philip Winston Pillsbury went to Yale College, where he starred as a guard on the university's undefeated 1923 football team, was an All-American water polo player, and sang tenor in the glee club. Also in 1923, the family finally reacquired the milling business from the English syndicate; that summer Philip attended some of the negotiating sessions with the Pillsbury-Washburn representatives in London. His plans had been to pursue a medical career, but once the return of the properties was accomplished, his family persuaded him to cast his lot with the company. A year later, on graduation from Yale with an A.B., he became an employee of the company.

Pillsbury started work as a clerk in the "A" mill wheat department. Working at nearly every job in the mill, he stayed long enough in each job to understand and perform all the tasks required, from the receipt of the grain to shipment of the milled products. In 1928, at the age of twenty-five, he was elected a member of the board of directors—its youngest member in history. Having mastered the art and science of milling, Philip was transferred in 1932 to the sales department and was sent to Chicago, where he ultimately became branch manager. About a year after his marriage to Eleanor Bellows on 5 July 1934, he returned to Minneapolis to assume responsibility for the company's sales in the eastern United States.

It was not too long before Philip became a senior officer of the company. In 1940 he had mustered enough experience and clout to be appointed treasurer. Six months later, pleased with Philip's integrity, experience, and insight, the Pillsbury family urged the board to appoint him president and chief executive officer.

At the time Pillsbury took over the helm, the company's sales and profits were being threatened by competition. The company was in need of innovation, reorganization, and growth. The first major decision Pillsbury made as president was to acquire a large West Coast miller, Globe Grain & Milling Company. Moreover, he launched a comprehensive plan for research and development. The main objective was to develop derivative products that could be used by households instead of food-processing factories. During World War II, the Pillsbury labs pioneered the production of formula cattle feed and enriched flour. When the war

ended, the company started to introduce one "easy to prepare" food product after another, including pancakes, waffles, and biscuits, to be followed later by cake, pie, and roll mixes. By the mid-1950s, the combination of such innovative goods, along with intensive and clever advertising (such as the annual national "Bake Off" contest), made the Pillsbury Company a leader in bringing baking convenience to the American homemaker.

In 1952 Pillsbury retired from the presidency and immediately became chairman of the board, a position he held until 1965. He continued as a director until 1974. At the time, the company's net sales were $315 million, more than seven times the level of sales at the beginning of his presidency. He now had more time to spend with family and friends and to pursue philanthropic and civic endeavors. He took a long trip to Egypt with his wife and children—Philip Winston, Jr., and Henry Adams—in 1955. The government of France named Pillsbury Honorary French Consul for the upper Midwest from 1960 to 1979 and decorated him as an officer of the Legion of Honor in recognition of his contribution to improved relations between the two countries. After the death of his wife in 1971, he married Corinne Griffith in 1977. Pillsbury died of cancer at the Abbott-Northwestern Hospital in Minneapolis, Minnesota.

Although family connections and an Ivy League education were instrumental in his rise to power, Pillsbury proved, in the course of his career, to be the right man to lead the Pillsbury Company. He oversaw the company's transformation from a milling business to a giant diversified food concern. In the process, he became a leader in introducing easy-to-prepare food products to the American household.

★

National Cyclopedia of American Biography (1964), pp. 128–129, provides a comprehensive list of Pillsbury's business activities. John. N. Ingham, ed., *Biographical Dictionary of American Business Leaders* (1983), contains biographies of Pillsbury family members. William J. Powell, *Pillsbury's Best: A Company History from 1869* (1985), gives good coverage of Pillsbury's presidency period. A tribute produced by the Pillsbury Company, *A Man for All Seasons* (1974), contains several photos. An obituary is in the *New York Times* (16 June 1984).

MOJTABA SEYEDIAN

PLOUGH, Abe (*b.* 27 December 1891 in Tupelo, Mississippi; *d.* 14 September 1984 in Memphis, Tennessee), corporate entrepreneur and philanthropist who built a giant over-the-counter drug company.

Born to Eastern European Jewish immigrant parents, Mose Plough and Julia Isaacs, Abe was one of eight children supported by the family's retail business in small town Mississippi and later in Memphis. Abe finished through the

Abe Plough. PRESS-SCIMITAR PHOTO/MISSISSIPPI VALLEY COLLECTION/UNIVERSITY OF MEMPHIS LIBRARIES

eighth grade in the Memphis public schools and then went to work for the family business.

He soon left the family furniture and clothing trade but retained the valuable entrepreneurial skills that he learned from his father's other business as a salvage dealer of Illinois Central Railroad's unclaimed freight. If Abe could find a way to dispose of used tombstones (with the names of other people carved on them), he could sell anything. Plough also enjoyed early and continued financial backing from his father. He recalled Mose saying: "Son, even though I have eight children and the going is pretty tough, I have notified the bank that you may sign your name to my checks."

Abe entered business for himself in 1908 by borrowing $125 from his father to purchase a wagon, a barrel of liniment, some small bottles, and printed labels that read: "Plough's Antiseptic Healing Oil." Abe peddled this mystery mixture, which actually contained linseed oil, camphor, and carbolic acid, to every drug and general store in the Memphis area. Every evening, in a room over his father's store, Abe filled twenty-five bottles, which was about the number he could sell in a day. If his customers did not have cash, he traded his product for other medicines, acquiring a broader supply of health remedies.

In 1916, Plough acquired his first drugstore, Battier's,

for $15,000 that he borrowed. That same year, he earned his first real capital from the sale of the drug stock from a bankrupt wholesale drug company that he bought for $1,400 borrowed against his father's insurance policy. He sold the acquired drug stock for $33,500.

Plough acquired Black & White Cosmetics in 1917 and then, in 1920, Gerstle Medicine Company, from which Plough acquired the St. Joseph trade name. He successfully applied the name to aspirin, offering twelve St. Joseph tablets for ten cents, less than half the price of Bayer, whose exclusive patent on aspirin had recently expired. An aggressive national advertising campaign in 400 newspapers, with a small seven-line ad for "The largest selling aspirin in the world for 10 cents," made Plough a national drug company.

Plough Chemical became a publicly traded company in 1923 to allow Abe to expand his enterprise. He pushed his company beyond the United States. In 1926 Plough hired Ramon R. Diaz of Puerto Rico as foreign-sales manager to expand sales from Mexico to forty-three other countries.

Abe married Jocelyn Cohn and fathered two daughters. As a young millionaire, Plough was able to make a dramatic gesture in 1926, when his father-in-law's American Savings Bank failed in Memphis. Plough stepped forward with money to return $235,000 to the owners of Christmas savings deposits with the bank. Abe's marriage was broken in the early 1930s when he moved into the Peabody Hotel to live alone for the next four decades.

The rapid growth of Plough Chemical came from acquisition rather than from product development. To be sure, Plough created the first children's aspirin in 1947 and put the first safety caps on St. Joseph's Children's Aspirin ten years later. The most successful creation of his research chemists was Di-Gel antacid. But greater energy was focused on a bold expansion policy, acquiring thirty companies in all, including radio stations, Coppertone sun lotion in 1957, Paas Easter Egg color kits in 1959, and Maybelline eye cosmetics in 1967. By 1971, Plough marketed 100 different products, including prescription, over-the-counter, and proprietary medicines; cosmetics; toiletries; and household goods. When the eighty-year-old entrepreneur began to tire, he arranged a merger with Schering pharmaceutical of New Jersey and relieved himself of his management duties. The sales of the newly formed Schering-Plough were $500 million the first year and $1.5 billion a decade later. Plough served as chairman of the board for five years and then resigned in 1976 to devote himself to philanthropy.

Plough had generously contributed to a variety of Memphis charities and causes under the name of "Mr. Anonymous." The Memphis Zoo was a special concern to which he had given more than $1 million. But much of his wealth went into the Plough Foundation, which he endowed with

$51 million dollars, creating the largest philanthropic foundation in Memphis.

During his last decade, Plough lived in the high-rise Edenborough on South Highland in Memphis. He died at ninety-two after entering Baptist Hospital with bleeding ulcers; he was buried at Temple Israel Cemetery in Memphis.

★

Abe Plough avoided *Who's Who,* protected his private life, and wrote no autobiography. The best source is his *Press-Scimitar* clipping files and one manuscript box in the Mississippi Valley Archives, University of Memphis Library. An obituary is in the Memphis *Commercial Appeal* (15 Sept. 1984). For his place in the Memphis Jewish community, see Selma Lewis, *A Biblical People in the Bible Belt* (1998).

DAVID M. TUCKER

PONSELLE, Rosa Melba (*b.* 22 January 1897 in Meriden, Connecticut; *d.* 25 May 1981 in Green Spring Valley, Maryland), self-taught dramatic soprano whose career at the Metropolitan Opera in New York City (1918–1937) brought her world renown and gave her the nickname "Caruso in Petticoats."

Rosa Ponzillo was the third and last child of Italian immigrants Beniamino Ponzillo, proprietor of a grocery store and bakery run out of the ground floor of the family home,

Rosa Ponselle at Covent Garden, London, *c.* 1929. HULTON-DEUTSCH COLLECTION/CORBIS

and Maddalena Conti. She attended local public schools. Aside from singing in church choirs, Ponselle's first experience with music was piano lessons at age eight with Anna Ryan, who was giving singing lessons to Ponselle's older sister, Carmela. One day, when Ryan came to the Ponzillo home, she overheard Rosa singing and began giving her singing lessons as well.

In school, during music class, Rosa was allowed to play the pump organ because she could sight-read almost as well as the teacher. When she sang, she sounded like an adult, and the other children made fun of her voice. Because of family financial problems, she never finished high school and went to work at age fourteen, demonstrating sheet music on the piano at the local five-and-ten-cent store. At age sixteen she was offered a job by Richard Halliwell, owner of a chain of theaters, playing background piano for the silent films at the Star Theater in Meriden for $12 a week. She later moved to another of Halliwell's theaters, the Ansonia, where she played the piano and became a "slide singer," singing songs to accompany stills and leading the audience in sing-alongs.

Because of her popularity, Ponselle was moved to Halliwell's San Carlino Theater in New Haven, which had a large stage and an orchestra pit with an all-female orchestra. Ponselle usually sang four songs, two to please the Italian immigrants in the audience and two for the Yale students in attendance. It was through these students that James G. Ceriani, owner of a New Haven supper club, Cafeé Mellone, heard about Ponselle. Ceriani offered to double her salary to sing at his club. Ponselle became one of two soloists for his dinner concerts until 1915, when a family financial crisis made it imperative that Rosa and Carmela earn more money to rescue their parents from creditors. Carmela had already made a name for herself singing in cafés, vaudeville, operettas, and musical comedies. It was her idea that they perform a sister act in vaudeville.

When Gene Hughes, Carmela's agent, first saw Rosa, he said the five-foot, eight-inch, 195-pound singer was too fat. After he heard her sing, he said, "I don't give a goddam how fat she is! When can she open with you?" Thanks to a good corset and dieting, Rosa slimmed down, and the sisters first appeared together on stage at the Star Theater in the Bronx, New York, as the Ponzillo Sisters. A contract with the prestigious B. F. Keith organization soon followed, and the sisters, billed as the Italian Girls, played at the Royal Theater in the Bronx in the fall of 1915. Their twenty-minute "turn" included six numbers from opera and popular songs. For their finale they did the prison scene in Gounod's *Faust*. Following their debut, they performed at a number of other houses on the Keith circuit, traveling from Portland, Maine, to Atlanta, Georgia, and as far west as Chicago. Increasing fame resulted in two engagements at the Palace Theater in Times Square in New York City, the pinnacle of the vaudeville world. It was on the Keith circuit, traveling between theaters, sometimes doing eight shows a day, that Ponselle derived much of her self-confidence as a performer and learned the hard lessons of pacing and managing a career. Ponselle's vaudeville career lasted until 1918.

While playing Keith's Riverside Theater on the Upper West Side of Manhattan, she met William Thorner and Romano Romani. Thorner introduced Ponselle to people in the opera world, and in December 1917, he signed a contract to manage Ponselle for 10 percent of her future earnings, should he ever place her in opera. Romani, a conductor and composer who had been Puccini's protégé, became Ponselle's coach in 1918 and remained so throughout her career.

Thorner introduced Ponselle to operatic tenor Enrico Caruso, who, after hearing her sing, predicted that she would soon sing with him. Caruso implemented his prediction by suggesting Ponselle to Giulio Gatti-Casazza, the general manager of the Metropolitan Opera in New York City, for the lead soprano role in a new production of Verdi's *La Forza del Destino*. She auditioned with the arias "Pace, pace mio Dio" from *Forza* and "Casta diva" from Bellini's *Norma*. Gatti-Casazza, amazed by the beauty of her voice, and the fact that she had no professional training, hired her on the spot. Ponselle studied the opera for five months with Romani and at this time changed her last name to Ponselle. She debuted at the Metropolitan on 15 November 1918, singing Leonora to Caruso's Don Alvaro, and became a star overnight. Critics described her voice as "vocal gold." Ponselle was the first American-born and American-trained soprano with no prior European experience to sing at the Metropolitan. Even more astounding was the fact that she had never sung opera anywhere until she debuted at the Met. The following month she sang in a revival of Weber's *Oberon* and later that season was in the world premier of Joseph Breil's *The Legend*.

Ponselle sang nineteen seasons with the Metropolitan Opera, giving 465 performances in twenty-three roles. One of the outstanding roles of her career was as the title character in the 1927 revival of *Norma,* a rarely performed opera because of its difficulty for singers. The title role has been called the "ultimate test" for great sopranos. Ponselle took two years to prepare for the role, and her performance was a triumph.

On 26 December 1931 Ponselle became part of radio history when NBC broadcast *Norma,* beginning a tradition of live Saturday broadcasts from the Met. By the time Ponselle was heard in *Norma,* she was already experienced in radio. She had made her radio debut on New Year's Day in 1927 on *The Victor Talking Machine Hour,* appearing with John McCormack. A number of radio shows followed, in-

cluding *The Chesterfield Hour* (1934–1938) with Andre Kostelanetz. Radio suited Ponselle. Singing a couple of arias, in any key she wished, and doing two or three ballads to complete her program did not seem like work to the vaudeville veteran.

Although Ponselle toured with the Met's annual spring tours, she did not enjoy traveling, which aggravated her recurrent stage fright. Her first trip to Europe was in 1924, during which she sang for the dying Puccini at his home. She sang for three seasons, from 1929 to 1932, at London's Covent Garden, debuting in *Norma* to rave reviews. In 1933 she sang Giulia in Spontini's *La Vestale* at the inaugural of the Maggio Musicale Fiorentino in Florence, Italy. An encore following an opera is usually unheard of, but in her second performance the public demanded that Ponselle repeat the prayer from the second act. After the audience rose to their feet and refused to allow the opera to continue, the angry conductor permitted the encore. Her performances were broadcast throughout Europe. Although she had numerous offers from a variety of foreign opera companies, Ponselle never traveled abroad again.

At the Metropolitan, standout performances included the title roles in Verdi's *Aida* and Ponchielli's *La Gioconda,* as well as Donna Anna in Mozart's *Don Giovanni* and Santuzza in Mascagni's *Cavalleria rusticana.* Ponselle had always wanted to play the lead in Bizet's *Carmen,* but her initial Metropolitan performance, in 1935, in the title role was a disappointment. Most of the press and the audience found her interpretation vulgar. Later versions were toned down and were favorably received. Ponselle tried for some years to have Hollywood produce *Carmen* with her as the star. Her trips to Hollywood caused some friction with the management of the Met. Ponselle was also unhappy with the Metropolitan's refusal to allow her to sing Cilea's *Adriana Lecouvreur,* and at the age of forty-one she retired. Her last appearance on the stage at the Metropolitan was 15 February 1937, as Carmen. Ponselle's retirement may have also been a result of her continuing stage fright and a developing unease concerning hitting the high notes needed for certain roles. The self-taught Ponselle possibly lacked the technical training to adjust to changes in her voice.

Ponselle married Carle A. Jackson, the son of the mayor of Baltimore, on 13 December 1936. Childless, they divorced in 1949. Following her retirement from the Metropolitan, Ponselle did a series of concert tours from 1937 to 1939, and during subsequent years some teaching and coaching. Among her students were William Warfield, Sherrill Milnes, Beverly Sills, and James Morris. She served as artistic director of the Baltimore Civic Opera from 1950 to the late 1970s. She also worked on a memoir with James Drake, *Ponselle: A Singer's Life,* published posthumously in 1982.

During her career Ponselle made more than 100 recordings, first for Columbia, then at Victor. In 1954, after a public silence of nearly seventeen years, she was persuaded to record from her Maryland home, Villa Pace. Over seven days, Ponselle recorded sixty songs and arias, many requiring several takes. The resulting LPs that RCA produced, *Rosa Ponselle Sings Today* and *Rosa Ponselle in Song,* reveal a voice still exceptional for its velvet tones.

Four years before her death, Ponselle drew up a will, creating the Rosa Ponselle Foundation to provide scholarships for aspiring musicians. Ponselle died of a heart attack at her home in Green Spring Valley, Maryland, near Baltimore. She is buried beside her sister Carmela at Druid Ridge Cemetery in Green Spring Valley.

Ponselle was a groundbreaker, singing at the Metropolitan Opera when American singers, generally, were not welcome there. Her voice, with its richness and clarity, remains a standard by which singers measure their capabilities. Soprano Maria Callas said Ponselle was "probably the greatest singer of us all."

★

A collection of Ponselle's scrapbooks, clippings, and letters is at the New York Public Library for the Performing Arts, Lincoln Center. James A. Drake, *Rosa Ponselle: A Centenary Biography* (1997), and Mary Jane Phillips-Matz, *Rosa Ponselle: American Diva* (1997), are two biographies published to celebrate the centennial of her birth. Drake includes a chronology of performances by Thomas G. Kaufman, a bibliography by Andrew Farkas, and a discography by Bill Park. Chapters dedicated to Ponselle can be found in Gladys Davidson, *A Treasury of Opera Biography* (1955), and in Henry Pleasants, *The Great Singers from the Dawn of Opera to Our Own Time* (1966). Articles include Walter Legge, "Rosa: An Eightieth Birthday Homage," *Opera News* (12 Mar. 1977); Thomas Pasatieri, "From the Villa Pace: Rosa Ponselle Tells Her Story," *Opera News* (12 Mar. 1977); Mary Jane Phillips-Matz, "Sister Act: The Vaudeville Roots of Carmela and Rosa Ponselle," *Opera News* (11 Jan. 1997); and Martin Bernheimer, "The Golden Soprano," *Opera* 48 (Feb. 1997). An obituary is in the *New York Times* (26 May 1981).

MARCIA B. DINNEEN

POOL, Ithiel de Sola (*b.* 26 October 1917 in New York City; *d.* 11 March 1984 in Cambridge, Massachusetts), pioneering political scientist, communications theorist, and author who predicted that the technology of communications would be more influential than governmental policies in shaping the social and political landscape of the future.

Pool was one of two children of Rabbi David de Sola Pool, the spiritual leader of the Sephardic Congregation in New York City, and Tamar (Hirshenson) de Sola Pool, the Palestinian-born daughter of a rabbi. Both parents were highly educated. His father earned a Ph.D. from the University of Heidelberg, Germany, and his mother was educated at Hunter College in New York City and the Sorbonne in Paris. She was a teacher of classical languages at Hunter and later joined her husband as an author and lecturer.

Pool was educated at Fieldston, an Ethical Culture school in New York City, and at the University of Chicago, where he received a B.A. degree in 1938, M.A. degree in 1939, and a Ph.D. in political science in 1952. His mentor was the noted educator Robert Maynard Hutchins, who was president of the University of Chicago from 1929 to 1945, a period in which it spawned the field of social science in America. In 1938 Pool married Judith Graham in Chicago; they would have two sons. The family lived at 5738 Maryland Avenue and later at 22 Delancy Drive in Chicago while Judith obtained her doctorate in physiology from the University of Chicago.

A tall, trim, professorial figure with Mediterranean features and dark, curly hair, Pool had the complex personality and humor of a brilliant visionary. He was an advocate of open-mindedness and nonjudgmental analysis who nevertheless was impatient with disagreement about his observations and conclusions. Politically, although he had been a Trotskyite at the University of Chicago, after his student years he became disenchanted with the ideas of revolutionary politics and denounced attempts by governments to restrict or control the freedoms of individual citizens.

In 1942 he began teaching at Hobart and William Smith College in Geneva, New York, where he served as chairman of the Division of Social Sciences until 1949. Prior to joining Hobart, he collaborated with two of his teachers, Harold Lasswell and Nathan Leites, in Washington, D.C., on research into Nazi and communist propaganda and the symbols of freedom used in speeches by political leaders. In 1942 he and Leites published *Communist Propaganda in Reaction to Frustration.* In 1944 his career was threatened by tuberculosis, but he recovered fully during a year in a Geneva, New York, sanatorium.

In September 1949 Pool joined the Hoover Institution on War, Revolution, and Peace, a conservative think tank at Stanford. At Hoover, he held a faculty appointment at Stanford as assistant professor of political science and was assistant director of research for Hoover's RADIR (Revolution and the Development of International Relations) Project. In April 1952 he began splitting his time between the Hoover Institution and the RAND Corporation. Judith ultimately joined the faculty at the Stanford Research Institute. The family lived at 1301 Sherman Avenue in Menlo Park, California, until the couple divorced in April 1953.

Pool left Stanford in 1953 to become an associate professor of political science at the Massachusetts Institute of Technology; he became a full professor in 1957. On 3 March 1955 he married Dr. Jean MacKenzie, who held a

Professor Ithiel Pool meeting with students in a sit-in at the Center for International Studies, Massachusetts Institute of Technology, 1969. UPI/Corbis-Bettmann

Ph.D. in psychology; they would have one son. The family resided at 105 Irving Street in Cambridge, Massachusetts.

Pool was instrumental in the establishment of MIT's political science department, which he chaired from 1959 to 1961 and 1965 to 1969. He helped to create the interdisciplinary Research Program on Communications Policy and in later years would hold the Ruth and Arthur Sloan professorship in political science. The president of MIT, Paul E. Gray, called Pool "the leading figure in the development of political science at MIT and an inspiring force in its growth as a field of study into a major department with an international reputation." Although the leftist politics of his student years brought challenges to his security clearances, he also served as a member of the Council on Foreign Relations and advised the U.S. government in several other capacities during the cold war.

Pool was the author of more than two dozen books and more than a hundred articles and reviews in professional journals and publications. *American Business and Public Policy,* published in 1963, won the Woodrow Wilson Award as the year's best book in political science. Writing in 1987 of Pool's *Technologies of Freedom* (1983), the media specialist Stewart Brand wrote that Pool, "like no one before or since . . . saw the world of communications whole and with up-to-the-second knowledge in depth," adding that the book's value was becoming more evident with each passing year.

"The first defensive tactic by the owners of an old medium against competition by a new one," Pool wrote in *Technologies,* "is to have the new one prohibited. If this does not work, the next defensive tactic is to buy into the attacker." Thus this early user of the Arpanet seemed to fore-

tell the phenomenal growth and impact of its successor, the Internet.

"People who think about social change in traditional political terms cannot begin to imagine the changes that lie ahead," wrote Pool in an article entitled "Development of Communication in the Future Perspective" (1983). "Conventional reformers cast their programs in terms of national policies, or in terms of laws and central planning. But in the end, what will shape the future is a creative potential that inheres in the new technologies."

Pool continued to lecture and write even after cancer was diagnosed in 1980. In 1983, the year before his death, he published not only *Technologies of Freedom* but also twenty articles and *Forecasting the Telephone: A Retrospective Technology Assessment of the Telephone,* an analysis of predictions about the telephone between 1860 and 1940.

Communication Flows (1984) appeared after his death. Pool died of cancer at Mount Auburn Hospital in Cambridge, Massachusetts, and was buried in that city.

Pool's writings express a vision of freedom in triumph through technology over the restrictions and boundaries imposed by governments, political philosophies, and nations. He envisioned citizens, utilizing simple and affordable tools of communication to breach the artificial lines drawn by political entities, in the active process of transforming and redefining their social and political lives.

★

In addition to the works mentioned above see *The Handbook of Communication* (1973), a collection edited by Pool that analyzes public opinion, and his *The Social Impact of the Telephone* (1977). See also Lloyd S. Etheridge, ed., *Politics in Wired Nations: Collected Papers by Ithiel de Sola Pool* (1998).

CHARLES A. ROND IV

POPE, James Soule, Sr. (*b.* c. 1900 in Zebulon, Georgia; *d.* 13 December 1985 in Panama City, Florida), newspaper editor who was instrumental in the enactment in 1966 of the Freedom of Information Act (FOIA).

Born in Zebulon, Georgia, Pope began his career as a railway clerk and in the automobile business after graduating from Emory University. In 1926 he got a job as a reporter for the *Atlanta Journal.* He advanced to city editor in 1930 and managing editor in 1939 before joining the *Courier-Journal* in Louisville, Kentucky, in 1940. Shortly after joining the Louisville paper, Pope was named managing editor. In 1952 he became the executive editor of both the *Courier-Journal* and the *Louisville Times,* and he held the position until retiring in 1962.

Throughout his thirty-six-year career in journalism, Pope fought doggedly for freedom of the press and for the public's access to government information and documents. In a speech in 1949 at the University of Georgia, Pope explained his philosophy as a crusading editor: "The good editor—and perhaps any good and useful leader—has to wake up angry every morning," Pope said. "He does not wait for the moment to crusade on a spectacular scale." Despite his belief in newspaper crusades as a means to bring about social reform, Pope did not support a common trend of the 1950s known as "interpretive reporting." This style of journalism had several causes, the most important being the argument that Americans were now receiving their news first from radio or television, and thus the role of newspapers had shifted from informer to interpreter. Pope criticized this notion, believing that reporters should deliver the news impartially, without their own analysis built into the story.

James S. Pope. THE COURIER-JOURNAL

The *Courier-Journal* was one of the leading regional papers during Pope's era, and under the direction of owner Barry Bingham, Sr., and general manager Mark Ethridge, the newspaper's editorial page campaigned for many liberal causes, particularly for the rights of African Americans in an era before integration. Pope's most important contribution, however, came from his work in the 1950s in trying to secure access for the public and press to government information and documents. Before the freedom of information (FOI) law was passed, the public could get information about the government only on an ambiguously defined "need to know" basis, a policy that had been in effect for more than 150 years.

Pope and two other editors, Basil "Stuffy" Walters of the *Chicago Daily News* and J. Russell Wiggins of the *Washington Post,* were the first three chairmen of the American Society of Newspaper Editors' committee on freedom of information. Originally, ASNE wanted to promote free flow of information throughout the world, but the committee soon discovered that access to government information was not just a problem overseas but in the United States as well. Pope recruited a former newspaper lawyer, Harold L. Cross, to write a book about recent statutes and court decisions that had limited access to government information. The resulting volume, *The People's Right to Know* (1953), became the bible of the FOI movement and the foundation for federal legislation. After his term chairing the ASNE's freedom of information committee, Pope served as the organization's president from 1953 to 1954.

The U.S. Congress took up the FOI issue in 1954, when John Moss, a freshman Democratic representative from California, was named chairman of a new subcommittee to investigate obstacles to openness. This move effectively began the government debate about FOI. Pope, representing ASNE, was a member of the panel of journalists at the subcommittee's first hearing in November 1955.

President Lyndon B. Johnson signed the FOI act into law on 4 July 1966, almost twenty years after ASNE had begun its campaign. It took effect one year later and was amended in 1974. It is essential to investigative reporting today, although some journalists, researchers, and citizens argue that it still does not allow enough access. Similar laws have since been enacted at the state and local levels.

Pope retired as executive editor of the *Courier-Journal* and the *Louisville Times* at a relatively young age, at sixty-one, saying that his energy and capacity for being editor had waned and that he had been considering early retirement for a long time. Several *New York Times* writers, however, in a book about Bingham, argue that Pope was fired by Ethridge for opposing the hiring of a black intern. In addition, the authors state that Pope had banned all pictures of blacks in the newspaper's women's and society sections.

For his FOIA work, Pope received honors named for some of the most famous journalists in American history. In 1957 he was awarded the John Peter Zenger Freedom of the Press Award by the University of Arizona, honoring the newspaper publisher victorious in one of the earliest cases establishing the freedom of the press in American history. Pope was also the first winner of the Elijah Lovejoy Fellowship, awarded by Colby College in Waterville, Maine, in honor of an editor who campaigned against slavery until he was murdered by a mob in Alton, Illinois, in 1837. Pope was also an original inductee into the American Society of Newspaper Editors FOIA Hall of Fame.

Pope and his wife, Geraldine, had three sons. Pope moved to Florida after his retirement in January 1962. He worked as a consultant on urban research projects for the Ford Foundation for about three years. He died at the age of eighty-five after a series of strokes.

Though Pope was a journalist, his contribution to American society did not come from his operation of his newspaper. Instead, his fierce determination to gain access for the press and public into the records of government helped lead to the creation of the Freedom of Information Act, from which the press and many average citizens have benefited.

★

Information about the *Louisville Courier-Journal* and Pope's reason for leaving is contained in Susan E. Tifft and Alex S. Jones, *The Patriarch: The Rise and Fall of the Bingham Dynasty* (1991). Good information about the FOIA can be found in L. G. Sherick, *How to Use the Freedom of Information Act* (1978). Obituaries may be found in the *Louisville Courier-Journal, Washington Post,* and *New York Times* (all 15 Dec. 1985).

BRADLEY J. HAMM

POWELL, Eleanor Torrey ("Ellie") (*b.* 21 November 1912 in Springfield, Massachusetts; *d.* 11 February 1982 in Beverly Hills, California), film and stage performer who as a tap dancing sensation left her mark in such film extravaganzas as *Rosalie* (1937), *Broadway Melody of 1940* (1940), and *Ship Ahoy* (1942).

Powell was the daughter of Blanche and Clarence Powell. Her father, who was engaged in the family business of roof restoration, divorced his teenage wife and abandoned his daughter when she was only two years old. Eleanor was raised by her grandmother, while her mother worked as a bank teller and a hotel chambermaid. When Eleanor was nine her grandmother enrolled her in the local ballet school, where she continued to take classes for the next five years.

In 1924, when she was eleven years old, Powell went

Eleanor Powell. ARCHIVE PHOTOS

with her mother and grandmother to Atlantic City for the summer. Gus Edwards, then show producer at the luxury Ambassador Hotel, saw her doing acrobatics on the beach and hired her for a spot in the hotel's dinner show, in which she performed in a revue headlined by future movie star Lola Lane. She returned to Atlantic City the next two summers, appearing in various nightclubs. In the summer of 1926 she was earning $75 a week as a dancer and occasional mistress of ceremonies at Martins, the top supper club in Atlantic City, which was frequented by such Broadway personalities as Jack Benny and Eddie Cantor, who urged her to seek her fortune in New York City.

In the summer of 1927 the family went to New York, with the understanding that if Powell did not land a part in a major show within the three months of the school vacation, she would go back to Springfield to continue her education. She was not yet fifteen years old. Her New York debut was at Ben Bernie's Club. Auditioning for Broadway shows in the daytime, Powell soon discovered that there was little call for ballet dancers in New York, in an era when the tap dance craze had swept the country. Powell enrolled in a dance school where she took tap lessons from Jack Donahue.

Bill Grady of the William Morris Agency caught Powell's act at Ben Bernie's Club, signed her as a client, and booked her for twenty-four performances at the Casino de Paris midnight show, *The Optimists,* on the Ziegfeld Roof beginning in January 1928. Grady then booked her as a tap dancer for a twenty-week vaudeville tour, for which she was paid $100 a week. She next appeared in *Follow Through,* a Broadway musical comedy starring Jack Haley that opened on 9 January 1929 and ran for 403 performances. She had her first leading role in a Broadway musical comedy in *Fine and Dandy,* which ran from September 1930 to May 1931 and went on a seven-city tour. In 1930 Powell and costar Maurice Chevalier, in his first performance in the United States, appeared with the George White band in a concert at Carnegie Hall. Powell was the first dancer so honored.

In the winter of 1932 Powell starred in the Broadway revue *Hot Cha!,* at the Ziegfeld Theater. Her next Broadway appearance was in *Yasha Bunchik's Third Birthday,* which opened in June 1932. During 1933 Powell appeared in several shows, among them the Broadway revues *George White's Music Hall Varieties* (1932–1933), *George White's Scandals,* and the road company of *Crazy Quilt.* In 1934 she was the principal headliner at Billy Rose's Cafe de Paris for seventeen weeks.

Powell's film career began when George White took his band and main headliners to California to film *George White's Scandals* (1935) at Twentieth Century. Louis B. Mayer of Metro-Goldwyn-Mayer (MGM) saw her performance and gave her a screen test, together with young Hollywood hopeful Robert Taylor. Mayer signed them both to seven-year contracts. Powell soon became one of MGM's top moneymakers. Movies gave her a worldwide audience and millions of new fans. Before beginning her film work, Powell returned to New York, where she was under contract to the Shubert brothers to star in *At Home Abroad* at the Winter Garden Theater. She stayed with the show for four months then returned to Hollywood.

Her first film for MGM was *Born to Dance* (1936), produced by Jack Cummings, directed by Roy del Ruth, and costarring Jimmy Stewart in his first leading role. Featuring the music of Cole Porter, *Born to Dance* established Powell as a major film star. She was noted in the press for her exhilarating tap dances and the smart way she looked in tails and top hat. The box-office success of the film convinced MGM that they had found their leading star for *Broadway Melody of 1936,* the long awaited sequel to *Broadway Melody* (1929) starring Ruby Keeler. The film costarred Robert Taylor and Jack Benny, and again featured the music of Cole Porter. Its wide appeal, however, was due to Powell's "eloquent feet" and dazzling performance, as she danced with "giddy delight, unusual candor, and engaging

charm." That year the Dancing Masters of America named Powell the "World's Greatest Feminine Tap and Rhythm Dancer."

For the leading roles in *Rosalie* (1937), MGM picked Nelson Eddy and Powell. One of her most important films, it told the story of a West Point cadet (Eddy) who falls in love with a Balkan princess (Powell). Stunning sets and lavish costumes, as well as Porter's elegant and sophisticated melodies, enhanced Powell's masterful footwork and Eddy's lilting baritone. The film was an overnight hit.

In recognition of her accomplishment the Dance Troupers of America named Powell the "Foremost Dancer in the World." On 23 December 1937, her hand and shoe prints were placed in cement in front of Grauman's Chinese Theater.

Her next film had a tropical island setting, a fad evidenced in many Hollywood musicals of the period. In *Honolulu* (1939), which costarred Robert Young, George Burns, and Gracie Allen, Powell danced in a Hawaiian straw skirt and abbreviated Spanish costumes. The film evoked sharp protests from the Hawaiian Society at Columbia University, which complained that Powell's hula dance was "too hot" and insulted the Hawaiian people who revered the dance as an important part of their culture. When the management of Capitol Theater, where the movie was premiered, refused to cut the dance segment from the film, members of the society picketed in front of the box office, which only succeeded in giving the film free publicity.

About this time MGM became interested in dancer-actor Fred Astaire, who in 1940 signed a three-year contract with the studio. In Astaire's first movie for MGM he was paired with Powell in the landmark musical *Broadway Melody of 1940,* which features some of the most elaborate tap dances ever seen on the screen. The high point of the movie is a tap pas de deux executed by Powell and Astaire, choreographed by Powell to the music of Porter's "Begin the Beguine." The intricate choreography showcased Powell's skill. Her rapid tap, regal ballet posture, and gently coaxing movements of her arms and shoulders gave the appearance of two dances being executed simultaneously by one dancer. Fans were fascinated with Powell's ability to gracefully coordinate two so disparate rhythms between her lower and upper limbs. Next to her, even the great Astaire found himself overshadowed; he did not renew his contract with MGM. From that point on Mayer sought to curb Powell's star power. Instead of the romantic duos she had become accustomed to, she was now cast as a member of a foursome or in cameo roles in multistar films, such as *Lady Be Good* (1941).

In 1942 the producer Jack Cummings, in defiance of Mayer, allowed Powell once again to dominate a movie. *Ship Ahoy,* costarring Bert Lahr and Red Skelton, was a merry comedy with a wartime background. Backed up by

Tommy Dorsey's orchestra, Powell invented some of her most imaginative choreography for the film.

In 1943 Powell returned to the all-star spectacular with *I Dood It,* directed by Vincente Minnelli and costarring Red Skelton, Sam Levene, Lena Horne, and John Hodiak, with a host of MGM stars in cameo roles. *Thousands Cheer* (1943), Powell's first color picture, was another multistar entertainment.

In 1943 Powell's contract with MGM expired and was never renewed. Paramount Pictures hired Powell to appear in *Sensations of 1945* with Dennis O'Keefe and C. Aubrey Smith. The film extravaganza featured vaudeville acts, orchestra bits, and dance. Powell performed two notable tap routines. She made two additional films before retiring from the movie industry, *King Morgan* (1945) and *Duchess of Idaho* (1950). In 1974 Fred Astaire and Gene Kelly produced a musical collage, *This Is Entertainment: MGM Golden Anniversary.* Included among their clippings are the Astaire-Powell tap pas de deux from *Broadway Melody of 1940* and excerpts of Powell's dances in *Born to Dance, Rosalie,* and *Ship Ahoy.*

Powell's war effort as an entertainer was exceptional. Throughout 1942 and 1943 she toured army camps. In April 1942 she took part in the Hollywood Victory Caravan, a well-publicized multicity benefit tour. On 24 June 1942, she appeared with nearly forty major movie stars at the Hollywood Bowl, perhaps the highlight of the entertainment war effort. On 23 October 1943 Powell married actor Glenn Ford, whom she divorced in 1959. They had one child.

Following World War II, Powell returned to the supper club circuit. In 1948 she took her "Symphony in Rhythm" to the Flamingo Hotel in Las Vegas. The following year she brought her nightclub act to Glasgow and London, opening a three-week engagement at the Palladium on 21 March. From 1951 to 1956 Powell hosted a weekly syndicated television show called *Faith of Our Children.* Conceived by Powell as a Sunday school of the air, the program featured Powell teaching children from various Catholic, Jewish, and Protestant denominations. The show garnered a total of six Los Angeles–area Emmy Awards, including five for Powell as the most outstanding female personality on television.

Powell made various other television appearances throughout the 1950s and 1960s, being interviewed in 1957 by Edward R. Murrow on *Person to Person* and on the *Tonight Show* with Johnny Carson.

In 1961 Powell made a notable comeback on the supper club circuit, taking a new act, "An Evening with Eleanor Powell," to Las Vegas and New York. She was now forty-nine years old and still a powerhouse of tap and rhythm. She played to capacity crowds, dazzling critics and fans alike. In 1963 and 1964 Powell returned to Las Vegas, with

new sets and ravishing costume designs. On 7 August 1964 Powell danced at a command performance for Princess Grace of Monaco. It was her last professional appearance as a dancer. In 1965, after a forty-year career, Powell retired to private life.

The Berlin International Film Festival presented Powell with its Silver Cup and held a ten-film retrospective of her films in 1976. On 10 September 1979 the Academy of Motion Picture Arts and Sciences awarded her the Best Dance Direction Salute. In October 1981 the National Film Society created the Ellie Award, named after Powell, to be given annually for dance performance in film. Powell was the award's first recipient. In 1982 the second Ellie Award was presented to Fred Astaire.

Following her death from cancer, in February 1984 a star bearing her name was installed on the Hollywood Walk of Fame. In 1993 the Hollywood Hoofers enshrined Powell as a Dance Legend. She is buried in the Hollywood Memorial Park Cemetery.

★

"Eleanor Powell" in John Kobal, *People Will Talk* (1985), is a transcription of a tape-recorded overview of Powell's life told in her own words without editing or omissions. Margie Schultz, *Eleanor Powell: A Bio-Biography* (1994), is an indispensable source book for anyone researching her career. A chapter on Powell is included in James R. Parish and Michael R. Pitts, *Hollywood Songsters: A Biographical Dictionary* (1990). Obituaries are in the *Los Angeles Times* and *New York Times* (both 12 Feb. 1982). A tribute by Charles Champlin is in the *New York Times* (13 Feb. 1982).

SHOSHANA KLEBANOFF

POWELL, William Horatio (*b.* 29 July 1892 in Pittsburgh, Pennsylvania; *d.* 5 March 1984 in Palm Springs, California), actor who is best remembered for his screen portrayals of the rambunctious Man of the World (the title of one of his movies), the self-assured sophisticate who flouted the rules of decorum; his signature role was Nick Charles in the *Thin Man* movies, a series of frothy whodunits.

The only child of Horatio Warren Powell, an accountant, and Nettie (Brady) Powell, William Powell moved with his parents to Kansas City, Missouri, at around the age of ten. After high school he circumvented his parents' wishes (they wanted him to be a lawyer) by appealing to a wealthy aunt back east for money to pursue an acting career. On the strength of a twenty-three-page letter sent by Powell, she lent him $700 to attend the American Academy of Dramatic Arts in New York City, where his classmates included Edward G. Robinson.

After graduating from the Academy in 1912, Powell slogged through several years of low-paying stage roles. In

William Horatio Powell, *c.* 1940. HULTON-DEUTSCH COLLECTION/
CORBIS

1914 he married actress Eileen Wilson, with whom in 1925 he had his only child, William David Powell; the marriage ended in divorce in 1931. By the age of thirty, Powell had played more than 200 stage roles, but he and his wife were still barely getting by. Director Albert Parker asked him to appear in the film *Sherlock Holmes* (1922), with John Barrymore as the sleuth. Powell found the work congenial, a relief from the rigors of the stage. After making several more movies, he signed a contract with Paramount in 1924.

"You don't look like anyone else," Parker had told him, and with his parrot-beak nose and pouchy eyes, Powell was not an obvious ladykiller. But for all its imperfections, it was a strong, expressive face. His painstaking preparation and intense concentration (his acting was analytical rather than instinctual) and the self-confidence won from all those years in the theater served him well. He progressed gradually but surely from villain to comedian to romantic comedian to full-fledged leading man. With the advent of sound in the late 1920s, Powell's resonant, stage-trained voice became a distinct plus.

On 26 June 1931 he married actress Carole Lombard, who at twenty-two was a generation younger than he (she matured into one of Hollywood's most polished comediennes). Although the marriage did not last long, Powell was always civilized about matters of the heart, and the two remained good friends. In fact, William Powell—the actor and the man—was naturally uxurious. Time and again, at Paramount and then at MGM, in silent movies and talkies, he was paired repeatedly with a particular actress: Evelyn Brent, Bebe Daniels, Kay Francis (with whom he made the classy weeper *One Way Passage,* 1932), Lombard herself (their best work together is in the screwball comedy *My Man Godfrey,* 1936), and above all Myrna Loy.

Loy played Nick's wife, Nora, in the *Thin Man* movies, and they worked so well together that fans had trouble believing they were not married in real life. They "met cute," as couples often do in romantic comedies: nobody at MGM had bothered to introduce them before she stepped into his character's car for their first scene together in *Manhattan Melodrama* (1934). She recalled that "right from the start there was this marvelous thing between us." *The Thin Man,* released later that year, reinforced their teamwork; five sequels followed (the last came out in 1947), all with the term "Thin Man" in the title, even though Powell was not notably thin and the sobriquet had belonged to a character who died in the first movie. Apart from the series, Powell and Loy costarred seven other times, and Loy made a cameo appearance in another film starring Powell, for a grand total of fourteen joint appearances.

The best of their "non-Thins" is the romantic comedy *Libeled Lady* (1936), also starring Spencer Tracy and Jean Harlow, which features the most brilliant set piece of Powell's career: a slapstick fly-casting sequence that ends up with him, a clumsy novice, landing a legendarily elusive fish. Altogether 1936 was Powell's banner year: in addition to *Libeled Lady* and *My Man Godfrey,* he had the title role in *The Great Ziegfeld,* made the second *Thin Man* movie with Loy, and costarred with Jean Arthur in *The Ex-Mrs. Bradford,* a winsome romantic mystery.

Powell had been secretly engaged to Harlow when she died in 1937. In 1940 he made the lasting marriage he had always seemed suited for, to starlet Diana Lewis. In the meantime, a bout with rectal cancer had slowed his career. Pronounced cured, he nonetheless had to pace himself afterward. Although his movies of the 1940s tend to be less impressive, there are exceptions: the comedies *I Love You Again* (1940) and *Love Crazy* (1941), both with Loy; and *Life with Father* (1947), in which he plays the eponymous autocrat.

He took character roles in the 1950s, notably a Texas tycoon in *How to Marry a Millionaire* (1953), with Marilyn Monroe; and a ship's doctor in *Mister Roberts* (1955), his last film. He and his wife retired to a quiet life in Palm Springs, where he died of respiratory failure at the age of ninety-one.

At his best, Powell managed to be both debonair and something of an anarchist. In the original *Thin Man,* for example, he takes time out from detection and badinage with Loy for indoor target practice, using an air gun to shoot ornaments off the Christmas tree. His acting has aged well because he often underplayed, letting spare gestures and controlled facial expressions carry a moment that other actors might have attacked at full throttle; and because he flavored his comic performances with a detached amusement that makes him look hip. He and Loy are an immortal couple because their long-running screen marriage resembles not the tiring life-sentence satirized in so many jokes and sitcoms but a witty adventure for spirited adults.

★

The only full-length biography, *Gentleman: The William Powell Story,* by Charles Francisco (1985), is solid, if uninspired. Lawrence J. Quirk, *The Complete Films of William Powell* (1986), has a useful biographical introduction and a brief discussion of every movie Powell made. *Myrna Loy: Being and Becoming,* which the actress cowrote with James Kotsilibas-Cavis (1987), gives an inside view of her celebrated partnership with Powell. Dennis Drabelle's "The Thin Man on Parnassus," *Film Comment* (May/June 1993), expands upon some of the themes in this entry. An obituary is in the *New York Times* (6 Mar. 1984).

DENNIS DRABELLE

PRICE, T(homas) Rowe, Jr. (*b.* 16 March 1898 in Glyndon, Maryland; *d.* 20 October 1983 in Baltimore, Maryland), investment manager who pioneered the growth-stock approach and helped build the mutual-fund industry.

The son of Thomas Rowe Price, Sr., a physician, and Ella S. Black, a homemaker, young Thomas attended Swarthmore College, where he earned a B.A. degree in chemistry in 1919. He worked as a chemist for the DuPont Company from 1919 to 1921, then switched to the world of stocks and bonds as a salesman for various brokerage houses in Baltimore. From 1925 to 1937 he was manager of the investment department and director of the investment management department at Mackubin, Legg, and Company, Baltimore. In 1937 he launched his own investment counseling firm, T. Rowe Price and Associates, with five employees.

Price built his business by rejecting the conventional wisdom of stock picking. Many Depression-era investors regarded stocks as cyclical investments, to be bought and sold based on swings in price. Price's growth-stock methodology transcended this short-term thinking. He favored acquiring and holding shares of promising firms in growing industries. Price's approach, refined at a time when business conditions were anything but stable, became the basis for a new school of investment practice in the boom years of the American economy after World War II.

Stock shares, Price reasoned, were not so different from businesses themselves. An owner would not continually

T. Rowe Price. T. ROWE PRICE ASSOCIATES, INC.

buy and sell his business with every swing in its fortunes. He would, rather, develop the business over time, sticking with it through occasional hard times as long as its prospects remained bright. Invoking another metaphor, Price stated that investors must seek out "fertile fields for growth," then possess both the patience and the vigilance to monitor their holdings over time. Above all, Price emphasized that he could not predict the course of the stock market and that trying to do so would only divert attention from the more important task of choosing individual stocks. "Change is the investor's only certainty," he stated in 1937, an oft-repeated comment that became a virtual mantra for his investment philosophy.

During his firm's early years, Price carefully spelled out his definition of a growth company and his criteria for buying and selling stocks. Industries, he believed, went through life cycles of growth, maturity, and decline. The key was to identify growth industries, and to choose the best-positioned companies within those sectors. Price sought to identify such companies while they were small and before they had been glamorized by Wall Street investors. Indeed, his distaste for the "herd instinct" was so great that he steadfastly refused to move his growing firm from Baltimore to the nation's financial center in New York. The formula incorporated quantitative measures, particularly the price-to-earnings ratio, which is a fundamental yardstick of how costly a stock is relative to the market. But its main thrust was qualitative, relying on factors such as the competence of a company's management, its competitive position, and its ability to plan for future growth.

Price applied his principles to a number of mutual funds, allowing middle-class investors to join wealthy clients in profiting from the growth-stock strategy. (A mutual fund is a pool of investments, professionally managed, in which individuals may buy shares.) The T. Rowe Price Growth Stock Fund was launched in 1950 amid a rising market. Its initial investment was in shares of the International Business Machines Corporation, which would become the nation's dominant maker of computers. The New Horizons Fund followed in 1960, investing in small companies including a then-obscure Xerox Corporation. In 1969, concerned with the effects of inflation on investors' wealth, Price introduced the New Era Fund, which bought stocks in gold mines, energy companies, and other inflation hedges.

Coworkers described Price as a hard-driving man who focused on investments to the exclusion of almost everything else. Price favored self-deprecating humor, once commenting that he was "not very bright," but he made up for any supposed lack of intelligence through rigid self-discipline. He often began work as early as 4 A.M., believing that his mind operated best in the uncluttered hours before sunrise. He disliked delegating authority and demanded strict allegiance from his employees. Even a newsletter issued by Price's own company reported, some years after his death, that the boss had often been thought "enigmatic, autocratic, and contentious."

Price sold out his stake in his firm by 1970 and retired in 1971. Afterward he was openly critical of his successors at the company, saying they had forsaken his principles by paying excessive price-to-earnings multiples for shares in fast-growing companies. Price's warnings were borne out by the disastrous bear market of 1973–1974, in which the prices of some growth stocks tumbled as much as 80 percent.

Price married Eleanor B. Gherky on 18 September 1926. They had two children. Following a long and active retirement spent tending his own family's investments, Price died of a stroke. After cremation, his ashes were buried at Druid Ridge Cemetery in Pikesville, Maryland.

At the time of his death, the firm bearing his name had more than 400 employees and was managing $13 billion, about half of it in mutual funds and the other half in private accounts. Price's legacy also included an influential school of investment thought, and a memorable example of the power of applying reason, intuition, and sheer hard work to the challenge of making money.

★

John Train, *The Money Masters* (1980), devotes an entire chapter to Price's investment approach, also offering clues to his enigmatic personality. The Price method of selecting stocks is detailed point-by-point in Maria Crawford Scott, "The T. Rowe Price Approach to Investing in Growth Stocks," *American Association of Individual Investors Journal* 18, no. 1 (Jan. 1996): 20–23. For an appreciation by a journalist who knew him for a quarter century, see James W. Michaels, "Thomas Rowe Price, 1898–1983," *Forbes* (21 Nov. 1983). An obituary is in the *New York Times* (22 Oct. 1983).

JAMES KATES

PRICHARD, Edward Fretwell, Jr. (*b.* 21 January 1915 in Paris, Kentucky; *d.* 23 December 1984 in Paris, Kentucky), attorney, Supreme Court clerk, appointee to several prominent positions in the New Deal administration of President Franklin D. Roosevelt, political adviser, and advocate for civil rights and higher education whose leadership of a citizens' committee to recommend improvements in Kentucky's higher education institutions resulted in significant reform and expansion of public higher education in that state.

Detail of a portrait of Edward F. Prichard, Jr., 1982. PORTRAIT BY AND © CHRISTINA SCHLESINGER

Prichard was the elder of two sons of Allene (Power) Prichard and Edward ("Big Ed") Prichard, Sr., a well-to-do Bourbon County farmer, horse breeder, farm-equipment dealer, and beer distributor who was involved in state and local politics. Prichard attended public schools in Paris, Kentucky, where he was a top student. He attended Princeton University, graduating summa cum laude at the age of nineteen. In 1935 he entered Harvard Law School, where, upon graduating, he worked for the law school's dean, Felix Frankfurter. When Frankfurter was named an associate justice of the United States Supreme Court, Prichard accompanied him to Washington and served as his clerk. During his years in the federal government, Prichard distinguished himself as a Washington wunderkind, associating with prominent jurists, lawyers, and New Deal policymakers. At Hockley, the Virginia house where Prichard lived with several other rising stars, some of Washington's most celebrated officials were entertained. One of his Hockley roommates was Philip Graham, a law clerk to Justices Stanley Reed and Frankfurter. Graham later married Katharine Meyer, whose family owned the *Washington Post,* where Graham, and then his wife, served as publisher. In her autobiography, *Personal History* (1993), Katharine Graham, who remained Prichard's friend all his life, recounted the names of some of those invited to Hockley, including Dean Acheson, Archibald Cox, and Frankfurter.

After leaving his Supreme Court clerkship, Prichard served as assistant attorney general in the Justice Department and as a member of the War Production Board. In 1942, when he was twenty-seven, he was named legal counsel to President Roosevelt. Amid some controversy over his draft-eligibility status, Prichard was drafted in the fall of 1943 but spent most of his time ill in the hospital at Fort Custer. Receiving a medical discharge in the spring of 1944, he returned to his White House position in June 1944. Before returning to Kentucky in 1945, he assisted Secretary of the Treasury (and later Chief Justice) Fred Vinson for several months in a reorganization of the Treasury Department.

Back in Kentucky, Prichard opened a law firm in Lexington with his Paris High School classmate Philip Ardery and involved himself in Democratic party politics. He was viewed as a potential gubernatorial candidate. In February 1947, he married Lucy Elliott; they had three children. Meanwhile, he retained his contacts and involvement in national politics, serving as legal counsel to the Democratic National Committee in 1946 and 1947.

In the midst of this flourishing career, scandal erupted in 1949 when he was indicted and convicted of vote fraud conspiracy for stuffing the ballot box in a 1948 statewide election. Prichard was found guilty, and his various appeals, including one to the Supreme Court, were denied. He served five months in federal prison before his two-year sentence was commuted by President Harry S. Truman on Christmas Day, 1949.

After nearly a decade of absence from public life, Prichard served as a political strategist and consultant for several Kentucky governors in the 1960s and 1970s. He was widely respected for his intellectual acuity, his political instincts and judgments, his legal abilities, and his progressive views on civil rights, state constitutional reform, and public education. Prichard worked behind the scenes to advance civil rights in the state; Kentucky was the only state in the South to enact civil rights legislation in the 1960s, an accomplishment for which he was acknowledged as an important contributor. But his stature remained tarnished by his conviction, and he never sought elective office himself.

Prichard's most significant contributions emerged in the mid-1960s with his appointment by Governor Edward Breathitt to the State Council on Higher Education. He served numerous terms as vice chairman of the council. In 1980 he was asked to head a committee to recommend improvements in the state's higher education institutions, programs, and policies. The report of the Committee on Higher Education in Kentucky's Future, *In Pursuit of Excellence* (1981), called public attention to inadequate financial support for Kentucky colleges and to ineffective planning procedures. The report was acknowledged by educators, politicians, and citizens' advocacy groups as comprehensive, ambitious, feasible, and well balanced. Several states openly advocated developing similarly focused reports, using *In Pursuit of Excellence* as a model.

Prichard's name became indelibly associated with efforts to improve higher education in Kentucky when the committee renamed itself the Prichard Committee in 1981. By 1983, committee members, angry at the failure of the state to move ahead with many of its recommendations, formed a privately funded, independent organization to build popular support to improve education in the state. In recognition of Prichard's advocacy and leadership, the new group was named the Prichard Committee for Academic Excellence. The committee's report, *The Path to a Better Life* (1985), published shortly after Prichard's death, argued forcefully for increased funding and reform of the educational system, especially in the area of early childhood education. Many state educators and legislators believed that the 1990 Kentucky Education Reform Act was the result of efforts initiated by Prichard.

In his later years, Prichard continued to practice law in Frankfort, Kentucky, while maintaining contact with friends and associates from his time spent in Washington. He and his family lived in a refurbished house called Heartland, in Versailles, Kentucky, near Paris. His health was severely impaired during the last decades of his life, and he suffered from glaucoma, diabetes (which led to blindness), and kidney disease, but he remained active and involved, particularly in matters relating to education. He died in Paris, Kentucky. The funeral was held in Lexington, and Prichard was buried in the Paris cemetery.

Many friends and admirers viewed Prichard as a person of extraordinary talent and ability, whose potential to become a national leader was thwarted by the events of the vote fraud scandal of 1948. Katharine Graham said of him: "My relationship with [Prich] always remained a great privilege, but with sad overtones. . . . He was widely talked about and written about as a future governor of Kentucky, or even president, so great were his political acumen, understanding of public issues, and sense of people. In the end, he may have had too much charm and talent for his own good. Along with all his assets, he had fatal liabilities."

★

Two longtime Kentucky associates wrote vivid and revealing descriptions of Prichard: John Ed Pearce, "The Kentuckian Who Might Have Been President," *Louisville Courier-Journal Magazine* (24 Oct. 1976), and Philip Ardery, "Prich," *Filson Club History Quarterly* 68, no. 4 (Oct. 1994). Arthur Schlesinger, James Wechsler, and Katharine Graham, all of whom knew Prichard in the heyday of Hockley and New Deal Washington, have reminisced about him: Arthur Schlesinger, Jr., "'Prich': A New Deal Memoir," *New York Review of Books* (28 Mar. 1985); James Wechsler, "Kentucky's Prichard Brightest of Roosevelt's Young Aides," *New York Post* (Feb. 1979); and Katharine Graham, *Personal History* (1997).

FREDERIC JACOBS

PRIMROSE, William (*b.* 23 August 1904 in Glasgow, Scotland; *d.* 1 May 1982 in Provo, Utah), virtuoso violist and pedagogue whose career helped to raise awareness of the viola as a solo instrument in its own right.

In his autobiography, *Walk on the North Side* (1978), Primrose states that his earliest musical memories were of watching his violinist father teaching in their home. The eldest of three chidren born to John Primrose and Margaret McInnis Whiteside, William was given a quarter-sized violin to play at the age of four. He quickly demonstrated prodigious musical ability by imitating almost exactly the sounds and motions he had observed in his father's studio. John Primrose realized that it was not appropriate for him to serve as his son's teacher and in 1908 enrolled him in the studio of Camillo Ritter, an Austrian violinist who had studied with Joseph Joachim and Oscar Ševčik.

Primrose made his public concert debut at the age of twelve, performing Felix Mendelssohn's Violin Concerto in E minor, op. 64, in Saint Andrew's Hall in Glasgow. During the next few years he performed regularly in various venues in the city, from the local Congregational church to the Palette Club, a private club for people interested in the

arts. In addition to his musical studies, Primrose attended regular school and indulged in what would become his lifelong passions of reading and sports. He played soccer and even boxed and claims that he was fortunate not to have injured his hands.

The city of Glasgow provided a relatively rich cultural environment for Primrose, with frequent performances by the Scottish Orchestra (in which his father played) and visiting guest artists. In 1919 Primrose was invited to play for Landon Ronald, the orchestra's conductor. Impressed by his obvious skill and talent, Ronald arranged for Primrose to be given a scholarship to the Guildhall School of Music in London. The entire Primrose family took this opportunity to relocate.

At the Guildhall School, Primrose studied violin under Max Mossel, whom he found to be a rather uninspiring teacher. He was also bored by his required secondary piano and theory lessons, and frequently missed classes. Born with perfect pitch and innate musical instincts, Primrose did avail himself of London's rich musical life and was inspired by performances of Jascha Heifetz, Fritz Kreisler, Pablo Casals, and many other notable artists. Despite his somewhat lackluster enthusiasm for his studies at Guildhall, Primrose graduated in 1924 with a gold medal, the school's highest honor.

William Primrose. PRIMROSE INTERNATIONAL VIOLA ARCHIVE, BRIGHAM YOUNG UNIVERSITY

Primrose made his London performance debut in 1923, playing Édouard-Victor-Antoine Lalo's Symphonie espagnole, op. 21, and Edward Elgar's Violin Concerto in B minor, op. 61, in Queens Hall with an orchestra conducted by Ronald. Following his graduation from Guildhall, he performed frequently in England and also participated in a large number of radio broadcasts. After two years of this type of concertizing, Primrose found that his performances remained uninspired and his violin playing was not improving. In 1926 he was advised by his good friend, pianist Ivor Newton, to travel to Belgium to study with Eugène Ysaÿe, one of the century's greatest violinists.

Primrose was indeed inspired by Ysaÿe's teaching and studied with him sporadically for three years. Although Primrose's violin playing improved dramatically, Ysaÿe prophetically encouraged him to switch to the viola, an idea that Primrose had entertained for many years. As a child he had secretly played his father's Brothers Amati viola. Although finding the sound to be preferable to a violin sound, he knew that his father would strongly disapprove of his son playing what the elder Primrose considered to be a secondary instrument.

Primrose's switch to the viola provided him with important opportunities as a chamber music player. In March 1930 he was invited to join the London String Quartet during the last part of its tour of the Americas. He joined the quartet for concerts in South America and played with the group until it disbanded in 1935, because of the Great Depression. Primrose's years with the London String Quartet provided him with his first exposure to international audiences and the rigors of a hectic touring schedule. He thoroughly enjoyed playing with his colleagues in the quartet and flourished as a professional touring musician. After the quartet's dissolution he performed frequently throughout Europe, taking advantage of every opportunity from performances with theater pit orchestras to playing William Walton's Viola Concerto with Sir Thomas Beecham and the Royal Philharmonic Society.

Primrose's next important opportunity came in 1937, when he heard that Arturo Toscanini would be conducting the newly formed NBC Symphony. Primrose was anxious to play in a symphony orchestra, especially under a conductor of Toscanini's stature. He was invited to join the Symphony, but was not its principal violist, as is frequently misstated. In fact, he shared the first desk with another violist, Carlton Cooley. In 1938, on the suggestion of the NBC music department, he formed the Primrose Quartet, which included violinists Oskar Shumsky and Josef Gingold and cellist Harvey Shapiro.

In 1941 Primrose heard that Toscanini might leave the NBC Symphony. Because he had joined the group in part to perform under the maestro's direction, he decided that it might be time to move on to a solo career. By chance, he ran into the tenor Richard Crooks while walking on Fifty-seventh Street in New York City, and Crooks invited Primrose to join him on an upcoming tour. Primrose toured successfully with the tenor for four years and was given equal billing on their joint programs. His career as a solo violist began to flourish, and in 1943 he was signed as a solo artist by the influential manager Arthur Judson.

Primrose performed as a soloist throughout Europe and the United States in the years that followed, playing both solo recitals and works with orchestras under such conductors as Maurice Abravanel, Sir John Barbirolli, Sir Thomas Beecham, Sir Adrian Boult, Wilhelm Furtwängler, Serge Koussevitzky, Charles Munch, and Sir Malcolm Sargent. He championed new repertoire for the instrument and commissioned or inspired works for viola by such composers as Peter Racine Fricker, Edmund Rubbra, Benjamin Britten, Darius Milhaud, and George Rochberg. In 1945 he commissioned Béla Bartók's Viola Concerto, which was left unfinished at the composer's death in September of that year. Bartók's associate Tibor Serly completed the work from the sketches, and Primrose premiered it with the Minneapolis Symphony under the baton of Antal Dorati on 2 December 1949.

In addition to his extensive solo activities, Primrose continued to play chamber music with many of the most notable artists of his generation, in groups such as the Festival Piano Quartet (1954–1962), which included Victor Babin, piano, Szymon Goldberg, violin, and Nicolai Graudon, cello; the Heifetz-Primrose-Feuermann Trio (Jascha Heifetz, violin, and Emanuel Feuermann, cello); the Heifetz-Primrose-Piatigorsky Trio (Heifetz, violin, and Gregor Piatigorsky, cello); and the Schnabel-Szigeti-Primrose-Fournier Piano Quartet (Artur Schnabel, piano, Joseph Szigeti, violin, and Pierre Fournier, cello). He made more than seventy recordings of solo, chamber, and orchestral works.

Primrose became a U.S. citizen in 1955. In 1963 he suffered a major heart attack, which greatly curtailed his concert appearances. He then focused his energies on teaching. He had taught at the Curtis Institute of Music in Philadelphia in the early 1940s and at the Juilliard School from 1955 to 1957. Primrose had begun teaching at the University of Southern California with Heifetz and Piatigorsky in 1961 and continued to 1965. He then taught at Indiana University from 1965 to 1972 and at Brigham Young University from 1979 until his death. He also gave master classes and lessons at the Aspen School in Colorado and at summer festivals in Toronto, Montreal, Geneva, Banff, and Santa Barbara. In 1971 and 1972 he traveled to Japan and was associated with the Tokyo University of Fine Arts and Music and the Toho Gakuen School, also in Tokyo. With his third wife, Hiroko, he also participated in the work of Shinichi Suzuki's institute in Matsumoto, Japan.

His published pedagogical writings include *The Art and Practice of Scale Playing on the Viola* (1954); *Technique Is Memory* (1960); *Violin and Viola,* with Yehudi Menuhin and Denis Stevens (1976); and *Playing the Viola: Conversations with William Primrose,* with David Dalton (1988).

Primrose had developed a hearing problem in 1946 that worsened over the years and gradually affected his ability to hear parts of the musical scale. Because he had perfect pitch, this affliction was particularly difficult. His first wife, Dorothy Friend, died of cancer in 1950; a second marriage, to Alice French, ended in divorce. In 1970 he married the Japanese musician Hiroko Sawa, who had three children from a previous marriage. Although a cancer diagnosed in 1977 gradually limited most of his activities, he continued to teach privately and coach chamber music until his death from cancer. His body was cremated and his ashes placed in the columbarium of Saint Mark's Cathedral in Salt Lake City, Utah.

Primrose was an enormously accomplished musician who brought viola playing to new heights of artistry. Described by friends and colleagues as a "no-nonsense Scotsman," an engaging raconteur, and a concerned humanitarian, he thoroughly enjoyed all of the opportunities presented to him and seemed to face obstacles with unflinching practicality and determination. He served as an inspiration for many of the twentieth century's most successful violists and string players.

★

Primrose's papers are housed at the Primrose International Viola Archive at Brigham Young University in Provo, Utah. The collection also includes Primrose's library of viola music. His autobiography, *Walk on the North Side: Memoirs of a Violist* (1978), was prepared with the assistance of his former student and close friend David Dalton and includes a discography of Primrose's recordings. Dialogue between Primrose and Dalton is in *Playing the Viola: Conversations with William Primrose* (1988), which contains Primrose's commentary on all aspects of viola playing. Memorial tributes and reminiscences of Primrose were published for the tenth anniversary of his death in a special commemorative edition of the *Journal of the American Viola Society* 8, no. 1 (1992). An obituary is in the *New York Times* (4 May 1982). A thirty-minute-video documentary on Primrose is titled *William Primrose: A Violist's Legacy* (1979). Also available commercially is a twenty-one-minute video titled *William Primrose, Violist* (1987), which includes a black-and-white film of Primrose in recital in 1947. The Brigham Young University Music Department Web site (http://www.lib.byu.edu/˜music/) includes substantial information on Primrose and the Primrose International Viola Archive, including a gallery of photographs.

JANE GOTTLIEB

PRITIKIN, Nathan (*b.* 29 August 1915 in Chicago, Illinois; *d.* 21 February 1985 in Albany, New York), noted inventor and self-taught nutritionist who changed the American concept of health by advocating a low-fat diet and aerobic exercise.

Pritikin, the oldest of three children of Jacob I. Pritikin and Esther Levitt, was born into a working-class family. His father was a sign salesman whose desire for privacy, distrust of authority, and propensity for hard work were strong and lasting influences on Pritikin. In 1929 Pritikin entered Proviso High School in Chicago. While he excelled in science and math, he barely passed English, a subject he had little interest in. He also began his lifelong informal study of human anatomy and physiology.

At the age of fifteen, Pritikin saved for and bought a camera, unwittingly propelling himself into the first of many careers. After graduating from high school in 1933, Pritikin received a scholarship to the University of Chicago. Meanwhile, Pritikin and his younger brother, Albert, started their own business, Pritikin Photographers. Soon the business, renamed Flash Foto, was so successful that Pritikin withdrew from the university after only two years of study in order to concentrate on work full time. He never returned to formal education. As a photographer, Pritikin

Nathan Pritikin. UPI/CORBIS-BETTMANN

was often called upon to photograph medical conferences. He used these opportunities to listen to lectures and thus augmented his readings in medicine and health.

At the age of twenty-one, Pritikin met his first wife, Roslyn "Babe" Smith. Adventurous and fun-loving, Smith was a marked contrast to the serious Pritikin. The young couple eloped in April 1937. The marriage, however, soon deteriorated, and six years later Smith and Pritikin divorced. They had one child.

During this period, Pritikin secured a government contract to help produce bombsights for air force bombers, an activity that exempted Pritikin from military duty during World War II and gave him access to classified documents. Among the records he studied were mortality reports of the civilian populations of Europe. Scientific thinking at that time held that heart disease was caused, in part, by stress. Pritikin felt that if that were true, the incidence of heart disease should have increased during the war, but to his surprise, death rates due to heart attack, even among concentration camp survivors, fell. After much research, Pritikin began to formulate his own theory of diet and cardiovascular health.

In the spring of 1945, Pritikin met Ilene Robbins, whose personality closely matched his; they married on 1 November 1947 and remained together for the rest of Pritikin's life. In addition to raising the son from his first marriage, they had four children together: Janet, Robert, Ralph, and Kenneth.

Settled into a successful career as a freelance inventor and a happy family life, Pritikin continued to research the causes of heart disease. In 1955, while planning to move his family and business to southern California, Pritikin met a Los Angeles cardiologist, Lester Morrison, who was studying arterial sclerosis, or hardening of the arteries. Pritikin learned from Morrison that he had a high blood cholesterol count but was reassured that the count was still within normal range. Nevertheless, Pritikin resolved to find a healthier way to live.

Although, Pritikin began cutting back on fat in his diet, in 1958 he suffered an angina attack and was diagnosed with heart disease. He was given a standard treatment of the day, the drug Atropine, to stimulate blood flow to the heart, and he was advised to restrict his exercise. Dissatisfied with the results he was getting with this regimen and having more faith in his own ability to find a cure than in doctors, Pritikin stopped taking the drug and, when he was refused help from the nutritionists he consulted, began to experiment with his diet. For more than ten years, he tracked the effects of dietary changes in his body by having his blood and urine tested regularly. In February 1966 Pritikin took a cardiovascular stress test and showed no sign of heart disease.

Although occasionally rebuffed for his lack of formal training, Pritikin began dispensing advice to family members, friends, and others informally referred to him who had symptoms that did not respond to traditional treatment. In 1974, after seeing favorable results with his regimen of diet and exercise, Pritikin published the first of his six books, *Live Longer Now,* and began explaining his plan to the medical community. While Pritikin gained the support of many physicians, he did not receive the backing of the medical establishment. His lack of medical credentials, the controversy he generated in the medical community, and his knack for self-promotion, especially when he opened his Wellness Centers, counted against him.

In 1976, Pritikin opened his first Wellness Center in southern California. The program at the centers included weekly physical exams by staff physicians, smoking cessation, exercise (especially walking), lectures, and eight meals/snacks a day designed to keep participants well-fed and in social contact. Pritikin immediately came under investigation by the California Board of Medical Quality Assurance for practicing medicine without a license. He was eventually cleared of the charges, but other groups, such as the American Heart Association, attacked Pritikin's diet, saying it did not demonstrate lasting benefit and was not a practical plan to follow over a lifetime. Pritikin criticized physicians for being more interested in collecting fees for open-heart surgeries than in warning the public about the dangers of poor nutrition. It was not until 1984 that the National Heart, Lung, and Blood Institute released the results of a ten-year trial that conclusively demonstrated a correlation between the concentration of fats in the blood and the risk of heart disease. This validation of Pritikin's work helped to make him respectable to the rest of the medical community, and on 27 April 1984 he addressed nearly 400 doctors at the Mount Sinai Medical School as the featured speaker. A thin and wiry man with dark hair, Pritikin dressed simply and looked more like a university professor than a hard-driving businessman.

Unfortunately, Pritikin's good fortune was short-lived. In 1957 he had been given radiation treatments for a fungal infection. Pritikin maintained that those treatments had contributed to his contracting leukemia. The disease went into remission but resurged twenty-seven years later. By January 1985, Pritikin was declining rapidly and responding poorly to chemotherapy. Growing more and more depressed, Pritikin nevertheless attempted to complete work on a machine that could remove fats from the blood quickly and without the use of drugs. On 21 February, weakened and despondent both from the disease as well as from the treatments that destroyed his kidneys, Pritikin committed suicide at the Albany Medical Center. He was buried in Santa Monica, California.

Pritikin held more than two dozen patents in physics, chemistry, and electrical engineering, and his development of ideas for such corporations as Honeywell, General Electric, and Corning made him rich. Often criticized for his lack of education, he succeeded because of his ability to find unconventional solutions.

★

Tom Monte, *Pritikin: The Man Who Healed America's Heart* (1988), is a biography cowritten with Pritikin's wife. A memorial is in the *Annual Obituary* (1985). Obituaries are in the *New York Times* and *Washington Post* (23 Feb. 1985), *Time* and *Newsweek* (4 Mar. 1985), and *People* (11 Mar. 1985).

NANCY M. FINN

QUINLAN, Karen Ann (*b.* 29 March 1954 in Scranton, Pennsylvania; *d.* 11 June 1985 in Morris Plains, New Jersey), young woman who, as the subject of the famous legal case involving the so-called right to die, sparked public awareness about medical decision-making in hopeless situations.

Karen Ann Quinlan was born Mary Ann Monahan at a hospital for unwed mothers in Scranton, Pennsylvania. She never knew her birth mother. At four weeks of age she was adopted by Joseph Quinlan, a shipping supervisor at a pharmaceutical company, and his wife Julia Quinlan, who renamed her Karen Ann and brought her to their home in Roxbury Township, New Jersey. Karen and her younger siblings, a sister and a brother, were raised in a strict Catholic family. Prior to her graduation in 1972, Karen was an average student at Morris Catholic High School in Denville, New Jersey, who enjoyed volleyball, basketball, and camping.

In 1975, at the age of twenty-one, Karen Ann Quinlan was a lab technician planning to attend college and living with a group of friends in Bryam Township, New Jersey. On 14 April of that year, following an evening with friends during which she drank several alcoholic beverages while taking mild tranquilizers, Karen lost consciousness for two short intervals and was admitted to Saint Clare's Hospital in Denville.

Initially, Karen's parents took all possible steps to save and prolong their daughter's life. However, approximately five months after Karen became comatose, they concluded that she was in a persistent vegetative state (PVS), and on 31 July 1975 they requested that her respirator be disconnected. When the attending physicians refused to take this action, the Quinlans, with the support of their parish priest, petitioned the Superior Court of New Jersey on 17 September 1975 to direct Karen's doctors to remove her life-support system and to allow Karen to die with "grace and dignity." On 10 November 1975 Judge Robert Muir, Jr., of

Karen Ann Quinlan. UPI/CORBIS-BETTMANN

the Superior Court of New Jersey ruled against the Quinlans and refused her father's request that he be appointed Karen's guardian. The Quinlans appealed this decision to the Supreme Court of New Jersey.

Richard Joseph Hughes, the chief justice of the New Jersey Supreme Court and former governor of the state, mindful of the suffering of the Quinlan family, moved quickly and the court rendered its decision, *In the Matter of Karen Quinlan, an Alleged Incompetent*, on 31 March 1976. Based on the right to privacy, the court ruled that "no compelling interest of the state could compel Karen to endure the unendurable." While acknowledging a state interest in the preservation of a human life, the court reasoned that the state interest weakens and the individual's constitutional right to privacy grows as the degree of bodily invasion increases and the prognosis for recovery decreases. Eventually, this balance sways and the rights of the individual outweigh the state interest. Further, the court ruled that the decision to withdraw life-support apparatus must be based on a finding that no reasonable possibility exists that the patient will emerge from a comatose condition to a cognitive, sapient state. The guardian and family as well as the attending physician must concur in the decision, which should be made in consultation with the hospital ethics committee. In the event that the life-support system is withdrawn, no participant in the decision-making process would incur civil or criminal liability. The decision became a touchstone case in influencing the legal definition of death in several states.

During the month of May 1976 Karen Ann Quinlan was weaned from her respirator. She continued breathing on her own for nine years. During this period, she was visited every day by her family. On 11 June 1985 Karen died of pulmonary failure caused by pneumonia and heart disease related to her vegetative state at the Morris View Nursing Home in New Jersey. She was thirty-one years old.

The decision in this case ignited interest in and awareness of the limitations that physicians and patients have when making critical medical decisions. The case became known under the catchphrase "right to die." The true issues were whether a patient has the right to refuse unwanted medical treatment and determining who can make the decision to refuse care when a patient is incompetent or unable to communicate. Karen's case "pointed to a new direction in human cognition" said Paul W. Armstrong, the Quinlans' attorney. "Karen's case, as it has for medicine, law and science really became a polestar for medical treatment decision making all across the country." Since the Quinlan decision, numerous "right to die" cases have been brought. In addition, the landscape of the law in the area changed; all states instituted "living will" statutes to allow people to specify the medical procedures they would want performed in case they are rendered incompetent. Following this decision, mechanisms were established to protect physicians from civil and criminal liability, and hospital ethics committees have routinely dealt with questions involving incompetent patients and appropriate medical treatment.

The Quinlan case changed the way that both the legal profession and the medical profession view death. Before the Quinlan case, the Harvard Ad Hoc Committee of 1968 published a definition of death that could be implemented in cases involving organ donations. The standard set forth four elements of death that had to be met to remove life-support from the patient: (1) a flat electroencephalogram for a twenty-four-hour period; (2) no response to external stimuli; (3) no spontaneous breathing; and (4) pupils fixed and dilated. This published standard thus made removing a patient in PVS from life-support a criminal offense. The decision in the Quinlan case permitted the removal of life-support systems in some cases that did not meet this standard without criminal liability.

Karen's parents continued to raise public awareness after the decision and the death of Karen. With the proceeds from a 1977 television movie, *In the Matter of Karen Ann Quinlan,* and the book *Karen Ann: The Quinlans Tell Their Story,* the Quinlans opened the Karen Ann Quinlan Center for Hope in Sussex, New Jersey, a hospice providing counseling and bereavement services for patients and families. "It is rewarding for us that so much good has come out of Karen's suffering" said Julia Quinlan, Karen's mother. "Before we went to court, there was really little discussion on prolongation of life. People weren't aware that they had the right to make decisions regarding their own bodies."

For some the case of Karen Ann Quinlan represented a right to die with dignity, and set boundaries for the medical profession and medical technology. For others the case represented the start of a "right to die" campaign that could ultimately lead to legal euthanasia. Clearly, the case of Karen Quinlan raised consciousness concerning the limits of medical technology and an individual's right to privacy without bodily invasion.

★

Joseph and Julia Quinlan, with Phyllis Battelle, *Karen Ann: The Quinlans Tell Their Story* (1977), provides a biographical sketch and an account of the events from the point of view of the parents of Karen Quinlan. For the legal perspective, see *In the Matter of Karen Quinlan,* vol. 1: *The Complete Legal Briefs, Court Proceedings, and Decision in the Superior Court of New Jersey* (1975). Tina M. L. Stevens, "The Quinlan Case Revisited: A History of the Cultural Politics of Medicine and the Law," *Journal of Health Politics, Policy, and Law* (spring 1996): 347–366, explores the cultural politics of medicine and law through a historical examination of the Karen Ann Quinlan case. George J. Annas, "The Duquesne University School of Law Institute for Judicial Education and the Supreme Court of Pennsylvania's Conference on Science and the Law: The 'Right to Die' in America: Sloganeering from Quinlan and Cruzan to Quill and Kevorkian," *Duquesne Law Review* 34 (summer 1996): 875–897, is a comprehensive discussion on so-called right to die litigation commencing with the case of Karen Ann Quinlan. See also Elizabeth Mehren, "The Agony Persists for Quinlans a Decade Later," *Los Angeles Times* (18 Mar. 1985), and Donna Leusner, "Quinlan Study Case Revisited Sheds Light on Brain," *Star Ledger, New Jersey* (25 May 1994). Obituaries are in the *New York Times* (12 June 1985) and *Time* (24 June 1985).

ELIZABETH F. DEFEIS

R

RAFFERTY, Max(well) Lewis, Jr. (*b*. 7 May 1917 in New Orleans, Louisiana; *d*. 13 June 1982 in Troy, Alabama), conservative educator and author who served as California state superintendent of public instruction from 1963 to 1971.

Rafferty's father, Maxwell Lewis Rafferty Sr., was in the paint business, and his mother, DeEtta Cox, was a homemaker; the family was Episcopalian. When young Max, an only child, was four years old, the family moved to Sioux City, Iowa. Rafferty's mother taught him to read when he was three, exposing him to history, music, and literature; as a result he excelled in school, skipping two grades. In 1931 the Great Depression prompted the family to move to southern California, where Rafferty entered Beverly Hills High School, graduating two years later. Enrolling at the University of California at Los Angeles, Rafferty majored in history, minored in English, was president of the Sigma Pi fraternity and manager of the football and rugby teams, and began his career of conservative activism as a member of the UCLA Americans, which sought to unite fraternity members and athletes to, as he put it, "counterbalance the leftists" on campus. Participating in so many activities may have hurt his academic record; he graduated in 1938 with a C-plus average.

After briefly working in a gas station, Rafferty decided to enter the teaching profession. Returning to UCLA for education credits, he was appalled by the dogmatism of the followers of John Dewey's "progressive education" on its faculty and by having to outwardly express agreement with their views. In 1940 he began his teaching career in the Trona Lake, California, school district, where he taught for eight years. During World War II he was excused from military service, reportedly for flat feet. On 4 June 1942 Rafferty married Frances Luella Longman. They had three children. In 1949 he received his M.A. in education from UCLA; the previous year he had become principal of Big Bear High School in Big Bear Lake, California. From 1951 to 1955 Rafferty was district superintendent of schools of the Saticoy, California, school district, and from 1955 to 1961 of the Needles, California, school district. Meanwhile, in 1956 Rafferty had received his doctorate in education from the University of Southern California. At Needles, a doctrinal conflict between partisans of progressive and traditional education resulted in a victory for the traditionalists, who brought in Rafferty to, as they put it, restore order. He introduced a program for gifted students and improved academic and athletic programs. The result was nationwide recognition, with Rafferty being awarded the Shankland Memorial Research Award by the American Association of School Administrators in 1955.

In 1961 Rafferty, newly appointed superintendent of schools of the La Canada, California, school district, addressed a public meeting of the school board on "The Pass-

Max Rafferty, 1962. UPI/CORBIS-BETTMANN

at Troy State University in Troy, Alabama. He continued his activities in support of conservative educational and political causes, frequently making speeches in California and elsewhere. *Max Rafferty on Education,* a collection of his newspaper columns, appeared in 1968, and *Classroom Countdown* in 1970. Rafferty coauthored with Emory Stoops *Practices and Trends in School Administration* (1961) and wrote *A Handbook on Educational Administration* (1975). In 1971 Rafferty became dean of education at Troy State University. Ten years later he was appointed Sorrell Distinguished Professor of Education there. On 13 June 1982 Rafferty was driving a friend of his granddaughter home when his car slipped off the side of an earthen dam into a pond near Troy. The passenger escaped almost unhurt, but Rafferty, trapped underwater for more than nine minutes, died before reaching the hospital. He is buried in Green Hills Memorial Park in Troy.

Rafferty symbolizes the conservative reaction in American education following the 1957 launch of the Soviet space satellite *Sputnik,* an event seen by many as demonstrating the impact on science and technology of the failure of progressive education, introduced in the early twentieth century by John Dewey and widely prevalent in American public schools when Rafferty's career began. Standing for patriotism and traditional values in a state that had seen radical social change after a depression, a war, and massive migrations to mushrooming suburbs, Rafferty attracted the support of working- and middle-class Californians and other Americans who felt that elitist teachers and school administrators were teaching their children to reject what their own parents stood for in favor of what were seen as nihilistic, anti-individualistic ideas that emphasized "adjustment" over learning. Although the educational establishment and elements of the university-educated upper middle class might have regarded Rafferty's conservative ideas as dangerously retrograde, by the end of the twentieth century, when the generation that grew up in the 1960s was concerned with its own children and a Democratic president, Bill Clinton, could express support for school uniforms, reexamination of these ideas was arguably appropriate. Although many moderates claimed to be repelled by what they saw as Rafferty's intemperate rhetoric (during his senatorial campaign he called for shooting looters in urban riots and suggested using nuclear weapons in Vietnam), his opponents were often no less outspoken and extreme.

★

A reminiscence by Rafferty's campaign director of the educator's successful 1962 race for California state superintendent of public instruction is in the *Los Angeles Times* (17 June 1982). Obituaries are in the *Los Angeles Times* and *New York Times* (both 14 June 1982).

STEPHEN A. STERTZ

ing of the Patriot." In the speech, later reprinted in *Reader's Digest,* he stated that "life adjustment" had replaced traditional standards in the schools, leaving young people rootless and open to Soviet propaganda. The conservative Citizens Advisory Committee on Education persuaded Rafferty to run for the elected office of California state superintendent of public instruction. In 1962 he narrowly defeated a well-known progressive educator. After attacking Harold Wentworth and Stuart B. Flexner's *Dictionary of American Slang* (1960), placed in many school libraries, for including obscenities, and strongly advocating conservative educational ideas in his books *Suffer, Little Children* (1962) and *What They Are Doing to Your Children* (1964), Rafferty was reelected in a landslide in 1966.

In 1968 Rafferty defeated the incumbent liberal U.S. senator Thomas H. Kuchel in the Republican primary but lost in the general election to Democrat Alan Cranston. In 1970 the more liberal Wilson Riles defeated Rafferty for reelection as state education superintendent. In the following year Rafferty became dean of the School of Education

RAINEY, Homer Price (*b*. 19 January 1896 in Clarksville, Texas; *d*. 19 December 1985 in Boulder, Colorado), critic of the American educational system best known for being ousted by the Board of Regents as president of the University of Texas in 1944.

The son of Edward Rainey, a rancher, and Jenny Price, Homer Price Rainey was ordained as a Baptist minister at the age of eighteen. A year later, in 1915, he enrolled in Austin College in Sherman, Texas. He graduated in 1919 with an A.B. degree, then began playing professional baseball as a pitcher for the Galveston franchise of the Texas League. Although he was offered a contract with the St. Louis Cardinals, he declined, deciding instead to join the faculty at Austin College. He married Mildred Collins of Lovelady, Texas, in 1920 and in 1922 enrolled in the graduate school of the University of Chicago, from which he earned an M.A. (1923) and then a Ph.D. in education (1924). He went to teach at the University of Oregon at Salem in 1924 as associate professor of education; two years later, he was promoted to full professor. Meanwhile, he wrote two monographs on educational financing: *A Study of School Finance in Oregon* (1925) and *The Distribution of School Funds in Oregon* (1926). A third monograph, *The Achievement of Elementary School Pupils in Oregon,* was published in 1927.

In 1927 Rainey was appointed president of Franklin

Homer Price Rainey addressing the Texas convention of Young Democrats, 1945. AP/WIDE WORLD PHOTOS

College in Franklin, Indiana. During his four-year administration, the college revised its requirements for the baccalaureate degree, making mathematics and foreign languages optional, except for students majoring in education, engineering, and science. In 1931, Bucknell University in Lewisburg, Pennsylvania, hired Rainey as its president. He served for four years in that capacity, supervising the revision of the undergraduate curriculum to include more courses in art, music, and literature. In 1935 he was appointed to the American Youth Commission by George Frederick Zook, the director of the American Council on Education. The fourteen-member commission elected Rainey as its director, and, under his leadership, undertook investigations of the correlation between education and employment, asserting the need for vocational education and guidance programs for the nation's youth. The commission's recommendations were published in *How Fare American Youth?* (1937).

In December 1939 Rainey was appointed president of the University of Texas. Within a year, problems arose between Rainey and the nine-member Board of Regents. In 1942 the American Association of University Professors censured the university for the dismissal of three economics professors who had attempted at a public meeting to correct misstatements about the minimum wage law and work stoppages in defense plants in Texas. Rainey opposed the professors' dismissals and increased the hostility between himself and the Board of Regents by opposing both the board's prohibition of books on campus on grounds of obscenity, particularly John Dos Passos's *U.S.A.,* and their refusal to allot funds for a school of social work. In October 1944 Rainey brought the conflict to a head when he read to the faculty a sixteen-point statement in which he outlined "the restrictive measures actual and attempted" by the Board of Regents to curtail academic freedom. On 1 November 1944 the Board of Regents dismissed Rainey after he refused to retract his accusations. Subsequently, the University of Texas was placed on probation by the Southern Association of Colleges and Secondary Schools. After a series of public hearings held by the Texas senate, Governor Coke Stevenson dismissed the allegations of Rainey and his supporters. In March 1946 the Southern Association of Colleges and Secondary Schools lifted the censure on the University of Texas, citing changes "in the attitudes and procedures of the Board of Regents."

Rainey ran for the Democratic nomination for governor of Texas in July 1946. Political pundits declared him the front runner on account of his liberal agenda, which included establishing a state-supported university for African Americans, increasing taxes on petroleum and natural gas to pay for programs of public health and education, and expanding public welfare. Rainey lost in a runoff election to Beauford H. Jester.

In November 1946 Rainey became president of Stephens College for Women in Columbia, Missouri. In 1956, he was hired by the University of Colorado as professor of education. Rainey died at the age of eighty-nine in Boulder, Colorado, the city in which he resided the last three decades of his life. Memorial services were held at the First Baptist Church in Boulder, followed by a private burial in Boulder.

Homer Price Rainey sacrificed his position as president of the University of Texas over the issue of academic freedom. He charged Governor W. Lee ("Pappy") O'Daniel and his successor, Governor Coke Stevenson, of appointing businessmen to the Board of Regents who had interlocking business interests and held similar conservative educational and political views. Rainey was accused by his detractors of being a radical and dangerous educator. Rainey made his position clear on a radio broadcast while running for the Democratic nomination for governor of Texas: "It is more important to protect the principles of democracy and the integrity of these principles than to be president [of the University of Texas]."

★

The Homer P. Rainey Papers are in the Department of Special Collections at the University of Chicago Library. Contemporary news accounts of his ouster are in "Trouble in Texas," *Time* (13 Nov. 1944), and Clarence Edwin Ayre, "Academic Freedom in Texas," *New Republic* (4 Dec. 1944). Alice Carol Cox, *The Rainey Affair: A History of the Academic Freedom Controversy at the University of Texas, 1938–1946* (1970), delineates the history of restrictive measures on academic freedom during World War II. David L. Brown, *Homer Price Rainey and the Campaign of 1946* (1989), discusses the gubernatorial campaign in which Rainey was accused of being soft on communism and deficient in religion. Jack Lala, *Academic Freedom Under Duress: A Political Witch Hunt at the University of Texas, 1939–1952* (1994), discussed the Board of Regents' attempt to restrict academic freedom. An obituary is in the *New York Times* (20 Dec. 1985).

P. DALE ROREX

RAND, Ayn (*b.* 2 February 1905 in St. Petersburg, Russia; *d.* 6 March 1982 in New York City), novelist and philosopher whose best-selling novels *The Fountainhead* and *Atlas Shrugged* promoted her philosophy of objectivism, a heroic advocacy of unfettered capitalism, self-centered individualism, and reason, and made her one of the seminal figures of the conservative revival of the 1960s.

It would be hard for a novelist of even the most extravagant imagination to conceive a life as dramatic (or melodramatic) as Ayn (rhymes with "fine") Rand's, unless that novelist were Ayn Rand herself. Born Alyssa Rosenbaum in St. Petersburg in 1905 into a middle-class Jewish family, she had governesses, tutors, and summers abroad. Her fa-

Ayn Rand. OSCAR WHITE/CORBIS

ther, Fronz Rosenbaum, was a prosperous druggist; her mother, Anna Kaplan, was a housewife. The Bolshevik Revolution thrust the family into poverty and danger, and when her father's chemist shop was nationalized, Alyssa and her two sisters fled with their parents to White-held Odessa. In 1921, with the communist capture of the Crimea, the family returned to St. Petersburg, then Petrograd, to sink deeper into misery.

By then Alyssa had discovered the world of ideas that would be her true home for the rest of her days: first in the detective stories she read in French children's magazines, then in romantic novels by her favorite authors—Victor Hugo's *Les Misérables* and *The Man Who Laughs* (echoed in *The Fountainhead*'s opening, "Howard Roark laughed"); Alexandre Dumas's *The Count of Monte Cristo;* Rostand's *Cyrano de Bergerac.* Her heroes were headstrong, brave, and handsome, ready to avenge themselves on the world for its insults. When she could not find such heroes in real life, she began to create them—and worlds for them to conquer—in the ideas for novels and plays she sketched while still in school. At the University of Petrograd (by the time she graduated, in 1924, the city had been renamed Leningrad), she absorbed Aristotle's view of man and the universe as rational and logical. From Nietzsche she derived an understanding of the hero as being devoted to "a purpose which is for his own sake, for his own happiness and his own selfish motives." One would not go too far astray in defining the Randian hero as an Aristotelian *Übermensch*.

Miserable under communism, Rosenbaum resolved to escape. She had been mesmerized by American movies, particularly shots of the New York skyline. She enrolled in the state institute for cinema: her intention was to go to the United States to write movies. She arranged for an invitation to visit America from relatives in Chicago, and in January 1926 Alyssa Rosenbaum left the Soviet Union with a newly self-chosen first name, Ayn, and a Remington-Rand typewriter that would suggest her new last name. After a short stay in Chicago, she set off for Hollywood with an introduction from a relative to a publicist in the Cecil B. DeMille Studio. There she met DeMille himself, who put her to work as an extra in *The King of Kings,* and Frank O'Connor, another DeMille extra, whom she married in 1929. She then began her first novel, *We the Living* (1936), a story of life in Russia immediately after the Revolution. Its heroine becomes the mistress of an idealistic young communist in order to pay for her lover's treatment for tuberculosis. When the two men learn of her sacrifice, the communist blames communism and commits suicide; her lover betrays her for a wealthy woman; Rand's heroine is shot and killed trying to escape to freedom.

From the same period came a similar story, a screen treatment called *Red Pawn,* about a woman who becomes the mistress of a Soviet concentration camp commandant to free her husband, one of the prisoners. Universal Pictures bought the story, but the film was never made. Rand achieved Broadway success with *Night of January 16th* (originally titled *Penthouse Legend*), a murder mystery whose jury was drawn from each night's audience; it ran in 1935 for 283 performances. With the royalties from this play, Rand tried to rescue her family from Russia, but the Soviets refused to let them leave; her parents were killed during the German siege of Leningrad in World War II. In 1939 George Abbott produced a Broadway version of *We the Living* as *The Unconquered,* a production deemed an artistic disaster by both Rand and the critics—and a financial failure as well.

Very much in the anticommunist vein of *We the Living* was her dystopian novelette *Anthem* (1938), set in a future when individualism has been suppressed; "we" has replaced the first-person singular "I." Unlike Yevgeny Zamyatin's *We* (1920) and George Orwell's *1984* (1949), with which *Anthem* is often compared, Rand's story rejects the usual assumption of a totalitarian society as being technologically advanced—since she believed that technological progress depends on intellectual and economic freedom, a society that opposes these freedoms must be envisioned as

shabby and backward. In 1940 Rand, who had become associated with a small group of conservative intellectuals in New York and Hollywood, put aside work on her new novel to write and speak for Wendell Willkie in his presidential campaign against Franklin D. Roosevelt.

Rand had begun work on *The Fountainhead* in 1937. When it was published in 1943 it established her as one of the most popular and controversial novelists in American history. The theme of the book was, she said, "individualism versus collectivism, not in politics, but in man's soul," as mirrored in the struggle of a great architect to build housing for the masses. Howard Roark's speech to a jury after he dynamited his buildings when his plans were compromised encapsulates the philosophy of militant egoism, materialism, and atheism that Rand would call objectivism. The Warner Brothers film version of *The Fountainhead* appeared in 1949, directed by King Vidor, with Gary Cooper as Roark playing opposite Patricia Neal.

In Hollywood, Rand joined the board of the conservative anticommunist Motion Picture Alliance for the Preservation of American Ideals, and wrote its "Screen Guide for Americans," which appeared on the front page of the *New York Times* drama section. During the House Un-American Activities Committee's October 1947 hearings in Hollywood, Rand testified as a friendly witness about communist influence in the industry. She opposed government controls, but called for a boycott against entertainment-industry communists: "we do not owe them jobs and support to advocate our own destruction at our own expense."

Atlas Shrugged, Rand's last major work, appeared in 1957. It tells of a strike by the creative men and women of the world, led by the mysterious John Galt, who assembles them all in a remote "Galt Gulch" to wait for civilization's collapse. In view of Galt's famous oath—"I swear by my life and my love of it that I will never live for the sake of another man, nor ask another man to live for mine"—it is ironic that a Library of Congress poll in 1991 found *Atlas Shrugged* to be second only to the Bible as the book American readers considered most influential in their lives.

Rand and her followers were seen as pernicious nuisances by religiously oriented conservatives such as William F. Buckley, Jr., whose *National Review* gave *Atlas Shrugged* one of the most brutal reviews ever penned: Whittaker Chambers, under the title "Big Sister Is Watching You," wrote that "from almost any page of *Atlas Shrugged,* a voice can be heard, from painful necessity, commanding: 'To a gas chamber—go!' "

In January 1958 Nathaniel Branden, a young friend and follower of Rand's, founded the Nathaniel Branden Institute to promote her philosophy—one of the lecturers was the economist Alan Greenspan. By 1965 the institute, with offices in the Empire State Building in Manhattan (Rand's symbol, along with the dollar sign, of America), was running courses in eighty cities and publishing a magazine, *The Objectivist*. Whether the NBI, as it was called, was a cult is still a matter of debate. Rand was becoming something of a celebrity, appearing on talk shows and being interviewed in *Playboy*.

Then, in 1968, Rand discovered that Nathaniel Branden (twenty-four years her junior), with whom she had been sexually involved since 1954, had fallen in love with a younger woman. In what Rand took pains to explain was a rational response to betrayal, and not the uncontrollable and inextinguishable jealousy it might appear to the unenlightened, she excommunicated Branden from the movement, closed down the Nathaniel Branden Institute, and demanded that her friends and followers choose between them. The "great schism" was the end of objectivism as a quasi–mass movement, although Rand's literary heir Leonard Peikoff organized the Ayn Rand Institute in Marina del Rey, California, to carry on the work, and the apostate Nathaniel Branden had a subsequent career as a guru in the California-based self-esteem movement.

Rand devoted her last years to philosophical writings. She cared for her ill husband, who had embarked on a career as a painter after their marriage, until his death in 1979, and on 6 March 1982, after treatment for lung cancer (she was a lifelong heavy cigarette smoker), she died of heart failure. Rand was buried in Kensico Cemetery in Westchester County, just north of New York City.

The large and steady sales of Rand's books (more than 20 million copies by the mid-1990s) suggest that her novels will continue to play an important role in the process of self-realization, inspiring fervent debate about the meaning of life among those who believe that the question can be settled by debate. Organized Ayn Randism, however, seems of a day gone by. Resembling in some ways the movements that inexplicably gathered around now-unreadable authors such as Karl Marx, Edward Bellamy, Henry George, and Robert Welch, the objectivist movement seems rooted in a moment of history when modernism was destroying religious certitude and creating a hunger for a rational, commonsensical, and all-embracing explanation of the universe accessible to average intelligences, for whom traditional religion was inadequate and modern science unsettling.

★

Rand's voluminous papers are housed at the Ayn Rand Institute. See also *Letters of Ayn Rand,* edited by Michael S. Berliner (1995), and *Journals of Ayn Rand,* edited by David Harriman (1997). Barbara Branden, *The Passion of Ayn Rand* (1986), is a full-length biography by Rand's longtime friend, and wife of Rand's lover, Nathaniel Branden, who himself wrote *Judgment Day: My Years with Ayn Rand* (1989). The two Brandens had collaborated earlier on *Who Is Ayn Rand? An Analysis of the Novels of Ayn Rand* (1962). Jerome Tuccille wrote a jaundiced view of Rand's influence on the New Right, *It Usually Begins with Ayn Rand* (1972).

Ronald E. Merrill has written a sympathetic but not uncritical guide to Rand's philosophy, *The Ideas of Ayn Rand* (1991). An obituary is in the *New York Times* (7 Mar. 1982).

RICHARD GID POWERS

REXROTH, Kenneth Charles Marion (*b.* 22 December 1905 in South Bend, Indiana; *d.* 6 June 1982 in Montecito, California), poet, painter, and man of letters who presided over San Francisco's literary scene in the 1950s and served as godfather to the Beat Generation.

The only child of Charles Marion Rexroth, a pharmacist and wholesale drug salesman, and Delia Reed, Rexroth was raised in a household that valued art, literature, and social responsibility. He was proud of his descent from a long line of socialists, suffragettes, and abolitionists. Several business reversals and his father's alcoholism strained the Rexroth marriage and introduced an element of instability into Kenneth's childhood. By his tenth year, he had lived in Elkhart, Indiana; Battle Creek, Michigan; and Chicago; he also traveled briefly in Europe. Rexroth attended public school sporadically and was educated chiefly by his mother until her death from a lung ailment in 1916. Afterward, Charles took Kenneth to live with his grandmother, Mary Moore Rexroth, in Toledo, where Charles found factory work. Kenneth's grandmother regularly beat him with her cane, and when Charles learned of this, he found a small apartment and raised Kenneth as best he could until his own death on 25 April 1919.

Minnie Monahan, Delia's sister, then brought Kenneth to live with her family on Chicago's South Side. In Sep-

Kenneth Rexroth with his daughter Mary. ARCHIVE PHOTOS

tember 1920, after briefly attending the Edmund Burke Grammar School, Kenneth began classes at Englewood High School. He worked after school at Vause's Drug Store, where he became the model for Kenny the drugstore clerk in James T. Farrell's *Studs Lonigan* (1935). During several summers, Rexroth found employment at Kinsolving and Granisson, his father's pharmaceutical company employer. Leo Eliel, a major stockholder in the firm, offered to pay for Kenneth's education and buy him into the business, but Rexroth rejected the offer to pursue painting and literature.

Expelled from high school on 28 May 1922, after a dispute with the principal over military training, Kenneth turned for his education to the Field Museum, the Art Institute, and the Bughouse Square in Washington Square Park, Chicago's answer to London's Hyde Park. The radicals he heard in the park reinforced his anarchist leanings and helped him to sharpen his speaking skills. In Bohemian tearooms, such as the Dill Pickle Club and the Green Mask, Rexroth made the acquaintance of some of Chicago's leading figures, including Clarence Darrow, Maxwell Bodenheim, and Sherwood Anderson. At this time, he also began a romance with Leslie Smith, a young social worker assigned to investigate his truancy.

Rexroth struck out on his own in 1923, investing a small inheritance in the Green Mask. He worked as a reporter, first for the City News Service, then for the *Journal of Commerce* and for the *Herald and Examiner*. His newspaper jobs and his financial involvement in the tearoom brought Rexroth into contact with the fringes of Chicago's underworld. Unfortunately, his interest in the Green Mask led to trouble after police raided the club during a risqué poetry reading and arrested the poet, as well as the club's owners, on obscenity charges. He was sentenced to a year in jail and a $1,000 fine.

Prior to his release, Rexroth had followed Leslie first to Smith College and then to New York City. He celebrated their love affair in a series of poems later published in *The Homestead Called Damascus* (1963). In New York, Rexroth spent time with radical writers associated with the *New Masses* and the *Liberator*. In 1926 he met the anarchists Niccola Sacco and Bartolomeo Vanzetti, who had been convicted of murder in 1921. Deeply affected by the anarchists' cause and doubting their guilt, he wrote several poems about them, including his memorable "Climbing Milestone Mountain, August 22, 1939" and "Fish Peddler and Cobbler." After Rexroth's release from jail, Smith looked for a way to gently end their affair. When his relationship with Leslie soured, Rexroth traveled extensively in America and abroad. On his return to Chicago, he met Andrée Dutcher (a pseudonym for Myrtle Schafer), a talented painter three years his senior who suffered from epilepsy.

After a whirlwind courtship, they were married in early January 1927 at the Church of the Ascension.

The newlyweds traveled cross-country for several months, then settled in San Francisco, where Kenneth engaged in union activities, helped establish West Coast branches of the John Reed Club, and participated in the Federal Writers Project. His poems began to appear in literary reviews, and he was featured in Louis Zukofsky's seminal work, *An "Objectivists" Anthology* (1932). Rexroth's budding reputation led to a meeting with Dorothy Van Ghent, a young graduate student interested in his work. Before long, Dorothy and her husband, Roger, were involved in affairs with Kenneth and Andrée, which took their tolls on both marriages. The strains on the Rexroth marriage, aggravated by Andrée's descent into mental illness, resulted in a divorce on 29 April 1938. Kenneth meanwhile had fallen in love with Marie Kass, a nurse he met through union activity. They married on 6 July 1940 at the Olivet Presbyterian Church, three months before Andrée's death.

Rexroth's career was on the rise. His first two books of poems, *In What Hour* (1940) and *The Phoenix and the Tortoise* (1944), won California Literature Silver Medal awards. Nevertheless, Rexroth, a conscientious objector, spent World War II working in a psychiatric ward, networking with pacifist groups, and assisting Japanese Americans threatened with internment. The Rexroths' Potrero Hill home at 692 Wisconsin Street became a center for discussions on radical politics and literature. His penchant for extramarital affairs continued unabated, and his second marriage began to unravel.

In 1948, with the aid of a Guggenheim Fellowship, Rexroth left for Europe, where he worked on *The Dragon and the Unicorn* (1952). He urged his lover, Marthe Larsen, to meet him in France, where they were married in a civil ceremony in the summer of 1949, after Rexroth lied about his divorce. Marie obtained a divorce from Rexroth on 13 September 1955, and Marthe and Rexroth married legally in June 1958 (already having had two daughters), less than three years before their tempestuous relationship ended in January 1961.

In the 1950s Rexroth published nearly a dozen volumes of poems, essays, and translations including *The Signature of All Things* (1950), *One Hundred Poems from the Japanese* (1955), and *Bird in the Bush: Obvious Essays* (1959). Rexroth had his own weekly book review show on Pacifica radio's KPFA, beginning in 1951, and wrote a regular column for the *Nation*. A pioneer in jazz poetry and a mentor to such young West Coast poets as Gary Snyder and Philip Lamantia, Rexroth seemed a likely ally to Allen Ginsberg, who sought to organize a poetry reading at San Francisco's Six Gallery. Rexroth agreed to serve as master of ceremonies at the reading on 7 October 1955, where Ginsberg's electrifying reading of *Howl* made literary history and launched the Beat Generation. Much to his later dismay, Rexroth's name would be forever linked to the Beat movement. Although he defended *Howl* (1956) in the obscenity trial the year after its publication, Rexroth turned against the Beats, particularly Jack Kerouac, in later years. Whether he did so because he was jealous of the younger writers, because he believed that they had sold out to the establishment, or because he blamed Kerouac for poet Robert Creeley's affair with Marthe remains a matter of conjecture.

Rexroth's reservations notwithstanding, his association with the Beats garnered the older poet greater attention. In 1957 he received the Eunice Tietjens Memorial Prize; the following year he received the $1,000 Shelley Memorial Award and an Amy Lowell fellowship, a $2,000 stipend that allowed him to travel to Europe, where he worked on his autobiography. In 1960 he began writing a weekly column for the *San Francisco Examiner* and touring the college lecture circuit. In 1964 he was invited to teach a poetry workshop at San Francisco State College and was poet-in-residence at the University of Wisconsin. New Directions published his collected works in two volumes: *The Collected Shorter Poems* (1966) and *The Collected Longer Poems* (1968). In May 1969, he was elected to the National Institute of Arts and Letters.

Rexroth remained active throughout the 1970s. From 1968 to 1974, he taught at the University of California at Santa Barbara, where he took part in Vietnam War protests. In August 1974, he married Carol Tinker, a young poet who arrived at 250 Scott Street in 1963 to serve as Rexroth's housekeeper and secretary. That same year, he received the Copernicus Award, a prize of $10,000 in recognition of lifetime achievement in poetry. He made several trips to Japan and continued to publish collection after collection of poems, essays, and translations, including, among others, *The Elastic Retort: Essays in Literature and Ideas* (1973), *New Poems* (1974), and *The Burning Heart: The Women Poets of Japan* (1977).

In December 1980, Rexroth suffered a major heart attack. Although he recovered enough to continue work on the second half of his autobiography, his health remained precarious. He survived two strokes, finally succumbing to a massive heart attack. Like his parents before him, Rexroth converted to Roman Catholicism shortly before his death, although he was also a follower of Buddhism. He was buried in the Santa Barbara Cemetery, following a funeral mass at the Mount Carmel Catholic Church.

In his distinguished career, Rexroth published more than fifty books, exhibited his paintings in numerous one-man shows, and was associated with three major literary movements: the Objectivists, the San Francisco Renaissance, and the Beat Generation. A cofounder of the San Francisco Poetry Center with Ruth Witt-Diamant, Rexroth

influenced a host of younger poets including Gary Snyder and Denise Levertov. His interest in jazz poetry paved the way for Beat experiments in this vein. Rexroth's literary achievements might have been more celebrated had it not been for his arrogant and abrasive personality. (In his 1962 book *Contemporaries*, Alfred Kazin labels him an "old-fashioned American sorehead.") Rexroth's outspoken contempt for the Academy and for the East Coast literary establishment did little to advance his national reputation. Nevertheless, he produced a substantial body of work and left an enduring mark on twentieth-century poetry.

★

Manuscripts and papers are located at the University of California at Los Angeles and the University of Southern California. Rexroth's *An Autobiographical Novel* (1966) provides an account of his life through 1926; at the time of his death, Rexroth was working on a sequel, a portion of which was published as *Excerpts from a Life* (1981). Sections also appear in *Conjunctions* 4 (1983): 96–114, and *Sagetribe* 2 (winter 1983): 9–17. "A Crystal out of Time and Space: The Poet's Diary" is included in *Conjunctions* 8 (1985): 62–85. A revised and expanded edition of *An Autobiographical Novel*, edited by Linda Hamalian, was published in 1991.

Linda Hamalian's *A Life of Kenneth Rexroth* (1991) is the most detailed and accurate portrait of the poet. *Kenneth Rexroth and James Laughlin: Selected Letters* (1991), edited by Lee Bartlett, provides a glimpse of how difficult Rexroth could be, even with friends. *Sagetribe* 2, no. 3 (winter 1983), a special issue dedicated to Rexroth, includes tributes and memorials by Thomas Parkinson, Eliot Weinberger, and others.

Obituaries are in the *New York Times* and the *Los Angeles Times* (both 8 June 1982). Recordings include *San Francisco Poets* (1950), *Poetry Readings in "The Cellar"* (1957), *Kenneth Rexroth at the Black Hawk* (1960), and *A Sword in a Cloud of Light* (1979).

WILLIAM M. GARGAN

REYNOLDS, Frank (*b.* 29 November 1923 in East Chicago, Indiana; *d.* 20 July 1983 in Washington, D.C.), American Broadcasting Company television news reporter and anchor.

Reynolds was one of four children of Helen Duffy and Frank James Reynolds, a mid-level steel-industry executive. The Reynoldses raised Frank and his three sisters in a Roman Catholic household; Reynolds continued to attend church regularly into adulthood.

After studying liberal arts at Indiana University and Wabash College, Reynolds entered the U.S. Army, where from 1943 to 1945 he served as an infantryman in the European theater of operations, stationed in France and Germany. He suffered a wound to the leg in Kassel, Germany, for which he received a Purple Heart and was taken out of combat.

Frank Reynolds. FRANK REYNOLDS PAPERS, SPECIAL COLLECTIONS DIVISION, GEORGETOWN UNIVERSITY LIBRARY, WASHINGTON, D.C.

He returned to Indiana, married Henrietta Mary Harpster on 23 August 1947, and took his first television anchor job at WJOB in Hammond, where he worked until 1950. He then moved to Chicago to anchor for WBKB-TV (later WLS-TV) and one year later went to WBBM, the Columbia Broadcasting System (CBS) affiliate in Chicago.

The American Broadcasting Company (ABC) hired Reynolds in 1963, first in Chicago as a correspondent and two years later in Washington, D.C., as White House correspondent during President Lyndon Johnson's administration. Reynolds turned down an offer to become the network anchor in New York City and later described his time as White House correspondent as a highlight of his career: "It was such a fascinating time at the White House.... There was Vietnam, the turmoil in the streets. I felt that what I was doing was far more important and personally satisfying than anchoring would be."

In Washington, Reynolds gained national esteem, and in 1968 ABC convinced him to come to its New York City headquarters as co-anchor, with Howard K. Smith, of its expanded, half-hour nightly news program. As Reynolds had expected, the anchor job bored him: "I remember reading the daily situation report ... about here is Joe in Bangkok and Anita is out in Abu Dhabi and somebody else is on the campaign trail, and there I was sitting on 66th Street and not really having very much fun."

Frequent editorials on events and politicians, including the Vietnam War and President Richard Nixon, livened up the job for Reynolds. Although many ABC officials considered Reynolds accurate and fair, some of the affiliates viewed him as liberal and opinionated. When Vice President Spiro Agnew criticized the press for being elite, negative, and biased, Reynolds fought back on the air. His 1969 commentary, which blasted Agnew and his opinions on the press, won Reynolds a George Foster Peabody Award. On another on-air occasion, Reynolds called John Ehrlichman, Nixon's domestic-affairs assistant, "a convicted Watergate felon."

When interviewed by Barbara Matusow for the *Washington Journalism Review* in 1980, Reynolds said he was most proud of his commentaries on the government's critique of the press: "I believe they [Nixon and Agnew] made a serious effort to undermine the freedom of the press.... Anyway, I did quite a few [editorials] on Agnew's attack on the press. And management was approached to get me to tone them down."

In 1970 ABC wooed Harry Reasoner over from CBS and sent Reynolds back to Washington. Reynolds said he felt he had been punished for stating his opinions. "I was taken off the air," he said. "Howard K. Smith was retained and he endorsed Agnew's views." Back in Washington, Reynolds covered the presidential campaigns of George McGovern in 1972 and Ronald Reagan in 1976.

In ABC's eyes, Reynolds built his credibility back up while reporting in Washington. When *World News Tonight* adopted a new format in 1978, network officials wanted Reynolds's camera-savvy face and voice. The nightly news show now boasted three anchors: Peter Jennings from the foreign desk in London, Max Robinson from the domestic desk in Chicago, and Reynolds from the national desk in Washington. Reynolds opened and closed the show and introduced his co-anchors but did not like sharing the twenty-two-minute newscast with two others. With this new format, ABC's ratings rose, surpassing those of CBS in 1980, but again, ABC executives had their qualms about Reynolds's performance. Roone Arledge, the new president of ABC News, wanted to soften up Reynolds's austere appearance. Reynolds came across like an elder statesman, formal and stern, while Arledge wanted a gentler and warmer figure. Reynolds balked, charging that Arledge paid too much attention to style.

Reynolds's demeanor fit his attitude toward his work—serious, concerned, determined. He introduced the first show of the revitalized *World News Tonight* with these words: "I promise you an accurate, responsible, meaningful report on events at home and abroad."

In 1979, when the American embassy in Tehran was

taken hostage, ABC ran a special program titled *The Iran Crisis: America Held Hostage,* which Reynolds anchored until his fifty-sixth birthday, when he took the day off because he felt ill. Newcomer Ted Koppel stepped in and eventually took over the lead anchoring position for the show that would become *Nightline.*

Unknown to everyone except his wife, five sons, and a few close friends, Reynolds's health had begun to decline. Although he was battling bone-marrow cancer, he continued to anchor for ABC and missed few days of work. But in January 1983 he hurt his leg during a Florida vacation. Soon after, he reinjured it and underwent surgery, during which he contracted viral hepatitis from infected blood. On 20 July 1983 Reynolds died at Sibley Hospital in Washington, D.C. He was buried at Arlington National Cemetery; ABC televised the funeral and produced an elaborate tribute. Reynolds's colleagues and friends said that had he been alive the extremely private man would not have approved of the hoopla, which included praise from President Ronald Reagan and Pope John Paul II. "I don't want to become more important than the message that I'm bearing," Reynolds had once said. "It's not the messenger who's important."

Although some would argue that Reynolds was a self-important television news personality who wanted the public to be very aware of him and his beliefs, others would argue that he was a responsible newsman who cared deeply about the news and the role of the press in society.

★

The majority of Frank Reynolds's papers, photographs, commentaries, and viewer responses are in the Special Collections Division of Georgetown University's Lauinger Library. Barbara Matusow, "How Frank Reynolds Viewed the News, Networks, and Notoriety," *Washington Journalism Review* (5 Sept. 1983), is the transcript of her in-depth interview with Reynolds, conducted when researching her book *The Evening Stars: The Making of the Network News Anchor* (1983). Marc Gunther's *The House That Roone Built: The Inside Story of ABC News* (1994) includes substantial information on Reynolds's personal background and professional career. Leonard H. Goldenson and Marvin J. Wolf, *Beating the Odds: The Untold Story Behind the Rise of ABC—The Stars, Struggles, and Egos That Transformed Network Television by the Men Who Made It Happen* (1991), also includes information on the struggles between Reynolds and ABC News. Robert Goldberg and Gerald Jay Goldberg, *Anchors: Brokaw, Jennings, Rather, and the Evening News* (1990), and Desmond Smith, "The Wide World of Roone Arledge," *New York Times Magazine* (24 Feb. 1980), have background information on Reynolds as anchor. ABC has the televised funeral and tribute in its tape archive.

ANNA GORMAN

RICE, Helen Steiner (*b.* 19 May 1900 in Lorain, Ohio; *d.* 23 April 1981 in Cincinnati, Ohio), author of more than fifty popular books of inspirational prose and poetry, including thirty-nine collections published posthumously, who was hailed as "poet laureate" of the greeting card industry.

Rice was one of the two daughters of John A. Steiner, a Baltimore and Ohio Railway engineer, and Anna Bieri Steiner, a designer-seamstress. Her childhood in Lorain, Ohio, a lake port and steel-mill town by Lake Erie, was a happy one, in which the Christian scriptures and spirituality played important roles. Also important in Rice's upbringing were the strong role models provided by her mother and grandmother, who showed that women could love and respect men without being dependent on them. Self-assured and popular at Lorain High School, Rice was encouraged to write by suffragette teacher Edith Wilker, with whom she remained friends for decades. An exceptional student, Rice graduated six months early, in January 1918.

Rice's first job was designing lampshades at Lorain Electric Light and Power Company. Her father's sudden death during the influenza epidemic, on 17 October 1918, ended her plans to attend college. Examining career options, she coerced reluctant supervisors to train her in bookkeeping.

Helen Steiner Rice. THE HELEN STEINER RICE FOUNDATION

Next, she persuaded them to let her do window displays to improve sales, and she eventually won the company national recognition in a window-display contest. Soon after she was promoted to advertising manager of the Ohio Public Service Company, of which Lorain Electric Light had become a branch. When asked to speak in her new capacity at the Ohio Electric Light Association convention, Rice later wrote, she "spoke to the God who means everything to me. . . . 'I don't know what to do, Father—You tell me.'" Comforted then, she made eye contact with audience members individually until she won them over.

In 1924 Rice's first article, which blended practical public-relations advice with an emphasis on service and positive thinking, was published in *Electric Light and Power* magazine. She then became the Ohio chairman of the Women's Public Information Committee of the National Electric Light Association. In that same year she won a prize from *Forbes* magazine for an article on public relations and, after a tornado struck Lorain, was nicknamed the "Lorain Tornado," her first national recognition.

From that time on, Rice received many invitations to speak at various events and to give interviews, with a focus always on public relations and service issues. Her speeches affirmed that even petite, attractive young women such as herself could be intelligent and valuable employees, a new and growing theme for the time. Often wearing distinctive hats, she used the fashion sense instilled in her by her mother to enhance her commanding presence. "If there were a hundred people in the room and she walked in," her cousin Jane Steiner recalled, "she would be the absolute center of attention." In 1927, after being photographed with President Calvin Coolidge at her address to the American Electric Railway Convention and with encouragement from publisher B. C. Forbes, Rice developed a number of speeches, printed up promotional material, and embarked on a whirlwind national lecture tour. In Dayton, Ohio, in June 1928 to deliver her speech "Living and Working Enthusiastically" to a group of bankers, she was welcomed by Dayton Savings and Trust vice president Franklin D. Rice, a handsome former military pilot from a wealthy, respected family. Their wedding on 30 January 1929 featured a reception at the Plaza Hotel in New York City, followed by a Caribbean honeymoon cruise. The happy newlyweds then briefly lived luxuriously in Dayton.

In October 1929 the stock market crash forced Franklin's bank to close. Franklin, despite his insistence on supporting his wife, was unable to find other work. Helen began teaching bridge. She wrote a letter inquiring about the direct purchase of playing cards to J. R. Gibson of the Gibson Art Company, in which she mentioned a plan for increasing sales of the company's Christmas seals. Gibson was so impressed, he hired her. During the 1931 Christmas season, Rice learned all she could about greeting card sales as troubleshooting consultant to the Gibson Art Company. In January 1932 she took a room at Cincinnati's Gibson Hotel, where she would reside until 1974. Her husband refused to leave their extravagant house in Dayton but visited on weekends. Gibson sales manager Sam Heed, familiar with Rice's earlier career, sent her to tour Gibson offices. She suggested many vital strategic changes, including a focus on gift wrapping, a tiny market she foresaw as a booming industry.

As Rice's career blossomed again, her husband was named in a lawsuit connected to his former bank work. On 13 October 1932 he was found dead from carbon monoxide poisoning in the car in their garage; he left his wife an apologetic letter dated three days earlier. Rice turned to religion and to her numerous friends, especially Cincinnati city councilman Willis D. Gradison, his wife, Dorothy, and their children, with whom she developed a familylike relationship that was lifelong. She also helped in Gradison's political campaigns, devotedly writing his speeches, campaign slogans, and literature from 1933 to 1947.

Rice, who claimed she was only asked to compose poetry for cards due to a vacancy at Gibson, and that until that moment she had not penned a verse, became editor of Gibson card lines when previous editor Ethel Brainerd, whose work she had admired, died. Beginning in 1934 and widely acknowledged by 1939, Rice wrote definitive poetry for greeting cards. Many of her works were still popular decades later, such as *Birthdays Are a Gift from God*: "For birthdays are a stepping-stone, / To endless joys as yet unknown, / So fill each day with happy things, / And may your burdens all take wings." Other popular titles include *God Bless America, Heart Gifts, Daily Prayers Dissolve Your Cares, Let Us Pray on This Holy Christmas Day, Fathers Are Wonderful People, A Tribute to All Daughters, Hush-a-Bye Honey* (set to music by Carl Portune), *There's Sunshine in a Smile, A Thankful Heart,* and *In Hours of Discouragement God Is Our Encouragement.*

Rice's work dramatically improved the quality and success of inspirational greeting cards. Poems of hers, including *The Priceless Gift of Christmas* and *The Praying Hands,* were read on national television on the *Lawrence Welk Show* in the 1960s. The show was routinely viewed by millions of families, and Rice received and personally handled abundant nationwide fan mail. The huge demand led to published collections of her works by 1963. She was one of the first greeting card authors to have her name printed on cards, because buyers recognized and sought them.

After 1971 Rice was a consultant to Gibson Greeting Cards, Inc., as the company was now named. In 1974, when the Gibson Hotel was torn down, she moved to the Cincinnati Club. She never completely recovered from a fall in 1980, but on 14 March 1981 she was awarded an honorary doctorate of humane letters from the College of Mount St.

Joseph in a private ceremony at Franciscan Terrace Nursing Home. Just over a month later she died and was buried at Elmwood Cemetery in Lorain next to her parents.

Rice's writings, addressed to the millions of people she felt were confused by increasingly complicated and dangerous times, speak of faith through great trials, sincere love, prayer, and simple hope. Even after her death her work continued to resonate with many. As the 1990s neared their end, more than 6 million books featuring Rice poems had been sold, and her poems were still popular in Gibson greeting cards.

★

Helen Steiner Rice, *Heart Gifts from Helen Steiner Rice: A Special Selection of Her Poems and a Pen Portrait of Her as a Person* (1968), and Rice, as told to Fred Bauer, *In the Vineyard of the Lord* (1979), are personal reflections. Ronald Pollit and Virginia Wiltse, *Helen Steiner Rice: Ambassador of Sunshine* (1994), is the definitive, well-researched biography authorized by the Helen Steiner Rice Foundation. An obituary is in the *New York Times* (25 Apr. 1981).

J. S. CAPPELLETTI

RICHTER, Charles Francis (*b.* 26 April 1900 near Hamilton, Ohio; *d.* 30 September 1985 in Altadena, California), seismologist best known for his development of the earthquake magnitude scale, commonly called the Richter scale.

Richter was reticent about his parents. Without naming them, he revealed to an interviewer that they divorced soon after his birth, that his mother resumed her maiden name (which was Lillian A. Richter), and that he took her family name. He, his mother, and his older sister lived with his maternal grandparents on a farm near Hamilton, Ohio, until his grandmother died in 1907; two years later the family moved to Los Angeles, California.

Richter attended a preparatory school associated with the University of Southern California in Los Angeles, and he enrolled in that college for the 1916–1917 school year. He developed an early interest in science, especially astronomy, and participated in a natural history club whose members enjoyed hiking and plant collecting in nearby mountains. In 1917 he transferred to Stanford University and received an A.B. in physics in 1920. Under a strain that he called "a definite nervous breakdown," he returned to Los Angeles, sought treatment from a psychiatrist, and held nominal jobs near home.

In a 1920 reorganization, the California Institute of Technology (Caltech) in Pasadena was established from Throop College of Technology and was headed by physicist Robert A. Millikan. Impressed by Millikan's lectures and interested in atomic theory, Richter enrolled at Caltech for graduate studies in 1923 and pursued physics under Paul Epstein on a project suggested by Millikan on the hydrogen

Charles F. Richter. COURTESY OF THE ARCHIVES, CALIFORNIA INSTITUTE OF TECHNOLOGY

atom with a spinning electron. In 1928 he completed his Ph.D. in theoretical physics. Wanting to remain in the intellectually stimulating Caltech environment, Richter had accepted an offer in 1927 from Millikan to work at the new Seismological Laboratory installed by Caltech in a Pasadena mansion. The original laboratory in Pasadena had been established by the Carnegie Institution of Washington in 1921, under the direction of seismologist Harry O. Wood, who continued to head the new facility. While some of its funding was from Caltech, the laboratory's administration remained in the hands of the Carnegie Institution, which paid Richter until 1937. He married Lillian Brand on 18 July 1928; they had no children.

As research assistant for Wood at the Seismological Laboratory, Richter was assigned to catalog the distribution of earthquakes in southern California in order to identify all significant local faults. The laboratory was establishing a network of recording stations with newly developed Wood-Anderson torsion seismographs, effective for recording nearby earthquakes. Wood and Richter soon determined that there was no apparent correlation between the distribution of small earthquakes and major fault structure.

In 1930 Beno Gutenberg, an internationally known German seismologist, was hired by Millikan on a Caltech appointment, located at the Seismological Laboratory. His interest was determining the earth's inner structure by means of seismic waves from worldwide earthquake records. He became Richter's mentor, and the latter's first collaboration with Gutenberg was writing the text to accompany data that Gutenberg had analyzed and wanted to publish in English.

The comparative methods of ranking earthquake size in 1930, such as the Mercalli intensity scale, were all based on damage to structures, which was not satisfactory for comparison between countries or under the ocean. Seismologists recognized that earthquakes that did not produce an especially large record on paper sometimes caused great loss of life and damage to structures, depending upon the type of construction and local geology. Wood, Richter, and Gutenberg were all interested in a more accurate comparison. Following a suggestion in a paper by Japanese seismologist Kiyoo Wadati, Richter in the early 1930s began plotting earthquake records in terms of measured amplitudes on instruments at the seven widely separated recording stations near Pasadena, with a correction for distance to the earthquake epicenter (the point on the surface immediately above the earthquake's origin).

The range from small to large earthquakes, however, proved to be "unmanageably great" on paper, said Richter, until Gutenberg suggested that handling the data logarithmically would simplify the presentation. A change of 1.0 in the logarithmic scale corresponded to a change of ten points in the amplitude of shaking. This worked well. Then Wood "insisted that this new quantity should be given a distinctive name to contrast it with the intensity scale," recalled Richter, who continued, "My amateur interest in astronomy brought out the term *magnitude,*" similar in some ways to stellar magnitudes, which are also on a logarithmic scale. Later he said, "I think it was Professor [Perry] Byerly [at the University of California, Berkeley] who started referring to it as the Richter Scale in public." That designation has stuck, although Richter felt that Gutenberg also deserved credit. In 1932 the Seismological Laboratory began using the magnitude scale in reports. Because it was based on instrumental records, magnitudes could be assigned to earlier earthquakes for which there were records (for example, the 1906 San Francisco earthquake), with an appropriate correlation between types of recorders.

To determine the distribution of local earthquakes, Richter wanted to take portable recorders to the site of an earthquake to record aftershocks. He had one recorder available at the time of the destructive Long Beach, California, earthquake of 1933, and it contributed to the understanding of that event. His concern with the impact of earthquakes on various types of construction probably began with that one, which destroyed a number of schools and led to the first building code for earthquake construction in California. Richter obtained more portable recorders

during the next few years and used them at sites of other nearby earthquakes.

The arrangement between the Carnegie Institution and Caltech changed in 1937, so that Caltech now administered the Seismological Laboratory, with limited support from the Carnegie Institution through 1941. In 1937 Richter became assistant professor of seismology at Caltech; he advanced to associate professor in 1947 and professor in 1952. He taught undergraduate and graduate courses in seismology at Caltech.

Richter's continuing fruitful collaboration with Gutenberg resulted in a series of papers called "On Seismic Waves" during the 1930s; other coauthored papers; and *Seismicity of the Earth* (1941; 2d ed. 1954), a classic compendium.

During World War II most international exchanges of earthquake information ended. Richter contributed to a war-related Caltech project concerning theoretical problems associated with the use of rockets against enemy submarines, through the Office of Scientific Research and Development. He also provided information to U.S. military forces on the earthquake risk at potential locations for building facilities.

Richter contributed, in chapters with Gutenberg, to the second edition of *Internal Constitution of the Earth* (1951), edited by Gutenberg and sponsored by the National Research Council. He wrote *Elementary Seismology* (1958), a well-received textbook useful to the layman and the specialist. In it he presented considerable information on the effects of earthquakes on structures. That was also one of his major themes in public lectures or conversations with the press. In 1977 he said that he had "a horror of predictions and of predictors" of earthquakes, but later acknowledged that carefully done research toward that goal might provide greater understanding of earthquakes.

In 1959 and 1960 Richter visited Japan on a Fulbright scholarship; there he enjoyed exchanging information with colleagues. He visited New Zealand several times, another country with frequent earthquakes. In 1970 he retired from Caltech. The following year he began his association with the Glendale, California, consulting firm of Lindvall, Richter, and Associates, which advised agencies of the city and county of Los Angeles on the safety of dams and reservoirs. The firm also advised on the earthquake safety of sites of tall buildings and nuclear power facilities.

Richter was of medium build, five-feet-eight-inches tall and about 150 pounds. He was clean shaven, and had thinning hair in his late years. His well-dressed appearance in the morning was somewhat rumpled by midday and his hair rather fly-about. He always had a ready smile for a visitor or friend and just a bit of stammer when hurried. Richter was a delightful conversationalist in small-group settings, helpful to colleagues and his few graduate students, and patient when explaining earthquakes to laypersons. Familiar with the nuances of the English language, he enjoyed collecting examples of abuses of it. Colleagues were in awe of his phenomenal memory, aware of his ineptness with tools and equipment, and amused at his maintaining a seismograph in his living room at home. His Altadena house was located in a grove of eucalyptus trees; visitors reported that he was not especially concerned about tidiness. One of his favorite activities was long, solitary hikes in the mountains. Richter was president of the Seismological Society of America in 1959 and 1960 and was awarded its medal in 1977. He died of coronary disease and is buried at Mountain View Cemetery in Altadena, California.

In their day, Richter and Gutenberg established the seismic geography of the earth, on which others could build. Richter's magnitude scale proved useful for comparing earthquakes worldwide. Through the years he resisted suggestions by other seismologists that the scale be defined in terms of energy, which he felt would necessitate continuous theoretical revisions. To him the magnitude scale was a measure derived by a simple computation from the records of a calibrated seismograph. By the 1980s the scale was being derived by a more complex calculation, but still as the Richter magnitude scale.

★

Richter's personal and professional papers are at the California Institute of Technology in Pasadena, California, as is an oral history. Richter describes his scale in "An Instrumental Earthquake Scale," *Bulletin of the Seismological Society of America* 25 (1935): 1–35. Judith R. Goodstein, *Millikan's School: A History of the California Institute of Technology* (1991), describes the establishment and early years of the Seismological Laboratory in Pasadena. Kate Holliday, "Charles Richter: 'Earthquake Man,' " *Smithsonian* 1 (Feb. 1971), is an account of Richter's career and personality for a popular audience. "Second Award of the Medal of the Seismological Society of America," *Bulletin of the Seismological Society of America* 67 (1977): 1243–1247, contains biographical information and a summary by Richter of the early years of the Seismological Laboratory. See also Clarence Allen, "Charles F. Richter: A Personal Tribute," *Bulletin of the Seismological Society of America* 77 (1987): 2234–2237. Obituaries are in the *Los Angeles Times* and *New York Times* (both 1 Oct. 1985).

ELIZABETH NOBLE SHOR

RIDDLE, Nelson Smock, Jr. (*b.* 1 June 1921 in Oradell, New Jersey; *d.* 6 October 1985 in Los Angeles, California), composer, conductor, music director, and arranger for such popular singers as Nat King Cole, Linda Ronstadt, and Frank Sinatra; he composed numerous scores for television and film, including the score for *The Great Gatsby* (1974), for which he won an Academy Award.

The son of Nelson Smock Riddle, Sr., a commercial artist an amateur trombone player and ragtime pianist, and Marie Albertine Rieber, Riddle began piano lessons at age eight. When he was fourteen, he switched to the trombone, and three years later was a member of the New Jersey State Orchestra. In his junior year of high school he met Bill Finegan, an arranger for Tommy Dorsey and Glenn Miller. Finegan taught Riddle the rudiments of arranging and served as Riddle's mentor. In 1938 Riddle wrote his first arrangement, for the song "I See Your Face Before Me."

In 1939, after graduating from high school, Riddle got his first job with a national band, led by Tommy Reynolds. Riddle worked primarily as a section trombonist and also did some arrangements. In December 1940 Riddle joined the Charlie Spivak band as trombonist and arranger. At age twenty-two, in 1943, Riddle enlisted in the merchant marine to play in the band. He had been told, erroneously, that by serving with that branch for a year, he could avoid being drafted into the regular army. Riddle served in a band stationed at Sheepshead Bay, Brooklyn, and later remembered this as the time that he learned to write for strings. After his discharge from the merchant marine, Riddle

Nelson Riddle at the "Hong Kong Bar" in the Century Plaza Hotel, Los Angeles, 1972. FOTOS INTERNATIONAL/ARCHIVE PHOTOS

joined the Tommy Dorsey band in May 1944 as trombone player and arranger. As trombonist, he played on such hit single records as "Sunny Side of the Street" and "Opus No. 1." Riddle worked for eleven months with Dorsey. Regarding his work as an arranger, Dorsey told Riddle that he was making the strings too important; consequently, Riddle adjusted his arrangements to include more instruments characteristic of a big-band sound.

During his time with Dorsey, Riddle made an important career decision, encouraged by Finegan. Riddle's skill as a trombonist was enabling him to solo occasionally, but he knew he would never distinguish himself as an instrumentalist. He was, however, becoming an excellent arranger. Finegan argued that as long as Riddle was working as a musician, bandleaders would treat his writing as more a hobby than a profession. A freak accident finally ended his career as a trombonist. In April 1945 Riddle was drafted into the regular army; he was assigned to lead a band for the officers' club in Fort Knox, Kentucky. During that time his front teeth were knocked out in an accident involving a garage door. The artificial crowns he was fitted with to replace his front teeth prevented him from playing trombone again.

On 10 October 1945 Riddle married Doreen Moran; the first piece of furniture the newlyweds bought was a piano. They would have seven children. Following his discharge from the army in June 1946, Riddle, with the encouragement of his wife, resolved to arrange full-time. He wrote for Dorsey, Spivak, and Larry Elgart. When Elgart's first band folded, in 1946, Riddle relocated to Los Angeles. Bob Crosby was looking for an arranger and, as Riddle said, "I sort of foisted myself on him." Riddle wrote for records and radio, and his first steady job was at NBC Radio in 1947 as an arranger under music director Henry Russell. From Russell, Riddle "learned to work fast and, I hope, well." It was said that Riddle would write for anybody, often being paid $100 to $150 an arrangement. Also during this time Riddle took advantage of the GI bill to study string orchestration with the Italian-born composer Mario Castelnuovo-Tedesco.

The first commercial recording company to give Riddle a job as an arranger for popular singers was Decca, for which he wrote more than twenty-five arrangements for Bing Crosby as well as for other singers. In 1950 he went to work for Capitol Records, where he was music director from 1951 to 1962. It is unknown how much Riddle wrote during his early years at Capitol, since he never received credit. He did not begin to emerge from anonymity until late 1950, when he was hired by Les Baxter to write arrangements for a Nat King Cole album. As a subcontractor, Riddle received no credit for his arrangements for "Too Young" and "Mona Lisa," both blockbuster hits. Cole discovered that Riddle had done the arranging, and in August

1951 Riddle began arranging and conducting regularly under his own name for Cole. Within a few months Riddle was writing for other Capitol singers, including Mel Tormé, Kate Smith, and Ella Mae Morse, a novelty blues singer for whom Riddle concocted the hit "Blacksmith Blues." By 1952 the word was out concerning Riddle's skill as an arranger, and he began writing for singers from a variety of labels. From 1963 to 1985 he was music director for Reprise Records.

Riddle's association with Frank Sinatra began in 1953 and lasted thirty years. He wrote more than 300 recorded orchestrations for Sinatra and arranged twenty-one albums. Riddle's unique combination of swing rhythm from his big-band background and his expertise with strings suited Sinatra's style. Riddle's two favorite albums with Sinatra were *Songs for Swingin' Lovers* (1956) and *Only the Lonely* (1958). It was during the recording of the 1956 album that Sinatra began to realize that Riddle intuitively understood what he wanted. The best Sinatra-Riddle tracks were crafted in what Riddle called "the tempo of the heartbeat." Many consider the albums Sinatra made with Riddle each man's best work.

In addition to arranging, Riddle was also a composer. His instrumental "Lisbon Antiqua" (1956) won a Gold Record, and "Cross Country Suite," eleven sketches of various parts of the United States, won a Grammy in 1958. Riddle received Grammy nominations for two albums with Sinatra and one with Oscar Peterson. He did numerous scores for film and television. His first full-length film score was for *Johnny Concho* (1956), with its distinctive theme "Wait for Me." He scored *St. Louis Blues* in 1958 and *Lolita* in 1962, which includes the popular instrumental "Lolita Ya-Ya." Riddle was nominated for an Academy Award for his scoring of *Li'l Abner* (1959), *Can-Can* (1960), *Robin and the Seven Hoods* (1964), and *Paint Your Wagon* (1969). He won an Oscar in 1974 for his original score of *The Great Gatsby*. For television he wrote the theme music for several shows, including *The Untouchables* (1959) and *Naked City* (1962); his theme song to *Route 66* was thirtieth on the *Billboard* pop charts in 1962 and received two Grammy nominations. It was one of the first television show themes to be recorded and commercially released.

Riddle worked as music director for a number of television programs, television specials, and special events, including the inaugurations of President John F. Kennedy (1961) and President Ronald Reagan (1985). Television shows included *The Frank Sinatra Show* (1957–1958), *The Julie Andrews Hour* (1972–1973), and *The Smothers Brothers Comedy Hour* (1967–1969). He also did the music to a number of Frank Sinatra and Bing Crosby specials, as well as *The Diahann Carroll Special* (1971), *The Don Rickles Special* (1975), and *The Lucille Ball Special* (1975 and 1976). He provided the music, which received an Emmy nomination, to *Our Town*, with Frank Sinatra (1955), and a documentary, *Bogart* (1967). Later work included a *Natalie Cole Special* (1978), *The Carpenters* (1980), and *Linda Ronstadt in Concert* (1984).

Always working to improve his skills, Riddle took conducting lessons from Victor Bay, conductor of the Santa Monica Symphony. Riddle conducted his own orchestra, was guest conductor for a number of artists, and regularly conducted at the Hollywood Bowl from 1954 to 1985; he conducted a concert for Ella Fitzgerald at this venue one month before his death.

Riddle divorced his first wife in the early 1970s and married his longtime secretary, Naomi. A serious liver condition resulted in an operation in 1980, and Riddle attempted to retire, working on a book, *Arranged by Nelson Riddle: The Definitive Study of Arranging,* which was published posthumously in 1985. The chance to work on an album with Linda Ronstadt brought him out of retirement. The result, *What's New* (1983), sold a half million copies within a month of its release and was the third-best-selling album in the nation that year. The album brought a second Grammy for Riddle. A series of concerts with Ronstadt and Riddle and his orchestra was critically acclaimed. The second Ronstadt-Riddle album, *Lush Life* (1984), was also successful, and a third album, *For Sentimental Reasons* (1986), was released after Riddle's death. He died from cardiac and kidney failure at Cedars-Sinai Medical Center in Los Angeles.

Over his long career Riddle worked with musicians as diverse as Nat King Cole, Rosemary Clooney, Judy Garland, Peggy Lee, Ella Fitzgerald, and Kiri Te Kanawa. He has been called the most celebrated vocal arranger and musical director in history.

★

In addition to his book on arranging, Riddle wrote a number of articles, including "Nelson Riddle Talking," *Crescendo International* 6, no. 1 (1967): 10–12, and "Branching Out from the Sound," *Crescendo International* 6, no. 2 (1967): 20–22. Will Friedwald, *Sinatra! The Song Is You: A Singer's Art* (1995), includes a chapter on Riddle. Interviews with Riddle by Les Tomkins are in *Crescendo International* 20, no. 1 (1981): 20–22, and *Crescendo International* 20, no. 2 (1981): 24–25. See also Harvey Siders, "Nelson Riddle: Arranger-Composer-Conductor," *International Musician* 71 (June 1973): 9 ff., and Todd Gold, "A Riddle Named Nelson Gives the Answer to Linda Ronstadt's Oldies LP *What's New,*" *People Weekly* (7 Nov. 1983). Tributes include Charles Champlin, "Riddle: A Master at His Craft," *Los Angeles Times* (10 Oct. 1985), and Steven Smith, "The Heartbeat Behind Sinatra's Songs," *Los Angeles Times* (13 Oct. 1985). Obituaries are in the *Los Angeles Times* and *New York Times* (both 7 Oct. 1985) and the *Atlanta Constitution* and *Boston Globe* (both 8 Oct. 1985).

MARCIA B. DINNEEN

RIDDLEBERGER, James Williams (*b.* 21 September 1904 in Washington, D.C.; *d.* 16 October 1982 in Woodstock,

Virginia), U.S. ambassador to Yugoslavia, Greece, and Austria.

The oldest of five children of Frank Belew Riddleberger, a salesman, and Anne Williams, a public school teacher, James Riddleberger attended public schools and Massanutten Academy, all located in Woodstock, Virginia. His grandfather, Harrison Holt Riddleberger, served as a U.S. senator from Virginia between 1883 and 1889. At seventeen, James went to Randolph-Macon College in Ashland, Virginia, graduating with an A.B. in 1924. He then attended Georgetown University, earning an A.M. in 1926. In 1926 and 1927 he took graduate courses at American University, but he proceeded no further in his formal education.

Riddleberger held a variety of jobs in his lifetime, working during his early youth as a farmhand, bricklayer, and housepainter. From 1924 to 1927 he was employed as a research assistant in the legislative reference service of the Library of Congress, and from 1927 to 1929 he worked for the U.S. Tariff Commission as a foreign tariffs expert. Between 1926 and 1929 he also was an assistant professor of international relations at Georgetown University's School of Foreign Service.

In 1929 Riddleberger entered the U.S. Foreign Service, first serving as vice-consul in Geneva, Switzerland, in 1930. He was promoted to full consul in 1935. On 20 March 1931, while in Geneva, Riddleberger married Amelie Johanna Sophie Otken, the daughter of a physician at The Hague. The couple had three children. In 1936 Riddleberger was

James Riddleberger. MR. PETER RIDDLEBERGER

transferred to Berlin, serving initially as third secretary, then as second secretary in the American embassy there between 1937 and 1941.

When war in Europe broke out, the United States, still neutral, transferred diplomats away from Eastern Europe and families away from Europe as a whole, and Riddleberger found himself in Germany alone. He became acquainted with another family man alone in Germany at this time, George Kennan, and he learned to enjoy the opera in Berlin. Riddleberger later told his youngest son that he had disliked his assignment in Nazi Germany, but that he believed some Germans had resisted Nazi propaganda in subtle ways, such as with humor, at that time.

A few months before the United States entered World War II, Riddleberger was recalled to Washington, D.C. From 1941 to 1943 he was on the Board of Economic Warfare as an alternate member of the reviews and appeals commission on export applications, chairman of the commission on neutral trade, and the liaison officer to the State Department. Riddleberger became second secretary and consul at the American embassy in London, England, in September 1942, becoming first secretary there in August 1943. The State Department then recalled Riddleberger, making him chief of its division on Central European affairs early in 1944.

He served as U.S. representative at the initial meeting between the United States and the United Kingdom on bizonal arrangements for vanquished Germany, held in Washington, D.C., in 1946. The following year Riddleberger became counselor of the embassy and chief of the political sections of the American military government in Berlin. He was in Berlin in 1948 and 1949 during the Berlin airlift. After the American military government was replaced by the U.S. High Commission for Germany, Riddleberger became director of the office of political affairs under John J. McCloy, U.S. high commissioner, in Frankfurt am Main in August 1949.

Riddleberger left the State Department in September 1950 to serve as political adviser at the headquarters of the Economic Cooperation Administration in Paris. He then served as a political adviser to U.S. ambassador William H. Draper, Jr., working particularly with the issue of coordination of U.S. military, economic, and political policies in Europe. Riddleberger returned to the State Department in May 1952, becoming director of a special bureau of German affairs at the rank of assistant secretary of state.

In July 1953 Riddleberger was appointed by President Dwight D. Eisenhower as U.S. ambassador to Yugoslavia, a post he held until January 1958. During his tenure there, Yugoslavia and Italy settled their differences over the Adriatic port of Trieste. Riddleberger was one of the Western diplomats who assisted in the negotiations that led to the signing of the compromise agreement in October 1954. He also is credited with helping to persuade Marshal Josip Broz

Tito to resist inducements by Nikita S. Khrushchev to return to the Soviet orbit, from which Yugoslavia had broken away in 1948. At a reception for Premier Khrushchev in Belgrade in May 1955, Riddleberger engaged in a noteworthy discussion with Khrushchev on the use of force in foreign affairs. At the beginning of June, Riddleberger was recalled to Washington, D.C., where he conferred with the Foreign Affairs Committee of the House of Representatives, recommending economic and military assistance to Marshal Tito. When he returned to Belgrade later in the month, he attended a meeting with British, French, and Yugoslav officials to review diplomatic relations between Yugoslavia and the West. While Riddleberger was on home leave in Washington, D.C., in October 1956, President Eisenhower decided in favor of continued aid, with limitations, to Tito's government, so Riddleberger returned to Belgrade, handling aid negotiations until he was transferred away from Yugoslavia in January 1958.

Riddleberger became ambassador to Greece in February 1958. While in that position, he attempted to improve relations between Greece and Turkey over Cyprus. In February 1959, he was appointed director of the International Cooperation Administration (a forerunner of the Agency for International Development) in charge of foreign economic aid. In 1961 he became chairman of the development assistance committee of the Organization for Economic Cooperation in Paris. He was then appointed U.S. ambassador to Austria in 1962, retiring in 1967 as a career ambassador, the highest rank in the Foreign Service.

After his retirement Riddleberger moved to his family home in Woodstock, Virginia. He served as president of DACOR (Diplomatic and Consular Officers Retired) and as honorary chairman of the Population Crisis Committee. He died of a heart attack and is buried in Woodstock. His religious affiliation was with the Methodist Church. He was a member of the University and Metropolitan Clubs.

James Riddleberger, despite his modest beginnings, rose rapidly in his career and was present at some of the most important political and military crises of the twentieth century. His presence in Germany during the Nazi period, in Washington, D.C., during World War II, and in Europe immediately after the war allowed him to influence the postwar institutions that remained decades later. Further, he served in important positions as ambassador during the cold war, particularly in Yugoslavia.

★

Riddleberger left a small collection of his papers, including a few speeches and conference reports, at the George C. Marshall Research Foundation Library in Lexington, Virginia. An obituary is in the *Washington Post* (19 Oct. 1982). He also left oral histories at the Marshall Library and at Princeton University, Princeton, New Jersey.

MICHELLE C. MORGAN

RIGGS, Ralph Smith (*b.* 20 June 1895 in Paris, Texas; *d.* 29 April 1981 in Bethesda, Maryland), vice admiral of the U.S. Navy who achieved fame for his heroism as a destroyer commander during World War II.

Riggs was one of four children born to Joseph Newton and Minnie Little Riggs. In 1914 he entered the U.S. Naval Academy at Annapolis, Maryland, graduating in 1917 with a B.S. degree. Riggs then served as a lieutenant aboard the cruiser *Minneapolis,* the dreadnought *Dante Alighieri,* and the destroyer *Manley,* which escorted U.S. troopships headed to France during World War I. After the armistice in 1918, Riggs had several shore-based assignments, which included studying at the Naval War College (1929–1930) and then working at the Naval Bureau of Personnel. He later served aboard several warships, including the battleships *Utah* (as an aide to the commander of cruiser divisions, Scouting Fleet, Yangtze Patrol), *Texas* (as an aide to Combat Division No. 1), and *West Virginia* (as a navigator). He also served as commanding officer aboard the destroyer *Zane* and the storeship *Arctic.* On 3 December 1929 Riggs married Kathryn Pew, with whom he had one son, Ralph S. Riggs, Jr.

In October 1941 Riggs transferred into Command Destroyer Squadron No. 1 as commander, Destroyer Division No. 2, in which capacity he remained through August 1942. His hard work in this his third command assignment, composed of the destroyers *Aylwin* (the flagship), *Dale, Farragut,* and *Monaghan,* paid off when the Japanese made their attack on Pearl Harbor on 7 December 1941. Riggs's ships, berthed near the battleship *Utah* at Buoy X-18, began moving as early as 8:28 A.M. *Monaghan* helped the destroyer *Ward* sink a Japanese minisubmarine; *Dale* and *Farragut* made it out of the harbor into open water; and *Aylwin,* minus most of its commanding officers, took up a patrol station near the harbor mouth. Riggs was credited with having an outstanding unit and was praised for its heroic efforts during the Japanese attack.

Riggs's first naval action as commander of Destroyer Division No. 2 was a raid on Rabaul with the carrier *Lexington.* The group, Task Force 11, launched an attack against Japanese forces on the atoll. Japanese scout planes discovered the raiding party before it could strike, and in the ensuing battle, Riggs's ship helped keep the Japanese planes from doing any damage to the American force. Riggs also participated in the historic 1942 naval battles at Coral Sea and Midway. During the Coral Sea engagement, Japanese aircraft attacked his group, and two planes attempted suicide runs against the carrier *Yorktown,* which he was protecting. To prevent damage to the aircraft carrier, Riggs ordered the *Aylwin* to steer close to the carrier, enabling "his ships' devastating gunfire to blast both planes into the

Rear Admiral Ralph S. Riggs, 1949. UPI/CORBIS-BETTMANN

sea." For this action and for defeating an enemy night air attack, and screening the U.S. task force at Midway, Riggs was awarded a Bronze Star Medal.

In 1942 Riggs was promoted to captain and placed in command of Destroyer Squadron No. 14, comprising the new destroyer *Bailey* and the *Coghlan, Dale,* and *Monaghan.* He was charged with blockading the Alaskan island of Attu, which the Japanese had recently captured. Soon thereafter, the Japanese sent a flotilla under Vice Admiral Moshiro Hosogaya to break through the American fleet. The group consisted of two heavy cruisers, the *Nachi* and *Maya,* the light cruisers *Abukuma* and *Tama,* the armed merchantmen *Asaka Maru* and *Sakito Maru,* and the destroyers *Wakaba, Hatsushimo, Ikazuchi,* and *Inazuma.* The *Coghlan* spotted the closest enemy warships on its radar at 7:30 A.M. on 26 March 1943. During the sea duel that developed, Captain Riggs was ordered by Admiral Charles H. McMorris to take command of all Task Group 16.6 destroyers. At 11:25 A.M. one of McMorris's cruisers, *Salt Lake City,* abruptly halted, damaged by salvos from the Japanese warships. McMorris ordered Riggs's destroyers to launch a torpedo attack to fend off the enemy warships. This order was rescinded when *Salt Lake City* got under way again a few minutes later at 11:38. But at 11:54, *Salt Lake City* lurched to a halt once more. This time, salt water had fouled the oil lines to the ship's boilers. As the hapless cruiser slid to a halt,

McMorris again ordered Riggs to launch a torpedo attack against the Japanese cruisers. Riggs's destroyers, which had already been laying a smoke screen for the American task group and had just aborted their first attack, swung into action. Following orders from Riggs to "Get the big boys!" *Dale* provided screening for the *Salt Lake City*, while Riggs, who was aboard *Bailey*, ordered the three remaining ships to launch a bold attack against the enemy ships. According to the naval unit commendation that Riggs received for his actions, his destroyers laid smoke and fought an enemy that was "twice his strength." *Bailey*, despite the havoc wreaked by Japanese fire, scored several hits on the lead Japanese cruiser *Nachi*. Due in large part to the persistent hounding by the U.S. destroyers, Admiral Hosogaya ordered his ships to retire. Riggs's bravery and quick thinking at the Komandorski Islands conflict led to the saving of an American cruiser, and he was awarded a naval unit commendation.

In July 1943 Riggs became chief of staff and aide to the commander of destroyers, Pacific Fleet. He continued in that post until March 1944. During this period, Riggs won a Legion of Merit for "contributing to the reliability and efficiency of destroyers in carrying out extensive operations [against Japanese-held islands]." At this time, he was named captain of the battleship *South Dakota*, in which capacity he received a Gold Star in lieu of a second Legion of Merit. During his term as commander of *South Dakota*, the battleship participated in the Battle of the Philippine Sea.

He continued as captain until November 1944, when he became the commander of Cruiser Division No. 12, a cover-and-support group of light cruisers and destroyers. Promoted to rear admiral on 12 December 1944, he saw action in the southern Philippines at the U.S. naval landing operations at Puerto Princesa Harbor on Palawan Island during February 1945. He earned Gold Stars (one in lieu of a third Legion of Merit, another in lieu of a second Bronze Star Medal) for his participation in these actions, and he received the British Order of Orange Nassau with Sword for his actions at Balikpapan in Borneo.

At the end of World War II, Vice Admiral Riggs took command of Cruiser Division No. 14 until 1946. He then returned to the United States and settled in Potomac, Maryland. Riggs continued in military life, serving as assistant chief of naval operations for the U.S. Naval Reserve. He was subsequently promoted to director of the naval reserves and served in this position until he retired from military service in 1951. He then became a general partner in the stock brokerage firm of Burton, Cluett, and Dana, establishing an office in Washington, D.C., for this company. Riggs continued to work in this capacity until he retired in 1966. In addition to his professional activities, Riggs maintained membership in the Army and Navy Club. He was also a member in several local social clubs, including the Metropolitan, the Chevy Chase, and the Burning Tree. He was also a life member of the Naval Academy Alumni Association.

Riggs lived a quiet life in Bethesda, Maryland, until February 1981, when he was involved in a traffic accident that left him with serious chest injuries. During his hospitalization at the National Naval Medical Center in Bethesda, Maryland, his wife of fifty-two years, Kathryn, died. Riggs succumbed to respiratory arrest due to complications from his injuries on 29 April 1981, approximately one month afterward. He was buried at Arlington National Cemetery with full military honors.

★

Theodore Roscoe, *United States Destroyer Operations in World War II* (1953), contains detailed information regarding Riggs's actions, especially during the Komandorski operation. Told from the perspective of the U.S. Navy destroyer command, it provides a unique view of the Pacific campaign. Robert Ross Smith, *Triumph in the Philippines* (1963; repr. 1991), includes brief information about Riggs's actions in the Philippines. See also Samuel Eliot Morison, *History of United States Naval Operations in World War II*, vol. 4: *Coral Sea, Midway, and Submarine Actions, May 1942–August 1942* (1949), vol. 7: *Aleutians, Gilberts, and Marshalls, June 1942–April 1944* (1964), and vol. 13: *The Liberation of the Philippines: Luzon, Mindanao, the Visayas, 1944–1945* (1965), and Walter Karig et al., *Battle Report*, vol. 3: *Pacific War: Middle Phase* (1947), vol. 4: *The End of an Empire* (1948), and vol. 5: *Victory in the Pacific* (1949). Both Morison and Karig provide detailed histories of the Pacific campaign, but from a more balanced view than the Roscoe book provides. Included in these multivolume sets are unique and detailed maps, charts, photographs, and orders of battle. Morison's works are particularly helpful for their brief biographical sketches. Brian Garfield, *The Thousand-Mile War: World War II in Alaska and the Aleutians* (1969; repr. 1983) is a critical analysis of the Alaskan campaign, including the Komandorski Island battle. See also the chapter "The Battle of the Komandorskis" in the U.S. Navy publication *The Aleutians Campaign: 1942–August 1943* (1943; repr. 1993). Samuel Eliot Morison, *The Two-Ocean War: A Short History of the United States Navy in the Second World War* (1963), has a brief sketch of Riggs. Obituaries are in the *Washington Post* (1 May 1981) and *New York Times* (2 May 1981).

BRIAN B. CARPENTER

RIPLEY, Elmer Horton (*b.* 21 July 1891 in Staten Island, New York; *d.* 29 April 1982 in Staten Island, New York), basketball coach and player who coached nearly thirty years at Georgetown, Yale, Columbia, and Notre Dame Universities and was elected to the Basketball Hall of Fame in 1972.

Born and raised on Staten Island in New York Harbor, Ripley was the oldest of the three children of William

Elmer Ripley, *c.* 1946. LAUINGER LIBRARY, GEORGETOWN UNIVERSITY

Ripley, owner of a sand and gravel business that made deliveries by horse and dray, and Ida Clark, a homemaker. Working with his father, Ripley and his younger brother developed massive upper bodies and strong legs that were great assets in playing sports. Ripley was a natural all-around athlete but was attracted early on to basketball, which had been invented the year he was born. He began playing on church league teams on Staten Island, particularly the Christ Episcopal Church team in New Brighton. He attended Curtis High School in St. George on Staten Island and graduated in 1908. He did not play basketball at his high school, and he did not attend college, despite unsubstantiated allusions to his acceptance or attendance at Brown University.

In 1907, shortly after his sixteenth birthday, Ripley was asked to join a barnstorming team from Hoboken, New Jersey, which had just played against his church team on Staten Island. From that time until 1928, the peripatetic Ripley was an active professional, performing for more than twenty-five teams and earning acclaim from writers of that period as one of the ten greatest players of all time. Initially he played with the Hoboken team, but he soon performed in the old Hudson River League. When that league folded in 1912, Ripley began playing for Troy of the New York State League, where he played regularly for at least two years. His teammates included Ed Wachter, Lew Wachter, Marty Ingils, and Andy Suils.

In 1914 Ripley played on an independent New York team that won a so-called national championship and ended its season, which was played entirely on the road, with a victory at the Panama-Pacific Exposition in San Francisco. Throughout this time he also played on various other independent teams, as was characteristic of the best professional players of the time. Ripley was known as "the Blond Adonis" of the pro game because of his forty-seven-inch chest and his thirty-two-inch waist.

Beginning in 1915, Ripley played on teams in the Interstate, Pennsylvania State, Metropolitan, Eastern, and American Leagues. Since the leagues generally played on different nights during the week, he often played with more than one team at a time. He also played for independent teams from 1918 to 1919, when most leagues shut down because of World War I.

Ripley's Carbondale (Pennsylvania) team won the Pennsylvania State League championship in 1917. His Scranton team won the league title in the 1920–1921 season and then went on to defeat Albany, the New York State League champion, in a five-game series. During the 1920–1921 season, Ripley also played on the Germantown (Pennsylvania) team, which won the title in the Eastern League. Ripley was only five feet, eight inches tall, but because players were generally not over six feet tall at that time, he was not considered short. He was initially a top scorer in a low-scoring game. He finished third in scoring in the Pennsylvania State League in the 1920–1921 season, sixth in the Pennsylvania State League in 1919–1920, eighth in Eastern League first half scoring in 1921–1922, and fourth in scoring in the first year of the American Basketball League while playing for Brooklyn in the 1925–1926 season. Despite his scoring, Ripley was best known as a tough defender, and he stressed that aspect along with team passing while he was a coach.

In 1922, while still an active player, Ripley began coaching at Wagner College in Staten Island. A few other pros also coached, most notably Nat Holman, who coached at City College of New York. Ripley was Wagner's first coach, and he remained in that position for three seasons. In 1924 Ripley was invited to join the greatest team of the era, the Original Celtics, based in New York City. Even though he was no longer the player he had once been, he was an excellent complement to John Beckman, Holman, Joe Lapchick, "Dutch" Dehnert, Chris Leonard, and Pete Barry. Ripley played as the seventh man on the club, but his knowledge of the game and of the opposing players was invaluable as the team lost only 6 games of the more than 100 it played. The next year he joined the Brooklyn franchise of the new American Basketball League. He played with Washington, Fort Wayne, and Cleveland in that league before finally retiring as an active player after the 1927–1928 season. The next year he appeared in three games for Fort Wayne.

Ripley wound down his playing career before resuming his coaching career at Georgetown University. He coached the Georgetown Hoyas three different times, first from 1927 to 1929, then from 1938 to 1943, and again from 1946 to 1949. He compiled a record of 133 wins and 82 losses, including a loss to Wyoming in the National Collegiate Athletic Association (NCAA) finals in the 1942–1943 season. He coached at Yale from 1929 to 1935, at Columbia from 1943 to 1945, and at Notre Dame from 1945 to 1946. While at Notre Dame, he converted to Roman Catholicism, influenced by the players to whom he was closest. He left Notre Dame when Edward "Moose" Krause, a former Notre Dame coach, returned from military service and expressed a desire to return to coaching. Ripley, who had left Georgetown only because the school had dropped basketball during World War II, eagerly returned there.

Ripley coached at John Carroll University from 1949 to 1951 and at the U.S. Military Academy (West Point) from 1951 to 1953. His collegiate teams compiled a record of 298–228. (This record does not include his freshman coaching at Regis College.) During the early 1950s he coached the Harlem Globetrotters for three years. Also notable were his international experiences. In 1956 the U.S. State Department sent him to Israel to help the Israeli youth prepare for the Olympics in Melbourne that fall. While Ripley was in Israel, the first Middle East war broke out, which prevented the Israeli team from going to the Olympics. In 1960 Ripley coached the Canadian Olympic basketball team, which competed in Rome that summer. He also led coaching clinics in the Far East, the Middle East, and South America under the aegis of the U.S. State Department. In 1962 he accepted a position at Englewood High School in Englewood, New Jersey, where he continued to coach into his eighties. In 1972 Ripley was elected to the James A. Naismith Memorial Basketball Hall of Fame as a contributor to the game. He retired from coaching in 1973.

Ripley, who never married and had no children, lived in New Jersey until his health worsened, then returned to Staten Island in 1976. He died of natural causes in Doctor's Hospital on Staten Island. His remains were cremated, and his ashes were scattered on the grounds of the Basketball Hall of Fame in Springfield, Massachusetts.

Elmer Ripley was one of the pioneers of basketball. From his earliest years as a professional at the age of sixteen, he studied the game and became one of the greatest players of his era. He played with or against all of the top players from 1910 to 1930. He was an astute coach who produced winning teams and well-known players in his nearly thirty years of college coaching. He also was a "goodwill ambassador" for both the United States and the game of basketball through his international coaching. His election to the Basketball Hall of Fame was richly deserved.

★

The Elmer Ripley file in the Naismith Memorial Basketball Hall of Fame is the single best resource for information on Ripley. A brief biography is in D. L. Porter, ed., *Biographical Dictionary of American Sports: Basketball and Other Indoor Sports* (1989). His coaching records are in William Mokray, *Ronald Encyclopedia of Basketball* (1963). Obituaries are in the *New York Times* (30 Apr. 1982) and *Sporting News* (17 May 1982).

MURRY R. NELSON

ROBBINS, Marty (*b.* 26 September 1925 near Glendale, Arizona; *d.* 8 December 1982 in Nashville, Tennessee), country singer best known for writing and recording the crossover pop hit "A White Sport Coat (and a Pink Carnation)" and the western folk saga "El Paso," which in 1960 won the first Grammy ever awarded a country song.

Robbins, one of nine children of John G. Robinson and Emma Caveness Heckle, was born Martin David Robinson and spent the first twelve years of his life in the rural desert area just outside the small town of Glendale. His father, a first-generation Pole originally named Mazinski, drank excessively, was given to sudden rages, and bounced from job to job, moving the family abruptly from one tumbledown rental home to another. He did play the harmonica, however, and was an early musical influence in Robbins's life.

From age six on, Robbins spent many hours with Texas Bob Heckle, his maternal grandfather and a traveling-medicine-show barker, listening to stories of the Old West and learning the art of spinning a tale. Many years later, Robbins's song "Big Iron" (1959) was composed around a story the charismatic Heckle had told him of being a Texas Ranger.

In 1937, when Robbins was twelve, his mother divorced his father and moved to Phoenix, Arizona, with the children, where she worked at various housekeeping jobs. Not a good student, Robbins spent enough time stealing and fighting around town that he nearly wound up in reform school. He also cultivated interests in amateur boxing, herding wild horses, and hanging out at the stock-car races, an activity that ignited a lifelong passion for racing cars. From 1966 to 1982, Robbins raced on the National Association for Stock Car Auto Racing (NASCAR) circuit, surviving several accidents and becoming friends with racing legends like Bobby Allison and Richard Petty.

During childhood Robbins loved the films of Gene Autry. He would pick cotton and do odd jobs to get the price of admission to the local theater. As he admitted later in an interview: "I first started praying to be a country singer.

Marty Robbins. ARCHIVE PHOTOS

Robbins's musical versatility, the secret of his career success, began to surface on these programs, as he covered the songs and styles of successful artists in various pop and country genres. In 1951 country star Little Jimmy Dickens, on a tour of the Southwest, guested on *Western Caravan*. When he reached Los Angeles, Dickens recommended Robbins to Columbia Records' artists and repertory (A&R) man Art Satherly, who signed him on 25 May 1951. On 14 November 1951, at Radio Recorders Studio in Hollywood, California, Marty Robbins rejected the songs Columbia had sent him and instead cut four of his own tunes, the first being "Love Me or Leave Me Alone." None of these records made the charts, but "I'll Go On Alone," recorded on 3 June 1952 at Jim Beck Studios in Dallas, did go to number one on the country charts in January 1953. On the basis of this success, Fred Rose of Nashville-based Acuff-Rose Publishers signed Robbins to a songwriting contract, and in 1953 Robbins was made a member of radio station WSM's *Grand Ole Opry*. He moved to Nashville.

Robbins's songs of the early 1950s were mainly ballads, sung in a smooth, Eddy Arnold–like voice with no trace of a southern accent, and earned him the name "Mister Teardrop." By 1954 Elvis Presley and rock and roll were heavily affecting the country music industry. Robbins, one of the few Nashville artists versatile enough to handle the new styles, cut country versions of Elvis's "That's All Right, Mama" and Chuck Berry's "Maybelline" in 1955. Both shot high on the country charts.

Switching musical styles once again, Robbins recorded Melvin Endsley's "Singin' the Blues" in 1956, which topped the country charts for thirteen weeks and climbed into the top twenty pop charts as well. Based on this record, Robbins was invited to New York City, where he recorded "A White Sport Coat (and a Pink Carnation)" (1957) for Mitch Miller, head of Columbia's pop A&R division. The record went to number one in country and number two in pop and has become a musical icon of that era in American popular culture.

In 1958 Robbins wrote and recorded the theme for Gary Cooper and George C. Scott's Western film *The Hanging Tree*. In 1959 he released "El Paso," a four-and-a-half-minute-long folk saga of the Old West, recorded in Nashville's Owen Bradley Studios, that in 1960 earned the first Grammy ever given a country song. With its length, the song shattered radio programmers' under-three-minute broadcasting convention, paving the way for radio play of the longer pop and country songs of the 1960s. "El Paso" was also the centerpiece of Robbins's classic *Gunfighter Ballads and Trail Songs* (1959), the first country album to go gold, in 1965, and a key launching pad, image-wise, for the country "outlaw" movement of the late 1960s and early 1970s. From 1959 and "El Paso" until late 1962, every record Robbins released went into the top one hundred world-

I wanted to be like Gene Autry. I wanted to ride off into the sunset."

Instead, in 1942, at age seventeen, he joined the U.S. Navy, driving World War II landing craft onto Pacific beaches during the Solomon Islands campaign. He also learned to play the guitar and composed his first songs in the service. During a stop in Hawaii, he fell in love with the "local" tourist/Hawaiian music, which inspired him later to record two albums—*Song of the Islands* (1957) and *Hawaii's Calling Me* (1963). Discharged from the navy in 1945, Robbins returned to Phoenix, where he worked construction jobs and gained stage experience by playing guitar for a local singer named Frankie Starr. He also began dating Marizona Baldwin, a Glendale waitress who became his wife on 27 September 1948. They had two children.

During the 1940s Robbins began appearing on radio programs on KTYL in Mesa, Arizona, and KPHO in Phoenix, and in 1951, when KPHO opened Phoenix's first television station, he was given his own fifteen-minute show, *Western Caravan*. Robbins later appeared on many nationally broadcast television shows, including the *Marty Robbins Show* in 1969 and *Marty Robbins Spotlight* in 1975.

wide, a feat duplicated only by Elvis Presley and Fats Domino at the time.

In 1970 Robbins earned his second Grammy, for "My Woman, My Woman, My Wife," which he wrote to underscore Marizona's support, especially during the still-experimental heart-bypass surgery he underwent. On 28 March 1970 he returned to a thunderous ovation at the Grand Ole Opry, where for thirty years he was one of its best-loved performers. In 1975 he was named to the Nashville Songwriters Hall of Fame. In 1981 he suffered a second heart attack but rebounded quickly. On 11 October 1982 Robbins was inducted into the Country Music Hall of Fame by his friend Eddy Arnold.

Throughout his career, Robbins appeared in several films, including *Buffalo Gun* (1959), with Webb Pierce and Carl Smith; *Ballad of a Gunfighter* (1963); and *Hell on Wheels* (1967), a stock-car story. On 2 December 1982 he was to screen Clint Eastwood's new film *Honky Tonk Man,* in which he sang and played a part. Instead, Robbins was hospitalized with severe chest pains. Although he survived quadruple-bypass surgery, his lungs and kidneys failed, and he died. His funeral took place in Nashville on 11 December, with interment at Woodlawn Memorial Park in that city.

A highly energetic man confident of his own abilities, Robbins blazed new trails for country entertainers. In an era of tunes authored in-house, he insisted on recording his own material. Although he loved country music, he refused to be shackled by its 1950s conventions and, because of his musical versatility and media-friendly image, was a trailblazer in connecting country music to a worldwide pop audience.

★

The Country Music Hall of Fame in Nashville has a good deal of manuscripts and audiovisual materials, including a re-created display of Robbins's study in its museum. Barbara J. Pruett, *Marty Robbins: Fast Cars and Country Music* (1990) is a better-than-average fan-based, pop-audience-oriented book; it has less depth and analysis than could be hoped for but is still worthwhile. Alanna Nash, *Behind Closed Doors: Talking with the Legends of Country Music* (1988), is a collection of interviews with country stars; a too-brief, but perceptive, interview with Robbins appears on pages 436–454. Rich Kienzle, *The Essential Marty Robbins: 1951–1982* (1991) is the extensive (twenty-three pages) liner notes to the Columbia Records box set of Robbins's work and a good overview of his life and music.

GEORGE H. LEWIS

ROBINSON, Julia Bowman (*b.* 8 December 1919 in St. Louis, Missouri; *d.* 30 July 1985 in Oakland, California), mathematician who is best known for her work that led to the solution of Hilbert's Tenth Problem; she was also the first woman mathematician to be elected to the National Academy of Sciences and the first woman president of the American Mathematical Society.

Julia Robinson was the second of two daughters born to Ralph Bowers Bowman and Helen Hall Bowman. Neither of her parents had gone to college, but her mother had attended a business school after graduating from high school. Ralph Bowman owned a successful tool and equipment shop in St. Louis.

When Robinson was two years old, her mother died. Robinson and her sister, Constance, were sent to live with their grandmother in a small desert community outside Phoenix, Arizona, near Camelback Mountain. After the death of his wife, Ralph Bowman lost interest in his business. He sold the shop and moved with his new wife, Edenia Kridelbaugh, to join his children in Arizona in 1923. In 1925 the family moved to Point Loma on San Diego Bay so that the girls, now ages five and seven, could attend school. Robinson, from infancy, had been slow to speak, and when she did talk, others had difficulty understanding her. Her older sister became her "interpreter." The small school they attended housed several grades together, enabling the younger students to learn from the older ones.

Julia Robinson. COURTESY OF CONSTANCE REID

In 1928 Robinson, now nine years old, contracted scarlet fever followed by rheumatic fever and chorea, a nervous disorder. She was quarantined and missed more than two years of schooling. Her parents hired a private tutor, and in one year she covered the syllabuses for grades five through eight. In 1932 she entered the ninth grade at Theodore Roosevelt Junior High School in San Diego, and the following year she entered San Diego High School. She was introduced to algebra, and her two women math teachers soon discovered that she excelled in math and science. She was hampered in her studies, however, since at this time there were not accelerated or advanced-placement courses. Robinson was shy by nature, an avid baseball fan who was particularly adept at keeping box scores of the games she attended, and also exhibited an interest in horseback riding and enjoyed target practice with her father.

Robinson graduated from San Diego High School in 1936 with honors in math and science. She entered San Diego State College (now San Diego State University) that year, at age sixteen. E. T. Bell's *Men of Mathematics,* published in 1936, gave Robinson a glimpse into the world of mathematicians, about which she knew nothing. San Diego State was largely a teacher-preparatory college with few Ph.D.s (and none in math) and no research mathematicians. For this reason Robinson transferred to the University of California at Berkeley in 1939. For the first time in her life, she experienced a sense of belonging, as there were other bright women at Berkeley who were as excited about mathematics as she was. She received her A.B. degree in 1940 and remained at the university to complete her M.A. degree in 1941.

Julia Robinson met her future husband, Raphael Mitchel Robinson, a number theorist who had been one of Julia's professors at Berkeley. They were married in Berkeley on 22 December 1941. Meanwhile, Julia continued to take courses and joined other faculty wives in the statistics laboratory at Berkeley, working to fulfill the government contracts that the university received during World War II. During this period she learned that she had a weakened heart, a residual effect of the rheumatic fever that she had suffered as a child. Because of the heart condition she was unable to have children.

In 1947 Robinson began work on her Ph.D. at Berkeley under the direction of Alfred Tarski, the noted Polish logician who had joined the Berkeley faculty during the war. Her thesis, "Definability and Decision Problems in Arithmetic," was accepted in 1948. In that same year she began to work on a problem connected with David Hilbert's Tenth Problem, one of twenty-three unsolved problems proposed by Hilbert at the Second International Congress of Mathematics in Paris in 1900. The Tenth Problem involved devising a general method of determining by a finite number of operations whether a given Diophantine equation has a solution in rational integers. This problem consumed most of Robinson's professional career, but she found time to work on other projects, such as one on elementary game theory in 1950. Her solution and the theorem she developed proved that a fictitious game problem has a convergent solution.

Many mathematicians had attempted to find a solution to the Tenth Problem, but it was Robinson's work (and she was given credit for it by the world of mathematics) that led to the ultimate solution in 1970, by Yuri Matijasevič, that there is no universal method for deciding the solvability of a Diophantine equation. The solution made Robinson famous and earned her a full professorship at Berkeley in 1975. The following year she became the first woman mathematician elected to the National Academy of Sciences, and in 1983 she became the first woman president of the American Mathematical Society. Other honors included an honorary degree from Smith College in 1979. In 1980 Robinson was the second woman in fifty years to deliver the prestigious Colloquium Lectures of the American Mathematical Society. In 1983 she was awarded a MacArthur Foundation Fellowship for five years in recognition of her contributions to mathematics.

In the summer of 1984, Robinson learned that she had leukemia. After a brief period of remission, she died in Oakland, California. Her cremated remains were buried in Santa Cruz, California.

★

Julia Robinson's papers, writings, and correspondence are in the Bancroft Library at the University of California at Berkeley. See *Julia: A Life in Mathematics* by Constance Reid, Robinson's sister (1996). "The Autobiography of Julia Robinson," a profile written by Constance Reid that also appears in *Julia,* is in *More Mathematical People: Contemporary Conversations,* edited by Donald J. Albers, G. L. Alexanderson, and Constance Reid (1990). An additional profile is in *Women of Mathematics: A Biobibliographic Sourcebook,* edited by Louise S. Grinstein and Paul J. Campbell (1987). Solomon Feferman, ed., *The Collected Works of Julia Robinson* (1996), also includes Feferman's memoir of her. See also Ronald Calinger, ed., *Classics of Mathematics* (1982), and Victor J. Katz, *A History of Mathematics* (1992). Obituaries are in the *New York Times* (2 Aug. 1985) and *Notices of the American Mathematical Society* (Nov. 1985).

BETTY B. VINSON

ROCK, John Charles (*b.* 24 March 1890 in Marlborough, Massachusetts; *d.* 4 December 1984 in Peterborough, New Hampshire), obstetrician and gynecologist who was an expert in human fertility, the first to fertilize a human egg in the laboratory, and one of the developers of the birth control pill.

Dr. John Rock, *c.* 1948. ARCHIVE PHOTOS

Rock was named for his paternal grandfather, of County Armagh, Ireland, and Marlborough. Rock's father, Frank Sylvester Rock, and Rock's uncle, John, managed to squeeze a profit out of their father's heavily mortgaged land and buildings. They owned a drugstore, a liquor store, commercial real estate, and a theater. Rock's father owned a racetrack, bred horses, and organized a semiprofessional baseball team. His mother, the former Ann Jane Murphy, raised Rock, his twin sister, and three other children. Preferring his twin to his sports-loving brothers, John learned to crochet and sew, which became useful in his later career as a surgeon. Despite his "sissy" ways, Rock got along well with his close-knit, affectionate family. The Catholic faith was integral to his outlook. During later disputes with the church, he never forgot the words of a priest who advised him always to listen to his own conscience, not what others told him.

Rock graduated from the High School of Commerce in Boston in 1909. After working on a banana plantation in Guatemala and at a Rhode Island engineering firm, Rock decided he had no future in business, and in 1912 entered Harvard College. A middling student, he acquired a taste for martinis, acted in Hasty Pudding theatricals, and be-

came interested in neurology and Freudian psychiatry. He agreed with Freud that traditional medicine had neglected the central role of sex in human well-being. He graduated with a B.S. degree in 1915 and received an M.D. degree from Harvard in 1918.

Rock tried to enlist in the U.S. Army during World War I, but as a medical student he needed a recommendation from his school. Rock's advisory professor would not write one, believing that he should accept a surgical residency offered him at Massachusetts General Hospital. Rock opted for additional residencies in obstetrics and gynecology at Boston Lying-in Hospital and the Free Hospital for Women in Brookline, Massachusetts.

Rock was appointed an assistant in obstetrics at Harvard Medical School in 1922. Meantime, he was courting Anna Thorndike, a Bryn Mawr College math graduate who was the socialite daughter of a Boston urologist. Their marriage, conducted at Boston's Immaculate Conception Cathedral by William Cardinal O'Connell on 3 January 1924, received extensive newspaper attention. For most of their lives the Rocks lived in a large stucco house on Quail Street in West Roxbury, Massachusetts, adjoining the Harvard Arboretum. Soon their five children were scampering permissively about the house. Rock was a fastidious dresser and highly sociable. He and his wife commanded attention wherever they went, and he belonged to the "best" clubs.

In 1924 Rock established the Fertility and Endocrine Clinic at the Free Hospital in Brookline, and he served as its director until 1956. He became the nation's leading expert on infertility and developed new ways to reduce its incidence. In the 1920s prevailing medical custom was to tell women requesting birth control information to stop trying to avoid their biological destiny and to raise a family. Rock was always pro-sex and pro-family, but he came to see the need for birth control when further pregnancies would endanger a woman's life. In 1931 he was the only Catholic to sign a petition of fifteen Boston physicians urging repeal of a Massachusetts law forbidding the sale of contraceptives. He was reviled by some for flouting Catholic doctrine, which opposed "unnatural methods" of preventing conception.

For some fifteen years after 1938, Rock and Dr. Arthur Hertig sought to retrieve early fertilized human eggs from discarded hysterectomy tissue. Over that time they found thirty-four fertilized eggs, providing new knowledge about human conception. Aiding them in the search was Harvard physiologist Gregory Pincus. In 1938 Rock also hired technician Miriam Menkin to try to extract and fertilize human eggs in his laboratory. After hundreds of efforts, Menkin produced the first laboratory-fertilized, two-cell human egg on 6 February 1944. The feat attracted national attention, to Harvard's discomfort.

In the early 1940s Harvard doctors were experimenting

with DES (diethylstilbestrol), a nonsteroid compound with estrogenic effects as a proposed aid to pregnancy. Rock gave DES to a number of his infertility patients, with some success. Around 1950 Pincus suggested he switch to progesterone. It halted ovulation (thus preventing overlapping pregnancies) and pregnancy occurred in a statistically significant sample of infertile women. Apparently the progesterone induced a more regular menstrual cycle, the result of a "rebound" effect.

In 1950 birth control pioneer Margaret Sanger persuaded Katherine McCormick, an International Harvester heiress, to fund research on a birth control pill. McCormick decided in 1951 to finance Pincus, Min-Chueh Chang, and Rock in an effort to produce a progesterone-based birth control pill. Cheap new synthetic steroidal sex hormones were then available, made from wild Mexican yams. McCormick paid for the new Rock Reproductive Study Center in Brookline to facilitate the task. Chang tested hundreds of synthetic progesterones on rabbits and rats; in 1954 Rock tried them on humans, some of them psychotic patients in the state mental hospital at Worcester, Massachusetts. The group settled on two synthetic progesterones, produced by the Syntex and Searle Corporations, for extensive human tests beginning in April 1956 among a poverty population in a suburb of San Juan. Rock went to Puerto Rico to help Dr. Edris Rice-Wray of the University of Puerto Rico conduct the tests. Near the end of 1956 Rice-Wray was forced to take another job in Mexico because of the objections of Puerto Rico's secretary of health.

In 1957 the U.S. Food and Drug Administration (FDA) approved the birth control pill for menstrual disorders. In 1960 the FDA approved the Searle pill, Enovid, for contraception, after Rock personally went to FDA headquarters to criticize its initial foot-dragging. The FDA approved the Syntex pill in 1962.

Rock's wife, Anna, died of cancer in 1961 in the midst of controversy over the pill. Although in his seventies, Rock strenuously defended the pill. In endless public appearances and many writings, including his book, *The Time Has Come: A Catholic Doctor's Proposals to End the Battle over Birth Control* (1963), Rock helped create a worldwide dialogue on the morality of "safe" sex, urging his church to approve the pill as an extension of nature and as "a morally permissible variant of the rhythm method." In 1964 Pope Paul VI named a Papal Commission on Population, the Family, and Natality to consider the question. In 1968 Paul VI ignored the findings of his own commission and warnings that "the church could not stand another Galileo" and denounced "new" methods such as the pill and the plastic intrauterine device (IUD). Instead, the pope advised couples seeking to limit births to acquire "perfect self-mastery." In an interview, Rock said he was "scandalized" by the encyclical.

In the meantime, Rock, whose notoriety irked the Harvard medical hierarchy, was being shunted out of the new Boston Hospital for Women, to which his clinic was joined in 1966. His patrons Sanger and McCormick having died in 1966 and 1967, respectively, he was unable to establish himself elsewhere. Forcibly retired by the university, Rock sold his practice. Virtually his sole source of income was a modest consultant's fee from Searle. Radical feminists began denouncing the pill and asking Congress to investigate it as a dangerous male-inspired assault on women. Lower doses of progesterone and estrogen in the pill, however, made it more acceptable to some. In 1971 Rock, who might have earned a fortune from his research had he not neglected his finances, was almost penniless. He moved near his daughter Ellen, living in an old clapboard house on an isolated hillside in Temple, New Hampshire. There he skinny-dipped and studied the habits of birds and squirrels. Rock died of a heart attack.

Regardless of Rock's personal setbacks, Catholics and many priests around the world disregarded the church's anti-contraception stance, although it was reiterated repeatedly by Pope John Paul II in the last decades of the twentieth century. "John Rock beat the Pope," said the Jesuit writer Andrew Greeley.

★

Some of Rock's files and laboratory notes are in Harvard University's Countway Library in Cambridge, Massachusetts. Loretta McLaughlin, *The Pill, John Rock, and the Church: The Biography of a Revolution* (1982), is a biographical account of Rock's life and career. For detailed information about Rock's work, see Sophie D. Aberle and George W. Corner, *Twenty-Five Years of Sex Research: History of the National Research Council Committee for Research in Problems of Sex, 1922–1947* (1953), and James Reed, *From Private Vice to Public Virtue: The Birth Control Movement and American Society Since 1830* (1978). A biographical sketch appears in Charles Moritz, ed., *Current Biography 1964* (1965). An obituary is in the *New York Times* (5 Dec. 1984).

JAMES STOUDER SWEET

ROSENBERG, Anna Marie Lederer (*b.* 19 June 1902 in Budapest, Hungary; *d.* 9 May 1983 in New York City), government officeholder, including assistant secretary of defense, considered the most influential woman in the nation's public affairs for more than a quarter of a century and a leading public relations executive.

Anna was the daughter and only child of Albert Lederer, a prosperous manufacturer in Budapest, and Charlotte Bacskai, a successful writer of juvenile fiction. After the family lost its fortune because the Hungarian government would not pay for the furniture they had already provided, Anna emigrated with the family to the United States in 1912. She

Assistant Secretary of Defense Anna Rosenberg in confrontation with Senator Lyndon B. Johnson, 1951. UPI/CORBIS-BETTMANN

attended Wadleigh High School in Manhattan, New York City, where her classmates described her as "an ignited Roman candle darting into space." She early displayed her flair for dramatizing her activities in public life as chief speaker at a demonstration against military drill while in high school.

At the age of nineteen Anna became a naturalized citizen and in 1919 married a young serviceman, Julius Rosenberg, later a rug merchant. While her husband was overseas, she did volunteer work in a state hospital. During the early 1920s Anna Rosenberg entered politics as a volunteer party worker and became active in settlement work. By 1924 her political network enabled her to become a public relations, personnel, and labor consultant. She was so successful in handling labor unions that Governor Franklin D. Roosevelt often consulted her.

In 1934 Rosenberg was appointed assistant to the regional director of the National Recovery Administration for New York City and regional director the next year. She became a member of the New York City Industrial Relations Board in 1937, at which time Mayor Fiorello H. La Guardia said of her, "She knows more about labor relations and human relations than any man in the country."

During World War II Rosenberg occupied several positions, including director of the Office of Defense, Health, and Welfare Services and regional director of the War Manpower Commission. In July 1944 President Roosevelt sent her as a personal observer to the European theater, primarily to report on soldier morale. The next summer President Harry S. Truman assigned her a similar mission to report on the problems occurring in repatriating and demobilizing American troops.

In the mid- and late 1940s Rosenberg was on numerous federal panels. In September 1946 she became a member of the Advisory Committee of the War Mobilization and Reconversion Board's subcommittee studying wage stabilization policy. Two months later she was named to the presidential committee on Universal Military Training.

From 1946 to 1950 Rosenberg was a member of the U.S. Commission for UNESCO and served as an alternate delegate in 1947 at Mexico City. In August 1950 the chairman of the National Security Resources Board, W. Stuart Symington, appointed her to a twelve-member committee to advise him on mobilization policy for the Korean War.

In November 1950 Secretary of Defense George C. Marshall offered Rosenberg the position of assistant secretary of defense in charge of coordinating the department's manpower activities, a job in which she would be the highest-ranking woman in the military establishment to that time. The Senate Armed Services Committee approved the nomination but then took back its approval as a result of accusations by Benjamin Freedman and former communist Ralph de Sola that Rosenberg had once been associated with communist front groups. Freedman later said he had confused her with another woman with the same name. Witnesses could not corroborate de Sola's accusations. Consequently, the committee unanimously reapproved the nomination in December 1950.

As assistant secretary of defense from 1950 to 1953, Rosenberg was responsible for preparing a universal military service and training bill for submission to Congress. Its main provision called for drafting eighteen-year-olds to enlarge the armed forces for the Korean conflict. She believed this to be the best method for supplying a pool of trained soldiers for the next decade, because it would occasion the least dislocation of national economic life and reduce government expense, because payments to dependents would be virtually eliminated. The Universal Military Training and Service Act was passed by a 79–5 vote in the Senate in March 1951. The final version, passed later that year, raised the draft age to eighteen and one-half and barred drafting anyone under nineteen until the twenty-six-year-old manpower pool was filled.

In 1952 Rosenberg initiated a drive to increase the number of women in the military. She was quoted as saying that "when men are being drafted and women are not, women should insist upon and assume some equality of rights." She also called for the improved use of women, saying that the military should offer women recruits a sufficient variety of activities to make full use of their skills.

President Dwight D. Eisenhower replaced her in 1953. After leaving office she resumed her personnel management practice; among her clients were the American Cancer Society, the American Hospital Association, the American College of Hospital Administrators, Encyclopaedia Britannica, and Merriam-Webster.

In 1955 and 1956 Rosenberg was cochairman of the Stevenson for President Committee in New York City and was throughout the Eisenhower years a leading liberal Democrat in New York State. In 1962 she was divorced from Julius Rosenberg and on 19 July 1962 married Paul G. Hoffman, a Republican who was the first administrator of the Marshall Plan after World War II and later head of the United Nations Development Program. He died in 1974.

During the 1960s and 1970s Rosenberg continued her membership on the boards of a number of organizations dealing with civil rights, the United Nations, and municipal problems. While occasionally antagonizing people, she was noted for her great charm and her ability to make friends of businesspeople, union executives, political figures, high-ranking military officers, and presidents. She was highly respected as a source of ideas and as an enter-

prising mediator. It was Rosenberg who was credited with obtaining for Nelson A. Rockefeller his first federal position as coordinator in the State Department's Office of Inter-American Affairs in 1940.

In 1955 Mayor Robert F. Wagner appointed her to the New York City Board of Hospitals. She was made chair of a three-member panel named in 1959 to mediate between the Transit Authority and two unions. During the early 1960s she served on the New York City Board of Education. While performing her duties in positions at the highest level, Rosenberg maintained energetically her associations with volunteer organizations and foundations, including the Albert and Mary Lasker and John Hay Whitney Foundations.

In 1945 Rosenberg was awarded the highest civilian honor, the Medal of Freedom, and in 1947 received the Medal of Merit. She received honorary doctorates from Tufts and Columbia Universities.

Rosenberg died of pneumonia in her Manhattan apartment after a year's bout with cancer.

★

Sketches of Rosenberg appear in Maxine Block, ed., *Current Biography 1943* (1944), and Anna Rothe, ed., *Current Biography 1951* (1952). See also "Bill of Health, Fiscal," *Time* (18 May 1942). An obituary is in the *New York Times* (10 May 1983).

HENRY WASSER

ROSZAK, Theodore (*b.* 1 May 1907 in Poznan, Poland; *d.* 3 September 1981 in New York City), painter and sculptor who was a significant early constructivist of sculptures of welded metal parts.

Roszak's father, Kaspar Roszak, was a farmer; his mother, Praxeda Swierczynska, was a fashion designer who had been employed by the court of the Hohenzollerns in Berlin. She encouraged Theodore, one of seven children, to draw at an early age. In 1909 the family emigrated from Poland to the United States, settling in Chicago, where there was a large Polish community. In Chicago Roszak's father worked in a foundry and then as a pastry chef. Young Roszak attended Chicago public schools and evening classes at the Art Institute of Chicago, where he enrolled full time following graduation from high school. In 1919 he became a U.S. citizen.

In 1926, after traveling to New York, he studied with Charles Hawthorne at the National Academy of Design and privately with George Luks, then returned to the Art Institute, where he studied with John Norton. In 1928 he visited museums in the East and studied lithography at Woodstock, New York. In 1929, during an eighteen-month sojourn in Europe, he set up a studio in Prague, and traveled through Austria, Germany, and Italy. At this time he

Theodore Roszak in his workshop at 1 St. Luke's Place, New York City, firing a garland for an aluminum eagle sculpture commissioned for the U.S. Embassy in London. UPI/CORBIS-BETTMANN

came under the influence of cubism, surrealism (particularly the metaphysical paintings of Giorgio de Chirico), and the teachings of the Bauhaus.

Back in the United States, Roszak married Florence Sapir in 1931 and settled on Staten Island in New York City; he remained there until 1934, when he moved to 241 E. Thirty-third Street in Manhattan. The couple had one child. Roszak's paintings of the early through the mid-1930s featured street scenes with buildings reassembled in a cubist manner and tiny figures in a vast space set next to tall towers, reminiscent of de Chirico. He bought a lathe and began making machine-tooled geometric constructions of metal, glass, Plexiglas, and wood, suggestive of Bauhaus work. During the Great Depression he was employed in various Works Progress Administration (WPA) projects, until in 1938 he joined the faculty of the Laboratory School of Industrial Design. In 1940 he went to work as a designer of aircraft with the Brewster Aircraft Corporation, and he worked in this capacity through World War II.

The year 1940 was a watershed in Roszak's development as an artist, when thirty of his geometric constructions, shown simultaneously in two New York galleries, were greeted with little enthusiasm. Thereafter he worked in welded steel, producing pieces that were more curvilinear

and organic. From 1941 to 1956 he taught two- and three-dimensional design at Sarah Lawrence College in suburban Bronxville. According to one of his students, Margot Williamson-Litt, he never showed his own work to the class, nor did he convey that he was an important artist. He provided a sense of how to handle various materials and how to work in different techniques, welding among them, but he never insisted that his female students experiment with welding.

On the Sarah Lawrence faculty at that time was Joseph Campbell, whose interest in early myths may have had some impact on Roszak. Brazing his surfaces with applications of bronze or brass, the sculptor produced rough forms evoking strange sea plants or animals. In his *Spectre of Kitty Hawk* of 1946–1947 (Museum of Modern Art), the shapes push upward as well as turn in upon themselves. One can make out, following Roszak's explanation, the fusion of certain suggested images: a preening prehistoric bird of prey and the landing struts of an airplane. Aviation interested him greatly. He commented on the piece: "The *Spectre* is the pterodactyl, an early denizen of the air, both savage and destructive. Present-day aircraft has come to resemble this beast of prey. . . . I think it interesting . . . that Orville Wright . . . died a disillusioned man, and the Myth of Icarus completes another circle, tangent to pragmatic America." It is noteworthy that this sculpture was made at the end of the war, when European cities lay in devastation from aerial bombardment. His *Thorn Blossom* of 1947 (Whitney Museum), made on the eve of the birth of his daughter Sara-Jane, presented forms suggestive of delicate buds surrounded by elements appearing as sharp, protective thorns. In the welded metal work, then, as opposed to the earlier Bauhaus-influenced work, Roszak fashioned his sculpture in ways that encouraged metaphoric and poetic interpretations. In *The Whaler of Nantucket* of 1952–1953 (Art Institute of Chicago) a longitudinal jawlike form (the whale?) merges with a vertical element, an apparently standing figure (the whaler?). The suggestion is made that the whaler and whale, the pursuer and pursued, become one, as is set forth in Herman Melville's novel *Moby-Dick*, which made a great impact on him. The best known of Roszak's public sculptures is the 2,000-pound eagle (1960) commissioned by the architect Eero Saarinen for the U.S. embassy in London.

Another eagle was executed for the federal courthouse in New York. Throughout his career, Roszak continued to draw in styles often independent of that of his sculpture. In the 1950s came drawings of stars, sunbursts, and meteors, executed in an expressionist manner, and in the 1960s, images of wastelands and storms, drawn with a ballpoint pen.

With Alexander Calder, David Smith, Ibram Lassaw, Seymour Lipton, and Herbert Ferber, Roszak was prominent in making welded metal constructions before midcentury and after. He preferred spiky, pitted forms, which appeared both aggressive and delicate. As was common with the contemporary abstract expressionist painters and some of the other metal constructivists, Roszak sought to express through his work certain universal truths and insisted that he was guided by moral imperatives. He was engaged by the duality of things, the meanings beyond appearances. He insisted that his works were "blunt reminders of primordial strife and struggle, reminiscent of those brute forces that not only produced life, but in turn threaten to destroy it."

Roszak died of heart failure in New York City.

★

H. H. Arnason, *Theodore Roszak* (1956), a solid but brief text published by the Walker Art Center in Minneapolis in collaboration with the Whitney Museum of American Art in New York City, contains ample illustrations of welded pieces. Howard E. Wooden, *Theodore Roszak: The Early Works, 1929–1943* (1986), demonstrates that Roszak's constructivist pieces were not as strong as his later welded metal ones. Joan M. Marter, *Theodore Roszak: The Drawings* (1992), shows a side of the artist not adequately appreciated and includes many statements of the artist. See also Beth Urdang, *Theodore Roszak Constructions, 1932–1945* (1978), and Joan Seaman Robinson, *The Sculpture of Theodore Roszak: 1932–1952* (Ph.D. diss., Stanford University, 1979). An obituary is in the *New York Times* (4 Sept. 1981).

ABRAHAM A. DAVIDSON

Arthur Rubinstein, *c.* 1968. HULTON-DEUTSCH COLLECTION/CORBIS

RUBINSTEIN, Arthur (*b.* 28 January 1887 in Lodz, Poland; *d.* 20 December 1982 in Geneva, Switzerland), pianist who won international acclaim as an interpreter of the classical piano repertoire; he is widely considered one of the greatest musicians of the twentieth century.

Rubinstein, the last of seven children of Isaak Rubinstein and Felicja Heyman, was born in Lodz, a manufacturing town dominated by German- and Jewish-owned factories. Although Lodz was under the jurisdiction of the Russian czar, many Jewish families, like the Rubinsteins, emigrated there because of the liberal policies toward Jews. Isaak's small textile factory enabled his family to live comfortably in a spacious apartment in the center of town. Arthur was playing the family piano when he was three and was at this time taken to Berlin to perform for the famed violinist Joseph Joachim. This meeting transformed Rubinstein's world. Joachim, who had himself been a child prodigy, proved to be a loving and judicious adviser to Arthur until Joachim's death in 1907. Felicja was told not to force Arthur into a career as a child prodigy, but to allow his musical talents to develop naturally.

Arthur Rubinstein remained in Lodz for the next five years. He was given piano lessons and played publicly for the first time at a charity concert on 14 December 1894. Three years later he auditioned for Joachim. He played Mozart's Rondo in A Minor, which so pleased Joachim that he agreed to be responsible for Rubinstein's musical and general education, and he established a special fund for this purpose. Rubinstein's mother then departed for Lodz, leaving ten-year-old Arthur alone in Berlin. Feelings of abandonment and not being loved for himself were to plague him for the rest of his life. He never returned to his family. Joachim arranged for Rubinstein to study music with Heinrich Barth, a severe Prussian taskmaster who demanded nothing less than perfection. It was Barth who shaped the unique Rubinstein sound, teaching the boy to sit straight at the keyboard and use his arms and elbows in performance. The result was a sound described by one critic as "a firm, clear, colorful sonority that is one of the miracles of twentieth-century pianism." Rubinstein's debut took place on 1 December 1900, at the Beethoven Saal with the Berlin Philharmonic. He played Mozart's Concerto in A Major, Schumann's *Papillons*, and Chopin's Scherzo no. 1

in B Minor. He ended with Camille Saint-Saëns' Concerto no. 2 in G, which became a signature piece for the rest of his career. Rubinstein recalled that his "nerves were on edge." In the audience were Joachim, Max Bruch, Leopold Godowsky, members of his family, and possibly Engelbert Humperdinck and Richard Strauss. The performance was an unqualified success. A critic wrote: "Arthur Rubinstein made his appearance, evoking the most vivid amazement, and rightly so. He played everything, not as a child prodigy, but as a mature, adult musician. He has been formed in Heinrich Barth's severe school, and this method favors artistic legitimacy and inner musicality over virtuosity."

Legendary concerts ensued. In the spring of 1900 Rubinstein played Mozart's Concerto in B-flat Major for the Mozart Society in Dresden. The seventy-four-year-old Aloys Schmitt, born just before the deaths of Beethoven and Schubert, conducted. Thus Rubinstein's early training forged a direct link with the titans of European music. His debut later that year with the Warsaw Philharmonic, under the direction of Emil Mlynarski (whose youngest daughter he would later marry), was also a triumph. Critics wrote of his "highly developed technique and his exceptionally beautiful tone that penetrates to the depths of the listener's soul."

These successful ventures gave him the courage to leave Barth and strike out on his own. He befriended Jules Edward Wertheim, the scion of a wealthy musical Polish family. It was Wertheim, Rubinstein maintained, who taught him the "true, real, authentic Chopin." He participated in the Wertheims' musical salons and later fell in love with Jules's sister, Lily Wertheim Radwan, who was at least six years older than Rubinstein and already married, with two small daughters. The affair lasted until the beginning of World War I. While still in his teens, Rubinstein played for the Polish pianist Ignacy Paderewski at his villa, and signed his first contract in Paris with Gabriel Astruc, who would later become the storied impresario.

He played a successful season in Paris and then sailed to New York City in 1906, where his debut was underwritten by William Knabe, the piano manufacturer. It was only a moderate success. The critics found him, at nineteen, to be immature. He was not asked back. He gave seventy-five concerts throughout the United States and then sailed back to Paris. When he arrived he was flat broke, having gambled away all of the concert proceeds. Thus began, according to Rubinstein, "the excruciating life of someone constantly short of money, constantly in debt." Chastened by his lukewarm reception in New York, he stopped playing in public for four years. He had no career and no money. His psychological depression mounted, until a failed suicide attempt in Berlin miraculously renewed his zest for life. He led a roller-coaster existence during the decade that preceded World War I; although he was still under contract

with Astruc, he was often penniless (once he had to sleep on a park bench), while other times he basked in luxury with the cream of artistic and aristocratic Europe. He was featured in extravagant galas in Paris and became involved with the French premiere of Strauss's *Salome,* composing a concert version of the opera, which he performed to enthusiastic audiences for 500 francs. (He and Emmy Destinn, the opera singer who played Salome, had an ongoing liaison for years.) He had successful debuts in Rome, London, and Vienna, and journeyed to St. Petersburg to play in the Anton Rubinstein competition. He did not win, but he did make a fruitful and lasting contact with the conductor Serge Koussevitzky. He became a regular at the musical soirees given by Paul and Ruth Draper in London, where he played chamber music with the most renowned artists of his time. The composer Igor Stravinsky befriended Rubinstein and wrote a special piano version of his ballet *Petrushka* for him.

When World War I began in 1914 Rubinstein managed to get a special document exempting him from military service. He secured a booking in Spain that proved to be the turning point of his career. There was an immediate rapport between Rubinstein and the Spanish people, who understood and responded to his passionate and improvisatory nature. He quickly learned the language and mastered the works of the great Spanish composers. Within a short time he was being hailed as the greatest interpreter of Spanish music. The works of Manuel de Falla, Isaac Albéniz, and Enrique Granados became permanent features of his repertoire. A widely acclaimed South American tour followed, where Rubinstein met Heitor Villa-Lobos in Brazil and became fascinated with his music. The triumphs in Spain and South America gave Rubinstein some financial security and a sense of belonging. However, in later years when he looked back on that time of wild popularity and adoring audiences, he said, "I gave the people what they wanted, but there was a void in my heart. Musically I was leading a double life."

Returning to Paris in 1920, Rubinstein succumbed to the postwar artistic and social frenzy, booking one international tour after another. But then he rented a house in Montmartre, at 15 rue Ravignan, and began to court Aniela ("Nela") Mlynarski. He was more than forty; she was eighteen. They were married on 27 July 1932 in London. Their first of four children was born in 1933. At about this time Rubinstein decided to devote the summer to perfecting his technique. He rented a farmhouse in a small French village and spent six to ten hours a day at the keyboard. "Slowly and excruciatingly I became a pianist," he recalled. His brother-in-law, the pianist Wiktor Labunski, agreed. "The change in his performance was spectacular. In place of an enormously gifted and promising artist, he became the great master he is now."

Then touring resumed. Rubinstein and Nela went to Asia for six months and then sailed to New York City under his first contract with impresario Sol Hurok. His 1937 concert at Carnegie Hall was touted as the event of the season, and it was an unqualified triumph. But Rubinstein never forgave New York for waiting until he was almost fifty to give him full recognition. Nevertheless, the political events of 1939 found him sailing back to Manhattan with his family to flee the Nazi occupation of France. They settled at the Buckingham Hotel, and later purchased an apartment on Park Avenue. During the summer of 1941 the family visited southern California and decided to put down roots there as well, buying a house in Brentwood.

Rubinstein was now a wealthy man. In addition to his regular concertizing, he had become a popular recording artist with a constantly expanding audience. He settled down to a life in California of lavish entertaining. In the 1940s he played the piano sound tracks for several films, made frequent appearances on television, and looked forward to sellout performances. As World War II raged on he assumed a prominent role in Polish relief projects and assisted many of his countrymen who were living in exile. In 1941 he delivered a radio address urging Americans to purchase U.S. savings bonds. He learned, after the war, that almost all of his family had been annihilated in Europe. This renewed, with iron conviction, the pledge he had made thirty years earlier never to play in Germany again. When he and Nela returned to Paris, they discovered that their house on avenue Foch, which they had been forced to vacate in 1939, had been plundered by the Nazis. The furniture, rare art, books, and treasured mementos were stolen.

In the late 1940s Rubinstein became a fervent supporter of the new state of Israel, traveling there frequently as an honored guest and performing without charge. In 1974 he established the Arthur Rubinstein International Piano Master Competition in Tel Aviv. Emanuel Ax, a Polish pianist, won the first prize that year. By the late 1950s Rubinstein had achieved a larger-than-life status. He could easily have retired and lived off his royalties, but these years were full of activity. Although he became an American citizen in 1946, he preferred Paris as his base of operations. He later purchased a house in Marbella, Spain, where, through the late 1960s and early 1970s, Rubinstein began to write his memoirs, eventually published as *My Young Years*. This volume became a Book of the Month Club selection and a best-seller. But playing for audiences was his true passion. During the 1966–1967 season, nearing eighty, he gave 114 concerts worldwide. The truth was that he became restless if he remained home for more than three months. Many of these concerts were benefits, the proceeds of which were devoted to numerous causes, including the National Association for the Advancement of Colored People, the Mu-

sician's Emergency Fund, the United Jewish Appeal, and the Mannes School of Music in New York City. He was also the recipient of many awards. Universities bestowed honorary doctorates on him, and in France he was made a commander of the Legion of Honor. In 1971 he was elected to the Académie des Beaux-Arts of the Institut de France, and on 1 April 1976, President Gerald Ford gave Rubinstein the Medal of Freedom, "the highest civilian honor that it is within the power of a President of the United States to bestow." Ford proclaimed Rubinstein to be "a giant among men."

By that time Rubinstein's sight was seriously failing. He had been suffering since 1969 from a macular disorder that eventually forced him to end his public career. His last New York appearance was at Carnegie Hall, in March 1976, and his farewell performance was in London, at Wigmore Hall, in May of that year. He could no longer see the keyboard.

Rubinstein's last years were spent traveling with Annabelle Whitemore, who had been his agent since 1969. He fully occupied himself, giving master classes, listening to his favorite recordings, receiving devoted friends, and dictating *My Many Years*, the sequel to *My Young Years*, to Annabelle. He died peacefully in his sleep, of cancer, on 20 December 1982 in Geneva. His ashes were taken to Israel, where they were interred in the Rubinstein Panorama, a pine forest that had been dedicated to him in Jerusalem.

Bon vivant, womanizer, opportunist, and confirmed egoist, Rubinstein possessed a generosity of spirit and an irrepressible passion for life. Above all else, he will be remembered for his success in communicating the joy of music to an ever appreciative audience.

★

The Rubinstein Collection is in the music division of the New York Public Library for the Performing Arts at Lincoln Center. Harvey Sachs, *Rubinstein: A Life* (1995), is an authoritative and comprehensive biography, painstakingly researched and written with wit and compassion. It includes a valuable discography compiled by Donald Manildi. Eva Hoffman, *Lost in Translation: A Life in a New Language* (1990), contains a vivid and compelling firsthand description of Rubinstein's first concert in Poland, in 1956, when the author was a twelve-year-old music student. An obituary, and an accompanying tribute by Harold C. Schonberg, is in the *New York Times* (21 Dec. 1982).

LORRAINE MARX-SINGER

RYAN, John Dale (*b*. 10 December 1915 in Cherokee, Iowa; *d*. 27 October 1983 in San Antonio, Texas), four-star general who served as U.S. Air Force chief of staff during the Vietnam War.

The youngest of five children of Edward Thomas Ryan, a railroad conductor, and Mabel Catherine Dubel, the

John D. Ryan. U.S. AIR FORCE PHOTO

daughter of a blacksmith, John Ryan graduated from high school in 1932 and attended Cherokee Junior College before being appointed to the United States Military Academy in 1934. He graduated in 1938 and was commissioned a second lieutenant in the field artillery. Ryan then entered flight training at Randolph and Kelly Fields, Texas, and after earning his wings in August 1939 he transferred to the Army Air Corps. On 26 August 1939 he married Jo Carolyn Guidera, the daughter of an Air Corps officer; they had three children.

From 1939 to 1943 Ryan served in various positions with the Air Corps Technical Training Command in the United States, including director of training, Advanced Bombardment School at Midland Army Air Field, Texas, in 1942 and 1943 and operations officer of the Second Air Force during the last half of 1943. In early 1944, now holding the rank of lieutenant colonel, he was appointed commander of the Second Bombardment Group, which was part of the Fifteenth Air Force in Italy. During the next months Ryan led fifty-eight combat missions against German targets. On one mission his left index finger was shot off, leading friends to dub him "three-fingered Jack." Later Ryan served as operations officer for the Fifth Bombardment Wing.

In February 1945 Ryan returned to the United States and, after again serving with the Air Training Command, he was assigned to the Fifty-eighth Bombardment Wing in

1946. For most of the next twenty-one years Ryan served with the Strategic Air Command while rising to the rank of full general. Between 1946 and 1948 he was assistant chief of staff for planning with the Fifty-eighth Bombardment Wing and then director of operations with the Eighth Air Force. From 1948 to 1951 Ryan led the 509th Bombardment Wing, and from 1951 to 1956 he commanded successively the 810th Air Division and the Nineteenth Air Division. Ryan then was made director of matériel for the Strategic Air Command, a post he held until 1960. His next assignment was as commander of the Sixteenth Air Force in Spain, and from 1961 to 1963 he was in charge of the Second Air Force. Following a year as inspector general of the U.S. Air Force, Ryan was recognized as one of the nation's major air power strategists. He was appointed vice commander of the Strategic Air Command in August 1964; three months later he became commander of the Strategic Air Command.

In 1967 Ryan was appointed commander of the Pacific Air Forces (PACAF), headquartered in Hawaii. His primary responsibility was the direction of Air Force operations in the Vietnam War. Like other airmen, Ryan was frustrated by the restrictions President Lyndon B. Johnson and Secretary of Defense Robert S. McNamara had placed on Operation Rolling Thunder, the air campaign that the United States had been waging against North Vietnam since March 1965. Officials in Washington regularly specified the targets, the types of forces, and the height, direction, and timing of attacks, an approach Ryan thought to be militarily unsound. While accepting without reservation civilian control of the military, he believed the actual conduct of air operations should be entrusted to professional leaders, who favored an unrelenting air assault against North Vietnam. As the war progressed, General Ryan became increasingly bitter toward the civilian leadership in Washington, blaming the country's political leaders for bringing on the war and then lacking the moral courage to fight it through to a successful conclusion.

After a year as PACAF, Ryan was named vice chief of staff of the Air Force. In July 1969 President Richard M. Nixon appointed General Ryan to the post of chief of staff, the highest position in the Air Force. In this post Ryan concerned himself with the continuing air war in Southeast Asia, which reached a crescendo in 1972 with the Linebacker I and Linebacker II air offensives against North Vietnam. He was deeply concerned with the need to maintain a strong strategic deterrent against the Soviet nuclear threat and to modernize the aircraft fleet, responsibilities that involved him in the development of new missiles and aircraft, such as the F-15 and F-16 fighters, and required him to testify regularly before congressional committees to explain Air Force policy and to defend budget requests.

The most controversial aspect of General Ryan's tenure

involved the secret bombing of North Vietnam between November 1971 and March 1972 carried out by General John Lavelle, commander of the Seventh Air Force, in violation of presidential and Joint Chiefs of Staff guidelines. Learning of the unauthorized raids in March 1972, Ryan promptly relieved Lavelle, a longtime friend, of his command, and a month later, after rejecting Lavelle's claim that he had the tacit approval of Admiral Thomas Moorer, chairman of the Joint Chiefs, and General Creighton Abrams, commander of American forces in Vietnam, Ryan forced his retirement at reduced rank. Later that year General Ryan testified before the House and Senate Military Affairs Committees about the affair, and despite initial skepticism from some congressmen and senators, they accepted his explanation that no one in the chain of command above Lavelle was involved in the bombing. The incident persuaded Ryan that the Vietnam experience was scarring the Air Force and that the service was in need of a major overhaul that emphasized, among other things, command authority.

In 1973 Ryan testified before the Senate Armed Services Committee about Operation Menu, the secret bombing in Cambodia carried out under the orders of President Nixon in 1969 and 1970. In providing the committee with details about the bombing, Ryan admitted he had been aware of the raids, but under sharp questioning he denied ever knowingly submitting false information to Congress in his periodic reports about the air war.

Ryan retired when his term as chief of staff expired on 1 August 1973 and took up residence in San Antonio, Texas, where he became a bank director. He died of a heart attack in 1983 at the Lackland Air Force Base Hospital and was buried in the cemetery of the United States Air Force Academy in Colorado Springs, Colorado.

Just under six feet tall, with piercing blue eyes, Ryan was an intense, straightforward leader who combined firmness with compassion. He is best remembered for his role in the disclosure of the secret bombings in Vietnam and Cambodia.

★

Ryan's papers are located in the United States Air Force Historical Research Agency, Maxwell Air Force Base, Alabama. References to Ryan's service during the Vietnam War are in Jack Broughton, *Going Downtown: The War Against Hanoi and Washington* (1988), and Mark Perry, *Four Stars* (1989). Ryan's involvement in the Lavelle affair is described in George C. Wilson, "Washington: The Lavelle Case," *Atlantic* (December 1972) and the *New York Times* (17 May; 11, 12, 13, and 22 June; 19, 26, and 27 Sept.; 7 and 8 Oct.; and 19 Dec. 1972). His involvement in Operation Menu is described in the *New York Times* (21 and 26 July 1973). A tribute, including a summary of his career, is in *Assembly* (March 1985): 137–138. Obituaries are in the *New York Times* (28 Oct. 1983) and the *Washington Post* (29 Oct. 1983). An oral history is in the Air Force Historical Agency.

JOHN KENNEDY OHL

RYSKIND, Morrie (*b.* 20 October 1895 in Brooklyn, New York; *d.* 24 August 1985 in Arlington, Virginia), playwright, screenwriter, and columnist who made groundbreaking contributions to musical theater between the world wars and won a Pulitzer Prize for his work on the Gershwin musical *Of Thee I Sing.*

The only son among the four children of Abraham and Ida (Etelson) Ryskind, Russian-Jewish immigrants, Morrie Ryskind grew up in New York City, where his father ran a cigar store in the Washington Heights neighborhood of Manhattan. He graduated in 1912 from Townsend Harris High School and then attended the Columbia University School of Journalism. Several weeks before Ryskind was due to graduate with the class of 1917, however, he was expelled because of articles he had written in school publications that were critical of the university's president, Nicholas Murray Butler. Columbia eventually awarded Ryskind an honorary bachelor's degree after he won the Pulitzer Prize.

Bald and slightly built, and outgoing despite his rather bookish appearance, Ryskind wrote for newspapers and worked as a press agent early in his career. He and Ira Gershwin, the lyricist and brother of George Gershwin, were among the youngest contributors to the well-known humor columns of Franklin P. Adams. Ryskind reported for the *New York World* until 1921 and published a volume of light verse, *Unaccustomed as I Am.*

Ryskind's early theatrical endeavors included sketches and lyrics for *The '49ers* in 1922, *The Garrick Gaieties* in 1925, and, in collaboration with Howard Dietz, *Merry Go Round* in 1927. Ryskind's first musical-comedy assignment was to write the words to Charles Rosoff's score for *Pardon Me,* which flopped. More successful were his collaborations with the playwright and screenwriter George S. Kaufman, with whom he shared a knack for satirizing corporate, political, and social institutions. They capitalized on their combined talents with the Marx brothers and Gershwin brothers.

Ryskind and Kaufman are considered the Marx Brothers act's most successful writing team. Ryskind was Kaufman's uncredited coauthor of *The Cocoanuts,* a 1925 play starring Groucho Marx as a swindling Florida hotel owner. In 1928 the writers got double billing for *Animal Crackers,* with Groucho Marx as the wacky African explorer Captain Jeffrey T. Spaulding. Ryskind adapted both shows for film, and wrote screenplays for *A Night at the Opera* (1935) and

Morrie Ryskind, 1932. UPI/CORBIS-BETTMANN

Room Service (1938). Groucho was best man in Ryskind's wedding to Mary House, a University of Chicago graduate, on 19 December 1929. Ryskind and Marx were friends for life.

Ryskind had befriended George and Ira Gershwin prior to 1920 and was a regular at Greenwich Village social gatherings where they sometimes tried out new material. With them Ryskind created three satirical stage works that differed radically from earlier musicals. Instead of focusing on interpersonal relationships, the plays spoofed war and political parties. *Strike Up the Band* reflected disillusion with American intervention in World War I. The show bombed at its 1927 tryout, perhaps owing to Kaufman's dark libretto. Audiences responded more favorably to the 1930 revival, with a book adapted by Ryskind. The team collaborated on *Of Thee I Sing,* which satirized the failings of American politics during the Great Depression. The story followed bachelor John P. Wintergreen's presidential campaign on a platform of love, an issue chosen for its voter appeal and lack of substance. Opening in 1931 at the Music Box Theatre, *Of Thee I Sing* ran for more than 400 performances. It won Ryskind, Kaufman, and Ira Gershwin a

Pulitzer Prize for drama and was the first musical ever to do so. *Let 'Em Eat Cake,* their 1933 sequel to *Of Thee I Sing,* closed after 90 performances. Ryskind's political humor found success on the stage again in 1940, when he adapted the libretto for the Irving Berlin hit musical *Louisiana Purchase,* a loose satire of Louisiana governor Huey Long. It played for more than 400 performances at the Imperial Theatre.

As a screenwriter, Ryskind was nominated twice for Academy Awards, for the screenplays to *My Man Godfrey* (1936), a sophisticated comedy about a butler vying for his female employer's affections, and *Stage Door* (1937), about a hotel full of aspiring actresses. Ryskind also wrote screenplays for *Penny Serenade* (1941) and for the Jack Benny comedies *Man About Town* (1939) and *It's in the Bag* (1945).

After World War II Ryskind left show business. He claimed Hollywood had ostracized him professionally after he testified in 1947, before the House Un-American Activities Committee that communists had infiltrated the Screenwriters' Guild. Ryskind again turned to journalism, and his satire now reflected a shift to conservatism. In 1954 he began raising money and hosting receptions to launch *National Review,* the right-wing periodical that got off the ground in November 1955. Ryskind served as a director and wrote a tongue-in-cheek piece on psychoanalysis for the inaugural issue. Three decades later, *National Review* editor William F. Buckley, Jr., acknowledged in a eulogy for Ryskind that the journal might not have begun without him. In his columns Ryskind zealously took on California lawmakers, the national debt, President John F. Kennedy, Fidel Castro, and Nikita Khrushchev. He began writing for the *Los Angeles Times* syndicate in 1960, and early in that association, newspapers in about two dozen cities carried his pieces. Ryskind resigned from the syndicate in 1971 and then wrote for the *Los Angeles Herald Examiner* until he retired in 1978.

Ryskind had lived in Beverly Hills, California, since 1937 but moved shortly before he died to Arlington, Virginia, to be near his children and grandchildren. He was buried in Mount Hebron Cemetery in Queens, New York. Mary Ryskind, his wife of more than fifty-five years and a longtime Republican party activist in California, survived him, as did his daughter Ruth Ohman and son Alan Ryskind, who both became writers and editors.

Whether he was satirizing World War I, supporting Kaufman's liberal leanings, lampooning aristocrats with the Marx Brothers, or advancing conservative causes, Ryskind reveled in voicing sharp, outspoken opinions riddled with thorny humor. Although *Of Thee I Sing* and Ryskind's other musical theater works are seldom revived, his Marx Brothers scripts became classics, and the political journal he helped found lives on.

★

Deena Rosenberg, *Fascinating Rhythm: The Collaboration of George and Ira Gershwin* (1991), delves into Ryskind's partnership with the Gershwin brothers and draws on the author's 1978 interview with Ryskind. See also Edwin McDowell, "On the Beach with Morrie Ryskind," *National Review* (Apr. 1963); Paul D. Zimmerman and Burt Goldblatt, *The Marx Brothers at the Movies* (1968); Steven Suskin, *Show Tunes 1905–1985: The Songs, Shows, and Careers of Broadway's Major Composers* (1986); and Kurt Ganzl, *The Encyclopedia of the Musical Theatre* (1994). Obituaries are in the *New York Times* (25 Aug. 1985), *Washington Post* (25 Aug. 1985), and *National Review* 37 (20 Sept. 1985).

WHITNEY SMITH

S

SAMUELS, Howard Joseph ("Howie the Horse") (*b.* 3 December 1919 in Rochester, New York; *d.* 26 October 1984 in New York City), wealthy industrialist who was a four-time Democratic party candidate for the gubernatorial nomination in New York State and the first president of the New York Off-Track Betting Corporation.

Samuels, one of two children of Harry L. Samuels and Bertha Levy and the grandson of Russian immigrants, was raised with his older brother, Richard M. Samuels, in Rochester. Samuels's father owned a small electrical-appliance manufacturing company, Samson-United, that produced private-label toasters, waffle irons, and rubber-bladed fans. Both boys attended local public schools, P.S. 23 and Monroe High School, where Howard was captain of the tennis team and winner of four city championships. At the Massachusetts Institute of Technology, the slim, athletic Samuels played soccer and tennis and was captain of the MIT basketball team, graduating in 1941 with a B.S. degree in business engineering administration. After graduation, Samuels enlisted as a private in the army, eventually serving with General George Patton's Third Army in the European theater. He was one of the soldiers who liberated the Nazi death camp at Buchenwald. This experience made a significant impression on Samuels, causing him to make an enduring commitment to the Zionist movement in Israel and to the civil rights movement in the United States. Samuels was discharged from the army as a lieutenant colonel in 1945.

Samuels's senior thesis for MIT had been titled "The Manufacturing and Distribution Problems of Vinyl-Coated Sisal Rope," written under his adviser, Professor E. Kirk Miller. As an undergraduate, Howard Samuels had distributed lengths of vinyl-coated clothesline to 100 housewives. After his military service, he returned to the study's original survey population and discovered that the women continued to prize their sample clotheslines for helping to keep wet clothes clean. With $15,000 borrowed against their father's life insurance policy and with the support of their family, Howard and Richard Samuels founded the Kordite Company (later Corporation) in 1946 in a Victor, New York, schoolhouse that they rented for $35 a month. With three employees, Samuels began manufacturing plastic brooms and plastic-covered clothesline. Richard Samuels, as president, called on chemical companies and sales representatives while Howard Samuels, as executive vice president, oversaw the construction and operation of machines that would extrude polypropylene resin into plastic film. Eventually, Kordite became the leading manufacturer of plastic packaging, plastic bags, and plastic foam products. In 1952 the Samuels brothers moved the plant to Macedon, New York, and began to open other manufacturing plants in Illinois, Texas, and California. In 1955 the brothers sold Kordite to Textron Corporation for $2 million, stock in Textron, and a ten-year agreement to continue running the company.

Kordite, under Samuels's leadership, created products that changed American life. Because of the expense and potential contamination of cleaning metal refuse cans at Tompson Memorial Hospital in Canandaigua, New York, where Howard Samuels served on the board of trustees, Samuels oversaw the creation of disposable plastic garbage bags made from polyethylene film. By extruding polypropylene resin into plastic film, Samuels's products replaced cellophane and changed the packaging and distribution of hundreds of products used commercially, in industry, and in American homes. The success of Kordite products, marketed under the brand names Kordite and Hefty, and Kordite Corporation's growth and diversity made a significant impact on the small upstate New York community where the factory was located. Samuels was as committed to good business practices as he was to creative involvement in his community. Tuition benefits for employees and their children, regular profit-sharing bonuses for all employees, and the opportunity for factory workers to act on their management potential created for Samuels and Kordite a reputation for community activism.

In 1958 National Distillers bought Kordite, selling the company to the plastics division of Mobil Corporation in 1962. In twelve years, Kordite Company, with Richard Samuels as chairman of the board and Howard Samuels as president, had grown to employ a workforce of 9,000 people with annual earnings in excess of $50 million. Shortly after the transfer of his business to the Mobil Corporation, Howard Samuels took a leave from his position as vice president of Mobil Chemical to begin a career in public service. Samuels made four attempts to secure the Democratic nomination for governor of New York State. He lost the primary in 1962 to Frank D. O'Connor, the New York City Council president from Queens. In 1966 Samuels secured the Democratic nomination for lieutenant governor (after a failed attempt to win the gubernatorial nomination) and ran on a ticket with Frank O'Connor against the ultimately successful Republican team of Nelson A. Rockefeller and Malcolm Wilson. In 1970 Samuels made his third attempt to win the Democratic nomination for governor and lost to Arthur Goldberg. Never a favorite of Democratic party bosses because he took positions that reflected his interest in good government over party politics, Samuels had alienated powerful downstate party regulars. He retired from active political life in 1974 after his fourth unsuccessful bid for the gubernatorial nomination in the New York State Democratic primary elections, losing this last time to Hugh L. Carey.

In 1966 Samuels was appointed undersecretary of commerce by President Lyndon B. Johnson and in 1968 he took the position of chief administrator of the Small Business Administration. In 1971 Howard Samuels was named the first president of the New York Off-Track Betting Corporation. Samuels's enthusiasm for using a statewide system of pari-mutuel, off-track betting sites as a vehicle for gen-

Howard J. Samuels, 1965. ARCHIVE PHOTOS

erating money for public educational and social programs, his high visibility as "Howie the Horse," and his superb administrative skills helped make this public benefit corporation a model in the 1970s for public service funding.

In October 1973 Samuels's marriage to his first wife, Barbara J. Christie, whom he had married in 1942, ended. In the course of their thirty-one years together, the couple had eight children. Two months later, in December 1973, Samuels married Antoinette Chautemps, the daughter of Camille Chautemps. (Camille Chautemps had been the premier of France four times between 1920 and 1940 before the family fled advancing German troops for the United States.) Samuels and his second wife had two children.

Howard Samuels died of a heart attack in his Manhattan apartment early in the morning of Friday, 26 October 1984. After funeral services at Temple Rodeph Sholom in Manhattan, Samuels was buried in Southampton, New York. Samuels was eulogized by New York governor Mario Cuomo as a "gentle, compassionate man who possessed a unique talent for bonding his own personal sense of humanity with an intelligent and practical view of business and government."

★

An editorial recounting Samuels's contributions to Ontario County, New York, is in the *Canandaigua* (New York) *Daily Messenger* (1 Nov. 1984). News clippings related to the growth, sales, and buyouts of the Kordite Corporation and to Samuels's political career are available in the Rochester Public Library. The *New York Times, Business Week,* and the *Wall Street Journal* reported on Samuels's political, business, and personal life between 1955 and 1984. Two books about Rochester, B. McKelvey, *A Panoramic History of Rochester* (1979), and K. Gerling, *Smugtown, USA* (1957), outline Samuels's remarkable success in establishing Kordite Corporation. Obituaries are in the *New York Times,* the *Rochester* (New York) *Democrat and Chronicle,* and the *Canandaigua* (New York) *Daily Messenger* (all 27 Oct. 1984).

WENDY HALL MALONEY

SAROYAN, William (*b.* 31 August 1908 in Fresno, California; *d.* 18 May 1981 in Fresno, California), prolific dramatist and story writer best known for his play *The Time of Your Life* and screenplay *The Human Comedy.*

Saroyan was the fourth and last child born to Armenian parents, Armenak and Takoohi Saroyan, who had immigrated to California shortly after the turn of the century to escape the persecution of the Turks. After the death of his father, a minister and farmworker, in 1911, Saroyan and his siblings lived for five years in an Oakland, California, orphanage, while their mother worked at menial jobs in San Francisco. Later, he attended the Fresno public schools, although he dropped out of high school after multiple expulsions. In 1926 he quit his job as a telegram messenger and moved to San Francisco to become a writer. He published his first story in the *Overland Monthly* in 1928, then moved to New York City for a few months before returning to San Francisco. "I took to writing at an early age to escape from meaninglessness, uselessness, unimportance, insignificance, poverty, enslavement, ill health, despair, madness, and all manner of other unattractive, natural, and inevitable things," he later reminisced.

In 1933, under the pseudonym Sirak Goryan, Saroyan published "The Broken Wheel" in *Hairenik,* a Boston newspaper for Armenian Americans, and it was subsequently reprinted in *Best Stories of 1934.* With the stream-of-consciousness narrative "The Daring Young Man on the Flying Trapeze" (*Story,* February 1934), he won sudden literary fame and commercial success. His first collection of twenty-six stories, *The Daring Young Man on the Flying Trapeze and Other Stories,* published that October was an immediate best-seller. In its preface Saroyan set down three rules for writers: "Do not pay attention to the rules other people make. Forget Edgar Allan Poe and O. Henry and write the kind of stories you feel like writing. Learn to typewrite, so you can turn out stories as fast as Zane Grey." In 1935 he traveled to the Soviet Union, specifically to Armenia, and to Mexico, and in 1936 he was briefly employed in Hollywood, first by B. P. Schulberg and later at Columbia Pictures, as a writer at a salary of $250 to $300 a week.

By 1941 Saroyan had published eight volumes of short fiction, including the best-seller *My Name Is Aram* (1940), and had written five staged plays, even though he had no formal training as playwright, actor, or director. The first of these plays, *My Heart's in the Highlands,* was produced by the Group Theatre in New York City in April 1939 and was based on one of his early short stories. *The Time of Your Life,* which he scripted in only six days while living in a New York City hotel, opened on Broadway in October 1939. Set in a San Francisco waterfront saloon, the play features a cast of lovable if stereotypical eccentrics, including a barroom philosopher, a cowboy down on his luck, and a whore with a heart of gold. Saroyan received both the New York Drama Critics Circle Award and the Pulitzer Prize in 1940—the first playwright to receive both awards for the same play—although he declined the Pulitzer because, as he wrote, "commerce had no business patronizing art." His ballet, *The Great American Goof,* opened in January 1940; his play *Love's Old Sweet Song* opened on Broadway in April 1940; and his play *The Beautiful People* opened on Broadway a year later.

Although he was at the height of his fame as a playwright early in the 1940s, Saroyan had mixed success as a screenwriter in Hollywood. He sold the script of *The Human Comedy,* which he claimed to have written in only

William Saroyan. ARCHIVE PHOTOS

eleven days, to Metro-Goldwyn-Mayer for $60,000 in 1941, but when the studio refused his demand to direct the film, Saroyan denounced the production in *Variety*. Ironically, he would receive an Academy Award for the screenplay. Saroyan also turned the scenario into a novel, which became his most popular publication and a Book-of-the-Month Club selection. He would also bitterly satirize his experience in the play *Get Away, Old Man,* about a dictatorial movie mogul modeled on Louis B. Mayer, first produced in 1943 and the last of his plays to be staged on Broadway for more than a decade.

In 1942 Saroyan rented the Belasco Theatre on Broadway, changed its name to the Saroyan Theatre, and began to produce his own plays, including *Across the Board on Tomorrow Morning,* first staged at the Pasadena Playhouse in February 1941. His company was evicted from the theater for nonpayment of rent a few weeks later. He was elected to the National Institute of Arts and Letters in 1943. On 20 February of that year he married the actress and former debutante, Carol Marcus; they had two children.

Drafted into the U.S. Army in 1942 and stationed in New York as an information-services writer, Saroyan was so unsuited to military discipline that he was briefly hospitalized and observed for evidence of mental incompetence. Reassigned to England in 1944 in anticipation of the Allied invasion of Europe, he wrote his picaresque antimilitary novel *The Adventures of Wesley Jackson* while billeted in the Savoy Hotel in London for thirty-eight days. The novel, a satire of army bureaucracy, was not published until 1946. After the liberation of France, Saroyan was temporarily reassigned to Paris, although he spent most of the duration of the war hospitalized with back trouble in California. He was honorably discharged from the army in September 1945. "Three years in the army and a stupid marriage had all but knocked me out of the picture and, if the truth is told, out of life itself," he later wrote.

Although he was often compared to Ernest Hemingway in the early 1940s, Saroyan's popularity declined sharply after World War II. In part as a result of his compulsive gambling, he eventually owed the Internal Revenue Service back taxes and penalties totaling $50,000. His plays *Don't Go Away Mad, Sam Ego's House,* and *A Decent Birth, a Happy Funeral* were published in a single volume in 1949. The Saroyans divorced in 1949, remarried in 1951, and divorced a second time the next year. Temperamental and iconoclastic, Saroyan blamed many of his problems on theatrical agents and the Dramatic Guild. "I'm a failure, but the others are a bankruptcy," he wrote.

He spent the rest of his life largely on the margins of the theatrical mainstream. He claimed coauthorship with his cousin Ross Bagdasarian of the popular song "Come On-a My House," recorded by Rosemary Clooney in 1951, and he wrote a number of television plays, mostly for *Om-nibus*. His play *A Lost Child's Fireflies* was staged by an African-American dramatic company in Dallas in 1954, and his absurdist play *The Cave Dwellers,* which he wrote in only eight days, opened on Broadway in October 1957. Seeking relief from his tax debt, he moved to a working-class neighborhood of Paris in 1959. The next year his play *The Dogs; or, The Paris Comedy* (1959) was staged in Vienna, and *Sam, the Highest Jumper of Them All; or, The London Comedy* (1961) opened in London. *Settled Out of Court,* written in collaboration with Henry Cecil, also opened in London. In 1961 he was writer-in-residence at Purdue University, where he wrote the rarely performed scripts *High Time Along the Wabash, Hanging Around the Wabash,* and *Death Along the Wabash.* He then virtually disappeared from the theatrical scene for more than a decade.

Late in life, after returning to Fresno to live in the late 1960s, Saroyan wrote a series of memoirs, including *Here Comes, There Goes, You Know Who* (1961), *Not Dying* (1963), and *Places Where I've Done Time* (1972). In 1974 his play *Armenians* opened in New York, and the next year his play *The Rebirth Celebration of the Human Race at Artie Zabala's Off-Broadway Theatre* opened off-Broadway. His last play to be produced professionally, *Play Things,* opened in Vienna in 1980.

In a statement released after his death from cancer, Saroyan laconically remarked, "Everybody has got to die, but I have always believed an exception would be made in my case. Now what?" At his request there was no funeral. Half of his ashes were interred a year later in a monument in Yerevan, Armenia.

Although he sympathized with the underclass, Saroyan refused to join proletarian associations or support their causes, preferring to describe himself as "a spiritual anarchist." Remarkably prolific, he wrote hundreds of stories and sketches in addition to more than 250 scripts for theater, movies, television, and radio. More a stylist than a craftsman, many of his writings, especially the plays, tend to formlessness. As Thelma J. Shinn noted, "The non-plot symbolic dramas of Pinter, of Beckett, of Ionesco with their usually unrelieved pessimism are remarkably similar to the 'romantic fantasies' of Saroyan." Whereas his early plays were often sentimental in theme and vaudevillian in their theatricality, with spare or lyrical dialogue, his later plays were more rhetorical and didactic, peopled by hard-boiled or skeptical characters who occasionally rant or preach to the audience.

★

Most of Saroyan's literary remains are owned by the William Saroyan Foundation. The Bancroft Library at the University of California at Berkeley holds the largest collection of his manuscripts available in a public archive. Lawrence Lee and Barry Gifford, *Saroyan: A Biography* (1984), is by far the most detailed chronicle of his life, superior certainly to the memoirs by his son,

Aram Saroyan, *Last Rites: The Death of William Saroyan* (1982) and *William Saroyan* (1983). David Stephen Calonne, *William Saroyan: My Real Work Is Being* (1983), is the best available bio-critical study, superseding Howard Russell Floan, *William Saroyan* (1966). Jon Whitmore, *William Saroyan: A Research and Production Sourcebook* (1994), is an essential reference guide to Saroyan's dramatic writing. Among the most valuable articles on Saroyan's writings is Thelma J. Shinn, "William Saroyan: Romantic Existentialist," *Modern Drama* 15 (1972): 185–194. A lengthy obituary is in the *New York Times* (19 May 1981).

GARY SCHARNHORST

SAVITCH, Jessica Beth (*b.* 1 February 1947 in Wilmington, Delaware; *d.* 23 October 1983 in New Hope, Pennsylvania), broadcast journalist who, as an anchorwoman for NBC News, was one of the most recognizable television personalities in America and helped extend credibility to women in the role of national news anchor; after her accidental death at age thirty-six she was seen as emblematic of both the underside of celebrity and the ratings-driven values of television news.

Raised in the middle-class community of Kennett Square, Pennsylvania, Savitch was the oldest of three daughters of David Savitch and Florence Goldberger. Her father ran one of several clothing stores owned by Jessica's paternal grandparents, Russian Jewish immigrants who had achieved social and economic prominence in the community. A precocious and outgoing child, Jessica attended the local public grade school. Her primary identification was with her father, who regularly engaged her in discussions of current events; to prepare for these discussions, she became an avid watcher of television news. A year after David Savitch died in May 1959 from kidney disease, Savitch's mother moved the family to Margate, New Jersey, and resumed her career as a registered nurse.

Savitch attended Atlantic City High School from 1960 to 1964. From 1962 to 1964 she worked as a weekend disc jockey and news reader at radio station WOND-AM in Pleasantville, New Jersey. In 1964 Savitch entered Ithaca College as a communications major. She supported herself by working as a radio disc jockey for WBBF-AM in Rochester, New York, and by modeling for print ads and making television commercials. After graduating with a B.A. from Ithaca in 1968, she moved to New York City and was hired by CBS as a clerical worker and gofer. In 1969 she became an administrative assistant for the network and then at WCBS Radio. There she had access to the technical facilities required to make a television demo tape, which helped her land her first reporting job, in June 1971, at the CBS affiliate KHOU-TV in Houston, Texas.

Hired as an on-air reporter, within three months at

Jessica Savitch. ARCHIVE PHOTOS

KHOU Savitch became anchor of the Sunday night newscast, aided by a 1971 ruling by the Federal Communications Commission prohibiting discrimination in the hiring and promotion of women in broadcasting; she was featured in *TV Guide* as the first female anchor in the South. Her telegenic looks—high cheekbones, blond hair, broad smile, and light blue eyes that turned down slightly at the outer corners—as well as her aggressive reporting style, impressed local viewers and caught the attention of the major networks.

From 1972 to 1977 Savitch worked for station KYW-TV in Philadelphia, NBC's largest affiliate station. As weekend anchor from 1973, she became a local celebrity, featured in regional publications and in demand as a public speaker. In July 1974 she became cohost of the daily *Newswatch 5:30* broadcasts. By 1975 KYW was the number-one-rated news station in Philadelphia, a development attributed largely to Savitch.

In September 1977 Savitch moved to NBC as Senate correspondent and anchor for the Sunday edition of *NBC Nightly News* and for the *NBC News Digest*, sixty-second updates delivered in two prime-time segments every evening, providing Savitch with an unprecedented amount of national exposure for a broadcast journalist. Based in Washington, D.C., she commuted to New York City on weekends to deliver her Sunday newscast. She also served as a contributing correspondent of the NBC news magazine *Prime Time Sunday* (later *Prime Time Saturday*) in 1979 and 1980, as a substitute anchor on *Today*, and as a guest reporter on *Meet the Press*, and she filled in occasionally on the weekday *Nightly News*, the first woman at NBC to anchor the weekday newscast.

Savitch, who had a great facility as a news reader and projected a competent, self-assured image on the television screen, had less success as an issues-oriented reporter. Criticized for her lack of analytical skills, she was taken off the Senate beat early in 1979. The demotion, however, did not affect the public perception that she was highly valued by the network; in January 1979 she was described in *Newsweek* magazine as NBC's "Golden Girl," and she received good notices as podium correspondent for the 1980 national conventions.

Savitch's personal life, however, was plagued with problems. Her marriage to Philadelphia advertising executive Melvin Korn on 6 January 1980 ended in divorce ten months later. On 21 March 1981 she married Donald R. Payne, a physician; he suffered from depression and committed suicide in their Washington townhouse the following August. Savitch then relocated to New York City, where she lived alone in an apartment on East Fifty-sixth Street. The most significant personal relationship of her adult life was with William Ronald ("Ron") Kershaw, a reporter for a rival network in her Houston days who went on to a career as a news director. They were briefly engaged in 1972, and their intense and at times physically combative relationship continued intermittently until her death.

Savitch's recreational use of drugs, which began in the early 1970s, reportedly escalated to cocaine addiction in the early 1980s. She was granted a partial leave of absence from NBC in 1982 to host the new PBS documentary series *Frontline*, and by 1983 she had been phased out of almost all her NBC duties except the nightly prime-time updates (she had been replaced as weekend anchor by Connie Chung in May). During the first update broadcast on 3 October 1983, she appeared dazed on the air and slurred her delivery. Three weeks later she was killed when a car driven by Martin Fischbein, a *New York Post* executive whom she had recently started dating, plunged into a canal of the Delaware River behind a Pennsylvania restaurant. In heavy fog, Fischbein apparently mistook a towpath leading from the restaurant for an exit. The cause of death for both was determined to be asphyxiation by drowning; ironically, neither drugs nor alcohol was determined to have played a part in the accident. Savitch was cremated and her ashes scattered over the Atlantic Ocean.

Savitch, who publicly decried the entertainment aspects of broadcast news and strove to be taken seriously as a journalist, acknowledged in her 1982 autobiography that television is "a visual industry, and exterior packaging plays an incontrovertible role." Hired by NBC for her ability to attract a viewing audience, she was pushed by the network into roles for which she had not been sufficiently prepared, in order to establish her credibility as a news anchor. She contributed to the perception held by critics that she was not a serious journalist by cultivating a star persona both on and off the set. After her death, accounts of Savitch's rapid rise to fame and tumultuous personal life found a ready audience in the millions of viewers to whom she was already a cultural fixture. The sense of inevitability surrounding her death gave rise to popular books and television movies based on her life, in which she was depicted as both a product and a victim of the visual medium of television news.

★

The best-selling autobiography *Anchorwoman* (1982) was characterized in the *New York Times Book Review* (7 Nov. 1982) as a celebration of Savitch's "limited accomplishments." Two full-length biographies, Alanna Nash, *Golden Girl: The Story of Jessica Savitch*, and Gwenda Blair, *Almost Golden: Jessica Savitch and the Selling of Television News*, both published in 1988, envision Savitch as a desperately insecure, self-absorbed woman who was mishandled by a broadcast news industry in disarray. Obituaries are in the *New York Times* and the *Washington Post* (25 Oct. 1983), and in *Time* magazine (7 Nov. 1983).

MELISSA A. DOBSON

SCARNE, John (*b.* 4 March 1903 in Niles, Ohio; *d.* 7 July 1985 in Englewood, New Jersey), card and gambling expert, magician, and authority on modern games.

Scarne's parents, Fiorangelo Scarnecchia, a factory worker, and Maria Giuseppa, were Italian immigrants, who relocated with their two children to New Jersey. Christened Orlando Carmelo Scarnecchia, he changed his first name to John shortly after enrolling at Guttenberg Grammar School and shortened his last name to Scarne (pronounced SCAR-ney) after beginning a career as a magician.

Scarne developed an interest in gambling after observing a group of card cheats playing at Columbia Amusement Park in North Bergen. He soon began attracting attention in gambling circles as one of the state's best card mechanics, or someone who could manipulate cards without being detected. He also turned a talent for mathematics to his advantage in gambling pursuits, allowing him to compute the odds for any gambling circumstance with lightning speed. Because of his strong religious beliefs, however, he swore to avoid cheating. He was deeply affected after he exposed a card cheat in a basement game, leading to the offender's being stabbed in an ensuing brawl.

Master gamesman and card manipulator John Scarne, 1938. UPI/Corbis-Bettmann

In spite of good scholarship, Scarne quit school after the eighth grade to devote all his time to magic and card manipulation. After a brief time as a factory worker, Scarne got a job working in a diner. He waited on tables and also performed magic tricks. He also visited the reading room at the New York Public Library to read everything he could about games and magic. While still a teenager, he worked with the local Fairview, New Jersey, police department to spot cheating in visiting carnivals.

Scarne began to perform card tricks for professional gamblers in New York City. In the early 1920s he was sent to Chicago and found himself doing tricks for the gangster Al Capone and his associates. As one of his tricks, Scarne was able to deal four aces to any position in a poker table, no matter how many times the cards had been cut or shuffled. By now, Scarne was a full-time performer, who practiced for hours each day. As his reputation grew, he impressed Harry Houdini and the two magicians became friends until Houdini's death in 1926. Scarne emulated Houdini's promotional abilities by billing himself as "the magician who fools other magicians." Scarne also started performing escape stunts but quit after nearly drowning in the Hackensack River.

In the early 1930s Scarne was invited to entertain the recently elected president Franklin D. Roosevelt during a visit to New Jersey. The president's favorite trick was one where he chose a card, marked it, and put it back in the deck. When asked to pull the card back out of the deck, Roosevelt could not find it. Scarne then produced it from his mouth.

When World War II broke out, Scarne was concerned that the newly mobilized soldiers were going to be systematically exploited by gambling cheats. This impression grew when he visited a factory in Chicago that could not keep up with the increased demand for marked cards and loaded dice. Scarne decided to devote himself to lecturing the troops about how to spot cheating. An article in *Life* magazine about his activities led to an invitation to serve as the first civilian writer for *Yank,* a weekly newspaper published by the army. While his work for the troops was sometimes controversial, particularly with proprietors who operated near military installations, he was awarded official commendations and invited to do a magic show for a gathering of generals and British dignitaries in Washington, D.C. On that occasion, he found himself temporarily in possession of papers detailing the secret plans for the D-day invasion. He managed to return it to the unwitting official later in the show.

After World War II, Scarne visited the new gambling mecca in Las Vegas, Nevada. At that time, blackjack games were dealt from a single deck and Scarne could consistently win by counting the number of high cards played. He went to each casino one night and calmly told the manager that he would win $1,000 and then leave. He did just as he predicted and was promptly banned from ever gambling in Las Vegas again. Some of his friends were upset, but Scarne was delighted at the compliment.

Although he had started writing guides to gambling in the 1930s, the fame that resulted from his work with the army opened publishing doors for him. His first major work, *Scarne on Dice,* was published in 1945. This publication was followed by other books on cards and other games, making Scarne the undisputed modern expert on games. He also hoped to invent a modern game that would become a classic, but his invention Teeko failed to capture the public's imagination.

On 23 March 1956 Scarne married Steffi ("Storm") Kearney, his longtime secretary. A son was born to them later that year. Meanwhile, casino owners were happy to have Scarne work as a consultant in gambling security. In the 1950s and 1960s he advised state-run casinos in Puerto Rico and Panama. The latter was particularly dangerous, because Scarne fired the entire casino staff and the president left the country while the aggrieved employees were protesting. The situation was defused when the former employees who could get endorsements from public officials were rehired. Scarne was working for the Hilton hotel in Havana at the time of the Cuban revolution in 1959. He helped avoid another dangerous situation by making his hotel the host for Fidel Castro's victorious forces, while the other hotels in the city were being looted.

Scarne dressed in double-breasted suits in the manner of movie detectives and developed a heavy cigar habit early in life. While he achieved considerable success as a magician, author, and consultant, he lived in his hometown of Fairview, New Jersey, throughout his life. He died in Englewood, New Jersey, and was buried in nearby Fort Lee.

★

Scarne's writings include *The Odds Against Me* (1966); *Scarne's Encyclopedia of Games* (1973); *Scarne's New Complete Guide to Gambling* (1974); and *Scarne's Guide to Casino Gambling* (1978). An obituary is in the *New York Times* (9 July 1985).

TERRY BALLARD

SCHACHT, Al(exander) (*b.* 11 November 1892? in the Bronx, New York; *d.* 14 July 1984 in Waterbury, Connecticut), baseball player, coach, and comedian who, as the self-described "Clown Prince of Baseball," performed his pantomimes at World Series games over a thirty-year period.

Al Schacht was born in 1892 (according to his autobiography; some sources list his date of birth as 1894) in the Bronx, not far from where Yankee Stadium would be built thirty years later. His parents, Saul and Ida Schacht, were Jewish immigrants to America. He had an older brother and a younger sister.

Al Schacht, "Clown Prince of Baseball," wears a catcher's mitt that is thirty inches wide and a fan cover as a mask. NATIONAL BASEBALL HALL OF FAME LIBRARY, COOPERSTOWN, N.Y.

As a child, Al would go to the Polo Grounds in Manhattan to run errands for his heroes, manager John J. McGraw and the members of the New York Giants. Schacht himself soon showed promise as a pitcher, helping his public school team win the New York City championship in 1908. He pitched for the High School of Commerce team in 1911 until it was learned that he had played in a summer league for $4 a week, whereupon he lost his amateur standing and was expelled from Commerce.

Al was given a tryout by Cincinnati, but the Reds turned him down, whereupon John McGraw allowed him to work with the Giants as an unpaid batting-practice pitcher; he played semipro baseball in New York as well. After a brief fling with the unsuccessful Federal League and another year of semipro games, Schacht finally got his first organized baseball contract with the famed Newark (New Jersey) Bears of the International League. There he showed the talent for clowning that would be the basis for his professional success. Once when he was on first base, an attempted pickoff throw landed on the ground beneath him. He retrieved the ball, put it in his pocket, and ran around the bases. He was fined for this violation of the rules, but the fans loved it. Later that season, as the starting pitcher in a game, Schacht rode to the pitching mound on an old horse.

While playing for Newark, Al began suffering injuries that would seriously shorten his pitching career, beginning with a sore arm. Despairing of ever making the major leagues, Schacht joined the U.S. Army in 1918, serving at Fort Slocum, New York. Discharged early in 1919, Schacht had his most successful minor league season that year, winning twenty games for the Jersey City Skeeters. This achievement inspired Clark Griffith to bring Schacht to the Washington Senators at the conclusion of the 1919 season.

Schacht had some pitching successes in the next three years, notably a 1921 game against the New York Yankees, in which he appeared as a last-minute substitute for the great Walter Johnson and pitched a complete game, winning 4–1. Unfortunately, an injury to his pitching shoulder suffered in a baserunning accident ended his career, his record a meager 14–10 for parts of three seasons.

But by this time Schacht had developed a popular clown act, characterized by a battered top hat, an old frock coat, and an oversized baseball glove. In 1921 Schacht joined forces with Senators coach and former pitcher Nick Altrock, already a noted clown, and the two of them were hired to perform before the games of the 1921 World Series. This began a string of over thirty years in which Schacht performed at every World Series except those during World War II, when he was overseas entertaining the troops. The Senators put him on the payroll as a coach, a role in which he performed successfully for the next twelve years, gaining praise for his skill at third-base coaching. In 1934, when

Senators manager Joe Cronin moved to the Boston Red Sox, he took Schacht along with him.

But by this time Schacht was better known as a clown than as a coach. He and Altrock performed together until 1933, although they did not get along well with each other, and for the last few years did not speak to one another. His success as a clown at the World Series and during the off-season, along with offers for his work from a variety of sources, inspired him to leave coaching and become a full-time clown, appearing at major- and minor-league ball-parks around the country. In 1941 he published his first autobiography, *Clowning Through Baseball* (written with Murray Goodman), in which he mentioned that clowning was bringing him $30,000 a year, five times his highest salary as a player. The book's lighthearted anecdotal style made it popular.

In 1941 two occurrences influenced his career. He opened an eating establishment, Al Schacht's Restaurant, on East Fifty-second Street in New York City. With its base-ball theme, it became a popular meeting place for sports personalities and fans for many years. After the Japanese bombed Pearl Harbor, Schacht went on a series of USO tours. He traveled extensively, giving hundreds of perfor-mances in Africa, Europe, and the Pacific.

In 1944 he published *Al Schacht's Dope Book,* a collec-tion of baseball anecdotes, facts, and figures. In 1945 he followed that with *GI Had Fun,* a memoir of his military tours, also written with Murray Goodman. The next year, Schacht tried the stage, appearing in a baseball comedy entitled *Second Guesser.* This show played briefly in Chi-cago, then closed. He returned to live in the Bronx, with his widowed mother.

Schacht appeared in his last World Series in 1952 and retired from clowning in 1958. Another autobiography, *My Own Particular Screwball* (edited by Ed Keyes), was pub-lished in 1955. Schacht retired to the life of a restaurateur and died, after a short illness, in Waterbury, Connecticut.

Al Schacht played a unique role in baseball. Of minor importance as a player, he became a beloved figure for his clowning and the publications in which he told his story. While the self-deprecating humor of his books has been echoed by later figures such as Bob Uecker, the role of baseball clown no longer exists, and perhaps the game is poorer for it.

★

See Schacht's memoir, written with Murray Goodman, *Clown-ing Through Baseball* (1941). *GI Had Fun* (1946), also written with Murray Goodman, is an account of his World War II tours with the USO. Al Schacht and Ed Keyes, *My Own Particular Screwball* (1955), provides a more complete account of his life. *Current Bi-ography 1946* has a thorough discussion of Schacht's life up to that time. An obituary is in the *New York Times* (16 July 1984).

ARTHUR D. HLAVATY

SCHLAMME, Martha Haftel (*b.* 25 September 1922 in Vienna, Austria; *d.* 6 October 1985 in Jamestown, New York), folksinger and actress known for her renditions of music by Kurt Weill and her belief that the music and peo-ple of different countries had much in common.

Martha Schlamme said that her parents were refugees all their lives; they fled from Russia and Poland to settle in Vienna in 1921; when Adolf Hitler annexed Austria in 1938, they left for France and then England where they were placed in an internment camp on the Isle of Man during World War II. Meier Haftel and his wife, Gisa Bra-ten Haftel, ran a kosher restaurant in Vienna. An only child, Martha sang for their international clientele. Her grandfather said it was a pity she wasn't a boy because then she might grow up to be a cantor.

As anti-Semitism became more blatant in Vienna, a syn-agogue in the building where the family lived was burned, and they decided to leave. Martha was sent to stay with relatives in France, while her mother got a job cooking for a family in England, where, after several months, she suc-ceeded in reuniting the family, her husband being hired as a butler. Having attended public school in Vienna, Martha was enrolled in England in a Jewish school, but when her parents were interned as "enemy aliens" on the Isle of Man, she chose to join them. There, she decided to sing the music of many countries. Watching a performance in several lan-

Martha Schlamme. ARCHIVE PHOTOS

guages by Icelandic folksinger Engel Lund, Martha was "dumbfounded" to learn that someone from a different culture could re-create the music her grandfather had sung to her in Vienna. She resolved to become an international folksinger: "I have always felt that people are very much alike all over the world. . . . The same holds true for the music of different peoples." She was convinced that what mattered most in singing music of other countries was to capture the spirit and character of the song. "I can never have been born in Yugoslavia, and I can never be a Russian Gypsy or Scottish lass, but in my effort to be an artist, I have glimpses of their worlds, and the joy I derive from trying to re-create them for listeners is indescribable."

After the war, Martha married Hans Schlamme, and, in 1948, they left for the United States. She found work singing at a Jewish resort in the Catskill Mountains in New York. She developed her singing career and through the 1950s made some 1,000 appearances at colleges and clubs throughout the country. She also became a popular recording artist, producing fifteen record albums for such labels as Vanguard, Folkways, MGM, and Columbia Records, including *German Folk Songs* (n.d.), *Israeli Folk Songs* (1953), *Martha Schlamme Sings Jewish Folk Songs* (1957), *Martha Schlamme Sings Folk Songs of Many Lands* (1958), *Martha Schlamme Sings Jewish Folk Songs, Vol. 2* (1959), *Martha Schlamme in Concert* (1961), *The World of Kurt Weill in Song* (1962), and *A Kurt Weill Cabaret* (1963).

During this time, many agreed with a *Chicago Tribune* critic who wrote that "Miss Schlamme lifts the folk song to a high art." A *Los Angeles Times* critic pointed out: "She is not only an expert linguist but also brings something special and unexpected in the way of interpretation to each song in general and each verse in particular. This she has in common with the best Lieder singers." As her music developed, Schlamme studied voice with Lieder singer Emmy Heim (in London), with Marinka Gurewich, Hans Heinz, and, eventually, Jennie Tourel and her teacher, Olga Ryss. Later, she herself became a teacher of song interpretation and acting, at the Aspen Music Festival in Colorado, and in New York at the Circle in the Square Theater School and the H. B. Studio.

Schlamme frequently gave benefit performances, such as one for the National Association for the Advancement of Colored People, and met well-known figures, such as Pete Seeger, involved in leftist politics. At a fundraiser for the defense of Julius and Ethel Rosenberg, she met attorney and Democratic politician Mark Lane (later investigator of the assassination of John Kennedy). Her first marriage had ended in the early 1960s, and Schlamme married Lane, but they eventually separated because she felt he was too preoccupied with politics to make a personal commitment. Later, she was involved in several long-term relationships, but, she said, "didn't bother" to marry again.

In 1963 Schlamme had scheduled sixteen concerts in South Africa, but canceled the tour because some of the songs on her programs made her liable to imprisonment. She said, "I cannot tailor my repertoire to a political climate." Through the 1960s, her performances drew larger audiences to more distinguished venues, including Town Hall in New York City, Hancock Hall in Boston, and the Wilshire-Ebell Theater in Los Angeles, and her interest in theater grew, with performances at such clubs as the Village Gate in New York City, the Gate of Horn in Chicago, and the Ash Grove in Hollywood. In such appearances, Schlamme impressed audiences with what a *New York Times* critic referred to as "her powers of projection and her gift for conjuring up the characters of the people she sang about."

In the early 1960s, she studied acting with actor Morris Carnowsky, who suggested that the songs of Kurt Weill might serve as an appropriate vehicle for her acting skills as well as for her singing. She began including Weill's songs in her concerts. Her first full Weill program had been at a café in Edinburgh, Scotland, called the Howff in 1959, and when Welsh owner-actor Robert Guest opened a second Howff in New York City (near the Bowery), Schlamme was featured with scriptwriter Will Holt in *The World of Kurt Weill in Song*. The show was enthusiastically reviewed and moved to One Sheridan Square in the West Village, then to the Vaudeville Theatre in London, and was recorded by Metro-Goldwyn-Mayer.

She starred as Jenny in *The Three-Penny Opera* at New York's City Center and was featured in *Mahogonny* at the Stratford Festival in Ontario in 1965. Schlamme and actor-director Alvin Epstein sang together in *A Kurt Weill Cabaret* at the Ravinia Music Festival (1967) and in revivals, when the show was sometimes called *Whores, Wars, and Tin Pan Alley*. In just over eighteen years, they played sixty-five engagements, touring the United States and also appearing in Argentina, Brazil, and Israel. Schlamme had made a career of Weill, and, as a *New York Times* critic put it, "These are songs that she has . . . polished to such an extent that every phrase has settled into a consistently revealing interpretation . . . excitement on a level rarely achieved."

On Broadway she debuted as Golde in *Fiddler on the Roof* and also in 1968 in *Solitaire, Double Solitaire* and *A Month of Sundays,* and she acted with the Long Wharf Theater in New Haven, Connecticut, in several productions and at the Edinburgh Festival (1971). By the mid-1970s, she had begun appearing in a one-woman show, "Martha Schlamme in Concert," which she continued to perform for a decade. In 1978 Schlamme underwent a hip operation for a limp she had developed—but observers said she never limped onstage, or when she was folkdancing. When not on tour, Schlamme lived on the Upper West Side of Manhattan. She was five feet six inches, weighed 130 pounds, and had brown eyes. In free moments she liked to play Ping-Pong and bridge—she said she hadn't played enough as a child.

After a successful engagement with Epstein at the Israel Festival in Jerusalem in the summer of 1985, Schlamme returned to Chautauqua, New York, to another performance of her one-woman show. Three thousand tickets had been sold to the amphitheater. When her aged mother died in London on 5 August, Schlamme had to decide whether to return for the funeral or to do the concert on 7 August. Her mother was by then senile and no longer recognized her, so she opted for the latter, and, while onstage, singing a number from *Candide* ("I Am So Easily Assimilated"), she suffered a stroke and went into a coma from which she never recovered. She was hospitalized nearby in Jamestown, New York, and died there.

Memorial services were held at Riverside Church and at Circle in the Square Theater in Manhattan; she was buried at Riverside Cemetery in Saddle Brook, New Jersey. A performance was given in her honor in 1988 to benefit the Martha Schlamme Scholarship Fund at Circle in the Square Theater School.

In an interview in August 1979, Schlamme said, "I prefer songs that have some bite. . . . The truth is that much of it is a comment on the tragedy of war and the insensitivity of governments. . . . Onstage I sing cynical songs [but] I have a deep-seated faith that everything will be all right. . . . I try to communicate this to audiences." Deeply affected by the nationalism that was such a factor throughout her youth, Schlamme made a major contribution to the radical internationalization of the folksong genre and the successful transplantation to America of middle-European cabaret culture.

★

"The Art of Folk Singing," *Music Journal* (May 1963), describes Schlamme's approach to international folksinging. See also Debra Weiner, "Martha Schlamme: Surrealistic Journey," *Soho Weekly News* (25 May 1978); and Allen Robertson, "Martha Schlamme: Triumphant Survival," *Minnesota Daily* (5 Jan. 1979). Jane Katz, *Artists in Exile* (1983), is a book based on a 1979 interview of Schlamme conducted in Aspen, Colorado. Obituaries are in the *New York Times* (8 Oct. 1985), *Daily Variety* (8 Oct. 1985), and the *Times* of London (15 Oct. 1985).

VERNE MOBERG

SCHNEIDER, Alan (*b.* 11 December 1917 near Kharkov, Ukraine; *d.* 3 May 1984 in London, England), stage director famed for his productions of Samuel Beckett, Edward Albee, and Harold Pinter.

The only child of physicians Leopold Victorovich Schneider and Rebecka Samoilovna Malkin, Abram Leopoldovitch

Alan Schneider, 1964. AP/WIDE WORLD PHOTOS

Schneider spent his early childhood in Rostov-on-Don, USSR. After moving to Moscow in 1921, the family emigrated to America in 1923, settling in Hartford, Connecticut, and then in Sabillasville, Maryland. The family, naturalized in 1928, moved to Baltimore in 1930, where Schneider attended Forest Park High School. In 1935 he entered Johns Hopkins University to study physics, but switched a year later to the University of Wisconsin, Madison, where he majored in political science and graduated magna cum laude in 1939. Preoccupied with college theatricals, he directed his first play, Valentin Katayev's *Squaring the Circle,* in 1938.

After college he worked in summer stock, staged plays for a black high school, was an announcer at radio station WBAL in Baltimore, was public relations director for the Washington (D.C.) Civic Theatre, and wrote speeches for U.S. Postmaster General James Farley. He earned an M.A. in theater from Cornell University in 1941, writing his thesis on theater artist-theorist Nikolai Evreinov. That year he received a draft deferment for physical reasons.

Schneider, although Jewish, joined the faculty of Catholic University in 1941, where he worked part and full time through 1953, teaching speech and theater and directing twenty-one plays, classic and modern. He enjoyed exploring the parameters of the "theater theatrical" associated with Vsevolod Meyerhold and Evgeni Vakhtangov, a brand of theater that expressly draws attention to its own artifice and conventionality. He later joined the Actors Studio, where Lee Strasberg's "method" became equally influential, teaching him to avoid external "results" in favor of an actor's inner truth and a script's subtextual life. He liked to believe that his work combined the best ideas of Strasberg and theatricalist Tyrone Guthrie.

Meanwhile, Schneider worked for various government agencies during World War II, including the Office of War Information, Public Health Service, and Treasury Department, and acted in a Broadway flop called *Storm Operation* (1944). He began to direct professionally in the summer of 1947 at the 6,000-seat outdoor Cain Park Theater, Cleveland, debuting with George S. Kaufman and Moss Hart's *You Can't Take It with You*. His first New York production was a showcase of Tennessee Williams's one-act *The Long Goodbye* (1947), for Studio 63, a group he founded. He followed with a noncommercial Broadway staging of *A Long Way from Home* (1948), Randolph Goodman and Walter Carroll's all-black adaptation of Maxim Gorky's *The Lower Depths*. In 1949 Schneider spent six months teaching and directing at Dartington Hall, a cultural center in England. He remained more interested in artistic expression than commercial ventures. His developing ideas were often revealed in lectures and magazine and newspaper articles.

In England, Schneider in 1949 married a woman whose anonymity he preserved after their marriage was annulled the following year. He married Eugenie Rosa Muckle on 23 March 1953. They had two children and from 1959 lived mostly in Hastings-on-Hudson, New York.

Schneider's nonuniversity assignments accumulated in the early 1950s, when he directed on Cape Cod, off-Broadway, and in Houston. Most significantly, in 1951 he became involved with Washington's new Arena Stage, whose inception he claimed to have inspired and where he formed a lasting relationship with Arena's cofounder, Zelda Fichandler. At the Arena he directed everything from Williams's *The Glass Menagerie* (1951), his maiden effort and one he believed among his career's best, to Michael Weller's *Loose Ends* (1979). The thirty-six other plays he directed at the Arena included mainly twentieth-century plays by Eugene O'Neill, Thornton Wilder, William Saroyan, Bertolt Brecht (an outstanding 1961 production of *Caucasian Chalk Circle*), Arthur Miller, Anton Chekhov, Beckett, Albee, and Gorky, among others. He loved the challenges of moving actors about within the three-dimensionality of theater-in-the-round and became one of its leading practitioners; being a true eclectic, however, he staged plays in all available venues, large and small.

Schneider's commercial Broadway debut was a production of Liam O'Brien's comedy *The Remarkable Mr. Pennypacker* (1953); it was a hit and he subsequently staged close to thirty other Broadway productions, only a few succeeding with audiences. The longest runs belonged to *Pennypacker;* Guy Bolton's *Anastasia* (1954); Albee's *Who's Afraid of Virginia Woolf?* (1962), for which Schneider won a Tony award; and Robert Anderson's *You Know I Can't Hear You When the Water's Running* (1967). But hating the Broadway rat race, where his occasional attempts at moneymakers lost as often as did more serious choices, and yearning to do only plays he cared for, he willingly worked off-Broadway, in far-flung regional and university theaters, and in foreign countries. In short, he went wherever a project stimulated his intellectual juices. His total output came to more than 200 plays, in addition to eight television works and one movie, the prize-winning *Film* (1964), written by Samuel Beckett and starring Buster Keaton.

Schneider's relationship with Beckett began with the American premier of *Waiting for Godot* (1956), a fiasco as a result of the producer's decision to open it in Miami—a poor choice where few understood it—and taken over by someone else for Broadway, although Schneider later staged several other versions. Schneider became the Irish playwright's designated American interpreter and introduced all of Beckett's dramas to the United States, including *Endgame* (1958), *Krapp's Last Tape* (1960), and *Happy Days* (1961), often staging the same play on several occasions. He had a similarly close connection with other towering playwrights, principally Albee, ten of whose plays he staged, and Britain's Harold Pinter, whose *The Birthday Party* (1967) was one of nine plays by the dramatist that Schneider directed. Michael Weller and Robert Anderson were others with whose plays Schneider was associated. He preferred elusive plays to those whose meanings were readily understandable, but he insisted on asking playwrights dozens of questions to help him in his preparations. His productions usually sought to express the playwright's ideas, not his own conceptualizations, and exemplified so-called invisible direction.

Schneider's dense career included a stint as critic for the *New Leader* (1962–1963), the headship of the Juilliard Theatre Center (1976–1979), and various university professorships, including running the graduate directing program at the University of California, San Diego (1979–1984). When he died, from head injuries after being struck by a motorcycle while in London to direct a play, he was president of Theatre Communications Group. Schneider's ashes were scattered at sea.

The bespectacled, youthful-looking Schneider was a demanding, often fiery tempered yet deeply humane man, known for his erudition (he received several prestigious research grants), for his ever-present baseball or Greek fisherman's cap, and for frequently firing actors. He was important in establishing arena staging, in developing America's regional theaters, in demonstrating how a noteworthy directorial career could be built by dedicating oneself to the work instead of to the dollar sign, and for furthering the acceptance of Beckett, Albee, and Pinter.

★

Schneider's excellently detailed posthumous autobiography is *Entrances: An American Director's Journey* (1986), which ends before 1970; a second volume had been planned. One of many interviews is Richard Schechner, "Reality Is Not Enough," *Tulane Drama Review* (spring 1965). Among Schneider's numerous articles are "Director As Dogsbody," *Theatre Quarterly* (April–June 1973), and "What Does a Director Do?" *New York Theatre Review* (spring/summer 1977). Further information is in John W. Frick and Stephen M. Vallillo, *Theatrical Directors: A Biographical Directory* (1994); Samuel L. Leiter, *The Great Stage Directors: 100 Distinguished Careers of the Theatre* (1994). See also Gerald Weales, "Alan Schneider on Broadway," *Journal of American Drama and Theatre* (fall 1995). An obituary is in the *New York Times* (4 May 1984).

SAMUEL L. LEITER

SCHWARTZ, Arthur (*b.* 25 November 1900 in Brooklyn, New York; *d.* 3 September 1984 in Kintnersville, Pennsylvania), composer best known for his many popular songs.

Schwartz was the son of Solomon Samuel Schwartz, a lawyer, and Dora Grossman, homemaker. Ironically, his father allowed his elder son to have a musical education but forbade the young Schwartz to study music and insisted that he become a lawyer. Nonetheless, he taught himself to play the harmonica and the piano, becoming good enough at the latter by age fourteen to become an accompanist for silent films at a Brooklyn movie house. He also began to invent tunes at an early age. He graduated from Boys High School in Brooklyn in 1916. He received a B.A. degree in English in 1920 from New York University and a master's degree in English literature from Columbia University the following year. He taught English at a New York City high school while studying law at Columbia. After earning his law degree in 1924, he practiced law in New York City.

Schwartz published his first song in 1923; it bore the awkward title "Baltimore Md., You're the Only Doctor for Me." The following year he collaborated with the budding lyricist Lorenz Hart in writing songs for shows at a boys' camp in the Adirondack Mountains; several of the songs were later inserted in Broadway shows. He had three songs in an off-Broadway revue, *The Grand Street Follies,* in 1926; a year later he contributed songs to another revue, *The New Yorkers.* In 1928 he gave up the practice of law to take his chances as a full-time songwriter.

At first, Schwartz worked primarily as an anonymous creator of vaudeville show scores and troubleshooter for foundering musicals. In 1929, however, he began a long-

Arthur Schwartz. FRANK DRIGGS/ARCHIVE PHOTOS

time collaboration with another New Yorker, Howard Dietz, then the director of advertising and publicity for the Metro-Goldwyn-Mayer movie studio and an aspiring, part-time lyricist. Together they wrote most of the songs for *The Little Show,* a successful musical revue of that year. Their contributions included a tribute to a famous New York mercantile establishment, "Hammacher Schlemmer I Love You," and the romantic ballad, "I Guess I'll Have to Change My Plans," often cited as Schwartz's first important song. They next wrote lyrics and music for *The Second Little Show* in 1930 but that production was unsuccessful. They then collaborated on another revue of 1930, *Three's a Crowd.* This show included Dietz and Schwartz's enduring classic song "Something to Remember You By."

In 1931 Dietz and Schwartz wrote the score for the highly successful revue *The Band Wagon,* often considered to be their finest collaboration. The show included the songs "New Sun in the Sky," "High and Low," "Confession," "I Love Louisa," and, above all, "Dancing in the Dark," often considered to be Schwartz and Dietz's finest song and certainly by far their best-known creation. Still another revue, *Flying Colors,* appeared in 1932. It included several notable songs, including "Alone Together," "A Shine on Your Shoes," and "Louisiana Hayride." In 1934 Dietz and Schwartz created their first musical with an integrated plot or "book." Titled *Revenge with Music,* it was based upon the Spanish novel *El Sombrero de Tres Picos* (The Three-Cornered Hat) by Pedro de Alarcón. It included two hits, "You and the Night and the Music" and "If There Is Someone Lovelier Than You." In July 1934 Schwartz married the actress Katherine Carrington; they had a son. In 1935 the revue *At Home Abroad,* which included the song "Love Is a Dancing Thing," was produced. Two years later Dietz and Schwartz collaborated on the book musical *Between the Devil,* which included "By Myself" and "I See Your Face Before Me."

Schwartz was forced to seek new collaborators in the late 1930s when Dietz found himself obliged to spend more time on his movie publicizing career. Schwartz wrote the musical show *Virginia* with the lyricist Albert Stillman in 1937; it was not a success. He then began working with the experienced and talented lyricist Dorothy Fields. Their collaboration produced *Stars in Your Eyes* (1939), a musical comedy satire on the making of a Hollywood musical, which included the songs "This Is It" and "The Lady Needs a Change." Between 1939 and 1946 Schwartz worked in Hollywood, writing songs for a series of films, including *Thank Your Lucky Stars* (1943) and *The Time, the Place, and the Girl* (1946). He also produced the movies *Cover Girl* (1944) and *Night and Day* (1946), a film biography of Cole Porter.

Schwartz returned to the New York stage in 1946, when he collaborated with Ira Gershwin on the musical *Park Avenue,* which was unsuccessful. He worked again with Dietz on the revue *Inside U.S.A.,* which ran on Broadway for more than a year beginning in 1948. He next collaborated again with Fields in writing *A Tree Grows in Brooklyn* (1951) and *By the Beautiful Sea* (1954). Although *A Tree* in particular was considered to have a fine score, neither of these book musicals was a commercial success. Following the death of his wife in 1954, Schwartz married Mary O'Hagon Scott that same year; they had one child. In 1958 he became a director of the American Society of Composers, Authors, and Publishers (ASCAP), a licensing organization to ensure the commercial rights of composers and authors; he held the post for twenty-five years.

In 1961 Dietz and Schwartz created the musical comedy *The Gay Life,* based on Arthur Schnitzler's *Affairs of Anatol.* Although it too was considered to be an excellent score, it was not commercially successful. Schwartz and Dietz's final collaboration was the musical *Jennie* in 1963, which was not a success. Schwartz moved to London, England, in 1969. He sang a selection of his own songs on a phonograph recording released in 1976. He returned to the United States and settled in Kintnersville, Pennsylvania, where he died after suffering a stroke.

Despite his lack of formal musical education, the self-taught Schwartz became in his lifetime a consummate professional and a highly respected composer of popular songs. Stanley Green has observed that Schwartz's numerous book musicals were all largely unsuccessful, primarily because he never found a good librettist. His most successful creations therefore were, and will probably remain, the collections of songs that he wrote with Howard Dietz for the musical revues of the 1930s. The finest and most perceptive tribute to Schwartz was made by Alec Wilder in his book *American Popular Song:* "Arthur Schwartz wrote some splendid songs. They have the character and sinew of the best of theater music. None of these songs concern themselves with anything but the American musical atmosphere of the time."

★

Howard Dietz, *Dancing in the Dark* (1974), an anecdotal autobiography, has disappointingly little detail about his longtime collaboration with Schwartz. Stanley Green, *The World of Musical Comedy,* 3d ed. (1974), has a brief history of the collaborations of Schwartz with Dietz and with Dorothy Fields. Alec Wilder, *American Popular Song: The Great Innovators, 1900–1950* (1972), offers a perceptive, if somewhat technical, analysis of what the author considers Schwartz's best songs. The best biographical sketch of Schwartz is in *Current Biography Yearbook* for 1979. Obituaries are in the *New York Times* and *Variety* (both 5 Sept. 1984).

JOHN E. LITTLE

SCOTT, Austin Wakeman (*b.* 31 August 1884 in New Brunswick, New Jersey; *d.* 9 April 1981 in Boston, Massachusetts), trusts expert, legal scholar, and one of Harvard Law School's most prominent professors.

Scott was one of seven children of Austin and Anna Prentiss (Stearns) Scott. His father was a prominent educator at Rutgers College in New Brunswick, New Jersey, and enjoyed a forty-year career in higher education as a professor of history, political economy, and constitutional law and as president of Rutgers for fifteen years (1891–1906). Austin's father inspired in his son a keen interest in education and scholarly activities. Austin once stated that he was the son of a "poor but respectable college president." He and his three brothers and three sisters were educated at home prior to their formal education. Austin attended Rutgers Preparatory School from 1890 until 1899, then entered Rutgers College that fall. He excelled in his studies and graduated in 1903 with a B.A. degree in mathematics and a Phi Beta Kappa key.

Upon graduation from Rutgers, Scott accepted a teaching position at his alma mater, Rutgers Preparatory School,

Austin Scott. NYT PICTURES/NYT PERMISSIONS

where he taught mathematics for three years (1903–1906). In addition to teaching young students at the prep school, Scott was called upon by his former Rutgers classmates, many of whom had entered law school, to assist them with their legal studies. He read law books and reinterpreted the treatises for his former classmates; he thus began teaching law long before he entered law school. Prompted by his successful tutoring and his fascination with the law, Scott entered Harvard Law School in 1906.

Scott was both "delighted and excited" by the study of law, sentiments that were documented in the many letters he wrote to his family in New Brunswick. Scott was on the editorial board of the prestigious *Harvard Law Review* during 1907 and 1908. He excelled in his studies and impressed his fellow students and the faculty alike. Scott graduated in 1909 and became a clerk at the New York firm of Winthrop and Stimson. He was admitted to the New York bar in 1910 and the Massachusetts bar in 1911.

In January 1910, Dean James Barr Ames of Harvard Law School died. Scott was asked by a former law professor of his if he would consider taking over the dean's teaching duties. He accepted the position and was appointed to the Harvard Law School faculty as an instructor. Throughout the first semester of his appointment at Harvard, he continued his employment at the law firm of Winthrop and Stimson, commuting from New York to Boston. In 1910, at the end of his first spring semester, he was promoted to assistant professor; he left his New York law firm and thus began his career at Harvard in earnest. He would teach over twelve different classes throughout his long career at Harvard, but he developed a particular interest in the study and teaching of trusts, the area of law in which property is administered for another person.

In the 1911–1912 academic year Scott took a leave of absence from Harvard to serve as dean of the college of law at Iowa State University in Iowa City. He returned to Harvard in 1914 and was promoted to full professor. In 1915 Scott was asked to serve as acting dean of Harvard Law School, a post he filled for half a year. Scott was subsequently asked by Harvard to assume the role of dean several times, but he declined any additional invitations and chose teaching over administrative responsibilities.

Scott married Esther Kendall on 12 June 1914. They had two sons, Austin Wakeman Scott, Jr., and Gordon Kendall Scott. Both of his sons attended Harvard College, were honor graduates of Harvard Law School, and chose careers in higher education. Austin taught trusts at the University of Colorado, and Gordon Kendall became a law professor at Stanford University in California.

Scott joined Company K of the Harvard Regiment ROTC in 1918 and served as a major. The following year Harvard honored Scott by naming him Story Professor of Law, a position he held from 1920 to 1928. In 1928 he was elected president of the Association of Law Schools. He was honored once again by Harvard in 1938 when he was named Dane Professor of Law. While his popularity as both teacher and colleague grew, he continued to devote many hours to the study of trusts. In 1939 Scott wrote *Scott on Trusts,* which in its fourth edition (1987) comprises nine volumes and is considered an authority on its subject. Harvard University Law School awarded Scott with its highest faculty distinction, the Ledlie Prize, for the second edition of his *Treatise on Trusts* in 1956. In addition to these publications, Scott wrote, coauthored, and edited articles in legal and scholarly journals throughout his career at Harvard. Included among his many publications are *Cases on Civil Procedure* (1914), *Fundamentals of Procedure in Actions at Law* (1922), and *Cases on Trusts* (1951). He was also a reporter for trusts for the American Law Institute.

Students and faculty at Harvard informally referred to Scott as "Scotty" and "Mr. Harvard Law School." He was fond of saying that there were three wishes he had for his career: to teach, to teach the law of trusts, and to teach the law of trusts at Harvard Law School. He exceeded even his own expectations. He was nearly seventy-six years of age at his retirement from Harvard's faculty in 1961. Harvard granted him emeritus status on 1 July 1961. Although retired, he maintained an office at Harvard, where he continued his scholarly work, revising his many publications. In 1974 the university named a professorship after Scott. In addition to the honors Harvard bestowed on Scott, he was also a fellow of the American Academy of Arts and Sciences and a member of the Academie Internationale de Droit Compare. He was granted an honorary membership in the Society of Public Teachers of Law in Great Britain and Northern Ireland.

Scott died following a brief illness resulting from gastric carcinoma at Brigham and Women's Hospital in Boston. Although his funeral was private, memorial services were held at Harvard's Memorial Church two weeks following his cremation. On the momentous occasion of his retirement from Harvard in 1961, when asked to summarize his lengthy and distinguished career, Scotty stated, "You can say of me, as Chaucer said of his Clerk of Oxenford, 'And gladly would he learn and gladly teach.' "

★

Austin Wakeman Scott, *Scott on Trusts,* 4th ed. (1987), is considered the standard work of authority on the topic of trusts. Among Scott's other significant works are *Cases on Trusts* (1951), *Treatise on Trusts* (1956), and *Letters from a Law Student to His Family, 1906–1908* (1974). Two major tributes by his colleagues and former students include *Perspectives of Law: Essays for Austin Wakeman Scott* (1964), edited by Roscoe Pound, Erwin N. Griswold, and Arthur E. Sutherland; and *Austin Wakeman Scott: Some Reminiscences of Students, Colleagues, and Friends* (1974), a pamphlet published by Harvard Law School to raise funds for the endowment of a professorship of law to honor Scott. Obituaries are in the *New York Times* (10 Apr. 1981) and *Newsweek* and *Time* (both 20 Apr. 1981).

LOIS CHEREPON

SCOTT, Hazel Dorothy (*b.* 11 June 1920 in Port of Spain, Trinidad; *d.* 2 October 1981 in New York City), pianist, singer, and civil rights activist known for her distinctive piano style, her outspoken views on racism, and her marriage to the controversial congressman Adam Clayton Powell, Jr.

Hazel Scott was the only child of R. Thomas Scott and Alma Long Scott. Her father, a black scholar from Liverpool, England, emigrated to Trinidad to teach at St. Mary's College. Her mother, a Trinidad native and the daughter of a prominent architect, was a talented musician.

A gifted child, Hazel was reading at age three and playing piano by ear at four. In 1924 the family emigrated to Harlem in New York City, where they lived in a four-story private house and Alma Scott tutored her precocious daughter on piano. At age eight, Hazel auditioned at the

Hazel Scott performing in Brooklyn, 1940s. JOSEPH SCHWARTZ COLLECTION/CORBIS

Juilliard School of Music. Although she was too young to enroll, her performance of a Rachmaninoff Prelude so impressed Professor Paul Wagner that he accepted her as his private student. In 1933 she played her first formal piano recital in New York City.

Her mother supplemented the family income by teaching piano and playing saxophone in various jazz bands. Billie Holiday, Art Tatum, Bud Powell, and Lester Young often visited the Scott home and influenced Hazel's musical development. After her husband died in 1934, Alma Scott formed her own all-female band, featuring Hazel on piano; thus, Hazel spent much of her childhood in the adult world of music. In 1938 she made her Broadway debut in *Sing Out the News.* In 1939 she was a featured performer at the New York World's Fair; she also made her recording debut that year with the Sextet of the Rhythm Club of London.

A turning point came in 1939 when Barney Josephson hired her to play at Cafe Society, his Greenwich Village nightclub, notable at that time for its integrated clientele. Scott's unique way with classical works by Chopin and Liszt, first playing them straight, then interjecting swinging rhythms and hints of boogie-woogie, quickly gained her a following. When Josephson opened his posh Cafe Society Uptown on East Fifty-eighth Street in 1940, she became his star performer. Soon she was "swinging the classics" at

New York's Paramount and Roxy theaters; she made her Carnegie Hall debut in December 1940.

An attractive woman with large dark eyes and a winning smile, Scott exuded glamour, performing in elegant evening gowns. She returned to Broadway in *Priorities of 1942* and appeared in several films: *I Dood It, The Heat's On,* and *Something to Shout About* (all 1943), *Broadway Rhythm* (1944), and *Rhapsody in Blue* (1945). By then her recordings, "Swinging the Classics," "Mighty Like the Blues," "Calling All Bars," and "Boogie-Woogie," had earned her national acclaim.

Throughout the 1940s Scott was an outspoken proponent of civil rights. She refused to appear before segregated audiences. During World War II she often performed at war bond and civil rights rallies and became romantically involved with a powerful Abyssinian Baptist minister and rising liberal Harlem politician, Adam Clayton Powell, Jr. In 1944 Powell was elected to the U.S. House of Representatives and, though still married to his first wife, brought Scott with him to Washington, D.C., for his swearing-in ceremony in January 1945. The Powells divorced, and on 1 August 1945 Powell married Hazel Scott in Stamford, Connecticut, amid media fanfare.

After the honeymoon, Scott departed on a national concert tour, but Powell urged her to perform in Washington. She sought an October 1945 concert date at Constitution Hall, but the Daughters of the American Revolution (DAR) controlled the bookings and refused to allow Scott to perform because she was black. Recalling that in 1939 First Lady Eleanor Roosevelt had resigned from the DAR after a similar incident involving Marian Anderson, Powell asked President Harry Truman to intercede, but he demurred. When First Lady Bess Truman subsequently attended a DAR social function, Powell publicly referred to her as the "last lady of the land." The incident drew extensive media attention and caused a rift between Powell and Truman that continued throughout Truman's presidency.

For a time after the birth of their son, Adam Clayton Powell III, in July 1946, Scott curtailed her performances. Then, perhaps due to her appearances at civil rights rallies and her marriage to the controversial Powell, Scott's name appeared on a list of entertainers alleged to be communist sympathizers. On 22 September 1950 she testified before the House Un-American Activities Committee. In a prepared statement she said: "I will maintain my fight for the application of our liberties to all regardless of color and creed. . . . [T]he fact that communists pretend to stand for the causes for which I stand will not make me abandon the battle." Asked if she was a member of the Communist party, she said: "I am not now, never have been, have never entertained the idea, and never will become a member."

Nonetheless, her career suffered, and during the 1950s she found more opportunities in Europe. By 1956 her marriage was foundering; in 1957 she moved to Paris with her son. She performed widely in Europe and appeared in a French film, *Disorder in the Night* (1958). In December 1960 she obtained a Juarez, Mexico, divorce from Powell, but they remained friends until his death on 4 April 1972. While living in Paris, she married Ezio Bedin, a white European; their brief marriage also ended in divorce.

Scott returned to the United States in 1967 and appeared in such television series as *Julia* and *CBS Playhouse 90*. During the 1970s she performed in New York City nightclubs and in 1972 issued the recording *Hazel Scott Live at the St. Regis Hotel*. In 1978 she was inducted into the Black Filmmakers Hall of Fame. She continued working until shortly before her death from pancreatic cancer.

Although Scott launched her career by "swinging the classics," her later work featured blues, jazz, rock, and show tunes that displayed her consummate piano technique and jubilant personality. According to *New York Times* jazz critic John Wilson, she had "an unusual ability to . . . find the right interpretive qualities, whether she's singing a ballad or a blues or making her piano jump." Scott took great pride in her African roots, fought for racial justice throughout her career and helped pave the way for other black women artists.

★

Donald Bogel, *Brown Sugar: Eighty Years of America's Black Female Superstars* (1980), contains photographs and a short biography; D. Antoinette Handy, *Black Women in American Bands and Orchestras* (1981), contains a short entry on Scott. Arthur Taylor, *Notes and Tones: Musician-to-Musician Interviews* (1993), an expanded edition of his 1982 book, includes his 1972 interview with Scott. Charles V. Hamilton, *Adam Clayton Powell, Jr.: The Political Biography of an American Dilemma* (1991), includes some material on Scott, but a more extensive treatment is in Wil Haygood's *King of the Cats: The Life and Times of Adam Clayton Powell, Jr.* (1993). L. Robinson, "Hazel Scott Comes Home to the Action," *Ebony* (Mar. 1968), offers an interview with and photos of Scott after her return from Paris; other articles on Scott are in *Ms.* (Nov. 1974) and *Essence* (Nov. 1978).

A newsclip file on Scott is located at the Institute of Jazz Studies, John Cotton Dana Library, at the Newark campus of Rutgers, the State University of New Jersey. An obituary appears in the *New York Times* (3 Oct. 1981). Audio materials include *Hazel Scott Boogie-Woogie Piano Transcriptions* (1943), which has a classical and a boogie-woogie version of each piece; *Forty Years of Women in Jazz: A Double Disc Feminist Retrospective*, which has one cut of a Scott solo piano (1952); and *The Women: Classic Female Jazz Artists, 1939–1952,* which has two cuts of Scott on piano with the Sextet of the Rhythm Club of London (1939). A videotaped interview with Scott is in *Hazel Scott Remembers* (1980), directed by Peter Pontillo and produced by Orde Coombs. In the film, she speaks of her Hollywood career, her marriage to Powell, and her life in Paris in the early 1960s.

SUSAN FLEET

SCOURBY, Alexander (*b.* 13 November 1913 in Brooklyn, New York; *d.* 22 February 1985 in Boston, Massachusetts), stage, radio, film, and television actor and narrator who recorded more than 500 Talking Books for the American Foundation for the Blind.

Alexander Scourby was one of four children of Constantine Nicholas Scourby, a successful restaurateur and baker, and Betsy Pataskos, both immigrants from Greece. He grew up in Brooklyn, where he belonged to a Boy Scout troop. Later, he was a cadet with the 101st National Guard Cavalry Regiment. He attended public and private elementary schools in Brooklyn. After a short stay at Polytechnic Prep School, he completed his secondary education at Brooklyn Manual Training High School, graduating in 1931. At Manual Training he was coeditor of the school magazine and yearbook and a member of the dramatic society. His first stage appearance was at Manual, in *The Meanest Man in the World.* Intending to study journalism, Scourby matriculated at West Virginia University in Morgantown, West Virginia. Because of his father's death, however, Scourby

Alexander Scourby demonstrating one of his Talking Book Records, 1951. UPI/Corbis-Bettmann

stayed only until the beginning of his second semester, leaving in 1932 to help operate the family's pie bakery.

Shortly after his return to Brooklyn, Scourby served as an apprentice at Eva Le Gallienne's Civic Repertory Theatre on West Fourteenth Street in Manhattan. There he studied dance, speech, and makeup. His first Broadway role, at the Imperial Theatre on 10 November 1936, was as the Player King in *Hamlet,* starring Leslie Howard. Over the years he had many stage roles in plays by Shakespeare, Jean-Paul Sartre, Federico Garcia Lorca, George Bernard Shaw, and others. Usually, he played the suave villain. Norman Nadel, drama critic for the *New York World Telegram and Sun,* commented on his interpretation of Gorotchenko in *Tovarich,* a 1963 Broadway musical: "The signal tribute to Alexander Scourby . . . was the hearty hissing opening night as he strolled on stage. In polished villainy, he has no peer." Scourby played Tami Giacopetti, a tough racketeer, in *Detective Story* in 1949; Peter Cauchon, bishop of Beauvais, in *Saint Joan* in 1951; and Rakitin in *A Month in the Country* in 1956. He won critical acclaim in 1961 for his portrayal of King Claudius in *Hamlet,* one of his final appearances on the New York stage. He later acted in plays staged by the Hartford Stage Company, for whom in 1979 he played the title role in Bertolt Brecht's *Galileo.*

In addition to the stage, Scourby was active in radio, television, and film. In the 1940s he had major radio roles in serial melodramas and narrated the André Kostelanetz musical program as well as many dramatic shows, including *The Eternal Light* and *Superman.* During World War II he worked for the Office of War Information, broadcasting in both English and Greek.

Although he maintained contact with the stage, partly through summer stock, and with radio as well, he turned more and more to television and film. In television he worked as both actor and narrator. He had major television roles in dramas presented by *Playhouse 90, Circle Theater,* and *Studio One* and occasional parts in series such as *Daniel Boone* and *The Defenders.* He narrated such programs as "The World of Maurice Chevalier," "The World of Jacqueline Kennedy," "The World of Bob Hope," and "The Body Human."

Scourby also narrated the scripts for numerous nature and historical documentaries, as well as drama and musical show commentaries. He hosted national opera broadcasts and provided the voice-overs for television commercials. He narrated the script for both a 1952 movie version of *Victory at Sea* and a condensed ninety-minute version of the television series of the same name, broadcast in 1960. He hosted the Metropolitan Opera's *Live from the Met* on public television.

Beginning in the 1950s Scourby became known for his film roles, appearing with Glenn Ford in *Affair in Trinidad* (1952), *The Big Heat* (1953), and *Ransom* (1956); as a Greek officer in the Korean War in *The Glory Brigade* (1953); and in *The Silver Chalice* (1959), *The Big Fisherman* (1959), and *Confessions of a Counterspy* (1960). Perhaps his greatest role was as the old Mexican ranch foreman in *Giant* (1956).

It was for his sensitive interpretation and precise, resonant bass voice that Scourby was most famous. "Everybody talks about my voice," he said in a 1966 interview. "Oh, I suppose they mean it as a compliment. But what actor wants to be known as a voice?"

But it is for his voice that Scourby will be best remembered. Rich and mellifluous, his voice widened the horizons of the blind by making available to them the great works of literature. Scourby had been introduced to the Talking Books Program of the American Foundation for the Blind in 1937 by Wesley Addy, a fellow cast member of Leslie Howard's *Hamlet*. At first Scourby was given small parts in plays, but later he narrated novels. "That was the beginning," he noted. "The recordings for the blind are perhaps the greatest achievement." In time the foundation would award him its Certificate of Merit.

Over more than forty years, Scourby narrated more than 500 books, including *The Iliad, War and Peace, Les Misérables, The Great Gatsby,* and *Leaves of Grass.* However, his best-loved and most famous recording was the King James Bible. He prepared meticulously for the reading of each of its sixty-six books, taking four years to record the set, which was released in 1966 and became a best-seller. His expressive bass voice enhanced the profound meaning of the scriptures, and he became known as the "Voice of the Bible." Scourby's narration was used for *The New Scenic Wonders Video Bible,* which depicts beautiful nature scenes, accompanied by original music. The entire New Testament, on eleven videos, won the 1994 Angel Award from the Video of the Month Club.

On 12 May 1943, Scourby married Lori von Eltz, an actress known to television, stage, and film audiences as Lori March. They had residences in Manhattan and in Newtown, Connecticut. The couple had one child. A slim five feet, ten and one-half inches, Scourby had black hair and blue-green eyes. An amateur photographer and an avid reader, he had a compassionate heart and a creative imagination. He usually voted Democratic. Although not affiliated with any particular religion, he was baptized in the Greek Orthodox Church and married in the Episcopal Church.

Scourby was in Boston, Massachusetts, hosting a National Public Radio production of Handel's opera *Semele* when he died suddenly of cardiac arrest. He is interred in a columbarium in "The Little Church Around the Corner" (Church of the Transfiguration) on East Twenty-ninth Street in Manhattan.

Scourby's prodigious work on stage, radio, television, and screen may no longer be readily available, but his vibrant rendering of the classics of literature will continue to bring joy and satisfaction to multitudes, especially to the blind.

★

Scourby's papers are in the New York Public Library and include correspondence, scripts, clippings, and photographs. A sketch can be found in Charles Moritz, ed., *Current Biography 1965* (1966). See also *Who's Who in the Theatre,* 17th ed., vol. 1 (1981). *Narrated by Alexander Scourby: A Tribute to Mr. Scourby* (1986) is an audiocassette issued by the American Foundation for the Blind. An obituary is in the *New York Times* (24 Feb. 1985).

RUTH S. KENNEY

SEASONGOOD, Murray (*b.* 27 October 1878 in Cincinnati, Ohio; *d.* 21 February 1983 in Cincinnati, Ohio), lawyer and mayor of Cincinnati who won national recognition as a good-government reformer.

The youngest of four children of Alfred Seasongood, a Jewish immigrant from Bavaria and prominent clothing merchant in Cincinnati, and Emily Fechheimer, Murray attended public elementary schools and began his secondary education at Cincinnati's Woodward High School. In 1895 the family embarked on an extended tour of Europe, during which Murray and his brother attended Edgebor-

Murray Seasongood, 1929. COURTESY OF JON HOFFHEIMER

717

ough School in Guildford, England. In 1896 Murray enrolled in Harvard University, graduating magna cum laude four years later. At Harvard, he was a member of the debate team, and in 1900 he was elected Ivy Orator and chosen one of the commencement speakers. After receiving his A.B. degree, Seasongood remained at Harvard, earning an A.M. degree in 1901 and an LL.B. in 1903.

Returning to Cincinnati, Seasongood was admitted to the bar in 1903 and joined the firm of Paxton and Warrington. During the next two decades he established his reputation as one of Cincinnati's leading attorneys. On 28 August 1912 he married Agnes Senior; they had one child.

During the second decade of the twentieth century, Seasongood became involved in public affairs, serving as a member of the Ohio Commission for the Blind from 1915 to 1925. In 1915 he was also appointed a member of the executive and advisory committee of the local Republican party. Composed in part of leading citizens, this committee was supposed to provide a respectable facade for the city's Republican organization, led by Rudolph K. Hynicka. The head of a chain of burlesque theaters, Hynicka had succeeded the notorious political boss George B. Cox as Republican leader of Cincinnati and had continued to dole out city and county jobs on the basis of party loyalty. Angered by this violation of the merit system, Seasongood resigned from the executive and advisory committee after a year of service and became an increasingly outspoken foe of Hynicka and his organization.

In 1923 Seasongood stepped up his opposition when he denounced a tax-levy proposal sponsored by the Hynicka-backed city administration. In a debate before the Cincinnatus Association, a local civic group, Seasongood attacked the corruption and inefficiency of Cincinnati's city government and urged voters to reject the levy in the upcoming referendum. "It is a crime what the people of Cincinnati are undergoing," Seasongood told the assembled group, "not only in the matter of receiving nothing for their money, but in being drugged into a state of lethargy that is fast making the city a laughing stock." Local newspapers reported these charges, and Seasongood's attack was soon labeled "the shot heard 'round the wards." Seasongood conducted a one-man crusade against the levy, and on election day the proposal suffered defeat.

This defeat of the Republican organization galvanized other reform-minded Cincinnatians, and in 1924 the City Charter Committee, which included Seasongood, proposed a new framework of government for Cincinnati. Under the proposed charter, the city would be governed by a nonpartisan city manager and a small council elected by proportional representation. Seasongood again applied his oratorical talents to the cause of reform, and after a vigorous campaign, Cincinnati's electorate approved the city-manager charter by a vote of 92,000 to 41,000. The Charter

Committee then proposed a slate of candidates for the first council under the new charter, and in 1925 this Charterite ticket carried six of the nine council seats. Among those elected to the council was Seasongood. Following the election, the council's Charterite majority chose Seasongood as the first mayor under the city-manager plan. As mayor he chaired the council and performed the ceremonial functions of city executive, while the manager, C. O. Sherrill, was in charge of administering the municipal departments.

From 1926 to 1930 Seasongood held the mayor's office, and during these years Cincinnati won a reputation as the nation's best governed city. The pace of street construction and repair increased notably, a new electric franchise secured lower rates for Cincinnati consumers, civil service rules were strictly enforced, and the city tax rate dropped. In 1929 Seasongood chose not to run for reelection, but by the close of his service he had won a nationwide reputation as a municipal reformer.

Building on this reputation, Seasongood served as president of the National Municipal League from 1931 to 1934. In 1932 he was selected to deliver the Godkin Lectures on government at Harvard; these lectures were published in book form as *Local Government in the United States: A Challenge and an Opportunity* (1933). While continuing his law practice, he also taught at the University of Cincinnati Law School from 1925 to 1959 and was visiting professor of law at Harvard from 1947 to 1948. Moreover, he compiled a widely used casebook on municipal corporations and wrote innumerable articles and delivered countless speeches on municipal reform. Government and law, however, were not his only concerns. Devoted to his Jewish heritage, Seasongood served as a member of the Hebrew Union College board of governors from 1913 to 1942 and as a member of the executive committee of the American Jewish Committee from 1938 to 1947.

A man of seemingly indefatigable energy, Seasongood continued to go to his law office until he was 100. He died at the age of 104 and was buried at United Jewish Walnut Hills Cemetery in Cincinnati.

Murray Seasongood was one of the most articulate and effective municipal reformers of the first half of the twentieth century. Imbued with a Progressive-era devotion to honesty and efficiency in government, he conducted a righteous crusade against bossism in Cincinnati and throughout America. During his long life, his devotion to good government never flagged as he sought to teach the nation as a whole the lessons learned in his native city.

★

Seasongood's papers are in the Cincinnati Historical Society. In *Local Government in the United States: A Challenge and an Opportunity* (1933), Seasongood described his reform efforts in Cincinnati. Charles P. Taft, *City Management: The Cincinnati Experiment* (1933), offers the best account of the charter movement. In her foreword to *Selections from Speeches (1900–1959) of Murray Seasongood* (1960), Agnes Seasongood presents a brief sketch of her husband's life and achievements. The best article on his life and work is William A. Baughin, "Murray Seasongood—Cincinnati's Civic Warrior," *Queen City Heritage* 46 (winter 1988): 35–39. A tribute to Seasongood marking his 100th birthday appears in the *National Civic Review* 67 (Oct. 1978): 393–394, 396–401. Obituaries are in the *New York Times* (23 Feb. 1983) and *National Civic Review* 72 (Mar. 1983): 126.

JON C. TEAFORD

SERT, José Luis (*b.* 1 July 1902 in Barcelona, Spain; *d.* 15 March 1983 in Barcelona, Spain), architect, urban planner, and teacher of design whose work integrated individual buildings with their surroundings and adapted the enlivening features characteristic of Mediterranean architecture.

Sert was the son of Francisco Sert and Genara López, and the nephew of the muralist José Maria Sert. The Catalan form of his name is Josep Lluis Sert. No record of any siblings exists. He started out as a painter but in 1921 enrolled at the Escuela Superior de Arquitectura in Barcelona. Influenced by the proposals of Le Corbusier for an archi-

José Luis Sert. ARCHIVE PHOTOS

tecture for "the city of tomorrow," Sert and his fellow students began to protest against their formal beaux arts training and to work on designs more responsive to urban social needs. In 1929 Sert received his master's degree in architecture and went to Paris to work in Le Corbusier's atelier, where they collaborated on plans, never realized, for the League of Nations headquarters. During his stay in Paris, Sert established lifelong friendships with such artists as Pablo Picasso and Joan Miró, both fellow Catalonians; Fernan Léger; and the American sculptor Alexander Calder.

Later in 1929 Sert set up a practice in Barcelona. He became an active member of the International Congresses for Modern Architecture (CIAM) and helped prepare the influential manifesto known as the Athens Charter of 1933, a codification of CIAM precepts for modern urban redesign. His earliest buildings include the Casa Bloc, a Barcelona complex of 200 low-rent apartments and social service facilities (1934–1936), and a tuberculosis clinic (1935). Between 1933 and 1935 Sert worked with Le Corbusier on a master plan for his native city, calling for its rezoning and the eradication of slums.

After the start of the Spanish civil war in 1936, the government appointed Sert codesigner, with Luis Lacasa, of the Spanish Pavilion for the Paris Exposition of 1937. His building, with its movable partitions and uncluttered spaces, served as an effective backdrop for art exhibitions and dramatic presentations that revealed the suffering of the Spanish people. For this pavilion, Picasso painted *Guernica* (1937), and Miró created a mural of an embattled Catalonian peasant. As Sert later affirmed, the relationship between the visual arts and architecture was always basic to his work. In 1938, he married Ramona Longás; they had one daughter. With the fall of the republic in 1939, he and his wife immigrated to the United States.

Settling in New York City, Sert, a bespectacled man who spoke with a pronounced accent that he never lost, established a group practice, Town Planning Associates, with Paul Lester Wiener and Paul Schulz. Between 1939 and 1942 they drew up plans for various cities in Latin America, taking into account the social needs of the urban underclass and, as far as possible, preserving the natural surroundings. During the 1944–1945 academic year, Sert taught city planning at Yale University. In 1945, the Brazilian government commissioned Sert and his associates to generate Cidade dos Motores (Motor City), a new industrial town to be built near Rio de Janeiro. From 1947 to 1956, Sert, who was respected for his tactful leadership, served as CIAM president.

In 1948 Sert's firm designed a workers' community in Chimbote, Peru. Ranging in scale from small, single-family houses to a civic center, the units were all conceived on the patio plan in Mediterranean style. Between 1949 and 1953, his group drew up plans for the cities of Cali, Medellín, and, in collaboration with Le Corbusier, Bogotá, Colombia. In 1951, Sert became a naturalized U.S. citizen. He joined the Harvard University faculty in 1953 as professor of architecture and dean of the Graduate School of Design. Appointed consultant to the Cuban government planning office, Sert worked from 1955 to 1958 on a redevelopment plan for Havana that provided for the capital's growth while preserving the old city center. Also in 1955, the U.S. State Department commissioned him to design the American embassy building in Baghdad, which was completed in 1960.

In 1958 Sert opened a new design partnership in Cambridge, Massachusetts, Sert, Jackson, and Associates. "An urban campus," Sert once declared, "is a cultural center within a city, and should set an example of good planning and . . . design. . . . It is, in a way, a micro-city." According to this concept, he designed Harvard's Holyoke Center (1958–1965), a multifacility office and shopping complex serving both town and campus; and Peabody Terrace (1963–1965), high-rise dormitories for married students that were sited and provided with public facilities to create a sense of community. Sert's university architecture also includes Boston University's Charles River Campus (1960–1967) and structures for Guelph University in Ontario (1964–1966).

In 1969 Sert retired from Harvard as professor emeritus. He designed the Harvard Undergraduate Science Center in 1970. In the 1970–1971 academic year he lectured at the University of Virginia in Charlottesville as the Thomas Jefferson Memorial Foundation Professor of Architecture. He next turned his attention to two apartment complexes in the New York area that were built between 1971 and 1975. Eastwood Housing, on Roosevelt Island in the East River, and Riverview Housing, a publicly assisted project along the Hudson River in Yonkers, demonstrated his guiding principle that high-rise, multiunit housing could provide both privacy and a feeling of community. In 1977, the American Institute of Architects awarded Sert's partnership its Architectural Firm Award. Working again in Cambridge, he planned the West Campus housing complex for the Massachusetts Institute of Technology (1981).

Sert's smaller, more intimate structures are strongly reminiscent of the architecture of his native region. Built with central courtyards, patios, open plans, and sunscreens to filter light, they employ natural materials and often include bright-colored ceramic exterior tiles. In this style, he built a studio for Miró in Palma de Mallorca, Spain (1955–1956); his own home in Cambridge, adapted for a northern setting (1958); the Fondation Maeght Museum in Saint-Paul-de-Vence, France (1959–1964); and the Center for the Study of Contemporary Art, built for the Miró Foundation in Montjuïc Park, Barcelona (1972–1975).

In 1982 José Luis Sert returned to Spain and completed his last project, the Porta Catalana Road Service building complex, along the border with France. He died of cancer in Barcelona.

Sert was the recipient of international professional honors. Among them, he was awarded the Gold Medal of the American Institute of Architects in 1981 for designs, in the words of the citation, "so influential and far-reaching . . . that the social awareness and concepts of artistic collaboration that he brought to the practice of architecture have become almost commonplace."

★

A file of Sert's papers from 1952 to 1982 is maintained in Harvard University's Loeb Design Library. He was the author of *Can Our Cities Survive? An ABC of Urban Problems, Their Analysis, Their Solutions* (1942), based on the 1933 Athens Charter; and coauthor with James Johnson Sweeney of the monograph *Antoni Gaudí* (1961; rev. 1970). He contributed numerous articles to American architectural journals. A biographical sketch of Sert is in Muriel Emanuel, ed., *Contemporary Architects,* 3d ed. (1994). Studies in English of his work include Knud Bastlund, *José Luis Sert: Architecture, City Planning, Urban Design* (1967), with an introduction by S. Giedion; Maria Lluïsa Borràs, ed., *Sert: Mediterranean Architecture* (1975); Katsuhiko Ichinowatari, ed., *Josep Lluis Sert: His Works and Ways* (1982); J. Freixa, *Josep Ll. Sert,* 3d ed. (1995); and J.M. Davern, "AIA Gold Medalist, 1981: Josep Lluis Sert," *Architectural Record* 169 (May 1981): 96–101. Obituaries are in the *New York Times* (17 Mar. 1983) and by Willo von Moltke in *Progressive Architecture* 64 (June 1983): 27.

ELEANOR F. WEDGE

SESSIONS, Roger Huntington (*b.* 28 December 1896 in Brooklyn, New York; *d.* 16 March 1985 in Princeton, New Jersey), Pulitzer Prize–winning composer and educator who, though his works were considered difficult for general audiences to appreciate, had a major influence on the development of twentieth-century music.

Roger Sessions was the third of four children of Archibald L. Sessions and Ruth Gregson Huntington Sessions, who married in 1887. Both of his parents descended from an established New England family that had been in America since the early seventeenth century; they were second cousins.

Ruth Sessions was trained as a musician and had studied at the Leipzig Conservatory. An accomplished writer, she was also active in a variety of political causes throughout her life. Archibald Sessions was trained as a lawyer but gave up his practice to pursue a literary career when Roger was around four years old. The dissolution of Archibald's law practice caused financial hardship for the family, and Ruth Sessions decided to move with her children to her ancestral home of Hadley, Massachusetts, where she ran an off-

Roger Sessions. REPRODUCED COURTESY OF THE SIMON & SCHUSTER CORPORATE DIGITAL ARCHIVE. © CLEVELAND PUBLIC LIBRARY.

campus house for Smith College students in neighboring Northampton. Sessions's parents thus remained married but lived apart for the next twenty-five years, a situation that Roger Sessions later described as rather puzzling for the children.

Roger began taking piano lessons at the age of four. In 1906 he was sent to the Cloyne boarding school in Newport, Rhode Island, but he was uncomfortable with the school's highly regimented program and left after three months. From 1908 to 1911 he attended the Kent School in Kent, Connecticut. In 1909 he began to compose, and in 1910 he completed an opera titled *Lancelot and Elaine,* based on Tennyson's *Idylls of the King.* At this time he also declared his intention to be a composer to his parents, who offered encouragement.

Sessions entered Harvard University in 1911, at the age of fourteen. During his four years at Harvard he discovered the music of other contemporary composers, including Arnold Schoenberg, Igor Stravinsky, Claude Debussy, and Aleksandr Scriabin. He also wrote and edited articles for the *Harvard Musical Review,* a short-lived periodical that

existed from 1912 to 1916. He graduated from Harvard with a B.A. in 1915, at the age of eighteen.

In the fall of 1915 Sessions entered Yale University, where he began the study of composition with Horatio Parker. He received a B.Mus. degree from Yale in 1917, and also received Yale's Steinert Prize for the first movement of his Symphony in D Major. Following his graduation from Yale he was offered a teaching position at Smith College. He met his first wife, Barbara Foster, while at Smith; they were married in 1920.

Sessions found the musical and academic environment at Smith to be less than inspiring for his compositional development, and he left in 1921 to become Ernest Bloch's assistant at the Cleveland Institute of Music. Sessions had first met Bloch in 1919, and acknowledged him to be his most influential and significant composition teacher. When Bloch was asked to leave the faculty of the Cleveland Institute in 1925, Sessions resigned along with him.

In 1923 Sessions was commissioned by Smith College to compose music for a production of Leonid Andreyev's 1908 play, *The Black Maskers.* The incidental music was premiered at Smith in June 1923 under the composer's direction, and is considered to be his first major work.

From 1925 to 1933 Sessions lived primarily in Europe, receiving financial support from his father (who died in 1927), as well as two Guggenheim Fellowships (1926, 1927), an American Academy in Rome fellowship (1928), and a Carnegie Foundation grant (1931). Unlike the many American artists who centered themselves in Paris in the years preceding World War II, Sessions resided primarily in Florence (which he found to be particularly agreeable), in Rome, and in Berlin. From 1928 until 1931 he also collaborated with Aaron Copland on the Copland-Sessions concerts, which presented performances of contemporary music to audiences in New York. Sessions was in Berlin in 1933 when Adolf Hitler came to power. He was profoundly affected by the events he witnessed there, and wrote passionately about the dangers of fascism and the Nazi terror.

Sessions quickly reestablished his teaching career upon his return to the United States in August 1933, teaching briefly at the Malkin Conservatory, the Boston Conservatory, the New School for Social Research, and the Dalcroze School in New York. In 1935 he joined the faculty at Princeton University, where he remained until 1944. From 1945 until 1953 he was professor of music at the University of California, Berkeley. He returned to Princeton as William Shubael Conant Professor of Music in 1953, remaining there until 1965, when he was forced to step down at the mandatory retirement age of sixty-eight. He then joined the faculty of the Juilliard School in Manhattan, and also held the positions of Ernest Bloch Professor at Berkeley from 1966 to 1967 and Charles Eliot Norton Professor at Harvard from 1968 to 1969. Over the course of his career,

Sessions taught some of the most noted American composers, including Milton Babbitt, David Diamond, Andrew Imbrie, Earl Kim, Leon Kirchner, Eric Salzman, and Ralph Shapey.

Sessions and his first wife became estranged in the early 1930s and divorced in September 1936. On 26 November 1936 he married Sarah Elizabeth Franck, a librarian and relative of the composer César Franck. They had two children. Sarah Sessions (who was known as Lisl) died on 9 July 1982.

Sessions composed over forty works in all genres, including nine symphonies, a Violin Concerto (1930–1935), a Piano Concerto (1955–1956), a Concerto for Violin, Cello, and Orchestra (1970–1971), the operas *The Trial of Lucullus* (1947) and *Montezuma* (1947–1963), three piano sonatas, two string quartets, and the cantata *When Lilacs Last in the Dooryard Bloom'd* (1964–1970). The latter is considered to be his most accessible work. He tended to favor large compositional forms, and wrote relatively few minor works. He received numerous honors and awards, including a special career citation from the Pulitzer Prize Committee in 1974, and the 1982 Pulitzer Prize for his Concerto for Orchestra.

Sessions also wrote numerous important articles and books, including *The Musical Experience of Composer, Performer, Listener* (1950), *Harmonic Practice* (1951), *Reflections on the Music Life in the United States* (1956), and *Questions About Music* (1970). A number of his essays were collected by Edward T. Cone as *Roger Sessions on Music: Collected Essays* (1979).

Sessions taught at the Juilliard School until 1983. During the last years of his life he resided in Princeton and continued to compose. He suffered a stroke in February 1985, and died of pneumonia in a Princeton hospital on 16 March. He was cremated and his remains were interred in the Old Hadley Cemetery in Hadley, Massachusetts, near the graves of his parents.

Although many of Sessions's works were commissioned and performed by major orchestras and soloists during his lifetime, and were highly respected by his fellow composers, his music was difficult for general audiences to appreciate. As the music critic Donal Henahan wrote in Sessions's *New York Times* obituary, "Mr. Sessions enjoyed such esteem among his fellow composers and other musicians that it was once remarked by one of his colleagues that 'everybody loves Roger Sessions except the public.' " Despite the lackluster popular reception of his music, Roger Sessions had a significant influence on twentieth-century musical life.

★

The manuscripts of Sessions's compositions are housed primarily in Princeton University, the Library of Congress, and the New York Public Library. The most substantial documentary work on Sessions has been published by Andrea Olmstead in *Roger Sessions and His Music* (1985), which contains a bibliography, *Conversations with Roger Sessions* (1987), and *The Correspondence of Roger Sessions* (1992). The latter source includes extant letters to and from Sessions written over the course of his lifetime. There is an entry on Sessions in *The New Grove Dictionary of American Music* (1986), edited by H. Wiley Hitchcock and Stanley Sadie. A tribute with contributions by many of Sessions's fellow composers and students is in *Perspectives of New Music* 23, no. 2 (spring-summer 1985). An obituary by Donal Henahan is in the *New York Times* (18 March 1985). Oral history interviews with Sessions are in Columbia University's Oral History Collection and at Yale University.

JANE GOTTLIEB

SEYMOUR, Whitney North (*b.* 4 January 1901 in Chicago, Illinois; *d.* 21 May 1983 in New York City), lawyer, civic leader, and president of the American Bar Association, a self-described "simple, barefoot Wall Street lawyer."

Seymour was one of two sons of Margaret Lucinda Rugg and Charles Walton Seymour, a New York lawyer who ceased practice in 1888 to pursue a life of reading history and lecturing. Whitney was born in Chicago but raised in Faribault and Madison, both in Wisconsin, where he enjoyed an idyllic childhood, working on farms to earn money

Whitney North Seymour, 1951. ARCHIVE PHOTOS

and spending one summer as a Yellowstone Park ranger. At the University of Wisconsin (1916–1920), Seymour excelled in debate and served in the student senate but lost his bid for the senior class presidency to the future actor Fredric March. At Columbia Law School, Harlan Fiske Stone, the school's dean and future associate justice of the U.S. Supreme Court, was among Seymour's many friends, one of many Supreme Court justices he came to know. Before his 1923 graduation, Seymour taught constitutional and administrative law at the City College of New York, and on 17 June 1922 the busy scholar married Lola Virginia Vickers. Their apartment at 170 Sullivan Street in Greenwich Village was for years a kind of salon for lawyers and academics.

After graduation from Columbia in 1923 the new attorney joined Simpson, Thacher, and Bartlett, his firm for the rest of his career. He rose rapidly in the firm while teaching law at New York University (1925–1931), making partner in 1929. From 1931 to 1933 Seymour was assistant solicitor general in President Herbert Hoover's administration, and argued thirty-five cases before the Supreme Court during that time. Seymour considered his Washington tenure the "most fascinating" time of his life, remembering both appearances before the Court and having tea with the justices. Reluctantly resuming New York practice, Seymour, a Republican, was asked in 1934 by Democratic friends to handle the appeal of Angelo Herndon, a black communist sentenced to twenty years on a chain gang for leading a march of unemployed Georgians on Atlanta. Although his first appeal failed on procedural grounds, Seymour persevered and in 1937 won the case *Herndon* v. *Lowry* by a 5–4 vote. Herndon's actions posed no danger to society, the Court ruled; therefore, the Reconstruction-era anti-insurrection statute under which he was prosecuted did not apply to him. Georgia's other evidence, the communist literature in his possession, did not warrant conviction because, according to the Court, merely to advocate communism was not insurrectionary. Seymour's concern for civil liberties also involved him in the *Kessler* v. *Strecker* decision (1939) barring deportation of communists and put him "on the fringe" of the Scottsboro case. His lifelong commitment to First Amendment liberties included service on the board of the American Civil Liberties Union from 1938 to 1953. Delivering the Charles Evans Hughes Lecture before the New York County Lawyers' Association in 1970, Seymour declared that seeking "equal justice" for all Americans was the key to his life.

Legal expertise and high ideals made Seymour's professional rise almost meteoric. Replacing Thurman Arnold, he taught New York Practice at Yale University from 1935 to 1945, but his first love was litigation. "I am a court lawyer. ... I have spent all my life in the courtroom," he once observed, and despite his claim never to have written out

an argument, his presence at legal proceedings was Olympian. Serving the profession became Seymour's hallmark, and during his career he at least twice rejected proffered judgeships. From 1941 to 1942 he led the executive committee of the Association of the Bar of the City of New York. His affection for the group's landmark structure on West Forty-fourth Street was legendary and for years he chaired its house committee. Seymour believed lawyers must serve all members of society, and he served as president of the Legal Aid Society of New York between 1945 and 1950. In 1950 he began his two-year term as president of the Association of the Bar just as McCarthyism appeared on the scene. Seymour used his presidential letter to condemn annual loyalty oaths for lawyers and, during a time of self-described "spiritual schizophrenia," maintained the independence of his profession. Equally ardent was his belief that judges ought never to be popularly elected.

During the 1950s both honors and duties accrued to Seymour. He served as president of the American Arbitration Association (1953–1955) and was a member of New York's Temporary Commission on the Courts led by Harrison Tweed (1953–1958). His 1954 American Bar Association (ABA) study on the interaction of personal rights and national security helped create the Uniform Code for Congressional Investigations (1955). Always aware of police abuses, he chaired a special ABA committee that insisted on court orders for all electronic eavesdropping and recommended that evidence gathered without warrants be dismissed; the ABA accepted the recommendation in 1958. Seymour was far ahead of his age in recognizing that television coverage of trials created a "circus atmosphere," as he called it in 1958, that was incompatible with justice. When in 1960 he became president of the American Bar Association, the *New York Times* noted the triumph of "a New Yorker who once successfully defended a Negro Communist." Seymour used his Annual Address in August 1961 to laud the "unity of the bar" and extol legal brotherhood. His personal credo declared that the "first duty of a lawyer is to nourish and preserve and defend an independent bench and bar."

Despite decades of achievement, Seymour never sought elective office. Believing it "useful to have a few Republicans" active in New York City politics, he willingly served on Mayor John V. Lindsay's judicial appointments committee. However, he confined his own elective ambitions to presidencies of the American Bar Foundation (1960–1964), the American College of Trial Lawyers (1963–1964), and the Institute for Judicial Administration (1968–1969). After he cochaired the Lawyer's Committee for Civil Rights Under Law (1965–1967), the Columbia Law School Alumni Association in 1968 awarded him a medal of excellence, its highest award, lauding his "staunch defense of the rights of the accused to a fair trial and able counsel."

Seymour also led the Council on Library Resources; served Freedom House from 1951 to 1983, including a stint as chairman of the board (1954–1959); and was immensely proud of his work at the William Nelson Cromwell Foundation, which published the legal papers of John Adams and Daniel Webster.

Seymour's courtroom personality was austere but in private he was gregarious and even a bit eccentric. He habitually wore a bowler to work, replacing it in summer with a boater straw hat. In college he had played a single performance with Sarah Bernhardt, and he parlayed that feat into membership in the Players Club. He was eminently clubbable, belonging to the Century Association in New York and the Metropolitan Club in Washington, among others. He enjoyed a drink and at times could be persuaded to perform magic tricks, a lifelong hobby. He was an Episcopalian. Seymour worked to preserve monuments of New York's past, such as Grand Central Terminal and the United States Customs House, and helped draw up the legislation that created the city's Landmarks Commission. His marriage lasted for fifty-three years (his wife died in 1975), and his two sons made successful careers in law and academe. Leslie Ten Eyck, his companion during his last years, was at Seymour's side as he received a medal from the Municipal Art Society in 1976 and had an award named in his honor by the American Arbitration Association in 1977. After his death from cancer, his firm financed a Whitney North Seymour room at the Association of the Bar in 1984, an enduring tribute this "lawyer's lawyer" would have relished. He is buried in Green-Wood Cemetery in Brooklyn.

★

The New York Public Library has Seymour's papers; they are restricted until 2008. Eleanor M. Fox, comp. and ed., *A Visit with Whitney North Seymour* (1984), includes a memoir by Seymour and excerpts from his speeches that reflect his public values. See also *Simpson, Thacher, and Bartlett, the First One Hundred Years, 1884–1984* (1988). An obituary is in the *New York Times* (22 May 1983). Seymour's oral history, recorded in 1977, is available at Columbia University.

GEORGE J. LANKEVICH

SHAW, Irwin Gilbert (*b.* 27 February 1913 in the Bronx, New York; *d.* 16 May 1984 in Davos, Switzerland), playwright, short story writer, and best-selling novelist.

Irwin Shaw was the first of two children born to William Shamforoff, a hat-trimmings salesman, and Rose Tompkins. In 1920 the Shamforoffs moved to Brooklyn, where William changed the family name to Shaw and opened a real estate business. When the real estate market collapsed in 1928, the Shaws were lucky to at first save their home at 2036 Brown Street, but they would lose it before the

Irwin Shaw. HORST TAPPE/ARCHIVE PHOTOS

Great Depression ended. The poverty of these years remained an ever-painful memory for Shaw and provided the theme for "Second Mortgage," an early story.

A precocious student, Irwin graduated from James Madison High School at age fifteen, enrolling in the newly established Brooklyn College in 1929. The young freshman's college dreams were shattered, however, when he was expelled for failing calculus and Latin. Shaw spent the next year working at odd jobs and going to night school, hoping to redeem himself. With the help of Lew Oshins, the football coach, he was readmitted to Brooklyn College the following year. Shaw wrote and was features editor for the school newspaper, edited the yearbook his senior year, participated in the dramatic society, and played quarterback on the football team. After receiving his B.A. in 1934, Shaw found a job in radio, writing scripts for two popular serials—*Dick Tracy* and *The Gumps*. His play *Bury the Dead*, meanwhile, premiered in two benefit performances for the New Theatre League at the Forty-sixth Street Theatre on the weekend of 14 March 1936. The reviews were sensational. Sensing the play's promise, a group of Broadway producers moved it to the Barrymore Theatre where it opened on 18 April 1936 and ran for 110 performances. An overnight success, Shaw was invited to Hollywood to work on a football movie, *The Big Game* (1936). Screenwriting, however, did not deter him from more serious work. Some of Shaw's finest stories, including "The Girls in Their Summer Dresses" and "Main Currents of American Thought," appeared in the *New Yorker* during this period. In 1939 Random House published *Sailor off the Bremen and Other Stories.* That same year, *The Gentle People,* Shaw's last successful play, ran on Broadway. It was later transformed into a popular film, *Out of the Fog* (1941), starring John Garfield and Ida Lupino. While in Hollywood, Shaw met a young actress, Marian Edwards. They married in Beverly Hills on 13 October 1939 and had one child, Adam.

In July 1942, Shaw entered the army, serving in the Signal Corps' moving-picture unit under director George Stevens. While not directly involved in combat, Shaw arrived shortly before or after major battles in North Africa, France, and Germany. Just missing the invasion of Normandy, he was present, along with Ernest Hemingway, when the Allies liberated Paris on 25 August 1944. At Stevens's recommendation, Shaw was promoted to warrant officer before being discharged on 13 October 1945. The war provided Shaw with material for several short stories, including "Walking Wounded," the winner of the 1944 O. Henry Memorial Award First Prize. It also served as the basis for *The Young Lions* (1948), the blockbuster novel that made Shaw famous.

In October 1945, Shaw returned to New York just four days before his play *The Assassin* opened and flopped on Broadway. He served as drama critic for the *New Republic,* taught briefly at New York University, and returned to screenwriting. In 1951 *The Troubled Air,* Shaw's best-selling novel exploring McCarthyism's chilling effect on the entertainment industry, was published. In June of that year, Shaw left for a vacation in France, little knowing that Europe would become home for the next twenty-five years.

In Europe, the Shaws divided their time between Paris and the small ski village of Klosters, Switzerland. Shaw became the center of a group of expatriates that included writer Peter Matthiessen, photographer Robert Capa, and writer James Jones. In 1954 Hollywood bought the movie rights to *The Young Lions* for $100,000; the film rights for *Lucy Crown* (1956) sold for four times that amount two months before the book's publication. Shaw purchased a house in Klosters, which he called Chalet Mia. He had found the perfect spot to work in the morning, ski in the afternoon, and entertain in the evening.

Shaw's critical reputation suffered in the 1960s. Critics complained that he had lost touch with the American scene and had abandoned the idealistic principles of his early work. *Two Weeks in Another Town* (1960), *Voices of a Summer Day* (1965), and *Love on a Dark Street* (1965), Shaw's first collection of stories in eight years, all failed to live up to the high expectations of reviewers. The 1960s also saw

the end of his relationship with Random House and publisher Bennett Cerf, as well as the collapse of his marriage. Tired of Shaw's infidelities, Marian had an affair of her own and announced late in 1967 that she wanted a divorce.

Shaw took his separation from Marian in stride. Despite acrimonious divorce proceedings over the next few years, he produced some of his most popular novels. In September 1970, shortly before the divorce became final, Delacorte Press published *Rich Man, Poor Man.* It remained on the *New York Times* best-seller list for thirty-three weeks and was turned into a television miniseries (1976) seen by more than 50 million viewers. The novels that followed, *Evening in Byzantium* (1973), *Nightwork* (1974), and *Beggarman, Thief* (1977), were all commercially successful.

In May 1975 Shaw returned to New York and settled in the Hamptons on Long Island. He was drinking heavily and his health was deteriorating. Still, there were some bright spots. In 1978 *Short Stories: Five Decades,* a monumental compilation of Shaw's best short fiction, appeared. That same year, Brooklyn College awarded its distinguished alumnus an honorary doctor of literature degree. Encouraged by his son, Shaw and Marian attempted a reconciliation. After a prostate operation in July 1981, Shaw learned he had cancer. He and Marian, who remarried on 3 May 1982 in Klosters, kept his illness secret until his death. As stipulated in his will, the body was cremated and no formal funeral service was held.

In a writing career spanning half a century, Shaw wrote a dozen novels, five published plays, and eighty-four short stories. His books, he once boasted, were "published in twenty-five languages, including Icelandic and Macedonian." Critics had high praise for early stories like "Sailor off the Bremen" and "The Eighty-Yard Run," works that are still widely anthologized and continue to serve as models for undergraduate writing seminars. After *The Young Lions,* however, critics and reviewers, taking their cue from John W. Aldridge (*After the Lost Generation,* 1951), turned against him. Shaw was viewed as a minor writer, a gifted storyteller who had betrayed his art for commercial gain. Shaw lamented his lack of recognition by the American Academy of Arts and Letters, but he bore that neglect more easily after the success of later works, such as *Rich Man, Poor Man* and *Beggarman, Thief.* Asked about his critical reputation by *People* magazine in 1975, he answered: "I don't want to be remembered—I want to be read." At the time of his death, there were 14 million copies of his books in print.

★

The Pierpont Morgan Library in New York City holds the manuscript of *The Young Lions;* typescripts for *Lucy Crown* and *The Troubled Air,* as well as college writings, are available at the Brooklyn College Library. The Random House collection at Columbia University's Butler Library contains substantial correspondence between Shaw and his editors. Additional materials are housed at Boston University's Mugar Memorial Library and at the Harry Ransom Humanities Research Center at the University of Texas, Austin. "The Education of a Brooklyn Son," *New York Times* (12 Sept. 1971), provides autobiographical information on Shaw's early years; "What I've Learned About Being a Man," *Playboy* (Jan. 1984), covers his later life. Interviews appear in the *Paris Review* 1 (1953): 27–49, and 21 (spring 1979): 248–262 (reprinted in *Writers at Work: The Paris Review Interviews,* 5th ser. 1981). Michael Shnayerson, *Irwin Shaw: A Biography* (1989), is a detailed, full-length study. James R. Giles, *Irwin Shaw* (1983), primarily a critical overview, also contains some biographical material. James Slater, "Winter of the Lion," *Esquire* (July 1989), is a moving memoir of his friendship with Shaw. Obituaries are in the *New York Times* and *Washington Post* (both 17 May 1984).

WILLIAM M. GARGAN

SHEARER, (Edith) Norma (*b.* 11 August 1902 in Westmount, Quebec, Canada; *d.* 12 June 1982 in Woodland Hills, California), actress in almost sixty American silent and sound films, six-time Academy Award nominee and one-time winner, and wife of MGM executive Irving Thalberg.

Active in outdoor winter sports as well as swimming, Shearer enjoyed her early years with her parents, Andrew Shearer and Edith Mary Fisher, and her brother and sister. Her father was president of a family lumber and construction company. After home schooling and piano lessons, she enrolled in the Montreal High School for Girls in 1912 and Westmount High in 1914. At age fifteen she won a local beauty contest; captivated by Pearl White's silent film series, *The Perils of Pauline,* Shearer aspired to a film career.

Economic misfortunes in 1919 caused the family's financial downfall and necessitated the sale of their middle-class home; Shearer did not graduate from high school but went to work in sheet music stores. In early 1920 Edith Shearer moved with her daughters to New York City and the three attractive women appeared as extras in *The Flapper* (1920), *The Restless Sex* (1920), and *Way Down East* (1920). The director of the last of these, D. W. Griffith, warned Shearer that her blue eyes would look "blank" in close-ups on film, and Florenz Ziegfeld predicted that her five-foot, two-inch height and lack of dancing ability would preclude a career. Nevertheless, the strong-willed Shearer remained undaunted. Her agent, the future film producer Edward Small, found several roles for her in films, including *The Stealers* (1920), her first full-length feature, and *The Sign on the Door* (1921), with Norma Talmadge (although final editing deleted Shearer's part).

Returning to Montreal in early January 1921, Shearer began modeling for fur coat layouts. In February she re-

Norma Shearer. ARCHIVE PHOTOS

turned to New York, where she modeled for commercial artists Rolf Armstrong, James Montgomery Flagg, and Charles Dana Gibson. A ten-foot poster of her promoting the Springfield Tire and Rubber Company as "Miss Lotta Miles" loomed over Columbus Circle. She later considered these experiences useful in developing a resourceful variety of facial expressions for her silent films.

Small secured two early episodes for Shearer in *The Leather Pushers* series (1922–1924). She appeared in nine feature films released during 1922 and 1923, including her first leads in such films as *Channing of the Northwest* (1922) and *A Clouded Name* (1923). The career break began in 1923, when she signed a contract with the Mayer Company (later Metro-Goldwyn-Mayer, or MGM, after a 1924 merger), one of the top West Coast studios. It provided for a screen test for the lead in *The Wanters* (1923), six months' salary at $250 a week with an option to renew, and transportation for her and her mother to California. Her screen test for *The Wanters* secured only third billing, but her second film, *Pleasure Mad* (1923), entailed a larger role. She soon learned that Irving Thalberg, Louis B. Mayer's new vice president and production assistant, had been impressed with "Miss Lotta Miles," *The Stealers,* and *The Leather*

Pushers and also had been responsible for an earlier offer to her from Universal.

While on loan to other studios for more than a year, she filmed *Broadway After Dark* (1924) for Warner Brothers and *The Wolf Man* (1924) for Fox, her first of three films with John Gilbert. Shearer's first film for the new MGM, released at the end of 1924, was the successful *He Who Gets Slapped,* starring Gilbert and Lon Chaney, Sr. A succession of MGM films followed quickly, including a well-acclaimed performance in *The Snob* (1924) and a dual role in *Lady of the Night* (1925). A 1925 polling of American movie theater owners named Shearer as the fourth biggest box-office attraction, after Marion Davies, Ramon Novarro, and Gilbert.

Three of Shearer's films were released in 1926; the following year she appeared in what some consider one of her finest silent performances, as Kathi, in *The Student Prince,* directed by Ernst Lubitsch. This box-office hit with Novarro was released one week before Shearer's wedding to Thalberg on 29 September 1927. They honeymooned just briefly, then in February 1928 began their first trip together to Europe. They had two children: Irving Grant Thalberg, Jr., and Katharine. Shearer became an American citizen in 1932. *The Latest from Paris* and *The Actress,* both with Ralph Forbes, and *A Lady of Chance,* all released in 1928, were notable among her final silent films. During those early years directors Monta Bell and Sidney Franklin were especially important influences on her acting skills.

When Mayer and Thalberg finally decided to bring MGM into the sound era, Shearer's voice proved ideal and she starred in MGM's second sound picture (and first non-musical talkie), *The Trial of Mary Dugan* (1929). Her second talkie was *The Last of Mrs. Cheyney* (1929), which included costumes by Adrian, who designed most of Shearer's screen wardrobe. With Gilbert and Lionel Barrymore, she did serious and spoof versions of the balcony scene in *Romeo and Juliet* as a Technicolor sequence in *The Hollywood Revue of 1929* (1929). She appeared in *Their Own Desire* (1929), the first of five films with Robert Montgomery, and *The Divorcée* (1930), for which she won the Academy Award for best actress in 1930. Continuing one custom from the days of silent films, she had a pianist and violinist play music on the set. Although she began her silent screen career at $25 per day, by the early 1930s Shearer's contracts with MGM made her one of the highest-salaried actresses of the Great Depression era.

The 1931 box-office hit *A Free Soul* placed Clark Gable, in his first major role at MGM, opposite Shearer, Leslie Howard, and Lionel Barrymore. Shearer acted in screen versions of Noël Coward's *Private Lives* (1931) and Eugene O'Neill's *Strange Interlude* (1932). Fredric March, Howard, and she were popular in their respective dual roles in *Smilin' Through* (1932), for which she was billed as the "First Lady of the Screen." She starred in *Riptide* (1934), her hus-

band's first film as an independent producer at MGM. One of her most important films was *The Barretts of Wimpole Street* (1934), with March and Charles Laughton.

After another extensive absence from acting to care for her husband and children, Shearer and Howard starred in George Cukor's grand-scale direction of *Romeo and Juliet* (1936). Less than a month after the film's New York opening on 20 August, Thalberg, sickly since birth with a weak heart, died.

Weakened herself by pneumonia, Shearer originally intended to retire, but, although the $10 million estate inherited by her and the children made her one of the wealthiest women in the country, she worked out a compromise with the Mayer Group (with which Thalberg had made an unwritten agreement) to assure equitable profits for her children. In 1937 she signed a six-film contract that paid $150,000 per film. The first of the six was *Marie Antoinette* (1938), which was based on the biography by Stefan Zweig and which Thalberg, his wife, and studio production staff had been long preparing. In September she repeated some of the Marie Antoinette role on the *Maxwell House Coffee Radio Hour.* When David O. Selznick revealed in 1937 that Shearer might play Scarlett in his production of *Gone with the Wind,* her fans protested that she was too gracious and gentle to be Scarlett. (The part eventually went to Vivien Leigh.) The other five films were based on well-known plays: *Idiot's Delight* (1939), the highly acclaimed *The Women* (1939), *Escape* (1940), *We Were Dancing* (1942), and the not too favorably received *Her Cardboard Lover* (1942). She retired in 1942.

On 23 August 1942 Shearer married a ski instructor and promoter of Squaw Valley, Martin Jacques Arrougé. When she married Thalberg, she had converted from Christianity to Judaism; before marrying Arrougé at the Church of the Good Shepherd, Beverly Hills, she was instructed in Catholicism but did not renounce her 1927 conversion. By prenuptial agreement, Arrougé had no claim to the Thalberg estate. They traveled with her children in the United States and abroad, and she had a special interest in skiing until she broke her leg in a 1957 skiing accident. Shearer participated in certain Hollywood activities, such as her first presentation of the Irving G. Thalberg Memorial Award in 1945 and the tribute to Mayer as recipient in 1952 of the Screen Producers Guild's second Milestone Award. She also helped to select the actor to play Thalberg in Universal's film about Lon Chaney, Sr., *Man of a Thousand Faces* (1957).

During the late 1970s Shearer's eyesight began to fail, and in September 1980 she became a permanent resident of the Motion Picture Country House and Lodge, in Woodlands, California, where she died of bronchial pneumonia. As prearranged with Arrougé, she was buried next to Thalberg at Forest Lawn Cemetery in Glendale, California.

Norma Shearer graced the silent and sound movie screens of the late 1920s and the 1930s as one of the most lovely and beloved stars; American and British film polls frequently ranked her first in popularity among film actresses. Professionally, she enjoyed a reputation for in-depth study of her roles. Shearer preferred extensive rehearsal time and retakes, an approach that did not always please her directors. She was admired by critics and fans for her gracious charm and feminine dignity, gracefulness in diction and movements, versatility and spontaneity in performing diverse roles, and stunning elegance. Her radiant face complemented the rich and sincere tones of her voice. Behind and on the set she was a sharp businesswoman and technical craftswoman, but the result was an apparently effortless, honest, and durable interpretation.

★

A first-person account is "I'm Tame As a Lion," *American Magazine* (July 1935). Although no exhaustive biographical study of Shearer has been written, two full-length biographies have appeared: Lawrence J. Quirk, *Norma: The Story of Norma Shearer* (1988), and Gavin Lambert, *Norma Shearer: A Life* (1990). Other books with substantial information about Shearer are Joe Franklin, *Classics of the Silent Screen: A Pictorial Treasury* (1959); Bob Thomas, *Thalberg: Life and Legend* (1969); James Robert Parish and Ronald L. Bowers, *The MGM Stock Company: The Golden Era* (1973); Jack Jacobs and Myron Braum, *The Films of Norma Shearer* (1976), consisting of a brief biography and a filmography; Peter Hay, *MGM: When the Lion Roars* (1991); Roland Flamini, *Thalberg: The Last Tycoon and the World of MGM* (1994); and Robert A. Osborne, *Sixty-five Years of the Oscar: The Official History of the Academy Awards* (1994). Informative articles include Jack Jacobs, "Norma Shearer: Her Beauty and Marriage to Thalberg Made Her a Decorative Star," *Films in Review* (1960), and Richard Schickel, "Norma Shearer and Irving G. Thalberg: The Santa Monica Beach House of a Hollywood Genius and His Leading Lady," *Architectural Digest* (Apr. 1990). Obituaries are in the *Los Angeles Times* (13 and 14 June 1983), *New York Times* (14 June 1983), and *Variety* (15 June 1983).

MADELINE SAPIENZA

SHEED, Francis Joseph ("Frank") (*b.* 20 March 1897 in Sydney, Australia; *d.* 20 November 1981 in Jersey City, New Jersey), Catholic writer, lecturer, publisher, and street preacher who, with his wife, Maisie Ward, established the firm of Sheed and Ward, a New York- and London-based publisher that specialized in Catholic theology.

Sheed was one of two sons of Irish parents, John Sheed, a Marxist, who battled alcoholism and worked sporadically as a draftsman, and Mary Maloney, a Catholic of intense

Francis J. Sheed. UPI/CORBIS-BETTMANN

religious faith. His father, of Presbyterian background, had the young Sheed attend Methodist Sunday school but Sheed fell under the religious influence of his mother. His early encounter with Protestantism and Marxism, however, served him well in his writing and lecturing. After graduating from Sidney High School, he attended the University of Sydney, where he earned a law degree in 1922.

Sheed soon after traveled to England on what was intended to be a temporary visit. There he became a member of the Catholic Evidence Guild, whose members distributed pamphlets and spoke in defense of the church in London's Hyde Park and other places. It was while he was a member of the guild that Sheed met Mary Josephine ("Maisie") Ward, a founder of the guild and member of a prominent English Catholic family. They were married in April 1926 and had two children: Wilfrid, a well-known novelist, and Rosemary, a prizewinning translator.

The following October the couple founded Sheed and Ward, which became famous as a vehicle for Catholic writers, including Sheed himself, who wrote dozens of titles under its imprint, including *Communism and Man* (1938),

Theology and Sanity (1947), and translations of Saint Augustine and other Catholic thinkers. His *Communism and Man,* unlike other Catholic books on the subject, which tended toward the polemical, was praised by scholars and even some Marxists for its objective view of communism. Early on Sheed and Ward's writers included Hilaire Belloc, G. K. Chesterton, Sigrid Undset, François Muriac, Hans Kung, Edward Schillebeeckx, and Henry de Lubac. Later writers included the American Catholic social activists Dorothy Day and Catherine de Hueck Doherty, as well as the noted preacher and television personality Bishop Fulton J. Sheen and the movie director John Farrow. Sheed and Ward "serviced the incurably brainy and kept them orthodox" by promoting the view that Catholics could be both intellectual and faithful to the teachings of the church, according to Wilfrid Sheed.

"They were very hard parents to explain," Wilfrid wrote about his parents. His father, he recalled, would trudge to Hyde Park in London and publicly pray for rain and preach the truth of Catholicism, often arguing with hecklers including communists and Bible-quoting Protestants. Sheed claimed to have learned much from his street-preaching days, pointing out that a speaker should not seek victory and should not attack his listeners' beliefs. J. M. Cameron described Sheed's approach as "Catholic apologetics at its best" and praised him for avoiding pompous language in his arguments. "For Frank anything that was worth saying was worth saying as plainly as the subject manner permitted," Cameron wrote in an article in the *New York Review of Books* (8 May 1986).

In 1933 Sheed and Ward opened an office in New York City. Sheed soon became a fixture on the American Catholic lecture circuit, drawing large crowds at parish halls and colleges for his scholarly discourses on church teaching. The family moved to the United States in 1940, living at various times in New York City, Jersey City, and Pennsylvania (Sheed never became a U.S. citizen, however).

Sheed assisted British intelligence in prewar America, as a counterforce to the influence of Father Charles E. Coughlin, a popular Detroit radio preacher and anti-Semite who vehemently opposed U.S. support for Britain and was eventually silenced by his bishop after pressure from Franklin D. Roosevelt's administration was brought to bear on the Catholic hierarchy. Sheed traveled throughout the United States, Britain, Europe, and Australia, directing the publishing firm and lecturing.

In a church dominated by clericalism, Sheed brought a different perspective into American Catholicism by his very presence. It was rare—particularly when Sheed began speaking to American Catholic audiences—for a layman to discuss theology publicly. His devotion to the church and his intelligent orthodoxy proved that laypeople could articulate and credibly defend and explain the faith. Chal-

lenged to defend Catholic teaching on the permanence of marriage and responding to charges that the church dissolved marriages only involving the wealthy and the privileged, Sheed wrote *Nullity of Marriage* (1959), a defense of church doctrine on what constitutes a permanent marital bond, comparing it to the concept of nullity in civil law.

A staunch defender of the British Empire even in the postwar era, Sheed was a critic of Britain's welfare state. He generally refrained from political comment, however, because he published the views of many sides and believed that saving souls was more important than scoring political points. He was a strong proponent of the Catholic church's renewal and opening to the world at the Second Vatican Council (1963–1965) and saw the council as a ratification of what Sheed and Ward's publishing efforts represented.

He soon grew disillusioned with many of the theological reformers who flourished after the council, however, and argued that they were tinkering with basic Catholic beliefs concerning the Eucharist and the nature of the church. He expressed alarm about the exodus of clerics in the 1960s and early 1970s who left the priesthood in order to marry. He also criticized conservatives who reacted against changes brought by the council, such as celebrating the Mass in the vernacular instead of Latin.

Sheed promoted loyalty to the church. In *Meeting Christ,* published three years before his death, Sheed argued that both Catholic reformers and traditionalists had lost their bearings by arguing "without reference to Christ, simply forming their own view of what needs doing, and either not adverting to Christ or assuming his agreement."

His wife, Maisie, died in 1975. Sheed, a man with a ruddy complexion and wispy hair who wore rumpled suits, was beset by his own ill health. He sold Sheed and Ward, but continued to write, publishing *Christ in Eclipse* in 1978. In this final book he ruminates on how Christ himself seems to be missing from modern Christianity.

Upon his death, Sheed was widely recognized for providing a reasoned view of the Catholic faith animated by a love for Scripture and church teaching. According to Cameron, Sheed's lay status, combined with his wit and scholarship, challenged "the fundamental ethos of American Catholicism, an ethos represented by Father or Sister knows best." He is buried in Jersey City, New Jersey.

★

Sheed's papers are at Notre Dame University in South Bend, Indiana. His *The Church and I* (1974) is considered to be the most autobiographical of his writings. Besides those works mentioned, he wrote more than forty books, including *Society and Sanity* (1953) and *To Know Christ* (1962). The most detailed account of his life is *Frank and Maisie: A Memoir with Parents* (1985) by his son, Wilfrid Sheed. Obituaries are in the *New York Times* (21 Nov. 1981) and *London Times* (24 Nov. 1981).

PETER FEUERHERD

SHEPPARD, Eugenia Benbow (*b.* ca. August 1900 in Columbus, Ohio; *d.* 11 November 1984 in New York City), fashion editor and syndicated columnist who revolutionized the style of fashion writing.

Sheppard's parents were James Taylor Sheppard and Jane Benbow. Her father's profession is unknown, and her mother was a professional singer who gave up her career in favor of marriage. Sheppard graduated from the Columbus School for Girls, then graduated cum laude with a B.A. degree from Bryn Mawr College in Bryn Mawr, Pennsylvania, in 1921. Throughout her life, Sheppard declined to disclose her age and spoke little about her background. She did admit that she began to write at the age of seven and that writing was what she always wanted to do. Of her days at Bryn Mawr, she commented, "It's either for students or girl athletes and I wasn't either one." In one of her articles, "The Party Peak" (*Harper's Bazaar,* November 1968), Sheppard hinted at the season of her birth when she spoke of coming to a party dressed as her sign of the zodiac, "roaring like a lion."

Sheppard's first job after graduation from college was for the *Columbus Evening Dispatch* in Columbus, Ohio. She was assigned to the society pages. In 1921 she married Samuel Black; they had one child. Active in the local Junior League, Sheppard published two short plays in the Junior League Plays series: *Cinderella: A Play for Children in Three Acts* (1928); and *The Pink Fox: A Comedy in Four Acts* (1932). After divorcing Black, Sheppard married Preston Wolfe. That marriage also ended in divorce, in 1938. In 1938 Sheppard moved to New York to become a fashion writer at *Women's Wear Daily.* Always eager to succeed, Sheppard gladly accepted even the worst assignments. One rainy night she was the only *Women's Wear Daily* reporter to travel to a fashion show in Brooklyn in bad weather. There she met Katherine (Kay) Vincent, fashion editor of the *New York Herald Tribune.* Six months later, in 1940, she was offered the job of covering home furnishings for the *Herald Tribune.*

Gradually, Sheppard added articles on beauty and fashion, until by 1946 she produced both the daily and the Sunday women's pages. She used the pseudonym "Sara Sutton" for the beauty column that appeared on Wednesdays. During this time Sheppard married her third husband, Walter Millis, assistant chief editorial writer of the *Herald Tribune* and a military historian. In the fall of 1947 Sheppard was named fashion editor, replacing Kay Vincent. In 1949 she started a daily woman's page in the *Herald Tribune.*

In 1956 Sheppard introduced her famous "Inside Fashion" column. At first it ran twice a week; eventually it ran every day. Standard fashion reportage of the day chronicled details about hemlines, necklines, and silhouettes to inform

Eugenia Sheppard. ARCHIVE PHOTOS

women about the latest styles from Paris. Sheppard decided to have some fun. While other publications reverently discussed the wedding dress and trousseau of Grace Kelly for her marriage to Prince Rainier of Monaco, Sheppard divulged the fact that the princess-to-be's lingerie color was yellow. "Inside Fashion" pioneered the frank, sometimes tongue-in-cheek, approach to fashion writing. If Sheppard did not like something, she said so. When the waistless chemise came into fashion in 1957, she pronounced it "just a gunnysack with diamonds." Master of the catchy phrase, Sheppard gained a wide readership and the respect of her peers for her outspoken style. Energetic and petite (four feet, eleven inches), Sheppard merited front-row seats at fashion shows, as much for her reputation as for her myopia. Even if some designers occasionally banned her from their shows in retaliation for her candor, Sheppard would enlist her friends in the fashion business to draw the clothes for her.

When the *New York Herald Tribune* became the *World Journal Tribune* in 1966, Sheppard stayed on as woman's editor. The *World Journal Tribune* collapsed a year later, but her column continued to be published in *Women's Wear*

Daily. The *New York Post* offered Sheppard a job as society editor in 1968. Her third husband, Walter Millis, died in the same year.

During the 1960s and 1970s, Sheppard not only wrote newspaper columns, but her articles were featured in magazines such as *Saturday Review, Saturday Evening Post, Holiday,* and *Ladies' Home Journal.* From 1968 until the middle of 1972, Sheppard wrote a monthly column for *Harper's Bazaar.* It was said that her readership consisted of not just women but men as well. When not reporting on the latest fashions, Sheppard gave readers glimpses into the lives of the rich and famous. Keen observation at parties in which she mingled with society, gaining the appellation of "socialite" herself, resulted in tidbits of inside information about how the wealthy really lived. Readers could be taken on board Aristotle Onassis's yacht or be told what Revlon cosmetics founder Charles Revson liked to eat.

Sheppard found more than eighty markets for her columns throughout the United States, Canada, and England. She had a reputation for spotting trends sooner than most. Names of celebrities sprinkled her writings, so it was natural that in her later years she would pair up with *Celebrity Register* publisher Earl Blackwell. Together they wrote two novels: *Crystal Clear* (1978), and *Skyrocket: A Novel About Glamour and Power* (1980). Sheppard was honored several times with the Annual Award of the Newspaper Women's Clubs. While dying of cancer, she continued to write her "Around the Town" column for Publishers Hall Syndicate, her distributor for the column.

Eugenia Sheppard's contribution to fashion journalism was to approach her subject as a theater critic would but in a light-hearted, personal style that would give her readers a feeling of involvement. The Council of Fashion Designers of America (CFDA) annually grants the Eugenia Sheppard Award for Fashion Journalism.

★

Sheppard's early start is covered in Helen M. Staunton, "Covered Story on a Bad Night: Landed H-T Job," *Editor and Publisher* (28 Feb. 1948). Sheppard was profiled in "Men Read Her," *Newsweek* (18 June 1962); "So They Say," *Mademoiselle* (Aug. 1963); and most significantly in Barbaralee Diamondstein, *Open Secrets: Ninety-four Women in Touch with Our Time* (1972). An obituary is in the *New York Times* (12 Nov. 1984).

THERESE DUZINKIEWICZ BAKER

SHIELDS, Cornelius (*b.* 7 April 1895 in St. Paul, Minnesota; *d.* 15 October 1981 in New Rochelle, New York), investment banker who was a cofounder of one of the largest securities brokerage firms in the United States; he had a second career as a competitive yachtsman.

Shields was the youngest of six children born into a Roman Catholic family. His father, Cornelius Shields, Sr., was vice president of the Great Northern Railroad Company in St. Paul at the time; his mother, Theresa McHugh Shields, was a homemaker. Six years after Cornelius was born, the family relocated to Sydney in Nova Scotia, Canada, where the elder Shields had accepted a lucrative position as president of the Dominion Iron and Steel Company. A few years later the family moved again, this time to Sault Sainte Marie, Ontario, Canada, where his father assumed the presidency of the Lake Superior Corporation.

In Sault Sainte Marie the young Cornelius lived in a house built on the banks of the St. Marys River, which links Lake Superior to the other Great Lakes. The river was the perfect place for Cornelius to learn his first lessons in sailing from his older brothers. But it was not until some years later that he acquired a true appreciation of the intricacies of sailing and developed a passion for boats.

Two years after Cornelius's father died in 1904, the family moved to suburban New Rochelle, New York, so that Mrs. Shields could be near her friends and relatives, especially her eldest daughter, who was married and living in New York. While Cornelius's brothers were busy with their careers, his older sisters assisted their mother in raising Cornelius. Cornelius benefited from his proximity to Long Island Sound, and spent his summers swimming in and wandering along the harbor. Occasionally his brothers took him sailing aboard the *Virginia,* the family boat that had been shipped down from Canada. As he grew older, Cornelius became increasingly interested in sailing, skippering the *Virginia* for pleasure and in competition and crewing for others on their boats.

In 1910 Cornelius Shields entered Loyola College in Montreal, Canada; he did not earn a degree. Three years later, upon returning to New Rochelle, he bought a boat—a Larchmont Interclub one-design ten-foot sloop. This craft enabled him to participate in more advanced sailing competitions. He won the prestigious championship of the Yacht Racing Association of Long Island Sound in 1916. In the same year he sailed a forty-four-foot craft to victory in the annual New York Yacht Club Cruise, competing for the first time in waters outside the sound.

When the United States entered World War I in 1917, Shields joined the navy. After completing several months of training, he became an ensign and was assigned to the armored cruiser *Montana.* Aboard the *Montana,* Cornelius crossed the North Atlantic sixteen times, escorting the ships that carried American troops to the battlefields of Europe.

After his discharge on 19 June 1919, Shields joined his brother Paul as a salesman in the New York real estate business, living for a time with Paul in suburban Great Neck, Long Island. That same year he sold his Larchmont Interclub to buy an engagement ring for his longtime sweetheart, Josephine ("Doe") Lupprian, and won the Victory Class Championship with a borrowed boat. Shields

Cornelius Shields in a twelve-foot dinghy, 1972. JAMES L. AMOS/CORBIS

and Lupprian were married on 1 January 1922; they had two children and maintained their principal residence in Larchmont.

By 1922 Cornelius and Paul were working with the investment company of Merrill Lynch—Paul as a partner and Cornelius a salesman. A year later the two brothers went into business for themselves, founding the investment firm of Shields and Company.

The new business grew steadily during the 1920s, as the brothers were able to capitalize on the economic uncertainties of the period. The business was almost 100 percent in cash prior to the great crash of 1929, and subsequently made numerous acquisitions. By 1940 Shields and Company was established as one of the more prosperous members of the New York Stock Exchange.

By 1953 Cornelius Shields had become an international celebrity in the sailing arena. In that year he won his most prestigious competition—the Mallory Cup, the North American men's sailing championship. A few years later, following a heart attack, the broad-shouldered, five-foot, ten-inch, stocky, deep-tanned Shields was warned by his doctors that the stress of competition could have serious ill effects on his health. By this time Shields had participated in more than 8,000 races. Despite the doctors' warning, he returned to international racing one more time. In 1958 he skippered the *Columbia* to victory during the final trials of the America's Cup. In 1964 he revealed his sailing secrets in a book, *Cornelius Shields on Sailing.*

By 1971 Shields and Company remained one of the major brokerage houses on Wall Street, ranking ninth among the top thirty-four Big Board houses in terms of commis-

sion revenue—a notable achievement, considering that the early 1970s were difficult for the investment banking business. This was a time when the New York Stock Exchange lost a major portion of its business to off-the-exchange markets, due to high fixed-commission costs.

In 1974 Shields and Company merged with Model Roland; this firm in turn was acquired in 1977 by Bache Group, Inc., to become Bache, Halsey, Stuart, Shields, Inc. At this time Shields was eighty-two years old, and his company was a $30 million private enterprise with some forty partners, twenty regional offices, and about 750 employees. Four years later Shields died of heart failure at New Rochelle Hospital. He is buried at St. Augustine's Cemetery in Larchmont, New York.

Cornelius Shields attained the pinnacle of success in two completely distinct endeavors. As an entrepreneur, Shields helped found an investment banking firm that survived the most violent stock market changes to become one of the largest securities firms in the United States. As a sportsman, Shields won almost every national and international sailing championship.

★

A revised edition of Shields's book on sailing, *Racing with Cornelius Shields and the Masters* (1974), contains a brief autobiography that concentrates on his sailing career. "Design for Living," *Time* (27 July 1953), provides some biographical information, though this source too focuses on Shields's career as a yachtsman. "Bache Group Set to Buy Shields Model Roland," *Wall Street Journal* (6 May 1977), contains information about Shields and Company at the time of the merger. "Shields and Company Says 1970 Results Compare Favorably with Brokerage Industry

Trends," *Wall Street Journal* (21 Jan. 1971), gives a historical account of Shields and Company. Richard E. Rustin, "How a Brokerage Firm Manages to Operate During a Postal Tie Up," *Wall Street Journal* (24 Mar. 1970), describes Shields and Company's management practices during the late 1960s. Rustin, "Back-Office Blues: How a Brokerage Firm Battles the Paperwork Trading Surge Creates," *Wall Street Journal* (6 Feb. 1964), is a good source of information on the business operations and personnel management practices of Shields and Company. An obituary is in the *New York Times* (17 Oct. 1981).

MOJTABA SEYEDIAN

SHIVERS, (Robert) Allan (*b*. 10 October 1907 in Lufkin, Texas; *d*. 15 January 1985 in Austin, Texas), a lawyer best known for his service in Texas state government from 1934 until 1957 as a senator, lieutenant governor, and governor.

Born to Robert Andrew Shivers and Easter Creasy, Allan (he did not use the name Robert) was the first of two children. His family moved from Lufkin to Woodville, Texas, when he was ten months old. His father was first a teacher, then a lawyer, and then a county judge. As a boy, Allan often went to the courthouse to hear his father argue

Allan Shivers, 1963. ARCHIVE PHOTOS

or hear a case. Because of his father's profession, there was a good deal of talk about politics in the Shivers home. Allan attended the Woodville public schools, which were not fully accredited at the time. Had he graduated from the Woodville high school, Allan would have had to take entrance examinations to enter college. Therefore, his parents moved to Port Arthur, in southeast Texas. Allan graduated from Port Arthur High School in 1924 and entered the University of Texas at Austin that fall.

Financial circumstances forced Shivers to drop out of the university after only one year, and he returned to Port Arthur and took a job at the Texaco refinery in 1925. By 1928 Shivers had been promoted from laborer to office manager and was making the princely sum of $165 per month. He later said, "It was one of the hardest decisions I ever had to make, to quit that good job and go back to the university." But Shivers had the political bug and becoming a lawyer seemed to him the best road to public office.

At the University of Texas, Shivers made his first public bid for office and was elected president of the student association. He received his law degree in 1933 and returned to Port Arthur to begin a law practice and wait for a political opening. Shivers won his first workmen's compensation case in 1934 and used his earnings to run for the state senate. Through his support for old-age pensions and considerable political acumen, Shivers won all four counties in his district from the incumbent, Senator W. R. Cousins, in the Democratic primary. In a solidly Democratic Texas, winning the Democratic primary was tantamount to election, and Shivers won easily in the general election.

In 1933 Shivers met the love of his life, Marialice Shary, the adopted daughter of John Shary, a self-made man who began as a drugstore proprietor and who became one of the early land developers of the Lower Rio Grande Valley in south Texas. By the time Allan and Marialice met, Shary had sold $55 million worth of real estate. After John Shary's death, Shivers presided over the Shary family business until his death. He and Marialice were married on 5 October 1937; they had three children.

By 1946 Shivers was the dean of the Texas senate and was the near-unanimous choice of his colleagues to run for the lieutenant governor's slot, to which he was easily elected. Beauford Jester was elected governor. As lieutenant governor Shivers ran the senate with an iron hand, and by the time he left office, it was a far stronger body. He had his legislators create the Legislative Budget Board, which created a budget the legislators themselves took seriously, as well as the Legislative Council, a research arm for lawmakers. The most important act of Shivers's lieutenant governorship, however, was his creation of the Gilmer-Aikin Committee to study the needs of public schools. When its recommendations were enacted in 1949, it gave the state a greater role in financing public schools and was the most comprehensive education reform the legislature had ever passed.

In July 1949 Governor Jester died, and Shivers became governor of Texas. He was considered a conservative Democrat but not an ideologue; he did not want the federal government involved in what he considered state business but was pragmatic enough to realize that if the state did not take care of certain matters, the federal government was likely to move in. Soon after he took office, he called in powerful oil and gas businessmen and told them that money would have to be raised for education and social services. At that time, Texas was nearly at the bottom of the list in state spending in these areas. Shivers told a meeting of the Texas Manufacturers Association, "If the state doesn't do the things the people want done, the federal government will."

In 1950 Shivers was elected governor in his own right. He was elected three more times and led Texas during some stormy times in its political history. He persuaded the legislature to significantly increase funding for public education and hospitals.

In the summer of 1951, Governor Shivers signed a bill allowing candidates of one party to cross-file as candidates of other parties. This allowed Texans to vote for the Republican presidential nominee, Dwight Eisenhower, rather than the Democratic nominee, Adlai Stevenson, in 1952. The main issue of the campaign for Texans was whether Texas or the federal government had the right to the revenue produced by the Texas tidelands. When the Republic of Texas entered the Union, the federal government gave Texas domain over its public lands and, in exchange, Texas assumed its own debts. This seemed like a good deal for the national government at the time, but not when oil was discovered in Texas. By then, technology allowed oilmen to exploit the oil-rich tidelands, a Texas misnomer for a seabed that was never exposed by the tide but was ten miles offshore. Texas claimed the right to the tidelands, but President Harry Truman claimed them for the federal government. This wounded Texas pride and its economy.

Shivers met with Adlai Stevenson during the 1952 campaign and asked if he would support the Texas position on the tidelands. Stevenson said he would not, and Shivers responded by leading a faction of Democrats for Eisenhower in Texas. Eisenhower carried Texas that year; his victory set the stage for a nascent Republican party to grow in Texas. In 1960 Senator John Tower became the first Republican since Reconstruction to win statewide office.

During Shivers's eight years as governor, Joseph McCarthy began and ended his mean-spirited and unfair political tactics. Shivers profited from the political atmosphere of fear and extremism, especially when he claimed during a campaign to have exposed a "communist-dominated union" in Port Arthur and crippled the union's "well-laid plans to spread its tentacles along the Gulf Coast and eventually into your community."

In 1954 the *Brown* v. *Board of Education of Topeka* decision came down from the Supreme Court, overturning the 1896 *Plessy* v. *Ferguson* "separate but equal" doctrine. This was not Shivers's finest political hour. He urged his fellow Texans to resist desegregation and asserted that he would, as governor, "interpose" the state between Texas citizens and the federal government and refuse to enforce this law in Texas.

After he left the governor's office in 1957, Shivers continued to be active in many endeavors. In 1967 he became president of the United States Chamber of Commerce. Under his presidency, the chamber had a better relationship with government than before because of his friendship with President Lyndon B. Johnson. He died of a heart attack and was buried in the state cemetery in Austin.

Even given his mistakes, Shivers was considered a good governor and a towering presence in Texas politics during the 1950s. He was such a strong governor that one conservative columnist said, "He practically dictated all major actions of the legislature." Despite his notorious red-baiting, Shivers kept the state from abandoning all restraint during the extreme right-wing atmosphere in Texas in the 1950s. Ironically, the conservative governor was later most proud of his accomplishments in the areas of increased appropriations for eleemosynary institutions, prisons, highways, and old-age pensions. He strengthened the office of governor and made the office of lieutenant governor a powerhouse in Texas. Although unable to rise above some of the meaner passions of his times, he did a great deal to bring Texas out of its provincialism and into the twentieth century.

★

The papers of Governor Shivers are in the Texas State Archives. The collection consists of general, personal, campaign, and clippings files of Shivers in his capacities as state senator, lieutenant governor, and governor of Texas. Sam Kinch and Stuart Long, *Allan Shivers: The Pied Piper of Texas Politics* (1973), is an account of Shivers's life with few criticisms. George Norris Green, *The Establishment in Texas Politics: The Primitive Years, 1938–1957* (1979), devotes a chapter to Shivers's political career that is more balanced and critical than that of Kinch and Long. Good contemporary articles are Ronnie Dugger, "What Corrupted Texas?," *Harper's* (Mar. 1957), and D. B. Hardeman, "Shivers of Texas: A Tragedy in Three Acts," *Harper's* (Nov. 1956). The Center for American History in Austin has a biographical file on Shivers containing clippings from his early political career through his death. The Lyndon Baines Johnson Library and Museum in Austin contains an interview with Shivers, but more helpful and extensive interviews are at North Texas State University.

CHRISTIE L. BOURGEOIS

SHOOK, Karel Francis Antony (*b*. 29 August 1920 in Renton, Washington; *d*. 25 July 1985 in Englewood, New Jersey), dancer, choreographer, writer, ballet master, and co-founder and associate artistic director of the Dance Theatre of Harlem, notable for his encouragement of black dancers in the formerly all-white world of ballet.

The oldest of three children of Walter Burnell Shook, an American World War I soldier-machinist with the British forces, and Ida Maria Teresa Tack, a Belgian war bride, Shook was born into a family with a Baptist grandmother, Pennsylvania Dutch forebears, and no dancers. A bright youngster who learned to read at age four, Karel (pronounced "Karl") became a child actor with the Seattle Repertory Theater. At age thirteen his talent and determination won him a scholarship to the Cornish School of Allied Arts in Seattle. There, Merce Cunningham was a dance student, John Cage taught music, and founder Nellie Cornish steered Shook toward ballet; he became her protégé.

When the Ballet Russe de Monte Carlo came to Seattle in 1937, Shook was asked to join that company by Léonide Massine. He appeared with the Seattle Civic Opera Ballet and ultimately accepted Massine's offer. Shook relocated to New York City and toured with such shows as *The Chocolate Soldier* and *Song of Norway*. He also studied at the School of American Ballet in 1939. In 1949 he danced with the New York City Ballet but did not enjoy the experience and rejoined the Ballet Russe. He was engaged as director of ballet at the Katherine Dunham School from 1952 to 1954 and was in charge of ballet at the June Taylor School from 1957 to 1959. In the intervening years, 1954–1957, Shook opened his own school, Studio Dance Arts, with black dancers Alvin Ailey and Arthur Mitchell among the teachers.

Leaving the United States for nine years, 1959–1968, Shook was ballet master of the Dutch National Ballet. In addition to this position, he taught in many major European cities, experimented with mime, and choreographed twenty-four works for film, television, and opera, as well as the stage. These included *Alceste* (1966), an opera-ballet for television, *Jazz-Nocturne* (1959), *Tales of Hoffman,* and *Da Capo*. A television program based on *Da Capo* documented the creation of a ballet.

In 1968 Mitchell, a New York City Ballet dancer whom Shook had taught, asked Shook to join him in developing the Dance Theatre of Harlem, which became the first permanently established black ballet company in the United States. Shook returned to the United States "to consolidate black ballet and bring it in full force across the threshold of classicism. . . . [The company] was, from its inception, firmly based on a school with high standards and an effective way of teaching." In the school, racial stereotypes were

Karel Shook. DANCE THEATRE OF HARLEM

rejected as traditional dance was taught to nontraditional students, and the company became known for its teamwork and spirit as well as its dancing. Shook also restaged *Don Quixote* (1974) and *Le Corsaire* (1972) for the company. He especially espoused the importance of experienced ballet teachers for elementary-level pupils. He also served as an adviser to the American Academy of Ballet in Tonawanda, New York.

Shook's slim manual on dance teaching "as practiced in the school of the Dance Theatre of Harlem," *Elements of Classical Ballet Technique* (1977), includes historical background, a firm pedagogical philosophy, and a syllabus of lessons. Shook also wrote poetry and many articles, including "Dancers as Ambassadors" (1978). *Beyond the Mist* (1968), a portfolio of his poems, was published in a limited edition with lithographs by the black painter Sam Middleton. Somewhat short, with white hair from his fifties on, Shook was a Renaissance man talented in writing, sculpting, and cooking, as well as teaching and dance. For many years he lived in different locations in New York City's Greenwich Village.

Shook died after a long bout with lung cancer; he had never married. A memorial service on 27 August 1985 at the Cathedral of St. John the Divine in New York City included dance and song, remarks by prominent dancers, and readings of his poetry.

Shook received the Presidential Award for Excellence and Dedication in Education in 1980 from President Jimmy Carter. Shook believed that teaching was an inborn gift, a "medium through which tradition will be transmitted." When Shook, a white man, began to teach black dancers in the 1950s, he did so as part of his job rather than out of principle, yet he was a pioneer who insisted color did not matter, that "skin shades and ethnic backgrounds have little or nothing to do with" dance. Some of his black students—including Alvin Ailey, Carmen de Lavallade, Geoffrey Holder, Donald McKayle, Dudley Williams, and Billy Wilson—became prominent in dance in America and worldwide.

Shook was simultaneously a strict disciplinarian and a humanist, a man concerned with tradition and a visionary, aloof and yet passionate about dancers and dance. Although he was best known to the general public as cofounder and codirector of the Dance Theatre of Harlem, Shook wished to be remembered as a teacher.

★

Jennifer Dunning, "A Man Who Championed Blacks in Ballet," *New York Times* (11 Aug. 1985), is a paean to Shook's role in encouraging black dancers and discusses American dance history and racial integration in ballet. The obituary in the *New York Times* (27 July 1985) includes Shook's comments on the young Arthur Mitchell. The obituary in *Dance Magazine* (Oct. 1985) includes quotations by Arthur Mitchell and Alvin Ailey.

RACHEL SHOR

SHORE, Edward William ("Eddie") (*b.* 25 November 1902 in Fort Qu'Appelle, Saskatchewan, Canada; *d.* 16 March 1985 in Springfield, Massachusetts), professional hockey player with the Boston Bruins who was the first marquee defenseman in the National Hockey League (NHL).

Shore was one of the seven children of John T. Shore, a rancher, and Katherine Spanier. As a youth he toughened himself by taming wild horses, herding cattle, and performing other chores of the typical western Canadian farmer, managing early in life to handle jobs that just about any other man would consider too difficult.

Shore did not entertain thoughts of playing hockey until his brother Aubrey challenged him to try out for the team at Manitoba Agricultural College in Winnipeg. At first, hockey was just a game for Shore, until the family's financial reverses in the early 1920s required that he leave school and search for a job. He became a professional hockey player for teams in Regina, Edmonton, and Victoria, all of the Pacific Coast Hockey League. When the league terminated operations at the end of the 1925–1926 season, a number of excellent players, including Shore, became available to the eight-year-old National Hockey League. To

Eddie Shore as a Boston Bruin, *c.* 1931. UPI/CORBIS-BETTMANN

stock his floundering Boston Bruins team, owner Charles F. Adams purchased a seven-man package for $50,000 that included future Hall of Famers Frank Boucher, Duke Keats, and Shore.

Shore was an artistic performer who could accomplish more on ice than any other individual player. His strong, long strides enabled him to skate the length of the 200-foot rink faster than any other player, and although he was a defenseman, he possessed the attacking prowess of a forward. But he was renowned most of all for his Bunyanesque physique and ability to consistently deliver crunching body checks.

As a player for the Bruins from 1926 to 1939, Shore dazzled audiences with his multiple skills while intimidating the opposition with his brutish deportment. At a time when defensemen were confined to their own end of the rink, located there strategically to blunt enemy attacks, Shore was a revolutionary in his offensive maneuvers. During the 1928–1929 season he scored twelve goals and seven assists to place sixth in scoring in the American Division of the NHL, ahead of such scoring notables as Bill Cook of the New York Rangers and Herbie Lewis of the Detroit Red Wings. In his fourteen seasons with the Bruins he played in 553 games, had 105 goals, made 179 assists, and racked up 1,047 penalty minutes.

But Shore's scoring ability never quite overshadowed his defensive work, which spanned the spectrum. He could poke check and hook check with finesse and, most important of all, could body check with ferocity. Shore usually hit his opponents cleanly, as there was no need to do otherwise because his clean checks were so devastating. The check for which he was best remembered was, in the view of most observers, on the other side of the rule book, however. It was a block he threw at Ace Bailey, a Toronto Maple Leaf forward, on 12 December 1933. Shore, who mistook Bailey for another player, struck him so violently that the Leaf forward was upended in a backward somersault. He landed on the ice with a loud report, knees raised, and legs twitching as if his neck was broken. Bailey, near death, miraculously recovered but his career was over. Shore was suspended for sixteen games, and the repercussions from the Shore-Bailey incident, as it came to be known, severely damaged the reputation of hockey. It remains one of the most controversial episodes in the history of the game.

The episode typified Shore's rugged style of hockey. It had many critics, but many more fans supported the macho, "hockey-is-war" attitude prevalent during the 1930s. One episode in particular reveals Shore's consummate courage. Once, after a collision, Shore's left ear was mashed to such an extent doctors advised him he would never hear out of it again. When asked by a medic what kind of anesthetic he wanted, Shore recounted, he "told him just to give me a small mirror. That way, I could watch the kind of stitching he did. I made him change the very last stitch. If I had not done that, he'd have left a scar. I told him I was just a farm boy who did not want his looks messed up."

Shore played on two Stanley Cup–winning teams in Boston before the close of the 1930s. After a feud with management, he was traded to the New York Americans in December 1939 and retired soon thereafter. In his playing career he had been chosen seven times as a member of the NHL's All-Star Team and was voted four times its most valuable player. His jersey number 2 was retired by the Bruins. Added to these honors, he managed to acquire more than 900 stitches in his face and body and fracture his back, hip, and collarbone. His nose was broken fourteen times and his jaw was cracked four times.

In 1939 Shore purchased the Springfield Indians of the American Hockey League. He was its president, owner, manager, and, often over the years, its coach. Fiercely independent, Shore ran a tight and frugal ship, often antagonizing players because of fiscal constraints. In December 1966 his players went on strike to better their conditions, forcing Shore to make concessions. Following the strike he sold the Springfield players to the Los Angeles Kings of the NHL's West Division.

Shore married Catherine Macrae in 1929; they had one son, Eddie Shore, Jr., and in 1945 Catherine Shore died. In 1952 Shore married Carol Ann Gaba; the two remained together until her death in 1981. He became a naturalized U.S citizen in 1946. Shore died of natural causes and was buried in Springfield, Massachusetts.

Shore truly lived up to his nickname the "Babe Ruth of Hockey": to the extent that Ruth "built" Yankee Stadium, Shore practically built the whole NHL. He was an obvious choice for the first class of players to be inducted into the Hockey Hall of Fame in 1947. Still, in reaction to the persistent criticism that was heaped on him, Shore became unusually defensive. "I'll tell you what's the matter," he once declared. "Shore has always been in the wrong. He doesn't mean to but he gets in people's bad graces. He's been outspoken even if it hurts. But his shoulders are fairly broad. Most of us are a little crazy in one way or another. Some of us admit it. As for me, I'm not sorry about anything I've done in my life."

★

For additional information see Stan Fischler, *Bad Boys: The Legends of Hockey's Toughest, Meanest, Most-Feared Players* (1991). An obituary is in the *New York Times* (18 Mar. 1985).

STAN FISCHLER

SHOUP, David Monroe (*b.* 30 December 1904 near Battle Ground, Indiana; *d.* 13 January 1983 in Alexandria, Virginia), military officer and Medal of Honor recipient who served as commandant of the Marine Corps from 1960 to 1963.

David Shoup, who would gain a near legendary reputation as a combat leader, was born on his father's farm, three miles north of the battleground in Tippecanoe County, Indiana, where General William Henry Harrison fought the Shawnees in 1811. David was one of four children born to John Lamar Shoup, a farmer, and Mary Layton Shoup, a homemaker. His early education took place in a one-room schoolhouse, followed by high school in Covington, Indiana, and enrollment at DePauw University in Greencastle, Indiana, in the fall of 1921. Shoup worked his way through college, taking a year off to serve as principal of a small elementary school. He majored in mathematics, ran the marathon on the track team, completed the Reserve Officers' Training program, and received his degree in 1926. He served for a month in the Army Infantry Reserve before being commissioned as a Marine second lieutenant on 20 July 1926. Shoup stood five feet, eight inches tall and had a stocky build; his weight varied from 150 to 200 pounds during his adult years. In 1932 he wed Zola De Haven; they were married until Shoup's death fifty-one years later and had two children.

Shoup's career was typical for the interwar Marine Corps: slow promotions (he was not promoted to major until April 1941), overseas duty (stints in China in 1927 and 1934–1936), and the standard range of Marine Corps

Major General David Shoup. ARCHIVE PHOTOS

assignments (although his service with the Civilian Conservation Corps, in 1933–1934, was atypical). In May 1941 Major Shoup was sent to Iceland with the Sixth Marines, serving there until March 1942, three months after the Japanese attack on Pearl Harbor. Promoted to lieutenant colonel, Shoup shipped out to New Zealand the following month. He served as operations and training officer of the Second Marine Division until 9 November 1943, when he was promoted to colonel and charged with commanding the Second Marines in their assault on Tarawa in the Gilbert Islands, in the west Pacific Ocean.

On 20 November 1943 the attack commenced on Betio, the largest of the Tarawa atoll's forty-seven islands. The well-entrenched Japanese defenders had largely survived the massive naval and air bombardment preceding the assault. Marines, coming in on Higgins boats that often became lodged on coral reefs, had to wade in for hundreds of yards in the face of withering fire. Shoup, as senior officer ashore, directed the costly suppression of Japanese resistance. At 4:00 P.M. of the second day of unrelenting battle, Colonel Shoup radioed his command ship: "Casualties: many. Percentage dead: unknown. Combat efficiency: we are winning." The following day, with Betio secured,

Shoup, with serious leg wounds suffered early in the battle, and exhausted after sixty hours without sleep, was relieved. His Second Marine Division had suffered 1,027 killed and 2,292 wounded.

Shoup's heroism on Tarawa earned him the Medal of Honor. On 22 January 1945 Secretary of the Navy James V. Forrestal presented the award to Shoup, with a citation noting that by "his brilliant leadership, daring tactics, and selfless devotion to duty, Col. Shoup was largely responsible for the final decisive defeat of the enemy."

Shoup steadily rose through the ranks of the postwar Marine Corps, taking on responsibilities in training, fiscal reorganization, and logistics. Shoup became a brigadier general in April 1953, and on 12 August 1959 he was nominated by President Dwight D. Eisenhower to be the twenty-second commandant of the Marine Corps. After Senate confirmation, Shoup assumed that position on 1 January 1960, along with a promotion to four-star rank.

Shoup's leadership of the Marines brought both symbolic and substantive change. He eliminated the use of swagger sticks and minimized base ceremonies during commandant visits, and he also upgraded the combat readiness of all Marine units. Vietnam became a pressing policy issue during this time, and Shoup opposed any commitment of U.S. combat forces in Southeast Asia. At the end of his term as commandant, 31 December 1963, David Shoup retired at the age of fifty-nine from the Marine Corps. His skepticism about involvement in Vietnam deepened and became public. In a 1966 speech, Shoup asserted that he did not believe that, "as related to the present and future safety and freedom of this country . . . the whole of Southeast Asia was worth a single American life." Two years later, in a ceremony at Tarawa marking the twenty-fifth anniversary of that battle, Shoup paid tribute to his fellow Marines, but also to all those on both sides who fell in that desperate encounter. He concluded: "Please God, may our ships of state sail on and on in a world forever at peace."

David Shoup died of a heart ailment in Alexandria, Virginia, at the age of seventy-eight. He was buried in Arlington National Cemetery. Shoup will be remembered for his personal heroism, his flinty integrity, and his early and continuing warnings about the danger of Vietnam.

★

The papers of General David M. Shoup are located at the Hoover Institution on War, Revolution, and Peace at Stanford University. See David M. Shoup, *The Marines in China, 1927–1928*, edited by Howard Jablon (1987), and Edward F. Murphy, *Heroes of World War II* (1990). Audiotapes of interviews Shoup gave are in the John F. Kennedy Library Oral History Program (1967) and the Columbia University Oral History Research Office (1972). Obituaries are in the *Washington Post* (15 Jan. 1983) and the *New York Times* (16 Jan. 1983).

JOHN O'SULLIVAN

SILLMAN, Leonard Dexter (*b.* 9 May 1908 in Detroit, Michigan; *d.* 23 January 1982 in New York City), actor, playwright, Broadway producer, and director who launched the careers of many actors, primarily with his numerous *New Faces* revues on Broadway.

Leonard Sillman was one of two children of May Grosslight and Morton Sillman, a jeweler. Sillman attended local public and private schools and was frequently disciplined for his precocious but disruptive behavior. With the financial support of his family, he moved to New York City in 1923, at the age of fifteen, to become an actor.

Sillman lived with his aunt and uncle in Mount Vernon, New York, while studying acting and dance at the Ned Wayburn studio in Manhattan. His first job was playing Lew Field's son in a vaudeville act, in which Field shoved chocolate down Sillman's throat. In 1925 he played the role originated by Fred Astaire in the touring company of *Lady Be Good*. Sillman's first principal role on Broadway was in *Merry-Go-Round* (1927), and in 1928 he appeared in a vaudeville revue at the Palace Theater with Imogene Coca. He also performed with Frances Gershwin, sister of the composer George Gershwin, and appeared in another vaudeville revue, *Temptations of 1930*.

In the early 1930s Sillman moved to Hollywood and opened his own dance studio, teaching such stars as Ruby Keeler. In 1932 he appeared in a revue, *Hullabaloo*, at the Pasadena Community Playhouse. When the show moved to Hollywood's El Capitan Theater, the agent Ivan Kahn discovered Sillman and procured small roles for him in movies, most notably *The Blonde Bombshell* (1933), starring Jean Harlow. Sillman returned to the Pasadena Playhouse to produce a new revue, *Low and Behold,* which featured Tyrone Power and Eve Arden. The show was a success and moved to Broadway in March 1934 as the first of Sillman's *New Faces* revues; featuring Coca, Henry Fonda, and Sillman (who also produced and codirected), *New Faces* was an instant hit.

Established as an actor, producer, and director, Sillman's next venture was the revue *Fools Rush In.* The show opened in December 1934 to mixed reviews, but the backers withdrew their support and it closed quickly thereafter. In 1935 Sillman acted in *The Ugly Runts* in Ann Arbor, Michigan; he returned to Broadway in 1936 with another *New Faces* revue. *New Faces of 1936* featured Coca, Van Johnson, and thirty-nine other performers, but Sillman himself was not in the cast. Although he would act again (*New Faces of 1943, Leonard Sillman's New Faces of 1968,* and *The Madwoman of Chaillot* in 1970), he increasingly turned his energies to directing and producing.

During the late 1930s and the 1940s, Sillman suffered a string of failures. The revue *Who's Who* opened in 1938 to negative reviews, which Sillman blamed on his backer, Elsa Maxwell. His next production, *Journey's End* (1939), was a revival of a drama about British soldiers in the trenches of World War I. Unfortunately, the play opened the night that Poland fell to Nazi Germany, and reviewers commented that the escalating tensions of international conflict overshadowed the dramatics of the play. The following month Sillman staged another revival, *They Knew What They Wanted,* again to mixed reviews and disappointing box office. *All in Fun,* which opened in 1940 and featured Bill "Bojangles" Robinson, was, according to Sillman, the most expensive flop of his career, and *New Faces of 1943* worsened his financial situation to near bankruptcy. He went to Hollywood to produce the film *An Angel Comes to Brooklyn* (1945) but returned to Broadway in 1946 with a musical retelling of the Cinderella story, *If the Shoe Fits,* which closed almost immediately. In 1948 Sillman brought his *New Faces* to NBC radio; this production lasted one year. Back on Broadway in 1950, Sillman produced Burgess Meredith's *Happy as Larry,* another flop, which closed after two nights.

The string of failures ended with *New Faces of 1952;* it was a huge success and played for a year on Broadway. Featuring Alice Ghostley, Eartha Kitt, and Paul Lynde, the 1952 incarnation of *New Faces* received rave reviews and

Leonard Sillman, 1937. UPS/Corbis-Bettmann

was made into a movie in 1954. After this success, Sillman had another disappointment in 1956 with *Mrs. Patterson,* which starred Eartha Kitt; *New Faces of 1956,* although less critically successful than the previous *New Faces,* was another hit and introduced Maggie Smith to the American stage.

Unfortunately, more flops came on the heels of these successes. *Mask and Gown,* premiering in 1957 and featuring female impersonator T. C. Jones, failed to win over the critics, and *Miss Isobel* (also 1957), starring Shirley Booth, lost $72,000. In the 1960s Sillman produced *A Second String* (1960), *The Family Way* (1965), and *The American Hamburger League* (1969), all of which opened to negative reviews. His *New Faces of 1962* and *New Faces of 1968* were also unfavorably received; both were found lacking in comparison to the success and energy of *New Faces of 1952.* In 1970 Sillman financed and appeared in *The Madwoman of Chaillot* and produced a revival of Noël Coward's *Hay Fever,* neither of which were well received. Efforts to stage a *Best of the New Faces* revue in the 1970s failed, but in 1977 Sillman hosted a retrospective of his career at the Ballroom Theater.

Sillman's personal and professional life were inseparable from each other. Although he never married, he was close with his family, particularly his sister, June Sillman Carroll. The two collaborated throughout their careers, with Carroll often acting in and writing lyrics for his shows. Sillman died of old age at Mount Sinai Hospital in New York City after a long illness. Although his career was riddled with disappointments, Sillman considered himself an innovator of the Broadway stage, declaring that "I've always been a pioneer. I'm always way ahead of myself; that's why so many of my shows are flops." As a Broadway fixture for much of the twentieth century, Sillman's contributions are apparent in the sheer volume both of shows produced and celebrities discovered. As he was fond of saying, "About the only talent I have is knowing talent."

★

Sillman's autobiography, *Here Lies Leonard Sillman: Straightened Out at Last* (1959), provides an entertaining and humorous account of his childhood and Broadway career. Obituaries are in the *New York Times* (24 Jan. 1982) and *Time* and *Newsweek* magazines (both 8 Feb. 1982).

WILLIAM WHITE TISON PUGH

SILVERS, Phil (*b.* 11 May 1911 in Brooklyn, New York; *d.* 1 November 1985 in Century City, California), actor and comedian who performed on stage and in film for more than sixty years and who is best known for his role as the bespectacled, ever-scheming Master Sergeant Ernest T. Bilko in the television series *You'll Never Get Rich* (later retitled the *Phil Silvers Show*).

Silvers, born Philip Silversmith, was the eighth and youngest child of Russian-Jewish immigrant parents Saul Silversmith, an ironworker, and Sarah Silversmith. He grew up in the Brooklyn neighborhoods of Brownsville and Bensonhurst, where protective shelters for a child were few, but he was assured of the affection of his family. He began singing at family social events before the age of six and wrote years later of how much he loved it. He attended public schools until the age of twelve. As a boy Silvers was drawn to the local theater where the organist accompanied the silent films. Once, when the film reel broke, Silvers surprised the impatient audience with an impromptu performance of his own. He captivated them with his high tenor voice and earned a reputation as the reel-breaker-down singer.

Soon thereafter he took a job at a local drugstore with the weekly objective of earning the fifty cents required for entry into Brooklyn's Bushwick Theater. He attended nearly every Saturday matinee, less to be entertained than to study the methods and learn the songs of the performers. He put his new material to use in a nearby beer hall and in children's shows. When Silvers was twelve the vaudevillian Gus Edwards noticed him singing on the boardwalk at Coney Island, invited him to try out at the Brighton

Phil Silvers. POPPERFOTO/ARCHIVE PHOTOS

Beach Theater, and later hired him to sing at the Palace Theater in New York City. Once his mother adjusted to the idea, he was permitted to leave school and travel with the act to other cities on the East Coast. As Silvers grew older, the quality of his singing voice faded and his tour with Gus Edwards ended. Gradually, however, he excelled at comedy skits and joined the vaudeville team of Morris and Campbell for five years.

In 1931 Silvers tried unsuccessfully to secure work in Times Square. After being turned down for a part in a vaudeville routine managed by Herman and Sammy Timberg, he stayed to watch the rehearsal and concluded that the finale was weak. On the way home that night he developed a new ending and returned the next morning to present it to a receptive Herman Timberg, who hired Silvers and his idea on the spot.

Life in the theater during the Great Depression was nothing if not mobile. After his stint in Manhattan, Silvers headed for the summer resorts in the Catskill Mountains northwest of New York City. He was called upon to assist a patronizing emcee who placed Silvers as a losing second fiddle. Silvers approached the emcee as he delved into his act downstage, and with a gesture of feigned caution said: "Excuse me, don't stand too close to the footlights. I smell ham burning." Silvers spent the rest of the 1930s in burlesque. He traveled with the Minsky Burlesque Troupe from 1934 to 1939, trying out new ideas, developing the intricacies of comedy, and refining his ability to improvise while gaining the advantage of increasing confidence.

In 1939 Silvers landed a part in the Broadway show *Yokel Boy*. In the audience one evening was the Metro-Goldwyn-Mayer mogul Louis B. Mayer, who offered Silvers a contract to work in film. The excitement of a new career in Hollywood was short-lived, however, because Silvers was never cast in a film. It was only when Darryl F. Zanuck of Twentieth Century–Fox engaged him a year after his MGM option expired that he began to emerge on screen.

His credits with Twentieth Century–Fox included *Tom, Dick, and Harry* (1941), *You're in the Army Now* (1941), *Cover Girl* (1944), *A Thousand and One Nights* (1945), and nineteen other films by the end of the decade. Silvers usually depicted comedic characters who supported the leading man. As work was more readily accessible, his personal life improved. On 2 March 1945 he married Jo-Carroll Dennison, the 1942 Miss America.

Silvers returned to Broadway in 1947 to star in the musical *High Button Shoes*, which ran for 727 performances. In 1951 Silvers starred in another successful musical, *Top Banana*, for which he won a Tony Award. A long road show ensued in 1953, and Silvers played the lead in the film version of *Top Banana* in 1954. His marriage did not fare as well as his career. In 1950 he and his wife had divorced. They had no children.

Silvers achieved his greatest acclaim and popularity in the 1955 television series *You'll Never Get Rich*. It became the highest-rated program on television, and its title was later changed to the *Phil Silvers Show*. Silvers filled the leading role as the charming if mischievous army sergeant, Ernie Bilko, who constantly tried to lure his men into money-making schemes. He was a chameleon of emotion as befit the occasion—feigning innocence before the chaplain, enthusiastic support in front of his colonel, and devilish when immersed in a gainful plot. After many years of experience, Silvers had perfected his craft to create a very funny underdog who appealed to a wide audience. The series ran until 1959 and won six Emmy Awards.

On 21 October 1956 Silvers married Evelyn Patrick. They had five daughters and lived in Beverly Hills. When the *Phil Silvers Show* ended, Silvers went back and forth between New York and Hollywood. In 1960 he starred on Broadway in the successful production of *Do Re Mi*. He returned to television in 1963 in the *New Phil Silvers Show* but unwittingly antagonized viewers in the role of a troublemaker who did not garner sympathy. The series lasted only one season. Silvers then appeared in a number of movies, such as *Forty Pounds of Trouble* (1963), *It's a Mad Mad Mad Mad World* (1963), *A Guide for the Married Man* (1967), and *Buona Sera, Mrs. Campbell* (1968). In 1971 he acted in his first serious role, opposite Sandy Dennis in the Broadway play *How the Other Half Loves*. In 1972 he reprised his film role in *A Funny Thing Happened on the Way to the Forum* (1966) on Broadway and won a Tony Award; the show was forced to close when Silvers suffered a minor stroke.

Privately, Silvers's life was infused with struggle—against gambling, a habit he acquired as a teenager, and depression, which haunted him in later life. His second marriage ended after ten years. Even at his most difficult times, however, Silvers was convinced that as long as he could work he would have a gratifying life. He continued to work until his death from natural causes during an afternoon nap at his home in Century City. He is buried at Mount Sinai Memorial Park in Los Angeles.

Silvers believed that his hardships had enhanced his ability as a comedian by way of personal insight. He was commended for his unmistakably talented work by the Donaldson Award for Theatre Excellence. He was also voted Entertainer of the Year by the Television Editors of America in 1957.

★

See Phil Silvers with Robert Saffron, *This Laugh Is on Me: The Phil Silvers Story* (1973). A clippings file is at the New York Public Library for the Performing Arts. An obituary is in the *New York Times* (2 Nov. 1985).

STEPHEN MCKAY

SKOLSKY, Sidney (*b.* 2 May 1905 in New York City; *d.* 3 May 1983 in Los Angeles, California), entertainment reporter and film producer best known for his widely syndicated column "Tintypes"; Skolsky achieved fame as a Broadway and Hollywood insider during a career that spanned more than fifty years.

Sidney Skolsky was the son of Louis Skolsky, who owned a dry-goods store, and Mildred Arbeit Skolsky. He and his brother were raised in New York City's Hell's Kitchen, located only a few blocks from Broadway. After graduating from DeWitt Clinton High School, Skolsky attended New York University, where he majored in journalism (B.A. degree, 1926).

He first became interested in the glitz and glamour of the world of theater and vaudeville as a child, when he would spend hours walking up and down Broadway hoping to catch a glimpse of the stars of the Great White Way. His first writing job on Broadway was as an assistant to Alex Yonkel, who handled publicity for many theatrical productions. In this capacity, Skolsky learned the intricacies of show business, met many people working in the business,

Sidney Skolsky, 1937. UPI/Corbis-Bettmann

and wrote press releases and arranged interviews for such stars as Humphrey Bogart, Gene Raymond, the Marx Brothers, Victor Moore, and George Jessel. Striking out on his own, he worked for a year and a half doing publicity for musical revue impresarios Earl Carroll and George White. Skolsky married Estelle Lorenz on 27 August 1928; they had two children.

Skolsky broke into the newspaper business by coming up with an idea for a column, "Tintypes," which was eventually bought by the *New York Sun*. The column, based on Skolsky's ability to obtain confidences from people and to ferret out the news about Broadway stars, consisted of vignette biographies, some gossip, and a great deal of interesting facts. The authenticity of the reportage garnered Skolsky instant acclaim. The *Sun* published the column for two years, and then Skolsky was signed by the *New York Daily News* to take columnist Mark Hellinger's place in 1929. Over the years, the column moved to the *New York Daily Mirror* and finally in 1943 to the *New York Post*, where it ran six days a week. Eventually in syndication, Skolsky became one of the most widely read columnists in the United States.

"Tintypes" contained pithy comments about everyone who was anyone in the world of entertainment, past and present. About George Gershwin, Skolsky wrote, "He is bashful about playing the piano at parties. He has to be coaxed. Once he starts, however, you can't stop him." Commenting on the actress Texas Guinan, he quipped, "Recently she abandoned the expression, 'Hello, sucker!' because customers began to take her seriously." As for William Shakespeare: "It's claimed that he stole his ideas. He doesn't deny it. Believes there's nothing new under the sun. Hopes that someday people will steal from him."

Skolsky's love for the Broadway scene inspired him to write a popular song, "It's a Fake, It's a Phoney, but It's My Broadway," which captured the color and pathos of the theatrical life. The song contains the lyric "A painted smile, a hard luck tale; a helping hand, they're all for sale; on Broadway, Broadway." In 1932 Skolsky switched the focus of his column from the coverage of the theater to that of film. The first New York columnist to go to Hollywood, he remained there for the rest of his life. While continuing with his column, Skolsky worked as a story editor for the producer Darryl F. Zanuck and cowrote the original story of the 1935 Fox release *The Daring Young Men*. He also produced two films of his own, based on the lives of his close friends: *The Jolson Story,* which was nominated for an Academy Award for best picture of 1946, and *The Eddie Cantor Story* in 1953.

Skolsky also had a weekly radio broadcast, which originated from Pickfair, the home of his friends Mary Pickford and Douglas Fairbanks. In 1954 Skolsky became one of the first entertainment reporters to have his own television show, a weekly series on ABC. His image was distinct: he was barely five feet tall, weighed only ninety pounds, and wore large horn-rimmed glasses. After his national television exposure, he became as widely recognizable as the celebrities he covered in his column. In the film *Sunset Boulevard* (1950), he played himself interviewing the character played by William Holden.

Asked if he would ever leave Hollywood, Skolsky gave his answer in one of his columns: "The boys have set up a big toy for my amusement. Here I can see W. C. Fields and Jack Benny playing in comedy; Fred Astaire and Ginger Rogers dancing; hear the best bands and entertainment that nobody on earth can buy. Why should I leave it? I love Hollywood." That last line eventually became his sign-off to all of his columns and broadcasts; sometimes, however, the kicker had an ironic twist, because he would occasionally present a biting critique of Hollywood.

Skolsky became friends with such stars as Hedy Lamarr, Marilyn Monroe, Jean Seberg, and Cary Grant. He had phenomenal accuracy in handicapping the annual Oscars, predicting, for example, that the best actor award would go to Marlon Brando in 1955 for *On the Waterfront*, and accurately naming virtually all of the eventual winners in 1981. Skolsky also had a role in naming the famed Oscar statuette. When a librarian of the Academy of Motion Picture Arts and Sciences remarked that the trophy somewhat resembled her Uncle Oscar, Skolsky mentioned it in his column the next day, and the name "Oscar" fell into common usage. One of the biggest scoops of Skolsky's career was the report in 1958 that Eddie Fisher would divorce Debbie Reynolds and marry Elizabeth Taylor.

His pen was always active. In addition to his column, his broadcasts, and the screenplays he worked on, Skolsky authored several books: *The Best Motion Pictures of 1937*; *Times Square Tintypes: Being Typewriter Caricatures of Those Who Made Their Names Along the Not So Straight and Very Narrow Path of Broadway* (1930); and a memoir, *Don't Get Me Wrong, I Love Hollywood* (1975). He was also the editor of a semiannual magazine, *This Was Hollywood*.

Skolsky's reportage of the vagaries of the Hollywood scene was informative and good-natured, a refreshing contrast to some of his competitors such as Louella Parsons and Hedda Hopper, who were often more acerbic. He was one of the most knowledgeable people in Hollywood, with information about what was happening on the lots and in the studios and production companies. He also displayed a deep understanding of the business and history of the art of motion pictures. Skolsky died of Parkinson's disease.

★

Profiles of Sidney Skolsky have appeared in newspapers over the years, with *Variety* being the most consistent chronicler of his career (see especially 28 Jan. 1976). Information and an appraisal of his life can be found in Gilbert W. Gabriel's introduction to Skolsky's book, *Times Square Tintypes*, and in the *ABC Program Service Bulletin* (24 Oct. 1937). Obituaries are in the *New York Times* (5 May 1983), the *New York Post* (4 May 1983), and *Variety* (11 May 1983).

FRANK BRADY

SLOANE, Eric (*b.* 27 February 1905 in New York City; *d.* 6 March 1985 in New York City), painter, author, illustrator, and meteorologist best known for his luminous landscapes and sky paintings and his series of books on Americana, all reflecting a busy career devoted to creating, documenting, and preserving emblems and souvenirs of early American farm life.

Sloane was born Everard Jean Hinrichs to George Francis Hinrichs, a wholesale meat dealer, and Marietta O'Brien. He learned painting from his neighbor, Fred Goudy, a sign painter. An only child, Sloane left home with his father's blessing immediately after the death of his mother. Driving westward through the American countryside at the age of nineteen, Sloane developed what would become an enduring affinity for meteorology and "skyscapes." While returning east from Taos, New Mexico, he wrote a series of notes and sketches on the subject of weather. This interest in

Eric Sloane stands before one of his meteorological displays, 1945. AP/ WIDE WORLD PHOTOS

what he called "airology" later led to the publication of his book *Clouds, Air, and Wind* in 1941.

Back east, he enrolled briefly in the meteorology program at the Massachusetts Institute of Technology, and in 1929 he studied at the Yale School of Fine Arts before returning to New York City. An avid autodidact, Sloane spent much of his time visiting local airfields, eventually writing a manual on weather and aviation that was accomplished enough to be adopted by a local division of the Army Air Corps. Working for a time as a mural and sign painter at the Coney Island amusement park in Brooklyn, he had frequent contact with members of the Ashcan school of painting, including Everett Shinn and John Sloan. So deeply impressed was he with Sloan that he began studying under him at the Art Students League in 1935 and shortly thereafter adopted his teacher's last name, with the addition of an "e." The name "Eric" was formed, according to his autobiography, *Eighty* (1985), by knocking off the "first and last two letters of American." In 1939 he married Myriam Heyne-Bailey ("Mimi"), also an artist, and the couple set up homes and studios in Santa Fe, New Mexico, and Cornwall Bridge, Connecticut.

Shortly after World War II, Sloane persuaded the American Museum of Natural History in New York City to allow him to create the Willets Memorial Hall of Atmosphere (1949), the first such atmospheric installation of its kind in the United States. This glass-encased, three-dimensional model of weather demonstrated the movements of clouds, fronts, and pressure systems and remained on display in the New York museum for nearly three decades. The project won him a Gold Medal from the National Academy of Design. In the 1940s, he also enjoyed a very brief stint on a local New York station as one of the first television weathermen. *Skies and the Artist* (1948), *Eric Sloane's Weather Book* (1952), and *Folklore of American Weather* (1963) grew out of his ongoing scientific, aesthetic, and spiritual reflections on the subject of weather, which he viewed as largely neglected. Starting in 1950 and continuing until his death, Sloane was the director of Weathermen of America, and he lectured widely on the subject, spreading what he called "the gospel of the upward glance."

In the 1950s Sloane began publishing books about early America, drawing upon his ever-growing collection of old farm tools, almanacs, and diaries. He toured continuously throughout New England and the Southwest, producing a wide body of sketches and paintings of old stone farmhouses, covered wooden bridges, enormous barns, sun-drenched pueblos, adobe villages, and sweeping, ominous cloud formations over meadows, hillsides, and valleys. Popular books from this period include *American Barns and Bridges* (1954); *Diary of an Early American Boy: Noah Blake* (1962), an account of domestic life, labor, and craft on the American frontier in 1805; and his encyclopedic volume, *ABC of Early Americana* (1963). In 1969 he donated his vast collection of American farm tools to the Sloane-Stanley Museum in Kent, Connecticut, and in 1974 he built an authentic early American cabin as an extension to the museum, which also houses the Kent Iron Furnace, a leading producer of pig iron for industrial America in the nineteenth century.

In addition to his books and paintings, Sloane undertook a number of commissions for corporations and public institutions, including a mural in the Morton Salt Building in Chicago, and, most notably, at the age of seventy-five, a seventy-foot-high, block-long skyscape in the Smithsonian Institution's National and Air Space Museum.

In an era in which American artists are largely identified by competing artistic agendas and expressionistic and often disparate styles, Sloane's art reflects a deliberate turning away from urban and academic solipsism in favor of a quiet, deeply personal embrace of American spaces. His books are invaluable but never simply nostalgic appreciations of the unfashionable traditions of rural architecture, farm labor, and tool-making crafts. Clearly indebted to the Hudson River school, his paintings demonstrate a uniquely sharp, often startling sense of how sunlight and shadow, atmosphere, and foreground can alter and enrich perspectives, endowing even the most stark landscapes with complexity and strangeness. His paintings are featured among the holdings of over thirty different museums and galleries worldwide, and most of his thirty-five books, all rich in the enduring American traits of ingenuity, curiosity, and humor, remain in print. His writings repeatedly emphasize a nearly religious devotion to naive and spontaneous creation over mannered self-consciousness—in life as much as in art.

While visiting New York City for a career retrospective at the Hammer Galleries, Sloane suffered a heart attack while walking the streets of his native city and died shortly afterward in Roosevelt Hospital. He was buried near his home in Connecticut.

★

There are no biographies of Sloane and his work has been lately ignored by art historians. His autobiography and monograph, *Eighty: An American Souvenir* (1985), is an invaluable mixture of personal reminiscences and artistic statements and includes vivid, full-color reproductions of his major paintings. His compilations *Reverence for Wood* (1965), *An Age of Barns* (1966), and *I Remember America* (1971) are also important documents. An obituary is in the *New York Times* (8 Mar. 1985).

TIM KEANE

SMITH, Ada Beatrice Queen Victoria Louisa Virginia See Bricktop.

SMITH, Walter Wellesley ("Red") (*b.* 25 September 1905 in Green Bay, Wisconsin; *d.* 15 January 1982 in Stamford, Connecticut), sportswriter who won the Pulitzer Prize for distinguished commentary in 1976 while a columnist for the *New York Times.*

Born to Ida Richardson Smith and Walter Philip Smith, a grocer, Walter Smith grew up in Green Bay with an older brother and a younger sister. Walter, nicknamed "Brick" for his shock of red hair, began reading at age five and developed an interest in sports as a youth, following especially the Green Bay minor league baseball team in the Class C Wisconsin-Illinois league. Smith attended East High School in Green Bay, graduating with a B average. One year later, in 1923, he entered Notre Dame University. While at Notre Dame he first displayed his talent in journalism, writing for the *Notre Dame Daily* and editing the college yearbook, *The Dome,* in his junior year.

After graduating from Notre Dame on 5 June 1927, Smith began a journalism career that spanned fifty-five years. His first job, as a general-assignment cub reporter for the *Milwaukee Sentinel,* brought in $24 per week. He worked there for ten months before landing a $40-a-week copy editor position with the *St. Louis Star,* composing headlines and rewriting stories hastily compiled by other reporters. After a few months he was offered a job as a sportswriter—a position that he did not seek but took because he wanted to be out reporting. He covered boxing, basketball, and track for a few months before taking an assignment in 1929 to report on the St. Louis Browns baseball team full-time. Two years later, in 1930, Smith was promoted to covering the St. Louis Cardinals, a team he reported on for three seasons.

During the early years of his career, Smith worked hard and developed a rich personal life. He socialized often with ballplayers and reporters (he became famously linked with fellow sportswriters Frank Graham and Grantland Rice, with whom he was close friends), and successfully courted Catherine ("Kay") M. Cody, whom he married on 11 February 1933. Smith was a dutiful husband and father. Throughout the Great Depression, he often worried about money; after gaining some experience he made about $50 a week at the *Star,* but he felt that this salary was far from enough to raise a family. Still, he turned down a public relations position with Southwest Bell Telephone Company that would have paid $10 a week more. "I only wanted to be a newspaperman," he said later. "I was attached to the newspaper like an undernourished barnacle."

In 1936 Smith moved to the *Philadelphia Record,* attracted by a higher salary. He covered the Philadelphia Phillies for the *Record,* and in 1936 he was first identified in a byline as "Red" Smith, a moniker that stuck for the remainder of his career. At the *Record,* as at the newspapers that followed, Smith kept himself very busy: a typical autumn weekend had him covering college football on Friday night and again on Saturday afternoon, professional football on Sunday, and then writing a weekend wrap-up about the local high school championships. Near the end of his life, Smith estimated that he had written about 10,000 columns.

The key to Smith's success was his ability to write well and get to the heart of a story while avoiding the usual excesses and clichés of sportswriting. He wrote to an aspiring journalist in 1937: "About the only requisites I could name for a sportswriter are those of any ordinary reporter—intelligence, common sense, and an impersonal viewpoint. By the latter I mean the ability to stand a little apart, take no sides, and merely report what happens. The good sportswriter needs one thing more—a degree of writing ability, the capacity to put a little freshness and originality into his stories." To that end, Smith said in one of his most famous quotes, "Writing is easy. I just open a vein and bleed."

Smith did not take sides—except for those of the athletes when they came in conflict with the owners—until the late 1960s, when he became increasingly aware of the political aspects of sports. During the last fifteen years of his career he wrote about baseball's reserve clause, the hypocrisy of the International Olympic Committee (IOC) during the 1972 Munich Olympic Games (which were not halted even after eleven Israelis, five terrorists, and a policeman were killed during a terrorist incident), and other issues.

Amplifying his feeling that sports "are just little games that little boys can play, and it really isn't important to the future of civilization whether the Athletics or the Browns win," Smith criticized the IOC during the 1972 Olympics: "Walled off in their dream world, appallingly unaware of the realities of life and death, the aging playground directors who conduct this quadrennial muscle dance ruled that a little bloodshed must not be permitted to interrupt play.... The men who run the Olympics are not evil men. Their shocking lack of awareness can't be due to callousness. It has to be stupidity."

Although Smith was on the road almost constantly throughout his career, he was a family man, the father of two children, one of whom, Terence ("Terry") Fitzgerald, went on to become a reporter for the *New York Times.* Smith, who often frequented bars with friends, players, and fellow reporters, led a balanced lifestyle marked mostly by devotion to his family, work, and fishing, in that order; a Roman Catholic, Smith attended church on a regular basis.

Smith was serious about his work, but he found plenty of time for his favorite pastime, fishing. Conveniently, fishing could also be fodder for a sports column, and he seemed to enjoy writing about fishing as much as about the major sports. (In 1963 a collection of his columns entitled *Red Smith on Fishing* was published.)

In September 1939 Smith became a full-time sports columnist due to his skill at covering baseball and a range of other events, and his popularity with readers. In 1944 he published his first magazine article, "Don't Send My Boy to Halas," for the *Saturday Evening Post.* He would also

Red Smith, 1951. UPI/CORBIS-BETTMANN

write for *Collier's, Liberty,* and *Holiday,* and in 1945 he published his first book, *Terry and Bunky Play Football,* aimed at the juvenile market.

In September 1945 Smith joined the staff of the *New York Herald Tribune,* attaining a goal he had been working for since the beginning of his career—writing for a New York daily. He began writing a regular column for the *Herald Tribune* on 5 December 1945 and was an immediate success, winning the National Headliners Club Award for excellence in newspaper writing the following year. In 1946 his column went into syndication, and in 1954, after the death of Grantland Rice, it became the most widely circulated sports column in the country. Smith's last column, on 11 January 1982, appeared in 275 U.S. newspapers and 225 newspapers abroad.

By the late 1940s Smith was an institution, widely considered to be one of the best sportswriters in the country. His columns were considered worthy of study at major universities. One of his stories, about a heavyweight fight between Joe Louis and Rocky Marciano, was the only sports story and the only piece of journalism anthologized in the college textbook *A Quarto of Modern Literature.*

Smith wrote for the *Herald Tribune,* with his column "Views of Sport" appearing six times weekly until the paper folded, publishing its last issue on 17 August 1965. He continued writing for the *Tribune*'s syndicate, and then the newly created *New York World Journal Tribune.* Less than two years later—in May 1967—that paper also folded, and

he was again relegated to writing for the Publishers-Hall Syndicate. Finally, in 1971, Smith accepted an offer to write a column for the *New York Times,* where he would continue to write his column, "Sports of the Times," four times weekly until just before his death.

Throughout the late 1960s Smith's personal life went through changes as well. In 1967 his wife Kay died of liver cancer. They had been married for thirty-four years. On 2 November 1968, Smith married an artist, Phyllis Warner Weiss, a widow with five children.

Smith's columns and magazine articles were collected in nine separate anthologies; the first, entitled *Out of the Red,* was published in 1950. *The Red Smith Reader* and *To Absent Friends* were released in 1982. Smith also edited a collection entitled *Sports Stories* in 1949.

Red Smith died of congestive heart failure and kidney failure on Friday, 15 January 1982, at Stamford Hospital in Stamford, Connecticut. His ashes were buried at the Long Ridge Cemetery, also in Stamford.

Smith's greatness as a writer was recognized during his lifetime, not just by prize-givers like the Pulitzer committee. "Red Smith was, quite simply, the best sportswriter. Put the emphasis on writer," began a story by fellow *New York Times* columnist Dave Anderson the day after Smith died. "Virtually all of today's sportswriters grew up reading Red Smith's column. He was their idol and their inspiration. And their friend."

Smith's importance extended beyond the world of sports

and journalism; in awarding only the second Pulitzer Prize ever to a sportswriter, the Pulitzer committee called his work "unique in the erudition, the literary quality, the vitality and the freshness of viewpoint." This high quality brought non–sports fans to read his column, and some thought it more than a coincidence that shortly after he called for a boycott of the 1980 Moscow Olympics because of the Soviet Union's invasion of Afghanistan, the United States followed suit.

★

Ira Berkow, *Red: A Biography of Red Smith* (1986), is the definitive biography, written by a younger *New York Times* sportswriter whose career overlapped that of Smith's. A cover story by Roger Kahn, "Red Smith of the Press Box," is in *Newsweek* (21 Apr. 1958). Donald Hall, "First a Writer, Then a Sportsman," *New York Times Book Review* (18 July 1982), is an appreciation by a poet and a sports fan. A tribute by Dave Anderson, a colleague of Smith's, and an obituary by Berkow, Smith's biographer, are in the *New York Times* (16 Jan. 1982).

JEFF MERRON

SNYDER, John Wesley (*b.* 21 June 1895 in Jonesboro, Arkansas; *d.* 8 October 1985 in Seabrook Island, South Carolina), banker and Treasury secretary who advised President Harry Truman on postwar demobilization and reconstruction of the international economy.

Snyder was one of two sons of Jerre Hartwell Snyder, a druggist, and Ellen Hatcher. He graduated from Jonesboro High School in 1914 and attended Vanderbilt University for one year before dropping out to work for his uncle, Judge E. A. Rolfe who managed farming, timber, and banking interests. After American entry into World War I, Snyder joined the army, was commissioned an artillery captain in 1917, and served in France with the American Expeditionary Forces.

After demobilization in 1919, Snyder spent the next decade working at various banks in Arkansas and Missouri. On 5 January 1920 he married Evelyn Cook; they had a daughter. Snyder was also active in the military reserve, where he formed a strong friendship with fellow reserve officer Harry S. Truman. After the stock market crash of 1929, Snyder became a national bank receiver in the Office of the Comptroller of the Currency, where he oversaw the liquidation of insolvent banks. In 1937 he became manager of the St. Louis Loan Agency of the Reconstruction Finance Corporation (RFC), and in 1940 he returned to Washington, D.C., as executive vice president of the RFC and director of the Defense Plant Corporation, responsible for the rapid construction of mobilization facilities.

When Truman ran for the U.S. Senate in 1934 and in 1940, Snyder was a strong supporter and an active fund-

Secretary of the Treasury John Snyder in 1948 with a check for $7.5 billion, the largest check that the U.S. government had ever issued to that time. UPI/CORBIS-BETTMANN

raiser. Snyder also lobbied President Franklin D. Roosevelt to name Truman as his running mate in the 1944 election.

In 1943 Snyder left Washington to become vice president of the First National Bank of St. Louis, but after Truman succeeded to the presidency in April 1945, he appointed Snyder as head of the Federal Loan Administration, where he was involved in the initial planning for postwar demobilization. Three months later Truman named Snyder as director of the Office of War Mobilization and Reconversion. In June 1946 President Truman appointed Snyder secretary of the Treasury to replace Fred Vinson. During the following six years, Snyder was one of Truman's closest advisers in the planning of U.S. domestic and foreign policy. He oversaw the diminution of the government that accompanied demobilization, when annual federal expenditures declined from $98 billion to $33 billion, and then the subsequent increase to $65 billion with the onset of the cold war and the permanent semimobilization of the economy that followed the outbreak of the Korean War in 1950.

Unlike President Roosevelt, who financed World War II largely through deficit spending, President Truman sought to finance the Korean War and the cold war on a pay-as-you-go basis. Snyder supported Truman's efforts to raise taxes, because he shared Truman's belief that continued deficit spending would permanently harm the national economy.

Even while the government embarked upon semimobilization and expensive programs of foreign aid and military assistance, Snyder undertook the diminution of the then-unprecedented government debt of $269 billion that had financed World War II. He also engaged in a longstanding dispute with the Federal Reserve Board over the extent of permissible inflation, and he won an increase in the prime rate.

Snyder took an active role in the formulation of international policy, both as Truman's personal friend and in his official capacities. He was the U.S. representative on the International Monetary Fund and the International Bank for Reconstruction and Development, as well as a member of the NATO Council from 1949 to 1953 and the National Security Council from 1951 to 1952.

As an ex-officio member of the National Security Council, Snyder was involved in every major foreign policy decision between 1946 and 1952. Truman consulted Snyder, along with Secretary of State Dean Acheson and Secretary of Defense Robert Lovett, regarding the insubordination of General Douglas MacArthur during the Korean War; Snyder recommended MacArthur's removal. During the 1951 debate over wage and price controls and the president's seizure of the steel mills in 1951, Snyder strongly advised against the seizure.

In the final years of the Truman administration, Snyder was subjected to accusations of cronyism after various newspapers published stories about corruption and bribery involving Internal Revenue Service inspectors. Despite the fact that all the corrupt officials had been appointed during the Roosevelt administration, the scandal damaged the reputations of both Truman and Snyder and contributed to the election of Republican Dwight Eisenhower in 1952.

After working on a transition team to facilitate the transfer of power to the Republicans in 1953, Snyder returned to private life as president from 1953 to 1966 of the Overland Corporation, an investment company based in Toledo, Ohio. Snyder also engaged in a number of philanthropic activities; he was one of the originators of the Harry S. Truman Scholarship Foundation and chair of its board of trustees, and was one of the guiding forces behind the financing of the Truman library. Snyder died of old age and cancer. His body was cremated and the ashes interred in the crypt of the National Cathedral in Washington, D.C.

Snyder was a midwestern banker who attained high office on the basis of his lifelong friendship with fellow midwesterner Harry Truman. Although criticized by liberals for being a conservative and by anti-Trumanites for being a Fair Dealer, Snyder was valued by Truman for his common sense, which the president believed was frequently lacking in others who appeared more brilliant or were more photogenic. As a fiscal conservative, Snyder favored balanced budgets, less government spending, and reduction of the government debt. While advising Truman in the new postwar environment, however, Snyder opted for higher interest rates to promote economic growth and later cold war mobilization and supported an active American role in international economic matters, including foreign aid and international reconstruction. He took his greatest pride, however, in having reduced the national debt during three of his six years in office, lowering it from $269 billion to $259 billion, a record that was not met by any other Treasury secretary during the subsequent half-century.

★

Snyder's papers and an extensive oral history interview are located at the Harry S. Truman Library, Independence, Missouri. Snyder's role in the Truman administration is discussed in Harry S. Truman, *Memoirs*, 2 vols. (1955–1956); Dean G. Acheson, *Present at the Creation: My Years in the State Department* (1969); Chester Bowles, *Promises to Keep: My Years in Public Life, 1941–1969* (1971); and Marriner S. Eccles, *Beckoning Frontiers: Public and Personal Recollections*, edited by Sidney Hyman (1951). Snyder's role in the cabinet is discussed in Alonzo L. Hamby, *Beyond the New Deal: Harry S. Truman and American Liberalism* (1973), and Robert J. Donovan, *Tumultuous Years: The Presidency of Harry S. Truman, 1949–1953* (1982). His role in domestic economic policy is discussed in Herbert Stein, *The Fiscal Revolution in America* (1969); A. E. Holmans, *United States Fiscal Policy, 1945–1959: Its Contribution to Economic Stability* (1961); Darrel Cady, "The Truman Administration's Reconversion Policies, 1945–1947" (Ph.D. diss., University of Kansas, 1974); and Maeva Marcus, *Truman and the Steel Seizure Case: The Limits of Presidential Power* (1977). His role in international economic policy is discussed in Richard N. Gardner, *Sterling-Dollar Diplomacy: The Origins and the Prospects of Our International Economic Order* (rev. ed., 1969); Alfred E. Eckes, Jr., *A Search for Solvency: Bretton Woods and the International Monetary System, 1941–1971* (1975); and Robert A. Pollard, *Economic Security and the Origins of the Cold War, 1945–1950* (1985). See also Francis H. Heller, ed., *Economics and the Truman Administration* (1981). Obituaries are in the *New York Times* and the *Washington Post* (both 9 Oct. 1985).

STEPHEN MARSHALL

SPANEL, Abram Nathaniel (*b.* 15 May 1901 in Odessa, Russia; *d.* 31 March 1985 in Princeton, New Jersey), founder of International Latex Company, manufacturer of Playtex products.

The son of Heyman Spanel, a tailor, and Hannah Sarokskaya, a laundress, Abram moved with his parents and sister to Paris in 1904 to escape the oppression of Jews in Russia. In 1910 the father moved the family to Rochester, New York, which was a major men's clothing manufacturing center. Spanel attended public schools in Rochester and, as a youth, became a citizen by virtue of his parents' natural-

Abram Spanel, 1957. UPI/Corbis-Bettmann

ization. He matriculated at the University of Rochester, from which he graduated with a chemical engineering degree in 1924.

After graduation, Spanel invented and patented the Vacuumizer, a garment bag that attached to a vacuum cleaner and mothproofed clothing. He sold the apparatus to the Eureka Company, and with the money he founded the International Latex Company in Rochester in 1932. The company's first product was women's swimming caps. Spanel was disappointed by the seasonal nature of the swimming cap business, and soon expanded the product line to rubber gloves, baby bibs, aprons, and makeup caps and capes, sold under the name "Play-Tex." Spanel moved the company to Dover, Delaware, in 1937 to avoid union organizing that was taking place in Rochester. At the same time, he changed the corporate name to Playtex International.

In 1947 Spanel launched the Playtex "Living Girdle." At that time, women's girdles were produced by dipping forms into vats of latex, then perforating the latex band with small holes to allow the skin to breathe. Unfortunately, the girdles tore easily. Spanel patented a form that put an extra bead of latex at the edges and other critical parts of the girdle that added strength and resisted tearing.

The success of Playtex girdles owed as much to imaginative marketing practices as to the improved manufacture of the garments. Spanel borrowed classic package-goods techniques to sell the apparel product. First, he gave the girdle a catchy brand name, the Playtex Living Girdle. Second, he provided an alternative to the common store practice of hanging girdles on hangers or keeping them behind a counter. Spanel packaged the girdles in attractive, self-service, clear plastic tubes that made it easy for consumers to select the garment without the aid of a salesclerk behind a counter. Women also liked the package because the girdle had not been handled and did not appear shopworn. Spanel encouraged retailers to incorporate eye-catching Playtex display racks in their stores, and he believed in extensive advertising.

In 1954 Playtex introduced the Living Bra and followed it with the Eighteen Hour Girdle, Cross Your Heart Bra, and other brand-name girdles and bras. Playtex, whose women's undergarments were the first to be advertised on television (beginning in 1955), employed celebrity spokeswomen like Jane Russell and later Eve Arden in television commercials. Playtex became a household word, and, in a brand-awareness survey conducted by Fairchild Publications, Playtex was the most recognized innerwear brand among consumers in 1993.

At the time Playtex moved to Dover, the town was primarily a farming community. The company quickly became an economic force in the area, employing about 3,000 people at its height. Employees who knew Spanel said that while he could be difficult, workers were devoted to him. A small man given to wearing bow ties and who possessed a booming voice, he could terrorize workers one minute, then sit quietly reminiscing with them the next. He was known for handing out vitamins gratis to all the workers and was one of the first industrialists to offer medical insurance to employees and to have production areas air-conditioned. Playtex provided company picnics and Christmas bonuses long before other firms adopted these practices. In 1951 the U.S. Department of Labor cited Playtex for its practice of hiring the handicapped. A patriotic man, Spanel returned to the U.S. government over $1 million in profits the company had earned on contracts supplying material for World War II.

In 1954 Stanley Warner, a member of the Warner moviemaking family, purchased a majority share of Playtex, which by then was valued at $30 million a year. Spanel welcomed the access to the financial resources of Warner Brothers and wrote to a friend that the infusion of money gave him "seven league boots" to embark on new ventures. The infusion of cash enabled Playtex to expand its operations to Europe, Canada, Australia, and South America.

Spanel probably gained as much notoriety as a writer of editorials as he did as an industrialist, writing more than 100 columns that he paid to have published in newspapers and magazines across the country. He began writing editorials early in his career, initially to counter Nazi propaganda being spread in the United States before World War II. After the war, Spanel continued to write on a wide range of subjects. He urged America to pay closer attention to South America, children's health issues, education, and the plight of Russian Jews; he opposed American isolationism and supported the State of Israel. He also advocated closer ties with France at a time when Franco-American relations were strained. The French government rewarded Spanel by naming him a commander of the French Legion of Honor. The City of Paris made him an honorary member of its municipal council, and several French cities and towns made him an honorary citizen. The Bolivian government bestowed its Condecoration Condor de los Andes on him.

Spanel's writing eventually embroiled him in a slander suit. When syndicated columnist Westbrook Pegler labeled Spanel "pro-Red," Spanel sued Pegler for $6 million and eventually forced Pegler to publish a retraction of the charge in 1949.

Spanel donated large sums of money for medical research, particularly to research on children's health and childhood diseases, and to cancer research. He was also generous in his support of Franco-American ties and the State of Israel.

After his retirement from the chairmanship of Playtex in 1975, Spanel remained active in Dover, devoting his time to Spanel International, Ltd., a company that he founded to exploit products he had invented. He remained chairman of ILC Dover and Reichold Chemical Co., spin-offs of the Playtex Industrial division, and to the Spanel Foundation. At the time of his death, he held over 2,000 patents.

Spanel was living in Princeton, New Jersey, when he died of congestive heart failure. He was survived by his wife, Margaret (a graduate of Smith College who also held a master's degree from Columbia), a son, David Louis, from a first marriage and a daughter, Ann, from his second marriage.

★

The Alexander Library at Rutgers University in New Brunswick, N.J., has a collection of approximately sixty-five boxes of Spanel's papers. The Playtex Apparel Corporation, a division of Sara Lee, in Stamford, Conn., and Playtex Personal Products in Dover, Del., maintain records on Playtex International. Obituaries are in the *New York Times, Delaware State News,* and *Womens' Wear Daily* (all 2 Apr. 1985).

WILLIAM J. MALONEY

SPARKMAN, John Jackson (*b.* 20 December 1899 near Hartselle, Alabama; *d.* 16 November 1985 in Huntsville,

Alabama), longtime Democratic congressman and senator from Alabama and Adlai Stevenson's vice presidential running mate in 1952.

The seventh of eleven children of Whitten Joseph Sparkman, a tenant farmer, and Julia Mitchell Kent, Sparkman grew up in the Tennessee River valley of rural northern Alabama. After attending a one-room, one-teacher school near his home, he went to Morgan County High School in Hartselle, graduating in 1917. He then entered the University of Alabama at Tuscaloosa, where he supported himself with part-time work until he was awarded a teaching fellowship during his junior year. He served as student-government president, edited the college newspaper, was a member of Phi Beta Kappa, and joined the Students' Army Training Corps. In 1921 he received an A.B. and a reserve commission in the Coast Artillery.

Unable to find suitable employment, Sparkman remained at the University of Alabama, earning an LL.B. (1923) and an A.M. (1924). On 2 June 1923 he married Ivo Hall, a graduate of the school; the couple had one daughter. In 1925 Sparkman was admitted to the Alabama bar and moved to Huntsville, where he practiced law, taught at Huntsville College, and became a civic leader.

When in 1936 the representative from Alabama's Eighth District announced he would not seek reelection to Congress, Sparkman entered a crowded Democratic primary, gained his party's nomination in a runoff election, and went on to win the general election. In the House of Representatives (1937–1946) he supported legislation to aid tenant farmers and concerned himself with issues of importance to his home district, such as the Tennessee Valley Authority; he served on the House Military Affairs Committee, which had jurisdiction over that agency. After war broke out in Europe in 1939, Sparkman consistently supported President Franklin D. Roosevelt's military and foreign policies and in 1944 advocated a fourth term for Roosevelt. In 1945 Sparkman was elected majority whip by House Democrats.

In July 1946, having already won renomination to his House seat, Sparkman entered and won a special Democratic primary to fill the unexpired term of Senator John H. Bankhead, who had died in June. Alabama's election law would not permit a new Democratic primary to choose another candidate for Sparkman's House seat, so he remained in that race to prevent the election of a Republican by default. In November, Sparkman was reelected to his House seat and elected to the U.S. Senate as well—the only person in history to be elected simultaneously to both houses of Congress. Sparkman immediately resigned from the House and took his seat in the Senate, where he remained until 1979, having been reelected in 1948, 1954, 1960, 1966, and 1972.

In 1947 Sparkman told a reporter that southerners

Senator John Sparkman at Andrews Air Force Base on his return from Moscow for the signing of the Nuclear Test Ban Treaty, 1963. ARCHIVE PHOTOS

would never accept President Harry S. Truman as a candidate for reelection because of his support of civil rights measures. But in 1948 Sparkman refused to join other southern leaders in splitting the Democratic party by backing the third-party candidacy of Strom Thurmond of South Carolina (the so-called Dixiecrat movement). Sparkman remained loyal to the national party and joined his fellow Alabama senator, Lister Hill, in battling Dixiecrats for control of the state Democratic party.

Sparkman's loyalty to the national party was soon rewarded. Although he worked to gain the 1952 Democratic presidential nomination for Senator Richard Russell of Georgia, the eventual nominee, Governor Adlai Stevenson of Illinois, chose Sparkman as his running mate in an unsuccessful bid for the White House. Some pundits believed his association with the liberal Stevenson would hurt Sparkman's chances for reelection to the Senate in 1954. Sparkman campaigned vigorously, convinced Alabamians he was "still the same tenant farmer's son they had always known," and was easily reelected, despite efforts to smear him through the use of doctored photographs, purporting

to show him with "Negro friends," and leaflets, supposedly issued by the "Communist Party of Alabama," calling for his reelection.

In the Senate, Sparkman gained a reputation for getting things done with minimal controversy and confrontation. Although he frequently spoke on the Senate floor, he preferred to work on legislation in committee. The seniority system and Democratic control of the Senate during most of his long tenure combined to give Sparkman the chairmanship of powerful committees. As chairman of the Senate Select committee on Small Business (1949–1953, 1955–1969), he sponsored the legislation creating the Small Business Administration.

In January 1949 Sparkman became chairman of the Subcommittee on Housing of the old Senate Committee on Banking and Currency (he was also chairman of the full committee, 1967–1970) and pushed through the Housing Act of 1949. Long before he became chairman (1971–1974) of the new Senate Committee on Banking, Housing, and Urban Affairs, Sparkman was known as "Mr. Housing," for, as Robert Sherrill wrote in 1965, "no major piece of housing legislation has passed Congress since World War II that Sparkman did not either originate or modify."

Sparkman also took a deep interest in foreign affairs. Long a member of the Senate Foreign Relations Committee (1951–1974), he assumed its chairmanship (1975–1978) when J. William Fulbright of Arkansas left the Senate after being defeated in the Democratic primary in 1974. Some critics charged that Sparkman, who was then seventy-five, allowed the power of that committee to decline. As the *Washington Post* editorialized, Sparkman's commitment to bipartisan foreign policy and his belief that the president, not Congress, should direct foreign affairs had become "casualties of the war in Southeast Asia."

In January 1978, at age seventy-eight, Sparkman announced he would not seek another term. In 1979, after forty-two years in Congress, he returned to Huntsville to open a law practice with his only grandson. He died of a heart attack at the Big Springs Manor Nursing Home in Huntsville, where he was undergoing therapy for an artificial hip joint, and was buried in that city.

Perhaps the most controversial aspect of Sparkman's long career concerns his position on civil rights. Like most southern congressmen, he consistently voted against civil rights legislation, but unlike many southern politicians, such as Alabama governor George Wallace, Sparkman avoided race as an election issue. When asked in 1974 to define the major change in southern politics during his lifetime, Sparkman replied, "the elimination of the civil rights question as a political issue." Surely what progress has been made in race relations in the South was due largely to moderates like Sparkman, who refused to descend to racist rhetoric and demagoguery in their quest for political office.

★

Sparkman's papers are in the W. S. Hoole Special Collections Library at the University of Alabama at Tuscaloosa. Ivo Hall Sparkman published two books on her overseas travels with him: *Over the Senator's Shoulder: A Glance at the East* (1966) and *Journeys with the Senator* (1977); these chatty works focus on the writer's impressions of people and places, but they provide occasional glimpses of Sparkman's views on specific foreign-policy issues. William Bridge, "John J. Sparkman: Democratic Senator from Alabama" (part of the Ralph Nader Congress Project, 1972) provides an assessment of Sparkman's effectiveness as a legislator. Although the tributes by legislators tend to be repetitious, *Memorial Addresses and Other Tributes in the Congress of the United States on the Life and Contributions of John Sparkman* (Senate document no. 99-26, 1986) reprints several useful newspaper accounts of Sparkman's career. "John Sparkman and the Civil Rights Issue," *New Republic* (18 Aug. 1952), and Robert Sherrill, "Portrait of a 'Southern Liberal' in Trouble," *New York Times Magazine* (7 Nov. 1965), grapple with Sparkman's position on the race issue. William D. Barnard, *Dixiecrats and Democrats: Alabama Politics, 1942–1950* (1974), deals briefly with Sparkman's relations with loyalist Alabama Democrats who fought Dixiecrats for control of the state party. Obituaries are in the *New York Times, Birmingham* (Ala.) *News,* and *Huntsville* (Ala.) *Times* (all 17 Nov. 1985).

ROMAN ROME

SPIEGEL, Sam(uel) (*b.* 11 November 1901 in Jarosław, Austria [now Poland]; *d.* 31 December 1985 on St. Martin, West Indies), film producer.

Spiegel was the second child of Simon Spiegel, a tobacco wholesaler, and Regina Spiegel. Samuel was rebellious and a disinterested student with a talent for languages. In 1919 the family fled to Vienna, Austria, to escape the postwar chaos and anti-Semitism in Poland. In the early 1920s, Spiegel left his family and migrated to Palestine, where he joined a kibbutz. In 1922 he married Rachel Agronovich, a Canadian immigrant. They had one daughter. In 1926, poor health forced Spiegel to move to Jerusalem, where he filed for a divorce a few months later. In 1927 he traveled to the United States to make his fortune. Heading to California, he left a trail of bad checks that finally caught up with him in San Francisco in 1929, leading to five months in jail and deportation to Poland. While in California, however, he got his first work in the movie business as a translator in 1927.

In 1930 Spiegel was employed by Universal Studios in Berlin to work on European distribution of their films, including *All Quiet on the Western Front.* He helped win the right to screen that film in Germany in 1930. Soon he produced his first film, *Marriage Unlimited.* In response to Nazi persecution of Jews, Spiegel fled Berlin for Paris in 1933 and then went to London in 1935. He quickly got to

Sam Spiegel, 1964. UPI/CORBIS-BETTMANN

work producing *The Invader* (1936), starring Buster Keaton, who was well past his popularity as a silent film star. (The film was released in the United States as *An Old Spanish Custom.*) While keeping the production afloat, Spiegel wrote bad checks and was arrested. He served three months and was deported in 1937. He then headed to Mexico, where he was soon in trouble with that government for his finances. In 1939, he entered the United States as an illegal alien under the name S. P. Eagle. Friends described him as a short, paunchy man with a powerful chest built up during his years at the kibbutz. He was affable and persuasive, with an urbanity that belied his lack of formal education.

Spiegel's first Hollywood film, *Tales of Manhattan* (1942), boasted a cast that included Henry Fonda, Paul Robeson, and Ginger Rogers. After the success of the film, he hired lawyers to battle his immigration problems. He won his case in 1947 and that year he married Lynn Baggett, an actress. After a few minor films, Spiegel achieved major success with *The African Queen* (1952), which starred Humphrey Bogart and Katharine Hepburn and was directed by his friend John Huston. To finance the international production, Spiegel mortgaged his house in Hollywood. Despite hardships of terrain, weather, and disease while on location in the Congo, the film cost only $4 million and was almost on budget. It was a huge success, grossing ten times its cost.

Spiegel next worked with the director Elia Kazan and the writer Budd Schulberg to produce *On the Waterfront* (1954) and took a major role in reworking the script. The resulting film, starring Marlon Brando and Eva Marie Saint, bore Spiegel's mark in every aspect of production and won him his first Academy Award for best picture. In 1955, his marriage ended in divorce.

Spiegel's next major project was an adaptation in 1957 of Pierre Boulle's novel *Bridge on the River Kwai,* the story of a bridge built during World War II by British prisoners of war held in a Japanese camp. Spiegel's choice of director was David Lean, an Englishman who was in a slump at the time. Spiegel tried to sign Laurence Olivier for the lead but eventually picked Alec Guinness. The movie was filmed on location in Ceylon, and Lean's meticulous work caused it to go over budget. Spiegel stayed in England until the filming of the finale, in which an actual bridge was demolished as a train crossed. The spectacular scene helped the movie become a major hit, winning eight Academy Awards, including Spiegel's second for best picture. In 1957, just before the charity premiere of *Bridge on the River Kwai,* Spiegel married Betty Benson, a model.

Spiegel's next film, *Suddenly Last Summer* (1959), was modestly successful, but he is best remembered for his second collaboration with Lean, *Lawrence of Arabia* (1962). The two men wanted to work on a film biography of Mahatma Gandhi but settled on the World War I exploits of the legendary British officer Thomas Edward Lawrence. Although Spiegel had obtained the film rights to Lawrence's war memoir, *Seven Pillars of Wisdom* (1926), from his brother Arnold Lawrence, he faced competition from a group centered around Terence Rattigan, who had written a play about Lawrence's later years. Early in 1961 Spiegel got the go-ahead.

Once again, Spiegel wanted to rely on location footage for realism. Lean insisted on Jordan, where some of Lawrence's adventures had actually taken place. The complication of a Jewish film producer working in Jordan was smoothed over with the assistance of Anthony Nutting, a career diplomat. In casting the lead, Spiegel first approached Brando, but they never came to terms. Albert Finney was offered the role, but he eventually turned down Spiegel's deal. Finally, the relatively unknown Irish actor Peter O'Toole tested for the part, and he completely won over Lean. The tall, athletic actor played a man who had only stood five feet, six inches tall, but O'Toole bore a striking facial resemblance to Lawrence.

The location filming was beset by difficulties, but the footage of desert storms and sunrises was some of the most striking imagery ever seen on film. *Lawrence of Arabia* premiered in December 1962 and created a sensation with audiences and critics, despite a running time of more than three hours. It won eight Oscars, including Spiegel's third best picture award. During the final days of filming, Spiegel and Lean had a falling out from which they never recovered. Spiegel later won the Irving G. Thalberg Award for lifetime achievement.

Lawrence of Arabia was Spiegel's high-water mark. Later films, such as *The Night of the Generals* (1967) and *The Chase* (1966), were disappointments, as the producer lost his touch for influencing a film without squelching other talent. He died of a sudden heart attack in a hotel room on St. Martin.

One critic wrote that Spiegel was the master of the multilayered deal in lining up a big cast. He lured an actor by saying that a second actor was already on board, then told the second actor that the first one would sign if he or she did. Another critic noted that Spiegel's long list of awards proved he could make films that lived up to Hollywood's idea of what movies should be.

★

Further information on Spiegel and his movies is in Andrew Sinclair, *Spiegel: The Man Behind the Pictures* (1987); Katharine Hepburn, *The Making of "The African Queen"; or, How I Went to Africa with Bogart, Bacall, and Huston and Almost Lost My Mind* (1987); and L. Robert Morris and Lawrence Raskin, *"Lawrence of Arabia": The Thirtieth-Anniversary Pictorial History* (1992). An obituary is in the *New York Times* (1 Jan. 1986).

TERRY BALLARD

STANFORD, Sally (*b.* 5 May 1903 in Baker City, Oregon; *d.* 1 February 1982 in Greenbrae, California), San Francisco madam and restaurateur who became mayor of Sausalito, California.

Born Mabel Janice Busby, Sally Stanford was the second of six children born to poor farmers. Sally termed her father "ineffectual but well-intentioned." Her mother was a religious woman who had once been a schoolteacher and a homesteader of 360 acres of land. Sally despised living in poverty and helped support the family by taking a golf caddying job at the age of seven. Frequent moves left the family with little stability. Sally left school after the third grade to work in a truck garden and on subsequent moves took in ironing and was a housekeeper. In the fall of 1917, Sally left for Santa Paula, California, to care for her recently orphaned cousins.

Sally returned to her family in Medford, Oregon, within a year. She met Dan Goodan, an auditor for a lumber company, while waitressing; the pair eloped in 1919 and settled in Colorado. In July 1920 Goodan was arrested for signing unauthorized checks from a former employer. Sally unknowingly cashed one of the checks to buy an iron and was arrested for obtaining goods under false pretenses. Sentenced to two years at the Oregon State Penitentiary, Sally lived with the warden's family because the prison held no other female inmates. (She received a pardon in 1947.)

After her parole in September 1921, Stanford returned to Santa Paula and manufactured bathtub gin. Calling herself Marsha Busby, she conducted the bootlegging business alone to avoid being caught and read extensively to educate herself. In 1927 she married criminal attorney Ernest Spagnoli and moved to his home in San Francisco. The two separated and in 1929 Stanford bought a hotel at 693 O'Farrell Street. Sally wrote that she ran a legitimate hotel, but after police charged her with operating a brothel, she decided that as long as she had been accused of being a madam she would become one. Spagnoli obtained an annulment from Sally in 1933. To avoid embarrassing him she took the name Sally Stanford.

In 1934 she married Louis Rapp and divorced him seven years later. At one time she owned four bordellos, two of her most famous being a turreted mansion on Russian Hill and her residence at 1144 Pine Street on Nob Hill, where she lived and operated a brothel from 1941 to 1949. Referred to as "the Fortress" because of its austere exterior and large wrought-iron gate, the Pine Street mansion's lavish interior boasted a sunken marble pool, a spotlighted fountain, and fireplace within a Pompeian Court. A glass ceiling allowed for plenty of sunlight to illuminate Stanford's collection of antiques. Among her clientele were politicians, diplomats, and movie stars. While living on Pine Street, she adopted two orphaned children and took the children's last name, becoming Marcia Owen.

Following World War II, police surveillance made it difficult for Stanford to operate her business. In 1947 two masked and armed robbers broke into her home and beat her. After receiving threatening phone calls, she went out of business in 1949. In 1948, however, Stanford began restoring the Valhalla, an 1870s waterfront saloon in Sausalito, California, and reopened it in 1950 as an elegant Victorian restaurant. A petite woman with chestnut hair, Sally ushered in her diners dressed in lavish evening gowns and displaying a glittering array of diamonds. In April 1951 she married wealthy Oriental art dealer Robert Livingston Gump. They separated the following December. In 1954 she married Robert Kenna, owner of a Fresno trucking company; they divorced in 1956.

While Stanford's marriages were short-lived, her restaurant flourished. When officials refused to let her put up an electric sign, she ran for one of two vacant city council seats in 1962. In typical Stanford fashion, she adorned her campaign headquarters with Tiffany lamps and Oriental rugs

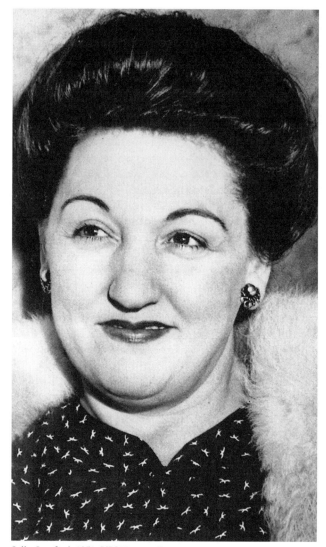

Sally Stanford, 1951. UPI/CORBIS-BETTMANN

and campaigned with Loretta, her pet parrot, on her shoulder. Included in her platform were promises to "keep Sausalito Sausalito" and to "live and let live." Other pledges included building a hospital, establishing a youth program, and stopping the development of high-rise apartment buildings. After five unsuccessful attempts, and after legally changing her name to Sally Stanford in 1971, Republican Stanford finally won a seat on the city council in 1972.

In the 1976 election she dispensed with the usual campaign literature and sent out valentines that said "I love you." After being elected to another four-year term, she stated that people voted for her "because they've got common sense." A high margin of votes (1,203) automatically gave her a two-year term as mayor. In 1978 she served as vice mayor and was named vice mayor for life by the council in 1980. One Sausalito businessman, commenting on the council, said, "She was really the only one ... who knew what she was talking about."

Reported to have had a total of twenty-two names, Stanford was arrested seventeen times, convicted twice, but never fined more than $1,500. She believed in a higher force and reincarnation and through mail-order was ordained a minister of the Kirby Hensley's Universal Life Church and occasionally officiated at marriages. After leaving Nob Hill, she lived in Pacific Heights and on a fifty-acre ranch in Sonoma County. In 1966 she wrote her autobiography, *Lady of the House,* which became the basis of a 1978 television movie. She survived eleven heart attacks and surgery for colon cancer; she died of heart failure and was buried in San Raphael, California.

Outspoken but always a woman of class, she took pride in her profession as a madam but would be horrified if strangers asked her to reveal details and refused to discuss business in mixed company. A collector of homeless pets, Stanford was a "woman of impulsive charity," who sent money anonymously to disaster victims or paid for funerals of indigent persons whose obituaries she had read. She campaigned against the death penalty for a number of women and filed a lawsuit to prevent the hunting of female deer. She won the hearts of Sausalito's voters and the backing of its Good Government League. She rose from madam to mayor and declared she loved money, the flag, and America, a place "where everybody can get ahead."

★

The California Historical Society and the History Room at the San Francisco Library have newspaper clips on Stanford's life. Although some information is missing and it contains some errors, Stanford's life is best detailed in her autobiography *The Lady of the House* (1966). Curt Gentry, *The Madams of San Francisco: An Irreverent History of the City by the Golden Gate* (1964), offers an account of the lives of various madams, and fills in some facts omitted in Stanford's biography; Carol Dunlap, *California People* (1982), provides an overview of numerous Californians; Terrance A. Sweeney, *God &* (1985), contains an interview that delves into Stanford's connection to God; and Harriet Swift, *The Virago Woman's Travel Guide to San Francisco* (1994), is an overall guide with mentions of Stanford. The article "Miss Stanford Weds Mr. Gump," *Life* (7 May 1951), summarizes her fourth marriage. Obituaries are in the *San Francisco Chronicle* and *New York Times* (both 2 Feb. 1982).

MARILYN ELIZABETH PERRY

STEIN, Aaron Marc (*b.* 15 November 1906 in New York City; *d.* 29 August 1985 in New York City), journalist and author of more than one hundred detective novels.

The son of Max Stein and Fannie Blumberg, Aaron attended the Ethical Culture School (1916–1923) in Man-

hattan before enrolling as an archaeology major at Princeton University. He received his A.B. (summa cum laude and Phi Beta Kappa) in 1927. Stein then became a reporter and columnist for the *New York Evening Post* (1927–1938) and a contributing editor at *Time* (March 1938–January 1939). He wrote fiction in his spare time and in 1939 he began devoting himself exclusively to his own writing. His writing career was interrupted by service in World War II, during which he worked for the Office of War Information (Bureau of Intelligence) in 1942 and 1943 and then served in the U.S. Army from 1943 to 1945 as a language specialist.

Returning to civilian life and his New York City base, Stein resumed his writing career. With the recommendation of Theodore Dreiser, Stein's first novel, *Spirals,* had been published in 1930, a critical if not popular success. Stein described his early attempts at fiction as "radical experiments in style, stream-of-consciousness novels." Prompted by his publishers to write fiction that was more commercial, he had written a popular romance, *Bachelor's Wife* (1932), under the pseudonym George Bagby. Although this book was moderately more successful, Stein did not enjoy writing it, and he turned to detective stories. A long convalescence in the 1930s had given him the opportunity to read many detective-fiction writers. Some he labeled "execrable"; he was convinced that he could write better mysteries. Under the pen name George Bagby, he wrote *Murder at the Piano* (1935) and launched his prolific career as a writer of detective fiction.

Stein kept the Bagby byline for one series featuring Bagby as a freelance writer who chronicled the homicide cases solved by New York police inspector Schmidt. Manhattan is prominently featured in most of the books, revealing Stein's familiarity with the city and detailing its landmarks: the New York Public Library, subway tunnels, seedy bars, exclusive men's clubs, tenements, and mansions. Under his own name he wrote one nonseries novel, *Lock and Key* (1973), and also created two series that reflected his lifelong penchant for travel: in 1940, the adventures of Tim Mulligan and Elsie Mae Hunt, archaeologists, in foreign locales; and in 1959, the escapades of construction engineer Matt Erridge. Under yet another pseudonym, Hampton Stone, Stein created a series featuring New York assistant district attorney Jeremiah X. "Gibby" Gibson, whose partner was Mac, another assistant district attorney. Because their homicide investigations were necessarily centered in New York City, Manhattan locations again provided local color.

Despite their various investigators, a few characteristics can be traced throughout Stein's novels. He provided an excellent sense of location, whether the novel is placed in Manhattan, Paris, Mexico, rustic Maine, or on a transatlantic passenger superliner. All feature unusual titles, such as Stein's *Shoot Me Dacent* (1951) and *Death Meets 400*

Rabbits (1953); Bagby's *The Corpse with the Purple Thighs* (1939), *The Corpse with Sticky Fingers* (1952), and *Mysteriouser and Mysteriouser* (1965); or Stone's *The Murder That Wouldn't Stay Solved* (1951) and *The Real Serendipitous Kill* (1964). Stein's sense of humor invaded not only the titles but also often enlivened the dialogue.

Some of Stein's early interest in narrative method can be discerned in his use of first-person narrators; Matt Erridge addresses the reader as "Charlie," perhaps in an attempt to involve the reader, but at its worst extension it is an annoying mannerism. Stein's main concern was the plot; he was dedicated to creating plots demanding his investigator's intelligence and concentration. As he once said, "I don't go in for descriptions of what police labs do and that sort of thing. My books pretty much depend on the mental process of the detective." This dependence marks the quality of his best books but also reveals the flaws of the weaker books. The solution can be too suddenly revealed, as Anthony Boucher remarked in his review of Bagby's *Another Day, Another Death* (1968), when the plot is "resolved largely by happenstance." Because he produced so many works, some of his books contained clever plots but were too thin to sustain the novels. Newgate Callendar described Stein's eightieth mystery, *The Cheating Butcher* (1980), as "a short story worked up to a novel."

The general quality of the novels, however, and the obvious professionalism Stein maintained are a tribute to his life's work. With the exception of his travels and a lifelong interest in archaeology, Stein dedicated his life to his writing, avoiding even family ties. Although Stein published several fine short stories (never collected) and critical essays, almost all of the more than one hundred books he wrote were mystery novels. He was an enthusiastic member of Mystery Writers of America and served as its president in 1974. He was named Grand Master by the association in 1979, cited for "his contribution over a period of many years to the craft of mystery writing." He aptly summarized his own literary contribution on the occasion of this presentation: "I make no claims to grandeur, but I have always aspired to mastery."

His aspiration persisted to the end of his career. He published his last novel, *The Most Wanted* (1983), under his Bagby pen name two years before his death from cancer in Lenox Hill Hospital.

★

Stein's manuscript collection is at the Firestone Library at Princeton University, Princeton, New Jersey. Helpful, if brief, biographical entries are in Christopher Steinbrunner and Otto Penzler, eds., *Encyclopedia of Mystery and Detection* (1976); Ann Evory, ed., *Contemporary Authors,* New Revision Series, vol. 6 (1982); and William L. DeAndrea, *Encyclopedia Mysteriosa* (1994). An obituary is in the *New York Times* (30 Aug. 1985).

ELIZABETH R. NELSON

STEIN, Julian Caesar ("Jules") (*b.* 26 April 1896 in South Bend, Indiana; *d.* 29 April 1981 in Los Angeles, California), entertainment tycoon who abandoned a promising career as an eye surgeon to convert a youthful business booking jazz orchestras into the show-business giant MCA Inc.

Stein's father, M. Louis Stein, owned a dry goods and shoe store in Indiana. His mother, Rosa Cohen, was an invalid whose illness kept the family in financial crisis. Both parents were Orthodox Jews. The second of five children, Julian was supporting himself at age twelve by playing the violin and saxophone, and at age fourteen he had his own band and was booking other orchestras. A hardworking student, Stein skipped several grades and received his high school degree from an academy at Winona Lake, Indiana, in 1912.

Stein attended the University of West Virginia (1912 and 1913), the University of Chicago (Ph.B., 1915), Rush Medical College (M.D., 1921), and the University of Vienna

Jules Stein. UPI/CORBIS-BETTMANN

(1922). After an ophthalmology residency at Cook County Hospital in Chicago, he entered private practice in that city in 1923. Stein's 1924 manual on telescopic spectacles became a standard reference. Meanwhile, he found time to complete a correspondence course on business and serve as a first lieutenant in the U.S. Army medical reserve. While trying to focus his principal attention on his eye patients, Stein was also booking dance bands into hotels and gangster-era nightclubs in Chicago. In 1924 Stein and William R. Goodheart founded the Music Corporation of America; Stein's brother William was executive vice president of the firm until his death in 1943. In 1925 Julian Stein took "temporary" leave from his practice with another Chicago ophthalmologist and became Jules Stein, president of the growing firm. Stein would later link his medical training with his ability to deal with show-business clients.

On 16 November 1928 Stein, once described by the Associated Press as a "small, slender ... man with genial brown eyes and a chipper manner," married Doris Jones in New York; he had met her while leading a band in Kansas City. They had two daughters.

Jules and William Stein, Goodheart (who eventually left the firm, shortly before World War II), and several early employees, particularly David A. "Sonny" Werblin, Lew Wasserman, and Taft Schreiber, introduced semi-monopolistic practices into the music business. This involved booking the firm's impressive roster of popular bands and requiring customers to accept a "block booking" package that included lower-grossing attractions. Client bands were required to deal exclusively through MCA. To obtain the most lucrative attractions, dance halls, theaters, nightclubs, and hotels also had to book attractions exclusively through MCA. Supplementing the customary practice of booking bands for extended stays in a few big-city venues, Stein and his associates increased revenues by also routing them through a series of "one-night stands," single performances. This generated sometimes violent opposition from local musicians, but Stein consistently enjoyed the support of James Petrillo's American Federation of Musicians. The firms also supplied business management, publicity, insurance, transportation, lodging, liquor, and even confetti to clients. In effect MCA tended to become the producer as well as the booker of musical entertainment, and later of radio, film, and television programs, often attracting adverse attention from federal antitrust officials. Soon half of the country's top-grossing bands became clients, beginning in 1928 with the popular Guy Lombardo and Eddie Duchin. Stein, a union musician, got the permission of Petrillo's national union to both represent and employ musicians. Petrillo became a millionaire, allegedly through MCA deals. MCA also produced a substantial number of entire programs and series for the growing mass radio audience, such as the *Lucky Strike Hit Parade*.

In 1938 Stein sent Wasserman to Hollywood to open a film division of MCA. The firm's first important film client was Bette Davis. Under Stein, Wasserman, and Schreiber's tight management, MCA came to dominate films as it had radio. Stein, who had owned a mansion in Chicago, moved to Beverly Hills, California. Under MCA's rules, film producers, in order to get the firm's top stars, would also have to hire MCA-managed directors and writers. A movie industry tradition was the seven-year contract by which a studio would engage, develop, and promote promising talent. If the actor became a big star, he or she would have to work for low pay until the contract ended. After World War II, the big studios saw their revenues declining as audiences increasingly turned to television, and they became more interested in hiring big revenue-generating stars for specific productions than long-term contract players. By negotiating single-package deals, MCA helped reduce the power of the big studios. In 1940 Petrillo and the Justice Department put pressure on the three major radio networks to cease booking talent as well as employing it. MCA bought the CBS network's representation of bands for a reported $500,000. A large factor in the firm's success was its subsequent purchase of Leland Hayward's agency with its roster of 300 stars, writers, and directors in 1945.

In 1946 Jules Stein, always the largest shareholder in the company, turned the presidency of MCA over to Wasserman. Stein remained chairman and continued planning business strategy. After World War II, MCA introduced a new practice that gave major stars a percentage of a film's box-office receipts and got them production deals. The landmark was James Stewart's *Winchester 73* (1950), which made Stewart rich.

With the advent of television MCA sought to create products for the new medium, as it had for radio. Ronald Reagan, president of the Screen Actors Guild (SAG) and an MCA client, negotiated an exclusive blanket agreement with SAG in 1952 that gave MCA an exclusive, unlimited right to both represent and hire actors. Because the major studios refused to produce films for their competitor, television, MCA's Revue Productions, established in 1959, quickly became the dominant supplier of network television productions.

In 1959 the Music Corporation of America legally became MCA Inc. and began issuing stock to the general public. Stein allowed Wasserman and Schreiber to buy large blocks of MCA stock at a bargain price, giving them a substantial share in the company. He set aside another block of his stock for a profit-sharing plan for employees. Also in 1959 MCA bought Decca Records and its subsidiary Universal-International Studios. It merged Revue Productions and Universal into Universal Pictures. MCA subsequently absorbed a music publisher, a Denver savings and loan association, Spencer Gifts, book publisher G. P. Putnam's Sons, and the Yosemite Land and Curry Company. It built a new sixteen-story black steel and glass headquarters tower (1963) in Universal City, California, north of Hollywood. (The austere tower was furnished with uncomfortable antique English furniture, which Stein collected.) MCA also began to develop commercial real estate sites in the area.

In 1962 the Antitrust Division of the Department of Justice, joined by SAG, no longer headed by Reagan, forced the firm to opt out of its talent-agency business. Reagan, called before a congressional committee, could not remember much about his role in obtaining for MCA the waiver to produce films. Six years later Stein tried to sell his extensive MCA holdings for a large profit to Westinghouse Electric, which owned radio and television stations, but the Justice Department intervened and the deal was abandoned in 1969. When Firestone Tire and Rubber offered to buy MCA, Wasserman opposed the sale because he did not want to work for a tire company. By the early 1970s MCA was known as "the factory" because of its large volume of television programs and feature films. Notable Universal films included *Airport* (1970), *The Sting* (1973), *Jaws* (1975), *The Deer Hunter* (1978), and *E. T.—The Extraterrestrial* (1982). Among MCA's television programs were *General Electric Theater,* with Ronald Reagan introducing the productions and taking part in and producing some of the programs, the *Ed Sullivan* and *Jack Benny* shows, *Wagon Train, Wells Fargo, M Squad, Alfred Hitchcock Presents, Leave It to Beaver, McHale's Navy,* and *Marcus Welby, M.D.* The company's tour of the Universal Cities studios became a top tourist attraction.

In his later years Stein focused on promoting vision research. In 1960 he helped found Research to Prevent Blindness, Inc., which supplies research funds to promising young scientists. Through his efforts, laser therapy and vitreous surgery were supported in their pioneer stages. Causative factors in cataract formation were ascertained and chemical therapy was developed. Diabetic blindness was contained. Corneal transplants, artificial lens implants, and an array of new drugs were introduced.

The Jules Stein Eye Institute at the University of California at Los Angeles, dedicated in 1966, became the only eye center among many that Stein and his wife endowed to bear his name. It began with several millions in seed money, attracted some $4 million more from show-business associates, and received major public and private research funds. In fact, Stein became a principal source of funds for eye research around the country. He also helped get Congress to establish the National Eye Institute in 1968 as a separate entity within the National Institutes of Health in Bethesda, Maryland. In 1969 and 1970 Stein underwent major intestinal surgery, which required a lengthy hospitalization. He recovered and continued his active interest

in business, political, and philanthropic affairs. A Republican, Stein had supported Richard M. Nixon's 1960 presidential bid. Stein and Schreiber helped raise money for Reagan's California gubernatorial campaigns in the 1960s and 1970s.

In 1973 Stein turned over the MCA chairmanship to Wasserman, but as the principal stockholder continued to help shape company policy, which included an unsuccessful attempt to market films on phonograph-like electronic discs. In the late 1970s President Jimmy Carter's Justice Department forced MCA, with other major producers, to abandon an effort to establish a cable television channel, Premier, that would have had first call on their films. (Under President Reagan's more business-friendly Justice Department, the firm later became a co-owner of the USA cable network.) Stein, a successful investor, was a major shareholder in Paramount Pictures. He was a member of the New York Stock Exchange and owned several New York antique stores.

When Stein died of a heart attack, President Reagan was among seventy-six honorary pallbearers from show business, medicine, and business, along with James Petrillo, Mervyn LeRoy, Hal Wallis, James Stewart, and Cary Grant. Interment was in Forest Lawn Memorial Park, Glendale, California. He left an estate worth $150 million.

★

The Stein family files, a useful newspaper clipping file on Stein and his family, are in the Local History/Genealogy Collection at the Saint Joseph County Public Library in South Bend, Indiana. Dan Moldea, *Dark Victory: Ronald Reagan, MCA, and the Mob* (1986), is heavy on guilt by association with a touch of conspiracy theory but contains a lengthy bibliography on MCA, Stein, and Reagan and on organized crime in the music, radio, film, and television industries. See also Walter Davenport, "Heat Wave," *Collier's* (Mar. 1934). Newspaper articles are Murray Schumach, "Hollywood's 'Music' Mogul: Jules C. Stein, of MCA, Discusses His Past, Industry's Future," *New York Times* (21 July 1963), and Earl C. Gottschalk, Jr. "Entertaining Giant: If It's Show Business, MCA Inc. Is Deeply Involved in It," *Wall Street Journal* (10 July 1973). Research to Prevent Blindness, Inc. published *A Remembrance of Julius Stein, M.D.* Obituaries are in the *New York Times* (30 Apr. 1981) and *Variety* (6 May 1981).

JAMES STOUDER SWEET

STERLING, J(ohn) E(wart) Wallace (*b.* 6 August 1906 in Linwood, Ontario, Canada; *d.* 1 July 1985 in Woodside, California), historian and fifth president of Stanford University, who led Stanford to high rank among American universities.

The second child of three born to William Sterling, a Methodist minister and recent immigrant from England to Canada, and Annie Wallace, a pianist and church organist,

Wallace Sterling, 1949. UPI/CORBIS-BETTMANN

young Sterling attended Ontario public schools, pitched hay, worked on a construction gang, and under his mother's tutelage learned to play the piano. In 1923 he entered the University of Toronto, where he majored in history. Over six feet tall and powerfully built, he was a member of the Victoria College basketball team and played end and guard on the university's rugby team until he suffered a serious back injury. Although he later recalled that he was a better athlete than he was a scholar during his undergraduate career, he became interested in the study of history, was elected president of the student body, and received his baccalaureate degree in 1927.

In his senior year at the University of Toronto, he courted a classmate, Ann Marie Shaver, vice president of the student body and about to graduate as a dietician. Shaver had been appointed to the faculty at the University of Alberta, in Edmonton, and Sterling applied there himself, unsuccessfully, settling instead for a year teaching history at Regina College in Saskatchewan. There he played guard on the town football team, which won the provincial championship. "Seldom," he wrote later, "have I burned more midnight oil to stay a chapter or two ahead of my students."

In the spring of 1928 the University of Alberta, Edmon-

ton, offered Sterling simultaneous appointments as instructor in history, director of physical education, and coach of the football and basketball teams. It was an opportunity to be near Shaver, and he accepted promptly. During the next two years, his basketball team did well, and his football team won the Western Canadian Intercollegiate Championship. In 1930 the University of Alberta awarded his M.A. in history.

Because his football team had been so successful he was offered a position as coach of the Calgary Tigers, but he declined at first, having applied for graduate fellowships at the universities of London and Wisconsin, as well as at Harvard and Stanford. Wisconsin and Harvard responded favorably, but Stanford did not. Stanford was where he wanted to study, however, because of the resources in European history at the Hoover Library. Shaver suggested that he accept the Calgary coaching job during the fall and enroll at Stanford for the other three quarters, returning to Calgary for the 1931 football season. The town fathers of Calgary were amenable to this arrangement, and Sterling took on two temporary summer jobs, one organizing the papers of Alberta pioneer William Pierce in the provincial archives, the other selling parimutuel tickets at a Calgary racetrack.

Wallace and Ann were married on 7 August 1930. He coached the Calgary Tigers through the fall season (losing the final game and the Western Championship), and in mid-December the newlyweds arrived at Stanford. He later recalled: "The Depression which then struck this country was a year late in reaching Canada, but reach Canada it did. The result was that my second year of coaching was cancelled, and in the final settlement with the Calgary Tigers I received 15% of that once handsome-looking contract." Ann found work as assistant manager of the freshman women's dining hall, and Hoover Library director Harold Fisher made Sterling a part-time research assistant. In 1935 he became an instructor in history, continuing his research in the Hoover Library on his dissertation and on the translation of V. I. Gurko's *Features and Figures of the Past,* in which he assisted Xenia Eudin and Harold H. Fisher. In January 1938, after acceptance of his dissertation, *Austrian-Hungarian Diplomacy and the Austro-Hungarian Press,* Stanford conferred his Ph.D. in history.

In the fall of 1937, Sterling was appointed assistant professor of history at the California Institute of Technology in Pasadena. In 1939 he took a year's leave and returned to Canada, where, supported by a Social Science Research Council grant he studied European immigration to Canada. In September of that year, after Great Britain declared war against Germany, he volunteered for military service but was rejected because of his college football injuries.

He returned to Caltech as an associate professor. In 1941 he was elected secretary of the faculty and the next year became a full professor and chairman of his department. From 1944 to 1946 he was chairman of the faculty and a member of the Caltech executive committee. He had filed his first citizenship papers in 1941, and in 1947 both Wallace and Ann Sterling became U.S. citizens. During the years 1942–1948, Sterling was a radio news analyst for the Columbia Broadcasting System; among his national broadcast assignments was covering the 1945 United Nations Conference in San Francisco. In the fall of 1947 he lectured at the National War College in Washington, D.C.

In July 1948 Sterling became director of the Henry E. Huntington Library and Art Gallery in nearby San Marino, but his brief tenure there ended with his election in November to the presidency of Stanford University, which he assumed on 5 April 1949.

"The first year after I came back I didn't know what it was all about," he recalled, "then I realized that what you need to get a university rolling is dollars, and the way to attract dollars is to get some shows going." One of his early achievements was to build an outstanding chemistry department in a new building, followed by a pioneering astrophysics program; its large dish antenna dominated the hills above the campus. In 1959 the Ford Foundation offered the university $25 million if it could raise $75 million to match it, and in three years total contributions had reached $113 million. Beginning in 1959 the Atomic Energy Commission funded the mile-long Stanford Linear Accelerator Center, which was completed in 1966. The will of Senator Leland Stanford forbade selling any of the Stanford Farm, 8,800 prime acres in the center of the fast-developing San Francisco peninsula, but the university began leasing some of the land in a carefully planned industrial park south of the campus and in a shopping center at its northeast corner, between Menlo Park and Palo Alto. One of the biggest, and most controversial, of Sterling's decisions was to move the Stanford Medical School from San Francisco to a new campus building designed by Edward Durrell Stone, also in 1959. Although critics called the move Wally's Folly, the new facility, attracting both gifts and distinguished faculty, was soon flourishing.

During Sterling's presidency, Stanford's student body increased from 3,500 to more than 11,000, the faculty from 360 to more than 900, and the board of trustees from fifteen to thirty-five (eight elected by alumni). In addition to the medical school, new laboratories, dormitories, and professional school facilities were built and the first of several small campuses in Europe and Asia were established. Sterling received more than twenty honorary degrees, including Stanford's Degree of Uncommon Man, and the title of chancellor upon retirement. He was knighted by Queen Elizabeth II in 1976.

The Sterlings had three children, and the family lived in the Lou Henry Hoover House on the Stanford campus,

a gift of President Herbert Hoover. After retiring in 1968, Sterling served on the Stanford board of trustees and was active in raising funds for the university. He died of cancer in nearby Woodside, where he and his wife had made their home.

★

Sterling's papers, including his dissertation, are in the University Archives, Stanford University Library. Biographical sketches include J. E. Wallace Sterling, *A Canadian Comes to Stanford, Written Especially for the First Fifty Life Members of the Associates of the Stanford University Libraries* (1982); and Frank J. Taylor, "Stanford's Man with the Midas Touch," *Saturday Evening Post* (3 Dec. 1960). The Sterling years figure prominently in Peter C. Allen's university history, *Stanford, from the Foothills to the Bay* (1980). An obituary is in the *New York Times* (3 July 1985).

DAVID W. HERON

STERN, Curt (*b.* 30 August 1902 in Hamburg, Germany; *d.* 23 October 1981 in Orinda, California), geneticist and cytologist who made significant discoveries and wrote extensively on human genetics.

Stern's father, Barned Stern, operated a dental supply business, and his mother, Anna Liebrecht, was a schoolteacher in Hamburg. Early family life nurtured an interest in nature; the young Stern, an only child, was fascinated by microscopic views of pond water. He entered the University of Berlin in 1920, the youngest student to enter the university to that time, and three years later earned his Ph.D. While in Berlin he studied at the Kaiser Wilhelm Institute under protozoologist Max Hartmann, writing his thesis on cell division in the protozoan *Heliozoa*.

In 1924 Stern was granted a fellowship to study in the United States by the International Education Board of the Rockefeller Foundation. He traveled to Columbia University in New York City to join the research team of Professor T. H. Morgan, whose worldwide reputation was based on his work describing the cellular mechanisms of heredity.

Morgan studied the fruit fly, *Drosophila,* and his Columbia laboratory, known as the "fly room," was remarkably productive. This could be credited to Morgan's leadership, broad knowledge, and brilliant collaborators, including Alfred Sturtevant, Calvin Bridges, and Hermann Muller. Fly cultures were bred to establish pure strains for particular genes. The short generations and many offspring in each culture yielded easily observable mutations, useful as markers, allowing the researchers to correlate the appearance of inherited traits with the behavior of chromosomes in the cell divisions of dissected flies. The work of drosophilists like Morgan and Stern (and other geneticists who worked with maize) revealed that genes were carried as a linear array of units on chromosomes that were sorted and recombined in the reproduction process. This work prepared the way for the later explanation of heredity at the chemical level by those who discovered the structure and function of DNA.

Returning to Berlin in 1926, Stern established his own fly lab and continued his successful research, combining the breeding techniques he had learned from Morgan with his expertise in microcytology. His work won him a second Rockefeller Foundation grant to rejoin Morgan's group, which had in the meantime relocated to the California Institute of Technology in Pasadena. In 1932 Stern traveled to Pasadena with his American wife, Evelyn Sommerfield, whom he had married on 29 October 1931 and with whom he had three children. Stern would not return to Germany for forty years; he became a U.S. citizen in 1939. After a temporary appointment at Western Reserve University in early 1933, he joined the faculty at the University of Rochester. He remained there until 1947, serving as chair of the Zoology Department and of the Division of Biological Sciences. While at Rochester, Stern demonstrated the very rare occurrence of crossing-over in mitotic (somatic) cell division and continued building a catalog of discoveries concerning chromosomes and heredity. He also began giving a course on the principles of human genetics.

In 1947 Stern became professor of zoology at the University of California, Berkeley. The work done in his research laboratory at Berkeley cast light on such topics as the extent of cell autonomy in gene expression, the genetic control of differentiation in *Drosophila* larvae, and the effects of low-level radiation on chromosomes. This last topic was the subject of some controversy and political implications in the postwar period. The conclusion published by Delta Emma Uphoff and Stern that "there is no threshold below which radiation fails to produce mutations" earned Stern a term on the Advisory Committee to the Division of Biology and Medicine of the U.S. Atomic Energy Commission (1950–1953). During this period he was editor of the journal *Genetics* (1947–1951). Stern retired in 1970. After eleven years of active retirement despite declining health caused by Parkinson's disease, Stern died of cardiac failure brought on by the disease.

Stern was remembered by students and colleagues as a small man with large principles and a generous spirit. Students received the hospitality of his home and the encouragement of a demanding and caring teacher. Honors accrued in abundance during the latter stages of his career. He was president of the Genetics Society of America in 1950, the American Society of Human Genetics in 1957, the American Society of Naturalists in 1962, and the Thirteenth International Congress of Genetics in 1973. He was elected to the National Academy of Sciences in 1948, the American Philosophical Society in 1954, and the American Academy of Arts and Sciences in 1959. The National Acad-

emy of Sciences awarded the Kimber Medal to Stern in 1963 for achievements in the science of genetics. In 1965 he delivered the Prather Lectures at Harvard University summarizing the discoveries of his career.

Stern's broadest scientific influence came from his writing and teaching. The first edition of his textbook, *Principles of Human Genetics,* was published in 1949, with revised editions appearing in 1960 and 1973. Stern's intimacy with the principles of genetics was hard-won in the fly lab, but he was determined to apply scientific knowledge to human concerns. Stern seized the opportunity to educate and is most widely remembered for contributing to the field of human genetics.

★

The Curt Stern papers are in the American Philosophical Society Library in Philadelphia. See James V. Neel, "Curt Stern," *Biographical Memoirs of the National Academy of Sciences,* 56 (1987): 443–473. Robert E. Kohler, *Lords of the Fly* (1994), describes the work of geneticists, including T. H. Morgan and his colleagues. See also Ernst Mayr, *The Growth of Biological Thought: Diversity, Evolution, and Inheritance* (1982), and the entry in *Dictionary of Scientific Biography,* vol. 18, supp. II: 860–867. An obituary is in the *New York Times* (31 Oct. 1981).

MICHAEL F. HAINES

STEWART, Potter (*b.* 23 January 1915 in Jackson, Michigan; *d.* 7 December 1985 in Hanover, New Hampshire), associate justice of the U.S. Supreme Court (1958–1981), best known as a "swing justice" whose vote was often decisive in a closely divided Court.

One of three children, Stewart came from a distinguished Cincinnati family. His father, James Garfield Stewart, had been mayor of Cincinnati and served on the Ohio Supreme Court; his mother, Harriet Loomis Potter, was a leader in the League of Women Voters and the Cincinnati reform movement. Potter Stewart grew up in Cincinnati and attended the University School there and the prestigious Hotchkiss School in Connecticut, toward the end on a scholarship after the Great Depression had an adverse effect upon family finances. He attended Yale College on a scholarship, supplemented by summer employment at a Cincinnati newspaper. After graduating cum laude and Phi Beta Kappa in 1937, Stewart studied at Cambridge University under a fellowship. He entered Yale Law School and graduated with an outstanding record in 1941.

Stewart then worked at the Wall Street law firm of Debevoise, Stevenson, Plimpton, and Page, but after less than a year his career there was interrupted by World War II, when he joined the navy. He served as an officer on tankers operating in the Atlantic and Mediterranean until his 1945 discharge. He described his service as "floating around in a sea of 100 octane gas, bored to death ninety-nine percent of the time and scared to death one percent." During the war he met Mary Ann Bertles, whom he married on 24 April 1943. They had three children.

After his discharge Stewart returned to his New York firm, but soon left to join Dinsmore, Shohl, Sawyer, and Dinsmore, a leading Cincinnati law firm. He had a thriving practice, including litigation and service as court-appointed counsel for criminal defendants, two of them charged with murder. He became active in municipal politics, with two terms on the Cincinnati City Council; he also served as vice mayor.

In 1954 Stewart was appointed by President Dwight D. Eisenhower to the Sixth Circuit U.S. Court of Appeals; at thirty-nine he was then the youngest federal judge. Stewart developed a reputation as a leading federal judge, noted for the careful reasoning and readability of his opinions. On the circuit bench he displayed the gift for the apt phrase that was to be his judicial trademark. In a dissent from the conviction of a defendant arrested, tried, and found guilty on the same day, he asserted, "swift justice demands more than just swiftness."

Stewart's best-known circuit opinion was in *Garland* v. *Torre* (1958), a libel suit by the actress Judy Garland against a columnist. Stewart wrote that the First Amendment did not confer a right to refuse to answer questions about the source of a defamatory column. Torre had to divulge the source or go to jail. Freedom of the press, Stewart stated, "must give place under the Constitution to a paramount interest in the administration of justice."

On 14 October 1958, two weeks after his *Garland* opinion, Stewart was appointed to the Supreme Court by President Eisenhower. At forty-three, Stewart was the second-youngest justice appointed in more than a century. Because the Senate was not in session, the new justice received a recess appointment, which meant that while awaiting confirmation he could vote and write opinions. Confirmation came 5 May 1959 by a 70–17 vote. (The negative votes were cast by southern senators because of his opinion in a circuit decision ordering immediate school integration.)

The Supreme Court to which Stewart was appointed was closely divided, a situation that continued until Chief Justice Earl Warren secured a firm majority with the 1962 retirement of Justice Felix Frankfurter. Before then Stewart usually cast the deciding vote in important cases. He would vote sometimes with the Warren (usually termed liberal) wing and somewhat more often with the Frankfurter (termed conservative) wing. Stewart defied traditional labeling. He called terms like liberal and conservative "fatuous"; when asked whether he was a liberal or a conservative, he answered, "I am a lawyer." He went on, "I have some difficulty understanding what those terms mean in the field of political life.... And I find it impossible to

Potter Stewart. ARCHIVE PHOTOS

know what they mean when they are carried over to judicial work."

Under Chief Justice Warren E. Burger, Stewart continued as a moderate with a pragmatic approach to issues that polarized others. In a 1986 interview Justice Harry A. Blackmun characterized Stewart as "in the [Court's] middle." He was essentially a pragmatist, without an agenda or overriding philosophy. Instead, he was motivated by case-by-case judgments on how to make a workable judicial accommodation that would resolve a divisive controversy. Inevitably, the Stewart decisions did not make for a logically consistent corpus. They reflected less an overriding calculus of fundamental values than lawyerlike attempts to resolve the given controversy.

Stewart took a less activist approach than colleagues such as Justices Hugo Black and William Brennan. Thus, he voted to uphold the constitutionality of laws that he would have voted against as a legislator. He upheld death-penalty laws, even though he said after retirement that he opposed capital punishment and would vote against it were he in the legislature. In his dissent in *Griswold* v. *Connecticut* (1965), he stated that the ban on contraceptives that was at issue was "an uncommonly silly law" but not unconstitutional.

Stewart, however, did not hesitate to strike down laws that he considered invalid. One of his first major opinions was in *Shelton* v. *Tucker* (1960), ruling that an Arkansas law requiring teachers to list organizations to which they belonged was an invalid interference with associational freedom. The question for Stewart was not constitutionality in the abstract but whether the particular law as applied to the facts of the case impinged upon a specific constitutional right.

This idea is also seen in *Rideau* v. *Louisiana* (1963), which Stewart once named his favorite case. His opinion there was the first reversing a murder conviction because of pretrial television publicity. Stewart called the TV broadcast of the defendant confessing to the sheriff "kangaroo court proceedings": "For anyone who has ever watched television the conclusion cannot be avoided that this spectacle, to the tens of thousands of people who saw and heard it, in a very real sense *was* [the] trial. . . . Any subsequent court proceedings in a community so pervasively exposed to such a spectacle could be but a hollow formality."

Stewart consistently opposed racial discrimination. He was particularly proud of his opinion in *Jones* v. *Alfred H. Mayer Co.* (1968), which imposed a sweeping ban on housing discrimination. Next to *Brown* v. *Board of Education* (1954), *Jones* was the most far-reaching Warren Court civil rights decision and the theory behind it was raised in neither the arguments nor the Court's conference but was worked out by Stewart himself.

Stewart also opposed what he considered religious discrimination, although he often spoke on that issue in dissent. When the Court in *McGowan* v. *Maryland* (1961) upheld a Sunday closing law, Stewart wrote that it forced an Orthodox Jew who wanted to observe his Sabbath and do business on Sunday "to choose between his religious faith and economic survival."

Stewart also dissented in *Engel* v. *Vitale* (1962), where the Court struck down voluntary prayer in the public schools. To Stewart, the majority acted on the basis of a "ritualistic application" of the abstract principle of "government neutrality" to refuse to let "those who want to say a prayer say it." In Stewart's view, "to deny the wish of these schoolchildren to join in reciting this prayer is to deny them the opportunity of sharing in the spiritual heritage of our nation." All that the state had done was "to recognize and to follow the deeply entrenched and highly cherished spiritual traditions of our nation—traditions which come down to us from those who almost 200 years ago avowed their 'firm reliance on the protection of divine Providence' when they proclaimed the freedom and independence of this brave new world."

Stewart firmly protected constitutional rights that he found based in the Bill of Rights. He wrote the opinion striking down New York's refusal to allow distribution of the film *Lady Chatterley's Lover* (1981) as violative of the First Amendment: "What New York has done, therefore, is to prevent the exhibition of a motion picture because that picture advocates an idea—that adultery under certain circumstances may be proper behavior. Yet the First Amendment's basic guarantee is of freedom to advocate ideas. The State, quite simply, has thus struck at the very heart of constitutionally protected liberty."

Stewart also joined the opinion in the Burger Court's most notable First Amendment case, *New York Times Co.* v. *United States* (1971), known as the Pentagon Papers case, ruling out injunctions against newspaper publication of a classified history of the Vietnam war. The Stewart concurring opinion stated the now-prevailing rule that only publication of material that would cause "direct, immediate, and irreparable damage to the nation or its people" might be restrained.

Stewart's Fourth Amendment opinions were typical of his judicial approach. A 1961 opinion, *Silverman* v. *United States,* ruled that the police had violated the amendment by driving a "spike mike" through the wall of a house to overhear conversations of gamblers. The police had physically trespassed upon private property, the traditional dividing line. "But we refuse to go beyond it, by even a fraction of an inch," Stewart wrote. But, deeming it necessary for protection in an electronic age, Stewart did go beyond it six years later, when he held that "bugging" without any physical trespass violated the Fourth Amendment. The Stewart opinion summed it up in a pithy phrase: "The Constitution protects people, not places."

On the other hand, Stewart refused to join the Court in protecting rights not enumerated in the Bill of Rights. He dissented in *Griswold* v. *Connecticut* (1965), refusing to recognize a right to privacy not specified in the Constitution. He concurred in *Roe* v. *Wade* (1973), feeling bound by precedent to include abortion within substantive due process. Nevertheless, in a letter to Justice Blackmun, author of the *Roe* opinion, Stewart decried the majority's action "to make policy judgments" that were "more legislative than judicial," a criticism that others have since made of the *Roe* decision.

On the Supreme Court, Stewart wrote 304 of its opinions—173 concurring and 225 dissenting opinions. His influence as a justice was not, however, confined to his opinions. Stewart's center position enabled him to play a pivotal role in the Warren and Burger Courts. The other justices tended to turn to him because they trusted his judgment as a lawyer. Thus, Stewart cast the deciding vote in *Baker* v. *Carr* (1962), the legislative apportionment case that Warren himself called the most important case decided by his Court. In the *Swann* school busing case (1971), it was Stewart who led the successful opposition to Chief Justice Burger's draft opinions, which sharply limited busing as a desegregation remedy and ensured that the final opinion firmly endorsed busing as a means of ending dual school systems. Similarly, in *United States* v. *Nixon,* the 1974 Watergate tapes case, Stewart fought the Burger attempt to take a more expansive view of presidential power. Stewart redrafted the portion of the opinion that ensures presidential subordination to the rule of law.

The Stewart hallmark remains the clarity and brevity of his opinions. He was the greatest Court master of the pungent phrase since Justices Robert H. Jackson and Oliver Wendell Holmes. His statement in a 1964 case, that he could not define pornography, but "I know it when I see it," is now a classic phrase but one that he correctly lamented would become his epitaph.

When in 1975 the Court upheld the right of a defendant to represent himself without a lawyer, Stewart wrote, "To force a lawyer on a defendant can only lead him to believe that the law contrives against him." The same year he held that the states may not confine supposedly mentally ill individuals involuntarily if they are not dangerous and can live safely out of institutions. Stewart stated: "The term 'mental illness' is notoriously vague and variable. To permit incarceration upon a criterion with such uncertain dimensions invites evils too obvious to require cataloguing." Explaining his vote in *Furman* v. *Georgia* (1972) against the death penalty, Stewart declared, "These death sentences are cruel and unusual in the same way that being struck by lightning is cruel and unusual."

Stewart was known as a freedom of the press advocate. When the Court upheld a publisher's obscenity conviction in *Ginzburg* v. *United States* (1966) under a novel "pandering" theory, Stewart indicated that the material published was "worthless." That did not, however, prevent him from urging in dissent that censorship would lead to "government by Big Brother. . . . The First Amendment protects us all with an even hand. It applies to Ralph Ginzburg with no less completeness and force than to G. P. Putnam's Sons." Putnam was the publisher whose right to publish the eighteenth-century erotic novel *Fanny Hill* was upheld the same day.

In 1969, amid press speculation that he might be elevated to replace the retiring Earl Warren, Stewart made a secret call on President Richard M. Nixon. He told the president that it was unwise to promote associate justices and that a chief justice should be named from outside the Court. After Nixon disclosed the meeting, Stewart explained that he had spoken to the president to put aside any personal ambition he might harbor, keeping a promise to himself not to seek any higher office once he had reached the Court.

Stewart retired from the Court at age sixty-six in 1981, one of the youngest justices to do so. He left to spend more time with his family and because he feared the example of

justices who had remained on the bench despite poor health and even senility. With typical pithiness he observed, "It's better to go too soon than to stay too long." In retirement, Stewart remained active by sitting in selected cases in courts of appeals (he delivered a rare dissent by a retired justice in one such case in 1982) and as chairman of an international arbitration commission, as well as serving on two presidential commissions. He also appeared in a television series on the Constitution aired by the Public Broadcasting System.

Stewart died after suffering a stroke while visiting his daughter in Vermont. He was buried in Arlington National Cemetery.

★

No Stewart biography has thus far been published. His work on the Warren and Burger Courts is discussed in two books by Bernard Schwartz: *Super Chief: Earl Warren and His Supreme Court: A Judicial Biography* (1983), and *The Ascent of Pragmatism: The Burger Court in Action* (1990). Biographical articles are in Clare Cushman, ed., *The Supreme Court Justices: Illustrated Biographies, 1789–1993* (1993), and Leon Friedman and Fred L. Israel, eds., *The Justices of the Supreme Court, 1789–1969,* vol. 4 (1969). An obituary is in the *New York Times* (8 Dec. 1985).

BERNARD SCHWARTZ

STOKES, Colin (*b.* 4 April 1914 in Winston-Salem, North Carolina; *d.* 14 December 1984 in Winston-Salem), tobacco company executive and humanitarian best known for supervising the diversification of R. J. Reynolds Tobacco Company from a manufacturer of tobacco products to an international conglomerate.

Colin Stokes, the oldest of three children, was the son of Henry Straughan and Eloise (Brown) Stokes. He attended the McCallie School in Chattanooga, Tennessee, from which he received a high school diploma in 1931. In September of that year he enrolled in the University of North Carolina at Chapel Hill and graduated in 1935 with a B.S. degree in commerce with honors. In Colin's senior year, his father, the superintendent of leaf processing for R. J. Reynolds, prodded his son into taking a part-time position as tag boy, a worker who puts company labels on baskets of tobacco as they enter warehouses. Upon graduating from the university, Stokes joined Reynolds as a foreman. This association was to last nearly half a century. During World War II, Stokes served with distinction in the U.S. Army, rising steadily through the ranks from private to captain. Before being transferred overseas, on 1 January 1943 Stokes married Mary Louise Siewers, with whom he had three children.

After his discharge from the military, Stokes rejoined Reynolds as assistant to the superintendent of manufactur-

Colin Stokes, 1973. AP/WIDE WORLD PHOTOS

ing. In 1953 he was appointed the assistant superintendent of manufacturing and was promoted to superintendent of manufacturing three years later. The following year he was elected to the board of directors of Reynolds, a post he occupied until his death. He became a corporate vice president in 1959 and served as executive vice president from 1961 to 1970.

As a member of the board of directors of Reynolds, Stokes was instrumental in organizing and overseeing a diversification committee that was commissioned to execute a feasibility study on investing in nontobacco areas and in expanding of tobacco operations overseas. The implementation of the committee's recommendations ushered in a period of unparalleled growth and diversification in nontobacco areas. In 1963 Reynolds purchased Pacific Hawaiian Products; in 1966 it bought Chun King for $63 million. Stokes recommended that the nontobacco acquisitions of Reynolds be placed under the direction of a subsidiary; R. J. Reynolds Foods was created in 1966. To accentuate the diversification of Reynolds into nonfood areas, the board of directors, at Stokes's behest, established a new corporate name, R. J. Reynolds Industries, which in 1969 purchased Sea-Land Industries, a containerized shipping business. In the following year Aminoil, a domestic crude oil and natural gas exploration firm, was acquired for $600 million.

In 1964 the U.S. Surgeon General issued a report that linked smoking to lung cancer and heart disease. Stokes's reaction to the subsequent assault of the U.S. Congress on the tobacco industry—which required health warnings on cigarette packs, banned cigarette advertisements from radio and television, and doubled the federal tax on cigarettes— was to establish R. J. Reynolds Tobacco International, a subsidiary that developed foreign tobacco markets. In 1970, as chairman of the board of R. J. Reynolds Industries, Stokes supervised the corporation's reorganization into a structure of three subsidiaries: R. J. Reynolds Tobacco, R. J. Reynolds Tobacco International, and R. J. Reynolds Foods. In 1972 he was elected president of R. J. Reynolds Industries. When he retired from the presidency two years later, Stokes was reappointed chairman of the board of directors.

In the 1970s Reynolds faced intensive competition from Philip Morris. By 1976 Marlboro, the leading brand of cigarettes manufactured by Philip Morris, had surpassed Reynolds's Winston as the number one cigarette in domestic sales. To regain market share, Stokes introduced two new low-tar brands, Doral and Vantage, which were successfully marketed as an effort to improve the health image of Reynolds. In 1979 Stokes retired as chairman of the board of directors of R. J. Reynolds Industries but continued as a board member until his death.

Throughout his career Stokes worked tirelessly with social organizations and educational institutions in his native state. From 1946 to 1952 he was director of the YMCA of Winston-Salem. He was the campaign chairman of the United Fund of Forsyth County in 1957 and director of the United Fund of Forsyth County from 1957 to 1959. As a Baptist, Stokes was involved in activities of community improvement that were sponsored by his faith. He was a trustee of the North Carolina Baptist Hospitals from 1958 to 1961, and in 1959 he was chairman of the financial commission of the North Carolina Baptist Hospitals. In 1961 he was elected chairman of the board of the North Carolina Baptist Hospitals, a position to which he was reelected in 1969 and 1970. From 1958 to 1964 he was director of the William and Kate B. Reynolds Memorial Park, and from 1959 to 1961 he was director of the Child Guidance Clinic. Stokes served as chairman of the Wake Forest University board of trustees from 1971 to 1975 and again in 1978; he was chairman of Wake Forest University from 1980 to 1981. His advocacy of equal access to higher education in North Carolina led to his election to the board of the Independent College Fund of North Carolina, on which he served from 1979 to 1981. Stokes was also a member of the Institutional Development Foundation of the University of North Carolina.

Stokes's interests in the corporate world extended beyond Reynolds. He was a member of the Winston-Salem Chamber of Commerce and its director from 1951 to 1955 and again from 1968 to 1970. He was on the board of directors of the North Carolina National Bank Corporation and was director of the First Home Federal Savings and Loan Association of Winston-Salem. Stokes was also a member of the board of directors of the Integon Corporation. He died of cancer at the North Carolina Baptist Hospital, and memorial services were held at the First Baptist Church of Winston-Salem, of which he was deacon. Interment was in Salem Cemetery.

★

Bryan Burrough and John Helyar, *Barbarians at the Gate: The Fall of RJR Nabisco* (1990), delineates the history of the leveraged buyout of the heir to R. J. Reynolds Industries, and Nannie M. Tilley, *The R. J. Reynolds Tobacco Company* (1985), provides an in-depth history of the firm. An obituary is in the *New York Times* (16 Dec. 1984).

P. DALE ROREX

STRASBERG, Lee (*b.* 17 November 1901 in Budzanow, Galicia, Austria-Hungary [now Budanov, Ukraine]; *d.* 17 February 1982 in New York City), actor, director, and acting teacher who propagated method acting.

Lee Strasberg was born Israel Strassberg, the youngest of four children born to Baruch Meier Strassberg, a stonecutter who worked in the garment industry in New York City, and Chaia (Ida) Diner. In 1909 he was the last of his family to emigrate to New York but did not become a citizen until 1936. The family lived on the Lower East Side of Manhattan, where Israel attended local public schools and studied at the Jewish National Radical School. As a teenager, he acted in amateur Yiddish theatricals at the Progressive Dramatic Club. He was admitted to Townsend Harris High School in the Bronx, New York, a school for intellectually gifted children, but dropped out after a brother's death in 1918.

The scholarly youth spent much of his time reading, eventually assembling a notable collection of books on the theater. He later credited his studies of ancient religions with indirectly teaching him how to interpret the inner life of playscripts. Soon after joining the Students of Arts and Drama (SAD) at the Chrystie Street Settlement, he became their teacher and director. He also changed his name to I. Lee Strasberg, later dropping the first initial.

In 1923 the Moscow Art Theatre, led by Konstantin Stanislavsky, toured the United States. Its performance at the Fifty-ninth Street Theater in New York City had a profound influence on Strasberg, who was overwhelmed by how fully each character, no matter how insignificant, had been believably embodied by the ensemble. Strasberg decided to become a professional actor, and he left his position at a wig business to study at the Clare Tree Major School of the Theatre. This training, however, proved too conventional, and he enrolled in 1924 at the American Laboratory

Lee Strasberg, 1975. WILLIAM E. SAURO/NEW YORK TIMES/ARCHIVE PHOTOS

Theatre, newly founded by two former Moscow Art Theatre members, Richard Boleslavsky and Maria Ouspenskaya. There he imbibed the principles of the Stanislavsky system of acting that he would eventually transform into an Americanized version, widely termed "the method," and of which he became the master teacher. He learned to reveal "true emotion" through the principles of sensory memory, improvisation, concentration, relaxation, listening, motivation, and, most important to his later beliefs, affective memory. This last principle taught an actor to stimulate the emotions required in a role by recalling analogous personal experiences the actor had undergone or by remembering related ones whose emotional reactions could be substituted for those demanded. Exercises were created to tap the actor's subconscious and to help the actor abandon traditional methods and clichés that led to artificiality. In addition, an essay by the Russian director Eugeni Vakhtangov guided Strasberg to believe that an actor must express his or her own temperament on stage, and not that of the character.

Strasberg played small roles for the Theatre Guild, acting in *Processional* (1925), *The Garrick Gaieties* (1925, 1930),

Goat Song (1926), *The Chief Thing* (1926), *Four Walls* (1927), *Red Dust* (1929), *Green Grow the Lilacs* (1931), and others, also working in assistant stage managerial positions. He directed for the amateur Lenox Hill Players and SAD and experimented with various directorial styles. In 1926 he married actress Nora Z. Krecaun; she died three years later.

Strasberg, a short, bespectacled intellectual with traces of his foreign origins in his speech, seemed anything but an actor to Harold Clurman, with whom Strasberg and Cheryl Crawford cofounded the Group Theatre in 1931. This company, organized on collective principles, was intended to emulate the Moscow Art Theatre. It was devoted to the ensemble over the star and to humanistic new plays of social—and, occasionally, political (the Group had a communist cell)—significance. Strasberg, a disciplinarian and perfectionist who demanded total commitment, trained (at first) religiously devoted actors in his evolving method. He taught mainly at the company's annual summer sessions set up at country resorts and camps. His Group directorial efforts included Paul Green's *The House of Connelly* (1931), with Crawford, Paul and Claire Sifton's *1931* (1931), Maxwell Anderson's *Night over Taos* (1932), John Howard Lawson's *Success Story* (1932), Sidney Kingsley's *Men in White* (1933), Melvin Levy's *Gold Eagle Guy* (1934), Erwin Piscator and Lina Goldschmidt's *The Case of Clyde Griffiths* (1936), and Paul Green's *Johnny Johnson* (1936). He also staged several outside productions. Perhaps his most creative directing was in the medical drama *Men in White,* which had a beautifully choreographed scene of doctors at work in an operating room. Strasberg's work was noteworthy for its insistence on reality from even the smallest roles and for its increasing reliance on theatricalist devices, as in *Men in White*'s operating scene pantomime.

The Group was important in American theater history because it demonstrated the power of the new method-acting techniques, producing a number of important artists, including Franchot Tone, Morris Carnovsky, Stella Adler, Luther Adler, and John Garfield. But Strasberg, the company's acting guru, found himself challenged on a number of fronts, mainly when Stella Adler, who believed his interiorized technique was artistically and emotionally destructive, returned in 1936 from a brief period of study with Stanislavsky in Paris. She insisted that Strasberg's emphasis on emotional recall was a distortion of the Russian's thinking, which had shifted to a belief that the actor should be more concerned with using his imagination and playing "the given circumstances" of his role than with eliciting emotions through personalized psychological exercises. Strasberg long disputed the viability of Stanislavsky's altered views.

Possessed of intellectual rigidity, emotional aloofness in personal relations (including with his first two children), a furious temper during artistic disputes, and what some considered a tyrant's hatred of having his authority questioned, Strasberg was often at the center of internecine squabbles. In 1937 he resigned from the Group, taking with him Paula Miller, a Group actress he had married on 16 March 1934. Their honeymoon had been spent on a subsidized trip to the Soviet Union, where Strasberg observed local theater art. The couple eventually had a daughter, Susan, who became a successful actress, and a son, John, an acting teacher. Paula Strasberg became a major adjunct of Strasberg's teaching career until her death in 1966.

In the 1940s, Strasberg, struggling financially, taught at the American Theatre Wing, the Dramatic Workshop, and Yale University; spent time in Hollywood in 1941 under contract to MGM to learn filmmaking and direct screen tests; and occasionally got a Broadway directing assignment. The latter included Benjamin A. Glazer and Ernest Hemingway's *The Fifth Column* (1940), Clifford Odets's *Clash by Night* (1941), revivals of James Barrie's *A Kiss for Cinderella* (1942), Karel Capek's *R.U.R.* (1942), Jan de Hartog's *Skipper Next to God* (1948), Odets's *The Big Knife* (1949), and Henrik Ibsen's *Peer Gynt* (1951). None were outstanding. He made his greatest mark on American theater when he took over in 1951 as artistic director of the Actors Studio, a workshop for professional actors established in 1947 by former Group Theatre members Elia Kazan, Cheryl Crawford, and Robert Lewis, and where Strasberg had occasionally lectured since 1948. For three decades, the top stage and film actors studied with him, including Julie Harris, James Dean, Paul Newman, Marilyn Monroe, Al Pacino, and Meryl Streep. Numerous famous directors also came under Strasberg's tutelage. While he had many detractors, most notably Stella Adler, who claimed that his psychologically probing methods could be harmful to sensitive natures and that his students were poorly trained in vocal and physical techniques, Strasberg reigned as America's most influential acting teacher. He was known for his perceptive but complex, ruthless, and rarely complimentary assessments of actors' problems; performers were known to throw up before showing him their work.

At the Actors Studio, he did a number of workshop stagings of plays; several were later moved by others to independent productions. Many thought the studio's natural destiny was to be a producing organization, even a national theater. Strasberg was disgusted when Elia Kazan in 1964 neglected to incorporate the studio into the new Lincoln Center Repertory Company, of which Kazan was named codirector. In 1964 the studio produced a series of flops, culminating in Strasberg's own star-studded staging of Anton Chekhov's *The Three Sisters* (1964). An artistic success in New York, it turned into an organizational shambles when produced in London in 1965, losing the allegiance of many studio stalwarts and squashing any hopes of the studio as a production center. Strasberg's last production work was his supervision of Martin Fried's revival of Odets's *The Country Girl* (1966).

On 7 January 1968 Strasberg married Anna Mizrahi, who, like Paula Strasberg, became a helpful aide in disseminating his ideas. They had two sons. In 1969, Strasberg, who had given private lessons and lectured at home and abroad but received little from his studio activities, founded the Lee Strasberg Theatre Institute in New York and Hollywood, California. The venture—after initial hardships—proved an economic windfall and he became a bicoastal teacher. His career moved in another direction in 1974, when he returned to acting, playing gangster Hyman Roth in the movie *The Godfather, Part II,* garnering an Academy Award nomination for best supporting actor. He also had roles in the movies *The Cassandra Crossing* (1977), *Boardwalk* (1979), *And Justice for All* (1979), and *Going in Style* (1979) and parts in two television movies, *The Last Tenant* (1981) and *Skokie* (1981).

Strasberg died in his Central Park West apartment of a heart attack that some believe attributable to his having cavorted in a chorus line at a Radio City Music Hall *Night of 100 Stars* benefit three nights earlier. His interment was at Westchester Hills Cemetery, Hastings-on-Hudson, New York. He will be remembered for cofounding the Group Theatre, arguably the most influential American theater company of the century, and for establishing method acting, despite the controversy surrounding it, as the technique shared by more outstanding American actors than any other.

★

The sole biography is Cindy Adams, *Lee Strasberg: The Imperfect Genius of the Actors Studio* (1980). Biographical material from Strasberg's children is available in Susan Strasberg, *Bittersweet* (1980) and *Marilyn and Me* (1992), and John Strasberg, *Accidentally on Purpose: Reflections on Life, Acting, and the Nine Natural Laws of Creativity* (1996). Brief career descriptions are in John W. Frick and Stephen M. Vallillo, eds., *Theatrical Directors: A Biographical Dictionary* (1994), and David Pickering, ed., *International Directory of Theatre—3: Actors, Directors, Designers* (1996). The Group Theatre is covered in Harold Clurman, *The Fervent Years: The Story of the Group Theatre and the Thirties* (1945), and Wendy Smith, *Real Life Drama: The Group Theatre and America, 1931–1940* (1990). For Strasberg's teaching, see Robert H. Hethmon, ed., *Strasberg at the Actors Studio: Tape-Recorded Sessions* (1965); David Garfield, *A Player's Place: The Story of the Actors Studio* (1980); and Foster Hirsch, *A Method to Their Madness: The History of the Actors Studio* (1984). Strasberg summed up his ideas in "Acting and the Training of the Actor," in *Producing the Play,* edited by John Gassner (1941), and the posthumous *A Dream of Passion: The Development of the Method* (1987). See also S. Loraine

Hull, *Strasberg's Legacy* (1988). An obituary is in the *New York Times* (18 Feb. 1982).

SAMUEL L. LEITER

STRATTON, Monty Franklin Pierce ("Gander") (*b.* 21 May 1912 in Celeste, Texas; *d.* 29 September 1982 in Greenville, Texas), major league baseball pitcher who made a comeback in the minor leagues after losing a leg and inspired a popular, award-winning motion picture.

Stratton was one of nine children born to Lee Aster Stratton and Minnie McElyes Stratton, a rural farm family in northeast Texas. Stratton was a gifted athlete, pitching for his grade school in nearby Wagner. He grew to be six feet, five inches and 195 pounds, and his long neck earned him the nickname "Gander." While pitching for an amateur team in Van Alstyne, Texas, his fastball caught the eye of Chicago White Sox scout Roy Kargentk. Stratton signed a minor league contract in 1934, pitching 40 innings for Galveston and appearing in 23 games for Omaha of the Western League before being promoted to the St. Paul Saints of the American Association. Stratton showed major promise in his second year with the Saints. He fanned 120 batters and walked only 63 on his way to a 17–9 record in 1935, making

Monty Stratton, *c.* 1938. UPI/CORBIS-BETTMANN

him the leading prospect in the White Sox farm system that year.

Stratton was called up by the White Sox at the end of the 1934 and 1935 seasons, and in 1936 got into 16 games, with a 5–7 win-loss record before being slowed by an appendectomy. The season's highlight was Stratton's hitting a home run in one of his first at bats in the big leagues. His breakthrough season was 1937. He won 15 games and lost only 5, pitching 164 innings in 21 starts, while throwing 5 shutouts and posting a remarkable 2.40 earned run average. His .750 winning percentage and his earned run average were second in the American League that year, outpacing perennial stars Bob Feller, Lefty Gomez, Lefty Grove, Bobo Newsom, and Red Ruffing. He averaged only two walks per nine innings, the best in the league. His imposing size, combined with an explosive fastball that broke in to right-handed batters and sank when thrown to lefties, made him nearly unhittable. The lanky right-hander pitched through arm problems in 1938, again winning 15 games and losing 9. Stratton tenaciously completed 17 of 22 starts and had a .625 winning percentage that was fourth in the American League, despite hurling for a sixth-place club. It confirmed his status as one of the league's best young pitchers.

Stratton married Ethel Milberger on 6 January 1936, and they made their home in Greenville, Texas, during the off-season. On 27 November 1938 Stratton, while hunting rabbits, slipped and fell as he was going downhill toward a creek. His holstered revolver accidentally discharged, the bullet creasing his right thigh and severing a major artery. Dallas doctors were forced to amputate Stratton's right leg the following day. During a long and difficult convalescence in which he was fitted with a wooden leg, Stratton continued his association with baseball. He served as a coach and batting-practice pitcher for the White Sox for two years. On 1 May 1939, White Sox management gave Stratton a $25,000 check following an exhibition game against the team's crosstown rivals, the Cubs. Everyone who entered Comiskey Park on that day had paid to see the game, including reporters, umpires, and players. Stratton's payment included these admission fees and the profits from all concessions, parking lots, scorecards, and refreshments.

Rejected when he tried to enlist in the army during World War II, Stratton managed a minor league team in Lubbock in 1942. He kept his arm limber with tosses to his two sons and even had Ethel serve as his catcher. He still had a good velocity and could throw strikes. Privately, Stratton nurtured the hope that he could return to pitching. "I still wanted to pitch and needed someone to give me a chance," he recalled.

Stratton organized a Greenville sandlot team in 1945 and pitched in a semipro all-star game that year in Houston, blanking the opposition 2–0 on three hits, while driving in both runs with a single off the center-field fence. He continued his comeback in 1946 with Sherman in the Class C East Texas League and compiled a record of 18–7. The effort won national praise and led the Philadelphia Sports Writers Association to name Stratton the Most Courageous Athlete of 1946.

Hollywood screenwriter Douglas Morrow became fascinated by Stratton's comeback and felt a film on his life would encourage World War II amputees. Metro-Goldwyn-Mayer bought the project and production began on the movie, *The Stratton Story* (1949). Ronald Reagan, then under contract with Warner Brothers, actively campaigned to play the part, but studio heads, convinced the project had little box-office appeal, refused to loan their star to a rival studio. James Stewart was given the lead and June Allyson costarred. The film was the highest-grossing picture of 1949, and won Photoplay's Gold Medal for best movie of the year and the Protestant Award for the most inspiring film of 1949.

Stratton had a 7–7 record with Waco of the Big State League in 1947. Two years later he lost his only start for Temple in the Big State League but threw a shutout in a single appearance for Vernon in the Longhorn League. "I got to where I could field bunts pretty well," Stratton said, "but I wasn't able to get any spring off the mound." The result was that "I didn't have the fastball I once had." Exhibition games around the country followed. At the age of thirty-eight Stratton posted a 4–0 record during a brief comeback in 1950, while pitching for Greenville, Corpus Christi, Sherman-Denison, and Brownsville. Record crowds came to see Stratton wherever he pitched.

Eventually, Stratton and his family settled into a fifty-two-acre farm outside Greenville. There he kept busy baling hay, running cattle, fly-fishing for bass on his six-acre lake, and answering letters from fans and those seeking encouragement. On 18 June 1950 he was honored by Greenville with a special day. In the years that followed Stratton became a leader in the Ex-Professional Baseball Players Association. In 1961 he was inducted into the Texas Sports Hall of Fame, in Dallas, only the fifth former major leaguer to earn the honor. In 1980 the soft-spoken Stratton was elected to the Texas Baseball Hall of Fame, in Waco. He died of cancer and was buried in Greenville.

Stratton never spoke of what might have been. "I've always been someone who accepted what comes along," he would tell interviewers. His quiet determination to beat the odds made him a symbol to the suffering. Each year he received hundreds of letters from amputees and others who sought his good counsel. At his death his Texas neighbors and the nation's sportswriters remembered the positive force of his example and the unparalleled courage that had made him a self-effacing celebrity.

★

The Stratton Story (1949) is a largely accurate motion-picture chronicle of Stratton's life. Substantial files on his life and career are available through the Texas Baseball Hall of Fame, in Dallas, and the Texas Sports Hall of Fame, in Waco, as well as the Public Relations Department of the Chicago White Sox and the W. Walworth Harrison Public Library in Greenville, Texas. Stratton interviews are in Clifford Bloodgood, *Baseball Magazine* (Sept. 1938), and Chuck Pickard, "A Visit with Monty Stratton," *Baseball Bulletin* (May 1975). Stratton's career statistics are in *The Baseball Encyclopedia,* 8th ed. (1986). An appreciation appears in the (Greenville) *Herald Banner* (30 Sept. 1982). An obituary is in the *New York Times* (30 Sept. 1982).

BRUCE J. EVENSEN

STRUBLE, Arthur Dewey (*b.* 28 June 1894 in Portland, Oregon; *d.* 1 May 1983 in Chevy Chase, Maryland), four-star admiral of the U.S. Navy best known as an expert on amphibious troop landings during World War II and the Korean War.

Struble, one of five children (four boys and one girl) of Walter Burr Struble, an accountant, and Hannah Wadsworth Fairchild, was educated in the public schools of Portland, Oregon, before being appointed to the United States Naval Academy in 1911. He graduated with a B.S. degree in 1915 and was commissioned an ensign. During the next

Vice Admiral Arthur D. Struble, Commander of the Seventh Fleet (*left*), and General Douglas MacArthur near Inchon, Korea, 1950. UPI/CORBIS-BETTMANN

six years Struble served successively aboard the battleship *South Dakota,* the cruiser *St. Louis,* the supply ship *Glacier,* and the destroyers *Stevens, Shubrick,* and *Meyer.* On 4 January 1918 he married Hazel Laura Ralston, the daughter of a real estate investor; they had three children.

During the years from 1921 to 1941 Struble rose in rank from lieutenant to captain while holding a variety of assignments at sea and on shore that prepared him for high command. They included service as an instructor in marine engineering and naval construction at the Naval Academy from 1921 to 1923, on the battleship *California* from 1923 to 1925, as a staff officer with the Battle Fleet from 1925 to 1927, in the Office of Naval Communications in Washington, D.C., from 1927 to 1930, as a staff officer with Battleship Division Three from 1930 to 1932, as gunnery officer on the battleship *New York* from 1932 to 1933, as communications officer of the Twelfth Naval District, San Diego, California, from 1933 to 1935, as damage control officer for the cruiser *Portland* and then for the Scouting Force from 1935 to 1937, in the Office of the Chief of Naval Operations in Washington from 1937 to 1940, and as executive officer of the battleship *Arizona* from 1940 to 1941. At the time of the Japanese attack on Pearl Harbor, Struble was commanding the cruiser *Trenton* in the southeast Pacific Ocean.

In the spring of 1942 Struble was assigned to intelligence work in the Office of the Chief of Naval Operations, and in November 1943, now holding the rank of rear admiral, he was appointed chief of staff for Rear Admiral Alan G. Kirk, commander of the Western Task Force, or Task Force 122, the Allied naval force charged with landing the United States First Army in Normandy, France. During the next months Struble directed the planning for the landings at Omaha and Utah beaches, and on 6 June 1944 he helped oversee the landings and the subsequent reinforcement, supply, and gunfire support of the beachheads.

Now recognized as an expert on amphibious landings, Struble in August 1944 was given command of Group Two, Seventh Amphibious Force, in the Southwest Pacific Area. His first major operation came during the Leyte campaign in the Philippine Islands on 7 December 1944 when he landed the Seventy-seventh Division behind the Japanese lines at Ormoc Bay to help speed the American conquest of the island. Shortly afterward, Struble was charged with landing 27,000 troops on Mindoro Island. While en route kamikazes, or suicide planes, attacked Struble's task group. One crashed into the cruiser *Nashville,* Struble's flagship, killing 133 men and forcing Struble to transfer to a destroyer. On 15 December 1944 he landed the troops without ground opposition. However, for the next weeks Struble's resupply convoys were attacked regularly by kamikazes that sunk or damaged a number of his vessels. After American forces invaded Luzon Island, Struble on 29 January 1945 landed the Eleventh Army Corps in the vicinity of Subic Bay to outflank the Japanese main body defending Luzon, and on 15 February he directed an operation to seize Mariveles on the Bataan Peninsula. A month later, his task group, renamed Group Nine, landed troops on Panay Island, and afterward he directed several other landings in the Philippines.

At the war's end, Struble was given command of Mine Craft, Pacific Fleet, and in 1945 and 1946 his minesweepers cleared the ports and channels in the western Pacific, where the Japanese and the Allies had laid mines. In June 1946 Struble was appointed commander of the Amphibious Forces, Pacific Fleet, and beginning in April 1948, now holding the rank of vice admiral, he served as deputy chief of naval operations in Washington, D.C., until May 1950, when he was given command of the Seventh Fleet.

When North Korea invaded South Korea in June 1950, Struble was ordered to prevent Communist China from attacking the island of Formosa. After American forces were committed to the defense of South Korea at the end of the month, Struble, in effect, was in charge of the combat operations of the major American naval forces in the war. In September 1950 he also assumed personal command of Task Force Seven, which was created to land the Tenth Corps at Inchon on the west coast of South Korea to outflank the North Koreans. The operation was risky because of the narrow channel leading to Inchon, the heavy guns of Wolmi Do Island that guarded the channel, the thirty-foot tidal range, and the need to disembark troops in a city that was garrisoned by the enemy. Despite these difficulties, Struble's 261-ship armada successfully landed the Tenth Corps beginning on 15 September, and within days United Nations troops had recaptured the nearby city of Seoul, South Korea's capital, and forced the North Koreans to evacuate South Korea. A month later Admiral Struble landed Tenth Corps troops at Wonsan on the eastern coast of North Korea, and in December 1950, after the Chinese Communists entered the war, he oversaw the evacuation of the Tenth Corps through the port of Hungnam, an operation that included nearly 100,000 troops and an equal number of Korean refugees.

Struble was transferred to command of the Pacific Fleet in March 1951, and during the first half of 1952 he commanded the Eastern Sea Frontier, Atlantic Fleet. From the summer of 1952 until his retirement in July 1956 with the rank of full admiral, Struble chaired the United States Military Staff Mission to the United Nations. In retirement he was an adviser to the Hamilton Watch Company and a director of the New York Shipbuilding Corporation. Struble's wife died in April 1962, and in March 1967 he married Margaret Avery Ringle. Struble died from pneumonia sixteen years later and was buried at Arlington National Cemetery.

A diminutive, irascible, and highly skilled naval practitioner, Admiral Struble stands out for his leading role in the planning and execution of several major amphibious landings in World War II and the Korean War.

★

A small collection of Struble's papers is located in the Naval Historical Center, Washington, D.C. For references to Struble's service during World War II and the Korean War see Samuel Eliot Morison, *History of United States Naval Operations in World War II,* vol. 7: *Leyte: June 1944–January 1945* (1958) and vol. 8: *The Liberation of the Philippines: Luzon, Mindanao, the Visayas* (1959); D. Clayton James, *The Years of MacArthur,* vol. 2: *1941–1945* (1972) and vol. 3: *Triumph and Disaster, 1945–1964* (1985); Robert W. Love Jr., *History of the U.S. Navy,* vol. 2: *1942–1991* (1992); and James A. Field, *History of United States Naval Operations: Korea* (1962). Obituaries are in the *New York Times* (4 May 1983) and the *Washington Post* (3 May 1983). An interview is located in the Special Collections Department, Mitchell Memorial Library, Mississippi State University.

JOHN KENNEDY OHL

STUART, Jesse Hilton (*b.* 8 August 1908 in W-Hollow, Kentucky; *d.* 17 February 1984 in Ironton, Ohio), poet, short-story writer, novelist, essayist, and educator who created a remarkable literary landscape from his life in the Appalachian region of Kentucky.

Born in a one-room log shack in W-Hollow, Greenup County, Kentucky, Jesse Stuart was the first son and second child of Martha Hilton and Mitchell Stuart's seven children. His father was illiterate and worked variously as a seasonal coal miner, railroad laborer, and tenant hill farmer. During his early years at the one-room Plum Grove School, Jesse was frequently hired out to work at odd jobs. Because he spent only twenty-two months in school between 1912 and 1922, he was required to pass an entrance exam to attend high school. The teacher who graded the test gave him an extra point, enabling him to pass the English composition section with a 60. Later on, Stuart would regard this special consideration as the most important "turning point" in his life.

After graduating from Greenup High School in 1926, Stuart hitchhiked around Kentucky traveling to personal interviews in an effort to gain admission to college. That fall he enrolled at Lincoln Memorial University in Harrogate, Tennessee, where he was encouraged to write by Professor Harry Harrison Kroll and was intellectually stimulated by classmates James Still and Don West, who later became noted American writers themselves. Stuart graduated in three years and two summers.

In September 1929 Stuart became a teacher and principal at Warnock High School, and the following year

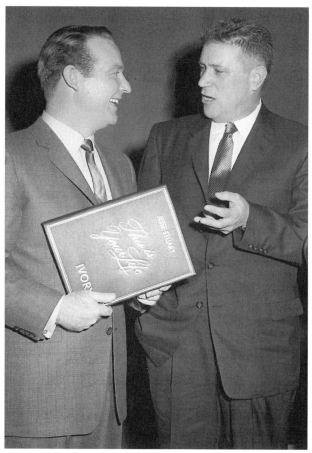

Jesse Stuart (*right*) with Ralph Edwards, host of *This Is Your Life,* 1958. AP/WIDE WORLD PHOTOS

served as principal of Greenup High School, from which he had graduated only four years earlier. A slightly fictionalized version of his experience in these two schools figures prominently in *The Thread That Runs So True* (1949), Stuart's most influential book about American education.

Stuart entered graduate school at Vanderbilt University in 1931. There he struggled financially, surviving on one meal a day. During one eleven-day period, Stuart wrote a 322-page autobiographical term paper for Professor Edward Mims which was published seven years later as *Beyond Dark Hills: A Personal Story* (1938). During his second semester, his clothing, poems, and a nearly completed M.A. thesis in English were destroyed in a house fire, and Stuart subsequently left Vanderbilt without his master's degree. While there, however, he met John Crowe Ransom, Allen Tate, Robert Penn Warren, and Donald Davidson, all founders of the literary journal *The Fugitive.* Known as the Southern Agrarians, this core group started a critical movement that attacked social ills intrinsic to industrialization and advocated formalism in literary criticism. Professor Davidson, himself a poet and critic, encouraged Stuart and

personally championed his artistic worth to editors of other influential literary journals. To Davidson, Stuart's writing was like a natural force, a "river of poetry."

Jesse Stuart left Vanderbilt at the age of twenty-six to become the superintendent of schools for Greenup County; he was the youngest superintendent in the state. At the height of the Great Depression he found himself thrust into the politics of the Kentucky educational system, which seemed to him a "cradle of copperheads." Working and writing at a furious pace, he produced essays, short stories, novels, and poetry. In 1933 he attracted national attention with his poems in H. L. Mencken's literary journal, *American Mercury,* and Stringfellow Barr's *Virginia Quarterly Review.* The following year, the *New Republic* published "Kentucky Hill Dance," Stuart's first short story to appear in a major literary magazine. Also in 1934, E. P. Dutton published *Man with a Bull-Tongue Plow,* an elaborate sequence of 703 sonnets that depicts the aspirations and struggles of the people of Appalachia and evokes the rich and vigorous beauty of the land. Never before had the form and spirit of the people of this region been so well expressed by one of its native sons. These poems, some of which Stuart claimed to have written on the backs of poplar leaves, established him as a literary talent worthy of serious national attention. During the Great Depression, he was the most frequently published author in *Esquire* magazine, a major outlet for popular literature during that era.

A Guggenheim grant allowed Stuart to live and write in Scotland in 1937 and 1938. During his stay he visited more than twenty European countries and viewed firsthand the growing tensions that would lead to World War II. Upon his return to the United States, he published *Beyond Dark Hills.* That same year Stuart started teaching high school in Portsmouth, Ohio, and on 14 October 1938 he married Naomi Deane Norris, his high school sweetheart and a fellow teacher. They had one child.

Stuart's *Taps for Private Tussie* (1943), a Book-of-the-Month Club selection, sold over one million copies and won the Thomas Jefferson Southern Award for best Southern book of the year. In the tradition of American humor, the novel portrays a bizarre family squabble over a windfall inheritance caused by a bungled report of a soldier's death.

Stuart's dual commitments to education and writing resulted in many awards. In 1949, Charles Scribner's Sons published *The Thread That Runs So True,* a chronicle of his early years as a country teacher and school administrator. Selected by the National Education Association as the best education book of the year, it was further praised by that association's president as "the best book on education written in the last fifty years." Frequently required reading in many colleges of education, it brought Stuart more mail than all of his other books combined.

Stuart became the poet laureate of Kentucky in 1954. That same year he suffered a near-fatal heart attack. His arduous recovery and the spiritual reawakening that accompanied it is recounted in *The Year of My Rebirth* (1956). His conviction that education is essential to the success of American democracy and his passion for teaching were undiminished throughout his life. A later book, *To Teach, to Love* (1970), is a continuing autobiographical account of Stuart's readings, lectures, and teaching experiences at numerous colleges. Stuart shared his fame by frequently using his appearances at universities to secure scholarships for talented and needy students in his schools.

As a social critic, Stuart complained about the influence of politics on education and noted with irony that while Kentucky's colleges prepared some of the nation's finest teachers, it lost them to other states where working conditions and salaries were more enticing.

The 1960s continued to expand Jesse Stuart's horizons. He became a fellow of the Academy of American Poets; he crisscrossed the country and traveled abroad extensively. He taught at the American University in Cairo and lectured for the U.S. State Department in the Near, Middle, and Far East.

On 18 February 1984, following a series of heart attacks and strokes and, after more than a year in a coma, Stuart died in the Jo-Lin Health Care Center in Ironton, Ohio. He is buried next to his parents in a family plot in the Plum Grove Cemetery near W-Hollow in Greenup County, Kentucky.

Stuart published more than 60 books, 450 short stories, and 2,000 poems during his life. At one point, he was one of America's most frequently anthologized authors. His works have been translated into more than thirty-three foreign languages. Collectively, Stuart's literary works constitute a vigorously imagined natural and social history of the people of Kentucky and the Appalachian region.

In the final sentence of Stuart's *God's Oddling* (1960), his moving biography of his father, Jesse Stuart mused, "He is still a part of this valley, just as it is still a part of him." This sentiment might equally serve as a fitting epitaph to Jesse Stuart's life and works.

★

Most of Stuart's papers and and manuscripts are housed in the Forrest C. Pogue Special Collections Library, Murray State University, Murray, Kentucky. Some additional materials and memorabilia can be found at Morehead State University, Morehead, Kentucky. Works by Jesse Hilton Stuart not mentioned in the text include *Head o' W-Hollow* (1936); *Hie to the Hunters* (1950); *The Seasons of Jesse Stuart: An Autobiography in Poetry* (1976); *Dandelion on the Acropolis: A Journal of Greece* (1978); and *If I Were Seventeen Again, and Other Essays* (1980).

Biographies include Ruel E. Foster, *Jesse Stuart* (1968); Harold E. Richardson, *Jesse: The Biography of an American Writer, Jesse Hilton Stuart* (1984); and Jerry A. Herndon and George Brosi, *Jesse Stuart: The Man and His Books* (1988). "Jesse Stuart," a half-hour documentary broadcast on 6 August 1986, is available from Kentucky Educational Television in Lexington, Kentucky. "Jesse Stuart Remembered" (1986), an hour-long videotape of family reminiscences, is available from the Jesse Stuart Foundation in Ashland, Kentucky.

JOSEPH G. FLYNN

STURGEON, Theodore (*b.* 26 February 1918 in Staten Island, New York; *d.* 8 May 1985 in Eugene, Oregon), science fiction and fantasy writer who also used the pseudonyms Frederick R. Ewing, E. Waldo Hunter, and E. Hunter Waldo.

Theodore Sturgeon was born Edward Hamilton Waldo, the youngest of two sons of Edward Waldo, who worked in oil production, and Christine Hamilton, who earned a living as a writer, artist, and musician. When Sturgeon was five, his father left the home, and the couple divorced in 1927. Two years later, after his mother married William D. Sturgeon, the head of the Romance Languages Department at Drexel Institute, young Edward adopted his stepfather's surname and legally changed his name to Theodore Hamilton Sturgeon. In 1929 the family moved to Philadelphia, where Sturgeon spent his high school years.

Even though his mother and stepfather were teachers who made every effort to instill a love of learning in their children, Sturgeon took little interest in formal education. He attended Overbrook High School near Philadelphia, where, at the age of twelve, he was introduced to gymnastics. Sturgeon so enjoyed the sport that he became the team captain within a year and was eventually allowed to instruct his class.

Sturgeon's dream to become a gymnast ended abruptly, however, when he suffered rheumatic fever at the age of fifteen; his illness saddled him with a permanently enlarged heart. Unable to pursue gymnastics, Sturgeon let his grades drop, but despite poor work, he was eventually "released" from Overbrook. Whether he actually graduated remains unclear, because he later claimed that he did not receive a diploma.

In 1935 Sturgeon spent one term at the Pennsylvania Nautical School, after which he gained passage aboard a ship as an engine-room wiper. It was at sea that Sturgeon began his writing, and in 1937 he sold "Heavy Insurance," a short story, to McClure's Syndicate for $5. The story was published in the *Milwaukee Journal* on 16 July 1938.

Despite this breakthrough, Sturgeon continued to work at sea. Within a year, however, he had written a sizable amount of short fiction. From 1937 to 1939, he sold about forty stories to *McClure's,* although none of the stories was science fiction or fantasy. He then published "The Ether Breather" in *Astounding Science-Fiction* in September 1939. This humorous tale depicts mischievous beings who interfere with television transmissions. "Ether Breather" was published as part of Sturgeon's first book, *Without Sorcery* (1948), which featured an introduction by noted science-fiction author Ray Bradbury.

In November 1939 Sturgeon sold "A God in a Garden" to *Unknown,* a fantasy magazine managed by John W. Campbell, Jr., who also edited *Astounding Science-Fiction.* Sturgeon would publish more highly regarded works, but this sale established him in the science-fiction field. He forged a closer relationship with *Unknown* because it freed him from the more technical orientation of *Astounding.*

From the time that he sold "A God in a Garden" until the end of 1940, Sturgeon sold six more stories to Campbell. In 1940 Sturgeon married Dorothy Fillingame, his high-school sweetheart. On their honeymoon, Sturgeon wrote for about ten hours, and he published the resulting short story, "It," in the August 1940 issue of *Unknown.* This nightmarish horror story displayed his talent as a gifted storyteller.

Sturgeon and Dorothy had two children, but, ultimately, Sturgeon's financial hardships took their toll. After a failed attempt to manage a resort hotel in the British West Indies (1940–1941), Sturgeon tried to be a door-to-door salesman. When that work proved fruitless, he took a job with the U.S. Army at a military gas station and tractor lubrication center. Sturgeon developed a strong interest in earth-moving machines, and from 1942 to 1943 he operated a bulldozer in Puerto Rico.

In 1944 the military base where Sturgeon worked was closed. Once more unemployed, Sturgeon wrote and sold a few stories based on his experiences. "Killdozer!" (*Astounding,* 1944), for example, earned Sturgeon the most he had ever received for a story: $545. For unknown reasons, however, Sturgeon soon developed writer's block. After he spent ten months away from home while struggling to write, his wife asked for a divorce in 1945.

Sturgeon became a literary agent in 1946. By helping other writers, Sturgeon regained his own ability to write. In 1947 he won the *Argosy* Prize for "Bianca's Hands," a terrifying story that some had considered too perverse for publication. In 1948 he published *Without Sorcery,* a short-story collection. Sturgeon dedicated that book to Mary Mair, a singer who became his second wife in 1949. This marriage was also short-lived and ended in divorce in 1951. Sturgeon married Marion Sturgeon in 1951; they had four children.

In the 1950s, under the influence of Horace L. Gold, the editor of *Galaxy Magazine,* Sturgeon learned to craft his stories more carefully, and his writing then showed a depth that earned him recognition. The most obvious sign of

Sturgeon's maturity as a writer was *More Than Human* (1954), his best-known work. This novel, built around three shorter stories—including "Baby Is Three" (*Galaxy,* 1952)—won the International Fantasy Award for 1954.

In the 1950s and 1960s Sturgeon added to his body of work: *The Dreaming Jewels* (1950; published in 1957 as *The Synthetic Man*), *E Pluribus Unicorn* (short stories, 1953), *The Cosmic Rape* (science-fiction novel, 1958), *Aliens 4* (short stories, 1959), *Venus Plus X* (science-fiction novel, 1960), and *The Joyous Invasions* (short stories, 1965). In 1966, Sturgeon moved to Los Angeles to write teleplays, most notably for *Star Trek*—"Shore Leave" (1966) and "Amok Time" (1967). On 16 April 1969 Sturgeon married Wina Golden. They had one son. In his later years he sported a gray mustache and goatee and was given to wearing turtlenecks and sports jackets.

Although he wrote in a variety of forms, the mainstay of Sturgeon's work was always his short fiction; his collection *Theodore Sturgeon Is Alive and Well . . .* (1971) contains "Slow Sculpture" (1970), which won the 1970 Nebula Award and the 1971 Hugo Award. After 1970, Sturgeon wrote relatively few stories. He did remain active as an editor and a workshop leader training new writers. Sturgeon died as a result of lung ailments.

Much of Sturgeon's early fiction carried a pessimistic and misanthropic tone. Over the years, Sturgeon could be either intensely prolific and effective or blocked and uninspired, depending on his emotional condition. Yet Sturgeon grew into a literary craftsman and created stories that successfully intertwined scientific speculations with musings on the human heart. His work explores especially the themes of loneliness, love, and sex. He wrote about taboo subjects such as androgyny and homosexuality when few others dared, not for shock value but to create stories that displayed the issues people deal with but may not speak of.

★

Listings of Sturgeon's works can be found in Lahna F. Diskin, *Theodore Sturgeon: A Primary and Secondary Bibliography* (1980), and in Diskin, *Theodore Sturgeon* (1981), which also includes descriptions of his major novels and short stories. Lucy Menger, *Theodore Sturgeon* (1981), is a full-length biography. Other works with extensive coverage of Sturgeon are four volumes of his stories edited by Paul Williams: *The Ultimate Egoist* (1994), *Microcosmic God* (1995), *Killdozer!* (1996), and *Thunder and Roses* (1997). These collections include extensive notes that provide publishing anecdotes and excerpts from Sturgeon's own letters and notes. See also Sam Moskowitz, "Theodore Sturgeon," in *Seekers of Tomorrow* (1966); Beverly Friend, "The Sturgeon Connection," in *Voices of the Future* (1976), edited by Thomas Clareson; and Brian M. Stableford, "Theodore Sturgeon," in *Science Fiction Writers* (1982), edited by E. F. Bleiler. The entire March 1991 issue of *Lan's Lantern,* a specialized science-fiction magazine, is devoted to articles on Sturgeon. See also Stephen King, "Theodore Sturgeon (1918–

1985)," *Washington Post Book World* (26 May 1985), and Brian W. Aldiss, "Sturgeon: Mercury Plus X: Farewell to a Master," in *And the Lurid Glare of the Comet* (1986). Obituaries are in the *New York Times* (11 May 1985) and *Publishers Weekly* (31 May 1985).

LEROY GONZALEZ

SUTTON, Carol (*b.* 29 June 1934 in St. Louis, Missouri; *d.* 19 February 1985 in Louisville, Kentucky), journalist who became the first woman to serve as managing editor of a major American newspaper, the *Louisville Courier-Journal*.

Raised in St. Louis, Sutton was the daughter of Dallas Monroe Sutton, a railroad conductor, and Marie (Marler) Sutton, an employment agent. After her graduation in 1955 from the University of Missouri at Columbia, where she had majored in journalism, Sutton went to work for the *Louisville Courier-Journal*, as secretary to James S. Pope, Sr., executive editor of the newspaper. This put her in a position to observe the dynamics of the news operation on a daily basis.

Within a year, Sutton was promoted to general assignment reporter, in which capacity she covered everything from city hall to local floods, from political campaigns to the Kentucky Derby. She mastered the hierarchical

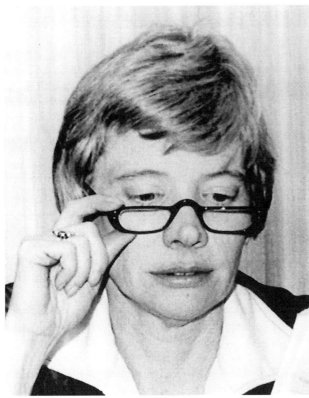

Carol Sutton, 1975. UPI/CORBIS-BETTMANN

traditions of Southern politics and quickly became known as a tough but fair-minded reporter who was serious in purpose, had a great sense of humor, and was bristling with ideas. She developed strong skills in uncovering facts and connecting events. On 23 November 1957 Sutton married Charles E. Whaley, director of communications at the Kentucky Education Association; they had two children.

In 1963, at the age of twenty-nine, Sutton became editor of the *Courier-Journal*'s "Women's World" section, transforming what had been a compilation of lighthearted household tips and society gossip into a trenchant features section that reflected the social concerns of the day, addressing such issues as abortion, poverty, violence, and unemployment. Soon after taking charge of the section, she renamed it "Today's Living." As Sutton explained, "We could not justify saying these were women's interests alone. It was the feeling that the word 'women's' was an arbitrary barrier to men." Her innovation was followed by newspapers all over the country and had an effect on the women's movement itself.

In 1973 Sutton won the Penney-Missouri award for an investigative story she crafted about the fashion industry's practice of giving lavish gifts to reporters who covered New York fashion shows. Her competitive nature, combined with her ability to create imaginative feature articles and photographic essays and to recognize important news stories, brought her to the attention of the newspaper's top editors.

In 1974 Sutton was appointed managing editor of the *Louisville Courier-Journal*, becoming the first woman to head the news operation of a major U.S. daily newspaper. Under her leadership, the *Courier-Journal* won a Pulitzer Prize in 1975 for photographic coverage of the city's desegregation crisis. For six tension-filled weeks the paper reported on the issues resulting from the busing of schoolchildren to achieve integration.

Her position as managing editor brought Sutton much recognition. In 1976 she appeared on the cover of *Time* magazine with eleven other movers and shakers as *Time*'s "Women of the Year," and subsequently she found herself something of a national celebrity, with frequent invitations to appear on television and radio talk shows. She was quoted as saying, "I'm not in any way a traditional, tough-talking managing editor. I don't go around banging shoes on desks or yelling at reporters across the city desk." She did, however, inspire and teach her reporters, and she began the tradition of outstanding investigative reporting for which the paper was renowned. But her zealous manner and noble intentions did not conflict with her gaiety. "She found fun in everything," said Barry Bingham, Jr., owner and chairman of the board of the *Louisville Courier-Journal* at the time of Sutton's death.

As senior editor of the *Courier-Journal* from 1979, Sutton

insisted on the recruitment of minority journalists, stating that the *Courier-Journal* had to follow in its offices what it preached on its editorial pages. As a result of her efforts, the representation of minority reporters and editors at the newspaper rose from 3 to 10 percent. Gaining even more national publicity for her civil rights efforts, Sutton was the subject of a *Time* magazine story in 1983; she was also named the first white member of the National Association of Black Journalists.

Sutton not only influenced the *Louisville Courier-Journal*, but she left her mark on national journalism as well. She was a discussion leader on ethics for the American Press Institute and was chairman of Pulitzer Prize committees in 1975 and 1976. Additionally, she was a member of the selection committee for the Nieman Fellows in Journalism at Harvard University and was one of two women regents of the Associated Press Managing Editors.

A small woman, known for her tremendous energy and refreshing personality, Sutton was committed to social justice. While in college she had worked as a counselor of underprivileged children. In retrospect, she said of this experience, "I got caught up in their problems—so caught up, it was eating me up. I just wasn't suited for that." But she was geared to help young journalists, especially women, and she served as an inspiration and unofficial guide for a generation of cub reporters trying to find their way in the pressure-filled world of newspaper publishing.

Sutton spoke fluent Spanish and was an avid collector of books, artifacts, and artwork from Latin America. Whenever possible, she vacationed in South America. She spent a summer in Quito, Ecuador, and in the Andes, where she served, pro bono, as an adviser to Latin American newspapers. In 1984 she was elected a member of the Kentucky Hall of Fame.

Carol Sutton died of cancer at her Louisville home at the age of fifty-one. She was cremated. As a continuing memorial to her excellence, her portrait hangs in the Kentucky state capitol.

★

An obituary is in the *New York Times* (20 Feb. 1985).

FRANK BRADY

SWANSON, Gloria (*b.* 27 March 1899 in Chicago, Illinois; *d.* 4 April 1983 in New York City), actress who was an icon of sophistication and glamour during the silent era of motion pictures and remained popular for several decades, making an unmistakable impact on the fashions and mores of her time.

Born Gloria May Josephine Svensson, she was the only child of Joseph Theodore Svensson and Adelaide Klanowski, a homemaker. Her father was a civilian official of

Gloria Swanson, 1920s. POPPERFOTO/ARCHIVE PHOTOS

the army transport service, stationed at various times in Florida, Texas, and Puerto Rico, and Gloria thus attended more than a dozen schools in various locations. Swanson's early life was relatively uneventful until she was fifteen and in her first year of high school, when a relative took her to the Chicago studio of the Essanay Company, where they were making "new-fangled" movies. She was hired as an extra and attracted the attention of a rising young actor named Wallace Beery, who persuaded her to come to California, where the movie business was booming, six months later. Her formal education ended, and she changed her name to Gloria Swanson in 1916.

After working in primitive one-reelers, Swanson met filmmaker Mack Sennett, who teamed her with Bobby Vernon in a series of romantic comedies. (She was never a Sennett bathing beauty and deplored the knockabout vulgarity of his slapstick comedies.) She married Beery in 1916, just days before her seventeenth birthday, but they were divorced in 1919. In 1918 she found her way to the Famous Players–Lasky Company and the director Cecil B. DeMille of Paramount Pictures. A diminutive girl (four feet, eleven inches tall) with an iron determination to succeed, she rose to stardom within a few years.

Beginning with *Don't Change Your Husband* (1919), Swanson's large blue eyes, sloping nose, and expressive mouth fascinated audiences, as did her stylish gowns and dresses. In movies such as *For Better, for Worse* (1919), *Male and Female* (1919), and *Why Change Your Wife?* (1920), under the direction of either DeMille or Sam Wood, she excelled at playing dressed-to-the-hilt society wives or playgirls caught up in romantic dilemmas. In December 1919 she married Herbert K. Somborn, a film distributor and later restaurateur, with whom she had a daughter, Gloria. She bought a mansion in Beverly Hills, California, in 1922, and they adopted a son, Joseph. They were divorced in 1925.

By the early 1920s, Swanson was the screen's foremost box-office attraction, although critics often reviewed her costumes more than her performances. Films such as *Beyond the Rocks* (1922), with Rudolph Valentino, *The Impossible Mrs. Bellew* (1922), and *Prodigal Daughters* (1923) allowed her to appear as high-spirited, upper-bracket women in extravagant costumes. She then moved into more challenging roles that required her to be more than a clotheshorse. In *Manhandled* (1924), *Wages of Virtue* (1924), and other films, often under the direction of Allan Dwan, she was able to play lower-class women with the same verve and distinction. Fans who still longed to see her in beautiful gowns were rewarded with a lavish display of costumes in *Her Love Story* (1924).

In 1925 she went to France to make a film called *Madame Sans-Gêne,* based on Victorien Sardou's 1893 play. While negotiating for the right to produce what was the first major Hollywood movie made in Europe, Swanson met and married on 28 January 1925 the handsome Marquis Henri de la Falaise de la Coudraye. Back in America, her popularity continued unabated with *Stage Struck* (1925), *Fine Manners* (1926), and other movies. In 1926, eager to have greater control over her films, Swanson joined with Mary Pickford, Douglas Fairbanks, Charlie Chaplin, and others in forming United Artists (UA), primarily a distribution company for the films of the actor-shareholders. She created Gloria Swanson Productions for her films, which were distributed by UA (the company was dissolved in 1932).

At the height of her fame, Swanson received as many as 10,000 fan letters a week, and her innovative coiffures were copied by millions of women around the world. She was also a major trendsetter in fashion, wearing clothing from her own designs and created exclusively for her by such famous designers as Paul Iribe, Gabrielle ("Coco") Chanel, René Hubert, Herbert de Givenchy, and Edith Head. Her striking appearance and offbeat beauty caught the attention of the most notable portrait photographers of the day, in-

cluding Cecil Beaton, George Hurrell, Karl Struss, Clarence Sinclair Bull, Phillipe Halsman, and Baron Adolph De Meyer.

In November 1927, Swanson met Joseph P. Kennedy, a wealthy, intensely ambitious banker with a wife and seven children. They began a clandestine romance, and Kennedy, eager to venture into the film business, took charge of Swanson's career. He helped her make *Sadie Thompson* (1928), for which she won an Academy Award nomination as Somerset Maugham's feisty South Seas prostitute, and he also oversaw and financed her trouble-plagued, never-completed expensive production of *Queen Kelly,* under the direction of the gifted but erratic Erich von Stroheim. Eventually, Swanson and Kennedy became estranged under cloudy circumstances.

As the luster of her star began to fade with the coming of sound pictures, Swanson ended her marriage to the marquis in 1930, and on 16 August 1931 she married Irish sportsman Michael Farmer, with whom she had a daughter, Michelle (they were divorced in 1934). Always an astute businesswoman, in 1938 she formed Multiprises, Inc., a company designed to market the inventions of German scientists in America. She starred in plays on the summer "straw-hat" circuit, and her first sound film, *The Trespasser* (1929), won her another Academy Award nomination. Others, including *Tonight or Never* (1931), *Perfect Understanding* (1933), and *Music in the Air* (1934), were disappointing, however. In 1945, she was married for one month to stockbroker William Davey; they officially divorced three years later. In 1948 she pioneered in television with her own talk show, *The Gloria Swanson Hour.*

In 1950, after being away from films for nine years, Swanson was asked to star in Billy Wilder's production of *Sunset Boulevard.* At first reluctant, she finally agreed to play Norma Desmond, a once-glittering silent film star, whose life disintegrates into madness and murder. The movie's harsh, acrid attitude toward the film business alienated some viewers, particularly those in the business themselves, but Swanson's bravura performance was widely admired, and she received an Academy Award nomination for best actress.

Although she would never again play a film or stage role as prestigious or as complex as Norma Desmond, Swanson remained a busy actress for many years after *Sunset Boulevard,* working in theater, radio, and television, living in New York City in a Fifth Avenue apartment. Her interests, however, extended far beyond acting. In 1957 she created and marketed her own line of clothing under the label Forever Young. She also became intensely concerned around 1944 with the nutritional habits of Americans, and, with a crusader's zeal, she argued tirelessly against chemically treated—or what she termed "make-believe" foods.

Swanson continued to make sporadic appearances up to

the 1970s, acting on Broadway in *Butterflies Are Free* in 1971 and in the movie *Airport 1975* (1974), in which she played herself. In 1976, she married a journalist named William Dufty, whom she divorced in 1981. Swanson died in New York Hospital of a heart ailment.

Glamorous, imperious, and dedicated to her work and to her multitude of fans, Gloria Swanson was also a tough-minded and determined woman, liberated many years before the feminist movement. Her obituary in the *Washington Post* states: "She was a sex symbol of one day, a Great Lady of another."

★

The Gloria Swanson Papers are in the library of the University of Texas at Austin. In addition to her autobiography, *Swanson on Swanson* (1980), see Richard M. Hudson and Raymond Lee, *Gloria Swanson* (1970); Lawrence J. Quirk, *The Films of Gloria Swanson* (1984), and Axel Madsen, *Gloria and Joe* (1988). An article by Swanson, "I Am Not Going to Write My Memoirs!," appeared in *Sight and Sound* (spring 1969). An obituary is in the *New York Times* (5 Apr. 1983).

TED SENNETT

T

TANNY, Vic(tor) Anthony (*b.* 18 February 1912 in Rochester, New York; *d.* 11 June 1985 in Tampa, Florida), body builder and health club pioneer.

Vic Tanny was the third of five children born to Ostilio Iannidinardo, a tailor, and Angelina Fiorito, both native Italians. Ostilio later Americanized his surname to Tanny. Vic Tanny's athletic abilities were evident from childhood. He was the strongest boy in his grammar school class, captain of the boxing team at John Marshall High School, and a competitive weight lifter in college. He was a testament to the benefits of strength training and to the dietary practices of his mother, who served her family plenty of vegetables while banishing sugars and dessert. Tanny stood five feet, ten inches and throughout his life maintained a weight lifter's build, with a fifty-two-inch chest and a thirty-four-inch waist.

After graduating with the class of 1935 from the Brockport State (New York) Teachers College, Tanny taught junior high school history and opened his first gymnasium, in a space over a bowling alley on West Ridge Road in Rochester. He believed that many people had the desire to improve their appearance through exercise, but most of the inhabitants of his hometown were unwilling to do so in public. He sold the gymnasium in 1938 and went west, where he met with greater success in body-conscious southern California.

In August 1940 Tanny started a new gymnasium on Second Street in Santa Monica, near the famed Muscle Beach. On 6 May 1941 he married Florence Shirley Grastorf, a Rochester native, in Las Vegas, Nevada. They had four children, Jacqueline, Jeanne, Candace, and Victor, Jr., before their divorce in 1953. In 1948 Tanny opened a branch of his gym in Long Beach. By the mid-1950s he had forty gyms in California; at his peak in 1962 he owned ninety-two of his Vic Tanny's Gym and Health Clubs across the United States and Canada.

Tanny believed that good health could be merchandised just like automobiles. His innovations brought record numbers of Americans, particularly weight-conscious women, into gymnasiums for the first time. Fitness advertisements up to that time typically appeared in the back pages of magazines that appealed to young men. The reader would be promised amazing results in the privacy of his own home through a mail-order purchase of some product. Tanny developed television commercials to overcome the natural reluctance of those with less-than-perfect shapes to exercise in public. His advertisements showed ordinary men and women of all ages and sizes working out together and enjoying themselves while reducing.

Before Tanny, gymnasiums were thought to be dank, malodorous places primarily inhabited by prizefighters and their hangers-on and particularly uninviting to women. Tanny's establishments featured thick red carpets and indirect lighting. Muzak was piped throughout the building, and there were massage rooms, swimming pools, steam baths, and sun rooms decorated in charcoal gray and pink. The elaborate exercise equipment, which Tanny invented and manufactured in his California factory, was plated in gleaming chromium.

Americans were accustomed to installment-plan purchasing and Tanny adopted this concept to make his gymnasiums affordable. He offered annual and lifetime membership options, with a variety of special promotions, all heavily publicized on television. Tanny owned all the gymnasiums in his chain as well as six other companies that supplied his clubs with everything from health foods to exercise apparatus. His firm, Vic Tanny Enterprises, Inc., was headquartered in Beverly Hills, California. He financed new clubs largely with borrowed funds. In 1961 he launched an aggressive membership campaign to raise money for expansion. To sign up new members, he employed door-to-door salesmen and rented storefronts in busy locations such as Times Square in New York City, where his employees gave demonstrations for passersby.

Tanny got into financial difficulty when many of these new members defaulted on their club dues. He attempted a public stock offering in his company, but this effort failed. In 1962 his creditors assumed ownership of the gyms when he did not have enough cash for loan payments and his $1.2 million monthly payroll. By the end of 1963 Tanny had succeeded in franchising about ten gymnasiums under his name, notably in the Midwest and Canada; other clubs remained open under new management, but more than half closed.

From 1963 to the end of his life, Tanny's companion was Carole Archer Tanny. After Tanny relinquished ownership of the gymnasium chain, he and Carole spent a year in Europe. They returned to California in 1964 and remained based there while they traveled around the country in a motor home visiting his family and the clubs franchised under his name. In 1980 they relocated to Florida. Tanny died on 11 June 1985, at age seventy-three, due to complications from a stroke he suffered two years earlier. He died in the University Community Hospital in Tampa, Florida, and his body was cremated.

Vic Tanny's passion was enlisting new people to the world of body-sculpting, as he called it. Even in the final months of his illness he coached his nurses in an exercise program he devised. His popular slogan, "Take it off, build it up, make it firm," successfully persuaded thousands of Americans to head for Vic Tanny's in their never-ending quest to achieve physical perfection, or at least to lose weight.

★

See Peter Bunzel, "Health Kick's High Priest," *Life* (29 Sept. 1958); Robert Alden, "Advertising: Hard Sell or Muscle Flexing," *New York Times* (5 June 1960); "Vic Tanny: A Biographical Portrait," *Wisdom* (May 1961); and Thomas Buckley, "State Is Studying Vic Tanny Losses," *New York Times* (11 Dec. 1963). An obituary is in the *Los Angeles Times* (12 June 1985).

KENNETH R. COBB

Vic Tanny. ARCHIVE PHOTOS

TARSKI, Alfred (*b*. 14 January 1902? in Warsaw, Poland; *d*. 27 October 1983 in Berkeley, California), mathematician and philosopher best known for his contributions to set theory, model theory, general algebra, and logic.

Tarski was the son of Ignacy Tajtelbaum, a shopkeeper, and Rose Prussak Tajtelbaum. He changed his name to Tarski sometime around 1924 because, according to his son, he felt that the Polish-sounding Tarski would be held in greater regard than the Jewish name Tajtelbaum. Tarski earned his Ph.D. in 1924 at the University of Warsaw, where he studied under Stanisław Leśniewski, the great Polish mathematician. His dissertation was entitled "The Primitive Term of Logistic." He married Maria Witkowski on 23 June 1929; they had two children.

After receiving his Ph.D., Tarski taught at the University of Warsaw. He left in 1939 for a lecture tour in the United States. That September, while he was in the United States, war broke out in Europe and Tarski remained in America, separated from his wife and children, who were now in German-occupied Poland. He was a research associate in mathematics at Harvard University until 1941, then moved to the Institute for Advanced Study at Princeton, New Jersey, during the 1941–1942 academic year. In 1942 he obtained a permanent teaching post at the University of California at Berkeley. His family joined him there in 1946, the year after he became a naturalized citizen. Tarski was appointed a professor of mathematics in 1949, and in 1958 he established the Group in Logic and Methodology of Science, which brought together philosophers, mathematicians, and other scholars. Although Berkeley remained his home, he held visiting positions at a number of institutions including University College, London (Sherman memorial lecturer in 1950 and 1966), Institut Henri Poincaré (lecturer in 1955), and the University of California at Los Angeles (Flint Professor of philosophy in 1967). Tarski was research professor at the Miller Institute of Basic Research in Science at the University of California at Berkeley from 1958 to 1960. After becoming professor emeritus at Berkeley in 1968, he continued to teach for five more years and was an active researcher until his death.

Among the many honors and awards Tarski received were a Rockefeller Fellowship (1935) and two Guggenheim Fellowships (1941–1942, 1955–1956). He received honorary doctorates from the Catholic University of Chile (1975) and the University of Marseilles (1977).

Tarski was both a mathematician and a philosopher, and many of his results in mathematics had ramifications for the development of logic in the postwar United States. In the 1930s Tarski did his foundational work in semantics, formulating the semantic method for which he is widely known. Semantics, broadly, is concerned with meaning in language. Previously the focus had been on syntax—or pure structure. Tarski shifted analysis of scientific language to "truth," seeking to define truth in a formalized language. The fundamental question is: What makes a given sentence in a language "true"? This discussion occurs in a metalanguage rather than the first-order language—a distinction that allowed Tarski to postulate a solution to the famous Liar's Paradox.

Although Tarski limited his investigations to logic and mathematics, the semantic method turned out to be important to the philosophical understanding of truth. His work on semantics greatly influenced Rudolph Carnap in developing a more formal approach to semantics. W. V. Quine was among the logicians who benefited from Tarski's work. In 1971 Karl Popper wrote: "I asked Tarski to explain to me his theory of truth, and he did so in a lecture of perhaps twenty minutes on a bench (an unforgotten bench) in the *Volksgarten* in Vienna. . . . No words can describe how much I learned from all this. . . . I looked upon him as the one man whom I could truly regard as my

teacher in philosophy. I have never learned so much from anybody else."

One of Tarski's greatest contributions to mathematics is contained in a paper written with Stefan Banach on the decomposition of the sphere, "Sur la décomposition des ensembles des points en parties respectivement congruentes" (1924). The Banach-Tarski paradox is that a sphere can be broken down into a finite number of pieces and then reassembled into a larger sphere. Tarski also did considerable work on cardinal numbers. With Paul Erdös he made the distinction between a strongly compact cardinal and a weakly compact cardinal. He worked on undecidability (expanding on Kurt Gödel's work on incompleteness theorems), algebra, and, particularly at the end of his career, cylindrical algebras.

In addition to his professional interests, Tarski had a passion for biology, which he had apparently intended to specialize in at college. However, his immense talent in logic put an end to that plan. Tarski also had broad interests in art, literature, and gardening. Tarski was a brilliant and incisive thinker and an inspiring teacher. His original work in logic and mathematics, as well as the quality of his instruction, made him one of the most influential logicians of the twentieth century. Tarski is credited with developing logic as a discipline at Berkeley at a time when it had little stature among mathematicians. Tarski's influence was felt not only through his numerous publications, but also through his students, many of whom went on to become distinguished in their own right. Among his students were Solomon Feferman, Dana Scott, Haim Gaifman, and Julia Robinson. Tarski continued to be an effective teacher to the end of his career and is credited with being particularly generous in suggesting problems for students and helping them with their work. His publications, professional activities, and teaching created strong ties between logic and mathematics. His work in semantics and metamathematics created new lines of research for future logicians and philosophers of mathematics.

Tarski died in Berkeley, California.

★

Tarski wrote hundreds of articles and books in Polish, German, French, and English. Among the most important are *Geometry* (1935); "The Semantic Conception of Truth and the Foundations of Semantics," in *Philosophy and Phenomenological Research* (1944); *A Decision Method for Elementary Algebra and Geometry* (1948); *Undecidable Theories* (1953); and *Logic, Semantics, Metamathematics* (1956). A complete bibliography is provided in Tarski's *Collected Papers*, edited by Steven Givant (1986). Leon Henkin et al., eds., *Proceedings of the Tarski Symposium* (1974), a tribute to Tarski on the occasion of his seventieth birthday, contains a bibliography of his work and a list of dissertation students. The *Journal of Symbolic Logic*, beginning with vol. 51 (Dec. 1986), published a survey of Tarski's work and a series of expository essays. A brief biography of Tarski appears in *Biographical Dictionary of Mathematicians,* vol. 4 (1991). An obituary is in *The Annual Obituary* (1984).

JULIA DRIVER

TAYLOR, Glen Hearst (*b.* 12 April 1904 in Portland, Oregon; *d.* 28 April 1984 in Burlingame, California), U.S. senator from Idaho (1945–1951) who was the vice presidential candidate on the Progressive party ticket in the presidential election of 1948.

Glen H. Taylor was the twelfth of thirteen children born to Pleasant John and Olive (Higgins) Taylor. John Taylor, a minister, was also involved in farming, acting, and law enforcement. Glen Taylor grew up in Kooskia, Idaho, on the Clearwater River. He left school at age twelve and worked as a sheepherder and metalworker for about four years. The Taylor family, which enjoyed acting, singing, and traveling, organized a stock company that toured throughout the West. In 1924 Taylor married Olive Nitkowskie in New Mexico; they had one child before divorcing in 1929. In the late 1920s, as talking movies became the rage, the Taylor Players struggled to survive. Taylor married Dora M. Pike in 1930 and joined his brother Paul in another stock company, the Glendora Players, which fea-

Senator Glen H. Taylor, 1954. UPI/CORBIS-BETTMANN

tured country-and-western singing as well as vaudeville. Throughout the Great Depression, the Taylors traveled from village to village in order to get food and gas money to get to the next town. In 1938 they bought a small frame home in Pocatello, Idaho, and Taylor decided to make a living as a politician.

Taylor was an ardent New Dealer, and he believed that the government needed to guarantee a good quality of life for its citizens. Interested in farmer-labor politics, he decided to run for Congress as a Democrat in 1938. Using the Glendora format, he played music and spoke throughout Idaho. Vardis Fisher, the novelist, ranked him as second to President Franklin D. Roosevelt as a political orator. Although he lost in 1938, he did secure the Democratic senatorial nomination in both 1940 and 1942. He was unsuccessful in these races as well, but he continued to develop a strong following and finally won a Senate seat in 1944.

In Washington, Taylor supported Harry S. Truman's domestic program and became an advocate of such Fair Deal measures as national health insurance, the GI Bill, and the Columbia Valley Authority. He fought for civil rights legislation and went to jail protesting discrimination in Birmingham, Alabama, in 1948. However, Taylor did not agree with the Truman foreign policy of containment. His primary concern was that the United States and the Soviet Union were drifting toward a nuclear war. Consequently, he adamantly opposed the Truman Doctrine, the Marshall Plan, and the North Atlantic Treaty Organization. He opposed universal military training and the peacetime draft. A supporter of the new United Nations, Senator Taylor believed that the United Nations deserved a chance to solve international disputes. Taylor's fear of possible war led him to make a decision that essentially ended his political career.

In 1948 Taylor became Henry A. Wallace's running mate on the Progressive party ticket. Wallace, like Taylor, felt that Truman's policies spelled disaster and that a liberal peace party would provide a legitimate alternative. Taylor realized that a crusade such as the Progressive party was waging made reelection virtually impossible, but the issue of peace or war made his decision to join Wallace easy. Of course, Taylor loved the spotlight and enjoyed performing on a national stage. President Truman and others attacked the Progressives as being dominated by communists, and in the general election they received more than a million votes, or less than 2 percent of the total. Taylor returned to the Senate and continued to support Truman's domestic agenda.

Taylor failed in his bid for reelection in 1950 when he lost the Democratic primary. He then made unsuccessful attempts to represent Idaho in the Senate in 1954 and 1956. Victimized by McCarthyism in both the 1950 and 1954 campaigns, Taylor was painted as a communist sympathizer who had supported leftist causes. Idahoans responded by defeating him, even though John Corlett, the political editor of the *Idaho Daily Statesman,* called Taylor the "best errand boy senator Idaho ever had."

Taylor moved to the San Francisco Bay Area in 1956, and with his wife, Dora, he established Taylor Topper, Inc. This men's toupee manufacturing company grew from Dora's ability to create a toupee for Taylor, who became bald in his late twenties. The Taylors were joined in the new enterprise by their children. Glen and Dora lived above the manufacturing plant and remained active in the business. He died in 1984 at age eighty of Alzheimer's disease, and he was buried in Skylawn Cemetery in Millbrae, California.

★

Glen H. Taylor wrote an autobiography, *The Way It Was with Me* (1974). F. Ross Peterson, *Prophet Without Honor: Glen H. Taylor and the Fight for American Liberalism* (1974), is the only full-length biography. See also Peterson's "Glen H. Taylor: Idaho's Liberal Maverick," in *Idaho Heritage,* edited by Richard W. Etolain and Bert W. Marley (1974). An obituary is in the *New York Times* (5 May 1984).

F. ROSS PETERSON

TERRY, Luther Leonidas (*b.* 15 September 1911 in Red Level, Alabama; *d.* 29 March 1985 in Philadelphia, Pennsylvania), physician who, as surgeon general of the U.S. Public Health Service, issued a landmark report in 1964 linking lung cancer and other health problems to smoking.

Terry was one of the three children of James Edward Terry, a physician, and Lula Durham Terry, a nutritionist. He earned a B.S. degree at Birmingham-Southern College in 1931, followed by an M.D. degree at Tulane University in 1935. After interning at the Hillman Hospital in Birmingham and serving a residency in Cleveland, Ohio, he moved to Washington University in St. Louis in 1939 as an instructor in medicine and research fellow in pneumonia. He subsequently served as instructor and then as assistant professor of preventive medicine and public health at the University of Texas in Galveston from 1940 to 1942. He married Beryl Janet Reynolds on 29 June 1940. The couple had three children.

In 1942 Terry joined the staff of the Public Health Service Hospital in Baltimore, becoming chief of medical services there the following year. His interest in cardiovascular research led him to accept the position of chief of general medicine and experimental therapeutics at the National Heart Institute of the National Institutes of Health in Bethesda, Maryland, in 1950, at first on a part-time basis while continuing his work at the Baltimore hospital. When the National Institutes of Health's Clinical Center opened in

Luther Terry. PROGRAM SUPPORT CENTER, DEPARTMENT OF HEALTH AND HUMAN SERVICES

1953, Terry's Heart Institute program was moved to the new facility, and he devoted his full time to the job. He also served as the first chairman of the medical board of the Clinical Center (1953–1955) and was instructor and then assistant professor at the Johns Hopkins University School of Medicine from 1944 to 1961. Terry and his team laid the foundations for what has been called the golden era of cardiovascular clinical investigation. In 1958 he became the assistant director of the National Heart Institute. Terry came to public prominence in 1961, when President John F. Kennedy selected him as surgeon general of the Public Health Service, a position he held from 2 March 1961 to 1 October 1965.

Although there had long been an awareness that smoking might be detrimental to health, it was not until the 1950s that researchers published significant scientific evidence suggesting that cigarette smoking causes lung cancer and other diseases. At the end of the decade, the Royal College of Physicians in Britain appointed a committee to investigate the relationship between smoking and health. The committee's report, issued on 7 March 1962, clearly indicted cigarette smoking as a cause of lung cancer and bronchitis, and argued that smoking probably contributed to cardiovascular disease as well.

Shortly after the release of this report, Terry established

783

the Surgeon General's Advisory Committee on Smoking and Health, which he chaired, to produce a similar report for the United States. *Smoking and Health: Report of the Advisory Committee to the Surgeon General of the Public Health Service,* released on 11 January 1964, concluded that lung cancer and chronic bronchitis are causally related to cigarette smoking. The report also noted that there was suggestive evidence, if not definite proof, for a causative role of smoking in other illnesses such as emphysema, cardiovascular disease, and various types of cancer. The committee concluded that cigarette smoking was a health hazard of sufficient importance to warrant appropriate remedial action.

This landmark report on smoking and health stimulated increased concern about tobacco on the part of the American public and government policy makers and led to a broad-based antismoking campaign. It also motivated the tobacco industry to intensify its efforts to question the scientific evidence linking smoking and disease. The report was also responsible for the passage of the Cigarette Labeling and Advertising Act of 1965, which mandated that health warnings appear on cigarette packaging.

Terry continued to play a leading role in the campaign against smoking after leaving the post of surgeon general in 1965. He chaired the National Interagency Council on Smoking and Health, a coalition of government agencies and nongovernment organizations, from 1967 to 1969, and served as a consultant to groups such as the American Cancer Society. Terry helped to obtain a ban on cigarette advertisements on radio and television in 1971. Late in his life he led the effort to eliminate smoking from the workplace.

When Terry retired from government service in 1965, he became vice president for medical affairs as well as professor of medicine and community medicine at the University of Pennsylvania. He managed the university's health sciences schools, comprising some 40 percent of the university's budget, until 1971, when he left the vice presidency. He retained his professorial appointment until 1975, when he became adjunct professor, and then in 1982 emeritus professor. From 1970 to 1983 he also served as president of University Associates, a nonprofit consulting firm based in Washington, D.C.

Terry's last years were spent as corporate vice president for medical affairs for ARA Services of Philadelphia (1980–1983) and then as a consultant. He died of congestive heart failure and was buried in Arlington National Cemetery, Virginia.

In addition to being a pioneer of clinical cardiovascular research, Terry served as a successful administrator of government and academic medical programs. He is most remembered for his role in the campaign against smoking. The 1964 surgeon general's report brought the issue of smoking and health to the attention of the American public on a widespread basis and laid the foundation for increased government regulation of cigarette labeling and advertising. Terry himself described the study as "probably having the greatest impact of any government report ever issued." For the rest of his life Terry continued to speak out about the health hazards of cigarette smoking and to fight the tobacco lobby.

★

The personal papers of Luther Terry at the National Library of Medicine document his career primarily from 1966 until his death. The records of the Public Health Service include his official correspondence during his tenure as surgeon general. The National Archives holds substantial material related to the work of the Advisory Committee on Smoking and Health. Discussions of the 1964 surgeon general's report and its impact may be found in Susan Wagner, *Cigarette Country: Tobacco in American History and Politics* (1971), and Richard Kluger, *Ashes to Ashes: America's Hundred-Year Cigarette War, the Public Health, and the Unabashed Triumph of Philip Morris* (1996). There is as yet no full-length biography of Terry. See Jonathan E. Rhoads, "Luther Leonidas Terry, 1911–1985," *Transactions and Studies of the College of Physicians of Philadelphia,* series 5, 7 (1985): 291–294. Other obituaries are in the *Philadelphia Inquirer,* the *New York Times,* and the *Washington Post* (all 31 Mar. 1985).

JOHN PARASCANDOLA

TERRY, Walter (*b.* 14 May 1913 in Brooklyn, New York; *d.* 4 October 1982 in the Bronx, New York), dance critic whose career paralleled the development of concert dance in the United States and whose reviews, lectures, and books on the subject helped to popularize the field.

The son of Walter Matthews and Frances Lindsay Gray, Terry grew up in suburban New Canaan, Connecticut; he had one sister. Terry's interest in the performing arts blossomed at the University of North Carolina, where he majored in drama and minored in music. There, Terry wrote, directed, and acted in plays and was a principal dancer in the student company. He also wrote for college publications. Following graduation in 1935, Terry continued his dance training, studying ballet and modern, ethnic, and popular dance forms. His writing career began in 1936, when the *Boston Herald* hired him as a dance critic. One of his first assignments was to cover the activities of Jacob's Pillow, a summertime dance school founded by the dancer Ted Shawn and located in the rolling Berkshire Mountains of western Massachusetts. Throughout his career, Terry remained a patron of Jacob's Pillow, and when Shawn died in 1972 he took over as artistic director.

Early on, Terry played an ambassadorial role that would define his career. In 1939 he publicized protests of the Mas-

Walter Terry, 1980. AP/WIDE WORLD PHOTOS

Her Life, Her Art, Her Legacy (1964), *The Ballet Companion* (1968), *Miss Ruth: The "More Living Life" of Ruth St. Denis* (1969), *Ballet: A Pictorial History* (1970), *Ted Shawn: Father of American Dance* (1976), *I Was There* (1978), *Great Male Dancers of the Ballet* (1978), and *The King's Ballet Master: A Biography of Denmark's August Bournonville* (1979).

Throughout his career, Terry was in great demand as a speaker at colleges and universities, dance festivals and competitions, public functions, and on radio and television. After World War II he served as a cultural ambassador on State Department–sponsored tours of Eastern and Western Europe. In the 1950s he made several television appearances and in 1953 and 1954 helped select dances and dancers for such productions as *Camera 3* on the Columbia Broadcasting System. He taught courses in dance history and criticism at Southern Connecticut State College (1974–1975) and Yale University (1975). He was a judge at the International Ballet Competition held in Varna, Bulgaria, and served as vice president of the U.S. chapter of UNESCO's International Dance Council. He also helped develop regional ballet companies by writing about or adjudicating nationwide competitions.

For his dedication to the livelihood of dance he received numerous honors as well as an honorary degree from Ricker, College of the Northeast, in Houlton, Maine (1968). In 1976 Queen Margrethe II of Denmark made him a Knight of the Order of Dannebrog in recognition of his support of the Royal Danish Ballet and for promoting the Danish choreographer Auguste Bournonville in the United States. The dance-wear company Capezio acknowledged Terry with an award in 1980. Terry died at Montefiore Hospital in the Bronx after a brief illness. He never married and had no children.

Scholars and critics agree that, along with John Martin of the *New York Times,* Terry brought the subject of dance into the minds and homes of many who had never seen it before. Perhaps Terry's greatest contribution was his effort to bridge the gap between performance and the everyday experiences of his readers. Familiar with the movers and shakers of the dance world, he combined accounts of formal aspects of choreography with trivia and anecdotes about its creators and performers; he concentrated equally on evaluation and explanation.

Terry's commentary on twenty-three-year-old Rudolf Nureyev's U.S. debut at the Brooklyn Academy of Music in 1962 exemplifies his personalization of the art of dance:

> [Nureyev] is not so much an attractive and gifted young man as he is a creature, a mysterious being who works magic on the stage whether he is soaring through space, awaiting explosive action or, in curtain calls, permitting a boyish grin to dissolve an otherwise enigmatic expression. . . . This is an artist, al-

sachusetts blue laws by such venerated arts aficionados as balletomane Lincoln Kirstein and Nathaniel Saltonstall, president of the Museum of Modern Art, which prohibited dance concerts on Sundays. In 1940 he hosted a radio program, *Invitation to Dance,* and in 1942 he taught dance at Adelphi College in Garden City, New York.

Terry worked for the *Boston Herald* until 1939, when he was hired as dance critic and dance editor of the *New York Herald Tribune.* Following entry of the United States into World War II, Terry was drafted by the army in 1942, ultimately serving in Africa. Even while abroad he pursued his ambassadorial calling, spending his spare time teaching modern dance to Egyptian students at the American University in Cairo, lecturing on American dance to Allied forces based there, and performing as the principal dancer in a British production of the operetta *Rose Marie* in 1943.

After the war, Terry returned to the United States and dedicated himself to increasing the public's understanding and interest in dance. As a critic, he wrote for the *New York Herald Tribune* from 1945 until its demise in 1966, the *New York World Journal Tribune* from 1966 to 1967, and the *Saturday Review* from 1967 to 1982. He contributed to a number of magazines and published twenty-two books in which he portrayed dance and dancers as subjects to which general audiences could relate. Some of the best known are *Ballet: A New Guide to the Liveliest Art* (1959), *Isadora Duncan:*

ready brilliant, who is at the threshold of what could be the most phenomenal dance career of our age.

Terry is remembered not only for his criticism but also for his enthusiastic advocacy of dance and dancers. As critic Clive Barnes said, "He was unsparing in the service of the art he loved, and extraordinarily helpful not only to dancers and choreographers, but also to younger critics." Barnes's claim is supported by critic Deborah Jowitt, who recalled, "There were many nights when I'd be sitting in a theater battling fatigue and despondency, and I'd look up to see Walter sailing down the aisle, plump and rosy and bright-eyed, always looking as if he'd just been laundered."

★

Walter Terry, *I Was There: Selected Dance Reviews and Articles, 1936–1976* (1978), offers an autobiographical account of Terry's career; Anna Kisselgoff's introduction to *I Was There* gives perspective on Terry's contribution to dance criticism and to the development of concert dance in the United States. Tributes to Terry that offer many personal anecdotes about him, as well as information about his contributions and career milestones, include: Christine Temin, "Terry 'Was There,' Wherever There Was Dance," *Boston Globe* (9 Oct. 1982); Deborah Jowitt, "Walter Terry, 1913–1982," *Village Voice* (19 Oct. 1982); Clive Barnes, "Walter Terry, 1913–1982," *Dance Magazine* (Dec. 1982); Kitty Cunningham, "Walter Terry: An Appreciation," *Dance News* (Nov. 1982); and Ernestine Stodelle, "Dance World Honors Late Critic Terry," *New Haven Register* (20 Feb. 1983). Illuminating obituaries that examine Terry's life and work from the perspective of the dance community are in the *New York Times* (6 Oct. 1982) and *Dance News* (Nov. 1982).

REBEKAH KOWAL

THOMAS, Lowell Jackson (*b.* 6 April 1892 in Woodington, Ohio; *d.* 29 August 1981 in Pawling, New York), broadcaster and world traveler who had the longest-running evening news program (1930–1976) in the history of radio.

Thomas was raised in Victor, Colorado, to which his father, Harry George Thomas, a physician and surgeon, and his mother, Harriet Wagner, a teacher, migrated in 1900. A sister born in 1901 died in infancy; another sister was born in 1904.

Thomas's lifelong quest for adventure began in childhood, exploring the scenic territory around Victor in the Cripple Creek gold-mining district. His intellectual growth was nurtured by his father, whom he called "the most persistent scholar I ever knew." Educated in Victor's public schools, he read books from his father's three-thousand-volume personal library and relished miners' stories about the Klondike gold rush. His father, who believed in the importance of elocution, had him memorize poems and

Lowell Thomas. ARCHIVE PHOTOS

orations and recite them in public, thus fostering the development of his phenomenal speaking talents.

Thomas graduated from Victor High School, where he edited the student newspaper, in 1909. In that year he matriculated at Valparaiso University in Indiana and received B.S. and A.B. degrees in 1910 and 1911, respectively. After working as a reporter and editor for the Victor *Daily Record* and *Daily News,* he enrolled at the University of Denver, where he earned an A.B. degree in 1913 and an A.M. in 1914. He was also a reporter for the *Rocky Mountain News* and *Denver Times.* Deciding to become a lawyer, Thomas enrolled at the Chicago–Kent College School of Law. Its president, impressed by his public-speaking background, gave him a position teaching forensic oratory while he pursued his studies (he did not earn a law degree). He also worked as a reporter for the *Chicago Evening Journal.*

At the University of Denver, Thomas had been attracted to one of his fellow students, Frances Ryan. Although they had never dated, he proposed marriage to her in the summer of 1914 while going to San Francisco to see the Panama-Pacific Exposition. Thomas visited Alaska and the Yukon Territory in the summer of 1915, photographed historic and scenic attractions, and reveled in the lore of the

Klondike. He visited Ryan in Denver on his trip back. Awaiting him in Chicago was a letter of admission to graduate study at Princeton University. Aided by an anonymous donor, he studied history and politics there in the 1915–1916 academic year and received an M.A. in 1916, when Princeton appointed him to an instructorship in public speaking.

In 1917 Franklin K. Lane, secretary of the interior, asked Thomas to make a speaking campaign promoting national parks. This tour did not materialize because of America's entry into World War I, but Thomas secured permission from Washington officials to go to Europe and make a propaganda film. Thomas raised money among Chicago backers to finance the venture and hired a veteran cameraman, Harry Chase, to assist him. On 4 August 1917 he married Ryan, who accompanied him on his voyage to Europe.

Leaving his wife temporarily in Paris, Thomas filmed trench warfare on the western front and then went to Italy, where he observed ski units fighting in the Alps. In December 1917, after his wife had rejoined him in Italy, he learned that General Sir Edmund H. H. Allenby had captured Jerusalem, and he secured permission from British authorities to go there. In Egypt, on his way to Palestine, Thomas took his first airplane flight and began a lifelong role as a promoter of aviation. He was also intrigued by reports about an enigmatic Englishman, T. E. Lawrence, who had led guerrilla raids against Turkish forces. After arriving in Jerusalem, Thomas met Lawrence in February 1918 and interviewed him at length. More than anyone else, Thomas created the blend of myth and reality that made Lawrence of Arabia famous.

After the war ended, Thomas wanted to observe revolutionary developments in Germany at first hand. Ignoring Allied restrictions against unauthorized entry by journalists like himself, he sneaked into Germany by way of Switzerland with reporter Webb Waldron. They were the first Western newsmen to cover the chaotic birth of the Weimar Republic. After talking to Karl Liebknecht, Rosa Luxemburg, and other leaders, they made their way furtively to Paris and returned to the United States aboard a captured German ocean liner.

When a U.S. speaking tour using his war footage failed to fulfill his expectations, Thomas went to England at the invitation of an impresario, Percy Burton, and scored a remarkable success giving illustrated lectures about the exploits of Allenby and Lawrence. The publicity embarrassed Lawrence, who asked him to cancel the tour. Undeterred, Thomas continued giving presentations in Great Britain and the United States. After accepting an invitation to continue his tour in Australia and New Zealand, where he attracted large audiences, he went on to speak in Malaya, Burma, and India. He also scored a journalistic coup by securing permission to enter Afghanistan, whose borders were closed, and interview its ruler, Amanullah Khan.

Thomas and his wife came home by way of London, where she gave birth to their only child, Lowell Thomas, Jr., on 6 October 1923. After returning to America, Thomas published *With Lawrence in Arabia* (1924), which became a best-seller. When the Army Air Service organized a flight around the world in 1924, he became official historian and wrote a book about the mission, *The First World Flight* (1924); he also published *Beyond Khyber Pass* (1925), an account of his visit to Afghanistan. In 1926 he decided to fly every commercial air route in Europe. Traveling 25,000 miles, he survived a crash in Spain and wrote *European Skyways* (1927), a book about his experiences.

Securing a publisher's advance to write more books, Thomas bought a thirty-two-room house seventy miles north of Manhattan in Pawling, New York, where he and his wife entertained lavishly. Aided by freelance writer Prosper Buranelli, he wrote several true adventure stories, including *The Wreck of the Dumaru: A Story of Cannibalism in an Open Boat* (1930). Another book describes raids on Allied shipping conducted during World War I by Count Felix von Luckner, a German mariner who took Thomas, his wife, and others on a Caribbean cruise in 1929 in his schooner, *Vaterland*.

In 1930 the *Literary Digest* asked Thomas to replace radio commentator Floyd Gibbons on a fifteen-minute evening news program aired by both the Columbia Broadcasting System (CBS) and the National Broadcasting Company (NBC). When the *Literary Digest* stopped sponsoring the program in 1932, the Sun Oil Company picked it up and Thomas continued the series on NBC. Thomas's organlike voice, folksy manner, and politically nonpartisan approach made him an instant success, although some critics thought him too bland. For almost a half century, his voice was reputedly "heard by more people than any other in the history of mankind, around a hundred and twenty-five billion." His opening salutation, "Good evening, everybody," and his closing words, "So long until tomorrow," became world famous.

Thomas began broadcasting in 1930 from a studio at Madison Avenue and Fifty-second Street in New York City. In 1932 his nightly show was moved to the RCA Building in Rockefeller Center. As his popularity grew, however, he arranged with NBC to give his nightly newscasts from wherever was most convenient to him, including a studio that he built behind his barn. He received an enormous amount of fan mail—for example, 265,567 telegrams after one program. His following continued to grow when he became the voice of *Fox-Movietone News,* which made newsreels shown in motion-picture theaters. NBC also chose Thomas to present the first news program ever shown on television on 21 February 1940.

During World War II, Thomas continued giving news broadcasts from his New York studios but made periodic trips to places outside the United States to report directly on military operations as they took place. Late in the war he joined a group of prominent newsmen on a tour organized by General H. H. "Hap" Arnold, chief of the Army Air Forces. Following U.S. units into Germany, Thomas flew over the bombed-out ruins of Berlin as Soviet tanks closed in on the bunker where Hitler committed suicide, had lunch with General Mark Clark on the day Benito Mussolini was killed in a nearby Italian village, and interviewed Pope Pius XII at the Vatican. Soon after Germany surrendered he went to Asia, flew the "hump" from India to China, and interviewed Generalissimo Chiang Kai-shek. On his way home, he and General Arnold toured the Pacific Islands, including Tinian, the base from which B-29s took off to drop atomic bombs on Japan.

Habitually indifferent about money, Thomas experienced increasing financial problems as he built private golf courses, went on expensive skiing expeditions, and poured money into improving his estate on Quaker Hill. After rejecting a financial arrangement with his sponsor, Sun Oil Company, that would have compromised his political independence, he sought help from a friend, Frank M. Smith, who devised a plan under which Thomas switched from NBC to CBS, acquired a new sponsor, and paid off his debts.

Thomas's zest for adventure continued unabated in the postwar era. In 1949 he traveled to Tibet, where the Dalai Lama granted him an interview. Crossing the Himalayas on his return, Thomas was thrown by a horse and suffered multiple hip fractures. In an agonizing ordeal, he was carried across tortuous terrain on a litter and brought to safety by a party led by his son. Making a remarkable recovery, he was glacier skiing in Alaska within a year.

Soon after his recovery, Thomas and Smith joined inventor Fred Waller, film director Merian C. Cooper, and producer Mike Todd in developing a new wide-screen film technique called Cinerama. This venture led to further trips to faraway places creating spectacular footage for such productions as *This Is Cinerama, The Seven Wonders of the World,* and *Search for Paradise.* The last of these projects took him to Nepal, where he officially represented President Dwight Eisenhower while filming the coronation of a new monarch.

After selling at least part of their stake in Cinerama, Thomas and Smith bought television station WROW in Albany, New York, and built a large, diversified media empire, Capital Cities Communications. Fearing that a regular television news program would tie him down, Thomas clung to radio and traveled as much as ever. He did, however, host *High Adventure,* a series of television specials that took him to remote locations, including New Guinea. He went to the Australian desert, where he found the remains of an explorer who had disappeared three decades earlier. Doing another film for the series, he flew over the North Pole from Alaska to Greenland and was marooned for two days and nights on a drifting ice pack. In 1963 he crossed the South Pole with naval aviators flying from South Africa to New Zealand.

Shortly after arriving home from his Antarctic flight, Thomas collapsed from exhaustion caused by repeated jet lag. Following his recovery he became more careful about planning his itineraries but continued to make trips to remote areas. In 1970 he went to Siberia to report on progress being made by the Soviet Union in developing its resources. He also took his wife, who was in poor health, on trips to Europe, Africa, and South America.

Thomas's wife died on 16 February 1975 after a long illness. On 14 May 1976 he made his final radio broadcast for CBS, but he continued to work on a television series based on his earlier films of faraway places and momentous events. In 1977 in Hawaii, he married Marianna Munn, who had worked for him for a decade in supporting the Spafford Children's Hospital in Jerusalem. The day after their wedding, leaving her temporarily on Maui, he flew to Washington, D.C., where he received the Medal of Freedom. They then took an around-the-world honeymoon to many of the places Thomas had visited in the past and returned to the United States from London on the Concorde supersonic jet airliner.

Thomas continued traveling, skiing, writing, and speaking for four more years. At age eighty-nine he died of a heart attack and was buried on Quaker Hill after a funeral service at Christ Church. At a memorial service at St. Bartholomew's Episcopal Church in New York City, clergyman Norman Vincent Peale characterized him as "a restless man eager always to do more and feeling that there was not enough time in his life for everything he wanted to do."

★

Thomas's papers are at the Lowell Thomas Communications Center, Marist College, Poughkeepsie, New York. He published a two-volume autobiography, *Good Evening Everybody: From Cripple Creek to Samarkand* (1976) and *So Long Until Tomorrow: From Quaker Hill to Kathmandu* (1977). See also his books *The First World Flight* (1925), *European Skyways: The Story of a Tour of Europe by Airplane* (1927), and *History as You Heard It* (1957). An obituary is in the *New York Times* (30 Aug. 1981), as is an account of his memorial service (4 Sept. 1981). See also Douglas Edwards, "Lowell Thomas Was Truly the Granddaddy of Us All," *New York Times* (20 Sept. 1981). Interviews with Lowell Thomas, Jr., and Fred D. Crawford, who is writing a biography of Lowell Thomas, and the records of various educational institutions that Thomas attended yielded valuable information for this essay.

W. David Lewis

THOMPSON, (Ira) Randall (*b.* 21 April 1899 in New York City; *d.* 9 July 1984 in Boston, Massachusetts), composer and educator, best known for his many choral compositions.

Thompson was one of three children of Daniel Varney Thompson, an English teacher, and Grace Brightman Randall, a homemaker. He grew up in Lawrenceville, New Jersey, where his father was a faculty member of the Lawrenceville School, a private preparatory school. Randall entered that institution in 1911, graduating in 1916. There he began to study piano and organ with the school organist. He matriculated at Harvard University in 1916 and received a B.A. in 1920, majoring in music and concentrating on the theoretical studies needed to become a composer. While at Harvard he served in the naval reserve during World War I. Following graduation Thompson lived in New York City for a year, studying privately with the Swiss-American composer Ernest Bloch. In 1922 he received an M.A. from Harvard.

In 1922 Thompson won a Prix de Rome that financed three years as a composer-in-residence at the American Academy in Rome. There he became a protégé of the Italian composer Gian Francesco Malipiero, who impressed upon the young American the importance of vocal, and especially

Randall Thompson, *c.* 1920. UPI/CORBIS-BETTMANN

choral, music. Under Malipiero's influence Thompson composed his first important choral work, *Five Odes of Horace,* in the years 1924–1925. Other important compositions of his Rome period were a piece for string quartet, *The Wind in the Willows,* and an orchestral prelude, *The Piper at the Gates of Dawn,* both written in 1924. In the autumn of 1925 he returned to the United States, settling in New York City. He married Margaret Quayle Whitney, daughter of a wealthy family of Montclair, New Jersey, on 26 February 1927. They would have four children. From 1927 to 1929 Thompson was assistant professor of music, choir director, and organist at Wellesley College in Massachusetts. He resigned in 1929 to spend the next two years composing with the aid of a Guggenheim Fellowship in Francestown, New Hampshire, Paris, and Gstaad, Switzerland. His major compositions during this period were the First and Second Symphonies, completed in 1929 and 1931, respectively, and first performed in Rochester, New York, in 1930 and 1932. The First Symphony was well received but the Second became his most popular orchestral work.

Thompson returned to New York City in the spring of 1931 and lived there until 1936. During 1931 and 1932 he directed the choir at the Juilliard School of Music. In 1932 he was appointed to head a committee formed by the Association of American Colleges to examine the state of higher education in music in the United States and spent much of the next three years traveling, interviewing, and collecting written material for a comprehensive report on the subject. The result was a book, *College Music* (1935), which proved to be highly influential and led to major revisions of college and university music curricula all over the country. The report strongly reflected Thompson's views that music should be an integral part of the liberal arts curriculum and that college credit should not be given for practical studies in singing or the playing of a musical instrument. Later in 1935 he composed his first important religious choral work, *The Peaceable Kingdom,* based upon verses from the Old Testament Book of Isaiah.

He returned to Wellesley College as an assistant professor in 1936–1937. He served from 1937 to 1939 as professor of music and director of the university chorus at the University of California at Berkeley. In 1939 he accepted the directorship of the Curtis Institute of Music in Philadelphia, an odd decision in view of his well-known dislike of the trade-school atmosphere of music conservatories. He immediately attempted to broaden and reform the institute's curriculum. He soon found himself at odds with the school's more conservative faculty members, and in February 1941 Mary Louise Curtis Bok, the institute's founder and chief financial backer, forced him to resign. Despite his troubles at Curtis, Thompson found the time and energy to compose one of his best-known choral works, *Alleluia,* which Serge Koussevitzky had requested in 1940 for the opening exercises of the new Berkshire Music Center at Tanglewood in Lenox, Massachusetts. In 1941 he wrote his First String Quartet.

In May 1941 Thompson was appointed professor and head of the department of music at the University of Virginia in Charlottesville; he remained there until 1945. His one composition during this period was *The Testament of Freedom,* a choral work based on four passages from the writings of Thomas Jefferson, completed and first performed in 1943. Written during the height of American patriotic fervor during World War II, it became probably the best known and most frequently performed of all Thompson's works. Thompson was a professor of music at Princeton University from 1946 to 1948. His major composition during this period was his Third Symphony.

In 1948 Thompson became professor of music at Harvard University, where he remained until his retirement in 1965. From about 1949 to the end of his life Thompson wrote primarily choral works, most of them on commission from various choral organizations; he became by far the most popular composer of sacred and secular choral music of his time. He wrote only one more orchestral work, the symphonic fantasy, *A Trip to Nahant* (1954), and a Second String Quartet (1967). In addition to many smaller choral pieces, he produced four major works: *The Mass of the Holy Spirit* (1955); *Requiem* (1958); *The Passion According to St. Luke: An Oratorio* (1964); and *Twelve Canticles* (1983). Plagued by increasingly ill health from 1975, when he suffered a stroke, he died of natural causes.

Throughout his lengthy academic career, Thompson, a slender man of average height and a dapper dresser, was regarded as an excellent, influential, and popular teacher. His significance as a composer is more problematical. In an era during which classical music was becoming ever more complex, dissonant, and difficult for nonmusicians to understand and appreciate, Thompson remained determinedly committed to traditional forms and straightforward melodies. Consequently, the musical avant-garde viewed him as both reactionary and irrelevant. His obituary in the *New York Times* described him as "music's Norman Rockwell, distilling the traditional values of his audience and reflecting them in uncomplicated, immediately comprehensible and endearing terms." Thompson would probably have regarded this as a compliment, if also perhaps an oversimplification. He took pride in being an expert musical craftsman who wrote most of his works on commission from performing individuals and groups. He insisted that his music be simple enough for amateurs to perform. Consequently, his enduring legacy probably lies in his many choral compositions, which still remain popular with amateur and professional singers alike.

★

Randall Thompson's musical manuscripts are in the Houghton Library at Harvard University. The fullest biographical essay to date is contained in Caroline Cepin Benser and David Francis Urrows, *Randall Thompson: A Bio-Bibliography* (1991), which also includes complete lists of his compositions and prose writings as well as a comprehensive bibliography of writings about Thompson. A briefer biographical sketch, bibliography, and list of compositions appears in H. Wiley Hitchcock and Stanley Sadie, eds., *The New Grove Dictionary of American Music,* vol. 4 (1986). Alfred Mann, ed., *Randall Thompson: A Choral Legacy* (1983), is a collection of articles by Thompson and others on his music. Obituaries appear in the *Boston Globe* (10 July 1984) and the *New York Times* (10 July 1984).

JOHN E. LITTLE

TILLSTROM, Burr (*b.* 13 October 1917 in Chicago, Illinois; *d.* 6 December 1985 in Palm Springs, California), puppeteer and television personality best known for his innovative, entertaining television series *Kukla, Fran, and Ollie.*

The second son of Bert F. Tillstrom, a physician, and Alice Burr Tillstrom, a pianist, Burr became interested in puppetry while still a child. Encouraged by a sister of the noted puppeteer Tony Sarg, at age fourteen he put on his first "paid" performance with his own puppet creations in her garden. He graduated from Senn High School in 1935, won an honor scholarship to the University of Chicago, and left after one semester to follow a career as a puppeteer.

After a stint handling marionettes with the WPA-Chicago Parks District Theatre, Tillstrom performed at state fairs, carnivals, and nightclubs. During 1939 he put on a weekly Saturday morning puppet show for children at the Marshall Field department store in Chicago and participated in an experimental television show. In 1939 and 1940 RCA used Tillstrom and his puppets at the New York World's Fair to demonstrate the potentialities of television. During World War II, after an unsuccessful attempt to enlist, Tillstrom worked with the United Service Organizations and gave benefit performances at many midwestern hospitals.

From 1936 he had been developing a colorful cast of puppet characters, the first being Kukla (the Russian word for "doll," the puppet being so named by a Soviet ballet dancer). A solemn, bulb-nosed, gentle worrier, Kukla was followed by a whole array of Kuklapolitans (as Tillstrom characterized his creations), including Oliver J. Dragon (better known as Ollie), a mild, carefree, extroverted, snaggle-toothed creature, and Beulah Witch, who buzzed around doing mischief on a jet-propelled broomstick equipped with radar. Ultimately the Kuklapolitans numbered ten, all distinct, engaging characters. Tillstrom's puppets, which he made by hand, had cloth heads stuffed

Burr Tillstrom displays his puppetry technique for Fran Allison (*right*) on the set of the *Kukla, Fran, and Ollie* show. GENEVIEVE NAYLOR/CORBIS

with cotton and attached to hollow bodies which were an arm's length so that he could manipulate the puppets from below without being seen. He not only created the puppets but voiced all the characters. It was unthinkable for him that anyone else would handle his creations, and with great dexterity during performances he would move from character to character.

When the Kuklapolitans made their commercial television debut on Chicago's WBKB-TV on 13 October 1947, they were joined by Fran Allison, a radio actress, singer, and former Iowa schoolteacher who was a master at ad-libbing. The show, first known as *Junior Jamboree,* was an instant success. Renamed *Kukla, Fran, and Ollie,* it became part of NBC's programming on 29 November 1948, airing Monday through Friday for a half hour at 7 P.M. Eastern Standard Time. As network television spread from coast to coast in the late 1940s and early 1950s, the show became a nationwide hit. Critics raved about the show and about Tillstrom. ("Genius," said *Variety;* "outrageously talented," exulted Harriet Van Horne.)

Tillstrom, who preferred spontaneity, laid out the general direction of the show just a bit before it went on the air. Usually, the show was done live, mainly unscripted, and with minimal rehearsal. The puppets performed for the camera on a miniature stage. Tillstrom stood erect behind a translucent screen, voicing and operating his characters, with his puppet-clad arms resting on a ledge. He monitored what was happening on a television off to the side. In front of the stage stood Fran, who for much of the show interacted with the puppets in conversation, song, plays, gentle

satire, and musical productions. A favored annual feature was a version of Gilbert and Sullivan's *The Mikado,* with Kukla as Nanki Poo, Fran as Yum Yum, and Ollie as the Lord High Executioner.

The show and Tillstrom won high ratings and nineteen awards in 1949 alone. In 1954 it received an Emmy from the National Academy of Television Arts and Sciences for Best Children's Program of 1953. Tillstrom's efforts charmed adults as well as children. In 1950 it was estimated that 60 percent of his national viewing audience consisted of adults. In the show's heyday during the early 1950s it was seen by more than 10 million viewers from coast to coast on fifty-seven stations, and at one point drew 6,000 letters weekly. Sponsors, however, proved indifferent to children's programming in prime time. As a result, in November 1951 the show was cut from a half hour to fifteen minutes, and the next year NBC relegated it to Sunday afternoons, which caused a huge outcry. (Adlai Stevenson likened it to "assassination.")

The fledgling ABC network, anxious to beef up its new status as a network with quality programming, broadcast the show from Monday through Friday for fifteen minutes at 7 P.M. Eastern Standard Time from September 1954 through August 1957. Thereafter, *Kukla, Fran, and Ollie* only appeared sporadically: as a five-minute weekday spot on NBC (1961–1962); on PBS (1969–1971), winning another Emmy; and in a syndicated version (1975–1976). Tillstrom in 1960 also staged on Broadway *An Evening with Kukla, Fran, and Ollie,* but with indifferent success because it lacked the intimacy of the television format.

Tillstrom managed to do well without the Kuklapolitans. During the 1964–1965 television season he became a regular on the bitingly satirical *That Was the Week That Was,* winning an Emmy as well as a prestigious Peabody Award for his imaginative and stirring artistry, especially a moving hand ballet about the emotional conflicts resulting from the erection of the wall dividing Berlin.

Slim, blue-eyed, with brown hair (often worn in a crew cut during his *Kukla, Fran, and Ollie* days), the five-foot, eleven-inch Tillstrom was unassuming, almost diffident, except when it came to his creations, about which he was "commanding" and "sure." His interest in puppetry never waned. He had an excellent collection of books on the subject. Tillstrom kept active until his death, holding seminars, writing, and engaging in various special projects. His creativity and artistry were recognized by more than fifty major awards (including five Emmys). Tillstrom died of a heart attack. At the time of his death he was scheduled to be inducted into the Television Academy Hall of Fame. He never married and had no children.

Kukla, Fran, and Ollie still remains popular: cassettes of the shows sell well, and reruns on cable television achieve respectable ratings. Tillstrom contributed substantially to TV; it is unfortunate that ultimately network television had no room for the Kuklapolitans.

★

Discussions of Tillstrom and *Kukla, Fran, and Ollie* include Richard Gehman, "Mr. Oliver J. Dragon . . . and Friends," *Theatre Arts* (Oct. 1950), and Harriet Van Horne, "The Chicago Touch," *Theatre Arts* (July 1951). Obituaries are in the *New York Times* (8 Dec. 1985) and *Variety* (11 Dec. 1985).

DANIEL J. LEAB

TRIPPE, Juan Terry (*b.* 27 June 1899 in Sea Bright, New Jersey; *d.* 3 April 1981 in New York City), a pioneer in commercial aviation.

Trippe was the son of Charles White Trippe, a senior partner in White, Weld, and Company, a New York investment house, and Lucy Adeline Terry. Trippe graduated from the Hill School in Pottstown, Pennsylvania, and entered Yale College in 1917. His college career was interrupted when he joined the U.S. Navy that December. He received a commission as an ensign and learned to fly in Florida but he did not go overseas. After the war he returned to Yale, where one of his major interests was a flying club that he organized. Upon graduating in 1922 with a Ph.B. degree, he worked briefly for Lee, Higginson, and Company as a bond salesman. But when he learned that the navy was selling surplus planes, he bought seven trainers with the help of some Yale friends and started an air charter service at Rockaway Beach, Long Island. Opinions varied concerning Trippe's personality. Some considered him aloof;

Juan Terry Trippe. NATIONAL AIR AND SPACE MUSEUM

others considered him shy. At prep school his quiet manner brought him the nickname "Mummy." Most would agree, however, that he was adept at developing useful friends in college, business, and government.

In 1925 Trippe and his associates convinced Congressman Clyde Kelly, chairman of the House Post Office Committee, of the benefits that could accrue from private contractors' flying airmail. Kelly introduced a bill for that purpose and it was passed. The outcome, with the help of such friends as Cornelius Vanderbilt Whitney, Percy Rockefeller, and William H. Vanderbilt, was the establishment of Colonial Air Transport, which operated between New York and Boston under the first U.S. airmail contract.

Two years later the imaginative Trippe saw more profitable possibilities in flying to Cuba and Latin America. With help from many of the same friends, he left Colonial and expanded Pan American Airways, a wholly owned subsidiary of the Aviation Corporation of the Americas. Trippe managed the company, but some of his friends owned more stock than he did. Pan Am, with the first international airmail contract from Key West to Havana, began service in October 1927 with an eight-passenger trimotor Fokker land plane. An effective negotiator, Trippe soon received an extension of Pan Am's contract route from Key West to the more populated Miami, which doubled daily mail revenues.

On 16 June 1928 Trippe married Elizabeth Stettinius, daughter of a J. P. Morgan partner and sister of Edward Stettinius, later secretary of state; they had four children.

Pan Am bought the New York, Rio, and Buenos Aires Line in 1930 and became the "chosen instrument" for carrying the U.S. flag abroad. Pan Am suddenly operated 20,000 miles of routes in twenty Latin American countries. Each route was a U.S. Post Office contract route. With the approval of Postmaster General Walter Brown, the companies emerged as the world's largest airline. Trippe's dream of Pan Am's becoming the sole American-flag carrier in the world was never realized.

Following the survey flights of Charles and Anne Lindbergh to the Orient in 1931, Trippe began construction of island bases in the Pacific. By 1933 *Time* magazine described Trippe as an "anomalous combination of visionary and hardheaded businessman; genial socialite and phlegmatic plodder." Trippe began flights from San Francisco to the Philippine Islands in 1936 with the China Clipper, a Martin M-130 flying boat. Three years later transatlantic service began with the Yankee Clipper flights from Port Washington, New York, to Lisbon and Marseilles in Europe.

After the Japanese attack on Pearl Harbor in December 1941, Pan Am served as a contract carrier for the U.S. government during World War II. In performing these duties, Pan Am planes flew more than 90 million miles and made 19,000 transoceanic crossings. President Harry Truman awarded Trippe the Medal of Merit in 1946 for his organizing capacity, management skills, and cooperation with representatives of the United States.

After World War II the company continued to expand; in 1949 Pan American Airways became Pan American World Airways when the holding and operating companies merged. As chief operating officer, Trippe developed a global network of 80,000 air miles linking the United States with eighty-five countries by 1968. For many years Trippe paid himself a salary of $10,000 a year. When he retired, his total salary and incentive compensation amounted to only $187,400.

Under Trippe, Pan Am began tourist-class service between the United States and Europe, led the way to using land planes for overseas flights, and in 1955 ordered the first commercial jet planes. Forty-five jet planes were purchased for $269 million, and in 1958 Pan Am operated transatlantic service with the Boeing 707.

Throughout the world Trippe was recognized as the leading force in commercial international air travel and was said to have been decorated by more foreign governments than any other U.S. citizen. He also received numerous honorary degrees and was on the Board of Visitors of Harvard Business School and Johns Hopkins University. He was a member of the corporate boards of the Chrysler Corporation and the Metropolitan Life Insurance Company. The air trophies that he received were the Robert Collier Trophy (1947), the Harmon Aviation Trophy (1937), and the Frye Airline Performance Trophy (1954).

Problems loomed on the horizon, however, because of the enormous capital expenditures required to purchase equipment. In 1966 a $600 million order was placed for Boeing 747s. By 1968 Pan Am had assets of more than $1 billion, operated a chain of international hotels, and was the prime contractor for airlift support for the U.S. government. But competition in international flight was increasingly corrosive because many foreign airlines were government-owned and not as concerned with making a profit.

After forty-one years as chief operating officer of Pan Am, Trippe retired on 7 May 1968. He remained an active board member until 1975. He was an authentic pioneer in international commercial aviation, and nothing could detract from his vision and achievements in aviation as an instrument of peace. He died of complications from a massive cerebral hemorrhage he suffered seven months earlier.

★

Biographical files are in the National Air and Space Museum, Washington, D.C. See Carl Solberg, *Conquest of the Skies: A History of Commercial Aviation in America* (1979); Robert Daley, *An American Saga: Juan Trippe and His Pan Am Empire* (1980); Marylin Bender and Selig Altschul, *The Chosen Instrument: Pan Am and Juan Trippe, the Rise and Fall of an American Enterprise* (1982), and Ann Crittenden, "Juan Trippe's Pan Am," *New York Times* (3 July 1971). An obituary is in the *New York Times* (4 Apr. 1981).

ERNEST A. MCKAY
STEPHEN MCKAY

TRUMAN, Bess Wallace (*b.* 13 February 1885 in Independence, Missouri; *d.* 18 October 1982 in Independence, Missouri), wife of President Harry S. Truman.

Bess Truman's father, David Willock Wallace, held various appointive political offices in Jackson County, Missouri, the county of Independence and Kansas City. Her mother, Margaret Elizabeth Gates, was a housewife. Margaret's father owned the Waggoner-Gates Milling Company, which produced Queen of the Pantry flour, a well-known cake and biscuit product sold throughout the Middle West. Bess, born Elizabeth Virginia Wallace, was the oldest of four children. She and her three brothers grew up at 608 North Delaware Street, Independence's leading residential avenue. After graduating from Independence High School in 1901, she helped her mother with household tasks. Her father committed suicide in 1903, after which the family spent a year in Colorado Springs and returned to live with the widowed mother's parents at 219 North Delaware, a two-and-a-half-story, seventeen-room house built by her

First Lady Bess Truman and President Harry Truman at the Army-Navy game, 1950. MORGAN COLLECTON/ARCHIVE PHOTOS

maternal grandfather. A member of Independence's social elite, Bess attended the Barstow School, a finishing school for girls in Kansas City, Missouri, in 1905 and 1906. Bess remained with the family until her marriage to Harry Truman on 28 June 1919. The couple had met in 1890 in Sunday school at the Presbyterian church in Independence and had seen each other in grade and high school, but their courtship did not begin until 1910. After a brief wedding trip, the couple returned to live in the house at 219 North Delaware, which after the death of Bess's mother in 1952 was purchased by the Trumans.

In the 1920s Bess Truman remained a housewife. A diminutive woman, round-faced, pleasant, quiet, even retiring, she believed that her task as the wife of a rising politician was to keep her mouth shut and her hat on straight. She took only a small part in her husband's political affairs, appearing during campaigns only when necessary. During the 1920s and early 1930s her husband was a judge on the Jackson County Court, a three-person board of county

commissioners. Their only child, (Mary) Margaret, was born to the couple in 1924.

In the early 1930s Bess remained in Independence, where her husband's office was just a three-minute walk away, in the courthouse. Upon his election to the U.S. Senate in 1934, where he served until 1944, life changed considerably. Until the war years of 1941–1945, Bess and Margaret spent half the year in Washington, D.C., and the other half in Independence, the senator coming home when possible. After Margaret entered George Washington University in Washington in 1942, the family spent their entire time together in the nation's capital. During the early Senate years they had lived in a series of apartments until settling in 1941 into a two-bedroom apartment at 4701 Connecticut Avenue, N.W.

The senatorial years of Harry Truman were a trial for Bess, who at the outset found Washington society standoffish and, perhaps a better word, cold. Beyond a small circle of senatorial wives, friendships proved difficult. Gradually, social life became more attractive, but the interludes in Independence were always reassuring, for Bess could rejoin a longtime group of woman friends who constituted a bridge club and otherwise took part in Episcopal Church and other activities similar to those she had known for years.

In the late spring of 1944 rumor arose that her husband was a leading candidate for the vice-presidential nomination in a fourth-term campaign by President Franklin D. Roosevelt, taking the place of then–vice president Henry A. Wallace. Bess Truman did not favor her husband's elevation. When he was chosen at the Democratic National Convention in Chicago in July 1944, Bess put the best possible public face on the matter. But according to her daughter's recollection, she was angry over her husband's decision to join the ticket and when the three Trumans drove back from Chicago to Independence, the temperature in the automobile was "close to Arctic."

Harry Truman had been vice president for only a few weeks early in 1945 when he became president on 12 April upon the death of President Roosevelt. Bess Truman suddenly found herself installed in the White House with the title of First Lady. As she had done earlier in her marriage, she took up her new duties with thoroughness but without any sense that she needed to be politically active. When returning from Roosevelt's burial at Hyde Park she asked Secretary of Labor Frances Perkins whether it was necessary to hold press conferences with female members of the press corps. Upon assurance that such conferences were unnecessary, she announced she would hold none. She presided over teas and luncheons and attended whatever other functions were essential, with or without her husband as the case dictated. She handled these matters with a single assistant, Reathel Odum, formerly a secretary in her husband's senatorial office. Odum took calls from reporters, who would ask such questions as, "What is the First Lady wearing for the dinner this evening?" Odum would ask the caller to hold the line while she made an inquiry. She then would turn to the First Lady, sitting next to her, and inquire. Bess Truman would answer, "It's none of her damned business." Odum would remove her hand from the receiver and reply to the caller, "Mrs. Truman has not yet made up her mind what she will wear this evening."

In the years after the presidency, Bess and Harry Truman resided again at 219 North Delaware Street in Independence in a quiet way. Bess hoped to live to be 100. She outlived her husband by ten years, dying of cardiovascular disease at the age of ninety-seven; she lived longer than any preceding First Lady. She was buried beside her husband in the courtyard of the Harry S. Truman Library, at the north end of Delaware Street.

Any appraisal of Bess Truman has to be tentative, for she was so much a private person that she left very few records of her activities, not to mention her inner thoughts.

After her husband's death, 1,268 letters from him to her were discovered in the Truman house. The letters showed the extraordinary devotion of at first her suitor, then her husband. On his trips, or during occasions when Bess was in Independence, he in Washington, Harry Truman wrote regularly and voluminously, relating not merely what he was doing but what amusing things caught his attention, and always asking for letters from her. For many years it appeared that her letters had not survived, save for two dozen or so, most of them short and uncommunicative. But in 1998 the Truman Library in Independence exhibited new letters from Bess Truman to her husband and announced that well over 100 more were in the possession of the Trumans' daughter, Margaret. These letters did not begin to display the detail and humor of the "Dear Bess" letters, but they had their moments, as in Bess's advice to her fiancé then in the U.S. Army in France in 1919: "You may invite the entire 35th Division to our wedding if you want to. . . . I guess we might as well have the church *full* while we are at it." In 1942, when her husband, then a senator, made a radio broadcast she congratulated him: "Dear Harry, Your speech last night was really 'something'—I think it was the best radio speech I have heard you make. . . . In your 'spare time' it really would be a good idea to take a few *speech lessons* if you are going to be on the radio from now on. *But* if you keep on doing as well as you did last night you won't need any."

Perhaps the largest question about Bess Truman's life has been why she disliked the White House. Some part of the reason doubtless was because of the need to care for her aged mother, who lived with the Trumans in the White House and died there in December 1952; the mansion was not as convenient as the house on North Delaware Street. Another reason for her dislike might have been concern for the well-being of Margaret, for the White House was a goldfish bowl and no place to raise a daughter. Another might have been sensitivity to the fact that her husband had placed her on his senatorial payroll in 1941 at a salary that became $4,500 per annum, a high salary in those days. This fact quickly came out in 1944, a few days after her husband's nomination for the vice presidency. Her duties in the Senate office, of course, had been nominal. Still another possible reason for her dislike of her husband's advancement beyond the Senate may have been a belief that her father's suicide would become public knowledge, because as late as the 1940s suicide frequently was considered a family disgrace. When Bess's husband was nominated for the vice presidency the couple's daughter had not yet been told what had happened to her maternal grandfather in 1903.

★

Apart from a small collection of letters in the Truman Library, the best biographical sources are daughter Margaret Truman's *Bess*

W. Truman (1986), and Robert H. Ferrell, ed., *Dear Bess: The Letters from Harry to Bess Truman, 1910–1959* (1983). A biographical sketch is in Anne Rothe, ed., *Current Biography 1947* (1948). An obituary is in the *New York Times* (22 Oct. 1982).

ROBERT H. FERRELL

TUBB, Ernest Dale (*b.* 9 February 1914 near Crisp, Texas; *d.* 6 September 1984 in Nashville, Tennessee), country music singer known as "The Texas Troubadour" and *Grand Ole Opry* cast member.

Ernest Tubb was the son of Calvin Robert Tubb, a farmer, and Sarah Ellen Baker, a homemaker. One of five children, Ernest grew up on a succession of farms operated by his father before his parents' separation; he then lived with older siblings. Frequent family moves limited his formal education to seventeen months in schools in Benjamin, Texas, and at Phoenix School in Kemp, Texas, leading to a fourth-grade proficiency.

Tubb worked in various fields of manual labor, including farming and road work, and as a salesman of beer and mattresses until he became an established entertainer. Jimmie Rodgers, a prominent country recording artist in the 1920s and 1930s until his death in 1933, became the idol Tubb attempted to emulate in his singing career. In 1933 Tubb acquired his first guitar with money intended to pay

Ernest Tubb. FRANK DRIGGS/ARCHIVE PHOTOS

for a trip to San Antonio, then had to return to work while he learned to play it and sing in the Jimmie Rodgers style.

After moving to San Antonio, Tubb married Lois Elaine Cook on 26 May 1934. In mid-1935 he met Carrie Rodgers, widow of Jimmie Rodgers, who arranged performance tours for Tubb in south Texas and used her influence to gain him his first recording contract, with Bluebird Records, a division of RCA. He made his first recordings on 27 October 1936, and his first royalty check was for $1.27.

For several years Tubb worked as a country singer in honky-tonks and for various local radio stations in Texas and for sponsors of his radio programs, sometimes as a route salesman and sometimes with personal appearances from a sound truck. Such work rarely lasted long, and the itinerant nature of his life meant that Elaine Tubb and their two children often lived in San Antonio while he was on the road. The couple lost a third child in infancy as a result of an auto accident.

Carrie Rodgers continued as Tubb's sponsor and eventually gave him one of her husband's famed Martin guitars with Rodgers's name inlaid in mother-of-pearl. Tubb's career as a recording artist produced sufficient success in the jukebox market for him to be noticed by promoters of country music shows in Alabama, Georgia, and eventually Nashville, home of the *Grand Ole Opry,* a network radio show, which meant ultimate success in Tubb's field. His first guest appearance on the *Opry* came in January 1943, and he became a regular cast member on 13 February of that year.

In addition to Carrie Rodgers's sponsorship, Tubb's career was based on his successful songwriting, sincerity of delivery on stage, indefatigable touring schedule that continued past his sixtieth year, and genuine friendships with fans and fellow performers. The only payment Carrie Rodgers asked for her sponsorship was that Tubb help others attempting a similar career. Among the beneficiaries of Tubb's help were such country music stars as Hank Williams, Loretta Lynn, Willie Nelson, Stonewall Jackson, and Hank Thompson. In addition, Tubb provided financial assistance to Rodgers for the remainder of her life, and did the same for several households of relatives in Texas.

Tubb's best-known songs, including "Walking the Floor Over You," were inspired by his hard life. Frequent separations from his family while on tours eventually led to a divorce from Lois Elaine Tubb in 1948. On 3 June 1949 he married Olene Adams, with whom he had five children; they separated in 1975, but remained married until Tubb's death.

Tubb recorded for Decca Records for more than forty years and appeared on the *Opry* even longer. In addition to the tours that occupied most of each year with frequent returns for Saturday *Opry* performances, Tubb opened the Ernest Tubb Record Shop in Nashville in 1947. A year later he began using it to stage *Midnite Jamboree,* a program that followed the *Opry* at 12:00 A.M. on radio station WSM. The record shop at first specialized in mail-order sales, then moved to retail sales; the weekly radio program promoted Tubb's tours, record sales, and new talent, including an appearance by Elvis Presley in 1954.

For many years Tubb toured in a seven-passenger limousine, but eventually he bought a bus for his Texas Troubadour band, which included a roster of well-known country musicians. Few of them remained with the band for extended periods. The primary reasons for a heavy turnover in musicians were the grueling schedule on which Tubb thrived but that wearied others and Tubb's irascible nature when drinking excessively. He achieved sobriety later in life and also succeeded in abstinence from smoking. Perhaps these habits kept his weight below 150 pounds for most of his life, although even when he stopped using alcohol and tobacco he remained slender. Tubb was six feet tall with dark brown hair and blue eyes; he almost always wore a white cowboy hat.

Tubb's stage costumes carried over to daily dress, including boots and Western hat and clothes. He was himself a devoted fan of country music who led an effort to gain respectability for his genre. In 1965 he was honored as the sixth inductee of the Country Music Hall of Fame. Tubb died of emphysema in Nashville.

Tubb's best-known recordings include his signature "Walking the Floor Over You" (1941), "I'll Get Along Somehow" (1940), "Soldier's Last Letter" (1944), "Time Changes Everything" (1945), "It's Been So Long Darling" (1945), "There's a Little Bit of Everything in Texas" (1945), and "Waltz Across Texas" (1965). He recorded more than 250 songs and sold at least 30 million records.

★

The most recent and thoroughly researched source on Tubb's career is Ronnie Pugh, *Ernest Tubb: The Texas Troubadour* (1996). For a general review of the history of country music and Tubb's role in its commercial development, see Bill C. Malone, *Country Music, U.S.A.* (1968; rev. ed., 1985), and Bill C. Malone and Judith McCulloh, *Stars of Country Music: Uncle Dave Macon to Johnny Rodriguez* (1975), which contains a chapter on Tubb. Obituaries are in the *New York Times* and *Washington Post* (both 7 Sept. 1984).

ARCHIE P. MCDONALD

TULLY, Grace (*b.* 9 August 1900 in Bayonne, New Jersey; *d.* 15 June 1984 in Washington, D.C.), secretary to President Franklin D. Roosevelt.

Tully was one of four children of James F. Tully, a wholesale merchant, and Alice Lee Galligan, an actress. She was named for Grace George, a well-known actress of that day. Her father died when she was a young girl. Beginning at

Grace Tully, 1949. UPI/CORBIS-BETTMANN

age three, Tully attended a succession of parochial schools, including St. Vincent's in Newark, New Jersey; Ladycliffe-on-the-Hudson near New York City; and Mrs. Disbrow's School in Easton, Pennsylvania. At age nine she entered Our Lady of Lourdes School in the Washington Heights section of Manhattan, and later completed her secondary education at the Convent of the Holy Child there. She then decided to prepare for a secretarial career by taking classes at the Grace Institute for business training, an institution established by the Grace Steamship Company in New York and operated by the Catholic Sisters of Charity.

In 1918 Tully took her first position, working in Manhattan as a secretary to Bishop (later Cardinal) Patrick Joseph Hayes, by whom she was employed for ten years. Seeking a change of pace in 1928, she found work as a secretary for the Democratic National Committee in New York City and was initially assigned to work with Malvina Thompson, secretary to Eleanor Roosevelt. Following Franklin D. Roosevelt's nomination for governor in the fall of 1928, Tully was often borrowed from his wife's staff and installed as one of his secretaries in New York City. After his victory she continued working for him, assisting Marguerite "Missy" LeHand in New York City, at the Roosevelt home in Hyde Park, New York, and at the health facility at Warm Springs, Georgia, purchased by Roosevelt in 1926. These arrangements were soon made permanent, and LeHand and Tully became good friends. They ultimately spent most of their professional lives in Franklin Roosevelt's service. LeHand was ill for part of 1928 and had to recuperate in Warm Springs for several months. Tully was pressed into service as her temporary replacement. In 1929 Tully joined the Roosevelts in Albany, the capital of New York State, following Franklin Roosevelt's election as governor. By 1929 she had become a firm fixture in his official family.

In the winter of 1931–1932 Tully developed tuberculosis, and was only able to work on a sporadic or part-time basis during Roosevelt's successful presidential campaign of 1932. She did not return to work full-time until the summer of 1934. As LeHand did little speech and mail dictation and not much typing, Tully, who referred to herself as "number two girl," assumed responsibilities in these areas almost from the beginning of the White House years. Roosevelt was much intrigued by the script of *I'd Rather Be Right,* the George M. Cohan comedy about the presidency then playing on Broadway, although he never saw a performance. Borrowing from the script, he would often begin dictation sessions with Tully by saying, "Take a law, Grace." One of Tully's sisters, Paula, a struggling actress, joined her at the White House in 1933, helping out with various secretarial assignments until 1940.

When LeHand suffered a stroke in 1941 and was forced into semiretirement, Tully took over as the president's principal secretary. She was always a key staff member on campaign trips, often working around the clock with limited sleep. She and her assistants were sometimes obliged to prepare numerous speech drafts in relays. Seven or eight versions were not unusual, although the number could sometimes exceed ten. She worked well with the president's speechwriters and advisers, and was often present with them during FDR's working lunches and dinners. During World War II her hours were long, and the duties sometimes onerous. Normal work days ran from ten in the morning until 6:30 or 7 in the evening. Sometimes, however, Tully would remain on duty until 10 P.M., and on occasion until three in the morning.

By her own admission, Tully was blunter in her dealing with FDR than was LeHand, but she has been described as having had "a machinelike efficiency which was amazing." Her ability to handle myriad details was outstanding and she was extremely knowledgeable about the president's files. In 1943, together with Harry Hopkins, several times a cabinet officer, and Samuel I. Rosenman, the president's counsel, Tully was selected by FDR to begin a review of his papers to determine which should go to the family, which should be made available for immediate use by researchers,

and which should be released to the public at a later date. This formidable assignment was taken over by the staff of the National Archives in 1949.

An attractive, high-spirited, and cheerful woman with a marvelous sense of humor, she was devoted to Roosevelt and he greatly depended upon her. Variously addressed as "Tully" or "Grace" by members of the White House staff, she was sometimes called "little Tully" by the president's mother, Sara Delano Roosevelt, and "child" by the president himself. She in turn usually referred to FDR as "the boss." She was very often included in Roosevelt picnics and other family activities. Judge Rosenman later wrote that she came closer to filling the void left by Missy LeHand's departure from the White House in 1941 than anyone else could have done, although she was "more detached and businesslike" than LeHand. She was present when Roosevelt died at Warm Springs on 12 April 1945.

In her affectionate 1949 memoir, *FDR: My Boss,* Tully described her seventeen years with the Roosevelts and their many friends and associates. Tactfully, she made no mention of the many intrafamily stresses and strains to which she doubtless had been privy. She was, however, quite outspoken about FDR's political foes.

For more than forty years Tully lived in the same Connecticut Avenue apartment in Washington, first with her widowed mother and then by herself. She became executive secretary of the FDR Memorial Foundation following Roosevelt's death. From 1955 to 1965 she was a staff member with the Senate Democratic Policy Committee, first under Senator Lyndon B. Johnson and later with Senator Mike Mansfield. Tully never married and had no children. She retired in 1965 and died in Washington after a long illness nearly two decades later.

★

Tully's *FDR: My Boss* (1949) is a useful account of her association with the Roosevelt family. A biographical sketch is in Otis L. Graham, Jr., and Meghan Robinson Wander, eds., *Franklin D. Roosevelt, His Life and Times: An Encyclopedic View* (1985). Tully was interviewed in the *New York Times* (3 Aug. 1980). An obituary is in the *New York Times* (16 June 1984).

KEIR B. STERLING

TUPPER, Earl Silas (*b.* 28 July 1907 in Berlin, New Hampshire; *d.* 3 October 1983 in San José, Costa Rica), inventor of Tupperware, a line of exceptionally durable and popular bowls, cups, and utensils that became a ubiquitous feature in American kitchens.

Tupper was a small-town farm boy. His parents, Earnest Leslie Tupper and Lulu Clark, farmed small acreages first in New Hampshire and then in Massachusetts. Like many marginal farmers of the era, the family accepted boarders,

Earl Tupper and Brownie Wise, the head of the Tupperware sales force. COURTESY OF THE BROWNIE WISE AND EARL TUPPER COLLECTION, NATIONAL MUSEUM OF AMERICAN HISTORY, SMITHSONIAN INSTITUTION

and Tupper's mother took in laundry to supplement the family income (Tupper was one of five children). Tupper's father was an avid but only partly successful inventor who passed on this love to his son.

The family moved to the village of Shirley, Massachusetts, when Tupper was a child. His formal schooling ended with his graduation from nearby Fitchburg High School in 1925. He then worked in the family greenhouses until 1928, when, after taking a course in tree surgery, he opened his own business, Tupper Tree Doctors. The business prospered for a time, giving Tupper, who had married Marie Whitcomb Smith in 1931, the means to pursue a career as an inventor. His interest grew out of both a love of inventing and a belief that this could be his path to riches.

Events in 1936 were pivotal for Tupper. The loss of his business that year reinforced Tupper's belief that his greatest chance for success on a grand scale lay in his inventions. Consequently he began to focus on bringing some of his projects to market. In the process he met Bernard Doyle, a founder of the Viscoloid company. Viscoloid was a plastics pioneer firm located in nearby Leominster, a manufacturing center already becoming known as "plastic city." The

chemical-manufacturing firm Du Pont had purchased the company in 1928, and Tupper, apparently with Doyle's support, joined Du Pont Viscoloid as a designer and chemist in 1937. Tupper would later recall that "my education really began" at Du Pont. In his year there Tupper gained the practical chemical, design, and manufacturing experience, as well as the contacts, that enabled him to successfully strike out on his own. In 1938 he founded the Earl S. Tupper Company, which initially operated primarily as a Du Pont subcontractor. The company prospered during World War II, manufacturing gas-mask parts and signal lamps. Although the company continued to do defense work for a few years after the war, Tupper's main interest had shifted to the civilian market.

Initially he favored his prewar strategy of making goods for others. Early contracts included items such as an order for 700,000 cups from American Thermos and 300,000 cigarette cases for Camel. But he also began making his own products, such as the "Wonderlier bowl" that he sold under the Tupperware trade name. Tupper distinguished himself from competitors primarily through the superior quality of his plastic. In 1938, he had developed Poly-T, a variant of the polyethylene he had first seen at Du Pont. Polyethylene had been invented in England in 1931 but attracted little interest until World War II, when researchers discovered it provided very effective insulation for the electrical wiring in radar units. Tupper's Poly-T was an unusually durable variant ideally suited to kitchen use. It was shatterproof, bendable, heat resistant, odorless, and inexpensive. This alone probably would have been enough to make Tupper a success, but in 1947 he introduced his patented airtight seal, which gave him a unique and powerful advantage over his competitors.

Tupper's seal, modeled after the lip typically found on paint cans, is the main reason Tupperware has been called "the first major [kitchen] storage breakthrough since the glass canning jar." Its partial vacuum kept foods fresh, and it was simple to use. Moreover, its Poly-T construction meant that it was also durable and inexpensive. Despite these advantages, however, sales lagged due to the lack of a suitable way to demonstrate it to the public.

Tupper found the solution to his marketing problems when Stanley Home Products, a Massachusetts firm that had developed the home-demonstration party in the 1930s, added Tupperware to its line. Some of Stanley's salespeople were enjoying great success with Tupperware, and with sales stalled in traditional retail outlets Tupper took notice. In 1948 he met with a group of Tupperware's best distributors, including a number of Stanley agents, to discuss how best to market his product. The group convinced Tupper that the product needed to be demonstrated and that the home party was its best venue. Modeled closely on the Stanley system, Tupper's marketing strategy and organization evolved between 1948 and 1951, when Tupper decided to pull Tupperware from retailer's shelves and sell it exclusively through in-home-sales parties.

Tupper chose Brownie Wise to head his new sales company, Tupper Home Parties, Inc. Much of Tupperware's phenomenal success in the 1950s can be attributed to Wise, who proved to be a skilled organizer, motivator, and spokesperson. In her first three years the sales force expanded from roughly 200 dealers to 9,000. Total sales doubled in the first full year of the new plan and tripled the following year.

By the mid-1950s Tupper had achieved his boyhood dream of wealth on a grand scale, and as he had once hoped, his inventions were the root of his success. Other factors, however, had also played a part. Doyle's faith in Tupper's real but unschooled abilities had given him the chance he needed to develop his creations. Wise's ability to tap and inspire the 1950s housewives who were both Tupper's market and his sales force had provided the difference between covering the market and dominating it. Overproduction of polyethylene in the early and mid-1950s had assured low prices and production that kept pace with demand.

In 1958 Tupper sold the business to Dart Industries for $16 million. He stayed on as chairman of the board of directors until 1973, when he retired and moved with his family to Costa Rica, where he became a citizen (ostensibly for tax reasons) and lived until his death, from a heart attack.

★

Tupper's personal and business papers are held by the Archives Center of the National Museum of American History, Smithsonian Institution. These include outlines and early drafts of Tupper's uncompleted autobiography and much of the research for a never-completed biography by Neil Osterweil.

Although his name became a household word, Tupper himself made infrequent appearances in the press. The most useful articles are: "Tupperware," *Time* (8 Sept. 1947), which provides the best interview of his early career; and "Selling a Party Line," *Business Week* (16 Jan. 1954), and "How Brownie Wise Whoops up Sales," *Business Week* (17 Apr. 1954), which describe Tupperware's rapid expansion. A brief obituary appears in the *New York Times* (7 Oct. 1983).

TOM DICKE

TURNER, Joseph Vernon ("Big Joe") (*b.* 18 May 1911 in Kansas City, Missouri; *d.* 24 November 1985 in Inglewood, California), one of the most prominent "blues shouters," who as a representative of the Kansas City style straddled the boundaries between blues, jazz, and rhythm and blues for half a century and was influential in each genre.

Joe Turner, *c.* 1951. FRANK DRIGGS/ARCHIVE PHOTOS

One of two children of Georgie, a laundress, and Joseph Turner, a cook and fisherman, Joe Turner grew up in Kansas City and as a child seemed interested only in listening to and making music. He learned his first tunes from his uncles but received most of his education on the street, accompanying blind blues singers as he was ducking school. Turner also sang in African-American church choirs and could be found "busting music" with friends. At this time, the mid-1920s, a distinctive Kansas City jazz and blues style was being formed from a unique, local interaction between country blues, ragtime, and orchestral dance music. Turner paid close attention to all these forms as well as to records by Ethel Waters, Bessie Smith, Leroy Carr, Lonnie Johnson, and others.

When he was about sixteen Turner made an arrangement with a local record store to listen to new records in order to introduce the artists' material in local clubs in which he had begun to perform well before reaching the legal age of admission. One of his early engagements was at the Backbiters Club, where one day he heard the piano player Pete Johnson perform. According to one story, Turner sneaked inside to ask Johnson for permission to sing with him and persuaded the club's owner to overlook his young age. Over succeeding decades Johnson and Turner would be regular partners, appearing together at performances and recording sessions all over the United States.

In many of his jobs at Kansas City clubs, Turner combined bartending with singing. Evenings at the clubs often turned into long, improvised jam sessions, with Turner making up new, often sexually loaded lyrics for hours in his half-sung, half-shouted trademark style of singing. Through his participation in after-hours sessions and the large annual local band competition, Turner contributed as much to the Kansas City style as he took from it. Through his entire career, Turner, at six feet, two inches and 250 pounds, was able to hold his own in front of a big band but also excelled in smaller, more intimate settings.

During the 1930s Turner, together with Pete Johnson and bands like Count Basie's, traveled to Chicago, St. Louis, Omaha, and New York City, but his big break came in 1938 when John Hammond recruited him for the groundbreaking "From Spirituals to Swing" presentations at New York City's Carnegie Hall. Turner made his first recording, "It's All Right Baby," at that show. It was not, however, released for decades. A commercial recording followed the same year, when Turner and Johnson cut "Goin' Away Blues" and "Roll 'Em Pete" for Vocation Records.

Hammond next got Turner an engagement at Cafe Society in New York City in 1938. On opening night he performed as a member of the renowned early regulars of the club: Billie Holiday, Meade Lux Lewis, Frankie Newton and band, Albert Ammons, and Pete Johnson. Turner would work on and off at the cafe for five years. His return to New York in 1938 was also the beginning of a long string of enduring recordings for a great many labels but particularly Decca between 1940 and 1944 and, later, National Records with its innovative rhythm and blues orientation. Turner's first work with Duke Ellington dates from 1941, in the latter's "Jump for Joy" revue in Hollywood. From the early 1940s Turner and other Kansas City stars were eventually forced to take their brand of jazz and blues on the road, because the vibrant local club scene had vanished with the collapse of Kansas City's Pendergast political machine in 1939.

The postwar decade with its rising prosperity and changing lifestyles for both whites and blacks brought unprecedented popularity for jazz, blues, and other kinds of black music. Turner, who married Lou Willie Brown in 1945, tried to ride the emerging rhythm and blues wave with a chart success. Initially he was unsuccessful, but his fortune changed after he moved to Atlantic Records in 1951. Atlantic's operators and producers, Ahmet Ertegun and Herb Abrahamson, helped Turner forge a highly effective sound from, on the one hand, his considerable talents and experience, and, on the other, the new, more polished rhythm and blues style. A string of classic hits testifies to Turner's success at Atlantic, the most important of which

are "Chains of Love" (1951), "Honey Hush" (1952), and "Shake Rattle and Roll" (1954).

The last tune was soon turned into an even bigger commercial success by the rock and roll band Bill Haley and the Comets, an event not devoid of symbolic meaning, because after the mid-1950s Turner had no more chart successes. Like so many other blues originals, his true heyday—in terms of creativity, innovation, and commercial success—was, after the 1930s, between the late 1940s and the mid-1950s. After that, Turner lost out to the next wave of modern popular music, rock and roll, even though, in his own view, it was just a different name for the kind of music he had been making all his life. This is only partly true, as can be seen by comparing Turner's style with that of a rock and roller like Chuck Berry, a younger black performer who, although firmly grounded in traditional jazz and blues, through his music, lyrics, and performing style made it his purpose to connect with a mass audience of predominantly white teenagers. Joe Turner always remained the traditional, black blues shouter/jazz singer.

Although his career as a producer of hits was over after the mid-1950s, the opposite was true of other sides of Turner's artistry. During the long autumn of his career, Turner remained the highly respected and much-acclaimed "boss of the blues." Until his death from a stroke, he was always in high demand as a stage performer and for films and television and never stopped recording. Turner toured extensively in the United States as well as abroad, performed with innumerable jazz and blues artists and bands, and was the recipient of several prestigious music awards. He also began a second marriage, in 1969 to Patricia Sims. He is buried in Roosevelt Cemetery, Gardena, California.

The lasting legacy of Joe Turner's work is that it is one of the best representations of the Kansas City jazz and blues style as it emerged and flourished during the 1920s and 1930s and merged with and evolved into new directions after World War II.

★

For Turner's own words see the interviews in *Jazz Beat* 2, no. 7 (1965) and *Living Blues* no. 10 (autumn 1972). Biographical information is in Ian Carmichael, Digby Fairweather, and Brian Priestly, *Jazz: The Essential Companion* (1987); "Majesty: Joe Turner," in Whitney Balliett, *American Singers: Twenty-seven Portraits in Song* (1988); William Barlow, *"Looking Up at Down": The Emergence of Blues Culture* (1989); and Sheldon Harris, comp., *Blues Who's Who* (1989). For Turner's recordings see Ron Wynn, ed., *The All Music Guide to Jazz* (1994). An obituary is in the *New York Times* (25 Nov. 1985).

RUUD VAN DIJK

TWINING, Nathan Farragut (*b.* 11 October 1897 in Monroe, Wisconsin; *d.* 29 March 1982 near San Antonio, Texas), U.S. Air Force officer who served as a bomber commander during World War II, as Air Force chief of staff, and as chairman of the Joint Chiefs of Staff, the nation's highest military position.

Twining, the sixth of eight children of Clarence Twining, a banker, and Maize Barber, attended public school in Monroe. After the death of his mother and the remarriage of his father, the family moved to Portland, Oregon, where he completed high school. In 1915 Twining enlisted in the Oregon National Guard as a private, and in 1916 he served along the Mexican border during the crisis with Mexico. Committed to a military career, Twining gained an appointment to the U.S. Military Academy at West Point, New York, in 1917. He graduated on 1 November 1918 after an accelerated course, because of U.S. entry into World War I, regraduated on 11 June 1919 after a postgraduate course, and was commissioned a second lieutenant in the infantry. Following a brief assignment in Germany, Twining was a student, with the rank of first lieutenant, at the Infantry School at Fort Benning, Georgia, from 1919 to 1920. He then served with the school's demonstration platoon until 1922, when he became the aide of the commander of the Fourth Infantry Brigade at Camp Travis, Texas.

By the early 1920s, Twining had developed an interest in flying, and in 1923 he entered flight training at Brooks Field, and later Kelly Field, both in Texas. An excellent pilot, he earned his wings in 1924, and until 1930 he was a flight instructor at Brooks Field; Duncan Field, Texas; and March Field, California. From 1930 to 1932, Twining was assigned to the Eighteenth Pursuit Group in Hawaii. While there, he married Maude McKeever, the daughter of a plantation owner, on 9 March 1932; they had three children. Twining served with the Third Attack Group at Fort Crockett, Texas, from 1932 to 1935 and then briefly as assistant operations officer with the Third Wing at Barksdale Field, Louisiana. Promoted to captain, Twining from 1935 to 1937 was a student at the Air Corps Tactical School at Maxwell Field, Alabama, and at the Command and General Staff School at Fort Leavenworth, Kansas. During the next three years, Twining was the technical supervisor at the San Antonio Air Depot, and between 1940 and 1942 he rose from the rank of major to brigadier general while serving in Washington, D.C., in staff positions in the Office of the Chief of Staff of the Air Corps (later the Army Air Forces).

In the summer of 1942, Twining was appointed chief of staff for Major General Millard F. Harmon, Jr., commander of Army Forces in the South Pacific, and in January 1943 he was named commander of the Thirteenth Air Force, which had administrative control over air force units in the South Pacific. That same month Twining was aboard a B-17 that was forced to ditch at sea during a flight from Guadalcanal to Espiritu Santo, and he and fourteen others were adrift on rafts for six days before being rescued. On 25 July 1943 Twining, now a major general, was appointed commander, Aircraft, Solomon Islands, a command that included all land-based air units in the Solomons. During the next months he directed operations in the northern Solomons that effectively destroyed Japanese air strength in the area.

Twining, now highly regarded as an aggressive, dependable, and hard-working officer, was transferred to the Mediterranean theater at the end of 1943 to command the Fifteenth Air Force. Over the next seventeen months, he sent his bombers against German targets in northern Italy, the Balkans, Hungary, Austria, and Germany, becoming in the process a fervent devotee of the use of strategic air power to destroy an enemy's industrial and urban centers. In the summer of 1945, Twining, promoted to lieutenant general, went to the Pacific to command the Twentieth Air Force, which was in charge of the strategic air campaign against Japan and dropped the atomic bombs on Japan in August 1945.

In December 1945 Twining was appointed head of the

Lieutenant General Nathan F. Twining in Guam, 1945. ARCHIVE PHOTOS

Air Technical Service Command (later the Air Materiel Command) at Wright Field, Ohio, and from October 1947 to May 1950 he was commander of the Alaska Command. After a brief tour as the air force's acting deputy chief of staff for personnel, Twining became air force vice chief of staff with the rank of general in October 1950. In this post he managed the daily affairs of the air force during the height of the Korean War.

By 1952, with the failing health of air force chief of staff General Hoyt Vandenberg, Twining was de facto chief of staff, and in 1953 President Dwight D. Eisenhower appointed him as Vandenberg's successor. During the next years, Twining advocated an expanded Strategic Air Command and the continued development and deployment of nuclear weapons, in the belief that they were the best deterrent to aggression by the Soviet Union. He also advocated the use of tactical nuclear weapons against the Vietminh at the time of the Dien Bien Phu crisis in Indochina in 1954. Within the Joint Chiefs of Staff (JCS), Twining strongly supported Eisenhower's New Look defense policy, which called for reduced spending for army ground forces and an emphasis on air power and nuclear weapons.

While Twining was an ardent air force partisan, Eisenhower was impressed with his even-tempered manner, conciliatory stance on divisive interservice issues, and candor, and in August 1957 he named Twining chairman of the JCS. In this capacity Twining continued to emphasize that a strong nuclear-war capability was the best deterrent to aggression and earned Eisenhower's high esteem for his advice on JCS matters and U.S. military capabilities. He retired in September 1960, after an operation for lung cancer in 1959.

In retirement Twining was vice chairman of Holt, Rinehart and Winston, a publishing house, and an unsuccessful Republican candidate for the U.S. Senate from New Hampshire in 1966. He also retained an active interest in defense matters, and in *Neither Liberty Nor Safety* (1966),

he explained his views on the development of postwar defense policy. Twining died of a heart attack at Lackland Air Force Base and was buried with full military honors at Arlington National Cemetery in Virginia.

A sturdy-looking, white-haired airman whose trademark was a large cigar, Twining was an able professional whose career mirrored the growth of the air force from biplanes to jet planes and missiles. He stands out for his combat leadership during World War II and his unswerving advocacy of air power and nuclear weapons.

★

An extensive collection of Twining's papers is located in the Library of Congress. J. Britt McCarley, "General Nathan Farragut Twining: The Making of a Disciple of American Strategic Air Power, 1897–1953" (Ph.D. diss., Temple University, 1989), is a thorough examination of Twining's career up to his appointment as Air Force chief of staff. Donald J. Mrozek, "Nathan F. Twining: New Dimensions, a New Look," in John L. Frisbee, ed., *Makers of the United States Air Force* (1987), provides a good summary of Twining's career and his role as air force chief of staff and chairman of the JCS. Clay Blair, Jr., "The General Everybody Loves: An Affable Airman with an Exceptional Talent for Calming Belligerent Brass Hats—That's Nate Twining, New Boss of the Joint Chiefs of Staff," *Saturday Evening Post* (17 Aug. 1957), and Roger Butterfield and Frank Gibney, "The Twining Tradition: A Heritage of U.S. Service from Muskets to Missiles Culminates in Joint Chiefs' New Boss and a Top Marine," *Life* (26 Aug. 1957), look at the personal side of Twining. Obituaries are in the *New York Times* and *Washington Post* (both 30 Mar. 1982). Oral histories are located at the Oral History Research Office, Columbia University, New York City; Albert F. Simpson Historical Research Center, Maxwell Air Force Base, Alabama; John Foster Dulles Oral History Project, Seeley G. Mudd Library, Princeton University, Princeton, N.J.; and the Murray Green Collection, U.S. Air Force Academy Library, Colorado Springs, Colo.

JOHN KENNEDY OHL

U-V

ULAM, Stanislaw Marcin (*b*. 13 April 1909 in Lwów, Poland [now part of the Ukraine]; *d*. 13 May 1984 in Santa Fe, New Mexico), mathematician and physicist who played a key role in the development of the hydrogen bomb.

Ulam, of Jewish ancestry, was the oldest of three children of Josef Ulam, a lawyer, and Anna Auerbach; he was descended from a family of industrialists. As a high school student, he was bored by the formalities of school mathematics but read on his own in the areas of set theory and number theory, which fascinated him. In 1927 he was admitted to the Polytechnic Institute in Lwów after taking a three-day series of examinations. He wanted to study electrical engineering, but his mathematical abilities soon came to the forefront, as he studied under Stefan Banach and others; his first mathematical paper was published in 1928. The Polytechnic Institute awarded him the M.A. degree in 1932 and the D.Sc. degree in 1933, both in mathematics.

The lack of opportunity for mathematicians in Poland and the already unstable political situation in central Europe inspired Ulam to seek employment elsewhere. After a 1935 visit to England, during which he lectured at the University of Cambridge, Ulam was invited by the great mathematician John von Neumann, with whom he was destined to work in many areas, to teach at the Institute for Advanced Study in Princeton, New Jersey.

The next year Ulam was invited to join the Society of Fellows at Harvard University, where from 1936 to 1939 he worked in the areas of set-theoretical topology and analysis

of real functions. He returned to Poland during the summers, but in 1939 he left Poland for the last time, traveling to America with his brother Adam. In the academic year 1939–1940, Ulam lectured in mathematics at Harvard. In 1941 he became a U.S. citizen and took a position in the mathematics department at the University of Wisconsin in Madison. There he met C. J. Everett, who became his collaborator in mathematical papers. On 14 August 1941 he married a French woman named Françoise Aron, whom he had met at Cambridge; they had a daughter.

Although his background was almost entirely in pure mathematics, in 1943 Ulam was invited, again at the recommendation of von Neumann, to join the physicists working on the atomic bomb at Los Alamos, New Mexico. He arrived in Los Alamos in February 1944 and collaborated with such well-known scientists as Hans Bethe, Enrico Fermi, and Edward Teller.

With the successful end of the war, which his researches had helped bring about, Ulam took a position at the University of Southern California (USC), moving to Los Angeles in September 1945. In January 1946 he was stricken with encephalitis. At first it was feared that he would suffer a loss of brain function, but he recovered fully and was able to make important scientific contributions in the ensuing years. Ulam was unhappy at USC, and while he was recuperating from encephalitis he received an offer to return to Los Alamos, which he eagerly accepted, going back in May 1946.

At this point, the first electronic computer, ENIAC, had

Stanislaw Marcin Ulam. LOS ALAMOS NATIONAL LABORATORY/CORBIS

just been built, and Ulam became one of the first scientists to use a computer for research. Everett joined him at Los Alamos in 1947, and they developed the Monte Carlo method, a way of using computer-generated random numbers to approximate the behavior of subatomic particles.

In 1949 the Russians tested their first atomic bomb, and President Harry Truman ordered the scientists of Los Alamos to research the hydrogen bomb. Ulam soon concluded that Teller's plan for causing the fusion of hydrogen atoms would not work, a conclusion supported by von Neumann's computer studies. He suggested an alternative approach, the details of which are still classified secret, and he and Teller were able to design a working bomb.

Ulam was a visiting professor at Harvard (1951–1952), at the Massachusetts Institute of Technology (1956–1957), and at the University of Colorado (1961–1962), while serving as research adviser to Norris Bradbury, the director of Los Alamos. Ulam returned to the University of Colorado in 1965, and, after formally retiring from Los Alamos in 1967 (although he retained connections with it for the rest of his life), he became chairman of Colorado's mathematics department, where he remained until his retirement in 1975.

After his retirement from the University of Colorado, Ulam remained active, with visiting professorships at the Rockefeller Institute (1980–1984) and University of Cali-

fornia, Davis (1982–1983). In 1968 he and Mark Kac published the survey *Mathematics and Logic,* and in 1974 his collected papers were published under the title *Stanislaw Ulam: Sets, Numbers, and Universes.* He died of a heart attack.

Ulam was remarkable for the breadth of his interests. He not only worked in such strictly mathematical areas as number theory and topology, but also contributed to mathematical physics, biomathematics, and the early applications of computers to scientific and mathematical research. The Monte Carlo method has found applications in a number of scientific areas, and while the exact extent of his work on the hydrogen bomb has not yet been revealed to the general public, he is known to have made a significant contribution. He was also remarkable for his ability to convey to the nonscientist reader something of what it is like to be a scientist.

★

Stanislaw Ulam, *Adventures of a Mathematician* (1976), was assembled by his wife from his tape-recorded reminiscences and is Ulam's account of his life and ideas. His *Science, Computers, and People: From the Tree of Mathematics* (1986), edited by Gian-Carlo Rota and Mark C. Reynolds, is a collection of his nontechnical writings and includes further reminiscences and comments. Necia Grant Cooper, ed., *From Cardinals to Chaos: Reflections on the Life and Legacy of Stanislaw Ulam* (1989), originally published as a special issue of the journal *Los Alamos Science* in 1987, includes reminiscences of Ulam and discussions of his ideas by his colleagues; Gian-Carlo Rota's personal memoir, "The Lost Cafe," is particularly valuable. George Gamow, *My World Line* (1970), is a memoir, including his work with Ulam at Los Alamos and a foreword by Ulam. D. Sharp and M. Simmons, eds., *Mathematics at Los Alamos* (1989), is a collection of reports on the Los Alamos project by Ulam and others. An obituary is in the *New York Times* (15 May 1984).

ARTHUR D. HLAVATY

UREY, Harold Clayton (*b.* 29 April 1893 in Walkerton, Indiana; *d.* 5 January 1981 in La Jolla, California), physical chemist, cosmic scientist, geophysicist, and Nobel Prize winner for his discovery of deuterium, an isotope of hydrogen, which led to the production of nuclear weapons.

Urey was one of three children of Samuel Clayton Urey and Cora Rebecca Reinoehl. His ancestors had been pioneers in the Walkerton area. His father was a schoolteacher and a minister of the Church of the Brethren and his mother was a housewife. Both of his parents were pacifists. In 1899, when Harold was six years old, his father died. Subsequently, his mother married a widowed clergyman with two children. He attended rural elementary schools in De Kalb County, Indiana. Later, he attended high

Harold Urey. ARCHIVE PHOTOS

schools in Kendalville and Walkerton in Indiana. Urey graduated from high school in 1911 and spent the next three years teaching in rural schools of Indiana and Montana.

In 1914 Urey matriculated at Montana State University in Missoula. There, he majored in zoology and minored in chemistry. Funds were in short supply for Urey, so he lived off campus in a rather spartan manner. He worked during summers on a road gang laying railroad tracks in the Northwest. These adverse conditions generated in him characteristics of efficiency and extreme frugality, traits that would carry over into his scientific work. Urey was awarded a B.S. degree in zoology in 1917. Although his major contribution would be in the physical sciences, his initial project was studying the protozoa in the Missoula River and his interest in bioscience would continue.

After the United States entered World War I, Urey went to work for Barrett Chemical Company, which was engaged in making war materials. He helped the war effort only as a duty to his country. He is reputed to have said that this experience turned him away from industry and toward academic work as a career option. After the war he returned

to Montana State University in 1919 to continue his teaching career as an instructor of chemistry.

In 1921 Urey began graduate work at the University of California at Berkeley. He studied thermodynamics under the preeminent thermodynamicist Gilbert Newton Lewis and minored in physics. While working under Lewis, he developed his interest in mathematical chemistry. Urey received his Ph.D. in physical chemistry in 1923. His thesis dealt with the calculation of the rotational contribution to the entropy of diatomic gases from molecular spectra, which was not well understood at the time. Urey's calculated entropies agreed with experimental values, quite a significant accomplishment. Urey's method of calculating the entropies was the model upon which are based current methods used to calculate thermodynamic functions and properties from measured spectroscopic data.

In 1923, as an American-Scandinavian Foundation fellow, Urey attended the Institute for Theoretical Physics at the University of Copenhagen in Denmark. He studied there for one year under Niels Bohr, who was conducting pioneering work in the theory of atomic structure. During this period Urey met and became friends with some of the most prominent scientists of the time as he involved himself in the international development of atomic and molecular physics. Several of the scientists with whom he was then associated either had or would receive the Nobel Prize: Albert Einstein (1921); Bohr (1922); Werner Heisenberg (1932); George von Hevesy (1943); and Wolfgang Pauli (1945).

In 1924 Urey returned to the United States, bringing with him a vast knowledge of quantum mechanics acquired in Copenhagen. For the next five years he served as an instructor of chemistry at Johns Hopkins University in Baltimore. While on a visit to Seattle, Urey met Freida Daum, a bacteriologist working in a doctor's office. Urey and Daum were married on 12 June 1926. He had a very stable family, which he treasured, including four children.

In 1929 Urey joined the faculty of Columbia University in New York City as an associate professor of chemistry; he was promoted to full professor in 1934. During this period his research was focused on experimental and theoretical work in spectroscopy and quantum mechanics. Also during this time he coauthored, with Arthur Edward Ruark, *Atoms, Molecules, and Quanta* (1930), one of the first comprehensive English-language textbooks on quantum mechanics. The book treated the new discoveries in quantum mechanics made by, among others, Louis de Broglie (matter-wave concept), Heisenberg (the uncertainty principle), Erwin Schrödinger (wave equation), Max Born, and Paul Dirac (all Nobelists).

Urey was intensely interested in atomic, molecular, and nuclear properties of any kind. Reflecting the breadth, depth, and vast scope of his knowledge, he had students, including Charles Bradley, engaged in several kinds of fundamental research. The potential energy function used by Urey and Bradley for a polyatomic molecule is considered one of the most satisfactory functions for a molecule with tetrahedral symmetry. This function is termed the Urey-Bradley function. In addition, Urey collaborated with a Columbia University colleague, R. H. Crist, in an attempt to separate the chlorine isotopes by a photochemical method.

With George M. Murphy, Urey studied the relative abundance of nitrogen and oxygen isotopes, theorizing that isotopic ratios were a function of sample origin. Urey proposed a systematic arrangement of nuclear species to be used as a guide to ascertain their existence. At the time, it was thought that the nucleus consisted of protons (positive charge, a relative mass of one) and electrons (negative charge, relative mass of zero); the neutron (zero charge, relative mass of one) had not been discovered. A plot of the number of electrons versus the number of protons would yield a line along which one could look for stable isotopes. Thus, the chart Urey kept in his laboratory showed hydrogen two (H^2), hydrogen three (H^3), helium five (He^5), lithium five (Li^5), and beryllium eight (Be^8).

What prompted Urey to search for H^2 was a *Physical Review* article by Edward Birge and Donald Menzel suggesting that the discrepancy in the atomic mass of H^1 could be due to isotopes of hydrogen. There existed two atomic weight scales: the chemist scale was based on oxygen sixteen (O^{16}) for the naturally occurring mixture of O^{16}, O^{17}, and O^{18}; the physicist scale was based on the isotopic masses and their relative abundance. Birge and Menzel speculated that the heavier isotope would be rather scarce, one part in 4,500. Urey concentrated his efforts on finding H^2. He knew that he was in a race with other scientists to be the first to prove its existence. He used the well-known Balmer equation (the frequency of a line in the spectrum of hydrogen is inversely proportional to the difference in the square of two integers, one integer being constant) to calculate the expected positions of the lines in the spectrum of H^2. (The atomic spectrum would be much less complex than the molecular spectrum.) The separations of the H^2 lines from H^1 were within the range of his grating spectrograph. However, he thought that the concentration of H^2 in H^1 would be too small to detect, so a concentrated solution was needed. There being no source of liquid hydrogen in New York State, Urey collaborated with his former student Ferdinand G. Brickwedde of Washington, D.C., who was an expert on low-temperature research. Initially as a quick test, Urey took the spectra of regular tank hydrogen and, surprisingly, found weak lines at the positions calculated for H^2. From vapor pressure calculations, Urey and Murphy speculated that the hydrogen molecule with greater mass would distill from the liquid hydrogen last. They were correct. The spectrum of the concentrated sample agreed with the calculated positions. Moreover, the lines were well resolved and intense. These results were obtained on Thanksgiving Day in 1931. Hydrogen of mass two definitely existed.

The first public announcement of the discovery was at the American Association for the Advancement of Science (AAAS) meeting in New Orleans, Louisiana, in 1931. Because of the expense, Urey had hesitated about going. A colleague, Bergen Davis, prevailed upon the president of Columbia, Nicholas Murray Butler, to grant Urey funds because Davis knew of the paper's importance. Urey received a prize for the best paper presented at the AAAS meeting. The discovery of hydrogen two, called deuterium, won the Nobel Prize in chemistry for Urey in 1934. His 14 February 1935 Nobel paper was titled "Some Thermodynamic Properties of Hydrogen and Deuterium." The discovery of deuterium has been called one of the most significant achievements of modern science. Scientists have used deuterium in a variety of ways, which has had an enormous impact on biology, chemistry, medicine, and physics. For example, in medicine it was the first tracer used to study physiological changes in the body. The difference in mass, two to one, between deuterium and light hydrogen was unique.

Urey and his group continued to study deuterium. Seeking ways of obtaining more concentrated samples, they tried fractional distillation, chemical exchange, electrolysis, and gaseous diffusion. Their efforts resulted in making deuterium, heavy water (D_2O), and other compounds readily available and inexpensive. Urey's group also continued to study theoretical and experimental aspects of isotopic chemistry. The group separated the isotopes of carbon, nitrogen, oxygen, and sulfur and then studied their medical and biological applications.

In 1933 Urey became the first editor of the *Journal of Chemical Physics*. The American Institute of Physics published this journal because of the great interest in subatomic and molecular spectroscopy and structure. He served for eight years and made it the leading journal in the new field of chemical physics. In 1934 Urey became professor of chemistry at Columbia University; from 1939 to 1942 he was the executive officer, or chairman, of the Chemistry Department.

In the 1930s Urey was a member of various political groups opposed to Francisco Franco's rebellion against the republican government in Spain. Always he was an advocate of the peace process over armed conflict. He was a registered Democrat throughout his career.

When World War II began, Urey was one of the first Americans to recognize that powerful atomic weapons could be made. Although opposed to war, Urey joined the Uranium Committee of the Manhattan Project. The U.S. Army had overall responsibility for atomic weapons development through the Manhattan Project. In 1940 Urey was recruited by the government to serve as director of this program at Columbia University, where he was director of war research for the Special Alloy Materials (SAM) Laboratories. He worked on the separation of bomb-grade uranium (U^{235}) from unenriched uranium (U^{238}) and the production of heavy water (deuterium oxide).

Various methods were tested to produce quantities of U^{235}. Most physicists opted for large-scale mass spectrometric methods as contrasted to Urey's statistical methods of gaseous and thermal diffusion, ultracentrifugation, distillation, exchange reactions, and electrolysis. Urey's statistical method was proven correct. The gaseous diffusion process, in which different isotopes of uranium were prepared in gaseous form (uranium hexafluoride, UF_6) and then diffused through membranes, was a major contribution to science. Although Urey was awarded the Medal of Merit for his contribution to the war effort, his aversion to oaths and secret work, as well as his concern for the destructiveness of nuclear weapons, caused him to leave the project.

Despite having aided in the development of nuclear weapons, Urey was always concerned about the social responsibility of scientists. After the United States used atomic bombs against Japan in World War II, he joined prominent scientists such as Einstein and Leo Szilard to form the Emergency Committee of Atomic Scientists. This committee was dedicated to enunciating the ethical and moral problems of atomic weapons and to indicating the devastating results that might follow from their use. Urey always spoke his mind and did not endear himself to some politicians and administrators, but graduate students were gratified by his bluntness and honesty. He was always neatly dressed, in suit and tie, sometimes complete with vest, until his very last years. A giant in figurative stature, he was just five feet, seven inches tall and weighed 178 pounds. He impressed upon his students the idea of using the quantitative approach to doing science. "Make the calculations," he exhorted. He insisted that "the whole problem be treated" rather than a specialized part or subject. Chemist Joel H. Hildebrand said that throughout his scintillating career, Urey had demonstrated the excitement of science to a degree seldom seen.

The Manhattan Project exceeded the available space at Columbia, so it was moved to Chicago, and in 1945 Urey joined the faculty of the University of Chicago, where he helped to establish the Institutes of Nuclear Studies. Collaborators were Enrico Fermi, Edward Teller, Leo Szilard, Joseph Mayer, Marie Goeppert Mayer, and other prominent scientists. The institute was supported in part by funding Urey obtained from corporations. In 1946 Urey participated in Operations Crossroads, a major and awesome nuclear bomb test that devastated parts of Bikini Atoll and rendered the island uninhabitable for decades.

Urey joined with Szilard and some other scientists in opposing the administration of nuclear power by the U.S. military. The congressional bill granting the military control of future atomic research was defeated through their efforts. Urey resigned from the Atomic Energy Commission in 1950. He vehemently opposed Senator Joseph McCarthy and McCarthyism. He also tried to save Ethel and Julius Rosenberg, who were convicted and executed for espionage. Urey read the trial records in their entirety and wrote letters to the trial judge, the media, and President Harry Truman urging clemency but to no avail. In a letter to Urey, Einstein wrote, "Your intervention in the Rosenberg case has been one of my most heartening experiences in the human sphere."

From 1952 through 1958 Urey was the Martin A. Ryerson Distinguished Service Professor at the University of Chicago. Although Urey did work on tritium (another isotope of hydrogen with a mass three times that of light hydrogen) as it related to hydrogen bomb construction, he was still an advocate of peaceful resolutions of conflicts. Because of the serious problem of nuclear wastes, he was an early proponent of alternative energy sources not requiring nuclear reactors.

Urey stated that a scientist should always choose significant problems that have meaning and depth. For his new research he chose the areas of geochemistry and cosmology. He applied his extensive knowledge of isotopes to measure with precision isotopic oxygen fractionation between ocean water and carbonates precipitated by belemnites (cigar-shaped fossil shells of an extinct kind of cuttlefish). His initial publication in this area was said to be the foundation for the embryonic field of isotopic geochemistry. Also while at Chicago, Urey and a small group of other scientists there began work that led to the development of the field of cosmochemistry. Urey and Hans Seuss derived chemical abundance tables of the isotopes as they occur and develop in nature, which led to Urey's contemplation of the origin of the solar system. His studies of meteorites led to their correct classification. A short article on his theory about the formation of the earth showed the sequence: primordial dust coagulation to protoplanets to planetesimals to planets. A detailed discussion is in his book *The Planets: Their Origin and Development* (1952).

In 1951 Urey's expansive knowledge and varied interests in elemental abundance, biology, and the origin of the solar system were joined in an imaginative landmark experiment with his graduate student Stanley L. Miller. The Urey-Miller experiment was a model of earth's primordial state (hot, simple molecules and a reducing atmosphere), demonstrating how complex molecules and eventually life could form from simple molecules. In the Urey-Miller experiment, electrical discharges were passed through a heated mixture of hydrogen (H_2), ammonia (NH_3), water

(H_2O), and methane (CH_4), with the resulting formation of amino acids, the building blocks of proteins. When Urey was asked what he expected to find in the mixture, he said "Beilstein!" (Beilstein is the best compendium of all known organic compounds.) This experiment was indicative of how Urey thought. It was this insightfulness that prompted him to say of himself, "There are a lot of people around who are smarter than me, but I pick only the most important problems."

Nearing retirement age, Urey accepted a position in 1958 as professor at large at the University of California's Scripps Institute of Oceanography at La Jolla, California. Scripps's director was Roger Revelle, a colleague of Urey at Operations Crossroads in 1946. Revelle was engaged in building what was to become the University of California at San Diego. Many of Urey's colleagues at Chicago moved west with him and established a chemistry program that became the leading center in cosmochemistry. The development of the center of cosmochemistry represented another career venture for Urey. He became an active participant in the space program and a strong advocate for fiscally responsible programs of clearly designed purpose. Urey was a founding member of the National Academy of Sciences Space Science Board and in 1958 he chaired the Committee on Chemistry of Space and Exploration of the Moon and Planets. Simultaneously, he chaired the University of California's statewide Advisory Committee on Space Science (1959–1961). Following the formation of the National Aeronautics and Space Administration (NASA) in 1958, he served as a consultant to the director, Robert Jastrow. He convinced Jastrow of the importance of Moon exploration, calling the Moon the Rosetta stone of the solar system. Urey was involved with many decisions concerning aspects of the Moon research and space missions, especially the Ranger and Apollo missions. He analyzed samples of Moon rock returned by various missions. The results did not support his theory about the Moon's history.

In 1966 the California Board of Regents voted to name the University of California at San Diego's first academic building Harold and Freida Urey Hall in honor of both Urey and his wife, an activist in the San Diego community. In 1970 Urey was named university professor, a newly created title. He became professor emeritus in 1972.

Urey continued his efforts on nuclear arms control, becoming a member of the Union of Concerned Scientists, a group of more than 23,000 members including numerous Nobel laureates. In 1975 the union petitioned President Gerald Ford to decrease the production of nuclear power plants. Urey was concerned about nuclear wastes and the possibility that the multiplication of nuclear power plants would increase the likelihood of the spread of nuclear weapons.

Urey received numerous major honors and awards, both domestic and foreign. He was awarded more than twenty honorary doctorates and fifteen medals, including the Willard Gibbs Medal of the American Chemical Society (1934), the Davy Medal from the Royal Society, London (1940), the Research Institute of America Silver Medal (1936 and 1960), the Joseph Priestley Award (1955), the Medal of the University of Paris (1964), the National Medal of Science (1964) from President Lyndon Johnson for his work on the space program, and the Gold Medal from the Royal Astronomy Society of London (1966). He was a member or fellow of more than two dozen academic institutions and societies in countries around the globe. Urey died from an apparent heart attack. He was buried in La Jolla, California, where he had made his home.

Urey was one of the foremost American-born scientists. He was brilliantly innovative. His discoveries of deuterium and heavy water helped the United States to become the first to develop nuclear weapons. He developed new fields of science but was humble enough to teach undergraduate physical chemistry to the end of his extraordinary career. He produced brilliant doctoral students who gained international fame. Most important, he was an active advocate for human and social justice, peaceful resolution of conflicts between nations, and the social responsibility of scientists. Urey's impact on the twentieth century was as dramatic as the nuclear bomb explosions that he helped to create. His imprint, though large on Earth, extends to the Moon and beyond.

★

The Harold Clayton Urey Papers, 1929–1981, which consist of articles about Urey and his own papers and correspondence, are at the University of California at San Diego. See also Frederick L. Holmes, ed., *Dictionary of Scientific Biography,* vol. 18 (1990), and Carl Sagan, "Obituary, Harold Clayton Urey: 1893–1981," *Icarus* 48, no. 3 (Dec. 1981): 348–352. Other obituaries are in the *New York Times* and the *Washington Post* (both 7 Jan. 1981).

SAMUEL VON WINBUSH

URIS, Harold David (*b.* 26 May 1905 in New York City; *d.* 28 March 1982 in Palm Beach, Florida), major New York City commercial real estate developer and philanthropist who, with his elder brother and partner, Percy Uris, reshaped the skyline of midtown Manhattan.

The Uris Buildings Corporation began as a modest family business. The founder, Harris Urias (later Uris) was born in Dunaburg, Latvia, around 1867. In 1892 he emigrated to New York where he found work in a plant that fabricated ornamental iron. Less than ten years later he bought the plant and renamed it the H. Uris Iron Works. Later he extended his efforts into residential, commercial, and hotel construction.

Harold and Percy Uris. COURTESY OF SUSAN U. HALPERN, ESQ.

Soon after arriving in New York, Harris Urias married Sadie Copland, an aunt of the composer Aaron Copland. The couple had four children: Percy (born in 1899), Madeline (1900), Gertrude (1904), and Harold. Harold and his older brother were educated at Ivy League colleges. In 1920 Percy graduated from Columbia University with a Phi Beta Kappa key and a B.S. degree in business administration. He immediately went to work in the family firm. Harold attended Cornell and graduated in 1925 with a degree in civil engineering. "When I got out of college," he once recalled, "I never bothered to come home; I went straight to the office." In later years he said that he had always been sure that he would join his father and brother and that they would construct large buildings together.

The first of their major New York City projects was One University Place, an upscale apartment house on Washington Square built in the 1920s. In 1925 came the Buckingham Hotel on West Fifty-seventh Street, built by the "Harper Organization," an acronym for Harold (or Harris) and Percy. In the autumn of 1930 the "Harper Organization" opened the thirty-eight-story, thousand-window St. Moritz Hotel on Central Park South. On 14 July 1935, Harold married Ruth Chinitz. They had four daughters: Judith, Susan, Linda, and Jane.

The Great Depression of the early 1930s was a difficult time for the Uris firm, but during the years just prior to the attack on Pearl Harbor they constructed two luxurious apartment buildings at desirable Manhattan addresses: Two Sutton Place on East Fifty-seventh Street and 930 Fifth Avenue, overlooking Central Park. During World War II, the firm provided low-cost housing for defense workers. With the coming of peace they constructed 880 Fifth Avenue, one of New York's first posh postwar co-ops. Then they turned away from residential projects to build many large office buildings.

Between 1947 and 1971 the Uris brothers were among the leaders of the New York office building industry, with new structures totaling more than 13 million square feet of space. In 1960 their fast-growing partnership went public as the Uris Buildings Corporation, but the brothers continued to exercise control and retained their private ownership of certain properties. In the same year they finished Two Broadway, and in 1961 they opened the doors of the ITT Building at 320 Park Avenue and Western Publishing at 850 Third Avenue. The next year saw the completion of the Sperry-Rand Building, followed in 1963 by the towering New York Hilton Hotel on the Avenue of the Americas adjacent to Rockefeller Center.

In 1964, the firm of J. C. Penney moved into a new Uris-built headquarters on the Avenue of the Americas. The next Uris projects were the American Tobacco Building on Park Avenue in 1967, the National City Bank Center at 111 Wall Street in 1968, and in 1970 the Uris Building at 1633 Broadway, which also housed the Uris Theater, later renamed the Gershwin. The final major Uris project was a downtown office tower at 55 Water Street. Fifty-six stories tall, it is one of the largest private office buildings in the world and was financed by a record-breaking $150 million mortgage.

During these years of enormous growth the Uris brothers remained an effective, close-knit team. "Neither of us ever raised his voice to the other," Harold maintained. Percy handled the financial side, negotiating huge loans, acquiring, selling, and swapping properties with a sureness and finesse that won the respect of major banks and insurance companies. He was a witty, cultivated man who played contract bridge at a near-professional level. He understood the odds. Harold ran the construction side of the company. In his own words, "Percy was the financial genius, and he ran the show, but I was the builder, and we bought and built faster than anyone else." An impeccably dressed man who was physically larger than Percy, Harold jokingly told a *New Yorker* magazine reporter in 1972 that he had been in the building business for all of his sixty-seven years. "The way I learned the alphabet, B stands for bulldozer," he declared.

The Uris firm had a talent for marketing. The company offices became showrooms to demonstrate the advantages of humidity control, fluorescent lighting, movable partitions, matched wood paneling, built-in sliding drawers, and other features not always found in large commercial structures of the day. Prospective customers readily "stepped up" to these features, resulting in greater profit to the builder. Not all the Uris buildings were in Manhattan. In Philadelphia the firm put up one million square feet as part of the Penn Center Plaza. In the nation's capital they built the Washington Hilton Hotel; five of its twelve stories were underground to conform with local height restrictions.

Most of the Uris buildings were essentially big, efficient boxes, and the brothers were often criticized for the plainness of their designs. They replied that their policy was to create the greatest space at the lowest cost, and that they had succeeded in doing so. Harold maintained that the satisfaction of those working inside a building was more important than the opinions of passersby.

When Percy Uris died on 20 November 1971, Harold decided not to continue in business alone. In July 1973, in a declining market, he sold his and Percy's interest in the Uris Building Corporation to the National Kinney Corporation.

The brothers were active philanthropists. As early as 1956 they established the Uris Foundation, primarily to funnel grants to educational institutions, hospitals, and performing arts organizations. Each of the brothers' alma maters was a substantial beneficiary of their largesse. Cornell received funds in support of the renamed Uris Undergraduate Library, and between 1963 and 1973, Columbia received donations for a building to house the Graduate School of Business, as well as a swimming center in a new gymnasium. Both the Columbia and Cornell campuses contain Uris Halls. The Uris Wing of Lenox Hill Hospital received very considerable support, and in 1971 a major grant went to the Metropolitan Museum of Art for its Junior Museum and programs.

Among their many volunteer positions, Percy and Harold Uris served as trustees of Columbia and Cornell universities, respectively. Harold was also a trustee of the Federation of Jewish Philanthropies and the City Center for Music and Drama. In 1972 New York City mayor John V. Lindsay honored Harold Uris and his family for preserving "the preeminence of New York City as the financial, commercial, and cultural capital of the world." Harold Uris died of a heart ailment in St. Mary's Hospital in Palm Beach, Florida. His remains were cremated following a service at Temple Emanu-El in New York City.

★

B. H. Friedman, *Coming Close* (1982), is called fiction but provides much data about the Uris family (particularly Percy) and the firm's business culture. Its author, Percy Uris's nephew, was an executive at Uris Buildings Corporation until he resigned to write full-time. W. Parker Chase, *New York 1932: The Wonder City* (1983), gives brief descriptions and photos of One University Place, the St. Moritz Hotel, and the Buckingham Hotel. Articles

include "Builder," *New Yorker* (2 Dec. 1972); "The $2 Billion Building Boom," *Fortune* (Feb. 1960); "Harold Uris Recollects with Pride," *New York Times* (9 Nov. 1981); and *Business Week* (19 Nov. 1960). Harold Uris's obituary is in the *New York Times* (29 Mar. 1982).

FRANK VOS

VAN BROCKLIN, Norm(an) ("The Dutchman") (*b.* 15 March 1926 in Eagle Butte, South Dakota; *d.* 2 May 1983 in Monroe, Georgia), Hall of Fame football quarterback whose determined leadership, football intuition, and explosive temper also made him a controversial coach.

Van Brocklin was the eighth of the nine children of Mac and Ethel Van Brocklin, struggling farmers. The family moved to California in 1929, "when those awful winds blew all the dirt away," Norm later recalled. Mac Van Brocklin became a watchmaker. From the age of eleven, Norm had to earn his own money to pay for clothing and all other personal items. At Acalanes Union High School in Walnut Creek, California, just outside Oakland, he lettered in baseball, his first love, as well as basketball and football. He was more determined than athletic. "They timed me in the 100-yard dash," he later quipped, "by the calendar." Van Brocklin entered the U.S. Navy in 1943, after graduating from high school, and spent three years ingloriously "swabbing the deck and the ship's head" without seeing combat.

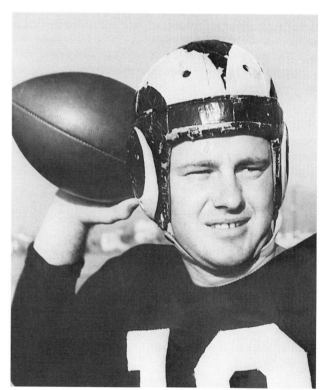

Norm Van Brocklin, 1951. UPI/CORBIS-BETTMANN

In 1946 Van Brocklin became the only member of his family to attend college when he used the GI Bill to enroll in the University of Oregon and joined the football team. At six feet, one inch and 200 pounds, he struggled "as a fifth-string back" in the Oregon Ducks' run-oriented, single-wing attack. He played only three minutes all season and failed to qualify for a letter. In 1947 Jim Aiken arrived from the University of Nevada and installed the T-formation. Van Brocklin became the conference's leading quarterback. In March 1947, he married his biology teacher, Gloria May Schiewe; they had six children. They lived in a campus trailer house "on short rations" and "didn't have the price of a weekend at Muscle Beach." Van Brocklin guided Oregon to a 9–1 record in 1948 and an appearance in the Cotton Bowl. He completed his B.S. degree in physical education in three years.

The Los Angeles Rams drafted Van Brocklin in 1949 as an $8,000 backup to their all-pro quarterback Bob Waterfield. On his first day in a Ram uniform, Van Brocklin completed 13 of 18 passes for 3 touchdowns. In his first major action of the season, he threw 4 touchdown passes as the Rams battered the Redskins 53–27. The hardworking quarterback supplemented his salary by selling real estate, running a beer distributorship, and working in a sawmill during the off-season. Van Brocklin quickly tired of carrying a clipboard, certain he could throw better than anyone the Rams had under contract. In 1950 he and Waterfield shared the quarterback job, with Van Brocklin finishing first and Waterfield second as the league's leading passers. Under Clark Shaughnessy and Joe Stydahar, the Rams were inventing the modern passing game. Van Brocklin and Waterfield threw to ends Tom Fears, Elroy "Crazy Legs" Hirsch, and Glenn Davis, a former halfback star for Army. Their 64 touchdowns and 466 points in a twelve-game schedule set new records, including 70-point and 65-point outpourings against Baltimore and Detroit in midseason. The Rams scored 4 touchdowns in their 1950 championship game, but for the second straight year, they were beaten by Cleveland, this time 30–28.

In 1951 Van Brocklin earned his master's degree in physical education from the University of Oregon. Also that year he edged out Waterfield as the Rams' starting quarterback, and he became the team's punter. He celebrated the promotion with a record 554 yards in passing against the New York Yankees. Backed by the "bull elephant" backfield of Dan Towler, Tank Younger, and Dick Hoerner and an improved defensive line, Van Brocklin led the Rams to their third consecutive conference title and again met the Cleveland Browns in the championship game. Stydahar started Waterfield in retaliation for Van Brocklin's refusal to call a running play in a late-season game against Green Bay. But with the title game on the line and the score tied, Van Brocklin was back on the field. He had Fears run down the sideline and cut across the middle on a spectacular 73-yard, fourth-quarter touchdown pass. The Rams won 24–17. It was the first major championship for a West Coast team, and it marked the beginning of the modern shape of professional football. The wire services, for the first time, named separate all-pro teams for offense and defense. Thanks to Van Brocklin and the Rams, the era of the two-way player was ending, and the era of the specialist was beginning.

Van Brocklin was an intense, unorthodox football general. He knew the book but preferred to trust his football instincts. "The time to throw the long one," he noted, "is when you're deep in your own territory, with second down and a yard to go." This conviction, based on intuition, opened up the National Football League (NFL) passing game and made the Rams the decade's dominant passing offense. If a play did not work, Van Brocklin would obstinately call it again until the offense got it right. One coach observed that Van Brocklin was a perfectionist at practice who "threw at a dime instead of a blanket." He had the strongest arm in the league, but tossed the touch pass so beautifully that Hirsch likened it to "reaching for a bubble." Van Brocklin challenged any teammate he sensed was dogging it and admitted to a tattoo on his left arm depicting a dagger imbedded in a skull. A bit bunchy around the middle, with thick arms and stubby hands, the persistent Dutchman three times became the NFL passing leader and was twice the league's top-rated punter. He passed for more than 2,000 yards in six seasons, played in ten professional bowl games, and guided Los Angeles to the championship game in 1955. But Sid Gillman, the new Rams coach, and the hot-tempered Van Brocklin had a highly publicized split over who was in control of the team's offense. Gillman wanted to call plays from the sidelines; Van Brocklin insisted on calling plays in the huddle. When Van Brocklin threatened to retire, Gillman traded him to the Philadelphia Eagles before the 1958 season. There, his leadership and precision passes to veterans Tommy McDonald, Pete Retzlaff, and Bobby Watson helped transform the Eagles from a 2–9–1 doormat to a respectable 7–5.

The 1960 season was the highlight of Van Brocklin's remarkable career. Philadelphia began the season with a 41–24 loss to the Cleveland Browns and a 2-point victory over the expansion Dallas Cowboys. This was the beginning of a surprising nine-game winning streak, in which Van Brocklin sparked five second-half comebacks. The 10–2 Eagles played Vince Lombardi's Green Bay Packers in the NFL championship game. The Eagles defense, led by Chuck Bednarik, Don Burroughs, and Maxie Baughan, overcame 2 Philadelphia fumbles deep inside their own territory, and Van Brocklin took over from there. He marched the Eagles downfield on 6 straight completions in a fourth-quarter drive that brought Philadelphia a 17–13 victory, the only championship game ever lost by Lombardi's Packers. It was Philadelphia's first championship in eleven years. Van Brocklin, at age thirty-four, was named the league's most valuable player. He retired from the game with 23,611 yards thrown and 173 touchdowns, and he had never missed a game because of injury. As one veteran sports writer observed, "What Ted Williams was to hitting, Norm Van Brocklin was to the forward pass."

Despite fears about Van Brocklin's legendary combative style, in 1961 the Minnesota Vikings expansion team made the Dutchman their first coach, the first time in the modern era that a pro football player had moved directly into a head coaching position. The Vikings won three games in their inaugural season, including a stunning 37–13 defeat of the Chicago Bears in their first league game. In his six years with the Vikings, Van Brocklin earned the grudging respect of critics for his patient, professorial molding of a young team and its talented quarterback, Fran Tarkenton. Center Mick Tingelhoff, linebacker Roy Winston, cornerback Ed Sharockman, defensive end Jim Marshall, tackle Grady Alderman, fullback Bill Brown, wide receiver Paul Flatley, and halfback Tommy Mason joined Tarkenton in giving Van Brocklin a core group of talented youngsters who responded well to his sweet talk and whiplash. Over time, however, Van Brocklin became estranged from some of his players, and he did not return in 1967.

After a one-year sabbatical, Van Brocklin returned to coaching, taking over the expansion Atlanta Falcons three games into the 1968 season. His seven seasons with the Falcons mirrored his early success with the Vikings, but when the 1974 team became mired in a losing streak, Van Brocklin's combative disposition and what some considered his imperial coaching style caused him to be fired. He had nurtured two expansion teams to NFL respectability and title contention and had only two bitter exits to show for it. His win-loss record in thirteen years as an NFL coach was 66–100, with 7 ties.

After he left coaching, Van Brocklin was football analyst for the Turner network, and his rough-hewn honesty made him a fan favorite. He lived in Social Circle, Georgia, where he was a pecan farmer. In 1979, the year of his induction into the Pro Football Hall of Fame, he assisted football coach Pepper Rodgers in restoring Georgia Tech to national prominence. Declining health led to two surgeries in 1979 and the end of his association with football after thirty-one remarkable and highly controversial years. He died of a heart attack in Monroe, Georgia, and was buried in Social Circle, Georgia.

Looking back at his career, Van Brocklin had once acknowledged that "football, unlike nuclear physics, is an inexact, often emotional science." But that did not stop him from inspiring an incontestable determination in his teams. His own determination and intuitive grasp of the game inspired the 1960 Eagles and the expansion Vikings and Falcons to play well above their anticipated abilities.

★

Vertical files on Van Brocklin's life and career are in the Pro Football Hall of Fame in Canton, Ohio, and the front offices of the St. Louis Rams, the Philadelphia Eagles, the Minnesota Vikings, and the Atlanta Falcons. Van Brocklin's playing and coaching philosophy are described in Norm Van Brocklin, *Norm Van Brocklin's Football Book: Passing, Punting, Quarterbacking* (1961), written with Hugh Brown.

Biographical pieces include Dave Anderson, *Great Quarterbacks of the NFL* (1965); Murray Olderman, *The Pro Quarterback* (1966); George Sullivan, *The Gamemakers: Pro Football's Great Quarterbacks—From Baugh to Namath* (1971); Murray Chass, "Norm Van Brocklin," in Lud Duroska, ed., *Great Pro Quarterbacks* (1974); Richard Rainbolt, *Football's Clever Quarterbacks* (1975); John D. McCallum, *Pac-10 Football: The Rose Bowl Conference* (1982); William A. Gudelunas, "Norman Van Brocklin," in David L. Porter, ed., *Biographical Dictionary of American Sports: Football* (1987); Myron J. Smith, Jr., *Professional Football: The Official Pro Football Hall of Fame Bibliography* (1993); Ralph Hickok, *A Who's Who of Sports Champions* (1995); Tex Maule, "The Dutchman Had a Feeling," *Sports Illustrated* (28 Nov. 1953); Harry T. Paxton, "Norm Van Brocklin: The NFL's Most Outspoken Coach," *Saturday Evening Post* (27 Oct. 1962); and Tex Maule and M. L. Sharnik, "The Dutchman Is Half an Inch Away," *Sports Illustrated* (13 Sept. 1965). His playing records are summarized in David S. Neft et al., *The Sports Encyclopedia: Pro Football* (1974). His coaching record is analyzed in David S. Neft, Richard M. Cohen, and Richard Korch, *The Sports Encyclopedia: Pro Football, the Modern Era, 1960–1992* (1993). Obituaries are in the *Los Angeles Times* and *New York Times* (both 3 May 1983).

BRUCE J. EVENSEN

VANDERBILT, William Henry (*b.* 24 November 1901 in New York City; *d.* 14 April 1981 in Williamstown, Massachusetts), politician, businessman, and philanthropist who served as governor of Rhode Island when the state's first civil service law was enacted.

Vanderbilt was a great-great-grandson of Commodore Cornelius Vanderbilt, who began the family transportation fortune by establishing ferry, river and transatlantic steamship, and railroad lines. William was the only child of Alfred Gwynne Vanderbilt, president of the National Horse Show Association, and Ellen Tuck French, who was active in civic affairs and a member of the Republican National Committee from Rhode Island from 1930 to 1944. His parents were divorced in 1908; his mother, after winning a $10 million divorce settlement and custody of William, moved to Harbourview, her family's home in Newport, Rhode Is-

William Henry Vanderbilt, c. 1925. COURTESY OF THE RHODE ISLAND HISTORICAL SOCIETY, #RHI (X3) 3083

land. His father remarried in 1911 and had two additional sons before he died on 7 May 1915 on the ocean liner *Lusitania,* which was torpedoed by Germans. Vanderbilt attended St. George's Preparatory School in Middletown, Rhode Island, from 1913 until his graduation in 1917. During World War I he served as a midshipman in the Naval Coast Defense and on the destroyer USS *Evans* from April 1917 through September 1919. While on the *Evans,* he met Paul FitzSimons, who married his mother on 3 April 1919. Vanderbilt was the best man at their wedding. After the war he attended Princeton University in the fall of 1919, then the Evans School in Mesa, Arizona, from 1919 to 1921.

At age twenty-one Vanderbilt began to control his inheritance of $5 million and his family's Oakland Farm in Portsmouth, Rhode Island. He ran Oakland Farm as a working farm raising poultry and used it as his residence until 1946.

On 1 November 1923 Vanderbilt married Emily O'Neil Davies at Grace Episcopal Church in New York City. They had one child and were divorced in 1927; he received custody of his daughter. Vanderbilt married Anne Gordon Colby on 27 December 1929 at her parents' home in North

Orange, New Jersey. They had three children and were divorced in 1969.

Vanderbilt began his business career in 1922 with the United States Trust Company in New York City. From 1923 to 1924 he worked as a bank messenger, runner, and student in the bond school of Lee, Higginson, and Company of Boston, Massachusetts. He completed management training as a boxcar detective (searching for missing railroad cars) for the New York Central Railroad from 1924 to 1925.

On 3 October 1925 Vanderbilt organized the Automotive Transportation Company, to own and control his bus, freight, and ferry holdings. He decided that buses could fill a niche moving people and freight short distances outside large cities and between small cities and towns that were not served by railroads and trolleys. By 1930 he was running the largest nonrailroad passenger transportation system in New England. He operated all his bus companies under the name The Short Line. In 1931 he set up the Short Line, Inc., to run his New England routes. In May 1944 he sold all his shares to the company treasury.

In 1928 Vanderbilt was elected as a Republican to the Rhode Island state senate from Portsmouth and served from 1929 to 1935. During his first term he was a member of the Committee on the Judiciary and chair of the Committee on Fisheries. He was one of his party's leaders during his second and third terms, serving as chairman of the Committee on Rules and Orders, chairman of the Committee on Finance, and president pro tempore of the senate. At times he demonstrated an independent streak, announcing that he would not be bound by the decisions of the party caucus. Although nominated for reelection by the Portsmouth Republican Town Committee in 1934, he declined, citing his wife's ill health.

Opposed by party leaders who did not think they could control him, Vanderbilt made an unsuccessful bid for the Republican nomination for governor of Rhode Island in 1936. Nominated by acclamation at a state GOP convention two years later, he pledged to end graft and corruption, run the government impartially and fairly, create a merit-based civil service, reform election laws, secure life tenure for state superior and supreme court justices, and ban the practice of dual-office-holding by members of the Rhode Island General Assembly who also sat on state boards and commissions. On 8 November 1938, he led a statewide sweep: Republicans captured all general offices, both seats in the U.S. House of Representatives, and the state senate and house. His victory reflected a split in the Rhode Island Democratic party between Governor Robert E. Quinn and Walter E. O'Hara, who led a third-party challenge for governor.

In 1935 the Democrats had substantially increased the appointment power of the Rhode Island governor, and Vanderbilt was the first Republican to benefit from that reform. He proposed and pushed through the General Assembly a merit-based civil service for state employees, and discovered that the major opposition was from state GOP leaders. He used a radio address to rally support. The legislature authorized a reorganization of state government that enabled him to abolish some boards and commissions and cut at least 800 jobs from the state payroll. Reduced spending permitted him to balance the budget and submit a budget more than $1 million below that of his predecessor.

Vanderbilt, however, did not get everything he wanted from the Republican legislature. He failed to obtain life tenure for members of the judiciary or a ban on dual-office-holding. He also appointed or retained Democrats in office, sought out those not active in politics for some jobs, and irritated GOP leaders who did not receive the patronage they expected.

In 1939 the General Assembly created a joint committee to investigate voter fraud in the 1938 election. When the governor was told the following year that there were no funds to pay the committee's expenses to investigate Pawtucket and Central Falls, he offered to pay for the investigation himself. The legislature responded by funding the committee.

A more serious incident occurred when Vanderbilt secretly hired and personally paid Frank B. Bielaski's Seabord Bureau, a New York City detective agency, to assist the state attorney general office, in its investigation of voter fraud. During the investigation some private detectives installed telephone taps on the lines of Pawtucket mayor Thomas P. McCoy and Attorney General Louis V. Jackvony. Vanderbilt denied knowledge of the taps, but it led to an investigation by U.S. attorney J. Howard McGrath, who at the end of his investigation announced that the taps violated no existing federal laws and that Vanderbilt had in fact hired and paid the Seabord Bureau.

Vanderbilt was defeated for reelection in 1940 by McGrath. The phone taps were not the only issue that cost him the election. It was a Democratic year: Franklin D. Roosevelt was elected president for a third time, and the Democrats captured all the state general offices, both houses of the General Assembly, a seat in the U.S. Senate, and both seats in the U.S. House of Representatives. State Republican leaders did little to help his reelection bid.

Following his defeat, Vanderbilt, who held a commission in the navy reserve, applied for active duty. Appointed a lieutenant commander, he was sent to Panama in June 1941, where he served as an intelligence officer. In December 1941 he was ordered to New York City, where he worked in the Office of the Coordinator of Information, which moved to Washington, D.C., in May 1942 and became the Office of Strategic Services (OSS). In the OSS he served as executive officer for Special Operations, second in com-

mand of the branch that trained and sent three- to five-person teams behind enemy lines to conduct sabotage. Vanderbilt was promoted to commander in March 1943 and was posted to San Francisco in August 1943. He joined Admiral Chester W. Nimitz's staff in May 1944 as a civil affairs officer in charge of organizing military governments in Allied-occupied islands in the Pacific. He was promoted to captain in November 1944 and placed on inactive duty in June 1945.

In 1939, during his first year as governor, Vanderbilt had bought Cricket Creek Farm in Williamstown, Massachusetts, to serve as a weekend retreat and vacation home. It was a working farm and in 1948 became his legal residence. In December 1951 he and his brother, Alfred Gwynne Vanderbilt, Jr., bought a 35,000-acre cattle ranch in Charlotte County, Florida.

Leaving Rhode Island marked the end of Vanderbilt's elective political career. In 1945 he declared that he had no interest in running either for the U.S. Senate or for governor, and he was critical of the national Republican party because it continued to oppose the New Deal without offering any alternatives. Noting that he voted for President Roosevelt in 1944, he suggested that state GOP leaders would not support him if they knew his views. He supported Harold Stassen for the 1948 Republican presidential nomination, and Dwight D. Eisenhower for the 1952 nomination but switched his support to Democratic nominee Adlai E. Stevenson during the 1952 campaign. After that he supported the Democrats and by 1964 conceded that he was himself a Democrat.

In addition to farming, real estate, and politics, Vanderbilt actively managed his family's investments. In 1947, he was elected to the board of directors of the New York Central Railroad, founded by Cornelius Vanderbilt. He served until 1954, when a stock proxy fight ousted the railroad's management. In 1955 he helped establish the Monte Marine Laboratory in Placida, Florida, and was a director there from 1955 to 1981. The laboratory investigated problems such as red tide and conducted research on sharks. He was appointed chairman of the Board of Visitors of the U.S. Naval Academy in 1963 and served until 1965. He was a trustee of Vanderbilt University, Nashville, Tennessee, from 1963 to 1981. On 18 January 1970 Vanderbilt married Helen Cummings Cook of Williamstown, Massachusetts.

Vanderbilt established the South Forty Corporation in 1969, and was its president and a director until 1981. It was a nonprofit organization that sponsored programs to rehabilitate prisoners in New York and Massachusetts. His programs encouraged inmates to seek education and training while in prison and provided assistance in finding employment and housing once they had been released. In October 1978 Vanderbilt bought the Five Corners Grocery Store and Exxon Station in South Williamstown, Massachusetts, because he did not want a fast-food chain to buy and close them. He worked in the grocery store and gas station with his wife for the rest of his life. Vanderbilt was diagnosed with lung cancer on his birthday in 1980 and died five months later. He was buried in South Williamstown.

Vanderbilt was described as a dark-haired, square-chinned, blue-eyed individual who was quiet not boisterous. He was wealthy and never pretended otherwise, but he used his wealth for philanthropic as well as business and political activities. He seemed to thrive on hard work, driving his farm tractors and buses or staying up all night reviewing the state budget. He was politically independent, appointing Democrats, the unaffiliated, and his Republican supporters to public office. He was perhaps too independent for state GOP leaders, but he recognized this and drifted from the Republican party after World War II.

★

Vanderbilt's papers, 1936–1941, chiefly concerned with his term as governor of Rhode Island, are located in Special Collections in the University of Rhode Island Library, Kingston, Rhode Island. The Special Collections/University Archives in the Jean and Alexander Heard Library of Vanderbilt University, Nashville, Tennessee, also has a limited collection of his papers. Dorothy Kelly MacDowell, *Commodore Vanderbilt and His Family: A Biographical Account of the Descendants of Cornelius and Sophia Johnson Vanderbilt* (1989), contains a biographical sketch; Duane Lockard, *New England State Politics* (1959), puts his administration in historical context; and Rhode Island, State Bureau of Information, *The Book of Rhode Island: An Illustrated Description of the Advantages and Opportunities of the State of Rhode Island* (1930), contains a biographical sketch of his early life. Thomas E. Murphy, "Rhode Island's Vanderbilt," *Current History* 51 (Oct. 1939): 50–52, 61, and S. J. Woolf, "A Vanderbilt Says, 'The Public Be Served,'" *New York Times Magazine* (6 Aug. 1939), contain information from his first year as governor. *The Providence Journal,* the major newspaper in Rhode Island, is essential for information on his career and is indexed in the "Rhode Island Index," created and maintained by the staff of the Providence Public Library, Providence, Rhode Island. Obituaries are in *Providence Journal, New York Times,* and *Boston Globe* (all 16 Apr. 1981).

WILLIAM A. HASENFUS

VanDerZee, James Augustus Joseph (*b.* 29 June 1886 in Lenox, Massachusetts; *d.* 15 May 1983 in Washington, D.C.), photographer of twentieth-century Harlem society.

VanDerZee was one of six children born to John VanDerZee and Susan Egberts VanDerZee, skilled servants of wealthy residents of a local resort, including former president Ulysses S. Grant. From childhood James VanDerZee showed a deep absorption in imagery. As a teenager, he

James VanDerZee, Self-Portrait, *c.* 1920. PHOTOGRAPHER JAMES VANDERZEE. COPYRIGHT © BY DONNA MUSSENDEN VANDERZEE.

earned his first camera by selling ladies' sachet powder; he honed his photographic skills by taking pictures of family members and summer residents of the resort. After leaving school in 1900, VanDerZee worked as a waiter at various resorts. In 1905 he and a brother joined their father, who had gone to New York City to begin a new job. As the family divided over the decision to move there, VanDerZee worked as a waiter and elevator operator and lived in a boardinghouse at Twenty-fourth Street and Seventh Avenue in the Tenderloin, a black neighborhood. Marriage to Kate L. Brown in 1907 and the birth of a daughter that year prompted a temporary move to Brown's hometown in Phoebus, Virginia, near Norfolk. There, VanDerZee renewed his interest in photography, creating images of the Whittier Academy, where he took classes in music, and of Slabtown, a black community founded by escaped slaves. VanDerZee worked at the Chamberlin, a famous resort.

Chafing under Virginia segregation, VanDerZee and his family returned to New York City and moved into an apartment at 138th Street near Lenox Avenue in Harlem, a burgeoning black neighborhood in upper Manhattan. He worked as a waiter and elevator operator because of his wife's opposition to his opening a photography studio. A second child was born in 1908 but died within a year.

VanDerZee began working as a photographer's assistant in Newark, New Jersey, in 1911 and began a career as a portraitist with images of Blanche Powell, daughter of the Reverend Adam Clayton Powell, Sr. His marriage broke up in 1916 over his desire to continue his photography, a form of employment Kate did not regard as promising. Next, VanDerZee met and wooed Gaynella Greenlee, a German-Spanish woman. As neither was divorced, James and Gaynella opened a photography studio in 1917 using the fiction that he was her employee. To avoid further controversy she passed as a light-skinned African American. They married within a year following the opening of the studio, after VanDerZee obtained a divorce and Gaynella's husband died.

Their union and the shop, the Guarantee Photo Studio (later the GGG Photo Studio), located at 109 West 135th Street, were both successes. His World War I images of warbound soldiers and, later, returning veterans, were cornerstones to local fame. Soon, VanDerZee was photographing families, fraternal organizations, women's clubs, social groups, funerary portraits, cab drivers for their license pictures, and Harlem street scenes. His portrait methods were often derived from celebrity magazine images. Backdrops evoked an air of gentility and prosperous warmth. VanDerZee became skilled at manipulating a negative to improve the appearance of the subject. He also excelled at photojournalism; his archive of images of Marcus Garvey's Universal Negro Improvement Association is unsurpassed. His daughter Rachel died in 1927.

By the mid-1930s the Great Depression was cutting down on his business. It did not fail, however, despite massive unemployment and poverty in Harlem. The wedding photos he took in this period show an ostentatious expense and demonstrate his mastery of photographic technique. During World War II, VanDerZee ensured prosperity by continuing to take license photos of cab drivers as well as photos of security guards and small tradesmen. Autopsy photos proved another consistent source of income. Also, many soldiers wanted their photos taken. In March 1943 Gaynella and he began renting a twelve-room brownstone at 272 Lenox Avenue, where they resided, had their studio, and ran a boardinghouse; two years later they purchased the property.

VanDerZee's business declined after the end of World War II, partially because of the rise of inexpensive snapshots, the gradual movement of the black middle class out of Harlem, and the fact that his style remained mired in older eras. VanDerZee tried photographic restoration to raise money; Gaynella and he also took out additional mortgages on their property. By the early 1960s they were broke, their business was exhausted, and foreclosure seemed imminent. Into this deteriorating situation came photographic researcher Reginald McGhee, who was collecting material for a Metropolitan Museum of Art exhibit called *Harlem on My Mind*. McGhee quickly realized the potential of VanDerZee's archives of thousands of images. Despite opposition from black artists who derided the inclusion of photographs, McGhee made VanDerZee's work central to the exhibition, which opened in January 1969, and to the accompanying book. Further controversy arose over the perception of anti-Semitism in the book's introduction. VanDerZee was not part of the rancor, and despite the uproar the show was a major success and broadened VanDerZee's fame.

In 1969 McGhee and VanDerZee established the James VanDerZee Institute, which sponsored exhibits of his work and published two monographs, *The World of James VanDerZee* (1969) and *James VanDerZee* (1973). VanDerZee also found a collector's market for his photographs, selling them for a few hundred dollars apiece. Still, he and Gaynella, having been evicted from 272 Lenox Avenue, lived largely on welfare payments in a squalid apartment. Gaynella's mental health collapsed and she was an invalid when she died in 1976. To raise money VanDerZee collaborated with artist Camille Billops on *The Harlem Book of the Dead* (1978) and charged $50 to portrait sitters happy to have their pictures taken by VanDerZee. In 1977 the VanDerZee Institute collapsed in acrimony as the photographer blamed McGhee for his financial troubles.

In June 1978 VanDerZee married Donna Mussenden, a young gallery owner fascinated by his work. She rejuvenated his life, organized exhibitions, and started a celebrity portrait business, including such luminaries as Muhammad Ali, Bill Cosby, and Miles Davis. The majority of his collection was transferred to the Studio Museum in Harlem; despite a dispute between VanDerZee and the museum, it is now the major repository of his work. He died in Washington during a trip to receive an honorary doctorate of humane letters from Howard University. VanDerZee is important for his photographic chronicle of a half century of Harlem life, for his participation in the *Harlem on My Mind* exhibit, and for opening American eyes to the world of black photography.

★

Jim Haskins, *James VanDerZee: The Picture Takin' Man* (1991), is a full-length biography. Deborah Willis-Braitwaite, *VanDerZee: Photographer, 1886–1983* (1993), offers a fifty-page biography preceding a collection of VanDerZee's photographs. Reginald McGhee, comp., *The World of James VanDerZee: A Visual Record of Black Americans* (1969), has an interview with VanDerZee followed by photographs. Liliane De Cock and Reginald McGhee, eds., *James VanDerZee* (1973), is a collection of photographs preceded by a short introduction on his work.

GRAHAM RUSSELL HODGES

VAN NIEL, Cornelis Bernardus See Niel, Cornelis Bernardus van.

VARGAS, Alberto ("Varga") (*b.* 9 February 1896 in Arequipa, Peru; *d.* 30 December 1982 in Los Angeles, California), artist whose paintings of women for magazines became known as Varga Girls.

Vargas was the eldest of the six children of Max Vargas, a professional photographer, and Margarita Chávez, a housewife. His full name was Joaquín Alberto Vargas y Chávez. Although he was expected to follow in his father's footsteps as a photographer, his mother encouraged his artistic ventures from the age of seven. Max Vargas took Alberto and another son to Europe for their education in 1911.

He went to Zurich later in 1911 and began a formal apprenticeship at the Julien Photographic Studios in Geneva in 1915. In 1916 he moved to Sarony Court Photographers in London. World War I ended his formal training in Europe, and he sailed for New York in mid-1916. Fascinated by the beauty of American women, he defied his father's wish that he return to Peru. Remaining in New York, Vargas earned a living drawing hats, retouching photographs, and painting illustrations for newspapers and magazines.

Soon after arriving in New York, Vargas met Anna Mae Clift, a showgirl at the Greenwich Follies. She was the model for some of his paintings long before their marriage on 9 June 1930; they had no children.

Vargas's career advanced when he became the official

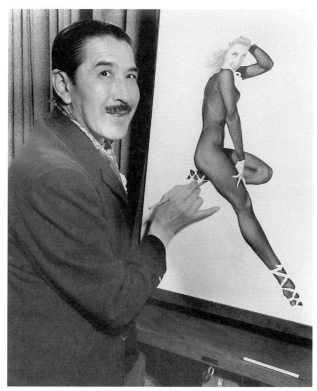

Alberto Vargas, 1946. UPI/CORBIS-BETTMANN

portrait painter for Florenz Ziegfeld in 1919. Remaining in that post for almost ten years, he painted posters of the stars of the *Follies*. In 1934 he moved to California at the request of Winfield Sheehan of the Fox Movie Studios, to paint portraits of that company's stars. His Hollywood work was varied and included set designs for several studios, especially Warner Brothers. His set for *Juarez* (1939) is considered his best movie work.

When Vargas joined some of his fellow studio artists in a union walkout in 1939, he was blacklisted by the studios. He then returned to New York, seeking work as an advertising illustrator. A friend sent him to the office of *Esquire* magazine.

Previously *Esquire* had used George Petty as an illustrator, and he had become famous for the Petty Girl layouts. However, David Smart, owner and publisher of *Esquire,* felt that Petty was asking for too much in a new contract and sought a replacement. In June 1940 he signed Vargas to a three-year contract.

Under terms of the contract, Vargas and his wife moved to Chicago, headquarters of *Esquire.* The first of his paintings, clothing added to an earlier nude, appeared in the October 1940 issue of *Esquire.* Smart felt that the term Varga Girl was not euphonious and convinced the artist to allow the name to be changed to Varga. The Varga Girls were youthful and healthy, usually scantily clad, with extremely long legs and slim figures.

With Petty due to leave *Esquire* as soon as his final one-year contract expired, the magazine went to great lengths promoting the work of its new artist. Smart proposed including a calendar with a dozen Vargas paintings in the December 1940 issue. Although only two of his paintings had appeared in print, this first calendar sold more than 300,000 copies by mail. During the *Esquire* years Vargas also worked on material for various advertisers. By the summer of 1941 *Esquire* offered a set of Varga playing cards.

American involvement in World War II increased Vargas's popularity. The Varga gatefolds epitomized the concept of the pinup. Even a cursory glance at Gary Valant's *Vintage Aircraft Nose Art* (1987) yields dozens of copies of Varga art on military aircraft. *Esquire* also printed an edition without advertising for servicemen; each of these included a different Varga Girl.

By 1943 Vargas's reputation as a popular artist rivaled that of Norman Rockwell, although their styles and subject matter were radically different. His notoriety increased when the Post Office threatened to cancel *Esquire*'s fourth-class mailing privileges, citing Vargas's work as one of the reasons. The resulting publicity, and *Esquire*'s victory in the case, increased the artist's reputation. He signed a contract to do a series of paintings for *American Weekly* and a major advertising campaign for Jergens beauty products.

Vargas's work schedule reached a peak in 1944. For *Esquire* alone, he produced forty-nine paintings. These were for the magazine's regular run, its military edition, the calendar, and the playing cards. He also began a number of paintings for personal satisfaction that were not finished until years later.

An artist rather than a businessman, Vargas signed a new contract in 1944 that would have required more work for probably less pay. The matter resulted in four years of litigation, beginning in the spring of 1946. Vargas's last paintings in *Esquire* appeared without a signature. When the suits and countersuits ended in 1950, the magazine was awarded exclusive rights to the name "Varga" and all products bearing it.

Vargas had little work for the rest of the 1940s and into the 1950s. After a few of his works appeared in the recently founded *Playboy* magazine, he signed a contract to produce work for that organization. Over the next two decades close to 200 of his paintings appeared in *Playboy*.

His wife, who had survived cancer surgery in 1950, died in 1974. The following year the *Chicago Tribune* planned a series of bicentennial paintings. When Americans who had served overseas in World War II were asked their memories, the Varga Girl was one of the two most frequent responses. Vargas's feeling of separation from Anna Mae can be seen in the painting that appeared in the *Tribune* on 7 December 1975. The painting is a back view, with the subject holding a purple heart, and is infused with a sense of poignancy and loss.

Although the fire was gone from his life, Vargas managed to contribute to a book on his career at the end of the 1970s. He continued painting and illustrated covers for record albums. Just after returning from a European tour, Vargas died of a stroke. His body was cremated.

Alberto Vargas built his reputation as an artist devoted to depicting female beauty, a fascination that lasted his entire life. The subject matter overshadows the quality of his work, which is meticulous and tasteful. Until the end he espoused a philosophy learned from Ziegfeld, who taught him the difference between nudity and a portrait with class and style. Because of his heavy work schedule, he became a master of technique, particularly with the airbrush.

Those who downgrade Vargas because of his subject matter often overlook his careful attention to details. Historians should find his work especially interesting because it reflects changing standards of beauty in America as seen in faces and hairstyles. Although his paintings focus on the female form, fashion historians can find much in his exquisite attention to the details of clothing and accessories.

★

Alberto Vargas and Reid Austin, *Vargas* (1978), is one of the more complete accounts of Vargas's life. *Playboy's Vargas Girls* (1972) contains seventy paintings, as they appeared in *Playboy*, from the first dozen years of the artist's association with that magazine. Reid S. Austin, *Varga* (1987), contains virtually all of the work produced for *Esquire*. *Vargas, 20s–50s* (1990) contains a number of his works not in other books. Tom Robothan, *Varga* (1995), contains selected works from the *Esquire* years, including a few of the calendar paintings.

ART BARBEAU

VARIPAPA, Andrew ("Andy") (*b.* 31 March 1891 in Carfizzi, Italy; *d.* 25 August 1984 in Huntington, New York), champion bowler and trick bowling shot performer whose exhibitions and instructional activities helped promote the sport of bowling during the first half of the twentieth century.

Varipapa was one of two sons born to Theodore and Constanza (Firco) Varipapa. His father, a farmer, died when he was three, and his mother subsequently married Jake Cardamone; they had five children. Varipapa came to the United States with his family in 1902 and grew up in Brooklyn, New York, where he attended Eastern District High School. At the age of thirteen he became interested in bowling partly because of the influence of his neighbor Jimmy Smith, later an American Bowling Congress All Events Champion. In 1914 he became a naturalized citizen.

Varipapa worked as a steelworker and machinist in the

Andy Varipapa. ARCHIVE PHOTOS

Brooklyn Navy Yard, while training as a professional fighter. He also played semiprofessional baseball under the name of Andy Bell. His fielding and hitting were good, and he had a tryout with the Brooklyn Dodgers. He might have had a chance of becoming a major league player except that his work schedule did not provide enough time for practice. In June 1917 he married Alice DeMartino; they had three children.

After World War I, Varipapa became especially active as a bowler. Phil Spinella put him on a major league team, which enabled him to take part in his first American Bowling Congress tournament as a member of Spinella's Orpheum team. At first, fellow members of this team did not think Varipapa was equal to their ability, but he soon proved them wrong and became one of the top bowlers of the New York City area. At this time he also became associated with Joe Falcaro, a leading bowler in the East and future match-game bowling champion, and the two were doubles partners during the next ten years, producing many local records. Their 1930 victory over a Philadelphia duo in a challenge match gained Varipapa national recognition. He also learned some of his trick shots from Falcaro.

By the mid-1930s Varipapa had developed trick-shot bowling to perfection. His repertoire of shots included a "boomerang ball" that moved down the lane in a skipping motion and returned to him, converting 4–6 and 7–9–10 leaves with confidence, and obtaining strikes while blindfolded or with his back to the pins. He also developed the conversion of the 7–10, 4–6, and 6–10 using two balls released at the same time from each hand. While performing these tricks, he tried to make them entertaining and colorful by constantly talking, boasting of his feats, or jumping in the air when making a strike. As a result of his skill at trick shots and his increasing fame as a bowler, he starred in the first movie short on bowling, *Strikes and Spares,* made by Pete Smith in 1934. The film earned an Oscar nomination. Varipapa went on to make twenty-six shorts, including *Set 'Em Up* (1939), which also starred Ned Day; he made more movies than any other bowler. Varipapa also presented numerous trick-shot exhibitions and served as one of the foremost bowling instructors from the 1930s onward. He was the first to make nationwide tours in these capacities and thus did much to promote bowling around the country at a time when the sport was just beginning to attract more people. He helped take bowling from the environment of makeshift facilities and launch it into today's more extensive recreational centers. Bowling was also kind to him; the income from exhibition and instructional classes enabled him to take a machinist course at Pratt Institute, while the earnings from movies permitted him to send his children to college.

Varipapa's trick-shooting activities, however, hindered his development as a competitive bowler; he had little time for tournaments and matches. Although he did win some local titles between 1928 and 1936, including three Metropolitan New York All Events titles, some of his peers viewed him more as a "vaudeville man," rather than as a serious bowler. He only came in third in the 1942 and 1945 National Match Game championships, but in 1946 at Chicago, at the age of fifty-five, he finally placed first in these championships, demonstrating competitive form and achieving the national title after a five-year quest. His 213.34 average for the sixty-four games played during the four-day finals was the second highest for this event. Varipapa repeated his victory the next year with a 210 average and became the first bowler to win successive national all-star (Match Game) championships. In both 1947 and 1948 he and his partner, Lou Campi, won the Bowling Proprietors Association of America doubles championship. These latter accomplishments helped him win the National Bowling Writers Association Bowler of the Year Award in 1948. Varipapa took part in the 1948 Match Game championships, finishing second.

Honors came to Varipapa in subsequent years. In 1951 he was chosen for the New York Hall of Fame, and in 1957 he was elected to the American Bowling Congress Hall of Fame. He received the John O. Martino Award in 1977 from the Bowling Writers Association of America for his distinguished contributions to bowling. In 1980 he was the first bowler to be inducted into the Italian-American Hall of Fame.

Varipapa had the physique of an athlete, weighing 180 pounds, standing five feet, six inches, and possessing a barrel chest and bowlegs. He had "bullwhip wrists" that helped him in his performance of trick shots. At the age of seventy-five, physical problems forced him to bowl with his left hand, but within three years his average as a southpaw was 180.

Varipapa was a colorful bowler, whose trick shots, movies, instructional classes, and travels within and outside the United States helped increase the popularity of bowling and improve its image. He was a friendly man with a strong sense of self-esteem who liked being in the limelight. He was a Roman Catholic and lived on Long Island from the 1940s on. He died of natural causes and is buried in Holy Rood Cemetery, Westbury, Long Island.

★

Frank Litsky, *Superstars* (1975), and Herman Weiskopf, *The Perfect Game: The World of Bowling* (1978), contain data on Varipapa's trick shots, as well as some brief biographical details and pictures. Pat McDonough, "You Can't Stop Andy," *Bowling* 14 (Sept. 1947): 8, presents information on Varipapa's early bowling career. "Handy Andy," *Newsweek* (23 Dec. 1946), briefly discusses Varipapa's 1946 all-star victory and presents a little data on his life and career. Ken Boylan, "Varipapa Elected to Hall of Fame," *Bowling* 23 (Apr. 1957): 26–28, also gives biographical data. There is a Hall of Fame profile for Varipapa that contains data on his bowling career, including titles won and other significant statistics in *Bowling* 36 (Sept. 1969): 126. George Iden, "I'll Never Forget," *Bowling* 44 (Aug. 1977): 6, gives an account of the author's experiences with Varipapa during a weeklong exhibition tour in 1945. Obituaries are in the *New York Times* (27 Aug. 1984) and *Bowling* 51 (Oct. 1984): 36.

ALLAN NELSON

VELDE, Harold Himmel (*b.* 1 April 1910 near Parkland, Illinois; *d.* 1 September 1985 in Sun City, Arizona), Republican congressman from Illinois who gained a national reputation during the 1950s as chairman of the House Committee on Un-American Activities.

One of three sons of Henry Jacob Velde, a farmer of German and East Frisian ancestry, and Laura Amanda (Himmel) Velde, Harold Velde was born on a farm in Tazewell County, Illinois. He played on the basketball and track teams at Manito High School and graduated in 1927. He then attended Bradley University in Peoria, Illinois, for two years before transferring to Northwestern University in Evanston, Illinois, where his student activities included base-

Harold Velde at his desk in Washington, D.C., 1954. UPI/CORBIS-BETTMANN

ball and playing in the school band. He earned a B.A. degree in 1931.

Velde began his professional life as a teacher and coach at the Hillsdale Community High School in Illinois. On 6 June 1931 he married Olive Pfander, with whom he had two children. He then entered the University of Illinois College of Law, where he received his LL.B. in 1937.

For five years Velde practiced law in Pekin, Illinois. In 1942 he volunteered for the Army Signal Corps, and from 1943 to 1946 he served as a special agent in the Federal Bureau of Investigation (FBI), where he was assigned to the sabotage and the counterespionage division. As an FBI agent, Velde gained the praise of a House Un-American Activities Committee investigator, who credited his "tenacity and firsthand knowledge" in the indictment of a former University of California physicist accused of passing atomic secrets to Russia.

After World War II, Velde returned to Illinois and was elected a county judge from Tazewell County in 1946. He served until 1949. Velde threw his hat into the congressional ring in 1948. Campaigning under the slogan "Get the Reds out of Washington and Washington out of the red," Velde demonstrated the anticommunist zealotry and fiscal conservatism that would mark his ensuing four terms in Washington. Winning election as a Republican to the Eighty-first Congress in 1948, Velde was eager to root out the communist subversives he felt were lurking in the halls of government, in the laboratories of the scientific community, and in the film studios of Hollywood.

Appointed to the House Un-American Activities Committee (HUAC) in January 1949, Velde served with fellow Republican Richard M. Nixon on the Democratically controlled committee. While HUAC had already become an acronym widely known to the American public during its Hollywood hearings in 1947 and the Whittaker Chambers–Alger Hiss hearings in 1948, it began its busiest and widest-ranging investigations when Velde became a member.

For Velde's next two terms, HUAC focused on the communist movement in labor unions and at the Radiation Laboratory at the University of California. While Velde felt his calling as an investigative congressman was useful to HUAC, his first two years on the committee saw few national headlines. He constantly agitated for wider-reaching inquiries, but was continually blocked by the Democratic majority on the committee.

In 1952, however, Republican Dwight D. Eisenhower won in a landslide presidential election and led his fellow Republicans to a majority in the House of Representatives. Velde was named chairman of HUAC in January 1953. Freed from the constraints placed on his investigative initiatives, Velde and his Republican majority looked to the coming session with fervor. Velde instituted HUAC subcommittee hearings throughout the country, returning to previously investigated turf such as Hollywood and labor unions. He was widely quoted during the Hollywood phase of the committee's work as saying that he was "certain that communist propaganda had been put into films—perhaps not in an open manner, but in the way the writers think if they are communists." He also led the committee into two new areas, education and religion. Hauling numerous professors, clergymen, and leaders of the National Council of the Churches of Christ before the committee, Velde attempted to prove that communists had infiltrated every aspect of American life.

Instead, Velde succeeded in making HUAC, and himself as chairman, look vindictive and overreaching. Few communists were discovered, and no dubious plots were uncovered. Frustrated, Velde saw a chance to bring back relevance and prominence to HUAC's investigations in November 1953, when he issued congressional subpoenas to former president Harry S. Truman, former secretary of state James Byrnes, and former attorney general Thomas C. Clark. Velde claimed that all three men had ties to Harry Dexter White, a government official accused of having communist ties. President Eisenhower made his displeasure with Velde's actions publicly known, and Truman, Byrnes, and Clark refused to heed the subpoena. Velde did not pursue the matter further.

In the 1954 elections, the Democrats regained the majority in Congress and Velde lost his chairmanship of HUAC. He served his last term in Congress unable to pursue the issue about which he cared most, the communist menace. He did not seek reelection in 1956. Velde's first wife, Olive Pfander, died in 1952. He married Dolores B. Harrington in 1954; they were divorced in 1956 and then remarried in 1957.

Velde returned to private law practice in Washington and then in Illinois. In 1969 he was named a regional counsel with the General Services Administration. Velde also served as a delegate to the 1981 White House Conference on Aging. After retiring from both politics and law, Velde moved to Sun City, Arizona, in 1974, where he died in Boswell Hospital at the age of seventy-five. He was cremated and his ashes interred in Pekin, Illinois.

Velde's chairmanship of the House Committee on Un-American Activities highlighted his career. Shadowing the efforts of the higher-profile Senate panel headed by Joseph McCarthy, Velde and HUAC served as chief instruments in the onset of the McCarthy era. Anticommunist fervor gripped the nation, and Velde ensured that HUAC would be at the forefront of this movement. The belief that no aspect of American life was safe from communist infiltration dominated Velde, HUAC, and much of the nation. From Hollywood to the clergy, Velde led HUAC into investigations that history has judged to be witch hunts. The tone set for the entirety of the ensuing McCarthy era was evident during the tenure of Velde's chairmanship.

★

While the number of sources documenting the House Un-American Activities Committee is plentiful, Robert K. Carr's *The House Committee on Un-American Activities: 1945–1950* (1952) and especially Walter Goodman's *The Committee: The Extraordinary Career of the House Committee on Un-American Activities* (1968) detail Velde's role more than other accounts. The journal *Pathfinder* 59, no. 17 (17 Dec. 1952), contains an account of Velde's tenacious investigative spirit, and Velde was quoted frequently during his tenure on HUAC in national newspapers; see, for example, the *New York Times* (7 May 1949 and 8 Nov. 1952). Obituaries are in the *New York Times* (6 Sept. 1985) and *Washington Post* (8 Sept. 1985).

IRVING DILLIARD
MARK E. SCHUSKY

VIDOR, King Wallis (*b.* 8 February 1894 in Galveston, Texas; *d.* 1 November 1982 in Paso Robles, California), pioneering filmmaker who won an honorary Academy Award for life achievement in 1979.

Vidor was a third-generation Texan. His grandfather, Charles Vidor, was a Hungarian immigrant who settled in

King Vidor. ARCHIVE PHOTOS

Galveston, Texas, in 1865 and worked as a cotton factor. His son, Charles Shelton Vidor, became a timber magnate who owned a forest in the Dominican Republic and sawmills in East Texas and Louisiana. Vidor, Texas, was named after the family in 1910. Charles Shelton Vidor married Kate Wallis, a homemaker, who was a descendant of Davy Crockett's wife, Elizabeth. They had one child in addition to King.

King Vidor attended grade school at Peacock Military Academy in San Antonio, Texas. He also attended Galveston High School and the Jacob Tome Institute in Port Deposit, Maryland, but he dropped out at sixteen to work as a ticket taker and substitute projectionist for a nickelodeon in Galveston.

He made his first film in 1913, using a friend's homemade camera to shoot a tropical storm in Galveston. He also filmed a troop parade in Houston, selling the footage to the Mutual Weekly newsreel, and made a two-reel comedy, *In Tow*. With Edward Sedgwick he formed the Hotex Motion Picture Company and made several comedy-adventures. In October 1914 Vidor went to New York City to find a distributor for Hotex. He made a deal with Sawyer, Inc., but the firm went bankrupt. Vidor also married Florence Arto in October 1914; they had one child.

Seeking better opportunities, the Vidors moved to Hollywood in 1915. Florence worked as an actress for Vitagraph, while Vidor worked as a prop boy, script clerk, and actor. He sold his first script, for *When It Rains, It Pours* (1916), to Vitagraph for $30. His first directing job came from Willis Brown, a former juvenile court judge who made films about saving wayward boys. Vidor directed ten two-reelers for him in 1918. Then he made his first feature, *The Turn in the Road* (1919), for Brentwood Films; it was his first national success.

After directing *The Jack-Knife Man* (1920) and *The Sky Pilot* (1921), Vidor built Vidor Village, a fifteen-acre studio on Santa Monica Boulevard in Hollywood, but financial problems forced its sale in January 1923. In 1922 Vidor directed Florence in three features and then gave up direction of a fourth, *Alice Adams* (1923), because their marriage was dissolving; they were divorced in 1924.

Working for Goldwyn studios, Vidor directed *Three Wise Fools* (1923), starring Eleanor Boardman. After directing other pictures for Metro-Goldwyn-Mayer (MGM), he made *The Big Parade* (1925), a thrilling World War I spectacle. The highest-grossing silent film ever made, this movie established MGM as well as Vidor. It employed a technique Vidor called "silent music," a visual rhythm created by editing the film according to the movement within the scene. In September 1926 Vidor married Boardman at Marion Davies's Beverly Hills home. The couple had two children.

Vidor then made *La Bohème* (1926), at the request of

Lillian Gish, and *The Crowd* (1928). During the advent of the "talkies," Vidor made *Hallelujah* (1929), an African American melodrama, and *The Champ* (1931), which received an Academy Award nomination for best picture. While directing *Bird of Paradise* (1932) for RKO, Vidor began an affair with Elizabeth Hill, his script clerk. He divorced Eleanor in 1933 and carried on a stormy relationship with Hill, who collaborated on his scripts. On 26 July 1937, after breaking off an announced engagement to Hollywood columnist Sheilah Graham, he married Hill.

During the early 1930s Vidor made a back-to-the-land trilogy, of which *Our Daily Bread* (1934) is the most prominent. Expressing populist sentiments, the film uses a powerfully choreographed ditch-digging sequence as a climax. After poor box-office returns, *Variety* ran the following headline in 1934: "Sticks Nix Hick Pix."

From 1935 to 1945 Vidor's work was troubled by production conflicts. After making *Stella Dallas* (1937), a feminist melodrama, he had a chance to finish *Gone with the Wind* (1939) but directed parts of *The Wizard of Oz* (1939) instead. Vidor's best film of this period, *Northwest Passage* (1940), was also his first color film. During World War II, Vidor made *An American Romance* (1944), a patriotic semi-documentary that was reedited by MGM, causing Vidor to leave the studio.

The postwar period saw a decline in Vidor's prestige. Seeking tranquillity, he bought the 1,200-acre Willow Creek Ranch, in Paso Robles, California, in 1946. He also directed parts of *Duel in the Sun* (1946), a Western that was bollixed up by producer David O. Selznick. In addition to *The Fountainhead* (1949), based on the Ayn Rand novel and starring Gary Cooper, he made film noir melodramas like *Beyond the Forest* (1949) and *Ruby Gentry* (1952) and directed an underappreciated Western, *Man Without a Star* (1955).

Vidor's last two features were *War and Peace* (1956) and *Solomon and Sheba* (1959), epic costume dramas that now seem dull or pretentious. During the 1960s he turned to sixteen-millimeter filmmaking, creating *Truth and Illusion: An Introduction to Metaphysics* (1964), a twenty-five-minute exploration of aesthetics, metaphysics, ontology, and film. He then examined the imagery of painter Andrew Wyeth in the forty-minute *Metaphor* (1980).

In 1969 Vidor began working with the cinema department at the University of Southern California as artist-in-residence. He published a book, *On Film Making* (1972), and wrapped up his career by acting in James Toback's *Love and Money* (1982). Vidor was a squarely built man with heavy jowls, who usually had a lively, affable look in his eyes. He enjoyed the fruits of his Hollywood success, traveling and spending time on his ranch. Vidor, who was sympathetic to Christian Science throughout his life, died of congestive heart failure at his ranch.

Vidor's career spanned the development of the Hollywood film industry. A master of composing shots and choreographing action, he helped to create the classic Hollywood style. Known as a dependable, talented director, he received the Christopher Award, the D. W. Griffith Award, and the Outstanding Achievement Award from the Directors Guild of America, all in 1957; the Golden Thistle Award at the Edinburgh Film Festival in 1964; and the Academy Award in 1979. All told, Vidor acted in three or more productions, wrote at least fifteen scripts, produced fifteen features, and directed fifty-six films.

★

King Vidor's unpublished scripts, correspondence, and writings are on deposit in the Special Collections at the University of Southern California in Los Angeles. A smaller group of papers is on deposit at the University of California at Los Angeles. King Vidor, *A Tree Is a Tree* (1953), offers an autobiographical look at his early career. King Vidor, *On Film Making* (1972), is an autobiographical view of Vidor's films and approaches to filmmaking. John Baxter, *King Vidor* (1976), is a dated but still useful full-length biography. Nancy Dowd and David Shepard, *King Vidor* (1988), is a book-length interview with Vidor; it contains details not available elsewhere. Raymond Durgnat and Scott Simmon, *King Vidor, American* (1988), is an accurate overview of Vidor's life and insightful analysis of his films. Sidney D. Kirkpatrick, *A Cast of Killers* (1986), discusses Vidor's solution of a 1922 Hollywood murder case; it also offers some biographical information. Robert Lang, *American Film Melodrama: Griffith, Vidor, Minnelli* (1989), contains a worthwhile discussion of Vidor's melodramas. An obituary is in the *New York Times* (2 Nov. 1982).

SETH BOVEY

VINSON, Carl (*b.* 18 November 1883 near Milledgeville, Georgia; *d.* 1 June 1981 in Milledgeville, Georgia), politician who, as a longtime member of the U.S. House of Representatives, was one of the most influential members of Congress in creating a formidable military establishment prior to World War II and expanding it in the subsequent cold war era.

Born on a farm to Edward Story Vinson and Annie Morris Vinson, Carl was one of seven children. While he was still a toddler, the family moved into Milledgeville so that the children could have better access to schools. Edward Vinson continued to run the family farm, providing his wife and children with a simple lifestyle. As a boy, Carl Vinson was a natural storyteller, a diligent student, and an energetic worker whose jobs included drugstore soda jerk and newspaper delivery boy.

Vinson's secondary education was completed at Georgia Military College in Milledgeville. In 1900 he entered the law school of Mercer University in Macon, Georgia. Upon

Carl Vinson. ARCHIVE PHOTOS

his graduation in 1902 he returned to Milledgeville and became a law partner with Edward Hines, a local county judge who headed a small firm. Because business was limited, Vinson sought and won an appointment in 1904 as Baldwin county court solicitor. Four years later he was elected to the Georgia General Assembly; in 1911 and 1912 he served as speaker pro tempore.

Like virtually all elected officials in the Deep South of that era, Vinson was a Democrat. He lost his bid for a third term in the assembly in 1912, and with his eyes on the U.S. House of Representatives, Vinson bided his time by securing an appointment in 1913 as a county judge. The following year, he won a special election as U.S. congressman from the Tenth District, replacing Thomas W. Hardwick, who resigned. On 3 November 1914, with Woodrow Wilson serving in the White House and the United States edging toward involvement in World War I, Vinson was sworn in as the youngest member of the House.

Although representing a landlocked district, Vinson was deeply interested in the United States Navy and national defense issues; his first speech on the floor of the House emphasized the centrality of defense policies. In 1917 he obtained an appointment to the House Naval Affairs Committee. Because members of Congress with little seniority had minimal power, it could have taken years for Vinson to become a truly influential figure in national politics. However, during his first seven years on the committee, eight of its Democratic members retired, died, or were defeated for reelection. By 1923 Vinson was the ranking Democrat on the committee; by 1932 he was its chairman. For all but four of the following forty-two years, he chaired that committee or its successor, the House Armed Services Committee, which was created in 1947. Those four years were rare periods when Republicans held majorities in the House, following the elections of 1946 and 1952. On 6 April 1921 Vinson married Mary Green McGregor; they had no children.

Like most southern Democrats serving in the Congress during the early and middle periods of the twentieth century, Vinson faced no serious opposition from Republicans and little competition from Democrats for his seat. Since he gained seniority early in his career and served for many decades, Vinson's political influence was predictable, though the way he carried out his congressional duties was not. Holding office during two world wars and during all or part of two "limited wars" (Korea and Vietnam) in the cold war years, Vinson saw firsthand the rise of the modern presidency, beginning with Franklin D. Roosevelt's administration. While congressional deference to presidential leadership on many issues, especially those concerning international affairs, was common, Vinson was self-assured of his ability to understand and shape defense policies, and exerted an extraordinary amount of control on the legislative process in this area.

The significance of Vinson's career can be seen by examining the political roots of the United States' military capabilities from the 1920s through the 1960s. Vinson served as the only Democratic congressman on the President's Aircraft Board (known as the Morrow Board), a nine-person committee appointed by President Calvin Coolidge in 1925 to examine the nation's military aviation capabilities. Vinson authored a number of the board's eventual proposals. This followed the highly publicized charges by Brigadier General William ("Billy") Mitchell that such defenses were scandalously inadequate, charges that led to Mitchell's being court-martialed. The board recommended a number of pieces of legislation (all enacted into law) that reformed and improved the management and extent of the nation's air defenses. One such law created the Army Air Corps.

In the 1930s, chairing the Naval Affairs Committee, Vinson was a fierce advocate of building up the sea and air capabilities of the navy. In President Roosevelt, a former assistant secretary of the navy, Vinson found a sympathetic ally. In 1940 and 1941 Vinson urged naval leaders to prepare for an expansion of air and sea capabilities while simultaneously pushing the necessary legislation through Congress, quite an accomplishment at a time when the country was generally isolationist in outlook. Historians credit Vinson with building up the navy to the extent that the 1941 Japanese attack on Pearl Harbor was survivable.

In the post–World War II era, which quickly became the cold war period, Vinson fought against those (including Presidents Harry S. Truman and Dwight D. Eisenhower) who favored cutbacks in manpower or armaments for the U.S. Army, Navy, Air Force, and Marines Corps, which challenged the perception of Vinson, who was chidingly referred to at times as "admiral," as someone who looked out for the interests of the navy exclusively. In fact, the fiscally conservative Vinson was notorious among military leaders for his willingness to reduce or increase expenditures in the budgets of any of the military services. In committee hearings, he rarely showed deference to those generals or admirals who testified. He was known to congressional colleagues as "Uncle Carl" and the "Swamp Fox" for his wily political skills. Outside of Capitol Hill, Vinson rarely sought publicity. Many members of Congress with less seniority than he received far more coverage in the press. Few Americans knew, for example, that Vinson (as Armed Services chairman) was one of a small number of congressional overseers of the secretive Central Intelligence Agency in the 1940s, 1950s, and 1960s.

In 1964 Vinson announced that he would retire at year's end to live in Georgia (he owned a 600-acre plantation just outside Milledgeville in addition to a house in town). He wanted "to wear out, not rust out," he said. Four years later, President Lyndon Johnson honored him with a White House party celebrating his eighty-fifth birthday. Said Johnson (who served under Vinson on the Naval Affairs Committee), "Uncle Carl was my chairman, my tutor, and my friend." On 15 March 1980 the ninety-six-year-old Vinson became the first living American to have a United States naval ship—an aircraft carrier—named for him.

Vinson died of heart disease in Milledgeville, thirty-one years after the death of his wife. He was buried in Milledgeville after a ceremony attended by a large congressional delegation that included his grandnephew, Senator Sam Nunn of Georgia, who subsequently emulated Vinson by chairing the Senate's Armed Services Committee from 1987 through 1994.

★

No biography of Vinson has been published, nor is one likely. Much to the frustration of archivists and historians, Vinson's congressional papers seem not to have been preserved. Two good journalistic profiles are Russell Baker, "Again Vinson Mounts the Ramparts," *New York Times Magazine* (4 May 1958), and Louis R. Stockstill, "Backstage Boss of the Pentagon," *Army Navy Air Force Journal* 98, no. 25 (1961): 1; 22–28. Tributes paid to Vinson upon his retirement are included in U.S. Eighty-eighth Congress, second session, *Tributes in the House of Representatives to Carl Vinson, Representative from Georgia, October 2, 1964* (1965). Susan Landrum, "Carl Vinson: A Study in Military Preparedness" (M.A. thesis, Emory University, 1968), looks at Vinson's role in the nation's military defense. A modern historical work that recognizes Vinson's importance in shaping naval affairs is Michael T. Isenberg, *Shield of the Republic: The United States Navy in an Era of Cold War and Violent Peace* (1993). An obituary is in the *New York Times* (2 June 1981).

DAVID M. BARRETT

VOORHIS, Horace Jeremiah ("Jerry") (*b.* 6 April 1901 in Ottawa, Kansas; *d.* 11 September 1984 in Claremont, California), educator and congressman remembered for losing a reelection bid against Richard M. Nixon in a bitter contest marred by red-baiting and distortions of the incumbent's record.

Voorhis's father, Charles Brown Voorhis, was a wealthy businessman; his mother, Ella Ward (Smith) Voorhis, was a homemaker. An only child, Voorhis attended public schools in Kansas, Colorado, Oklahoma, Missouri, and Michigan as his father established new enterprises. He

Jerry Voorhis. REPRODUCED FROM THE COLLECTIONS OF THE LIBRARY OF CONGRESS

graduated Phi Beta Kappa from Yale College in 1923 and promptly became a foreign representative in Germany for the Young Men's Christian Association (YMCA). A religious man, Voorhis was throughout his life a lay reader in the Episcopal Church. He worked as a cowboy in Wyoming and on an auto assembly line in Charlotte, North Carolina. In 1924 he married Alice Louise Livingston. They had three children.

Voorhis taught school at Allendale Farm School in Lake Villa, Illinois, in the 1925–1926 academic year, and the following year he became head of a cottage at the Home for Boys in Laramie, Wyoming. In 1928 he opened the Voorhis School for Boys in San Dimas, California, where his charges learned mechanical arts and "the fundamentals of Christian citizenship." He was headmaster for ten years, while earning an M.A. degree in education at Claremont College in 1928. In 1938 he gave the Voorhis school to the state of California, which converted it into a branch of the state university. Voorhis taught labor history at Pomona College between 1930 and 1935 and was active for a time in the Socialist party.

Voorhis entered politics in 1934, when he lost a race for the California state assembly as a Democratic candidate. In 1936 he ran for Congress as a Democrat. Questioned about his past Socialist party registration, Voorhis explained that "Mr. Roosevelt has made it possible for me to be a Democrat with a clear conscience." He was elected by 8,589 votes in what was the predominantly Republican Twelfth District, which encompassed Whittier and other suburban areas outside of Los Angeles. He was able to retain his seat despite gerrymandering by the Republican state legislature after the 1940 census.

Voorhis was one of the most liberal members of Congress. In 1938 he attacked the House Committee on Un-American Activities, also known as the Dies Committee, for making irresponsible charges and smearing people unfairly for political advantage. He urged that the committee be disbanded, thus earning the enmity of the Republican right wing. In 1939 the Speaker of the House put him on the committee, hoping that Voorhis would moderate its strident tone, which he did in its 1940 report. His major piece of legislation was the Voorhis Act of 1940, requiring the registration of foreign-controlled political organizations whose purpose was to establish, control, conduct, seize, or overthrow a democratic government by force or threat of force. He also called for the deportation of members of organizations directed by foreign governments. These measures were aimed primarily at front organizations for Nazi Germany and were considered preparedness measures for U.S. involvement in World War II. They were also aimed at the Communist Party of the USA, which never registered under the Voorhis Act.

Congressman Voorhis took the side of unions in labor-management issues. In 1945, when Representative Frances Case proposed a bill providing for a thirty-day cooling-off period before any walkouts, judicial injunctions against strikes (despite the protections of the Norris–La Guardia Labor Relations Act), a prohibition against organized boycotts, union liability for breach of employment contracts, and denial of National Labor Relations Board coverage to foremen and supervisory personnel, Voorhis offered a much milder substitute, which was rejected by the House, 101–183. President Harry S. Truman vetoed the Case bill and was sustained by the Democratic Congress, although the Republican-controlled Congress that followed passed the Taft-Hartley Act with similar provisions. Voorhis was voted hardest-working legislator by other members of the House in 1945, and in 1946 he was voted the member of Congress with the greatest integrity by the Washington press corps.

In 1946 Voorhis faced Richard M. Nixon, who had been recruited by a committee of prominent local Republicans to win the seat back from the Democrats. Nixon's strategy, developed by campaign manager Murray Chotiner, was to refer to Voorhis as a "former registered Socialist," to claim that Voorhis was associated with left-wing groups, to criticize Voorhis's liberal voting record, and to claim that his legislative career paralleled that of Vito Marcantonio, a representative from New York who was a member of the American Labor party and who was allied with the communists in New York City. The Nixon campaign claimed that Voorhis had the backing of CIO-PAC, labor's political campaign organization, referred to by the Nixon campaign as an organization "with . . . communist principles." Nixon's slogan was "Had enough?" Voorhis denied having CIO-PAC support, and in fact he had not been endorsed by the group. The California CIO had refused to back Voorhis because he was not far enough to the left. As for the parallel with Marcantonio, both their voting records were similar to the voting patterns of about 100 liberal Democrats.

The crucial event in the campaign was a debate between the two candidates on 13 September 1946 in Pasadena, a Republican stronghold. Nearly 1,000 people attended the debate, sponsored by the Independent Voters of South Pasadena, at the South Pasadena–San Marino High School auditorium. Before the event began, handouts had been distributed among the crowd, declaring that Voorhis "votes straight down the line for the socialization of our country." During the debate, Nixon claimed that the Los Angeles chapter of the National Citizens Political Action Committee, and by extension the communists in the CIO, some of whose directors served in both organizations, had endorsed Voorhis; Nixon asserted that the two organizations were "the same thing, virtually, when they have the same directors." Voorhis never recovered his composure from the allegation, from the booing and jeering of the crowd, and from the way Nixon played fast and loose with the facts. Most observers believed that Nixon won the debate, and his favorable press coverage thereafter kept Voorhis on the defensive.

Nixon also took out campaign ads in the local newspapers, stating that "Voorhis is a former registered Socialist and his voting record in Congress is more Socialistic and Communistic than Democratic." All Voorhis could do was put out an advertisement saying that "deception of the voter has no place in American politics." Nixon won 57 percent of the electorate and defeated Voorhis by 15,000 votes.

After leaving Congress, Voorhis became a registered lobbyist for the Cooperative League of the USA, which set up food cooperatives for low-income people. He served as executive director from 1947 to 1965 and as president until 1967. He was also active in consumer protection groups. He became chairman of the Co-Op Foundation in 1967. Voorhis entered a retirement home in Claremont, California, where he died of emphysema. He was buried in Claremont.

In a 1972 biography of Nixon, Voorhis claimed that the future president had smeared him and said that Nixon's accusing him of following the communist line had been "unworthy of a responsible politician." But Voorhis also blamed the defeat on himself, saying he had "let the country down" by not fighting harder and by underestimating his opponent's willingness to use dirty tricks to win.

★

Jerry Voorhis summarized his career in an autobiography, *Confessions of a Congressman* (1947). Voorhis's *The Strange Case of Richard Milhous Nixon* (1972) is a psychobiography of Nixon, in which Voorhis charges him with underhanded campaign tactics. Roger Morris, *Richard Milhous Nixon: The Rise of an American Politician* (1990), contains a thorough discussion of the Nixon campaign against Voorhis. An obituary is in the *New York Times* (12 Sept. 1984).

RICHARD M. PIOUS

W

WALKER, Edward Patrick ("Mickey"; "The Toy Bulldog") (*b.* 13 July 1901 in Elizabeth, New Jersey; *d.* 28 April 1981 in Freehold, New Jersey), boxer who held world welterweight and middleweight titles.

The first of the three children of Michael Patrick Walker, a bricklayer, and Elizabeth Higgins, Walker was raised in an Irish-American Catholic household. He showed a flair for fighting at an early age and earned the nickname Mickey because of his Irish pug nose. He attended Sacred Heart Grammar School until his expulsion in the eighth grade as a disciplinary problem. In 1916 he began training as an architect at George B. Post and Company in New York City, where he worked his way up to draftsman before he was fired in 1918 for flooring a coworker who had played a practical joke on him. During this period he also studied at the Mechanics Institute in New York City at night but left before earning a degree.

Too young to enlist when World War I began, Walker found work in Berley's Shipyard in Staten Island, New York. There he got into a fight with a professional boxer, Eddie McGill. Walker knocked out his opponent but was again fired for fighting. After another similar episode (and firing) at Moore's Shipyard in Elizabeth, New Jersey, he decided to become a professional boxer.

Walker's debut was a no-decision bout against Dominic Orsini in 1919. A string of victories followed, most by knockout. In 1921 he challenged the welterweight cham-

pion Jack Britton. The bout ended in a no-decision, but in a rematch on 1 November 1922 Walker defeated Britton to become welterweight champion. While training for a fight in 1922, Walker met Maude Kelly. They married in June 1923 and settled in suburban Rumson, New Jersey. They had two children. Despite his marriage, Walker remained a self-admitted hell-raiser with a fondness for liquor, philandering, and gambling.

Walker defended his title four times in 1923 and 1924. Boxing writer Francis Albertanti dubbed him the "Toy Bulldog" because of his aggressive and tenacious style. Walker epitomized the spirit of the Roaring Twenties, with his tough-guy stance and brawling ring technique. On 7 January 1925 Walker fought Mike McTigue for the light-heavyweight championship, but the bout ended in a no-decision. At the time, Walker weighed only 150 pounds and was the lightest man to fight for that title. On 2 July 1925 he fought Harry Greb for the middleweight title. Greb was a formidable opponent, the only man ever to defeat the future heavyweight king Gene Tunney. The match was a brutal affair, and Walker lost a fifteen-round decision. Later that night Walker met Greb in a Broadway nightclub. As they were leaving, Walker made a remark that angered Greb, and a second fight erupted on the street. According to Walker, he flattened Greb while the middleweight was taking off his jacket and so deserved the "win" in their sidewalk rematch.

On 20 May 1926 Walker lost his welterweight title to

Mickey Walker, *c.* 1930. HULTON-DEUTSCH COLLECTION/CORBIS

Pete Latzo in Scranton, Pennsylvania. But in December 1926, Walker won the middleweight championship in a ten-round decision over Theodore "Tiger" Flowers, who had won the title from Greb. In 1927 Walker traveled to England to defend his title against the British champion, Tommy Milligan. Upon learning that he was a 4–1 underdog, Walker and his manager, Jack "Doc" Kearns, who had once managed heavyweight champion Jack Dempsey, bet their entire purse on the outcome. They won more than $600,000 when Walker defeated Milligan with a knockout. In 1929 Walker again fought for the light-heavyweight title but lost on points to champion Tommy Loughran.

Aiming for larger purses, Walker relinquished his middleweight crown in 1931 to battle the heavyweights, even though he stood only five feet, seven inches and never weighed more than 170 pounds. That year Walker fought Jack Sharkey, a leading heavyweight contender, to a controversial draw. Also in 1931, Walker and his wife divorced. Three months later he married Clara Hellmers; they had one son. In 1932 Walker fought Max Schmeling, who had lost the heavyweight crown to Sharkey. By the end of the eighth round, Walker was so badly beaten and bloodied that Kearns refused to let him continue.

The high life had finally caught up with Walker, and he was through as a big-time boxer. In 1933 he made a last attempt to wrest the light-heavyweight crown from "Slapsie" Maxie Rosenbloom but lost on points. In 1935, after being stopped by the lightly regarded Eric Seelig, Walker finally hung up his gloves.

Walker had spent most of the millions he had earned, so he opened the Toy Bulldog, the first of his many saloons, in New York City. He and Clara separated in 1936 and divorced in 1939. Later that year he married Eleanor Marvil, and they had a son. Walker also worked as a nightclub entertainer, a columnist for the *Police Gazette,* and a salesman for a liquor distributor. He eventually stopped drinking, discovered art, and became a primitive painter of some renown. He participated in many exhibitions and had a one-man show at the American Contemporary Artists Gallery in New York City in 1945 and another at the Associated American Artists Gallery in 1955. In 1946 Walker divorced Eleanor to remarry his second wife, Clara, who again divorced him in 1948. Later that year he remarried his first wife, Maude, to be close to his daughter, Pat. They divorced in 1955. Finally, on 21 January 1956 Walker married Martha Chudy Gallagher.

Walker was diagnosed with Parkinson's disease in 1974 and spent his declining years in various nursing homes. He died of Parkinson's in Freehold Area Hospital in Freehold, New Jersey. His remains were cremated.

Mickey Walker's illustrious ring career spanned seventeen years. His final record was 163 bouts, 94 won, 19 lost, 4 draws, 1 no-contest, 45 no-decisions, and 61 knockouts. He held both the welterweight title (1922–1926) and the middleweight title (1926–1931), and he defended each several times. He also fought many of the best light-heavyweights and heavyweights of his time, usually acquitting himself well. In an age when boxing's popularity was at its zenith, Walker more than held his own with such fistic luminaries as Dempsey, Tunney, and Greb. His rollicking lifestyle and bruising fists ensured his popularity with the fans. In 1955 he was elected to the Boxing Hall of Fame and in 1990 to the International Boxing Hall of Fame.

★

Mickey Walker, *The Will to Conquer* (1953), covers Walker's life in and out of the ring. Mickey Walker with Joe Reichler, *Mickey Walker: The Toy Bulldog and His Times* (1961), includes more details and is more up-to-date than the earlier volume. Peter Heller, *In This Corner . . . ! Forty World Champions Tell Their Stories* (1973), contains a reminiscence by Walker. An obituary is in the *New York Times* (29 Apr. 1981).

MICHAEL MCLEAN

WALKER, Fred ("Dixie") (*b.* 24 September 1910 in Villa Rica, Georgia; *d.* 17 May 1982 in Birmingham, Alabama), baseball player whose eighteen-year major league career was highlighted by his nine seasons as a Brooklyn Dodger (1939–1947); acclaimed by the fans at Ebbets Field as "The

People's Cherce," he was one of the most popular players in franchise history.

Walker shared the nickname "Dixie" with his father, Ewart Gladstone Walker, who was a pitcher for the Washington Senators from 1909 to 1912. His mother, Flossie Vaughn Walker, was a homemaker, and Fred had one brother, Harry.

Walker began his professional baseball career at age twelve, earning $5 per game playing for a Calvert, Alabama, semiprofessional team coached by his father. After he had batted .401 for Greenville, South Carolina, in the South Atlantic League in 1930, the New York Yankees bought his contract in midseason for a then-record $25,000. Envisioned by the Yankees as the successor to Babe Ruth, Walker batted .350 for the Newark Bears of the International League. Although he was a pull hitter with fine defensive skills and a strong throwing arm, he did not fulfill his promise, largely as a result of career-threatening injuries. A shoulder injury sustained while crashing into a fence impaired his throwing. Although corrected by surgery, the injury recurred on a slide into second base. Following the arrival of Joe DiMaggio, Yankee manager Joe McCarthy traded Walker to the Chicago White Sox for outfielder Gerald Holmes ("Gee") Walker.

At the conclusion of the 1937 season, Walker was traded to the Detroit Tigers, for whom he hit .308 in 1938 and

Fred ("Dixie") Walker, 1941. UPI/Corbis-Bettmann

.305 in forty-three games in 1939 before being traded to Brooklyn, where he hit his stride. He hit .280 in the sixty-one remaining games of the 1939 season, but his season batting average dipped under .300 only once in his next eight seasons as a Brooklyn Dodger (.290 in 1942). A career .306 batter, Walker won the National League batting title with a .357 average in 1944, and he led the league in RBIs with 124 in 1945. In 1944 the *Sporting News* named Walker to its Major League All-Star Team, and he represented the National League in four All-Star games (1943, 1944, 1946, and 1947). In 1943 and 1947 Walker was joined on the All-Star team by his brother, Harry ("The Hat"). The brothers had a composite lifetime batting average of .303, making them one of only six brother combinations in baseball history to surpass the .300 lifetime average.

In 1947, when the Dodgers broke baseball's color barrier by signing Jackie Robinson, Walker became a figure of some controversy. When it was announced that Robinson was going to be brought up from the minors, Walker wrote to Branch Rickey, the club president, asking to be traded. Walker acknowledged prior to his death that he had been put under pressure by people in Alabama, where he lived in the off season, not to play with Robinson. Toward the end of his life Walker denied being a ringleader in an attempt to prevent Robinson from playing for the Dodgers. He said he came to respect Robinson for the way he handled the abuse hurled at him and called him "as outstanding an athlete as I ever saw."

Following two years with the Pittsburgh Pirates, during which he hit .316 and .282, Walker managed teams for Atlanta, in the Southern Association (1950–1952); Houston, in the Texas League (1953–1954); and Rochester and Toronto, in the International League (1955–1956, 1957–1959). He was a coach for the St. Louis Cardinals (1953, 1955) and for the Milwaukee Braves (1963–1965). He continued in baseball as a scout for the Milwaukee Braves (1960–1962) and the Atlanta Braves (1966–1968) and as a batting instructor in the Los Angeles Dodgers organization (1968–1978).

In the Faber Rating System's category Best Player Born Each Year 1870–1958, Walker is best player born in 1910, and in the category Major League All-Star Teams by Decades, he joins Enos Slaughter and Ralph Kiner in the National League outfield for 1941–1950.

Walker married Estelle Shea in May 1936; they had five children. Walker died of cancer and was buried in Elmwood Cemetery in Birmingham, Alabama.

★

Stanley Frank, "Nobody Wanted Him but the Fans—Yes, It's Dixie Walker—Ask Any Brooklynite," *Saturday Evening Post* (14 Feb. 1942), and William B. Mead, *Even the Browns* (1978), provide information on Walker. Statistical works include C. C. Johnson Spink, Paul A. Rickart, and Clifford Kachline, comps., *The Sport-*

ing News Official Baseball Dope Book (1965); Larry Wigge, ed., *The Sporting News Official Baseball Guide* (1983); Charles F. Faber, comp., *Baseball Ratings: The All-Time Best Players at Each Position* (1985); David L. Porter, ed., *Biographical Dictionary of American Sports: Baseball* (1987); *The Baseball Encyclopedia,* 8th ed. (1990); and Tot Holmes, ed., *Dodgers Blue Book: 1890–1990* (1990). An obituary is in the *New York Times* (18 May 1982).

JAMES A. CASTAÑEDA

WALLACE, (William Roy) DeWitt (*b.* 12 November 1889 in Saint Paul, Minnesota; *d.* 30 March 1981 in Mount Kisco, New York), and **WALLACE, Lila (Bell) Acheson** (*b.* 25 December 1889 in Virden, Manitoba, Canada; *d.* 8 May 1984 in Mount Kisco, New York), cofounders of the *Reader's Digest,* a conservative, patriotic monthly of practical advice and moral uplift that reached tens of millions of readers worldwide, and distributors of billions of dollars to educational, civic, and cultural institutions throughout the United States.

Lila and DeWitt Wallace, *c.* 1965. ARCHIVE PHOTOS

Called Roy by his mother, Willie by his siblings, and, in adult life, Wally by his friends, DeWitt Wallace was one of seven children born to James T. Wallace and Janet Davis. His father was a professor of Greek and Old English at Macalester College, a small, nearly bankrupt Presbyterian school founded in Saint Paul in 1885. Named the college's president in 1894 during a major depression, James Wallace devoted most of his time and energy to keeping the institution afloat and often traveled about the country for months on end in search of funds and students. At those times his wife, a homemaker, and his children remained behind or lived with her parents in Ohio, where her father, a licensed lay Presbyterian preacher, was the librarian of Wooster College. Like her husband, who suffered bouts of depression, Janet Wallace was given to fits of emotional instability that sometimes required institutional care, so the children, with their mother ill and their father absent, were often thrown back on their own resources.

Young DeWitt was high-spirited, energetic and bright, difficult to control, and undeterred by his parents' religious and political conservatism. In later life, although nominally a Presbyterian, he was largely indifferent to formal religion but accepting of its moral constraints as essential to social order; he championed the "positive thinking" doctrines of religious popularizers like Norman Vincent Peale. As a youngster DeWitt embraced the rule that everyone contribute to the family's finances, and from his earliest years he proved himself imaginative in devising successful money-making schemes, such as raising chickens and selling the eggs. Enrolled in a private elementary school in Saint Paul, he skipped two grades, but at Macalester Academy, a private preparatory school, he quickly developed a reputation as a

cutup and earned a series of failing grades. In desperation, his father sent him off to Northfield, Massachusetts, for the strict discipline provided by Mount Hermon Boys' School, which was founded by evangelist Dwight L. Moody. Within three months, however, the seventeen-year-old Wallace and a friend were punished for a dormitory prank. They left the school, heading for San Francisco and a year of hard work in construction.

In 1907 he was admitted to Macalester College but, as in his prep school years, was indifferent to the academic demands of the classroom and concentrated instead on athletics and a boisterous social life. He withdrew from school in 1909, and after a summer of semiprofessional baseball with a team in Leeds, North Dakota (Wallace played second base), he clerked in his uncle's bank in Monte Vista, Colorado. Through the next year he whiled away the evening hours reading magazines and early on developed the habit of noting on index cards the most interesting facts he had discovered. He entered the University of California at Berkeley as a freshman in September 1910 and that Christmas accompanied Barclay Acheson, an old friend from Macalester, to the Acheson family home in Tacoma, Washington. There he met Lila Bell Acheson, the woman who would become his wife.

Lila was one of five children born to Thomas Davis Acheson and Mary Eliza Huston. At the time of her birth, her father was a student at the University of Manitoba, preparing for the Presbyterian ministry. Her mother was a homemaker. In the years following Thomas Acheson's ordination, the family moved through a succession of small-town parishes in North Dakota, Minnesota, Illinois, and Washington. Despite his limited cash income, they enjoyed a comfortable standard of living because the parishes provided decent housing, occasional live-in help, and other amenities. Lila Acheson attended public grammar schools in Marshall, Minnesota, and graduated from Lewistown (Illinois) Community High School in 1907. With funds her mother had inherited, she went first as an English major to Ward-Belmont College (a two-year institution) in Nashville, Tennessee, and then to the University of Oregon, where she graduated from the School of Social Services with a B.A. in 1911.

Her first job was teaching in a one-room Washington schoolhouse on Fox Island in Puget Sound (1911–1913). She taught English at a junior high school in Puyallup, Washington (1913–1915), and at the high school level in Eatonville (1915–1917). When World War I broke out, she left teaching to work for the Young Women's Christian Association (YWCA) as a supervisor of social workers who were helping newly hired young women adjust to the demands of wartime production. Sent to a DuPont munitions plant in Pompton Lakes, New Jersey, where a number of serious accidents had been caused by inexperienced and fatigued workers, the diminutive Lila Acheson (five feet, two inches tall and weighing perhaps 100 pounds) immediately took charge of thirty colleagues and dramatically improved working conditions, lowered the injury rate, and created a recreational program for employees that became a model for factories elsewhere in the country.

In 1918 the YWCA sent her to New Orleans, where she set up programs to improve working conditions for women in tobacco factories and cotton mills, winning over the mill owners in the bargain. By 1920 she was back in New York, working simultaneously for the Board of Home Missions of the Presbyterian Church, the YWCA, and the Inter-Church World Movement, ranging across the country to short-term assignments along the San Francisco waterfront, in Minnesota mining camps, and among migrant workers in New York State and New England. This would be her last long-term connection to organized religion. In later years she, like her husband, was a nonpracticing Presbyterian.

DeWitt Wallace, in the meantime, had left Berkeley at the end of his sophomore year in 1912. He never returned to school and in the years ahead was seldom excited by intellectual issues, but he had developed a lifelong interest in practical information that could be translated into career advancement or a better life. As in his Colorado days, he continued to read widely in magazines (books were too long) and keep notes of what he had read. From 1912 to 1916 he worked as a sales-letter writer for the Webb Publishing Company in Saint Paul, which specialized in self-help books for farmers. During that time, as part of his work for Webb, he discovered that the U.S. Department of Agriculture published dozens of free pamphlets on every aspect of farming and farm life. In 1916, using money borrowed from his employer, he compiled and printed a 128-page pamphlet, *Getting the Most Out of Farming,* that listed the hundreds of bulletins the government had available as well as bits of practical farm information he had gleaned from his own reading. Traveling through Minnesota, North Dakota, Montana, Oregon, and Washington, he sold 100,000 copies to banks and seed stores to offer their customers as premiums. At some point along the way he hit on the idea of publishing condensations of general magazine articles as a convenience for American readers who had little time for reading but a desire to find information that might improve their lives. The idea was put on hold, and he became a calendar salesman for Brown and Bigelow in Saint Paul.

Now fully grown, Wallace had a strong physical presence. At slightly over six feet, he radiated self-confidence and good health. Always trim, he moved with athletic grace even in his declining years and always appeared to be far younger than he really was. His friends thought him handsome. He had a ready wit and a lifelong penchant for practical jokes. He was a ferocious poker player and loved baseball and fast cars. All his life, especially after accumulating his great wealth, he remained remarkably modest and somewhat withdrawn on public occasions. His courtesy and kindness toward his employees at every level were legendary.

In April 1917 he enlisted in the U.S. Army and after a year volunteered for duty overseas. He was seriously wounded in the groin by an exploding shell during the Meuse-Argonne offensive in France on 29 September 1918. In the long months of recovery that followed at Aix-les Bains, Sergeant Wallace practiced condensing articles from magazines like *Scribner's* and *Saturday Evening Post.* Back in the United States in April 1919, he spent six months in the Minneapolis Public Library preparing the first edition of a magazine to be called *Reader's Digest.* Dated January 1920, the prototype contained thirty-one articles, one for each day of the month. They were taken from ten-year-old copies of popular magazines and selected, according to the cover, for their "enduring value and lasting interest." Condensed by as much as three-quarters of their original length, each article offered some kind of practical advice on matters like personal health or career advancement. Wallace printed several dozen copies and sent them to publishers across the United States, but the few who replied said the venture had no chance of success.

DeWitt spent the next year writing advertising copy for Westinghouse in Pittsburgh until he lost his job in the depressed economy of 1921. Determined to control his own business, he went to New York to publish the *Digest* on his own, having been encouraged to do so by Lila Acheson, with whom he had recently resumed correspondence. On 15 October 1921 the two were married by her brother Barclay, a Presbyterian minister, in Pleasantville, New York. In the weeks before the wedding, Wallace had sent out thousands of circulars to potential subscribers; on return from their honeymoon, the newlyweds found they had sold 1,500 subscriptions at three dollars a year each.

The 64-page first edition of the *Reader's Digest,* of which 5,000 copies were printed, appeared in February 1922. The magazine's offices were in a basement room at 1 Minetta Lane in Greenwich Village, and the Wallaces lived nearby at 76 Macdougal Street at Bleecker. The *Digest* was an almost immediate success; by year's end Wallace moved his operation to a rented garage and pony shed in Pleasantville, thirty miles north of New York City. Until then he and Lila had handled all the editorial, publishing, and mailing duties on their own, but now they added additional staff. By 1929 the publication had 216,190 subscribers and a gross income of $600,000 a year. In the next decade they doubled its size to 128 pages, added newsstand sales to their marketing strategy, paid for the articles they condensed, and after 1933 printed original articles they had commissioned or planted in leading magazines for later use in the *Digest.* In 1938 Wallace published the first British edition and made plans for Spanish and Portuguese editions to be sold in Europe and South America. In 1939, having outgrown all the available space in Pleasantville, the *Digest* offices were moved to Chappaqua, New York. There they were located on an eighty-acre estate, in a handsome, three-story, red-brick Georgian building. For sentimental reasons, the Wallaces maintained the magazine's mailing address in Pleasantville.

The design and the decoration of the new headquarters were overseen by Lila Wallace. The same was true of High Winds, the 100-acre estate the Wallaces now owned in Mount Kisco, New York.

Lila's name continued to appear on the *Digest* masthead as coeditor, but in reality she had little to do with editing or publishing the magazine after its first year, beyond the pointed suggestions she gave to her husband either in private or in sharply worded memos. Nonetheless, until her health declined she visited her office almost daily to carry out the duties she had adopted as her own, the first of which, as she saw it, was to provide her husband and his editors with a creative environment and to humanize the workplace for the *Reader's Digest* staff.

A gracious if demanding employer, she was especially attentive to the needs of her women employees, who made up the bulk of the noneditorial workforce. For many years *Digest* employees were given subsidized meals in the cafeteria and subsidized fares on the private buses the Wallaces operated to bring them to work from the small towns of Westchester and Putnam counties, where no public transportation was available. At her direction, generous medical and dental programs were provided at all levels of employment.

Conscious of her mother's delight in decorating the various Acheson homes with her own sketches and drawings, Lila Wallace kept the greater part of her priceless collection of French impressionist art on public display in the reception areas, corridors, cafeteria, and offices in the *Digest* headquarters, because, she said, she wanted to surround her employees with beauty. The pictures included important paintings by Cézanne, Corot, Degas, Manet, Pissarro, Rouault, Sisley, and Utrillo, as well as works by Braque, Chagall, Gauguin, Matisse, and Modigliani. A passionate gardener, she regularly placed fresh flowers throughout the *Digest* building, often in arrangements she herself made with blooms from her own gardens. (One of her final gifts to the Metropolitan Museum of Art in New York City was a fund to provide in perpetuity fresh-cut flowers daily in the entrance hall.)

In the years after World War II the *Reader's Digest*'s monthly circulation was the largest of any publication in the United States and remained so until the late 1970s, when it was surpassed by *TV Guide*. The magazine's success was a result of DeWitt Wallace's near-intuitive understanding of his audience and his unswerving adherence to the original editorial formula that joined articles of practical advice and moral uplift to political and social commentary. It was an effective though curious mix because featured articles on such topics as birth control and the dangers of smoking were often socially progressive, while the political viewpoint was unrelentingly right-wing and often regressive. The *Digest* gave unquestioned support to the Republican party, to free-market capitalism, and to anticommunism at home and abroad. It regularly featured articles on the dangers of big government as exemplified by the New Deal. It attacked trade unionism and public-welfare programs, suggesting that both were riddled with corruption and undermined the quality of American life. Because the magazine had no letters page and never ran retractions, opposing points of view were unacknowledged and unpublished.

By the early 1950s DeWitt Wallace had added condensed books, reference works, and recordings to the *Digest* enterprise. In April 1955 he accepted advertising for the first time in order to maintain the magazine's three-dollar annual subscription price. At its high point in 1972 the *Digest* claimed 100 million readers worldwide, 50 million of them in the United States, where one family in four was a *Digest* subscriber and 18 million copies were sold each month. Twelve million copies in thirty-seven editions and fifteen languages were sold in 162 countries overseas. (In February

1981, the year of DeWitt Wallace's death, the magazine added Hindi to its list of languages, bringing the total to sixteen.) In addition, the *Digest* each quarter sold as many as 2 million condensed books (featuring three or four best-selling titles per volume), along with millions of special-interest books, such as guides to home repair and medical reference books. Their contents were determined by extensive market testing of target audiences, a practice also used in compiling *Digest* collections of classical and popular music.

Beginning in the late 1930s, as the *Reader's Digest* operations expanded and more and more money flowed in, both DeWitt and Lila Wallace, who were childless, turned their attention to philanthropic projects. They both believed that wealth should be used wisely for the public good. Each of them pursued separate interests, she inclining toward art and cultural activities, he toward educational enterprises. Even after her death, the Lila Wallace/Reader's Digest Fund remained the largest private source of cultural grants in the nation and continued the support she had begun years earlier of local museums, music and dance schools, and community orchestras in small towns and cities across the United States. The DeWitt Wallace/Reader's Digest Fund underwrote programs for improving teaching in the public schools, expanding library services, especially in inner city and rural school districts, and providing after-school tutoring programs in poor neighborhoods. The fund gave stocks eventually worth $42 million to Spelman College in Atlanta in 1981. All of the Wallaces' gifts were made quietly, and a good number of them anonymously, without the fanfare that often accompanies corporate philanthropy. They were especially generous to the town of Mount Kisco, helping to finance park and hospital facilities and underwriting youth activities there and elsewhere in the New York Metropolitan area. DeWitt Wallace was an important benefactor of Macalester College, although he briefly withdrew his support in the late 1960s, when he believed the faculty and student body had become too radical and the college "too affluent." Lila Wallace gave substantial gifts to the University of Oregon, the Juilliard School of Music, and the Metropolitan Opera in New York.

In the months before DeWitt Wallace's death, seven so-called "conduit trusts" were established to channel about two-thirds of the Wallace estate (including Lila Wallace's share) to seven specific beneficiaries: Macalester College, Colonial Williamsburg, the Metropolitan Museum of Art, Lincoln Center for the Performing Arts, the Bronx Zoo, Sloan-Kettering Cancer Center, and an environmental group dedicated to preserving the Hudson Highlands in New York State. The conduit trusts (or support organizations) were designed to allow the estate to maintain control of the principal, assure the stability of the *Reader's Digest* organization, and satisfy the federal tax code with respect to charitable gifts, which in the case of the Wallace trusts were valued in excess of $3 billion in 1995. The separate Lila Wallace and DeWitt Wallace funds in 1994 had a combined value of nearly $2 billion.

DeWitt Wallace died at home of pneumonia three weeks after undergoing abdominal surgery at Columbia-Presbyterian Hospital in New York. Lila Acheson Wallace died at home of heart failure. Both Wallaces were cremated and their ashes strewn through the rose garden at High Winds. A subsequent buyer of the estate paved over the gardens to make a play area for his children in 1986.

★

The Wallace Family Papers (including photographs and letters of Lila Acheson) are at Macalester College, Saint Paul, Minnesota, where the archives also hold an unpublished biography of DeWitt Wallace by James Playsted Wood. DeWitt Wallace's papers and journals are held by the Wallace Estate and the Reader's Digest Foundation in Pleasantville, New York. The most satisfactory of the several published biographies is John Heidenry, *Theirs Was the Kingdom: Lila and DeWitt Wallace and the Story of the Reader's Digest* (1993). The Wallace legacy and what happened to it after their deaths is the subject of a former *Digest* editor, Peter Canning, in *American Dreamers: The Wallaces and Reader's Digest, An Insider's Story* (1996). The oldest of the critical evaluations of the magazine and its role in American life is John Bainbridge, *Little Wonder; or, The Reader's Digest and How It Grew* (1945). See also James Playsted Wood, *Of Lasting Interest: The Story of the Reader's Digest* (1958), and Samuel A. Schreiner, Jr., *The Condensed World of Reader's Digest* (1977). Charles Ferguson, a longtime associate of the Wallaces and a *Digest* editor, wrote an unpublished biography, "Unforgettable DeWitt Wallace," portions of which appeared in *Reader's Digest* (Feb. 1987). The *New York Times* ran obituaries of DeWitt Wallace (1 Apr. 1981) and Lila Acheson Wallace (9 May 1984).

ALLAN L. DAMON

WALLENSTEIN, Alfred Franz (*b.* 7 October 1898 in Chicago, Illinois; *d.* 7 February 1983 in New York City), one of the first American-born conductors to achieve national and international renown.

The son of Franz Albrecht von Wallenstein and Anna Klinger, both of Austrian-German ancestry, Wallenstein claimed that he was a direct descendant of Albrecht von Wallenstein, the famed German leader of Europe's Thirty Years' War in the seventeenth century. The Wallensteins moved from Chicago to Los Angeles when Alfred was a child. Both of his parents were amateur musicians. At the age of eight Alfred was asked to choose either a bicycle or a cello as a birthday gift. He chose the cello and was sent to take lessons with the mother of the jazz composer and arranger Ferde Grofé. He began to play professionally at age ten, performing in theater pit orchestras and accompanying silent films. At fifteen he toured with the Orpheum vaudeville circuit and was presented as "The Wonder Boy Cellist." He played with the San Francisco Symphony Orchestra in 1916 and in 1917 toured South and Central America with the dancer Anna Pavlova, playing the cello solo for her performances in *Swan Lake*. During the 1919 season he played with the Los Angeles Philharmonic and again toured South America, this time with the dancer Maud Allen.

In 1920 Wallenstein traveled to Leipzig to study cello with the German cellist and composer Julius Klengel. At the request of his father he also undertook medical studies at the University of Leipzig but soon found that music occupied all of his time. He returned to the United States in 1922 and was appointed principal cellist with the Chicago Symphony Orchestra (1923–1929) under the musical direction of Frederick Stock. Stock composed a cello concerto for him, which Wallenstein premiered on 25 January 1929. He also taught at the Chicago Musical College, where he met his wife, Virginia Wilson, who was a piano student; they were married on 10 May 1924. The couple had no children.

In 1929 Arturo Toscanini invited Wallenstein to become principal cellist of the New York Philharmonic. He left Chicago and played with the Philharmonic until 1936, when Toscanini resigned as the orchestra's conductor. Toscanini was very impressed with Wallenstein's musicianship and encouraged him to try conducting. In 1931 Wallenstein was asked to step in at the last minute and conduct a concert for the Mutual Broadcasting System's radio station WOR in New York City. In 1932 he appeared both as guest soloist and conductor at the Hollywood Bowl. In 1933 he formed the Wallenstein Sinfonietta for WOR and from 1935 to 1945 served as the station's music director. During his tenure he presented many works heard for the first time on American radio: a complete cycle of Bach cantatas, scheduled on the Sundays for which they were composed; cycles of Mozart piano concertos and Haydn symphonies; a series of Mozart operas; an American Opera Festival; and a significant number of works by contemporary composers. Wallenstein's creative radio programming was recognized in 1942 when he received the first George Peabody Award from the University of Georgia for "pioneering in a quiet way for good music and encouraging and originating various unique broadcasts."

In 1943 Wallenstein was appointed music director of the Los Angeles Philharmonic; he was the first American-born conductor of that group. He remained in this position until 1956 and also served as music director of the Hollywood Bowl from 1952 to 1956. Among his notable outreach activities was a series of young people's concerts for the Los Angeles public schools. In 1956 he led the Los Angeles

Alfred Wallenstein. AMERICAN STOCK/ARCHIVE PHOTOS

Philharmonic on a ten-week tour of Asia under the auspices of the U.S. State Department. Works by American composers were presented throughout this tour.

Wallenstein resigned from the Los Angeles Philharmonic after the 1956 tour. During the years that followed he appeared as a guest conductor with orchestras in the United States and abroad. He had made his operatic debut in 1951, conducting Beethoven's *Fidelio* with the San Francisco Opera. He served as music director of the Caramoor Festival in suburban Katonah, New York, from 1958 to 1961, and conducted the Symphony of the Air (formerly the NBC Symphony) in seven concerts in New York's Carnegie Hall during the 1961 season.

From 1968 to 1976 Wallenstein was a member of the conducting faculty of the Juilliard School in New York City. He was also involved with the Juilliard Repertory Project, which was sponsored by the U.S. Department of Education and was an effort to make high quality music available for teaching children. He gave his last public performance on 26 January 1979, at the age of 81, leading the Juilliard Orchestra in a program of works by Wagner, Beethoven, Dohnanyi, and Ravel in New York's Alice Tully Hall. He was found dead in his New York City apartment, at 200 East Sixty-sixth Street, by his housekeeper.

Wallenstein was a distinguished musician who did much to promote the works of contemporary American composers and bring classical music to the wider public.

★

Wallenstein's personal papers are not extant. The Alfred Wallenstein Collection, housed at the University of Maryland at College Park, contains the working library of radio station WOR from the 1920s to the 1950s, including sheet music and scores used for Wallenstein's performances as WOR's music director. Extensive chapters on Wallenstein are found in David Ewen, *Dictators of the Baton* (1943), and Hope Stoddard, *Symphony Conductors of the U.S.A.* (1957). Entries on Wallenstein are found in major music dictionaries and encyclopedias, including *Baker's Biographical Dictionary of Musicians,* 8th ed. (1992); *The New Grove Dictionary of American Music* (1986); and John Holmes, *Conductors on Record* (1982). An obituary by Allen Hughes appears in the *New York Times* (10 Feb. 1983). An oral history with Wallenstein concerning musical life in southern California in the 1930s and 1940s is housed at the California State University Library in Long Beach, California, as part of its Oral History of the Arts Archive.

JANE GOTTLIEB

WANER, Lloyd James ("Little Poison") (*b.* 16 March 1906 in Harrah, Oklahoma; *d.* 22 July 1982 in Oklahoma City, Oklahoma), baseball player and member of the National Baseball Hall of Fame, best known for his lifetime batting average of .316 during an eighteen-year major league career.

Lloyd Waner. NATIONAL BASEBALL HALL OF FAME LIBRARY, COOPERSTOWN, N.Y.

Lloyd was the son of Ora Lee Waner and Etta Lenora Beavers. Both parents were members of prosperous farming families that migrated from Germany to the Midwest and later to Oklahoma during the land rush of 1889. Lloyd was raised in a devoutly religious Methodist family. His father, a successful farmer, was asked to run for public office but declined. Lloyd graduated from McLoud High School in 1922 and then spent not quite three years at East Central State College in Ada, Oklahoma. He had two siblings, one of them an older brother, Paul, also a Hall of Fame baseball player.

At five feet, nine inches tall and 145 pounds, Lloyd was by no means a physically imposing player. But inspired by his father, a semiprofessional player in the old Western League in 1898, and encouraged by Paul, Lloyd came to love the game of baseball. While growing up on the farm, Paul and Lloyd were constantly seen playing baseball. "We were always pitching to each other," Lloyd recalled, "be it one of those old rag-and-twine balls, or else corncobs. . . . We would break them in two and then soak them in water so they'd go farther when we hit them."

Lloyd, who batted left and threw right, dropped out of college to follow in his brother's footsteps. He signed a contract with the San Francisco Seals of the Pacific Coast League in 1925. When the Seals reneged on its verbal commitment to a $1,500 signing bonus, Lloyd was granted his release at the start of the 1926 season. He was immediately picked up by the Pittsburgh Pirates on Paul's recommendation. Playing for Columbia, South Carolina, of the South Atlantic League, Lloyd hit .345 and was named the league's most valuable player.

Lloyd came up to the major leagues in 1927, playing center field for the Pirates. His speed and quick batting wrists proved to be his greatest assets. He and Paul accumulated the most hits, 5,611, of any brother combination in major league history. They were only the second set of brothers to be inducted into the Hall of Fame, following George and Harry Wright, players of the late nineteenth century.

Lloyd was known as Little Poison and Paul as Big Poison. According to Lloyd, they acquired the nicknames as Pirate teammates when a sportswriter misunderstood a fan's foreign-accented shout about "the big person and the little person" directed at the brothers. Spanning the years 1927–1945, Lloyd totaled 2,459 hits with a lifetime batting average of .316. He played for the Pirates from 1927 through 1940. Hall of Famer and former New York Giants pitcher Carl Hubbell once said of the Waners that "they killed you with jillions of doubles and triples." Lloyd was also hard to strike out. Sportswriter Bob Broeg said of him: "He had a sharp batting eye, a chocked grip, and flying feet. Especially on the anthracite infield of the Pirates' home park, he would pound a pitch into the ground and often arch a high-hopping grounder for a hit if the ball didn't skip through the infield." Remarkably, he struck out an average of just once every forty-five times at bat. He holds the major league record for fewest strikeouts by an outfielder with 500 or more at bats. He struck out only eight times in 1933; in 1941 he went seventy-seven straight games before being struck out. In his nineteen seasons he fanned only 173 times, and his ratio of one strikeout per 44.9 at bats remains second best in major league history.

Because of his speed, Lloyd was also a gifted outfielder. He led the National League in putouts four times. In a 1935 doubleheader he set a record with eighteen putouts, but it was his hitting skills, marked by an unorthodox style, that set him apart. He rested the bat on his shoulders until the pitcher began his delivery. Once the ball was released, Lloyd would step into the pitch, often with a chopping motion. He led the National League in singles four times. In his first year with the Pirates he established a modern record with 198 singles, breaking Jack Tobins's modern record of 179 set in 1921. During his rookie year of 1927 he also collected 223 hits while batting .355. In the 1927 World Series, in which the Pirates lost four straight to Babe Ruth and the New York Yankees, Lloyd batted .400 with six hits.

In his first three seasons with the Pirates he hit .355, .335, and .353, and averaged 226 hits; in 1929 he led the league with twenty triples. He hit .362 in 260 times at bat in a 1930 season foreshortened due to appendicitis. In 1931 he returned to full strength with a .314 average and a league-leading 214 hits.

After the 1929 season the Waners held out for new contracts. Rumor had it that the New York Giants were willing to go as high as $225,000 for both players. The Pirate management, however, refused to allow them to sign with another team. Paul was offered a new contract, which he signed; Lloyd quickly followed. Lloyd remained a consistent hitter. Between 1932 and 1938 his batting average dipped below .300 only twice. From 1935 to 1938 he batted .309 or better. The 1935 season was marked by a twenty-three-game hitting streak, his best, and in 1938 he managed to hit in twenty-two straight games. In his first six seasons with the Pirates he hit over .300.

By 1939 the Pirates were interested in bringing up younger outfielders. Lloyd started in only ninety-two games that year, and forty-two the next year. In 1941 he was traded to the Boston Braves. "I can tell you the saddest day in my career," he stated. "It was the day in 1941 when the Pirates traded me to Boston for pitcher Nick Strincevich. I never thought I'd get over it." A month after the trade, Boston shipped him to the Cincinnati Reds, where he batted .256; for the season overall he hit .292. He then spent brief stints with the Phillies and Dodgers before finishing his career with the Pirates in 1945.

After retiring as a player, he worked as a Pirates scout from 1946 to 1949 and for the Baltimore Orioles in 1955. His post-baseball career included duties as a field clerk with the Oklahoma City government from 1950 until his retirement in 1967.

Waner never made more than $13,500 a season as a ballplayer. During his era players were wont to barnstorm during the off-season in order to pick up additional money. The Waners' success in the 1927 World Series, in which they outhit Babe Ruth and Lou Gehrig, .367 to .357, led to a certain degree of fame. After the series the brothers went on a national vaudeville tour, earning $2,000 a week. Lloyd recounted: "We were a vaudeville act. We traveled on the Loew's Orpheum circuit. We played ten weeks, going from St. Louis to Baltimore to New York . . . then on to Pittsburgh and San Francisco and Los Angeles. . . . We'd come out on the stage in our uniforms and play catch and tell some jokes about Babe Ruth and the World Series. . . . Then we played some music. You see, when we were going to school Paul took some lessons on the saxophone and I tried the violin. . . . So after the jokes and the running around on stage, the orchestra would strike up and we'd get our instruments and play along with them."

On 17 September 1929 Lloyd married Frances Mae Snyder of Pittsburgh. They had two children. The family resided in Pittsburgh until his baseball career ended and then relocated to Oklahoma City. In 1967 he was elected to the National Baseball Hall of Fame, fifteen years after Paul's enshrinement. With Paul, Lloyd helped popularize the game of baseball as the national pastime. Yet despite his achievement, recalled pitcher Waite Hoyt, Lloyd was "very self-effacing, quite modest, never given to boasting."

Lloyd Waner died at Oklahoma City's Presbyterian Hospital of complications related to emphysema. He was buried in Oklahoma City. Prior to his death he was fond of telling admirers, "The fans in Pittsburgh always looked forward to the 'Waner Act'—as leadoff man I'd get on base and Paul being cleanup hitter would score me."

★

A scrapbook collection and memorabilia on Waner's professional career are at the National Baseball Hall of Fame in Cooperstown, New York. A brief, unrewarding autobiographical account is in Donald Honig, *The October Heroes: Great World Series Games Remembered by the Men Who Played Them* (1970). Other books with information on Waner are Lee Allen, *The National League Story: The Official History* (1961); Harold Seymour, *Base-*

ball: The Early Years (1960); and Seymour's *Baseball: The Golden Age* (1971). Newspaper articles discussing Waner's career are Lee Allen, "Memory Can Play Some Tricks," *Cooperstown Corner* (8 May 1965), and Nick Seitz, "Modesty, Thy Name Is Lloyd Waner," *Sporting News* (18 Feb. 1967). Statistical accounts are in *The Baseball Encyclopedia* (1974) and Hy Turkin and S. C. Thompson, *Official Encyclopedia of Baseball* (3d ed., 1963). Obituaries are in the *New York Times* (23 July 1982) and the *St. Louis Post Dispatch* (26 July 1982). See also Bob Broeg, "'Poison' Brothers Would Have Loved the Turf," *St. Louis Post Dispatch* (26 July 1982).

CHARLES F. HOWLETT

WARD, John William (*b.* 21 December 1922 in Boston, Massachusetts; *d.* 3 August 1985 in New York City), historian and college president who attracted national attention for an act of civil disobedience.

Bill Ward, the son of John Joseph Ward, a physician, and Margaret Carrigan, grew up in the Dorchester and Brighton neighborhoods of Boston. He took pride in the fact that all four of his grandparents were Irish Americans. The

John William Ward. AMHERST COLLEGE ARCHIVES AND SPECIAL COLLECTIONS. BY PERMISSION OF THE TRUSTEES OF AMHERST COLLEGE.

youngest of the three siblings, he had two older sisters. He attended both parochial and public schools, notably Boston Public Latin School, where he captained the football team. Admitted to Harvard College in 1941, he enlisted in the Marine Corps in the fall of 1942, rising to first lieutenant and participating in the Allied landings in France. Back at Harvard in 1946, he was influenced by the teaching of F. O. Matthiessen and Perry Miller, and he shifted his studies from premedical to history and literature.

After receiving his B.A. from Harvard in 1947, Ward entered the University of Minnesota's pioneering program in American Studies and enjoyed the opportunity to study under Henry Nash Smith. Leo Marx soon joined the faculty. Smith, Marx, and Ward became linked as central figures in the myth and symbol school of American Studies. Ward's principal contribution to the movement was his doctoral dissertation, published as *Andrew Jackson: Symbol for an Age* (1955). Financial support for his advanced study came from the GI Bill and the secretarial work of his wife, Barbara Carnes. They were married on 19 March 1949 and had three sons. Ward earned his M.A. in 1950 and his Ph.D. in 1953.

In 1952 Ward became an instructor in English at Princeton University. After winning tenure, he shifted to the history department and became head of the program in American Civilization, but he concluded that American Studies was underappreciated at Princeton. During a year at the Center for Advanced Study in the Behavioral Sciences in Stanford, California (1963–1964), Ward was offered a professorship by Stanford University, but he accepted instead an offer from Amherst College, where Leo Marx was teaching. In 1967 and 1968 Ward held both a Fulbright lectureship at the University of Reading in Britain and a John Simon Guggenheim fellowship (his second, following one in 1956 and 1957). In 1969 he collected his essays into *Red, White, and Blue: Men, Books, and Ideas in American Culture.*

At Amherst, Ward's gregariousness and intense personal concern for others attracted both students and faculty to him. He was a popular and demanding teacher, and as student activism mounted, he proved gifted at communicating with protesters. Elected by his colleagues to a search committee for a new president, he found to his surprise that he was the choice. He took office as president of Amherst College in 1971.

In his first year as president the issue of social activism in the academic community was dramatized by his announcement on 10 May 1972, in reaction to President Nixon's escalation of the Vietnam War, that he would the next day join an ongoing series of sit-ins blocking the main entrance gate at Westover Air Force Base in Chicopee, near Amherst. Within hours the faculty voted to grant students joining protest activities extensions on their course deadlines. Ward was accompanied to the sit-in by some twenty faculty members and close to five hundred others—students from Amherst and other colleges in the area and by townspeople, including his wife. He was among those arrested and paid a fine for disturbing the peace. The incident was widely debated in the media. Ward insisted that he acted as an individual and not as the president of the college.

Although some students and faculty disagreed with his participation in the protests, there was more serious opposition among trustees and alumni. Ward rode out the storm, but not without leaving a residue of ill will. This rancor made it more difficult for him to lead the movement—strongly supported by faculty and students but resisted by many trustees and alumni—for admission of women as degree candidates. (Some women already attended as exchange students.) After much argument and data collection, the trustees finally decided to admit women to Amherst in 1975. Although favoring the change, Ward was more a mediator in the debate than an advocate of the shift.

Protests against racial inequalities, led by African-American students, intensified during Ward's presidency, resulting on two occasions in the seizure of academic buildings. Ward took the lead in steps to address the African-American students' criticisms. A black student culture center and a Black Studies department were developed and efforts to enroll African-American students accelerated. Ward did, however, oppose demands for Amherst College to divest its stock portfolio of companies doing business in apartheid-era South Africa.

Amherst's faculty had a tradition of assertiveness, and having one of their own elevated to the presidency did not please all Ward's colleagues. At faculty meetings Ward sometimes reacted angrily to criticisms. Strained relations hampered the adoption in 1976 of a modest curricular restructuring to replace the free elective system. The issue of faculty compensation (suffering in an era of stagflation) and allegations that Ward had not adequately consulted professors on budgetary matters led to a highly charged confrontation. This clash, along with an approaching fund drive that was in jeopardy because of Ward's shaky relations with alumni, influenced his decision to resign the presidency, effective in June 1979.

The resignation was made easier for Ward because, in May 1978, Governor Michael Dukakis had appointed him to chair the awkwardly named Special Commission Concerning State and County Buildings (later known as the Ward Commission), created by the state legislature to investigate corruption in public construction projects. Although the position was unpaid and intended to be part-time, Ward moved to Boston and threw himself into the undertaking. Backed by dedicated fellow commissioners, an able staff, and subpoena powers, Ward made headlines and supervised the writing of a twelve-volume report, released on 31 December 1980, that detailed bribes, kickbacks, conflicts of interest, and inordinate cost overruns. Throughout the hearings he sought to differentiate between family, ethnic, and neighborhood loyalties, which he valued, and illegal activities rationalized by those loyalties. The legislature adopted the commission's recommendations for a new office of inspector general and for alterations in the state's regulations for letting contracts.

During the commission's hearings Ward supported his family largely from his personal savings. He hoped to find work that would keep him in Boston, where he delighted in the return to his roots, but a desired appointment to head the Boston Chamber of Commerce failed to materialize. He taught briefly at Harvard's Kennedy School of Government, served for six months as a social science consultant for the American Express Company, and then in 1982 was appointed as president of the American Council of Learned Societies (ACLS), headquartered in New York City. Salient in the functions of the ACLS was the negotiation of scholarly exchange programs with communist nations, whose state-run academies had no close counterpart in the United States. His involvement with these exchange programs provided Ward with what he called a "free adult education course" and travel to the Soviet Union, China, and Hungary. In May 1985 he received the honorary degree Doctor of Humane Letters from the University of Minnesota.

Later that year, while staying at the Harvard Club in New York City, Ward committed suicide. Friends, some of whom had observed recent evidence of depression, now recalled a dark side that sometimes broke through his characteristic ebullience as well as his frequent references to irony and paradox. Indeed, his life included some striking paradoxes. He was a Marine Corps volunteer who joined in direct action to protest a war. He identified with both the tough spirit of city streets and the careful thought of scholars. He craved deep and widespread affection, but relished a fight. The contradiction between individual self-assertion and social obligation was not merely an area of study for Ward, but something of intense and troubling personal relevance.

Ward's principal influence was in the academic world. He advanced the emerging field of American Studies, and his analysis of a single historic person as a symbolic figure was widely imitated. His exploration of individualism, though it did not lead to the book he had long planned, reached a wide audience through his teaching, addresses, and articles. As president of Amherst College he added moral fervor and intellectual complexity to a major recasting of the institution's role, and despite the brevity of his tenure at the ACLS, he elevated its international stature and joined in easing cold war tensions. He relished the unpredictability of his career. Most surprising was his role in public life as chair of the Ward Commission. Although not as effective as he had hoped, it brought structural changes in state contract-letting and undercut the widespread attitude that corruption was inescapably part of "the system."

Physically vigorous, dark-haired, and long-chinned, Ward liked unfiltered cigarettes, a strong drink, and a good anecdote, especially if told by himself. Even his critics admitted the conviviality of this "blend of John F. Kennedy and Johnny Carson." Although quick to oppose any negative stereotyping of Roman Catholics, as an adult he never practiced the religion in which he was reared. His characteristic farewell "Keep the faith!" had a broader, humanistic referent. His body was cremated and the ashes scattered.

★

An extensive collection of clippings and addresses is in the John William Ward file in the Amherst College archives. A faculty colleague's perspective appears in William H. Pritchard, *English Papers: A Teaching Life* (1995). From the extensive press coverage, see especially "Books, Ideas, and Talk," *New Yorker* 47 (5 Feb. 1972): 27–28; Susan Trausch, "The Experiment Is John Ward," *Boston Globe* (9 Sept. 1980): 31, 41; Paul Desruisseaux, "John William Ward: A Boston 'Street Fighter' Defends the Humanities," *Chronicle of Higher Education* (7 July 1982): 7–8; Suzanne Wilson, "In Consideration of the Late John William Ward," *Daily Hampshire Gazette* (30 Aug. 1985): suppl., 6–9, 27; and Philip Bennett, "A Life of Individualism Cut Short by a Suicide," *Boston Globe* (15 Sept. 1985): 1, 24. Audio and video tapes, notably an oral history interview of 19 June 1979, are in the Amherst College archives.

HUGH HAWKINS

WARING, Fred(eric) Malcolm (*b.* 9 June 1900 in Tyrone, Pennsylvania; *d.* 29 July 1984 in Danville, Pennsylvania), choral conductor, showman, and music educator known as the "man who taught America how to sing."

Fred Waring was one of five children of Frank Waring, a banker in Tyrone, and Jessie Calderwood Waring, a homemaker. Both parents were music lovers. They held musicales in their home on Sunday evenings in which friends, relatives, and neighbors sang and performed. This was a definite influence on Waring, who made his first stage appearance at the age of five and later became leader of the local Boy Scout Drum Corps. As a teenager he took up the banjo and joined a quartet called the Waring-McClintock Snap Orchestra, which included his younger brother, Tom, on piano, as well as two friends, banjo player Freddie Buck and drummer Poley McClintock.

In 1918 Waring entered Penn State University to pursue a degree in architectural engineering. The band changed

Fred Waring. METRONOME COLLECTION/ARCHIVE PHOTOS

its name to Waring's Banjo Orchestra and toured colleges playing fraternity parties, proms, and local dances. In 1922 Waring left school without graduating to became full-time leader of the band, which by then included a dozen performers. The group's reputation grew as it played the theater circuit in Michigan and later participated in the opening of Grauman's Metropolitan Theatre in Hollywood in January 1923.

Adopting the name "Waring's Pennsylvanians," Waring and his band met with increasing success as they played movie theaters from coast to coast. In April 1928 they performed in shows by Cole Porter at the Café des les Ambassadeurs in Paris, then returned to the States to appear on Broadway in the stage show *Hello Yourself*. Between performances they made the first all-musical sound motion picture, *Syncopation*. From November 1930 to May 1931 they were featured in the Cole Porter revue *The New Yorkers*. The following year the Pennsylvanians, grown now to a fifty-five-piece jazz orchestra, scored a great theatrical success with an unprecedented five-month run at New York's Roxy Theatre.

During this period they were also becoming well-known recording artists. Waring and the band had recorded "Sleep," his theme song, for the Victor Talking Machine Company back in 1923. They made the first vocal dance recording ("Memory Lane Waltz") in 1924 and one of the first electronic recordings ("Collegiate") in 1925. Waring anticipated major musical trends by being the first leader of a popular orchestra to use a female singer on a recording, to feature vocalists with an orchestra, and to combine an orchestra and glee club.

In the 1930s and 1940s the Pennsylvanians had a successful string of network radio programs, including *The Old Gold Show* (1933–1934), the *Ford Dealers Show* (1934–1936), and award-winning programs for Chesterfield (1939–1944). They filmed *Varsity Show* for Warner Bros. in 1937, and Waring continued to keep his band on the cutting edge of new media by appearing on the first experimental television broadcast at the 1939 New York World's Fair.

Waring's enthusiastic embrace of technological advances in the entertainment industry was perhaps not surprising in an artist who had once majored in architectural engineering. His mechanical bent showed itself even more clearly in 1937, when he developed and marketed the "Waring Blendor," which soon became a staple of homes across America, as well as an instant steam iron. Always considered a very handsome man, Waring had thick wavy hair that in later years became "silver." He was a dominant personality, loyal to his employees but demanding competence and precision at all times.

From an early age Waring had written songs on every imaginable subject, from his radio theme, "I Hear Music," to patriotic and college fight songs. During World War II he turned his attention to composing nearly thirty songs for branches and units of the armed services, including "Roll Tanks Roll," "Look Out Below," and "Miss Victory."

While many of the popular jazz orchestras of the era broke up or fell into obscurity after the war, Waring and the Pennsylvanians continued to thrive. In 1947 he organized the Fred Waring Choral Workshop with the stated purpose of fostering better singing techniques and sharing his knowledge about the entertainment business. He would teach and supervise the workshop staff for thirty-nine years, literally to the day he died. He also established Shawnee Press, Inc., which became one of the world's largest publishers and sellers of choral music.

The Pennsylvanians entered regular, prime-time television when Fred Waring introduced weekly "spectaculars" for General Electric on CBS-TV in April 1949. The series, which ran through 1954, captured numerous awards for Best Musical Show. Although popular music tastes changed radically in the 1960s and 1970s, Fred Waring kept the Pennsylvanians busy by touring some 40,000 miles every year, mostly by bus, a schedule that earned him the nickname "King of the Road." He nevertheless managed to make time for golf, a sport he enjoyed so much that he established the Fred Waring 4 of Kind 4 Ball tournament at the Shawnee Inn and Country Club, a place he owned for thirty years, located in Shawnee-on-Delaware, Penn-

sylvania. In all he completed sixty-nine continuous years in the entertainment business, a record unequaled in the field.

On 15 December 1983, President Ronald Reagan presented Waring with the Congressional Gold Medal at a White House ceremony. Up to that time the medal had been awarded to only five entertainers in its hundred-year history. Inscribed on the medal was this statement:

> Medal of Congress presented to Fred Waring expressing the nation's pride and gratitude for his achievements as composer-musical director-educator [and] for the pleasure given countless admirers through music and song.

Just after videotaping a concert with the Pennsylvanians and completing his summer workshops at Penn State, on 29 July 1984, Fred Waring suffered a stroke and died at Geisinger Hospital in Danville, Pennsylvania. He is buried in the cemetery of the Shawnee Presbyterian Church in Shawnee-on-Delaware, Pennsylvania.

Fred Waring was recognized as one of the nation's leading music educators. He was honored by the Association of Professional Vocal Ensembles, the Music Educators National Conference, and the American Choral Directors Association. Many contemporary choral conductors, including his protégé Robert Shaw, have called him the primary influence on the American public's appreciation of choral singing. He pioneered and set standards in the fields of recording, radio broadcasting, television, stage productions, motion pictures, and the concert stage.

★

Waring's collection of memorabilia, music library, photographs, correspondence, business records, personal papers, cartoons, costumes, golf paraphernalia, oral histories, films, videotapes, and sound recordings spanning seven decades is at the University Libraries Special Collections Department of Pennsylvania State University. A full biography by his widow, Virginia Waring, is *Fred Waring and the Pennsylvanians* (1997), and a full listing of his recordings can be found in Peter Kiefer, comp., *Discography of Fred Waring and the Pennsylvanians* (1996). Articles include William McKenna, "Fred Waring Is Alive and Making Music," *Record Collectors Journal* 2, no. 1 (1976): 1, 6–7, 20; and two tributes by Peter Kiefer, "Fred Waring: He Taught America How to Sing," *Pop, Jazz & Show Choir Magazine* no. 3 (1985): 5–9, and "Fred Waring: A Master 'Blendor,' " *Choral Journal* (Nov. 1996): 35–36.

PETER T. KIEFER

WARREN, Harry (*b.* 24 December 1893? in Brooklyn, New York; *d.* 22 September 1981 in Los Angeles, California), composer whose numerous songs for Hollywood musicals became popular standards.

Harry Warren, 1929. FRANK DRIGGS/ARCHIVE PHOTOS

Details about Warren's family are sparse. He claimed that he had been named Salvatore Guaragna, the eleventh of twelve children of a bootmaker, also named Salvatore Guaragna, who had emigrated from Calabria, Italy, to New York City in 1885. But the New York Municipal Archives has no record of Warren's birth on Christmas Eve, the date he claimed to be his birthday. Although one of his brothers and a sister entered vaudeville and the stage, Warren's father discouraged Harry's musical interests and urged him to learn a trade. Warren taught himself how to play the accordion and drums. He received informal piano lessons from a barber and sang in his church choir. He later told an interviewer: "When I was a kid, I had a great craving for music. Once I went to the Armory to hear the Boston Symphony and damned near died at the sound. I'd never heard an orchestra before." He attended local public and parochial schools but dropped out after his freshman year at Commercial High School in Brooklyn in order to work as a drummer in his grandfather's touring carnival show.

He returned to New York City to work as a stagehand at a silent movie theater in the Brownsville neighborhood of Brooklyn. He then became an extra at New York's Vitagraph Studio. He played the piano to provide inspiration for the actors and eventually became an assistant director.

After the United States entered World War I, Warren enlisted in the navy. He was stationed in Long Island, New York, where he produced plays and musical entertainment for the troops. He married Josephine ("Jo") Wensler in 1917; they had two children. After his discharge in 1918,

he worked as an insurance investigator and a piano player in theaters and restaurants. In 1922, he became a pianist and song plugger with music publishers Stark and Cowan. That firm published his first popular song, "Rose of the Rio Grande" (1922). Other hit songs he composed during the 1920s include "Back Home in Pasadena," "I Love My Baby," and "Nagasaki."

During the early 1930s, Warren was under contract as a songwriter with Remick Music Company. He also composed scores for Broadway shows: Billy Rose's *Sweet and Low* and *Crazy Quilt,* and Ed Wynn's *Laugh Parade,* which included "I Found a Million Dollar Baby in a Five and Ten Cent Store."

In 1932 Warner Brothers bought the Remick Music Company and invited Warren to Hollywood, where he worked with lyricist Al Dubin on the score for *42nd Street* (1933). The musical included several songs that became standards: "Shuffle Off to Buffalo," "You're Getting to Be a Habit with Me," and "42nd Street." During the rest of the 1930s, Warren and Dubin turned out numerous other hits for Warner Brothers films, including: "We're in the Money" and "Shadow Waltz" for *Gold Diggers of 1933* (1933); "Keep Young and Beautiful" for *Roman Scandals* (1933); "Honeymoon Hotel" and "Shanghai Lil" for *Footlight Parade* (1934); "I Only Have Eyes for You" for *Dames* (1934); "Lullaby of Broadway" (which won him his first Academy Award in 1935) for *Gold Diggers of 1935* (1935); "About a Quarter to Nine" for *Go Into Your Dance* (1935); "With Plenty of Money and You" in *Gold Diggers of 1937*

(1936); and "September in the Rain" for *Melody for Two* (1937).

In 1938 Warren became a member of the board of directors of the American Society of Composers, Authors, and Publishers (ASCAP). That same year he left Warner Brothers to join Twentieth Century–Fox, where he worked primarily with the lyricists Johnny Mercer and Mack Gordon. His hit songs from this period include: "Jeepers Creepers" for *Going Places* (1938); "You Must Have Been a Beautiful Baby" for *Hard to Get* (1938); the theme song for *Down Argentine Way* (1940); "I Yi Yi Yi Yi" for *That Night in Rio* (1941); "Chattanooga Choo-Choo" for *Sun Valley Serenade* (1941); "Serenade in Blue" and "I've Got a Gal in Kalamazoo" for *Orchestra Wives* (1942); "I Had the Craziest Dream" for *Springtime in the Rockies* (1942); and "You'll Never Know" (which won him his second Oscar) for *Hello, Frisco, Hello* (1943).

Warren had little difficulty producing songs to order for any film. After viewing an individual scene to ascertain its mood, he would select a sequence of notes on his studio piano that embodied that mood. He frequently began with a series of fast eighth or quarter notes and then ended the theme with whole notes, as in "You're Getting to Be a Habit with Me," "42nd Street," and "Shuffle Off to Buffalo." After expanding the sequence into a song, he would then collaborate with a lyricist to add appropriate words.

In 1944 Warren joined Metro-Goldwyn-Mayer (MGM), where he worked with lyricists Leo Robin, Arthur Freed, and Ira Gershwin, collaborating on "The More I See You" for *Billy Rose's Diamond Horseshoe* (1945) and "On the Atchison, Topeka, and the Santa Fe" (which won him his third Oscar) for *The Harvey Girls* (1946). In 1953, he left MGM and went to Paramount Studios.

Throughout the late 1940s and 1950s, as movie audiences declined and Hollywood musicals went out of fashion, an increasing amount of Warren's work went into composing songs for dramatic films, such as *The Rose Tattoo* (1955) and *An Affair to Remember* (1957), and comedies, including *The Caddy* (1953), *Artists and Models* (1955), *Cinderfella* (1960), and *The Ladies' Man* (1961). He had few popular hits during this period, although Dean Martin's rendition of Warren's composition "That's Amore" (from *The Caddy*) sold more than 3 million records. He also composed the themes for two television programs, *The Legend of Wyatt Earp* and *The Californians*.

When Warren retired in 1961, he was wealthy. He owned several music companies, his ASCAP royalties amounted to hundreds of thousands of dollars each year, and he had used his studio salary (which exceeded $200,000 annually in the 1940s) to invest in the real estate market in Beverly Hills, where he lived. He alternated his time between a daily golf game and serious musical composi-

tions: a Latin "Mass," in 1962, and "Piano Vignettes" in 1970–1975.

After Warren was elected to the Songwriters Hall of Fame in 1973, he told an interviewer: "There just isn't a market for the kind of old-fashioned numbers I used to do and which I still love to create. . . . When rock and roll first became popular I was convinced that it was a passing fad and that another age of ballads would return as an inevitable reaction. But I was wrong. Rock music is bigger than ever—just look at those best-selling lists of current records—and only occasionally does the old-fashioned type of love ballad make an impression on the public."

Numerous regional theater revues began featuring Warren's songs in the 1970s and 1980s. *Lullaby of Broadway,* based entirely on his songs, opened off-Broadway on 27 November 1979, and the following year David Merrick produced *42nd Street.* The show opened on 25 August 1980 to sold-out audiences at Broadway's Winter Garden Theater and had an eight-year run, in the midst of which Warren died of kidney failure.

Despite the popularity of his songs, Warren himself remained unknown to the general public. After a performance of *42nd Street,* pianist Michael Feinstein talked to members of the departing audience and discovered that none knew who had composed the show's music. Feinstein stated: "What should have been the crowning achievement of a six-decade career turned out to be the final karmic joke on a man whose life's work never brought him proper credit." Industry professionals, however, recognized his genius, which was characterized by singer Mel Tormé in the April 1994 issue of *Down Beat:* "Harry Warren was an absolute giant. He's one of the songwriting gods to me. I'd lump him with Kern, Rodgers and Hart, Gershwin, Porter, Berlin."

★

The Harry Warren Collection of musical folios is at the University of California, Los Angeles, Archive of Popular Music. The most comprehensive discussion is Tony Thomas, *Harry Warren and the Hollywood Musical* (1975). See also David Ewen, *Great Men of American Popular Song* (1970); Max Wilk, *They're Playing Our Song* (1973); Alec Wilder, *American Popular Song: The Great Innovators, 1900–1950* (1972); Ethan Calder, "The Songsmith Nobody Knows," *American Record Guide* (July 1977); Michael Feinstein, "Can't Get His Tunes Out of Our Heads. But Who Was He?," *New York Times* (26 Dec. 1993); and Wilfred Sheed, "Harry Warren," *New Yorker* (20 Sept. 1993). Obituaries are in the *New York Times* (23 Sept. 1981) and *Washington Post* (24 Sept. 1981).

STEPHEN MARSHALL

WASHINGTON, Chester Lloyd, Jr. ("Chet") (*b.* 13 April 1902 in Pittsburgh, Pennsylvania; *d.* 31 August 1983 in Culver City, California), journalist, author, and publisher, best known as a humanitarian and president of Central News–

Wave Publications, at one time America's largest African American–owned weekly newspaper chain.

Washington was the son of Chester Lloyd Washington and Bessie Willis. He received his B.A. degree from Virginia Union University in 1928. He did postgraduate work at Virginia Union, the University of Pittsburgh, Los Angeles City College, and the University of Southern California. On 25 June 1950 he married Alma Graham. They had two children.

Washington embarked on his journalistic career after graduating from Virginia Union University in 1928. In 1935 he became the sports editor of the African American–owned *Pittsburgh Courier.* He became the paper's West Coast bureau chief in 1949, a position he held until 1955, when he left the *Pittsburgh Courier* to join the editorial department of the *Los Angeles Mirror-News.* He was that publication's first full-time African-American reporter. He left the *Mirror-News* in 1960 and moved on to the *Los Angeles Sentinel,* the city's oldest African American–owned weekly newspaper. Starting as a reporter in 1960, he was the *Sentinel*'s editor from 1961 until 1965 and then editor in chief until he resigned in 1966.

In 1966 Washington became a newspaper publisher when he purchased the *Central News* and the *Southwest News,* weekly newspapers in south-central Los Angeles. He was head of the combined Central News–South West News company until 1971. In that year Washington purchased the five California weekly Wave newspapers from the Hicks Deal chain. Washington purchased additional newspapers and created the thirteen-newspaper Central News–Wave Publications, with himself as president. By 1974 Washington's weekly chain had a combined circulation of 200,000. By 1979 his company had become so successful that it was listed by *Black Enterprise* magazine as among the top 100 black-owned businesses in the United States.

As an author, Washington was a ghostwriter for former world heavyweight champion Joe Louis's autobiography, *My Life Story* (1947). He was also an associate editor of the sixty-four-page illustrated *The ABC Picture Book of Eminent Negroes, Past and Present* (1959).

In addition to his interests in journalism and the business of newspaper publishing, Washington was deeply involved in civic and humanitarian activities devoted to the betterment of African Americans and the general public. A great deal of his time and energy went into unpaid voluntary positions. It was through his humanitarian activities and concerns that Washington achieved his greatest recognition during his lifetime. He was a member of the National Association for the Advancement of Colored People and the Urban League. He served as chairperson of the Los Angeles County Parks and Recreation Commission and was a member of the California State Bicentennial Commission, the Los Angeles City Council, and the Chambers of Commerce of Crenshaw and Central. Other organizations in which Washington was active included the Brotherhood Crusade, the Crenshaw Young Men's Christian Association, the South Area Boys Club, Women for Good Government, Women at Work, and Women for Good Media. In 1975 Washington cochaired Afro-American History Week.

Washington's social concerns naturally spilled over into his journalism. This was reflected in comments appearing in *Jet* magazine in January 1974, regarding an awards banquet given in Washington's honor: "Regarded as a humanitarian and a crusader for racial equality, Washington has accomplished his goal of promoting and printing positive Black news, and Black progress in all aspects." This event, officially called "Salute to Chester L. Washington," took place in Los Angeles, California, in January 1974. Awards presentations and testimonials were made by Mayor Tom Bradley of Los Angeles, Secretary of State Edmund G. Brown, Jr., U.S. representatives Augustus Hawkins and Yvonne Burke of California, and other state political leaders.

As a writer, publisher, and tireless activist in worthy causes, Washington received numerous honors including citations from governmental bodies, charities, and other associations and institutions. In 1974 he was awarded the congressional Medal of Merit. He also received the Robert S. Abbot Best Editorials Award from the National Newspaper Publishers' Association in 1979, and the Greater Los Angeles Press Club bestowed upon him the Best Editorial Award.

Washington died of cancer.

★

Information on Washington can be found in *Who's Who in the West* (1978); Hal May, ed., *Contemporary Authors,* vol. 110 (1984); and *Who's Who Among Black Americans, 1992/1993* (1993). See also "Solons, City Officials Salute Noted Los Angeles Publisher," *Jet* (24 Jan. 1974). Obituaries are in the *Los Angeles Times* (1 Sept. 1983) and *New York Times* (2 Sept. 1983).

ALEX SHISHIN

WATERFIELD, Robert Staton ("Bob"; "Rifle") (*b.* 26 July 1920 in Elmira, New York; *d.* 25 March 1983 in Burbank, California), Hall of Fame college and professional football player, coach, and scout who is considered by some experts to be the greatest all-around football player of the post–World War II era.

Waterfield was the only child of Jack Waterfield, who ran the Van Nuys Transfer and Storage Company when the family moved from New York to Los Angeles, California, and Frances Waterfield, a nurse. His father died when Bob was only nine, and his mother supported the family. Wa-

Bob Waterfield. Pro Football Hall of Fame

terfield was a gifted athlete, tall, 155 pounds, and taciturn. He competed in football and gymnastics at Van Nuys High School, from which he graduated in 1937, at the age of sixteen. He worked for three years after high school to pay family debts, but at age nineteen he followed his mother's urging and enrolled at the University of California at Los Angeles (UCLA), where he majored in physical education.

Waterfield did not play freshman football, but in his sophomore year, when Coach Babe Horell switched the UCLA Bruins to the T-formation attack, Waterfield made first-string quarterback. Under the tutelage of Bernie Masterson, Waterfield, now six feet, one inch and 190 pounds, became a West Coast sports celebrity. In the spring of 1942 he competed on the undefeated Bruins gymnastics team in the long horse, rings, and hand balancing. In the fall of 1942 he passed, ran, and kicked the Bruins football team to their first-ever victory over crosstown rival Southern California and a trip to the Rose Bowl.

Working as a double for the movie actor Michael O'Shea, Waterfield made enough money to date his high school sweetheart, Jane Russell. She found him "cool, detached," and confident, a "green-eyed cat" to her mouse. In 1943 Waterfield and Russell married, and that year Waterfield was sent to Officers Training School at Fort Benning, Georgia. He was commissioned a second lieutenant in the infantry, but he never saw combat. An old football injury led to a medical discharge from the army in 1944.

Later that year, he reentered UCLA, became team cocaptain, and finished his college career as the school's leading passer, punter, and placekicker. A sensational appearance in the East-West Shrine Game on New Year's Day, in which Waterfield passed for the winning touchdown, ran the ball for 6 yards a carry, and averaged 59 yards a punt, won him headlines and, after graduation in 1945, a contract with the Cleveland Rams of the National Football League (NFL).

Waterfield's rookie season was one of the most remarkable in NFL history. Local columnists complained that Cleveland's $7,500 contract with Waterfield was excessive. Since joining the NFL in 1937, the Rams had never finished above .500 and had briefly disbanded in 1943 because of manpower shortages. But with Waterfield, the Rams raced to four straight victories in 1945, including a 27–14 pasting of the NFL champions, the Green Bay Packers. Waterfield methodically dissected the opposition by throwing the long ball, by tossing a short possession pass, or by running the bootleg. He inspired his teammates with gritty determination and mental toughness. His heroic performance against the Detroit Lions, when he threw for more than 300 yards while playing with three cracked ribs, clinched the Western Conference championship, and the Rams finished the regular season 9–1. Waterfield was their all-pro quarterback, a star defensive halfback with 6 interceptions, and one of the league's leading punters and placekickers. These talents were on display when the Rams played the veteran Washington Redskins in the league's championship game. Waterfield's 37-yard touchdown pass to Jim Benton in the second quarter and his 53-yard touchdown toss to Jim Gillette in the third quarter gave the Rams a surprising 15–14 victory and made Waterfield the first rookie quarterback in NFL history to take his team to a championship. In recognition of this feat, Waterfield was named the league's most valuable player. He then signed a three-year contract for $20,000 a season, which made him the NFL's highest-paid player.

In 1946 the Rams became the first major sports franchise to move to the West Coast. During the next seven years, the Los Angeles Rams never finished below .500. They won divisional championships in 1949, 1950, and 1951 and tied for the divisional crown in 1952. The Rams won a second NFL title in 1951. That year Waterfield was for the second time the league's leading passer and was again voted most valuable player. Waterfield, who was thirty-one, shared quarterbacking duties with twenty-five-year-old Norm Van Brocklin. They threw to all-pro wide receivers Tom Fears and Elroy "Crazy Legs" Hirsch and handed off to a "bull elephant" backfield of Dan Towler, Dick Hoerner, and Tank Younger. The Rams scored 392 points in a twelve-game season and set up a memorable championship game against the 11–1 Cleveland Browns, which the Rams won when Van Brocklin threw a fourth-quarter, 73-yard touchdown pass to Fears.

Rams fans divided over the quarterback competition between Waterfield and Van Brocklin. Waterfield remained the team leader, but Van Brocklin's flair for the dramatic won him a large following. When the Rams opened the 1952 season at 1–3, Coach Joe Stydahar was forced to resign, and his replacement, Hank Camp, installed Van Brocklin as starting quarterback. Waterfield took his highly publicized demotion as a professional, but he decided the 1952 season would be his last. Waterfield's 813 career completions for 11,849 yards and 98 touchdowns rated him among the league's all-time passers. In addition, his 315 punts for an average 42.4 yards, his 498 points on field goals and points after touchdowns, combined with his 13 touchdowns running the ball to give him a 573-point total, which was then third among the all-time leaders. To this he added 20 interceptions, which he returned for 228 yards during his first five years in the league. Waterfield's all-pro receiver Hirsch considered that "Bob Waterfield was the best football player who ever played the game." In 1965 Waterfield was unanimously elected into the Pro Football Hall of Fame.

After a brief stint as a Rams assistant coach, Waterfield finished the 1950s as a producer in his wife's film company. Jane Russell had become a major Hollywood star following the release of *The Outlaw* in 1943, a film produced by Howard Hughes that capitalized on her seductive figure. Box-office hits with Robert Mitchum, Bob Hope, and Marilyn Monroe followed. The couple built a beautiful home in Sherman Oaks with a breathtaking view of the San Fernando Valley and adopted three children. Russell thought Waterfield was a "wonderful" if sometimes "crabby" father. The couple established their offices in Hollywood. Waterfield sought properties, read scripts, hired production teams, and oversaw the operations of Russ-Field.

When Russell's film career wound down, Waterfield accepted an offer in 1960 to coach the Rams, who had fallen to a record of 2–10 the year before. Although Waterfield's patient rebuilding through the draft brought the Rams four victories in 1960 and four more in 1961, the fans and the press grew weary of waiting. Midway through the 1962 season, Waterfield left coaching to devote his full time to scouting. Under his supervision, the Rams found and began to develop future stars, such as David "Deacon" Jones, Merlin Olsen, Roman Gabriel, Roosevelt Grier, Lamar Lundy, Joe Scibelli, Charlie Cowan, and Jack Pardee.

With their careers winding down, Waterfield and Russell drank and argued more. Their stormy separation in 1967 and their divorce a year later proved personally painful and publicly embarrassing. The press gave wide play to their charges of infidelity. Russell had found Waterfield alternately "darling, dynamic, witty, extremely bright" and "as stubborn as they come." He retained custody of the couple's youngest child and later married Jan Mangus. By the mid-1970s, after years in the media spotlight, Waterfield avoided publicity and lived quietly with his family. He became a sensitive, emotionally vulnerable, occasionally controlling family man who liked to shoot pool, fish, play racquetball, and hunt. He admitted to a lifelong affliction of being unable to say what he felt most deeply. "There never was anything else," he once told an interviewer. "Just football." Brilliance on football's battlefield had been the language with which he seemed most comfortable. Waterfield died of a respiratory ailment in Burbank, California. He was cremated, and his ashes were scattered in Caliente, California.

There may have been better passers, stronger kickers, more elusive runners, and more cunning ball handlers than Bob Waterfield in NFL history, but no single player ever did all these things as well as he. Combined with an usurpassed will to win, those skills made him perhaps the most complete player in the history of pro football.

★

Vertical files on Waterfield's career are in the Pro Football Hall of Fame in Canton, Ohio, and the press office of the St. Louis Rams. Waterfield wrote of his career in *My Greatest Day in Football*, ed. by Murray Goodman and Leonard Lewin (1948). Insights into Waterfield's personal life and personality are described in Jane Russell's autobiography, *My Paths and My Detours* (1985). Biographical pieces are in Robert H. Shoemaker, *Famous Football Players* (1953); Murray Olderman, *The Pro Quarterback* (1966); William Heuman, *Famous Pro Football Stars* (1967); George Sullivan, *The Gamemakers: Pro Football's Great Quarterbacks—from Baugh to Namath* (1971); David L. Porter, ed., *Biographical Dictionary of American Sports: Football* (1987); and Ralph Hickok, *A Who's Who of Sports Champions: Their Stories and Records* (1995). Waterfield's playing records are chronicled in David S. Neft, Richard M. Cohen, and Jordan A. Deutsch, *Pro Football: The Early Years: An Encyclopedic History, 1895–1959* (1978); and Bill Barron et al., eds., *The Official NFL Encyclopedia of Pro Football* (1982). Obituaries are in the *Los Angeles Times* and *New York Times* (both 26 Mar. 1983).

BRUCE J. EVENSEN

WATERS, Muddy (*b.* 4 April 1915 near Rolling Fork, Mississippi; *d.* 30 April 1983 in Westmont, Illinois), blues singer, musician, and composer who developed and personified the influential post–World War II Chicago blues style.

Muddy Waters, whose real name was McKinley Morganfield, was one of two children of Ollie Morganfield, a farmer and musician, and Bertha Jones. After the separation of his parents and his mother's death, he was raised by his maternal grandmother, Della Jones, from age three. In 1918 he and his grandmother, who gave him the name Muddy Waters because he liked to play in muddy streams and put the mud in his mouth, moved to the Stovall plantation outside of Clarksdale, Mississippi. There Muddy lived, worked, and made music until 1943.

At an early age Waters began to play the harmonica and by his own account became quite good at it. When he was seventeen, however, he switched to the guitar. He taught himself how to play, using the recordings of Mississippi blues men such as Charley Patton, Robert Johnson, and Son House as examples. From the latter he received personal instruction in playing "bottleneck" style. Like House, Muddy Waters was influenced by what he took in at church. Although he worked a full day five or six days a week at the plantation, Waters always thought of himself as a musician. "I always felt like I could beat plowing mules, chopping cotton, drawing water. I did all that, and I never liked none of it. Sometimes they'd want us to work Saturday, but . . . they'd look for me and I'd be *gone,* playing [my guitar] in some little town or in some juke joint," he told Robert Palmer years later. As a teenager Waters teamed up with a friend to play at country suppers. Later he performed as a member of the Son Sims Four. By 1940 he was well-known in the Clarksdale area, while blues people in Chicago also had heard of, in Waters's own words, "Stovall's famous guitar picker."

As he received more recognition, Muddy Waters's ambition grew. Like the musicians he admired and friends like Robert Nighthawk, he wanted to cut a record and get a real career in music under way. Then, in August 1941, two representatives from the Library of Congress field recording project, Alan Lomax and John Work, came to make a recording of Waters's music. Although this was not the kind of recording Waters had been looking for, the event still had tremendous significance for his career because, for the first time, he heard himself play. He was now convinced that he was as good as anybody else and became even more restless for a way out of plantation life. One Friday afternoon in May 1943, he finally boarded the four o'clock train out of Clarksdale to Memphis. From there it was straight on to Chicago.

At this time in his life, Muddy had been married twice—to Mabel Berry in 1932 and Sally Ann Adams in 1942. It is not clear if or when these marriages were broken off. In 1934 he fathered one child with yet another woman. In late 1948 he married Geneva Wade, and this marriage lasted until Geneva's death in 1973. While Muddy did not have any children with Geneva, he did father three more children with two of his many girlfriends. On 5 June 1979, Muddy married for a fourth time, to Marva Jean Brooks. Even though it is known that his wife Geneva was hurt by

Muddy Waters. FRANK DRIGGS/ARCHIVE PHOTOS

Muddy's many affairs, his children remember him as a caring and responsible father. In any case, Muddy's personal life was always secondary to his quest for musical glory and perfection.

In wartime Chicago jobs were easy to come by, and Muddy took one at a paper factory. Back in Mississippi he had received an exemption to the draft because of his work on the cotton plantation, which was deemed essential for the war effort. Shortly after arriving in Chicago, he was called up again, but this time he avoided service because of his illiteracy and poor eyesight. The exemption allowed him to concentrate fully on his musical career. Thanks to the help of Big Bill Broonzy, who was prominent in the Chicago blues scene, Muddy soon began to play at house parties, where he met and played with such musicians as John Lee ("Sonny Boy") Williamson and Eddie Boyd, and, with a changing cast of musicians, he began to build his own band and develop a personal sound.

Muddy's sound consisted of four major elements: a band consisting of a singer, lead guitar, rhythm guitar, harmonica, bass, drums, and piano; a tempo more energetic than a lot of traditional blues; amplification or "electrification" producing not only a louder but also a fuller sound; and, despite all the innovation, a firm grounding in the traditions of the Mississippi Delta, or "country" blues. Of course, none of this would have mattered much had Muddy and his men not been such skilled musicians, gifted songwriters, and ambitious, hard workers. It would, however, take until 1950–1951 before Muddy's record company—Aristocrat, later Chess—let the entire band record their revolutionary material. Muddy himself had begun to record as early as 1946, with the Aristocrat sides "I Can't Be Satisfied" (1948) and "Feel Like Going Home" (1948) as his first solo successes.

The period 1950–1955 was the most important of Muddy Waters's career. He was a reputable and accomplished musician before he came to Chicago, and he produced great work after 1955 but, in terms of opportunity, creativity, and success, circumstances never equaled those of the early 1950s. This was a time of rising prosperity for all groups in American society, including blacks—the almost exclusive audience for the blues at this time. It was also before the advent of rock and roll, a kindred competitor that, together with soul music, would consign the blues to the margins of the music business. Finally, the early 1950s was the period during which Muddy Waters formed his legendary bands, transformed his "deep"—that is authentic and intense—country blues into an equally deep but now electric and urban style, and thus defined what from then on would be known as Chicago blues.

With band members such as guitarist Jimmy Rogers, harmonica player "Little" Walter Jacobs (followed by Junior Wells and "Big" Walter Horton), drummer Elgin Evans (followed by Francis Clay), pianist Otis Spann, and such bass players as Willie Dixon, the Muddy Waters Band produced a string of rhythm and blues chart successes, including "Rolling Stone," "Walking Blues," "Louisiana Blues," "She Moves Me," and in the top year 1954 "Hoochie Coochie Man," "I'm Ready," and "Just Make Love to Me (I Just Want to Make Love to You)." The new, integrated sound supported Muddy's powerful, intense, and sophisticated singing, and the band members reinforced each others' strengths while preserving their own, often brilliant, individual input. The sound also evolved from being fairly close to Muddy's Library of Congress recordings to something a good deal more hard-driving and macho, as especially demonstrated by the 1954 hits. These three songs, signature Muddy Waters numbers, were all written by Willie Dixon, who had keenly tracked Muddy Waters's development since his arrival in Chicago. "There was quite a few people around singin' the blues, but most of 'em was singin' all *sad* blues. Muddy was givin' his blues a little pep, and ever since I noticed him givin' his blues this kinda pep feelin', I began tryin' to think of things in a peppier form," Dixon explained later.

Starting in 1954, with the arrival of such stars as Elvis Presley, Chuck Berry, Little Richard, Ray Charles, and Fats Domino, black popular music became a good deal peppier as well as—and more important—much more accessible for a large, racially mixed audience. Although Muddy Waters was not against some experimentation, and even though he later became immensely popular with white musicians and audiences in Europe and the United States, he always remained a creator of "deep" Chicago blues with long, Mississippi Delta roots. Like virtually every other blues performer, he would not, nor could he really, become a rock and roll star. Around 1955 Muddy Waters's rise began to level off. Rock and roll and soul performers scored commercial successes that blues musicians could not even dream of, and it became ever more difficult to score a chart hit. On top of that, Muddy's sound was fully developed by now. It appeared that where the likes of Chuck Berry and James Brown were making great creative strides, Muddy and his colleagues were basically offering the same old fare. Muddy continued to record, and he was never without opportunities to perform, but, both commercially and creatively, the future looked less exciting than during the early 1950s.

Thanks to the so-called folk music and blues revivals of the late 1950s and 1960s, Muddy Waters did become a popular figure with younger, well-educated, and mainly white audiences during the final two decades of his life. A frequent performer at folk and blues festivals in the United States and Europe, Muddy and his ever-changing but consistently excellent band helped a great many new blues aficionados establish a link between the blues-based rock music of a host of British and American artists and the "deep" country blues of the Mississippi Delta. His work continues to function as a bridge. Unfortunately, it was the British and American rock musicians who had the big hits and made fortunes with what can be seen as the intellectual property of "originals" like Muddy Waters. Still, the young white stars were frequently generous in paying tribute to their blues examples and many were also eager to perform and record with them. Nonetheless, Little Walter, Willie Dixon, and Muddy Waters were never as successful with mass audiences as the Rolling Stones or Eric Clapton.

Waters's recording career sagged for most of the 1960s and early 1970s, but he made a strong comeback toward the end of his life with the help of the white blues man and producer Johnny Winter. Along with three strong studio albums, Waters and Winter also produced what is probably the most impressive live album of Muddy's career—*Muddy "Mississippi" Waters Live*. At the time of his death of a heart attack, following a year-long struggle with lung cancer, Muddy Waters, a winner of several Grammy awards along with numerous other honors, was the undisputed "boss" of the Chicago blues. Because this music in its vibrant form is tied to a specific historic era, it is a title that will forever be tied to his name.

★

Invaluable are the interviews Alan Lomax and John Work conducted with Muddy Waters in 1941 and 1942 on the Stovall plantation. They can be heard on *Muddy Waters: The Complete Plantation Recordings,* a Chess/MCA reissue (1993), and have been transcribed in part in the otherwise also informative Alan Lomax, *The Land Where the Blues Began,* (1993). Essential reading is Sandra B. Tooze, *Muddy Waters: The Mojo Man* (1997), a fine biography that includes a complete discography compiled by Phil Wright and Fred Rothwell. For Muddy's own words see James Rooney, *Bossmen: Bill Monroe and Muddy Waters* (1971); and Robert Palmer's interview in *Rolling Stone* (5 Oct. 1978). Also indispensable is Robert Palmer, *Deep Blues* (1981). Also useful are Charles Keil, *Urban Blues* (1966); Paul Oliver, *The Story of the Blues* (1969); Mike Rowe, *Chicago Blues* (1981); and Sheldon Harris, *Blues Who's Who: A Biographical Dictionary of Blues Singers* (1979, 1989). An obituary is in the *New York Times* (1 May 1983).

RUUD VAN DIJK

WATTS, John Everett (*b.* 16 July 1930 in Cleveland, Tennessee; *d.* 2 July 1982 in New York City), composer known for his early use of synthesizers and founder of the electronic music program at the New School for Social Research in New York City.

Information on John Watts's early life is not readily available. Watts attended the University of Tennessee, receiving a B.A. degree in 1949, and the University of Colorado, earning the M.Mus. degree in 1953. His doctoral work took place at the University of Illinois (1955–1956), Cornell University (1958–1960), and the University of California at Los Angeles (1961–1962). His primary teachers and mentors were John Krueger, David Van Vactor, Cecil Effinger, Burrill Phillips, Robert Palmer, and Roy Harris. A clarinetist early in his career, he performed with the orchestra of the U.S. Army Special Services at Knoxville, Tennessee, and with the Colorado Springs Symphony. He later served as assistant to the conductor of the Youngstown (Ohio) Philharmonic.

Watts moved to New York City and in 1964 founded the Composers Theatre, a contemporary music organization that would perform the works of some 250 composers during his eighteen-year tenure as its director. At the same time, he began to branch out in new directions in his own compositional work. Early pieces such as his *Piano Sonata* (1958; revised 1960) made use of traditional instruments and classical forms. As electronic instruments became increasingly sophisticated in the 1960s, however, Watts's interests turned to synthesizers. He taught himself how to play the Moog synthesizer, designed by the electrical engineer Robert Moog, and later switched to the ARP synthesizer, an instrument he used so ingeniously he was called "wizard of the ARP."

Watts also brought his expertise with this new media into an academic setting. Having joined the faculty of the New School for Social Research in 1967, he founded the electronic music program there two years later. He supervised some twenty-five workshops and courses and helped make the school a well-known center for electronic music and audio engineering.

By the early 1970s Watts was a well-known figure in the New York avant-garde arts community, which was pioneering new forms of mixed media, conceptual and performance art, and music that often incorporated Japanese, Balinese, and other non-Western influences. Watts used synthesizers to expand the sound spectrum in works such as *Elegy to Chimney: In Memoriam* (1972). Combining trumpet, tape, and synthesizers, this meditative and moving piece creates sounds that the critic Tom Johnson described as "a sumptuous electronic whirring," likening it to the sound of wind. Indeed, part of the appeal of Watts's music is that he sought to "humanize" his electronic media rather than simply using them for effects. In *Laugharne* (1974), a live orchestra is combined with prerecorded tape to achieve a lush, romantic sound that one critic described as "intoxicating."

Watts appeared in solo concerts and guest-composer residencies and took part in series and festivals devoted to new music, including those at the Museum of Modern Art (1973–1975) and ART NOW '74, a national interdisciplinary festival of the arts at the Kennedy Center, where he appeared with artists such as Andy Warhol, Robert Wilson, Richard Foreman, and Philip Glass. He produced about 100 works in all, including numerous scores for film, video, theater, and dance. He frequently collaborated with his wife, the choreographer Laura Foreman, in such works as the films *Time-Coded Woman I, II, and III* (1981). (Watts and Foreman had a daughter.) Another collaboration was *MAS* (1976), written for the dancer Satoru Shimazake. Described as a twenty-seven-track "study in density" based on traditional gagaku (the ancient court music of Japan), it was first performed at the Japan House in New York City and was considered by Watts to be his best work. In accordance with the spirit of the times, he and Laura Foreman also collaborated on a bit of conceptual art called *Wallwork* (1981), in which they "orchestrated" waves of posters and press releases announcing a sold-out, but totally imaginary, concert. He wrote the score for the film *War,* which won the Gold Medal for documentaries at the 1966 New York International Festival, as well as music for theatrical productions of *Faust, The Madwoman of Chaillot,* and several children's theater pieces. He even made a foray into commercial television with the theme music to the NBC show called *Station Exchange.*

In April 1982 the Brooklyn Philharmonic performed a work of his as part of its "Meet the Moderns" program. Three months later, he fell ill and died at his home in Manhattan at the age of fifty-two.

John Watts was a proponent of electronic music at an important moment in its development. At a time when electronic media were regarded in many quarters as alienating, he did much to expand both the musical vocabulary and expressive possibilities of these instruments. Through his work as a composer and teacher he helped bring electronic music into the mainstream.

★

Papers concerning John Watts, including lists of major works, are on file at Composers Theatre, Inc., New York City; additional papers and musical scores are on file at the American Music Center, New York City. An obituary is in the *New York Times* (3 July 1982).

JOHN-FORREST BAMBERGER

WEBB, John Randolph ("Jack") (*b.* 2 April 1920 in Santa Monica, California; *d.* 23 December 1982 in Los Angeles, California), actor, producer, and writer for television, motion pictures, and radio, best known for the television series *Dragnet*.

Webb was the only child of Samuel Chester Webb and Margaret Smith. Samuel Webb abandoned his wife and infant child and disappeared, leaving Jack, as he was called from birth, to be raised by his impoverished mother and grandmother, Emma Smith, in downtown Los Angeles. A sickly child who suffered from asthma, Webb did not attend school until the age of nine because of his poor health. His grandmother taught him his letters from the cereal and salt cartons on the kitchen table, and from there he graduated to reading the newspaper. After his health improved he went on to grade school and then to Belmont High School, where he graduated in 1938. At Belmont, Webb showed skill at cartooning and illustrated his class yearbook. He also helped stage a series of variety shows to raise money to buy uniforms for the school football team. As the producer and master of ceremonies, Webb gained both show-business experience and schoolwide recognition. Persuaded by his friends to run for student-body president, he won the election by defeating the captain of the football team.

Webb was offered an art scholarship to the University of Southern California but turned it down in order to help support his mother and grandmother. He went to work as a sales clerk at Silverwoods, a prominent men's clothing store in downtown Los Angeles, where he worked his way up to be store manager. With the U.S. entry into World War II, however, he felt he had to help in the war effort. Initially he gained a draft deferment because he was the main financial support for his family and went to work for a defense plant as a stamp operator making parts for anti-tank guns. By 1943, having convinced his mother that he had to fight, he enlisted in the Army Air Forces. To his

Jack Webb. ARCHIVE PHOTOS

disappointment, he neither earned his pilot's wings nor went overseas, but instead helped to train B-26 bomber pilots at Laughlin Field in Del Rio, Texas, and hosted some base United Service Organizations (USO) shows. Frustrated with these duties, he obtained a dependency discharge early in 1945. Of his World War II service, Webb wrote, "I went in with a dream. I came out with a blank page."

Returning to Los Angeles, Webb tried to land a job in radio, where he hoped to take advantage of his experience as master of ceremonies in his high school and USO shows. After some initial rejections, his persistence paid off, and in April 1945 he took an announcing job with radio station KGO, the American Broadcasting Company's station in San Francisco, where he reported on the conference that would organize the United Nations. Various announcing assignments followed: he was a "man on the street" interviewer on V-J Day, a station-break announcer, and host of an early morning record show that featured jazz. He was skilled enough to be kept on despite the influx of returning servicemen.

Webb's next step up in radio came in 1946, when he was cast in the title role of *Pat Novak for Hire,* a weekly half-hour radio drama about the adventures of a tough private detective. Written by his friend Richard Breen, the show ran for twenty-six weeks, and Webb was deemed a success. After Breen left KGO for Hollywood to pursue his writing career, Webb followed his friend in search of greater opportunities. Radio work came quickly at first, including roles on *The Johnny Modero Show, The Whistler,* and *This Is Your F.B.I.,* and he landed bit parts in films such as *The Hollow Triumph* (1948) and *He Walked by Night* (1948). Gradually, however, acting jobs were fewer and fewer, so he decided to take the initiative and create his own opportunities. Recalling the suggestion of Sergeant Marty Wynn of the Los Angeles Police Department that there should be a radio drama that focused on the work of real policemen rather than on glamorous private eyes, Webb set out to create his own show. Wynn provided Webb with the access necessary to research Los Angeles Police Department files, interview officers, and ride along in a squad car. He wrote a series of radio plays that, based on these experiences, authentically dramatized the work of an average policeman in a routine and workaday style.

After rejecting other titles, Webb chose *Dragnet.* As he tells it, "The title came first. The name *Dragnet* popped up after I had discarded several others, and as time proved, it was the perfect name for the show." He developed a lead character who would represent the dedicated, hardworking peace officer of law-enforcement departments throughout the country. Webb named the character Joe Friday because "I wanted a name that had no connotations at all. He could be Jewish, or Greek, or English, or anything. He could be all men to all people in their living rooms." Friday's partner also bore an Everyman name, Officer Frank Smith.

Dragnet was given the official approval of the Los Angeles Police Department, which needed its image improved after a series of scandals. The National Broadcasting Company accepted the drama as a summer replacement beginning on 3 June 1949. Webb produced the show, cowrote the scripts with his friend Jim Moser, and starred as Joe Friday. Borrowing the narrative documentary style from *He Walked by Night,* Webb and Moser contributed *Dragnet*'s terse, clipped dialogue and quality of understatement.

Initially a sustaining show with no sponsor, *Dragnet* was given a four-week guarantee and was then continued on a week-to-week basis. Fourteen weeks later the tobacco company Liggett and Myers became the sponsor. Within two years *Dragnet* became the most popular drama on radio; it ran until 1955.

Along with his work on *Dragnet,* Webb obtained parts in motion pictures: *Appointment with Danger* (1949), *Sunset Boulevard* (1950), *United States Mail* (1950), *Dark City* (1950), *The Men* (1950), and *Halls of Montezuma* (1950).

Bosley Crowther, the film reviewer for the *New York Times,* singled out Webb for excellence in his supporting role as a paraplegic in *The Men,* playing alongside Marlon Brando in the latter's screen debut.

As television replaced radio as the national medium, Webb followed the example of other radio producers and created a television version of *Dragnet.* The pilot episode, which Webb produced and starred in, aired on Liggett and Myers's *Chesterfield Sound Off Time* on 16 December 1951. The realism and documentary style were a sharp contrast to the live vaudeville format and slapstick situation comedies of early television. *Dragnet* became a regular series on 3 January 1952. It quickly became a hit, achieving the number-two A. C. Nielsen rating behind Lucille Ball's *I Love Lucy* in the 1953–1954 season with an estimated 68 million viewers. The series lasted until 1958.

A feature motion-picture version of *Dragnet* was released in 1954 with Webb starring and directing and with a screenplay by Richard Breen. Webb went on to direct and star in a number of other films, including *Pete Kelly's Blues* (1955), a film about a Dixieland band leader in the early 1930s; *The DI* (1957), about a U.S. Marine Corps drill instructor; and *30,* about a night on a big-city newspaper. All were shot with the gritty realism that Webb had pioneered in *Dragnet.*

Webb had established his own production company, Mark VII, to produce *Dragnet.* The earnings, enhanced by the sale of *Dragnet* for syndication, enabled Webb to produce and direct other television series, including *Noah's Ark* (1956–1958), *Pete Kelly's Blues* (1959), and *The D.A.'s Man* (1959).

In 1962 Webb went to Warner Brothers, where he produced and narrated an anthology series, *General Electric True,* which was based on actual incidents. He was then put in charge of television for the studio, but soon wanted to get back to directing and acting. As Webb explained, "I must admit there is a lot of satisfaction in performing a role." In 1967 he revived *Dragnet* under his Mark VII Productions with the title *Dragnet 67.* It aired until 1970. He also found time to create and produce *Adam 12* (1968–1975), a television series about two squad-car officers.

Driven by Webb's tireless energy and penchant for work, Mark VII produced *O'Hara, U.S. Treasury* (1971–1972), *Emergency* (1972–1977), *Hec Ramsey* (1973–1974), *Escape* (1973), *Chase* (1973–1974), and *Project U.F.O.* (1978–1979). During his career Webb also found time to write *The Badge* (1958), a book on police work; and to narrate four record albums. Webb was developing a new police series titled *The Department* when he died suddenly of a heart attack at his home in Los Angeles.

Webb's workaholic lifestyle gave him little time for a home life, and three of his marriages ended in divorce. His first, to the singer and starlet Julie London, lasted from

16 July 1947 to 1954; they had two daughters. He married Dorothy Towne shortly after the divorce; they were divorced on 15 May 1957. Jackie Loughery, a former Miss USA, became his third wife on 23 June 1958; they were divorced on 24 March 1964. Three years before his death, on 31 December 1979, he married his bookkeeper, Opal Gates.

Jack Webb's staccato narration, catch phrases such as "This is the city" and "Just the facts, ma'am," and the opening "Dum-de-dum-dum" of *Dragnet*'s theme music, became part of American popular culture. His terse documentary style influenced many future television dramas and motion pictures. More significantly, he changed the Hollywood image of policemen—and the public's perception of them—from that of inept, comic figures such as Mack Sennett's Keystone Kops to that of hardworking, respectable individuals engaged in the often thankless task of law enforcement.

★

Newspaper, magazine, and trade-paper clippings plus studio biographies on Jack Webb and his work can be found in the Margaret Herrick Library of the Academy of Motion Picture Arts and Sciences in Beverly Hills, California. Useful articles appear in the *American Weekly* (12 Sept., 19 Sept., and 3 Oct. 1954); *Saturday Evening Post* (5 Sept., 12 Sept., and 19 Sept. 1959), by Dean Jennings; and *Los Angeles Times West Magazine* (2 July 1967), by Jane Ardmore. An obituary is in the *New York Times* (24 Dec. 1982).

KELLAM DE FOREST

WECHSLER, David (*b.* 12 January 1896 in Lespedi, Romania; *d.* 2 May 1981 in New York City), pioneer psychologist involved in both clinical and experimental work, most widely identified with intelligence scales for adults, children, and preschoolers.

The youngest of seven children, Wechsler emigrated to the United States in 1902; the family settled in New York City. He graduated from City College of New York with an A.B. degree in 1916 and received an M.A. from Columbia University in 1917, followed by a Ph.D. from Columbia in 1925. During his years at Columbia his primary training was in experimental psychology; he studied with such major figures as Robert S. Woodworth, J. McKeen Cattell, E. L. Thorndike, and Thomas Hunt Morgan.

An emerging interest in clinical work, a field then barely in its infancy, was fostered after Wechsler was inducted into the U.S. Army in 1917 and subsequently assigned as a psychologist at the Army Military School on Long Island, New York, and later at Camp Logan, Texas. While at Camp Logan he was involved with individualized testing of inductees who, despite adequate adjustment in civilian life, had failed standardized group tests used by the armed

forces to assess intellectual ability. He began to question the limitations of the then commonly accepted definitions of intelligence and the suitability of the Stanford-Binet Intelligence Test for use with adults, especially foreign-born persons who did not comprehend English.

Wechsler's next military assignment, at the University of London, brought him into contact with Charles Spearman and Karl Pearson, both important influences in his development as a psychologist. Although Spearman's concept of *G* (a general intelligence factor) was later deemed insufficient by Wechsler, it played a significant role in his theorizing. From Pearson, Wechsler gleaned the potential of correlational techniques that could allow the assessment of relationships among variables. Following his discharge from the army in 1919, Wechsler accepted a scholarship to the University of Paris, where he studied under Henri Piéron and Louis Lapique and conducted the research that formed the basis of his doctoral work at Columbia on psychogalvanic response, an area unique in the United States.

Wechsler's long-term alliance with the Psychological Corporation began soon after his return to the United States in 1922. He began developing and applying tests, in particular a series for the Yellow Cab Company that included measurements of mental alertness and general intelligence. These endeavors were followed by a stint as psychologist with the new Bureau of Child Guidance in New York City (1922–1924) and private practice as a clinical psychologist (1927–1932). In 1932 Wechsler was appointed chief psychologist at Bellevue Psychiatric Hospital in New York City, a position he held until 1967. During that same period he served on the faculty at the New York University College of Medicine.

Despite his clinical work in the 1920s and early 1930s, Wechsler's devotion to his experimental roots were most evident during that period. However, the focus of his research began to change in 1930 with the publication of "The Range of Human Capacities," an article on the comparative similarities of human beings. His book with the same title, published in 1935 (updated in 1952 and republished in 1971), expanded on the theme of limited variability by examining available data on human traits and abilities for which quantitative data existed. This article and book are among his major works.

Wechsler's position at Bellevue provided the impetus for what are generally acknowledged to be his best-known contributions to psychology: the development of intelligence scales (that bear his name) for adults, children, and preschoolers, and the use of a deviation quotient, based on the concept of comparing an individual's (raw) intelligence score against those of others of the same chronological age rather than basing an intelligence quotient (IQ) on chronological age divided by mental age (with a ceiling of fif-

David and Lazar Wechsler, 1953. HULTON-DEUTSCH COLLECTION/CORBIS

teen years). In this way he acknowledged the difference between evaluating adult and juvenile intelligence.

The Wechsler-Bellevue Scale (Bellevue I), published in 1939—as was *The Measurement of Adult Intelligence* (a major work that became *The Measurement and Appraisal of Adult Intelligence* in its fourth edition in 1958, enlarged in 1972)—was a response to a need for a valid instrument to test the diverse and multilingual adult patient population referred to Bellevue Hospital. Reflecting Wechsler's contention that intelligence, rather than being a unitary trait, is composed of many abilities, Bellevue I produced full-scale verbal and performance IQs based on ten verbal and performance subtests. He also believed that the subtests could provide clinical information about the functioning and personality of the individual.

With the advent of World War II, Wechsler was engaged by the secretary of war as a consultant; this led to the development of the Army Wechsler Scale (Bellevue-Wechsler II) in 1942 and subsequent service with the Veterans' Administration. Following a comparable multiple-subtest design, Wechsler continued his exploration of measurement of human intelligence with the Wechsler Intelligence Scale for Children (WISC, 1949), Wechsler Adult Intelligence Scale (WAIS, 1955), and Wechsler Preschool and Primary Scale of Intelligence (WPPSI, 1967). These tests, which have undergone periodic restandardization and revision, remain among the most widely used psychological instruments. Wechsler was a multifaceted researcher and prolific

author. His numerous honors included the American Psychological Association's (APA) Award for Distinguished Contribution to Clinical Psychology (1960) and the APA Award for Distinguished Professional Contribution (1973). The American Association on Mental Deficiency hailed his contributions to the study of mental deficiency in 1972. In addition he was involved in the development of Hebrew University in Jerusalem and helped found its Psychology Department; he served as the director of the American Friends of Hebrew University for three decades and was a member of the university's board of governors.

In 1939 Wechsler married Ruth Halpern; they had two children. He died in New York City.

Although he is best known for his development of tests, Wechsler successfully melded clinical and experimental perspectives throughout his career. His conception of intelligence as a global entity encompassing nonintellective qualities broadened the understanding of intelligence; he asserted that assessment of an individual is more broad-based than testing. When he accepted the American Psychological Association Professional Contribution award in 1975, Wechsler explained, "What we measure with tests is not what tests measure—not information, not spatial perception, not reasoning ability. These are only means to an end. What intelligence tests measure, what we hope they measure, is something much more important: the capacity of an individual to understand the world about him and his resourcefulness to cope with its challenges." His guiding principle is seen in his 1939 definition: "Intelligence is the aggregate or global capacity to act purposefully, think rationally, and deal effectively with the environment."

★

Allen J. Edwards, ed., *Selected Papers of David Wechsler* (1974), is a collection of articles dating from 1917 that illustrate the wide scope of Wechsler's research and philosophy. There are many detailed explanations of his tests, for example Allen J. Edwards, *Individual Mental Testings* (1971). Obituaries are in the *New York Times* (3 May 1981); *American Psychologist* 36 (Dec. 1981): 1542–1543, by Joseph Matarazzo; and *Journal of the History of the Behavioral Sciences* 18 (1982): 78–79, by Allen J. Edwards.

MYRNA W. MERRON

WECHSLER, James Arthur (*b.* 31 October 1915 in New York City; *d.* 11 September 1983 in New York City), editor and columnist for the *New York Post* and outspoken liberal.

Wechsler was one of the two children of Samuel Wechsler, an attorney, and Anna Weisberger. He always knew that he wanted to be a journalist. His boyhood heroes were H. L. Mencken, the *Baltimore Sun* columnist, and Heywood Broun, a liberal reporter. "I somehow mated the cynicism of one and the passion of the other into a single image of virtuous valor," Wechsler wrote. "Under the spell of such rebellious spirits," he asserted, he became the editor of the

James Wechsler, 1953. UPI/CORBIS-BETTMANN

Townsend Harris High School newspaper, the *Stadium,* and began demonstrating the combative nature, independent spirit, and concern for the powerless that characterized his career. An outstanding student, he graduated from high school in 1931 and enrolled at Columbia University that year, just short of his sixteenth birthday.

Entering college at the height of the Great Depression, Wechsler became more interested in the larger issues of the day, from fascism in Europe to the millions of unemployed on New York's streets, than he was in his studies. He also became deeply involved in the university's daily newspaper, the *Columbia Spectator.* He joined a strike protesting the expulsion of the paper's editor, Reed Harris, for writing editorials that called for an end to football at Columbia and greater concern for the unemployed. The strike, partially organized by campus communists, was one of a series of events that gradually lured Wechsler into the communist fold. His complicated relationship with communism was as crucial as his journalistic abilities in forming his identity. By his senior year at Columbia, Wechsler was both a member of the Young Communist League and the editor of the *Spectator.* On 5 October 1934 he married Nancy Fraenkel, a student at Columbia's Teachers College and the daughter of an American Civil Liberties Union lawyer, whom he had met at an anti-Nazi rally. They had two children.

After graduating with a B.A. degree in 1935, Wechsler worked full-time for the Young Communist League, where his first assignment was to write a book on the national student protest movement, *Revolt on the Campus* (1935). He served as the editor of the communist-front National Student League (NSL) magazine and was director of publications for the American Student Union, a merger of the NSL and the Socialist Student League for Industrial Democracy, from 1936 to 1937. Eventually, Wechsler became a member of the executive committee of the Young Communist League. At the same time, however, he began to turn away from communism, in part because of the 1937 Moscow show trials and the Communist party's insistence on rigidly adhering to each twist and turn in doctrine.

At age twenty-two, Wechsler resigned from the Young Communist League to become a professional journalist. He worked first for the *Nation* from 1938 to 1939. In 1940 he joined the staff of the short-lived daily *PM,* where he served as a labor reporter and editor and eventually as Washington bureau chief. During this period, he also wrote a biography of the United Mine Workers union chief John L. Lewis, *Labor Baron* (1944). Although Wechsler admired the paper's attempts to break the journalistic mold, he was far less enamored of its internecine politics. By now a committed anticommunist, he railed against what he saw as sugarcoated news of the Soviet Union and attempts by the publisher, Ralph Ingersoll, to restore a leftist Popular Front in the United States.

In 1947 Wechsler resigned from *PM* and became involved in a new political organization and a new journalistic venture. Together with such liberal anticommunists as Averell Harriman and Arthur Schlesinger, Jr., Wechsler founded Americans for Democratic Action, an organization that favored an assertive foreign policy to counter the Soviets and a liberal domestic policy. Also in 1947, Wechsler joined the Washington bureau of the *New York Post,* where he worked for the rest of his life. In 1949 Wechsler became editor of the *Post,* a position he held until 1961. In his first editorial for the *Post,* he outlined the journalistic philosophy that guided him throughout his life, "the deep belief that there is no conflict between our craft responsibilities and our social responsibilities." He wrote, "We are convinced we will be better newspapermen because we are liberals; and—in the most profound sense—better liberals because we are newspapermen."

His values led Wechsler into the most dramatic period of his life. Senator Joseph McCarthy of Wisconsin, angered by *Post* editorials and articles challenging his anticommunist crusade of the early 1950s and disturbed by Wechsler's communist past, brought the *Post* editor in for questioning before his Committee on Government Operations. Wechsler's reply to the accusations was curt: "Senator, let's face it. You are saying that an ex-Communist who is for McCarthy is a good one and an ex-Communist who is against McCarthy is a suspect. I will stand on that distinction."

After the McCarthy hearings, Wechsler continued espousing his liberal views as editor and editorial page editor of the *Post* and in his 1960 book *Reflections of an Angry Middle-Aged Editor.* In 1969 Wechsler's son Michael, who had a history of mental illness and drug abuse, died at age twenty-six from an overdose of barbiturates. Wechsler, his wife, and his daughter, Holly W. Karpf, chronicled Michael's story in a book, *In a Darkness,* published in 1972.

In 1980 Wechsler became a columnist as the paper's new publisher, Rupert Murdoch, put a more conservative stamp on the publication. Wechsler continued writing columns until just before his death from cancer in New York City, where he was buried.

Wechsler's ultimate influence was limited by both his time period and the *Post*'s readership. Wechsler's *Post* was a paper of local rather than national influence, and because he wrote in liberal New York City, he was often preaching to the converted. Nevertheless, the *New York Times* correctly editorialized that Wechsler's "most memorable time" was when he had shown "clarity and courage" in resisting both communism and anticommunist hysteria. With the cold war over, many of these efforts can seem dated or irrelevant, but the humane skepticism that Wechsler demonstrated in abundance is timeless.

★

James A. Wechsler, *The Age of Suspicion* (1953), chronicles his journey into and out of communism and culminates with his testimony before McCarthy's committee. Obituaries are in the *New York Times* (12 Sept. 1983), *Newsweek* (26 Sept. 1983), *Time* (26 Sept. 1983), and *Rolling Stone* (27 Oct. 1983).

MILES A. POMPER

WEINER, Lazar (*b.* 24 October 1897 in Cherkassy, near Kiev, Ukraine; *d.* 10 January 1982 in New York City), composer of Yiddish art songs and Jewish liturgical music who is best known for the Yiddish cantatas he wrote and produced as director of the Workmen's Circle Chorus between 1930 and 1965.

Weiner, who had four brothers and two sisters, was the son of Samuel Weiner, a shoemaker, and Gussie Weiner, a housewife. He became familiar with the Jewish liturgical tradition as a singer in two synagogue choirs, first in Cherkassy and later in Kiev, following his family's relocation to

Lazar Weiner. NYT PICTURES/NYT PERMISSIONS

that city when he was ten. In 1910 his parents enrolled their musically talented son in the State Conservatory in Kiev, where he studied piano and music theory until 1914. Anti-Semitism posed an ongoing threat to the family, and after a Jewish neighbor was accused of murdering a Gentile child, the Weiner family immigrated in 1914 to the United States and settled in New York City. Lazar Weiner, who was seventeen, became a naturalized U.S. citizen that year.

Weiner continued his musical pursuits almost immediately. He took a job as a piano accompanist for a voice teacher and performed in concert with featured vocalists. In the 1920s he deepened his already extensive knowledge of the European classical tradition by studying with the noted composers Robert Russell Bennett, Frederick Jacobi, and, most significantly for his career, Joseph Schillinger. During much of this period of study, however, Weiner concentrated his efforts on absorbing literary Yiddish and setting Yiddish poetry to music. Through a violinist named Nahum Baruch Minkoff, who wrote poetry and moved in Yiddish avant-garde circles, Weiner met other Yiddish artists and quickly became intrigued by the literary uses of the language and the possibility of incorporating it into musical composition. His new companions enhanced his personal life as well as his artistic one. The playwright Peretz Hirschbein introduced Weiner to Sarah Naomi Shumiatcher, who was Hirschbein's sister-in-law. In 1921 Weiner and Shumiatcher married. They had two sons, one of whom, Yehudi Wyner, also became a successful composer and performer of Jewish music.

In 1922 Weiner sent several of his first art songs to the noted composer Joel Engel, who was living in Berlin at the time. Engel found Weiner's songs promising in their compositional sophistication but lacking a Jewish musical sensibility. This response drove Weiner to establish contact with the St. Petersburg Society for Jewish Folk Music and several of its members, including Lazare Saminsky and Joseph Achron, both of whom had recently arrived in the United States. As a result of his exposure to these composers, Weiner situated his songs firmly in an Ashkenazic musical tradition and commenced his cultivation of the Yiddish art song in the American context. Unlike most of the composers influenced by the St. Petersburg Society, Weiner was committed to Yiddish over Hebrew texts, and his compositions were characterized by their close attention to Yiddish linguistic rhythms.

Weiner gained a wider public recognition through his leadership of several Yiddish choruses in the New York area, including the New York Freiheit Gesangs Verein, the Yiddish Culture Chorus, and the International Ladies' Garment Workers' Union Chorus. His greatest accomplishments as conductor, however, came with the Workmen's Circle Chorus, which he directed between 1930 and 1965. As leader of this chorus, he vastly expanded the range

of music performed in the Yiddish language. He translated the libretti of classical European choral works by composers such as Beethoven, Rossini, Mozart, Mendelssohn, and Schubert; he composed and produced his own cantatas, including *Legend of Toil* (1933), *To Thee America* (1944), and *Prologue to the Golem* (1951); and he performed the songs of other Yiddish composers. During this peak period of his career, Weiner wrote the score to the opera *The Golem* (1956) and hosted the weekly radio program *The Message of Israel,* which exposed new audiences to Jewish music.

Weiner was also a major contributor to the development of liturgical music for the Jewish Reform service. His prominence as a composer and conductor earned him the position of musical director at New York's Central Synagogue, where, between 1930 and 1974, he helped to revise the service by replacing the music of secular composers with melodies from a Jewish liturgical tradition. Many of these chants were his own compositions, while others were the work of his peers, such as Achron and Ernest Bloch. A Manhattan resident, Weiner continued to promote Jewish music until the end of his life by teaching classes and giving lectures at the Hebrew Union College, the Jewish Theological Seminary, the Juilliard School of Music, and the Ninety-second Street YM-YWHA. Weiner died of heart failure in New York City following a mishandled treatment of arteriosclerosis. He was buried in Cedar Park Cemetery in Paramus, New Jersey.

Lazar Weiner made significant contributions to the development of Reform Judaism in the United States, but he is best remembered for his sustained promotion of music and poetry in the Yiddish language. Despite his relatively late acquaintance with literary Yiddish, he was deeply committed to publicizing its beauty and potential as an artistic medium. He used his knowledge of various musical traditions and his acquired ear for the nuances of the language to establish the Yiddish art song as a credible art form. Through his work as conductor, teacher, and radio host, he provided the Yiddish art song with a foundation for further development.

★

Irene Heskes, "Lazar Weiner: In Service of the Jewish Musical Heritage," in *The Historic Contribution of Russian Jewry to Jewish Music: Supplement* (1968), written by a noted music historian with a specialty in Jewish music, is a sound biographical source with some occasional analysis. The most sustained discussion of Weiner's formal innovations is in Israel Rabinovitch, *Of Jewish Music Ancient and Modern* (1952). Albert Weisser, *The Modern Renaissance of Jewish Music: Events and Figures Eastern Europe and America* (1954), provides a strong though brief commentary on Weiner's importance in relation to other Yiddish songwriters. Aron Marko Rothmüller, *The Music of the Jews: An Historical Appreciation* (1967), contains limited information on Weiner's life but some detailed analysis of his music. Two crucial sources for biographical detail are Albert Weisser, "Lazar Weiner: A Tribute," *Congress Bi-Weekly* 34 (20 Nov. 1967): 16, written by the former president of the American Society for Jewish Music; and Marsha Bryan Edelman, "In Memoriam: Lazar Weiner (1897–1982)," *Musica Judaica: Journal of the American Society for Jewish Music* 4, no.1 (1981–1982): 99–112, which includes a comprehensive list of Weiner's published compositions. For an obituary with illuminating quotations, see Susan Chira, "Lazar Weiner, 84, Composer and Teacher of Jewish Music," *New York Times* (11 Jan. 1982).

PHILIP JOSEPH

WEISSMULLER, John Peter ("Johnny") (*b.* 2 June 1904 in Freiburg, Austria-Hungary [near present-day Timişoara, Romania]; *d.* 20 January 1984 in Acapulco, Mexico), two-time Olympic swimmer who won five gold medals and was voted most outstanding swimmer of the first half of the twentieth century by the Associated Press; after his athletic successes he gained even greater fame by portraying Tarzan, lord of the jungle, in twelve movies.

Weissmuller was born Petr Janos Weiszmuller, the elder of two sons of Peter and Elizabeth Weiszmuller, poor Austrian immigrants who lived a short time in Windber, Pennsylvania. (Some sources give Windber as Weissmuller's birthplace.) When Johnny was young the family moved to 1921 North Cleveland Avenue in Chicago, where the elder Weissmuller was a brewmaster. Weissmuller's introduction to swimming was therapeutic rather than competitive. After a series of childhood illnesses had rendered him thin and frail, a physician prescribed swimming to improve his health. He began dog-paddling with his brother Peter in the muddy Des Plaines River on the western edge of Chicago. Eventually he ventured into the cleaner water of Lake Michigan. Because swimming was a prescription and not a pleasant diversion, Weissmuller entertained himself by mimicking the strokes of faster swimmers he observed in Chicago's public pools.

Weissmuller also spent time as an altar boy at St. Michael Roman Catholic Church at 458 West Eugenie Avenue in Chicago. He attended the parish school but dropped out during the eighth grade. His swimming skills met the requirements for the Chicago Park District's lifeguard corps. In 1920 he attracted the attention of the great Illinois Athletic Club swim coach, Bill Bachrach. The famed coach immediately recognized Weissmuller's potential, but also realized that his crude, powerful stroke needed refinement. Bachrach kept his protégé out of competition until his starts, techniques, and speed were improved. On 6 August 1921, Coach Bachrach introduced his discovery to competition. Swimming in open water in Duluth, Minnesota, he sprinted 100 yards in fifty-two seconds, one second faster than the world record. Prevailing weather conditions, however, prevented official recognition of his achievement (before pools proliferated over the landscape, swimming meets were often held in oceans and lakes, or "open water"). On 21 September 1921 he achieved his first international record at New York's Brighton Baths in the 100-yard freestyle race. In that same meet he won the 150-yard backstroke and the 50-yard freestyle races.

By the time Weissmuller was eighteen years of age, he was the most outstanding freestyle swimmer in the world. At six feet, three inches tall and weighing 170 pounds, the superbly conditioned athlete exemplified the classic physique of a swimmer's broad shoulders, muscular torso, and narrow hips. His flexible knee joints executing deep leg action were perfect for the six-beat flutter kick; this, combined with his extraordinary speed, high position in the water, strong arms, and determination, set the champion apart from other competitors. On 9 July 1922 he made history upon becoming the first person ever to swim 100 meters in less than one minute.

In 1923, a year before the Paris Olympic Games, a pall was cast over Weissmuller's career when he was hospitalized after a swimming meet in Decatur, Illinois. He had competed in five races and had broken the world record in the 500-meter race. Physicians diagnosed a heart leakage and recommended complete rest. Reluctantly, he refrained from competing in the 1923 National Amateur Athletic Union championships but by September of that year he had reentered competitive swimming and won the 440-yard freestyle event.

Weissmuller began his quest for a berth on the 1924 Olympic team with a world-record performance in the 50-meter freestyle at the Olympic trials in Indianapolis, Indiana. On 5 June 1924, the final day of the swimming trials, he defeated the legendary Duke Kahanamouku of Hawaii in the 100-meter freestyle. Weissmuller's reputation preceded his arrival in Paris, and he entered the competition as the most feared swimmer of the 1924 Olympic Games. He won individual gold medals in the 100- and 400-meter freestyle events and anchored the gold medal 4 × 200 meter relay team. He was also a member of the bronze medal water polo team.

Weissmuller returned to the United States and after a brief rest continued setting records. His proudest moment came when he carried the American flag during the Opening Ceremonies of the 1928 Amsterdam Olympic Games. There, he overcame a near-disastrous gulp of water during the turn in the 100-meter freestyle, regained his composure, and claimed another gold medal. The fifth and last gold medal of his Olympic career came in Amsterdam on 11 August 1928, when he again anchored the 4 × 200 meter relay team. Weissmuller swam in his final amateur race on 3 January 1929, in an exhibition at the Illinois Athletic Club.

Johnny Weissmuller. POPPERFOTO/ARCHIVE PHOTOS

In 1930 Weissmuller was offered $500 a week to advertise swimsuits for the BVD Underwear Company. One of his photographs was noticed by a Hollywood agent, and he was invited to try out for the part of Tarzan. First appearing in that role in *Tarzan, the Ape Man* (1932), the carefree, casual Weissmuller was appropriately cast as an athletic man who befriended animals and survived jungle life. His character was likened to a Superman of the jungle and protector of his family, which included his wife Jane (played by Maureen O'Sullivan), son Boy, and pet chimpanzee Cheetah. He accentuated his jungle demeanor with his famous elephant call and his chest-thumping victory yell. In later Tarzan films, Olympians Clarence ("Buster") Crabbe, Herman Brix (also known as Bruce Bennett), and Glenn Morris would follow the Weissmuller prototype, but none achieved his fame in that role.

On 28 February 1931 Weissmuller married his first of five wives, musical comedy actress Bobbe Arnst, whom he divorced on 4 October 1932. On 20 June 1934 he exchanged vows with Mexican film actress Lupe Vélez. Their marriage ended 15 August 1938. On 20 August 1939 Weissmuller married San Francisco socialite Beryl Scott Ginter; they had three children and were divorced on 29 January 1948. Immediately after this divorce he married golfer Allene Gates

on 30 January 1948. After divorcing Gates, he married his fifth wife, Maria Gertrudis, in 1963.

Following his last Tarzan film, *Tarzan and the Mermaids* (1947), Weissmuller made a series of Jungle Jim movies and played that role on television for ten years. With Weissmuller by then in his mid-forties, the Jungle Jim character donned pants and a shirt and was a more modern jungle dweller. During the 1960s Weissmuller was vice president of the General Pool Corporation of Addison, Illinois, near Chicago. He then worked as a greeter at Caesars Palace in Las Vegas before suffering a series of strokes in 1977. His health steadily deteriorated and he and his wife moved to Acapulco, Mexico, in 1979. He died in Acapulco of pulmonary edema, or lung blockage, and was buried there.

Weissmuller consistently broke freestyle records during the 1920s, the golden age of sport. He was never seriously challenged in any of his swimming races and was credited with advancing the popularity of swimming to new heights. While many of the athletes who had established sport's golden age were quickly forgotten, Weissmuller's film appearances extended his reputation into the 1960s. Although his detractors made light of the limited verbal exchanges in the films, his Tarzan movies were immensely popular.

★

The Henning Library at the International Swimming Hall of Fame in Fort Lauderdale, Florida, has a collection of Weissmuller's pictures, papers, and memorabilia. "A Boy Who Has Broken All Swimming Records," *Literary Digest* (27 May 1922), details Weissmuller's early career and influence of his coach. Johnny Weissmuller, "My Methods of Training," *Saturday Evening Post* (8 Mar. 1930), is an analysis of his training methods and stroke execution. "Personal Glimpses: Swim, Said the Doctors, and Johnny Swam," *Literary Digest* (4 July 1931), includes his introduction to swimming and Olympic Games performances. Weissmuller's films are treated in Gabe Essoe, *Tarzan of the Movies: A Pictorial History of More Than Fifty Years of Edgar Rice Burroughs' Legendary Hero* (1968), and David Fury, *Kings of the Jungle: An Illustrated Reference to "Tarzan" on Screen and Television* (1994). Obituaries are in the *Chicago Tribune* (22 Jan. 1984) and *New York Times* (22 Jan. 1984).

PAULA D. WELCH

WELCH, Robert Henry Winborne, Jr. (*b.* 1 December 1899 near Chowan, North Carolina; *d.* 6 January 1985 in Winchester, Massachusetts), founder of the John Birch Society, which warned in the 1950s and 1960s of a communist conspiracy infiltrating government, schools, business, and other facets of national life.

Robert Welch, Jr., was the first of six children born to Robert Welch, Sr., a prosperous cotton farmer, and Lina Welch, a former schoolteacher. They were both college graduates

Robert Welch, 1953. ARCHIVE PHOTOS

and, largely because of the inaccessibility of public schools, Lina taught her children at home, sending them away to high school for their last two years. Robert Welch experienced a fundamentalist religious upbringing, tracing his ancestry to Baptist preachers. As a child, he was a "boy wonder," learning to read when he was three years old. He knew arithmetic and basic algebra at six, read Latin at seven, and graduated from high school at twelve. Welch entered the University of North Carolina in 1912 and graduated with an A.B. in the top third of his class in 1916. In an interview, Welch said of himself that he spent much of his time trying to impress people with how smart he was, and that in college he "was probably the most insufferable little squirt that ever tried to associate with his elders."

After graduation, Welch began a master's degree at the university, but dropped out a few months later, moving to Durham, North Carolina. There he got a job as a clerk, but in 1917 received an appointment to the U.S. Naval Academy. Spending only two years at Annapolis, Welch dropped out and tried his luck writing a column for newspapers. By 1921 Welch was back in academia, this time at Harvard Law School. After only two years there, Welch dropped out, disillusioned with academia and ready to go into business for himself.

Welch had started a candy company while at law school because he felt it was the one field "in which it seemed least impossible to get a start without either capital or experience." After purchasing a fudge recipe from a local candy-store owner, Welch launched the Oxford Candy Company. By 1924 his business was doing moderately well with its product Avalon Fudge. With the addition of two new candies, Oxford Candy prospered for the next five years before succumbing to the financial difficulties of the Great Depression. Oxford Candy was eventually sold to Daggett Chocolate Company.

The sale of Oxford Candy did not mean the end of the candy business for Welch. In 1932 he joined the staff of the largest candy manufacturer in the United States, E. J. Brach, at whose company he stayed for two years. He then moved on to his brother's candy business, the James O. Welch Company, in Massachusetts, as sales manager and vice president. As sales manager he increased sales from $20,000 in 1935 to $20 million in 1956. Welch wrote a how-to book in 1941 entitled *The Road to Salesmanship,* and was awarded the annual Kettle Award by *Candy Industry* magazine in 1947 for his achievements.

His position with the James O. Welch Company, along with his other positions as director of a local bank and several business organizations, allowed Welch to travel extensively throughout the nation and world. One of his trips took him to Great Britain in the late 1940s, where he spent several weeks studying the socialist government. Never one to trust collectivism, Welch told a group of American businessmen when he returned that there was "no reason on earth why we should import, or let ourselves be infected by, such disease of social old age as socialism and Communism and other ideological cancers." Soon after his trip, having had some experience in politics campaigning for Governor Robert F. Bradford of Massachusetts in 1946, Welch made a bid for lieutenant governor in 1950 as a Republican. He put his whole heart into the campaign, exhibiting a tremendous drive and commitment to "principle." Although he did not win, he made a strong showing and put his efforts in campaigning for presidential candidate Robert A. Taft in 1952. When Taft lost to Dwight Eisenhower as the Republican nominee, Welch and other conservatives were bitterly disappointed.

Welch spent the next six years writing books espousing his many ideas on communism and the liberal establishment. *May God Forgive Us* (1952) criticized President Harry Truman's dismissal of General Douglas MacArthur from his command of UN forces in Korea. In 1954, while researching for an article, Welch discovered the story of John Birch, an American military intelligence officer and Baptist missionary who was killed by the Chinese Communists just days after World War II ended. Welch was inspired by Birch's last words: "It doesn't matter what happens to me. But it is of utmost importance that my country learn now whether [the Chinese] are friend or foe." For Welch, John Birch was a model for every American, an uncompromising patriot, and a paragon of morality. He immortalized him in the book *The Life of John Birch* (1954) and established the John Birch Society in 1958, pledging to combat what was perceived to be the infiltration of communism into American life.

Welch spent the rest of his life devoted to his organization, which claimed a membership of 100,000 by the early 1960s. He continued to write about the communist conspiracy in his magazine, *American Opinion,* and he openly attacked President Eisenhower in the privately published book *The Politician* (1963). Other powerful members of government who were similarly accused by the Society as "dedicated, conscious agents of the Communist conspiracy" were CIA director Allen Dulles and Chief Justice Earl Warren. Welch was fond of saying "education is our total strategy, and truth is our only weapon." The John Birch Society was able to gain popular support from many conservatives throughout the 1950s and 1960s, but as the years passed, the Society's popularity and influence waned.

Welch had married Marian Lucille Probert on 2 December 1922, while he was still in the candy business. She stood by her husband through all of his ventures; they had two sons. Marian helped her husband with his society at the offices in Belmont, Massachusetts, where the Welches lived. The couple was active in the organization until he suffered a stroke in 1983.

Described by friends as a gregarious man with restless blue eyes and a fringe of white hair, Welch had to step down as president in March 1983. He became a chairman emeritus of the Society but remained in poor health for the duration of his life. He died in Winchester, Massachusetts, and was buried in Belmont.

The legacy of Robert Welch lies with the John Birch Society. His radical right-wing organization has been labeled by critics as extreme, while proponents of the Society have called Welch a prophet with a vision. The John Birch Society took its commitment to an extreme, suspecting communists in every government department, public school, and arts organization, using "red smear" tactics that functioned by spreading suspicion in an era during which cold war fears ran high.

★

G. Edward Griffin, *The Life and Words of Robert Welch* (1975), is a rather subjective biography. J. Allen Broyles, *The John Birch Society: Anatomy of a Protest* (1964), gives a good overview of the early days of the Society. Obituaries are in the *New York Times* (8 Jan. 1985) and *National Review* (8 Feb. 1985).

VALERIE L. DUNHAM

WELLES, Orson (*b.* 6 May 1915 in Kenosha, Wisconsin; *d.* 9 October 1985 in Los Angeles, California), flamboyant film director and actor and virtuoso of radio and theater, best known for his controversial film *Citizen Kane* and for his panic-producing radio broadcast of *War of the Worlds.*

Welles was one of two sons of Richard Head Welles, an inventor, and Beatrice (Ives) Welles, an amateur pianist and patron of the arts. Welles made his professional debut at the age of two as the child in the Chicago Lyric Opera's production of *Madame Butterfly,* but he was dismissed when he gained too much weight and the singers complained about having to lift the bulky child.

Welles's mother died when he was six. Welles was raised by his father for several years, traveling on several adventurous trips around the world until Welles's father, too, died. The orphaned Welles then was reared by a guardian, Dr. Maurice Bernstein, a friend of the family who loved the boy very much. Bernstein introduced the young Orson to great literature and to the cultural life of Chicago. He also encouraged Welles in various artistic areas and provided him with a violin, painting supplies, a magic kit, a puppet theater, and even a conductor's baton. After testing the boy's intelligence, psychologists reported that he was a genius.

At the age of ten Welles entered Todd School in Woodstock, Illinois, and was greatly influenced by the school's headmaster, Roger Hill, a relationship that would last for

Orson Welles, *c.* 1938. ARCHIVE PHOTOS

more than sixty years. As a student at Todd, Welles directed and played the Soothsayer in *Julius Caesar* and went on to become involved in dozens of plays and skits. In 1930, while still at Todd, he directed and acted in his first film, a four-minute avant-garde set piece called *Hearts of Age.* Filmed in sixteen-millimeter, it had an amateurish and rough-hewn look but nevertheless displayed elements of the great film director to come. He and Hill wrote and edited a series of textbooks, *Everybody's Shakespeare,* which made suggestions as to the interpretation, staging, and acting of the Bard's plays and became widely used prompt-books in high-school English and drama classes across the nation.

At the age of sixteen Welles went on a painting and sketching trip through Ireland. Short of funds, he auditioned for a job with the renowned Gate Theater in Dublin, attempting to appear older by smoking a cigar and telling the managers, the famous actor-directors Hilton Edwards and Micheál Mac Liammóir, that he had acted with the Theater Guild on the New York stage. Although they didn't believe him, they discerned a wealth of talent under Welles's braggadocio and hired him. He made his professional acting debut in November 1931 as the Duke of Würtemburg in *Jew Süss* and completed the season with the Gate Theater in a number of other featured parts. Leaving Dublin, he embarked on a short tour of England, Spain, and Morocco, but, after attempting without success to land any kind of job in the theater in Europe, he returned to Chicago, where he played, among other parts, the title role in a stock production of *Hamlet.*

In 1933 Welles was invited to join Katharine Cornell's eminent touring company, playing a highly praised Mercutio in *Romeo and Juliet;* Marchbanks in *Candida*; and Octavius Moulton-Barrett in *The Barretts of Wimpole Street.* His Broadway debut consisted of two parts, Tybalt and the Chorus, in Cornell's *Romeo and Juliet.* Generally praised for his acting (despite occasional criticisms that he was too histrionic), Welles nevertheless let it be known to all members of the company that he hoped to become a director. He married the Chicago socialite and aspiring actress Virginia Nicholson in 1934; they would have one daughter before divorcing in 1940.

In 1936, Welles began his directing career working in New York City with the Federal Theatre Project of the Works Progress Administration, a New Deal program established to stimulate employment in the theater community. Together with producer John Houseman, Welles produced and directed such works as *Horse Eats Hat; Dr. Faustus,* with Welles in the title role; and *Macbeth,* with an all-black cast. Dubbed the "Voodoo *Macbeth,*" the production caused a national sensation; on opening night more than 10,000 people crammed the streets around the Lafayette Theater in Harlem, attempting to purchase tickets.

The following year the two men founded the Mercury Theater. Welles directed and starred as Brutus in a version of *Julius Caesar* that was set in contemporary fascist Italy and drew clear parallels between the character of Caesar and the Italian dictator, Benito Mussolini. Welles infused in the play much of the speed and violence it had had on the Elizabethan stage. Contending that Shakespeare knew little of the speech of the Romans and so gave *Julius Caesar* the contemporary speech patterns of the playwright's own Elizabethan London, Welles rewrote Shakespeare so that the play sounded like the New York of Welles's day.

The Mercury Theater also produced such distinguished plays as *The Cradle Will Rock, The Shoemaker's Holiday, Heartbreak House,* and *Danton's Death,* most with Welles directing and appearing in a starring role and all with powerful and unusual stagings. The theater world was so thrilled about the Mercury performances that on 9 May 1938, *Time* published a cover story about the twenty-three-year-old Welles. It concluded: "The brightest moon that has risen over Broadway in years, Welles should feel at home in the sky, for the sky is the only limit his ambitions recognize."

At the same time Welles was dazzling Broadway with his theatrical productions he was also establishing a national reputation as a radio actor. On the dramatized news documentary *The March of Time,* he impersonated dozens of famous people of the day. But imitation was only a small part of Welles's radio métier. His voice had been resoundingly commended in virtually every stage performance over the years. On radio, his command of diction and tone—a rich, mellifluous sound delivered with a slight Oxonian accent—was thought of as the essence of his persona.

Welles became familiar to millions as the sepulchral voice of the weekly radio series *The Shadow* ("Who knows what evil lurks in the hearts of men?"), about a playboy detective named Lamont Cranston who could become invisible in order to confuse and foil criminals. The actress Agnes Moorehead served as Cranston's loyal assistant, Margot Lane. As a result, Welles and Moorehead established a creative relationship on radio and in film that lasted for many years.

Over the course of his lifetime Welles hosted or appeared in literally thousands of radio programs. In 1938 he and Houseman established the Mercury Theater of the Air, which presented weekly adaptations of classics. The parts were played mainly by the actors in their legitimate theater troupe, with Welles writing, directing, narrating, and starring. On 11 July the series premiered on CBS with *Dracula,* followed by such works as *A Tale of Two Cities, Rebecca, Les Misérables, Jane Eyre,* and *Arrowsmith.* His use of crisp writing, believable sound effects, overlapping dialogue, precision timing, and stellar acting raised the art of radio drama to a new level. Welles became such a popular radio star and had so much broadcasting work that he often hired an ambulance, with siren blasting and red lights flashing, to transport him from studio to studio across the traffic-snarled streets of Manhattan in order to arrive on time for his live broadcasts.

On 30 October 1938, Welles presented a radio dramatization of H. G. Wells's *War of the Worlds,* which relates the story of a Martian invasion of Earth. Orson Welles contemporized the tale, moving its locale to New Jersey and using fictitious news bulletins and reporters from the field in which the alien spaceship had supposedly landed. Many listeners tuned in late and did not hear the announcement that the show was a dramatization. So authentic was the presentation of flash bulletins and other effects that tens of thousands of Americans thought the invasion was real. Panic ensued, especially in New Jersey. People armed themselves, fled their homes, and went to local police stations and churches looking for safety. The CBS switchboard was flooded with thousands of calls from all over the country; within a few hours, news of the panic had spread around the world. Welles woke the next morning to find himself an international celebrity of sorts as the show produced front-page headlines and commentary at home and abroad. As a result of the *War of the Worlds* panic a special law was initiated by the Federal Communications Commission preventing the broadcast of dramatized news shows if they were so real as to be believable.

Welles's artistic triumphs and the enormous publicity now led a number of motion-picture producers to try to lure him to Hollywood. In the summer of 1939, Welles signed a contract with RKO Pictures to write, produce, direct, and star in three motion pictures, the subjects of which were to be determined. Few people, with the exception of Charlie Chaplin, had had the opportunity to write, produce, direct, and star in their own film. Welles's arrangement was touted as the most lavishly attractive and unrestrictive contract in motion-picture history. The *New York Times* of 20 August reported that Welles was to be paid $100,000 per film and that "it is understood that the studio will exercise no supervision over the picture, merely footing the bill." However, there were restrictions put on Welles's relationship to RKO that were not made public at the time, such as the studio's right to approve the idea before filming began and to edit, cut, dub, or change the film for censorship purposes.

After considering a number of ideas and test-shooting scenes for several films, Welles decided on a screenplay he wrote with Herman J. Mankiewicz. Titled *Citizen Kane,* it was an impressionistic biography of a newspaper tycoon who had fallen from grace, and it strongly suggested the career of the real-life publisher William Randolph Hearst.

As he did with radio and theater, Welles mastered the art of motion-picture making. Many critics regard *Citizen Kane* as the greatest American motion picture ever made. In order to learn the craft of filmmaking, Welles spent long hours at the studio absorbing the craft of every department, from costuming and makeup to special effects and cinematography. He also ordered a copy of John Ford's *Stagecoach* from the Museum of Modern Art and screened the movie more than forty times to learn the syntax and grammar of film. Welles wanted the viewer to see his film as "reality": to enter the film, become a part of it, and remain there to its conclusion.

Although Welles introduced nothing new from a technical standpoint, he synthesized techniques used by some of the great masters of filmmaking to create an artistic statement that has rarely been equaled. Flashbacks, chronological tampering, sets with ceilings, deep-focus cinematography, radical editing, and unusual camera angles were used to present the subject of alienation in a realistic manner, perhaps the first American film ever to do so. Welles's elliptical style was that of disorientation, a departure from the linear way of telling a story in which time proceeds in chronological, cause-and-effect fashion. He broke cinematic tradition with *Citizen Kane,* and all his later films would be infused with the same originality and tension.

When Hearst saw an advance screening of *Citizen Kane* he was horrified. He believed that the character of Charles Foster Kane was nothing less than a caustic cinema à clef of himself and that the alcoholic character of Susan Alexander Kane was clearly intended to be a characterization of his longtime beloved mistress, the actress Marion Davies. Through intermediaries Hearst attempted to buy all prints of *Citizen Kane* for what it cost to produce plus a modest profit, with the idea of destroying them so that the American public could never see the movie. When RKO refused Hearst's offer, successful attempts were made to block the showing of the film in selected theaters. Welles threatened to have large tents put up in cities across the nation and then to project the film under canvas to the public, perhaps for free admission. Eventually, on 8 May 1941, *Citizen Kane* opened in a limited number of theaters to mostly favorable reviews. The *New Yorker* stated: "Something new has come to the movie world at last." The *New York Times* claimed "it comes close to being the most sensational film ever made in Hollywood." And the *New York World-Telegram* held *Citizen Kane* "to be a masterpiece."

Despite its critical acclaim, *Citizen Kane* did not do well at the box office. Welles (and Mankiewicz) received the Academy Award that year for best screenplay, and Welles was nominated for best director and best actor. Years later, the British critic Kenneth Tynan summed up the importance of Welles's first film: "Nobody who saw *Citizen Kane* at an impressionable age will ever forget the experience; overnight, the American cinema had acquired an adult vocabulary."

Having been divorced for several years, Welles married the film star Rita Hayworth in 1943. The marriage was a tempestuous affair widely reported on in the press. The couple had a daughter, Rebecca, before divorcing in 1948. His third marriage, to the Italian actress Paola Mori, La Comtesse di Girafalco, lasted from 1956 until his death and produced Welles's third daughter, Beatrice, named after Welles's mother.

Welles went on to make a number of films, both independently and in Hollywood, that had the imaginative Wellesian touch, although none were particularly successful at the box office. He directed and starred in three Shakespeare films: *Macbeth* (1948), which he shot in three weeks; *Othello* (1951); and *Chimes at Midnight* (1966). He was influential in defining the film-noir genre with *The Lady from Shanghai* (1948), *Mr. Arkadin* (1954), and *Touch of Evil* (1958); proved that he could direct and star in typical Hollywood productions with *Journey into Fear* (1942) and *The Stranger* (1946); and demonstrated that he was still at home with the adaptation of classic literature by directing films based on works by Franz Kafka (*The Trial,* 1962) and Isak Dinesen (*The Immortal Story,* 1968).

In addition to directing films of his own, Welles spent more than forty years acting in other motion pictures, playing such characters as Napoleon, Cesare Borgia, Cagliostro, and Rochester in *Jane Eyre* (1944). Many people remember Welles best as the evil but charming Harry Lime in *The Third Man* (1949), directed by Sir Carol Reed. In England he went on to direct and star in a radio series based on the Lime character, which was popular for several years.

Because of tax problems, and because it was less expensive to make his own films in Europe, Welles spent many years living there. He moved back to the United States eventually, and lived out the last two decades of his life doing voice-overs for radio and television commercials, acting in occasional films, appearing on television talk shows, and unsuccessfully attempting to mount a major film of one of his screenplays, such as *Don Quixote, King Lear, The Big Brass Ring,* and *The Other Side of the Wind.*

During his lifetime Welles was continually in the process of being transformed into a legend. Festivals of his motion pictures were frequently held in the United States and abroad, books and articles about his life and films were published regularly, and aspiring filmmakers beat a path to his favorite restaurant to meet him, hoping to learn the secrets of the screen. But no one would give him the financial backing he needed to continue to direct and make films. It was argued that he was too much of a maverick and just not commercial enough.

It is ironic that Welles could not find backing during the last years of his life, for few could dispute that he placed, indelibly, his creative stamp on the theater, radio, and film.

In the United States, and perhaps internationally, there can be no history of cinema, no archive of broadcasting, no chronicle of the stage, that can fail to include among its pages the name of Orson Welles as one of its most illustrious talents. He invented his own unmistakable and controversial style, the mark of a true original.

Orson Welles died of a heart attack late one evening, alone in Hollywood, California. He had been sitting at his typewriter, writing a screenplay. He is buried in Ronda, Spain.

★

A wealth of biographies, studies of his work, and articles about Welles appeared in the years following his death in 1985. Some major ones are: Frank Brady, *Citizen Welles* (1985), a biography by the film scholar; John Russell Taylor, *Orson Welles* (1986), a celebration by the film critic of the *London Times*; Harlan Lebo, *Citizen Kane* (1990), a fiftieth-anniversary album; Orson Welles and Peter Bogdanovich, *This Is Orson Welles* (1992), a transcript of many talks between the two directors; Lynne Piade, *Citizen Kane* (1992), a photo album of the picture; Robert Carringer, *The Magnificent Ambersons* (1993), a reconstruction of the film; Simon Callow, *Orson Welles: The Road to Xanadu* (1995), a biography by the actor; David Thomson, *Rosebud* (1996), an impressionistic biography; and Orson Welles, *Les Bravades* (1996), a sketchbook of pictures Welles drew for his daughter Rebecca. Also to be noted are *Persistence of Vision* no. 7 (1989), an issue devoted to Welles's life and career; and Vassili Silovic, *Orson Welles: The One Man Band* (1995), a documentary film that offers a fascinating glimpse of Welles's final years.

FRANK BRADY

WEST, (Mary) Jessamyn (*b.* 18 July 1902 near North Vernon, Indiana; *d.* 23 February 1984 in Napa, California), writer best known for her narratives about midwestern Quakers, such as the short stories collected in *The Friendly Persuasion* (1945).

Jessamyn West was a "birthright Quaker," the eldest of four children of Eldo Ray and Grace Anna (Milhous) West. She lived on a southern Indiana farm until the family moved to southern California in 1909, going from the horse-and-buggy era directly into the automobile age, as she later described the transition. Her father was a teacher and amateur poet as well as a farmer, but West was more influenced by her maternal grandmother, Mary Frances McManaman Milhous, who told wonderful stories about her Quaker relatives.

The West family settled in the new town of Yorba Linda in Orange County, California, and achieved modest prosperity growing lemons and oranges. Jessamyn's second cousin, Richard Milhous Nixon, who was ten years her

Jessamyn West, 1976. UPI/CORBIS-BETTMANN

junior, also lived in Yorba Linda. West graduated from Whittier College with a degree in English, and some weeks later, on 16 August 1923, she married Harry Maxwell Mc-Pherson, a fellow student who had not yet graduated. She taught for several years in a one-room rural school while her husband worked on a nearby ranch. In 1929 they both enrolled at the University of California in Berkeley, where Max McPherson earned a doctorate in education. West flourished as a graduate student in the American studies division of the English department, but her academic career ended suddenly in 1931 when she was diagnosed with advanced tuberculosis. In the sanatorium she contemplated suicide, and her condition was so desperate that she was sent home to die in the company of her family. To help pass the time, her mother told her many stories of earlier generations of Quaker relatives back in Indiana.

Jessamyn West read eagerly from an early age, but she began to write fiction only during her prolonged recuperation, what she called "the lost ten years of my life." Not until 1940 were she and her husband able to move into a home of their own in Napa, California. Writing was a very private experience for West, and only at the repeated urging of her husband did she submit a dozen short stories to various little magazines in 1939. Her first published stories were set in tuberculosis hospitals, but she turned increasingly to stories of mid-nineteenth-century Indiana and early-twentieth-century southern California. Her first story appeared in the leftist *New Masses* under the name of Jessamyn McPherson, but for fear that association with this sort of publication might cause political difficulty for her husband, by then a school superintendent, she wrote thereafter as Jessamyn West. Through the 1940s and 1950s her stories appeared in such distinguished magazines as *Atlantic, Harper's,* and the *New Yorker*, as well as more popular magazines such as *Collier's* and *Ladies Home Journal.*

Fourteen stories of a Quaker family in southern Indiana before and during the Civil War were brought together in *The Friendly Persuasion* (1945). The book was an immediate success both financially and critically, and it firmly established Jessamyn West's reputation and popularity. Although she returned on occasion to Quaker themes, especially *Except for Me and Thee* (1969), West firmly resisted efforts to characterize her as a "Quaker writer." Her first novel, *The Witch Diggers* (1951), told of disappointed love in turn-of-the-century Indiana, but offended some by its sexual frankness. In *The Massacre at Fall Creek* (1975), West turned to a sensational murder trial in frontier Indiana, the first occasion in which white men were hanged for the murder of Native Americans. Its graphic violence and open sexuality startled readers who knew only her Quaker stories, but West proudly defended the novel's realism.

The first collection of West's California stories appeared in *Cress Delahanty* (1953), a Book-of-the Month Club selection. West drew on her own girlhood memories for stories of a teenager's life in Orange County. *South of the Angels* (1960) is also set in southern California, but presents a view of adolescence that some reviewers found downright bawdy. *Love, Death, and the Ladies' Drill Team* (1955) brings together a group of West's finest California stories.

The Life I Really Lived (1979) is a novel set in both Indiana and California. The plot is strongly sexual, but in language and events the work is quite subdued. It was not well received. Far more successful was West's excursion into science fiction, in the satirical and wildly humorous story "The Pismire Plan" (1948). Sometimes described as a "California fantasy," it skillfully exploited the stranger aspects of southern California culture.

A Matter of Time (1966) is a controversial novel about euthanasia, drawn from West's loving care of her sister Carmen, who suffered from inoperable cancer. Years later West revealed that she had assisted in her sister's suicide. In her turn, Jessamyn West directed that her body be cremated without any funeral service and that the ashes be buried in her backyard.

Frank Capra purchased the film rights to *The Friendly Persuasion* in 1945, but it was director William Wyler who brought it to the screen ten years later. He persuaded West to develop the script, although she did not receive the official screen credit. She wrote two later films but never sought a career in Hollywood. Film rights for *The Massacre at Fall Creek* brought substantial payments, but it has never been made into a film. Her short story "Learn to Say Goodbye" was produced for television in 1960 by Ronald Reagan.

Although her health was never robust after her recovery from tuberculosis, West enjoyed public speaking. She always refused to read from her own stories but did occasionally recite her poems, which were published as *The Secret Look: Poems by Jessamyn West* (1974). During the 1950s and 1960s she taught writing courses at several colleges and universities, including Indiana, Stanford, and Wellesley.

Jessamyn West never wrote an autobiography as such, but four books are drawn in part from the journals she kept for most of her life. She describes herself as growing up as a Quaker in sheltered rural environments, an avid reader who became a teacher and a journalist and who turned to writing only in her thirties. She carefully guarded her privacy and avoided the entertaining expected of a school superintendent's wife. Her marriage was happy. The McPhersons had no children of their own, but they took an impoverished Irish girl into their home in 1955. Legal difficulties were eased by Vice President Nixon, and this was the only occasion West ever asked her cousin for a political favor. Max McPherson legally adopted Ann McCarthy Cash in 1990.

Jessamyn West described herself as "a plain woman" and often told those who asked about her life, "If you want to know me, read my works." She was always conscious of her dual heritage, saying, "I am by all I know a Californian, and by all I imagine a Hoosier." The homes of her heart were southern Indiana and southern California: "I only live in northern California," she explained. Readers who knew only *The Friendly Persuasion* were sometimes startled by the realistic view of sexuality and the frank language of West's other works. She often described strong women characters, only some of them Quakers, for she was herself a vigorous personality who accepted risks without fear. Although half her stories are set in California, Jessamyn West is better known and more highly regarded as an Indiana writer. She died of a stroke in 1984.

★

The Jessamyn West Collection at Wardman Library, Whittier College, includes manuscripts for all her books and several hundred letters. Her journals were burned as she instructed. West revealed many aspects of her life in four volumes drawn from her journals: *To See the Dream* (1957), *Hide and Seek: A Continuing Journey* (1973), *The Woman Said Yes: Encounters with Life and Death—Memoirs* (1976), and *Double Discovery: A Journey* (1980). Alfred S. Shivers, *Jessamyn West, Revised Edition* (1992), is the best critical study. It offers only a brief biography but includes a complete bibliography of her books and short stories. Ann Dahlstrom Farmer, *Jessamyn West* (1982), is a short critical study emphasizing the California stories, while John T. Flanagan, "The Fiction of Jessamyn West," *Indiana Magazine of History* 67 (Dec. 1971): 299–316, covers her works set in Indiana. Catherine E. Forrest Weber presents a more personal view in "Writer Jessamyn West: The Storyteller's Daughter," *Traces of Indiana and Midwestern History* (summer 1994): 42–47. An obituary is in the *New York Times* (24 Feb. 1984).

PATRICK J. FURLONG

WHEELER, Raymond Milner (*b.* 30 September 1919 in Farmville, North Carolina; *d.* 17 February 1982 in Charlotte, North Carolina), physician, civil rights activist, and advocate of better health care and nutrition for the poor, especially in the South.

Wheeler was the son of George Raymond Wheeler, a school superintendent in Farmville, North Carolina, and Sallie Kate Collins. Raymond Wheeler received a certificate in medicine from the University of North Carolina in 1941 and a medical degree from Washington University in St. Louis, Missouri, in 1943. He served his internship at Barnes Hospital in St. Louis in 1943 and 1944.

In June 1942 Wheeler married Mary Lou Browning. They had three children. The marriage ended in divorce in 1956. He married Julie Buckner Carr on 6 June 1958. They had no children.

Wheeler served in the U.S. Army Medical Corps from 1944 to 1946; he left at the rank of captain. Wheeler was awarded the Silver Star and Purple Heart for rescuing two wounded soldiers in the Battle of the Bulge in Europe. From 1946 to 1948 Wheeler was an assistant resident in medicine at North Carolina Baptist Hospital in Winston-Salem. In 1948 he entered private practice in internal medicine with the Charlotte Medical Clinic. He served as chairman of the department of medicine at the Charlotte Memorial Hospital from 1961 to 1963 and as clinical associate professor of medicine in the University of North Carolina Medical School from 1966 to 1970.

Wheeler recognized the connection between poverty and the medical problems he saw in his patients, and he became known as a champion of the rights of the poor. In 1956 Wheeler joined the Southern Regional Council, a civil rights organization whose work resulted in the registration of millions of black voters. Wheeler served as chairman of its executive committee from 1964 to 1969 and as president from 1969 to 1974. He also served as president of the North Carolina Council for Human Relations from 1957 to 1961.

In 1967 Wheeler was a member of a team of six physicians supported by the Field Foundation who studied the health and living conditions of black children in Mississippi. Its findings were published by the Southern Regional Council as *Hungry Children* (1967).

Wheeler and another physician, Harvard University child psychiatrist Robert Coles, took their findings to Senator Robert Kennedy of New York. The senator told them that their reports would have no real value unless they were willing to testify before hostile Senate committees. Kennedy suggested that Wheeler be the spokesman for the group because he had a southern accent. In June 1967 the doctors appeared before the Employment, Manpower, and Poverty Subcommittee of the Senate Labor and Public Welfare Committee, describing the conditions they found in the 600 to 700 children examined. Wheeler told the committee that even though he had been born and raised in the South, he had not been prepared for what he had observed in Mississippi. Wheeler described seeing children suffering from hunger and disease and directly or indirectly dying from them. What the doctors had seen was not malnutrition but starvation, he stated.

Raymond Wheeler testifies before the Senate subcommittee on migratory labor, 1970. UPI/CORBIS-BETTMANN

Mississippi's senators, James Eastland and John Stennis, responded angrily to Wheeler's morning testimony. Senator Stennis called Wheeler's statements "gross libel and slander." Senator Eastland denounced them as "totally untrue." After the lunchtime recess Wheeler responded to the senators' criticisms. Speaking calmly and without notes he said,

> I reported what I saw because it is intolerable to me that this situation should exist in the region I love. . . . For the past twenty years, I have worked in the South, my birthplace and home. During that time I have come to know in depth the white and the Negro—their problems, their sorrows, their joys. Throughout those years, my heart has wept for the South, as I have watched the southern black man and white man walk their separate ways, distrusting each other, separated by false and ridiculous barriers—doomed to a way of life tragically less than they deserve, when, by working together, they could achieve a society finer and more successful than any which exists in this country today.

Wheeler later told a friend, "I never enjoyed myself so much in my life."

Wheeler sat on the Citizens Board of Inquiry into Hunger and Malnutrition in the United States, which published *Hunger, U.S.A.* in 1968. This report formed the basis for a CBS prime-time documentary, "Hunger in America" (1968) and helped spur the expansion of the federal food stamp program. Over the next few years Wheeler participated in several tours to investigate the health conditions of the poor, including migrant farm workers in Texas and Florida.

Wheeler continued his work for social justice until the end of his life. During the 1970s he was active in the Voter Education Project, the Children's Foundation, the North Carolina Hunger Coalition, the National Sharecroppers' Fund, and Southerners for Economic Justice. In each of these organizations he served for a time as president, chairman of the board of directors or executive committee, or as a board member. In 1979 the North Carolina Civil Liberties Union honored him with the Frank Porter Graham Award in recognition of his distinguished service.

Wheeler was a member of the Unitarian Fellowship. In 1970 he told an interviewer that he did not know what had sparked his interest in social problems. He did, however, recall an unusual friendship he developed as a child with a black man, Jim Thigpen, who worked as a janitor in the Farmville school that Wheeler, who was white, attended. They took long bike rides together on Saturdays. Wheeler admired the man for his sense of personal dignity despite the discrimination and lack of opportunity he had endured.

Later, Wheeler went back to visit Thigpen and learned

that he had died at home of pneumonia without medical treatment. It was something Wheeler never forgot.

Wheeler died of a heart attack. In keeping with his wishes, no funeral or memorial service was held.

Wheeler enjoyed gardening and reading, but these hobbies took a back seat to his other pursuits. A colleague at the Charlotte Medical Clinic said of him, "Human rights are to Ray Wheeler what golf is to the rest of us."

Wheeler is remembered for his dedication, courage, and unassuming manner. He was good-humored but reserved and shunned public recognition for his work. Robert Coles called Wheeler "one of the greatest figures in the civil rights struggle that we don't know about because of his shyness and modesty."

★

Papers relating to Wheeler's social justice activities are housed in the Southern Historical Collection of the University of North Carolina at Chapel Hill. William S. Powell, ed., *Dictionary of North Carolina Biography,* vol. 6 (1996), includes a summary of Wheeler's life and accomplishments. "N.C. Doctor: 'My Heart Has Wept for the South,'" *Raleigh News and Observer* (29 July 1970), describes Wheeler's role as a spokesman for the South's poor and recounts the story of his childhood friendship with Jim Thigpen. Rick Warner, "A Quiet, One-Man Crusade for Social Justice," *Raleigh News and Observer* (22 June 1980), features Wheeler as the "Tar Heel of the Week" and chronicles his life and career. Tributes in the *Charlotte Observer* at the time of his death include Frye Gaillard, "Dr. Raymond Wheeler Shook Southern Sensibilities of '60s" (19 Feb. 1982), and "Dr. Wheeler: A Life Devoted to Healing" (19 Feb. 1982). Another tribute, "Raymond M. Wheeler," was published in the *Greensboro Daily News* (23 Feb. 1982). Obituaries are in the *Charlotte Observer* (18 Feb. 1982) and the *New York Times* (20 Feb. 1982).

ROBYN K. BURNETT

WHITAKER, Rogers E(rnest) M(alcolm) ("E. M. Frimbo") (*b.* 15 January 1900 in Arlington, Massachusetts; *d.* 11 May 1981 in the Bronx, New York), writer and editor for the *New Yorker* magazine, best known for his articles about football, nightclubs, and railroads.

Rogers Whitaker's father, Charles Harris Whitaker, was a tough yet perceptive taskmaster. Nicknamed "the Skipper" by his family, the elder Whitaker was an architectural critic and the first editor of the *Journal of the American Institute of Architects.* He made astute but unorthodox decisions concerning the educations of his two sons. When, in 1922, at the age of fifteen, Rogers's younger brother, Francis, came home from school complaining that he had learned how to compute how much work a laborer could do but knew nothing of what a laborer's life was like, his father got him a job as a helper with Samuel Yellin of Philadelphia, Amer-

ica's premier ironsmith. Francis loved the work from the start, never returned to school, and went on to assume his mentor's mantle as America's greatest teacher of ironsmiths and as a designer and producer of decorative ironwork.

Charles Whitaker sent his elder son to Princeton University, but after Rogers's sophomore year the father abruptly refused to pay his tuition, giving him instead $40 and letters of introduction to three New York publishers. Rogers took the challenge, moved to New York, and looked for work in publishing, taking whatever jobs he could get at first and learning as much as he could. Whitaker's mother had helped equip him by teaching him to cook and sew when he was still a child. She was also an active suffragist. His father required that he be independent; his mother showed him how.

Whitaker loved New York from the moment he arrived in 1920. A large man, solid and six feet, two inches, with a gruff drawl, an independent manner, and a fondness for good clothes (his handmade Bernard Weatherill tweed sportscoat is in the Costume Institute of the Metropolitan Museum of Art), Whitaker immediately began moving about the city with assurance and curiosity. He lived at first in a theatrical boardinghouse just down the hall from the actress Mae West and later in a Greenwich Village apartment with fifteen cats.

At first he sold advertising for a trade magazine and did fact checking for the *New York Times.* In 1925 he bought the first issue of the *New Yorker* and decided that was the publication for which he wanted to work. A year later, he got a job at the magazine as head of the makeup department and for the next six years he directed layout and, with art editor Rea Irvin, helped editor Harold Ross develop the magazine's format. Whitaker also worked with copy editor Hobart G. Weekes in setting up the *New Yorker*'s famously meticulous fact-checking department. His attention to detail, his devotion to the magazine, and his rigorous, mercilessly ironic, but patient manner with writers led Ross to promote him first to chief proofreader and then head of the copy desk.

In 1934, while continuing to carry out various editorial chores, Whitaker began writing a college football column for the magazine, something he did for the next forty-six years. Whitaker inherited the column when the writer John O'Hara, assigned to a Harvard game, became too inebriated to write the story (or so the story went at the *New Yorker*). Whitaker covered mainly Ivy League contests because he believed the players, who did not receive athletic scholarships, were more likely to be playing for love of the game. The beat enabled him to return to Princeton, where he showed up for games decked out in a real tiger-skin vest under a large raccoon coat. His football column was published over the initials "J. W. L.," ostensibly because an early

Rogers E. M. Whitaker, 1955. UPI/Corbis-Bettmann

the *New Yorker* with his office mate, Anthony Hiss. The two of them collected some of this work in a 1974 book, *All Aboard with E. M. Frimbo.* By himself, Whitaker wrote *Decade of the Trains: The 1940s* (1977) and was consulting editor for *Fodor's Railways of the World* (1977), for which he wrote the preface. A musical, *Frimbo,* written and directed by John Haber and based on Whitaker's travels, ran at Grand Central Terminal in 1980. Whitaker served as a major in the U.S. Army during World War II, routing troop trains, and later was a consultant to Amtrak. In 1970 he was a key witness at an Interstate Commerce Commission hearing that denied Penn Central permission to shut down many of its long-distance passenger trains.

Married and divorced three times, Whitaker died of cancer. He had no children. Whitaker's ashes were scattered by his brother in the Cumbres Pass in southern Colorado, which at 10,022 feet is the highest point traversed by passenger trains in the United States.

Rogers Whitaker was possessed of particular passions. He made them his work and in so doing helped celebrate and preserve certain essential twentieth-century American traditions—amateur football, Manhattan nightlife, efficient and comfortable train travel, and well-crafted sentences.

★

Whitaker's collected papers and correspondence are in the Rogers E. M. Whitaker Collection, American Heritage Center, University of Wyoming, Laramie, Wyoming. Rogers E. M. Whitaker and Anthony Hiss, *All Aboard with E. M. Frimbo, World's Greatest Railroad Buff* (1974), is a compilation of Whitaker's railroad features, most of which appeared first in the *New Yorker.* Rogers E. M. Whitaker, with photos and commentary by Don Ball, Jr., *Decade of the Trains: The 1940s* (1977), is a photoessay of trains in their heyday drawing on Whitaker's experiences. Brendan Gill, *Here at the New Yorker* (1975), contains numerous in house anecdotes about Whitaker as editor and character. Tony Hiss, "Frimbo's Peak," *New Yorker* (8 Aug. 1983), is an article about the Whitaker brothers by Rogers Whitaker's longtime *New Yorker* office mate and collaborator. Obituaries are in the *New Yorker* (1 June 1981) and the *New York Times* (12 May 1981).

NED STUCKEY-FRENCH

managing editor liked how those letters looked typographically.

In the early 1930s he also began writing short reviews of supper clubs and cabarets for the "Goings On About Town" section in the front of the magazine. This work eventually led to a second column, when in 1943 he took over the "Table for Two" reviews, which had been pioneered by Lois Long. This column, written by Whitaker for twenty years, carried profiles of nightclub entertainers and enabled him to become friendly with many performers, especially Bobby Short, Duke Ellington, and the composer Cy Coleman. Known as "Popsie" among show-business people because of his prematurely gray hair, Whitaker helped launch many careers with his influential reviews.

When Whitaker was only nine, his father told him he was old enough to ride a train by himself, and from that point he became obsessed with them, eventually riding, he said, every mile of passenger track in the United States and all of the world's great lines. He calculated that he had logged 2,748,636.81 miles on trains during his lifetime—more than 50,000 miles a year for more than fifty years—riding mostly at night, during weekends, and on vacations. Under the moniker "E. M. Frimbo, the world's greatest railroad buff," he collaborated on articles about trains for

WHITE, E(lwyn) B(rooks) (*b.* 11 July 1899 in Mount Vernon, New York; *d.* 1 October 1985 in North Brooklin, Maine), essayist and children's author best known for his association with the *New Yorker* magazine, the essay "Once More to the Lake," the children's novel *Charlotte's Web,* and the short writing guide *The Elements of Style.*

E. B. White was one of six children of Samuel Tilly White, vice president, and later president, of Horace Waters and Company, piano manufacturers; and Jessie Hart, a housewife. Much younger than his siblings, White often felt iso-

E. B. White, *c.* 1960. UPI/CORBIS-BETTMANN

lated in the spacious house at 101 Summit Street in suburban Mount Vernon. He learned to read by sounding out words in the *New York Times,* and his earliest letters reveal a distinctive voice and a deft ear for language. He attended Lincoln Elementary School and from childhood was rewarded for writing about what he observed. He published a poem on a mouse in *Women's Home Companion* at age ten, won a silver medal in 1911 and a gold medal in 1914 from *St. Nicholas Magazine* for dog stories, and later published poems, stories, and editorials in the *Mount Vernon High School Oracle.*

White entered Cornell University in 1917 and wrote for the *Cornell Daily Sun,* becoming editor-in-chief and an award-winning editorialist by his senior year. As an English major in the Manuscript Club, a creative writing group, and as a college journalist, White wrote light verse and humorous sketches in the manner of New York columnists Franklin P. Adams (F.P.A.), Don Marquis, and Christopher Morley. Cornell reinforced White's self-image as a writer, developed his talents as an observer and commentator, and encouraged brevity, immediacy, wit, and self-expression in his writing.

He graduated in 1921 and worked briefly in turn for the United Press, a silk-mill house magazine, and the Ameri-

can Legion News Service. He also submitted material to popular columns but succeeded only in placing one poem in Morley's. Discouraged, in the spring of 1922, White and a college friend, Howard Cushman, drove across the United States in White's Model T Ford. White took a job with the *Seattle Times* and for three months ran a classified-section column mixing poetry, paragraphs, and humor as Marquis and F.P.A. did. Fired in June 1923, he returned to New York, supporting himself with a series of jobs in advertising and submitting poetry to F.P.A.'s "Conning Tower" column.

On 18 April 1925, White was published for the first time in the *New Yorker,* Harold Ross's new weekly magazine. At the urging of the fiction editor, Katharine Sergeant Angell, Ross hired White as a staff writer in 1927. White's association with the *New Yorker* changed every aspect of his life, and he would continue to publish there for the next fifty years. He wrote poetry and sketches as well as funny column-fillers called "Newsbreaks," cartoon captions, theater reviews, and advertising copy; he also edited the Talk of the Town section. Eventually he became the anonymous principal author of Notes and Comment, a section of untitled paragraphs in Talk of the Town, and gave the magazine its editorial voice.

On 13 November 1929 he married Angell, who was recently divorced, and moved from his apartment at 23 West Twelfth Street into her larger apartment at 16 East Eighth Street, where they were visited by her children, Nancy and Roger. The Whites' only child, Joel, was born in 1930.

Early in his career White was known principally as a humorist, his reputation established by a collection of light verse, *The Lady Is Cold* (1929), and by a parody of psychological self-help books, *Is Sex Necessary?* (1929), written with and illustrated by James Thurber, then a friend and fellow *New Yorker* writer. Thurber credited White with introducing him as an artist. Between 1927 and 1937, White was thoroughly involved in the editorial life of the *New Yorker,* and his subsequent books reprinted magazine material: newsbreaks in *Ho Hum* (1931) and *Another Ho Hum* (1932); Notes and Comment paragraphs in *Every Day Is Saturday* (1934); a long essay about his cross-country trip in *Farewell to Model T* (1936); more light verse in *The Fox of Peapack and Other Poems* (1938); and casuals, stories, and satirical pieces in *Quo Vadimus? or, The Case for the Bicycle* (1939).

Increasingly restless under the limitations and demands of the Comment assignment, in 1937 he took a year's leave of absence from the *New Yorker* to do other kinds of writing. He moved with his family in 1938 to North Brooklin, Maine, where they began living year-round on the farm they had purchased in 1933. Katharine continued to edit part-time for the magazine and White continued to write Comment, but he also contributed "One Man's Meat," a monthly four-page column, to *Harper's Magazine*. More personal and introspective than Comment and written in the first person singular ("the only grammatical implement I am able to use without cutting myself"), the columns established White as an essayist of passion and insight and were reprinted as *One Man's Meat* (1942; enlarged 1944). A reflective rural life overshadowed by World War II broadened and deepened White's writing. *A Subtreasury of American Humor* (1941), an anthology coedited with Katharine, virtually concluded his role as a humorist, and *Four Freedoms* (1942), a political pamphlet in which he edited texts by Malcolm Cowley, Reinhold Niebuhr, and Max Lerner, reintroduced him as a political writer. Wanting to write more regularly and immediately about the war and its aftermath, he ended the popular monthly column at *Harper's* and in 1943 returned full time to New York City to resume weekly responsibilities at the *New Yorker*.

The Whites lived at 229 East Forty-eighth Street for the next fourteen years. By the early 1950s, under White's influence, Notes and Comment had been transformed from a lighthearted multiple-item page to a single-subject editorial. White's editorials argued for world government and against McCarthy-era witch-hunting, nuclear arms, pesticide use, and pollution. His postwar nonfiction books were all reprints of magazine work, including world-government editorials in *The Wild Flag* (1946), a travel essay in *Here Is New York* (1949), and poems, stories, essays, and Comment in *The Second Tree from the Corner* (1954). In the same period, returning to a project begun years earlier, he completed and published *Stuart Little* (1945), his first children's book, a whimsical, picaresque story of a mouse born to a human family. With his second children's book, *Charlotte's Web* (1952), the story of a friendship between a pig and a spider, White established his place as a children's author.

In 1957 the Whites retired to Maine. White wrote more sporadically, much distracted by family health problems. Yet the freedom from regular magazine work gave him time to revise the work of his onetime college professor William Strunk, *The Elements of Style* (1959; 2d ed. 1972; 3d ed. 1979), a great success as both trade book and textbook. It has remained popular because of its clear and direct pronouncements about usage and its common-sense approach to style from a writer's perspective. He also composed infrequent but sustained and developed essays for a *New Yorker* series reprinted as *The Points of My Compass* (1962) and wrote his final children's novel, *The Trumpet of the Swan* (1970). His last projects were retrospective anthologies, including *Letters of E. B. White* (1976), *Essays of E. B. White* (1977), and *Poems and Sketches of E. B. White* (1981), along with new editions of *One Man's Meat* (1983) and *The Second Tree from the Corner* (1984). Katharine White died on 20 July 1977 of congestive heart failure, and E. B. White succumbed to Alzheimer's disease on 1 October 1985.

Their ashes are buried in Brooklin Cemetery in Brooklin, Maine.

E. B. White received many honorary degrees and literary awards, among them the Presidential Medal of Freedom in 1963, the Laura Ingalls Wilder Award in 1970, the National Medal of Literature in 1971, the American Academy of Arts and Letters gold medal for essays and criticism in 1973, and a special Pulitzer Prize for the body of his work in 1978. His themes and personae are difficult to separate from the writer himself. White's children's novels had strong autobiographical components including the values that the principal characters came to hold. *Charlotte's Web* celebrates the natural cycle of life, the importance of friendship, and the power of language, and its closing lines were often said of White: "It is not often that someone comes along who is a true friend and a good writer. Charlotte was both." White's Comment and editorials for the *New Yorker* were admired for their sharp observation, inventive expression, and principled common sense. He extolled both the pastoral and the urbane, and the very attributes that grated on his critics—his surprising whimsical twists and his refusal to polemicize in editorials—endeared him to admirers. White also was preeminent among American personal essayists, and even critics of White's unassuming persona and persistent sense of loss have admired the artistic achievement of "Once More to the Lake," which simultaneously celebrates timelessness and acknowledges mortality.

All of White's writing, regardless of genre or audience, was marked by his prose style. He claimed once that he "wrote mainly by ear," and his language exhibits grace, rhythm, balance, vigor, and clarity whatever his subject or audience. He maintained a flexible but consistent voice throughout his work and advised that "the whole duty of a writer is to please and satisfy himself, and the true writer always plays to an audience of one." He claimed to feel "charged with the safekeeping of all unexpected items of worldly or unworldly enchantment," but he also believed that when the writer approaches style "it is himself he is approaching, no other." In *Charlotte's Web* and "Once More to the Lake" he crafted prose that no textbook can teach and that arose from his own particular feeling for language and for the world.

★

White's manuscripts are in the Department of Rare Books, Cornell University Library, and are described in Katherine Romans Hall, *E. B. White: A Bibliographic Catalogue* (1979). Katharine S. White's papers are in the Rare Books Room, Bryn Mawr College Library. Much autobiographical material is in Dorothy Lobrano Guth, ed., *Letters of E. B. White* (1976), and in his essay collections. The standard biography is Scott Elledge, *E. B. White: A Biography* (1984). Beverly Gherman, *E. B. White: Some Writer!* (1992), a biography for children, and Linda H. Davis, *Onward and Upward: A Biography of Katharine S. White* (1987), are also valuable.

Edward C. Sampson, *E. B. White* (1974), covers White's career. John W. Griffith, *Charlotte's Web: A Pig's Salvation* (1993); Peter F. Neumeyer, *The Annotated "Charlotte's Web"* (1994); and Lucien L. Agosta, *E. B. White: The Children's Books* (1995), treat his children's novels. Robert L. Root, Jr., ed., *Critical Essays on E. B. White* (1996), collects reviews and criticism. Especially valuable are Dennis Rygiel, "Stylistics and the Study of Twentieth-Century Literary Nonfiction," in Chris Anderson, ed., *Literary Nonfiction: Theory, Criticism, Pedagogy* (1989): 29–50; and Carl H. Klaus, "The Chameleon 'I': On Voice and Personality in the Personal Essay," in Kathleen Blake Yancey, ed., *Voices on Voice: Perspective, Definitions, Inquiry* (1994): 111–129. Peter F. Neumeyer examines manuscripts of the children's books in *The Horn Book* (Oct. and Dec. 1982; Jan./Feb. 1985; Sept./Oct. 1988). Rebecca M. Dale, ed., *Writings from the New Yorker, 1925–1976* (1990), collects unreprinted pieces.

An obituary is in the *New York Times* (2 Oct. 1985). Tributes appear in *Time* (14 Oct. 1985), the *Nation* (12 Oct. 1985), and the *New Yorker* (14 Oct. 1985).

ROBERT L. ROOT, JR.

WHITEHEAD, Don(ald) Ford (*b.* 8 April 1908 in Inman, Virginia; *d.* 12 January 1981 in Knoxville, Tennessee), journalist and author, noted Associated Press correspondent during World War II, and winner of two Pulitzer Prizes for reportage on the Korean War.

Don Whitehead, 1952. UPI/CORBIS-BETTMANN

One of the three children of Harry Ford Whitehead, a merchant originally from Kent County, England, and the former Elizabeth Bond, of Virginia, Don Whitehead grew up in Harlan, Kentucky, from the age of five. He played baseball, basketball, and football in high school and was editor of the sports section of his school newspaper. His English teacher and his older brother, Kyle, then studying journalism at the University of Kentucky, encouraged his journalistic aspirations. After graduating from high school in 1926 Whitehead enrolled at the university to study journalism. He worked on the student paper, played football, and visited the horsetrack so often he was dubbed "clocker" Whitehead.

On 20 December 1928, during his junior year, Whitehead married Marie Patterson, a fellow journalism student; they would have one child. After marrying he left college to work for his brother, who was publishing a small weekly, the *La Follette Press,* in Tennessee. In 1930 Whitehead took a job as managing editor of the weekly *Harlan* (Kentucky) *American.* He was made city editor when the newspaper merged with another to become the *Daily Enterprise.* He began his association there with the *News-Sentinel* of Knoxville, Tennessee, serving as area correspondent and receiving attention for his coverage of a bloody episode in a Kentucky coal field labor strike.

In 1934 Whitehead joined the *Knoxville Journal;* a year later he moved to Memphis, Tennessee, as night editor for the Associated Press (AP). This was the beginning of a twenty-one-year career with the wire service. He later was appointed correspondent for Knoxville. The quality of his reporting earned him a promotion in 1941 to AP's prestigious news features office in New York City.

When World War II broke out in Europe in 1939, Whitehead lobbied to be sent overseas as a correspondent. In September 1942 AP assigned him to India. In Cairo, Egypt, however, his trip was canceled when the Germans captured an AP reporter. Instead, Whitehead was sent to join General Bernard L. Montgomery's British Eighth Army for a 1,700-mile chase of German field marshal Erwin Rommel's tank corps across North Africa. Whitehead filed gripping eyewitness reports of battles and refugees. In July 1943 Whitehead joined U.S. troops for the amphibious assault on Sicily, followed by invasions of Italy at Salerno and Anzio. In 1944 AP sent Whitehead to England. On 6 June 1944 Whitehead landed with the First Infantry Division at Omaha Beach. He later told an interviewer that the D-day landing was his worst experience of the war, recalling that with so many men being killed around him he resigned himself to death and finally lost his fear. He continued moving with the troops inland and borrowed a Jeep to accompany the Allied army into liberated Paris. Whitehead filed the first news story from Paris, pounding out a 1,600-word article in forty-five minutes.

A close friend of Pulitzer Prize–winning correspondents Hal Boyle and Ernie Pyle, Whitehead was nominated for a Pulitzer Prize for his war coverage in Europe. In 1945 he was one of nineteen correspondents honored with the army's Medal of Freedom. From 1945 to 1948 Whitehead was AP bureau chief in Hawaii, where he covered the atomic bomb tests at Bikini Island. In 1948 he joined AP's Washington, D.C., bureau. In July 1950 Whitehead was assigned to cover the Korean War. For almost a year he lived with American soldiers, carrying his typewriter on his back. He witnessed the American fight to hold the Naktong line against the North Koreans, landed on the Inchon beachhead, and crossed the Han River with U.S. marines in the campaign to retake Seoul, South Korea's capital. A centerpiece of his coverage was a story about a marine sergeant who carried two white rabbits into battle as mascots and used the bunnies to befriend two sobbing Korean children on the battlefield. Whitehead followed the army north and was present when U.S. and South Korean troops seized P'yongyang, the capital of North Korea. As part of an armored task force with another reporter, he discovered an infamous massacre of sixty-eight American prisoners. His stories on the army's inadequate winter clothing for troops led to the airlifting of warm clothes for soldiers.

In 1951 Whitehead was awarded the Pulitzer Prize for international affairs reporting, specifically for his stories on the crossing of the Han River. In 1952 Whitehead covered the U.S. presidential campaign. His acquaintance with Dwight D. Eisenhower and his knowledge of Korea led to his selection as one of three news service reporters to accompany the president-elect on a secret flight in December 1952 to Korea to lay the groundwork for ending the fighting. Whitehead filed a 4,400-word article that won him a second Pulitzer Prize in 1953.

From 1956 to 1957 Whitehead served as Washington bureau chief for the *New York Herald Tribune.* In 1956 he wrote the first of his six books, *The FBI Story: A Report to the People,* a best-seller with a foreword by FBI director J. Edgar Hoover. It was later made into a movie. In 1959 Whitehead returned to Knoxville and, working from home, wrote a column three times a week for the *News-Sentinel.* He also wrote the books *Journey into Crime* (1960), *Border Guard: The Story of the U.S. Customs* (1963); *The FBI Story for Young Readers* (1964), *The Dow Story: The History of the Dow Chemical Company* (1968), and *Attack on Terror: The FBI Against the Ku Klux Klan in Mississippi* (1970). The last book, about the murder of three young civil rights workers, was the basis for a two-part television movie in 1975.

Whitehead ended his popular *Knoxville News-Sentinel* column on 25 June 1978, after a run of eighteen years and eight months. The column had become a local classic by lampooning liquor raids on Knoxville country clubs in 1961 and spoofing citizens for hypocritically "drinking wet but voting dry." He wrote in his farewell: "One of the most satisfying parts of writing the column was the curious feeling that there was an invisible link between me and those who were reading. ... At times, a reader would want to know, 'Why don't you use your talent to write about serious national and world problems?' To tell the truth, I never felt qualified to lecture the world or even a next-door neighbor."

His wife died in September 1979. Lonely, Whitehead resumed his column briefly in January 1980, but he was ill and died of lung cancer a year later. He donated his body to the University of Tennessee School of Medicine in Memphis.

Tom Siler, a close friend and fellow war correspondent, wrote that Whitehead was a sensitive, modest man and a fierce competitor at golf and fishing. Tall, dark-haired, and sporting a mustache, Whitehead fit the image of the dashing war correspondent. As a newspaperman of fifty years Whitehead, Silar said, was "a craftsman who wrote from the heart, writing as if he were there talking to you about how you make beaten biscuits, or to tell you about this dandy little roadside restaurant he had found, or to poke fun at some bit of bureaucratic nonsense." Carson Brewer, another friend and a fellow columnist for the Knoxville newspaper, said: "He was a very quiet and very likable and competent man. He didn't have the demeanor of a star, but was one anyhow."

★

The Don Whitehead Collection at the Hoskins Library, University of Tennessee at Knoxville, contains his correspondence, manuscripts, scrapbooks, clippings, and columns. A biographical sketch is in Marjorie Dent Candee, ed., *Current Biography 1953* (1954). Information on his writings and his life can be found in James M. Ethridge and Barbara Koppala, eds., *Contemporary Authors,* vols. 11–12 (1965). In an interview in the *Knoxville News-Sentinel* (25 June 1978), columnist Carl Brewer summarizes Whitehead's career. Journalist Tom Siler offers a remembrance in the *Knoxville News Sentinel* (18 Jan. 1981). A lengthy obituary appears in the *Knoxville News-Sentinel* (13 Jan. 1981). The obituary in the *New York Times* (14 Jan. 1981) gives a trenchant account of Whitehead's career.

RICHARD GILBERT

WHITNEY, John Hay (*b.* 17 August 1904 in Ellsworth, Maine; *d.* 8 February 1982 in Manhasset, New York), newspaper publisher, diplomat, art collector, and philanthropist who presided over the *New York Herald Tribune* from 1961 to 1967 and served as ambassador to Great Britain from 1956 to 1961.

Whitney was the son of William Payne Whitney, a millionaire sportsman, and Helen (Hay) Whitney, the daughter of the distinguished author and diplomat John Hay and a well-published poet in her own right. His paternal grandfather was William C. Whitney, secretary of the navy under President Grover Cleveland. Named John Oliver Whitney at birth and christened John Hay Whitney ten months later, he was born to great wealth and earned his living by choice rather than necessity. Known as "Jock" to acquaintances, he was called "Johnny" among the family. Whitney had one sibling, a sister who was fourteen months older.

Whitney was raised in luxurious surroundings and taught by governesses until he entered school, first at Miss Chapin's and then St. Bernard's, small private schools in New York City. At thirteen he entered Groton School in Groton, Massachusetts, graduating in 1922. At Yale, Whitney distinguished himself in dramatics and as a junior varsity oarsman, and graduated with a B.A. degree in 1926. He enrolled the next year at Oxford to study history and literature, and he spent considerable time in London and visiting country houses. His father presented Whitney with two thoroughbred horses for his twenty-second birthday, beginning his lifelong involvement in horse racing in both England and America.

When Payne Whitney died unexpectedly in 1927, John Whitney's inheritance exceeded $30 million. Whitney lived well and enjoyed the benefits of great wealth, but avoided

John Hay Whitney in his Rockefeller Center offices, 1956. UPI/CORBIS-BETTMANN

extravagant display. Whitney later described himself at this period as a participant rather than a leader. His chief role was to provide capital, his supporting role was to provide good advice, but he was never asked to play the lead. Tall and handsome as well as rich, he was often regarded as shy.

Three weeks before the Great Crash on Wall Street in October 1929, Whitney took a position as a junior clerk for the investment banking firm of Lee, Higginson, and Company. Having gained some practical business experience, he left the firm after a year and served actively as a director of Pan American Airways and Freeport Sulphur throughout the 1930s. He became a leading figure in what came to be called New York's café society, along with his first cousin C. V. Whitney, with whom he was sometimes confused. Most of Whitney's life passed in the glare of publicity, whether in his role as a championship polo player, a companion of Broadway and Hollywood actresses, or a movie producer. Whitney's marriage to Mary Elizabeth Altemus on 25 September 1930 was a society event of that year. It was Whitney, as chairman of the board of Selznick International from 1936 to 1940, who purchased the screen rights to *Gone with the Wind* (1936).

Whitney had begun collecting modern art in 1929 and began his lifelong service as a trustee of the Museum of Modern Art a year later. His personal art collection was particularly strong in works of the French impressionists and postimpressionists. Beginning in 1935 Whitney also played a major role in the development of the museum's film library. In 1940 he was among the investors who supported the innovative New York City newspaper *PM,* but he sold his interest within a few months because he disagreed with the paper's increasingly liberal slant. Also in 1940, Whitney was divorced from his first wife, with whom he had had no children. On 1 March 1942 he married Betsey Cushing Roosevelt, the former wife of James Roosevelt. The couple had no children together, but in 1949 Whitney adopted his second wife's two daughters from her previous marriage.

By the summer of 1940 Whitney was supporting several interventionist organizations and had attended the military training program at Plattsburg, New York. A few months later his friend Nelson A. Rockefeller named Whitney as head of the Motion Picture Division at the Office of the Co-ordinator of Inter-American Affairs. In 1942 Whitney was commissioned a captain in the Army Air Forces and assigned to staff intelligence duties in England. In August 1944, while on assignment with the Office of Strategic Services (OSS) in a newly liberated area of southern France, Colonel Whitney was captured by German troops. After eighteen days in enemy custody he managed to escape with the help of French Resistance forces. For perhaps the first time in his life, Jock Whitney had found himself in circumstances where his wealth and influence were of no value.

Whitney returned to civilian life in 1945 with a new determination to use his talent and his wealth to better purpose. He became active in venture capital investments through J. H. Whitney and Company, which he founded in 1946; that same year, he established the John Hay Whitney Foundation, which made innovative grants in education and social welfare. From 1950 onward Whitney sponsored a variety of fellowships, particularly for minority students and for high school teachers.

After the war Whitney also began to show interest in politics, supporting Jacob Javits's first campaign for Congress in 1946. Whitney was an early backer of General Dwight D. Eisenhower for president, and he became finance committee chairman of Citizens for Eisenhower-Nixon in 1952. Whitney declined offers of minor government positions during Eisenhower's first term, but his success in raising campaign funds for Eisenhower was rewarded with an appointment as ambassador to Great Britain, a position once held by his grandfather John Hay. Whitney assumed his duties in February 1957 in the aftermath of the Anglo-American disagreements over the Suez Canal crisis. He had the charm and talent for an endless round of speeches, and the wealth to entertain graciously and often, while his close relationship with the president allowed him to be more involved in policy than the typical noncareer diplomat.

When Whitney returned to New York in January 1961, it was to take up his most ambitious business project, saving the *New York Herald Tribune*. The paper had been in financial trouble for years, although it maintained its reputation for lively writing and moderate Republican editorial views. A Whitney loan rescued the *Herald Tribune* in 1958, but only in 1961 did Whitney become majority shareholder, publisher, and editor in chief. Through Whitney Communications Corporation, he controlled a group of successful magazines and small newspapers, as well as several radio and television stations, but his heart was with the *Herald Tribune*. Whitney described its closing in 1966 as "the emptiest day of my life," and he never again played an active public role in business.

Whitney was a board member and financial supporter of the Museum of Modern Art, the National Gallery of Art, and especially Yale University. He maintained an estate in Manhasset, Long Island, New York; apartments in Manhattan and London; summer residences at Fishers Island, Connecticut, and at Saratoga, a horse farm in Kentucky; a vacation estate in Greenwood, Georgia; as well as a yacht, a private airliner, and a private Pullman car. Whitney died of congestive heart failure at North Shore Hospital on Long Island in 1982. He is buried at Christ Church (Episcopal) in Manhasset.

★

Whitney's correspondence with President Eisenhower is at the Dwight D. Eisenhower Library in Abilene, Kansas. Official papers concerning his service as a Yale trustee are in the Yale University Archives. E. J. Kahn, Jr., *Jock: The Life and Times of John Hay Whitney* (1981), is a complete biography by a longtime friend, written with Whitney's cooperation. Richard Kluger, *The Paper: The Life and Death of the New York Herald Tribune* (1986), provides a full account of his association with the *Herald Tribune*. John Rewald, *The John Hay Whitney Collection* (1983), describes many of the paintings in Whitney's personal collection. Detailed obituaries are in the *New York Times* (9 and 13 Feb. 1982), *Thoroughbred Record* (10 Feb. 1982), and *Art in America* (Apr. 1982).

PATRICK J. FURLONG

WILKINS, Roy (*b.* 30 August 1901 in St. Louis, Missouri; *d.* 8 September 1981 in New York City), executive director of the National Association for the Advancement of Colored People (NAACP) who was a major force behind the Civil Rights Act of 1964 and the Voting Rights Act of 1965.

Wilkins's paternal grandparents, Asberry and Emma Wilkins, had been slaves in Mississippi. His father, William D.

Roy Wilkins, 1955. NEW YORK TIMES CO./ARCHIVE PHOTOS

Wilkins, was a graduate of Rust College who had to settle for work as a porter in Mississippi; he was later employed as a tender at a brick kiln in East St. Louis, Illinois. Wilkins's mother, Mayfield Edmondson Wilkins, a housewife, died of tuberculosis when Roy was four. Since William Wilkins was incapable of taking care of Roy and his younger sister and brother, the children moved from St. Louis to St. Paul, Minnesota, where a maternal aunt, Emma Williams, and her husband, Samuel, chief steward on the Great Northern Pacific Railroad, raised them in modest but secure circumstances.

Blacks were few in St. Paul and segregation was nonexistent, so Wilkins grew up in a mostly white neighborhood and attended mostly white schools. In high school Wilkins edited the literary magazine and his class's yearbook. He was the class salutatorian.

In 1919 Wilkins entered the University of Minnesota in Minneapolis. He became the first black reporter for the university newspaper. While a senior, he edited the *St. Paul Appeal,* a weekly black newspaper. During his university years he also worked in a munitions factory, in a slaughterhouse, and as a railroad dining car waiter. In 1922 Wilkins joined the St. Paul branch of the NAACP and became its secretary.

Racism was comparatively muted in Minnesota, but Wilkins wrote later in his autobiography that during the summer of 1920, "I lost my innocence on race once and for all." Then, three black circus roustabouts, wrongly suspected of raping a young white woman, were lynched in Duluth, Minnesota, as a mob of thousands cheered.

Having obtained his B.A. degree in the spring of 1923, Wilkins became news editor for the *Kansas City* (Missouri) *Call,* a black weekly, the following October. Not long after, he became managing editor. Wilkins was angered by the rigid racial segregation in Kansas City, something he had not previously experienced. Consequently, he used the *Call,* previously known for its lurid crime stories, to fight housing and school segregation as well as both police brutality and inadequate police protection. He also led a boycott of segregated theaters. Wilkins condemned most black leaders for their failure to pursue racial equality, while also opposing black nationalist Marcus Garvey's racial separatism.

During the 1920s Wilkins became secretary of the Kansas City NAACP. In 1930 he led the local version of that organization's successful national campaign against Senate confirmation of a segregationist U.S. Supreme Court nominee. Wilkins's effort brought him to the attention of Walter White, the NAACP's national assistant secretary. After White became the organization's national executive secretary—its day-to-day leader—in March 1931, he brought Wilkins to New York City to fill his old post.

Wilkins, who became assistant secretary in August 1931, felt that in the NAACP national office he could contribute more actively to the cause of racial justice than as a newspaperman. He was also drawn to the task by the status and comfortable New York lifestyle his position in America's leading civil rights organization would afford. He was particularly happy to settle in at one of Harlem's most prestigious addresses, 409 Edgecombe Avenue, atop Sugar Hill, where he had a panoramic view overlooking the Harlem River.

But Wilkins had to, and gladly did, work hard and long for what he received. His responsibilities included administrative work in the national office; speaking to NAACP chapters and other organizations; forming new chapters; political lobbying; investigating civil rights violations; conducting public relations; and raising money. The fact that he and his wife, Aminda ("Minnie") Badeau, whom he married on 15 September 1929, had no children made it easier for Wilkins to work long hours.

In December 1932 White sent Wilkins south to investigate reports that black workers on the federally funded Mississippi Flood Control Project were suffering from pay discrimination and abusive treatment. Wilkins and black journalist George Schuyler, working out of Memphis, Tennessee, spent about three weeks visiting some twenty Mississippi River levee work camps posing as laborers. Had their real identities become known, they could have been in grave, even mortal, danger. Wilkins's report verified earlier accounts and helped convince the federal government to end pay discrimination and improve wages and working conditions for all unskilled workers on the Mississippi.

In 1934 the black historian and sociologist W. E. B. Du Bois, editor of the NAACP's monthly magazine, *The Crisis,* left the organization in a policy dispute. Wilkins became editor, a post he held until 1949. Whereas the intellectual Du Bois had tried to keep the magazine at a very elevated level, the practical Wilkins tried to make it more accessible by giving the publication a more journalistic flavor and by including stories about popular black artists and sports figures.

That year Wilkins also organized a demonstration in Washington, D.C., after U.S. Attorney General Homer S. Cummings excluded lynching from the agenda of a national crime conference. In connection with the protest, Wilkins was jailed for the first time. Throughout the 1930s he and White lobbied unsuccessfully for a federal antilynching law, then the NAACP's major goal.

An opponent of what he believed was the American Communist Party's antidemocratic ideology, its peculiar twists and turns of policy, and its pro-Soviet agenda, Wilkins fought against communist influence in the civil rights community during the immediate post–World War II years. He excluded communists from a national civil rights mobilization for a federal Fair Employment Practices Commission that he organized in 1949. At the NAACP's national conference in 1950, he played a leading role in putting through a resolution rescinding the charters of local chapters under communist control. (It has been estimated that 20 percent of the chapters were so controlled.)

When Walter White went on a one-year leave of absence in 1949, Wilkins became acting executive secretary. White died in March 1955, and the following month Wilkins was chosen to the post of executive secretary (renamed executive director in 1965). The year before, the U.S. Supreme Court had struck down school segregation in its renowned *Brown v. Board of Education* decision. Wilkins believed that the NAACP's long work on behalf of racial equality was nearing its culmination. Lobbying in Congress for civil rights legislation, along with continued litigation, he felt, would achieve the NAACP's long-standing goal.

But Wilkins's first years as executive secretary were frustrating. Southern resistance and Eisenhower administration indifference blocked most progress toward school integration. Meanwhile, in 1957 Southern Democrats in Congress weakened an already modest administration voting rights bill. Against prevailing liberal opinion, Wilkins decided to back the Civil Rights Act of 1957 because it represented an advance, however small, and a possible steppingstone to further legislation. But amendments in 1960, supposedly to strengthen the 1957 law, were so ineffectual that Wilkins dismissed them as "a fraud."

In the meantime the *Brown* decision, and the slow pace of progress in its wake, sparked new civil rights movements and strategies. Wilkins had a mixed and complex reaction to the direct, mass action campaigns that had begun with the 1955–1956 Montgomery bus boycott in Alabama, led by the Reverend Martin Luther King, Jr., and resumed with the student lunch-counter sit-ins of 1960.

Wilkins believed that the legal strategy of the NAACP, guided by its professional lobbyists and lawyers familiar with the political system and the law, was the surest route to equality. Direct mass action, he believed, could not long be sustained; besides, it could easily slip into careless militancy, costing the needed support of moderates. Therefore, for example, he did not endorse the Prayer Pilgrimage to Washington, D.C., in 1957 until it was framed as an appeal for civil rights legislation rather than a protest against the president or Congress. Six years later Wilkins would not associate himself with the March on Washington for Jobs and Freedom until civil disobedience and the mass lobbying of Congress were dropped from the agenda, and until plans to make civil rights leader Bayard Rustin, a homosexual and former communist, the march director were abandoned.

Yet Wilkins did not flatly oppose direct action; rather, he felt it should be used selectively and cautiously as a tactic subordinate to the legal struggle. Just two months after the first student sit-in at a Greensboro, North Carolina, lunch counter in February 1960, Wilkins announced that the NAACP would conduct wade-ins to integrate publicly supported beaches. Sparked by King's demonstrations in Birmingham, Alabama, in the spring of 1963, the NAACP's Medgar Evers organized similar protests in Jackson, Mississippi. Arriving there in May 1963 to participate, Wilkins was arrested for the first time since 1934. Also, the NAACP consistently provided free legal representation and financial assistance to the direct action organizations.

Clearly, though, Wilkins was more deliberate than many other civil rights leaders, and he was sometimes criticized for his counsels of caution and patience: for example, when he urged the biracial Mississippi Freedom Democratic party delegation to the 1964 Democratic Convention to accept a compromise giving it just two at-large seats, or when he urged a moratorium against demonstrations during the 1964 presidential election to prevent a backlash that might hurt President Lyndon B. Johnson's campaign.

Nevertheless, Wilkins reached the peak of his influence during the 1960s, and he did so on his own terms, within the framework of the NAACP's legal strategy. Because of his sophisticated understanding of the deployment of power and the NAACP's depth of resources, contacts, and experience, President Johnson made him the chief mobilizer of support for the Civil Rights Act of 1964, banning segregation in public facilities, employment discrimination, and discrimination in federally funded programs, and for the Voting Rights Act of 1965, which provided for voter registration in the South by federal examiners. He had complete access to Johnson, who constantly called Wilkins for strategic advice. Wilkins did not get all he wanted—he felt the 1964 legislation should have included a school integration deadline and anti–housing discrimination provisions—but he recognized that the two laws were enormous strides forward.

Just at this point of triumph, troublesome new issues materialized. The black power movement emerged in the spring of 1966. Many of its followers—mostly young Northern blacks—tended toward racial separatism, hostility toward whites, and sympathy with the use of violence, all anathema to Wilkins. At the 1966 NAACP annual convention, he denounced black power as "a reverse Mississippi, a reverse Hitler, a reverse Ku Klux Klan."

A few days after President Johnson signed the Voting Rights Act in August 1965, massive rioting began in the Watts section of Los Angeles, a prelude to widespread black urban rioting over the next several summers. Wilkins denounced the riots as a disaster that would sharply reduce support for further civil rights legislation and for President Johnson's War on Poverty. But as one of the eleven members of President Johnson's National Advisory Commission on Civil Disorders, also called the Kerner Commission, Wilkins wholeheartedly supported the panel's 1968 report condemning white racism as the source of the violence.

Wilkins saw the Vietnam War as another issue threatening to divide the civil rights coalition, and he refused to take a stand on the conflict during the latter half of the 1960s. In 1966 and 1967 he unsuccessfully urged Martin Luther King not to speak out against the war. In 1968 he watched with distress as the war contributed to the defeat of pro–civil rights presidential candidate Hubert H. Humphrey at the hands of the much less sympathetic Richard M. Nixon.

Regarding the Nixon administration as possessed of "malignant indifference on issues of civil rights and race," Wilkins opposed presidential policy on many occasions. In 1969 the NAACP helped block two Nixon nominees to the Supreme Court, neither of whom were friendly toward civil rights. Wilkins also fought with considerable success against Nixon's efforts to give Southern schools more time to desegregate, to stop school busing for the purpose of integration, and to water down the Voting Rights Act in 1970. In 1974 and 1975 he convinced the administration of Nixon's Republican successor, President Gerald Ford, not to side in court with Boston parents resisting court-ordered busing.

In the 1970s, then, the NAACP retained considerable clout; indeed, it was the only civil rights organization that still did. Yet the NAACP was past its prime. Membership had peaked at more than 500,000 in the 1960s but fell close to 400,000 during the 1970s. This emboldened a faction within the NAACP, opposed to what they considered Wilkins's autocratic leadership, to pressure him to resign. Nevertheless, Wilkins, who had planned to leave in 1972, postponed his departure several times, finally resigning because of failing health at the end of July 1977.

In his retirement, Wilkins wrote a syndicated newspaper column and his autobiography. While hospitalized for a heart condition, he died of kidney failure. Wilkins, who had been a member of the African Methodist Episcopal Church, was buried at Pinelawn Cemetery in Farmingdale, New York.

The tall, thin, dapper Wilkins was a well-spoken man who always appeared poised and self-assured. His confidence as a public figure stemmed in part from being certain of his goals as a civil rights leader. Having grown up in an integrated community, he believed from an early age that race prejudice could be overcome. From his days at the *Kansas City Call* onward, he took the same stand, condemning both those blacks accepting racial discrimination and those advocating revolutionary or black nationalist views. Some thought him too cautious, but while a philosophical, temperamental, and strategic moderate, Wilkins was throughout his adult life adamant, outspoken, and tenacious in his pursuit of racial equality.

★

The Roy Wilkins Papers and the NAACP papers, at the Library of Congress, are the most important manuscript collections for Wilkins's career. Roy Wilkins, with Tom Mathews, *Standing Fast: The Autobiography of Roy Wilkins* (1982), both reveals and hides much, and is most interesting for Wilkins's pre-NAACP years. Cleophus Charles, "Roy Wilkins, the NAACP, and the Early Struggle for Civil Rights" (Ph.D. diss., Cornell University, 1981), a well-researched effort, is the only major attempt at a Wilkins biography. Taylor Branch, *Parting the Waters: America in the King Years, 1954–1963* (1988), and David J. Garrow, *Bearing the Cross: Martin Luther King, Jr., and the Southern Christian Leadership Conference* (1986), contain valuable information concerning both Wilkins's views and his relations with other civil rights leaders. The same is true, though to a lesser degree, of *Lay Bare the Heart: An Autobiography of the Civil Rights Movement* (1985), by former CORE leader James Farmer, and *A Man's Life: An Autobiography* (1982), by Wilkins's nephew Roger Wilkins. Melvin Drimmer's "Roy Wilkins and the American Dream," *Phylon* 45, no. 2 (June 1984): 160–163, contains astute insights into Wilkins's mind-set. Obituaries are in the *New York Times* and the *Washington Post* (both 9 Sept. 1981).

Michael L. Levine

WILLIAMS, John Bell (*b*. 4 December 1918 in Raymond, Mississippi; *d*. 26 March 1983 in Brandon, Mississippi), congressman and governor of Mississippi who paved the way for the development of two-party politics in the South.

The firstborn of the two children of Graves Kelly Williams, a pharmacist, and Maude Elizabeth Bedwell, John Bell Williams grew up in the small town of Raymond, Mississippi, and attended Hinds Junior College in his hometown. He studied at the University of Mississippi in Oxford from 1936 to 1938, leaving without a degree, then enrolled in the Jackson School of Law, from which he received his LL.B. in 1940.

Admitted to the bar in 1940, Williams established a law practice in his hometown. The next year he learned to fly. When he joined the military service on 5 November 1941, he selected the Army Air Corps, which trained him to be a bomber pilot. Flying his B-26 to North Africa, Williams crashed in British Guiana on 15 March 1943. The only member of the crew to survive, he experienced multiple injuries, including the loss of the lower part of his left arm. The accident ended his military career.

After his release from the military hospital in Atlanta, Williams returned to Raymond, where he met Elizabeth Ann Wells, a member of the Women's Army Corps (WAC), at a Baptist church revival. They were married on 12 October 1944 and had three children.

In 1944 Williams was appointed by the governor to serve

John Bell Williams. REPRODUCED FROM THE COLLECTIONS OF THE LIBRARY OF CONGRESS

as prosecuting attorney for Hinds County. He held that position until he was elected to the U.S. House of Representatives in 1946. Twenty-seven years of age, he was the youngest person ever elected to represent Mississippi. To get to Congress, Williams had to defeat an incumbent in the Democratic primary, which was tantamount to election in the one-party state. Williams characterized his opponent as a do-nothing politician and himself as an energetic young man eager to serve the public. Dark-haired and handsome, Williams was the picture of youthful vigor, excepting the very obvious absence of part of his left arm. Never hesitant to demonstrate the sacrifice that he had made in the service of his country, Williams would use his artificial hand, made of steel, to adjust the microphone at rallies, causing a "bloodcurdling squeal" according to one witness and reminding the audience of his war injury.

Williams took his seat on the Democratic side of the House of Representatives in the Eightieth Congress in January 1947. From the first he found himself agreeing more frequently with the Republicans on policy matters than with his own party.

Although he took an active role on the Commerce Committee in writing legislation on aviation and railroads, and even organized a congressional flying club, Williams was better known in Congress for his virulent opposition to communism, foreign aid, and civil rights than for his contributions to policy. In his first term he voted against the Marshall Plan, even though President Harry Truman considered it essential to his efforts to insulate Western Europe from communism. Williams declared that half of the aid recipients had been "running bayonets through the bellies of good American soldiers" only three years earlier.

Such vitriolic rhetoric became the hallmark of Williams's congressional style. The Civil Rights Act of 1964, which would open restaurants, hotels, and other public accommodations to black people, was "literally crawling with vermin, snakes, and worms of every sort and kind," he told the House. He termed the Voting Rights Act of 1965, which opened voting booths to black citizens, a "rape of the Constitution."

Elected to Congress eleven times as a Democrat, Williams never supported a Democratic candidate for president. He joined the Dixiecrat revolt against Truman in 1948 but generally stayed quiet in presidential elections until 1964, when he supported Republican candidate Barry Goldwater against his own party's Lyndon Johnson. As a result the House Democratic Caucus voted in 1965 to take away Williams's seniority, effectively depriving him of influence in his committee, where he had been the second-ranking Democrat. Two years later, when the Commerce Committee chairman resigned to become a federal judge, Williams mounted an unsuccessful campaign to regain his seniority and thereby become chairman of the committee. Rejecting invitations from the Republicans to switch parties, Williams decided to return to Mississippi to seek the governorship.

Denouncing the federal government, the civil rights movement, and his opponents at every campaign stop, Williams won the Democratic nomination for governor, then defeated Republican Rubel Phillips in the general election. When he assumed the governorship on 16 January 1968, however, his inaugural address attracted notice for its moderate tone. He denounced the perpetrators of racial violence and advocated the aggressive pursuit of federal grants despite the federal control that accompanied them.

Governor Williams modernized government in a state where the past was cherished. He created an Office of Federal-State Programs to seek and coordinate federal grants and initiated the state's participation in the federal Medicaid program to bring medical care to the poorest citizens. He won teachers their largest pay increase in history, funded by sales and income tax increases that created surpluses in the state treasury and funded other needed modernization efforts. Although Williams often appeared inattentive and detached from day-to-day government, he won praise from all sides for his personal coordination of relief efforts when the Mississippi Gulf Coast was devastated by Hurricane Camille in August 1969. After his term as governor ended in 1972, Williams established a law office in Jackson. He obtained a divorce from his wife in 1973.

While he never became a Republican, Williams tirelessly campaigned for Republican candidates for national office and for his former congressional seat. His fiery rhetoric never diminished. Campaigning for Republican presidential candidate Gerald Ford in 1976, he recklessly described Democrat Jimmy Carter as "a man who put aside Jefferson and picked up Karl Marx." Happiest flying small airplanes or drinking and sharing stories with a small group of "salty old cronies," Williams practiced little law but cultivated his political and personal relationships in retirement. He was a Baptist. He died unexpectedly of a heart attack in his town house and was buried in Raymond, Mississippi.

John Bell Williams stands as a transitional figure in regional and national politics. He loosened the ties that had kept white southerners in the Democratic Party and demonstrated the value of the conservative southern vote to the Republicans, paving the way for the advent of two-party politics in the Deep South and the rise of southern leadership in the Republican party. Having run an openly racist campaign for governor, he accommodated himself and Mississippi's state government to the gains made by the civil rights movement and modernized state government for more effective delivery of services to the public.

★

Williams's papers are housed in the George M. McClendon Library of Hinds Community College, Raymond, Mississippi, and the Mississippi Department of Archives and History in Jackson. The Department of Archives and History also has an extensive subject file, consisting primarily of newspaper clippings. Sandra Stringer Vance analyzes the congressional portion of Williams's political career in "The Congressional Career of John Bell Williams, 1947–1967" (Ph.D. diss., Mississippi State University, 1976). Earl Black, *Southern Governors and Civil Rights: Racial Segregation as a Campaign Issue in the Second Reconstruction* (1976), examines Williams's gubernatorial campaign and performance in the context of racial politics in the South. Obituaries are in the *New York Times* and the *Washington Post* (both 27 Mar. 1983).

VAGN K. HANSEN

WILLIAMS, Mary Lou (*b.* 8 May 1910 in Atlanta, Georgia; *d.* 28 May 1981 in Durham, North Carolina), pianist, arranger, composer, and premier figure of jazz who participated in its evolution from smoky bars and brothels to concert halls and cathedrals.

Born Mary Elfrieda Scruggs, Williams was the second child of Virginia Scruggs. Her father, whose name and occupation are unknown, abandoned the family. Virginia Scruggs

Mary Lou Williams. CORBIS-BETTMANN

had difficulty caring for her children, but she managed to keep her family together by doing domestic work. She played piano and organ, and Williams learned by sitting on her mother's lap and picking out notes. In 1913 the family moved from Georgia to Pittsburgh, where Williams's talent flourished. She attended Lincoln Public School in Pittsburgh and often entertained the teacher and other students with her pianistic genius.

Williams's childhood was relatively happy, and despite her poverty, she never thought of herself as poor. She was noted for her occasional pranks. Once she was challenged to jump over a series of boxes, and in doing so, she fell and broke her wrist. As a child, she developed a stuttering impediment that she never completely conquered. By age six, Williams was a favorite in neighbors' homes. She earned money by playing at local churches, thus supplementing her mother's meager earnings. Williams's youthful celebrity brought her to the attention of the prominent Mellon family, who asked her to perform at one of their parties.

In 1926, at age sixteen, Williams left Westinghouse High School and joined Seymour and Jeanette, a vaudeville band. That year she married the band's saxophonist, John Williams. They had no children. Touring with the vaudeville band, Williams attracted the attention of Thomas "Fats" Waller and Duke Ellington. After a few weeks, John Williams left the band to form the Syncopaters. He soon left that band also, but Mary Lou remained with the Syncopaters, led by Andy Kirk after 1929. She became popular playing boogie-woogie tunes, such as "Froggy Bottom," which was one of her standards. Under Kirk's tutelage, she learned how to arrange music and quickly became one of the band's principal arrangers. In 1930 she made her first professional recording with Andy Kirk's Twelve Clouds of Joy. She performed with Kirk's band for twelve years while independently arranging for Benny Goodman and Ellington. Her long separations from her husband led to their divorce in 1940.

The 1940s began a period of small groups of players or combos, called the bebop era. Along with Charlie "Bird" Parker, Dizzie Gillespie, Max Roach, Bud Powell, and Thelonious Monk, Williams was at the center of this jazz evolution. In 1942, when the Kirk band was working in New York City, Williams left it and went home to Pittsburgh. She stayed with her sister, but her semiretirement was short-lived. Art Blakey, a drummer, pestered Williams to form her own group. That year she established a sextet that included alumni from the Kirk band, among them Harold "Shorty" Baker, a trumpet player. About 1942, she married Baker because, she said, she fell "in love with the sound of his horn." The marriage ended in 1944; they had no children.

During her marriage, Williams toured with the Duke Ellington Band and arranged some of the band's music. She also performed as a soloist, playing to sellout crowds. Always eager to experiment, she opened her New York apartments to gatherings of old and new jazz performers. "I loved them," she said. "I learned a great deal about their chord changes and style of expression. The old blues took on a new look. The bop era blues chords added a great richness and more technique."

Williams embraced other interests. A humanitarian, she devoted much time to benefits supporting the World War II effort. Maturing as a composer, she wrote music for big-time stage revues, such as *The Victory Bandwagon* (1944). In 1944 her musicianship and popularity were recognized by Paul Whiteman, a bandleader and host of the NBC *Philco Hall of Fame,* who awarded Williams a citation for her achievements. Generosity was characteristic of Williams. For example, in Pittsburgh she was once introduced to the young Erroll Garner, whose incipient genius was as unlearned as hers had been. She offered to help him learn to read music, but he was not interested. "I realized," she recalled, that Garner was "born with more than most musicians could accomplish in a lifetime."

During the 1940s, Williams's genius in performing and composing blossomed. In 1945 she introduced her ambitious work *The Zodiac Suite.* Late in the decade, however, despite her success, a sense of isolation troubled her. In the early 1950s, she traveled throughout Europe, and while performing in a Paris club in 1954 she suffered an emotional breakdown. She walked off the set, left the club, and retreated to a friend's French villa to take stock of her life.

Williams returned to New York City in 1954, and in 1957, feeling the need for a spiritual center to her life, she became a Roman Catholic. In 1957, she established the Bel Canto Foundation to help needy musicians. She supported the foundation by opening a thrift shop and with proceeds from her record company, Mary Records. Encouraged by a young priest, Father Peter O'Brien, and by Dizzie Gillespie's wife, Williams performed at selective forums, such as the Newport Jazz Festival.

By the 1960s Williams was more focused and more secure in her faith than earlier. She began a series of religious compositions, using a liturgical base with a jazz motif. In 1962, she created *St. Martin de Porres: Black Christ of the Andes,* a jazz hymn. Williams's sense of music as mission turned her toward young people, whom she hoped to inspire with the knowledge and history of jazz. About 1966, she began teaching jazz theory in a parochial school in Pittsburgh.

In 1977 the chairman of the Duke University music department in Durham, North Carolina, offered Williams a position as artist in residence, which, at age sixty-seven, she accepted. A year later she learned she had cancer. According to Father O'Brien, Williams took her illness in stride, using "her music [to] ease her pain." In 1980 Williams played her last concert, in Tallahassee, Florida. After radiation treatments she insisted on performing one of her masses at Sacred Heart Cathedral in Raleigh, North Carolina, in November 1980. A few weeks later, she was confined to her bed. On 10 May 1981, Duke University honored Williams with its Trinity Award, "praising her accomplishments as an artist and humanitarian." At her death in Durham, most of the major figures in the jazz world paid tribute to her. She was buried in Pittsburgh.

Mary Lou Williams was admired and respected as a preeminent figure of what is known as America's only indigenous music. Deeply in need of adulation, she craved a life of simplicity and solitude but needed to be useful to others. A strong feature of Williams's life was her uncompromising attitude toward her art. Often she chastised her fellow musicians about their lack of seriousness. Along with her musical gifts, she was recognized for her humanity, which was as instinctive as her musical skills. Her genius encompassed much more than her musical legacy.

★

Williams's notable recordings include *A Mass for the Lenten Season* (1968), *Mass: Music for Peace* (1969), *Zoning* (1974), and with Cecil Taylor, *Embraced* (1978). Her work is discussed in Whitney Balliett, *American Musicians: Fifty-six Portraits in Jazz* (1986), and *Improvising: Sixteen Musicians and Their Art* (1977); Len Lyons, *The Great Jazz Pianists* (1983); and Mary Unterbrink,

Jazz Women at the Keyboard (1983). An obituary is in the *New York Times* (30 May 1981).

WILLIAM F. BROWNE

WILLIAMS, Thomas Lanier, III ("Tennessee") (*b.* 26 March 1911 in Columbus, Mississippi; *d.* 25 February 1983 in New York City), playwright who vitalized the postwar theater with dramas combining poetic language, psychological realism, and unconventional music and lighting techniques in brief scenes of lyric intensity. By creating immortal characters, such as Amanda Wingfield in *The Glass Menagerie* (1945) and Blanche DuBois in *A Streetcar Named Desire* (1947), Williams dominated the Broadway stage for more than two decades and earned international acclaim as one of the best American dramatists of the twentieth century.

Williams's father, Cornelius Coffin Williams, was a traveling salesman and spent long periods of time away from home. Williams, along with his mother, Edwina Dakin, and his older sister, Rose, therefore lived with his maternal grandparents in the various communities where Edwina's father, the Reverend Walter Dakin, served as an Episcopal

Tennessee Williams at the Morosco Theater in New York City for the opening of *Cat on a Hot Tin Roof*, 1955. UPI/CORBIS-BETTMANN

minister. In 1913 the family moved with the Dakins from Columbus to Nashville, Tennessee, returning to Mississippi in 1915, spending only a few months in Canton, before settling for the next two and a half years in Clarksdale. In the summer of 1916 Williams suffered a nearly fatal attack of diphtheria, followed by a crippling case of Bright's disease, which left him unable to walk for nearly eighteen months. During his convalescence, Williams listened as his mother read to him, providing an introduction to Shakespeare and other classic works of literature, early preparation for his career as a writer.

In July 1918 the Williams family moved to St. Louis, where Cornelius Williams had accepted a managerial post with the International Shoe Company, trading their relatively spacious home with the Dakins in an Episcopal rectory for a much more confining but affordable St. Louis apartment. The sensitive, young Williams adjusted with difficulty to the urban environment, becoming more conscious of the family's limited economic means and suffering the indignity of ridicule in the public schools. Shy and introspective following his illnesses, Williams became even more so when St. Louis schoolchildren teased him because of his slow, southern speech and mocked him because of his small size and physical frailty. His boisterous and sometimes tyrannical father taunted him as well. Alienated from his father and distant in age from his brother (born in 1919), Williams turned for companionship to his sister, with whom he formed a close, emotional attachment, a relationship reflected in his many autobiographical plays and especially in *The Glass Menagerie.*

Williams attended St. Louis public schools, graduating in June 1929 from University City High School. The following September he enrolled at the University of Missouri at Columbia. With financial aid from his father and maternal grandparents, Williams completed two years of the general liberal arts curriculum and one year studying journalism, the program his father prescribed for him as the most practical, given his son's impractical interest in writing poetry and fiction. Williams distinguished himself by publishing a short story, "A Lady's Beaded Bag," in the university's literary magazine and by winning honorable mention for *Beauty Is the Word* in a one-act play contest.

Although Williams performed well enough academically to remain in school, his father, a veteran of the Spanish-American War, became increasingly dismayed by his son's repeated failures in the Reserve Army Training Corps. Claiming financial hardship, Cornelius refused to support his son beyond his junior year and instead put him to work. From 1932 to 1935, Williams was employed at a branch of the International Shoe Company in St. Louis, performing routine tasks—dusting shoes, typing factory orders, carrying shoe samples—chores he detested. At night and on weekends, Williams wrote lyric poetry and short stories. Overwork, coupled with poor eating and sleeping habits, contributed to Williams's eventual collapse from exhaustion in the spring of 1935. Hospitalized briefly, Williams thereafter quit his job and spent the summer recuperating with his grandparents in Memphis. That summer, in collaboration with a next-door neighbor, Williams wrote a comedy called *Cairo! Shanghai! Bombay!,* which was performed in July by the Memphis Garden Players. The success of the production convinced Williams to begin writing seriously for the theater.

Although his father refused to support him, Williams returned to college in September 1935 at Washington University in St. Louis. During his first year Williams audited classes. When his grandparents paid his tuition the following year, he took classes for credit, but because he failed to take physical education at the University of Missouri, a requirement at Washington, he entered as a nondegree student. While he continued to write poetry and short fiction, Williams showed greater promise as a playwright. In April 1936 his *Magic Tower* won a contest sponsored by the Webster Groves Theatre Guild in St. Louis and was staged the following October. His first full-length play, *Candles to the Sun,* was performed in March 1937 by an amateur theatrical group in St. Louis. In order to graduate, Williams transferred to the University of Iowa in the fall of 1937. On 5 August 1938, he received his B.A. degree.

Soon after graduation, Williams looked for support from the Works Progress Administration, traveling first to Chicago and then to New Orleans. Unsuccessful, Williams secured odd jobs to support himself, at the same time enjoying the freedom afforded by an independent life in cosmopolitan New Orleans. Uncertain about his own sexual identity during his college years, Williams shunned intimacy, except for a brief affair with a more experienced woman at the University of Iowa. In New Orleans, Williams lost his inhibitions, adopting a homosexual lifestyle that he maintained throughout his life.

In February 1939 Williams entered a play-writing contest sponsored by the Group Theatre in New York, submitting a collection of sketches called *American Blues.* To meet the eligibility requirements, Williams lied about his age, giving his date of birth as 1914. In subsequent years, he often repeated the lie, to the confusion of many biographers. Although Williams failed to win first prize, the panel of judges, including Molly Day Thacher (the wife of the director Elia Kazan), awarded Williams a special prize of $100. Recognizing Williams's talent, Thacher also recommended his work to the agent Audrey Wood. When Williams hired Wood, she acted quickly on his behalf, arranging for the publication of "The Field of Blue Children" in *Story* magazine. Printed in the September–October 1939 issue, it was the first of his published works to bear the name "Tennessee Williams." For more than thirty years

thereafter, Wood loyally managed Williams's professional career.

With Wood's assistance, Williams obtained a $1,000 Rockefeller Foundation grant, awarded in December 1939. That winter in New York, under John Gassner's tutelage at the New School for Social Research, Williams completed a one-act play, *The Long Goodbye,* and continued revising *Battle of Angels,* his first play to be selected for major production. Optioned by the Theatre Guild, *Battle of Angels* opened in Boston on 30 December 1940, starring Miriam Hopkins. Considered blasphemous by some critics and still needing substantial revision, *Battle of Angels* failed to win the support of the Theatre Guild for a New York production.

Despite the failure of *Battle of Angels,* Williams continued revising and writing, aided by another Rockefeller Foundation grant of $500 in January 1941. Rejected for military service during World War II because of poor vision, Williams obtained temporary jobs that suited his itinerant lifestyle. After graduating from college, Williams seldom stayed in any one place for more than a few months, although he would eventually own homes in both Key West, Florida, and New Orleans.

In the spring of 1943, his financial resources exhausted, Williams returned to St. Louis. Open hostility between his parents, the result of their deteriorating marriage, made for inhospitable living conditions. His parents separated in 1947. Adding to the family's turmoil, in January 1943 Williams's sister had undergone a prefrontal lobotomy as a treatment for mental illness. In August 1937 she had been institutionalized at Farmington State Hospital, but various treatment measures, including insulin shock treatment, had failed to improve her condition. The news of her operation contributed to Williams's strong sense of guilt, feelings reflected in *The Glass Menagerie,* the play that he began writing at about this time.

To Williams's relief, Audrey Wood found work for him in Hollywood, as a screenwriter for Metro-Goldwyn-Mayer. His efforts to write for the actress Lana Turner and the child actress Margaret O'Brien, however, proved unsatisfactory to his employers. Twice during his six months in Hollywood, he was suspended without pay before finally losing his position in October 1943.

Williams's first successful major production, *The Glass Menagerie,* opened on 26 December 1944 in Chicago and on 31 March 1945 on Broadway. But for the enthusiastic reviews of Ashton Stevens and Claudia Cassidy praising the performance of Laurette Taylor as Amanda, the show might never have reached New York. Described by Cassidy as a "fragile" drama, *The Glass Menagerie* nevertheless endured, becoming a classic in the American theater.

The success of *The Glass Menagerie* secured Williams's financial future, but critics waited to see whether Williams could sustain the promise heralded by his first Broadway play. Startled and somewhat dismayed by his success, Williams shunned the limelight, choosing to undergo a cataract operation, his fourth since 1941. In April 1945, when he was sufficiently recovered to travel, Williams journeyed to Mexico, where he resumed writing what would later become *A Streetcar Named Desire.*

In June 1947 Williams rented a cottage in Provincetown, Massachusetts, where he worked on revisions to another play, *Summer and Smoke.* Opening on 8 July 1947 at the Gulf Oil Playhouse in Dallas, *Summer and Smoke* could have preceded *A Streetcar Named Desire* to Broadway. Instead, it followed Williams's masterpiece to New York and suffered by comparison with it. In Provincetown, although Williams shared living quarters with Pancho Rodriguez y Gonzalez, he met and had an affair with Frank Merlo, hastening the end of Williams's relationship with Rodriguez. Afterward, with Merlo, Williams developed the only long-lasting romantic relationship of his life. They lived together until Merlo's death from lung cancer in September 1963. Avoiding the explicit treatment of homosexuality in his plays, Williams kept his homosexuality a secret from the general public until he came out publicly in a 1970 televised interview with David Frost.

With the production of *A Streetcar Named Desire* in December 1947, critics no longer doubted Williams's talent. Winning both the Drama Critics' Circle Award and the Pulitzer Prize, *A Streetcar Named Desire* earned for Williams a permanent place among America's finest dramatists. Widely produced around the world, *A Streetcar Named Desire* is recognized not only as Williams's finest play, but as one of the best on the world stage.

In February 1948, Williams traveled with Merlo to Italy and Sicily, returning to New York for the October opening of *Summer and Smoke.* Later Williams would recall his pleasant experience in Sicily, writing a comic play, *The Rose Tattoo,* about a Sicilian widow and her clownish suitor. Opening on Broadway on 3 February 1951, *The Rose Tattoo* convinced critics that Williams could effectively write both tragedy and comedy. Following the success of *The Rose Tattoo,* Williams tried a bolder experiment with *Camino Real* (1953), an expansion of an earlier play, "Ten Blocks on the Camino Real." Critics failed to appreciate its mixture of fantasy and romance. Audiences and critics alike found it difficult to understand, resulting in a rare box-office failure for Williams.

Even when successful, Williams suffered from a lack of confidence, leading some critics to speculate that Williams too easily gave in to directors, Elia Kazan for example, and compromised his artistic integrity for commercial success. Despite his insecurities and his increasing dependence upon alcohol and prescription medications, Williams continued to produce extraordinary work. *Cat on a Hot Tin Roof,* which opened on Broadway on 24 March 1955, won both the Drama Critics' Circle Award and the Pulitzer Prize. It would be Williams's most successful play of the decade, running for a remarkable 694 performances.

In the late 1950s, Williams began to fear that his plays no longer appealed to theater audiences. His 1956 screenplay, *Baby Doll,* received harsh criticism and was condemned as immoral from the pulpit by Francis Cardinal Spellman of New York. When *Orpheus Descending* (1957), a remake of *Battle of Angels,* closed after just 68 performances, Williams lost confidence in his ability to write. Already suffering from depression and hypochondria, Williams felt even more dismayed when he learned of his father's death in May 1957. A month later Williams began psychoanalysis. After about a year in treatment, Williams ended the sessions, ignoring his doctor's advice to quit writing.

Critics responded with shock to Williams's *Suddenly Last Summer* (1958), a play that probed topics close to Williams's psyche—homosexuality and art, madness and truth—but reviewers responded more favorably to *Sweet Bird of Youth,* helping to restore Williams's confidence. Soon after the Broadway premier of *Sweet Bird of Youth* on 10 March 1959, Williams traveled to Cuba, where he met Fidel Castro and Ernest Hemingway. The following August he embarked with Merlo on a worldwide tour. When they returned, Williams made Key West his most frequent stopping place until November 1960, when the opening of *Period of Adjustment* brought him back to New York. Billed as a serious comedy, the play was neither a critical nor a commercial success. In 1961, with the Broadway production of *The Night of the Iguana,* Williams returned to the kind of poetic lyricism that characterized his earlier work. Many critics praised this play as his best since *Cat on a Hot Tin Roof* (1955). It earned for Williams his fourth Drama Critics' Circle Award.

The demands of repeated Broadway productions gradually affected Williams adversely. Suffering from hypochondria and paranoia, Williams resorted to the use of alcohol and drugs, creating tension between Williams and those people closest to him, including Merlo. Merlo's death in September 1963 added loneliness to Williams's general sense of personal despair.

With the production of *The Milk Train Doesn't Stop Here Anymore,* which opened on Broadway in January 1963, Williams ended a long run of Broadway successes. After a revival attempt failed the following January, Williams next tried writing an experimental kind of drama, intended for the off-Broadway theater. *Slapstick Tragedy* (1966), a double bill featuring two nonrealistic plays, *The Gnadiges Fraulein* and *The Mutilated,* was the immediate result, to which critics responded negatively. Reviews of the more conventional *Kingdom of Earth (The Seven Descents of Myrtle),* which opened on Broadway on 27 March 1968, were also unfavorable, and it closed within a month. *In the Bar of a Tokyo Hotel,* produced at the Eastside Playhouse in May 1969, similarly failed to appeal to a wide audience.

By the end of the decade, Williams had experienced an unusual number of failures. In a surprising move, in January 1969 Williams converted to Catholicism. His spiritual transformation could not reverse, however, the effects of alcohol and drug use. In the fall of 1969 Williams's condition had deteriorated to the point that his brother intervened, convincing Williams to admit himself to Barnes Hospital in St. Louis for treatment. As a result of his confinement there, Williams temporarily enjoyed better health and soon resumed his usual habit of traveling, punctuated by stops where his plays were in production. In July 1971 he was in Chicago for the production of *Out Cry,* a revised version of his earlier *Two-Character Play,* first performed in London in 1967. In Chicago, Williams quarreled with Audrey Wood, with the result that their once amiable professional relationship ended.

During the last decade of his life, Williams traveled frequently, with only occasional prolonged visits to his home in Key West or to New York. His output of plays continued unabated, but none displayed the poetic lyricism of his earlier triumphs. *Small Craft Warnings* opened in New York on 2 April 1972. In March 1973 *Out Cry* opened and closed in New York after only twelve performances at the Lyceum Theatre. *The Red Devil Battery Sign* (1975), *Vieux Carré* (1978), *A Lovely Sunday for Creve Coeur* (1979), and *Tiger Tail* (1979) all failed to win critical or popular acclaim. In December 1979, despite recent failures, Williams was honored for his achievements at the Kennedy Center in Washington, D.C., and the following April was awarded the Medal of Freedom by President Jimmy Carter.

From 1980 until his death, Williams wrote unfailingly, as was his habit, even when audiences judged his work harshly. *Clothes for a Summer Hotel,* a play based on the lives of Zelda and F. Scott Fitzgerald, opened at the Cort Theatre in New York on 26 March 1980. On 24 August 1981 *Something Cloudy, Something Clear,* a play about Williams's experiences at Provincetown, opened at the Bouwerie Theater in New York. *A House Not Meant to Stand,* the last play to open during Williams's lifetime, premiered on 27 April 1982 at the Goodman Memorial Theatre in Chicago.

Early in the morning on 25 February 1983, Williams died in his suite at the Elysée Hotel in New York City. Apparently he choked to death when a cap from a bottle of eye drops lodged in his throat. The cause of death was asphyxiation. Despite Williams's expressed wish to be interred at sea, in the vicinity where his favorite poet, Hart Crane, had drowned, he was buried in St. Louis.

The name Tennessee Williams is synonymous with the Broadway theater of the 1940s and 1950s. Gifted with an insightful understanding of human nature and a talent for creating realistic psychological portraits, Williams fashioned such immortal characters as Amanda Wingfield, Blanche DuBois, Stanley Kowalski, Big Daddy Pollitt, and Maggie "the cat." The themes of his plays—the inability to communicate, the seductive allure and bitter disappointment of material wealth, the emotional bankruptcy of life without love, and the fear of death—reflect some of the social ills that continue to plague modern society. Aiming to replace "the exhausted theatre of realistic conventions," with a more "plastic" theater, Williams offered audiences an alternative point of view, refracted through the prism of his "poetic imagination." Critically acclaimed as one of the best American dramatists of his century, Williams also enjoyed widespread popular appeal, owing to the successful film adaptations of many of his remarkable dramas.

★

Significant collections of Williams's papers and manuscripts are housed at the Harry Ransom Humanities Research Center at the University of Texas at Austin, Columbia University, and Harvard University. Supplementing Williams's *Memoirs* (1975), Lyle Leverich, *Tom: The Unknown Tennessee Williams* (1995), provides a comprehensive account of Williams's life through the production of *The Glass Menagerie* in 1945. A projected second volume by Leverich will complete the life otherwise documented by Benjamin Nelson, *Tennessee Williams: The Man and His Work* (1961); Donald Spoto, *The Kindness of Strangers: The Life of Tennessee Williams* (1985); and Ronald Hayman, *Tennessee Williams: Everyone Else Is an Audience* (1993). George W. Crandell, *Tennessee Williams: A Descriptive Bibliography* (1995), provides a comprehensive listing of Williams's published work through 1991. An obituary is in the *New York Times* (26 Feb. 1983).

GEORGE W. CRANDELL

WILLSON, (Robert Reiniger) Meredith (*b.* 18 May 1902 in Mason City, Iowa; *d.* 15 June 1984 in Santa Monica, California), composer, musical director, musician, and writer best known for his Broadway musical *The Music Man* (1957), which won five Tony awards.

Meredith Willson was the son of John David Willson and Rosalie Reiniger. His father was a member of the first law class at Notre Dame University and played cornet in the Notre Dame band. He never practiced law, however, instead following his own father, Alonzo, into real estate. Willson's mother, by many accounts a social activist, started Mason City's first kindergarten and was director of the Sunday school at the First Congregational Church. She also acted in community theater. Meredith grew up in Mason City, the youngest of three children in a moderately prosperous family. He was immersed in the arts, especially

Meredith Willson, 1946. UPI/Corbis-Bettmann

ing I went down to Brooks Brothers to get measured for my Sousa uniform." He toured with Sousa from 1921 to 1923, traveling to Europe, Mexico, and Cuba. Willson also studied privately with flutist Georges Barrère from 1920 to 1929 and Henry Hadley from 1923 to 1924. In 1924 his first important composition, *Parade Fantastique,* was performed. The same year Willson was invited to join the Philharmonic Society of New York as third chair flute; Arturo Toscanini was director. On his first night, he arrived to find the second chair had quit and the first chair was out sick with appendicitis. Suddenly he was first chair flute. It was the kind of luck that seemed to characterize his career. Willson remained with the orchestra until 1929.

In 1929 Willson decided he wanted to compose and conduct. He went to Seattle to conduct the Seattle Symphony, but the experience was unsuccessful. From 1929 to 1930 he was musical director for the northwest division of ABC radio. After a short-lived return to New York, he moved to California and began work scoring films. His first two were *Peacock Alley* (1930) and *The Lost Zeppelin* (1930). He found more permanent work as musical director of the NBC radio network, and from 1932 to 1936 he was based in San Francisco. He wrote his first two symphonies, both important compositions, in 1936: *San Francisco* and *The O. O. McIntyre Suite.* His work has been characterized by a sprightly use of rhythm and rich instrumental colors.

During the 1930s Willson was intensely active. He worked on such radio shows as *America Sings, Waltz Time,* and *House of Melody,* which attracted and introduced him to major stars. He also organized a show called *Maxwell House Coffee Time.* He frequently conducted the Seattle, San Francisco, and Los Angeles symphony orchestras. Continuing to work in the movie industry, Willson composed and arranged for Charlie Chaplin's *The Great Dictator* (1940) and wrote the music for Lillian Hellman's *The Little Foxes* (1941). Willson enlisted in the U.S. Army in 1942. He was made a major and from 1942 to 1945 was head of the music division for the Armed Forces Radio Service. He was responsible for such GI shows as *Command Performance* and *Mail Call.* Following his discharge, with the rank of major, he continued in radio. He was host of *The Big Show* with Tallulah Bankhead and in 1950 wrote its popular theme song, the hymnlike "May the Good Lord Bless and Keep You." The song, based on his mother's favorite parting words, became a sensation, selling half a million copies of sheet music in four months, a record for theme music. His other popular tunes include "You and I," and "Two in Love." Divorced in 1947, Willson married Ralina ("Rini") Zarova, a singer, on 13 March 1948.

Willson rose steadily through the ranks, eventually making it big on Broadway with the smash-hit musical that put his hometown of Mason City on the map and earned him the moniker of Iowa's Music Man. Willson, fifty-six at the

music, from a young age. His mother played the piano, and several of his aunts and uncles played musical instruments as well. He had years of piano, flute, and piccolo lessons and was a member of the Mason City High School band and orchestra, where he was known for his ability to play a variety of instruments. He ordered his first flute through the mail, becoming the first person in Mason City to play one. Willson later recalled in a whimsical memoir, *And There I Stood with My Piccolo* (1948), that he was surprised to discover that "you had to play it sideways . . . where you couldn't see what was going on." Meanwhile, he had been composing music from the time he could pick up a pencil.

Willson had a less than happy relationship with his father, and after graduation from Mason City High School in 1919 he left home to pursue a musical career in New York City. (His parents divorced the following year.) He was just seventeen, but his background and experience made it possible for him to attend the Institute of Musical Art (now the Juilliard School) from 1919 to 1922. On 29 August 1920 he married Elizabeth Wilson, his high school sweetheart. At age nineteen Willson was hired to play flute in John Philip Sousa's band, a coup for someone so young. "I had scaled the heights," he wrote of landing his first job. "Nobody will ever feel more important than I did the morn-

time, was the composer, librettist, and lyricist of *The Music Man* (1957) which ran for 1,375 performances on Broadway and won the New York Drama Critics Circle Award and a Tony for outstanding musical of the 1957–1958 season. (The movie sound track won an Oscar in 1962.) Willson spent eight years writing the musical, which grossed over $10 million on Broadway. A movie version of the same name was released in 1962. None of his subsequent works brought him the fame or attention that *The Music Man* did, but *The Unsinkable Molly Brown* (1960) was a Broadway hit and also became a movie. He also wrote the commercially successful *Here's Love* (1963). It was based on *Miracle on 34th Street* and was noted for the song "It's Beginning to Look a Lot Like Christmas." At one point all three musicals were running simultaneously on Broadway.

The Music Man told the story of a likable but unethical traveling salesman in Iowa who sold band uniforms and instruments to schoolchildren, promising their parents he would teach his pupils to play. Rather than form a band, however, the salesman tried to pull a disappearing act, making off with the money. Willson drew not only on his small-town Iowa background for the story, but his wide experience in music for the score. "Seventy-six Trombones," the musical's exuberant highlight, evokes his tenure with Sousa. The lilting "Lida Rose" and "It's You" show his fondness for the barbershop quartets he had heard as a boy. A *New York Times* review at the time called Willson's music as American as apple pie, and indeed his score is a celebration of homespun values and midwestern gumption.

Wilson, who towered above many at six feet, was known for his perpetual optimism and lighthearted manner. He had friends throughout the music business. As far as Iowa was concerned, he was a "one-man chamber of commerce," according to a longtime friend. His colorful stories changed with each telling. He once explained that the inspiration for *The Music Man* was the second bass clarinet in Sousa's band during Willson's tenure: he had not played a note in five years and was undiscovered until he moved to first chair. In another telling the inspiration became a traveling salesman who passed through Mason City and tried to sell musical instruments to all the local schoolchildren.

Throughout his career the multitalented Willson wrote books as well as music. These include three memoirs: *And There I Stood with My Piccolo* (1948), *Eggs I Have Laid* (1955), and *"But He Doesn't Know the Territory"* (1957). He also wrote two novels: *Who Did What to Fedalia?* (1952) and *The Music Man, a Novel* (1962).

Ralina Zarova Willson died of cancer in 1966. Willson married his third wife, Rosemary Sullivan, on 14 February 1968. He made his home in the Brentwood section of Los Angeles. Willson was a Congregationalist. He died of apparent heart failure and is buried in Elmwood Cemetery in Mason City. He had no children.

Willson made Mason City famous as the fictional River City in *The Music Man*. Much of his music survives him. His boyhood home is now a museum, and across the street the Mason City Public Library houses a large collection of Willson memorabilia. A Mason City footbridge featured in the movie version of that musical was renamed the Meredith Willson Footbridge in 1962.

★

The Lee P. Loomis Archive in the Mason City Public Library includes many personal papers and photographs of the Willson family and recordings of Willson's radio shows, as well as magazine and newspaper articles. The Iowa Writers Collection at the University of Iowa contains original scores and manuscripts of Willson's work, as well as clippings, reviews, and letters. Willson's three memoirs, although written in a humorous vein, include many anecdotes about his personal life and career. A sketch appears in Charles Moritz, ed., *Current Biography, 1958* (1959). Biographical information is in Clare D. Kinsman, ed., *Contemporary Authors,* vols. 49–52 (1975), and H. Wiley Hitchcock and Stanley Sadie, eds., *The New Grove Dictionary of American Music,* vol. 4 (1986). With the success of *The Music Man* came articles about Willson in *Newsweek* (30 Dec. 1957), *Time* (30 Dec. 1957), and *Life* (20 Jan. 1958). An obituary is in the *New York Times* (17 June 1984).

TERRY ANDREWS

WINOGRAND, Garry (*b.* 14 January 1928 in New York City; *d.* 19 March 1984 in Tijuana, Mexico), photographer whose innovations changed the way the "street photo" was taken.

Winogrand was born in the Pelham Parkway section of the Bronx to Abraham and Bertha Winogrand. His father was a leather worker and his mother worked part-time as a seamstress. As a youth Winogrand was full of restless energy, and he was frequently absent from school. He joined the Army Air Forces in his senior year of high school and served for eighteen months.

Supported by the GI bill, Winogrand enrolled in 1946 at the City College of New York, where he studied painting. After one year he transferred to Columbia University, where he studied until 1951 but did not earn a degree. In 1948 a friend introduced him to photography, and so began a bond between Winogrand and the camera. For most of his career Winogrand would shoot with a Leica brand camera.

By the early 1950s photojournalism had become a field of great interest. Magazines were publishing photos of the American social landscape that were highly popular with readers. The photojournalist's life appealed to young artists because of its seemingly authentic work. Many of these young photographers rejected the carefully planned photo in favor of a more candid, "honest" snapshot.

Winogrand began working for the Pix Agency in 1951. Having developed an interest in things that moved, he photographed boxers at a training gym and at numerous fight clubs. In January 1952 he married Adrienne Lubow, an aspiring dancer; they had two children, Laurie and Ethan.

On the recommendation of a colleague, Winogrand went to work for Brackman Associates. He began to be published more frequently in magazines such as *Collier's, Redbook, Gentry, Men,* and *Sports Illustrated.* Two of his photographs were chosen by the photographer and curator Edward Steichen for inclusion in the landmark show "The Family of Man" at the Museum of Modern Art in 1955.

In 1955 Winogrand decided to take a trip across the United States with his wife, hoping to capture images different from the East Coast city subjects he knew so well. Before leaving, a friend showed him Walker Evans's book *American Photographs.* This book changed the way Winogrand thought about photography.

The early 1960s was a transitional time in Winogrand's personal and professional lives. Winogrand began to focus his nervous, almost electrical energy onto his art. In 1963, after years of troubled marriage and numerous informal separations, he and his wife legally separated; they were divorced in 1966.

In 1963 forty-five of Winogrand's photographs were included in the exhibit "Five Unrelated Photographers" at the Museum of Modern Art. That year he also applied for a Guggenheim Fellowship, which was awarded in the spring of 1964. He exhibited again at the Museum of Modern Art in the 1967 show "New Documents." By this time, Winogrand was accepted as a leading photographer of his generation. The casual, seemingly indifferent composition of his images broke with the traditional design of earlier artists.

In the 1960s magazines began to run fewer photo stories and to print more advertisements. Winogrand shot promotional ads but found the work banal and emotionally unrewarding. In 1967 he married Judy Teller, an advertising copywriter. By 1969 they were divorced and Winogrand had given up shooting ads.

The Animals (1969), a book of photos taken at the Central Park Zoo in New York City, documented interactions between the animals and the humans. These photos were neither sentimental scenes of lovable creatures nor testaments to the sadness of caged lives, but unpretentious candid moments.

Winogrand often used a wide-angle lens that allowed for a close shot with more pictorial elements. His method of tilting the frame diagonally disrupted the standard structure of photographs.

In 1971 Winogrand was offered a teaching position at the Chicago Institute of Design. The next year he married Eileen Adele Hale; they had one child, Melissa. In 1973

Garry Winogrand, New Jersey, 1983. COURTESY FRAENKEL GALLERY, SAN FRANCISCO. © 1983 EILEEN ADELE HALE. ALL RIGHTS RESERVED.

they moved to Austin, where Winogrand had accepted a job in the Photography Department at the University of Texas. *Stock Photographs* (1980), commissioned by the Fort Worth Art Museum, documented that city's Fat Stock Show and Rodeo.

In 1975 Winogrand was diagnosed with a thyroid condition that required surgery. Later that year, while shooting at the University of Texas–Texas A&M football game, he suffered a broken leg after being trampled by a player.

In 1976 Winogrand compiled photographs for the book *Public Relations* (1977), the fruit of a Guggenheim Fellowship he received in 1969. This work, which was intended to show the effects of the media on events, offered alternative depictions of situations seen mostly on television or in newspapers.

Winogrand resigned his teaching position at Texas and moved to Los Angeles in 1978. That year he also received a third Guggenheim Fellowship, an extraordinary achievement. Adding a motor-driven frame advance to his camera enabled Winogrand to shoot considerably more photos in a given time. He spent hours feeding his camera image after image. Early in 1984 he was diagnosed with cancer of the gall bladder. His health quickly weakened, and he died at the Gerson Clinic in Tijuana, Mexico.

At the time of his death Winogrand had left nearly a third of a million exposures untouched. Many rolls of film were not even developed, and he had never looked at most of them. This is understandable, considering his method of photography. Winogrand would shoot many frames of the same scene from many angles. After developing the film he would often choose only a few shots to make into a final print. Winogrand claimed that this process of editing, which he called a "process of discovery," interested him more than the images themselves.

Winogrand was one of the most influential photographers of his era. His prints, employing rapid, unplanned exposures, defined the snapshot aesthetic of a street photographer. Winogrand was not interested in social or moral issues. He avoided critical analysis, fearing it might bias his visual judgment. Winogrand continually sought out new angles, distances, and movements. His technical experiments, combined with scenes of public behavior, produced fresh images that allowed for a variety of interpretations.

★

Winogrand's *Women Are Beautiful* (1975), with an essay by Helen Gary Bishop, is a compilation of photos of a subject on which Winogrand focused for years. Tod Papageorge, *Garry Winogrand: Public Relations* (1977), is the catalog that accompanied the exhibition of the same name; Ron Tyler, *Stock Photographs: The Fort Worth Fat Stock Show and Rodeo* (1980), consists of Winogrand's photographs commissioned by the Fort Worth Art Museum; John Szarkowski, *Winogrand: Figments from the Real World* (1988), is the biographical catalog that accompanied the exhibition of the same name at the Museum of Modern Art. Articles include "Monkeys Make the Problem More Difficult: A Collected Interview with Garry Winogrand," *Image* (July 1972); Charles Hagen, "An Interview with Garry Winogrand," *Afterimage* (December 1977); and Andy Grundberg, "Life Seized on the Fly," *New York Times* (23 Dec. 1984), on Winogrand's life and work. An obituary is in the *New York Times* (22 Mar. 1984).

RENÉE COPPOLA

WOOD, Natalie (*b.* 20 July 1938 in San Francisco, California; *d.* 29 November 1981 near Santa Catalina Island, California), movie star who appeared in *Rebel Without a Cause* (1955), *West Side Story* (1961), and *Splendor in the Grass* (1961) and whose image projected a healthy vitality and romanticism.

Natalie Wood was born Natasha Gurdin to Russian immigrant parents associated with the entertainment industry. Her father, Nicholas Gurdin, was a set designer and her mother, Maria (Kuleff) Gurdin, was a former ballerina. Natalie was the middle child of three daughters. She attended studio and public schools and worked her way up through the ranks of the film industry.

In 1943 Natalie began working as a child actress, appearing with her mother in *Happy Land,* which was produced by Twentieth Century–Fox and directed by Irving Pichel. Pichel then gave her a major role opposite Orson Welles in RKO's *Tomorrow Is Forever* (1946). For this film her name was changed to "Natalie," and she had earlier

Natalie Wood as she appeared in *All the Fine Young Cannibals,* 1960. ARCHIVE PHOTOS

been given "Wood" as a last name because the directors wished to honor a deceased director and friend, Sam Wood. In 1947 she appeared in *Miracle on 34th Street, Driftwood,* and *The Ghost and Mrs. Muir;* in 1948 she appeared in *Scudda-Hoo! Scudda-Hay!;* in 1949, *Chicken Every Sunday, Father Was a Fullback,* and *The Green Promise.* In the 1950s, she starred in *No Sad Songs for Me, The Jackpot, Our Very Own, Never a Dull Moment* (1950); *The Blue Veil* (1951); *Dear Brat, Just for You, The Rose Bowl Story* (1952); *The Star* (1953); and *The Silver Chalice* (1954).

Her first great role was in *Rebel Without a Cause* (1955). This film dealt with upper- and middle-class juvenile delinquency, a common theme after World War II as the children of the postwar period were beginning to mature. The teenagers portrayed in this movie had everything yet lacked self-discipline and "rebelled" against constraints. In a sense, it was a morality play as the "rebel" reforms and is enlightened by a developing social conscience. Sal Mineo, who also starred in this film, spoke to the film's desire to inspire social responsibility in young people of different ethnic groups. This film was a watershed in Wood's career, and she was nominated for her first Oscar. She and James Dean personified the teenage generation's search for meaning and focus, and she, like Dean, was idolized by teenagers.

Throughout the 1950s, Wood seemed to be, in the words of Gene Kelly, "the teenagers' teenager, the one girl they all identify with." She appeared with such male leads—sometimes as a youthful companion and sometimes as a lover—as John Wayne in *The Searchers* (1956) and Tab Hunter in *The Burning Hills* (1956) and *The Girl He Left Behind* (1956). Again, these roles carried social messages, with Wood playing roles of virtuous young women setting an example. Often, she depicted a youth growing up in turbulent times. In *Marjorie Morningstar* (1957) she was herself in transition. As the director, Irving Rapper, commented: "Natalie started this film as a teenager, but she completes it as an important star." She also appeared in *Bombers B-52* and *No Sleep Until Dawn* in 1957. In 1958 she starred with Frank Sinatra in *Kings Go Forth*, and in 1959 she appeared in *Cash McCall.*

Natalie dated James Dean, Elvis Presley, and Nicky Hilton before marrying Robert Wagner on 28 December 1957. She starred with Wagner in *All the Fine Young Cannibals* in 1960. They divorced in 1962. In 1969 she married Richard Gregson, with whom she had a daughter, Natasha. After they were divorced in 1972, Wood remarried Robert Wagner. They had a daughter, Courtney.

The 1961 film *West Side Story* told the story of inner-city gang warfare. Again, Wood worked with minority actors and actresses such as Rita Moreno. Wood performed the intricate dance routines herself but her singing was dubbed with the voice of Marni Nixon. Due to the success of this film, Natalie Wood had her hand and foot prints preserved in cement in the forecourt of Hollywood's Grauman's Chinese Theater. *West Side Story* marked an early high in her career.

Splendor in the Grass (1961) changed Wood's image to that of a mature love interest appealing to an older generation. As before, she made this transition in her life easily, and she received wide acclaim as a serious actress after this film's release. She portrayed a young woman whose natural sexual desire was constrained by social mores. This role spoke to young adult women as yet unmarried. For her performance Wood was nominated for the second time for an Oscar. Meanwhile, Wood's life story and biography appeared in numerous magazines, such as *Look, Newsweek, Saturday Evening Post,* and *Parade* throughout the 1950s and 1960s.

From the 1960s until her death, she starred in *Gypsy* (1962); *Love with the Proper Stranger* (1963), which earned her a third Oscar nomination; *Sex and the Single Girl* (1964); *The Great Race* (1965); *Penelope, This Property Is Condemned,* and *Inside Daisy Clover* (1966); *Bob and Carol and Ted and Alice* (1969), which was her first try at comedy; *The Candidate* and *I'm a Stranger Here Myself* (1972); *The*

Affair (1973); *Peeper* (1975); *Meteor* and *The Cracker Factory* (1979); *The Last Married Couple in America* (1980); and *Brainstorm* (1981), released after her death.

Natalie Wood also starred in two television miniseries, *The Pride of the Family* (1953–1954) and *From Here to Eternity* (1979). She died by drowning after paddling away in a dinghy from her cabin cruiser on which she was staying with Wagner and *Brainstorm* costar Christopher Walken. She is buried in Westwood Memorial Park in Los Angeles.

Natalie Wood will be remembered especially for her roles in *Rebel Without a Cause* (1955) and *West Side Story* (1961). She will be linked to the pouting James Dean, who also died young. Natalie Wood will also be remembered for playing in films with social messages and setting a virtuous example for the young generation growing up after World War II. In a career spanning nearly forty years, Wood transformed herself very easily from a child star into a teenage idol and then mature female lead. Her durability and versatility as an actress make her an important figure in the history of American cinema.

★

Kirk Crivello, *Fallen Angels: The Lives and Untimely Deaths of Fourteen Hollywood Beauties* (1988), has perhaps a view different from all the other biographies in the field, such as Warren G. Harris, *Natalie and R.J.: Hollywood's Star-Crossed Lovers* (1988), and John Parker, *Five for Hollywood* (1991). Christopher Nickens, *Natalie Wood: A Biography in Photographs* (1986), has excellent film shots and publicity photos at various stages of her career. Amy L. Unterburger, *International Dictionary of Films and Film Makers: Actors and Actresses,* 3d ed. (1997), has a chronological list of Wood's films. Lana Wood, *Natalie: A Memoir by Her Sister* (1984), is the best insider's view. An obituary is in the *New York Times* (30 Nov. 1981).

Barbara Bennett Peterson

WOODRUFF, Robert Winship (*b.* 6 December 1889 in Columbus, Georgia; *d.* 7 March 1985 in Atlanta, Georgia), business executive and civic leader who guided the Coca-Cola Company to a predominant position in domestic and international soft drink markets.

Eldest of the four sons born to Ernest Woodruff and Emily Caroline Winship, Robert Woodruff was four years old when his family moved to Atlanta. There his father built a business empire that included banking, coal and ice, steel, and cotton ginning enterprises. In 1919 the family's prominence was further enhanced when Ernest Woodruff led a group of investors in wresting control of the growing Coca-Cola Company from Asa G. Candler.

As a boy and young adult, Robert was constantly at odds with his authoritarian father. A poor student, possibly because of undiagnosed dyslexia, he attended Georgia Mili-

Robert Wilson Woodruff in his office at the Coca-Cola Company, late 1970s. UPI/CORBIS-BETTMANN

tary Academy after failing at Atlanta Boys' High School, and there he excelled in organizing events and managing organizations, while barely getting by academically. After Robert's graduation in 1908, his father sent him to Emory College (now Emory University), at the time a small two-year institution in Oxford, Georgia. He was in college only one semester before the school's president advised his father that Robert should not return for another term.

In February 1909 Woodruff began working in a blue-collar job in an Atlanta foundry. In the hope that Robert would soon marry, his father gave him a job as purchasing agent for his Atlanta Ice and Coal Company. On 17 October 1912 Robert married Nell Kendall Hodgson, who was from a wealthy Athens, Georgia, family. They had no children.

As purchasing agent, Woodruff decided to replace the company's mule-drawn wagons with trucks, buying a fleet from White Motor Company without his father's knowledge. In retaliation, the elder Woodruff reneged on a pay raise he had promised his son, and Robert quit his job, going to work as a salesman for the White Motor Company in 1913. His rise in that company was meteoric. He sold the company's trucks across the South, won a federal contract for tourist buses at Yellowstone National Park, and developed the first troop-carrying motor vehicles in World War I. He and his wife moved to Cleveland, Ohio, the

corporate headquarters, and Woodruff shuttled regularly to New York City, where he established an office. He lived extravagantly and joined clubs where he could associate with the country's wealthiest and most powerful businessmen. His personality and skills attracted their confidence. By 1921 he was a vice president of White Motor Company and a protégé of its president, Walter White.

The legendary Walter Teagle soon offered Woodruff the presidency of Standard Oil Company. But Woodruff returned to Atlanta in 1923 to accept the presidency of the Coca-Cola Company, which had come through serious financial difficulties and was still suffering from internal divisions caused by its hostile takeover, four years earlier, by the group of investors led by Ernest Woodruff. As president until 1939 and chairman of the board thereafter until his retirement in 1955, Robert Woodruff would lead the company in its ascent to the status of American icon, and he would continue to dominate it for another thirty years after his nominal retirement.

As president, Woodruff quickly took control of the company, marginalizing the rival Candler family and their supporters and placing executives of his own choice in positions of prominence. His father, who died in 1944, was his only persistent rival for influence. Known as "the Boss," Robert Woodruff maintained a gruff demeanor and distanced himself from all but the highest tier of executives. A stocky six feet even, Woodruff's physique and domineering personality combined to create a commanding presence in any room.

During the 1920s Coca-Cola prospered as an alternative to the alcoholic beverages forbidden by nationwide Prohibition. It benefited from saturation advertising overseen by the brilliant "idea man" Archie Lee, whose brand-image campaign associated the soft drink with energy, wholesomeness, and respite from the hectic pace of twentieth-century life. Lee covered billboards and magazine pages with the work of artists such as Norman Rockwell and Haddon Sundblom, who communicated visually the message he wanted to convey. Under Lee's guidance, Coke promoted itself as "the pause that refreshes."

Woodruff worked closely with Lee on building the image of Coca-Cola while driving competitors from the field with trademark-infringement lawsuits. Standardizing the product was an obsession for Woodruff. Determined that Coca-Cola would have the same taste everywhere and a reputation for purity, Woodruff sent inspectors regularly to soda fountains to test their product, and he encouraged bottlers, whose contracts with the company allowed them a great deal of independence, to improve sanitation and quality control. He converted the sales force into a corps of service personnel to work with dealers in solving their problems, and he created a statistical department, which pioneered market research.

As the seller of an inexpensive item, Coca-Cola weathered the Great Depression better than most corporations. Woodruff refused to cut salaries as other corporations did, and the company's stock actually hit a new high in 1935. Sales of Coca-Cola in bottles increased as refrigeration became available in more homes.

In World War II Woodruff masterminded a plan to make Coca-Cola available, at five cents per bottle, to American troops, wherever they might be. Production of Coke in the United States remained high as the company won exemption from sugar rationing on drinks sold for consumption by military personnel, and Coca-Cola "technical officers" followed military units into combat zones, setting up and operating bottling plants and soda fountains for the thirsty troops.

The World War II experience and the ensuing cold war helped Woodruff to realize another of his goals, worldwide marketing of Coca-Cola. Despite Woodruff's determined efforts, prewar campaigns to sell the soft drink outside the United States had been successful only in Canada, Cuba, and Germany. After the war, Coca-Cola courted elites all over the world—save in the Communist countries, where Coca-Cola was officially despised as a symbol of American imperialism—and awarded bottling contracts to prominent citizens of many countries. By the early 1950s, one-fourth of Coca-Cola's sales were outside the United States; a decade later foreign sales accounted for over half of the company's revenues.

Politics, of necessity, became one of Woodruff's chief activities. To fend off government regulation and secure access to foreign markets, Woodruff employed skillful lobbyists in Washington and other capitals. Coke won many battles, including exemption from a Food and Drug Administration regulation that would have required Coke labels to reveal the addition of caffeine to the product. A Georgia Democrat, Woodruff joined the Republican business leaders who helped General Dwight D. Eisenhower win the presidency, and he took great pride in his easy access to the Eisenhower White House. He also enjoyed close relationships with Presidents Lyndon B. Johnson and Jimmy Carter.

Always preferring the background to the public eye, Woodruff made skillful use of his 30,000-acre South Georgia hunting retreat, Ichauway, to cultivate relationships with political figures. In what was then the male-only world of big business and high politics, hunting, card games, cigars, and alcohol facilitated Woodruff's access to the men who held, or aspired to hold, political power. Ichauway was one of four Woodruff residences. His Atlanta home was a white-columned mansion on elegant Tuxedo Road. He spent much of his time in New York City, where he owned a duplex apartment in Manhattan's exclusive River House, overlooking the East River. In Wyoming he vacationed at his T. E. Ranch near Cody, once the property of Buffalo Bill Cody.

In Atlanta, Coca-Cola was a major employer, a source of civic pride, and inevitably a major player in local politics. And Robert Woodruff was Atlanta's first citizen. He regularly convened the leading businessmen of the city to decide issues of public importance. Political officials generally followed their lead. No issue was more important to a southern city in the 1950s and 1960s than race, and Woodruff and his associates decided that Atlanta must accommodate itself to black aspirations for civil rights. Segregation policies were changed gradually—and Atlanta, billing itself as "the city too busy to hate"—escaped the turmoil that engulfed Little Rock, Birmingham, and other southern cities.

Woodruff donated immense sums of money—much of it given anonymously—to educational, artistic, and social service institutions in Atlanta. His gift of $105 million to Emory University in 1979 was the largest private donation ever made to a university up to that time. In all he gave Emory at least $225 million during his lifetime and donated an estimated $100 million to other Atlanta institutions, including the Robert W. Woodruff Arts Center, a complex that was renamed for him in 1982. Raised a Methodist, Woodruff had little interest in religion as an adult.

In spite of Woodruff's political and business acumen, Coca-Cola's market lead over its chief rival, Pepsi-Cola, slipped from approximately 400 percent at the end of World War II to only 4 percent by the mid-1980s. A conservative man, Woodruff regularly rejected his subordinates' recommendations to adjust the product to changing markets. For years he refused to put Coca-Cola into larger bottles to compete with Pepsi's ten-ounce bottles, or into cans, or to develop a diet version of Coke, or to produce fruit-flavored beverages. Unwilling to allow his handpicked CEOs to make strategic decisions for the company, Woodruff kept the pace of corporate innovation slow and only reluctantly approved the diversification of Coca-Cola's products and packaging.

Only his final illness, brought on by old age, removed Woodruff for the last two weeks of his life from corporate decision-making at Coca-Cola. He died in Atlanta's Emory University Hospital and is buried in the city's Westview Cemetery.

An unquestioned genius as a manager, Woodruff often declared: "It's easy to see down the valley and up the slope, but it's tough as hell to see over the next hill." Through his understanding of changing lifestyles and consumer expectations, Woodruff made Coca-Cola a part of American culture, then won the soft drink a place in markets around the world. After the age of seventy, he no longer could see so clearly over the next hill, but he refused to trust his subordinates to make decisions in the best interests of the company. As a result Coca-Cola's market supremacy was eroded.

Woodruff's contributions to the city of Atlanta are immeasurable. His donations to Emory University and other civic enterprises strengthened the cultural life of the city, and his leadership of the business community provided direction to Atlanta's emergence as a major business center. Woodruff's early recognition of the importance of eliminating racist policies moved Atlanta a step ahead of other Southern cities and helped to keep it peaceful in an era of turmoil.

★

Woodruff's papers are in the Robert W. Woodruff Library at Emory University. There is one authorized biography, *Mr. Anonymous: Robert W. Woodruff of Coca-Cola* (1982), by Charles Elliott, published originally in 1979 as *A Biography of the "Boss": Robert Winship Woodruff*. Histories of the Coca-Cola Company, including Mark Pendergrast, *For God, Country, and Coca-Cola: The Unauthorized History of the Great American Soft Drink and the Company That Makes It* (1993), and Frederick Allen, *Secret Formula: How Brilliant Marketing and Relentless Salesmanship Made Coca-Cola the Best-Known Product in the World* (1994), provide extensive coverage of the career of the man who dominated the company for six decades. Pendergrast's work is the bolder of the two; Allen's is more respectful in tone and relies on interviews with corporate insiders. Obituaries are in the *Atlanta Constitution* and the *New York Times* (8 Mar. 1985).

VAGN K. HANSEN

WRIGHT, Louis Booker (*b.* 1 March 1899 in Phoenix, South Carolina; *d.* 26 February 1984 in Chevy Chase, Maryland), scholar and library director who guided the Folger Shakespeare Library in Washington, D.C., through its development into a major research institution for early modern literature and history.

Louis Wright was one of three children of Thomas Fleming Wright, a schoolmaster who directed and taught in a small country school, and Lena Booker Wright, a homemaker. The family lived in Greenwood County, South Carolina.

Louis Wright (who pronounced his name in the French style) attended public schools in the region and entered Wofford College in Spartanburg, South Carolina. Following the outbreak of World World I, he left Wofford to join the Students' Army Training Corps, in spite of his short, wiry build. After the Armistice he returned to Wofford and also took flying instruction from a local veteran of the Army Air Corps, with whom he went into partnership to purchase a small plane to engage in contract deliveries for the government mail service.

Wright graduated with an A.B. in chemistry from Wofford in 1920, then worked in several capacities for the

Dr. Louis B. Wright, 1960. UPI/CORBIS-BETTMANN

Greenwood (S.C.) *Index-Journal*, serving as office boy, reporter, and city editor before returning to academia for graduate studies. He received an M.A. degree in literature from the University of North Carolina in 1924 and the Ph.D. in 1926. While in graduate school he married Frances Marion Black, from Spartanburg, South Carolina, on 10 June 1925; their son, Louis Christopher, became chief of the Loan Division at the Library of Congress.

Louis Wright taught at the University of North Carolina at Chapel Hill from 1926 to 1932, first as instructor and then as associate professor. He also was Johnston Research Scholar at Johns Hopkins University (1927–1928) and a Guggenheim Research Fellow at the British Museum (1930). In 1931 he began research at the Henry E. Huntington Library and Art Gallery in San Marino, California. From 1932 to 1948 he was on the library's research staff and chaired its committee on fellowships, among other responsibilities. His work in developing the Huntington as a research institution, along with his writing, professional memberships, and other scholarly activities, led to his appointment in 1948 as director of the Folger Shakespeare Library.

A diplomatic man with a passion for tradition and cultural literacy and yet without pretension, Wright was well suited to direct the library. The Folger's holdings included the world's largest collection of Shakespeare folios and the Harmsworth collection of primary works in early modern literature and history. However, as Wright later remarked, "a collection of books is not a library, and the transformation of a collector's acquisitions into an efficient research library is a slow and sometimes tedious process requiring expert knowledge and patience."

Wright's directorship of the Folger (1948–1968) transformed an arcane collection into an accessible scholarly resource. During his tenure the library modernized its physical plant, constructed a new wing, and purchased photographic and other technical equipment. The Reading Room was cleared of seldom-read eighteenth- and nineteenth-century editions of Shakespeare and stocked with a reference collection modeled on that of the Huntington—that is, works purchased by the library itself and used on the premises rather than sending readers to borrow from the Library of Congress across the street. The library's cataloging system was overhauled and the library staff augmented by, among others, an assistant to the director in charge of acquisitions and an administrator for the Reading Room.

In its expanded role as a research center, the library developed and participated in publication and fellowship programs, traveling exhibitions to other libraries and schools, on-site exhibitions, performances at its theater, and seminars and professional meetings. According to the tribute compiled by the Folger staff at Wright's retirement, "the three main areas of function for the Library under his direction have consisted of (1) its operation as a research center; (2) its encouragement to scholarship; and (3) its publication program. On each of these fronts advancements have been made that can only be described as astonishing."

Wright's own professional development was no less impressive. Both his scholarship and his directorship pursued the study of major literary figures in historical context. His scholarly publications on English and American history and literature—monographs, articles, reviews, and editions—numbered 314 at his retirement in 1969; notable among these were *New Interpretations of American Colonial History* (1959) and *The Folger Library: A Decade of Growth, 1950–1960* (1960). He participated extensively on advisory boards of universities and other institutions, including the Winterthur Museum and the Guggenheim Foundation, and he was a lifetime trustee of the Shakespeare Birthplace Trust, Stratford-upon-Avon. He received honorary degrees from twenty-three universities including Amherst, Bucknell, Princeton, Yale, Northwestern, and UCLA. He also was decorated as an Officer of the British Empire and received the Benjamin Franklin medal of the Royal Society of the Arts (1969).

After his retirement from the Folger, Wright remained at his Chevy Chase residence, maintaining his membership in learned societies and other professional organizations. He died at home, of cardiovascular disease.

★

Wright's autobiographical *Barefoot in Arcadia: Memories of a More Innocent Era* (1974) provides a familiar approach to his youth and early career, while his *Of Books and Men* (1976) chronicles his experience as a scholar, including chapters on the Huntington and the Folger. Folger Shakespeare Library staff, *Louis B. Wright: A Bibliography and an Appreciation* (1968), narrates Wright's accomplishments as a scholar and lists his publications.

MARGIE BURNS

WRIGHT, Olgivanna Lloyd (*b*. 27 December 1896 in Cetinje, Montenegro; *d*. 1 March 1985 in Scottsdale, Arizona), composer, dancer, educational administrator, and author, best known as the collaborator and wife of architect Frank Lloyd Wright.

Olgivanna was born Olga Ivanovna Lazovich to Ivan and Militza Milianova Lazovich in Montenegro. Her father was chief justice of Montenegro's highest court for more than thirty years. Her maternal grandfather was Marco Milianov, a Montenegran duke and celebrated general who fought for his country's independence. Milianov's home was a virtual shrine to his heroism, and this is where Olgivanna resided up until she went to live with her sister's family at age nine. Olgivanna attended school internationally: she was educated in Belgrade, in Batumi of the Russian Caucasus, and in Turkey. In 1915 she married Vladimir Hinzenberg, an architectural draftsman and friend of the Lazovich family; they had one child. In less than a year they had separated, Hinzenberg emigrating to the United States while Olgivanna trained as a dancer at the Gurdjieff Institute, in Fontainebleau, France. A friend of Katherine Mansfield, who also attended the school, Olgivanna studied religious dancing and was also indoctrinated into Georgi I. Gurdjieff's philosophy, containing metaphysical ideas as well as "learning-through-work" practices.

Olgivanna traveled to the United States with Gurdjieff in 1924, ostensibly to perform with his company in Carnegie Hall but also to acquire a divorce from Hinzenberg. While in the United States, Olgivanna taught rhythmic exercise and dance in New York and Chicago and was a patron of the performing arts. She met the architect Frank Lloyd Wright through a mutual acquaintance while attending the Russian ballet in Chicago and, although she was thirty years his junior, they quickly became intimate friends.

In April 1924, upon obtaining a divorce from Hinzenberg, Olgivanna moved in with Wright, despite the fact that he was still married to his second wife, Miriam Noel. Olgivanna and Wright lived at Taliesin, Wright's architectural

Olgivanna Lloyd Wright (*center*) with her husband Frank Lloyd Wright and their youngest child Iovanna, 1957. UPI/CORBIS-BETTMANN

workshop and office in Spring Green, Wisconsin. They had one child, born in 1925, but the years immediately following this event were full of obstacles for Olgivanna and Wright, including the foreclosure of Taliesin (he regained possession of the complex in 1928), government charges brought against Olgivanna citing the Mann Immigration Act, and continual harassment by Miriam Noel, who enlisted the aid of Olgivanna's former husband in her hostile campaign against the couple. On 25 August 1928, after three years of turmoil, they began to live prosperously together when Olgivanna became Frank Lloyd Wright's third wife.

In 1933 Olgivanna Lloyd Wright attained her U.S. citizenship. Together, the preceding year, the Wrights had founded the Taliesin Fellowship, an architectural school dedicated to Frank Lloyd Wright's ideals, based at Taliesin. Olgivanna oversaw the administrative responsibilities of the school, interviewing students for admission, planning the curriculum, and serving as a counselor to many of the apprentices of the school. She employed many of the teachings she acquired at the Gurdjieff school as well as Wright's concepts of organic architecture. Beginning in 1941 she also acted as vice president of the Frank Lloyd Wright Foundation.

Olgivanna influenced many Frank Lloyd Wright and Taliesin Associated Architects projects during Wright's most prolific period, helping with the interior design and color coordination on Fallingwater (the Kaufmann House) and on the Guggenheim Museum, among others. Olgivanna utilized her fine arts training as well, composing numerous works for chamber orchestra, including sonatas, trios, and quartets. She organized and composed orchestral music for the Taliesin Festivals of Music and Dance. In addition, she authored a handful of books during her lifetime. *The Struggle Within* was published in 1955. She also published four works about Frank Lloyd Wright and his work: *Our House* (1959), *The Shining Brow: Frank Lloyd Wright* (1960), *Roots of Life* (1963), and *Frank Lloyd Wright: His Life, His Work, His Words* (1966).

Upon Wright's death in 1959, Olgivanna became the guardian of his ideals, assuming her husband's responsibilities as president of the Frank Lloyd Wright Foundation and the Frank Lloyd Wright School of Architecture, and as the president of Taliesin Associated Architects. Her tenure in these roles and her influence over Frank Lloyd Wright's legacy continued for more than twenty-five years. Critics accused her of wielding too much power over Wright's interests, calling her domineering and dictatorial in her supervision of the Taliesin School and Architects. Olgivanna considered herself merely "strict," keeping close watch on both Taliesin and Taliesin West in Arizona by shuttling between them and reviewing projects and publications affiliated with the fellowship and firm. In 1984, Olgivanna received a citation from the Association of Interior Architects in recognition of her efforts in the field of interior design, as well as for her contributions to architectural education.

The month before she died of a heart attack at Taliesin West, she transferred leadership of Taliesin, the school and architecture firm, to William Wesley Peters, an associate of Wright and the former husband of her daughter from her first marriage.

Olgivanna Lloyd Wright is a significant figure both for her efforts in the performing arts and in architectural education and for continuing the work of Frank Lloyd Wright. Acting as the administrator of the Taliesin workshop, she made a great impact on the many students and associates identified with Taliesin and Wright, perpetuating his ideas and practices after his death.

★

The Frank Lloyd Wright Foundation maintains an archive of documents and correspondence from both Olgivanna and Frank Lloyd Wright. Peter Kihss, "Custodian of a Tradition," *New York Times* (24 Feb. 1972), and David Sheff, "In the Arizona Desert, Frank Lloyd Wright's Widow Keeps the Architect's Flame Burning and Her Students Building," *People* (31 Jan. 1983), discuss Olgivanna's background and the role she played both as Wright's

inspiration and as the protector of his legacy. Loudon Wainwright, "Guardian of a Great Legacy," *Life* (11 June 1971) elaborates on the practices at Taliesin and Olgivanna's role as its perpetuating force. An obituary is in the *New York Times* (2 Mar. 1985).

WENDI ARANT

WURF, Jerome (*b.* 18 May 1919 in New York City; *d.* 10 December 1981 in Washington, D.C.), union organizer under whose leadership the American Federation of State, County and Municipal Employees (AFSCME) became the largest union in the American Federation of Labor–Congress of Industrial Organizations (AFL-CIO).

Jerry Wurf was one of two sons of Jewish immigrants, Sigmund Wurf, a textile jobber, from Hungary, and Frieda Tennenbaum from Austria. He attended public schools in the Bronx, Brooklyn, and suburban Nassau County. Wurf's political beliefs were formed early in his life, and he attributed them to the strong left-wing influence of his predominantly working-class Brighton Beach neighborhood. Becoming an anticommunist socialist, Wurf was active with Socialist party youth organizations. As he entered adulthood, he became convinced that dramatic changes were needed in the country's political and economic system.

Wurf entered New York University in 1938 but dropped out in 1940. He soon began his first union job, organizing for the Hotel and Restaurant Employees Union (HREU). In 1941 he married Sylvia Spinrad; they had one child, Linda Susan, who later became an AFSCME organizer. Wurf's confrontations with the HREU leadership over the administration and finances of the union led to his dismissal and a difficult few years, during which he held a number of jobs, including coownership of a delicatessen with his younger brother, Al.

In 1947 Wurf was hired by AFSCME president Arnold Zander to work for his organization, then a union of only 73,000 members nationwide. Wurf began organizing public employees in New York City but became frustrated with the entrenched union leadership and almost quit. In 1948 Zander persuaded him to stay by appointing him head of District Council 37, giving him de facto control of all New York City AFSCME locals. Wurf's new position, however, brought new difficulties; half of DC 37's membership defected to the Teamsters shortly after his appointment, the defectors following union traditionalists who feared that Wurf was a threat to their own power bases.

At that time, public employees had no legal right to strike, no official mechanism for collective bargaining, and no dues checkoff (meaning organizers had to collect dues personally rather than have the dues automatically deducted from earnings). Nevertheless, Wurf used aggressive and unorthodox tactics, including illegal strikes and protest marches, to win concessions. He capitalized on dissatisfaction with the low salaries of public workers to increase union membership. In 1958 Wurf convinced New York City mayor Robert Wagner to grant municipal employees the legal right to unionize. From 1948 to 1964 Wurf increased DC 37 membership from about 1,000 members to more than 100,000. From 1960 to 1965 alone, DC 37 grew 10 percent annually.

During this time, Wurf's marriage had begun to fail. He and his wife divorced in 1954. Wurf then became involved with Mildred Kiefer, a woman who had left graduate school to work for AFSCME as Wurf's assistant. They married in 1960 and had two children.

By the late 1950s, Wurf become frustrated with Zander's refusal to democratize the union and grant districts and locals more control of their own affairs. In 1962 Wurf decided to run against Zander for the AFSCME presidency. He was unsuccessful that year, but in 1964, Wurf pulled off an upset victory, sweeping into office with a reform slate of regional vice presidents.

Once in office, Wurf found that AFSCME's finances were in shambles, and a housing program started by Zander was rife with corruption. He also learned that the

Jerome Wurf calls for a one-day strike by New York City municipal workers, 1959. UPI/CORBIS-BETTMANN

union's international projects were covers for Central Intelligence Agency (CIA) operations, through which AFSCME funneled CIA funds to anticommunist unions in Latin America. He sold off the union's national headquarters, ended the housing program, and severed connections with the CIA. Meanwhile, Wurf began a massive, nationwide organizing drive, bringing his aggressive tactics to municipalities across the country. In the first two years of his presidency, the union grew 16.5 percent nationally, four times the average growth rate of other unions at the time.

In 1968 AFSCME became involved in a strike by African-American sanitation workers in Memphis, Tennessee. Memphis mayor Henry Loeb refused to allow sanitation workers to unionize, leading to a walkout that brought AFSCME together with leaders of the civil rights movement. After Martin Luther King, Jr., came to Memphis for a march in support of the sanitation workers (and was assassinated on 4 April 1968), federal mediation eventually resolved the strike, while Wurf and AFSCME gained a national reputation for tenacity and militancy. The cost of the Memphis strike, both financially and in human terms, led Wurf to turn against the use of strikes in favor of arbitration.

The remarkable growth of AFSCME (in 1969 it had more than 400,000 members and was growing at a rate of 1,000 members weekly), and Wurf's indefatigable lobbying led in 1969 to his appointment to the AFL-CIO Executive Council by its president, George Meany. Wurf soon became a thorn in Meany's side, clashing with him over support of the Vietnam War, the AFL-CIO's failure to endorse a candidate in the 1972 U.S. presidential election, and Meany's reluctance to give public employees a greater voice in the AFL-CIO. Taking progressive positions, Wurf was often the lone vote against Meany and his allies.

Although a backlash against public employees in the 1970s because of rising property taxes and municipal financial problems led to increased resistance to unionization by elected officials, Wurf negotiated a merger between AFSCME and the Civil Service Employees Association of New York, which gave AFSCME more than 1 million members and made it the largest union in the AFL-CIO. Meanwhile, AFSCME distinguished itself within the labor movement by aggressively recruiting women and minorities. Wurf maintained control of AFSCME at its 1980 convention but was challenged for leadership of the union by Victor Gotbaum, a former protégé. Wurf's health had begun to deteriorate, and by the summer of 1981 he was quite sick. He nevertheless walked picket lines in support of striking air traffic controllers and made his final speech at an AFL-CIO–sponsored solidarity march in September of 1981, railing against President Ronald Reagan's economic policies. Three months later he died from a heart attack and was buried in Washington D.C.

Wurf was a tireless organizer, demanding of both himself and his employees. While his manner alienated some around him, he was successful in winning membership drives and negotiating contracts. As Wurf gained institutional power, and as public employee unions won legal recognition, he came to favor arbitration over strikes as a means of settling contract disputes. He will be remembered for his leadership of AFSCME during that union's remarkable rise, but his dedication to the dignity of all workers is his true legacy. As Wurf himself said, "I like to tell our training institutes what most organizers don't realize. They think they're peddling better wages and working conditions, but essentially they're offering dignity. And sometimes the worker who doesn't articulate this very easily has more awareness than the professional organizer."

★

The AFSCME archives for much of Wurf's presidency are located in the Walter P. Reuther Library at Wayne State University in Detroit. Joseph C. Goulden, *Jerry Wurf: Labor's Last Angry Man* (1982), is an authorized biography of Wurf. Wurf's time in DC 37 and as AFSCME president is detailed in Mary H. Maier, *City Unions: Managing Discontent in New York City* (1987); Jewel and Bernard Bellush, *Union Power and New York City* (1984); and Richard N. Billings and John Greenya, *Power to the Public Worker* (1974). See also Fred Shapiro, "How Jerry Wurf Walks on Water," *New York Times Magazine* (11 Apr. 1976). An obituary is in the *New York Times* (11 Dec. 1981).

JIM O'LOUGHLIN

WYLER, William ("Willi") (*b.* 1 July 1902 in Mülhausen/ Mulhouse, [German-annexed] Alsace; *d.* 27 July 1981 in Beverly Hills, California), Academy Award–winning director of such films as *Wuthering Heights, The Best Years of Our Lives,* and *Ben-Hur.*

Willi Wyler—the name he went by all his life—was the second of three sons of the haberdasher Leopold Wyler. The family were Swiss-German Jews, but from his mother, Melanie Auerbach Wyler, young Willi also absorbed the French culture that was a strong undercurrent in Alsace-Lorraine. Willi struck all observers as less likely to succeed than his handsome and studious older brother, Robert. He followed Robert to the Institut Bloch in Lausanne, Switzerland, but was expelled from that elite school in 1919 and later dropped out of the École Supérieure de Commerce in the same city. Quickly tiring of work in the family's hat shop, Willi opted for commercial experience in Paris, where he held several department-store jobs and also briefly studied the violin, displaying a minor talent that he would demonstrate throughout his life. It was Melanie Wyler who furthered her son's career by urging him upon a visiting cousin, "Uncle" Carl Laemmle, who had emigrated to America in 1884 to become one of Hollywood's founding moguls and the head of Universal Pictures. Laemmle

William Wyler. ARCHIVE PHOTOS

agreed to sponsor the feckless youth, and young Willi Wyler sailed to New York in 1920 to begin clerical duties in Universal's international film-exchange office. His first friend there was a German-speaking contemporary named Paul Kohner. The two became lifelong friends, and Kohner went on to establish one of Hollywood's most successful talent agencies.

Wyler's own career was slower to blossom, even after he wangled a transfer to Hollywood in 1922. As a studio errand boy he failed to impress the head of production, Irving G. Thalberg, who dubbed him "worthless Willie." Only through a slow apprenticeship would Wyler become a director, starting on Universal's "Mustang" Westerns in 1925. These two-reel, twenty-four-minute shorts were formula product, shot in three days and released to fill out an evening's program. Wyler made twenty-one Mustangs between 1925 and 1927 and six five-reelers in the Blue Streak series (1926–1927). His first feature was *Anybody Here Seen Kelly?* (1928), produced by his brother Robert, who had come to America in 1923 and eventually became a minor film executive. Several silent and sound features followed, but Wyler did not become a major director until 1933 with *Counsellor at Law,* starring John Barrymore. This screen version of Elmer Rice's Broadway play set a career pattern from which Wyler rarely varied: prestigious literary adaptations involving major stars.

Restless under the Universal administration of Carl Laemmle, Jr., Wyler leapt at the chance to join the Samuel Goldwyn organization in 1935. Goldwyn's need for "prestige" pictures made the increasingly meticulous Wyler an asset to the studio, even though the two men often clashed over artistic matters. For Goldwyn, Wyler made a string of successes that raised him to the top echelon of Hollywood directors: *These Three* (based on Lillian Hellman's controversial play *The Children's Hour*) and *Dodsworth* (both 1936), *Dead End* (1937), *Wuthering Heights* (1939), *The Westerner* (1940), and *The Little Foxes* (1941). During the same period Wyler also directed *Jezebel* (1938) and *The Letter* (1940) for Warner Brothers and *Mrs. Miniver* (1942) for MGM.

Wyler established several important relationships during the Goldwyn years. The playwright and scenarist Lillian Hellman became a lifelong friend and occasional collaborator. The cinematographer Gregg Toland went on to make seven films with Wyler. Together they developed a technique of "composition in depth" that allowed complex relationships to be enacted in a single shot, with a minimum of cutting. And the strong-willed Bette Davis always credited Wyler as her best director. The two had an intense love affair but quarreled bitterly over all three of the films they made together, *Jezebel* (for which Davis received an Oscar), *The Letter,* and *The Little Foxes.* After prolonged conflict on the last film, the two never worked together again.

Wyler married actress Margaret Sullavan on 25 November 1934, as they worked on *The Good Fairy.* They were divorced after fifteen tempestuous months. The short, tough-looking Wyler was a lifelong hellraiser, ladies' man, and daredevil motorcyclist who once motored off a friend's diving board into a swimming pool. Many thought him unsuitable for marriage. But his wedding to the young starlet Margaret Tallichet on 23 October 1938 brought out the family man in Wyler, and their long union became one of Hollywood's notable successes. They had five children, including a son who died in childhood.

The Nazi threat made Wyler increasingly conscious of his Jewish heritage, and, having become a U.S. citizen in 1928, he volunteered for military service in 1942. He was at the peak of his career after the pro-British *Mrs. Miniver* had won seven Academy Awards and the personal endorsements of President Franklin D. Roosevelt and Prime Minister Winston Churchill. Assigned to the Signal Corps, Wyler flew on four combat missions over Europe, suffered a nearly catastrophic hearing loss, and produced two memorable documentaries, including *The Memphis Belle* (1944), a dramatic film about an American bomber crew flying dangerous missions over Germany, for which President Roosevelt ordered the widest possible circulation. Wyler also narrowly avoided court-martial after punching a civilian who made an anti-Semitic remark.

Sobered by his war experience, Wyler returned to make one last film for Goldwyn. *The Best Years of Our Lives* (1946), a warm and uniquely personal account of three returning veterans, is usually considered Wyler's masterpiece. Of it James Agee wrote in the *Nation,* "William Wyler has always seemed to me an exceedingly sincere and good director; he now seems one of the few great ones." The film received seven Oscars, including best picture and best director, and enabled Wyler to sever his troubled relationship with Sam Goldwyn and become an independent producer. With George Stevens and Frank Capra he helped found Liberty Films.

Ironically the pressures of independence in Hollywood's competitive postwar environment seemed to constrict Wyler's career. He soon affiliated with a studio (Paramount), and his films of the postwar decade are generally less memorable than those made for Goldwyn. *The Heiress* (1949) won an Oscar for best actress (Olivia de Havilland), as did *Roman Holiday* (1953) for Audrey Hepburn's first starring role. But the social criticism of *Carrie* (1952, after Theodore Dreiser's *Sister Carrie*) was blunted by studio interference at the height of Hollywood's anti-Communist panic. Wyler, a lifelong liberal and close friend of Lillian Hellman's, had been active in the controversial Committee for the First Amendment in 1947. He was at risk during the nervous 1950s, but Paramount shielded its star director from the blacklist even as it restrained his creative freedom.

Again seeking independence, Wyler made two pictures with pacifist themes. *Friendly Persuasion* (1956), for Allied Artists, won the Palme d'Or at the Cannes Film Festival. The epic-scaled Western *The Big Country* (1958), for United Artists, was another troubled production. But Wyler showed his unflagging energy by agreeing to direct *Ben-Hur* (1959) for MGM. At the time the most elaborate production in Hollywood history, *Ben-Hur* commenced a yearlong Italian shooting schedule without a satisfactory screenplay in place. Wyler worked desperately with Christopher Fry and other writers to improve the script and became de facto producer of the gigantic project when Sam Zimbalist died suddenly amid the rising pressures of Hollywood's desperate gamble. MGM's confidence in Wyler was rewarded when the picture went on to become the studio's greatest success in a generation. *Ben-Hur* was praised for bringing intimacy and dignity to the biblical genre and for its mastery of wide-screen composition. It won twelve Academy Award nominations and an unprecedented eleven Oscars and has remained a popular classic.

Wyler's later films drew mixed reviews. A more explicit remake of Hellman's *The Children's Hour* (1961) misfired, but *The Collector* (1965) was a critical success, earning unprecedented double acting awards for its two unknown leads, Terènce Stamp and Samantha Eggar, at the Cannes Festival. *Funny Girl* (1968) launched Barbra Streisand's film career with yet another Oscar-winning performance. Wyler's last film was the racial drama *The Liberation of L. B. Jones* (1970). Tired of the strains of filmmaking, Wyler withdrew from a commitment to direct *Patton* and retired in order to travel with his family and friends. Lifetime awards from the Academy, the Director's Guild, and the American Film Institute confirmed him as the industry's most honored filmmaker. Although the French-based "auteurist" school of film criticism began to disparage his allegedly impersonal brand of craftsmanship, Wyler was forthright about his skills. He never originated a script and claimed only to be seeking the most effective way of telling a variety of stories.

Wyler's famously exacting craftsmanship led to countless tales of "forty-take Wyler" or even "ninety-take Wyler." Some actors nursed grudges against him, and a few even alleged a sadistic streak. Around town, Wyler was a much-loved family man and popular dinner guest. But as David Niven put it, he "became a fiend the moment his bottom touched down in his director's chair." Uncompromising on the set and impatient with star egos, Wyler could infuriate actors with his inarticulate perfectionism. After dozens of takes of a scene in *Wuthering Heights,* Laurence Olivier exploded at Wyler and demanded to know what the director was after. "I want you to be better" was the only answer. Such aloofness wounded some stars, but Wyler's technique

regularly earned performers the highest acting honors. In addition to his three Academy Awards for best picture and best direction (*Mrs. Miniver, Best Years of Our Lives,* and *Ben-Hur*), Wyler was responsible for thirteen Oscar-winning performances and thirty-eight acting nominations—numbers that have no parallel. Laurence Olivier got over his frustration, gave a powerful performance as Heathcliff, and eventually became one of many filmmakers to credit Willi Wyler as a friend and mentor. Wyler died of heart failure and was buried in Forest Lawn Cemetery in Los Angeles.

★

Axel Madsen, *William Wyler* (1973), is the authorized biography, for which Wyler shared the copyright. Jan Herman, *A Talent for Trouble* (1995), offers a more objective account, with full documentation. Sharon Kern surveys the critical literature in *William Wyler: A Guide to References and Resources* (1984). The chief critical study is Michael A. Anderegg, *William Wyler* (1979). Catherine Wyler's documentary film *Directed by William Wyler* (1986) contains numerous interviews; the unedited transcripts are a prime biographical source. Tributes and recollections are assembled in a special issue of *American Film* (April 1976) celebrating the American Film Institute's Lifetime Achievement Award. Innumerable Hollywood memoirs feature recollections of Wyler. The most substantial are by Charlton Heston: *The Actor's Life* (1978), excerpting his *Ben-Hur* journals, and *In the Arena* (1995), a full autobiography.

JOHN FITZPATRICK

Y-Z

YOST, Charles Woodruff (*b.* 6 November 1907 in Watertown, New York; *d.* 22 May 1981 in Washington, D.C.), a career ambassador and author who served as assistant and then chief U.S. delegate to the United Nations; he was a participant in several important conferences that established post–World War II international institutions.

An only child, Yost was born to Nicholas Doxtater Yost, a banker in Watertown, New York, and his wife, Gertrude Cooper. He graduated from the Hotchkiss School in 1924 and then attended Princeton University, earning his A.B. degree in 1928. He proceeded to do postgraduate work at the University of Paris between 1928 and 1929.

Entering the Foreign Service in 1930, Yost was the vice consul in Alexandria, Egypt, from 1931 to 1932. He served in the same position in Warsaw, Poland, from 1932 until 1933, when he left the Foreign Service to work as a freelance foreign correspondent in Europe and to write poetry and fiction. Meanwhile, he married Irena Oldakowska on 8 September 1934; they eventually had two sons and a daughter. Yost returned to the Foreign Service in 1935, working at the Department of State in Washington, D.C., between 1935 and 1945.

During World War II, Yost worked at the Dumbarton Oaks Conference, which established an international monetary policy for the postwar world, between August and October 1944. He wrote one of the articles of the United Nations Charter during the San Francisco Conference between April and June 1945, when he served as the assistant to the chairman of the U.S. delegation. He then became secretary-general for the U.S. delegation at the Potsdam Conference from July to August 1945, which set Allied policy on the future of Germany.

At the war's end, Yost served as chargé d'affaires to the U.S. legation in Bangkok, Thailand, from 1945 to 1946. In 1946, with the formation of the United Nations, Yost became the political adviser to the U.S. delegation, which benefited from his intimate knowledge of the UN framework. In the following year, he became the first secretary at the American embassy in Prague, Czechoslovakia, where he was a witness to the cold war battles in Eastern Europe. From 1947 to 1949, Yost served as a counselor for the American legation in Vienna, Austria. Next, Yost was the special assistant to the ambassador-at-large in the Council of Foreign Ministers and the UN General Assembly in 1949. He then was appointed minister-counselor at the U.S. embassy in Athens, Greece, from 1950 to 1953, during the end of the Greek civil war.

He became deputy high commissioner to Austria in 1953, staying in that position until 1954. Then, he was appointed U.S. minister to the Kingdom of Laos from 1954 to 1955 and minister to Paris, France, from 1956 to 1958. In 1958, he was given the rank of full ambassador, and he served in that capacity in Syria. He became U.S. ambassador to Morocco from 1958 to 1961, where he had to conduct difficult negotiations over the U.S. withdrawal from military bases.

In 1961, Yost became the U.S. deputy representative to

Charles W. Yost, 1971. ARCHIVE PHOTOS

the UN, working first under Ambassador Adlai Stevenson. During that year, Yost announced the American refusal to admit Outer Mongolia to the United Nations, appealed to France and Tunisia to end hostilities, and presented a resolution calling for international cooperation in the exploration of outer space. In 1963, Yost urged the United Nations to press peace efforts in Yemen to prevent the fighting there from spreading, announced American approval of the restoration of Hungary to full accredited status, voted for an embargo on arms shipments to South Africa, and denounced the Soviet Union for its refusal to condemn Syria for the ambush of two Israeli farmers. In May 1964, he defended the United States in a UN debate against Soviet charges of U.S. military aggression in Cambodia. Yost received the Rockefeller Public Service Award in 1964. That same year, he published his first book, *The Age of Triumph and Frustration: Modern Dialogues,* which treated the errors and successes of diplomacy.

In 1965, Yost represented the United States in the UN Special Committee on Peace-Keeping Operations. He also led the U.S. delegation in the June 1965 Security Council discussion of the Dominican Crisis. In December 1965 he headed the delegation debating continued UN mediation of the Cyprus dispute.

Yost resigned from the UN delegation in April 1966,

retiring with the title "career ambassador," a rare honor. He became a senior fellow with the Council on Foreign Relations that year and proceeded to write another book, *The Insecurity of Nations: International Relations in the Twentieth Century,* published in 1968. In 1969, President Richard M. Nixon asked Yost to come out of retirement to serve as the U.S. ambassador to the UN, which Yost did until 1971. He then taught at Columbia University, where he wrote his third book, *The Conduct and Misconduct of Foreign Affairs,* published in 1972. From 1973 to 1975, he served as president of the National Committee on U.S.-China Relations. He also worked for the Brookings Institution in 1975. In 1976, he became special adviser of the Aspen Institute. The year before his death in 1981 witnessed the publishing of his memoirs, *History and Memory.* Charles Woodruff Yost succumbed to cancer in May 1981 and was buried in Watertown, New York.

Personally and professionally, Yost had an abiding interest in the United Nations, an organization that he hoped would facilitate the coming of world peace. Yost felt strongly about ending war and supported nuclear disarmament. He was also deeply interested in the Middle East, having been posted there three times, more than any other place. While Yost had strong beliefs that he defended, he always felt there were two sides to any question. This characteristic allowed him to remain a moderate in an age of extremes, and it explains his earning the title of "career ambassador." He was a born diplomat.

★

Beyond the four books Yost wrote, he left a few personal papers and an unpublished draft of his autobiography, all of which are in the possession of the Yost family. He also wrote numerous magazine and newspaper articles during his lifetime. His obituary is in the *New York Times* (23 May 1981). Additionally, he left two oral history interviews, one at Columbia University and one at Princeton University.

MICHELLE C. MORGAN

YOUNG, Claude, Jr. ("Buddy") (*b.* 5 January 1926 in Chicago, Illinois; *d.* 4 September 1983 near Terrell, Texas), diminutive halfback who, despite standing only five feet, four inches, gained a combined 5,430 rushing and receiving yards in the All-American Football Conference (AAFC) and the National Football League (NFL); he later became the first African American hired for a major sports league executive position when he joined the NFL Commissioner's Office.

Young and his twin sister, Claudine, were raised on Chicago's South Side; they had seven siblings. Young's parents separated when he was eight, and his father, Claude, a Pullman car porter, had little contact with the family.

Young's mother, Lillian Young, a pianist and choir director in the local African Methodist Episcopal (AME) church, exerted the most powerful influence on his life, making sure that he was "more a good boy than a bad boy." Young's church experience also gave him a permanent sense that all people, no matter their race or social status, were equal in the eyes of God. His Christian faith provided him with his sense of determination to succeed in both football and society.

Young started playing football as a ten-year-old on a team that sometimes performed during halftime at Chicago Bears games in Wrigley Field. Determined to play football in high school, despite standing only five feet, two inches as a sophomore, Young claimed residence with an aunt in a neighboring school district and ran four miles to Wendell Phillips High School every day to play. As a senior he won the city football scoring championship. Inspired by the African-American heroes of the 1936 Olympics, including Jesse Owens and Ralph Metcalfe, Young also excelled in track for his high school.

Young enrolled at the University of Illinois in 1944 on a track scholarship. Recruited to play varsity football because of the shortage of players during World War II, Young scored thirteen touchdowns in his first year, tying the immortal Red Grange's school record for touchdowns in a season. Averaging 8.8 yards per carry, Young rushed for 841 yards in a season that saw the Fighting Illini compete against both college and more powerful military teams. On the track Young won both the 100-yard and 220-yard NCAA outdoor championships in 1944, and the national Amateur Athletic Union 100-meter race the same year. Overall, he took first place in twenty-four of the twenty-seven races he entered, tying a then world record for the indoor 60-yard dash with a time of 6.1 seconds.

Young spent 1945 in the merchant marine, starring on the powerful Fleet City Merchant Marine football team in California. That experience, competing against many players who would later play professional football, convinced Young that he could succeed despite his size.

Returning to the University of Illinois for the 1946 season, Young was the star of the January 1947 Rose Bowl. Against undefeated and heavily favored UCLA, he scored two touchdowns to lead Illinois to an unexpected 45–14 rout. He was named most valuable player of the game and his scintillating performance earned him a three-year contract for $10,000 a year with the New York Yankees of the AAFC at the end of January. Recently married to his high school sweetheart, Geraldine, and supporting his first of four children on the $90 per month that military veterans in school received, Young left school because he believed that professional football provided him with the best way to support his family. His success in the Rose Bowl and

during his first season at Illinois led to his induction in the National College Football Hall of Fame in 1968.

Young took time off from summer training with his new professional team to play in the college all-star game in Chicago. Playing before 100,000 fans at Soldier Field, Young was named the team's most valuable player in a shocking 16–0 upset over the NFL champion Chicago Bears.

Young joined the Yankees during a bidding war for players between the AAFC and the NFL, but the AAFC lasted only four years (1946–1949) before financial losses forced it into a merger with the more powerful NFL. Young joined the AAFC with six other African-American players in 1947, preceded in the league only by Marion Motley and Bill Willis, both of the Cleveland Browns. While Young could recount experiences like a trip to Baltimore where he was met by fans in blackface outside the locker room, he continually maintained that football was "a great marketplace to weed out the prejudice and bigotry in life." Nevertheless, Jim Crow laws sometimes forced Young to stay in separate hotels during team trips to the South and Midwest.

In Young's three-year career with the AAFC Yankees, he earned 1,452 rushing yards, finishing ninth on the all-time list of AAFC rushing leaders. He attributed his college and

Claude ("Buddy") Young, 1947. UPI/Corbis-Bettmann

professional success to his size, arguing that his opponents hated "to miss the little man, who can make them look foolish, so they hesitate." He packed an average of 170 pounds on his short frame with powerful legs, creating a low center of gravity that enhanced his speed and quickness on the field.

The New York Yankees joined the NFL in 1950, finishing a respectable 7–5–0 in their first season before falling to 1–9–2 in 1951. The undersized but speedy Young continued to star for the Yankees, prompting Pittsburgh Steelers owner Art Rooney to claim that he had "never seen an athlete arouse a crowd the way Buddy Young can." Young's size, combined with his ability to make larger men grasp at air in their effort to tackle him, made him a popular player among fans. In addition to his play as a halfback, he specialized in exciting punt and kickoff returns, often dazzling crowds with his ability to elude tacklers in the open field.

Despite Young's popularity, however, the Yankees could not compete in the New York City market against the more established New York Giants, and Young followed the woeful Yankees to Dallas in 1952, where they were renamed the Dallas Texans. Although Young remained a strong player, leading the Texans in scoring and total offense, the team failed miserably in Dallas with a 1–11–0 record, ending the season as a road club based in Hershey, Pennsylvania.

The beleaguered franchise shifted to Baltimore at the end of the 1952 season, and Young finished his career as a Baltimore Colt. Voted the team's most popular player in 1953 by the Baltimore fans, he used his popularity to establish a brief off-season career as a disc jockey for a local radio station in the same year. Eventually, he served as general manager and sportscaster for WEBB in Baltimore. Young also continued to excel on the field, setting the Colts record for a kickoff return with a 104-yard runback against the Philadelphia Eagles on 15 November 1953. He was named to the Pro Bowl in 1954. While his rushing numbers fell off significantly to eighty-seven yards in his final season, Young was a productive receiver even at the end of his career, averaging a gaudy 22.4 yards per reception in 1955.

Promised a job in the Colts front office, Young retired as a player at the start of the 1956 season. He was so popular in Baltimore that many local citizens, both black and white, worked to convince him to run for mayor of the city. Instead, he served as a football scout for the Colts, with a special talent for recruiting promising black players, such as Gale Sayers and Jim Parker, who became an All-Pro offensive lineman for the organization. Young also worked briefly in public relations for Baltimore. In 1956 the Colt organization retired his jersey number 22 in recognition of his ability on the field as a player and his success in promoting Colts football to the fans.

Young joined the NFL Commissioner's Office in 1964, hired as a special assistant to Commissioner Pete Rozelle. While Young called himself a Christian first, an American second, and a black man third, one of his earliest projects in the Commissioner's Office was to help African-American athletes find new careers after their retirement from football. He also founded the Buddy Young Football League in Harlem in New York City, providing a place to learn the game for more than a thousand boys ages nine to twenty. He believed that black players needed to give something back to the African-American community and to teach children that "the system can work for them."

After he joined the NFL office, Young moved his family from Baltimore to Hartsdale, New York, in Westchester County. By 1983 he had risen to the position of director of player relations for the NFL.

Young was on official NFL business when he died. Returning from a funeral in Louisiana for Joe Delaney, an NFL player who had drowned, Young lost control of his car near Terrell, Texas, and was killed when his automobile crashed into a ditch.

Young made his mark on professional football as both a player and an executive, proving that African Americans could successfully play and lead in the NFL. After he joined the NFL Commissioner's Office in 1964, a time of profound social and racial unrest, Young was called an "Uncle Tom" by some in the black community, but he argued that "if we don't move together, we won't move at all." While he did not discount the racism that he and his fellow African-American players encountered, especially in the early years of professional football, he insisted that black players had to work within the system to change it.

★

The University of Illinois Sports Information Department, Urbana-Champaign, and the Pro Football Hall of Fame in Canton, Ohio, maintain files on Young's life and career. Brief write-ups, with special attention to Young's on-the-field exploits, are available from two out-of-print books: Larry Fox, *Little Men in Sports* (1968), and Murray Olderman, *The Running Backs* (1969). Arthur Ashe's groundbreaking work on African-American athletes, *Hard Road to Glory* (1988), mentions Young as an early pioneer in professional football. Obituaries are in the *New York Times* and *Washington Post* (both 6 Sept. 1983).

KATHRYN A. JOHNSON

YOUNG, Stephen Marvin (*b.* 4 May 1889 in Norwalk, Ohio; *d.* 1 December 1984 in Washington, D.C.), Ohio Democratic congressman and senator known for a bellicose style of discourse, who championed liberal causes throughout his political career.

The fourth of five children born to Stephen M. Young and Belle M. Wagner, Stephen Marvin Young grew up in the town of Norwalk, Ohio, where his father was an attorney and county court judge and his mother a homemaker. After attending Kenyon College in Gambier, Ohio, from 1908 to 1910, he entered Western Reserve University in Cleveland, where he received a law degree in 1912. He then began private practice in Cleveland. He married Ruby Louise Dawley on 18 January 1911; they had two sons, Stephen and Richard, and one daughter, Marjorie. In 1952 Ruby Young died of lung cancer, and on 28 March 1957 Young married Rachel Louise Bell of North Carolina, who died in 1982.

Young's political career developed over an extended period of time, and was interspersed with spans when he served in the military or practiced law. He experienced several political defeats as well as victories and was not always on the best terms with Democratic party leaders, often preferring to run as a political outsider. In 1912 he became the youngest person ever elected to the Ohio House of Representatives, where he served two terms. Young was defeated in his first race for a U.S. House seat in 1916, in part because he had volunteered for military service in the expedition against Mexico and had little opportunity to campaign. From 1917 to 1921 he served as assistant prosecutor

Stephen M. Young. REPRODUCED FROM THE COLLECTIONS OF THE LIBRARY OF CONGRESS

for Cuyahoga County (Cleveland), again with an interruption for military duty in World War I, in which he served with the Field Artillery. After defeat in a race for Ohio attorney general in 1922, Young resumed his law practice in Cleveland.

The Great Depression in the 1930s gave new political life to Democrats in Ohio and throughout the nation, as they rallied to the banner of President Franklin D. Roosevelt and the New Deal. As a result of congressional reapportionment in 1932, following the 1930 census, Ohio received two additional House seats, which were to be elected at large. Young and another Democrat won the seats in 1932 and were reelected by even wider margins in 1934. As a young New Dealer, Young strongly supported Roosevelt's policies during those four years, especially ones that brought direct relief to the unemployed and poverty stricken. Young was more skeptical of efforts to stabilize corporations and agricultural interests. In 1936 Harry L. Hopkins and other administration officials urged him to give up Congress to run for governor of Ohio against an incumbent Democrat who was not strongly supportive of Roosevelt. Young did so, but lost in the primary. He lost again in 1938 in a bid to return to Congress, but was successful in 1940, as President Roosevelt was being elected to a third term.

After the 1940 census Ohio's at-large congressional seats were reduced from two to one, and in 1942 Young was forced to run against the other incumbent at-large representative, Republican George Bender, who defeated him. Young immediately volunteered for World War II military duty, and became an army major assigned to the invasion of Italy under General Mark W. Clark. During the subsequent U.S. occupation of Italy he served as a judge advocate general and military governor of the province of Reggio nell'Emilia. For his service he received the Bronze Star and other commendations. Returning to Cleveland after the war to resume legal practice, Young found the lure of politics irresistible and won the Democratic nomination for Congress in 1948, beating his old rival George Bender in the fall election for an at-large seat. During what would prove to be his last term as a House member, he supported President Harry S. Truman's foreign policy initiatives (NATO, the Marshall Plan, foreign aid) and various liberal and labor causes at home, including repeal of the Taft-Hartley Act. Young's defeat in 1950, again to George Bender, was the result of voter frustrations with the Korean War, the Democrats' poor showing in Ohio that year, and the fact that he did not spend much time campaigning.

Now in his sixties, Young's political career would have seemed over, but in fact his greatest achievements were still ahead. In 1958 two-term U.S. senator John Bricker, a popular vote-getter, seemed destined for reelection, and Ohio Democrats concentrated on other races. Young chose to run without strong party support because he had long opposed Bricker's conservative record, and he scored an upset victory that surprised most prognosticators. A big turnout of labor union members to defeat an Ohio right-to-work amendment, also on the 1958 ballot, contributed to Young's victory. In the Senate, Young quickly identified with a bloc of liberal Democrats who attacked the conservative domestic policies of the Dwight D. Eisenhower administration. He opposed increased civilian defense expenditures, which he regarded as wasteful, and tax breaks for the wealthy. During his Senate career Young served on the Aeronautical and Space Sciences, Agriculture and Forestry, Armed Services, and Public Works committees.

A lifetime of vigorous physical exercise helped Young maintain a trim, youthful appearance and vigorous energy despite his age. After some uncertainty he decided to run for reelection in 1964. A potential primary challenge from astronaut John Glenn ended after Glenn suffered a head injury in a fall during the campaign season. (Glenn would eventually be elected to the Senate from Ohio in 1974.) In the 1964 general election Young rode President Lyndon B. Johnson's coattails to squeak out an extremely narrow victory (50.2–49.8 percent) over Robert A. Taft, Jr., who would also later be elected to the Senate.

Throughout his career, but especially as a senator, Young never shied away from controversy, and he developed a reputation for tart, even provocative, replies to colleagues and constituents who attacked his liberal stands. He once told a lawyer: "Don't give me any more of this unsolicited advice. I know it costs nothing, but that is exactly what it is worth." One of his frequent responses to a harsh letter from a constituent was to suggest that some "crackpot" was using that person's name and address.

Young was a strong supporter of President John F. Kennedy and was especially proud of Kennedy's initiatives in arms control and civil rights, which led to the Nuclear Test Ban Treaty of 1963 and the Civil Rights Act of 1964. He also supported President Johnson's Great Society programs, having worked with Johnson several years before in the Senate. He finally broke with the president in 1966 over the Vietnam War. Young had characteristically harsh words to describe the South Vietnamese leaders who seemed unable to win the support of their own people in that conflict. Choosing not to seek reelection in 1970, Young lived in Washington in retirement until his death from a blood disorder in 1984. He was buried in Arlington National Cemetery. He had the pleasure of seeing his former campaign manager, Howard Metzenbaum, win election to the Senate in 1976; Metzenbaum championed many of the same liberal causes that Young had espoused.

Stephen Young's political career spanned the years from the Progressive Era to the Great Society, from the social needs of inner-city Cleveland to the space race and America's difficult role as world policeman. Never one to avoid controversy, he followed an independent course. In so doing he enjoyed the respect of colleagues on both sides of the political aisle for his candor, integrity, and energetic devotion to public service.

★

A collection of Stephen Marvin Young Papers is housed at the Western Reserve Historical Society in Cleveland. There is no published biography, but Young published an informative autobiography, *Tales Out of Congress* (1964). Aspects of Young's senatorial career are analyzed in Barbara Sinclair, *The Transformation of the U.S. Senate* (1989), especially chapter 3: "The Impact of a Change in Membership: The Democratic Classes of 1958–1964." Alexander P. Lamis, ed., *Ohio Politics* (1994), and John J. Grabowski, ed., *The Encyclopedia of Cleveland History* (1991), provide background on the local setting of Young's political and legal careers. See also "Taft vs. Young," *Newsweek* (26 Oct. 1964). An obituary is in the *New York Times* (2 Dec. 1984).

JOHN B. WEAVER

ZIMBALIST, Efrem Alexandrovich (*b.* c. 9 April 1889 in Rostov-on-Don, Russia; *d.* 22 February 1985 in Reno, Nevada), world-class violin virtuoso considered an exemplar of the Auer school of czarist Saint Petersburg.

Zimbalist was the son of Maria Litvinoff and Alexander Zimbalist, the conductor of the Rostov Opera Orchestra. He exhibited an early propensity for music. Under his father's tutelage, he was able by the age of nine to join his father's orchestra as first-chair violinist. In 1901 he entered the Saint Petersburg Conservatory and studied under Leopold Auer. During his six years at the conservatory, Zimbalist also studied composition with Nikolay Rimsky-Korsakov, whose home he frequently visited to play in string quartets. When Zimbalist graduated from the conservatory in 1907, he was awarded the school's gold medal for his playing and the Rubinstein Prize (which came with an honorarium of 1,200 rubles).

Zimbalist began performing that same year. His debut performance occurred in Berlin on 7 November 1907, where he performed the Brahms violin concerto with the Berlin Philharmonic Orchestra. The next month, Zimbalist debuted in London. For the following few years he toured Germany, England, and Belgium. In 1910 he performed the Tchaikovsky violin concerto at Leipzig Gewandhaus under the direction of Arthur Nikisch.

On 27 October 1911 Zimbalist arrived in the United States for his American debut, which took place in Boston. He performed the American premier of Alexander Glazunov's Concerto in A minor with the Boston Symphony Orchestra. Zimbalist enjoyed critical success in America and decided to remain in the country. He met his first wife,

Efrem Zimbalist. UPI/CORBIS-BETTMANN

Alma Gluck, on a ferry to New Jersey during his first visit to New York. The young violinist was immediately smitten with the beautiful Metropolitan Opera soprano and courted her for the next three years. During this time the couple often shared the stage. Zimbalist proposed several times before Gluck finally accepted. They were married on 15 June 1914 and Zimbalist became a U.S. citizen.

The Zimbalists bought a house on the West Side of Manhattan, moving a few years later to a brownstone on Park Avenue. They continued performing together and spent their summers at a cottage on Fishers Island off Long Island in New York State. The couple had two children. Their son, Efrem Zimbalist, Jr., went on to become a well-known actor in film and on television. A granddaughter, Stephanie Zimbalist, also became a popular television and film actor.

The family remained in New York for more than ten years, during which time he composed a score for a successful Broadway musical comedy called *Honeydew*. The operetta opened on 6 September 1920 at the Casino Theater in New York and ran for 231 performances.

Alma Gluck retired from the stage in 1925, and in 1928 Zimbalist relocated the family to Philadelphia, where he joined the teaching faculty in the violin department of the Curtis Institute of Music. Auer, who had followed his students to America, died a few years later, and Zimbalist assumed the position as head of the violin department. In addition to his teaching, Zimbalist gave performances around the world.

On 3 March 1936 the first version of Zimbalist's *American Rhapsody* for orchestra was performed in Chicago. In 1938 Zimbalist's wife died. Three years later he was appointed director of the Curtis Institute, a position he held for twenty-seven years. Five years after Alma died, Zimbalist married Mary Louise Curtis Bok, the widow of Edward W. Bok and the founder of the Curtis Institute. They married on 6 July 1943, three months after a revised version of Zimbalist's *American Rhapsody* was performed in Philadelphia on 5 February 1943. Zimbalist and his second wife set up housekeeping on Delancey Place in Philadelphia.

On 7 December 1945 Zimbalist's orchestral tone poem, *Portrait of an Artist,* debuted in Philadelphia. In 1947 and 1948 Zimbalist performed five programs in New York, covering 400 years in the history of violin music. On 14 November 1949 he gave his farewell performance in New York and retired from the stage. In 1951 Zimbalist published *Solo Violin Music of the Earliest Period* as a result of the five programs he had performed in 1947 and 1948.

Zimbalist came out of stage retirement in 1952 to perform the debut of Gian Carlo Menotti's violin concerto, a concerto Menotti had dedicated to Zimbalist. He continued to perform sporadically until his performance with the Philadelphia Orchestra of Beethoven's violin concerto in 1955. On 6 April 1956 Zimbalist's opera *Landara* was performed in Philadelphia. Although Zimbalist had slowed down somewhat from the frantic schedule he kept in the 1930s and 1940s, he remained active and served on the juries of the 1962 and 1966 Tchaikovsky competitions in Moscow.

Zimbalist retired from performing and teaching for good in 1968 and moved to Reno, Nevada. His second wife, Mary, died in 1970. Even in retirement Zimbalist continued to compose music and practiced the violin every day. In November 1984 he completed what would be his final work, a revision of one of his earlier works, *Sarasateana*.

Poised and courtly, Zimbalist was a keen-witted man with a passion for gambling, bargain hunting, and collecting, and will be remembered alongside Mischa Elman and Jascha Heifetz as one of the Auer school's most gifted alumni and one of America's greatest violinists. His virtuoso style on the violin was as dignified, reverent, and sincere as the man himself. He personified the same refined understatement that he brought to his music, and he left behind a long, successful history as a violinist, teacher, and composer.

★

Biographical information can be found in David Ewen, comp. and ed., *Musicians Since 1900: Performances in Concert and Opera* (1978); Stanley Sadie, ed., *The New Grove Dictionary of Music and Musicians* (1980); and Bruce Bohler, ed., *The International Cyclopedia of Music and Musicians,* 11th ed. (1985). Obituaries are in the *New York Times* and *Washington Post* (both 23 Feb. 1985).

KEVIN ALEXANDER BOON

ZWORYKIN, Vladimir Kosma (*b.* 30 July 1889 in Murom, Russia; *d.* 29 July 1982 in Princeton, New Jersey), scientist who invented the original technology for transmitting and receiving television pictures.

The son of Kosma and Elaine Zworykin, Zworykin benefited from the relative wealth of his father, who owned a string of riverboats in Murom, about 200 miles east of Moscow—Zworykin was able to attend the Saint Petersburg Institute of Technology. While studying there with Professor Boris Rosing, Zworykin was introduced to the technology of the cathode-ray tube, which had been invented by the German-born physicist Karl F. Braun in 1897. Professor Rosing theorized that images could be displayed on such a tube; simultaneously, the English physicist A. A. Campbell-Swinton was adopting a similar approach. Neither of these scientists, however, dared the bold step Zwor-

Vladimir Zworykin holds an RCA Image Orthicon tube. His inventions helped make television possible. ARCHIVE PHOTOS

ykin was to take. He realized that a moving beam of electrons (the main element of the cathode-ray tube) might not only display a visual image, it might record one as well. This recognition was the basis of television.

Zworykin obtained a degree in electrical engineering from Saint Petersburg in 1912 and enrolled in the Collège de France in Paris; there he studied X rays under Paul Langevin. His stay was cut short by the outbreak of World War I, which forced him to return home and enroll in the Signal Corps. His expertise in wireless transmission spared him from combat service; instead he was assigned to work with the Marconi Company. Zworykin married Tatiana Vasilieff on 17 April 1916; they had two children. When the November 1917 Revolution took place, Zworykin decided to leave Russia; he fled north, to the Arctic Ocean, then worked his way through Scandinavia to England, and from there to the United States, which he reached in 1919 after a year and a half of effort. Ironically, his first job in the United States was as a bookkeeper for the Russian embassy's financial agents.

In 1920, having learned sufficient English, Zworykin took a job with the Westinghouse Electric Corporation in Pittsburgh. He also became a U.S. citizen in 1924 and received a Ph.D. from the University of Pittsburgh in 1926. At Westinghouse, Zworykin studied a number of aspects of the burgeoning electrical industry, from photoelectric cells—the subject of his doctoral work—to mercury rectifiers. All these interests converged on his development of television. As early as 1923, Zworykin completed a working iconoscope, or television camera, and applied for a patent.

The first practical iconoscope was essentially similar in design to the human eye. A lens focused an image on a plate (equivalent to the retina) covered with tiny photoelectric cells (the rods and cones), each of which generated a current proportional to the intensity of the light falling on it. An electron beam scanned the back of the plate in a series of horizontal lines every thirtieth of a second, producing a signal (along the electronic equivalent of the optic nerve) that changed in proportion to the current of each cell. The result was not dissimilar to a photogravure image in a newspaper, made up of tiny dots of varying intensity of light and dark. By using photoelectric cells to collect the light and then discharging them every thirtieth of a second, Zworykin achieved far greater light-gathering power than any previous instrument; even though his iconoscope would eventually be supplanted by the more efficient image-orthicon camera, the principles of television remain the ones Zworykin developed in the early 1920s. Zworykin also applied for a patent on a color television camera in 1925; he received that patent in 1928, and his patent for the iconoscope was belatedly granted in 1938. He demonstrated this camera for Westinghouse executives in 1924, but the image that resulted was still quite dim, and for financial reasons his work was not given high priority.

Zworykin also developed a kinescope, or picture tube, which fulfilled his early studies with the cathode-ray tube. An electron beam, focused by electrical or magnetic fields, is modulated by the changing picture signal so that it hits a series of fluorescent dots on the screen with greater or less intensity; as long as this beam is synchronized with the iconoscope's transmitting scan, the result will be an exact replica of the transmitted image. Zworykin's first kinescope traced fewer than 200 lines, but he steadily improved the focus of his beam to produce 240, then 343, then 441 lines per image; for comparison, modern television tubes still trace only 525 lines per image. With more lines available, the size of the screen could also be enlarged; from the original cathode-ray tube size of about 4 inches square, Zworykin developed a screen as large as 7.5 inches by 12 inches, which is roughly the same image size as that provided by a standard 14-inch computer screen.

Zworykin demonstrated his system in 1929 to the Institute of Radio Engineers in Rochester, New York, and among those impressed was another Russian emigré, David Sarnoff, general manager of the Radio Corporation of America (RCA). In a meeting that would become famous in later years, Sarnoff asked Zworykin how much it would take to make television commercially profitable, and was told it could be done for "about $100,000." It would ultimately take fifty times that amount. Because Westinghouse was a major stockholder in RCA, Sarnoff was able to have Zworykin and his team transferred to the electronics research division of RCA in Camden, New Jersey, where they worked for the next ten years, transforming what were little more than scientific instruments into commercially viable products. In addition to television imaging, Zworykin also worked on methods of converting infrared and ultraviolet rays into visible light, what he excitedly described as "seeing the heretofore invisible."

In 1936 a complete program was transmitted from the RCA building in Rockefeller Center in New York City through an antenna atop the Empire State Building and was received as much as forty-five miles away; the technology of television was complete. However, RCA would not receive approval from the Federal Communications Commission to begin broadcasting until July 1941, when war was imminent; as a result, the first commercial television did not go on sale until the fall of 1946.

After the commercialization of his inventions was complete, Zworykin's career moved to other, related areas of investigation. In 1940 he recruited James Hillier to his development team, and in three months Hillier had developed the electron microscope. During the war, Zworykin developed the electron-image tube, a camera a hundred times more powerful than the iconoscope; it became the first night-vision camera, variously called the sniperscope and the snooperscope. The microscopic photoelectric cells in his iconoscope were incorporated into the scintillation counter, a vital tool for the measurement of radioactivity. Most interestingly, he worked with the mathematician John Von Neumann on the development of the computer; although his contribution, based as it was on vacuum-tube technology, was soon superseded by the transistor, at the time it represented a twenty-five-fold increase in computational ability. From 1947 until his retirement in 1954, Zworykin held the title of vice president and director of electronic research for RCA.

After retirement, Zworykin continued to work at his own laboratory in Princeton, New Jersey. He developed the endoradiosonde, a tiny transmitter that could be swallowed to allow doctors to monitor processes inside the body. He also developed the ultraviolet microscope, which bathes specimens in ultraviolet light in order to provide maximum detail, then corrects the colors into the visible spectrum for display on a television screen. Zworykin also served as director of the Medical Electronics Center of Rockefeller University in New York.

Zworykin's first marriage ended in divorce in 1950. The next year, he married Dr. Katherine Polevitzky. He was coauthor of four books: *Photocells and Their Application* (1934; reprinted in 1949 as *Photoelectricity and Its Applications*); *Television: The Electronics of Image Transmission in Color and Monochrome* (1940); *Electron Optics and the Electron Microscope* (1945); and *Television in Science and Industry* (1958). Among his numerous awards were election to both the National Academy of Sciences (1943) and the National Academy of Engineering (1965), the Faraday Medal from the British Institute in 1965, the Presidential Medal of Science in 1966, and the National Medal of Science in 1967. Zworykin died of natural causes.

In his later life Zworykin expressed his deep ambivalence about the effects his invention had wrought on life in America and throughout the world. In an interview a year before his death, he summed up American television as "awful," claiming it was one of the leading causes of juvenile delinquency. Nevertheless, he was proud of television's positive effects in areas ranging from politics to news to transportation.

★

See Albert Abramson, *Zworykin: Pioneer of Television* (1994). Zworykin's life was sketched in John Lear, "Merchant of Vision," *Saturday Review* (1 June 1957). Those interested in a more technical presentation can consult Albert Abramson, "Pioneers of Television: Vladimir Kosma Zworykin," *SMTE Journal* (July 1981). An obituary is in the *New York Times* (1 Aug. 1982).

HARTLEY S. SPATT

OCCUPATIONS INDEX

Acting Coach
  Strasberg, Lee
Actor (Film)
  Adler, Luther
  Albertson, Jack
  Baxter, Anne
  Belushi, John
  Bergman, Ingrid
  Brooks, (Mary) Louise
  Brynner, Yul
  Carmichael, Howard Hoagland
    ("Hoagy")
  Coogan, John Leslie, Jr. ("Jackie")
  Crabbe, Clarence Linden
    ("Buster")
  Douglas, Melvyn
  Fetchit, Stepin
  Fonda, Henry Jaynes
  Gaynor, Janet
  Gordon, Ruth
  Hamilton, Margaret
  Holden, William
  Hudson, Rock (Roy Scherer, Jr.)
  Jessel, George Albert ("Georgie")
  Kelly, Grace Patricia (Princess
    Grace)
  Lawford, Peter Sydney Vaughn
  Lenya, Lotte
  Lodge, John Davis
  Markham, Dewey ("Pigmeat")
  Massey, Raymond Hart
  Merman, Ethel
  Montgomery, Robert
  Nelson, Eric Hilliard ("Rick")
  O'Brien, William Joseph, Jr. ("Pat")
  Pidgeon, Walter
  Powell, William Horatio

  Shearer, (Edith) Norma
  Silvers, Phil
  Swanson, Gloria
  Webb, John Randolph ("Jack")
  Weissmuller, John Peter
    ("Johnny")
  Welles, Orson
  Wood, Natalie
Actor (Radio)
  Ace, Goodman
  Gosden, Freeman Fisher
  Jessel, George Albert ("Georgie")
  Livingstone, Mary
  Strasberg, Lee
  Welles, Orson
Actor (Stage)
  Adler, Luther
  Albertson, Jack
  Astaire, Adele Marie
  Beck, Julian
  Bergman, Ingrid
  Brynner, Yul
  Douglas, Melvyn
  Fetchit, Stepin
  Fonda, Henry Jaynes
  Fontanne, Lynn
  Gordon, Ruth
  Hamilton, Margaret
  Jessel, George Albert ("Georgie")
  Lenya, Lotte
  Lodge, John Davis
  Markham, Dewey ("Pigmeat")
  Massey, Raymond Hart
  Merman, Ethel
  Montgomery, Robert
  Schlamme, Martha Haftel
  Scourby, Alexander

  Sillman, Leonard Dexter
  Silvers, Phil
  Welles, Orson
Actor (Television)
  Ace, Goodman
  Albertson, Jack
  Belushi, John
  Diamond, Selma
  Kaufman, Andrew G. ("Andy")
  Livingstone, Mary
  Markham, Dewey ("Pigmeat")
  Massey, Raymond Hart
  Montgomery, Robert
  Nelson, Eric Hilliard ("Rick")
  Scourby, Alexander
  Silvers, Phil
  Tillstrom, Burr
  Webb, John Randolph ("Jack")
Admiral. *See* NAVAL OFFICER.
Air Force Officer
  Ryan, John D.
  Twining, Nathan Farragut
Anthropologist
  Coon, Carleton Stevens
  Davis, (William) Allison
Architect
  Breuer, Marcel
  Fuller, R(ichard) Buckminster
  Owings, Nathaniel Alexander
  Sert, José Luis
  Wright, Olgivanna Lloyd
Army Officer
  Bradley, Omar Nelson
  Clark, Mark Wayne
  Gruenther, Alfred Maximilian
Art Critic
  Canaday, John Edwin

Art Dealer
  Parsons, Elizabeth Pierson
    ("Betty")
Artist (Painter)
  Benn, Ben
  Ernst, Hans-Ulrich ("Jimmy")
  Krasner, Lee
  Okada, Kenzo
  Rexroth, Kenneth Charles Marion
  Sloane, Eric
  Vargas, Alberto ("Varga")
Artist (Sculptor)
  Parsons, Elizabeth Pierson
    ("Betty")
  Roszak, Theodore
Athlete (Auto Racing)
  Parsons, Johnnie
Athlete (Baseball)
  Averill, Howard Earl ("Rock")
  Coveleski, Stanley Anthony
    ("Covey")
  Cronin, Joseph Edward
  Dean, Paul ("Daffy")
  Grimes, Burleigh Arland
  Hoyt, Waite Charles ("Schoolboy")
  Kelly, George Lange
    ("Highpockets")
  Lindstrom, Frederick Charles, Jr.
    ("Lindy")
  Maris, Roger Eugene
  McCormick, Frank Andrew
  Paige, Leroy Robert ("Satchel")
  Schacht, Al(exander)
  Stratton, Monty Franklin Pierce
  Walker, Fred ("Dixie")
  Waner, Lloyd James ("Little
    Poison")
Athlete (Basketball)
  Cooper, Charles Henry
    ("Chuck")
Athlete (Bowling)
  Varipapa, Andrew ("Andy")
Athlete (Boxing)
  Dempsey, William Harrison
    ("Jack")
  Louis, Joe
  Walker, Edward Patrick ("Mickey";
    "The Toy Bulldog")
Athlete (Football)
  Battles, Clifford Franklin ("Gyp")
  Crisler, Herbert Orin ("Fritz")
  Engle, Charles Albert ("Rip")
  Friedman, Benjamin ("Benny")

  Kinard, Frank Manning
    ("Bruiser")
  McNally, John Victor ("Johnny
    Blood")
  Van Brocklin, Norm(an) ("The
    Dutchman")
  Waterfield, Robert Staton ("Bob";
    "Rifle")
  Young, Claude, Jr. ("Buddy")
Athlete (Golf)
  Demaret, James Newton
    ("Jimmy")
Athlete (Hockey)
  Shore, Edward William ("Eddie")
Athlete (Running)
  Fixx, James Fuller
Athlete (Swimming)
  Crabbe, Clarence Linden
    ("Buster")
  Weissmuller, John Peter
    ("Johnny")
Author (Drama)
  Burrows, Abe
  Chase, Mary Coyle
  Chayefsky, Sidney Aaron
    ("Paddy")
  Gershwin, Ira
  Gordon, Ruth
  Hellman, Lillian Florence
  Levin, Meyer
  Loos, Anita
  MacLeish, Archibald
  Maltz, Albert
  Ryskind, Morrie
  Saroyan, William
  Shaw, Irwin Gilbert
  Sillman, Leonard Dexter
  Williams, Thomas Lanier, III
    ("Tennessee")
Author (Fiction)
  Adams, Harriet Stratemeyer
  Algren, Nelson
  Barnes, Djuna Chappell
  Boylston, Helen Dore
  Brautigan, Richard
  Caldwell, (Janet Miriam) Taylor
  Capote, Truman
  Cheever, John
  Dick, Philip Kindred
  Gardner, John Champlin, Jr.
  Halper, Albert
  Himes, Chester Bomar
  Levin, Meyer

  Loos, Anita
  Macdonald, Ross
  MacInnes, Helen Clark
  Maltz, Albert
  Rand, Ayn
  Saroyan, William
  Shaw, Irwin Gilbert
  Stein, Aaron Marc
  Sturgeon, Theodore
  West, (Mary) Jessamyn
  White, E(lwyn) B(rooks)
  Williams, Thomas Lanier, III
    ("Tennessee")
Author (Nonfiction)
  Ace, Goodman
  Atkinson, (Justin) Brooks
  Bainton, Roland Herbert
  Barnes, Djuna Chappell
  Barr, Stringfellow
  Beard, James Andrew
  Brodie, Fawn McKay
  Canaday, John Edwin
  Capote, Truman
  Chase, Stuart
  Coon, Carleton Stevens
  Crowther, (Francis) Bosley, Jr.
  Daniels, Jonathan Worth
  de Man, Paul
  Denby, Edwin Orr
  Deutsch, Helene Rosenbach
  Durant, Ariel
  Durant, Will(iam) James
  Engel, A. Lehman
  Fielding, Temple Hornaday
  Fixx, James Fuller
  Fossey, Dian
  Friedrich, Carl Joachim
  Gardner, John Champlin, Jr.
  Golden, Harry
  Grosvenor, Melville Bell
  Hellman, Lillian Florence
  Hicks, Granville
  Hoffer, Eric
  Holt, John Caldwell
  Hughes, Emmet John
  Jacoby, Oswald ("Ozzie")
  Jessel, George Albert ("Georgie")
  Kahn, Herman
  Kardiner, Abram
  Ladd, George Eldon
  Langer, Susanne Katherina
  Levin, Meyer
  Logan, Rayford Whittingham

Lynd, Helen Merrell
Macdonald, Dwight
Mays, Benjamin Elijah
Milgram, Stanley
Monroe, Marion
Murray, Anna Pauline ("Pauli")
Nearing, Scott
Niel, Cornelis Bernardus van
Pool, Ithiel de Sola
Rand, Ayn
Scott, Austin Wakeman
Sheed, Francis Joseph ("Frank")
Shook, Karel Francis Antony
Sloane, Eric
Stuart, Jesse Hilton
Terry, Walter
Welch, Robert Henry Winborne, Jr.
West, (Mary) Jessamyn
White, E(lwyn) B(rooks)
Whitehead, Don(ald) Ford
Wright, Olgivanna Lloyd

Author (Poetry)
Brautigan, Richard
Fitzgerald, Robert Stuart
MacLeish, Archibald
Oppen, George
Rexroth, Kenneth Charles Marion
Rice, Helen Steiner
Stuart, Jesse Hilton

Author (Screenplays)
Chayefsky, Sidney Aaron ("Paddy")
Foreman, Carl
Goodrich, Frances
Ryskind, Morrie

Author (Television)
Diamond, Selma

Author (Translation)
Fitzgerald, Robert Stuart
Levin, Meyer

Banker. *See* BUSINESS EXECUTIVE (BANKING INDUSTRY).

Baseball Manager. *See* SPORTS COACH (BASEBALL).

Baseball Player. *See* ATHLETE (BASEBALL).

Basketball Player. *See* ATHLETE (BASKETBALL).

Biochemist
Cori, Carl Ferdinand
Moore, Stanford
Niel, Cornelis Bernardus van

Biologist
Claude, Albert
Delbrück, Max Ludwig Henning
Dubos, René Jules
Niel, Cornelis Bernardus van

Bishop. *See* CLERGY.

Boxer. *See* ATHLETE (BOXING).

Business Executive (Advertising Industry)
Bernbach, William

Business Executive (Aviation Industry)
Beebe, William Thomas
Douglas, Donald Wills
Grumman, Leroy Randle ("Roy")
Mackey, Joseph Creighton
Mitchell, John James, Jr.
Northrop, John Knudsen ("Jack")
Trippe, Juan Terry

Business Executive (Banking Industry)
Morgan, Henry Sturgis ("Harry")
Shields, Cornelius
Snyder, John Wesley

Business Executive (Broadcast Industry)
Hagerty, James Campbell

Business Executive (Chemical Industry)
Plough, Abe

Business Executive (Construction Industry)
Brown, George Rufus

Business Executive (Courier Industry)
Casey, James E.

Business Executive (Entertainment Industry)
Dietz, Howard
Knott, Walter
Stein, Julian Caesar ("Jules")

Business Executive (Financial Services Industry)
Johnson, Edward Crosby, 2d
Mitchell, John James, Jr.
Morgan, Henry Sturgis ("Harry")
Price, T(homas) Rowe, Jr.

Business Executive (Food Industry)
Austin, John Paul
Black, William
Cohen, N(ehemiah) M(yer)
Knott, Walter
Kroc, Ray(mond) Albert

Lay, Herman W.
Magowan, Robert Anderson
Marriott, J(ohn) Willard
Morton, Thruston Ballard
Pillsbury, Philip
Samuels, Howard Joseph
Woodruff, Robert Winship

Business Executive (Greeting Card Industry)
Hall, Joyce Clyde

Business Executive (Hotel Industry)
Marriott, J(ohn) Willard

Business Executive (Insurance Industry)
Kemper, James Scott
Kennedy, William Jesse, Jr.

Business Executive (Manufacturing Industry)
Spanel, Abram Nathaniel
Tupper, Earl Silas

Business Executive (Mining Industry)
Hirshhorn, Joseph Herman

Business Executive (Petroleum Industry)
Pauley, Edwin Wendell

Business Executive (Physical Fitness Industry)
Tanny, Victor Anthony ("Vic")

Business Executive (Public Relations Industry)
Rosenberg, Anna Marie Lederer

Business Executive (Real Estate Industry)
Uris, Harold David

Business Executive (Sports Industry)
Halas, George
Irish, Edward Simmons, Sr. ("Ned")

Business Executive (Steel Industry)
Blough, Roger Miles

Business Executive (Tobacco Industry)
Stokes, Colin

Cardinal. *See* CLERGY.

Cartoonist
Gould, Chester
Vargas, Alberto ("Varga")

Chef
Beard, James Andrew

Chemist
Flory, Paul John
Giauque, William Francis

Chemist (*cont.*)
Kistiakowsky, George Bogdan
Urey, Harold Clayton

Choreographer
Balanchine, George
Shook, Karel Francis Antony

Circus Executive
Feld, Irvin
North, John Ringling

Civic Worker
Johnson, Rachel Harris
McNamara, Margaret Craig

Civil Rights Activist
Baldwin, Roger Nash
Blackwell, Randolph Talmadge
Golden, Harry
Groppi, James Edward
Harris, Patricia Roberts Fitzgerald
Hays, Lee
Holland, Jerome Heartwell
("Brud")
Murray, Anna Pauline ("Pauli")
Scott, Hazel Dorothy
Wheeler, Raymond Milner
Wilkins, Roy

Clergy (Episcopal)
Murray, Anna Pauline ("Pauli")

Clergy (Methodist)
Mueller, Reuben Herbert

Clergy (Mormon)
Kimball, Spencer Woolley

Clergy (Roman Catholic)
Cody, John Patrick
Cooke, Terence James
Groppi, James Edward
Medeiros, Humberto Sousa

Clergy (Southern Baptist)
King, Martin Luther, Sr. ("Daddy King")

Coach. *See* SPORTS COACH.

Comedian
Kaufman, Andrew G. ("Andy")
Markham, Dewey ("Pigmeat")
Schacht, Al(exander)
Silvers, Phil

Communications Theorist
Pool, Ithiel de Sola

Composer (Broadway)
Engel, A. Lehman
Moross, Jerome
Willson, (Robert Reiniger) Meredith

Composer (Classical)
Barber, Samuel
Hanson, Howard Harold
Moross, Jerome
Sessions, Roger Huntington
Thompson, (Ira) Randall
Watts, John Everett
Wright, Olgivanna Lloyd

Composer (Jazz)
Blake, James Hubert ("Eubie")
Monk, Thelonious Sphere

Composer (Liturgical)
Weiner, Lazar

Composer (Popular)
Carmichael, Howard Hoagland ("Hoagy")
Jenkins, Gordon Hill
Marks, John D. ("Johnny")
Martin, Freddy
Riddle, Nelson Smock, Jr.
Schwartz, Arthur

Conductor. *See* MUSICIAN (CONDUCTOR).

Congressman/woman. *See* POLITICIAN (REPRESENTATIVE, SENATOR).

Cook. *See* CHEF.

Costume Designer
Head, Edith

Crime Figure
Boyle, William Anthony ("Tony")
Demara, Ferdinand Waldo ("Fred")
Lansky, Meyer
Patriarca, Raymond
Stanford, Sally

Cytologist
Stern, Curt

Dancer. *See also* CHOREOGRAPHER.
Astaire, Adele Marie
Balanchine, George
Powell, Eleanor Torrey ("Ellie")
Shook, Karel Francis Antony

Designer. *See* ENGINEER, FASHION DESIGNER, FURNITURE DESIGNER.

Diplomat
Armour, Norman
Bunker, Ellsworth
Eisenhower, Milton Stover
Harris, Patricia Roberts Fitzgerald
Holland, Jerome Heartwell ("Brud")

Lodge, Henry Cabot, Jr.
Lodge, John Davis
Riddleberger, James Williams
Whitney, John Hay
Yost, Charles Woodruff

Director (Film)
Cukor, George
Foreman, Carl
Montgomery, Robert
Peckinpah, David Samuel ("Sam")
Vidor, King Wallis
Welles, Orson
Wyler, William

Director (Stage)
Beck, Julian
Montgomery, Robert
Schneider, Alan
Sillman, Leonard Dexter
Strasberg, Lee
Welles, Orson

Director (Television)
Liebman, Max

Doctor. *See* PHYSICIAN.

Dramatist. *See* AUTHOR (DRAMA).

Economist
Chase, Stuart
Hoyt, Homer
Koopmans, Tjalling Charles
Kuznets, Simon Smith
Snyder, John Wesley

Editor (Crossword Puzzles)
Farrar, Margaret Petherbridge

Editor (Magazines)
Fixx, James Fuller
Grosvenor, Melville Bell
Levin, Meyer
Macdonald, Dwight

Editor (Newspapers)
Canham, Erwin Dain
Catledge, Turner
Knight, John Shively
Pope, James Soule, Sr.
Sheppard, Eugenia
Sutton, Carol
Wechsler, James Arthur

Educator
Albion, Robert G.
Bainton, Roland Herbert
Barr, Stringfellow
Billington, Ray Allen
Bloch, Felix
Breuer, Marcel
Brodie, Fawn McKay

de Man, Paul
Eisenhower, Milton Stover
Engel, A. Lehman
Fletcher, Harvey
Galarza, Ernesto, Jr.
Gardner, John Champlin, Jr.
Hanson, Howard Harold
Harris, Patricia Roberts Fitzgerald
Hicks, Granville
Holland, Jerome Heartwell
 ("Brud")
Holt, John Caldwell
Hughes, Emmet John
Kline, Nathan Schellenberg
Koopmans, Tjalling Charles
Kuznets, Simon Smith
Langer, Susanne Katherina
Logan, Rayford Whittingham
Lynd, Helen Merrell
MacLeish, Archibald
Mays, Benjamin Elijah
Monroe, Marion
Moos, Malcolm Charles
Nagel, Ernest
Neyman, Jerzy
Niel, Cornelis Bernardus van
Padover, Saul Kussiel
Perkins, Dexter
Primrose, William
Rafferty, Max(well) Lewis, Jr.
Rainey, Homer Price
Scott, Austin Wakeman
Sessions, Roger Huntington
Strasberg, Lee
Thompson, (Ira) Randall
Ward, John William
Waring, Fred(eric) Malcolm
Wright, Olgivanna Lloyd
Engineer (Architectural)
Fuller, R(ichard) Buckminster
Engineer (Audio)
Fletcher, Harvey
Engineer (Aviation)
Grumman, Leroy Randle ("Roy")
Link, Edwin Albert
Northrop, John Knudsen ("Jack")
Engineer (Communications)
Zworykin, Vladimir Kosma
Engineer (Nuclear)
Ulam, Stanislaw Marcin
Engineer (Rocket Science)
Debus, Kurt Heinrich

Environmentalist
Adams, Ansel Easton
Dubos, René Jules
Holden, William
Kieran, John Francis
McCall, Thomas William Lawson
Nearing, Scott
Fashion Designer
Gernreich, Rudi
Head, Edith
Film Director. *See* DIRECTOR (FILM).
Film Producer. *See* PRODUCER
 (FILM).
Financier. *See* BUSINESS EXECUTIVE
 (FINANCIAL SERVICES
 INDUSTRY).
First Lady
Truman, Bess Wallace
Football Player. *See* ATHLETE
 (FOOTBALL PLAYER).
Furniture Designer
Breuer, Marcel
Games Expert
Jacoby, Oswald ("Ozzie")
Scarne, John
Geneticist
Stern, Curt
Geographer
Grosvenor, Melville Bell
Golfer. *See* ATHLETE (GOLF).
Government Official
Bane, Frank B.
Corcoran, Thomas Gardiner
Debus, Kurt Heinrich
DiSalle, Michael Vincent
Fortas, Abe
Gates, Thomas Sovereign, Jr.
Hanks, Nancy
Harris, Patricia Roberts Fitzgerald
Hoyt, Homer
Lilienthal, David
MacLeish, Archibald
Moses, Robert
Myer, Dillon Seymour
Prichard, Edward Fretwell, Jr.
Rosenberg, Anna Marie Lederer
Samuels, Howard Joseph
Snyder, John Wesley
Terry, Luther L.
Governor. *See* POLITICIAN
 (GOVERNOR).
Guitarist. *See* MUSICIAN.

Historian. *See also* EDUCATOR.
Albion, Robert G.
Bailey, Thomas A.
Billington, Ray Allen
Brodie, Fawn McKay
Butterfield, Lyman Henry
Durant, Ariel
Durant, Will(iam) James
Logan, Rayford Whittingham
Moos, Malcolm Charles
Padover, Saul Kussiel
Perkins, Dexter
Sterling, J(ohn) E(wart) Wallace
Ward, John William
Humorist
Ace, Goodman
Golden, Harry
Illustrator. *See* ARTIST.
Inventor
Fuller, R(ichard) Buckminster
Link, Edwin Albert
Margulies, Lazar
Olin, John Merrill
Rock, John Charles
Tupper, Earl Silas
Journalist (Art Critic)
Canaday, John Edwin
Journalist (Broadcast)
Collingwood, Charles Cummings
Garroway, David Cunningham
Reynolds, Frank
Savitch, Jessica Beth
Thomas, Lowell Jackson
Journalist (Dance Critic)
Denby, Edwin Orr
Terry, Walter
Journalist (Drama Critic)
Atkinson, (Justin) Brooks
Journalist (Fashion Columnist)
Sheppard, Eugenia
Journalist (Film Critic)
Crowther, (Francis) Bosley, Jr.
Journalist (Magazines)
Cowles, Gardner ("Mike")
Hughes, Emmet John
Ingersoll, Ralph McAllister
Ryskind, Morrie
Stein, Aaron Marc
Journalist (Newspapers)
Canham, Erwin Dain
Catledge, Turner
Daniels, Jonathan Worth
Dedmon, Emmett

Journalist (Newspapers) *(cont.)*
Knight, John Shively
Lodge, Henry Cabot, Jr.
Pope, James Soule, Sr.
Ryskind, Morrie
Skolsky, Sidney
Stein, Aaron Marc
Sutton, Carol
Wechsler, James Arthur
Whitehead, Don(ald) Ford

Journalist (Sportswriter)
Irish, Edward Simmons, Sr.
("Ned")
Kieran, John Francis
Smith, Walter Wellesley ("Red")
Whitaker, Rogers E(rnest)
M(alcolm) ("E. M. Frimbo")

Judge. *See* JURIST.

Jurist
Ferguson, Homer Samuel
Fortas, Abe
Stewart, Potter

Labor Leader
Boyle, William Anthony ("Tony")
Curran, Joseph Edwin
Dubinsky, David
Fitzsimmons, Frank Edward
Galarza, Ernesto, Jr.
McBride, Lloyd
Miller, Arnold Ray
Petrillo, James Caesar
Wurf, Jerome

Lawyer
Berman, Emile Zola
Bernard, Anna Jones
Cohen, Benjamin Victor
Corcoran, Thomas Gardiner
Fortas, Abe
Jaworski, Leon
Johnson, Paul Burney
Murray, Anna Pauline ("Pauli")
Prichard, Edward Fretwell, Jr.
Seymour, Whitney North
Shivers, (Robert) Allan

Legal Scholar
Scott, Austin Wakeman

Librarian
Mumford, Lawrence Quincy
Wright, Louis Booker

Literary Critic
de Man, Paul
Gardner, John Champlin, Jr.
Hicks, Granville

Lyricist (Popular). *See also*
SONGWRITER.
Dietz, Howard
Gershwin, Ira
Harburg, Edgar Yipsel ("Yip")
Willson, (Robert Reiniger)
Meredith

Madam
Stanford, Sally

Magician
Scarne, John

Marine Corps Officer
Shoup, David Monroe

Maritime Worker
Hoffer, Eric

Mathematician
Kahn, Herman
Neyman, Jerzy
Robinson, Julia Bowman
Tarski, Alfred
Ulam, Stanislaw Marcin

Mayor. *See* POLITICIAN (MAYOR).

Medicine. *See* PHYSICIAN.

Meteorologist
Charney, Jule Gregory
Sloane, Eric

Military Personnel. *See* AIR FORCE,
ARMY, MARINE CORPS, NAVY,
SOLDIER, etc.

Minister. *See* CLERGY.

Miscellaneous
Demara, Ferdinand Waldo
("Fred")
Quinlan, Karen Ann

**Motion Picture Actor, Director,
Producer, etc.** *See* ACTOR,
DIRECTOR, PRODUCER, etc.

Museum Director
Barr, Alfred Hamilton, Jr.

Museum Founder
Hirshhorn, Joseph Herman

Museum President
Burden, William

Musical Arranger
Bennett, Robert Russell
Jenkins, Gordon Hill
Riddle, Nelson Smock, Jr.

Musician (Big Band)
Machito (Frank Raúl Grillo)
Martin, Freddy
Riddle, Nelson Smock, Jr.

Musician (Blues)
Hopkins, Sam ("Lightnin'")

Hunter, Alberta
Turner, Joseph Vernon ("Big Joe")
Waters, Muddy

Musician (Broadway)
Bennett, Robert Russell
Engel, A. Lehman
Merman, Ethel

Musician (Cabaret)
Bricktop (Ada Smith)

Musician (Choral Director)
Waring, Fred(eric) Malcolm

Musician (Classical)
Peerce, Jan
Ponselle, Rosa Melba
Primrose, William
Rubinstein, Arthur
Schlamme, Martha Haftel
Zimbalist, Efrem Alexandrovich

Musician (Conductor)
Bennett, Robert Russell
Hanson, Howard Harold
Jenkins, Gordon Hill
Martin, Freddy
Ormandy, Eugene
Riddle, Nelson Smock, Jr.
Wallenstein, Alfred Franz

Musician (Country)
Robbins, Marty
Tubb, Ernest Dale

Musician (Folk)
Chapin, Harry Forster
Hays, Lee
Schlamme, Martha Haftel

Musician (Jazz)
Barrett, Emma ("Sweet Emma")
Basie, William James ("Count")
Clarke, Kenny ("Klook")
Cole, William R. ("Cozy")
Greer, William Alexander
("Sonny")
Hines, Earl Kenneth ("Fatha")
James, Harry Haag
Machito (Frank Raúl Grillo)
Manne, Sheldon ("Shelly")
Monk, Thelonious Sphere
Scott, Hazel Dorothy
Williams, Mary Lou

Musician (Liturgical)
Weiner, Lazar

Musician (Popular)
Carpenter, Karen
Downey, Morton
Gaye, Marvin Pentz

Jenkins, Gordon Hill
Mercer, Mabel
Musician (Rock)
Haley, William John Clifton, Jr. ("Bill")
Nelson, Eric Hilliard ("Rick")
Narrator
Scourby, Alexander
NASA Administrator
Debus, Kurt Heinrich
Naval Officer
McCain, John Sydney, Jr.
Riggs, Ralph Smith
Struble, Arthur D.
Nutritionist
Pritikin, Nathan
Painter. *See* ARTIST (PAINTER).
Philanthropist
Black, William
Casey, James E.
Frick, Helen Clay
Harkness, Rebekah West
Hirshhorn, Joseph Herman
Marriott, J(ohn) Willard
McNamara, Margaret Craig
Olin, John Merrill
Phillips, Marjorie Acker
Stokes, Colin
Vanderbilt, William Henry
Wallace, (William Roy) DeWitt
Wallace, Lila (Bell) Acheson
Whitney, John Hay
Philosopher
Friedrich, Carl Joachim
Hoffer, Eric
Langer, Susanne Katherina
Nagel, Ernest
Rand, Ayn
Tarski, Alfred
Photographer
Adams, Ansel Easton
Kertész, André (Andor)
VanDerZee, James Augustus Joseph
Winogrand, Garry
Physician (Anatomist)
Corner, George Washington
Physician (Angiologist)
Gruentzig, Andreas Roland
Physician (Endocrinologist)
Corner, George Washington
Physician (Nephrologist)
Merrill, John Putnam

Physician (Neurologist)
Geschwind, Norman
Physician (Nutritionist)
Terry, Luther L.
Wheeler, Raymond Milner
Physician (Obstetrician/ Gynecologist)
Margulies, Lazar
Rock, John Charles
Physician (Physiologist)
Enders, John Franklin
Hartline, Haldan Keffer
Physician (Surgeon)
Cooper, Irving Spencer
Merrill, John Putnam
Ochsner, (Edward William) Alton
Stein, Julian Caesar ("Jules")
Physicist
Bloch, Felix
Dirac, Paul Adrien Maurice
Kahn, Herman
Ulam, Stanislaw Marcin
Urey, Harold Clayton
Physicist (Acoustician)
Fletcher, Harvey
Pianist. *See* MUSICIAN.
Playwright. *See* AUTHOR (DRAMA).
Poet. *See* AUTHOR (POET).
Political Activist
King, Martin Luther, Sr. ("Daddy King")
Mueller, Reuben Herbert
Nearing, Scott
Welch, Robert Henry Winborne, Jr.
Political Adviser
Hughes, Emmet John
Kahn, Herman
Political Scientist
Padover, Saul Kussiel
Pool, Ithiel de Sola
Voorhis, Horace Jeremiah ("Jerry")
Politician (Governor)
Benson, Elmer Austin
Clements, Earle C.
DiSalle, Michael Vincent
Grasso, Ella Rosa Giovanna Oliva Tambussi
Johnson, Paul Burney
Jordan, Leonard Beck
Lodge, John Davis
McCall, Thomas William Lawson
Shivers, (Robert) Allan

Vanderbilt, William Henry
Williams, John Bell
Politician (Mayor)
Corning, Erastus, 2d
DiSalle, Michael Vincent
Hofheinz, Roy Mark
Seasongood, Murray
Stanford, Sally
Politician (Party Leader)
Bernard, Anna Jones
Bliss, Ray Charles
Politician (Presidential Adviser)
Hagerty, James Campbell
Pauley, Edwin Wendell
Politician (Presidential Secretary)
Snyder, John Wesley
Tully, Grace
Politician (Representative)
Arends, Leslie Cornelius
Burton, Phillip
Celler, Emanuel
Hays, (Lawrence) Brooks
Hill, (Joseph) Lister
Lodge, John Davis
Morton, Thruston Ballard
Sparkman, John Jackson
Velde, Harold Himmel
Williams, John Bell
Young, Stephen M.
Politician (Senator)
Aiken, George David
Benson, Elmer Austin
Case, Clifford P.
Church, Frank Forrester
Clements, Earle C.
Ervin, Samuel James, Jr.
Ferguson, Homer Samuel
Jackson, Henry Martin ("Scoop")
Jenner, William Ezra
Jordan, Leonard Beck
Lodge, Henry Cabot, Jr.
Morton, Thruston Ballard
Sparkman, John Jackson
Taylor, Glen Hearst
Politician (State Senator)
Shivers, (Robert) Allan
Politician (Vice-Presidential Candidate)
Sparkman, John Jackson
Taylor, Glen Hearst
Preacher. *See* CLERGY.
Priest. *See* CLERGY.

Producer (Film)
Foreman, Carl
Hecht, Harold
Skolsky, Sidney
Spiegel, Sam(uel)
Producer (Stage)
Jessel, George Albert ("Georgie")
Sillman, Leonard Dexter
Producer (Television)
Liebman, Max
Professor. *See* EDUCATOR.
Psychiatrist
Kline, Nathan Schellenberg
Psychoanalyst
Deutsch, Helene Rosenbach
Kardiner, Abram
Psychologist
Clark, Mamie Phipps
Davis, (William) Allison
Hathaway, Starke Rosencrans
Milgram, Stanley
Monroe, Marion
Wechsler, David
Public Opinion Researcher
Gallup, George Horace
Public Relations Executive. *See*
BUSINESS EXECUTIVE.
Publisher (Books)
Boni, Albert
Brett, George Platt, Jr.
Knopf, Alfred Abraham
Sheed, Francis Joseph ("Frank")
Wallace, (William Roy) DeWitt
Wallace, Lila (Bell) Acheson
Publisher (Magazines)
Cowles, Gardner ("Mike")
Wallace, (William Roy) DeWitt
Wallace, Lila (Bell) Acheson
Publisher (Newspapers)
Dedmon, Emmett
Golden, Harry
Ingersoll, Ralph McAllister
Knight, John Shively
Loeb, William
Washington, Chester Lloyd, Jr.
("Chet")
Whitney, John Hay
Puppeteer
Tillstrom, Burr
Radio Personality
Garroway, David Cunningham

Godfrey, Arthur (Morton)
Kaufman, Murray ("Murray
the K")
Kieran, John Francis
Religious Leader (Presbyterian)
Blake, Eugene Carson
Religious Leader (Southern Baptist)
Hays, (Lawrence) Brooks
Representative. *See* POLITICIAN
(REPRESENTATIVE).
Restaurateur
Dempsey, William Harrison
("Jack")
Kroc, Ray(mond) Albert
Stanford, Sally
Rock Star. *See* MUSICIAN (ROCK).
Runner. *See* ATHLETE (RUNNING).
Scholar. *See* EDUCATOR, HISTORIAN,
LEGAL SCHOLAR.
Scientist. *See* individual fields.
Sculptor. *See* ARTIST (SCULPTOR).
Seismologist
Richter, Charles Francis
Senator. *See* POLITICIAN (SENATOR).
Singer. *See* MUSICIAN.
Sociologist
Goffman, Erving Manual
Lynd, Helen Merrell
Soldier
Kelly, Charles E. ("Commando")
Songwriter (Blues). *See also*
LYRICIST.
Hopkins, Sam ("Lightnin'")
Songwriter (Popular). *See also*
LYRICIST.
Carmichael, Howard Hoagland
("Hoagy")
Gershwin, Ira
Harburg, Edgar Yipsel ("Yip")
Harkness, Rebekah West
Hays, Lee
Hunter, Alberta
Marks, John D. ("Johnny")
Schwartz, Arthur
Warren, Harry
Sports Coach (Baseball)
Alston, Walter Emmons
Grimes, Burleigh Arland
Kelly, George Lange
("Highpockets")
Schacht, Al(exander)
Sports Coach (Basketball)
Bee, Clair Francis
Ripley, Elmer Horton

Sports Coach (Boxing)
D'Amato, Constantine ("Cus")
Sports Coach (Football)
Bryant, Paul William ("Bear")
Crisler, Herbert Orin ("Fritz")
Engle, Charles Albert ("Rip")
Friedman, Benjamin ("Benny")
Halas, George
Kinard, Frank Manning ("Bruiser")
Van Brocklin, Norm(an) ("The
Dutchman")
Waterfield, Robert Staton ("Bob";
"Rifle")
Sports Coach (Track and Field)
Elliot, James Francis ("Jumbo")
Sports Commentator (Baseball)
Hoyt, Waite Charles ("Schoolboy")
Sports Executive (Baseball)
Cronin, Joseph Edward
Lane, Frank Charles
Sportswriter. *See* JOURNALIST
(SPORTSWRITER).
Statistician
Gallup, George Horace
Kuznets, Simon Smith
Neyman, Jerzy
Supreme Court Justice
Fortas, Abe
Stewart, Potter
Swimmer. *See* ATHLETE
(SWIMMING).
Teacher. *See* EDUCATOR.
Television Personality
Garroway, David Cunningham
Godfrey, Arthur (Morton)
Theologian
Ladd, George Eldon
Mays, Benjamin Elijah
Translator. *See* AUTHOR
(TRANSLATION).
Union Official. *See* LABOR LEADER.
University President
Mays, Benjamin Elijah
Rainey, Homer Price
Sterling, J(ohn) E(wart) Wallace
Urban Planner
Sert, José Luis
Violinist. *See* MUSICIAN.
Yachtsman
Morgan, Henry Sturgis ("Harry")
Shields, Cornelius
Zoologist
Fossey, Dian

DIRECTORY OF CONTRIBUTORS

ADAMS, EARL W.
Allegheny College
    Koopmans, Tjalling Charles
    Kuznets, Simon Smith
ADAMS, RAYMOND L.
Baptist Bible College, Springfield, Mo.
    Bricktop (Ada Smith)
    Lawford, Peter Sydney Vaughn
ALEXANDER, THOMAS G.
Brigham Young University
    Kimball, Spencer Woolley
    Marriott, J(ohn) Willard
ALINDER, MARY STREET
Independent Scholar, Gualala, Calif.
    Adams, Ansel Easton
ALLIN, LAWRENCE CARROLL
Maritime Historian, Norman, Okla.
    Gruenther, Alfred Maximilian
    Mackey, Joseph Creighton
ANDREWS, DAVID A.
State University of New York Maritime College
    Gardner, John Champlin, Jr.
ANDREWS, TERRY
Freelance Writer, Warrenton, Oreg.
    Willson, (Robert Reiniger) Meredith
ANNUNZIATA, FRANK
Rochester Institute of Technology
    Hughes, Emmet John
ARANT, WENDI
Humanities Librarian, Texas A&M University
    Wright, Olgivanna Lloyd
ARETAKIS, JONATHAN G.
Editorial East, Pembroke, Maine
    Fixx, James Fuller
AURAND, HAROLD W.
Pennsylvania State University, Capital College
    Battles, Clifford Franklin ("Gyp")
    McNally, John Victor ("Johnny Blood")

AVERY, GLEN EDWARD
Houghton College
    Barr, Stringfellow
BADER-BOREL, PHYLLIS
State University of New York at Albany
    Barber, Samuel
BAKER, JAMES T.
Western Kentucky University
    Hays, (Lawrence) Brooks
BAKER, THERESE DUZINKIEWICZ
Western Kentucky University
    Sheppard, Eugenia
BALLARD, TERRY L.
Librarian, Quinnipiac College
    Blake, James Hubert ("Eubie")
    Massey, Raymond Hart
    Scarne, John
    Spiegel, Sam(uel)
BAMBERGER, JOHN-FORREST
Writer, Amherst, Mass.
    Watts, John Everett
BARBEAU, ART
West Liberty State College
    Fossey, Dian
    Vargas, Alberto ("Varga")
BARRETT, DAVID M.
Villanova University
    Vinson, Carl
BARTHEL, THOMAS
Herkimer County Community College, N.Y.
    Coveleski, Stanley Anthony ("Covey")
    Kelly, George Lange ("Highpockets")
BENEDICT, ANNETTE
Ramapo College of New Jersey
    Kardiner, Abram
BERNSTEIN, DAVID
California State University, Long Beach
    Averill, Howard Earl ("Rock")

BIRD, DONALD ALLPORT
Long Island University
Collingwood, Charles Cummings

BLICKLEY, MARK A.
Brooklyn College, City University of New York
Goodrich, Frances

BOON, KEVIN ALEXANDER
State University of New York Maritime College
Albertson, Jack
Marks, John D. ("Johnny")
Zimbalist, Efrem Alexandrovich

BORNSTEIN, JERRY
Baruch College, City University of New York
Gallup, George Horace

BORRIES, MICHAEL S.
Office of Library Services, City University of New York
Durant, Will(iam) James and Ariel

BOSKY, BERNADETTE
Writer and Teacher, Yonkers, N.Y.
Caldwell, (Janet Miriam) Taylor

BOURGEOIS, CHRISTIE L.
Briarcliff, Texas
Shivers, (Robert) Allan

BOVEY, SETH
Louisiana State University at Alexandria
Vidor, King Wallis

BOYLES, MARY
University of North Carolina at Pembroke
Golden, Harry

BRADY, FRANK
St. John's University, New York
Skolsky, Sidney
Sutton, Carol
Welles, Orson

BRAUCH, PATRICIA
Brooklyn College, City University of New York
Coon, Carleton Stevens

BROWNE, WILLIAM F.
Brooklyn College, City University of New York
Himes, Chester Bomar
Williams, Mary Lou

BRUNS, ROBERT T.
Boston College
Canham, Erwin Dain
Demaret, James Newton ("Jimmy")

BRUUN, ERIK
Great Barrington, Massachusetts
Frick, Helen Clay

BURDICK, CAROL
State University of New York at Alfred
Boylston, Helen Dore
Farrar, Margaret Petherbridge

BURNETT, ROBYN K.
Missouri Department of Health
Wheeler, Raymond Milner

BURNS, MARGIE
University of Maryland, Baltimore County
Wright, Louis Booker

BUSTER, ALAN
Harvard-Westlake School, Los Angeles
Hofheinz, Roy Mark

CALHOUN, RICHARD B.
Editorial Consultant, Merrill Lynch
Burden, William
Kahn, Herman

CAMPBELL, JIM
Bucknell College
Crisler, Herbert Orin ("Fritz")
Friedman, Benjamin ("Benny")
Kinard, Frank Manning ("Bruiser")

CAPPELLETTI, J. S.
Songwriter and Writer, New York City
Fletcher, Harvey
Geschwind, Norman
Rice, Helen Steiner

CARP, DAVID M.
Carl Fischer, Inc.
Mercer, Mabel

CARPENTER, BRIAN
Sterling C. Evans Library, Texas A&M University
Riggs, Ralph Smith

CARSTENSEN, FRED
University of Connecticut
Kennedy, William Jesse, Jr.
Lay, Herman W.

CASTAÑEDA, JAMES A.
Rice University
Brown, George Rufus
Walker, Fred ("Dixie")

CASTLE, ALFRED L.
The Samuel N. and Mary Castle Foundation
Perkins, Dexter

CHEREPON, LOIS
St. John's University, New York
Scott, Austin Wakeman

CICARELLI, JULIANNE
Early Childhood Educator, Arlington Heights, Ill.
Monroe, Marion

COBB, KENNETH R.
New York City Municipal Archives
Tanny, Victor Anthony ("Vic")

COLBERT, THOMAS BURNELL
Marshalltown Community College
Cowles, Gardner ("Mike")

COLETTA, PAOLO E.
Professor Emeritus, United States Naval Academy
    Gates, Thomas Sovereign, Jr.
COLL, BLANCHE D.
Department of Health and Human Services (Retired)
    Bane, Frank B.
CONTINELLI, LOUISE
The Buffalo News
    Boyle, William Anthony ("Tony")
COOPER, DIANE E.
Maritime Museum of San Diego
    Albion, Robert G.
    Feld, Irvin
    North, John Ringling
COPPOLA, RENÉ
Museum of Modern Art
    Barr, Alfred Hamilton, Jr.
    Winogrand, Garry
COREY, DAVID
New York City
    Kelly, Grace Patricia (Princess Grace)
CRADDOCK, BRIAN
Writer and Pilot, U.S. Naval Reserves, Burtonsville, Md.
    Mitchell, John James, Jr.
CRANDELL, GEORGE W.
Auburn University
    Williams, Thomas Lanier, III ("Tennessee")
DAHLSTROM, W. GRANT
University of North Carolina at Chapel Hill
    Hathaway, Starke Rosencrans
DAMON, ALLAN L.
Horace Greeley High School, Chappaqua, N.Y.
    Cooke, Terence James
    Demara, Ferdinand Waldo ("Fred")
    Hoyt, Homer
    Wallace, (William Roy) DeWitt and Lila (Bell)
        Acheson
DAVIDMAN, RICHARD
Downtown Financial Network, New York City
    Belushi, John
DAVIDSON, ABRAHAM A.
Tyler School of Art, Temple University
    Roszak, Theodore
DEDERICK, WARREN E.
Brooklyn College, City University of New York
    Burrows, Abe
DEFEIS, ELIZABETH F.
Seton Hall University Law School
    Quinlan, Karen Ann
DE FOREST, KELLAM
De Forest Research Service, Santa Barbara, Calif.
    Webb, John Randolph ("Jack")

DICK, BERNARD F.
Farleigh Dickinson University
    Maltz, Albert
DICKE, THOMAS
Southwest Missouri State University
    Tupper, Earl Silas
DILLIARD, IRVING
Collinsville, Illinois
    Velde, Harold Himmel
DINNEEN, MARCIA B.
Bridgewater State College
University of Massachusetts at Dartmouth
    Haley, William John Clifton, Jr. ("Bill")
    Jenkins, Gordon Hill
    Lynd, Helen Merrell
    MacInnes, Helen Clark
    Ponselle, Rosa Melba
    Riddle, Nelson Smock, Jr.
DiRUSSO, BEN
York College, City University of New York
    Claude, Albert
DOBSON, MELISSA A.
Freelance Writer, Newport, R.I.
    Savitch, Jessica Beth
DOENECKE, JUSTUS D.
New College of the University of South Florida
    Chase, Stuart
DOYLE, ANDREW
Winthrop University
    Bryant, Paul William ("Bear")
DRABELLE, DENNIS
Washington Post
    Powell, William Horatio
DRIVER, JULIA
Brooklyn College, City University of New York
    Tarski, Alfred
DROBNICKI, JOHN A.
York College Library, City University of New York
    Hanson, Howard Harold
DUNHAM, VALERIE L.
Ph.D. Candidate, University of New Hampshire
    Corning, Erastus, 2d
    Douglas, Donald Wills
    Welch, Robert Henry Winborne, Jr.
EKBLADH, DAVID
Columbia University
    Mumford, Lawrence Quincy
ELTSCHER, LOUIS R.
Rochester Institute of Technology
    Grumman, Leroy Randle ("Roy")
EMANUEL, EDWARD
California State University, Fresno
    Chayefsky, Sidney Aaron ("Paddy")

EMANUEL, EDWARD
(Continued)
    Fontanne, Lynn
ENGELBRECHT, LLOYD C.
University of Cincinnati
    Breuer, Marcel
EVENSEN, BRUCE J.
DePaul University
    Crowther, (Francis) Bosley, Jr.
    Dempsey, William Harrison ("Jack")
    Godfrey, Arthur (Morton)
    Stratton, Monty Franklin Pierce
    Van Brocklin, Norm(an) ("The Dutchman")
    Waterfield, Robert Staton ("Bob"; "Rifle")
FERRELL, ROBERT H.
Indiana University, Bloomington
    Hagerty, James Campbell
    Truman, Bess Wallace
FEUERHARD, PETER
Long Island Catholic
    Sheed, Francis Joseph ("Frank")
FINN, NANCY M.
*Graduate Student, State University of New York at Stony
    Brook*
    Margulies, Lazar
    Pritikin, Nathan
FISCHER, WILLIAM E., JR.
U.S. Air Force
    Elliot, James Francis ("Jumbo")
    Grosvenor, Melville Bell
FISCHLER, STAN
Fischler Hockey Service, New York City
    Shore, Edward William ("Eddie")
FISHER, JAMES T.
Saint Louis University
    Kaufman, Murray ("Murray the K")
    Parsons, Johnnie
FITZPATRICK, JANE BRODSKY
*Stephen B. Luce Library, State University of New York
    Maritime College*
    Cooper, Charles Henry ("Chuck")
FITZPATRICK, JOHN
Charles Scribner's Sons
    Moross, Jerome
    Wyler, William
FLEET, SUSAN
Berklee College of Music
    Scott, Hazel Dorothy
FLYNN, JOSEPH G.
State University of New York College of Technology, Alfred
    Stuart, Jesse Hilton

FRIGUGLIETTI, JAMES
Montana State University, Billings
    Brodie, Fawn McKay
FRISCH, PAUL
Washington and Jefferson College
    Alston, Walter Emmons
FURLONG, PATRICK J.
Indiana University South Bend
    West, (Mary) Jessamyn
    Whitney, John Hay
GAAR, GILLIAN G.
Freelance Writer, Seattle, Wash.
    Carpenter, Karen
GARGAN, WILLIAM M.
Brooklyn College, City University of New York
    Rexroth, Kenneth Charles Marion
    Shaw, Irwin Gilbert
GENTILE, RICHARD H.
South Easton, Massachusetts
    Cronin, Joseph Edward
    Lodge, John Davis
    Loeb, William
GERBER, BARBARA L.
Brooklyn College, City University of New York
    Gernreich, Rudi
    Head, Edith
GIGLIO, FRANCES T.
Ozark Technical Community College, Springfield, Mo.
    Gaynor, Janet
GILBERT, RICHARD
Ohio University
    Whitehead, Don(ald) Ford
GIOIA, DANA
Poet and Critic, Santa Rosa, Calif.
    MacLeish, Archibald
GNEUHS, GEOFFREY B.
Writer, New York City
    Cody, John Patrick
GOLDMAN, ALEXANDER
Charles Scribner's Sons
    Hoffer, Eric
GONZALEZ, LEROY
Columbia University Graduate School of Business
    Sturgeon, Theodore
GORMAN, ANNA
Fremont Argus
    Reynolds, Frank
GOTTLIEB, JANE
The Juilliard School
    Primrose, William
    Sessions, Roger Huntington
    Wallenstein, Alfred Franz

GOULD, LEWIS L.
University of Texas at Austin
  Catledge, Turner
  Garroway, David Cunningham
  Petrillo, James Caesar
GRAFF, HENRY F.
Columbia University
  Paige, Leroy Robert ("Satchel")
GRAYBAR, LLOYD J.
Eastern Kentucky University
  Baxter, Anne
  Pidgeon, Walter
GREENBERG, DAVID
Columbia University
  Ervin, Samuel James, Jr.
  Jaworski, Leon
  Macdonald, Dwight
GRIFFITH, JEAN W., JR.
Crowder College
  Halas, George
HADLER, MONA
*Brooklyn College and the Graduate Center, City University
    of New York*
  Ernst, Hans-Ulrich ("Jimmy")
HAINES, MICHAEL F.
Dominican College, Orangeburg, N.Y.
  Stern, Curt
HAMM, BRADLEY J.
Elon College
  Pope, James Soule, Sr.
HANDLER, JACK
*Adjunct Faculty, Antioch New England Graduate School,
    Massachusetts College of Liberal Arts*
  Blackwell, Randolph Talmadge
  Dubinsky, David
HANSEN, VAGN K.
High Point University
  Austin, John Paul
  Engel, A. Lehman
  Johnson, Paul Burney
  Pauley, Edwin Wendell
  Williams, John Bell
  Woodruff, Robert Winship
HARRIS, RICHARD C.
Webb Institute
  Knopf, Alfred Abraham
HARRISON, MARJORIE FREEMAN
Independent Scholar, Merrick, N.Y.
  Bliss, Ray Charles
HART, JOHN E.
Albion College, Albion, Mich.
  Halper, Albert

HASENFUS, WILLIAM A.
Community College of Rhode Island
  Vanderbilt, William Henry
HASSEN, MARJORIE
University of Pennsylvania
  Ormandy, Eugene
HAWKINS, HUGH
Amherst College
  Ward, John William
HAWLEY, ELLIS W.
University of Iowa
  Cohen, Benjamin Victor
HAYES, DAVID J., JR.
Spotswood (New Jersey) High School
  Bee, Clair Francis
HEALY, JOHN DAVID
William Paterson University
Interstate Commerce Commission (Retired)
  Casey, James E.
HENNESSEY, THOMAS J.
Fayetteville State University
  Basie, William James ("Count")
HENRIQUES, DIANA B.
New York Times
  Johnson, Edward Crosby, 2d
HERON, DAVID W.
University of California, Santa Cruz
  Boni, Albert
  Sterling, J(ohn) E(wart) Wallace
HERRINGTON, NANCY J.
Syracuse University
  Charney, Jule Gregory
HILL, MARILYNN WOOD
Bronxville, New York
  Grasso, Ella Rosa Giovanna Oliva Tambussi
  Holland, Jerome Heartwell ("Brud")
HLAVATY, ARTHUR D.
Yonkers, New York
  Schacht, Al(exander)
  Ulam, Stanislaw Marcin
HODGES, GRAHAM RUSSELL
Colgate University
  VanDerZee, James Augustus Joseph
HOGAN, DAVID W.
U.S. Army Center of Military History
  Bradley, Omar Nelson
HOOGENBOOM, LYNN
New York Times News Service
  Ingersoll, Ralph McAllister
  Macdonald, Ross

HOWLETT, CHARLES F.
Adelphi University
Amityville Public Schools
    Waner, Lloyd James ("Little Poison")

HULSEY, BYRON C.
University of Texas at Austin
    Morton, Thruston Ballard

JACOBS, FREDERIC
American University
    Prichard, Edward Fretwell, Jr.

JACOBS, JOHN
McClatchy Newspapers, Sacramento, Calif.
    Burton, Phillip

JALENAK, NATALIE
Playhouse on the Square, Memphis, Tenn.
    Adler, Luther
    Bennett, Robert Russell

JOHNSON, KATHRYN A.
Barnard College
    Young, Claude, Jr. ("Buddy")

JOSEPH, PHILIP
Ph.D. Candidate, State University of New York at Buffalo
    Weiner, Lazar

KASS, JUDITH M.
Freelance Researcher and Writer, New York City
    Fonda, Henry Jaynes

KATES, JAMES
Milwaukee Journal Sentinel
    Groppi, James Edward
    Price, T(homas) Rowe, Jr.

KAUFMAN, ROBERT GORDON
University of Vermont
    Jackson, Henry Martin ("Scoop")

KEANE, TIM
Writer, Mt. Vernon, N.Y.
    Sloane, Eric

KELLY, MATTHEW
The Patriot Ledger, Quincy, Mass.
    Medeiros, Humberto Sousa

KELLY, ROBERT J.
Brooklyn College and The Graduate School, City University of New York
    Lansky, Meyer
    Patriarca, Raymond

KENNEY, RUTH
Mater Christi High School, Astoria, N.Y. (Retired)
    Scourby, Alexander

KHAN, SYED M. A.
O'Neill Library, Boston College
    Merrill, John Putnam

KHATUN, SAIYEDA
University of Rhode Island
    Harkness, Rebekah West

KIEFER, PETER T.
Fred Waring's America Collection, Pennsylvania State University
    Waring, Fred(eric) Malcolm

KIRSHNER, RALPH
Independent Scholar, Chapel Hill, N.C.
    Olin, John Merrill

KLEBANOFF, SHOSHANA
Writer, Santa Monica, Calif.
    Hecht, Harold
    Powell, Eleanor Torrey ("Ellie")

KLOTTER, JAMES C.
Kentucky Historical Society
    Clements, Earle C.

KOTULAK, THOMAS D.
Indiana University Southeast
    Jenner, William Ezra

KOWAL, REBEKAH
Ph.D. Candidate, New York University
    Denby, Edwin Orr
    Terry, Walter

KREMPEL, DANIEL S.
Syracuse University
    Atkinson, (Justin) Brooks
    Gordon, Ruth

KUTULAS, JUDY
St. Olaf College
    Baldwin, Roger Nash
    Hicks, Granville

LAHOOD, MARVIN J.
Buffalo State College
    Algren, Nelson

LAKIN, PAMELA ARMSTRONG
Herrick Memorial Library, Alfred University
    Kertész, André (Andor)

LANKEVICH, GEORGE J.
Professor of History Emeritus, City University of New York
    Montgomery, Robert
    Seymour, Whitney North

LASSER, MICHAEL
Harley School, Rochester, N.Y.
    Carmichael, Howard Hoagland ("Hoagy")
    Harburg, Edgar Yipsel ("Yip")

LAUNIUS, ROGER D.
Chief Historian, National Aeronautics and Space Administration
    Debus, Kurt Heinrich

LEAB, DANIEL J.
Seton Hall University
    Tillstrom, Burr

LEARY, WILLIAM M.
University of Georgia
    Link, Edwin Albert

LEITER, SAMUEL L.
Brooklyn College and The Graduate Center,
*   City University of New York*
Lenya, Lotte
Merman, Ethel
Schneider, Alan
Strasberg, Lee

LETTIERI, RONALD
Mount Ida College
Holt, John Caldwell

LEVINE, MICHAEL
Freelance Writer and Editor,
*   New York City*
Wilkins, Roy

LEVY, SHARONA A.
Baruch College, City University of
*   New York*
Berman, Emile Zola

LEWIS, GEORGE H.
University of the Pacific
Robbins, Marty

LEWIS, W. DAVID
Auburn University
Thomas, Lowell Jackson

LITTLE, JOHN E.
Princeton University
Dietz, Howard
Gershwin, Ira
Schwartz, Arthur
Thompson, (Ira) Randall

LORD, TOM FORRESTER
Rice University
Housing Corporation of Greater Houston
Bainton, Roland Herbert

LUEBBERING, KEN
Lincoln University of Missouri
Hall, Joyce Clyde

LYNCH, G. ANDREW
Falmouth, Massachusetts
Langer, Susanne Katherina

MACAULEY, NEILL
University of Florida
Bunker, Ellsworth

McCARTHY, TIMOTHY P.
Columbia University
Gaye, Marvin Pentz

McDONAGH, DON
State University of New York at Purchase
New York University
Balanchine, George

McDONALD, ARCHIE P.
Stephen F. Austin State University
Tubb, Ernest Dale

McDOWELL, MARKUS H.
Pepperdine University
Fuller Theological Seminary
Ladd, George Eldon

McKAY, ELIZABETH
The New York and Presbyterian Hospital
Dubos, René Jules

McKAY, ERNEST A.†
University of South Carolina at Aiken
Trippe, Juan Terry

McKAY, STEPHEN
Burlington, Vermont
Silvers, Phil

McLAUGHLIN, MARILYN SAUDER
Ypsilanti, Michigan
Ferguson, Homer Samuel

McLEAN, MICHAEL
Independent Scholar, New York City
Walker, Edward Patrick ("Mickey"; "The Toy
    Bulldog")

MALONEY, WENDY HALL
Brooklyn College, City University of New York
Samuels, Howard Joseph

MALONEY, WILLIAM J.
Bilateral Credit Corporation, New York City
Spanel, Abram Nathaniel

MANNING, PHILIP
Cleveland State University
Goffman, Erving Manual

MARC, DAVID
Newhouse School of Public Relations, Syracuse University
Jessel, George Albert ("Georgie")

MARKGRAF, SARAH
Fort Lee, New Jersey
Machito (Frank Raúl Grillo)

MARSHALL, STEPHEN
Lincoln Park, New Jersey
Cukor, George
McCain, John Sydney, Jr.
Morgan, Henry Sturgis ("Harry")
Snyder, John Wesley
Warren, Harry

MARX-SINGER, LORRAINE
New York City
Rubinstein, Arthur

MAYO, LOUISE A.
County College of Morris
Lindstrom, Frederick Charles, Jr. ("Lindy")

MEACHAM, JACK
State University of New York, Buffalo
Clark, Mamie Phipps

MEAD, CHRISTOPHER B.
London & Mead, Washington, D.C.
Louis, Joe

MEANOR, PATRICK H.
State University of New York, College at Oneonta
    Cheever, John

MENNINGER, MARGARET E.
Harvard University
    Friedrich, Carl Joachim

MERRON, JEFFREY M.
State University of West Georgia
    Smith, Walter Wellesley ("Red")

MERRON, MYRNA W.
Mount Dora, Florida
    Wechsler, David

MILLER, JAMES P.
ACA Publications, Alexandria, Va.
    Brett, George Platt, Jr.

MOBERG, VERNE
Columbia University
    Schlamme, Martha Haftel

MORGAN, ANN LEE
Princeton, New Jersey
    Hanks, Nancy

MORGAN, MICHELLE C.
Ph.D. Candidate, Columbia University
    Armour, Norman
    Riddleberger, James Williams
    Yost, Charles Woodruff

MORROW, FRANK
San Francisco
    Kaufman, Andrew G. ("Andy")

MOWER, SUSAN
Albert S. Cook Library, Towson State University
    Astaire, Adele Marie
    Diamond, Selma

MUGLESTON, WILLIAM F.
Floyd College
    Logan, Rayford Whittingham

MYERS, R. DAVID
New Mexico State University
    Galarza, Ernesto, Jr.

NEAL, STEVE
Chicago Sun-Times
    Case, Clifford P.
    Dedmon, Emmett
    Eisenhower, Milton Stover
    McCall, Thomas William Lawson

NELSON, ALLAN
Caldwell College, Caldwell, N.J.
    Billington, Ray Allen
    Varipapa, Andrew ("Andy")

NELSON, ELIZABETH R.
St. Peter's College
    Stein, Aaron Marc

NELSON, MURRY R.
Pennsylvania State University
    Ripley, Elmer Horton

NEUSE, STEVEN
University of Arkansas
    Lilienthal, David

NEWMAN, ROGER K.
School of Law, New York University
    Fortas, Abe
    Hill, (Joseph) Lister

NOEL, THOMAS J.
University of Colorado at Denver
    Chase, Mary Coyle

OHL, JOHN KENNEDY
Mesa Community College
    Ryan, John D.
    Struble, Arthur D.
    Twining, Nathan Farragut

O'LOUGHLIN, JIM
Pennsylvania State University, Erie,
    The Behrend College
    Wurf, Jerome

O'SULLIVAN, JOHN
Florida Atlantic University
    Kelly, Charles E. ("Commando")
    Shoup, David Monroe

PACHECO, MARIA
Buffalo State College
    Moore, Stanford
    Niel, Cornelis Bernardus van

PARASCANDOLA, JOHN
U.S. Public Health Service
    Terry, Luther L.

PARKER, JUDITH A.
Graduate Student, Baylor University
    Martin, Freddy

PARRIS, LaROSE T.
Graduate Student, City College of
    New York
    Bernard, Anna Jones
    Harris, Patricia Roberts Fitzgerald

PERRY, MARILYN ELIZABETH
Independent Scholar, Prospect Heights, Ill.
    McNamara, Margaret Craig
    Stanford, Sally

PETERSON, BARBARA BENNETT
University of Hawaii
    Wood, Natalie

PETERSON, F. ROSS
Utah State University
    Jordan, Leonard Beck ("Len")
    Taylor, Glen Hearst

PIEHL, CHARLES K.
Mankato State University
    Canaday, John Edwin
    Hirshhorn, Joseph Herman

PINN, ANTHONY B.
Macalaster College
    King, Martin Luther, Sr. ("Daddy King")
    Murray, Anna Pauline ("Pauli")

PIOUS, RICHARD M.
Adolph and Effie Ochs Professor, Barnard College, and The
    Graduate Faculties, Columbia University
    Aiken, George David
    Church, Frank Forrester
    Voorhis, Horace Jeremiah ("Jerry")

POLLNER, FRAN
The NIH Catalyst, National Institutes of Health
    Gruentzig, Andreas Roland

POLLOT, NAN
State University of New York College at Geneseo
    Davis, (William) Allison
    Johnson, Rachel Harris

POMPER, MILES A.
Washington, D.C.
    Wechsler, James Arthur

PORTER, DAVID L.
William Penn College
    Engle, Charles Albert ("Rip")
    Grimes, Burleigh Arland
    Irish, Edward Simmons, Sr. ("Ned")

POTTER, BARRETT G.
State University of New York College of Technology, Alfred
    Hunter, Alberta

POWERS, RICHARD GID
College of Staten Island and The Graduate Center, City
    University of New York
    Rand, Ayn

PUGH, WILLIAM WHITE TISON
University of Oregon, Eugene
    Sillman, Leonard Dexter

REDMAN, NICK
Santa Monica, California
    Holden, William

REED, JAMES W.
Rutgers University
    Corner, George Washington

REICHARD, GARY W.
California State University, Long Beach
    Lodge, Henry Cabot, Jr.

REILLY, KEVIN P.
University of Wisconsin–Extension, Madison
    O'Brien, William Joseph, Jr. ("Pat")

REYNOLDS, CLARK G.
College of Charleston
    Cole, William R. ("Cozy")
    Fuller, R(ichard) Buckminster
    Hines, Earl Kenneth ("Fatha")
    James, Harry Haag

RIDGLEY, RONALD H.
Coastal Georgia Community College
    Hoyt, Waite Charles ("Schoolboy")
    Ochsner, (Edward William) Alton

RILEY, HARRIS D., JR.
Vanderbilt Children's Hospital, Vanderbilt University
    Delbrück, Max Ludwig Henning
    Enders, John Franklin

ROBERSON, GLORIA GRANT
Adelphi University
    Mays, Benjamin Elijah

ROBINSON, GREG
Jazztimes
    Monk, Thelonious Sphere

ROME, ROMAN
State University of New York Maritime College
    Clark, Mark Wayne
    Sparkman, John Jackson

ROND, CHARLES A., IV
Computer Consultant, Center for Earthquake Research and
    Information, University of Memphis
    Cooper, Irving Spencer
    Giauque, William Francis
    Pool, Ithiel de Sola

ROOT, ROBERT L., JR.
Central Michigan University
    White, E(lwyn) B(rooks)

ROREX, P. DALE
Seiwa College
    Rainey, Homer Price
    Stokes, Colin

ROSEN, JEFFREY S.
Spotswood (New Jersey) High School
    Greer, William Alexander ("Sonny")

ROSS, PHILIP
New York School of Industrial and Labor Relations, Cornell
    University
    Curran, Joseph Edwin

ROYCE, BRENDA SCOTT
Editor, Renaissance Books, Los Angeles
    Hudson, Rock

ROZAKIS, LAURIE
State University of New York College of Technology at
    Farmingdale
    Capote, Truman

RUTLAND, ROBERT ALLEN
University of Virginia
    Butterfield, Lyman Henry

ST. ANDRE, KENNETH E.
Phoenix Public Library
    Dick, Philip Kindred

SAPIENZA, MADELINE
Independent Scholar, Washington, D.C.
    Brynner, Yul
    Shearer, (Edith) Norma

SCHARNHORST, GARY
University of New Mexico
    Saroyan, William

SCHERER, JOHN L.
Minneapolis, Minnesota
    Moos, Malcolm Charles

SCHONDELMEYER, BRENT
Independence, Missouri
    Daniels, Jonathan Worth

SCHUSKY, MARK E.
Edwardsville, Illinois
    Arends, Leslie Cornelius
    Velde, Harold Himmel

SCHWARTZ, BERNARD†
University of Tulsa School of Law
    Stewart, Potter

SCHWARTZ, JOEL
Montclair State University
    Moses, Robert

SCOTT, BONNIE KIME
University of Delaware
    Barnes, Djuna Chappell

SEARL, MARJORIE B.
Memorial Art Gallery, University of Rochester
    Krasner, Lee

SEEMAN, COREY
National Baseball Hall of Fame Library
    Dean, Paul ("Daffy")
    Lane, Frank Charles

SENNETT, TED
Author, Closter, N.J.
    Bergman, Ingrid
    Douglas, Melvyn
    Hamilton, Margaret
    Liebman, Max
    Swanson, Gloria

SEYDOR, PAUL
University of Southern California Film School
    Peckinpah, David Samuel ("Sam")

SEYEDIAN, MOJTABA
State University of New York, College at Fredonia
    Pillsbury, Philip
    Shields, Cornelius

SHARP, NICHOLAS A.
Virginia Commonwealth University
    Ace, Goodman
    Gosden, Freeman Fisher

SHISHIN, ALEX
Akashi City, Hyogo Prefecture, Japan
    Washington, Chester Lloyd, Jr. ("Chet")

SHOR, ELIZABETH NOBLE
Scripps Institution of Oceanography, University of California San Diego, La Jolla (Retired)
    Richter, Charles Francis

SHOR, RACHEL
York College, City University of New York
    Shook, Karel Francis Antony

SILVERBERG, MARK
Dalhousie University
    Oppen, George

SILVERMAN, GILLIAN
Ph.D. Candidate, Duke University
    Deutsch, Helene Rosenbach

SMID, LAURA KATHLEEN
Charles Scribner's Sons
    Chapin, Harry Forster

SMITH, ROBERT J.
East Amherst, New York
    Miller, Arnold Ray

SMITH, WHITNEY
The Commercial Appeal, Memphis, Tenn.
    Barrett, Emma ("Sweet Emma")
    Beebe, William Thomas
    Kemper, James Scott
    Magowan, Robert Anderson
    Nelson, Eric Hilliard ("Rick")
    Ryskind, Morrie

SNYDER, RACHEL
Independent Scholar, Boulder, Colo.
    Cohen, N(ehemiah) M(yer)

SOLON, LEONARD R.
Physicist and Educator, Fort Pierce, Fla.
    Bloch, Felix
    Dirac, Paul Adrien Maurice
    Kistiakowsky, George Bogdan
    Neyman, Jerzy

SPATT, HARTLEY S.
State University of New York Maritime College
    Jacoby, Oswald ("Ozzie")
    Northrop, John Knudsen ("Jack")
    Owings, Nathaniel Alexander
    Zworykin, Vladimir Kosma

STAHL, MARTIN
Empire State College, State University of New York
    Celler, Emanuel

STEBENNE, DAVID L.
Ohio State University
    Blough, Roger Miles
STENSTROM, CHRISTINE
*LaGuardia Community College, City University of
    New York*
    Parsons, Elizabeth Pierson ("Betty")
STERLING, KEIR B.
Ordnance Branch Historian, U.S. Army Ordnance Corps
    Tully, Grace
STERNER, INGRID
Writer, New York City
    Brautigan, Richard
STERTZ, STEPHEN A.
Dowling College
Mercy College
    Rafferty, Max(well) Lewis, Jr.
STOLOFF, SAM
Cornell University
    Coogan, John Leslie, Jr. ("Jackie")
STUCKEY-FRENCH, NED
University of Iowa
    Whitaker, Rogers E(rnest) M(alcolm)
        ("E. M. Frimbo")
SWEET, JAMES STOUDER
Writer and Editor, Silver Spring, Md.
    Rock, John Charles
    Stein, Julian Caesar ("Jules")
TAKOOSHIAN, HAROLD
Fordham University
    Milgram, Stanley
TAMBORRINO, VICTORIA
St. John's University, New York
    Kline, Nathan Schellenberg
TAPPER, JOHN
The Brockton Enterprise, Boston
    Knight, John Shively
TASSINARI, EDWARD J.
Scarsdale, New York
    Maris, Roger Eugene
TAYLOR, JON E.
National Park Service
    DiSalle, Michael Vincent
TEAFORD, JON C.
Purdue University
    Seasongood, Murray
THAYER, CINDY
Organic Farmer and Writer, Gouldsboro, Maine
    Nearing, Scott
THOMPSON, GAIL STRANGE
Falmouth, Maine
    Hopkins, Sam ("Lightnin'")

TINO, RICHARD L.
University of New Haven
    Bernbach, William
TISCHLER, BARBARA L.
Horace Mann School
Columbia University
    Hays, Lee
TOMASINO, ADRIANA C.
*Ph.D. Candidate, Graduate School and University Center,
    City University of New York*
    Hartline, Haldan Keffer
TOMKO, ANDREW S.
Bergen Community College
    McCormick, Frank Andrew
TUCKER, DAVID M.
University of Memphis
    Plough, Abe
TURTELL, STEPHEN
Brooklyn College, City University of New York
    Cori, Carl Ferdinand
    McBride, Lloyd
    Markham, Dewey ("Pigmeat")
TUTOROW, NORMAN
*Visiting Fellow, 1996–1998, Hoover Institution on War,
    Revolution, and Peace, Stanford University*
    Benson, Elmer Austin
TUTTLE, ANN LESLIE
Silhouette Books
    Adams, Harriet Stratemeyer
    Beard, James Andrew
TYTELL, JOHN
Queens College
    Beck, Julian
UROFSKY, MELVIN I.
Virginia Commonwealth University
    Corcoran, Thomas Gardiner
VAN DIJK, RUUD
Ohio University
    Kieran, John Francis
    Turner, Joseph Vernon ("Big Joe")
    Waters, Muddy
VANDOREN, SANDRA SHAFFER
Archivist, Balch Institute for Ethnic Studies, Philadelphia
    de Man, Paul
VARNER, JIM
New York State College of Ceramics at Alfred University
    Flory, Paul John
VINSON, BETTY B.
Freelance Writer, Mobile, Ala.
    Robinson, Julia Bowman
VON WINBUSH, SAMUEL
State University of New York at Westbury
    Urey, Harold Clayton

VOS, FRANK
Stamford, Connecticut
  Kroc, Ray(mond) Albert
  Uris, Harold David

WALD, MALVIN
School of Cinema/Television, University of Southern California
  Foreman, Carl

WARD, NATHAN
Library Journal
  Clarke, Kenny ("Klook")
  D'Amato, Constantine ("Cus")

WASSER, HENRY
Academy for Humanities and Sciences, City University of New York
  Nagel, Ernest
  Rosenberg, Anna Marie Lederer

WATTEL, HAROLD L.
Hofstra University
  Padover, Saul Kussiel

WATTS, JILL
California State University, San Marcos
  Fetchit, Stepin

WEAVER, JOHN B.
Sinclair Community College, Dayton, Ohio
  Blake, Eugene Carson
  Mueller, Reuben Herbert
  Young, Stephen M.

WEDGE, ELEANOR F.
Freelance Writer and Editor, New York City
  Benn, Ben
  Downey, Morton
  Fitzgerald, Robert Stuart
  Manne, Sheldon ("Shelly")
  Sert, José Luis

WEIGOLD, MARILYN E.
Pace University, Pleasantville, N.Y.
  Black, William

WEINSTEIN, HONORA RAPHAEL
Brooklyn College, City University of New York
  Peerce, Jan

WEISBLAT, LEIGH BULLARD
Independent Art Historian, New York City
  Okada, Kenzo
  Phillips, Marjorie Acker

WEISBLAT, TINKY "DAKOTA"
Independent Scholar, Hawley, Mass.
  Brooks, (Mary) Louise
  Livingstone, Mary
  Loos, Anita

WELCH, PAULA D.
University of Florida
  Crabbe, Clarence Linden ("Buster")
  Weissmuller, John Peter ("Johnny")

WESTON, MARY ANN
Northwestern University
  Gould, Chester

WILSON, THEODORE A.
University of Kansas
  Bailey, Thomas A.
  Myer, Dillon Seymour

WITHAM, BARRY B.
University of Washington
  Hellman, Lillian Florence

WITWER, DAVID S.
Lycoming College
  Fitzsimmons, Frank Edward

WONG, AMY ANMEI B.
Nassau Community College
  Knott, Walter

ZHANG, TIAN XIAO
St. John's University, New York
  Fielding, Temple Hornaday
  Levin, Meyer

ENCYCLOPEDIA OF AMERICAN LIVES

SCS